THE
MOTION PICTURE
GUIDE

THIS VOLUME IS DEDICATED TO
PAUL MUNI
LESLIE HOWARD
FREDRIC MARCH
PAUL NEWMAN
HENRY FONDA
JAMES STEWART
CARY GRANT
JOHN GARFIELD
MARLON BRANDO
CLARK GABLE
TYRONE POWER
ERROL FLYNN
LAURENCE OLIVIER
KIRK DOUGLAS
BURT LANCASTER
ROBERT REDFORD
WILLIAM POWELL
ROBERT DENIRO
WILLIAM HOLDEN
and all the leading men

Publishers: Jay Robert Nash, Stanley Ralph Ross; **Associate Publisher:** Kenneth H. Petchenik; **Executive Editor:** Jim McCormick; **Senior Editor:** David Tardy; **Associate Editors:** Oksana Lydia Creighton, Jeffrey H. Wallenfeldt; **Senior Staff Writer:** James J. Mulay; **Staff Writers:** Arnie Bernstein, Daniel Curran, Phil Pantone, Michael Theobald, Brian Brock; **Director of Production:** William Leahy; **Production Editor:** Shelby Payne; **Production Assistants:** Jeanette Hori, Michaela Tuohy; **Chief Researcher:** William C. Clogston.

Editorial and Sales Offices: CINEBOOKS, 990 Grove, Evanston, Illinois 60201.

Library of Congress Catalog Card Number: 85-071145
ISBN: 0-933997-00-0 THE MOTION PICTURE GUIDE (10 Vols.)
       0-933997-09-4 THE MOTION PICTURE GUIDE, Vol. IX (W–Z)

Printed in the United States
First Edition
This volume contains 4,184 entries.

1 2 3 4 5 6 7 8 9 10

THE
MOTION PICTURE
GUIDE

W-Z

1927-1984

Jay Robert Nash
Stanley Ralph Ross

CINEBOOKS, INC.
Chicago, 1987
Publishers of THE COMPLETE FILM RESOURCE CENTER

HOW TO USE INFORMATION IN THIS GUIDE

ALPHABETICAL ORDER

All entries have been arranged alphabetically throughout this and all subsequent volumes. In establishing alphabetical order, all articles (A, An, The) appear after the main title (AFFAIR TO REMEMBER, AN). In the case of foreign films the article precedes the main title (LES MISERABLES appears in the letter L) which makes, we feel, for easier access and uniformity. Contractions are grouped together and these will be followed by non-apostrophized words of the same letters. B.F.'s DAUGHTER is at the beginning of the letter B, not under BF.

TITLES

It is important to know what title you are seeking; use the *complete* title of the film. The film ADVENTURES OF ROBIN HOOD, THE, cannot be found under merely ROBIN HOOD. Many films are known under different titles and we have taken great pains to cross-reference these titles. (AKA, also known as) as well as alternate titles used in Great Britain (GB). In addition to the cross-reference title only entries, AKAs and alternate titles in Great Britain can be found in the title line for each entry. An alphabetically arranged comprehensive list of title changes appears in the Index volume (Vol. X).

RATINGS

We have rated each and every film at critical levels that include acting, directing, script, and technical achievement (or the sad lack of it). We have a *five-star* rating, unlike all other rating systems, to signify a film superbly made on every level, in short, a masterpiece. At the lowest end of the scale is *zero* and we mean it. The ratings are as follows: *zero* (not worth a glance), *(poor), **(fair), ***(good), ****(excellent), *****(masterpiece, and these are few and far between). Half-marks mean almost there but not quite.

YEAR OF RELEASE

We have used in all applicable instances the year of United States release. This sometimes means that a film released abroad may have a different date elsewhere than in these volumes but this is generally the date released in foreign countries, not in the U.S.

FOREIGN COUNTRY PRODUCTION

When possible, we have listed abbreviated names of the foreign countries originating the production of a film. This information will be found within the parenthesis containing the year of release. If no country is listed in this space, it is a U.S. production.

RUNNING TIME

A hotly debated category, we have opted to list the running time a film ran at the time of its initial U.S. release but we will usually mention in the text if the film was drastically cut and give the reasons why. We have attempted to be as accurate as possible by consulting the most reliable sources.

PRODUCING AND DISTRIBUTING COMPANIES

The producing and/or distributing company of every film is listed in abbreviated entries next to the running time in the title line (see abbreviations; for all those firms not abbreviated, the entire firm's name will be present).

COLOR OR BLACK-AND-WHITE

The use of color or black-and-white availability appears as c or bw following the producing/releasing company entry.

CASTS

Whenever possible, we give *the complete cast and the roles played* for each film and this is the case in 95% of all entries, the only encyclopedia to ever offer such comprehensive information in covering the entire field. The names of actors and actresses are in Roman lettering, the names of the roles each played in Italic inside parentheses.

SYNOPSIS

The in-depth synopsis for each entry (when such applies) offers the plot of each film, critical evaluation, anecdotal information on the production and its personnel, awards won when applicable and additional information dealing with the production's impact upon the public, its success or failure at the box office, its social significance, if any. Acting methods, technical innovations, script originality are detailed. We also cite other productions involving an entry's personnel for critical comparisons and to establish the style or genre of expertise of directors, writers, actors and technical people.

REMAKES AND SEQUELS

Information regarding films that have sequels, sequels themselves or direct remakes of films can be found at the very end of each synopsis.

DUBBING AND SUBTITLES

We will generally point out in the synopsis when a foreign film is dubbed in English, mostly when the dubbing is poor. When voices are dubbed, particularly when singers render vocals on songs mimed by stars, we generally point out these facts either in the cast/role listing or inside the synopsis. If a film is in a foreign language and subtitled, we signify the fact in a parenthetical statement at the end of each entry (In Italian, English subtitles).

CREDITS

The credits for the creative and technical personnel of a film are extensive and they include: p (producer, often executive producer); d (director); w (screenwriter, followed by adaptation, if any, and creator of original story, if any, and other sources such as authors for plays, articles, short stories, novels and non-fiction books); ph (cinematographer, followed by camera system and color process when applicable, i.e., Panavision, Technicolor); m (composer of musical score); ed (film editor); md (music director); art d (art director); set d (set decoration); cos (costumes); spec eff (special effects); ch (choreography); m/l (music and lyrics); stunts, makeup, and other credits when merited. When someone receives two or more credits in a single film the credits may be combined (p&d, John Ford) or the last name repeated in subsequent credits shared with another (d, John Ford; w, Ford, Dudley Nichols).

GENRES/SUBJECT

Each film is categorized for easy identification as to genre and/or subject and themes at the left-hand bottom of each entry. (Western, Prison Drama, Spy Drama, Romance, Musical, Comedy, War, Horror, Science-Fiction, Adventure, Biography, Historical Drama, Children's Film, Animated Feature, etc.) More specific subject and theme breakdowns will be found in the Index (Vol. X).

PR AND MPAA RATINGS

The Parental Recommendation provides parents having no knowledge of the style and content of each film with a guide; if a film has excessive violence, sex, strong language, it is so indicated. Otherwise, films specifically designed for young children are also indicated. The Parental Recommendation (**PR**) is to be found at the right-hand bottom of each entry, followed, when applicable, by the **MPAA** rating. The PR ratings are as follows: **AAA** (must for children); **AA** (good for children); **A** (acceptable for children); **C** (cautionary, some objectionable scenes); **O** (completely objectionable for children).

KEY TO ABBREVIATIONS

Foreign Countries:

Arg.	Argentina
Aus.	Australia
Aust.	Austria
Bel.	Belgium
Braz.	Brazil
Brit.	Great Britain (GB when used for alternate title)
Can.	Canada
Chi.	China
Czech.	Czechoslovakia
Den.	Denmark
E. Ger.	East Germany
Fin.	Finland
Fr.	France
Ger.	Germany (includes W. Germany)
Gr.	Greece
Hung.	Hungary
Ital.	Italy
Jap.	Japan
Mex.	Mexico
Neth.	Netherlands
Phil.	Philippines
Pol.	Poland
Rum.	Rumania
S.K.	South Korea
Span.	Spain
Swed.	Sweden

Key to Abbreviations (continued)

Switz.	Switzerland
Thai.	Thailand
USSR	Union of Soviet Socialist Republics
Yugo.	Yugoslavia

Production Companies, Studios and Distributors (U.S. and British)

AA	ALLIED ARTISTS
ABF	Associated British Films
AE	Avco Embassy
AEX	Associated Exhibitors
AH	Anglo-Hollandia
AIP	American International Pictures
AM	American
ANCH	Anchor Film Distributors
ANE	American National Enterprises
AP	Associated Producers
AP&D	Associated Producers & Distributors
ARC	Associated Releasing Corp.
Argosy	Argosy Productions
Arrow	Arrow Films
ART	Artcraft
Astra	Astra Films
AY	Aywon
BA	British Actors
B&C	British and Colonial Kinematograph Co.
BAN	Banner Films
BI	British Instructional
BIFD	B.I.F.D. Films
BIP	British International Pictures
BJP	Buck Jones Productions
BL	British Lion
Blackpool	Blackpool Productions
BLUE	Bluebird
BN	British National
BNF	British and Foreign Film
Boulting	Boulting Brothers (Brit.)
BP	British Photoplay Production
BPP	B.P. Productions
BRIT	Britannia Films
BRO	Broadwest
Bryanston	Bryanston Films (Brit.)
BS	Blue Streak
BUS	Bushey (Brit.)
BUT	Butchers Film Service
BV	Buena Vista (Walt Disney)
CAP	Capital Films
CC	Christie Comedy
CD	Continental Distributing
CHAD	Chadwick Pictures Corporation
CHES	Chesterfield
Cineguild	Cineguild
CL	Clarendon
CLIN	Clinton
COL	COLUMBIA
Colony	Colony Pictures
COM	Commonwealth
COMM	Commodore Pictures
COS	Cosmopolitan (Hearst)
DE	Dependable Exchange
DGP	Dorothy Gish Productions
Disney	Walt Disney Productions
DIST	Distinctive
DM	DeMille Productions
DOUB	Doubleday
EAL	Ealing Studios (Brit.)
ECF	East Coast Films
ECL	Eclectic
ED	Eldorado
EF	Eagle Films
EFF & EFF	E.F.F. & E.F.F. Comedy
EFI	English Films Inc.
EIFC	Export and Import Film Corp.
EL	Eagle-Lion
EM	Embassy Pictures Corp.
EMI	EMI Productions
EP	Enterprise Pictures
EPC	Equity Pictures Corp.
EQ	Equitable
EXCEL	Excellent
FA	Fine Arts
FC	Film Classics
FD	First Division
FN	First National
FOX	20TH CENTURY FOX (and Fox Productions)
FP	Famous Players (and Famous Players Lasky)
FRP	Frontroom Productions
Gainsborough	Gainsborough Productions
GAU	Gaumont (Brit.)
GEN	General
GFD	General Films Distributors
Goldwyn	Samuel Goldwyn Productions
GN	Grand National
GOTH	Gotham
Grafton	Grafton Films (Brit.)
H	Harma
HAE	Harma Associated Distributors
Hammer	Hammer Films (Brit.)
HD	Hagen and Double
HM	Hi Mark
HR	Hal Roach
IA	International Artists
ID	Ideal
IF	Independent Film Distributors (Brit.)
Imperator	Imperator Films (Brit.)
IP	Independent Pictures Corp.
IN	Invincible Films
INSP	Inspirational Pictures (Richard Barthelmess)
IV	Ivan Film
Javelin	Javelin Film Productions (Brit.)
JUR	Jury
KC	Kinema Club
KCB	Kay C. Booking
Knightsbridge	Knightsbridge Productions (Brit.)
Korda	Alexander Korda Productions (Brit.)
Ladd	Ladd Company Productions
LAS	Lasky Productions (Jesse L. Lasky)
LFP	London Films
LIP	London Independent Producers
Lorimar	Lorimar Productions
LUM	Lumis
Majestic	Majestic Films
Mascot	Mascot Films
Mayflowers	Mayflowers Productions (Brit.)
Metro	Metro
MFC	Mission Film Corporation
MG	Metro-Goldwyn
MGM	METRO GOLDWYN-MAYER
MON	Monogram
MOR	Morante
MS	Mack Sennett
MUT	Mutual
N	National
NG	National General
NGP	National General Pictures (Alexander Korda, Brit.)
NW	New World
Orion	Orion Productions
Ortus	Ortus Productions (Brit.)
PAR	PARAMOUNT
Pascal	Gabriel Pascal Productions (Brit.)
PDC	Producers Distributors Corp.

Key to Abbreviations (continued)

PEER	Peerless
PWN	Peninsula Studios
PFC	Pacific Film Company
PG	Playgoers
PI	Pacific International
PIO	Pioneer Film Corp.
PM	Pall Mall
PP	Pro Patria
PRC	Producers Releasing Corporation
PRE	Preferred
QDC	Quality Distributing Corp.
RAY	Rayart
RAD	Radio Pictures
RANK	J. Arthur Rank (Brit.)
RBP	Rex Beach Pictures
REA	Real Art
REG	Regional Films
REN	Renown
REP	Republic
RF	Regal Films
RFD	R.F.D. Productions (Brit.)
RKO	RKO RADIO PICTURES
Rogell	Rogell
Romulus	Romulus Films (Brit.)
Royal	Royal
SB	Samuel Bronston
SCHUL	B.P. Schulberg Productions
SEL	Select
SELZ	Selznick International (David O. Selznick)
SF	Selznick Films
SL	Sol Lesser
SONO	Sonofilms
SP	Seven Pines Productions (Brit.)
SRP	St. Regis Pictures
STER	Sterling
STOLL	Stoll
SUN	Sunset
SYN	Syndicate Releasing Co.
SZ	Sam Zimbalist
TC	Two Cities (Brit.)
T/C	Trem-Carr
THI	Thomas H. Ince
TIF	Tiffany
TRA	Transatlantic Pictures
TRU	Truart
TS	Tiffany/Stahl
UA	UNITED ARTISTS
UNIV	UNIVERSAL (AND UNIVERSAL INTERNATIONAL)
Venture	Venture Distributors
VIT	Vitagraph
WAL	Waldorf
WB	WARNER BROTHERS (AND WARNER BROTHERS-SEVEN ARTS)
WEST	Westminster
WF	Woodfall Productions (Brit.)
WI	Wisteria
WORLD	World
WSHP	William S. Hart Productions
ZUKOR	Adolph Zukor Productions

Foreign

ABSF	AB Svensk Film Industries (Swed.)
Action	Action Films (Fr.)
ADP	Agnes Delahaie Productions (Fr.)
Agata	Agata Films (Span.)
Alter	Alter Films (Fr.)
Arch	Archway Film Distributors
Argos	Argos Films (Fr.)
Argui	Argui Films (Fr.)
Ariane	Les Films Ariane (Fr.)
Athos	Athos Films (Fr.)
Belga	Belga Films (Bel.)
Beta	Beta Films (Ger.)
CA	Cine-Alliance (Fr.)
Caddy	Caddy Films (Fr.)
CCFC	Compagnie Commerciale Francais Einematographique (Fr.)
CDD	Cino Del Duca (Ital.)
CEN	Les Films de Centaur (Fr.)
CFD	Czecheslovak Film Productions
CHAM	Champion (Ital.)
Cinegay	Cinegay Films (Ital.)
Cines	Cines Films (Ital.)
Cineriz	Cinerez Films (Ital.)
Citel	Citel Films (Switz.)
Como	Como Films (Fr.)
CON	Concordia (Fr.)
Corona	Corona Films (Fr.)
D	Documento Films (Ital.)
DD	Dino De Laurentiis (Ital.)
Dear	Dear Films (Ital.)
DIF	Discina International Films (Fr.)
DPR	Films du Palais-Royal (Fr.)
EX	Excelsa Films (Ital.)
FDP	Films du Pantheon (Fr.)
Fono	Fono Roma (Ital.)
FS	Filmsonor Productions (Fr.)
Gala	Fala Films (Ital.)
Galatea	Galatea Productions (Ital.)
Gamma	Gamma Films (Fr.)
Gemma	Gemma Cinematografica (Ital.)
GFD	General Film Distributors, Ltd. (Can.)
GP	General Productions (Fr.)
Gray	(Gray Films (Fr.)
IFD	Intercontinental Film Distributors
Janus	Janus Films (Ger.)
JMR	Macques Mage Releasing (Fr.)
LF	Les Louvre Films (Fr.)
LFM	Les Films Moliere (Fr.)
Lux	Lux Productions (Ital.)
Melville	Melville Productions (Fr.)
Midega	Midega Films (Span.)
NEF	N.E.F. La Nouvelle Edition Francaise (Fr.)
NFD	N.F.D. Productions (Ger.)
ONCIC	Office National pour le Commerce et L'Industrie Cinematographique (Fr.)
Ortus	Ortus Films (Can.)
PAC	Production Artistique Cinematographique (Fr.)
Pagnol	Marcel Pagnol Productions (Fr.)
Parc	Parc Films (Fr.)
Paris	Paris Films (Fr.)
Pathe	Pathe Films (Fr.)
PECF	Productions et Editions Cinematographique Francais (Fr.)
PF	Parafrench Releasing Co. (Fr.)
PIC	Produzione International Cinematografica (Ital.)
Ponti	Carlo Ponti Productions (Ital.)
RAC	Realisation d'Art Cinematographique (Fr.)
Regina	Regina Films (Fr.)
Renn	Renn Productions (Fr.)
SDFS	Societe des Films Sonores Tobis (Fr.)
SEDIF	Societe d'Exploitation ed de Distribution de Films (Fr.)
SFP	Societe Francais de Production (Fr.)
Sigma	Sigma Productions (Fr.)
SNE	Societe Nouvelle des Establishments (Fr.)
Titanus	Titanus Productions (Ital.)
TRC	Transcontinental Films (Fr.)
UDIF	U.D.I.F. Productions (Fr.)
UFA	Deutsche Universum-Film AG (Ger.)
UGC	Union Generale Cinematographique (Fr.)
Union	Union Films (Ger.)
Vera	Vera Productions (Fr.)

(NOTE: 1984 releases appear in this Volume)

W zero   (1974) 95m Bing Crosby Productions/Cinerama c (AKA: I WANT HER DEAD)

Twiggy [Leslie Hornby] (*Katie Lewis*), Michael Witney (*Ben Lewis*), Eugene Roche (*Charles Jasper*), Dirk Benedict (*William Caulder*), John Vernon (*Arnie Felson*), Michael Conrad (*Lt. Whitfield*), Alfred Ryder (*Investigator*), Carmen Zapata (*Betty*), Dave Morick (*Paul*), Ken Lynch (*Guard*), Peter Walker (*Prison Official*).

Twiggy, newly married to her real-life husband Witney, is the victim of a succession of near-fatal "accidents" always prefaced by the initial "W." That letter of the alphabet corresponds to the given name of first-husband Benedict, who is supposedly in prison, convicted of Twiggy's "murder." The amnesiac housewife, thought to be dead, has actually established a new identity. Her memory regained, she bug-eyes her way through the horrors of this slow-paced, ill-plotted picture in a manner which evokes little audience sympathy.

p, Mel Ferrer; d, Richard Quine; w, Gerald Di Pego, James Kelly (based on a story by Ronald Shusett, Kelly); ph, Jerry Hirschfeld (DeLuxe Color); m, Johnny Mandel; ed, Gene Milford; art d, Cary Odell.

Thriller   Cas.   (PR:C MPAA:PG)

W.C. FIELDS AND ME***   (1976) 111m UNIV c

Rod Steiger (*W.C. Fields*), Valerie Perrine (*Carlotta Monti*), John Marley (*Harry Bannerman*), Jack Cassidy (*John Barrymore*), Bernadette Peters (*Melody*), Dana Elcar (*Dockstedter*), Paul Stewart (*Florenz Ziegfeld*), Billy Barty (*Ludwig*), Allan Arbus (*Gregory La Cava*), Milt Kamen (*Dave Chasen*), Louis Zorich (*Gene Fowler*), Andrew Parks (*Claude*), Hank Rolike (*Leon*), Kenneth Tobey (*Parker*), Paul Mantee (*Edward*), Elizabeth Thompson (*Woman Patient*), Eddie Firestone (*Private Detective*), Linda Purl (*Ingenue*), Clay Tanner (*Assistant Director*), George Loros (*Schmidt*).

Though the great comedian would have hated this film, this movie biography of W.C. Fields has a certain appeal, thanks to Steiger's handling of the lead role. The story opens in 1924. Steiger is appearing in the Ziegfeld Follies, but Stewart (as Flo Ziegfeld) grows angry with the comedian's ribald humor. Steiger is hit with a double blow when his mistress, Peters, runs off with another man, and his broker ends up losing Steiger's life savings. With nothing to keep him in New York, Steiger talks his diminutive friend Barty into financing a trip for the two to California. After operating a wax museum in Santa Monica, Steiger is given a chance to appear in the movies. Soon he is a star comedian, as well as one of the film community's most notorious drinkers. At a party with friends John Barrymore (Cassidy), Gene Fowler (Zorich), Dave Chasen (Kamen), and an agent (Elcar), Steiger meets Perrine, a struggling actress. The inebriated group plays a joke on her, telling the eager Perrine that she is invited to Steiger's home to discuss a possible film role. Though Perrine knows this is a hoax, she goes to the comedian's home the next day. Steiger offers her a position as live-in secretary, which she accepts. She quickly becomes his confidant and sympathetic ear, but refuses to give up her dream of becoming an actress. Steiger arranges a screen test, with the agreement that Perrine will be told she is terrible. Producer Marley thinks she shows some talent, but Steiger threatens to quit Paramount studios if Perrine is encouraged. After returning from an alcoholic binge in Mexico, Steiger has a fight with Marley, and Perrine learns the truth. She angrily goes to New York, but returns to comfort Steiger when Cassidy suddenly passes away. Perrine pushes Steiger for marriage, but on the set of MY LITTLE CHICKADEE she learns the reason why he so stubbornly refuses. Visiting the set is Steiger's son, Parks, who tells the surprised Perrine about Steiger's past marriage that has never been legally dissolved. Though hurt, Perrine continues to stay with this exasperating personality as his heavy drinking continues to deteriorate his health. Steiger enters a hospital, and Perrine takes a room as well to be near him. Finally, after much physical pain, Steiger passes away on Christmas Day (ironically, a day Fields hated with a passion), 1946. Though Fields purists undoubtedly will be outraged with the many inaccuracies in the film, Steiger gives an intelligent performance as the bulbous-proboscised comedian. The makeup job certainly helps him look the part, but the key to Steiger's portrait is avoiding any imitation of Fields. Fields' voice arguably is one of the world's most often imitated (and usually with only passable results at best) but Steiger doesn't just mimic the comedian's vocal tones and inflections. Rather than ape Fields, Steiger creates his own interpretation of the man, capturing subtle nuances that create a better rounded character. Carlotta Monti, whose self-serving, ghost-written autobiography served as the film's basis, was given credit as technical consultant, and makes a cameo appearance as well, sitting near Cassidy when Perrine is first introduced. On the whole, the great man's admirers would be better advised to be in Philadelphia rather than watching this litany of misanthropy. Fields' talent– his art–was comedy, an element that is completely lacking in the picture. Two of the crony-characterization actors died shortly after the film's release: Milt Kamen from a heart attack, and Jack Cassidy (husband of actress Shirley Jones, father of actor- singer David Cassidy) in a fire in his home. This was the last picture show for both.

p, Jay Weston; d, Arthur Hiller; w, Bob Merrill (based on the book by Carlotta Monti with Cy Rice); ph, David M. Walsh (Panavision, Technicolor); m, Henry Mancini; ed, John C. Howard; prod d, Robert Boyle; set d, Arthur Jeph Parker; cos, Edith Head, Bill Jobe; spec eff, Albert Whitlock; makeup, Stan Winston.

Biography   (PR:C MPAA:PG)

W.I.A. (WOUNDED IN ACTION)*½   (1966) 87m Myriad bw

Steve Marlo (*Pvt. Joe Goodman*), Maura McGiveney (*Lt. Marietta Dodd*), Leopoldo Salcedo (*Maj. Armando De Leon*), Mary Humphrey (*Lt. Joan Marsh*), Albert Quinton (*Maj. Slater*), Victor Izay (*Sgt. Roman*), Bella Flores (*Carmen*), John Horn (*Cpl. Bliss*), Peter Deuel (*Pvt. Myers*), Joe Sison (*Sanchez*), Brennan Wood (*Capt. Ed Bill*), Romy Brion (*Ruther*).

A behind-the-scenes look at the goings-on in an Army hospital in the Philippines during WW II. This mostly takes the form of developing affairs between the wounded soldiers and the nurses, with occasional lapses into the tension-filled working routine. Some interest, but not enough to overcome the burdensome script, ineffective camera work, and inexperienced acting.

p, Irving Sunasky, Samuel Zerinsky; d&w, Sunasky; ph, Enrique Rogales; m, Leopold Silos; ed, Gregorio Caraballo.

War Drama   (PR:A MPAA:NR)

"W" PLAN, THE**   (1931, Brit.) 87m BIP/RKO bw

Brian Aherne (*Col. Duncan Grant*), Madeleine Carroll (*Rosa Hartmann*), Gordon Harker (*Pvt. Waller*), Gibb McLaughlin (*Pvt. McTavish*), George Merritt (*Ulrich Muller*), Mary Jerrold (*Frau Muller*), C. M. Hallard (*Commander-in-Chief*), Frederick Lloyd (*Col. Jervois*), Norah Howard (*Lady of the Town*), Milton Rosmer (*President of Court Martial*), Alfred Drayton (*Prosecution*), Charles Paton (*Defence*), Cameron Carr (*Otto Geddern*), Robert Harris (*Subaltern*), Clifford Heatherley (*Proprietor*), Wilhelm Koenig, Austin Trevor, B. Gregory, Arthur Hambling.

Gripping WW I yarn in which Aherne plays a British officer given the assignment of infiltrating the German ranks to destroy a Nazi plan to blow up various towns and villages within the British domain. Although action footage is poorly staged and the dialog is stiff, the picture retains interest through the tension and suspense of its plot. After the picture's release, Aherne made his first trip to the U.S. to star in a Broadway play.

p&d, Victor Saville; w, Saville, Miles Malleson, Frank Launder (based on the novel by Graham Seton); ph, Rene Guissart, F. A. Young, Werner Brandes; ed, P. MacLean Rogers.

War   (PR:A MPAA:NR)

W. W. AND THE DIXIE DANCEKINGS**½   (1975) 94m FOX c

Burt Reynolds (*W. W. Bright*), Conny Van Dyke (*Dixie*), Jerry Reed (*Wayne*), Ned Beatty (*Country Bull*), James Hampton (*Junior*), Don Williams (*Leroy*), Richard D. Hurst (*Butterball*), Art Carney (*Deacon Gore*), Sherman G. Lloyd (*Elton Bird*), Bill McCutcheon, Mel Tillis, Fred Stuthman (*Gas Station Attendants*), Furry Lewis (*Uncle Furry*), Mort Marshall (*Hester Tate*), Sherry Mathis (*June Ann*), Hal Needham (*Patrolman*), Nancy Andrews (*Rosie*), Peg Murray (*Della*), Tootsie (*Herself*).

In Nashville during the mid-1950s confidence man Reynolds has been getting even with a large oil company by robbing gas stations. A thief with heart, Reynolds always gives part of the take back to the underpaid attendants, his philosophy being that they are getting pennies while the oil companies are raking an absurd amount of money into their pockets. When pursuit gets too intense, in the form of Carney as a detective-evangelist preacher, Reynolds hooks up with a struggling country music band as manager. Through his manipulative abilities, Reynolds is able to land the band a gig at the Grand Ole Opry, himself going through a change due to his association with the band. Reynolds is perfect as the sweet-talking hustler who doesn't take himself or anything else very seriously, a highly likable individual. Also featured is a rare performance by the ancient blues singer Furry Lewis. Van Dyke is charming in her screen debut.

p, Stanley S. Canter; d, John G. Avildsen; w, Thomas Rickman; ph, James Crabe (DeLuxe Color); m, David Grusin; ed, Richard Halsey, Robbe Roberts; prod d, Larry Paull; set d, Jim Berkey; spec eff, Milt Rice; Stunts, Hal Needham.

Comedy   (PR:A MPAA:PG)

WABASH AVENUE***½ (1950) 92m FOX c

Betty Grable (Ruby Summers), Victor Mature (Andy Clark), Phil Harris (Uncle Mike), Reginald Gardiner (English Eddie), James Barton (Hogan), Barry Kelley (Bouncer), Margaret Hamilton (Tillie Hutch), Jacqueline Dalya (Cleo), Robin Raymond (Jennie), Hal K. Dawson (Healy), Irving Bacon (Harlan), Marie Bryant (Elsa), Colette Lyons (Beulah), Charles Arnt (Carter), Walter Long, Billy Daniel (Dancers), Marion Marshall (Chorus Girl), Percy Helton (Ship's Captain), Dorothy Neumann (Reformer), Alexander Pope (Charlie), Henry Kulky (Joe), Dick Crockett (Bartender), John "Skins" Miller (Drunk), Harold Cornsweet (Bartender), George Beranger (Wax Museum Attendant), David Clarke (Workman), Paul "Tiny" Newlan (Bouncer), Ruby Dale Hearn, Barbara A. Pellegrino (Tumbling Act), Michael Ross, Mickey Simpson (Policemen), Douglas Carter (Ferris Wheel Operator), Claire Carleton (Tessie), Bill Phillips (Attendant), Peggy Leon (Hairdresser), Dick Wessel (Electrician).

Grable had such success with her film CONEY ISLAND (1943) that she was cast in virtually the same plot, remade with a Chicago setting, during the 1893 Columbian Exposition. She's a singer and dancer, employed at a Wabash Avenue casino (hence the title). Harris is the casino's owner, who wants Grable to keep working there, though she aspires to bigger things. Mature is a producer and pal of Harris. The two have a friendly rivalry going, and this is compounded by Mature falling for Harris' singing-and-dancing star. Mature wants to bring her to New York and put her into an important show, but Harris will stop at nothing to keep her. Through some cons and tricks, things get a little sticky, but of course love wins out in the end. Though the plot is better suited to a 1940s musical, this certainly has its moments of charm, and Grable at the age of 34 shows she can still dance up a storm. Harris and Mature have a good-natured chemistry, and while the story may be slight, this is a highly enjoyable musical. Plenty of good musical numbers here, including:"I Wish I Could Shimmy Like My Sister Kate" (Armand J. Piron, Peter Bocage), "Walking Along with Billy," "Baby Won't You Say You Love Me," "Wilhelmina," "May I Tempt You with a Big Red Rosy Apple?" "Clean Up Chicago," "Down on Wabash Avenue" (Mack Gordon, Josef Myrow), "I've Been Floating Down the Old Green River" (Bert Kalmar, Joe Cooper), "I Remember You" (Victor Schertzinger, Johnny Mercer), and a dozen or so other oldies.

p, William Perlberg; d, Henry Koster; w, Harry Tugend, Charles Lederer; ph, Arthur E. Arling (Technicolor); ed, Robert Simpson; md, Lionel Newman; art d, Lyle Wheeler, Joseph C. Wright; ch, Billy Daniel.

Musical   (PR:A MPAA:NR)

WAC FROM WALLA WALLA, THE** (1952) 83m REP bw (GB: ARMY CAPERS)

Judy Canova (Judy), Stephen Dunne (Lt. Tom Mayfield), George Cleveland (Gramps Canova), June Vincent (Doris Vail), Irene Ryan (Sgt. Kearns), Roy Barcroft (Mr. Prentiss), Allen Jenkins (Mr. Redington), George Chandler (Jud Canova), Elizabeth Slifer (Betty Mayfield), Thurston Hall (Col. Mayfield), Sarah Spencer (Recruiting Sergeant), Dick Wessel (Sgt. Malone), Pattee Chapman (Lizzie), Republic Rhythm Riders (Themselves), Dick Elliott (Sheriff), Carl Switzer (Pvt. Cronkheit), Tom Powers (General), Jarma Lewis, Emlen Davies, Virginia Carroll (Specialists), Evelynne Smith (Judo Instructor), Phyllis Kennedy (WAC Technical Sergeant).

Lifeless Canova vehicle in which the popular hillbilly comedienne accidentally enlists in the Army. Not to let down the long line of soldiers in her family, she proves capable of toting the uniform after foiling the attempts of Barcroft and Jenkins to make off with top-secret plans on guided missiles. Not very funny. Songs include: "Lovey," "If Only Dreams Came True," "Boy, Oh Boy," "Song of the Women's Army Corps."

p, Sidney Picker; d, William Witney; w, Arthur T. Horman; ph, Jack Marta; m, R. Dale Butts; ed, Tony Martinelli; art d, Fred A. Ritter; set d, John McCarthy, Jr., James Redd; spec eff, Howard and Theodore Lydecker; m/l, Jack Elliott, Harold Spina.

Comedy   (PR:A MPAA:NR)

WACKIEST SHIP IN THE ARMY, THE**½ (1961) 99m COL c

Jack Lemmon (Lt. Rip Crandall), Ricky Nelson (Ens. Tommy Hanson), John Lund (Comdr. Vandewater), Chips Rafferty (Patterson), Tom Tully (Capt. McClung), Joby Baker (Josh Davidson), Warren Berlinger (Sparks), Patricia Driscoll (Maggie), Mike Kellin (Chief Mate MacCarthy), Richard Anderson (Lt. Foster), Alvy Moore (Johnson), Joe Gallison (Cameo), Teru Shimada (Maj. Samada), George Shibata (Capt. Shigetsu), Richard Torrence (Horse), Naaman Brown (Goroka).

During WW II, Lemmon is given the command of a broken-down ship called the Echo which has a crew as adept at making a vessel seaworthy as a penguin is at flying. They are given the mission of escorting an Australian through Japanese-occupied waters, including minefields, to get him to a point where he can witness enemy craft movement. This slight premise was an excuse to exploit the comic genius of Lemmon; here placed in a seemingly hopeless situation (as in so many of his more successful roles), he goes through his chores with a look of exasperation and confusion, his boundless energy lifting this picture out of total tedium to create mild entertainment. Without Lemmon there would have been no chance of creating any type of

picture with this predictable material and the other performers can only feed off their star. Lemmon had wanted to do this picture since 1959, but the production had been delayed as a result of conflicting schedules. His widely successful THE APARTMENT was released in the interim, and completely overshadowed this little effort. Nelson, in the role of the inept ensign, gets a chance to sing "Do You Know What It Means to Miss New Orleans" (Louis Alter, Eddie De Lange), which was originally introduced--sung by Billie Holiday--in the film NEW ORLEANS (1947). The film later served as the source of a short-lived TV series.

p, Fred Kohlmar; d, Richard Murphy; w, Murphy, Herbert Margolis, William Raynor (based on a story by Herbert Carlson); ph, Charles Lawton, Jr. (CinemaScope, Eastmancolor); m, George Duning; ed, Charles Nelson; art d, Carl Anderson.

Comedy   **Cas.**   (PR:A MPAA:NR)

WACKIEST WAGON TRAIN IN THE WEST, THE*½ (1976) 86m Topar c

Bob Denver, Forrest Tucker, Jeannine Riley, Lori Saunders, Ivor Francis, Lynn Wood, Bill Cort.

On the western trail, a wagon train of seven people goes through a series of "zany" adventures. The group includes wagonmaster Tucker and bumbling sidekick Denver; rich Bostonian Francis and his wife, Wood; Riley, a would-be showgirl; teacher Saunders; and bachelor Cort in a big-screen version of a minor television sit-com called "Dusty's Trail." The premise will be even more familiar to fans of the ridiculous TV sit-com "Gilligan's Island." That one featured seven similar castaways on a deserted island. The Schwartzes, who had an overseeing hand in this production, also produced those television programs, as well as the WASP nightmare, "The Brady Bunch." Only television cultists might find anything worth watching here.

p, Elroy Schwartz; d, (uncredited); w, Elroy Schwartz, Sherwood Schwartz, Brad Radnitz, Howard Ostroff, Sherwood Friedman.

Comedy/Western   **Cas.**   (PR:A MPAA:G)

WACKO zero (1983) 84m Jensen Farley c

Joe Don Baker (Harbinger), Stella Stevens (Marg Graves), George Kennedy (Dr. Graves), Julia Duffy (Mary Graves), Scott McGinnis (Norman), Andrew Clay (Tony), Elizabeth Daily (Bambi), Michele Tobin (Rosie), Anthony James (Zeke), David Drucker (Looney), Sonny Davis (Weirdo), Victor Brandt (Dr. Moreau), Jeff Altman (Harry), Charles Napier (Patrick), Wil Albert (Dr. Denton), Michael Lee Gogin (Damien).

Everything conceivable was thrown into this spoof on teenage slasher horror films, starting with a weird rendition of the Norman Bates of PSYCHO, through CARRIE, and ending with gags from more modern pictures that have been filling the market ad nauseam. There's even a football game between the Hitchcock Birds and the De Palma Knives. It attempts to be clever but is just a rehash of gags with nothing to bond them together. The joke is carried on much too long.

p&d, Greydon Clark; w, Dana Olsen, Michael Spound, M. James Kauf, Jr., David Greenwalt; ph, Nicholas von Sternberg; m, Arthur Kempel; ed, Earl Watson, Curtis Burch; art d, Chester Kaczenski, Jay Burkhart; spec eff, Joe Quinlavin, Dana Rheaume; makeup, Allan Apone, Kenny Myers.

Comedy   **Cas.**   (PR:C MPAA:PG/R)

WACKY WORLD OF DR. MORGUS, THE* (1962) 83m Calongne-Sevin

Sid Noel [Noel Rideau] (Dr. Alexander Morgus), Dana Barton (Pencils McCane), Jeanne Teslof (Mona Speckla), David Kleinberger (Bruno), Thomas George (Chopsley), Bob Nelson, Marshall Pearce, Chris Owens, Wayne Mack.

Silly cheapie independent in which Noel plays a mad scientist who comes up with an invention that breaks down a person's molecular structure and then revives it. The thing gets into the wrong hands and is used to position anti-American spies. Dumb! Star Noel hosted a TV horror-picture show in New Orleans, where many scenes were filmed. Made by the director of the forgettable OKEFENOKEE.

p, Eugene T. Calongne, Jules Sevin; d, Roul Haig; w, Noel and Roul Haig; m, Corelli Jacobs.

Horror   (PR:A MPAA:NR)

WACKY WORLD OF MOTHER GOOSE, THE,**½ (1967) 81m Videocraft/EM c

Voice of Margaret Rutherford (Mother Goose).

A combination of secret agents and well-known storybook characters from Sleeping Beauty to Tom Thumb are dished up in this animated children's feature. The adventures in Never-Never-Land are definitely aimed for a juvenile audience or the child in us all. Passable for its type, but no great shakes.

p, Arthur Rankin, Jr.; d, Jules Bass; w, Romeo Muller (based on characters created by Charles Perrault in the book *Mother Goose Tales*); ph, (Pathe Color); m/l, George Wilkins, Bass.

Animation/Children's   **Cas.**   **(PR:AAA MPAA:NR)**

WACO**½   (1952) 68m Silvermine/MON bw (GB: THE OUTLAW AND THE LADY)

Wild Bill Elliott (*Matt Boone*), I. Stanford Jolley (*Curly Ivers*), Pamela Blake (*Kathy Clark*), Paul Fierro (*Lou Garcia*), Rand Brooks (*Al*), Richard Avonde (*Pedro*), Pierce Lyden (*Farley*), Lane Bradford (*Wallace*), Terry Frost (*Richards*), Stanley Price (*Sheriff of Waco*), Stanley Andrews (*Judge*), Michael Whalen (*Barnes*), Ray Bennett (*Bull Clark*), Rory Mallinson (*Crawford*), Richard Paxton (*Ace Logan*), Russ Whiteman (*Sheriff of Pecos*), House Peters, Jr (*Doctor*), Ray Jones, Edward Cassidy.

Unusual series western starring Elliott as a tough-talking, hard-drinking outlaw who is hired by the people of Waco to clean up their town. He does so in short order and is given the sheriff's job permanently. While the action is fairly routine, the fact that the *hero* is seen drinking and swearing is quite a departure from the average oater. Release prints were sepia-toned.

p, Vincent M. Fennelly; d, Lewis Collins; w, Dan Ullman; ph, Ernest Miller; m, Raoul Kraushaar; ed, Sam Fields; art d, Martin Obzina.

Western   **(PR:A MPAA:NR)**

WACO**   (1966) 85m A.C. Lyles/PAR c

Howard Keel (*Waco*), Jane Russell (*Jill Stone*), Brian Donlevy (*Ace Ross*), Wendell Corey (*Preacher Sam Stone*), Terry Moore (*Dolly*), John Smith (*Joe Gore*), John Agar (*George Gates*), Gene Evans (*Deputy Sheriff O'Neill*), Richard Arlen (*Sheriff Billy Kelly*), Ben Cooper (*Scotty Moore*), Tracy Olsen (*Patricia West*), De Forest Kelley (*Bill Rile*), Anne Seymour (*Ma Jenner*), Robert Lowery (*Mayor Ned West*), Willard Parker (*Pete Jenner*), Jeff Richards (*Kallen*), Reg Parton (*Ike Jenner*), Fuzzy Knight (*Telegraph Operator*), Russ McCubbin, Dan White, Red Morgan, King Johnson, Barbara Latell.

Tired of living under the thumb of a gang of crooks, the people of Emporia, Wyoming, hire mercenary ex-convict Keel to come and drive the bad guys out. When he arrives he is surprised to find that his former flame, Russell, is now married to a preacher, Corey. There is some romantic tension between the two former lovers, but Keel avoids a rendevous. Seeing that cleaning up the town will be a bigger job than he anticipated, Keel sends for his former riding buddy, Donlevy, a black-clad gunslinger, to help out. Eventually Keel wipes out the killers in a big showdown which sees Corey shot dead while trying to stop the violence. An interesting pairing of absorbingpairs in the two female leads, Russell and Moore, both busty one-time proteges of Howard Hughes.

p, A. C. Lyles; d, R. G. Springsteen; w, Steve Fisher (based on the novel *Emporia* by Harry Sanford, Max Lamb); ph, Robert Pittack (Techniscope, Technicolor); m, Jimmie Haskell; ed, Bernard Matis; art d, Hal Pereira, Al Roelofs; set d, Robert R. Benton, Chuck Pierce; cos, Edith Head; m/l, Hal Blair Haskell (sung by Lorne Greene).

Western   **(PR:C MPAA:NR)**

WAGA KOI WAGA UTA   (SEE: SONG FROM MY HEART, THE, 1970, Jap.)

WAGES OF FEAR, THE****   (1955, Fr./Ital.) 140m Filmsonor-CICC-Vera-Fono Roma/Int ernational Affiliates bw (LE SA-LAIRE DE LA PEUR)

Yves Montand (*Mario*), Charles Vanel (*Jo*), Vera Clouzot (*Linda*), Folco Lulli (*Luigi*), Peter Van Eyck (*Bimba*), William Tubbs (*Bill O'Brien*), Dario Moreno (*Hernandez*), Jo Dest (*Smerloff*), Centa (*Camp Chief*), Luis de Lima (*Bernardo*), Jeronimo Mitchell (*Dick*).

In the sweaty, dusty Central American village of Las Piedras, poverty is seen wherever one looks. The men bake in the hot sun while the women tend to chores, and half-naked children play in the muddy, unpaved streets. The town is controlled by an oil firm–Southern Oil Company (SOC)–whose concerns lie with making a profit at the expense of the villagers' safety. However, a job with SOC is still valued by those who feel the wages are worth the danger. Three hundred miles from Las Piedras a well-fire burns out of control. The firm's callous American boss, Tubbs, puts out a call for drivers willing to haul a load of highly volatile nitroglycerine across the long stretch of trecherous terrain. The wages for this suicidal mission–$2,000, just enough to buy them a ticket out of the Latin American hellhole which traps them. In order to improve his odds of success, Tubbs plans to send two trucks, expecting that only one will survive the trek. After testing their skills behind the wheel, Tubbs chooses his men–Montand, a French-raised Corsican; Lulli, his husky Italian roommate; Van Eyck, a cold and egostistical German; and Dest. Vanel, a fugitive French gangster with a dangerous veneer, is overlooked, much to the dismay of Montand, who has come to respect his fearlessness. Although Tubbs has respect for Vanel, he explains that he is too old for the job. As the men prepare for their odyssey,

they notice that Dest has not yet arrived. Conveniently, and rather suspiciously, Vanel arrives under the pretense that he is bidding his friends farewell. Since Dest seems to have vanished, Vanel is given the job. After the nitro is loaded on board, the trucks (which have been modified to handle the shock, but are still highly unsafe) depart. With a half-hour safety distance separating them, Montand and Vanel lead the way, and Van Eyck and Lulli follow. Vanel is behind the wheel of the truck, which creeps along at an overly cautious snail's pace. Although he previously appeared to possess nerves of steel, Vanel is stricken with fear and tries to pass it off as a case of malaria. Before long, Van Eyck has closed the gap between the trucks and has opted to assume the lead spot. Their first harrowing obstacle occurs at the edge of a mountain road. In order to make a turn, the trucks have to back onto a rickety wooden support suspended over a deep ravine. Van Eyck's lighter truck completes the turn with little trouble. Montand, is now steering the much larger rig. As he backs onto the support, boards creek beneath his wheels. He backs up too far and knocks Vanel over the edge. Thinking he has killed his partner, Montand searches below only to find Vanel scurrying away like a frightened rabbit. As he tries to drive back onto the road, Montand is unable to prevent the tires from sliding about on the oily surface of the support. He succeeds but barely escapes death when the wooden structure completely gives way just as his tires reach safety. Disillusioned with Vanel, Montand considers abandoning him but decides to give him a second chance. The next obstacle is a giant boulder which has blocked the road. Since the rock is far too large to move, Van Eyck decides to use the only effective tool he has at hand–the nitroglycerine. After ingeniously devising a relatively safe method of exploding the rock, the trucks are again on their way. In the meantime, Vanel has again taken off in a fit of cowardice. Montand chases him down and mercilessly beats him, ordering him to continue as his partner. Their destination is not far off and once more the safety gap separates the trucks. Suddenly, in the distance, Montand and Vanel see the lead truck destroyed in a thunderous explosion. When they finally reach the sight they find that a crater caused by the explosion has filled with oil from a busted pipeline. Vanel, chest-deep in the oil, bravely guides Montand and the truck through. While trying to move a tree branch, Vanel gets entangled in the path of the truck. Unable to stop, Montand runs over his partner's leg. With the help of a winch, the truck makes it through. Montand loads the dying Vanel into the vehicle and continues the final leg of his journey, He arrives at the well-fire, but only after Vanel has succumbed to the pain. As Montand receives his payment, word travels back to Las Piedras that he has survived. A cafe full of his friends bursts into a joyful dance. Overcome with the exhilaration of his success, Montand jubilantly drives home along the mountain road. On his dashboard sits his lucky Metro ticket. Montand, however, loses control of the truck and it plunges over the edge. A superb suspenser which eats at one's nerves during the entire last half, WAGES OF FEAR can almost be thought of as two movies. While the final portion is devoted to the safe passage of the trucks and is dependent on visuals, the beginning half spends its time building characters and an atmosphere. It is this detailing of man's human nature which proved essential to the film's success. From the opening shot–four frantic beetles which have been strung together by a mischievous child–it is clear that the four characters are prisoners of Las Piedras. The wages they are paid amount to $2,000 apiece, which in turn can buy them their freedom. Their freedom, it turns out, is not easily attained. Three of the four die in the process (although Lulli is convinced that death is better than another day in the village). For Montand to succeed he must trudge through the oil (not unlike the "underworld" of so many myths) to emerge a free man. Unable to handle this freedom, Montand is driven to his death in the very truck he so carefully maneuvered before. Employing each of the character's native tongues (the film, primarily in French, is subtitled), director Clouzot had an epic on his hands with the possibility of internation-al success. Commenting on his own film, Clouzot said, "A significant setting, complex human material, and the gripping accessory of a truck loaded with nitroglycerin allowed me to develop not the picturesque story, but the epic qualities; yes, this is an epic whose main theme is courage. And the opposite." This masterful success was awarded with Best Picture honors at both the 1953 Cannes Film Festival and the British Academy Awards. Cannes also awarded Vanel a Best Actor prize. Although the film had a positive critical reception in England and the U.S., it was cut severely. Its Cannes showing ran 155 minutes, but by the time it reached American shores it had been whittled away to 106 minutes losing much of the first half. It was finally restored to a 140-minute version in 1967. In 1977, director William Friedkin (THE FRENCH CONNECTION; THE EXORCIST) brought a remake to the screen, SORCERER, which added nothing except a harrowing finale across a swaying rope bridge.

p&d, Henri G. Clouzot; w, Clouzot, Jerome Geronimi (based on the novel by Georges Arnaud); ph, Armand Thirard; m, Georges Auric; ed, Henri Rust, Madeleine Gug, Etiennette Muse; prod d, Rene Renoux; md, Auric.

Adventure/Drama   **Cas.**   **(PR:O MPAA:NR)**

WAGES OF FEAR, 1977   (SEE: SORCERER, 1977)

WAGNER***   (1983, Brit./Hung./Aust.) 540m London Trust Cultural/Alan Landsburg c

Richard Burton (*Richard Wagner*), Vanessa Redgrave (*Cosima Wagner*), Gemma Craven (*Minna*), Laszlo Galffi (*King Ludwig II of Bavaria*), John

Gielgud (*Pfistermeister*), Ralph Richardson (*Pfordten*), Laurence Olivier (*Pfeufer*), Ekkerhard Schall (*Franz Liszt*), Ronald Pickup (*Friedrich Nietzsche*), Miguel Herz-Kestranek (*Hans von Bulow*), Richard Pasco (*Otto Wesendonck*), Marthe Keller (*Mathilde Wesendonck*), Gwyneth Jones (*Malvina von Carolsfeld*), Peter Hoffmann (*Schnorr von Carolsfeld*), Franco Nero (*Crespi*), Joan Greenwood (*Frau Dangl*), William Walton (*Friedrich August II*), Corin Redgrave (*Dr. Pusinelli*), Barbara Leigh-Hunt (*Queen Mother*), Joan Plowright (*Mrs. Taylor*), Christopher Gable (*Peter Cornelius*), Cyril Cusack (*Sulzer*), Patrick Rollin (*Eugene Laussot*), Liza Goddard (*Jessie Laussot*), Sigfrit Steiner (*King Ludwig I*), Bill Fraser (*Mayor of Bayreuth*), Arthur Lowe (*Meser*), Vernon Dobtcheff (*Giacomo Meyerbeer*), Jean Luc Moreau (*Petipa*), Bernadette Schneider (*Judith Gautier*), Prunella Scales (*Frau Pollert*), Daphne Wagner (*Princess Metternich*), Matyas Usztics (*Franz*), Andrew Cruickshank (*Minister Bar*), Stephen Oliver (*Richter*), Niall Toibin (*Lutz*), Gabriel Byrne (*Karl Ritter*), Stephan Paryla (*Rockel*), John Shrapnel (*Semper*), Arthur Denberg (*Paul Taxis*), Manfred Jung (*Unger*), Jess Thomas (*Albert Niemann*), Adele Leigh-Enderl (*Frau Heim*), Edith Rujsz (*Natalie*), Laszlo Horvath (*Dr. Hanslick*), Brook Williams (*Joukowsky*).

An epic film biography in every sense of the term. Director Palmer became interested in filming the life of the German composer Richard Wagner in 1974 and after seven years was able to begin production. The resulting work took two years to complete, with a running time of nine hours, making this one of the longest works in cinema history. The film begins with Wagner's death in 1883. In flashback, every major event in the composer's life is chronicled, from the writing of his operas to personal episodes in Wagner's relations with those surrounding him. Burton in the lead and Redgrave as his wife give life to their parts despite the seemingly overwhelming task of playing such austere roles over the course of nine hours. The film itself is handsome to look at with an authentic air that is complemented by some 2,000 separate costumes and 200 different locations. Wagner's music is conducted by Sir Georg Solti, the internationally renowned conductor. The term "Wagnerian" has come to mean anything long and grandiose, something this biography certainly is. Consequently, it may have a difficult time maintaining the interest of anyone other than those who have little trouble sitting through the composer's "Ring" operas. Other versions, including one of 208 minutes and one of 300 minutes, also exist but understandably don't have the same feeling. A fine cast of supporting players including Olivier, Richardson, and Gielgud adds to the proceedings, as does the marvelous photography by Storaro. Though the film certainly has a limited audience, those with an interest in the man and his music might find this well worth their time.

p, Alan Wright: d, Tony Palmer; w, Charles Wood; ph, Vittorio Storaro; m, Richard Wagner; ed, Graham Bunn; prod d, Kenneth Carey; art d, Terry Pritchard, Andras Langmar; cos, Shirley Russell.

Biography   **Cas.**   **(PR:C-O MPAA:NR)**

WAGON MASTER, THE*½   (1929) 70m UNIV bw

Ken Maynard (*The Rambler*), Edith Roberts (*Sue Smith*), Tom Santschi (*Jake Lynch*), Jack Hanlon (*Billie Hollister*), Al Ferguson (*Jacques Frazalle*), Bobby Dunn (*Buckeye Pete*), Frank Rice (*Grasshopper*), Frederick Dana (*Bill Hollister*), Whitehorse (*Stuttering Sam*).

The first Maynard talkie makes great use of the new audio medium by emphasizing every possible sound effect from hand-clapping to villain Santschi's whip-snapping. With a vocal chorus behind him, Maynard plays both guitar and violin. Maynard plays a guide hired to take a wagon of miners to their future work site. Santschi is the whip-toting bad guy out to stop the miners at all costs. Exciting footage of the wagon train thundering over the desert was re-used several times in other films including MYSTERY MOUNTAIN (1934) and THE MIRACLE RIDER (1935).

P, Ken Maynard; d, Harry Joe Brown; w, Marion Jackson, Lesley Mason; ph, Ted McCord; ed, Fred Allen.

Western   **(PR:A MPAA:NR)**

WAGON TEAM*½   (1952) 61m COL bw

Gene Autry (*Gene Autry*), Pat Buttram (*Pat Buttram*), Gail Davis (*Connie Weldon*), Dick Jones (*Dave Weldon*), Gordon Jones (*U.S. Marshal Taplan*), Harry Harvey ("*Doc*" *Weldon*), Henry Rowland (*Mike McClure*), George J. Lewis (*Carlos de La Torre*), John Cason (*Sim*), Fred S. Martin (*Fred Cass*), Bert Dodson (*Bert Cass*), Jerry Scoggins (*Jerry Cass*), Gregg Barton (*Gandy*), Pierce Lyden (*Mangrum*), Carlo Tricoli (*Dr. Kunody*), Syd Saylor, Sandy Sanders, Champion, Jr, the Horse.

Pretty slow Autry oater which sees Gene as a special stagecoach agent who goes under cover posing as a medicine-show singer so that he can get the goods on a gang of crooks who have hijacked an Army payroll. Eventually, the crooks make a costly mistake, enabling Autry to bring them in. One of six Autry oaters released by the studio in 1952.

p, Armand Schaefer; d, George Archainbaud; w, Gerald Geraghty; ph, William Bradford; ed, James Sweeney; md, Mischa Bakaleinikoff; art d, Charles Clague; set d, James Crowe.

Western   **(PR:A MPAA:NR)**

WAGON TRACKS WEST*½   (1943) 55m REP bw

Wild Bill Elliott (*Wild Bill Elliott*), George "Gabby" Hayes (*Gabby Whittaker*), Tom Tyler (*Clawtooth*), Anne Jeffreys (*Moonbush*), Rick Vallin (*Fleetwing*), Robert Frazer (*Robert Warren*), Roy Barcroft (*Laird*), Charles Miller (*Brown Bear*), Tom London (*Lem Martin*), Cliff Lyons (*Matt*), Jack Rockwell (*Sheriff Summers*), Kenne Duncan, Minerva Urecal, Hal Price, William Nestell, Frank Ellis, Hank Bell, Jack O'Shea, Ray Jones, Jack Ingram, Curley Dresden, Frank McCarroll, Marshall Reed, Ben Corbett, Jack Montgomery, Tom Steele, J. W. Cody, Roy Butler.

Elliott, Hayes, and their pal Vallin (an educated Indian who has returned to the reservation after attending medical school back East) team up to rid the friendly redskins of crooked Indian agent Frazer and bogus medicine man Tyler. Tyler and Frazer are in cahoots with rancher Barcroft and his men, who have been digging an illegal irrigation project which has polluted the Indians' drinking water.

p, Louis Gray; d, Howard Bretherton; w, William Lively; ph, Reggie Lanning; m, Mort Glickman; ed, Charles Craft; art d, Russell Kimball.

Western   **(PR:A MPAA:NR)**

WAGON TRAIL**½   (1935) 55m Ajax bw

Harry Carey (*Sheriff Hartley*), Gertrude Messinger (*Joan Collins*), Ed Norris (*Hartley, Jr.*), Earl Dwire (*Bob Collins*), Roger Williams (*Deputy Sheriff*), Chuck Morrison (*Collins' Henchman*), Chief Thundercloud, John Elliott, Roger Williams, Dick Botiller, Lew Meehan, Francis Walker, Silver Tip Baker, Allen Greer.

Carey plays a noble sheriff who is unjustly fired after his son, who was sent to prison and sentenced to death after a stagecoach robbery, breaks out of jail and disappears. The townsfolk assume Carey must have had something to do with the escape, so they relieve him of his duties. In his place, the citizens install Dwire as sheriff. Unfortunately, Dwire is a gambler and–secretly–the outlaw chief responsible for the stagecoach robbery. Eventually Carey returns to the town, exposes the crook, clears his son's name, and reassumes his job as sheriff. Dwire shoots himself rather than face a lynch mob.

p, William Berke; d, Harry Fraser; w, Monroe Talbot; ph, Robert Cline; ed, Arthur A. Brooks.

Western   **(PR:A MPAA:NR)**

WAGON TRAIN*   (1940) 62m RKO bw

Tim Holt, Ray Whitley, Emmett Lynn, Martha O'Driscoll, Bud McTaggart, Cliff Clark, Ellen Lowe, Wade Crosby, Ethan Laidlaw, Monte Montague, Carl Stockdale, Bruce Dane, Glenn Strange.

Seeking a cheap replacement for oater star George O'Brien, who hung up his spurs at RKO upon completion of TRIPLE JUSTICE (1940), the studio decided to put young Tim Holt in the saddle. Perhaps because they were unsure of their new star, RKO moguls barely spent a dime on the production, and it shows. Holt plays the leader of a supply train that delivers essential provisions to outlying settlements. The job isn't easy as Holt must fight off constant Indian attacks, but he does find time to uncover his father's killer and rescue O'Driscoll from the clutches of the evil man's son. Songs, mostly delivered off-camera by Ray Whitley, include: "Wagon Train," "A Girl Just Like You," "Why Shore," "Farewell" (Ray Whitley, Fred Rose).

p, Bert Gilroy; d, Edward Killy; w, Morton Grant (based on a story by Bernard McConville); ph, Harry Wild; m, Paul Sawtell; ed, Frederic Knudtson, Harry Marker; art d, Van Nest Polglase.

Western   **(PR:A MPAA:NR)**

WAGON TRAIN, 1952   (SEE: WAGON TEAM, 1952)

WAGON WHEELS**   (1934) 56m PAR bw (AKA: CARAVANS WEST)

Randolph Scott (*Clint Belmet*), Gail Patrick (*Nancy Wellington*), Billy Lee (*Sonny Wellington*), Leila Bennett (*Hetty Masters*), Jan Duggan (*Abby Masters*), Monte Blue (*Murdock*), Raymond Hatton (*Jim Burch*), Olin Howland (*Bill O'Meary*), J. P. McGowan (*Couch*), James Marcus (*Jed*), Helen Hunt (*Mrs. Jed*), James B. "Pop" Kenton (*Masters*), Alfred Del Cambre (*Ebe*), John Marston (*Orator*), Sam McDaniel (*Black Coachman*), Howard Wilson (*Permit Officer*), Michael S. Visaroff (*Russian*), Julian Madison (*Lester*), Eldred Tidbury (*Chauncey*), E. Alyn Warren (*The Factor*), Fern Emmett (*Settler*), Clara Lou [Ann] Sheridan (*Extra*), Lew Meehan (*Listener*), Harold Goodwin (*Nancy's Brother*), Pauline Moore.

Unused footage from Gary Cooper's FIGHTING CARAVANS (1931) was put to good use in this remake of the same Zane Grey novel. Scott stars as the leader of a wagon train of settlers out to homestead the state of Oregon. Blue plays an evildoer out to stop the wagon train who is employed by fur traders who don't want the settlers invading their territory. To ensure that progress is halted, Blue stirs up trouble with the Indians and sends them out to attack the pioneers. Eventually all the obstacles are surmounted and the settlers make it to Oregon.

p, Harold Hurley; d, Charles Barton; w, Jack Cunningham, Charles Logue, Carl A. Buss (based on the novel *Fighting Caravans* by Zane Grey); ph, William C. Mellor; ed, Jack Dennis; art d, Earl Hedrick; m/l, "Wagon Wheels," Billy Hill.

Western   (PR:A   MPAA:NR)

WAGON WHEELS WESTWARD**   (1956) 56m REP bw

"Wild Bill" Elliott *(Red Ryder)*, Bobby [Robert] Blake *(Little Beaver)*, Alice Fleming, Linda Stirling, Roy Barcroft, Emmett Lynn, Jay Kirby, Dick Curtis, George J. Lewis, Bud Geary, Tom London, Kenne Duncan, George Chesebro, Tom Chatterton, Frank Ellis, Bob McKenzie, Jack Kirk.

When the duchess has some problems with her stage line, Elliott and his eager sidekick, Blake, come on the scene. Arriving at the isolated town their old friend is living in, the two stop the nefarious types in the usual fashion. (See RED RYDER series, Index.)

p, Sidney Picker; d, R. G. Springsteen; w, Earle Snell (based on a story by Gerald Geraghty); ph, William Bradford; ed, Fred Allen; md, Richard Cherwin; art d, Frank Hotaling.

Western   (PR:AA   MPAA:NR)

WAGONMASTER*****   (1950) 86m Argosy/RKO bw

Ward Bond *(Elder Wiggs)*, Ben Johnson *(Travis Blue)*, Harry Carey, Jr. *(Sandy Owens)*, Joanne Dru *(Denver)*, Charles Kemper *(Uncle Shiloh Clegg)*, Jane Darwell *(Sister Ledeyard)*, Alan Mowbray *(Dr. A. Locksley Hall)*, Ruth Clifford *(Fleuretty Phyffe)*, Russell Simpson *(Adam Perkins)*, Kathleen O'Malley *(Prudence Perkins)*, James Arness *(Floyd Clegg)*, Fred Libby *(Reese Clegg)*, Hank Worden *(Luke Clegg)*, Mickey Simpson *(Jesse Clegg)*, Francis Ford *(Mr. Peachtree)*, Cliff Lyons *(Sheriff of Crystal City)*, Don Summers *(Sam Jenkins)*, Movita Castenada *(Navajo Woman)*, Jim Thorpe *(Navajo)*, Chuck Hayward *(Jackson)*.

When asked by Peter Bogdanovich to comment on WAGONMASTER during their famous interview in 1966, director Ford replied that he thought the film, "Along with THE FUGITIVE and THE SUN SHINES BRIGHT... came closest to being what I had wanted to achieve." Written by the director's son Patrick and Frank Nugent, based on a story by Ford himself, WAGONMASTER is a deceptively simple tale about a wagon train of Mormons led by their elder, Bond, who are headed for the promised land. The religious sectarians have been forced out of Crystal City because their beliefs are too different for the majority Christians to tolerate, so the Mormons gather up their belongings and push westward. Bond, a pragmatic man who knows how to bend the rules when it will benefit the group, tries to persuade two young horse traders, Johnson and Carey, to "give the Lord a hand," and help guide the wagon train through the treacherous territory they are likely to encounter on the way to Utah. The young men are a bit wary at first, but the narrow-minded sheriff's attitude toward the Mormons finally convinces Johnson that he would rather travel with them than stay in such an intolerant town. Carey and Johnson join up with the Mormons, though some of the settlers express dismay at the fact that the young men do not share their religious beliefs. On the trail the wagon train comes upon Mowbray, Clifford, Francis Ford, and Dru, the members of a traveling medicine show who were also kicked out of Crystal City and have been stranded in the desert. All four are obviously drunk, which shocks the Mormons, until they learn that the four had been dying of thirst and were forced to drink what they had on hand–the "medicine." The introduction of the show people causes conflict among the Mormons. Their guiltless enjoyment of life scares and intimidates the settlers who have spent a lifetime trying to repress such desires. Bond, however, recognizes that the show people share a common goal with the Mormons–to live in peace–and he allows them to join the wagon train, despite the fact that the deacon, Simpson, continually voices the fears of the Mormons. In an effort to end the dissension, Bond tells Simpson (loud enough for the others to hear), "The way I see it, the Lord went to an awful lot of trouble to put these people in our way...and if I were Him, I wouldn't want anybody messing up my plans!" This logic seems to convince Simpson and, therefore, the rest of the Mormons. Johnson doesn't need any convincing and finds himself very attracted to the vivacious and uninhibited Dru. He is fascinated by her tough demeanor and spunky impulsiveness, while she is challenged by his steady calmness. The pair spar romantically throughout the film. This relationship is contrasted with that of Carey and Mormon girl O'Malley, who flirt like school children. Meanwhile, another threat to the settlers takes shape. In a pre-credits sequence, we see a sleazy band of varmints known as the Clegg family (Kemper, Arness, Libby, Worden, and Mickey Simpson) rob an express office and murder the clerk. While the Mormons head West, Kemper and his evil brood are shown riding the same trail, trying to escape a posse. Eventually the Cleggs and the Mormons intersect, and the killers force the pacifist Mormons to turn over their guns. When the posse catches up with the wagon train, the Mormons must plead ignorance of the Cleggs' whereabouts, even though the criminals are hiding among them. Soon after, the travelers encounter a band of Navajo Indians. Though the Cleggs are ready to blast them, Bond walks forward and greets the Indians as friends. The Indians accept Bond's offer of friendship, and that night both tribes make camp nearby and join in a fireside celebration. The joyous but controlled dancing of the Mormons is contrasted with the more

primordial dance of the Indians. The celebration is stopped, however, when it is learned that a young Indian maiden has been molested by Libby, one of Kemper's boys. Fully aware that his next action can cost lives, Bond immediately orders the culprit tied to a wagon wheel and whipped. This proves to be the smartest move, and even Kemper knows it, for had Bond refused to punish the evildoer, the Indians would have slaughtered the lot of them, including the Cleggs (though the Mormon who whipped Libby is later shot dead by the Cleggs to "preserve the family honor"). Back on the trail, Johnson and Carey go about their duties, all the time waiting for an opportunity to rid the wagon train of the Cleggs. When the Mormons finally reach the last mountain that leads to the valley of the promised land, the Cleggs decide to get revenge by killing Bond and dumping the settler's vital grain. The pacifist Mormons choose to do nothing but watch in horror. Luckily, they are saved by Carey, who recovers a gun and tosses it to Johnson, who quickly guns down the whole heinous family. When the deed is done, Johnson disgustedly throws the gun away and rejoins the caravan as they move to the peak of the mountain and get their first glimpse of the promised land. WAGONMASTER is pure poetry. Ford was not concerned with telling an exciting story brimming with plot twists, he simply brought us into the lives of a group of characters and allowed us to observe. The film is filled with wonderful moments of character observation and naturalness that tumble forth with amazing ease and simplicity. As the clannish Mormons are exposed to a world from which they have tried to shy away, they begin to learn how to adapt to others and deal with the reality around them, something that Bond, had learned to do a long time ago. Bond is a practical man and knows how to adapt, but even he has limits to what actions he can take and therefore he needs Johnson and Carey–who are outsiders–to help him get his people to the promised land. The process of rejection and eventually full acceptance of the show people by the Mormons is telling and finally heart-warming. Upon the introduction of the Cleggs, the Mormons finally realize that it is not the carefree, uninhibited attitudes of the show people that threaten to destroy their world; the sick, incestuous, perverted "family" the Cleggs have become is the true evil. WAGONMASTER is a film about solidarity, sacrifice, adaptability, acceptance, bravery, courage, faith, and love. In short, it is an uplifting film about life which affirms that we can achieve the ultimate dream and make it to the promised land–if we have the strength and courage to see ourselves as we are, identify our faults, and endeavor to improve. Ford executes his ideal with consummate skill, from the brilliant visual compositions right down to the casting of the bit players. The relaxed, refreshing naturalness of WAGONMASTER is achieved chiefly through the casting of minor players in major roles, with no actual "stars" present. John Wayne is too big and established a personality to fit in this small, intimate Ford film. By putting his supporting players in lead roles, Ford was able to exploit the fact that his actors had new, yet familiar, faces. Thus he was able to develop their characters in a fresh and unexpected way because their screen personalities were not yet written in stone. The final effect is such that audience members feel they have entered the lives of real people who do not seem to be *acting*, but simply living their lives before us. Bond, Johnson, and Dru are nothing less than brilliant here, each turning in a superior performance. All the beloved Fordian trademarks are here: breathtaking scenery, dancing, songs, bits of business, and a warm sense of humor mesh into a seemingly effortless whole. This is one of the master's most perfect films.

p, John Ford, Merian C. Cooper; d, Ford; w, Frank S. Nugent, Patrick Ford (based on a story by John Ford); ph, Bert Glennon; m, Richard Hageman; ed, Jack Murray; art d, James Basevi; set d, Joe Kish; cos, Wes Jeffries, Adele Parmenter; spec eff, Jack Caffee; m/l, "Wagons West," "Rollin' Shadows in the Dust," "Song of the Wagon Master,' "Chuck-A-Walla-Swing," Hageman, Stan Jones (sung by The Sons of the Pioneers).

Western   Cas.   (PR:A   MPAA:NR)

WAGONS ROLL AT NIGHT, THE***   (1941) 84m WB-FN bw

Humphrey Bogart *(Nick Coster)*, Sylvia Sidney *(Flo Lorraine)*, Eddie Albert *(Matt Varney)*, Joan Leslie *(Mary Coster)*, Sig Rumann *(Hoffman the Great)*, Cliff Clark *(Doc)*, Charles Foy *(Snapper)*, Frank Wilcox *(Tex)*, John Ridgely *(Arch)*, Clara Blandick *(Mrs. Williams)*, Aldrich Bowker *(Mr. Williams)*, Garry Owen *(Gus)*, Jack Mower *(Bundy)*, Frank Mayo *(Wally)*, Tom Wilson, Al Herman, George Riley, Cliff Saum *(Barkers)*, Eddie Acuff *(Man)*, George Guhl *(Deputy Sheriff)*, Jimmy Fox *(Customer)*, Grace Hayle *(Mrs. Grebnick)*, Beverly Quintanilla, Barbara Quintanilla *(Baby)*, Richard Elliott *(Mr. Paddleford)*, John Dilson *(Minister)*, Ted Oliver *(Sheriff)*, Fay Helm *(Wife)*, Anthony Nace *(Husband)*, Freddy Walburn, Buster Phelps, Bradley Hall, Tom Braunger, Robert Winkler, Harry Harvey, Jr., George Ovey *(Boys)*.

This remake of the Edward G. Robinson-Humphrey Bogart vehicle of 1937, KID GALAHAD, transfers the action from the boxing world to the circus world. Bogart is the owner of a run-down carnival which he desperately tries to keep his convent-schooled sister, Leslie, away from. By keeping her on a distant farm, Bogart feels that he can protect her from the evils that the carnival atmosphere breeds. The carnival runs into trouble when the perpetually soused lion tamer, Rumann, inadvertently lets one of the cats loose. It wanders into a nearby general store clerked by Albert, who calmly corners the animal with a pitchfork. Bogart, impressed with Albert's ease around lions, offers him a job with the circus, replacing the embittered Rumann. It's not long, however, before Albert meets Bogart's sister and falls for her. In the meantime, Bogart is involved in his own romance with

Sidney, a fortune teller who bills herself as "Madame Florina." When Bogart learns of Albert's meddling in his previously well- secured private life, he plots to kill him. He forces Albert into the lion's cage with Caesar, the most ferocious lion in the circus. When Sidney sees what has happened she rushes to Leslie for help. Albert survives the battle with the beast when Bogart has a change of heart and enters the cage to aid the troubled lion tamer. Bogart, however, falls victim to the animal. After surviving the fight with Caesar, Albert finds himself up against Rumann, who has returned to the circus brandishing a gun with the intent of taking revenge on Bogart and Albert. Albert emerges from this battle alive, as well, taking Leslie with him, while Sidney remains behind with her crystal ball and tarot cards. An entertaining but predictable picture which was quickly forgotten, mainly because it was bookended by two of Bogart's finest–HIGH SIERRA and THE MALTESE FALCON.

p, Harlan Thompson; d, Ray Enright; w, Fred Niblo, Jr., Barry Trivers (based on the novel *Kid Galahad* by Francis Wallace); ph, Sid Hickox; m, Heinz Roemheld; ed, Frederick Richards; art d, Hugh Reticker; spec eff, Byron Haskin, H.F. Koenekamp.

Crime Drama   (PR:A   MPAA:NR)

WAGONS WEST**   (1952) 70m MON c

Rod Cameron (*Jeff Curtis*), Noah Beery, Jr (*Arch Lawrence*), Peggie Castle (*Ann Wilkins*), Michael Chapin (*Ben Wilkins*), Henry Brandon (*Clay Cook*), Sara Haden (*Mrs. Cook*), Frank Ferguson (*Cyrus Cook*), Anne Kimbell (*Alice Lawrence*), Wheaton Chambers (*Sam Wilkins*), Riley Hill (*Gaylord Cook*), I. Stanford Jolley (*Slocum*), Almira Sessions, Effie Laird (*Old Maids*), Harry Tyler (*Old Man*), Glenn Strange (*Joplin Marshal*), Harry Strang (*Territorial Marshal*), John Parrish (*Chief Black Kettle*), Charles Stevens (*Kaw Chief*).

Routine Cameron vehicle which sees the lead in charge of a wagon train headed for California. Though warned that the Cheyennes have been sold rifles by mysterious gunrunners and are on the warpath, Cameron guides his settlers through the rough spots and fends off several Indian attacks. Eventually he discovers that three of the settlers, Ferguson, Brandon, and Hill, are the gunrunners and wastes no time taking appropriate action. As in others of this one's ilk, the homesteader situation provides ample opportunities for domestic subplots and comedy relief.

p, Vincent M. Fennelly; d, Ford Beebe; w, Dan Ullman; ph, Harry Neumann (Cinecolor); m, Marlin Skiles; ed, Walter Hannemann.

Western   (PR:A   MPAA:NR)

WAGONS WESTWARD**   (1940) 70m REP bw

Chester Morris (*David Cook/Tom Cook*), Anita Louise (*Phyllis*), Buck Jones (*Sheriff McDaniels*), Ona Munson (*Julie*), George "Gabby" Hayes (*Hardtack*), Guinn "Big Boy" Williams (*Hardman*), Douglas Fowley (*Marsden*), Wayne Hull (*David as a Boy*), Warren Hull (*Tom as a Boy*), John Gallaudet (*Blackie*), Virginia Brissac (*Angela Cook*), Trevor Bardette (*Alan Cook*), Selmer Jackson (*Maj. Marlowe*), Charles Stevens (*Pima*), Joe McGuinn, Tex Cooper.

Morris plays twin brothers, one good, the other evil, in this sporadically interesting oater which also boasts the surprising casting of Buck Jones as a bad guy. When his evil brother is sent to jail, the good Morris–a government agent–assumes his sibling's identity in order to trap a couple of crooks played by Williams and Fowley. While he succeeds in his law-enforcement duties, he is cornered by his brother's girl friend, Louise, a dance-hall cutie whom his brother had promised to marry. This development sends the good Mr. Morris' girl friend, Munson, into a tizzy and Morris must do some of his fanciest maneuvering to get himself out of that jam.

p, Armand Schaefer; d, Lew Landers; w, Harrison Jacobs, Joseph M. March; ph, Ernest Miller; ed, Murray Seldeen, Ernest Nims; md, Cy Feuer; cos, Adele Palmer.

Western   (PR:A   MPAA:NR)

WAHINE   (SEE: MAEVA, 1961)

WAIKIKI WEDDING***   (1937) 89m PAR bw

Bing Crosby (*Tony Marvin*), Bob Burns (*Shad Buggle*), Martha Raye (*Myrtle Finch*), Shirley Ross (*Georgia Smith*), George Barbier (*J. P. Todhunter*), Leif Erickson (*Dr. Victor Quimby*), Grady Sutton (*Everett Todhunter*), Granville Bates (*Uncle Herman*), Anthony Quinn (*Kimo*), Prince Lei Lani (*Priest*), Mitchell Lewis (*Koalani*), George Regas (*Muamua*), Nick Lukats (*Assistant Purser*), Kuulei De Clercq (*Lani*), Nalani De Clercq (*Maile*), Miri Rei (*Specialty Dancer*), Spencer Charters (*Frame*), Alexander Leftwich (*Harrison*), Harry Stubbs (*Keith*), Augie Goupil (*Specialty Dancer*), Ralph Remley (*Tomlin*), Pierre Watkin (*John Durkin*), Iris Yamaoka (*Secretary*), Jack Chapin (*Photographer*), Pedro Regas (*Cab Driver*), David Newell (*Radio Operator*), Emma Dunn (*Tony's Mother*), Robert Emmett O'Connor, Lalo Encinas (*Policemen*), Sojin, Jr (*Bellboy*), Ray Kinney (*Singer*), Maurice Liu (*Kaiaka*), Raquel Echeverria (*Mahina*).

Charming South Seas musical comedy starring Crosby as a public relations man for a pineapple conglomerate who is given the task of accompanying

contest winner Ross on a tour of the Hawaiian Islands. Ross insists on bringing her friend Raye along, so Crosby drafts his goofy pal Burns to come along as another escort. Crosby's heart really isn't in his work and Ross soon becomes bored and books passage to return to the mainland. This development sends the pineapple executives into a frenzy and Crosby is forced to take drastic measures to get Ross to stay. He hires a group of local natives led by Quinn to "kidnap" the foursome. Quinn and his men pretend to be after a sacred jewel and they capture the group and accuse them of possessing it. Instead of being scared by their predicament, Ross begins to develop romantic feelings for Crosby, who leads them through their "escape." Eventually Ross learns that the whole adventure was just a trick and she angrily prepares to leave the islands. At this point Crosby discovers that he has fallen in love with her and he tries a number of tricks to prevent her departure. Luckily Raye and Burns have also fallen in love and announce their wedding. This news softens Ross and she says yes to Crosby's marriage proposal. The song "Sweet Leilani" won an Oscar for its author Harry Owens. Other songs included: "Sweet Is the Word for You," "In a Little Hula Heaven," "Blue Hawaii," "Okolehao," and "Nani Ona Pua" (Ralph Rainger, Leo Robin).

p, Arthur Hornblow, Jr.; d, Frank Tuttle; w, Frank Butler, Don Hartman, Walter DeLeon, Frances Martin (based on a story by Butler, Hartman); ph, Karl Struss; ed, Paul Weatherwax; md, Boris Morros; set d, A. E. Fruedeman; cos, Edith Head; spec eff, Farciot Edouart; LeRoy Prinz; m/l, Leo Robin, Ralph Rainger, Harry Owens, Jimmy Lovell.

Musical   (PR:A   MPAA:NR)

WAIT 'TIL THE SUN SHINES, NELLIE**½   (1952) 108m FOX c

David Wayne (*Ben Halper*), Jean Peters (*Nellie*), Hugh Marlowe (*Ed Jordan*), Albert Dekker (*Lloyd Slocum*), Helene Stanley (*Eadie Jordan*), Tommy Morton (*Ben Halper, Jr. at Age 20*), Joyce MacKenzie (*Bessie Jordan*), Alan Hale, Jr (*George Oliphant*), Richard Karlan (*Kava*), Merry Anders (*Adeline*), Jim Maloney (*Austin Burdge*), Warren Stevens (*McCauley*), Charles Watts (*Mr. Burdge*), David Wolfe (*Sam Eichenbogen*), Dan White (*Doc Thomas*), Erik Nielsen (*Ben Halper, Jr. at Age 8*), Jerrylyn Flannery (*Nellie at Age 5*), Noreen Corcoran (*Adeline Halper at Age 6*), William Walker (*Trooper*), James Griffith (*Ollie*), Kermit Echols (*Hotel Clerk*), Eugene Mazola (*Ben Halper, Jr. at Ages 2 and 4*), Tony Barr (*Broidy*), Maude Prickett (*Mrs. Burdge*), Mary Hain (*Adeline at Age 2*).

Sentimental small-town drama starring Wayne as a barber in love with the rural, slow-paced life he leads. His wife, Peters, hates the small town and longs to move to the big, more exciting city. The difference in their temperaments causes a rift in the marriage and Peters soon takes on a lover and leaves Wayne. Soon after, both Peters and her lover, Marlowe, are killed in a railway accident, leaving Wayne a widower with two children. As the years progress Wayne is disappointed to learn that his son has become a Chicago gangster heavily involved in a bloody gang struggle. Once again tragedy strikes when Wayne's son is killed; then his barber shop burns down. Luckily, the old barber's loyalty to the community pays off and the townsfolk band together to help him rebuild. When the small town celebrates its 50th anniversary, Wayne is made the guest of honor. Though the trials and tribulations of Wayne's life are piled on a bit thick in spots, WAIT 'TIL THE SUN SHINES, NELLIE has several heartwarming moments and Wayne turns in a fine performance as he ages 50 years during the course of the film.

p, George Jessel; d, Henry King; w, Allan Scott, Maxwell Shane (based on the novel *I Heard Them Sing* by Ferdinand Reyher); ph, Leon Shamroy (Technicolor); m, Alfred Newman; ed, Barbara McLean; art d, Lyle R. Wheeler, Maurice Ransford; cos, Renie.

Drama   (PR:A   MPAA:NR)

WAIT UNTIL DARK***½   (1967) 107m WB c

Audrey Hepburn (*Susy Hendrix*), Alan Arkin (*Roat*), Richard Crenna (*Mike Talman*), Efrem Zimbalist, Jr. (*Sam Hendrix*), Jack Weston (*Carlino*), Samantha Jones (*Lisa*), Julie Herrod (*Gloria*), Frank O'Brien (*Shatner*), Gary Morgan (*Boy*), Jean Del Val (*The Old Man*).

A real edge-of-your-seat thriller adapted from a Broadway stage hit written by Frederick Knott, author of DIAL M FOR MURDER. Zimbalist, a commercial artist who has just returned to New York City from a business trip in Montreal, is stopped at the airport by fashion model Jones who asks him to hold a toy doll for her. Moments later the woman vanishes and the bemused Zimbalist brings the doll home to his Greenwich Village apartment and gives it to his wife, Hepburn, who is blind. Meanwhile, two criminals, Crenna and Weston, arrive to meet with Jones, but find Arkin, a crazed criminal mastermind who employs all manner of disguises. Arkin informs the men that he has just murdered Jones because she tried to double-cross them. The doll, which has a fortune in heroin hidden inside it, must be recovered at all costs. After dumping Jones' body in the river, the men hatch a plan to get Zimbalist out of his apartment so that they can steal the doll. Crenna pretends to be an ex-Marine who served in Zimbalist's unit who would like to get together and reminisce about the old days. Zimbalist goes off to New Jersey on a wild goose chase to meet with his "buddy." Crenna, however, stays in New York, and together with Arkin and Weston tries to con Hepburn into letting them into the apartment by using a variety of disguises. Posing as detectives, Weston and Arkin convince Hepburn that they are investigating the murder of Jones, and that Zimbalist may have had something to do with the crime. To keep their facts straight, the men write notes and hold them up for each other to read, unbeknownst to the blind Hepburn who thinks they are simply taking notes regarding the investigation. The men ask Hepburn if she could hand over the doll, for it might provide a clue. Unfortunately, Herrod, the child of a neighbor, has taken the doll and the concerned Hepburn can't find it. When Herrod returns the doll, Hepburn phones Crenna (who she believes is her husband's friend) only to discover that the number is that of a phone booth across the street. Now realizing the men were impostors who want the doll, Hepburn sends Herrod to meet Zimbaist at the train station (he having returned from his misadventure in New Jersey) while she tries to phone the police. Much to her shock, the phone line has been cut, and Crenna shows up at the door. Feeling a bit guilty, Crenna confesses he just wants the doll and the story about her husband's involvement with Jones is untrue. At that moment the psychotic Arkin bursts in and, having already murdered Weston, kills Crenna as well. In an attempt to even her odds with Arkin, the terrified blind woman smashes all the light bulbs in the apartment and plunges the killer into complete darkness. Now having the advantage because she knows the apartment by touch, Hepburn tries to hide. Arkin stumbles to the kitchen where he opens the refrigerator door for some light and is stabbed with a kitchen knife by Hepburn. As Arkin pulls the knife out of his body and tries to use it on Hepburn, the blind woman scrambles behind the refrigerator and pulls the plug, once again putting the odds in her favor. The tension is unbearable as the wheezing, bleeding Arkin tries to find Hepburn in total darkness. Just then, Zimbalist and the police arrive to find Arkin dead on the floor, only inches from the cornered Hepburn. Expertly directed by veteran British helmsman Young (Arthur Penn had directed the stage version), WAIT UNTIL DARK is an exciting, original chiller. Hepburn turns in a strong, realistic performance as the terrorized blind woman–a role she researched diligently with the help of two young blind women from the Lighthouse for the Blind school. For weeks the actress (and director Young) wore a special shade over her eyes and learned how to use a cane properly, to feel the texture of different objects, and how to listen carefully to distinguish the quality and distance of sounds. Hepburn's husband, Mel Ferrer, produced the film, though their marriage was about to collapse. Rumor had it that Ferrer was spending weeks interviewing dozens of sexy New York models for the small role of the girl who hands Zimbalist the doll that starts all the trouble. Studio head Jack Warner found the whole project exasperating, especially Hepburn, who first wanted the film shot in Europe, and when that was refused, insisted that the production be halted every day at 4 p.m. for a tea break. Since director Young was British, he concurred, and the art department built a tea garden set right next to the apartment set. Despite her off-screen eccentricities, Hepburn carries the film by herself, with able assistance from Crenna and Weston. Unfortunately, Zimbalist is a bit stiff, and Arkin chews on the scenery a few times too often to retain much credibility. The film was a tremendous success at the box office, and for added effect, some theater owners turned the house lights off completely during the final 15 minutes.

p, Mel Ferrer; d, Terence Young; w, Robert Carrington, Jane-Howard Carrington (based on the play by Frederick Knott); ph, Charles Lang (Technicolor); m, Henry Mancini; ed, Gene Milford; art d, George Jenkins; set d, George James Hopkins; m/l, "Wait Until Dark," Mancini, Jay Livingston, Ray Evans (sung by Bobby Darin); makeup, Gordon Bau.

Thriller   Cas.   (PR:O   MPAA:NR)

WAITING AT THE CHURCH   (SEE: RUNAROUND, THE, 1931)

WAITING FOR CAROLINE**   (1969, Can.) 83m National Film Board
                                        of Canada-Canadian Broadcasting Corp./Lopert c

Alexandra Stewart (*Caroline*), Francois Tasse (*Marc*), Robert Howay (*Peter*), Sharon Acker (*Emily*), William Needles (*Stephen*), Aileen Seaton (*Lally*), Paul Guevremont (*Mons. Simard*), Daniel Gadouas (*Jean-Pierre*), Lucie Poitras (*Mme. Simard*), Monique Mercure (*Yvette*), Reginald McReynolds (*Hagan*), Paul Buissoneau (*Louis*).

Stewart stars as the daughter of rich Canadian businessman Needles. She moves to Quebec and takes up with Tasse, an aspiring actor. Trouble arises when Howay–Stewart's former lover–arrives proposing marriage. The men compete with each other for Stewart's affections but it quickly becomes apparent that it is her father whom she truly loves. When Stewart learns that her father intends to marry a young college friend of hers, she flies to Vancouver to attend the engagement party, dragging Tasse and Howay with her. At the party it becomes clear to her lovers that they can never compete with her father for her affections so they both depart, leaving Stewart very alone.

p, Walford Hewitson; d, Ron Kelly; w, George C. Robertson, Kelly; ph, Denis Gillson (DeLuxe Color); m, Eldon Rathburn, The Jaybees; ed, Barnie Howells; art d, Earl Preston.

Drama   (PR:C   MPAA:NR)

WAITING FOR THE BRIDE   (SEE: RUNAROUND, THE, 1931)

WAITING WOMEN   (SEE: SECRETS OF WOMEN, 1961, Swed.)

WAITRESS*   (1982) 88m Troma c (AKA: SOUP TO NUTS)

Carol Drake (*Andrea*), Jim Harris (*Jerry*), Carol Bevar (*Jennifer*), Renata Majer (*Lindsey*), David Hunt (*Bill*), Anthony Sarrero (*Moe*), Ed Fenton (*Mr. Bellerman*), Augie Grompone (*Piebalt*), Bonnie Horan (*Mrs. Bellerman*), Fred Salador (*Cavendish*), Wendy Stuart (*His Assistant*), Bill Kirksey (*Alfred*), Katya Colman (*Mrs. Alfred*).

Awful low-budget comedy which takes place in a New York City restaurant and follows the lives of three women who work there. Majer, the daughter of the owner, is forced to work at the restaurant against her will after being expelled from prep school. Bevar is a lusty-looking blonde working as a waitress in order to research an article she is writing on how to meet men, and Drake is the proverbial actress working as a waitress in order to pay the bills until she is discovered. There isn't much of a plot, just a bunch of fitfully amusing episodes revolving around the parade of characters who make their way through the restaurant.

p, Lloyd Kaufman, Michael Herz; d, Samuel Weil, Herz; w, Michael Stone, Charles Kaufman; ph, L. Kaufman; ed, Dan Lowenthal; art d, Barry Shapiro.

Comedy   (PR:O   MPAA:PG/R)

WAJAN*   (1938, South Bali) 60m Tomfilms bw

Nodonk (*The Witch*), Wajan (*Son of the Witch*), Sari (*His Sweetheart*), Lombos (*Her Father*), Boarang (*The God of Good*), Rangda (*The God of Evil*).

The ceremonies of the Balinese get a trivialized movie treatment in this borderline documentary that throws an intrusive story line on to island legends. The thin plot has a witch causing havoc as her son falls for the girl next door. To save the romance (in addition to wiping out a plague) the witch is exorcised and killed. The filmmakers show no respect for their subject, resulting in a condescending piece of tripe. Ironically, the movie had its New York opening at a former striptease emporium.

p, Dr. Frederick Dalsheim, Victor Baron Von Plessan; d, Walter Spies, Gdeh Ray; w, (uncredited) m, Wolfgang Zeller.

Drama   (PR:A   MPAA:NR)

WAKAMBA!**   (1955) 65m American Museum of Natural
                                              History/RKO c

Paul E. Prentiss (*Narrator*).

A hunter in Africa wants to marry the daughter of the local village chief. The head tribesman agrees, but only if the hunter can fetch the tusks off of a local bull elephant. This simple premise, held together with a rather stiff narration, is really just an excuse to stitch some good wildlife footage together for the American Museum of Natural History. Why the museum would endorse a simplistic jungle film remains a mystery, but the results are okay. It gives a slightly more realistic look at the native African life than most jungle pictures, and the stock animal footage holds some moments of interest.

p&d, Edgar M. Queeny; w, Charles L. Tedford; ph, Queeny, Fort B. Guerin, Jr., Richard E. Bishop, Fred Wardenburg, Donald I. Ker, S.B. Eckert, E.G.S. Blanckart (Technicolor); m, Howard Jackson; ed, V. C. Lewis.

Adventure   (PR:AA   MPAA:NR)

WAKAMONO TACHI   (SEE: LIVE YOUR OWN WAY, 1970, Jap.)

WAKARE   (SEE: FAREWELL, MY BELOVED, 1969, Jap.)

WAKARETE IKURU TOKI MO   (SEE: ETERNITY OF LOVE, 1961,
                                              Jap.)

WAKE ISLAND***   (1942) 78m PAR bw

Brian Donlevy (*Maj. Caton*), MacDonald Carey (*Lt. Cameron*), Robert Preston (*Joe Doyle*), William Bendix (*Smacksie Randall*), Albert Dekker (*Shad McClosky*), Walter Abel (*Comdr. Roberts*), Mikhail Rasumny (*Probenzky*), Don Castle (*Pvt. Cunkel*), Rod Cameron (*Capt. Lewis*), Bill Goodwin (*Sergeant*), Barbara Britton (*Sally Cameron*), Damian O'Flynn (*Capt. Patrick*), Frank Albertson (*Johnny Rudd*), Phillip Terry (*Pvt. Warren*), Philip Van Zandt (*Cpl. Goebbels*), Keith Richards (*Sparks Wilcox*), Willard Robertson (*Col. Cameron*), Marvin Jones (*Tommy*), Jack Chapin (*Squeaky Simpkins*), Rudy Robles (*Triunfo*), John Sheehan (*Pete Hogan*), Charles Trowbridge (*George Nielson*), Mary Thomas (*Cynthia Caton*), Mary Field (*Miss Pringle*), Richard Loo (*Mr. Saburo Kurusu*), Earle Tex Harris (*Tex Hannigan*), Hillary Brooke, Patty McCarty (*Girls at Inn*), William Forrest (*Maj. Johnson*), Jack Mulhall (*Dr. Parkman*), Ivan Miller (*Colonel*), Hugh Beaumont (*Captain*), Edward Earle (*Commander*), James Brown (*Wounded Marine*), Angel Cruz (*Rodrigo*), Anthony Nace (*Gordon*), Hollis

Bane 'Mike Ragan' (1st Lieutenant), Frank Faylen (Wounded Marine), Dane Clark (Marine), Alan Hale, Jr. (Sight Setter).

The heroic but doomed defense of Wake Island against the Japanese in the opening days of WW II joined such gallant last stands as Bataan and Corregidor as the only things Americans could feel proud about even as the war went badly for them. The first film to capitalize on the last-ditch stands of the early war, WAKE ISLAND was immensely popular and garnered several Academy Award nominations. Wake is a small island in the middle of the Pacific, used mostly as a refueling station for the clipper planes that plied the airways between the U.S. and the Orient. As the film opens, the tiny American garrison there is visited by a Japanese diplomat on his way to the U.S. He is treated to a dinner with full honors, but he seems intent on having a good look around at the facilities. A running dispute continues between Donlevy, commander of the island, and Dekker, a construction supervisor building up the island's defenses. Then, on December 7, 1941, almost as soon as word has come over the radio of the attack on Pearl Harbor, waves of Japanese planes begin bombing the island, reducing almost every structure to rubble. The men move out into foxholes and machine gun nests and hunker down to wait for the inevitable attack. When the first invasion barges appear offshore, Donlevy orders the few pieces of artillery left intact to wait until they come in close. When he finally gives the word to fire, the Japanese, caught totally by surprise by the intensity of the opposition, withdraw with heavy losses. Donlevy sends a now-famous message back to America: "Send more Japs." Unfortunately, that is exactly what they get, as wave after wave of Imperial Marines swarm the beaches, only to be fought back time and again with machine guns, rifles, and bayonets. For two weeks the men hold on, but with no help coming and ammunition running low, they are doomed and they know it. In the end Donlevy and Preston go down in a blaze of glory and a hail of machine gun bullets as a leering Jap runs up and kills the pair. Americans never surrender. The film hit the perfect note for an audience that had heard nothing but defeats for the American forces in the Pacific, showing that even in defeat there was victory (a lesson the British have long understood). All the performers are good, particularly Donlevy, whose calm in the face of overwhelming odds is nothing short of amazing. The film was widely shown to soldiers at training camps all over the country, and it never failed to rouse cheers from the men who would soon have to go out and take Wake back. Shot on an impressively accurate looking location on the shores of the Salton Sea in the California desert, the film was a smash success and was nominated for no less than four Academy Awards for Best Picture, Best Director, Best Supporting Actor (Bendix), and Best Original Screenplay.

p, Joseph Sistrom; d, John Farrow; w, W.R. Burnett, Frank Butler; ph, Theodor Sparkuhl; m, David Buttolph; ed, LeRoy Stone; art d, Hans Dreier, Earl Hedrick.

War						**(PR:A MPAA:NR)**

### WAKE ME WHEN IT'S OVER*** 					(1960) 126m FOX c

Ernie Kovacs (Capt. Charlie Stark), Margo Moore (Lt. Nora McKay), Jack Warden (Doc Farrington), Nobu McCarthy (Ume), Dick Shawn (Gus Brubaker), Don Knotts (Sgt. Warren), Robert Strauss (Sam Weiscoff), Noreen Nash (Marge Brubaker), Parley Baer (Col. Hollingsworth), Robert Emhardt (Joab Martinson), Marvin Kaplan (Hap Cosgrove), Richard Tyler (Lt. William Pincus), Ralph Dumke (Sen. Gillespie), Tommy Nishimura (Pvt. Jim Hanigawa), Raymond Bailey (Gen. Weingang), Robert Burton (Col. Dowling), Frank Behrens (Maj. Biglow), Linda Wong (Kaiko), Caroline Richter (Mrs. Hollingsworth), Robert Peoples (Connorton), Ron Hargrave (Hawaiian Singer), David Bedell (Capt. Arthur Finch), Jay Jostyn (Col. Mulhern), Byron Morrow (Maj. Horace Tillman), Michael Quinn (Capt. John Guevara), Owen Cunningham.

A funny but slightly elongated peacetime service comedy directed by LeRoy, who had already shown his ability with men in uniform by helming MR. ROBERTS and NO TIME FOR SERGEANTS. Shawn is a veteran of the fracas known as WW II and is comfortably ensconced in a new career as a restaurateur when he is redrafted in error and shipped off to the lonely Pacific island of Shima, where tedium and ennui are rampant. It's all a bureaucratic mistake but those things take time to rectify so Shawn has to make the best of it while governmental red tape strangles his requests to be released. Kovacs is the commander of the radar station that dominates the island and he does his best to keep his men amused by arranging sports tournaments, classes in ornithology, anything to maintain their morale. Shawn arrives and meets McCarthy, the mayor's daughter. She informs him of a natural spa that pours warm, healthy water forth with a never-ending supply and Shawn conceives the idea of building a luxury hotel that will bring tourists and revenue to the island as well as keep everyone from letting the devil find work for their idle hands. There are piles of surplus equipment and supplies just lying around so Shawn convinces Kovacs, and the servicemen are recruited to build the hotel. Warden is the base physician and requests the presence of Moore, a nurse in the Air Force. She arrives and her main job is to keep Kovacs in line because too much time on the island has caused him to become eccentric. Kovacs finds Moore to his liking and forgets about the fact that they are coworkers as love blossoms. Shawn is married to Nash, who is in the U.S. and he could probably get out sooner but once he begins the project of the hotel, he's determined to complete it. The local natives had been carping about the U.S. personnel and now they

see that they are to be the recipients of the U.S. largesse. The hotel opens with the natives working as busboys, bellhops, etc., and it is a smash and soon the jewel of the area. Everyone is making money and there is a smile on the face of each islander. Then trouble comes on the horizon when an article is published that says this is lots more than just a hotel and offers more pleasures than are usually found. It's all a base canard (as opposed to a tenor canard) but an immediate investigation of the allegations is called for. A blow-hard senator (Dumke) and some muckety-mucks in the Air Force are dispatched to Shima and the result is an instant court-martial of Shawn. Warden is called in to act as Shawn's defense attorney and the courtroom scenes are a riot. At the end, Shawn, who never should have been in service in the first place, is allowed to leave when the mistake that brought him in is discovered. Before that happens, though, we have laughed ourselves silly as Kovacs and the others cavort in a fine satire of life in the service. Shawn had appeared in 1956's THE OPPOSITE SEX but this was his first large role and he knew what to do with it, wringing every last laugh out of the schnook character he portrayed. Knotts had appeared for LeRoy in NO TIME FOR SERGEANTS and was again called on by the director for this. Strauss was already a veteran of service movies after having been in SAILOR BEWARE (Navy), JUMPING JACKS (Paratroopers), STALAG 17 (prisoner of war), THE BRIDGES OF TOKO-RI (Naval aviator), and ATTACK (infantry). Marvin Kaplan scores in a brief comedy role and Tommy Nishimura is hysterical as an Asian who speaks superb Yiddish. If the voice of Col. Mulhern sounds familiar to older readers, that's because it belongs to Jay Jostyn, who was "Mr. District Attorney" on the radio for many years. The idea of building a hotel using extra material from the U.S. forces had already been seen before in THE TEAHOUSE OF THE AUGUST MOON, but this is sufficiently different to make it worth your while.

p&d, Mervyn LeRoy; w, Richard Breen (based on a novel by Howard Singer); ph, Leon Shamroy (CinemaScope, DeLuxe Color); m, Cyril J. Mockridge; md, Lionel Newman; art d, Lyle Wheeler, John Beckman; ed, Aaron Stell; cos, Bill Thomas; m/l, "Wake Me When It's Over," Sammy Cahn, James Van Heusen (sung by Andy Williams).

Comedy					**(PR:A MPAA:NR)**

### WAKE OF THE RED WITCH***½ 				(1949) 106m REP bw

John Wayne (Capt. Ralls), Gail Russell (Angelique Desaix), Gig Young (Sam Rosen), Adele Mara (Teleia Van Schreeven), Luther Adler (Mayrant Ruysdaal Sidneye), Eduard Franz (Harmenszoon Van Schreeven), Grant Withers (Capt. Wilde Youngeur), Henry Daniell (Jacques Desaix), Paul Fix (Antonio "Ripper" Arrezo), Dennis Hoey (Capt. Munsey), Jeff Corey (Mr. Loring), Erskine Sanford (Doktor Van Arken), Duke Kahanamoku (Va Nuke), John Wengraf (Prosecutor), Henry Brandon (Kurinua, a Native), Myron Healey (Seaman on "Red Witch"), John Pickard (2nd Diver), Harlan Warde (Seaman Handling Diving Line), Fernando Alvarado (Maru), Jose Alvarado (Taluna), Carl Thompson (Hekkim, Cabin Boy), Mickey Simpson (2nd Officer), Grant Means (Dirk), Jim Nolan (1st Diver), Harry Vejar (Jarma), David Clarke (Mullins), Fred Fox (Ship's Surgeon), Al Kikume (Native Servant), Leo C. Richmond (Native Priest), Harold Lishman (Kharma), Fred Libby (Sailor, Lookout), Robert Wood (Young Sailor), Fred Graham (Sailor, Fight), Rory Mallinson (Officer), Norman Rainey (Lawyer), Wallace Scott (Sailor), Kuka Tuitama, George Pliz (Natives).

A strong seafaring adventure that's long on action and short on credibility. The studio shots were obviously that and the sea sequences left a bit to be desired. Nevertheless, it was rip-snorting good and Wayne showed that he could do other things besides leading cavalry charges. There are two long flashbacks that add nothing and the movie would have been better with a linear progression. Wayne is a seaman who has incurred the wrath of some natives in the South Seas. He is saved when he manages to get aboard a ship owned by Adler, a man who is a tycoon in the shipping industry. Wayne says he knows where there is a fortune in pearls to be found but he will only take Adler there if he can captain the ship. Adler agrees, then, as they are approaching the island where the pearls can be found, Adler has Wayne clapped in irons below decks. They arrive at the island, Wayne is released, and they go off to find the gems, which are hidden in a chest and secreted in a cavern that is overseen by a huge octopus that has taken the lives of many who've attempted to retrieve the pearls. Daniell is the man who runs the island for the French and his daughter is Russell. Both Wayne and Adler find her attractive and she falls for Wayne, although Adler strikes a deal with Daniell for her hand. Wayne finds out about this and is thrown into a depression, drowning himself in alcohol. He battles with his own men and appears to be about to hit Russell for what she's done, although she has no idea that her father and Adler have made such an arrangement. Then Wayne singlehandedly takes on the octopus and beats the creature. With the pearls in his possession, Wayne returns to Russell and plans their future together but Daniell has him arrested for stealing the pearls. This occasions a battle between Wayne and Daniell and the older man is killed when he falls into a fire. Russell marries Adler, seven years pass, and she can't forget the love she had for Wayne. Wayne is running Adler's ship, the Red Witch, and then Adler appears to be jealous of Russell's affections for Wayne and plans to get rid of him. Wayne moves more quickly and sinks the ship, with a cargo of more than $5 million in gold aboard, and since he knows where it is, he now has a pawn in the chess game with Adler, a man who loves money more than anything. Russell falls ill with a mysterious disease and there is no hope of recovery. Wayne would like to spend her remaining days with her and agrees to show Adler where the scuttled boat is if Adler agrees to release Young (Wayne's first mate, who has been held hostage) and Mara, Young's girl friend. The boat is perched on a reef below the ocean's surface and is in terrible danger of plunging over the edge to the depths as a terrible storm is roiling the sea. Wayne dies in the storm and the final image of the film is that of Wayne and Russell aboard the *Red Witch* as it sails to a world far better than the one they had occupied. A bit of fantasy, good action, and a first-rate acting job by Wayne, who was not known for that sort of thespian range. In a small role, note British actor Dennis Hoey, who was best known as the bumbling Inspector Lestrade in the SHERLOCK HOLMES series of films which starred Rathbone and Bruce. Another noteworthy addition to the cast was famed Hawaiian Duke Kahanamoku, who was an athletic star in the islands long before they became the 50th state.

p, Edmund Grainger; d, Edward Ludwig; w, Harry Brown, Kenneth Gamet (based on the novel by Garland Roark); ph, Reggie Lanning; m, Nathan Scott; ed, Richard L. Van Enger; art d, James Sullivan; spec eff, Howard Lydecker, Theodore Lydecker.

Adventure   Cas.   (PR:A-C MPAA:NR)

WAKE UP AND DIE½   (1967, Fr./Ital.) 102m
Sanson-Castoro-CIPRA/Rizzoli c (LUTRING ... REVEILLE-TOI ET MEURS; SVEGLIATI E UCCIDI [LUTRING])

Robert Hoffmann (*Luciano Lutring*), Lisa Gastoni (*Yvonne Lutring*), Gian Maria Volonte (*Inspector Moroni*), Claudio Camaso, Renato Nicolai, Ottavio Fanfani, Giovanni De Luca, Corrado Olmi, Aldo Suligoi, Augusto Bonardi.

Decent crime thriller starring Hoffmann as a petty thief who pulls a daring escape from Italian police and suddenly finds himself splashed across the newspapers as some sort of daring criminal mastermind. Unfortunately, Hoffmann makes the mistake of believing his own press, and he begins living up to his print reputation as a killer. Eventually, Hoffmann's wife Gastoni sets him up in order to stop the killing and have him put away. At the last minute she changes her mind and tries to help Hoffmann escape, but he is too far gone to listen to reason and stupidly tries to take on the police, who wound and capture him.

p, Joseph Fryd, Carlo Lizzani; d, Lizzani; w, Ugo Pirro (based on a story by Lizzani, Pirro); ph, Armando Nannuzzi (Eastmancolor); m, Ennio Morricone; ed, Franco Fraticelli.

Crime   (PR:C MPAA:NR)

WAKE UP AND DREAM**   (1934) 75m UNIV bw

Russ Columbo (*Paul Scotti*), Roger Pryor (*Charley Sullivan*), June Knight (*Toby Brown*), Catharine Doucet (*Mme. Rose*), Henry Armetta (*Cellini*), Andy Devine (*Egghead*), Spencer Charters (*Earl Craft*), Wini Shaw (*Mae LaRue*), Gavin Gordon (*Seabrook*), Richard Carle (*Babcock*), Paul Porcasi (*Polopolis*), Maurice Black (*Tom Romero*), Clarence H. Wilson (*Hildebrand*), Arthur Hoyt (*George Spelvin*), Philip Dakin (*John Richards*), Jane Darwell (*Woman*).

Dull musical starring Columbo, Pryor, and Knight as members of a vaudeville trio trying to make it big. The men both love Knight, but in the end she chooses Columbo just as he was about to bow out of the picture. A tragic footnote: popular singer Columbo was killed in a bizarre shooting accident shortly after filming was completed. Some sources state that Columbo was at the home of a friend who struck a match on one of a pair of dueling pistols that were being used as decorative paperweights on a desk and accidentally fired the gun (which was supposed to have been empty). The bullet ricocheted off the desk and struck Columbo in the head, killing him. Songs include: "Too Beautiful for Words" (Bernie Grossman, Russ Columbo, Jack Stern), "When You're in Love," "Wake Up and Dream," "Let's Pretend" (Grossman, Stern, Grace Hamilton).

p, B. F. Ziedman; d, Kurt Neumann; w, John Meehan, Jr.; ph, Charles Stumar; ed, Daniel Mandell; m/l, Russ Columbo, Jack Stern, Bernie Grossman, Grace Hamilton.

Musical   (PR:A MPAA:NR)

WAKE UP AND DREAM, 1942   (SEE: WHAT'S COOKIN', 1942)

WAKE UP AND DREAM**   (1946) 92m FOX c

John Payne (*Jeff*), June Haver (*Jenny*), Connie Marshall (*Nella*), Clem Bevans (*Henry Pecket*), Charlotte Greenwood (*Sara March*), John Ireland (*Howard Williams*), Charles Russell (*Lt. Coles*), Lee Patrick (*The Blonde*), Oliver Blake [Prickett] (*Mr. Agrippa*), George Cleveland (*Prof. Feverfew*), Charles D. Brown (*Lieutenant Commander*), Irving Bacon (*Toll Gate Attendant*), Minerva Urecal (*Mrs. Lucash*), Eddie Acuff (*Bus Driver*), Charles Smith (*Carl*), Francis Ford (*Old Man at Counter*), Milton Kibbee (*Mailman*), Frank Orth (*Milkman*), Kathryn Sheldon (*Mrs. Kroot*), John Russell (*Pilot*), Stanley Andrews (*Conductor*), William "Billy" Newell (*Extra in Cafe*).

Marshall stars as a young girl who sets out on a strange adventure in search of her brother, Payne, who was listed as missing in action in WW II. Accompanied by Payne's girl friend, Haver, Marshall, knowing that Payne

had once said that he would go to a remote island if he were missing, boards eccentric old man Bevans' boat–which is on dry land 300 miles from the sea–and asks him to take her to her "dream" island. A storm comes up, creating a flood which carries the boat out to sea. The adventure having gone sour, the small crew is rescued by the Coast Guard, which brings them together with Payne, who has returned home after all. Songs include: "Give Me the Simple Life," "I Wish I Could Tell You," "Into the Sun" (Harry Ruby, Rube Bloom), and "Who Knows?" (Don Raye, Gene De Paul).

p, Walter Morosco; d, Lloyd Bacon; w, Elick Moll (based on the novel The *Enchanted Voyage* by Robert Nathan); ph, Harry Jackson (Technicolor); m, Cyril Mockridge; ed, Robert Fritch; md, Emil Newman; art d, Lyle Wheeler, J. Russell Spencer.

Adventure   (PR:A MPAA:NR)

WAKE UP AND LIVE**   (1937) 91m FOX bw

Walter Winchell (*Himself*), Ben Bernie and Band (*Themselves*), Alice Faye (*Alice Huntley*), Patsy Kelly (*Patsy Kane*), Ned Sparks (*Steve Cluskey*), Jack Haley (*Eddie Kane*), Grace Bradley (*Jean Roberts*), Walter Catlett (*Gus Avery*), Leah Ray (*Cafe Singer*), Joan Davis (*Spanish Dancer*), Douglas Fowley (*Herman*), Miles Mander (*James Stratton*), The Condos Brothers (*Specialty*), The Brewster Twins (*Themselves*), Etienne Girardot (*Waldo Peebles*), Paul Hurst (*McCabe*), George Givot (*Manager*), Barnett Parker (*Foster*), Charles Williams (*Alberts*), Warren Hymer (*1st Gunman*), Ed Gargan (*Murphy, Doorman*), William Demarest, John Sheehan (*Attendants*), Rosemary Glosz (*Singer*), Robert Lowery (*Chauffeur*), George Chandler (*Janitor*), Gary Breckner (*Announcer*), Elyse Knox (*Nurse*), Ellen Prescott (*Girl*), Harry Tyler (*Buick Driver*), Andre Beranger (*Accompanist*).

Radio was big-time show business in 1937 and this was an excellent satire of the industry, one of the best. Columnist Walter Winchell and bandleader Ben Bernie play themselves and seek to capitalize on their well-known "feud" (a manufactured grudge which was erected to help raise the ratings, not unlike the Jack Benny-Fred Allen "feud" which was also a total fabrication) in his slap-happy musical with lots of music. The whole country is tuning in to the "Old Maestro's" show to hear what he has to say about Winchell and to Winchell's radio program to hear the retorts. (Winchell began his radio shows with "Good evening Mr. and Mrs. North and South America and all the ships at sea...let's go to press!") While this is happening, entertainers Haley and Bradley come to New York to find a niche in radio. Haley's sister, Kelly, works for Winchell and she gets the duo an audition for the powerful newsman. They arrive at the audition and Haley watches the nervousness of an operatic performer who faints because of "mike fright." Haley and Bradley approach the microphone and he falls prey to the same fear so they never do get their audition. Bradley takes a singing job on her own and Haley has to content himself with gainful employment as a tour guide at the radio station. While leading some rubberneckers around, Haley meets Faye, a radio star who oversees a daily program of various kinds of advice. Faye thinks that Haley has to gain confidence before he can perform in front of the electric device so she has him practice in a studio at a mike that's "off." As luck, fate, and the contrivance of screenwriters would have it, Haley is practicing one day while Bernie's show is on the air. He's singing to the Bernie orchestra background and somehow his microphone is switched "on" and his singing voice is sent out over the airwaves. (Actually, Haley was dubbed by Buddy Clark, who sang "Linda" and had many hits before perishing in a private plane crash in Los Angeles.) The huge listening audience falls in love with the voice and phone calls and wires flood the station to find out who owns those dulcet tones. Bernie sees that he has a winner and tags Haley as "The Phantom Troubador" (at one time in radio, there was a man known as "The Masked Tenor"), a ruse that is immediately seen through by Winchell when Bernie tries to use another singer in Haley's stead. The whole city is looking for Haley. Kelly's boy friend is stoic Sparks, who also toils for Winchell, and he is busily searching for Haley as well. When Faye's radio show is dumped, she contacts Mander, the boss, and says that she can get the singer to perform but only on the proviso that the microphone is set up in her apartment on a remote broadcast basis. The reason for this is she knows Haley will be able to sing as long as he thinks the microphone is dead. Bradley comes back into the picture. She knows Haley's identity and tells agent Catlett, who promptly kidnaps Haley in the hopes of adding him to his client roster. At the conclusion, Faye lures Haley to the nightclub where Bernie's band is appearing and he screws up enough courage to sing into a mike. Sparks and Kelly are united (he'd been loath to make a commitment past lunch) and Faye and Haley are soon renowned as the "latest" singing duo in radio. Winchell and Bernie shake hands and call off their feud and all ends well. Lots of good tunes and specialties abound. Mack Gordon and Harry Revel contributed all the new songs, which include: "There's a Lull in My Life" (sung by Faye), "I Love You Too Much Muchacha" (sung by Leah Ray, then hysterically danced by Joan Davis), "Wake Up and Live" (Faye), plus "Never in a Million Years," "It's Swell of You," "Red Seal Malt," "I'm Bubbling Over," "Oh, But I'm Happy," and "De Camptown Races," which was written, you should know by now, by Stephen Foster. Haley was sensational in his role and wrought every last ounce of humor from his lines and was convincing as he moved his lips to Clark's singing. Haley had a pleasant singing voice of his own, as he demonstrated in several movies, not the least of which was THE WIZARD OF OZ. Good tap dancing from The Condos Brothers and a lot of fun from fade in to fade out. Older readers will enjoy the re-creation of a Winchell broadcast because his Sunday night show was very popular and must listening for everyone in the country in those years. Winchell, who had begun his show business career as one of the kids in the old Gus Edwards "School Days" act, knew his way around a sound stage and later became the narrator on "The Untouchables" TV show, receiving a reported $25,000 per episode for his voice. As popular as he was with the public, that's how feared Winchell was in New York for his power. It is alleged that he was the model for the character Burt Lancaster played in SWEET SMELL OF SUCCESS and, as anyone who has seen that movie will testify, this was hardly a beloved human being.

p, Darryl F. Zanuck; d, Sidney Lanfield; w, Harry Tugend, Jack Yellen (based on an original story by Curtis Kenyon and the book by Dorothea Brande); ph, Edward Cronjager; ed, Robert Simpson; md, Louis Silvers; art d, Mark-Lee Kirk; set d, Thomas Little; cos, Gwen Wakeling; ch, Jack Haskell.

Musical Comedy   (PR:AA MPAA:NR)

WAKE UP FAMOUS**   (1937, Brit.) 68m Premier-Stafford/RKO bw

Nelson Keys (*Alfred Dimbleden*), Gene Gerrard (*Fink*), Bela Mila (*Agatha Dimbleden*), Josephine Huntley Wright (*Daisy*), Fred Conyngham (*Jack*), H.F. Maltby (*Sir Weatherby Watts*), Joan White, Leo Von Kokorny, Bruno Barnabe.

Innocent hotel clerk Keys is framed by a gang of thieves for a jewel robbery. He is forced to flee the country, along with his wife, Mila. On arriving in France, the hapless clerk is mistaken for a songster by phony movie producer Gerrard; then he encounters the gang he was fleeing from in the first place. He manages to thwart their plans and captures them, and then a song he has written becomes a hit. The comedy takes one unbelievable twist after another, but the pace almost covers this up. The plot does catch up at last, causing the laughs finally to thin out.

p, John Stafford; d, Gene Gerrard; w, Basil Mason; ph, James Wilson.

Comedy   (PR:A MPAA:NR)

WALK A CROOKED MILE**½   (1948) 91m Edward Small/COL bw

Louis Hayward (*Philip Grayson*), Dennis O'Keefe (*Daniel O'Hara*), Louise Allbritton (*Dr. Toni Neva*), Carl Esmond (*Dr. Ritter von Stolb*), Onslow Stevens (*Igor Braun*), Raymond Burr (*Krebs*), Art Baker (*Dr. Frederick Townsend*), Lowell Gilmore (*Dr. William Forrest*), Philip Van Zandt (*Anton Radchek*), Charles Evans (*Dr. Homer Allen*), Frank Ferguson (*Carl Bemish*), Jimmy Lloyd (*Alison*), Bert Davidson (*Potter*), Paul Bryar (*Ivan*), Howard J. Negley (*Feodore*), Crane Whitley (*Curly*), Grandon Rhodes (*Adolph Mizner*), Keith Richards (*Miller*), Tamara Shayne (*Landlady*), Ray Teal (*Police Sergeant*), Arthur Space (*Mr. North, FBI Official*), John Hamilton (*G. W. Hunter, FBI Official*), Reed Hadley (*Narrator*).

Fast-paced espionage drama presented in a documentary style that details the mechanics employed by the FBI and Scotland Yard as they go after a ring of Communist spies trying to steal America's atomic secrets. O'Keefe plays the FBI agent and Hayward the Scotland Yard investigator hot on the trail of Communist agent Stevens who heads up a spy ring trying to get A-bomb secrets from prominent scientists.

p, Grant Whytock; d, Gordon Douglas; w, George Bruce (based on a story by Bertram Millhauser); ph, George Robinson; m, Paul Sawtell; ed, James E. Newcom; art d, Rudolph Sternad; set d, Howard Bristol; makeup, Norbert Miles.

Spy Drama   (PR:A MPAA:NR)

WALK A CROOKED PATH*½   (1969, Brit.) 90m Hanover/Cavalcade c

Tenniel Evans (*John Hemming*), Faith Brook (*Elizabeth Hemming*), Christopher Coll (*Bill Colman*), Patricia Haines (*Nancy Colman*), Clive Endersby (*Philip Dreaper*), Georgina Simpson (*Elaine*), Margery Mason (*Mildred*), Georgina Cookson (*Imogen*), Peter Copley (*Dr. Oberon*), Paul Dawkins (*Inspector*), Barry Perowne (*Unwins*).

Misfired psychological drama starring Evans as a tenured teacher in an exclusive boys' school who is shocked to learn that school officials have once again ignored him for the job of headmaster after many years of loyal service. Seeking a change in his life and tiring of his marriage to his independently wealthy wife Brook, Evans cooks up a bizarre scheme to inherit her fortune. He pays an unscrupulous male student, Endersby, to claim that he was homosexually abused by Evans, thus creating a shocking and embarrassing scandal. Then, with the help of Haines, his mistress, Evans humiliates Brook so badly that she commits suicide. The plan works, but justice soon catches up with the crazed schoolteacher.

p&d, John Brason; w, Barry Perowne.

Crime   (PR:O MPAA:NR)

WALK A TIGHTROPE**   (1964, U.S./Brit.) 69m
Parroch-McCallum-Associated Producers /PAR bw

Dan Duryea (*Lutcher*), Patricia Owens (*Ellen*), Terence Cooper (*Jason*), Richard Leech (*Doug*), Neil McCallum (*Counsel*), Trevor Reid (*Inspector MacMitchell*), A.J. Brown (*Magistrate*), David Bauer (*Ed*), Jack Melford.

Convoluted mystery starring Owens as an American woman married to British businessman Cooper. One day Owens becomes convinced she is being followed and shares her fears with her husband and his friend Leech. The three go to Owens' and Cooper's home, and when Leech goes upstairs to make a phone call, a killer, Duryea, enters the house and murders Cooper. When Leech runs downstairs to see what has happened, he overhears Duryea request his payment from Owens. Eventually, Duryea is captured by police and makes a full confession, claiming that Owens had hired him to kill her husband. The court refuses to believe him, however, because Duryea had recently been released from an insane asylum. Though Leech believes he knows that Owens is responsible for the murder, he keeps his mouth shut. Soon after the trial Leech learns that Owens was being blackmailed by her American ex-husband who claimed that they were never divorced. Despite the fact that she was pressured into the killing Leech phones the police and informs them of what he knows.

p, Jack Parsons; d, Frank Nesbitt; w, Neil McCallum (based on a story by Mann Rubin); ph, Basil Emmott; m, Buxton Orr; ed, Robert Winter; art d, Harry White.

Mystery   (PR:A-C MPAA:NR)

WALK, DON'T RUN***   (1966) 114m Granley/COL c

Cary Grant (*Sir William Rutland*), Samantha Eggar (*Christine Easton*), Jim Hutton (*Steve Davis*), John Standing (*Julius P. Haversack*), Miiko Taka (*Aiko Kurawa*), Ted Hartley (*Yuri Andreyovitch*), Ben Astar (*Dimitri*), George Takei (*Police Captain*), Teru Shimada (*Mr. Kurawa*), Lois Kiuchi (*Mrs. Kurawa*), Bob Okazaki (*Plant Manager*), James Yagi (*Rutland's Driver*), Craig Matsunaga (*Boy*), Patty Siu (*Girl*), Miyoshi Jingu (*Woman*), Ishimoto, Frank Kumagai (*Plain Clothesmen*), William Saito (*Japanese Athlete*), C. K. Yang (*Chinese Athlete*), Sonya Harrison, Kenneth Parker, Gail Peters, Mel Profit (*American Athletes*), Bert Santos, Isabel Boniface (*Mexican Athletes*), Holger Abro, Alex Rodine, David Draper, Sonja Haney (*Swedish Athletes*), Peggy Rea (*Russian Shot Putter*), Ilona Wilson, Andre Hemmers (*German Athletes*), Wendee Tochihara, Jodee Tochihara (*Japanese Twins*), Jane Tochihara (*Japanese Mother*), Noriko, Mori Moto, Anna Shin, Irene Mizushima, Yuki Tani (*Bath Attendants*), Susan Ikeda, June Kawai, Miko Mayama (*Japanese Waitresses*), Randy Okazaki (*Cab Driver*), George Matsui, Roy Taguchi (*Desk Clerks*), Kay Shimatsu, Bob Kino (*Assistant Managers*), Rollin Moriyama (*Manager*), Sheri Yamasaki (*Hostess*), Vickey Cason (*Contortionist*), Alan Chee, Lei Kim, Lukas Shimatsu, Roy Ogat, Yangi Kitadani, Monty O'Grady (*Ad Libs*).

Cary Grant's last film, which is a remake of THE MORE THE MERRIER (1943), sees him cast as a British industrialist who arrives in Tokyo on business but is unable to find a hotel due to the crowds brought in by the upcoming Olympic Games. Willing to do anything for accommodations, Grant fast-talks his way into the apartment of a young British embassy secretary, Eggar, who has a room to rent. The next day Grant meets Hutton, a member of the U.S. Olympic walking team, who is also in desperate need of a room. Taking a liking to the young man, Grant invites him to stay at Eggar's apartment as well. Though Eggar is miffed by Grant's impertinence, she does become vaguely attracted to Hutton (after all, *no one* in film history could stay mad at Cary Grant for long) and allows them to stay. Seeing that a possible romance could bloom between the two youngsters, Grant (who thinks Eggar's fiance, Standing, is a bore), sets out to play matchmaker. Everything proceeds smoothly until the Soviet security forces arrest Eggar and Hutton and accuse them of being spies. Standing panics because he thinks that if word leaks out that his fiancee is a Soviet spy living with two men, his career will be ruined. Grant shows up and gets the young couple out of jail. To placate Standing's fears (and further his own Cupid-like plans), Grant arranges a wedding for Hutton and Eggar so everything will appear to be on the up and up. Standing immediately agrees to the scheme, playing right into Grant's hands. After the wedding, Hutton and Eggar realize they love each other and decide to stay married. Happy that everything has turned out well for the young lovers, Grant boards a plane and returns to England.

p, Sol C. Siegel; d, Charles Walters; w, Sol Sak (based on a story by Robert Russell, Frank Ross; ph, Harry Stradling (Panavision, Technicolor); m, Quincy Jones; ed, Walter Thompson, James Wells; prod d, Joe Wright; set d, George R. Nelson, Robert Priestley; cos, Morton Haack; makeup, Ben Lane.

Comedy   (PR:A MPAA:NR)

WALK EAST ON BEACON***   (1952) 98m COL bw (GB: THE CRIME OF THE CENTURY)

George Murphy (*Inspector Belden*), Finlay Currie (*Prof. Kafer*), Virginia Gilmore (*Millie*), Karel Stepanek (*Alex*), Louisa Horton (*Elaine*), Peter Capell (*Gino*), Bruno Wick (*Danzig*), Karl Weber (*Reynolds*), Rev. Robert Dunn (*Dr. Wincott*), Jack Manning (*Vincent Foss*), Vilma Kurer (*Mrs. Ross*),

Michael Garrett (*Terrence*), Robert Carroll (*Boldany*), Ernest Graves (*Martin*), Rosemary Pettit (*Mrs. Martin*), George Roy Hill (*Wilben*), Bradford Hatton (*Mason*), Eva Condon (*Landlady*), Paul Andor (*Helmuth*), Lotte Palfi (*Mrs. Kafer*), Ann Thomas (*Philadelphia Suspect*), Nancy Heyl (*Mrs. Belden*), Suzanne Moulton (*Sherry Belden*), John Farrell (*Taxi Driver*), Stephen Mitchell (*Samson*).

A solid pseudo-documentary follow-up to the far superior THE HOUSE ON 92ND STREET, also produced by Rochemont. Based on a *Reader's Digest* story allegedly written by FBI topper J. Edgar Hoover, it's a penetration into the "Red Menace" that is more of a commercial for the FBI than anything else. Graves is a spy who was born in the U.S. and is now working for the Soviets. His job has been to secure valuable information on a new project known as "Falcon." When he fails to do this, he is replaced by Stepanek, the best spy in the USSR. Graves is spirited away on a Polish ship and his wife, Pettit, who is totally innocent, immediately contacts the FBI to find out what's happened to her missing hubby. Agent Murphy is put on the job, and together with his Boston-based sub-agents, uncovers the plot. Currie is a refugee scientist (sort of like Albert Einstein). He is busily contemplating weighty matters about time and space (never fully explained) and the Russkies go after him. His son is in Europe and they use the threat of killing the lad to attempt to extract information from him. But Currie notifies Murphy and a plan is concocted to feed the spies the wrong data. Stepanek didn't just fall off the vodka truck and he is soon hip to the duplicity and eventually lays his hands on the real material. The FBI pounces and arrests all of Stepanek's men, but he manages to get away and nab Currie. He intends taking the old man back to Russia in a sub that's moored off the Massachusetts shore. Before that can happen, the Coast Guard joins up with the FBI and the spy ring is cracked. Borden Mace and Lothar Wolff acted as Rochemont's associates on this picture that gave a good indication of how spies operate and eschewed phony dramatics and suspense for as accurate a depiction as they could show without betraying official secrets. Three writers were brought in to punch up Rosten's script so it's difficult to discern who wrote what. Rosten will also be recalled for his compendiums on Yiddish as well as his funny stories about Hyman Kaplan which he wrote under the name of "Leonard Q. Ross."

p, Louis de Rochemont; d, Alfred Werker; w, Leo Rosten, Virginia Shaler, Emmett Murphy, Leonard Heidemann (based on the magazine article "The Crime of the Century" by J. Edgar Hoover); ph, Joseph Brun; ed, Angelo Ross; md, Jack Shaindlin; art d, Herbert Andrews.

Spy Drama   **(PR:A   MPAA:NR)**

WALK IN THE SHADOW***   (1966, Brit.) 93m Allied Film
                                                    Makers/CD bw (GB: LIFE FOR RUTH)

Michael Craig (*John Harris*), Janet Munro (*Pat Harris*), Patrick McGoohan (*Dr. Brown*), Paul Rogers (*Hart Jacobs*), Megs Jenkins (*Mrs. Gordon*), Maureen Pryor (*Teddy's Mother*), John Barrie (*Mr. Gordon*), Basil Dignam (*Mapleton*), Leslie Sands (*Clyde*), Ellen McIntosh (*Duty Sister*), Frank Finlay (*Teddy's Father*), Michael Aldridge (*Howard*), Malcolm Keen (*John's Father*), Lynne Taylor (*Ruth Harris*), Freddy Ramsey (*Teddy*), Michael Bryant (*John's Counsel*), Norman Wooland (*Crown Counsel*), Walter Hudd (*Judge*), Maurice Colbourne (*Vicar*), John Welsh (*Marshal*).

Powerful drama which examines the question of religious freedom when it may cause harm to others. When little Lynne Taylor is hurt in a boating accident and taken to a hospital, her parents, Craig and Munro, are informed that only a blood transfusion will save her life. However, the procedure is forbidden by Craig, who is a member of a strict religious sect that does not allow believers to be operated on by doctors. Munro, who has tolerated her husband's religious convictions throughout their marriage, is outraged and returns to the hospital to grant the doctor, McGoohan, permission to proceed with the transfusion. Unfortunately, the go-ahead comes too late and the girl dies. McGoohan, an agnostic, decides to press manslaughter charges against Craig and the matter soon ends up in the courts. Now alone (Munro has left him), Craig finds a friend in a Jewish lawyer, Rogers, who volunteers to defend him. After a lengthy and emotional trial, Craig is eventually acquitted. Though a free man, Craig has been forced to question his faith and realizes that it was a mistake to put so much trust in God to perform miracles. Deeply depressed because he now blames himself for his daughter's death, Craig attempts suicide. McGoohan, who now sees that Craig needs help as well, goes to the distraught father and helps him face life. Realizing that she still loves her husband, and that he needs her, Munro returns to Craig.

p, Michael Relph; d, Basil Dearden; w, Janet Green, John McCormick (based on a play by Green); ph, Otto Heller; m, William Alwyn; ed, John D. Guthridge; md, Muir Mathieson; art d, Alex Vetchinsky; set d, Arthur Taksen; makeup, Harry Frampton.

Drama   **(PR:A   MPAA:NR)**

WALK IN THE SPRING RAIN, A**   (1970) 98m COL c

Anthony Quinn (*Will Cade*), Ingrid Bergman (*Libby Meredith*), Fritz Weaver (*Roger Meredith*), Katherine Crawford (*Ellen Meredith*), Tom Fielding (*Boy Cade*), Virginia Gregg (*Ann Cade*), Mitchell Silverman (*Bucky*).

Soapy melodrama starring Bergman as the bored, middle-aged wife of dry college professor Weaver, who accompanies her husband on a sabatical from New York City to the back roads of Tennessee. Finding the rural life refreshing, Bergman soon becomes enamored of local married man Quinn, whose simple vibrancy is in marked contrast to the musty intellectual musings of her husband. Quin returns her affections and soon the middle-aged pair begin a doomed romance. When Bergman's selfish daughter arrives in Tennessee announcing her acceptance by Harvard Law School, she demands that her mother return to New York to care for young Silberman, her son, and Bergman's grandson. Not wanting to leave Quinn, Bergman refuses. Soon afterward, Quinn disturbed son, Fielding, who knows of the illicit romance, tries to rape Bergman. Quinn arrives on the scene and accidentally kills his son while attempting to stop him. The incident brings the relationship to a bitter conclusion as Bergman and Weaver return to New York. While the presentation of a middle-aged romance was more than welcome on the screen in 1970 (after years of youth-oriented pictures), not even Bergman and Quinn could save the insipid meanderings of th contrived script. Though not totally embarrassing, A WALK IN THE SPRING RAIN is a major disappointment for all involved.

p, Stirling Silliphant; d, Guy Green; w, Silliphant (based on the novel by Rachel Maddux); ph, Charles lang (Panavision, Technicolor); m, Elmer Bernstein; ed, Ferris Anderson, Jr.; m/l, Bernstein, Don Black.

Romance   **(PR:C   MPAA:M/PG)**

WALK IN THE SUN, A*****   (1945) 117m FOX bw (GB: SALERNO
                                                                    BEACHHEAD)

Dana Andrews (*Sgt. Tyne*), Richard Conte (*Rivera*), John Ireland (*Windy*), George Tyne (*Friedman*), Lloyd Bridges (*Sgt. Ward*), Sterling Holloway (*McWilliams*), Herbert Rudley (*Sgt. Porter*), Norman Lloyd (*Archimbeau*), Steve Brodie (*Judson*), Huntz Hall (*Carraway*), James Cardwell (*Sgt. Hoskins*), Chris Drake (*Rankin*), Richard Benedict (*Tranella*), George Offerman, Jr. (*Tinker*), Danny Desmond (*Trasker*), Victor Cutler (*Cousins*), Anthony Dante (*Giorgio*), Harry Cline (*Cpl. Kramer*), Jay Norris (*James*), Al Hammer (*Johnson*), Don Summers (*Dugan*), Malcolm O'Guinn (*Phelps*), Grant Maiben (*Smith*), John Kellogg (*Riddle*), Dick Daniels (*Long*), Matt Willis (*Sgt. Halverson*), George Turner (*Reconnaissance*), Robert Lowell (*Lt. Rande*).

One of the best films to emerge from the final days of WW II (actually, the three best films of the war all appeared almost simultaneously shortly after the end of hostilities: THE STORY OF G.I. JOE, THEY WERE EXPENDABLE, and A WALK IN THE SUN). A WALK IN THE SUN is the story of one infantry platoon on one morning, from the time they hit the beach at Salerno to the time they reach and capture their objective: a farmhouse six miles inland. Before they even get ashore things go badly and the green lieutenant in command is killed. A sergeant takes over for a time, but the stress proves too great and he cracks. The men encounter a German armored car for which they set up an ambush, raining it with grenades as it passes down the road in one long, sweeping tracking shot. The men start walking again with Andrews in command. Several times German planes swoop down and strafe the men, killing many. When they reach the objective, they find it bristling with machine guns. Andrews sends one group around to ford a river and attack the position from the rear, while Andrews and the main force move up through a cornfield. Finally they rush out of the corn, shown in another fabulous tracking and panning shot, throwing grenades and taking more losses. Finally, though, they achieve their objective. Ireland, the company philosopher, states–as the men leave the farmhouse, writing a letter to his wife aloud, as is his habit–"Dear Frances. We just took a farmhouse in Italy," and then adds ironically, "it was so terribly easy." Throughout the film, as it follows the men in battle, the soundtrack picks up their thoughts, sometimes in first person, sometimes in third person. The men think about their place in the great scheme of the war, about their fear of being killed, and about the hard, dirty, tedious, and dangerous job of being a front-line foot soldier. Milestone set out to make the WW II equivalent of his masterpiece ALL QUIET ON THE WESTERN FRONT and he more than succeeded (he would also make the masterpiece of the Korean War, PORK CHOP HILL). The characters assembled in the platoon are convincing in their various foibles, Andrews as the sergeant who never liked to travel but who gets his job done professionally; Ireland as the son of a minister, constantly off alone and thinking to himself; and Lloyd, the skeptic of the unit, who thinks they will still be fighting in 1958, probably in Tibet. A langorous sense of resignation holds sway over all the men. They are there to do a job, and although they don't even understand what part they play in the big picture, they go and do it anyway, even at the cost of their lives. The dialog in the film is brilliantly written by Rossen, and Milestone's masterful direction employs all the fluid movements for which he was known, especially his marvelous trucking and dolly shots to keep pace with the constantly moving men, techniques he developed when directing ALL QUIET ON THE WESTERN FRONT. When the film was released here, it was immediately seen as a great film, but it was not released in Britain for six years because of the furor caused by OBJECTIVE: BURMA, which the British took offense to because it showed Erroll Flynn winning the war in Burma all but single-handed (THEY WERE EXPENDABLE was held up for British release for the same reason). In the years since A WALK IN THE SUN was made, a great many movies have dealt with the same themes, but none of them has come so near the truth as this film.

p&d, Lewis Milestone; w, Robert Rossen (based on a story by Harry Brown); ph, Russell Harlan; m, Frederic Efrem Rich; ed, Duncan Mansfield; art d, Max Bertisch; m/l, Millard Lampell, Earl Robinson.

War   Cas.   (PR:C MPAA:NR)

WALK INTO HELL*½   (1957, Aus.) 93m Southern International-Discfilm/Patric c

Chips Rafferty (*Steve McAllister*), Francoise Christophe (*Dr. Dumarcet*), Reginald Lye (*"Sharkeye" Kelly*), Pierre Cressoy (*Jeff Clayton*), Sgt. Maj. Somu (*Towalaka*), District Officer Fred Kaad (*Himself*).

Low-budget adventure saga starring Rafferty as a brave bush explorer hired to take entrepreneur Lye and French woman doctor Christophe into the wilds of New Guineain search of oil. Once oil is discovered, Rafferty must clear a patch of land and build a small airfield before the rainy season sets in. One day the small troupe runs across white hunter Cressoy, who has killed a white bird sacred to the natives, and is now running for his life. This of course, brings the angry natives right down the throats of Rafferty and company, but the clever explorer is able to fend them off.

p, Chips Rafferty; d, Lee Robinson; w, Rex Rienits; ph, Carl Kayser (Eastmancolor); m, Georges Auric; ed, Alex Ezard.

Adventure   (PR:A MPAA:NR)

WALK LIKE A DRAGON**   (1960) 95m PAR bw

Jack Lord (*Line Bartlett*), Nobu McCarthy (*Kim Sung*), James Shigeta (*Cheng Lu*), Mel Torme (*The Deacon*), Josephine Hutchinson (*Ma Bartlett*), Rudolph Acosta (*Sheriff Marguelez*), Benson Fong (*Wu*), Michael Pate (*Will Allen*), Lilyan Chauvin (*Mme. Lili Raide*), Don Kennedy (*Masters*), Donald Barry (*Cabot*), Natalie Trundy (*Susan*).

Miscegenation in the Old West as visiting cowboy Lord, in Chinatown, purchases the beautiful Chinese slave girl McCarthy to save her from certain sale to a San Francisco brothelkeeper. Discovering that she will be no better off with freedom, as she has few possessions or pretensions, humanitarian Lord brings the girl home to serve as live-in maid for himself and his less tian pleased mother, Hutchinson. Gradually, the two fall in love, to the discomfiture of local immigrant Shigeta, a disaffected, proud young man. Shigeta wants to learn to handle a gun as an egalitarian gesture; he enlists the services of itinerant preacher gunslinger Torme, a black-garbed mystery man, as mentor. Graced with great reflexes, Shigeta ultimately guns down his teacher, Torme. McCarthy elects to leave the household of the round-eyes and go away with her fellow oriental Shigeta despite her love for Lord, apparently deciding that the entire affair was only occidental. A fascinating view of the schism between whites and oriental immigrants in the turn-of-the-century West. Mainly a product of Clavell's talents; he would go on to greater fame in a similar vein as the author of the East-meets-West epic novel *Shogun.*

p&d, James Clavell; w, Clavell, Daniel Mainwaring; ph, Loyal Griggs; m, Paul Dunlap; ed, Howard Smith; art d, Hal Pereira, Ronald Anderson; m/l, Mel Torme (sung by Torme).

Western   (PR:O MPAA:NR)

WALK ON THE WILD SIDE*½   (1962) 114m Famous Artists/COL bw

Laurance Harvey (*Dove Linkhorn*), Capucine (*Hallie*), Jane Fonda (*Kitty Twist*), Anne Baxter (*Teresina Vidarverri*), Barbara Stanwyck (*Jo Courtney*), Joanna Moore (*Miss Precious*), Richard Rust (*Oliver*), Karl Swenson (*Schmidt*), Donald "Red" Barry (*Dockery*), Juanita Moore (*Mama*), John Anderson (*Preacher*), Ken Lynch (*Frank Bonito*), Todd Armstrong (*Lt. Omar Stroud*), Lillian Bronson (*Amy Gerard*), Adrienne Marden (*Eva Gerard*), Sherry O'Neil (*Reba*), John Bryant (*Spence*), Kathryn Card (*Landlady*), Nesdon Booth (*1st Van Driver*), Steve Benton (*2nd Van Driver*), Pat Tiernan (*Georgia*), Barbara Hines, Elaine Martone, Virginia Holden, Florence Wyatt (*Girls*), Marl Young (*Piano Player*), Ted Jacques (*Sheriff*), Joni Morris (*Little Girl*), Paul Maxey (*Auctioneer*), Cordy Clark (*Fat Woman*), Ray Walker (*Salesman*), Miss Masters (*Tony*), Murray Alper (*Simon*), Bill Walker (*Black Man*), Edward Mallory (*Sidekick*), Alexander Lockwood (*Doctor*), Chester Jones (*Black Waiter*), Crahan Denton, Willard Waterman.

Harvey travels from Texas to New Orleans looking for his missing love, Capucine. As soon as he hops off the freight train that brought him to Louisiana, he meets Fonda, a girl of few morals, and together they make their way into town. Harvey soon lands a job in a restaurant run by Baxter. Eventually he discovers Capucine working in the Doll's House, a brothel run by Stanwyck, whose interest in Capucine is something more than professional. Harvey tries to get Capucine to come back to the farm with him, but she refuses, and when Stanwyck discovers his intentions toward her object of affection, she has some of her bouncers beat him to a pulp. Fonda, who is also working for Stanwyck by this time, takes him back to Baxter's restaurant where he is bandaged up. Fonda tells Capucine what has happened to Harvey and she goes to see him. Stanwyck and one of her goons (Rust) follow and a shootout at the restaurant ensues. Capucine is hit by a stray bullet and she dies in Harvey's arms. Bearing no resemblance to its namesake novel by Nelson Algren, the film is mostly an exercise in luridness

and suggested deviance, without ever daring to face up to what it hints at. Stanwyck's lesbian interest in Capucine is so delicately suggested one might not even notice it, although prudish critics proclaimed it a new low in cinematic perversion. Much more interesting than the tensions between the characters were the tensions on the set. Producer Feldman was living with Capucine at the time and although the setting of the film was 1931, he insisted that she only wear the latest Cardin designed gowns. Director Dmytryk could only shoot around this glaring flaw as best he could. Fonda also contributed to the tensions on the set by turning up for shooting with a personal "secretary," a Greek ex-dancer who would advise Fonda on aspects of her performance. Together with Capucine they formed a sort of cabal that would return to where Feldman and Capucine were staying and discuss the day's shooting. On one of the last days of shooting, matters finally came to a head. They had rehearsed Capucine's death scene extensively the day before and it was all ready to go in front of the cameras, but when Capucine arrived in the morning, she announced she had been thinking about the scene and now wanted to do it another way. She proceeded to act out an embarrassingly bad death that Dmytryk later said looked like something out of an amateur ballet. As Dmytryk began to give a point-by-point critique, Capucine defended herself, and Harvey, who had been trying to keep his temper the whole time, finally exploded. Dmytryk restored order on the set, banished Fonda's advisor for the duration of the shooting, as well as the New York art director who was another "conspirator." After that the rest of the shooting went smoothly. The script of the film also had tangled problems. Feldman sent it to seemingly dozens of writers for rewrites, including Clifford Odets, who told Dmytryk: "I can make any scene interesting, even though it may have nothing to do with the story." His scenes were indeed interesting, but they do not appear in the film. Ben Hecht also did work on the script, but after a careful and total rewrite, Feldman decided it wasn't "sexy" enough. Even during the shooting, Feldman was almost daily sending over rewritten scenes which Dmytryk would discuss with the actors, then discard. The final film certainly shows all the problems of its production. On the positive side, the film's title song received an Academy Award nomination, and Saul Bass designed a terrific opening credit sequence using a cat walking through shadowy alleys.

p, Charles K. Feldman; d, Edward Dmytryk; w, John Fante, Edmund Morris (based on the novel by Nelson Algren); ph, Joe MacDonald; m, Elmer Bernstein; ed, Charles J. Rice; art d, Richard Sylbert; set d, William Kiernan; cos, Charles LeMaire; m/l, title song, Mack David, Bernstein (sung by Brook Benton).

Drama   (PR:O MPAA:NR)

WALK PROUD**   (1979) 102m UNIV c (AKA: GANG)

Robby Benson (*Emilio*), Sarah Holcomb (*Sarah Lassiter*), Henry Darrow (*Mike Serrano*), Pepe Serna (*Cesar*), Trinidad Silva (*Dagger*), Ji-Tu Cumbuka (*Sgt. Gannett*), Lawrence Pressman (*Henry Lassiter*), Domingo Ambriz (*Cowboy*), Brad Sullivan (*Jerry Kelsey*), Irene De Bari (*Mrs. Mendez*), Gary Cervantes (*Carlos*), Eloy Phil Casados (*Hugo*), Tony Alvarenga (*Paco*), Daniel Faraldo (*El Tigre*), Panchito Gomez (*Manuel*), Joe D. Jacobs (*Store Owner*), Bill Lopresto (*Ice Cream Vendor*), Stephen Morrell (*Hippo*), Benjie Bancroft (*Police Guard*), Lee Fraser (*Johnny*), Tim Culbertson (*Guard*), Claudio Martinez (*Vincente*), Rod Masterson, Dennis O'Flaherty (*Policemen*), Patricia A. Morales (*Church Singer*), Rose Portillo (*Katie*), Luis Reyes (*El Espanol*), Eduardo Ricard (*Priest*), Angel Salazar (*Angel*), Judith Searle (*Abigail Lassiter*), Tony Steinhart (*Interrogation Officer*), Felipe Turich (*Prayer Maker/Stuntman*), Eddie Hice, Rafael E. Lopez, Thomas Rosales, Jr, Rick Sawaya (*Stuntmen*).

The tamest and most "socially relevant" youth-gang film of 1979 (THE WARRIORS and BOULEVARD NIGHTS were also released that year) sees white-as-a-lily Robby Benson, the Anthony Quinn of the juvenile set, cast as a confused Chicano gang member. With all the maturity, insight, and plausibility of an ABC-TV "After School Special", WALK PROUD follows Benson through his rites of passage with his street gang and an unlikely romance with a rich white girl, Holcomb, who begs him to stop running with the pack. Infused with Latin machismo, Benson refuses, but his point of view changes after a visit back to Mexico for the funeral of his grandmother. Once in Mexico, Benson's mother inexplicably decides to introduce her son to his long-lost father, Sullivan, an alcoholic gringo with no redeeming qualities whatsoever. For some reason, this revelation snaps Benson back to his senses and he forsakes the street gang for the love of Holcomb (but not before he is beaten practically to a pulp by his buddies). Surprisingly, Benson isn't as bad as you'd think, but the hypocrisy of his casting didn't exactly endear the filmmakers to the Latin community. While the gang-related details are fascinating (the script was written by Evan Hunter, who had penned one of the earliest gang movies—THE BLACKBOARD JUNGLE—nearly 25 years before), the human drama is a bit on the soap opera side.

p, Lawrence Turman; d, Robert Collins; w, Evan Hunter; ph, Bobby Byrne (Panavision, Technicolor); m, Don Peake, Robby Benson; ed, Douglas Stewart; art d, William L. Campbell.

Drama   (PR:C MPAA:PG)

WALK SOFTLY, STRANGER**½

(1950) 81m Vanguard-RKO/RKO bw

Joseph Cotten (*Chris Hale*), [Alida] Valli (*Elaine Corelli*), Spring Byington (*Mrs. Brentman*), Paul Stewart (*Whitey*), Jack Paar (*Ray Healey*), Jeff Donnell (*Gwen*), John McIntire (*Morgan*), Howard Petrie (*Bowen*), Frank Puglia (*A. J. Corelli*), Esther Dale (*Thompson*), Marlo Dwyer (*Mabel*), Robert Ellis (*Boy*).

Cotten is a crooked gambler trying to escape his past by relocating in a small Ohio town. He moves into a boarding house Byington runs, then takes a job in a shoe factory owned by Puglia. Puglia's daughter Valli is a bitter young woman, confined to a wheelchair as the result of a skiing accident. Cotten sees a chance to bilk some money out of Valli by pretending to court her, but surprises himself by really falling in love. Romance blossoms, but this is threatened when some of Cotten's old cronies arrive in town. Cotten is once more under their thumb but this time he extricates himself by causing the villains' automobile to crack up after a thrilling chase. In the end Cotten must go to prison, but Valli promises to wait while he does his time. The film develops like a checklist, using every conceivable cliche that fits these characters and situations. Despite good performances by Cotten and Valli, it quickly grows boring with an easily predictable progression. Production had been completed two years prior to release but RKO held off on this, waiting for the popularity of Cotten and Valli in 1949's THE THIRD MAN to help sell the film. And to no avail, for this was the studio's biggest bomb of the year, losing some $775,000. Moroni Olsen originally played the shoe factory owner but during retakes it was decided to replace him with Puglia. This also marked the last film famed producer Dore Schary worked on for RKO. Following disagreements with studio head Howard Hughes, Schary went back to his old offices at MGM.

p, Robert Sparks; d, Robert Stevenson; w, Frank Fenton (based on a story by Manny Seff, Paul Yawitz); ph, Harry J. Wild; m, Frederick Hollander; ed, Frederic Knudtson; md, C. Bakaleinikoff; art d, Albert D'Agostino, Alfred Herman.

Drama   (PR:C   MPAA:NR)

WALK TALL**

(1960) 60m FOX c

Willard Parker (*Capt. Ed Trask*), Joyce Meadows (*Sally Medford*), Kent Taylor (*Ed Carter*), Russ Bender (*Col. Stanton*), Ron Soble (*Leach*), Alberto Monte (*Carlos*), Bill Mims (*Jake*), Felix Locher (*Chief Black Feather*), Dave DePaul (*Buffalo Horn*).

Parker plays an Army captain assigned to bring psychotic killer-Indian hater Taylor to justice in order to prevent the angry Shoshone Indians from going on the warpath over him. Unfortunately for Parker, Taylor's gang shows up on the trail and attempts to rescue their leader. Luckily, the noble Shoshones arrive and help Parker fend off the outlaws. Pretty dull.

p&d, Maury Dexter; w, Joseph Fritz; ph, Floyd Crosby (CinemaScope, DeLuxe Color); m, Richard D. Aurandt; ed, Eddie Dutko.

Western   (PR:A   MPAA:NR)

WALK THE ANGRY BEACH*½   (1961) 74m John Patrick Hayes bw

Anthony Vorno (*Tony*), Rue McClanahan (*Sandy*), Paul Bruce (*Nick*), Ernest Macias (*Ernest*), John Barrick (*Tom*), Leslie Moorhouse (*Shakespearean*), Doug Rideout (*Fitz*), Joanne Stewart (*Patti*), Lea Marmer (*Mrs. McVea*).

Grim Hollywood drama starring Vorno as a young man who hits the skids after his wife leaves him. Soon after, Vorno's junkyard business folds up and he is forced to join some crooks in a waterfront holdup. Vorno meets and falls in love with McClanahan, a young woman willing to bed producers to get her big break in Hollywood. After a disagreement with his criminal cohorts, Vorno is stabbed and dies in McClanahan's arms. A depressing character study done with little finesse. Limited release.

p,d&w, John Patrick Hayes; ph, Vilis Lapenieks; m, Bill Marx; ed, Esther Poche, Ronald Thorne.

Crime   (PR:C   MPAA:NR)

WALK THE DARK STREET**

(1956) 74m Valor/Associated
Artists-Dominant c

Chuck Connors, Don Ross, Regina Gleason, Eddie Kafafian, Vonne Godfrey, Ewing Brown, Don Orlando, Fred Darian, LaRue Malouf, Ernest Dominy, Jay Lawrence.

Weird action drama starring Connors as a somewhat crazed big-game hunter who challenges Army officer Ross (whom he blames for his soldier-brother's death by heart attack) to a duel by giving each man a camera-gun he has invented and forcing each to defend himself in the streets of Los Angeles during a "simulated" manhunt. In a none-too-original twist, Connors finds himself cornered by Ross and realizes that his rival accidentally has the gun with the real bullets, leaving him defenseless. Of course, Connors panics and dies of a heart attack.

p,d&w, Wyott Ordung; ph, Brydon Baker; m, Paul Dunlap; ed, Leon Barsha; md, Dunlap.

Adventure   (PR:C   MPAA:NR)

WALK THE PROUD LAND**½   (1956) 88m UNIV c

Audie Murphy (*John P. Clum*), Anne Bancroft (*Tianay*), Pat Crowley (*Mary Dennison*), Charles Drake (*Tom Sweeney*), Tommy Rall (*Taglito*), Robert Warwick (*Eskiminzin*), Jay Silverheels (*Geronimo*), Eugene Mazzola (*Tono*), Anthony Caruso (*Disalin*), Victor Millan (*Santos*), Ainslie Pryor (*Capt. Larsen*), Eugene Iglesias (*Chato*), Morris Ankrum (*Gen. Wade*), Addison Richards (*Gov. Safford*), Maurice Jara (*Alchise*), Frank Chase (*Stone*), Ed Hinton (*Naylor*), Marty Carrizosa (*Pica*).

Slow screen biography starring Murphy as John P. Clum, famed Indian agent responsible for talking Geronimo (played by Silverheels again) into surrendering to the authorities. The film sees Murphy as a noble ex-soldier working diligently at setting up a system so that the Apaches will be allowed self-government. Into the drama are thrown marital difficulties between Murphy and his wife Crowley. Crowley doesn't take kindly to widowed squaw Bancroft's attentions to her husband, and she would like nothing better than to move back East. The climax, where Silverheels surrenders to Murphy, is less than thrilling.

p, Aaron Rosenberg; d, Jesse Hibbs; w, Gil Doud, Jack Sher (based on the biography *Apache Agent* by Woodworth Clum); ph, Harold Lipstein (CinemaScope, Technicolor); ed, Sherman A. Todd; md, Joseph Gershenson; art d, Alexander Golitzen, Bill Newberry; cos, Bill Thomas.

Western   (PR:A   MPAA:NR)

WALK THE WALK*   (1970) 95m HQZ/Hallmark of Hollywood c

Bernie Hamilton (*Mike*), Honor Lawrence (*Pusher*), David Steinbuck, Bert Hoffman, Eric Weston, Steve Lavigne.

Low-budget antidrug evangelism starring Hamilton as a black college student addicted to heroin. Despite his efforts to break the habit, Hamilton sinks deeper and deeper into the seedy underworld of junkies and pushers. Eventually he overcomes his addiction, but after suffering an injury that requires doctors to inject him with painkillers, Hamilton once again winds up a junkie. The despair of starting over drives Hamilton to hang himself. Ineptly executed, pure exploitation.

p,d&w, Jac Zacha; ph, Stu Stallsmith (Movielab Color).

Drama   (PR:O   MPAA:R)

WALK WITH LOVE AND DEATH, A**   (1969) 90M FOX c

Anjelica Huston (*Lady Claudia*), Assaf Dayan (*Heron of Foix*), Anthony Corlan (*Robert*), John Hallam (*Sir Meles*), Robert Lang (*Pilgrim Leader*), Guy Deghy (*Priest*), Michael Gough (*Mad Monk*), George Murcell (*Captain*), Eileen Murphy (*Gypsy Girl*), Anthony Nicholls (*Father Superior*), Joseph O'Connor (*St. Jean*), John Huston (*Robert the Elder*), John Franklin (*Whoremaster*), Francis Heim (*Knight Lieutenant*), Melvyn Hayes (*1st Entertainer*), Barry Keegan (*Peasant Leader*), Nicholas Smith (*Pilgrim*), Antoinette Reuss (*Charcoal Woman*), Gilles Segal, Med Hondo, Luis Masson (*Entertainers*), Eugen Ledebur (*Goldsmith*), Otto Dworak (*Innkeeper*), Max Sulz (*Peasant*), John Veenenbos (*Monk*), Dieter Tressler (*Major Domo*), Paul Hoer (*Peasant Boy*), Myra Malik (*Peasant Girl*), Michael Baronne, Yvan Strogoff (*Soldiers*).

Both Anjelica Huston and her father John would like to forget they ever made this film, which was designed as Anjelica's debut in motion pictures. Unfortunately Miss Huston wasn't quite ready for the silver screen (she's getting better--see PRIZZI'S HONOR) and the results are spotty at best. Set in the Middle Ages during the Hundred Years War, the film opens as Dayan (son of Israeli soldier-politician Moshe) wanders the French countryside trying to avoid the death and destruction around him. Soon he meets Huston, the young daughter of a nobleman, and the pair fall in love. They decide to flee the country together, but the war overcomes them and they are eventually killed in a monastery after performing their own wedding ceremony. While not a total disaster (director Huston successfully creates an accurate portrayal of life in the Middle Ages), the performances of Anjelica and Dayan are not strong enough to carry the film.

p, Carter De Haven III; d, John Huston; w, Dale Wasserman, Hans Koningsberger (based on the novel by Koningsberger); ph, Ted Scaife (DeLuxe Color); m, Georges Delerue; ed, Russell Lloyd; md, Delerue; prod d, Stephen Grimes; art d, Wolf Witzemann; set d, Josie Macavin; cos, Leonor Fini; m/l, Delerue, Gladys Hill.

Drama   (PR:C   MPAA:M)

WALKABOUT***½   (1971, Aus./U.S.) 95m FOX c

Jenny Agutter (*Girl*), Lucien John (*Brother*), David Gumpilil (*Aborigine*), John Meillon (*Father*), Peter Carver (*No Hoper*), John Illingsworth (*Husband*), Barry Donnelly (*Australian Scientist*), Noelene Brown (*German Scientist*), Carlo Manchini (*Italian Scientist*).

A lyrical adventure film from director Nicolas Roeg (DON'T LOOK NOW, INSIGNIFICANCE) which stars Agutter and John as a brother and sister left stranded in the Australian outback by their father who goes insane and kills himself (we're really never sure why). Armed only with a transistor radio for survival, the children wander the wasteland with little hope of rescue. One day a young aborigine, Gumpilil, finds them and he shows them how to survive in the desert. There is a sexual attraction between Gumpilil and Agutter, and the white girl even encourages the aborigine to pursue her. One night Gumpilil performs a strange ritual mating dance for Agutter, but she rejects him and the next morning she and her brother find the aborigine dead–an apparent suicide. Eventually the children make their way back to civilization and we see that the whole film has been a flashback for Agutter while she lies in the arms of her white Australian husband. While the narrative is a bit ambiguous and heavily laden with allegory and metaphor, the visuals are stunning and the musical score by John Barry is beautiful and haunting. A powerful film if one lets it work its magic. Songs and musical numbers include "Electronic Dance" (Billy Mitchell), "Gasoline Alley" (Rod Stewart), "Los Angeles" (Warren Marley), and excerpts from "Hymen" (Karl Heinz Stockhausen).

p, Si Litvinoff; d, Nicolas Roeg; w, Edward Bond (based on the novel by James Vance Marshall); ph, Roeg (Eastmancolor); m, John Barry; ed, Antony Gibbs, Alan Patillo; md, Barry; prod d, Brian Eatwell; art d, Terry Gough; m/l, Billy Mitchell, Rod Stewart, Warren Marley, Karl Heinz Stockhausen; makeup, Linda Richmond.

Drama   **(PR:C MPAA:R/GP)**

WALKING DEAD, THE*½**   (1936) 66m WB bw

Boris Karloff (John Ellman), Ricardo Cortez (Nolan), Warren Hull (Jimmy), Robert Strange (Merritt), Joseph King (Judge Shaw), Edmund Gwenn (Dr. Evan Beaumont), Marguerite Churchill (Nancy), Barton MacLane (Loder), Henry O'Neill (Warner), Paul Harvey (Blackstone), Joseph Sawyer (Trigger Smith), Eddie Acuff (Betcha), Ruth Robinson (Mrs. Shaw), Addison Richards (Prison Warden), Kenneth Harlan (Stephen Martin), Miki Morita (Sako), Adrian Rosley (Florist), Milt Kibbee, Bill Elliott, Wade Boteler.

Creepy horror film starring Karloff as a gentle ex-convict on the road to reform when he is framed for the murder of an important judge (who just happens to be the one who sent him to prison) by a group of gangsters led by corrupt attorney Cortez. Though the evidence is mainly circumstantial, Karloff is convicted and sentenced to die in the electric chair. Learning that Karloff is indeed innocent about 30 seconds after he has been executed, the authorities allow scientist Gwenn to try bringing Karloff back to life using his new "Lindbergh Heart" gadget (the Lindbergh Heart was an actual mechanical circulating system developed by famed flier Charles A. Lindbergh with the help of several doctors including Nobel Prize winner Dr. Alexis Carrel). The experiment succeeds and Karloff lives again, though his face has taken on a distinctly Frankenstein-monsterish look and his hair has developed a massive white streak. Though definitely alive, Karloff seems more zombie-like than human and does not seem to enjoy his reanimated state. Gwenn becomes convinced that Karloff has gained some sort of supernatural knowledge while dead and tries to get his reticent subject to tell what he knows. At night, Karloff confronts those who sent him to the electric chair and scares them to death (all the killings are self-inflicted; Karloff never touches them). Eventually the two surviving crooks, MacLane and Cortez, track Karloff down in a graveyard (where the living-dead man feels the most at home) and kill him a second time, but on their getaway their car veers off the road and crashes into a power line, electrocuting them both. Gwenn finds the dying Karloff and asks him "what is death?" and Karloff replies "peace" before he passes on again. While the story is basically just a variation on the FRANKENSTEIN themes, director Curtiz infuses the film with a moody visual style full of low-key lighting and interesting camera angles that make this the best of Karloff's many "living-dead" movies (the list includes THE MAN WHO LIVED AGAIN [1936], THE MAN THEY COULD NOT HANG [1939], THE MAN WITH NINE LIVES [1940], BEFORE I HANG [1940], and THE DEVIL COMMANDS [1941]).

p, Lou Edelman; d, Michael Curtiz; w, Ewart Adamson, Peter Milne, Robert Andrews, Lillie Hayward (based on a story by Adamson, Joseph Fields); ph, Hal Mohr; ed, Thomas Pratt; art d, Hugh Reticker; cos, Cary Odell, Orry-Kelly; makeup, Perc Westmore.

Horror   **Cas.**   **(PR:A MPAA:NR)**

WALKING DOWN BROADWAY, 1935 (SEE: HELLO SISTER, 1935)

WALKING DOWN BROADWAY**   (1938) 75m FOX bw

Claire Trevor (Joan Bradley), Phyllis Brooks (Vicki Stone), Leah Ray (Linda Martin), Dixie Dunbar (Tiny Bronson), Lynn Bari (Sandra De Voe), Jayne Regan (Jerry Lane), Michael Whalen (Peter Claybourne), Thomas Beck (Tom Douglas), Douglas Fowley (Ace Wagner), Walter Woolf King (Jeff Hoffman), Jed Prouty (F. R. Randall), Robert Kellard (Bob Randall), Joan Carol (Sunny), Leon Ames (Frank Gatty), William "Billy" Benedict (Eddie), Maurice Cass (Mr. Wentwhistle).

Trevor, Brooks, Ray, Dunbar, Bari, and Regan star as six Broadway chorus girls who, when the revue they have been performing in closes, vow to have a reunion exactly one year from that day. We follow their lives during that period and watch as one is jailed for murder, two are killed in accidents, one

marries her childhood sweetheart, another marries for money, and Trevor becomes a happy, successful businesswoman.

p, Sol M. Wurtzel; d, Norman Foster; w, Robert Chapin, Karen DeWolf (based on the story "Six Girls and Death" by Mark Hellinger); ph, Virgil Miller; ed, Norman Colbert; md, Samuel Kaylin; art d, Bernard Herzbrun, Lewis H. Creber; m/l, Sidney Clare, Harry Akst.

Drama   **(PR:A MPAA:NR)**

WALKING HILLS, THE**   (1949) 78m COL bw

Randolph Scott (Jim Carey), Ella Raines (Chris Jackson), William Bishop (Shep), Edgar Buchanan (Old Willy), Arthur Kennedy (Chalk), John Ireland (Frazee), Jerome Courtland (Johnny), Josh White (Josh), Russell Collins (Bibbs), Charles Stevens (Cleve), Houseley Stevenson (King), Reed Howes (Young King).

A fine low-budget western (director Sturges' first) has a band of treasure seekers looking for a wagon train full of gold that had been buried years before somewhere in Death Valley. Of course the closer the group gets to the gold, the higher the tension among them gets until several members of the party are killed. When a vicious sandstorm kicks up, the remaining treasure hunters scatter, but the winds reveal the location of the gold. Raines and Scott nab the treasure and then Scott, who is wanted for murder, nobly rides to town to give himself up. Black singer White provides some fine blues numbers and folk songs, accompanying himself on the guitar in his inimitable way.

p, Harry Joe Brown; d, John Sturges; w, Alan LeMay, Virginia Roddick; ph, Charles Lawton, Jr.; m, Arthur Morton; ed, William Lyon; md, Morris W. Stoloff; art d, Robert Peterson; set d, James Crowe; cos, Jean Louis; makeup, Dave Grayson.

Western   **(PR:A MPAA:NR)**

WALKING MY BABY BACK HOME**   (1953) 95m UNIV c

Donald O'Connor (Jigger Millard), Janet Leigh (Chris Hall), Buddy Hackett (Blimp Edwards), Lori Nelson (Claire), Scatman Crothers (Smiley), Kathleen Lockhart (Mrs. Millard), George Cleveland (Col. Wallace), John Hubbard (Rodney Millard), Norman Abbott (Doc), Phil Garris (Hank), Walter Kingsford (Henry Hall), Sidney Miller (Walter Thomas), Paula Kelly, The Modernaires, The Sportsmen.

A disappointing musical comedy that starts nowhere and goes rapidly in the same direction. O'Connor is a well-to-do young man who is mustered out of the Army and who uses his inheritance to back his own band made up of his pals from the service. They soon find that their kind of music has little appeal so O'Connor disbands the aggregation and takes a job in a minstrel show run by Kingsford, who is the uncle of the beauteous Leigh. But that kind of entertainment is long past its prime and the minstrel show quickly goes into bankruptcy. Now it's time to do some heavy thinking and O'Connor comes up with an idea only scriptwriters could have imagined; he takes the classics and swings them in a Dixieland fashion. It's only minutes before he's on top of the musical world with the girl of his dreams at his side. In concept and execution, the movie was more like a 30s film than something from the 50s, and therein was the problem. O'Connor dances, sings, mugs, and does everything asked of him, but not enough was asked of him. Buddy Hackett makes his film debut and gets the chance to do his patented racial stereotype routine as a Chinese waiter. It was this comedy sketch that brought him national attention on TV and they repeated it in the movie, although the rest of his dialog was so heavily Brooklynese that it was not easy to understand. O'Connor's long-time nightclub partner, Sidney Miller, does well as a sleazy agent. Songs from a raft of writers include: "Man's Gotta Eat" (Scatman Crothers, F.E. Miller, sung by Crothers), "Walkin' My Baby Back Home" (Roy Turk, Fred Ahlert, Sr., sung by O'Connor), "Glow Worm" (Johnny Mercer, Paul Lincke), "Honeysuckle Rose" (Andy Razaf, Thomas "Fats" Waller), "South Rampart Street Parade" (Ray Bauduc, Bob Haggart, Steve Allen), "Muskrat Ramble" (Ray Gilbert, Kid Ory), "De Camptown Races" (Stephen Foster), as well as "Liebestraum" (arranged by Shorty Rogers), "Hi Lee, Hi Low," and "Largo Al Factotum Della Citta." Paula Kelly of The Modernaires dubbed Leigh's voice as well as used her own and the Jack Benny singing group known as "The Sportsmen" were also seen. The production numbers were lackluster and the direction was bland.

p, Ted Richmond; d, Lloyd Bacon; w, Don McGuire, Oscar Brodney (based on a story by McGuire); ph, Irving Glassberg (Technicolor); ed, Ted J. Kent; md, Joseph Gershenson; art d, Bernard Herzbrun, Emrich Nicholson; ch, Louis Da Pron.

Musical   **(PR:A MPAA:NR)**

WALKING ON AIR**   (1936) 70m RKO bw

Gene Raymond (Pete Quinlan), Ann Sothern (Kit Bennett), Jessie Ralph (Evelyn Bennett), Henry Stephenson (Mr. Bennett), Gordon Jones (Joe), George Meeker (Tom Quinlan), Maxine Jennings (Flo Quinlan), Alan Curtis (Fred Randolph), Anita Colby (Ex-Mrs. Randolph), Patricia Wilder (Reception Girl), George Andre Beranger (Albert), Charles Coleman (Butler), A. S. Byron, Frank Jenks, Manny Harmon, Arthur Hoyt, Robert

Graves, J. Maurice Sullivan, Jack Rice, Fred Stanley.

Pleasant musical comedy starring Sothern as an independent young woman who hires college student Raymond to pose as a rude French count whom she brings home as her new boy friend in order to drive her father, Stephenson, and her aunt, Ralph, crazy enough to approve of her relationship with the man she really loves, the recently-divorced Curtis. Of course as the film progresses Sothern falls in love with Raymond and dumps Curtis. Lively performances and a fast pace keep this one bouncing along. Songs include: "Cabin on a Hilltop" (Bert Kalmar, Harry Ruby), "Let's Make a Wish," and "My Heart Wants to Dance" (Kalmar, Ruby, Sid Silvers).

p, Edward Kaufman; d, Joe Santley; w, Bert Kalmar, Harry Ruby, Viola Brothers Shore, Rian James (based on a story by Francis M. Cockrell); ph, J. Roy Hunt; m, Ruby; ed, George Hively; cos, Bernard Newman.

Musical   **(PR:A MPAA:NR)**

WALKING ON AIR*   (1946, Brit.) 61m Marylebone/Piccadilly bw

Johnny Worthy (Johnny), Bertie Jarrett (Bertie), Susan Shaw, Billy Thatcher, Jasmine Dee, Maudie Edwards, Miki Hood, Gordon Edwards, Jill Allan, Sonny Thomas, Carol Fenton, Lauderic Caton, Coleridge Goode, Freddie Crump, The Skating Avalons, The Ray Ellington Quartet.

Shaw is the south end of a horse for an ice show, but she longs to be a ballerina. With hard work it looks like she will achieve that goal, but will her oversized ego get in her way? Plenty of dancing and skating, but the story skims along on thin ice.

p, Michael H. Goodman; d, Aveling Ginever; w, Ginever, John Worthy, Val Guest; ph, Stanley Clinton; m/l, Worthy, Peter Noble.

Drama   **(PR:AAA MPAA:NR)**

WALKING STICK, THE½**   (1970, Brit.) 101m Winkast/MGM c

David Hemmings (Leigh Hartley), Samantha Eggar (Deborah Dainton), Emlyn Williams (Jack Foil), Phyllis Calvert (Erica Dainton), Ferdy Mayne (Douglas Dainton), Francesca Annis (Arabella Dainton), Bridget Turner (Sarah Dainton), Dudley Sutton (Ted Sandymount), John Woodvine (Bertie Irons), David Savile (David Talbot), Derek Cox, Harvey Sambrook (Guards), Gwen Cherell (Mrs. Hartley), Walter Horsburgh (Maitland), Basil Henson (Inspector Malcolm), Anthony Nicholls (Lewis Maude), Nan Munro (Mrs. Stevenson), Donald Sumpter (Max), David Griffin (Benjy), Susan Payne (Deborah as a Child).

Eggar stars as a beautiful young antiques appraiser crippled by polio who succumbs to the charms of Hemmings, a struggling young painter who tries to woo her. Eventually, the romance blossoms into love for Hemmings and she moves in with him. Not long after, Hemmings approaches Eggar with the suggestion that she help him and his partner Williams rob the antique shop where she works. Blinded by her love, Eggar agrees to help, assuming that Hemmings will use the money to start their own antique shop. With Eggar's help the robbery is a success, but it quickly becomes apparent to her that her whole relationship with Hemmings was designed by him in order to rob the shop. Crushed, Eggar turns herself in to the police and informs on Hemmings and Williams.

p, Alan Ladd, Jr.; d, Eric Till; w, George Bluestone (based on the novel by Winston Graham); ph, Arthur Ibbetson (Panavision, Metrocolor); m, Stanley Myers; ed, John Jympson; prod d, John Howell; art d, John Graysmark; set d, Pamela Cornell; cos, Sue Yelland, Mia Fonssagrives, Vicki Tiel.

Crime   **(PR:C MPAA:GP)**

WALKING TALL½**   (1973) 125m BCP/Cinerama c

Joe Don Baker (Buford Pusser), Elizabeth Hartman (Pauline Pusser), Gene Evans (Sheriff Al Thurman), Noah Beery, Jr (Grandpa Carl Pusser), Brenda Benet (Luan Paxton), John Brascia (Prentiss Parley), Bruce Glover (Grady Coker), Deputy, Arch Johnson (Buel Jaggers), Felton Perry (Obra Eaker, Deputy), Richard X. Slattery (Arno Purdy), Rosemary Murphy (Callie Hacker), Lynn Borden (Margie Ann), Ed Call (Lutie McVeigh), Sidney Clute (Sheldon Levine), Douglas V. Fowley (Judge Clarke), Don Keefer (Dr. Lamar Stivers), Sam Laws (Willie Rae Lockman), Pepper Martin (Zolan Dicks), John Myhers (Lester Dickens), Logan Ramsey (John Witter), Kenneth Tobey (Augie McCullah), Lurene Tuttle (Grandma Pusser), Wanea Wes (Singer), Leif Garrett (Mike Pusser), Dawn Lyn (Dwana Pusser), Dominick Mazzie (Bozo), Russell Thorson (Ferrin Meaks), Gil Perkins, Gene Lebell (Bouncers), Carey Loftin (Dice Player), Warner Venetz (Stickman), Del Monroe (Otie Doss), Lloyd Tatum (Prosecutor), Vaudie Plunk (Jury Foreman), Pearline Wynn (Hassie Berlson), Ted Jordan (Virgil Button), Red West (Sheriff Tanner), Andrew J. Pirtle (Prisoner).

Baker stars as the legendary real-life Tennessee sheriff Buford Pusser, whose one-man battle against gambling, moonshine whiskey, and prostitution in his county elevated him to folk-hero stature in three movies (WALKING TALL, PART 2 and FINAL CHAPTER–WALKING TALL followed this one) and a shortlived TV series. Basically the story of an angry redneck with a big stick (his favored weapon–gives him a sort of homey air, doesn't it?); Baker pounds his way through the film smashing all illegal activities in his jurisdiction, much to the dismay of the criminal kingpins in

Tennessee. Not being ones to take things lying down, the crooks band together in an effort to eliminate the troublesome sheriff. After several life-threatening beatings and the murder of his wife, Hartman, Baker finally gets really mad, grabs his stick, and cleans out the whole town, killing several people. Though the audience is supposed to side with Baker (after all, it seems as though the man is being beaten up by baddies through the whole movie) throughout his noble HIGH NOON-ish quest, the body count inflicted by him on the crooks would justify sending everybody in the movie to prison. Incredibly, the film grossed over $17 million at the box office, and the sequels were already in the works.

p, Mort Briskin; d, Phil Karlson; w, Briskin; ph, Jack A. Marta (DeLuxe Color); m, Walter Scharf; ed, Harry Gerstad; prod d, Stan Jolley; cos, Oscar Rodriguez, Phyllis Garr; spec eff, Sass Bedig; m/l, Scharf, Don Black; makeup, Jack H. Young; stunts, Gil Perkins, Carey Loftin.

Crime   **Cas.**   **(PR:O MPAA:R)**

WALKING TALL, PART II*   (1975) 109m BCP-Fuqua-Wometco/AIP c

Bo Svenson (Buford Pusser), Luke Askew (Pinky Dobson), Noah Beery, Jr (Carl Pusser), John [Davis] Chandler (Ray Henry), Robert Doqui (Obra Eaker, Deputy), Bruce Glover (Grady Coker, Deputy), Richard Jaeckel (Stud Pardee), Brooke Mills (Ruby Ann), Logan Ramsey (John Witter), Angel Tompkins (Marganne Stilson), Leif Garrett, Dawn Lyn (Pusser Children), William Bryant (FBI Agent), Lurene Tuttle (Grandma Pusser).

The second film in the Buford Pusser saga which was supposed to have starred Pusser himself in the lead role, but the Tennessee sheriff was mysteriously killed in a car crash just before the film was shot. This called for a replacement and since WALKING TALL star Joe Don Baker was unavailable (or uninterested), the studio hired big blond Bo Svenson in his stead. If one isn't paying close attention to the actors, one might think they were watching the first film again. This one picks up just as the Tennessee-Mississippi crime conglomerate sends out more assassins to kill the ever-resilient supersheriff, Svenson. The big lug survives another half-dozen attempts on his life and manages to pull himself together enough to take his big stick and bash a few more heads. Not as violent as WALKING TALL, but it's even dumber. Believe it or not, a third film followed, FINAL CHAPTER–WALKING TALL, which was about the events that led to the making of this film.

p, Charles A. Pratt; d, Earl Bellamy; w, Howard B. Kreitsek; ph, Keith Smith (DeLuxe Color); m, Walter Scharf; ed, Art Seid; art d, Phil Jeffries; stunts, Carey Loftin.

Crime   **Cas.**   **(PR:O MPAA:PG)**

WALKING TARGET, THE**   (1960) 74m Zenith/UA bw

Joan Evans (Gail Russo), Ronald Foster (Nick Harbin), Merry Anders (Susan), Robert Christopher (Dave), Berry Kroeger (Hoffman), Harp McGuire (Max Brodney), Bill Couch (Thug), George Sawaya (Driver), Norman Alden (Russo), William Fawcett (Packy), Charles Seel (Editor), Robert Brubaker (Brenner), James Callahan (Al Kramer), J. Edward McKinley (Warden), Barbara Mansell (Stenographer), Burt Wenland (Cameraman), Jack Kenney (Gas Station Owner), Harvey Parry (Jerry), James Parnell (Worker), Guy Wilkerson (Lank), Madge Cleveland (Mrs. Haley), Ralph Barnard (Lieutenant).

Foster is fresh out of prison after serving five years for armed robbery. Now he wants to collect the $260,000 he stashed away before being sent up the creek, but this is no easy pickup. The law still wants him, as do his former pals. He's beaten up, loses the cash, and is double-crossed by former girl friend Anders. But Foster isn't totally unhappy by the film's end, for Evans, his late partner's widow, has taken up with him. Plenty of hard drinking and tough action are interspersed with gangster movie cliches, all done with more originality more often than in this production.

p, Robert E. Kent; d, Edward L. Cahn.

Crime   **(PR:C MPAA:NR)**

WALKOVER***   (1969, Pol.) 77m Syrena-Film Polski/New Yorker bw
                                                        (WALKOWER)

Aleksandra Zawieruszanka (Teresa), Jerzy Skolimowski (Andrzej Leszczyc), Krzysztof Chamiec (Director), Franciszek Pieczka (Activist), Elzbieta Czyzewska (Girl at Train Station), Andrzej Herder (Pawlak), Joanna Jedlewska (Designer), Tadeusz Kondrat (Old Man), Stanislaw Zaczyk ("Priest"), Henryk Kluba (Trainer Rogala), Teresa Belczynska (Director's Secretary), Krzysztof Litwin (Miecio), Janusz Klosinski, B. Dec, S. Przedwojewski, A. Turcewicz, J. Fedorowicz, S. Kaminska, M. Waskowski, S. Tym.

Polish director Jerzy Skolimowski's third film stars himself as a 30-year-old boxer who runs into Zawieruszanka, an old acquaintance from his college days. Learning that his sole source of income is from boxing, Zawieruszanka introduces Skolimowski to the director of a new industrial development project in Plock. Taking a liking to the boxer, the director offers him a job as an engineer. Skolimowski hesitates to make a decision until he is told that the company has its own boxing team and would be happy to have him as one of the contestants in an upcoming fight. Skolimowski wins the first fight of the boxing tournament, but he and Zawieruszanka decide to leave Plock. His opponent in the previous match stops his departure and persuades him to fight again. When Skolimowski enters the ring he is surprised to discover he has won the match by forfeit because his opponent did not show up. Later that evening the rival boxer shows up and demands half the prize money, explaining that the trainer told him to throw the fight. Skolimowski doesn't pay the man and challenges him to another bout. The man accepts and beats Skolimowski easily. As a youth, director-writer-actor Skolimowski had been a boxer; his first directorial effort, a documentary, was about boxing.

d&w, Jerzy Skolimowski; ph, Antoni Nurzynski; m, Andrzej Trzaskowski; ed, Barbara Kryczmonik; art d, Zdzislaw Kielanowski.

Drama   (PR:C MPAA:NR)

WALKOWER   (SEE: WALKOVER, 1969, Pol.)

WALL, THE   (SEE: PINK FLOYD-THE WALL, 1982, Brit.)

WALL FOR SAN SEBASTIAN (SEE: GUNS FOR SAN SEBASTIAN, 1968, U.S./Fr./Ital./Mex.)

WALL OF NOISE**½**   (1963) 112m WB bw

Suzanne Pleshette (*Laura Rubio*), Ty Hardin (*Joel Tarrant*), Dorothy Provine (*Ann Conroy*), Ralph Meeker (*Matt Rubio*), Simon Oakland (*Johnny Papadakis*), Jimmy Murphy (*Bud Kelsey*), Murray Matheson (*Jack Matlock*), Robert F. Simon (*Dave McRaab*), George Petrie (*Mr. Harrington*), Jean Byron (*Mrs. Harrington*), Fred Carson (*Adam Kasper*), Bill Walker (*Money*), Napoleon Whiting (*Preacher*), Kitty White (*Singer*), Jim Murray (*Sportswriter*).

The lives and loves behind the scenes at the racetrack are detailed in this thoroughbred soap opera. Hardin stars as an ambitious young trainer who enters into an illicit affair with his boss' wife, the hot-to-trot Pleshette, so that he may someday have enough dough to buy his own horses and become an owner. The husband, Meeker, suspects what is going on and fires Hardin. Desperate, Hardin borrows money from his old girl friend's boss, Oakland, to buy a promising horse. When the horse wins big in a preliminary race, Meeker offers to buy the steed, but Hardin declines. In the next big race, however, Hardin's horse loses, leaving him stuck with no way to pay back Oakland. Hardin's ex-girl friend Provine offers her boss her life's savings, and her body, to bail out her old beau and Oakland accepts. Luckily things don't go that far and Oakland is kind enough to die of a heart attack before demanding payment. Meanwhile, Hardin's horse is injured, and, learning the news, Provine reunites with Hardin while he tends to his sick animal.

p, Joseph Landon; d, Richard Wilson; w, Landon (based on the novel by Daniel Michael Stein); ph, Lucien Ballard; m, William Lava; ed, William Ziegler; art d, Hilyard Brown; set d, John P. Austin; cos, Howard Shoup; makeup, Gordon Bau.

Drama   (PR:A MPAA:NR)

WALL STREET**   (1929) 68m COL bw

Aileen Pringle (*Ann Tabor*), Ralph Ince (*Roller McCray*), Sam De Grasse (*John Willard*), Philip Strange (*Walter Tabor*), Ernest Hilliard (*Savage*), Jimmy Finlayson (*Andy*), Freddie Burke Frederick (*Richard Tabor*), George MacFarlane (*Ed Foster*), Camille Rovelle (*Miss Woods*), Grace Wallace (*Bonnie Tucker*), Hugh McCormack (*Jim Tucker*), Marshall Ruth (*Billy*), Ben Hall (*Cliff*), Billy Colvin (*Hoffman*), Frederick Graham (*Baring*), Louise Beavers (*Magnolia*), Andy Cairn.

Ince plays an ex-steelworker who has played his cards right and grabbed enough power to make himself a wealthy businessman. Having destroyed whomever got in his path to power, Ince opens himself up to attacks from vengeful rivals. Pringle, the wife of one of the men Ince drove to suicide, sets out to destroy him by wooing her way into his confidence and then ruining him financially. She does so, but in the end realizes that she indeed loves Ince. A bit overblown, but not bad.

d, R. William Neill; w, Norman Houston (based on a story by Paul Gangelin, Jack Kirkland); ph, Ted Tetzlaff; ed, Ray Snyder; art d, Harrison Wiley.

Drama   (PR:A MPAA:NR)

WALL STREET COWBOY*½   (1939) 66m REP bw

Roy Rogers (*Himself*), George "Gabby" Hayes (*Gabby*), Raymond Hatton (*Chuckwalla*), Ann Baldwin (*Peggy*), Pierre Watkin (*Hammond*), Louisiana Lou (*Herself*), Craig Reynolds (*Tony*), Ivan Miller (*Niles*), Reginald Barlow (*Bainbridge*), Adrian Morris (*Gillespie*), Jack Roper (*Ducky*), Jack Ingram (*McDermott*), Fred Burns, Paul Fix, George Chesebro, Ted Mapes, Trigger the Horse.

Rogers and company leave the ranch and wander into the big city out East to stop the efforts of a powerful Wall Street conglomerate to strip Roy and his pals of their land. The power brokers are interested in the sagebrush because valuable molybdenum (a mineral used in the mining of steel) has been discovered on the property. With the help of Hayes and Hatton, Rogers

sets the three-piece-suiters straight.

p&d, Joseph Kane; w, Gerald Geraghty, Norman Hall (based on a story by Doris Schroeder); ph, Jack Marta; ed, Lester Orlebeck; md, Cy Feuer.

Western   (PR:A MPAA:NR)

WALLABY JIM OF THE ISLANDS**   (1937) 61m GN bw

George Houston, Ruth Coleman, Douglas Walton, William Von Brincken, Mamo Clark, Colin Campbell, Syd Saylor, Juan Torena, Nick Thompson, Warner Richmond, Wilson Benge.

Danger looms for the swaggering captain of a pearl fishing boat in the South Seas when he is forced to deal with pirates who are after his valuable cargo. Singing and roistering help pad out this tale of the sea and make sitting through it a comfortable hour.

p, Bud Barsky; d, Charles Lamont; w, Bennett R. Cohen, Houston Branch (based on a story by Albert Richard Wetjen); ph, Ira Morgan; ed, Guy Thayer; md, Arthur Kaye; art d, Paul Palmentola; m/l, "Ia-O-Ra-Na," "Hi-Ho-Hum," Felix Bernard, Irving Bibo.

Adventure   (PR:A MPAA:NR)

WALLET, THE**   (1952, Brit.) 64m Sunset/Archway bw (AKA: BLUEPRINT FOR DANGER)

John Longden (*Man with Pipe*), Chil Bouchier (*Babs*), Roberta Huby (*Dot Johnson*), Alfred Farrell (*Harry Maythorpe*), Hilda Fenemore (*Alice Maythorpe*), Diana Calderwood (*May Jenkins*), John Gatrell, Leslie French, Peter Prowse, Shawn O'Riordan, Robert Moore, Leslie Parker, Geoffrey Denys, Bernard Davies, Hilary Dean, Wanda Rands, Jimmy Brown.

During a fight between police and enemy agents, a wallet containing a sum of money and priceless microfilm is flung from a window. It's found by a passing stranger, Longden, and the wallet takes a strange trip of it's own. First it goes to a dancer, then a cashier, and finally a blackmailing clerk. The wallet at last finds its way back to Longden, who is arrested–it seems he was the head of the enemy ring. The idea is intriguing but the execution falls short of tense entertainment.

p&d, Morton M. Lewis; w, Ted Willis; ph, Brendan J. Stafford.

Crime   (PR:A MPAA:NR)

WALL-EYED NIPPON**½**   (1963, Jap.) 90m Toho c (YABUNIRAMI NIPPON)

Akira Takarada (*Shin Moriyama*), Yumi Shirakawa (*Momoko*), Jerry Ito (*John Machihei*), Muza Kemanai (*Meery Sweett*), E.H. Eric (*Lafcadio Yearn*), Akiko Wakabayashi (*Nashiko*).

Ito plays a Japanese-American nuclear scientist who visits Japan in search of a docile Japanese wife who will serve his every whim back in the States in this Japanese romantic comedy. His female guide, Shirakawa, tips her friend Takarada, a newspaper reporter, on the story. Seeking to help Ito, Shirakawa introduces him to Kemanai, a modernized Japanese woman. Instead of Ito falling for Kemanai, Takarada does. Ito is amazed by traditional Japanese culture and becomes enamored of Shirakawa. In the end the partners switch, Shirakawa and Takarada staying in Japan, and Ito and Kemanai traveling to the West.

p, Seitan Kaneko; d, Hideo Suzuki; w, Nagaharu Okuyama; ph, Taiichi Kankura (Tohoscope, Eastmancolor).

Romance/Comedy   (PR:A MPAA:NR)

WALLFLOWER**½**   (1948) 77m WB bw

Robert Hutton (*Warren James*), Joyce Reynolds (*Jackie Linnett*), Janis Paige (*Joy Linnett*), Edward Arnold (*Mr. Linnett*), Barbara Brown (*Mrs. Linnett*), Jerome Cowan (*Mr. James*), Don McGuire (*Stevie*), Ann Shoemaker (*Mrs. Jones*), Lotte Stein (*Minna, Servant*), Walter Sande (*Officer*), Angela Greene (*Miss Walsh*).

Strong cast helps this otherwise undistinguished comedy starring Reynolds and Paige as sisters competing for the affections of dashing young man Hutton. Paige has the unfair advantage of good looks and sparkling personality, but she's something of a dim-wit. Eventually Reynolds wins out due to her intelligence and good sense. Arnold and Brown play the girls' parents.

p, Alex Gottlieb; d, Frederick de Cordova; w, Phoebe Ephron, Henry Ephron (based on the stage play by Reginald Denham, Mary Orr); ph, Karl Freund; m, Frederick Hollander; ed, Folmar Blangsted; md, Leo F. Forbstein; art d, Hugh Reticker; set d, G. W. Bernsten; cos, Leah Rhodes; spec eff, William McGann, Wesley Anderson; m/l, "I May Be Wrong (But I Think You're Wonderful)," Harry Ruskin, Henry Sullivan (sung by Janis Paige); makeup, Perc Westmore, John Wallace.

Comedy   (PR:A MPAA:NR)

WALLS CAME TUMBLING DOWN, THE** (1946) 82m COL bw

Lee Bowman (Gilbert Archer), Marguerite Chapman (Patricia Foster), Edgar Buchanan (George Bradford), George Macready (Matthew Stoker), Lee Patrick (Susan), Jonathan Hale (Capt. Griffin), J. Edward Bromberg (Ernst Helms), Elisabeth Risdon (Catherine Walsh), Miles Mander (Dr. Marko), Moroni Olsen (Bishop Martin), Katherine Emery (Mrs. Stoker), Noel Cravat (Rausch), Bob Ryan (Detective Regan), Charles LaTorre (Bianca).

Bowman plays a Broadway columnist intent on finding out who murdered his friend, a priest, who was found hanged in his rectory. The cops declare it suicide and close the case, but Bowman knew his friend better than that and sets out to uncover the killer. The trail takes him to the door of Chapman, an icy socialite from Boston. This leads him to a mysterious art dealer, Bromberg, a crooked lawyer, Buchanan, and the motive–the theft of two Bibles and a painting.

p, Albert J. Cohen; d, Lothar Mendes; w, Wilfrid H. Pettitt (based on the novel by Jo Eisinger); ph, Charles Lawton, Jr.; m, Marlin Skiles; ed, Gene Havlick; md, M.W. Stoloff; art d, Stephen Goosson, A. Leslie Thomas; set d, Robert Priestley.

Mystery (PR:A MPAA:NR)

WALLS OF GOLD* (1933) 74m FOX bw

Sally Eilers (Jeanie Satterlee), Norman Foster (Barnes Ritchie), Ralph Morgan (J. Gordon Ritchie), Rosita Moreno (Carla Monierez), Rochelle Hudson (Joan Street), Frederick Santley (Tony Van Raalte), Marjorie Gateson (Cassie Street), Mary Mason ("Honey" Satterlee), Margaret Seddon (Mrs. Satterlee).

Ridiculous melodrama which shows young businesswoman Eilers and her fiance Foster inflicting some pretty serious emotional pain on themselves and others after Foster gets drunk and marries Eilers' sister, Mason. Seeking vengeance, Eilers weds Foster's old and rich uncle, Morgan, and basks in the good life. Months later, Mason dies during childbirth and Morgan passes on from a heart attack, leaving the former lovers able to reunite and live comfortably.

d, Kenneth MacKenna; w, Wallace Sullivan, Edmond Seward, Lester Cole (based on the novel by Kathleen Norris); ph, George Schneiderman.

Drama (PR:C MPAA:NR)

WALLS OF HELL, THE** (1964, U.S./Phil.) 88m
Filipinas-Hemisphere/Hemisphere bw (INTRAMUROS)

Jock Mahoney (Lt. Jim Sorenson), Fernando Poe, Jr (Nardo), Michael Parsons (Papa), Cecilia Lopez (Tina), Oscar Roncal (Joker), Vance Skarstedt (The Captain), Paul Edwards, Jr (Murray), Claude Wilson (The Major), Ely Ramos, Jr, Angel Buenaventura, Carpi Asturias, Arsenio Alonso, Pedro Navarro, Tommy Romulo, Fred Galang, Alex Swanbeck, Jess Montalban, Ben Sanchez, Reynaldo Sibal (The Guerrillas).

Another WW II epic set in the Philippines from low-budget director Eddie Romero. This one shows desperate Japanese troops cornered in an ancient walled city in Manila and holding thousands of Filipino civilians hostage. American lieutenant Mahoney leads his band of guerrilla forces into the city aided by Filipino freedom fighter Poe to defeat the Japs. You can count on the standard Romero thrills.

p, Eddie Romero; d, Gerardo de Leon, Romero; w, Ferde Grofe, Jr., Cesar J. Amigo, Romero; ph, Felipe J. Sacdalan; m, Tito Arevalo.

War (PR:A MPAA:NR)

WALLS OF JERICHO**½ (1948) 106m FOX bw

Cornel Wilde (Dave Connors), Linda Darnell (Algeria Wedge), Anne Baxter (Julia Norman), Kirk Douglas (Tucker Wedge), Ann Dvorak (Belle Connors), Marjorie Rambeau (Mrs. Dunham), Henry Hull (Jefferson Norman), Colleen Townsend (Marjorie Ransome), Barton MacLane (Gotch McCurdy), Griff Barnett (Judge Hutto), William Tracy (Cully Caxton), Art Baker (Peddigrew), Frank Ferguson (Tom Ransome), Ann Morrison (Nellie), Hope Landin (Mrs. Hutto), Helen Brown (Mrs. Ransome), Norman Leavitt (Adam McAdam), Whitford Kane (Judge Foster), J. Farrell MacDonald (Bailiff), Dick Rich (Mulliken), Will Wright (Dr. Patterson), Daniel White (Loafer), Les Clark (Photographer), William Sheehan (Reporter), Gene Nelson, Jack Gargan (Assistant Prosecutors), James Metcalfe (Court Clerk), Douglas Carter (Intern), Paul Palmer (Policeman), Oliver Hartwell (Bootblack), Edward Clark (Barber), Joe Forte, Charles Marsh, Lou Mason, Ralph Littlefield, William H. Gould (Politicians), Dorothy Granger, Ann Doran (Gossips), Cecil Weston (Head Nurse), Gene Collins (Harmonica Player), Patricia Morison (Mrs. Landon), Brick Sullivan (Iceman), David Hammond (Messenger Boy), Guy Beach (Hack Driver), Robert Filmer, Wallace Scott, Herbert Heywood, Fred Graff (Toughs), Morgan Farley (Proprietor), Kay Riley (Woman), Oliver Blake (Mr. Reynolds), Ed Peil, Sr. (Court Reporter), Tom Moore (Man), Milton Parsons (Joe).

A cross-blend of a soap opera and a biblical tale set in an agricultural area just after the turn of the century, it has all the deadly sins Sunday school teachers have always warned about: envy, greed, hate, murder, and the list goes on. It's 1908 in Kansas and Wilde is a local lawyer in the town of Jericho. His wife, Dvorak, is an inebriate, and doesn't much care who knows it. The problems of this marriage are legion and the Wilde-Dvorak relationship is further muddled by his love for Baxter, another attorney, and the fact that his best friend (Douglas) has a wife (Darnell) who is making eyes at him. Wilde can't handle three women at once so he spurns Darnell (he didn't want to be a cad and, as we all know, a cad is "a married man who cheats on his girl friend"). She gets steamed and sets Douglas against Wilde. It seems her favorite way of passing time is stirring up trouble, like a rouged witch stirring a cauldron. Douglas runs a newspaper and, under Darnell's prodding, he begins a smear campaign against Wilde's alleged transgressions, thus throwing any political ambitions Wilde may have had into a cocked hat. Wilde decides that the town of Jericho is no longer friendly so he packs up his gear and exits. With Wilde out of the way and with Darnell spurring him on, Douglas goes into politics, wins the election, and departs for D.C. With hubby out of the way, Darnell continues weaving her web of influence in the town, a fact that Douglas is unaware of. Wilde and Baxter meet again later when a mutual friend is convicted of a capital offense. The newspaper headlines proclaim that Dvorak is suing Wilde for divorce on the grounds of adultery and Baxter is cited as being the woman who made it all happen. Darnell keeps agitating matters, pouring oil on a fire, and gets Dvorak so angry that the souse grabs a gun and plugs Wilde. He is taken to the hospital, near death as Baxter, trouper that she is, goes into court, stifles her emotions, pleads the case, and gets her client sprung from the manslaughter charge, thereby convincing herself that she has what it takes to be a big-time counselor. Later, when Dvorak has dried out, she admits that her accusations in the press and her subsequent violent behavior were caused by Darnell's needles. Douglas comes to the realization that he has been married to a shrew and calls a halt to their life together. Baxter visits the hospital and lets Wilde know what's happened, telling him Douglas has tossed Darnell aside. Good triumphs over evil in an ending that offers no surprises. A few individual scenes but the characterizations are too broadly drawn with nary a smidgen of subtlety. Douglas is basically a supporting actor and he carries it off well in this, his fifth movie. MacLane is the murder victim and Townsend turns in a good performance as the accused killer. The theme of virtue beating evil is predictable and trite and might have been more exciting if any of several permutations could have been added.

p, Lamar Trotti; d, John M. Stahl; w, Trotti (based on the novel by Paul I. Wellman); ph, Arthur Miller; m, Cyril J. Mockridge; ed, James B. Clark; md, Lionel Newman; art d, Lyle R. Wheeler, Maurice Ransford; set d, Thomas Little, Paul S. Fox; cos, Kay Nelson; spec eff, Fred Sersen; makeup, Ben Nye, Henry Vilardo, Allan Snyder.

Drama (PR:C MPAA:NR)

WALLS OF MALAPAGA, THE*** (1950, Fr./Ital.) 91m
Francoriz/Films International bw (AUDELA DES GRILLES)

Jean Gabin (Pierre), Isa Miranda (Marta), Vera Talchi (Cecchina), Andrea Checchi (Manfredini), Robert Dalban (Bosco), Ave Ninchi (Maria), Carlo Tamberlani (Superintendent of Police).

A fine French-Italian coproduction directed by Frenchman Clement in a neorealistic style. Gabin stars as a wanted killer (he had murdered his mistress) who stows away on a ship and disembarks in Genoa, looking for a dentist to cure his toothache. There he meets a little girl, Talchi, and is introduced to her beautiful mother, Miranda, who works as a waitress. A romance blossoms between the Frenchman and the Italian, but their happiness ends when the authorities catch up with Gabin and arrest him. The film was shot in war-torn Genoa, which was in the midst of rebuilding. Gabin is, once again, outstanding, as are Miranda and Talchi. (In French and Italian; English subtitles.)

p, Alfredo Guarini; d, Rene Clement; w, Jean Aurenche, Pierre Bost (based on a story by Suso Cecchi d'Amico, Guarini, Cesare Zavattini); ph, Louis Page; m, Roman Vlad; ed, Mario Serandrei.

Drama (PR:A MPAA:NR)

WALPURGIS NIGHT**½ (1941, Swed.) 82m AB Svenskfilmindustri
bw (VALBORGSMASSOAFTON)

Lars Hanson (Johan Borg), Karin Carlsson (Clary Borg), Victor Seastrom (Fredrik Bergstrom), Ingrid Bergman (Lena Bergstrom), Erik Berglund, Sture Lagerwall, Georg Rydeberg, Georg Blickingberg, Rickard Lund, Stig Jarrel, Marie-Louise Sorbon, Gabriel Alw, Carl-Gunnar Wingard, Aino Taube, Torsten Hillberg, Anders Hendriksson, Torsten Winge, Greta Berthels, Ake Uppstrom, Linnea Hillberg, Ivar Kage, Lill-Acke, Olaf Widgren, Hjalmar Peters, Pecka Hagman, Harry Hednoff.

A fairly controversial film at the time, WALPURGIS NIGHT deals with the scandal of abortion. Bergman plays the loyal secretary of businessman Hanson, whom she loves from afar. Hanson is married to Carlsson, a cold and unemotional woman who refuses to bear children because she fears the effects pregnancy and childbirth would have on her body. Much to her dismay, Carlsson becomes pregnant and decides to have an abortion rather than tell her husband, who would gladly welcome a child. Unfortunately, the abortionist's medical records fall into the hands of a blackmailer and he comes calling on Carlsson. There is a struggle for the papers and Carlsson accidentally shoots the blackmailer. Unable to deal with the crisis, Carlsson kills herself. Soon the whole scandal is splashed across the newspapers, even the one owned by Bergman's father, Seastrom. Hanson, seeking solace from the publicity, joins the Foreign Legion. Bergman waits faithfully until Hanson returns and marries him, bearing several children and finally giving Hanson the happiness he was denied.

d, Gustaf Edgren; w, Oscar Rydquist, Edgren; ph, Martin Bodin.

Drama   **(PR:A-C MPAA:NR)**

WALTZ ACROSS TEXAS**   (1982) 99m Aster/Atlantic c

Anne Archer (*Gail Weston*), Terry Jastrow (*John Taylor*), Noah Beery [Jr.] (*Joe Locker*), Mary Kay Place (*Kit Peabody*), Josh Taylor (*Luke Jarvis*), Richard [Dick] Farnsworth (*Frank Walker*), Ben Piazza (*Bill Wrather*).

A lame attempt at resurrecting the romantic comedies of the 1930s and the 1940s starring the husband and wife team of Archer and Jastrow (who also wrote the original story) who just don't have the magic needed to spark interest in the hackneyed material. Archer plays a cool intellectual East Coast geologist out to find black gold. Jastrow plays a tough-but-lovable Texas wildcatter who plays on his instincts and scoffs at science. You guessed it, they fall in love *and* strike it rich. No surprises here.

p, Martin Jurow, Scott Rosenfelt; d, Ernest Day; w, Bill Svanoe (based on a story by Terry Jastrow, Anne Archer); ph, Robert Elswit (Metrocolor); m, Steve Dorff; ed, Jay Lash Cassidy; prod d, Michael Erler; m/l, title song (sung by Waylon Jennings).

Romance   **Cas.**   **(PR:A-C MPAA:PG)**

WALTZ OF THE TOREADORS***   (1962, Brit.) 104m Independent Artists/CD c (AKA: THE AMOROUS GENERAL)

Peter Sellers (*Gen. Leo Fitzjohn*), Dany Robin (*Ghislaine*), Margaret Leighton (*Emily Fitzjohn*), John Fraser (*Robert*), Cyril Cusack (*Dr. Grogan*), Prunella Scales (*Estella*), Denise Coffey (*Sidonia*), Jean Anderson (*Agnes*), Raymond Huntley (*President of the Court Martial*), Cardew Robinson (*Midgeley, the Undertaker*), John Glyn-Jones (*Innkeeper*), John Le Mesurier (*Vicar*), Vanda Godsell (*Mrs. Bulstrode*), Catherine Feller (*Rosemary*), Guy Middleton, Humphrey Lestocq (*Huntsmen*).

Sellers is outstanding as a retired general looking to escape a bleak existence with his shrewish wife Leighton in this fine adaptation of Jean Anouilh's bittersweet stage comedy. The film opens just before the outbreak of WW I. Sellers has retired from the Army and now lives on his manor (the wealth of which belongs to his wife) with Leighton whom he can no longer stand. Tortured by loneliness, Sellers pines for the days when he had a platonic affair with a beautiful young French girl, Robin, 17 years before. Surprisingly, Robin arrives at the manor claiming fidelity to Sellers and demanding that they consummate the relationship. Sellers jumps at the chance, but circumstances force a postponement of their rendezvous and the general leaves Robin under the care of his aide, Fraser. In two days, Fraser succeeds where Sellers has failed and the angry general puts the young soldier in for a court-martial. During the trial Sellers learns that Fraser is actually his illegitimate son, so he stops the proceedings and allows his son and Robin to marry. Unhinged by the reality that he is stuck with Leighton for the rest of his life, Sellers puts a gun to his head to end it all, but at that moment a gorgeous new maid arrives and he changes his mind.

p, Peter de Sarigny; d, John Guillermin; w, Wolf Mankowitz (based on the play by Jean Anouilh); ph, John Wilcox (Eastmancolor); m, Richard Addinsell; ed, Peter Taylor; prod d, Wilfrid Shingleton; md, Muir Mathieson; art d, Harry Pottle; cos, Beatrice Dawson; makeup, William Partleton, Stuart Freeborn.

Comedy   **Cas.**   **(PR:A-C MPAA:NR)**

WALTZ TIME**   (1933, Brit.) 83m GAU bw

Evelyn Laye (*Rosalinde Eisenstein*), Fritz Schultz (*Fritz Eisenstein*), Gina Malo (*Adele, Maid*), Jay Laurier (*Frosch, Gaoler*), Parry Jones (*Alfred the Dove*), George Baker (*Orlovsky*), Frank Titterton (*Fiacre Driver*), Ivor Barnard (*Falke the Bat*), D. A. Clarke-Smith (*Meyer*), Edmund Breon (*Judge Bauer*), Kenneth Buckley, Jane Cornell, Joe Spree, Diana Cotton, Joyce Kirby.

Loose film adaptation of Strauss' opera "Die Fledermaus" starring Schultz as a writer who travels to Vienna on the pretext of researching his new book. Of course his wife, Laye, suspects he is having affairs with fancy ladies (and she's right) so she trips him up at a masquerade ball.

p, Herman Fellner; d, William Theile; w, A.P. Herbert, Louis Levy (based on the opera "Die Fledermaus" by Johann Strauss).

Musical   **(PR:A MPAA:NR)**

WALTZ TIME*½   (1946, Brit.) 98m BN/Anglo-American bw

Carol Raye (*Empress Maria*), Peter Graves (*Count Franz von Hofer*), Patricia Medina (*Cenci Prohaska*), John Ruddock (*Count Prohaska*), Harry Welchman (*Count Rodzanka*), Thorley Walters (*Stefan Ravenne*), George

Robey (*Vogel*), Wylie Watson (*Josef*), Anne Ziegler, Webster Booth, Hans May (*Gypsy Troubadours*), Albert Sandler (*Orchestra Leader*), Richard Tauber (*Shepherd*), Toni Edgar Bruce (*Augustine*), Hay Petrie (*Minister of War*), Hugh Dempster (*Ferdinand Hohenlohe*), Brefni O'Rorke (*Emperor*), Kay Kendall (*Lady-in-Waiting*), Ferdi Mayne, Cecil Bevan, David Keir, Billy Matthews, Charles Paton, Roy Russell, Ivan Samson, Marie Ault, Dick Francis, Charles Doe, Basil Jason, Charles Peters, John Howard, Gordon Edwards, Joyce Linden, Ruthene Leclerc, Eileen Moore, Dawn Bingham.

Dull musical set in Old Vienna starring Raye as a powerful empress who wants to marry Graves, an officer in her guard. Her ministers forbid the marriage because Graves has a reputation as a womanizer. The ministers are proven correct when Graves begins a mild flirtation with Raye's best friend Medina, so the empress decides to set her soldier straight by posing as Medina at a masked ball and catching him in the act. Pretty awful stuff with some inexplicable cut-aways to singer Richard Tauber, who performs a few musical numbers by himself in locations unrelated to the story.

p, Louis H. Jackson; d, Paul L. Stein; w, Montgomery Tully, Jack Whittingham (based on an idea by Karl Rossier); ph, Ernest Palmer; m, Hans May.

Musical   **(PR:A MPAA:NR)**

WALTZES FROM VIENNA   (SEE: STRAUSS' GREAT WALTZ, 1934, Brit.)

WANDA*½**   (1971) 101m Foundation for Filmmakers/Bardene International c

Barbara Loden (*Wanda*), Michael Higgins (*Mr. Dennis*), Charles Dosinan (*Dennis' Father*), Frank Jourdano (*Soldier*), Valerie Manches (*Girl in Roadhouse*).

Barbara Loden (who was married to Elia Kazan) wrote, directed, and starred in this moving and insightful film which was shot on 16mm, blown up to 35mm, and brought in at a budget of $115,000. The result is a powerful character study of an uneducated Pennsylvania coal-country woman who allows her husband a divorce and custody of her two children because she admits, "I'm just no good." She leaves her home town and drifts into a series of one-night stands with traveling salesmen she meets in bars. One day she wanders into a tavern while it is being held up by a neurotic thief, Higgins, who kidnaps her and makes her his hostage. Loden takes a liking to the disturbed man and she accompanies him on his petty criminal escapades. Eventually he grows to like her as well and allows her to assist him. He buys her a dress and even compliments her when she does particularly well on a robbery. After a while, Higgins becomes tired of his life style and decides to pull one last job, a bank, and then retire. Giving Loden the job of getaway driver, Higgins enters the bank and is killed by the police. Loden gets away. Alone again, Loden wanders into another roadside dive and the film ends with a freeze frame on her vacant face. Well worth seeing. This film won acclaim at several film festivals, including the International Critics' Prize for Best Film at the 1970 Venice Film Festival.

p, Harry Shuster; d&w, Barbara Loden; ph&ed, Nicholas T. Proferes (Kodachrome).

Drama/Crime   **(PR:C MPAA:GP)**

WANDA NEVADA*   (1979) 105m Panda/UA c

Peter Fonda (*Beaudray Demerille*), Brooke Shields (*Wanda Nevada*), Fiona Lewis (*Dorothy Deerfield*), Luke Askew (*Ruby Muldoon*), Ted Markland (*Strap Pangburn*), Severn Darden (*Merlin Bitterstix*), Paul Fix (*Texas Curly*), Henry Fonda (*Old Prospector*), Fred Ashley (*Barber*), Jason Clark (*Alonzo*), Larry Golden (*Card Hustler*), John Denos (*Gas Station Greaser*), Bert Williams (*Sherman Krupp*), Robert V. Walker, H. Samuel Hackin (*Poker Players*), Charles Lawry (*Drunk*), Jack Caddin (*Trucker*), Teri Shields (*Clerk*), Benny Dobrofsky, Craig Pinkard, Tiny Wells, Bert, J.D. Clark, Danny Zapein, Geno Silva, Carol Norton, Ramona Richards, Melvin Todd, Tim James, Riley Hill, Lon Carli.

Brooke Shields is simply awful in this already weak modern day (1950) western directed by and starring Peter Fonda. Fonda plays a gambler who wins young Brooke in a poker game. Suddenly stuck playing babysitter to an adolescent cowgirl, Fonda drags her with him as he searches for gold hidden in the Grand Canyon. A gang of baddies have the same plan, which forces Fonda and Shields to play cat-and-mouse throughout the rest of the film. Pretty bad, with a brief cameo by Peter's dad Henry as a grizzled desert rat being the only point of interest (it was their only screen appearance together).

p, Neal Dobrofsky, Dennis Hackin; d, Peter Fonda; w, Hackin; ph, Michael Butler (Panavision, Technicolor); m, Ken Lauber; ed, Scott Conrad; art d, Lynda Paradise.

Western   **(PR:A-C MPAA:PG)**

WANDER LOVE STORY   (SEE: WANDERLOVE, 1970)

WANDERER, THE½   (1969, Fr.) 103m Madeleine-Awa/Leacock
Pennebaker c (LE GRAND MEAULNES)

Brigitte Fossey (*Yvonne de Galais*), Jean Blaise (*Augustin Meaulnes*), Alain
Libolt (*Francois Seurel*), Alain Noury (*Frantz de Galais*), Juliette Villard
(*Valentine Blondeau*), Christian de Tiliere (*Ganache*), Marcel Cuvelier
(*Mons. Seurel*), Therese Quentin (*Mme. Seurel*), Serge Spira (*Mouche
Boeuf*), Bruno Castan (*Delouche*), Elizabeth Guy, Henri Alain Dmurtal.

Turn-of-the-century romance starring Blaise and Noury as two romantic
youths searching for the young women they have fallen in love with. One
of them, Villard, stood Noury up at the altar and disappeared. The other,
Fossey, Noury's sister, is simply missing after all the excitement surrounding the called-off wedding. Eventually Blaise finds Fossey and the two are
married, but his happiness is brief because Noury pleads with him to help
continue the search for Villard. Blaise reluctantly leaves his new bride and
after many months they find Villard, but when Blaise returns he discovers
that his wife has died in childbirth.

p, Gilbert de Goldschmidt; d, Jean-Gabriel Albicocco; w, Albicocco, Isabelle
Riviere (based on "Le Grand Meaulnes" in "Nouvelle Revue Francaise" by
Alain Fournier); ph, Quinto Albicocco (Techniscope, Eastmancolor); m,
Jean-Pierre Bourtayre; ed, Georges Klotz; art d, Daniel Louradour; cos,
Sylvie Poulet.

Drama   (PR:A   MPAA:G)

WANDERER OF THE WASTELAND½   (1935) 62m PAR bw

Dean Jagger (*Adam Larey*), Gail Patrick (*Ruth Virey*), Edward Ellis
(*Dismukes*), Benny Baker (*Piano Player*), Larry "Buster" Crabbe (*Big Ben*),
Trixie Friganza (*Big Jo*), Monte Blue (*Guerd Larey*), Raymond Hatton
(*Merryvale*), Fuzzy Knight (*Deputy Scott*), Anna Q. Nilsson (*Mrs. Virey*),
Tammany Young (*Paducah*), Jim Thorpe (*Charlie Jim*), Charles Waldron,
Sr (*Mr. Virey*), Stanley Andrews (*Sheriff Collinshaw*), Pat O'Malley (*Jed*),
Glenn [Leif] Erickson (*Lawrence*), Marina Schubert, Kenneth Harlan, Al St.
John, Bud Osborne, Robert Burns, Alfred Delcambre.

Tedious western starring Jagger as a miner on the lam after he thinks he
has killed his brother. Jagger wanders into Death Valley and is nearly dead
until prospector Ellis finds him and saves his life. Brought back to his senses
by his gal, Patrick, Jagger agrees to turn himself in, only to discover that
his brother isn't dead after all.

p, Harold Hurley; d, Otho Lovering; w, Stuart Anthony (based on the novel
by Zane Grey); ph, Ben Reynolds; ed, Everett Douglass.

Western   (PR:A   MPAA:NR)

WANDERER OF THE WASTELAND**   (1945) 67m RKO bw

James Warren (*Adam Larey*), Richard Martin (*Chito Rafferty*), Audrey
Long (*Jean Collinshaw*), Robert Clarke (*Jay Collinshaw*), Robert Barrat
(*Uncle Collinshaw*), Harry Woods (*Guerd Eliott*), Minerva Urecal (*Mama
Rafferty*), Harry D. Brown (*Papa Rafferty*), Tommy Cook (*Chito as a Boy*),
Harry McKim (*Adam as a Boy*), Jason Robards, Sr (*Dealer*).

A supposed adaptation of the Zane Grey novel of the same title which bears
no resemblance to the book or the two films already based on it. Warren
plays the young hero on a vendetta to find the killer of his father. When he
finally tracks down the dirty dog he opts not to kill him because he has fallen
in love with the bad man's niece, Long. As luck would have it, the villain is
killed anyway and Warren is blamed. In the end Warren clears his name and
gets the girl.

p, Herman Schlom; d, Edward Killy, Wallace Grissell; w, Norman Houston
(based on the novel by Zane Grey); ph, Harry J. Wild; m, Paul Sawtell; ed,
J.B. Whittredge; md, C. Bakaleinikoff; art d, Albert S. D'Agostino, Lucius
Croxton; set d, Darrell Silvera.

Western   (PR:A   MPAA:NR)

WANDERERS, THE**   (1979) 113m Orion c

Ken Wahl (*Richie*), John Friedrich (*Joey*), Karen Allen (*Nina*), Toni Kalem
(*Despie Galasso*), Alan Rosenberg (*Turkey*), Jim Youngs (*Buddy*), Tony
Ganios (*Perry*), Linda Manz (*Peewee*), William Andrews (*Emilio*), Erland
Van Lidth de Jeude (*Terror*), Val Avery (*Mr. Sharp*), Dolph Sweet (*Chubby
Galasso*), Michael Wright (*Clinton*), Burtt Harris (*Marine Recruiter*),
Samm-Art Williams (*Roger*), Dion Albanese (*Teddy Wong*), Olympia Duka-
kis (*Joey's Mom*), George Merolle, Terri Perri, John Califano, Richard Price,
Linda Artuso, Earlie J. Butler III, Rafael Cabrera, Brian Colleary, Rose-
mary DeAngelis, Lorna Erickson, Ken Foree, Sally Anne Golden, Leon
Grant, Jery Hewitt, Adam Kimmel, Tara King, Faith Minton, Bruce Nozick,
Michael Pasternak, Sheryl Posner, Bert Samuel, Konrad Sheehan, Harry
Benjamin, Alan Braunstein, Mark Lesly, Farrel R. Tannenbaum, Anthony
Tirico.

The best of the gang films to be released in 1979 (the list includes THE
WARRIORS, WALK PROUD, and BOULEVARD NIGHTS), THE WAND-
ERERS is a strangely compelling film directed with flair by Phil Kaufman

(INVASION OF THE BODY SNATCHERS, 1978, THE RIGHT STUFF,
1983). While basically just a string of vignettes strung together about a gang
of Italian-American teenagers living in the Bronx circa 1963, the film has an
air of authenticity in its episodes, as if they were all based on fact or
adolescent recollections. The performances in the film are uniformly strong,
with Wahl, showing a great screen promise he has never fulfilled (FORT
APACHE, THE BRONX, and THE SOLDIER being dismal wastes of his
talent), as the film's focus character. Little Linda Manz (a superb young
actress who also shines in DAYS OF HEAVEN and OUT OF THE BLUE)
nearly steals the film as a pint-sized tough gal who is the girl friend of Van
Lidth de Jeude, the giant leader of a rival street gang known as "The
Fordham Baldies." Kaufman infuses the film with a wistful sadness for an
era about to end (and most of the characters realize that it is slipping out
of their grasps) with the assassination of JFK. Many incidents will stick with
the viewer, including the very funny sequence where the entire membership
of The Fordham Baldies gets drunk and joins the Marines, and the haunting,
almost surrealistic battle with the mysterious and violent rival gang known
as "The Ducky Boys." All in all a fascinating film with an outstanding
musical score consisting of juke box hits from the period.

p, Martin Ransohoff; d, Philip Kaufman; w, Rose Kaufman, P. Kaufman
(based on the novel by Richard Price); ph, Michael Chapman (Technicolor);
ed, Ronald Roose, Stuart H. Pappe; art d, Jay Moore; cos, Robert de Mora.

Drama   Cas.   (PR:O   MPAA:R)

WANDERERS OF THE WEST**   (1941) 58m MON bw

Tom Keene (*Tom Mallory/Arizona*), Sugar Dawn (*Sugar Lee*), Slim An-
drews (*Slim*), Betty Miles (*Laura Lee*), Tom Seidel (*Westy Mack/Waco
Dean*), Stanley Price (*Jack Benson*), Gene Alsace (*Bronco*), Tom London
(*Sheriff*), James Sheridan [Sherry Tansey] (*Jeff Haines*), Fred Hoose
(*Saloonkeeper*), Rusty the Horse.

When rustlers kill rancher Keene's father, the angry cowpoke vows revenge
and chases the baddies from Montana to Arizona. Unfortunately, Keene
knows only the killer's name because he has never seen his face. The killer
has never seen his pursuer, either. The deadly foes meet finally but they
don't realize the identity of the other until the end of the movie.
Unnecessarily confusing story, as phony as they come.

p, Robert Tansey; d, Robert Hill; w, Robert Emmett [Tansey]; ph, Jack R.
Young; m, Frank Sanucci; ed, Fred Bain.

Western   (PR:A   MPAA:NR)

WANDERING JEW, THE**½   (1933) 68m Jafa bw

Jacob Ben-Ami, Ben Adler, Jacob Mestel, Abraham Teitelbaum, Natalie
Browning, M.B. Samuylow.

This adaptation of the "wandering Jew" legend is a haunting look at events
to come, though the filmmakers couldn't have realized it at the time. Filmed
in Yiddish, the story deals with a young Jewish artist living in Germany in
the early 1930s. Engaged to a gentile girl, the artist has just completed a
portrait of his father entitled "The Eternal Jew." A friend warns him that
the painting may be excluded from the Academy of Art because of the
artist's Jewish heritage. Below his studio the man hears Nazis marching
through the streets, belittling the Jews as they go. Soon his world falls apart
as the painting is rejected and his fiancee leaves him because of his
Jewishness. The artist, a veteran of WW I, is enraged that all this is
happening simply because of his religion. He takes a knife and prepares to
destroy the portrait, but is stopped when his father's image steps out of the
picture. The old man gives his son a brief history of the Jews' ability to
survive from Babylonian times to the Spanish Inquisition to Tsarist times
in Russia. The son realizes his destiny and considers migrating from
Germany, and the film ends with a massive anti-Nazi rally held in Madison
Square Garden. The story is riveting, the evils of Nazism speaking for
themselves. What is perhap s the most gripping and ironic point to the film
is how prophetic it turned out to be. And yet, in another irony, Ben-Ami's
father shows his son how good things are for Jews in the Soviet Union.
Considering what has been discovered in the post-Stalinist era about the
Soviet government's treatment of Jews, the film's message becomes all the
more poignant. (In Yiddish; English subtitles.)

d, George Roland; w, Jacob Mestel; ph, Frank Aukor, Bergi Contner.

Drama   (PR:A   MPAA:NR)

WANDERING JEW, THE**½   (1935, Brit.) 85m
GAU/Twickenham/Olympic bw

Conrad Veidt (*The Wandering Jew*), Phase I: Veidt (*Matathias*), Marie Ney
(*Judith*), Cicely Oates (*Rachel*), Basil Gill (*Pontius Pilate*), Phase II: Veidt
(*The Unknown Knight*), Anne Grey (*Joanne de Beaudricourt*), Bertram
Wallis (*Boemund*), Prince of Tarentum, Hector Abbas (*Issachar*), Dennis
Hoey (*De Beaudricourt*), Jack Livesey (*Godfrey*), Duke of Normandy,
Takase (*Phirous*), Phase III: Veidt (*Matteos Battadios*), Joan Maude
(*Gianella*), John Stuart (*Pietro Morelli*), Arnold Lucy (*Andrea Michelotti*),
Phase IV: Veidt (*Matteos Battadios*), Peggy Ashcroft (*Olalla Quintana*),
Frances L. Sullivan (*Juan de Texeda, Inquisitor General*), Felix Aylmer
(*Ferera*), Ivor Barnard (*Castro*), Abraham Sofaer (*Zapportas*), Stafford

Hilliard *(Juan)*, Robert Gilbert *(1st Monk)*, Conway Dixon *(2nd Monk)*.

Odd British film starring Veidt as a Jew who, during the trials of Christ, demanded that Barabbas be released from prison and that Christ be crucified. As punishment for his behavior, Veidt is condemned by God to live forever, wandering through the ages. The film follows Veidt on his travels through various countries and occupations over 13 centuries until he is finally released from his torture when Christ allows him to die during the Spanish Inquisition after the Jew embraces his teachings. While the film has aged poorly, it has some fantastic sequences and deserves a look.

p, Julius Hagen; d, Maurice Elvey; w, H. Fowler Mear (based on a play by E. Temple Thurston); ph, Sydney Blythe; m, Dr. Hugo Reisenfeld.

Drama   **(PR:A MPAA:NR)**

WANDERING JEW, THE*   (1948, Ital.) 97m Globe bw (L'EBREO
                                                            ERRANTE)

Vittorio Gassman *(Matthew Blumenthal)*, Valentina Cortese *(Esther)*, Noelle Norman *(Blumenthal's Mistress)*, Inge Gort *(Sarah)*, Pietro Sharov *(Prof. Epstein)*, Harry Feist *(Hans)*, Armando Francioli *(David)*, Hans Hinrich *(Dr. Schuster)*, Antonio Crast *(German Officer)*, Amilcare Olivieri *(Deschamps)*, Egisto Olivieri *(Maquisard)*, Cesare Polacco, Giovanni Hinrich, Angelo Calabrese, Fosca Freda.

Loose adaptation of the "wandering Jew" legend starring Gassman as a wealthy, but cursed, Parisian Jew who willingly assists the Nazis against his own people during WW II. He has a change of heart and allows himself to be shipped off to a concentration camp with his people, only to escape with the woman he loves, Cortese. When Gassman learns that the Nazis will slaughter the remaining prisoners unless he returns, the escaped prisoner turns himself in to save the others' lives. In the end, Gassman is machine-gunned by the Nazis, ending his curse.

d, Goffredo Alessandrini; w, Alessandrini, Ennio De Concini, Anton Giulio Majano (based on a story by G.B. Angioletti); ph, Vaclav Vich; m, Enzo Massetti; art d, Arrigo Equini.

War   **(PR:O MPAA:NR)**

WANDERLOVE* (1970) 95m Fine Products c (AKA: WANDER LOVE
                                                            STORY)

Jamie Michaels *(Judy)*, Fletcher Fist *(P.G.)*, Norman Cole, Gerrie Grant, Lisa Tennele, Adam Wade, The Hot Soup, Year 2000, The Runaway Pancake.

Exploitation film starring Michaels as the proverbial girl from the Midwest who travels to Hollywood to become a movie star. There she meets swinging film director Fist and she does what it takes to become a star. Eventually, Michaels gets fed up with the abuse Hollywood and Fist heap on her and she boards the next bus back home with Fist running alongside professing his love. Ambition and disillusionment at a low level, indeed. Songs include: "Archie's Theme" (Jeff Barry), "Gettin' in My Way Again" (Frank Carillo), "Baby's Wearing Blue," "Farewell, Sweet Papa," "Groovy Feelin'," Oh, No, Not Again," "Once Before" (Mario Castellanos), "I'm Working So Hard."

p, Fletcher Fist, Gerald Fine; d&w, Fist; ph, Robert Maxwell (Eastmancolor); m/l, Jeff Barry, Frank Carillo, Mario Castellanos.

Drama   **(PR:O MPAA:R)**

WANDERLUST   (SEE: MARY JANE'S PA, 1935)

WANT A RIDE LITTLE GIRL?   (SEE: IMPULSE, 1975)

WANTED, 1929   (SEE: HIGH VOLTAGE, 1929)

WANTED, 1933   (SEE: POLICE CALL, 1933)

WANTED½   (1937, Brit.) 69m Sound City bw

ZaSu Pitts *(Winnie Oatfield)*, Claude Dampier *(Henry Oatfield)*, Mark Daly *(Mr. Smithers)*, Norma Varden *(Mrs. Smithers)*, Finlay Currie *(Uncle Mart)*, Kathleen Harrison *(Belinda)*, Billy Holland *(Harry the Hick)*, Stella Bonheur *(Baby Face)*, Billy Bray *(Sparrow Hawkins)*, Arthur Goulet *(Bonelli)*, Arthur Wellesley *(Lord Hotbury)*, Mable Twenlow *(Lady Hotbury)*, D.J. Williams *(Capt. McTurk)*, Brian Herbert *(Police Constable Gribble)*.

A amusing comedy starring Dampier as an unassuming shipping clerk and Pitts as his wife, who are mistaken for a pair of famed jewel thieves by gangsters who hire them to steal some gems. Pushed into the crime, Pitts and Dampier find themselves at a fancy party where the jewels are located. During the festivities, the pair realize that the real thieves are also at the party and they round up the crooks and receive a large reward.

p&d, George King; w, H.F. Maltby (based on the play by Brock Williams); ph, Jack Parker.

Comedy   **(PR:A MPAA:NR)**

WANTED BY SCOTLAND YARD**
       (1939, Brit.) 60m Pathe/MON bw (GB: DANGEROUS FINGERS)

James Stephenson *("Fingers")*, Betty Lynne *(Doris)*, Leslie Perrins *(Standish)*, Nadine March *(Mabel)*, Sally Stewart *(Molly)*, D. A. Clarke-Smith *(Inspector Williams)*, George Merritt *(Charlie)*, Bryan Herbert *(Sherlock)*, Florence Groves *(Maud)*, Phil Ray *(Ben)*.

Contrived crime drama starring Stephenson as a suave thief who, while on a job which requires the theft of some rubies, discovers that his victim, Perrins, is the man who drove his former love to suicide. Obsessed with the thought of revenge, Stephenson lets his guard down and is trapped by Perrins, but is saved by another thief, Ray, who kills Perrins. Ray, in turn, is killed by the cops. Stephenson escapes and flees to South America with his new girl friend, Lynne.

p, John Argyle; d, Norman Lee; w, Vernon Clancey (based on the novel *Man Hunt* by Clancey); ph, Bryan Langley; ed, E.G. Richards.

Crime   **(PR:A MPAA:NR)**

WANTED BY THE POLICE*½   (1938) 59m MON bw

Frankie Darro *(Danny)*, Lillian Elliott *(Mrs. Murphy)*, Robert Kent *(Mike)*, Evalyn Knapp *(Kathleen)*, Matty Fain *(Williams)*, Don Rowan *(Owens)*, Sam Bernard *(Stinger)*, Mauritz Hugo *(Marty)*, Thelma White *(Lillian)*, Willy Costello *(Russo)*, Walter Merrill *(Trigger)*, Ralph Peters *(Jess)*.

Standard good-kid-gone-bad film starring Darro as the plucky Irish-American youngster who falls in with a bad crowd and begins stealing cars. When his mom, Elliott, learns what her Danny-boy's been up to she gets her daughter's boy friend, Kent, who is a cop, to set the kid straight.

p, Lindsley Parsons; d, Howard Bretherton; w, Wellyn Totman (based on a story by Don Mullaly, Renaud Hoffman); ph, Bert Longnecker.

Crime   **(PR:A MPAA:NR)**

WANTED FOR MURDER**   (1946, Brit.) 91m FOX bw (AKA: A
                                                      VOICE IN THE NIGHT)

Eric Portman *(Victor Colebrooke)*, Dulcie Gray *(Anne Fielding)*, Derek Farr *(Jack Williams)*, Roland Culver *(Inspector Conway)*, Stanley Holloway *(Sgt. Sullivan)*, Barbara Everest *(Mrs. Colebrooke)*, Kathleen Harrison *(Florrie)*, Jenny Laird *(Jeannie McLaren)*, Bill Shane *(Detective Ellis)*, Bonar Colleano *(Cpl. Mappolo)*, John Salew *(Walters)*, Moira Lister *(Miss Willis)*, Viola Lyel *(Mrs. Cooper)*, John Ruddock *(Tramp)*, George Carney *(Boatman)*, Edna Wood, Wilfrid Hyde-White, Gerhardt Kempinski, Mary Mackenzie, Caven Watson, Beatrice Campbell, Wally Patch.

Silly thriller about a young man, Portman, obsessed with the fact that his father was a hangman in Victorian times. The obsession drives him insane, and Portman spends much of the film strangling young ladies. Even a psycho can fall in love, however, and Portman falls hard for the beautiful Miss Gray. Unfortunately, he cannot control his homicidal impulses and he attempts to strangle his love. The police arrive before he gets too far and rather than be captured, Portman drowns himself. Portman is very good in a complex role.

p, Marcel Hellman; d, Lawrence Huntington; w, Emeric Pressburger, Rodney Ackland, Maurice Cowan (based on the play by Percy Robinson, Terence de Marney); ph, Max Greene [Mutz Greenbaum], R. Frankie; m, Mischa Spoliansky; ed, E.B. Jarvis.

Crime   **(PR:C MPAA:NR)**

WANTED: JANE TURNER**   (1936) 67m RKO bw

Lee Tracy *(Mallory)*, Gloria Stuart *(Doris)*, Judith Blake *(Jane)*, John McGuire *(Jerry)*, Frank M. Thomas *(Banks)*, Patricia Wilder *(Babe)*, Barbara Pepper *(Marge)*, Willard Robertson *(Davies)*, Irene Franklin *(Ruby)*, Paul Guilfoyle *(Crowley)*.

Based on an actual 1926 crime case pulled from the files of the United States Postal Service, this less-than-thrilling crime story stars Tracy as the head investigator of the post office out to smash a gang that has robbed a mail truck and murdered the driver. "Jane Turner" is the phony name the crooks use to fool the post office into delivering their loot. When a real Jane Turner shows up, the law and the crooks both sink under the weight of the confusion.

p, Cliff Reid; d, Edward Killy; w, John Twist (based on a story by Edmund L. Hartmann, Julius Klein); ph, Robert De Grasse; ed, Ted Cheesman.

Crime   **(PR:A MPAA:NR)**

WANTED MEN, 1931   (SEE: LAW OF THE RIO GRANDE, 1931)

WANTED MEN, 1936   (SEE: WOLVES, 1936, Brit.)

WANTED WOMEN   (SEE: JESSIE'S GIRLS, 1976)

WANTON CONTESSA, THE   (SEE: SENSO, 1968, Ital.)

WAR   (SEE: RAT, 1960, Yugo.)

WAR AGAINST MRS. HADLEY, THE***   (1942) 85m MGM bw

Edward Arnold (*Elliott Fulton*), Fay Bainter (*Stella Hadley*), Richard Ney (*Theodore Hadley*), Jean Rogers (*Patricia Hadley*), Sara Allgood (*Mrs. Michael Fitzpatrick*), Spring Byington (*Cecilia Talbot*), Van Johnson (*Michael Fitzpatrick*), Isobel Elsom (*Mrs. Laura Winters*), Frances Rafferty (*Sally*), Dorothy Morris (*Millie*), Halliwell Hobbes (*Bennett*), Connie Gilchrist (*Cook*), Horace [Stephen] McNally (*Peters*), Miles Mander (*Dr. Leonard V. Meecham*), Rags Ragland (*Louie*), Mark Daniels (*Bob*), Carl Switzer (*Messenger Boy*).

A well-done piece of American WW II propaganda starring Bainter as a rich society woman who refuses to change her comfortable life style to help the war effort. She comes to realize that by making some minor sacrifices now, she is aiding the boys overseas in their battle to ensure that she may continue living in a free country. The cast does well with the material,and the film remains an interesting look at how America drove some messages home to those stateside during WW II.

p, Irving Asher; d, Harold S. Bucquet; w, George Oppenheimer; ph, Karl Freund; m, David Snell; ed, Elmo Veron; art d, Cedric Gibbons.

Drama   (PR:A   MPAA:NR)

WAR AND PEACE****   (1956, Ital./U.S.) 208m Ponti-DD/PAR c

Audrey Hepburn (*Natasha Rostov*), Henry Fonda (*Pierre Bezukhov*), Mel Ferrer (*Prince Andrei Bolkonsky*), Vittorio Gassman (*Anatole Kuragin*), John Mills (*Platon Karatsev*), Herbert Lom (*Napoleon*), Oscar Homolka (*Gen. Mikhail Kutuzov*), Anita Ekberg (*Helene, later Pierre's First Wife*), Helmut Dantine (*Dolokhov*), Barry Jones (*Count Ilya Rostov*), Anna Maria Ferrero (*Mary Bolkonsky*), Milly Vitale (*Lise, Prince Andrei's Wife*), Jeremy Brett (*Prince Nicholas Rostov*), Lea Seidl (*Countess Rostov*), Wilfred Lawson (*Prince Nicholas Bolkonsky*), Sean Barrett (*Petya Rostov*), Tullio Carminati (*Prince Vasili Kuragin*), May Britt (*Sonya Rostov*), Patrick Crean (*Vasili Denisov*), Gertrude Flynn (*Peronskaya*), Teresa Pellati (*Masa*), Maria Zanoli (*Mayra*), Alberto Carlo Lolli (*Rostov's Major-Domo*), Mario Addobati (*Young Servant at Rostov's*), Gualtiero Tumiati (*Pierre's Father*), Clelia Matania (*Mlle. Georges*), Gianni Luda, Eschilo Tarquini, Alex D'Alessio, Alfredo Rizzo (*Soldiers During the Rostovs' Exile*), Mauro Lanciani (*Young Prince Nicolai Bolkonsky*), Ina Alexeiva (*His Governess*), Don Little (*Young Dancing Partner of Natasha*), John Horne (*Old Gentleman Dancing with Natasha*), Sdenka Kirchen (*Old Maid at Rostov's*), Nando Gallai (*Count Bezukhov's Servant*), Michael Tor (*Pope*), Piero Pastore (*Andrei Bolkonsky's Servant*), Vincent Barbi (*Balaga, Dolokhov's Coachman*), John Douglas, Robert Stephens (*Officers Talking with Natasha During Exile*), Luciano Angelini (*Young Soldier at Borodino*), Charles Fawcett (*Russian Artillery Captain*), Piero Palermini (*Russian Artillery Lieutenant*), Angelo Galassi, David Crowley, Patrick Barrett, Michael Billingsley (*Russian Soldiers*), Aldo Saporetti, Dimitri Konstantinov, Robin White Cross, Lucio de Santis (*Young Officers at Orgy*), Robert Cunningham (*Pierre's Second at Duel*), Andrea Eszterhazy (*Dolokhov's Second*), Marianne Leibl (*Servant at Bolkonsky's*), Marisa Allasio (*Matriosa, Dolokhov's Servant*), Stephen Garrett (*Coachman/Doctor*), Micaela Giustiniani (*Woman*), Cesare Barbetti (*Young Boy*), Francis Foucaud (*French Soldier*), Savo Raskovitch (*Czar Alexander I*), George Brehat (*French Officer at Execution*), Gilberto Tofano (*Young Dying Soldier*), Umberto Sacripante (*Old Man*), Paole Quagliero (*Young Girl Protected by Pierre*), Christopher Hofer (*French Officer During Retreat*), Carlo Delmi (*Young Guard*), Enrico Olivieri (*French Drummer*), Eric Oulton, Archibald Lyall, John Stacey, Mino Doro (*Russian Generals*), Alan Furlan, Joop van Hulsen (*Russian Officers*), Giovanni Rossi-Loti (*Young Russian Officer at Austerlitz*), Giacomo Rossi-Stuart (*Young Cossack*), Guido Celano (*Napoleon's Officer*), Jerry Riggio, Geoffrey Copplestone, Mimmo Palmara, Giorgio Constantini (*French Officers*), Richard McNamara (*De Beausset*), Andrea Fantasia (*Constand, Napoleon's Valet*), Stephen Lang (*Tichon, Old Servant at Bolkonsky's*), Carlo Dale, Paul Davis (*Young French Officers*).

A mammoth undertaking, WAR AND PEACE seems short at more than three hours in its condensation of the more than 600,000-word novel that Tolstoy took nearly six years to write. Filmed at a cost of more than $6 million in Rome and environs, it ranked as the best adaptation of Tolstoy until the 1968 six-hour version directed by and starring Sergei Bondarchuk, which had the unlimited funds of the Soviet government to back the production. Although deftly using thousands of Italian soldiers as extras, Vidor was hampered by a cast that mixed their accents (British, American, German, Swedish, French, Italian, and everything else, it seemed) and caused the suspension of disbelief, so necessary in historical epics, to be shattered. Lom is Napoleon ("The Little Corporal") and he is about to make his ill-fated attack on Mother Russia in his megalomaniacal effort to be emperor of all Europe. Fonda is a gentle and liberal man of the aristocratic class. He pays a call on his friend, Jones, and Jones' daughter, Hepburn, and falls in love with the elegant young woman, but finds himself unable to declare his love because he is the illegitimate son of a count and therefore feels unworthy. The count dies shortly thereafter and leaves Fonda an inheritance as well as legitimizing Fonda's birth. Before Fonda can approach Hepburn, he meets Ekberg, a luscious woman with a scheming brain. She soon entices Fonda and his naivete causes him to marry her. On the war front, Fonda's best comrade, Ferrer, is battling for the country's sake under his general, Homolka. Ferrer has been injured in the service and comes home to have some peace but when his wife dies giving birth, he is depressed and nearly suicidal. Fonda learns that Ekberg has been seeing other Russians on the side and dispenses with her, but he is so loyal to Ferrer that he arranges an introduction between him and Hepburn to help assuage the man's grief. Hepburn and Ferrer fall in love and plan to marry but Fate steps in and Ferrer is ordered to go back to war to help stem the French tide. Fonda decides to go to the front as well, but more as an observer than a warrior. Fonda is stunned by the actuality of war as seen at the battle of Borodino (brilliantly directed by Mario Soldati) and is so personally incensed by the blood-letting that he promises himself he will never sleep soundly until the perpetrator is killed by his hand. And so, with that, the timid Fonda resolves to personally kill Lom. Later, Fonda goes home to Moscow and watches as Homolka oversees the evacuation of the capital. Just before Lom marches in with his men, all of the troops are ordered out of the city so the French encounter no resistance. Ferrer has been wounded badly and has only a short while to live. Jones and Hepburn find a place to hide at an old religious retreat outside Moscow and she and Ferrer are together briefly before he succumbs of his wounds. Meanwhile, Fonda has attempted to kill Lom but failed and he is taken prisoner and will be marched back to France. Lom's forces are cut off from their supply lines and the bitter Soviet weather begins taking a huge toll in lives. The French are hardly used to fighting in this kind of weather and terrain and Fonda watches as the men drop like frozen flies. At the same time, the Russian forces have been reuniting and begin to chase the beleaguered French. Thousands perish in the flight from Moscow to France and Fonda barely holds on to his own life. At Berezina, the remaining forces of the Russians swoop down on the tired, cold, and poorly supplied French and administer the *coup de grace*. Fonda gets away from the French and makes his way to Moscow where he is soon involved with the returning soldiers and civilians in the process of putting the country back to normal. In the end, Fonda and Hepburn, who have been star-crossed from the beginning, are happy when they meet again and can fulfill the love that was hinted at some three hours before. Cardiff's lensing was superb and he was nominated for an Oscar, although Aldo Tonti was responsible for the second unit, which was every bit as distinguished. Vidor was also nominated for an Oscar but 1956 was a year for spectacular movies and this film was overshadowed by the success of AROUND THE WORLD IN 80 days, THE KING AND I, ANASTASIA, WRITTEN ON THE WIND, and GIANT, all huge pictures. Several plots ran through the scenario and never seemed to get confusing. It was complex, but never too much so. The movie didn't make much money and more's the pity. Cecil B. DeMille made THE TEN COMMANDMENTS this same year and that picture, plus the other large films, siphoned off whatever profits a movie such as WAR AND PEACE might have earned in another year. It was in preproduction for almost a decade and the actual shooting took almost two more years. Fonda never believed he was right for the part and tried to get the feeling of Pierre's intellectuality by insisting he wear small eyeglasses, which he did in about half the film. In later years, such as in the 1980s, a movie of this magnitude would have cost nearly 10 times the amount. Tolstoy scholars may argue that much of the classic novel has been omitted, but anyone who knows the exigencies of moviemaking will appreciate the adaptation and the selection of which stories were told. Hepburn is glorious, totally believable and the definitive Natasha. This was the second version of the story, the first having been done in Russia in 1916, only six years after Tolstoy died. The Bondarchuk version is far more enveloping because he told his story in about seven hours (although it was cut somewhat for U.S. distribution) and used about the same number of extras as Napoleon had troops. Mike Todd, David O. Selznick, and MGM had their own plans for the book and all thought of Hepburn as the lead but once Vidor got to work, the other films were abandoned. It was not an easy shoot, with constant battles among the producers, hassles with the actors, and some internecine script squabbles (Irwin Shaw had his name removed from the credits because of the manner in which he was rewritten). Despite all of that, this is a superior motion picture of a very difficult and vast story that everyone said could not be done well. Texan Vidor became famous again years after his death when his notes on a projected screenplay about the life and times and death of director William Desmond Taylor were uncovered by his biographer and published in 1986 as *Cast of Killers*. That book named Charlotte Shelby, mother of the tragic Mary Miles Minter, as the killer of Taylor, although there is still some doubt of that. Vidor would go on to make SOLOMON AND SHEBA before being considered "too old" by the studio chiefs.

p, Dino De Laurentiis; d, King Vidor; w, Bridget Boland, Robert Westerby, Vidor, Mario Camerini, Ennio De Concini, Ivo Perilli, (uncredited) Irwin Shaw (based on the novel by Leo Tolstoy); ph, Jack Cardiff, Aldo Tonti (VistaVision, Technicolor); m, Nino Rota; ed, Stuart Gilmore, Leo Cattozzo; md, Franco Ferrera; art d, Mario Chiari, Franz Bachelin, Giani Polidori; set d, Piero Cherardi; cos, Maria De Matteis.

Historical Drama   **Cas.**   (PR:A-C MPAA:NR)

WAR AND PEACE½** (1968, USSR) 373m Mosfilm/CD c (VOINA I MIR)

Lyudmila Savelyeva (*Natasha Rostova*), Sergei Bondarchuk (*Pierre Bezukhov*), Vyacheslav Tikhonov (*Andrey Bolkonskiy*), Viktor Stanitsyn (*Ilya Andreyevich Rostov*), Kira Golovko (*Countess Rostova*), Oleg Tabakov (*Nikolay Rostov*), Nikolay Kodin, Seryozha Yermilov (*Petya Rostov*), Irina Gubanova (*Sonya*), Anatoliy Ktorov (*Nikolay Andreyevich Bolkonskiy*), Antonina Shuranova Princess Marya, Anastasia Vertinskaya (*Liza Bolkonskaya*), Boris Smirnov (*Prince Vasiliy Kuragin*), Irina Skobtseva (*Helene Kuragin*), Vasiliy Lanovoi (*Anatole Kuragin*), Oleg Yefremov (*Dolokhov*), N. Tolkachyov (*Count Bezukhov*), Yelena Tyapkina (*Marya Akhrosimova*), K. Polovikova (*Princess Anna Drubetskaya*), Eduard Martsevich (*Drubetskoy*), A. Stepanova (*Anna Scherer*), D. Firsova (*Catiche*), G. Kravchenko (*Julie Karagina*), Boris Zakhava (*Gen. Kutuzov*), Nickolay Trofimov (*Tushin*), Gyuli Chokhonelidze (*Prince Bagration*), Nikolay Rybnikov (*Denisov*), V. Murganov (*Tsar Aleksandr I*), Vladislav Strzhelchik (*Napoleon Bonaparte*), V. Sofronov (*Emperor Franz*), N. Bubnov (*Gen. Mack*), I. Solovyov (*Shinshin*), Yu. Chekulayev (*Nesvitskiy*), Pyotr Savin (*Timokhin*), A. Smirnov (*Staff Officer*), V. Badayev (*Regiment Commander*), Aleksandr Borisov (*Uncle Mikhail*), Nonna Mordyukova (*Anisya Fyodorovna*), A. Syomin (*Nikolushka*), G. Zommer (*Bennigsen*), Ya. Grantinsh (*Woltzogen*), D. Eysentals (*Karl von Clausewitz*), Mikhail Khrabrov (*Karatayev*), Stanislav Chekan (*Tikhon Shcherbatyy*), Jean-Claude Balard (*Ramballe*), Georgiy Millyar (*Morel*), Boris Molchanov (*Marshal Louis Davout*), L. Polyakov (*Lauriston*), G. Shapovalov, N. Smorchkov, I. Turchenkov, A. Boldyrev, N. Khryashchikov, A. Degtyar, A. Lebedev, D. Sivakov, N. Sorokin, V. Prikhodko, D. Netrebin, A. Bakhar, Ye. Shalamov, M. Vorobyov (*Russian Soldiers*), Ye. Stroyeva, S. Uspenskaya, M. Dobrovolskaya, N. Fogel, L. Borisenko, V. Matissen, Ye. Yelina, N. Lebedev, A. Fadeyev, N. Kollen, V. Renin, Z. Smirnova-Nemirovich, A. Rebane, Yu. Ovsyannikov, Yu. Dioshi, E. Knausmyuller, A. Barushnoy, G. Kurovskiy, V. Maslatsov, P. Alekseyev, Yu. Rossinol, V. Lutsekovich, A. Ponomarenko, A. Kin, V. Mashchenko, V. Smirnov, Z. Dvizhkova, V. Polonskaya, L. Kramareskiy, Yelena Vanke, A. Begak, D. Begak, A. Sezemann, N. Sibeykin, G. Ivanov, V. Vagina, Yu. Chuveleva, S. Makovskaya, V. Yermilov, Yu. Grigoryev, Ye. Khovanskaya, O. Mikhaylova, G. Rybakov, V. Lapin, Ye. Lyutsau, N. Grinko, Sergey Nikonenko, L. Vidavskiy, A. Gruzinskiy, A. Mombelli, G. Svetlani, T. Makhova, Yu. Vetrov, V. Matov, A. Glazyrin, L. Nedovich, T. Kazankova, R. Aleksandrov, V. Islavin, Yu. Kryuchkov, I. Vasilenko, B. Batashov, V. Fromgoldt, G. Shostko, Z. Zaks, G. Mityakov, G. Edzhubov, A. Komissarov, V. Levchenko, Vladimir Likhachyov, A. Yachnitskiy, S. Konovalova, V. Kosarikhin, I. Labina, N. Afrikyants, N. Avetisova, V. Alakhverdova, N. Aparin, V. Seleznyov, P. Kiryutkin, R. Chumak, Norman Rose (*English Narrator*).

Quite possibly the most expensive and ultimately the most mediocre epic ever put on film. State-favored director Bondarchuk pulled together the vast resources of the Soviet Union and staged what is perhaps one of the most monumental productions ever assembled at a cost the Russians claim to have been $100 million. Unfortunately, the human scope of the film is all but lost in this gigantic display of bravado. The Russian adaptation of Tolstoy's novel is a mammoth, ponderous white-elephant of a movie with splashes of sheer, breathtaking visuals. The English version (which is dubbed rather than subtitled–a deadly mistake that makes this even harder to sit through) was released in two parts shown back to back. Part one runs 3 hours and 15 minutes, part two, 2 hours and 58 minutes. This, believe it or not, is the cut version! The uncut version runs an incredible 507 minutes, almost nine hours, and was released in four parts. Just digesting the length alone is a chore. The film is sporadically successful at best, with epic battle scenes (the battle of Borodino runs nearly an hour) that stunningly portray the scope and inhumanity of war, contrasted with equally epic scenes of the glamor and wealth found at an elite, upper-class ball. In between these successes are dismal failures of dramatic finesse, pacing, and characterization which pull the film back down to earth with a thud. Most of the film's problems stem from an all-too-faithful obsession with the novel. While this may be admirable in literary circles, it does not allow for good filmmaking. Regardless, it is a film oddity that should warrant some attention.

p&d, Sergei Bondarchuk; w, Bondarchuk, Vasiliy Solovyov (based on the novel *Voyna i Mir* by Leo Tolstoy); ph, Anatoliy Petritskiy (Sovcolor); m, Vyacheslav Ovchinnikov; ed, Tatyana Likhachyova; art d, Mikhail Bogdanov, Gennadiy Myasnikov; set d, G. Koshelyov, V. Uvarov; cos, Mikhail Chikovani, Vladimir Burmeyster; makeup, Mikhail Chikiryov.

Drama (PR:A-C MPAA:NR)

WAR AND PEACE** (1983, Ger.) 85m TeleCulture c (KRIEG UND FRIEDEN)

Jurgen Prochnow (*Kevin*), Gunther Kaufmann (*Mac*), Manfred Zapatka (*Nikotai*), Karl-Heinz Merz (*Ivan*), Heinz Bennett (*Joe*), Edgar Selge (*Oscar*), Angela Winkler (*Margot*), Michael Gahr (*Albert*), Hans Michael Rehberg (*General*), Dieter Traier (*Interviewer*), Axel-Torg Gros (*Narrator*).

Strange little film that is made up of a series of antinuclear vignettes told with a sure sense of black humor and directed by some of West Germany's "New Wave" talent. One skit sees a group of U.S. astronauts in one spaceship, and a group of Russian cosmonauts in another, discussing the results of WW III. Other episodes deal with nuclear fallout, contamination,

and the stress put on Europe by the Americans and Russians who insist on planting their missile bases on European soil. A scattershot (excuse the expression) effort that only occasionally succeeds. (In German; English subtitles.)

p, Eberhardt Junkersdorf, Theo Hinz; d&w, Volker Schlondorff, Heinrich Boll, Alexander Kluge, Stefan Aust, Axel Angstfeld (based on the novel *From the Standpoint of the Infantry* by Kluge); ph, Franz Rath, Igor Luther, Werner Luring, Thomas March, Bernd Mosblech; ed, Dagmar Hirtz, Beate Mainka-Jellinghaus, Carola Mai, Barbara von Weitershausen; English subtitles, Boll.

Comedy/War (PR:C MPAA:NR)

WAR AND PIECE (SEE: HAREM BUNCH, OR WAR AND PIECE, THE, 1969)

WAR ARROW½** (1953) 78m UNIV c

Maureen O'Hara (*Elaine Corwin*), Jeff Chandler (*Maj. Howell Brady*), John McIntire (*Col. Jackson Meade*), Suzan Ball (*Avis*), Noah Beery, Jr (*Sgt. Augustus Wilks*), Charles Drake (*Sgt. Luke Schermerhorn*), Henry Brandon (*Maygro*), Dennis Weaver (*Pino*), Jay silverheels (*Satanta*), James Bannon (*Capt. Roger Corwin*), Brad Jackson (*Lieutenant*), Steve Wyman (*Capt. Neil*), Lance Fuller, Bill Ward (*Troopers*), Dee Carroll (*Hysterical Woman*), Roy Whatley (*Lieutenant*), Darla Ridgeway (*Crying Child*).

Chandler plays a clever Army officer recruiting Seminole Indians in his fight against the troublemaking Kiowa tribe. Chandler's peers think he's crazy to trust the Seminoles, but in the end he's proved correct and wins the heart of O'Hara. Supposedly based on a historical incident.

p, John W. Rogers; d, George Sherman; w, John Michael Hayes; ph, William Daniels (Technicolor); ed, Frank Gross; md, Joseph Gershenson; art d, Bernard Herzbrun, Alexander Golitzen; set d, Russell A. Gausman, Joseph Kish; cos, Edward Stevenson.

Western **Cas.** (PR:A MPAA:NR)

WAR BETWEEN MEN AND WOMEN, THE½** (1972) 105m NG c

Jack Lemmon (*Peter Wilson*), Barbara Harris (*Terry Kozlenko*), Jason Robards, Jr. (*Stephen Kozlenko*), Herb Edelman (*Howard Mann*), Lisa Gerritsen (*Linda Kozlenko*), Moosie Drier (*David Kozlenko*), Severn Darden (*Dr. Harris*), Lisa Eilbacher (*Caroline Kozlenko*), Lucille Meredith (*Mrs. Schenker*), Ruth McDevitt (*Elderly Woman*), Joey Faye (*Florist Delivery Man*), Alan DeWitt (*Man*), John Zaremba (*Minister*), Rick Gates (*Bernie*), Lea Marmer (*Old Hag*), Janya Brannt (*Nurse*), Dr. Joyce Brothers (*Herself*), William Hickman (*Large Gentleman*), Olive Dunbar, Margaret Muse (*Women at Literary Tea*), Danny Arnold (*Manhattan Policeman*).

An amiable comedy that may appeal more to fans of James Thurber than to anyone else, although they will take umbrage at some of the smarmy jokes, the sappy sentimentality, and the tacked-on happy ending. Lemmon is a writer-cartoonist who discovers that he's losing his vision. After a visit to his opthamologist (Darden), he trips over the attractive legs of divorcee Harris who is cooling her heels in the waiting room. Lemmon has a few acerbic remarks for Harris but they serve to intrigue, rather than repel her. After Lemmon exits with a lurch, Harris asks the doctor the details of Lemmon's eye woes. It being a small world, Harris and Lemmon meet again at a literary cocktail party. He loses his spectacles in a pitcher of martinis and is forced to down the contents to find them. Now drunk and reeling, Lemmon is swaying on a Manhattan street and having a battle with a belligerent lamp post. Lemmon's nose is bloodied as Harris arrives. She offers to administer first aid and he agrees to submit. She leads him to her residence where he meets her three children, Gerritsen, Drier, and Eilbacher, as well as the family pooch. All four take an immediate dislike to this nearsighted trespasser. Despite the enmity of the family and dog, Harris and Lemmon are attracted to each other and he eventually proposes to her. She accepts and wonderment abounds among Lemmon's acquaintances, who know that he is a confirmed woman, child, and dog hater. The wedding day dawns and Harris' ex-husband arrives. This is Robards, a much-traveled photojournalist and the shining hero to his adoring trio of children. After the honeymoon, Harris and Lemmon rent a house at a beach that soon turns into Vicksburg as Lemmon's attempts at stepfatherhood cause the rift between him and the children to widen into a chasm. Robards appears again for a visit and things get worse. With a father and a stepfather in the same house, the kids are getting confused. Late one night, both Lemmon and Robards are awakened by the sounds of what they perceive to be an intruder. They jump the person and it turns out to be Eilbacher, who is on her way home from a date and guilty of staying out well past her deadline. Harris thinks that Eilbacher must be made to understand that this is something not to be taken lightly but Robards and Lemmon shrug it off, thereby enraging both mother and daughter, who stalk off to their respective bedrooms, leaving Robards and Lemmon to sit around and get soused as they talk the night away. The next day, Lemmon notices a strong deterioration in his vision and goes to the city to see his doctor, while Robards departs on an assignment in Thailand. Lemmon learns that he has to have surgery performed right away if he is to keep any part of his sight. When Harris admits that she knew how bad his eyes were, Lemmon wonders if she didn't marry him more out of pity than love. The surgery is done and Harris comes to see Lemmon while he's recovering. He advises her to return to Robards, it might be better for all if the family were united once more. Then Harris drops the bombshell that Robards has been killed in Asia. Lemmon can barely see but if he draws on large enough paper, he can still do his cartoons. Gerritsen is the problem child. She is a terrible stutterer and the loss of Robards has caused her to stutter even worse than she had. At the request of Harris, Lemmon has a tete-a-tete with Gerritsen and encourages her, then baits her into venting her anger. Next, he relates the story of his latest book, a parable titled "The Last Flower," in which he details the cycle of humanity's self- destruction due to war and the ability of mankind to be redeemed by the regenerative power of love. He shows her that his cartoons and her late father's photographic equipment are two means of achieving the same ends and she is relieved to learn that Lemmon is not the ogre that she first thought him to be, and her stutter vanishes. Later, at a party launching Lemmon's new book, he finally realizes that Harris married him out of love and nothing more. The Thurber overtones ran all the way through the movie but, while the artist-writer managed to write and draw about his lack of vision and never once descended into maudlin stickiness, the movie aims for it in a big way. Thurber-type drawings appear in the opening credits and as fillers, and, at one point, they are animated. Lemmon hadn't acted in a movie for two years prior to this, only accepting his one directorial assignment on KOTCH. He admitted that the script by director Shavelson and TV mogul Arnold ("Barney Miller") read a lot funnier than the film turned out. Arnold does a cameo performance as a police officer, and Dr. Joyce Brothers is seen as herself. Whimsy, to work, should be sliced thin. This is thicker than a slab of Smithfield ham at a farmer's breakfast and when one adds the gooey sentiment, it tends to drown whatever humor was in the story. Shavelson was later involved with the Thurber-based TV series "My World and Welcome to It," which starred William Windom as the myopic master. Thurber was tough; Lemmon plays him grumpy but essentially soft. There are enough laughs in the movie to designate this as a comedy, but just barely.

p, Danny Arnold; d, Melville Shavelson; w, Arnold, Shavelson (based on the writings and drawings of James Thurber); ph, Charles F. Wheeler (Panavision, Technicolor); m, Marvin Hamlisch; ed, Frank Bracht; prod d, Stan Jolley; set d, Robert Benton; cos, Jerry Woods, Lambert Marks; anim, Robert Dranko, Dale Case; m/l, "You and Me," Hamlisch, Howard Liebling (sung by Barbara Harris, Jason Robards, Jr.); makeup, Harry Ray, Gary D. Liddiard.

Comedy (PR:A-C MPAA:PG)

WAR BETWEEN THE PLANETS zero (1971, Ital.) 80m
Fanfare/Mercury c (MISSIONE PLANETE ERRANTE; IL PIANETA ERRANTE; AKA: PLANET ON THE PROWL)

Jack Stuart [Giacomo Rossi-Stuart], Amber Collins [Ombretta Colli], John Barta, Enzo Fiermonte, Alina Zalewska, Freddy Urger, Vera Dolen, Marco Bogliani.

Poor Italian science-fiction effort which dredges up the old story about the scientists who try to save the Earth before a wild asteroid collides with it, and does absolutely nothing to illuminate the story. Stuart heads the team that meets the asteroid and blows it out of the heavens before it can reach Earth. Special effects rank high as do the relatively imaginative sets, but the script and dubbing both are so poor as to nullify the good points.

p, Joseph Fryd, Antonio Margheriti, Walter Manley; d, Anthony Dawson [Antonio Margheriti], Manley; w, Ivan Reiner, Renato Moretti; ph, Riccardo Pallottini; m, Francesco Lavagnino.

Science Fiction (PR:A MPAA:G)

WAR CORRESPONDENT (1932) 76m COL bw (GB: SOLDIERS OF FORTUNE)

Jack Holt (Jim Kenyon), Ralph Graves (Franklyn Bennett), Lila Lee (Julie March), Victor Wong (Wu Sun), Tetsu Komai (Fang).

Graves plays the title character who tries to cover the war in Shanghai while maintaining a detached perspective. Holt plays the hotshot mercenary pilot who competes with the reporter for the affections of a reformed prostitute, Lee. In the end Graves finally gets emotionally involved when he helps Holt save Lee from the enemy's evil clutches and sees his rival die in the effort.

d, Paul Sloane; w, Jo Swerling (based on a story by Keene Thompson); ph, Benjamin Kline; ed, Gene Havlick.

War (PR:A MPAA:NR)

WAR DOGS (1942) 64m MON bw (AKA: UNSUNG HEROES)

Billy Lee, Addison Richards, Kay Linaker.

To do his part for the war effort, a boy gives up his beloved pooch to the Army. A plaintive reminder to the folks back home that war is sacrifice. Tall and dignified character actor Richards performed in the four-star U.S. Air Army Corps picture AIR FORCE the next year.

p, George W. Weeks; d, S. Roy Luby; w, John Vlahos (based on a story by

Ande Lamb); ph, Robert Cline; ed, Roy Claire.

War/Children's Film (PR:A MPAA:NR)

WAR DRUMS½ (1957) 75m UA c

Lex Barker (Mangas Coloradas), Joan Taylor (Riva), Ben Johnson (Luke Fargo), Larry Chance (Ponce), Richard Cutting (Judge Bolton), James Parnell (Arizona), John Pickard (Sheriff Bullard), John Colicos (Chino), Tom Monroe (Dutch Herman), Jil Jarmyn (Nona), Jeanne Carmen (Yellow Moon), Mauritz Hugo (Clay Staub), Ward Ellis (Delgadito), Fred Sherman (Dr. Gordon), Paul Fierro (Fiero), Alex Montoya (Manuel), Stuart Whitman (Johnny Smith), Barbara Parry (Mary Smith), Jack Hupp (Lt. Roberts), Red Morgan (Trooper Teal), Monie Freeman.

Barker plays the noble Indian chief who reluctantly wages war on the white man after a broken treaty which promised his people peace. When a brief and bloody war threatens to doom Barker and company, sympathetic white man Johnson aids the chief in escaping to the hills rather than see them forced onto a reservation. Noble but dull.

p, Howard W. Koch; d, Reginald LeBorg; w, Gerald Drayson Adams; ph, William Margulies (DeLuxe Color); m, Les Baxter; ed, John A. Bushelman; cos, Paula Giokaris.

Western (PR:A MPAA:NR)

WAR GAMES, 1970 (SEE: SUPPOSE THEY GAVE A WAR AND NO ONE CAME? 1970)

WAR GAMES, 1983 (SEE: WARGAMES, 1983)

WAR GODS OF THE DEEP (SEE: CITY UNDER THE SEA, 1965, Brit.)

WAR HEAD (SEE: OPERATION SNAFU, 1965, Brit.)

WAR HERO, WAR MADNESS (SEE: WAR IS HELL, 1964)

WAR HUNT***½ (1962) 81m T-D Enterprise/UA bw

John Saxon (Pvt. Raymond Endore), Robert Redford (Pvt. Roy Loomis), Charles Aidman (Capt. Wallace Pratt), Sydney Pollack (Sgt. Van Horn), Gavin MacLeod (Pvt. Crotty), tommy Matsuda (Charlie), Tom Skerritt (Cpl. Showalter), Tony Ray (Pvt. Fresno).

After years of apprenticeship on the stage and in television, Robert Redford finally made his feature film debut in this odd, low-budget war film. He plays the new man, a replacement sent to a front-line platoon in Korea commanded by Aidman. Under the tutelage of the other men, many of them veterans of WW II, Redford quickly loses his illusions about war and heroism. He also meets Saxon, a private who goes on solitary nocturnal patrols, his face blackened, stalking and killing North Koreans in the darkness. The other men keep their distance from Saxon, and Aidman, who finds his prowlings a useful source of information, leaves him alone. Saxon's only companion is an 8-year-old Korean orphan, Matsuda. When Redford, worried about Saxon's influence on the boy, tries to befriend him, Saxon threatens to kill him if he doesn't keep away. One night Redford spots Saxon after he has killed another unwary Korean. In the light of a flare he sees Saxon crouch by the body as if in meditation, then do a strange dance around it. Now it is clear that Saxon is insane. A cease-fire is declared and that night the platoon celebrates. Saxon, though, can't stop killing so easily and goes off again, taking Matsuda with him. Redford, Aidman, and sergeant Pollack go out after him and find the pair in a bombed-out bunker. Completely unhinged, Saxon attacks the three with his stiletto and Aidman kills him. Matsuda puts his hands over his ears and runs off into no-man's land. One of the few films to deal with the uncomfortable subject of homicidal psychopaths in war (NIGHT OF THE GENERALS [1966! is another), the film has intelligence and production values that belie its $250,000 budget and 15 day shooting schedule. The film, in addition to being rather successful financially, also proved a major breeding ground for new talent. Francis Ford Coppola helped drive the Army trucks. Noel Black, who went on to direct PRETTY POISON (1968), helped with the lights. Sydney Pollack soon abandoned his acting career and, thanks to the friendship he formed with Redford during this shoot, the two would work together many times, including JEREMIAH JOHNSON (1972), THREE DAYS OF THE CONDOR (1976), THE ELECTRIC HORSEMAN (1979), and OUT OF AFRICA (1985).

p, Terry Sanders; d, Denis Sanders; w, Stanford Whitmore; ph, Ted McCord; m, Bud Shank; ed, John Hoffman, Edward Dutko; art d, Edgar Lansbury.

War **Cas.** (PR:C MPAA:NR)

WAR IS A RACKET (1934) 90m Cummings-Koepel/eureka bw

Col. Harry K. Eustace (The Munitions Maker), Hershell Mayall (The Economist), Gertrude Clemens (The Gold Star Mother), Frank Jacquet (Minister), June Leslie (Young Wife), Williard Dashiell (Business Man), Jacques Koerpel (Editor), Paul Owen (Ex-Soldier), A.L. Alexander (The

Reporter).

An editor sends out reporter Alexander to discover what any thinking individual could have told him: war is big money to many people at the expense of young lives. Alexander interviews many people, including a Gold Star mother (Clemens), a minister (Jacquet), and an economist (Mayall). Each tells their respective story which serves as voice-over for a poorly edited mixture of real-life war footage. It's as simple as that, continually hammering its message out well past any reasonable point. As a 10-minute short, this might have been effective, but at 90 minutes it ends up negating itself. In addition, the film is poorly edited, with an often pale imitation of Soviet style montage. Another shining example of why good intentions need thought and talent to make message films with impact.

p&d, Samuel Cummings, Jacques Koerpel; w, Vincent Valentini.

Drama   (PR:A-C MPAA:NR)

WAR IS HELL**   (1964) 81m AA bw

Tony Russel *(Sgt. Keefer)*, Baynes Barron *(Sgt. Garth)*, Burt Topper *(Lt. Hallen)*, Judy Dan *(Yung Chi Thomas)*, Tony Rich *(Miller)*, J.J. Dahner *(Koller)*, Wally Campo *(Laney)*, Bobby Byles *(Gresler)*, Michael Bell *(Seldon)*, Russ Prescott *(Bender)*, Robert Howard *(Connors)*, Paul Sherriff *(Thurston)*, Kei Chung *(Korean Lieutenant)*, Audie Murphy *(Narrator of Introduction)*.

Cowardly sergeant Russel stays behind and watches as his men bravely storm a Communist bunker in the midst of the Korean conflict. Most of the men are killed, but the rest succeed in capturing the stronghold with Russel taking all the credit (he expects a medal) and claiming to his superior officers that the surviving soldiers are all cowards. One of the officers suspects the truth, but Russel kills the man to ensure his silence. Russel goes even further to plant his name in military history by leading his men on a slaughter of Communist troops who have honored a cease-fire and disarmed themselves. Eventually the Communists have had enough of this nonsense and they kill Russel.

p, Burt Topper, Ross Hahn; d&w, Topper; ph, Jacques Marquette; m, Ronald Stein; ed, Ace Herman; spec eff, Pat Dinga.

War   (PR:A-C MPAA:NR)

WAR IS OVER, THE   (SEE: LA GUERRE EST FINIE, 1967, Fr./Swed.)

WAR ITALIAN STYLE** (1967, Ital.) 74m AIP c (DUE MARINES E UN GENERALE)

Buster Keaton *(Gen. Von Kassler)*, Franco Franchi *(Frank)*, Ciccio Ingrassia *(Joe)*, Martha Hyer *(Lt. Inge Schultze)*, Fred Clark *(Gen. Zacharias)*, Franco Ressel, Tommaso Alvieri, Barbara Loy, Alessandro Sperli, Alfredo Adami, Ennio Antonelli.

Poor comedy starring Keaton, in one of his last film appearances, as a German general stationed in Italy on the eve of the Allied invasion in WW II. Two American soldiers, Franchi and Ingrassia, plot to steal the Nazi offensive strategy plans, but the Nazis plant a false set of documents for the m. Luckily for the Allies, the Germans had accidentally planted the real invasion plans, which makes the invasion all the easier. When the Allies arrive on Anzio, the two soldiers are captured by Keaton's men, but, donning disguises of Hitler and an SS general, they fool the befuddled old general and escape. Taking pity on Keaton, the men dress him up as a scarecrow and help him escape as well.

p, Fulvio Lucisano; d, Luigi Scattini; w, Franco Castellano, Pipolo (based on an idea by Lucisano); ph, Fausto Zuccoli (Techniscope, Technicolor); m, Piero Umiliani.

Comedy/War   (PR:A MPAA:NR)

WAR LORD, THE, 1937   (SEE: WEST OF SHANGHAI, 1937)

WAR LORD, THE**   (1965) 123m court/UNIV c

Charlton Heston *(Chrysagon)*, Richard Boone *(Bors)*, Rosemary Forsyth *(Bronwyn)*, Maurice Evans *(Prist)*, Guy Stockwell *(Draco)*, Niall MacGinnis *(Odins)*, Henry Wilcoxon *(Frisian Prince)*, James Farentino *(Marc)*, Sammy Ross *(Volc)*, Woodrow Parfrey *(Piet)*, John Alderson *(Holbracht)*, Allen Jaffe *(Tybald)*, Michael Conrad *(Rainault)*, Dal Jenkins *(Dirck)*, Johnny Jensen *(Boy Prince)*, Forrest Wood *(Chrysagon Man)*, Belle Mitchell *(Old Woman)*.

This accurate accont of medieval life opens with Heston, an 11th-Century Morman knight, driving off a group of Frisians intent on invading a primitive Druid town. Heston, lord of the town, later spies Forsyth as she bathes in a stream. Forsyth is engaged to Farentino, son of the town's leader MacGinnis. Using the law of *le droit du seigneur* (a custom which allows a lord to take any bride he desires on her wedding night), Heston has his way with Forsyth. In the course of the evening Heston and Forsyth fall in love. When she refuses to leave the knight, her spurned husband vows revenge. Farentino goes to the Frisians, telling them their king's son is a prisoner in his village. Stockwell, Heston's brother, tries to take over as lord and the siblings engage in a duel. Stockwell is killed and Heston returns the captive

prince to the Frisians. The band also takes in Forsyth for her own safety. Heston is attacked by Farentino's men and, though wounded, the knight is able to get away to the woman he loves. This period piece is a fine example of cinema's ability to recreate long-gone eras. The period detail is exact, from costuming to the imposing tower from which Heston rules the village. The violence is brutal and bloody, with a savagely relistic climactic battle. Heston is fine in his role, and is given excellent support by an ensemble that never stoops to his trionics. Stockwell, actor Dean Stockwell's brother, made his acting debut in this movie, as did Farentino. In one fight sequence Heston engages in some well choreographed swordplay with Joe Canutt, son of legendary Hollywood stuntman Yakima Canutt. Despite its many excellent qualities, THE WAR LORD did only moderate box office in the U.S. Misunderstood by studio officials, director Schaffner's final cut was subjected to further editing despite his wishes. Shaffner claimed these imposed cuts removed "those fragile but always terribly consequential subtleties that you put into a film, so important to character, motivation, and reaction." Heston also was disappointed with the final results, though the movie remained one of his personal favorites. In his autobiography *The Actor's Life* Heston wrote "...the studio was convinced from the beginning that they had the ingredients for a huge tits-and-armor piece. If we'd been allowed to shoot in the English marshes with an English cast, away from the studio's enthusiastic urgings that we spend more money on flaming siege towers, I think we'd have the film we envisioned." Be that as it may, the essence of the filmmakers' intentions was not removed. THE WAR LORD remains an intelligent historical drama, exciting and atmospheric while never losing sight of the human passions that are its driving force.

p, Walter Seltzer; d, Franklin J. Schaffner; w, John Collier, Millard Kaufman (based on the play "The Lovers" by Leslie Stevens); ph, Russell Metty (Panavision, Technicolor); m, Jerome Moross; ed, Folmar Blangsted; art d, Alexander Golitzen, Henry Bumstead; set d, John McCarthy, Oliver Emert; cos, vittorio Nino Novarese; ch, Kenny Williams; makeup, Bud Westmore.

Drama   (PR:O MPAA:NR)

WAR LOVER, THE**   (1962, U.S./Brit.) 105m COL bw

Steve McQueen *(Buzz Rickson)*, Robert Wagner *(Ed Bolland)*, Shirley Ann Field *(Daphne Caldwell)*, Gary Cockrell *(Lynch)*, Michael Crawford *(Junior Sailen)*, Billy Edwards *(Brindt)*, Chuck Julian *(Lamb)*, Robert Easton *(Handown)*, Al Waxman *(Prien)*, Tom Busby *(Farr)*, George Sperdakos *(Bragliani)*, Bob Kanter *(Haverstraw)*, Jerry Stovin *(Emmet)*, Edward Bishop *(Vogt)*, Richard Leech *(Murika)*, Bernard Braden *(Randall)*, Sean Kelly *(Woodman)*, Charles De Temple *(Braddock)*, Neil McCallum *(Sully)*, Viera *(Singer)*, Justine Lord *(Street Girl)*, Louise Dunn *(Hazel)*, Arthur Hewlett *(Vicar)*.

McQueen is an American bomber pilot stationed in Britain who has found his niche and is thoroughly enjoying himself as the combat continues. His crew members, including copilot Wagner, don't especially like him, but they all respect his flying ability. Wagner takes up with English girl Field, and McQueen decides that he will add her to his list of conquests, but she sees through his thin facade of bravado and realizes that McQueen is incapable of a mature relationship with a woman. He and Wagner clash over her and over the pleasure McQueen is taking in his job. Finally, on a mission over Germany, the B-17 is hit by flak and struggles back to England. Over the English Channel McQueen makes everyone bail out, then tries to bring the plane in by himself. He doesn't make it, though, and the plane crashes into the Dover cliffs. A not altogether successful film that tries to probe the veneer of heroism to find the psychopathic, childish, and suicidal impulses beneath the acts. McQueen is better than he has any right to be, given the script, and he actually makes his rather despicable character a real and likable fellow. Wagner is also much better than he usually is, though he has often been so bad this achievement seems only a minor lapse. While filming in Britain, McQueen took advantage of lulls in the shooting to indulge his passion of race car driving. He was nearly badly hurt when his car spun out on a wet track, but he emerged with nothing worse than a split lip. The stitches in his lip showed up badly, and director Leacock let McQueen do all his scenes in the cockpit of the plane with an oxygen mask on to cover the scar. The plane used for the filming was one of the few (less than a half-dozen) B-17s still flying in serviceable condition. The same plane appeared in several films, including TWELVE O'CLOCK HIGH.

p, Arthur Hornblow, Jr.; d, Philip Leacock; w, Howard Koch (based on the novel by John Hersey); ph, Bob Huke; m, Richard Addinsell; ed, Gordon Hales; md, Muir Mathieson; art d, Bill Andrews; set d, Andrew Low; cos, Julie Harris; spec eff, Wally Veevers, Ted Samuels; makeup, George Partleton.

War Drama   Cas.   (PR:C-O MPAA:NR)

WAR MADNESS   (SEE: WAR IS HELL, 1969)

WAR NURSE½**   (1930) 79m MGM bw

Robert Montgomery *(Wally)*, Robert Ames *(Robin)*, June Walker *(Babs)*, Anita Page *(Joy)*, ZaSu Pitts *(Cushie)*, Marie Prevost *(Rosalie)*, Helen Jerome Eddy *(Kansas)*, Hedda Hopper *(Matron)*, Edward Nugent *(Frank)*, Martha Sleeper *(Helen)*, Michael Vavitch *(Doctor)*.

Badly handled war melodrama detailing the love lives of a corps of Army war nurses stationed in France during WW I. Montgomery plays the handsome fighter pilot, but brings little freshness to the role. Page is a nurse engaged in an illicit affair with soldier Ames, who's a married man (and he dies for his sins). Pitts performs her usual comedic bits and the rest of the cast does little of interest. Based on a sensational anonymous autobiography.

d, Edgar Selwyn; w, Becky Gardiner, Joe Farnham (based on the book *War Nurse: The True Story of a Woman Who Lived, Loved and Suffered on the Western Front* [anonymous]); ph, Charles Rosher; ed, William Levanway; art d, Cedric Gibbons; cos, Rene Hubert.

War   (PR:A   MPAA:NR)

WAR OF THE ALIENS   (SEE: STARSHIP INVASIONS, 1978, Can.)

WAR OF THE BUTTONS***   (1963 Fr.) 92m Bronston/Comet bw LA GUERRE DES BOUTONS)

Martin Lartique (*Tigibus*), Andre Treton (*Lebrac*), Michel Isella (*Aztec*), Jacques Dufilho (*Aztec's Father*), Pierre Trabaud (*Teacher*), Jean Richard (*Lebrac's Father*), Yvette Etievant (*Lebrac's Mother*), Michel Galabru (*Balatier*), Pierre Tchernia, Michele Meritz, Paul Crauchet, Claude Confortes, Henri Labussiere, Robert Rollis, Louisette Rousseau, Yves Peneau.

Interesting French anti-war film about two groups of boys who wage war against each other. The prizes in battle are the buttons of the enemy and during the fighting the boys strip each other of their buttons. Cleverly, one side enters the next battle naked and resoundly defeats their opponents. One boy on the winning team turns traitor and during the victory celebration the enemy stages a sneak attack and wins. The traitor is discovered and punishment is meted out to him. Seeking revenge, the boy runs home to his parents and tells on his companions. The children are rounded up by the adults and punished, but their leader escapes. Eventually he is caught and sent to reform school, along with the leader of the rival army of boys, for waging war without permission. (In French; English subtitles.)

p, Yves Robert, Daniele Delorme; d, Robert; w, Francois Boyer, Robert (based on the book *La Guerre des Boutons* by Louis Pergaud); ph, Andre Bac; m, Jose Berghmans; ed, Marie Josephe Yoyotte; md, Rene-Pierre Chouteau; art d, Pierre Thevenet; English subtitles, Noelle Gillmor.

Comedy   (PR:A   MPAA:NR)

WAR OF THE COLOSSAL BEAST*½
(1958) 68m AIP bw/c (GB: THE TERROR STRIKES)

Sally Fraser (*Joyce Manning*), Dean Parkin (*Col. Glenn Manning*), Roger Pace (*Maj. Baird*), Russ Bender (*Dr. Carmichael*), Charles Stewart (*Capt. Harris*), George Becwar (*Swanson*), Robert Hernandez (*Miguel*), Rico Alaniz (*Sgt. Luis Murillo*), George Alexander (*Army Officer*), George Navarro (*Mexican Doctor*), John McNamara (*Neurologist*), Bob Garnet (*Correspondent*), Howard Wright (*Medical Corps Officer*), Roy Gordon (*Mayor*), George Milan (*Gen. Nelson*), Warren Frost (*Switchboard Operator*), Bill Giorgio (*Bus Driver*), Loretta Nicholson (*Joan*), June Jocelyn (*Mother*), Jack Kosslyn (*Newscaster*), Stan Chambers (*TV Announcer*).

Silly sequel to THE AMAZING COLOSSAL MAN stars Parkin as the unfortunate GI who was caught in an atomic blast and grew into a rampaging giant. The end of the first film saw the hapless giant shot into Boulder Dam, where he met almost certain doom. The opening of this film, however, sees Parkin very much alive, sporting a half-skull face with one eye missing, and angry at those who tried to kill him. The Army eventually captures him and holds him captive in an airplane hanger, but he escapes and starts stomping on cars and killing people again. Finally, his sister, Fraser, catches up with him, scolds him for causing so much havoc, and drives the big guy to suicide. Not as good as the original (which wasn't all that good anyway), and with special effects just as unspectacular.

p&d, Bert I. Gordon; w, George Worthing Yates (based on a story by Gordon); ph, Jack Marta; m, Albert Glasser; ed, Ronald Sinclair, spec eff, Gordon.

Science Fiction   (PR:A   MPAA:NR)

WAR OF THE GARGANTUAS, THE zero
(1970, Jap.) 93m Toho/Maron c (FURANKENSHUTAIN NO KAIJU-SANDA TAI GAILAH; SANDA TAI GAILAH; AKA: DUEL OF THE GARGANTUAS)

Russ Tamblyn (*Dr. Paul Stewart*), Kumi Mizuno (*His Assistant*), Kipp Hamilton (*Singer*), Yu Fujuki (*Army Commander*), Kenji Sahara, Hiroshi Sekita, Jun Tazaki.

Trashy Japanese giant monster film that was supposed to be a sequel to the equally trashy FRANKENSTEIN CONQUERS THE WORLD, but minds were changed at the last minute and whatever vague connections this had with the previous film were removed. THE WAR OF THE GARGANTUAS tells the tale of a pair of twin monsters, sort of ape-like creatures, one brown (good) and one green (evil). The green monster wants to destroy Japan and his brown brother spends the rest of the move trying to stop him. After much

destruction the army shoots the green monster down and the brown one takes pity on his sibling and nurses him back to health, in the hope that he will abandon his war on humans. Unfortunately, once the green guy is healthy again he sets out to wreak new havoc on Tokyo, forcing his usually passive sibling to finally stand up and fight it out. The results of the battle are never seen because a volcano conveniently explodes, smothering them both. Russ Tamblyn as the American scientist hangs around between bouts of very effective special effects.

d, Inoshiro Honda; w, Kaoru Mabuchi, Honda; ph, Hajime Koizumi (Tohoscope, Eastmancolor); m, Akira Ifukube; spec eff, Eiji Tsuburaya; song, "The Words Get Stuck In My Throat."

Science Fiction   (PR:A   MPAA:G)

WAR OF THE MONSTERS**   (1972, Jap.) 89m Toho c (GOJIRA TAI GAIGAN; GOJIRA TAI GIGAN; AKA: GODZILLA ON MONSTER IS-LAND: GODZILLA VS. GIGAN)

Hiroshi Ichikawa, Yuriko Hishimi, Tomoko Umeda, Minoru Takashima, Kunio Murai, Susumu Fujita, Toshiaki Nishizawa, Haruo Nakajima (*Godzilla*), Yukietsu Omiya (*Angurus*), Kanta Ina (*Ghidorah*), Kengo Nakayama (*Gaigan*).

Godzilla returns, this time as a good guy, to do battle with a bunch of cockroach-like aliens who have hired the notorious giant monster Ghidorah (obviously a mercenary) and another big monster, Gaigan (this one's got a *chainsaw* in his chest!), to help them conquer Earth. Godzilla and his buddy Anzilla leave monster island and travel to Japan to rid the world of these rancid creatures. Better than the usual Godzilla farc.

p, Tomoyuki Tanaka; d, Jun Fukuda; w, Shinichi Sekizawa; ph, Kiyoshi Hasegawa; spec eff, Shokei Nakano.

Science Fiction   (PR:A   MPAA:NR)

WAR OF THE PLANETS*   (1977, Jap.) 86m Toho c (NAKUSEI DAISENSO; AKA: WAR IN SPACE; COSMOS: WAR OF THE PLA-NETS)

Kensaku Morita, Yuke Asano, Ryo Ikebe, William Ross, Masaya Oki.

Another attempt by the Japanese to capitalize on the STAR WARS craze, this one details a fight for the fate of the planet Earth fought by two spaceships located just outside of Venus. Lots of familiar elements, none of which are handled too well.

p, Tomoyuki Tanaka, Fumio Tanaka; d, Jun Fukuda: w, Ryuzo Nakanishi; ph, Jo [Yuzuru] Aizawa: spec eff, Shokei Nakano.

Science Fiction   (PR:A   MPAA:NR)

WAR OF THE RANGE*   (1933) 59M Monarch/Freuler bw

Tom Tyler, Caryl Lincoln, Lane Chandler, Lafe McKee, Slim Whitaker, Ted Adams, Charles K. French, William Nanlan, Fred Burns, Billy Franey, Wesley Giraud.

Tyler stars as a cowpoke in love with a rancher's daughter, Lincoln, but he must compete with the tough ranch foreman for her hand. French plays the girl's father adequately, with some touches of humanness to make him real. However, this one is for diehard lovers of westerns only.

p, Burton King; d, J.P. McGowan; w, Oliver Drake; ph, Edward Kull; ed, Fred Bain.

Western   (PR:A   MPAA:NR)

WAR OF THE SATELLITES*   (1958) 66m AA bw

Dick Miller (*Dave Royer*), Susan Cabot (*Sybil Carrington*), Richard Devon (*Dr. Van Pander*), Eric Sinclair (*Dr. Lazar*), Michael Fox (*Akad*), Robert Shayne (*Hodgkiss*), Jerry Barclay (*John*), Jay Sayer (*Jay*), Mitzi McCall (*Mitzi*), John Brinkley, Beech Dickerson (*Crew Members*).

Legendary Corman science fiction stinker cranked out in two weeks to capitalize on the launching of Sputnik by the USSR. Earthlings are frustrated when they learn that their first manned spaceflight is going to be prevented by an angry alien who warns them that he will destroy the planet if they attempt such a stunt. Never being one to let themselves be pushed around, the UN decides to go ahead with the plan, putting all its hopes in the hands of space scientist Devon. Unfortunately, Devon gets himself killed in a car crash. The world mourns and its hopes now center on another scientist, Miller. Surprisingly, Devon shows up at the UN very much alive and warns the assembled nations not to tamper with outer space. Miller suspects a trick and after a bit of digging discovers that the hostile aliens have resurrected the dead scientist and turned him into a mindless zombie. Nevertheless, he is allowed on the first space flight and, once in orbit, the zombie-scientist tries to crash the ship. Luckily Miller prevents this disaster and the mission is a success. Pretty weak and it looks as though it was conceived and shot in two weeks. Corman would have better luck with LITTLE SHOP OF HORRORS which he shot in even less time.

p, Roger Corman, Jack Rabin, Irving Block; d, Corman; w, Lawrence Louis

Goldman (based on the story by Block,'Rabin); ph, Floyd Crosby; m, Walter Greene; ed, Irene Morra; art d, Dan Haller; spec eff, Jack Rabin, Irving Block, Louis DeWitt.

Science Fiction   (PR:A MPAA:NR)

WAR OF THE WILDCATS   (SEE: IN OLD OKLAHOMA, 1943)

WAR OF THE WIZARDS*½   (1983, Taiwan) 76m 21st
Century/Eastern Media c (AKA: THE PHOENIX)

Richard Kiel, Charles Lang, Betty Noonan.

Once again Earth is attacked by an evil lady from outer space, determined to rule our fair planet. She comes equipped with a variety of gimmicks, including fire-breathing capabilities, the power to change her size from normal to gigantic, and a magic fan that can whip up a nasty tidal wave. Of course, there's a superhero come to save the world from her destruction, but not before a variety of monsters, laser rays, and delightfully ludicrous dialog pass by. Though not in the "so bad it's wonderful" class, this does have some agreeably bad moments that fans might want to catch.

d, Sadamasa Arikawa, Richard Caan; w, F. Kenneth Lin, Rudolph Marinelli, Richard Vetere; ph, mike Tomioka; m, Lawrence Borden; spec eff, Arikawa.

Science Fiction   Cas.   (PR:C MPAA:PG)

WAR OF THE WORLDS, THE**   (1953) 85m PAR c

Gene Barry (*Dr. Clayton Forrester*), Ann Robinson (*Sylvia Van Buren*), Les Tremayne (*Gen. Mann*), Lewis Martin (*Pastor Matthew Collins*), Robert Cornthwaite (*Dr. Pryor*), Sandro Giglio (*Dr. Bilderbeck*), William Phipps (*Wash Perry*), Paul Birch (*Alonzo Hogue*), Jack Kruschen (*Salvatore*), Vernon Rich (*Col. Heffner*), House Stevenson, Jr. (*General's Aide*), Paul Frees (*Radio Announcer*), Henry Brandon (*Cop*), Carolyn Jones (*Bird-Brained Blonde*), Pierre Cressoy, John Mansfield, Eric Alden (*Men*), Nancy Hale (*Young Wife*), Virginia Hall, Patricia Iannone (*Girls*), Walter Sande (*Sheriff Bogany*), Charles Gemora (*Martian*), Alex Frazer (*Dr. Hettinger*), Ann Codee (*Dr. Duprey*), Ivan Lebedeff (*Dr. Gratzman*), Robert Rockwell (*Ranger*), Alvy Moore (*Zippy*), Frank Kreig (*Fiddler Hawkins*), John Maxwell (*Doctor*), Ned Glass (*Well-Dressed Man During Looting*), Russell Conway (*Rev. Bethany*), Cliff Clark (*Australian Policeman*), Edward Colmans (*Spanish Priest*), Jameson Shade (*Deacon*), David McMahon (*Minister*), Gertrude Hoffman (*News Vendor*), Freeman Lusk (*Secretary of Defense*), Don Kohler (*Colonel*), Sydney Mason (*Fire Chief*), Peter Adams (*Lookout*), Ted Hecht (*KGEB Reporter*), Teru Shimada (*Japanese Diplomat*), Herbert Lytton (*Chief of Staff*), Ralph Dumke (*Buck Monahan*), Edgar Barrier (*Prof. McPherson*), Wally Richard, Morton C. Thompson, Jerry James (*Reporters*), Ralph Montgomery (*Red Cross Leader*), Russell Bender (*Dr. Carmichael*), Douglas Henderson (*Staff Sergeant*), Anthony Warde (*MP Driver*), Bud Wolfe (*Big Man*), Jimmie Dundee (*Civil Defense Official*), Joel Marston (*MP*), Bill Meader (*P.E. Official*), Al Ferguson (*Police Chief*), Rudy Lee, Waldon Williams (*Boys*), Gus Taillon (*Elderly Man*), Ruth Barnell (*Mother*), Dorothy Vernon (*Elderly Woman*), George Pal, Frank Freeman, Jr. (*Bums*), Hugh Allen (*Brigadier General*), Stanley W. Orr (*Marine Major*), Charles J. Stewart (*Marine Captain*), Freddie Zendar (*Marine Lieutenant*), Jim Davies (*Marine Commanding Officer*), Dick Fortune (*Marine Captain*), Edward Wahrman (*Cameraman*), Martin Coulter (*Marine Sergeant*), Hazel Boyne (*Screaming Woman*), Cora Shannon (*Old Woman*), Mike Mahoney (*Young Man*), David Sharpe, Dale Van Sickel, Fred Graham (*Looters*), Sir Cedric Hardwicke (*Narrator*).

One of the key science fiction films of the 1950s, and one that continues to be extremely popular (when it was released on videotape it quickly became one of the top 20 in sales), George Pal's THE WAR OF THE WORLDS is a magnificent adaptation of the classic H.G. Wells novel. The film opens as the voice of Paul Frees explains how weapons of warfare have become more powerful, destructive, and deadly during the 20th Century. Then the British voice of Hardwicke tells us how the inhabitants of the planet Mars have had to abandon their dying world and search for a place to populate. The action then shifts to the small California town of Linda Rosa where a large meteor lands in a field. Barry, and two other scientists from Pacific Tech, go to the scene to investigate. A small crowd has gathered around the meteor, including Robinson, the niece of the local minister. Discovering that the meteor is still too hot to get near, Barry decides to stay in town and wait. Three men are left to stand guard, and before long a strange sound is heard, the meteor's top unscrewing. When the top is off, a long, snakelike probe resembling the head of a cobra emerges. The three men decide to show the visitor that they are peaceful, and advance on the machine waving a white flag. A piercing noise is heard and the men are instantly disintegrated in the flash of an alien heat- ray. Suddenly the small town is in the grip of the Martian machines. Out of the meteor emerges a huge flying ship shaped like a manta ray, which has the heat-ray-spraying snakelike neck mounted on top of it. The alien machine destroys whatever comes near it, and the Army is called in. Soon after, two more Martian machines appear, and the three ships fly in formation. While the military waits for the machines to make their move, Robinson's uncle, the minister, slips past the soldiers and tries to appeal to the Martians on a Christian level. Bible in hand, the minister is blasted by the machines. The troops immediately open fire on the Martian machines, but their shells do no damage. The heat-ray, however, sprays

death and destruction wherever it is aimed. Barry and Robinson find an abandoned small airplane and attempt to fly to safety. Flying low to avoid the Air Force jets, Barry is forced to crash land rather than hit one of the Martian machines. The couple seek shelter in a deserted farmhouse and enjoy a few moments of relaxation before a new meteor crashes into the house. A new machine rises from the meteor and its snakelike probe moves into the house looking for signs of life. Barry and Robinson hide from the probe. Out of the corner of her eye, Robinson spots one of the Martians. As they come out of hiding to investigate, the probe appears right in front of them. Barry grabs and ax and cuts the head of the probe off. As Barry examines the "eye" of the probe, a long, thin hand with three suckered fingers touches Robinson's shoulder. Robinson turns to face one of the Martians. She screams and Barry turns, shining his flashlight at the creature. The alien tries to shield its eye from the light. Barry hits it with a length of pipe and the Martian emits a horrible, high- pitched scream and scampers off. Taking the head of the probe, which seems to be leaking blood, Barry and Robinson escape the farmhouse. Meanwhile, the rest of the world is fighting against the deadly domination of the Martians. Thousands of the machines are shown destroying famous landmarks throughout the world. By the time the Martians have advanced on Los Angeles, the decision is made to drop the atomic bomb on them. The Martian machines emerge from the radioactive mushroom cloud unscathed. Panic hits Los Angeles as thousands of people begin running, looting, or cowering in buildings. The chaos interrupts Barry's research- he's trying to find a way to combat the Martians, not the machines–and he is forced to flee. As the alien machines fly slowly through the streets of Los Angeles destroying everything in their path, Barry runs from church to church in search of Robinson. Eventually he finds her huddled together with dozens of other people. As the crowd cowers and prays, waiting for death, the noise of the Martian machines slows and then stops. The sound of crashing is heard. Barry and Robinson go outside to see that one of the ships has crashed across the street. A trap door opens on the bottom of the ship and a skinny Martian arm slowly claws its way out, briefly shudders, and then falls limp. Barry surmises that the Martians have no immunity to Earth's bacteria, and it is the bacteria that are killing the creatures. As we are shown scenes of Martian machines crashed and silent throughout the world, the voice of Hardwicke returns and informs us that though all of man's weapons had failed against the invaders, "...it is the littlest things that God in his wisdom had put upon the Earth that save mankind." Producer and special effects wizard George Pal, who was responsible for such science fiction classics as DESTINATION MOON (1950), WHEN WORLDS COLLIDE (1951), and later, THE TIME MACHINE (1960), was amazed to find that Paramount had owned the rights to H.G. Wells' *The War of the Worlds* since 1925, when Cecil B. DeMille had planned to film the novel. When DeMille lost interest in the project, Paramount gave it to Russian director Sergei Eisenstein in 1930, but this, too, fell through. By the 1950s, supported by DeMille, who still possessed great influence at Paramount, Pal began production of THE WAR OF THE WORLDS. Three days into shooting, Paramount's legal department discovered that the studio only owned the silent movie rights to film the novel, not the sound rights. The author's son, Frank Wells, was contacted and he quickly agreed to sell them the sound rights for a small fee. Pal's THE WAR OF THE WORLDS owes more to Orson Welles' infamous radio broadcast than to H.G. Wells' novel. To keep costs low, Pal had screenwriter Lyndon update the story and set it in California (the novel took place in England circa 1898). Welles' radio script was also set in the then present (1939) and had the Martians first land in New Jersey. Though special-effects master Gordon Jennings worked to create the Martians' walking tripod machines found in the novel, Pal decided that the effect would be too expensive and difficult to make realistic on screen. It was then decided to have the Martians man flying saucers which could be suspended and manipulated by invisible wires (though the wires are not always so invisible if one watches the film closely). The scenes of mass destruction in THE WAR OF THE WORLDS are unparalleled and were achieved through a complex series of glass paintings, miniatures, and matte work (an eight-foot-high replica of Los Angeles' City Hall was constructed and then blown up with dynamite). Perhaps the most distinctive and overall effective aspect of the special effects is the sounds that the Martian machines make. The piercing sound of the heat-ray was done by making a recording of specific notes played on three electric guitars which was then replayed backward. The sounds of explosions, buildings collapsing, the meteor unscrewing, and even the Martian's scream (which was a combination of dry ice scraped across a microphone and a woman's scream played backward) were all done with skill and flair by sound recordists Harry Lindgren and Gene Garvin. Pal originally wanted the last part of the film (from the atomic explosion to the conclusion) shot in 3D, but Paramount thought 3D a fad and nixed the idea. Filmed on a meager budget of $2 million ($1.3 million went to special effects), Pal's THE WAR OF THE WORLDS was a solid box office hit. The film presents the special effects, an intelligent script, and romantic melodrama at such a fast pace that the audience barely has time to catch its breath before the next alien onslaught. Gordon Jennings' special effects won him an Oscar, but the cinematic wizard didn't live to see it because he died soon after the filming of his masterpiece was completed.

p, George Pal; d, Byron Haskin; w, Barre Lyndon (based on the novel by H.G. Wells); ph, George Barnes (Technicolor); m, Leith Stevens; ed, Everett Douglas; art d, Hal Pereira, Albert Nozaki; set d, Sam Comer, Emile Kuri; cos, Edith Head; spec eff, Gordon Jennings, Paul Lerpae, Wallace Kelly, Ivyl Burks, Jan Domela, Irmin Roberts, Walter Hoffman, Chesley Bonestell;

stunts, Dale Van Sickel, David Sharpe, Fred Graham; makeup, Wally Westmore.

Science Fiction   Cas.   (PR:C MPAA:NR)

WAR OF THE WORLDS--NEXT CENTURY, THE**
(1981, Pol.) 98m Zespoly Filmowe/Perpekty Unit c (WOJNA SWAITOW—
                                           NASTEPNE STULECIE)

Roman Wilhelmi, Krystyna Janda, Mariusz Dmochowski, Jerzy Stuhr,
Bozena Dykiel, Morek Walcewski.

Interesting variation on the Orson Welles "War of the Worlds" radio
broadcast in the 1930s and the furor it created. Wilhelmi stars as a television
reporter in the year 1999 who sees Martians invade Earth but finds that no
one will believe him. The government knows the truth, but the officials
make Wilhelmi appear as if he were mad. More a statement about the media
than a science fiction film, THE WAR OF THE WORLDS–NEXT CENTURY
is provocative and fascinating.

d&w, Piotr Szulkin; ph, Zygmunt Samosiak.

Science Fiction   (PR:C MPAA:NR)

WAR OF THE ZOMBIES, THE   (1965 Ital.) 85m AIP c (ROMA
             CONTRO ROMA; AKA: NIGHT STAR; GODDESS OF ELECTRA)

John Drew Barrymore (Aderbal), Susy Andersen (Tullia), Ettore Manni
(Gaius), Ida Galli (Rhama), Mino Doro (Lutetius), Philippe Hersent (Azer),
Ivano Staccioli (Sirion), Matilda Calnan, Antonio Corevi, Giulio Maculani,
Livia Contardi, Rosy Zichel.

Fairly entertaining sword and sandal-horror epic starring Manni as the
brave warrior sent by his people to retrieve a treasure trove that was stolen
en route to Rome. The trail takes Manni to the lair of Barrymore, the leader
of a mysterious cult who has been collecting the bodies of dead soldiers in
order to resurrect them as a zombie army with which he can rule the world.
Manni learns that Barrymore's mystic power is tied to a powerful idol and
after several battles he manages to destroy the statue and Barrymore's
plans. Suspenseful sequences and some good battle scenes make this one
well worth watching.

p, Ferruccio De Martino, Massimo De Rita; d, Giuseppe Vari; w, Piero
Pierotti, Marcello Sartarelli (based on an idea by De Martino, De Rita); ph,
Gabor Pogany (Colorscope, Eastmancolor); m, Roberto Nicolosi; ed, Vari; art
d, Giorgio Giovannini; cos, Tina Grani; spec eff, Ugo Amadoro.

Adventure   (PR:C-O MPAA:NR)

WAR PAINT½**   (1953) 89m UA c

Robert Stack (Lt. Billings), Joan Taylor (Wanima), Charles McGraw (Sgt.
Clarke), Keith Larsen (Taslik), Peter Graves (Tolson), Robert Wilke (Sgt.
Grady), Walter Reed (Allison), John Doucette (Charnofsky), Douglas Kenne-
dy (Clancy), Charles Nolte (Cpl. Hamilton), James Parnell (Martin), Paul
Richards (Perkins), William Pullen (Jeb), Richard Cutting (Kirby).

Stack is assigned to deliver a peace treaty to an Indian leader before a
deadline elapses and fighting begins again. He leads a pack of cavalrymen
through Death Valley while fending off attacks which make the trip
treacherous. The sharp, able direction by Selander is one of the picture's
bright spots.

p, Howard W. Koch; d, Lesley Selander; w, Richard Alan Simmons, Martin
Berkeley (based on a story by Fred Friedberger, William Tunberg); ph,
Gordon Avil (Pathe Color); m, Emil Newman; ed, John F. Schreyer; song,
Johnny Lehmann, Newman: "Elaine."

Western   (PR:A MPAA:NR)

WAR PARTY**   (1965) 72m Steve Productions/FOX bw

Michael T. Mikler (Johnny Hawk), Davey Davison (Sarah), Donald Barry
(Sgt. Chaney), Laurie Mock (Nicoma), Dennis Robertson, Charles Horvath,
Michael Carr, Guy Wilkerson, Fred Krone.

With a cavalry unit trapped by Comanches, Mikler and Barry lead a patrol
attempting to deliver a message which will save the soldiers from a
massacre. An Indian girl informs them of a passage they should take and
eventually the message is delivered, the soldiers are rescued, but only
Mikler and Davison, the daughter of a pastor, survive the patrol.

p, Hal Klein; d, Lesley Selander; w, George Williams, William Marks; ph,
Gordon Avil; m, Richard LaSalle; ed, John F. Schreyer; cos, Frank R. Budz;
spec eff, Joe Lombardi; makeup, Gustaf M. Norin.

Western   (PR:A MPAA:NR)

WAR SHOCK   (SEE: WOMAN'S DEVOTION, A, 1956)

WAR WAGON, THE*½**   (1967) 101m Batjac/UNIV c

John Wayne (Taw Jackson), Kirk Douglas (Lomax), Howell Keel (Levi
Walking Bear), Robert Walker, Jr (Billy Hyatt), Keenan Wynn (Wes Catlin),
Bruce Cabot (Frank Pierce), Joanna Barnes (Lola), Valora Noland (Kate
Catlin), Gene Evans (Hoag), Bruce Dern (Hammond), Terry Wilson (Sheriff
Strike), Don Collier (Shack), Sheb Wooley (Dan Snyder), Ann McCrea
(Felicia), Emilio Fernandez (Calito), Frank McGrath (Bartender), Chuck
Roberson (Brown), Red Morgan (Early), Hal Needham (Hite), Marco
Antonio (Wild Horse), Perla Walter (Rosita), Jose Trinidad Villa (Townsman
at Bar), Miko Mayama Midori, Margarite Lune.

An energetic and humorous western which casts Wayne and Douglas as
friendly rivals who put aside their differences and decide to work together
on a heist. Wayne is released from prison after being framed by the
malevolent Cabot, a greedy mine owner. Determined to get revenge, Wayne
plans to knock off a $500,000 Cabot gold shipment. He persuades Douglas
to team up with him, but Douglas has already received an offer of $10,000
(later upped to $12,000) from Cabot to kill Wayne. Douglas' share of the heist
would be $100,000, however, so he decides to go where the money is, but
consistently reminds Wayne of his other offer. Their relationship is sealed
when two of Cabot's henchman see that he's in cahoots with Wayne. The
henchmen bravely pull their guns on Douglas and Wayne only to take a
bullet and hit the ground. Douglas smartly remarks to Waynr, "Mine hit the
ground first." Wayne retorts calmly, "Mine was taller." They begin
organizing their operation, gathering together three additional hands–Keel,
a wisecracking Indian; Walker, an alcoholic explosives expert; and Wynn, a
crotchety old employee of Cabot's who wants to hurt his employer. Things
are made difficult when Cabot reveals the "war wagon," an iron-plated
stagecoach armed with a Gatling gun and guarded by dozens of gunmen on
horseback. Wayne and his men carry out their intricate plan with the
assistance of the Indian nations that are angry at Cabot for his attempts to
relocate their reservations. The Indians descend on the war wagon, causing
the men on horseback to chase after them, separating the guards from the
coach. Meantime, traps have been set and nitroglycerin prepared to blow up
a bridge as the war wagon passes. The coach crosses the bridge as planned,
the bridge explodes, and the guards are left behind, unable to cross the
ravine. The war wagon continues on its way with a handful of guards firing
from inside. Cabot, trying to save his fortune, stands at the Gatling gun
frantically firing rounds. Eventually the war wagon is sent crashing to the
ground and Wayne retrieves the sacks of gold dust. Wynn hides them in
barrels of flour which his wagon is carrying, stashing a couple of sacks of
gold away for himself. The Indians turn on Wayne and his men but soon fall
victims to one last bottle of nitro. Wynn's wagon is pulled out of control by
a frightened horse as Wynn falls victim to a shotgun blast. The horse takes
off through Indian territory as barrels of flour and gold break open at the
feet of the grateful Indians. The riches that Cabot had mined from the
Indian territory are now returned to where they came from, as Wayne and
his men are left with only one-fifth of their predicted fortune. The picture
is at its best when it lets Wayne and Douglas play off each other using their
rapport and humor to its fullest. Director Kennedy filled this endeavor with
the utmost action, especially in a charged barroom brawl scene which
features Douglas nonchalantly swinging from a chandelier. A thoroughly
enjoyable way to spend 101 minutes.

p, Marvin Schwartz; d, Burt Kennedy; w, Clair Huffaker (based on the novel
Badman by Huffaker); ph, William H. Clothier (Panavision, Technicolor); m,
Dimitri Tiomkin; ed, Harry Gerstad; art d, Alfred Sweeney; set d, Ray
Moyer; cos, Oscar Rodriguez; m/l, "Ballad of the War Wagon," Tiomkin,
Ned Washington (sung by Ed Ames); makeup, Donald W. Roberson, Dave
Grayson, Bud Westmore.

Western   Cas.   (PR:A MPAA:NR)

WARD 13   (SEE: HOSPITAL MASSACRE, 1982)

WARE CASE, THE½**   (1939, Brit.) 72m EAL-ASSOCIATED Talking
                              Pictures-Capad-Associated Star/FOX bw

Clive Brook (Sir Hubert Ware), Jane Baxter (Lady Margaret Ware), Barry
K. Barnes (Michael Adye), C.V. France (Judge), Francis L. Sullivan (Attorney
General), Frank Cellier (Skinner), Edward Rigby (Tommy Bold), Peter Bull
(Eustace Ede), Dorothy Seacombe (Mrs. Slade), Athene Seyler (Mrs. Pinto),
Elliot Mason (Impatient Juror), John Laurie (Hewson), Wally Patch (Taxi
Driver), Glen Alyn (Clare), Ernest Thesiger (Carter), Peggy Novak (Lucy),
Harold Goodwin, Wallace Evennett, J. R. Lockwood, Alf Goddard, Charles
Paton.

Brook stars as a bourgeous financier who finds himself on trial when his
brother-in-law's body floats to the top of the garden pond. He is acquitted
but returns home to find a romance blossoming between his wife and his
lawyer. He confronts his lawyer with the truth–that he really was
guilty–and then leaps to his death from a balcony. Strong, tense drama with
convincing motivations.

p, Michael Balcon; d, Robert Stevenson; w, Stevenson, Roland Pertwee,
E.V.H. Emmett (based on the play by George Pleydell Bancroft); ph, Ronald
Neame; m, Ernest Irving; ed, Charles Saunders; art d, Oscar Werndorff.

Crime Drama   (PR:A MPAA:NR)

WARGAMES*** (1983) 113m MGM/UA c

Matthew Broderick (David), Dabney Coleman (McKittrick), John Wood (Falken), Ally Sheedy (Jennifer), Barry Corbin (Gen. Beringer), Juanin Clay (Pat Healy), Kent Williams (Cabot), Dennis Lipscomb (Watson), Joe Dorsey (Conley), Irving Metzman (Richter), Michael Ensign (Beringer's Aide), William Bogert (Mr. Lightman), Susan Davis (Mrs. Lightman), James Tolkan (Wigan), David Clover (Stockman), Drew Snyder (Ayers), John Garber (Corporal in Infirmary), Duncan Wilmore (Maj. Lem), Billy Ray Sharkey (Radar Analyst), John Spencer (Jerry), Michael Madsen (Steve), Erik Stern (Commander), Gary Bisig (Deputy), Garcy Sexton, Paul V. Picerni, Jr (Technicians), Jason Bernard (Capt. Knewt), Frankie Hill (Airman Fields), Jessie Goins (Sergeant), Alan Blumenfeld (Mr. Liggett), Len Lawson (Boy's Vice Principal), Maury Chaykin (Jim Sting), Eddie Deezen (Malvin), Stephen Lee (Sgt. Schneider), Lucinda Crosby (Nurse in Infirmary), Stack Pierce (Airman), Art LaFleur (Guard), Brad David Berwick (Flight Pilot Leader), Martha Shaw (Vice Principal Secretary), Howie Allen (Boy in Arcade), Mike Adams (Travis), James Ackerman (Joshua), Jim Harriott (Newscaster), Tom Lawrence (Sgt. Sims), Frances Nealy (Visitor), Charles Akins (Maj. Ford), Glenn Standifer (Maj. Wenstin), Edward Jahnke (Norad Officer).

A slick but forgettable box office hit that capitalizes on two national obsessions, video games and nuclear war. Broderick is very likable as the teenage computer whiz who taps into a top-secret Pentagon computer and sets in motion what he innocently belives is a war game entitled "Global Thermonuclear War," but in reality is the real thing. The best minds at the Pentagon can't do a thing to stop the computer from sending bombers to Russia so they find the kid and drag him in to try and stop them. After some effective suspense scenes the computer gives up, stating that Global Thermonuclear War is "a strange game," wherein the only way to win is "...not to play." A simple message, but effective.

p, Harold Schneider; d, John Badham; w, Lawrence Lasker, Walter F. Parkes; ph, William A. Fraker (Metrocolor); m, Arthur B. Rubinstein; ed, Tom Rolf; prod d, Angelo P. Graham; art d, James J. Murakami; set d, Jerry Wunderlich; cos, Barry F. Delaney, Linda Matthews; spec eff, Joe DiGaetano; stunts, Tom Elliott, Marguerite Happy, Al Jones.

Drama   **Cas.**   **(PR:A MPAA:PG)**

WARKILL**½ (1968, U.S./Phil.) 100m Balut-Centaur/UNIV c

George Montgomery (Col. John Hannegan), Tom Drake (Phil Sutton), Conrad Parham (Pedring), Eddie Infante (Dr. Fernandez), Henry Duval (Willy), Paul Edwards, Jr (Mike Harris), Bruno Punzalan (Maj. Hashiri), David Michael (Sgt. Johnson), Joaquin Fajardo (Max), Bert La Fortesa (Dr. Namura), Claude Wilson (U.S. Major), Ken Loring.

Set in the Philippines near the end of WW II, WARKILL tells the story of Montgomery, a hardened, animalistic colonel in charge of Filipino guerrillas, and Drake, a journalist who has made a hero out of the colonel without ever meeting him. At their first encounter Drake is shocked at Montgomery's war credo–never take a prisoner and savagely kill the enemy. Drake soon learns that Montgomery's rage is not without cause and asks to join him on a guerilla raid against small groups of Japanese occupation troops. Montgomery dies a hero's death and before Drake meets the same fate he is saved by reinforcements who arrive and fend off the enemy. A hard-hitting war actioner with few false moments.

p,d&w, Ferde Grofe, Jr.; ph, Remegio Uoung (DeLuxe Color); m, Gene Kauer, Douglas Lackey; ed, Phillip Innes; spec eff, Enrique Ledesma.

War   **(PR:O MPAA:NR)**

WARLOCK**** (1959) 121m FOX c

Richard Widmark (Johnny Gannon), Henry Fonda (Clay Blaisdell), Anthony Quinn (Tom Morgan), Dorothy Malone (Lilly Dollar), Dolores Michaels (Jessie Marlow), Wallace Ford (Judge Holloway), Tom Drake (Abe McQuown), Richard Arlen (Bacon), De Forest Kelley (Curley Burne), Regis Toomey (Skinner), Vaughn Taylor (Richardson), Don Beddoe (Dr. Wagner), Whit Bissell (Mr. Petrix), J. Anthony Hughes (Shaw), Donald Barry (Edward Culhoun), Frank Gorshin (Billy Gannon), Ian MacDonald (MacDonald), Stan Kamber (Hutchinson), Paul Comi (Friendly), Mickey Simpson (Fitzsimmons), Robert Osterloh (Professor), James Philbrook (Cade), David Garcia (Pony Benner), Robert Adler (Foss), Joel Ashley (Murch), Joe Turkel (Chet Haggin), Saul Gorss (Bob Nicholson), Ann Doran (Mrs. Richardson), Bartlett Robinson (Slavin), L.Q. Jones (Jiggs), Henry Worth (Burbage), June Blair (Dance Hall Girl), Walter Coy (Deputy Thompson), Wally Campo (Barber), Hugh Sanders (Sheriff Keller).

A unique and often overlooked "adult" western that goes much deeper than most movies in this genre. What is happening on screen is on one level and what can be perceived by incisive audiences forms the subtler side. For example, on the surface this would seem to be a fairly standard story. The folks who live in the small town of Warlock are a kind and God-fearing lot who exist in dread because a group of brawling cowboys, led by Drake, like to come into town from time to time and shoot up the place. Several lawmen have departed due to these rowdies and the town is livid. They hire Fonda, a well-known gunslinger, and he's given the job of local marshal, which he accepts on the proviso that he can run the local gambling and dance parlor as part of the deal. Fonda's faithful companion is clubfooted Quinn, a man who worships Fonda the way Tonto loved the Lone Ranger or Robin adored Batman. Quinn, who plays the role with a blond dye job on his raven hair, loves Fonda in a manner that almost borders on the unspeakable, although that is hinted at rather than blatantly explored. Fonda soon finds Michaels, a local filly, and an attraction grows. It's 1881 and men of Fonda's type are either dying of old age or being shot down by younger, faster cowboys, so he is somewhat of an anachronism. Drake and his cohorts mosey into Warlock with all intentions of having some fun at the town's expense. With them is Widmark, who is rapidly becoming disenchanted with Drake and his rowdies so he quits the gang and decides to remain in Warlock and become a deputy to Fonda. Fonda manages to get Drake and his raucous ranch hands out of town and there appears to be some law and order for a brief spell. The townsfolk reckon that they don't need a professional gunslinger anymore, now that Drake and the others have been cowed. This is not lost on Quinn, who suggests that they move on and out of Warlock. Quinn is quite jealous of the relationship being established by Fonda and Widmark, and Michaels and would like to put a stop to it. Malone arrives in Warlock with fire in her eyes. She'd been Quinn's woman at one time, and after they broke up Quinn murdered the man she'd intended marrying. She means to get even. Malone and Widmark become enamored of each other and discuss the fact that Fonda is running the town his own way and must be taught a lesson. Drake and his men come into town for a confrontation and Fonda wants to go out and face them but Quinn points a gun at him and makes him stay put so Widmark will have to face the gang by himself. The townsfolk who were every bit as cowardly as the people in Gary Cooper's town in HIGH NOON, finally decide to stand up for their rights and back up Widmark in his battle with his former compadres. It works and this causes Quinn to look with new eyes at Fonda. His idol may not be the fastest gun in the West any longer. In order to make sure Fonda remains top dog, Quinn decides to kill Widmark, but Fonda tries to talk him out of it and says that it might be more advantageous to all if Quinn left. Fonda means to stay in Warlock and settle in with Michaels. Quinn can't handle the rejection from the only person he ever really cared about and there is a gun battle between the two that leaves Quinn's boots turned up. Widmark tells Fonda that he must leave the now-peaceful town of Warlock as there is no room for him there any longer. Before the conclusion, there is a quick-draw scene between Fonda and Widmark. They draw twice and, in both cases, Fonda gets his guns out first but does not fire. Satisfied that he is still the best in the business, Fonda tosses his gold-plated Colts in the dust at Widmark's feet and rides out of town to seek whatever adventures are left. Partly made in Utah, although there was not all that much of the glorious scenery utilized. Instead, they concentrated on the story within the confines of the small town and the multi-layered stories going on between the principals. There's a dollop of Grecian tragedy here, blended with morsels of psychology and overlaid with a patina of brooding, none of which might seem apt for an oater. Yet, under Dmytryk's strong direction of the Aurthur adaptation, it all works to great advantage. Fonda had bombed in two movies previous to this and had to get back into mainstream movies. While this was hardly the usual kind of western, it did re-establish him in the eyes of the movie-going public as more than the effete Easterner seen in STAGE STRUCK and 12 ANGRY MEN (although Fonda was born, as everyone knows, in the Midwest). Lots of action punctuates the excellent dialog and several strong supporting actors each have their turn. They include Gorshin, Turkel, and the three "B's" - Barry, Bissell, and Beddoe.

p&d, Edward Dmytryk; w, Robert Alan Aurthur (based on the novel by Oakley Hall); ph, Joe MacDonald (CinemaScope, Technicolor); m, Leigh Harline; ed, Jack W. Holmes; md, Lionel Newman; art d, Lyle R. Wheeler, Herman Blumenthal; set d, Walter M. Scott, Stuart A. Reiss; cos, Charles LeMaire; spec eff, L.B. Abbott; makeup, Ben Nye.

Western   **Cas.**   **(PR:C MPAA:NR)**

WARLORD OF CRETE, THE (SEE: MINOTAUR, THE, 1961 Ital.)

WARLORDS OF ATLANTIS** (1978, Brit.) 96m EMI/COL c (AKA: SEVEN CITIES TO ATLANTIS)

Doug McClure (Greg Collinson), Peter Gilmore (Charles Aitken), Shane Rimmer (Capt. Daniels), Lea Brodie (Delphine), Michael Gothard (Atmir), Hal Galili (Grogan), John Ratzenberger (Fenn), Derry Power (Jacko), Donald Bisset (Prof. Aitken), Ashley Knight (Sandy), Robert Brown (Briggs), Cyd Charisse (Atsil), Daniel Massey (Atraxon).

McClure and the father-and-son exploration team of Bisset and Gilmore take a jaunt under the ocean to the lost continent of Atlantis. They encounter all sorts of obstacles including a gigantic octopus until their adventure takes them to high priestess Charisse, playing a cameo role at age 57. It's silly but harmless and won't offend anyone under 12 years of age.

p, John Dark; d, Kevin Connor; w, Brian Hayles; ph, Alan Hume (Technicolor); m, Mike Vickers; ed, Bill Blunden; art d, Jack Maxsted; prod d, Elliott Scott; spec eff, John Richardson, Roger Dicken, George Gibbs.

Science Fiction/Adventure   **Cas.**   **(PR:AA MPAA:PG)**

WARLORDS OF THE DEEP (SEE: CITY UNDER THE SEA, 1965, Brit.)

WARLORDS OF THE 21ST CENTURY (SEE: BATTLETRUCK, 1982)

WARM BODY, THE (SEE: THUNDER IN THE BLOOD, 1962, Fr.)

WARM CORNER, (1930, Brit.) 104m Gainsborough/ID bw

Leslie Henson (*Charles Corner*), Heather Thatcher (*Mimi Price*), Connie Ediss (*Adela Corner*), Austin Melford (*Peter Price*), Belle Chrystal (*Peggy Corner*), Kim Peacock (*Count Toscani*), Alfred Wellesley (*Thomas Turner*), Toni Edgar Bruce (*Lady Bayswater*), George de Warfaz (*Waiter*), Merle Oberon.

Henson plays a corn plaster tycoon who takes off for a vacation in Monte Carlo. There, with the encouragement of pal Wellesley, be flirts with Thatcher. Trouble looms, though, for on his return home he discovers that the girl is the secret wife of a friend's nephew. Disaster is averted for the millionaire when Thatcher claims Wellesley was her lover. Average comedy, featuring an early appearance by 19-year-old Oberon in a minor role.

p, Michael Balcon; d, Victor Saville; w, Angus MacPhail, Saville (based on the play Franz Arnold, Ernst Bach, Arthur Wimperis, Lauri Wylie); ph, Alex Bryce, F. A. Young; art d, Walter Murton.

Comedy (PR:AA MPAA:NR)

WARM DECEMBER, A** (1973, Brit.) 99m First Artists/NGP c

Sidney Poitier (*Dr. Matt Younger*), Esther Anderson (*Catherine*), Yvette Curtis (*Stefanie Younger*), George Baker (*Henry Barlow*), Earl Cameron (*Ambassador George Oswandu*), Johnny Sekka (*Myomo, Ambassador's Aide*), Hilary Crane (*Marsha Barlow*), John Beardmore (*Burberry*), Milos Kirek (*Gen. Kuznovski, Russian Diplomat*), Ann Smith (*Carol Barlow*), Stephanie Smith (*Janie Barlow*), Letta Mbulu (*Club Singer*).

Poitier is an American doctor living in England who comes to the aid of Anderson, the niece of an African ambassador. She is being followed by an unknown group of people, who turn out to be concerned that her sickle-cell anemia may flare up. What appears at first to be some kind of espionage thriller rather unsuspectingly turns into a disease picture. Poitier's performance is standard for him–emotionally engrossing at points while bordering on super-sensitivity.

p, Melville Tucker; d, Sidney Poitier; w, Lawrence Roman; ph, Paul Beeson (Technicolor); m, Coleridge-Taylor Perkinson; ed, Pembroke Herring, Peter Pitt; art d, Elliott Scott; set d, Norman Reynolds.

Drama (PR:C MPAA:PG)

WARM IN THE BUD* (1970) 57m Filmmakers bw

Robert Mont (*Mortiz*), Dean Stricklin (*Melchior*), Toni Hamilton (*Martha*), Bruce Johnson (*Ernst*), John Goetz (*Hanchen*), Mary Rivard (*Wendla*), Nuala Willis (*Ilse*), John Carmody (*Otto*), Barry Peterson (*George*), David Martini (*Robert*), Lynne Alpert (*Ina*), Sage Cowles (*Mother*).

A pair of sensitive young men in the late 1800's deal with their approaching manhood in different ways–one kills himself and the other enters a fantasy world with a mock trial. Heavy on the metaphysics and symbolism–Both common mistakes of independent features (this one is shot on 16mm) that have come out of the 1960s–but overall a sincere attempt to define youth probing for a grip on maelstrom-spinning world.

p,d&w, Rudolph Caringi (based on the play "Spring's Awakening" by Franz Wedekind); ph, John Walsh, Dahl Delu; m, Don Carlo Gesualdo (Latin Madrigals); ed, Caringi.

Drama (PR:A MPAA:NR)

WARN LONDON!**½ (1934, Brit.) 68m BL bw

Edmund Gwenn (*Dr. Herman Krauss*), John Loder (*Inspector Yorke/Barraclough*), Leonora Corbett (*Jill*), D.A. Clarke-Smith (*Dr. Nicoletti*), Garry Marsh (*Van Der Meer*), John Turnbull (*Inspector Frayne*), Raymond Lovell (*Prefect*), Douglas Stewart (*Davis*).

Solid crime thriller stars Gwenn as a famed German criminologist who finds himself the victim of a con game which wipes out his savings. He seeks revenge and, aided by opportunistic theif Loder, plans a perfect robbery which will net him millions. Before the robbery is committed however, Loder reveals himself to be a Scotland Yard detective and foils Gwenn's plans.

p, Herbert Smith; d, T. Hayes Hunter; w, Charles Bennett, Billie Bristow (based on the novel by Denison Clift); ph, Alex Bryce.

Crime (PR:A MPAA:NR)

WARN THAT MAN** (1943, Brit.) 82m ABPC/Pathe bw

Gordon Harker (*George Hawkins*), Raymond Lovell (*Hausemann/Lord Buckley*), Finlay Currie (*Capt. Andrew Fletcher*), Philip Friend John Cooper, Jean Kent (*Frances Lane*), Frederick Cooper (*Charles/Frampton*), Carl Jaffe (*Schultz*), John Salew (*Wilson*), Veronica Rose (*Miss Conway*), Anthony Hawtrey (*Brent*), Antony Holles (*Waiter*), Pat Aherne (*Mellows*), Frederick Richter, Leonard Sharp, Frank Bagnall.

A fanciful WW II espionage thriller which sees German Commandos parachute into England and take over Buckley Hall. The resident Lord is kidnaped and a look-alike actor takes his place (both men played by Lovell). The mansion is then staffed with Nazi soldier posing as domestic help, all awaiting the arrival of a very important man who, one assumes, is Winston Churchill. Luckily Lovell's niece, Kent, has managed to hide in another part of the mansion and summons help. Before "that man" arrives the British army descends on Buckley Hall and the Nazis are defeated. Despite the ludicrous premise, of WARN THAT MAN, the film manages to be exciting. Thirty-three years later a strikingly similiar film starring Robert Duvall and Michael Caine was released entitled THE EAGLE HAS LANDED (1976).

p, Warwick Ward; d, Lawrence Huntington; w, Vernon Sylvaine, Huntington (based on the play by Sylvaine); ph, Gunther Krampf.

War (PR:A MPAA:NR)

WARNING FORM SPACE (SEE: MYSTERIOUS SATELLITE, THE, 1956, Jap.)

WARNING SHOT***½ (1967) 100m Bob Banner/PAR c

David Janssen (*Sgt. Tom Valens*), Ed Begley (*Capt. Roy Klodin*), Keenan Wynn (*Sgt. Ed Musso*), Sam Wanamaker (*Frank Sanderman*), Lillian Gish (*Alice Willows*), Stefanie Powers (*Liz Thayer*), Eleanor Parker (*Mrs. Doris Ruston*), George Grizzard (*Walt Cody*), George Sanders (*Calvin York*), Steve Allen (*Perry Knowland*), Carroll O'Connor (*Paul Jerez*), Joan Collins (*Joanie Valens*), Walter Pidgeon (*Orville Ames*), John Garfield, Jr. (*Police Surgeon*), Bob Williams (*Judge Gerald Lucas*), Jerry Dunphy (*TV Newscaster*), Romo Vincent (*Ira Garvin*), Vito Scotti (*Designer*), Jean Carson (*Cocktail Waitress*), Donald Curtis (*Dr. James Ruston*), Brian Dunne (*Rusty*), Norma Clark (*Shari Sherman*).

A knockout cops-and-killers yarn that starts fast and gets faster. Janssen, just coming off his "Fugitive" TV series, is a police sergeant who is searching for a killer. He's lurking on the grounds of an apartment complex when he spies a man racing across the grass. Janssen duly warns the man to stop, then is forced to shoot the runner when the man draws a gun. The dead body turns out to be that of Curtis, a well-known physician who had spent a great deal of time and effort on behalf of downtrodden Mexicans in the area south of San Diego. Janssen and the other cops try to find the gun Janssen swears he saw, but it appears to have vanished. The press has a field day and accuses Janssen of being just another one of the trigger-happy cops who prowl the streets of Los Angeles. He is immediately suspended from duty and it seems as though he will be facing charges of manslaughter. Janssen knows that he didn't just imagine the gun so he begins a campaign to clear his name and become reinstated in his job. Now on his own, Janssen returns to the scene of the "crime" and starts his investigation. First, he encounters aged Gish (who was celebrating her 55th year in the movies at the time this film was made) and learns that Curtis was her doctor and often stopped by her efficiency apartment and brought various toys for her late dog. Janssen continues to question the people who inhabit the apartments and meets Grizzard, an airline pilot who offers to help. He also finds the dead corpse of an attractive young woman who perished during an illegal abortion operation. Janssen continues by quizzing Curtis' nurse, Powers, who informs him that the late medical man was the recent recipient of several checks in large amounts. The sender of the money was Sanders, who had been the stockbroker servicing Curtis. Powers is then found dead and there is an attempt on Janssen's life. Digging more deeply, Janssen recalls that Gish had made mention of the fact that her pet dog was interred with all of the trinkets and toys that Curtis had given the animal. Janssen calls upon Grizzard for help and the two men remove the pet's coffin from the resting place and find the "weapon" Janssen thought he'd seen. It isn't a real gun at all. Rather, it is a kid's pistol that has an even deadlier content than bullets; it is filled with heroin! Now the pieces all come together. Grizzard, Curtis, and Sanders are all part of a nationwide narcotics organization, with Grizzard being the man who transported the stuff around the country in his capacity as an airlines pilot. Grizzard pulls a revolver and wounds Janssen, who fires back and sends Grizzard reeling into the dog's grave at the close. Solid direction and production and a no-nonsense script all contribute to making this an excellent way to spend 100 minutes. Joan Collins is seen briefly as Janssen's soon-to-be-ex-wife, Steve Allen scores as a TV broadcaster who is always seeking to stir up controversy, and Vito Scotti gets his share of chuckles as a dress designer who is light in his moccasins. The all-star cast also included John Garfield, Jr., making his film debut, as well as such luminaries as Carroll O'Connor, Walter Pidgeon, Sam Wanamaker, Keenan Wynn, Ed Begley, and Eleanor Parker in small, but important roles. The movie was coproduced by Texas-born TV veteran Bob Banner who alternates his time between show business and teaching at his alma mater, Southern Methodist University.

p, Buzz Kulik, Bob Banner; d, Kulik; w, Mann Rubin (based on the novel *711 Officer Needs Help* by Whit Masterson); ph, Joseph Biroc (Technicolor); m, Jerry Goldsmith; ed, Archie Marshek; art d, Hal Pereira, Roland Anderson; set d, Robert R. Benton, George R. Nelson; cos, Edith Head; spec eff, Paul K. Larpae; makeup, Wally Westmore.

Crime Drama   **Cas.**   **(PR:A-C MPAA:NR)**

WARNING TO WANTONS, A**½ (1949, Brit.) 104m Aquila/GFD bw

Harold Warrender (*Count Anton Kardak*), Anne Vernon (*Renee de Vaillant*), David Tomlinson (*Count Max Kardak*), Sonia Holm (*Maria*), Hugh Cross (*Pauli*), Marie Burke (*Therese*), Judy Kelly (*Mimi de Vaillant*), Ellen Pollock (*Baroness de Jammes*), Andre Van Gyseghem (*Oblensky*), Bruce Belfrage (*Archimandrite*), Denis Vance (*Franklin Budd*), Jack Melford (*Maurice Lugard*), Vincent Ball (*Footman*), Brian Oulton, Stanley Ratcliffe, Aletha Orr, Ida Patlanski, Olwen Brookes, Kenneth Firth, John Warren, Mela White, Alexander Field, Betty Thomas, Frank Cochrane, Nancy Roberts, Grace Denbigh-Russell, Margaret Damer, Michael Bazalgette, Patricia Davidson, David Keir, Herbert C. Walton, Peter Faber, Pauline Loring, Mary Midwinter, Claud Frederic, Joan Denver, Caldwell Mason, Harriet Petworth.

A spirited romantic comedy about a 17-year-old runaway from a convent who finds refuge with a count. She disrupts his socially proper lifestyle by getting involved with his son, much to the displeasure of the fellow's fiancee, who puts up a battle for what she is bargaining for. In the end the runaway runs away again, but this time with a peasant boy, turning her back on high society.

p&d, Donald B. Wilson; w, Wilson, James Laver (based on the novel by Mary Mitchell); ph, George Dudgeon Stretton; ed, Sidney Hayers.

Romance/Comedy   **(PR:A MPAA:NR)**

WARPATH**½   (1951) 95m PAR C

Edmond O'Brien (*John Vickers*), Dean Jagger (*Storekeeper Sam Quade*), Charles Stevns (*Courier*), Forrest Tucker (*Sgt. O'Hara*), Harry Carey, Jr (*Capt. Gregson*), Polly Bergen (*Molly Quade*), James Millican (*Gen. George Armstrong Custer*), Wallace Ford (*Pvt. Potts*), Paul Fix (*Pvt. Fiore*), Louis Jean Heydt (*Herb Woodson*), Paul Lees (*Cpl. Stockbridge*), Walter Sande (*Sgt. Parker*), Charles Dayton (*Lt. Nelson*), Bob [Robert] Bray (*Maj. Comstock*), Douglas Spencer (*Kelso*), James Burke (*Oldtimer*), Chief Yowlachie (*Chief*), John Mansfield (*Sub-Chief*), Monte Blue (*1st Emigrant*), Frank Ferguson (*Marshal*), Cliff Clark (*Bartender*), Paul Burns (*Bum*), John Hart (*Sgt. Plennert*).

O'Brien is bent on vengeance as he tracks down the three men who brutally murdered his fiance. He kills one and traces another's path to the Seventh Cavalry. There he finds the man, Tucker, now a sergeant in the Army, and the third man, Jagger, a storekeeper, but before he can kill them, all three are taken prisoner by the Indians. Tucker gives up his life so the other two can escape, and Jagger rides off to warn Gen. Custer (Millican) of an ambush. He is killed, thusallowing Bergen, his daughter, and O'Brien to carry on their romance with a clear conscience. Neatly descripted and colored with some of the best cavalry-Indian battle sequences ever put on film.

p, Nat Holt; d, Byron Haskin; w, Frank Gruber; ph, Ray Rennahan (Technicolor); m, Paul Sawtell; ed, Philip Martin; art d, John Goodman.

Western   **(PR:A MPAA:NR)**

WARREN CASE, THE*   (1934, Brit.) 75m BIP/Pathe bw

Richard Bird (*Louis Bevan*), Nancy Burne (*May Clavering*), Diana Napier (*Pauline Warren*), Edward Underdown (*Hugh Waddon*), Iris Ashley (*Elaine de Lisle*), A. Bromley Davenport (*Sir Richard Clavering*).

Languid murder mystery starring Bird as an insane crime reporter who strangles his girl friend and then frames Underdown, the fiance of his boss' daughter. Underdown manages to persuade the police to continue the investigation until the truth is revealed. Lacks plausibility, thrills, or style.

p, Walter C. Mycroft; d&w, Walter Summers (based on the play "The Last Chance" by Arnold Ridley); ph, Jack Parker.

Crime   **(PR:A MPAA:NR)**

WARRING CLANS**½ (1963, Jap.) 97m Toho bw (SENGOKU YARO)

Yuzo Kayama, Yuriko Hoshi, Makoto Sato.

Matter-of-course samurai actioner about a warrior who resigns his position as bodyguard to the head of clan after learning that members of the clan have been smuggling weapons to a rival army. Those samurai still loyal to the clan try to win the honorable warrior back, but war breaks out when the corrupt samurai rebel. Some stunning swordplay scenes deftly directed by Okamoto highlight this samurai film which examines the disintegration of the *Bushido* code, which prescribes strict rules of conduct for warriors.

p, Tomoyuki Tanaka; d, Kichachi Okamoto.

Martial Arts   **(PR:C MPAA:NR)**

WARRIOR AND THE SLAVE GIRL, THE**½
        (1959, Ital.) 89m COL c (LA RIVOLTA DEL GLADIATORI)

Gianna Maria Canale (*Princess Amira*), Georges Marchal (*Asclepio*), Ettore Manni (*Marcus Numidius*), Rafael Calvo (*Lucanus*), Vera Cruz (*Zahar*).

Canale is the Queen of Armenia, a wicked ruler who is trying to poison her own brother, the rightful heir to the throne. When the Romans hear of her plan they send troops out to thwart it, destroying her and her allies and deposing the lawful king in his ruling seat. It looks great and is a step or two above most of gladiator spectacles imported into the U.S., but is flawed by poor dubbing and editing that in parts looks like butchers were turned loose on it with cleavers.

p, Virgilio De Blasi; d, Vittorio Cottafavi; w, Ennio De Concini, Francesco De Feo, Gian Paolo Callegari, Francesco Thellung; ph, (SupercinemaScope, Eastmancolor).

War/Adventure   **(PR:A MPAA:NR)**

WARRIOR EMPRESS, THE*   (1961, Ital./Fr.) 101m
        Orsay-Documento/COL c (SAFFO, VENERE DI LESBO; SAPHO)

Kerwin Mathews (*Phaon*), Tina Louise (*Sappho*), Riccardo Garrone (*Hyperbius*), Antonio Batistella (*Paeone*), Enriso Maria Salerno (*Melanchrus*), Susi Golgi (*Actis*), Alberto Farenese (*Laricus*), Strelsa Brown (*Priestess*), Annie Gorassini (*Dyla*), Lilly Mantovani (*Cleide*), Aldo Fiorelli (*Man with Scar*), Elda Tattoli (*Sappho's Nurse*), Isa Crescenzi (*Peasant Woman*).

An ancient Roman costume adventure which has the people of Mytilene revolting against their government--a monarchy which unfairly taxes the citizens. Mathews and graceful Louise (later to play the movie star on the *Gilligan's Island* television program) star as the picture's romantic hero and heroine. Post-dubbing burdens the picture which is filled with stereotypes and, incidentally, beautiful women cavorting around the notorious Temple of Aphrodite.

p, Gianni Hecht Lucari; d, Pietro Francisci; w, Ennio De Concini, Francisci, Luciano Martini (based on a story by Francisci); ph, Carlo Carlini (CinemaScope, Eastmancolor); m, Angelo Francesco Lavagnino; ed, Nino Baragli; art d, Giulio Bongini; cos, Gaia Romanini.

Adventure   **(PR:O MPAA:NR)**

WARRIORS, THE*** (1955) 85m AA c (GB: THE DARK AVENGER)

Errol Flynn (*Prince Edward*), Joanne Dru (*Lady Joan Holland*), Peter Finch (*Count de Ville*), Yvonne Furneaux (*Marie*), Patrick Holt (*Sir Ellys*), Michael Hordern (*King Edward III*), Moultrie Kelsall (*Sir Bruce*), Robert Urquhart (*Sir Philip*), Vincent Winter (*John Holland*), Noel Willman (*Du Gueselin*), Frances Rowe (*Genevieve*), Alastair Hunter (*Libeau*), Rupert Davies (*Sir John*), Ewen Solon (*D'Estell*), Richard O'Sullivan (*Thomas Holland*), Jack Lambert (*Dubois*), John Welsh (*Gurd*), Harold Kasket (*Arnaud*), Leslie Linder (*Francois Le Clerc*), Robert Brown, John Phillips (*French Knights*), Sam Kydd.

Flynn's final swashbuckler was a rousing costumer shot in Hertfordshire, England, which doubled as 14th Century France. Hordern is King Edward and his men have trounced the French in the Hundred Years' War. Hordern comes back to England and allows his son, Flynn, to stay behind and keep watch over the Empire's new acquisitions in Aquitaine. The French *roi* is a captive but his countrymen still don't accept the defeat and have decided to commence a counterattack. Since Hordern returned to England with a great many troops, there is but a skeleton crew in France and the rebels know it. Further, the chief of the French, Finch, has taken Dru, a British noblewoman, as a hostage. Finch is no great patriot, though, and he wants to take back Aquitaine for selfish reasons. He's a count with a mean disposition and cunning ways and he hies Dru to a castle where she will be kept until the war is finally over. He thinks this plot will cause Flynn to walk right into a trap with his men. Flynn, however, has other ideas. He masquerades as an itinerant knight, joins Finch's army, and, once inside, gathers information as to the weaknesses of Finch's forces. The final sequence is exciting as Flynn leads his men in a defense of Hordern's castle. This was the same castle used in IVANHOE, which was also shot at the Elstree studio in England and had been left standing, rather than razed. Dru is rescued and Flynn, once again, is at the forefront of a revision of history. The picture looks totally authentic, the dialog is sparse when it should be and never becomes over-blown; it's a good example of the genre, although Flynn, at age 46, was becoming a bit wrinkled and grizzled for this type of role. Yvonne Furneaux sings "Bella Marie," and while it's a pleasant air, it has nothing to do with the picture and seems to have been shoehorned in.

p, Walter Mirisch; d, Henry Levin; w, Daniel B. Ullman, (uncredited) Phil Park; ph, Guy Green (CinemaScope, Technicolor); m. Cedric Thorpe Davie; ed, E.B. Jarvis; md, Louis Levy; art d, Terence Verity; set d, Harry White; cos, Elizabeth Haffenden; m/l, Davie, Christopher Hassall; makeup, L.V. Clark.

Historical   **Cas.**   **(PR:A-C MPAA:NR)**

WARRIORS, THE, 1970   (SEE: KELLY'S HEROES, 1970)

WARRIORS, THE***½   (1979) 90m PAR c

Michael Beck (Swan), James Remar (Ajax), Thomas Waites (Fox), Dorsey Wrights (Cleon), Brian Taylor (Snow), David Harris (Cochise), Tom McKitterick (Cowboy), Marcelino Sanchez (Rembrandt), Terry Michos (Vermin), Deborah Van Valkenburgh (Mercy), Roger Hill (Cyrus), David Patrick Kelly (Luther), Lynn Thigpen (D.J.), Ginny Ortiz (Candy Store Girl), Edward Sewer, Ron Ferrell, Fernando Castillo, Hubert Edwards, Larry Sears, Mike James, Gregory Cleghorne, George Lee Miles, Stanley Timms, John Maurice, Jamie Perry, Winston Yarde (Gramercy Riffs), Joel Weiss, Harold Miller, Dan Bonnell, Dan Battles, Tom Jarus, Michael Garfield, Chris Harley, Mark Baltzar (Rogues), J.W. Smith, Cal St. John, Joe Zimmardi, Carrotte, William Williams, Marvin Foster, John Barnes, Ken Thret, Michael Jeffrey (Turnbull A.C.'s), Paul Greco, Apache Ramos, Tony Michael Pann, Neal Gold, James Margolin, Chuck Mason, Andy Engels, Ian Cohen, Charles Serrano, Charles Doolan (Orphans), Jerry Hewitt, Bob Ryder, Joseph Bergman, Richard Ciotti, Tony Latham, Eugene Bicknell, T.J. Mcnamara, Steven James, Lane Ruoff, Harry Madsen, Billy Anagnos, John Gibson (Baseball Furies), Lisa Maurer, Kate Klugman, Dee Dee Benrey, Jordan Cae Harrell, Donna Ritchie, Doran Clark, Patty Brown, Iris Alahanti, Victoria Vanderkloot, Laura DeLano, Suki Rothchild, Heidi Lynch (Lizzies), Craig Baxley, A.J. Bajunas, Gary Baxley, Konrad Sheehan, Eddie Earl Hatch, Tom Huff, Leon Delaney (Punks), Irwin Keyes, Larry Silvestri, Sonny Landham, Frank Ferrara, Pat Flannery, Leo Ciani, Charlie McCarthy (Police).

Kinetic is a word overused when describing visually exciting films, but there is no better word for the films of director Walter Hill. Where Hill's films may lack complex characterizations and stunning thespian performances (a charge that only really applies to THE DRIVER and THE WARRIORS), he makes up for these deficiencies with pure, stunning visual panache. Noted for the stir it caused in theaters across the country on its release (flareups between rival gang members in theaters) due to its advertising slogan, "These are the Armies of the Night. They are 100,000 strong. They outnumber the cops five to one. They could run New York City," THE WARRIORS developed an unenviable reputation as a thoughtless incitement to gang violence. Of course, Hill intended no such thing, and those who criticized the film probably never saw it. THE WARRIORS is loosely based on Sol Yurick's 1965 novel about a reprehensible New York street gang, which in the end is shown to be composed of nothing but a bunch of babies. The gang is trapped outside of their turf and must make it back home through enemy territory, a plot-line taken from the story "Anabasis" in Greek mythology. Where Yurick barely gave a nod to his source material, Hill cuts out all of Yurick's fairly tiresome social content and instead creates a memorable, modern-day adaptation of the Greek myth. Hill's heroes are very similar to their mythological counterparts. Each gang member lives by his wits and physical skill, with only a strong loyalty to each other to guide them. THE WARRIORS opens (after a marvelous credits sequence that sets the mood for the movie) at a massive rally held by the ambitious leader of a gang known as the "Riffs," Hill (not the director), who seeks to unite all the different street gangs into one giant army. Each gang has sent a handful of representatives to the meeting and all agree that no one will come "packed" (i.e., no weapons). Of course, there is one psycho in the bunch, Kelly, the leader of a gang called the "Rogues," and he pulls a gun, kills Hill, and frames the "Warriors" for the crime. The film then turns into a battle for the Warriors to make it home through enemy territory with every rival gang in the city out to get them. The Warriors finally "bop" their way back to Coney Island where the truth is revealed, leaving Kelly and his gang in the hands of a very angry group of "Riffs." THE WARRIORS is a delight to look at. Director Hill fills the frame with vibrant colors, bright lights, and nonstop motion. The uniforms of the various gangs are unique, funny, fearsome, and more than a bit theatrical. These are not real street kids and they are not meant to be taken as such (most of the actors were actually dancers). The exciting fight scenes are brilliantly choreographed and instead of focusing on the violence, Hill concentrates on pure movement. Inside of all this glitz there are a few moments of tender insight into these characters. In a simple but effective scene, The Warriors are spread out in a subway car exhausted. At one stop two teenage couples fresh from a prom enter and sit opposite gang-leader Beck and his girl, Valkenburgh. The street kids stare at the tuxedos, prom dresses, and flowers of the "wholesome" kids, and there is a sense of melancholy, regret, and loss for the members of the Warriors because they have missed out in life, and were denied a normal adolescence.

p, Lawrence Gordon; d, Walter Hill; w, David Shaber, Hill (based on the novel by Sol Yurick); ph, Andrew Laszlo (Panavision, Movielab Color); m, Barry De Vorzon; ed, David Holden; art d, Don Swanagan, Bob Wightman; set d, Fred Weiler; cos, Bobbie Mannix, Mary Ellen Winston; stunts, Craig Baxley.

Drama   Cas.   (PR:O MPAA:R)

WARRIORS FIVE**   (1962), Fr./Ital.) 91m Italian International Film-S. N.C./AIP bw (LA DERNIERE ATTAQUE; LA GUERRE CONTINUA)

Jack Palance (Jack), Giovanna Ralli (Italia), Serge Reggiani (Libero), Folco

Lulli (Marzi), Venantino Venantini (Alberto), Franco Balducci (Conti), Miha Baloh (Sansone), Vera Murco (Mafalda), Vida Levstik (Ida), Ajsa Mesic (Luisa), Valeria Sila (Old Woman), Isabella Chiurco (Carla), Guido Bertone (Carlo), Bruno Scipioni (Angelino).

Palance stars in this dubbed European coproduction as an American soldier who parachutes behind enemy lines on an espionage mission, only to be imprisoned by the enemy. He escapes with four Italian prisoners, enlisting their aid in exploding a bridge. By the finale he and Ralli, an Italian prostitute, are the only ones left alive and continuing to fight.

p, Fulvio Lucisano; d, Leopoldo Savona; w, Gino De Santis, Ugo Pirro, Savona (based on a story by Lino Del Fra); ph, Claudio Racca; m, Armando Trovajoli; ed, Gabriele Varriale; art d, Gastone Carsetti.

War   (PR:A MPAA:NR)

WARRIOR'S HUSBAND THE***   (1933) 75m FOX bw

Elissa Landi (Antiope), Marjorie Rambeau (Hippolyta), Ernest Truex (Sapiens), David Manners (Theseus), Helen Ware (Pomposia), Maude Eburne (Buria), John Sheehan (Pokus), Lionel Belmore (Homer), "Tiny" Sandford (Hercules), Helene Madison (Captain of the Guards), Ferdinand Gottschalk (Sapiens, Sr.), Claudia Coleman (Heroica).

An innovative satire about a dominant group of Amazonian women and the whimpering men they control. Rambeau is the chesty Amazon queen who rules over Pontus in 800 B.C. When Rambeau decides to take a husband, Truex, it is not because he is manly but because his mother makes generous contributions to the Treasury. Like most men living in Pontus, Truex is a full-fledged pansy. He dresses in effeminate clothing made of silk and satin, curls his beard, and cowers whenever confronted by women. It is the women who are the forceful ones—laboring, fighting, and heading the government. Although Rambeau is in charge, it is Landi, her beautiful sister, who gets the attention, especially when Pontus is invaded by a Greek army headed by Manners, who is intent on stealing Rambeau's "magic girdle." The sight of Manners, with his Greek Adonis posings, comes as quite a shock to the Amazonian women. It doesn't take Manners very long to realize that Landi is the girl for him. When he first kisses Landi, she resists because she is unaccustomed to being wooed. After a few more kisses Landi likes it and, although she won't admit it, falls in love with Manners. As they discover the benefits of having real men, the Amazonian women gladly allow them to take control. In an attempt to add some sort of social relevance to THE WARRIOR'S HUSBAND, a final subtitle reads: "In 1933 A.D. nothing has changed. Women are still fighters and think man's place is in the home." Surprisingly racy in its portrayal of male and female roles, THE WARRIOR'S HUSBAND managed to sneak into movie houses before the Hays Code made pictures like this obsolete.

p, Jesse Lasky; d, Walter Lang; w, Lang, Ralph Spence, Sonya Levien (based on the play by Julian Thompson), ph, Hal Mohr; md, L. E. DeFrancesco.

Comedy   (PR:C MPAA:NR)

WASHINGTON B.C.   (SEE: HAIL, 1973)

WASHINGTON COWBOY   (SEE: ROVIN' TUMBLEWEEDS, 1939)

WASHINGTON MASQUERADE*½   (1932) 75m MGM bw (GB: MAD MASQUERADE)

Lionel Barrymore (Jeff Keane), Karen Morley (Consuela Fairbanks), Diane Sinclair (Ruth Keane), Nils Asther (Henri Brenner), Reginald Barlow (Sen. Withers), William Collier, Sr (Babcock), William Morris (Sen. Hodge), Rafaela Ottiano (Mona), C. Henry Gordon (Hinsdale, Lobbyist), Burton Churchill (Sen. Bitler), Henry Kolker (Stapleton).

Melodrama isn't strong enough a word to describe WASHINGTON MASQUERADE. Barrymore stars as a widowed senator who marries the coniving Morley, a beautiful bombshell of a lobbyist. She does her lobbying in the bedroom, however, and convinces her husband to take a bribe and pass a water rights bill. He is found out, confesses to the corruption and ends up dying because of the scandal. Lionel did well in the part as he had appeared in the stage version on Broadway in 1921.

d, Charles Brabin; w, John Meehan, Samuel Blythe (from the play "The Claw" by Henri Bernstein); ph, Gregg Toland; ed, Ben Lewis.

Drama   (PR:A MPAA:NR)

WASHINGTON MELODRAMA**   (1941) 78m MGM bw

Frank Morgan (Calvin Claymore), Ann Rutherford (Laurie Claymore), Kent Taylor (Hal Thorne, Editor), Dan Dailey, Jr (Whitney King), Lee Bowman (Ronnie Colton), Fay Holden (Mrs. Claymore), Virginia Grey (Teddy Carlyle), Anne Gwynne (Mary Morgan), Sara Haden (Mrs. Harrigan), Olaf Hytten (Parry), Douglas Dumbrille (Donnelly), Cliff Clark (Simpson), Hal K. Dawson (Logan), Thurston Hall (Sen. Morton), Joseph Crehan (Phil Sampson), Frederick Burton (Dean Lawford), Howard Hickman (Bishop Chatterton), Virginia Brissac (Mrs. Curzon).

Morgan is a multi-millionaire who is trying to get the Senate to pass a bill that would send relief monies to Europe's starving children, but his goodwill image is shattered when he has a murder pegged on him. A platonic female companion, Gwynne, is found dead in her apartment and since Morgan had just left he is naturally accused. It turns out that blackmailer Dailey is the guilty one, a vile night club host who packs a memorable wallop, knocking Gwynne to the ground in one scene. As expected Morgan is cleared by the finale and the hungry kids get a belly full. Includes the easily forgotten song "Fishing for Suckers" (Earl Brent).

p, Edgar Selwyn; d, S. Sylvan Simon; w, Marion Parsonnet, Roy Chanslor (based on the play by L. du Rocher Macpherson); ph, Harold Rosson; m, Davis Snell; ed, Gene Ruggiero; art d, Cedric Gibbons; ch, Sammy Lee; water ballet, Lottie Horner.

Drama/Crime   **(PR:A MPAA:NR)**

WASHINGTON MERRY-GO-ROUND*   (1932) 78M COL bw (GB: INVISIBLE POWER)

Lee Tracy (*Button Gwinnett Brown*), Constance Cummings (*Alice Wylie*), Alan Dinehart (*Norton*), Walter Connolly (*Sen. Wylie*), Clarence Muse (*Clarence, Valet*), Arthur Vinton (*Beef Brannigan*), Frank Sheridan (*Kelleher*), Clay Clement (*Conti*), Sam Godfrey (*Martin*), Arthur Hoyt (*Willis*), Ernie Woods (*Beauchard*).

This sugary Washington soap opera casts Tracy as a crusading Mr. Smith-type congressman who attempts to stop a corrupt group of politicians. In order to shut him up, the crooks stage a phony recount and get Tracy booted out of his governmental seat. With the help of elder statesman Connolly and his granddaughter Cummings, Tracy not only regains his seat but makes the halls of justice squeaky clean. The film takes its title from a best-selling novel and the syndicated news column by Drew Pearson and Jack Anderson.

d, James Cruze; w, Jo Swerling, (based on a story by Maxwell Anderson); ph, Ira Morgan, Teddy Tetzlaff; ed, Richard Cahoon.

Drama   **(PR:A MPAA:NR)**

WASHINGTON STORY½**   (1952) 81m MGM bw (GB: TARGET FOR SCANDAL)

Van Johnson (*Joseph T. Gresham*), Patricia Neal (*Alice Kingsly*), Louis Calhern (*Charles W. Birch*), Sidney Blackmer (*Philip Emery, Lobbyist*), Philip Ober (*Gilbert Nunnally, Columnist*), Patricia Collinge (*Miss Galbreth*), Moroni Olsen (*Speaker*), Elizabeth Patterson (*Miss Dee*), Reinhold Schunzel (*Peter Kralik*), Fay Roope (*Caswell*), Dan Riss (*Bill Holmby*), Joan Banks (*Mrs. Varick*), Raymond Greenleaf (*John Sheldon*), Gregory Marshall (*Rodney Delwick*), Perry Sheehan (*Secretary*), Jimmie Fox (*Mr. Watkins, Mailman*), Katherine Warren (*Mrs. Birch*), Don Beddoe, Hugh Beaumont, Willis Bouchey, Carleton Young, Larry Dobkin, Emory Parnell.

Johnson is an honest, hard-working senator of the sort that only exists in the movies. When a journalist wrongly accuses him of being less honorable than he appears, Johnson prepares a slander suit. Neal comes up with the idea of writing a series of articles in favor of the job that politicians do and in the process falls in love with the senator. Filmed, in part, in Congress and the Pentagon.

p, Dore Schary; d&w, Robert Pirosh; ph, John Alton; m, Conrad Salinger; ed, John Dunning, John Durant; art d, Cedric Gibbons, Daniel B. Cathcart; cos, Helen Rose.

Drama   **(PR:A MPAA:NR)**

WASP WOMAN, THE*   (1959) 73m Filmgroup/AA bw

Susan Cabot (*Janice Starling*), Fred [Anthony] Eisley (*Bill Lane*), Barboura Morris (*Mary Dennison*), Michael Marks (*Dr. Eric Zinthrop*), William Roerick (*Arthur Cooper*), Frank Gerstle (*Hellman*), Bruno Ve Sota (*Night Watchman*), Frank Wolff.

This laughable Corman quickie was the first product produced by his company Filmgroup. In her search for eternal youth and beauty Cabot uses a potion concocted by crazed scientist Marks which is made of wasp (the bug, not the social group) enzymes. By day she is a gorgeous young woman, but when night falls she buzzes around town killing people. She discovers her Achilles heel, the inability to fly, the hard way.

p&d, Roger Corman; w, Leo Gordon; ph, Harry C. Newman; m, Fred Katz; ed, Carlo Lodato; prod d&art d, Daniel Haller.

Science Fiction   **Cas.**   **(PR:A MPAA:NR)**

WASTREL, THE*½   (1963, Ital.) 84m Lux Film-Tiberia/Medallion bw (IL RELITTO)

Van Heflin (*Duncan Bell*), Ellie Lambetti (*Liana*), Franco Fabrizi (*Rudi Veronese*), Michael Stellman (*Cam*), Fosco Giachetti (*Jug Hardy*), Tiberio Mitri (*Macniff*), Paul Muller (*Fatso*), Clelia Matania (*Betsy*), Aldo Pini (*Doc*), Annie Gorassini (*Monique*), Alix Talton.

Greek Director Cacoyannis uses a boat explosion as an excuse to have his main character Heflin think back over his life while clinging to the debris

with his 10-year-old son. We learn about his problematic romance with wife Lambetti, his attempt to sail around the world in his yacht, and his bout with alcoholism. This brush with death causes him to straighten up and sail forward.

p, Angelo Ferrara; d, Michael Cacoyannis (with Giovanni Paolucci); w, Cacoyannis, Frederic Wakeman, Suso Cecchi D'Amico (based on the novel by Wakeman); ph, Piero Portalupi; m, Angelo Francesco Lavagnino, Mario Zafred; ed, Alberto Gallitti; art d, Arrigo Equini; set d, Ferdinando Ruffo; cos, Gaia Romanini.

Drama   **(PR:C MPAA:NR)**

WASTRELS, THE   (SEE: VITELLONI, 1956, Ital.)

WATASHI GA SUTETA ONNA   (SEE: GIRL I ABANDONED, THE, 1970, Jap.)

WATCH BEVERLY*½   (1932, Brit.) 80m Sound City/But bw

Henry Kendall (*Victor Beverly*), Dorothy Bartlam (*Audrey Thurloe*), Francis X. Bushman (*President Orloff*), Frederic de Lara (*Rachmann*), Charles Mortimer (*Sir James Briden*), Patrick Ludlow (*Patrick Nolan*), Colin Pole (*George*), Antony Holles (*Arthur Briden*), Ernest Stidwell (*Inspector Roberts*), Aileen Pitt Marsden (*Anne Markham*), Vincent Clive, Edith Barker Bennett.

Flaccid comedy starring Kendall as a diplomat who is outraged to discover that a rich British businessman has agreed to pay a large sum of money to a foreign dictator in exchange for some lucrative oil drilling rights. To divert the money back to Britain, Kendall poses as the dictator, takes the money, and gives it to charity. Too tame to be funny.

p, Ivar Campbell; d, Arthur Maude; w, N.W. Baring Pemberton, John Cousins (based on a play by Cyril Campion); ph, George Dudgeon Stretton.

Comedy   **(PR:A MPAA:NR)**

WATCH IT, SAILOR!*½   (1961, Brit.) 81m Cormorant-Hammer/COL bw

Dennis Price (*Lt./Comdr. Hardcastle*), Marjorie Rhodes (*Emma Hornett*), Irene Handl (*Edie Hornett*), Liz Fraser (*Daphne*), Vera Day (*Shirley Hornett*), John Meillon (*Albert Tufnell*), Cyril Smith (*Henry Hornett*), Miriam Karlin (*Mrs. Lack*), Graham Stark (*Carnoustie Bligh*), Frankie Howerd (*Organist*), Bobby Howes (*Drunk*), Brian Reece (*Solicitor*), Renee Houston (*Mrs. Mottram*), Arthur Howard (*Vicar*).

Wearisome farce starring Price as a young sailor whose impending marriage appears dashed when he receives a telegram containing a bogus paternity accusation. His bride-to-be's mother makes his life hell until all the usual misunderstandings and tiresome complications are sorted out.

p, Maurice Cowan; d, Wolf Rilla; w, Falkland Cary, Philip King (based on the play by Cary, King); ph, Arthur Grant; m, Douglas Gamley; ed, James Needs, Alfred Cox; art d, Bernard Robinson, Don Mingaye.

Comedy   **(PR:A MPAA:NR)**

WATCH ON THE RHINE***   (1943) 114m WB bw

Bette Davis (*Sara Muller*), Paul Lukas (*Kurt Muller*), Geraldine Fitzgerald (*Marthe de Brancovis*), Lucile Watson (*Fanny Farrelly*), Beulah Bondi (*Anise*), George Coulouris (*Teck de Brancovis*), Donald Woods (*David Farrelly*), Henry Daniell (*Phili von Ramme*), Donald Buka (*Joshua Muller*), Eric Roberts (*Bodo Muller*), Janis Wilson (*Babette Muller*), Helmut Dantine (*Young Man*), Mary Young (*Mrs. Mellie Sewell*), Kurt Katch (*Herr Blecher*), Erwin Kalser (*Dr. Klauber*), Robert O. Davis 'Rudolph Anders' (*Overdorff*), Clyde Fillmore (*Sam Chandler*), Frank Wilson (*Joseph*), Clarence Muse (*Horace*), Violett McDowell (*Belle*), Joe Bernard, Jack Mower (*Trainmen*), Creighton Hale (*Chauffeur*), William Washington (*Doc*), Elvira Curci (*Italian Woman*), Anthony Caruso (*Italian Man*), Michele Fehr (*Baby*), Jean DeBriac (*Mr. Chabeuf*), Leah Baird (*Miss Drake*), Howard Hickman (*Cyrus Penfield*), Frank Reicher (*Admiral*), Robert O. Fischer (*German Ambassador*), Walter Stahl (*German Embassy Butler*), Glen Cavender (*German Embassy Servant*), Joe deVillard (*Spanish General*), Wedgwood Nowell (*American Diplomat*), Hans Tanzler (*German Diplomat*), Herma Cordova, Gretl Dupont (*Women*), Alan Hale, Jr. (*Boy*), Garry Owen (*Taxi Driver*), Hans von Morhart (*German*).

One of those rare instances where the movie surpasses the play from whence it was drawn. Hellman's successful and lauded stage drama was adapted for the screen by herself and her boy friend, Dashiell Hammett, and then handed to the same man who directed it in New York, Herman Shumlin. The result was a powerful drama that was nominated as Best Picture, for Best Script, and had Lucile Watson nominated as Best Supporting Actress. None of those Oscars were bestowed, but Paul Lukas, repeating his role on the stage, did win the Best Actor nod from the Motion Picture Academy. Davis and Lukas are married and the parents of Buka, Roberts, and Wilson. They are on a train from Mexico to Washington, D.C., for a visit to Davis' mother, Watson, who has not seen her daughter for 18 years and has never met her grandchildren. Davis married Lukas years before and they moved to Europe, where they stayed until the dangerous situation caused them to come back to the U.S. Watson is all a twitter about having her daughter and grandchildren come to visit. Her excitement is shared by her son, Woods, and her housekeeper, Bondi. Staying at Watson's home for the time being are Coulouris, a Rumanian peer, and his American-born wife, Fitzgerald. Coulouris is a villainous type whom we suspect may be a spy. (Although released in 1943 as a film, the play had been seen on Broadway during the 1940-41 season, before the world was totally at war.) The family arrives and hugs and kisses abound for a while. Later, Davis tells her mother and brother that Lukas has not been well and is only staying in the U.S. until his health improves. Later, he will go back to Europe as his "business" is important. Watson doesn't quite know what her son-in-law does for a living and presses Davis for an answer but receives only vague mumblings about him being involved in engineering. It's because of that peripatetic job that he has to travel so much; because the family is close-knit, they travel with him. Coulouris wonders if there may be more to the gentle Lukas than meets the eye so he pries open a briefcase belonging to Lukas and raises his eyebrows as he sees a great deal of money in it, fresh U.S. bills. Coulouris likes to spend his time at the German Embassy, although the Teutons think little of him. He plays poker with the Germans and they enjoy taking his money. At one of the regular games, Coulouris hears of an underground leader having been captured in Europe. But the man would not crack under the sadistic bludgeonings of the Gestapo and the Nazis are at a loss to get the information they need which would crack the underground ring. Coulouris believes that Lukas may be the U.S. contact for the underground leader and tells Katch, a German intelligence officer attached to the legation, that he might be able to help their cause, if they are willing to pay him a fee. Later, Coulouris confronts Lukas and says that he knows the truth about what the man does but he is willing to keep mum about it, if Lukas forks over $10,000. Upon hearing this, Fitzgerald is shocked and tells her husband that she can't believe what she's just heard. Coulouris tells her to mind her own business, then reveals that he "knows" she and Woods are romantically involved. The cash that Coulouris saw in Lukas' briefcase has been gathered by him for the express purpose of fighting the fascists. People who have to share meals and wear old shoes have donated their money and there is no way that he can ever hand it to a scoundrel like Coulouris for blackmail. Watson and Woods will give Coulouris the money to keep him quiet but Lukas knows that once a victim gets into the web of a blackmailer, the spider will bleed the fly dry. So Lukas kills Coulouris rather than allow that to happen. Now a murderer, Lukas is forced to flee to Mexico. He is assured by Watson and Woods that they will not contact the authorities about Coulouris until after he has had enough time to cross the border. Lukas kisses Davis and his children farewell and departs to attempt the rescue of the underground leader by using the money he's collected and spreading it around in the right places. Months pass and no one knows if Lukas made it or not, then Buka announces that he is going off to Europe to continue the battle against the fascists. Lukas, Watson, Coulouris, Roberts, and Wilson were in the stage version which also starred Mady Christians (in the Davis role) and Helen Trenholme (in the Fitzgerald part). Shumlin's direction was superb and what might have been an excessively talky piece was never that at all. This was the very first movie made in the U.S. that showed the dark side of fascism as an ideal, rather than as a war machine. Davis took the small role as the wife (although she received top billing) and never stepped out of line to do a star turn. Rather, she was content to submerge some of her accustomed histrionics in favor of being one of the ensemble, a wise decision. At the time, the Production Code insisted that a movie could not be made in which a killer did not get punished for the crime, no matter how heinous the victim. To placate the Code administrations, a new ending was written in which Lukas got his due punishment, but the actor never showed up at the studio to shoot it (a slap in the face to the Code and its stupidity) and so the ending of his "disappearance" or possible capture was tacked on. What one must recall is that fascism, even as late as 1939, still held several prominent Americans in its sway because the news of what the Nazis were doing had not yet reached these shores, at least not for the public. So Hellman's play broke new ground and showed the dangers of complacency by introducing the problem into what might have been a typical household. The following year, it was dealt with once more in TOMORROW THE WORLD.

p, Hal B. Wallis; d, Herman Shumlin; w, Dashiell Hammett, Lillian Hellman (based on the play by Hellman); ph, Merritt Gerstad, Hal Mohr; m. Max Steiner; ed, Rudi Fehr; md Leo F. Forbstein; art d, Carl Jules Weyl; set d, Julia Heron; cos, Orry-Kelly; spec eff. Jack Holden, Edwin B. DuPar.

Drama   **Cas.**   **(PR:A MPAA:NR)**

WATCH THE BIRDIE½   (1950) 70m MGM bw

Red Skelton (Rusty Cameron/Pop Cameron/Grandpop Cameron), Arlene Dahl (Lucia Corlane), Ann Miller (Miss Lucky Vista), Leon Ames (Grantland D. Farns), Pam Britton (Mrs. Shanway), Richard Rober (Hugh Shanway), Dick Wessel (Man Who Undresses), Jacqueline Duval, Paula Drew, Georgia Pelham (Starlets).

Wacky adventures are multiplied by three as Skelton plays a news cameraman, his father, and his grandfather. He inadvertently films a business scam while on location at a new building's opening ceremony. Dahl, the project's financier, is the victim of a scheme that would cause her to file

for bankruptcy, putting the building up for sale at a rock bottom price. Skelton, after a wildly silly chase scene, hands the crooks over to the authorities. Clips from BOOM TOWN with Clark Gable and Claudette Colbert, and from JOHNNY EAGER with Lana Turner and Robert Taylor, are mixed in.

p, Harry Ruskin; d, Jack Donohue; w, Ivan Tors, Devery Freeman, Ruskin (based on a story by Marshall Neilan, Jr.); ph, Paul C. Vogel; m, Georgie Stoll; ed, Robert Watts; art d, Cedric Gibbons, Eddie Imazu; set d, Edwin B. Willis, Keogh Gleason; spec eff, A. Arnold Gillespie, Warren Newcombe; makeup, William J. Tuttle.

Comedy   **(PR:A MPAA:NR)**

WATCH YOUR STERN**   (1961, Brit.) 88m G.H.W./Magna bw

Kenneth Connor (O/S Blissworth), Eric Barker (Capt. David Foster), Leslie Phillips (Lt. Comdr. Fanshawe), Joan Sims (Ann Foster), Hattie Jacques (Agatha Potter), Spike Milligan (Dockyard Matey), Eric Sykes (2nd Dockyard Matey), Sidney James (C.P.O. Mundy), Ed Devereaux (Comdr. Phillips), David Lodge (Security Sergeant), Victor Maddern (1st Sailor), Noel Purcell (Adm. Sir Humphrey Pettigrew), Robin Ray (Flag Lieutenant), George Street, Michael Brennan (Security Guards), Peter Howell (Admiral's Secretary), Arch Taylor (Coxswain), Richard Bennett (Officer of the Day), Leila Williams (Wren Driver), Eric Corrie (Engineer Officer), Rory MacDermot (3rd Security Guard).

A couple of naval dunderheads mess up during the testing of a prototype torpedo and end up losing the plans, making much-needed modification of the weapon impossible. They try to prevent their admiral from discovering their mistake by presenting him with plans for the ship's refrigeration system instead. When word leaks out that a female inspector has been assigned to the testing, Connor dresses in drag and impersonates the woman, which leads to him and his foolish partner Barker getting booted out of the Navy. From the folks responsible for the CARRY ON series.

p, Peter Rogers; d, Gerald Thomas; w, Alan Hackney, Vivian A. Cox (based on the play "Something About a Sailor" by Earle Couttie); ph, Ted Scaife; m, Bruce Montgomery; ed, John Shirley; art d, Carmen Dillon; set d, Peter Lamont; cos, Joan Ellacott; makeup, Alex Garfath.

Comedy   **(PR:A MPAA:NR)**

WATCHED**   (1974) 93m Penthouse c

Stacy Keach (Mike Mandell/Sonny), Harris Yulin (Gordon Pankey), Bridget Pole (Informer), Turid Aarstd (Blonde), Valeri Parker (Hitchhiker), Denver John Collins (Hippie).

Another in the series of paranoia-conspiracy films that leaped to the screen around the time of Watergate. This one stars Keach as a fanatical government agent whose by-the-book handling of cases erodes his support among fellow agents. In addition, Keach also has a split personality which turns him into a mafia gangster. Of course these opposing instincts cause Keach mental turmoil and he begins to feel that fellow agent Yulin is out to get him. WATCHED is a confused and at times even ludicrous film that tries too hard to be socially significant while indulging in some irritating camerawork that distracts from the story. Unfortunately, not even such solid actors as Keach and Yulin can rescue this film from the bog of self-importance it is mired in. The musical score was written and performed by the popular jazz-fusion group Weather Report.

p, David Goldman; d&w, John Parsons; ph, Hart Perry, Ed Lynch, Keavin Keating, Jack Wright; m, Weather Report; ed, Ed Deitch; m/l, Bob Carpenter.

Crime   **Cas.**   **(PR:O MPAA:R)**

WATCHER IN THE WOODS, THE½
                                        (1980, Brit.) 100m Disney/BV c

Bette Davis (Mrs. Aylwood), Carroll Baker (Helen Curtis), David McCallum (Paul Curtis), Lynn-Holly Johnson (Jan Curtis), Kyle Richards (Ellie Curtis), Ian Bannen (John Keller), Richard Pasco (Tom Colley), Frances Cuka (Mary Fleming), Benedict Taylor (Mike Fleming), Eleanor Summerfield (Mrs. Thayer), Georgina Hale (Young Mrs. Aylwood), Katherine Levy (Karen Aylwood).

A disappointing attempt by Disney to get into another field, this tepid horror-ghost story is splayed all over the place and never focuses on a story or the target audience. Baker and McCallum are the parents of Johnson and Richards. They are an American family renting an old mansion in England that is owned by Davis, who lives in a small guest house on the property and depends on the rental from the large house to survive. The place is surrounded by dark woods that seem to encroach on the building. There are indications from the start that this is no ordinary glen, teeming with flora, fauna, and cute little Disney squirrels. While Johnson and Richards explore the area, Davis also seems to be on a pursuit. She is looking for a daughter lost 30 years ago when the child was a teenager. The conclusion has her child, Levy, being discovered as having been trapped in another dimension when she was somehow misplaced there by Hale (playing Davis at a younger age). The original ending had something to do with an alien planet and a huge "being" from that planet in an "other world" sequence. After spending a fortune on the special effects for that sequence, the studio junked the idea (it was briefly seen in previews and audiences had to hold their sides from laughter) and opted for the new ending, which was directed, without credit, by long-time Disney veteran Vincent McEveety. A bland attempt at a horror story that needed, but didn't get, some spice. Johnson had previously been seen in the James Bond film FOR YOUR EYES ONLY, which was the first Bond film that original author Ian Fleming received no credit for. The screenwriters and the directors failed to take advantage of a potentially interesting situation. Hough had already done some interesting movies like LEGEND OF HELL HOUSE, EYE WITNESS, TWINS OF EVIL, and BRASS TARGET, but he was found wanting on this effort. Even though mild by comparison to many other films of this ilk, children may have a problem with some of the scenes and would be well-advised to skip this.

p, Ron Miller; d, John Hough, (uncredited) Vincent McEveety; w, Brian Clemens, Harry Spalding, Rosemary Anne Sisson (based on the novel bw Florence Engel Randall); ph, Alan Hume (Technicolor); m, Stanley Myers; ed, Geoffrey Foot; prod d, Elliott Scott, Harrison Ellenshaw; art d, Alan Cassie; cos, Emma Porteous; spec eff, John Richardson, Art Cruickshank, Bob Broughton, David Mattingly, Dick Kendall, Don Henry.

Horror/Science Fiction   Cas.   (PR:C MPAA:PG)

WATER BABIES, THE½**   (1979, Brit.) 93m Ariadne/Pethurst International c

James Mason (Grimes), Billie Whitelaw (Mrs. Doasyouwouldbedoneby), Bernard Cribbins (Masterman), Joan Greenwood (Lady Harriet), David Tomlinson (Sir John), Paul Luty (Sladd), Tommy Pender (Tom), Samantha Gates (Ellie).

This enchanting children's adventure mixes live action with animated underwater sequences. Pender is a 12-year-old apprentice chimney sweep to veteran sweep Mason, who tends to hit the bottle. When the youngster is wrongly accused of stealing he flees and takes a leap into a pool. While under the water he meets an assortment of characters and rescues the water babies–children being held captive by an eel and a shark. He eventually gets to return to dry land where his name has been cleared of any wrongdoing. Not especially interesting for adults, nor is the animation all that wonderful, but kids will probably get a kick out of it.

p, Peter Shaw; d, Lionel Jeffries; w, Michael Robson (based on the novel by Charles Kingsley); ph, Ted Scaife; ed, Peter Weatherley; art d, Herbert Westbrook; cos, Phyllis Dalton; m/l, Phil Coulter, Bill Martin; animators, Miroslaw Kijowicz, J. Stokes.

Children's Adventure/Anim. Cas.   (PR:AAA MPAA:NR)

WATER CYBORGS   (SEE: TERROR BENEATH THE SEA, 1966)

**WATER FOR CANITOGA*   (1939, Ger.) 109m Bavaria-Filmkunst bw
(WASSER FUR CANITOGA)**

Hans Albers, Charlotte Susa, Hilde Sessak, Peter Voss, Josef Sieber, Andrews Engelman.

Albers stars as a German pioneer who leads his fellow settlers in search of a water supply. When he cannot come up with enough cash to complete a pipeline and his American backers fall through, he loses the respect of his followers. Since this is a propaganda film, his death makes him an Aryan martyr.

d, Herbert Selpin; w, Emil Burri, Peter Francke; ph, Franz Koch, Josef Illig.

Western   (PR:A MPAA:NR)

WATER GIPSIES, THE   (SEE: WATER GYPSIES, THE, 1932, Brit.)

WATER GYPSIES, THE   (1932, Brit.) 76m Associated Talking Pictures/RKO bw

Ann Todd (Jane Bell), Sari Maritza (Lily Bell), Ian Hunter (Fred Green), Peter Hannen (Bryan), Richard Bird (Ernest), Frances Doble (Fay), Anthony Ireland (Moss), Barbara Gott (Mrs. Green), Moore Marriott (Mr. Pewtar), Harold Scott (Mr. Bell), Charles Garry (Mr. Green), Betty Shale (Mrs. Higgins), Lilli Anne, Kenneth Carlisle, Raymond Raikes.

The life of gypsies living in barges along the Thames is examined when one of them is asked to sit for a well-known society artist. Todd, the beautiful gypsy girl, gets a taste of a better life, to the chagrin of the artist's fiancee. Her life takes a turn for the worse when she accidentally drowns the fiancee. The movie is surprisingly realistic in many sequences, adding an appealing atmosphere to the picture.

p, Basil Dean; d, Maurice Elvey; w, Dean, Miles Malleson, Alma Reville, John Paddy Carstairs (based on the novel by A.P. Herbert); ph, Robert Martin, Robert de Grasse.

Romance   (PR:A MPAA:NR)

WATER RUSTLERS*½   (1939) 54m Coronado/GN bw

Dorothy Page (Shirley Martin), David O'Brien (Bob Lawson), Vince Barnett (Mike), Ethan Allen (Tim Martin), Leonard Trainer (Jurgens), Merrill McCormick (Sheriff), Stanley Price (Robert Weylan), Warner Richmond (Wiley), Lloyd Ingraham (Judge).

Page is a ranch owner who takes over her father's property when he is killed by outlaws. With the help of her foreman and sweetheart, O'Brien, she keeps her property safe and avenges her father's death. The second of three pictures in Page's short cowgirl series which began with RIDE 'EM COWGIRL and finished up with THE SINGING COWGIRL.

p, Don Liegerman; d, Samuel Diege; w, Arthur Hoerl; ph, Mack Stengler; ed, Guy V. Thayer, Jr.; m/l, Al Sherman, Walter Kent, Milton Drake.

Western   Cas.   (PR:A MPAA:NR)

WATERFRONT*   (1939) 60m WB bw

Gloria Dickson (Ann Stacey), Dennis Morgan (Jim Dolan), Marie Wilson (Ruby Waters), Larry Williams (Frankie Donahue), Sheila Bromley (Marie Cordell), Aldrich Bowker (Father Dunn), Frank Faylen (Skids Riley), Ward Bond (Mart Hendler), Arthur Gardner (Dan Dolan), George Lloyd (Joe Becker).

Morgan is given the tough job of trying to make his longshoreman character appealing in this melodrama set on a dingy, steamy waterfront. He leads an unenviable life of drinking and fighting, spending half his days in jail. Upon meeting a priest, however, he is instantly and unrealistically converted to a decent, loving husband, with Dickson as his wife. His nasty side creeps out when a longtime enemy kills his brother. Instead of cooperating with the police, he gets revenge himself over the protests of his peace-loving wife. Not even the most illiterate dock worker would accept this is as being true to life.

p, Bryan Foy; d, Terry Morse; w, Lee Katz, Arthur Ripley (based on the play "Blind Spot" by Kenyon Nicholson); ph, James Van Trees; ed, Louis Hesse; cos, Milo Anderson.

Drama   (PR:A MPAA:NR)

WATERFRONT   (1944) 65m PRC bw**

John Carradine (Victor Marlowe), J. Carroll Naish (Dr. Carl Decker), Maris Wrixon (Freda Hauser), Edwin Maxwell (Max Kramer), Terry Frost (Jerry Donovan), John Bleifer (Zimmerman, Saloonkeeper), Marten Lamont (Mike Gorman), Olga Fabian (Mrs. Hauser), Claire Rochelle (Maisie), Billy Nelson (Butch).

Set against the background of San Francisco's waterfront, Naish, a local optometrist, heads the area's Nazi espionage ring. His power comes from secret information he keeps in his "little black book," and his persuading other German-Americans to help the cause. He is challenged by Nazi spy Carradine, who wants the book (and the power) for himself. Naish is killed, but before Carradine can enjoy his position he is nabbed by the authorities. The espionage incidents defy logic but entertain all the same.

p, Arthur Alexander; d, Steve Sekely; w, Martin Mooney, Irwin R. Franklyn (based on the story by Mooney); ph, Robert Cline; ed, Charles Henkle, Jr; md, Lee Zahler; art d, Paul Palmentola; set d, Harry Reif.

Spy Drama   Cas.   (PR:A MPAA:NR)

WATERFRONT, 1952   (SEE: WATERFRONT WOMEN, 1952, Brit.)

WATERFRONT AT MIDNIGHT½   (1948) 63m PAR bw**

William Gargan (Mike Hanrohan), Mary Beth Hughes (Ethel Novack), Richard Travis (Socks Barstow), Richard Crane (Denny Hanrohan), Cheryl Walker (Helen Hanrohan), Horace McMahon (Hank Bremmer), John Hilton (Woody), Douglas Fowley (Joe Sargus), Paul Harvey (Commissioner Ryan), Keye Luke (Loy).

A swiftlypaced crime story with Gargan as a tough-as-nails cop who sets his sights on busting Travis, a mobster who deals in stolen goods. Gargan's investigation hits a snag when his brother, Crane, joins up with the mobster, causing the cop to shoot with caution. Fine suspense story carried nicely along by a competent cast and sharp direction.

p, William Pine, William Thomas; d, William Berke; w, Bernard Girard; ph, Ellis W. Carter; m, Harry Lubin; ed, Howard Smith; md, David Chudnow; art d, Lewis H. Creber; set d, Alfred Kegerris; makeup, Paul Stanhope.

Crime   (PR:A MPAA:NR)

WATERFRONT LADY*½   (1935) 68m Mascot-REP bw

Ann Rutherford (Joan O'Brien), Frank Albertson (Ronny), J. Farrell MacDonald (O'Brien), Barbara Pepper (Gloria), Grant Withers (Tod), Charles C. Wilson (McFee), Purnell Pratt (District Attorney), Jack LaRue (Tom), Mary Gordon (Mrs. O'Flaherty), Paul Porcasi, Ward Bond, Mathilda Comont, Victor Potel, Naomi Judge, Dorothy Ates, Robert Emmett O'Connor, Wally Albright, Carlotte Miles, Smiley Burnette, Clarence H. Wilson, Norma Taylor.

Another waterfront yarn made distinctive by sequences in a houseboat fishing colony. Here, Albertson takes the blame when his partner in a gambling ship operation accidentally kills his lookout after a raid. A muddy ending tends to spoil the story, with Albertson figuring he can beat the charge by using his pull. It is a thin story and depends mostly on locale to keep up interest, a sure indication of a draggy story line.

p, Nat Levine; d, Joseph Santley; w, Wellyn Totman, Joseph Fields; ph, Ernest Miller, Jack Marta; ed, Ray Curtiss.

Crime Drama (PR:A MPAA:NR)

WATERFRONT WOMEN** (1952, Brit.) 74m Conqueror/GFD bw (GB: WATERFRONT)

Robert Newton *(Peter McCabe)*, Kathleen Harrison *(Mrs. McCabe)*, Avis Scott *(Nora McCabe)*, Susan Shaw *(Connie McCabe)*, Robin Netscher *(George Alexander)*, Richard Burton *(Ben Satterthwaite)*, Kenneth Griffith *(Maurice Bruno)*, Olive Sloane *(Mrs. Gibson)*, James Hayter *(Ship's Captain)*, Charles Victor *(Bill)*, Michael Brennan *(Engineer)*, Allan Jeayes *(Prison Officer)*, Hattie Jacques *(Singer)*, Duncan Lamont, Anthony Oliver.

A bleak drama about an angry, alcoholic seaman who leaves his pregnant wife and two children and returns home 14 years later. He's just as drunk as ever, gets thrown out of his house, slits the throat of a former fellow worker, and winds up in jail. His wife pays him a visit and shows him the teenage child he had never met. An early film of Burton's.

p, Paul Soskin; d, Michael Anderson; w, John Brophy, Soskin (based on the novel *Waterfront* by Brophy); ph, Harry Waxman; ed, Michael Charlton; md, Muir Mathieson; set d, Alex Vetchinsky.

Drama (PR:A MPAA:NR)

WATERHOLE NO. 3*** (1967) 95m Blake Edwards-Geoffrey/PAR c

James Coburn *(Lewton Cole)*, Carroll O'Connor *(Sheriff John Copperud)*, Margaret Blye *(Billee Copperud)*, Claude Akins *(Sgt. Henry Foggers)*, Timothy Carey *(Hilb)*, Bruce Dern *(Deputy)*, Joan Blondell *(Lavinia)*, James Whitmore *(Capt. Shipley)*, Harry Davis *(Ben Agajanian)*, Roy Jenson *(Doc Quinlen)*, Robert Cornthwaite *(George, Hotel Clerk)*, Jim Boles *(Cpl. Blyth)*, Stephen Whittaker, Ted Markland *(Soldiers)*, Rupert Crosse *(Prince)*, Jay Ose *(Bartender)*, Buzz Henry *(Cowpoke)*.

Blake Edwards was the *eminence grise* behind this farcical oater and it might have been better if he had come forth and taken an active role, rather than just overseeing matters. Some good laughs, adult dialog, and a passel of action in an attempt to capture the same audience which flocked to see CAT BALLOU. It's 1888 or so and Akins, a renegade cavalry sergeant, robs a fortune in gold from his Army post. His chief aide in this is scowling Carey and they are also toting a reluctant hostage, Davis. The bullion is interred in a waterhole in the midst of a vast desert and duly marked on a map. Later, Coburn arrives on the scene. He's the hero, but just barely, as he doesn't mind cheating and killing to get what he wants, and he wants that map. He kills to get it, then makes his way to the small town of Integrity, Arizona (an inside joke, no doubt), where he steals a horse, after locking up O'Connor, the sheriff, in his own jail. Then Coburn stops long enough to make love to O'Connor's comely daughter, Blye, and rides away to find the gold. Blye is incensed that she gave in so easily to Coburn and now the bounder has tossed her aside. So instead of telling the truth (that she allowed herself to be made love to), she screams that she has been forcibly raped and joins O'Connor in the chase to bring Coburn to justice. Coburn finds the gold in the waterhole just as O'Connor and Blye catch up to him. The two men explore the idea of halving the gold and it looks as though that might transpire until Akins shows up and takes the glittering yellow metal away from both of them. Coburn returns to the town of Integrity and finds Akins and his compatriots having a marvelous time at the brothel owned by Blondell. She's a breezy bordello boss who makes sure that her clients get the best service in her place of business. Coburn wants to have that gold and he and O'Connor join forces to have a shootout with Akins and his men. In the ensuing fracas, Blondell talks Davis into grabbing the gold and putting it safely into the ground at a location far from the small town. Blye learns where the gold is and arrives there moments before Coburn. Once they are together, he works with considerable charm on the gorgeous young woman, gets her to remove her clothes, then he takes the gold and rides away with her clothes and the fortune. She screams like a banshee as the picture ends and Coburn makes his way to Mexico where he fully intends to spend all of his money getting drunk and drunker. The major problem with this comedy is that it takes too long to get started and audiences spend the first 20 minutes wondering if it is for real or for fun. And when people can't tell if it's a comedy or not, it's not. After years in the TV world ("Batman," etc.) director Graham took his plunge into movies and the result was hit and miss, with a few more misses than hits. Shot in the Mojave Desert in California, it could have used about 10 minutes less time on screen and about 20 more good jokes to put it into the CAT BALLOU or BUTCH CASSIDY AND THE SUNDANCE KID category. Davis, who was so superb in Elia Kazan's AMERICA, AMERICA, has appeared in many movies but never repeated his success in the aforementioned. Good secondary work from Dern, Markland (who was also a stand-up comedian at the time), Whitmore (in a stereotypical role as an officer), and Crosse. The cowpoke was Buzz Henry, who starred in many films before he was a teenager as "Buzzy" Henry. In later years, he became a stunt coordinator. The bartender was played by Jay Ose, one of the best sleight-of-hand magicians in history and a man who was one of the founding members of Hollywood's "Magic Castle" before his untimely death.

p, Joseph T. Steck; d, William Graham; w, Steck, Robert R. Young; ph, Robert Burks (Techniscope, Technicolor); m, Dave Grusin; ed, Warren Low; art d, Fernando Carrere; set d, Reg Allen, Jack Stevens; cos, Jack Bear; spec eff, Paul K. Lerpae; m/l, "The Code of the West," Grusin, Robert Wells (sung by Roger Miller); makeup, Emile Lavigne.

Western/Comedy Cas. (PR:C MPAA:NR)

WATERLOO** (1970, Ital./USSR) 123m DD-Mosfilm/PAR c

Rod Steiger *(Napoleon Bonaparte)*, Orson Welles *(Louis XVIII)*, Virginia McKenna *(Duchess of Richmond)*, Michael Wilding *(Sir William Ponsonby)*, Donal Donnelly *(Pvt. O'Connor)*, Christopher Plummer *(Duke of Wellington)*, Jack Hawkins *(Gen. Thomas Picton)*, Dan O'Herlihy *(Marshal Michel Ney)*, Terence Alexander *(Lord Uxbridge)*, Rupert Davies *(Lord Gordon)*, Ivo Garrani *(Marshal Soult)*, Gianni Garko *(Gen. Drouot)*, Eughenj Samoilov *(Vicomte Pierre Cambronne)*, Ian Ogilvy *(William De Lancey)*, Sergei Zakhariadze *(Marshal Gebhard Blucher)*, Philippe Forquet *(Le Bedoyere)*, Andrea Checchi *(Sauret)*, Irina Skobzeva *(Maria)*, John Savident *(Gen. Muffling)*, Susan Wood *(Sarah)*, Peter Davies *(Lord Richard Hay)*, Oleg Vidov *(Tomlinson)*, Charles Millot *(Marquis Grouchy)*, Vladimir Druzhnikov *(Gerard)*, Andre Esterhazy *(Duke of Richmond)*, Orazio Orlando *(Constant)*, Jeffrey Wickham *(Sir John Colborne)*, Willoughby Gray *(Capt. Ramsay)*, Adrian Brine *(Capt. Normyle)*, Roger Green *(Duncan)*, Karl Liepinsc *(Gen. August Gneisenau)*, Richard Heffer *(Capt. Mercer)*, Colin Watson *(McKevitt)*, Charles Borromel *(Mulholland)*, Franco Fantasia *(Delessart)*, Giorgio Sciolette *(Marshal Berthier)*, Jean Louis *(Oudinot)*, Vasili Livanov *(Percy)*, Victor Murganov *(Somerset)*, Veronica De Laurentiis *(Madeleine Hall)*, Rodolfo Lodi *(Joseph Fouche)*, Giuliano Raffaelli *(McDonald)*, Filippo Perego *(Saint-Cyr)*, Valentin A. Koval *(MacMahon)*, Boris Molcianov *(Gen. Bertrand)*, Attilio Severini *(Boudin)*, Massimo Dello Torre *(Cambaceres)*, Ghennadj Judin *(Chactas)*, Andrei Jurenev *(Corporal)*, Aldo Cecconi *(Charles X)*, Vasili Plaksin *(Maitland)*, Valentino Skulme *(Tamburo Maggione)*, Camillo A. Rota *(De Vitrolles)*, Fred Jackson *(Prince of Brunswick)*, Rotislav Jankowski *(Flahaut)*, Oleg Machajlov *(Green)*, Lev Poliakov *(Kellerman)*, Christian Janakiev *(Larrey)*, Armando Bottin *(Legros)*, Gheorghy B. Rybakov *(Taylor)*, Vaslav Bledis *(Colson)*, Sergei Testori *(Marbot)*, Antonio Anelli *(Molien)*, Franco Ceccarelli *(Rumigus)*, Felix Eynas *(Patsy)*, Guglielmo Ambrosi *(1st Sergeant)*, William Slater *(2nd Sergeant)*, Alan Elledge *(3rd Sergeant)*, Volodia Levcenko *(Drummer)*, Alexander Paromenko *(Wounded Officer)*, Guidarino Guidi *(Fat Man)*, Valerij Gurjev *(Fainting Soldier)*, Paul Butkevic *(Officer with Wellington)*, Igor Jasulovic *(Officer of the 13th Square)*, Isabella Albonica *(Lady Webster)*, Andrea Dosne *(Lady of the Court)*, Ivan Milanov *(Soldier with Ney)*, Vladimir Butenko *(Lancer with Napoleonic Hat)*, Rino Bellini *(Coulincourt)*.

Rod Steiger adds his name to the distinguished list of actors who played Napoleon Bonaparte, but this performance is not nearly as good as many of the others. Rather, it is a method actor's way of showing the innards of the complex Corsican, and the result is a lot of strutting, fretting, and sweating but no indication as to what's going on inside the Little Corporal's fevered brow. Filmed on location in the Ukraine and Italy, with interiors done at Cinecitta Studios in Rome, it travels familiar ground that has been seen too many times before. Steiger is under heavy pressure to leave his throne as the French monarch. Every other king and queen in Europe fears his power hunger and he finally agrees to step down. In a touching goodbye to his men, Steiger indicates a smidgen of how the man felt, then goes off to that island that occasioned the most famous of all palindromes...."Able was I ere I saw Elba." That exile doesn't last long and soon Welles (as Louis XVIII in what must have been, at most, a two-day cameo) and his court learn that Steiger had fled the small island and is already at work gathering some of his loyal men in an attempt to take control once more. O'Herlihy, who was at one time an ally of Steiger's, promises to catch the man and bring him back. When O'Herlihy and his men face Steiger and his men, the former's troops refuse to let their rifles go at their beloved commander. O'Herlihy sees the power of Steiger's presence, tosses his saber to the ground, and joins his former chief. United, the troops arrive in Paris and occupy the city without a shot fired or a sword wielded. Welles gets away and Steiger takes over his former position as emperor, a fact that does not escape the eagle eyes of the leaders of Russia, England, Austria, and Prussia, all of whom fear Steiger. They decide that this man must be stopped at once so they unite in the battle. Plummer (as Wellington) leads his men to a meeting on the Belgian plains with Zakhariadze (as the Prussian marshal, Blucher) and his regiments. Steiger is on to their unification and launches an attack on Zakhariadze's men after first driving a wedge into Plummer's forces. The Prussians fall back immediately and race toward Waterloo but O'Herlihy, leading the wing of Steiger's troops, doesn't go after them. Plummer is at Waterloo and reckons he has to stay there and not retreat another foot. The weather has been wet, thus causing Steiger's cannons to be mired in the mud, so he plans to wait until the earth dries out. Steiger is not well and must command his men from the rear, so he is depending on information from couriers that is less than accurate. Time passes and the morning of June 18, 1815, dawns. By that day, all of the Prussians have made it back to Waterloo and they represent a much larger force than Steiger had expected. The French march in and are decimated by the combined troops of Plummer and Zakhariadze. After the battle is over and Steiger has been defeated, Plummer rides through the field and his nose crinkles as he smells the stench of death and ruminates that losing a battle is just slightly worse than winning one. The director, Bondarchuk, was the same man responsible for the most expensive picture ever shot, the Russian version of WAR AND PEACE. Since the government was footing the bill on that film, he spent what might have been $100 million. On WATERLOO the Russians put up half the money and Bondarchuk had to be content with losing as much as $40 million (nobody will own up to the real cost but it looks like that on screen). The technical advisor, Willoughby Gray, is one of those people who lives for minutiae and his own grandfather fought on the British side and left behind copious notes. Paramount distributed the picture in the U.S. but Columbia sent it out to other parts of the world, except for the Iron Curtain countries, which were handled by Mosfilm. Steiger was the main thorn in this movie and failed to convince in the role. His rotund face under the tri-cornered hat made him look more like comedian Shecky Greene doing his impression of Hugh Herbert. And his acting was in fits and starts, something that caused Steiger and Bondarchuk to have off-screen battles that made the Waterloo sequence look like patty-cake. When Steiger is good, he is an Oscar winner. When he is bad, he is aromatic as a week-old ham. While the battle scenes employed thousands, there was something basically wrong with all the chaos as it was not easy to discern who was killing whom, although that may have been deliberate on the part of Bondarchuk in an attempt to say "War is hell" and everyone dies. Other men who played Napoleon include Marlon Brando (DESIREE), Herbert Lom (King Vidor's WAR AND PEACE), Vladislav Strzhelchik (Bondarchuk's WAR AND PEACE), Charles Boyer (CONQUEST), Jean-Louis Barrault (MLLE. DESIREE), and Albert Dieudonne (Abel Gance's NAPOLEON). Steiger, it is alleged, wanted the name of the movie changed to "Napoleon" so there was no mistaking who was the star. For all the money lavished on the huge battle scenes, it seemed pound-foolish to use rear-screen projections in other sequences because they appeared to be so obviously that. The movie was far longer in the Russian version (each country had the right to edit it the way it liked) and the scenes clipped from the U.S. release print might have helped explain some of the erratic behavior from the actors. It was a monstrous bomb at the box office and deserved a better fate, if only for the spectacle.

p, Dino De Laurentiis; d, Sergei Bondarchuk; w, H.A.L. Craig, Bondarchuk, Vittorio Bonicelli; ph, Armando Nannuzzi (Panavision, Technicolor); m, Nino Rota; ed, E.V. Michajlova; prod d, Mario Garbuglia; md, Rota; art d, Ferdinando Giovannoni; set d, Emilio D'Andria, Kenneth Muggleston; cos, Maria De Matteis, Ugo Pericoli; spec eff, V.A. Likhachov; ch, Gino Landi; makeup, Alberto De Rossi; military consultant, Willoughby Gray.

Historical Drama **Cas.** **(PR:C MPAA:G)**

WATERLOO BRIDGE*½** (1931) 72m UNIV bw

Mae Clarke *(Myra)*, Kent Douglas 'Douglass Montgomery' *(Roy)*, Doris Lloyd *(Kitty)*, Ethel Griffies *(Mrs. Hoble)*, Enid Bennett *(Mrs. Wetherby)*, Frederick Kerr *(Mr. Wetherby)*, Bette Davis *(Janet)*, Rita Carlisle *(Old Woman)*, Billy Bevan.

A sensitive and haunting drama, directed with sympathy for the tawdry subject, features Clarke as a London chorus girl who loses her job at the onset of WW I. Desperation forces her into prostitution. When air raids hit the city, Clarke takes cover under the Waterloo Bridge. There she meets Douglas, a Canadian soldier whose furlough has put him in London at the time of the bombing. Douglas falls in love, not realizing Clarke is a streetwalker, and proposes to her shortly before he is sent off to the war. Clarke returns his affection and without revealing her past, accepts Douglas' offer. On the weekend before Douglas leaves, the couple goes to his family home in the country. They are met by his uncle Kerr, widowed mother Bennett, and Douglas' sister, Davis. Kerr is a former army man himself who has now retired from the service. Davis, a simple and contented young woman, is delighted to meet her brother's fiancee, but Clarke is torn by conflicting emotions. When Douglas goes back to join his fellow soldiers, Clarke has a heart-to-heart conversation with Bennett, confessing about her streetwalking days. Clarke goes back to London, where she takes to the streets once again. During another air raid, Clarke once more finds herself near Waterloo Bridge. This time she does not take cover, and is killed in the bombing. Whale handles this delicate material with compassion. His first film for Universal (he was to follow it three months later with FRANKENSTEIN), Whale fills the story with small moments, letting the drama flow naturally and letting its own inherent emotions build to the tragic ending. The director's background was rooted in theater, but with WATERLOO BRIDGE Whale shows his growing command of the film medium. His camera movements, unlike those in other films of the era, are numerous and fluid, making some interesting use of overhead shots as well. Whale also makes some forays into the use of off-screen sound which, while now commonplace, was considered revolutionary in 1931. Clarke is marvelous in the lead role, creating a sympathetic character whose situations drive her to desperate measures. Some parts of the story walk that fine line between good drama and soap opera, and her performance gives the script's intelligent aspects the needed edge. Clarke, a contract player at Universal who was given a chance by Whale with this picture, admired the director and his working methods. "He wouldn't say *how* to do it, he would tell you *what* was happening," she later recalled. Sherwood, whose original play served as a basis for the story, was highly impressed with her performance, and autographed a photograph for the actress with the inscription: "For Mae Clarke–who did right by WATERLOO BRIDGE." Davis, in her last film for Universal before going to Warner Bros., reportedly cared little for Whale or his working methods, unaware of the director's theatrical background. Though her role is minor, Davis gives a good performance that shows the promise of what was to come. In the book *Mother Goddam* by Whitney Stine, Davis commented that she "yearned all during (the) shooting of the film to play Myra. I *could* have!" The production took a brief 26 days to film, and Whale brought the film in under budget, knocking off $25,000 from the original $252,000 spending projection. For many years WATERLOO BRIDGE was unavailable for screening, and it appeared the film had been lost forever. After 40 years, a print of the missing work was found (in 1977), hidden amidst the wealth of material stored in the MGM vaults. Remade twice, first in 1940 with Vivien Leigh and Robert Taylor, then in 1956 (under the title GABY) with Leslie Caron and John Kerr.

p, Carl Laemmle, Jr.; d, James Whale; w, Benn W. Levy, Tom Reed (based on the play by Robert E. Sherwood); ph, Arthur Edeson; ed, Whale; art d, Charles D. Hall; makeup, Jack P. Pierce.

Drama **(PR:C MPAA:NR**

WATERLOO BRIDGE**** (1940) 103m MGM bw

Vivien Leigh *(Myra Lester)*, Robert Taylor *(Capt. Roy Cronin)*, Lucile Watson *(Lady Margaret Cronin)*, C. Aubrey Smith *(Duke)*, Maria Ouspenskaya *(Mme. Olga)*, Virginia Field *(Kitty)*, Leo G. Carroll *(Policeman)*, Clara Reid *(Mrs. Bassett)*, Steffi Duna *(Lydia)*, Leonard Mudie *(Parker)*, Herbert Evans *(Commissionaire)*, Halliwell Hobbes *(Vicar)*, Ethel Griffies *(Mrs. Clark)*, Gilbert Emery *(Colonel)*, David Clyde *(Barnes the Butler)*, Janet Shaw *(Maureen)*, Virginia Carroll *(Sylvia)*, Florence Baker *(Beatrice)*, Elsie Prescott *(Cockney Woman)*, Bob Winkler *(Boy)*, Norma Varden *(Hostess)*, Fred Sasbsoni *(Newsboy)*, Kathryn Collier *(Barmaid)*, Dennis d'Auburn *(Generous Man)*, Wilfred Lucas *(Elderly Huntsman)*, Janet Waldo *(Elsa)*, Leda Nicova *(Marie)*, Marjorie Manning *(Mary)*, Frances MacInerney *(Violet)*, Eleanore Stewart *(Grace)*, Janet Shea, Jimmy Aubrey, Leonard Mudie.

In London during WW II, a British colonel, Taylor, is caught in a blackout in his chauffeured army sedan. His passage to Waterloo Station–and, eventually, to combat in France–thus interrupted, Taylor steps from the vehicle to tread the pavement of the famed Waterloo Bridge (rebuilt following its destruction during WW I.) As he paces, the middle-aged officer fondles a tiny figurine, reminiscing about days long past. In flashback, Taylor is on the old Waterloo Bridge of 1917, now a handsome young captain in the regiment commanded by his uncle, Smith. As an air-raid siren shrieks, a group of attractive, vivacious women passes; one of them, Leigh, inadvertently drops her purse, spilling its contents on the pavement. The gallant young captain helps the girl, Leigh, pick up her scattered belongings and then accompanies her to an air-raid shelter, where she reveals her background and her aspirations to him. The Birmingham-born young woman is a dancer in an internationally known ballet troupe headed by Ouspenskaya. The smitten soldier attends the ballet that same evening, where his longing for Leigh is heightened by her performance in "Swan Lake." He invites her to join him for a late snack, and over supper they confess their mutual adoration, so strong though so sudden. Leigh accepts Taylor's proposal of marriage, a proposal that proves to conflict with military regulations. Taylor importunes his uncle, Smith–a peer of the realm as well as his commanding officer–to bend the rules and permit him to wed, and Smith–despite some reservations–agrees. Before the nuptials can take place, the regiment is called to the front. Leigh abandons her performance to bid her lover a solemn-visaged farewell at Waterloo Station–a true theatrical transgression–and is fired from the ballet company. Leigh's loyal friend and roommate, Field, quits the company in support, and the two ballerinas seek alternative employment. They descend into poverty; desperate, Field becomes a prostitute. Attempting to sustain her hopes, Leigh continues her association with Taylor's wealthy family. Joining Taylor's mother Watson for tea at a restaurant, Leigh spots a casualty list bearing her fiance's name. Leigh valiantly conceals her grief from the dead-presumably–officer's mother. Despondent and destitute, Leigh joins her friend Field's profession, plying her trade on the Waterloo Bridge (historically, the bridge *was* a hooker haven during wartime, the streetwalkers soliciting soldiers funneling into London via the overpath after disentraining). On the bridge, months later, seeking a client, she meets the returning Taylor– who had spent the intervening time as a prisoner of war–and, thinking fast, conceals her profession during the shocking reunion. Their romance continues; it appears that her degradation was no more than a nightmare, best forgotten. She and Taylor travel to the country estate of his mother, Watson. Slowly, Leigh begins to realize that her indiscretions will come to light one day, besmirching the aristocratic name of her fiance and his family. Leigh recounts her recent history to Watson, imploring the latter to keep it a secret, and departs. Taylor searches for her, but in vain; he finds only the crushed body of his suicidal enamorata, her life lost under the tires of a truck at the Waterloo Bridge. The film flashes forward as the older Taylor– the blackout ended–leaves to rejoin his regiment during another world war. Leigh is stunning in this second cinematic version of author Sherwood's hit play. WATERLOO BRIDGE was Leigh's first movie following the record-breaking David Selznick production of GONE WITH THE

WIND, which had made her the most visible, most desirable actress in the world. Selznick had loaned Leigh's services to MGM for the picture in repayment for help that studio's head had given him for the previous picture. Leigh was in the midst of a divorce from her husband Leigh Holman at the time, her romance with Laurence Olivier–also wed at the time–a continuing scandal. She and Olivier had both invested every farthing they had in their planned theatrical production–in which they were both to star–William Shakespeare's "Romeo and Juliet," and both were desperately in need of money. Olivier accepted the male lead in PRIDE AND PREJUDICE, and the lovers were forced to separate temporarily. Leigh was irate about the parting, believing that Olivier should have gotten the role assigned to Taylor. In a letter, she wrote, "...it was written for Larry 'Olivier', it's a typical piece of miscasting. .." Taylor drew kudos for his mature, restrained performance, which revitalized his then-fading career by demonstrating that he was more than just another pretty face, although critics were none too tolerant of his "Nebraska accent." Of all his seventy-plus screen performances, this was Taylor's personal favorite. WATERLOO BRIDGE had been filmed in 1931, starring Mae Clarke and Kent Douglass 'Douglass Montgomery', and was to be filmed again in 1956 as GABY, a disappointing version starring Leslie Caron and John Kerr.

p, Sidney Franklin; d, Mervyn LeRoy; w, S.N. Behrman, Hans Rameau, George Froeschel (based on the play by Robert E. Sherwood); ph, Joseph Ruttenberg; m, Herbert Stothart; ed, George Boemler; art d, Cedric Gibbons, Urie McCleary; set d, Edwin B. Willis; cos, Adrian, Gile Steele; ch, Ernst Matray.

Drama   (PR:C   MPAA:NR)

WATERLOO ROAD**   (1949, Brit.) 77m Gainsborough/GFD-EL bw

John Mills (*Jim Colter*), Stewart Granger (*Ted Purvis*), Alastair Sim (*Dr. Montgomery*), Joy Shelton (*Tillie Colter*), Beatrice Varley (*Mrs. Colter*), Alison Leggatt (*Ruby*), Leslie Bradley (*Mike Duggan*), Jean Kent (*Toni*), George Carney (*Tom Mason*), Wylie Watson (*Tattooist*), Arthur Denton (*Fred*), Vera Frances (*Vera Colter*), Ben Williams (*Cpl. Lewis*), Anna Konstam (*May*), Wallace Lupino (*Uncle*), Dennis Harkin, Johnnie Schofield, Frank Atkinson, Mike Johnson, Dave Crowley, John Boxer, George Merritt, Amy Dalby, Nellie Bowman.

The war separates Mills from his wife, Shelton, who stays with Mills' mother and sister. When she becomes involved with Granger, a spineless cheat who used fake medical papers to stay out of the service, Mills gets word and goes AWOL. After getting beaten into the ground by Granger's friends, he turns around and does the same to Granger, winning back his wife. The final fight sequence is terrific as bombs drop during an air raid while the two men slug it out.

p, Edward Black; d, Sidney Gilliat; w, Val Valentine (based on a story by Gilliat); ph, Arthur Crabtree, Phil Grindrod; m, Bob Busby; ed, Alfred Roome; md, Louis Levy; art d, Alex Vetchinsky.

Drama   (PR:A   MPAA:NR)

WATERMELON MAN½**   (1970) 97m Johanna/COL c

Godfrey Cambridge (*Jeff Gerber*), Estelle Parsons (*Althea Gerber*), Howard Caine (*Mr. Townsend*), D'Urville Martin (*Bus Driver*), Mantan Moreland (*Counterman*), Kay Kimberly (*Erica*), Kay E. Kuter (*Dr. Wainwright*), Scott Garrett (*Burton Gerber*), Erin Moran (*Janice Gerber*), Irving Selbst (*Mr. Johnson*), Emil Sitka (*Delivery Man*), Lawrence Parke (*1st Passenger*), Robert Dagny (*2nd Passenger*), Ray Ballard (*3rd Passenger*), Karl Lukas (*2nd Policeman*), Paul H. Williams (*Employment Office Clerk*), Ralph Montgomery (*Drugstore Boss*), Charles Lampkin (*Dr. Catlin*), Vivian Rhodes (*Gladys*), Erik Nelson (*Doorman*), Matthias Uitz (*Cab Driver*), Rhodie Cogan (*Mrs. Johnson*), Donna Dubrow (*Receptionist*), Frank Farmer (*Andy Brandon*), Hazel Medina (*Widow*).

An often funny film that fails to sustain the premise over the length of the entire movie and may have been better suited as a "Saturday Night Live"-type sketch. Cambridge is hilarious in his role but many of the gags are cliched, uninspired, and just what one might have expected from the situation. And comedy, in order to work, must have surprise. Cambridge is a bigoted white insurance agent married to Parsons and father of Garrett and Moran. (The white makeup applied to Cambridge's very brown face was not convincing and he looked like a minstrel man as seen on a negative print.) The family's life is a placid one with all the usual suburban problems, none of which can compare to what is about to happen to Cambridge. One morning he wakes up to find that, due to some bizarre inner occurrence in his body, he is now totally and irrefutably a black man! At first, he thinks he might have remained under his sun lamp for too long, then he frantically attempts to wash off the pigment with hot showers, skin lighteners, milk baths, anything to cleanse the color away. It's all to no avail and he suddenly feels how it is to be the butt of bigotry. He goes to see his physician, Kuter, who suggests that he might feel more comfortable consulting a black doctor instead. His neighbors take up a collection in order to get him to leave the area, fearful that his presence will drive real estate prices down and cause an influx of other blacks to parade in. Caine is Cambridge's boss at the insurance agency and he can't believe his eyes when the new black walks in so he consults his optometrist to see if something has gone awry with his contact lenses. Later, when Caine realizes what's happened, he comes up

with the thought that perhaps Cambridge could be used to tap the lucrative black insurance market. Cambridge is accepted by bus driver Martin and counterman Moreland (appearing in what was reputed to be his 310th film) as one of them and feels slightly better that *someone* has accepted him. His curvy Norwegian secretary, Kimberly, who never had anything beyond a perfunctory boss-steno relationship with him, is suddenly attracted to him and Cambridge sees that this reverse bigotry is just as distasteful as the obvious bias he's encountered. At the conclusion, after Parsons has taken the children and moved to her mother's home in Indiana, Cambridge decides he can't fight it so he'll accept himself. He moves into a black neighborhood, tosses aside his conservative togs, opens an insurance agency of his own, and registers to join a self- defense unit for blacks. WATERMELON MAN has problems in balancing the themes because it plays hard for laughs, then spends about half the time going for the emotional jugular and making salient points about racial prejudice. The combination of the two is oil and water and the film feels awkward and whatever impact was intended is dispelled. This marked Van Peebles' debut as a major studio director and it was also one of the first films done by a black director in the modern era. Van Peebles later did SWEET SWEETBACK'S BAADASSSSS SONG with the money he made from this one. Cambridge was a gifted comedian who showed that he could act in this film as well as in several others, such as COTTON COMES TO HARLEM, COME BACK, CHARLESTON BLUE, and SCOTT JOPLIN, which was released after his death in 1976, at the age of 43. The candid language and a few questionable scenes mark this as a no-no for kids. Without them, it might have been good family fare and made a point with youngsters about the color of a person's skin having nothing to do with the quality of the human being.

p, John B. Bennett; d, Melvin Van Peebles; w, Herman Raucher; ph, W. Wallace Kelley (Eastmancolor); m, Van Peebles; ed, Carl Kress; art d, Malcolm C. Bert, Sydney Z. Litwack; set d, John Burton; makeup, Ben Lane.

Comedy   **Cas.**   (PR:C   MPAA:R)

WATERSHIP DOWN***   (1978, Brit.) 92m Nepenthe/AE c

Voices of: John Hurt (*Hazel*), Richard Briers (*Fiver*), Michael Graham-Cox (*Bigwig*), John Bennett (*Capt. Holly*), Simon Cadell (*Blackberry*), Roy Kinnear (*Pipkin*), Richard O'Callaghan (*Dandelion*), Terence Rigby (*Silver*), Sir Ralph Richardson (*Chief Rabbit*), Denholm Elliott (*Cowslip*), Zero Mostel (*Kehaar*), Mary Maddox (*Clover*), Hannah Gordon (*Hyzenthlay*), Lyn Farleigh (*Cat*), Harry Andrews (*Gen. Woundwort*), Nigel Hawthorne (*Campion*), Clifton Jones (*Blackavar*), Joss Ackland (*Black Rabbit*), Michael Hordern (*Narrator*).

Expertly and realistically animated, this version of the popular novel doesn't seem to have an audience. It's much too violent and bloody for kids (who won't be too fond of seeing little rabbits with blood gushing from their furry little bodies), and it's not the type of picture that an adult would go out and see, in part because it is animated. The spirit of the book is captured here as the rabbits, faced with problems of ecology, are forced to find a new home. Their trek is filled with surprises and adventures, as well as bloodshed. The job of personifying the rabbits is nicely achieved due to expert readings by the cast.

p,d&w, Martin Rosen (based on the novel by Richard Adams); ph, (Technicolor); m, Angela Morley, Malcolm Williamson; ed, Terry Rawlings; animation supervisor, Philip Duncan; animation director, Tony Guy; m/l, Mike Batt.

Animated Drama   **Cas.**   (PR:C-O   MPAA:PG)

WATTS MONSTER, THE   (SEE: DR. BLACK, MR. HYDE, 1976)

WATUSI*½   (1959) 85m MGM c

George Montgomery (*Harry Quartermain*), Taina Elg (*Erica Neuler*), David Farrar (*Rick Cobb*), Rex Igram (*Umbopa*), Dan Seymour (*Mohamet*), Robert Goodwin (*Jim-Jim*), Anthony M. Davis (*Amtaga*), Paul Thompson (*Gagool*), Harold Dyrenforth (*Wilhelm von Kentner*).

Using leftover footage from 1950's KING SOLOMON'S MINES, this picture, weak in comparison, stars Montgomery in the role vacated by Stewart Granger. Set in 1919, Montgomery leads an expedition into the Dark Continent in search of the legendary mines, eventually locating chests overflowing with diamonds and jewels. The hard part is staying alive, something they don't all do. Kurt Neumann, the director of countless B movies and in 1958 the science fiction classic THE FLY, died before this picture was released, ending a 30-year career. Scripted by James Clavell, who authored the blockbuster novel *SHOGUN*. Watusi tribesmen are in reality UCLA basketball players.

p, Al Zimbalist; d, Kurt Neumann; w, James Clavell (based on the novel *Return To King Solomon's Mines* by H. Rider Haggard); ph, Harold E, Wellman (Technicolor); ed, William B. Gulick; art d, William A. Horning, Malcolm Brown.

Adventure   (PR:A   MPAA:NR)

WATUSI A GO-GO (SEE: GET YOURSELF A COLLEGE GIRL, 1964)

WAVE, A WAC AND A MARINE, A*½
                                    (1944) 70m Sabastian Cristillo MON bw

Elyse Knox (*Marian*), Sally Eilers (*Margaret Ames*), Ramsay Ames (*Betty*),

Ann Gillis (*Judy*), Alan Dinehart (*Producer R.J.*), Marjorie Woodworth (*Eileen*), Henny Youngman (*Henny*), Charles ""Red" Marshall (*Red*), Connie Haines (*Singer*), Richard Lane (*Marty Allen*), Cy Kendall (*Mike*), Aileen Pringle (*Newswoman*), Freddie Rich and Orchestra, The Music Maids. Broadway talent agent Youngman — in his feature-film debut-makes a big slip-up when he signs the wrong ladies for the cast of a show: he mistakes understudies Knox and Gillis for the legitimate actresses, Ames and Woodworth. But everything turns out fine when the two understudies have enough talent to attract the interest of a Hollywood studio. Although not billed as such, this was Lou Costello's executive producing debut: Sebastian Cristillo is his father's name. Songs include: ""Time Will Tell," "" Gee, I Love My G.I. Guy," and ""Carry On" (Eddie Cherkose, Jacques Press, Freddie Rich).

p, Edward Sherman; exec p, Sebastian Cristillo; d, Phil Karlstein òKarlsonÖ; w, Hal Fimberg (based on the story by Lillian Planer, Dick Hyland); ph, Maury Gertsman; m, Freddie Rich; ed, William Austin; md, Rich; m/l, Rich, Eddie Cherkose.

Comedy   **(PR:A MPAA:NR)**

WAVELENGTH**   (1983) 88m New World c

Robert Carradine (*Bobby Sinclaire*), Cherie Currie (*Iris Longacre*), Keenan Wynn (*Dan*), Cal Bowman (*Gen. Milton Ward*), James Hess (*Col. James MacGruder*), Terry Burns (*Capt. Hinsdale*), Eric Morris (*Dr. Vernon Cottrell*), Bob McLean (*Dr. Benjamin Stern*), Eric Heath (*Dr. Sidey*), Robert Glaudini (*Dr. Wolf*), George O. Petrie (*Dr. Savianno*), George Skaff (*Gen. Hunt*), Milt Kogan (*Pathologist*), Dov Young (*Gamma*), Joshua Oreck (*Beta*), Christina Morris (*Delta*), Jim Elk (*Fleming*), Ivan Naranjo (*Warren*), Alan Koss (*Military Attache*), Brooke Hudson (*Undercover Cop*), Kent Butler (*Young Lieutenant*).

A science-fiction tale which has some promise but is held back by some especially uninteresting performances and cliched dialog. Carradine, a drippy Warren Beatty look-alike, meets dumb blonde Currie, who has a special sense and can hear things others cannot. The pair venture into an airshaft which is on the property of a U.S. air base where military advisors and scientists are performing an autopsy on an alien creature while three others are stored in frozen containers. It turns out that Currie is able to communicate telepathically with the little fellows–actually three naked young boys. Some military and governmental mumbo-jumbo leads to panic and mysterious deaths which the aliens are responsible for. All they want is sunlight and their freedom, so Currie and Carradine help them escape. The search is on but since the pair look a little conspicuous with three naked boys they gather up some clothes because, as Carradine puts it, "We can't run around with three naked kids, not even in Hollywood." They make it to the desert and, before the military can attack, the aliens get away in some sort of spaceship-glowing orb. The film's saving grace is a sense of morality in its depiction of aliens, but Carradine's struggling California musician scenes are pitiful, as is the sensitive and homey narration that ruins the beginning and end. Wynn's performance is okay given his material, but he serves as nothing more than a mouthpiece spouting out the film's expository information. Tangerine Dream, which supplied the music for SORCERER and THIEF, adds another fine score to its filmography.

p, James Rosenfield; d&w, Mike Gray; ph, Paul Goldsmith; m, Tangerine Dream; ed, Mark Goldblatt, Robert Leighton; art d, Linda Pearl; cos, Jack Buehler; makeup, Jim Gillespie; spec eff, Mike Menzel, Joseph Wallikas.

ScienceFiction   **Cas.**   **(PR:C MPAA:PG)**

WAY AHEAD, THE**½**   (1945, Brit.) 106m TC/FOX bw (AKA: THE
                                                       IMMORTAL BATTALION)

David Niven (*Lt. Jim Perry*), Raymond Huntley (*Davenport*), Billy [William] Hartnell (*Sgt. Fletcher*), Stanley Holloway (*Brewer*), James Donald (*Lloyd*), John Laurie (*Luke*), Leslie Dwyer (*Beck*), Hugh Burden (*Parsons*), Jimmy Hanley (*Stainer*), Renee Ascherson [Asherson] (*Marjorie Gillingham*), Penelope Dudley-Ward (*Mrs. Perry*), Reginald Tate (*Commanding Officer*), Leo Genn (*Company Commander*), Mary Jerrold (*Mrs. Gillingham*), Raymond Lovell (*Garage Proprietor*), Alf Goddard (*Instructor*), A.E. Matthews (*Col. Walmsley*), Peter Ustinov (*Rispoli*), Tessie O'Shea (*Herself*), Jack Watling (*Marjorie's Boy Friend*), John Ruddock, A. Bromley Davenport, Johnnie Schofield, John Salew, Lloyd Pearson, Grace Arnold, Eileen Erskine, Esma Cannon.

In the aftermath of the Dunkirk evacuation, Niven trains a troop of soldiers who are ordinary British civilians conscripted into the service. He toughens them up over loud protests and leads them in battle against Rommel's crack troops in North Africa. An engrossing character study that is aptly handled by Reed's assured directorial skill, THE WAY AHEAD blends fiction with a documentary-like account of wartime military training. In the process, it proved to be a useful educational tool for the British army. Niven, who conceived the idea for the film after watching a short training film, was an officer in the army at the time.

p, John Sutro, Norman Walker; d, Carol Reed; w, Eric Ambler, Peter Ustinov (based on a story by Eric Ambler); ph, Guy Green; m, William Allwyn; ed, Fergus McDonell; md, Muir Mathieson; art d, David Rawnsley.

War Drama   **Cas.**   **(PR:A MPAA:NR)**

WAY BACK HOME**   (1932) 81m RKO bw (GB: OLD GREATHEART;
                                                       AKA: OTHER PEOPLE'S BUSINESS)

Phillips Lord (*Seth Parker, Preacher*), Effie L. Palmer (*Ma Parker*), Mrs. Phillips Lord (*Liz*), Bennett Kilpack (*Cephus*), Raymond Hunter (*Captain*), Frank Albertson (*David Clark*), Bette Davis (*Mary Lucy*), Oscar Apfel (*Wobblin*), Stanley Fields (*Rube Turner*), Dorothy Peterson (*Runaway Rosie*), Frankie Darro (*Robbie Turner*).

A fair piece of entertainment which has Lord taking the role of a Maine preacher who shelters Darro from the boy's alcoholic father, Fields. The preacher intends to adopt the boy but Fields takes him back only to meet a gruesome end as a train smashes into him during a chase in a railroad yard. The boy is saved and adopted by Lord. Bette Davis (working three weeks for only $900) and Frank Albertson, both unknowns at the time, were cast as young lovers, mixed up in the battle for Darro's custody. The story is based upon characters created by Lord for his popular radio show of the time.

p, Pandro S. Berman; d, William A. Seiter; w, Jane Murfin (based on the radio characters created by Phillips H. Lord); ph, J. Roy Hunt; m, Max Steiner; art d, Max Ree.

Drama   **(PR:A MPAA:NR)**

WAY DOWN EAST**   (1935) 80m FOX bw

Rochelle Hudson (*Anna Moore*), Henry Fonda (*David Bartlett*), Slim Summerville (*Constable Seth Holcomb*), Russell Simpson (*Squire Bartlett*), Spring Byington (*Mrs. Bartlett*), Edward Trevor (*Lennox Sanderson*), Margaret Hamilton (*Martha Perkins*), Sara Haden (*Cordelia Peabody*), Andy Devine (*Hi Holler*), Astrid Allwyn (*Kate*), William Benedict (*Amos*), Clem Bevans (*Doc Wiggin*), Seymour and Corncob (*Rube Comedians*), Phil La Toska (*Abner*), Al Lydell (*Hank Woolwine*), Ann Doran (*Hired Girl*), Nora Cecil (*Woman*), George B. French (*Man*), Ray Hoback (*Violinist*), Kay Hammond (*Mrs. Stackpole*), Vera Lewis (*Mrs. Poole*), Florence Gill, Lucille Ward, Brenda Fowler, claire Whitney (*Women for Quilting Party*), Louis King (*Minister*), William Borzage (*Musician*), Harry C. Bradley (*Mr. Peabody*).

A remake of the classic D. W. Griffith-Lillian Gish-Richard Barthelmess silent of 1920, WAY DOWN EAST here shows that its material is rather dated. Hudson, taking over the lead role from Janet Gaynor (reportedly involved in a car accident, but some say there was a personal conflict), stars as the poor waif who wanders around penniless after being duped into a false marriage to the wealthy Trevor and having a child by him. The baby soon dies and Hudson is taken in by a farm family headed by the puritanical Simpson, where she falls in love with his son, Fonda. Word of Hudson's spotted past eventually gets out and she is banished from the farm. While trying to cross a frozen river the ice breaks apart and she begins floating toward a waterfall. Fonda, leaping from ice floe to ice floe, saves Hudson and agrees to marry her. The final climactic scene, one of the most famous in silent cinema, still can raise one's heartbeat, but Hudson is nothing in comparison to Gish. As hokey as the film is, Fonda delivers the persona that has made him one of the screen's great actors–the film's saving grace.

p, Winfield R. Sheehan; d, Henry King; w Howard Estabrook, William Hurlbut (based on the play by Lottie Blair Parker); ph, Ernest Palmer; m, Oscar Bradley; ed, Robert Bischoff; art d, William Darling; cos, William Lambert.

Drama/Romance   **(PR:A MPAA:NR)**

WAY DOWN SOUTH*½   (1939) 62m Principal Productions/RKO bw

Bobby Breen (*Tim Reid, Jr.*), Alan Mowbray (*Jacques Bouton, Innkeeper*), Ralph Morgan (*Timothy Reid*), Clarence Muse (*Uncle Caton*), Steffi Duna (*Pauline*), Sally Blane (*Claire*), Edwin Maxwell (*Martin Dill, Lawyer*), Charles Middleton (*Cass*), Robert Greig (*Judge Ravenal*), Lillian Yarbo (*Janie*), Stymie Beard (*Gumbo*), Jack Carr (*Luke*), Marguerite Whitten (*Lulu*), The Hall Johnson Choir.

Set in pre-Civil War Louisiana, WAY DOWN SOUTH tells the melodramatic tale of a youngster who is orphaned and plans on taking control of his late father's plantation. It has since fallen into the hands of corrupt lawyer Maxwell and cruel Middleton, who mercilessly drives the slaves into the ground. The young Breen makes everything turn out hunky-dory by the finish. A rare general-release film with a major distributor co-authored by black artists. Poet Hughes and veteran black actor Muse (around whom much of the action revolves) collaborated on the screenplay. Director Vorhaus, born in Germany, was in his second year in Hollywood; he had made his mark directing early British talkies. Songs: "Good Ground," "Louisiana" (Clarence Muse, Langston Hughes), plus the Negro spirituals "Nobody Know De Trouble I Seen," "Sometimes I Feel Like a Motherless Child," "Lord If You Can't Come Send One Angel Down."

p, Sol Lesser; d, Bernard Vorhaus; w, Clarence Muse, Langston Hughes; ph, Charles Schoenbaum; ed, Arthur Hilton; md, Victor Young; art d, Lewis J. Rachmil; spec eff, Vernon L. Walker.

Musical   **(PR:A MPAA:NR)**

WAY FOR A SAILOR*   (1930) 83m MGM bw

John Gilbert (*Jack Berley*), Wallace Beery (*Tripod McMasters*), Leila Hyams (*Joan Jones*), Jim Tully (*Ginger*), Polly Moran (*Mamie*), Doris Lloyd (*Flossy*),

Lena Malena, Desmond Roberts (Bits), Pat Moriarity (Mate), Sojin (Proprietor of Shanghai House), John George (Dwarf), Leo White (Sailor), Raymond Milland (Canadian Ship's Officer).

Miscast again in his second sound feature release, Gilbert plays a scruffy British merchant sailor who, with shipmates Beery and Tully, loves the liberty and licentiousness of his seafaring life. Smitten by shipping clerk Hyams, who pays him little notice and tends to stay upwind, Gilbert finally bathes, shaves, and attires himself in a shorebound suit to pursue the courtship. After the wedding, he confesses that he lied to her about his presumed dry-land job and they separate. The disconsolate Gilbert pulls himself together and becomes a ship's officer, complete with natty uniform. The equally disconsolate Hyams, emigrating from Blighty to Canada, finds herself traveling on the same ship as the neatly accoutered officer. A shipwreck occurs, giving the principals a chance to demonstrate their courage, and love blossoms once again. The film is choppily edited and, with its multitude of collaborating screenwriters– conditions allegedly necessitated by the censor's scissors–difficult to follow. The action scenes at sea are excellent and Beery steals all his scenes. Gilbert fails to fit the type as the Liverpool Lothario with fancy ladies Moran and Lloyd in a cheap waterfront dive. His voice is fine, but the persona is wanting; drawing rooms are more his style. Comic foil Tully, better known as a writer than as an actor, is a none-too-satisfactory sailor sidekick.

d, Sam Wood; w, Laurence Stallings, W.L. River, Charles MacArthur, Al Boasberg (based on the novel Way of a Sailor by Albert Richard Wetjen); ph, Percy Hilburn; ed, Frank Sullivan; art d, Cedric Gibbons.

Romance   **(PR:A   MPAA:NR)**

WAY OF A GAUCHO½   (1952) 91m FOX c

Rory Calhoun (Martin), Gene Tierney (Teresa), Richard Boone (Salinas), Hugh Marlowe (Miguel), Everett Sloane (Falcon), Enrique Chaico (Father Fernandez), Jorge Villoldo (Valverde), Roland Dumas (Julio), Lidia Campos (Tia Maria), Hugh Mancini, Nester Yoan (Army Lieutenants), Raoul Astor (Police Lieutenant), John Paris (Foreman), Alex Peters (Driver), John Henchley (Gaucho Tracker), Kim Dillon (Sentry), Lia Centeno (Lady Guest), Claudio Torres (Florencio), Douglas Poole (Pall Bearer), Mario Abdah (Horse Dealer), Teresa Acosta, Oscar Lucero (Dancers), Anthony Ugrin.

A sharply photographed western set and filmed in Argentina amidst the Andes Mountains which greatly benefits from its picturesque quality. Calhoun is a fugitive who flees from a stint in the army, where he was sent as an alternative to serving a prison term. He and a gang of outlaws make it tough on a railroad which cuts through Argentina's pampas, causing a railroad policeman–Calhoun's former commanding officer, Boone–to give chase. For the finish Calhoun promises to straighten up his act and in return Boone lets him keep his freedom and his lady, Tierney.

p, Philip Dunne; d, Jacques Tourneur; w, Dunne (based on the novel by Herbert Childs); ph, Harry Jackson (Technicolor); m, Sol Kaplan; ed, Robert Fritch; md, Alfred Newman; art d, Lyle Wheeler, Mark-Lee Kirk; set d, Thomas Little, Bruce MacDonald; cos, Charles LeMaire.

Western   **Cas.**   **(PR:A   MPAA:NR)**

WAY OF ALL FLESH, THE*   (1940) 86m PAR bw

Akim Tamiroff (Paul Kriza, Bank Cashier), Gladys George (Anna Kriza), William Henry (Paul Kriza, Jr.), John Hartley (Victor Kriza), Marilyn Knowlden (Julie Kriza), Betty McLaughlin (Mitzi Kriza), James West (Paul Jr., as a Child), Darryl Hickman (Victor as a Child), June Heden (Julie as a Child), Norma Nelson (Mitzi as a Child), Tommy Bupp (Timothy as a Child), Muriel Angelus (Mary Brown), Berton Churchill (Reginald L. Morten), Fritz Leiber (Max), Roger Imhof (Franz Henzel), James Seay (Varno), Douglas Kennedy (Timothy), James Burke (Frisco), Torben Meyer (Sandor Nemzeti), Stanley Price (Lefty), John Harmon (Pete), Leonard Penn (Joe).

Those hoping to see a filmed version of Samuel Butler's famed semi-autobiographical novel will be very disappointed in this picture, which has nothing to do with that classic of literature. This film is a saccharine tearjerker about an honest businessman who ventures to the big city only to wind up on the skids, mistakenly believed to be dead. Many years later he returns to his country home, where his wife and family have aged but not forgotten his memory. C. B. DeMille filmed the first version silently in 1918 as THE WHISPERING CHORUS and a second silent version appeared in 1927 with Emil Jannings.

p, Eugene Zukor; d, Louis King; w, Lenore Coffee (based on a story by Lajos Biro, Jules Furthman); ph, Theodor Sparkuhl; ed, Stuart Gilmore.

Drama   **(PR:A   MPAA:NR)**

WAY OF ALL MEN, THE*½   (1930) 69m FN-WB bw (GB: SIN FLOOD)

Douglas Fairbanks, Jr (Billy Bear), Dorothy Revier (Poppy), Robert Edeson (Swift), Anders Randolf (Frazer), Ivan Simpson (Higgins), William Orlamond (Nordling), Henry Kolker (Sharp), Louis King (Levee Louie), William Courtenay (Preacher), Noah Beery, Sr (Stratton), Wade Boteler (Charlie), Dorothy Mathews (Edna), Pat Cummings (Dick), Alona Marlowe (Gwen), Eddie Clayton (Jack).

A sunken-submarine drama without the submarine. Fired by boss Randolf,

Fairbanks, Jr. allies himself with the wealthy Edeson and makes millions in the market, then goes to a basement speakeasy in New Orleans to arrange a victory party. Present at the illegal watering-hole are a variety of wealthy people, bums, and shady ladies such as Fairbanks, Jr.'s one-time love interest Revier, a former actress and now a woman of the streets. The floodwaters of the Mississippi River threaten to burst a levee and inundate the establishment, so quick-thinking proprietor Beery closes the airtight doors of the gin mill (doors installed for just such an eventuality). One of the assemblage, a down-and-outer, is a former scientist who reminds the distinguished company that all are jeopardized not only by the threat of drowning, but also ultimately by suffocation in the tightly closed confines. Another of the bums is a half-crazed former clergyman who regains his calling and urges them to make their peace with their maker. A mass confession of past remissnesses ensues as each of the merrymakers tries to outdo the other in a veritable free-for-all of terminal good will. Fairbanks, Jr., recants his rejection of Revier and prepares to die with her, finally demanding that the doors be opened to let the floodwaters take them. The doors are indeed opened, and lo, the sun is shining: the levee didn't give way after all! Played straight, but good for some laughs.

d, Frank Lloyd; w, Bradley King (based on Henning Berger's play "Sin Flood"); ed, Ray Curtiss

Drama   **(PR:A   MPAA:NR)**

WAY OF LIFE, THE   (SEE: THEY CALL IT SIN, 1932)

WAY OF LOST SOULS, THE**   (1929, Brit.) 94m Charles Whittaker/WB bw (GB: THE WOMAN HE SCORNED)

Pola Negri (Louise), Warwick Ward (Maxim), Hans Rehmann (John), Cameron Carr (Magistrate), Margaret Rawlings (Woman).

Famed silent screen vamp Negri made her British film debut in this melodrama which sees her as a prostitute longing to abandon her seedy life style and settle down. She leaves the gambler she has been supporting and marries a lighthouse keeper in Cornwall. Her idyllic existence is shattered, however, when the gambler becomes a fugitive and seeks asylum in the lighthouse. Negri hides her former lover, but the gambler is killed despite her efforts. When Negri's husband learns the truth, he leaves her. Rejected and alone, Negri drowns herself. Originally filmed silent, THE WAY OF LOST SOULS was pulled from distribution, sound was added, and the film was re-released. Unfortunately for Negri, sound was to herald the decline of her career. Hampered by a thick Polish accent, studios stopped casting her, forcing the former Hollywood sex queen to return to Germany during WW II where she made a few more films before retiring.

p, Charles Whittaker; d, Paul Czinner; w, Whittaker.

Drama   **(PR:C   MPAA:NR)**

WAY OF THE WEST, THE*½   (1934) 51m Empire/Superior bw

Wally Wales, Marla Bratton, Bobby Nelson, William Desmond, Fred Parker, Sherry Tansey, Art Mix, Bill Patton, Tex Jones, Harry Beery, Helen Gibson, Tiny Skelton, Gene Raymond, Jimmy Aubrey.

Yet another tedious western adventure which sees the ever-put-upon cattle ranchers forced to wage a fierce little war against those pesky sheepherders whose livestock nibble away all the good grazing land. A classic western feud premise with, unfortunately, an ordinary presentation.

p&d, Robert Emmett [Tansey]; w, Al Lane (based on a story by Barry Barringer).

Western   **(PR:A   MPAA:NR)**

WAY OF YOUTH, THE*   (1934, Brit.) 66m British and Dominions/PAR British bw

Aileen Marson (Carol Bonnard), Irene Vanbrugh (Mme. Bonnard), Sebastian Shaw (Alan Marmon), Henry Victor (Sylvestre), Diana Wilson (Grace Bonnard), Robert Rendel (Sir Peter Marmon), Leslie Bradley (Lt. Burton), The Western Brothers.

Feeble crime drama starring Shaw as a young man with a weakness for gambling. Accompanied by his fiancee, Marson, Shaw goes on a whirlwind gambling spree at a casino run by Marson's grandmother, Vanbrugh. Shaw loses his shirt and the unscrupulous casino manager, Victor, tries to blackmail the husband-to-be. Luckily Marson comes to the rescue by alerting Veanbrugh and she puts a stop to the plot. Plodding, unimaginative, and poorly produced.

p&d, Norman Walker; w, Sherard Powell (based on the play "Wayward Youth" by Amy Kennedy Gould, Ralph Neale).

Crime   **(PR:A   MPAA:NR)**

WAY OUT, THE*½   (1956, Brit.) 86m Todon-Merton Park/RKO bw (GB: DIAL 999)

Gene Nelson (Greg Carradine), Mona Freeman (Terry Carradine), John Bentley (Detective Sgt. Seagrave), Michael Goodliffe (John Moffat), Sydney Tafler (Alf Cressett), Charles Victor (Tom Smithers), Arthur Lovegrove (George), Cyril Chamberlain (Anderson), Paula Byrne (Vera Bellamy), Kay Callard (Blonde), Michael Golden (Inspector Keyes), Charles Mortimer (Mr. Harding), Margaret Harrison (Policewoman Larkins), Clifford Buckton

(Farmer), Tony Simpson, Jack MacNaughton.

Nelson kills a man in a barroom brawl in cold blood and convinces wife Freeman and her brother Goodliffe to help him escape. Both driving trucks, they manage to evade Scotland Yard authorities by shifting Nelson from one vehicle to the other. They become aware that the murder wasn't accidental as Nelson claimed. Nelson meets his demise by colliding with a bus while trying to escape on foot, freeing his wife, Freeman, to carry on with detective Bentley. The quick pace and compelling action sequences aren't enough to overshadow the weak cast and script flaws.

p, Alec Snowden; d&w, Montgomery Tully (based on the novel by Bruce Graeme); ph, Philip Grindrod; ed, Geoffrey Miller; md, Richard Taylor; art d, Wilfred Arnold.

Crime   **(PR:A   MPAA:NR)**

WAY OUT*   (1966) 102m Valley Forge/Premiere c

Frank Rodriguez *(Frankie)*, James Dunleavy *(Jim)*, Sharyn Jiminez *(Anita)*, Jerry Rutkin *(Jerry)*, Starr Ruiz *(Stella)*, Gilbert Mesa *(Fats)*, Cecil White *(Che Che)*, Louis Colon *(Louie)*, Rudy Rosado *(Rudy)*, John Giminez *(Pop)*, Eddie James *(Harlem Man)*, Naomi Perez *(Anita's Mother)*, Eric Hutson *(Narco)*, J. R. Helton *(Snuffy)*, Norman Yager *(Pusher)*, Chuck Painter *(Policeman)*, Louis Sager *(Guard)*.

One of a spate of drug-addiction films of the 1960s, this features amateur actors, some of whom demonstrate real ability. Set where much of it was filmed, in the Puerto Rican slums of the Bronx, the story follows Rodriguez, whose despair has led him to addiction. Forced to kick his habit when jailed, he emerges from imprisonment to find only more trauma, which leads him to try to renew his therapeutic addiction. An ex-dope peddler turned evangelist attempts to prevent him from renewing his habit, but he persists in his quest for the habit-forming anodyne. Pursued by police, he seeks refuge in a church, where he prays for peace. At the film's conclusion, each of the principal actors addresses the audience to explain that Jesus Christ is the WAY OUT. Producer- director Yeaworth had been responsible for a number of evangelist Billy Graham's specials.

p&d, Irvin S. Yeaworth, Jr.; w, Jean Yeaworth, Rudy Nelson, Shirley Nelson (based on the play "The Addicts" by John Giminez); ph, Thomas E. Spalding; m, Kurt Kaiser; ed, John Bushelman; art d, Jasper Brinton; m/l, "Lament," Giminez (sung by Roy Hamilton).

Drama   **(PR:O   MPAA:NR)**

WAY OUT LOVE   (SEE: TOUCH OF HER FLESH, THE, 1967)

WAY OUT, WAY IN*½   (1970, Jap.) 84m Daiei c (KOKOSEI BANCHO)

Yoko Namikawa *(Miho Sakai)*, Ichiro Ogura *(Hiroto Miyagawa)*, Saburo Shinoda *(Yuji Shibata)*, Kozaburo Onogawa *(Kenta Namiki)*, Akiko Naruse *(Yuki Nohara)*, Eiko Yanami *(Taeko)*, Sumire Mikasa.

This Japanese youth-gang movie deals with the class differences between full-time high-school day students (generally children of the moneyed) and the less affluent night students (who must work for their keep) who, unseen by one another, occupy the same school desks at different times of day. Female day student Namikawa leaves a note for her lower-class counterpart, whom she has never met. Offended by what she believes to be a rich girl's condescension, night student Onogawa returns her kindness with a gross obscenity. This starts the equivalent of a night-and-day war, which ultimately brings the day side in intimate contact with the night side, seduction and rape reducing the alienation of the two camps. The two most aggressive students finally attain a day-for-night conciliation through a motorcycle-racing competition.

d, Michihiko Obimori; w, Katsuya Suzaki; ph, Yoshihisa Nakagawa (Daiei Scope, Fuji Color); m, Harumi Ibe; art d, Shigeo Mano.

Drama   **(PR:O   MPAA:NR)**

WAY OUT WEST**   (1930) 71m MGM bw

William Haines *(Windy)*, Leila Hyams *(Molly)*, Polly Moran *(Pansy)*, Cliff Edwards *(Trilby)*, Francis X. Bushman, Jr *(Steve)*, Vera Marsh *(La Belle Rosa)*, Charles Middleton *(Buck)*, Jack Pennick *(Pete)*, Buddy Roosevelt *(Tex)*, Jay Wilsey *[Buffalo Bill, Jr.] (Hank)*.

The first talkie send-up of the western genre, this benchmark picture features the fast-talking Haines as a carnival trickster forced into ranch work by his victims, a group of tough cowboys. Trusted by innocent blonde ranch owner Hyams, Haines is sent off in her automobile to make a large cash deposit in her bank. After wrestling with his conscience, the suave swindler decides that he likes the girl too much to follow his nature, so he returns to the ranch. Jealous top hand Bushman, Jr. engages Haines in some fisticuffs, but in the end the rascal redeems himself, saving Hyams in a sandstorm and winning her heart and the respect of his former adversaries.

d, Fred Niblo; w, Alfred Block, Ralph Spence, Joe Farnham, Byron Morgan (based on the story "Easy Going" by Block, Morgan); ph, Henry Sharp; ed, William S. Gray, Jerry Thoms; art d, Cedric Gibbons; cos, David Cox.

Western/Comedy   **(PR:A   MPAA:G)**

WAY OUT WEST**   (1937) 65m Hal Roach/MGM bw

Stan Laurel, Oliver Hardy *(Themselves)*, James Finlayson *(Mickey Finn)*, Sharon Lynne *(Lola Marcel)*, Stanley Fields *(Sheriff)*, Rosina Lawrence *(Mary Roberts)*, James Mason *(Anxious Patron)*, James C. Morton, Frank Mills, Dave Pepper *(Bartenders)*, Vivien Oakland *(Stagecoach Passenger/ Molly, Sheriff's Wife)*, Harry Bernard *(Man Eating at Bar)*, Mary Gordon, May Wallace *(Cooks)*, Avalon Boys Quartet: 'Chill Wills, Art Green, Walter Trask, Don Brookins' *(Themselves)*, Jack Hill *(Worker at Mickey Finn's)*, Sam Lufkin *(Stagecoach Baggage Man)*, Tex Driscoll *(Bearded Miner)*, Flora Finch *(Maw, Miner's Wife)*, Fred "Snowflake" Toones *(Janitor)*, Bobby Dunn, John Ince, Fritzi Brunette, Frank Montgomery, Fred Cady, Eddie Borden, Bill Wolf, Denver Dixon 'Art Mix', Ben Corbett, Buffalo Bill, Jr. 'Jay Wilsey', Cy Slocum *(Audience at Saloon)*, Lester Dorr *(Cowboy)*, Dinah the Mule.

Hal Roach presented this film on which Laurel was the producer and the attention that Laurel paid to the movie is evident in every frame as it turned out to be one of the comedy team's best movies and surely must rank up there in the pantheon of Laurel and Hardy. In a scant 65 minutes, more laughs and joy are crammed in than can be found in a dozen modern comedies as Laurel and Hardy do their first, and only, western spoof and cause sides to split. The boys are on their faithful mule and going to the town of Brushwood Gulch where they are to deliver a gold mine deed to the daughter of their departed partner. They are hopelessly lost and come to a crossroads where a signpost keeps being switched by the force of the wind, thus confusing them even further. (This sequence was only in the European version of the film.) They were just as popular on the other side of the Atlantic and numbered Winston Churchill, Joseph Stalin, and Marshal Tito among their greatest fans.) Aboard the mule, they make the mistake of crossing a small stream that appears to be safe until they go right to the bottom of a hidden hole. Later, they flag a ride on a passing stagecoach when Laurel lifts his pant leg (the same way Claudette Colbert did it in IT HAPPENED ONE NIGHT) and they climb aboard. Once on the stagecoach, Hardy does his best to be civil to a traveling woman, Oakland, but his conversation is so banal that it is hilarious, with bon mots like: "We've been having a lot of weather lately." She tries to be pleasant but it's obvious she wishes Hardy would clam up. Upon arriving in the town, Oakland's husband, sheriff Fields, is told by her that she had a nice enough trip except that Hardy kept bothering her. Fields casts an eye on Laurel and Hardy and tells them that they'd better be on the next coach out of town. Since that's not due for a while, the boys tarry a bit in front of the local saloon and go into a soft shoe routine--done in front of a rear projection screen. They are accompanied by the Avalon Boys (look closely and you'll see Chill Wills among them). They are on a hush-hush mission but Laurel errs by telling bartender Finlayson of their task. The woman they want, Lawrence, works as a scullery maid for Finlayson, but he deliberately steers them wrong, to Lynne, who is his wife. She's a blonde hussy type and is so obviously not the right person that everyone in the audience can see right through her phony tears at hearing of her "father's" death. Everyone, that is, except Laurel and Hardy. After they've handed over the document, they learn that Lawrence is the true heiress and they enter the saloon again and demand the return of the deed. Finlayson and Lynne refuse to hand it over and the slapstick commences as there is a protracted tug of war over the paper. Laurel gets the deed and Lynne chases him into her boudoir. He slips the deed into his shirt and she chases him around the room, then begins tickling him until he can't breathe from laughing and she gets her mitts on the deed. Later, Lynne and Finlaysone cache the deed in their safe, thinking that it is now impervious to Laurel and Hardy. They are wrong. Later that night, the boys devise a pulley to raise them to the second floor but that doesn't work out. They tie the rope to their mule and Hardy takes a moment out to spit on his fingers like a baseball player approaching the plate. The moment Hardy does that, Laurel crashes to the ground, thus alerting Finlayson, who comes storming out of the house with a shotgun. A chase takes them in and out of the house, finds them hiding in a huge grand piano that finally collapses due to their combined weight. At the conclusion, Laurel and Hardy capture Finlayson, get his gun, force him to open the safe and hand them the deed, then tie him up. Laurel and Hardy and Lawrence flee the town of Brushwood Gulch and will presumably run their mine until it taps out. Lots of good gags, some reminiscent but not direct steals of other Laurel and Hardy films. Laurel is seen eating his hat and lighting his finger in order to get his pipe going; Hardy does his famous "camera takes" where he looks out at the audience for sympathy. Finlayson also looks at the camera but in a fashion that dares the audience to shout back at the screen to warn Laurel and Hardy of his villainy. Beginning with their first short, PUTTING PANTS ON PHILLIP, Laurel and Hardy made more than 60 shorts and 27 features. They were able to make the move from silents to talkies without any of the same problems encountered by Buster Keaton, Harry Langdon, Charlie Chaplin, and the others who faded the moment Hollywood found a voice. Laurel was 36 and Hardy was 34 when they met and a more enduring partnership has yet to be found. The songs were "Trail of the Lonesome Pine" (Harry Carroll, Ballard MacDonald) and "Commence to Dancing" (J.L. Hill). While Hardy had a pleasant baritone, Laurel's singing was dubbed by Chill Wills. Many years later, a record of "Trail of the Lonesome Pine" was released from the film's soundtrack. It went right into the Top Twenty in England, a fact that surprised everyone as Hardy had been gone more than 20 years at the time and Laurel more than 10. The lone Oscar nomination for the film went to Marvin Hatley for his score. This film and

SONS OF THE DESERT are a must for any Laurel and Hardy collector.

p, Stan Laurel; d, James W. Horne; w, Charles Rogers, Felix Adler, James Parrott (based on a story by Jack Jevne, Rogers); ph, Art Lloyd, Walter Lundin; m, Marvin Hatley, LeRoy Shield, Egbert Van Alstyne, Leonard-Munson, J.L. Hill, Carroll-MacDonald, Nathaniel Shilkret, Irving Berlin, Franz von Suppe; ed, Bert Jordan; md, Hatley; art d, Arthur I. Royce; set d, William L. Stevens; spec eff, Roy Seawright; makeup, Jack Dawn.

Comedy/Western   **Cas.**   **(PR:AAA MPAA:NR)**

WAY TO LOVE, THE*½   (1933) 80m PAR bw

Maurice Chevalier (Francois), Ann Dvorak (Madeleine), Edward Everett Horton (Prof. Gaston Bibi), Arthur Pierson (Mons. Joe), Minna Gombell (Suzanne), Blanche Frederici (Rosalie), Douglas Dumbrille (Agent Chapusard), John Miljan (Marco), Sidney Toler (Pierre), George Hagen (Wladek, the Mighty), George Rigas (Pedro, Knife-Thrower), Nydia Westman (Anna-Marie), Billy Bevan (Mons. Prial), Jason Robards, Sr (Guide), Grace Bradley (A Sunburned Lady), Arthur Housman (A Drunk), Mutt (Casanova, a Dog).

One of the least interesting of Chevalier's pictures, THE WAY TO LOVE originally co-starred Sylvia Sidney (who left after two-and-a-half weeks, claiming sickness), was foisted on Carole Lombard (who read the script and vehemently declined), and ended up with Dvorak. She plays a carnival knife-throwing target who falls in love with Chevalier, an aspiring tour guide in Paris, who makes his money by traipsing up and down the boulevard wearing an advertisement: "Is Your Heart Happy? NO? Consult Professor Bibi, 17 Rue Canton." After fighting off the professor's maritally inclined niece, Westman, Chevalier ends up with Dvorak in his arms. Chevalier, after this picture, was lured to MGM by Irving Thalberg, leaving the troubled Paramount in the lurch like so many of the studio's other stars. About to drift into bankruptcy, the studio was saved only by the enormous success of Mae West's SHE DONE HIM WRONG. A French-language version of THE WAY TO LOVE was shot simultaneously, with Chevalier also in the lead, but with virtually all the other actors replaced. Titled L'AMOUR GUIDE, this Hollywood-made picture played in French-speaking lands. Songs: "Lover of Paree," "Lucky Guy," "In a One-Room Flat," "The Way to Love," "It's Oh, It's Ah, It's Wonderful" (Ralph Rainger, Leo Robin).

p, Benjamin Glazer; d, Norman Taurog; w, Gene Fowler, Glazer, Claude Binyon, Frank Butler (based on the story "Laughing Man" by Fowler, Glazer); ph, Charles Lang; ed, William Shea; md, Nathaniel W. Finston; art d, Hans Dreier.

Musical/Romance   **(PR:A MPAA:NR)**

WAY TO THE GOLD, THE**½   (1957) 94m FOX bw

Jeffrey Hunter (Joe Mundy), Sheree North (Hank Clifford, Waitress), Barry Sullivan (Marshal Hannibal), Walter Brennan (Uncle George), Neville Brand (Little Brother Williams), Jacques Aubuchon (Clem Williams), Ruth Donnelly (Mrs. Williams), Tom Pittman (Sid Songster, Jr.), Philip Ahn (Mr. Ding, Cafe Owner), Geraldo A. Mandia (Brokaw), Alan Jeffrey (Brokaw's Driver), Ted Edwards (Sid Songster, Sr.), Ken Scott (Intern), Jonathan Hale (Mr. Felton), Frank Mazzola (Teenager).

Hunter is released from prison with information on a hidden cache of gold worth $250,000 which was buried by a now-dead convict some 30 years earlier. He is followed in his search by an eccentric family that wants a share of the gold, and along the way picks up waitress North, with whom he falls in love. Disappointment sets in when they discover that the buried loot is covered by the man-made Lake Mead. The eccentric clan tries to kill the young lovers but Sullivan, the town sheriff, comes to their aid. Songs: "Strange Weather," "Drive-In Rock" (Lionel Newman, Carroll Coates).

p, David Weisbart; d, Robert D. Webb; w, Wendell Mayes (based on the novel by Wilbur Daniel Steele); ph, Leo Tover (CinemaScope); m, Lionel Newman; ed, Hugh S. Fowler; art d, Lyle R. Wheeler, Addison Hehr; cos, Adele Balkin; spec eff, Ray Kellogg.

Drama   **(PR:A MPAA:NR)**

WAY TO THE STARS, THE   (SEE: JOHNNY IN THE CLOUDS, 1945, Brit.)

WAY...WAY OUT* (1966) 101m Jerry Lewis-Coldwater-Way Out/FOX c

Jerry Lewis (Peter Mattemore), Connie Stevens (Eileen Forbes, Astronomer), Robert Morley (Harold Quonset), Weather Bureau Chief, Dennis Weaver (Hoffman), Howard Morris (Schmidlap), Brian Keith (Gen. Hallenby), Dick Shawn (Igor), Anita Ekberg (Anna Soblova), William O'Connell (Ponsonby), Bobo Lewis (Esther Davenport), Milton Frome (Russian Delegate), Alex D'Arcy (Deuce), Linda Harrison (Peggy), James Brolin (Ted Robertson), Michael Jackson (TV Announcer), Col. John "Shorty" Powers (Narrator).

Lewis stars in this almost worthless science-fiction comedy set in 1994. He marries–in name only–a fellow weathernaut, Stevens, and together they man a space station on the moon adjacent to one occupied by a Russian pair, Shawn and Ekberg. Lewis and Stevens (who married him, under orders, only seconds before their space vessel blasted off) are to replace a pair of male moon-dwellers, Weaver and Morris, who have–appropriately enough–become lunatics. The contention of their superiors in the service is that the lunacy resulted from the frustration of being in close proximity to the buxom Ekberg, thus the requirement of a married pair of replacements. A space-based sex farce that's not very funny (even for those diehard Lewis fans) mainly because of a "who-cares" script. The only person in the cast to glean a couple of laughs is Morley as the man in charge of the weather service. A clip from James Whale's FRANKENSTEIN (1931) is included, and is better than the rest of the picture. The title tune, penned by Lalo Schifrin and Hal Winn, is sung by Gary Lewis (Jerry's kid) and The Playboys.

p, Malcolm Stuart; d, Gordon Douglas; w, William Bowers, Laslo Vadnay; ph, William H. Clothier (CinemaScope, DeLuxe Color); m, Lalo Schifrin; ed, Hugh S. Fowler; md, Schifrin; art d, Jack Martin Smith, Hilyard Brown; set d, Walter M. Scott, Stuart A. Reiss; cos, Moss Mabry; spec eff, L.B. Abbott, Emil Kosa, Jr., Howard Lydecker; makeup, Ben Nye.

Science Fiction/Comedy   **(PR:C-O MPAA:NR)**

WAY WE LIVE, THE***   (1946, Brit.) 64m TC/GFD bw

Peter Willes, Francis Lunt, Verena Chaffe, Patsy Scantlebury, June Riddols, Beryl Rosekelly, Mrs. MacMillan, Pat Lang, James Robson, Lt. Hutchinson, Sir Patrick Abercrombie, James Paton-Watson.

A well-produced post-WW II drama which details the resurrection of the city of Plymouth which had been razed during the blitz. The film follows a typical British family as it moves from one area to another seeking shelter. After becoming entangled in the frustrating bureaucratic red tape of temporary housing services, the family joins thousands of other displaced souls in a march demanding that a proposed redevelopment plan be activated immediately. The protest works and Plymouth is rebuilt. THE WAY WE LIVE provides a fascinating look at the reconstruction problems facing Britain after the war is a valuable document for those interested in the effects of WW II on civilians.

p,d&w, Jill Craigie; ph, Laurie Friedman.

Drama   **(PR:A MPAA:NR)**

WAY WE LIVE NOW, THE*   (1970) 110m East Coker/UA c

Nicholas Pryor (Lionel Aldridge), Joanna Miles (Amelia), Lois Smith (Jane Aldridge), Linda Simon (Rosalind Leopoldo), Pat McAneny (Laurie), Rebecca Darke (Martha), Sydney Walker (Lincoln), Linda Blair (Sara Aldridge), Samantha Jones (Samantha), Eugene Wood (Mr. Aldridge), Miriam Phillips (Mrs. Aldridge), Morris Strassberg (Mr. Leopold), James McMurray.

Pryor plays a disaffected Madison Avenue advertising executive in mid-life crisis who leaves his wife Smith and young daughter Blair. He initiates a series of unsatisfactory love affairs with professional dancer McAneny, with TV executive Simon, and with one-time girl friend–now married matron–Miles. Learning of his liaisons, wife Smith seeks a divorce. Pryor consoles himself once more with McAneny, who promptly has a nervous breakdown. He looks again to Miles, but finds her occupied with minor domestic difficulties. Breathing a sigh of relief, Pryor realizes that he can do without the distaff side. Slickly filmed as a first feature by long-time TV commercial maker Brown, the length of the picture exceeds its slim content.

p&d, Barry Brown; w, Brown, Daniel Tamkus (based on the novel by Warren Miller); ph, Brown (Deluxe Color); m, Nate Sassover, Tamkus; ed, Brown.

Drama   **(PR:O MPAA:NR)**

WAY WE WERE, THE***   (1973) 118m Rastar/COL c

Barbra Streisand (Katie Morosky), Robert Redford (Hubbell Gardiner), Bradford Dillman (J.J.), Lois Chiles (Carol Ann), Patrick O'Neal (George Bissinger), Viveca Lindfors (Paula Reisner), Allyn Ann McLerie (Rhea Edwards), Murray Hamilton (Brooks Carpenter), Herb Edelman (Bill Verso), Diana Ewing (Vicki Bissinger), Sally Kirkland (Pony Dunbar), Marcia Mae Jones (Peggy Vanderbilt), Don Keefer (Radio Actor), George Gaynes (El Morocco Captain), Eric Boles (Army Corporal), Barbara Peterson (Ash Blonde), Roy Jenson (Army Captain), Brendan Kelly (Rally Speaker), James Woods (Frankie McVeigh), Connie Forslund (Jenny), Robert Gerringer (Dr. Short), Susie Blakely (Judianne), Ed Power (Airforce), Suzanne Zenor (Dumb Blonde), Dan Seymour (Guest), Dorian Cusick (Professor's Wife), Don Koll (Officer Dining), Bob Dahdah (Officer Passing Plaza).

Most critics panned it but the public loved it to the tune of more than a $30 million gate the first time around. Redford had to be cajoled into doing the movie and resented the fact because he didn't want to be typed as a romantic idol. He preferred demonstrating that he could act, rather than just be a foil to the powerful Streisand. Toward the end of shooting in New York City, California, and at the Union College in Schenectady, the atmosphere on the set was described as "doing overtime at Dachau." Redford is a handsome WASP college student in the late 1930s. He yearns to be a writer, spends his spare time in mindless social activities, and is as neutral as a Swiss herdsman when it comes to politics. Streisand is a Jewish radical student who joins every political organization and parades, marches, and waves flags for them. She is the essential "True Believer" (Eric Hoffer's brilliant treatise which states that it is the person who is attracted to the cause rather than the cause that attracts the person. Thus the ardent communist is more easily turned to become a conservative and the most zealous atheist is quicker to convert to piety). Streisand is the butt of many jokes at the college and the sharpest needles come from Redford's pals but he doesn't feel the same way and reserves comment. They meet briefly at a dance and there is an attraction, but that's put on the back burner for the nonce. Years pass, and WW II begins. Streisand is on the radio talking about her favorite subject– politics–and Redford is now a member of the armed forces. They meet again and he is drunk so she takes him back to her apartment where there is a failed attempt at intimacy that ends when he passes out on top of her. Another time, another place, and they spend an evening together. He's now a published author and she has a copy of his novel. They discuss the book and it's evident to both that the attraction they felt in college is still there so they begin to date. Redford's snobbish friends again try to wreck the relationship, a fact that she resents and lets him know. She won't put up with their attitudes and Redford decides this might be the time to end their romance. But, as in all love stories, they are reconciled. The two marry and move to California where Redford has received a screenplay assignment to adapt his novel into a film. Enter the "Red Scare"–that insidious moment in Hollywood's history when anyone caught wearing a red tie or red shoes was thought to be in the direct employ of the Kremlin. The storybook marriage of Redford and Streisand is beginning to fall apart. She goes off to Washington to fight against the House Un-American Activities Committee. Streisand had always been in fear that Redford was selling out his talent for money and he starts to agree with her and is soon in trouble with the studio toppers. Dillman, an old buddy of Redford's, is the wishy-washy producer assigned to the project and he wants certain changes in the script that Redford is loath to make. The usual Hollywood types are seen, with O'Neal as the director, Lindfors as a local literary doyenne, McLerie as an agent, and Edelman as the radio producer who backs Streisand. (Edelman and Redford were great pals, and the tall, bald comic actor appeared often with Redford, starting with their Broadway work in "Barefoot in the Park.") While Streisand is away, Redford seeks balm and solace in the arms of an ex-girl friend. Streisand is distraught and pregnant and thinks it might be better if they call an end to their marriage, something Redford does not want. They will wait until after their child has been born, then part amicably. Years later, they meet again in New York. Redford has now sold out totally and makes his living writing for TV. Streisand has remarried and they meet in the area near Central Park where they have their final conversation. They still do love each other but their worlds began far apart and have gotten no closer. In a rather predictable ending, they bid each other farewell and she walks away handing out "Ban the Bomb" leaflets as he shakes his head and calls out after her: "You never give up, do you?" Streisand, cinematographer Stradling, designer Grimes, composer Hamlisch, and lyricists Alan and Marilyn Bergman were Oscar-nominated, with the music and the song gaining the Academy Awards. Most of the secondary roles were shallow, as it was a true "star vehicle" for the pairing of Redford and Streisand. Redford did get an Oscar nomination this same year, but it was for THE STING. The title song was a smash and will be recalled more easily than the plot of the picture. Howard Koch, Jr., who was hired to run Ray Stark's production company in the 1980s, was assistant director and the associate producer, Richard Roth, went on to great success with his own productions in later years. After an Oscar nomination for the period piece THEY SHOOT HORSES, DON'T THEY?, director Pollack was hired for this film and did a few movies with Redford, culminating in the successful OUT OF AFRICA. It was Pollack's insistence on Redford over Ryan O'Neal (who'd starred with Streisand in WHAT'S UP, DOC?) that finally convinced Redford to take the role, after he had originally turned thumbs down on the Laurents script. There were many behind-the-scenes woes taking place during shooting. Columbia's management was being replaced, the script was rewritten daily, Pollack and Redford disagreed with Stark, and Streisand never seemed to leave well enough alone by putting herself smack in the middle of production matters that don't usually concern hired actors. Perhaps it is that quest for perfection that caused Streisand to become her own director, something her former directors always felt she was doing anyway.

p, Ray Stark; d, Sydney Pollack; w, Arthur Laurents, (uncredited) Alvin Sargent, David Rayfiel (based on the novel by Laurents); ph, Harry Stradling, Jr. (Panavision, Eastmancolor); m, Marvin Hamlisch; ed, Margaret Booth; prod d, Stephen Grimes; set d, William Kiernan; cos, Dorothy Jeakins, Moss Mabry; ch, Grover Dale; m/l, title song, Hamlisch, Marilyn Bergman, Alan Bergman (sung by Barbra Streisand); makeup, Donald Cash, Jr., Gary Liddiard.

Romance   **Cas.**   **(PR:C MPAA:PG)**

WAY WEST, THE**½   (1967) 122m Harold Hecht/UA c

Kirk Douglas (*Sen. William J. Tadlock*), Robert Mitchum (*Dick Summers*), Richard Widmark (*Lije Evans*), Lola Albright (*Rebecca Evans*), Michael Witney (*Johnnie Mack*), Stubby Kaye (*Sam Fairman*), Sally Field (*Mercy McBee*), Katherine Justice (*Amanda Mack*), Michael McGreevey (*Brownie Evans*), Connie Sawyer (*Mrs. McBee*), Harry Carey, Jr (*McBee*), Elisabeth Fraser (*Mrs. Fairman*), William Lundigan (*Michael Moynihan*), Anne Barton (*Mrs. Moynihan*), Roy Barcroft (*Masters*), Eve McVeagh (*Mrs. Masters*), Paul Lukather (*Turley*), Peggy Stewart (*Mrs. Turley*), Stefan

Arngrim (*Billy Tadlock, Jr.*), Jack Elam (*Weatherby*), Hal Lynch (*Big Henry*), Timothy Scott (*Middle Henry*), John Mitchum (*Little Henry*), Roy Glenn (*Saunders*), Patric Knowles (*Col. Grant*), Nick Cravat (*Calvelli*), Gary Morris (*Paw-Kee-Mah*), Michael Lane (*Sioux Chief*), Eddie Little Sky, Michael Keep (*Sioux Braves*), Clarke Gordon (*Caleb Greenwood*), Ken Murray (*Hank*), Paul Wexler (*Barber*), Mitchell Schollars (*Indian Boy*), Jack Coffer, Everett Creach, James Burk, Gary McLarty (*Cattlemen*).

An extraordinarily predictable and uninviting western directed by McLaglen in the John Ford vein but with none of the Ford atmosphere, complexity, characterization, or inventiveness. Only in its visualization of the western expanse and picturesque rendering of Oregon Trail country does it come close to its goal. The story–based on a Pulitzer Prize-winning novel (though you'd never know it)–is of a wagon trek of pioneers from Independence, Missouri to Oregon. Douglas, a widowed senator, leads the pack with Mitchum, a trail scout with poor eyesight, second in command. The main conflict centers on the escapades of newlywed husband Witney, who ignores his frigid wife and succumbs to the lure of the slatternly Field (in her first film role). He gets deeper into trouble when he accidentally kills an Indian boy camouflaged in a wolf skin, thinking he is a real wolf. In order to avoid a battle with the Sioux, Douglas orders Witney hanged, shocking his fellow pioneers. The bitter widow gets revenge on Douglas later as she cuts his rope as he descends a deep gorge. There are enough shallow subplots here to keep daytime TV happy for weeks (or months...or years), and have western fans squirming in their seats until the end credits roll. The only saving grace is the fine (though admittedly uninspired) cast and the awesome photography. Costing over $5 million to produce, THE WAY WEST grossed a dismal $1.67 million at the box office, which goes to show that audiences don't *always* see whatever's thrown into their laps.

p, Harold Hecht; d, Andrew V. McLaglen; w, Ben Maddow, Mitch Lindemann (based on the novel by Alfred Bertram Guthrie, Jr.); ph, William H. Clothier (Panavision, DeLuxe Color); m, Bronislau Kaper; ed, Otho Lovering; md, Andre Previn; art d, Ted Haworth; set d, Robert Priestly; cos, Norma Koch; spec eff, Danny Hays; m/l (title song) Kaper, Mack David, sung by The Serendipity Singers; stunts, Hal Needham; makeup, Frank McCoy.

Western   **Cas.**   **(PR:A MPAA:NR)**

WAYLAID WOMEN   (SEE: INDECENT, 1962, Ger.)

WAYS OF LOVE*****   (1950, Ital./Fr.) 119m Joseph Burstyn bw

"A Day in the Country": Sylvia Bataille (*Henriette*), Gabriel (*Mons. Doufour*), Jeanne Marken (*Mme. Doufour*), Georges St. Saens (*Henry*), Bordan (*Anatole*), Jacques Borel (*Rudolph*), Gabrielle Fontane (*Grandmother*), Jean Renoir (*Innkeeper*), Marguerite Renoir (*Waitress*), Federico Fellini (*The Stranger*), Annie Toinon (*Barbe*), Tyrand (*The Priest*), A. Robert (*The Teacher*), Henri Poupon (*Fonse*), Charles Blavette (*Antonin*), Odette Roger (*Marie*).

A peculiar masterpiece since it is actually a compilation of three brilliant short films–Jean Renoir's A DAY IN THE COUNTRY (1946), Roberto Rossellini's THE MIRACLE (1948), and Marcel Pagnol's JOFROI (1933). Compiled by foreign film importer Joseph Burstyn, WAYS OF LOVE has only been shown on U.S. screens for the benefit of those Americans who would not otherwise get a chance to see them. Renoir's film is one of his most perfect, adapting a Guy de Maupassant story about a burgeois mother and daughter who get involved with two oarsmen. Rossellini's picture was originally released in Italy in a diptych entitled L'AMORE and was meant as a vehicle for Magnani. Besides being Fellini's only acting credit, THE MIRACLE was also the film that paved the way for free speech in motion pictures. When New York's Cardinal Spellman saw the picture he was morally outraged and attempted to have it banned. As is always the case, the U.S. Justice Department had enough good sense to let it play. The final episode, JOFROI, is a tale of a peasant who sells his land and then tries to prevent the owner from cutting down the olive trees that grow on it. All three episodes have been released as short films and are masterpieces in their own right. (In French and Italian; English subtitles.)

"A Day in the Country": p, Pierre Braunberger; d&w, Jean Renoir (based on a story by Guy de Maupassant); ph, Claude Renoir, Jean Bourgoin; m, Joseph Kosma; ed, Marguerite Renoir; "The Miracle": d, Roberto Rossellini; w, Rossellini, Tullio Pinelli (based on a story by Federico Fellini); m, Renzo Rossellini; "Jofroi": d, Marcel Pagnol (based on the story "Jofroi De La Maussan" by Jean Giono).

Drama   **(PR:C-O MPAA:NR)**

WAYSIDE PEBBLE, THE**   (1962, Jap.) 104m Tokyo Eiga/Toho bw
                                                    (ROBO NO ISHI)

Hiroyuki Ota (*Goichi Aikawa*), Setsuko Hara (*Oren Aikawa*), Hisaya Morishige (*Shogo Aikawa*), Tatsuya Mihashi (*Tsugino*), Kyu Sazanka (*Chusuke*), Yusuke Takita, Masao Oda.

A young Japanese boy longs to attend a private school but his father cannot afford the expense. When a local businessman offers to send the boy to the school, his father sells the boy to an uncaring merchant. The boy eventually runs away and boards a train to Tokyo in the hope of starting anew.

d, Seiji Hisamatsu; w, Kaneto Shindo; ph, Shojiro Sugimoto (Tohoscope); m, Ichiro Saito.

Drama   **(PR:A   MPAA:NR)**

WAYWARD*½   (1932) 71m PAR bw

Nancy Carroll (*Daisy Frost*), Richard Arlen (*David Frost*), Pauline Frederick (*Mrs. Frost*), John Litel (*Bob Daniels*), Margalo Gillmore (*Louisa Daniels*), Burke Clarke (*Uncle Judson*), Dorothy Stickney (*Hattie, Maid*), Sidney Easton (*George*), Gertrude Michael (*Mary Norton*).

Carroll stars as the wife of the wealthy Arlen, who becomes a victim of her mother-in-law's (Frederick's) wicked ways. Frederick, who thinks Carroll isn't good enough for her boy, tries to break up the marriage, and also takes away the couple's child. Carroll fights back, takes her child, and eventually is reunited with her husband, dismissing the rumors that she ran off with Litel. Similar in plot to both EAST LYNNE and THE SOCIAL REGISTER, but lacking any of their finer qualities. Song: "What's the Difference?" (Edward Heyman, John W. Green), accompanied by The Claude Hopkins Orchestra.

d, Edward Sloman; w, Gladys Unger, William Day (based on the novel *Wild Beauty* by Matee Howe Farnham); ph, William Steiner; ed, Arthur Ellis.

Drama   **(PR:A   MPAA:NR)**

WAYWARD BUS, THE**   (1957) 89m FOX bw

Joan Collins (*Alice Chicoy*), Jayne Mansfield (*Camille*), Dan Dailey (*Ernest Horton*), Rick Jason (*Johnny Chicoy*), Betty Lou Keim (*Norma*), Dolores Michaels (*Mildred Pritchard*), Larry Keating (*Pritchard*), Robert Bray (*Morse*), Kathryn Givney (*Mrs. Pritchard*), Dee Pollock (*Pimples*), Will Wright (*Dan Brunt*).

This adaptation of John Steinbeck's novel barely scratches its surface in terms of characterizations, but still turns up as mildly entertaining. Jason is a bus driver who takes his passengers on a journey which is spotted by storms of both the emotional and meteorological kind. In both cases disaster is barely averted. Jason is reunited with hard-drinking, jealous wife, Collins, while stripper Mansfield and traveling salesman Dailey become an unlikely pair.

p, Charles Brackett; d, Victor Vicas; w, Ivan Moffat (based on John Steinbeck's novel); ph, Charles G. Clarke (CinemaScope); m, Leigh Harline; ed, Louis Loeffler; md, Lionel Newman; art d, Lyle R. Wheeler, Walter M. Simonds; cos, Mary Wills; spec eff, L. B. Abbott.

Drama   **(PR:C   MPAA:NR)**

WAYWARD GIRL, THE*   (1957) 71m REP bw

Marcia Henderson (*Judy Wingate*), Peter Walker (*Tommy Gray*), Katharine Barrett (*Frances Wingate*), Whit Bissell (*Ira Molson*), Rita Lynn (*Midge Brackett*), Peg Hillias (*Big Hilda*), Tracey Roberts (*Dot Martin*), Ray Teal (*Sheriff*), Ric Roman (*Eddie Nolan*), Barbara Eden (*Molly*), Grandon Rhodes (*District Attorney*), Francis DeSales (*Investigator Butler*), John Maxwell (*Parole Agent*).

Henderson becomes the victim of an unkind stepmother (as well as an equally unkind scriptwriter) whose ready-and-willing boy friend makes a move on the girl. Henderson retaliates by smacking him with an iron and winds up in jail for murder. It turns out that her stepmom actually finished the lecher off after Henderson had left. All is revealed in a confession that the stepmother was carrying as she fell down a flight of stairs, a victim of too much boozing. In the interim, Henderson has been paroled in the care of lonely-hearts club operator Bissell, who actually runs a white slavery ring.

Drama   **(PR:A   MPAA:NR)**

WE ACCUSE   (SEE: J'ACCUSE, 1945, Fr.)

WE ARE ALL MURDERERS**½   (1957, Fr.) 113m Union General Cinematographique/King sley International bw (NOUS SOMMES TOUS DES ASSASSINS; GB: WE ARE ALL MURDERERS?)

Marcel Mouloudji (*Rene Le Guen*), Raymond Pellegrin (*Gino*), Antoine Balpetre (*Dr. Albert Dutoit*), Claude Laydu (*Philippe Arnaud, a Counsel*), Amedeo Nazzari (*Dr. Albert Detouche*), Georges Poujouly (*Michel Le Guen*), Julien Verdier (*Marcel Bauchet*), Louis Seigner (*Abbe Roussard*), Andre Reybas (*Father Simon*), Juliette Faber (*Madame Sautier*), Yvonne Pierreux (*Yvonne Le Guen*), Jerome Goulven (*Noblet*), Charles Lemontier (*Prosecutor*), Francois Joux (*Sautier*), Henri Valbert (*Counsel Mousset*), Line Noro (*Louise Arnaud*), Marcel Peres (*Malingre*), Sylvie (*Gino's Mother*), Renee Gardes (*Le Guen's Mother*), Yvette Etievant (*Bauchet's Wife*), Leonce Corne (*Captain at the Military Court*), Lucien Nat (*Leading Counsel*), Henri Cremieux (*Bauchet's Counsel*), Jean-Paul Moulinot (*Governor of the Sante Prison*), Jean-Marc Tennberg (*Fred*), Jacques Morel (*"Gros" Charles*), Anouk Ferjac (*Agnes*), Louis Arbessier (*Deputy Prosecutor*), Guy Decomble (*Police Inspector*), Charles Bouillaud (*Policeman*), Alexandre Rignault (*Gendarme*), Liliane Maigne (*Rahel*), Daniel Mendaille (*Chief Warden*), Rene Lacourt (*Balloon Seller*).

A polemical picture, deliberately made by cowriter/director Cayatte to influence an audience's views about the efficacy of capital punishment as a deterrent to murder, which poses the question "If you were the President of the Republic, would you want this man to die?" The film details, in case-history fashion, the stories of five condemned murderers. The five prisoners await the guillotine nervously, listening for the small sounds that will announce the coming of the stocking-footed guards hoping to seize them unawares (a stratagem that passes for mercy, the men never knowing the moment of their final torment) and transport them to their terminal rites. The condemned Pellegrin is a Corsican trapped by an archaic tradition of family honor and vengeance, within which he killed a transgressor, adhering to a law older than the judicial system that condemned him. Balpetre, a physician, has been convicted on circumstantial evidence of poisoning his wife. Verdier, an illiterate peasant, murdered his infant daughter because her crying interfered with his sleep. Peres, victim of a brain tumor–since surgically removed–raped and murdered a child. In the most detailed of the histories, Mouloudji's, the progress of this much-brutalized slum child is depicted through his adulthood and his small-arms training and recruitment into the Resistance during the occupation of WW II, a time when he found social rewards and admiration to be connected with killing. Cayatte, himself an attorney, presents his case against judicial murder fairly; he deliberately avoids highly charged emotional scenes, preferring to undertake the method espoused by theatrical theorist Berthold Brecht: giving his viewers a chance to use their own minds. One of four "judicial" films directed by Cayatte. In Britain, the film's title received a question mark, avoiding Cayatte's apparent presumption of guilt.

d, Andre Cayatte; w, Cayatte, Charles Spaak; ph, Jean-Serge Bourgoin; m, Raymond Legrand; ed, Paul Cayatte; art d, Jacques Colombier.

Drama   **(PR:C   MPAA:NR)**

WE ARE ALL NAKED*   (1970, Can./Fr.) 82m
Citel-Canada-Eurocitel/Citel-USA bw (ILS SONT NUS)

Alain Saury (*Stranger*), Jacques Normand (*Father*), Rita Maiden (*Mother*), Catherine Ribeiro (*Niece*), Gerard Desalles (*Son*), Isabelle Pierson (*Daughter*), Georges Beauvilliers (*Worker*), Max Montavon (*Crony*), Rene Roussel (*Young Seaman*), Boniface (*Old Seaman*).

Stranger Saury disrupts the troubled existence of a disturbed family in a small French fishing village. The father, Normand, who had been a successful and well-regarded fisherman, has become a drunk. Maiden, his wife, has turned slattern, visiting sexual favors upon the more physically fit men of the community. Pierson is the troubled daughter of the unfortunate pair, Desalles the retarded son, and Ribeiro a visiting teen-aged niece. Saury makes love to Maiden in the sand, unaware that they are observed by her son. When seen, the brain-damaged boy runs off; his mother pursues him into quicksand, where both are drowned in the incoming tidal waters. Saury consoles himself with niece Ribeiro; the two leave the community together. A depressing film.

p&d, Claude Pierson; w, Huguette Boisvert (English dialog, Jack Curtis); ph, Jean-Louis Picavet (Totalscope); m, Jean-Paul Mengeon; m/l, Mengeon, Arnold Drake (title song sung by Charles Duval).

Drama   **(PR:O   MPAA:NR)**

WE ARE IN THE NAVY NOW   (SEE: WE JOINED THE NAVY, 1962, Brit.)

WE ARE NOT ALONE**½   (1939) 112m WB bw

Paul Muni (*Dr. David Newcome*), Jane Bryan (*Leni-Krafft*), Flora Robson (*Jessica Newcome*), Raymond Severn (*Gerald Newcome*), Una O'Connor (*Susan*), Alan Napier (*Archdeacon*), James Stephenson (*Sir William Clintock*), Montagu Love (*Maj. Millman*), Henry Daniell (*Sir Ronald Dawson*), Stanley Logan (*Mr. Guy Lockhead*), Cecil Kellaway (*Judge*), Crauford Kent (*Dr. Stacey*), E.E. Clive (*Major*), Eily Malyon (*Archdeacon's Wife*), Doris Lloyd (*Mrs. Jaeggers*), May Beatty (*Mrs. Patterson*), Clarence Derwent (*Stage Manager*), Billy Bevan (*Mr. Jones*), Charles Irwin (*Working Man*), Douglas Scott (*Tommy Baker*), John Powers (*Charley*), Colin Kenny (*George*), Joseph Crehan (*American*), David Clyde (*Ticket Collector*), Sidney Bracey (*The Lamplighter*), Viola Moore, Phyllis Barry (*Chorus Girls*), Lowden Adams, Leyland Hodgson (*Detectives*), Harry Cording, Cyril Thornton (*Men*), Douglas Gordon (*Mr. Selby*), Olaf Hytten (*Mr. Clark*), Rita Carlyle (*Mrs. Deane*), Barlowe Borland (*Tom Briggs*), Egon Brecher (*Mr. Schiller*), Lillian Kemble-Cooper (*Mrs. Stacey*), Holmes Herbert (*Inspector*), Boyd Irwin (*Police Officer*), Ethel Griffies (*Mrs. Raymond*), Keith Kenneth (*Policeman*), Thomas Mills (*Judge's Chaplain*).

This was not a hit with the war-conscious U.S. in 1939 but star Muni felt it was one of his greatest roles and who are we to argue? This time he's a country doctor in England with a penchant for the violin. (In the film, Muni played his own violin after studying some time to be able to reproduce sounds on the instrument.) He's married to neurotic Robson and they have a precocious son, Severn. The movie begins in 1914 as the physician treats an Austrian dancer, Bryan, for a broken wrist. (The part was originally cast with Dolly Haas but when she and Muni had those old, familiar "creative differences," she was replaced with tyro Bryan after three weeks' shooting had been completed.) Bryan is sad enough with her lot to attempt suicide but Muni comes to her aid and helps her find a place to stay while she searches for work. She becomes the child's governess and Muni hies Severn away from Robson so she can't exert her powerful influence during the day while he is out calling on patients. Bryan and Severn like each other very much but Robson steps in and tells Muni she wants Bryan fired after learning that the sweet young thing had been a dancer and had also attempted to kill herself. Robson takes the lad and sends him off to live with her pious brother, Napier, an archdeacon. It's all veddy British and stiff upper lip as the camera examines life in the quiet English town, but then things begin popping. Muni is irate at Robson for what she's done and continues to see Bryan, who now enters a music school. One day, Severn sneaks back to his house to find a small pocket knife Robson had confiscated earlier. In his foraging, he accidentally knocks over some pill bottles belonging to Muni. Several of the bottles are broken and, in a panic, Severn stuffs the pills into whatever bottles remain, not realizing that they are now mislabeled and the result could be fatal. WW I breaks out and the angry townspeople go wild, breaking windows and trashing shops owned by anyone with even a vaguely German-sounding name. Muni, realizing that Bryan is in danger due to her Austrian heritage, gets her to another town from whence she can travel back to her country. Meanwhile, Robson develops a headache and takes some tablets from Muni's medicine cabinet, not knowing that their son has fouled matters earlier. She soon dies, the result of downing the wrong medication. Muni and Bryan are arrested on the charge of murder, tried, then convicted and finally sentenced to death. The only one who could accurately solve the crime is Severn but, at his father's insistence, the boy knows nothing. During the trial, Muni comes to love Bryan and, on the eve of the execution, the two are allowed some time together. It is here that they bare their love for each other and they go to their deaths confident that they will be together in some other time and place. Even with the downbeat conclusion, the picture has a certain dignity and conviction and is a moving experience. It was Muni's tenth and final picture for Warner Bros. and a fine bow-out to the contract that saw him appear as Louis Pasteur, Benito Juarez, and Emile Zola. The studio did well in its creation of the atmosphere of a small English village of the period. Excellent acting in this, one of the more than 400 films either produced or supervised by Hal Wallis, who died in October, 1986, at age 88.

p, Henry Blanke; d, Edmund Goulding; w, James Hilton, Milton Krims (based on a novel by Hilton); ph, Tony Gaudio; m, Max Steiner; ed, Warren Low; spec eff, Byron Haskin, H.F. Koenekamp.

Drama   (PR:A-C MPAA:NR)

WE DIVE AT DAWN*½   (1943, Brit.) 98m Gainsborough/GFD bw

Eric Portman (James Hobson), John Mills (Lt. Freddie Taylor), Reginald Purdell (CPO Dicky Dabbs), Niall MacGinnis (PO Mike Corrigan), Joan Hopkins (Ethel Dabbs), Josephine Wilson (Alice Hobson), Louis Bradfield (Lt. Brace), Ronald Millar (Lt. Johnson), Jack Watling (Lt. Gordon), Caven Watson (CPO Duncan), Leslie Weston (Tug Wilson), Norman Williams (Canada), Lionel Grose (Spud), Beatrice Varley (Mrs. Dabbs), Frederick Burtwell (Sidney Biggs), Marie Ault (Mrs. Metcalfe), John Salew (Drake), Philip Friend (Humphries), David Peel (Oxford), Philip Godfrey (Flunkey), Robert Wilton (Pincher), John Slater, Kenneth Evans, Charles Russell, Gerik Schjelderup, Molly Johnson, Franklin Bennett, Bryan Powley, Merle Tottenham, Joan Sterndale, George Cross, John Redmond, Johnnie Schofield.

More underwater action, this time from the British. The crew members of the Sea Tiger return to port after a long patrol and go home on leave. Portman comes home to find his wife, Wilson, has left him. The personal joys and anguishes of the various crewmen are put aside when they are suddenly recalled to their sub. The German battleship Brandenburg is making a run from its home port in Bremerhaven for the Baltic via the Kiel Canal across the base of the Danish penninsula, and Mills, the youthful commander of the Sea Tiger, is assigned to sink the enemy dreadnought before she can reach the safety of the canal. Along the way they sink an enemy radio buoy and capture some prisoners, but when they reach the entrance of the canal they find they are too late. Mills decides to go quickly around Denmark and sink the ship when she emerges from the other end of the canal. They have to negotiate a treacherous minefield across the entrance to the Baltic but they make it safely and eventually find the Brandenburg. They fire their torpedoes and crash dive, not knowing whether they hit the target or not. They lie on the bottom "playing dead" to avoid the German destroyers searching for them and then carefully make their way for home. They discover, however, that their fuel is almost exhausted. Portman, who can speak German, puts on the uniform of one of the prisoners aboard and goes ashore on a Danish island to search for fuel. He finds a docked tanker and signals the sub to come in. While they refuel, the Germans occupying the island find them and a battle breaks out. Danish partisans come to the aid of the submariners and they manage to get away and eventually back home. As they enter port they learn that the Brandenburg was sent to the bottom by their torpedoes and Portman finds Wilson has come back to him and is waiting dockside. Above average submarine movie manages to avoid most of the cliches of the genre and generates quite a lot of tension. The performances are all good, and Mills prepared for his role by actually riding a submarine down the river Clyde. Mills was struck by the youthfulness of the crew–the captain was only 21 and his first officer all of 19. When the

submarine crash-dived, Mills recalls in his autobiography Up in the Clouds, Gentlemen Please: "The ship then seemed to stand on her nose and I felt her speeding like an arrow towards the sea bed; charts and crockery went flying in all directions; I hung on to a rail near the periscope trying to look heroic and totally unconcerned; the only thing that concerned me was the fact that I was sure my face had turned a pale shade of pea-green."

p, Edward Black; d, Anthony Asquith; w, J.B. Williams, Val Valentine, (uncredited) Frank Launder; ph, Jack Cox; ed, R.E. Dearing; md, Louis Levy; art d, W. Murton.

War Drama   **Cas.**   (PR:A MPAA:NR)

WE GO FAST*   (1941) 65m FOX bw

Lynn Bari (Rose Coughlin), Alan Curtis (Bob Brandon), Sheila Ryan (Diana Hempstead), Don Deforest [Defore] (Herman Huff), Ernest Truex (Harold Bruggins), Gerald Mohr (Nabob), Paul McGrath (Carberry), Thomas [Tom] Dugan (Dimwit), Arthur Hohl (Thin Man), James Flavin (Lt. Bardette), Arthur Loft (Frank Futter), Charles Arnt (Salesman), Charles Trowbridge (Lawyer), George Lessey (J.P. Hempstead).

About as awkward as its title, this lame tale has waitress, Bari, falling for a foreign businessman, Mohr, while receiving affection from a pair of motorcycle cops, Curtis and Deforest. She soon realises that Mohr is actually a crook, and goes back to flirting with her fast cop friends.

p, Lou Ostrow; d, William McGann; w, Thomas Lennon, Adrian Scott (based on a story by Doug Welch); ph, Harry Jackson; ed, Fred Allen; md, Emil Newman; cos, Herschel.

Drama   (PR:A MPAA:NR)

WE HAVE ONLY ONE LIFE*   (1963, Gr.) 116m Finos/Greek Motion Pictures bw (MIA ZOI TIN ECHOME)

Dimitri Horn (Kleon), Yvonne Sanson (Bibi), Basil Avlonitis (Guard), Christ Tzagneas (Bank President).

Along with Michael Cacoyannis and Nikos Kondourous, Tzavellas is one of Greece's big three on the international film scene. However, WE HAVE ONLY ONE LIFE doesn't add much to his reputation. It's a familiar tale of a bank clerk who steals a fortune in bank funds and shows his girl the good life. The cash soon runs out and the bank clerk finds himself in prison. Released in Greece in 1958.

d&w, George Tzavellas; ph, Dinos Katsouridis; m, Manos Hadjidakis.

Drama   (PR:A MPAA:NR)

WE HAVE OUR MOMENTS*   (1937) 65m UNIV bw

Sally Eilers (Mary Smith), James Dunn (John Wade), David Niven (Joe Gilling), Mischa Auer (Enrico Mussetti), Warren Hymer (Smacksey, Bodyguard), Marjorie Gateson (Mrs. Rutherford), Thurston Hall (Frank Rutherford), Virginia Sale (Miss Koltz), Grady Sutton (Clem Porter), Ray Brown (The Captain), Franklin Pangborn (Bartender), George Davis, Gunnis Davis (Waiters), Margaret McWade (Woman in Stateroom), Olaf Hytten (Steward), Alice Ardell (Stewardess), Alphonse Martell (Headwaiter), Jerry Larkin (Assistant Purser), Adrienne d'Ambricourt (Maid), Jack Chefe (Croupier), Joyce Compton (Carrie, School Teacher), John Maurice Sullivan (Bank Manager).

Eilers is a schoolteacher on a boat bound for Europe who becomes entangled with crooks who hide their stolen cash in her baggage. Meantime, French private eye Auer is trying to find the loot along with American detective Dunn, who falls for Eilers while doing so. WE HAVE OUR MOMENTS has its moments, but most of them have been done better in other pictures.

p, Edmund Grainger; d, Alfred L. Werker; w, Bruce Manning, Charles Grayson (based on the story by Charles F. Belden, Frederick Stephani); ph, Milton Krasner; ed, Frank Gross; md, Charles Previn; art d, Jack Otterson.

Crime/Romance   (PR:A MPAA:NR)

WE HUMANS   (SEE: YOUNG AMERICA, 1942)

WE JOINED THE NAVY*½   (1962, Brit.) 109m ABF/WB Pathe c (AKA: WE ARE IN THE NAVY NOW)

Kenneth More (Lt. Comdr. Badger), Lloyd Nolan (Vice Adm. Ryan), Joan O'Brien (Carol Blair), Mischa Auer (Colonel/President), Jeremy Lloyd (Dewberry), Dindsdale Landen (Bowles), Derek Fowlds (Carson), Denise Warren (Collette), John Le Mesurier (Dewberry, Sr.), Lally Bowers (Mrs. Dewberry), Laurence Naismith (Adm. Blake), Andrew Cruickshank (Adm. Filmer), Walter Fitzgerald (Adm. Thomas), John Phillips (Rear Admiral), Ronald Leigh-Hunt (Commander Royal Navy), Arthur Lovegrove (Chief Petty Officer Froud), Brian Wilde (Petty Officer Gibbons), Paul Maxwell (Comdr. Spelling U.S.N.), Nicholas Stuart (Comdr. Hurley U.S.N.), John Barrard (Consul), Esma Cannon (Consul's Wife), Kenneth Griffith (Orator), Hank (Albert), Dirk Bogarde (Dr. Simon Sparrow), Sidney James, Michael Bentine.

A tired service comedy about lieutenant commander More's sinking reputation among his fellow officers. He is sent to Dartmouth to train naval cadets and winds up at sea with three air-headed midshipmen. Everything runs off course and More's men get mixed up in a revolution, but soon all order is restored. Bogarde makes a guest appearance in a role out of DOCTOR AT SEA.

p, Daniel M. Angel; d, Wendy Toye; w, Arthur Dales (based on a novel by John Winton); ph, Otto Heller (CinemaScope, Eastmancolor); m, Ron Granier; ed, Richard Best; art d, John Howell; cos, Julie Harris.

Comedy   **(PR:A   MPAA:NR)**

WE LIVE AGAIN****   (1934) 85m UA bw

Anna Sten (*Katusha Maslova*), Fredric March (*Prince Dmitri Nekhlyudov*), Jane Baxter (*Missy Kortchagin*), C. Aubrey Smith (*Prince Kortchagin*), Sam Jaffe (*Gregory Simonson*), Ethel Griffies (*Aunt Maria*), Gwendolyn Logan (*Aunt Sophia*), Mary Forbes (*Mrs. Kortchagin*), Jessie Ralph (*Matrona Pavlovna*), Leonid Kinskey (*Simon Kartinkin*), Dale Fuller (*Yaphemia Batchkova*), Morgan Wallace (*Colonel*), Davison Clark (*Tikhon*), Crauford Kent (*Lt. Schonbock*), Barron Hesse (*Kortchagin's Butler*), Cecil Cunningham (*Theodosia*), Jessie Arnold (*Korbalova*), Edgar Norton, Michael S. Visaroff (*Judges*), Fritzi Ridgeway (*Redhead*), Newton House (*Aunt's Footman*), Akin Dobrynin (*Aunt's Coachman*), Serge Temoff (*Specialty Dancer*), Halliwell Hobbes, James Marcus, Gilbert Clayton, Alex Kandyba, Harry Cording, John Ince, George Burr MacAnnan, Jack Kenny, Theodore Lorch, Stanley Blystone, Bud Fine, Gordon DeMain, Harry Myers, Edwin Mordant, Dick Alexander, Anders Van Haden, Tom Wilson, Edward Gargan, Roger Gray, Agnes Steele.

This fine adaptation of Tolstoy's oft-filmed novel *Resurrection* opens in the countryside of Czarist Russia where a prince (March) grows up with Sten, a peasant servant girl. The two feel like social equals and Sten falls in love with the dashing March. He goes into the service and returns after two years to find Sten's affections unchanged. They attend Easter mass at a Russian Orthodox church and afterwards take a walk in the trees near March's aunts' home. There March seduces the adoring Sten, then slips out the next morning. He forgets all about the poor girl, who is now expecting their child. Sten tries to recapture his heart, and at one point runs through a storm after a train to catch his attention. March continues playing cards with fellow army officers, oblivious to the girl's efforts. Later, her child dies and Sten, accompanied only by another servant, buries the tiny coffin in unconsecrated ground. Seven years pass and March (now with a beard) is engaged to marry Baxter, daughter of a fellow Russian prince, Smith. Smith invites March to sit in as juror on a murder case he is trying, involving a prostitute charged with murder. The accused is none other than Sten, who has turned to a life of ill repute following the emotionally devastating events of her life. Sten is innocent of the crime, and March realizes that he is the cause of her downfall. March presses for acquittal, but the Russian legal system is strict. Through a miswording of the verdict, Sten is found guilty and sentenced to exile in Siberia. March tries to get Sten released, but she only mocks her former lover's efforts. March decides he must pay for the suffering he has caused Sten, and consequently gives up all his land to his retainers. After selling all of his possessions as well, March joins Sten on her long journey to Siberia, telling her, "All I ask is to live again with your forgiveness and your help and your love." This classic story of redemption is beautifully told under Mamoulian's strong direction. March and Sten are excellent as the tragic lovers, giving their roles depth and intensity. The photography, by master lensman Toland, gives the film a moody, atmospheric look which further enhances the strong emotions of the story. Tolstoy's novel had been filmed three times in the silent era: first by D.W. Griffith in 1909, then in 1918 with Pauline Frederick, and again in 1927 with Dolores Del Rio and Rod LaRocque. Lupe Velez also appeared in a 1931 sound version shot in both Spanish and English. But producer Goldwyn, in typical fashion, dismissed these previous outings, exclaiming, "It has not been made until I make it." Goldwyn was furiously trying to promote Sten, an actress he considered to be "the Russian Garbo." This was her follow-up to NANA, and though she again gave an admirable performance, Sten never caught on as Goldwyn had hoped. Anderson and Praskins both receive credit for the screenplay along with Sturges, though neither writer made contributions to the final script. Both had written drafts which were unacceptable by Goldwyn's standards, and though the producer was essentially distrustful of Sturges, the future director was finally given the assignment after Mamoulian's urgings. Condensing a 400-page novel into an 85-minute film proved to be a difficult but not insurmountable task, and Sturges turned out his script in a surprisingly short amount of time. Thornton Wilder made a small, uncredited contribution to the screenplay as well. According to some reports, Goldwyn was highly impressed with the Russian Orthodox Easter service portrayed in the film, though the music was accidentally recorded backwards. Because of Goldwyn's enthusiasm for the scene, no one dared to tell him of the error and the sequence stayed as is. Other complaints rose from Goldwyn's seeming misunderstanding of the story. At one point the noted mogul observed of March's character: "This Dmitri. He is a horse's ass!" An ad campaign for the film boasted "the directorial genius of Mamoulian, the beauty of Sten, and the producing genius of Goldwyn have combined to make the world's greatest entertainment." Goldwyn reportedly was pleased with this hook, exclaiming: "That's the kind of ad I like. Facts. No exaggeration." Two more versions of Tolstoy's novel followed, a 1943

Mexican adaptation and a 1958 German-French coproduction, AUFER-STEHUNG, featuring Horst Buchholz in the March role.

p, Samuel Goldwyn; d, Rouben Mamoulian; w, Maxwell Anderson, Leonard Praskins, Preston Sturges, (uncredited) Thornton Wilder (based on the novel *Resurrection* by Leo Tolstoy); ph, Gregg Toland; m, Alfred Newman; ed, Otho Lovering; prod d, Sergei Sudeikin; md, Newman; art d, Richard Day; cos, Omar Kiam.

Drama   **(PR:C   MPAA:NR)**

WE OF THE NEVER NEVER**½   (1983, Aus.) 132m
                                              Adams-Packer-Mainline/Triumph c

Angela Punch McGregor (*Jeannie*), Arthur Dignam (*Aeneas Gunn*), Tony Barry (*Mac*), Tommy Lewis (*Jackeroo*), Lewis Fitz-Gerald (*Jack*), Martin Vaughan (*Dan*), John Jarratt (*Dandy*), Tex Morton (*Landlord*), Donald Blitner (*Goggle Eye*), Kim Chiu Kok (*Sam Lee*), Mawuyul Yanthalawuy (*Rose*), Cecil Parkee (*Cheon*), Brian Granrott (*Neaves*), Danny Adcock (*Brown*), John Cameron (*Jimmy Dodd*), Sibina Willy (*Bett Bett*), Jessie Roberts (*Nellie*), Christine Conway (*Judy*), Ray Pattison (*Johnny Wakelin*), George Jadarku (*Charly*), Sally McKenzie (*Carrie*), Sarah Craig (*Liz*), Fincina Hopgood (*Dot*), Lise Rodgers, Dayle Alison, Jenni Cunningham (*Friends*).

A visually stunning film, WE OF THE NEVER NEVER richly details the period flavor of Australia in a cinematic handling of the memoirs of the first white women to travel the aborigine wilderness known as the "Never Never." It is so impressive to look at that one can recommend it solely on that basis. However, by now the Australian landscape is becoming quite familiar and an overlong, weakly-scripted picture such as WE OF THE NEVER NEVER doesn't do much for one's faith in that country's output.

p, Greg Tepper, John B. Murray; d, Igor Auzins; w, Peter Schreck (based on the book by Jane Taylor Gunn); ph Gary Hansen (Technovision, Eastmancolor); m, Peter Best; ed, Clifford Hayes; prod d, Josephine Ford; cos, Camilla Rountree, May Botterill, Fiona Nicolls.

Drama/Adventure   Cas.   **(PR:C   MPAA:G)**

WE SHALL RETURN** (1963) 92m United International/Cari-Cinema
                                                       Video International bw

Cesar Romero, Tony Ray, Linda Libera, Ramon Rodrigues, Mario Rodrigues, Nina Ortiz, Paul Daniel.

Wealthy Cuban landowner Romero flees his Fidel Castro-led country with his son and his son's fiancee. In Miami he meets his older son, a member of the "Free Cuba" pro-Castro forces who plan to sabotage the Bay of Pigs invasion. The boy is killed by his father, who wants to prevent betrayal and preserve the spirit of Cuba.

p, Robert M. Carson; d, Philip S. Goodman; w, Pat Frank; ph, Ted Saizis, Vincent Saizis; m, Edgar Summerlin; ed, David Tucker.

Drama   **(PR:A   MPAA:NR)**

WE SHALL SEE* (1964, Brit.) 61m Merton Park/Anglo Amalgamated
                                                                                       bw

Maurice Kaufmann (*Evan Collins*), Faith Brook (*Alva Collins*), Alec Mango (*Ludo*), Alex McIntosh (*Greg Thomas*), Hugh Paddick (*Connell*), Talitha Pol (*Jirina*), Bridget Armstrong (*Rosemary Layton*), William Abney (*Shaw*), Donald Morley.

Predating THE DEADLY BEES by three years, WE SHALL SEE is theoretically the first "killer bee" movie. The deranged wife of an airline pilot is killed when someone throws a hive of bees into her bedroom, knowing that she is allergic to bee stings. The rest of the picture is a standard crime tale as the murderous hive-tosser is tracked down and caught.

p, Jack Greenwood; d, Quentin Lawrence; w, Donal Giltinan (based on a novel by Edgar Wallace); m, Bernard Ebbinghouse; ed, Derek Holding; art d, Peter Mullins.

Crime   **(PR:C   MPAA:NR)**

WE STILL KILL THE OLD WAY**½ (1967, Ital.) 92m Cemo/Lopert
                                              c (A CIASCUNO IL SUO)

Gian Maria Volonte (*Prof. Paolo Laurana*), Irene Papas (*Luisa Roscio*), Gabriele Ferzetti (*Rosello*), Salvo Randone (*Prof. Roscio*), Luigi Pistilli (*Arturo Manno*), Mario Scaccia (*Priest*), Laura Nucci (*Paolo's Mother*), Leopoldo Trieste (*Member of Parliament*), Franco Tranchina (*Dr. Antonio Roscio*), Luciana Scalise (*Rosina*), Anna Rivero (*Manno's Wife*), Giovanni Pallavicino (*Raganae*), Orio Cannarozzo (*Police Inspector*), Carmelo Oliviero (*Archpriest*), Tanina Zappala.

An intriguing crime melodrama about Volonte's attempts to uncover the real reasons behind the deaths of two town figures, one of whom was having an affair with a peasant girl. Everyone asssumes this to be the reason for the murders, but Volonte unearths a diary which points to involvement in the Mafia and a plot to incriminate Mafia leaders. Volonte's life is spared since he has the diary, but he finally becomes the victim of Sicilian assassins, which permanently covers up the facts behind the case. Director Petri would soon win an Academy Award for his INVESTIGATION OF A CITIZEN ABOVE SUSPICION, a superior crime meller. (In Italian; English subtitles.)

p, Giuseppe Zaccariello; d, Elio Petri; w, Petri, Ugo Pirro (based on the novel by Leonardo Sciascia); ph, Luigi Kuveiller (Technicolor); m, Luis Enriquez Bacalov; ed, Ruggero Mastroainni; art d, Sergio Canevari; cos, Luciana Marinucci; makeup, Pier Antonio Mecacci.

Crime Drama   (PR:C   MPAA:NR)

WE THREE   (SEE: COMPROMISED, 1931)

WE WANT TO LIVE ALONE   (SEE: FATHER CAME TOO, 1966, Brit.)

WE WENT TO COLLEGE**   (1936) 64m MGM bw (GB: THE OLD SCHOOL TIE)

Charles Butterworth (Glenn Harvey), Walter Abel (Phil Talbot), Hugh Herbert (Professor), Una Merkel (Susan), Edith Atwater (Nina), Walter Catlett (Sen. Budger), Charles Trowbridge (President Timlin), Tom Ricketts (Grandpop).

Butterworth leads the comic escapades in this one as he returns to his college in hopes of recapturing the youthful exuberance of his school days. During football homecoming week, a victim of too much alcohol, he finds his way onto the field and tries to prevent his team from being scored against. Abel takes the role of a snooty contractor who sees nothing but dollar signs and Herbert is a lame-brained professor, both of whom also return to their old stomping grounds.

P, Harry Rapf; d, Joseph Stanley; w, Richard Maibaum, Maurice Rapf (based on a story by George Oppenheimer, Finley Peter Dunne, Jr.); ph, Lester White; m, Dr. William Axt; ed, James E. Newcom; art d, Frederic Hope; cos, Dolly Tree.

Comedy   (PR:A   MPAA:NR)

WE WERE DANCING½**   (1942) 95m MGM bw

Norma Shearer (Vicki Wilomirsky), Melvyn Douglas (Nicki Prax), Gail Patrick (Linda Wayne), Lee Bowman (Hubert Tyler), Marjorie Main (Judge Sidney Hawkes), Reginald Owen (Maj. Tyler-Blane), Alan Mowbray (Grand Duke Basil), Florence Bates (Mrs. Vanderlip), Sig Rumann (Baron Prax), Dennis Hoey (Prince Wilomirsky), Heather Thatcher (Mrs. Tyler-Blane), Connie Gilchrist (Olive Hansome), Florence Shirley (Mrs. Charteris), Paul Porcasi (Manager of Duquesne), John Piffle (Dutchman), Lionel Pape (Englishman), Philip Ahn (Chinaman), George H. Reed (Butler at Blane's House), Ottola Nesmith (Mrs. Quimby), Mary Forbes (Mrs. Sandys), Thurston Hall (Sen. Quimby), Douglas Wood (Col. Sandys), Alan Napier (Capt. Blackstone), Martin Turner (Red Cap), Pierre Watkin (Mr. Bentley), Bryant Washburn, Sr. (Mr. Lambert), Nella Walker (Mrs. Bentley), Helene Millard (Mrs. Lambert), Florence Wix (Sporting Woman), Alfred Hall (Butler), Alex Callam (Clerk), Dick Elliott (Mr. Platt), Jessamine Newcombe (Mrs. Platt), Betty Hayward (Debutante), John Roche (Mr. Fox), Duncan Renaldo (Sam Estrella), Russell Hicks (Bryce- Carew), Norma Varden (Mrs. Bryce-Carew), Anthony Marsh (Tommy Brooke), Willy Castello (Felucci), Emmett Vogan (Bailiff), Harry Hayden (Clerk), Polly Bailey (Flower Woman), Tim Ryan (Traffic Cop), Jean Fenwick (Girl), Fred Santley (Clerk), Harold Minjir (Beverly), Ian Wolfe (Reggie), Barlowe Borland (McDonough), Dick Alexander (Moving Man), Alex Pollard (Ransome's Butler), Jacques Vanaire (Beverly's Assistant), Gino Corrado (Headwaiter in Inn), Esther Michelson (Headwaiter's Wife), Meeka Aldrich (Housemaid), Henry Roquemore (Mr. Ransome), Charles Sullivan (Train Announcer), Bill Fisher (Train Conductor), John "Buddy" Williams (Red Cap), John Holland, Herbert Rawlinson (Friends), Ava Gardner (Girl).

Loosely based on two of the nine plays that made up Noel Coward's 1937 hit, "Tonight at 8:30," this film marked Shearer's return to the screen after a layoff of more than a year. She'd turned down the role of "Scarlett" in GONE WITH THE WIND and "Mrs. Miniver" in the film of the same name and it was hard to believe she'd find this script preferable over those. This time she's a poor Polish princess who meets Douglas, an Austrian baron who is all title and no cash. Shearer is at a party in South Carolina celebrating her upcoming marriage to socialite Bowman at Bowman's family home, which is overseen by his parents, Owen and Thatcher. Douglas and Shearer meet at the party, dance one waltz, and she is soon aware that he is the man for her. Douglas has no business at the party but has crashed it with such debonair aplomb that he seems to be in the right spot. Love happens instantly and Douglas and Shearer run off to be married, each thinking that the other is filthy rich. The rest of the guests are thunderstruck at this turn of events, led by Bowman and his dumbfounded parents. Once married, they finally come to understand that they are cut from the same cloth and are little more than professional sharpers who have managed to eke out existences by being charming and suave. They decide to pretend being single but continue to see each other on the sly. When Patrick, a rich decorator who had been Douglas' lover some time before, finds out they are married, she lets the world know, thereby ruining their entries into the homes of the rich

and famous in the East. Now unable to attend the soignee soirees of Newport, Rhode Island, New York, Palm Beach, and other watering holes, Douglas and Shearer, still very much in love, make their way to the relatively unsophisticated climes of the Midwest. They manage to insinuate themselves in the home of some nouveau riche people and are living well but the thought that they don't actually *do* anything begins to nag at Shearer and she prevails on Douglas to find a career. Patrick arrives and still carries a torch for Douglas so she sets her cap for him. This behavior enrages Shearer and she sues for divorce-- exactly what Patrick wants. Bowman enters again and he and Shearer plan the marriage that went out the window in the first reel. Douglas goes to see Patrick at her decorating studio and demonstrates that he has a good knowledge of the business and excellent taste. Patrick has accepted the assignment of decorating Bowman's residence in preparation for his marriage to Shearer and Patrick gives Douglas the task of taking care of the details, a mistake that everyone in the audience knew would lead to the eventual reunion of Shearer and Douglas. He arrives at the Bowman home and does a smashing job of putting the place in order. Shearer watches his work in awe and is infuriated by the fact that Douglas acts as though he were a hired hand (which he is) and pays scant attention to her. The date of the marriage comes closer and Douglas breaks down her reserve and pleads with her to abort the wedding. Shearer feels awful about that and can't bear to leave Bowman in the lurch twice in a row. At the home of Bowman's mother, a repeat of the earlier betrothal scene is going on. Douglas tells Shearer that he understands how she feels and says his last farewell but pleads for one final dance. The orchestra plays the same waltz heard in the first reel and the music works a magic spell. Shearer and Douglas dance, kiss, and take off again as the movie ends. In small roles, note Alan Napier, who became famous as "Alfred the Butler" on "Batman," and Philip Ahn, who later opened a successful restaurant in Los Angeles, and Ava Gardner in her film debut. Everyone in the picture was dressed to the teeth and there were more tuxedos in this movie than the average debutante ball at the Plaza. What was missing was any semblance of the delicious dialog of Coward. It was a comedy of manners and morals with one straight line after another and hardly a punch line to be found. And since the country was in the deepest, darkest throes of the war, this kind of movie seemed outdated and old hat when compared to the headlines in every day's newspaper.

p, Robert Z. Leonard, Orville O. Dull; d, Leonard; w, Claudine West, Hans Rameau, George Froeschel (based on the play "Tonight at 8:30" by Noel Coward); ph, Robert Planck; m, Bronislau Kaper; ed, George Boemler; art d, Cedric Gibbons; cos, Adrian, Robert Kalloch.

Comedy   (PR:A   MPAA:NR)

WE WERE STRANGERS*½**   (1949) 106m Horizon/COL bw

Jennifer Jones (China Valdes), John Garfield (Tony Fenner), Pedro Armendariz (Armando Ariete), Gilbert Roland (Guillermo), Ramon Novarro (Chief), Wally Cassell (Miguel), David Bond (Ramon), Jose Perez (Toto), Morris Ankrum (Bank Manager), Tito Renaldo (Manolo), Paul Monte (Roberto), Leonard Strong (Bombmaker), Robert Tafur (Rubio), Alexander McSweyn, Alfonso Pedroza (Sanitation Men), Ted Hecht (Enrico), Santiago Martinez (Waiter), Joel Rene (Student), Argentina Brunetti, Mimi Aguglia (Mamas), Robert Malcolm (Priest), Roberta Haynes (Lolita), Lelia Goldoni (Consuelo), Paul Marion (Truck Driver), Felipe Turich (Spy), Fred Chapman (Altar Boy), Julian Rivero (Flower Vendor), Rod Redwing, Charles Granucci, Herschel Graham, Abdullah Abbas, Gertrude Chorre, Thomas Quon Woo, Spencer Chan, Edwin Rochelle, Rodolfo Hoyos, Billy Wilson, Tina Menard, Joe Sawaya (Bits), Harry Vejar (Watchman), Fred Godoy (Contreras), Peter Virgo (Contreras' Chauffeur).

Huston's follow-up film to THE TREASURE OF THE SIERRA MADRE and KEY LARGO doesn't measure up to either of these classics, but is certainly an entertaining picture in its own right. It is 1933 and Garfield is an American citizen, returning to his native Cuba to help his people in revolution. Knowing that some government officials are about to attend a funeral, Garfield plans to assassinate them by detonating some explosives hidden in an underground tunnel beneath a cemetery (an idea that was successfully used in real life to blow up the automobile of an heir to Spain's Generalissimo Francisco Franco). Garfield and three comrades begin to build the tunnel, though one of the men, Roland, nearly ruins the plan. He comes to realize that innocent people might be killed, but Garfield is insistent that their work is for the good of the revolution. The plan falls apart, though, when officials change the location of the funeral and the police descend on the revolutionaries. Garfield dies in a terrific gun battle, but not before hearing the sounds of his people beginning their own revolt in the nearby streets. This starts out strong, but the film never succeeds in fulfilling its promising beginnings. The Huston theme of male bonding under dangerous conditions, ultimately leading to death, permeates the picture, but his direction never pulls the material together with the needed excitement. Political themes introduced in the beginning are almost entirely forgotten by the film's end. Still, Huston does know how to tell a story, and this holds viewer interest throughout. Garfield is good, though at times he seems uncomfortable with the part. Jones, as one of Garfield's revolutionary comrades, uses a Cuban accent as though it was her second nature, delivering a nice supporting performance. Garfield and Huston both had another actress in mind for the role: the then unknown Marilyn Monroe. Huston set up a color screen test, with Garfield to play opposite her, but, for inexplicable reasons producer Spiegel canceled this. Huston ended up using Monroe in his next film, THE ASPHALT JUNGLE. For some second-unit photography to be done in Havana, Huston and co- writer Viertel went down to Cuba to scout locations. While there, the two men looked up Viertel's friend Ernest Hemingway, and took in a few days on the writer's boat, *Pilar*. Though this was a serious film, the shooting was not without some lighter moments. As a gag, Huston planted a prop hand in a grave, then, under moody lighting, instructed Jones to dig. The effect was perfect, giving the actress quite a scare. It was the director's intention for this film to be a political allegory aimed at the House Un-American Activities Committee, but this was missed by both right- and left-wing political factions. The conservative *Hollywood Reporter* accused Huston of serving up "...the heaviest dish of Red theory ever served to audiences outside the Soviet Union." The American Communist Party newspaper *Daily Worker*, on the other hand, dismissed the film as "capitalistic propaganda." "I was," wrote Huston in his autobiography *An Open Book*, "able to laugh the whole thing off as utter nonsense." Viewers of both political persuasions were uninterested in the film, however, and Columbia pulled it from release shortly after its premiere because of the poor turnout at the box office.

p, S.P. Eagle 'Sam Spiegel'; d, John Huston; w, Huston, Peter Viertel (based on the novel *Rough Sketch* by Robert Sylvester); ph, Russell Metty; m, George Antheil; ed, Al Clark; md, M.W. Stoloff; art d, Cary Odell; set d, Louis Diage; cos, Jean Louis; makeup, Robert Shiffer.

Adventure/Drama   (PR:C   MPAA:NR)

WE WHO ARE ABOUT TO DIE**   (1937) 82m RKO bw

Preston Foster *(Mathews)*, Ann Dvorak *(Connie)*, John Beal *(John)*, Ray Mayer *(Bright Boy)*, Gordon Jones *(Slim Tolliver)*, Russell Hopton *(Mac)*, J. Carroll Naish *(Nick)*, Paul Hurst *(Tip Fuller)*, Frank Jenks *(Clyde)*, John Wray *(Jerry)*, Barnett Parker *(Barkly)*, Willie Fung *(Kwong)*, John Carroll *(Joe Donahue)*, DeWitt Jennings *(Watchman)*, Landers Stevens *(Warden)*, John "Skins" Miller *(Macy)*, Howard Hickman *(Prison Chaplain)*, Robert Emmett O'Connor *(Mitchell)*, Frank M. Thomas *(Carter)*.

San Quentin is the setting for this prison drama about an inmate sentenced to die, and the extent to which others go to prove his innocence. Girl friend Dvorak and private eye Foster get Beal released with almost no time to spare as he walks through the halls of Death Row toward the chair. Based on the true life story of a prisoner who spent 13 months in San Quentin before winning a reprieve.

p, Edward Small; d, Christy Cabanne; w, John Twist (based on the story by David Lamson); ph, Robert Planck; ed, Arthur Roberts; cos, Edward Stevenson.

Prison Drama   (PR:A   MPAA:NR)

WE WHO ARE YOUNG**½   (1940) 80m MGM bw

Lana Turner *(Margy Brooks)*, John Shelton *(William Brooks)*, Gene Lockhart *(C.B. Beamis)*, Jonathan Hale *(William Braddock)*, Grant Mitchell *(Jones)*, Henry Armetta *(Tony)*, Irene Seidner *(Mrs. Weinstock)*, Clarence Wilson *(R. Glassford)*, Charles Lane *(Perkins)*, Hal K. Dawson *(Salesman)*, Richard Crane *(Bellboy)*, John Butler *(Peabody)*, Horace McMahon *(Foreman)*, Ian Wolfe *(Judge)*, Dorothy Adams *(Nurse)*, Don Castle, Jack Rice *(Clerks)*, Harry Hayden *(Examiner)*, Bill Lally, Edgar Dearing, Ralph Dunn *(Policemen)*, Hal Price *(Bartender)*, Truman Bradley *(Commentator)*, Grady Sutton *(New Father)*, Charles McMurphy *(Mover)*.

Dalton Trumbo's screenplay gave the formerly glamorous Turner an opportunity to strut her stuff as a serious actress and the result was a toning down of the blazing blonde to wistful brunette. The audience much preferred the glitz to the drama and the studio changed the ad campaign to reflect a poll they took so the movie's ads did not truly reflect the nature of the story (so what else is new?). Turner and Shelton are coworkers who meet, fall in love, and marry. They toil in an accounting office where it is forbidden for people to marry coworkers so they must keep their union a secret or lose their positions. They soon find themselves in the same situations as most newlyweds face: financial woes, approaching parenthood, etc. Set in New York City, the movie darts quickly as their marriage is disclosed, Turner loses her job, their furniture is repossessed, and, when Shelton gets involved with some loan sharks, he loses his job as well. They are forced to seek aid. Shelton tries to find other work to no avail and whatever problems that can befall a young couple are heaped upon their shoulders. Grouch Lockhart, who runs the office, finally helps them. The final scene shows a desperate Shelton stealing a car so he can drive the very pregnant Turner to the hospital in time to deliver twins. (Someone must have felt the picture needed a bang-up ending so they handed us two children for the price of one.) This was but one of many "love against all odds" films of the 1940s and comparisons between this movie and others of the period were inevitable. Shelton was good and great hopes were placed on him but the studio didn't groom him in the same fashion they'd done with others and he faded from sight. Turner showed that she was more than a bust and a smile and this role helped convince the powers at the top that she had what it took to be a real actress. Lockhart was excellent in his role, as were all the others. It's slow, somewhat predictable, but pleasant for mature audiences or for anyone who has been through the troubles of being young and in love.

p, Seymour Nebenzahl; d, Harold S. Bucquet; w, Dalton Trumbo (based on a story by Trumbo); ph, Karl Freund; m, Bronislau Kaper; ed, Howard O'Neill; art d, Cedric Gibbons, Wade B. Rubottom; set d, Edwin B. Willis; cos, Dolly Tree.

Romance   (PR:A-C   MPAA:NR)

WE WILL REMEMBER**   (1966, Jap.) 134m Toho/Official Films c
                                  (SENJO NI NAGARERU UTA)

Hisaya Morishige *(Kiyoshi Kodama)*, Chang Mei Yao *(Yoichi Mashio)*, Keiju Kobayashi *(Masaya Nihei)*, Daisuke Kato *(Akira Kubo)*, Kon Omura, Yuzo Kayama, Kiyoshi Kodama, Yoichi Mashio, Yukihiko Gondo, Kazuo Suzuki, Chutaro Togin, Yoko Fujiyama.

With WW II approaching its end, a group of youthful Japanese volunteer for duty with an army band in the hope that doing so will keep them from combat. They are soon sent to the Chinese front to help boost morale and are attacked and brutally beaten by the Chinese with the survivors ending up in a POW camp. Interesting for the glimpses of Japanese basic training during the war and life in a combat zone.

p, Sanezumi Fujimoto; d&w, Zenzo Matsuyama (based on a story by Ikuma Dan); ph, Asaichi Nakai (Tohoscope, Eastmancolor); m, Dan.

War   (PR:AC-O   MPAA:NR)

WEAK AND THE WICKED, THE**   (1954, Brit.) 88m Marble
                                          Arch/ABF-AA bw

Glynis Johns *(Jean Raymond)*, John Gregson *(Michael)*, Jane Hylton *(Babs)*, Diana Dors *(Betty)*, Sidney James *(Sid Baden)*, A.E. Matthews *(Harry Wicks)*, Anthony Nichols *(Chaplain)*, Athene Seyler *(Millie)*, Olive Sloane *(Nellie Baden)*, Sybil Thorndike *(Mabel)*, Barbara Couper *(Doctor)*, Joyce Heron *(PO Arnold)*, Ursula Howells *(Pam)*, Mary Merrall *(Mrs. Skinner)*, Rachel Roberts *(Pat)*, Marjorie Rhodes *(Susie)*, Josephine Griffin *(Miriam)*, Simone Silva *(Tina)*, Josephine Stuart *(Andy)*, Edwin Styles *(Seymour)*, Cecil Trouncer *(Judge)*, Paul Carpenter *(Joe)*, Eliot Makeham *(Grandad)*, Jean Taylor-Smith *(Grange Warden)*, Sandra Dorne, Bessie Love *(Prisoners)*, Joan Haythorne, Thea Gregory, Tom Gill, Irene Handl, Marjorie Stewart, Hannah Watt, Kathleen Michael, Maureen Pryor, Ruth Denning, Margaret Diamond.

Johns is sent to jail for one year after failing to pay her gambling debts and she befriends a number of inmates, including Dors, who is taking a rap for her boy friend. Prison life (an "open" prison where good behavior is all-important) is given a glorified depiction and by the finale Johns has done her time and her beau has returned. Based on the real-life prison stay of author Joan Henry.

p, Victor Skutezky; d, J. Lee Thompson; w, Thompson, Anne Burnaby, Joan Henry (based on the book *Who Lie in Gaol* by Henry); ph, Gilbert Taylor; ed, Richard Best.

Prison Drama   (PR:A   MPAA:NR)

WEAKER SEX, THE**   (1949, Brit.) 89m RANK-TC/EL bw

Ursula Jeans *(Martha Dacre)*, Cecil Parker *(Geoffrey Radcliffe)*, Joan Hopkins *(Helen Dacre)*, Derek Bond *(Nigel)*, Lana Morris *(Lolly Dacre)*, John Stone *(Roddy)*, Thora Hird *(Mrs. Gaye, Servant)*, Digby Wolfe *(Benjie Dacre)*, Marian Spencer *(Harriet Lessing)*, Dorothy Bramhall *(Mrs. Maling)*, Bill Owen *(Soldier)*, Kynaston Reeves *(Capt. Dishart)*, Eleanor Summerfield *(Clippie)*, Gladys Henson *(Woman)*, Basil Appleby, Vi Kaley, Campbell Cotts, Merle Tottenham, Rosemary Lomax, Evelyn Moore, Helen Goss, Joan White, Kathleen Boutall, Josephine Ingram.

The title is ironic and applies to the life of a housewife on the eve of D-Day in Europe during WW II. Jeans is the housewife widow who gives lodgings to a pair of navy men, while her two daughters lend a hand as Wrens and her son fights in Europe. She and one daughter get involved with the sailors and marry them, while worrying that the son in the family may never return. D-Day arrives, the war is finally over, and the son comes home, with all of them ostensibly facing the horrible fact that a third world war is a distinct possibility. The picture lacks action but makes up for it in its good characterizations and obvious sincerity.

p, Paul Soskin; d, Roy Baker; w, Esther McCracken, Soskin (based on the play "No Medals" by McCracken); ph, Erwin Hillier, Eric Besche; m, Arthur Wilkinson; ed, Michael Joseph Stirling; md, Muir Mathieson; art d, Alex Vetchinsky.

War Drama   (PR:A   MPAA:NR)

WEAPON, THE**½   (1957, Brit.) 80m Periclean/REP bw

Steve Cochran *(Mark Andrews)*, Lizabeth Scott *(Elsa Jenner)*, Herbert Marshall *(Inspector Mackenzie)*, Nicole Maurey *(Vivienne)*, Jon Whiteley *(Erik Jenner)*, George Cole *(Joshua Henry)*, Laurence Naismith *(Jamison)*, Stanley Maxted *(Colonel)*, Denis Shaw *(Groggins)*, Fred Johnson *(Fitzsimmons)*, John Horsley *(Johnson)*, Basil Dignam, Richard Goolden, Arthur Lovegrove, Felix Felton, Joan Schofield, Myrtle Reed, Roland Brand, Ryck Rydon, Vivan Matalon, Peter Augustine, George Bradford, Peter Godsell,

Fraser Hines, Joe Aston & Renee.

A neat suspense story about a youngster, Whiteley, who accidentally shoots his playmate with a gun he finds, hiding it after the incident and running away. The gun turns out to be the murder weapon in a case involving a U.S. Army officer 10 years earlier. CID officer Cochran is in pursuit of the boy, as is the murderer of the army man. The killer tries to force the boy to dig up the weapon, but has to flee when Cochran closes in. The chase leads to a gutted building and the killer falls to his death. A well-crafted, energetic thriller.

p, Hal E. Chester, Frank Bevis; d, Val Guest; w, Fred Frieberger (based on a story by Frieberger, Chester); ph, Reg Wyer; m, James Stevens; ed, Peter Rolfe Johnson; art d, John Stoll.

Drama/Crime   **(PR:C   MPAA:NR)**

WEARY RIVER*½   (1929) 84m FN/WB bw

Richard Barthelmess (*Jerry Larrabee*), Betty Compson (*Alice*), William Holden (*Warden*), Louis Natheaux (*Spadoni*), George Stone (*Blackie*), Raymond Turner (*Elevator Boy*), Gladden James (*Manager*).

Barthelmess is cast as a gangster who winds up in jail after another crook squeals on him. While in prison, Barthelmess discovers a knack for singing. He joins the prison band and takes his jailhouse routines to the top of the charts. The governor, impressed with his voice and his amiable personality, arranges for his release. A good excuse to use sound but after warbling the same tune three times one wishes he could turn off Barthelmess' voice.

d, Frank Lloyd; w, Bradley King, Tom J. Geraghty (based on a story by Courtney Ryley Cooper); ph, Ernest Haller; ed, Edward Schroeder, Paul Perez; art d, John J. Hughes; cos, Max Ree; m/l, "Weary River," Louis Silvers, Grant Clarke.

Prison Drama/Musical   **(PR:A   MPAA:NR)**

WEATHER IN THE STREETS, THE*½   (1983, Bri.) 133m
                                    Rediffusion-BBC TV-BritanniaT V c

Michael York (*Rollo*), Lisa Eichhorn (*Olivia*), Joanna Lumley (*Kate*), Rosalind Ayres (*Etty*), Faith Brook (*Lady Spencer*), Isabel Dean (*Mrs. Curtis*), Sebastian Shaw (*Mr. Curtis*).

An overlong between the wars tale about a gorgeous young woman, Eichhorn, who has an affair with the married York, only to become pregnant and lose him, as well as the child, to end up a sadder but wiser woman. All very cliched and mannered and excrutiatingly slow-paced, none of it adding up to much. Eichhorn, who turned in a virtuoso performance in CUTTER'S WAY, again does so here, proving to be the only thing worth watching in THE WEATHER IN THE STREETS.

p, Alan Shallcross; d, Gavin Millar; w, Julian Mitchell (based on novel by Rosamond Lehmann); ph, John Hooper; m, Carl Davis; ed, Angus Newton; art d, Don Homfray; cos, Amy Roberts.

Drama   **(PR:C   MPAA:NR)**

WEB, THE*   (1947) 87m UNIV bw

Ella Raines (*Noel Faraday*), Edmond O'Brien (*Bob Regan*), William Bendix (*Lt. Damico*), Vincent Price (*Andrew Colby*), Maria Palmer (*Martha Kroner*), John Abbott (*Charles Murdoch*), Fritz Leiber (*Leopold Kroner*), Howland Chamberlin (*James Nolan*), Tito Vuolo (*Emilio Canepa*), Wilton Graff (*District Attorney*), Robin Raymond (*Newspaper Librarian*), Ed Begley (*Man*), Joe Kirk, William Haade, Ethan Laidlaw (*Plainclothesmen*), Patricia Alphin (*Secretary*), Pierre Watkin (*Mr. Griswold*), Alex Frazer (*Medical Examiner*), Jack G. Lee (*Maintenance Man*), Lorin Baker (*Assistant*), Lee Phelps (*Policeman*), Ted Stanhope (*Clerk*), Russell Conway (*Mike the Fingerprint Man*), Bob Allen (*Office Boy*), Jack Gargan (*Ticket Man*), Gino Corrado (*Waiter*), Lee Shumway (*Cop*), Ralph Montgomery (*Photographer*).

An absorbing crime drama which casts Price as a wealthy business tycoon who hires attorney O'Brien to work as his bodyguard. When he gets entangled in Price's venomous scheme to snare a stolen $1 million, O'Brien backs off, thinking he may be a fall guy. He enlists the aid of tough police lieutenant Bendix and together they trick Price into a confession. Packed with suspense and a script that delivers with a wallop, not to mention outstanding performances from O'Brien and Bendix.

p, Jerry Bresler; d, Michael Gordon; w, William Bowers, Bertram Milhauser (based on the story by Harry Kurnitz); ph, Irving Glassberg; m, Hans J. Salter; ed, Russell Schoengarth; art d, Bernard Herzbrun, James Sullivan; set d, Russell A. Gausman, William L. Stevens; cos, Yvonne Wood.

Crime   **(PR:A   MPAA:NR)**

WEB OF DANGER, THE   (1947) 58m REP bw

Adele Mara (*Peg Mallory*), Bill Kennedy (*Ernie Reardon*), Damian O'Flynn (*Bill O'Hara*), Richard Loo (*Wing*), Victor Sen Yung (*Sam*), Roy Barcroft (*Monks*), William Hall (*Slim*), J. Farrell MacDonald (*MacKronish*), Michael Branden, [Archie Twitchell] (*Ramsey*), Ed Gargan (*Dolan*), Chester Clute (*Customer*), Ralph Sanford (*Peterson*), Russell Hicks (*Gallagher*).

Stamped out of a familiar mold, THE WEB OF DANGER is set against a backdrop of bridge building with Kennedy and O'Flynn as part of a construction crew. Their rivalry is enhanced by their mutual interest in Mara, but a flood and an urgency to finish the bridge to help refugees flee the inundated valley brings them together and puts Mara on the back-burner.

p, Donald H. Brown; d, Philip Ford; w, David Lang, Milton M. Raison; ph, Alfred S. Keller; ed, William Thompson; md, Mort Glickman; art d, Gano Chittenden; set d, John McCarthy, Jr., George Suhr; spec eff, Howard Lydecker, Theodore Lydecker.

Action   **(PR:A   MPAA:NR)**

WEB OF EVIDENCE   (SEE: BEYOND THIS PLACE, 1959, Brit.)

WEB OF FEAR½**   (1966, Fr./Span.) 92m Luxor Capitole Balcazar
                            P.C./Comet bw (CONSTANCE AUX ENFERS; UN BALCON SOBRE EL
                                                                    INFIERNO)

Michele Morgan (*Constance*), Dany Saval (*Pascale*), Simon Andreu (*Hugo*), Maria Pacome (*Marie-Cecile*), Claude Rich (*Student*), Georges Rigaud (*Sartori*), Carlos Casarvilla (*Detective*).

An intriguing murder mystery with enough plot switches to throw most audiences off its trail. Morgan, a widow who lives alone in her Paris apartment, is able to watch the promiscuous affairs of a female neighbor. One evening she witnesses the girl's strangulation and then is forced to let the murderer, Andreu, hide out in her apartment. She soon becomes Andreu's lover, but unexpectedly falls victim to a blackmail plot. She pays out her entire savings to keep the blackmailer from revealing the identity of her guest, then learns that the "dead" neighbor is very much alive and is part of the blackmail plot. To get back at Andreu, Morgan pretends that another blackmailer exists and leads him to believe that he is being double-crossed by the "dead" girl. Andreu, by now thoroughly confused, attempts his own act of revenge and actually strangles the blackmailing girl out of jealousy, leaving Morgan pleased that her counter attack was a success. Released in Paris in 1964.

p, Gerard Ducaux-Rupp, Almos Mezo; d, Francois Villiers; w, Jacques Siguard, Jean-Pierre Ferriere (based on a novel by Ferriere); ph, Manuel Berenguer; m, Claude Bolling; ed, Christian Gaudin; art d, Pierre Thevenet.

Crime Drama/Mystery   **(PR:C   MPAA:NR)**

WEB OF PASSION**   (1961, Fr.) 101m Paris-Titanus/Times c (A
                        DOPPIA MANDATA; A DO UBLE TOUR; AKA: LEDA)

Madeleine Robinson (*Therese Marcoux*), Antonella Lualdi (*Leda Mortoni*), Jean-Paul Belmondo (*Laszlo Kovacs*), Jacques Dacqmine (*Henri Marcoux*), Jeanne Valerie (*Elizabeth Marcoux*), Bernadette Lafont (*Julie*), Andre Jocelyn (*Richard Marcoux*), Mario David (*Roger the Milkman*), Laszlo Szabo (*The Hungarian*), Raymond Pelissier, Andre Dino.

The third film from "New Wave" director Claude Chabrol, which also marked his first use of color–a garish sort that soon became an identifying mark of his films. Again Charol finds himself concerned with murder and its effect on an upper middle-class family as a son (Jocelyn) kills his father's lover. Dacqmine, the head of the household, upsets the suburban balance by falling in love with his exotically beautiful neighbor, Lualdi. After tearing apart his family with his extracurricular activities, Dacqmine plans to leave with his mistress, but before their wish is fulfilled Lualdi is found murdered. Suspicions run high and eventually Jocelyn, upset over a parental dispute, is revealed as the criminal. A mediocre crime thriller which pales in comparison with the other "New Wave" films of 1959 (LEDA'S French release date)–Truffaut's 400 BLOWS, Godard's BREATHLESS, and Resnais' HIROSHIMA MON AMOUR. Those who remember Belmondo's character in BREATHLESS, note that his alias in that film, "Laszlo Kovacs," has again been used. Yet another tidbit of "New Wave" information: working as assistant director on LEDA was Philippe de Broca, who would soon make his mark with pictures like THAT MAN FROM RIO, which also starred Belmondo.

p, Robert Hakim, Raymond Hakim; d, Claude Chabrol; w, Paul Gegauff (based on the novel *The Key to St. Nicholas Street* by Stanley Ellin); ph, Henri Decae (Eastmancolor); m, Hector Berlioz (from "Romeo and Juliet"), Wolfgang Amadeus Mozart (from "Serenade In B-Flat Major"), Paul Misraki; ed, Jacques Gaillard; art d, Jacques Saulnier, Bernard Evein; set d, Maurice Bourbotte; cos, Jeannine Germes-Vergne; makeup, Louis Bonnemaison.

Crime   **(PR:C   MPAA:NR)**

WEB OF SUSPICION*½   (1959, Brit.) 70m Danziger/PAR bw

Philip Friend (*Bradley Wells*), Susan Beaumont (*Janet Shenley*), John Martin (*Eric Turner*), Peter Sinclair (*Tom Wright*), Robert Raglan (*Inspector Clark*), Peter Elliott (*Watson*), Ian Fleming (*Forbes*), Rolf Harris (*Ben*), Hal Osmond (*Charlie*), John Brooking, Diana Chesney, Jack Melford, Vivienne Lacey, Carol White, Ann Taylor, The Girls of the Corona Stage School.

Friend, a gym teacher at a girl's school, is accused of murder and nearly lynched by the angry townspeople. With the help of his art teacher girl friend, Beaumont, he discovers that the actual killer is a demented music teacher, Martin. Together they clear Friend's name and save the school from another tragedy.

p, Edward J. Danziger, Harry Lee Danziger; d, Max Varnel; w, Brian Clemens, Eldon Howard; ph, Jimmy Wilson.

Crime   **(PR:A   MPAA:NR)**

WEB OF THE SPIDER**   (1972, Ital./Fr./Ger.) 93m Cinema Shares c (NELLA STRETTA M ORSA DEL RAGNO; IN THE GRIP OF THE SPIDER; DRACULA IN THE CASTLE OF BLOOD; AND COMES THE DAWN...BUT COLORED RED)

Klaus Kinski (Edgar Allan Poe), Tony Franciosa (Alan Foster), Michele Mercier (Elizabeth), Karin Field (Julia), Paolo Goslino, Irinia Maleva.

A remake of CASTLE OF BLOOD (1964) with director Margheriti once again trying to spook us with the tale of a man, Franciosa, who spends the night in a haunted house in order to disprove an age-old legend. During the night the dead come back to life and he realizes what a foolish mistake he had made. He flees the house and accidentally kills himself. This version lacks the enigmatic Barbara Steele, of CASTLE OF BLOOD, but does have Klaus Kinski playing Edgar Allan Poe–the only reason to watch it.

p, Giovanni Adessi; d, Anthony Dawson [Antonio Margheriti]; w, Margheriti, Adessi (based on the story "Danse Macabre" by Edgar Allan Poe); ph, Sandro Mancori; m, Riz Ortolani.

Horror   **(PR:O   MPAA:NR)**

WEB OF VIOLENCE**   (1966, Ital./Span.) 90m Liber Hesperia/Governor c (TRE NOTTI VIOLENTE; TRES NOCHES VI-OLENTAS)

Brett Halsey (Walter), Margaret Lee (Cristina), Pepe Calvo, Julio Pena, Daniele Vargas, Iran Eory, Emilio Messina, Enzo Cerusico, Mirko Ellis, Aldo Cristiani, Renato Chiantoni, Valentino Macchi, Renzo Palmer.

A standard crime picture about a journalist, Halsey, who sees a former girl friend get kidnaped and sets out to discover who was responsible and why. The girl soon turns up dead and Halsey solicits help from Lee. The guilty party is the head of a smuggling ring who is gunned down by the finale as a result of Halsey's determined investigation.

p, Ottavio Poggi; d, Nick Nostro; w, Fernando Cerchio, Mino Giardo, Juan Cobos, Poggi (based on a story by Sergio Donati); ph, Emilio Foriscot (Eastmancolor); m, Franco Pisano; ed, Magdalena Pulido; art d, Carlos Viudes.

Crime Drama   **(PR:C   MPAA:NR)**

WEBSTER BOY, THE**   (1962, Brit.) 83m RF bw (AKA: MIDDLE OF NOWHERE)

Jon Cassavetes (Vance Miller), Elizabeth Sellars (Margaret Webster), David Farrar (Paul Webster), Richard O'Sullivan (Jimmy Webster), Niall MacGinnis (Headmaster), Geoffrey Bayldon (Charles Jamison), Karl Lanchbury (Michael Johnson), John Bull (Alfred Baxter), Norman Rodway (Donald Saunders), Harry Brogan (Grant), John Geary (Alvin Roberts), Seymour Cassel (Vic), Aideen O'Kelly (Mary).

Cassavetes plays a gambler who, after a prison term, returns to an old flame, Sellars, only to be treated to the news that she is married and has a 14-year-old son. Cassavetes is persistent and before long the boy isn't sure whether Farrar or Cassavetes is his real father. Sellars is emotionally torn between the men and her responsibilities as a mother, but it is the youngster, O'Sullivan, who is tormented by his classmates and a particularly vile schoolmaster, Bayldon.

p, Emmett Dalton; d, Don Chaffey; w, Ted Allen (based on a story by Leo Marks); ph, Gerrard Gibbs; m, Wilfred Joseph; ed, John Trumper.

Drama   **(PR:A   MPAA:NR)**

WEDDING, A*   (1978) 125m Lion's Gate/FOX c

The Groom's Family: Lillian Gish (Nettie Sloan, Grandmother), Ruth Nelson (Beatrice Sloan Cory, Her Sister), Ann Ryerson (Victoria Cory, Beatrice's Granddaughter), Desi Arnaz, Jr. (Dino Corelli, the Groom), Belita Moreno (Daphene Corelli, His Twin), Vittorio Gassman (Luigi Corelli, Groom's Father), Nina van Pallandt (Regina Corelli, Groom's Mother), Virginia Vestoff (Clarice Sloan, Groom's Aunt), Dina Merrill (Antoinette Sloan Goddard, Groom's Aunt), Pat McCormick (Mackenzie Goddard, Groom's Uncle), Luigi Proietti (Little Dino, Groom's Uncle), The Bride's Family: Carol Burnett (Tulip Brenner, Bride's Mother), Paul Dooley (Snooks Brenner, Bride's Father), Amy Stryker (Muffin Brenner, the Bride), Mia Farrow (Buffy Brenner, Her Sister), Dennis Christopher (Hughie Brenner, Her Brother), Mary Seibel (Aunt Marge Spar, Snook's Sister), Margaret Ladd (Ruby Spar, Marge's Daughter), Gerald Busby (David Ruteledge, Tulip's Brother), Peggy Ann Garner (Candice Ruteledge, David's Wife), Mark R. Deming (Matthew Ruteledge, David's Son), David Brand, Chris

Brand, Amy Brand, Jenny Brand, Jeffrey Jones, Jay D. Jones, Courtney MacArthur, Paul D. Keller III (Ruteledge Children), Houseman, Robert Fortier (Jim Habor, Gardener), Maureen Steindler (Libby Clinton, Cook), The Wedding Staff: Geraldine Chaplin (Rita Billingsley, Coordinator), Mona Abboud (Melba Lear, Her Assistant), Viveca Lindfors (Ingrid Hellstrom, Cateress), Lauren Hutton (Flo Farmer, Film Producer), Allan Nicholls (Jake Jacobs, Cameraman), Maysie Hoy (Casey, Sound Person), John Considine (Jeff Kuykendall, Chief of Security), Patricia Resnick (Redford, Guard), Margery Bond (Lombardo, Guard), Dennis Franz (Koons, Guard), Harold C. Johnson (Oscar Edwards, Chef), Alexander Sopenar (Victor, Photographer), The Friends and Guests: Howard Duff (Dr. Jules Meecham), John Cromwell (Bishop Martin), Bert Remsen (William Williamson, Only Guest), Pamela Dawber (Tracy Dawber, Groom's Ex-Girl Friend), Gavan O'Hirlihy (Wilson Briggs, Groom's Ex-Roommate), Craig Richard Nelson (Capt. Reedley Roots, Teacher from Groom's School), Jeffrey S. Perry (Bunky Lemay, Groom's Friend), Marta Heflin (Shelby Munker, Bridesmaid), Lesley Rogers (Rosie Bean, Bridesmaid), Timothy Thomerson (Russell Bean, Rosie's Husband), Beverly Ross (Nurse Janet Schulman), David Fitzgerald (Kevin Clinton, Cook's Son), Susan Kendall Newman (Chris Clinton, Kevin's Bride), Ellie Albers (Gypsy Violinist), Tony Llorens (Pianist), Chuck Banks' Big Band with Chris La Kome.

One of the worst of Altman's films in his post-NASHVILLE slump, A WEDDING is extraordinarily self-indulgent, even more so than many of Altman's other excesses. Here, Altman examines the wedding between the daughter of a Southern parvenu family and the scion of another family that is a combination of old money and the Mafia. Inside this, Altman trots more than 50 characters across the screen in what must have been an attempt to prove that he felt "short" with the 24 stars he used in NASHVILLE. There are so many people and so many snippets of stories that you can't tell the actors without a program and since no programs were handed out at the theater, it became as complex as playing "Dungeons and Dragons." The movie has no thrust, just a gathering of scenes, vignettes, moments, as Altman examines the families, the household staff, the friends of the families, and the single guest who shows up, Remsen. (Remsen, who works half the time as a casting director, does a good deal of acting for Altman.) Gish was making her 100th appearance and the movie opens with her but she is killed off about midway in the first reel. Arnaz, the groom, is set to marry Stryker, the brace-toothed bride. Stryker's sister Farrow has already had an affair with Arnaz and is pregnant. Stryker's mother is Burnett. She is bored with husband Dooley (another Altman favorite who played Wimpy in POPEYE) and has a sexual liaison with Arnaz's uncle, McCormick (the well-known comedy writer whose off-screen exploits are legend). Arnaz's mother is van Pallandt, a confirmed heroin addict. (Van Pallandt was also the amour of Cliff Irving when he pulled off the famous Howard Hughes biography scam, then wrote a book about it.) The wedding coordinator is lesbian Chaplin (isn't anyone straight here?) and Cromwell is the senile priest who forgets his lines and is so myopic that he speaks to a corpse and wonders why his remarks go unanswered. Duff is a drunken doctor who tries to feel every woman who walks past his blood-shot eyes and still they come. But enough, there's just no reason to continue. Gish is the only one of the bunch who gets what Rodney Dangerfield has screamed for. The finale has a young couple killed in an auto accident in an attempt to trick the audience. It's not the honeymooners at all, just another duo who die. When the parents of the bride and groom realize that it isn't their children, they are relieved, and thus show their callousness at the loss of two innocents. Gassman, the father of Arnaz, exits at the conclusion (but not before many in the audience left), sick of being his wife's pawn. Altman uses Leonard Cohen's "Bird on a Wire" as Gassman leaves. He favors Cohen and used his tunes in MCCABE AND MRS. MILLER. Here, the song makes no sense, as the picture makes no sense. A smug exercise, a waste of time and talent, and proof that Altman is the most hit-and-miss director of his era. Since there is no one to care about in the movie, how can we care at all about the movie?

p&d, Robert Altman; w, John Considine, Patricia Resnick, Allan Nicholls, Altman (based on a story by Considine, Altman); ph, Charles Rosher (Panavision, DeLuxe Color); m, John Hotchkis; ed, Tony Lombardo.

Comedy/Drama   **Cas.**   **(PR:C   MPAA:PG)**

WEDDING BELLS   (SEE: ROYAL WEDDING, 1951)

WEDDING BREAKFAST   (SEE: CATERED AFFAIR, THE, 1956)

WEDDING GROUP   (SEE: WRATH OF JEALOUSY, 1936, Brit.)

WEDDING IN WHITE**½   (1972, Can.) 106m Dermet/AE c

Carol Kane (Jeannie), Donald Pleasence (Jim), Doris Petrie (Mary), Leo Phillips (Sandy), Christine Thomas (Sarah), Paul Bradley (Jimmie), Doug McGrath (Billy), Bonnie Carol Case (Dolly).

A powerful subject is admirably handled as Pleasence, a former soldier, must face the fact that his teenage daughter, Kane, has been raped and (as they soon find out) impregnated by an Army pal of her brother's. Set during WW II times, the atmosphere is sharply detailed and great care is given to the father and daughter characters, brilliantly played by Pleasence and

Kane, portraying the circumstances as they would most logically develop during that period. Designated Best Picture of the Year by the 1972 Canadian Film Awards.

p, John Vidette; d&w, William Fruet (based on his play); ph, Richard Leiterman (Panavision, DeLuxe Color); m, Milan Kymlicka; ed, Tony Lower; art d, Karen Bromley-Watkins; set d, Ted Watkins; cos, Patty Unger.

Drama   (PR;:O MPAA:NR)

WEDDING NIGHT, THE***   (1935) 82m UA bw

Gary Cooper (Tony Barrett), Anna Sten (Manya Nowak), Ralph Bellamy (Fredrik Sobieski), Helen Vinson (Dora Barrett), Sigfried 'Sig' Rumann (Jan Nowak), Esther Dale (Kaise Nowak), Leonid Snegoff (Mr. Sobieski), Eleanor Wesselhoeft (Mrs. Sobieski), Milla Davenport (Grandmother), Agnes Anderson (Helena), Hilda Vaughn (Hezzie Jones), Walter Brennan (Bill Jenkins), Douglas Wood (Heywood), George Meeker (Gilly), Hedi Shope (Anna), Otto Yamaoka (Taka), Violet Axzelle (Frederica Sobieski), Ed Ebele (Uncle), Robert Bolder (Doctor), Alphonse Martell (Waiter), Robert Louis Stevenson II (Man at Party), Richard Powell (Truck Driver), Auguste Tollaire, Dave Wengren, George Magrill, Bernard Siegel, Harry Semels (Men at Wedding), Miami Alvarez, Constance Howard, Jay Eaton, Jay Belasco (Party Guests).

Cooper stars as a troubled writer (reportedly modeled after F. Scott Fitzgerald) whose latest manuscript fails to impress. On the advice of his publisher he retreats to a Connecticut farmhouse with his devoted wife, Vinson, where he hopes to get back in touch with his roots as a writer. He soon meets a Polish farm girl, Sten, and is enthralled by her simple ways and philosophies. Their talks become more frequent, and when Vinson complains of the confines of the country, Cooper suggests that she return home to New York City for a while. Cooper becomes increasingly interested in Sten and decides to use her and her heritage as the basis of his new novel. He then learns that she has been betrothed by her puritanical father, Rumann, to the rather drab Bellamy. Sten has no feelings of love for her betrothed, so she sets her sights on Cooper, spending time cleaning his house and listening to the drafts of his latest chapters. One day a particularly violent snowstorm brews; Sten is forced to spend the night with Cooper, who makes romantic advances but decides instead to retreat to his bedroom alone. Rumann, in a fit of rage, rushes through the snow to Cooper's and drags his daughter back. Convinced that she is up to no good, Rumann demands that she marry Bellamy within the next two days. Sten is determined to fight her father's wishes and returns to Cooper's farmhouse, where she finds that Vinson has also come back. After reading the draft of Cooper's novel, Vinson easily deduces that the lead character, "Sonya," is really Sten and convinces the farmgirl that she will not be able to lure Cooper away. Sten relents and marries Bellamy, but rebukes his advances on their wedding night when he suggests that she has lost her virginity to Cooper. In a drunken rage, Bellamy heads for Cooper's. Sten goes along to warn Cooper. The confrontation comes to a head at Cooper's on a staircase. In the midst of the brawl between the two men, Sten falls down the stairs and dies as Cooper admits his love for her. A love triangle with a high tragedy ending, THE WEDDING NIGHT just didn't make much of an impression on the Depression-era audiences. Although the film has a great deal of artistic merit-Goldwyn's influence, Vidor's directorial skill, and Toland's sharp photography-it fell victim to indifference on the part of moviegoers. Goldwyn had been determined to make his Russian-born discovery, Sten, a star of the magnitude of Greta Garbo or Marlene Dietrich, and there was no real reason he shouldn't have succeeded. He commissioned his friend Knopf to write a scenario specifically for Sten, hoping to succeed where her previous vehicles-NANA and RESURRECTION-had failed. Goldwyn even found himself on the set to help pack a Cooper-Sten love scene with all the sexual energy it could muster. Stepping into Vidor's shoes for a while, Goldwyn began to coach the actors, exclaiming "If this scene isn't the greatest love scene ever put on film, then the whole goddamned picture will go right up out the sewer!" Well, it wasn't, and though the film didn't "go right up out the sewer," it did, unfortunately for Sten and Goldwyn, leave the audience unimpressed. Sten was soon gone from Hollywood, remembered only as "Goldwyn's Folly" or "The Edsel of the Movie Industry." THE WEDDING NIGHT did mark a momentous return for Cooper to Goldwyn's company, who 10 years previously let Cooper slip away to Paramount. In addition to dealing with Sten's thick accent (she received endless vocal coaching to subdue it), director Vidor had Cooper's laconic delivery to worry about. "I remember well the first day I directed him..." Vidor recalled in his book King Vidor on Film Making. "He had difficulty remembering or speaking two or three sentences consecutively. We had to stop the camera again and again and put the scene together piecemeal. This was one of his early speaking parts: he had not needed words before to communicate." The Goldwyn-Cooper marriage was short-lived, however, as the actor returned to Paramount for his very next picture, THE LIVES OF A BENGAL LANCER. It would be another eight years before Cooper would return to Goldwyn in THE ADVENTURES OF MARCO POLO (opposite Goldwyn's next discovery Sigrid Gurie) and 14 years before he would reunite with Vidor in the THE FOUNTAINHEAD.

p, Samuel Goldwyn; d, King Vidor; w, Edith Fitzgerald (based on a story by Edwin H. Knopf); ph, Gregg Toland; m, Alfred Newman; ed, Stuart Heisler; art d, Richard Day; cos, Omar Kiam.

Drama   (PR:A MPAA:NR)

WEDDING NIGHT*   (1970, Ireland) 99m Ardmore-Krasne/AIP c
(AKA: I CAN'T...I CAN'T)

Dennis Waterman (Joe O'Reilly), Tessa Wyatt (Mady), Alexandra Bastedo (Gloria), Eddie Byrne (Tom), Martin Dempsey (Father Keegan), Maire O'Donnell (Kate), Patrick Laffan (Dr. Farnum), Garden Odyssey Enterprise (Rock Group), Peter Mayock, Eileen Page, Trevor Bailey, Chris Curran, Vernon Hayden, Cecil Nash, Christian Lyons, Martin Lyons.

Young Irish Catholic girl Wyatt's marriage to Waterman is marred by her mother's miscarriage and consequent death on the very day of the wedding. One of seven children, Wyatt blames her father's lustful nature for her mother's death; unable to consummate her own marriage because of her fears, she rebuffs the gentle physical advances of her new husband. Waterman, hoping that time will overcome his bride's fears, leaves for London where he has secured a job as a commercial artist. Wyatt remains in Dublin, caring for her younger siblings in the absence of her deceased mother. When another family member agrees to take over the chores of the household, Wyatt joins Waterman in London. Frustrated by the long delay, he attempts to force his attentions on her, causing her to hysterically flee back to her family. As Waterman seeks the solace proffered by sexy Bastedo, a one-time girl friend, Wyatt rejects the counsel of a doctor, Laffan, that she explore the use of contraceptives. Her hidebound priest, Dempsey, citing dogma of the church, forbids her the use of the pill. In desperation, she asks his help in having her unfulfilled marriage annulled, but he refuses. The distraught girl collapses and is hospitalized, where she makes a suicide attempt. Hearing of her plight, Waterman comes to her bedside, where the two vow to attempt to overcome her fears through mutual love and understanding. A well-made film dealing fairly with a topical issue, the picture caused quite a stir on release in its country of origin.

p, Philip N, Krasne; d, Piers Haggard; w, Robert I. Holt, Lee Dunne, Haggard (based on a story by Holt); ph, Ray Sturgess (Eastmancolor); m, Cyril Ornadel; ed, Kenneth Crane; md, Ornadel; art d, James Weatherup; m/l, "Mady," Haggard, sung by Scott Peters.

Drama   (PR:O MPAA:M/PG)

WEDDING OF LILLI MARLENE, THE*
(1953, Brit.) 87m Monarch bw

Lisa Daniely (Lilli Marlene), Hugh McDermott (Steve Moray), Sidney James (Fennimore Hunt), Gabrielle Brune (Maggie Lennox), Jack Billings (Hal Marvel), Robert Ayres (Andrew Jackson), Joan Heal (Linda), Wally Patch (Wally), Irene Handl (Daisy), John Blythe (Holt), Mairhi Russell, Tom Gill, Ernst Ulman, Ben Williams, Dandy Nichols, Ann Bennett, Jacques Cey, Patricia Somerset, Jacqueline Mackenzie, Ann Duran, Lou Matto, Charmian Buchel.

Daniely plays the famed WW II favorite who found a place in every soldier's heart through the song "Lilli Marlene." She's in love with American reporter McDermott but refuses to marry until she becomes a success. She soon gets a lead role in a chorus when Brune drops out. Brune returns on opening night and sends Daniely into a tailspin. Eighth Army boys rally round her and she becomes an instant favorite. Great subject, tediously told and stiffly acted.

p, William Gell; d, Arthur Crabtree; w, John Baines; ph, Arthur Grant.

Musical/Drama   (PR:A MPAA:NR)

WEDDING PARTY, THE*   (1969) 90M Powell-Ondine/Ajay bw

Jill Clayburgh (Josephine Fish), Charles Pfluger (Charlie), Valda Setterfield (Mrs. Fish), Raymond McNally (Mr. Fish), Jennifer Salt (Phoebe), John Braswell (Rev. Oldfield), Judy Thomas (Celeste, Organist), Sue Ann Converse (Nanny), John Quinn (Baker), Robert De Niro (Cecil), William Finley (Alistair), Richard Kollmar, Jr (Jean-Claude/I. Singh/Klaus), Helmuth Pfluger (Charlie's Father), Jane Odin (Carol), Penny Bridgers, Nancy Reeder, Joanna Chapin, Cynthia Munroe (Bridesmaids), Kitty Gallagher (Mrs. Lovett), Clara Gallagher (Mrs. Greely), Vivian Muti (Mrs. Thackery), Andra Akers, Laurie Kennedy, Tony Converse, Louisa Youell, Susan Fowler, Jared Martin, Diana Welles, Robert Groves, Lena Tabori (Wedding Guests).

A coming-of-age comic nightmare in which young Pfluger, accompanied by two close friends, journeys to the posh estate of fiancee Clayburgh's parents two days before his nuptials. Revelations of reality beflood the youth as he is alternately ignored by his busy future in-laws and darkly counseled by his friends. Portents of his future life cause him to attempt to evade it: he tries to get Clayburgh back together with former suitor Kollmar, Jr., and then courts discovery while making a pass at the plain-visaged organist, Thomas. Despite all his evasions, he finds himself propelled inexorably towards his impending marriage; desperate for freedom, he makes a run for it. Pursued and captured, he is brought to the altar in time for the ceremony. A student project at Sarah Lawrence College, made by graduate student De Palma-his first feature-in collaboration with fellow student Munroe and faculty member Leach, this landmark film marks the first screen appearances of Clayburgh (a Sarah Lawrence alumna with a well-to-do background, like that of her character) and of De Niro (spelled "De Nero" in the film's credits). Completed in 1967, the film's release was delayed; two of De Palma's other features preceded this one in release. Technically well done, the picture is episodic, partly ad-libbed to an outline screenplay.

p,d&w, Brian De Palma, Cynthia Munroe, Wilford Leach; ph, Peter Powell; m, John Herbert McDowell; ed, De Palma, Munro, Leach; cos, Ellen Rand, Nancy Reeder; spec eff, B&O Film Specialists.

Comedy   Cas.   (PR:O   MPAA:NR)

WEDDING PRESENT**   (1936) 80m PAR bw

Joan Bennett (Monica "Rusty" Fleming), Cary Grant (Charlie Mason), George Bancroft (Stagg), Conrad Nagel (Dodacker), Gene Lockhart (Archduke), William Demarest ("Smiles" Benson), Inez Courtney (Mary Lawson), Edward Brophy (Squinty), Purnell Pratt (Van Dorn), Douglas Wood (Willett), George Meeker (Blaker), Lois Wilson (Laura Dodacker), John Henry Allen (Jonathan), George Offerman, Jr. (Sammy Smith), Damon Ford (Haley), Heinie Conklin, Billy Engel, Ray Hanson (German Band), Jack Mulhall, Chuck Hamilton, Cy Ring, Charles Williams, Marshall Ruth, Eddie Phillips, Eddie Borden, Ted Thompson, Charles Sherlock, Eddie Fetherston, Dagmar Oakland, Allen Fox (Reporters), Bradley Page (Givens), Torben Meyer (Winternitz), Charles Middleton (Turnbull), Clarence H. Wilson (Simmons), Katherine Perry Moore (Miss Chandler), Harry C. Bradley (Ticket Seller), Frank Darien (Cashier), Otto Hoffman (Printer), Hal K. Dawson (Furniture Salesman), Harry Tyler (Marriage License Clerk), Richard Powell (Hotel Room Waiter), George Davis (Cafe Waiter), Russ Powell (Beer Wagon Driver), Edd Russell (Telegraph Editor), Lee Shumway (Police Captain), Eddy Baker (Motorcycle Cop), Charles Meakin (Pompous Man), Ralph McCullough (Timid Man), Ernie Shields (Man with Key), Walter Long, Jimmy Dundee, Charles Sullivan (Gangsters), Milton Kahn, Rex Moore (Office Boys), Estelle Eterre, Frances Morris (Switchboard Operators), Charles McAvoy (Fire Chief), Jack Cheatham (Ambulance Attendant).

A newspaper screwball comedy that didn't have enough screwballs or enough comedy. This bears about the same amount of resemblance to the truth about journalists as NIGHT AND DAY (also starring Grant) bore to the truth about Cole Porter's life. Bennett and Grant (just coming off their success in BIG BROWN EYES) are cast as a duo of reporters working for city editor Bancroft. Grant's practical-joking antics cause Bancroft to lose his voice and finally exit his job, so Grant is elevated to the position of boss. He changes into an ogre and cracks the whip over his pals in the reporters room. His pomposity causes Bennett to wave bye- bye and leave. She soon announces that she's going to marry stick-in-the-mud Nagel, a writer who specializes in inspirational books. Grant tries to win her back but she is adamant. Grant begins drinking and now worries about what to buy for a wedding present. He knows she likes excitement like fires and police calls, so he sends black-and-whites, fire engines, and hearses to the home where Bennett and Nagel are to be wed. At the conclusion, he arrives in a wagon from a psychiatric hospital and kidnaps her. (A similar scene was also in THE GRADUATE, if you recall.) The movie ends with the two united, something that wasn't doubted by the audience for one second. It was Grant's final film in his five-year contract with Paramount although he came back several more times on a single-movie basis. Ed Brophy gets whatever laughs there are as a punchy pal. Ben Hecht and Charles MacArthur did it far better with their recreation of newspapering in their play, "The Front Page."

p, B.P. Schulberg; d, Richard Wallace; w, Joseph Anthony (based on a story by Paul Gallico); ph, Leon Shamroy; ed, Robert Bischoff; art d, Hans Dreier, Earl Hedrick.

Comedy   (PR:A   MPAA:NR)

WEDDING PRESENT, 1963   (SEE: TURKISH CUCUMBER, THE, 1963, Ger.)

WEDDING REHEARSAL**½   (1932, Brit.) 84m LFP/ID bw

Roland Young ("Reggie, Marquis Of Buckminster), George Grossmith (Lord Stokeshire), John Loder ("Bimbo"), Maurice Evans ("Tootles"), Wendy Barrie (Lady Mary Rose Wroxbury), Joan Gardner (Lady Rosemary Wroxbury), Merle Oberon (Miss Hutchinson), Lady Tree (Lady Stokeshire), Kate Cutler (Dowager Marchioness of Buckminster), Edmund Breon (Lord Fleet), Lawrence Hanray (News Editor), Diana Napier (Mrs. Dryden), Morton Selten (Maj. Harry Roxbury), Rodolfo Mele.

The titled Young, who has evaded his grandmother's frequent importunities that he marry by matchmaking all of her many candidates with his male friends, finally succumbs to the charms of a commoner. His choice is the beautiful Oberon–his mother's secretary–who, without her glasses, proves to be perfectly smashing. This pleasant comedy scores a number of historical firsts. It is the first production to be made by producer-director Alexander Korda's own independent company, London Film Productions, Ltd.; Korda had settled in England only the year previously, where he had directed a film for Paramount British, after successes in Hollywood and in France. His company was to become one of the most successful in Europe, employing talented directors such as Orson Welles, Carol Reed, and Anthony Asquith. This was actress Oberon's first featured role; she had just been "discovered" by her future husband, A. Korda, after playing a number of bit parts using the name Estelle Thompson. Stage actress Barrie also had her first featured

film role here, as did Gardner, future wife of the producer-director's brother (also a well-known director), Zoltan Korda. London Film had a record of creative nepotism which more than matched anything Hollywood had to offer; A. Korda's talented designer brother Vincent did well here, as he did on many other films made by his brothers.

p&d, Alexander Korda; w, Arthur Wimperis, Helen Gardom (based on a story by Lajos Biro, George Grossmith); ph, Leslie Rowson; m, Kurt Schroeder; ed, Harold Young; art d, O. F. Werndorff, Vincent Korda.

Comedy   Cas.   (PR:A   MPAA:NR)

WEDDING RINGS*½   (1930) 74m FN-WB bw

H. B. Warner (Lewis Dike), Lois Wilson (Cornelia Quinn), Olive Borden (Eve Quinn), Hallam Cooley (Wilfred Meadows), James Ford (Tim Hazleton), Kathleen Williams (Agatha), Aileen Manning (Esther Quinn).

Warner is the subject of two sisters' affections, but ends up falling for the less responsible of the two. He weds Borden, who is more interested in social standing and dashing parties than her more likable sister Wilson. In the end, however, Wilson charms Warner and takes him away from Borden. A familiar plot with some unconvincing performances by the miscast players. Song: "That's My Business," sung by Borden.

d, William Beaudine; w, Ray Harris (based on the novel The Dark Swan by Ernest Pascal); ph, Ernest Haller.

Drama/Romance   (PR:A   MPAA:NR)

WEDDINGS AND BABIES***   (1960) 81M FOX bw

Viveca Lindfors (Bea), John Myhers (Al), Chiarina Barile (Mama), Leonard Elliott (Ken), Joanna Merlin (Josie), Chris (Tony), Gabriel Kohn (Carl), Mary Faranda (Mrs. Faranda).

An ambitious independent feature shot on location in New York's Little Italy area by Engel who, a few years previously, delivered the superb THE LITTLE FUGITIVE (1953). Myhers stars as a photographer (Engel's background is still photography and he shot this picture) who is debating whether or not to marry his assistant Lindfors, who not only wants marriage but babies, too. The story is kept bare, allowing Engel to concentrate on the situation without much interference. Reportedly, WEDDINGS AND BABIES was the first feature to be shot with a portable camera that had a synchronous sound attachment (Engel's own design). Winner of the Critics Prize at the 1958 Venice Film Fest and one of Time magazine's top 10 films of 1960.

p&d, Morris Engel; w, Engel, Mary-Madeleine Lanphier, Blanche Hanalis, Irving Sunasky (based on a story by Engel); ph, Engel; m, Eddy Manson; ed, Stan Russell, Michael Alexander.

Drama   (PR:A   MPAA:NR)

WEDDINGS ARE WONDERFUL**   (1938, Brit.) 79m
                                       Canterbury/RKO bw

June Clyde (Cora Sutherland), Esmond Knight (Guy Rogers), Rene Ray (Betty Leadbetter), Bertha Belmore (Mrs. Leadbetter), Frederick Lloyd (Mr. Leadbetter), Bruce Seton (John Smith), Antony Holles (Adolph), George Carney (Rogers), Charles Paton, Michael Ripper, Valentine Dunn.

A marital comedy in which wackiness abounds as sluttish showgirl Clyde gets tangled in affairs with the married Lloyd as well as with Knight, who plans to marry Lloyd's daughter. When Clyde entertains at the engagement party and sees a number of familiar masculine faces the farce takes off.

p, A. George Smith; d, Maclean Rogers; w, Kathleen Butler, H. F. Maltby (based on the play "Peaches" by Sidney Blow, Douglas Hoare); ph, Geoffrey Faithful.

Comedy   (PR:A   MPAA:NR)

WEDNESDAY CHILDREN, THE*½   (1973) 88m Venture c

Marji Dodril (Mrs. Miller), Donald E. Murray (Mr. Miller), Tom Kelly (Scott Miller), Carol Cary (Mrs. Edith Berlow), Al Miskell (Mr. Fenton), Robert D. West (Minister).

Young Kelly is among the leaders of a group of country children who, mistreated by their parents and other elders, are full of woe. Visiting their complaints on a sympathetic farmhand, Miskell–whose satanic bearded visage bodes no good–the children are offered a Faustian bargain. By embracing demonism, they are made to be able to cast a spell which eradicates their tormentors. Simultaneously, having acquired their new found powers, they assume many of the characteristics of the latter. An ambitious social allegory, the first and only production by an independent group formed on the banks of the blazing Cuyahoga River near the city of Cleveland, this is a surprisingly professional job.

p, Homer Baldwin, Cal Clifford; d&w, Robert D. West; ph, Baldwin; m, Tom Baker, Dene Bays; ed, Baldwin.

Drama/Horror   (PR:C   MPAA:NR)

WEDNESDAY'S CHILD** (1934) 69M RKO bw

Frankie Thomas (*Bobby Phillips*), Edward Arnold (*Ray Phillips, His Father*), Karen Morley (*Kathryn Phillips, His Mother*), Shirley Grey (*Louise*), Robert Shayne (*Howard Benson*), David Durand (*Chick*), Paul Stanton, Richard Barbee, Tom Franklin [Frank M. Thomas], Mona Bruns, Elsa Janssen, Frank Conroy.

Hackneyed now, but a novelty in its time, this picture's plot deals with the consequences of divorce. Thomas is the woeful 11-year-old who is placed in a military academy while father Arnold and mother Morley squabble about a settlement, and who is made to testify in court. Young Thomas played the role on stage in a production that deviated substantially from the course of the film; the latter has a relatively happy ending, with Arnold reuniting with his son for a sunny finale typical of Hollywood's self-censorship. Actor Thomas' real-life father, Franklin (who later appeared in many of the studio's releases under his real name) has a small role. In a remake, CHILD OF DIVORCE (1946), the studio made a gender switch, putting a girl in the part of the victimized youngster.

p, Kenneth Macgowan; d, John S. Robertson; w, Willis Goldbeck (based on the play by Leopold L Atlas); ph, Harold Wenstrom; ed, George Hively; cos, Walter Plunkett.

Drama (PR:A MPAA:NR)

WEDNESDAY'S CHILD (SEE: FAMILY LIFE, 1971, Brit.)

WEDNESDAY'S LUCK* (1936, Brit.) 68m British and Dominions/PAR British bw

Wilson Coleman (*Stevens*), Susan Bligh (*Sheila*), Patrick Barr (*Jim Carfax*), Moore Marriott (*Nobby*), Paul Neville (*Waddington*), Linden Travers (*Mimi*), George Dewhurst (*Wood*), Ernest Borrow, Eric Hales, George Bailey.

Barr is a detective who pretends to be an ex-convict in order to jail Coleman, a notorius fence. Barr finds enough evidence to lock up his man, and in the meantime falls in love with Coleman's niece.

p, Anthony Havelock-Allan; d, George Pearson; w, Ralph Neale (based on the story by Edythe Pryce).

Crime (PR:A MPAA:NR)

WEE GEORDIE*** (1956, Brit.) 93m Argonaut/Times (GB: GEORDIE)

Alistair Sim (*The Laird*), Bill Travers (*Geordie MacTaggart, Gamekeeper*), Norah Gorsen (*Jean Donaldson*), Molly Urquhart (*Geordie's Mother*), Francis de Wolff (*Henry Samson*), Jack Radcliffe (*Rev. McNab*), Brian Reece (*Dick Harley*), Raymond Huntley (*Rawlins*), Miles Malleson (*Lord Paunceton, Olympic Squad Head*), Jameson Clarke (*Geordie's Father*), Doris Godard (*Helga*), Danish Shot-Putter, Stanley Baxter (*Postman*), Duncan Macrae (*Schoolmaster*), Paul Young (*Young Geordie*), Anna Ferguson (*Young Jean*), Margaret Boyd (*Laird's Housekeeper*), Alex McCrindle (*Guard*), Alex MacKenzie, Eric Woodburn, Jack Short, John Lang, Frank Taylor, Michael Ripper.

Set in the "past and present, with a wee glimpse into the future," this tender tale about a youngster's rise to fame is photographed against the picturesque Scottish highlands. Geordie (Young) is a frail lad who takes a ribbing from his schoolmates because of his size, or lack of it. After seeing a muscleman ad in a magazine, he begins to get himself into shape. Entering manhood (now played by Travers), his pains begin to pay off when he is selected for Britain's Olympic squad in the hammer-throwing event in Australia. Leaving his local lassie, Gorsen, he embarks for down under, with a muscular Danish damsel, Goddard, pouncing on her reticent cocompetitor. Travers extracts himself from prospective Viking pillage and returns to his highland lassie Gorsen. A characteristically fine performance from Sim as the laird who emplys Travers-Young's gamekeeper father. Gorsen is striking in her screen debut; a critic of the time said: "Remember her name–you will be encountering it with increasing frequency." As far as we know, this is her only feature film. A pleasant comedy with likable people from the consistent team of Launder and Gilliat.

p, Frank Launder, Sidney Gilliat; d, Launder; w, Launder, Gilliat (based on a novel by David Walker), ph, Wilkie Cooper (Technicolor); m, William Alwyn; ed, Thelma Connell; md, Muir Mathieson; art d, Norman Arnold; cos, Anna Duse.

Drama (PR:A MPAA:NR)

WEE WILLIE WINKIE*** (1937) 103m FOX bw

Shirley Temple (*Priscilla Williams*), Victor McLaglen (*Sgt. MacDuff*), C. Aubrey Smith (*Col. Williams*), June Lang (*Joyce Williams*), Michael Whalen (*Lt. "Coppy" Brandes*), Cesar Romero (*Khoda Khan*), Constance Collier (*Mrs. Allardyce*), Douglas Scott (*Mott*), Gavin Muir (*Capt. Bibberbeigh*), Willie Fung (*Mohammet Dihn*), Brandon Hurst (*Bagby*), Lionel Pape (*Maj. Allardyce*), Clyde Cook (*Pipe Maj. Sneath*), Lauri Beatty (*Elsie Allardyce*), Lionel Braham (*Maj. Gen. Hammond*), Mary Forbes (*Mrs. MacMonachie*), Cyril McLaglen (*Cpl. Tummel*), Jack Pennick (*Soldier Guard*), George

Hassell (*MacMonachie*), Pat Somerset (*Capt. Stuart*), Hector V. Sarno (*Coach Driver*), Noble Johnson (*Sikh Policeman*), Scotty Mattraw (*Merchant*), Louis Vincenot (*African Chieftain*).

Temple brings her charms to India in this starring vehicle very loosely based ona story by Rudyard Kipling and directed by, of all people, John Ford. At the turn of the century, Temple and her widowed mother Lang are sent to live with her grandfather, Smith, on a British army base in India. She goes through maneuvers with the troops, donning a darling pint-sized uniform. She manages to win over everyone she comes in contact with including rebel leader Romero. The entire political situation is reduced to Shirley asking why the two factions are mad at each other, which brings about a peaceful resolution. An interesting film to see listed on Ford's filmography and, not surprisingly, Temple's presence was seen then (and now) as the reason for the film, delivering few or none of the familiar Ford themes.

p, Gene Markey; d, John Ford; w, Ernest Pascal, Julien Josephson (based on a story by Rudyard Kipling), ph, Arthur Miller; m, Louis Silvers; ed, Walter Thompson; md, Alfred Newman; art d, William Darling; set d, Thomas Little; cos, Gwen Wakeling.

Drama/Comedy (PR:AA MPAA:NR)

WEEKEND** (1964, Den.) 84m Cinema-Video International bw (AKA: WEEK-END)

Jens Osterholm (*Lars*), Birgit Bruel (*Tove*), Willy Rathnov (*Kjeld*), Elsebet Knudsen (*Bet*), Jesper Jensen (*Knud*), Bente Dessau (*Ilse*), Erik Kuhnau (*Jan*), Lotte Tarp (*Birthe the Maid*), Jorgen Beck (*Innkeeper*), Carl Joha n Hviid (*Herr Cornelius*), Inga Reim (*Fru Cornelius*), Hugo Herrestrup (*Shooting Gallery Attendant*), Tove Bang (*Cloakroom Attendant*), Erik Paaske (*Man on the Beach*), Masja Dessau (*Tanja*), Tine Kjaerulff-Schmidt (*Tine*), Morten Kjaerulff-Schmidt (*Morten*), Jens Oliver Henriksen.

Three young married couples and a party-minded bachelor get together for a spouse-swapping-plus-one beach cottage weekend, letting it all hang out after pigging out TOM JONES-style. Suddenly seized by whim, the sybaritic Scandinavians drive to a nearby roadhouse, where their boisterousness gets them barred. Comes the dawn and the left-out husband Rathnov, miffed at having managed to avoid the assorted adulteries, goes to the beach where he happens upon attractive teenaged Tarp, who had been baby sitting for the revelers. Having missed much of the night's fun, he tries to make amends by raping the half-clad beauty. Although he fails in his attempt, he returns to the cottage to the scorn and contempt of the others, who are shocked by his transgression of the rules they have established. The quarreling couples–plus one–then motor back to their workaday weekday world. A theme resembling that of Jean Renoir's THE RULES OF THE GAME (1961), but lacking either the tragedy or any of that great director's grace and style. No pastry, this. (In Danish; English subtitles.)

p, Bent Christensen; d, Palle Kjaerulff-Schmidt; w, Klaus Rifbjerg; ph, Georg Oddner; m, Erik Moseholm; ed, Maj Soya; art d, Erik Aaes.

Drama (PR:C MPAA:NR)

WEEKEND*** (1968, Fr./Ital.) 103m Comacico-Copernic-Lira-Ascot/Grove Press c (LE WEEK-END)

Mireille Darc (*Corinne*), Jean Yanne (*Roland*), Jean-Pierre Kalfon (*Leader of the FLSO*), Valerie Lagrange (*His Moll*), Jean-Pierre Leaud (*Saint-Just/ Man in Phone Booth*), Yves Beneyton (*Member of FLSO*), Paul Gegauff (*Pianist*), Daniel Pommereulle (*Joseph Balsamo*), Yves Alfonso (*Gros Poncet*), Blandine Jeanson (*Emily Bronte/Girl in Farmyard*), Juliette Berto (*Girl in Car Crash/Member of FLSO*), Anne Wiazemsky (*Girl in Farmyard/ Member of FLSO*), Virginie Vignon (*Marie-Madeleine*), Jean Eustache (*Hitchhiker*), J. C. Guilbert (*Tramp*), Ernest Menzer (*Cook*), Georges Staquet (*Tractor Driver*), Laszlo Szabo (*The Arab Speaking for His Black Brother*), Michel Cournot (*Man from Farmyard*), Mons. Jojot, Isabelle Pons.

A stunning film which stacks analogy upon analogy, allegory upon allegory in an episodic odyssey of an unpleasant upper-class Parisian pair out for a weekend trip to visit the wife's mother. Opening with a psychiatric-session monolog by the delicate Darc, clad only in panties and perched, respectively, on a desk and on a refrigerator as she hesitantly describes a sexual encounter involving an egg and an orifice, the movie quickly moves to the carnage of the roadways during a sunny weekend. A bumper-to-bumper carnival of cars, honking, careening, crashing, overturning, and burning along with their grotesque occupants ensues as Darc and Yanne wend their way motherward. Social values are explored in myriad ways: a wailing woman seeks to re-enter a blazing automobile, screaming of the loss of her beloved Gucci bag; a young socialite woman excoriates the fat, phlegmatic farmer who, with his tractor, survived the crash that killed her lover, stating that the farmer killed him because he was young and handsome and drove a sports car; following the loss of their own vehicle, Darc uncomplainingly piggybacks her husband cross-country as they continue their journey. Yanne demonstrates the uncaring insouciance of the self-centered male when Darc, unable to extricate herself from a ditch, is raped by a passing tramp (who, first, politely asks her husband if he minds) as he meditates about his own financial difficulties. Static political monologs jarringly interrupt the flow of the bloody trip, which suddenly shifts to a beautiful pastoral scene with a gigantic hog, its pristine human flesh-like hide gleaming amidst the greenery, being formally, ritually slaughtered with an axe. The carnage continues as the peripatetic pair arrive at the home of Darc's mother, only to murder her when she refuses to give them the money they request (the motive for their terrible trip). On their return journey, the two encounter a band of disenfranchised radicals who kill Yanne. Darc elects to join the band, taking, as her first meal in their company, a stew which includes her husband's remains. Curiously, a connective thread runs through this seemingly disjointed tale, which is alternately terrifying, funny, disgusting, and dull, but always paranoid. The closing titles suggest something of Godard's possible feeling toward this picture: the words "End of Film" are followed by the further words "End of Cinema". Just as the painter Marcel Duchamp, after giving up the plastic arts, wrote only one poem–which he viewed as definitive and terminal, the last poem necessary– so might Godard have felt upon completion of this powerful picture. Certainly this film was the apogee of his *oeuvre;* his later works never approached this one. The director's mother died in a road accident in 1954, and he himself was seriously injured in a motorcycle crash in 1975. (In French; English subtitles.)

d&w, Jean-Luc Godard; ph, Raoul Coutard (Eastmancolor); m, Antoine Duhamel, Wolfgang Amadeus Mozart (Piano Sonata K.576); ed, Agnes Guillemot; m/l, "All, Allo, Tu m'Entends?" Guy Beart; English subtitles, Sonja Mays Friedman.

Drama   **(PR:O   MPAA:NR)**

WEEKEND A ZUYDCOOTE   (SEE: WEEKEND AT DUNKIRK, 1966, Fr./Ital.)

WEEKEND AT DUNKIRK**   (1966, Fr./Ital.) 102m
Paris-Interopa/FOX c (WEEKEND A ZUYDCOOTE)

Jean-Paul Belmondo (*Sgt. Maillat*), Catherine Spaak (*Jeanne*), Georges Geret (*Pinot*), Jean-Pierre Marielle (*Father Pierson*), Pierre Mondy (*Dhery*), Marie Dubois (*Helene*), Francois Perier (*Alexandre*), Kenneth Haigh (*Atkins*), Ronald Howard (*Robinson*), Nigel Stock (*Burnt Man*), Albert Remy (*Virrel*), Francois Guerin (*Lieutenant*), Jean-Paul Roussillon (*Blackguard*), Michel Barbey (*Cirilli*), Christian Barbier (*Giant*), Pierre Vernier (*Happy Undertaker*), Raoul Delfosse (*Infrantryman*), Marie-France Mignal (*Antoinette*), Marie-France Boyer (*Jacqueline*), Christian Melsen (*1st German Parachutist*), Rolf Spath (*2nd German Parachutist*), Robert Bazil, Julien Verdier, Gerard Darrieu, Robert Deslandes, Dominique Zardi, Alan Adair, Donald O'Brien, Anthony Stuart, Robert Napier, Rene Penetra, Paul Preboist, Robert Rollis, Charles Bouillaud.

In June, 1940, German troops, tanks, and airplanes force the British to evacuate their troops from the Continent at Dunkirk. French soldiers, who also want to join the withdrawal in order to continue the fight against the invaders, must wait on the beaches; the British have priority on the boats. Spaak refuses to leave her home despite the carnage; she befriends some of the waiting French soldiers, including Belmondo, who saves her from rape by killing two of his fellow *poilus.* The waiting French suffer terrible attrition as they are slowly picked off. Electing to depart at last, Spaak approaches the waiting Belmondo, only to see him die on the beach. This showcase for Belmondo's cynical style has little to recommend it except for a few good battle scenes.

p, Robert Hakim, Raymond Hakim; d, Henry Verneuil; w, Francois Boyer (based on the novel by Robert Merle); ph, Henri Decae (CinemaScope, DeLuxe Color); m, Maurice Jarre; ed, Claude Duran md, Jarre; art d, Robert Clavel; set d, Pierre Charron; cos, Jean Zay, Leon Zay; spec eff, Karl Baumgartner.

War Drama   **Cas.**   **(PR:A   MPAA:NR)**

WEEKEND AT THE WALDORF***   (1945) 130m MGM bw

Ginger Rogers (*Irene Malvern*), Walter Pidgeon (*Chip Collyer*), Van Johnson (*Capt. James Hollis*), Lana Turner (*Bunny Smith*), Robert Benchley (*Randy Morton*), Edward Arnold (*Martin X. Edley*), Leon Ames (*Henry Burton*), Warner Anderson (*Dr. Campbell*), Phyllis Thaxter (*Cynthia Drew*), Keenan Wynn (*Oliver Webson*), Porter Hall (*Stevens*), Samuel S. Hinds (*Mr. Jessup*), George Zucco (*Bey of Aribajan*), Xavier Cugat and His Orchestra (*Themselves*), Lina Romay (*Juanita*), Bob Graham (*Singer*), Michael Kirby (*Lt. John Rand*), Cora Sue Collins (*Jane Rand*), Rosemary DeCamp (*Anna*), Jacqueline De Wit (*Kate Douglas*), Frank Puglia (*Emile*), Charles Wilson (*Hi Johns*), Irving Bacon (*Sam Skelly*), Miles Mander (*British Secretary*), Nana Bryant (*Mrs. H. Davenport Drew*), Russell Hicks (*McPherson*), Ludmilla Pitoeff (*Irma*), Naomi Childers (*Night Maid*), Moroni Olsen (*House Detective Blake*), William Halligan (*Chief Jennings*), John Wengraf (*Alix*), Ruth Lee (*The Woman*), William Hall (*Cassidy the Doorman*), Jack Luden, Mel Shubert (*Clerks*), Ruth Warren, Jean Carpenter, Hope Landin, Karen Lind, Gertrude Short (*Telephone Operators*), Byron Foulger (*Barber*), Harry Barris (*Anna's Boy Friend*), Dorothy Christy (*Cashier*), Bess Flowers, Ella Ethridge, Franklyn Farnum, Sandra Morgan, Dick Gordon, Oliver Dross (*Guests*), Gladden James (*Assistant Manager*), Carli Elinor (*Orchestra Leader*), Dick Crockett (*Bell Captain*), Wyndham Standing (*Literary Type*), Rex Evans (*Pianist*), Arno Frey (*Maitre d'Hotel*), Gordon Richards (*Headwaiter*), Dick Hirbe (*Newsboy*), Shirley Lew, Billie Louie (*Chinese Girls*), Charles Madrin (*Assistant Hotel Manager*), Kenneth Cutler (*Desk Clerk*),

Frank McClure (*Florist*), Estelle Etterre (*Assistant Florist*), Barbara Bowers (*Cigarette Girl*).

An updated version of GRAND HOTEL screenplayed by the Spewacks and zippily directed by Leonard. The famed Park Avenue hotel management asked for no money for the right to the story and was content with the sensational publicity the film generated. It was among the top grossers of 1945 and was just the ticket for war-weary moviegoers who wanted to have some laughs, some tears, and some relaxation. All of the action takes place at Lucius Boomer's Waldorf-Astoria in the time frame of a weekend, and several stories are told at once, plus a couple of tunes tossed in. Rogers is a noted movie actress who is unhappy despite her success and popularity. (In GRAND HOTEL, this was Garbo.) Her maid, DeCamp, is involved with a man Rogers thinks may be a crook, so Rogers decides to talk to the lad and try to change his ways. By mistake, she confuses tired war reporter Pidgeon with the apprentice malfeasant and he is so charmed by Rogers that he doesn't tell her she's wrong and, instead, encourages the deception by pretending to be a man named "Duke." (John Barrymore did this in GRAND HOTEL but he was a real crook in that.) When the truth is uncovered, the two, by that time, have fallen in love. (There is no attempt at masking the fact that this is a remake of GRAND HOTEL and upon hearing a line of Pidgeon's that sounds familiar, Rogers says, "That's right out of GRAND HOTEL." Also, in homage to another MGM hit, Rogers says to Pidgeon, whose name is "Chip Collyer" in the film, "Goodbye, Mr. Chip...Collyer." A bit of inside humor that let audiences in on the gags and nobody minded. In another story, slim Thaxter is to marry fiance Anderson, a doctor, but is about to abort the wedding because she thinks that the medical man is in love with Rogers. To forestall that, Rogers tells Thaxter that she is secretly wed to Pidgeon (a lie) and it's not long before that rumor races through the Waldorf. On another floor, the hotel stenographer, Turner (Joan Crawford played her as an amoral woman in the original), dreams of marrying a fella from Park Avenue, where she works, rather than from 10th Avenue, where she lives. She meets Air Corps man Johnson, who is about to go in for delicate surgery to remove shrapnel lodged near his heart and the odds are slim. (This role was done by Lionel Barrymore in GRAND HOTEL and is the major alteration from that script.) Turner would like nothing better than to become that... mistress of wealthy tycoon Arnold (Wallace Beery in GRAND HOTEL) but her heart won't let her and, after an evening with Johnson atop the hotel in the nightclub, she allows her emotions to outweigh her pragmatism. Complications ensue but are all smoothed over by the end of the film as Thaxter and Anderson go on their honeymoon, Rogers and Pidgeon make plans to meet in England and get married, Johnson discovers that he may survive the operation, and Arnold's plan to bilk wealthy Arab Zucco is sidetracked due to the efforts of cub reporter Wynn, who is helped by Pidgeon in the unmasking. Along the way, as a comedy runner, we also meet Benchley, a besotted gossip-monger fretting over his pregnant Scotch terrier. The dog finally gives birth to triplets. Although four more films with Benchley were yet to be released, he died before this one was previewed. Cugat and his orchestra perform "Guadalajara" (written by Pepe Guizar). The other tune was Sammy Fain and Ted Kohler's "And There You Are." Kay Thompson handled the vocal arrangements and Johnny Green the orchestral chores. With all of those plots, they actually shot even more, and one sequence featuring Constance Collier as a former opera singer on her way to a retirement home had to be scissored. The gowns by Irene were superb and hairstyles by Sydney Guilaroff were equally tasteful. In the original, Crawford and Garbo never met and audiences wondered why. They had the chance to rectify that with Rogers and Turner but chose to keep the two characters apart as well. Lots of fun and one of the best advertising commercials ever made.

p, Arthur Hornblow, Jr.; d, Robert Z. Leonard; w, Sam Spewack, Bella Spewack, Guy Bolton (based on the play "Grand Hotel" by Vicki Baum); ph, Robert Planck; m, Johnny Green; ed, Robert J. Kern; md, Green; art d, Cedric Gibbons, Daniel B. Cathcart; set d, Edwin B. Willis, Jack Bonar; cos, Irene; spec eff, Warren Newcomb; ch, Charles Walters.

Musical Drama/Comedy   **Cas.**   **(PR:A   MPAA:NR)**

WEEKEND BABYSITTER   (SEE: WEEKEND WITH THE BABYSITTER, 1970)

WEEKEND FOR THREE**   (1941) 65m RKO bw

Dennis O'Keefe (*Jim Craig*), Jane Wyatt (*Ellen Craig*), Philip Reed (*Randy Bloodworth*), Edward Everett Horton (*Fred Stonebraker*), ZaSu Pitts (*Anna*), Franklin Pangborn (*No. Seven*), Marion Martin (*Mrs. Weatherby*), Hans Conried (*Desk Clerk*), Mady Lawrence (*Miss Bailey*).

A harmless marital comedy which offers an occasional laugh when an athletic, obnoxious visitor, Reed, drops in on newlyweds O'Keefe and Wyatt. Initially Wyatt sees Reed as a way to make her hubbie jealous, but when he stays on well past his allotted weekend she helps O'Keefe in a plan to get rid of him.

p, Tay Garnett; d, Irving Reis; w, Dorothy Parker, Alan Campbell (based on a story by Budd Schulberg); ph, Russell Metty; ed, Desmond Marquette.

Comedy   **(PR:A   MPAA:NR)**

WEEKEND IN HAVANA½   (1941) 80m FOX c

Alice Faye *(Nan Spencer)*, Carmen Miranda *(Rosita Rivas)*, John Payne *(Jay Williams)*, Cesar Romero *(Monte Blanca)*, Cobina Wright, Jr *(Terry McCracken)*, George Barbier *(Walter McCracken)*, Sheldon Leonard *(Boris)*, Leonid Kinskey *(Rafael)*, Billy Gilbert *(Arbolado)*, Chris-Pin Martin *(Driver)*, Hal K. Dawson *(Mr. Marks)*, William B. Davidson *(Capt. Moss)*, Hugh Beaumont *(Officer)*, Maurice Cass *(Tailor)*, Leona Roberts, Harry Hayden *(Passengers)*, Maj. Sam Harris *(Gambler)*.

One of a spate of lavish south-of-the-border musicals, this pre-Fidel Castro tomfoolery has Faye as a Macy's salesgirl who saves her pennies to take a Caribbean cruise, only to have her ship run aground. Refusing to sign a waiver of responsibility document profferred by the shipping company's attorneys, she is awarded an expense-paid tour of the title city, with shipping-line official Payne as her escort. Her reluctant guide--who would prefer to be attending his long-planned nuptial ceremony with fiancee Wright, Jr., in New York--grudgingly shepherds her about the bistros and casinos of pre-revolution Cuba. They meet broke gambler Romero and his fiery girl friend, entertainer Miranda; to the latter's discomfiture, Romero makes a play for blonde Faye, believing her to be a wealthy heiress. After the customary romantic intrigues, Payne discovers Faye to be the girl of his dreams. Faye, recently married to bandleader-actor Phil Harris, was pregnant at the time of filming. She had won the role despite serious competition from Betty Grable. Miranda was a hit in the third of her 14 screen appearances, and Romero was an eminently likable Latin rascal. Censors viewing the movie apparently missed some action in a production number near the end of it, when a male dancer fondled the breast of his partner, to her considerable consternation. Such was the real Havana in those palmy days. Faye gives a jubilant portrayal, as does Miranda (reportedly earning $5,000 a week). Faye performed two tunes with Romero: "Romance and Rhumba" (Mack Gordon, James V. Monaco) and "Tropical Magic" (Gordon, Harry Warren). A third song, "The Man with the Lollipop Song" (Gordon, Warren), sung by Gilbert is only briefly heard though it was intended to play in its entirety. Other songs by Miranda include "The Nango," "A Weekend in Havana," "When I Love, I Love" (Gordon, Warren). Other songs are "Maria Inez" (L. Wolfe Gilbert, Eliseo Grenet), "Rebola a Bola" (Oliviera, Almaro).

p, William Le Baron; d, Walter Lang; w, Karl Tunberg, Darrell Ware; ph, Ernest Palmer (Technicolor); ed, Allen McNeil; md, Alfred Newman; art d, Richard Day, Joseph C. Wright; set d, Thomas Little; cos, Gwen Wakeling; makeup, Guy Pearce; ch, Hermes Pan.

Musical   (PR:A   MPAA:NR)

WEEKEND, ITALIAN STYLE   (1967, Fr./Ital./Span.) 90m Ultra-Les Films du Siecle-Altura/G.G.-Marvin c (L'OMBRELLONE; EL PARASOL; AKA: WEEKEND WIVES)

Enrico Maria Salerno *(Enrico Marletti)*, Sandra Milo *(Giuliana Marletti)*, Jean Sorel *(Sergio)*, Daniela Bianchi *(Signora Dominici)*, Trini Alonso *(Clelia Valdemari)*, Alicia Brandet *(Swedish Vamp)*, Lelio Luttazzi *(Count Bellanca)*, Raffaele Pisu *(Pasqualino)*, Leopoldo Trieste *(Ferri)*, Ana Castor *(Signora Pellini)*, Pedro Rodriguez de Quevedo *(Gustavo Valdemari)*, Veronique Vendell, Helga Line, Pepe Calvo, Liselotte Pulver.

A typical Italian marital farce in which Salerno, an engineer in Rome, heads for the seaside in order to be with his vacationing wife, Milo. He hopes to find relaxation but instead his wife exposes him to a life of parties and swinging couples. He becomes suspicious of a playboy whom he catches with Milo, but is soon convinced of his wife's fidelity and returns home to Rome for some rest. Song: "Take a Weekend Italian Style" (Bob Swanson, performed by the Beejays).

d, Dino Risi; w, Risi, Ennio De Concini; ph, Armando Nannuzzi (Eastmancolor); m, Lelio Luttazzi; ed, Franco Fraticelli; art d, Mario Chiari.

Comedy   (PR:A   MPAA:R)

WEEK-END MADNESS   (SEE: AUGUST WEEK-END, 1936)

WEEK-END MARRIAGE   (1932) 66m FN-WB bw (GB: WEEKEND LIVES; AKA: WORKING WIVES)

Loretta Young *(Lola Davis)*, Norman Foster *(Ken Hays)*, George Brent *(Peter Acton)*, Aline MacMahon *(Agnes)*, Vivienne Osborne *(Shirley)*, Sheila Terry *(Connie)*, J. Farrell MacDonald *(Davis)*, Louise Carter *(Mrs. Davis)*, Grant Mitchell *(Doctor)*, Harry Holman *(Judge)*, Luis Alberni *(Louis)*, J. Carrol Naish *(Joe)*, Richard Tucker *(Jameson)*.

Foster loses his job, while his wife, Young, retains hers. A predictable role reversal occurs, with Foster rebelling at his submissive position and taking a mistress. Young finally wins him back by re-feminizing, in effect choosing to chain herself to the stove.

d, Thornton Freeland; w, Sheridan Gibney (based on the novel *Part-Time Wives* by Faith Baldwin); ph, Barney McGill; ed, Herbert Levy.

Comedy   (PR:A   MPAA:NR)

WEEKEND MILLIONAIRE   (1937, Brit.) 62m BIP/GAU bw (GB: ONCE IN A MILLION)

Buddy Rogers *(Pierre)*, Mary Brian *(Suzanne)*, W.H. Berry *(Gallivert)*, John Harwood *(Dupont)*, Norah Gale *(Princess)*, Billy Milton *(Prince)*, Charles Carson *(President)*, Aubrey Mallalieu *(Hotel Manager)*, Veronica Rose *(Caroline)*, Nadine March *(Josette)*, Reginald Smith *(Maier)*, Iris Hoey *(Mrs. Fenwick)*, Jimmy Godden *(Plume)*, Haver and Lee *(Joe and Chief)*.

Clerk Rogers pretends to be a millionaire in this bright comedy when he makes it to the bank with his firm's receipts after the bank is closed and he is forced to keep the cash over the weekend. He impresses phony countess Brian with his supposed wealth and romance quickly blooms. Then, to his surprise, he is given a hero's welcome on Monday when he learns that the bank was robbed over the weekend. Paris background is just for show; charming as Brian and Rogers are, their accents are strictly Anglo.

p, Walter C. Mycroft; d, Arthur Woods; w, Jack Davies, Geoffrey Kerr, Max Kester; ph, Ronald Neame, Ernest Steward; ed, George Black, Jr.; cos, Norman Hartnell.

Comedy   (PR:A   MPAA:NR)

WEEKEND MURDERS, THE   (1972, Ital.) 98m Jupiter Generale/MGM c (CONCERTO PER PISTOLA SOLISTA; AKA: CONCERT FOR A SOLO PISTOL)

Anna Moffo *(Barbara)*, Lance Percival *(Inspector Grey)*, Gastone Moschin *(Sgt. Thorpe)*, Eveline Stewart [Ida Galli] *(Isabelle)*, Peter Baldwin *(Anthony)*, Giacomo Rossi Stuart *(Ted)*, Christopher Chitell *(Georgie)*, Marisa Fabbri *(Aunt Gladys)*, Beryl Cunningham *(Pauline)*, Quinto Parmeggiana *(Lawrence)*, Orchidea De Santis *(Maid)*, Robert Hundar *(Valet)*, Franco Borelli *(Stranger)*, Ballard Berkeley *(Butler)*, Richard Caldicott *(Lawyer)*, Harry Hutchinson *(Gardener)*.

An Italian-produced programmer takes stabs at the standard murder mystery in which members of the family gather for a will reading at a British estate and then are murdered one by one, leaving Metropolitan Opera soprano Moffo the sole beneficiary. An incredibly dumb Scotland Yard detective gets Moffo to confess that she is guilty of the murders and that a second will exists which she hid. The best moment has Moffo commenting, after finding the butler's corpse, "At least for once no one will be able to say the butler did it." Black sexpot Cunningham and nympho maid De Santis gave the picture an "R" rating, but their antics were muted and the rating should have been a "G".

p, Franco Committeri, Federico Ippolito; d, Michele Lupo; w, Fabio Pittorru, Massimo Felisatti, Sergio Donati; ph, Guglielmo Mancori (Techniscope, Technicolor); m, Francesco De Masi, "First Piano Concerto" by Peter Ilich Tchaikovsky; ed, Vincenzo Tomassi; art d, Ugo Sterpini; set d, Bonaventura Fraulo.

Mystery/Comedy   (PR:O   MPAA:R)

WEEKEND OF FEAR*   (1966) 63m JD bw

Micki Malone *(Judy)*, Kenneth Washman *(Young Deaf-Mute)*, Tory Alburn *(Tom)*, Ruth Trent *(Mrs. Harris)*, Dianne Danford *(Connie)*, James Vaneck *(Jack)*, Kurt Donsbach *(Man in Car)*, Jill Banner *(Carol)*.

A stagnant horror picture about a crazed widow who wants a younger boy friend and chooses Alburn, who already is taken by Danford. Malone, the demented widow, hires an equally demented deaf-mute to frighten away her competition, eventually causing her death. Rock-bottom product on all counts.

p,d&w, Joe Danford; ph, Saul N. Leyton; m, William H. Lockwood; ed, Danford.

Horror   (PR:C   MPAA:NR)

WEEKEND OF SHADOWS   (1978, Aus.) 94m Samson-South Australian/Roadshow c

John Waters *(Rabbit)*, Melissa Jaffer *(Vi)*, Wyn Roberts *(Sgt. Caxton)*, Barbara West *(Helen Caxton)*, Graham Rouse *(Ab Nolan)*, Graeme Blundell *(Bernie Collins)*, Bill Hunter *(Bosun)*, Keith Lee *(David Wayne)*, Les Foxcroft *(Badger)*, Kit Taylor *(Ryan)*, Mark Gaweda *(The Pole)*.

A trenchant murder drama which is mixed with a sufficiently convincing tale about lynch mob fury. Waters joins a posse determined to catch a Polish immigrant farmhand whom they believe killed a rancher's wife. The mob is led by police sergeant Roberts, whose sole purpose in hunting down the fugitive is to regain his stature as a cop after he had caused the deaths of two youngsters. The posse is on the hunt for the weekend and soon grows weary, a condition hurried along by its drunkenness. Waters finds himself identifying with the supposed criminal and is eventually the one to defend the man's innocence. Keenly directed and with a fresh conception of its characters, this Australian entry has universal appeal.

p, Tom Jeffrey, Matt Carroll; d, Jeffrey; w, Peter Yeldham (based on a novel by Hugh Atkinson); ph, Richard Wallace (Eastmancolor); m, Charles Marawood; ed, Rod Adamson; art d, Christopher Webster.

Crime Drama   Cas.   (PR:C MPAA:NR)

WEEKEND PASS**   (1944) 65m UNIV bw

Martha O'Driscoll (Barbara), Noah Beery, Jr (Johnny), George Barbier (Bradley), Andrew Tombes (Constable), Irving Bacon (Sheriff), Dennis Moore (Ray), Edgar Dearing (Motor Cop), Pierre Watkin (Kendall), Lotte Stein (Hilda), Eddie Acuff (Waikowsky), Jack Rice (Jenkins), Perc Launders (Murphy), Carol Hughes (Maisie), Grady Sutton (Pajama Man), Eddie Dunn (Proprietor), Donald Kerr (Hobo), Lew Diamond and His Harmonaires, The Delta Rhythm Boys, The Mayris Chaney Dancers, The Sportsmen.

A dry programmer which offers little humor or good music, the two things it strives to achieve. O'Driscoll is a debutante who has hopes of joining the WACS but meets opposition from her grandfather. She runs away, meeting and falling head over heels in love with Beery, a shipyard worker on leave for the weekend. The pair live it up for a while but soon return home–O'Driscoll to her granddad and Berry to the docks. The Delta Rhythm Boys deliver "All or Nothing at All" (Jack Lawrence, Arthur Altman). Other songs: "I Like to Be Loved" (Everett Carter, Milton Rosen, sung by Driscoll), "We Build 'Em, We Sail 'Em" (Carter, Rosen, sung by The Sportsmen), "I Am, Are You?," "She's a Girl a Man Can Dream Of" (Carter, Rosen), "We're in the Navy" (Don Raye, Gene de Paul).

p, Warren Wilson; d, Jean Yarbrough; w, Clyde Bruckman (based on a story by Wilson); ph, William Sickner; ed, Edward Curtiss; md, Don George; art d, John B. Goodman; cos, Vera West.

Musical   (PR:A MPAA:NR)

WEEKEND WITH FATHER***½   (1951) 83m UNIV bw

Van Heflin (Brad Stubbs), Patricia Neal (Jean Bowen), Gigi Perreau (Anne Stubbs), Virginia Field (Phyllis Reynolds), Richard Denning (Don Adams), Jimmy Hunt (Gary Bowen), Janine Perreau (Patty Stubbs), Tommy Rettig (David Bowen), Gary Pagett (Eddie Lewis), Frances Williams (Cleo), Elvia Allman (Mrs. G.), Forrest Lewis (Innkeeper), Maudie Prickett (Maid), Robert Rockwell, Martha Mears.

A charming tale of adults vs. children and urban life vs. nature is told by melodramatist Sirk as he casts Heflin and Neal as husband-and-wife-to-be. They meet while bringing their children to a summer camp and, learning that they've both been widowed, fall in love. Their children, however, are against the idea, preferring, instead, their parent's recent marital prospects- -for Heflin it is a hot-shot TV personality, while for Neal it is the athletic camp counselor. The mischievous youngsters led by Perreau (a Sirk regular) succeed in breaking the couple apart, but when Perreau sees just how much in love they really are the kids again work to get them back together. The children become the focal point in WEEKEND WITH FATHER, taking the lives of the adults in their own hands, substituting for fate. Sirk stresses the importance of the children by claiming he made the picture "only for the children." Themes from this picture also crop up again in Sirk's work, most notably in ALL THAT HEAVEN ALLOWS, which has the impending marriage of Rock Hudson and Jane Wyman controlled by her selfish children and a snobbish society crowd. While Sirk makes light of a number of the characters in WEEKEND WITH FATHER, he seems to have the most fun with the health-nut camp counselor, Denning. Oddly, Sirk became a vegetarian during this picture and Denning's character, in Sirk's words, "was, therefore, a bit of a self-satire."

p, Ted Richmond; d, Douglas Sirk; w, Joseph Hoffman (based on a story by George F. Slavin, George W. George); ph, Clifford Stine; m, Frank Skinner; ed, Russell Schoengarth; art d, Bernard Herzbrun, Robert Boyle; set d, Russell A. Gausman, Rudy R. Levitt; cos, Bill Thomas.

Comedy/Romance   (PR:A MPAA:NR)

WEEKEND WITH LULU, A**½   (1961, Brit.) 91m Hammer/COL bw

Bob Monkhouse (Fred Scrutton), Leslie Phillips (Timothy Gray), Alfred Marks (Comte de Grenoble), Shirley Eaton (Dierdre Proudfoot), Irene Handl (Florence Proudfoot), Sidney James (Cafe Patron), Kenneth Connor (British Tourist), Sydney Tafler (Stationmaster), Russ Conway (French Pianist), Eugene Deckers (Inspector Larue), Graham Stark (Chiron), Harold Berens (Card Seller), Tutte Lemkow (Leon), Stuart Hillier (Flying Corsican), Andreas Malandrinos (Lodge Keeper), Ernst Walder (Count's Chauffeur), Judith Furse (Mme. Bon-Bon), Denis Shaw (Bar Patron), Keith Pyott (Count's Butler), Gordon Rollings (Humper), Edie Martin (Lodgekeeper's Wife), Harold Kasket (Bon Viveur), Alexis Bobrinskoy (Mayor), Heidi Erich (Lulubelle), Marie Devereux, Eve Eden, Sally Douglas, Janette Rowsell.

An enjoyable comedy about a pair of young lovers, Phillips and Eaton, who attempt to take off on a romantic weekend for two in his pal's ice cream truck, affectionately called "Lulu." When Eaton's mother comes along, Phillips' plans are somewhat altered. A ferry boat mixup finds the threesome (foursome, counting Lulu) in France where they run into a variety of unwelcome guests, including a whorehouse madam and a man who sells dirty postcards, before the van is rushed back to England on an airplane.

p, Ted Lloyd; d, John Paddy Carstairs; w, Lloyd (based on a story by Lloyd, Val Valentine); ph, Ken Hodges, Jack Mills; m, Tony Osborne, Trevor H.

Stanford; ed, Tom Simpson; art d, John Howell; cos, Maude Churchill; makeup, Dick Bonnor-Moris.

Comedy   (PR:A MPAA:NR)

WEEKEND WITH THE BABYSITTER*   (1970) 93m Dundee/Crown
International c (AKA: WEEKEND BABYSITTER)

George E. Carey (Jim Carlton), Susan Romen (Candy Wilson), James Almanzar (Rich Harris), Luanne Roberts (Mona Carlton), Anthony Victor (Sancho), Bob Bernard (A.K.), Guy Edwards (Leon), Steve Vinovich (Snitch), Annik Borel (Doris), Gloria Hill (Mary Mary), James E. McLarty (Smitty), Patrick Whyte (Salesman), Pat Welch (Waitress), Ellen Bailey (Operator), Susan L. Stoner (Marge), Easton Herd (Michael Carlton).

A melodrama so far-fetched it's hard to believe it's not the product of some bizarre drug trip. Carey is a director-screenwriter in Hollywood whose wife, Roberts, and child are on the way to a weekend with her mother. Due to a mixup, Romen, their baby sitter, arrives and Carey invites her to stay. He lets her read his new youth-oriented script. She thinks it is full of bunk, and offers to take him to a party to see how the kids really live. Marijuana and sex follow, but in the meantime they learn that Roberts, a secret heroins addict, is tangled up in a scheme to smuggle drugs into the U.S. from Mexico. Romen leads a gang of motorcyclists to help Roberts, while Carey buzzes the boat they are on in his private plane. The police arrive, husband and wife are reunited, and the baby sitter hits the road with a lighthearted "ciao."

p, George E. Carey; d, Don Henderson; w, James E. McLarty (based on a story by Henderson, Carey); ph, Jack Steeley (DeLuxe Color); m, Robert O. Ragland; ed, Dick Elliott; m/l, Ragland, Marcia Waldorf (performed by The Opposition).

Drama   (PR:O MPAA:NR)

WEEKEND WIVES   (SEE: WEEKEND, ITALIAN STYLE, 1967,
Fr./Ital./Span.)

WEEK-ENDS ONLY**   (1932) 65m FOX bw

Joan Bennett (Venetia Carr), John Halliday (Arthur Ladden), Ben Lyon (Jack Williams), Halliwell Hobbes (Martin), Henry Armetta (Washroom Attendant), Berton Churchill (Mr. Carr), John Arledge (Ted), John Elliott (Bartender), Walter Byron (Mr. Brigg), Bud Flanagan [Dennis O'Keefe].

Bennett, formerly rich and presently poor, takes a job as a hostess in a nightclub and meets wealthy and elegant Halliday, who hires her to help pep up his private weekend bashes. She accepts and is soon leading the life she is used to–wearing furs and diamonds and living in a penthouse. the only problem is that her sweetheart, poor artist Lyon, doesn't know about her "other" life. He soon finds out and nearly loses the girl, but the clinch comes in the final moments. Artificiality is the dominant characteristic in this bit of fluff.

d, Alan Crosland; w, William Counselman, Warner Fabian (based on the novel Week-End Girl by Fabian); ph, Hal Mohr; cos, Earl Luick.

Drama/Comedy   (PR:A MPAA:NR)

WEIRD LOVE MAKERS, THE*   (1963, Jap.) 75m Nikkatsu/Audubon
bw (KYONETSU NO KISETSU; AKA: WILD LOVE-MAKERS)

Tamio Kawaji (Al), Noriko Matsumoto (Fumiko), Yuko Chiyo (Yuki), Hiroyuki Nagato (Kashi).

The influence of the "cool" modern jazz age takes over in this bizarre Japanese melodrama about a man and a woman living in a jazz bar–he a pickpocket and she a prostitute who relishes foreigners. One day they are betrayed by another couple to the police, and after serving a jail sentence they plot revenge. The pickpocket rapes the woman who betrayed him, and his girl seduces her fiance, both women becoming pregnant. In the hospital to which both women go for an abortion, the victims are told who the real fathers are, and at the finale the cruel laughter of the pickpocket and the prostitute rings from the screen.

d, Koreyoshi Kurakara; w, Nobuo Yamada; ph, Yoshio Mamiya (Cinema-Scope); m, Toshiro Mayuzumi; ed, Akira Suzuki.

Drama   (PR:O MPAA:NR)

WEIRD ONES, THE zero   (1962) 76m Crescent-Colonial bw

Mike Braden, Rudy Duran, Phyliss Warren, Lee Morgan.

A feature which is just too brainless to be reckoned with. For the record, a pair of press agents try to capture an "Astronik" which has come from space to torture and kill women. To capture the alien, they hire a "cosmos-cutie" to lure it into a trap. Celluloid looniness.

p,d&w, Pat Boyette.;

Science Fiction/Comedy   (PR:C MPAA:NR)

WEIRD WOMAN**½   (1944) 62m UNIV bw

Lon Chaney, Jr (*Prof. Norman Reed*), Anne Gwynne (*Paula Reed*), Evelyn Ankers (*Ilona Carr*), Ralph Morgan (*Prof. Millard Sawtelle*), Elisabeth Risdon (*Grace Gunnison*), Lois Collier (*Margaret Mercer*), Elizabeth Russell (*Evelyn Sawtelle*), Harry Hayden (*Prof. Septimus Carr*), Phil Brown (*David Jennings*), Jackie Lou Harding (*Student*), Hanna Kaapa (*Laraua*), William Hudson (*Student*), Chuck Hamilton (*Carpenter*), Kay Harding.

A fun programmer with a great title that stars Chaney as a college professor who returns from an island vacation with an exotic bride, Gwynne, who was reared by the natives. Former girl friend Ankers has a jealous streak which gets the better of her and she spreads rumors that Gwynne is an evil spirit who practices island voodoo rites. When a couple of deaths follow, the neighbors begin to believe the whisperings. The finale, however, proves Ankers to be the one responsible, causing her to scream (one of her juiciest), leap off a roof, and hang herself from some vines. Remade as BURN, WITCH, BURN in 1962, and WITCH'S BREW (1980).

p, Oliver Drake; d, Reginald LeBorg; w, Brenda Weisberg, W. Scott Darling (based on an Inner Sanctum radio program mystery from the novel *Conjure Wife* by Fritz Leiber, Jr.); ph, Virgil Miller; ed, Milton Carruth; md, Paul Sawtell; art d, John B. Goodman, Richard Riedel; cos, Vera West.

Mystery   (PR:A   MPAA:NR)

WELCOME DANGER**½   (1929) 112m PAR bw

Harold Lloyd (*Harold Bledsoe*), Barbara Kent (*Billie Lee*), Douglas Haig (*Buddy Lee*), Noah Young (*Officer Patrick Clancey*), Charles Middleton (*John Thorne/The Dragon*), William Walling (*Capt. Walton*), Jimmy Wang (*Dr. Chang Gow*), Nelson McDowell (*1st Train Passenger*), E.H. Calvert (*Chief Jim Bledsoe [wall photo]*), Edgar Kennedy (*Desk Sergeant*), James Mason (*Dick the Dude/Barry Steele*), Eddy Chandler (*Cop*), Tetsu Komai (*Florist Henchman*), James Leong (*Florist Henchman/High Priest*), Leo Willis (*Cop*), Wang Lee (*Chinaman with Queue*), Soo Hoo Sun (*Dead Chinaman*).

Brilliant silent comedian Lloyd made the transition to sound with this box office smash (his highest grosser at the time) which cast him as a botany student expected to fill the shoes of his recently deceased San Francisco police chief father. He succeeds in smashing a ring of drug dealers led by the mysterious "Dragon," who later turns out to be Middleton, the pillar of the community. Amidst the criminal comedy is a dose of romantic comedy as Lloyd bullies Kent, who has disguised herself as a boy. One humorous moment has Lloyd taking his picture in a photo booth with a picture of Kent sitting next to him. He becomes enamored with her face, failing to notice her beside him. Originally filmed as a silent by Mal St. Clair, WELCOME DANGER was largely reshot and turned into a talkie by Bruckman. Its running time, however, was just short of three hours–a long film by today's standards, and an unheard of epic in 1929. An hour was cut from the footage and though it was still too long it was a smash hit. Lloyd's character had changed somewhat (as had audience expectations and needs), making him a less identifiable comic than in his previous outings. He was no longer "one of us" but a funny man on the screen and his popularity would never match what it had been in SPEEDY (1928) and the classic SAFETY LAST (1923).

p, Harold Lloyd; d, Clyde Bruckman; w, Paul Gerard Smith (based on a story by Felix Adler, Lex Neal, Bruckman); ph, Walter Lundin, Henry L. Kohler; m, C. Bakaleinikoff; ed, Bernard Burton, Carl Himm; art d, Liell K. Vedder; m/l, "Billie," Lynn Cowan; "When You Are Mine," Paul Titsworth, Cowan.

Comedy/Crime   (PR:A   MPAA:NR)

WELCOME HOME*½   (1935) 73m FOX bw

James Dunn (*Richard Foster*), Arline Judge (*Gorgeous*), Raymond Walburn (*Giltedge*), Rosina Lawrence (*Susan Adams*), William Frawley (*Painless*), Charles Sellon (*Anstruther*), Charles Ray (*Andrew Carr*), Frank Melton (*Willis Parker*), George Meeker (*Edward Adams*), James Burke, Arthur Hoyt, Dave O'Brien, Spencer Charters, Harry Holman, Sarah Edwards.

When con man Dunn is elected to his home town's chamber of commerce he returns to the town with three slick friends of his. The friends aren't welcome unless they pay off a debt for some bad bonds they sold the town. Dunn wins a fortune at the track, pays the debt, befriends a wealthy New Yorker, and he and his friends win a mint in a shell game. A lot happens but the story rambles around and finally staggers to a finish without anything much being said or done that makes sense.

p, B.G. DeSylva; d, James Tinling; w, Marion Orth, Arthur Horman, Paul Gerard Smith (based on the story by Horman); ph, Arthur Miller; md, Oscar Bradley; cos, William Lambert.

Drama/Comedy   (PR:A   MPAA:NR)

WELCOME HOME   (SEE: SNAFU, 1945)

WELCOME HOME, SOLDIER BOYS*   (1972) 91m FOX c (AKA: FIVE DAYS HOME)

Joe Don Baker (*Danny*), Paul Koslo (*Shooter*), Alan Vint (*Kid*), Elliott Street (*Fatback*), Jennifer Billingsley (*Broad*), Billy "Green" Bush (*Sheriff*), Geoffrey Lewis (*Francis Rapture, Motel Owner*), Francine York (*Lydia*), Timothy Scott (*Mike*), Lonny Chapman (*Danny's Father*), Florence MacMichael (*Danny's Mother*), Cherie Foster (*Gloria*), Beach Dickerson (*Used Car Salesman*), Ted Markland (*Hick*), Joel Lawrence (*Trooper*), Luanne Roberts (*Charlene*), Damienne Oliver (*Ruby*).

A pretentious antiwar picture about four Vietnam vets who pool their money and take off for California by car. By the time they get to New Mexico they've blown all but $69 of their original $9,000 stake. They help themselves at a gas station and get shot at by the owner, causing the vets to unload from the car an arsenal of weapons. They put on their Green Beret uniforms, shoot up the town (heavy-handedly called Hope), and then await the battle that is expected when the authorities arrive. Another series of post-Nam movies that are most notable for their depressing themes.

ed, Patrick Kennedy; art d, Hilyard M. Brown; cos, William Lambert; spec eff, Cliff Wenger; m/l, Ronee Blakely, The Country Gazette; makeup, Dan Striepeke.

Drama   (PR:O   MPAA:R)

WELCOME KOSTYA!**   (1965, USSR) 75m Mosfilm/Artkino bw
(DOBRO POZHALOVAT; DOBRA POZHALOVAT ILI POSTORONNIM VKHOD VOSPRESHCHEN)

Vitya Kosykh (*Kostya*), Yevgeniy Yevstigneyev (*Camp Director*), Lida Smirnova (*The Informer*), A. Aleynikova (*Camp Nurse*), I. Rutberg, A. Smirnov, Yura Bondarenko, Lida Volkova, Boris Demb, Seryozha Kokorev, Igor Kryukov, Sasha Moshovets, Tanya Prokhorova, Lida Smeyan, Slava Tsaryov, T. Barysheva, A. Lagranskiy, I. Mazurova, V. Uralskiy, N. Shatskaya, Vova Bordukov, Sasha Zhiveynov, Alik Miniovich, Seryozha Shappu, Sasha Baykov.

Kosykh is cast as the title character, a Soviet boy who gets kicked out of summer camp because he is too unruly. He sneaks back in, however, and is hidden from the counselor by his friends until the counselor turns out not to be a bad guy after all, and welcomes him back.

d, E. Klimov; w, S. Lungin, I. Nusinov; ph, Anatoliy Kuznetsov; m, Mikhail Tariverdiyev, I. Yakushenko; art d, V. Kamskiy, B. Blank; spec eff, I. Felitsyn, N. Zvonaryov.

Drama/Comedy   (PR:AA   MPAA:NR)

WELCOME, MR. BEDDOES   (SEE: MAN COULD GET KILLED, A, 1966)

WELCOME, MR. WASHINGTON**½   (1944, Brit.) 90m BN/Anglo American bw

Barbara Mullen (*Jane Willoughby*), Donald Stewart (*Lt. Johnny Grant*), Peggy Cummins (*Sarah Willoughby*), Leslie Bradley (*Capt. Abbott*), Roy Emerton (*Selby*), Martita Hunt (*Miss Finch*), Arthur Sinclair (*Murphy*), Graham Moffatt (*Albert*), Shelagh Frazer (*Millie*), Beatrice Varley (*Martha*), George Carney (*Publican*), Louise Lord (*Katherine Willoughby*), Paul Blake (*Vernon*), Drusilla Wills (*Mrs. Curley*), Irene Handl, Julian d'Albie, Alexander Field, Victor Woods, Tony Quinn, Tommy Palmer, Hal Gordon, John MacLaren, Danny Green, Gordon Begg, Elsie Wagstaffe, Herbert Lomas, Johnnie Schofield.

A satisfying British drama about the encroachment of U.S. troops on English country life during WW II. Stealing the picture is Cummins as a youngster who, with her sister, Mullen, farms the land left behind by their father. They find themselves at odds with a crotchety tenant-farmer who is angry that the U.S. soldiers chose his property for an airfield instead of theirs. He tries to rally community support against the Americans, but finds his fellow countrymen are in favor of the soldiers.

p, Elizabeth Hiscott; d, Leslie Hiscott; w, Jack Whittingham (based on a story by Noel Streatfield); ph, Erwin Hillier.

Drama   (PR:A   MPAA:NR)

WELCOME STRANGER, 1941   (SEE: ACROSS THE SIERRAS, 1941)

WELCOME STRANGER***   (1947) 107m PAR bw

Bing Crosby (*Dr. Jim Pearson*), Joan Caulfield (*Trudy Mason*), Barry Fitzgerald (*Dr. Joseph McRory*), Frank Faylen (*Bill Walters*), Elizabeth Patterson (*Mrs. Gilley*), Robert Shayne (*Roy Chesley*), Larry Young (*Dr. Ronnie Jenks*), Percy Kilbride (*Nat Dorkas*), Charles Dingle (*Charlie Chesley*), Don Beddoe (*Mort Elkins*), Thurston Hall (*Congressman Beeker*), Lillian Bronson (*Miss Lennek*), Mary Field (*Secretary, Boston*), Paul Stanton (*Mr. Daniels*), Pat McVey (*Ed Chanock*), Milton Kibbee (*Ben, Bus Driver*), Clarence Muse (*Clarence, Steward*), Charles Middleton (*Farmer Pinkett*), Margaret Field (*Cousin Hattie*), John Ince, Franklyn Farnum (*Friends*), Erville Alderson (*Train Companion*), John Westley (*Mr. Cartwright*),

Edward Clark (*Mr. Weaver*), Clarence Nordstrom (*Man*), Brandon Hurst (*Man*), Ethel Wales (*Mrs. Sims*), Frank Ferguson (*Mr. Crane*), Elliott Nugent (*Dr. White*), Bea Allen (*Telephone Operator*), Julia Faye (*Woman*), Gertrude Hoffman (*Miss Wendy*), Douglas Wood (*Principal, Mr. Tilson*), Fred Datig, Jr. (*Al*), John "Skins" Miller (*Citizen*).

"Unwelcome Stranger" might have been a better title for this film which united Crosby and Fitzgerald again in the same kind of heart-warming comedy with music they scored with in GOING MY WAY. This time, they've doffed the collar and cassock in favor of stethoscopes and scalpels and, instead of Crosby saving Fitzgerald's church, he saves the man's life, with four tunes by Johnny Burke and Jimmy Van Heusen tossed in for good measure. Fitzgerald runs a clinic in a small town. He's a curmudgeon (as usual) and doesn't take kindly to Crosby, a young medico who has come to town to help. Fitzgerald doesn't cotton to Crosby's penchant for singing and thinks that any doctor who uses his vocal chords to warble can't be trusted. Caulfield is a young teacher who helps out at the clinic and Crosby is immediately attracted to her but she shows him scant attention and explains that she is betrothed to the local druggist. Crosby feels the resentment from Fitzgerald, the coolness from Caulfield, and the general malaise of the people toward him so he opts to depart. When Patterson, who is Fitzgerald's maid, learns of Crosby's decision, she prevails upon the younger sawbones to bare his thoughts to Fitzgerald and see if they can straighten these matters out. Crosby takes her advice and approaches Fitzgerald and it isn't long before the two men begin to like and respect each other and Fitzgerald persuades Crosby to stay. A few weeks later, the older man has a near-fatal attack of appendicitis and, through the deft skill of Crosby (who is just as handy with a lancet as he is with a lyric), he is saved and Crosby becomes a local hero. During the aforementioned, town council topper Dingle has arranged for snobbish young doctor Young to be given the job of chief of surgery at the village's new hospital, a position originally promised to Fitzgerald. News breaks that a terrible illness has hit a quartet of young boys at the local school. Young rushes in to make his diagnosis and states that the boys are definitely suffering from equine encephalitis, a viral brain fever contracted from diseased horses. Crosby and Fitzgerald don't see it that way at all and think there's another answer to the stupor that the young boys are in. They search the school and wind up in the locker room where they come upon the real answer, four half-smoked cigars the boys puffed which laid them low. With Young being discredited, the way is open for Fitzgerald and Crosby to take over the running of the new medical facility. The message of the movie is clear at once: never judge a book by its cover or a doctor by his singing (though der Bingle's singing is above reproach). Hendrix chimes in with a neat portrayal as a teenager swooning over Crosby, and Patterson and Kilbride are charming as flinty New Englanders. The tunes are pleasant and there is one production number for "Country Style" that gets toes to tapping as the actors go into a square dance. The romance between Caulfield and Crosby takes a back seat to the drama in front and the scenes between them are not on a par with the ones between Crosby and Fitzgerald. Despite the minor faults, there's lot to like in the film and some very funny lines in Sheekman's screenplay (with good reason, as Sheekman had been a Marx Brothers writer at one time). It's refreshing to see a nostalgic film about a time in history when doctors were average people without God complexes and when the word "malpractice" was seldom heard. Director Nugent does a cameo as a doctor.

p, Sol C. Siegel; d, Elliott Nugent; w, Arthur Sheekman, N. Richard Nash (based on a story by Frank Butler); ph, Lionel Lindon; ed, Everett Douglas; md, Robert Emmett Dolan; art d, Hans Dreier, Franz Bachelin; set d, Sam Comer, John McNeil; cos, Edith Head; m/l "Smile Right Back at the Sun," "Country Style," "My Heart Is a Hobo," "As Long As I'm Dreaming," "Smack in the Middle of Maine," James Van Heusen, Johnny Burke (sung by Bing Crosby).

Comedy/Drama   **Cas.**   **(PR:A MPAA:NR)**

WELCOME TO ARROW BEACH   (SEE: TENDER FLESH, 1976)

WELCOME TO BLOOD CITY zero   (1977, Brit./Can.) 96m Blood
                                                City/EMI-FP c

Jack Palance (*Sheriff Frendlander*), Keir Dullea (*Lewis*), Samantha Eggar (*Katherine*), Barry Morse (*Supervisor*), Hollis McLaren (*Martine*), Chris Wiggins (*Gellor*), Henry Ramer (*Chumley*), Allan Royale (*Peter*), John Evans (*Lyle*).

A blatant rip-off of the vastly superior WESTWORLD which again has a colony of robot-people living in a Wild West setting. Dullea is zapped into this world and forced to fight for his survival or die. The big man in town is Palance, who has been deemed "Immortal" because he has killed more people than anyone else–a status symbol in this society. One can drive a fleet of trucks through the holes in the script, the direction is anemic, the acting is amateurish and the production quality appears cheap. Nothing to celebrate here.

p, Marilyn Stonehouse; d, Peter Sasdy, w, Stephen Schenck, Michael Winder; ph, Reginald H. Morris; m, Roy Budd; ed, Keith Palmer; prod d, Jack McAdam; art d, Tony Hall.

Science Fiction/Western   **Cas.**   **(PR:O MPAA:NR)**

WELCOME TO HARD TIMES**   (1967) 103m MGM c (AKA: KILLER
                                                        ON A HORSE)

Henry Fonda (*Will Blue*), Janice Rule (*Molly Riordan*), Keenan Wynn (*Zar*), Janice Paige (*Adah*), John Anderson (*Ezra/Isaac Maple*), Warren Oates (*Jenks*), Fay Spain (*Jessie*), Edgar Buchanan (*Brown*), Aldo Ray (*Man from Bodie*), Denver Pyle (*Alfie*), Michael Shea (*Jimmy Fee*), Arlene Golonka (*Mae*), Lon Chaney, Jr (*Avery*), Royal Dano (*John Bear*), Alan Baxter (*Jack Millay*), Paul Birch (*Mr. Fee*), Dan Ferrone (*Bert Albany*), Paul Fix (*Maj. Munn*), Elisha Cook (*Hanson*), Kalen Liu (*China*), Ann McCrea (*Flo*), Bob Terhune (*1st Drinker*), Ron Burke (*Young Miner*).

A depressing, stark western set in the hopeless town of Hard Times. Fonda is the spineless mayor of the town, who gets walked all over by Ray, an evil wretch who kills as he pleases, leaving his mark behind him on a number of gravestones, wherever he goes. The town is left no choice but to rebuild after Ray leaves, burning the town to a cinder as a final vile gesture. The town's future begins to look up when Wynn arrives and sets up a saloon populated by a collection of women. But Ray, known only as "The Man from Bodie," returns and this time Fonda, conscious that he must confront him, dissolves the town's fear with a well-aimed bullet. Director Kennedy (SUPPORT YOUR LOCAL SHERIFF, THE ROUNDERS, THE WAR WAGON) attempted something different with this picture, a bleak look at the west's dark side, but never really succeeded, though some fine supporting performances by Wynn, Chaney, Jr., Oates, Cook, and others helped tremendously.

p, Max E. Youngstein, David Karr; d, Burt Kennedy; w, Kennedy (based on the novel by E.L. Doctorow); ph, Harry Stradling, Jr. (Metrocolor); m, Harry Sukman; ed, Aaron Stell; art d, George W. Davis, Carl Anderson; set d, Henry Grace, Joseph J. Stone; cos, Frank Roberts, Rose Rockne; makeup, William Tuttle, Gene Bartlett.

Western   **(PR:O MPAA:NR)**

WELCOME TO L.A.½**   (1976) 106 UA c

Keith Carradine (*Carroll Barber*), Sally Kellerman (*Ann Goode*), Geraldine Chaplin (*Karen Hood*), Harvey Keitel (*Ken Hood*), Lauren Hutton (*Nona Bruce*), Viveca Lindfors (*Susan Moore*), Sissy Spacek (*Linda Murray*), Denver Pyle (*Carl Barber*), John Considine (*Jack Goode*), Richard Baskin (*Eric Wood*), Allan Nicholls (*Dana Howard*), Cedric Scott (*Faye*), Mike Kaplan (*Russell Linden*), Diahann Abbott (*Jeannette Ross*).

Although heralded by some as one of the most original and innovative directorial debuts of the 1970s, Alan Rudolph's WELCOME TO L.A., like his REMEMBER MY NAME, seems better suited to cult status than anything else. It takes a pretentious look at a self-important group of weirdos from Los Angeles as they realize how worthless their lives are. Contemporary sexual relationships abound as does an excess of drinking and driving (though not necessarily at the same time). Carradine and his fellow Altman veterans just seem to wander around a lot and the film's success or failure depends almost entirely on how much you like them. Although the players for both Altman and Rudolph are the same–Carradine (NASHVILLE), Hutton, Chaplin, Considine (A WEDDING), Kellerman (M.A.S.H.), Keitel (BUFFALO BILL), etc.–the comparisons between them are unfair. Altman has since drifted off into the nowhere land of filmed theater, while Rudolph has continued to push forward, releasing CHOOSE ME in 1985, his best film to date and one of the finest releases of the year.

p, Robert Altman; d&w, Alan Rudolph (based on the music suite "City of the One Night Stands" by Richard Baskin); ph, David Myers (DeLuxe Color); m, Baskin; ed, William A. Sawyer, Thomas Walls; set d, Dennis Parrish; cos, Jules Melillo; makeup, Monty Westmore; m/l, "At the Door," "When the Arrow Flies," "Night Time," "After the End," Baskin (sung by Baskin, Keith Carridine).

Drama   **Cas.**   **(PR:O MPAA:R)**

WELCOME TO THE CLUB*½   (1971) 88m COL c

Brian Foley (*Lt. Andrew Oxblood*), Jack Warden (*Gen. Strapp*), Andy Jarrell (*Robert E. Lee Fairfax*), Kevin O'Connor (*Harrison W. Morve*), Francesca Tu (*Hogan*), David Toguri (*Hideki Ikada*), Al Mancini (*Pt. Marcantonio*), Art Wallace (*Col. Buonocuore*), Marsha Hunte (*Leah Wheat*), Joyce Wilford (*Shawna O'Shay*), Lon Satton (*Marshall Bowles*), Christopher Malcolm (*Pvt. Henry Hoe*), John Dunne-Hill (*Pvt. O'Malley*), Lee Meredith (*Betsy Wholecloth*), Louis Quinn (*Capt. Sigmus*), Lionel Murton (*Col Ames*), Christopher Malcolm (*Pvt. Henry Hoe*), Jeanne Darville (*Mrs. Oxblood*), Anisha (*Chita*), Claus Ersbak (*Schultz*), Ueda (*Headwaiter*), Robert Kidd (*Becker*), Oliver Norman (*Tom*), Eva Marie Petryshen (*Ann*).

An unfunny comedy set, of all places, in Hiroshima in 1945 which casts Foley as a crusading Quaker morale officer who is determined to get his black friends better treatment. He tries to get a black singing combo billeted in the officers' club but, having no luck, grows increasingly upset with the prejudice displayed by his fellow soldiers. Underneath this mushroom cloud of pretension there seems to be a message about the human condition, but it's not worth the trouble digging through the wreckage to find.

p, Sam Lomburg, Walter Shenson; d, Shenson; w, Clement Biddle Wood (based on the novel by Wood); ph, Mikael Salomon (Eastmancolor); m, Ken

WELL, THE-

Thorne; ed, Jim Connock; art d, Maurice Fowler; m/l, "A Song for Them," Brian Foley (sung by Foley).

Comedy   (PR:O   MPAA:R)

WELL, THE***   (1951)85m UA bw

Gwendolyn Laster (*Carolyn Crawford*), Richard Rober (*Sheriff Ben Kellogg*), Maidie Norman (*Mrs. Crawford*), George Hamilton (*Grandfather*), Ernest Anderson (*Mr. Crawford*), Dick Simmons (*Mickey*), Lane Chandler (*Stan*), Pat Mitchell (*Peter*), Margaret Wells (*Schoolteacher*), Wheaton Chambers (*Woody*), Michael Ross (*Frank*), Russell Trent (*Chet*), Allen Mathews (*Hal*), John Philips (*Fred*), Walter Morrison (*Art*), Christine Larson (*Casey*), Jess Kirkpatrick (*Quigley*), Roy Engel (*Gleason*), Alfred Grant (*Gaines*), Ed Max (*Milkman*), Guy Beach (*Baggageman*), Robert Osterloh (*Wylie*), Henry [Harry] Morgan (*Claude Packard*), Barry Kelley (*Sam Packard*), Walter Kelly (*Chip*), Mary Ellen Kay (*Lois*), Beverly Jons (*Sally*), Elzie Emanuel (*Student*), Tom Powers (*Mayor*), Bill Walker (*Dr. Billings*), Douglas Evans (*Lobel*), Sherry Hall (*Manners*).

An intense drama boldly addressing the racial issue when a young black girl disappears and a white man, Morgan, is jailed for kidnaping her. She is located in a well, however, and efforts begin to dig her out. The rescue mission builds to an explosive point when machines begin boring holes into the ground. Crowds of curious townsfolk arrive, as both blacks and whites peacefully await word of the girl's fate. Morgan, meanwhile, is released when it is discovered that he has been telling the truth. Rober, the town sheriff, asks Morgan for some of his construction experience in digging the shaft, but a bitter Morgan refuses. He reconsiders and shows up at the rescue sight when it appears that all hope is lost. Morgan volunteers to go into the shaft and with some difficulty rescues the girl, who is only barely alive. A suspenseful picture which builds to a powerful climax as the boring machines rhythmically drive into the ground with an accelerated pace that is heightened by a pounding musical score and fierce, frenetic editing. Released the same year as Billy Wilder's THE BIG CARNIVAL, which took a cynical look at the same situation.

p, Harry M. Popkin, Clarence Greene; d, Leo Popkin, Russell Rouse; W, Rouse, Greene; ph, Ernest Laszlo; m, Dimitri Tiomkin; ed, Chester Schaeffer.

Drama   (PR:A   MPAA:NR)

WELL DONE, HENRY*   (1936, Brit.) 86m BUT bw

Will Fyffe (*Henry McNab*), Cathleen Nesbitt (*Mrs. McNab*), Charles Hawtrey (*Rupert McNab*), Iris March (*Mary McNab*), Donald Gray (*Jimmy Dale*), Marjorie Taylor (*Celia Canford*), Edward Wild (*Peter Dill*), Hugh McDermott (*Sevier*), Paul Sheridan (*Leroux*), Torin Thatcher (*George Canford*), Gordon Bailey, Fred Schwartz, Wensley Russell, MacArthur Gordon, Ben Wright, Gerald Pring, Douglas Stewart, Ann Campbell, Rags the Dog.

Matter-of-course comedy has Fyffe a meek bank clerk who is bullied by his nagging wife and shunned by his spoiled children. He catches some crooks who had schemed to filch some bonds, thus saving his bank, and then helps his daughter elope. Suddenly he has won new respect and takes charge.

p, Neville Clark; d, Wilfred Noy; w, Noy, A. Barr-Smith (based on a story by Selwyn Jepson); ph, Jack Parker.

Comedy   (PR:A   MPAA:NR)

WE'LL GROW THIN TOGETHER* (1979, Fr.) 100m Alpes Cinema-Le Goff/ Silenes c (NOUS MAIGRIRONS ENSEMBLE)

Peter Ustinov (*Victor*), Bernadette Lafont (*Corinne*), Catherine Alric (*Patricia*), Sylvie Joly (*Doctor*).

Ustinov stars as an obese film director whose career takes a downward slide as his weight climbs upward. His romantic life fluctuates between the devoted Lafont and the wealthy Alric, he finally shares a house with. A big fat waste of time and energy and an embarrassment for Ustinov.

p, Jean-Pierre Le Moine, Sybil Le Goff; d&w, Michel Vocoret; ph, Georges Barsky; m, Pierre Perret; ed, Claudio Ventura.

Comedy   (PR:C   MPAA:NR)

WE'LL MEET AGAIN**½   (1942, Brit.) 84m COL British bw

Vera Lynn (*Peggy Brown*), Geraldo (*Gerry*), Patricia Roc (*Ruth*), Ronald Ward (*Frank*), Donald Gray (*Bruce McIntosh*), Frederick Leister (*Mr. Hastropp*), Betty Jardine (*Miss Bohne*), Brefni O'Rorke (*Dr. Drake*), Marian Spencer (*Mrs. Crump*), Lesley Osmond (*Sally*), John Watt, John Sharman, Alvar Liddell, Molly Raynor, Aubrey Mallalieu, Geraldo's Orchestra.

Loosely based on the real-life career of Vera Lynn, the "Forces' Sweetheart" of British troops in WW II, WE'LL MEET AGAIN follows Lynn's career as an aspiring singer to her rise as a BBC radio star. Along the way she falls in love with Gray, a Scottish soldier, but the romance ends when he falls for her best friend. She leaves London and devotes her talents to entertaining military forces through Europe. A fine morale booster which served its purpose in 1942.

p, Ben Henry, George Formby; d, Phil Brandon; w, James Seymour, Howard Thomas (based on the story by Derek Sheils); ph, Stephen Dade.

Musical   (PR:A   MPAA:NR)

WE'LL SMILE AGAIN**½   (1942, Brit.) 93m BN/Anglo-American bw

Bud Flanagan (*Bob Parker*), Chesney Allen (*Gordon Maxwell*), Meinhart Maur (*Herr Steiner*), Phyllis Stanley (*Gina Cavendish*), Peggy Dexter (*Googie*), Horace Kenney (*George, Makeup Man*), Gordon McLeod (*MacNaughton*), Alexander Kardan (*Holtzman*), Julian Vedey (*Hoffman*), Charles Austin (*Butler*), Edgar Driver, Wally Patch (*Porters*), C. Denier Warren (*Waiter*), Gwen Catley, Billy Mayerl, Malcolm "Mr. Jetsam" McFachern, Nuala Barrie, Trevor Denis, Charles Doe, Mary Eaton, Hal Gordon, Harry Herbert, Henry Hilliard, Gerchardt Kempinski, Joe E. Lee, Patrick Ludlow, Ruth Maitland, Andrea Malandrinos, Ernest Metcalfe, Peter Newman, Hilde Palmer, Stanley Pasken, Ethel Royale, Brookes Turner, Bombardier Billy Wells, Ben Williams, George Merritt.

A witty and fresh comedy about Nazi spies who infiltrate a film studio where Allen is employed. Flanagan is hired as his dresser but is fired shortly after attempting to break up the ring. It seems that the Nazis are sending codes through the films, a plot which Flanagan successfully uncovers, causing Gordon to hire him back. An elaborately staged musical comedy which, while minor, often hits the mark with its bright gags and all too human touches.

p&d, John Baxter; w, Austin Melford, Barbara K. Emary, Bud Flanagan; ph, Jimmy Wilson; m/l, Kennedy Russell, Desmond O'Connor.

Musical/Comedy   (PR:A   MPAA:NR)

WELL-DIGGER'S DAUGHTER, THE**½   (1946, Fr.) 122m Pagnol/Siritzky bw (LA FILLE DU PUISATIER)

Raimu (*Pascal*), Fernandel (*Felipe*), Josette Day (*Patricia*), Charpin (*Mons. Mazel*), George Grey (*Jacques Mazel*), Line Noro, Milly Mathis, Tramel.

Day becomes pregnant by her aviator lover who promptly goes off to war, leaving the girl and her child behind with her well-digger father, Raimu. Her father is less than compassionate and kicks her out of the house in order to preserve the innocence of his other daughters. Raimu finally comes around and makes peace with his daughter and with the aviator's parents. As theatrical as Pagnol's films sometimes are, THE WELL-DIGGER'S DAUGHTER is surprisingly realistic, especially since it was filmed under the watchful eye of the newly instated Vichy government. Filmed in 1940, THE WELL-DIGGER'S DAUGHTER was, in fact, the first film to be completed after France's defeat and the resumption of the French film industry.

p,d&w, Marcel Pagnol; m, Vincent Scotto: ed, Charles Clement.

Drama   (PR:C   MPAA:NR)

WELL-GROOMED BRIDE, THE**   (1946) 75m PAR bw

Olivia De Havilland (*Margie Dawson*), Ray Milland (*Lt. Dudley Briggs*), Sonny Tufts (*Lt. Torchy McNeil*), James Gleason (*Capt. Hornby*), Constance Dowling (*Rita Sloane*), Percy Kilbride (*Mr. Dawson*), Jean Heather (*Wickley*), Jay Norris (*Mitch*), Jack Reilly (*Buck*), George Turner (*Goose*), Tom Fadden (*Justice*), Donald Beddoe (*Hotel Clerk*), William Forrest (*Maj. James Smith*), Dale Van Sickel, James Millican (*Shore Police*), Frank Faylen (*Taxi Driver*), Noel Neill, Roberta Jonay (*Waves*), Jean Carlin (*Elevator Girl*), Eddie Laughton (*Waiter*), Tom Dillon (*Mr. Bennett*), William [L.] Haade, Roger Creed, Charles Mayon, Charles Eggleston, Stan Johnson, Walter Wilson (*MPs*), Larry Thompson (*Lt. Cutler*), Luke Chan (*Chinaman*), Minerva Urecal (*Woman*).

An uneventful comedy which, despite its fine cast, fails to produce anything out of the ordinary. Milland is an Army lieutenant who must locate some champagne in San Francisco to christen a French vessel. For some reason, De Havilland is the only one who has any, and she's saving it for her wedding to Tufts, a conceited former football player. Milland tries everything to get the champagne but to no avail. In all his efforts he finds himself growing fond of De Havilland and romance bubbles. In the process, Milland finally gets the champagne. Made during a contract dispute with Warner Bros., De Havilland took this minor Paramount project just to get back on the screen after nearly a three-year absence. A Supreme Court decision in 1945 ruled for De Havilland and she was freed of her seven-year contract to Warners. She almost didn't get the part in THE WELL-GROOMED BRIDE but was cast when Paramount's first choice, Paulette Godard, became pregnant.

p, Fred Kohlmar; d, Sidney Lanfield; w, Claude Binyon, Robert Russell (based on the story by Russell); ph, John F. Seitz; m, Roy Webb; ed, William Shea; art d, Hans Dreier, Earl Hedrick; set d, Kenneth Swartz; spec eff, Gordon Jennings.

Romance/Comedy   (PR:A   MPAA:NR)

WELLS FARGO****   (1937) 115m PAR bw

Joel McCrea (Ramsay MacKay), Bob Burns (Hank York), Frances DeeJustine, Lloyd Nolan (Del Slade), Porter Hall (James Oliver), Ralph Morgan (Mr. Pryor), Mary Nash (Mrs. Pryor), Robert Cummings (Trimball), Henry O'Neill (Henry Wells), John Mack Brown (Talbot Carter), Jane Dewey (Lucy Dorsett Trimball), Peggy Stewart (Alice MacKay), Bernard Siegel (Pawnee), Stanley Fields (Abe), Frank McGlynn (Lincoln), Jack Clark (William Fargo), Clarence Kolb (John Butterfield), Granville Bates (Bradford the Banker), Harry Davenport (Ingalls the Banker), Frank Conroy (Ward the Banker), Brandon Tynan (Edwards the Newspaper Publisher), Hal K. Dawson (Correspondent), Lucien Littlefield (San Francisco Postmaster), Jimmy Butler (Nick, Jr.), Willie Fung (Wang), Sheila Darcy (Lola Montez), Spencer Charters (Jethrow), Robert Emmett O'Connor (Sea Captain).

An episodic epic tracing the fictionalized history of the famed express company through the actions of one of that company's loyal activists, played by McCrea. Each segment of the film has a prolog superimposed title giving the time and place as the characters age appropriately while spreading messages into the West. The opening sequence sets the stage for the rest of the coach-and-six saga as barrels of fresh oysters are off-loaded from a railway car in Batavia, New York–where the rails end–and transferred to a waiting stagecoach. In a furious race against the possible culturing of salmonella bacteria in the mussels, the coach horses gallop off to Buffalo where waiting gourmandizers will safely gorge themselves on the slimy delicacies. The master of this orchestrated motion is O'Neill, the founder of the famed company. Segment two traces the Westward transit of emigrating settlers, served only–at the time–by ships sailing the many tedious miles around the Horn. Forward-thinking entrepreneur O'Neill envisages a time-saving landward passage and dispatches his sturdy second, McCrea, to California, where he happens upon segment three, the Gold Rush. Recruiting a buckskinned bumpkin, Burns, and his Indian companion, Siegel, McCrea hastens to set up the western arm of segment four, the Overland Mail, which is threatened by both meretricious bankers and the customary robber bands and Indian war parties. The famed Pony Express races by at something more than its legendary speed in the brief fifth episode. The sixth sees the outbreak of the Civil War, a conflict which separates the chief protagonists, McCrea and wife Dee, whose sympathies lie with different camps. Indeed, when a valuable gold bullion shipment intended to pay for provisioning the Union forces is hijacked by Confederates, McCrea comes to believe that Dee has leaked the location of the cache to the Confederacy. Husband and wife part coldly as a result. The singing wires of the emergent telegraph, stringing Westward, grace segment seven, while in the final episode the iron horse connects the country's coasts as the seventeenth birthday of their son reunites McCrea and Dee. A small thing in great compass, the film covers far too much history to deal with any of it fairly. Burns functions as a translator of sorts, his laconic comments punctuated by an occasional "Ugh!" in rejoinder by his taciturn Indian friend. Dee is good in her part as McCrea's wife (a part she played in life; the two celebrated their golden wedding anniversary in 1983). Most of the other roles are fragmentary, their characters lacking the screen time needed for real development. The tribulations of the two leading players are the focus; crowd scenes are at a minimum. In this, the picture more resembles the series of "historical" dramas produced by Darryl F. Zanuck for 20th Century-Fox than anything Paramount had done to that date. (see THE HOUSE OF ROTHSCHILD, 1934, LLOYD'S OF LONDON, 1936.) The tale is really an amalgam of anecdotes about many different express companies, which competed fiercely in their mutual race to remain in front of the railroad and telegraph which dogged their trails so relentlessly. The true story of these companies–which consolidated, broke up, and re- merged at a breakneck pace–might have been more interesting than this film flawed by its all-inclusive excess. Wells, Fargo and Company–founded in 1851 with the chartered intent to "forward Gold Dust, Bullion, Specie, Packages, Parcels & Freight of all kinds, to and from New York and San Francisco$e-3and all the principal towns of California and Oregon"–proved to be too big a subject in its total context.

p&d, Frank Lloyd; w, Paul Schoefield, Gerald Geraghty, Frederick Jackson (based on a story by Stuart N. Lake); ph, Theodore Sparkuhl; m, Victor Young; ed, Hugh Bennett; md, Boris Morros; art d, Hans Dreier, John Goodman; m/l, Burton Lane, Arthur Freed.

Historical Drama   (PR:A   MPAA:NR)

WELLS FARGO GUNMASTER**   (1951) 60m REP bw

Allan "Rocky" Lane (Himself), Chubby Johnson (Skeeter Davis), Mary Ellen Kay (Carol Hines), Michael Chapin (Tommy Hines), Roy Barcroft (Brick Manson), Walter Reed (Ed Hines), Stuart Randall (John Thornton), William Bakewell (Charlie Lannon), George Meeker (Croupier), Anne O'Neal (Mrs. Feathergill), James Craven (Henry Mills), Forrest Taylor (Doctor), Lee Roberts (Townsman), Black Jack the Horse.

Lane is hired by Wells Fargo to investigate a rash of holdups. He goes undercover and stages his own heist in order to get in good with the crooks, who have been getting killed at a frequent pace as they try to fence their stolen properties. He nearly gets himself killed while snooping around but finally hauls in the guilty parties.

p, Gordon Kay; d, Philip Ford; w, M. Coates Webster; ph, John MacBurnie;

m, Stanley Wilson; ed, Robert W. Leeds; art d, Frank Hotaling.

Western   (PR:A   MPAA:NR)

WENT THE DAY WELL?   (SEE: 48 HOURS, 1944, Brit.)

WE'RE GOING TO BE RICH**   (1938, Brit.) 80m FOX bw

Gracie Fields (Kit Dobson), Victor McLaglen (Dobbie Dobson), Brian Donlevy (Yankee Gordon), Coral Browne (Pearl), Ted Smith (Tim Dobson), Gus McNaughton (Broderick), Charles Carson (Keeler), Syd Crossley (Jake), Hal Gordon (Charlie), Robert Nainby (Judge), Charles Harrison (Rat Face), Tom Payne (Kinch), Don McCorkindale (Killer), Joe Mott (Manager of Corona Mine), Alex Davies (Kimberly Kid), D.H. Williams, Victor Fairley, Charles Castella.

Set in South Africa in the 1880s, WE'RE GOING TO BE RICH details the attempts made by drunken, brawling McLaglen and wife Fields to strike it big in an empty gold mine. To tide them over, Fields takes a singing job in a local saloon run by Donlevy and the pair fall in love, but she returns to her shiftless but lovable husband and they make another attempt to find a prosperous vein. Music is almost completely made up of old ballads that were popular in the 1890s.

p, Samuel G. Engel; d, Monty Banks; w, Sam Hellman, Rohama Siegel (based on a story by James Edward Grant); ph, Mutz Greenbaum; ed, James Clarke; cos, Joe Strassner; m/l, Lew Pollack, Sidney D. Mitchell, Harry Parr-Davies, Will Haynes, Jim Harper, Noel Forrester, Greatrex Newman, Howard Flynn, Ralph Butler.

Musical/Drama   (PR:A   MPAA:NR)

WE'RE IN THE ARMY NOW   (SEE: PACK UP YOUR TROUBLES, 1939)

WE'RE IN THE LEGION NOW*½   (1937) 56m GN c

Reginald Denny (Dan Linton), Esther Ralston (Louise Rillette), Eleanor Hunt (Honey Evans), Vince Barnett (Spike Conover), Claudia Dell (Yvonne Cartier), Robert Frazer (Capt. Henri Rillette), Rudolph Amendt (Sgt. Groebner), Francisco Maran (Abdul Ben Abou), Merrill McCormick (Ali), Frank Hoyt (Adjutant Cartellini), Manuel Pelufo (Military Prisoner), Charles Moyer (Recruit Ringleader), Lou Hicks (Perrelli).

Denny and Barnett are American gangsters who flee to Paris when rival racketeers threaten to kill them. They are spotted again and decide to join the French Foreign Legion as a means of escape. They don't respond too well to the Legion's rules and regulations, and end up in a series of slapstick situations, an idea which would be taken further in Laurel and Hardy's 1939 FLYING DEUCES.

P, Georges A. Hirliman; d, Crane Wilbur; w, Roger Whateley, Wilbur (based on the story by J.D. Newsom); ph, Mack Stengler (Magnacolor).

Comedy   (PR:A   MPAA:NR)

WE'RE IN THE MONEY**½   (1935) 65m WB bw

Joan Blondell (Ginger Stewart), Glenda Farrell (Dixie Tilton), Ross Alexander (C. Richard Courtney), Hugh Herbert (Homer Bronson, Lawyer), Henry O'Neill (Stephen Dinsmoor), Hobart Cavanaugh (Max), Anita Kerry (Claire LeClaire), Phil Regan (Phil Ryan, Singer), Lionel Stander (Butch), Man Mountain Dean (Himself), Edward Gargan (O'Rourke), Joseph King (Mr. Blank), E.E. Clive (Jevons), Myron Cox (Chief Pontiac), Virginia Sale (Maid), Sam McDaniel (Attendant), Gene Morgan (Band Leader), Frank Moran, John Kelly (Mugs), Joseph Crehan, Mayo Methot (Bits), Walter Brennan (Wedding Witness), Al Hill (Bodyguard), Billy Wayne (Process Server), Frank Marlowe (Sailor), Edwin Mordant (Judge), Harlan Briggs (Justice of the Peace), Chief Little Wolf (Wrestler).

Golddiggers Blondell and Farrell zero in on a playboy Blondell has fallen for, who is a defendant in a breach-of-promise suit. Silly contrivances abound as the scriptwriters make the two poor women go through every absurd trick in the book to provoke a laugh, and seldom score deeply enough to care.

p, Harry Joe Brown; d, Raymond Enright; w, F. Hugh Herbert, Brown Holmes (based on the story by George R. Bilson); ph, Arthur Todd; ed, Owen Marks; md, Leo F. Forbstein; art d, Carl Weyl; m/l, "So Nice Seeing You Again," Mort Dixon, Allie Wrubel.

Comedy   (PR:A   MPAA:NR)

WE'RE NO ANGELS***   (1955) 106m PAR c

Humphrey Bogart (Joseph), Aldo Ray (Albert), Peter Ustinov (Jules), Joan Bennett (Amelie Ducotel), Basil Rathbone (Andre Trochard), Leo G. Carroll (Felix Ducotel), John Baer (Paul Trochard), Gloria Talbott (Isabelle Ducotel), Lea Penman (Mme. Parole), John Smith (Arnaud), Louis Mercier (Celeste), George Dee (Coachman), Torben Meyer (Butterfly Man), Paul Newlan (Port Captain), Ross Gould (Foreman), Victor Romito, Jack Del Rio (Gendarmes), Joe Ploski (Customs Inspector).

A rare excursion into comedy for the king of the curled lip, Bogart, but he proves that he could handle a comic line with the same aplomb he showed when handling a gat. Based on a French play (and having nothing to do with the 1953 Bella and Samuel Spewack play "My Three Angels" although that play and this movie both credit Husson's play as their source), it's a little too talky for its own good and one wishes that there might have been a bit more cinematic action but the performers are all delicious and the fun they were having is evident in every frame. Bogart, Ustinov, and Ray escape Devil's Island. All three are life- termers, with Bogart having been incarcerated for forgery and Ray and Ustinov being convicted killers. Ray keeps a pet poisonous snake, Adolphe, and brings him along as they flee the prison on Christmas Eve. In order to mask their identities, they must secure new clothing and plan to steal the togs from the store owned by Carroll and his spouse, Bennett. Their daughter is Talbott and Carroll thinks that they are paroled convicts who have been sent to his place to help fix their leaking roof. Once the criminals meet Carroll and family, they are immediately taken by their charm and naivete, and decide that robbing and killing this lovely family might spoil their Christmas. It isn't long before the hoodlums spot how badly Carroll is running his business and how they might make it operate more efficiently. Rather than race away (and hoping to have a place to hide until the heat of their escape is off), they remain at Carroll's and put the place in order. In no time, the bills, long overdue, are being paid off, customers are charmed into buying items they never thought they needed when they first walked in, and the whole place is running like a well-oiled clock. Now they learn that Carroll doesn't own the store, he merely manages it for his nasty relative, Rathbone, who arrives with nephew Baer on a surprise visit to audit the store's books. Carroll has been no great shakes at keeping records and Rathbone believes that Carroll has been siphoning off money. This is patently untrue and Bogart, Ustinov, and Ray know it. Rather than allow the villainous Rathbone to press charges against Carroll, they believe they must take matters into their own hands. Ray puts Adolphe into a basket and Rathbone, in his foraging for evidence, makes the mistake of sticking his hand in that basket. The result is a bite and instant death (although that occurs offscreen). Baer enters and finds Rathbone dead and, being the greedy and voracious type that he is, Baer begins to search through Rathbone's pockets. Instead of money, Baer finds Adolphe who takes a bite of him and the result is two down, none to go. With them out of the way, Carroll, Bennett, and Talbott have inherited the store and the rest of Rathbone's holdings, and all problems are apparently solved, except for finding an acceptable suitor for Talbott, who seems hopelessly single at first glance. Fate (and script contrivance) enters with the appearance of Smith, a medical officer, who is immediately attracted to Talbott. Their work complete, the trio decide to leave the island and make for freedom on the mainland, but they begin to have misgivings about the way life is outside the prison and choose to go back behind bars where they believe it is safer and there are fewer criminals than in the outside world. It's a bit macabre in spots but good fun most of the way. Bogart, Ray, and Ustinov worked well together opposite Carroll and Bennett. Since the deaths of Rathbone and Baer happen away from the audience's eyes, it won't frighten anyone who is repelled by murder and/or snakes. Bogart and Ustinov became good friends while making this. Bogart would star in three more films before his death at 58 in January, 1957. Ustinov stayed away from Hollywood four years before returning. He never liked the place and called it "A gigantic world's fair they haven't had the time to tear down." Curtiz had also directed Ustinov's prior movie, THE EGYPTIAN.

p, Pat Duggan; d, Michael Curtiz; w, Ranald MacDougall (based on the play "La Cuisine des Anges" by Albert Husson); ph, Loyal Griggs (VistaVision, Technicolor); m, Frederick Hollander; ed, Arthur Schmidt; art d, Hal Pereira, Roland Anderson; set d, Sam Comer, Grace Gregory; cos, Mary Grant; spec eff, John P. Fulton; m/l," Sentimental Moments," Hollander, Ralph Freed, "Ma France Bien-Aimee," G. Martini, Roger Wagner; makeup, Wally Westmore.

Comedy   Cas.   (PR:A-C MPAA:NR)

WE'RE NOT DRESSING*   (1934) 63m PAR bw

Bing Crosby (*Stephen Jones*), Carole Lombard (*Doris Worthington*), George Burns (*George*), Gracie Allen (*Gracie*), Ethel Merman (*Edith*), Leon Errol (*Hubert*), Jay Henry (*Prince Alexander Stofasi*), Raymond Milland (*Prince Michael Stofani*), John Irwin (*Old Sailor*), Charles Morris (*Captain*), Ben F. Hendricks (*1st Ship's Officer*), Ted Oliver (*2nd Ship's Officer*), Ernie Adams (*Sailor*), Stanley Blystone (*Doris' Officer*).

The second of many adaptations of J.M. Barrie's "The Admirable Crichton," this had the distinction of having songs added to the familiar story and an all-star cast that took advantage of every last bit of comedy in the script. First made by Cecil B. DeMille as MALE AND FEMALE (with Tom Meighan and Gloria Swanson), it was later remade twice in England and the plot has been "appropriated" several more times without due credit. Lombard is a fabulously wealthy heiress who has invited a group of friends to join her on a leisurely trip to the South Seas. Also aboard are royalists Milland and Henry, plus Errol and his fiancee, Merman. There's a full crew but the one member we care about is Crosby, a deckhand, whose main job is taking Lombard's pet bear for a walk around the yacht's decks. Errol thinks he can pilot the yacht, takes control of the helm, and the result is that the huge vessel is wrecked and the passengers are tossed on the small island nearby. None of the crew survives the experience except Crosby (a convenience for the plot and totally implausible). The nature of the power

shifts once they are on the island because all of the passengers are ill-suited for the rigors of a Robinson Crusoe existence. Crosby takes over as the leader of the pack and whips them all into shape so they share the chores needed to survive. The servant becomes the master and that forms much of the comedy. On another part of the island, Burns and Allen are a pair of botanists who set fantastic traps to catch animals (a satire of the "Rube" Goldberg cartoons which were so popular in that era). Naturally, Crosby loves Lombard and, after the usual turns, she reciprocates when they are rescued at the finale. Mark Gordon and Harry Revel wrote all of the pleasant tunes, and other than "It's Just a New Spanish Custom" (sung by Merman and Errol), the songs were all done by Crosby. They include: "It's a Lie," "Once in a Blue Moon," "Let's Play House," "Goodnight, Lovely Little Lady," "Love Thy Neighbor," "May I?" "She Reminds Me of You," "I'll Sing About the Birds and the Bees," and "Riding Round in the Rain." "Love Thy Neighbor" stepped out to become a hit. Burns and Allen got the lion's share of the laughs with their brief bit, most of which was devoted to showing how dense Allen was. At one point, Burns speaks of "flora and fauna" and Allen thinks that they are a vaudeville duo. If it all sounds a bit like "Gilligan's Island," you're right.

p, Benjamin Glazer; d, Norman Taurog; w, Horace Jackson, Francis Martin, George Marion, Jr. (based on a story by Glazer from the play "The Admirable Crichton" by J.M. Barrie); ph, Charles Lang; ed, Stuart Heisler; art d, Hans Dreier, Ernst Fegte; m/l, Mack Gordon, Harry Revel.

Musical Comedy   (PR:A   MPAA:NR)

WE'RE NOT MARRIED½   (1952) 85m FOX bw

Ginger Rogers (*Ramona*), Fred Allen (*Steve Gladwyn*), Victor Moore (*Justice of the Peace*), Marilyn Monroe (*Annabel Norris*), David Wayne (*Jeff Norris*), Eve Arden (*Katie Woodruff*), Paul Douglas (*Hector Woodruff*), Eddie Bracken (*Willie Fisher*), Mitzi Gaynor (*Patsy Fisher*), Louis Calhern (*Freddie Melrose*), Zsa Zsa Gabor (*Eve Melrose*), James Gleason (*Duffy*), Paul Stewart (*Attorney Stone*), Jane Darwell (*Mrs. Bush*), Tom Powers (*Attorney General*), Victor Sutherland (*Gov. Bush*), Alan Bridge (*Detective Magnus*), Harry Golder (*Radio Announcer*), Kay English (*Wife*), Lee Marvin (*Pinky*), O.Z. Whitehead (*Potman*), Marjorie Weaver (*Ruthie*), Forbes Murray (*Mississippi Governor*), Maurice Cass (*Organist*), Margie Liszt (*Daughter on Radio*), Maude Wallace (*Autograph Hound*), Richard Buckley (*Mr. Graves*), Alvin Greenman, Eddie Firestone (*Men in Radio Station*), Phyllis Brunner (*Wife*), Steve Pritko, Robert Dane (*MPs at Railroad Station*), James Burke (*Master Sgt. Nuckols*), Robert Forrest, Bill Hale (*MPs*), Ed Max (*Counterman*), Richard Reeves (*Brigadier General*), Ralph Dumke (*Twitchell*), Harry Antrim (*Justice of the Peace*), Byron Foulger (*License Bureau Clerk*), Harry Harvey (*Postman*), Selmer Jackson (*Dr. Ned*), Harry Carter (*Chaplain Hall*), Dabbs Greer (*Man at Miss Mississippi Contest*), Emile Meyer (*Beauty Contest Announcer*), Henry Faber, Larry Stamps (*State Troopers*).

WE'RE NOT MARRIED is the perfect TV movie, made in the days before they produced TV movies. Though many people might rejoice in the knowledge that their marriages were not valid and they had the opportunity to remedy their lives, that is not the case here. This plot had been seen before in other films (Norman Krasna and Alfred Hitchcock's MR. AND MRS. SMITH being the most notable example). It was segmented into five separate stories for this movie which was not unlike O. Henry's TALES OF MANHATTAN (which Rogers also worked in) and O. HENRY'S FULL HOUSE, which saw Monroe as one of the participants. Moore is an elderly and befuddled judge who learns too late that he'd married a number of lovers after his license had expired. He must now track down the couples and inform them of the situation. The movie follows a quintet of couples through the stages of solving the dilemma of living in sin, without benefit of proper clergy or civil ceremony. Rogers and Allen are a radio Mr. and Mrs. team who appear to be, on the air, the perfect couple. When the red light goes off, they are at each other's throats and their only dialog is coated with acid. Monroe is married to Wayne and they have a new baby but their happiness is jeopardized when Monroe wins the "Mrs. Mississippi" contest (thus giving her the opportunity to show her figure in a swimsuit) and she becomes eligible for the big award as "Mrs. America." Wayne resents this new situation and feels that it is threatening the sanctity of their marriage and her duties as mother and wife. Gabor and Calhern are on the verge of divorce. He's a millionaire and Gabor is planning to take him to the cleaners when Calhern opens the letter from Moore telling him that they were never married at all. Gabor and her avaricious lawyer are thrown for a loop when they find out what's happened. Bracken is a soldier and his wife, Gaynor, is awaiting the birth of their child as he is ordered to fight in the Korean "police action" and he must depart before they can remarry. The final couple is Arden and Douglas, a duo who seldom communicates, and Douglas is about to begin nosing around for other feminine companionship. That's the story, so to speak, five couples who must decide whether the news that they are not really married is to their benefit. The possibilities seem limitless but they aren't as the denouements are just about what one might expect. The ennui problems of Douglas and Arden are the most believable while the Gaynor-Bracken story is the weakest in the link. The much-married Gabor (in real life) plays her role as if she knows what she's doing, but the kudos must be handed to Allen and Rogers who walk away with the comedic applause, handling their witty lines with aplomb. Monroe was appearing in her fourteenth film and did a good job playing Monroe. It's the kind of mindless romp that the TV networks were specializing in during the

1970s and 1980s, though far more sophisticated than the material allowed by network censors. Good fun for adults.

p, Nunnally Johnson; d, Edmund Goulding; w, Johnson, Dwight Taylor (based on a story by Gina Kaus, Jay Dratler); ph, Leo Tover; m, Cyril J. Mockridge; ed, Louis Loeffler; md, Lionel Newman; art d, Lyle R. Wheeler, Leland Fuller; set d, Thomas Little, Claude Carpenter; cos, Charles Le Maire, Elois Jenssen; makeup, Ben Nye.

Comedy (PR:A MPAA:NR)

WE'RE ON THE JURY** (1937) 71m RKO bw

Victor Moore (*J. Clarence Beaver*), Helen Broderick (*Mrs. Jonathan Ashley Dean*), Philip Huston (*Steve*), Louise Latimer (*Mrs. Clyde*), Vinton Haworth (*M. Williams, Defense Attorney*), Robert McWade (*Judge Prime*), Maxine Jennings (*Clara Simpson*), Frank M. Thomas (*D. Van Cobb, Prosecutor*), Colleen Clare (*Mrs. Patterson*), Billy Gilbert (*E. Allen*), Charles Lane (*Horace Smith*), Charles Middleton (*B.J. Martin*), Jean Howard (*Marion Gordon*), Leonid Kinskey (*Nicholas Krakin*), Sarah Edwards (*Evelyn Bottomley*), Hal K. Dawson (*J. Weatherman*), George Irving (*Clerk of Court*), Edward Gargan (*Officer Clark*), Earle Foxe (*Thomas Jeffreys*), Roy James (*Dr. Fields*), Georgette Rhodes (*Antoinette*), George Cooper (*Taxi Driver*), Jack Adair (*Radio Cop*).

An innocuous comedy stars Broderick as a daffy member of a jury who is certain that the defendant is innocent and won't give in until the other 10 jurors see it her way. She dismisses legal mumbo-jumbo for common sense and facts, finaly becoming responsible for clearing the defendant's name. She does so with the help of childhood pal Moore (whom she affectionately refers to as Pudgy), a real estate salesman who is also on the jury. A remake of 1932's LADIES OF THE JURY.

p, Lee Marcus; d, Ben Holmes; w, Franklin Coen (based on the play "Ladies of the Jury" by John Frederick Ballard); ph, Nick Musuraca; ed, Ted Cheesman; cos, Edward Stevenson.

Comedy/Drama (PR:A MPAA:NR)

WE'RE ONLY HUMAN** (1936) 67m RKO bw

Preston Foster (*Det. Sgt. Pete McCaffrey*), Jane Wyatt (*Sally Rogers, Reporter*), James Gleason (*Danny Walsh, Policeman*), Arthur Hohl (*John Martin, Lawyer*), Johh Arledge (*Johnny O'Brien*), Jane Darwell (*Mrs. Walsh*), Moroni Olson (*Inspector Curran*), Mischa Auer (*William "Lefty" Berger, Gangster*), Harold Huber (*Tony Ricci*), Christian Rub (*William Anderson, Bookkeeper*), Rafaela Ottiano (*Mrs. Anderson*), Delmar Watson (*Tommy*), Effie Ellsler (*Grandma*), Charles Wilson (*Morgan, City Editor*), James Donlan (*Casey*), Lee Phelps (*Detective*), Hattie McDaniel (*Molly, Martin's Maid*), Ward Bond (*Henchman*), John Dilson (*Ballistics Expert*).

A standard entry finds Foster as a tough lone wolf cop who likes to muss up his prisoners and is not afraid of gangster bullets. He is told by his superior to follow the rules and stop trying to catch all the bad guys in town by himself. However, Foster roars on to a shooting climax where he succeeds in capturing a big gang leader, with the help of his girl friend, newspaper reporter Wyatt. Lots of slam-bang pistol action but nothing of account otherwise.

p, Edward Kaufman; d, James Flood; w, Rian James (based on the story "Husk" by Thomas Walsh); ph, J. Roy Hunt; ed, Archie F. Marshek.

Crime (PR:A MPAA:NR)

WE'RE RICH AGAIN* (1934) 73m RKO bw

Edna May Oliver (*Maude*), Billie Burke (*Mrs. Page*), Marian Nixon (*Arabella*), Reginald Denny (*Booky*), Joan Marsh (*Carolyne Page*), Larry "Buster" Crabbe (*Erp*), Grant Mitchell (*Wilbur Page*), Gloria Shea (*Victoria*), Edgar Kennedy (*Healy, Process Server*), Otto Yamaoka (*Fugi*), Lenita Lane (*Charmion*), Dick Elliott, Andreas De Segurola.

Denny and Marsh are husband and wife-to-be who never make it to the altar because of some senseless comedy antics involving the bride's formerly wealthy family. The Depression-era family is too concerned with scraping together $25,000 for a stock market gamble to pay much attention to a wedding. Nothing is credible here, especially the polo-playing grandmother, Oliver, and the end result is annoying.

d, William A. Seiter; w, Ray Harris (based on a play by Alden Nash); ph, Nick Musuraca; m/l, "Senorita," Albert Hay Malotte; cos, Walter Plunkett.

Comedy (PR:A MPAA:NR)

WEREWOLF, THE*½ (1956) 83m COL bw

Steven Ritch (*Duncan March/The Werewolf*), Don Megowan (*Jack Haines*), Joyce Holden (*Amy Standish*), Eleanore Tanin (*Helen Marsh*), Kim Charney (*Chris Marsh*), Harry Lauter (*Clovey*), Larry J. Blake (*Dirgus*), Ken Christy (*Dr. James Gilchrist*), James Gavin (*Fanning*), S. John Launer (*Dr. Emery Forrest*), George M. Lynn (*Dr. Morgan Chambers*), George Cisar (*Hoxie*), Don C. Harvey (*1st Deputy*), Ford Stevens (*1st Reporter*), Marjorie Stapp (*Min*), Jean Charney (*Cora*), Jean Harvey (*Old Woman*).

A blase retelling of the age-old werewolf tale which this time has a family man, Ritch, being turned into the monster after taking an experimental serum. The year 1956 and this picture were the starting point for the resurgence of gothic horror onto the silver screen with the rise of American International and Hammer Films, both of which specialized in digging up Frankenstein, Dracula, the mummy, and the werewolf and giving them new treatments.

p, Sam Katzman; d, Fred F. Sears; w, Robert E. Kent, James B. Gordon; ph, Edwin Linden; m, Mischa Bakaleinikoff; ed, Harold White; art d, Paul Palmentola.

Horror (PR:C-O MPAA:NR)

WEREWOLF IN A GIRL'S DORMITORY zero
(1961, Ital./Aust.) 82m Royal/MGM-Altura bw (LYCANTHROPUS); (AKA: THE GHOUL IN SCHOOL)

Barbara Lass (*Brunhilde*), Carl Schell (*Prof. Julian Olcott*), Curt Lowens (*Mr. Swift*), Maurice Marsac (*Sir Alfred Whiteman*), Maureen O'Connor (*Leonor McDonald*), Mary McNeeran (*Mary Smith*), Grace Neame (*Sandy*), Alan Collins (*Walter*), Anni Steinert (*Sheena Whiteman*), Joseph Mercer (*Porter*), Anne Marie Avis, Elizabeth Patrick, Lucy Derleth, Patricia Meeker, Herbert Diamonds, Martha Marker.

In its original language this rehash of the werewolf theme mixed with teenagers may have been only moderately worthless, but with a dubbing job that could have been better executed by a blind man WEREWOLF IN A GIRL'S DORMITORY is totally bad. Lowens is in charge of a home for wayward girls but he has this terrible problem which turns him into a hairless wolfman. Growling, mMurder, and screaming girls follow. Everything is saved, however, by Maximilian Schell's brother Carl, a heroic teacher, who discovers that the werewolf is the schoolmaster himself.

p, Jack Forrest; d, Richard Benson [Paolo Heusch]; w, Julian Berry [Ernesto Gastaldi]; ph, George Patrick; m, Francis Berman; ed, Julian Attenborough; art d, Peter Travers; m/l, "The Ghoul in School," Marilyn Stewart, Frank Owens (sung by Adam Keefe).

Horror (PR:AC-O MPAA:NR)

WEREWOLF OF LONDON, THE***½ (1935) 75m UNIV bw

Henry Hull (*Dr. Glendon*), Valerie Hobson (*Lisa Glendon*), Warner Oland (*Dr. Yogami*), Lester Matthews (*Paul Ames*), Lawrence Grant (*Sir Thomas Forsythe*), Spring Byington (*Miss Ettie Coombes*), Clark Williams (*Hugh Renwick*), J.M. Kerrigan (*Hawkins*), Charlotte Granville (*Lady Forsythe*), Ethel Griffies (*Mrs. Whack*), Zeffie Tilbury (*Mrs. Mancaster*), Jeanne Bartlett (*Daisy*), Reginald Barlow (*Dr. Phillips*), Louis Vincenot (*Head Cooley*), Eddie Parker, Tempe Pigott, Egon Brecher, Harry Stubbs, David Thursby.

Though not as popular or as well known as the 1941 horror classic THE WOLF MAN, this chiller from Universal is, nevertheless, the original werewolf movie and a surprisingly exotic exercise in the bizarre. The film opens in Tibet as Hull, a famed British botanist, begins a treacherous expedition into the mountains to search for the elusive Marifasa Lumina Lupina plant which blossoms only in the light of a full moon. After a difficult climb, Hull spots the precious plant and moves forward toward it only to find a strange and savage creature about to pounce. It seems the creature, a werewolf, wants the plant as well and it attacks and bites Hull. Hull manages to scare the werewolf off and take the plant back to civilization. Back in London, Hull experiments with the plant in his laboratory. To simulate the light of the full moon, the botanist rigs up special lamps to shine on the flower. One day Hull is visited by Oland, an oriental scientist who informs the botanist that the juice from the Marifasa plant in full bloom can cure the curse of lycanthropy (i.e., becoming a werewolf). Hull dismisses Oland's claims as ridiculous, until the mysterious Oriental reveals that it was he, as a werewolf, who had attacked Hull in Tibet. Oland also informs Hull that the bite he suffered will transform him into a werewolf upon the next full moon. Soon after this strange meeting, the moon does become full and Hull finds himself transformed into a werewolf (the transformation scene–achieved through a series of dissolves–is surprisingly smooth and fluid). More like Robert Louis Stevenson's Mr. Hyde than a crazed beast, Hull dons a large overcoat and a checkered cap and takes to the street in search of blood. He kills a lonely prostitute that night, and the next morning–having returned to his human state– is plagued with visions of what he has done. Hull works feverishly to get the Tibetan plant to bloom before the next full moon. His efforts fail. Knowing what will happen upon nightfall, Hull checks himself into a flophouse and locks the door in an effort to imprison the beast. That evening two drunken Cockney landladies, Griffies and Tilbury, listen outside the door as Hull undergoes another hideous transformation. The werewolf then escapes this prison and runs through the streets in search of more blood. The next morning the papers are full of news about the horrible series of murders in London. Hull realizes that he cannot be responsible for all the killings and that Oland (as a werewolf) must be terrorizing the streets as well. Eventually Hull's efforts with the Marifasa plant pay off and the flower blooms. His victory is short-lived, however, when Oland arrives and attempts to steal the blossom. As the moon begins to rise, the two men battle each other over possession of the plant that will cure them. Hull kills Oland, but it is too late and he is transformed into a werewolf and attacks his wife, Hobson. Before he has a chance to hurt her, Hull is shot down by the police and reverts back to his human form. Full of imagination, innovation, and style, THE WEREWOLF OF LONDON was a fine addition to Univeral's stable of monsters. The werewolves are portrayed as creatures to be pitied, men who hate what they become and are driven to desperate means to try to stop it. The viewer's sympathies are torn between both Hull and Oland for they are both afflicted with the same horrible malady. Whereas Hull's performance is a bit cold and distant, Oland is right on the mark with his ability to mix mystery, villainy, pathos, and tragedy. It is one of Oland's best performances. Hull, a famed stage actor who had appeared in director Walker's previous film, GREAT EXPECTATIONS, was chosen to replace Boris Karloff–the original choice for the role. As this was the actor's first starring role, *and* he was given the unenviable task of filling the shoes of Universal's top horror draw, Hull turned in a commendable performance. Some critics and horror movie fans criticize the somewhat perfunctory werewolf makeup done by Universal's master makeup magician Jack Pierce. This is a short-sighted complaint, evidenced by the fact that none of Pierce's special makeup jobs before or since THE WEREWOLF OF LONDON have the look of a lazy, uninspired artist. The problem with the makeup job was actor Hull, who refused to sit still for hours while Pierce worked his magic. Since the actor disdained any heavy makeup, Pierce was forced to minimize his creation. However disappointing the werewolf makeup may be, the transformation scenes are remarkably smooth and creative. In one sequence, the camera tracks Hull as he walks down the street and is occasionally obscured by a series of pillars in the foreground. As Hull passes each pillar, his transformation progresses to the point to where he becomes the werewolf. The scene is shot in such a way that it appears that Hull has been transformed during one long, uninterrupted tracking shot (though the camera was stopped at the point where the pillar obscured the lens, additional makeup was applied to Hull, and then the camera continued to the next pillar where it was stopped again and more makeup was added to the actor). THE WEREWOLF OF LONDON simply looks different when compared to the other Universal horror films of the era. The exotic opening scenes in Tibet and Hull's rather modern, clinical, uncluttered laboratory certainly don't belong in a Tod Browning or James Whale horror film. Because of its peculiar nature, THE WEREWOLF OF LONDON is a fascinating and somewhat obscure gem of a horror film that deserves more attention than it has received. The better-known THE WOLF MAN (1941) is not a sequel or a remake, but a wholly original film.

p, Stanley Bergerman; d, Stuart Walker; w, John Colton, Harvey Gates (based on a story by Robert Harris); ph, Charles Stumar; ed, Russell Schoengarth; art d, Albert S. D'Agostino; spec eff, John P. Fulton; makeup, Jack Pierce.

Horror   **(PR:C MPAA:NR)**

WEREWOLF OF WASHINGTON*   (1973) 90m Millco/Diplomat c

Dean Stockwell (*Jack Whittier*), Biff McGuire (*The President*), Clifton James (*Attorney General*), Beeson Carroll (*Comdr. Salmon*), Jane House (*Marion*), Michael Dunn (*Dr. Kiss*), Barbara Siegel (*Girl Hippie*), Stephen Cheng (*Chinese Foreign Minister*), Nancy Andrews (*Mrs. Captree*), Ben Yaffe (*Judge Captree*), Jacquiline Brooks (*Publisher*), Thurman Scott (*Boy Hippie*), Tom Scott (*Reporter*), Dennis McMullen (*Astronaut*), Jack Waltzer (*Appointments Secretary*), Randy Phillips (*Federal Agent*), Glenn Kezer (*Admiral*).

The laughs are few and far between in this horror spoof-political satire about a White House press secretary, Stockwell, and the situations that arise when he turns into a werewolf. It's such a bizarre idea that one really wants it to be funny, but the promise is never fulfilled and the picture ultimately disappoints.

p, Nina Schulman; d&w, Milton Moses Ginsberg; ph, Bob Baldwin; m, Arnold Freed, ed, Ginsberg; art d, Nancy Miller-Corwin; makeup, Bob Obradovich.

Horror/Satire   **Cas.**   **(PR:C MPAA:PG)**

WEREWOLF VS. THE VAMPIRE WOMAN, THE*½
(1970, Span./Ger.) 82m Plate-Ellman (La NOCHE DE WALPURGIS; GB: SHADOW OF THE WEREWOLF)

Paul Naschy [Paul Nash] (*Waldemar Daninsky/Werewolf*), Gaby Fuchs (*Elvire*), Barbara Capell [Kapell] (*Genevieve*), Patty Sheppared (*Wandesa Darvula de Nadasdy*), Velena Samarine, Julio Pena, Andres Resino [Andrew Reese].

This Paul Naschy horror vehicle went over big in Europe but isn't all that great. He stars as a part-time wolfman who travels with a pair of female students in the search of a witch's tomb. One girl is turned into a vampire woman and then the battle starts between the monsters. One of the first successful Spanish horror pictures.

d, Leon Klimovsky [Leon Klim]; w, Jacinto Molina, Hans Munkell; ph, Leopoldo Villasenor (Eastmancolor); m, Anton Garcia Abril; ed, Antonio Jimeno; art d, Ludwig Orny; spec eff, Antonio Molina; makeup, Jose Luis Morales.

Horror   **(PR:O MPAA:R)**

WEREWOLVES ON WHEELS*   (1971) 85m Fanfare c

Stephen Oliver (*Adam*), Severn Darden (*One, High Priest*), D.J. [Donna] Anderson (*Helen*), Duece Barry (*Tarot*), Billy Gray (*Bill*), Gray Johnson (*Movie*), Barry McGuire (*Scarf*), Owen Orr (*Mouse*), Anna Lynn Brown (*Shirley*), Leonard Rogel (*Gas Station Operator*), Dan Kopp, Ingrid Grunewald, N. A. Palmisano, John Hull, Carl Lee, Tex Hall, Keith Guthrie, Marilyn Munger, Bart Smith.

A biker movie in which the leather-clad motorcyclists turn into werewolves thanks to a satanic spell cast by high priest Darden. Lots of sex, violence, and wide-open desert highways. The cast includes Barry McGuire, whose hit, "Eve of Destruction," topped the charts in the mid-1960s with its antiwar message. McGuire eventually "born-again" and moved to New Zealand where he recorded for a religious record label.

p, Paul Lewis; d, Michel Levesque; w, Levesque, David M. Kaufman; ph, Isidore Mankofsky (DeLuxe Color); m, Don Gere; ed, Peter Parasheles; art d, Allen Jones; stunts, Chuck Bell.

Horror/Action   **Cas.**   **(PR:O MPAA:R)**

WEST 11*½   (1963, Brit.) 93m ABF/WB-Pathe bw

Alfred Lynch (*Joe Beckett*), Kathleen Breck (*Ilsa Barnes*), Eric Portman (*Richard Dyce*), Diana Dors (*Georgia*), Kathleen Harrison (*Mrs. Beckett*), Finlay Currie (*Mr. Cash*), Freda Jackson (*Mrs. Hartley*), Peter Reynolds (*Jacko*), Harold Land (*Silent*), Marie Ney (*Mildred Dyce*), Sean Kelly (*Larry*), Patrick Wymark (*Father Hogan*), Alan McClennard (*Mr. Royce*), Francesca Annis (*Phyl*), Una Stubbs, Virginia Weatherall, Ken Collyer and Tony Kinsey with Their Bands.

Lynch is a young man living a wasted life who makes the acquaintance of Portman, an ex-army man. Lynch agrees to murder Portman's aunt, believing that he needs an emotional shock to get back on the main road of life. He prepares to kill the old woman but loses his nerve and accidentally pushes her down a flight of stairs, killing her. After a witness reports to the police, Lynch loses whatever nerve he has left and turns himself in. Never is any sympathy given to either character, allowing for little or no audience involvement in their situation. Songs include: "West 11," Stanley Black, Acker Bilk, "What a Gas," Tony Kinsey, "I'm Traveling," "La Harpe Street Blues," "Creole Bob," "Gettysburg," arranged by Ken Colyer.

p, Daniel M. Angel; d, Michael Winner; w, Keith Waterhouse, Willis Hall (based on the novel *The Furnished Room* by Laura Del Rivo); ph, Otto Heller; m, Stanley Black; ed, Bernard Gribble; art d, Bob Jones.

Crime   **(PR:C MPAA:NR)**

WEST OF ABILENE**   (1940) 58m COL bw (GB: THE SHOWDOWN)

Charles Starrett (*Tom Garfield*), Marjorie Cooley (*Judith Burnside*), Bruce Bennett (*Frank Garfield*), William Pawley (*Christ Matson*), Don Beddoe (*Forsyth*), George Cleveland (*Bill Burnside*), Forrest Taylor (*Sheriff*), William A. Kellogg (*Deputy*), Bob Nolan (*Bob*), Francis Walker (*Bat*), Eddie Laughton (*Poke*), Vestor Pegg (*Kennedy*), Bud Osborne (*Wilson*), Al Bridge, Frank Ellis, Sons of the Pioneers.

Starrett and Bennett are brothers who stake a claim "west of Abilene," but find themselves pitted against the gunslinging ways of Beddoe and his hired hand, Pawley. Starrett defends his claim and kills off his enemies, while Bennett romances Cooley.

p, Leon Barsha; d, Ralph Cedar; w, Paul Franklin; ph, George Meehan; ed, Charles Nelson; m/l, Bob Nolan.

Western   **(PR:A MPAA:NR)**

WEST OF BROADWAY*   (1931) 71m MGM bw

John Gilbert (*Jerry*), El Brendel (*Axel*), Lois Moran (*Dot*), Madge Evans (*Anne*), Ralph Bellamy (*Mac*), Frank Conroy (*Judge Barham*), Gwen Lee (*Maizie*), Hedda Hopper (*Mrs. Trent*), Ruth Renick (*Barbara*), Willie Fung (*Wing*), Richard Carlyle.

Gilbert is cast as a millionaire who likes to tip the bottle and, one night, after having a few too many drinks, he marries Moran. His boozing doesn't cease, however, and he loses her, only to win her back by the finale. A feeble outing for former superstar Gilbert, who at the time was still earning a fabulous $250,000 per picture.

d, Harry Beaumont; w, Gene Markey, J.K. McGuinness (based on the story by Ralph Graves, Bess Meredyth); ph, Merritt B. Gerstad; ed, George Hively.

Drama   **(PR:A MPAA:NR)**

WEST OF CARSON CITY**   (1940) 57m UNIV bw

Johnny Mack Brown (*Jim Bannister*), Bob Baker (*Nevada*), Fuzzy Knight (*Banjo*), Peggy Moran (*Millie Harkins*), Harry Woods (*Mack Gorman*), Robert E. Homans (*Judge Harkins*), Al K. Hall (*Lem Howard*), Roy Barcroft (*Bill Tompkins*), Charles King (*Drag*), Frank Mitchell (*Breed*), Edmund Cobb (*Sleepy*), Jack Roper (*Larkin*), Ted Wells (*Slim*), Jack Shannon (*Pete*),

Vice Potel, Kermit Maynard, Ernie Adams, Donald Kerr, Dick Carter, Al Bridge, The Four Singing Notables.

Brown leads a crusade against the illegitimate governing of a gold rush town by gamblers intent on cleaning out the prospectors. On the urging of some of the townsfolk and the mighty wallop of his fists, he does the cleaning out instead and the villains bite the dust. Excellent photography leads the generally superior production values.

d, Ray Taylor; w, Milton Raison, Sherman Lowe, Jack Bernhard (based on a story by Raison); ph, Jerry Ash; m/l, "On the Trail of Tomorrow," Milt Rosen, Everett Carter.

Western   **(PR:A   MPAA:NR)**

WEST OF CHEYENNE*½   (1931) 56m SYN/States Rights bw

Tom Tyler, Josephine Hill, Harry Woods, Robert Walker, Ben Corbett, Fern Emmett.

Tyler sets out to square matters with a gang of outlaws who murdered his father, and joins the gang undercover to do so. The action takes place at a ghost town west of Cheyenne, Wyoming, called Ghost City, where the hero throws off his mantle of desperado and slugs it out with the bad men, giving them what they deserve.

d, Harry Webb; w, Oliver Drake, Bennett Cohen; ph, William Nobles; ed, Carl Himm.

Western   **(PR:A   MPAA:NR)**

WEST OF CHEYENNE*½   (1938) 59m COL bw

Charles Starrett (Brad Buckner), Iris Meredith (Jean Wayne), Bob Nolan (Bob), Pat Brady (Pat), Dick Curtis (Link Murdock), Edward J. LeSaint (J.B. Wayne), Edmund Cobb (Dirkin), Art Mix (Cinch), Ernie Adams (Shorty), Jack Rockwell (Sheriff), John Tyrrell (Trigger), Tex Cooper, Sons of the Pioneers.

A familiar oater plot about a gang of cattle rustlers given a fight by Starrett and his boys, which seems to exist more for the sake of the Sons of the Pioneers than for the star. The five man singing combo is thoroughly listenable but cannot sustain the creaking plot line.

d, Sam Nelson; w, Ed Earl Repp; ph, Benjamin Kline; ed, William Lyon; md, Morris W. Stoloff; m/l, Bob Nolan.

Western   **(PR:A   MPAA:NR)**

WEST OF CIMARRON**   (1941) 56m REP bw

Bob Steele, Tom Tyler, Rufe Davis, Lois Collier, James Bush, Guy Usher, Hugh Prosser, Cordell Hickman, Roy Barcroft, Budd Buster, Mickey Rentschiler, John James, Bud Geary, Cactus Mack, Stanley Blystone.

The Mesquiteers take on carpetbaggers robbing the populace in post-Civil War Texas. Routine series entry in an above average series, with plenty of action and two-fisted fights, good scenery, and beautiful horses. (See THREE MESQUITEERS series, Index.)

p, Louis Gray; d, Les Orlebeck; w, Albert DeMond, Don Ryan, (based on characters created by William Colt MacDonald); ph, Ernest Miller; ed, Howard O'Neill.

Western   **(PR:A   MPAA:NR)**

WEST OF EL DORADO**   (1949) 58m MON bw

Johnny Mack Brown (Johnny), Max Terhune (Alibi), Reno Browne (Mary), Teddy Infuhr (Larry), Milburn Morante (Brimstone), Terry Frost (Stone), Marshall Reed (Barstow), Boyd Stockman (Joe), Kenne Duncan (Steve), Bud Osborne (Jerry), William Norton Bailey (Sheriff), Artie Ortego (Indian), Bill Potter (Phil), Bob Woodward.

An appealing Brown western which has him taking custody of an orphaned youngster after he kills the boy's outlaw brother in a stage holdup. The boy discovers his brother's hidden cash and soon becomes the target of a greedy band of robbers. Brown comes to the boy's aid and puts the outlaws in their place.

p, Barney A. Sarecky; d, Ray Taylor; w, Adele Buffington; ph, Harry Neumann; ed, John C. Fuller; md, Edward J. Kay.

Western   **(PR:A   MPAA:NR)**

WEST OF MONTANA   (SEE: MAIL ORDER BRIDE, 1964)

WEST OF NEVADA**   (1936) 57m Colony/FD bw

Rex Bell (Jim Lloyd), Joan Barclay (Helen Haldain), Al St. John (Walla Walla), Steve Clark (Milt Haldain), Georgia O'Dell (Rose Gilhuly), Dick Botiller (Bald Eagle), Frank McCarroll (Slade Sangree), Forrest Taylor (Steven Cutting), Bob Woodward.

Bell lends a hand to a band of Indians who are being victimized by a gang that wants to walk off with their gold. Bell, however, won't see to it and lets

his fists do the talking, tossing the black hats in jail with the help of the Indians.

p, Arthur Alexander; d, Robert Hill; w, Rock Hawkey [Robert Hill] (based on the story "Raw Gold" by Charles Kyson); Robert Cline.

Western   **(PR:A   MPAA:NR)**

WEST OF PINTO BASIN**   (1940) 60m MON bw

John King (Dusty), Ray Corrigan (Crash), Max Terhune (Alibi), Gwen Gaze (Joan), Tristram Coffin (Harvey), Dick Thane (Hank), George Chesebro (Lane), Carl Mathews (Joe), Bud Osborne (Sheriff), Phil Dunham (Summers), Budd Buster (Jones), Jerry Smith (Jerry, Stagecoach Guard), Dick Cramer, Jack Perrin.

King, Corrigan, and Terhune combine their talents again in a flight against Coffin's gang of stagecoach robbers. The heroes work closely with female bank president Gaze and discover that a bank employee has been supplying the gang with information. (See RANGE BUSTERS series, Index.)

p, George W. Weeks; d, S. Roy Luby; w, Earle Snell (based on the story by Elmer Clifton); ph, Ed Linden; ed, Roy Claire; md, Frank Sanucci; m/l, "That Little Prairie Gal of Mine," Johnny Lange, Lew Porter (sung by John King), "Rhythm of the Saddle," "Ridin' the Trail Tonight" (sung by Jerry Smith.)

Western   **(PR:A   MPAA:NR)**

WEST OF RAINBOW'S END**   (1938) 57m Concord/MON bw

Tim McCoy (Tim), Kathleen Eliot (Joan), Walter McGrail (Johnson), Frank LaRue (Ed), George Chang (Elmer), Mary Carr (Mrs. Carter), Ed Coxon (Joel Carter), Goerge Cooper (Happy), Bob Kortman (Speck), Jimmy Aubrey (Postmaster), Reed Howes, Ray Jones, Sherry Tansey.

McCoy plays a retired railroad investigator who picks up his gun again to stalk down a gang who killed both his foster father and his best pal. A flurry of bullets brings about the enemy's downfall, and McCoy is left with enough energy to take himself a bride by the finale.

p, Maurice Conn; d, Alan James; w, Stanley Roberts, Gennard Rea (from the story by Robert Emmett (Tansey)); ph, Jack Greenhalgh; m, Connie Lee.

Western   **(PR:A   MPAA:NR)**

WEST OF SANTA FE**   (1938) 60m COL bw

Charles Starrett (Lawlor), Iris Meredith (Madge), Dick Curtis (Taylor), Robert Fiske (Parker), Leroy Mason (McLain), Bob Nolan (Bob), Hank Bell (Hank), Edmund Cobb (Barlow), Clem Horton (Hager), Richard [Dick] Botiller (Foley), Eddie [Edward] Hearn (Crane), Edward J. LeSaint (Conway), Buck Connors (Hardpan), Bud Osborne, Blackie Whiteford, Hal Taliaferro, Sons of the Pioneers.

Starrett comes to the aid of the troubled Meredith who is left to fight cattle rustlers after her father is killed by the gang. The outlaws then try to blame the murder on the girl. Starrett defends the poor lass and gives the villains a dose of their own sour medicine. Plenty of action and some pleasantries from the Sons of the Pioneers.

d, Sam Nelson; w, Bennett R. Cohen; ph, Allen Siegler; ed William Lyon; m/l, "When the Prairie Sun Says Good Morning," "Song of the Prairie," "Tumblin' Tumbleweed," Bob Nolan, "Hellow Way Up There," Nolan, Lloyd Perryman.

Western   **(PR:A   MPAA:NR)**

WEST OF SHANGHAI**½   (1937) 65m FN WB bw (AKA: THE WARLORD)

Boris Karloff (Gen. Wu Yen Fang), Beverly Roberts (Jane Creed), Ricardo Cortez (Gordon Creed), Gordon Oliver (James Hallett), Sheila Bromley (Lola Galt), Vladimir Sokoloff (Gen. Chou Fu Shan), Gordon Hart (Dr. Abernathy), Richard Loo (Mr. Cheng), Wy Yen Fang's Bodyguard, Douglas Wood (Myron Galt), Chester Gan (Capt. Kung Nui), Luke Chan (Chan), Selmer Jackson (Hemingway), James B. Leong (Pao), Tetsu Komai (Gen. Mu), Eddie Lee (Wang Chung), Maurice Lui (Conductor), Mia Ichioaka (Hua Mei).

Karloff stars in this third remake of the Porter Emerson Browne play which had been filmed silently in 1923, then again in 1930, both under the title THE BAD MAN. While those two were set in Mexico with a bandit named Pancho Lopez as the kind-hearted title character, WEST OF SHANGHAI tried to capitalize on a rising interest in the East because of the Sino-Japanese war and transposed the story to that area. Karloff is Gen. Wu Yen Fang, "The White Tiger," a bandit general who controls much of northern China. He takes over the village in which Oliver and Roberts are fighting against some greedy Americans who want to foreclose on Oliver's oil interests, especially since his sweetheart (Roberts) is the estranged wife of Cortez, one of the Americans. Karloff, remembering that Oliver had once saved his life, has his vile nemesis killed, an action which brings the government down on him. Karloff's future is a firing squad, but he willingly faces the gun barrels, knowing that Oliver and Roberts will end up husband and wife. An attempt to spruce up the Chinese backgrounds is only moderately successful, but at least they used actual Chinese extras, not a common practice at the time.

p, Bryan Foy; d, John Farrow; w, Crane Wilbur (based on Porter Emerson Browne's play "The Bad Man"); ph, L. William O'Connell; ed, Frank Dewar; cos, Howard Shoup; makeup, Perc Westmore.

Drama   (PR:A   MPAA:NR)

WEST OF SINGAPORE**   (1933) 65m MON bw

Betty Compson (Lou), Weldon Heyburn (Dan Manton), Margaret Lindsay (Shelby Worrell), Noel Madison (Degama), Tom Douglas (Glenn Worrell), Clyde Cook (Ricky), Harvey Clark (Scrub), Ernie Adams (Watson).

Violence and romance go hand in hand in this island story about an oil man working in the island's swamps who comes under the spell of an English upper-class lady, although he has a lovely blonde on the island. The woman's brother falls for the oil man's blonde and shoots the oil man for interfering. The Britons then flee, leaving the blonde and the recovering oil man to clinch in the end.

p, Trem Carr; d, Al Ray; w, Elizabeth Meehan, Adele Buffington, (based on the story by Houston Branch); ph, Harry Neumann, Robert Clive; ed, Carl Pierson.

Drama   (PR:A   MPAA:NR)

WEST OF SONORA**   (1948) 55m COL bw

Charles Starrett (Steve Rollins/The Durango Kid), Smiley Burnette (Himself), Steve Darrell (Black Murphy), George Chesebro (Sheriff Jeff Clinton), Anita Castle (Penelope Clinton), Hal Taliaferro (Sandy Clinton), Bob [Robert] Wilke (Brock), Emmett Lynn (Jack Bascom), Lynn Farr (Dickson), Lloyd Ingraham, The Sunshine Boys.

Starrett brings together the young Castle's two feuding grandfathers, one of whom believes the other to be an outlaw. The heroic cowboy proves the old man wrong when he rounds up the real bandit after a long lynch mob chase. (See DURANGO KID series, Index.)

p, Colbert Clark; d, Ray Nazarro; w, Barry Shipman; ph, Ira H. Morgan; ed, Jerome Thoms; art d, Charles Clague; set d, George Montgomery.

Western   **Cas.**   (PR:A   MPAA:NR)

WEST OF SUEZ   (SEE: FIGHTING WILDCATS, THE, 1957, Brit.)

WEST OF TEXAS**   (1943) 59M PRC-EL bw (AKA: SHOOTIN' IRONS)

Dave "Tex" O'Brien (Tex Wyatt), Jim Newill (Jim Steele), Guy Wilkerson (Panhandle Perkins), Frances Gladwin (Marie Moenette), Marilyn Hare (Ellen Yeager), Tom London (Steve London), Henry Hall (Bart Yaeger), Jack Rockwell (Gabe Jones), Roy Butler (Sheriff), Jack Ingram (Blackie), Art Fowler (Clem), Robert Barron (Bert Calloway).

O'Brien and Newill head west of the Lone Star state and set up a Texas Ranger organization in New Mexico. Battles wage and tempers rage as they try to clean up against the railroads, which are unscrupulous in their acquisition of the ranchers' lands. In the end the fellows come out on top in terms of the law and their love lives. The duo also delivers a trio of tunes: "Whistle a Song," "El Lobo," and "Tired of Rambling" (O'Brien, Newill). (See TEXAS RANGERS series, Index.)

p, Alfred Stern, Arthur Alexander; d&w, Oliver Drake; ph, Ira Morgan; ed, Charles Henkel, Jr.; md, Lee Zahler.

Western   (PR:A   MPAA:NR)

WEST OF THE ALAMO*½   (1946) 57m MON bw

Jimmy Wakely (Jimmy), Lee "Lasses" White (Lasses), Iris Clive (Jane Morgan), Jack Ingram (Clay Bradford), Rod Holton (Emmet), Budd Buster (Shotgun), Eddie Majors (Dean), Ray Whitley, Early Cantrell, Betty Lou Head, Billy Dix, Ted French, Bill Hamilton, Steven Keys, Jack Rivers, Ray Jones, Rudy Bowman, Arthur "Fiddlin'" Smith Trio, The Saddle Pals.

Heavy on the oat-tunes, this prairie programmer has Wakely making a feeble attempt at a starring role as a ranger going undercover to stop a streak of bank robberies. He uncovers a plot by the bank president, Ingram, who implicates a pair of sisters in the thefts and a murder. Nothing here to make you sit up and take notice.

p&d, Oliver Drake; w, Louise Rousseau; ph, Harry Neumann; ed, William Austin; md, Frank Sanucci; set d, Vin Taylor.

Western/Musical   (PR:A   MPAA:NR)

WEST OF THE BRAZOS**   (1950) 58m Lippert bw

Jimmy [James] Ellison (Shamrock), Russ Hayden (Lucky), Raymond Hatton (Colonel), Fuzzy Knight (Deacon), Betty [Julie] Adams (Ann), Tom Tyler (Sam), George Lewis (Manuel), John Cason (Cyclone), Stanley Price (Marshal), Stephen Carr (Rusty), Dennis Moore (Ricco), George Chesebro (Deputy), Bud Osborne (Stage Driver), Jimmy Martin (Joe), Gene Roth (Attorney), Judy Webster (Judy).

Ellison and Hayden are cast as Shamrock and Lucky, a duo of Irish cowboys who saddle up in the West. They show up on a ranch which has been willed to them only to find it occupied by a deceptive Cason. Unknown to them, but known to Cason, the ranch sits on a field of black gold and Cason is just waiting to get rid of the Irish lads before he puts up his oil rigs. Justice is soon served, however, and Ellison and Hayden get what's rightfully theirs. The first in a series which was supposed to last five years at six pictures per annum. Lippert instead made the first six in a one-month period and the film's production quality looks it. The film does, however, benefit from some natural acting performances from the leads.

p, Ron Ormond, Murray Lerner; d, Thomas Carr; w, Ormond, Maurice Tombragel; ph, Ernest Miller; m, Walter Greene; ed, Hugh Winn; md, Greene; art d, Fred Preble.

Western   (PR:A   MPAA:NR)

WEST OF THE DIVIDE**½   (1934) 54m Lone Star/MON bw

John Wayne (Ted Hayden), Virginia Brown Faire (Fay Winters), Lloyd Whitlock (Gentry), George ["Gabby"] Hayes (Dusty Rhodes), Yakima Canutt (Hank), Billy O'Brien (Spud), Lafe McKee (Winters), Blackie Whiteford (Hutch), Earl Dwire (Red), Dick Dickinson (Joe), Tex Palmer, Artie Ortego, Horace B. Carpenter, Hal Price, Archie Ricks.

One of John Wayne's better programmers has him seeking vengeance on the man who killed his mother and father years earlier. Not only does he find the culprit, he also locates his missing brother and falls in love with a tough but tender ranch girl. A remake of 1931's PARTNERS OF THE TRAIL.

p, Paul Malvern; d&w, Robert N. Bradbury; ph, Archie J. Stout; ed, Carl Pierson.

Western   **Cas.**   (PR:A   MPAA:NR)

WEST OF THE GREAT DIVIDE   (SEE: NORTH OF THE GREAT DIVIDE, 1945)

WEST OF THE LAW**½   (1942) 60m MON bw

Buck Jones, Tim McCoy, Raymond Hatton, Evelyn Cook, Milburn Morante, Harry Woods, Roy Barcroft, George DeNormand, Bud McTaggart, Jack Daley, Bud Osborne, Lynton Brent, Silver.

McCoy goes undercover as a minister to help Jones in this fine addition to the ROUGH RIDERS Series, fighting against Barcroft, a pillar of the community who is really the mastermind of a gold heist ring. Full of western cliches, but these cliches are only used so often because they work so well. (See ROUGH RIDERS series, Index.)

p, Scott R. Dunlap; d, Howard Bretherton; w, Jess Bowers (Adele Buffington); ph, Harry Neumann; ed, Carl Pierson.

Western   **Cas.**   (PR:A   MPAA:NR)

WEST OF THE PECOS***   (1935) 68 RKO bw

Richard Dix (Pecos Smith), Martha Sleeper (Terrell), Samuel S. Hinds (Col. Lambeth), Fred Kohler (Sawtelle), Louise Beavers (Mauree), Maria Alba (Dolores), Pedro Regas (Manuel), Sleep 'n' Eat [Willie Best] (Jonah), G. Pat Collins, Russell Simpson, Maurice Black, George Cooper, Irving Bacon.

An unusually sexual western for its time which has Sleeper masquerading in boy's clothes while traveling through post-Civil War Texas. Dix thinks her a man until one day he has to rescue her from the Pecos River. Her clinging wet apparel is a dead giveaway for Dix, who agrees to keep her secret. An even odder scene occurs when Alba, interested in the masculine version of Sleeper, makes a not-to-subtle pass at the girl. The idea is no different than that of a picture like TOOTSIE (1982) which probably raised just as many eyebrows as WEST OF THE PECOS. The story, which in comparison seems elementary, has Dix trying his darndest to restore peace to the lawless Pecos region. Based on a novel by Zane Grey and remade in 1945 with Robert Mitchum and Barbara Hale.

p, Cliff Reid; d, Phil Rosen; w, Milton Krims, John Twist (based on the novel by Zane Grey); ph, James Van Trees, Russell Metty; ed, Archie Marshek.

Western   (PR:A-C   MPAA:NR)

WEST OF THE PECOS***   (1945) 66m RKO bw

Robert Mitchum (Pecos Smith), Barbara Hale (Rill Lambeth), Richard Martin (Chito Rafferty), Thurston Hall (Col. Lambeth), Rita Corday (Suzanne), Rill's French Maid, Russell Hopton (Jeff Stinger), Bill Williams (Tex Evans), Harry Woods (Brad Sawtelle), Bruce Edwards (Clyde Morgan), Perc Launders (Sam Sawtelle), Bryant Washburn (Doc Howard), Philip Morris (Marshal), Martin Garralaga (Don Manuel), Sammy Blum, Robert Anderson (Gamblers), Italia DeNubila (Dancer), Ethan Laidlaw (Lookout), Jack Gargan (Croupier), Larry Wheat (Butler), Carmen Grenada (Spanish Girl), Ariel Sherry, Virginia Wave (Mexican Girls), Allan Lee (Four-Up Driver).

10 years after the first version of the Zane Grey tale, RKO again did right

by western viewers with Mitchum bringing Richard Dix's Pecos Smith character to the screen in an admirable way. A stagecoach robbery brings him together with Hale, disguised as a boy for reasons of safety, who is on her way to the family ranch in Texas. She's a gentle high society girl, but underneath the vest and hat Mitchum doesn't even notice, that is, until he playfully tosses her into the Pecos River. She comes out soaking wet with her clinging clothes giving away the secret of her feminine anatomy. They continue to make their way to the ranch where Mitchum has been offered work, battling outlaws along the way. They safely reach their destination and agree to an expected wedding. Mitchum first came to the attention of critics and the public in this promising picture, which appeared to presage his stardom. He disappeared from films for a time shortly before the film's release, serving in the Army during WW II.

p, Herman Schlom; d, Edward Killy; w, Norman Houston (based on the novel by Zane Grey); ph, Harry J. Wild; m, Paul Sawtell; ed, Roland Gross; md, Constantin Bakaleinikoff; art d, Albert S. D'Agostino, Lucius Croxton; set d, Darrell Silvera, William Stevens.

Western   **(PR:A   MPAA:NR)**

WEST OF THE ROCKIES zero   (1929) 63m Exhibitors Film Exchange
                                                                       bw

Art Mix (Bob Strong), Horace B. Carpenter (Hair-Trigger Strong), George Edward Brown (George), Cliff Lyons (Snakey Rogers), Bud Osborne (Juan Escobar), Fontaine LaRue (Celia de la Costa), Inez Gomez (Rosita), Ione Reed (Beth Lee), Alfred Hewston (Tex), Pete Crawford (Sheriff), Antonio Sanchez (Pedro), Henry Roquemore.

A worthless oater which displays the typical story of good-guy-defeats bad-guy-and-wins-girl-while-making-pop-proud. Super-theatrical in its acting and cursed with a horrible soundtrack, which gives it the appearance of being a dubbed silent. The villain does all the evil sneering you could ever want and stops just short of curling his mustache.

p, J. Charles Davis; d, Horace B. Carpenter; w, Philip Schuyler; ph, E. L. McManigal.

Western   **(PR:A   MPAA:NR)**

WEST OF THE ROCKIES zero   (1931) 60m Road Show bw

Ben Lyon (Kit Carson), Marie Prevost, Gladys Johnston, Anders Randolph, Russell Simpson.

Perhaps it has something to do with the title, but this substandard oater is just as bad as the previous, like-titled entry. Lyon leads a wagon train of settlers across the plains and into the Rockies while fending off all sorts of typical obstacles–Indians, outlaws, etc. Prevost has her eyes on Lyon and nearly loses him to Johnston but things work out in the end. Most people couldn't wait that long, however. Technically a shambles and possibly a leftover from the silents which attempted to get a shot in the arm from the addition of a dubbed soundtrack.

p, Lew Gater, Al Dezer; ph, King Gray, H. H. Brounell.

Western   **(PR:A   MPAA:NR)**

WEST OF THE SUEZ   (SEE: FIGHTING WILDCATS, 1957, Brit.)

WEST OF TOMBSTONE**   (1942) 59m COL bw

Charles Starrett (Steve Langdon), Russell Hayden ("Lucky" Barnet), Cliff Edwards (Harmony Haines), Marcella Martin (Carol Barnet), Gordon DeMain (Wilfred Barnet), Clancey Cooper (Dave Shurlock), Jack Kirk (Sheriff), Budd Buster (Wheeler), Tom London (Morris), Francis Walker, Ray Jones, Eddie Laughton, Lloyd Bridges, Ernie Adams, George Morrell.

A bandit attack on a stagecoach driven by Hayden leads the local people to renew the long-standing legend that Billy the Kid still lives. Scoffing at their renewal of the old story, deputy marshal Starrett opens the kid's grave, only to find it empty. As he ruminates in the graveyard, a masked horseman takes a shot at Starrett. Later, the latter recognizes the horse ridden by rspectable middle-aged businessman DeMain as the mount of the phantom shootist. DeMain admits his old identity–he'd shot toward the marshal to divert him from the empty grave–but protests his innocence of any recent crimes. Starrett arrests Hayden–DeMain's son, unbeknownst to Starrett–for suspected complicity in the stagecoach robbery. Hoping to clear his son of the charges, DeMain buckles on his guns and goes after the real outlaws. Ambushed by the latter, DeMain is surrounded by them and subjected to punishing gunfire. In the nick of time, Starrett releases Hayden and the two rush to the rescue of Hayden's beleaguered father. The basic premise was ripped off for a later picture, Lash LaRue's SON OF BILLY THE KID (1949), a laughable premise considering just how ruthless the real-life William "Billy the Kid" Bonney was. Picturing him as a successful businessman is as ludicrous as it is humorous. Songs: "Midnight Blues," "Get Along Little Pony," "We'll All Be Together."

p, William Berke; d, Howard Bretherton; w, Maurice Geraghty; ph, George Meehan; ed, Mel Thorsen; art d, Lionel Banks.

Western   **(PR:A   MPAA:NR)**

WEST OF WYOMING*½   (1950) 57m MON bw

Johnny Mack Brown (Johnny), Gail Davis (Jennifer), Myron Healey (Brody), Dennis Moore (Dorsey), Stanley Andrews (Simon), Milburn Morante (Panhandle), Mary Gordon (Nora), Carl Mathews (Ray), Paul Cramer (Terry), John Merton (Sheriff), Holly Bane [Mike Ragan] (Chuck), Steve Clark (Dalton), Frank McCarroll, Bud Osborne.

A malicious cattle baron, Andrews, makes life uncomfortable for homesteaders new to his region, but Brown comes along and acts in the name of the law, putting down Andrews' scoundrelly ways. WEST OF WYOMING is so filled with familiar situations everyone involved could have slept through the filming. And why not, the audiences probably did. Once-brawny star Brown was getting beefy by the time this one was made.

p, Eddie Davis; d, Wallace W. Fox; w, Adele Buffington; ph, Harry Neumann; ed, John C. Fuller; md, Edward J. Kay.

Western   **(PR:A   MPAA:NR)**

WEST OF ZANZIBAR**   (1954, Brit.) 94m
                                                    EAL-Balcon-Schlesinger/UNIV c

Anthony Steel (Bob Payton), Sheila Sim (Mary Payton), William Simons (Tim Payton), Orlando Martins (M'Kwongwi), Edric Connor (Chief Ushingo), David Osieli (Ambrose), Bethlehem Sketch (Bethlehem), Martin Benson (Lawyer Dhofar), PEter Illing (Khingoni), Edward Johnson (Half Breed), Juma (Juma), R. Stuart Lindsell (Col. Ryan), Howard Marion Crawford (Wood), Alan Webb (Senior Official), Roy Cable, Sheik Abdullah, Joanna Kitau, Fatuma.

Relying too much on its scenic African location, this British adventure moves along slowly as game warden Steel breaks up a ring of ivory smugglers. The gang's leader Benson, had given an African tribe land in return for the tusks, but he is repaid for his scheming when the tribe turns on him. A sequel to IVORY HUNTERS (1951). Although the film takes the side of the native population against economic exploitation, it was banned by the government of Kenya, which considered its approach too paternalistic. Sim, as Steel's wife, gets wardrobe changes that suggest that Christian Dior may be hiding in the nearby bush.

p, Leslie Norman; d, Harry Watt; w, Jack Whittingham, Max Catto; (based on a story by Watt); ph, Paul Beeson (Technicolor); m, Alan Rawsthorne; ed, Peter Bezencenet; art d, Jim Morahan.

Adventure   **(PR:A   MPAA:NR)**

WEST POINT OF THE AIR**   (1935) 100m MGM bw

Wallace Beery (Big Mike), Robert Young (Little Mike), Maureen O'Sullivan (Skip Carter), Lewis Stone (Gen. Carter), James Gleason (Joe Bags), Rosalind Russell (Dare), Russell Hardie (Phil Carter), Henry Wadsworth (Pettis), Robert Livingston (Pipinger), Robert Taylor (Jaskerelli), Frank Conroy (Capt. Cannon), G. Pat Collins (Lt. Kelly), Ronnie Cosby (Little Mike as a Boy), Bobbie Caldwell (Phil as a Boy), Marilyn Spinner (Skip as a Girl), Richard Tucker (Club Manager).

Considering the fine cast, this peacetime service melodrama never delivered what was promised as Beery turned in his typecast tough-father role to Young's carefree son. Dad wants his boy to grow up to be the best flyer in the world's best army, but junior would rather make eyes at the sultry Russell. By the finale he redeems himself and pairs up with O'Sullivan, the army commandant's "nice" daughter. For some reason both women characters are given rather ludicrous names–Young is "Skip" and Russell is "Dare." Taylor had only one or two lines but, as always, he looked pretty.

p, Monta Bell; d, Richard Rosson; w, Frank Wead, Arthur J. Beckhard (based on the story by James K. McGuinness, John Monk Saunders); ph, Clyde DeVinna, Charles Marshall, Elmer Dyer; m, Charles Maxwell; ed, Frank Sullivan; art d, Cedric Gibbons, H. R. Campbell; cos, Dolly Tree.

Drama   **(PR:A   MPAA:NR)**

WEST POINT STORY, THE*½**   (1950) 107m WB bw (GB: FINE
                                                                       AND DANDY)

James Cagney (Elwin Bixby), Virginia Mayo (Eve Dillon), Doris Day (Jan Wilson), Gordon MacRae (Tom Fletcher), Gene Nelson (Hal Courtland), Alan Hale, Jr. (Bull Gilbert), Roland Winters (Harry Eberhart), Raymond Roe (Bixby's "Wife"), Wilton Graff (Lt. Col. Martin), Jerome Cowan (Jocelyn), Frank Ferguson (Commandant), Russ Saunders (Acrobat), Jack Kelly (Officer-in-Charge), Glen Turnbull (Hoofer), Walter Ruick (Piano Player), Lute Crockett (Senator), Victor Desney (French Attache), Wheaton Chambers (Secretary), James Dobson, Joel Marston, Bob Hayden, DeWitt Bishop, John Hedloe, Don Shartel, James Young (Cadets).

Cagney is a down-on-his-luck Broadway director who is offered a job from producer Winters to put on a show at West Point. Although he dislikes Winters, he accepts the job. The show has been written by Winters' nephew (MacRae) and Winters thinks he can have a hit on Broadway with it if he can only persuade MacRae to resign from the Academy. Cagney, along with his girl friend, Mayo, travel to West Point and begins putting the show together. Although Cagney tries to convince MacRae to leave the Academy, he always refuses. Constantly frustrated by the Academy rules that wreak havoc with his rehearsal schedules, Cagney seethes until one day he explodes and strikes a cadet. To continue work on the show (and keep Mayo, who is threatening to leave him) he is told he must become a cadet–a rather well-fed and graying sight in dress grays–and be subject to all the rules of discipline of the Academy. The cadets now haze him like the greenest plebe but he takes all they can dish out, tough guy that he is. One of the stars he has brought in for the show is Day, and her charms succeed where Cagney has failed; when she goes back to Hollywood, a lovesick MacRae follows her, going AWOL. Cagney goes after him in order to save MacRae's military career, but when he returns MacRae is arrested and the show cancelled. Cagney manages to find an odd twist in the Academy rules that allows visiting dignitaries to ask for and receive pardons for cadets under punishment, and using the French decoration he received in an earlier war, he persuades the French Attache to visit and get MacRae out of the pokey in time for the show to go on. MacRae is reunited with Day, the show is a big hit, with Cagney stepping in at the last minute to dance in the "It Could Only Happen in Brooklyn" number with Mayo, and a grateful MacRae gives the rights to the show to Cagney. Mostly a dull and overlong film, it does have an energetic performance by Cagney, who always put everything he had into his song-and-dance parts. But as a follow-up to one of his best roles ever, Cody Jarrett in WHITE HEAT (1949), Cagney's Elwin Bixby can't help but be a disappointment. During the rehearsals, Cagney worked out his dance routines with a young dancer whom he could easily lift and who could perform the more rigorous parts of his number, but when the time came to perform the routine with Virginia Mayo, Cagney found her quite a bit heavier than his rehearsal partner. Also complicating Cagney's dancing was the fact that the dance director, LeRoy Prinz, in Cagney's words:"...didn't know one foot from the other. He hated me...he knew I was on to him." Everything conspired to make this one of the most leaden musicals ever, and certainly the weakest of Cagney's song-and-dance movies. Songs by Jule Styne and Sammy Cahn included: "Ten Thousand Sheep," "You Love Me" (sung by Doris Day), "By the Kissing Rock," ""Long Before I Knew You" (sung by MacRae), "Brooklyn," "It Could Only Happen in Brooklyn" (sung by Cagney), and "Military Polka" (sung by Cagney, Mayo, Day, MacRae). Music director Ray Heindorf received an Academy Award nomination for his scoring.

p, Louis F. Edelman; d, Roy Del Ruth; w, John Monks, Jr., Charles Hoffman, Irving Wallace (based on the story "Classmates" by Wallace); ph, Sid Hickox; ed, Owen Marks; md, Ray Heindorf; art d, Charles H. Clarke; set d, Armor E. Marlowe; cos, Milo Anderson, Marjorie Best; spec eff, Edwin DuPar; ch, LeRoy Prinz, Johnny Boyle, Jr.; makeup, Otis Malcolm.

Musical Comedy   **(PR:A MPAA:NR)**

WEST POINT WIDOW**   (1941) 63m PAR bw

Anne Shirley (Nancy Hull), Richard Carlson (Jimmy Krueger), Richard Denning (Rhody Graves), Frances Gifford (Daphne), Maude Eburne (Mrs. Willits, Housekeeper), Janet Beecher (Mrs. Graves), Cecil Kellaway (Dr. Spencer), Archie Twitchell (Joe Martin), Lillian Randolph (Sophie), Patricia Farr (Miss Hinkle), Sharon Lynne, Deanna Jean Hall (Jennifer), Eddy Conrad (Mr. Metapoulos), Jack Chapin (Bill), Charles Coleman (Mr. Appleton), Jean Phillips (Betty), Eleanor Stewart (Pearl), Catherine Craig (Hilda), Keith Richards, Richard Webb, Jack Luden (Internes), Nina Guilbert (Supervisor of Nurses), Kate Drain Lawson (Elderly Nurse), Ethel Clayton, Gloria Williams (Nurses), Ray Cooke (Father in Hospital), Nell Craig (Switchboard Operator), Grace Hayle (Dowager), Rita Owin (Beauty Operator), Harry McKim, Robert Winkler (Fresh Kids), Lee Shumway (Cop), Sam Ash (Pedestrian), Mike Frankovich (Announcer at Football Game), Lillian West (Manageress), Gladys Blake (Salesgirl), Marjorie Deanne (Young Girl at Bar), Catherine Wallace (Woman at Bar), Gilbert Wilson, Louis Natheaux (Men at Bar), Leonard Carey (Simpson), Frances Raymond (Old Lady at Beach), Herbert Holcombe (George), Matt McHugh (Drunk at Football Game), Harry Barris (Hot Dog Vendor), Audra Siddons (Girl at Football Game).

Hospital nurse Shirley, briefly wed to a West Point cadet football hero, has had her marriage annulled (in a most unlikely plot line) despite her resulting pregnancy in order to protect her husband's budding military career. Her secret plan is to remarry the gridiron great following his graduation from the military academy, which bans marriage for cadets. She keeps her own counsel about the child that resulted from her legitimate, but all too brief, union. Interne Carlson, smitten with Shirley, discovers the secret of her baby daughter. He maintains silence until her one-time husband graduates from the academy. Discovering that the husband has found new interests, Carlson succeeds in winning Shirley's heart and hand. Co-writer Herbert functioned as dialog director for Siodmak, who made his U.S. helming debut in this picture after a successful career in France, Producer Siegel's first job for Paramount after a long stint at Republic.

p, Sol C. Siegel; d, Robert Siodmak; w, F. Hugh Herbert, Hans Kraly (based on the story "The Baby's Had a Hard Day" by Anne Wormser); ph, Theodor Sparkuhl; ed, Archie Marshek; art d, Hans Dreier, Haldane Douglas.

Romance   **(PR:A MPAA:NR)**

WEST SIDE KID**   (1943) 57m REP bw

Donald [Don "Red"] Barry (Johnny April), Henry Hull (Sam Winston), Dale Evans (Gloria Winston), Chick Chandler (Shoelace), Matt McHugh (The Worrier), Nana Bryant (Mrs. Winston), Walter Catlett (Ramsey Fensel), Edward Gargan (Donovan), Chester Clute (Gwylim), Peter Lawford (Jerry Winston), George Metaxa (Dr. Kenton).

An innocuous little drama about a gangster Barry, who is hired to kill Hull, a newspaper publisher, for the hefty purse of $25.00. He discovers that Hull is paying to have the job done as a way to get out of his ungrateful family situation, and takes it upon himself to straighten everything out. In the meantime, Barry falls for Evans, Hull's spoiled daugther. A rare chance to see both Barry and Evans away from their customary western ranch settings. Director Sherman had "discovered" Barry in the conventional Hollywood manner (in Shwab's drugstore) in 1939, and had directed him in a number of westerns; this was their first deviation as a team from that genre. Barry, who grew up in a Houston slum, makes quite a convincing gangster. This was the singing Evans' first straight dramatic role; the following year she was to team for the first time with Roy Rogers.

p&d, George Sherman; w, Albert Beich, Anthony Coldeway; ph, Jack Marta; ed, Ernest Nims; md, Morton Scott; art d, Russell Kimball.

Drama   **(PR:A MPAA:NR)**

WEST SIDE STORY****   (1961) 153m Mirisch-Seven Arts-Beta/UA c

Natalie Wood (Maria), Richard Beymer (Tony), Russ Tamblyn (Riff), Rita Moreno (Anita), George Chakiris (Bernardo), The Jets: Tucker Smith (Ice), Tony Mordente (Action), Eliot Feld (Baby John), David Winters (A-Rab), Burt Michaels (Snowboy), Robert Banas (Joyboy), Scooter Teague (Big Deal), Tommy Abbott (Gee-Tar), Harvey Hohnecker (Mouthpiece), David Bean (Tiger), Sue Oakes (Anybodys), Gina Trikonis (Graziella), Carole D'Andrea (Velma), The Sharks: Jose De Vega (Chino), Jay Norman (Pepe), Gus Trikonis (Indio), Robert Thompson (Luis), Larry Roquemore (Rocco), Jaime Rogers (Loco), Eddie Verso (Juano), Andre Tayir (Chile), Nich Covvacevich (Toro), Rudy Del Campo (Del Campo), Suzie Kay (Rosalia), Yvonne Othon (Consuelo), Joanna Miya (Francisca), Adults: Simon Oakland (Lt. Schrank), Bill Bramley (Officer Krupke), Ned Glass (Doc), John Astin (Glad Hand, Social Worker), Penny Santon (Mme. Lucia).

Winner of 10 Academy Awards, including Best Picture, WEST SIDE STORY is a triumph of style over substance. The thin story was a transplant of "Romeo and Juliet," which was conceived for the stage by Jerome Robbins, who also gets a "codirector" credit in the film although he and Robert Wise battled and Robbins left the production after choreographing only four numbers, "I Feel Pretty," "America," "Cool," and the prolog. The play opened in September, 1957, and enjoyed a run of 734 performances at New York's Winter Garden Theatre and has since been successfully revived several times. Even as you read this, it's playing somewhere. The movie hews closely to Laurents' book for the musical, although Ernest Lehman (who also did THE SOUND OF MUSIC for the screen) made enough alterations to merit his credit. (Abby Mann won the Oscar that year for his adaptation of JUDGMENT AT NUREMBERG.) It begins with a remarkable opening shot from a helicopter so the West Side of Manhattan (specifically the "Hell's Kitchen" area) is seen as a series of geometric patterns. It then zooms in to one particular area as if to say "We've chosen this section, but if we opted for another neighborhood, the story would have been different, but equally interesting." The Saul Bass credits are indicated as graffiti scrawled on walls and set the tone immediately. Then we are plunged into the tragic tale of two lovers from separate worlds. There is great racial tension aboil between the established Anglo gang, the Jets, and the Puerto Ricans, known as the Sharks. They are all teenagers (or supposed to be) in conflict over "turf" in their area. The Sharks are lead by Chakiris (who won a Best Supporting Actor Oscar), whose tempestuous girl friend is Moreno (also an Oscar winner as Best Supporting Actress). There is sort of an armed truce between the two gangs and when Chakiris' sister, Wood, arrives from Puerto Rico, she is warned by Moreno to stay away from the Anglos. It doesn't work as Wood meets Beymer, a Polish boy who is one of the Jets. The young lovers fall hard for each other, thus incurring the wrath of both gangs (which, after a fashion, represent the warring Montagues and Capulets of Shakespeare's tragedy). There are warnings and threats and the result is a final showdown between the gangs. Wood tries to stop the impending battle by influencing Beymer into a show of peace but it fails and the leader of the Jets, Tamblyn, dies in a knife fight with Chakiris. Beymer has been calm and cool during the movie but at seeing his pal stabbed, he grabs a knife and stabs Chakiris to death. Now he races to Wood's side and pleads with her to understand why he did what he did and how there was no way out. He also asks that she go away with him to a better place. They are about to leave when Beymer is tracked down by the surviving members of the Sharks and trapped in a playground, then killed by the gang. Wood kneels beside Beymer and cries bitterly while members of both gangs watch and the trio of deaths starts to register on them. In the end, the gangs join forces to haul the dead Beymer out of the playground and there is a faint glimmer of hope that the carnage may have ceased with demise. Made at a price of about $6 million, WEST SIDE STORY went on to become one of the most popular film musicals in history, along with MY FAIR LADY, THE SOUND OF MUSIC, MARY POPPINS, and GREASE. It's a melange of fantasy and reality and doesn't always work. The sets were obvious sets and the streets were obvious streets, thus jarring the senses somewhat. They might have done better had they remained with one style rather than attempting to blend them. The greatest asset to the play and the film was the dancing by Robbins. It's a combination of ballet, acrobatics, and jazz, and even though the picture of tough gang members doing obvious steps brought laughter to the street-wise youngsters in New York, that didn't seem to matter to the rest of the country, who had no idea what the gang life was like in reality. On the stage, Harold Prince and Robert Griffith were able to convey with their production a sense of power without having to expand the confines of the Winter Garden. But when the screen expands to 70 millimeters, there is little left to the imagination so what is up there must be accurate. Robbins used the palette of the screen to create even more spectacular dance numbers than had been seen on stage and the result is exciting showmanship in every scene he personally oversaw. This was not the case in some of the other sequences, especially the love moments between the miscast Wood and Beymer. Wood was a wonderful actress but had some trouble maintaining the accent, and Beymer, while handsome enough, didn't appear to have the power to make him one of the leaders of such a tough gang. There's no question where the sympathy is placed—directly on the backs of the Puerto Ricans. They are the underdogs from the start and so the story is stacked against the Anglos, who are seen as a boorish lot of louts. The costumes are also on the fanciful side and hardly indicated that the real people who live in the area might wear. Tamblyn's casting as the Sharkmaster was also an error, not that he isn't a good actor and a fine dancer, he just didn't look right in the role of a hard-boiled type. The film rights were acquired by the Mirisch Company who produced it with Seven Arts and released it though United Artists. On a radio interview, Sondheim was quoted years later as saying that, although the play received wonderful notices from the New York critics, the score did not. Hardly anyone mentioned his lyrics or Bernstein's music and all they raved about was the staging and dancing. It wasn't until this movie was about to be released and the power of a large studio got behind it that the tunes began to be plugged on the radio and the result was several hits. Their songs were: "Prologue" (the Jets and the Sharks), "Jet Song" (Tamblyn, the Jets), "Something's Coming" (Beymer), "Dance at the Gym" (Wood, Beymer, Jets, Sharks), "Maria" (Beymer), "America" (Moreno, Chakiris, Sharks, and Female Sharks), "Tonight" (Wood, Beymer), "One Hand, One Heart" (Wood, Beymer), "Gee, Officer Krupke" (Tamblyn, Jets), "Quintet" (Beymer, Wood, Moreno, Sharks, Jets), "Rumble" (Jets, Sharks), "Cool" (Tucker Smith, Jets), "I Feel Pretty" (Wood, Suzie Kaye, Yvonne Othon, Joanne Miya), "Somewhere" (Beymer, Wood), "A Boy Like That," "I Have a Heart" (Wood, Moreno). Although we have listed Wood and Beymer as singing the songs, neither of their voices were on the sound track. Wood's "voice" was actually done by veteran Marni Nixon, who also sang for Audrey Hepburn in MY FAIR LADY. And Beymer's voice was substituted by Jimmy Bryant. Since Wood was not a singer or a dancer, some creativity had to be exercised to make it appear she was. Using someone else's voice as the singer is easy enough but faking the dancing required some careful planning and so she was handed some easy steps to do but through excellent camera planning, it appeared that she was doing more than she actually was. Other than the previously mentioned Oscars, statuettes were handed to Wise and Robbins for their co-direction, Daniel Fapp's cinematography, Boris Leven's art direction, Victor Gangelin's set direction, Irene Sharaff's costume design, Thomas Stanford's film editing, the musical scoring (which integrates direction and arrangement) by Johnny Green, Sid Ramin, Irwin Kostal, and associate producer Saul Chaplin, the sound by the Todd-AO company (Fred Hynes, director) and the Samuel Goldwyn sound department (Gordon E. Sawyer, director), and a special honorary Oscar to Robbins for "his brilliant achievements in the art of choreography on film in WEST SIDE STORY." As a sidelight, three of the dancers in the film went on to become directors; David Winters, Gus Trikonis, and Tony Mordente, who married Chita Rivera, who appeared in the stage production but was bypassed for the movie. Making his motion picture debut as the social worker was John Astin, who later achieved great success on TV in "I'm Dickens, He's Fenster" and "The Addams Family." A number of eminent jazz musicians worked on the soundtrack, including Al Viola, Red Mitchell, Jack Dumont, Shelly Manne, and Pete Candoli. Everything about the movie was first-rate. It fell just short, however, of being a classic because one always had the feeling of watching a movie, and the status of classic occurs when all disbelief is suspended and we are plunged totally into the action on screen, as though we are part of it, rather than merely observers. Anyone who grew up in that era and in that area will recognize the falseness of the language and the settings and some of the characters, all of which detract from the totality of the experience.

p, Robert Wise; d, Wise, Jerome Robbins; w, Ernest Lehman (based on the stage play by Arthur Laurents, based on a conception by Jerome Robbins, inspired by a play by William Shakespeare); ph, Daniel L. Fapp (Panavision, Technicolor); m, Leonard Bernstein; ed, Thomas Stanford; prod d, Boris Leven; md, Johnny Green, Saul Chaplin; set d, Victor Gangelin; cos, Irene Sharaff; ch, Jerome Robbins; makeup, Emile La Bigne; m/l Bernstein, Stephen Sondheim.

Musical   **Cas.**   **(PR:A-C MPAA:NR)**

WEST TO GLORY*½   (1947) 61m PRC bw

Eddie Dean (*Himself*), Roscoe Ates (*Soapy*), Dolores Castle (*Marta*), Gregg Barton (*Barrett*), Jimmy Martin (*Cory*), Zon Murray (*Avery*), Alex Montoya (*Juan*), Harry Vejar (*Don Lopez*), Carl Mathews (*Vincente*), The Sunshine Boys: Casey MacGregor, Billy Hammond, Ted French.

Sheriff Dean may be traveling "west to glory," but he's sure doing it at a snail's pace. This molasses-paced oater has the lead helping a Mexican rancher keep his jewels out of the hands of bandits. He also belts out a trio of ballads, "Cry, Cry, Cry," "I'm Ridin' West," "In the Shadow of the Mission."

p, Jerry Thomas; d, Ray Taylor; w, Elmer Clifton, Robert B. Churchill; ph, Milford Anderson; ed, Hugh Winn; m/l, Eddie Dean, Hal Blair, Pete Gates.

Western   **(PR:A MPAA:NR)**

WESTBOUND**   (1959) 72M WB c

Randolph Scott (*John Hayes*), Virginia Mayo (*Norma Putnam*), Karen Steele (*Jeannie Miller*), Michael Dante (*Rod Miller*), Andrew Duggan (*Clay Putnam*), Michael Pate (*Mace*), Wally Brown (*Stubby*), John Day (*Russ*), Walter Barnes (*Willis*), Fred Sherman (*Christy*), Mack Williams (*Col. Vance*), Ed Prentiss (*James Fuller*), Jack Perrin (*Man*), Creighton Hale, Gertrude Keeler (*Passengers*), Walter Reed (*Doctor*), Buddy Roosevelt, Charles Morton (*Stock Tenders*), Rory Mallinson, Rudi Dana, Tom Monroe, Kermit Maynard, May Boss, William A. Green, Jack E. Henderson, Felice Richmond, Jack C. Williams, Gerald Roberts, John Hudkins, Don Happy, Bobby Heron, Fred Stromscoe.

In the midst of a number of fine Westerns Boetticher churned out this barely sufficient actioner which has little of the energy of his other projects. Scott is a Union officer assigned the task of starting a coach line and delivering gold shipments to the North from California. Duggan is trying to intercept the line and send the gold to the Confederates, but eventually gets killed trying to defend Scott against his own (Duggan's) men. His dying wish is that Mayo, his soon-to-be widow, be taken care of by Scott. Steele, who also appeared in THE RISE AND FALL OF LEGS DIAMOND, (1960) was at the time Boetticher's wife. WESTBOUND, if nothing else, demonstrates the importance of Ranown, the production company begun by Scott and producer Harry Joe Brown, which took the scripts of Burt Kennedy (also, like Brown, absent from this picture) and turned them into Boetticher masterpieces. Without their assistance Boetticher's stature as one of the greatest directors of the modern Western seems to fall by the wayside.

p, Henry Blanke; d, Budd Boetticher; w, Berne Giler (based on the story "The Great Divide No. 2" by Giler, Albert Shelby LeVino); ph, J. Peverell Marley (WarnerColor); m, David Buttolph; ed, Philip W. Anderson; art d, Howard Campbell; set d, Gene Redd; cos, Howard Shoup; makeup, Gordon Bau.

Western   **(PR:A MPAA:NR)**

WESTBOUND LIMITED**   (1937) 76m UNIV bw

Lyle Talbot (*Dave Tolliver*), Polly Rowles (*Janet Martin*), Henry Brandon (*Joe Forbes*), Frank Reicher (*Pop Martin*), Henry Hunter (*Howard*), William Lundigan (*Dispatcher*), William Royle (*Messenger*), Tom Steele (*Brakeman*), Charles Murphy (*Freight Brakeman*), Monte Vandegrift (*Freight Conductor*), J. P. McGowan (*Freight Engineer*).

An exciting, but minor, railway tale about a railroad agent blamed for a train crash who was actually trying to prevent a gunman from taking over the train. He flees the authorities and helps out a struggling family, in the meantime discovering the identity of the culprit. He not only brings in the guilty party, but prevents a second collision from occurring.

p, Henry MacRae, Ben Koenig; d, Ford Beebe; w, Maurice Geraghty (based on a story by Beebe); ph, Elwood Bredell; ed, Phil Cahn.

Adventure   **(PR:A MPAA:NR)**

WESTBOUND MAIL**   (1937) 57m COL bw

Charles Starrett (*Jim Bradley/Mule Skinner*), Rosalind Keith (*Marion Saunders*), Edward Keane (*Gun Barlow*), Arthur Stone (*Andy*), Ben Welden (*Steve Hickman*), Al Bridges (*Bull Feeney*), George Chesebro (*Slim*), Art Mix (*Shorty*).

A lively horse opera which benefits more from the extensive footage of thundering hoofs than from the wooden performances of the leads. Starrett doesn't put much effort into his law officer role as he helps postmistress Keith round up a gang of bandits that has been preying on her mail runs. Their real object is to get the lovely lady to sell her land, which is adjacent to villain Keane's mined-out gold diggings (she promised her late father she wouldn't sell). The plot line has vagrant mule skinner Starret an undercover agent for—ready for this?—the FBI during pioneer days. "Perilous days with the pioneers...when every load of letters spelled a message of death," read the poster.

d, Folmer Blangsted; w, Francis Guihan (based on a story by James P. Hogan); ph, Benjamin Kline; ed Richard Fantl.

Western   (PR:A MPAA:NR)

WESTBOUND STAGE**   (1940) 57m MON bw

Tex Ritter *(Tex)*, Nelson McDowell *(Rawhide)*, Muriel Evans *(Jean)*, Nolan Willis *(Lane)*, Steve Clark *(Butch)*, Tom London *(Parker)*, Reed Howes *(Greer)*, Frank Ellis *(Spider)*, Chick Hannon, Kenne Duncan, Frank LaRue, Chester Gan, Hank Bell, Phil Dunham.

Ritter is in pursuit of Howes, a fugitive gang leader who's broken loose from the Kansas penitentiary in order to wreak havoc in the West. Ritter gets his man by tricking him into hijacking a coach carrying a $30,000 gold shipment and then ambushing him. Along the way, he croons a couple of ballads.

p, Ed Finney; d, Spencer Gordon Bennett; w, Robert Emmett [Tansey] (based on a story by John Foster); ph, Marcel LePicard; m, Frank Sanucci; ed, Fred Bain; md, Sanucci; m/l, Johnny Lange, Lew Porter.

Western   (PR:A MPAA:NR)

WESTERN CARAVANS**   (1939) 59m COL bw

Charles Starrett *(Carson)*, Iris Meredith *(Joyce)*, Dick Curtis *(Mort)*, Russell Simpson *(Thompson)*, Hal Taliaferro [Wally Wales] *(Jed)*, Hank Bell *(Hank)*, Bob Nolan *(Bob)*, Sammy McKim *(Matt)*, Edmund Cobb *(Tex)*, Ethan Laidlaw *(Tip)*, Steve Clark, Herman Hack, Charles Brinley, The Sons of the Pioneers.

Starrett brings peace to the valley when homesteaders begin to descend on the ranchers and foul play hangs over the West like a rain cloud ready to burst. He prevents a storm and offers the audience a little romance with Meredith and some music with Nolan and his boys. They sing "Serenade to the Night Bird" and "Westward, Ho" (Bob Nolan, Tim Spencer).

d, Sam, Nelson; w, Bennett R. Cohen; ph, George Cooper; ed, William Lyon.

Western   (PR:A MPAA:NR)

WESTERN COURAGE**½   (1935) 61m COL bw

Ken Maynard *(Ken Baxter)*, Geneva Mitchell *(Gloria Hanley)*, Charles K. French *(Mr. Hanley)*, Betty Blythe *(Mrs. Hanley)*, Cornelius Keefe *(Eric)*, Ward Bond *(LaCrosse)*, Captain E. H. Calvert *(Col. Austin)*, Renee Whitney *(Betty Johns)*, Dick Curtis, Bob Reeves, Wally West, Roy Bucko, Buck Bucko, Bud McClure, Bart Carre, Arkansas Johnny, "Tarzan.".

A fresh program western which is blessed, for once, with a female lead who actually has some screen presence and knows the meaning of the phrase "to act." Mitchell is a rich, spoiled brat from the city who gives dude ranch foreman Maynard a tough time, getting him in trouble with an outlaw gang that nearly kills him. Luckily for Maynard he's the star and can't die, so the finale has Maynard and the girl, making a strong improvement in her attitude, staying together as sweethearts. Not too bad for only six days of shooting.

p, Larry Darmour; d, Spencer Gordon Bennett; w, Nate Gatzert (based on a story by Charles Francis Royal); ph, Herbert Kirkpatrick; ed, Dwight Caldwell.

Western   Cas.   (PR:A MPAA:NR)

WESTERN CYCLONE**   (1943) 62m PRC bw

Buster Crabbe *(Billy The Kid)*, Al St. John *(Fuzzy Q. Jones)*, Marjorie Manners *(Mary Arnold)*, Karl Hackett *(Governor Arnold)*, Milton Kibbee *(Senator Peabody)*, Glenn Strange *(Dirk Randall)*, Charles King *(Ace Harmon)*, Hal Price *(Sheriff)*, Kermit Maynard *(Hank)*, Frank Ellis, Frank McCarroll, Artie Ortego, Herman Hack, Al Haskell.

Crabbe has to fight for his own neck when a gang of outlaws frames him for murder and then kidnaps Manners, pinning that crime on him too. With the help of the governor, Hackett, Crabbe is able to prove himself innocent before he finds himself hanging from a tree. Given a fair share of laughs by the inclusion of St. John into the cast. Re-edited in 1947 and released as a 40-minute featurette called FRONTIER FIGHTER. (See BILLY THE KID series, Index.)

p, Sigmund Neufeld; d, Sam Newfield; w, Patricia Harper; ph, Robert Cline; m, Leo Erdody; ed, Holbrook N. Todd.

Western   (PR:A MPAA:NR)

WESTERN FRONTIER**   (1935) 56m COL bw

Ken Maynard *(Ken)*, Lucile Browne *(Mary)*, Nora Lane *(Goldie)*, Robert Henry *(Pewee)*, Frank Yaconelli *(Haw Haw)*, Otis Harlan *(Cook)*, Harold Goodwin *(Morgan)*, Frank Hagney *(Link)*, Gordon S. Griffith *(Steve)*, Jim Marcus *(Bat)*, Tom Harris, Nelson McDowell, Frank Ellis, Art Mix, Slim Whitaker, William Gould, Dick Curtis, Budd Buster, Herman Hack, Horace B. Carpenter, Oscar Gahan, Joe Weaver, "Tarzan".

Maynard is a decent cowboy whose family was obliterated in an Indian attack when he was a child, although–unknown to him–a young sister also survived and was raised by Indians. Later Maynard is called on to lead an

attack against a gang of outlaws who he discovers are led by his sister. Quickly paced and filled from beginning to end with action. Maynard's first film for Columbia after moving there from Universal.

p, Larry Darmour; d, Al Herman; w, Nate Gatzert (based on a story by Ken Maynard); ph, James s. Brown, Jr., Herbert Kirkpatrick; ed, Dwight Caldwell.

Western   (PR:A MPAA:NR)

WESTERN GOLD*   (1937) 57m Principal FOX bw (GB: THE
                                                     MYSTERIOUS STRANGER)

Smith Ballew *(Bill Gibson)*, Heather Angel *(Jeannie Thatcher)*, Leroy Mason *(Fred Foster)*, Ben Alexander *(Bart)*, Otis Harlan *(Jake)*, Victor Potel *(Jasper)*, Frank McGlynn, Sr *(President Abraham Lincoln)*, Howard Hickman *(Thatcher)*, Alan [Al] Bridge *(Holman)*, Bud Osborne *(Steve)*, Wesley *(Girard (Bud)*, Lew Kelly *(Ezra)*, Tom London *(Clem)*, Horace Murphy *(Squatter)*, Steve Clark, Paul Fix, Art Lasky.

Lacking the necessary element of action, this Civil War oater falls from memory as Ballew is chosen from among the Union ranks to make a trip to California and find out why the gold shipments aren't making it to the North. He discovers that Mason, an old school chum, is behind the scheme. WESTERN GOLD is notable only because Ballew, the "hero," doesn't get to kill the bad guy; someone else gets him first. Ballew, in his first starring role, had been selected by producer Lesser as George O'Brien's replacement when the latter shifted his allegiance to RKO. Ballew, who allegedly dubbed John Wayne's singing voice in his SINGIN' SANDY series of westerns, gets a chance here to warble a number of familiar songs of the era: "The Battle Hymn of the Republic" (Julia Ward Howe), "Camptown Races" and "Jeannie with the Light Brown Hair" (Stephen Collins Foster).

p, Sol Lesser; d, Howard Bretherton; w, Earle Snell, Forrest Barnes (based on the novel *Helen of the Old House* by Harold Bell Wright); ph, Harry Neumann; ed, Carl Pierson; md, Arthur Lange; art d, Frank Sylos.

Western   (PR:A MPAA:NR)

WESTERN HERITAGE**   (1948) 61m RKO bw

Tim Holt *(Ross Daggett)*, Nan Leslie *(Beth Winston)*, Richard Martin *(Chito Rafferty)*, Lois Andrews *(Cleo)*, Tony Barrett *(Trigg)*, Walter Reed *(Joe Powell)*, Harry Woods *(Arnold)*, Richard Powers [Tom Keene] *(Spade)*, Jason Robards, Sr *(Judge Winston)*, Robert Bray *(Pike)*, Perc Launders *(Sheriff)*, Emmett Lynn.

An average oater entry which has Holt fighting a gang of outlaws who have tricked unsuspecting ranchers into falling for the "phony Spanish land grant" trick. The culprits' scheme of rustling cattle and taking over ranches is foiled when Holt catches on. Lovely Leslie is Holt's leading lady for the third time in a row. Song "If You Happen to Find My Heart" (sung by Lois Andrews).

p, Herman Schlom; d, Wallace A. Grissell; w, Norman Houston; ph, Alfred Keller; m, Paul Sawtell; ed, Desmond Marquette; md, Constanti Bakaleinikoff; art d, Albert S. D'Agostino, Lucius O. Croxton; set d, Darrell Silvera, Adolph Kuri; spec eff, Russell A. Cully; make up, Jack Barron.

Western   (PR:A MPAA:NR)

WESTERN JAMBOREE**   (1938) 60 REP bw

Gene Autry *(Gene)*, Smiley Burnette *(Frog)*, Jean Rouverol *(Betty Haskell)*, Esther Muir *(Duchess)*, Joe Frisco *(Frisco)*, Frank Darien *(Dad Haskell)*, Margaret Armstrong *(Mrs. Gregory)*, Harry Holman *(Doc Trimble)*, Edward Raquello *(Don Carlos)*, Bentley Hewlett *(Kimball)*, Kermit Maynard *(Slim)*, George Walcott *(Walter Gregory)*, Ray Teal *(McCall)*, Frank Ellis, Eddie Dean, Davison Clark, Jack Perrin, Jack Ingram, "Champion".

Autry's westerns often had fantastic or superby topical story lines, and this is no exception. Failing in their attempt to purchase the ranchland that Autry straw-bosses, a gang of crooks secretly lays a pipeline to leach off the valuable helium gas which lies beneath its surface. (Remember, the German dirigible "Hindenberg" which used flammable hydrogen in its gas bags had burst into flames during its landing approach in New Jersey the previous year, causing interest in non-flammable helium to jump sharply.) Autry discovers the pipeline and rounds up the gang. Variety artist Frisco, a stuttering wonder, does well here. Autry manages to work in a few songs, including "November Moon."

p, Harry Grey; d, Ralph Staub; w, Gerald Geraghty (based on a story by Pat Harper); ph, William Nobles; ed, Lester Orlebeck.

Western   (PR:A MPAA:NR)

WESTERN JUSTICE**   (1935) 55m Supreme/William Steiner bw

Bob Steele, Renee Bordon, Julian Rivero, Jack Cowell, Perry Murdock, Vane Calvert, Lafe McKee, Arthur Loft.

A gang of land-grabbers is terrorizing the settlers, so Steele arrive on the scene to see that justice prevails. Acceptable horseback actioner with sidekick humor to keep the wheels spinning and derring-do in the saddle.

p, A.W. Hackel; d&w, Robert N. Bradbury.

Western   (PR:A MPAA:NR)

WESTERN LIMITED*   (1932) 65m MON bw (GB: THE NIGHT EXPRESS)

Estelle Taylor, Edmund Burns, Lucien Prival, Gertrude Astor, Eddie Kane, James Burtis, John Vosburgh, Mahlon Hamilton, Crauford Kent, Adaline Asbury, Arthur Millett, J.L. Palmer.

An unimpressive murder mystery which takes place mostly on a train after a woman's jewels are stolen at a party the night before. In keeping with tradition, everyone on the train (the conductor is the only exception) is suspected and an insurance company detective unearths the clues to the mystery.

d, Christy Cabanne; w, C.E. Roberts (based on story by Evelyn Campbell); ph, Lou Physioc.

Mystery   (PR:A MPAA:NR)

WESTERN MAIL*½   (1942) 54m MON bw

Tom Keene (Tom), Frank Yaconelli (Lopez), Leroy Mason (Gordon), Jean Trent (Julia), Fred Kohler, Jr (Lucky), Glenn Strange (Collins), Gene Alsace (Rod), James Sheridan (Cheyenne), Karl Hackett (Rivers), Tex Palmer, Prince the Horse.

Nothing special in this standard pony-programmer which has Keene going undercover in order to gain the trust of a nefarious outlaw. He gets close to the bandit and guns him down before the finish. Yaconelli is the picture's highlight as he plays his guitar, and with his pet monkey.

p&d, Robert Tansey; w, Robert Emmett [Tansey], Frances Kavanaugh; ph, Marcel LePicard; ed, Fred Bain; md, Frank Sanucci.

Western   (PR:A MPAA:NR)

WESTERN PACIFIC AGENT**   (1950) 61m Lippert bw

Kent Taylor, Sheila Ryan, Mickey Knox, Robert Lowery, Morris Carnovsky, Frank Richards, Sid Melton, Dick Elliott, Anthony Jochim, Lee Phelps, Ted Jacques, Vera Marshe, Carla Martin, Margia Dean, Gloria Gray.

Taylor is the title agent hired to capture an outlaw who committed a robbery and killed two people in the process. Along the way he falls in love with Ryan, the sister of one of the murdered men, and eventually brings down the fugitive killer. Newfield's direction concentrates more on the violent aspects of the picture than on any other facet.

p, Sigmund Neufeld; d, Sam Newfield; w, Fred Myton (based on the story by Milton Raison); ph, Ernest W. Miller; m, Albert Glasser; ed, Carl Pierson.

Western   (PR:A MPAA:NR)

WESTERN RENEGADES**   (1949) 56m MON bw

Johnny Mack Brown (Johnny), Max Terhune (Alibi), Riley Hill (Joe Gordon), Jane Adams (Judy Gordon), Steve Clark (Dusty), Marshall Bradford (Paul Gordon), Hugh Prosser (Laren), Marshall Reed (Frank), Constance Worth (Annie), James H. Harrison (Bill), Terry Frost (Carl), William H. Ruhl (Curly), Myron Healey (Gus), Milburn Morante (Jenkins), John Merton Blacksmith, Dee Cooper (Cook), Chuck Roberson (Jones), Bill Potter (Bob), Lane Bradford.

Brown stars as a lawman in Gordontown defending his townspeople against the shenanigans of Prosser, who unsuccessfully attempts to make the town his own by killing Bradford, its chief figure. A muddled sub-plot has Bradford's children arriving in town to be duped by Prosser aide de camp Worth, who pretends to be their mother. Despite a corpulence that might dismay many of his fans, Brown cavorts around quite nimbly in doing the best he can with the material he is given.

p, Eddie Davis; d, Wallace Fox; w, Adele Buffington; ph, Harry Neumann; m, Edward J. Kay; ed, John C. Fuller.

Western   (PR:A MPAA:NR)

WESTERN TRAILS*½   (1938) 58m UNIV bw

Bob Baker (Bob Mason), Marjorie Reynolds (Alice), Carlyle Moore (Rudd), John Ridgely (Ben), Franco Corsarro (Indian Joe), Jack Rockwell (Bartender), Forrest Taylor (Williams), Bob Burns (Dad Mason), Wimpy (Smoky), Apache (Apache), Jack Ingram, Jack Montgomery, Tex Palmer, Oscar Gahan, Herman Hack, Hank Worden.

Baker cleans up a Wild West town which is terrorized by Moore. After the usual punch 'em out, shoot 'em up antics Baker hits the trail with Reynolds and his dog Wimpy by his side. Weak acting and an even weaker script don't lend much to this forgettable oater, which is redeemable only by Baker's singing and the smart antics of Wimpy, some of them admittedly incredible.

p, Paul Malvern; d, George Waggner; w, Norton S. Parker; ph, Harry Neumann; ed, Charles Craft.

Western   **Cas.**   (PR:A MPAA:NR)

WESTERN UNION****   (1941) 93m FOX c

Randolph Scott (Vance Shaw), Robert Young (Richard Blake), Dean Jagger (Edward Creighton), Virginia Gilmore (Sue Creighton), John Carradine (Doc Murdoch), Slim Summerville (Herman), Chill Wills (Homer), Barton MacLane (Jack Slade), Russell Hicks (Governor), Victor Kilian (Charlie), Minor Watson (Pat Grogan), George Chandler (Herb), Chief Big Tree (Chief Spotted Horse), Chief Thundercloud (Indian Leader), Dick Rich (Porky), Harry Strang (Henchman), Charles Middleton (Stagecoach Rider), Addison Richards (Capt. Harlow), Irving Bacon (Barber), Francis Ford, Eddy Waller (Stagecoach Drivers), James Flavin, Frank Mills, Ralph Dunn (Men), Cliff Clark, Paul E. Burns.

After the success of his first western, THE RETURN OF FRANK JAMES, German director Lang was assigned to do another, this one based on the construction of the Western Union telegraph line from Omaha, Nebraska, to Salt Lake City, Utah. Scott stars as an outlaw looking to reform his wicked ways. While trying to escape a posse, he spies a fresh horse and goes to steal it. The owner of the animal, Jagger, is injured (broken ribs) and it looks as though he'll die if he doesn't get help. Scott takes pity on the man and helps him to the nearest cabin. Jagger is grateful to the outlaw and lets him take his horse. As it turns out, Jagger is in charge of constructing the Western Pacific telegraph line which must be raised to help the Union stay in contact with the West during the Civil War. When he recovers, he begins hiring dozens of men for the job. Months later, Jagger is surprised to find that his foreman has hired Scott to be their scout. Jagger knows Scott was an outlaw–and Scott offers to quit–but he lets the man keep his job because he knows Scott is a decent man. To help in the telegraph office in Omaha, Jagger brings in his beautiful sister, Gilmore, who knows the Morse Code inside out. Scott and Gilmore are attracted to each other and they begin a very gentle courtship. One day an Eastern dandy, Young, arrives to report for work. The son of a rich man who helped fund the project, Jagger agrees to take Young on to "make a man" of him. To everyone's surprise, Young proves himself to be an able horseman and a valuable asset to the crew. Unfortunately, he also proves to be romantic competition for Gilmore's affections and he and Scott both try to steal a few extra moments with the woman. Finally the crew has been picked and trained and the wagons begin to roll into the territory. Construction goes smoothly with poles being raised and wire strung at a rapid pace. Then one night the company's cattle is stolen by Indians. Scott rides off to investigate and discovers that the men aren't Indians at all, but his brother, MacLane, and his old outlaw gang dressed up as Indians. MacLane tells Scott that he and the boys have joined up with the Confederate Army and are now working as guerrillas. Their orders are to sabotage the Western Union telegraph line. It is obvious to Scott, however, that his brother is using the war as an excuse to make big money by looting and then reselling. Scott agrees to keep his mouth shut about the cattle, but then warns MacLane to stay away from the Western Union project. A few days later Indians attack the camp and run off the company's horses. Contrary to Scott's orders to hold fire, Young shoots and wounds an Indian brave. This proves to be trouble because the chief–who claims that white men got the young braves drunk and talked them into the raid–becomes angry that his son was injured and tells Western Union that they can no longer string their "singing wire" through their territory. Jagger tells the Indians that the wire can be bad medicine for them and he proves it by electrically shocking 10 of the chief's strongest braves. The Indians agree that the wire is powerful and when Jagger promises them that it can be used to defeat their enemies, the chief lets them continue their work. Later, Jagger, Young, and Scott ride through a nearby town and spot their horses in a corral. Tending to the animals is MacLane, and he offers to sell them back for $5,000. Having no time to fight him physically or legally, Jagger pays MacLane off and gets the horses back–though both he and Young begin to suspect Scott is involved. One night in camp, one of MacLane's gang sneaks in and lures Scott to their hideaway. There MacLane gives his brother one more chance to join the gang. Scott refuses and MacLane has him tied up. The gang has orders from the Confederacy to burn down the Western Union camp. The villains ride off leaving Scott hog-tied. To free himself of his bonds, Scott has no choice but to hold his hands over the campfire. His hands are horribly burned, but the flames burn through the rope and he is freed. Meanwhile, MacLane and his gang have spread coal oil all around the camp and set it ablaze. Chaos erupts as the workers scramble to save lives and equipment. Scott arrives in time to help, but when the disaster is over Jagger demands an explanation of his whereabouts. Scott keeps his silence and Jagger is forced to fire him. His hands bandaged from the burns, Scott rides off to face his brother. He catches up with MacLane in a nearby town. MacLane is in a barber shop getting a shave and he orders the gang to take up posts in and around the shop to protect him (he knows Scott's coming for him). Scott arrives, hitches his horse nearby, and removes the bandages from his hands. He then painfully flexes his gun hand to see if he can draw. Satisfied, he goes to the barber shop. A bloody gun battle erupts and Scott manages to kill every gang member but his brother. MacLane has a better vantage point however, and he kills Scott. As he stands over Scott's body, Young shows up and draws his gun. MacLane wounds Young, but Young manages to kill MacLane. Scott is buried on boot hill and the Western Union telegraph is completed. The most epic and beautiful of Lang's westerns (it was the director's personal favorite), WESTERN UNION is an outstanding entry in the genre.

Lang, who loved the American West and spent much time traveling there, researched the period thoroughly and took great pride in the attention to detail he demonstrated. Having studied Indians for some time, he was delighted with the opportunity to present Indians in their full glory, with accurate warpaint and battle gear photographed in beautiful Technicolor. While the director paid close attention to accuracy, the story of the construction of the Western Union telegraph line was not the stuff of high drama. Research showed that things went smoothly in 1861 and the only problems encountered were that the company ran out of wood poles and that the poles already raised were being knocked over by buffalo who were scratching themselves on them. Screenwriter Carson took the title of a Zane Grey story (and tossed out the rest of the material) and developed a plot that concentrated on the human drama during the construction. Lang did not like the original script and made changes, but studio head Zanuck overruled the director and made him return to the original script. Scott's character is distinctly Langsian however. He is a bad man turned good and has gone far to reform, but his dark side is always there, lurking in the woods in the form of his brother, MacLane. Scott is fully aware of his destiny and he ruefully tells Gilmore that if he had met her a few years before his life would be different. When asked why he says he has made some mistakes in his life. When she responds that some mistakes can be fixed, he responds that it is too late. Events beyond his control draw Scott to his violent end and he accepts his fate with honor. Scott's tragic tale is told in an utterly entertaining manner. The color photography by Cronjager is some of the most beautiful work of the 1940s, and the cast is filled with outstanding character actors such as Carradine, Wills, Summerville, and Killian. There is much humor in WESTERN UNION, most of it centering around Summerville, the timid cook scared witless of the "Wild West." Lang would make only one more western, RANCHO NOTORIOUS (1952), yet another superior entry from a German director working in a distinctly American genre.

p, Darryl F. Zanuck; d, Fritz Lang; w, Robert Carson (based on the novel by Zane Grey); ph, Edward Cronjager, Allen M. Davey (Technicolor); m, David Buttolph; ed, Robert Bischoff, (uncredited) Gene Flowler, Jr.; art d, Richard Day, Wiard B. Ihnen; set d, Thomas Little; cos, Travis Banton.

Western   **Cas.**   **(PR:A MPAA:NR)**

WESTERNER, THE**   (1936) 60m COL bw (AKA: THE FIGHTING WESTERNER)

Tim McCoy (Tim Addison), Marion Shilling (Juanita Barnes), Joseph Sauers [Joe Sawyer] (Bob Lockhart), John H. Dilson (Sen. Lockhart), Hooper Atchley (Wallace), Edward J. Le Saint (Zack Addison), Harry Todd (Uncle Ben), Edmund Cobb (Joe Allen), Albert J. Smith (Sheriff), Bud Osborne, Slim Whitaker, Lafe McKee, Merrill McCormick.

McCoy stars as a rodeo cowboy who buys himself a ranch only to find himself in the middle of a battle with a cattle rustler. Not only is the culprit taking his horses, but those of Shilling, a neighboring ranch owner and the rustler's boss. A murder is pinned on McCoy but after plenty of scrapping and shooting he clears his name and paves the way for a future with Shilling.

d, David Selman; w, Harold Shumate (based on the story by Walt Coburn); ph, George Meehan; ed, Ray Snyder

Western   **(PR:A MPAA:NR)**

WESTERNER, THE*****   (1940) 100m UA bw

Gary Cooper (Cole Hardin), Walter Brennan (Judge Roy Bean), Doris Davenport (Jane-Ellen Mathews), Fred Stone (Caliphet Mathews), Paul Hurst (Chickenfoot), Chill Wills (Southeast), Charles Halton (Mort Borrow), Forrest Tucker (Wade Harper), Tom Tyler (King Evans), Arthur Aylesworth (Mr. Dixon), Lupita Tovar (Teresita), Julian Rivero (Joan Gomez), Lillian Bond (Lily Langtry), Dana Andrews (Bart Cobble), Roger Gray (Eph Stringer), Jack Pennick (Bantry), Trevor Bardette (Shad Wilkins), Bill Steele (Tex Cole), Blackjack Ward (Buck Harrigan), James "Jim" Corey (Lee Webb), Buck Moulton (Charles Evans), Ted Wells (Joe Lawrence), Joe De La Cruz (Mex), Frank Cordell (Man), Philip Connor (John Yancy), Capt. C.E. Anderson (Hezekiah Willever), Art Mix (Seth Tucker), William Gillis (Leon Beauregard), Buck Connor (Abraham Wilson), Dan Borzabe (Joe Yates), Speed Hanson (Walt McGary), Gertrude Bennett (Abigail), Miriam Sherwin (Martha), Annabelle Rousseau (Elizabeth), Helen Foster (Janice), Connie Leon (Langtry's Maid), Charles Coleman (Langtry's Manager), Lew Kelly (Ticket Man), Heinie Conklin (Man at Window), Lucien Littlefield (A Stranger), Corbet Morris (Orchestra Leader), Stanley Andrews (Sheriff), Phil Tead (Prisoner), Henry Roquemore (Stage Manager), Bill Bauman (Man Getting Haircut), Hank Bell (Deputy).

A superior western that mixes fine cinematography, terrific performances, and a script of higher intelligence than most to produce a film still fondly remembered today. Cooper is a drifter who runs afoul of the law when he is falsely accused of stealing a horse. He is taken in front of Brennan, who serves as a justice of the peace and "Law west of the Pecos," as a cemetery full of his victims will attest. He tries Cooper in a hasty mockery of justice and sentences him to hang, but Cooper, knowing Brennan's admiration and even love for stage star Lily Langtry (after whom Brennan has named his town), he convinces the judge that he is a personal friend of Langtry's and

will obtain a lock of her hair for the judge if he lets him go. Brennan is so love-struck that he sees through this obvious lie, and the two men soon become friends of a sort. That night, Cooper steals Brennan's gun and escapes, stopping at the farm of Stone and his daughter, Davenport. Brennan is conducting a campaign, through his henchmen with badges, aimed at driving the homesteaders off the range. Cooper, who has become smitten with Davenport, decides to stay in the area and be the advocate of the homesteaders with Brennan. For a time things go smoothly, and Cooper gives Brennan a lock of Davenport's hair, telling him it is from Langtry, but then Brennan's terrorizing of the farmers takes on new fervor, and Stone is murdered. Cooper sets out for a reckoning with Brennan, but learns that the judge has left Langtry to travel to Fort Davis, where he has bought every seat in the theater to see Langtry in person for the first time. The curtain rises, and it is Cooper who is standing there, guns at the ready. The two men shoot it out in the gaslit hall, and Cooper finally manages to mortally wound Brennan. Dying, Brennan is taken backstage by Cooper to finally meet his dream, played here by Bond, whose hand he kisses before dying. Cooper was initially reluctant to take his part here, thinking it too minor for an actor of his stature. Director Wyler shamed him out of that attitude, though, with a variation of the "no small parts, only small actors" bit, and he gave Cooper enough good scenes to make the actor happy, and he is indispensible to the narrative. It is Brennan, however, who steals the picture, making Judge Roy Bean one of the most unforgettable characters ever seen in a western film. Writer Niven Busch recalled: "I met Walter coming back from lunch one day on the Goldwyn lot and as soon as he saw me he twisted his neck to one side and stood there with his chin cocked around at a strange angle. He was in costume for the role, but I never connected this with the cramped attitude he'd assumed, and when he continued his awkward attitude I inquired 'Did you do something to your neck, Walter?' 'Well, no,' he said,'not my neck. You know the story about Bean. He was hanged one time but they cut him down and saved him. That would have given him a crick in the neck, wouldn't it?' He was just showing us how Bean's must have looked. I had never read anything about this–but Brennan had–and his research gave us the running gag of the dislocated neck which afflicts Brennan throughout the film: his adversary-buddy Cooper has to repair it for him by poking him in the jaw." Cinematographer Toland's work is superb, filling his western skies with gnarled trees and amazing clouds, and maintaining a strangely somber tone to the story. The score by Tiomkin was completely scrapped at the last minute and a new one written by Alfred Newman, though he did not receive screen credit. Dana Andrews and Forrest Tucker made their debuts here. A major success, the film earned Brennan his third Oscar as Best Supporting Actor, the first performer ever to take home three of the awards.

p, Samuel Goldwyn; d, William Wyler; w, Jo Swerling, Niven Busch (based on a story by Stuart N. Lake); ph, Gregg Toland; m, Dimitri Tiomkin (uncredited, Alfred Newman); ed, Daniel Mandell; art d, James Basevi; set d, Julia Heron; cos, Irene Saltern; spec eff, Archie Stout, Paul Eagler.

Western   **Cas.**   **(PR:A MPAA:NR)**

WESTLAND CASE, THE**   (1937) 62m UNIV bw

Preston Foster (Detective Bill Crane), Carol Hughes (Emily Lou), Barbara Pepper (Miss Hogan), Frank Jenks (Doc Williams), Astrid Allwyn (Brentino), George Meeker (Bolston), Theodore Von Eltz (Robert Westland), Clarence Wilson (Frazee), Russell Hicks (Woodbury), Rollo Lloyd (Sprague), Selmer Jackson (Warden), Thomas Jackson (Strom), Ben Lewis (Havemeyer), Charlie Murphy (Bookkeeper), Eddie Kane (Pedro), Thomas Quinn (Mannie Grant), Arthur Hoyt, Bryant Washburn.

With an innocent man heading for the electric chair detective Foster is called in to solve the case before it's too late. The case itself is a tough one–a girl is killed in a room which has all the windows and doors locked from the inside–but not too tough for Foster. Unfortunately the story is a bit muddled and often forgets to fill the audience in on what evidence Foster is gathering, leaving a chink yards wide in the interest area.

p, Larry Fox, Irving Starr; d, Christy Cabanne; w, Robertson White (based on the novel Headed for a Hearse by Jonathan Latimer); ph, Ira Morgan; md, Charles Previn; art d, Ralph Berger; cos, Vera West; spec eff, John P. Fulton.

Mystery   **(PR:A MPAA:NR)**

WESTMINSTER PASSION PLAY--BEHOLD THE MAN, THE**
(1951, Brit) 75m Film Reports-Companions of the Cross/Philomena bw

Charles P. Carr (Jesus Christ).

Earnest adaptation of the death of Christ from the annual play staged at Westminster Abbey. A religious-cultural event which is a moving experience to everybody who has seen it, with nothing much lost in the filming.

p, Susan Dallison; d, Water Rilla; w, Walter Meyjes, Rilla (based on the play "Ecce Homo" by Meyjes, Charles P. Carr).

Religious Drama   **(PR:A MPAA:NR)**

WESTWARD BOUND**½   (1931) 65m SYN bw

Buffalo Bill, Jr *(Bob Lansing)*, Buddy Roosevelt *(Frank)*, Allene Ray *(Marge Holt)*, Yakima Canutt *(Jim)*, Ben Corbett *(Ben)*, Tom London *(Dick)*, Fern Emmett *(Emma)*, Robert Walker *(Steve)*, Pete Morrison.

A fine program western which is better than most from the period, both in terms of freshness of story and technical achievement. Bill gets mixed up in a publicity incident in a speakeasy and rescues Ray from what turn out to be fake crooks. His senator father sends him out west with chauffeur Roosevelt to accompany him. Once there, however, they run into Ray again and this time save her from a real gang of rustlers.

p, Harry S. Webb, F.E. Douglas; d, Webb; w, Carl Krusada; ph, William Nobles; ed, Fred Bain.

Western   (PR:A   MPAA:NR)

WESTWARD BOUND*   (1944) 54m MON bw

Ken Maynard *(Ken)*, Hoot Gibson *(Hoot)*, Bob Steele *(Bob)*, Betty Miles *(Enid Barrett)*, John Bridges *(Ira Phillips)*, Harry Woods *(Roger Caldwell)*, Karl Hackett *(Henry Wagner)*, Weldon Heyburn *(Albert Lane)*, Hal Price *(Jasper Tuttle)*, Roy Brent *(Will)*, Frank Ellis *(Judd)*, Curley Dresden *(Monte)*, Al Ferguson, Dan White.

Shoddy formula-type entry in which Maynard, Gibson, and Steele play the heroes in a valley where Woods and Hackett are trying to scare the existing ranchers off their land. Production standards were so low that the makers stooped to borrowing footage for the dynamiting climax. An astute viewer (though this is by no means a prerequisite) may catch proof of the slack production techniques in a scene where a stick of dynamite that is supposed to cause an explosion is kept in full view of the camera while the explosion takes place. The stick of dynamite remains intact throughout this shot. (See Trail Blazers Series, Index.)

p&d, Robert Tansey; w, Frances Kavanaugh; ph, Marcel LePicard; ed, John C. Fuller; md, Frank Sanucci.

Western   (PR:A   MPAA:NR)

WESTWARD DESPERADO**   (1961, Jap.) 107m Toho bw
(DOKURITSU GURENTAI NISHI-E)

Yuzo Kayama, Makoto Sato, Kumi Mizuno, Frankie Sakie, Ichiro Nakayama, Akihiko Hirata, Sachio Sakai, Shoji Ooki, Tatsuji Ebara, Yasushi Yamamoto, Akira Kubo, Tadao Nakamaru, Mayumi Tamura, Michiyo Yokoyama, Ichiro Nakatani.

Japanese army resorts to the most daring tactics, many not up to the standards of soldierly ethics, in order to infiltrate Communist China to retrieve the flag of a regiment defeated in battle. A Japanese flag-waver virtually drowning in soy sauce.

d, Kihachi Okamoto; w, Shinichi Sekizawa, Okamoto; ph, Yuzuru Aizawa (Tohoscope).

War   (PR:C   MPAA:NR)

WESTWARD HO*½   (1936) 60m REP bw

John Wayne *(John Wyatt)*, Sheila Mannors *(Mary Gordon)*, Frank McGlynn, Jr *(Jim Wyatt)*, Jack Curtis *(Ballard)*, Yakima Canutt *(Red)*, Bradley Metcalfe *(Young John)*, Hank Bell *(Mark Wyatt)*, Mary McLaren *(Hannah Wyatt)*, Jim Farley *(Lafe Gordon)*, Dickie Jones *(Young Jim)*, Glenn Strange *(Carter)*.

As in many of Wayne's early westerns, he plays a man set on revenge against the crooks responsible for the murder of his parents. While Wayne was still a budding youth, the hoods, lorded over by McGlynn, took the hero's brother as a captive, integrating him into the gang. Wayne heads a vigilante group known as a "The Singing Riders," and as such must be shown warbling a tune, a ridiculous thing to watch as the Duke lip-synchs to a voice obviously not his own.

p, Paul Malvern; d, Robert N. Bradbury; w, Lindsley Parsons, Robert Emmett [Tansey], Harry Friedman (based on the story by Parsons); ph, Archie Stout; ed, Carl Pierson.

Western   (PR:A   MPAA:NR)

WESTWARD HO**   (1942) 56m REP bw

Bob Steele *(Tucson Smith)*, Tom Tyler *(Stony Brooke)*, Rufe Davis *(Lullaby Joslin)*, Evelyn Brent *(Mrs. Healey)*, Donald Curtis *(Rick West)*, Lois Collier *(Anne Henderson)*, Emmett Lynn *(Sheriff)*, John James *(Jimmy Henderson)*, Tom Seidel *(Wayne Henderson)*, Jack Kirk *(Deputy)*, Budd Buster *(Coffee)*, Kenne Duncan, Milton Kibbee, Edmund Cobb, Monte Montague, Al Taylor, Bud Osborne, Jack Montgomery, Horace B. Carpenter, John L. Cason, Jack O'Shea, Ray Jones, Tex Palmer, Curley Dresden.

An oddity for westerns has a woman crook, Brent, as the town banker who doubles as the mastermind behind a gang of thieves. Steele, Tyler, and Davis in their customary roles as the THREE MESQUITEERS bring the gang to bay, but only after Davis has an extremely close brush with death. An action-filled, well-paced effort. (See THE THREE MESQUITEERS Series, Index.)

p, Louis Gray; d, John English; w, Morton Grant, Doris Schroeder (based on the story by Grant from characters created by William Colt MacDonald); ph, Reggie Lanning; ed, William Thompson; art d, Russell Kimball.

Western   (PR:A   MPAA:NR)

WESTWARD HO THE WAGONS!**   (1956) 86m Disney/BV c

Fess Parker *(John "Doc" Grayson)*, Kathleen Crowley *(Laura Thompson)*, Jeff York *(Hank Breckenridge)*, David Stollery *(Dan Thompson)*, Sebastian Cabot *(Bissonette)*, George Reeves *(James Stephen)*, Doreen Tracey *(Bobo Stephen)*, Barbara Woodell *(Mrs. Stephen)*, John War Eagle *(Wolf's Brother)*, Cubby O'Brien *(Jerry Stephen)*, Tommy Cole *(Jim Stephen)*, Leslie Bradley *(Spencer Armitage)*, Morgan Woodward *("Obie" Foster)*, Iron Eyes Cody *(Many Stars)*, Anthony Numkena *(Little Thunder)*, Karen Pendleton *(Myra Thompson)*, Jane Liddell *(Ruth Benjamin)*, Jon Locke *(Ed Benjamin)*, Brand Stirling *(Tom Foster)*.

Done in the truest of Disney fashion in that it promotes goodwill and provides plenty of scenic and light atmosphere, yet never excites much interest in terms of story to sink one's teeth into. Parker plays a scout on a wagon train bound for Oregon, whose biggest fear is an Indian attack. After surviving one such, in which the wagoners came out on top by staging a horse stampede, they come into contact with another, more friendly tribe. A peaceful relationship is cemented when the chief's son injures himself, with Parker able to administer the proper aid to save his life, doing it in a diplomatic manner to make the tribal medicine man appear as if he had part in the undertaking. Though sure to make many viewers feel good in its attitudes of human understanding, something is missing. Yakima Canutt, villain and stuntman in a countless number of westerns, served as the second unit director, staging the attack sequences. Songs include: "John Colter," "Westward Ho the Wagons!" (George Bruns, Tom Blackburn), "Pioneer's Prayer" (Paul J. Smith, Gil George), "Wringle Wrangle" (Stan Jones), "I'm Lonely My Darling" (Bruns, Fess Parker).

p, Bill Walsh; d, William Beaudine; w, Tom Blackburn (based on the novel by Mary Jane Carr); ph, Charles Boyle (CinemaScope, Technicolor); m, George Bruns; ed, Cotton Warburton; art d, Marvin Aubrey Davis; set d, Emile Kuri, Bertram Granger; cos, Chuck Keehne, Gertrude Casey; makeup, David Newell.

Western   (PR:A   MPAA:NR)

WESTWARD PASSAGE**½   (1932) 72m RKO-Pathe/RAD bw

Ann Harding *(Olivia Van Tyne)*, Laurence Olivier *(Nick Allen)*, ZaSu Pitts *(Mrs. Truesdale)*, Irving Pichel *(Harry Lenman)*, Juliette Compton *(Henrielle)*, Irene Purcell *(Diane Van Tyne)*, Emmett King *(Mr. Ottendorf)*, Florence Roberts *(Mrs. Ottendorf)*, Ethel Griffies *(Lady Caverly)*, Bonita Granville *(Little Olivia)*, Don Alvarado *(The Count)*, Florence Lake *(Elmer's Wife)*, Edgar Kennedy *(Elmer)*, Herman Bing *(The Dutchman)*, Julie Haydon *(Bridesmaid)*, Joyce Compton *(Girl)*, Nance O'Neil *(Mrs. Van Tyne)*, Lee Phelps *(Bartender)*.

A lightweight romance which pairs Harding and Olivier as two young lovebirds. Olivier, living at the poverty line, is a struggling author given to nasty displays of anger. When he's with Harding, however, his love for her is a sure remedy. Although they can barely support themselves, Harding and Olivier marry. Shortly thereafter Harding presents her husband with news that she's in a family way. At first Olivier is charmed by his new daughter, but as she grows older and more mischievous (she likes to tie ribbons on Olivier's typewriter) his patience wears thin. The last straw comes when she spills tea all over Olivier's latest manuscript. He decides to do his writing away from home, leading to the break-up of their marriage. Harding sues for divorce and rebounds by marrying Pichel, a staid businessman who can offer financial security and who will willingly adopt Harding's daughter. Years later Harding and Olivier meet again in Europe, both now enjoying a more secure and luxurious life. Olivier has finally become the successful writer he dreamed of being. Harding, however, must soon return to the States by boat. As a surprise, Olivier gets himself a ticket on the same ship, and the two travel together. The love they once held for each other again fills their hearts. When they reach land they are given a chance to continue their romance. Harding's husband is too busy to meet her at the boat so Olivier offers to escort her. They decide to stop at an inn run by Pitts–the same inn where they stayed when they were first married. Their love is fully renewed and Harding and Oliver vow to remain together. Although WESTWARD PASSAGE sometimes comes across as overly theatrical (especially in Harding's performance) it still manages to engage and entertain much in the same way as the works of Noel Coward, whose "Private Lives" it resembles.

p, Harry Joe Brown; d, Robert Milton; w, Bradley King, Humphrey King (based on the novel by Margaret Ayer Barnes); ph, Lucien Andriot; ed, Charles Craft; md, Mac Steiner; art d, Carroll Clark; cos, Margaret Pemberton, Josette De Lima.

Romance   (PR:A   MPAA:NR)

WESTWARD THE WOMEN*** (1951) 116m MGM bw

Robert Taylor (Buck Wyatt), Denise Darcel (Fifi Danon), Hope Emerson (Patience Hawley), John McIntire (Roy Whitman), Julie Bishop (Laurie Smith), Beverly Dennis (Rose Meyers), Marilyn Erskine (Jean Johnson), Lenore Lonergan (Margaret O'Malley), Renata Vanni (Mrs. Moroni), Henry Nakamura (Ito), Guido Martufi (Antonio Moroni), Bruce Crowling ("Cat"), Frankie Darro, George Chandler.

The novel idea of having a wagon train full of woman trek across the rugged West from Chicago to sunny California makes for a very entertaining vehicle. With an old pro like Wellman at the helm, an evenly paced plot develops into a hard-hitting climax, with eccentricities unusual for a western spliced in along the way. Taylor plays a scout escorting 150 women from Chicago to California to help populate a verdant valley owned by McIntire. Hazards along the way include the men hired to accompany the women who are unable to control their passions and attack the women at every opportunity. These helpers dwindle as Taylor ruthlessly punishes them, leaving only the women and him to fight off Indian attacks, rough weather, and the harshness of the terrain. One woman even delivers a baby during the trip. By the end of the journey the women prove every bit as rugged as men, a slick reversal of the image that has been a part of western fare since the beginning of the genre.

p, Dore Schary; d, William A. Wellman; w, Charles Schnee (based on the story by Frank Capra); ph, William C. Mellor; m, Jeff Alexander; ed, James E. Newcom; art d, Cedric Gibbons, Daniel B. Cathcart; set d, Edwin B. Willis, Ralph S. Hurst; cos, Walter Plunkett; m/l, "To the West, To the West!" Alexander.

Western (PR:A MPAA:NR)

WESTWARD TRAIL, THE* (1948) 56m PRC/EL bw

Eddie Dean (Eddie), Roscoe Ates (Soapy), Phyllis Planchard (Ann), Eileen Hardin (Mrs. Benson), Steve Drake (Tom), Bob Duncan (Larson), Carl Mathews (art), Lee Morgan (Sheriff), Bob Woodward (Stage Driver), Budd Buster (Benson), Charles "Slim" Whitaker (Bartender), Frank Ellis (Taggart), Andy Parker and The Plainsmen, Copper the Horse.

Drab sagebrusher that has singing cowboy Dean going undercover to help Planchard, as well as several others, keep their ranches from falling into the hands of Duncan. Dean sings several songs which don't help matters much, including "When Shorty Plays the Schottische."

p, Jerry Thomas; d, Ray Taylor; w, Robert Alan Miller; ph, Ernie Miller; m, Walter Greene; ed, Hugh Winn; m/l, Pete Gates, Hal Blair, Eddie Dean.

Western (PR:A MPAA:NR)

WESTWORLD***½ (1973) 91m MGM c

Yul Brynner (Gunslinger), Richard Benjamin (Peter Martin), James Brolin (John Blane), Norman Bartold (Medieval Queen), Dick Van Patten (Banker), Linda Scott (Arlette), Steve Franken (Technician), Michael Mikler (Black Knight), Terry Wilson (Sheriff), Majel Barrett (Miss Carrie), Anne Randall (Servant Girl), Julie Marcus (Girl in Dungeon), Sharyn Wynters (Apache Girl), Anne Bellamy (Middle-aged Woman), Chris Holter (Stewardess), Charles Seel (Bellhop), Wade Crosby (Bartender), Nora Marlowe (Hostess), Will J. White, Ben Young, Tom Falk (Workmen), Orville Sherman, Lindsay Workman, Lauren Gilbert, Davis Roberts, Howard Platt (Supervisors), Jared Martin, Richard Roat, Kenneth Washington, Robert Patten, David Frank, Kip King, David Man, Larry Delaney (Technicians), Lin Henson (Ticket Girl).

The idea of having robots become lost to the control of their creations was hardly a new theme when WESTWORLD was made, yet no earlier film seemed to touch upon an area so close to the movie entertainment business itself. The title refers to a futuristic Disney-type fantasy land where the over-civilized denizens of the modern world have a chance to actually live their fantasies. In this case the Old West, where robots are supplied with characteristics of western figures designed to please and entertain the human visitors. Benjamin and Brolin are two businessman who come to WESTWORLD to live out their fantasies of classic western heroes, with Brynner as the robot Benjamin kills in a saloon fight. Suddenly everything goes haywire, with the robots turning about and stalking the visitors. Brynner guns down Brolin, then goes on a chase after Benjamin that exceeds the boundaries of the fantasy world. An extremely chilling film that shocks the viewer, WESTWORLD could very easily be correlated to the everyday usage of the cinema, a place where fantasies are lived out without having one's security destroyed. As a robot, Brynner is very good, his austere presence and unflinching intent making him seem indestructible. The film grossed a healthy $3.4 million in the U.S. and Canada and was the last release from MGM before it dissolved its releasing company. Ten minutes have been deleted from the original footage to allow WESTWORLD's present PG rating instead of its original R. The gardens of movie comedian Harold Lloyd's estate were used for some of the amusement park sequences. Followed by sequel: FUTUREWORLD (1976).

p, Paul N. Lazarus III; d&w, Michael Crichton; ph, Gene Polito (Panavision, Metrocolor); m, Fred Karlin; ed, David Bretherton; art d, Herman Blumenthal; set d, John Austin; spec eff, Charles Schulthies.

Fantasy Cas. (PR:C MPAA:PG)

WET PARADE, THE**½ (1932) 120m MGM bw

Dorothy Jordan (Maggie May), Lewis Stone (Col. Roger Chilcote), Neil Hamilton (Roger Chilcote, Jr.), Emma Dunn (Mrs. Chilcote), Frederick Burton (Judge Brandon), Reginald Barlow (Maj. Randolph), John Larkin (Moses), Gertrude Howard (Angeline), Robert Young (Kip Tarleton), Walter Huston (Pop Tarleton), Jimmy Durante (Abe Schilling), Wallace Ford (Jerry Tyler), Myrna Loy (Eileen Pinchon), Joan Marsh (Evelyn Fessenden), John Miljan (Maj. Doleshal), Clarence Muse (Taylor Tibbs), Clara Blandick (Mrs. Tarleton), Forrester Harvey (Mr. Fortesque), John Beck (Mr. Garrison), Ben Alexander (Dick), Cecil Cunningham (Mrs. Twombey).

A lengthy expose based on an Upton Sinclair novel which shows the evils both of drinking and the Prohibition law. Divided into two parts–"The Parade in the South" and "The Parade in the North"–the film centers on two families. The Northern family is the Tarletons, headed by Huston a hard drinker who spends his time in New York bars. The Southern clan, the Chilcotes, is headed by the gentlemanly Stone, who drinks as much as Huston and runs a bootlegging operation. Stone is married to Dunn and is the father of two: Hamilton, who plans to go to New York and become a writer, and Jordan, a beautiful and decent daughter. Stone downs some bad hootch, is sent into a maddening depression, and slits his throat while in a pigsty. Meanwhile, up North, Huston has been tipping the bottle once too often. When his wife Blandick angrily breaks a bottle of expensive liquor, Huston kills her and is sent to prison for life. His son, Young, later joins the FBI and with his partner, Durante, tracks down a gang of bootleggers. Before long Young and Jordan have fallen in love and married. Jordan's brother Hamilton has also married, becoming a successful playwright in New York and wedding Loy. Booze takes its toll on Hamilton who, like his father, pays no attention to Prohibition. After downing an excess of rotgut liquor Hamilton goes blind and loses the less-than-faithful Loy. Young and Durante continue their pursuit of the lawbreakers and their illegal stills. They get close but before they can foil the operation Young is kidnaped. Durante locates his partner and in the ensuing battle is killed trying to save Young's life. Oddly, THE WET PARADE never really takes a stand. It shows the evils of drinking–Huston and Stone both suffer, as do their families–but it also proves the ineffectiveness of Prohibition. At one point, the agents complain that the law is counter-productive, but they must do their job and continue their crackdown. It's not exceptionally well done, but some fine performances (Durante is a standout who, with his humor, adds some much-needed life to the production) and its honest treatment of an explosive issue make it worthwhile. The film, which begins in 1916, devotes much of its screen time to the historical issues of the day, including footage of the presidential campaign between Woodrow Wilson and Charles Evans Hughes and coverage of WW I. Even more time, however, is spent on the process of making bootleg mash–from the cleaning and labeling of the bottles to shipping.

p, Hunt Stromberg; d, Victor Fleming; w, John Lee Mahin (based on the novel by Upton Sinclair); ph, George Barnes; m, Dr. William Axt; ed, Anne Bauchens; md, Oscar Radin; art d, Cedric Gibbons.

Drama (PR:C MPAA:NR)

WETBACKS** (1956) 120 BAN c

Lloyd Bridges (Jim Benson), Nancy Gates (Sally Parker), Barton MacLane (Karl Shanks), John Hoyt (Steve Bodine), Harold Peary (Juan Ortega), Nacho Galindo (Alphonse), Robert Keys (Reeser), David Colmans (Pedro), Jose Gonzales Gonzales (Wetback), Louis Jean Heydt (Coast Guard Commander), Scott Douglas (Immigration Officer), Wally Cassell (Coast Guard Lieutenant), Richard Powers [Tom Keene] (Highway Patrol Inspector), Salvador Baguez (Mexican Policeman).

Bridges plays the owner of a fishing boat that is the center of attraction for a couple of smugglers who want to use it to ship illegal immigrants across the Mexican border. Members of the U.S. Immigration Department, in the guise of Gates and MacLane, are also interested in Bridges to help them nab Hoyt and Peary. Script badly needs reworking, relying t oo much on old tricks, such as the chase across the water, to make it work. Bridges performs in the manner he is most remembered for, the confident yet careful adventurer of the television series "Sea Hunt."

p&d, Hank McCune; w, Pete LaRoche; ph, Brydon Baker (Eastmancolor); m, Les Baxter; ed, Ronald V. Ashcroft.

Adventure/Drama (PR:A MPAA:NR)

WE'VE NEVER BEEN LICKED*** (1943) 103m UNIV bw (AKA: FIGHTING COMMAND)

Richard Quine (Brad Craig), Anne Gwynne (Nina Lambert), Martha O'Driscoll (Deedee Dunham), Noah Beery, Jr. (Cyanide Jenkins), Edgar Barrier (Nishikawa), William Frawley (Fat Man), Harry Davenport (Pop Lambert), Bob 'Robert' Mitchum (Panhandle Mitchell), Samuel S. Hines (Col. Jason Craig), Moroni Olsen (Col. J. Armstrong), Allen Jung (Kubo), Bill Stern (Himself), George Putnam (Announcer), Malcolm McTaggart (Chip Goodwin), William Blees, Paul Dubov, David Street, Dick Chandlee, Michael Moore, Danny Jackson, Roger Daniel, Dick Morris, Herbert Gunn,

Henry Rogers, John Forrest, William Lechner, Bob Lowell, Michael Towne, Bill Nash, Jack Ray, Ward Wood, Jack Edwards, Jr. (Students), Cliff Robertson (Adams), Gordon Wynne (Hank James), Bill Walker (Shotgun), Kenneth MacDonald (Captain), Mantan Moreland (Willie), Frank Tang (Yoshida), John Frazer (Flight Commander), Henry Hall (Conductor), Phil Warren (Soldier), Kendall Bryson (Deck Officer), Franco Corsaro (Italian Mentor), Walter Bonn (German Mentor), Beal Fong (Japanese Mentor), Alfredo DeSa (Fortunio Tavares), Bruce Wong (Japanese Messenger), Alex Havier (Japanese Sniper), Paul Langton (Naval Officer), Richard Gunn (Officer), Students of the Texas State College for Women (Girls), Big Willie Zapalec (Football Player), William Kuhl, Sammy McKim, John James, Dean Benton, Don McGill.

It's the Texas Aggies versus the Japs in this rah-rah piece of wartime silliness. Quine is a student at Texas A&M in the prewar days whose sympathies toward the Japanese cause and friendliness toward Japanese students at the school make him an outcast among the other students. Accused of stealing the secret formula for a poison gas antidote from a professor and turning it over to spymaster Frawley, Quine is expelled. He goes to Japan with his new friends, and when war is declared he begins making propaganda broadcasts on their behalf. He is not really a traitor, though. Having long plotted to ingratiate himself with the Japanese in order to spy for the U.S., he uses his position to learn the Japanese war plans. He manages to tip the Americans off to the impending invasion of the Solomons, and later talks his way onto a Japanese bomber on its way to bomb the American aircraft carrier where most of his old college buddies are now aviators. On the way, though, he overpowers the crew, and, taking over the controls, he leads his old chums back to the Japanese carrier flagship and dives in, kamikaze style, to his death. The American planes finish off the ship, ending the Japanese threat. A simplistic propaganda message was all audiences demanded of their wartime film fare, and this film certainly fit the bill, even tossing in such items as Aggie fight songs ("Spirit of Aggieland," "Aggie War Hymn," "I'd Rather Be a Texas Aggie"), football games, and a romance between Gwynne and Quine. Mitchum appears as one of Quine's fellow students in one of seventeen (!) films he made that year. Quine, a former child actor, made his adult debut here, but soon abandoned acting for directing, helming such films as THE SOLID GOLD CADILLAC (1956), BELL, BOOK, AND CANDLE (1958), and MY SISTER EILEEN (1955). Nothing inspired here in any department, but more than adequate for the time.

p, Walter Wanger; d, John Rawlins; w, Norman Reilly Raine, Nick Grinde (based on a story by Raine); ph, Milton Krasner; m, Frank Skinner; ed, Phil Cahn; md, Charles Previn; art d, John B. Goodman, Alexander Golitzen; m/l, "Me for You, Forever," Harry Revel, Paul Francis Webster; tech adv, Col. J.K. Boles, Lt. Comdr. John S. Thach.

War Drama   **(PR:A   MPAA:NR)**

WHALE OF A TALE, A**   (1977) 90m Luckris c

William Shatner, Marty Allen, Abby Dalton, Andy Devine, Richard Arlen, Scott Kolden.

A killer whale at Marine Land is trained to perform in the main tank by an eager young tyke. Scarcely a whale of a tale, as the title promises, but some of the whale's antics border on the fantastic.

p&d, Ewing M. Brown; w, (uncredited); m, Jonathan Cain.

Drama   **Cas.**   **(PR:AAA   MPAA:G)**

WHALERS, THE**½   (1942, Swed.) 79m A.B. Svenski Film/Scandia
                                                     bw (VALFANGARE)

Allan Bohlin (Allan Blom), Eric Bergland (Blom, Sr.), Hank Aabel (Jensen, Sr.), Tutia Rolf (Sonja), Titus Vihe-Mueller (Jensen, Jr.), Arthur Rolen (Nisse), Georg Loekkeberg (Norse Lieutenant), Lilieba Bouchette (Solveig), Johann Hange (The Minister), Karl Holter (Captain S.S. Kosmos II), Oscar Egede-Nissen (Olav Lykke), Arthur Barking (Big Knut), Gunnar Hoeglund (Little Knut), Arthur Fischer (Alfred), Gunnar Sjoeberg (Tore), Carl-Gunnar Wingard (Cook), Einar Fagstad (Steward).

Playboy Bohlin turns into just another one of the boys as he hunts whales off the icy Arctic shores, spending his free time competing with the whaler boat captain for the affections of good looking Rolf. The incredible footage of the whale hunting, as well as the Arctic sceneray, make this odd Swedish production well worth seeing as the softie transforms into a he-man. (In Swedish and Norwegian; English sub-titles.)

d, Anders Henrikson; w, Weyler Hildebrand (based on the story by Tancred Ibsen).

Adventure/Drama   **(PR:A   MPAA:NR)**

WHARF ANGEL*½   (1934) 65m PAR bw

Victor McLaglen (Turk), Dorothy Dell (Toy), Preston Foster (Como), Alison Skipworth (Mother Bright, Saloonkeeper), David Landau (Moore), John Rogers (Goliath), Mischa Auer (Sadik), Alfred Delcambre (Steve), James Burke (Brooklyn Jack), Frank Sheridan (The Skipper), Don Wilson (Slim), John Northpole (Vasil), Max Wagner, Frank Rice, Russell Powell, Joseph

Sauers [Sawyer], A.S. Byron, Jill Dennett, Alice Lake, Miami Alvarez, Florence Dudley, Marie Green, Charles Brinley, Al Hill, Frederik Vogeding, Ivan Linow, Jack Cheatham, Charles McAvoy.

Bland story in which streetwalker Dell falls for fugitive Foster, deciding to reform in the name of love. An interesting subtheme never fully developed is the friendship that erupts between Foster and McLaglen, the latter as the captain of the tramp steamer used to hide the crook, who also has desires for Dell. All of which is worked out in the end, which seems to never come.

d, William Cameron Menzies, George Somnes; w, Samuel Hoffenstein, Frank Partos, Stephen Morehouse Avery (based on the story by Frederick Schlick); ph, Victor Milner.

Drama   **(PR:A   MPAA:NR)**

WHAT!**   (1965, Fr./Brit./Ital.) 90m
Francinor-PIP-Vox-Leone/Futuramic c (LA FRUSTA E IL CORPO: LE CORPS ET LE FOUET; AKA: NIGHT IS THE PHANTOM)

Daliah Lavi (Nevenka), Christopher Lee (Kurt Menliff), Tony Kendall [L. Stella] (Christian Menliff), Isli Oberon (Katia), Harriet White (Giorgia), Dean Ardow (Count Vladimir), Alan Collins [Luciano Pigozzi] (Manservant), Jacques Herlin (Priest).

This picture stirred quite a controversy when first released. Italy refused to have it shown within its borders, while just about every place else required that the shearing scissors go to work. A horror flick that relies almost totally on eerie atmosphere, including the shady personalities of Lee and Lavi. Lee plays the son of a wealthy count, who forces him to flee when a servant girl commits suicide after being seduced by the young man. When good son Kendall is about to marry Lavi, he asks for Lee to return to the castle. Lee immediately tries to seduce his brother's new wife, going so far as to whip her when he discovers her alone on the beach. After Lee is murdered, and several other bodies pop up, the locals suspect supernatural forces are at work, namely that Lee has continued with his terrorizing behavior even after death. A shock ending discloses that Lavi was really the person responsible for all the violence. Just about everyone who worked on this production did so under a pseudonym, which may be some indication of censorship problems and the resulting mutilation of the original.

p, Richard G. Yates; d, John M. Old [Mario Bava]; w, Julian Berry [Ernesto Gastaldi], Robert Hugo [Ugo Guerra], Martin Hardy [Luciano Martino]; ph, David Hamilton [Ubaldo Terzano] (Technicolor); m, Jim Murphy [Carlo Rustichelli]; ed, Bob King; art d, Dick Grey [Ottavio Scotti]; cos, Peg Fax.

Horror   **(PR:O   MPAA:NR)**

WHAT?   (SEE: CHE? 1973, Ital./Fr./Ger.)

WHAT A BLONDE*½   (1945) 71m RKO bw

Leon Errol (Fowler), Richard Lane (Pomeroy, Butler), Michael St. Angel (Andrew), Elaine Riley (Cynthia), Veda Ann Borg (Pat), Lydia Bilbrook (Mrs. Fowler), Clarence Kolb (Mr. Dafoe), Ann Shoemaker (Mrs. Dafoe), Chef Milani (Gugliemi), Emory Parnell (McPherson), Larry Wheat (Watson), Dorothy Vaughan (Annie), Jason Robards Sr (Redmond).

Lingerie tycoon Errol has a host of showgirls move into his mansion when he finds that he can't make do with his allotted number of gas rationing coupons. In this way he'll get more coupons from the government under the "share the ride" incentive, but its really just an excuse to create an absurd situation and the consequent laughs. It comes off as pretty forced and seldom is funny.

p, Ben Stoloff; d, Leslie Goodwins; w, Charles E. Roberts (based on the story by Oscar Brodney); ph, J. Roy Hunt; m, Leigh Harline; Edward W. Williams; md, C. Bakaleinikoff; art d, Albert S. D'Agostino, Lucius Croxton; cos, Edward Stevenson.

Comedy   **(PR:A   MPAA:NR)**

WHAT A CARRY ON!*   (1949, Brit.) 94m Film Studios
                                                     Manchester/Mancunian bw

Jimmy Jewell (Jimmy Jervis), Ben Warriss (Ben Watts), Josef Locke (Sgt. Locke), Terry Randall (Cpl. Joan Watts), Anthony Pendrell (Capt. Derek Whitfield), Kitty Blewett (Maid), Eva Eacott (Daisybell).

Poor service comedy has Jewell and Warriss joining the army and getting into all sorts of mischief. Clumsily done, with radio personalities Jewell and Warriss exhibiting little talent for acting, and certainly none for the slapstick this one is loaded with.

p&d, John E. Blakeley; w, Anthony Toner; ph, Ernest Palmer.

Comedy   **(PR:A   MPAA:NR)**

WHAT A CARVE UP!**   (1962, Brit.) 87m New World/EM bw (AKA:
                                                     NO PLACE LIKE HOMICIDE)

Kenneth Connor (Ernie Broughton), Sidney James (Syd Butler), Shirley Eaton (Linda Dickson), Donald Pleasence (Everette Sloane, Solicitor),

Dennis Price *(Guy Broughton)*, Michael Gough *(Fisk, Butler)*, Valerie Taylor *(Janet Broughton)*, Michael Gwynn *(Malcolm Broughton)*, Esma Cannon *(Aunt Emily)*, Philip O'Flynn *(Arkwright/Gabriel Broughton)*, Timothy Bateson *(Porter)*, Frederick Piper *(Hearse Driver)*, Adam Faith *(Himself)*.

An uneven spoof in which the eccentric members of a rich man's family are gathered together in an eerie-looking mansion for the reading of his will. These include Connor, a proofreader with an overactive imagination acquired from his hours of reading cheap horror novels. In this case, his fears turn out to be justified when several people turn up dead, the murderer being none other than the supposed dead man, who feigned death to get a laugh at the rest of the family. The fast pace keeps the material and indifferent performances from becoming too bogged down.

p, Robert S. Baker, Monty Berman; d, Pat Jackson; w, Ray Cooney, Tony Hilton (based on the novel *The Ghoul* by Frank King); ph, Berman; m, Muir Mathieson; ed, Gordon Pilkington; art d, Ivan King; cos, Jean Fairlie; makeup, Alex Garfath.

Comedy **(PR:A MPAA:NR)**

WHAT A CHASSIS! (SEE: LA BELLE AMERICAINE, 1961, Fr.)

WHAT A CRAZY WORLD*½ (1963, Brit.) 88m Capricorn/WB-Pathe bw

Joe Brown *(Alf Hitchens)*, Susan Maughan *(Marilyn)*, Marty Wilde *(Herbie Shadbolt)*, Harry H. Corbett *(Sam Hitchens)*, Avis Bunnage *(Mary Hitchens)*, Michael Ripper *(Common Man)*, Grazina Frame *(Doris Hitchens)*, Monty Landis *(Solly Gold)*, Michael Goodman *(Joey Hitchens)*, Larry Dann *(Chas)*, Brian Cronin *(Harry)*, Barry Bethel *(Dave)*, David Nott *(Lenny)*, Alan Klein *(Jervis)*, Fanny Carby *(Dolly)*, Bill Fraser *(Milligan)*, Freddie and The Dreamers, The Bruvvers, The Happy Wanderers, Tricky Dicky.

The atmosphere of East Side London filled with rough humor and gutsy vitality is created for the exposure of a barrage of early 1960s London Rockers. Brown is a kid from a working class family who is expected to go out and find a job and continue in the same manner as the rest of his family. Instead he decides that music is the path for him, so he sets out trying to peddle a song. In this way he hopes to avoid the despair of his forebears. Unfortunately, the unfolding is done in a form as predictable as that of the usual poor-boy-seeking-independence story.

p&d, Michael Carreras; w, Alan Klein, Carreras (based on the play by Klein); ph, Otto Heller; ed, Max Benedict; m/l, Klein.

Musical/Drama **(PR:A MPAA:NR)**

WHAT A LIFE** (1939) 75m PAR bw

Jackie Cooper *(Henry Aldrich)*, Betty Field *(Barbara Pearson)*, John Howard *(Mr. Nelson)*, Janice Logan *(Miss Shea, Secretary)*, Vaughan Glaser *(Mr. J.C. Bradley, Principal)*, Lionel Stander *(Frank Ferguson, Detective)*, Hedda Hopper *(Mrs. Aldrich)*, James Corner *(George Bigelow)*, Dorothy Stickney *(Miss Wheeler)*, Kathleen Lockhart *(Miss Pike)*, Lucien Littlefield *(Mr. Patterson)*, Sidney Miller *(Pinkie Peters)*, Andrew Tombes *(Prof. Abernathy)*, George Guhl *(Janitor)*, Arthur Aylesworth *(MacGowan, Pawnbroker)*, Wilda Bennett *(Miss Doolittle)*, Bennie Bartlett *(Butch Williams)*, Kay Stewart *(Marjorie, Drum Majorette)*, Leonard Sues *(Harold)*, Eddie Brian *(Don Bray)*, Janet Waldo *(Gwen)*, Betty McLaughlin *(Jessie)*, Douglas Fahy *(Tony Milligan)*, Roberta Smith *(Gertie)*, Nora Cecil *(Miss Eggleston)*.

Enjoyable and somewhat interesting look at the formative years of high school has Cooper as the lad struggling with grades and his natural inclination to get into hot water. The added pressure of a dad who expects his son to continue in the vein of his own fine performance at Princeton doesn't make things any easier for Cooper. The youth is finally given a chance to prove what he is made of and comes out with shining colors. It was said during the filming of this picture that the writing team of Wilder and Brackett had little respect for producer-director Reed. Consequently, when they saw which way Reed was taking the film, they tried to get their names removed from the credits, without success. Ironically, WHAT A LIFE took off and developed into the popular Henry Aldrich series which, never to become the fabulous grosser of the somewhat similarly themed Andy Hardy pictures, still remains to this day a nostalgic touchstone for millions of moviegoers. (See HENRY ALDRICH series, Index.)

p&d, Jay Theodore Reed; w, Charles Brackett, Billy Wilder (based on the play by Clifford Goldsmith); ph, Victor Milner; ed, William Shea; art d, Hans Dreier, Earl Hedrick.

Comedy/Drama **(PR:A MPAA:NR)**

WHAT A MAN*½ (1930) 72m Sono-Art-Worldwide bw (GB: THE GENTLEMAN CHAUFFEUR)

Reginald Denny *(Wade Rawlins)*, Miriam Seegar *(Eileen Kilbourne)*, Harvey Clark *(Mr. Kilbourne)*, Lucile Ward *(Mrs. Kilbourne)*, Carlyle Moore *(Kane Kilbourne)*, Anita Louise *(Marion Kilbourne)*, Norma Drew *(Elsie Thayer)*, Christiane Yves *(Marquise de la Fresne)*, Greta Granstedt *(Hanna, Maid)*, Charles Coleman *(William, English Butler)*.

Tepid romance between the family chauffeur, really a decorated war hero who took up the job to avoid a bootlegging career, and one of the young misses of the family. There is never doubt from the opening sequence that the two will get together once it is revealed that the driver is actually acceptable marrying material.

d, George J. Crone; w, Harvey H. Gates, A.A. Kline (based on the novel *The Dark Chapter* by E.J. Rath); ph, Arthur Todd; ed, Harry Chandlee.

Drama **(PR:A MPAA:NR)**

WHAT A MAN!** (1937, Brit.) 74m Independent Films-Phoenix/BL bw

Sydney Howard *(Samuel Pennyfeather)*, Vera Pearce *(Emily Pennyfeather)*, Ivor Barnard *(Mayor)*, Jenny Laird *(Daisy Pennyfeather)*, Frederick Bradshaw *(Walter Walkeling)*, H.F. Maltby *(Sgt. Bull)*, John Singer *(Harold Bull)*, Robert Adair *(Lord Bromwich)*, Frank Cochrane *(Simpkins)*, Sybil Grove, Alfred Wellesley, Francesca Bahrle.

Howard is a photographer given some village funds for safekeeping. He stashes the bundle in an old dresser, which his unknowing wife sells to a junk dealer. While he searches for the items, he discovers an old charter that helps save the village from being spoiled by developers. Mediocre entertainment that Howard valiantly tries to make better.

p, Hugh Perceval; d, Edmond T. Greville; w, Basil Mason, Jack Marks (based on a story by Mason); ph, Ernest Palmer.

Comedy **(PR:A MPAA:NR)**

WHAT A MAN, 1941 (SEE: NEVER GIVE A SUCKER AN EVEN BREAK, 1941)

WHAT A MAN!** (1944) 67m MON bw

Johnny Downs *(Henry Burrows)*, Wanda McKay *(Jean Rankin)*, Robert Kent *(Steve Jackson)*, Etta McDaniel *(Beulah)*, Harry Holman *(Prewitt)*, Lillian Bronson *(Constance)*, Wheeler Oakman *(Detective)*, John Ince *(Doctor)*, I. Stanford Jolley *(Parsons)*, Jack Gardner *(Boyle)*, Betty Sinclair, Dick Rush, Jim Farley, Henry Hull, Ralph Cathey.

Downs plays an office clerk who has an unexpected visitor to his apartment in McKay, the lady feigning illness to extend her stay until she feels it's safe to show her face on the street again and not get picked up by the police. Downs doesn't seem to mind much and takes the girl to the altar once the coast is clear. Well-conceived and acted piece of entertainment.

p, Barney A. Sarecky; d, William Beaudine; w, William X. Crowley, Beryl Sachs; ph, Marcel LePicard; ed, Carl Himm; md, Edward J. Kay; art d, David Milton.

Drama **(PR:A MPAA:NR)**

WHAT A NIGHT!* (1931, Brit.) 58m BIP/FN-Pathe bw

Leslie Fuller *(Bill Grimshaw)*, Molly Lamont *(Nora Livingstone)*, Frank Stanmore *(Mr. Livingstone)*, Charles Paton *(Grindle)*, Syd Courtenay *(Mr. Merry)*, Ernest Fuller *(Landlord)*, Molly Hamley-Clifford *(Landlady)*, Olivette *(Rose)*, Lola Harvey.

Broad slapstick has Fuller a traveling salesman who stops at an allegedly haunted inn for the night and ends up nabbing a burglar. Not worth losing any sleep over.

p&d, Monty Vanks; w, Syd Courtenay, Lola Harvey.

Comedy **(PR:A MPAA:NR)**

WHAT A WAY TO GO*½ (1964) 111m FOX c

Shirley MacLaine *(Louisa)*, Paul Newman *(Larry Flint)*, Robert Mitchum *(Rod Anderson)*, Dean Martin *(Leonard Crawley)*, Gene Kelly *(Jerry Benson)*, Bob Cummings *(Dr. Stephanson)*, Dick Van Dyke *(Edgar Hopper)*, Reginald Gardiner *(Painter)*, Margaret Dumont *(Mrs. Foster)*, Roy Gordon *(Minister)*, Phil Arnold *(Publicity and Press Agent)*, Dick Wilson *(Driscoll)*, Lou Nova *(Tentino)*, Fifi D'Orsay *(Baroness)*, Maurice Marsac *(Rene)*, Wally Vernon *(Agent)*, Jane Wald *(Polly)*, Lenny Kent *(Hollywood Lawyer)*, Sid Gould *(Movie Executive)*, Paula Lauc *(Movie Executive's Girl)*, Army Archerd *(TV Announcer)*, Tracy Butler *(Movie Star)*, Anton Arnold *(Mr. Foster)*, Burt Mustin *(Crawleyville Lawyer)*, Pamelyn Ferdin *(Geraldine Crawley at Age 4)*, Jeff Fithian *(Jonathan Crawley at Age 5)*, Billy Corcoran *(Leonard Crawley at Age 7)*, Helen F. Winston *(Doris)*, Jack Greening *(Chester)*, Queenie Leonard *(Lady Kensington)*, Tom Conway *(Lord Kensington)*, Barbara Bouchet *(Girl on Plane)*, Marjorie Bennett *(Mrs. Freeman)*, Milton Frome *(Lawyer)*, Anthony Eustrel *(Willard)*, Marcel Hillaire *(French Lawyer)*, Eugene Borden *(Neighbor)*, Chris Connelly *(Ned)*, Lynn Borden, Cleo Ronson, Pat O'Moore, Justin Smith.

Former press agent Arthur Jacobs always felt that "bigger was better" so for this, his first venture into film producing, he decided to do a huge comedy, filled with stars, surrounded by huge sets and colorful costumes, and it all went to prove that bigger was worse. MacLaine is a many-times widow who it telling her story to her psychiatrist, Cummings (who must have thought this was a comedy because he used the billing of "Bob" rather than "Robert," which he reserved for dramas). The tale she spins is unbelievable to the analyst. She has offered her huge $200 million fortune to the IRS because she feels the moolah is cursed. They have declined the cash thinking she's nuts and that accepting it would cause a huge brouhaha. The story spins back to when MacLaine, daughter of Dumont, a money-mad mother, turns down wealthy Martin and marries Van Dyke, a poor shopkeeper. Martin is incensed and pokes fun at Van Dyke and his humble ways. Van Dyke counters by putting in a Herculean effort, becoming a prince, and promptly dying from the effort, thereby leaving MacLaine a fortune. MacLaine goes to France to forget her lost love and meets Newman, a struggling artist. Newman has devised a new contraption that paints mechanically. It is moved by sound waves and the metal arms of the machine are attached to paint brushes aimed at a canvas. MacLaine falls in love with Newman and marries him. Then she comes up with a brainstorm: since the machine operates on sound, what if some really good classical music were fed into it? What kind of art would the machine produce? Well, the result is that the paintings take the art world by storm and Newman becomes an instant Picasso. He is now a rich man but his happiness is short-lived as he is killed when the metal arms of the painting machine go berserk and crush out his life. MacLaine is now even richer. She next meets Mitchum, who is already a moneybags and she figures that her dangerous Midas touch won't affect him as he has made his pile. Mitchum marries MacLaine and they go off to the rural life and decide to operate a small farm while communing with nature. Mitchum pays little attention to his business and that lack of interest causes his conglomerate to prosper. He really has no idea of dairy farming and is killed when foolishly attempting to milk a bull, who responds the way any self-respecting bull might have responded. Now a widow for the third time, MacLaine goes to a night spot where she spies Kelly, a first-rate entertainer working in a fifth rate locale. He is known by his penchant for the color pink and has no ambitions other than what he's doing. He dresses up as a clown and audiences reward him with mild applause. After MacLaine and Kelly marry, everything changes. He gets to the club late and doesn't have time to don his makeup and gear so he walks on stage and changes his act to a straighter one. The audience loves it and the following montage depicts a succession of triumphs as he becomes a huge Hollywood star and director, the kind of man who appears in big, overblown musicals. He continues his love of pink and that's his trademark as he reaches the top of the heap and is eventually trampled to death by a horde of adoring fans. She finishes her story to Cummings and he then gets a call from the IRS corroborating her tale. Upon hearing that the IRS is now willing to take the money, Cummings faints. In walks Martin, now the janitor at the building where Cummings keeps his office. Martin has lost everything in a series of business reversals and he and MacLaine marry to live in dire poverty, but with smiles on their faces. The size of the production was awesome. Head had half a million dollars to play with for the more than 70 MacLaine costumes, and jeweler Harry Winston lent a bauble collection of almost $4 million to the production. A musical extravaganza number featured Kelly and MacLaine in a satire of every nautical musical ever made. Comden, Green, and Jule Styne collaborated on "Musical Extravaganza" and "I Think You and I Should Get Acquainted." Several styles were used in Thompson's shooting. In the Van Dyke episode, it's almost a silent movie. The Newman section is shot as French film, right down to the English subtitles. The Mitchum section is like a Doris Day-Rock Hudson Universal glosser, and the Gene Kelly piece looks as though it were directed by Busby Berkeley. On paper, this picture seemed to have everything going for it. Unfortunately, movies are made on film, not paper, and it sank. Some interesting cameos include veteran players like Dumont (in last film after having been the Marx Brothers' foil), former boxer Lou Nova, Tom Conway (in his last role. He is the former "Falcon" of the movies and brother of George Sanders), and comics Lenny Kent, Sid Gould, and Wally Vernon. A real flopperoo that proves excess, for its own sake, means little or nothing to movie audiences.

p, Arthur P. Jacobs; d, J. Lee Thompson; w, Betty Comden, Adolph Green (based on a story by Gwen Davis) (CinemaScope, DeLuxe Color); m, Nelson Riddle; ed, Marjorie Fowler; art d, Jack Martin Smith, Ted Haworth; set d, Walter M. Scott, Stuart A. Reiss; cos, Edith Head, Moss Mabry; spec eff, L.B. Abbott, Emil Kosa, Jr.; ch, Gene Kelly, Richard Humphrey; makeup, Ben Nye, Frank Westmore, Dick Smith, Toby Skarstedt.

Comedy   (PR:A-C   MPAA:NR)

WHAT A WHOPPER*½   (1961, Brit.) 89m Viscount/RF bw

Adam Faith (Tony Blake), Sidney James (Harry), Carole Lesley (Charlie Pinner), Terence Longdon (Vernon), Clive Dunn (Mr. Slate), Freddie Frinton (Gilbert Pinner), Marie France (Marie), Charles Hawtrey (Arnold), Spike Milligan (Tramp), Wilfred Brambell (Postie), Fabia Drake (Mrs. Pinner), Harold Berens (Sammy), Ewan Roberts (Jimmy), Archie Duncan (Macdonald), Terry Scott (Sergeant), Anne Gilchrist (Grace), Lloyd Reckord (Jojo), Lance Perceval (Policeman), Mollie Weir (Teacher), Fyffe Robertson (Commentator), Graham Stuart (Man Lover), Eileen Gourlay (Girl Lover).

Basically a vehicle that tried to capitalize on the popularity of once prominent pop singer Faith, starring here as a writer who wants to sell a book about the Loch Ness monster to help himself and four beatnik friends make ends meet. When publishers refuse to buy, the group makes its own

monster, photographs it, and goes to Scotland to try and convince the locals that their photograph is actually of the legendary monster. Faith proved to be a much better singer than actor, and can be grateful that he received amiable support from other members of the cast who had more experience.

p, Teddy Joseph; d, Gilbert Gunn; w, Terry Nation (based on the story by Trevor Peacock, Jeremy Lloyd); ph, Reginald Wyer; m, Laurie Johnson; ed, Bernard Gribble; m/1, "What a Whopper," "The Tire Has Come," Johnny Worth.

Comedy   (PR:A   MPAA:NR)

WHAT A WIDOW*½   (1930) 90m UA bw

Gloria Swanson (Tamarind Brooks), Owen Moore (Gerry), Lew Cody (Victor), Margaret Livingston (Valli), William Holden (Mr. Lodge), Herbert Braggiotti (Jose Alvarado), Gregory Gaye (Bastikoff), Adrienne D'Ambricourt (Paulette), Nella Walker (Marquise), Daphne Pollard (Masseuse).

Reportedly the picture that caused a split between multi-millionaire Joseph Kennedy, Sr., and Swanson, the final break coming over a car, which Kennedy said he paid for but which Swanson found charged to her account, given to the man who thought up the title to this mash. Kennedy mustered every bit of his will power to see this picture through to production, thinking it a good idea. Though Swanson knew how dreadful it was destined to be, she went along to please her sugar daddy. A lot of money and hard work could have been saved had she used better judgment and refused. Swanson is a widow who discovers herself to be very rich on the death of her elderly husband. So she sets off around the world on what seems like one long shopping spree, a good way to have her display as many clothes as possible, amd that's about it, though she does fall for another man and take him to the altar.

p, Joseph P. Kennedy; d, Allan Dwan; w, James Gleason, James Seymour (based on the story by Josephine Lovett); ph, George Barnes; ed, Viola Lawrence; md, Josiah Zuro; art d, Paul Nelson; cos, Rene Hubert; m/1, "Love, Your Magic Spell Is Everywhere," "Edmund Goulding," "Love Is Like a Song," "Say Oui, Cherie," "You're the One," Vincent Youmans, Hugo Felix.

Comedy   (PR:A   MPAA:NR)

WHAT A WOMAN   (SEE: THERE'S THAT WOMAN AGAIN, 1939)

WHAT A WOMAN!*½   (1943) 94m COL bw (GB: THE BEAUTIFUL CHEAT)

Rosalind Russell (Carol Ainsley), Brian Aherne (Henry Pepper), Willard Parker (Michael Cobb), Alan Dinehart (Pat O'Shea), Edward Fielding (Sen. Ainsley), Ann Savage (Jane Hughes), Norma Varden (Miss Timmons), Douglas Wood (Dean Shaeffer), Grady Sutton (Clerk), Lilyan Irene (Minna), Frank Dawson (Ben), Irving Bacon (Newsman), Shelly Winters (Girl Actress), Isabel Withers (Telephone Operator), Hobart Cavanaugh (Mailman), Edward Earle (Livingstone Lawyer), Shimen Ruskin (Gadajalski), Bess Flowers (Dawson), Hal K. Dawson (Foster), Barbara Brown (Receptionist), Byron Foulger (Desk Clerk), Doris Lloyd (Dramatic Coach), Pierre Watkin (Senator), Mary Forbes (Senator's Wife), Gertrude Hoffman (Night Maid), Selmer Jackson (Bruce), Ken Carpenter (Radio Announcer).

Agent Russell is given the task of trying to find the male lead for the Hollywood production of the book she has just sold. Her main prospect turns out to be strongman Parker, the author of the book who has kept his identity secret. Only the comic skill of Russell keeps this from being a failure.

p&d, Irving Cummings; w, Therese Lewis, Barry Trivers (based on the story by Erik Charell); ph, Joseph Walker; ed, Al Clark; md, Morris W. Stoloff; art d, Lionel Banks, Van Nest Polglase; set d, William Kiernan; cos, Travis Banton.

Comedy   (PR:A   MPAA:NR)

WHAT A WOMAN!   (SEE: BEAUTIFUL CHEAT, THE, 1946)

WHAT AM I BID?**   (1967) 92m Liberty International/Emerson c

LeRoy Van Dyke (Pat Hubbard), Kristin Nelson (Beth Hubbard), Stephanie Hill (Maggie Hendricks), Bill Craig (Mike Evans), Leland Murray (Bus Ticket Clerk), Billy Benedict (Clem), Robert Boylan (Capt. Harrigan), Andy Davis (Tractor Salesman), Muriel Landers (Concert Fan), Sid Rushakoff (Fenster), J.B. Towner (Publisher), Jack McCall (Hal Cook), Darrell McCall (Darrell), Lea Marmer (Secretary), Al Hirt, Tex Ritter, Johnny Sea, Faron Young.

Country singer Van Dyke tries to avoid becoming famous, despite the efforts of Hill and Craig to push him into the limelight. His reasons being that his father led a disastrous personal life as a result of his fame. But a persistent Hill sees that Van Dyke is not to spend his entire life around cattle. A good way of providing for a number of tunes including: "We've Got the Best There Is," "Don't Look Back," "I'll Make It Up to You," "Auctioneer," "What Am I Bid?" "When a Boy Becomes a Man" (Nash), "I Never Got to Kiss the Girl" (Tex Ritter).

p, Wendell Niles, Jr.; d&w, Gene Nash; ph, Ralph Woolsey (Techniscope, Technicolor); ed, Terry O. Morse; md, Ernie Freeman; art d, Archie Bacon; set d, Harry Reif; ch, George Jack.

Musical/Drama   (PR:A MPAA:NR)

WHAT BECAME OF JACK AND JILL?*½
(1972, Brit.) 93m Amicus/FOX c (AKA: ROMEO AND JULIET, 1971–A GENTLE TALE OF SEX, VIOLENCE, CORRUPTION AND MURDER)

Vanessa Howard (Jill), Mona Washbourne (Gran), Paul Nicholas (Johnny/ Jack), Peter Copley (Dickson), Peter Jeffrey (Dr. Graham), Patricia Fuller (Frankie), George A. Cooper (Trouncer), Renee Roberts (Woman in Street), Lillias Walker (Dickson's Secretary), Angela Down (Jehovah's Witness), George Benson (Vicar).

Scheming Howard and Nicholas plan to murder the latter's grandmother and collect on her will. Their idea is to scare her by telling the woman, Washbourne, that the young of the world have decided that the aged should be killed for causing too much trouble for the people who must look over them. The elderly lady does die when a protest group marches past her house, but she has the last laugh by having made a change in her will before she died, cutting off Nicholas. Excellent art direction and photography fail to save this clinker, whose biggest shame is involving stage veteran Washbourne in the project.

p, Max J. Rosenberg, Milton Subotsky; d, Bill Bain; w, Roger Marshall (based on the novel The Ruthless Ones by Laurence Moody); ph, Gerry Turpin (Deluxe Color); m, Carl Davis, George Howe; ed, Peter Tanner; art d, Tony Curtis; set d, Helen Thomas.

Horror   (PR:C-O MPAA:PG)

WHAT CHANGED CHARLEY FARTHING?*
(1976, Brit.) 82m Stirling Gold c (AKA: BANANAS BOAT)

Hayley Mills, Doug McClure, Lionel Jeffries, Warren Mitchell, Dilys Hajlett, Fernando Sancho.

An inferior comedy-action picture has McClure a free-living sailor in Havana who steals a boat to escape when the revolution comes. A total misfire.

p, Sidney Hayers, Tristam Cones; d, Hayers; w, David Pursall, Jack Seddon (based on a novel by Mark Hebdon); ph, Graham Edgar; m, Angela Arteaga.

Adventure   (PR:C MPAA:PG)

WHAT DID YOU DO IN THE WAR, DADDY?*   (1966) 116m UA c

James Coburn (Lt. Christian), Dick Shawn (Capt. Cash), Sergio Fantoni (Capt. Oppo), Giovanna Ralli (Gina Romano), Aldo Ray (Sgt. Rizzo), Harry Morgan (Maj. Pott), Carroll O'Connor (Gen. Bolt), Leon Askin (Kastorp), Henry Rico Cattani (Benedetto), Jay Novello (Romano), Kurt Kreuger (German Captain), Vito Scotti (Federico), Johnny Seven (Vittorio), Art Lewis (Pfc. Needleman), William Bryant (Capt. Minow), Robert Carricart (Cook), Ralph Manza (Waiter), Danny Francis (Bus Boy), Herb Ellis (Sgt. Lumpe), Ken Wales (Blair), Rex Morhan (American General), Carl Ekberg (Adolf Hitler), Richard Niles (Jeep Driver), Karla Most, Ivana Kislinger (Italian Girls), Mina Darno (Madame), Giovanna Coppola, Louise De Carlo, Sondra Farrell, Emily La Rue, Jeanne Ranier (Village Women Employed by Madame), Eric Anderson, Ken Del Conte, Thomas Hunter, Kelly Johnson (American Soldiers), Hern Andreas (German Lieutenant), Horst Graf (German Officer), Vincent Barbi, Joe Lo Presti, Benito Prezia, Cosimo Renna, Neil Rosso, Philip Garris (Italian Soldiers), Mario Cimino, James Lanphier, Jerry Martin, Joe Polina (Italian Villagers).

The best things one can say about this lame comedy are that it is inane, silly, and contrived. Blatty's screenplay and the direction by Edwards are appallingly dumb and this must rank as one of the worst attempts at a war comedy ever. It's 1943 in Sicily and a war-weary Shawn is the commanding officer of a troop unit about to take over a small village. Insofar as wars go, this is a sensible thing and the U.S. troops don't want to make any trouble. The locals are quite willing to go along with being occupied and will offer no resistance but there are some stipulations which must be met if the takeover is to be bloodless. There is an annual soccer game about to be played and, following that, the wine festival. If the U.S. is willing to wait until those have ended, all will go smoothly. And it is with that that the movie goes over into the absurd. Shawn thinks he may not have done right by agreeing to the deal but his second in command, Coburn, convinces him that all they will lose is a brief time and many lives may be saved. This decided, the Americans and Italians join forces for an orgy of partying, a round-the-clock bacchanalia that would have pleased Nero. While the fun is going on, both the Germans and the U.S. send scout planes overhead and, from up there, it looks like resistance fighting rather than fun and games. The Germans radio to their troops to attack the town and they find Americans there, wearing every sort of uniform, including German togs. American flags fly high over the town and the Germans begin to gather all the drunken troops. The U.S. forces have been alerted and a unit is sent to rescue the first group. They pop in and out of catacombs like moles and eventually manage to capture all of the Germans. This, of course, leads to another celebration, which is every bit as mindless as the first one was. It's

hard to understand how some superior talents like Edwards and Blatty could have been involved with this tripe. Most people think of Blatty and his success with THE EXORCIST but he also had his licks in comedy, having written THE MAN FROM THE DINER'S CLUB, and JOHN GOLDFARB, PLEASE COME HOME. You couldn't fault the acting as a corps of fine characters paraded their wares including Carroll O'Connor (who was doing more and more of these brass-bottom military parts until he got his career break in "All in the Family"), Vito Scotti, Jay Novello, and Johnny Seven. But all of the actors' efforts are wasted on this poor excuse for a comedy that had none of the elan, eclat, and verve of Edwards' other works. True, there are a few genuinely funny "takes" on the part of Shawn, who is a genuinely funny man, but sitting through 116 minutes of alleged humor in the hopes of garnering a smile is a bit too much punishment. This movie was made between Edwards' efforts on THE GREAT RACE and GUNN, so maybe it was just a respite and left his brains in second gear. Blatty worked on GUNN as well as Edwards' other huge disaster, DARLING LILI, before hitting it big with THE EXORCIST, which he also produced.

p&d, Blake Edwards; w, William Peter Blatty (based on a story by Edwards, Maurice Richlin); ph, Philip Lathrop (Panavision, DeLuxe Color); m, Henry Mancini; ed, Ralph E. Winters; prod d, Fernando Carrere; set d, Reg Allen, Jack Stevens; cos, Jack Bear; spec eff, Danny Lee; ch, Carey Leverett; m/l, "In the Arms of Love," Mancini, Jay Livingston, Ray Evans.

War Comedy   (PR:A-C MPAA:NR)

WHAT DO WE DO NOW?**   (1945, Brit.) 74m GN bw

George Moon (Wesley), Burton Brown (Lesley), Gloria Brent (Diana), Jill Summers (Birdie Maudlin), Ronald Frankau (Drunk), Leslie Fuller (Cabby), Barry Lupino (Jeff), Harry Parry's Swing Band, Edmundo Ros' Conga Band, Steffani and His Silver Songsters, Monte Crick, Gail Page.

Thin musical comedy which sees comedians Moon and Brown becoming amateur detectives in order to trace the whereabouts of a missing brooch. Nothing much to recommend aside from the fairly engaging musical numbers.

p, Maurice J. Wilson; d, Charles Hawtrey; w, George A. Cooper.

Musical   (PR:A MPAA:NR)

WHAT EVER HAPPENED TO AUNT ALICE?***
(1969) 101m Palomar/Cinerama c

Geraldine Page (Mrs. Claire Marrable), Ruth Gordon (Mrs. Alice Dimmock), Rosemary Forsyth (Harriet Vaughan), Robert Fuller (Mike Darrah), Mildred Dunnock (Miss Tinsley), Joan Huntington (Julia Lawson), Peter Brandon (George Lawson), Michael Barbera (Jim Vaughn), Peter Bonerz (Mr. Bentley), Richard Angarola (Sheriff Armijo), Claire Kelly (Elva), Valerie Allen (Dottie), Martin Garralaga (Juan), Jack Bannon (Olin), Seth Riggs (Warren), Lou Kane (Telephone Man), Howard Wright (Mourner).

Robert Aldrich proved that his callousness and cruelty did not end with WHAT EVER HAPPENED TO BABY JANE?, as he once again resorts to the murder of the helpless elderly in this dark mystery. Page is a widow who can't cope with being poor, so she kills the maids who come to work for her, then steals their savings. One maid, Gordon, applies for the position in the hopes of uncovering the mystery behind the recent disappearance of a friend. She is aided by her nephew, Fuller, who becomes attached to the woman living next door to Page. Gordon eventually is killed and Fuller unmasks the sick lady. Both Page and Gordon are excellent, at one point humorous as they deliver lines filled with cruel cuts, and the next menacing and suspenseful. One last thrust is made when it is revealed that Page never had to go through with her cruel murders, the stamp collection her husband left her being worth over $100,000.

p, Robert Aldrich; d, Lee H. Katzin; w, Theodore Apstein (based on the novel The Forbidden Garden by Ursula Curtiss); ph, Joseph Biroc (Metrocolor); m, Gerald Fried; ed, Frank Urioste; art d, William Glasgow; set d, John W. Brown; cos, Renie, makeup, Bill Turner.

Mystery/Drama   Cas.   (PR:C MPAA:M/PG)

WHATEVER HAPPENED TO BABY JANE?****
(1962) 132m Aldrich Associates/Seven Arts/WB bw

Bette Davis (Jane Hudson), Joan Crawford (Blanche Hudson), Victor Buono (Edwin Flagg), Anna Lee (Mrs. Bates), Maidie Norman (Elvira Stitt), Marjorie Bennett (Mrs. Della Flagg), Dave Willock (Ray Hudson), Anne Barton (Cora Hudson), Barbara D. Merrill (Liza Bates), Julie Allred (Young Jane), Gina Gillespie (Blanche as a Child), Bert Freed (Producer), Wesley Addy (Director), Debbie Burton (Singing Voice), William Aldrich, Ernest Anderson, Don Ross, Russ Conway, James Seay, Maxine Cooper, John Shay, Robert Cornthwaite, Jon Shepodd, Michael Fox, Peter Virgo, Jr., Bobs Watson.

A superb gothic horror film that revitalized the careers of Davis and Crawford while introducing a new Laird Cregar in the person of Victor Buono. The picture drew heavily on the real movies of the women and provided an opportunity to see clips from Davis' PARACHUTE JUMPER and EX-LADY (both 1933) as well as Crawford's SADIE MCKEE (1934).

Davis received her 10th Oscar nomination for her role and Buono his first. Haller's excellent camerawork also received a nomination. Davis and Crawford (together for the first time in a film) are sisters and actresses living in a rotting mansion in the Hancock Park area of Los Angeles, where the old money still resides. Davis had been a Shirley Temple-type but as crow's feet surrounded her eyes, her career faded. Crawford went into pictures and became a huge star, Hollywood's best, and Davis would only get the odd role if Crawford insisted upon it. The picture begins as the women are old. They live together in hatred and maid Norman is watching closely as Davis drinks more and more and threatens Crawford, who is now in a wheelchair and paralyzed due to a car crash years before. Davis is obviously mad and when she learns that Crawford is planning to dispose of the mansion and put her in a sanitarium, she becomes irate. What now begins is a reign of terror as Davis proceeds to terrorize Crawford, who is immobile. She serves her dead rats and birds in elegant dishes, she cuts her off from the outside world, and she teases Crawford unmercifully. It's all an assertion of power on the part of Davis and she is getting even for all the years when her sister was top dog. Davis is now totally deranged due to drink but she plans to go back on the stage in the vaudeville act she did so many years before. She places an ad in one of the trade papers for an accompanist and the only person who answers is Buono, a mother-dominated fatso who hopes to use Davis as a meal ticket. Davis is made up as a grotesque parody of the child star she once was and she begins practicing her act with Buono at the keyboards. She sings the haunting and tasteless "I've Written a Letter to Daddy" (written by Frank DeVol, longtime associate of director Aldrich). Crawford is locked in her room while Davis practices her awful act. When Crawford tries to escape, Davis ties and gags her. Later, Crawford is found by cleaning woman Norman who frees her. Davis finds out about that and she kills Norman. Still later, Buono hears Crawford struggling and goes upstairs to find her close to death. He leaves and when Davis thinks that Buono has gone to call the police, she takes Crawford to Malibu where she plans to bury her crippled sister alive in the sand. Norman is reported missing and her body is finally found by the police. Meanwhile, at the beach, Crawford tells Davis that she takes full responsibility for the life they've had. She planned the accident that took place out of jealousy and made a miscalculation that left her crippled. All this time, Davis believed the accident was her own fault and has lived with the guilt. The cops are hot on the trail of the sisters as this denouement continues. Crawford goes on to say that she deliberately manipulated Davis' frail mind into thinking that the accident was her fault. The cops arrive and Davis has fallen apart and madness has totally taken over. Davis goes into the cutesy act she did in her youth to the amazement of the cops as the movie ends. This film is thought to be the SUNSET BOULEVARD of the 1960s, a look into Hollywood's crumbling myths. As in the best Alfred Hitchcock movies, suspense, rather than actual blood and gore, was the key to the success. There are several holes in the story that could have used caulking but they are bypassed in the dark rush of images that come flying off the screen. Among the more blatant is the fact that Crawford makes no attempt to call for help from the family next door. The most memorable scene is shot from a camera above in Crawford's room as she races her wheelchair around like a caged rat when her mind snaps temporarily. Davis, as is the usual case, plays her role broadly and proves a dynamic counterpoint to Crawford's understated portrayal of the more sensible sister. Two such mannered performers in one film might have made for a chewing-up-the-scenery contest but Aldrich wisely kept the personalities so apart from each other that both actresses had the opportunity to operate on different levels, much to the benefit of the movie. Davis' film after this was DEAD RINGER and Crawford's was STRAIT-JACKET. Aldrich later worked with Davis on HUSH HUSH...SWEET CHARLOTTE, an attempt to secure the same kind of audience response. It didn't work as well as this one. Buono was only 24 at the time and looking much older due to the enormous weight he carried around with him. The weight was also responsible for his early death, not long after he turned 40. Buono was an excellent actor who achieved some of his finest moments in TV's "Batman." The worst part of the film has to do with the copout twist ending that was unsatisfying as the rest was not. The same year that Crawford and Davis were united for the first time, Joel McCrea and Randolph Scott teamed up for the first time in RIDE THE HIGH COUNTRY, an excellent western. The movie is a tad long, although don't blame the superior editing of Luciano because he kept matters hopping. But when two great ladies of the screen are at last together, they must be given their moments and there are moments galore in WHATEVER HAPPENED TO BABY JANE? Even though there is only one killing (Norman), the terror is so intense that children are not advised to see it.

p&d, Robert Aldrich; w, Lukas Heller (based on the novel by Henry Farrell); ph, Ernest Haller; m, Frank DeVol; ed, Michael Luciano; art d, William Glasgow; set d, George Sawley; cos, Norma Koch; spec eff, Don Steward; ch, Alex Romero; makeup, Jack Obringer, Monte Westmore.

Drama/Horror Cas. (PR:C MPAA:NR)

WHAT EVERY WOMAN KNOWS** (1934) 92m MGM bw

Helen Hayes (Maggie Wylie), Brian Aherne (John Shand), Madge Evans (Lady Sybil Tenterden), Lucile Watson (Comtesse), Dudley Digges (James Wylie), Donald Crisp (David Wylie), David Torrence (Alick Wylie), Henry Stephenson (Venables, Political Leader), Boyd Irwin (Tenterden).

A film version of the play Hayes had starred in eight years earlier has her as the ever faithful and patient woman behind Aherne, a Scotsman recently elected to the British Parliament. The naive theme behind this picture is that it takes a woman to balance out a man's gross errors in judgment. But it does so in a light enough manner, with the right touches added by Hayes, to keep from offending anyone. Previously made twice as silents (1917 and 1921).

d, Gregory LaCava; w, Monckton Hoffe, John Meehan (based on the play by Sir James Matthew Barrie); ph, Charles Rosher; ed, Blanche Sewell.

Comedy (PR:A MPAA:NR)

WHAT EVERY WOMAN WANTS** (1954, Brit.) 86m Advance/Adelphi bw

William Sylvester (Jim Barnes), Elsy Albiin (Jane), Brenda de Banzie (Sarah), Patric Doonan (Mark), Dominic Roche (Bill), Joan Hickson (Polly Ann), Brian Rix (Herbert), Joan Sims (Doll), Beckett Bould (Tom), Prunella Scales (Mary), Douglas Ives (Sam), Edwin Richfield (Frank).

Realistic drama in which cramped living conditions force Albiin to flee the home of her husband and family to pursue a whimsical affair with her Korean, war-wounded cousin, Sylvester. But she comes back to her husband under the promise of the pair gaining their independence from the rest of the family. Delicate problems in England at the time, housing and employment shortages, were treated in a mature and effective manner without appearing preachy.

p, David Dent; d, Maurice Elvey; w, Talbot Rothwell (based on the play "Relations Are Best Apart" by Edwin Lewis); ph, Wilkie Cooper; m, Edward Astley; ed, Robert Jordan Hill.

Drama (PR:A MPAA:NR)

WHAT EVERY WOMAN WANTS**½ (1962, Brit.) 69m Danziger/UA bw

William [James] Fox (Philip Goodwin), Hy Hazell (Jean Goodwin), Dennis Lotis (Tom Yardley), Elizabeth Shepherd (Sue Goodwin), Guy Middleton (George Barker), Andrew Faulds (Dereck Chadwick), Patsy Smart (Hilda), Ian Fleming (Nelson), George Merritt (Maxwell).

Having grown frustrated and disgusted with their unresponsive spouses, Hazell and her married daughter Shepherd set in motion a strange scheme to change the personalities of their men. Surprisingly amusing family-oriented comedy.

p, Brian Taylor; d, Ernest Morris; w, M.M McCormack.

Comedy (PR:A MPAA:NR)

WHAT HAPPENED THEN?** (1934, Brit.) 62m BIP/Wardour bw

Richard Bird (Peter Bromley), Lorna Storm (Alicia Deverton), Francis L. Sullivan (Richard Bentley, King's Counsel), Geoffrey Wardwell (Raymond Rudford), Richard Gray (Robert), Cecil Ramage (Defense), George Zucco (Inspector Hull), J. Fisher White (Judge), Stella Arbenina (Mrs. Bromley), Lawrence Hanray (Dr. Bristol), Kathleen Harrison, Quinton McPherson, Raymond Huntley, Alec Finter.

Wardwell is a sculptor convicted on charges of murder. His guardian has been killed, and although he is found guilty, Storm, his fiancee, goes to the murdered man's nephew, Bird, in hopes of freeing Wardwell. Bird agrees to help, but only if Storm will marry him instead of her intended. It turns out that Bird is a psycho who has plotted the entire thing, including murdering his uncle, in order to marry Storm. Skillfull little mystery with some good twists.

p, Walter C. Mycroft; d&w, Walter Summers (based on a play by Lilian Trimbler Bradley); ph, James Wilson.

Crime (PR:A MPAA:NR)

WHAT HAPPENED TO HARKNESS** (1934, Brit.) 53m WB-FN bw

Robert Hale (Sgt. McCabe), James Finlayson (Police Constable Gallun), Brember Wills (Bernard Harkness), John Turnbull (Inspector Marlow), Clare Harris (Mrs. Millett), Wally Patch (Bullett), Morland Graham (Billy), Veronica Brady (Mrs. Bullett), Aubrey Mallalieu (Dr. Powin), Kathleen Kelly (Pat), Douglas Jeffries, Geoffrey Wardwell, S.A. Cookson, D.J. Williams.

When a local miser and his maid disappear, a pair of cops, Hale and Finlayson, try to top each other in figuring out what happened. Evidence points to murder but it turns out the missing duo have merely eloped. Some mildly amusing moments. Finlayson is better remembered as a nemesis for Laurel and Hardy in some of their silent shorts.

p, Irving Asher; d, Milton Rosmer; w, Brock Williams (based on a story by Roland Brown).

Comedy (PR:AAA MPAA:NR)

WHAT LOLA WANTS								(SEE: DAMN YANKEES, 1958)

WHAT MEN WANT**								(1930) 65m UNI bw

Pauline Stark *(Lee)*, Ben Lyon *(Kendall Phillips)*, Barbara Kent *(Betty)*, Robert Ellis *(Howard)*, Hallam Cooley *(Bunch)*, Carmelita Geraghty *(Mabel)*.

Problems arise for a debonair playboy, Ellis, when his mistress swoons for another man, Lyon. When her sister comes to town, the plot thickens and becomes a good edible stew. Lyon went from WHAT MEN WANT into the classic HELL'S ANGELS, in which he piloted his own craft and shot some of the unforgettable air combat scenes.

d, Ernst Laemmle; w, John B. Clymer, Dorothy Yost (based on a story by Warner Fabian); ph, Roy Overbaugh.

Drama											**(PR:A MPAA:NR)**

WHAT NEXT, CORPORAL HARGROVE?***		(1945) 95m MGM bw

Robert Walker *(Cpl. Marion Hargrove)*, Keenan Wynn *(Pvt. Thomas Mulvehill)*, Jean Porter *(Jeanne Ouidoc)*, Chill Wills *(Sgt. Cramp)*, Hugo Haas *(Mayor Ouidoc)*, William "Bill" Phillips *(Bill Burk)*, Fred Essler *(Marcel Vivin)*, Cameron Mitchell *(Joe Lupot)*, Ted Lundigan *(Curtis)*, Dick Hirbe *(Neilson)*, Arthur Walsh *(Ellerton)*, Maurice Marks *(Gilly)*, Paul Langton *(Capt. Drake)*, James Davis *(Sgt. Hill)*, John Carlyle *(Lt. Morley)*, Walter Sande *(Maj. Kingby)*, Theodore Newton *(Capt. Parkson)*, Robert Kent *(Lt. Dillon)*, Matt Willis *(Sgt. Staple)*, Richard Bailey *(Chaplain Mallowy)*.

Walker and Wynn play a couple of GIs stationed in Europe toward the end of WW II, whose incompetence even manages to mess up the simple task of garbage duty. When they are given charge of an artillery truck, the two men become detached from the rest of their company, winding up in even more hot water as they attempt to make up for lost time. This includes a trip to a small French village followed by one to Paris. A sequel to the similar SEE HERE, PRIVATE HARGROVE (1944), played only for laughs.

p, George Haight; d, Richard Thorpe; w, Harry Kurnitz (based on characters created by Marion Hargrove); ph, Henry Sharp; m, David Snell; ed, Albert Akst; art d, Cedric Gibbons, Leonid Vasian; set d, Edwin B. Willis, Keogh Gleason; spec eff, A. Arnold Gillespie, Warren Newcombe.

Comedy										**(PR:A MPAA:NR)**

WHAT! NO BEER?**								(1933) 70m MGM bw

Buster Keaton *(Elmer J. Butts)*, Jimmy Durante *(Jimmy Potts)*, Roscoe Ates *(Schultz)*, Phyllis Barry *(Hortense)*, John Miljan *(Butch Lorado)*, Henry Armetta *(Tony)*, Edward Brophy *(Spike Moran)*, Charles Dunbar *(Mulligan)*, Charles Giblyn *(Chief)*.

Neither the comic talents of Durante nor of Keaton could do much to save this farce about two men who attempt to set up a brewery toward the end of Prohibition. But it still isn't legal, so they wind up having to give all their stock away. Though it has its moments, these are few and far between, one of the major problems being Keaton's real-life bout with the bottle which left him too despondent for any form of acting.

d, Edward Sedgwick; w, Carey Wilson, Jack Cluett (based on a story by Robert E. Hopkins); ph, Harold Wenstrom; ed, Frank Sullivan.

Comedy										**(PR:A MPAA:NR)**

WHAT PRICE BEAUTY?							(SEE: FALSE FACES, 1932)

WHAT PRICE CRIME?*							(1935) 63m Beacon bw

Charles Starrett *(Allen Gray)*, Noel Madison *(Douglas Worthington)*, Virginia Cherrill *(Sondra Worthington)*, Charles Delaney *(Armstrong)*, Jack Mulhall *(Hopkins)*, Nina Guilberg, Henry Roquemore, Gordon Griffith, John Elliott, Arthur Loft, Earl Tree, Jack Cowell, Arthur Roland, Edwin Argus, Al Baffert, Monte Carter, Lafe McKee.

Western star Starrett is out of the saddle and into the streets in this unmemorable outing in which he plays an undercover FBI Agent–his disguise being that of a prizefighter–to get the goods on a gang smuggling artillery stolen from the government. Lacks punch.

p, Max Alexander; d, Albert Herman; w, Al Martin; ph, Harry Forbes; ed, S. Roy Luby.

Crime										**(PR:A MPAA:NR)**

WHAT PRICE DECENCY?*½						(1933) 67m EQ bw

Dorothy Burgess *(Norma)*, Alan Hale *(Klaus van Leyden)*, Walter Byron *(Tom O'Neil)*, V. Durant *(Pimp)*, Henry Durant *(Matizzi)*.

Forced to implicit indecorous conduct by impecunity, the beauteous Burgess accompanies bestial Hale abroad his equator-bound ship and finds herself an unwilling stowaway when the vessel sets sail. She excoriates the tricky brute for permitting the unwanted passage to occur, and to make amends

he asks for her hand in marriage, offering her a lifetime of comfort as mistress of a luxurious tropical home. Arranging a false wedding ceremony at sea, he takes her to his rain-drenched, dreary shack, where he makes his living trading pearls and abusing gullible natives. Burgess becomes a virtual slave to Hale until the arrival of a young, handsome man, appropriately named Byron. When Burgess announces her impending departure from Hale, he sneers, pointing out that she was never his wife. Enraged, she beats him with a leather thong, blinding the bully. Confessing her clouded past to her new-found Galahad, she departs with him for a better life. Sex and sado-masochism in the 1930s, probably patterned after the Walter Huston vehicle KONGO, released the previous year. Hale is no Huston, and the entire production–particularly the dialog–seems slapdash.

d&w, Arthur Gregor.;

Drama										**(PR:O MPAA:NR)**

WHAT PRICE GLORY?***							(1952) 111m FOX c

James Cagney *(Capt. Flagg)*, Corinne Calvet *(Charmaine)*, Dan Dailey *(Sgt. Quirt)*, William Demarest *(Cpl. Kiper)*, Craig Hill *(Lt. Aldrich)*, Robert Wagner *(Lewisohn)*, Marisa Pavan *(Nicole Bouchard)*, Casey Adams *(Lt. Moore)*, James Gleason *(Gen. Cokely)*, Wally Vernon *(Lipinsky)*, Henry Letondal *(Cognac Pete)*, Fred Libby *(Lt. Schmidt)*, Ray Hyke *(Mulcahy)*, Paul Fix *(Gowdy)*, James Lilburn *(Young Soldier)*, Henry Morgan *(Morgan)*, Dan Borzabe *(Gilbert)*, Bill Henry *(Holsen)*, Henry Kulky *(Company Cook)*, Jack Pennick *(Ferguson)*, Ann Codee *(Nun)*, Stanley Johnson *(Lt. Cunningham)*, Luis Alberni *(The Great Uncle)*, Barry Norton *(Priest)*, Torben MeyerZ *(Mayor)*, Alfred Zeisler *(English Colonel)*, George Bruggeman *(English Lieutenant)*, Sean McClory *(Lt. Austin)*, Scott Forbes *(Lt. Bennett)*, Charles Fitzsimons *(Capt. Wickham)*, Louis Mercier *(Bouchard)*, Mickey Simpson *(M.P.)*, Olga Andre, Tom Tyler.

This was an unusual departure for Ford, but his strong direction and some fine performances from his cast make this often strange comedy work. It is WW I, and Cagney is a marine captain doing his military duty in France. He and Dailey, Cagney's top sergeant, are assigned to take a company of older men, as well as some boys, from the home in a small French village to the brutal reality of the war in the trenches. In addition to battling German forces, Cagney and Dailey must fight one another when it comes to attracting the attentions of Calvet, the pretty daughter of a French innkeeper. A remake of Raoul Walsh's 1926 silent feature, Ford's film was generally raked over the coals by critics when it was first released, though WHAT PRICE GLORY? has found its audience over the years. Ford makes an interesting use of artificial looking colors to achieve mood, giving, at times, a dream-like affect to the proceedings. There is a slightly surreal edge to the film, reflecting the insanity of the war that has caused the situation in the first place. Though atypical for Ford, WHAT PRICE GLORY? still remains a fascinating film to watch, an unusual work that uses some of Ford's favorite themes. Originally this was to be a musical, and seven songs were written with this in mind. Ford cared little for this idea, and told surprised studio officials "if you want music, *you* put it in!" Two songs by Jay Livingston and Ray Evans, "My Love, My Life," and "Oui, Oui, Marie," did make it into the final cut however. Cagney, looking somewhat portly, plays with spirit and is well complemented by Dailey's talents. Norton, who is seen here as a priest, also appeared in Walsh's film, essaying the part of a disturbed soldier. Problems developed on the set when scriptwriters Henry and Phoebe Ephron overheard some of Ford's off-color, though good natured, wisecracks. They misinterpreted Ford's jokes for anti-Semitism and refused to come back to the set. Ford was subsequently forced to complete the film without them. For one sequence, Cagney was required to leap into a sidecar of a motorcycle, then take off at a furious pace. "Do you really want to ride with this guy," Ford asked Cagney. "Why not?" was the actor's reply. Demarest was to drive the motorcycle off, and Cagney had complete faith in him, knowing that Demarest had actually driven motorcycles during WW I combat. Ford continued to question the safety factor, but Cagney was insistent. Ford asked Cagney if he always did what the script called for. Cagney replied no, but insisted on his confidence in the sequence. "Well," Ford told him, "all right. But *I* wouldn't" Little did Cagney or Demarest realize that the motorcycle's brake pads had worn away. The motorcycle careened out of control and Demarest ended up breaking both his legs. He and an electrician were taken to the hospital, though Cagney was able to escape the accident with only a few scratches. In his autobiography, Cagney recalled: "...I limped up the hill to find John Ford standing there, quietly sucking on his dudeen pipe. As I drew abreast of him, he looked meditatively at me and said, 'What'd I tell ya?'"

p, Sol C. Siegel; d, John Ford; w, Phoebe Ephron, Henry Ephron (based on the play by Maxwell Anderson, Laurence Stallings); ph, Joseph MacDonald (Technicolor); m, Alfred Newman; ed, Dorothy Spoencer; art d, Lyle R. Wheeler; set d, George W. Davis, Thomas Little, Stuart A. Reiss.

War/Comedy				**Cas.**			**(PR:C MPAA:NR)**

WHAT PRICE HOLLYWOOD?***						(1932) 88m RKO-Pathe/RKO bw

Constance Bennett *(Mary Evans)*, Lowell Sherman *(Maximilian Carey)*, Neil Hamilton *(Lenny Borden)*, Gregory Ratoff *(Julius Saxe)*, Brooks Benedict *(Muto)*, Louise Beavers *(Bonita the Maid)*, Eddie "'Rochester'" Anderson *(James)*, Bryant Washburn *(Washed-Up Star)*, Florence Roberts *(Diner)*,

Gordon DeMain (Yes Man), Heinie Conklin (Car Owner), Eddie Dunn (Doorman at Grauman's Chinese Theatre), Phil Teal (Jimmy, Assistant Director).

The first big success for director Cukor, and also the first talking picture to take a jaundiced look at Hollywood, WHAT PRICE HOLLYWOOD? opens in the famed Brown Derby restaurant. Bennett is a waitress there, determined to break into show business as an actress. One night Sherman, a film director, enters the Brown Derby and Bennett switches stations with another waitress so she can serve him. The well-dressed Sherman is quite inebriated, but takes a liking to his ambitious waitress. Sherman invites Bennett to attend a Hollywood premiere at Grauman's Chinese Theatre, but rather than arrive in a fancy, chauffeur driven limousine, the couple make their entrance in a beat-up vehicle. The shocked parking attendant doesn't know what to do, especially when Sherman gives him the jalopy as a tip. To Sherman, this is all part of the advice he had earlier given Bennett: "Remember our motto–'It's all in fun'...Always keep your sense of humor and you can't miss." That evening Sherman introduces Bennett to Ratoff, a producer, then takes the hopeful woman home with him. The next morning, when Sherman wakes up, the previous evening is a blank. Bennett reminds Sherman that he had promised her a screen test. She worries about his excessive drinking, flippant attitudes, and solitary lifestyle, but Sherman simply shrugs off Bennett's concerns. Later he directs her screen test, which proves the would-be actress has more ambition than talent. Bennett rehearses the scene by herself, then pleads for just one more chance. Ratoff sees this new test and decides Bennett has some potential. He has her signed up, and Bennett's rise is meteoric. Sherman, on the other hand, is convinced that his talents and career are on the decline. He decides not to become personally involved with Bennett, lest he harm her career. After Bennett becomes a full-fledged movie star, she meets Hamilton, a polo-playing plutocrat. Hamilton falls in love, though Bennett is more amused than anything else. The wealthy playboy arranges a fancy dinner for her, complete with full orchestra, but Bennett fails to show up. Hamilton is enraged. He storms over to the star's home and, pulling her from her bed, brings Bennett to the dinner. She finally agrees to marry Hamilton, though Ratoff and Sherman are convinced this is a mistake. Their predictions on the marriage's longevity prove correct when the honeymoon is interrupted so Bennett can get back to a movie set. Hamilton grows angry when he must wait for hours while Bennett is doing her day's shooting, but this is only the beginning. He begins badgering Bennett about the articles Hollywood fan magazines publish about her. Hamilton finally blows his stack when one writer wants to portray the couple in a series called "Great Lovers of Today." Hamilton walks out on Bennett, and Sherman bitterly comforts her by saying: "I made you what you are today–I hope you're satisfied." Sherman's own career is sinking fast, undermined by his growing dependence on alcohol. After her divorce from Hamilton is final, Bennett realizes she is pregnant but her hopes are lifted after winning the Oscar for Best Actress. She bails out Sherman after he is arrested for drunk driving, then takes the failed director home. Despite Bennett's encouragement, Sherman's attitudes are as cavalier as ever. "I'm washed up, it's all gone," he says without a hint of remorse. Later, alone in Bennett's dressing room, Sherman stares at his sorry reflection in the mirror, comparing it with a photograph from his happier days. He makes a few ironic jokes, then finds a handgun in a drawer. With no feelings of self-pity, Sherman decides to end his misery and kills himself with a bullet to the chest. After the corpse is discovered, Bennett falls victim to scandal and gossipmongers. A reporter callously asks Bennett if she thinks Hamilton will be awarded custody of her son. The personal and professional anguish is more than she can bear, so Bennett takes her child and flees to France. Hamilton learns where they are staying and comes to see the boy. He realizes how wrong he was in abandoning his wife and asks forgiveness. Bennett, with hopes for the future, reconciles with Hamilton. Though the conclusion is a pat romantic ending, this is a strong drama that shows the real Hollywood behind the glamorous facades. Bennett gives an excellent performance, making her turn from ingenue to hardened star wholly believable. Bennett later stated she felt this was the best performance of her career, although she also conceded that she was "no Sarah Bernhardt." Sherman's portrait of a director on the skids is powerful, playing the drunken man in a straightforward manner, accepting of his self-induced fate. The scene of his suicide is incredible, cutting swiftly from flashes of his past to his sorry present, shot at weird angles. When he shoots himself, the fall is in slow-motion, anticipating the slow-motion violence of THE WILD BUNCH by almost 40 years. This unsettling montage was apparently the work of Slavko Vorkapich, a Yugoslavian immigrant who contributed memorable scenes to a number of films, including the frightening wraiths zooming through the canyons of New York in CRIME WITHOUT PASSION (1934). Unfortunately the romance between Hamilton and Bennett remains in the film's spotlight while Sherman's fascinating disintegration is kept a subplot. Hamilton's role was one he was well-accustomed to, and there is nothing new or revealing in his character that adds to the film's plot or ambience. Cukor, after numerous forgettable directing and codirecting jobs, finally came into his own with this work here. Producer Selznick conceived the idea of making a film that accurately portrayed Hollywood. He contacted Adela Rogers St. John and told her, "It's time we made a really good picture about Hollywood, so why don't you go and find us a story?" She came up with a story approximately based on the experiences of Colleen Moore and her husband, alcoholic producer John McCormick. She further based Sherman's role on the life and death of director Tom Forman, who had shot himself in

the chest after a nervous breakdown, and Sherman himself based some of his performance on his own brother-in-law, John Barrymore. The script that St. John submitted was entitled "The Truth About Hollywood" and it was to star Clara Bow in her talkie comeback, but Bow, already an alcoholic, had put on too much weight and couldn't lose it before production began, so she was replaced by Bennett. The picture was quite successful and five years later Selznick reworked the film into A STAR IS BORN, directed by William Wellman and starring Janet Gaynor and Fredric March. Cukor also returned to the material with his version of A STAR IS BORN in 1954, featuring Judy Garland and James Mason (in 1976 Barbara Streisand was featured in a rock 'n' roll version of the story that was a pale shadow of the other films). Selznick remained fond of WHAT PRICE HOLLYWOOD? and, in his book Memo From David O. Selznick, recounted his motivations in making the film: "I believed that the whole world was interested in Hollywood and that the trouble with most films about Hollywood was that they gave a false picture...that they were not true reflections of what happened in Hollywood...Ninety-five percent of the dialog in that picture was actually straight out of life and was straight 'reportage,' so to speak."

p, David O. Selznick; d, George Cukor; w, Jane Murfin, Ben Markson, Gene Fowler, Roland Brown (based on a story by Adela Rogers St. John); ph, Charles Rosher; ed, Jack Kitchin; md, Max Steiner; art d, Carroll Clark; cos, Margaret Pemberton.

Drama   Cas.   (PR:C MPAA:NR)

WHAT PRICE INNOCENCE?*   (1933) 64m COL bw (GB: SHALL
                                                          THE CHILDREN PAY?)

Willard Mack (Dr. Dan Davidge), Minna Gombell (Amy Harper), Jean Parker (Ruth Harper), Betty Grable (Beverly Bennett), Bryant Washburn (John Harper), Ben Alexander (Tommy Harrow), Beatrice Banyard (Mrs. Bennett), Louise Beavers (Hannah).

This early plea for sex education has kindly old family physician Mack making house calls and observing the lives of the children he delivered becoming shambles upon their adolescence. Parker is the tremulous teen whose mother, Gombell, believes that the less said about sex, the better. The innocent ingenue, pregnant, is deserted by her much older seducer, Alexander, and commits suicide. This tour-de-force by actor-writer-director Mack seems too clinical in its inexorable do-good story line to be a feature film, but it might do well in sex-education classrooms. Interesting for an early glimpse of the 17-year-old Grable in one of her few nonmusical films of the time.

d&w, Willard Mack; ph, Joseph A. Valentine; ed, Arthur Hilton.

Drama   (PR:A MPAA:NR)

WHAT PRICE MELODY?   (SEE: LORD BYRON OF BROADWAY,
                                                                        1930)

WHAT PRICE VENGEANCE?*½   (1937) 60m Rialto bw

Lyle Talbot (Tom Connors), Wendy Barrie (Polly Moore), Marc Lawrence (Pete Brower), Eddie Acuff (Tex McGirk), Lucille Lund (Babe Foster), Robert Rideout (Slim Ryan), Reginald Hincks (Inspector Blair), Wally Albright (Sandy MacNair), Lois Albright (Mary Connors), Arthur Kerr (Bill MacNair).

An exciting opening sequence is followed by pure tedium, as Talbot plays a copper who fakes a resignation from the force under the proposition that he can't shoot at a living target. This somehow allows him to become involved with a gang of bank robbers in the hope of blowing their operation. In between potshots, he romances waitress Barrie over lunch.

p, Kenneth J. Bishop; d, Del Lord; w, J. P. McGowan; ph, Harry Forbes; William Beckway; ed, William Austin.

Crime   (PR:A MPAA:NR)

WHAT SHALL IT PROFIT   (SEE: HARD STEEL, 1941, Brit.)

WHAT THE BUTLER SAW**   (1950, Brit.) 63m Hammer/Exclusive
                                                                          bw

Edward Rigby (The Earl), Henry Mollison (Bembridge), Mercy Haystead (Lapis), Michael Ward (Gerald), Eleanor Hallam (Lady Mary), Peter Burton (Bill Fenton), Anne Valery (Elaine), Tonie MacMillan, Mollie Palmer, Howard Charlton, Alfred Harris, George Bishop, Norman Pitt.

A delightful comedy with a cast of amiable actors in a story of an earl, Rigby, who retires as governor on a tropical island and returns to live in England. He soon discovers, however, that an island princess, Haystead, has come to England to be with the earl's butler, Mollison. Rigby goes to great pains to ship the princess back, and in the end she and the butler begin a life together.

p, Anthony Hinds; d, Godfrey Grayson; w, A.R. Rawlinson, Edward J. Mason (based on the story by Roger Good, Donald Good); ph, Walter Harvey.

Comedy   (PR:A MPAA:NR)

WHAT THE PEEPER SAW   (SEE: NIGHT HAIR CHILD, 1971)

WHAT WIVES DON'T WANT   (SEE: VIRTUOUS HUSBAND, 1931)

WHAT WOMEN DREAM½   (1933, Ger.) 81m Super
Film/Bayerische-Film bw (WAS FRAUEN TRAUMEN)

Nora Gregor (*Rina Korff*), Gustav Frohlich (*Walter Konig*), Otto Wallburg
(*Kleinsilber*), Peter Lorre (*Fussli*), Kurt Horwitz (*Levassor*).

Two German expatriats who were to score highly in Hollywood were
involved in this production, Peter Lorre as an actor and Billy Wilder as a
screenwriter. Both would flee Germany later that year when the Nazis came
to power. Yarn centers around a beautiful kleptomaniac who has a yen for
expensive jewelry, but each time she steals, a mysterious man is quick to pay
for it. Detective Lorre gets on the case. More a bumbler than a sleuth, he
uses the lady's lost glove to trace her. The scent of the perfume on the glove
is a very expensive one which Lorre's friend Frohlich recognizes as
belonging to nightclub singer Gregor. Frohlich immediately falls in love
with the thief, but must fight for her affections with Horwitz, the wealthy
international criminal who has paid for the jewelry she swiped. When
Horwitz is turned over to the police, Frohlich has sole claim on the girl.
Unfortunately, only one print of WHAT WOMEN DREAM remains in
existence, and that one is locked up in a vault in Switzerland, so the odds
of having a chance to see it are quite slim.

p, Julius Haimann; d, Geza von Bolvary; w, Franz Schulz, Billie [Billy]
Wilder; ph, Willy Goldberger; m, Robert Stolz; art d, Emil Hasler; m/l, Stolz,
Robert Gilbert.

Drama/Comedy   (PR:A   MPAA:NR)

WHAT WOULD YOU DO, CHUMS?½
                        (1939, Brit.) 75m BN-Anglo bw

Syd Walker (*Himself*), Jean Gillie (*Lucy*), Cyril Chamberlain (*Mike*), Jack
Barty (*Joe*), Wally Patch (*Tom*), Gus McNaughton (*Harry*), Peter Gawthorne
(*Sir Douglas Gordon*), Julien Vedey (*Mossy*), Arthur Finn (*Slim*), Leonard
Morris, Andrea Malandrinos, George Street.

Radio personality Syd Walker stars as a junk dealer who gives fatherly
advice to a young girl, Gillie, when she falls in love with spineless criminal,
Chamberlain. Gillie tries to get Chamberlain to go straight, but his period
of reform is cut short when he gets caught robbing a bank. Unusual
hankie-grabber for a story about a junk dealer.

p, John Corfield; d, John Baxter; w, David Evans, Geoffrey Orme, Con West
(based on the radio series "Mr. Walker Wants to Know" by Gordon Crier);
ph, James Wilson.

Crime   (PR:A   MPAA:NR)

WHAT WOULD YOU SAY TO SOME SPINACH***
(1976, Czech.) 90m Studio Barrandov c (COZ TAKHLE DAT SI SPE-
NAT; AKA: A NICE PLATE OF SPINACH)

Vladimir Mensik, Jiri Sovak, Josef Somr, Peter Kostka, Eva Treytnorova.

A mad but inspired scientist creates a machine that can rejuvenate the
aging. Since all is vanity, the prototype of the popular mechanism is quickly
stolen by a beauty shop entrepreneur, who plans to make a fortune by
putting spring in the step of the patrons. Unfortunately, not all of the
wrinkles have been ironed out of the wrinkle-reducing mechanism; if it isn't
precisely adjusted, it tends to reduce the dimensions of its user. Moreover
(shades of Popeye), the machine has a selective affinity for people who have
recently ingested spinach. Such pecadilloes plague the would-be Ponce de
Leon, resulting in numerous contretemps. One of a number of fine comic
fantasies from the same talented team.

d&w, Vaclav Vorlicek, Milos Makourek; ph, Frantisek Uldrich.

Fantasy/Comedy   (PR:A   MPAA:NR)

WHAT'S BUZZIN COUSIN?*½   (1943) 75m COL bw

Ann Miller (*Ann Crawford*), Eddie "Rochester" Anderson (*Rochester*), John
Hubbard (*Jimmy Ross*), Freddy Martin (*Himself*), Leslie Brooks (*Josie*), Jeff
Donnell (*Billie*), Carol Hughes (*May*), Theresa Harris (*Blossom*), Roy
Gordon (*Jim Langford*), Bradley Page (*Pete Hartley*), Warren Ashe (*Dick
Bennett*), Dub Taylor (*Jed*), Betsy Gay (*Saree*), Louis Mason (*Hillbilly*),
Eugene Jackson (*Bellboy*), Jessie Arnold (*Mrs. Hillbilly*), Erville Alderson
(*Gas Station Attendant*), Harry Tyler (*Hotel Clerk*), Walter Soderling (*Mr.
Hayes*), Eddie Fetherstone (*Radio Repairman*), John Tyrrell, Craig Woods
(*Henchmen*), Freddy Martin's Orchestra.

Anything to show Ann Miller's legs dancing seemed to be the sole motivation
behind this rather ridiculous story in which the beautiful girl inherits a hotel
in a ghost town. She and three friends set out for the place with the dream
of making it into a hot spot, and are given assistance in shaping it up by a
band of musicians, who just happen to be stuck there. A false gold discovery
makes the place a minor success, with Miller able to sell at a large profit.
No harm done. Songs and musical numbers include: "$18.75" (Wally

Anderson), "Ain't That Just Like a Man," "Short, Fat and 41" (Don Raye,
Gene De Paul), "Nevada" (Mort Greene, Walter Donaldson), "Knocked Out
Nocturne" (Jacques Press). Other songs by Walter Samuels, Saul Chaplin,
Charles Newman, Lew Pollack, and Eddie Cherkose include: "By Order of
the Interceptor Command," "Three Little Mosquitoes," "In Grandpa's
Beard, "They're Countin' in the Mountains," "Where Am I Without You,"
"Taffy".

p, Jack Fier; d, Charles Barton; w, Harry Sauber, John P. Medbury (based
on a story by Aben Kandel); ph, Joseph Walker; ed, James Sweeney; md, M.
W. Stoloff; art d, Lionel Banks; set d, Joseph Kish; ch, Nick Castle; makeup,
Clay Campbell.

Musical   (PR:A   MPAA:NR)

WHAT'S COOKIN'?*½   (1942) 69m UNIV bw (GB: WAKE UP AND
                                               DREAM)

The Andrews Sisters (*Maxene, Patty, La Verne*), Jane Frazee (*Anne*), Robert
Paige (*Bob*), Gloria Jean (*Sue*), Leo Carrillo (*Marvo*), Charles Butterworth
(*J. P. Courtney*), Billie Burke (*Agatha*), Grace McDonald (*Angela*), Donald
O'Connor (*Tommy*), Peggy Ryan (*Peggy*), Franklin Pangborn (*Prof. Bistell*),
Susan Levine (*Tag-a-long*), Woody Herman and His Orchestra, The Jivin'
Jacks and Jills.

Another of the "we don't need a theater, kids" potpourris, in which
Universal showcases some of its younger talents, blending them with
established musical stars. The slender story line has to do with the efforts
of a number of young hopefuls who try to make it big in radio. Songs and
musical numbers include "What To Do" (Sid Robin, sung by The Andrews
Sisters), "Blue Flame" (James Noble, played by Woody Herman and His
Orchestra), "Woodchopper's Ball" (Joe Bishop, Herman, played by Herman
and His Orchestra), "I'll Pray for You" (Arthur Altman, Kim Gannon, sung
by Gloria Jean, The Andrews Sisters, Jane Frazee), "Amen [Yea-Man]"
(Roger Segure, Bill Hardy, Vic Schoen, played by Herman and His
Orchestra), "You Can't Hold a Memory in Your Arms" (Hy Zaret, Altman,
sung by Frazee), "If," "Love Laughs at Anything" (Don Raye, Gene De
Paul).

p, Ken Goldsmith; d, Edward F. Cline; w, Jerry Cady, Stanley Roberts,
Haworth Bromley (based on the story "Wake Up and Dream" by Edgar
Allan Woolf); ph, Jerome Ash; ed, Arthur Hilton; md, Charles Previn; art d,
Jack Otterson; ch, Johnny Mattison.

Musical   (PR:A   MPAA:NR)

WHAT'S GOOD FOR THE GANDER
                        (SEE: WHAT'S GOOD FOR THE GOOSE, 1969, Brit.)

WHAT'S GOOD FOR THE GOOSE*   (1969, Brit.) 104m
                                        Tigon/National Showmanship c

Norman Wisdom (*Timothy Bartlett*), Sally Geeson (*Nikki*), Sarah Atkinson
(*Meg*), Terence Alexander (*Frisby*), Sally Bazely (*Margaret Bartlett*), Derek
Francis (*Harrington*), David Lodge (*Hotel Porter*), Paul Whitsun-Jones
(*Clark*), Stuart Nichol (*Bank Manager*), Hilary Pritchard (*Cashier in
discotheque*), H. H. Goldsmith (*Policeman*), Thelma Falls-Hand (*Bank
Clerk*), Duncan Taylor (*Other Banker*), Jonathan Cox, Patrick Goggin (*Sons*),
Sally Beglin (*Daughter*), George Meaton (*3rd Speaker*), Karl Lanchbury
(*Peter*), The Pretty Things.

Popular British comedian Wisdom, noted for his roles as the little man
confronted with everyday problems, here arrives at mid-life crisis. On his
way to a bankers' convention, staid bank manager Wisdom picks up pretty
young persons Geeson and Atkinson. Bored by the conference, and
doubtlessly influenced by the after-hours carousals of the customarily
upright conventioneers, he seeks the company of his young traveling
companions. Exhausting himself dancing with Geeson at a discotheque, he
brings her to his hotel room for some hanky-panky. Staving off his
impending climacteric, he begins garbing himself in youthful attire. He runs
on the beach and swims in the altogether with the nubile naiad, and finally
sets her up in her own flat. Returning one evening, he finds a wild party in
progress, with the gold-digging girl in bed with one of her peers. Disappointed but undefeated, Wisdom reunites with his wife, Bazely, and attempts to
interest her in adopting a similarly youthful demeanor. Their efforts prove
inadequate, and the two end up apologizing to one another for their mutual
failure. Geeson (younger sister of actress Judy Geeson) gets to evidence full
frontal nudity in this, her first starring role. Motion picture merchandiser
Golan–who, with his partner Yoram Globus, became a legend at making big
bucks with low budgets with their Cannon Films company–made his British
directorial bow with this film after a start in his native Israel.

p, Tony Tenser, Norman Wisdom; d, Menahem Golan; w, Wisdom, Golan,
Christopher Gilmore; ph, William Brayne (Eastmancolor); m, Reg Tilsley;
ed, Dennis Lanning; art d, Hayden Pearce; m/l, Tilsley, Howard Blaikley,
The Pretty Things.

Comedy   (PR:O   MPAA:R)

WHAT'S IN IT FOR HARRY? (SEE: TARGET: HARRY, 1980)

WHAT'S NEW, PUSSYCAT?***½ (1965, U.S./Fr.) 108m Famous Artists-Famartists/UA c (QUOI DE NEUF, PUSSYCAT?)

Peter Sellers (Dr. Fritz Fassbender), Peter O'Toole (Michael James), Romy Schneider (Carole Werner), Capucine (Renee Lefebvre), Paul Prentiss (Liz), Woody Allen (Victor Shakapopulis), Ursula Andress (Rita), Eddra Gale (Anna Fassbender), Katrin Schaake (Jacqueline), Eleonore Hirt (Mrs. Sylvia Werner), Jean Paredes (Marcel), Jacques Balutin (Etienne), Jess Hahn (Perry Werner), Howard Vernon (Doctor), Michel Subor (Philippe), Sabine Sun (Nurse), Nicole Karen (Tempest O'Brien), Jacqueline Fogt (Charlotte), Daniel Emilfork (Gas Station Man), Tanya Lopert (Miss Lewis), Barbara Somers (Miss Marks), Robert Rollis (Car Renter), Annette Poivre (Emma), Richard Saint-Bris (Le Maire), Marion Conrad (1st Stripteaser), Maggie Wright (2nd Stripteaser), Louis Falavigna (Jean), Jean-Yves Autrey, Pascal Wolf, Nadine Papin (Fassbender's Children), Colin Drake (Durell), Norbert Terry (Kelly), Gordon Felio (Fat Man), Louise Lasser (The Nutcracker), F. Medard (Nash), Francoise Hardy (Secretary), Douking (Concierge at Renee's Apartment), Richard Burton (Man in Bar).

A most significant film to buffs as it marks the first time Woody Allen appeared on screen in a script drawn from his own typewriter. Until this time, he'd been a successful nightclub and TV variety show comic and WHAT'S NEW PUSSYCAT? gave a wider audience to his patented neuroses. It's a good example of the "swinging sixties" style under the broad direction of Clive Donner who had begun his career in films as an assistant director. O'Toole, fresh from his triumphs in LAWRENCE OF ARABIA and BECKET, shows that he can deliver the goods comedically as well as dramatically in the role of a lover of gorgeous women who fears nothing in this world save marriage. Sellers is a freaked- out, Beatle-wigged analyst who is attempting to help O'Toole deal with his problems but is so lecherous himself that he is of little value to the disturbed O'Toole. Allen is seen as the intellectual nebbish whose life is a perpetual attempt to learn why he can't attract women. He toils as a dresser (or, rather, an "un-dresser") for exotic dancers at a Parisian nightspot (the famed "Crazy Horse Saloon") and his propinquity to the femmes drives him mad. O'Toole needs a Louisville Slugger to keep the women away from him. The coterie is led by Schneider, an English teacher and pal of Allen's, who is the sanest in the lot of fatales who flock to O'Toole's side. She loves O'Toole and would enjoy becoming his wife, but there is no way she would ever put up with his compulsive Don Juan behavior, as his attitude appears to be "too many women, and not enough time." One of the patients at a Sellers group therapy session is the radiant Capucine, who is sex mad for O'Toole, much to the chagrin of her jealous husband, Paredes. Prentiss is a stripper at the club where Allen toils in frustration and perspiration and she, too, chases O'Toole. She becomes suicidal over her passion for O'Toole and reaches for her overdose of sleeping pills the way other women might reach for Kleenex. Just as O'Toole has made the supreme sacrifice and decided to marry Schneider, Andress skies down from overhead in a parachute to test O'Toole's mettle. She almost succeeds in breaking O'Toole's will power but he winds up with the comely Schneider at the conclusion when there is a raucous scene at a French country chateau and all the protagonists unite for a final madcap merry-go-round. It's this crazy scene where we get our first indication of Allen's penchant for Marxian slapstick (Groucho, Harpo and Chico, not Karlo) as action speaks louder than the sometimes-too-many words. All of the women in O'Toole's life are seen in Feydeau-like fashion as they race yon and hither, hide in closets, run around the countryside in Go-Karts, lie in wait under covers and, in general, try to capture O'Toole, who sincerely wants to avoid them (albeit half-heartedly at times) because he knows what kind of complications would ensue if he allowed himself to be seduced by any of the bevy. O'Toole marries Schneider but scant moments after the service, another "pussycat" (which he calls all of his women) emerges in the form of license clerk Hardy. The sight of her sends a jolt into O'Toole's just-married baby blue eyes. WHAT'S NEW, PUSSYCAT? is a classic comedy of its time and captures the period in sight and sound. It doesn't wear as well as a true classic, though, and many of the gags would feel dated 20 years later. Sets and costumes are superb, as are the scenes at the "Crazy Horse." Burt Bacharach's music and Hal David's lyrics helped immensely with the title tune being Oscar-nominated and reaching No. 3 in pop music polls that year. The movie was a box- office success, appealing, no doubt, to those who doubted the sexual "double standard" as well as the Teutonic psychiatrist so aptly portrayed by Sellers. Richard Burton does a cameo, as does Allen's wife at the time, Louise Lasser. By showing O'Toole as the editor on a Paris fashion magazine, the tale was able to move with lighting speed and also justify his coming into contact with so many gorgeous women–every man's dream and, most particularly, Woody Allen's. Other songs by Bacharach and David include: "Here I Am" (sung by Dionne Warwick), and "Little Red Book" (sung by Paul Jones), "What's New Pussycat?" (sung by Tom Jones).

p, Charles K. Feldman; d, Clive Donner; w, Woody Allen; ph, Jean Badal (Technicolor); m, Burt Bacharach; ed, Fergus McDonell; md, Charles Blackwell; art d, Jacques Saulnier; set d, Charles Merangel; cos, Gladys de Segonzac, Mia Fonssagrives, Vick Tiel; spec eff, M. MacDonald; ch, Jean Guelis; makeup, Charles Parker.

Comedy Cas. (PR:C MPAA:NR)

WHAT'S NEXT?** (1975, Brit.) 60m Kingsgate/Children's Film Foundation-Rank c

Peter Robinson, Perry Benson, Lynn White, James Cossins, Laurence Carter, Jerold Wells, Derek Deadman, Charles Cork, Allan O'Keefe, Janet Davies, David Webb, Peter Smart, Alan Collins.

Made with only the juvenile population in mind, this tells of a London lad who is able to foretell a crime before it takes place. In this way he pins down the kingpin behind a crime organization, who just happens to be a highly respected citizen. The cause of young Robinson's portents is a nasty knock on the head. Rather naive but not without its moral merits, making it a good thing to stick in front of a youngster for an hour.

p, Carole Smith; d, Peter Smith; w, Derek Hill; ph, Ray Orton; m, Carl Davis; ed, Brian Tomkins; art d, Evan Hercules.

Drama (PR:AAA MPAA:NR)

WHAT'S SO BAD ABOUT FEELING GOOD?** (1968) 94m UNIV c

George Peppard (Pete), Mary Tyler Moore (Liz), Don Stroud (Barney), Susan Saint James (Aida), Dom De Luise (J. Gardner Monroe), Nathaniel Frey (Conrad), John McMartin (The Mayor), Charles Lane (Dr. Shapiro), Jeanne Arnold (Gertrude), George Furth (Murgatroyd), Monty Gunty (Sgt. Gunty), Joe Ponazecki (Officer Ponazecki), Frank Campanella (Capt. Wallace), Emily Yancy (Sybil), Joey Faye (Zoo Keeper), Thelma Ritter (Mrs. Schwartz), Arny Freeman (1st Mate), Martin O'Hara (TV Newscaster), John Ryan (Roger), Cleavon Little (Phil), Gillian Spencer (The Sack), Donald Hotten (Sam), Robert Moore (Board Member), Marc Seaton, Vicki Racimo, Mina Kolb, Peter Turgeon, Kay Turner, Moses Gunn, Bob Kaliban, Ira Lewis, George Petrie, Hugh Franklin, Hy Anzell, Peter Gumeny, Eda Reiss Merin, Jara Kohout, Nat Polan, Barbara Minkus, Salem Ludwig, Franklin Cover, Louis Zorich, George Sperdakos, Albert Henderson, Lincoln Kilpatrick, Tom Ahearne.

Psittacosis becomes salubrious as a foreign toucan slips through customs in New York and infects the native population of muggers, malcontents, and self-centered strivers with a virus that causes happiness and good will. Peppard, a disaffected dropout artist, is the first to be contaminated by the euphoria bug. He and his live-in girl friend, Moore, harbor the feathered carrier, which they name "Amigo". Recognizing the source of the delightful disease, the two conspire to spread it. Soon, happiness alters the face of the city, resulting in an economic crisis: sales of cigarettes, alcoholic beverages, and tranquilizers have plummeted. Hoping to save his city from financial disaster, bland mayor McMartin–with the assistance of Presidential envoy De Luise–distributes face masks to the populace. Peppard and pals find a way to infect the masks with the virus. Counterstrike follows counterstrike as Amigo is captured and an antidote is found. Soon the city is itself again: rude, vicious, self-centered people shove, shout at, maim, rob, and kill one another. Peppard gives up his evangelic quest to rid the Big Apple of its worms, realizing that he wants only Moore who, already angelic, was unchanged by the infection. A pleasant, well-made comedy with fine lead performances and support.

p&d, George Seaton; w, Seaton, Robert Pirosh (suggested by the novel I Am Thinking of My Darling by Vincent McHugh); ph, Ernesto Caparros (Techniscope, Technicolor); m, Frank De Vol; ed, Alma Macrorie; art d, Alexander Golitzen, Henry Bumstead; set d, John McCarthy; cos, Edith Head; m/l, Jerry Keller, Dave Blume; makeup, Bud Westmore.

Comedy (PR:A MPAA:NR)

WHAT'S THE MATTER WITH HELEN?** (1971) 101m Filmways-Raymax/UA c

Debbie Reynolds (Adelle Bruckner), Shelley Winters (Helen Hill), Dennis Weaver (Lincoln Palmer), Agnes Moorehead (Sister Alma, Evangelist), Micheal MacLiammoir (Hamilton Starr), Samee Lee Jones (Winona Palmer), Robbi Morgan (Rosalie Greenbaum), Helene Winston (Mrs. Greenbaum), Molly Dodd (Mrs. Rigg), Peggy Rea (Mrs. Schultz), Yvette Vickers (Mrs. Barker), Paulle Clark (Mrs. Plumb), Pamelyn Ferdin (Kiddy M.C.), Debbie Van Den Houten (Sue Anne Schultz), Tammy Lee (Charlene Barker), Teresa De Rose (Donna Plumb), Swen Swenson (Gigolo), Timothy Carey (Tramp), Harry Stanton (Malcolm Hays), James Dobson (Cab Driver), Logan Ramsey (Detective West), Peggy Lloyd Patten (Ellie Banner), Gary Combs (Matt Hill), Sallie Delfino (Midget Lady), Annette Davis (Spinster), Helene Heigh (Widow), Peter Brocco (Old Man), Minta Durfee Arbuckle (Old Lady), Peggy Walton (Young Girl), Douglas Deane (Fanatical Man), Sharon Hisamoto, Stacy Hollow, Marcia Garcia, Bambi Meyers, Roxanne Meyers, Vicki Schreck, Keri Shuttleton, Sian Winship, Shawn Steinmann, Madelon Tupper (Dance School Students).

Another in a substantial series of vehicles for aging actresses who still possess some box-office drawing power, this film–while following the "which one is the psychotic killer?" formula–deviates from others scripted by Farrell (who appears to want to keep doing it until he gets it right), such as WHAT EVER HAPPENED TO BABY JANE? (1962) and HUSH... HUSH, SWEET CHARLOTTE (1965). It contains a number of Hollywood insider jokes (one is the employment of Fatty Arbuckle's divorced wife in a small role) and it effectively recreates an interesting bygone era. Opening with a 1930s-newsreel style title sequence, the picture recounts the travails of the mothers–Reynolds and Winters–of two Leopold-Loeb-like convicted killers. Chased from town by threatening telephone calls following the trial of their sons, the two travel to the Hollywood of early sound days and establish a dancing school for Shirley Temple clones. Reynolds is the dance instructor, while Winters belts out the music–mostly "Goody-Goody" (Johnny Mercer, Matt Malneck) on the untuned upright. The curly-topped moppets go through their routines under the fond observance of their watchful studio moms. This idyllic new life is despoiled by reminders of the prior one: a mysterious stranger wearing a raincoat who keeps the studio under silent observation; more strange telephone calls. Reynolds finds romance with wealthy westerner Weaver, but Winters finds adjustment difficult and turns to radio evangelist Moorehead (a thinly disguised Aimee Semple McPherson characterization). Ham actor MacLiammoir joins the school as an elocution instructor (and a red herring for the subsequent events). The Mackintoshed mystery man invades the studio while Winters is alone there one evening; she pushes him down the staircase to his death. The two aging pedants then drag the corpse through the rain to a hiding place. Winters discloses that her husband's "accidental" death under the blades of a farm harrow was no accident. The finale has the trussed, costumed, smiling corpse of Reynolds, complete with Jean Harlow hairdo, puppet-strung into a dancing pose in the studio as the weird Winters tinkles out a mad rendition of "Goody-Goody" on the upright. The film is flawed by a predictable story line following a fast start. Reynolds does well in her role; she reportedly invested $800,000 in the picture, so she had a high stake in its success. The contrapuntal musical score is smashing, and the muted-color visuals evoke the era well.

p, George Edwards; d, Curtis Harrington; w, Henry Farrell; ph, Lucien Ballard (DeLuxe Color); m, David Raksin; ed, William H. Reynolds; art d, Eugene Lourie; set d, Jerry Wunderlich; cos, Morton Haack; ch, Tony Charmoli; makeup, William Tuttle.

Crime   **(PR:O   MPAA:GP)**

WHAT'S UP, DOC?*   (1972) 94m Saticoy/WB c

Barbra Streisand *(Judy Maxwell)*, Ryan O'Neal *(Prof. Howard Bannister)*, Madeline Kahn *(Eunice Burns)*, Kenneth Mars *(Hugh Simon)*, Austin Pendleton *(Frederick Larrabe)*, Sorrell Booke *(Harry)*, Stefan Gierasch *(Fritz)*, Mabel Albertson *(Mrs. Van Hoskins)*, Michael Murphy *(Mr. Smith)*, Graham Jarvis *(Bailiff)*, Liam Dunn *(Judge)*, Phil Roth *(Mr. Jones)*, John Hillerman *(Mr. Kaltenborn)*, George Morfogen *(Rudy the Headwaiter)*, Randall R. 'Randy' Quaid *(Prof. Hosquith)*, M. Emmet Walsh *(Arresting Officer)*, Eleanor Zee *(Banquet Receptionist)*, Kevin O'Neal *(Delivery Boy)*, Paul Condylis *(Room Service Waiter)*, Fred Scheiwiller, Carl Saxe, Jack Perkins *(Jewel Thieves)*, Paul B. Kililman *(Druggist)*, Gil Perkins *(Jones' Driver)*, Christa Lang *(Mrs. Hosquith)*, Stan Ross, Peter Paul Eastman *(Musicologists)*, John Byner *(Head)*, Eric Brotherson *(Larrabee's Butler)*, Elaine Partnow *(Party Guest)*, George R. Burrafato *(Eunice's Cabdriver)*, Jerry Summers *(Smith's Cabdriver)*, Morton C. Thompson *(Airport Cabdriver)*, John Allen Vick *(Airport Driver)*, Donald T. Bexley *(Skycap)*, Leonard Lookabaugh *(Painter on Roof)*, Candace Brownell *(Ticket Seller)*, Sean Morgan *(Banquet Official)*, Patricia O'Neal *(Elderly Lady on Plane)*, Joe Alfasa *(Waiter in Hall)*, Chuck Hollom *(Pizza Cook)*, William M. Niven *(Painter)*, Paul Baxley, Bud Walls, Glenn H. Randall, Jr., Bill Hickman, Alex Sharp, Wally Rose, Marvin James Walters, John Angelo Moio, Ernest Robinson, Ted M. Grossman, Richard E. Butler, Loren Janes, George N. Robotham, Victor Paul, Patty Elder, Paul Stader, Donna Garrett, Jack Verbois, Gerald Brutsche, Craig Baxley, Ted Duncan, Fred Stromsoe, Bob Harris, Dean Jeffries, Richard A. Washington, Joe Pronto, Joe Amsler.

Peter Bogdanovich's attempt to restore the genre of screwball comedy is, unfortunately, more of an imitation than an *homage*, especially if you've seen Howard Hawks' classic BRINGING UP BABY. Streisand and O'Neal are also no match for Cary Grant and Katharine Hepburn but there is enough good 1930s slapstick and cartoon humor to merit your attention and to justify Bugs Bunny's famed opening line (which serves as the title) and Porky Pig's equally famed closing line of "Th-th- that's all, folks," which closes the movie. O'Neal is a clumsy and shy professor from Iowa who hopes to win a $20,000 fellowship in musicology that Pendleton is offering in San Francisco. (We know that O'Neal is shy and clumsy and intellectual by the eyeglasses he wears, but props do not always a characterization make.) In a plaid suitcase, he carries some ancient rocks which demonstrate his theory on the beginnings of music back in the days when–in the movies–cave men and dinosaurs vied for territorial rights over the earth, even though the two never coexisted. (The similarity here to BRINGING UP BABY is obvious because Grant was searching for an archaeological grant by reconstructing a dinosaur skeleton with one bone still missing.) O'Neal arrives in San Francisco with his fiancee, Kahn (in her film debut) and they check into separate rooms because that's only fitting and proper for unmarrieds from Iowa to do. O'Neal walks into a pharmacy later and meets Streisand, who is chomping on a carrot and opens the conversation with "What's Up, Doc?" At the same time, two other guests with duplicate suitcases are checking into rooms on the same floor as O'Neal (you just *know* there will be a suitcase switch). Albertson's suitcase is filled with her jewels that house dick Booke and receptionist Gierasch are planning to steal. Murphy's suitcase contains stolen government documents that federal agent Roth is planning to retrieve. Streisand also moves into a vacant room on the floor (without paying for it) and she carries the same type of valise. (There must have been a huge sale on those as it seems everyone has a copy. However, if that were

not the case, there would have been no plot. As it is, the plot is so slim it is anorexic.) That night, at the musicologists' convention banquet, Streisand pretends to be Kahn and works on Pendleton to give O'Neal the grant, thus infuriating Croation contender Mars, another money suitor. (Mars, who played a German in THE PRODUCERS and YOUNG FRANKENSTEIN, is exceptionally adroit at *mittel-European* accents.) At the same time, Booke and Gierasch are stealing the wrong suitcases (as one might have expected). O'Neal hadn't planned on what Streisand did but he is enthralled by her charm and since her efforts on his behalf have borne fruit, he doesn't blow the whistle. When Kahn finally does arrive, O'Neal tells everyone that she is an imposter and she is dragged away, screaming at the top of her ample lungs. Later, O'Neal attempts to pacify Kahn but Streisand has gone to O'Neal's room to have a bath and there's no way he can explain that. Mars calls the police, trying to create a scandal. Everyone charges into the room; the TV set is knocked off the table and a fire begins. Streisand tries to hide by hanging from a ledge outside the room and if that all sounds confusing, that's the way screwball comedy is supposed to sound. The following morning, Kahn searches for O'Neal and, instead, finds Booke being tortured by mobsters because he stole O'Neal's rocks instead of Albertson's jewels. (Albertson's name in the film is Mrs. Van Hoskins, thereby identifying her as wealthy. Screenwriters seem to think that anyone with a "Van" in front of their last name must be wealthy, except, of course, for Van Gogh, whose poverty made church mice seem rich.) The three gangsters, Schweiller, Saxe, and Perkins, force Kahn to take them to Pendleton's mansion where the award for musicology is about to be handed to O'Neal, with Streisand at his side, again pretending to be Kahn. There's a shoot-out and O'Neal and Streisand flee with all four suitcases in tow. An auto chase through the San Francisco streets ensues and everyone winds up in the Bay and is later hauled into court in front of tyrannical judge Dunn, who just happens to be Streisand's father! (Coincidence is the fulcrum upon which this, and many other comedies, swings.) O'Neal loses the grant due to his behavior in the eyes of the conservative Pendleton and his peers. He also loses Kahn to Pendleton as the two of them are prigs who were born to be with each other. Mars gets the grant but Streisand steps in and proves that Mars has plagiarized his thesis so the award swings back to O'Neal. Later, O'Neal is returning on the plane to Iowa with Streisand at his side and he apologizes profusely for the manner in which he treated her earlier. Steisand replies: "Love means never having to say you're sorry" (a parody of O'Neal's successful appearance in LOVE STORY). O'Neal replies: "That's the silliest thing I've ever heard," like Groucho. They embrace and watch Bugs Bunny and Elmer Fudd sing, then Porky breaks through the screen with his patented closing line. The movie grossed nearly $30 million, pleased a few critics, and delighted the public. Streisand and O'Neal were to do a film called "A Glimpse of Tiger" which had been developed for her ex-husband, Elliot Gould, at Fox. It was dropped and Bogdanovich wanted to do a picture with his two stars so he wrote a story, hired Benton and Newman to do the script (the team had written Warner's box-office bonanza BONNIE AND CLYDE) then brought in Buck Henry to rewrite. The Writers Guild Arbitration Committee must have felt that Henry's work was important because they awarded him first position in the credits. Splendid second banana work from several actors who went on to successful careers. Note John Hillerman ("Magnum, P.I.), Randy Quaid (THE LAST DETAIL, PAPER MOON, MIDNIGHT EXPRESS), Michael Murphy (MANHATTAN, AN UNMARRIED WOMAN) and others. Stan Ross, who appears as one of the musicologists, is the man who used to be with Milton Berle and Jackie Gleason as a comedy foil and is not to be confused with Stanley Ralph Ross, co-author of *The Motion Picture Guide*, who also acts from time to time and was seen in TONY ROME, ROMANTIC COMEDY, SLEEPER, and many TV shows. WHAT'S UP, DOC? was shot on location in San Francisco and Kovacs' cinematography made the city look like a jewel. The director was only 32 at the time and, other than PAPER MOON and THE LAST PICTURE SHOW, never had this kind of commercial success. He declared bankruptcy in 1986.

p&d, Peter Bogdanovich; w, Buck Henry, David Newman, Robert Benton (based on a story by Bogdanovich); ph, Laszlo Kovacs (Technicolor); m, Artie Butler; ed, Verna Fields; md, Butler; prod d, Polly Platt; art d, Herman A. Blumenthal; set d, John Austin; cos, Nancy McArdle, Ray Phelps; spec eff, Robert MacDonald; m/l, "You're the Top," Cole Porter, sung by Barbara Steisand, Ryan O'Neal, "As Time Goes By," Herman Hupfeld, sung by Streisand; makeup, Don Cash.

Comedy   **Cas.**   **(PR:AA   MPAA:G)**

WHAT'S UP FRONT*   (1964) 83m Delta/Fairway-International c
                    (AKA: THE FALL GUY; A FOURTH FOR MARRIAGE)

Tommy Holden *(Homer L. Pettigrew)*, Marilyn Manning *(Candy Cotton)*, Carolyn Walker *(Pamela Johnson)*, William Watters [Arch Hall, Sr.] *(Cash Johnson)*, Carmen Bonacci *(August Poe)*, Mary Jane Neese *(Joan)*, Barbara Ballar *(Mable)*, Jack Sword *(Alf)*, Robert Wheeler *(Gen. Smythe)*, Nancy Czar *(Mrs. Smythe)*, Joan Howard, David Reed, Rick Dennis, Addalyn Fay, Sam Chiodi.

This low-budget bra-burner by the creator of the unforgettable camp classic EEGAH! (1963) has meek salesman Holden gaining employment with Watters' brassiere manufacturing company by suggesting that he can increase sales using door-to-door methods. Succeeding beyond his wildest dreams–to the discomfiture of sales manager Bonacci, who is trying to get ahead by romancing Walker, the boss' daughter–Holden is sent to the sticks by Bonacci. Tenacious to the last, Holden manages to sell even the airline flight attendants on an uplifting experience during his flight to West Virginia, where he brings brassieres to the buxom farm girls. Bonacci tries to take credit for the successes of his rival and reports the returning salesman to government authorities as a mad bomber. FBI agents arrest Holden at the airport, but discover nothing more sinister than D cups in his luggage. Bonacci is arrested at the altar as he is about to marry Walker and Holden takes his place as groom. Hall, Sr., served as executive producer on this one-joke film which he financed, cowrote, and acted in.

p, Anthony M. Lanza; d, Bob Wehling; w, Wehling, Arch Hall, Sr. (based on the story by Hall); ph, William Zsigmond (Technicolor); ed, Lanza; art d, David Reed III; cos, Frederick's of Hollywood.

Comedy   **(PR:C   MPAA:NR)**

WHAT'S UP, TIGER LILY?**½   (1966) 80m Toho-Benedict/AIP c

Tatsuya Mihashi (*Phil Moscowitz*), Mie Hama (*Terri Yaki*), Akiko Wakabayashi (*Suki Yaki*), Tadao Nakamaru (*Shepherd Wong*), Susumu Kurobe (*Wing Fat*), Woody Allen (*Narrator/Host/Voice*), Frank Buxton, Len Maxwell, Louise Lasser, Mickey Rose, Julie Bennett, Bryna Wilson (*Voices*), The Lovin' Spoonful (*Themselves*), China Lee (*Herself*), Kumi Mizuno.

Woody Allen took a low-grade Japanese spy film called KAGI NO KAGI (Key of Keys) and dubbed in new dialog (improvised with Buxton, Maxwell, Lasser, Rose, Wilson, and Bennett) to create this wonderfully cockeyed movie. In a prolog Allen explains to an interviewer that this is the "definitive" spy picture. Allen was chosen to head the project because Hollywood knows that "death and danger are his various breads and various butters." The story tells the adventures of Phil Moscowitz, a Japanese James Bond who is searching for the world's greatest egg salad recipe. The balance of world power hangs on whether or not Moscowitz can keep this recipe–"so delicious you could *plotz*"–from falling into the wrong hands. After much pluck and derring Moscowitz confronts Shepherd Wong, the evil mastermind trying to get the recipe for his own nefarious doings. Moscowitz defeats Wong's henchmen and then returns to his loves, Suki and Terri Yaki. They eagerly await his arrival, "bringing with him the constant promise of joy and fulfillment in its most primitive form," but alas Moscowitz is now under the delusion that he is a Pan Am jet! WHAT'S UP, TIGER LILY?, more than any of Allen's films, is beyond the realm of synopsis. It's cleverly devised, with an incredible sense of the absurd. Allen and his cohorts make good use of situations, turning KEY OF KEYS' obvious cliches into some wonderful parodic gems. The one-liners spew out like popcorn popping and as a result this wears a little thin towards the end. This is a film to see only once, for the wild humor loses its punch with repeated viewings. Footage of the pop group The Lovin' Spoonful edited into the story also detracts from the pell-mell pacing. Though Allen had limited control over the visual content, the beginnings of specific themes and ideas he would later develop in such films as LOVE AND DEATH and HANNAH AND HER SISTERS are clearly evident within the dialog. Allen plays around with sexual frustrations, psychiatry and neurosis, Judaism, and the influence of movies within the myriad of one-liners. Executive producer Saperstein paid only $66,000 for the rights to KEY OF KEYS and certainly got more than his money's worth when he turned this cover to the rising comedian. Heard on the soundtrack are Allen's second wife, Lasser, and Rose, who cowrote Allen's films TAKE THE MONEY AND RUN and BANANAS. A brief appearance in the closing credits is made by China Lee, a former Playboy centerfold and wife of comedian Mort Sahl. Songs include: "Pow," "Pow Revisited" (John Sebastian, Joe Butler, Steve Boone, Zalman Yanovsky, Skip Boone, sung by the Lovin' Spoonful), "Gray Prison Blues," "Unconscious Minuet," "A Cool Million," "Lookin' to Spy," "Phil's Love Theme" (Sebastian, Butler, Steve Boone, Yanovsky, sung by The Lovin' Spoonful), "Fishin' Blues" (arranged by Sebastian, sung by The Lovin' Spoonful), "Respoken" (Sebastian, sung by Sebastian), "Speakin' of Spoken" (Sebastian, sung by The Lovin' Spoonful).

p, Woody Allen; d, Senkichi Taniguchi; w, Kazuo Yamada, Allen, Frank Buxton, Len Maxsell, Louise Lasser, Mickey Rose, Bryna Wilson, Julie Bennett; ph, Yamada (Tohoscope, Eastmancolor); ed, Richard Krown; m, Jack Lewis, The Lovin' Spoonful.

Comedy   **Cas.**   **(PR:C   MPAA:PG)**

WHAT'S YOUR RACKET?*   (1934) 64m Mayfair bw

Regis Toomey (*Bert Miller*), Noel Francis (*Mae Cosgrove*), J. Carrol Naish (*Dick Graves*), Fred Malatesta (*Benton*), May Wallace (*Mrs. Cosgrove*), Lew Kelly (*Cameron*), David Callis (*Jones*).

Toomey is an undercover cop attempting to infiltrate a gang of mobsters. Francis is a "moll" who undertakes dangerous assignments–such as burglarizing the home of a rival hoodlum–for her mob. The denouement proves her to be the daughter of a one-time bank president who was framed and sent to prison by the gang. Together with Toomey, she cracks the case and frees her father. Made strictly as a second feature.

d, Fred Guiol; w, Barry Barringer (based on a story by George E. Rogan); ph, James S. Brown, Jr.; ed, Dan Milner.

Crime   **(PR:A   MPAA:NR)**

WHEEL OF ASHES*½   (1970, Fr.) 110/96m PBN/Film-Makers bw

Pierre Clementi (*Pierre*), Katinka Bo (*Anka*), Pierre Besancon (*David*), Members of the Living Theater.

The Living Theater enjoyed a brief spate of popularity during the 1960s with its then-novel near-nudity and audience involvement techniques. Associates of the group created this Parisian travelog centering on the karma-seeking quest of the introspective Clementi, who explores his inner self through contacts with the landmarks of Paris and through random sexual adventures. He gets Danish expatriate Bo pregnant, but deserts her, retreating to his room for a long session of contemplation filled with fantasies. Ultimately, he decides to effect certain compromises; he embraces both life and Bo while retaining his basic beliefs in mysticism. Pretentious pap filmed in 16 mm, available in that format at an overlong 96 minutes or in blown-up 35 mm at an even more exhausting 110 minutes.

d,w&ph, Peter Emanuel Goldman; ed, Joele Bleton.

Drama   **(PR:C   MPAA:NR)**

WHEEL OF FATE*   (1953, Brit.) 70m Kenilworth/GFD bw (GB: ROAD HOUSE GIRL)

Patric Doonan (*Johnny Burrows*), Sandra Dorne (*Lucky Price*), Bryan Forbes (*Ted Reid*), John Horsley (*Sgt. Simpson*), Johnnie Schofield (*Len Bright*), Martin Benson (*Riscoe*), Cyril Smith (*Perce*).

Doonan and Forbes are stepbrothers who co-operate a garage. Forbes, however, has few ambitions beyond spending his money at the dog track and chasing dance hall singer Dorne. When Dorne meets Doonan she falls for him, jilting Forbes. Forbes gets revenge by killing his invalid father and stealing his money. While trying to escape he is nearly hit by a train, but lives and is caught by the police.

p&d, Francis Searle; w, Guy Elmes (based on the play by Alex Atkinson); ph, Reginald Wyer.

Crime   **(PR:A   MPAA:NR)**

WHEEL OF FORTUNE   (SEE: MAN BETRAYED, 1941)

WHEEL OF LIFE, THE*   (1929) 55m PAR bw

Richard Dix (*Capt. Leslie Yeullat*), Esther Ralston (*Ruth Dangan*), O. P. Heggie (*Col. John Dangan*), Arthur Hoyt (*George Faraker*), Myrtle Stedman (*Mrs. Faraker*), Larry Steers (*Major*), Nigel de Brulier (*Tsering Lama, Buddhist Priest*), Regis Toomey (*Lt. MacLaren*).

Dix is a British officer on leave in London who falls in love with Ralston. Discovering that she is the vacationing wife of his commanding officer Heggie, he disavows his feelings and requests a transfer from his regiment. Returning to India, Dix goes to the rescue of Ralston and some other Britons who are trapped in a Buddhist monastery, besieged by hostile tribesmen. Believing themselves doomed, the lovers unite and confess their feelings for one another. Their terminal reveries are interrupted by Buddhist priest de Brulier, who lectures them about oriental mysticism. At the conclusion of the interminable theology lesson, reinforcements arrive, led by none other than the lady's husband, who declares his undying love for her. Husband Heggie is then conveniently killed by a stray bullet, which tells us something about his *karma*. Released in both silent and sound versions.

d, Victor Schertzinger; w, John Farrow, Julian Johnson (based on a story by James Bernard Fagan); ph, Edward Cronjager; ed, Otho Lovering.

Drama   **(PR:A   MPAA:NR)**

WHEELER DEALERS, THE**½   (1963) 106m Filmways/MGM c (GB: SEPARATE BEDS)

James Garner (*Henry Tyroon*), Lee Remick (*Molly Thatcher*), Phil Harris (*Ray Jay*), Chill Wills (*Jay Ray*), Louis Nye (*Stanislas*), John Astin (*Hector Vanson*), Jim Backus (*Bullard Bear*), Elliott Reid (*Leonard*), Patricia Crowley (*Eloise*), Pat Harrington, Jr (*Buddy Zack*), Joey Forman (*Buster Yarrow*), Charles Watts (*J. R.*), Vaughn Taylor (*Thaddeus Whipple*), Howard McNear (*Mr. Wilson*), Robert Strauss (*Fineberg*), Marcel Hillaire (*Giuseppe*), John Marley (*Achilles Dimitrios*), Don Briggs (*Len Fink*), Peter Leeds (*Arthur Watkins*), William Fawcett, Percy Helton, Dal McKennon (*The Whipples*), H. M. Wynant (*Bo Bluedog*), Walter Burke (*Billy Joe*).

A number of outrageously zany characterizations were gathered together in this spoof of Wall Street stock market ethics. Garner is the catalyst that sets the whole thing in motion when he comes to analyst Remick to invest some of his "millions." Though Garner hardly has a penny, Remick is told by her always business-minded boss, Backus, to sell him a totally worthless stock. As it turns out, the stock is actually worth tons when oil is discovered on property belonging to the company. A number of skeletons are brought out of the closet as Garner actually turns out to be a millionaire once the deal is completed, promptly asking for the hand of Remick. Both script and direction are aimed at keeping the pace moving swiftly, much in accordance with the practices of Wall Street and greater New York in general. Garner is the only character to show any depth, though all perform with comic intention.

p, Martin Ransohoff; d, Arthur Hiller; w, George J. W. Goodman, Ira Wallach (based on the novel by Goodman); ph, Charles Lang (Panavision, Metrocolor); m, Frank De Vol; ed, Tom McAdoo; art d, George W. Davis, Addison Hehr; set d, Henry Grace, Keogh Gleason; cos, Norman Norell; m/l, title song, Randy Sparks, sung by The New Christy Minstrels; makeup, William Tuttle.

Comedy   **(PR:A MPAA:NR)**

WHEELS OF DESTINY*½   (1934) 63m UNIV bw

Ken Maynard *(Ken Manning)*, Dorothy Dix *(Mary)*, Philo McCullough *(Rocky)*, Frank Rice *(Pinwheel)*, Jay Wilsey *(Buffalo Bill, Jr.)*, Ed Coxen *(Dad)*, Fred Sale, Jr *("Scalp-em-Alive")*, Fred McKaye *(Red)*, Jack Rockwell *(Ed)*, William Gould *(Deacon)*, Nelson McDowell *(Trapper)*, Merrill McCormick, Slim Whitaker, Hank Bell, Robert Burns, Artie Ortego, Wally Wales [Hal Taliaferro], Jack Evans, Helen Gibson, Bud McClure, Fred Burns, Chief Big Tree, Roy Bucko, Marin Sais, Chuck Baldra, Arkansas Johnny, Blackjack Ward, Bobby Dunn, Tarzan the Horse.

Miner Maynard hooks up with a wagon train of adventurers as he makes his trek back East with a map leading to his recently found claim. Among this group is a callous bunch whose intention is to ambush the wagons in order to gain access to Maynard's find. They do so by instigating an Indian uprising. Little variation from the accepted formula of oater material.

p, Ken Maynard; d, Allan James; w, Nate Gatzert; ph, Ted McCord; ed, Charles Harris.

Western   **(PR:A MPAA:NR)**

WHEN A FELLER NEEDS A FRIEND
                    (SEE: FELLER NEEDS A FRIEND, 1932)

WHEN A GIRL'S BEAUTIFUL*   (1947) 68m COL bw

Adele Jergens, Marc Platt, Patricia White, Stephen Dunne, Steven Geray, Mona Barrie, Jack Leonard, Paul Harvey, Lela Bliss, Nancy Saunders, Doris Houck, Amelita Ward, Peggie Call, Vera Stokes, Thomas Louden.

An one-line joke about young advertising man Platt, who creates a photograph of a woman by combining the best parts of a number of pictures of various models. He then must find a girl to fit the bill. A charming idea which ended up as a shallow picture. Songs include "I'm Sorry I Didn't Say I'm Sorry," "When a Girl's Beautiful" (Allan Roberts, Lester Lee).

p, Wallace MacDonald; d, Frank McDonald; w, Brenda Weisberg (based on a story by Henry K. Moritz); ph, Henry Freulich; ed, Jerome Thoms; md, Mischa Bakaleinikoff; art d, A. Leslie Thomas; set d, James Crowe.

Musical   **(PR:A MPAA:NR)**

WHEN A MAN RIDES ALONE*½   (1933) 60m Freuler/Monarch bw

Tom Tyler *(Tom Harris)*, Adele Lacey *(Ruth Davis)*, Al Bridge *(Slade)*, Bob Burns *(Sheriff)*, Frank Ball *(Jack Davis)*, Alma Chester *(Aggie Simpson)*, Barney Furey *(Deputy Sheriff)*, Lee Cordova, Lillian Chay, Jack Rockwell, Bud Osborne, Ed Burns, Jack Kirk, Herman Hack.

Robin Hood comes to the Old West in this tale of Tyler as a masked outlaw who robs the gold-shipment wagons of an unscrupulous mining firm and uses the proceeds to reimburse investors who have been cheated out of their fair profits. Inadvertently viewed by Lacey, he abducts her to protect his secret identity. Initially outraged, the lissome Lacey–daughter of one of the swindling company's victims–joins her abductor in bringing the wretches to justice. A superior western romance.

p, Burton King; d, J. P. McGowan; w, Oliver Drake (based on a story by F. McGrew Willis); ph, Edward Kull; ed, Fred Bain.

Western   **(PR:A MPAA:NR)**

WHEN A MAN SEES RED*½   (1934) 60m UNIV bw

Buck Jones, Dorothy Revier, Syd Saylor, Peggy Campbell, LeRoy Mason, Frank LaRue, Libby Taylor, Jack Rockwell, Charles K. French, Bob Kortman, William Steele.

More of a love story than usually found in the oater formula, with Jones being the foreman of a ranch recently inherited by Campbell. The two argue incessantly, as lovers always do, each trying to make the other jealous by shifting their attention elsewhere. But when things start getting tough, Campbell shows just how much she's been taken by the cowboy by shielding the wounded Jones with her own body.

p, Buck Jones; d&w, Alan James (based on a story by Basil Dickey); ph, Ted McCord, Joseph Novak.

Western   **(PR:A MPAA:NR)**

WHEN A MAN'S A MAN*   (1935) 60 Lesser-Zanft/FOX bw

George O'Brien *(Larry Knight)*, Dorothy Wilson *(Kitty Baldwin)*, Paul Kelly *(Phil Acton)*, Harry Woods *(Nick Cambert)*, Jimmy Butler *(Newsboy)*, Richard Carlisle *(Dean Baldwin)*, Clarence Wilson *(Garby)*, Edgar Norton *(Gibbs)*.

Down on his luck, tenderfoot easterner O'Brien heeds the advice of Horace Greeley. Once in the west, O'Brien attempts to prove himself by taming an irascible, unridden bronco, to the great amusement of the assembled ranchhands. Water rights threaten peaceful relations between adjacent ranchers, but O'Brien divines a well site for the arid side to save the day and win the hand of rancher's daughter Wilson. A predictable, overused story and limited action flaw this well-acted western.

p, Sol Lesser, d, Edward F. Cline; w, Agnes Christine Johnson, Frank M. Dazey, Dan Jarrett (based on a story by Harold Bell Wright); ph, Frank B. Good.

Western   **(PR:A MPAA:NR)**

WHEN A STRANGER CALLS***   (1979) 97m COL c

Carol Kane *(Jill Johnson)*, Rutanya Alda *(Mrs. Mandrakis)*, Carmen Argenziano *(Dr. Mandrakis)*, Kirsten Larkin *(Nancy)*, Charles Durning *(John Clifford)*, Bill Boyett *(Sgt. Sacker)*, Ron O'Neal *(Lt. Charlie Garber)*, Heetu *(Houseboy)*, Rachel Roberts *(Dr. Monk)*, Tony Beckley *(Curt Duncan)*, Colleen Dewhurst *(Tracy)*, Michael Champion *(Bill)*, Joe Reale *(Bartender)*, Ed Wright *(Retired Man)*, Louise Wright *(Retired Woman)*, Carol O'Neal *(Mrs. Garber)*, Dennis McMullen *(Maintenance Man)*, Wally Taylor *(Cheater)*, John Tobyansen *(Bar Customer)*, Sarah Dammann *(Bianca Lockart)*, Richard Bail *(Stevie Lockart)*, Steven Anderson *(Stephen Lockart)*, Lenora May *(Sharon)*, Randy Holland *(Maitre d')*, Trent Dolan, Frank Dielsi, Arell Blanton, DeForest Covan, Charles Boswell *(Policemen)*.

Unbearably scary in spots, WHEN A STRANGER CALLS begins with a sequence that will test anyone's threshold for fright. A baby sitter, Kane, arrives at the home of a doctor and his wife to begin what she thinks will be a quiet evening of work. She goes through the usual baby sitter routine–eating whatever she can find in the refrigerator and racking up the phone bill by calling her friends. She then gets a rather ominous phone call from a man who asks a rather ominous question, "have you checked the children?" Considering the children are safely tucked away upstairs in bed, Kane assumes the call to be a prank. The calls keep coming, however. She calls the police, who offer to trace them. After another phone call, the police contact Kane. They tell her the calls are coming from inside the house. As a menacing shadow approaches the top of the staircase, Kane frantically tries to unlock the front door (unlocking doors is a skill everyone in movies seems to lose when frightened). She opens it to find Durning, a police officer, standing in front of her. The childrens parents are notified that a madman has killed their two children. Unfortunately, the film comes to a screeching halt at this point, which comes as no surprise since the beginning was originally a short film called THE SITTER. Director Walton just decided to expand the premise (which is an ingenious one) into a feature. That also explains why Kane is absent from the film for the next hour. The story picks up seven years later with Durning resuming his interest in the case when he learns that the killer, Beckley, has escaped from a mental institution run by Roberts. After meeting Dewhurst in a bar (the familiar "Torchy's" from 1982's 48 HOURS), Beckley, who appears to be as gentle as a homeless puppy, begins to pursue her. He follows her back to her apartment and invites himself in, but he leaves peacefully. Durning follows the scent to Dewhurst and starts questioning her. She tries to keep from getting involved, but Durning persists. By now Durning is determined to find and kill Beckley. He gives chase but Beckley eludes him and escapes into the night. We then see Kane and her husband preparing to go out for the evening. The children are asleep upstairs and the baby sitter has just arrived. While at the restaurant, Kane is called to the phone. The voice on the other end asks, "have you checked your children?" Needless to say, Kane completely flips out. The baby sitter is warned and police are summoned to the house. No one is found, however, and the children are safe. Later that evening Kane is preparing for bed. As a precautionary method, her husband has pulled his shotgun out of the closet. Kane begins to hear noises. The power goes off. The phone has been disconnected. Frightened, she gets back into bed and hears a voice coming from the closet. Without revealing the truly heart-stopping end, it can be said that Kane survives, as do her children, with Durning arriving on the scene in the nick of time. As chilling as WHEN A STRANGER CALLS is, it can be unbelievably stupid at points, raising countless questions. Why does Durning decide to kill Beckley? He has been in an asylum for years and shows no sign of wanting to kill again. Why should we believe that Beckley, a seemingly harmless though maladjusted Britisher, has viciously ripped two children limb from limb years earlier? (The film is surprisingly bloodless, however.) Why does Durning try to kill Beckley with a ridiculous little needle instead of the more effective and popular .357 Magnum? Most importantly, why does Kane let her children sleep in another room after receiving such a threatening phone call? And why is her husband's shotgun al the way across the room instead of right next to the bed? Aside from all these logic lapses (which have become essential to horror films over the years), WHEN A STRANGER CALLS will still frighten the bejesus out of most audiences. The perfect film for mischievous parents to rent and leave in the video recorder for their baby sitter.

p, Doug Chapin, Steve Feke; d, Fred Walton; w, Feke, Walton; ph, Don Peterman; m, Dana Kaproff; ed, Sam Vitale; prod d, Elayne Barbara Ceder; m/l, "Space Race," Billy Preston (performed by Preston).

Horror   **Cas.**   **(PR:O   MPAA:R)**

WHEN A WOMAN ASCENDS THE STAIRS***
(1963, Jap.) 111m Toho bw (ONNA GA KAIDAN O AGARU TOKI)

Hideko Takamine (Keiko Yashiro), Masayuki Mori (Nobuhiko Fujisaki), Daisuke Kato (Matsukichi Sekine), Tatsuya Nakadai (Kenichi Komatsu), Reiko Dan (Junko Inchihashi), Keiko Awaji (Yuri), Eitaro Ozawa (Minobe), Ganjiro Nakamura (Goda).

Tragic story of a woman who works hard as a barmaid to avoid the alternative fate of becoming a prostitute. After a failed attempt at business, she accepts the fact that prostitution is the only means available for her to earn a living. As in all of Naruse's late period films, a depressing and fatalistic tone is maintained.

p, Ryuzo Kikushima; d, Mikio Naruse; w, Kikushima; ph, Masao Tami (Tohoscope); m, Toshiro Mayuzumi; ed, H. Ito; cos, Hideko Takamine.

Drama   **(PR:C   MPAA:NR)**

WHEN ANGELS DON'T FLY   (SEE: AWAKENING, THE, 1958, Ital.)

WHEN BLONDE MEETS BLONDE
(SEE: ANYBODY'S BLONDE, 1931)

WHEN DINOSAURS RULED THE EARTH**
(1971, Brit.) 96m Hammer/WB c

Victoria Vetri (Sanna), Robin Hawdon (Tara), Patrick Allen (Kingsor), Drewe Henley (Khaku), Sean Caffrey (Kane), Magda Konopka (Ulido), Imogen Hassall (Ayak), Patrick Holt (Ammon), Jan Rossini (Rock Girl), Carol-Anne Hawkins (Yani), Maria O'Brien (Omah), Connie Tilton (Sand Mother), Maggie Lynton (Rock Mother), Jimmy Lodge (Fisherman), Billy Cornelius, Ray Ford (Hunters).

Nearly naked prehistoric ladies wearing push-up bras and animated anachronisms are the major features of this follow-up to Hammer's last venture into prehistory, ONE MILLION YEARS B.C. (1966). The Venus-like Vetri's golden tresses are blamed by her Rock Tribe's elders for an eruption of the sun which causes the moon to break away from it. Condemned to be sacrificed to appease the creator of this unlikely natural phenomenon, Vetri leaps from a cliff into the sea. Rescued by muscular fisherman Hawdon and his Sand Tribe cohorts, she is again threatened when the pursuing Rock chief forms an alliance with the small-grained group. She takes refuge within a dinosaur eggshell. The appropriate maternal bonding ensues, and Vetri finds herself regarded as part of a mother dinosaur's brood. Protected by the saurian, she is found by the lovestruck Hawdon, who joins her for a happy romp. Returning to his people, Hawdon is menaced for his affiliation with Vetri and sentenced to the stake (these folks have discovered fire). In the nick of time, the orbiting gaseous solar breakaway solidifies to become the moon, creating a monstrous tidal wave. Vetri, Hawdon, and another pair of young lovers are the sole survivors. With a total of 27 coined words, the picture isn't exactly dialog heavy. Vetri, who inherited the mega-annum mantle of Carole Landis and Raquel Welch, was known as Angela Dorian when she was Playboy magazine's Playmate of the Year in 1968.

p, Aida Young; d&w, Val Guest (based on an idea by J.G. Ballard); ph, Dick Bush (Technicolor); m, Mario Nascimbene; ed, Peter Curran; art d, John Blezard; cos, Carl Toms; spec eff, Allan Bryce, Roger Dicken, Brian Johncock, Jim Danforth; makeup, Richard Mills.

Fantasy   **(PR:A   MPAA:G)**

WHEN EIGHT BELLS TOLL**   (1971, Brit.) 94m Winkast/Cinerama c

Anthony Hopkins (Philip Calvert), Robert Morley (Sir Arthur Arnold-Jones), Nathalie Delon (Charlotte), Jack Hawkins (Sir Anthony Skouras), Corin Redgrave (Hunslett), Derek Bond (Lord Charnley), Ferdy Mayne (Lavorski), Maurice Roeves (Helicopter Pilot), Leon Collins (Tim Hutchinson), Wendy Allnut (Sue Kirkside), Peter Arne (Imrie), Oliver MacGreevy (Quinn), Jon Croft (Durran), Tom Chatto (Lord Kirkside), Charlie Stewart (Sgt. MacDonald), Edward Burnham (Macullum), Del Henney (Dungeon Guard).

An incredibly convoluted thriller which has Hopkins on an underwater search to stop a mysterious gang of gold bullion pirates. Ordered to investigate the situation by his superior Morley, Hopkins and his assistant Redgrave pose as marine biologists in a Scottish coastal town. The area has been shaken by a number of unexplained murders believed to have been engineered by the wealthy Hawkins, who lives on a luxurious yacht with "wife" Delon (real-life ex-wife of Alain Delon) and advisor Mayne. Hopkins spends a great deal of his time investigating the ocean floor until he finds a cave hidden away under a cliffside castle. In the meantime, Redgrave is mysteriously drowned, his bloated corpse found tied to an anchor. Delon

informs on her "husband" and relays details about the pirating scheme to Hopkins. Further investigation turns up proof that the pirates are transferring the bullion from a sunken ship to Hawkins' nearby castle. It turns out that Delon is really married to Mayne and that the pair has blackmailed Hawkins into warehousing the bullion. The investigators and the villains battle it out at the cave and by the finale all the pirates are dead except for Delon. Hopkins, who has found a soft spot for Delon, lets her escape and even provides her with a gold ingot. WHEN EIGHT BELLS TOLL (the title refers to midnight, which is when the climax takes place), with all of its mysterious murders and helicopter explosions, has a certain visceral appeal, but on a level of logic it falls apart at the seams. The outcome is cliche-ridden and has all the depth of an adolescent mystery novel. Hopkins does an admirable job of creating a James Bond-type hero but the script is too concerned with plot mechanisms to pump much life into his character. An exquisitely photographed piece of escapism and nothing more.

p, Elliott Kastner; d, Etienne Perier, Paul Stader; w, Alistair MacLean (based on his novel); ph, Arthur Ibbetson (Panavision, Eastmancolor); m, Wally Stott; ed, John Shirley; md, Stott; art d, Jack Maxted; set d, Peter Lamont; cos, Sue Yelland; spec eff, Les Hillman; stunts, Bob Simmons.

Mystery/Crime   **(PR:C   MPAA:GP)**

WHEN G-MEN STEP IN*½   (1938) 61m COL bw

Don Terry (Frederick Garth), Jacqueline Wells [Julie Bishop] (Marjory Drake), Robert Paige (Bruce Garth), Gene Morgan (Neale), Paul Fix (Clip Phillips), Stanley Andrews (Preston), Edward Earle (Morton), Horace MacMahon (Jennings), Huey White (Turk).

Paige plays the government agent given the assignment of breaking up the racketeers who have his brother, Terry, as their kingpin, this racket having a hand in just about every type of crime possible. As it turns out Terry isn't as bad a guy as everyone had him figured to be. Routine, though the fast pacing keeps that from being too heavily noticed.

p, Wallace MacDonald; d, C.C. Coleman, Jr.; w, Arthur T. Horman (based on the story by Horman, Robert C. Bennett); ph, Henry Freulich; ed, Al Clark.

Crime   **(PR:A   MPAA:NR)**

WHEN GANGLAND STRIKES*½   (1956) 70m REP bw

Raymond Greenleaf, Marjie Miller, John Hudson, Anthony Caruso, Marian Carr, Slim Pickens, Mary Treen, Ralph Dumke, Morris Ankrum, Robert Emmett Keane, Addison Richards, John Gallaudet, Paul Birch, Richard Deacon, James Best, Jim Hayward, Peter Mamakos, Fred Siterman, Dick Elliott, Norman Leavitt, Jack Perrin.

A country prosecutor puts aside his duties and devotes his energy to saving his blackmailed daughter from danger. A less than memorable picture which mixes six-shooting with gangland crime. Remake of MAIN STREET LAWYER (1939).

p, William J. O'Sullivan; d, R.G. Springsteen; w, John K. Butler, Frederic Louis Fox; ph, John L. Russell, Jr.; ed, Tony Martinelli; md, Van Alexander; art d, Walter Keller; cos, Adele Palmer.

Crime   **(PR:A   MPAA:NR)**

WHEN GIRLS LEAVE HOME   (SEE: MISSING GIRLS, 1936)

WHEN HELL BROKE LOOSE*   (1958) 78m PAR bw

Charles Bronson (Steve Boland), Violet Rensing (Ilsa), Richard Jaeckel (Karl), Arvid Nelson (Ludwig), Robert Easton (Jonesie), Dennis McCarthy (Capt. Melton), Bob Stevenson (Capt. Grayson), Eddie Foy III (Brooklyn), Kathy Carlyle (Ruby), Ann Wakefield (Myra), John Morley (Chaplain), Ed Penny (Bertie).

Unoriginal Bronson outing in which he plays a bookie who joins the Army to escape the hands of the law, and not even the rigidness of a soldier's life can tame his rebellious ways. It requires a woman, Rensing, to give Bronson some form of respect. It is also this same woman who helps make him a hero when she tells him of an underground movement plotting to kill President Dwight Eisenhower. Performances looked so bad that even Bronson was a Laurence Olivier in comparison.

p, Oscar Brodney, Sol Dolgin; d, Kenneth G. Crane; w, Brodney (based on articles by Ib Melchior); ph, Hal McAlpin; m, Albert Glasser; ed, Asa Clark; set d, G. W. Bernstein; spec eff, Jess Davidson.

War   **(PR:A   MPAA:NR)**

WHEN I GROW UP**½   (1951) 90m Horizon/EL bw

1890 Sequence: Bobby Driscoll (Josh Reed), Robert Preston (Father Reed), Martha Scott (Mother Reed), Sherry Jackson (Ruthie Reed), Johnny McGovern (Duckface Kelly), Frances Cheney (Mrs. Kelly), Poodles Hanneford (Bobo), Ralph Dumke (Carp), Paul Guilfoyle (Doc), Paul Levitt (Carp's Assistant), Griff Barnett (Dr. Bailey), Margaret Lloyd (Volunteer Nurse), Modern Sequence: Bobby Driscoll (Denny Reed), Charles Grapewin (Grandpa Reed), Henry [Harry] Morgan (Father Reed), Elizabeth Fraser

(Mother Reed), Bobby Hyatt *(Binks)*, Robin Camp *(Bully)*, Ruth Lee *(Bully's Mother)*, Donald Gordon *(Harmonica Boy)*.

Touching story about a young boy, Driscoll, who can't seem to generate any warmth from his harried parents. The lad's grandfather, Grapewin, also lives with the boy's family, and kept a diary about similar feelings he had toward his parents back in the 1890s. He wanted to run away from home to join the circus, but was stopped when stricken with typhoid. His life was saved only through the tender care of his father, who died contracting the disease. Though given a saccharine treatment, a meaningful message is effectively made regarding people being unable to show their love.

p, S.P. Eagle [Sam Spiegel]; d&w, Michael Kanin; ph, Ernest Laszlo; m, Jerome Moross; ed, Edward Mann; m/l, (harmonica played by George Fields).

Drama   **(PR:AA MPAA:NR)**

WHEN IN ROME**½   (1952) 78m MGM bw

Van Johnson *(Father John Halligan)*, Paul Douglas *(Joe Brewster)*, Joseph Calleia *(Aggiunto Bodulli)*, Carlo Rizzo *(Antonio Silesto)*, Tudor Owen *(Father McGinniss)*, Dino Nardi *(Commissario, Genoa)*, Aldo Silvani *(Cabby)*, Mario Siletti *(Luigi Lugacetti)*, Argentina Brunetti *(Mrs. Lugacetti)*, Mimi Aguglia *(Rosa)*, Emory Parnell *(Ship's Captain)*, Alberto Lolli *(Father Segatini)*, Adriano Ambrogi *(Father Mariani)*, Amina Pirani Maggi *(Dove)*, Carlo Borrelli *(Monsignor)*, Giuseppe Pierozzi *(Baker)*, Guido Martufi *(Urchin)*, Joe Faletta *(Cab Driver)*, Charles Fawcett *(Mr. Cates)*, Angela Clarke.

The cathedrals of Rome serve as the backdrop for this pleasant, moving tale in which convict Douglas tries evading the law but winds up taking a pious path through his association with priest Johnson. The two men meet while traveling on a boat from the U.S. to Italy; Douglas has made a prison break, and Johnson is on a pilgrimage to the Holy City. The former steals the priest's cloak and identification in hopes of evading the law. Johnson eventually catches up with the thief, deciding not to turn him in immediately so Douglas can continue with a tour of Rome. The two men dodge police pursuers, and Douglas undergoes a change of heart through the sacred environment and companionship of Johnson. The great cinematographer William Daniels had a heyday in the picturesque Rome.

p&d, Clarence Brown; w, Charles Schnee, Dorothy Kingsley (based on the story by Robert Buckner); ph, William Daniels; m, Carmen Dragon; ed, Robert J. Kern; art d, Cedric Gibbons, Edward Carfagno.

Drama/Comedy   **(PR:A MPAA:NR)**

WHEN JOHNNY COMES MARCHING HOME*½
                                                       (1943) 74m UNIV bw

Allan Jones *(Johnny Kovacs)*, Gloria Jean *(Marilyn)*, Donald O'Connor *(Frankie)*, Jane Frazee *(Joyce)*, Peggy Ryan *(Dusty)*, Richard Davies *(Tommy Bridges)*, Clyde Fillmore *(Hamilton Wellman)*, Marla Shelton *(Diana Wellman)*, Olin Howlin *(Trullers)*, Constance Worth *(Woman)*, Emma Dunn *(Ma Flanagan)*, The Four Step Brothers, Phil Spitalny and His "Hour of Charm" All-Girl Orchestra with Evelyn and Her Magic Violin.

Lame story in which one-time singer Jones, a WW II GI back in the U.S. because of his heroics overseas, decides to avoid all the commotion he's been receiving by slipping off to his old boarding house. What he finds is a bunch of girls trying to get a musical act together, thus an excuse to exhibit some talent. Featured is the oddity of an all-woman orchestra. Songs and musical numbers include: "This is It," Say it With Dancing" (Don Raye, Gene De Paul). "This is Worth Fighting For" (Edgar De Lange, Sammy Stept), "When Johnnie Comes Marching Home" (Louis Lambert, adapted by Buddy Kaye), "One of Us Has Gotta Go" (Inez James, Buddy Pepper), "We Must Be Vigilant" (Edgar Leslie, Joe Burke).

p, Bernard W. Burton; d, Charles Lamont; w, Oscar Brodney, Dorothy Bennett; ph, George Robinson; m, Ted Cain; ed, Charles Maynard; md, Charles Previn; art d, John Goodman; ch, Louis Da Pron.

Musical   **(PR:A MPAA:NR)**

WHEN KNIGHTHOOD WAS IN FLOWER
                              (SEE: SWORD AND THE ROSE, THE, 1953)

WHEN KNIGHTS WERE BOLD**   (1942, Brit.) 57m CAP/FA bw

Jack Buchanan *(Sir Guy de Vere)*, Fay Wray *(Lady Rowena)*, Garry Marsh *(Brian Ballymote)*, Kate Cutler *(Aunt Agatha)*, Martita Hunt *(Aunt Esther)*, Robert Horton *(Cousin Bertie)*, Aubrey Mather *(The Canon)*, Aubrey Fitzgerald *(Barker)*, Robert Nainby *(Whittle)*, Moore Marriott *(The Tramp)*, Charles Paton *(The Mayor)*.

It seems that the best British farces come from mocking that land's rather stuffy customs. This picture takes that course and provides pleasing comedy by not taking itself so seriously. Buchanan is a soldier who finds himself the inheritor of his ancestral home. His ideas of nobility are quite different from those of his snobbish relatives, and a clash erupts when Buchanan prefers the company of the locals to that of his aged aunts. When the new lord is hit over the head with a suit of armor, he dreams of what his knightly ancestor would have done to his enemies. He wakes up and promptly sees

his relatives out the door. This was released in England six years earlier and ran 19 minutes longer.

p, Max Schach; d, Jack Raymond; w, Austin Parker, Douglas Furber (based on the play by Charles Marlowe); ph, Frederick A. Young.

Comedy   **Cas.**   **(PR:A MPAA:NR)**

WHEN LADIES MEET**   (1933) 73m MGM bw (AKA: TRUTH IS
                                                                STRANGER)

Ann Harding *(Clare Woodruff)*, Robert Montgomery *(Jimmie Lee)*, Myrna Loy *(Mary Howard)*, Alice Brady *(Bridget Drake)*, Frank Morgan *(Rogers Woodruff)*, Martin Burton *(Walter)*, Luis Alberni *(Pierre)*.

Harding and Loy play women with affections for the same man, book publisher Morgan, Harding as his wife and Loy as the novelist-mistress. They are wittingly brought together by Montgomery, without either knowing the other's identity; in this way, when she discovers her companion's true identity, Loy will understand that she has hooked up with an unhonorable man. Though the situation has built-in humor, it takes Brady to really cause the laughs--she plays the cynical hostess.

p, Lawrence Weingarten; d, Harry Beaumont; w, John Meehan, Leon Gordon (based on the play by Rachel Crothers); ph, Ray June; ed, Basil Wrangell; cos, Adrian.

Comedy   **(PR:A MPAA:NR)**

WHEN LADIES MEET**½   (1941) 105m MGM bw

Joan Crawford *(Mary Howard)*, Robert Taylor *(Jimmy Lee)*, Greer Garson *(Claire Woodruff)*, Herbert Marshall *(Rogers Woodruff)*, Spring Byington *(Bridget Drake)*, Rafael Storm *(Walter Del Canto)*, Max Willenz *(Pierre)*, Florence Shirley *(Janet Hopper)*, Leslie Francis *(Homer Hopper)*, Olaf Hytten *(Mathews the Butler)*, Mona Barrie *(Mabel Guiness)*, Mary Forbes *(Mother at Party)*, John Marlowe *(Violinist)*, Harold Minjir *(Clerk)*, Barbara Bedford *(Anna the Maid)*.

An entertaining piece of drawing-room fluff that had already been made once in 1933 starring Frank Morgan, Myrna Loy, Robert Montgomery, and Ann Harding in the roles played here by Herbert Marshall, Joan Crawford, Robert Taylor, and Greer Garson. Byington, who was in the 1932 stage play by Crothers, is also in this remake. Crawford is a novelist who has enjoyed great success with her work. She is also a forerunner of the women's liberation movement, with some modern concepts about what love and marriage entail. Marshall is Crawford's publisher--and her amour--and the fact that he is already married to Garson doesn't appear to enter into Crawford's thinking. Taylor loves Crawford and chases after her in an attempt to show that he is more suitable as the object of her affections than Marshall but, so far, he is having difficulty making his point. Crawford doesn't mind Taylor, and he is good for a smile every so often, but her mind is concentrated on her love for Marshall and her work. Crawford is a pragmatist and thinks hard about all of the ramifications of being the "other woman" and now decides that there is only one course of action to be taken: she must steal Marshall away from the unmet Garson, marry him, and be done with her second-class status. Taylor believes that Crawford would be making a mistake and that she is the victim of a mistress' rationalizations so he arranges a meeting between her and Garson at the country home of addlepated Byington, a friend. Crawford and Garson have never met and don't know a thing about each other or the relationship each has with Marshall. Once they meet at Byington's, they stay overnight and spend time with each other and are soon friends. When Crawford sees the kind of woman Garson is, she is impressed. In a long talk between the two, Garson reveals that Marshall is a long-time cheater and that Garson has known about it for years and has turned away and overlooked it. Crawford understands that she could never put up with Marshall if he didn't change his ways and she knows he's not about to do that for any single woman. Crawford decides that the affair is over and that Taylor, who has been waiting in the wings, is really the man for her. Good direction, sharp script, and the interesting sidelight backstage of Crawford being top-billed while Garson was an up-and-coming actress who was soon to take over Crawford's mantle as leading actress at MGM. The rivalry between the two adds a certain sharpness to their witty exchanges and Taylor shows that he has a way with comedy and is not merely a slick leading man with no depth.

p, Robert Z. Leonard, Orville O. Dull; d, Leonard; w, S.K. Lauren, Anita Loos (based on the play by Rachel Crothers); ph, Robert Planck; m, Bronislau Kaper; ed, Robert Kern; art d, Cedric Gibbons; cos, Adrian.

Comedy   **(PR:A-C MPAA:NR)**

WHEN LONDON SLEEPS** (1932, Brit.) 78m Twickenham/AP&D bw

Harold French *(Tommy Blythe)*, Francis L. Sullivan *(Rodney Haines)*, Rene Ray *(Mary)*, A. Bromley Davenport *(Col. Grahame)*, Alexander Field *(Sam)*, Diana Beaumont *(Hilda)*, Ben Field *(Lamberti)*, Barbara Everest *(Mme. Lamberti)*, Herbert Lomas *(Pollard)*.

French surmounts a large debt that he ran up at Sullivan's gambling den and gladly pays him off. Sullivan soon learns that French's girl friend, Ray, is his cousin and the only obstacle to a fortune that his dead uncle once held.

He kidnaps Ray, but a Scotland Yard raid foils his plans. A raging fire breaks out and French heroically rescues his girl from the roof of the burning building.

p, Julius Hagen; d, Leslie Hiscott; w, Bernard Merivale, H. Fowler Mear (based on a play by Charles Darrell).

Crime (PR:A MPAA:NR)

WHEN LONDON SLEEPS*½ (1934, Brit.) 70m Sound City/Reunion bw (GB: SABOTAGE; AKA: MENACE; WHILE LONDON SLEEPS)

Victor Varconi (Stephen Ronsart), Joan Maude (Lady Conway), D.A. Clarke-Smith (Sir Robert Conway), J. Hubert Leslie (Mr. Jones), Joan Matheson (Mrs. Jones), J.A. O'Rourke (O'Leary), Shayle Gardner (Commissioner), Wilfred Noy (Dean), Henry Longhurst, Cecil Bishop, George D'Arcy, Frank Barclay, Neil Boyd.

A troubled railroad executive, Clarke-Smith, causes numerous train accidents during spells of schizophrenia. Railway investigators finally discover that he is responsible before any more disasters occur. Originally titled MENACE in Britain but that tag was changed to avoid confusion with a Hollywood picture starring John Lodge and Ray Milland.

p, Norman Loudon; d, Adrian Brunel; w, Heinrich Fraenkel, A.R. Rawlinson (based on a story by Victor Varconi); ph, Claude Friese-Greene.

Drama (PR:A MPAA:NR)

WHEN LOVE IS YOUNG½** (1937) 75m UNIV bw

Virginia Bruce (Wanda Werner), Kent Taylor (Andy Russell), Walter Brennan (Uncle Hugo), Greta Meyer (Hannah Werner), Christian Rub (Anton Werner), William Tannen (Norman Crocker), Jean Rogers (Irene Henry), Nydia Westman ("Dotty" Leonard), Sterling Holloway (Orville Kane), David Oliver (Cudgy Wallace), Jack Smart (Winthrop Grove), Laurie Douglas (Laurie Sykes).

It's the nice-girl-pushed-about-makes-good story all over again; in this case Bruce is a small town Pennsylvania girl with visions of becoming a star. Her career at college is less than admirable as she is coolly pushed to the side. But when Taylor molds the girl into a successful Broadway performer, she returns to make her former tormenters eat their hearts out. Songs include: "When Love is Young," "Did Anyone Ever Tell You" (Harold Adamson, Jimmy McHugh).

p, Charles R. Rogers; d, Hal Mohr; w, Eve Greene, Joseph Fields (based on the story "Class Prophecy" by Eleanore Griffin); ph, Jerome Ash; ed, Bernard W. Burton; md, Charles Previn.

Drama (PR:A MPAA:NR)

WHEN LOVERS MEET (SEE: LOVER COME BACK, 1946)

WHEN MEN ARE BEASTS (SEE: WOMEN IN THE NIGHT, 1948)

WHEN MY BABY SMILES AT ME* ** (1948) 98m FOX c

Betty Grable (Bonny), Dan Dailey (Skid), Jack Oakie (Bozo), June Havoc (Gussie), Richard Arlen (Harvey), James Gleason (Lefty), Vanita Wade (Bubbles), Kenny Williams (Specialty Dancer), Robert Emmett Keane (Sam Harris), Jean Wallace (Sylvia Marco), Pati Behrs (Woman in Box), Jerry Maren (Midget), George "Beetlepuss" Lewis (Comic), Tom Stevenson (Valet), Sam Bernard (Process Server), Mauritz Hugo (Stage Manager), Frank Scannell (Vendor), J. Farrell MacDonald (Doorman), Les Clark, Harry Seymour (Troupers), Lee MacGregor (Call Boy), Charles Tannen (Intern), Robert Karnes (Attendant), George Medford (Conductor), Marion Marshall (Girl), Robert Patten (Sailor), Harry Carter (Man in Box), Kit Guard (Man), Tiny Timbrell (Musician), Ted Jordan (Sailor), Bee Stephens (Chorus Girl), Charles La Torre (Tony), Dorothy Babb, Joanne Dale, Lu Anne Jones, Noel Neill (Specialty Dancers), Lela Bliss (Woman), Tim Graham, Dave Morris (Painters), Edward Clark (Box-Office Man), Hank Mann (Man).

Based on the stage play "Burlesque" by Watters and Hopkins, this was the third screen version of the story. In 1929, Paramount had made THE DANCE OF LIFE and in 1937 Carole Lombard starred in SWING HIGH, SWING LOW, by the same studio. Fox acquired the rights and assigned the lead role to their prime lady, Grable, and gave the male lead to Dailey, who was sensational. George Jessel, when he wasn't performing, produced a number of films for Fox and this was one of the better ones. Grable and Dailey are a married vaudeville team, with Dailey being a putty-nosed comic. They are managed by Gleason and life is beer and skittles for them, with Dailey soon becoming a Broadway star. The quick success goes to the core of his ego and he takes to the bottle the same way he took to the stage. His drinking pushes them apart and he must finally be placed in Bellevue Hospital (where Stephen Foster actually died of the same ailment). Grable divorces Dailey and starts to be wooed by wealthy rancher Arlen. With the help of pals Oakie and Havoc, Dailey gets himself back together and onto the stage. It doesn't work at first, then Grable comes back to him, they team up again, and their act is a success once more. He is redeemed by the love of a good woman. A slim plot but lots of music to go along with the pathos and comedy. Joseph Myrow and Mack Gordon wrote the only new tunes for the picture, "What Did I Do?" (sung by Grable) and "By the Way" (also Grable, with production backrounds during the reprises). Other tunes were standards that included: "Say Si Si" (Al Stillman, Ernesto Lecuona), "When My Baby Smiles at Me" (Ted Lewis, Bill Munro, Andrew B. Sterling, sung by Dailey), "Oui, Oui, Marie" (Fred Fisher, Joseph McCarthy, Alfred Bryan), "Don't Bring Lulu" (Billy Rose, Lew Brown, Ray Henderson), "Shoe Shine Blues" (this was part of "Birth of the Blues" by Brown, Henderson, Buddy De Sylva), "The Daughter of Rosie O'Grady" (Walter Donaldson, M.C. Brice), and there were bits and pieces of several other tunes including "Bye Bye, Blackbird." Burlesque is seen to be an honorable way to earn a living and a family entertainment at that. Snappy direction, good dance routines by Seymour Felix, and a nice moral undertone help make this a pleasant way to spend 98 minutes.

p, George Jessel; d, Walter Lang; w, Elizabeth Reinhardt, Lamar Trotti (based on the play "Burlesque" by George Manker Watters, Arthur Hopkins); ph, Harry Jackson (Technicolor); ed, Barbara McLean; md, Alfred Newman; art d, Lyle Wheeler, Leland Fuller; ch, Seymour Felix.

Musical (PR:A-C MPAA:NR)

WHEN STRANGERS MARRY*½ (1933) 65m COL bw

Jack Holt (Steve Rand), Lillian Bond (Marian Drake), Arthur Vinton (Hinkle), Barbara Barondess (Antonia), Ward Bond (Billy McGuire), Gustav Von Seyffertitz (Van Wyck), Paul Porcasi (Phillipe), Harry Stubbs (Maj. Oliver), Rudolph Amendt (Von Arnheim), Charles Stevens (Chattermahl).

Routine action fare in which Holt plays a man working on a railroad at the straits of Malay, when he suddenly finds himself sharing a conjugal bed with the spoiled rich kid Bond. In true fashion, Vinton plays the romantic adversary who also has reasons for not wanting to see the railroad completed.

d, Clarence Badger; w, James Kevin McGuiness (based on a story by Maximalian Foster); ph, Benjamin Kline.

Drama (PR:A MPAA:NR)

WHEN STRANGERS MARRY*½** (1944) 67m King Brothers/MON bw (AKA: BETRAYED)

Dean Jagger (Paul Dean), Kim Hunter (Millie), Robert Mitchum (Fred), Neil Hamilton (Detective Blake), Lon Lubin (Hamilton), Milt Kibbee (Charlie), Dewey Robinson (Newsstand Man), Claire Whitney (Middle-Aged Woman), Edward Keane (Middle-Aged Man), Virginia Sale (Chambermaid), Dick Elliott (Prescott), Lee "Lasses" White (Old Man), Minerva Urecal (Landlady), Marta Mitrovich (Baby's Mother), Rhonda Fleming (Girl on Train), George Lloyd, Billy Nelson, Weldon Heyburn, Sam McDaniel.

If ever a movie deserved the designation of "sleeper," this is it. There is not a wasted frame in this tense, tight psychological thriller that offered Mitchum his first chance at a juicy role. Shot in a 10-day period, it is vastly superior to many of the other attempts at film noir that went on through the 1980s. Nobody thought it was much when it was completed, and they didn't even get a Manhattan theater for it. It opened at the Brooklyn Strand in November, 1944, but word of mouth caused patrons to flock to see it. Elliott is a drunken conventioneer in New York to attend the annual conclave of his fraternal order. He makes the mistake of flashing a wad of dough in a bar and meets a man, who is not identified. The mysterious stranger claims that he has no place to stay in the city so Elliott offers him the chance to share his hotel room. The two men exit the bar, and the next day, Elliott is found strangled and there is no sign of the other man. Hunter is a waitress from a tiny burg who has come to New York to unite with her new husband, Jagger, whom she wed after a brief courtship. Jagger doesn't show up and Hunter is worried as she spends the night in her hotel room alone. Earlier, she had met an old flame, Mitchum, who wished her well in her new marriage. In the morning, Hunter turns to Mitchum who suggests that she call the police right away. A short while later, Jagger phones Hunter and says that he's okay and that they must meet right away, but she is not to reveal his whereabouts to anyone and is to keep the whole matter mum. Hamilton is the cop on the Elliott murder case and he arrives in time to think that perhaps Mitchum might be Elliott's killer. Hamilton goes so far as to wonder aloud whether Mitchum is not telling everything he should be telling. Hunter has just joined Jagger and his surreptitious behavior makes her question her decision of having married him after only three instances together. The cops begin to chase Hunter and Jagger and he finally admits that he was in the bar with Elliott and that he did go back to the hotel room with the tipsy conventioneer, but that when he left the man, he was still alive. Now Hunter begins to wonder if Mitchum had anything to do with the murder. Jagger seems like a gentle man, although his very benign manner makes him suspect. Jagger is arrested and tells his story to Hamilton, who believes him. Now, with the help of Hamilton, Hunter entraps Mitchum and he is uncovered as the real killer when they catch him trying to slip the dead man's money into a post office mail slot. Mitchum comes clean and Hunter and Jagger are allowed to leave and have the honeymoon they've planned for so long. Director Castle was only 30 years old and on his sixth film, one of his best. The King brothers, Franklin and Maurice, were the force behind the movie. They opened their own production company and made several low-budget features before investing their money in various real estate properties and becoming incredibly wealthy. While their mother was alive (and she lived a long time), the brothers stayed single and took care of her and were a familiar sight along South Beverly Drive as they wheeled her down the street. This was their first venture into the gangster-type film as well as writer Yordan's, who went on to write ANNA LUCASTA, DETECTIVE STORY, THE HARDER THEY FALL, EL CID, KING OF KINGS, and many more. Another plus was the excellent mood music provided by Tiomkin, who had already done such important features as LOST HORIZON, YOU CAN'T TAKE IT WITH YOU, MR. SMITH GOES TO WASHINGTON, MEET JOHN DOE, and several others. He must have been intrigued by the subject matter in order to work for Monogram after having toiled in far more expensive vineyards. The suspense and the style of shooting, rather than any actual violence, may prove disturbing for younger viewers.

p, Franklin King; d, William Castle; w, Philip Yordan, Dennis J. Cooper (based on a story by George V. Moscov); ph, Ira Morgan; m, Dimitri Tiomkin; ed, Martin G. Cohn; art d, F. Paul Sylos.

Murder Mystery   (PR:C   MPAA:NR)

WHEN STRANGERS MEET*½   (1934) 72m Liberty bw

Richard Cromwell (*Paul Tarman*), Arline Judge (*Ruth Crane*), Lucien Littlefield (*Barney Crane*), Charles Middleton (*John Tarman*), Hale Hamilton (*Capt. Manning*), Sarah Padden (*Mrs. Tarman*), Maude Eburne (*Nell Peck*), Barbara Weeks (*Elaine*), Sheila Terry (*Dolly*), Ray Walker (*Steve*), Vera Gordon (*Mrs. Rosinsky*), Lee Kohlmar (*Sam Rosinsky*), Luis Alberni (*Nick*), Julie Haydon (*Mrs. Mason*), Herman Bing (*Mr. Schultz*), Arthur Hoyt (*Mr. Peck*), Franklyn Parker (*Ed Mason*), Sidney Miller (*Leon Rosinsky*), Bryant Washburn (*Mr. Pendleton*).

Sappy treatment of a mishmash of characters who are brought together through sharing a bungalow court, of all places. Some of the caricatures are interesting, but they aren't put to the best use.

d, William Christy Cabanne; w, Adele Buffington (based on the story "The Way" by Zona Gale); ph, Harry Neumann, Tom Galligan; ed, Mildred Johnston.

Drama   (PR:A MPAA:NR)

WHEN THE BOUGH BREAKS½**   (1947, Brit.) 81m
                                        RANK-Gainsborough/GFD bw

Patricia Roc (*Lily Bates*), Rosamund John (*Frances Norman*), Bill Owen [Rowbotham] (*Bill*), Brenda Bruce (*Ruby Chapman*), Patrick Holt (*Robert Norman*), Cavan Malone (*Jimmy*), Leslie Dwyer (*George*), Sonia Holm (*Nurse*), Torin Thatcher (*Adams*), Catherine Lacey (*Almoner*), Edith Sharpe (*Matron*), Muriel George (*1st Landlady*), Ada Reeve (*2nd Landlady*), Joan Haythorne (*Miss Brent*), Edie Martin (*Woman Customer*), Sheila Huntington (*1st Shop Assistant*), Mary Stone (*2nd Shop Assistant*), Gerald Case (*Doctor*), Jane Hylton (*Maid*), Noel Howlett (*Judge*).

Well-meaning project revolving around Roc's attempt to retrieve the baby she had given up for adoption, though without legal red tape, to John when she learned that the boy's father was married to her as well as to somebody else. Years after parting with the tot (and hubby), she has remarried and wants the boy back, taking John to court and proving her case. But the lad prefers his adopted mother to his real one, the latter being a virtual stranger. Unhappy, but devoted to her boy's well-being, Roc brings the laddy back to John. Designed to wring out one tear after another, it pulls o ut a final sob when Roc finally gets her wish and has another baby.

p, Betty E. Box; d, Lawrence Huntington; w, Peter Rogers, Muriel Box, Sydney Box (based on the story by Moie Charles, Herbert Victor); ph, Bryan Langley, Dudley Lovell; m, Clifton Parker; ed, Gordon Hales; md, John Hollingsworth; art d, John Elphick; cos, Yvonne Caffin; makeup, Len Garde.

Drama   (PR:A MPAA:NR)

WHEN THE BOYS MEET THE GIRLS*⅙
                                    (1965) 97m Four Leaf/MGM c (AKA: GIRL CRAZY)

Connie Francis (*Ginger*), Harve Presnell (*Danny*), Sue Anne Langdon (*Tess*), Fred Clark (*Bill*), Frank Faylen (*Phin, Mailman*), Joby Baker (*Sam*), Hortense Petra (*Kate*), Stanley Adams (*Lank*), Romo Vincent (*Pete*), Susan Holloway (*Delilah*), Russell Collins (*Stokes*), William T. Quinn (*Dean of Cody College*), Patti Moore (*Divorcee*), Louis Armstrong, Liberace, Pepper Davis, Tony Reese, Herman's Hermits, Sam the Sham & the Pharoahs (*Themselves*).

When a producer is looking for assured success at the box office, it's usually a safe bet to take some tired and true material, give it modern settings and situations, and release it to the public as something new. Katzman did just that by taking twice-made GIRL CRAZY, (once with Mickey Rooney and Judy Garland), inserting some then-popular tunes and old favorites, and having Francis and Presnell try to duplicate the energy of their predecessors. The result was a far cry from the originals, but not without merit, having ingeniously conceived comic routines and exceptional music performances. The plot is pure hokum. Presnell plays a millionaire trying to escape

the clutches of a money-grabbing chorus girl by fleeing to Nevada. He meets Francis who has a dad with a gambling habit so bad that he almost loses their broken-down ranch. Presnell comes up with the bright idea of converting the ranch into a place for divorcees to while away their time while waiting for their quickie divorces to go through. Songs include: "But Not for Me" (George Gershwin, Ira Gershwin, sung by Connie Francis, Harve Presnell), "I Got Rhythm" (Gershwin, Gershwin, sung by Francis, Presnell, Louis Armstrong), "Bidin' My Time" (Gershwin, Gershwin, sung by Herman's Hermits), "Embraceable You" (Gershwin, Gershwin, sung by Presnell), "Treat Me Rough" (Gershwin, Gershwin, sung by Sue Anne Langdon), "When the Boys Meet the Girls" (Jack Keller, Howard Greenfield, sung by Francis), "Mail Call" (Fred Karger, Ben Weisman, Sid Wayne, sung by Francis), "Monkey See, Monkey Do" (Johnny Farrow, sung by Sam the Sham & the Pharoahs), "Listen People" (Graham Gouldman, sung by Herman's Hermits), "Throw it Out of Your Mind" (Armstrong, Billy Kyle, performed and sung by Armstrong), "It's All in Your Mind" (sung by The Standells), "Aruba" (Liberace, played by Liberace). Louis Armstrong plays with Tyree Glenn (trombone), Buster Bailey (clarinet), Billy Kyle (piano), Buddy Catlett (bass), and Danny Barcelona (drums).

p, Sam Katzman; d, Alvin Ganzer; w, Robert E. Kent (based on the musical "Girl Crazy" by Guy Bolton, John McGowan); ph, Paul C. Vogel (Panavision, Metrocolor); m, Fred Karger; ed, Ben Lewis; md, Karger; art d, George W. Davis, Eddie Imazu; set d, Henry Grace, Keogh Gleason; spec eff, J. McMillan Johnson, Carroll L. Shepphird; ch, Earl Barton; makeup, William Tuttle.

Musical/Comedy   (PR:A   MPAA:NR)

WHEN THE CLOCK STRIKES*½
        (1961) 72m Harvard/UA bw (AKA: THE CLOCK STRIKES THREE)

James Brown (*Sam Morgan*), Merry Anders (*Ellie*), Henry Corden (*Cady, Lodge Owner*), Roy Barcroft (*Sheriff*), Peggy Stewart (*Mrs. Pierce*), Jorge Moreno (*Martinez*), Francis De Sales (*Warden*), Max Mellinger (*Postman*), Eden Hartford (*Waitress*), Jack Kenny (*Cafe Proprietor*).

Confusing and misguided crime melodrama in which a handful of people are gathered at a lodge near the prison where a man is to be executed at midnight. As the clock strikes, a man rushes in to confess that he is actually the criminal and is taken into custody. Everyone left thinks of ways to get their hands on leftover money hidden away in a safe-deposit box. After innumerable back-stabbings and lies being told, Brown figures that the best thing to do is call in the police and let them work this mess out. Someone sure has to.

p, Robert E. Kent; d, Edward L. Cahn; w, Dallas Gaultois; ph, Kenneth Peach, Sr.; m, Richard La Salle; ed, Grant Whytock; md, Lloyd Young; makeup, Harry Thomas.

Crime/Drama   (PR:A   MPAA:NR)

WHEN THE DALTONS RODE*½**   (1940) 80m UNIV bw

Randolph Scott (*Tod Jackson*), Kay Francis (*Julie King*), Brian Donlevy (*Grat Dalton*), George Bancroft (*Caleb Winters*), Broderick Crawford (*Bob Dalton*), Stuart Erwin (*Ben Dalton*), Andy Devine (*Ozark*), Frank Albertson (*Emmett Dalton*), Mary Gordon (*Ma Dalton*), Harvey Stephens (*Rigby*), Edgar Dearing (*Sheriff*), Quen Ramsey (*Wilson*), Dorothy Granger (*Nancy*), Bob McKenzie (*Photographer*), Fay McKenzie (*Hannah*), Walter Soderling (*Judge Swain*), Mary Ainslee (*Minnie*), Erville Alderson (*District Attorney Wade*), Sally Payne (*Annabella*), June Wilkins (*Suzy*), William Gould, Walter Long (*Deputies on Train*), Pat West (*Pete the Restaurant Owner*), Dorothy Moore (*Girl*), George Guhl (*Deputy in Baggage Car*), Robert Dudley (*Juror Pete Norris*), Ed Brady, Jack Clifford (*Deputies*), Bob Reeves (*Henchman*), Kernan Cripps (*Freight Agent*), Tom London (*Lyncher*), Mary Cassidy (*Girl*), Lafe McKee (*Doctor*), Russ Powell (*Engineer*), John Beck (*Native*), James Morton (*Juror Ed Pickett*), Edgar Buchanan (*Man at Livery Stable*), Harry Cording (*Sam Fleeson*).

Cinematic version of the legend of the Dalton Gang, abstractions included to make for more acceptable film entertainment. Crawford, Donlevy, Erwin, and Albertson are the four brothers run off their land by insensitive railroad people who then turn to a life of crime. although this was not their original intention, it becomes the only course after one of the boys accidentally kills a villainous land-grabber. Scott plays the lawyer who attempts to give the Daltons a fair court trial. An excellent job of directing by Marshall, effectively combining hard-hitting action, believable character development, and even a bit of humor.

d, George Marshall; w, Harold Shumate, Lester Cole, Stuart Anthony (based on the book by Emmett Dalton, Jack Jungmeyer, Sr.); ph, Hal Mohr; ed, Ed Curtiss; art d, Jack Otterson; cos, Vera West.

Western   (PR:A   MPAA:NR)

WHEN THE DEVIL WAS WELL*½   (1937, Brit.) 67m COL bw

Jack Hobbs (*Jack Lawson*), Vera Lennox (*Betty Painton*), Eve Gray (*Ann*), Gerald Rawlinson (*Bob*), Annie Esmond (*Mrs. Lawson*), Max Adrian (*David*), Aubrey Mallalieu (*Banks*), Bryan Powley (*Col. Piper*).

A simple plot which doesn't try to be anything more than a plain love story. Hobbs loves Lennox but his pushy mother wants him to get engaged to the rich and elegant Gray. He convinces mom that she is wrong and fixes his best friend Rawlinson up with her. By the time the finale rolls around, everyone is happy. Sometimes less is definitely more.

p, A. George Smith; d, Maclean Rogers; w, W. Lane Crawford; ph, Geoffrey Faithfull.

Comedy/Romance   (PR:A   MPAA:NR)

WHEN THE DOOR OPENED   (SEE: ESCAPE, 1940)

WHEN THE GIRLS MEET THE BOYS   (SEE: GIRL CRAZY, 1943)

WHEN THE GIRLS TAKE OVER*   (1962) 80m Trans-Oceanic/Parade
c

Robert Lowery (*Maximo Toro*), Marvin Miller (*Henri Degiere*), Jackie Coogan (*Capt. Toussaint*), Jimmy [James] Ellison (*Axel "Longhorn" Gates*), Ingeborg Kjeldsen (*Francoise Degiere*), Jeff Stone (*Steve Harding*), Don Durrell (*"Stoney" Jackson*), Tommy Cook (*Razmo*), True Ellison (*Melesa*), Gabe [Gabriel] Dell (*Henderson*), Paul Bailey (*Clutch*).

A bunch of has-beens gathered in Puerto Rico to make this spoof on Caribbean revolutions (perhaps inspired by the then-recent takeover in Cuba of Castro's regime), in which a plot to take over the small island of Hondo-Rico is spoiled when 26 pink Jeeps with wine, women, and food entice the revolutionist army away from continuing with their plans. Not a bad political strategy.

p&d, Russell Hayden; w, Samuel Roeca; ph, Arthur Arling (Technicolor); m, Ben Oakland; ed, Reg Browne, Maurice Max; md, Howard Jackson.

Comedy   (PR:C   MPAA:NR)

WHEN THE LEGENDS DIE**   (1972) 107m Sagaponack/FOX c

Richard Widmark (*Red Dillon*), Frederic Forrest (*Tom Black Bull*), Luana Anders (*Mary Redmond*), Vito Scotti (*Meo*), Herbert Nelson (*Dr. Wilson*), John War Eagle (*Blue Elk*), Tillman Box (*Young Tom Black Bull*), John Gruber (*Tex Walker*), Garry Walberg (*Superintendent*), Jack Mullaney (*Gas Station Attendant*), Malcolm Curley (*Benny Grayback*), Roy Engel (*Sam Turner*), Rex Holman (*Neil Swenson*), Mel Gallagher (*Cowboy*), Sondra Pratt (*Angie*), Verne Muehlstedt (*Harold*), Evan Stevens (*George*), John Renforth (*Old Man*), Rhoda Stevens (*Teacher*), Mel Flock (*Car Salesman*), Joyce Davis (*Mom*), Bennett Thompson (*Albert Left Hand*), Eldred Vigil, Jr. (*Luther Spotted Dog*), Terry Hutchison (*Waitress*), Doug Vold, Bart Brower (*Rodeo Hands*), Jiggs Beutler (*Stock Contractor*), Guy Pinecoos, Jr. (*Tribal Chairman*).

Seldom does a film which tries to depict the plight of the American Indian avoid the cliches of how badly white men treat their red brothers, causing disillusioned Indians to retreat to their reservations and fill themselves with alcohol. There is a bit of that in WHEN THE LEGENDS DIE, but it refrains from hitting the viewer over the head and filling him with guilt. Forrest plays a young Indian who makes his first contact with whites through the rodeo, and especially through his relationship with Widmark, a no-good drunkard who seems to have little respect for anything beyond his immediate pleasure. Widmark notes the skill with which Forrest handles horses, a skill he learned while a young boy in the reclusiveness of the Colorado mountains. The older man makes the youth a star bronco rider, and in no time he is winning rodeo after rodeo. But the chance of Widmark to make money soon comes into play, and he begins fixing events in order to make a killing gambling, the winnings of which he squanders without Forrest ever seeing a cent. Before long, Forrest resents Widmark's antics and takes off in search of success on his own. Allowing a driving desire for success to control him, Forrest makes it all the way to the World Championships. After a stint in the hospital to which Forrest is forced because of his recklessness in the ring, he makes his way back to Widmark, who is closing in on death but feeling rejuvenated by the mere presence of the youthful Indian. Rejuvenated enough, in fact, to steal the remains of Forrest's money and embark on one last spree, which leaves him hopelessly ill and destined to die shortly. Forrest has one last chance to see the man who treated him so badly, and despite Widmarks abuse, he feels genuine loss when Widmark dies, and performs an Indian ritual of burning Widmark's belongings. Forrest then returns to the reservation where he had always wanted to remain as a teacher of Indian customs, but it having been requested by the elders of the reservation that he first learn the ways of the white man; having done this Forrest can now lead a peaceful life on the reservation. WHEN THE LEGENDS DIE offers a lot of uncommon depictions to the cinema of the 1970s, from the rodeo ring to the broken-down existence of many towns of the West, but strongest among these is the friendship which develops between Widmark and Forrest. Almost fatherly in nature, it leaves as a mystery that which kept the men together. As always, Widmark is brilliant, his grizzled exterior fitting in perfectly with the hardened and heartless character he portrays.

p, Stuart Millar, Gene Lasko; d, Millar; w, Robert Dozier (based on the novel by Hal Borland); ph, Richard H. Kline (DeLuxe Color); m, Glenn Paxton; ed,

Louis San Andres; md, Lionel Newman; art d, Angelo Graham; set d, Jerry Wunderlich; m/l, "When You Speak to the Kids," "Summer Storm," "The Riderless Wagon," Glenn Paxton, Bo Goldman (sung by Freddie Hart, Kenni Huskey); stunts, Joe Canutt; makeup, Dan Striepeke, Bill Miller.

Drama   (PR:C   MPAA:PG)

WHEN THE LIGHTS GO ON AGAIN**   (1944) 74m PRC bw

Jimmy [James] Lydon (*Ted Benson*), Barbara Belden (*Arline Cary*), Grant Mitchell (*Mr. Benson*), Dorothy Peterson (*Mrs. Benson*), Regis Toomey (*Bill Regan, Reporter*), George Cleveland (*Pat Benson*), Harry Shannon (*Tom Carey*), Warren Mills (*Joey Benson*), Williard Jielson (*1st Marine*), Jac Turrell (*2nd Marine*), Bill Nelson (*3rd Marine*), Larry Thompson (*Medical Officer*), Myrtle Ferguson (*Middle Aged Woman*), Emmett Lynn (*Old Panhandler*), Jill Browning (*Peggy*), Roberta Carling (*Barbara*), Guy Blake (*Jim Bagby*), Al Stewart (*1st Farmer*), Elmo Lincoln (*2nd Farmer*), Joseph Crehan (*Engineer*), Luis Alberni, James Hope.

A well-conceived and produced dramatization of a wartime shell-shock victim's return home after a newspaper reporter escorts him from the front. The concentration is on the importance of the young's man family, first emphasized in flashback as he daydreams while on the train ride home. Then, these same people are shown actually helping the soldier to cope with his problem.

p, Leon Fromkess; d, William K. Howard; w, Milton Lazarus (based on a story by Frank Craven); ph, Ira Morgan; m, W. Franke Harling; ed, W. Donn Hayes; art d, Paul Palmentola; m/l, "When the Lights Go on Again (All Over the World)," Eddie Seiler, Sol Marcus, Bennie Benjamin, "Living a Dream," Alec Morrison.

Drama   (PR:A   MPAA:NR)

WHEN THE REDSKINS RODE*½   (1951) 78m COL c

Jon Hall (*Prince Hannoc*), Mary Castle (*Elizabeth Leeds*), James Seay (*George Washington*), John Ridgely (*Christopher Gist*), Sherry Morland (*Morna*), Pedro de Cordoba (*Chief Shingiss*), John Dehner (*John Delmont*), Lewis L. Russell (*Gov. Dinwiddle*), William Bakewell (*Appleby*), Gregory Gay (*St. Pierre*), Rusty Wescott (*Znueau*), Milton [B.] Kibbee (*Davey*), Rick Vallin (*Duprez*).

Set during the French-and-Indian War, the English are looking for an alliance from the Delaware Indians in their attempt to battle the savages who have sided with their European rivals. French spy Castle has other plans for the Delawares, as she attempts to seduce the chief's son. A heavy dosage of action but lacking in plot development.

p, Sam Katzman; d, Lew Landers; w, Robert E. Kent; ph, Lester White (Super Cinecolor); ed, Richard Fantl; md, Mischa Bakaleinikoff; art d, Paul Palmentola.

Western   (PR:A   MPAA:NR)

WHEN THE TREES WERE TALL*½   (1965, USSR) 100m
Gorky/Artkino bw (KOGDA DEREVYA BYLI BOLSHIMI)

Inna Gulaya (*Natasha*), Yuri Nikolin (*Kuzma Kuzmich Iordanov*), Lev Kuravlev (*Lenka*), Ye. Mazurova (*Anastasiya Borisovna*), Vasiliy Shukshin (*Chairman of the Kolkhoz*), Lea Chursina (*Zoya*), Ye. Korolyova (*Nyurka*), Ye. Melnikova, V. Trusov, P. Shalnov, V. Lebedev, O. Yakushev, A. Pashukhina, G. Shmovanov, T. Tishura, G. Binevskaya, Olya Petrova, G. Shapovalov, M. Gavrilko, I. Marks, D. Stolyarskaya, V. Orlova.

A sensitive story in which a war veteran who has turned to a life of drunkenness regains his self-respect through the affection he receives from a young woman. Posing as the girl's father, he leaves Moscow to dwell on a farming collective, at first taking advantage of the situation to continue his decadent ways, but eventually making a vital contribution to the community.

p&d, Lev Kulidzhanov; w, Nikolai Figurovsky (based on a story by V. Pogosheva); ph, Valeriy Ginzburg; m, Leonid Afansyev; ed, N. Loginova; md, G. Gamburg; art d, P. Galadzhev; cos, N. Baburina; m/l, Afansyev, A. Fatyanov; makeup, A. Ivanov.

Drama   (PR:A   MPAA:NR)

WHEN THIEF MEETS THIEF*½   (1937, Brit.) 85m
Criterion/UA-Anglo bw (GB: JUMP FOR GLORY)

Douglas Fairbanks, Jr (*Ricky Morgan*), Valerie Hobson (*Glory Howard*), Alan Hale (*Jim Dial/"Col. Fane"*), Jack Melford (*Thompson*), Anthony Ireland (*Sir Timothy Haddon*), Barbara Everest (*Mrs. Nolan*), Edward Rigby (*Sanders*), Esme Percy (*Robinson*), Basil Radford (*Defending Counsel*), Leo Genn (*Prosecuting Counsel*), Ian Fleming (*Coroner*), Frank Birch (*Vicar*).

One of director Walsh's few overseas ventures, the results of this trip were not particularly successful. Cat burglar Fairbanks grows extremely attached to one of his victims, Hobson, who just happens to be the fiancee of Hale, Fairbanks' one-time back-stabbing partner. Hale is now a successful, and apparently honest, businessman, but deep down he is still a two-bit crook. Hale is killed in a battle with Fairbanks, but the damning evidence points to Hobson as the guilty party. At the ensuing trial, the noble Fairbanks tries to get her out of the jam by taking the blame. Everything turns out hunky-dory when it appears as if Hale's death was a suicide brought on by a stock market crash. Except for Fairbanks' feats of daring, little else memorable occurs.

p, Marcel Hellman, Douglas Fairbanks, Jr.; d, Raoul Walsh; w, John Meehan, Jr., Harold French (based on the novel *Jump for Glory* by Gordon McConnell); ph, Victor Armenise, Cedric Williams; m, Percival Mackey; ed, Conrad von Molo; art d, Edward Carrick.

Drama   **(PR:A MPAA:NR)**

WHEN TIME RAN OUT zero   (1980) 121m International Cinema/WB c

Paul Newman (*Hank Anderson*), Jacqueline Bisset (*Kay Kirby*), William Holden (*Shelby Gilmore*), Edward Albert (*Brian*), Red Buttons (*Francis Fendly*), Barbara Carrera (*Iolani*), Valentina Cortesa (*Rose Valdez*), Veronica Hamel (*Nikki*), Alex Karras (*Tiny Baker*), Burgess Meredith (*Rene Valdez*), Ernest Borgnine (*Tom Conti*), James Franciscus (*Bob Spangler*), John Considine (*Webster*), Sheila Allen (*Mona*), Pat Morita (*Sam*), Lonny Chapman (*Kelly*), Darrell Larson (*Webster's Assistant*), Sandy Kenyon (*Henderson*), Marcus Mukai (*Wrangler*), Ted Gehring (*Durant*), Joe Papalimu (*Joe*), Jaylin Maureen Acol, Reed Derwin Acol, Ava Readdy, Glynn Rubin, Takayo Doran, James Gavin, M. James Arnett, Marcia Nicholson, Barbara Costello, Bill Smillie, Steven Marlo, Esmond Chung, Jeffrey McDevitt, John Springer, Jr..

Another turkey from the "Disaster Master," Irwin Allen, who thought that by putting a cast of stars into an impossible situation he could mine gold. This time it was "fool's gold" and the picture grossed about what one or two of the stars received in salary. It was but one in a long line of his mega-buck flops and was so laughably bad that audiences hooted at the screen. It's as though Allen hadn't learned from THE SWARM and BEYOND THE POSEIDON ADVENTURE. In his typical fashion, Allen throws his cast into a confined area to face a disaster. This time, it's an angry volcano on a luxurious resort island. The eruption spews lava and the entire island is in danger. Most of the vacationers ignore the bubbling but the smarter ones, the actors with some sense and top billing, join oil driller Newman on the island's highest landfall, the only area that offers refuge. With him is Bisset, the romantic lead; Holden, who owns the plush hotel; native Albert; elderly couple Meredith and Cortesa; swindler Buttons; and detective Borgnine. Both Borgnine and Buttons had appeared in one of Allen's rare successes, THE POSEIDON ADVENTURE, and became lifelong pals. Franciscus and Carrera don't heed Newman's warnings and, as one might expect, get theirs in the end. As the group ascends to safety, they meet potential death and destruction at every turn, but they do wind up at the top of the mountain, like some modern-day Noahs atop Ararat, watching everyone else drown in a sea of lava. Even the volcano isn't convincing when one considers that $20 million was spent on the film. With cheesy special effects and an even more hole-ridden script by two screen writers who should have known better (Silliphant and Foreman), there's precious little to like here. The trade ads taken by the studio proclaimed this as "the most important film of the decade." Puffery is one thing but that was downright nonsensical. The novel was *The Day the World Ended* and that was the first title for this film. It might have also been called "The Day Irwin Allen's Career Almost Ended." His hopes were encouraged by the coincidental eruption of Mount St. Helens just prior to the film's opening. When THE CHINA SYNDROME was being released, there was the nuclear scare at Pennsylvania's Three Mile Island, which, no doubt, helped the audiences identify with the problem. However, THE CHINA SYNDROME was a good film and this was not. Many of the film's stars had worked with Allen before so they knew exactly what was in store and they also knew that they would be paid incredible fees for their labors, much the same way Otto Preminger did with many of his bummers. Our only regret was that Preminger died before he could collaborate on a movie with Ross Allen. Now that would have been the disaster to end all disasters! In a small role, note comedian Pat Morita, long before he was acknowledged as an actor for his Oscar-nominated performance in THE KARATE KID. In another minor role, ex-Detroit Lion football player Alex Karras before he trimmed down and became a TV star on "Webster." After this, Allen took a respite for a while to design a theme park for Marineland in Southern California; then he came back to produce an all-star "Alice In Wonderland" for TV that showed he hadn't lost his touch for overblown tripe.

p, Irwin Allen; d, James Goldstone; w, Carl Foreman, Stirling Silliphant (based on the novel *The Day the World Ended* by Gordon Thomas, Max Morgan Witts); ph, Fred J. Koenekamp (Panavision, Technicolor); m, Lalo Schifrin; ed, Edward Biery, Freeman A. Davies; prod d, Philip M. Jefferies; art d, Russell C. Menzer; set d, Stuart Reiss; cos, Paul Zastupnevich; spec eff, L.B. Abbott.

Disaster   **(PR:C MPAA:PG)**

WHEN TOMORROW COMES**   (1939) 90m UNIV bw

Irene Dunne (*Helen*), Charles Boyer (*Philip Andre Durand*), Nydia Westman (*Lulu, Waitress*), Onslow Stevens (*Holden, Labor Organizer*), Fritz Feld (*Nicholas, Butler*), Barbara O'Neil (*Madeleine Durand*), Nella Walker (*Mme. Durand*), Constance Moore (*Bride*), Jerry Marlowe (*Groom*), Doris Weston, Frances Robinson, Bobbe Trefts, Helen Lynd, Myrtis Crinley, Kitty McHugh, Florence Lake, Dorothy Granger, Mary Treen, Inez Courtney, Helen MacKellar, Helen Brown, Ruth Warren, Dorothy Appleby, Virginia Sale, Mira McKinney, Claire Du Brey, Greta Granstedt, Diana Gibson, Jane Barnes, Sally Payne, Jennifer Gray, Claire Whitney, Mary Field (*Waitresses*), Harry C. Bradley (*Minister*), Milton Parsons (*Organist*), William B. Davidson (*Army Captain*), Addison Richards (*Refugee Leader*), Thom Dugan (*Bum*), Greta Meyer (*Madeline's Nurse Maid*), Howard Hickman (*Wealthy Man*), Natalie Moorhead, Margaret McWade, Gladys Blake (*Women*), Frank Darien (*Boathouse Caretaker*), George Humbert (*Vendor*), Wade Boteler (*Policeman*), Milburn Stone (*Busboy Head*), Emmett Vogan (*Headwaiter*), Gaylord "Steve" Pendleton (*Busboy*), Edward Keane Alden, Stephen Chase, Landers Stevens, John Dilson (*Men*), Vinton Haworth, Gordon Jones, Stanley Taylor (*Radio Technicians*), Philip Trent (*Serviceman*), James Flavin (*Coast Guard Man*), Eddie Acuff (*Bus Driver*), Edward Earle (*Assistant Manager*), Otto Hoffman (*Farmer*), Mickey Kuhn, Tommy Bupp, Ray Nicholas, Payne Johnson, Sonny Bupp, Delmar Watson (*Boys*), Hally Chester (*Newsboy*), Lillian Elliott (*Character Woman*), James Morton (*Chef*), Ed Piel, Jr (*Janitor*), George Offerman, Jr (*Farmer's Son*), Dick Winslow (*Accordian Player*).

An overly sentimental tear-jerker about the never-to-be love between a famous concert pianist and a waitress. Boyer, with his usual self-assured charm, is the pianist whose wife suffers fits of psychological instability, the result of a miscarriage. While grabbing a bite to eat at the restaurant where Dunne works, Boyer strikes up a friendship with the waitress that eventually results in a passionate romance. When Dunne is forced out of work because of a strike that she was instrumental in instigating, Boyer takes her on a trip to Long Island. A hurricane strands them, and after a session of tempestuous love making, Dunne learns of her lover's marital situation, humbly bowing out once the wife begs for sole ownership of her man. Though all the ingredients for a zesty romance are here, the direction and the players are too self-conscious, resulting in a glossy and empty effort. Remade twice as INTERLUDE (1957 and 1968).

p&d, John M. Stahl; w, Dwight Taylor (based on a story by James Cain); ph, John Mescall; ed, Milton Carruth; cos, Orry-Kelly.

Drama   **(PR:A MPAA:NR)**

WHEN TOMORROW DIES*   (1966, Can.) 91m Laurence Kent bw

Patricia Cage, Douglas Campbell, Neil Dainard, Lanny Backman, Nikki Cole, Diane Filer, Francesca Long, Rex Owen, Louise Payne, Patricia Wilson.

Affected and boring story of a wife's growing dissatisfaction with her life. She embarks on a brief affair, then breaks it off and ends up about where she began, nowhere. Director Kent's third low-budget feature, it shows much evidence of his having watched too many French films, and the movie is replete with jump cuts, grainy photography, and bad sound.

d, Laurence Kent; w, Kent, Robert Harlow; ph, Doug McKay; m, Jack Dale; ed, Hajo Hadeler.

Drama   **(PR:C MPAA:NR)**

WHEN WE ARE MARRIED**   (1943, Brit.) 98m BN/Anglo-American bw

Sydney Howard (*Henry Ormonroyd*), Lloyd Pearson (*Joe Helliwell*), Raymond Huntley (*Albert Parker*), Barry Morse (*Gerald Forbes*), Lesley Brook (*Nancy Holmes*), Olga Lindo (*Maria Helliwell*), Ethel Coleridge (*Clara Soppitt*), Patricia Hayes (*Ruby Birtle*), Marjorie Rhodes (*Mrs. Northrup*), George Carney (*Landlord*), Cyril Smith (*Fred Dyson*), Lydia Sherwood (*Lottie Grady*), Charles Victor (*Mr. Northrup*), Marian Spencer (*Annie Parker*), A. Bromley Davenport (*Mayor*), Ernest Butcher (*Herbert Soppitt*), Charles Doe, Charles Mortimer, Terry Randall.

Enjoyable farce in which three middle-aged busybodies, noted for their self-righteousness, discover after 25 years of happy matrimony that they were married by a minister who was not properly ordained. Thus their marriages were never legal, something they try to keep quiet, but which manages to leak out, causing the women to eat their pious words.

p, John Baxter; d, Lance Comfort; w, Austin Melford, Barbara K. Emary (based on the play by J.B. Priestley); ph, Jimmy Wilson, Arthur Grant.

Comedy   **(PR:A MPAA:NR)**

WHEN WE LOOK BACK   (SEE: FRISCO WATERFRONT, 1935)

WHEN WERE YOU BORN?*   (1938) 65m FN-WB bw

Margaret Lindsay (Doris Kane), Anna May Wong (Mary Lee Ling), Lola Lane (Nita Kenton), Anthony Averill (Larry Camp), Charles Wilson (Inspector Gregg), Frank Jaquet (Sgt. Kelly), Eric Stanley (Shields), James Stephenson (Philip Corey), Jeffrey Lynn (Davis), Leonard Mudie (Fred Gow), Maurice Cass (Dr. Merton), Jack Moore (Assistant District Attorney).

The rather novel idea of solving a murder mystery through the use of astrology may have seemed like a good way of heightening the sense of mystery; however, as handled here, it produces more tedium than suspense. An importer, Averill, is murdered when his ship docks in San Francisco. The police call in astrologer Wong to help with the investigation, but two more killings occur before the culprit is nabbed.

p, Bryan Foy; d, William McGann; w, Anthony Coldeway (based on a story by Coldeway, Manly P. Hall); ph, L.W. O'Connell; ed, Doug Gould; cos, Howard Shoup.

Mystery   (PR:A   MPAA:NR)

WHEN WILLIE COMES MARCHING HOME***½

(1950) 82m FOX bw

Dan Dailey (Bill Kluggs), Corinne Calvet (Yvonne), Colleen Townsend (Marge Fettles), William Demarest (Herman Kluggs), James Lydon (Charles Fettles), Lloyd Corrigan (Mayor Adams), Evelyn Varden (Gertrude Kluggs), Kenny Williams, Lee Clark (Musicians), Charles Halton (Mr. Fettles), Mae Marsh (Mrs. Fettles), Jack Pennick (Sergeant-Instructor), Mickey Simpson (M.P. Kerrigan), Frank Pershing (Maj. Bickford), Don Summers (M.P. Sherve), Gil Herman (Lt. Comdr. Crown), Peter Ortiz (Pierre), Luis Alberni (Barman), John Shulick, John McKee (Pilots), Clarke Gordon, Robin Hughes (Marine Officers), Cecil Weston (Mrs. Barnes), Harry Tenbrook (Joe, Taxi Driver), Russ Clark (Sgt. Wilson), George Spaulding (Judge Tate), James Eagle (Reporter), Harry Strang (Sergeant), George Magrill (Chief Petty Officer), Hank Worden (Choir Leader), Larry Keating (Gen. G. Reeding), Dan Riss (Gen. Adams), Robert Einer (Lt. Bagley), Russ Conway (Maj. J.A. White), Whit Bissell (Lt. Handley), Ann Codee (French Instructor), Ray Hyke (Maj. Crawford), Gene Collins (Andy), James Flavin (Gen. Brevort), David McMahon (Col. Ainsley), Charles Trowbridge (Gen. Merrill), Kenneth Tobey (Lt. K. Geiger), Maj. Sam Harris (Hospital Patient), Alberto Morin, Louis Mercier (Resistance Fighters), Paul Harvey (Officer), James Waters, Ken Lynch, Frank Baker, J. Farrell MacDonald, Vera Miles.

While director Ford always included moments of broad comedy in his "serious" films, he was never really allowed to direct an out-and-out comedy until 1950 when he helmed WHEN WILLIE COMES MARCHING HOME. Dailey stars as a the first man in Puxatawney, West Virginia to enlist upon the outbreak of WW II. The locals, led by Dailey's father Demarest, give the young recruit a huge, patriotic sendoff as he leaves for boot camp. When Dailey returns from training camp, the town throws a huge welcome home party. Unfortunately, the eager-to-fight Dailey has been assigned duty as a gunnery instructor at a new air base in his home town. Dailey becomes the joke of the town as he watches all the other young men go off to war and come back heroes. Even small dogs harass him on his way home. Dailey gets his big chance when the gunner of a B-17 becomes ill just before a secret mission. Picked to replace the gunner, an excited Dailey boards the plane and promptly falls asleep. When he awakes, Dailey finds the plane empty of all personnel except him (he failed to hear the order to bail out). The bewildered soldier jumps out of the plane and winds up getting his chute tangled in a tree. He hangs there until rescued by a group of French Resistance fighters who cut him down and then quiz him to prove he's an American. "What does the Lone Ranger say?" and "Who is Dick Tracy?" are the questions asked Dailey by the French. Once satisfied that Dailey is an ally, the Resistance fighters bring him along while they go to photograph a secret German V-2 base. During his adventure, Dailey becomes attracted to Calvet, a sexy French partisan, and almost forgets about Townsend, his wholesome girl back home. Faced with having to sneak Dailey out of the country, the Resistance fighters stage a mock wedding between the American gunner and Calvert to cover their tracks. Leaving Calvert behind, Dailey makes it to London where he is hailed a hero, given loads of liquor, and then kept awake and interrogated by every ranking officer from London to Washington. Finally, Dailey makes his way back to Puxatawney–only 36 hours after he left–drunk and tired. Finding himself locked out of his house, Dailey comes in through the window and is attacked by his own father, who mistakes him for a Nazi spy. Dailey soon discovers that the whole town thinks he went AWOL, and his tired and drunken state only confirms their suspicions. Sworn to secrecy by Washington regarding his mission, Dailey is helpless to protest and must endure the same abuse heaped upon him before he left. Eventually the powers that be at the Pentagon reveal the truth and MPs are dispatched to Puxatawney to escort the hero to Washington where he is to be decorated by the President. An extremely funny film, WHEN WILLIE COMES MARCHING HOME was based on a story (which was nominated for an Oscar) written by Sy Gomberg, who conveyed his own experience during WW II which saw him ship out on a Friday afternoon, shoot down a Japanese plane, get strafed, and return home the following Monday morning. The incident was expanded and stretched to allow for all the satirical social observation it was worth and Ford attacked it with his usual insightful gusto. The hypocrisy of small town life is pinpointed here and Ford gently condemns the people who would

make such a fuss to send a man off to war and then ridicule him when assigned to a local training post, even though his job was an important one that could mean the difference between life and death for most recruits. While the small town scenes are funny and treated in a satirical manner, the vision of war is very serious and no fun at all. Ford's visual style darkens when Dailey lands in France and the mission to photograph the V-2 is given a straight dramatic treatment, thus driving home how serious war is and highlighting the small town's ludicrous (and dangerous) attitude toward it. The balance between comedy and drama is a successful one and when asked why Ford chose to handle the war scenes in a straightforward manner, the director replied: "Well, that was my racket for a while, and there wasn't anything funny about it. I wonder what s.o.b. will be the first who makes a comedy about Viet Nam?"

p, Fred Kohlmar; d, John Ford; w, Mary Loos, Richard Sale (based on the story "When Leo Comes Marching Home" by Sy Gomberg); ph, Leo Tover; m, Alfred Newman; ed, James B. Clark; md, Lionel Newman; art d, Lyle R. Wheeler, Chester Gore; set d, Thomas Little, Bruce MacDonald; cos, Charles LeMaire; spec eff, Fred Sersen; ch, Kenny Williams.

Comedy/War   (PR:A   MPAA:NR)

WHEN WOMEN HAD TAILS zero   (1970, Ital.) Film Ventures
International c (QUANDO DE DONNE AVEVANDO LA CODA)

Senta Berger (Filli), Giuliano Gemma (Ulli), Frank Wolff (Grrr), Lando Buzzanca (Kao), Lino Toffolo (Put), Aldo Giuffre (Zug), Renzo Montagnani (Malue), Francesco Mule (Uto), Paolo Borboni.

This spoof on caveman epics has only the music of Ennio Morricone to make it bearable. Berger is the lone woman on a small island which has a sudden influx of seven cavemen. It doesn't take much to figure out what the presence of sexy Berger will do to seven animalistic men, even if she does sport a tail. Sequel: WHEN WOMEN LOST THEIR TAILS.

p, Silvio Clementelli; d, Pasquale Festa Campanile; w, Lina Wertmuller, Ottavio Jemma, Marcello Costa, Campanile; m, Ennio Morricone.

Comedy/Fantasy   (PR:O   MPAA:NR)

WHEN WORLDS COLLIDE**½   (1951) 81m PAR c

Richard Derr (Dave Randall), Barbara Rush (Joyce Hendron), Peter Hanson (Dr. Tony Drake), John Hoyt (Sydney Stanton), Larry Keating (Dr. Cole Hendron), Judith Ames (Julie Cummings), Stephen Chase (Dr. Dean George Frey), Frank Cady (Harold Ferris), Hayden Rorke (Dr. Emory Bronson), Sandro Giglio (Ottinger), Laura Elliot (Stewardess), Jim Congdon (Eddie Garson), Frances Sanford (Alice, Secretary), Freeman Lusk (Rudolph Marston), Joseph Mell (Glen Spiro), Marcel de la Brosse (Headwaiter), Queenie Smith (Matron), Leonard Mudie (British UN Representative), Art Gilmore (Paul), Keith Richards (Stanley), Gay Nelson (Leda), Rudy Lee (Mike), John Ridgely (Chief Airport Inspector), James Seay Donovan (Reporter at Airport), Harry Stanton (Dr. Zenta), Hassan Khayyam (Indian Chairman), Bill Meader (Clerk), Ramsay Hill (Frenchman), Gene Collins (Newsdealer), Sam Finn, Gertrude Astor, Estelle Etterre (Travelers), Mary Murphy, Stuart Whitman, Kirk Alyn, Robert Chapman, Charmienne Harker, Walter Kelley, Chad Madison, Dolores Mann, Robert Sully, Richard Vath (Students), Paul Frees (Narrator).

If the naive dramatic situations and trite idealism can be ignored, the viewer is in for an amazing spectacle of special effects. These were good enough to warrant an Academy Award in 1951, especially worth noting since THE THING and THE DAY THE EARTH STOOD STILL were also in the running. Yarn concerns the efforts to build a spaceship which will take 40 people to a new planet, actually the satellite of a planet that will eventually crash into the Earth. Keating is the scientist who verifies that a planet is running wild through the solar system. Though the government does not accept his hypothesis, the filthy rich Hoyt does, and helps commission the building of the ship. His purposes are totally selfish, so he and Keating can be unemotionally gotten out of the way to allow for the younger people to go to the new planet to rebuild the human population. The special effects include such hazards as New York being flooded, plus the actual takeoff of the ship and its landing on the new planet.

p, George Pal; d, Rudolph Mate; w, Sydney Boehm (based on the novel by Edwin Balmer, Philip Wylie); ph, John F. Seitz, W. Howard Greene (Technicolor); m, Leith Stevens; ed, Arthur Schmidt; art d, Hal Pereira, Al Nozaki; set d, Sam Comer, Ross Dowd; cos, Edith Head; spec eff, Gordon Jennings, Harry Barndollar.

Science Fiction   Cas.   (PR:A   MPAA:G)

WHEN YOU COME HOME*   (1947, Brit.) 98m Butcher Empire
Productions/BUT bw

Frank Randle (Himself), Leslie Sarony (Maestro), Leslie Holmes (Fingers), Diana Decker (Paula Ryngelbaum), Fred Conyngham (Mike O'Flaherty), Linda Parker (Singer), Jack Melford (Dr. Dormer Franklyn), Lily Lapidus (Mrs. Ryngelbaum), Tony Heaton (Mr. Ryngelbaum), Hilda Bayley (Lady Langfield), Lesley Osmond (Delia), Gus Aubrey (Designer), Ernest Dale (Fireman).

This lifeless comedy follows an old man reminiscing about his early days working backstage at a London theater; his granddaughter is the listener in the midst of the old gent's birthday celebration. More ridiculous than amusing.

p&d, John Baxter; w, David Evans, Geofrey Orme, Frank Randle; ph, Geoffrey Faithfull; m, Percival Mackey; ed, Ted Richards, art d, Charles Gilbert; ch, Fred Conyngham, Hazel Gee; m/l, Leslie Sarony, Leslie Holmes, Bruce Sievier.

Comedy   **(PR:A MPAA:NR)**

WHEN YOU COMIN' BACK, RED RYDER? zero (1979) 118m COL c

Candy Clark (Cheryl), Marjoe Gortner (Teddy), Stephanie Faracy (Angel Childress), Dixie Harris (Grandma Childress), Anne Ramsey (Rhea Childress), Lee Grant (Clarisse Ethridge), Hal Linden (Richard Ethridge), Peter Firth (Stephen Ryder), Pat Hingle (Lyle Striker), Bill McKinney (Tommy Clark), Alex Colon (Younger Mexican Man), Joe Hernandez (Older Mexican Man), Leon Russell (Radio Preacher), Audra Lindley (Ceil Ryder), Sherry Unger (Bar Floozy), Elaine Story (Bowling Alley Waitress), Riley Hill (Junior Ferguson), Carmen Ledoux (Mexican Waitress), Tiny Wells (Walter), Ron Sobel (Sheriff Garcia), Robert Easton (Customs Man), Barry Cahill (Customs Doctor), Mark Medoff (Faith Healer), Albert Pena (Mexican Father), Jamie Hilliard & the Countrymen, Hovie Lister & the Statesmen.

In this abysmal pseudo-psychodrama, Gortner plays a crazed Vietnam veteran who takes over a small Texas diner that contains the usual slice-of-life characters. Assisted by his hippie girl friend Clark, Gortner screams, yells, threatens, and intimidates the customers until at last someone finally shuts up the lout. In adapting his play to film, Medoff changed much of the original concept. Characters here are introduced so we know exactly who these nice people are who are being threatened by big, bad Gortner. Grant and Linden, looking hopelessly lost, are the stereotypical rich folks with a marriage on the rocks. Equally lost as the diner's short order cook is Firth, whose British accent would cause him to get knocked around by some good ol' Texas boys any day of the week. Gortner's tirade is nonstop and grows tiresome quickly. In a strange way, his portrayal is not unlike the real-life performance he gave as an evangelical minister in the documentary of the former child preacher's life, MARJOE. Filmed in a theatrical style, the film comes off as a loud and obnoxious marathon that refuses to let up. Repulsive.

p, Marjoe Gortner; d, Milton Katselas; w, Mark Medoff (based on his play); ph, Jules Brenner (Panavision); m, Jack Nitzsche; ed, Richard Chew; prod d, Ted Haworth; md, Nitzsche; cos, Joe J. Thompkins; m/l, "The Thrill Is Gone" (performed by B.B. King).

Drama   **(PR:O MPAA:R)**

WHEN YOU'RE IN LOVE★★★   (1937) 110m COL bw

Grace Moore (Louise Fuller), Cary Grant (Jimmy Hudson), Aline MacMahon (Marianne Woods), Henry Stephenson (Walter Mitchell), Thomas Mitchell (Hank Miller), Catherine Doucet (Jane Summers), Luis Alberni (Luis Perugini), Gerald Oliver Smith (Gerald Meeker), Emma Dunn (Mrs. Hamilton), George Pearce (Mr. Hamilton), Frank Puglia (Carlos), Barnett Parker (Butler), Marcelle Corday (Marie, Louise's Maid), Enrique de Rosas (Hotel Manager), William Pawley, Don Rowan (Bruisers), Billy Gilbert (Jose the Bartender), Romaine Callender (Waiter), Arthur Hoyt, Otto Fries, Harvey Leach (Men), Dewey Robinson, Bud Geary (Reporters), Pat West, Harry Holman (Babbitt Brothers), Edward Keane (Stage Manager), Peggy Stratford, Ruth Williard, May Wallace, Isabelle LaMal, Georgia Cooper, Helen Dickson (Women), Robert Emmet O'Connor, George Cooper (Assistant Immigration Officers), Emery D'Arcy (Scarpia), Herbert Ashley (Immigration Chief), Hector V. Sarno (Jail Guard), Antonio Vidal (Justice of Peace), Soledad Jimenez (Wife of Justice of Peace), Carmen Samaniego, Nena Sandoval, Robert Linden, Dave O'Brien, Jose Fernandez, Gene Morgan (Dancers), Fletcher Norton (Teacher), Lucille Ward (Music Teacher), Robert McKenzie (Charlie Perkins), Scotty Beckett (Boy), Henry Roquemore (Ticket Clerk), Arthur Stuart Hull (Business Man), Jean De Briac (Headwaiter), Ann Doran (Secretary), J.P. Lockney (Doorman), Bruce Sidney (Stage Manager), Frank Leyva, Raoul Lechuga (Mexican Policemen), Dick Botiller, Joe Dominguez (Mexicans), Wilson Millar (Italian), Joe Forte (Waiter's Assistant), Manuel Paris (Hotel Clerk), Gus Reid (Fat Waiter), Bess Flowers, Leyland Hodgson (Couple in Dressing Room), Louise Brooks (Chorus Girl), Chris-Pin Martin (Servant), C. Montague Shaw (Attorney), Alphonse Martel (Announcer), Chuck Hamilton (Tony, Assistant Stage Manager), Cyril Ring, Olive Morgan, Catherine Wallace, Carlos Montalban.

This musical romance is as light and sweet as cotton candy and probably just as memorable. Moore plays an Australian opera singer who remains in Mexico after her visa expires. U.S. immigration officials consequently detain the singer, along with her manager, MacMahon, and Moore's ever-present trio of groupies, Doucet, Alberni, and Smith. This puts in peril Moore's opportunity to sing at a music festival run by Stephenson, her old maestro. To get her star back into the states, MacMahon hits on the idea of arranging a marriage of convenience. Enter Grant, a witty young artist who agrees to wed and then divorce Moore for the right price. MacMahon and Moore's plot takes an unexpected twist when Grant actually falls for his new bride. He bursts into her home, demanding Moore get rid of cling-ons

Doucet, Alberni, and Smith. Eventually, Grant's charm wears down Moore's attitude, and she takes a ride with her unwanted husband to his farmhouse. Moore finally succumbs and agrees to run off with Grant. She changes her mind, however, after realizing she must sing at a music festival, and decides to follow through with the planned divorce. But Moore soon realizes she loves Grant too much and is utterly miserable without him. She refuses to perform at the festival, until Grant suddenly shows up backstage and forces her to go on. Moore and Grant realize their love for each other and decide to remain husband and wife as the film ends happily. This is a charming little musical, full of bright, witty moments and some enjoyable numbers. Though the plot is fairly predictable, Moore and Grant are an amusing team who give the film spark. Riskin's direction is fine for the material, moving this along at an easy pace. Normally a screenwriter (having won an Oscar for his script of Frank Capra's classic comedy IT HAPPENED ONE NIGHT), this was Riskin's only foray in the director's chair. Appearing in an insignificant part as a chorus girl is Louise Brooks, best known for her work in such classic silent films as DIARY OF A LOST GIRL and PANDORA'S BOX. She had retired from the movies after appearing in many European silents, which had consequently made her unpopular with Hollywood studios. Brooks attempted to make a comeback in 1936 but found little opportunity. The best she could get was this bit part in WHEN YOU'RE IN LOVE, which she graciously accepted in return for a screen test for the major role of another film. Columbia's publicity department heralded her return by releasing stills with a humiliating caption which read: "Louise Brooks, former star, who deserted Hollywood at the height of her career, has come back to resume her work in pictures. But seven years is too long for the public to remember, and Louise courageously begins again at the bottom." The film's songs include: "Our Song," "The Whistling Boy" (Jerome Kern, Dorothy Fields), "Minnie the Moocher" (Cab Calloway, Irving Mills, Clarence Gaskill), "In the Gloaming" (Meta Orred, Annie F. Harrison), "Siboney" (Dolly Morse, Ernest Lecuona), as well as "Serenade" and "The Waltz Song" from Franz Schubert's "Romeo and Juliet."

p, Everett Riskin; d, Robert Riskin; w, R. Riskin (based on an idea by Ethel Hill, Cedric Worth); ph, Joseph Walker; ed, Gene Milford; md, Alfred Newman; art d, Stephen Goosson; cos, Bernard Newman; ch, Leon Leonidof.

Musical   **(PR:A MPAA:NR)**

WHEN YOU'RE SMILING★½   (1950) 75m COL bw

Jerome Courtland (Gerald Durham), Frankie Laine (Himself), Lola Albright (Peggy Martin), Jerome Cowan (Herbert Reynolds), Margo Wood (Linda Reynolds), Collette Lyons (Nan Doran), Robert Shayne (Jack Lacey), Don Otis (Himself), Ray Teal (Steve), Jimmy Lloyd (Dave), Donna Hamilton (Margie), Edward Earle (Foster), Frank Nelson (Jeweler), Neyle Morrow (Carlo), Bob Crosby, Mills Brothers, Modernaires, Kay Starr, Billy Daniels.

A modest plot was the excuse for even more modest musical numbers, with only the appearances of such talents as Crosby, Laine, and the Mills Brothers to highlight them. Courtland is a cowpoke who comes to Hollywood with remote thoughts of getting into show business. Cowan is an owner of a recording company on the financial edge because of the boss' yen for gambling. Mistaking Courtland for a Texas millionaire, Cowan attempts to hitch him up with his daughter. But it doesn't take, the cowboy falling for Albright and becoming a recording star in the process. Songs include: "When You're Smiling" (Mark Fisher, Joe Goodwin, Larry Shay, sung by Frankie Laine, Jerome Courtland, the Modernaires), "That Old Black Magic" (Harold Arlen, Johnny Mercer, sung by Billy Daniels), "When the Wind Was Green" (Don Hunt, sung by Jerome Courtland), "Georgia on My Mind" (Stuart Garrell, Hoagy Carmichael, sung by Frankie Laine), "Up a Lazy River" (Sidney Arodin, Hoagy Carmichael, sung by the Mills Brothers), "Deed I Do" (Walter Hirsch, Fred Rose, sung by Billy Daniels), "Juke Box Saturday Night" (Al Stillman, Paul McGrane, sung by the Modernaires), "Mama Goes Where Papa Goes" (sung by Kay Starr), "If You Can't Get a Drum with a Boom, Boom, Boom" (performed by Bob Crosby and His Bobcats).

p, Jonie Taps; d, Joseph Santley; W, Karen DeWolfe, John R. Roberts; ph, Vincent Farrar; m, Morris W. Stoloff; ed, Edwin Bryant; art d, Harold MacArthur.

Musical   **(PR:A MPAA:NR)**

WHEN YOUTH CONSPIRES   (SEE: OLD SWIMMIN' HOLE, THE,
                                                                    1941)

WHEN'S YOUR BIRTHDAY?★★½   (1937) 77m David L. Loew/RKO
                                                                    bw-c

Joe E. Brown (Dustin Willoughby), Marian Marsh (Jerry Grant), Fred Keating (Larry Burke), Edgar Kennedy (Mr. Basscombe), Maude Eburne (Mrs. Basscombe), Suzanne Kaaren (Diane Basscombe), Margaret Hamilton (Mossy), Minor Watson (Regan), Frank Jenks (Lefty), Don Rowan (Steve), Granville Bates (Judge O'Day), Charles Judels (Headwaiter), Corky (Zodiac the Dog), Bull Montana.

In 1937 Joe E. Brown left Warner Bros. to work with independent producer Loew on what the two hoped would be a successful string of movie comedies. Though the venture never reached the level they hoped for, this first effort is amusing. The film opens with an animated piece showing the influence of the moon over the planets. We then meet Brown, an amiable sort who's working his way through astrology school as a boxer. Eventually his talents take Brown to a carnival midway, where he's hired as a fortune teller. Watson is a gambler who decides having an astrologer around could be a handy thing. He hires Brown, telling the stargazer to start picking winning horses and boxers for Watson to place wagers on. Marsh and Kaaren add to the hijinks as Brown's *two* romantic interests. In the end Marsh's charms win out as things wind up to a happy conclusion. The story is slight, but punched up with some good gags and a fine supporting cast. Kennedy, master of the slow burn, is funny as a newly rich plumber. Though the film is black and white, the opening sequence was animated in Technicolor. This charming cartoon was produced by Leon Schlesinger, better known for his work with the zanies over at the Warner Bros. animation department.

p, Robert Harris; d, Harry Beaumont; w, Harry Clork, Harvey Gates, Malcolm Stuart Boylan, Samuel M. Pike (based on a play by Fred Ballard); ph, George Robinson (cartoon sequence in Technicolor); ed, Jack Ogilvie; cartoon sequence, Leon Schlesinger.

Comedy   Cas.   **(PR:AA MPAA:NR)**

WHERE ANGELS GO...TROUBLE FOLLOWS*½   (1968) 95m COL c

Rosalind Russell (*Mother Superior Simplicia*), Stella Stevens (*Sister George*), Binnie Barnes (*Sister Celestine*), Mary Wickes (*Sister Clarissa*), Dolores Sutton (*Sister Rose Marie*), Susan Saint James (*Rosabelle*), Barbara Hunter (*Marvel Ann Clancy*), Alice Rawlings (*Patty*), Hilarie Thompson (*Hilarie*), Devon Douglas (*Devon*), Ellen Moss (*Tanya*), Cherie Lamour (*Cherie*), June Fairchild (*June*), Michael Christian (*Motorcycle Leader*), Jon Hill (*Cyclist*), John Findletter (*Jud Farriday*), Tom Logan (*Tom*), Mary Jo Begley (*Miss Ohio*), Barbara Boman (*Miss Missouri*), Janis Eaton (*Miss Oklahoma*), Patricia Eaves (*Miss New Mexico*), Betsy Gindele (*Miss Pennsylvania*), Vivian Gradin (*Miss Texas*), Suellen Helland (*Miss Illinois*), Cindy Lu Rumple (*Miss Indiana*), Milton Berle (*Film Director*), Arthur Godfrey (*Bishop*), Van Johnson (*Father Chase*), William Lundigan (*Mr. Clancy*), Robert Taylor (*Mr. Farriday*).

Here we have an attempt to create a drama around the conflict between the traditional, rigid values of the Roman Catholic church and the liberalism of the 1960s. As the mother superior, Russell represents the old ways, while the young, rebellious Stevens tries to introduce new teaching methods in their convent school. According to this picture, the major thing to emerge from this re-evaluation of traditions is that nuns get to wear shorter skirts. The shallowness of the story is an insult to the capable performers, who are never given an opportunity to demonstrate their talents. A sequel to THE TROUBLE WITH ANGELS (1966).

p, William Frye; d, James Neilson; w, Blanche Hanalis (based on characters created by Jane Trahey); ph, Sam Leavitt (Pathe Color); m, Lalo Schifrin; ed, Adrienne Fazan; prod d, Lyle Wheeler; set d, Frank Tuttle; co s, Moss Mabry; ch, Hannah Reiner; m/l, "Where Angels Go, Trouble Follows," Schifrin, Bobby Hart, Tommy Boyce (sung by Boyce, Hart); makeup, Ben Lane.

Drama   **(PR:C MPAA:NR)**

WHERE ARE YOUR CHILDREN?**   (1943) 73m MON bw

Jackie Cooper (*Danny*), Gale Storm (*Judy*), Patricia Morison (*Linda*), John Litel (*Judge Evans*), Gertrude Michael (*Nell*), Addison Richards (*Halstead*), Herbert Rawlinson (*Butler*), Betty Blythe (*Mrs. Cheston*), Anthony Warde (*Jim*), Charles Williams (*Caesar*), Evelyn Eaton (*Opal*), Jimmy Zaner (*Jerry*), Sarah Edwards (*Matron*), John Laurenz (*Petty Officer Jones*), Neyle Marx (*Herb*).

This well-meaning film explores the situations with the potential to lead teenagers to crime. In this case it's Storm who gets herself involved with an unruly bunch and one thing leads to another until she is inadvertently part of a murder. She is put behind bars, and Coogan, as the rich kid gone Navy, helps to see that Storm's true association with the crime is made known, letting her off the hook. Songs include: "Glad You're Dead, You Rascal", "Girl Of My Dreams" (Ronald Thomas).

p, Jeffrey Bernard; d, William Nigh; w, Hilary Lynn, George W. Sayre (based on the story by Lynn); ph, Mack Stengler, Ira Morgan; ed, Duncan Mansfield; md, Edward J. Kay.

Drama   **(PR:A MPAA:NR)**

WHERE DANGER LIVES***   (1950) 84m RKO bw

Robert Mitchum (*Jeff Cameron*), Faith Domergue (*Margo Lannington*), Claude Rains (*Frederick Lannington*), Maureen O'Sullivan (*Julie*), Charles Kemper (*Police Chief*), Ralph Dumke (*Klauber*), Billy House (*Mr. Bogardus*), Harry Shannon (*Dr. Maynard*), Philip Van Zandt (*Milo DeLong*), Jack Kelly (*Dr. Mullenbach*), Lillian West (*Mrs. Bogardus*), Ruth Lewis (*Nurse Collins*), Julia Faye (*Nurse Seymour*), Dorothy Abbott (*Nurse Clark*), Gaylord 'Steve' Pendleton, Joey Ray, Don House, Jerry James, Len Henry, Carl Saxe, Marvin Jones (*Policemen*), Lester Dorr (*Assistant Police Chief*), Art Dupuis (*Intern*), Stanley Andrews (*Dr. Mathews*), Jack Kruschen (*Casey*), Elaine Riley (*Nurse Bates*), Gordon Clark (*Attendant*), Geraldine

Wall (*Annie*), David Stollery (*Boy*), Sherry Jackson (*Girl in Iron Lung*), Clifford Brooke (*Butler*), Jim Dundee (*Taxi Driver*), Tol Avery (*Honest Hal*), Robert R. Stevenson (*Clerk*), Ethan Laidlaw, Earle Hodgins, William Bailey, Stuart Holmes, Frank Leyuda, Carl Sklover (*Men*), Gene Barnes (*Tipsy Youth*), Ray Teal (*Joe Borden*), Duke York (*Cowboy*), Marie Allison, Grace MacNaughton, Betty Hannon (*Girls*), Julian Rivero (*Pablo*), George Sherwood, John Sheehan (*Quartz Miners*), James Brick Sullivan, Carlos Albert, Mike Lally, Philip Ahlm (*Customs Officers*), Tina Menard (*Cashier*), Jeraldine Jordan, Hazel Boyne, Ann Zikal (*Women*), Erno Verebes, Allen Matthews (*Waiters*), Florence Hamblin, Amilda Cuddy (*Hawaiians*), Maxine Gates (*Girl in Act*), Phil Boutelje (*Pianist*), Herschel Daugherty (*Desk Clerk*), Linda Johnson (*Airport Announcer*), Marie Thomas, Gerry Ganzer (*Stewardesses*), Bob Coleman (*Airport Official*), Helen Brown (*Nurse*), William E. Green (*Doctor*), Frank Layva (*Mexican*).

A mediocre *film noir* which is saved only by Mitchum's fine performance as a reputable doctor whose relationship with O'Sullivan is disrupted when he falls for suicidal patient Domergue. Without realizing her weak mental state, Mitchum begins to get involved with her, eventually asking her father, Rains, for permission to marry her. When he finds out that Rains is actually her husband, a fight ensues resulting in a concussion for Mitchum. When he comes to, he finds Rains dead. Domergue explains that a brutal Mitchum punch killed him, but actually it was she who committed the murder, suffocating her unconscious husband. Domergue talks Mitchum into fleeing to Mexico with her, all the while being tracked by police. They devise a complicated plan to cross the border, but soon Mitchum starts doubting her. While Domergue still has a chance, she tries to suffocate Mitchum. Leaving him for dead, she heads for the border, only to be followed by Mitchum when he regains consciousness. She is ready to cross when Mitchum arrives. After a shootout, Mitchum is wounded, while Domergue is gunned down by the Border Patrol, clearing Mitchum of the murder with her final breaths, and thereby enabling him to resume his life with O'Sullivan. WHERE DANGER LIVES was Howard Hughes' effort to make Faith Domergue a star of the status of Jane Russell, his previous creation. After declaring that VENDETTA-Domergue's previous film and the one that was supposed to catapult her to stardom-was a washout, Hughes decided to postpone that film's release and star Domergue opposite someone of a greater stature than VENDETTA star George Dolenz, namely Robert Mitchum. Domergue's career peaked with WHERE DANGER LIVES and she was eventually relegated to such unmemorable films as PREHISTORIC PLANET WOMEN (1966), once again proving Hughes' lack of star-making ability.

p, Irving Cummings, Jr.; d, John Farrow; w, Charles Bennett (based on a story by Leo Rosten); ph, Nicholas Musuraca; m, Roy Webb; ed, Eda Warren; md, Constantin Bakaleinikoff; art d, Albert S. D'Agostino, Ralph Berger; set d, Darrell Silvera, John Sturtevant; cos, Michael Woulfe; makeup, Mel Berns.

Crime   **(PR:A MPAA:NR)**

WHERE DID YOU GET THAT GIRL?*½   (1941) 65m UNIV bw

Leon Errol (*MacDevin, Pawnshop Proprietor*), Helen Parrish (*Helen Bordon*), Charles Lang (*Jeff Grant*), Eddie Quillan (*Joe Olson*), Franklin Pangborn (*Digby*), Stanley Fields (*Crandall*), Tom Dugan (*Murphy*), Joe Brown, Jr (*Davey*), Leonard Sues (*Franky*), Kenneth Lundy (*Shrimp*), Joe Cobb (*Tubby*), Billy Jack Elliott (*Jack*), Peter Sullivan (*Pete*), Thurston Hall (*Stuyvesant*), Wade Boteler (*Connolly*), Nina Orla (*Singer*), Frank Mitchell (*Crook*), Tim Ryan (*Inspector*), Leon Belasco (*Hayden*), Kay Leslie (*Secretary*), Hope Lanlon (*Mrs. Olson*), Connie Leon (*Housewife*), Frank Jenks.

An unlikely bunch of musicians are brought together through their common poverty, resulting in the creation of a hit tune which lands them a contract. Lang is the composer whose works are tampered with by Quillan to be more acceptable to swing listeners. But Lang doesn't much mind this prostitution since he winds up with the singing beauty Parrish. Songs include: "Where Did You Get That Girl?" (Harry Puck, Bert Kalmar, sung by Helen Parrish), "Sergeant Swing," "Rug-Cuttin' Romeo" (Milton Rosen, Everett Carter).

p, Joseph G. Sanford; d, Arthur Lubin; w, Jay Dratler, Paul Franklin, Stanley Crea Rubin (based on the story by Dratler); ph, John Boyle; ed, Phil Cahn; md, Charles Previn; cos, Vera West.

Musical/Comedy   **(PR:A MPAA:NR)**

WHERE DO WE GO FROM HERE?**½   (1945) 77m FOX c

Fred MacMurray (*Bill*), Joan Leslie (*Sally*), June Haver (*Lucilla*), Gene Sheldon (*Genie/Ali*), Anthony Quinn (*Indian Chief*), Carlos Ramirez (*Benito*), Alan Mowbray (*Gen. George Washington*), Fortunio Bonanova (*Christopher Columbus*), Herman Bing (*Hessian Colonel*), Otto Preminger (*Gen. Rahl*), Howard Freeman (*Kreiger*), John Davidson (*Benedict Arnold*), Rosina Galli (*Old Lady*), Fred Essler (*Dutch Councilman*), Joseph Haworth, Scott Elliott, Robert Castaine, William Carter (*Service Men*), Arno Frey (*German Lieutenant*), Max Wagner (*Sergeant*), Larry Thompson (*Soldier*), Bob Stephenson, Will Kaufman, Walter Bonn (*Dutchmen*), Hans Von Morhart (*Blacksmith*), Bert Roach, Paul Weigel, Ferdinand Munier, Harry Holman, Harrison Greene (*Dutch Councilmen*), Joe Bernard (*Burgher*), Hope Landin (*Elderly Wife*), Dick Elliott (*Father*), Norman Field (*Minister*), Edward Clark (*Organist*), Cyril Ring (*Army Doctor*), Sam Bernard (*Warden*),

Ralph Dunn, Ralph Sanford (Policemen).

A whimsical musical fantasy that often borders on silliness but has enough historical merit and humor to make it pleasant fare. Everyone fantasizes about finding the genie in the lamp who will grant their trio of wishes. MacMurray finds that lamp and his genie is Sheldon. It's WW II time and the 4-F MacMurray would like nothing better than to join the armed forces and fight, but his physical problems (minor) keep him out, so he does the next best thing and goes to work for the USO. When a scrap drive is instituted, a lamp is donated and MacMurray, idly polishing it to bring back the metal's luster, is surprised when Sheldon pops up. Sheldon's magical powers are as rusty as the lamp and when MacMurray expresses a desire to join the service, he does get his wish, but finds himself in the 18th-Century equivalent of the U.S. Army and serving under the command of Mowbray (as the father of our country). From Valley Forge, he is whisked even further backward by the out-of-practice Sheldon, joining forces with Bonanova (as Christopher Columbus). From there, he is off to Manhattan Island where he is bargaining with Quinn, a recalcitrant Indian, who agrees to sell the island for the famed price of $24. Through all of his travels, MacMurray is surrounded by the same women who were around him in the 20th Century–Haver and Leslie. They continue to pop up in the same roles in various times. MacMurray thanks the memory of his former history teacher and gets the chance to warn Mowbray of the traitorous Benedict Arnold (Davidson). He is also armed with the 'mistaken' knowledge that the first landfall seen by the sailors on the Nina, Pina, and Santa Maria is not the shores of America, but the island of Cuba. With each new error, Sheldon attempts to rectify his mistakes and finally saves his reputation by bringing MacMurray back to the 20th Century and placing him in the Marines. The final scene has MacMurray marching along in tight formation as he waves to Haver and Leslie, who watch him proudly from the curb as the exonerated Sheldon marches alongside. It's pure fantasy so look not for logic. The scene on the Santa Maria is the best shot and staged and emerges as an opera. There are no step-out songs in the Weill-Gershwin score but they are serviceable enough, though not memorable. The tunes include: "Morale," "If Love Remains," "All at Once," "Song of the Rhineland," "Christopher Columbus," "The Nina, the Pinta, and the Santa Maria." Good color and some fine special effects. Quinn's role as the Indian showed a bit of comedy talent, but not much. Haver left show business about eight years after this film to enter a convent. That didn't last too long and when she emerged, she married MacMurray, thus granting him a fervent wish in real life.

p, William Perlberg; d, Gregory Ratoff; w, Morrie Ryskind (based on a story by Ryskind, Sig Herzig); ph, Leon Shamroy (Technicolor); m, David Raksin; ed, J. Watson Webb; md, Emil Newman, Charles Henderson; art d, Lyle Wheeler, Leland Fuller; set d, Thomas Little, Walter Scott; spec eff, Fred Sersen; ch, Fanchon; m/l, Kurt Weill, Ira Gershwin.

Musical Fantasy   **(PR:AA MPAA:NR)**

WHERE DOES IT HURT?*   (1972) 90m Josef Shaftel/Cinerama c

Peter Sellers (Albert T. Hopfnagel), Jo Ann Pflug (Alice), Rick Lenz (Lester Hammond), Harold Gould (Dr. Zerny), Hope Summers (Nurse Throttle), Eve Bruce (Nurse LaMarr), Kathleen Freeman (Mrs. Mazzini), Norman Alden (Katzen), Keith Allison (Hinkley), William Elliot (Oscar the Orderly), Jeanne Byron (Dr. Kincaid), Paul Lambert (Dr. Pinikhes), Brett Halsey (Dr. Quagliomo), Albert Reed (Dr. Radcliffe), J. Edward McKinley (Hospital Commissioner), Marvin Miller (Catering Manager), Pat Morita (Nishimoto), Jack Mullaney (Male Secretary).

Warning: The Surgeon General does not sanction this movie. Nor do the AMA, medical school graduates, insurance companies, ethnic groups, or sick people who are about to enter a hospital. Although it's not as plausible as THE HOSPITAL, the movie does make a few points as it shatters the business of medicine. Would that they had used a sharp scalpel instead of a scythe. Sellers is a rapacious hospital administrator whose major aim is making money. He goes about this in the traditional way by duping insurance companies, having surgery performed on patients who don't need it, padding the bills of his charges, falsifying reports, and even going so far as to hit a patient in the abdomen after surgery. One or two of the above would have been all that were needed to make the point but the authors and director thought that "more was better" so they laid it on with a trowel. Lenz is an out-of-work construction man who comes to Sellers' hospital for a chest X-ray and that's it. When Sellers learns through the admitting nurse, Pflug, that Lenz owns his own house, he conspires with Morita, the lab assistant, and Lenz is told that he must have his appendix removed. Later, when Lenz learns that he is now devoid of a part of his body that needed no removal, he is fit to be tied and ready to take action. Sellers fears that would close the hospital so he asks his girl friend, Pflug, if she would help get Lenz's mind off any lawsuit. That means that she has to seduce him. She doesn't want to at first but does it anyhow. Then she learns that the whole sexual liaison is being filmed by Sellers in the next room and she is irate. To get even with Sellers, she arranges a huge Mexican fiesta at the hospital, without Sellers' knowledge. The place turns into a Cinco de Mayo celebration and Pflug has her timing just right because she knows that the city hospital administrator, McKinley, is coming to the place to inspect the shenanigans. Sellers is fired right away and the hospital is kept open with Lenz now in charge as an investigator. Sellers goes to jail for a short time

but he has revenge in mind and comes back to the hospital after his jail term is completed. He masquerades as a patient and uses blackmail to get surgeon Lambert to plan to remove Sellers' appendix (unnecessarily) so Sellers can show up later and begin a malpractice suit. Sellers is in the operating room and the anesthesia is taking effect when Lambert gives the task to Gould, his bumbling brother-in-law. Gould is totally inept and has to ask where the appendix is, then begins the surgery by closing his eyes and pointing the scalpel in the general direction of Sellers' abdomen. The movie ends, and none too soon for most viewers. If there was one single ethnic minority that was not slandered here, it must have been Eskimo lesbians because it seems that everyone else got the knife at one time or another. The language is profane, the proceedings inane, and the story insane. True, there are a few laughs in the picture, but not enough to make up for the appalling lack of taste. They had a chance to lance the medical profession and it would have worked if subtlety had been employed. Morita does a neat turn as the lab technician, as does Lambert as the head surgeon. Director Amateau and executive producer Josef Shaftel had made an earlier exercise in bad taste called THE STATUE. Until this picture came out, that had to have been the nadir of major studio nonsense. This is even lower. If you hate doctors, Mexicans, homosexuals, blacks, females, Catholics, Jews, Italians, Japanese, insurance companies, hospitals, Poles and humanity, you just may love this movie. We didn't, even though they tried to sell it as a "black comedy." but there are two words in that phrase and one of them is "comedy," which means that something has to be funny. None of the above was.

p, Rod Amateau, William Schwartz; d, Amateau; w, Amateau, Budd Robinson (based on their novel The Operator); ph, Brick Marquard (Eastmancolor); m, Keith Allison; ed, Tony Mora, Stan Rabjohn; art d, Mike Haller; m/l, title song, Keith Allison, sung by Allison.

Comedy   **(PR:C-O MPAA:R)**

WHERE EAGLES DARE***½   (1968, Brit.) 155m Winkast/MGM c

Richard Burton (John Smith), Clint Eastwood (Lt. Morris Schaffer), Mary Ure (Mary Ellison), Patrick Wymark (Col. Turner), Michael Hordern (Vice Adm. Rolland), Donald Houston (Christiansen), Peter Barkworth (Berkeley), Robert Beatty (Cartwright Jones), William Squire (Thomas), Derren Nesbitt (Maj. von Hapen), Anton Diffring (Col. Kramer), Brook Williams (Sgt. Harrod), Neil McCarthy (MacPherson), Vincent Ball (Carpenter), Victor Beaumont (Col. Weissner), Richard Beale (Telephone Orderly), Ivor Dean (German Officer), Lyn Kennington (German Woman), Nigel Lambert (Young German Soldier), Michael Rooney (Radio Operator), Ernst Walder (Airport Control Officer), Ingrid Pitt (Heidi), Ferdy Mayne (Rosemeyer).

A high-powered, big-budget WW II espionage thriller starring Burton as the head of an elite group of commandos assigned to rescue an American general who has been captured by the Nazis and is being held in a castle high in the Bavarian Alps. Ably assisted by a young American lieutenant, Eastwood, Burton, and his crew of six don German uniforms and parachute into enemy territory. Upon landing, one of their number is found dead with a broken neck and Burton begins to suspect that one of his men is a double agent. Burton meets with an Allied contact, Ure, and she steers him to another female agent, Pitt. Pitt and Ure manage to infiltrate the castle and sneak the commandos in. When another commando is killed under mysterious circumstances, the group's position is compromised and they are forced to surrender. Burton and Eastwood escape, leaving the three others behind. The pair formulate a plan and return to the castle by crouching on the top of a cable car that serves as the only access to the fortress. The pair hook up with the three others and while searching for the American general, Burton reveals to Eastwood that the general isn't a military man at all, but an actor hired by the OSS to help flush out an organization of traitors who have infiltrated British Intelligence. The commandos locate the man, and then Burton reveals that he is a double agent and he confiscates Eastwood's gun. The other three commandos react favorably to Burton's revelation, thus showing themselves to be Nazi double agents. Burton then gives Eastwood his gun and the trick is complete–Burton has uncovered the traitors in his own ranks. Having accomplished what they came for, Burton, Eastwood, Ure, and the actor must make their daring escape amidst the violent explosions they have wired throughout the fortress. The four board a cable car and, with the Germans following close behind, they make their way down a canal and commandeer a bus which gets them to the airport where a plane awaits to take them back to England. Waiting for them in the airplane is Wymark, the British commander who assigned the mission. Once in the air, Burton attacks Wymark and forces him to confess that he is the head of the traitorous spy ring. Burton gives the spy a choice between a court-martial which could lead to an execution and scandal for his family name, or to die a hero by jumping out the plane without a parachute. Wymark jumps to his death and the commandos return to England. WHERE EAGLES DARE was made because Burton was looking for a popular vehicle which would get him away from the heavy dramas he had been appearing in at that point in his career. Urged by his children to play a "real hero" Burton looked to producer Kastner for the right material. Kastner contacted famed WW II espionage author Alistair MacLean. MacLean had no novels to offer for adaptation, so Kastner suggested he come up with an original screenplay that he could later turn into a novel. Six weeks later the script for WHERE EAGLES DARE was finished. For the foreboding and treacherous Nazi headquarters, Kastner secured permission to shoot in Schloss

WHERE LOVE HAS GONE

Hohenwerfen, a famous 11th Century castle in Austria nestled on the peak of a mountain. With the danger of blizzards, high winds, sub-zero temperatures and avalanches, production began. Famed stuntman Yakima Canutt handled the direction of the stunning action sequences and while observing the stuntmen do their dangerous work Eastwood quipped that the film's title should be "Where Doubles Dare." Risk and money paid off handsomely at the box office. WHERE EAGLES DARE was a big hit with the public, helped Burton's sagging career, and propelled Eastwood to new heights of popularity.

p, Elliott Kastner; d, Brian G. Hutton; w, Alistair MacLean; ph, Arthur Ibbetson (Panavision, Metrocolor); m, Ron Goodwin; ed, John Jympson; md, Goodwin; art d, Peter Mullins; set d, Arthur Taksen; spec eff, Richard Parker, Fred Hellenburgh; stunts, Yakima Canutt.

War   **Cas.**   **(PR:C   MPAA:M)**

WHERE HAS POOR MICKEY GONE?*   (1964, Brit.) 59m
                                       Ledeck-Indigo/Compton-Cameo bw

Warren Mitchell (*Emilio Dinelli*), John Malcolm (*Mick*), Raymond Armstrong (*Ginger*), John Challis (*Tim*), Christopher Robbie (*Kip*), Karol Hagar (*Girl*), Joseph Cook (*Boy*), Philip Newman (*Detective*).

A gang of minor-league punks led by Malcolm have nothing better to do with themselves than to go about making life miserable for everyone who dares cross their path. But they get more than they bargain for when they try to rob Mitchell's workshop. A magician, he uses his skills to make the ruffians disappear. Too bad he couldn't do the same for the picture.

p&d, Gerry Levy; w, Peter Marcus; ph, Alan Pusney; m, Graham Whettam; ed, Howard Lanning; m/l, "Where Has Poor Mickey Gone?" Ottilie Patterson (sung by Patterson).

Fantasy   **(PR:A   MPAA:NR)**

WHERE IS MY CHILD?*   (1937) 95m Abraham Leff bw

Celia Adler, Samuel Steinberg, Morris Silberkasten, Anna Lillian, Morris Strassberg, Rubin Wendorff, Blanche Bernstein, Leon Schactman, Murray Stuckoff, Celia Arnold, Esther Gerber.

A Yiddish production which is a lame piece of entertainment in any language. This tissue-thin plot has Adler looking for the child that she gave away 20 years earlier. She looks and cries, and then looks some more. She finally ends up in a sanatorium where her now-grown son discovers her and takes her away. She is so pleased, she cries some more. A weepie melodrama which leaves the audience crying in pain. (In Yiddish; English subtitles.)

p, Abraham Leff.;

Drama   **(PR:A   MPAA:NR)**

WHERE IS THIS LADY?*   (1932, Brit.) 77m Amalgamated/BL bw
                                     (AKA: WHERE IS THIS GIRL?)

Marta Eggerth (*Steffi Piringer*), Owen Nares (*Rudi Miller*), Gustl Linzer (*George K. Arthur*), Wendy Barrie (*Lucie Kleiner*), Gibb McLaughlin (*Dr. Schilling*), O.B. Clarence (*Dr. Peffer*), Ellis Jeffreys (*Frau Kleiner*), Robert Hale (*Herr Piringer*).

A typical musical about Nares, the chairman of a failing bank, who gets pushed into a relationship with the supposedly wealthy Barrie. They both fall in love with other people, placing the bank's financial woes second to romantic desires. The bank goes under but it is turned into a swinging nightclub. The British version of a German film ES WAR EINMAL EIN WALZER (1932) written by Billy Wilder who would, of course, become quite a name in Hollywood.

p, John Stafford; d, Laszlo Vajda, Victor Hanbury; w, Sydney Blow, John Stafford (based on the story by Billy Wilder); m, Franz Lehar.

Musical/Romance   **(PR:A   MPAA:NR)**

WHERE IT'S AT*   (1969) 104m T.F.T. Productions/UA c

David Janssen (*A.C. Smith*), Robert Drivas (*Andy Smith*), Rosemary Forsyth (*Diana Mayhew*), Brenda Vaccaro (*Molly Hirsch*), Don Rickles (*Willie*), Warrene Ott (*Betty Avery*), Edy Williams (*Phyllis Horrigan*), Vince Howard (*Ralph*), The Committee (*Voices*), Debbie Wickstrom.

The wheeler-dealer owner of Caesars Palace, Janssen, is given a lesson by his son, Drivas, when the latter visits his father after graduating from Princeton. Father wants son to be like dad, a man's man with a head for business, while Drivas seems to be taken in by the liberalism of the younger generation, and is even a bit effeminate. But he is certainly not gay, which is demonstrated when Janssen sends a chorus girl to look into the matter. Drivas proves to have an even more astute business sense than his father when he wrests total control of Caesars Palace from Janssen. But he does so only to let his old man rest easily knowing his son is capable of surviving in the world without his father. The flashiness of Las Vegas is reflected in the fast pace, glittering exterior, and hardened shallowness of the Janssen character.

p, Frank Ross; d&w, Garson Kanin; ph, Burnett Guffey (DeLuxe Color); m, Benny Golson; ed, Stefan Arnsten; art d, Albert Brenner; set d, Ralph S. Hurst; m/l, "Where It's At," Jeff Barry (sung by Barry); makeup, Emile La Vigne.

Drama   **(PR:O   MPAA:R)**

WHERE LOVE HAS GONE**   (1964) 111m EM-PAR/PAR c

Susan Hayward (*Valerie Hayden Miller*), Bette Davis (*Mrs. Gerald Hayden*), Michael Connors (*Luke Miller*), Joey Heatherton (*Danielle Valerie "Dani" Miller*), Jane Greer (*Marian Spicer*), DeForest Kelley (*Sam Corwin*), George Macready (*Gordon Harris*), Anne Seymour (*Dr. Sally Jennings*), Willis Bouchey (*Judge Murphy*), Walter Reed (*George Babson*), Ann Doran (*Mrs. Geraghty*), Bartlett Robinson (*Mr. Coleman*), Whit Bissell (*Prof. Bell*), Anthony Caruso (*Rafael*), Jack Greening, Olga Sutcliffe, Howard Wendell, Colin Kenny.

There's no denying that this film was inspired by the murder of gangster Johnny Stompanato by Lana Turner's teenage daughter. Novelist Robbins changed enough of the story to avoid legal problems. The actress became a sculptor, the restaurateur father became a building executive, and Los Angeles became San Francisco. Connors is meeting at his building firm when he learns that his teenage daughter, Heatherton, has been arrested for murder. Connors hasn't seen Heatherton for some time but that doesn't stop him from racing away from business to lend whatever help he can. It's not that Connors didn't want to see his daughter, it's just that he was forbidden by the terms of his divorce settlement from Heatherton's mother, Hayward. Hayward's attorney is Macready and he has asked for Connors because Heatherton is going to be presented to the juvenile court and her problems might be alleviated if the hearing committee could see Connors and Hayward on good terms. Heatherton has been accused of killing Hayward's current lover. Connors makes it clear that he feels Hayward has been unfit and once his daughter is out of this mess, he wants custody of her. Macready disagrees and feels that it will never happen. The newspapers are filled with the news and Connors begins to recall how this all came to pass in a flashback. He was a hero in WW II and, after being saluted in a parade, Connors met Hayward at a sculpture showing of her works. Later, he was asked to dinner by Hayward's mother, Davis, a calculating grande dame who is every bit as manipulative as Rosalind Russell in CRAIG'S WIFE. She is a woman of few words and makes Connors an offer of a large sum of money and a good job if Connors will marry Hayward. He is appalled by this flesh bargain and storms out. Then he runs into Hayward and tells her what happened. She thinks he's a heckuva guy for having walked out but she is unable to get out from under her mother's heavy thumb. They begin seeing each other and fall in love, then marry. Shortly thereafter, Connors has to return to the war that is still raging. An ex-boy friend, Kelley, cynically mentions that he believes the Hayward-Connors union will eventually be torn apart because no one man can keep Hayward's sexual desires replenished. The war ends and the young couple are given a well-furnished home by Davis. He is a good architect and has plans for a career, now that his service to his country is done. Davis wishes he would give up those ideas and come to work for her firm but he is adamant and plans to succeed on his own terms as a designer of low-cost housing for the millions of veterans who have come home to live in peace. Try as he may, Connors can get nowhere with the banking institutions, never realizing that Davis is behind all of his refusals for financing. He has to take a job now and accepts an executive position with the company owned by Davis just as Hayward tells him they are going to be parents. Soon, their daughter is born. Connors can't handle the fact that he is under both Davis and Hayward's influence and he finds solace in the bottle. Hayward takes to lovers like Connors has taken to drink and when he finds her in the muscular arms of one of her male models, Connors has had it and walks out. Davis gets her a sharp attorney to arrange for the divorce and Connors winds up with nothing, not even partial custody of their daughter. The daughter grows up to be gorgeous Heatherton as Hayward takes one lover after another in a vain attempt to slake her sexual thirsts. It's not long before some of the men are casting glances at Heatherton, something Hayward notes and despises. Back to the present as the hearings go on and the truth begins to emerge: Hayward is an unfit mother and is as much responsible for her lover's death as Heatherton. Hayward tries to patch it up with Connors but his pain is too deep and the wounds too fresh. Hayward's reason for wanting to reconcile with Connors is not so much that she loves him, she just wants to make certain Heatherton is not released into the custody of her shrewish mother. When it is determined that the lover had attacked Hayward and that Heatherton leaped to her defense, the case is tossed out as justifiable homicide. Now the custody hearing begins and Davis does as expected; she asks the court for Heatherton to be placed in her custody. Now Hayward makes a dramatic confession at the custody proceedings. It's true that Heatherton killed the man but he was trying to *save* Hayward. Heatherton wanted to kill her mother and the man was accidentally killed when he stepped between them. Heatherton loved the man and resented his affection for Hayward and was determined to stop her at all costs. With that off her chest, Hayward races out of the proceedings, goes home, and slashes a portrait of Davis. Then she takes her own life with her sculptor's chisel. At Hayward's funeral, Heatherton and Connors stand quietly together while Davis stands alone. Heatherton will go to jail for a while and Connors will be waiting for her when she exits the prison. A soap opera that smacked of what later came on TV with "Dynasty" and "Dallas." Good technical work, lots of good sets and costumes, but a wrong focus of attention. It was really Heatherton's story but Davis and Hayward were not about to relinquish their starring roles, so the movie revolved around them rather than the young Heatherton (who did quite well under Dmytryk's direction). Davis was only 10 years older than Hayward, who was 46. Hayward was so gorgeous that it wasn't a stretch of the imagination when we saw her 20 years before as a young bride. The title song was Oscar-nominated and lost that year to "Chim Chim Cheree" from MARY POPPINS, which was also about a meddlesome woman, after a fashion. Fireworks were reported on the set between Davis and Hayward, which is what one might have anticipated from such dynamic, headstrong women. Connors was making his 11th feature and acquitted himself well in a part that was sort of a fulcrum to the teeter-totter of the two women.

p, Joseph E. Levine; d, Edward Dmytryk; w, John Michael Hayes (based on the novel by Harold Robbins); ph, Joseph MacDonald (Techniscope, Technicolor); m, Walter Scharf; ed, Frank Bracht; art d, Hal Pereira, Walter Tyler; set d, Sam Comer, Arthur Kram; cos, Edith Head; spec eff, Paul L. Lerpae; m/l, title song, Sammy Cahn, James Van Heusen (sung by Jack Jones); makeup, Wally Westmore, Gene Hibbs.

Drama   **(PR:C MPAA:NR)**

WHERE NO VULTURES FLY   (SEE: IVORY HUNTER, 1952, Brit.)

WHERE SINNERS MEET*½   (1934) 73m RKO bw (GB: THE DOVER ROAD)

Diana Wynyard (*Anne*), Clive Brook (*Mr. Latimer*), Billie Burke (*Eustacia*), Reginald Owen (*Leonard*), Alan Mowbray (*Nicholas*), Gilbert Emery (*Dominic, Latimer's Butler*), Vernon Steele (*Saunders*), Phyllis Barry, Katherine Williams (*Maids*), Walter Armitage, Robert Adair (*Footmen*).

Far-fetched plot has millionaire Brook holding two eloping couples captive in his mansion, his object being to keep these young people from making grave mistakes. After two failed marriages, Brook firmly believes that wedlock is not all it's cracked up to be. Except for a couple of amusing situations it's a tedious picture.

d, J. Walter Ruben; w, H.W. Hannemann (based on the play "The Dover Road" by A.A. Milne); ph, Nick Musuraca; ed, George Hively; cos, Walter Plunkett.

Comedy   **(PR:A MPAA:NR)**

WHERE THE BLOOD FLOWS   (SEE: HORROR CASTLE, 1956, Ital.)

WHERE THE BOYS ARE**½   (1960) 99m Euterpe/MGM c

Dolores Hart (*Merritt Andrews*), George Hamilton (*Ryder Smith*), Yvette Mimieux (*Melanie*), Jim Hutton (*TV Thompson*), Barbara Nichols (*Lola*), Paula Prentiss (*Tuggle Carpenter*), Connie Francis (*Angie*), Chill Wills (*Police Captain*), Frank Gorshin (*Basil*), Rory Harrity (*Franklin*), John Brennan (*Dill*), Ted Berger (*Stout Man*), Vito Scotti (*Maitre d'*), Sean Flynn.

It's spring break, and college kids from around the country descend en masse to Fort Lauderdale, Florida. Hart, Mimieux, Prentiss and, Francis are four friends in search of sun, parties, and boys, though not necessarily in that order. The episodic plot line follows each girl in her respective success or failure with members of the opposite gender. Prentiss (in her film debut) is a scatterbrained lass who falls for Hutton, though the relationship takes a jealous turn when Hutton is briefly infatuated with Nichols, a nightclub entertainer who performs an underwater act in a glass tank. Francis, a well-known recording star, also makes her first film appearance capitalizing more on her vocal talents than acting ability. Francis' amorous adventures propel her–where else?–into the arms of a musician, Gorshin, a myopic bass fiddler. She also sings the film's title tune, which became a hit single in 1960. Hart is the group's sensible member. She had been reluctant to come along but, faced with expulsion from school for her in-class expounding on relationships, Hart realizes a vacation might do her some good. In Florida she meets Ivy Leaguer Hamilton, and romance blooms. Hamilton pressures her for sex but Hart refuses, winning both his respect and a promise of commitment in the end. Mimieux, the last girl in the quartet, is a firm believer in love at first sight. She is determined to get herself an Ivy Leaguer any way she can, mistaking sexual passion for true love. Harrity quickly catches onto the girl's idealism, and uses Mimieux for sex before passing her along to his fraternity brothers. She ends up emotionally wracked by the experience. Dazed, Mimieux wanders into traffic and is hit by a car. She winds up in the hospital, embittered by it all, then returns home to recuperate. WHERE THE BOYS ARE is judgmental in the moralistic attitudes it holds over the characters, yet the film is not without a naive sense of charm. A girl like Hart, who doesn't give in so easily to Hamilton, is the pinnacle of everything good and proper, while poor Mimieux gets exactly what she deserves for responding so swiftly to Harrity's importunities. This sexual moralizing is a bit much, portraying women as either good or bad while boys who chase them have just one thing on their collective minds. Fortunately, the black-and-white ethics are balanced out with the lighter involvements of the other couples. Prentiss and Hutton give their story a silly sweetness, going through predictable situations with fine comic

flair. Considering the radical movements that would sweep college campuses in the 1960s, this film holds some interest as a relic of sexual attitudes in the 1950s. A 1984 remake showed just how much Hollywood had changed in portraying sexual antics on screen in 24 years, though the later film has none of the original's appeal. Seen in a bit part is Sean Flynn, Errol Flynn's son by actress Lily Damita. He showed some promise as an actor but gave it up for a career as a photographer. In 1970 while on assignment as a Vietnam correspondent Flynn disappeared, presumably killed or captured by hostile forces. Hart also gave up her screen career, surprising her Hollywood cohorts by joining a Roman Catholic convent. In 1970 she completed her education, taking vows as a member of the Benedictine order. Francis didn't go far in the movies past this role. Though she had some appealing moments here, the singer never got another part that suited her talents. She made two look-alike films that tried to capitalize on her biggest success with the titles FOLLOW THE BOYS and WHEN THE BOYS MEET THE GIRLS, but these were minor B movies at best.

p, Joe Pasternak; d, Henry Levin; w, George Wells (based on the novel by Glendon Swarthout); ph, Robert Bronner (CinemaScope, Metrocolor); m, George Stoll, Pete Rugolo; ed, Fredric Steinkamp; art d, George W. Davis, Preston Ames; cos, Kitty Mager; ch, Robert Sidney; m/l, title song, "Turn on the Sunshine," Neil Sedaka, Howard Greenfield; Stella Unger, Victor Young.

Comedy   **Cas.**   **(PR:A-C MPAA:NR)**

WHERE THE BUFFALO ROAM*   (1938) 61m MON bw

Tex Ritter (*Tex Houston*), Dorothy Short (*Laddie Gray*), Horace Murphy (*Ananias*), Snub Pollard (*Pee Wee*), Richard Alexander (*Sellers*), Karl Hackett (*Rogel*), Dave O'Brien (*Jeff*), Ed Cassidy (*Hodge*), Charles King, Jr (*Bull*), Louise Massey's Westerners, Bob Terry, Blackie Whiteford, Denver Dixon, Ernie Adams, Hank Worden, John Merton, Curt Massey, White Flash.

In this dreadful oater entry Ritter is the U.S. marshal trying to keep a gang of outlaws from ruthless slaughter of the buffalo, in keeping with an agreement with the Indians to allow the giant beasts to roam the plains. These same crooks are also responsible for the death of Ritter's mother, allowing him to kill two birds with one stone. Songs include "Where the Buffalo Roam" (Ritter, Frank Harford, Frank Sanucci, sung by Ritter).

p, Edward Finney; d, Al Herman; w, Robert Emmett [Tansey]; ph, Francis Corby; ed, Fred Bain; md, Frank Sanucci.

Western   **(PR:A MPAA:NR)**

WHERE THE BUFFALO ROAM**   (1980) 96m UNIV c

Peter Boyle (*Lazlo*), Bill Murray (*Hunter S. Thompson*), Bruno Kirby (*Marty Lewis*), Rene Auberjonois (*Harris*), R.G. Armstrong (*Judge Simpson*), Danny Goldman (*Porter*), Rafael Campos (*Rojas*), Leonard Frey (*Desk Clerk*), Leonard Gaines (*Super Fan*), DeWayne Jessie (*Man No.1*), Mark Metcalf (*Dooley*), Jon Matthews (*Billy Kramer*), Joseph Ragno (*Willins*), Quinn Redeker (*Pilot*), Lisa Taylor (*Ruthie*), Danny Tucker (*Narcotics Agent*), Susan Kellermann (*Waitress*), John Acevedo, Phillip L. Allan, Juli Andelman, Janit Baldwin, Bruce Barbour, Marsha Bissler, Jack Caddin, David Castle, Linden Chiles, Suzanne Coltrin, Caesar Cordova, Michael Cornelison, Brian Cummings, Ron Cummings, Joshua Daniel, Sonny Davis, Richard M. Dixon, Suzanne Elliott, Les Engel, Reginald H. Farmer, Lou Felder, Randy Glass, Doris Hargrave, Jim Healy, Cork Hubbert, Doreen Jaros, Sunny Johnson, Garrie Kelly, Charles Konya, Marguerite Lamar, Jerry Maren, Miles McNamara, John Moio, Richard Seff.

This should have been a great movie. The life and crazy exploits of "Gonzo" journalist Hunter S. Thompson are prime ground for a funny, bitter, biting satire on the U.S. from Vietnam to Watergate, but something went wrong. Maybe it was the wholly unfocused script that never really seemed to have a handle on the area, the events, or the lunacy, let alone on Thompson himself. Maybe it was the meandering, thoughtless direction that lacked the kind of excitement needed to exploit the best of the Thompson legend. It certainly wasn't the casting. Murray is fine as Thompson, so fine, in fact, that when the first rushes were screened for Thompson's friends, they thought the reporter had wandered on to the set and gotten before the cameras. Thompson had allowed Murray to follow him around and study his movements, mannerisms, and voice, and Murray learned well. Unfortunately, Thompson got fed up with the way shooting was going (he hated the script) and disappeared from the set (presumably taking his bottle of Wild Turkey and cache of drugs with him), leaving the filmmakers to destroy whatever potential there was–and they did. Borrowing heavily from Thompson's books, *Fear and Loathing in Las Vegas* and *Fear and Loathing on the Campaign Trail '72*, the film is a series of disconnected incidents based on the highlights of the author's writing. In the end, one is left with a sporadically amusing, frustratingly scattershot look at Thompson's life and times. Read the books instead.

p&d, Art Linson; w, John Kaye (based on the writings of Hunter S. Thompson); ph, Tak Fujimoto (Technicolor); m, Neil Young; ed, Christopher Greenbury; prod d, Richard Sawyer; set d, Barbara Krieger; cos, Eddie Marks, Gilda Texter.

Comedy/Biography   **Cas.**   **(PR:O MPAA:R)**

WHERE THE BULLETS FLY**   (1966, Brit.) 88m Puck/EM c

Tom Adams (*Charles Vine*), Dawn Addams (*Felicity "Fiz" Moonlight*), Sidney James (*Mortuary Attendant*), Wilfrid Brambell (*Train Guard*), Joe Baker (*Minister*), Tim Barrett (*Seraph*), Michael Ripper (*Angel*), John Arnatt (*Rockwell*), Ronald Leigh-Hunt (*Thursby*), Marcus Hammond (*O'-Neil*), Maurice Browning (*Cherub*), Michael Ward (*Michael*), Bryan Mosley (*Connolly*), Terence Sewards (*Minister's Press Agent*), Heidi Erich (*Carruthers*), Suzan Farmer (*Caron*), Maggie Kimberley (*Jacqueline*), Sue Donovan (*Celia*), Julie Martin (*Verity*), Tom Bowman (*Russian Colonel*), Patrick Jordan (*Russian*), Gerard Heinz (*Venstram*), James Ellis (*Flight Lt. Fotheringham*), Charles Houston (*Copilot*), Tony Alpino (*Butler*), Michael Balfour (*Bandleader*), Garry Marsh (*Major*), Michael Graham Cox (*Lt. Guyfawkes*), Peter Ducrow (*Prof. Harding*), Barbara French (*Harding's Secretary*), John Horsley (*Air Marshal*), Michael Goldie (*Laborer*), Joe Ritchie (*Truck Driver*), John Watson (*Controller*), David Gregory (*RAF Sergeant*), Roy Stephens (*Staff Officer*).

As in its predecessor, THE SECOND BEST SECRET AGENT IN THE WHOLE WIDE WORLD, Adams plays a secret agent in the mold of James Bond, who defies death to save the British Parliament and battles communism in the name of democracy. Adams' main mission here is to keep double agent Ripper from access to a lightweight metal destined for the creation of aircraft. None of the proceedings demand serious criticism, and are directed at a fast, breezy pace, just for fun.

p, S.J.H. "James" Ward; d, John Gilling; w, Michael Pittock; ph, David Holmes (Eastmancolor); m, Kenneth Graham; ed, Ron Pope; md, Philip Martell; art d, George Lack; cos, Joanna Wright; spec eff, Pat Moore, Bowie Films; m/l, "Where the Bullets Fly," Bob Kingston, Ron Bridges (sung by Susan Maughan); makeup, Aldo Manganaro.

Comedy/Spy   **(PR:A MPAA:NR)**

WHERE THE HOT WIND BLOWS**½
        (1960, Fr., Ital.) 120m MGM bw (LA LEGGE; LA LOI; AKA: THE LAW)

Gina Lollobrigida (*Marietta*), Yves Montand (*Matteo Brigante*), Pierre Brasseur (*Don Cesare*), Marcello Mastroianni (*Engineer*), Melina Mercouri (*Donna Lucrezia*), Paolo Stoppa (*Tonio*), Raf Mattioli (*Francesco Brigante*), Vittorio Capriolli (*Attilio*), Nino Vingelli (*Pizzaccio*), Teddy Billis (*Guidice*), Lydia Alfonsi (*Giuseppina*), Edda Soligo (*Giulia*), Luisa Rivelli (*Elvira*), Anna-Maria Bottini (*Maria*), Bruno Carotenuto (*Balbo*), Marcello Giorda (*Priest*), Herbert Knippenberg (*Swiss Tourist*), Sonia Barbieri (*Tourist's Wife*), Anna Arena (*Anna*).

A peaceful Sicilian fishing village serves as the background for some not very pleasant hanky-panky in which Montand plays an unscrupulous gangster type who goes so far as to seduce his son's gal Mercouri in order to keep the two from marrying. Mercouri reacts by jumping to her death. The vivacious Lollobrigida meanwhile takes to raising money for her dowry by organizing a gang of kids to pick the pockets of tourists. At least her purpose, to marry engineer Mastroianni, is noble, and she does remain faithful to him despite everyone's advances. The film is poorly post-dubbed.

p, Jacques Bar; d, Jules Dassin; w, Dassin, Francoise Giroud (based on the novel *The Law* by Roger Vailland); ph, Otello Martelli; m, Roman Vlad; m/l, "Where the Hot Wind Blows," Jimmy McHugh, Buddy Kaye (sung by the Mills Brothers).

Drama   **(PR:O MPAA:NR)**

WHERE THE LILIES BLOOM**½   (1974) 96m Radnitz-Mattel/UA c

Julie Gholson (*Mary Call*), Jan Smithers (*Devola*), Matthew Burrill (*Romey*), Helen Harmon (*Ima Dean*), Harry Dean Stanton (*Kiser Pease*), Rance Howard (*Roy Luther*), Sudie Bond (*Miss Fleetie, Teacher*), Tom Spratley (*Mr. Connell*), Helen Bragdon (*Mrs. Connell*), Alice Beardsley (*Goldie Pease*).

Sincere and unglamourized look at the backwoods U.S. has four children left parentless when their father dies, but refusing to let his death be known to the proper authorities for fear of being separated and placed in an orphanage. Gholson, though not the eldest of the brood, takes on the role of the parent figure, protecting the kids from the frightful world of adults, especially Stanton as the landlord. Pacing and plot development are very slow, but effectively detail the changes the children undergo as they grow and learn to accept Stanton as a friend. The latter gives a strong performance as a crusty gent who really is pretty cool underneath it all.

p, Robert B. Radnitz; d, William A. Graham; w, Earl Hamner, Jr. (based on the book by Vera and Bill Cleaver); ph, Urs Furrer (DeLuxe Color); m, Earl Scruggs; ed, Nick Brown; m/l, "Where the Lilies Bloom," Barbara Mauritz (sung by Mauritz).

Drama   **(PR:A MPAA:G)**

WHERE THE RED FERN GROWS*   (1974) 97m Doty-Dayton c

James Whitmore (*Grandpa*), Beverly Garland (*Mother*), Jack Ging (*Father*), Lonny Chapman (*Sheriff*), Stewart Peterson (*Billy*), Jill Clark (*Alice*), Jeanna Wilson (*Sara*), Bill Thurman (*Sam*), Bill Dunbar (*Ben*), Rex Corley (*Rubin*), John Lindsey (*Rainie*), Gardland McKinney (*Pritchard*), Robert Telford (*Station Master*), Charles Seat (*Carl*), Roger Pancake (*Shopkeeper*), Marshall Edwards (*Preacher*).

A boy-and-his-dog story, actually two dogs, is here given the sappiest treatment this side of "The Waltons," as a poor Oklahoma lad, his pets, and his family struggle to get by on a 1930s farm. Competently made but highly contrived so as to evoke as many 'aws' and 'ahs' as could be compiled in an hour and a half, this movie is only for the extremely naive.

p, Lyman Dayton; d, Norman Tokar; w, Douglas Stewart, Eleanor Lamb (based on the novel by Wilson Rawls); ph, Dean Cundey (DeLuxe Color); m, Lex De Azevdo; ed, Bob Bring, Marsh Hendry; prod d, Michael D. Devine; m/l, The Osmonds (sung by Andy Williams).

Drama   **Cas.**   **(PR:A MPAA:G)**

WHERE THE RIVER BENDS   (SEE: BEND OF THE RIVER, 1952)

WHERE THE SIDEWALK ENDS***½   (1950) 95m FOX bw

Dana Andrews (*Mark Dixon*), Gene Tierney (*Morgan Taylor*), Gary Merrill (*Tommy Scalise*), Bert Freed (*Paul Klein*), Tom Tully (*Jiggs Taylor*), Karl Malden (*Lt. Bill Thomas*), Ruth Donnelly (*Martha*), Craig Stevens (*Ken Paine*), Harry von Zell (*Ted Morrison*), Robert F. Simon (*Inspector Nicholas Foley*), Don Appell (*Willie Bender*), Neville Brand (*Steve*), Grace Mills (*Mrs. Tribaum*), Lou Krugman (*Mike Williams*), David McMahon (*Harrington*), David Wolfe (*Sid Kramer*), Steve Roberts (*Gilruth*), Phil Tully (*Tod Benson*), Ian MacDonald (*Casey*), John Close (*Hanson*), John McGuire (*Gertessen*), Lou Nova (*Ernie*), Oleg Cassini (*Oleg the Fashion Designer*), Louise Lorimer (*Mrs. Jackson*), Lester Sharpe (*Friedman*), Chili Williams (*Teddy*), Robert Foulk (*Fenney*), Eda Reiss Merin (*Shirley Klein*), Mack Williams (*Jerry Morris*), Duke Watson (*Cab Driver*), Clancy Cooper (*Lt. Arnaldo*), Bob Evans (*Sweatshirt*), Joseph Granby (*Fat Man*), Harry Brooks, Anthony George (*Thugs*), Wanda Smith, Shirley Tegge, Peggy O'Connor (*Models*), Milton Gowman, Lee MacGregor (*Men*), Charles J. Flynn (*Schwartz*), Larry Thompson (*Riley*), Ralph Peters (*Counterman*), Robert B. Williams, John Marshall, Clarence Straight (*Detectives*), Bob Patten (*Medical Examiner*), Louise Lane, Kathleen Hughes (*Secretaries*), John Trebach (*Bartender*), Herbert Lytton (*Joe*), John Daheim, Tony Barr (*Hoodlums*), Fred Graham (*Attendant*).

Director Otto Preminger's second consecutive film based on a Ben Hecht screenplay (WHIRLPOOL was first) stars Andrews as a vicious police detective–the son of an infamous mobster–prone to beating confessions out of suspects. While trying to get information from a robbery suspect that will connect the crime with Merrill, a top mob boss, Andrews lets his violent nature spin out of control and he accidentally kills the suspect. Obsessed with nailing Merrill, Andrews fakes the evidence so it appears that the killing was a gangland slaying commited under Merrill's orders. Unfortunately, police conclude that an innocent cab driver, Tully, was the culprit because he had a score to settle with the victim who was his ex-son-in-law. When Andrews meets the victim's widow, Tierney, he begins to fall in love with her, which complicates matters (Andrews doesn't want to see his new love's father go to the chair for a crime he didn't commit). Desperate to save Tully and hang Merrill in one deft stroke, Andrews decides to force a confrontation with Merrill and his goons in the hope they will kill him. To clear Tully, Andrews leaves behind a letter confessing to the murder. The plot goes awry, however, when the gang gives up instead of killing Andrews. Despite his hero status within the department, Andrews is plagued by guilt over Tully's situation. Rather than live with himself and risk continuing a relationship with Tierney based on horrible lies, Andrews confesses to the police. The noble gesture only strenghtens Tierney's love and she vows to wait for him during his prison term. Hecht once again examines the fine line between cop and criminal with memorable results. Consumed with a desire to make up for his father's criminal reputation, Andrews demonstrates the same savagery–only this time wearing a badge. Blind to the fundamental contradiction between his quest and his methods, Andrews finally crosses the line that separates the hunters from the hunted. Andrews is man torn by conflicting emotions and the situation only gets worse when he begins to fall in love with the widow of the man he murdered. Andrews gives one of his best performances as this complicated, explosive man whose darker impulses begin dominating his personality.

p&d, Otto Preminger; w, Ben Hecht, Frank Rosenberg, Victor Trivas, Robert E. Kent (based on the novel *Night Cry* by Rosenberg and a book by William L. Stuart); ph, Joseph La Shelle; m, Cyril J. Mockridge; ed, Louis Loeffler; md, Lionel Newman; art d, Lyle R. Wheeler, J. Russell Spencer; set d, Thomas Little, Walter M. Scott; cos, Charles LeMaire, Oleg Cassini; spec eff, Fred Sersen; makeup, Ben Nye.

Crime   **(PR:C MPAA:NR)**

WHERE THE SPIES ARE½**   (1965, Brit.) 113m MGM c

David Niven (*Dr. Jason Love*), Francoise Dorleac (*Vikki*), John Le Mesurier (*Col. Douglas MacGillivray*), Cyril Cusack (*Peter Rosser*), Eric Pohlmann (*Farouk*), Richard Marner (*Josef*), Paul Stassino (*Simmias*), George Pravda (*1st Agent*), Noel Harrison (*Jackson*), Ronald Radd (*Stanislaus*), Alan Gifford (*Security*), Bill Nagy (*Aeradio*), George Mikell (*Assassin*), Nigel Davenport (*Parkington*), Reginald Beckwith (*Mr. Kahn*), Gabor Baraker (*2nd Agent*), Geoffrey Bayldon (*Lecturer*), Derek Partridge (*Duty Officer*), Robert Raglan (*Sir Robert*), Riyad Gholmieh (*1st Taxi Driver*), Muhsen Samrani (*2nd Taxi Driver*), Basil Dignam (*Maj. Harding*), Gordon Tanner (*Inspector*).

In this enjoyable spy spoof, Niven is a country doctor called to service by Le Mesurier because of espionage work he did in WW II. He is sent to Beirut (a beautiful city before it became a battleground) to dig up some information for which one agent had already been murdered. Enthusiastically, Niven reveals that the Communists plan on killing the Prince of Zahlouf, a man who leans toward Britain and whose death would be a serious threat to Britain's power in the Middle East. Niven thwarts the Russian attempts, with help from Dorleac as a sexy double agent mysteriously popping up to rescue him from one hot spot after another. Though far-fetched, the picture's tongue-in-cheek attitude allows the viewer to get involved without taking the story seriously.

p, Val Guest, Steven Pallos; d, Guest; w, Wolf Mankowitz, James Leasor, Guest (based on the novel *Passport to Oblivion* by Leasor); ph, Arthur Grant (Panavision, Metrocolor); m, Mario Nascimbene; ed, Bill Lenny; md, Alfredo Antonini; art d, John Howell; cos, Beatrice Dawson; makeup, Tony Sforzini.

Spy Drama/Comedy   (PR:A   MPAA:NR)

WHERE THE TRUTH LIES**   (1962, Fr.) 83m Marianne-S.N.E.
                                                     GAU/PAR bw (MALEFICES)

Juliette Greco (*Myriam Heller*), Jean-Marc Bory (*Francois Rauchelle*), Liselotte Pulver (*Catherine Rauchelle*), Mathe Mansoura (*Ronga*), Jacques Dacqmine (*Vial*), Jeanne Perez (*Mere Capitaine*), Georges Chamarat (*Malet*), Marcel Peres.

Bory is a veterinarian who falls in love with former African explorer Greco when he calls on her sickly cheetah. She wants him to return with her to Africa, but he refuses to leave his wife, Pulver. Pulver soon becomes the victim of a succession of strange accidents and Bory blames Greco, who has more than a passing interest in voodoo. In order to save his wife from falling under any more of Greco's curses, he agrees to accompany her to Africa. While driving through the Dark Continent, a flood sweeps Greco away. Bory has a chance to save her but opts to let her drown. Pulver later confesses that she had staged the accidents Bory had interpreted as voodoo. Stricken with guilt, Bory offers himself up to the police. A standard suspenser which suffers from uninspired direction.

d, Henri Decoin; w, Decoin, Claude Accursi, Albert Husson (based on the novel *Malefices* by Pierre Boileau, Thomas Narcejac); ph, Marcel Grignon (Dyaliscope); m, Pierre Henry; ed, Robert Isnardon, Monique Isnardon; set d, Paul-Louis Boutie.

Drama   (PR:A-C   MPAA:NR)

WHERE THE WEST BEGINS*½   (1938) 56m MON bw

Jack Randall (*Manning*), Fuzzy Knight (*Buzzy*), Luana Walters (*Lynne*), Arthur Housman (*Beano*), Budd Buster (*Sheriff*), Kit Guard (*Smiley*), Richard Alexander (*Barnes*), Ralph Peters (*Hawkins*), Joe Garcia (*Miller*), Ray Whitley/Ken Card and the Phelps Brothers (*the Six-Bar Cowboys*).

Without Fuzzy Knight around to supply the laughs this would be a very sad sagebrusher starring Randall, one of the worst singing cowboys ever to undertakethe role. He couldn't sing a chord, yet here he was responsible for three songs in 56 minutes. As the foreman of a ranch belonging to Walters, Randall discovers the lady's eagerness to sell her spread could lose her the rights to alarge sulfur deposit. Songs include: "I'm in Prairie Heaven," "That's My Idea of Fun," "Sleep, Little Cowboy, Sleep" (Connie Lee), and "Born to the Range" (Johnny Lange, Fred Stryker).

p, Maurice Conn; d, J.P. McGowan; w, Stanley Roberts, Gennaro Rea (based on the story by Roberts); ph, Jack Greenhalgh; ed, Carl Pierson.

Western   (PR:A   MPAA:NR)

WHERE THERE'S A WILL***   (1936, Brit.) 80m Gainsborough/GAU
                                                                          bw

Will Hay (*Benjamin Stubbins*), Gina Malo (*Goldie Kelly*), Hartley Power (*Duke Wilson*), Graham Moffatt (*Willie*), H.F. Maltby (*Sir Roger Wimpleton*), Norma Varden (*Lady Margaret Wimpleton*), Peggy Simpson (*Barbara Stubbins*), Gibb McLaughlin (*Martin*), Hal Walters (*Nick*), John Turnbull (*Sgt. Collins*), Mickey Brantford (*Jimmy*), Davina Craig (*Lucy*), Frederick Piper, Henry Adries, Eddie Houghton, Sybil Brooke.

Hay is a lawyer whose office is located directly above a bank. A gang of robbers comes into his office one day, knocks him out, and enters the bank through his office floor. He later spots the gang at a high-society Christmas

Eve party and notifies the police. Hay is in top form; and the script, which he cowrote, is a tightly knit comic achievement.

p, Michael Balcon; d, William Beaudine; w, Will Hay, Ralph Spence, Robert Edmunds, Beaudine (based on the story by Leslie Arliss, Sidney Gilliat); ph, Charles Van Enger; ed, Terence Fisher; md, Louis Levy; art d, Alex Vetchinsky; cos, Paula Newman.

Comedy/Crime   (PR:A   MPAA:NR)

WHERE THERE'S A WILL**   (1937, Brit.) 78m Gainsborough/GAU
                                                     bw (GB: GOOD MORNING, BOYS)

Will Hay (*Dr. Benjamin Twist*), Martita Hunt (*Lady Bagshott*), Peter Gawthorne (*Col. Willoughby-Gore*), Graham Moffatt (*Albert*), Fewlass Llewellyn (*The Dean*), Mark Daly (*Arty Jones*), Peter Godfrey (*Cliquot*), C. Denier Warren (*Henri Duval, Minister of Education*), Lilli Palmer (*Yvette*), Charles Hawtrey, Will Hay, Jr, Basil McGrail, Charles McBain, Terry Richardson.

Humorous crime picture starring Hay as the headmaster of a school near a prison, where he becomes the unwitting participant in the theft of the Mona Lisa from the Louvre. One of his charges is the son of a convict who escapes with the intention of stealing the famous painting. Not knowing the pupil's father is a convict, Hay allows the man to stay at the school and even innocently helps with the robbery. But in the final hour, he is hailed the hero as the school boys retrieve the masterpiece.

p, Edward Black; d, Marcel Varnel; w, Val Guest, Leslie Arliss, Marriott Edgard (based on a story by Anthony Kimmins); ph, Arthur Crabtree.

Crime/Comedy   (PR:A   MPAA:NR)

WHERE THERE'S A WILL**   (1955, Brit.) 79m Film Locations/Eros
                                                                          bw

Kathleen Harrison (*Annie Yeo*), George Cole (*Fred Slater*), Leslie Dwyer (*Alfie Brewer*), Ann Hanslip (*June Hodge*), Michael Shepley (*Mr. Cogent*), Dandy Nichols (*Maud Hodge*), Thelma Ruby (*Amy Slater*), Norman Macowan (*Cagey*), Hugh Morton (*Arscott*), Edward Lexy (*Mafeking*), Edward Woodward, Sam Kydd, Philip Ray, Bill Shine.

A bit of country corn from the British in this rustic comedy about a Cockney family that inherits a dilapidated farm in Devon. Though his sisters and lazy brother-in-law are extremely skeptical about moving to the country, Dwyer takes on the job and, aided by the farm's housekeeper, Harrison, he manages to rebuild the farm and make it a success. A harmless comedy with some charming touches.

p, George Maynard; d, Vernon Sewell; w, R.F. Delderfield (based on the play by Delderfield); ph, Basil Emmott.

Comedy   (PR:A   MPAA:NR)

WHERE THERE'S LIFE**½   (1947) 75m PAR bw

Bob Hope (*Michael Valentine*), Signe Hasso (*Gen. Katrina Grimovitch*), William Bendix (*Victor O'Brien*), George Coulouris (*Krivoc*), Vera Marshe (*Hazel O'Brien*), George Zucco (*Paul Stertorius*), Dennis Hoey (*Minister of War Grubitch*), John Alexander (*Herbert Jones*), Victor Varconi (*Finance Minister Zavich*), Joseph Vitale (*Albert Miller*), Harry Von Zell (*Joe Snyder*), Emil Rameau (*Dr. Josefsberg*), William Edmunds (*King Hubertus II*), Leo Mostovoy (*Minister of Interior Karakovic*), Norma Varden (*Mrs. Herbert Jones*), Roy Atwell (*Salesman*), Harlan Tucker (*Mr. Alvin*), Oscar O'Shea (*Uncle Phillip*), Crane Whitley (*Man with Cane*), Mary Field, Phyllis Kennedy (*Hotel Maids*), Fred Zendar (*Copilot*), Rene Dussaq, Charles Legneur (*Officers*), Mike Macy (*Peasant*), Edwin Chandler (*Officer*), George Bruggaman, George Magrill, Carl Saxe, Tom Costello (*Aides*), John Mallon, Charles Cooley, Ralph Gomez, Dario Piazza, Otto Reichow, Eugene Stutenroth [Gene Roth] (*Mordians*), Floyd Pruitt, Tom Coleman, Jack Clifford, William Haade, John Jennings, Pat Flaherty, Bud Sullivan (*O'Briens*), Erno Verebes (*Peter Gornics*), Dorothy Barrett (*Model in Window*), Edgar Dearing (*Desk Sergeant*), Ralph Peters, James Dundea, George Lloyd (*Cops*), Dorothy Barrett (*Girl*), Hans von Morhart (*Karl*), Edwin Chandler (*New York Policeman*), Eric Alden, Len Hendry (*Airport Attendants*), Guy Kingsford (*Mordian Pilot*), Lorna Jordan, Letty Light (*Salesgirls*), Lucille Barkley (*Salesgirl*), Brandon Hurst (*Floor Walker*).

This is one of those films whose appeal rests totally on the viewer's appreciation of its star, in this case Bob Hope, placed in a ridiculous situation to set up a nonstop barrage of wisecracks and the usual Hope antics. A happy-go-lucky New York disc jockey about to be married to the girl of his dreams, Marshe, Hope wakes up one day to find that he is the heir to the kingdom of Barovia, whose king has just been assassinated by revolutionaries. Hasso is the female general who convinces Hope that he is needed, though doing more so with her looks than powers of speech. This kicks off a mad chase through New York as Hope and Hasso try to avoid the Bolsheviks who have put him on their hit list. What's more, there's Marshe with her cop brother Bendix also on Hope's tail; they want him for the proposed wedding ceremony. Bendix wants it clear that no bum is gonna walk out on his sister. It's all Hope, and he delivers in his own particular style, enhanced by the efforts of his favorite writers. Next to Hope, Bendix is the only other performer allowed to shine; he's perfect as a dimwit cop, a role, to exaggerate a bit, it seems he was born to play.

p, Paul Jones; d, Sidney Lanfield; w, Allen Boretz, Melville Shavelson (based on a story by Shavelson); ph, Charles B. Lang, Jr.; ed, Archie Marshek; md, Irvin Talbot; art d, Hans Dreier, Earl Hedrick; set d, Sam Comer, Syd Moore; cos, Edith Head; spec eff, Gordon Jennings.

Comedy   **(PR:A   MPAA:NR)**

WHERE TRAILS DIVIDE*   (1937) 59m MON bw

Tom Keene, Eleanor Stewart, Warner Richmond, David Sharpe, Lorraine Randall, Charles K. French, Steve Clark, Hal Price, Dick Cramer, James Sheridan [Sherry Tansey], Bud Osborne, Horace B. Carpenter, Wally West, James Mason, Forrest Taylor, Oscar Gahan.

This unimpressive oater, surprisingly lacking in action, has Keene the U.S. Marshal posing as a lawyer to bring Richmond's gang of thieves to justice. He does so in the most boring manner possible. Only the ending, which features the bad guys dying of thirst in the Mojave Desert, leaves an impression.

p&d, R.N. Bradbury; w, Robert Emmett [Tansey]; ph, Bert Longnecker.

Western   **(PR:A   MPAA:NR)**

WHERE WERE YOU WHEN THE LIGHTS WENT OUT?**
                                                (1968) 90m MGM c

Doris Day (Margaret Garrison), Robert Morse (Waldo Zane), Terry-Thomas (Ladislau Walichek), Patrick O'Neal (Peter Garrison), Lola Albright (Roberta Lane), Steve Allen (Radio Announcer), Jim Backus (Tru-Blue Lou), Ben Blue (Man With a Razor), Pat Paulsen (Conductor), Dale Malone (Otis J. Hendershot, Jr.), Robert Emhardt (Otis J. Hendershot, Sr.), Harry Hickox (Detective Capt. Percy Watson), Parley Baer (Dr. Dudley Caldwell), Randy Whipple (Marvin Reinholtz), Earl Wilson (Himself).

Does life imitate art or is it the other way around? Although New York City suffered a power blackout 30 months before this film was released, it's based on a play that opened in Paris nine years before the November 9, 1965, blackout. Anyone who has ever experienced this type of problem knows that mixups, looting, boredom, and pregnancies can and do occur. Such was the case in real life and in the movie. Day is an actress married to O'Neal. Her Broadway show has closed for the night due to the power outage, and she arrives home to find O'Neal being interviewed in their apartment by sexy reporter Albright. In a jealous rage, Day leaves their Manhattan aerie and drives to their country home in Connecticut where, unable to sleep, she downs some sleeping liquid and conks out on the couch. Morse, an executive who is fleeing with several million of his company's dollars, comes to the Day house when his car breaks down during his getaway. He comes into the house, makes the mistake of taking some of Day's sleeping potion, and falls asleep next to Day. O'Neal, feeling deflated by Day's leaving, comes to the house and sees the two asleep and immediately becomes jealous. Meanwhile, Day has been planning to quit the stage and take it easy, something her greedy agent, Terry-Thomas, wishes she would reconsider. In order to keep her working (and his pockets lined with the 10 percent he takes), he fans the jealousy flame even further in O'Neal's fevered brain. O'Neal believes what he sees and starts back to Manhattan in haste, Morse wakes up, tries to leave, but the cops pick him up when the car he is driving is found to contain the purloined cash. He goes free, though, when the fast-thinking Morse explains that he had taken the money but only so it would be protected during the blackout. Morse is made chief executive of his company for his quick thinking but his happiness is short-lived when his boss' son runs off with the money that he brought back. O'Neal and Day reconcile and, as luck and fate and contrivance would have it, she gives birth nine months later to the child they always wanted but never took the time to conceive. A trifle, made somewhat better by the adroit acting that triumphed over the lacklustre script. As typical a Doris Day movie as could have been planned, it was coproduced by her late husband (and business manager) Martin Melcher. Years later, it was learned that Melcher had taken liberties with the Day bank account and she did not realize it at the time. Good comedy bits from Backus as a used car dealer, Steve Allen as a radio newsman, Ben Blue as a befuddled bystander, and Pat Paulsen as a subway conductor. Columnist Earl Wilson (New York Post) makes a cameo appearance, as does director Averback, who was a radio announcer before he went into directing. He was best known for his work on the Bob Hope radio program. The movie started out funnily enough, than sank into predictability. The baby boom that supposedly happened nine months after the blackout was not nearly as extensive as everyone thought. For a brief while, there was a mild flurry of a revival of the old song, "When the Lights Go on Again (All Over the World)" but that went by the boards about as fast as this movie did. Emhardt, as Morse's boss, and Malone, as the weasel son who steals the money, don't have much to do. Consolidated Edison took a lot of flak for the blackout but they can't be blamed for this movie. Day's long- time songwriter, Joe Lubin, chipped in with "Showtime" and it was about as distinguished as the title tune by Dave Grusin and Kelly Gordon, which is to say not at all. The title number was sung by The Lettermen.

p, Everett Freeman, Martin Melcher; d, Hy Averback; w, Freeman, Karl Tunberg (based on the play "Monsieur Masure" by Claude Magnier); ph,

Ellsworth Fredericks (Panavision, Metrocolor); m, Dave Grusin; ed, Rita Roland; art d, George W. Davis, Urie McCleary; set d, Henry Grace, Dick Pefferle; cos, Glenn Connelly; spec eff, J. McMillan Johnson, Carroll L. Shepphird; makeup, William Tuttle, Harry Maret.

Comedy   **(PR:A-C   MPAA:NR)**

WHERE'S CHARLEY?***½   (1952, Brit.) 97m WB c

Ray Bolger (Charley Wykeham), Allyn McLerie (Amy Spettigue), Robert Shackleton (Jack Chesney), Horace Cooper (Stephen Spettigue), Margaretta Scott (Dona Lucia), Howard Marion Crawford (Sir Francis Chesney), Mary Germaine (Kitty Verdun), Henry Hewitt (Brassett), H.G. Stoker (Wilkinson), Martin Miller (Photographer).

The picture itself is not that good. The sets are cheesy, the dialog often creaky, and the chorus ordinary. What makes the experience extraordinary is the incredible performance by Bolger, who was 48 years of age and playing a college student at Oxford! The creaky farce by Brandon Thomas had already been filmed in 1940 as CHARLEY'S BIG-HEARTED AUNT with Arthur Askey and Phyllis Calvert, then again in 1941 as CHARLEY'S AUNT with Jack Benny, Kay Francis, Laird Cregar, Felix Aylmer, and several others. The addition of music (by Frank Loesser) and Bolger make this stand out. Sydney Chaplin filmed it as a silent and Charlie Ruggles also did it in 1930, but only Benny's version comes close. Bolger and Shackleton are roommates at Oxford during the reign of Queen Victoria. The boys are in love with McLerie (reprising the stage role she played with Bolger) and Germaine and would like to have a date with them but dating without a chaperone was unheard of in those days. Bolger's wealthy, widowed aunt from Brazil ("where the nuts come from" is the key comedic phrase here) is due to arrive but when she is delayed, there is no chaperone and that could lead to all sorts of embarrassment for the young women. Bolger dresses up as his own aunt to save their faces. Cooper is the guardian of Germaine and McLerie's uncle (he was appearing in his first film at the age of 70, perhaps the oldest movie debut in history) and he takes an immediate shine to Bolger's feminine persona. Also intrigued by the supposed millions of the Brazilian is Shackleton's father, Crawford. Both oldsters are not above wooing the very rich "woman" and the scenes become hysterical as the graybeards attempt to act like rakehells. Eventually, the real aunt, Scott, does show up and the whole tempest in a teapot is calmed, but not before we've been treated to a tour de force performance by Bolger and several well-integrated songs by Loesser (who was already a major songwriter in his twenties). The songs include the classic "Once in Love with Amy" (sung by Bolger as he moons around the campus), "Make a Miracle," "The New Ashmolean Marching Society and Students Conservatory Band," "Better Get Out of Here," "At the Red Rose Cotillion," "My Darling, My Darling," and others. Butler, who was celebrating 35 years in movies, directed at a breakneck pace and kept matters moving when one considers the ancient derivation of the source material. Almost everyone connected with the film, save Bolger, was British and this was shot at the Warner Bros. studio in England as well as on actual location at venerable Oxford University. Bolger is no singer but his ebullience and elan more than make up for the lack of vocalizing and his dancing is a wonder to behold. Most of the dancers were local lads and lasses and they danced well enough under the sure hand of choreographer Kidd, but one wishes this could have been shot in the U.S. where the dancers, at that time, were better trained and more capable of stunning leg work. McLerie was born in Canada and began her career in WORDS AND MUSIC (1948), then did several more films after this. That Bolger could cavort this well while in his late forties was a marvel. In 1986, Bolger could still be seen walking the streets of Beverly Hills and was never too busy to talk to a youngster who recognized him as the Tin Man in THE WIZARD OF OZ. A true gentleman in every way, he continued to work well into his eighties.

p, Ernest Martin, Cy Feuer; d, David Butler; w, John Monks, Jr. (based on the musical play by Frank Loesser, George Abbott from the play "Charley's Aunt" by Brandon Thomas); ph, Erwin Hillier (Technicolor); ed, Reginald Mills; md, Louis Levy; art d, David Folkes; ch, Michael Kidd.

Musical Comedy   **Cas.**   **(PR:AA   MPAA:NR)**

WHERE'S GEORGE?   (SEE: HOPE OF HIS SIDE, THE, 1935, Brit.)

WHERE'S JACK?**   (1969, Brit.) 119m Oakhurst Productions/PAR c
                                                (AKA: RUN, REBEL, RUN)

Tommy Steele (Jack Sheppard), Stanley Baker (Jonathan Wild), Fiona Lewis (Edgworth Bess Lyon), Alan Badel (The Lord Chancellor), Dudley Foster (Blueskin), Noel Purcell (Leatherchest), William Marlowe (Tom Sheppard), Sue Lloyd (Lady Darlington), Harold Kasket (The King), Cardew Robinson (Lord Mayor), Esmond Knight (Ballad Singer), Eddie Byrne (Rev. Wagstaff), John Hallam (The Captain), Leon Lissek (Deeley), Iole Marinelli (Lady Clarissa), Carolyn Montagu (Mistress Barrow), Carla Challoner (Emma), Jack Woolgar (Mr. Woods), Roy Evans (Mr. Hind), Michael Elphick (Hogarth), Caroline Munro (Mme. Vendonne), Rona Newton-John (Countess Bethune), Bernadette Brady (Ballad Singer's Guide), Dafydd Havard (Clerk), Roc Brynner (Drunk), Skip Martin (Dwarf), Vernon Hayden (Deputy Marshal), Norman Smythe (Bosun), Cecil Nash (Storyteller), Howard Goorney (Surgeon), George Woodbridge (Hangman),

Clare Mullen (*Dwarf's Girl Friend*), Ivan Dixon (*Naval Officer*), Danny Cummins (*Barker*), Fred Johnson (*Merchant*), Loretta Clarke (*Lady Mayoress*), Danny Holland, Michael Douglas, Terry Plummer (*Constables*), Liam Sweeney (*Austin*), John Kelly (*Proprietor*), Mary Willoughby (*Poll Maggott*), John Morley (*Judge*), Paschal Perry (*Guard*).

This costume drama set in 18th-Century London chronicles the life of the notorious thief Jack Sheppard who became a legend in his own time for his stunning jailbreaks and other incredible feats. Steele plays the young locksmith who begins his life of crime to save his brother Marlowe from prison. He soon becomes the chief object of Baker, who makes his living setting up thieves in order to cash in on the reward for turning them in. The movie is packed with adventure, though delivered unevenly; Steele makes a good hero by keeping an aura of integrity throughout that is juxtaposed against Baker's greed.

p, Stanley Baker; d, James Clavell; w, Rafe Newhouse, David Newhouse; ph, John Wilcox (Eastmancolor); m, Elmer Bernstein; ed, Peter Thornton; prod d, Cedric Dawe; set d, Dorothy Elliott; cos, Cynthia Tingey; ch, Malcolm Goddard; makeup, Wally Schneiderman, Jill Carpenter; scenic artist, Ferdie Bellan; tech adv, Alan Dent.

Biography/Drama (PR:A MPAA:G)

WHERE'S POPPA?*½ (1970) 83m UA c (AKA: GOING APE)

George Segal (*Gordan Hocheiser*), Ruth Gordon (*Mrs. Hocheiser*), Trish Van Devere (*Louise Callan*), Ron Leibman (*Sidney Hocheiser*), Rae Allen (*Gladys Hocheiser*), Vincent Gardenia (*Coach Williams*), Joe Keyes, Jr. (*Gang Leader*), Alice Drummond (*Woman in Elevator*), Tom Atkins (*Policeman in Apartment*), Florence Tarlow (*Miss Morgiani*), Jane Hoffman, Helen Martin (*Job Applicants*), Barnard Hughes (*Col. Hendriks*), Paul Sorvino (*Owner of "Gus & Grace's Home"*), William Le Massena (*Judge*), Michael McGuire (*Army Lawyer*), Rob Reiner (*Roger*), Israel Lang (*Muthafucka*), Garrett Morris (*Garrett*), Arnold Williams (*Arnold*), Buddy Butler (*Buddy*), Martha Greenhouse (*Owner of "Happytime Farms"*), Jack Manning (*Lawyer for Memphis Maulers*), John Gilliar (*Policeman in Courthouse*), Rehn Scofield (*Bailiff*), John McCurry (*Policeman in Jail Cell*), April Geleta (*Taxi Lady*), Edward Brooks (*Sheldon Hocheiser*), W. Benson Terry (*Cab Driver*), Fuddles (*Shoeshine Man*), Stella Marrs.

Once again, George Segal is saddled with a difficult Jewish mother, as he was in NO WAY TO TREAT A LADY (mother played by Eileen Heckart) and LOST AND FOUND (mother played by Maureen Stapleton). This time mother is the ultimate as she is not only domineering, she is downright nuts. Robert Klane wrote the screenplay from his hysterical novel (which was actually funnier than the movie) and Reiner directed it but missed many of the jokes that played so well in the book. Segal is a New York attorney who lives with Gordon, his aged and quite senile mother. He has never married because she fouled up all of his relationships. She deserves to be in a home but Segal made a promise to his father as the man lay dying and so he can't bring himself to confine her, even though she is destroying him. At the start, he awakens to a local radio show, showers, shaves, puts on a gorilla suit, and races into Gordon's room. We're not sure if he wants to cheer her up or cause her to have a heart attack. She responds by punching him hard in the groin and saying, "You almost scared me to death," as she laughs. Segal, doubled over in pain, mumbles, "Almost is not good enough." Gordon prepares orange slices for Segal's breakfast, then eats them herself, along with Lucky Charms breakfast cereal smothered in Coca-Cola. Segal's brother Leibman is married to Allen and they live on the East Side, across Central Park. Leibman won't help in the care and odd feeding of Gordon so Segal hires a succession of nurses but none stay past noon because Gordon is impossible to deal with. Segal meets and hires Van Devere, a sweet nurse with a strange background. She's been married once, for 32 hours, then, after her first sexual experience with her husband, she was appalled to find that he'd defecated in bed. When she expressed shock, her husband shrugged and answered, "Doesn't everybody?" With that marriage by the wayside, Van Devere is thrilled to find a man like Segal and the two are soon in love. Segal invites Van Devere home for dinner, hoping that Gordon won't screw this up. He tells her that if she does, he will punch her heart out. It doesn't help. At the dinner, Gordon's behavior is reprehensible. She takes food from everyone else's plate and candidly talks about Segal's private parts. Van Devere leaves quickly and Segal begins to think that he can kill his own mother. To stop himself, he calls Leibman and insists that his brother come over right away or they will be orphans. Leibman runs across the park (too cheap to take a cab) and is beset by a gang of tough black youths led by Keyes. They take his clothing and he races nude to Segal's apartment building. Leibman promises Segal that he will take more of an active participation in the care of Gordon, and Segal calms down and gives Leibman the gorilla suit to wear home. On the street, Leibman hails a cab at the same time a well-dressed black woman is also after the same taxi. In a commentary on New York drivers, the hackie stops for the gorilla rather than the black woman. Van Devere comes back and they try to have dinner again but it's no use as Gordon pulls down Segal's pants and gives him a love bite on his rump (or his "tush" as she calls it). Segal calls Leibman again. He has just arrived home and is still in his gorilla suit. Segal threatens to kill Gordon so Leibman runs across the park again and gets stopped by the same group of muggers. They force him to join them in a gang rape of what turns out to be a male policeman in drag. Leibman is arrested and calls Segal

to get him out of jail. The cop sends Leibman flowers with a note, saying "Thank you for a lovely evening" and Leibman is touched because this is the first time anyone has ever sent him flowers. All the time, Segal is trying to keep his law practice going but the pressure of dealing with Gordon is making it impossible. His current case is Gardenia, a manic football coach who snatches 10-year-old boys off the street when he thinks he can turn them into players. While in court, Van Devere comes to see Segal and says that she is going home to the Midwest because there is no way she can deal with Segal's relationship with his mother. That does it for Segal. All through the movie, Gordon has been asking, "Where's Poppa?" although Segal keeps explaining that he's dead. Now he uses her question to advantage as he takes all of Gordon's gear, stows it in his car, and he and Van Devere take her to a terrible old age home run by Sorvino. It's so awful that there is no way Segal can leave Gordon there. They take her to another rest home and an old codger walks up to her and says, "Momma?" Gordon's eyes light up as she says, "Poppa?" Segal and Van Devere leap into their car before she can change her mind and drive off as the movie fades to black. There was another ending that was jettisoned because it was too downbeat. In that, Segal gets a call from Gordon, picks her up at the home, and eventually climbs into bed with her saying that he is "Poppa." That version was never seen and so we are only dealing in hearsay. What is funny in the film is very funny, but Reiner tries to sustain the pace without offering any respite and so the jokes sometimes fall flat because there is no contrast. His son, Rob, now a respected director in his own right, does a cameo. Klane, who also wrote The Horse is Dead (yet to be filmed), wrote a splendid screenplay but Reiner botched it up just enough to keep it from being a classic. Bluenoses will cringe at the lapses in taste and children would be well advised to stay away until they can understand the underlying theme and take the raw language. Filmed on location in New York City, WHERE'S POPPA? has taken on the status of a cult movie although television showings have been cut to ribbons and one must see the full version to appreciate it. Norman Gimbel and Jack Elliott collaborated on five tunes, none of which added a thing to the picture. The songs: "Freedom," "Move It!" (sung by June Jackson), "Pleasure Palace" (sung by Bright Cheerstrap), "The Goodbye Song" (sung by Harry "Sweets" Edison), "Where's Poppa?" (sung by Clydie King).

p, Jerry Tokofsky, Marvin Worth; d, Carl Reiner; w, Robert Klane (based on his novel); ph, Jack Priestley (DeLuxe Color); m, Jack Elliott; ed, Bud Molin, Chic Ciccolini; art d, Warren Clymer; set d, Herbert Mulligan; cos, Albert Wolsky.

Comedy Cas. (PR:C-O MPAA:R)

WHERE'S SALLY?** (1936, Brit.) 71m WB bw

Gene Gerrard (*Jimmy Findlay*), Claude Hulbert (*Tony Chivers*), Reginald Purdell (*Dick Burgess*), Renee Gadd (*Sally*), Chili Bouchier (*Sonia*), Violet Farebrother (*Mrs. Hickory*), Athole Stewart (*Lord Mullion*), Morland Graham (*Polkinhorne*), Ralph Roberts.

Tired of the philandering life style he's been leading, playboy Gerrard decides to settle down and marry his latest sweetheart, Gadd. At the reception his best friend, Hulbert, tells Gadd several colorful stories detailing Gerrard's past romantic rovings which upset the new bride. Before she can learn more, Gerrard hustles Gadd off on their honeymoon, but complications arise as they run into a variety of outlandish characters including Hulbert's wife, Bouchier, who has just left him. Throughout the honeymoon Gadd continually disappears and returns, unable to decide whether or not she wishes to stay married to Gerrard. The whole film is a bit silly, but the enthusiastic players do their best to make it all convincing and amusing.

p, Irving Asher; d, Arthur Woods; w, Brock Williams, Frank Launder; ph, Basil Emmott.

Comedy (PR:A MPAA:NR)

WHERE'S THAT FIRE?** (1939, Brit.) 73m FOX bw

Will Hay (*Capt. Benjamin Viking*), Moore Marriott (*Jerry Harbottle*), Graham Moffatt (*Albert Brown*), Peter Gawthorne (*Chief Officer*), Eric Clavering (*Hank Sullivan*), Hugh McDermott (*Jim Baker*), Charles Hawtrey (*Youth*).

Daft comedy starring Hay as the chief of an incompetent fire company whose latest call resulted in the total destruction of the town hall. Desperately wanting to redeem himself and his men, Hay learns of a plot to steal the crown jewels and decides to foil the plan. The firefighters and their chief venture to the Tower of London where they catch the crooks in the act and capture them, using a chemical foam extinguisher. Occasionally funny, but the film misses more than it hits.

p, Edward Black; d, Marcel Varnel; w, Marriott Edgar, Val Guest, J.O.C. Orton (based on a story by Maurice Braddell); ph, Derek Williams.

Comedy (PR:A MPAA:NR)

WHEREVER SHE GOES** (1953, Aus.) 80m EAL/Mayer-Kingsley bw

Eileen Joyce (*Herself*), Suzanne Parrett (*Eileen Joyce as a Young Girl*), Muriel Steinbeck (*Mother*), Nigel Lovell (*Father*), John Wiltshire (*Daniel*), George Wallace (*Stage Manager*), Tim Drysdale (*John Joyce*), Syd Chambers (*Mr. Hallohan*), Rex Dawe (*Hotel Keeper*), Sefton Daly (*Piano Player*), Jacqueline Cat (*Nun*).

Another musical screen-biography, this time the life of famed concert pianist Eileen Joyce that is trivialized to the point of banality. The film details the young girl's efforts to become a musician amidst the poverty of a Tasmanian mining town. To raise money, Parrett (who plays the young Joyce) tries to collect money by playing the harmonica for bar patrons and miners. She soon endears herself to the community with her tireless ambition and talent. With the help of the miners, Parrett enters a musical competition and wins a scholarship to study music in the city. In a few short years she is playing London's Albert Hall. While Parrett is charming as the teenaged Joyce, the film is filled with the tired rags-to-riches cliches and sheds no new light on the magic that brilliant musicians possess.

p, Eric Williams; d&w, Michael S. Gordon; ph, George Heath; md, Ernest Irving.

Biography   (PR:A   MPAA:NR)

WHICH WAY IS UP?* (1977) 94m UNIV c

Richard Pryor (*Leroy Jones/Rufus Jones/Rev. Thomas*), Lonette McKee (*Vanetta*), Margaret Avery (*Annie Mae*), Morgan Woodword (*Mr. Mann*), Marilyn Coleman (*Sister Sarah*), Bebe Drake-Hooks (*Thelma*), Gloria Edwards (*Janelle*), Ernesto Hernandez (*Jose*), Diane Rodrigues (*Estrella*), Danny Valdez (*Chuy Estrada*), Dewayne Jessie (*Sugar*), Morgan Roberts (*Henry*), Dolph Sweet (*The Boss*), Luis Valdez (*Ramon Juarez*), Pat Ast (*Hooker*), Timothy Thomerson (*Tour Guide*), Marc Alaimo (*Frankie*), Tony Alvarenga (*Errand Boy*), Victor Argo (*Angel*), Kathy Cronkite, Ron Cummins (*Photographers*), Evelyn J. Dutton (*Receptionist*), Carmen Filpi (*Wino*), Darrell Giddens, Eddie Smith (*Men at Picnic*), Cheryl Harvey, Julie Dorman, Louise Johnson, Yvonne Mooney (*Congregation Girls*), Sidney Lanier (*Rossi*), Tanya Lee (*Althea*), Terrence Locke (*Assassin*), Ted Markland, Blair Burrows, Ralph Montgomery, Hank Robinson, Bob Terhune (*Goons*), Paul Mooney (*Inspector*), Shane Mooney (*Alvin*), Harry Northup (*Chief Goon*), Korla Pandit (*Hindu*), Cliff Pellow (*White Boss*), Mark Robin, Dennis O'Flaherty (*Reporters*), Spo-de-odee (*Cripple*), Carol Trost (*Ms. Collins*), Joseph Turkel (*Harry*), Angela Wilson (*Dawn*), Hank Worden (*Flunky*), El Teatro Campesino.

Pryor made a name for himself with his bizarre caricatures that took advantage of supposed liberal attitudes toward racial differences during the 1970s. But the difference between his performance in this film and in GREASED LIGHTING and SILVER STREAK is immense. In those films his characters were funny and even a bit insightful, but here they are embarrassing and trite. Based on Lina Wertmuller's THE SEDUCTION OF MIMI, this film offers Pryor as a Southern California grove worker who suddenly finds himself involved politically in the lives of overworked and underpaid laborers. His position doesn't sit well with the owners, so Pryor is forced to flee to the city, where he picks up nasty habits which eventually leave him alone and friendless because of his incredible greed. The problem with this characterization is that the audience cannot possibly like this guy either; he just fails to evoke any form of sympathy, making it impossible for his situation to appear the least bit humorous. Pryor carries two other roles in this film which are just as ridiculous and hard to care about: an unscrupulous minister and the father of the orange-picking Pryor. It's a real shame to have to watch a person with Pryor's ability to captivate an audience wallow in such trash.

p, Steve Krantz; d, Michael Schultz; w, Carl Gottlieb, Cecil Brown (based on the film script THE SEDUCTION OF MIMI by Lina Wertmuller); ph, John A. Alonzo (Panavision, Technicolor); m, Paul Riser, Mark Davis; ed, Danford B. Greene; prod d, Lawrence G. Paul; set d, John M. Dwyer; m/l, "Which Way is Up?" Norman Whitfield (sung by Stargard); stunts, Allen Oliney.

Comedy   **Cas.**   (PR:O   MPAA:R)

WHICH WAY TO THE FRONT?*½ (1970) 96m WB c

Jerry Lewis (*Brendan Byers III*), Jan Murray (*Sid Hackle*), Willie Davis (*Lincoln*), John Wood (*Finkel*), Steve Franken (*Peter Bland*), Dack Rambo (*Terry Love*), Paul Winchell (*Schroeder*), Sidney Miller (*Adolf Hitler*), Robert Middleton (*Colonico*), Kaye Ballard (*Mayor's Wife*), Harold J. Stone (*Gen. Luther Buck*), Joe Besser (*Dock Master*), Gary Crosby, Artie Lewis, Mickey Manners (*SS Guards*), Danny Dayton (*Man in Car*), Kathleen Freeman (*Bland's Mother*), Neil Hamilton (*Chief of Staff*), Milton Frome (*Executive*), Bob Lauher (*Sergeant*), Bobo Lewis (*Bland's Wife*), George Takei (*Yamashita*), Martin Kosleck (*German Submarine Commander*), Fritz Feld (*Von Runstadt*), Ronald Lewis, Benny Rubin, William Wellman, Jr.

With all the fine comic impersonations Jerry Lewis has created, it's very sad to see him involved in such total trash as this. But he really has only himself to blame, except, perhaps, for the poorly conceived script, as Lewis took on both direction and production for this vehicle in which he starred. The result is a desperate attempt at trying to create humor out of totally ridiculous situations. Sometimes this can be a very effective form of humor, but when

lacking inventiveness or a satirical perspective, as in WHICH WAY TO THE FRONT, the results look very flat, and in this case, like an old clown who wants very much to entertain his audience but just lacks a sense of viewer appeal. Lewis plays a multimillionaire whose greatest desire is to do something to help the U.S. effort during WW II, but who has been declared unfit for service. So this millionaire gets together his own little army and undertakes to enter the war on the Allied side. A raggedy group sails to Italy to embark upon this goal, coming up with a plan to kidnap a high-ranking Nazi officer. In doing this Lewis takes over the Nazi's identity, getting himself into trouble when the Allied forces come marching into town. This film gives Lewis the chance to try his hand at playing a Nazi to comic effect, something done much more effectively by Charlie Chaplin in THE GREAT DICTATOR at a more fitting time in the course of world events. There is one enjoyable bit of humor supplied by Sidney Miller as Hitler, but it's wasted in the overall scheme of this picture.

p&d, Jerry Lewis; w, Gerald Gardner, Dee Caruso (based on a story by Gardner, Caruso, Richard Miller); ph, w. Wallace Kelley (Technicolor); m, Louis Y. Brown; ed, Russel Wiles; md, Brown; art d, John Beckman; cos, Guy Verhille; spec eff, Ralph Webb; makeup, Jack Stone, Fred Williams.

Comedy   (PR:A   MPAA:G)

WHICH WILL YOU HAVE? (SEE: BARABBAS THE ROBBER, 1949, Brit.)

WHIFFS* (1975) 90m Brut/FOX c

Elliott Gould (*Dudley Frapper*), Eddie Albert (*Col. Lockyer*), Harry Guardino (*Chops*), Godfrey Cambridge (*Dusty*), Jennifer O'Neill (*Scottie*), Alan Manson (*Sgt. Poultry*), Donald Barry (*Post*), Richard Masur (*Lockyer's Aide*), Howard Hesseman (*Gopian*), Matt Greene (*Sentry*), James Brown (*Trooper*).

A weak vehicle which tries to promote Gould (a la Jerry Lewis) as a comedian with a bent toward slapstick. He plays a man being used in an experiment on germ warfare (it's never to be believed that any nut would allow for such a thing) who suffers some very nasty side effects from the drug that leave him acting like a chimpanzee with only a small bit of human intelligence. Leave it to a character of this nature to plot to use this same gas to go about robbing banks. The scriptwriter must have taken a good dose of this same gas each time he sat down at his typewriter.

p, George Barrie; d, Ted Post; w, Malcolm Marmorstein; ph, David Walsh (DeLuxe Color); m, John Cameron; ed, Robert Lawrence; art d, Fernando Carrere; set d, Robert Signorelli; m/l, "Now That We're in Love," "You Can Do it Without the Army," George Barrie, Sammy Cahn.

Comedy   (PR:A   MPAA:PG)

WHILE I LIVE*½ (1947, Brit.) 85m FOX bw (AKA: THE DREAM OF OLWEN)

Tom Walls (*Nehemiah, Julia's Servant*), Clifford Evans (*Peter*), Carol Raye (*Sally Warwick*), Patricia Burke (*Christine*), Sonia Dresdel (*Julia Trevelyan*), John Warwick (*George Warwick*), Edward Lexy (*Selby*), Audrey Fildes (*Olwen Trevelyan*), Charles Victor (*Sgt. Pearne*), Enid Hewitt (*Ruth*), Ernest Butcher (*Ambrose*), Johnny Schofield (*Alfie*), John Martyn (*Onlooker*), Sally Rogers (*Hannah*), Brenda Cameron (*Mary*), Diana Lake (*Lucy*), Doreen Fischer (*Ethel*).

Too far-fetched a concept to be effective as dramatic filmmaking, this British feature revolves around Dresdel's belief in the reincarnation of her musician sister Fildes, whose death she feels responsible for. Apparently, Dresdel has pushed her sister to achieve, and when Fildes, obsessed with completing a piano composition, falls off a cliff during a sleepwalking episode, Dresdel latches onto the notion that the girl's soul has transmigrated. Twenty-five years later this belief seems to be given tangible evidence when amnesiac Raye wanders into Dresdel's home and sits down at the piano, in the manner of Fildes. Poor Raye almost meets the same cliffside fate as her predecessor, but is saved in the nick of time by her worried husband. Stiff performances and strained direction do little to help the plot's inadequacies.

p, Edward Dryhurst; d, John Harlow; w, Harlow, Doreen Montgomery (based on the play "This Same Garden" by Robert Bell); ph, Frederick A. Young; m, Charles Williams; ed, Douglas Robertson; art d, Bernard Robinson.

Drama   (PR:A   MPAA:NR)

WHILE LONDON SLEEPS (SEE: WHEN LONDON SLEEPS, 1934)

WHILE NEW YORK SLEEPS, 1934 (SEE: NOW I'LL TELL, 1934)

WHILE NEW YORK SLEEPS** (1938) 61m FOX bw

Michael Whalen (*Barney Callahan*), Jean Rogers (*Judy King*), Chick Chandler (*Snapper Doolan*), Robert Kellard (*Malcolm Hunt*), Joan Woodbury (*Nora Parker*), Harold Huber (*Joe Marco*), Marc Lawrence (*Happy Nelson*), Sidney Blackmer (*Ralph Simmons*), William Demarest (*Red Miller*), June Gale (*Kitty*), Cliff Clark (*Inspector Cliff Collins*), Edward

Gargan (Sgt. White), Minor Watson (Charles MacFarland), Robert Middlemass (Sawyer).

A die hard newspaper reporter with a knack for allowing romantic interests to get in the way of his duties resorts to some unethical methods in order to track down those responsible for a number of murders that have held the police at bay. One thing that is always amazing about these newspaper yarns is that the star reporter is always so much better than the detectives at pinning down the culprits. This picture is no exception, though it arrives at the inevitable with a greater amount of flair than most.

p, Sol M. Wurtzel; d, H. Bruce Humberstone; w, Frances Hyland, Albert Ray (based on a story by Frank Fenton, Lynn Root); ph, Lucien Andriot; ed, Norman Colbert; md, Samuel Kaylin; ch, Nicholas Castle, Geneva Sawyer; m/l, Sidney Clare, Arthur Johnston.

Crime   **(PR:A   MPAA:NR)**

WHILE PARENTS SLEEP*½   (1935, Brit.) 72m TRA-British and
                                              Dominions/UA bw

Jean Gillie (Bubbles Thompson), Ellis Jeffreys (Mrs. Hammond), Enid Stamp-Taylor (Lady Cattering), Mackenzie Ward (Jerry Hammond), Davy Burnaby (Lord Cattering), Athole Stewart (Col. Hammond), Romilly Lunge (Neville Hammond), Albert Rebla (Bedworth), Wally Patch (Taxi Driver), Billy [William] Hartnell (George).

Another tired comedy of manners from the British, this time starring Gillie as a poor-but-spunky shopgirl who sets out to teach a wealthy family a lesson in civility. Learning that her boy friend's brother is having a discreet affair with the upper-crust matron Stamp-Taylor, Gillie uses the information to her advantage by forcing the wealthy woman to accept and respect those from the lower class.

p, Paul Soskin; d, Adrian Brunel; w, Anthony Kimmins, Edwin Greenwood, John Paddy Carstairs, Jack Marks (based on the play by Kimmins); ph, Ernest Palmer.

Comedy   **(PR:A   MPAA:NR)**

WHILE PARIS SLEEPS½**   (1932) 66m FOX bw

Victor McLaglen (Jacques Costaud), Helen Mack (Manon Costaud), William Bakewell (Paul Renoir), Jack LaRue (Julot), Rita La Roy (Fifi), Maurice Black (Roca), Dot Farley (Concierge), Lucille La Verne (Mme. Golden Bonnet), Paul Porcasi (Kapas), Eddie Dillon (Concierge's Husband).

Effectively stark depiction of the white slave trade in Paris has McLaglen as an escaped convict journeying to the City of Lights to try to save his daughter from the clutches of lecherous pimps. One of the more striking scenes has the hoods taking care of an informant by sticking him into the burning oven of the bakery that serves as the front for their corrupt dealings.

p, William Sistrom; d, Allan Dwan; w, Basil Woon; ph, Glen MacWilliams; cos, Guy Duty.

Crime   **(PR:A   MPAA:NR)**

WHILE PLUCKING THE DAISIES   (SEE: PLEASE! MR. BALZAC,
                                              1957, Fr.)

WHILE THE ATTORNEY IS ASLEEP*½
   (1945, Den.) 80m A-S Palladium bw (MENS SAGFOR EREN SOVER)

Gunnar Lauring (Erik Jessen the Attorney), Beatrice Bonnesen (Else Jessen, Attorney's Daughter), Christian Arhoff (Magnus Stripp), Elith Pio (Robert Jensen), Gerda Neumann (Lilian Berner), Sam Besekow (Takituki the Butler), Poul Reichardt (Charlie), Freddy Albech (Joe), Gunnar Lemvigh (Mike), Per Gundmann (Sam), Valdemar Skjerning (Mr. Jorgensen), Knud Heglund (Tardini).

A Danish ripoff of Hollywood gangster yarns lacking the necessary effects, this revolves around four gangsters who leave the U.S. and return to their homeland, Denmark, to steal the Crown Jewels from Rosenborg Castle. They lure an attorney to their suite for a chat, drug him, and then make their move while he is asleep. In this way he is supposed to provide the perfect alibi: if questioned he will be unable to say that the gang wasn't with him when the crime occurred. But that's not the way things work out, leaving one wondering what the alibi was for this movie that makes the U.S. look like a land that breeds thugs.

d, Johan Jacobsen; w, Arvid Muller (based on the story by Gunnar Robert Hansen); ph, Einar Olsen; m, Kai Moller; ed, Edith Schlussel; art d, Erik Aaes.

Crime   **(PR:A   MPAA:NR)**

WHILE THE CITY SLEEPS**   (1956) 100m Thor/RKO bw

Dana Andrews (Edward Mobley), Rhonda Fleming (Dorothy Kyne), Sally Forrest (Nancy Liggett), Thomas Mitchell (John Day Griffith), Vincent Price (Walter Kyne, Jr.), Howard Duff (Lt. Burt Kaufman), Ida Lupino (Mildred

Donner), George Sanders (Mark Loving), James Craig (Harry Kritzer), John Barrymore, Jr. (Robert Manners), Vladimir Sokoloff (George Palsky), Robert Warwick (Amos Kyne), Ralph Peters (Meade), Larry Blake (Police Sergeant), Edward Hinton (O'Leary), Mae Marsh (Mrs. Manners), Sandy White (Judith Fenton), Celia Lovsky (Miss Dodd), Pitt Herbert (Bartender), David Andrews (Bar Pianist), Andrew Lupino, Carleton Young.

Lang's finest film since THE BIG HEAT and his last great success, WHILE THE CITY SLEEPS is a twisted crime drama which sends its lead actors on a perverse, dog-eat-dog journey into the unknown darkness of the underworld in a quest for success. The plot revolves around the aspirations of three newsmen—Mitchell, Sanders, and Craig—each of whom are in line for the job of editor-in-chief of a New York tabloid called The Sentinel. With the death of newspaper owner Warwick, his manipulative, dilettante son, Price, takes charge. The city is being terrorized by a sex murder known as "The Lipstick Killer" (played with conventional dementia by Barrymore), a mama's boy who, during the dark of night, preys on beautiful woman. In a kind of demented power game, Price offers the newspaper's top position to the man who can crack the case. Naturally, Mitchell, Sanders, and Craig become rivals, and are reduced to their most base. Mitchell, a leathery, hard-drinking Irishman, is clear about his motive—he needs the money that the position pays. Sanders, the head of the wire service, is a ruthless cad interested in the societal implications of being the boss. While photo-editor Craig tries to use his romantic link with Price's wife, Fleming, as his inroad to the top job, spending more time wooing her than investigating the crime. To help achieve his goal, Mitchell engages the help of streetwise reporter Andrews, who can only be interested after an offer of money. Each character's lack of moral values is soon made clear when they all employ the services of women to find the killer—risking the ladies' lives instead of their own. Mitchell agrees to Andrew's plan to use his fiancee, Forrest, as a decoy for the Barrymore. Sanders cons gutsy femme columnist Lupino into helping him secure information by seducing Andrews. While Craig continues working through Fleming and her influence over Price. In the process of working as a decoy, Forrest is nearly killed when Barrymore comes to her apartment and tries to gain entrance. A climactic chase leads to Andrews to the New York subway system, hot on the trail of the pathetic killer. A battle ensues between the pair, eventually ending up on the subway tracks. The roar of a northbound train thunders closer, while the lights of a southbound loom larger by the second. At the very last moment, Andrews is tossed past the oncoming train, landing safely, though Barrymore escapes up the stairs only to be apprehended by the police. Although viewed rather narrow-mindedly, by some as an unsuccessful thriller because Lang reveals the killer's identity too early in the film, WHILE THE CITY SLEEPS is clearly more than a thriller—as Lang's previous superb credits can attest. Lang's interest is not in the killer's motivation and methods, but in the equation of the ruthless, morally guilty minds of the journalists—men who are entrusted to uphold societal morals and protect a community—as they put other people in danger for their own benefit. This superbly constructed and multilayered film was, not surprisingly, Lang's second favorite film, following his 1936 U.S. masterpiece FURY. Produced independently, WHILE THE CITY SLEEPS was set for release by United Artists, though in the end it was distributed by RKO.

p, Bert E. Friedlob; d, Fritz Lang; w, Casey Robinson (based on the novel The Bloody Spur by Charles Einstein); ph, Ernest Laszlo (SuperScope); m, Herschel Burke Gilbert; ed, Gene Fowler, Jr.; art d, Carroll Clark; set d, Jack Mills; cos, Norma; m/l, "While The City Sleeps," Gilbert, Joseph Mullendore.

Crime   **Cas.**   **(PR:C   MPAA:NR)**

WHILE THE PATIENT SLEPT*   (1935) 67m FN-WB bw

Aline MacMahon (Sarah Keate, Nurse), Guy Kibbee (Lance O'Leary, Detective), Lyle Talbot (Deke Lonergan), Patricia Ellis (March Federie), Allen Jenkins (Jackson), Robert Barrat (Adolphe Federie), Hobart Cavanaugh (Eustace Federie), Dorothy Tree (Mittee Brown), Henry O'Neill (Elihu Dimuck), Russell Hicks (Dr. Jay), Helen Flint (Isobel Federie), Brandon Hurst (Grondal), Eddie Shubert (Muldoon), Walter Walker (Richard Federie).

A large number of friends and family are gathered in the mansion of a millionaire who suffers a stroke and takes to his bed for a good, long rest. This gathering of people filled with mutual animosity leads to a number of mysterious happenings, including a couple of murders that are accompanied by figures crawling through side panels and hidden doorways. The picture tried hard to be suspenseful, using antiquated spooky-old-house methods, but it was far from successful. The millionaire had the right idea when he stayed in bed.

p, Harry Joe Brown; d, Ray Enright, w, Robert N. Lee, Eugene Solow, Brown Holmes (based on the novel by Mignon G. Eberhart); ph, Arthur Edeson; ed, Owen Marks; art d, Esdras Hartley.

Thriller   **(PR:A   MPAA:NR)**

WHILE THE SUN SHINES*½   (1950, Brit.) 82m International Screenplays-ABF/MON-Straford bw

Barbara White (*Lady Elisabeth Randall*), Ronald Squire (*The Duke of Ayr and Sterling*), Brenda Bruce (*Mabel Crum*), Bonar Colleano [Jr.] (*Joe Mulvaney*), Michael Allan (*Colbert*), Ronald Howard (*The Earl of Harpenden*), Margaret Rutherford (*Dr. Winifred Frye*), Cyril Maude (*Old Admiral*), Garry Marsh (*Mr. Jordan*), Joyce Grenfell (*Daphne*), Amy Frank (*Mrs. Finckel*), Charles Victor (*Tube Train Conductor*), Wilfrid Hyde-White (*Male Receptionist*), Judith Furse (*Female Receptionist*), Clive Morton (*Guide*), Cecil Trouncer (*Naval Captain*), Vida Hope (*Elsie*), Geoffrey Sumner (*A Peer*), Aubrey Mallalieu (*Night Porter*), O.B. Clarence (*Old Gentleman*), Tamara Lees (*Manicurist*), Andrea Malandrinos (*Giovanni*), Beryl Measor (*Woman in Train*), Eric Messiter (*Man in Train*), Brian Peck (*Page Boy*), Patrick Bloomfield (*Lift Boy*), Wilfred Caithness (*Naval Officer*), Hugh Dempster (*Escort*), Hamilton Keene (*Reading Clerk in the House of Lords*), David Keir (*Man in Tube Train*), Gordon Begg (*Ancient Porter*), Richard Turner, Geoffrey Dunn (*Ushers in The House of Lords*), Russell Barry (*Clergyman*), Miles Malleson (*Horton*), Pat [Patricia] Owens.

A forced farce in which Colleano, a drunken American soldier, and Allan, a suave Frenchman, vie for White. The problem is that she is already engaged to Howard, a British sailor who also happens to be a wealthy earl. Matters are complicated because Colleano mistakes White for another woman after the kindly Howard takes him off the street. The direction never convinces the viewer that this story was meant to be told anywhere but on the stage. The son of the very talented Leslie Howard played the earl, proving that he would never have the ability to fill his father's shoes.

p, Anatole de Grunwald; d, Anthony Asquith; w, Terence Rattigan, de Grunwald (based on the play by Rattigan); ph, Jack Hildyard; m, Nicholas Brodsky; ed, Fred Wilson; md, Philip Green; art d, Tom Morahan; cos, Creed, Katja Krassin, M. Berman, Ltd.; m/l, "While the Sun Shines," Ian Grant.

Comedy   (PR:A   MPAA:NR)

WHIP HAND, THE**   (1951) 82m RKO bw

Carla Balenda (*Janet Koller*), Elliott Reid (*Matt Corbin*), Edgar Barrier (*Dr. Edward Koller*), Raymond Burr (*Steve Loomis*), Otto Waldis (*Dr. Willem Bucholtz*), Michael Steele (*Chick*), Lurene Tuttle (*Molly Loomis*), Peter Brocco (*Garr*), Lewis Martin (*Peterson*), Frank Darien (*Luther Adams, Storekeeper*), Olive Carey (*Mrs. Turner*), Jamesson Shade (*Sheriff*), Art Dupois (*Speedboat Pilot*), Robert Foulk, William Challee (*Guards*), Brick Sullivan, Robert Thom (*Rangers*).

Another in the list of Howard Hughes anti-Communist propaganda films, this was originally made as THE MAN HE FOUND and dealt with Adolf Hitler, alive and well and plotting away in the secure confines of a small town in the postwar U.S. After the production was wrapped, cut, and ready for release, Hughes opted for Communist bogeymen instead of Hitler, so it was back to the storyboards, and only a workmanlike effort by Menzies was able to create a decent picture despite the decrepit material. Reid, a vacationing journalist, gets a cold reception from the inhabitants of a tiny burg, provoking his curiosity and leading him to uncover a Communist plot to use the town as a base for germ warfare against the U.S. Considering that they remade almost the entire film, the cost was kept low at $376,000, but little of that investment was returned at the box office.

p, Lewis J. Rachmil; d, William Cameron Menzies; w, George Bricker, Frank J. Moss (based on a story by Roy Hamilton); ph, Nicholas Musuraca; m, Paul Sawtell; ed, Robert Golden; prod d, Menzies; md, Constantin Bakaleinikoff.

Thriller/Drama   (PR:A   MPAA:NR)

WHIPLASH**   (1948) 91m WB bw

Dane Clark (*Michael Gordon*), Alexis Smith (*Laurie Durant*), Zachary Scott (*Rex Durant*), Eve Arden (*Chris*), Jeffrey Lynn (*Dr. Arnold Vincent*), S.Z. Sakall (*Sam*), Alan Hale, Sr (*Terrance O'Leary*), Douglas Kennedy (*Costello*), Ransom Sherman (*Tex Sanders*), Fred Steele (*Duke Carney*), Robert Lowell (*Trask*), Don McGuire (*Harkus*), Clifton Young (*Gunman*), Sam Hayes (*Announcer*), Mike Lally (*Ring Announcer*), Howard Mitchell (*Fight Announcer*), Ralph Volkie (*Referee*), Donald Kerr (*Vendor*), Rudy Friml (*Orchestra Leader*), Jimmy Dodd (*Bill, Piano Player*), Charles Marsh (*Hotel Clerk*), I. Stanford Jolley (*Artist*), Kate Lawson (*Woman on Steps*), Maude Prickett (*Mrs. Gruman*), Jack Worth (*Doorman*), Richard Walsh (*Assistant Stage Manager*), Tommy Garland (*Rocky*), John Daheim (*Kid Lucas*), John Harmon (*Kid McGee*), Wally Scott (*Drunk*), Cliff Herd (*Waiter*), Howard Negley (*Policeman*), Larry McGrath (*Manager*), Bob Perry (*Timekeeper*), George Nokes, Norman Ollestad (*Boys*), Harvey Perry, Jim O'Catty (*Handlers*), Ray Montgomery, Harry Lewis (*Press Men*), Sam Shack, Charles Sullivan, Cy Malis, Sailor Vincent, Gene Delmont, George Suzanne, Joe LaBarba, Ray McDonald (*Seconds*), Joey Gray, Aldo Spoldi, Ceferino Garcia, Georgie Goodman, John Salvata, Artie Sullivan, Henry Vroom, Rito Funay, Wally Rose, Larry Anzalone, Paul Baxley, Buddy Wright (*Fighters*).

It's amazing how many Hollywood boxing tales center on a fighter who deep down inside is a sensitive and thoughtful person who would rather be doing something else, but has taken to the ring out of necessity. WHIPLASH uses this premise to the hilt, taking Clark away from his artist's canvas to get his

head knocked about after falling head-over-heels for Smith. Her husband is Scott, was a fighter, but because of an accident, had to retire and now runs a nightclub where his wife sings. After Smith mysteriously disappears from Clark's life, he tracks her down to this club. Scott then uses Clark to fulfill his dream of becoming the world champ. Eventually Scott gets wind of the affair between the artist-cum-fighter and his wife, and instead of supporting Clark in the ring, Scott does the best to see that he gets his brains knocked out. Pure hokum that relies upon unbelievable and overly sentimental situations.

p, William Jacobs; d, Lewis Seiler; w, Maurice Geraghty, Harriet Frank, Jr., Gordon Kahn (based on a story by Kenneth Earl); ph, Peverell Marley; m, Franz Waxman; ed, Frank Magee; md, Leo F. Forbstein; art d, Charles H. Clarke; set d, Jack McConaghy; cos, Milo Anderson; spec eff, William McGann, Edwin DuPar; m/l, Dick Redmond, Fausto Curbello, Johnny Camacho, Mack David, "Just for Now," Redmond (sung by Alexis Smith); makeup, Micki Marcelino.

Sports Drama   (PR:A   MPAA:NR)

WHIPPED, THE**   (1950) 89m UA bw (AKA: THE UNDERWORLD STORY)

Dan Duryea (*Mike*), Herbert Marshall (*Stanton*), Gale Storm (*Cathy*), Howard da Silva (*Durham*), Michael O'Shea (*Munsey*), Mary Anderson (*Molly*), Gar Moore (*Clark*), Melville Cooper (*Maj. Radford*), Frieda Inescort (*Mrs. Eldridge*), Art Baker (*Lt. Tilton*), Harry Shannon (*Parkie*), Alan Hale, Jr (*Schaeffer*), Stephen Dunne (*Lee*), Roland Winters (*Becker*), Sue England (*Helen*), Lewis L. Russell (*Calvin*), Frances Chaney (*Grace*).

Journalist Duryea buys into a small New England paper after being tossed off a big city daily for his unethical tactics. Right off the bat he finds himself immersed in a case involving the murder of the wife of a wealthy heir. Though all the evidence points to Anderson, the woman's maid, who even admits to the crime under pressure, Duryea goes with his hunch that she is innocent and eventually gathers enough evidence to grab the true culprit. As the black maid accused of murder, Anderson gives a sincerely emotional and moving performance that far outshines the other members of the cast.

p, Hal E. Chester; d, Cyril [Cy] Endfield; w, Henry Blankfort, Endfield (based on a story by Craig Rice); ph, Stanley Cortez; m, David Rose; ed, Richard Heermance; art d, Gordon Wiles.

Crime/Drama   (PR:A   MPAA:NR)

WHIP'S WOMEN*½   (1968) 73m Jode/CIP-Chellee c

Forman Shane (*Johnny Whipley*), Robin Flynn (*Ellen*), Cara Loren (*Louise*), San Gie (*Kate*), Lawrence Adams (*Inspector Parker*), Rubin Atkins (*Tattoo Artist*), Suzie Wong.

Strange tale of eroticism and murder that details the investigation of the death of Shane, a sadomasochist whose involvement with four women makes any one of them a likely suspect. The killer turns out to be Gie. Secretly married to Shane, she had put up with her husband's hanky-panky because of the strong hold he had on her until he went too far by announcing his engagement to another woman.

d, Jerry Denby; w, Perry Berg; m, The Duvals.

Crime/Drama   (PR:O   MPAA:NR)

WHIPSAW***   (1936) 78m MGM bw

Myrna Loy (*Vivian Palmer*), Spencer Tracy (*Ross McBryce*), Harvey Stephens (*Ed Dexter*), William Harrigan (*Doc Evans*), Clay Clement (*Harry Ames*), Robert Gleckler (*Steve Arnold*), Robert Warwick (*Wadsworth*), Georges Renavent (*Monetta*), Paul Stanton (*Chief Hughes*), Wade Boteler (*Humphries*), Don Rowan (*Curly*), John Qualen (*Dobson*), Irene Franklin (*Mme. Marie*), Lillianne Leighton (*Aunt Jane*), J. Anthony Hughes (*Bailey*), William Ingersoll (*Dr. Williams*), Charles Irwin (*Larry King*), Edward Peil, Sr. (*Bartender*), Frank De Voe (*Photographer*), Bert Moorhouse (*Reporter*), John Marston, John Kelly, Arthur Loft, William Pawley (*Patrolmen*), Cyril McLaglen (*Detective*), Charles Coleman (*Doorman*), Wallis Clark (*Claymore*), William Wagner (*Waiter*), Howard Hickman (*Hotel Clerk*), Frances Gregg (*Nurse*), Robin Adair (*Cummings*), John Sheehan (*Joe*), Carl Stockdale (*Farmer*), Halliwell Hobbes.

Although filled with plot holes and suffering from a mediocre script, WHIPSAW delighted audiences with the superb chemistry that existed between Spencer Tracy and Myrna Loy. Loy is one-third of a gangster trio, rounded out by Stephens and Clement, who steal some jewels in Europe and head for New York, only to have their booty lifted by two other crooks, Harrigan and Gleckler. Loy manages to reclaim the jewels and then leaves town with her new man, Tracy, whom she believes to be another thief. Tracy, however, is actually a G-man trying to locate the stolen gems. The pair take off on a cross-country journey, making a stop at the country home of Qualen where they help his wife deliver a set of twins. Stephens and Clement finally catch up and hold Tracy and Loy hostage. Loy convinces her former cohorts that the booty is still in New York and that they must return to get it. Later, Tracy lets his real identity be known, and after a nearly fatal battle, assists police in the capture of the thugs. Although Loy is brought to trial, Tracy still loves her and promises to help with her defense. Originally intended as a Loy-William Powell vehicle, WHIPSAW had to be recast when the actress went on strike to receive better wages and Powell ended up involved in another film. MGM production head Irving Thalberg suggested Tracy as a replacement, but before long Wood and Tracy were at serious odds–Tracy complaining that Wood needlessly wasted time and was reshooting excessively. When Thalberg heard of their inability to work together, he went to the set and confronted the director. According to Larry Swindell in his biography of Tracy, Thalberg asked, "Well, Sam, what's your opinion of Tracy?" After a moment, Thalberg received a direct answer, "I think the red-headed bastard is the best actor on the lot!" Although Tracy would never again work under Wood's direction, the two managed to complete WHIPSAW on friendly terms.

p, Harry Rapf; d, Sam Wood; w, Howard Emmett Rogers (based on a story by James Edward Grant); ph, James Wong Howe; m, William Axt; ed, Basil Wrangell; art d, Cedric Gibbons, William Horning; set d, Edwin B. Willis; cos, Dolly Tree.

Crime/Romance   **(PR:A   MPAA:NR)**

WHIRLPOOL½**   (1934) 73m COL bw

Jack Holt (*Buck Rankin*), Jean Arthur (*Sandra Morrison*), Allen Jenkins (*Mac*), Donald Cook (*Bob Andrews*), Lila Lee (*Helen Morrison*), Rita La Roy (*Thelma*), John Miljan (*Barney Gaige*), Willard Robertson (*Judge Morrison*), Ward Bond (*Farley*), Oscar Apfel (*Editor*).

One of the more interesting depictions of a father-daughter relationship that is woven into a variety of interesting settings. Holt plays the owner of a carnival saddled with a murder charge that leaves him with a 20-year sentence. His newlywed wife, who is pregnant, is led to believe that her husband has committed suicide, so she goes on to marry another man to provide a decent home for her child. Daughter Arthur grows up to become a beautiful woman, finally meeting her father in the nightclub that Holt has taken over after his release from prison. Holt is anxious to make up for all the lost time, but trouble can't seem to keep from crossing his path. This time a crooked lawyer discovers the ghosts in Holt's closet. To prevent his identity from being revealed, Holt murders the blackmailer, but even that doesn't bring an end to his problems. Though the picture tends to be a little sappy, for the most part, it is a well-scripted and finely tuned effort.

d, R. William Neill; w, Dorothy Howell, Ethel Hill (based on a story by Howard Emmett Rogers); ph, Benjamin Kline; ed, Richard Cahoon.

Drama   **(PR:A   MPAA:NR)**

WHIRLPOOL***   (1949) 97m FOX bw

Gene Tierney (*Ann Sutton*), Richard Conte (*Dr. William Sutton*), Jose Ferrer (*David Korvo*), Charles Bickford (*Lt. Colton*), Barbara O'Neil (*Theresa Randolph*), Eduard Franz (*Martin Avery*), Constance Collier (*Tina Cosgrove*), Fortunio Bonanova (*Feruccio di Ravallo*), Ruth Lee (*Miss Hall*), Ian MacDonald (*Store Detective Hogan*), Bruce Hamilton (*Lt. Jeffreys*), Alex Gerry (*Dr. Peter Duval*), Larry Keating (*Mr. Simms*), Mauritz Hugo (*Hotel Employee*), John Trebach (*Freddie*), Myrtle Anderson (*Agnes*), Larry Dobkin (*Surgeon Wayne*), Jane Van Duser (*Miss Andrews*), Nancy Valentine (*Taffy Lou*), Clancy Cooper, Eddie Dunn, Charles J. Flynn (*Policemen*), Randy Stuart (*Miss Landau*), Helen Westcott (*The Secretary*), Mack Williams (*Whorton*), Howard Negley (*Gordon*), Robert Foulk (*Andy*), Phyllis Hill (*Cocktail Party Guest*), Roger Moore (*Fingerprint Man*), Margaret Brayton (*Policewoman*), Sue Carlton (*Elevator Girl*), Ted Jordan (*Parking Attendant*).

A compelling and rather eerie melodrama which stars Tierney as a woman haunted by her habitual kleptomania. Although she is married to a highly successful psychiatrist she cannot break the hold that stealing has over her. When she snatches a brooch from a department store she is caught in the act. Ferrer, a bizarre hypnotist, comes to her aid and persuades the store not to prosecute Tierney. He acts not out of kindness but out of the malicious act of involving Tierney in an ingenious murder scheme. Having scammed a former mistress out of some money, Ferrer hypnoizes Tierney and sends her to the mistress' house. She is already dead, however, and when the police arrive, Tierney, though innocent, is nabbed as the murderer. Conte is convinced of his wife's innocence and, with the help of investigator Bickford, is able to disprove Ferrer's alibi–that he was in the hospital for an operation–by proving that he actually hypnotized himself, temporarily left the hospital, and committed the murder. Ferrer's guilt is sealed when he returns to the murder site, again under hypnosis, in search of evidence. After a shootout, he holds his pursuers at bay, but the wounded Ferrer soon dies from loss of blood. A strange suspenser which mixes the elements of murder and the subconcious state of hypnosis–Tierney, having been hypnotized, cannot be sure whether or not she is guilty, but the one who loves her, Conte, fights to prove her innocence. Penned by a blacklisted Ben Hecht under the pseudonym Lester Barstow, WHIRLPOOL bears a striking resemblance to another Hecht-penned suspenser, Alfred Hitchcock's SPELLBOUND. That film also mixes murder with a subconscious state–a psychoanalytic mental block–and a person innocently accused of murder, Gregory Peck, who is saved by a loved one, Ingrid Bergman. While WHIRLPOOL is gripping throughout, the material and Preminger's direction are simply a rehash of that which Hitchcock brought to the screen four

years earlier. Suspiciously, Preminger's autobiography makes no mention of the film which he no doubt spent months working on. Even stranger is a quote in Gerald Pratley's study *The Cinema of Otto Preminger* in which the director still seems stuck in a mental block about WHIRLPOOL: "I cannot remember anything about this film." Sure.

p&d, Otto Preminger; w, Lester Barstow 'Ben Hecht', Andrew Solt (based on the novel by Guy Endore); ph, Arthur Miller; m, David Raksin; ed, Louis R. Loeffler; md, Alfred Newman; art d, Lyle R. Wheeler, Leland Fuller; set d, Thomas Little, Walter M. Scott; cos, Charles Le Maire, Oleg Cassini; spec eff, Fred Sersen.

Crime Drama   **(PR:A   MPAA:NR)**

WHIRLPOOL*   (1959, Brit.) 95m RANK c

Juliette Greco (*Lora*), O.W. Fischer (*Rolph*), Marius Goring (*Georg*), Muriel Pavlow (*Dina*), William Sylvester (*Herman*), Richard Palmer (*Derek*), Lilly Kann (*Mrs. Steen*), Peter Illing (*Braun*), Geoffrey Bayldon (*Wendel*), Victor Brooks (*Riverman*), Arthur Howell (*Pilot*), Harold Kasket (*Stiebel*).

Dull, plodding drama in which non-actress sexpot singer Greco flees her crooked boy friend by stowing away on a river boat under the dominion of Fischer. It doesn't take too long before the vessel's captain begins to seek the affections of the girl. But her boy friend reenters the proceedings, sneaking aboard the boat in hope of claiming his girl. The police make their presence known as well, but not before Fischer has dealt with the crook in his own manner, tossing him overboard and allowing him to drown. Filming took place along the Rhine River, which was obviously of more interest to the photographer and director than the story, as lots of effort is put into capturing postcard-type shots and almost none into fleshing out the action. But that's okay, as it's doubtful that anything could have helped this script.

p, George Pitcher; d, Lewis Allen; w, Lawrence P. Bachmann (based on his novel "*The Lorelei*"); ph, Geoffrey Unsworth (Eastmancolor); m, Ron Goodwin; ed, Russell Lloyd.

Drama   **(PR:A   MPAA:NR)**

WHIRLPOOL OF FLESH   (SEE: WHIRLPOOL OF WOMAN, 1966, Jap.)

WHIRLPOOL OF WOMAN**   (1966, Jap.) 116m Nikkatsu/Toho bw
      (ONNA NO UZU TO FUCHI TO NAGARE; AKA: WHIRLPOOL OF FLESH);

Kuzako Inano (*Sugako*), Noboru Nakaya (*Husband*), Sadako Sawamura, Tamio Kawaji.

Kinky tale about the wife of a hard-working professor who looks for sexual satisfaction outside her marriage. Raped by her uncle as a child, she has developed an obsession with death that is bound up with sexual experience and comes to the fore every time she makes love.

d, Ko Nakahira; w, Masashige; ph, Yoshihiro Yamazaki (Nikkatsu Scope).

Drama   **(PR:O   MPAA:NR)**

WHIRLWIND*½   (1951) 70m Gene Autry/COL bw

Gene Autry (*Himself*), Smiley Burnette (*Himself*), Gail Davis (*Elaine Lassiter*), Thurston Hall (*Big Jim Lassiter*), Harry Lauter (*Wade Trimble*), Dick Curtis (*Lon Kramer*), Harry Harvey (*Sheriff Barlow*), Gregg Barton (*Bill Trask*), Tommy Ivo (*Johnnie Evans*), Kenne Duncan (*Slim*), Al Wyatt (*Bert*), Gary Goodwin (*Carl*), Pat O'Malley, Bud Osborne, Boyd Stockman, Frankie Marvin, Stan Jones, Leon DeVoe, Champion, Jr. the Horse.

The Singing Cowboy was reunited with his old sidekick Burnette, as the two teamed to bring the crooked Hall to justice for his part in forming a Western crime syndicate. Autry is a postal inspector, while Burnette plays an agent posing as a horse doctor, roles that only the charm of these two performers keep from being mundane stereotypes.

p, Armand Schaefer; d, John English; w, Norman S. Hall; ph, William Bradford; ed, Paul Borofsky; md, Mischa Bakaleinikoff; art d, Charles Clague.

Western   **(PR:A   MPAA:NR)**

WHIRLWIND½**   (1968, Jap.) 107m Toho c (DAI TATSUMAKI)

Toshiro Mifune (*Lord Akashi*), Somegoro Ichikawa (*Jubei*), Yuriko Hoshi (*Kozato*), Kumi Mizuno (*The Witch*), Yosuke Natsuki, Yoshiko Kuga, Makoto Sato.

Subtly handled and lushly photographed samurai epic in which Ichikawa is the fighter assigned the task of accompanying a lady-in-waiting and young prince from the court of a defeated warlord to a place of safety. Their path is one filled with numerous enemies who would like to see the prince dead, but Mifune comes to the rescue and easily mows down numerous adversaries without once deeming it necessary to draw his sword. Also coming to Ichikawa's aid is a witch, Mizuno, who threatens to discontinue her assistance unless Ichikawa gives his affection to her instead of the maiden he is escorting. Although Mifune has a secondary role, his appearance dominates the film with his incredible display of physical prowess. The whirlwind appearing at the end of the film was a creation of the same man responsible for Japanese movie monsters "Godzilla" and "Rodan".

d, Hiroshi Inagaki; w, Inagaki, Takeshi Kimura; ph, Kazuo Yamada (TohoScope, Eastmancolor); spec eff, Eiji Tsuburaya.

Martial Arts   **(PR:C MPAA:NR)**

WHIRLWIND HORSEMAN*   (1938) 58m GN bw

Ken Maynard (Ken Morton), Joan Barclay (Peggy Radford), Bill Griffith (Happy Holmes), Kenneth Harlan (Harper), Joe Girard (Jim Radford), Kenny Dix (Bull), Roger Williams (Ritter), Dave O'Brien (Slade), Walter Shumway (The Sheriff), Budd Buster (Cherokee), Lew Meehan (Hank), Glenn Strange, Tarzan the Horse.

The search for Maynard's gold prospector pal leads the cowpoke to the ranch owned by Girard, Maynard's chief suspect and a man with an eyeful of a daughter. Then the real villains turn up and the fists start to fly. This is one of those oaters in which Tarzan the horse is the most interesting presence on the screen and also the best performer, probably because he doesn't have to say anything.

p, Max and Arthur Alexander; d, Bob Hill; w, George Plympton.

Western   **(PR:A MPAA:NR)**

WHIRLWIND OF PARIS*   (1946, Fr.) 88m Les Films Albert
Lanzin/Jay Hoffberg bw (TOURBILLON DE PARIS)

Ray Ventura (Himself), Charpin (Charbonnier), Marguerite Pierry (Mme. Charbonnier), Mona Goya (Marie-Claude), Paul Misraki (Paul), Jean Tissier (Rosales), Mila Pitoeff (Mony), Coco [Gregoire] Aslan (Coco), Ray Ventura's Orchestra.

Ray Ventura's music is the only worthwhile thing in this French so-called musical about some army-bound cadets who form an orchestra and cause havoc. One horrible casting mistake has members of the orchestra popping up in places which should be reserved for trained actors, as cadets, for example. Not a very strategic method of constructing a film. (In French; English subtitles.)

d, Henri Diamant-Berger; w, Andre Hornez; m, Paul Misraki; English subtitles, Herman G. Weinberg.

Musical   **(PR:A MPAA:NR)**

WHIRLWIND RAIDERS*½   (1948) 54m COL bw (GB: STATE
POLICE)

Charles Starrett (Steve Lanning/The Durango Kid), Fred Sears (Tracy Beaumont), Smiley Burnette (Smiley Burnette), Nancy Saunders (Claire Ross), Little Brown Jug (Tommy Ross), Jack Ingram (Buff Tyson), Philip Morris (Homer Ross), Patrick Hurst (Bill Webster), Edwin Parker (Red Jordan), Lynn Farr (Slim), Arthur Loft, Doyle O'Dell and the Radio Rangers.

In his dual role as the "Durango Kid" and Steve Lanning, Starrett comes to the aid of ranchers harassed by a supposedly law-abiding group which name themselves "Texas State Police," though in actuality they are a front for numerous shady activities. Instrumental in bringing the culprits to justice is the appearance of Little Brown Jug, a real life 10-year old rodeo star, who is able to point out the leader of the gang. (See DURANGO KID series, Index)

p, Colbert Clark; d, Vernon Keays; w, Norman S. Hall; ph, M.A. Anderson; ed, Paul Borofsky; art d, Charles Clague; set d, David Montrose.

Western   **(PR:A MPAA:NR)**

WHISKY GALORE   (SEE: TIGHT LITTLE ISLAND, 1949, Brit.)

WHISPERERS, THE***½   (1967, Brit.) 105m Seven Pines/UA-Lopert
bw

Edith Evans (Mrs. Maggie Ross), Eric Portman (Archie Ross), Nanette Newman (Girl Upstairs), Gerald Sim (Mr. Conrad), Avis Bunnage (Mrs. Noonan), Ronald Fraser (Charlie Ross), Leonard Rossiter (National Assistance Official), Kenneth Griffith (Mr. Weaver), Harry Baird (Earl), Margaret Tyzack (Almoner), Clare Kelly (Prostitute), Robert Russell (Andy), Michael Robbins (Mr. Noonan), Penny Spencer, Kaplan Kaye (Noonan Children), Robin Bailey (Psychiatrist), Max Bacon (Mr. Fish), Sarah Forbes (Mrs. Ross as a Child), Peter Thompson (Publican), Tom Kempinski, George Spence, Terry Eliot, Roy Maxwell, Michael Lees.

An absolutely riveting performance by Dame Edith Evans (Oscar-nominated) lifts this downbeat story about old age into the ether reserved for UMBERTO D and a few other films about how it is to become feeble and ancient. Based on the 1961 novel Mrs. Ross, director-screenwriter Forbes has fashioned what he hoped would be an important work. It was, but not as much as had been expected. Evans lives alone in a dark, dank flat. She

has companions, though. She hears voices whispering to her through the walls, the pipes, the air. Married for years to Portman, who has left her some time before, she exists on the government dole although she'll never admit it. She prefers to think that the queen is just lending her a few bob to help her until the inheritance left her by her late father is finally distributed. It's all in her imagination, of course, as there is no money to be forthcoming. By day, she walks the streets, stopping by a soup kitchen for some sustenance, gathering some warmth at the local library, and going to the office where they give her the small stipend upon which she lives. Fraser is Evans and Portman's son, a chip off the old man's block, in that he is a thief and a rascal. He's just pulled a job and stashes the booty in her closet. When Evans finds it, her addled mind tells her that here, at last, is her father's gift to her. She races off to the government office to tell them that they need not "lend" her any more from this day forward. She makes the mistake of telling Bunnage, an avaricious neighbor, about her good luck after all these years. Bunnage asks Evans to stop by for some celebratory tea or sherry and once Evans gets there, she is drugged into a stupor, robbed, and tossed in a nearby alley. The following day, she is found by neighbor Newman (Mrs. Bryan Forbes) as she coughs and hacks with the beginnings of pneumonia. Evans is taken to a local hospital where she recovers her health while being tested psychologically. The authorities attempt to find Portman and when they do, they prevail on the scoundrel to come back to Evans. There is a pathetic scene as they attempt to rebuild what may have once been, but Portman reverts to type, takes the money that had been stolen by their son, and he disappears, leaving Evans to sit alone in the cramped, newspaper-strewn flat, as she listens to the whisperings and says, "Are you there?" This movie could make the toughest critic sob. It goes right for the tear ducts and doesn't stop jerking. Made on a very low budget, it was one of the few films made by Evans, who started in sound films in 1948 in THE QUEEN OF SPADES after having made a few appearances in the silent era. The location is Manchester, which is depressing enough. Add that to the problem of an aged woman flirting with insanity and then make it totally uncompromising and you can see why it wasn't a commercial success. To be old is bad enough. To be poor is terrible. To be old and poor is something that almost everyone has thought of and feared. In this movie, it is brutally depicted and one shudders that "there but for the grace of God, go I." Perhaps Evans might have found happiness if she'd met Carlo Battista (UMBERTO D), but that's another story. Evans died in 1976 at the age of 88 and her final films, NASTY HABITS and THE SLIPPER AND THE ROSE, had not yet been released. Yet, if she is to be recalled for anything, it must be for this searing portrait of an old woman struggling to stand tall in the face of a hurricane wind of ill fortune. Although there is no violence and no raw language, sensitive children will be moved to uncontrollable tears.

p, Michael S. Laughlin, Ronald Shedlo; d&w, Bryan Forbes (based on the novel Mrs. Ross by Robert Nicolson); ph, Gerry Turpin; m, John Barry; ed, Anthony Harvey; md, Barry; art d, RaySimm; set d, Peter James; makeup, Basil Newall.

Drama   **Cas.**   **(PR:C MPAA:NR)**

WHISPERING CITY***   (1947, Can.) 89m Quebec Production
Corp./EL bw

Helmut Dantine (Michel Lacoste), Mary Anderson (Mary Roberts), Paul Lukas (Albert Frederic), John Pratt (Mons. Edward Durant), Joy LaFleur (Blanche Lacoste), George Alexander (Police Inspector), Mimi d'Estee (Renee Brancourt), Henri Poltras (Assistant Police Inspector).

Intriguing yarn in which newspaper reporter Anderson tries to get the goods on a prosperous lawyer, Lukas, for a murder committed several years earlier before she finds herself another item in the obituaries. She is enlightened to the guilt of Lucas through the confessions of a woman on her deathbed, and then she becomes the target of composer Dantine, tricked into helping Lukas kill Anderson because Dantine's wife committed suicide while she was drunk. This ploy fails when the young composer falls in love with Anderson. Both script and direction effectively handle the pacing and mood to heighten suspense.

p, George Marton, Paul L'Anglais; d, Fedor Ozep; w, Rian James, Leonard Lee (based on the story by George Zuckerman, Michael Lennox); ph, Guy Roe, William Steiner; m, Jean Deslauriers; ed, Douglas Bagier; md, Jack Shaindin.

Crime/Drama   **(PR:A MPAA:NR)**

WHISPERING DEATH   (SEE: NIGHT OF ASKARI, 1976, Ger./South
Africa)

WHISPERING ENEMIES**   (1939) 62m COL bw

Jack Holt (Stephen Brewster), Dolores Costello (Laura Crandall), Addison Richards (Red Barrett), Joseph Crehan (George Harley), Donald Briggs (Fred Bowman), Pert Kelton (Virginia Daniels), Paul Everton (Warden).

Holt and Costello play rival owners of cosmetic companies. Though they are unaware of each other's identity, they go about trying to put their competitor out of business through the underhanded method of spreading nasty rumors about each other's products. The snappy dialog helps lift the story beyond tedium.

p, Larry Darmour; d, Lewis D. Collins; w, Gordon Rigby, Tom Kilpatrick (based on a story by John Rawlins, Harold Tarshis); ph. James S. Brown, Jr.; ed, Dwight Campbell.

Drama   (PR:A   MPAA:NR)

WHISPERING FOOTSTEPS**   (1943) 54m REP bw

John Hubbard (Marcus Borne), Rita Quigley (Brook Hammond), Joan Blair (Helene LaSalle), Charles Halton (Harry Hammond), Cy Kendall (Brad Doland), Juanita Quigley (Rose Murphy), Mary Gordon (Ma Murphy), Billy Benedict (Jerry Murphy), Matt McHugh (Cy Walsh), Marie Blake (Sally Lukens).

Bank clerk Hubbard spends a humble vacation in Indianapolis and returns home to the excitement of his Ohio boarding house. He hears a radio report about a girl found murdered in Indianapolis and a description of the killer. He, of course, fits the bill and is quickly looked upon with suspicion. The deaths of a couple more girls implicate him even further, weakening his alibi with each death. Everyone turns against him, firmly convinced that he is the murderer–perhaps the victim of some Jekyll and Hyde complex. His credibility hits bottom when another murder is committed, but before any action can be taken against him the real killer confesses. A compelling crime thriller which keeps one guessing until the end.

p, George Blair; d, Howard Bretherton; w, Gertrude Walker (based on her story); ph, Jack Marta; ed, Ralph Dixon; md, Morton Scott; art d, Russell Kimball.

Crime   (PR:A   MPAA:NR)

WHISPERING GHOSTS*½   (1942) 57m FOX bw

Milton Berle (H.H. Van Buren), Brenda Joyce (Elizabeth Woods), John Shelton (David Courtland), John Carradine (Nobert/Long Jack), Willie Best (Euclid White), Edmund MacDonald (Gilpin), Arthur Hohl (Inspector Norris), Grady Sutton (Jonathan Flack), Milton Parsons (Dr. Bascomb), Abner Biberman (Mack Wolf), Renie Riano (Meg), Charles Halton (Gruber), Harry Hayden (Conroy).

Listless spoof in which Berle plays a radio entertainer who solves crimes for his listeners. He investigates the murder of a sea captain which occurred aboard a vessel 10 years before, visiting the ship to try to find some clues and discovering that it appears to be haunted. This premise was not unlike the one used in the Red Skelton vehicle WHISTLING IN THE DARK, but lacks the same ingenuity in terms of plot development, wasting Berle's talent.

p, Sol M. Wurtzel; d, Alfred Werker; w, Lou Breslow (based on a story by Philip McDonald); ph, Lucien Ballard; ed, Alexander Troffey; md, Emil Newman; art d, Richard Day, Lewis Creber.

Mystery/Crime   (PR:A   MPAA:NR)

WHISPERING JOE**   (1969, Jap.) 90m Saito/Shochiku Films of
                                    America bw (SASAYASHI NO JOE)

Jin Nakayama (Joe), Reiko Asoo (Kanako), Manami Fuji (Woman), Akira Nishimura (Her Husband), Kinzo Shin (Tramp).

Nakayama plays a worthless young man with a willing meal ticket in a fashion model who goes to extremes to provide for her lover. When he finds himself in a sticky situation because of an affair with another woman that leads to murder, Nakayama comes up with the preposterous scheme of building a raft and sailing to Brazil, this being the land he feels holds his fate. It is very unlikely that he will ever reach its borders, but still he takes off on the flimsy raft.

p,d,w,ph&m, Koichi Saito (Shochiku Grandscope); art d, Kuninobu Yasuda.

Drama   (PR:O   MPAA:NR)

WHISPERING SKULL, THE**   (1944) 56m PRC bw

Tex Ritter, Dave O'Brien, Guy Wilkerson, Denny Burke, I. Stanford Jolley, Henry Hall, George Morrell, Edward Cassidy, Bob Kortman, Wen Wright.

This entry in the Texas Rangers series sees our heroes hot on the trail of a mysterious killer dubbed "The Whispering Skull" who rides at night to dispose of his enemies. When a small-town sheriff is murdered by the phantom rider, the rangers set out to capture the evildoer by disguising one of their members as the killer, thus forcing the real "Whispering Skull" to reveal himself. (See TEXAS RANGER series, Index.)

p, Arthur Alexander; d, Elmer Clifton; w, Harry Fraser; ph, Edward Kull; m, Lee Zahler; ed, Hugh Winn.

Western   (PR:A   MPAA:NR)

WHISPERING SMITH***½   (1948) 88m PAR c

Alan Ladd (Luke "Whispering" Smith), Robert Preston (Murray Sinclaire), Brenda Marshall (Marian Sinclaire), Donald Crisp (Barney Rebstock), William Demarest (Bill Dansing), Fay Holden (Emmy Dansing), Murvyn Vye (Blake Barton), Frank Faylen (Whitey DuSang), John Eldredge (George McCloud), Robert Wood (Leroy Barton), J. Farrell MacDonald (Bill Baggs), Don Barclay (Dr. Sawbuck), Will Wright (Sheriff McSwiggens), Eddy Waller (Conductor), Gary Gray (Boy), Bob Kortman (Gabby Barton), Ashley Cowan, Jimmie Dundee, Ray Teal.

A big box office success for Ladd, WHISPERING SMITH was billed by Paramount as being his first western and his first picture in color. He was cast as a real-life, gun-toting railroad detective whose low-voice and quiet demeanor earned him the monicker "Whispering Smith." The film opens with a spectacular credit sequence over a great western panorama–complete with green valleys, rolling hills, snow-capped mountains, and a powerful blue sky–into which Ladd rides on horseback. A gun enters the frame, takes aim at Ladd, and shoots his horse out from under him. We then learn from a group of railroad men of the legend of "Whispering Smith," the detective in charge of investigating a recent rash of train robberies. Ladd, without his horse, hops a ride from the train, and before long bandits strike. Ladd is wounded in the battle that ensues and is knocked from the train, landing unconscious on the ground. He is found by Marshall, who brings him home to her ranch where she tends to his wounds. It turns out that she is a past love of Ladd's, a secret which they both keep from her husband, Preston, a railway employee who keeps bad company. Preston offers to let Ladd stay on as ranch foreman, but Ladd declines. Instead, he begins investigating Preston, who suspiciously lives a comfortable ranch life on a meager railway salary. Before long, Preston is caught looting a wrecked railway car and is fired from his job, turning to a full- time life of crime as a member of the train robbing Rebstock gang led by Crisp. Preston gets deeper in trouble when one of Crisp's gang, the devilish Faylen, murders a postal employee and then kills Crisp himself. Ladd tracks Preston back to the ranch and they exchange gunfire. Ladd fills Preston with lead and is about to tend to the wound when the dying man pulls a concealed gun. Before he can squeeze the trigger, however, he collapses and dies, leaving Ladd to resume his past romance with Marshall. Pre-dating the quintessential Ladd western hero, SHANE, by five years, WHISPERING SMITH shows a striking similarity between the two–his calm but dangerous demeanor, his devotion to friends, and his ability to be gentle to women (both Marshall's and Jean Arthur's character names, coincidentally, are Marian) and children. While this was Ladd's first color feature, as Paramount boasted, it was not his first western. Ladd had appeared eight years earlier as a bit player in LIGHT OF WESTERN STARS and IN OLD MISSOURI. As in Spearman's novel, the characters of this film are drawn from whole cloth. Ladd is essaying the real-life super lawman Joe Lefors, while Preston's role is loosely based on the notorious badman Butch Cassidy, and Faylen, playing the albino, Whitey DuSang, is recreating one of the worst killer gunmen of the Old West, Harvey Logan, who followed Cassidy in a series of spectacular train and bank holdups committed by the infamous Wild Bunch.

p, Mel Epstein; d, Leslie Fenton; w, Frank Butler, Karl Kamb (based on the novel by Frank H. Spearman); ph, Ray Rennehan (Technicolor); m, Adolph Deutsch; ed, Archie Marshek; art d, Hans Dreier, Walter Tyler; spec eff, Gordon Jennings, Farciot Edouart; m/l, "Laramie," Jay Livingston, Ray Evans.

Western   (PR:A   MPAA:NR)

WHISPERING SMITH HITS LONDON
    (SEE: WHISPERING SMITH VERSUS SCOTLAND YARD, 1852, Brit.)

WHISPERING SMITH SPEAKS*½   (1935) 65m FOX bw

George O'Brien (Whispering Smith), Irene Ware (Nan Roberts), Kenneth Thomson (J. Wesley Hunt), Maude Allen (Mother Roberts), Spencer Charters (Cal Stone), Vic Potel (Bill Prouty), Edward Keane (Rebstock), Frank Sheridan (Gordon Harrington, Sr.), William V. Mong (Blake), Maurice Cass (C. Luddington Colfax).

An oater with a bent toward laughter has O'Brien the son of a president of a railroad who prefers to work for a living instead of taking the easy way out. This allows him to strike up a friendship with Ware as a woman all set on selling her land cheaply until O'Brien lets it be known that it is rich in tungsten ore and therefore very valuable.

p, Sol Lesser; d, David Howard; w, Dan Jarrett, Don Swift (based on the story by Frank H. Spearman); ph, Frank B. Good; ed, Robert Crandall.

Western   (PR:A   MPAA:NR)

WHISPERING SMITH VERSUS SCOTLAND YARD*½
    (1952, Brit.) 77m Hammer-Lesser/RKO bw (GB: WHISPERING SMITH
                                    HITS LONDON)

Richard Carlson (Whispering Smith), Greta Gynt (Louise), Herbert Lom (Ford), Rona Anderson (Anne), Alan Wheatley (Hector Reith), Dora Bryan (Miss La Fosse), Reginald Beckwith (Manson), Daniel Wherry (Dr. Taren), Michael Ward (Reception Clerk), Danny Green (Cecil Fleming), James Raglan (Superintendent Meaker), Stuart Nichol, Laurence Naismith, Christine Silver, Vic Wise, Middleton Woods, Ben Williams, Sidney Vivian, Tony Frost, June Bardsley, Michael Hogarth, John Wynn, Anthony Warner, Ian Wilson, Stanley Baker, Lionel Grose, John Kyle, John Singer.

One of the many yank-in-London tales so unremittingly popular with

Britons through the years, this has inept American detective Carlson–vacationing in England–recruited by a secretary, Anderson, to investigate the supposed suicidal death of her employer's daughter. He stumbles into the solution to the mystery, discovering that the "victim" is still alive, having visited her identity on a corpse in order to escape extortion charges. Faced with exposure, the "dead" Gynt tries to kill Carlson, but only succeeds in shooting her accomplice, Lom.

p, Anthony Hinds, Julian Lesser; d, Frances Searle; w, Steve Fisher (based on a story by John Gilling and the character created by Frank H. Spearman); ph, Walter Harvey; ed, James Needs; md, Frank Spencer.

Mystery   **(PR:A MPAA:NR)**

WHISPERING TONGUES*   (1934, Brit.) 55m REA/RKO bw

Reginald Tate (Alan Norton), Jane Welsh (Claudia Mayland), Russell Thorndike (Fenwick), Malcolm Keen (Inspector Dawley), Felix Aylmer (Supt. Fulton), Charles Carson (Roger Mayland), Tonie Edgar Bruce (Lady Weaver), Victor Stanley (Steward).

Rigid crime melodrama starring Tate as a young man who returns from a trip abroad to discover that his father has been driven to suicide by a group of men who wanted him dead. Gripped by an eye-for-an-eye fervor, Tate becomes determined to avenge his father. He falls in love with the daughter of the man responsible for his father's death and abandons the murderous aspects of his plan, settling for a financial revenge by stealing some valuable jewels from the evildoer. Silly and uninteresting.

p, Julius Hagen; d, George Pearson; w, H. Fowler Mear (based on a story by Bernard Mainwaring).

Crime   **(PR:A MPAA:NR)**

WHISPERING WINDS*   (1929) 65m TS bw

Patsy Ruth Miller (Dora), Malcolm McGregor (Jim), Eve Southern (Eve Benton), Eugenie Besserer (Jim's Mother), James Marcus (Pappy).

When his singing sweetheart (Southern) leaves fisherman McGregor and his Maine home town, he soon finds and marries Miller. She, however, is unconvinced of his love, and when Southern returns for a visit she fears that the old flame will reignite. Instead, Southern is aloof and condescending and McGregor becomes sure that he loves Miller. Only later does Miller discover that Southern was pretending not to care for McGregor so he would forget her and be happy. Not terribly interesting part-talkie.

d, James Flood; w, Charles Logue, Jean Plannette (Based on a story by Plannette); ph, Harry Jackson, Jack MacKenzie; m, Erno Rapee; ed, James Morley; m/l, "When I think of You," Vincent Rose.

Drama   **(PR:A MPAA:NR)**

WHISTLE AT EATON FALLS½**   (1951) 96m COL bw

Lloyd Bridges (Brad Adams), Dorothy Gish (Mrs. Doubleday), Carleton Carpenter (Eddie Talbot), Murray Hamilton (Al Webster), James Westerfield (Joe London), Lenore Lonergan (Abby), Russell Hardie (Dwight Hawkins), Helen Shields (Miss Russell), Doro Merande (Miss Pringle), Ernest Borgnine (Bill Street), Parker Fennelly (Issac), Diana Douglas (Ruth Adams), Anne Francis (Jean), Anne Seymour (Mary London), Joe Foley (Horace Dunbar), Donald McKee (Daniel Doubleday), Arthur O'Connell (Jim Brewster), Rev. Robert A. Dunn (Rev. Payson), Victor Sutherland (Glenn Sewell), Herbert J. Moss (Mr. Peabody), Lawrence Paquin (Ted Wagner), Andrew W. Donaldson (Mr. Gibson), Seth Arnold (Sheriff), Joe Sullivan (Pete), Verne Davenport (Verne), John Farrell (Fred), James Nolan (George Peck), William Kent (Dick Wagner), Bob Maher (Jack).

A well-meaning, though not entirely successful, story of labor-management relations opens in Eaton Falls, New Hampshire, where the president of the local plastics plant has been killed in a airplane crash. Bridges, a union leader, is promoted to the position and finds he has inherited a wealth of trouble. The plant needs to be more cost effective, and therefore faces the unpleasant task of laying off workers. Knowing what it is like to be on the workers' side of the fence, Bridges tries to help save some jobs, but the union, led by Hamilton, disagrees with his methods. Unable to come to an understanding, the factory is forced to close down. Eventually, and all too easily, the dispute is settled when big orders arrive for the company's products. This, coupled with some time-and-money-saving machinery, allows Bridges to bring back all the employees, settling all squabbles between union and management. The film presents some interesting problems and intelligent questions about the roles and relations between management and workers. Unfortunately, the script never delves deep enough into the issues it raises, opting for pat, simplistic solutions that just don't ring true. However, Siodmak's direction overcomes some of this with a gritty, documentary-style direction. Filmed on location in Eaton Falls, the production used local laborers as extras in factory scenes as well. Gish, as the president's widow who promotes Bridges, gives an intelligent presentation with her small part.

p, Louis deRochemont; d, Robert Siodmak; w, Lemist Esler, Virginia Shaler (based on the research of J. Sterling Livingston); ph, Joseph Brun; m, Louis Applebaum; ed, Angelo Ross; md, Jack Schaindlin; art d, Herbert Andrews;

m/l, "Ev'ry Other Day," Carleton Carpenter.

Drama   **(PR:A MPAA:NR)**

WHISTLE DOWN THE WIND*½   (1961, Brit.) 98m Beaver-Allied Film Makers/Pathe-America bw

Hayley Mills (Kathy Bostock), Bernard Lee (Mr. Bostock), Alan Bates (Arthur Blakey, the Man), Diane Holgate (Nan Bostock), Alan Barnes (Charles Bostock), Norman Bird (Eddie), Diane Clare (Miss Lodge), Patricia Heneghan (Salvation Army Girl), Elsie Wagstaff (Auntie Dorothy), John Arnatt (Teesdale), Hamilton Dyce (Reeves), Howard Douglas (Weaver), Roy Holder (Jackie), Gerald Sim (Wilcox), Ronald Hines (Police Constable Thurstow), Michael Lees, Michael Raghan (Civil Defense Workers), Barry Dean (Raymond), May Barton (Villager), Christine Ashworth, John Bodne, Doreena Clark, Keith Clement, Pamela Lonsdale, Judy Ollerneshaw, Robert Palmer, Lois Read, Nigel Stafford (The Disciples), Anne Newby, Julie Jackson (The Latecomers).

Bryan Forbes' directorial debut was a beauty. Not satisfied to cut his teeth on a proven commercial vehicle, he used the unique novel by Mary Hayley Bell as the basis for this unique film. In today's world, anyone proclaiming himself to be Jesus Christ would be whisked away by the authorities before many moments passed. And children today are a lot keener on life's realities than they were a quarter of a century ago, perhaps due to the increased power of television. But on a grim Lancashire farm 25 years ago, a man claiming to be Christ wins the trust of three motherless children who have been strongly influenced by their strict religious training. Mills is the eldest of Lee's children. The other two are Barnes and Holgate. The trio saves some cuddly kittens from drowning and decides to hide them in the family barn where they find a bearded man hiding. Beards are not common in that area and when Mills asks the wild-eyed fellow who he is, he replies, "Jesus Christ," more as a mutter than an answer. Then he falls to the straw from hunger and fatigue. The truth of the matter is that the man, played superbly by Bates, is a killer on the run but Mills has already been influenced earlier when Heneghan, a Salvation Army employee, told her that Jesus would take care of the kittens and that they would be safe from harm. So when Mills meets Bates in the barn and the kittens are nearby and still happily mewing, Mills is convinced. Word of Christ in the barn travels like wildfire and the other children in the village bring Bates food, wine, and other gifts, eager to get on his good side. The kids keep the secret from their parents in the wondrous way kids have of doing such things. They fear that the adults will take Christ away, the way it was done 2000 years before. Bates is betrayed by accident when, at Barnes' birthday party, Holgate blurts the secret out to her aunt, Wagstaff. The cops are called at once and move in on Bates. By this time, his attitude has mellowed under the love and adoration of the children and he surrenders meekly, rather than endanger the lives of any of the youngsters. He stretches his arms out in surrender and it almost looks as though he is to be crucified. It's done subtly but the obvious implication is there. Two children arrive as Bates is taken away, and Mills sagely says, "You missed him this time, but he'll come again." Mills had been a staunch believer in Bates' divinity but 6-year-old Barnes didn't buy it when one of the kittens died and Bates didn't prevent it. This could have been a mawkish movie if it had gone over the edge but Forbes kept matters realistic and still managed to enfold several bits of New Testament symbolism into the picture without hammering anyone on the head. The novel's author was Mills' mother (and wife of actor John Mills) and although there is no proof that she wrote the book with her daughter in mind, the youngster was surely the right choice for the role. It was her fourth movie, she having already completed TIGER BAY, POLLYANNA, and THE PARENT TRAP before this. Bates was wonderful in his difficult role. Prior to this, he had established himself as a stage actor and had appeared in THE ENTERTAINER the year before in his debut. Holgate and Barnes are so delicious in their naivete that they almost steal the film from Mills. It's an allegory and those are usually dull and dreadful but that's not the case in this, the second film produced by actor Richard Attenborough, who later became the Oscar-winning director of GANDHI.

p, Richard Attenborough; d, Bryan Forbes; w, Keith Waterhouse, Willis Hall (based on the novel by Mary Hayley Bell); ph, Arthur Ibbetson; m, Malcolm Arnold; ed, Max Benedict; md, Arnold; art d, Ray Simm; makeup, Geoffrey Rodway.

Drama   **Cas.**   **(PR:A MPAA:NR)**

WHISTLE STOP*½   (1946) 85m UA bw

George Raft (Kenny), Ava Gardner (Mary), Victor McLaglen (Gillo), Tom Conway (Lew Lentz), Jorga Curtright (Fran), Jane Nigh (Josie), Florence Bates (Molly Veech), Charles Drake (Ernie), Charles Judels (Sam Veech), Carmel Myers (Estelle), Jimmy Ames (The Barker).

A second-rate gangster film with a fine cast but no spark. Gardner is from a tank town. She's gone to the big city and come back with money in her purse and mink on her back. When she departed, she'd been having a torrid affair with low-life Raft but he wouldn't change his lazy ways, so she left him. Now, she hopes he's learned his lesson and will give up his play-cards-at night and sleep-all-day existence. Time hasn't changed Raft, though, and he is still mired in his ways, so Gardner turns her attention to Conway, the local club owner who has the money and the time to lavish his attentions on her.

Raft can't bear the relationship Gardner is having with Conway so he is easy fodder for McLaglen, Conway's former bartender. The two men conspire to ambush and kill Conway, but when Gardner finds out what's in the offing, she prevails on Raft to give up the idea and start life anew in a legitimate fashion. Now that Gardner has gone back to Raft, Conway becomes the heavy and the hotelkeeper-saloon boniface concocts a plan to eliminate both Raft and McLaglen. He plans a robbery of his own premises, kills his own bouncer, and makes it look as though Raft and McLaglen are the murderers. The police get to the scene of the crime and there's a shootout during which Raft is mildly wounded. McLaglen and Raft race away to the nearest big town in the Midwest, St. Louis, and they lay low. Then McLaglen, who suspects that Conway was behind the robbery-murder, returns to the whistle stop of Ashbury (the state is not mentioned). McLaglen gets to the cafe owned by Conway, there's a gun battle, and both men are killed. Raft is cleared and Gardner leaves the town to join Raft in St. Louis where they will start life anew. Only one of three pictures directed in the U.S. by Moguy, a Russian-born and French-educated filmmaker, it was not as good as his other two, PARIS AFTER DARK and ACTION IN ARABIA. After the war, he went back to France and wound up running the film department of the International Red Cross before his death at the age of 77. Silent screen star Carmel Myers, the daughter of a San Francisco rabbi and one of the many early movie stars of Jewish heritage, does a small role. She'd been off the screen for more than a decade (except for a cameo in LADY FOR A NIGHT, 1941). Actress Jorga Curtwright had a brief career before marrying writer Sidney Sheldon. Although Gardner had appeared in several movies and was already divorced after a brief marriage to Mickey Rooney, this was the film that gave her the opportunity to play in THE KILLERS and shoot to stardom.

p, Seymour Nebenzal; d, Leonide Moguy; w, Philip Yordan (based on the novel by Maritta M. Wolff); ph, Russell Metty; m, Dimitri Tiomkin; ed, Gregg Tallas; md, Dimitri Tiomkin; art d, Rudi Feld, George Van Marter; set d, Alfred Kegerris; spec eff, R.O. Binger; ch, Jack Crosby.

Crime Drama   Cas.   (PR:A-C MPAA:NR)

WHISTLER, THE***   (1944) 59m COL bw

Richard Dix (*Earl Conrad*), J. Carrol Naish (*The Killer*), Gloria Stuart (*Alice Walker*), Alan Dinehart (*Gorman*), Joan Woodbury (*Toni Vigran*), Cy Kendall (*Bartender*), Trevor Bardette (*The Thief*), Don Costello (*Lefty Vigran*), Clancy Cooper (*Briggs*), Byron Foulger (*Flophouse Clerk*), Robert E. Keane (*Charles McNear*), George Lloyd (*Bill Tomley*), Charles Coleman (*Jennings*), Robert E. Homans (*Dock Watchman*), Otto Forrest (*The Whistler*).

The popular radio series was brought to the screen in this low-budget programmer. Dix plays a rich industrialist who learns that his wife has drowned and, devastated, contacts Costello and has him put out a contract on his own life. Costello speaks with Naish, a professional killer, who takes up the contract. Soon after, Costello is killed by police and Dix learns that his wife is not dead after all, but held by the Japanese on a Pacific island. He tries to cancel the contract, but cannot. Now he must avoid the killer, who has decided that he will murder Dix by frightening him to death. Several times he narrowly escapes death when the mysterious sound of "The Whistler" warns him, although this figure, who also narrates the drama, is never seen. In the end Dix is rescued from his fate by his secretary, Stuart. Director Castle made his first big impression with this tense little B programmer. Assigned the script by Harry Cohn, Castle recalled in his autobiography: "I tried every effect I could dream up to create a mood of terror: low-key lighting, wide-angle lenses to give an eerie feeling, and a hand-held camera in many of the important scenes to give a sense of reality to the horror. To achieve a mood of desperation, I insisted that Dix give up smoking and go on a diet. This made him nervous and irritable, particularly when I gave him early-morning calls and kept him waiting on the set–sometimes for an entire–day before using him in a scene. He was constantly off-center, restless, fidgety, and nervous as a cat. When I finally used him in a scene, I'd make him do it over and over until he was ready to explode. It achieved the desired effect–that of a man haunted by fear and trying to keep himself from being murdered." The film got rave reviews and Castle, at the beginning of his career, and Dix, at the end of his, worked together on two more films in the series. Forrest is the disembodied voice, who never appeared in any of the seven subsequent films. Castle went on to direct a great many very forgettable schlock pictures (SLAVES OF BABYLON, THE LAW VS. BILLY THE KID, THIRTEEN FRIGHTENED GIRLS, etc.) along with a few memorable ones (THE HOUSE ON HAUNTED HILL, HOMICIDAL, and THE NIGHT WALKER), but never did anything else as effective as this. Dix is excellent as the man terrorized and unable to do anything to stop it. The production values, considering that the film was shot on a budget of less than $75,000, are excellent. A perfect example of the art that could be created within the strictures of studio B-unit production.

p, Rudolph C. Flothow; d, William Castle; w, Eric Taylor (based on a story by J. Donald Wilson, suggested by the radio program "The Whistler"); ph, James S. Brown; m, Wilbur Hatch; ed, Jerome Thoms; art d, George Van Marter; set d, Sidney Clifford.

Crime   (PR:A MPAA:NR)

WHISTLIN' DAN**   (1932) 65m TIF/SONO-Art-World Wide bw

Ken Maynard, Joyzelle Joyner, Georges Renevant, Don Terry, Harlan E. Knight, Jack Rockwell, Jessie Arnold, Bud McClure, Lew Meehan, Merrill McCormick, Roy Bucko, Buck Bucko, Frank Ellis, Hank Bell, Iron Eyes Cody, Wesley Giraud, Tarzan the Horse.

Decent western in which Maynard becomes part of a gang in order to avenge the murder of his brother at the hands of one of the outlaws. Quite a bit of effort went into establishing camera angles and developing a script that was not an exact replica of dozens of other outings.

p, Phil Goldstone; d, Phil Rosen; w, Stuart Anthony; ph, Ira J. Morgan; ed, Rose Loewinger.

Western   Cas.   (PR:A MPAA:NR)

WHISTLING BULLETS**   (1937) 58m Ambassador bw

Kermit Maynard (*Larry Graham*), Jack Ingram (*Tim Raymond*), Harlene [Harley] Wood (*Anita Saunders*), Maston Williams (*Ace Beldon*), Bruce Mitchell (*Capt. Saunders*), Karl Hackett (*Dave Stone*), Sherry Tansey (*Sam*), Cliff Parkinson (*Bart*), Cherokee Alcorn (*Karl*).

Better than average oater fare in which Maynard plays a Texas Ranger placed in prison to befriend a crook incarcerated for a spell, and thus to gain access to the rest of the gang as well as some missing money. Though made on an extremely limited budget, taut direction and a well developed script proves what can be accomplished when ingenuity instead of money is relied on.

p, Maurice Conn; d, John English; w, Joseph O'Donnell (based on a story by James Oliver Curwood); ph, Jack Greenhalgh; ed, Richard G. Wray; m/l, Connie Lee.

Western   Cas.   (PR:A MPAA:NR)

WHISTLING HILLS*½   (1951) 58m Frontier/MON bw

Johnny Mack Brown (*Johnny*), Jimmy [James] Ellison (*Dave Holland*), Noel Neill (*Beth Fairchild*), Lee Roberts (*Slade*), Stan [I. Stanford] Jolley (*Chet Norman*), Marshall Reed (*Claine*), Lane Bradford (*Cassidy*), Pamela Duncan (*Cora*), Bud Osborne (*Pete*), Pierce Lyden, Frank Ellis, Ray Jones, Merrill McCormack.

Nothing was added to distract from the usual formula as Brown plays a cowpoke who is pretty handy with the gun, offering his assistance to the stage line owner in order to run down a gang of masked highwaymen. Ellison plays the sheriff who must swallow his pride when receiving assistance from the guns of Brown. By this time in his career Brown was on a downswing, his physical attributes no longer those of an oater hero, and audiences were making more demands in terms of western entertainment.

p, Vincent M. Fennelly; d, Derwin Abrahams; w, Fred Myton (based on a story by Jack Lewis); ph, Ernest Miller; ed, Sammy Fields.

Western   (PR:A MPAA:NR)

WHISTLING IN BROOKLYN**   (1943) 87m MGM bw

Red Skelton (*Wally Benton*), Ann Rutherford (*Carol Lambert*), Jean Rogers (*Jean Pringle*), "Rags" Ragland (*Chester*), Ray Collins (*Grover Kendall*), Henry O'Neill (*Inspector Holcomb*), William Frawley (*Detective Ramsey*), Sam Levene (*Creeper*), Arthur Space (*Detective MacKenzie*), Robert Emmett O'Connor (*Detective Finnigan*), Steve Geray (*Whitey*), Howard Freeman (*Steve Conlon*), Tom Dillon (*Manager of the Beavers*), Garry Owen, Anthony Caruso, The Brooklyn Dodgers.

The third and final film in a series starring Skelton as a radio crime-solving pundit reprised many of the elements found in WHISTLING IN THE DARK (1941) and WHISTLING IN DIXIE (1942). A cop-killer with the cognomen "constant reader" preys on the police until screwball sleuth Skelton runs him down on the baseball diamond. As a bearded Brooklyn baseball player, the disguised detective delivers imperiled inspector O'Neill from the menacing murderer. Made by the same production team that was responsible for the first two entries in the series. (See WALLY BENTON series, Index.)

p, George Haight; d, S. Sylvan Simon; w, Nat Perrin, Wilkie Mahoney; ph, Lester White; m, George Basserman; ed, Ben Lewis; art d, Cedric Gibbons; spec eff, Warren Newcombe.

Comedy   (PR:A MPAA:NR)

WHISTLING IN DIXIE**   (1942) 74m MGM bw

Red Skelton (*Wally Benton*), Ann Rutherford (*Carol Lambert*), George Bancroft (*Sheriff Claude Stagg*), Guy Kibbee (*Judge George Lee*), Diana Lewis (*Ellamae Downs*), Peter Whitney (*Frank V. Baille*), "Rags" Ragland (*Chester Conway/Lester Conway*), Celia Travers (*Hattie Lee*), Lucien Littlefield (*Cpl. Lucken*), Louis Mason (*Lem*), Mark Daniels (*Martin Gordon*), Pierre Watkin (*Doctor*), Emmett Vogan (*Radio Producer*), Hobart Cavanaugh (*Panky*).

Skelton, as the radio series sleuth known as "The Wolf" (his airwave appearances are heralded by a vulpine howl), is vamped into traveling to Georgia by his sweetheart Rutherford, who hopes he can help a troubled ex-sorority sister. The latter's difficulty involves a hidden cache of gold dating from the Civil War and the efforts of a local band of insiders to keep quiet about the cache. Taken to be a treasure-seeker, Skelton is appropriately menaced and chased by backwoods bandits. Ragland plays a dual role as a reformed convict and a murderous escapee. Second in the slapstick series which includes WHISTLING IN THE DARK (1941) and WHISTLING IN BROOKLYN (1943). (See WALLY BENTON series, Index.)

p, George Haight; d, S. Sylvan Simon; w, Nat Perrin, Wilkie Mahoney; ph, Clyde de Vinna; ed, Frank Sullivan; art d, Cedric Gibbons.

Comedy   **(PR:A   MPAA:NR)**

WHISTLING IN THE DARK**   (1933) 78m MGM bw

Ernest Truex (Wallace Porter), Una Merkel (Toby Van Buren), Edward Arnold (Jake Dillon), John Miljan (Charlie), C. Henry Gordon (Ricco Lombardo), Johnny Hines (Slim Scanlon), Joseph Cawthorn (Otto Barfuss), Nat Pendleton (Joe), Tenen Holtz (Herman), Marcelle Corday (Hilda).

Aspiring detective-story writer Truex, eloping with Merkel, wanders into the den of a baron of booze, where–to impress his bride–he regales the crime kingpin and his henchmen with the plot for a perfect murder. The nabob of the underworld decides to use Truex's scheme to safely eliminate a rival salon of speakeasies. Realizing what they have unwittingly wrought, Truex and Merkel labor mightily to prevent the proposed crime and to escape from its presumed perpetrators. Truex's first talking picture is a fine farce. Writer-director Nugent was, at the time of production, himself a leading man at the studio.

d&w, Elliott Nugent (based on the play by Laurence Gross, Edward Childs Carpenter); ph, Norbert Brodine; ed, Ben Lewis.

Crime/Comedy   **(PR:A   MPAA:NR)**

WHISTLING IN THE DARK***   (1941) 77m MGM bw

Red Skelton (Wally Benton), Ann Rutherford (Carol Lambert), Virginia Grey (Fran Post), Conrad Veidt (Joseph Jones), "Rags" Ragland (Sylvester), Eve Arden (Buzz Baker), Don Douglas (Gordon Thomas), Don Costello (Moose Green), Paul Stanton (Jennings), William Tannen (Robert Graves), Reed Hadley (Beau Smith), Lloyd Corrigan (Harvey Upshaw), Henry O'Neill (Phillip Post), George Carleton (Deputy Commissioner O'Neill), Mariska Aldrich (Hilda), Will Lee (Herman), John Piccori (Gatekeeper), Joe Devlin (Taxi Driver), Ruth Robinson (Mrs. Robinson), John Wald (Announcer's Voice), Ken Christy (Inspector), Betty Farrington (Mrs. Moriarity), Paul Ellis (Captain), Dora Clement (Mrs. Upshaw), James Adamson (Attendant), Inez Cooper (Stewardess), Emmett Vogan (Producer), Barbara Bedford (Local Operator), Lester Dorr (Dispatcher), Mark Daniels (Copilot), Leon Tyler (Gerry), Mel Ruick (Engineer), Dorothy Adams (Mrs. Farrell), Jenny Mac (Mrs. Kendall), John Dilson (Vanderhoff), Billy Bletcher (Effects Man), Larry Steers (Studio Manager), Ronnie Rondell (Waiter), Brick Sullivan, Al Hill, Robert E. Homans (Policemen).

Red Skelton became a star with this surprise hit in which he plays a radio sleuth known as "The Fox" ("Ah-wooooo, I'm the Fox!"). The film opens with a spooky scene on the moonlit grounds of Silver Haven, a mansion where Veidt heads a phony religious cult. He conducts funeral ceremonies for one of his devotees, Clement, and believes that he is to collect her million dollar fortune. A spanner is thrown into the works, however, when Veidt learns that the money is still controlled by Corrigan, Clement's nephew, until his death. Ragland, another of Veidt's followers, suggests they murder Corrigan. Veidt hits upon the scheme of kidnaping Skelton, a famous radio detective, and forcing him to work out the perfect murder. To further convince Skelton, Veidt also abducts Rutherford, Skelton's radio actress girl friend, and Grey, the daughter of Skelton's sponsor. Unwillingly, Skelton plans a murder involving an undetectable poison to be put in Corrigan's toothpaste. Veidt's henchmen put the plan into operation, leaving Skelton, Rutherford, and Grey locked in a room at the mansion with the phone wires cut, and the door guarded by huge, ominous housekeeper Aldrich. The three work out a scheme in which they somehow connect the phone wires to the radio and do their broadcast and call the police from where they're held, putting in subtle (and not-so-subtle) warnings to Corrigan ("Do not ... brush... your teeth!") who is on an airplane flying across the country. The plan works, Corrigan doesn't brush his teeth, the police arrive to rescue Skelton and the others, and Veidt and his followers are carted off to the pokey. Skelton had been signed to an MGM contract a couple of years earlier and had made some appearances as comic relief in various vehicles, as well as creating a running character in the DR. KILDARE series, but this was his first starring vehicle, actually a remake of a 1933 film with Ernest Truex, and MGM found it had a surprise hit on their hands. Skelton is as good here as he ever got, clever and funny, and the others do their jobs well, especially Veidt and Arden, Skelton's manager. Two sequels followed, WHISTLING IN DIXIE (1942) and WHISTLING IN BROOKLYN (1943). (See WALLY BENTON series, Index.)

p, George Haight; d, S. Sylvan Simon; w, Robert MacGunigle, Harry Clork, Albert Mannheimer (based on the play by Laurence Gross, Edward Childs Carpenter); ph, Sidney Wagner; ed, Frank E. Hull; art d, Cedric Gibbons.

Comedy/Mystery   **(PR:A   MPAA:NR)**

WHITE ANGEL, THE*½   (1936) 75m FN/WB-FN bw

Kay Francis (Florence Nightingale), Ian Hunter (Fuller), Donald Woods (Charles Cooper), Nigel Bruce (Dr. West), Donald Crisp (Dr. Hunt), Henry O'Neill (Dr. Scott), George Curzon (Sir Sidney Herbert), Secretary of State, Phoebe Foster (Elizabeth Herbert), Charles Croker-King (Mr. Nightingale), Georgia Caine (Mrs. Nightingale), Billy Mauch (Tommy), Lillian Kemble-Cooper (Parthe Nightingale), Ara Gerald (Mrs. Ella Stevens), Montagu Love (Mr. Bullock, Under Secretary of War), Halliwell Hobbes (Lord Raglan), Frank Conroy (Mr. LeFroy), Eily Malyon (Sister Columbo), Egon Brecher (Pastor Fieldner), Barbara Leonard (Minna), Gaby Fay (Queen Victoria), Ferdinand Munier (Alexis Soyer, the Cook), Tempe Pigott (Mrs. Waters, the Nurse), Daisy Belmore, Alma Lloyd, May Beatty, Kathrin Clare Ward (Nurses), Lawrence Grant (Colonel), Nelson McDowell (Superintendent of Hospital), Eric Wilton (Servant), Robert Bolder, James May, Arthur Turner Foster (Doctors), Harry Cording (Storekeeper), Charles Irwin, Clyde Cook, Harry Allen, George Kirby (Soldiers), Vesey O'Davoren.

Another attempt by Hollywood to recreate a famous person, this follows the conventions of the genre in its humorless, arid approach, sanctifying its subject in the dullest possible way. The efforts of one brave, bullheaded woman to bring sterile conditions to the wounded during the Crimean War of the mid-19th Century, against the entrenched policies of the military-medical bureaucracy, might have been of surpassing interest save for the sterility of the script and direction. Francis is miscast as the Saint of Scutari, and the twisted history of the screenplay is little more than laughable in this bowdlerization of Strachey's biography. Worth seeing only for the coterie of fine character actors backing up the leading players.

p, Henry Blanke; d, William Dieterle; w, Michel Jacoby, Mordaunt Shairp (based on the biography by Lytton Strachey); ph, Tony Gaudio; ed, Warren Low; md, Leo F. Forbstein.

Historical Drama   **(PR:A   MPAA:NR)**

WHITE BANNERS**   (1938) 88m COS/WB bw

Claude Rains (Paul Ward), Fay Bainter (Hannah Parmalee), Jackie Cooper (Peter Trimble), Bonita Granville (Sally Ward), Henry O'Neill (Sam Trimble), Kay Johnson (Marcia Ward), James Stephenson (Thomas Bradford), J. Farrell MacDonald (Dr. Thompson), William Pawley (Joe Ellis), John Ridgely (Charles Ellis), Mary Field (Hester), Edward McWade (Sloan).

Rains is a kindly, mild-mannered chemistry professor who, with the assistance of student Cooper, invents a mechanism which causeth the iceman to goeth: an iceless icebox. The homeless Bainter, seeking shelter, is taken into Rains, domicile as cook and housekeeper. With her sagacious advice and happy homilies, she helps the lad and his mentor to overcome the crushing disappointment of the theft of their invention. With her encouragement, the two return to the workshop, where they perfect and patent an even better fridge. Bainter then makes her departure, never revealing that she is, in truth, young Cooper's mother. A truly frost-free story by inspirational author Douglas which first appeared in William Randolph Hearst's Cosmopolitan magazine and was promoted by the magnate for film adaptation by his similarly named Cosmopolitan Productions.

p, Hal B. Wallis, Henry Blanke; d, Edmond Goulding; w, Lenore Coffee, Cameron Rogers, Abem Finkel (based on the story by Lloyd C. Douglas); ph, Charles Rosher; m, Max Steiner; ed, Thomas Richards; md, Leo F. Forbstein; art d, John Hughes.

Drama   **(PR:A   MPAA:NR)**

WHITE BONDAGE*   (1937) 60m WB bw

Jean Muir (Betsy Ann), Gordon Oliver (David Graydon), Howard Phillips (Cal Sanders), Joseph King (Talcott), Harry Davenport (Pap Craig), Virginia Brissac (Sarah Talcott), Addison Richards (Kip Gillis), Cy Kendall (Rickets), Milt Kibbee (Joe Tawney), Trevor Bardette (Lon Huston), Gordon Hart (Huxley), Eddie "Rochester" Anderson (Glory), Bernice Pilot (Hannah), Vic Potel.

Crusading investigative reporter Oliver heads for the Bible Belt hoping to expose the shortweighting and usury that the wealthy planters use to virtually enslave the white sharecroppers in post-Emancipation Proclamation times. A worthy subject and an opportunity for stirring social comment are then bypassed as the film turns into a routine Bwestern-style chase picture. Oliver is saved from a ravening lynch mob by local beauty Muir–her hair colored brunette for this role, unusual for her–for the romantic but disappointing finish.

p, Bryan Foy; d, Nick Grinde; w, Anthony Coldeway (based on the story "Lords of the Land" by Coldeway); ph, L.W. O'Connell; ed, Frank Dewar.

Drama   **(PR:A   MPAA:NR)**

WHITE BUFFALO, THE*   (1977) 97m DD/UA c (AKA: HUNT TO KILL)

Charles Bronson (Wild Bill Hickok/James Otis), Jack Warden (Charlie Zane), Will Sampson (Crazy Horse/Worm), Kim Novak (Poker Jenny Schermerhorn), Clint Walker (Whistling Jack Kileen), Stuart Whitman (Winifred Coxy), Slim Pickens (Abel Pinkney), John Carradine (Amos Briggs), Cara Williams (Cassie Ollinger), Shay Duffin (Tim Brady), Douglas V. Fowley (Amos Bixby), Cliff Pellow (Pete Holt), Ed Lauter (Capt. Tom Custer), Martin Kove (Jack McCall), Scott Walker (Gyp Hook-Hand), Ed Bakey (Ben Corbett), Richard Gilliland (Cpl. Kileen), David Roy Chandler (Kid Jelly), Philip Montgomery (Wes Pugh), Linda Moon Redfearn (Black Shawl), Chief Tug Smith (Old Worm), Douglas Hume (Aaron Pratt), Cliff Carnell (Johnny Varner), Ron Thompson (Frozen Dog Pimp), Eve Brent (Frieda), Joe Roman (Silky Smith), Bert Williams (Paddy Welsh), Dan Vadis (Tall Man), Christopher Cary (Short Man), Larry Martindale (Cheyenne Bar Man), Scott Bryson, Will Walker, Gregg White (Frozen Dog Miners).

Bronson–as Wild Bill Hickock, using an alias–his sleep shattered by dreams of a gigantic albino buffalo, returns to the West, where he falls in with a number of cute character cameos and with Sampson as Chief Crazy Horse. The latter's small daughter has been killed by the buffalo, and Sampson seeks revenge. The two pursue the legendary white beast to the accompaniment of much specious philosophizing in this westernization of Herman Melville's novel *Moby Dick*. Bronson appears to have the Queequeg role to Sampson's Captain Ahab; the latter actually kills the beast with his knife when Bronson's rifle freezes during its terminal charge. Barring two made-for-TV films, this was Novak's first Hollywood feature in eight years; in the interim, she acquired an extra chin. Executive producer Dino De Laurentiis reportedly sank $5 million into this chip off the old buffalo. Not exactly confident about its reception, the producers released it in "test engagements," withholding it from formal review. Generally regarded as Bronson's worst picture to date.

p, Pancho Kohner; d, J. Lee Thompson; w, Richard Sale (based on his novel); ph, Paul Lohmann (DeLuxe Color); m, John Barry; ed, Michael F. Anderson; prod d, Tambi Larsen; set d, James I. Berkey; cos, Eric Seelig, Dennis Fill; spec eff, Richard M. Parker, Roy Downey; stunts, Ben Dobbins.

Western   Cas.   (PR:C-O MPAA:PG)

WHITE CAPTIVE   (SEE: WHITE SAVAGE, 1943)

WHITE CARGO*½   (1930, Brit.) 80 Neo-Art/Harold Auten bw

Leslie Faber (Weston), John Hamilton (Ashley), Maurice Evans (Langford), Sebastian Smith (Doctor), Humberstone Wright (Missionary), Henry de Vries (Skipper), George Turner (Mate), Tom Helmore (Worthing), Gypsy Rhouma (Tondelayo).

The old standard expatriate drama which has a weak-willed youngster among the Britons going to seed in the damp heat of a West African rubber plantation, boozing and consorting with native girls. In this polemic anent the evils of miscegenation, young English expatriate Evans initially attempts to bring civilization to the bush by hanging curtains in his hovel and keeping a stiff upper lip while the bibulous doctor, Smith, wonders how long the lad can last. Caustic plantation manager Faber taunts the boy who, in desperation, turns to sexy half-caste Rhouma. Striving to maintain a civilized veneer, Evans proposes marriage to the semi-savage girl. In the theatrical lexicon of the early 1900s, half a caste was worse than none, so the libidinous lady prepares to poison her new husband. Caught in the act by Faber, she is forced to drink the fatal potion herself. Broken in mind and spirit, young Evans is shipped homeward, the WHITE CARGO of the title. The Hollywood version of 1942 was better. The project had originally been scheduled for Hollywood production, but a zealous Hays Office forced it overseas.

p&d, J.B. Williams, Arthur Barnes; w, Williams (based on the play by Leon Gordon and the novel by Vera Simonton); ph, Karl Puth.

Drama   (PR:C MPAA:NR)

WHITE CARGO*   (1942) 90m MGM bw

Hedy Lamarr (Tondelayo), Walter Pidgeon (Harry Witzel), Frank Morgan (Doctor), Richard Carlson (Langford), Reginald Owen (Skipper), Henry O'Neill (Rev. Roberts), Bramwell Fletcher (Wilbur Ashley), Clyde Cook (Ted), Leigh Whipper (Jim Flash), Oscar Polk (Umeela), Darby Jones (Doctor's Houseboy), Richard Ainley (Worthing).

First this was a steamy book, then a play, then it hit the screens as an early British talkie. In 1942, it was remade as a vehicle for Hedy Lamarr, who proved to be at her sultry best. Pidgeon is working at an African rubber station. Carlson, his new assistant, is the replacement for Fletcher, whose mental and physical destruction rendered him incapable of helping Pidgeon. Carlson is determined not to let this happen to him, but this is easier said than done. Lamarr, a sexy jungle maiden Pidgeon had warned Carlson about, pays a call on this new man. Pidgeon finds her there, and tosses her out. Now Carlson finds himself in the same situation as Fletcher. The natives refuse to obey him, and Carlson is pining for the enticing Lamarr. She eventually returns, much to Carlson's delight. Though Pidgeon is

against it, Carlson is determined to marry her. Lamarr, thought to be a native, is actually the daughter of an Egyptian, making her a Caucasian, which eliminates any sort of racial prejudice against the marriage. After they are wed, Lamarr quickly grows bored with her new spouse. Carlson takes ill, and Lamarr sees the chance to be rid of him. She starts to give Carlson some deadly poison, but Pidgeon catches her in the act. He forces the vixen to drink the poison herself, then sends her into the jungle where she dies. Carlson returns home after regaining his strength, leaving Pidgeon in need of a new employee, though he no longer must fear any man's destruction at the hands of Lamarr. Lamarr, clad in sarong and dancing in an oh-so-sexy fashion, needless to say, is the main attraction in the film. She swings her hips and sashays around the floor, breaking not only Carlson's and Fletcher's hearts, but capturing the passions of any warm-blooded male viewing the film ("I know," Lamarr wrote in her autobiography *Ecstasy and Me*, 'in my cocoa-butter-smeared nudity I contributed to the war effort. Soldiers all over the world sent fan letters..."). Her male costars give Lamarr some fine support. Pidgeon (in a role played on stage by both Clark Gable and Spencer Tracy) is fine as the cynical plantation owner, while Morgan, as an alcoholic expatriate doctor, gives an intelligent portrait of a man fighting to retain his self- respect. For Lamarr, this film proved to be a turning point in her career. After WHITE CARGO, she was offered sexier roles. "There was so much sex in 'WHITE CARGO'," she wrote, "I couldn't resist the temptation to kill the 'marble goddess image' for good!"

p, Victor Saville; d, Richard Thorpe; w, Leon Gordon (from his stage play based on the book *Hell's Playground* by Ida Vera Simonton); ph, Harry Stradling; m, Bronislau Kaper; ed, Frederick Y. Smith; art d, Cedric Gibbons, Daniel B. Cathcart; set d, Edwin B. Willis; cos, Robert Kalloch; ch, Ernest Matray; makeup, Jack Dawn.

Drama   (PR:C MPAA:NR)

WHITE CHRISTMAS*   (1954) 120 PAR c

Bing Crosby (Bob Wallace), Danny Kaye (Phil Davis), Rosemary Clooney (Betty), Vera-Ellen (Judy), Dean Jagger (Gen. Waverly), Mary Wickes (Emma), John Brascia (Joe), Anne Whitfield (Susan), Richard Shannon (Adjutant), Grady Sutton (General's Guest), Sig Rumann (Landlord), Robert Crosson (Albert), Herb Vigran (Novello), Dick Keene (Assistant Stage Manager), Johnny Grant (Ed Harrison), Gavin Gordon (Gen. Carlton), Marcel De La Brosse (Maitre d'), James Parnell (Sheriff), Percy Helton (Conductor), Elizabeth Holmes (Fat Lady), Barrie Chase (Doris), I. Stanford Jolley (Station Master), George Chakiris (Specialty Dancer), Mike P. Donovan, Glen Cargyle, Lorraine Crawford, Joan Bayley, Lester Clark, Ernest Flatt, Bea Allen.

This eagerly awaited musical comedy had all the ingredients for success attached to it: two of the biggest box office draws, a solid director, and a score by America's treasure, Irving Berlin. And yet, it was not nearly as satisfying as it might have been, perhaps due to the predictable and cliched script by Krasna, Panama, and Frank. It seemed to borrow from every other movie of the same genre and the audiences yawned when the dialog was spoken, then smiled as the songs were sung and the dances danced. Kaye and Crosby meet during the war and team up afterward to become the hottest song-and-dance duo around. Not content with starring, they begin to mount their own shows and are enormously adroit at it. After five years of heady success, they think it's about time to take a vacation so, with their two lovelies, entertainers Clooney and Vera-Ellen, they travel to a New England hostelry for some rest and recuperation. Once there, they see that the place is in terrible financial condition and in desperate need of an infusion of money. The man who runs the hotel is their old Army topkick, Jagger. It's supposed to be a ski resort but there hasn't been any snow for almost a year so the place is about to topple. Crosby and Hope decide to aid Jagger by staging a benefit show which is, of course, a smash. The hotel is saved and the picture ends with Bing crooning to Clooney and Kaye cavorting with Vera-Ellen as the snow begins to fall. This was Paramount's first film in VistaVision, its answer to CinemaScope, and it lent a grand air to the trivial proceedings. Berlin had written "White Christmas" for HOLIDAY INN 12 years before and it became an instant standard. With that as the core, the script was fashioned, so to speak, and several more Berlin tunes were added. They include: "The Best Things Happen While You're Dancing" (sung by Kaye, Vera-Ellen), "Love, You Didn't Do Right By Me," (Clooney), "Choreography" (Kaye, John Brascia, Vera-Ellen), "Count Your Blessings Instead of Sheep" (Crosby, then reprised by Clooney), "What Can You Do With a General?" (Crosby), "Mandy" (an old Berlin tune done by Crosby, Kaye, Clooney, Vera-Ellen, and the ensemble), "The Minstrel Show" (snatches of various tunes done by just about everyone), "Sisters" (Clooney, Vera-Ellen, then mimed by Kaye and Crosby), "Heat Wave," "Blue Skies," "Let Me Sing" (Crosby, Kaye), "Abraham" (Brascia, Vera-Ellen), "Snow" (Crosby, Kaye, Clooney, Vera-Ellen), "The Old Man" (Crosby, Kaye), "Gee, I Wish I Was Back in the Army" (Crosby, Kaye, Clooney, Vera-Ellen), and, of course, "White Christmas" (Crosby, Kaye, Clooney, Vera-Ellen). Jagger does a good job as the old Army man and he is ably assisted by Wickes, as the hotel housekeeper. It grossed more than $12 million, making it one of the most profitable films of the year. Teaming Crosby and Kaye was an afterthought because Donald O'Connor was supposed to play the role but had to bow out due to an injury. With Kaye in the costarring role, someone had to come in and do the dance routines originally planned for O'Connor and that someone was Brascia, who later

3821 -WHITE DAWN, THE

teamed with his wife to become a successful nightclub dance act known as Brascia and Tybee. Look quickly and you'll see a very young George Chakiris as a specialty dancer, long before he scored in WEST SIDE STORY. Also seen as a dancer is Barrie Chase, who performed with Fred Astaire in his Emmy-winning TV specials. One of the other dancers, Ernest Flatt, later became a respected choreographer. VistaVision added height to the screen and reduced the grain of the film. It was accomplished by running the film past the lens in a horizontal position so that each frame occupied the space of two 35-millimeter frames. WHITE CHRISTMAS had terrific clarity and first-rate camerawork by Griggs but it still remains a curious disappointment as a total entertainment. Berlin was nominated for his umpteenth Oscar for "Count Your Blessings Instead of Sheep."

p, Robert Emmett Dolan; d, Michael Curtiz; w, Norman Krasna, Norman Panama, Melvin Frank; ph, Loyal Griggs (VistaVision, Technicolor); ed, Frank Bracht; md, Joseph J. Lilley; art d, Hal Pereira, Roland Anderson; set d, Sam Comer, Grace Gregory; cos, Edith Head; ch, Robert Alton; m/l, Irving Berlin.

Musical   **Cas.**   **(PR:AA MPAA:NR)**

WHITE CLIFFS OF DOVER, THE***½   (1944) 126m MGM bw

Irene Dunne (*Susan Dunn Ashwood*), Alan Marshall (*Sir John Ashwood*), Frank Morgan (*Hiram Porter Dunn*), Roddy McDowall (*John Ashwood II as a Boy*), Peter Lawford (*John Ashwood II at age 24*), Dame May Whitty (*Nanny*), C. Aubrey Smith (*Colonel*), Gladys Cooper (*Lady Jean Ashwood*), Van Johnson (*Sam Bennett*), John Warburton (*Reggie*), Jill Esmond (*Rosamund*), Brenda Forbes (*Gwennie*), Norma Varden (*Mrs. Bland*), Elizabeth Taylor (*Betsy at Age 10*), June Lockhart (*Betsy at Age 18*), Charles Irwin (*Farmer Kenney*), Jean Prescott (*Mrs. Kenney*), Tom Drake (*American Soldier*), Isobel Elsom (*Mrs. Bancroft*), Edmund Breon (*Maj. Bancroft*), Miles Mander (*Maj. Loring*), Ann Curzon (*Miss Lambert*), Steven Muller (*Gerhard*), Norbert Muller (*Dietrich*), Molly Lamont (*Helen*), Lumsden Hare (*The Vicar*), Arthur Shields (*Benson*), Emily Fitzroy (*Spinster in Boarding House*), Emily Massey (*Elegant Lady in Boarding House*), Guy D'Ennery (*Curate in Boarding House*), Lal Chand Mehra (*Indian Student in Boarding House*), Clifford Brooke (*Indian Major in Boarding House*), Ethel Griffies (*Woman on Train*), Elton Burkett, Eldon Burkett (*Twins in Boarding House*), Herbert Evans (*Footman*), Ian Wolfe (*Skipper*), Alec Craig (*Billings*), Clyde Cook (*Jennings*), Bunny Gordon (*John at 6 Months*), Leo Mostovoy (*Bandmaster*), Arthur Gould-Porter (*Capt. Portage*), Gavin Muir (*Capt. Griffiths*), Charles Coleman (*Capt. Davis*), Kay Deslys (*Blonde*), George Davis (*Boots*), Vera Graaf (*Duchess*), Anita Bolster (*Miller*), Wilson Benge (*Chauffeur*), Harry Allen (*English Cabby*), Nelson Leigh (*British Naval Officer*), Mabel Row (*Housemaid*), James Menzies (*Telegraph Boy*), George Kirby (*Old Man*), Matthew Boulton (*Immigration Officer*), Doris Lloyd (*Plump Lady at Boarding House*), Keith Hitchcock (*Duke of Waverly*).

Through the years, producers have found source material in many places: novels, plays, short stories, and even poems. Joseph Moncure March's epic poems were made into THE WILD PARTY and THE SET-UP and this feature was based on the narrative poem by Alice Duer Miller. It's a sentimental look at the ravages of war, one woman's courage, and the strength she demonstrates after losing both her husband and son in the two world wars that decimated this century. Dunne is a Red Cross supervisor in England, awaiting casualties of WW II. At her desk, she ruminates about her past and flashes back to a time in 1914, when she comes to England with Morgan–her father, a newspaper publisher in a medium-sized town in the U.S. In no time at all, Dunne meets, falls in love with, and marries wealthy and titled Marshal. They are ecstatic, but their happiness is brief as the assassination takes place at Sarajevo, war breaks out, and Marshal must serve his country in France. He has a short respite from the war and they get together for a few passionate hours, then he's off to war again. On November 11th, when the world is celebrating the end of "The War to End All Wars," Dunne is plunged into despair as she learns that Marshal will not be coming back. By this time, she has a son Marshal never met, and she opts to remain in England to raise the boy. Time passes and there is a new threat of war coming from Germany. Her mother-in-law, Cooper, is ill and Dunne is taking care of her. Morgan thinks Dunne would be safer in the U.S. but when Cooper dies, Dunne is left the estate and stays there with her son (played at first by McDowall and later by Lawford). She is afraid that her son might die the same way her husband did but stays on anyhow, thinking that Marshal would have wanted it that way. War breaks out and Dunne becomes a worker for the Red Cross assigned to a hospital in London. The wounded servicemen are brought in for repair and she is shocked to see that one of them is her son, Lawford, now 24. He is dying of his injuries and she is powerless to stop his death. At the conclusion, Dunne stands and looks out a window and describes a battalion of American soldiers as they march past, the first such warriors to reach the British shores. Lawford dies in the service of his country, just as his father did, and the tragedy is complete. With the advent of the war, MGM made several pro- English features, not the least of which was MRS. MINIVER, the tale of another spunky woman. That picture was a huge box-office winner and the studio wanted to make it happen again, but couldn't find the right material until producer Franklin happened on Miller's poem (which was given some additional words by Robert Nathan). Dunne was busy on A GUY NAMED JOE but the picture had to go on hiatus while Van Johnson recovered from an auto accident. In the meantime, this one began and when Johnson was able to get back before

the cameras more quickly than anyone had anticipated, Dunne found herself working on two major features at the same time. Beside MRS. MINIVER, MGM had already made GOODBYE, MR. CHIPS and RANDOM HARVEST, and was in danger of being classified as a strictly Anglophile studio. This movie didn't reach the public as widely as had been hoped but still managed a respectable gross of more than $4 million. Elizabeth Taylor will only be seen in the uncut version of this lengthy film as she plays a coquettish youngster in a scene with McDowall that was snipped from many TV prints. It was her fourth film after THERE'S ONE BORN EVERY MINUTE, LASSIE COME HOME, and JANE EYRE. Also recognizable in the film are Arthur Shields (who did *not* play a priest) and Tom Drake, who hit it big later the same year with MEET ME IN ST. LOUIS. Good acting, superior production values, sensitive direction, and one of Dunne's finest performances add to the film's overall success. In order to make the settings authentic, MGM hired Major Cyril Seys Ramsey-Hill as technical advisor and he must have done his job because Britons living in the U.S. sobbed at the showings. And so will youngsters when they see this, so be prepared with a handful of tissues.

p, Sidney Franklin; d, Clarence Brown; w, Claudine West, Jan Lustig, George Froeschel (based on the poem "The White Cliffs of Dover" by Alice Duer Miller, with additional poetry by Robert Nathan); ph, George Folsey; m, Herbert Stothart; ed, Robert J. Kern, Al Jennings; art d, Cedric Gibbons, Randall Duell; set d, Edwin B. Willis, Jacques Mesereau; cos, Irene; spec eff, Arnold Gillespie, Warren Newcombe; makeup, Jack Dawn; tech adv, Maj. Cyril Seys Ramsey-Hill.

War Drama   **(PR:A-C MPAA:NR)**

WHITE COCKATOO*   (1935) 73m WB bw

Jean Muir (*Sue Talley*), Ricardo Cortez (*Jim Sundean*), Ruth Donnelly (*Mrs. Felicia Byng*), Mina Gombell (*Grete Levscheim*), Walter Kingsford (*Marcus Levscheim*), John Eldredge (*Francis Talley*), Gordon Westcott (*Dr. Roberts*), Addison Richards (*David Lorn*), Pauline Garon (*Marianne*), Armand de Bordes (*Marcel*), Bentley Hewlett (*Michael Stravsky*), Andre Cheron (*Commissaire of Police*), Georges Renavent (*Pierre*), Noel Francis (*Elise*).

Dull and uninteresting drama in which heiress Muir's claim to a vast fortune causes several murders and other mysterious (though not really) acts as other people want to get at the money. A decent book was given a strictly routine treatment which highlighted stereotypes as a means of telling a story.

p, Henry Blanke; d, Alan Crosland; w, Ben Markson, Lillie Hayward (based on the novel by Mignon G. Eberhart); ph, Tony Gaudio; ed, Clarence Kolster; art d, John Hughes.

Mystery   **(PR:A MPAA:NR)**

WHITE CORRIDORS**   (1952, Brit.) 102m Vic/JARO bw

Googie Withers (*Dr. Sophie Dean*), James Donald (*Dr. Neil Marriner*), Godfrey Tearle (*Groom, Sr.*), Barry Jones (*Dr. Shoesmith*), Petula Clark (*Joan Shepherd*), Moira Lister (*Dolly Clark*), Jack Watling (*Dick Groom*), Mary Hinton (*Matron*), Avice Landone (*Sister Jenkins*), Helen Harvey (*Nurse Miller*), Lyn Evans (*Pedlar*), Timothy Bateson (*Dr. Cook*), Henry Edwards (*Phillip Brewster*), Brand Inglis (*Tommy Briggs*), Megs Jenkins (*Mrs. Briggs*), Basil Radford (*Civil Servant*), Fabia Drake (*Miss Farmer*), Jean Anderson (*Sister Gater*), Gerard Heinz (*Dr. Macuzek*), Dagmar [Dana] Wynter (*Marjorie Brewster*), H. F. Hills (*Tranter*), Jean Lodge (*Night Nurse*), Bernard Lee (*Burgess*), Bruce Seton, Johnnie Schofield, Grace Gaven, Helen Harvey, Patrick Troughton, Dandy Nichols, Deirdre Doyle, Mignon O'Doherty, Mary Minton, Philip Stainton, Joan Winmill, Humphrey Howarth.

A behind-the-scenes look at the goings-on in a hospital, not solely limited to matters dealing with medicine, though enough such matters are injected into the script to add a sense of realism. Prime among these are the efforts of Donald to develop a serum to combat an infectious disease. He gets the chance to test the serum when he is infected with the disease while treating a young lad destined to die; luckily, it proves to be an effective medicine. Though emphasis is placed upon heavy sentiment, direction capably interweaves the various dramas to create a fairly interesting outing.

p, Joseph Janni, John Croyden; d, Pat Jackson; w, Jackson, Jan Read (based on the novel *Yeoman's Hospital* by Helen Ashton); ph, C. Pennington Richards; ed, Sidney Havers; art d, Maurice Carter.

Drama   **(PR:A MPAA:NR)**

WHITE CRADLE INN   (SEE: HIGH FURY, 1947, Brit.)

WHITE DAWN, THE**½   (1974) 109m PAR bw-c

Warren Oates (*Billy*), Timothy Bottoms (*Daggett*), Lou Gossett (*Portagee*), Simonie Kopapik (*Sarkak*), Joanasie Salomonie (*Kangiak*), Pilitak (*Neevee*), Sagiaktok (*Shaman*), Munamee Sako (*Sowniapik*), Pitseolala Kili (*Sowniapik's Wife*), Meetook Mallee (*Ikuma*), Seemee Nookiguak (*Avinga*), Sakkeassie (*Dirty Boy*), Akshooyooliak (*Old Mother*), Neelak (*Panee*), Oolipika Joamie (*Mia*), Higa Ipeelie (*Evaloo*), Jacob Partridge (*Archer*),

Ashoona Kilabuck (*Shartok*), Namonai Ashoona (*Nowya*), Aupalotak Simonee, Atcheelak (*Hunters*).

Three whalers–Oates, Bottoms, and Gossett–become stranded in the Arctic and take refuge with a tribe of Eskimos. Gradually they take over the village, introducing liquor, gambling, thievery, and their style of sex to this isolated civilization. At first the natives tolerate this behavior but gradually resentment grows until the cultural clash becomes intolerable. The leads are very strong, particularly Oates as the meanest of the trio. The portrait of Eskimo life in the 1890s is sensitive and nicely detailed. The actual language of the tribe is used with English subtitles for translation, a technique that works well. However, the story tends to ramble in various directions and occasionally has some slow spots. This does not detract from the overall production, for it maintains interest throughout. THE WHITE DAWN is an example of a good film that could have been an excellent one if more care had been taken with the screenplay. The opening sequences are filmed in black and white, with the rest in color. This was only the third film in the history of moviemaking to be shot in the Arctic Circle, after NANOOK OF THE NORTH (1922) and ESKIMO (1932).

p, Martin Ransohoff; d, Philip Kaufman; w, James Houston, Tom Rickman, Ransohoff (based on the novel by Houston); ph, Michael Chapman (Movielab Color); m, Henry Mancini; ed, Douglas Stewart.

Drama   **Cas.**   **(PR:O   MPAA:R/PG)**

WHITE DEATH* (1936, Aus.) 78m Great Barrier/British Empire Film bw

Zane Grey, Nola Warren, John Weston, Alfred Frith.

The great Western writer Grey made his acting debut with this, but probably should have spent his time turning out another novel. WHITE DEATH involves Grey's minor adventures as he goes fishing off Australia's Great Barrier Reef. There's little excitement, and Grey's acting leaves much to be desired, to say the least. The messy and incompetent direction was by Grey's business manager.

d, Edward Bowen; w, Frank Harvey; ph, Arthur Higgins, H. C. Anderson.

Drama   **(PR:A   MPAA:NR)**

WHITE DEMON, THE*½   (1932, Ger.) 106m UFA bw (DER WEISSE DAMON; AKA: RAUSCHG IFT)

Hans Albers (*Heini Gildemeister*), Gerda Maurus (*Gerda Gildemeister*), Peter Lorre (*Hunchback*), Lucie Hoflich (*Gildemeister's Mother*), Trude von Molo (*Dora Lind*), Alfred Abel (*Gorre*), Hans Joachim Schaufuss (*Gorre's Son*), Raoul Aslan (*Dr. Urussew*), Hubert von Meyerinck (*Marquis d'Esquillon*).

After spending five years in Brazil, Albers returns to his family in Germany only to discover that his sister, Maurus, a noted opera singer, has become a morphine addict. He takes Maurus to a sanitarium so she can be freed from her addiction. However Lorre, the hunchbacked leader of the dope-smuggling outfit, fears Maurus will expose his operation, so he has her kidnaped. Albers teams up with von Molo, another opera singer whom he initially suspects to be a gang member, to discover what's going on. Later Albers finds that the opera company's makeup jars have been used to hide the drugs. He rescues his sister and exposes a well-known industrialist as the head of the operation. This is a strong story about the underworld of drug dealing which is headed by Albers' strong lead. He's given excellent support by Lorre, the evil opposite of Albers' hero. THE WHITE DEMON proved to be too controversial for German censors; the original film was re-cut, emphasizing the adventure aspects more than the drugs. This could not diminish the film's power, however, a well-acted and nicely photographed work of high drama. A French version of this film called NARCOTICS (FR: STUPEFIANTS) was shot concurrently with the German film, utilizing many of the same production team, with Lorre repeating his role.

p, Bruno Duday; d, Kurt Gerron; w, Lothar Mayring, Friedrich Zeckendorf; ph, Carl Hoffmann; m, Hans-Otto Borgmann; ed, Constantin Mick; art d, Julius von Borsody.

Drama   **(PR:C   MPAA:NR)**

WHITE DEVIL, THE** (1948, Ital.) 100m Manenti bw (IL DIAVOLO BIANCO)

Rossano Brazzi (*Prince Mdwani/The White Devil*), Annette Bach (*Countess Olga*), Roldano Lupi (*Gov. Alexis*), Lea Padovani (*Katiousha*), Harry Feist (*Col. Stanikow*), Mario Ferrari (*Prof. Ilya*), Armando Francioli (*Wassili*), Vittorio Sanipoli (*John*).

Evil despot Lupi tyrannizes over the people of his Caucasus province in the year 1850 as the fawning, mincing dandy, Brazzi, dances attendance to his every whim. Brazzi's fiancee, Bach, begins to have reservations about her impending marriage to this weakling, especially when she hears of the exploits of "The White Devil," the mysterious masked man who fights to save the people from oppression. When the outlaw savior unmasks, he proves to be none other than.... This is a big-budget ZORRO clone with good scenery and costumes and a fair amount of action. Brazzi had just signed a contract with David O. Selznick.

d, Nunsio Malasomma; w, Gaspare Cotaldo, Malasomma (based on a story by Cotaldo); ph, Rodolfo Lombardi; m, Ezio Carabella

Adventure   **(PR:C   MPAA:NR)**

WHITE DOG*½   (1982) 90m Edgar J. Scherick/PAR c (AKA: TRAINED TO KILL)

Kristy McNichol (*Julie Sawyer*), Paul Winfield (*Keys*), Burl Ives (*Carruthers*), Jameson Parker (*Roland Gray*), Lynne Moody (*Molly*), Marshall Thompson (*Director*), Bob Minor (*Joe*), Vernon Weddle (*Vet*), Christa Lang (*Nurse*), Tony Brubaker (*Sweeper Driver*), Samuel Fuller (*Charlie Felton*), Paul Bartel (*Cameraman*), Martine Dawson (*Martine*), Alex A. Brown (*Man in Church*), Parley Baer (*Wilbur Hull*), Karl Lewis Miller, Karrie Emerson, Helen J. Siff, Glenn D. Garner, Terrence Beasor, Richard Monohan, Neyle Morrow, George Fisher, Hubert Wells, Dick Miller, Robert Ritchie, Cliff Pellow, Sam Laws, Samantha Fuller, Jamie Crowe, Joseph R. Hornok.

One of the most famous "unseen" films, WHITE DOG never got a theatrical run in the U.S. even though it had a well known cast, a legendary director, and a powerful subject–racism. McNichol stars as a young actress who lives alone in a fabulous hillside house. One night, while out driving, she hits a beautiful white dog. She brings the ailing dog to a veterinarian and eventually brings it home with her. The dog is playful and gentle enough until a rapist breaks into McNichol's home. It viciously attacks and nearly tears the man limb from limb before the police arrive. The pride she has for her dog soon turns to fear when she learns that it has been trained to kill blacks. She brings the dog to an animal training center (specializing in Hollywood animals) run by Ives. He explains to McNichol that her dog has been beaten since birth by hired blacks (junkies and alcoholics in need of a fix) and is conditioned to attack only black skin. He begs her to put the dog to sleep since it can never be completely broken of its desire to kill. Before she is able to leave, however, Winfield–a black trainer–agrees to break the dog. Something of a renegade, Winfield finds the dog a challenge. He has failed in the past to break "white dogs" (a double-edged description which refers to the dog's color and its racist breeding) and wants to try again. He treats the dog with extreme kindness and is the only one allowed to feed it–proving to the dog that black skin can mean friendship as well as pain. The dog manages to escape one night and wanders into town where it mutilates a black man in a church. Winfield roams the streets in search of the dog, hoping to find it and bring it back for more training before the police kill it. Winfield continues to patiently break the dog and finally is able to gain the dog's affection and confidence. In the meantime, McNichol is confronted by a seemingly friendly old man with his two young granddaughters. When one of the girls (Samantha Fuller, Sam's charming daughter) asks, "Where's my dog?" McNichol flies into a rage, cursing the old man for raising a killer dog. It is a brilliant scene because one expects the owner to be a psychotic neo-Nazi instead of a "grampa." It's especially frightening to think of the two young girls having the dog as a pet when we know it could easily rip them apart. During a final "test" with Ives and McNichol present, the dog again turns vicious. Just when Winfield thinks he has "cured" the dog of its racism it lunges for Ives and kills him. Winfield fires bullets into the dog and kills it. Winfield stopped the dog from killing blacks, but could not stop it from killing completely. Not surprisingly, Paramount was frightened by the volatile subject–fearing that it would incite racial controversy. Based on an award-winning novella by Romain Gary, the story had been bought by Paramount 10 years before production began. A number of names were involved with the project, including Robert Evans, Robert Towne, and Roman Polanski (all of whom went on to different projects, notably CHINATOWN). The NAACP was even on the set (pressuring the filmmaker's with ridiculous demands and changes, such as wanting Winfield's character to have a college degree) to insure that there was no racist content in the picture. Fuller's version of the film is anything but racist. It is, in fact, a strong condemnation of racists and their perverse sense of morality. This version, however, never got a theatrical run. Test marketing in Detroit proved to Paramount that the film was a dud, which should come as no surprise since they failed to advertise the screening. They also ignored the fact that those who did see the film were hailing it as one of Fuller's best. Paramount president Michael Eisner insisted that they "never got a strong enough reaction to justify a major opening." When WHITE DOG finally opened in Paris and London it was hailed as a "masterpiece" by some critics. Oddly enough, the film wasn't titled WHITE DOG in Paris (where Romain Gary's novella was well known under that name), but as TRAINED TO KILL. The film finally did show up on cable television in January of 1984, but it was a re-edited version from Paramount which foolishly turned the dog from a killer to one that merely bites. WHITE DOG is one of the most obvious examples of a gross artistic injustice performed by a major studio on a superb director–an injustice that Sam Fuller should never forgive and that Paramount should never be allowed to forget.

p, John Davison; d, Samuel Fuller; w, Fuller, Curtis Hanson (based on the novella by Romain Gary); ph, Bruce Surtees (Metrocolor); m, Ennio Morricone; ed, Bernard Gribble; prod d, Brian Eatwell; set d, Geoff Hubbard.

Drama   **(PR:O   MPAA:PG)**

WHITE EAGLE**   (1932) 64m COL bw

Buck Jones (*White Eagle*), Barbara Weeks (*Janet*), Robert Ellis (*Gregory*), Jason Robards, Sr (*Dave Rand*), Robert Elliott (*Capt. Blake*), Jim Thorpe, Ward Bond, Frank Campeau, Bob Kortman, Clarence Geldert, Jimmie House, Frank Hagney, Russell Simpson, Silver the Horse.

Jones, to all appearances a native American Indian, becomes a Pony Express rider in the period just after the Civil War. Thieving white men, led by Ellis, have been stealing the organization's finest steeds and blaming their encroachments on neighboring Indians. The noble Jones uncovers Ellis' treachery and brings the gang to justice. In the process, he discovers that he himself is really a white man; he had been abducted and raised by Indians. This permits him to meet the anti-miscegenation code of the Hays Office and marry the beautiful blonde Weeks (who had been a brunette in her previous screen appearances).

d, Lambert Hillyer; w, Fred Myton; ph, L. William O'Connell.

Western   (PR:A   MPAA:NR)

WHITE ENSIGN**   (1934, Brit.) 84m Sound City/MGM bw

Anthony Kimmins (*Comdr. Falcon*), Molly Lamont (*Consul's Daughter*), Kenneth Villiers (*Terry*), Ivan Sampson (*Captain*), S. Victor Stanley (*Seaman Steele*), Ballard Berkeley (*Cortez*), Anthony Ireland (*Denton*), Ivo Dawson, Edgar Driver.

Standard seafaring actioner starring Kimmins as the commander of a cruiser who is sent to Santa Barbara to quell a revolt at an oilfield. Upon arrival, the sailors learn that oil company engineer Ireland has been involved in a power struggle with Berkeley, who has organized the locals against him. Kimmins and her majesty's navy put a stop to this nonsense and crush the uprising, leaving the commander to sail off with the British consul's daughter, Lamont. Yes, it's as unabashedly imperialistic as it sounds.

p, Ivar Campbell; d&w, John Hunt.

Adventure   (PR:A   MPAA:NR)

WHITE FACE***   (1933, Brit.) 70m Gainsborough-BL/Woolf and Freedman bw

Hugh Williams (*Michael Seeley*), Gordon Harker (*Sam Hackett*), Norman McKinnel (*Inspector Mason*), Renee Gadd (*Janice Harman*), Richard Bird (*Donald Bateman*), Nora Swinburne (*Inez Landor*), Leslie Perrins (*Louis Landor*), John H. Roberts (*Dr. Marford*), D.A. Clarke-Smith (*Dr. Rudd*), Gibb McLaughlin (*Sgt. Elk*), Jeanne Stuart (*Gloria Gaye*), Clare Greet (*Mrs. Albert*), George Merritt.

When a mysterious blackmailer who goes by the name "White Face" begins producing corpses, intrepid reporter Williams and police inspector McKinnel root around for clues. The crime fighters are assisted by Roberts, a doctor who suspects that one of his patients may be the killer, and inevitably the identity of "White Face" is revealed. Standard Edgar Wallace mystery helped immensely by a decent production and solid cast. Wallace's son Bryan, also a writer, helped adapt his father's play for the screen.

p, Michael Balcon; d, T. Hayes Hunter; w, Angus Macphail, Bryan Edgar Wallace (based on the play "Persons Unknown" by Edgar Wallace); ph, Bernard Knowles, Alex Bryce; art d, Norman Arnold.

Crime   (PR:A   MPAA:NR)

WHITE FANG**   (1936) 70m FOX bw

Michael Whalen (*Weedon Scott*), Jean Muir (*Sylvia Burgess*), Slim Summerville (*Slats*), Charles Winninger (*Doc McFane*), John Carradine (*Beauty Smith*), Jane Darwell (*Maud Mahoney*), Thomas Beck (*Hal Burgess*), Joseph Herrick (*Kobi*), George Ducount (*Francois*), Marie Chorie (*Nomi*), Lightning (*White Fang*).

Covering much the same territory as CALL OF THE WILD, which the studio had filmed the year previously–and which included some of author Jack London's plot from his sequel to the earlier tale, *White Fang*–this is a story of the gold rush days in the Far North. Muir and her brother Beck, heirs to a rich vein of the precious metal, are assisted to their mine by rough-hewn guide Whalen, owner of the title canine. Unable to withstand the rigors of the trip, weak-willed Beck commits suicide. An evil band of men led by Carradine tries to gain possession of the valuable mine by throwing suspicion on Whalen, Muir's protector, claiming him to be Beck's murderer. After some gunplay and some daring rescues by the dog, Beck's diary turns up, proving him to have killed himself. Excellent dialog and some fine comedy touches by Summerville and Winninger. Darwell shines as a north-country hotel keeper and Carradine, who paired so well with her in THE GRAPES OF WRATH (1940), is a wonderful villain. Unfortunately, leads Whalen and Muir don't come up to the charisma of the leads of THE CALL OF THE WILD, Clark Gable and Loretta Young. Audiences were pleased to notice that the dog, ostensibly wounded by a gunshot, favored one leg in an early scene and a completely different leg in a later one. Previously filmed in 1925.

p, Darryl F. Zanuck, Bogart Rogers; d, David Butler; w, Hal Long, Sam G.

Duncan (based on Jack London's novel); ph, Arthur Miller; ed, Irene Morra; md, Arthur Lange.

Adventure   (PR:A   MPAA:NR)

WHITE FEATHER***   (1955) 102m FOX c

Robert Wagner (*Josh Tanner*), John Lund (*Col. Lindsay*), Debra Paget (*Appearing Day*), Jeffrey Hunter (*Little Dog*), Eduard Franz (*Chief Broken Hand*), Noah Beery, Jr (*Lt. Ferguson*), Virginia Leith (*Ann Magruder*), Emile Meyer (*Magruder*), Hugh O'Brian (*American Horse*), Milburn Stone (*Commissioner Trenton*), Iron Eyes Cody (*Indian Chief*).

In 1877, the Cheyenne are persuaded to peacefully withdraw from their Wyoming hunting grounds to make way for white settlers. Army colonel Lund is assigned the task of resettling the redskins. He has the help of surveyor Wagner, whose friendship with young Indian stalwarts Hunter and O'Brian is of great assistance. Indian maiden Paget, betrothed to Hunter, develops a yen for Wagner; this threatens the success of the resettlement campaign. The resentful redskins forswear their friendship with Wagner and launch an arrow with a white feather attached as a sign that they intend to do battle with the whole cavalry troop. Wagner persuades his former friends to settle the matter in single combat and when O'Brian stoops to treachery in combat, Franz shoots him. Hunter is reconciled with Wagner at the intervention of Paget and then charges the lined-up soldiers whereupon they kill him. There is a beautiful scene showing Wagner arranging Hunter's body for proper Indian burial. Resigned to their fate, the Indians trek on to their reservation. Paget reprises the type of role she had in BROKEN ARROW (1950). The Indians are treated with considerable sympathy in this film, which is interesting despite its tepid direction.

p, Robert L. Jacks; d, Robert Webb; w, Delmer Daves, Leo Townsend (based on a story by John Prebble); ph, Lucien Ballard (CinemaScope, Technicolor); m, Hugo Friedhofer; ed, George Gittens; md, Lionel Newman; art d, Jack Smith; cos, William Travilla.

Western   (PR:A   MPAA:NR)

WHITE FIRE**   (1953, Brit.) 81m Tempean/Lippert bw (GB: THREE STEPS TO THE GALLOWS)

Scott Brady (*Gregor Stevens*), Mary Castle (*Yvonne Durante*), Gabrielle Brune (*Lorna*), Ferdy Mayne (*Sartago*), Colin Tapley (*Winston*), John Blythe (*Darry*), Lloyd Lamble (*James Smith*), Julian Somers (*John Durante*), Ballard Berkeley (*Inspector Haley*), Ronan O'Casey (*Crawson*), Johnnie Schofield (*Charley*), Paul Erickson (*Larry*), Bill Lowe, Hal Osmond, Dennis Chinnery, Ronald Leigh-Hunt, Arthur Lovegrove, Harcourt Nicholls, Russell Westwood, Laurie Taylor, Alastair Hunter, Michael Balfour.

Brady is a rough, tough officer of a U.S. cargo ship who, docking in London, discovers that his brother is to be executed for murder in just three days. The crime was pinned on the brother by a gang of diamond smugglers led by attorney Tapley, who defended the brother at his murder trial. Brady prowls the waterfront dives seeking a solution to the crime. Beset by thugs and beaten, he manages to meet Castle, a singer in one of the waterfront hangouts of the crooks. Working together, they solve the case and Brady embarks with Castle in his arms. A rather weak script is saved by some good cinematography in this routine thriller. The coproducers both served extensive time behind the camera. Apparently designed for the overseas market with its two American leading players, the picture opened in Britain two years after its U.S. release.

p, Robert S. Baker, Monty Berman; d, John Gilling; w, Gilling, Paul Erickson (based on a story by Erickson); ph, Berman; m, Stanley Black; ed, Marjorie Saunders; m/l, "No Way Out," Black, Barbara Killalee.

Crime   **Cas.**   (PR:A   MPAA:NR)

WHITE GODDESS*   (1953) 73m Lippert bw

Jon Hall, Ray Montgomery, M'Liss McClure, Ludwig Stossel, James Fairfax, Joel Fluellen, Darby Jones, Lucian Prival, Robert Williams, Millicent Patrick.

Laughable adventure film which chronicles the brave derring-do of a doctor who plunges himself into the wilds of deepest Africa in search of valuable medicinal herbs. En route he encounters a community of natives ruled by white women pretending to be goddesses so they can control the tribe. Silly, inept, and racist.

p, Rudolph Flothow; d, Wallace Fox; w, Sherman L. Lowe, Eric Taylor; m, Irving Gertz.

Adventure   (PR:A   MPAA:NR)

WHITE GORILLA zero   (1947) 62m Special Attractions bw

Ray "Crash" Corrigan, Lorraine Miller, Frank Merrill.

One of the all-time worst. To make a really cheap jungle adventure film, producer Weiss dug up a 1927 silent serial entitled PERILS OF THE JUNGLE starring Frank Merrill, pillaged the footage, and used the exciting sequences to build a framework onto which he hung his new footage. Renting a few ratty gorilla costumes, the writer and director went to work and fabricated this crazy-guilt film where actors filmed in 1927 are seen reacting to actors filmed in 1947. The story, such as it is, sees Corrigan as a misfit white gorilla who is ostracized by his black-haired peers for being the wrong color. Thrown out of his tribe, the white ape becomes lonely and embittered–a bitter hate for all two-legged erect and semi-erect creatures burning inside him. There are the obligatory greatwhite hunters on an expedition wandering through the brush who get in the way of the angry white ape. Finally there is a showdown between the king of the black apes and the disenfranchised white ape, which is basically just two men in bad costumes goofing around while the ever-serious narrator grimly describes how the fate of Africa hangs in the balance. All in all, this is an amazing film that is a delight to watch, filmmaking at its most basic. Take shot A and splice it to shot B, then make a story. As a finishing touch, slap on some voice-over narration to explain away any holes in the plot line and you've got yourself a movie that didn't cost much. The narrative gymnastics performed by the writer and editor of this picture to create a cohesive film deserves some recognition and none other than respected film historian William K. Everson has taken it upon himself to give it to them. Having fallen in love with the pure nerve and misguided panache of WHITE GORILLA back in 1947, Everson has been extolling its questionable virtues at film festivals and in print ever since. Of course he realizes that WHITE GORILLA is an awful film, but that is precisely the point. WHITE GORILLA is a wonderful example of how very basic filmmaking can be.

p, Adrian Weiss; d, Harry L. Fraser; w, Monro Talbot; ph, Bob Cline.

Adventure   Cas.   (PR:A MPAA:NR)

WHITE HEAT*½   (1934) 60m Seven Seas/Pinnacle bw

Virginia Cherrill (*Lucille Cheney*), Mona Maris (*Leilani*), Hardie Albright (*Chandler Morris*), David Newell (*William Hawks*), Arthur Clayton (*Armia*), Robert Stevenson (*Mac*), Whitney de Rahm (*Hale*), Naomi Childers (*Mrs. Cheney*), Nani Palsa (*Adam*), Kolimau Kamai (*Lono*), Kamaunani Achi (*Mrs. Hale*), Peter Lee Hyun (*Soong*), Nohili Naumu (*Leilani's Father*).

Another story of moral and physical degeneration in the tropics, so popular in the early 1930s. Sugar plantation manager Newell has settled into his job, finding a measure of happiness in the attentions of native girl Maris, but inner insecurity pushes him into marriage to San Francisco socialite Cherrill. His pampered wife's adjustment to island life fails to take. Bored by her lonely life and the daily rains, she nearly succumbs to the blandishments of a handsome native lad. In the nick of time, the vacationing Albright–a former admirer–turns up. Jealous husband Newell's attack on the hapless lover is diverted by Cherrill, who sets fire to the sugar cane in the fields. Deserted mistress Maris selflessly saves Newell from certain death in the flaming field of cane. Cherrill rejoins Albright and leaves the islands forever; Newell finds happiness once again with Maris. Filmed entirely in the Hawaiian Islands with native players in secondary roles (Maris, no native, came out of Hollywood). A rare independent production for the time with a woman director.

d, Lois Weber; w, Weber, James Bodrero (based on a story by Bodrero); ph, Alvin Wyckoff, Frank Titus.

Drama   (PR:O MPAA:NR)

WHITE HEAT*****   (1949) 114m WB bw

James Cagney (*Arthur Cody Jarrett*), Virginia Mayo (*Verna Jarrett*), Edmond O'Brien (*Hank Fallon/Vic Pardo*), Margaret Wycherly (*Ma Jarrett*), Steve Cochran (*Big Ed Somers*), John Archer (*Phillip Evans*), Wally Cassell (*Giovanni Cotton Valetti*), Fred Clark (*Daniel Winston the Trader*), Ford Rainey (*Zuckie Hommell*), Fred Coby (*Happy Taylor*), G. Pat Collins (*Herbert the Reader*), Mickey Knox (*Het Kohler*), Paul Guilfoyle (*Roy Parker*), Robert Osterloh (*Tommy Ryley*), Ian MacDonald (*Bo Creel*), Ray Montgomery (*Ernie Trent*), Jim Toney (*Brakeman*), Leo Cleary (*Fireman*), Murray Leonard (*Engineer*), Terry O'Sullivan (*Radio Announcer*), Marshall Bradford (*Chief of Police*), Milton Parsons (*Willie Rolf the Stoolie*), John Pickard, Eddie Phillips (*Government Agents*), Bob Foulk (*Guard at Plant*), Jim Thorpe (*Convict*), Eddie Foster (*Nat Lefeld*), Lee Phelps (*Tower Guard*), Perry Ivins (*Simpson the Prison Doctor*), Nolan Leary (*Gas Station Owner*), Grandon Rhodes, John McGuire (*Psychiatrists*), Harry Lauter (*Radio Patrolman Car A*), Ray Bennett, Harry Strang, Jack Worth, Bob Fowke, Art Foster, Arthur Miles (*Guards*), Sid Melton (*Russell Hughes*), Fern Eggen (*Margaret Baxter*), Sherry Hall (*Clerk*), Garrett Craig (*Ted Clark*), Larry McGrath (*Clocker*), George Spaulding (*Judge*), Buddy Gorman (*Popcorn Vendor*), Claudia Barrett (*Cashier*), De Forrest Lawrence (*Jim Donovan*), George Taylor (*Police Surgeon*), Stanton Herzog (*Accountant*), Carl Harbrough (*Foreman*).

None of Cagney's superlative gangster films of the 1930s approaches the supercharged production of WHITE HEAT. Here the great actor, under Walsh's masterly direction, brought the image of the gangster into the realm of psychopathic explosion. Never was Cagney so intense, electrifying, or lethal as in this incredible film. It opens as a train is robbed by Cagney and his gang. One of the members mentions Cagney's name in front of the engineer and he shoots both engineer and fireman to prevent them from later identifying him. But the dying engineer falls on a lever which releases

a steam valve and a gang member is horribly scalded while standing by the side of the train. The gang flees and hides out in a mountain cabin. There, the injured man, Rainey, suffers horribly from his wounds. The gang members, especially the rebellious Cochran, known as Big Ed, want to leave the cold cabin but Cagney orders them to stay where they are. His slut of a wife, Mayo, does nothing but sleep all day while his mother, Wycherly, looks after Cagney's well-being. Cochran and Mayo, it is obvious, have a yen for each other and are constantly exchanging suggestive looks. Cagney, a very savvy crook, is aware of Cochran's rebellious nature and secret ambitions to replace him. As he sits in the cabin contemplating his next move, Cagney looks at Cochran and says: "Big Ed...great big Ed. You know why they call him Big Ed? 'Cause he's got big ideas. One day he's gonna get a big idea about me...and it's gonna be his last!" While cleaning his revolver, Cagney suddenly gets one of his severe headaches and begins to fall forward, accidentally firing a shot which alarms everyone. Wycherly manages to steer Cagney into a bedroom so the gang will not see him go through the agony of his recurrent searing headaches. She massages his head and coolly talks to him until the seizure passes. "Now go out there and show 'em who's boss, son...Remember, top of the world!" Wycherly orders her son and Cagney marches into the outer room to tell everyone to start packing, that they are leaving for southern California. A gang member rushes inside to tell Cagney that he has just heard over the car radio that a storm is coming up. Cagney explodes, shouting at the henchman, "I thought I told you to stay off that radio?" He knocks the thug down and sneers at him, "If that radio is dead, it's gonna have company!" The gang clears out, but Rainey is left behind to freeze to death in the cabin. His friend, Cassell, is told to kill Rainey and runs back into the cabin as the gang members get into their cars. Cassell tells Rainey that he will send him help, and leaves him some cigarettes, firing his revolver into the air to make it sound as if he has carried out Cagney's execution order. He then runs outside and gets into the car. The gang flees south, Cagney taking mother Wycherly and wife Mayo with him. The other gang members leave in another car but before the cars take their separate paths, Mayo gives Cochran, at the wheel of the other car, a long, knowing look as he smiles back at her. Meanwhile, federal agent Archer is trying to piece together the identities of the train robbers and is having no luck. He then gets a report of Rainey being found frozen to death in the cabin, and when he learns that the dead man has been scalded he thinks it might have been from the steam engine in the train holdup. He orders everything in the cabin dusted for fingerprints. A report is teletyped to him that Cassell's prints have been found on the package of cigarettes in the dead man's pocket and Cassell is a "known member of the Jarrett gang." Archer now conducts a hunt for Cagney, realizing that Wycherly is the link to the man he wants, that "wherever Ma goes, Cody goes." One of his agents finds Wycherly buying fresh strawberries for her son, his favorite, at a fruit stand in downtown L.A. and he affixes a rag to the bumper of her car so the vehicle can be identified and followed, then calls Archer. The agent has his cars follow the woman to a motor court where Cagney is staying with Wycherly and Mayo. But only Archer, driving alone, enters the court and tries to stop the fleeing Cagney who shoots and wounds him before speeding away with Wycherly and Mayo. Cagney cleverly avoids pursuing police cars by driving into a drive-in movie where the trio nervously watch TASK FORCE (a Warner Bros. movie starring Gary Cooper). While sitting in the drive-in, Cagney realizes he must figure out a plan to clear himself of the train robbery. He has murdered two men and will face the death penalty if found guilty. He remembers a robbery in Illinois, done by "Scratch Morton," who has not been caught. He tells mother Wycherly that he is going to turn himself in for the Illinois robbery and get a lesser sentence than what the train robbery would bring and he will soon be out of prison, rejoining her and Mayo. "You're the smart one, Cody," beams Wycherly. Cagney confesses to the robbery in Illinois and is given a prison sentence. Archer, who has no witnesses that Cagney shot him, plants a police informant, O'Brien, in Cagney's cell. O'Brien overcomes Cagney's natural suspicion of strangers by covering for Cagney when the gangster has his seizures, becoming a surrogate Wycherly, and is taken into the gangster's confidence. Menawhile, Mayo, as expected, takes up with Cochran on the outside. Wycherly, visiting Cagney in prison, tells her son about Cochran's betrayal and how he should be careful inside the prison. Cagney rubs his head knowingly since he has almost been killed in a machine shop accident where one of Cochran's friends dropped a trash barrel from a crane, almost killing him. He realizes that the man, Guilfoyle, has tried to kill him on Cochran's orders. Before leaving the prison's visiting area, Wycherly promises Cagney that she will deal with Cochran and Cagney tries to stop her, clinging to the screen separating them, but Wycherly is gone. While eating in the mess hall with hundreds of other prisoners, Cagney gets the news that Wycherly is dead. He begins screaming wildly, jumps on the long table, staggers down it and off it and, when a guard rushes up, Cagney knocks him cold. Another guard and another run up to the berserk, screaming prisoner and he knocks them out despite taking brutal chops from their billy clubs. Several guards finally corner him and drag him screaming like the madman he has become from the mess hall. Cagney is put into a straitjacket and one of his men brings him some soup to eat, feeding him. Cagney whispers to the inmate, Osterloh, to bring the gun he has been hiding the next time he brings in food. When Osterloh returns at the next meal time, he unties Cagney's straitjacket and slips him the gun. The gangster rounds up the psychiatrists who have arrived in the prison clinic to take him to a mental hospital and also members of his gang, including O'Brien, escaping the prison in the doctors' car. Guilfoyle is taken along in the trunk of the car as Cagney's prisoner.

Once the gang is on the outside, Cagney stops at a farmhouse, changes clothes, and makes arrangements to rejoin his old gang. Before leaving for the coast, Cagney steps outside, passes the car, and hears Guilfoyle shouting from the trunk that he can't breathe. Cagney, chewing on a chicken drumstick, pulls out his automatic and shouts: "Stuffy in there, Parker? I'll give it some air!" He then blasts the trunk, killing Guilfoyle, and, just as casually, tosses away the bone from the drumstick and gets into another car. When Mayo hears that Cagney has escaped she runs out of a farmhouse in California and into a garage, leaving Cochran, who is preparing for Cagney's arrival by barricading the building. But in the garage Cagney grabs his slatternly wife and is about to kill her when she tells him that she has been held a virtual prisoner by Cochran. To get herself off the hook, Mayo lies and tells Cagney that it was Cochran who shot his mother in the back when she was the one who really killed Ma Wycherly. Cagney goes into the house, using Mayo as a decoy, and shoots Cochran. His gang members rush into the house and Cagney stands grinning at the top of the stairs with Mayo. At his feet is the dead Cochran. Cagney says, while looking down at his men and kicking Cochran's body down the stairs, "Here, catch!" O'Brien, still with the gang but unable to contact Archer and the other federal agents, tries to slip away one night but runs right into Cagney who steps from the woods, eyes glazed. He tells O'Brien that he was "out there...talking to Ma. I liked it, liked it a lot....Maybe I am nuts!" Later, Clark appears; he is the man who selects the robbery jobs for Cagney's gang. The gang is scheduled by Clark to loot a payroll from an oil refinery. Cagney, remembering the story of the Trojan Horse his mother told him as a boy, hides his men inside an empty oil truck and heads for the plant. But O'Brien has installed an oscillator on the bottom of the truck and its signal is picked up by Archer and his agents who trail the truck to the oil refinery. The driver of the truck, who is Clark's man and a recently released convict, MacDonald (MacDonald would later play Frank Miller in HIGH NOON), recognizes O'Brien as a federal agent and tells Cagney while the gang is inside the plant. Cagney screams that he trusted O'Brien like his own brother and shoots at him, but hits one of his own men. O'Brien escapes to join Archer and an army of police outside. Cagney and his men are trapped and one by one they are killed, leaving Cagney on top of a huge oil tank. Using a high-powered rifle with a telescopic lens while enormous lights play upon Cagney, O'Brien shoots him, but Cagney only laughs hysterically while he staggers around wounded, then lets go one of his shots which ignites the oil. Flames begin to shoot out of pipes as the police, realizing that the entire field can explode at any second, run for cover. Cagney keeps firing wildly, his shots going into the tank, and more flames appear. Dying from his wounds, Cagney suddenly stands upright, spreads his arms, and looks heavenward to shout at the top of his lungs: "Made it, Ma! Top of the world!" The oil tank then erupts with an ear-splitting explosion, killing Cagney and igniting the entire oil field. O'Brien looks on in awe, saying, "Cody Jarrett–he finally made it to the top of the world and it blew up in his face." The film ends as one titanic explosion after another is shown, flames shooting skyward in billowing bursts, fireballs looking like minature atom bombs going off. WHITE HEAT is undoubtedly the toughest and most explicit crime film ever made, brilliantly directed by Walsh who deftly guided Cagney to perform his virtuoso essay of a psychopathic gangster. Cagney is as lethal to his own kind as he is to people of law and order, a homicidal maniac whose insanity is certifiable, and he actually knows it. His role is based on Arthur "Doc" Barker, and Wycherly is playing the infamous "Ma" Barker, the earthshaking catalyst of his criminal pursuits. Cagney's mother fixation was graphically demonstrated when the actor, following one of his epileptic-type fits, is soothed by Wycherly. He gratefully moves toward her and then, a grown man, sits in her lap, to allow her to assure him that all is fine. This startling scene, like many another in this classic *film noir* entry, was Cagney's own idea. Again, to achieve the high level of intensity of his part and project the lunatic he had to make believable, Cagney called on his own experiences to provide impetus for his moments of insanity. He later stated: "I knew what deranged people sounded like, because, once as a youngster, I had visited Ward's Island where a pal's uncle was in the hospital for the insane. My God, what an education that was! The shrieks, the screams of those people under restraint. I remembered those cries, saw that they fitted, and I called on my memory to do as required." His portrayal is nothing short of spectacular and his final image in the film (shot in an actual oil refinery in Torrance, California), about to be blown skyward, calling out his warped triumph to his deceased mother, is probably Cagney's most memorable, next to scenes in YANKEE DOODLE DANDY.

p, Louis F. Edelman; d, Raoul Walsh; w, Ivan Goff, Ben Roberts (based on a story by Virginia Kellogg); ph, Sid Hickox; m, Max Steiner; ed, Owen Marks; art d, Edward Carrere; set d, Fred M. MacLean; cos, Leah Rhodes; spec eff, Roy Davidson, H.F. Koenekamp; makeup, Perc Westmore.

Crime Drama   **Cas.**   **(PR:C   MPAA:NR)**

WHITE HORSE INN, THE**½   (1959, Ger.) 99m Sam Baker
                                                                                Associates c

Johanna Matz *(Josepha)*, Johannes Heesters *(Dr. Siedler)*, Walter Mueller *(Leopold)*, Paul Westermeier *(Giesecke)*, Rudolf Forster *(Kaiser Franz Joseph)*, Marianne Wischmann *(Ottilie)*, Sepp Nigg *(Hinzelmann)*, Ingrid Pan *(Klarchen)*, Ulrich Beiger *(Sigismund)*, Klaus Pohl *(Loidl)*, Walter Koch *(Piccolo)*, Alfred Pongratz *(Burgermeister)*.

Matz is the lady owner of the famous White Horse Inn. She finds she's got

plenty on her hands, and not just with management duties. Mueller, the headwaiter, is madly in love with her, though she is more interested in Heesters. In the end, Heesters marries Wischmann, the daughter of one of his business rivals, leaving Matz at last returning Mueller's much offered affections. This minor musical is fluff at best, though enjoyable for what it is. (In German; English subtitles.)

p, Erik Charell; d, Willi Forst; w, Horst Budjuhn, Charell, Harry Halm (based on the operetta by Hans Mueller and Charell from a play by Oskar Blumenthal and Gustav Kadelburg); ph, Guenther Anders (Agfacolor); m, Ralph Benatzky.

Musical   **(PR:A   MPAA:NR)**

WHITE HUNTER**   (1936) 65m FOX bw

Warner Baxter *(Capt. Clark Rutledge)*, June Lang *(Toni Varek)*, Gail Patrick *(Helen Varek)*, Alison Skipworth *(Aunt Frederika)*, Wilfrid Lawson *(Michael Varek)*, George Hassell *(Valentine Ponosonby-Smith)*, Ernest Whitman *(Abdi)*, Forrester Harvey *(Pembrooke)*, Willie Fung *(Wong)*, Olaf Hytton *(Barton)*, Ralph Cooper *(Ali)*, Will Stanton *(Harry)*.

This is a quintessential safari picture with each cliche and stereo-type firmly in place. Because of a troubled past, explorer Baxter lives as an exile. He's hired by Lawson, the man responsible for his father's death, to lead an expedition into darkest Africa. All past deeds are forgotten when Baxter falls in love with Lawson's daughter Lang, who is along for the adventure. Through skillful editing of much stock footage, this studio-shot picture has a realistic look that makes its story more interesting than it deserves to be. The characters and dialog are exactly what one would expect, acted in the usual fashion by a competent cast. The audience always knows what's going to happen before the characters do (a leopard hiding in a tree is obvious to everyone but the seemingly knowledgeable guide and his party) but for what this is, it's not too bad. Probably worth a look for camp fans.

p, Darryl F. Zanuck; d, Irving Cummings; w, Sam Duncan, Kenneth Earl (based on a story by Gene Markey); ph, Chester Lyons; m, Arthur Lange; ed, Allen McNeil; md, Lange.

Drama   **(PR:A   MPAA:NR)**

WHITE HUNTER**   (1965) 86m Signal International/Herts-Lion
                                                                                International c

George Michael *(Narrator)*, David Georgiades, June Michael, John Haddad, Carole Michael, Roger Blake, Jack Hutcheson, Emile Georgiades.

Some big game hunters go off to the African wilderness and stalk the game. There are plenty of lions, giraffes, leopards, elephants, and even some baboons in what amounts to an African documentary with a simplistic fictional story line grafted on.

p,d&w, George Michael; ph, Tim Spring; John B. Kennard (Eastmancolor).

Adventure   **(PR:A   MPAA:NR)**

WHITE HUNTRESS*½   (1957, Brit.) 86m Summit/AIP c (GB:
                                                                                GOLDEN IVORY)

Robert Urquhart *(Jim Dobson)*, John Bentley *(Paul Dobson)*, Susan Stephen *(Ruth Meecham)*, Alan Tarlton *(Seth)*, Howarth Wood *(Meecham)*, Maureen Connell *(Elizabeth Johnson)*, Tom Lithgow *(Peter Johnson)*, Kip Kamoi *(Kip)*.

Bentley and Urquhart are a pair of brothers leading some settlers through the jungles of Africa. Both are smitten with the charms of Stephen, daughter of the settlers' leader. Later the colonists are joined by Tarlton, a killer on the run. He and Bentley attempt to change the group's course in a search for gold, but their path only leads this duo to death at the hands of local natives. A simplistic plot greatly hampered by a running time much longer than is sufferable.

p, John Croydon, Peter Crane, George Breakston, Ray Stahl; d, Breakston; w, Dermot Quinn; ph, John Lawrence (Technicolor); m, Philip Green.

Adventure   **(PR:A   MPAA:NR)**

WHITE LEGION, THE*½   (1936) 81m GN bw

Ian Keith *(Dr. Murray)*, Tala Birell *(Dr. Sterne)*, Ferdinand Gottschalk *(Dr. Fontaine)*, Rollo Lloyd *(The Colonel)*, Lionel Pape *(Dr. Travis)*, Teru Shimada *(Dr. Nogi)*, Suzanne Kaaren *(Gloria Blank)*, Ferdinand Munier *(Sen. Blank)*, Nigel de Brulier *(Father Gonzales)*, Nina Campana *(Maria)*, Warner Richmond *(Burke)*, Harry Allen *(McKenzie)*, Don Barclay *(Miggs)*, Snub Pollard *(Baker)*, Robert Warwick *(Capt. Parker)*, Edward Piel *(Dr. Moore)*, Jason Robards, Sr *(Kramer)*.

When yellow fever breaks out amidst the workers along the Panama Canal construction site it's up to Keith to discover the cause of the disease. After some standard trials and tribulations, including the death of one doctor, scandal with a senator's daughter, and a pet monkey nearly destroying the research, the dread disease is conquered and all ends up happy. Story development lacks the sense of urgency that might make this interesting. Keith isn't bad in the lead but the story is too predictable for him to conquer.

p, Bennie F. Zeidman; d&w, Karl Brown; ph, Harry Jackson; ed, Duncan Mansfield; md, Dr. Hugo Riesenfeld.

Drama   Cas.   (PR:A MPAA:NR)

WHITE LIES*   (1935) 63m COL bw

Walter Connolly (John Mitchell), Fay Wray (Joan Mitchell), Victor Jory (Terry Condon), Leslie Fenton (Dan Oliver), Irene Hervey (Mary Mallory), Robert Allen (Arthur Bradford), William Demarest (Roberts), Catherine Clare Ward, Robert Emmett O'Connor, Jessie Arnold, Mary Foy, Oscar Apfel.

Natty traffic cop Jory gives a ticket to a politically powerful newspaper publisher (Connolly). Connolly threatens to break the policeman but is given a tongue lashing by his daughter Wray. This will not stop Connolly, who continues to publish anything he wants. He does, however, arrange for Jory to get promoted and ends up being saved by the latter when an embezzler harmed by Connolly's yellow journalism enters his office with a gun. Later Wray is implicated in murder and arrested by Jory. Connolly is forced to print the story. Jory, again demoted due to Connolly's string pulling, goes after the murderer himself. WHITE LIES was produced after an agreement between the Hays Office and the Crime Commission in Washington D.C. that all movie policemen should be given a dignified portrayal. This film quickly espoused the new philosophy, making Jory a Yale graduate, snappy dresser, classical music lover, flower enthusiast, and attentive to his legal duties. It's a good thing no one at the Hays Office was able to see SERPICO or PRINCE OF THE CITY, which could have caused the censors cardiac arrest.

d, Leo Bulgakov; w, Harold Shumate (based on his story); ph, Benjamin Kline, ed, Otto Meyer.

Crime   (PR:A MPAA:NR)

WHITE LIGHTNIN' ROAD*   (1967) 95m J.R.T./Ormond c

Arline Hunter, Tim Ormond, Earl "Snake" Richards.

A Southern exploitation feature involving the genre's perennial favorite topics: shotgun weddings and car races. This one features a big moonshine car race. Produced by the Ormonds, who in addition to producing cheapies like this also worked on Lash LaRue westerns and in vaudeville.

p, June Ormond, Ron Ormond; d, R. Ormond.

Action/Drama   (PR:A MPAA:NR)

WHITE LIGHTING**   (1953) 61m AA/MON bw

Stanley Clements (Mike), Steve Brodie (Jack), Gloria Blondell (Ann), Barbara Bestar (Margaret), Lyle Talbot (Rocky), Frank Jenks (Benny), Paul Bryar (Stew), Lee Van Cleef (Brutus), Myron Healey (Nelson), Riley Hill (Norwin), Tom Hanlon (Announcer), Jane Easton (Girl), John Bleifer (Tailor), Duncan Richardson (Davey), Joel Marston.

When hotshot egomaniac Clements joins the Red Devils hockey team, the other players and coaching staff are willing to overlook his brash personality because of his talent on the ice. The team goes on a successful winning streak thanks to his abilities, but this causes some problems for his teammate Healey. The latter is being paid by some mobsters so the Red Devils will lose. Coach Brodie already is having problems with the fresh kid, and Clements seriously considers throwing games himself when confronted by the mob. But in the end honesty triumphs and he leads the team on to victory in an important game. The story is formula material but has good visual quality sometimes lacking in sports films.

p, Ben Schwalb; d, Edward Bernds; w, Charles R. Marion; ph, Lester White; m, Marlin Skiles; ed, Bruce Schoengarth; art d, David Milton.

Crime/Sports   (PR:A MPAA:NR)

WHITE LIGHTNING***   (1973) 101m UA c (AKA: MCKLUSKY)

Burt Reynolds (Gator Mcklusky), Jennifer Billingsley (Lou), Ned Beatty (Sheriff Connors), Bo Hopkins (Boy Boone), Matt Clark (Dude Watson), Louise Latham (Martha Culpepper), Diane Ladd (Maggie), R. G. Armstrong (Big Bear), Conlan Carter (Deputy), Dabbs Greer (Pa McKlusky), Lincoln Demyan (Supt. Simms), John Steadman (Skeeter), Iris Korn (Ma McKlusky), Stephanie Burchfield (Jenny), Barbara Muller (Louella), Robert Ginnaven (Harvey), Fay Martin (Sister Linda Fay), Richard Allin, Bill Bond (Treasury Agents), Glenn Wilder (Junior), Dick Ziker, Buddy Joe Hooker (Highway Patrolmen), Kathy Finley (Student), Sherry Boucher (Sherry Lynn).

Convicted of running moonshine whiskey, Reynolds is offered his release from prison if he will serve as an informer and help catch his one-time cohorts. Convinced that crooked sheriff Beatty has murdered his younger brother–a civil rights activist–Reynolds reluctantly agrees in order to be able to bring the killer to justice. Assisted by fellow informant Clark, Reynolds infiltrates the organization, finding that the head of the mob is his nemesis Beatty. Along the way, Reynolds manages to steal demon driver Hopkins' girl friend Billingsley, get in a few fights, and participate in some amazing stunt-driving chases. Generally regarded as the best of the

Reynolds-starring "good ol' boy" films, with fine, sensitive performances by the leads and a wonderful supporting cast. The vastly inferior sequel GATOR was released in 1976.

p, Arthur Gardner, Jules Levy; d, Joseph Sargent; w, William Norton; ph, Edward Rosson (DeLuxe Color), m, Charles Bernstein; ed, George Nicholson; spec eff, Cliff Wenger.

Action   Cas.   (PR:C MPAA:PG)

WHITE LILAC**   (1935, Brit.) 67m FOX British bw

Basil Sydney (Ian Mackie), Judy Gunn (Mollie), Claude Dampier (Percy), Percy Marmont (Tollitt), Gwenllian Gill (Muriel), Leslie Perrins (Iredale), Constance Travers (Jessie), Billy Holland (Harvey), Majorie Hume (Mrs. Lyall), Edward Dignon, Edward Ashley, Vashti Taylor.

A man is murdered in a small English village and everyone is a suspect. It seems the dead man was the town's most unpopular resident and each person in town has a motive for the crime. However, for every suspect there is an alibi, which makes this a difficult case to solve. Average mystery.

p, Ernest Garside; d, Albert Parker; w, (based on the play by Ladislas Fodor); ph, Alex Bryce.

Mystery   (PR:A MPAA:NR)

WHITE LINE, THE**   (1952, Ital.) 87m Lux bw

Gina Lollobrigida (Donata Sebastian), Raf Vallone (Domenico), Enzo Stajola (Pasqualino Sebastian), Erno Crisa (Stefano), Cesco Baseggio (Giovanni Sebastian), Ernesto Almirante (The Grandfather), Silvia Curetti (The Grandmother), Gianni Cavalieri (Pentecoste), Gino Cavalieri (The Priest), Fabio Neri (Gaspare), Mario Sestan (Lampadina), Antonio Catania (Acquasanta), Giordano Cesini (Cacciavite), Ray Morgan (English Narration).

Following WW II, the city of Trieste and surrounding villages were partitioned in accordance with a ruling of the International Peace Commission. Parts of the area came under Western-block Italian dominion and other parts under Eastern bloc Yugoslav control. A white line is drawn through a small community to delineate the division. The line meanders capriciously. A farmhouse is separated from its adjacent fields by the arbitrary division a priest retains his church while losing his oratory to a hostile regime. The line divides the slope down which the local children coast their wagons, to their dismay, so they decide to do something about it. Young Stajola steals one of the boundary-making stakes. Both regimes threaten reprisals unless the missing stake is restored. When the frightened boy secretly attempts to return the stolen stake, he is shot and killed by border guards. This tragedy unites the villagers on both sides of the border. Lollobrigida, who has been unable to choose between her East-bloc and West-bloc suitors–Vallone and Crisa–is finally able to maker her decision now that the populace is as one. The slight romance detracts from the story line in this picture which is at its best when dealing with the children. (In Italian; English subtitles, opening and closing narrative in English.)

p, Carlo Ponti; d, Luigi Zampa; w, Piero Tellini, Stefano Terra, Clare Cataleno (based on a story by Tellini); ph, Carlo Montuori; m, Carlo Rustichelli; md, Ugo Giancomozzi; set d, Aldo Buzzi.

Drama   (PR:C MPAA:NR)

WHITE LINE FEVER½**   (1975, Can.) 89m International Cinemedia Center/COL c

Jan-Michael Vincent (Carrol Jo Hummer), Kay Lenz (Jerri Hummer), Slim Pickens (Duana Haller), L. Q. Jones (Buck Wessle), Don Porter (Josh Cutler), Sam Laws (Pops Dinwiddie), Johnny Ray McGhee (Carnell), Leigh French (Lucy), R. G. Armstrong (Prosecutor), Martin Kove (Clem), Jamie Anderson (Jamie), Ron Nix (Deputy), Dick Miller (Birdie), Arnold Jeffers (Reporter), Curgie Pratt (Defense Lawyer), John David Garfield (Witness Miller).

Returning from a stint in the Air Force, Vincent borrows money to buy a truck, hoping to make enough money hauling produce to marry Lenz and set up housekeeping. Vincent gets a load from Pickens, but then discovers that the long-haul business is run by racketeers, and that smuggling is a routine part of the industry. Refusing to participate in such illicit activities, Vincent is beaten by Pickens' thugs. Recovered from the attack, he retaliates by getting a load from Pickens while holding him at gunpoint. Other independent truckers rally to his support and Pickens relents, giving him more cargo to carry. Big shipping boss Porter, his dominion threatened by the honest, charismatic young trucker, sends thugs to burn Vincent's home, but to no avail; he remains rigidly upright in his moral stance. Porter has the backsliding Pickens killed and, with the help of crooked public prosecutor Armstrong, tries to pin the crime on Vincent. Through all these travails, Lenz remains the saintly, supportive wife, concealing her pregnancy from her husband for as long as possible to prevent him from worrying about her. Good wins over evil as Vincent finally singlehandedly reforms the trucking industry–on acetate if not in life–in this quick-paced saga of Jack-the-Giant-Killer. Well acted and with excellent truck choreography by the talented stunt crew, the picture is a cut above most little-man-beats-the-system films. Director Kaplan's premiere effort at a nonsoft core sex film (he was responsible for Roger Corman's NIGHT CALL NURSES, 1972, among others).

p, John Kemeny; d, Jonathan Kaplan; w, Kaplan, Ken Friedman; ph, Fred Koenekamp (Metrocolor); m, David Nichtern; ed, O. Nicholas Brown; md, Billy Byers; art d, Sydney Litwack; set d, Sam Jones; stunt coordinator, Carey Loftin, Nate Long, Joe Hooker.

Action   Cas.   (PR:C MPAA:PG)

WHITE MAN, THE   (SEE: SQUAW MAN, THE, 1931)

WHITE NIGHTS*   (1961, Ital./Fr.) 106m CIAS-Vides-Intermondia/
United Motion Picture Organization bw (LE NOTTI BIANCHE; NUITS BLANCHES)

Maria Schell (*Natalia*), Marcello Mastroianni (*Mario*), Jean Marais (*Lodger*), Clara Calamai (*Prostitute*), Marcella Rovena (*Housewife*), Maria Zanolli (*Housekeeper*), Dick Sanders (*Dancer*), Giorgio Listuzzi (*Policeman*), Elena Fancora (*Cashier*), Alberto Carloni (*Bar Proprietor*), Ferdinando Gera (*Father*), Leonida Montesi (*Mother*), Anna Filippini (*Daughter*), Lanfranco Ceccarelli, Angelo-Galassi, Renato Terra, Corrado Pani.

Lonely, introspective clerk Mastroianni offers his assistance to the sobbing Schell, whom he spots standing on a canal bridge one winter evening. She explains that she awaits the return of the man she loves, a one-time lodger at the home of her blind grandmother, a seaman who had promised to return to her in one year. Suspecting that her tardy fantasy lover may have returned to a nearby hotel, she asks that Mastroianni take a note to him. Sorely smitten with Schell, Mastroianni wastes little time in destroying the note. Meeting her again the following evening at her place of assignment, Mastroianni importunes Schell to go to a dance with him. Following an evening of choreographic abandon, the enthused pair stroll homeward, Mastroianni uncharacteristically verbalizing his romantic fantasies of Schell to her. As they approach the bridge of assignation, she spots the silhouette of a man standing there. She runs to meet her sailor sweetheart, leaving Mastroianni in the company of a stray dog. Dostoyevsky's tale of the reality of fantasy was transposed by Visconti from mid-1800s St. Petersburg to a modern Italian town of meandering canals, its romantic mood counterpoised by a group of prostitutes, pickpockets, and motor scooters. Filmed entirely in the studio, the sombre, misty sets are reminiscent of the murky mood pieces of Marcel Carne. Illusory, dreamlike flashback memories mingle strangely with the realities of the rock 'n' roll cacophony of the dialog-free dance-hall scenes. A deliberately artificial exercise by a director who had previously specialized in "neorealism."

p, Franco Cristaldi; d, Luchino Visconti; w, Visconti, Suso Cecchi d'Amico (based on the story "Belye Nochi" by Fedor Mikhailovich Dostoyevsky); ph, Giuseppe Rotunno; m, Nino Rota; ed, Mario Serandrei; md, Franco Ferrara; art d, Mario Chiari; set d, Engo Eusepi; cos, Piero Tasi; ch, Dick Sanders; makeup, Alberto De Rossi.

Drama   (PR:O MPAA:NR)

WHITE ORCHID, THE**   (1954) 81m UA c

William Lundigan (*Robert Burton*), Peggie Castle (*Kathryn Williams*), Armando Silvestre (*Juan Cervantes*), Rosenda Monteros (*Lupita*), Jorge Trevino (*Arturo*), Alejandro de Montenegro (*Miguel*), Miguel A. Gallardo (*Pedro*).

Archeologist Lundigan and photographer Castle trek through the jungles of Mexico with the help of guide Silvestre hoping to find the remnants of a lost Toltec civilization, said to still be viable. Lush vegetation and credible old monumental ruins provide the most interest in this hackneyed expedition story, with the two male leads vying for Castle's favors until, finally, Silvestre sacrifices his life so that the two survivors may make it back to civilization. The Mexican players tend to outshine the Anglo leads, with honors going to Silvestre and Monteros as the girl who loves him. The film's one song is vocalized in Spanish by de Montenegro and Gallardo early in the picture, then reprised in English by the off-camera Durant.

p&d, Reginald Le Borg; w, David Duncan, Le Borg; ph, Gilbert Warrenton (Eastmancolor); m. Antonio Diaz Conde; ed, Jose W. Bustos; m/l, "Femme Fatale," Chuy Hernandez (sung by Don Durant).

Adventure   (PR:A MPAA:NR)

WHITE PARADE, THE½   (1934) 90m FOX bw

Loretta Young (*June Arden*), John Boles (*Ronald Hall III*), Dorothy Wilson (*Zita Scofield*), Muriel Kirkland (*Glenda Farley*), Sara Haden (*Miss Harrington*), Astrid Allwyn (*Gertrude Mack*), Joyce Compton (*Una Mellon*), June Gittelson (*Pudgy Lucy Stebbins*), Frances Carlon (*Diana Carter*), Rheta Hoy (*Mabel Wiley*), Polly Ann Young (*Hannah Seymour*), Ann Darcy (*Angie Duke*), Jane Barnes (*Miss Watkins*), Jane Darwell (*Miss "Sailor" Roberts*), Lillian West (*Miss Hudson*), Frank Melton (*Dr. Barnes*), Frank Conroy (*Dr. Thorne*), Walter Johnson (*Dr. Moore*), Fred Wallace (*Soda Jerk*), Sunny Ingraham (*Bit*), Edward Earle (*Bolger*), Noel Francis (*Clare*), Ben Bard (*Tony*).

Life at a nurses' training school in the Midwest is portrayed with the usual 1930s woman-picture conventions fully intact. Young, arriving at Fox after

a stint of romantic roles at Warner Bros., plays an unusually dramatic role as a woman who learns a few things about herself while studying for her nursing degree. Boles, a rich Boston boy, gives her a choice: a career or him. It's tough, but in the end she sticks by her trade, convinced that helping others truly will bring her the happiness she desires. The cast is strong as it goes about the usual complications, guided by even direction. THE WHITE PARADE is really nothing but a soap opera, but is well done for what it is.

p, Jesse L. Lasky; d, Irving Cummings; w, Rian James, Sonya Levien, Ernest Pascal, Lasky, Jesse L. Lasky, Jr. (based on the novel by James); ph, Arthur Miller; md, Louis de Francesco.

Drama   (PR:A MPAA:NR)

WHITE PONGO*   (1945) 74M PRC bw

Richard Fraser (*Bishop*), Maris Wrixon (*Pamela*), Lionel Royce (*Van Doorn*), Al Eben (*Kroegert*), Gordon Richards (*Sir Harry*), Michael Dyne (*Carswell*), George Lloyd (*Baxter*), Larry Steers (*Dr. Kent*), Milton Kibbee (*Gunderson*), Egon Brecher (*Old Doctor*), Joel Fluellen (*Mumbo Jumbo*).

The Neufeld-Newfield brothers bleached their NABONGA gorilla suit from the previous year to make this camp jungle drama. Undercover policeman Fraser goes on safari with a group of British biologists out to capture a mythic white primate believed to be the missing link. Fraser suspects the expedition's guide to be a killer. Sure enough, once in the wilds, the wicked guide suborns mutiny among the bearers, strands the scientists, abducts the beautiful daughter of the expedition's chief, and goes off to find some gold he's heard about. Unbeknownst to the bad man and his minions, his band has ambled into the abode of the blond title beast, which strangles the guide and–apparently hankering for a little female companionship–re-abducts Wrixon. Bearing the shrieking beauty–her blouse now in tatters–to his cave, the albino is confronted by a brunette counterpart. The two beasts battle over the battered beauty. As the pristine Pongo hurls his rival primate from a cliff, Fraser and the biologists arrive. They wound the surviving beast with rifle shots, cage him, and take him back to England for further study. Will these gorillas never learn to treat a girl with a little respect? The film is filled with irrelevant, mismatched stock shots of various African beasts.

p, Sigmund Neufeld; d, Sam Newfield; w, Raymond L. Schrock (based on his story); ph, Jack Greenhalgh; ed, Holbrook N. Todd; md, Leo Erdody; art d, Edward C. Jewell.

Adventure   Cas.   (PR:AA MPAA:NR)

WHITE RAT zero*   (1972) 76m Mulnik Films c

Hal Sherman (*Mike Capon*), Alisha Fontaine (*Alice Leasen*), Joe Petrullo (*Alexander Poultrez*), Carolyn Lenz (*Paula Davis*), Ray Fisher (*Lou Alton*), Christine Somerfield (*Cindy Capone*), Richie Closs (*Pimp*), High Bennet (*Krauss*).

Inept, amatuer trash about a private eye who goes on the trail of some baddies after his hoydenish blonde nightclub singer heartthrob turns up dead. The ending is a virtual blood bath, which the production team may have thought meant "dramatic conclusion." Supposedly made in just two weeks on a $25,000 budget, it sure looks that way. The acting, script, and direction are without merit. Surprisingly, the photography has its moments.

p, Nick Paindiris; d, Steve Mullen; w, Paindiris, Mullen; ph, Dave Axelrod; m, Tony Esposito; ed, James Stark.

Crime   (PR:O MPAA:NR)

WHITE, RED, YELLOW, PINK*   (1966, Ital.) 94m S.S.&B. Film/Seymour Borde c-bw

"White–The Inkindest Cut": Anita Ekberg (*Albachiaria*), Carlo Guiffre (*Vitaliano*), Sandro Dori (*The Mute*), "Red–Veni, Vidi, Vici": Carlo Guiffre (*Apollodorus*), Maria Grazia Buccella (*Poppaea*), Giancarlo Cobelli (*Nero*), Marcella Ruffini (*Sulpicia*), "Yellow–Suicides Anonymous": Carlo Guiffre (*Brighenti*), Agnes Spaak (*Enrichetta*), Claudia Gianotti (*Mrs. Brighenti*), "Pink–The First": Carlo Guiffre (*Johnny*), Yoko Tani (*Yoko*).

Most of the color of this episodic Italian sex farce is in the title, since only one of the four segments is filmed in Technicolor. A tour de force for the talents of Guiffre, who takes a disparate role in each episode, working with a number of actresses. In "White," veterinarian Guiffre has an impassioned fling with the voluptuous Ekberg, who proves to have the threatening profession of pig castrator. In "Red" –the one episode in color–he's diddling the wife of the fiddling Nero, bathing in milk with the beauteous Buccella before Cobelli burns Rome. In "Yellow," Guiffre finds himself between the two flags of wife Gianotti and mistress Spaak. In "Pink" his liaison with oriental Tani results in his pregnany; after the delivery, he begs his lustful companion to use protection. Heavy-handed direction and sledgehammer humor mar this farce. (In Italian; English subtitles.)

p, Francesco Mazzei; d, Massimo Midi; m, Piero Umliani.

Comedy   (PR:O MPAA:NR)

WHITE ROSE OF HONG KONG** (1965, Jap.) 110m Toho c
(HONKON NO SHIROIBARA)

Chang Mei Yao *(Yuli Rin)*, Tsutomu Yamazaki *(Shirio Matsumoto)*, Akira Takarada *(Susumu Uzuki)*, Kumi Mizuno *(Yoshiko Nakao)*, Kenjiro Ishiyama *(Syozo Tabe)*, Mar Chi *(Eidatsu Ki)*, Yu Fujiki *(Chief of Police Jin)*, Eijiro Yanagi *(Kiyoaki Hayashi)*.

A morphine smuggling ring operates out of Hong Kong. When a detective attempts to break up this operation he meets a Chinese woman and learns her family is behind the outfit.

p, Masumi Fujimoto; d, Jun Fukuda; w, Ichiro Okeda (based on a story by Shinobu Hashimoto); ph, Shinsaku Uno (Tohoscope, Eastmancolor); m, Sadao Bekku.

Crime (PR:O MPAA:NR)

WHITE SAVAGE, 1941 (SEE: SOUTH OF TAHITI, 1941)

WHITE SAVAGE** (1943) 75m UNIV c (GB: WHITE CAPTIVE)

Jon Hall *(Kaloe)*, Maria Montez *(Princess Tahia)*, Sabu *(Orano)*, Don Terry *(Gris)*, Turhan Bey *(Tamara)*, Thomas Gomez *(Sam Miller)*, Sidney Toler *(Wong)*, Paul Guilfoyle *(Erik)*, Constance Purdy *(Blossom)*, Al Kikume *(Guard)*, Frederick Brunn *(Sully)*, Pedro de Cordoba *(Candlemaker)*, Anthony Warde *(Clark)*, Jim Mitchell, Bella Lewitzky *(Specialty Dancers)*, John Harmon *(Williams)*, Minerva Urecal, Kate Lawson *(Native Women)*.

Hall is a fisherman who hunts sharks for the vitamin A in their livers. He seeks permission to fish in the waters surrounding Temple Island–ruled by princess Montez–by asking Sabu, the son of the princess' maid, to arrange a meeting. Sabu brings Hall to the island and the fisherman and Montez immediately fall in love. But when Hall asks to fish the local waters, she assumes that he is only out to get the treasure in the island's pool and orders him from the island, though they reconcile when Sabu arranges another meeting. Meanwhile, trader Gomez, who is after the treasure, involves Montez's brother Bey in a rigged card game, trying to make him lose the deed to the island. Hall, however, joins the game and wins the deed, angering Bey, who strikes him. The next day the inhabitants of Temple Island are celebrating the engagement of Montez and Hall when Gomez arrives with word that Bey has been murdered and that the evidence points to Hall. The shark hunter is locked up until Sabu helps him to escape and prove his innocence. Gomez arrives to plunder the treasure pool, but an earthquake topples the temple, crushing the villains, and Montez and Hall live on in wedded bliss. Not exactly what one would call a serious picture, it was, however, exactly what wartime audiences wanted to see, lightweight entertainment that had nothing to do with reality. In many ways WHITE SAVAGE is the quintessential second-rate adventure film. It features a ludicrous plot, silly dialog, lurid Technicolor, attractive women in sarongs, and two leads who together couldn't act their way out of a paper bag, but who look good. This was the second teaming of Hall and Montez (ARABIAN NIGHTS [1942] was the first).They would be reunited four more times, often with Sabu, mostly in vehicles even sillier than this, including the delightfully campy COBRA WOMAN (1944).

p, George Waggner; d, Arthur Lubin; w, Richard Brooks (based on a story by Peter Milne); ph, Lester White, William Snyder (Technicolor); m, Frank Skinner; ed, Russell Schoengarth; md, Charles Previn; art d, John B. Goodman, Robert Boyle; set d, R.A. Gausman, I. Webb; cos, Vera West.

Adventure (PR:A MPAA:NR)

WHITE SHADOWS IN THE SOUTH SEAS**½
(1928) 88m COS/MGM bw

Monte Blue *(Dr. Matthew Lloyd)*, Raquel Torres *(Fayaway)*, Robert Anderson *(Sebastian, a Merchant)*.

An early talkie, this film is also one of the first films to deal openly with the ill effects of imposed Western cultures on the natives of the Polynesian Islands. After alcohol, drugs, and the effects of prostitution begin taking their effects on the local tribes, doctor Blue attempts to stop the colonialists from completely destroying the lifestyles and cultural traditions of the natives. Anderson, a merchant who intends to profit from the natives, locks the doctor up in a sinking ship. Blue manages to escape and flees to a previously unknown island populated by Polynesians. There, he marries the daughter of the island chief. However, greed catches up with Blue as well: he tries to sell some of the island pearls to the colonials, who decide to take over the island. Blue tries to stop this but is ultimately killed in the effort. This film was begun as a project for Robert Flaherty, whose documentary MOANA (1925) had been an open, almost lyrical view of the Samoan islands. Flaherty, who also did NANOOK OF THE NORTH and would go on to do LOUISIANA STORY, was a hard-liner on realism. When it was decided to use professional actors in place of local natives, Flaherty left the picture rather than violate his artistic principles. He was replaced by Van Dyke, known in the industry as "One Take Woody" because of his quick, efficient style of direction. Though Van Dyke was really nothing more than a good workmanlike director, he was able to combine all the previously shot elements with his own work to produce a better-than-average picture that carried an important theme.

d, Woodbridge S. Van Dyke; w, Jack Cunningham (based on the novel by Frederick O'Brien); ph, Clyde De Vinna, George Nagle, Bob Roberts; m/l, "Flower of Love," William Axt, David Mendoza.

Drama (PR:A MPAA:NR)

WHITE SHEIK, THE**½ (1956, Ital.) 86m PDC-OFI/Janus-API bw
(LO SCEICCO BIANCO)

Alberto Sordi *(Fernando Rivoli, "The White Sheik")*, Brunella Bovo *(Wanda Cavalli)*, Leopoldo Trieste *(Ivan Cavalli)*, Giulietta Masina *(Cabiria)*, Lilia Landi *(Felga)*, Ernesto Almirante *(Director of "White Sheik" Strip)*, Fanny Marchio *(Marilena Vellardi)*, Gina Mascetti *("White Sheik's" Wife)*, Enzo Maggio *(Hotel Concierge)*, Ettore M. Margadonna *(Ivan's Uncle)*, Jole Silvani, Anna Primula, Nino Billi, Armando Libianchi, Ugo Attanasio, Elettra Zago, Giulio Moreschi, Piero Antonucci, Aroldino the Comedian, Giorgio Savioni, Antonio Acqua, Carlo Mazzoni, Rino Leandri, Guglielmo Leoncini.

The first solo directoral effort for Fellini (after codirecting VARIETY LIGHTS with Alberto Lattuada) is an enjoyable romp that shows the promise of what was to come later in the Italian director's career. Originally released in Italy in 1952, the story deals with newlyweds Bovo and Trieste who are honeymooning in Rome. The couple is a total mismatch, for Trieste lives by strict personal rules while his bride is full of spontaneous energy, eager to follow her dreams. When she learns that a popular photo strip romance magazine "The White Shiek" is being photographed nearby, Bovo splits from her betrothed, heading out to the world of her fantasies. Once Trieste realizes that his wife is missing he begins a frantic search all over Rome. Bovo, in the meantime, has gotten to the shooting site and met Sordi, the man of her dreams. Slowly she gets to know this decidedly unhandsome sheik and the more she learns, the more her dreams melt into reality. Meantime, Trieste has been forced into adopting a few fantasies of his own, constantly making excuses for his wife's absence to relatives in an effort to create an illusion of normalcy. Bovo, heartbroken over the death of her illusions, tries to commit suicide by leaping into the Tiber River, but since the water is low the effort is for naught. Finally husband and wife are reunited just in time to make it to a prearranged visit with the pope during this Holy Year. In THE WHITE SHEIK, Fellini plays with fantasy and reality between the married couple like a conductor with a symphony. Though each character is introduced with a distinct set of perceived realities, both end up changing their outlooks because of unusual circumstances. Trieste, the realist, is forced to create a fantasy, while the ever-dreaming Bovo finds her illusions shattered when coming face to face with fantasy. Where the film falters is in the pacing. The story moves slower than what would be best (the original Italian release ran at 105 minutes), with portions that overplay the dialog. The script originally was proposed as a project for Michaelangelo Antonioni, but producer Rover convinced Fellini that he should direct his own script. Masina, in a bit part as a whore, was the director's wife (and glorious leading lady in much of his work to follow) and was never considered for Bovo's role. Fellini had a strong dislike for the character's personality and thus cast Masina in a more sympathetic role. Though THE WHITE SHEIK is no masterwork by any means, it is certainly an interesting piece. In looking at Fellini's career, one can see the beginnings of what was to be in this piece. Remade as THE WORLD'S GREATEST LOVER (1977).

p, Luigi Rovere; d, Federico Fellini; w, Fellini, Tullio Pinelli, Ennio Flaiano (based on a story by Fellini and Pinelli from an idea by Michaelangelo Antonioni); ph, Arturo Galea; m, Nino Rota; ed, Rolando Bebedetti; art d, Raffaello Tolfo; makeup, Franco Titi.

Comedy (PR:C MPAA:NR)

WHITE SHOULDERS*½ (1931) 80m RKO bw

Mary Astor *(Norma Selbee)*, Jack Holt *(Gordon Kent)*, Ricardo Cortez *(Lawrence Marchmont)*, Sidney Toler *(William Sothern)*, Kitty Kelly *(Marie Fontaine)*, Nicholas Soussanin *(Head Waiter)*, Robert Keith.

Astor, down on her luck, meets multi-millionaire Holt, who plucks her from poverty. Meeting and marrying her in a single day, he-man Holt lavishes jewels and furs on the attractive Astor in a seemingly unending flow. Taking time off from his attendance to his bride, the phlegmatic business baron retreats to his mines to get more ready cash with which to regale his wife. In his absence, gigolo Cortez makes his appearance, wooing the worried wife. Astor succumbs to the bounder's blandishments, as Holt learns upon his return. Holt exacts a terrible revenge upon the two: he hires private detectives to ensure that they remain entwined. Each time Cortez attempts to escape with Astor's jewels, he is rounded up and returned to her; when Astor evades the cad, he is brought to her side. Finally, a convenient first–and never divorced– husband of Astor's is brought into the picture. He is murdered by the disgruntled Cortez. The latter convicted of the crime, the contrite Astor returns to Holt, her benevolent benefactor. A remake of the silent RECOIL (1924).

p, Henry Hobart; d, Melville Brown; w, J. Walter Ruben, Jane Murfin (based on the novel *Recoil* by Rex Beach); ph, Jack Mackenzie.

Drama (PR:A MPAA:NR)

WHITE SISTER, THE*** (1933) 110m MGM bw

Helen Hayes (*Angela Chiaromonte*), Clark Gable (*Lt. Giovanni Severi*), Lewis Stone (*Prince Guido Chiaromonte*), Louise Closser Hale (*Mina*), May Robson (*Mother Superior*), Edward Arnold (*Monsignor Saracinesca*), Alan Edwards (*Ernesto Severi*), Donald Ogden Stewart (*Rear End of a Horse*), Gino Corrado (*Chauffeur*), Nat Pendleton (*Corporal*), Frank Puglia (*Soldier*), Agostino Borgato (*Citizen*).

The third screen version of a popular wartime romance has Hayes a young woman of noble Italian breeding whose father has arranged a marriage to someone she does not love. Before the marriage can take place, though, she meets Gable at a religious festival and runs away to be with him. Later the war erupts and he goes off as a pilot. When he is reported dead, Hayes deep in grief, joins a convent. Gable is not dead, though, but in an Austrian prisoner of war camp, unable to get any word to her. After two years he escapes, steals an Austrian plane, and flies back to his own lines. He searches everywhere for Hayes, but when he finds her, she has already taken her final vows, vows from which only a special dispensation from the Pope can release her. Although Gable begs, she refuses to ask to leave the order. He kidnaps her, but still she remains obedient to her vows. Dejected but understanding, Gable returns her to the convent, only to be killed by an Austrian bomber outside the gates. He dies in Hayes' arms, accepting of her decision. Hayes and Gable are excellent, overcoming the melodramatic material with sturdy and heartfelt performances. Strong performances weren't enough, though. There simply isn't any chemistry between Hayes and Gable, who seems awkward and shy throughout the romance. Hayes would recall years later that Gable was always trying to hide "his big, scarred hands" from his demure costar. The story had its first incarnation as a successful Broadway play, was first filmed in 1915 with Viola Allen and Richard Travers, then again in 1923 with Lillian Gish and Ronald Colman.

p, Hunt Stromberg; d, Victor Fleming; w, Donald Ogden Stewart (based on the play by Walter Hackett from the novel by Francis Marion Crawford); ph, William Daniels; m, Herbert Stothart; ed, Margaret Mooth; art d, Cedric Gibbons.

Romance (PR:A MPAA:NR)

WHITE SISTER* (1973, Ital./Span./Fr.) 96m C.I.P.-Midega-Concordia-Champion/COL-WB c (BIANCO, ROSSO E...; AKA: THE SIN)

Sophia Loren (*Sister Germana*), Adriano Celentano (*Annibale Pezzi*), Fernando Rey (*Chief Physician*), Juan Luis Galiardo (*Guido*), Luis Marin (*Libyan Brigadier*), Giuseppe Maffioli (*Dr. Arrighi*), Sergio Fasanelli (*Dr. Filippini*), Pilar Gomez Ferrer (*Sister Teresa*), Patrizia de Clara (*Sister Caterina*), Teresa Rabal (*Lisa*), Valentine (*Martina*), Tina Aumont (*Mrs. Ricci*), Bruno Biassibetti (*Ottolenghi*), Antonio Alfonso (*Gigino*), Aldo Farina (*Valenzani*), Alessandra Mussolini (*Sister Germana as a Child*), Ezio Curti (*Attilio*), Franio Curti (*Pinin*), Bruno Sciponi (*Chiacchiera*), Massimiliano Filoni (*Giacomino*), Maria Marchi (*Giacomino's Mother*), Francesca Modigliani (*Lucia*), Carla Galletti (*Gina*), Angelo Bellia (*Sapigni*), Enzo Cannalvale (*Quinto*), Enzo Turchini (*Policemen*), Ettore Bussoli (*Policeman*), Guido Spadea (*Amilcare*), Mario Comaschi (*Solitario*), Dori Dorika (*Cook*), Merriana Henrique (*Arab Girl Mother*), Gianni Magni, Attilio Meanti, Carlo Gaddi (*Bandits*).

More wasted celluloid as Loren takes on the role of a nun with her usual Amazonian aplomb and lack of talent. As a tramp of the Libyan oil fields, she takes up the veil when her lover is killed. Returning to Italy, she assumes a position as head nurse at a church-run hospital in a city where the entire administration is Communist. This inevitably leads to conflicts, particularly when a handsome young Marxist (Celentano) is admitted and sets to running things his way. Celentano is a crude workingman who constantly intrudes into hospital operations, and only with time does Loren understand that he is a frustrated doctor. Something like love begins to grow between the two, but Loren is loyal to her vows and when Celentano realizes that their relationship can never be, he finally allows himself to be discharged from the hospital, only to die in an accident. Loren is slightly better than usual, though that's not saying much. She is simply not convincing as a woman of God. Celentano, an Italian singer, is better, but the script is just too silly for any decent performances. Loren as a young girl is played by her niece, Alessandra Mussolini, the granddaughter of the Italian dictator (Loren's sister, Maria, married Mussolini's jazz pianist son, Romano).

p, Carlo Ponti; d, Alberto Lattuada; w, Iaia Fiastri, Lattuada, Tonino Guerra, Ruggiero Maccari (based on a story by Guerra, Maccari); ph, Alfio Contini (Technicolor); m, Fred Bongusto; ed, Sergio Montanari; art d, Vincenzo del Prato; set d, Ennio Michtettoni; cos, Mario Ambrosino.

Drama (PR:O MPAA:PG)

WHITE SLAVE SHIP*½ (1962, Fr./Ital.) 92m Giorgio Agliani Cinematografica-Illiria-Gladiator-Champs Elysees/AIP c (LES REVOLTEES DE L'ALBATROS; L'AMMUTINAMENTO; AKA: THE MUTINY)

Pier Angeli (*Polly*), Edmund Purdom (*Dr. Bradley*), Armand Mestral (*Calico Jack*), Ivan Desny (*Capt. Cooper*), Michele Girardon (*Anna*), Franca Parisi Strahl, Mirko Ellis, Maria Pia Luzi, Paola Petrini, Ruth von Hagen, Ivy Holsen, Renato Speziali, Franco Capucci, Germana Francioli, Fiorella Ferrero, Letitia Bollante, Charles Borromel.

In the year 1675 British prisoner Angeli, along with a dozen other women, is shipped to the New World to be sold into slavery. She is put on the aptly named *Albatross* in secret with Purdom, a political prisoner. Traveling as passengers on the ship are some well-to-do people as well. The prisoners, freed by Angeli, take over the ship. After a storm, Desny takes back control of his ship with Purdom's help. Since mutiny is punishable by death in the New World, the mutineers try to re-route the course, tossing Desny and Purdom in the brig. Mestral wants to throw Angeli and her sister convicts overboard to save rations, but the women free Purdom and Desny to battle the mutineers. A British warship, hailed by Angeli, comes to the rescue. Desny exonerates Angeli and Purdom, leaving the latter and Girardon, the daughter of a murdered passenger, free to marry. A silly plot dished up with a good deal of hokum.

p, Giorgio Agliani, Rodolphe Solmsen; d, Silvio Amadio; w, Sandro Contineza, Marcello Coscia, Ruggero Jacobbi; ph, Aldo Giordani (Colorscope, Eastmancolor); m, Les Baxter; ed, Nella Nannuzzi; art d, Gianni Polidori; makeup, Otello Fava.

Adventure (PR:C MPAA:NR)

WHITE SQUAW, THE* (1956) 75m COL bw

David Brian (*Sigrod Swanson*), May Wynn (*Ectay-O-Wahnee*), William Bishop (*Bob Garth*), Nancy Hale (*Kerry Arnold*), William Leslie (*Thor Swanson*), Myron Healey (*Eric Swanson*), Robert C. Ross (*Knute Swanson*), Frank de Kova (*Yellow Elk*), George Keymas (*Yotah*), Roy Roberts (*Purvis*), Grant Withers (*Sheriff*), Wally Vernon (*Faro Bill*), Paul Birch (*Thad Arnold*), Neyle Morrow (*Swift Arrow*), Guy Teague (*Joe Hide*).

Wynn is a half-white woman who has grown up with the Sioux and now is one of them. In rides Brian, a Swedish immigrant who's trying to start a ranch in the area. He tries to drive the tribe off their land by poisoning the water their cattle drink. This starts a battle in which Birch, a white man and in reality Wynn's father, is killed. Bishop is the cattle-driving hero who helps out the tribe. The cruel Brian dies in a burning tepee. (As any real fan of westerns knows, buffalo-hide tepees don't burn.) Making the Indians heroic just doesn't work with the ridiculous stereotypes that pass off as characterizations here. As a western the picture is below standard; as a plea for Indian rights it is a failure.

p, Wallace MacDonald; d, Ray Nazarro; w, Les Savage, Jr. (based on the novel by Larabie Sutter); ph, Henry Freulich; m, Mischa Bakaleinikoff; ed, Edwin Bryant; md, Bakaleinikoff; art d, Ross Bellah.

Western (PR:A MPAA:NR)

WHITE STALLION** (1947) 54m Walt Mattox/Astor bw (AKA: HARMONY TRAIL)

Ken Maynard (*Himself*), Eddie Dean (*Himself*), Rocky Cameron (*Himself*), Max Terhune (*Himself*), Glenn Strange (*U.S. Marshal Taylor*), Ruth Roman (*Ann Martin*), Bob McKenzie (*Pop Martin*), Charles King (*Jim Sorrell*), Bud Osborne (*Tip*), Al Ferguson (*Red*), Dan White (*Bronco*), Fred Gildart (*Sleepy*), Jerry Shields (*Tex*), Hal Price (*Mr. Hodges*), John Bridges (*Sheriff*).

Working under Cameron's command, the other three leading players–using their own well-known names in the roles–join a medicine show in order to catch a gang of bank robbers. This gives them a chance to display their several talents: Maynard does roping and trick riding; Dean sings a few numbers; Terhune does his ventriloquist act. The volatile McKenzie adds humor as the proprietor of the traveling show. Roman is the very minor romantic interest, a role she essayed in a number of westerns before her critical success in CHAMPION (1949). Released briefly as HARMONY TRAIL in 1944.

p, Walt Mattox; d, Robert Emmett [Tansey]; w, Frances Kavanaugh (based on a story by Frank Simpson); ph, Edward Kull; m, Frank Sanucci; ed, Fred Bain; md, Sanucci.

Western (PR:A MPAA:NR)

WHITE TIE AND TAILS**½ (1946) 75m UNIV bw (AKA: THE SWINDLERS)

Dan Duryea (*Charles Dumont*), Ella Raines (*Louise Bradford*), William Bendix (*Larry Lundie*), Richard Gaines (*Archer Ripley*), Barbara Brown (*Mrs. Latimer*), Clarence Kolb (*Mr. Arkwright*), Donald Curtis (*Nate Romano*), Frank Jenks (*George*), Samuel S. Hinds (*Mr. Bradford*), John Miljan (*Mr. Latimer*), William Trenk (*Emil*), Scotty Beckett (*Bill Latimer*), Nita Hunter (*Betty Latimer*), Patricia Alphin [Audrey Young] (*Cynthia Bradford*), Joan Fulton [Shawlee] (*Virgie*), Beatrice Roberts (*Marie*), Lois Austin (*Agnes*), Rex Lease (*Briggs*), Bert Moorhouse (*Croupier*), Earl Keen (*Dog Impersonator*), Ralph Brooks (*Roger*), Bob Wilke (*Starter*), Roger Cole (*Cashier*), Leo Z. Gray, Albin Robeling (*Waiters*).

Despite the title, this is *not* a Fred Astaire vehicle (the top hat is missing) and hero Duryea does no dancing, although fully qualified. Butler Duryea, left alone with chauffeur-cum-crapshooter Jenks in the spacious mansion of his vacationing employers for 10 days, decides to sample a life of leisure. Since his master's vestments fit him, he assumes the guise of a millionaire, enlisting the services of Jenks and the family vehicle. Proceeding to a posh gambling club, he meets Raines, a troubled child of real wealth, whose sister owes a $100,000 gambling debt to tough but soft-hearted racketeer Bendix. To impress the ravishing Raines, dapper Duryea writes a check–using his employer's name–to cover the debt. As security until the check clears, Bendix takes some priceless paintings from Duryea's master's mansion. With only a few days to go, Duryea, Raines, and Jenks scramble frantically to get enough money to cover the forged check and retrieve the captive canvases. Dailey isn't quite right for his role in this pleasant little suspense comedy. The talented Bendix steals his every scene.

p, Howard Benedict; d, Charles T. Barton; w, Bertram Millhauser (based on the novel *The Victoria Docks at Eight* by Rufus King and Charles Beahan); ph, Charles Van Enger; m, Milton Rosen; ed, Ray Snyder; md, Rosen; art d, Jack Otterson, John De Cuir; cos, Yvonne Wood.

Comedy   **(PR:A   MPAA:NR)**

WHITE TOWER, THE*½   (1950) 98m RKO c

Glenn Ford *(Martin Ordway)*, 'Alida' Valli *(Carla Alton)*, Claude Rains *(Paul Delambre)*, Oscar Homolka *(Andreas)*, Sir Cedric Hardwicke *(Nicholas Radcliffe)*, Lloyd Bridges *(Mr. Hein)*, June Clayworth *(Mme. Astrid Delambre)*, Lotte Stein *(Frau Andreas)*, Fred Essler *(Knubel)*, Edit Angold *(Frau Knubel)*.

The pristine tower of this tale is the yet-unclimbed peak in the Swiss Alps, its elusive summit sought by a diverse group of travelers, whose personalities and motivations are explored during the quest. Set shortly after the end of WW II, a resort lodge nestled in the shadow of the shimmering peak serves as headquarters for the group, which includes Valli, who obsessively seeks to master the mountain that killed her climber father; a disillusioned, alcoholic French man of letters, Rains; aging British naturalist Hardwicke; and ex-Nazi German army officer Bridges. Accompanying the group is experienced Alpine guide Homolka, a bear of a man who has been higher on the peak than any other guide in the area. Recreational climber Ford–a Yankee ex- bomber pilot–is also staying at the lodge, making frequent forays against the gentler climbs in the vicinity. Knowing Ford to be an accomplished alpinist, Valli attempts to recruit the reluctant Ford for the planned climb, chiding him for his lack of vertical aspirations. Ford, who has planned to test his climbing skills only minimally while reflecting on the majesty of the mountains, finds the single-minded beauty sufficiently compelling to edge him into agreeing to help the ascent by carrying supplies up the first sections of the formidable peak. Guide Homolka tests his climbing ropes and, all found secure, the party sets off, boulder-hopping to the base of the initial cliff. Benighted on a broad ledge, the climbers shake off their belaying ropes and disperse, with botanist Hardwicke, exhausted, withdrawing his arms from the sleeves of his parka–keeping them inside the cotton body of the protective shell–gazing at the distant peaks in the fading light, his posture telling of his portent that this may be his final ascent. Marooned in a small space within the towering vista, the other climbers begin their self-revelatory ruminations, which further disclose their characters. Self-destructive Rains, filled with ennui, seeks to meet his maker nonsuicidally; Bridges is filled with hate and loathing for his fellow climbers, considering them beneath his dignity (significantly, he sports a German army field cap–an excellent item of headwear which actually enjoyed a spate of postwar popularity among climbers of many nationalities). Homolka is a stolid servant, secure in his abilities and at peace with his profession; Ford is attempting to find an appropriate destiny for himself in the maelstrom of postwar discontent; Valli begins to question her obsession. The climb continues in the morning, albeit with many mishaps. The party reaches the highest point yet trodden by a cleated boot: virgin snowfields lie beyond a final rocky barrier. The latter has served to turn away many such strivers. Homolka, reaching upward, trying to find a hold, discovers that a man's reach *does* exceed his grasp, and proclaims failure. "It won't go," he says. "It *must* go," states Bridges, unwilling to abort the attempt. Pushing Homolka from his position on the face, Bridges–in a desperate triumph of the will–finds a hold and pulls himself upward. The others follow closely. Ford has elected to remain with the by now death-depleted party as it inches toward the summit, but his plans had not included so high an ascent, so he finds himself without the requisite dark goggles. He suffers snow blindness on the glaring glacier. His plight persuades Valli that her obsessive quest is senseless, and she decides to abandon the attack on the peak. The German's obsession with victory is stronger than hers, and he forges ahead, vowing to succeed despite the weakness of his companions. Bridges must make a handhold transit across a stretch of rock, and his cold-weakened fingers begin to lose their grip. The blinded Ford reaches out, offering his supportive hand, which the arrogant Nazi scornfully rejects. Struggling on, Bridges loses his grip and falls to his death. The survivors wincingly return to the valley floor with Valli leading the blinded Ford, a new purpose now in her life. The best feature film about mountain climbing to its time, THE WHITE TOWER was filmed on location in the Swiss Alps. The best, unfortunately, was none too good. The picture was wincingly irritating to the climbing fraternity. The actors had been ill- coached in the ascent techniques prevalent at the time, and only a totally mad leader would have selected frail, ancient Hardwick–who puffed even on the lower slopes–as an appropriate companion on a difficult first ascent. At the time depicted, the Alps were crawling with climbers–they had begun to stink of human excrement–yet not a human figure other than those of the cast is to be seen

in all the footage. This was a high-budget production for the studio, and the Technicolor panoramas are superb. Only during the many claustrophobic medium and close shots of the actors doing their formula introspections does the picture really lose interest. The director managed to get lackluster performances out of a cast of excellent actors; only Homolka really shines. This may be due in large part to the plot line, which is more literary than cinematic.

p, Sid Rogell; d, Ted Tetzlaff; w, Paul Jarrico (based on the novel by James Ramsay Ullman); ph, Ray Rennahan (Technicolor); m, Roy Webb; ed, Samuel E. Beetley; md, C. Bakaleinikoff; art d, Albert D'Agostino, Ralph Berger.

Adventure   **Cas.**   **(PR:A   MPAA:NR)**

WHITE TRAP, THE**   (1959, Brit.) 58m
                                    Independent/Anglo-Amalgamated bw

Lee Patterson *(Paul Langley)*, Conrad Phillips *(Sgt. Morrison)*, Michael Goodliffe *(Inspector Walters)*, Jack Allen *(Dr. Hayden)*, Yvette Wyatt *(Ann Fisher)*, Gillian Vaughan *(Wendy)*, Felicity Young *(Joan Langley)*, Trevor Maskell *(Dr. Lucas)*, Harold Siddons, Charles Leno, Ian Colin, Helen Towers.

Patterson is a jailed war hero whose wife, Young, is about to give birth to their first child. He breaks out of his cell, then with the help of a war buddy reaches his wife despite the police lines and newsmen who surround the hospital. Patterson manages to get to Young's hospital ward, but all is for naught. Though a healthy baby boy is delivered, Young dies in childbirth. Though the suspense builds up towards the end, the plot is pretty unrelievedly downbeat.

p, Julian Wintle, Leslie Parkyn; d, Sidney Hayers; w, Peter Barnes; ph, Eric Cross.

Crime/Drama   **(PR:C   MPAA:NR)**

WHITE TRASH ON MOONSHINE MOUNTAIN
                          (SEE: MOONSHINE MOUNTAIN, 1964)

WHITE UNICORN, THE   (SEE: BAD SISTER, 1947, Brit.)

WHITE VOICES**   (1965, Fr./Ital.) 93m Franca-Federiz-Francoriz/
Rizzoli c (LE SEXE DES ANGES; LE VOCI BIANCHE; I CASTRATI;
                              AKA: UNDER COVER ROGUE)

Paolo Ferrari *(Meo)*, Sandra Milo *(Carolina)*, Graziella Granata *(Teresa)*, Anouk Aimee *(Lorenza)*, Vittorio Caprioli *(Matteuccio)*, Jeanne Valerie *(Maria)*, Philippe Leroy *(Ascanio)*, Barbara Steele *(Guilia)*, Leopoldo Trieste *(Oropreenobbi)*, Jacqueline Sassard *(Eugenia)*, Claudio Gora *(Marchionne)*, Jean Tissier *(Savello)*, Alfredo Bianchini, Francesco Mule, Luigi Basagalupi, Giulio Battiferri, Anita Durante, Jacques Herlin, Guglielmo Spoletini, Filippo Spoletini, Ugo Carbone, Rosalba Neri.

It's 18th-Century Rome and Ferrari, an improverished chamber pot salesman, tries to raise some money by selling his young brother to the Vatican choir. However, the brother escapes and Ferrari must take his place. Since he doesn't have the beautiful high voice of his young brother, Ferrari faces castration but bribes his way out of this most distressing predicament. He manages to talk his way into bed with girl friend Granta and then begins his choir training. The new job frustrates Ferrari until he finds it allows him entry into the homes of the affluent. The moneyed husbands don't mind his presence, for they think he's minus a few essential parts, a fact Ferrari uses to his advantage. Once more he meets Granata, now a nobleman's wife. He gets her pregant and Granata's angered husband threatens to see that Ferrari is beheaded unless he can prove he is a eunuch. He reluctantly goes for the operation though his brothers hurry to rescue him. Some good bawdy fun in this off-the-wall italian comedy. (In Italian; English subtitles.)

p, Luciano Perugia, Nello Meniconi; d, Pasquale Festa Campanile, Massimo Franciosa; w, Campanile, Franciosa, Luigi Magni; ph, Ennio Guarnieri (Techniscope, Technicolor); m, Gino Marinuzzi, Jr.; ed, Ruggero Mastroianni; cos, Pier Luigi Pizzi.

Comedy   **(PR:O   MPAA:NR)**

WHITE WARRIOR, THE*   (1961, Ital./Yugo.) 86m
Lovcen-Majestic/WB c (AGI MURAD, IL DIAVOLO BIANCO; BELI
                                                      DJAVO)

Steve Reeves *(Hadji Murad)*, Georgia Moll *(Sultanet)*, Renato Baldini *(Akmet Khan)*, Scilla Gabel *(Princess Maria)*, Gerard Herter *(Prince Sergei/Gen. Vorontzov)*, Nikola Popovic *(King Shamyl)*, Milivoje Zivanovic, Niksa Stefanini.

Muscleman Reeves meets literary giant Tolstoy in what ranks as one of the art world's most unusual pairings. This adaptation of the Russian novelist's tale finds Reeves leading a troop of mountain warriors against evil Czar Nicholas I. Baldini, his rival, also has a thing for Reeves' girl Moll. When he's double-crossed by Baldini, Reeves ends up in the hands of Herter, A Russian prince. Reeves won't sign a treaty and gets tortured for his trouble.

Herter's wife Gabel falls for Reeves, while Baldini kidnaps Reeves' son and threatens him with death unless Moll marries the brutish captor. With some help from a loyal aide, Reeves escapes and rescues his boy and Moll from Baldini's clutches. The two rivals engage in hand-to-hand combat with Reeves coming out on top. Once more he leads his men into their struggle against the Czar. Reeves is all muscle and fake beard, showing little talent in this turgid drama. The sluggish direction and a poor job of dubbing don't make things any easier for audiences.

d, Riccardo Freda; w. Gino De Santis, Akos Tolney (based on the novel *Khadzhi-Murat* by Leo Tolstoy); ph, Mario Bava, Frano Vodopivec (Dyaliscope, Technicolor); m, Robert Nicolosi; md, Pierluigi Urbini; art d, Aleksandar Milovic; cos, Filippo Sanjust.

Historical Drama   (PR:C   MPAA:NR)

WHITE WITCH DOCTOR***   (1953) 96m FOX c

Susan Hayward *(Ellen Burton)*, Robert Mitchum *(Lonni Douglas)*, Walter Slezak *(Huysman)*, Mashood Ajala *(Jacques)*, Joseph C. Narcisse *(Utembo)*, Elzie Emanuel *(Kapuka)*, Timothy Carey *(Jarrett)*, Otis Greene *(Bakuba Boy)*, Charles Gemora *(Gorilla)*, Paul Thompson, Naaman Brown *(Witch Doctors)*, Myrtle Anderson *(Aganza)*, Everett Brown *(Bakuba King)*, Dorothy Harris *(Chief's Wife)*, Michael Ansara *(De Gama)*, Michael Granger *(Paal)*, Leo C. Aldridge-Milas *(Council Member)*, Louis Polliman Brown *(Councilman)*, Floyd Shackelford *(Chief)*, Henry Hastings, John Iboko *(Men)*, Gabriel Ukaegbu *(Native)*, Anyaogu, Elechukwu N. Njakar, Nnaemeka Akosa, Chukemeka Okeke.

In the Belgian Congo of 1907, Hayward is a missionary nurse who sets out to minister to the feared Bakuba tribe. She hires guides Slezak and Mitchum to take her into the interior, but their motives are somewhat less altruistic than hers. They have heard stories of gold in Bakuba territory and plan to use Hayward's mission to learn of its whereabouts. As they travel through the jungle, Hayward stops to cure the wife of a native chief. This infuriates the local witch doctor, and he puts a tarantula in Hayward's bed in vengeance but she manages to escape its venom. Traveling on, Mitchum saves a boy from a lion, and the child turns out to be the son of the Bakuba chief. Mitchum and Slezak are also interested in the necklace of gold nuggets the boy wears around his neck. As the boy recovers under Hayward's care, the two men plan to use him to get the gold, but their scheme falls apart when six warriors from the tribe come and carry the boy off. The boy does not recover, though, and the chief sends for Hayward. Mitchum, who by now has fallen in love with Hayward, goes along, while Slezak gathers some armed men to take the gold by force. Bakuba pickets discover the preparations and Mitchum is accused of leading them to the village. He offers to go and tell Slezak there is no gold, while Hayward stays behind as a hostage. Slezak refuses to believe Mitchum and pulls a gun on him. There is a struggle. The gun goes off, and Slezak falls down dead. Mitchum quickly puts Slezak's cohorts to rout and returns to the village, where he and Hayward decide to remain to care for the tribesmen. Basically a routine jungle melodrama with big stars, WHITE WITCH DOCTOR did little for the careers of any of the principals. Hayward certainly did not enjoy working on the picture, as she disliked director Hathaway from their previous effort together, RAWHIDE (1951), and on the set even refused to have anything to do with anyone who was a friend of the director's. Nor did she especially like Mitchum, with whom she had previously worked in THE LUSTY MEN (1952). The film had a troubled production history, starting when Hayward learned that Mitchum disliked the script as much as she did. She approached Darryl F. Zanuck and stated that unless the script was rewritten, she and Mitchum would refuse to star in the film. Zanuck told her the studio couldn't afford a rewrite but she stood firm. Zanuck told Hathaway about the trouble with the stars, and Hathaway answered: "$e3I don't blame them. It's a lousy script." Hathaway then offered to do a rewrite himself in a couple of weeks and after some consideration of the money already invested in sets and the like–including $600,000 spent to send a second-unit crew to Africa for background shots and to pick up some genuine native artifacts for the picture–Zanuck agreed. During the shooting, Mitchum had a little fun at Hathaway's expense. He walked onto the set for one of the final days of shooting claiming to not know his lines (actually he had studied them thoroughly). While Hathaway raged at him for being unprepared, Mitchum calmly asked for a script, glanced over the six pages to be shot, then spoke his lines perfectly. Amazed, Hathaway later told Zanuck: "This S.O.B. is the most phenomenal actor I've ever seen. He glanced through the script and did six pages of dialog–four in solid African dialect–letter perfect, with every nuance."

p, Otto Lang; d, Henry Hathaway; w, Ivan Goff, Ben Roberts (based on the novel by Louise A. Stinetorf); ph, Leon Shamroy (Technicolor); m, Bernard Herrmann; ed, James B. Clark; art d, Lyle Wheeler, Mark-Lee Kirk; set d, Stuart Reiss; cos, Dorothy Jeakins; spec eff, Ray Kellogg; makeup, Ben Nye.

Adventure   (PR:A   MPAA:NR)

WHITE WOMAN*½   (1933) 68m PAR bw

Charles Laughton *(Horace Prin)*, Carole Lombard *(Judith Denning)*, Kent Taylor *(David von Eitz)*, Percy Kilbride *(Jakey)*, Charles B. Middleton *(Fenton)*, James Bell *(Hambley)*, Claude King *(Chisholm)*, Ethel Griffies *(Mrs. Chisholm)*, Jimmie Dime *(Vaegi)*, Noble Johnson *(Native Chief No. 1)*,

Marc Lawrence *(Connors)*, Gregg Whitespear *(Native Chief No. 2)*, Charles Bickford *(Ballister)*.

"Woman Hunger. Crazed Men Who Lived Without Love–Sly Whispers!" read the ads for this ridiculous "adults only" feature of the early 1930s that comes off today as great camp. Laughton, fresh from his role in ISLAND OF LOST SOULS, is the cruel head of a Malaysian rubber plantation. He marries Lombard, a singer about to be deported. Her life with Laughton provides little happiness until Taylor, a plantation worker, comes along to relieve her loneliness. Laughton becomes jealous and sends Taylor off to head-hunter country. The plantation owner considers Taylor a coward and is surprised when the man returns unharmed. Later there's a native revolt and Bickford, an escaped convict working for Laughton, helps Lombard and Taylor to safety. Knowing they're bound to die soon, Laughton and Bickford play poker. Laughton draws a great hand but becomes furious when Bickford is speared to death before they show their cards. Talk about sore winners! Perhaps they continue the game at that Great Card Table in the Sky, for Laughton is struck dead moments later. Laughton probably felt right at home in this film, as it employed sets from ISLAND OF LOST SOULS. The story is overblown hokum and unintentionally hysterical. Lombard, soon to emerge as the queen of screwball comedy, was cast here simply as a contractual obligation. At this point in her career she was merely a filler actress for parts the bigger names wouldn't take.

p, E. Lloyd Sheldon; d, Stuart Walker; w, Samuel Hoffenstein, Gladys Lehman, Jane Loring (based on a story by Norman Reilly Raine, Frank Butler); ph, Harry Fischbeck; art d, Hans Dreier, Harry Oliver; m/l, "Yes, My Dear," "A Gentleman and a Scholar," Harry Revel, Mack Gordon (sung by Carole Lombard).

Adventure   (PR:C   MPAA:NR)

WHITE ZOMBIE***   (1932) 73m UA bw

Bela Lugosi *(Murder Legendre)*, Madge Bellamy *(Madeline Short)*, John Harron *(Neil Parker)*, Joseph Cawthorn *(Dr. Bruner, Missionary)*, Robert Frazer *(Charles Beaumont)*, Clarence Muse *(Coach Driver)*, Brandon Hurst *(Silver, Servant)*, Dan Crimmins *(Pierre, Witch Doctor)*, John Peters *(Chauvin)*, George Burr McAnnan *(Von Gelder)*, John Printz, Claude Morgan, John Fergusson *(Zombies)*, Annette Stone, Velma Gresham *(Maids)*.

In the early 1930s the horror film enjoyed one of its most lucrative periods with such classics as DRACULA, FRANKENSTEIN, and DR. JEKYLL AND MR. HYDE. Strangely enough, WHITE ZOMBIE, one of the better horror films of the period, is all but forgotten today. The film opens with Bellamy and Harron passing a funeral in Haiti, the body being buried in the road. The driver explains that this will protect the corpse from ghouls. soon the coach the couple are riding in passes some strange creatures led by a mysterious figure (Lugosi, fresh from his immortal success in DRACULA). The driver hurries past and later explains these creatures are zombies, living dead who have been resurrected through voodoo. They arrive at Frazer's mansion, where the couple is to be married. Bellamy had met Frazer on a ship taking her to Haiti to join her fiance. The wealthy man had insisted the wedding be held in his home, though it is obvious his interests in the woman are less than honorable. Later he gets Lugosi to turn her into a zombie when his offers of love are refused. He realizes his mistake when she becomes one of the living dead, but Lugosi will not change her back. Harron grows feverish and falls ill. Lugosi orders Bellamy to stab her husband but is stopped by a hooded figure, who later turns out to be Cawthorn, a friend of the young couple. In the end Lugosi and Frazer fall over a cliff in a struggle and the newlyweds both recover. "Neil, I...I dreamed," says the dazed woman. WHITE ZOMBIE is a nightmare of dark and troubling matter. It was filmed on fantastic sets (a combination of leftover pieces from a wide range of pictures, including THE KING OF KINGS, 1927, DRACULA, 1931, and FRANKENSTEIN, 1931. Through use of wired camera setups and disorienting music (written in part by Xavier Cugat, of all people), the film's mise-en-scene is imaginative and atmospheric. The dialog is sparse to good effect. Like the then recently disappeared silent films, this is a movie that suggests horror with the visual rather than explaining everything with Hollywood's new toy. WHITE ZOMBIE is notable as the first film to deal with the zombie, a manifestation of the living dead introduced to the popular imagination in 1929 in William Seabrook's *The Magic Island*. Bellamy, who had been a major star in the silent era, was trying for a film comeback with this picture. Unfortunately her Cupid's bow mouth and stylized acting don't work, her performance often approaching a camp feeling. Lugosi, on the other hand, is magnificent. As in DRACULA, the star's Hungarian accent adds to his chilling characterization. The Halperin brothers, who produced the film, originally offered him only $500 for his work, though Lugosi's final salary was reportedly between $800 and $900. This fine actor was constantly abused throughout his career and he died a broke, bitter man. On its release WHITE ZOMBIE was blasted by the critics and was largely forgotten over the years. Though some of it is unintentionally comic, the film deserved a better fate. It was a wholly original work, imaginatively done and not soon forgotten by the viewer. Footage from this film later appeared in REVOLT OF THE ZOMBIES and in a compilation horror film, DR. TERROR'S HOUSE OF HORRORS.

p, Edward Halperin; d, Victor Halperin; w. Garnett Weston (based on the novel The Magic Island by William Seabrook); ph, Arthur Martinelli; m, Guy

Bevier Williams, Xavier Cugat, Nathaniel Dett, Gaston Borch, Hugo Riesenfeld, Leo Kempenski, H. Herkan, H. Maurice Jacquet; ed, Harold MacLernon; set d, Ralph Berger, Conrad Tritschler; spec eff, Howard Anderson; makeup, Jack P. Pierce, Carl Axcelle.

| Horror | Cas. | (PR:O MPAA:NR) |

WHITEFACE (SEE: WHITE FACE, 1933, Brit.)

WHO?**½ (1975, Brit./Ger.) 91m Lion International-Hemisphere-MacLean/Lorimar c (AKA: MAN WITHOUT A FACE; PRISONER OF THE SKULL; THE MAN IN THE STEEL MASK)

Elliott Gould (*Sean Rogers*), Trevor Howard (*Col. Azarin*), Joe Bova (*Dr. Lucas Martino*), Ed Grover (*Finchley*), James Noble (*Gen. Deptford*), John Lehne (*Haller*), Kay Tornburg (*Edith*), Lyndon Brook (*Dr. Barrister*), Joy Garrett (*Barbara*), Ivan Desny (*Gen. Sturmer*), Alexander Allerton (*Dr. Korthu*), Michael Lombard (*Dr. Besser*), John Stewart (*Frank Heywood*), Bruce Boa (*Miller*), Fred Vincent (*Douglas*), Dan Sazarino (*Uncle Lucas*), Craig McConnel (*Tonino*), Herb Andress, Del Negro, Frank Schuller (*FBI Agents*).

When American scientist Bova is nearly killed in an accident along the Russian border, Soviet doctors perform life-saving surgery that makes him half man-half machine. He wants to return to his top-secret work but American officials, led by Gould, must figure out whether Bova is now a mole for the USSR. Howard is the Russian spy trainer who wants to use Bova for this country's purposes. The film ends on a lackluster note, though, when Bova returns to his late parents' farm to spend his days rather than serve as a pawn for either country. Bova gives an intriguing performance in this combination spy-science fiction piece. However, the direction never amounts to much, paying more attention to stock chase sequences than to the unusual character development.

p, Barry Levinson; d, Jack Gold; w, John Gould [Jack Gold] (based on the novel by Algis Budrys); ph, Petrus Schloemp (Eastmancolor); m, John Cameron; ed, Norman Wanstall; art d, Peter Scharff; spec eff, Richard Richtsfeld; makeup, Colin Arthur.

| Spy Drama/Science Fiction | (PR:C MPAA:PG) |

WHO CAN KILL A CHILD (SEE: ISLAND OF THE DAMNED, 1976, Span.)

WHO DARES WIN (SEE: FINAL OPTION, THE, 1983, Brit.)

WHO DONE IT?**½ (1942) 75m UNIV bw

Bud Abbott (*Chick Larkin*), Lou Costello (*Mervyn Milgrim*), William Gargan (*Lt. Moran*), Louise Allbritton (*Jane Little*), Patric Knowles (*Jim Turner*), Don Porter (*Art Fraser*), Jerome Cowan (*Marco Holler*), William Bendix (*Brannigan*), Mary Wickes (*Juliet Collins*), Thomas Gomez (*Col. J.R. Andrews*), Ludwig Stossel (*Dr. Anton Marek*), Edmund MacDonald (*Jenkins*), Joe Kirk (*Thompson*), Walter Tetley (*Elevator Boy*), Crane Whitley (*Radio Actor*), Margaret Brayton (*Radio Actress*), The Pinas (*Acrobats*), Milton Parsons (*Coroner*), Edward Keane (*Carter*), Ed Emerson (*Announcer*), Buddy Twiss (*2nd Announcer*), Gladys Blake (*Telephone Operator*), Harry Strang (*Truck Driver*), Frank Penny (*Spinelli*), Jerry Frank (*Customer No. 2*), Bobby Barber (*Technician in Booth*), Shemp Howard (*Goof*), Paul Dubov, Duke York, Alice Fleming, Eddie Bruce.

One of Abbott and Costello's better outings finds them as a pair of would-be radio mystery writers who work as soda jerks. Their place of employment is in the same building as a major broadcasting studio, and when a network president is murdered the two pose as detectives. Surprisingly, everyone believes them to be private eyes, but problems arise when Bendix, a cop who is even dumber than Costello, bungles up their already bungled work. The film includes a riotous chase that finds Costello dangling high above the ground on the radio station's aerial. There are some good laughs, with old A & C routines worked handily into the script. As a screen comedy team, Abbott and Costello were passable at best but occasionally showed moments of brilliance. WHO DONE IT? contains its fair share of those moments, aided, no doubt, by the absence of musical numbers which tended to get in the way of the jokes. (See: ABBOTT AND COSTELLO series, Index.)

p, Alex Gottlieb; d, Erle C. Kenton; w, Stanley Roberts, Edmund Joseph, John Grant (based on a story by Roberts); ph, Charles Van Enger; m, Frank Skinner; ed, Arthur Hilton; art d, Jack Otterson.

| Comedy | (PR:A MPAA:NR) |

WHO DONE IT?** (1956, Brit.) 85m EAL/RANK bw

Benny Hill (*Hugo Dill*), Belinda Lee (*Frankie Mayne*), David Kossoff (*Zacco*), Garry Marsh (*Inspector Hancock*), George Margo (*Barakov*), Ernest Thesiger (*Sir Walter Finch*), Denis Shaw (*Otto Stumpf*), Frederick Schiller (*Gruber*), Thorley Walters (*Raymond Courtney*), Nicholas Phipps, Gibb McLaughlin, Ernest Jay, Harold Scott (*Scientists*), Irene Handl (*Customer*), Charles Hawtrey (*Disc Jockey*), Philip Stainton (*Frankie's Agent*), Jeremy Hawk (*Himself*), Warwick Ashton (*Police Constable Roberts*), Stratford

Johns (*Police Constable Coleman*), Arthur Lowe, Robert McDermott, Norah Blaney, Dagenham Girl Pipers, Fabian the Dog.

The popular but utterly sleazy British TV comic Hill makes his screen debut as an ice-rink sweeper who wins a good sum of money and a bloodhound in a contest. He gives up his old profession and opens up his own detective service, getting more than he had bargained for when one case leads him into cold war intrigue involving the planned assassination of some British scientists. Lee is the woman who helps Hill in his battle against the enemy agents. There are some moments of good humor and Hill's fans undoubtedly will enjoy this, but for the most part WHO DONE IT? is a mess. There are plenty of chases and car crashes substituting as humor, with more than the necessary number of corny jokes. Dearden directed this with plenty of life but it is ultimately shallow and not very funny. For fans only. This was the last of the Ealing comedies.

p, Michael Relph; d, Basil Dearden; w, T.E.B. Clarke; ph, Otto Heller; m, Philip Green; ed, Peter Tanner; art d, Jim Morahan; Cos, Anthony Mendleson.

| Comedy | (PR:C MPAA:NR) |

WHO FEARS THE DEVIL*** (1972) 89m Two's Company/Jack H. Harris c (AKA: THE LEGEND OF HILLBILLY JOHN; MY NAME IS JOHN)

Severn Darden (*Mr. Marduke*), Sharon Henesy (*Lily*), Honor Hound (*Himself*), Sidney Clute (*Charles*), Denver Pyle (*Grandpappy John*), White Lightnin' (*Themselves*), William Traylor (*Rev. Millen*), Harris Yulin (*Zebulon Yandro*), Susan Strasberg (*Polly Wiltse*), Alfred Ryder (*O.J. Onselm*), R.G. Armstrong (*Bristowe*), Chester Jones (*Uncle Anansi*), Val Avery (*Cobart*), Percy Rodrigues (*Capt. Lojoie H. Desplain IV*), Hedges Capers (*John*).

This interesting and novel film is based on various legends from the folklore of North and South Carolina. Capers, along with his grandfather, Pyle, is out to challenge the Devil. This frightens their Appalachian neighbors and ends in the strange death of the older man. It's up to Capers to continue their quest, a voyage that takes him through the modern-day U.S. all the way to Washington, D.C. There's some real imagination in this independent production, well cast with some talented character actors. The direction is a little slow to start, but once the unusual story and characters hit their stride, the film picks up and becomes most enjoyable.

p, Barney Rosenzweig; d, John Newland; w, Melvin Levy (based on the book *Who Fears the Devil?* by Manly Wade Wellman); ph, Flemming Olsen (Metrocolor); m, Roger Kellaway; ed, Russell Schoengarth.

| Fantasy | (PR:A MPAA:G) |

WHO GOES NEXT?**½ (1938, Brit.) 85m FOX British bw

Barry K. Barnes (*Maj. Hamilton*), Sophie Stewart (*Sarah Hamilton*), Jack Hawkins (*Capt. Beck*), Charles Eaton (*Capt. Royde*), Andrew Osborn (*F/O Stevens*), Frank Birch (*Capt. Grover*), Roy Findlay (*Lt. Williams*), Alastair Macintyre (*Lt. Mackenzie*), Meinhart Maur (*Commandant*), Viola Compton, Elizabeth Nolan, Charles Lancing, Kitty Kirwan, Francis James, Frances R. Mann, Wyndham Hewett.

During WW I a group of British soldiers held as POWs by the Germans plot an escape. Hawkins, a newly captured soldier, joins the group in their efforts to tunnel their way to freedom. Osborn, another member, cracks under pressure, forcing the group to leave ahead of schedule. In the end Hawkins comes to realize that Barnes, the group's leader, is his mistress' husband. Hawkins ultimately is killed, saving the life of the man he has cuckolded in the process. Some tense moments in this war drama make for good viewing. This was a predecessor of many such British war dramas involving men under pressure which were to follow in the next 20 years.

p, Ivor McLaren; d, Maurice Elvey; w, David Evans, Lawrence Green (based on the play by Reginald Simpson, James W. Drawbell); ph, Ronald Neame.

| War Drama | (PR:C MPAA:NR) |

WHO GOES THERE! (SEE: PASSIONATE SENTRY, THE, 1952, Brit)

WHO HAS SEEN THE WIND**½ (1980, Can.) 100m Souris River/Cinema World c

Brian Painchaud (*Brian*), Douglas Junor (*The Young Ben*), Gordon Pinsent (*Gerald O'Connal*), Chapelle Jaffe (*Maggie*), Jose Ferrer (*The Ben*), Charmion King (*Mrs. Abercrombie*), David Gardner (*Rev. Powelly*), Patricia Hamilton (*Miss MacDonald*), Helen Shaver (*Ruth Thompson*), Tom Hauff (*Digby*), Gerard Parkes (*Sean*), Nan Stewart (*Mrs. MacMurray*).

In a small prairie town in Saskatchewan a young boy must confront the reality of death as he sees his beloved pets and, finally, his father pass away. The story has some interesting moments, backed by some gorgeous photography and good support from a wonderful assortment of character actors. But the film is troubled by a somewhat tedious episodic development and a wavering score. Painchaud and Junor are marvelous as two youngsters caught in circumstances beyond their control and Ferrer gives a fine comic portrait as the town drunk.

p, Pierre Lamy; d, Allan King; w, Patricia Watson (based on the novel by W. O. Mitchell); ph, Richard Leiterman; m, Eldon Rathburn; ed, Arla Saare; art d, Anne Pritchard.

Drama   **Cas.**   **(PR:A MPAA:NR)**

WHO IS GUILTY?** (1940, Brit.) 69m Grafton/GN bw (GB: I KILLED THE COUNT)

Syd Walker (*Detective Inspector Davidson*), Ben Lyon (*Bernard Froy*), Terence de Marney (*Detective Sgt. Raines*), Barbara Blair (*Renee la Lune*), Athole Stewart (*Lord Sorrington*), Antoinettee Cellier (*Louise Rogers*), Leslie Perrins (*Count Mattoni*), David Burns (*Diamond*), Ronald Shiner (*Mullet, Porter*), Aubrey Mallalieu (*Johnson*), Kathleen Harrison (*Polly*), Gus McNaughton (*Martin*), Robert Adair.

A Scotland Yard murder mystery where four people confess to the same crime. Walker, on the day before his retirement, is assigned to investigate the murder of an Italian count. Three people, Stewart, Lyon, and Shiner, come forward and confess to the murder. Stewart's daughter, Cellier, was married to the count and she was mistreated by him. Lyon was in love with her and Shiner's reason for admitting to the crime is unclear. Cellier comes out of hiding and confesses that she was the one who really murdered her husband. As it actually happened, a neighbor accidentally killed the much-despised nobleman; the self-sacrificing confessors remain free to continue their lives, freed of the presence of the onerous aristocrat.

p, Isidore Goldschmidt; d, Fred Zelnik; w, Lawrence Huntington, Alec Coppel (based on a play by Coppel); ph, Bryan Langley.

Comedy/Mystery   **(PR:A MPAA:NR)**

WHO IS HARRY KELLERMAN AND WHY IS HE SAYING THOSE TERRIBLE THINGS ABOUT ME?** (1971) 108m Harry Kellerman-Cinema Center/NG c

Dustin Hoffman (*Georgie Soloway*), Barbara Harris (*Allison Densmore*), Jack Warden (*Dr. Moses*), David Burns (*Georgie's Father*), Dom DeLuise (*Irwin*), Gabriel Dell (*Sid*), Betty Walker (*Georgie's Mother*), Rose Gregorio (*Gloria*), Regina Baff (*Ruthie Tresh*), Ed Zimmermann (*Halloran*), Amy Levitt (*Susan*), Joseph R. Sicari (*Marty*), Rudy Bond (*Newsdealer*), Walter Hyman (*Flower Vendor*), Robyn Millan (*Samantha*), Josip Elic (*Chomsky*), James Hall (*Lemuel*), Candy Azzara (*Sally*), Susan Bell (*Sky Phone Operator*), Walter Hyman, Jr. (*Danny*), Sidney Armus (*Marvin*), Martin Greene (*Uncle Louis*), Shel Silverstein (*Pop Group Leader*).

An ambitious failure that suffers from the inability to make the surrealistic devices work and the diverse elements meld. The result is a film that is as confusing and overblown as the title. Hoffman is an extremely successful but depressed and lonely pop composer. He is approaching middle age and is frightened that it might stem his prodigious output which, the year before, was staggering and included more than 60 songs as well as various charitable works and a jingle for cancer. He is plagued with the delusion that someone named Harry Kellerman is bad-mouthing him across Manhattan and making crank middle-of-the-night phone calls. Hoffman lives in a triplex in the General Motors Building and decides to end it all. He writes a suicide note, tapes it to his awning, and leaps off the ledge. Instead of becoming pizza on the pavement, he lands on his analyst's couch (played by Warden). He tells Warden all the things that Kellerman has done to him but Warden offers no help and Hoffman leaves. In a series of stylized flashbacks, we get some insight into Hoffman as he thinks about his relationship with Baff at age 19 and the fact that he impregnated her, then fled after securing her an abortion. He next recalls his marriage to Gregorio that wound up in an angry divorce and two small sons. Hoffman is desperate for some friendly companionship and calls upon old pal Dell and accountant DeLuise but neither man offers him any help. He's hired a private eye to locate Kellerman and now has a lead on him so he hops into his limo and goes off searching for the man who is making his life a shambles. His current girl friend is Harris (in an Oscar-nominated role as Best Supporting Actress–she lost to Cloris Leachman in THE LAST PICTURE SHOW), a middle-thirties singer who has about three good notes in her vocal range. Harris met Hoffman while she was auditioning for his new show and found that she couldn't get her hand off the stage lamp while she was singing. The two fell in with each other and shared many of the same neuroses and when she enjoyed flying over New York in Hoffman's private airplane, he knew that she was the girl for him. But he's now frightened that Kellerman, who broke up several of his other relationships, will get to Harris and destroy this one. Hoffman's parents are Burns and Walker. They run a small luncheonette and when Hoffman arrives there one day he is thrilled to learn that they've named a triple decker sandwich after him, then he is distraught to find out that Burns is dying. Hoffman is frightened at what his life has to offer, leaps into his small plane, and takes to the skies, phoning all of his friends from the air. He finally gets Harrison on the radio-telephone and informs her that *he* is Harry Kellerman and he starts to tell her all of the bad things he is and does. The plane begins to nosedive and Hoffman sees the clouds as snow on the side of a mountain. The picture ends as Hoffman imagines Warden and himself skiing down the hill. Phew! We couldn't make head or tail out of the symbolism and the usually pragmatic Gardner (who wrote the screenplay from his own short story) was unable to transmit whatever he

was attempting to say. The whole idea of the film was specious, in that we have seen, all too often, the old cliches that "money can't buy happiness." Perhaps it can't but it sure makes living with misery a lot easier. To Hoffman's credit, he never ceases trying to expand his horizons and to try different roles. This picture was made between his remarkable portrayal of a 100-year-old Indian in LITTLE BIG MAN and the bloody STRAW DOGS. Coney Islander Gardner, who had his first success as a cartoonist, then wrote A THOUSAND CLOWNS, would go on to win the Tony for "I'm Not Rappaport" in 1986. Director Grosbard had already shown he could handle drama in THE SUBJECT WAS ROSES but comedy is evidently not his *metier*. The native-born Belgian had previously served as an assistant director on THE HUSTLER, THE PAWNBROKER, WEST SIDE STORY, and SPLENDOR IN THE GRASS, among others. Burns makes his last screen appearance. He died on March 12, 1971, while on the stage of a Philadelphia theater during a Broadway tryout of "70, Girls, 70"-the musicalization of MAKE MINE MINK. It's the way an actor would like to go, with a full audience in front of him and the last sound he hears being applause. Ray Charles is heard singing his "Don't Tell Me Your Troubles" and Shel Silverstein, who had a cameo as a pop group leader, wrote the tunes, none of which were more than incidental.

p, Ulu Grosbard, Herb Gardner; d, Grosbard; w, Gardner (based on his short story); ph, Victor J. Kemper (DeLuxe Color); ed, Barry Malkin; prod d, Harry Horner; set d, Leif Pedersen; cos, Anna Hill Johnstone; m/l, Shel Silverstein; makeup, Dick Smith.

Comedy/Fantasy   **(PR:C MPAA:GP)**

WHO IS HOPE SCHUYLER?* (1942) 55m FOX bw

Joseph Allen, Jr (*Tom Mason*), Mary Howard (*Diane Rossiter*), Sheila Ryan (*Lee Dale*), Richard Cortez (*Anthony Pearce*), Janis Carter (*Vesta Hadden*), Joan Valerie (*Phyllis Guerney*), Robert Lowery (*Robert Scott*), Rose Habart (*Alma Pearce*), Paul Guilfoyle (*Carl Spence*), William "Billy" Newell (*Perley Seymour*), Pat Flaherty (*Nash*), Charles Trowbridge (*Rossiter*), Frank Puglia (*Baggott*), Ed Stanley (*Stafford*), Edward Keane (*Judge*), Cliff Clark (*Lt. Palmer*).

Poorly constructed mystery features Cortez as an indicted district attorney. Allen is appointed as special prosecutor for the politically hot case. He has to find an astrologer named "Hope Schuyler" in order to solve a murder. Ryan is the newspaperwoman who helps him in the search and falls for the man as well. He's already romancing Howard, a judge's daughter, so this complicates matters. The film is without any interest whatsoever. The overly dramatic story is given a simplistic presentation, all wrong for its complicated plot twists. It quickly degenerates into a boring mess, directed without style and played without much feeling by its cast.

p, Sol M. Wurtzel; d, Thomas Z. Loring; w, Armaud d'Usseau (based on the novel *Hearses Don't Hurry* Stephen Ransome); ph, Virgil Miller; ed, Louis Loeffler; md, Emil Newman.

Mystery   **(PR:A MPAA:NR)**

WHO IS KILLING THE GREAT CHEFS OF EUROPE?*** (1978, US/Ger.) 112m Aldrich Lorimar-Geria-Bavaria/WB c (GB: TOO MANY CHEFS; AKA: SOMEONE IS KILLING THE GREAT CHEFS OF EUROPE)

George Segal (*Robby*), Jacqueline Bisset (*Natasha*), Robert Morley (*Max*), Jean-Pierre Cassel (*Kohner*), Philippe Noiret (*Moulineau*), Jean Rochefort (*Grandvilliers*), Luigi Proietti (*Ravello*), Stefano Satta Flores (*Fausto Zoppi*), Madge Ryan (*Beecham*), Frank Windsor (*Blodgett*), Peter Sallis (*St. Claire*), Tim Barlow (*Doyle*), John Le Mesurier (*Dr. Deere*), Joss Ackland (*Cantrell*), Jean Gaven (*Salpetre*), Daniel Emilfork (*Saint-Juste*), Jacques Marin (*Massenet*), Jacques Balutin (*Chappemain*), Jean Paredes (*Brissac*), Michael Chow (*Soong*), Anita Graham (*Blonde*), Nicholas Ball (*Skeffington*), David Cook (*Bussinghall*), Nigel Navers (*Counterman*), John Carlisle (*Actor*), Sheila Ruskin (*Actress*), Kenneth Fortescue (*Director*), Strewan Rodger (*Assistant Director*), Derek Smith (*Man in Corridor*), Marjorie Smith (*Receptionist*), Sylvia Kay (*Reporter*), Aimee Delamain (*Old Woman*), Lyall Jones (*Driver*), Eddie Tagoe (*Mumbala*), Caroline Langrishe (*Loretta*).

The title of this movie tells it all. Morley is a gourmand who must lose 140 pounds to protect his health. But how can he lose all this excess weight when his favorite chefs are still cooking up delectable dishes? Suddenly the finest of Europe's chefs mysteriously are done in with the most bizarre style of murder one might imagine. Each chef is killed in accordance with his specialty. A duck press crushes the head of one man; another is baked in his own oven. What's in store for Bisset, a dessert specialist and ex-wife of fast-food entrepreneur Segal? The string of murders takes the viewer on a rollicking trans-European chase with all the clues pointing to Morley. But is he the killer? There are some wonderful moments of black humor in this unusual comedy. The direction moves at a slick pace but keeps the tone light, with some witty results. Though the relationship between Segal and Bisset is a mite unbelievable, the three leads handle their roles well. Morley nearly steals the entire film. A good deal of fun in what ranks as one of the more macabre comedies of the 1970s.

p, William Aldrich; d, Ted Kotcheff; w, Peter Stone (based on the novel *Someone is Killing the Great Chefs of Europe* by Nan and Ivan Lyons); ph,

John Alcott (Metrocolor); m, Henry Mancini; art d, Werner Achmann; cos, Judy Moorcroft.

Comedy   **(PR:C MPAA:PG)**

WHO IS KILLING THE STUNTMEN?   (SEE: STUNTS, 1977)

WHO KILLED AUNT MAGGIE?**½   (1940) 70m REP bw

John Hubbard (*Kirk Pierce*), Wendy Barrie (*Sally Ambler*), Edgar Kennedy (*Sheriff Gregory*), Elizabeth Patterson (*Aunt Maggie Ambler*), Onslow Stevens (*Bob Dunbar*), Joyce Compton (*Cynthia Lou*), Walter Abel (*Dr. George Benedict*), Mona Barrie (*Eve Benedict*), Willie Best (*Andrew, Servant*), Daisy Lee Mothershed (*Bessie*), Milton Parsons (*Mr. Lloyd*), Tom Dugan (*Trooper Leroy*), William Haade (*Trooper Curtis*), Joel Friedkin (*Coroner Dodson*).

This fairly good comedy-mystery was an unusual outing for near-Poverty Row studio Republic. As it is, it's not bad, though viewed today the comic antics of Best play as typical Hollywood racism of the era. Bodies are dropping left and right in an old house and the eternally frustrated Kennedy is trying to investigate the cause. The mysterious "secret room" is apparently the cause of it all. Or is it? Some good direction and a fun script make this an enjoyable little outing.

p, Albert J. Cohen; d, Arthur Lubin; w, Stuart Palmer, Frank Gill, Jr., Hal Fimberg (based on the novel by Medora Field); ph, Reggie Lanning; m, Cy Feuer; ed, Edward Mann; md, Feuer; art d, John Victor Mackay; cos, Adele Palmer.

Comedy/Mystery   **(PR:A MPAA:NR)**

WHO KILLED "DOC" ROBBIN?**½
(1948) 51m Hal Roach/UA c (GB: SINISTER HOUSE; AKA: CURLEY AND HIS GANG IN THE HAUNTED MANSION)

Virginia Grey (*Ann Loring*), Don Castle (*Defense Attorney*), George Zucco (*Doc Robbin*), Whitford Kane (*Dan*), Claire Dubrey (*Housekeeper*), Grant Mitchell (*Judge*), Larry Olsen (*Curley*), Eilene Janssen (*Betty*), Ardda Lynwood (*Ardda*), Gerald Perreau [Peter Miles] (*Dudley*), Dale Belding (*Speck*), Renee Beard (*Dis*), Donald King (*Dat*).

After the first and second generations of the "Our Gang" kids grew up, Hal Roach, Jr., the namesake son of that series producer, attempted to create a new kiddie-comedy series, in which this was the second feature. This followup to THE ADVENTURES OF CURLEY AND HIS GANG has Zucco playing a mad scientist with "an atomic firing chamber." The youthful cast accidentally gets involved in his nefarious plans while looking for the local Mr. Fixit, played by Kane. Several slapstick sequences later, the minor mystery is solved. There isn't much to laugh at here and the film pales in comparison with those of the earlier Roach children. Particularly offensive are Beard and King, two small black kids dubbed "Dis" and "Dat." The film moves at the required quick pace, but ultimately it's not much.

p, Hal Roach, Jr., Robert F. McGowan; d, Bernard Carr; w, Maurice Geraghty, Dorothy Reid; ph, John W. Boyle (Cinecolor); ed, Arthur Seid; md, Heinz Roemheld; art d, Jerome Pycha, Jr.; set d, William Stevens; spec eff, Roy W. Seawright; makeup, Burris Grimwood.

Comedy   Cas.   **(PR:AAA MPAA:NR)**

WHO KILLED FEN MARKHAM?*½   (1937, Brit.) 76m St. Margarets/Ambassador bw (AKA: THE ANGELUS)

Anthony Bushell (*Brian Ware*), Nancy O'Neil (*June Rowland*), Eve Gray (*Maisie Blake*), Mary Glynne (*Sister Angelica*), Garry Marsh (*Fen Markham*), Zoe Wynn (*Gina Lock*), Richard Cooper (*Kenneth Blake*), Joyce Evans (*Jill Ware*), Charles Carson (*John Ware*), Amy Veness (*Mrs. Grimes*), Alice O'Day, Ernest Sefton, Jack Allen, John Turnbull.

O'Neil is an actress who is forced to give up boy friend Bushell, a wealthy banker's offspring, when her name is tainted by scandal. She then gets a part in a minor show where the manager (Marsh) takes a liking to her. Marsh is found murdered and the blame is pinned on O'Neil. Glynne, O'Neil's aunt, enters the scene at this point. She's a nun, temporarily on leave from the convent to help prove O'Neil's innocence (thus making this one of the highly limited "religious figure as detective" genre films). Of course this is done and what's more, O'Neil gets her old boy friend back. A boring mystery that has not aged at all well.

p, Julius Hagen; d, Thomas Bentley; w, Michael Barringer; ph, William Luff.

Crime   **(PR:A MPAA:NR)**

WHO KILLED GAIL PRESTON?**   (1938) 60m COL Bw

Don Terry (*Inspector Tom Kellogg*), Rita Hayworth (*Gail Preston*), Robert Paige (*Swing Traynor, Orchestra Leader*), Wyn Cahoon (*Ann Bishop*), Gene Morgan (*Cliff Connolly*), Marc Lawrence (*Frank Daniels*), Arthur Loft (*Jules Stevens*), John Gallaudet (*Charles Waverly*), John Spacey (*Patsy Fallon*), Eddie Fetherston (*Mike*), James Millican (*Hank*), Mildred Gover (*Maid*), Dwight Frye (*Mr. Owen*), John Dilson (*Curran*), Bill Irving (*Arnold*),

Vernon Dent (*Bill, Watchman*), Ruth Hilliard (*Cigarette Girl*), Jane Hamilton (*Hat-Check Girl*), Allen Brook, Jack Egan (*Radio Technicians*), James Burtis (*Headwaiter*), Nell Craig (*Society Woman*), Hal Craig (*Motor Cop*), Larry Fisher, Charles Hamilton, George Magrill, Billy Lally, E.L. Dale (*Cops*), Ralph McCullough (*Marshall*), Nick Copeland (*Louis*), Bruce Sidney (*Society Man*), Broderick O'Farrell (*Doctor*), Malcolm McTaggart (*Elevator Boy*), Lee Shumway (*Police Announcer*), Dick Curtis (*Jake*).

Hayworth is a nightclub singer who gets bumped off 20 minutes into the story. It takes the remaining screen time for Terry to discover that Gallaudet is the murderer and jealousy his motive. Not particularly memorable, the film is typical of the simplistic mystery programmers of the time. Hedy Lamarr was about to be loosed on the public in ALGIERS and Columbia anticipated the appeal her exotic looks would have by dressing Hayworth in a similar style for this film, capping her head with a dark wig and using makeup design that resembled Lamarr's features. Ironically, other studios would dress their starlets as Hayworth look-alikes after her success in BLOOD AND SAND. Hayworth had two musical numbers in the film: "It's Twelve O'Clock and All is Not Well" (Milton Drake, Ben Oakland), a mixture of her voice and Gloria Franklin's, and "The Greatest Attraction in the World," (Drake, Oakland), which was completely dubbed by Franklin.

p, Ralph Cohn; d, Leon Barsha; w, Robert E. Kent, Henry Taylor (based on the screen story "Murder in Swingtime" by Taylor); ph, Henry Freulich; ed, Byron Robinson; md, Morris W. Stoloff; art d, Stephen Goosson; cos, Robert Kalloch.

Mystery   **(PR:A MPAA:NR)**

WHO KILLED JESSIE?***   (1965, Czech.) 80m CFD bw (KDO CHCE ZABIT JESSU?; AKA: WHO WOULD KILL JESSIE? WHO WANTS TO KILL JESSIE?)

Jiri Sovak, Dana Medricka, Olga Shoberova [Olinka Berova], Karel Effa, Juraj Visny.

After inventing a machine that shows a sleeper's dreams on a screen, scientist Medricka uses it to see what goes on in her husband's (Sovak) head after hours. His dreams are populated by some cartoonish characters, including Shoberova, a Daisy Mae type who is chased by nasty cowpoke Effa. Also after her is Visny, a muscle-bound superhero. These dreams surprise the prim scientist and she tries to manipulate them with disastrous results. The machine malfunctions, causing the dream characters to appear in the flesh in the couple's apartment. This is marvelous comedy, full of unusual slapstick and some great inventive moments. It originally had been planned as a children's film, but as the script kept getting wilder, the production team changed its target audience. The film unfortunately is at a disadvantage in its black-and-white format, for this off-the-wall story surely would have benefitted greatly from color. The directing and writing team of Vorlicek and Makourek went on to create some of Czechoslovakia's best zany comedies, many with themes similar to this film.

d, Vaclav Vorlicek; w, Milos Makourek; ph, Jan Nemecek.

Comedy   **(PR:C MPAA:NR)**

WHO KILLED JOHN SAVAGE?**½   (1937, Brit.) 68m Teddington-WB-FN/WB bw

Nicholas Hannen (*John Savage*), Barry Mackay (*Anthony Benedict*), Edward Chapman (*Inspector Chortley*), Kathleen Kelly (*Kate Savage*), Henry Oscar (*Woolrich*), Ross Landon (*Smith*), George Kirby (*Prout*), Denier Warren (*Scruggs*).

At a synthetic rubber plant, Hannen, the senior business partner, is found dead. He had claimed before his death that a man named Marchetti had been threatening him, so a murder investigation is launched. Eventually it's discovered that Hannen had been terminally ill and faked his own murder so that bankrupt company would get his insurance money. Though slow to develop, this is an interesting mystery with some nicely detailed moments. Some good thesping by the ensemble overcomes the directorial sluggishness to create an unusual whodunit. This is a remake of the 1931 film RYNOX.

p, Irving Asher: d, Maurice Elvey; w, Basil Dillon (based on the novel *Rynox* by Philip MacDonald); ph, Basil Emmott, Robert Lepresle.

Mystery   **(PR:A MPAA:NR)**

WHO KILLED MARY WHAT'SER NAME?**
(1971) 90m Cannon c (AKA: DEATH OF A HOOKER)

Red Buttons (*Mickey Isadore*), Alice Playten (*Della Isadore*), Sylvia Miles (*Christine*), Sam Waterston (*Alex*), Donald Marye (*Leo*), Dick Williams (*Malthus*), Conrad Bain (*Val*), Norman Rose (*Dr. Barkunian*), David Doyle (*Boulting*), Ellen Gurin (*Angela*), Gilbert Lewis (*Officer Solomon*), Ron Carey (*Bartender*), Earl Hindman (*Whitey*), Antony Page (*Joe*), Sally Birkhead (*Snug Harbor Nurse*), Stella Longo (*1st Hooker*), Ellen Faison (*2nd Hooker*), Dee Timberlake (*Hospital Nurse*).

Despite an unusual premise this comedy murder mystery never goes anywhere. Buttons is a diabetic ex-boxer who becomes interested in the slaying of a Greenwich Village hooker. After his release from the hospital he begins his own investigation of the crime. With the help of Playten, his daughter, and residents of the Village, Buttons puts the clues together until he confronts the killer. In the end he succumbs to his disease when he slips into a diabetic coma. What keeps this sinking ship afloat is the excellent work of the supporting cast, Waterston, an unscrupulous filmmaker, Bain, an unemployed insurance salesman, and Lewis, the cop assigned to the case. They clearly deserved better than this contrived plot which has the additional handicap of endless holes in story logic.

p, George Manasse; d, Ernie Pintoff; w, John O'Toole; ph, Greg Sandor (DeLuxe Color); m, Gary McFarland; ed, Angelo Ross; makeup, Bill Pinkney.

Mystery   **Cas.**   **(PR:O   MPAA:GP)**

WHO KILLED TEDDY BEAR?*   (1965) 90m Phillips/Magna bw

Sal Mineo (*Lawrence*), Juliet Prowse (*Norah*), Jan Murray (*Bill Madden*), Elaine Stritch (*Billie*), Margot Bennett, Dan Travanty, Diane Moore, Frank Campanella, Bruce Glover, Tom Aldredge, Rex Everhart, Alex Fisher, Stanley Beck, Casey Townsend.

A thoroughly ugly potboiler has Prowse playing a discotheque hostess who is being harassed by an obscene phone caller. Murray, the very unfunny standup comic, is a police investigator who takes an interest in the case and acts so weird he makes Prowse think he's the culprit. Meanwhile, she becomes friendly with Mineo, a club busboy who actually is the caller. Mineo starts spying on her with binoculars and increasing his calls so the terrified woman moves in with Murray and his family. Stritch, the lesbian club owner, visits Prowse one evening and Mineo mistakes her for Prowse. He rapes and kills her, which sets off some old wounds in Murray as his wife was also a victim of a sex killer. He doubles his efforts while the unsuspecting Prowse gives Mineo a dance lesson at the club. He assaults her, revealing himself as the man behind the terror, and flees the club. The police chase the psychopath and shoot him down. Unpleasant and most unwatchable.

p, Everett Rosenthal; d, Joseph Cates; w, Leon Tokatyan, Arnold Drake (based on a story by Drake); ph, Joseph Brun; m, Charlie Calello; ed, Angelo Ross; art d, Hank Aldrich; m/l, Al Kasha, Bob Gaudio.

Drama   **(PR:O   MPAA:NR)**

WHO KILLED THE CAT?**   (1966, Brit.) 76m Eternal/GN bw

Mary Merrall (*Janet Bowering*), Ellen Pollock (*Ruth Prendergast*), Amy Dalby (*Lavinia Goldsworthy*), Mervyn Johns (*Henry Fawcett*), Vanda Godsell (*Eleanor Trellington*), Conrad Phillips (*Inspector Bruton*), Natasha Pyne (*Mary Trellington*), Ronald Adam (*Gregory*), Gregory Phillips (*Peter Parsons*).

When the beloved pussy cat of a trio of spinsters turns up dead, the three begin a search for the culprit. Their main suspect is the nasty old landlady, so a plan for a revenge poisoning is hatched. Strange idea, to say the least.

p, Maurice J. Wilson; d, Montgomery Tully; w, Wilson, Tully (based on the play "Tabitha" by Arnold Ridley, Mary Cathcart Borer).

Crime   **(PR:A-C   MPAA:NR)**

WHO KILLED VAN LOON?**½   (1984, Brit.) 52m Kyle/Exclusive bw

Raymond Lovell (*Johann Schmidt*), Kay Bannerman (*Anna Kreuger*), Robert Wyndham (*Inspector Oxley*), John Dodsworth (*Ian Ferguson*), Milton Rosmer (*Simmonds*), Patricia Laffan (*Peggy Osborn*), Graham Russell, Beth Ross, Paul Sheridan.

Lovell manages to free a Dutch diamond cutter from a Nazi prison camp, intending to use the man for some nefarious doings. Lovell has killed the Dutchman's ex-partner for his collection of uncut diamonds, and now threatens to frame the gem cutter's daughter, Bannerman, for murder unless he cuts them. Wyndham is a detective investigating the murder and, thanks to his persistence, Lovell's plans are foiled. Some good moments, backed by a nice directorial feel for the material.

p, Gordon Kyle, James Carreras; d, Kyle, Lionel Tomlinson; w, Peter Cresswell; ed, Douglas Myers.

Crime   **(PR:A   MPAA:NR)**

WHO RIDES WITH KANE?   (SEE: YOUNG BILLY YOUNG, 1969)

WHO SAYS I CAN'T RIDE A RAINBOW!**½
                                                    (1971) 85m Transvue c

Jack Klugman (*Barney Marcovitz*), Norma French (*Mary Lee*), Reuben Figueroa (*Angel*), David Mann (*David*), Kevin Riou (*Kevin*), Val Avery (*The Marshal*), Morgan Freeman (*Afro*), Skitch Henderson, Heather MacRae, Otis Stephens (*Themselves*), Ed Crowley, Nancy Davison, Lee Dowell, Dan Drake, Frank Durk, Laura Figueroa, Frances Foster, Roy Hill, Florence Kennedy, Virginia Kiser, Leib Lensky, Rick Moss, Bob Nielsen, Mervyn Nelson, David Polinger, Rod Rogers, Antonia Rey, Elliot Robins, Esther Rolle, Jack Strauss, Don Smith, Lee Steele, Douglas Watson, Barney Marovitz, Chichi Bonilla, Joey Vonilla, Nicky Brooks, Todd Hammer, Dara Mann, Eloy Mesa.

A charming film for children features Klugman as a man who is convinced that the hope of the world lies with its young people. He runs a pony farm/mini-zoo on a small plot of land in Manhattan so city kids can experience animals they might only see on television. His plans are upset when the real estate company which owns the property wants to put up a housing complex. The neighborhood rallies around him but to no avail. Klugman gives his animals to the neighborhood kids with some amusing results (two youngsters have an unusual time trying to keep a pony hidden from their parents), but finally he and his assistant, French (an aspiring singer who is taken with the man and his vision), relocate to the Bronx. The potential for this film to get overly sentimental is high but luckily the filmmakers never stoop to the obvious. The result is a warm-hearted tale, which occasionally suffers from a slow pacing and some repetitious moments. Klugman is surprisingly good in projecting genuine emotional honesty.

p, Jerry Hammer; d, Edward Mann; w, Mann, Daniel Hauer; ph, (DeLuxe Color); m, Bobby Scott; ed, Sid Katz; m/l, Scott, Danny Meehan, Richard Ahlert, Joe Scott (title song sung by Bobby Vinton).

Children's Film   **(PR:AAA   MPAA:G)**

WHO SLEW AUNTIE ROO?**½   (1971, U.S./Brit.) 89m
Hemdale-AIP/AIP c (GB: WHOEVER SLEW AUNTIE ROO?; AKA: GINGERBREAD HOUSE)

Shelley Winters (*Rosie Forrest*), Mark Lester (*Christopher*), Ralph Richardson (*Mr. Benton*), Lionel Jeffries (*Inspector Willoughby*), Judy Cornwell (*Clarine*), Michael Gothard (*Albie*), Hugh Griffith (*The Pigman/Mr. Harrison*), Chloe Franks (*Katy*), Rosalie Crutchley (*Miss Henley*), Pat Heywood (*Dr. Mason*), Jacqueline Cowper (*Angela*), Richard Beaumont (*Peter*), Charlotte Sayce (*Katherine*), Marianne Stone (*Miss Wilcox*).

An unusual bit of macabre humor features Winters (in a wonderfully hammy performance) as an ex-music hall singer who has become a recluse since the death of her only daughter years before. A la PSYCHO, she keeps the child's room exactly the same as when the girl was alive, rocking and singing to the cradle that holds the child's mummified remains. Every year she allows eight children from the local orphanage to spend Christmas with her, but one year 10 show up, the extra two being Lester and his sister, Franks, a pair of problem kids who snuck into the car bound for the mansion. Franks bears an uncanny resemblance to her late daughter so Winters allows them to stay, showing the girl more affection than any of the others. Lester gets jealous and goes prowling around the place after hours, discovering the mummy and Winters' unusual seance sessions with Richardson, a fake medium. Lester puts two and two together and decides that this is really the story of "Hansel and Gretel" come to life, and he is convinced that Winters is a witch who wants to eat him and his sister. When the children go back to the orphanage Franks is missing and Lester assumes his nightmare vision is true. He sneaks back and discovers Winters and his sister equally charmed with one another. She cooks the children a lavish supper but Lester, faithful to the "Hansel and Gretel" story, locks her in the pantry and sets fire to the house, fleeing with his sister and Winters' jewels. This film walks a fine line between good and bad taste, manipulating audience expectations and loyalties gleefully and shamelessly. It was an intentional updating of the gruesome fairy tale, which succeeds on its own strange level, but the child murderer may disturb some viewers. Definitely not for children.

p, Samuel Z. Arkoff, James H. Nicholson; d, Curtis Harrington; w, Robert Blees, James [Jimmy] Sangster, Gavin Lambert (based on a story by David Osborn); ph, Desmond Dickinson (Movielab Color); m, Kenneth V. Jones; ed, Tristam V. Cones; art d, George Provis; makeup, Eddie Knight, Sylvia Croft.

Drama/Satire   **Cas.**   **(PR:O   MPAA:GP)**

WHO WANTS TO KILL JESSIE?   (SEE: WHO KILLED JESSIE?,
                                                            1965, Czech.)

WHO WAS MADDOX?**   (1964, Brit.) 62m Merton/Anglo
                                                            Amalgamated bw

Bernard Lee (*Supt. Meredith*), Jack Watling (*Jack Heath*), Suzanne Lloyd (*Diane Heath*), Finlay Currie (*Alec Campbell*), Richard Gale (*Maddox*), James Bree (*Reynolds*), Dora Reisser (*Anne Wilding*), Christa Bergmann (*Greta*), Billy Milton (*Chandler*).

A rivalry at a publishing house leads to murder. The trail in discovering the culprit leads to a blackmail plot and some jewel thievery as well.

p, Jack Greenwood; d, Geoffrey Nethercott; w, Roger Marshall (based on the story "The Undisclosed Client" by Edgar Wallace).

Crime   **(PR:A   MPAA:NR)**

WHO WAS THAT LADY?***   (1960) 115m Ansark-Sidney/COL bw

Tony Curtis (*David Wilson*), Dean Martin (*Michael Haney*), Janet Leigh (*Ann Wilson*), James Whitmore (*Harry Powell*), John McIntire (*Bob Doyle*), Barbara Nichols (*Gloria Coogle*), Larry Keating (*Parker*), Larry Storch (*Orenov*), Simon Oakland (*Belka*), Joi Lansing (*Florence Coogle*), Barbara

Hines (Girl), Marion Javits (Miss Melish), Michael Lane (Glinka), Kam Tong (Lee Wong), William "Billy" Newell (Schultz), Mark Allen (Joe Bendix), Snub Pollard (Tattoo Artist).

This cute farce features Curtis as a Columbia University professor caught by his wife (Leigh) when he kisses a pretty student. Enraged at this dalliance, Leigh packs her bags and prepares to fly to Reno for a quickie divorce. Curtis, in sheer desperation, turns to his old pal Martin, a television writer, for some help. Martin concocts a wild story about Curtis being an undercover man for the FBI, and kissing this girl was part of a secret operation. Leigh falls for the story, then follows Curtis and Martin when they go to a Chinese restaurant with a pair of daffy blondes. Leigh surmises the two girls are also suspected spies, and tries to pass Curtis a blank gun he left at their apartment. This sets off a mini-riot that involves actual FBI agents and a television news crew that captures the action for that evening's news. Some genuine Russian spies come to believe Curtis really is an agent involved in a sensitive project being conducted at the university. Curtis, along with Leigh and Martin, is grabbed by the Soviets and taken to an underground room below the Empire State Building. There he is given truth serum and admits his deceit. Leigh is furious with her husband and manages to escape the spies' clutches. Curtis and Martin finally wake up, believing they are captive in an enemy submarine. The two patriotically decide to sink the ship, opening up the basement water valves. As the water pours in, Martin and Curtis bravely sing "The Star Spangled Banner," convinced they are about to die for their country. Some FBI men arrive to save the water-logged duo, as Leigh ultimately forgives Curtis for his errant ways. Though the premise is stretched a little too thin, this is an enjoyable comedy. Curtis and Leigh make good use of their well-known off-screen marriage, playing up the husband and wife roles for some fun moments. Martin, playing his affable drunk character, also gives a good comic performance and sings the movie's title song. Overall WHO WAS THAT LADY? is nothing special, but an enjoyable diversion. The three costars engaged in an on-set battle of sorts, involving water pistols fired at each other. For the climactic flood scene, Leigh decided to carry the joke one step further, employing director Sidney's help. After Curtis and Martin were finished with the scene, Leigh recalled in her autobiography There Really Was a Hollywood, Sidney "gave me the signal and kept the camera rolling. I let myself be caught in the stream and then blithely swam by them, nonchalantly waving hello. Their reaction was unintelligble, unrepeatable, and unmatchable. I was victorious!" Making a small appearance as a tattoo artist is former Mack Sennett clown, Snub Pollard.

p, Norman Krasna; d, George Sidney; w, Krasna (based on the play "Who Was That Lady I Saw You With?" by Krasna); ph, Harry Stradling; m, Andre Previn; ed, Viola Lawrence; art d, Edward Haworth; set d, James M. Crowe; cos, Jean Louis; m/l, Sammy Cahn, James Van Heusen; makeup, Ben Lane.

Comedy   **(PR:A MPAA:NR)**

WHO WOULD KILL A CHILD   (SEE: ISLAND OF THE DAMNED, 1976, Span.)

WHOEVER SLEW AUNTIE ROO?
                    (SEE: WHO SLEW AUNTIE ROO? 1971, Brit.)

WHOLE SHOOTIN' MATCH, THE*   (1979) 100m Cinema
                                              Perspectives bw

Lou Perry (Loyd), Sonny Davis (Frank), Doris Hargrave (Paulette), Eric Henshaw (Olan), David Weber (T. Frank), James Harrell (Old Man).

Perry and Davis are a pair of rural Texans, well past the 30th birthday benchmark, and still looking for their life work. They've tried raising small animals from frogs to chinchillas, and even flying squirrels. Now they want to go into the polyurethane business, dead set on making a fortune from well-off hippies. "There's money to be made from rich hippies..." Perry insists. Though technically this is not a great film, it is rich in characterizations and warmth. The duo are a charming team, giving portraits one can both laugh at and sympathize with. This independent feature was shot on a minuscule budget of $30,000, once again proving that big budgets aren't always a key to good movies. Though technically the film has its troubles, these aren't all that distracting. The film stock itself is sepia-toned, an imaginative old idea that further gives the film its special feeling.

p, Eagle Pennell, Lin Sutherland; d, Pennell; w, Pennell, Sutherland; ph, Pennell; m, Chuck Pennell; art d, Jim Rexrode.

Drama/Comedy   **(PR:C MPAA:NR)**

WHOLE TOWN'S TALKING, THE***   (1935) 95m COL bw

Edward G. Robinson (Arthur Ferguson Jones/Killer Mannion), Jean Arthur (Wilhelmina "Bill" Clark), Arthur Hohl (Detective Sgt. Mike Boyle), Wallace Ford (Healy), Arthur Byron (District Atty. Spencer), Donald Meek (Hoyt), Paul Harvey (J.G. Carpenter), Edward Brophy (Bugs Martin), Etienne Girardot (Seaver), James Donlan (Detective Sgt. Pat Howe), J. Farrell MacDonald (Warden), Effie Ellsler (Aunt Agatha), Robert Emmett O'Connor (Police Lt. Mac), John Wray, Joe Sawyer 'Savers' (Mannion's Henchmen), Frank Sheridan (Russell), Clarence Hummel Wilson (President

of the Chamber of Commerce), Ralph M. Remley (Ribber), Virginia Pine (Seaver's Private Secretary), Ferdinand Munier (Mayor), Cornelius Keefe (Radio Man), Francis Ford (Reporter at Dock), Lucille Ball (Girl), Ben Taggart (Traffic Cop), Walter Long (Convict), Mary Gordon (Landlady), Bess Flowers (Secretary), Charles King, Gordon DeMain (Men), Robert E. Homans (Detective), Grace Halo (Sob Sister), Al Hill (Gangster), Sam Flint (City Official), Emmett Vogan (Reporter), Tom London (Guard).

One of the most underrated of Ford's early films, THE WHOLE TOWN'S TALKING is a marvelous gangster film told in a comic vein and sporting a superb performance from Robinson. Robinson plays a timid clerk working for a hardware company. He has a superlative work record with the company and has been punctual every morning for eight years. He is in love with one of his coworkers, Arthur, from afar. While he is having lunch with her, the police arrive and arrest him. They have mistaken him for Public Enemy No.1, Killer Mannion, who has recently escaped from prison and is Robinson's exact double. After much confusion over his identity, the district attorney is satisfied that Robinson isn't the gangster they are looking for and he issues the clerk an identity card he can show police to avoid being arrested by mistake again. Unfortunately, the news about Robinson's misadventure hits all the newspapers--due in part to Robinson's boss who urges his employee to write about Mannion for the papers--and the real Killer Mannion (also played by Robinson) reads the story. The gangster shows up at the clerk's house and demands that the identity card be turned over to him every evening so that he can move about more freely. The gangster also begins dictating the details of his sordid life to the clerk to be included in the newspaper column. To ensure the clerk's cooperation, the gangster kidnaps Arthur and the clerk's aunt, Ellsler. Posing as the clerk, the gangster and his thugs commit several robberies in the area and the police put the innocent Robinson in jail for his own protection. To kill two birds with one stone, the gangster decides to pose as the clerk, get into jail, kill a stoolie that once double-crossed him, and then send the clerk out on a bank job where he is sure to be killed--thus "Killer Mannion" would be dead and "Arthur Ferguson" could be released. The clerk heads for the bank, but when he realizes that he's forgotten his gun, he goes back to the gang's hideout. Before entering, he overhears the gangsters joking about the setup. The clerk then decides to act like the gangster, and when the real gangster enters the room, the clerk orders the men to kill him (they think their boss is the clerk). The clerk then gets the drop on the gang with a Tommy gun and rescues Arthur and his aunt. The police arrive and take the gang away and a newly confident Robinson asks Arthur to marry him. Based on a story by W.R. Burnett (who wrote the novel Little Caesar) which was adapted by screenwriters Swerling and Riskin, THE WHOLE TOWN'S TALKING is a masterful balance of comedy and drama with a very dark subtext. Robinson the clerk and Robinson the gangster are two sides of the same coin. The clerk is a milquetoast who can't bring himself to tell the woman he loves how he feels about her, but once he dons the identity of the gangster and orders a man to be killed, he is suddenly infused with self-confidence and power which finally enable him to speak his mind and take action. Though the film is essentially a comedy and there is enough motivation for Robinson the clerk's actions for his character to remain sympathetic, it is an undeniably chilling and ambiguous moment. Robinson handles the role beautifully, bringing several shadings and subtleties to a double role that could have easily gone the way of gimmicky silliness. Because of the ambiguity and subtle handling of the darker aspects of the story, director Ford and actor Robinson turned what could have been dismissed as just another light, frivolous entertainment into an evocative work of art.

p, Lester Cowan; d, John Ford; w, Jo Swerling, Robert Riskin (based on the novel by William R. Burnett); ph, Joseph August; ed, Viola Lawrence.

Comedy/Crime   **(PR:A MPAA:NR)**

WHOLE TRUTH, THE½   (1958, Brit.) 84m COL bw

Stewart Granger (Max Paulton), Donna Reed (Carol Paulton), George Sanders (Carliss), Gianna Maria Canale (Gina Bertini), Michael Shillo (Inspector Simon), Richard Molinas (Gilbert), Peter Dyneley (Willy Reichel), John Van Eyssen (Archer), Philip Vickers (Jack Leslie), Jimmy Thompson (Assistant), Hy Hazell (American Woman), Carlo Justini (Leading Man), Agnes Lauchlan (Englishwoman), Jacques Cey (Barman), Hugo De Varnier (Hotel Receptionist), Yves Chanteau (Rouget), Jean Driant (Male Servant), Joan Benham, Mignon O'Doherty, Jan Holden, Laurie Main (Party Guests).

Movie producer Granger is bored in his marriage with Reed. He has an affair with Canale, a temperamental actress, but decides he prefers Reed's company. After he dumps Canale, the star turns up with a knife in her back and all clues point toward Granger as the killer. When he meets Canale, quite alive in a chalet, he discovers the "detective" assigned to the murder case, who told him Canale was dead, was her cuckolded husband, Sanders. The actress is then really murdered and this time Granger is arrested. But Reed, loyal to the end, proves Sanders is the killer and he is killed while fleeing in his car. Well acted and briskly directed. Canale, who has the film's smallest role, proves to be its most intriguing player.

p, Jack Clayton; d, John Guillermin; w, Jonathan Latimer (based on the stage and television play by Philip Mackie); ph Wilkie Cooper; m, Mischa Spoliansky; ed, Gerry Hambling; md, Lambert Williamson; art d, Tony Masters; makeup, Roy Ashton.

Mystery/Thriller   (PR:A   MPAA:NR)

WHO'LL STOP THE RAIN?***½   (1978) 125m UA c

Nick Nolte (Ray), Tuesday Weld (Marge), Michael Moriarty (John), Anthony Zerbe (Antheil), Richard Masur (Danskin), Ray Sharkey (Smitty), Gail Strickland (Chairman), Charles Haid (Eddy), David O. Opatoshu (Bender).

Even though every other review lists the co-screenwriter as "Judith Roscoe," we can assure you that there is no such person in the Writers Guild and that the real credit should be given to Judith Rascoe, a novelist and screenwriter who is kin to the late Burton Rascoe, a superb sportswriter of a generation ago. This is an excellent and somewhat overlooked film about the disillusionment of America in the late 1960s. Moriarty is a journalist who has been traumatized by the war in Vietnam. He decides to smuggle heroin back into the U.S. and hires his pal Nolte to be the courier. Nolte is in the Merchant Marine and has better access through customs. He'd smuggled marijuana in the past but is reluctant to do this at first. He finally decides to take the chance as the reward will be great. Nolte is to bring in the heroin, meet Moriarity's pill-popping wife, Weld, and then wait until her husband returns so they can sell the goods. Nolte has been followed by a pair of gunmen so he races off with Weld in tow as the men come after him. The men, Sharkey and Masur, are in the employ of Zerbe, a corrupt narcotics agent. Moriarty comes back to the U.S. and is kidnaped and tortured by Zerbe's henchmen. Nolte is on the run with Weld and they meet Haid, a trendy drug dealer who caters to up-scale California clients. Nolte wants to dump the white stuff with Haid. Masur and Sharkey find out where Nolte and Weld are. They're holing up in a semi- abandoned old hippie commune and when Masur and Sharkey arrive, there is a shoot-out. Nolte is shot and left to die on the railroad tracks as the picture ends, in a most depressing fashion. It does an excellent job of symbolizing the death of idealism in the late 1960s through corruption, loss of faith in one's leaders, and the war. Reisz was making his second U.S. film (his first was THE GAMBLER). He is the author of the textbook The Technique of Film Editing, a must for anyone interested in that field. The film was originally to be called "Dog Soldiers" (after the novel) but was changed to the current title, which is the name of a Creedence Clearwater Revival song used on the soundtrack. A well-made, tough movie that might have been a 1940s film noir. The subject matter and the bloody violence make this off limits for children under 16.

p, Herb Jaffe, Gabriel Katzka; d, Karel Reisz; w, Judith Rascoe, Robert Stone (based on the novel Dog Soldiers by Stone); ph, Richard H. Kline; m, Laurence Rosenthal; ed, John Bloom; m/l, John Fogerty, Creedence Clearwater Revival.

Drama/Crime   Cas.   (PR:C   MPAA:R)

WHOLLY MOSES zero   (1980) 109m COL c

Dudley Moore (Harvey/Herschel), Laraine Newman (Zoe/Zerelda), James Coco (Hyssop), Paul Sand (Angel of the Lord), Jack Gilford (Tailor), Dom DeLuise (Shadrach), John Houseman (Archangel), Madeline Kahn (Sorceress), David L. Lander (Beggar), Richard Pryor (Pharaoh), John Ritter (Devil), Richard B. Shull (Jethro), Tanya Boyd (Princess), Ruth Manning (Landlady), Walker Edmiston (Voice of God), Andrea Martin (Zipporah), Stan Ross (Mohammed), William Watson, Sam Weisman, Jeffrey Jacquet, Howard Mann, Charles Thomas Murphy, Hap Lawrence, David Murphy, Tom Baker, Sandy Ward, Lee Wilkof, Maryedith Burrell, Rod McCary, Brion James, Lois Robbins, Shelley Johnson, Michael Champion, Lauren Frost, Ion Teodorescu, Nick Mele.

Absolute claptrap. An alleged comedy with religious overtones has Moore as a phony religious prophet back in the days of Moses. He hears Moses get God's words and the fun starts. Moore and Newman begin as a pair of tourists who find the long-missing "Book of Herschel" which recounts, in flashback, the terrible existence of Coco, a slave, and his son, Moore, as he goes from sculptor of idols up to the top of the mountain where Moses hears the voice of God (played by famous voice-over actor Edmiston). From there, it's a hop, skip, and jump to the court of Pryor, pharaoh of Egypt. There are several cameo appearances by a number of TV and film stars, none of whom can help this film rise above stupidity. How the distinguished John Houseman could have been induced to play an archangel is beyond us. Either he didn't read the script or needed the money badly. Whatever it is, he earned it. DeLuise does his usual predictable turn and even the gifted Madeline Kahn is at a loss to be anything but dull, given the script by fledgling Thomas and the direction by first-timer Weis. Various sections of the California desert doubled for the Holy Land. The executive producer was David Begelman, who used to run Columbia Studios until he was caught playing games with certain financial documents. The story of Begelman's shenanigans was well-documented in a later book, Indecent Exposure. The Stan Ross who plays Mohammed is no relation to the coauthor of The Motion Picture Guide, thank goodness.

p, Freddie Fields; d, Gary Weis; w, Guy Thomas; ph, Frank Stanley (Panavision, Metrocolor); m, Patrick Williams; ed, Sidney Levin; prod d, Dale Hennesy; set d, Diane Wager; cos, Guy Verhille.

Comedy   Cas.   (PR:C   MPAA:PG)

WHOM THE GODS DESTROY**½   (1934) 75m COL bw

Walter Connolly (John Forrester), Robert Young (Jack Forrester), Doris Kenyon (Margaret Forrester), Macon Jones (Jack at Age 14), Scotty Beckett (Jack at Age 4), Rollo Floyd (Henry Braverman), Hobart Bosworth (Alec), Maidel Turner (Miss Henrietta Crossland), Gilbert Emery (Prof. Weaver), Hugh Huntley (Jamison the Ship's Officer), Akim Tamiroff (Morotoft), Henry Kolker (Carlos), George Humbert (Niccoli), Yale Puppeteers (Puppets), Reginald Mason (Behan), Charles D. Middleton (Constable Malcolm), Walter Brennan (Clifford), Mary Carr (Old Actress), Jack Mulhall (Lead Man in Show), Betty Francisco (Lead Woman in Show), Tom Ricketts (Charlie), Bud Geary (Sailor), Arthur "Pop" Byron (Stagehand).

When an ocean liner strikes a derelict ship and begins to sink, Connolly, a noted theatrical figure, helps save the women and children, and then dresses as a woman to save his own skin. Oh returning home, he finds that he is assumed dead and is mourned as a hero, and he is forced to remain "dead" to save his family from disgrace and himself from charges of cowardice. This spotty drama swings between ludicrousness and sincerity, but Connolly gives an excellent performance as the tortured lead. Implausibilities abound in the script and finally become ridiculous. Look for an appearance by Beckett, one of the "Our Gang" kids, in a minor role.

d, Walter Lang; w, Fred Niblo, Jr., Sidney Buchman (based on a story by Albert Payson Terhune); ph, Benjamin Kline; ed, Viola Lawrence.

Drama   (PR:A   MPAA:NR)

WHOM THE GODS LOVE   (SEE: MOZART, 1940, Brit.)

WHOOPEE***½   (1930) 94m UA c

Eddie Cantor (Henry Williams), Eleanor Hunt (Sally Morgan), Paul Gregory (Wanenis), John Rutherford (Sheriff Bob Wells), Ethel Shutta (Mary Custer), Spencer Charters (Jerome Underwood), Chief Caupolican (Black Eagle), Albert Hackett (Chester Underwood), William H. Philbrick (Andy McNabb), Walter Law (Judd Morgan), Marilyn Marsh 'Marian Marsh' (Harriet Underwood), Dean Jagger (Deputy), George Morgan and His Orchestra (Specialty), Joyzelle Jacques Cartier, Betty Grable, Virginia Bruce, Muriel Finley, Jeanne Morgan, Ruth Eddings, Ernestine Mahoney, Christine Maple, Dorothy Knapp, Claire Dodd, Jane Keithley, Mary Ashcraft, Betty Stockton, Georgia Lerch (Goldwyn Girls), Theodore Lorch, Budd Fine, Gene Alsace, Frank Rice, Edmund Cobb, Martin Faust, Arthur Dewey, William J. Begg, John Ray, Frank Lanning, Paul Panze.

"Another bride, another groom, another sunny honeymoon, another season..." that was the reason for making WHOOPEE. After the smash hit Broadway show in 1928-29 finished its long run, Sam Goldwyn joined forces (temporarily) with Flo Ziegfeld to recreate this stage winner for one of the first Technicolor films. It made Cantor a Goldwyn star and the hit song, "Making Whoopee" (Walter Donaldson and Gus Kahn), became a standard. Cantor sings it in one of the longest single film sequences on record. Cantor is a state-of-the-art hypochondriac whose imagined poor health causes him to bring many hilarious situations upon his person. He lives in the East and is convinced that he needs to go West to survive so, with his nurse-companion Shutta, he travels across the country and winds up on an Arizona ranch. He is somewhat of a busybody and when he meets Hunt, he gets involved in her affairs. Hunt is engaged to the local sheriff, Rutherford, but she really loves Indian brave Gregory, who lives in the general area. Cantor manages to extricate Hunt from Rutherford and place her firmly in the arms of Gregory. Later, it is learned that Gregory isn't a redskin at all, rather a paleface who had been abandoned and raised by the local Indians. Not much more than that by way of plot but several splendid Busby Berkeley production numbers, a bevy of Goldwyn's girls (one of whom was a very young Betty Grable), and super art direction by Capt. Richard Day, for which he was Oscar-nominated by the Motion Picture Academy. The key to the film was, of course, Cantor, just as it was Danny Kaye when Goldwyn remade this movie as UP IN ARMS 14 years later. Hypochondriacs have always been great comedy fodder and this is no exception. Cantor's largest laugh comes when he blithely explains that he could die from any of his sextet of diseases right on the spot. Many in the cast were from the stage play, including Hunt (who was a chorus girl), Gregory, Rutherford, Shutta (in her only film role here), Charters, Hackett, and several others. This was the first time since 1923 that Goldwyn had worked with a partner and it didn't wear well with either Sam or the tempestuous Flo. This story had been filmed silently before in 1926, being taken from the Owen Davis play "The Nervous Wreck" which had, in turn, been adapted from a serial in Argosy/All Story magazine by Robert W. Davis and Edith R. Rath. Goldwyn and Ziegfeld broke up when Ziegfeld wanted his name first in the billing of the company, something Goldwyn's ego couldn't handle, and Ziegfeld was not allowed on the sound stage during shooting. Songs by Donaldson and Kahn were "The Song of the Setting Sun," "Mission Number," "Makin' Waffles," "A Girlfriend of a Boyfriend of Mine" (Cantor), "My Baby Just Cares for Me" (Cantor). One extra tune, "I'll Still Belong to You," was written by Edward Eliscu and Nacio Herb Brown. "Nacio" means "born" in Spanish and Brown's real name was Ignacio Moreno (Moreno means "brown") and that's how he came to use that name. Berkeley showed here a taste of what was yet to come in his Warner Bros. heyday as he used geometric patterns, closeups on the chorus girls, and the various abstract forms that would become his trademark. Before Berkeley, there would be several camera crews shooting the same sequence and later editing it. Berkeley kept only one camera, preferring to shoot the scene over and over from different angles in the hopes that he would get better performances in later takes. Actor Hackett later became a renowned screenwriter with his wife, Frances Goodrich, and they wrote screenplays for SEVEN BRIDES FOR SEVEN BROTHERS, LADY IN THE DARK, FATHER OF THE BRIDE, and THE DIARY OF ANNE FRANK among many others. Goldwyn opened this movie in the nadir of the Depression and charged $5 per ticket, a price that was the equivalent of a day's pay back then. Remade in 1944 as UP IN ARMS.

p, Samuel Goldwyn, Florenz Ziegfeld; d, Thornton Freeland; w, William Conselman (based on the Ziegfeld musical "Whoopee" by William Anthony McGuire, Walter Donaldson, Gus Kahn, the comedy "The Nervous Wreck" by Owen Davis, and the story "The Wreck" by E.J. Rath); ph, Lee Garmes, Ray Rennahan, Gregg Toland; ed, Stuart Heisler; md, Alfred Newman; art d, Capt. Richard Day; cos, John Harkrider; ch, Busby Berkeley; m/l, Walter Donaldson, Gus Kahn, Nacio Herb Brown, Edward Wliscu.

Musical Comedy   **Cas.**   **(PR:AA MPAA:NR)**

WHO'S AFRAID OF VIRGINIA WOOLF?****   (1966) 131m WB bw

Elizabeth Taylor (*Martha*), Richard Burton (*George*), George Segal (*Nick*), Sandy Dennis (*Honey*).

A very good film but it falls short of greatness. As in so many of the Burton-Taylor movies, the backstage stories are sometimes more intriguing than what's going on in front of the camera. Albee's play opened in October, 1962, and shocked even the blase Broadwayites with the language and the dark subject matter. It's two in the morning in New England. Burton is a defeated history professor who is married to Taylor, a shrew and harridan whose father is the president of the college at which Burton lectures. They have been married two decades and their union is alternately loving and vicious. Taylor adores comparing her weakling husband with her strong father (who is never seen), something that she knows rankles Burton so she keeps doing it. They have created a son they never had and talk about him as though he actually exists. Earlier that night, they'd attended a faculty party where they met Segal and Dennis. Segal is a self-proclaimed ladies man and Dennis is a mouse in blonde's clothing. The older couple have invited the younger duo to their comfortable home for a nightcap. Enter Segal and Dennis. She is already tipsy and when she has another drink she becomes woozy. Taylor is behaving boorishly and makes some overt advances toward Segal while Burton does nothing to stop her. Dennis becomes sick to her stomach and Segal gets increasingly drunk. While in his cups, Segal admits to Burton that he was trapped in this marriage because she had lied and told him she was expecting a child. The late evening drags into early morning as Taylor takes Segal up to her bedroom. Burton stands in the yard below and watches their shadows in the window. Later, Segal mentions the fact that Burton and Taylor have a "son" and Burton explodes. That was supposed to be *their* secret....He retaliates by "murdering" their son and running a Latin funeral service for the child that never was. Taylor is near madness at that. The light begins to dawn and Segal and Dennis leave. Both Taylor and Burton are mentally and physically spent. They share a moment of silence before they go to bed and we are left with the feeling that this is just a typical day in their lives. Lehman's screenplay left most of Albee's play intact, something that shocked many in the movie audience who were not accustomed to hearing those kinds of four- letter words cannonading off the screen. At first, the Production Code seal was denied to the movie but Jack Warner used every bit of his personal clout to make sure the picture finally did get it when he argued that the raw dialog was totally in context and not merely there to incite a prurient interest on the part of the audience. The play had been bought for half a million dollars after it opened on the New York stage with Arthur Hill and Uta Hagen in the leads. Bette Davis wanted to play "Martha" and Taylor does a bit of an impression of Davis in one of the scenes when she berates Burton for not knowing which movie had Davis saying the famous line, "What a dump." Taylor and Burton were each paid a reported million dollars. Add that to the half million for the rights and there wasn't much left over to make the movie on the $5 million budget. It grossed large numbers at the box office, nearly $15 million the first time around, due, in part, to the draw of the stars. When Oscar time came around, 13 nominations were awarded and it won five, for Taylor (Best Actress), Dennis (Best Supporting Actress in her second role after a small part in SPLENDOR IN THE GRASS). The other Oscars went to Sylbert and Hopkins for their black-and-white art direction, Sharaff for her black-and-white costumes, and Wexler for his black-and-white cinematography (he replaced Harry Stradling during production). It was assumed that the rough words in the play script would have to be excised or diluted, but they somehow managed to keep faith with Albee and it was shot almost as it was written for the stage. Taylor did some of her best acting in the movie although one wonders if she received her Oscar for that or for the fact that she allowed herself to be seen in such a blowzy role, with lots of excess weight and wild hair. Both Burton and Taylor did win British Oscars for their work. The fine details are in the dialog, much of which is not able to be represented here because of its candor. Hiring Nichols to direct was a risk in the minds of many because the former nightclub comic (with Elaine May) had only done lighter work. He proved he was the right choice by keeping a tight rein on the film and providing the audience with a smashing directorial debut. Lehman was

making his producing debut as well and the decision was made to rehearse this film as though it were a play, so three weeks were allocated for that before a camera ever turned. A heavy film and definitely not for children, it could have shed 20 minutes of the third act with no loss in impact.

p, Ernest Lehman; d, Mike Nichols; w, Lehman (based on the play by Edward Albee); ph, Haskell Wexler, Harry Stradling; m, Alex North; ed, Sam O'Steen; prod d, Richard Sylbert; set d, George James Hopkins; cos, Irene Sharaff; makeup, Gordon Bau, Ron Berkeley.

Drama   **Cas.**   **(PR:O MPAA:NR)**

WHO'S BEEN SLEEPING IN MY BED?**   (1963) 103m PAR c

Dean Martin (*Jason Steel*), Elizabeth Montgomery (*Melissa Morris*), Carol Burnett (*Stella Irving*), Martin Balsam (*Sanford Kaufman*), Jill St. John (*Toby Tobler*), Richard Conte (*Leonard Ashley*), Macha Meril (*Jacqueline Edwards*), Louis Nye (*Harry Tobler*), Yoko Tani (*Isami Hiroti*), Jack Soo (*Yoshimi Hiroti*), Dianne Foster (*Mona Kaufman*), Elliott Reid (*Tom Edwards*), Johnny Silver (*Charley*), Elisabeth Fraser (*Dora Ashley*), Steve Clinton (*Sam Jones*), Daniel Ocko (*Lawyer*), Allison Hayes (*Mrs. Grayson*), James O'Rear (*Policeman*).

Martin, an actor who portrays a doctor on a top-rated TV show, must deal with his legion of women fans and the wives of his poker playing buddies, who call him and make passes, many of which he accepts. This begins to wear him down and he postpones his marriage to lovely Montgomery. She, in turn, appeals to her friend, Burnett (making her screen debut), who is the secretary ot one of Martin's poker-playing friends, a psychoanalyst, and Burnett arranges a phony marriage for Montgomery, hoping the threat will bring Martin around to thoughts of a wedding again. It works and he goes to the same analyst for treatment. While under the influence of sodium amytal he admits to his affairs with his pals' wives, which Burnett overhears, and she rushes to Montgomery to tell her the news. Martin goes to Montgomery's fake wedding reception, feeling free of guilt, but soon afterwards she shows up at his door in the same manner as his pals' spouses. Once more he proposes and now she must fake a divorce. When he discovers the plot Martin breaks off the engagement again but Burnett manages to get the two back together. Psychoanalysis was a popular sex comedy topic in the early 1960s but is carried off with little wit or style here, the film relying instead on sex humor for laughs–at one point Burnett must do a striptease to pay for a check in a restaurant. The result is a workmanlike comedy with little humor to speak of. The usually smarmy Martin is surprisingly good, though.

p, Jack Rose; d, Daniel Mann; w, Rose; ph, Joseph Ruttenberg (Panavision, Technicolor); m, George Duning; ed, George Tomasini; art d, Hal Pereira, Arthur Lonergan; set d, Sam Comer, Arthur Krams; cos, Edith Head; ch, Stephen Peck; makeup, Frank Westmore.

Comedy   **(PR:C MPAA:NR)**

WHO'S GOT THE ACTION?**   (1962) 93m PAR c

Dean Martin (*Steve Flood*), Lana Turner (*Melanie Flood*), Eddie Albert (*Clint Morgan*), Nita Talbot (*Saturday Knight*), Walter Matthau (*Tony Gagoots*), Margo (*Roza*), Paul Ford (*Judge Boatwright*), Lewis Charles (*Clutch*), John McGiver (*Judge Fogel*), Dan Tobin (*Mr. Sanford*), Alexander Rose (*Mr. Goody*), Jack Albertson (*Officer Hodges*), Hillary Yates (*Hoxie*), Mack Gray, John Indrisano (*Hoods*), Ned Glass (*Baldy*), George Dee (*Waiter*), Alphonse Martell (*Maitre d'*), Joseph Vitale (*Bartender*), Eddie Quillan (*Dingo the Phone Repairman*), Ralph Montgomery (*Street Cleaner*), Charles LaRocca (*Doorman*), Wilbur Mack (*Groom/Octogenarian*), Len Hendry, Lee Sabinson (*Lawyers*), House Peters, Jr (*Cop in Elevator*), June Wilkinson (*Bride*).

In an unusual teaming, Martin and Turner are husband and wife. He loves to play the ponies so she arranges, via Martin's law partner, Albert, to become his bookie, thus keeping his losses in the family. However, the plan is a bust and she finds herself forced to sell her diamonds and antiques to pay off Martin's winnings. When his pals start putting bets through Martin, Turner is really in trouble. Eventually Martin becomes curious as to the identity of this new bookie, as do his cronies and Matthau, a mob boss. Turner confesses but Martin finds that Matthau's girl (Talbot) could turn the mobster over to the cops. He suggests to Matthau that perhaps he should marry the nightclub singer so she can't testify against him. Matthau takes the advice and hands over $18,000 in legal fees, which just happens to be the amount needed to cover Turner's debts. This comedy of errors has its moments but for the most part it's a flat story without much style. The direction moves sluggishly and the result is an often strained humor with only flashes of wit. The Martin-Turner team is okay but both clearly were cast in the wrong film. Oddly enough, this light comedy was from the director of such heavy-duty dramas as BUTTERFIELD 8, THE ROSE TATTOO, and I'LL CRY TOMORROW.

p, Jack Rose; d, Daniel Manne; w, Rose (based on the novel *Four Horseplayers are Missing* by Alexander Rose); ph, Joseph Ruttenberg (Panavision, Technicolor); m, George Duning; ed, Howard Smith; md, Duning; art d, Arthur Lonergan; set d, Darrell Silvera; cos, Edith Head; song, "Who's Got the Action," sung by Nita Talbot; makeup, Del Armstrong, Loren Cosand, Mary Hadley.

Comedy   (PR:A MPAA:NR)

WHO'S GOT THE BLACK BOX?**½   (1970, Fr./Gr./Ital.) 85m Les
Films La Boetie-Compagnia Generale Finanziaria Cinematografica-
Orion/RAF c (LA ROUTE DE CORNITHE)

Jean Seberg (Shanny), Maurice Ronet (Dex), Christian Marquand (Robert Ford), Michel Bouquet (Sharps), Saro Urzi (Kalhides/Skolikides), Antonio Passalia (Killer), Paulo Justi (Josio), Claude Chabrol (Alcibiades).

When U.S. radar installations in Greece are jammed, Marquand, a NATO security man, is assassinated–he had been looking into some strange black boxes found to have electronic devices inside. Seberg, his widow, is blamed for the murders, and Bouquet, who had desired her sexually in the past, demands she leave the base. Ronet is assigned to follow her, since they know she will search for the real killer. She escapes his constant shadowing and meets Chabrol (the film's director in a cameo) who had been her husband's informant. He tells her that Urzi was the killer, so that night Seberg goes to the marble quarry where Urzi works. She is caught and held prisoner but finally gets away. She's saved by a trucker who also ends up dead. In desperation, Seberg meets Ronet and asks him to go back to the quarry with her. They find that the black boxes are being sent out hidden in marble statues, though Bouquet finds this unbelievable. Seberg is kidnaped by Chabrol's goons and taken to a secret island to be killed. Ronet arrives in time to save her and kills Chabrol in the process.

p, Andre Genoves; d, Claude Chabrol; w, Claude Brule, Daniel Boulanger (based on the novel La Route de Cornithe by Claude Rank); ph, Jean Rabier (Eastmancolor); m, Pierre Jansen; ed, Jacques Gaillard, Monique Fardoulis; art d, Marilena Aravantinou.

Thriller   (PR:O MPAA:M/PG)

WHO'S MIDING THE MINT?***½   (1967) 98m COL c

Jim Hutton (Harry Lucas), Dorothy Provine (Verna Baxter), Milton Berle (Luther Burton), Joey Bishop (Ralph Randazzo), Bob Denver (Willie Owens), Walter Brennan (Pop Gillis), Victor Buono (Captain), Jack Gilford (Avery Dugan), Jamie Farr (Mario), David Stewart (Samson Link), Corinne Cole (Doris Miller), Jackie Joseph (Imogene Harris), Bryan O'Byrne (Maxwell), Robert Ball (Grayson), Dodo Denney (Bertha), Luther James (Jess), Mickey Deems (Drunk), Lennie Bremen (Man in Window), Cordy Clark (Woman in Window), Thom Carney (1st Guard), Khalil Bezaleel (2nd Guard), Peanuts the Dog (Inky).

Great zany fun has Hutton a money checker for the U.S. Mint. He lives a high life by arranging accounts with various department stores to get fancy gadgets on a trial basis, then switches his accounts to other stores. One day he's given some fudge by Provine, an admiring coworker, and he accidentally stuffs $50,000 in the bag as well. The fudge is awful and he tosses it into the garbage disposal only to discover his mistake too late. Hutton talks Brennan, a retired money printer, into sneaking back at night so they can print up some cash to cover the loss. Gilford, a deaf safecracker, is hired to help them get at the plates if only he can get a hearing aid. The trio go to a pawnshop run by Berle, who wants $2,000 for his "management" services. The only way to get into the mint is via the city sewers, so Buono is hired to build an underground boat. Denver is an ice cream truck driver who covers them as they enter the underground. At long last with all the hands needed to pull off the task, Hutton realizes he'll need a lot more than $50,000 to pay off everyone–the total comes to one million dollars per person! On the night of the scheme everything that can go wrong does, including Brennan's tag-along pregnant beagle who proceeds to deliver her litter. The scheme somehow is pulled off but further hijinks find the money accidentally tossed out to sea. Hutton manages to save his $50,000 and realizes he loves Provine. The remaining gang members go skindiving for the rest of the loot. A wild and off-the-wall comedy of errors, this works thanks to its overall fine production qualities. The ensemble players are good, keeping pace with each new twist they meet. The direction never lets the material get away, always keeping the loonies in firm control.

p, Norman Maurer; d, Howard Morris; w, R.S. Allen, Harry Bullock; ph, Joseph Biroc (Technicolor); m, Lalo Schifrin; ed, Adrienne Fazan; art d, John Beckman; set d, Morris Hoffman, Budd S. Friend; spec eff, Richard Albain; makeup, Ben Lane.

Comedy   **Cas.**   (PR:A MPAA:NR)

WHO'S MINDING THE STORE?**   (1963) 90m PAR c

Jerry Lewis (Raymond Phiffier), Jill St. John (Barbara Tuttle), Agnes Moorehead (Phoebe Tuttle), John McGiver (Mr. Tuttle), Ray Walston (Mr. Quimby, Store Manager), Francesca Bellini (Shirley), Nancy Kulp (Mrs. Rothgraber), John Abbott (Roberts), Jerry Hausner (Smith), Peggy Mondo (Lady Wrestler), Mary Treen (Mattress Customer), Isobel Elsom (Hazel, a Dowager), Richard [Dick] Wessel (Cop), Fritz Feld (Irving Cahastrophe, Gourmet Manager), Kathleen Freeman (Mrs. Glucksman), Milton Frome (Francois the Driver), Richard Deacon (Tie Salesman), Barbara Pepper (Client at Sale), Sheila Rogers (Nurse), Mike Ross, Jerry Gordet (Caretakers), Fifi, Bosley (The Poodles).

Typical Lewis nonsense finds him a bumbling poodle sitter in love with St.

John. Her well-to-do mother, Moorehead, disapproves of St. John's beau and, determined to break up the romance, hires Lewis to work in her department store. Despite the impossible requests of Walston, the store manager, Lewis manages to do an admirable job in his own slapstick manner, and becomes buddies with St. John's dad, McGiver, but he nearly causes an in-store riot when he manhandles a vacuum cleaner demonstration. Moorehead fires him but henpecked McGiver stands up and tells her off. The family is reunited in apologizing to Lewis and, happy at last, the two lovebirds walk their poodles accompanied by St. John's parents. Lewis, who ranks as possibly the worst comedy talent ever to appear in films, goes through his typical antics predictably, but the direction keeps him under control. As his own director, Lewis' films were little more than ego fests (witness THE NUTTY PROFESSOR), but under Tashlin's steady hand the madcap comic shows occasional glimmers of talent. Undoubtedly the French will love this.

p, Paul Jones; d, Frank Tashlin; w, Tashlin, Harry Tugend (based on a story by Tugend); ph, W. Wallace Kelley (Technicolor); m, Joseph J. Lilley; ed, John Woodcock; art d, Hal Pereira, Al Roelofs, Roland Anderson; set d, James Payne; cos, Edith Head; spec eff, Paul K. Lerpae; makeup, Wally Westmore.

Comedy   (PR:A MPAA:NR)

WHO'S THAT KNOCKING AT MY DOOR?***
(1968) 90m Trimrod/Joseph Brenner bw (AKA: I CALL FIRST; J.R.)

Zina Bethune (The Young Girl), Harvey Keitel (J.R.), Lennard Kuras (Joey), Ann Colette (Young Girl in Dream), Michael Scala (Sally Gaga), Wendy Russell (Sally's Girl Friend), Philip Carlson (Mountain Guide), Robert Uricola ("Gunman" at Stag Party), Bill Minkin (Iggy/Radio Announcer), Marissa Joffrey (Rosie), Harry Northrup (Rapist), Saskia Holleman, Tsuai Yu-Lan, Marieka (Other Girls in Dream Fantasy), Catherine Scorsese (J.R.'s Mother), Vic Magnotta, Paul Di Bionde (Boys in Street Fight), Susan Wood (Susan), Martin Scorsese (Gangster), Thomas Aiello.

Director Martin Scorsese's feature film debut chronicles a brief time in the life of Keitel, an Italian-American who lives in New York's Little Italy. Keitel suffers under the contradictions of a strict Catholic upbringing, while forced to grow up in the harsh realities of New York City. In his early twenties, Keitel spends most of his time "hanging out" with his male buddies and getting into trouble. To satisfy their sexual urges, the young men simply pick up a couple of "broads" (women who are willing to have premarital sex) and take turns. "Broads" are never to be confused with the "nice girls" (virgins), whom the boys will someday marry and have children with. One day, while riding the Staten Island Ferry, Keitel meets a young blonde woman, Bethune, unlike anyone he has ever met. She is an art student, reads literature, speaks French, and is fascinated by European art films directed by people like Jean-Luc Godard. He is also stunned to learn that she lives alone, and doesn't even own a television set. She is equally fascinated by him. His ethic, urban demeanor, street smarts, and love of John Ford westerns hold her attention. During the next few days Keitel and Bethune grow close and she attempts to initiate intimate relations with him. Horrified that a woman he has been considering marrying would offer herself to him before marriage, Keitel declines. Still tied to his male friends, Keitel goes off on a short trip to the country with them. The urban boys are intimidated by the openess of the country and become terrified when climbing what they consider a "mountain" (it's barely a hill). Back in New York Keitel is shocked to hear Bethune confess that she was once raped by an old boy friend. Outraged that his "nice girl" is in reality a "broad," and had been lying to him, Keitel breaks off the relationship and returns to the safety of the neighborhood. He reasserts himself into his old life style with a vengeance, and after much carousing, begins to feel lonely and disgusted with himself. He attempts to return to Bethune, saying that he forgives her and will try to ignore the fact that she is not a virgin. Amazed and disappointed by Keitel's blind devotion to the codes of his upbringing, Bethune realizes that they can never maintain such a warped relationship and she breaks it off. Totally confused and angry over the rejection, Keitel wanders back to church, the place with all the answers, and finds it has none. This is the ultimate student film. The young Martin Scorsese began the film, under the title I CALL FIRST, while a student at New York University under the guidance of professor Haig Manoogian. With the exception of a few scenes, the resulting 58-minute film was deemed awful by most observers at the N.Y.U. film festival. It was decided by Scorsese and Manoogian that the script would be rewritten to incorporate the scenes that played well, and then reshot as a feature. The story is part of a trilogy which would chronicle the lives of a group of teenage boys who lived in New York's Little Italy. Scorsese had originally envisioned beginning the trilogy with a film to be called "Jerusalem, Jerusalem!" which would have shown kids at the age of 18 out on a church-sponsored religious retreat at a monastery in the woods. While reacting to the trees, space, and light of the forest, they would ponder the hypocrisy, contradiction, and guilt inherent in their Catholic upbringing. The weekend serving its purpose, the boys of the mean streets would effectively be infused with the fear of God. Because no one at N.Y.U. really wanted to see such a personal film dealing directly with Catholicism, "Jerusalem, Jerusalem!" was never shot. WHO'S THAT KNOCKING AT MY DOOR? was to be the second installment, with MEAN STREETS being the third and final chapter. Because "Jerusalem, Jerusalem!" was never filmed, Scorsese borrowed some aspects from it and inserted them into both WHO'S THAT KNOCKING AT MY DOOR? and MEAN STREETS. To film the feature version of WHO'S THAT KNOCK-ING AT MY DOOR?, Scorsese and Manoogian raised $35,000 and recalled Keitel (the only actor from the original who returned for the feature) to continue his role as J.R. Three years had passed since the original shooting, which posed some problems. Careful viewing can pinpoint shots and scenes from the original student film intercut with the new footage by looking for changes in Keitel's hair style. All the scenes between Keitel and the girl were reshot, and Bethune was cast in the female lead. The film is a fascinating, creative, ultra low-budget effort with a good sense of place and character. Scorsese presents a detailed look at the lives of these confused boys struggling to become men in an oppressive environment that threatens to strangle them. The trip to the country is truly telling, for the brief change of scenery and taste of the "outside" scares most of the boys, all of whom prefer the streets. It's what they know. While the writer-director has a good handle on his male characters, the women in the film are given scant attention. Bethune, although given plenty of screen time, is basically a plot device used to explore Keitel's character. While Scorsese's sense of character and environment is mostly precise, his experiments with visuals (some of the film was shot by Michael Wadleigh who would later direct WOODSTOCK and WOLFEN) and homages to the movies he loves betray his film school roots and date the film badly. The strong influence of the French New Wave filmmakers is felt, but the scenes where Scorsese introduces his love for the cinema by having characters refer to Godard, John Ford, THE SEACHERS, and RIO BRAVO are blatant and, therefore, clumsily handled because they seem gratuitous and out of place. Scorsese and Manoogian sent their movie to the Venice Film Festival to be considered for competition but after several weeks heard nothing from the judges. When a friend returned to New York from a trip to Rome, he asked Manoogian if he had worked on a film called I CALL FIRST (still under the original title). The professor said yes and was informed by the man that he had seen the cans of film just sitting in the Rome airport. Manoogian called Joseph Weiler, an attorney who helped raise money for the film, and sent him to Rome. Weiler found the cans of film, still sitting unattended at the Rome Airport, and brought them to the festival judges. The film was never shown at the Venice Film Festival, but it was screened at the Chicago Film Festival and got a rave review from critic Roger Ebert. Despite good press, WHO'S THAT KNOCKING AT MY DOOR? was having trouble getting distributed. As a concession to potential distributor Joseph Brenner, Scorsese inserted a lengthy nude love scene between Keitel and Colette. The young director agreed to shoot the scene while he was filming commercials in Amsterdam, Holland, and Keitel was flown over to participate. The woman, Colette, had appeared in Godard's short film ALL THE BOYS ARE CALLED PATRICK, making the scene another homage to the French New Wave. By Scorsese's own admission, the scene is the worst part of the film. Unmotivated and practically slapped into the middle of the story, its overactive camerawork and editing are out of place and annoying. Problems aside, this is a fascinating look at the creative development of one of the new American cinema's most important directors and is well worth a look.

p, Joseph Weill, Betzi Manoogian, Haig Manoogian; d, Martin Scorsese; w, Scorsese, Betzi Manoogian; ph, Michael Wadleigh, Richard Coll, Max Fisher; ed, Thelma Schoonmaker; art d, Vic Magnotta.

Drama   (PR:O   MPAA:R)

WHO'S YOUR FATHER?*   (1935, Brit.) 63m St. George's/COL bw

Lupino Lane (George Medway), Peter Haddon (Frank Steadley), Nita Harvey (Bina Medway), Jean Kent (Mary Radcliffe), Margaret Yarde (Mrs. Medway), James Carew (Elmer J. Radcliffe), Peter Gawthorne (Capt. Medway), James Finlayson, Eva Hudson.

Lane is about to be married and prepares to meet his wealthy father-in-law to be. But all appears to be disaster, for his mother has finally remarried, her new spouse being an undertaker. Next, Lane's father, long believed to have been lost at sea, turns up with his new wife, a black woman. Once upon a time this might have been considered funny but the racial overtones to the humor are not funny now. The film as a whole is simply boring.

p, Lupino Lane; d, Henry W. George; w, Lane, Arthur Rigby, Reginald Long (based on the play "Turned Up" by Mark Melford).

Comedy   (PR:A MPAA:NR)

WHO'S YOUR LADY FRIEND?   (1937, Brit.) 73m Dorian/ABF bw

Frances Day (Lulu), Vic Oliver (Dr. Mangold), Betty Stockfeld (Mrs. Mangold), Romney Brent (Fred), Margaret Lockwood (Mimi), Sarah Churchill (Maid), Marcelle Rogez (Yvonne Fatigay), Muriel George (Mrs. Somers), Frederick Ranalow (The Cabby).

Brent, the male secretary of a plastic surgeon, picks up a supposed new client of his boss. Instead he has mistakenly taken cabaret singer Day and is seen by his fiancee Lockwood, who naturally assumes he's fooling around. Stockfield, wife of the doctor, assumes the same of her husband (Oliver). All ends in a riot as a drunken Brent ends up in Stockfield's bedroom. Cute farce and one of the many British programmers Reed directed before moving up to bigger features.

p, Martin Sabine; d, Carol Reed; w, Anthony Kimmins, Julius Hoest (based

on the play "Der Herr Ohne Wornung" by Oesterreicher and Jenbach); ph, Jan Stallich.

Comedy   (PR:A MPAA:NR)

WHOSE LIFE IS IT ANYWAY?*   (1981) 119m MGM/UA c

Richard Dreyfuss (Ken Harrion), John Cassavetes (Dr. Michael Emerson), Christine Lahti (Dr. Clare Scott), Bob Balaban (Carter Hill), Kenneth McMillan (Judge Wyler), Kaki Hunter (Mary Jo), Thomas Carter (Orderly John), Alba Oms (Nurse Rodriguez), Janet Eilber (Pat), Kathryn Grody (Mrs. Boyle), George Wyner (Dr. Jacobs), Mel Stewart (Dr. Barr), Ward Costello (Mr. Eden), Alston Ahern (Day Nurse), Betty Cole (ICU Nurse), Lyman Ward (Emergency Room Doctor), Juli Andelman (Stella, Student Nurse), Abigail Hepner (Lissa), Alan Stock (3rd Year Student), Jeffrey Combs (1st Year Intern), Steven Bourne (Hoffman), John Garber (Physiotherapist), Katie Guymon (Anesthesiologist), J.J. Johnston (Guard), Michael Steve Jones (Intern), Fred Slyter (Court Clerk), Tony Simotes (Orthopedic Surgeon), Robert Telford (Old Man), Roberta Jean Williams (Technician), Francine Henderson, Lissa Layng, Dorothy Meyer, Karla Pitti, Beth Renner (Nurses), Sebastian DeFrancesco, Thomas Collette, Duane F. Johnson, Larry D. Callaghan, William E. Townsend.

Looking for a light-hearted escape from reality? Then look further because this is not the movie you want to see. Based on a hit play that has starred both males and females as the lead (Tom Conti, Mary Tyler Moore), it's a movie with a lot of "what ifs?" to pique your brain. What if the person up there were me? What if I had to make the decision Dreyfuss makes? No matter how objective you may be and, understanding this is only a story, you'll still find yourself wondering, even subconsciously, how you would handle the situation posed. Dreyfuss is a happily married and talented sculptor with the world at his fingertips. His career and life are altered in one shattering car accident that makes the insouciant young man into a bed-ridden quadraplegic, totally dependent on life support systems and the kindness of others. The only part of his body not damaged is his brain. At first, he is just glad to be alive, until he realizes that living is much more than just an awareness of one's surroundings. Living means doing, sharing, loving, and he can do none of that. His bitterness at his plight multiplies and he becomes petulant, aggressive, annoying, and starts to believe that he is a burden to everyone around him so he erects an impenetrable wall. His caustic humor regarding his condition is often tough for those around him to take. When he isn't spewing insults, he isolates himself from everyone and everything and even forbids his wife from visiting him, telling her to go out and find someone else, someone who can satisfy her needs. His prognosis is life as a vegetable. It's made even more apparent when nurse trainee Hunter, attempting to make the bed with him in it, is distracted for a moment and Dreyfuss slips out of bed and onto the floor, helpless to do anything. His doctor is Lahti and she does her best to make his life comfortable, going so far as to force him to recall the good times he had, the talent he still possesses (although he can do nothing with it) and, in general, tries to improve his attitude. It's to no avail. Dreyfuss opts to end his own life. (This actually happened in California when a female patient petitioned the courts to allow her to starve herself. She lost and was still alive after two years of hassles.) He is fought every step of the way by hospital administrator Cassavetes, a crusty type who goes strictly by the book. Cassavetes argues that life is sacred and must be preserved at all costs, even if the patient doesn't think so. Dreyfuss hires a lawyer Balaban to plead his case, requesting to be allowed to die, in the court of judge McMillan. In a stirring courtroom scene, Balaban and Dreyfuss win their case and Dreyfuss is allowed to leave the hospital and spend the rest of his life, if he chooses to live, in any manner he wishes. So, in effect, there is a happy ending because Dreyfuss gets what he wants. You don't know if one should rejoice or have remorse. Dreyfuss is such an engaging character that you hate the thought that he may take his own life but it might be the right solution for him. McMillan gives an excellent performance as the understanding jurist, and Balaban, who seemed to be in every movie in 1981, chips in with a finely etched portrayal. In a small, but telling role, Carter is seen as a hospital orderly who takes Dreyfuss down to the hospital's basement to hear his combo play Jamaican music and allows Dreyfuss to smoke a huge joint and get stoned. That the play was a large success in an age when Broadway seemed to want little more than mindless comedies and frothy musicals was a marvel. The picture did not fare that well. WHOSE LIFE IS IT ANYWAY? is thought-provoking, has moments of black humor, and is a tribute to Dreyfuss' acting, in that he does most of his work with his eyes.

p, Lawrence P. Bachmann; d, John Badham; w, Brian Clark, Reginald Rose (based on the play by Clark); ph, Mario Tosi (Panavision, Metrocolor); m, Arthur B. Rubinstein; ed, Frank Morriss; prod d, Gene Callahan; art d, Sydney Z. Litwack; cos, Marianna Elliott; ch, Marge Champion.

Drama   Cas.   (PR:C-O MPAA:R)

WHY ANNA?   (SEE: DIARY OF A SCHIZOPHRENIC GIRL, 1970, Ital.)

WHY BOTHER TO KNOCK*½   (1964, Brit.) 88m
Haileywood-Associated British/Seven Arts c (GB: DON'T BOTHER TO KNOCK)

Richard Todd (*Bill Ferguson*), Nicole Maurey (*Lucille*), Elke Sommer (*Ingrid*), June Thorburn (*Stella*), Rik Battaglia (*Giulio*), Judith Anderson (*Maggie Shoemaker*), Dawn Beret (*Harry*), Scott Finch (*Perry*), Eleanor Summerfield (*Mother*), John Le Mesurier (*Father*), Colin Gordon (*Rolsom*), Kenneth Fortescue (*Ian*), Ronald Fraser (*Fred*), Tom Duggan (*Al*), Michael Shepley (*Colonel*), Joan Sterndale-Bennett (*Spinster*), Kynaston Reeves (*Neighbor*), John Laurie (*Taxi Driver*), Warren Mitchell (*Waiter*), Robert Nichols, Jerry Stovin, Gary Cockrell (*U.S. Sailors*), Sara Luzita, Pirmin Trecu (*Flamenco Dancers*).

British actor Todd makes the transition to producer in this minor bedroom farce starring himself. As an Edinburgh travel agent who has a fight with fiancee Thorburn, he travels to the continent and gives keys to his apartment to nearly every woman he meets in his travels. On his return to Scotland, he patches up his quarrel with Thorburn, only to have a drove of European beauties descend on his flat. Predictable complications abound as Todd tries to hide this invasion from Thorburn.

p, Frank Godwin, Richard Todd; d, Cyril Frankel; w, Denis Cannan, Frederick Gotfurt, Frederic Raphael (based on the novel *Love From Everybody* by Clifford Hanley); p, Geoffrey Unsworth (CinemaScope Technicolor); m, Elisabeth Lutyens; ed, Anne V. Coates; md, John Hollingsworth; art d, Tony Masters; makeup, Bob Clark.

Comedy   (PR: MPAA:NR)

WHY BRING THAT UP?**½   (1929) 80m PAR bw

George Moran (*Moran*), Charles Mack (*Mack*), Evelyn Brent (*Betty*), Harry Green (*Irving*), Bert Swor (*Bert*), Freeman S. Wood (*Powell*), Lawrence Leslie (*Casey*), Helene Lynch (*Marie*), Selmer Jackson (*Eddie*), Jack Luden (*Treasurer*), Monte Collins, Jr (*Skeets*), George Thompson (*Doorman*), Eddie Kane (*Manager*), Charles Hall (*Tough*).

Moran and Mack, white comics who wore burnt cork on their faces and billed themselves as "The Two Black Crows," re-create some of their best vaudeville routines in this loosely plotted comedy. The two weave their sketches around a story involving Brent, who attempts to take Moran to the cleaners. She and her boy friend try their best but the "Crows" manage to come through in the end. In between are some of the team's best known comedy routines including "Head Man," "Let's Not Talk About That," and the popular "Early Bird Gets the Worm." Like Amos and Andy to follow Moran and Mack were funny in their day but seem crudely racist today. Still, for a simple comedy this is well put together and an important historical record of what vaudeville comedy was like a long time ago.

d, George Abbott; w, Abbott, Hector Turnbull (based on a story by Octavus Roy Cohen); ph, J. Roy Hust; ed, William Shea; m/l, "Do I Know What I'm Doing While In Love," Richard A. Whiting, Leo Robin, "Shoo Shoo Boogie Boo," Whiting, Sam Coslow.

Comedy   (PR:A MPAA:NR)

WHY CHANGE YOUR HUSBAND?
(SEE: GOLD DUST GERTIE, 1931)

WHY DOES HERR R. RUN AMOK?***½   (1977, Ger.) 88m
Maran-Film/New Yorker c (WARUM LAUFT HERR R. AMOK?)

Kurt Raab (*Herr R*), Lilith Ungerer (*His Wife*), Amadeus Fengler (*Their Son*), Franz Maron (*The Boss*), Harry Baer, Peter Moland, Lilo Pampeit (*Colleagues at Office*), Hanna Schygulla (*School Friend*), Mr. Sterr (*Father*), Mrs. Sterr (*Mother*), Peer Raben (*School Friend*), Eva Pampuch (*Salesgirls in Record Shop*), Ingrid Caven, Doris Mattes, Irm Hermann, Hannes Gromball (*Neighbors*), Peter Hamm, Jochen Pinkert (*Inspectors*), Eva Madelung (*Boss's Sister*).

Rainer Werner Fassbinder's fourth film, WHY DOES HERR R. RUN AMOK? was first shown in Germany in 1970 when the director was only 24 years old. Raab stars as an industrial draftsman who leads a mundane life with his mundane, chatty wife and his mundane child. Improvisational scenes of Raab at work, at dinner with his boss, out with his family, and at a record store fill the first 80 minutes of the film. The result is often boring, but that is precisely Fassbinder's desired effect. The camera doesn't budge–letting characters walk in and out of frame, and the sound is often garbled or barely audible. Within this tedium, however, Fassbinder captures a frustrating and uneventful existence. The audience begins to feel the frustration Raab feels in his life and his job. At the picture's end, Raab is watching television in his living room visibly annoyed at his wife's conversation with a friend. As their talk continues, Raab methodically walks to the television, grabs a heavy candelabra, and proceeds to bludgeon his family. The following day Raab goes into his bathroom at work and hangs himself. The emotional impact of the final minutes of the film is extremely powerful only in light of the tedium that precedes the murder. Because the audience members feel a need to release tension they are drawn into Raab's killing spree. The murders come as a shock and one leaves the theater suffering from an emotional drain. Considerably less stylized than his other

films, WHY DOES HERR R. RUN AMOK? is a product of Fassbinder's involvement with a group tagged "anti-theater"–which believed in a Socialist means of making films. This accounts for Fassbinder sharing a codirection credit with Fengler (who later acted as a producer for Fassbinder). The result, however, is most definitely a Fassbinder film. A dark and bitter film which is difficult for some viewers and fascinating for others. (In German; English subtitles.)

d, Rainer Werner Fassbinder, Michael Fengler; w, Fassbinder, Fengler; ph, Dietrich Lohmann; m, Christian Anders; ed, Franz Walsch; prod d, Kurt Raab; m/l, "Geh Nicht Vorbei," Christian Anders; English titles, Fassbinder, Fengler.

Drama/Crime   (PR:O   MPAA:NR)

WHY GIRLS LEAVE HOME*½   (1945) 69m PRC bw

Lola Lane (*Irene*), Sheldon Leonard (*Chris Williams*), Pamela Blake (*Diana Leslie*), Elisha Cook, Jr (*Jimmie Lobo*), Paul Guilfoyle (*Steve Raymond*), Constance Worth (*Flo*), Claudia Drake (*Marien*), Virginia Brissac (*Mrs. Leslie*), Thomas Jackson (*Reilly*), Evelynne Eaton (*Alice*), Peggy Lou Bianco (*Peggy Leslie*), Fred Kohler, Jr (*Ted Leslie*), Walter Baldwin (*Wilbur Harris*), Robert Emmett Keane (*Ed Blake*).

Unhappy about her life with her parents, Blake strikes out for the sophisticated world of night clubs. She gets a job singing but soon is caught up with the thugs who run the place. When she learns too much her boss, Lane, decides to kill her and make it look like suicide. A reporter suspects the truth and pursues the story until the facts are made public. Dull, poorly plotted programmer that shows some skill by its cast, but the direction and script are clearly below their talents.

p, Sam Sax; d, William Berke: w, Fanya Foss Lawrence, Bradford Ropes (based on a story by Lawrence); ph, Mack Stengler; ed, Carl Pierson; md, Walter Greene; art d, Edward C. Jewell; set d, Glenn P. Thompson; m/l, Jay Livingston, Ray Evans.

Crime   (PR:C MPAA:NR)

WHY LEAVE HOME?**½   (1929) 70m FOX bw

Dixie Lee (*Billie*), Jean Barry (*Jackie*), Sue Carol (*Mary*), Richard Keene (*Jose*), David Rollins (*Oscar*), Jed Prouty (*George*), Walter Catlett (*Elmer*), Gordon DeMain (*Roy*), Ilka Chase (*Ethel*), Dot Farley (*Susan*), Laura Hamilton (*Maude*), Nick Stuart (*Dick*).

Enjoyable comedy finds three husbands, their wives, three bachelors, and their girl friends all getting mixed up in a nightclub and garden. It moves with the frantic pacing of a Mack Sennett comedy, with some surprisingly good lines for an early talkie. Innocent fun and charming in its simplicity.

p, Malcolm Stuart Boylan; d, Raymond Cannon; w, Robert S. Carr, Walter Catlett (based on the play "The Cradle Snatchers" by Russell G. Medcraft, Norma Mitchell); ph, Daniel Clark; ed, Jack Murray; m/l, "Doing the Boom-Boom," "Look What You've Done to Me," "Bonita," "Old Soldiers Never Die" (Con Conrad, Archie Gottler, Sidney Mitchell).

Comedy   (PR:A MPAA:NR)

WHY MUST I DIE?**½   (1960) 86m AIP bw

Terry Moore (*Lois King*), Debra Paget (*Dottie Manson*), Bert Freed (*Adler*), Julie Reding (*Mitzi*), Lionel Ames (*Eddie*), Richard LePore (*Sinclair*), Selette Cole (*Peggy Taylor*), Dorothy Lovett (*Mrs. Benson*), Phil Harvey (*Kenny Randall*), Fred Sherman (*Red King*), Robert Shayne (*Charlie Munro*), Damian O'Flynn (*Dennison*), Holly Harris (*Mrs. Bradley*), Mark Sheeler (*Jim*), Jhean Burton (*Trixie*), Abigail Shelton (*Dawn*).

Interesting thriller finds Moore the daughter of Sherman, an over-the-hill safecracker. She's involved with Ames, a small-time gangster who, like her father, continually promises a big score. She goes along with the pair on a safecracking job as lookout, but the two prove to be incompetent. Moore goes back to singing in night clubs and gets involved with Harvey, a club owner. Meanwhile, her father has taken up with Paget, a lady safecracker. Moore is forced to accompany her father and his enamorata on a job, and Harvey comes along and is shot by Paget. Moore is convicted for the crime and sentenced to the electric chair. As she is about to be electrocuted, Paget comes shrieking into the death chamber. She has been convicted of killing a blind news vendor and now wants to make amends. Though the story is a formula plot, there is a wonderful intensity to the film, particularly in its final moments. The acting is fine throughout.

p, Richard Bernstein; d, Roy Del Ruth; w, George W. Waters, Bernstein (based on a story by Waters); m, Dick LaSalle; cos, Marjorie Corso.

Crime   (PR:C MPAA:NR)

WHY NOT?   (SEE: POURQUOI PAS, 1979, Fr.)

WHY PICK ON ME?** (1937, Brit.) 64m GS Enterprises/RKO bw

Wylie Watson (Sam Tippett), Jack Hobbs (Stretton), Sybil Grove (Mrs. Tippett), Max Adrian (Jack Mills), Isobel Scaife (Daisy Mog), Elizabeth Kent (Bubbles), Michael Ripper.

Watson is a sheepish bank clerk (like all bank clerks in movies) who woefully mutters the title phrase to himself much too often. One evening, while his wife is away visiting a sick aunt, Watson goes out with some friends to a seedy nightclub. The police raid the club and Watson is carted off to prison. Oddly enough, he is also charged with robbing his own home. He finally clears up his predicament when he realizes that he has a double wandering the streets. Simple-minded but enjoyable.

p, A. George Smith; d, Maclean Rogers; w, H.F. Maltby, Kathleen Butler (based on the story by Con West, Jack Marks); ph, Geoffrey Faithfull.

Comedy (PR:A MPAA:NR)

WHY ROCK THE BOAT?***½ (1974, Can.) 112m National Film Board of Canada/COL c

Stuart Gillard (Harry Barnes), Tiiu Leek (Julia Martin), Ken James (Ronny Waldron), Budd Knapp (Fred O'Neill), Henry Beckman (Philip L. Butcher), Sean Sullivan (Herb Scannell), Patricia Gage (Isobel Scannell), Ruben Morena (Senor Gomez), Cec Linder (Carmichael), Henry Ramer (Club President), Maurice Podbrey (Guest Speaker), Barrie Baldaro (Benson), Patricia Hamilton (Hilda), Ian deVoy (Smith), Basil Fitzgibbon (Ridley), Ann Reiser (Irene), Robert Rivard (Saint-Onge), Don MacIntyre (Harrison), J. Leo Gagnon (Bartender), Jean-Pierre Masson (Lapierre), Marie-France Beaulieu (Suzanne), Mary Morter (Miss Stevens), Peter MacNeill (Peterson), Thomas Donohue (Pierre Beaulac), Benoit Lepine (Ski Instructor), Kirk McColl (Policeman).

In the 1940s Gillard is a bumbling but eager cub reporter for a big newspaper whose dreams are quickly dashed by the hard-bitten reporters who surround him. Leek is another reporter and his main competitor whom he falls hopelessly in love with. His city editor's nymphomaniac wife helps Gillard lose his virginity before he finally impresses Leek by getting drunk and campaigning for the union on the paper. A gentle comedy with some wonderful moments. Gillard projects the right qualities of earnestness and innocence to make his reporter believable in every way. A great supporting cast, particularly Gage as his seductress, are a definite asset.

p, William Weintraub; d, John Howe; w, Weintraub (based on his novel); ph, Savos Kalogeras; m, John Howe; ed, Marie-Helene Guillemin; art d, Denis Boucher; set d, Boucher, Earl Preston, Ronald Fauteux; cos, Philippa Wingfield; m/l, Howe.

Comedy (PR:O MPAA:NR)

WHY RUSSIANS ARE REVOLTING* (1970) 91m Mutual Releasing bw

Neil Sullivan (Cyrus Barnwhistle Diner), Ed Maywood (Vladimir Flynn), George Badera (Henry Sabotage), Seneca Ames (Tootsie Fahrenheit), D. F. Barry (Leon Trotsky), Herbert Boland (Peter Tobashin), Ralph Hebel (Conductor), Saul Katz (Stalin), Wes Carter (Rasputin), Cookie Vazzana, Janet Wood (Girls in Bar), Frank Walker (Man in Bar), John Connelly, Don Nevene (High Rollers), Andy "Slugger" Loremus, Larry O'Dea (Saloon Singers), Edward Walsh, Robert Hennessy, Joseph Marchese (Other Singers).

An inept "comedy" has Sullivan (who also served as producer, director, and writer) playing a W.C. Fields type, complete with the great comic's accent (badly imitated) and a Fieldsian name, going back in time to pre-revolutionary Russia. There he encounters various historical figures from Lenin, Trotsky, and Stalin to Adolf Hitler, who apparently was visiting the wrong dictatorship. It's hard to tell which is worse, Sullivan's acting ability or his behind-the-camera talent. Some footage from the silent 1920 verson of DR. JEKYLL AND MR. HYDE is tossed in with little effect.

p,d&w, Neil Sullivan; ph, William Glass, James Cozart (UniScope); ed, Jay Fitzgerald; spec eff, EFX Unlimited; m/l, "Those S.O.Bs Upstairs," "Shall My Soul Pass Through Old Ireland," Robert Hennessy, Neil Sullivan.

Comedy (PR:O MPAA:NR)

WHY SAILORS LEAVE HOME*½ (1930, Brit.) 70m BIP/Wardour bw

Leslie Fuller (Bill Biggles), Peter Barnard (George), Eve Gray, Gladys Cruickshank (Slave Girls), Dmitri Vetter (Multhasa), Frank Melroyd (Captain), Syd Courtenay (Sheik Sidi Ben), Lola Harvey (Maya), Gerard Lyley, Bob Johnson, Olivette, Marika Rokk.

Fuller assumes his Bill Biggles character, a halfwit Cockney, in this cliched comedy. A sailor sent overseas, he winds up heading a harem.

p, John Maxwell; d, Monty Banks; w, Val Valentine (based on a story by Syd Courtenay, Lola Harvey); ph, James Rogers.

Comedy (PR:A MPAA:NR)

WHY SAPS LEAVE HOME*½ (1932, Brit.) 63m BIP/Power bw

Henry Kendall (Percy Lloyd), Betty Norton (Betty Woods), Margot Grahame (Lil), Bernard Nedell (Tony Costello), Binnie Barnes (Peg Guinan), Ben Welden (Spike Guinan), Charles Farrell (Smiler), Wallace Lupino, Cyril Smith, Ernest Sefton, Peter Bernard, Val Guest (Gangsters), Maurice Beresford.

Kendall, a quiet Englishman, inherits a Chicago dairy business from his uncle. He finds himself caught up in the underworld when he learns that the business is really a front for gangster operations. The mixing of styles–the American gangster film and the British comedy–makes for some interesting moments but nothing much comes of it.

p&d, Lupino Lane; w, Lane, Leslie Arliss (based on the play "The Milky Way" by Reginald Simpson, J.W. Drawbell); ph, H.E. Palmer, ed, Leslie Norton.

Comedy (PR:A MPAA:NR)

WHY SHOOT THE TEACHER*** (1977, Can.) 96m Fraser-Lancer/Ambassador-Quartet c

Bud Cort (Max Brown), Samantha Eggar (Alice Field), Chris Wiggins (Lyle Bishop), Gary Reineke (Harris Montgomery), John Friesen (Dave McDougall), Michael J. Reynolds (Bert Field), Dale McGowan (Jake Stevenson).

During the Depression Cort is sent to a small town in Saskatchewan, Canada, to serve as a teacher in a one-room schoolhouse. He has little training for the job and faces many problems. Students prove to be uncooperative, there is no money for his salary, and he grows lonely. Eggar is the mother of three students who is just as lonely as Cort. A sensitive film that gives an accurate portrait of life in Depression-era Canada with its small town life well detailed and showing how the townspeople survive the harshness of winter. Very human, very warm, and honest enough for universal appeal.

p, Lawrence Hertzog; d, Silvio Narizzano; w, James DeFelice (based on the novel Why Shoot the Teacher by Max Braithwaite); ph, Marc Champion; m, Ricky Hyslop; ed, Bruce Nyznik, Ian McBride, Peter Thillaye; art d, Karen Bromley.

Drama Cas. (PR:C MPAA:NR)

WHY SPY (SEE: MAN CALLED DAGGER, A, 1968)

WHY WOULD ANYONE WANT TO KILL A NICE GIRL LIKE YOU? (SEE: TASTE OF EXCITEMENT, 1969, Brit.)

WHY WOULD I LIE*½ (1980) 105m MGM/UA c

Treat Williams (Cletus), Lisa Eichhorn (Kay), Gabriel Swann (Jeorge), Susan Heldfond (Amy), Anne Bryne (Faith), Valerie Curtin (Mrs. Bok), Jocelyn Brando (Mrs. Crumpe), Nicolas Coster (Walter), Severn Darden (Dr. Barbour), Sonny Davis (Paul), Jane Burkett (Natalie), Kay Cummings (Edith), Mia Bendixsen (Thelma), Ilene Kristen (Waitress), Harriet Gibson, Gynthia Hoppenfeld, Mitzi Hoag, Natalie Core, Shirley Slater, Elizabeth Kerr, Michael Shane, Eric Haims, Marcia Nicholson, Sheila Kandlbinder, Gino Ardito, Martin Cassidy, Susan Elliot, Lonnie Lloyd, Mary Kay Pupo, Jan D'Arcy, Marian Gants, Joe Gillis, Ron Graves.

A talented cast flounders under a script well below its talents in this low-quality porridge. Williams is a thoroughly unlikable character who wants to keep the $1 million inheritance his parents have left him and his siblings. Inexplicably this repugnant individual is hired as a social worker and gets caught up with Swann, a young client taken from his wrongfully jailed mother and placed in a foster home. He's about to be adopted but instead Williams takes the boy home. Then Williams meets Eichhorn, a feminist retreat worker who has met Swann's mother. The film lumbers on toward its predictable finish without much interest and with more corn than one would find in popcorn. Williams is obnoxious yet his chemistry with Eichhorn works. Swann is probably the best the film has to offer, making a good screen debut as the maligned child.

p, Pancho Kohner; d, Larry Peerce; w, Peter Stone (based on the novel The Fabricator by Hollis Hodges); ph, Gerald Hirschfeld (Metrocolor); m, Charles Fox; ed, John C. Howard; art d, James Schoppe; cos, Al Lehman.

Comedy-Drama (PR:C MPAA:PG)

WICHITA***½ (1955) 81m AA c

Joel McCrea (Wyatt Earp), Vera Miles (Laurie), Lloyd Bridges (Gyp), Wallace Ford (Whiteside), Edgar Buchanan (Doc Black), Peter Graves (Morgan Earp), Keith Larsen (Bat Masterson), Cal Benton Reid (Mayor), John Smith (Jim Earp), Walter McCoy (McCoy), Walter Sande (Wallace), Robert Wilke (Ben Thompson), Jack Elam (Al), Mae Clark (Mrs. McCoy), Gene Wesson (1st Robber), Rayford Barnes (Hal Clements).

Wyatt Earp is the most legendary lawman of the Old West, and his exploits have been celebrated in countless movies, from Walter Huston in LAW AND ORDER (1931) to Henry Fonda in MY DARLING CLEMENTINE (1946) and

Burt Lancaster in GUNFIGHT AT THE O.K. CORRAL (1957). In WICHITA Earp is portrayed by McCrea, and as the film opens he is hired by the town elders to bring some law and order to the wide-open cow town. His first act is to ban all guns within the city limits, a move that does not endear him to anyone, but after Clark, the wife of the local banker, is killed, they go along with him. Eventually peace settles on the town after McCrea gets rid of Buchanan, the local outlaw chief. This could have been another routine oater but for the skillful direction of Tourneur, who built a career on making strong films out of mediocre scripts. The film has visual style and moves at a fast enough pace to distract from the plot deficiencies. McCrea gives a strong central performance, and the supporting players are uniformly excellent, including Bridges as a young gunslinger, Ford as the town newspaper editor, Larsen as Bat Masterson, and especially Buchanan in one of his all-too-few bad- guy roles. Earp's authorized biographer, Stuart N. Lake, served as technical advisor, but still the film bears little relation to real events.

p, Walter Mirisch, Richard Heermance; d, Jacques Tourneur; w, Daniel Ullman; ph, Harold Lipstein (CinemaScope, Technicolor); m, Hans Salter; ed, William Austin; md, Salter; art d, David Milton; m/l, title song, Salter, Ned Washington, sung by Tex Ritter; tech adv, Stuart N. Lake.

Western   Cas.   (PR:A MPAA:NR)

WICKED**   (1931) 55m FOX bw

Elissa Landi (Margot Rande), Victor McLaglen (Scott Burrows), Theodore Von Eltz (Tony Rande), Una Merkel (June), Alan Dinehart (Blake), Oscar Apfel (Judge Luther), Irene Rich (Mrs. Luther), Blanche Payson (Matron), Kathleen Kerrigan (Miss Peck), Eileen Percy (Stella), Mae Busch (Arlene), Blanche Frederici (Mrs. Johnson), Lucille Williams, Alice Lake (Prisoners), Ruth Donnelly (Fanny), Edmund Breese.

Pregnant Landi is sent to prison after accidentally killing a policeman, this just after her husband was killed in a bank robbery. There she gives birth and unwittingly signs away the child. Two and a half years later, Landi attempts to escape to be with her child, and does succeed in a reunion at the end. A surprisingly good cast succeeds in keeping attention on all this hokum, but the story is too depressing for its own good nevertheless.

d, Allan Dwan; w, Kenyon Nicholson, Kathryn Scola (based on a story by Adela Rogers St. John); ph, Peverell Marley; ed, Jack Dennis; cos, Dolly Tree.

Drama   (PR:A MPAA:NR)

WICKED AS THEY COME (SEE: PORTRAIT IN SMOKE, 1957, Brit.)

WICKED DIE SLOW, THE*   (1968) 75m Cannon c

Gary Allen (The Kid), Steve Rivard (Bart Lenoir), Jeff Kanew (Armadillo), Sussanah Campbell (The Kid's Girl), Yolanda (Herself), Richard Palenske (Her Father), Helen Stewart (Bart's Girl), Samantha Worthington (Bar Girl), Racine (Indian Maiden).

After his girl friend Campbell is raped, Allen and his partner, Kanew, go riding through the post-Civil War West to find the four Indians responsible. They meet some outlaws beating up an old man and his daughter and rescue the pair. The outlaws are killed later when they are caught raping another woman and Allen gets revenge. This western was shot in New Jersey, of all places.

p, Donald C. Dennis; d, William K. Hennigar; w, Gary Allen, Jeff Kanew; ph, Amin Chaudhri; m, Robert Schwartz; ed, George Thomas;

Western   (PR:O MPAA:NR)

WICKED DREAMS OF PAULA SCHULTZ, THE*½
                                                   (1968) 113m Theme/UA c

Elke Sommer (Paula Schultz), Bob Crane (Bill Mason), Werner Klemperer (Klaus, Propaganda Minister), Joey Forman (Herbert Sweeney), John Banner (Weber), Leon Askin (Oscar), Maureen Arthur (Barbara Sweeney), Robert Carricart (Rocco), Theo Marcuse (Owl), Larry D. Mann (Grossmeyer), John Myhers (Boss), Chanin Hale (Hilda), Barbara Morrison (Kalbfus), Benny Baker (Cab Driver), Fritz Feld (Kessel), Adele Claire (Coach).

Sommer, a discontented East German athlete, takes to wearing miniskirts instead of the dowdy prescribed uniform of her teammates. Klemperer, in a nasty and amusing role, lusts after her and to escape him Sommer pole-vaults over the Berlin Wall. Crane, a black marketeer, agrees to help the Communists get her back for some spot cash and hides her in the apartment occupied by old Army pal Forman, who works for the CIA, and his wife. He is all set to turn Sommer over to the Reds when he realizes that he loves her and junks his plans. Still needing money, however, he tries to induce his pal Forman to hire her for the CIA. When Sommer learns that he is using her to make some money, she sadly give herself up to the Communists and goes home. But love conquers all, as a bewigged Crane sneaks into East Germany to prove his devotion. Sommers sees her man in drag and realizes that she does indeed love him, so the two flee back to the free world. A witless comedy played without style by a cast pirated from the "Hogan's Heroes" TV series. Klemperer provides the only really good

moments, and those are few.

p, Edward Small; d, George Marshall,; w, Burt Styler, Albert E. Lewin, Nat Perrin (based on a story by Ken Englund); ph, Jacques Marquette (DeLuxe Color), m, Jimmie Haskell; ed, Grant Whytock; art d, Edward L. Ilou; set d, Raymond Paul; cos, Marjorie Corso; spec eff, Robert Overbeck; makeup, Hal Lierley.

Comedy   (PR:C MPAA:NR)

WICKED GO TO HELL, THE***   (1961, Fr.) 74m Fanfare bw LES
                                            SALANDS VONT EN ENFER)

Marina Vlady (Eva), Henri Vidal (Macquart), Serge Reggiani (Rudel), Robert Hossein (Fred), Guy Kerner, Martha Mercadier.

After escaping from prison Vidal and Reggiani take refuge in an out-of-the way cabin along the shore line in this French film dubbed in English. There they find an artist and Vlady, his mistress. The artist is quickly despatched and Vlady becomes their prisoner. She learns to manipulate the two with her charms so they each grow to desire her, then they grow jealous of each other and, provoked by Vlady, they quarrel. The tension builds and the two finally die in quicksand. An interesting psychological drama, well acted by the three leads. The suspense is tight, thanks to well-detailed direction.

p, Jules Borkon; d, Robert Hossein.

Drama   (PR:O MPAA:NR)

WICKED LADY, THE*½   (1946, Brit.) 98m Gainsborough/UNIV, bw

Margaret Lockwood (Barbara Worth/Lady Skelton), James Mason (Capt. Jerry Jackson), Patricia Roc (Caroline), Griffith Jones (Sir Ralph Skelton), Enid Stamp-Taylor (Henrietta Kingsclere), Michael Rennie (Kit Locksby), Felix Aylmer (Hogarth, Family Retainer), David Horne (Martin Worth), Martita Hunt (Cousin Agatha Trimble), Amy Dalby (Aunt Doll), Beatrice Varley (Aunt Moll), Helen Goss (Mistress Betsy), Francis Lister (Lord Kingsclere), Emrys Jones (Ned Cotterell), Jean Kent (Doxy).

Lockwood is an aristocratic woman during the reign of Charles II. Bored with the country, she takes to highway robbery for spice in her life, and has an affair with Mason, a fellow highway robber. Ultimately, Aylmer, the family retainer, discovers Lockwood's secret but she swears him to secrecy on the promise that she'll reform. Jones, the man she was promised to, realizes he loves Roc, his original intended. However, Rennie has asked Roc for her hand in marriage. Lockwood, who also loves Rennie, is determined to destroy their happiness. Mason is nearly hanged thanks to Lockwood's two-timing, but he manages to make a cunning escape. After committing more crimes, Lockwood reaches her ultimately tragic ending. This lushly costumed drama is surpisingly boring, but Mason stands out with his swagger and gusto while the rest of the cast member are sadly unconvincing. Despite being bombarded by the critics and the problems inherent in the film, THE WICKED LADY proved to be England's top box office draw for 1946. For American release it required re-shooting, as the ladies' decolletage proved to be more than American censors would allow.

p, R. J. Minney; d, Leslie Arliss; w, Arliss, Aimee Stuart, Gordon Glennon (based on the novel The Life and Death of the Wicked Lady Skelton by Magdalen King-Hall); ph, Jack Cox; m, Louis Levy; ed, Terence Fisher; art d, John Bryan.

Adventure   (PR:A MPAA:NR)

WICKED LADY, THE*   (1983, Brit.) 99m MGM/UA c

Faye Dunaway (Lady Barbara Skelton), Alan Bates (Capt. Jerry Jackson), John Gielgud (Hogarth, Family Servant), Denholm Elliott (Sir Ralph Skelton), Prunella Scales (Lady Kingsclere), Oliver Tobias (Kit Locksby), Glynis Barber (Caroline), Joan Hickson (Aunt Agatha Trimble), Helena McCarthy (Moll), Mollie Maureen (Doll), Derek Francis (Lord Kingsclere), Marina Sirtis (Jackson's Girl), Nicholas Gecks (Ned Cotterell), Hugh Millais (Uncle Martin), Guinevere John (Landlady at Inn), John Savident (Squire Thorton), Dermot Walsh (Lord Marwood), Marc Sinden (Lord Dolman), Glynis Brooks (Ned's Wife), Mark Burns (King Charles II), Teresa Codling (Nell Gwynne), David Gant (Clergyman at Church), Ewen Solon, Roger Brierley (Clergymen at Tyburn Prison), Arthur Whybrown (Storyteller at Tyburn), Tony Martin (Vendor at Tyburn), John Pierce Jones (Ringleader at Tyburn), Robert Putt (Man at Tyburn), Terence Mountain (Law Officer), Cyril Conway (Doctor), Malcolm Mudie (Courtier), Celia Imrie (Servant at Inn), Ellen Pollack (Mrs. Munce), Lisa Mulidore (Village Girl), Douglas Milvain, Pamela Cundell, Patrick Brock (Coach Passengers), Marianne Stone, Catherine Neilson (Customers in Shop), Fiona McArthur, Judi Maynard, Francine Morgan, Lucy Hornak, Maggie Rennie (Bridesmaids).

This remake of the 1945 film sinks below the original in poor moviemaking qualities. The low-cut gowns which so offended the American censors in the original give way here to ladies, outfits with pop-open tops. Plenty of breast jiggling and protruding nipples make up for the lack of plot or talent in this mess. Dunaway is the aristocratic lady turned highway robber, with Bates as her highwayman lover. How actors of this quality (to say nothing of Gielgud) ever were persuaded to appear in such garbage is a mystery. There's plenty of sophomoric racy humor to cover the skimpy plot and the ensemble is clearly better than the weak material. The photography is lush, however, making good use of the English countryside. A controversy arose over a scene in which Dunaway and Sirtis go at each other with horsewhips. Dunaway manages to tear her opponent's dress to ribbons with a few breast-whipping shots tossed in for good measure. This greatly offended the censors but director Winner protested it was art and rounded up such notable figures as author Kingsley Amis, John Schlesinger, Karel Reisz, and Lindsay Anderson to back him up. The scene remained. Arliss, who directed the original 1945 mess, contributed his talents to the script for this remake.

p, Menahem Golan, Yoram Globus; d, Michael Winner; w, Winner, Leslie Arliss (based on the novel *The Life and Death of the Wicked Lady Skelton* by Magdalen King-Hall); ph, Jack Cardiff; m, Tony Banks; ed, Arnold Crust; art d, John Blezard; cos, John Bloomfield; ch, Madeleine Inglehearn; spec eff, Albert J. Whitlock.

Adventure   **Cas.**   **(PR:O   MPAA:R)**

WICKED, WICKED*   (1973) 95m MGM c

David Bailey (*Rick Stewart*), Tiffany Bolling (*Lisa James*), Randolph Roberts (*Jason Gant*), Scott Brady (*Sgt. Ramsey*), Edd Byrnes (*Hank Lassiter*), Diane McBain (*Dolores Hamilton*), Roger Bowen (*Manager*), Madeleine Sherwood (*Lenore Karadyne*), Indira Danks (*Genny*), Arthur O'Connell (*Hotel Engineer*), Jack Knight (*Bill Broderick*), Patsy Garrett (*Housekeeper*), Robert Nichols (*Day Clerk*), Kirk Bates (*Owen Williams*), Maryesther Denver (*Organist*).

Not too exciting thriller that takes place at a California seaside resort. Three blonde female guests are found murdered. It turns out that the hotel's handyman (Roberts) is donning a kiddie Halloween mask and hacking up the guests. Brady, a retired cop who now works as the house detective, tracks him down to the bloody end. This strange feature employed "Duo-Vision," the split-screen technique that so nicely built up suspense in Brian De Palma's terror film, SISTERS. Unfortunately, none of the skill shown in that film is evident here and the technique is reduced to a gimmick. The music was the original organ score from the 1925 silent classic PHANTOM OF THE OPERA. WICKED, WICKED was written, produced, and directed by the house director of the 1960s TV comedy series "Green Acres."

p,d&fw, Richard L. Bare; ph, Frederick Gately (Metrocolor); m, Philip Springer; ed, John F. Schreyer; art d, Walter McKeegan,

Thriller   **(PR:O   MPAA:PG)**

WICKED WIFE**   (1955, Brit.) 75m Talisman-George Minter/AA bw
                                     (GB: GRAND NATIONAL NIGHT)

Nigel Patrick (*Gerald Coates*), Moira Lister (*Babs Coates*), Beatrice Campbell (*Joyce Penrose*), Betty Ann Davies (*Pinkie Collins*), Michael Hordern (*Inspector Ayling*), Noel Purcell (*Philip Balfour*), Leslie Mitchell (*Jack Donovan*), Barry MacKay (*Sgt. Gibson*), Colin Gordon (*Buns Darling*), Gibb McLaughlin (*Morton*), Richard Grayden (*Chandler*), May Hallatt (*Hoskyns*), George Sequira (*George*), Ernest Jay, Russell Waters, George Rose, Harold Goodwin, Arthur Howard, Edward Evans, Maria Mercedes.

Competent British thriller shot in the north country and starring Patrick as a horse owner whose pony is entered in the Grand National. Unfortunately for Patrick he accidentally kills his dipsomaniac wife, Lister, and, in a panic, stuffs her body in the trunk of another man's car. When the cops come to investigate, Patrick denies any knowledge of the events. The horse owner's neck is saved from the noose with a hackneyed, theatrical plot device that destroys the film's credibility.

p, Phil C. Samuel; d, Bob McNaught; w, McNaught, Val Valentine (based on the play "Grand National Night" by Dorothy and Campbell Christie); ph, Jack Asher; m, John Greenwood; ed, Anne V. Coates; md, Muir Mathieson; art d, Fred Pusey; cos, Beatrice Dawson.

Crime   **(PR:O   MPAA:NR)**

WICKED WOMAN, A**½   (1934) 72m MGM bw

Mady Christians (*Naomi Trice*), Jean Parker (*Rosanne*), Charles Bickford (*Pat Naylor*), Betty Furness (*Yancey*), William Henry (*Curtis Trice*), Jackie Searle (*Curtis as a Boy*), Betty Jane Graham (*Yancey as a Girl*), Marilyn Harris (*Rosanne as a Girl*), Paul Harvey (*Ed Trice*), Zelda Sears (*Gram Teague*), Robert Taylor (*Bill Renton*), Sterling Holloway (*Peter*), George Billings (*Neddie*), Dewitt Jennings (*Sheriff*).

Christians is married to a sadistic drunk whom she ends up killing to protect her children. She hides the body in a nearby swamp and moves her family to a new location. After 10 years guilt catches up with her and she confesses to the crime. Bickford, a newsman covering the trial, falls for her and the two are united after her children testify that the murder was committed in self defense. Christians gets off and all is well again. Essentially this was just soap opera, but Christians, a noted Viennese actress, conveys an honesty that gives the material a dramatic boost. Parker, her daughter, gets involved with Taylor in one of the film's subplots. Taylor was making his feature debut here after working in a much hailed short, BURIED LOOT. As the caddish young man he shows none of the talents for which he would

later be acclaimed.

p, Harry Rapf; d, Charles Brabin; w, Florence Ryerson, Zelda Sears (based on the novel by Anne Austin); ph, Lester White; ed, Ben Lewis.

Drama   **(PR:C   MPAA:NR)**

WICKED WOMAN**   (1953) 77m UA bw

Beverly Michaels (*Billie Nash*), Richard Egan (*Matt Bannister*), Percy Helton (*Charlie Borg*), Evelyn Scott (*Dora Bannister*), Robert Osterloh (*Mr. Lowry*), William Phillips (*Gus*), Frank Ferguson (*Mr. Porter*), Bernadene Hayes (*Mrs. Walters*), Herb Jeffries.

A seamy little number finds Michaels in the title role as a bar girl who works for Egan and his wife, Scott. She and Egan plan to chuck it all and head for Mexico but this falls through and she is forced into an affair with Helton, the local tailor, so he won't squeal about the husband's transgressions to Scott. Egan catches the pair in an embrace which subsequently ends his romance with the waitress. He goes back to his nagging wife and Michaels catches the next bus leaving town. Despite the lack of pleasant characters the drama is delivered without resorting to cliche situations. The film's eroticism pales by modern standards, but it was considered very salacious in its time. Directed in a straightforward manner with performances to suit the material.

p, Clarence Greene; d, Russell Rouse; w, Greene, Rouse; ph, Edward Fitzgerald; m, Buddy Baker; ed, Chester Schaeffer; m/l, "Wicked Woman," Baker, Joe Mullendore (sung by Herb Jeffries), "One Night In Acapulco," Baker, Mullendore.

Drama   **(PR:O   MPAA:NR)**

WICKER MAN, THE***½   (1974, Brit.) 102m BL/WB c

Edward Woodward (*Sgt. Neil Howie*), Christopher Lee (*Lord Summerisle*), Diane Cilento (*Miss Rose, Schoolteacher*), Britt Ekland (*Willow MacGregor*), Ingrid Pitt (*Librarian-Clerk*), Lindsay Kemp (*Alder MacGregor, owner of "Green Man" Pub*), Russell Waters (*Harbormaster*), Aubrey Morris (*Old Gardener-Gravedigger*), Irene Sunters (*May Morrison*), Walter Carr (*Schoolmaster*), Roy Boyd (*Broome*), Ian Campbell (*Oak*), Leslie Mackie (*Daisy*), Geraldine Cowper (*Rowan Morrison*), Kevin Collins (*Old Fisherman*), Donald Eccles (*T. H. Lennox*), Jennifer Martin (*Myrtle Morrison*), Leslie Blackwater (*Hairdresser*), Barbara Ann Brown (*Woman with Baby*), S. Newton Anderson (*Landers*), Penny Cluer (*Gillie*), Myra Forsyth (*Mrs. Grimmond*), John Hallam (*Police Constable McTaggart*), Alison Hughes (*Sgt. Howie's Fiancee*), John MacGregor (*Baker*), Charles Kearney (*Butcher*), Fiona Kennedy (*Holly*), Jimmie MacKenzie (*Brian*), Tony Roper (*Postman*), Lorraine Peters (*Girl on Grave*), John Sharp (*Dr. Ewan*), John Young (*Fishmonger*), Richard Wren (*Ash Buchanan*), Ross Campbell, Ian Wilson (*Communicants*), Juliette Cadsow, Helen Norman, Elizabeth Sinclair (*Villagers*), Peter Brewis, Ian Cutler, Michael Cole, Bernard Murray, Andrew Tompkins (*Musicians*).

Film history is replete with examples of misunderstood works receiving minor and perfunctory releases if not being shelved outright. THE WICKER MAN unfortunately is an excellent example of such treatment. This well-told tale of mounting horror was completely mishandled on its initial release and it is only through perseverance along with some good fortune that the complete director's version was finally released. Woodward plays a devoutly Christian policeman and lay minister, still an unmarried virgin though middle-aged. He anonymously receives a photograph of a girl (Cowper) in the mail with a note stating she has mysteriously vanished. Woodward heads out to Summerisle, an island community within his jurisdiction, in his search for the girl. No one there has heard of Cowper, not even Sunters, whom Woodward suspects to be Cowper's mother. Sunters' young daughter shows Woodward a picture she says she has drawn of the supposed missing girl, but the drawing is that of a hare. Woodward takes a room at an inn run by Kemp and his daughter, Ekland. He is shocked by the ribald songs sung by customers of the inn's pub and even more so when he observes couples making love in a cemetery as he takes an evening walk. On his return, Woodward is further shaken when he sees Lee, the lord of the island, bringing Ekland a young boy for sexual initiation. The next morning Woodward heads to the local school in search of Cowper. There he finds Cilento teaching the children about phallic symbols, including a phallic maypole dance. Woodward finds Cowper's name on the school roster and Cilento explains that the girl had died but returned in another form. His frustration mounting, Woodward goes to Lee's mansion for permission to exhume Cowper's grave, suspecting murder. Though Lee is a perfect host, Woodward is angered by his pagan attitudes. Woodward removes the girl's coffin from the grave and is shocked to find the corpse of a hare. He surmises that these pagan people have kidnaped Cowper and are going to sacrifice her in May Day festivities. As the costumed procession begins, Woodward knocks out Kemp and steals his jester's outfit. The parade around the island is colorful and gay, full of costumes representing nature. Woodward spots Cowper being led for an apparent sacrifice and attempts to rescue her. He is quickly surrounded and it is only then he discovers the truth: Cowper's disappearance was simply a ruse to lure the good Christian man to Summerisle for a ritual sacrifice. Feverently offering up prayers to Jesus, Woodward is placed inside a giant wicker man that is set afire against the setting sun. THE WICKER MAN consistently plays with audience loyalties and expectations, revealing information in small chunks before Woodward finally realizes his fate. The setting of Summerisle is hardly that of horror. It is populated with genuinely happy individuals. Though their life on the island is unusual (and not nearly so abhorrent as the devout Woodward finds it) it is not entirely unattractive. It is a world full of light and color, in contrast to the darker outfits worn by Woodward. Only in the end is Summerisle's true nature revealed. It is here that the building tension between Woodward and Lee's people explodes in a horrifying crescendo. THE WICKER MAN was written by Anthony Shaffer, best known for his play "Sleuth." This was his first original screenplay, which was to be financed by British Lion in an attempt to revive that studio's former status. Despite some problems on the set (including a pregnant Ekland who continually argued with director Hardy) the final cut, running 102 minutes, looked to be a promising film. Though Hardy wasn't entirely pleased, Lee thought the film represented the best of his work. However, shortly before its release British Lion was taken over by EMI, whose film division head clearly didn't know (or care) about the project. After talking over it's American possibilities with Roger Corman, EMI's Michael Deeley cut the film by 15 minutes, which caused some drastic changes in plot logic. This version was released in England in 1973, with the American debut a year later in Atlanta and San Diego. The rights for distribution had been bought by a tax-shelter group, which gave not an iota whether or not the film made money. It was advertised as straight horror when eventually Warner Bros. took over the distribution, but this ad campaign was all wrong for the film. Horror fans looking for special effects and gore were disappointed and the film was quickly pulled. Two years later a pair of New Orleans film buffs bought the distribution rights. After conferring with the much disillusioned Hardy, they learned the original director's cut might exist in negative. Though this led to dead ends and outright deception by EMI, a full version of the film turned up at the Corman offices. A new negative was struck from this print, restoring Hardy's original film. When looking at the film, one can't help but wonder why all the controversy began in the first place. THE WICKER MAN is an intelligent entertainment that takes its subject seriously without resorting to gratuitous effects to make a point. It remains a fine example of occult horror that remains with the viewer well past its conclusion.

p, Peter Snell; d, Robin Hardy; w, Anthony Shaffer; ph, Harry Waxman; m, Paul Giovanni; ed, Eric Boyd-Perkins; art d, Seamus Flannery; cos, Sue Yelland; ch, Stewart Hopps; song, "Corn Rigs," sung by Paul Giovanni; makeup, Billy Partleton.

Occult Horror   **Cas.**   **(PR:O   MPAA:R)**

WICKHAM MYSTERY, THE*½   (1931, Brit.) 84m Samuelson/UA bw

Eve Gray (*Joan Hamilton*), John Longden (*Harry Crawford*), Lester Matthews (*Charles Wickham*), Sam Livesey (*Inspector Cobb*), Walter Piers (*George Beverley*), John Turnbull (*Howard Clayton*), Wally Bosco (*Edward Hamilton*), Doris Clemence (*Mrs. Wickham*), Elsie Moore, Ormonde Wynne.

Inventor Matthews is the victim of a robbery, losing a valuable necklace and some top secret plans of a new aircraft. His neighbor is suspected, but daughter Gray does some snooping and proves that a notorious gang of crooks is responsible. Not much of a mystery.

p, E. Gordon Craig; d, G.B. Samuelson; w, (based on the play "The Paper Chase" by John McNally).

Crime   **(PR:A   MPAA:NR)**

WIDE BOY*½   (1952, Brit.) 67m Merton Park/Anglo-Amalgamated bw

Sydney Tafler (*Benny*), Susan Shaw (*Molly*), Ronald Howard (*Inspector Carson*), Melissa Stribling (*Caroline*), Colin Tapley (*Mannering*), Laidman Brown (*Pop*), Helen Christie (*Sally*), Martin Benson (*Rocco*), Glyn Houston.

Tafler is a petty crook who steals in order to satisfy his sweetheart's desire for luxury. He lifts a wallet that gets him entangled in a blackmail scheme. He is ultimately killed and his girl, Shaw, tracks down the guilty party.

p, W.H. Williams; d, Ken Hughes; w, Rex Rienits; ph, Jo Amber.

Crime   **(PR:A   MPAA:NR)**

WIDE OPEN**½   (1930) 69m WB c

Edward Everett Horton (*Simon Haldane*), Patsy Ruth Miller (*Julia Faulkner/Doris*), T. Roy Barnes (*Bob Wyeth*), Louise Fazenda (*Agatha Hathaway*), Edna Murphy (*Nell Martin*), Vera Lewis (*Agatha's Mother*), E. J. Ratcliffe (*Trundle*), Louise Beavers (*Easter*), Frank Beal (*Faulkner*), Vincent [Vince] Barnett (*Dvorak*), Lloyd Ingraham (*Doctor*), bobby Gordon (*Office Boy*), Fred Kelsey (*Detective*), Robert Dudley (*Office Worker*), B.B.B (*Richards*).

A charming comedy has Horton playing a timid, bumbling employee of a big company who is brimful of workable new ideas but is too shy to express them. Enter the boss' daughter, Miller, who knows exactly how to go about putting Hordon's ideas across. A wild series of complications follow during which the firm's superintendent is fired, Horton's ideas are adopted, and he and Miller march off to the altar. In spite of plenty of naughty dialog which Horton puts across with his inimitable nervous innocence, there is a naive

quality to the story which has allowed it to age well. Horton and Miller are an excellent team and Fazenda works in a funny song along the way.

d, Archie Mayo; w, James A. Starr, Arthur Caesar (based on the novel *The Narrow Street* by Edward Bateman Morris).

Comedy   **(PR:A   MPAA:NR)**

WIDE OPEN FACES**   (1938) 67m COL bw

Joe E. Brown (*Wilbur Meeks*), Jane Wyman (*Betty Martin*), Alison Skipworth (*Auntie*), Lyda Roberti (*Kitty*), Alan Baxter (*Tony*), Lucien Littlefield (*P.T. "Doc" Williams*), Sidney Toler (*Sheriff*), Berton Churchill (*Mr. Crawford*), Barbara Pepper (*Belle*), Joseph Downing (*Stretch*), Stanley Fields (*Duke*), Horace Murphy (*Mr. Schultz*).

Some stolen cash is missing so every public enemy around moves into an inn run by Wyman and her aunt Skipworth while a search is initiated. Brown, a soda jerk, outwits the mobsters, gets them all behind bars, and wins Wyman in the process. He collects the reward money and turns up the missing loot as well. The comedy moves at a brisk pace, hiding the fact that this really isn't much to begin with. Brown is okay but for the most part WIDE OPEN FACES is a corn fest with predictable situations.

p, David Loew; d, Kurt Neumann; w, Earle Snell, Clarence Marks, Joe Bigelow, Pat C. Flick (based on a story by Richard Flournoy); ph, Paul C. Vogel; ed, Jack Ogilvie; md, Dr. Hugo Riesenfeld.

Comedy   **(PR:A   MPAA:NR)**

WIDE OPEN TOWN***   (1941) 78m PAR bw

William Boyd (*Hopalong Cassidy*), Russell Hayden (*Lucky Jenkins*), Andy Clyde (*California Jack*), Evelyn Brent (*Belle Langtry*), Victor Jory (*Steve Fraser*), Morris Ankrum (*Jim Stuart*), Kenneth Harlan (*Tom Wilson*), Bernice Kay (*Joan Stuart*), Roy Barcroft (*Red*), Glenn Strange (*Ed Stark*), Ed Cassidy (*Brad Jackson*), Jack Rockwell (*Rancher*), Bob Kortman, George Cleveland.

One of the best "Hopalong Cassidy" films and also one of the longest running times for a series western. Brent dominates a town being plagued by rustlers. She also serves as a front for the gang, which is led by Jory. Boyd and his Bar 20 boys decide to clean things up so the cowpoke hero gets elected sheriff and leads in chasing the bad guys from the area and jailing Brent. The story is no different from many westerns but the players perform with conviction under the taut direction of Selander. (See HOPALONG CASSIDY series, Index.)

p, Harry Sherman; d, Lesley Selander; w, Harrison Jacobs, J. Benton Cheney (based on characters created by Clarence E. Mulford); ph, Sherman A. Rose; ed, Carroll Lewis; md, Irving Talbot, John Leopold; art d, Ralph Berger

Western   **(PR:A   MPAA:NR)**

WIDOW AND THE GIGOLO, THE
              (SEE: ROMAN SPRING OF MRS. STONE, THE, 1961)

WIDOW FROM CHICAGO, THE*   (1930) 64m FN-WB bw

Alice White (*Polly Henderson*), Neil Hamilton (*Swifty Dorgan*), Edward G. Robinson (*Dominic*), Frank McHugh (*Slug O'Donnell*), Lee Shumway (*Cris Johnston*), Brooks Benedict (*Mullins*), John Elliott (*Detective Lt. Finnegan*), Dorothy Mathews (*Cora*), Ann Cornwall (*Mazie*), E.H. Calvert (*Capt. Davis*), Betty Francisco (*Helen*), Harold Goodwin (*Jimmy Henderson*), Mike Donlin (*Desk Man*), Robert E. Homans (*Patrolman*), Al Hill (*Johnston's Henchman*), Mary Foy (*Neighbor Woman*), Allan Coran (*Sgt. Dunn*).

A weak gangster epic that doesn't show off Robinson or anyone else. Elliott and Goodwin are New York police officers who have learned that Hamilton, a hood from the Windy City, is coming to New York to do some work for Robinson, a gangland vice czar. Elliot and Goodwin want to get to Hamilton before he gets off the train and is lost in the crowded city. The train is coming into New York when the cops board and Hamilton apparently leaps off as it goes over a bridge. With Hamilton dead, the cops think they've done their job. Goodwin sends a story to the papers that Hamilton has eluded the cops, then he assumes Hamilton's identity because nobody in New York knows what the killer is supposed to look like. Goodwin joins Robinson's gang and is immediately accepted. Goodwin is waiting in a doorway for one of Robinson's cars to pick him up when he is suddenly shot down in cold blood. The killing is seen by Goodwin's sister, White, and she swears to wreak revenge on whoever pulled the trigger. She arrives at Robinson's nightclub and says that she is Goodwin's widow. That's good enough for the gangster and she is given a job to tide her over. Now we learn that Hamilton never died at all. He arrives and White gets to him before he can spill the beans. She prevails on him to keep mum and he is soon in love with her, so much so that he is planning to go straight. Robinson and his boys have been having trouble with a rival nightclub and decide to put it out of business right away with a holdup. When a detective tries to shoot Hamilton, White gets her hands on a gun and shoots the man, thereby allowing Robinson and his men to flee. Later, Robinson admits that he's killed his share of cops in his day, including her late brother. White had fixed the phone so that cops could hear the entire conversation at the local police station. After he finishes his bragging, Robinson notes that the phone is off the hook and he tries to make a getaway but cops have already surrounded his place. Robinson uses White's curvy body as a shield against police bullets and he almost escapes, but Hamilton arrives and there's a gun battle with Robinson eventually giving up. White and Hamilton leave to start their life afresh. This is almost the plot of JOHNNY DANGEROUSLY and bordered on parody. Even Robinson's snarl was out of place, and Hamilton, who had always been a matinee idol type before aging gracefully into a character actor, is not well cast. Too much coincidence in the script and too much emoting from top-billed White whose rise to stardom was swift but her fall to bit parts was even swifter.

d, Edward Cline; w, Earl Baldwin; ph, Sol Polito; ed, Edward Schroeder.

Crime Drama   (PR:A-C MPAA:NR)

WIDOW FROM MONTE CARLO, THE*½   (1936) 63m WB bw

Warren William (Chepstow), Dolores Del Rio (Inez), Louise Fazenda (Mrs. Torrent), Colin Clive (Eric), Herbert Mundin (Mr. Torrent), Warren Hymer (Dopey), Olin Howland (Eaves), E. E. Clive (Lord Holloway), Mary Forbes (Lady Holloway), Eily Malyon (Lady Maynard), Ann Douglas (Joan), Andre Cheron (Croupier), Charles Fallon (Foreigner), Billy Bevan (Officer), Charles Coleman (Barker the Torrent's Butler), John G. Spacey (Kilted Man), Ferdinand Schumann-Heink (Chauffeur), May Beatty (Dowager), Boyd Irwin, Sr (Desk Sergeant), Alphonse Martell (Emil), Olaf Hytten, Norman Ainsley (Englishmen), Viva Tattersall (Joan), Herbert Evans (Butler).

Social climber Fazenda, at Monte Carlo on holiday, seeks to extort the friendship of glamorous widowed duchess Del Rio by purloining a compromising letter. Colin Clive is the impossibly snobbish English fiance whose marriage to Del Rio is threatened by possible revelation of the contents of the missing missive. American thief Hymer is recruited to steal the letter back on behalf of his duchess "pal." All the while, suave suitor William never flags in his amorous pursuit of beautiful Del Rio. A contrapuntal course is followed as the scene shifts from the storied casino at Monte Carlo to the vulgar amusement park of Margate, where the dazzling but doughty duchess is tumbled in a barrel ride and Fazenda's skirts are blown to mid-thigh. The comical comedown of the high and mighty leads to the altar for William and the newly humanized Del Rio. Too unrelentingly contrived to be truly funny, this little romantic comedy is further marred by the wooden performance of the very decorative Del Rio.

p, Bryan Foy; d, Arthur Greville Collins; w, F. Hugh Herbert, Charles Belden, George Bricker (based on the play "Meet the Duchess" by Ian Hay and A. E. W. Mason); ph, Warren Lynch; ed, Thomas Pratt; md, Leo F. Forbstein; art d, Hugh Reticker; cos, Orry-Kelly.

Comedy   (PR:A MPAA:NR)

WIDOW IN SCARLET*   (1932) 64m Mayfair bw

Dorothy Revier (Baroness Orsani), Kenneth Harlan (Peter Lawton-Bond), Lloyd Whitlock (Mandel), Glenn Tryon (Spuffy), Myrtle Stedman (Alice Lawton-Bond), Lloyd Ingraham (Bradley), Harry Strang (Hymie), Hal Price, Arthur Millet, William V. Mong, Phillips Smalley, Wilfred North, Erin LeBessoniere.

Idiosyncratic Revier bets that she will be able to pinch the stuffy Stedman's jewelry under the very noses of the well-informed constabulary. Clever crook Whitlock, posing as a policeman, helps with the theft. An inadequate script spoils what might have been a fine female equivalent to RAFFLES (1930). Revier's performance is insufficiently flamboyant for the character she plays; with 10 other features to her credit during the year, she may simply have been tired. Uncharacteristically fine production values for a low-budget independent feature.

p, Ralph M. Like; d, George B. Seitz; w, Norman Battle; ph, Jules Cronjager; ed, Byron Robinson.

Crime   (PR:A MPAA:NR)

WIDOW IS WILLING, THE   (SEE: VIOLENT SUMMER, 1961, Fr./Ital.)

WIDOW'S MIGHT**   (1934, Brit.) 77m WB-FN bw

Laura La Plante (Nancy Tweesdale), Yvonne Arnaud (Princess Suzanne), Garry Marsh (Barry Carrington), George Curzon (Champion), Barry Clifton (Cyril Monks), Margaret Yarde (Cook), Davina Craig (Amelia), Joan Hickson (Burroughs), Hugh E. Wright (Peasgood), Hay Plumb (Sgt. Dawkins).

Widow La Plante, on the urging of her best friend, widow Arnaud, fakes a robbery in order to win back her one-time sweetheart. They con butler Curzon into confessing to the "crime" but their plan goes awry. Trouble is averted at the finale, and romance takes its place.

p, Irving Asher; d, Cyril Gardner; w, Roland Brown, Brock Williams (based on a play by Frederick Jackson).

Comedy   (PR:A MPAA:NR)

WIDOWS' NEST**   (1977, U.S./Span.) 119m Navrarro c

Patricia Neal (Lupe), Valentina Cortese (Dolores), Susan Oliver (Isabel), Yvonne Mitchell (Elvira), Jadwiga Baranska (Carmen), Jerzy Zelnik (Carlos), Lila Kedrova (Mother), Angel del Pozo (Victor), Helen Horton (Ana), Jorge Lago (Rafael), Ricardo Palacios, Pepe Yepes, Juan Lombardero, Yelena Samarina.

Cortese, Mitchell, and Baranska are three sisters who might have stemmed from Shakespeare's "Macbeth" in this gothic tale of aging ladies who reside in a house in the Cuba of the 1930s with their one-eyed maidservant Neal. The arrival from Spain of swinging in-law Oliver and presumed "brother" Zelnik triggers flashbacks of past social and sexual traumas on the part of the hitherto cloistered sisters. The picture proceeds in episodic fashion, detailing the denigration of each in turn until the final demise of the fragile household structure. A Harold Pinter-like plot with some good, if woefully overacting, players is ruined by utter humorlessness. Producer-director-writer Navarro lost a backer in mid-shoot and was unable to find a reputable releasing company. Gina Lollobrigida had signed for the role played by Neal, but had wisely withdrawn. Filmed in Spain, the land of low production costs.

p,d&w, Tony Navarro; ph, John Cabrera; m, Francis Lai; ed, Juan Serra; art d, Jose A. De La Guerra; set d, Edda Dorini; cos, Tony Pueo, Luis Lopez, Adela Velasco; m/l, Lai, Paul Taylor.

Drama   Cas.   (PR:O MPAA:NR)

WIEN, DU STADT DER LIEDER (SEE: VIENNA, CITY OF SONGS, 1931, Ger.)

WIEN TANZT   (SEE: VIENNA WALTZES, 1961, Aust.)

WIFE, DOCTOR AND NURSE**½   (1937) 85m FOX bw

Loretta Young (Ina), Warner Baxter (Dr. Judd Lewis), Virginia Bruce (Steve, Lewis' Nurse), Jane Darwell (Mrs. Krueger, Housekeeper), Sidney Blackmer (Dr. Therberg), Maurice Cass (Pomout), Minna Gombell (Constance, Nurse), Margaret Irving (Mrs. Cunningham), Gordon [William "Wild Bill"] Elliott (Bruce Thomas), Elisha Cook, Jr (Glen Wylie), Brewster Twins (Specialty), Paul Hurst (Bill), Hal K. Dawson (Dr. Hedges), George Ernest (Red), Georges Renavent (Nick), Spencer Charters (Uncle), Claire duBrey (Miss Farrell), Lon Chaney, Jr (Chauffeur), Charles Judels (Chef), Stanley Fields (Delivery Man), Olin [Howlin] Howard (Doorman), Jan Duggan (Superintendent of Nurses), Lynn Bari (Girl at Party), Robert Lowery (Intern).

When socialite Young marries Park Avenue doctor Baxter she finds that Bruce, his nurse, also loves and has devoted her life to the physician. Young becomes jealous and has Bruce sent away. The married couple continue their life but Baxter's work begins to suffer without his operating-room partner. He also begins neglecting Young, who realizes that Baxter can't cope without the other woman. Bruce returns as the two women declare a peaceful agreement and all ends happily. The material isn't much but the direction has a light touch that gives this just the right tone needed to work. Baxter is fine in his role, with Young countering him well. As the nurse, Bruce brings much more emotion to her role than another actress might, giving the part a unique quality.

p, Raymond Griffith; d, Walter Lang; w, Kathryn Scola, Darrell Ware, Lamar Trotti; ph, Edward Cronjager; ed, Walter Thompson; md, Arthur Lange; art d, David Hall.

Comedy   (PR:A MPAA:NR)

WIFE, HUSBAND AND FRIEND***   (1939) 80m FOX bw

Loretta Young (Doris Blair Borland), Warner Baxter (Leonard Borland), Binnie Barnes (Cecil Carver), Cesar Romero (Hugo), George Barbier (Maj. Blair), J. Edward Bromberg (Rossi), Eugene Pallette (Mike Craig), Ruth Terry (Carol the Secretary), Helen Westley (Mrs. Blair), Alice Armand (Sally Bostwick), Iva Stewart (Miss Carver's Secretary), Dorothy Dearing (Mrs. Price), Helen Ericson (Mrs. Spalding), Kay Griffith (Nancy Sprague), Harry Rosenthal (Wilkins), Edward Cooper (Butler), Renie Riano (Mrs. Craig), Lawrence Grant (Hertz), Charles Williams (Jaffee), Howard Hickman (Concert Manager), George Irving (Doctor), Harry Hayden (Hotel Manager), Robert Kellard (Bank Teller), Cecil Weston (Dresser), Robert Lowery, Arthur Rankin (Interns).

Venal vocal coach Romero, against all contrary evidence, persuades housewife Young that her singing ability is such that she should pursue a career as a vocalist. Businessman Baxter, Young's husband, is dismayed by his wife's pretensions, but goes along with her plans. Young's theatrical debut is a debacle, but unknown to her, Baxter–encouraged by his opera-singing girl friend Barnes–has secretly taken singing lessons. Baxter scores small successes at private concerts and is importuned by Barnes to appear with her in a grandopera performance. When Baxter's ineptitude turns the opera into slapstick, he and Young come to their senses and decide to duet only for amusement. Baxter, Barnes, and Young perform beautifully under Ratoff's finely timed direction. Associate producer Johnson remade the story in 1949 as EVERYBODY DOES IT. Some operatic arias, and

Baxter mouths a few songs dubbed by an uncredited vocalist, including the Rudyard Kipling classic "The Road to Mandalay" and "Drink from the Cup of Tomorrow" (Samuel Pokrass, Walter Bullock).

p, Nunnally Johnson; d, Gregory Ratoff; w, Johnson (based on novel *Career in C Major* by James M. Cain); ph, Ernest Palmer; ed, Walter Thompson; md, David Buttolph; art d, Richard Day, Mark Lee Kirk; set d, Thomas Little; cos, Royer; m/l, Samuel Pokrass, Walter Bullock, Armando Hauser.

Musical Comedy   **(PR:A   MPAA:NR)**

WIFE OF GENERAL LING, THE½   (1938, Brit.) 72m
Premier-Stafford/GAU bw (AKA: REVENGE OF GENERAL LING)

Griffith Jones (*John Fenton*), Valery Inkijinoff (*Gen. Ling/Wong*), Adrianne Renn (*Tai*), Alan Napier (*Governor*), Anthony Eustrel (*See Long*), Jino Soneya (*Yuan*), Hugh McDermott (*Tracy*), Gibson Gowland (*Mike*), Gabrielle Brune (*Germaine*), Lotus Fragrance (*Tai's Maid*), Marion Spencer (*Lady Buckram*), Billy Holland (*Police Sergeant*), George Merritt (*Police Commissioner*), Howard Douglas (*Doctor*), Kenji Takase.

When British armaments are being smuggled into China it's up to Secret Service agent Jones to find out who's behind it all. Russian actor Inkijinoff plays a wealthy Chinese merchant-philanthropist who is the the main suspect. Jones theorizes that Inkijinoff is in cahoots with General Ling, a noted Chinese warlord terrorist, not realizing that the two are one and the same. Renn plays Inkijinoff's wife, who once was a sweetheart of Jones. When she finds out what her husband has been doing she helps her old flame rig a trap. Inkijinoff is killed and the two former lovers rekindle their romance. Despite the unbelievable coincidences within the plot structure this is a tight, well-made picture. Inkijinoff is strong as the villain, a performance matched by Jones' characterization. The direction has good pacing, helped greatly by some smartly written dialog.

p, John Stafford; d, Ladislas Vajda; w, Akos Tolnay, Reginald Long (based on the story by Peter Cheyney, Dorothy Hope); ph, James Wilson; ed, R. Thomas.

Drama/Adventure   **(PR:A   MPAA:NR)**

WIFE OF MONTE CRISTO, THE   (1946) 80m PRC bw

John Loder (*De Villefort, Prefect of Police*), Lenore Aubert (*Haydee, Countess of Monte Cristo*), Charles Dingle (*Danglars*), Fritz Kortner (*Maillard*), Eduardo Ciannelli (*Antoine*), Martin Kosleck (*Count of Monte Cristo*), Fritz Feld (*Bonnett*), Eva Gabor (*Mme. Maillard*), Clancy Cooper (*Baptiste*), Colin Campbell (*Abbe Faria*), John Bleifer, Egon Brecher, Anthony Warde, Crane Whitley.

As this picture has it, rather than retiring to his island estates following his revenge on his persecutors, the famed count of the Alexandre Dumas romance revisits Paris, where–his true identity concealed–he avenges the sufferings of the poor in the post-revolution period of the early 1800s. Loder is the smooth, crafty, Robespierre-like prefect of police who tries to catch the crusading count, Kosleck. As a diversionary tactic, to throw Loder off the scent of his prey, Aubert takes up the sword. In masculine attire (encased in tights, her shapely figure betrays her gender), the countess proves an able substitute for her husband. Loder is fine as the wry and witty villain bent on entrapment, and Kosleck (whose rodent's face was customarily employed to play Josef Goebbels or some other high-ranking Nazi) is surprisingly effective and graceful in a rare heroic role. The salon sets and costumes are well executed and there is action apace. This is generally regarded to be the most prestigious picture to emerge from poverty-row producer PRC. It was the last personal production of that studio's production chief, Fromkess. It made the company more than a million dollars, its biggest grosser ever.

p, Leon Fromkess; d, Edgar G. Ulmer; w, Dorcas Cochran (based on the story "Thanks, God, I'll Take it from Here" by Ulmer and Franz Rosenwald, based on characters created by Alexandre Dumas); ph, Adolph Edward Kull; ed, Douglas Bagier; md, Paul Dessau; art d, Edward C. Jewell; set d, Glenn P. Thompson.

Adventure   **(PR:A   MPAA:NR)**

WIFE OR TWO, A   (1935, Brit.) 63m BL bw

Henry Kendall (*Charles Marlowe*), Nancy Burne (*Margaret Marlowe*), Betty Astell (*Mary Hamilton*), Fred Duprez (*Sam Hickleberry*), Garry Marsh (*George Hamilton*), Ena Grossmith, Wally Patch, Leo Sheffield.

A divorced couple, Kendall and Astell, are remarried to Burne and Marsh, respectively. To please a rich uncle who frowns on divorce they must pretend to still be married to each other. The two couples visit the uncle's cottage, leading to comic results.

p, Herbert Smith; d, P. Maclean Rogers; w, Rogers, Kathleen Butler (based on the play by C.B. Poultney, Roland Daniel).

Comedy   **(PR:A   MPAA:NR)**

WIFE SWAPPERS, THE   (SEE: SWAPPERS, THE, 1970, Brit.)

WIFE TAKES A FLYER, THE   (1942) 86m COL bw (GB: A YANK IN DUTCH)

Joan Bennett (*Anita Woverman*), Franchot Tone (*Christopher Reynolds*), Allyn Joslyn (*Maj. Zellfritz*), Cecil Cunningham (*Countess Oldenburg*), Roger Clark (*Keith*), Lloyd Corrigan (*Thomas Woverman*), Lyle Latell (*Muller*), Georgia Caine (*Mrs. Woverman*), Barbara Brown (*Maria Woverman*), Erskine Sanford (*Jan*), Chester Clute (*Adolphe Bietjelboer*), Hans Conried (*Hendrik Woverman*), Romaine Callender (*Zanten*), Aubrey Mather (*Chief Justice*), William Edmunds (*Gustav*), Curtis Railing (*Mrs. Brandt*), Nora Cecil (*Miss Updike*), Kurt Katch (*Capt. Schmutnick*), Margaret Seddon, Kate MacKenna (*The Twins*), Gordon Richards (*Maj. Wilson*), Fredric Bolton (*Cpl. Heidne*), Lloyd Bridges (*German Sergeant*), Gohr Van Vleck (*Court Attendant*), James Millican, Manart Kippen, Steven Geray, Cy Kendall (*Gestapo*), Erik Rolf (*Gestapo Leader*), Carl Ekberg (*Adolf Hitler*), Bert Roach (*Guldreschts*), Lloyd Whitlock (*Head Waiter*), Collin Blair (*Man*), John Vosper (*German Sergeant*), Hallene Hill, Mary Young (*Old Ladies*), Gertrude W. Hoffman (*Mrs. Gruyson*), Mary Bertrand, Josephine Allen, Belle Johnstone, Nellie Farrell, Phoebe Rudd, Agnes Steel, Stella LeSant, Eleanor Wood, Marie Spingold, Minnie Steel, Lucille Isle, Elsie Bishop (*Women*), Marie Blake (*Frieda*), Henry Zynda, Hugh Beaumont (*Officers*), Joe McGuinn (*Lieutenant*), Wheaton Chambers (*Chaplain*), Vernon Downing, Leslie Denison (*English Officers*), Max Hoffman, Jr, Max Wagner (*Sergeants*), Frank Alten (*German Orderly*), Charles Hamilton, David Newell, Arno Frey, George Turner, William Yetter, Walter Stiritz, Pat Lane, Chris Frank, John Peters (*German Officers*), Henry Victor (*Col. Bosch*).

Tone is a British-based pilot whose plane is downed over Nazi-occupied Holland during WW II. He finds refuge in the home of Bennett, a Dutch woman who is nearing divorce. She passes Tone off as her mentally deranged, but not dangerous, husband. Nazi major Joslyn has been billeted in Bennett's spacious home and the slapstick interactions between Joslyn and Tone comprise the bulk of the film. Tone finally steals a German plane and escapes to England with Bennett. The rude, crude, forced satires of a dangerous enemy enraged some viewers at the time of the film's release. The Nazis were slaughtering noncombatants, and were not to be taken lightly. Ernst Lubitsch's TO BE OR NOT TO BE, released earlier that same year, was a far better film in the same vein. Joslyn's comic characterization is the best thing in this picture.

p, B. P. Schulberg; d, Richard Wallace; w, Gina Kaus, Jay Dratler, Harry Segall (based on a story by Kaus); ph, Franz F. Planer; m, Werner R. Heymann; ed, Gene Havlick; md, M. W. Stoloff; art d, Lionel Banks; cos, Irene.

Comedy   **(PR:A   MPAA:NR)**

WIFE VERSUS SECRETARY½   (1936) 88m MGM bw

Clark Gable (*Van Stanhope*), Jean Harlow (*Helen "Whitey" Wilson*), Myrna Loy (*Linda Stanhope*), May Robson (*Mimi*), Hobart Cavanaugh (*Joe*), James Stewart (*Dave*), George Barbier (*Underwood*), Gilbert Emery (*Simpson*), Margaret Irving (*Edna Wilson*), William Newell (*Tom Wilson*), Marjorie Gateson (*Eve Merritt*), Leonard Carey (*Taggart*), Charles Trowbridge (*Hal Harrington*), John Qualen (*Mr. Jenkins*), Hilda Howe (*Mary Connors*), Mary MacGregor (*Ellen*), Gloria Holden (*Joan Carstairs*), Tommy Dugan (*Finney*), Jack Mulhall (*Howard*), Frank Elliott (*Mr. Barker*), Greta Meyer (*German Cook*), Aileen Pringle (*Mrs. Barker*), Frank Puglia (*Hotel Clerk*), Myra Marsh (*Miss Clark*), Holmes Herbert (*Frawley*), Frederick Burton (*Trent*), Harold Minjir (*Williams*), Maurice Cass (*Bakewell*), Tom Herbert (*Business Man*), Frederick Guy D'Ennery (*Cuban Waiter*), Niles Welch (*Tom Axel*), Richard Hemingway (*Bridegroom*), Paul Ellis (*Raoul*), Tom Rowan (*Battleship*), Edward Le Saint, Helen Shipman (*Bits*), Clay Clement (*Herbert*), Tom Mahoney (*Policeman*), Nena Quartaro (*Telephone Operator*), Charles Irwin (*Information Clerk*), Andre Cheron (*Frenchman*), Eugene Borden (*Ship's Officer*), Hooper Atchley (*Postal Clerk*), Lucille Ward (*Scrub Woman*), Clifford Jones 'Phillip Trent' (*Elevator Boy*).

In lesser hands this might have been a mediocre soap opera, but under Brown's skilled direction and the talents of his cast, WIFE VERSUS SECRETARY is an entertaining, intelligent drama. Gable plays a magazine publisher married to Loy, whom he dearly loves. Because of the hectic nature of his job, Gable must have a secretary available to him at a moment's notice. That job is Harlow's, and although she has a close working relationship with her boss, there is not an iota of romantic interest between the two. Still, Gable's mother, Robson, finds something suspicious about such an arrangement and makes this very clear to Loy. Harlow's boy friend Stewart tries to push her into marriage, but to Harlow the career comes first. The two argue and Stewart breaks up with her. Gable must go on a business trip to Havana, and explains to Loy that he simply cannot bring her along. Loy is hurt by this, and the seed planted in her head by Robson grows into full-blown anger when she finds Harlow has also gone to Cuba. Gable had sent for her because she had some important information regarding his business. After making a successful deal, Harlow and Gable celebrate. Of course Loy is unaware of this, and places a call to her husband when Gable does not call as promised. Harlow answers the telephone–convincing Loy the two are involved–and she decides to legally separate from Gable. Loy wants to forget her sorrows by taking a cruise to Europe, but before the ship leaves port she is confronted by an angry Harlow. Harlow tells Loy how foolish she is being, and if she is not careful she will lose Gable forever. It seems Gable has asked Harlow to accompany him to Bermuda, and she is ready to take him up on the offer. She goes back to the office, where Gable tells her to pick up some new clothes for the trip. Suddenly Loy enters the office, falling into Gable's forgiving arms. Harlow leaves, finding Stewart still waiting for her. The casting on this couldn't be better. Gable and Harlow, in their fifth film appearance together, make this pairing more unusual in the lack of sexual chemistry between them. They definitely have warmth and affection for one another, but in a good natured brother- sister type relationship. It was an unusual partnership for the two, but it worked with complete believability. Loy, as the jealous wife, also makes some intelligent acting choices in creating her character. She makes the role more than a jealous wife, giving her a range of complex, frightened emotions. Loy enjoyed the part, later stating she played the wife as a woman who "had one foot in bed all the time." Stewart, in only his fourth film, makes the most of his lesser role, and enjoyed playing opposite Harlow. In the biography *Everybody's Man* by Jhan Robbins, Stewart recalled: "Clarence Brown, the director, wasn't too pleased by the way I did the smooching. He made us repeat the scene about half a dozen times...I botched it up on purpose. That Jean Harlow sure was a good kisser. I realized that until then I had never been really kissed!" The script, by Krasna, Miller, and Mahin, is packed with witty and realistic dialog. The scene in which Harlow puts an inebriated Gable to bed, played without a hint of sexual play, is a marvelous bit of work that deliberately works against the images of the two stars. Brown's direction is straightforward, moving the story along nicely with an intelligent, respectful feeling for the material and the cast. This clearly was designed by MGM to be a moneymaker, and it was, a reward it richly deserved.

p, Hunt Stromberg; d, Clarence Brown; w, Norman Krasna, Alice Duer Miller, John Lee Mahin (based on the story by Faith Baldwin); ph, Ray June; m, Herbert Stothart; ed, Frank E. Hull; art d, Cedric Gibbons; cos, Adrian.

Drama   **(PR:A   MPAA:NR)**

WIFE WANTED*   (1946) 73m MON bw

Kay Francis (*Carole Raymond*), Paul Cavanagh (*Jeffrey Caldwell*), Robert Shayne (*Bill Tyler*), Veda Ann Borg (*Nola Reed*), Teala Loring (*Mildred Hayes*), John Gallaudet (*Lee Kirby*), Barton Yarborough (*Walter Desmond*), Selmer Jackson (*Lowell Cornell*), Bert Roach (*Arthur Mayfield*), John Hamilton (*Judge*), Jonathan Hale (*Philip Conway*), Anthony Warde (*Man*), Sara Berner (*Agnes*), Will Stanton (*Squint*), Paul Everton (*Toland*), Buddy Gorman (*Newsboy*), Shelby Payne (*Secretary*), Mabel Todd (*Florist*), Tim Ryan (*Bartender*), Barbara Woodell (*Miss Sheldon*), Valerie Ardis (*Nurse*), Wilbur Mack (*Doctor*), Bud Fine (*Cop*), Joe Greene (*Hector*), Maurice Prince, Bob Alden (*Messengers*), Charles Marsh, Claire Meade (*Tenants*), Edgar Hayes, Elaine Lange, George Carleton.

Fading film star Francis plays a fading film star in her last film, a low-budget crime drama about a lonely hearts club used as a front for criminal activities. Of little interest save to diehard Francis fans.

p, Jeffrey Bernerd, Kay Francis; d, Phil Karlson; w, Caryl Coleman, Sidney Sutherland (based on a story by Robert Callahan); ph, Harry Neumann; ed, Richard Curriers, Ace Herman; md, Edward J. Kay; art d, Dave Milton.

Crime   **(PR:A   MPAA:NR)**

WIFEMISTRESS**½   (1979, Ital.) 101m Vides/Quartet c
                                         (MOGLIAMANTE; AKA: LOVER, WIFE)

Laura Antonelli (*Antonia De Angelis*), Marcello Mastroianni (*Luigi De Angelis*), Leonard Mann (*Dr Dario Favella*), Olga Karlatos (*Dottoressa Pagano*), Annie Belle (*Clara*), Gastone Moschin (*Vincenzo*), William Berger (*Count Brandini*), Stefano Patrizi (*Clara's Fiance*), Helen Stollaroff (*Innkeeper*).

Sequestered middle-class housewife Antonelli experiences a social and sexual awakening when her husband, Mastroianni, is threatened with arrest for his political activities and forced to seek asylum with a neighbor. Looking over her absent husband's private papers and tracing his footsteps kindles the frail recluse's interest in his politics, his business activities, and–to her suprise–his philandering. The bosomy Antonelli blossoms, virtually assuming the identity of her departed husband: writer of political tracts, philosopher, rakehell. She engages in casual sexual encounters and begins an affair with Mann, a dedicated young doctor. Closeted in an attic room in the adjacent house, Mastroianni–with a view of his wife's bedroom–turns unwilling voyeur, witnessing Antonelli's sexual peccadiloes. Beautiful muted color photography characterizes this steamy story of a woman's awakening. Antonelli is gorgeous but offers little in the way of acting ability; the talented Mastroianni is wasted in his entirely reactive loneliness.

p, Franco Cristaldi; d, Marco Vicario; w, Rodolfo Sonego; ph, Ennio Guarnieri (Technicolor); m, Armando Trovajoli; ed, Nino Baragli; art d, Mario Garbuglia; cos, Luca Sabatelli.

Drama   **Cas.**   **(PR:O   MPAA:R)**

WIFE'S FAMILY, THE   (SEE: MY WIFE'S FAMILY, 1931, Brit.)

WILBY CONSPIRACY, THE**½   (1975, Brit.) 101m UA c

Sidney Poitier (*Shack Twala*), Michael Caine (*Jim Keogh*), Nicol Williamson (*Maj. Horn*), Prunella Gee (*Rina Van Niekirk, Defending Counsel*), Persis Khambatta (*Dr. Persis Ray*), Saeed Jaffrey (*Dr. Anil Mukerjee, Dentist*), Ryk De Cooyer (*Van Heerden*), Rutger Hauer (*Blaine Van Niekirk*), Joseph De Graf (*Wilby*), Helmut Dantine (*Prosecutor*), Brian Epsom (*Judge*), Abdulla Sunadu (*Headman in Masai Village*), Freddy Achiang (*Shepherd Boy*), Patrick Allen (*District Commissioner*), Archie Duncan (*Gordon*), Peter Pearce (*Highway Policeman*).

In the midst of South Africa's apartheid government Poitier, a political agitator, links up with Caine, an Englishman in trouble with the law. The two are pursued by Williamson, a bigoted cop. He wants them to lead him to De Graf, the head of the black activist movement. The film essentially is a well-done chase picture that says little about the political turmoil raging in South Africa at the time. However, the actors give real life to their characters, which fleshes out the story to some extent. Direction is routine action filmmaking with no originality at all. This manages to be both exciting and flat all at once. Actor Dantine, long absent from films, plays a small part as a prosecutor; he was the picture's executive producer.

p, Martin Baum; d, Ralph Nelson; w, Rod Amateau, Harold Nebenzal (based on the novel by Peter Driscoll); ph, John Coquillon (DeLuxe Color); m, Stanley Myers; ed, Ernest Walter; prod d, Harold Pottle; art d, John Hoesli; set d, Denise Exshaw; cos, Rosemary Burrows; spec eff, Phil Stokes, Kit West; stunts, Robert Simmons; makeup, Freddie Williamson.

Action   **Cas.**   **(PR:C   MPAA:PG)**

WILD AFFAIR, THE**½   (1966, Brit.) 88m Seven
                                         Arts-Bryanston/Goldstone bw

Nancy Kwan (*Marjorie Lee*), Terry-Thomas (*Godfrey Deane*), Jimmy Logan (*Craig*), Bud Flanagan (*Sgt. Bletch*), Gladys Morgan (*Mrs. Tovey*), Betty Marsden (*Mavis Cook*), Paul Whitsun-Jones (*Tiny Hearst*), Donald Churchill (*Andy*), David Sumner (*Ralph*), Joyce Blair (*Monica*), Victor Spinetti (*Quentin*), Bessie Love (*Marjorie's Mother*), Joan Benham (*Assistant*), Bernard Adams (*Bone*), Diane Aubrey (*Jill*), Sheila Bernette (*Tea Trolley Girl*), Sidonie Bond (*Sue Blair*), Patience Collier (*Woman in Travel Agency*), Paul Curran (*Father*), Frank Finlay (*Drunk*), Penny Morrell (*Tart*), Claire Neilsen (*Blonde Assistant*), Fred Stone (*Head Waiter*), Frank Thornton (*Manager*).

Before she settles down in marriage Kwan decides to have one last fling at single flirtation at her office Christmas party. She wears a sexy little dress which gets the desired results. Her boss, Terry-Thomas, and Logan, a sales manager for this cosmetics company, are both suitably impressed. After accepting a dress from Logan, Kwan meets him for lunch in his hotel room but runs when he makes a pass. She goes back to the party, bringing some booze to liven it up a bit. Her fiance Churchill arrives and is promptly booted out. Everyone becomes inebriated and quite physically friendly with one another, much to Kwan's dismay. She sets off the office sprinkler system to cool things down. The crowd's dampened spirits are uplifted when word comes that one worker's wife has just given birth. Kwan makes up with Churchill and leaves the party. A strange, sexy, somewhat interesting comedy though Kwan is all wrong for the lead.

p, Richard L. Patterson; d&w, John Krish (based on the novel *The Last Hours of Sandra Lee* by William Sansom); ph, Arthur Ibbetson; m, Martin Slavin; ed, Russell Lloyd, Norman Savage; md, Slavin; prod d, John Box; art d, Terence Marsh, Wallis Smith.

Comedy   **(PR:O   MPAA:NR)**

WILD AND THE INNOCENT, THE**½   (1959) 84m UNIV c

Audie Murphy (*Yancey*), Joanne Dru (*Marcy Howard*), Gilbert Roland (*Sheriff Paul Bartell*), Jim Backus (*Cecil Forbes, Store Owner*), Sandra Dee (*Rosalie Stocker*), George Mitchell (*Uncle Hawkes*), Peter Breck (*Chip Miller*), Strother Martin (*Ben Stocker*), Wesley Marie Tackitt (*Ma Ransome*), Betty Harford (*Mrs. Forbes*), Mel Leonard (*Pitchman*), Lillian Adams (*Kiri*), Val Benedict (*Richie*), Jim Sheppard, Ed Stroll, John Qualls, Frank Wolff (*Henchmen*), Rosemary Eliot, Barbara Morris, Louise Glenn (*Dancehall Girls*), Stephen Roberts (*Bouncer*), Tammy Windsor (*Townswoman*).

The monastic Murphy plays prodigal when crusty old fur-trapper Mitchell, injured by an angry bear, is forced to send his nephew into town to trade beaver pelts for supplies. Along the way Murphy passes the isolated cabin of Martin, who persuades Murphy to permit his tattered daughter, Dee, to travel with him. The innocents reach the wicked community, where they are befriended by town boss-cum-sheriff Roland, who appears to take an untoward interest in the spruced-up Dee. Naively, Murphy thanks ruffian Roland for finding Dee a job in the local "dance hall." Impressed by painted lady Dru, a "hostess" in the establishment, Murphy begins a romance with her. With the counsel of storekeeper Backus, the light soon dawns, and Murphy races to the rescue of Dee, preventing her despoilation. Unusually light on gunplay, this comic western wanders aimlessly. Murphy seems a little long in the tooth to be playing so juvenile a role.

p, Sy Gomberg; d, Jack Sher; w, Gomberg, Sher (based on a story by Gomberg); ph, Harold Lipstein (CinemaScope, Eastmancolor); m, Hans J. Salter; ed, George Gittens; md, Joseph Gershenson; art d, Alexander Golitzen, Robert Clatworthy; m/l "A Touch of Pink," Diane Lampert, Richard Loring (sung by Audie Murphy).

Comedy/Western   **(PR:C MPAA:G)**

WILD AND THE SWEET, THE   (SEE: LOVIN' MOLLY, 1974)

WILD AND THE WILLING, THE
                  (SEE: YOUNG AND WILLING, 1962, Brit.)

WILD AND WILLING   (SEE: RAT FINK, 1965)

WILD AND WONDERFUL**½   (1964) 88m UNIV c

Tony Curtis (*Terry Williams*), Christine Kaufmann (*Giselle Ponchon*), Larry Storch (*Rufus Gibbs*), Pierre Olaf (*Jacquot*), Mary Ingels (*Doc Bailey*), Jacques Aubuchon (*Papa Ponchon, Giselle's Father*), Sarah Marshall (*Pamela*), Marcel Dalio (*Dr. Reynard*), Jules Munshin (*Rousseleau, TV Director*), Marcel Hillaire (*Inspector Duvivier*), Cliff Osmond (*Hercule, Giselle's Uncle*), Fifi D'Orsay (*Simone*), Vito Scotti (*Andre*), Steven Geray (*Bartender*), Stanley Adams (*Mayor of Man La Loquet*), Monsieur Cognac (*The Poodle*), Shelly Manne, Paul Horn (*Musicians*), Maurice Marsac (*Announcer*), Guy De Vestel (*Gustav*), Louis Mercier (*Le Beque, The Policeman*), Danica d'Hondt (*Monique*), Dante Caesari (*Butler*).

Curtis is an American musician working in Paris. He meets Kaufmann, a film star, after she bumps into him while chasing her runaway poodle Monsieur Cognac. The dog is aptly named, for he loves liquor. So does Curtis, and the two end up going on a drinking spree! Kaufmann and her father Aubuchon find the two together. She falls in love with Curtis and they marry despite Aubuchon's objections. Monsieur Cognac has some objections of his own, becoming quite jealous of Curtis and destroying the wedding night. Kaufmann cannot give up the dog for the honeymoon, which causes the two humans to separate. Curtis saves his marriage, though, by finding Pink Poupee, a lady poodle that sets Monsieur Cognac's tail wagging. He and Kaufmann make up and all ends happily for both couples. This is an amiable comedy with enough cute elements to overcome the one-joke aspects of the screenplay. It's fun in its own way and of course the dog ends up stealing the show. Surprisingly, it took three writers to come up with the screenplay from a screen story by two others. Rather than shoot this in Paris, the producer decided to recreate Montmartre on the studio backlot. Curtis and Kaufmann–married in real life at the time–play well together. The scintillating score was composer Stevens' first.

p, Harold Hecht; d, Michael Anderson; w, Larry Markes, Michael Morris, Waldo Salt (screen story by Richard M. Powell, Phillip Rapp, based on an unpublished short story by Dorothy Crider); ph, Joseph LaShelle (Eastmancolor); m, Morton Stevens; ed, Gene Milford; art d, Alexander Golitzen, Edward S. Haworth; set d, Ruby Levitt; cos, Rosemary Odell; makeup, Bud Westmore; spec eff, Whitey McMahon; poodle trainer, Frank Weatherwax.

Comedy   **(PR:A MPAA:NR)**

WILD AND WOOLLY**½   (1937) 65m FOX bw

Jane Withers (*Arnette Flynn*), Walter Brennan (*Gramp Flynn*), Pauline Moore (*Ruth Morris*), Carl "Alfalfa" Switzer (*Zero*), Jack Searl (*Chaunce*), Berton Churchill (*Edward Ralston*), Douglas Fowley (*Blackie Morgan*), Robert Wilcox (*Frank Bailey, Editor*), Douglas Scott (*Leon Wakefield*), Lon Chaney, Jr (*Dutch*), Frank Melton (*Barton Henshaw*), Syd Saylor (*Lutz*).

A solidly cast Withers vehicle which overcomes its average scripting by its enjoyable characterizations. Brennan is Withers' granddad, the town's former sheriff and diehard enemy of local banker Churchill. Withers and a 6-year-old Switzer ("Alfalfa" of The Little Rascals) uncover a plot to stage a bank robbery during the town's 50th-anniversary celebration. The children warn Brennan, who gains the townspeople's respect by foiling the heist.

p, John Stone; d, Albert Werker; w, Lynn Root, Frank Fenton; ph, Harry Jackson; ed, Al De Gaetano; md, Samuel Kaylin; art d, Lewis Creber; m/l Sidney Clare, Harry Akst.

Western/Comedy   **Cas.**   **(PR:A MPAA:NR)**

WILD ANGELS, THE**   (1966) 83m AIP c

Peter Fonda (*Heavenly Blues*), Nancy Sinatra (*Mike*), Bruce Dern (*Loser [Joey Kerns]*), Lou Procopio (*Joint*), Coby Denton (*Bull Puckey*), Marc Cavell (*Frankenstein*), Buck Taylor (*Dear John*), Norman Alden (*Medic*), Michael J. Pollard (*Pigmy*), Diane Ladd (*Gaysh*), Joan Shawlee (*Mama Monahan*), Gayle Hunnicutt (*Suzie*), Art Baker (*Thomas*), Frank Maxwell (*Preacher*), Frank Gerstle (*Hospital Policeman*), Kim Hamilton (*Nurse*), Members of the Hell's Angels of Venice, California (*Themselves*), Peter Bogdanovich.

The first of the wave of biker movies that hit American screens in the latter half of the 1960s, starring soon-to-be cult hero Peter Fonda as the leader of a leather-clad biker gang. When one of the cyclists, Dern, gets injured and hospitalized Fonda and company kidnap him from his hospital bed. They toss the hospital up for grabs, rape a black nurse, and carry Dern back to their turf. He dies on the way, however, so they stage a funeral service for him in a local church, binding up the minister and carrying on a festive, drunken, drugged-out orgy. Their decadent life style is opposed by local townspeople who break up Dern's funeral procession, and are then aided by the police in stopping the bikers. Fonda's friends ride off, but their leader remains behind mumbling that there's nowhere to go. An excessively violent and brutal picture, THE WILD ANGELS became one of AIP's most successful films, grossing some $25,000,000 (on a production budget of $350,000) and drew almost exclusively negative response from the critics. A documentary feel pervades the screen in this expose of the country's direction towards nihilism. Audiences for the first time were able to see how outlaw bikers led their lives, making Marlon Brando's characterization in THE WILD ONES (1954) seem pure fiction. More accurately defining the sub-culture in that picture was Lee Marvin's vile, brutal hoodlum, replicated here by actual members of the Hells Angels bike club (nearly all of whom were wanted by the police during the shooting of the film, resulting in some subtle diplomacy on Corman's part). George Chakiris had originally been slated for the lead role and Fonda for the role of "Loser" (dead for nearly the entire film, Loser wasn't much of a part), but when Corman discover that Chakiris couldn't ride a motorcycle Fonda took top billing. Fonda also made a few changes (though his added acting responsibility was not met with a pay increase–he received the same $10,000 he would have been paid playing a corpse) in the lead role, starting with the character's name. "Heavenly Blues," a 1960s name if there ever was one, was a reference to a cheap high one got from crushing up flower seeds, though Fonda consented to Sinatra calling him "Henry" (?!) if she desired. Changes were also made in the script by Peter Bogdanovich, who was called in to rewrite Griffith's first-draft while also acting as Corman's assistant and playing a small role. Besides the familiar names of Michael J. Pollard (BONNIE AND CLYDE), Dern, and Diane Ladd, the editor of THE WILD ANGELS was director Monte Hellman, who later turned out the superb TWO-LANE BLACKTOP. Interestingly, European reception to the WILD ANGELS was more accepting than that of U.S. audiences and turned Corman into something of an artist in their eyes. They seemed more tolerant of and enthralled with the decadent side of America and invited Corman to bring the picture to the Venice Film Festival–making it the only U.S. picture that year to receive such an honor. Includes the song "Blue Theme" by The Arrows, which received a generous amount of airplay.

p&d, Roger Corman; w, Charles Griffith; ph, Richard Moore (Panavision, Pathe Color); m, Mike Curb; ed, Monte Hellman; prod d, Rick Beck-Myer; art d, Leon Erickson; makeup, Jack Obringer.; (PR:O MPAA:NR)

Drama/Action

WILD ARCTIC   (SEE: SAVAGE WILD, THE, 1970)

WILD BEAUTY**   (1946) 61m UNIV bw

Don Porter (*Dave Morrow*), Lois Collier (*Linda Gibson*), Jacqueline de Wit (*Sissy*), George Cleveland (*Barney*), Robert Wilcox (*Gordon Madison*), Robert "Buzzy" Henry (*Johnny*), Dick Curtis (*John Andrews*), Eva Puig (*Winnie*), Pierce Lyden (*Roy*), Roy Brent (*Gus*), Isabel Withers (*Mrs. Anderson*), Hank Patterson (*Ed*), Wild Beauty the Horse.

An Indian boy, Henry, and the title horse are befriended by a kindly doctor who saves the horse from having his hide skinned for profit. They foil the attempts of an unscrupulous capitalist who is killing off herds in order to build up his shoe manufacturing empire.

p&d, Wallace W. Fox; w, Adele Buffington; ph, Maury Gertsman; ed, Patrick Kelly; art d, Jack Otterson, Abraham Grossman.

Western Drama   **(PR:A MPAA:NR)**

WILD BILL HICKOK RIDES**   (1942) 81m WB bw

Constance Bennett (*Belle Andrews*), Bruce Cabot (*Wild Bill Hickok*), Warren William (*Harry Farrel*), Betty Brewer (*Janey Nolan*), Walter Catlett (*Sylvester Twigg*), Ward Bond (*Sheriff Edmunds*), Howard da Silva (*Ringo*), Frank Wilcox (*Martin*), Faye Emerson (*Peg*), Julie Bishop (*Violet*), Lucia Carroll (*Flora*), Russell Simpson (*Ned Nolan*), J. Farrell MacDonald (*Judge Hathaway*), Lillian Yarbo (*Daisy*), Cliff Clark (*Vic Kersey*), Trevor Bardette (*Sam Bass*), Elliott Sullivan (*Bart Hanna*), Dick Botiller (*Sager*), Ray Teal (*Jack Hanley*), Joseph Crehan (*Ray Trent*), Land Commissioner, Francis MacDonald, Paul E. Burns, Sarah Padden, Charles B. Middleton.

Cabot takes the title role of the legendary western character and helps homesteaders repel the greedy tactics of the villainous William and Bond. He has an easy time of it, leaving himself enough energy to romance Bennett, a tough dance-hall queen. Bennett, oddly miscast, does get to recite some great dialog, especially in a confrontation with the malicious William when she promises to "beat your brains out with the leg of a chair." Keep this woman away from the furniture.

p, Edmund Grainger; d, Ray Enright; w, Charles Grayson, Paul Gerald Smith, Raymond L. Schrock; ph, Ted McCord; m, Howard Jackson; ed, Clarence Kolster; spec eff, Byron Haskin, Willard Van Enger; ch, Matty King.

Western   (PR:A   MPAA:NR)

WILD BLUE YONDER, THE***
(1952) 98m REP bw (GB: THUNDER ACROSS THE PACIFIC)

Wendell Corey (*Capt. Harold Calvert*), Vera Ralston (*Lt. Helen Landers*), Forrest Tucker (*Maj. Tom West*), Phil Harris (*Sgt. Hank Stack*), Walter Brennan (*Maj. Gen. Wolfe*), William Ching (*Lt. Ted Cranshaw*), Ruth Donnelly (*Maj. Ida Winton*), Harry Carey, Jr (*Sgt. Shaker Schuker*), Penny Edwards (*Connie Hudson*), Wally Cassell (*Sgt. Pulaski*), James Brown (*Sgt. Pop Davis*), Richard Erdman (*Cpl. Frenchy*), Philip Pine (*Sgt. Tony*), Martin Kilburn (*Peanuts*), Hal Baylor (*Sgt. Eric Nelson*), Joe Brown, Jr (*Sgt. O'Hara*), Jack Kelly (*Lt. Jessup*), Bob Beban (*Sgt. Barney Killion*), Peter Coe (*Sgt. Pollio*), Hall Bartlett (*Lt. Jorman*), William Witney (*Gen. Curtis E. LeMay*), David Sharpe (*Sgt. "Red" Irwin*), Paul Livermore (*Sgt. Harker*), Jay Silverheels (*Benders*), Glen Vernon (*Crew Man*), Joel Allen (*Chaplain Goodrich*), Don Garner (*George*), Gayle Kellogg (*Pilot*), Gil Herman, Freeman Lusk, Reed Hadley (*Commanding Officers*), Richard Avonde (*Joe Wurtzel*), Robert Karnes (*Copilot*), Kathleen Freeman (*Nurse Baxter*), Jim Leighton, Ray Hyke (*Lieutenants*), John Hart, Paul McGuire, Robert Kent (*Generals*), Amy Iwanabe (*Tokyo Rose's Voice*), Andy Brennan (*Orderly*), Bob Morgan (*Engineer Schiller*), Steve Wayne (*Sergeant*), Stann Holbrook (*Bombardier*), Jack Sherman, Myron Healey (*Tower Voices*).

The B-29 Superfortress taking to the sky is the main reason behind this WW II picture starring Corey and Tucker as a pair of Army Air Corps officers assigned to bomb a South Pacific target. On the ground each tries to get Army nurse Ralston interested in him, but in the air their sights are set on the war. Tucker's nerves weaken before takeoff and it appears as if he won't fly with Corey. He finally does and the mission is a success, but he is wounded and dies upon the plane's return, leaving Corey to get the girl. Phil Harris sings "The Thing," Bill Ching delivers "The Man Behind the Armor-Plated Desk," with "The U.S. Air Force" and "The Heavy Bomber Song" tossed in for good patriotic measure. The studio had high hopes for this relatively high-budget picture with its many top-grade players. Studio head Yates personally produced and, as usual, cast his girl friend (later his wife), Ralston, in the lead. Sadly, the public failed to buy the formula plot.

p, Herbert J. Yates; d, Allan Dwan, w, Richard Tregaskis (based on the story by Andrew Geer, Charles Grayson); ph, Reggie Lanning; m, Victor Young; ed, Richard L. Van Enger; art d, James Sullivan; set d, John McCarthy, Jr., Charles Thompson; cos, Adele Palmer; spec eff, Ellis F. Thackery, Howard Lydecker, Theodore Lydecker; m/l, Robert Crawford, Young, Ned Washington, Dwan, Charles R. Green.

War Drama   (PR:A   MPAA:NR)

WILD BOY**   (1934, Brit.) 85m Gainsborough/GAU-British bw

Sonnie Hale (*Billy Grosvenor*), Mick the Miller (*Wild Boy*), Gwynneth Lloyd (*Maggie Warren*), Bud Flanagan, Chesney Allen (*Bookmakers*), Lyn Harding (*Redfern*), Leonora Corbett (*Gladys*), Ronald Squire (*Rollo*), Fred Kitchen (*Plumber*), Arthur Sinclair (*Murphy*), Cyril Smith (*Kennel Boy*).

Hale is a secretary at a greyhound track who works for the unscrupulous Harding. He uncovers some crooked dealings and ensures that dog owner Lloyd and her greyhound Mick the Miller get a fair shake at winning the Greyhound Derby. Of course, Mick takes first prize and Harding's criminal activities are justly dealt with.

p, Michael Balcon; d, Albert de Courville; w, Stafford Dickens (based on a story by de Courville, J.E. Bradford).

Sports Drama   (PR:A   MPAA:NR)

WILD BOYS OF THE ROAD*****   (1933) 77m WB-FN bw (GB: DANGEROUS AGE)

Frankie Darro (*Eddie Smith*), Dorothy Coonan (*Sally*), Edwin Phillips (*Tommy*), Rochelle Hudson (*Grace*), Ann Hovey (*Lola*), Arthur Hohl (*Dr. Heckel*), Grant Mitchell (*Mr. Smith*), Claire McDowell (*Mrs. Smith*), Sterling Holloway (*Ollie*), Charles Grapewin (*Mr. Cadmust*), Robert Barrat (*Judge White*), Ward Bond (*Red*), Adrian Morris (*Buggie Maylin*), Shirley Dunstead (*Harriet*), Minna Gombell (*Aunt Carrie*), Willard Robertson (*Captain of Detectives*).

Viewed both for its historical and entertainment value, WILD BOYS OF THE ROAD is a marvelous slice of Americana which now serves as a memory of the social confusion of the Depression Era. The film's two chief characters, Darro and Phillips, are California youths accustomed to a pleasant picket-fence life style living under the safety of their parents' roofs, surviving comfortably on their fathers' incomes. The Depression hits hard, however, and when their fathers lose their jobs, the boys decide to hop a freight train to Chicago to find work. They soon find that there are others just like themselves, hundreds, perhaps thousands, all looking for work, all hoping to fight the plague of economic depression that is destroying the country. Darro and Phillips not only find a number of other "wild boys" but also Coonan and Hudson, tough girls who take to the rails with them. Along the way, this moving city of innocent, naive vagrants, becomes a pack of outlaws when they kill a brakeman. It is first believed that the murder is politically and socially motivated, but it is then revealed that the brakeman earlier raped Hudson. The kids are finally forced off the tracks in Ohio, forming their own "sewer city," constructed from sewer pipes and supplies--

a city founded on new ideals and a commitment to equality. Their city, however, breeds theft in the nearby community, prompting the police and fire department to, literally, wash away the vagrants with fire hoses. They are opposed by hundreds of rock-throwing youths, but the opposition isn't strong enough to defeat the authorities. It turns out to be a benevolent authority, however, with one of the firemen admitting, "This is a rotten trick," as the city and vagrants alike are battered by the rushing water. His coworker responds, "How do you think I feel, with two kids of my own," as if his role as a father somehow absolves him of the guilt of his duty. The gang moves on, suffering through constant hardships, lack of money, lack of food, and a disastrous accident in which one of them loses a leg under the wheels of a train. By time they arrive in New York, Darro, Phillips, and Coonan have been almost completely broken in spirit, no longer looking for the sort of comfortable living they had in California, but merely trying to stay alive. They get involved in a theft ring, get arrested, and are hauled off to court. Coming before the judge, who sits proudly under the blue eagle of the National Recovery Administration, the young thieves are given the customary lecture. This one, however, smacks of Franklin Roosevelt's New Deal ideology: "Things are going to get better all over the country..." the judge confidently informs them, as if speaking directly for the President. "I know your father will be going back to work soon." Blasted by countless critics for its political stance, WILD BOYS OF THE ROAD, if naive politically, is still a superb entertainment which illustrates the plight of these Depression-Era youngsters in a socio-realistic approach. Andrew Bergman, author of *We're in the Money*, a study of Depression-Era America through its films, discusses the role of this "topical" genre: "The topicals were rooted in a longing for the old verities about work and success, but it seems pointless to blame them for lacking a 'constructive programme.' Films can help influence consciousness by depicting lifestyles or by dramatically revealing social inequities. They can present radically different models of behavior with greater skill than they can possibly present anything like a 'program.'" In WILD BOYS OF THE ROAD, rather than try to solve the problem of these "wild boys," Wellman simply presents the problem. It is not his job, but the politician's and social reformer's, to fix what is broken. Today, WILD BOYS OF THE ROAD presents with amazing accuracy the feeling of emptiness and apparent hopelessness that ran rampant in the country. Coming off the failure of his previous HEROES FOR SALE (a film too embarrassingly naive and narratively confused to be of any importance, except as a precursor to this picture), Wellman tackled a straightforward "road movie" structure and applied the simplest of New Deal ideas to it. For one to see WILD BOYS OF THE ROAD as the classic that it is, it must be viewed in a historical time frame. Wellman, like everyone else at the time, was in the middle of the Depression and simply doing his best to present a social condibtion. The chief problem with the film is its refusal to lay the blame for the Depression at anyone's feet. In Wellman's world there is a benevolent authority--no one means anyone any harm--and even the vagrants brought before the judge are let off the hook because they are just kids who don't really know any better. The feeling at the film's end, though technically a happy ending, is rather mindless, leaving the audience with a "don't worry everything will be fine" promise. Despite these faults, WILD BOYS OF THE ROAD is one of the finest films about youthful idealism to hit the screen. Costing $203,000 to produce, the film had only minimal success at the box office, though it has become more highly regarded with time. Cast as the comely, tomboyish freight-hopper is Coonan, Wellman's fourth and final wife. Looking like a doppelganger of the Louise Brooks freight-hopper in Wellman's 1928 BEGGARS OF LIFE, Coonan dons mens clothing and a cap but still manages to appear as feminine as if in formal wear. Besides the superb Coonan, the film is peopled with numerous teens, most of whom were, before and after the film, unknowns, adding to the authenticity of the film's atmosphere. The standout among the cast, however, is the pint- sized Darro who, throughout the entire picture, seems like a pack of dynamite ready to explode. This energy finally does burst forth in one of the most phenomenal scenes ever committed to celluloid as Darro turns himself upside-down and while standing on his head begins to spin around on the pavement, like a tornado ready to destroy anything in its path. It was scenes like this, combined with his tough punk image, that turned Darro, the son of circus aerialists (where he probably learned his great head- spinning display), into the foremost Depression-Era tough kid of the screen.

p, Robert Presnell; d, William A. Wellman; w, Earl Baldwin (based on the story "Desperate Youth" by Daniel Ahearn); ph, Arthur Todd; ed, Thomas Pratt; art d, Esdras Hartley; makeup, Perc Westmore.

Drama   (PR:A-C   MPAA:NR)

WILD BRIAN KENT*½   (1936) 60m FOX bw

Ralph Bellamy (*Brian Kent*), Mae Clarke (*Betty Prentice*), Helen Lowell (*Sue Prentice*), Stanley Andrews (*Tony Baxter*), Lew Kelly (*Bill Harris*), Eddie Chandler (*Jed*), Richard Alexander (*Phil Hanson*), Jack Duffy (*Old Timer*), Howard Hickman.

Bellamy takes the title role in this below-average programmer about a polo-playing leech who talks himself into living on Lowell's farm along with her daughter Clarke. Bellamy soon gets in the middle of their struggles to keep realtor Andrews from taking away their property. Bellamy proves himself to be more than merely a cad by preventing a fire from destroying the farm, thereby winning Clarke's hand.

p, Sol Lesser; d, Howard Bretherton; w, Earle Snell, Don Swift, James Gruen (based on the novel *The Re-Creation of Brian Kent* by Harold Bell Wright); ph, Harry Neuman; ed, Robert Crandall.

Drama/Western   **(PR:A   MPAA:NR)**

WILD BUNCH, THE*****   (1969) 143m WB c

William Holden *(Pike Bishop)*, Ernest Borgnine *(Dutch Engstrom)*, Robert Ryan *(Deke Thornton)*, Edmond O'Brien *(Sykes)*, Warren Oates *(Lyle Gorch)*, Jaime Sanchez *(Angel)*, Ben Johnson *(Tector Gorch)*, Emilio Fernandez *(Mapache)*, Strother Martin *(Coffer)*, L.Q. Jones *(T.C.)*, Albert Dekker *(Pat Harrigan)*, Bo Hopkins *(Crazy Lee)*, Dub Taylor *(Mayor Wainscoat)*, Jorge Russek *(Lt. Zamorra)*, Alfonso Arau *(Herrera)*, Chano Urueta *(Don Jose)*, Sonia Amelio *(Teresa)*, Aurora Clavel *(Aurora)*, Elsa Cardenas *(Elsa)*, Fernando Wagner *(German Army Officer)*, Paul Harper, Constance White, Lilia Richards.

A landmark film in many respects, Sam Peckinpah's THE WILD BUNCH became controversial not only because of its extreme, now legendary, slow-motion violence, but also because of the war started between the producer, Phil Feldman, and the director. As with the majority of Peckinpah's work, the studios and producers hacked the film apart to suit their needs (length, controversy, to prove their power over the ever-difficult Peckinpah) and distributed a vastly different film from the one the director had originally presented. The hatchet job on THE WILD BUNCH occurred when Peckinpah was on vacation in Hawaii, *after* his film had been shown *uncut* to reviewers on the East Coast (critic Vincent Canby displayed dismay when he went to see the film again and discovered scenes missing, but his protests were dismissed by Feldman who declared that if he, Canby, hadn't seen the missing scenes he wouldn't have missed them–a stunning piece of logic). Adverse reaction to the film did not spur Feldman to make the cuts (all the trimmed scenes contained important motivational information vital to the portrayals of the main characters, especially Holden's–none of them was particularly violent), but instead were made to bring the film's running time down to two hours so that theater owners would be able to cram in another show and sell more popcorn. The film takes place in Texas, 1913, as progress, old age, and the onset of WW I are killing off the Old West and its outlaws. As children sit on the outskirts of the small town of San Rafael and play a game where hundreds of red ants consume a scorpion, a group of men dressed as American soldiers ride by. The men enter the town and visit the bank. Before the clerk has a chance to ask what it is that the men want, their leader, Holden, pulls him out of his chair and pushes the man across the room. The rest of the "soldiers" brandish their weapons on the patrons inside. Holden glances around to make sure all is secure. It is. He utters a simple, deadly command, "If they move...kill 'em." The soldiers are in fact bank robbers. Borgnine, Oates, Hopkins, and Sanchez are dressed as cavalry, the rest of the gang is positioned throughout the town on lookout for anything suspicious. Once the dozens of heavy canvas bags filled with gold have been nestled away, the bunch prepare to leave. They stop dead in their tracks when Sanchez observes three rifles on the rooftop across the street. Members of the bunch stationed outside have noticed them as well and it becomes apparent to all that they have become trapped in an ambush. Holden quickly decides to make a run for it, and uses a temperance union that has begun marching down the middle of the street for cover. As a brief diversion, Holden kicks the bank manager out of the building and he is immediately blasted to bits by the overzealous bounty hunters. A horrible gunfight ensues between the bunch and the bounty hunters, with innocent men, women, and children taking most of the bullets. During the battle Holden sees that one of the posse is Ryan, an old friend. Ryan raises his rifle to shoot Holden. Holden draws his pistol. Both men lose their nerve and aim for targets nearby, sparing each other's lives. After losing several men in the battle, Holden is able to gather his forces and escape. Those left of the bunch, Borgnine, brothers Oates and Johnson, and Sanchez ride to their hideout in Mexico where the grizzled old desert rat O'Brien waits with fresh horses. When the bunch cut open their loot, they are shocked to find out that the canvas bags are filled with worthless metal washers. This nearly collapses the delicate balance of the group, with Holden's judgment seriously questioned by Oates and Johnson. Realizing that the whole thing was a setup by Holden's arch-enemy Dekker, a railroad baron, the leader of the bunch informs his old friend O'Brien that Ryan was among the bounty hunters who participated. O'Brien is surprised and saddened by the news–the three used to ride together–and the men decide to travel to Sanchez's village for a rest. Meanwhile, Ryan argues with Dekker about the ill-planned ambush that resulted in many civilian deaths. Bemoaning the fact that he is saddled with worthless, trigger-happy morons (the sleazy bounty hunters are picking over the corpses like vultures) Ryan demands better men. Dekker, delighting in the power he holds over Ryan (he got Ryan out of prison to help track Holden), gleefully informs the man that he must make do with what he has, and informs the other men that if any of them try to get away (with special emphasis on Ryan) he'll pay a ransom to the man who kills him. With that, the bounty hunters take off after the bunch. In Sanchez's village the bunch are treated with a wary respect by the locals. The village elder, Urueta, tells them that Mexico is in the throes of a civil war. Recently a ruthless army general, Fernandez, invaded the village, killed all the young men, and made off with Sanchez's girl friend, who went with them willingly. Sanchez wants to ride off and retrieve his girl, but Holden forbids it. The next day the bunch ride out of the village, having gained the respect of the people, who look upon them as saviors who will deliver them from the hands of Fernandez, though the bunch them-

selves are a bit confused by the adoration. Feeling pressure from Ryan's posse, the bunch decide to visit Fernandez's compound because the bounty hunters wouldn't dare follow. Suddenly a horn sounds and the startled outlaws turn to see a bright red automobile, carrying the general through the gate. Most of the men have never seen a car and are both scared and fascinated by it. By chance, Sanchez sees his girl friend happily presenting a pony to Fernandez. Overcome with rage, the impetuous Sanchez shoots his beloved while she is in the arms of Fernandez. This sudden outburst of violence startles everyone and the bunch immediately raise their hands in an effort to avoid annihilation by Fernandez's troops. The trick works and the men are spared, though Sanchez is taken away and beaten. Fernandez, who is being manipulated by a pair of German advisors, asks the bunch inside for a drink. There the Germans propose that the bunch rob a U.S. Army shipment of guns for the general. Once the price is agreed upon, and Sanchez returned to them, the bunch ride off to execute the robbery. The train robbery goes off without a hitch until Ryan, his men, and a trainload of incompetent cavalry soldiers enter the fray. To deal with just such an occurrence, Holden had laced the main bridge across the Rio Grande with a ton of dynamite, blowing Ryan and his men into the river. The haul is a bountiful one, including a machine gun, and Holden agrees to let Sanchez take a few cases of rifles for his people back in the village. Eventually Fernandez learns of this deception and when Sanchez and Borgnine ride into the general's fortress to collect their part of the loot, he has the young Mexican captured and tortured. Obviously outnumbered, Borgnine declares Sanchez a thief and rides back to the bunch where he pleads with them to rescue the boy. The idea is rejected by Holden, but when he sees that Ryan and his men are hot on their trail, and have shot and seriously wounded O'Brien, the leader of the bunch decides to return to Fernandez's stronghold (where a wild celebration over the guns is taking place) and wait it out. When they arrive, the remaining members of the bunch, Holden, Borgnine, Oates, and Johnson, are greeted by the sick sight of Sanchez being dragged around in the dirt, tied to the back of Fernandez's car. Swallowing the urge to shoot it out, the men accept the general's invitation to join the party and they all seek solace in the company of whores, save Borgnine, who waits outside. Disgusted with himself, his life, and the recent turn of events, Holden decides to get it over with. He enters another part of the whorehouse where Oates and Johnson are dickering with a single prostitute over her price. Holden looks Oates right in the eye with a steely determination. "Let's go." he states. Oates looks at his brother, then at Holden, and returns with a confident, "Why not?" The men gather their gear and meet Borgnine outside. Borgnine immediately realizes that a noble decision has been reached and arms himself to the teeth. The four men, laden with every gun they can carry, march across town to the place where Fernandez is holding court with the new machine gun proudly displayed on a table. The drunken soldiers demand to know what they want. Holden calmly states that they want the return of Sanchez. Fernandez smiles and agrees. He walks a near-dead Sanchez over to the men, cuts the bonds that tie his arms, and then sadistically slits the boy's throat. Holden immediately pulls his pistol and shoots Fernandez, as does Borgnine. The drunken troops stagger to their feet and reach for their weapons, but the bunch have actually managed to get the drop on hundreds of men. The silent standoff is almost painful. As the men whirl around, expecting an attack, not a soldier moves so much as a muscle. Johnson and Borgnine laugh at the thought that they might actually get away. Borgnine gives an encouraging smile to Holden, as if trying to convince his partner that they have won. Holden will have none of it. It is time to die. Choosing one of the German advisors as his next target, Holden takes deliberate aim and kills the man. This time, all hell breaks loose and the fortress erupts into an orgy of violence which sees the bunch eventually make their way to the machine gun where they are able to dig in and slaughter hundreds of Fernandez's troops. After a long and brutal fight, the bunch begin to die. First Oates and Johnson, then Holden, shot in the back by a child who can barely carry his gun. Borgnine stumbles to his friend's aid but it is too late. He, too, is gunned down and the men die side by side, Holden's hand still clutching the trigger of the machine gun. With Fernandez's troops wiped out, Ryan and his bounty hunters ride into town and begin to pick over the bodies with glee. Ryan looks sadly upon the corpse of his fallen friend, wishing that he went down in battle as well, rather than selling out to the railroad. While his men are grabbing rifles and boots, Ryan claims one trophy for himself, Holden's pistol. Hours later, with the remnants of the town leaving with what they can carry, Ryan tells his men he does not intend to return to the States with them. They shrug it off and ride into the distance with the wild bunch face down over their saddles. Ryan sits alone, listening to the dusty wind. In the distance a brief gunfight is heard and Ryan smiles with the knowledge that his charges didn't get very far. Moments later O'Brien, the elder from Sanchez's village, and a few other men armed with the guns Holden gave them ride up. O'Brien tells Ryan, "Me and the boys here got a job to do. Wanna come along? It ain't like it used to be, but it'll do." Ryan chuckles, mounts his horse, and rides off with O'Brien and his men. While THE WILD BUNCH is an incredibly violent film, it is also an honest one. Peckinpah's characters are bad, brutal men and no effort is made to soften their crimes. What separates them from the bounty hunters, Dekker, the railroad man, and "civilized" society is their sense of honor and commitment to themselves. Holden's character, Pike, is not just a mindless killer, he is an insecure man saddled with a mighty reputation, but wracked with doubt and self-loathing. Holden is getting old and making bad, thoughtless decisions that jeopardize the lives of those he is closest to. It is here that the mindless cuts by producer

Feldman hurt the most. Nearly every scene excised deals with Holden's guilt over his leadership (and all have finally been restored to the film via a new videotape release). The first scene details how Ryan was captured by the law and shows that it was an overconfident Holden's fault. While Ryan is hauled off to jail, it is Holden who escapes. The second scene is a brief exchange where O'Brien reveals that Hopkins (whom Holden had forgotten about and left to die in the opening massacre) was his grandson. The old man asks if the boy had served the bunch well, and a nervous Holden states that the kid did "Just fine." The third missing scene shows the origin of Holden's painful leg wound. When he was younger, Holden was having an affair with a married woman whose husband had left town for good. Holden had loved the woman, but his thoughtless disappearances put a strain on the relationship. One night, while they prepared to make love, the woman's husband returned, killed her, and wounded Holden. Holden was unable to shoot back and the man escaped with his life. These scenes are essential ingredients to Holden's motivation and subsequent actions. Holden feels as if he had ruined everything that was good in his life (his friendship with Ryan, the love of a woman) and the fiasco at San Rafael (where he thoughtlessly left one of his men behind) tends to confirm his failure. By accepting Fernandez' assignment, Holden has one last chance to redeem himself in the eyes of his men and to himself, and the train robbery is pulled off beautifully, but once again bad decisions cause the deaths of people close to him (Sanchez's capture and torture, O'Brien's apparently fatal wound). As the film reaches its climax, Holden has finally decided that the only way to redeem himself is to live up to his preachments on solidarity and friendship and sacrifice his life for an honorable cause–he had been dead for years anyway. The rest of the bunch sense that they can no longer exist in this brave new world of automobiles, machine guns, and airplanes, and they, too, willingly join the final battle. Without these flashbacks showing the events that have brought Holden to this place, his character is a meaningless monster, hell-bent on destruction. Other cuts by Feldman contributed to the perception that the film was filled with disgusting characters and mindless violence. Two important scenes which enlighten the Fernandez character were also excised. The first is a large battle scene (with little blood) showing the general and his troops besieged by Pancho Villa at a train station while awaiting word that Holden and his men have obtained the guns. Standing on the train tracks while his men are dying around him, a nervous Fernandez suppresses his urge to flee for the sake of a young boy who admires him. Not wanting to shatter the boy's illusions, Fernandez stands his ground and bravely salutes the little soldier and then together they slowly march to the safety of the train. The second scene shows a brief aftermath to the battle with Villa where a concerned Fernandez watches intently as the wounds of his soldiers are tended to. One of his men states, "With the new guns, this wouldn't have happened." Both these scenes show Fernandez as more than a cruel, heartless monster. He is vicious and brutal, but only to those who threaten his people. The general is shown to have a genuine concern for his men and their families, but with these scenes missing he appears to be a drunken buffoon unworthy of pity, respect, or understanding. Feldman's other cut is fairly minor, a bit of dancing by the bunch in Sanchez's village, but this, too, shows a more human side to the characters that is missing from the butchered version. Peckinpah never softens his perspective on these men–they are killers and thieves–but they are also human. They have wants and desires, they make mistakes, but they are also alive and vital. The difference between Peckinpah and other western directors is perfectly illustrated when THE WILD BUNCH is compared to a much safer film like BUTCH CASSIDY AND THE SUNDANCE KID, which was released the same year. While the latter is a marvelously well-made and entertaining western, it bathes its outlaw characters in a pleasant, romantic light. Butch and Sundance were also robbers, but they are portrayed as two basically likable rogues who happen to rob banks. By casting such appealing movie stars as Newman and Redford, the audience is immediately drawn to these men and will accept anything they do. While the robbers' careers weren't nearly so violent as the thieves in the THE WILD BUNCH are shown to be, George Roy Hill's characters are unabashedly romanticized and they are easy to get close to. By the end of the film, when the jig is up and they have to answer for their crimes, the film freeze-frames on their heroic faces, propelling them into movie lore unsullied by blood or death. These men have not earned our respect by the end of the film, they were already pristine examples of manhood when the film started. Peckinpah's men are more challenging, and therefore his is the greater artistic achievement. One can't go wrong with Newman and Redford. Holden, Borgnine, Oates, and Johnson are shown as violent killers from the beginning. We see (and through the director's complex visual style at times participate in) the carnage they cause. By the end of the film we have learned that they are honorable men clutching to the past, but finally compelled to enter the myth of the Old West by sacrificing their lives. We see them go down. We feel them die. There is a strange sense of loss. At the end of the film they have earned our respect and their place in legend. The reprise of the bunch's slow exit from Sanchez's home under the closing credits leaves little doubt that the villagers will be singing songs about the bunch to their grandchildren.

p, Phil Feldman; d, Sam Peckinpah; w, Walon Green, Peckingpah (based on a story by Green, Roy N. Sickner); ph, Lucien Ballard (Panavision,Technicolor); m, Jerry Fielding; ed, Louis Lombardo; art d, Edward Carrere; spec eff, Bud Hulburd; makeup, Al Greenway.

Western   Cas.   (PR:O MPAA:R)

WILD CARGO (SEE: WHITE SLAVE SHIP, 1952, Fr./Ital.)
WILD CHILD, THE* (1970, Fr.) 90m Films du Carrosse-Les Productions Artistes A ssocie/UA bw (L'ENFANT SAUVAGE)

Jean-Pierre Cargol (Victor the Boy), Francois Truffaut (Dr. Jean Itard), Jean Daste (Prof. Philippe Pinel), Francoise Seigner (Mme. Guerin), Paul Ville (Remy), Claude Miller (Mons. Lemeri), Annie Miler (Mme. Lemeri), Pierre Fabre (Orderly at Institute), Rene Levert (Police Offical), Jean Mandaroux (Itard's Doctor), Nathan Miler (Lemeri Baby), Mathieu Schiffman (Mathieu), Jean Gruault (Visitor at Institute), Robert Cambourakis, Gitt Magrini, Jean-Francois Stevenin (Peasants), Laura Truffaut, Eva Truffaut, Guillaume Schiffman, Frederique Dolbert, Eric Dolbert, Tounet Cargol, Dominique Levert, Mlle. Theaudiere (Children at Farm).

In the same vein as THE 400 BLOWS (1959) and SMALL CHANGE (1976) THE WILD CHILD is devoted to the perceptual honesty and the education of children. In this case Truffaut has made a clear and basic picture of mythic proportions (in the sense of Romulus and Remus or Tarzan) about the socialization of an orphaned boy discovered in the forest. Bsed on an actual case study published in 1806, THE WILD CHILD stars Cargol as a long-haired nature boy who, apparently abandoned in the woods by his parents years earlier, is placed in the Institute for the Deaf and Dumb in Paris. The boy is ridiculed and looked upon as a perverse outcast and freak by Daste, the professor in charge. Truffaut takes the role of Itard (the real-life professor who raised the boy), a patient, enlightened doctor concerned with the boy's well-being and growth. Instead of having the boy sent to an asylum, Truffaut cares for him in his country home. He teaches the boy (whom he has by now named Victor) how to communicate with the spoken word. In the end Truffaut is forced to inflict an unjust punishment on the child as a test of his moral sense. The boy is driven to tears and runs away, but eventually returns to his optimistic teacher. Truffaut, himself raised in an orphanage, had an affinity for children and expressed this in nearly all his pictures, consistently finding an appropriate role for a child to play. Again, like Victor, Truffaut himself had a teacher in the form of critic and Cahiers du Cinema editor Andre Bazin, who not only brought the delinquent Truffaut off the streets and taught him about film, but practically adopted him. Truffaut in turn offered the same sort of mentorship to Jean-Pierre Leaud, the star of THE 400 BLOWS, who went on to portray Truffaut's alter ego in many more films, most obviously the ANTOINE DOINEL series. THE WILD CHILD feels less like a fiction film than it does a documentary or even more an educational film. It is also a tribute to children–his fictional one, Leaud (to whom he dedicated the picture), and non-fictional ones (his own and those of his friends)–he has cast, in minor roles, his daughters Eva and Laura (named, incidentally, after films by Joseph Losey and Otto Preminger), as well as the children of long-time associate Suzanne Schiffman, prop master Jean-Claude Dolbert, and camera operator Philippe Theaudiere. Cargol, the boy of the title role, was spotted by Truffaut in the South of France and chosen for the role, filmed in summer in order to coincide with his school vacation. Some years before filming THE WILD CHILD (Truffaut had tried since 1962 to bring this story to the screen and had hoped to purchase the rights to the stage version of "The Miracle Worker," which were already owned by Arthur Penn), Truffaut expressed his feelings for children: "Even as a child, I loved children. I have very strong ideas about the world they inhabit. Morally, the child is like a wolf–outside society." In THE WILD CHILD, Truffaut displays this belief over and over again.

p, Marcel Berbeet; d, Francois Truffaut; w, Truffaut, Jean Gruault (based on the journals published by Jean-Marc Gaspard Itard, Memoire et Rapport sur Victor de L'Aveyron); ph, Nestor Almendros; m, Antonio Vivaldi, "Concerto for Mandolin," "Concerto for Flautino," recorder played by Michel Sanvoisin, mandolin by Andre Saint-Clivier; ed Agnes Guillemot; art d, Jean Mandaroux; cos, Gitt Magrini; makeup, Nicole Felix.

Drama   (PR:C-O MPAA:G)
WILD COMPANY*½   (1930) 71m FOX bw

Frank Albertson (Larry Grayson), H. B. Warner (Henry Grayson), Sharon Lynn (Sally), Joyce Compton (Anita), Claire McDowell (Mrs. Grayson), Mildred Van Dorn (Natalie), Richard Keene (Dick), Frances McCoy (Cora), Kenneth Thomson (Joe Hardy), Bela Lugosi (Felix Brown, Nightclub Operator), George Fawcett (Judge).

Pampered by permissive parents, wild Prohibition-era youth Albertson sponges sawbucks from his jewelry store-owning father, Warner, and spends them in a speakeasy mooning over singer Lynn. The songstress is the moll of gangster Thomson, who befriends the befuddled youth and then sets him up to take the blame for a murder he himself committed. Discovering his son's shame, Warner turns the lad over to the police. The trial is held before judge Fawcett, who sternly lectures the delinquent lad, then gives him a suspended sentence. Paroled in Warner's custody, the sobered son decides to sin no more. Every generation has its gap. Young Albertson, in an early starring role, turned into a fine character actor in the H. B. Warner mold. Lugosi, pre-cape and fangs, appears in a minor part. This is one of many flaming-youth films in which the protagonists have a lot of fun before the late-dawning moral message is delivered.

d, Leo McCarey; w, Bradley King (based on a story by King, John Stone); ph, L.W.O'Connell; ed, Clyde Carruth; cos, Sophie Wachner.

Drama   (PR:A MPAA:NR)

WILD COUNTRY*   (1947) 57m PRC bw

Eddie Dean (Himself), Roscoe Ates (Soapy), Peggy Wynn (Martha Devery), Douglas Fowley (Clark Varney), I. Stanford Jolley (Rif Caton), Lee Roberts (Josh Huckings), Forrest Mathews (Sam), Bill [William] Fawcett (Spindle), Henry Hall (Marshal Thayer), Charles Jordan (Brown), Richard Cramer (Guard), Gus Taute (Dilling), The Sunshine Boys, Flash the Horse.

A weak "Giddyupper" with Dean in the role of a U.S. Marshal in pursuit of Jolley, who is wanted for the murder of a sheriff. Dean prevents Jolley from causing trouble when he foils Jolley's plan to kill the late sheriff's daughter, Wynn, and lay claim to her ranch.

p, Jerry Thomas; d, Ray Taylor; w, Arthur E. Orloff; ph, Robert Cline; ed, Hugh Winn; m/l, Eddie Dean, Hal Blair, Pete Gates.

Western   **(PR:A MPAA:NR)**

WILD COUNTRY, THE**½   (1971) 100m Disney/BV c (AKA: THE NEWCOMERS)

Steve Forrest (Jim Tanner), Vera Miles (Kate Tanner), Jack Elam (Thompson), Ronny Howard (Virgil Tanner), Frank De Kova (Two Dog), Morgan Woodward (Ab Cross), Clint Howard (Andrew Tanner), Dub Taylor (Phil), Woodrow Chambliss (Dakota), Karl Swenson (Jenson), Mills Watson (Feathers), RAnce Howard (Cleve), Ben Miller (Shelby), Lawrence Mann (The Mashal).

A standard wilderness family adventure which is given the usual pleasantries by the Disney bunch. The Tanner family members headed by Forrest, leave their Pittsburgh surroundings behind them and set off for the Wyoming ranch that they've purchased. What they find is a dilapidated piece of property inhabited by mountain man Elam and his Indian sidekick De Kova. Forrest learns that a neighboring rancher has refused to allow the use of his water, forcing action to be taken by the Tanner clan. After struggling through a tornado and a fire, Forrest and his family get their water rights by shooting it out with Woodward, the evil cattle rancher. Ronny Howard is the real star of the film as the 15-year-old boy whose rite of passage into manhood is the killing, in defence of his father, of Woodward. One of the finer family wilderness films. A family affair, with Ronny's father Rance and his brother Clint also featured.

p, Ron Miller; d, Robert Totten; w, Calvin Clements, Jr., Paul Savage (based on the novel Little Britches by Ralph Moody); ph, Frank Phillips (Technicolor); m, Robert F. Brunner; ed, Robert Stafford; prod d, Robert Clatworthy; art d, John B. Mansbridge; set d, Emile Kuri, Hal Gausman; cos, Chuck Keehne, Emily Sundby; spec eff, Robert A. Mattey; makeup, Robert J. Schiffer.

Adventure   **(PR:AA MPAA:G)**

WILD DAKOTAS, THE*   (1956) 73m American Releasing bw

Will Williams, Coleen Gray, Jim Davis, John Litel, Dick Jones, John Miljan, Lisa Montell, I. Stanford Jolley, Wally Brown, Bill Dix, Iron Eyes Cody.

A war with the Indians is narrowly averted when a crazed wagonmaster wages a battle on an Indian-held valley. His actions are balked and instead of bloodshed there is peace in the valley.

p, Sigmund Neufeld; d, Sam Newfield; w, Thomas W. Blackburn.

Western   **(PR:A MPAA:NR)**

WILD DRIFTER   (SEE: BORN TO KILL, 1974)

WILD DUCK, THE**½   (1977, Ger./Aust.) 100m Solaris -Sascha-Westdeutscher Rundfunk/New Yorker c (DIE WILDENTE)

Jean Seberg (Gina), Peter Kern (Hjalmar), Bruno Ganz (Gregors), Anne Bennent (Hedwig), Martin Floerchinger (Old Ekdal), Heinz Bennent (Relling), Sonja Sutter (Mrs. Sorby), Robert Werner (Molvik), Guido Wieland (Petersen).

A faithful adaptation of Ibsen's play about the relationships between a mother (Seberg), her egotistical husband (Kern), and their daughter (Bennent) who sacrifices her own life, instead of that of a captive wild duck, to gain her unloving father's approval. Beautifully photographed by Robby Mueller, best known for his work with Wim Wenders. The following year Ganz, here cast as the childhood friend of Kern, and Mueller worked together on Wender's THE AMERICAN FRIEND. (In German; English subtitles.)

p, Bernd Eichinger; d&w, Hans W. Geissendoerfer (based on the play by Henrik Ibsen); ph, Robby Mueller; m, Nils Janette Walen; ed, Jutta Brandstaetter; cos, Edith Almoslino-Assmann, Lambert Hofer.

Drama   **(PR:A MPAA:NR)**

WILD DUCK, THE*½   (1983, Aus.) 96m Orion c

Liv Ullmann (Gina), Jeremy Irons (Harold), Lucinda Jones (Henrietta), John Meillon (Maj. Ackland), Arthur Dignam (Gregory), Michael Pate (George), Colin Croft (Mollison), Rhys McConnochie (Dr. Roland), Marion Edward (Bertha), Peter DeSalis (Peters), Jeff Truman (Johnson).

Nearly 100 years after Henrik Ibsen wrote his poetic and symbolic play "The Wild Duck," French-born Australian director Safran (THE STORM BOY) made the mistake of trying to film it. The story is of a young girl, Jones, whose birth is kept a secret, straining the relationship between Ullmann and Irons. The material is dated, the symbolism heavily laid on, and the performances by Ullmann and Irons are as calculated as can be. A very dull picture which will thrill only those fans who've been thrilled by Irons, Ullmann, and Ibsen in the past.

p, Phillip Emanuel, Basil Appleby; d, Henri Safran; w, Safran, Peter Smalley, John Lind (based on the play by Henrik Ibsen); ph, Peter James; m, Simon Walker; ed, Don Saunders; prod d, Darrell Lass.

Drama   **(PR:C MPAA:PG)**

WILD EYE, THE*½   (1968, Ital.) 91m Cavara/AIP c (L'OCCHIO SELVAGGIO)

Philippe Leroy (Paolo), Delia Boccardo (Barbara Bates), Gabriele Tinti (Valentino), Giorgio Gargiullo (Rossi), Lars Bloch (John Bates), Luciana Angelillo (Mrs. Davis), Gianni Bongioanni (The Hunter), Tullio Marini (Ruggero).

One of a number of films about filmmaking ethics. Documentarist Leroy, with Olympian detachment, photographs the miseries of others, which he has helped to foster. Seducing Bloch's wife Boccardo, he brings her to Bombay, where he films opium addicts undergoing a cure in which they are severely beaten. Finding fewer addicts than he feels the footage requires, Leroy recruits ringers to undergo the torment. Traveling to Bali, he records the denigration of deaf-mute prostitutes. He then unsuccessfully importunes a Buddhist priest to immolate himself for the benefit of his camera. In India, he cajoles a starving old deposed maharajah into eating insects in exchange for some canned goods. Finally fed up with Leroy's callous, impersonal attitude, Boccardo excoriates him for making money from misery. They proceed to Vietnam to film the atrocities of the war. When Leroy learns of Viet Cong plans to bomb a bar, he sets up a hidden camera and seeks safe haven. The bar is blasted, killing most of those inside, and Leroy retrieves his film. When he discovers the lifeless body of Boccardo amidst the ruins, he has his assistant, Tinti, focus on his own face to record his tears.

p, Georges Marci; d, Paolo Cavara; w, Cavara, Tonino Guerra, Alberto Moravia (based on the story by Cavara, Fabio Carpi, Ugo Pirro); ph, Raffaele and Marcello Masciocchi (Techniscope, Technicolor); m, Gianni Marchetti; ed, Sergio Montanari; art d, Pier Luigi Pizzi.

Drama   **(PR:O MPAA:NR)**

WILD FOR KICKS   (SEE: BEAT GIRL, 1962, Brit.)

WILD, FREE AND HUNGRY*   (1970) 88m Boxoffice c

Gary Graver (Dave), Barbara Caron (Cinthia), Jane Tsentas (Evelyn), Jon Stone (Frank), Monica Gayle (Diane), George Todd (Don), Michael Downing (1st Gangster), Rene Leeland (2nd Gangster), Butch Griswald (Hugo).

A mega-melodrama about a carnival owner who gets mixed up with the mob and a motorboat racer. Romance, violence, and fast-paced speedboating leave their scars on the carnival owner who eventually loses his wife, fortune, and carnival, while retaining his only true love, a carnival employee. A happy ending has all his lost property returned to him. Tune in next week for another episode of....

p, Gary Graver; d, H. P. Edwards; ph, Rahn Vickery (Eastmancolor).

Drama   **(PR:C MPAA:R)**

WILD FRONTIER, THE**½   (1947) 59m REP bw

Allan "Rocky" Lane (Himself), Jack Holt (Charles "Saddles" Barton), Eddy Waller ("Nugget" Clark), Pierre Watkin (Marshal Frank Lane), John James (Jimmy Lane), Roy Barcroft (Lon Brand), Tom London (Patrick MacSween), Sam Flint (Steve Lawson), Ted Mapes (Gunman), Budd Buster (Sam Wheeler), Wheaton Chambers (Doc Hardy), Bob Burns, Art Dillard, Bud McClure, Silver Harr, Black Jack the Horse.

A short, lightning-paced oater which has Lane taking over the sheriff's position from his murdered father, determined to get the men responsible for the killing. Sure enough it's Holt, in an unusual role as a villain, the pillar of the community, who's to blame, secretly heading an outlaw gang. Lane beats the man senseless and by doing so restores law and order to the town. The first of Lane's films where he used his own name for his character, marking the demise of the RED RYDER series.

p, Gordon Kay; d, Philip Ford; w, Albert DeMond; ph, Alfred S. Keller; ed, Les Orlebeck; md, Mort Glickman; art d, Fred Ritter.

Western   **Cas.**   **(PR:A MPAA:NR)**

WILD GAME   (SEE: JAIL BAIT, 1977, Ger.)

WILD GEESE, THE**   (1978, Brit.) 132m AA c

Richard Burton (Col. Allen Faulkner), Roger Moore (Shawn Flynn), Richard Harris (Rafer Janders), Hardy Kruger (Pieter Coetzee), Stewart Granger (Sir Edward Matherson), Jack Watson (R.S.M. Sandy Young), Winston Ntshona (President Limbani), John Kani (Jesse), Kenneth Griffith (Witty), Frank Finlay (The Priest), Barry Foster (Balfour), Jeff Corey (Mr. Martin), Ronald Fraser (Jock), Ian Yule (Tosh), Brook Williams (Samuels), Percy Herbert (Keith), Patrick Allen (Rushton), Glyn Baker (Esposito), Rosalind Lloyd (Heather), Jane Hylton (Mrs. Young), David Ladd (Sonny),

Paul Spurrier (*Emile*), Joe Cole (*Derek*), Sydney Chama (*Clark*), Ken Gampu (*Alexander*), Jazzer Jeyes (*Jones*), Graham Clark (*Gennaro*), Gordon Steel (*Cavendish*), Harry Magnus (*Williams*), Ryno Hattinga (*Finchley*), DeWet Van Rooyen (*Haigh*), Chris Gibbons (*Balland*), Trevor Lloyd (*Robertson*), Len Sparrowhawk (*Slate*), Colin Abraham (*Carpenter*), George Leech (*Stone*), Chris Chittel (*Philips*), James Bailey (*West*), Bernard Nathanson (*Smith*), Ernst Briemle (*Taffy*), Clive Curtis (*Randolf*).

A typical adventure film which offers no surprises and tries to get by on a name cast. Burton leads a force of mercenaries into an African nation in order to rescue a former president of that country and put him back in office. With Ntshona back in power British business interests will gain considerably. The first third of the picture has Burton rounding up the necessary men for the mission, followed by an intense training period. Too long and too talky.

p, Euan Lloyd; d, Andrew V. McLaglen; w, Reginald Rose (based on the novel by Daniel Carney); ph, Jack Hildyard (Panavision); m, Roy Budd; ed, John Glen; prod d, Syd Cain; art d, Bob Bell; m/l, Joan Armatrading.

Adventure   **Cas.**   **(PR:O MPAA:R)**

WILD GEESE CALLING*   (1941) 77m FOX bw

Henry Fonda (*John Murdock*), Joan Bennett (*Sally*), Warren William (*Blackie*), Ona Munson (*Clarabella*), Barton MacLane (*Pirate Kelly*), Russell Simpson (*Len Baker*), Iris Adrian (*Mazie*), James C. Morton (*Mack*), Paul Sutton (*Manager*), Mary Field (*Jennie*), Stanley Andrews (*Delaney*), Jody Gilbert (*Swede*), Robert Emmett Keane (*Headwaiter*), Michael 'Adrian' Morris (*Stout Guide*), George Watts (*Mahoney*), Charles Middleton (*Doctor*), Paul Burns (*Logger*), Jack Pennick (*Mug*), Nestor Paiva (*Manager*), George Melford (*Foreman*), Tom London, Alan Bridge (*Men*), Lee Phelps (*Clerk*), Capt. Anderson (*Trapper*), Joe Bernard (*Waiter*).

Fonda was coming off the high of having worked with Preston Sturges on THE LADY EVE and was understandably disappointed when Zanuck put him into this mediocre adventure set in the 1890s. He's a lumberjack with a yen to see the world so he quits his job and travels to Seattle where he tries to find his old pal, William, a con artist with a lust for life equaling Fonda's. He searches for William and meets Bennett, a happy-go-lucky dancer who works in one of the many saloons that dot the Seattle waterfront. Fonda and Bennett are soon mad about each other but she doesn't have the heart to tell him that she used to be the main squeeze of William. Fonda and Bennett marry and all seems well. Meanwhile, Fonda is not the only person looking for William. It seems that William used some loaded dice to win a ramshackle hotel away from tough MacLane and if MacLane finds him, William may not survive. Fonda eventually does locate William and the trio takes off for Alaska. William sees how much in love the two of them are and keeps his mouth shut about his one-time affair with Bennett. In Alaska, William asks Fonda to help in running the old hotel won from MacLane but Fonda prefers the free and easy outdoor life of the lumberjack after first helping William get out of MacLane's clutches. Bennett and Fonda move into a rough-hewn cabin in the wilderness, then Bennett befriends local hooker Munson, who has exactly what you'd expect, a heart of gold. Bennett is in town, notes MacLane, and goes to William to tell him to beware. William can't resist stealing a kiss from Bennett and it happens just as Fonda walks in. He is ready to leave his wife but stays when he learns that they are to have a child. Fonda no longer trusts his wife in the same way, even though she has been honest with him. Bennett is in heavy labor and Fonda goes to town to find the local sawbones. While there, MacLane sees him, and shoots and wounds him. William arrives and kills MacLane, then he and Munson get into a small boat and make it across raging waters to the cabin in the wilderness. Munson aids Bennett in the birth, and William tells Fonda that he is totally guilty of having forced himself on Bennett. All is forgiven and Fonda settles down to the life of a father and husband and will no longer heed the wild geese who formerly called him to make the annual trip to wherever. A tedious film that might have been exciting if directed at a swifter pace than Brahm used.

p, Harry Joe Brown; d, John Brahm; w, Horace McCoy (based on the novel by Stewart Edward White); ph, Lucien Ballard; m, Alfred Newman; ed, Walter Thompson.

Adventure   **(PR:A-C MPAA:NR)**

WILD GIRL½   (1932) 78m FOX bw (GB: SALOMY JANE)

Charles Farrell (*The Stranger*), Joan Bennett (*Salomy Jane Clay*), Ralph Bellamy (*Jack Marbury*), Eugene Pallette (*Yuba Bill*), Irving Pichel (*Rufe Waters*), Minna Gombell (*Millie*), Sarah Padden (*Lize*), Willard Robertson (*Red Pete*), Ferdinand Munier (*Col. Starbottle*), Louise Beavers (*Mammy Lou*), Morgan Wallace (*Phineas Baldwin*), James Durkin (*Madison Clay*), Murdock MacQuarrie (*Jeff Larabee*), Alphonse Ethier (*Sheriff*), Marilyn Harris (*Anna May*), Carmencita Johnson (*Mary Ann*), Delmar Watson (*Willie*), Will Stanton (*Bartender*), Mary Gordon (*Washwoman*), Stanley Blystone (*Deputy*), George Sowards (*Hangman*), Jack Padjan (*Posseman*), Iron Eyes Cody (*Indian*), Robert E. Homans (*Gambling Kibitzer*).

A well-crafted programmer which is set in the High Sierras at the close of the Civil War. Farrell is a former soldier who guns down the man who seduced his sister. He takes off with the comely Bennett and before long they are falling in love. Bennett isn't exceptionally wild, as the title suggests, but

she does have a certain attractive tomboyish flair. They film includes some interesting techniques for scene transitions. Instead of the usual fade out-fade in or cut, WILD GIRL uses a processed shot which simulates the turning of a page. A nice touch for an otherwise ordinary picture. In a supporting role is Irving Pichel who, the same year, codirected THE MOST DANGEROUS GAME with Ernest B. Schoedsack (who in turn went on to codirect KING KONG with Merian C. Cooper the following year). Silent films had been made from the same story in 1914 (starring Jack Holt) and again in 1923.

d, Raoul Walsh; w, Doris Anderson, Edwin Justus Mayer (based on the story "Salomy Jane's Kiss" by Bret Harte and the play by Paul Armstrong); ph, Norbert Brodine; ed, Jack Murray; md, Louis de Francesco; set d, Joseph Wright; cos, Earl Luick.

Drama   **(PR:A MPAA:NR)**

WILD GOLD*   (1934) 75m FOX bw

John Boles (*Steve Miller*), Claire Trevor (*Jerry Jordan*), Harry Green (*J. Lorillard Pushkin*), Roger Imhof (*Pop Benson*), Ruth Gillette (*Dixie Belle*), Monroe Owsley (*Walter Johnson*), Edward Gargan (*Eddie Sparks*), Suzanne Kaaren, Wini Shaw, Blanca Vischer, Elsie Larson, Gloria Roy, Myra Bratton.

With a backdrop of gold mining, WILD GOLD tells the tale of a romance between a showgirl on the run from her confidence-man husband and a dam engineer. Love blooms between the pair (Boles and Trevor) and tragedy strikes, conveniently, when Trevor's spouse is killed in a dam break. Includes some effective newsreel footage of the break and the flood that follows. Trevor sings the tune "You're On the Top of My List"... twice. The film uses flood footage from THE JOHNSTOWN FLOOD (1926).

p, Sol M. Wurtzel; d, George Marshall; w, Lester Cole, Henry Johnson (based on the story by Dudley Nichols, Lamar Trotti); ph, Joseph Valentine; cos, Royer.

Romance/Drama   **(PR:A MPAA:NR)**

WILD GUITAR*   (1962) 87m Fairway bw

Arch Hall, Jr (*Bud*), Nancy Czar (*Vicky*), William Watters [Arch Hall, Sr.], Cash Flagg [Ray Dennis Steckler], Marie Denn, Bob Crumb, Bill Lloyd, Mike Kannon, Hal Kenton, Jonathan Karle, Al Scott, Virginia Broderick, Paul Voorhees, Rick Dennis, Tony Flynn, Carol Flynn.

Hall, Jr. is interested in two things–his motorcycle and his guitar–both of them "wild." He gets signed by the bloodthirsty, money-hungry Watters, a promoter who incessantly cheats the singer. He becomes a dishwasher, but is kidnaped and brainwashed, only to be rescued by some restaurant employees. Directed by the 22-year old Steckler. Another attempt by the man with many names, Hall, Sr., to make his moonfaced boy a singing star, this film reportedly cost a mere $35,000 to make. Most of the cast members are amateurs. Another low-budget effort of 1962 from the same father-son team, EEGAH! introduced Richard Kiel to cult viewers.

p, Nicholas Merriwether [Arch Hall, Sr.]; d, Ray Dennis Steckler; w, Merriwether, Bob Wehling, Joe Thomas; ph, Joseph V. Mascelli; m, Alan O'Day; ed, Anthony M. Lanza; m/l, O'Day, Arch Hall, Jr.

Drama   **(PR:A MPAA:NR)**

WILD GYPSIES*   (1969) 85m Manson c

Todd Grange (*Anton*), Wayne Lundy (*Juan*), Gayle Clarke (*Maria*), Ray Rappa (*Armendero*), Laura Welcome (*Julia*), Winn Geary (*Helena*), Carmen Filpe (*Felipe*), Eli Hadash (*Victor*), Kay Dahlquist (*Anna*), Demian Oliver (*Paula*), Samantha Scott (*Marguerite*), Glen Jackobson (*Erik*), Ruth Marcus (*Mama*), Barry Michlin (*Amos*).

A band of gypsies is terrorized by one of its disenfranchised former members, who rapes and kills the women of the clan. He is eventually captured and killed by the most heroic member of the gypsy tribe. Of interest only for the camerawork of Burum, who's gone on to become one of Hollywood's best, lensing, among others, the poetically picturesque RUMBLEFISH.

p, Paul Mart; d&w, Marc B. Ray; ph, Steve Burum; md, Andre Brunner (performed by the Hollywood String Orchestra); art d, Ektor Carranza; set d, Tod Jonson; cos, John Brandt; ch, Joe Cassini; makeup, Scott Hamilton.

Drama   **Cas.**   **(PR:O MPAA:NR)**

WILD HARVEST*½   (1947) 92m PAR bw

Alan Ladd (*Joe Madigan*), Dorothy Lamour (*Fay Rankin*), Robert Preston (*Jim Davis*), Lloyd Nolan (*Kink*), Dick Erdman (*Mark Lewis*), Allen Jenkins (*Higgins*), Will Wright (*Mike Alperson*), Griff Barnett (*Hankin*), Anthony Caruso (*Pete*), Walter Sande (*Long*), Frank Sulley (*Nick*), Gaylord Pendleton (*Swanson*), Caren Marsh (*Natalie*), William Meader (*Drury*), Bob Kortman (*Sam*), Frances Morris (*Mrs. Swanson*), Chet Root, Tex Swan, Gordon Carveth, Pat Lane (*Madigan Crew*), Harry Wilson, Mike Lally, Danny Stewart, Frank Moran, Frank Hagney, Constantine Romanoff (*Alperson Crew*), Ian Wolfe (*Martin*), Eddy C. Waller (*Mr. Hatfield*), Edgar Dearing (*Man*), Al Ferguson, Bill Wallace (*Husky Farmers*), Vernon Dent (*Farmer*), Gloria Williams (*Girl*), Al Murphy (*Bartender*).

The wide-open spaces of the Midwest provide the backdrop for this Ladd outing which combines the heat of romance with violence en route from Texas to Canada. Ladd pours money into organizing a wheat harvesting combine crew, but runs into a financial crisis and must avoid being bought out by his rival, Wright. The fun-loving Preston enters the scene and agrees to front Ladd the necessary money. With Nolan and Erdman as the two chief assistants, Ladd's crew begins to make its way through the wheat fields. Along the way, in Kansas City, Ladd makes the acquaintance of farmer girl Lamour. Ladd, however, isn't nearly as interested in her as she is in him. Although he shuns her advances, she continues her pursuit. To stay in Ladd's company, Lamour manages to con Preston into marriage. While the pressure increases between Ladd and Wright, Preston spends more and more time with Lamour, succumbing to her desire for expensive gifts. In order to feed her expensive tastes, Preston starts skimming money from the wheat sales. When Ladd discovers the scheme, their friendship explodes into a two-fisted battle. Ladd and Preston eventually mend their differences and return the money to the farmers. Disgusted with Lamour's manipulative ways, Ladd and Preston leave her behind as they set off again with the combine. Garnett's follow-up to THE POSTMAN ALWAYS RINGS TWICE, WILD HARVEST (which had the pre-release title, THE BIG HAIRCUT) never quite achieves the level of passion that seeped from the pages of the James M. Cain original, but it does manage to show off three fine lead talents and a horde of commendable supporting names. Reuniting Preston with Ladd for the first time since THIS GUN FOR HIRE (1942) brought the film a certain chemistry to which Lamour adds fire. The closeness of the characters in the film comes perhaps not from the script but from the shooting conditions. During filming (December, 1946), the Studio Painters and Carpenters Union staged a walkout, forcing the film crew to remain on the set at all hours to avoid crossing the picket lines. Each day's shooting was capped off by an evening of partying and drinking. On one such evening, Ladd noticed a rather large, uninvited guest bullying people at the bar. Garnett, in his autobiography, recounts his conversation with Ladd, "I told him, 'That big mug is bad trouble and nobody has a line on him.'" Ladd toughly responded, "I know who he is. He's the big bastard who's leaving as of now." Ladd, who was only 5 feet 5 inches tall (to appear taller onscreen, he often would stand on wooden planks outside of the camera's view), was considerably shorter than the man. Ladd bravely approached him only to be greeted with the insult, "Hi, Shorty." Without backing off, Ladd told the man, "You weren't invited to this party." As the man prepared to pound Ladd into the pavement, Ladd turned to the crew and shouted, "Get my planks." Everyone burst into laughter except the man, who was shown to the door before he could attack Ladd.

p, Robert Fellows; d, Tay Garnett; w, John Monks, Jr. (based on a story by Houston Branch); ph, John Seitz; m, Hugo Friedhofer; ed, Billy Shea, George Tomasine; art d, Hans Dreier, Haldane Douglas; spec eff ph, Farciot Edouart.

Drama   (PR:A MPAA:NR)

WILD HARVEST*   (1962) 80m Hollywood Artists/Sutton bw

Dolores Faith (Rose), Dean Fredericks (Whitey), Susan Kelly (Madge), Robert Harrow (Tom Ludlow), Arlynn Greer (Julie), Ralph Camargo (Sam Ludlow), Kathleen Freeman (Goldie), Walter Winchell (Narrator), Ivy Thayer, Gordon Casell, Dave Dundon, Annette Foosamer, Echoe Jordan, L. Michelle Marx, Ramona Fulmore, Lynda Lee Harrison.

A brutal ranch foreman, Fredericks, treats his female migrant workers as pieces of meat, physically and sexually abusing them at will. He sneakily tries to gain control of the ranch, pounding owner Harrow nearly lifeless. The women unite and viciously mutilate Fredericks with pruning shears.

p, Aubrey Schenck; d, Jerry A. Baerwitz; w, Sid Harris (based on the novel by Stephen Longstreet); ph, Gordon Avil; m, Bert Shefter, Paul Sawtell; ed, Peter Zinner; cos, Oscar Rodriguez; spec eff, Howard Anderson; m/l, Shefter, Sawtell, Jack Ackerman, sung by Tommy Cooper; makeup, Rudolph Liszt.

Drama   (PR:O MPAA:NR)

WILD HEART, THE**   (1952, Brit.) 82m
    LFP-Vanguard/RKO-SELZNICK c (GB: GONE TO EARTH; AKA:
                                                                    GYPSY BLOOD)

Jennifer Jones (Hazel Woodus), David Farrar (Jack Reddin), Cyril Cusack (Edward Marston), Sybil Thorndyke (Mrs. Marston), Edward Chapman (Mr. James), Esmond Knight (Abel Woodus), Hugh Griffith (Andrew Vessons), George Cole (Albert), Beatrice Varley (Aunt Prowde), Frances Clare (Amelia Comber), Raymond Rollett (Landlord), Gerald Lawson (Roadmender), Bartlett Mullins, Arthur Reynolds (Chapel Elders), Ann Tetheradge (Miss James), Peter Dunlop (Cornet Player), Louis Phillip (Policeman), Valentine Dunn (Martha), Richmond Nairne (Mathias Booker), Joseph Cotten (Narrator), Owen Holder.

An odd misfire from the normally reliable team of Powell and Pressburger, this 1890s British-based film was taken from a fair novel and only barely came up to the novel's standards, despite an excellent and lively turn by Jones in the lead. She is an innocent Shropshire lass who lives in the country and takes care of the various little animals in the woods. She is especially devoted to her pet fox, a cute critter, and her main goal in life seems to be rescuing the equally innocents of the forest from the shotguns, and slings

and arrows of outrageous hunters searching for trophies. Farrar is the local landowner and he would love to marry Jones but she marries the clergyman, Cusack, instead. Cusack is a pleasant chap but has no sexual interest in his comely wife, something that causes the curvy Jones a great deal of frustration. This being the case, she takes up with Farrar, who satisfies her lust but, as it turns out, is cruel to animals, specifically her fox. She returns to husband Cusack who, while not being particularly virile, does have a sympathetic nature toward her pet. Farrar leads a hunt to find her fox and kill it so Jones tries to get the pet before the squire does. In doing so, she dies when she falls down a long, dark mine shaft. Not believable on any level, the movie came in at 110 minutes in the British version, then was recut by Selznick for the U.S. He added some scenes, directed by Rouben Mamoulian, plus a narration by Joseph Cotten in a vain attempt to make some sense out of the mish-mash story. Filmed near the Welsh border with additional scenes done in Hollywood. Two tasteful men, Selznick and Alexander Korda, financed it and that, plus the participation of Powell and Pressburger (who did THE RED SHOES, among others) should have insured that this had some merit. It had very little.

p, David O. Selznick; d&w, Michael Powell, Emeric Pressburger (based on the novel Gone to Earth by Mary Webb); ph, Christopher Challis (Technicolor); m, Brian Easdale; ed, Reginald Mills; prod d, Hein Heckroth; art d, Arthur Lawson.

Drama   (PR:C MPAA:NR)

WILD HERITAGE**   (1958) 78m UNIV c

Will Rogers, Jr (Judge Copeland), Maureen O'Sullivan (Emma Breslin), Rod McKuen (Dirk Breslin), Casey Tibbs (Rusty), Troy Donahue (Jesse Bascomb), Judy Meredith (Callie Bascomb), Gigi Perreau (Missouri Breslin), George "Foghorn" Winslow (Talbot Breslin), Gary Gray (Hugh), Jeanette Nolan (Ma Bascomb), Paul Birch (Jake Breslin), John Beradino (Arn), Phil Harvey (Jud), Lawrence Dobkin (Josh Burrage), Stephen Ellsworth (Bolivar Bascomb), Ingrid Goude (Hilda Jansen), Christopher Dark (Brazos), Guy Wilkerson (Chaco).

Two families, westward-bound in their covered wagons, come together to battle rustlers and gunmen. Sons from both families arm themselves, rid the land of a few more bad men, and make the West a better place to live. Rogers, Jr. is top-billed as a frontier jurist in what amounts to a very small role, one redolent of his father's JUDGE PRIEST (1934) characterization. He fails to come up to the original.

p, John E. Horton; d, Charles Haas; w, Paul King, Joseph Stone (based on a story by Steve Frazee); ph, Philip Lathrop (CinemaScope, Eastmancolor); m, Joseph Gershenson; ed, Edward Mann; md, Gershenson; art d, Alexander Golitzen, Robert Boyle; cos, Morton Haack.

Western   (PR:A MPAA:NR)

WILD HORSE*   (1931) 77m Allied-Astor bw (AKA: SILVER DEVIL)

Hoot Gibson, Alberta Vaughn, Stepin Fetchit, Neal Hart, Edmund Cobb, Skeeter Bill Robins, Glenn Strange, George Bunny, Edward Piel, Sr, Joe Rickson, Mutt the Horse.

An interesting example of Gibson's inability to adapt to the pacing of sound films, this picture–reportedly the star's favorite among his talkies–concentrates largely on the antics and abilities of his beloved Palomino horse, "Mutt". The capture of the beast occupies the bulk of the action in the picture.

p, M. H. Hoffman, Jr.; d, Richard Thorpe, Sidney Algier; w, John Francis Natteford (based on the story by Peter B. Kyne); ph, Ernest Miller; ed, Mildred Johnston.

Western   Cas.   (PR:A MPAA:NR)

WILD HORSE AMBUSH*   (1952) 54m REP bw

Michael Chapin (Red), Eilene Janssen (Judy), James Bell (Sheriff Tom White), Richard Avonde (Jalisco), Roy Barcroft (Big John Harkins), Julian Rivero (Enrico Espinosa), Movita (Lita Espinosa), Drake Smith (Mace Gary), Scott Lee (Shorty), Alex Montoya (Pedro), John Daheim (Turk), Ted Cooper (Spy), Wayne Burson.

Youngsters Chapin and Janssen topped off their fourth (and thankfully) final kiddie western with the self-explanatory WILD HORSE AMBUSH. A gang of counterfeiters is ambushing wild horses and smuggling phony loot by gluing it under the animals' manes. (See ROUGH RIDIN' KIDS series)

p, Rudy Ralston; d, Fred C. Brannon; w, William Lively; ph, John MacBurnie; m, Stanley Wilson; ed, Harold Minter; art d, Frank Arrigo.

Western   (PR:A MPAA:NR)

WILD HORSE CANYON*½   (1939) 57m MON bw

Jack Randall, Dorothy Short, Frank Yaconelli, Dennis Moore, Warner Richmond, Ed Cassidy, Walter Long, Charles King, Earl Douglas, Sherry Tansey, Hal Price, Rusty the Horse.

Rustlers make living tough for Cassidy, but when Randall starts shooting no one has anything to fear–except the guys wearing black. Outside of cleaning up the town, Randall has a personal stake in the chase–one of the outlaws killed his brother.

p, Robert Tansey; d, Robert Hill; w, Robert Emmett [Tansey]; ph, Bert Longnecker; ed, Howard Dillinger.

Western   (PR:A MPAA:NR)

WILD HORSE HANK** (1979, Can.) 94m Film Consortium of Canada c

Linda Blair (*Hank Bradford*), Michael Wincott (*Charlie Connors*), Al Waxman (*Jay Connors*), Richard Crenna (*Pace Bradford*).

Blair is a college girl with a fondness for wild horses that are doomed to be used as dog food. She bucks her father's authority and rides the animals to safety in a nearby wildlife reserve. Crenna turns in a sharp performance as Blair's father in this softhearted family picture.

p, Bill Marshall, Henk Van Der Kolk; d, Eric Till; w, James Lee Barrett (based on the novel *The Wild Horse Killers* by Mel Ellis); ph, Richard Leiterman; m, Paul Hoffert, Brenda Hoffert; ed, George Appelby.

Drama/Adventure   (PR:A MPAA:NR)

WILD HORSE MESA**½   (1932) 61m PAR bw

Randolph Scott (*Chane Weymer*), Sally Blane (*Sandy Melberne*), Fred Kohler, Sr (*The Horse Trapper*), Lucille LaVerne (*Ma Melberne*), James Bush (*Bent Weymer*), Charles Grapewin (*Sam Bass*), Jim Thorpe (*Indian Chief*), George ["Gabby"] F. Hayes (*Slack*), Buddy Roosevelt (*Horn*), E. H. Calvert (*Sheriff*).

Scott brings some justice to Blane's part of town when he puts an end to Kohler's trapping of wild stallions. Kohler puts up barbed wire to catch the animals, but in the end gets trampled to death by the wildest of the horses as Scott rides in front of the herd to deflect them from the barbed wire.

p, Harold Hurley; d, Henry Hathaway; w, Frank Howard Clark, Harold Shumate (based on the novel by Zane Grey); ph, Arthur Todd; art d, Earl Hedrick.

Western   (PR:A MPAA:NR)

WILD HORSE MESA**   (1947) 61m RKO bw

Tim Holt (*Dave Jordan*), Nan Leslie (*Sue Melbern*), Richard Martin (*Chito Rafferty*), Richard Powers [Tom Keen] (*Hod Slack*), Jason Robards, Sr (*Pop Melbern*), Tony Barrett (*Jim Horn*), Harry Woods (*Jay Olmstead*), William Gould (*Marshal Bradford*), Robert Bray (*Tex*), Richard Foote (*Rusty*), Frank Yaconelli.

Holt sets out to locate a herd of 2,000 horses which has been hidden in the mountains in Utah by an odious gang who killed the father of Holt's girl friend, Leslie. With Mexican cowpoke Martin at his side, Holt manages to locate the herd and whip the bad guys. A loose adaptation of Zane Grey's novel which had already come to the screen silently in 1925 and again in 1932.

p, Herman Schlom; d, Wallace A. Grissell; w, Norman Houston (based on the novel by Zane Grey); ph, Frank Redman; m, Paul Sawtell; ed, Desmond Marquette; md, Constantin Bakaleinikoff; art d, Albert S. D'Agostino, Lucius O. Croxton; set d, Darrell Silvera, Adolph Kuri.

Western   (PR:A MPAA:NR)

WILD HORSE PHANTOM*½   (1944) 56m PRC bw

Buster Crabbe (*Billy Carson*), Al "Fuzzy" St. John, Elaine Morey, Kermit Maynard, Budd Buster, Hal Price, Robert Meredith, Frank Ellis, Frank McCarroll, Bob Cason, John Elliott.

Once again an unscrupulous banker manages to wreak havoc in the Old West by coming up with yet another land-grabbing scheme. This time out the good ranchers arrive in town to deposit their money so they can pay the mortgage on their land. The banker, however, robs the bank and hides the funds so that he can foreclose on the ranches because payments are past due. Crabbe and St. John discover the truth, find the cash, and bring the banker to justice. (See BILLY CARSON series, Index.)

p, Sigmund Neufeld; d, Sam Newfield; w, George Milton; ed, Holbrook N. Todd.

Western   (PR:A MPAA:NR)

WILD HORSE RODEO*½   (1938) 55m REP bw

Bob Livingston (*Stony Brooke*), Ray Corrigan (*Tucson Smith*), Max Terhune (*Lullaby Joslin*), June Martel (*Alice*), Walter Miller (*Col. Nye*), Edmund Cobb (*Hank*), William Gould (*Harkley*), Jack Ingram (*Jim*), Dick Weston [Roy Rogers] (*Singer*), Henry Isabell (*Slim*), Art Dillard (*Bud*), Ralph Robinson (*Announcer*), Jack Kirk, Fred "Snowflake" Toones, Cyclone the Horse.

This MESQUITEERS entry has Livingston, Corrigan, and Terhune lending a hand to Martel, a woman writer and painter who manages a herd on the side. A horse, Cyclone, is the real star, however, as it kicks up some dust during a rodeo. The usual crooked baddies get in the way and, in the slam-bang finale, try to shoot the Mesquiteers from a plane. Corrigan proves

his prowess with a six-gun and brings the outlaws out of the sky with a single shot, sending the plane augering into the ground. The film includes a plea for freedom for wild horses, and also had in its cast an actor in a musical number named Weston, who would soon become the singing cowboy Roy Rogers. This was prolific George Sherman's first film as a director. (See THREE MESQUITEERS series, Index.)

p, Sol C. Siegel; d, George Sherman; w, Betty Burbridge (based on the story by Gilbert Wright, Oliver Drake); ph, William Nobles; ed, Lester Orlebeck.

Western   **Cas.**   (PR:A MPAA:NR)

WILD HORSE ROUND-UP**   (1937) 58m Ambassador bw

Kermit Maynard (*Jack Benson*), Betty Lloyd (*Ruth Williams*), Dickie Jones (*Dickie Williams*), John Merton (*Charlie Doan*), Frank Hagney (*Steve*), Roger Williams (*Pete*), Dick Curtis (*Bill*), Budd Buster (*Mopey*).

Average oater entertainment with Maynard cleaning up a western valley which has an outlaw cloud hanging over it. A nasty bunch plans on taking control of the town once they realise that a railroad is to be built through it, but rail plans change and the villains, like the herd of wild stallions, are rounded-up by the finale.

p, Martin G. Conn; d, Alan James; w, Joseph O'Donnell (based on a story by James Curwood); ph, Arthur Reed; ed, Richard G. Wray; m/l, "K-yippee," "Shadows on the Trail," "Men of the Saddle," Connie Lee.

Western   (PR:A MPAA:NR)

WILD HORSE RUSTLERS*½   (1943) 58m PRC bw

Bob Livingston (*Lone Rider Tom Cameron*), Al St. John (*Fuzzy*), Linda Johnson (*Ellen*), Lane Chandler (*Smokey Beckman/Hans Beckman*), Stanley Price (*Collins*), Frank Ellis (*Jake*), Karl Hackett (*Sheriff*), Jimmy Aubrey (*Deputy*), Kansas Moehring, Silver Harr.

An oater oddity which stars Chandler in a dual role as identical twins–one a patriotic ranch foreman, the other a Nazi agent (with a cowpoke accent!). The Army's horse procurement plan comes under fire by the scheming Nazi, but Livingston, with the help of St. John and Chandler (who, of course, gets blamed for his twin brother's deeds), straightens the mess out. (See LONE RIDER series, Index.)

p, Sigmund Neufeld; d, Sam Newfield; w, Joe O'Donnell; ph, Robert Cline; m, Leo Erdody; ed, Holbrook N. Todd.

Western   (PR:A MPAA:NR)

WILD HORSE STAMPEDE**   (1943) 58m MON bw

Ken Maynard (*Ken*), Hoot Gibson (*Hoot*), Betty Miles (*Betty Wallace*), Ian Keith (*Carson*), Don Stewart (*Donny*), Si Jenks (*Rawhide*), Bob Baker (*Cliff Tyler*), John Bridges (*Col. Black*), Glenn Strange (*Tip*), Reed Howes (*Tex*), Kenneth Harlan (*Borman*), Tom London, Tex Palmer (*Outlaws*), Forrest Taylor, I. Stanford Jolley, Kenne Duncan, Bob McKenzie, Chick Hannon.

When a tribe of Indians goes on the warpath against a group of railway workers, Maynard and Gibson investigate the goings-on. They quickly uncover a plot by some unscrupulous horse rustlers who've incited the redskins to cause trouble. Mediocre at best. (See TRAIL BLAZERS series, Index.)

p, Robert Tansey; d, Alan James; w, Elizabeth Beecher (based on a story by Francis Kavanaugh); ph, Marcel Le Picard; ed, Fred Bain; md, Frank Sanucci.

Western   (PR:A MPAA:NR)

WILD HORSE VALLEY*½   (1940) 57m Metropolitan bw

Bob Steele, Phyllis Adair, Buzz Barton, Lafe McKee, Jimmy Aubrey, Ted Adams, Bud Osborne, George Chesebro.

When a group of evil rustlers steal a beautiful Arabian stallion, Steele must give chase and reclaim the priceless steed. A few exciting moments of Steele and villain Chesebro duking it out, but this is a duller-than-average oater. It was the next-to-last film appearance of aging child cowboy star Buzz Barton, who retired from the movie business to join the Navy at the outbreak of WW II. Barton did return to Hollywood, but this time behind the scenes as a horse wrangler on major studio productions.

p, Harry S. Webb; d, Ira Webb; w, Carl Krusada.

Western   **Cas.**   (PR:A MPAA:NR)

WILD IN THE COUNTRY**   (1961) 112m FOX c

Elvis Presley (*Glenn Tyler*), Hope Lange (*Irene Sperry*), Tuesday Weld (*Noreen*), Millie Perkins (*Betty Lee Parsons*), Rafer Johnson (*Davis*), John Ireland (*Phil Macy*), Gary Lockwood (*Cliff Macy*), William Mims (*Uncle Rolfe*), Raymond Greenleaf (*Dr. Underwood*), Christina Crawford (*Monica George*), Robin Raymond (*Flossie*), Doreen Lang (*Mrs. Parsons*), Charles Arnt (*Mr. Parsons*), Ruby Goodwin (*Sarah*), Will Corry (*Willie Dace*), Alan Napier (*Prof. Larson*), Jason Robards, Sr (*Judge Parker*), Harry Carter (*Bartender*), Harry Shannon (*Sam Tyler*), Bob "Red" West (*Hank Tyler*).

Presley is a backwoods delinquent youngster who, after a fight, is paroled into the care of his crooked uncle, a tonic manufacturer. He also must pay weekly visits to psychiatrist Lange, a widow, who discovers a talent for writing in the young man and nurses it along, finally becoming attracted to him. In the meantime, Presley is carrying on with the pushy Weld and the more reserved Perkins. Instead of concerning himself with romance he concentrates on his education and leaves for college, presumably to become a literary giant. The well-versed fellow also manages a few tunes: "In My Way," "I Slipped, I Stumbled, I Fell" (Fred Weiss, Ben Weidman), "Lonely Man" (Bennie Benjamin, Sol Marcus), "Wild in the Country" (Hugo Peretti, Luigi Creatore, George David Weiss). Presley's character may be tough to swallow, but he makes the attempt in an enjoyable dramatic role amidst the typical swooning and singing pictures he churned out. One of the less than memorable efforts of screenwriter Odets, the once proletarian dramatist ("Golden Boy," "Awake and Sing") who turned to Hollywood in the middle 1940s after several successes on Broadway. Most of the critics of WILD IN THE COUNTRY called the premise—a country boy from the Shenandoah Valley in Virginia being groomed for a career in literature—unconvincing and romantic, without realizing that the author, J.R. Salamanca, may have based part of his story on the poet and novelist Jesse Stuart (*Taps for Private Tussy*), who came out of the hills of Kentucky to become the toast of New York literary circles in the 1930s and 1940s.

p, Jerry Wald; d, Philip Dunne; w, Clifford Odets (based on the novel *The Lost Country* by J.R. Salamanca); ph, William C. Mellor (CinemaScope, DeLuxe Color); m, Kenyon Hopkins; ed, Dorothy Spencer; art d, Jack Martin Smith, Preston Ames; set d, Walter M. Scott, Stuart A. Reiss; cos, Don Feld; makeup, Ben Nye.

Drama   Cas.   (PR:A MPAA:NR)

WILD IN THE SKY   (SEE: BLACK JACK, 1973)

WILD IN THE STREETS½**   (1968) 96m AIP c

Shelley Winters (*Mrs. Flatow*), Christopher Jones (*Max Flatow/Max Frost*), Diane Varsi (*Sally LeRoy*), Ed Begley (*Sen. Allbright*), Hal Holbrook (*Sen. John Fergus*), Millie Perkins (*Mary Fergus*), Richard Pryor (*Stanley X*), Bert Freed (*Max Jacob Flatow, Sr.*), Kevin Coughlin (*Billy Cage*), Larry Bishop (*Abraham*), May Ishihara (*Fuji Ellie*), Michael Margotta (*Jimmy Fergus*), Don Wyndham (*Joseph Fergus*), Kellie Flanagan (*Young Mary Fergus*), Salli Sachse (*Hippie Mother*), Paul Frees (*Narrator*), Walter Winchell, Melvin Belli, Kenneth Banghart, Louis Lomax, Dick Clark, Jack Latham, Pamela Mason, Allan J. Moll, Army Archerd, Gene Shacove (*Themselves*).

A teenage Jones leaves his home, blows up the family car, and sells LSD until he finally makes it big as a rock star named Max Frost. Rolling in the millions he's made, Jones accepts an offer to help Holbrook get elected to the office of U.S. senator, appealing to the nation's youth. Jones manages to get the voting age lowered to 14 and inevitably is himself elected President. The "Don't Trust Anyone Over 30" banner is waved as Jones legislates work camps for the adults in which they are fed LSD. His position is challenged, however, by those even younger than he who look at 14-year olds as "old." A humorous and inventive political satire which, aside from datedness and some technical flaws, is entirely watchable and witty. Songs: "The Shape of Things to Come," "Fifty-Two Per Cent," "Listen to the Music," "Sally LeRoy," "Fourteen or Fight" (Barry Mann, Cynthia Weil, sung by Christopher Jones, Paul Weiler, The Thirteenth Power).

p, James H. Nicholson, Samuel Z. Arkoff; d, Barry Shear; w, Robert Thom (based on his story "The Day it All Happened, Baby"); ph, Richard Moore (Pathe Color); m, Les Baxter; ed, Fred Feitshans, Eve Newman; art d, Paul Sylos; set d, Harry Reif; cos, Richard Bruno; makeup, Fred Williams.

Drama/Comedy/Satire   Cas.   (PR:C MPAA:R/GP)

WILD INNOCENCE**   (1937, Aus.) 72m Herman Garfield bw

Wendy Munro (*Margot*), Brian Abbott (*Tom Henton*), Ethel Saker (*Mrs. Saker*), Harry Abdy (*Shorty McGee*), Joe Valli (*McMeeker*), Ron Whelan, Sylvia Kellaway, Chute the Kangaroo.

American filmmakers have churned out scores of innocuous heart-warming films about stray dogs being adopted by kindly farmers. Australians employ the same tired formula but substitute kangaroos. In WILD INNOCENCE, good-hearted rancher Abbott comes across a baby kangaroo orphaned by the guns of two hunters. Abbott adopts the critter and teaches it to box. Unfortunately, this new talent lands the kangaroo in trouble when it falls into the hands of an unscrupulous circus owner. Mistreated in the circus, the kangaroo runs away and makes it back to Abbott's ranch where it is greeted with open arms. Only the animal and the backgrounds are different from other well-known dog stories.

p&d, Ken G. Hall; w, Edmund Deward (based on the story "Wilderness Orphan" by Dorothy Cottrell); ph, George Heath.

Drama   (PR:A MPAA:NR)

WILD IS MY LOVE*   (1963) 74m GEN/Mishkin bw

Elizabeth MacRae (*Queenie*), Paul Hampton (*Ben*), Ray Fulmer (*Aga*), Bob Alexander (*Zero*), Ralph Stanley (*Tony*), Gene Courtney (*Lola*), Carl Low (*Mr. Durrel*), Mary Harrigan, Mike O'Dowd, Richard Forstmann, Victoria

Ardiss, Jane Ross, Marge Randolph, "Jezebel.".

Three college students spend the summer studying for exams with one getting involved with a stripper, and the other two going through a rite-of-passage ritual by playing Chinese roulette. The finale has the three surviving their summer and renewing their friendship. Except for an occasional surprise in the candid bump-and-grind sequences, WILD IS MY LOVE is tame.

p&d, Richard Hilliard; w, Otto Lemming, Hilliard; ph, Emil Knebel, Louis McMahon; m, Wilford Holcombe; ed, Ray Pierce; md, Holcombe.

Drama   (PR:O MPAA:NR)

WILD IS THE WIND**   (1957) 114m PAR bw

Anna Magnani (*Gioia*), Anthony Quinn (*Gino*), Anthony Franciosa (*Bene*), Dolores Hart (*Angie*), Lili Valenty (*Teresa*), James Flavin (*Wool Buyer*), Joseph Calleia (*Alberto*), Dick Ryan (*Priest*), Joseph Vitale, Iphigenie Castiglioni, Ruth Lee, Frances Morris (*Party Guests*).

Weakly scripted and directed, WILD IS THE WIND succeeds thanks only to the excellent performances of Magnani and Quinn, both of whom received Academy Award nominations for their roles. Quinn is a Nevada sheepherder who travels home to Italy to marry Magnani, the sister of his deceased wife. He brings her back to his ranch, but struggles with the memory of his dead wife, even calling Magnani by her sister's name during a birthday toast. Magnani turns outside of her marriage to fulfill her needs and begins an affair with Franciosa, a ranch hand Quinn raised. Only then does Quinn realise how much he needs Magnani, pleading with her to stay at the ranch instead of returning home. The symbolism of wild horses is a bit heavy and the film's structure easily topples, but this is a case where the performers make it all worthwhile. Songs: "Wild Is the Wind" (Dimitri Tiomkin, Ned Washington, sung by Johnny Mathis), "Scapricciatiello" (Fernando Albano, Pacifico Vento, sung by Magnani). A remake of the Italian film FURIA, directed by Geoffredo Alessandrini. The intense emotional roles played by Franciosa and Magnani spilled over from the set into their private lives and the gossip churned up by the Hollywood rumor mills brought Franciosa's fiancee, mercurial Shelley Winters, flying from California to Nevada to put a halt to it. She did; they were married the same year, and remained so for three years.

p, Hal B. Wallis; d, George Cukor; w, Arnold Shulman (based on the novel "Furia" by Vittorio Nino Novarese); ph, Charles B. Lang, Jr. (VistaVision); m, Dimitri Tiomkin; ed, Warren Low; art d, Hal Pereira, Tambi Larsen; spec eff, John P. Fulton, Farciot Edouart.

Drama   (PR:A MPAA:NR)

WILD JUNGLE CAPTIVE   (SEE: JUNGLE CAPTIVE, 1945)

WILD LOVE-MAKERS   (SEE: WEIRD LOVE-MAKERS, 1963, Jap.)

WILD MAN OF BORNEO, THE**½** (1941) 78m MGM bw

Frank Morgan (*J. Daniel Thompson*), Mary Howard (*Mary Thompson*), Billie Burke (*Bernice Marshall, Boarding House Keeper*), Donald Meek (*Prof. Charles Birdo, Whistler*), Marjorie Main (*Irma*), Connie Gilchrist (*Mrs. Diamond*), Bonita Granville (*Francine Diamond*), Walter Catlett ("*Doc*" *Skelby*), Andrew Tombes ("*Doc*" *Dunbar*), Dan Dailey, Jr (*Ed LeMotte*), Joseph J. Green (*Mr. Ferderber*), Phil Silvers (*Murdock*), Joe Yule (*Jerry*), Henry Roquemore (*Sheriff*), Tom Conway (*Actor in Film Scene*), Karen Verne (*Actress in Film Scene*), Matt McHugh, Irving Bacon (*Cabbies*).

Morgan stars in this passable comedy as a medicine show barker who returns to his long-forgotten daughter when he learns that she has inherited a sizable fortune. He is mistaken, however, and discovers a daughter, Howard, who is poorer than he. Planning to continue the charade of wealth, they take off together for New York, boarding in the theatrical district until their deception is aired. As was par for the course, the finale found life taking a turn for the better for the two likable frauds.

p, Joseph L. Mankiewicz; d, Robert B. Sinclair; w, Waldo Salt, John McLain (based on the play by Herman J. Mankiewicz, Marc Connelly); ph, Oliver T. Marsh; m, David Snell; ed, Frank Sullivan; art d, Cedric Gibbons; cos, Dolly Tree, Gile Steele.

Comedy   (PR:A MPAA:NR)

WILD McCULLOCHS, THE**   (1975) 93m AIP c (AKA: THE McCULLOCHS; J.J. McCULLOCH)

Forrest Tucker (*J.J. McCulloch*), Julie Adams (*Hannah McCulloch*), Max Baer (*Culver Robinson*), Janice Heiden (*Ali McCulloch*), Dennis Redfield (*Steven McCulloch*), Don Grady (*R.J. McCulloch*), Chip Hand (*Gary McCulloch*), William Demarest (*Father Gurkin*), Harold J. Stone (*George*), Vito Scotti (*Tony*), Sandy Kevin (*Rad*), Lillian Randolph (*Missy*), Doodles Weaver (*Pop*), James Gammon (*Detective*), Candice Smith (*Marsha*), Mike Mazurki (*Randall*).

An uncomplicated family history features Tucker as a man whose domineering ways drive his children to hate him. One son dies in the Korean conflict; another ends up in jail for murder. Hand manages to get out of the family before he ends up like his older brothers, while Heiden is the daughter no man is good enough for. This instigates a climactic fight between Tucker and

Heiden's suitor. The latter is played by Baer, who also wrote, directed, and produced the film. The story never makes an attempt to grapple with any psychological issues, but merely is presented in a straightforward manner. Thus motivations remain dull and characters all fit stereotypes. Baer does do a neat job in re-creating the film's era (1949). Baer took up film direction after achieving some dubious success as the idiot farm boy, Jethro, on TV's "The Beverly Hillbillies."

p,d&w, Max Baer; ph, Fred Koenekamp (CFI Color); m, Ernest Gold; ed, David Berlatsky.

Drama (PR:O MPAA:PG)

WILD MONEY** (1937) 71m PAR bw

Edward Everett Horton (P.E. Dodd), Louise Campbell (Judy McGowan), Lynne Overman (Perry Brown), Lucien Littlefield (Bill Hawkins), Esther Dale (Jenny Hawkins), Porter Hall (Bill Court), Benny Baker (Al Vogel), Ruth Coleman (Mrs. West), Louis Natheaux (Mr. West), Billy Lee (Malcolm West), Howard Mitchell (Sheriff Jones), William Burgess (Spreckett), Gertrude Short (Miss Green), Colin Tapley, Nick Lukats, Wesley Barry.

Eccentric Horton and screen newcomer Campbell work on a newspaper, he as a stingy bookkeeper and she as a hard-as-nails reporter Horton is crazy about. One day on vacation Horton uncovers a kidnaping and phones the story in to his newspaper. As he is the paper's only representative around, he is ordered to stay on the job and keep the phone lines open to Campbell, which he does. He is also given a $25,000 expense account which he uses to sew up every means of communication around so that he can give his paper continuing scoops. He not only raises the paper's circulation, but cleans up on the crooks and wins the Brenda Starr as well. Agreeable little story but without enough substance to send Campbell into orbit.

d, Louis King; w, Edward T. Lowe, Marguerite Roberts, Eddie Welch (based on a story by Paul Gallico); ph, Henry Sharp; ed, Stuart Gilmore; md, Boris Morros.

Comedy/Drama (PR:A MPAA:NR)

WILD MUSTANG** (1935) 61m Ajax bw

Harry Carey (Norton), Barbara Fritchie (Jill), Del Gordon (Reno Norton), Cathryn Johns (Ma McClay), Robert Kortman (Utah Evans), George Chesebro, Dick Botiller, George Morrell, Milburn Morante, Francis Walker, Budd Buster, Chuck Morrison, Sonny the Marvel Horse.

Carey plays a sheriff determined to smash a ring of vicious criminals led by Kortman who sadistically brand their victims. Hoping to help his father, Carey's son, Gordon, volunteers to join the gang and set a trap. Things go awry, however, when Carey is captured and almost branded. Luckily he escapes and the crooks are dealt with harshly. A solid oater featuring a solid star.

p, William Berke; d, Harry Fraser; w, Weston Edwards (based on a story by Monroe Talbot); ph, Robert Cline; ed, Arthur A. Brooks.

Western (PR:A MPAA:NR)

WILD 90* (1968) 90m Supreme Mix bw

Norman Mailer (The Prince), Buzz Farbar (Cameo), Mickey Knox (20 Years), Beverly Bentley (Margie), Jose Torres (Kid Cha Cha), Mara Lynn (Lillian), Dick Adler (Lieutenant), Harold Conrad (Boots), Bryan Hamill (2R), Milt Machlin (Chief Inspector), Ramona Torres (Carmela), D.A. Pennebaker (Al).

Author Mailer's first plunge into filmmaking is not one that will guarantee his name on marquees around the country, but it does hold some brief interest. It is an improvised, cinema-verite study of three Mafia hoods holed up in a warehouse shooting the bull, drinking, arguing, cursing. Their wives pay them a visit, followed by their girl friends, prizefighter Jose Torres and a dog, and then, in the climax, the police. Photographed by documentarian D.A. Pennebaker, WILD 90 is as much a work of his as it is Mailer's. One could make all sorts of moral and ethical judgments about writers making films, but it might have been delightful if Ernest Hemingway or F. Scott Fitzgerald had preserved 90 minutes of wild conversation on film. Filmmaker Mailer certainly missed his calling as an actor.

p&d, Norman Mailer; w, (improvised); ph, D.A. Pennebaker; m, Charlie Brown; ed, Jan Welt, Mailer.

Drama (PR:O MPAA:NR)

WILD NORTH, THE** (1952) 97m MGM c (AKA: THE BIG NORTH)

Stewart Granger (Jules Vincent), Wendell Corey (Constable Pedley), Cyd Charisse (Indian Girl), Morgan Farley (Father Simon), J.M. Kerrigan (Callahan), Howard Petrie (Brody), Houseley Stevenson (Old Man), Lewis Martin (Sergeant), John War Eagle (Indian Chief), Ray Teal (Ruger), Clancy Cooper (Sloan), Henry Corden (Clerk), Robert Stephenson (Drunk), G. Pat Collins (Bartender), Russ Conklin (Indian), Brad Morrow (Boy), Emile Meyer (Jake), Henri Letondal (John Mudd), Holmes Herbert (Magistrate), Cliff Taylor, Rex Lease (Members of Quartette).

Granger is on the run in Mountie territory after committing a murder in self-defense. Corey is in pursuit, and when he finally catches him he is steered in the wrong direction by his prisoner. Granger, who knows the wild north like the back of his hand, leads his captor into treacherous blizzards

and a wolf pack. Corey is wounded and unconscious, but Granger carries him to safety, in the end restoring his health. Corey is convinced that Granger acted in self-defense and frees him. Charisse, as Granger's girl, is, as in any of her screen outings, the most watchable character in the film.

p, Stephen Ames; d, Andrew Marton; w, Frank Fenton; ph, Robert Surtees (Ansco Color); m, Bronislau Kaper; ed, John Dunning; art d, Cedric Gibbons, Preston Ames.

Western (PR:A MPAA:NR)

WILD ON THE BEACH* (1965) 77m Lippert/FOX bw

Frankie Randall (Adam), Sherry Jackson (Lee Sullivan), Jackie and Gayle, Sonny and Cher, The Astronauts, Cindy Malone, Sandy Nelson, Russ Bender, Booth Colman, Justin Smith, Jerry Grayson, Marc Seaton, Robert Golden, Larry Gust.

College students Randall and Jackson get their wires crossed and both descend on a beach house with their friends to spend the weekend. They agree to share and share alike, tossing a wild beach party complete with wild beach party music, chaperoned, of course, by "spies" from their college. Notable only for an appearance by Sonny and Cher. Songs: "It's Gonna Rain" (Sonny Bono), "Snap It" (Jimmie Haskell), "House on the Beach," "Gods of Love," "Run Away from Him" ("By" Dunham, Bobby Beverly), "Yellow Haired Woman (Tic-a-tic-a-tac)," "Rock the World," "Winter Nocturne" (Dunham, E. Davis), "Pyramid Stomp" (Dunham, Haskell), "Drum Dance" (Frank Warren, Joe Saracino).

p&d, Maury Dexter; w, Harry Spaulding (based on a story by Hank Tani); ph, Jack Marquette; m, Jimmie Haskell; ed, Jodie Copelan; cos, Joseph Dimmitt; makeup, Dan Greenway.

Musical/Comedy (PR:A MPAA:NR)

WILD ONE, THE**** (1953) 79m COL bw

Marlon Brando (Johnny), Mary Murphy (Kathie), Robert Keith (Harry Bleeker), Lee Marvin (Chino), Jay C. Flippen (Sheriff Singer), Peggy Maley (Mildred), Hugh Sanders (Charlie Thomas), Ray Teal (Frank Bleeker), John Brown (Bill Hannegan), Will Wright (Art Kleiner), Robert Osterloh (Ben), Robert Bice (Wilson), William Yedder (Jimmy), Yvonne Doughty (Britches), Keith Clarke (Gringo), Gil Stratton, Jr. (Mouse), Darren Dublin (Dinky), Johnny Tarangelo (Red), Jerry Paris (Dextro), Gene Peterson (Crazy), Alvy Moore (Pigeon), Harry Landers (Go-Go), Jim Connell (Boxer), Don Anderson (Stinger), Angela Stevens (Betty), Bruno VeSoto (Simmonds), Pat O'Malley (Sawyer), Timothy Carey (Chino Boy), Wally Albright (Cyclist), Eve March (Dorothy), Mary Newton (Mrs. Thomas), Ted Cooper (Racer).

The first and best biker movie begins as a group of 40 leather-jacketed motorcyclists roar down a lonely country road straight at the camera. The bikers, who call themselves The Black Rebels, invade a legitimate motorcycle race and try to join the competition, but they are soon thrown out by the mass of motorcycle enthusiasts. Before leaving, a gang member manages to snatch the first prize trophy and he presents it to their leader, Brando. With the trophy now strapped to his handle-bars, Brando leads his pack of rowdies into the small town of Wrightsville where they drag up and down the street forcing an old man to drive his car to a light pole. Many of the bikers pile into the local bar, Bleeker's Cafe, which is owned and operated by the sheriff of the little town, Keith. Keith is obviously overwhelmed by the disturbance and does little to calm things down as the bikers drink themselves into oblivion. Brando's minions amuse themselves by terrorizing the town, while he spots a good looking girl, Murphy, and follows her into the bar. To his surprise he learns that she is Keith's daughter, and he tries to impress her by giving her the stolen trophy. Though she is intrigued by this strange, somewhat withdrawn, brutish young man, she refuses the gift. More trouble soon thunders into town in the guise of Marvin, a former member of Brando's gang who has left and formed his own pack. Marvin enjoys goading his former chieftain and when he tries to snatch the trophy off of Brando's motorcycle, a savage fight erupts. The townsfolk mingle in with the dozens of bikers to get a good look at the brawl, but when a foolish man tries to drive his car through the mass of people, the bikers turn his car over. Realizing that the hoodlums have now gone too far, Keith works up enough nerve to arrest Marvin. A bit bemused by the situation, Marvin allows himself to be put in jail, confident that his gang can bust him out. Meanwhile, Murphy begins to see Brando as a way out of her dull small town existence and she begins to trust him, much to the annoyance of Doughty, a girl in Marvin's gang who carries a torch for Brando. When night falls, Marvin's gang erupts in a frenzy of activity. They destroy the phone lines in the police station to prevent Keith from calling for more help from the county sheriff and they then go on a rampage of destruction. Having lost control of the situation, Brando takes Murphy to safety in the local park. They talk for a while and when asked by Murphy what he's rebelling against, Brando replies: "What've ya got?" Torn between her desire for him and her fear of him, Murphy runs away from Brando. He chases her and when he catches up she whirls around and slaps him. She then breaks free and runs off. The incident is witnessed by several townspeople who assume that Brando has tried to rape the girl. Brando rides back to town alone, but he is attacked by a vigilante mob and beaten severely. Murphy sees what is happening and begs her father to stop it. Keith arrives with his pistol and orders the citizens to stop. Brando collects himself and decides to leave town, but as he rides off one of the townsfolk throws a tire iron at him. The object knocks Brando off his motorcycle and the rideless machine hits and kills an old man. The townsfolk's bloodlust in full boil, a lynching is suggested, but Brando is saved by the arrival of the county sheriff, Flippen. Order is restored to the town, but the matter of the killing needs to be settled. Murphy comes to Brando's defense and declares that he never attacked her, and another person admits that they saw someone hit Brando with the tire iron. Flippen sets Brando free with orders that he and his gang never enter the area again. Shocked and confused over Murphy, Keith, and some members of the community's kindness towards him, Brando tries to articulate his thanks, but the words don't come and he rides out of town. Inspired by an incident in 1947 where a gang of 4,000 motorcyclists took over the small town of Hollister, California for the 4th of July weekend and destroyed it, producer Kramer put together a film which he hoped would illustrate the frustration and alienation felt by a younger generation who rebelled by becoming nomadic wanders searching for something intangible. Instead of becoming the examination of a social ill that Kramer expected it to be, THE WILD ONE became an anthem for the very disaffected youth it sought to illuminate. Brando's gripping, totally engrossing performance enthralled audiences who became fascinated with his contradictory character who seemed powerful and brutal, but who demonstrated a sensitive, caring, and vulnerable side which he tried hard to repress. The rest of the bikers, including Marvin's wonderfully sleazy gang leader Chino, are merely indistinguishable rabble looking for cheap thrills. Brando rarely participates in their violent acts, preferring to talk with Murphy. When he loses control of the situation he seems ready to just leave them to their own fates and ride off with the girl. The only death in the film is an accident and it was caused by one of the victim's own neighbors, thus leaving Brando a sympathetic, if enigmatic, anti-hero–one that would pave the way for James Dean in REBEL WITHOUT A CAUSE. Brando is simply superb in the film. He perfectly captures the confusion which causes the inarticulate frustration of youth while trying to cover this vulnerability with macho bravado. We see both the child and the adult in his performance as each side wrestles for control. It is a powerful performance–one that would haunt him for the rest of his career. Of the film itself, Brando thought little, stating that he thought it failed to explore: "...why young people tend to bunch into groups that seek expression in violence, all that we did was show the violence." While Brando may have been right (the film was banned in England for 14 years for fear that would it incite British teenagers to riot), his portrayal of Johnnie would become an American youth-culture icon that would remain strong and vivid for decades–the eternal rebel.

p, Stanley Kramer; d, Laslo Benedek; w, John Paxton (based on a story by Frank Rooney); ph, Hal Mohr; m, Leith Stevens; ed, Al Clark; prod d, Rudolph Sternad; md, M.W. Stoloff; art d, Walter Holscher; set d, Louis Diage.

Drama   Cas.   (PR:C   MPAA:NR)

WILD ONES ON WHEELS zero   (1967) 92m Charles Bros./Emerson bw (AKA: DRIVERS TO HELL)

Francine York, Edmund Tontini, Robert Blair.

A good-for-unintentional-laughs-only film about a group of crazed young hot-rodders who meet and kill an ex-con who was about to venture into the Mojave Desert and dig up $240,000 in loot he had buried there. Learning of the treasure, the psychotic teenagers kidnap their victim's wife in the hopes that she will lead them to where the money is buried. Meanwhile, an insurance investigator infiltrates the gang's ranks and manages to get enough evidence to put them behind bars. Pretty awful.

p, Fred Charles; d, Rudolph Cusumano.

Crime   (PR:C-O   MPAA:NR)

WILD PACK, THE½**   (1972) 102m AIP c (AKA: THE SANDPIT GENERALS)

Kent Lane (Bullet), Tisha Sterling (Dora), John Rubinstein (Professor), Butch Patrick (No Legs), Mark De Vries (Dry Turn), Peter Nielsen (Lollypop), Alejandro Rey (Father Jose Pedro), Eliana Pittman (Dalvah), Ademir Da Silva (Big John), Guilherme Lamounier ("The Cat"), Dorival Caymmi (Voodoo Priest), Chris Rodriquez (Police Chief), Jimmy Fraser (Dora's Brother), Marisa Urban (Wealthy Woman), William Hobson (Husband), Macio (Ezequiel), Aloysio De Oliveira (Chancellor), Creusa Millet (Priestess), Freddie Gedeon (Almiro), The Girls from Bahia, Oscar Castro Neves.

Lane leads a group of wild children who live in South America, picking through garbage to find food and often having to battle stray animals for their keep. Sterling, the only woman in the gang, is brought in by Lane who must fight to keep her. They plan to rob a wealthy family but a rival gang leader threatens to inform and is subsequently killed by Lane in self-defense. On the run, the gang is plagued by poor health, accidents, and inevitably the successful pursuit by lawmen. Both Lane and Sterling are captured and, though they escape, Sterling falls prey to smallpox and dies in Lane's arms. While THE WILD PACK took top honors at the Moscow Film Fest it is not without problems, especially in the casting of a pair of blue-eyed blondes as Brazilians. Everything is very obvious and lacks the subtlety needed for a film like this to succeed. Songs: "When I See a Star" (Dorival Caymmi, Louis Oliveira), "When the Sun Starts Shining Through" (Guilherme Lamounier), "Sing with Me" (Lamounier), "Dora" (Caymmi, Oliveira).

p,d&w, Hall Bartlett (based on a story collection "Capitaes de Areia" by Jorge Amado); ph, Ricardo Aronovich (Panavision, CFI Color); m, Louis Oliviera; ed, Marshall M. Borden; makeup, Gilberto Marquez.

Drama   (PR:O   MPAA:R)

WILD PARTY, THE½**   (1929) 77m PAR bw

Clara Bow (Stella Ames), Fredric March (Gil Gilmore), Shirley O'Hara (Helen Owens), Marceline Day (Faith Morgan), Joyce Compton (Eva Tutt), Adrienne Dore (Babs), Virginia Thomas (Tess), Kay Bryant (Thelma), Alice Adair (Mazie), Jean Lorraine (Ann), Renee Whitney (Janice), Amo Ingram (Jean), Jack Oakie (Al), Marguerite Cramer (Gwen), Phillips Holmes (Phil), Ben Hendricks, Jr. (Ed), Jack Luden (George), Jack Raymond (Baloam).

Though the plot practically grows mold before the viewer's eyes, and some of the production qualities are laughable, THE WILD PARTY remains fascinating to watch from first reel to last. One of the popular happy-go-lucky college-based films of the era, this has an added benefit in featuring Bow in her talkie debut. She is, naturally, a wild party girl who's enrolled in college for the good times rather than to advance her education. Bow and her girl friends decide to take a class taught by March, not for his stunning classroom abilities, but because he's cute! March is a no-nonsense type and the course proves to be much more difficult than Bow and company had anticipated. To relieve this academic pressure, the coeds pull a few classroom pranks. Bow attends a ball, but is kicked out for wearing a low-cut dress. She later goes to a roadhouse, where an inebriated Hendricks tries to have his way with her. March, who inexplicably is also at the roadhouse, puts a stop to this, then gives Bow a lift. Compton, a fellow classmate of Bow's, sees the campus flirt leaving March's car, and her nimble mind immediately assumes there's funny business involved. Gossip spreads thick, so March chews out Bow in front of other students to prove they aren't an item. Bow angrily walks out of the classroom. She and roommate O'Hara go to a party (no one ever studies at this school), where O'Hara falls for Luden. Hendricks, still angry with March for the earlier altercation, finds the professor and shoots him. Bow tells the wounded March of her love for him, giving Compton more fuel for her gossip mill. A letter from O'Hara to Luden turns up, and its spicy contents create a scandal. Bow decides to take the fall for her pal, and leaves school in disgrace. She boards a train to leave town, but true love wins out in the end. March knows Bow is innocent and resigns his position to join her on the train. It's silly, but so what? Bow gives an energetic performance, her Brooklyn accent serving the "It" girl's well-known personality with absolute perfection. The advertising campaign played up on this with glee, claiming: "You've had an eyeful of IT...now get an earful!" March, in only his second film, takes his part seriously, which adds to the picture's inherent campiness. Bow was terrified of making a talkie, but she handled herself well in the funfest. Reportedly, her voice was so loud it blew meters on the sound equipment when she spoke her first line. At times her voice is muddled on the soundtrack, partly the fault of the new technology and partly due to her accent. In England, THE WILD PARTY was released as a silent film. Within a few years Bow would be gone from the screen forever, while March would become one of filmdom's most respected thespians.

d, Dorothy Arzner; w, E. Lloyd Sheldon, John V.A. Weaver, George Marion, Jr. (based on a story by Warner Fabian); ph, Victor Milner; ed, Otho Lovering; cos, Travis Banton; m/l, theme song "My Wild Party Girl," Leo Robin, Richard Whiting.

Comedy/Romance   (PR:A   MPAA:NR)

**WILD PARTY, THE*   (1956) 91m UA bw

Anthony Quinn (Big Tom Kupfen), Carol Ohmart (Erica London), Arthur Franz (Lt. Arthur Mitchell), Jay Robinson (Gage Freeposter), Kathryn Grant (Honey), Nehemiah Persoff (Kicks Johnson), Paul Stewart (Ben Davis), Barbara Nichols (Sandy), Jana Mason (Singer), William Phipps (Wino), Maureen Stephenson (Ellen), Nestor Paiva (Branson), Michael Ross (Bouncer), Carl Milletaire (Customer), James Bronte (Bartender), Joe Greene (Fat Man), The Buddy DeFranco Quartet Combo.

Not to be confused with the equally annoying picture of the same name that was made from Joseph Moncure March's less than epic poem, this one features sex, violence, loud jazz, and as reprehensible a group of thieves and brigands as have ever been seen on any screen. It's a quickie flick that hoped to cash in on the Beatniks who were occupying the media spotlight at the time. Quinn is an ex-football player who is now close to being an animal. He spends his time frequenting jazz clubs with his cadre of pals; Robinson, a drug-crazed knife man, Grant, and pianist Persoff. All are on drugs and need money to fill their veins. One night, the quartet goes out looking for someone to rob and winds up in a jazz club. There, they spot Ohmart and her betrothed, Franz, enjoying the sounds. Quinn moves in on the delicate Ohmart and makes a play for her that she welcomes at first, then turns away from when she realizes that he's a brute. Franz and Ohmart don't have a car and accept a lift from the foursome, not sensing that they are about to become victims. The four kidnap the couple but have no idea from whom to extract the ransom so they try to get it from club owner Stewart. When he refuses, Quinn gets the sappy idea of marrying Ohmart and taking her away from Navy man Franz. By doing that, Ohmart's family will be happy to get her back by paying Quinn money. Quinn tells Grant and Persoff to send Ohmart's family a telegram saying that she has eloped with him. Later, Robinson and Quinn battle, and Robinson is thrown down in the abandoned beach amusement building where they have taken the couple. Persoff, the only one with any sense, tries to explain that Quinn will bring them all ruin and it might be better to forget this caper. Grant agrees with him but she's only pretending. She tells Persoff to go back to the beach so she can warn Quinn that Persoff is a weakling. They get back and Quinn begins to throttle Persoff. Now Grant realizes that Quinn is bonkers and runs him down with her car, then drives off with Persoff as cops come and free Franz and Ohmart. A despicable picture peopled by despicable characters. The only saving grace was the superb jazz score by Bregman and the players, who included Buddy DeFranco, Teddy Buckner, and Pete Jolly, who did the fingering for Persoff. Other jazz players of note were Maynard Ferguson, Bud Shank, Barney Kessel, Ralph Pena, Georgie Auld, and Dave Pell. Ohmart had been touted as a new sex symbol in films and given a huge publicity campaign but it never happened, although she did appear in a number of films including BORN RECKLESS, ONE MAN'S WAY, and THE SPECTRE OF EDGAR ALLAN POE.

p, Sidney Harmon; d, Harry Horner; w, John McPartland; ph, Sam Leavitt; m, Buddy Bregman; ed, Richard C. Meyer; art d, Rudi Feld; cos, Richard Bachler, Gwen Fitzer.

Crime Drama   **Cas.**   **(PR:C-O   MPAA:NR)**

WILD PARTY, THE zero   (1975) 100m AIP c

James Coco (*Jolly Grimm*), Raquel Welch (*Queenie*), Perry King (*Dale Sword*), Tiffany Bolling (*Kate*), Royal Dano (*Tex*), David Dukes (*James Morrison*), Dena Dietrich (*Mrs. Murchison*), Regis Cordic (*Mr. Murchison*), Jennifer Lee (*Madeline True*), Marya Small (*Bertha*), Bobo Lewis (*Wilma*), Annette Ferra (*Nadine*), Eddie Laurence (*Kreutzer*), Tony Paxton (*Sergeant*), Waldo K. Berns (*Policeman*), Nina Faso (*Lady in Black*), Baruch Lumet (*Tailor*), Martin Kove (*Editor*), Ralph Manza (*Fruit Dealer*), Lark Geib (*Rosa*), Fredric Franklyn (*Sam*), J.S. Johnson (*Morris*), Michael Grant Hall (*Oscar D'Armano*), Skipper (*Phil D'Armano*), Don De Natale (*Jackie the Dancer*), Tom Reese (*Eddy*), Geraldine Baron (*Grace*), Jill Giraldi (*Crippled Girl*), Barbara Quinn (*Mildred*), Gloria Gadhoke (*Redhead*), Clea Ariell, Susan Arnold, Joe Arrowsmith, Jonathan Becker, Waldo K. Berns, Bob Buckingham, Jennifer Chessman, Chuck Comisky, Bill Dance, Dick Dano, Kathleen Dimmick, Mark David Jacobson, Rick Kanter, Kevin Matthews, Luke Matthiessen, Gordon Maus, Bill Merickel, Tommie Merickel, Tony Paxton, Anthony Pecoraro, Jack Sachs, Carmen Saveiros, Mark Swope, Ayesha Taft, Whitney Tower (*Party Guests*).

An absolutely dismal picture, THE WILD PARTY features Coco as a silent movie comedian whose career is falling apart as talking pictures arrive. His plan is to release one last, great silent epic and to that end, he invites several Hollywood bigwigs to his mansion in hopes of finding a distributor. Welch, his mistress, continues encouraging Coco, though it is obvious to everyone attending the soiree that the film is a bomb. Liquor starts flowing and Coco's mood grows worse with each drink. King, a rising young star, makes a pass at Welch, which infuriates Coco. Ferra, a dancer who hopes Coco will give her a break, finds her sister in a bed with another party guest. She is highly upset and turns to Coco for sympathy. She kisses the comedian, but another drunken guest is convinced Coco is a lecherous old man taking advantage of the girl. He starts beating on Coco, but King puts a stop to the fight. Coco is ungrateful, though, and Welch ends up in bed with King. Bolling, a friend of Welch's, tries to seduce Dukes, Coco's screenwriter, but she is rejected by him. She responds by angrily telling Coco that he is too old for the much younger Welch. Coco goes off the deep end, and when he sees Welch and King coming out of a bedroom, he shoots them both. Dukes is hurt as well, but survives, going on to write an epic poem about this wild night. THE WILD PARTY is obviously inspired by the infamous Fatty Arbuckle-Virgina Rappe case, though the true-life incidents and this film bear no resemblance to one another. Instead it rolls around in lurid glee, unfolding the ridiculous plot with one piece of sensationalism after another. The film originally had an 120-minute running time, but American International Pictures, realizing this would never do, cut some 20 minutes from the film. This 100-minute version was later pared down to 90 minutes, infuriating director Ivory. "The whole thing is a mess," he said. "Scenes have been cut and transposed and scenes which originally were cut have been restored. They removed a lot of the poetry and cut scenes which were important to establish characterizations." Whether Ivory's arguments had any merit will probably never be known, but the final film got exactly what it deserved. AIP gave this trash only a token release, and it quickly disappeared from the theaters. Songs include "The Wild Party," "Funny Man," "Not That Queenie of Mine," "Singapore Sally," "Herbert Hoover Drag," "Ain't Nothing Bad About Feeling Good," "Sunday Morning Blues" (Larry Rosenthal, Walter Marks).

p, Ismail Merchant; d, James Ivory; w, Walter Marks (based on the narrative poem by Joseph Moncure March); ph, Walter Lassally (Movielab Color); m, Larry Rosenthal, Louis St. Louis; ed, Kent McKinney; md, Rosenthal; art d, David Nichols; set d, Bruce David Weintraub; cos, Ron Talsky, Ralph Lauren, Ronald Kolodgie; spec eff, Edward Bash; ch, Patricia Birch; stunts, Teri McComas; makeup, Louis Lane.

Drama   **Cas.**   **(PR:O   MPAA:R)**

WILD RACERS, THE*   (1968) 79m Alta Vista-Filmakers/AIP c

Fabian (*Jo-Jo Quillico*), Mimsy Farmer (*Katherine*), Alan Haufrect (*Charlie*), Judy Cornwell (*British Girl*), Davis Landers (*Manager*), Warwick Sims (*Jo-Jo's Partner*), Talia Coppola [Shire], Ursule Pauly, Dick Miller, Ron Gans, Fabienne Arel, Patricia Culbert, Mary Jo Kennedy, Kurt Boon.

A meager race car picture which relies heavily on stock footage to tell its story, that of racer Fabian who is hired by an auto tycoon to do some driving. He really has a fondness for the girls, however, and chalks up them up faster than laps. Farmer is his favorite until she mentions marriage. He drops her like a hot radiator cap and finds someone else without any desire for a commitment. Francis Ford Coppola was the second unit director on this one, which is quite similar to the 1962 AIP picture THE YOUNG RACERS, on which Coppola was the soundman. In a minor role is Francis' sister Talia, who soon changed her name to Talia Shire and went on to appear in THE GODFATHER and ROCKY. Also notable is the photography by Almendros who is famous for his work for Francois Truffaut as well as for receiving three Oscar nominations in a row–DAYS OF HEAVEN (1978), winning the award, KRAMER VS. KRAMER (1979), and THE BLUE LAGOON (1980).

p, Joel Rapp; d, Daniel Haller; w, Max House; ph, Nestor Almendros, Daniel Lacambre (Pathe Color); m, Mike Curb; ed, Verna Fields, Dennis Jacob; m/l, Pierre Vassilu.

Action/Drama   **(PR:A-C   MPAA:NR)**

WILD REBELS, THE*   (1967) 90m Comet/Crown International c

Steve Alaimo (*Rod Tillman*), Willie Pastrano (*Banjo*), John Vella (*Jeeter*), Bobbie Byers (*Linda*), Jeff Gillen (*Fats*), Walter Philbin (*Lt. Dorn*), Robert Freund (*Detective*), Seymour A. Eisenfeld (*Walt Simpson*), Phil Longo (*1st Man*), Milton Smith (*Bartender*), Kurt Nagler, Steve Gellar, Chris Martell, Gary Brady (*College Boys*), Nora Alonzo (*Nori*), The Birdwatchers (*A Band*), Dutch Holland (*Driver*), Art Barker (*Gunshop Owner*), William P. Kelley (*Bank Teller*), Cosmo Lloyd (*Bank Guard*), Tom Frysinger, Emil Deaton (*Sheriffs*), Jamie Hickson, Nick Bontempo, Edward Wanisko, Aaron Deaton, Dennis French, Bob Sparks (*Policemen*).

A stereotyped biker picture which casts Alaimo as a former stock car driver who cooperates with the police in a scheme to capture some riders in the Satan's Angels motorcycle gang. Alaimo serves as a getaway driver (the Angels use a car instead of bikes to avoid detection) during a bank holdup, informs the police of the bikers' plans, and then takes part in the police ambush. Nothing wild about this one. Gang leader Pastrano is a former light heavyweight boxing champion.

d&w, William Grefe; ph, Clifford H. Poland, Jr., Harry Walsh (Technicolor); m, Al Jacobs; ed, Julio C. Chavez, Robert Woodburn; set d, Patrick Nielsen; m/l, "You Don't Know Like I Know," Al Jacobs (sung by Steve Alaimo; makeup, Marie Del Russo.

Action/Drama   **(PR:O   MPAA:NR)**

WILD RIDE, THE*   (1960) 63m Filmgroup bw

Jack Nicholson (*Johnny Varron*), Georgianna Carter (*Nancy*), Robert Bean (*Dave*).

Nicholson's admirable performance can't do much for this tired hot rod tale about a murderous roadster (Nicholson) who freely runs motorcycle cops off the road. He's also a miffed at one-time buddy Bean for going straight and giving up life in the fast lane in exchange for a possessive girl friend (Carter). He kidnaps Carter and in the process kills a few more coppers before biting the dust himself.

p&d, Harvey Berman; w, Ann Porter, Marion Rothman; ph, Taylor Sloane; ed, William Meyer.

Action/Drama   **Cas.**   **(PR:C   MPAA:NR)**

WILD RIDERS zero   (1971) 91m Tudor/Crown International c (AKA: ANGELS FOR KICKS)

Alex Rocco (*Stick*), Elizabeth Knowles (*Rona*), Sherry Bain (*Laure*), Arell Blanton (*Pete*), Ted Hayden (*Rona's Husband*), Jax Carroll (*Stud*), Steve Vincent (*Neighbor*), Bill Collins (*Kelly*), Gail Liddle (*Hippie Girl in Bar*), Ray Galvin (*Tom The "Fence"*), Linda Johanesen (*Crucified Girl*), Diana Jones (*Tom's Daughter*), Frank Charolla (*Biker*), Dirty Denney (*Bike Gang Leader*).

A pair of bikers break into the mansion of two attractive ladies who are as wealthy as they are sexy. Rape and violence follow until the outrageously inventive finale which has the husband of one of the women, a cellist, come home and kill the captors with his instrument. Good try in many ways with a deplorable script.

p, John Burrows, Edward Paramore III; d&w, Richard Kanter (based on a story by Sal Comstock); ph, Paul Hipp, Bob Maxwell, Scott Lloyd Davies (Eastmancolor); m, Alan Alper; ed, Marco Meyer; art d, Lee Fisher; m/l, "He's My Family," Arell Blanton; stunts, Frank Charolla; makeup, Ron Kenney.

Crime Drama   **(PR:O   MPAA:R)**

WILD RIVER****   (1960) 115m FOX c

Montgomery Clift (*Chuck Glover*), Lee Remick (*Carol Baldwin*), Jo Van Fleet (*Ella Garth*), Albert Salmi (*F.J. Bailey*), Jay C. Flippen (*Hamilton Garth*), James Westerfield (*Cal Garth*), Big Jeff Bess (*Joe John Garth*), Robert Earl Jones (*Ben*), Frank Overton (*Walter Clark*), Barbara Loden (*Betty Jackson*), Malcolm Atterbury (*Sy Moore*), Bruce Dern (*Jack Roper*), Judy Harris (*Barbara Baldwin*), Jim Menard (*Jim Baldwin, Jr.*), Jim Steakley (*Mayor Tom Maynard*), Patricia Perry (*Mattie*), John Dudley (*Todd*), Alfred E. Smith (*Thompson*), Mark Menson (*Winters*).

Not a great success at the box office because issue-oriented films were not what the public seemed to want in 1960. Nevertheless, this dramatic tug-of-war between progress and tradition remains a memorable example of Kazan at his best. It's the Tennessee Valley in the early 1930s. Clift is an agent for the Tennessee Valley Authority (TVA) which is in the process of clearing land to build much-needed dams across the area. This cannot be accomplished without the demolition of many homes and the relocation of their inhabitants. One of Clift's most unpleasant tasks is the removal of Van Fleet, an 80-year-old widow, from her home. It's a parcel of land she and her late husband had cleared and that she has lived on for more than a half century. Van Fleet refuses to leave, thus causing a major problem. As if Clift's plight isn't bad enough, the local townspeople look rightly upon him as an interloper and make his life in the area miserable. They sorely resent him and the job he must do. Further, since Clift is a liberal, he is hated for his attitude about treating the area's blacks the same way he does the whites, who are still reticent to admit that Lincoln freed the slaves. The locals go so far as to attempt beating some sense into Clift. During his sojourn, Van Fleet's young widowed granddaughter, Remick, falls in love with Clift and the courtship continues until they marry. In time, under the bludgeonings of progress, Van Fleet finally gives up her battle, the land is flooded, and she has the last laugh on all of them when she dies shortly after moving into her new home. It's an emotionally charged movie that offers little respite to the viewer. Skillfully scripted by Osborn from two novels, and masterfully directed by Kazan, it featured excellent acting and strong production values. Remick, who had appeared in Kazan's realization of Budd Schulberg's A FACE IN THE CROWD, was paged again for this, which continued the beginning of a long and distinguished career. Many nonprofessional Tennesseans were used in the film and that lent a realism seldom seen when Hollywood extras are employed. Kazan's wife, Barbara Loden, plays a small role and if you keep a weather eye out you'll see a very young Bruce Dern appearing in his first movie. Van Fleet's performance is a standout and it was expected that she would garner an Oscar for it, but that was not to be and the winner that year was Shirley Jones in ELMER GANTRY. Although playing an 80-year-old, it was a marvel of Ben Nye's makeup because she was only 41 at the time. But great acting comes from within and she was able to convey the tiredness and doggedness of an octogenarian with the subtlest of moves. Hopkins did a fine, spare score that never intruded and managed to make every dramatic point with a minimum of music. Shot on location in Tennessee at Lake Chickamauga, the Hiwassee River, and in the towns of Cleveland and Charleston, it was the end of a 25-year dream of Kazan's. He had been to the area in the mid-1930s and always wanted to do a movie about the subject but it took more than two decades to find a studio and the right script to fulfill his desire. Clift was never easy to work with, as he had several personal problems, not the least of which was his drinking and his difficulty in coming to grips with his homosexuality. He'd promised to stay off the sauce for the picture and kept his word until the final week when he went on a bender that almost submarined the movie. In a good turn as a racist, note Albert Salmi (whose real name is not Italian at all). It's Imlas, which is Salmi spelled backwards, another person in the entertainment business from Coney Island, which may have been the birthplace of more show people than any other area in the United States. It's a talky movie (ah, but what talk!) and the only action sequences are the battle between Clift and the rednecks and the scene just preceding it, when the yahoos run a car into Remick's house. Social drama has seldom been a moneymaker and the same held true for this, which looks better and better through the gauze of time.

p&d, Elia Kazan; w, Paul Osborn (based on the novels *Mud on the Stars* by William Bradford Huie, *Dunbar's Cove* by Borden Deal); ph, Ellsworth Fredricks (CinemaScope, DeLuxe Color); m, Kenyon Hopkins; ed, William Reynolds; art d, Lyle R. Wheeler, Herman A. Blumenthal; set d, Walter M. Scott, Joseph Kish; cos, Anna Hill Johnstone; makeup, Ben Nye.

Drama   Cas.   (PR:A-C MPAA:NR)

WILD ROVERS**   (1971) 106m MGM c

William Holden (*Ross Bodine*), Ryan O'Neal (*Frank Post*), Karl Malden (*Walter Buckman*), Lynn Carlin (*Sada Billings*), Tom Skerritt (*John Buckman*), Joe Don Baker (*Paul Buckman*), James Olson (*Joe Billings*), Leora Dana (*Nell Buckman*), Moses Gunn (*Ben*), Victor French (*Sheriff*), Rachel Roberts (*Maybell*), Charles Gray (*Savage*), Sam Gilman (*Hansen*), William Bryant (*Hereford*), Jack Garner (*Cap Swilling*), Caitlin Wyles (*Ross' Girl*), Mary Jackson (*Sada's Mother*), William Lucking (*Ruff*), Ed Bakey (*Gambler*), Ted Gehring (*Benson Sheriff*), Alan Carney (*Palace Bartender*), Ed Long (*Cassidy*), Lee De Broux (*Leaky*), Bennie Dobbins, Red Morgan (*Sheepmen*), Bob Beck (*Bathhouse Attendant*), Geoffrey Edwards (*Attendent's Son*), Studs Tanney (*Piano Player*), Hal Lynch (*Mack*), Dick Crockett

(*Deputy*), Bruno VeSota (*Cantina Bartender*).

Aging cowboy Holden and young O'Neal star as a pair of big, bad, but lovable ranch hands, employed by Malden, who are tired of their pointless existence. They decide to rob a bank in the hope that it'll ignite a spark in them and help them amount to something. They are soon on the run from a posse headed by Malden's two sons, Skerritt and Baker, chasing them along their Mexico-bound path. The downbeat ending has both men killed off, first O'Neal, then Holden. The actors try as they can with the uneven script–Holden extends his WILD BUNCH persona, and O'Neal tries to hide his LOVE STORY role–but some rather obvious symbolism and the unavoidable comparison to BUTCH CASSIDY AND THE SUNDANCE KID don't add much strength to Blake Edwards' corner.

p, Blake Edwards, Ken Wales; d&w, Edwards; ph, Philip Lathrop (Panavision, Metrocolor); m, Jerry Goldsmith; ed, John F. Burnett; art d, George W. Davis, Addison Hehr; set d, Robert Benton, Reg Allen; cos, Jack Bear; m/l, title song, Goldsmith, Ernie Sheldon; makeup, Tom Tuttle.

Western   (PR:C-O MPAA:GP)

WILD SCENE, THE zero   (1970) 96m Four Star Excelsior c

Richard Tate (*Jack*), Alberta Nelson (*Dr. Virginia Grant*), Gary Pillar (*Hal*), Anita Eubank (*Diana*), Berry Kroeger (*Tim*), Nancy Czar (*Clarette*), John Craven (*Morton*), Rita Lupino (*Faith*), Wendy Stuart (*Andrea*), Charles Terhune (*Paul*), Katherine Darc (*Sandra*), Margaretta Ramsey (*Kay*), Jarl Victor (*Dr. Jennings*), Suzanne Bragg (*Kathy*), Rick Bentley (*Student*), Kathie Zundel (*Janice*), Barbara Maneff (*Annabelle*), Jo Graff (*Nancy*), Anne Hershon (*Felicia*), Evanna Lynn (*Ella*), Jackie Kendall (*Alice*), Phyllis Sally (*Sally*).

A psychiatrist relates various case studies that include incest, impotency, voyeurism, masochism, prostitution, and a birth control racket, all with accompanying visuals, of course. In the meantime she and her daughter get involved in a campus riot, an orgy and an extortion scam, and the seamy visuals go on. A wildly disagreeable romp on the tawdry side, shot in Los Angeles, of course.

p, Sam Jacoby; d, William Rowland; w, Michael Kraike, William Keys (based on a story by Jacoby, Rowland); ph, Robert Caramico; m, Jaime Mendoza-Nava; ed, Sergei Goncharoff; m/l, "The Wild Scene," "It's You Alone," sung by Jimmie Reed; "I Just Want a Chance," performed by Carnival.

Drama   (PR:O MPAA:R)

WILD SEASON**½   (1968, South Africa) 92m Emil Nofal/UNIV c
                                                      (AKA: WILDE SEISOEN)

Gert Van den Bergh (*Dirk Maritz*), Marie Du Toit (*Martie Maritz*), Joe Stewardson (*1st Mate Tom Sheppard*), Janis Reinhardt (*Jess Sheppard*), Anthony Thomas (*Michael Maritz*), Johan Du Plooy (*Hennie de Waal*), Ian Yule (*Andy Wilson*), Michael Spalletta (*Maria*), Freddie Van Urk, Gerrit Van Urk, Hynie Slade, Shelley Trope, Don Leonard, Karel De Wet, Johan Koegelenberg.

Thomas is the son of ship fleet owner Van den Bergh, both of whom are affected by the death of another son. Van den Bergh tries to get Cambridge-educated Thomas to fill the dead boy's place, but has no success. At length, however, Thomas comes around, gets work at the port, begins a romance with first-mate Stewardson's leukemia-stricken daughter, and then uncovers evidence that proves Stewardson responsible for his brother's death. Thomas reveals his discovery to his father and the bond between the two is made even stronger, when, in the ensuing showdown, Thomas performs a heroic act at sea and proves himself to be an exceptional young man.

p, Jans Rautenbach; d&w, Emil Nofal; ph, Vincent Cox; m, Roy Martin; ed, Peter Henkel.

Drama   (PR:A MPAA:NR)

WILD SEED**½   (1965) 99m Pennebaker/UNIV bw

Michael Parks (*Fargo*), Celia Kaye (*Daffy*), Ross Elliott (*Mr. Collinge*), Woodrow Chambliss (*Mr. Simms*), Rupert Crosse (*Hobo*), Eva Novak (*Mrs. Simms*), Norman Burton (*Policeman*), Merritt Bohn (*Constable*), Anthony Lettier (*Bartender*).

Kaye heads for Los Angeles in search of her real parents, leaving behind her foster parents in New York. Her cross-country romp is accompanied by Parks, a drifter and opportunist who travels with her only to see what he can get out of the deal. By the time Kaye learns the truth about her past, however, she and Parks have fallen in love and decided to stay together, on Parks' part seemingly because he has nothing better to do. Phony upbeat ending characterizes the weakness of the entire film. Marlon Brando, Sr. acted as executive producer for this witlessly acted farrago.

p, Albert S. Ruddy; d, Brian G. Hutton; w, Les Pine (based on a story by Pine, Ike Jones); ph, Conrad Hall; m, Richard Markowitz; ed, Hugh S. Fowler; art d, Alexander Golitzen, George Webb; set d, John McCarthy, James S. Redd; cos, Ted Parvin; m/l, "That's Why," Hutton, Ruddy, Markowitz; makeup, Bud Westmore, Richard Cobos.

Drama   (PR:A MPAA:NR)

WILD STALLION½										(1952) 70m MON c

Ben Johnson (*Dan Light*), Edgar Buchanan (*Wintergreen*), Martha Hyer (*Caroline*), Hayden Rorke (*Maj. Callen*), Hugh Beaumont (*Capt. Wilmurt*), Orley Lindgren (*Young Dan Light*), Don Haggerty (*Sgt. Keach*), Susan Odin (*Caroline as a Child*), I. Stanford Jolley (*Bill Cole*), Barbara Woodell (*Mrs. Light*), John Halloran (*Mr. Light*), Don Garner.

An enjoyable little western programmer starring Johnson as a young cavalry lieutenant, recently graduated from West Point, who thinks back to the events that formed his character. In flashback we see Johnson as a young boy (played by Lindgren) on the day he is orphaned in an Indian attack. His prize colt escapes in the battle and runs off to join a herd of wild stallions. Alone and afraid, Johnson is taken in by wild horse hunter Buchanan who raises him at a cavalry outpost. As the boy grows older he becomes obsessed with recapturing his beautiful horse that has now become wild. Johnson at length finds his stallion, but then loses it to the Army. After he rescues a cavalry patrol from am Indian attack, the Army gratefully returns Johnson's horse to him and the pair are reunited. Standard stuff made watchable by a solid cast with Buchanan the standout. The assistant director on this film was Andrew McLaglen, son of Academy Award-winning Victor McLaglen who was a senior member of director John Ford's performing family.

p, Walter Mirisch; d, Lewis D. Collins; w, Dan Ullman; ph, Harry Neumann (Cinecolor); m, Marlin Skiles; ed, William Austin.

Western									(PR:A MPAA:NR)

WILD STRAWBERRIES***								(1959, Swed.) 90m Svensk
										Filmindustri/Janus bw SMULTRON- STALLET)

Victor Sjostrom [Seastrom] (*Prof. Isak Borg*), Bacteriologist, Bibi Andersson (*Sara*), Ingrid Thulin (*Marianne Borg*), Gunnar Bjornstrand (*Evald Borg*), Jullan Kindahl (*Agda*), Folke Sundquist (*Anders*), Bjorn Bjelvenstram (*Viktor*), Naima Wifstrand (*Isak's Mother*), Gunnel Brostrom (*Mrs. Berit Almann*), Gertrud Fridh (*Isak's Wife, Karin*), Ake Fridell (*Her Lover*), Sif Ruud (*Aunt*), Gunnar Sjoberg (*Alman*), Max von Sydow (*Akerman*), Yngve Nordwall (*Uncle Aron*), Per Sjostrand (*Sigfrid*), Gio Petre (*Sigbritt*), Gunnel Lindblom (*Charlotta*), Maud Hansson (*Angelica*), Anne-Mari Wiman (*Mrs. Akerman*), Eva Noree (*Anna*), Lena Bergman, Monica Ehrling (*Twins*), Per Skogsberg (*Hagbart*), Goran Lundquist (*Benjamin*), Helge Wulff (*Promoter*), Gunnar Olson, Wulff Lund.

Bergman's finest film and a staple in film history, WILD STRAWBERRIES not only serves as an example of what one of Sweden's greatest directors is capable of but of what importance a superb performance can hold. Sjostrom (another of Sweden's great directors, possibly the greatest) stars as old Uncle Isak Borg, a medical professor on his way to accept an honorary degree celebrating the 50th anniversary of his graduation from the university at Lund. He rides with his daughter-in-law, Thulin, who has decided to leave her husband, Bjornstrand, because he does not want her to have a child. An animosity exists between the opinionated Sjostrom (as Thulin sees him) and his daughter-in-law, mainly because the old man reminds her so much of her husband. En route they stop at Sjostrom's childhood house. He walks around and watches his family in the days of his youth (he, however, is not seen by the characters, nor is he present in this flashback). He sees his sweetheart, Andersson, picking wild strawberries to give to her deaf grandfather and carrying on semi-innocently with Sjostrom's brother. He watches the family as they eat dinner and finally he is awakened by a teenage girl (in the present) named Sara and again played by Andersson. She asks the old man for a ride, bringing her two male friends and admirers along for the trip. With five people in the car, they pick up another pair--a boisterous, loud, suffering couple whose car overturned in a near-fatal collision with Sjostrom's--and continue their journey. The bantering of the husband and wife turns sado-masochistic and they are kicked out of the car by Thulin. They stop for an outdoor meal and get engaged in a conversation about the existence of God. Andersson's companions give their philosophical disagreement a physical twist and begin a seemingly playful fight. The group continues on, stopping once again, however, to visit to Sjostrom's 95-year-old mother, a frightening old woman who complains that she has been cold as long as she can remember. In a dream sequence, Sjostrom enters an old house where he must prove that he is worthy of his award. He fails miserably, unable to diagnose a woman (the bickering wife from the car) as being dead. He finally receives his honorary degree and returns home where he comes to peace with Thulin, Bjornstrand, and his youth. The most striking sequence of the film occurs in the opening minutes, supplying cinema with one of its most haunting moments. Sjostrom, in a dream, walks through a desolate city which appears to have been designed by a German Expressionist. He is approached by a man without a face and notices a clock without hands. A funeral wagon makes its way through the echoing streets, but as it makes a turn it catches its rear wheel on a lamppost. The wheel comes off in a crash, the wagon continues on, and out of it slides a coffin onto the street. Sjostrom nears the coffin, it opens, Sjostrom extends his hands, church bells clang in the background, a hand reaches from the coffin and grabs his hand; a struggle ensues. Sjostrom, himself, is in the coffin--the dead Sjostrom fights with the living Sjostrom attempting to pull him into the afterlife. The symbolism is chilling, as are the visuals and the soundtrack, and the entire scene is perfectly integrated into the whole of the film. Sjostrom, in his final film, delivers, without

reservation, the finest performance in a Bergman film–a major accomplishment considering the virtuosity Bergman's actors consistently display. The usual annoying Bergman traits, however, still manage to surface–a deep concentration on symbols and psychoanalysis, over-intellectualizing, and the use of theater dramatics. Bergmaniacs love these traits, but time and reevaluation have not treated them so kindly. It is only in WILD STRAWBERRIES that these qualities seem unobtrusive. This, combined with Sjostrom's touching performance, is what makes WILD STRAWBERRIES such a wholly satisfying picture. (In Swedish; English subtitles.)

p, Allen Ekelund; d&w, Ingmar Bergman; ph, Gunnar Fischer, Bjorn Thermenius; m, Erik Nordgren; ed, Oscar Rosander; md, E. Eckert-Lundin; art d, Gittan Gustafsson; cos, Millie Strom.

**Drama						Cas.				(PR:O MPAA:NR)**

WILD WEED*	(1949) 90m Eureka bw (AKA: SHE SHOULD'A SAID
										NO; DEVIL'S WEED)

Lila Leeds (*The Girl*), Alan Baxter (*Markey*), Lyle Talbot (*Capt. Hayes*), Michael Whalen (*Treanor*), Mary Ellen Popel (*Rita*), Doug Blackley (*Lt. Mason*), David Holt (*Bob Lester*), Don Harvey (*Lt. Tyne*), David Gorcey (*Ricky*), Jack Elam (*Raymond*), Dick Cogan (*Edmunds*), Rudolph Friml, Jr (*Piano Soloist*), Knox Manning (*Narrator*).

Along the lines of REEFER MADNESS, this "evils of marijuana" film shows the cruel effects the drug can have on people. Leeds is a chorus girl who hits the "wild weed," becomes an addict, and at last kicks the habit. She then turns to the side of the law and helps the police crack a drug ring. WILD WEED offers a few laughs with its hallucinatory camera effects. The picture was an obvious and shameful attempt to cash in on the nationwide headlines generated by its beautiful blonde star and Robert Mitchum, who were arrested in Leeds' home on September 1, 1948, in a narcotics raid, and charged with conspiracy to possess marijuana.

p, Richard Kay; d, Sherman Scott; , w, Richard Landau (based on a story by Arthur Hoerl); ph, Jack Greenhalgh.

**Drama						Cas.				(PR:A-C MPAA:NR)**

WILD WEST*½			(1946) 73m PRC c (AKA: PRAIRIE OUTLAWS)

Eddie Dean (*Himself*), Roscoe Ates (*Soapy*), Al ["Lash"] LaRue (*Stormy*), Robert "Buzzy" Henry (*Skinny*), Sarah Padden (*Carrio*), Louise Currie (*Florabelle*), Jean Carlin (*Mollie*), Lee Bennett (*Butler*), Terry Frost (*Drake Dawson*), Warner Richmond (*Judge Templeton*), Lee Roberts (*Capt. Rogers*), Chief Yowlachie (*Chief Black Fox*), Bob Duncan (*Rockey*), Frank Pharr (*Doctor*), Matty Roubert (*Halfbreed Charlie*), John Bridges (*Constable*), Al Ferguson (*Kansas*), Bud Osborne (*Cactus*), Flash the Horse.

Prairie Caruso Dean and his fellow Texas Rangers hop on their horses and help in the laying of some telegraph lines. The familiar set of ruthless outlaws try to put a damper on the construction but are repulsed by the Rangers and a large force of U.S. Cavalry. Someone later (in 1948) came up with the idea of re-releasing this picture with 15 minutes excised and in black and white as PRAIRIE OUTLAWS.

p&d, Robert Emmett Tansey; w, Frances Kavanaugh; ph, Fred Jackson, Jr.; (Cinecolor); ed, Hugh Winn; md, Karl Hajos; art d, Edward C. Jewell; cos, Karlice; m/l, Dorcas Cochran, Charles Rosoff, Eddie Dean, Ruth Herscler, Louis Herscher.

**Western									(PR:A MPAA:NR)**

WILD WEST WHOOPEE zero		(1931) 57m Cosmos/Associated Film
										Exchange bw

Jack Perrin, Josephine Hill, Buzz Barton, Fred Church, Horace B. Carpenter, John Ince, George Chesebro, Henry Rocquemore, Ben Corbett, Charles Austin, Walt Patterson.

An incomprehensible oater which lacks intelligence, writing, camerawork, and acting. That doesn't leave much except for the standard rodeo tale of a rider who is sabotaged by a villain who wants his girl. The end follows suit and everything works out for hero Perrin.

p,d&w, Robert J. Horner; ph, Jules Cronjager; ed, Arthur A. Brooks.

**Western									(PR:A MPAA:NR)**

WILD WESTERNERS, THE*½			(1962) 70m Four Leaf/COL c

James Philbrook (*U.S. Marshal Jim McDowell*), Nancy Kovack (*Rose Sharon*), Duane Eddy (*Deputy Marshal Clint Fallon*), Guy Mitchell (*Deputy Johnny Silver*), Hugh Sanders (*Chief Marshal Reuben Bernard*), Elizabeth MacRae (*Crystal Plummer*), Marshall Reed (*Sheriff Henry Plummer*), Nestor Paiva (*Gov. John Bullard*), Harry Lauter (*Judas*), Bob Steele (*Deputy Marshal Casey Banner*), Ilse Burkert (*Yellow Moon*), Terry Frost (*Ashley Cartwright*), Hans Wedemeyer (*Wasna*), Don Harvey (*Hanna*), Elizabeth Harrower (*Martha Bernard*), Frances Osborne (*Lulu*), Tim Sullivan (*Rev. Thomas*), Pierce Lyden (*Jake*), Joe McGuinn (*Sam Clay*), Charles Horvath (*Moose*), Marjorie Stapp (*Lily*).

Philbrook is a U.S. Marshal in 1864 who, with the help of his tough wife

Kovack, fights Indians and an outlaw gang in order to get a gold shipment from Montana to the Union troops in the East. The local sheriff is in cahoots with the bandits and arranges the kidnap of Kovack, but Philbrook kills the outlaws and rescues his wife, her mettle through it all deepening his love for her. Rock 'n' roller Duane Eddy, who had a 1958 smash hit "Rebel Rouser," is third-billed as a deputy marshal and also sings the title tune.

p, Sam Katzman; d, Oscar Rudolph; w, Gerald Drayson Adams; ph, Gordon Avil (Eastmancolor); ed, Jerome Thoms; art d, Robert Peterson; set d, Sidney Clifford; m/l, title song, Duane Eddy, Lee Hazlewood, (sung by Eddy).

Western   **(PR:A   MPAA:NR)**

WILD WHEELS zero   (1969) 92m Kendall/Fanfare c

Don Epperson (Reb Smith), Robert Dix (King), Casey Kasem (Knife), Dovie Beams (Ann), Terry Stafford (Huey), Johenne Lemont (Cotton), Bruce Kimball (Boomer), Mac McLaughlin (Count), Bobby Clark (Gunner), Nancy Brock (Candy), Evelyn Guerrero (Sissy), Gordon Zimmerman (Bobo), Lois Jones (Helen), Randee Jensen (Joy), Phill Bartell (Lt. Ryan), Lee Parrish (Wright), Byrd Holland (Rich), Mike Perrotta (Store Owner), Alex Eliot (Hank), Marsha Jo Sandidge (Bikini Girl), Willis Martin (Policeman), Billie and Blue, Three of August, Saturday Revue, Thirteenth Committee.

A biker gang pushes a normally peaceful dune buggy gang too far when they rape the buggy leader's girl friend. The buggy drivers attack the bikers while the bikers are having a drunken orgy and pave the way for the police to arrest the troublemakers. Shot in 16mm, WILD WHEELS was originally released with an "X" rating, but with a snip snip here and a snip snip there it became an "R". They should never have stopped cutting.

p, Budd Dell; d, Kent Osborne; w, Osborne, Ralph Luce; ph, Ralph Waldo; m, Harley Hatcher; ed, Luce; stunts, Bobby Clark.

Action   **(PR:O   MPAA:R)**

WILD, WILD PLANET, THE*½   (1967, Ital.) 93m Mercury Film International-Souther n Cross/MGM c (I CRIMINALI DELIA GALASSIA; AKA, THE CRIMINALS OF THE GALAXY)

Tony Russell (Comdr. Mike Halstead), Lisa Gastoni (Connie Gomez), Massimo Serato (Nels Nurmi), Franco Nero (Jake), Charles Justin [Carlo Giustini] (Ken), Enzo Fiermonte (General), Umberto Raho (Maitland), Isarco Ravaioli (Hotel Agent), Moha Tahi (A.G. Chief), Freddy Unger (De Lauty), Lino Desmond (Schneider), Franco Ressel (Jeff), Victoria Zinny, Kitty Swan, Rosemary Martin, Annelise Stern (A.G. Agents), Giuliano Raffaelli (Francini), Rodolfo Lodi (Claridge), Renato Montalbano (Detective), Aldo D'Ambrosio (Fryd), Carlo Kechler (Werner), Margherita Orowitz (Edith Halstead), Sandro Mondini (Dr. Delfos), Vittorio Bonos (Dr. Delfos, Dwarf), Michel Lemoine, Aldo Conti, Franco Doria, Ivan Gilborne, Linda Sini.

Russell is assigned to investigate some strange goings-on during a series of shrinking experiments in this fun-filled, dubbed-into-English entry from Italy. The people responsible are from the planet Delphos and are making miniaturized world leaders to be transported back to their world. Don't fret, though, Russell saves civilization in a wooden piece of acting, and all the futuristic costumes are skintight for an unending display of muscles and curves.

p, Joseph Fryd, Antonio Margheriti; d, Anthony Dawson [Margheriti]; w, Ivan Reiner, Renato Moretti; ph, Richard Pallton [Riccardo Pallottini] (Eastmancolor); m, Angelo Francesco Lavagnino; ed, Angel Coly [Otello Colangeli]; art d, Piero Poletto; cos, Bernice Sparrow; ch, Archie Savage; makeup, Euclide Santoli.

Science Fiction   **(PR:A-C   MPAA:NR)**

WILD, WILD WINTER**   (1966) 80m UNIV c

Gary Clarke (Ronnie), Chris Noel (Susan), Don Edmonds (Burt), Suzie Kaye (Sandy), Les Brown, Jr (Perry), Vicky Albright (Dot), James Wellman (Dean), Steve Franken (John), Steven Rogers (Benton), Loren Janes (The Bear), Paul Geary (Larry), Val Avery (Fox), James Frawley (Stone), Dick Miller (Rilk), Mark Sturges (Danny), Anna Lavelle (Bus Bit Girl), Linda Rogers (Trisha), Buck Holland (McGee), Darryl Vaughan (Bob), Fred Festinger (Jake McCloskey), Jay and The Americans, The Beau Brummels, Dick and Dee Dee, The Astronauts, Jackie and Gayle.

If it's bikinis, snow, and surf music you're looking for, then WILD, WILD WINTER will wet your beach-blanket whistle. Clarke leads off the cast as a college kid who pretends to be a Hawaiian millionaire to score with Noel, the man-hating head of the sorority. A ton of mountain snow and Malibu sand is kicked around before he finally succeeds. That boppin' beach beat is heard in the following tunes: "Heartbeats" (Al Capps, Mary Dean, sung by Dick and Dee Dee), "Snowball," (Capps, Dean, sung by Jackie and Gayle), "Two of a Kind" (Victor Millrose, Tony Bruno, sung by Jay and The Americans), "Just Wait and See" (Ron Elliott, sung by The Beau Brummels), "A Change of Heart" (Chester Pipkin, Mark Gordon, sung by The Astronauts), "Wild, Wild Winter" (Pipkin).

p, Bart Patton; d, Lennie Weinrib; w, David Malcolm; ph, Frank Phillips (Techniscope, Technicolor); m, Jerry Long; ed, Jack Woods; set d, Victor

Gangelin; cos, Paula Giokaris, Walt Hoffman; makeup, Rolf Miller.

Comedy/Musical   **(PR:A   MPAA:NR)**

WILD, WILD WOMEN, THE   (SEE: ...AND THE WILD, WILD WOMEN, 1961, Fr./Ital.)

WILD WOMEN OF WONGO, THE zero   (1959) 80m Tropical c

Jean Hawkshaw (Omoo), Johnny Walsh (Engor), Mary Ann Webb (Mona), Cande Gerrard (Ahtee), Adrienne Bourbeau (Wana), Ed Fury (Gahbo), Val Phillips, Roy Murray, Rex Richards, Pat Crowley, Steve Klisanin.

THE WILD WOMEN OF WONGO is so bad it almost has to be seen to be believed. It includes some hilarious tribal dances (with some heavy gyrating), a hungry alligator, wild women, and sexually unsatisfied male tribe members. It seems the guys aren't pleased with their shapeless prehistoric wives and turn to the Wongo-ettes for some fun.

p, George R. Black; d, James L. Wolcott; w, Cedric Rutherford; ph, M. Walsh (Pathecolor); ed, D.J. Cazale; makeup, R. Liszt; ch, Olga Suarez.

Science-Fiction/Adventure   **(PR:C   MPAA:NR)**

WILD WORLD OF BATWOMAN, THE zero
                (1966) 70m ADP bw (AKA: SHE WAS A HIPPY VAMPIRE)

Katherine Victor (Batwoman), George Andre, Steve Brodie, Lloyd Nelson, Richard Banks, The Young Giants.

Unbelievable! Victor is a femme vampire who is forced to steal a hearing aid that doubles as an atomic bomb. A mad scientist has kidnaped a fellow bloodsucker and won't release her unless Victor comes up with the goods. The scientist uses laughing gas to get the bomb, but it explodes and he is caught red-handed. Warren was sued over the name "Batwoman," spent a bundle defending himself before renaming the film, and then retired from the movie business. Very weird.

p,d&w, Jerry Warren; m, The Young Giants

Science-Fiction/Crime   **(PR:C   MPAA:G)**

WILD YOUTH*   (1961) 73m Cinema Associates bw (AKA: NAKED YOUTH)

Robert Hutton (Maddo), John Goddard (Revis), Carol Ohmart (Madge), Jan Brooks (Donna), Robert Arthur (Frankie), Steve Rowland (Switch), Clancy Cooper (Erickson).

A decent kid, Arthur, gets entangled in a web of unlawful activities and finds himself in prison. He breaks out with the help of a fellow inmate and winds up near Mexico with a heroin addict who hides his stash in a doll. Government agents gun down the bad guys and Arthur learns a thing or two about the life of crime.

p, John Bushelman; d, John Schreyer; w, Robert J. Black, Jr., Lester William Berke, Dean Romano (based on a story by Berke, Gary Judis); ph, Lloyd Knechtel; m, Richard La Salle; ed, Dwight Caldwell; m/l, "Wild Youth," Steve Rowland.

Crime Drama   **(PR:C   MPAA:NR)**

WILDCAT**   (1942) 73M PAR bw

Richard Arlen (Johnny Maverick), Arline Judge (Nan Deering), William Frawley (Oliver Westbrook), Larry "Buster" Crabbe (Mike Rawlins), Arthur Hunnicutt ("Watchfob" Jones), Elisha Cook, Jr ("Chicopee" Nevins), Ralph Sanford ("Grits" O'Malley), Alec Craig (Joseph D. Campbell), John Dilson (Gus Sloane), Will Wright (Paw Smithers), Jessica Newcombe (Maw Smithers), Billy [William] Benedict (Bud Smithers), Ed Keane, Billy Nelson, Tom Kennedy, Fred Sherman, John Fisher, William Hall.

Penniless Arlen gets himself in a bind when he purchases a chunk of oil-rich land by selling half the rights to Cook. Cook is killed, however, and Arlen sweats it out until the oil begins to gush. Crabbe sabotages the rig but Arlen comes out on top.

p, William H. Pine, William C. Thomas; d, Frank McDonald; w, Maxwell Shane, Richard Murphy (based on a story by North Bigbee); ph, Fred Jackman, Jr.; ed, William Ziegler; art d, F. Paul Sylos.

Drama   **(PR:A   MPAA:NR)**

WILDCAT   (SEE: GREAT SCOUT AND CATHOUSE THURSDAY, THE, 1976)

WILDCAT BUS*   (1940) 63M RKO bw

Fay Wray (Ted Dawson), Charles Lang (Jerry Waters), Paul Guilfoyle (Donovan), Joseph Sawyer (Burke), Roland Drew (Davis), Leona Roberts (Ma Talbot), Oscar O'Shea (Charles Dawson), Frank Shannon (Sweeney), Warren Ashe (Joe Miller), Don Costello (Casey), Paul McGrath (Stanley Regan).

Lang, a down-and-out playboy, gets involved with a gang of racketeers who are attempting to sabotage O'Shea's bus line. Lang falls in love with O'Shea's daughter, Wray, and before long is helping to defeat the gangsters.

p, Cliff Reid; d, Frank Woodruff; w, Lou Lusty; ph, Jack Mackenzie; ed, George Crone; cos Renie; spec eff, Vernon L. Walker.

Crime Drama   (PR:A   MPAA:NR)

WILDCAT OF TUCSON*½   (1941) 59m COL bw

Bill Elliott (Wild Bill Hickok), Evelyn Young (Vivian), Stanley Brown (Dave), Dub Taylor (Cannonball), Kenneth MacDonald (McNee), Ben Taggart (Judge), Edmund Cobb (Seth), George Lloyd (Marshall), Sammy Stein (Logan), George Chesebro, Forrest Taylor, Francis Walker, Robert Winkler, Dorothy Andre, Bert Young, Johnny Daheim, Newt Kirby, Murdock MacQuarrie.

An uneventful western programmer which has Elliott searching for his mischievous brother, who is part of a claim-jumping racket. The standard good vs. bad confrontation comes when Elliott beats ring leader MacDonald to the draw. (See WILD BILL HICKOK series, Index.)

p, Leon Barsha; d, Lambert Hillyer; w, Fred Myton; ph, George Meehan; ed, Charles Nelson.

Western   (PR:A   MPAA:NR)

WILDCAT TROOPER**½   (1936) 60m Ambassador-Syndicate bw

Kermit Maynard (Gale), Hobart Bosworth (Dr. Martin), Fuzzy Knight (Pat), Lois Wilde (Ruth), Jim Thorpe (Indian), Yakima Canutt (The Raven), Eddie Phillips (Reynolds), John Merton (McClain), Frank Hagney (Foster), Roger Williams (Slim), Richard Curtis (Henri), Ted Lorch (Rogers), Hal Price (Buyer), Rocky the Horse.

Maynard investigates a feud between two rival fur traders in the great Northwest. Donning his familiar Mountie outfit, Maynard discovers that the feud is fueled by Bosworth, an apparently benign country doctor who really wants the furs for his own profit. Quick pacing and top-notch horse stunts are the high points. Note the presence of Olympic champion and football great Thorpe, who appeared in several films in the 1930s. Here the great native American athlete is cleverly cast as an "Indian."

p, Maurice Conn; d, Elmer Clifton; w, Joseph O'Donnell (based on the story "The Midnight Call" by James Oliver Curwood); ph, Arthur Reed; ed, Richard G. Wray; m/l, Didheart Conn.

Western   (PR:A   MPAA:NR)

WILDCATS OF ST. TRINIAN'S, THE*   (1980, Brit.) 91m Wildcat c

Sheila Hancock, Michael Hordern, Joe Melia, Thorley Walters, Rodney Bewes, Maureen Lipman, Ambrosine Philpotts.

There were several ST. TRINIAN'S films released and this inept piece was the last. This time out the schoolgirls, who seem to raise more hell than study for exams, organize themselves in a union, then grab an Arab's daughter hostage in order to bring themselves center stage. More wasted energy than anything else.

p, E.M. Smedley-Aston; d&w, Frank Launder; ph, Ernest Steward (Technicolor); m, James Kenelm Clarke.

Comedy   (PR:A   MPAA:NR)

WILDCATTER, THE*   (1937) 58M UNIV bw

Scott Colton ("Lucky" Conlon), Jean Rogers (Helen Conlon), Jack Smart (Smiley), Suzanne Kaaren (Julia Frayne), Russell Hicks (Tom Frayne), Ward Bond (Johnson), Wallis Clark (Torrance), Jack Powell (Joe Tinker).

Colton is an eager fellow named "Lucky" who tries his hand at the oil business. With wife Rogers not far behind and his sister taking care of the family roadside restaurant, he lights out for "black gold" country. There he gets involved with the daughter of an oil baron and is played for a fool, though he eventually exposes the tycoon as a cheat and returns to his wife's loving arms.

p, George Owen; d, Lewis D. Collins; w, Charles A. Logue (based on a story by Tom Van Dyke); ph, Stanley Cortez; ed, Frank Gross; md, Charles Previn.

Adventure/Drama   (PR:A   MPAA:NR)

WILDE SEISON   (SEE: WILD SEASON, 1968, S. Africa)

WILDERNESS FAMILY PART 2
   (SEE: FURTHER ADVENTURES OF THE WILDERNESS FAMILY-
                                            PART TWO, 1978)

WILDERNESS MAIL*½   (1935) 65m Ambassador bw

Kermit "Tex" Maynard, Fred Kohler, Sr, Doris Brook, Dick Curtis, Syd Saylor, Paul Hurst, Nelson McDowell, Kernan Cripps, Rocky the Horse.

Ken Maynard's less popular little brother Kermit stars as a Mountie who bravely paddles a canoe throughout the Pacific Northwest delivering mail to secluded outposts in this somewhat unusual outdoor adventure. Unusual, certainly, but about as exciting as it sounds.

p, Maurice Conn; d, Forrest Sheldon; w, Bennett Cohen, Robert Dillon (based on a story by James Oliver Curwood); ph, Arthur Reed; ed, Jack [John] English.

Adventure   Cas.   (PR:A   MPAA:NR)

WILDFIRE*½   (1945) 57m Action/Screen Guild c (GB: WILDFIRE: THE STORY OF A HORSE)

Bob Steele (Happy Hay), Sterling Holloway (Alkali), John Miljan (Pete Fanning), William Farnum (Judge Polson), Virginia Maples (Judy Gordon), Sarah Padden (Aunt Agatha), Eddie Dean (Johnny Deal), Wee Willie Davis (Moose Harris), Rocky Camron (Buck Perry), Al Ferguson (Steve Kane), Francis Ford (Ezra Mills), Frank Ellis, Hal Price.

Steele and Holloway, a couple of horse traders, are just passing through when they uncover horse thief Miljan's scheme to empty his neighbors' ranches of their herds. He's been trying to put the blame on a wild horse, but Steele and Holloway know better. Notable for an early appearance by Eddie Dean, a warbling cowboy who soon would gain fame in his own western series.

p, William B. David; d, Robert Tansey; w, Frances Kavanaugh (based on a story by William C. Tuttle); ph, Marcel Le Picard (Cinecolor); ed, Charles Henkel.

Western   (PR:A   MPAA:NR)

WILDFIRE; THE STORY OF A HORSE   (SEE: WILDFIRE, 1945)

WILDWECHSEL   (SEE: JAIL BAIT, 1977, Ger.)

WILL ANY GENTLEMAN?**½   (1955, Brit.) 84m Associated British/Stratford

George Cole (Henry Sterling), Veronica Hurst (Mrs. Sterling), Jon Pertwee (Charlie Sterling), James Hayter (Dr. Smith), Heather Thatcher (Mrs. Whittle), William Hartnell (Inspector Martin), Diana Decker (Angel), Alan Badel (The Great Mendoza), Joan Sims (Beryl), Sidney James (Mr. Hobson), Brian Oulton (Mr. Jackson), Alexander Gauge (Mr. Billing), Josephine Douglas (Receptionist), Peter Butterworth (Stage Manager), Wally Patch (Bookmaker), Lionel Jeffries (Mr. Frobisher), Richard Massingham (Stout Man), Wilfred Boyle, Jill Melford, Diana Hope, Martyn Wyldeck, Frank Birch, Arthur Howard, Brian Wilde, Nan Braunton, Lucy Griffiths, Harry Herbert, Russ Allen, Sylvia Russell, Jackie Joyner, Eleanor Fazan, Lillemor Knudsen.

Cole unwillingly agrees to take part in a hypnotist's stage show, leading to a series of comic adventures for the normally reserved bank clerk. Before the spell can be broken, Cole leaves the theater and begins to live a carefree existence. He cheats on his wife, frivolously spends his bank's cash, and makes a general fool of himself. On the brink of a marital breakup, the hypnotist finds Cole and snaps him out of his dangerous lifestyle.

p, Hamilton G. Inglis; d, Michael Anderson; w, Vernon Sylvaine (based on his play); ph, Erwin Hillier (Technicolor); m, Wally Stott; ed, Max Benedict.

Comedy   (PR:A   MPAA:NR)

WILL JAMES' SAND   (SEE: SAND, 1949)

WILL PENNY***½   (1968) 109m PAR c

Charlton Heston (Will Penny), Joan Hackett (Catherine Allen), Donald Pleasence (Preacher Quint), Lee Majors (Blue), Bruce Dern (Rafe Quint), Ben Johnson (Alex), Slim Pickens (Ike Wallerstein, Trail Cook), Clifton James (Catron), Anthony Zerbe (Dutchy), Roy Jenson (Boetius Sullivan), G.D. Spradlin (Anse Howard), Quentin Dean (Jennie), William Schallert (Dr. Fraker), Lydia Clarke (Mrs. Fraker), Robert Luster (Shem Bodine), Dal Jenkins (Sambo), Matt Clark (Romulus), Luke Askew (Foxy), Anthony Costello (Bigfoot), Gene Rutherford (Rufus Quint), Chanin Hale (Girl), Jon Francis (Horace Greeley Allen), Stephen Edwards (Town Boy).

Heston turns in a superb performance as an aging cowboy accepting and loving his life in the West. Set in Montana in the 1880s, WILL PENNY shows us the rugged details and the day-by-day hardships that cowboys encountered, concentrating less on the glory than on the guts. With winter approaching, Heston and fellow cowpokes Majors and Zerbe try to find employment. In the process, they are ambushed by Pleasence, a demented preacher with three sons, one of whom is killed by Heston. Pleasence vows to get revenge. Heston finds work, as well as romance, in the form of Hackett, who is traveling with her son to California to meet her husband.

Pleasence stages another ambush, wounding Heston. As he recovers, he grows fond of Hackett. Pleasence, determined to finish off Heston, captures him but cannot prevent him from escaping to save Hackett from the sexual yearnings of Pleasence's sons. Heston kills Pleasence, shoots his sons, and when Hackett asks him to stay with her and farm, refuses and rides on, proclaiming that he's a cowboy and he "don't know nothing else." WILL PENNY, with its fine direction, realistic atmosphere, stunning photography (Ballard in top form), and great performance by Heston, still failed to make even a dent at the box office, grossing only $1.3 million. The public instead preferred to check out another Heston picture released at the same time–PLANET OF THE APES.

p, Fred Engel, Walter Seltzer; d&w, Tom Gries; ph, Lucien Ballard (Technicolor); m, David Raksin; ed, Warren Low; art d, Hal Pereira, Roland Anderson; set d, Robert R. Benton, Ray Moyer; cos, John A. Anderson, Ruth Stella; spec eff, Paul Lerpae; m/l, "The Lonely Rider," Raksin, Robert Wells (sung by Don Cherry); makeup, Wally Westmore, Charles Blackman.

Western   **(PR:A-C   MPAA:NR)**

WILL SUCCESS SPOIL ROCK HUNTER?***

(1957) 94m FOX c (GB: OH! FOR A MAN!)

Jayne Mansfield (*Rita Marlowe*), Tony Randall (*Rock Hunter*), Betsy Drake (*Jenny*), Joan Blondell (*Violet*), John Williams (*Le Salle, Jr.*), Henry Jones (*Rufus*), Lili Gentle (*April*), Mickey Hargitay (*Bobo*), Georgia Carr (*Calypso Number*), Groucho Marx (*Surprise Guest*), Dick Whittinghill (*TV Interviewer*), Ann McCrea (*Gladys*), Lida Piazza (*Junior's Secretary*), Bob Adler, Phil Chambers (*Mailmen*), Larry Kerr (*Mr. Ezzarus*), Sherrill Terry (*Annie*), Mack Williams (*Hotel Doorman*), Patrick Powell (*Receptionist*), Carmen Nisbit (*Breakfast Food Demonstrator*), Richard Deems (*Razor Demonstrator*), Don Corey (*Voice of Ed Sullivan*), Benny Rubin (*Theater Manager*), Minta Durfee, Edith Russell (*Scrubwomen*), Alberto Morin, Louis Mercier (*Frenchmen*).

A frequently funny film from Frank Tashlin (he produced, directed, and wrote the screenplay) lampooning advertising and the quest for success. As in his other films and the cartoons Tashlin formerly directed at Warner Bros., his style here is brash and anarchistic and the result is numerous imaginative jokes. The laughs begin immediately as Randall introduces everyone in the film at the top (he also comes back midway to offer an intermission to viewers who are hooked on TV and need a break). He's an ad man at the agency owned by Williams, a place where the acknowledgement of power comes when an executive gets the key to the washroom. When Williams passes Randall in the hallway, he doesn't note him. Randall would like to move up and even buys a set of smoking pipes so he can get "that Gregory Peck look." The agency is about to lose the profitable Stay-Put lipstick account and that puts Randall and his immediate superior, Jones, in jeopardy. Randall is watching TV one day and sees movie star Mansfield at a reception. A flash of light over his head and Randall thinks that if he can get Mansfield to endorse the product (she has those "oh, so kissable lips,") then his future is assured. Randall goes to Mansfield's residence to plead for her endorsement and finds her quarreling with her beau, TV jungle man Hargitay (her real-life spouse). Randall pretends to be her new boy friend and the head of her production company. Mansfield goes along with the gag to make Hargitay jealous and she eventually agrees to put her seal of approval on Stay-Put lipstick, but only if Randall will continue his impersonation. Then Randall is in seventh heaven because everyone thinks he is Mansfield's lover. He saves the account, gets his own key to the executive washroom, and is covered with acclaim at the agency. The success begins to go to his head and he starts appearing in all the gossip columns. Exacting revenge, Randall does acknowledge Williams when they pass in the hall. He is soon pursued by teenage admirers and even gets his hand print in the courtyard at Grauman's Chinese Theater on Hollywood Boulevard (now Mann's Chinese Theatre). It's a hoot as his arm sinks into the cement up to his shoulder. All this time, his real girl friend has been his aide, Drake. She can't take the charade any longer and walks out on him. Randall now gets Williams' job as managing director of the agency as Williams has retired to grow roses. Randall's head is getting so large that his shoulders can barely support it. He pictures Mansfield covered in money as Georgia Carr sings Bobby Troup's "You Got It Made." Mansfield, ever looking for publicity, suggests a staged marriage between her and Randall and plans to pass out and be carried off on a stretcher due to the potency of Randall's kisses. Randall finally comes to his senses as he understands that he's been a success all along and that all average guys are successes because it is they that the advertisers and agencies always cater to and attempt to please. Randall gets back Drake and he leaves the agency to marry her and retire to a farm to raise chickens. Jones takes over the agency's management and Mansfield finds true love in the end with Groucho Marx. Throughout the film, Tashlin has a fine time ridiculing the media. The takeoffs on commercials are biting satire and at one point in the film the CinemaScope screen shrinks down to TV size so "the viewers can feel more at home." Mansfield's character is a thinly disguised version of herself but make no mistake, she was not a vacant woman. She had a good college education, played a mean violin, and knew exactly who she was and what she was and how to make the best of it. The film was based on George Axelrod's play but just barely. Tashlin rewrote it totally and it bears little resemblance to the play, which the studio purchased mainly for the title and the chance to get Mansfield. French critics enjoyed this immensely, and

Jean-Luc Godard, while he was still writing on film, had this movie on his 10 best list. In a small role as one of the scrubwomen, note Minta Durfee, former silent screen comedienne who worked with Charlie Chaplin, among others, and married Roscoe "Fatty" Arbuckle. The play was about the movie business and was made better by Tashlin's switch to the Madison Avenue milieu. Fox plugged many of its own films in the picture and TWA got a huge plug as well. While there is a whole industry on plugging products in films, this was a trifle blatant and stuck out every bit as much as all the Marlboro cigarette plugs in SUPERMAN.

p,d&w, Frank Tashlin (based on the play by George Axelrod); ph, Joe MacDonald (CinemaScope, DeLuxe Color); m, Cyril J. Mockridge; ed, Hugh S. Fowler; md, Lionel Newman; art d, Lyle R. Wheeler, Leland Fuller; cos, Charles LeMaire; spec eff, L.B. Abbott; m/l, Bobby Troup, "You Got It Made."

Comedy   **(PR:A-C   MPAA:NR)**

WILL TOMORROW EVER COME   (SEE: THAT'S MY MAN, 1947)

WILLARD**½

(1971 95m Bing Crosby/Cinerama c)

Bruce Davison (*Willard Stiles*), Elsa Lanchester (*Henrietta Stiles*), Ernest Borgnine (*Al Martin*), Sondra Locke (*Joan*), Michael Dante (*Brandt*), Jody Gilbert (*Charlotte Stassen*), Joan Shawlee (*Alice Rickles*), William Hansen (*Mr. Barskin*), J. Pat O'Malley (*Jonathan Farley*), John Myhers (*Mr. Carlson*), Helen Spring (*Mrs. Becker*), Pauline Drake (*Ida Stassen*), Almira Sessions (*Carrie Smith*), Alan Baxter (*Walter T. Spencer*), Sherry Presnell (*Mrs. Spencer*), Lola Kendrick (*Mrs. Martin*), Robert Golden (*Motorcycle Rider*), Minta Durfee Arbuckle, Arthur Tovey, Shirley Lawrence, Louise De Carlo (*Guest*).

WILLARD could have been a great horror film; instead, it will just make your flesh crawl, your brows sweat, and your feet avoid the theater floor for at least 95 minutes (in fact, theater patrons may have sat through the film a second time only because they were too repulsed to put their feet to the floor and walk out). With THE BIRDS, Hitchcock made famous this genre in which masses of creatures attack humans. Since that film we've witnessed enough bees and frogs and spiders and snakes to give even the bravest pet shop owner the shakes. Rats, however, are especially nasty, particularly when they are trained to kill by a psychotic youngster (Davison) whose widowed mother (Lanchester) looks like (and indeed had been) "The Bride of Frankenstein). Davison's office boy character is fed up with his pushy, conniving boss Borgnine. He decides to make friends with a couple of rats, whom he calls Ben and Socrates, and trains them to savagely rip the flesh from his enemies' bodies. Borgnine is the prime target, and in one of his most memorable roles, cowers in the corner of his office as the furry monsters stage a mass attack. Davison begins to neglect his rats when he falls in love with Locke, upsetting Ben, the most intelligent and independent of the rats. Davison plots to poison his former "friends," but Ben corrals his fellow rodents and they kill their one-time trainer. Ben survived the entire fiasco and later showed up in his own film titled, appropriately enough, BEN. Surprisingly (or maybe not) audiences were drawn to WILLARD, standing in line to see their worst fears come at them on the screen–the reason to see any horror film. Moe and Nora Di Sesso, the animal trainers, deserves special mention for getting the vermin to "act." Dozens of rats were used, each of them given specific skills (plank crawling, face chewing etc.), and assisted by, of all things, the Di Sessos' pet cat.

p, Mort Briskin; d, Daniel Mann; w, Gilbert A. Ralston (based on the novel *Ratman's* Notebooks by Stephen Gilbert); ph, Robert B. Hauser (DeLuxe Color); m, Alex North; ed, Warren Low; md, North; art d, Howard Hollander; set d, Ralph S. Hurst; cos, Eric Seelig, Dorothy Barkley; spec eff, Bud David; makeup, Gus Norin; animal trainers, Moe Di Sesso, Nora Di Sesso.

Horror   **(PR:O   MPAA:GP)**

WILLIAM COMES TO TOWN**

(1948, Brit.) 89m
Diadem/Alliance/UA bw (AKA: WILLIAM AT THE CIRCUS).

William Graham (*William Brown*), Garry Marsh (*Mr. Brown*), Jane Welsh (*Mrs. Brown*), A.E. Matthews (*Minister*), Muriel Aked (*Emily*), Hugh Cross (*Robert Brown*), Kathleen Stuart (*Ethel Brown*), Michael Medwin (*Reporter*), Jon Pertwee (*Superintendent*), Brian Roper (*Ginger*), James Crabbe (*Douglas*), Brian Weske (*Henry*), David Paige, Michael Balfour, Norman Pierce, Eve Mortimer, John Powe, Mary Vallange, Peter Butterworth, Donald Clive, John Warren, Alan Goford, Basil Gordon, Claude Bonsor, Ivan Craig, John Martell, Pinkie Hannaford, Jumble the Dog, Marquis the Chimpanzee.

William Graham stars in his followup to JUST WILLIAM'S LUCK (1947), an adaptation of the children's stories of Richmal Crompton which also made it to the screen in 1939 as JUST WILLIAM. In this adventure, Graham and his friends descend on the Prime Minister's home to demand shorter school hours and bigger allowances. By doing so, Graham almost ruins his chances of going to the circus (his parents made him promise to stay out of trouble) but he finally finds his way there.

p, John R. Sloan, David Coplan; d&w, Val Guest (based on the stories by Richmal Crompton); ph, Bert Mason.

Comedy   (PR:A   MPAA:NR)

WILLIAM FOX MOVIETONE FOLLIES OF 1929
                    (SEE: FOX MOVIETONE FOLLIES, 1929)

WILLIE AND PHIL**½   (1980) 116m FOX C

Michael Ontkean (*Willie Kaufman*), Margot Kidder (*Jeanette Sutherland*), Ray Sharkey (*Phil D'Amico*), Jan Miner (*Mrs. Kaufman*), Tom Brennan (*Mr. Kaufman*), Julie Bovasso (*Mrs. D'Amico*), Louis Guss (*Mr. D'Amico*), Kathleen Maguire (*Mrs. Sutherland*), Kaki Hunter (*Patti Sutherland*), Kristine DeBell (*Rena*), Laurence Fishburne III (*Wilson*), Ed Van Nuys (*Official Clerk*), Jill Mazursky (*Jill*), Alison Cass Shurpin (*Zelda Kaufman No. 4*), Christine Varnai (*Zelda Kaufman No. 3*), Walter N. Lowery (*Park Bum*), Jerry Hall (*Karen*), Helen Hanft (*Used Car Salesperson*), Hubert J. Edwards (*Black Kid*), Natalie Wood (*Herself*), Eivand Harum (*Igor*), Sol Frieder, Donald Muhich, Anne E. Wile, Allen C. Dawson, Alvin Alexis, Robert Townsend, Cynthia McPherson, Karen Montgomery, Tom Noonan, Ginny Ortix, Lionel Pina, Jr, Louis Cappetto, Karen Ford, Stephan Hart, Kitty Muldoon, Nikolas Irizarry, Madeline Moroff, R.M. Wexler, Mary-Pat Green.

A *menage-a-trois* involving Sharkey, Ontkean, and Kidder that, try as it might, fails to provide much insight into the changing attitudes of American culture during the 1970s. Though Mazursky has created a light and pleasant enough situation, he never really gets at what it is that makes these people tick, steering clear of matters that might cause the audience to feel too uncomfortable. At the decade's start, Sharkey and Ontkean become incredibly close friends, not even allowing their mutual attraction to Kidder to interfere with their feelings toward each other (or if it does, this is never shown in the film). Though Kidder is fond of both men, and they equally so of her (they all even sleep together once), she marries Ontkean. The setting switches from New York to California, the marriage fails, and Kidder takes up with Sharkey. WILLIE AND PHIL looks very much like a glossy remake of JULES ET JIM, although missing all the cinematic subtleties and human insight which filled the Truffaut work. There is even one instance in which the a portion of Delerue's score for the earlier film is used. It is almost impossible not to like the characters that Mazursky has created, making it all the more irritating as they go about making fools of themselves. Yet somehow one never really gets to know them, or to develop a very strong attachment to these aloof personalities.

p, Paul Mazursky, Tony Ray; d&w, Mazursky; ph, Sven Nykvist (DeLuxe Color); m, Claude Bolling, Georges Delerue, "Suite for Flute and Piano," "Picnic Suite," Bolling; ed, Donn Cambern; prod d, Pato Guzman; md, Bolling; set d, Ed Stewart, Ernie Bishop; cos, Albert Wolsky.

Drama   Cas.   (PR:O   MPAA:R)

WILLIE AND JOE BACK AT THE FRONT
                    (SEE: BACK AT THE FRONT), 1952)

WILLIE DYNAMITE**½   (1973) 102m UNIV c

Roscoe Orman (*Willie Dynamite*), Diana Sands (*Cora*), Thalmus Rasulala (*Robert Daniels*), Joyce Walker (*Pashen*), Roger Robinson (*Bell*), George Murdock (*Celli*), Albert Hall (*Pointer*), Norma Donaldson (*Honey*), Juanita Brown (*Sola*), Royce Wallace (*Willie's Mother*), Judy Brown (*Georgia*), Marilyn Coleman (*Connie*), Mary Wilcox (*Scatback*), Marcia McBroom (*Pearl*), Jack Bernardi (*Willie's Lawyer*), Ted Gehring (*Sergeant*), Ron Henriquez (*Cyrus*), Wynn Irwin (*Bailiff*), Richard Lawson (*Sugar*), Ken Lynch (*Judge No. 1*), Davis Roberts (*Judge No. 2*).

Orman stars as a New York City pimp in this atypical black exploitationer that follows him as he rises to the top of the hustling scene and then tumbles to the bottom. Many of the usual elements are included, especially the flashy-trash costumes, but underneath it all there is an air of morality. Sands (who died of cancer before the film's release) is believable in her role as a former prostitute-turned-social-worker who is hardened to the environment and tries to straighten out Orman's and Walker's lives. Songs include: "Willie D," "King Midas," "Keep On, Movin' On" (J.J. Johnson, Gilbert Moses III, sung by Martha Reeves and The Sweet Things).

p, Richard D. Zanuck, David Brown; d, Gilbert Moses III; w, Ron Cutler (based on a story by Cutler, Joe Keyes, Jr.); ph, Frank Stanley (Technicolor); m, J.J. Johnson; ed, Aaron Stell; art d, John T. McCormack; set d, Claire P. Brown.

Action/Drama   (PR:O   MPAA:R)

WILLIE MCBEAN AND HIS MAGIC MACHINE**½
       (1965, U.S./Jap.) 94m Dentsu-Videocraf t International/Magna c

Willie McBean; Voice of Larry D. Mann, Billie Richards, Alfred Scopp, Paul Kligman, Bunny Cowan, Paul Soles, Pegi Loder.

A delightful and technically superior puppet film about a mad scientist who travels in his time machine to the days of Christopher Columbus, King Tut, King Arthur, Buffalo Bill, and the cavemen to rewrite history. A schoolboy gets in his own time machine and prevents disaster by making the scientist

promise to be good. An early Rankin and Jules Bass (an associate producer on this film) effort.

p,d&w, Arthur Rankin, Jr.; ph, (AniMagic, Eastmancolor); m/l, Edward Thomas, Gene Forrell, James Polack.

Children's Film   Cas.   (PR:AAA   MPAA:NR)

WILLY**   (1963, U.S./Ger.) 73m ABA bw

Hubert Persicke (*Willy*), Hannelore Schroth (*Klara*), Edith Schultze-Westrum (*Grandmother*), Joseph Offenbach (*Herbst*), Peter Kuiper (*Scott*), Klaus Behrendt (*Teacher*), Reinhard Kolldehoff (*Brother*), Kurt A. Jung (*Agent*), Viktoria von Campe (*Secretary*), Wilhelm Fricke (*Herbert*), Arnfried Lerche (*Wolfgang*).

Produced for German television, WILLY stars Persicke as a youngster with a white German mother and a black American soldier father. He suffers from being the only black boy in his village and finally is allowed by his mother to leave for the more tolerant Hamburg.

p&d, Allan A. Buckhantz; w, Gunter Rudorf, Marcus Scholz (based on the play "The First Lesson" by Rudorf); ph, Ludwig Berger; m, Nicholas Carras; ed, Klaus Dudenhofer; art d, Mathias Matthies, Ellen Schmidt; m/l, "Willy," Carras, Ric Marlow.

Drama   (PR:A   MPAA:NR)

WILLY DYNAMITE   (SEE: WILLIE DYNAMITE, 1973)

WILLY WONKA AND THE CHOCOLATE FACTORY**½
                    (1971) 98m PAR c

Gene Wilder (*Willy Wonka*), Jack Albertson (*Grandpa Joe*), Peter Ostrum (*Charlie Bucket*), Michael Bollner (*Augustus Gloop*), Ursula Reit (*Mrs. Gloop*), Denise Nickerson (*Violet Beauregarde*), Leonard Stone (*Mr. Beauregarde*), Julie Dawn Cole (*Veruca Salt*), Roy Kinnear (*Mr. Salt*), Paris Themmen (*Mike Teevee*), Dodo Denny (*Mrs. Teevee*), Diana Sowle (*Mrs. Bucket*), Aubrey Wood (*Mr. Bill*), David Battley (*Mr. Turkentine*), Gunter Meissner (*Mr. Slugworth*), Peter Capell (*Tinker*), Werner J. Heyking (*Jopeck*), Ernest Ziegler (*Grandpa George*), Dora Altmann (*Grandma Georgina*), Franziska Liebing (*Grandma Josephine*).

A mean-spirited black comedy that has many wonderful moments and a jangly score that did produce one standard and one minor hit. Quaker Oats company put up part of the money for the film, their only venture in the movie industry. Wilder is Wonka, the world's greatest candy maker. He sells dandy candy bars and has hidden golden tickets in five of them. Whoever finds the tickets will be entitled to a tour of Wilder's facilities plus a lifetime supply of the stuff. Ostrum lives in the town where Wilder is located and he dreams of finding a ticket. His mother is Sowle and the house is also occupied by all four aged grandparents, led by a bedridden Albertson. The tickets are distributed in the candy bars and winners come from everywhere. Nickerson is the daughter of Stone, a car salesman from the U.S.; Salt is the mean little brat offspring of Kinnear, a British businessman who deals in peanuts; Themmen is a young lad who only cares about spending his life as a couch potato in front of the television; and Bollner is a rotund German boy. That takes care of four tickets. When the fifth ticket is claimed in South America, Ostrum is shattered. Then his hopes rise when that ticket turns out to be a forgery. Ostrum is elated as he opens one of the chocolate bars and learns that he's the recipient of the final ticket. Shortly thereafter, Ostrum is approached by Meissner, a man who is Wilder's number- one enemy because he runs an inferior candy company and yearns to be the best and the biggest. Ostrum is offered a bribe by Meissner to steal a particular item called an "Everlasting Gobstopper" from the factory while he is on the tour. Ostrum doesn't know how to handle this as his family could use the money, but it's not within his nature to do anything illegal. The other four children have already been approached by Meissner as well. According to the terms of the tour, each child may bring one adult to the factory and Ostrum opts for Albertson, his beloved grandfather. Albertson has been lying in bed for 20 years and will now step out for the first time. The other kids are joined by one of their parents and the tour begins as Wilder icily welcomes them to the factory telling them that if they touch anything at all, the lifetime chocolate supply deal is off. Further, he doesn't trust their words, so he induces them to sign an agreement to that effect. Once that's taken care of, the tour commences and Wilder shows them all the marvels inside the factory. There's a little vessel called the "S.S. Wonkatania" in which the kids ride on a river of chocolate; there's a room made of chocolate where everything--including the doorknobs--is edible; they visit the "Inventing Room" and each child gets an "Everlasting Gobstopper" which is far more than an all-day sucker, it's an all-life sucker that will never wear out; then they meet the little people who run the factory. It's a wonderful tour and the kids all love it but each of them, except Ostrum, runs afoul of Wilder's strict rules and they are asked to leave the factory, sans the lifetime chocolate supply. At the end, Ostrum is the one child who has not violated any of Wilder's insane edicts. Then even Ostrum and Albertson are told they must leave because they drank a special drink which sent them careening off the ceiling. Albertson is irate and tells Ostrum that Wilder is a rat who deserves to have his secret to the "Everlasting Gobstopper" unmasked. Ostrum still can't bear to do anything dishonest so he takes the sucker from his pocket and gives it to Wilder. Wilder smiles a broad smile. It was all an honesty test and he is delighted that Ostrum has passed it. Now Meissner enters and it seems that he's not a competitor at all. Rather, he is an agent in the employ of Wilder and his job was to see which of the five children was sincere. Wilder rewards Ostrum and Albertson by taking them on his "Great Glass Wonkavator" and they go soaring high over the small town and see the factory and the village. Wilder is so happy that Ostrum passed the test that he designates him as his official beneficiary and tells him that he and his family can now move into the factory and that he will eventually take over from Wilder and be the chocolate maker. The story meanders somewhat but the dialog is sharp and the performances by the kids are stand-outs. Wilder does his patented yelling routine (it was already getting tedious in 1971 but he continued doing it into the 1980s) but director Stuart manages to keep him somewhat in check. The movie only played for a week as a "showcase" but the box-office receipts were meager so it was taken out of the theaters and had a far better life on TV. The other four children are all seen as rotten; only Ostrum comes off as a sweet boy with no underlying selfish motives. Stuart's only previous feature works were IF IT'S TUESDAY, THIS MUST BE BELGIUM and I LOVE MY WIFE, neither of which had as much merit as this. In later years, Stuart would direct many segments of "Ripley's Believe It or Not" for producer Jack Haley, Jr. and become wealthy on the residuals. The production had a bit of shabbiness attached to it and the attempt at making another WIZARD OF OZ failed, even though there were many of the same elements, including dwarfs and midgets not unlike the "Munchkins." But Anthony Newley and Leslie Bricusse were no match for "Yip" Harburg and Harold Arlen (who wrote the tunes for the 1939 classic) and the score fell short. Tunes include "Willy Wonka, the Candy Man," "Cheer Up, Charlie," "I've Got a Golden Ticket," "Oompa-Loompa-Doompa-Dee-Doo," and "Pure Imagination" (one of the better ones). Where this picture shines is that it never talks down to the children who went to see it. They had an opportunity to watch a movie which allowed them to think, and not be lectured to. Younger tots had a problem figuring out why their older siblings and parents were laughing. Dahl did the adaptation from his own book and made many changes, including removing the boy's father and replacing him with a grandfather. Making Ostrum a lad without a male parent soldered the union between him and Wilder. All through the film, Wilder acts like a stern father and Ostrum is forever seeking his approval, thus adding another element to the deceptively simple story. Scharf and the score were Oscar-nominated.

p, David L. Wolper, Stan Margulies; d, Mel Stuart; w, Roald Dahl (based on his book *Charlie and the Chocolate Factory*); ph, Arthur Ibbetson (Technicolor); m, Walter Scharf; ed, David Saxon; md, Scharf; art d, Harper Goff; cos, Ille Sievers; spec eff, Logan R. Frazee; ch, Howard Jeffrey; makeup, Raimund Stangl.

Fantasy/Musical   **Cas.**   **(PR:A   MPAA:G)**

WILSON*   (1944) 154m FOX c

Alexander Knox (*Woodrow Wilson*), Charles Coburn (*Prof. Henry Holmes*), Geraldine Fitzgerald (*Edith Wilson*), Thomas Mitchell (*Joseph Tumulty*), Ruth Nelson (*Ellen Wilson*), Sir Cedric Hardwicke (*Henry Cabot Lodge*), Vincent Price (*William G. McAdoo*), William Eythe (*George Felton*), Mary Anderson (*Eleanor Wilson*), Sidney Blackmer (*Josephus Daniels*), Madeleine Forbes (*Jessie Wilson*), Stanley Ridges (*Adm. Grayson*), Eddie Foy, Jr. (*Eddie Foy*), Charles Halton (*Col. House*), Thurston Hall (*Sen. E.H. Jones*), J.M. Kerrigan (*Edward Sullivan*), James Rennie (*Jim Beeker*), Katherine Locke (*Helen Bones*), Stanley Logan (*Sec. Lansing*), Marcel Dalio (*Clemenceau*), Edwin Maxwell (*William Jennings Bryan*), Clifford Brooke (*Lloyd George*), Tonio Selwart (*Von Bernstorff*), Gilson Gowland (*Senator*), John Ince (*Sen. Watson*), Charles Miller (*Sen. Bromfield*), Anne O'Neal (*Jennie*), Arthur Loft (*Secretary Lane*), Russell Gaige (*Sec. Colby*), Jamesson Shade (*Sec. Payne*), Reginald Sheffield (*Sec. Baker*), Robert Middlemass (*Sec. Garrison*), Matt Moore (*Sec. Burleson*), George Anderson (*Sec. Houston*), Robert Barron (*Sec. Meredith*), Paul Everton (*Judge Westcott*), Arthur Space (*Francis Sayre*), George MacCready (*McCombs*), Roy Roberts (*Ike Hoover*), Frank Orth (*Smith*), Dewey Robinson (*Worker*), Francis X. Bushman (*Barney Baruch*), Reed Hadley (*Usher*), Cy Kendall (*Charles F. Murphy*), Maj. Sam Harris (*Gen. Bliss*), Hilda Plowright (*Jeannette Rankin*), Joseph J. Greene (*Chief Justice White*), Ralph Dunn (*La Follette*), Davidson Clark (*Champ Clark*), Ferris Taylor, Ken Christy, Guy D'Ennery, Antonio Filauri, Gus Glassmire, Tony Hughes, Isabel Randolph, Jess Lee Brooks, Gladden James, Frank Dawson, Larry McGrath, Josh Hardin, Ralph Linn, Russ Clark, Harold Schlickemeyer, Ed Mundy, Aubrey Mather, Jesse Graves, Del Henderson, John Ardell, George Mathews, John Whitney, Harry Tyler, William Forrest, Harry Carter, Jessie Grayson.

A lavish biography of Woodrow Wilson, this film was Darryl F. Zanuck's first production after he returned from war service in North Africa. Knox plays the president, first as the head of Princeton University and the author of books on political theory. He is chosen to run for Governor of New Jersey and makes such a success of that that he is soon running for president. During his first term WW I erupts in Europe, but he sturdily maintains U.S. neutrality, in keeping with the largely isolationist sentiment of the country. Eventually, though, German sinkings of U.S. merchant ships leads him to declare war, against the advice of his son-in-law and Secretary of the Treasury, Price. After the war is won, thanks to the massive infusion of fresh American boys into the exhausted and depleted Allied armies, Knox

goes to Versailles to help form the peace treaty. He conceives of the League of Nations and convinces most of the former combatants to join, but back in the U.S. he is unable to drum up support in the congress, isolationism still running strong. He goes on a cross-country campaign to bring his idea to the masses, but the trip only ruins his own health and the U.S. votes to stay out of the League. Zanuck staked a lot on this movie, saying at the time, "If WILSON fails, I will never make another picture without Betty Grable." More than $3 million was spent on the production, and the lavish sets included a nearly perfect re-creation of the White House. Henry Fonda and Gary Cooper were considered for the lead, but eventually an obscure contract player, Knox, was tagged for the role. Zanuck and Lamar Trotti wrote most of the script at Zanuck's home, surrounded by history books. Zanuck also oversaw the cutting, seeing that the film moves quickly depite its impressive length. When the film was finally ready, Zanuck told his wife, "I'm kind of proud of myself. I think it will win an Oscar." (It didn't, but when he did recieve one for GENTLEMAN'S AGREEMENT in 1947 he told the Academy in his acceptance speech, "I should have got this for WILSON.") Someone in the studio publicity department came up with the idea of premiering the film in Zanuck's hometown of Wahoo, Nebraska, as a sort of local-boy-makes-good affair. The producer, the stars, and their massive entourage chartered a private train to Wahoo, where Zanuck was honored with a parade, speeches, and the like. For him the trip was a great letdown. Wahoo seemed small and squalid compared to his memories, and osme of the sights brought back unpleasant recollections of a painful childhood. At the debut of the film that night, the house was packed. The next day, the theater was all but deserted. Zanuck asked a local, who told him "The people of Wahoo wouldn't have come to see Woodrow Wilson if he rode down Main Street in person, so why in hell should they pay to see him in a movie." Desperate to get out, Zanuck sent a telegram to Fox ordering them to send a telegram reading "Urgent: needed at studio." When it arrived he hastily packed his bags and never returned to Wahoo again. The reception of the film everywhere was similar to that of Wahoo; although critics praised the film lavishly, the public just wasn't interested, and it turned into a big money-loser.

p, Darryl F. Zanuck; d, Henry King; w, Lamar Trotti; ph, Leon Shamroy (Technicolor); m, Alfred Newman; ed, Barbara McLean; art d, Wiard Ihnen, James Basevi; set d, Thomas Little; cos, Rene Hubert; spec eff, Fred Sersen; makeup, Guy Pearce.

Biography   **(PR:A   MPAA:NR)**

WIN, PLACE AND SHOW   (SEE: CRAZY OVER HORSES, 1951)

WIN, PLACE, OR STEAL*   (1975) 88M Syn-Frank/Cinema National c
        (AKA: THREE FOR THE MONEY; JUST ANOTHER DAY AT THE
                                                              RACES)

Dean Stockwell, Russ Tamblyn, Alex Karras, McLean Stevenson, Alan Oppenheimer, Kristina Holland, Harry Dean Stanton, Liv Von Linden.

Comedy goes to the racetrack again, but this time hampered by a lame-brained script. Stockwell, Tamblyn, and Karras try to scheme their way into a fortune by using the parimutuel machine at the track. Better suited as a made-for-TV picture, especially since one could have seen it for free instead of plunking down cash at the box office.

p, Thomas D. Cooney; d, Richard Bailey; w, Anthony Monaco, Bailey; m, Tim McIntire.

Comedy   **Cas.**   **(PR:A   MPAA:PG)**

WINCHESTER '73**   (1950) 92m UNIV bw

James Stewart (*Lin McAdam*), Shelley Winters (*Lola Manners*), Dan Duryea (*Waco Johnny Dean the Kansas Kid*), Stephen McNally (*Dutch Henry Brown*), Millard Mitchell (*Johnny "High Spade" Williams*), Charles Drake (*Steve Miller*), John McIntire (*Joe Lamont*), Will Geer (*Wyatt Earp*), Jay C. Flippen (*Sgt. Wilkca*), Rock Hudson (*Young Bull*), John Alexander (*Jack Rider*), Steve Brodie (*Wesley*), James Millican (*Wheeler*), Abner Biberman (*Latigo Means*), Anthony 'Tony' Curtis (*Doan*), James Best (*Crater*), Gregg Martell (*Mossman*), Frank Chase (*Cavalryman*), Chuck Robertson (*Long Tom*), Carol Henry (*Dudeen*), Ray Teal (*Marshal Noonan*), Virginia Mullens (*Mrs. Jameson*), John Doucette (*Roan Daley*), Steve Darrell (*Masterson*), Chief Youilachie (*Indian*), Frank Conlan (*Clerk*), Ray Bennett (*Charles Bender*), Guy Wilkerson (*Virgil*), Bob Anderson (*Bassett*), Larry Olsen (*Boy at Rifle Shoot*), Edmund Cobb (*Target Watcher*), Forrest Taylor (*Target Clerk*), Ethan Laidlaw (*Station Master*), Bud Osborne (*Man*), Bonnie Kay Eddy (*Betty Jameson*), Jennings Miles (*Stagecoach Driver*), John War Eagle (*Indian Interpreter*), Duke Yorke (*First Man*), Ted Mapes (*Bartender*), Norman Kent (*Buffalo Hunter*), Norman Olestad (*Stable Boy*), Tony Taylor (*Boy*), Tim Hawkins (*Boy at Rifle Shoot*), Mel Archer (*Bartender*), Bill McKenzie (*Boy at Rifle Shoot*).

The first collaboration between director Mann and actor Stewart who would create a series of superior westerns that added a new dimension to the genre and its heroes. The Mann-Stewart westerns are revenge tales where the hero (Stewart) harbors a deep, dark secret that claws at his very core and consumes his being. His obsession threatens to destroy him and he pursues his quarry with a psychotic fervor. The line between hero and villain in the

Mann-Stewart westerns is a thin one. WINCHESTER '73 begins as Stewart, who is pursuing the murderer of his father, rides into Dodge City with his friend, Mitchell. It is the 4th of July and the whole town is celebrating in the streets under the watchful eye of the fatherly Wyatt Earp (Geer), who collects pistols from gun-toting strangers and keeps them in his office until they leave. Stewart enters the local saloon and orders a drink. Out of the corner of his eye he sees McNally and both men spastically grope for their sidearms, only to find empty holsters. Stewart's nerves are frazzled by the event and he leaves the saloon shaking. The two men square off again, this time in a shooting contest with a brand new "one of 1,000" Winchester '73 rifle as the first prize. The contestants are evenly matched and the fight for the coveted weapon is intense, but Stewart manages to best McNally and is awarded the rifle. Before Stewart can leave town with his prize, however, he is attacked by McNally and the rifle is stolen. Stewart pursues McNally with maniacal intensity. McNally loses the rifle to seedy Indian trader McIntire in a card game and the weapon again changes hands when the trader is killed by Indian chief Hudson who takes it for himself. When the Indians launch an attack on the U.S. Cavalry, Hudson loses the rifle to a cowardly homesteader, Drake, who is out to start a new life with dance hall girl Winters. Stewart, who has managed to stay one step behind the weapon, meets Winters during the Indian attack on the cavalry and she is attracted to him. When the smoke clears, however, Winters goes off with Drake. On the trail, the couple is attacked by a crazed bandit, Duryea, and he kills Drake and steals the Winchester. Duryea and his gang take refuge in a ranch house where they terrorize the settlers into submission. The home is burned to the ground to smoke out the outlaws, and Duryea is killed. The gun is then passed back to the hands of McNally–the original thief. Now accompanied by Winters, Stewart finally tracks down McNally and there is a dramatic confrontation amongst steep, craggy, windswept rocks. During the scene it is revealed that McNally is Stewart's brother and it is he who murdered their father. The men exchange gunfire, the bullets ricocheting off the rocks and kicking up clouds of dust. Obsessed with avenging the family name, Stewart kills McNally and reclaims the Winchester. Purged of his madness, Stewart makes his way back down the mountain and into the arms of Winters. WINCHESTER '73 was the first of the so-called "psychological" westerns that became the benchmark of the genre in the 1950s. Mann and Stewart present a hero who is possessed with a basic decency, dignity, and nobility, but forces in his past drive him to the brink of madness and his passion nearly consumes him. Mann's westerns are biblical in structure and feel, filled with brutality and violence, where those who lose their place in society are driven back to the brutal wilderness to purge their dark obsessions so that they may reenter the promised land. These tales are played out against the various landscapes of the West, each background reflecting the psychological condition of the main character. Stewart turns in one of his greatest performances in WINCHESTER '73, his manic intensity evoking both terror and pathos. The scene where older brother McNally first steals the rifle from sibling Stewart evokes the struggles the brothers must have had as children. Stewart's face becomes that of an upset, forever picked-on child trying desperately to retain his self-respect and dignity in the face of his bullying older brother. It is a horrible, telling moment. The supporting cast is fine as well, with both Tony Curtis and Rock Hudson appearing in small roles. WINCHESTER '73 was once a project for Fritz Lang, who worked on the script with Silvia Richards in 1948. Lang eventually walked away from the film and Mann took over at Stewart's suggestion. Beginning a collaboration that would last through two more westerns (BEND OF THE RIVER, 1952, and THE FAR COUNTRY, 1955) Mann rewrote the script with Borden Chase. WINCHESTER '73 was a great success at the box office and reestablished Stewart (who was suffering a decline in popularity) as one of Hollywood's top actors. In addition to providing both star and director with a career boost, the film launched a whole new series of adult westerns (directed by such notables as Mann, Budd Boetticher, Don Siegel, Sam Fuller, and Nicholas Ray) that explored, questioned, and analyzed the very nature of savagery, civilization, and heroism.

p, Aaron Rosenberg; d, Anthony Mann; w, Robert L. Richards, Borden Chase (based on the story by Stuart N. Lake); ph, William Daniels; m, Joseph Gershenson (assisted by Jesse Hibbs); ed, Edward Curtiss; art d, Bernard Herzbrun, Nathan Juran, Russell A. Gausman, A. Roland Fields; cos, Yvonne Wood.

Western   **Cas.**   **(PR:C   MPAA:NR)**

WIND, THE**   (1928) 74m MGM bw

Lillian Gish (Letty), Lars Hanson (Lige), Montagu Love (Roddy Wirt), Dorothy Cumming (Cora), Edward Earle (Beverly), William Orlamond (Sourdough), Laon Ramon, Carmencita Johnson, Billy Kent Schaefer (Cora's Children).

Gish is a naive girl from Virginia heading for Texas to live with her cousin. However, her cousin's wife, Cumming, takes a dislike to Gish when her husband and children dote on her and she forces her to leave. Having nowhere to go, Gish quickly marries Hanson, a roughneck cowboy she had earlier scorned. When he leaves for a wild horse roundup, Gish, left alone in the midst of a violent windstorm, is visited by Love, a married man who had earlier hinted at a possible marriage to Gish. He tries to rape her and Gish kills him with a pistol. With great effort she drags the body outside and tries to bury it but the wind and constantly shifting sands make this a near

impossible task. She watches in horror as the dead man's hand materializes from the grave when the unrelenting wind pushes back the sand. Gish's mind begins to turn and an almost hallucinatory white horse, a probable runaway, gallops past in the blowing wind. Hanson finally returns home to find his wife nearly mad but eventually he calms her. The two find renewed feelings for one another and decide to remain together. Like the film's title element, this is a story of unrelenting power continually pushing the characters in defiance of their hopes and beliefs. Gish's performance is powerful, as she fights back against the forces working on her psyche. The wind, which continually blows sand into the food, clothing, and bodies of its victims, is almost a character in and of itself. No matter where she turns or whom she meets, she must always deal with the unrelenting Texas winds, a metaphor for the unplanned circumstances and crises that never cease to plague her. Seastrom directs with a strong feeling for realism while fully objectifying the story's more hallucinatory qualities. Originally the film was to end with Gish, driven insane, wandering off into the desert. However, the studio chiefs at MGM demanded a happy ending as well as a soundtrack to capitalize on the new technology of talking pictures. This version was released in the U. S. to mixed reviews but did not deter Seastrom. His original cut, an undeniable classic in silent filmmaking, was released in Europe where it was met with much acclaim. The feeling for depth and space was common to many Scandinavian directors, but most peculiarly to Seastrom, who used it constantly to add the beauty of nature and the rhythm of poetry to his work.

d, Victor Seastrom [Sjostrom]; w, Frances Marion (based on the novel The Wind by Dorothy Scarborough); ph, John Arnold; ed, Conrad A. Nervig; set d, Cedric Gibbons; cos, Andre-ani; m/l, "Love Brought the Sunshine" Herman Ruby, William Axt, Dave Dreyer, David Mendoza.

Drama   **(PR:C   MPAA:NR)**

WIND ACROSS THE EVERGLADES**½
                              (1958) 93m Budd Schulberg WB c

Burl Ives (Cottonmouth), Christopher Plummer (Walt Murdock), Gypsy Rose Lee (Mrs. Bradford), George Voskovec (Aaron Nathanson), Tony Galento (Beef), Howard I. Smith (George), Emmett Kelly (Bigamy Bob), Pat Henning (Sawdust), Chana Eden (Naomi), Curt Conway (Perfesser), Peter Falk (Writer), Fred Grossinger (Slowboy), MacKinlay Kantor (Judge Harris), Sammy Renick (Loser), Toch Brown (One-Note), Frank Rothe (Howard Ross Morgan).

In this unusual effort for director Ray, Plummer plays an alcoholic conservationist with the Audubon Society, in the early 1900s. He's trying to protect the Florida Everglades from both real estate developers and poachers killing some of the wild life. Certain plume birds are in particular demand, as their tail feathers are used to decorate fashionable hats for women. Ives is the poachers' leader, engaging in a head-to-head battle with Plummer. Eventually Plummer is able to capture Ives, but the outlaw hunter is killed before Plummer can turn him over to authorities. The film has some engaging moments, but Schulberg's script meanders into varying subplots that hamper the overall drama of the story. Lee provides some fine comic moments as the madam of a brothel Plummer frequents. At best, though, this is a curio in both Schulberg's and Ray's filmographies. Falk, who would later star in the television series "Columbo," makes his film debut in a minor supporting role.

p, Stuart Schulberg; d, Nicholas Ray; w, Budd Schulberg (based on his story "Across the Everglades"); ph, Joseph Brun (Technicolor); ed, George Klotz, Joseph Zigman; art d, Richard Sylbert; cos, Frank Thompson.

Drama   **(PR:C   MPAA:NR)**

WIND AND THE LION, THE***½   (1975) 119m MGM/UA c

Sean Connery (Mulay el Raisuli), Candice Bergen (Eden Pedecaris), Brian Keith (Theodore Roosevelt), John Huston (John Hay), Geoffrey Lewis (Gummere), Steve Kanaly (Capt. Jerome), Vladek Sheybal (The Bashaw), Nadim Sawalha (Sherif of Wazan), Roy Jenson (Adm. Chadbwick), Deborah Baxter (Alice Roosevelt), Jack Cooley (Quentin Roosevelt), Chris Aller (Kermit Roosevelt), Simon Harrison (William Pedecaris), Polly Gottesman (Jennifer Pedecaris), Antoine St. John (Von Roerkel), Aldo Sambrell (Ugly Arab), Luis Barboo (Gayaan the Terrible), Darrell Fetty (Dreighton), Marc Zuber (The Sultan), Billy Williams (Sir Joseph), Shirley Rothman (Edith Roosevelt), Rusty Cox (Marine Sergeant), Larry Cross (Henry Cabot Lodge), Alex Weldon (Elihu Root), Akio Mitamura (Japanese General), Frank Gassman (President's Aide), Audrey San Felix (Miss Hitchcock), Ben Tatar (Sketch Artist), Michael Damian (President's Secretary), Leon Liberman (2nd Aide), Allen Russell (3rd Aide), Howard Hagan (Diplomat), Arthur Larkin (1st Secret Serviceman), James Cooley (2nd Secret Serviceman), M. Ciudad (3rd Secret Serviceman), Rupert Crabb (Mountain Man), Charles Stalnaker (1st Reporter), David Lester (2nd Reporter), Paul Rusking (3rd Reporter), Carl Rapp (1st Station Man), Jim Mitchell (Gummere's Aide), Anita Colby (Station Woman), Ricardo Palacois (Torres), Robert Case (U.K. Military Advisor), Felipe Solano (Pock-faced Arab), Charley Bravo (Decapitated Arab), Eduardo Bea (Philippe), Juan Cazalilla (Chef).

A stirring, if grossly inaccurate look at the dawn of U.S. as a world power willing to intervene in foreign countries. Keith is Teddy Roosevelt, looking for a way to establish himself in his own right after coming to office after the death of President McKinley. When a rebellious Arab chieftain (Connery) seizes an American woman (Bergen) and her children (Harrison and Gotteson), Keith prepares to send in the Marines. At the same time, the Germans are landing in force looking for a way to turn the situation to their advantage. Connery and Bergen talk a great deal of philosophy and the chieftain begins to take on heroic stature in the eyes of her son. Eventually, under pressure from Keith, for whom Connery gains great respect, he releases his hostages to the American Marines and is immediately arrested and imprisoned by the Germans. The Marines are none too happy about this development, especially as Keith had promised Connery his freedom if his prisoners were turned over, so they march into the town (in a scene almost directly stolen from THE WILD BUNCH) and shoot it out with the Germans. Connery is released and joins the battle, and, mounted on horseback, he kills the German commander with his sword. Afterward he sends a letter to Keith, comparing them. Connery likens himself to the lion, lord of his dominion, but helpless in the face of the wind, Keith. He goes on to say, though, that as the lion, he knows his place, but the wind can never know his. The film is certainly jingoistic to a fault, and its portrayal of the various factions is little above the cartoon level, but thanks to marvelous performances by Keith and Connery, the film works as a maker of myths. The real facts of the case were not so grand. Raisuli, a brigand chief, kidnaped Ion Perdicaris, a balding, overweight businessman who bore no resemblance to Candice Bergen, to embarrass the Sultan of Morocco, who was already having troubles in his relations with the U.S. Perdicaris was released after only a couple of days, but before that word was made public, the Republican party, looking for something to whip up some public support, announced that a telegram had been sent to the kidnaper, saying: "Perdicaris alive or Raisuli dead." No troops were landed. No one was killed. But historical truth isn't what's important here, heroes and myth are what's important, and this film delivers up two heroes in admirable fashion.

p, Herb Jaffe; d&w, John Milius; ph, Billy Williams (Panavision, Metrocolor); m, Jerry Goldsmith; ed, Robert L. Wolfe; prod d, Gil Parando; art d, Antonio Paton; cos, Richard E. LaMotte.

Adventure   **Cas.**   **(PR:C MPAA:PG)**

WIND BLOWETH WHERE IT LISTETH, THE
                                        (SEE: MAN ESCAPED, A, 1957, FR.)

WIND CANNOT READ, THE**½   (1958, Brit.) 115m RANK/FOX c

Dirk Bogarde (*Flight Lt. Michael Quinn*), Yoko Tani ("*Sabby*", *Suziki San*), Ronald Lewis (*Squadron Leader Fenwick*), John Fraser (*Flight Officer Munroe*), Anthony Bushell (*Brigadier*), Henry Okawa (*Lt. Nakamura*), Marne Maitland (*Bahadur*), Michael Medwin (*Flight Officer Lamb*), Richard Leech (*Hobson*), Anthony Wager (*Moss*), Tadashi Ikeda (*Itsumi San*), Yoichi Matsue (*Cpl. Mori*), Donald Pleasence (*Doctor*), Joy Michael, Avice Landone (*Nurses*).

Bogarde, a Royal Air Force officer in Burma during the early days of World War II, is transferred to India to learn Japanese so he can become an interrogator of prisoners of war. He falls in love with his instructor, Tani, the daughter of a Japanese liberal who fled his country during the rise to power of Tojo and his militants. The pair do a lot of sightseeing and, because the RAF would refuse him permission, they secretly marry. Soon after, Bogarde is sent to the front and in short order captured by the Japanese. Tani joins All India Radio, beaming British propaganda to the enemy, and from the camp where he has been tortured and humiliated, Bogarde listens intently. One day, though, Tani isn't broadcast and Bogarde learns from fellow prisoner Lewis that she is suffering from an incurable brain disease. Determined to see her again, Bogarde and Lewis stage a daring escape and make their way through dense jungles back to their own lines. In Delhi he is reunited with Tani and reaffirms his love for her just before she dies a lovely soft-focus death. A routine sentimental wartime romance is saved from maudlin excess by Bogarde's sincere performance and the exciting prison camp and escape sequences. Bogarde was just about the biggest star in Britain at this point and his indenture to Rank, which had kept him in bland, lightweight juvenile leads like the "Doctor" series, was soon to end.

p, Betty E. Box; d, Ralph Thomas; w, Richard Mason (based on his novel); ph, Ernest Steward (Eastmancolor); m, Angelo Lavagnino; ed, Frederick Wilson; art d, Maurice Carter; cos, Beatrice Dawson.

Drama   **(PR:A MPAA:NR)**

WIND FROM THE EAST*   (1970, Fr./Ital./Ger.) 92m
        Polifilm-Anouchka-CCC-Filmkunst/ New Line Cinema c (LE VENT
        D'EST; AKA: EAST WIND)

Gian Maria Volonte (*Soldier*), Anne-Wiazemsky (*Whore*), Daniel (*Cohn-Bendict*), Gotz George, Christian Tullio, Rick Boyd, Paolo Pozzesi, Allen Midgette, Glauber Rocha, Jose Varella, Marco Ferreri, Jean-Luc Godard.

One of Godard's many excursions into Marxist cinema, this one barely predated his Dziga Verto days and began his association with Gorin. Basically, it is about a group of filmmakers and actors discussing and trying to make political films. It barely resembles a western, much to the consternation of Italian producer Barcelloni who received a promise from Godard that WIND FROM THE EAST would be along the lines of Sergio

Leone's pictures. Anyone with a speck of knowledge about Godard would have realised that Barcelloni was indeed in for a surprise. Godard contacted Cohn-Bendit, a leading figure in France's 1968 riots, and proposed this project. Before long, Cohn-Bendit was no longer associated with the project due to creative disagreements (although he's listed in many cast lists, he does not appear in the film). Godard then took up with Brazilian filmmaker Glauber Rocha, but this time political differences had a positive effect on the film. The film's most memorable scene has Rocha standing at a crossroads, meant to symbolize the directions that political cinema could take. He is approached by a pregnant woman who says, "Excuse me for interrupting your class struggle, but could you please tell the way toward political cinema?" For the most part, WIND FROM THE EAST is unwatchable, even for die-hard Godard fans. There are, of course, some interesting moments, but all the Marxist-Maoist ideology that the film spouts comes across just as clearly (probably more so) on the printed page. Godard's problem with political cinema is most apparent in WIND FROM THE EAST–his attempts to bring politics to the masses, to the common working man, are so intellectualized and unentertaining that he instead alienates all but his most radical followers.

p, Gianni Barcelloni, Ettore Rosbach; d, Jean-Luc Godard, Daniel Cohn-Bendit, Jean-Pierre Gorin; w, Godard, Cohn-Bendit; ph, Mario Vulpiani (Eastmancolor); ed, Godard.

Drama   **(PR:C MPAA:NR)**

WIND OF CHANGE, THE**   (1961, Brit.) 64m Cresswell/Bry bw

Donald Pleasence (*Pop*), Johnny Briggs (*Frank*), Ann Lynn (*Josie*), Hilda Fenemore (*Gladys*), Glyn Houston (*Sgt. Parker*), Norman Gunn (*Ron*), Bunny May (*Smithy*), David Hemmings (*Ginger*).

A forgettable picture about a rebellious teen whose fellow gang members beat a black person to death. The violence hits home when the gang knifes the teen's sister, causing the lad to renounce gang life. A young and frail 20 year-old David Hemmings appears, six years before appearing older and frail in Michelangelo Antonioni's BLOW-UP.

p, John Dark; d, Vernon Sewell; w, Alexander Dore, John McLaren.

Crime   **(PR:A MPAA:NR)**

WINDBAG THE SAILOR**   (1937, Brit.) 85m Gainsborough/GAU bw

Will Hay (*Capt. Ben Cutlet*), Moore Marriott (*Jeremiah Harbottle*), Graham Moffatt (*Albert*), Norma Varden (*Olivia Potter-Porter*), Kenneth Warrington (*Yates*), Dennis Wyndham (*Maryatt*), Amy Veness (*Emma Harbottle*).

Hay, a seaman filled with hot air and tall tales, brags about his abilities and panics when he actually gets a chance to show them off. He is hired by a wealthy ship owner to take command of a vessel which, unbeknownst to Hay, is to be scuttled by its crew as part of an insurance scam. Hay, however, saves the day and proves his worth as a seaman.

p, Michael Balcon; d, William Beaudine; w, Marriott Edgar, Stafford Dickens, Will Hay, Robert Edmunds, Val Guest (based on a story by Robert Stevenson, Leslie Arliss); ph, Jack Cox; ed, R. E. Dearing, Terence Fisher; md, Louis Levy; art d, Alex Vetchinsky, A. Cox.

Comedy   **(PR:A MPAA:NR)**

WINDFALL**   (1935, Brit.) 65m EMB/RKO bw

Edward Rigby (*Sam Spooner*), Marie Ault (*Maggie Spooner*), George Carney (*Syd*), Marjorie Corbett (*Mary*), Derrick de Marney (*Tom Spooner*), Googie Withers (*Dodie*).

A hard-working old ironmonger, Rigby, inherits a large sum, allowing him to live the good life. His family soon takes advantage; his son becomes lazy and falls into bad company, while his brother-in-law gets mixed up in murder. To prove a point to them, Rigby returns to work and is nearly killed on the job. It takes this near-tragedy to straighten up the family.

p, George King, Randall Faye; d, King; w, Faye, Jack Celestin (based on a play by R.C. Sherriff).

Drama   **(PR:A MPAA:NR)**

WINDFALL**   (1955 Brit.) 64m Mid-Century/Eros bw

Lionel Jeffries (*Arthur Lee*), Jack Watling (*John Lee*), Gordon Jackson (*Leonard*), Avice Landone (*Mary Lee*), Brian Worth Michael Collins, Patricia Owens (*Connie Lee*), Cyril Chamberlain (*Clarkson*), Arthur Lowe, Erik Chitty, Alastair Hunter, Peter Swanwick.

Jeffries is a shop assistant who finds a briefcase containing a hefty sum of cash. His daughter's shifty boy friend steals the money but gets caught when it turns out to be counterfeit. Jeffries' luck takes a turn when the publicity gives a boost to his business. A young Jeffries is made up to appear elderly in this early film role.

p, Robert Baker, Monty Berman; d, Henry Cass; w, John Gilling; ph, Berman.

Comedy   **(PR:A MPAA:NR)**

WINDFLOWERS zero (1968) 75m Windflowers/Film-Maker's Distribution Center bw (AKA: WINDFLOWERS: THE STORY OF A DRAFT DODGER)

John Kramer (Henry Hawkins/"Paul Ramsey"), Pola Chapelle (Julie), Dino Narizzano (Clergyman), Joy Nicholson (Mother of a War Hero), Edward Rishon (Driver), Maxton Latham (Publisher), James Hunter (Newspaper Reporter), Dave Tice (Police Captain), Todd Everett (Police Rookie), Roger Briant (Student), Barbara Vary, Margaret Vary (The Twins), Tina Stoumen (Teenage Girl), Henry Calvert (Father), Ronnie Gilbert (Mother), William Traylor, Reathel Bean (FBI Agents), Harry Gantt (Office Manager), Karl Bissinger (Man in the Flower Shop), The Brown Family (Family), Adolfas Mekas (Card Player).

The final day in the life of a draft dodger is documented in this rambling anti-Establishment drama. Various scenes commenting on war are intercut with flashbacks to earlier episodes in Kramer's six-year life-on-the-run. The only positive aspect of this film is the avoidance of mentioning Vietnam, but then what other wars were American kids evading in the mid-1960s?

d&w, Adolfas Mekas; ph, Bruce Sparks; m, Mekas, Pola Chapelle; ed, Mekas; md, Dave Blume.

Drama (PR:C MPAA:NR)

WINDJAMMER, THE*½ (1931, Brit.) 75m Wardour/BIP-Pro Patria bw

Tony Bruce (Jack Mitchell), Michael Hogan (Bert Hodges), Hal Gordon (Alf), Roy Travers (Old Ned), Gordon Craig (Youth), Hal Booth, J. Baker, J. Cunningham, P. Russell, C. Christie, G. Thomas, Charles Levey.

A hobo joins the crew of a sailing ship embarking on a five-month journey from Australia to England, via Cape Horn. The film is a re-creation of an actual expedition by a pair of newsmen, one of whom–Walker–died at sea, the other having finished the voyage. The authentic feel of the camera work is of high merit, but the studio scenes are just awful.

p, H. Bruce Woolfe; d, John Orton; w, Orton, A. P. Herbert (based on the novel By Way of Cape Horn by A. J. Villiers); ph, Villiers, R. J. Walker, Jack Parker.

Adventure (PR:A MPAA:NR)

WINDJAMMER (1937) 60m Condor/RKO bw

George O'Brien (Lane), Constance Worth (Betty), William Hall (Morgan), Brandon Evans (Commodore), Gavin Gordon (Forsythe), Stanley Blystone (Peterson), Lal Chand Mehra (Willy), Ben Hendricks (Dolan), Lee Shumway (Captain), Frank Hagney (Slum), Sam Flint (Bishop).

O'Brien, a deputy state's attorney, is ordered to serve a subpena on wealthy yachtsman Evans. In order to do so, he must sign on for a race from California to Hawaii. En route, the yacht–with its mainly moneyed people–is wrecked by the gun-smuggling windjammer commanded by Hall. Rescued from the sea and taken aboard the gunrunning ship, the survivors–initially snobbish–come to rely on the muscular O'Brien for ultimate rescue. A departure from the western plains for the star.

p, George A. Hirliman, David Howard; d, Ewing Scott; w, Dan Jarrett, James Gruen (based on a story by Maj. Raoul Haig); ph, Frank B. Good; ed, Robert Crandall; md, Abe Meyer; art d, F. Paul Sylos.

Adventure/Crime (PR:A MPAA:NR)

WINDMILL, THE*½ (1937, Brit.) 62m WB-FN bw

Hugh Williams (Lt. Peter Ellington), Glen Alyn (Clodine Asticot), Henry Mollison (Gaston Lefarge), Anthony Shaw (Col. Richardson), George Galleon (Maj. Arbuthnot), William Dewhurst (Mons. Asticot), Winnifred Oughton (Mme. Asticot), John Laurie (Mons. Coutard), John Carol (Pvt. Goggle), Bruce Lister (Officer), Agnes Laughlan, Charlotte Parry, Robert Algar.

Williams is an English soldier fighting in WW I. He falls in love with an innkeeper's daughter, Alyn, whose German-born fiance is uncloaked as a German spy. Alyn is taken to a nearby windmill which her fiance uses to transmit secret messages. The climax has the spy burning to death in a fire at the windmill and Williams heroically rescuing Alyn.

p, Irving Asher; d&w, Arthur Woods (based on the novel by John Drabble); ph, Robert Lapresle.

War Drama (PR:A MPAA:NR)

WINDOM'S WAY (1958, Brit.) 108m RANK c

Peter Finch (Dr. Alec Windom), Mary Ure (Lee Windom), Natasha Parry (Anna Vidal), Robert Flemyng (George Hasbrook), Michael Hordern (Patterson), John Cairney (Jan Vidal), Marne Maitland (Belhedron), Gregoire Aslan (Lollivar), Kurt Siegenberg (Kasti), George Margo (Lansang), Sanny Bin Hussan (Amyan), Olaf Pooley (Col. Lupat), Martin Benson (Rebel Commander), John A. Tinn.

Finch is an idealistic, pacifistic doctor running a small hospital in the village of Selim, in northern Malaya. His estranged wife, Ure, arrives to try to patch up their failing marriage, but he doesn't seem interested, being more concerned with his fledgling affair with native nurse Parry. Political unrest increases in this tropic locale as native workers go on strike against rubber plantation owners. The conscientious doctor at first tries to mediate the dispute, but when the owners begin repressive measures backed by government policemen, he hides union leader Cairney in his hospital while continuing to work for a peaceful settlement. As the police come down on all dissent, most of the workers take to the hills. Finch goes up to talk to them but is captured by an insurgent and apparently Communist rebel army most of the strikers have joined. He escapes them and finds that the government, which had promised to give Finch time to talk the rebels down, has double-crossed him and called in the army to put down the uprising. Utterly disillusioned by betrayals all around him, he packs his bags to leave the country, but Ure convinces him to remain and care for the wounded while continuing to work for peace. Good, intelligent drama with an excellent, heartfelt performance by Finch. The film was indirectly based on the life on Dr. Gordon S. Seagrave, who was imprisoned in Burma for aiding Communist insurgents there.

p, John Bryan; d, Ronald Neame; w, Jill Craigie (based on a novel by James Ramsey Ullman); ph, Christopher Challis (Eastmancolor); m, James Bernard; ed, Reginald Mills; md, Muir Mathieson.

Drama Cas. (PR:A-C MPAA:NR)

WINDOW, THE**** (1949) 73m RKO bw

Barbara Hale (Mrs. Woodry), Bobby Driscoll (Tommy Woodry), Arthur Kennedy (Mr. Woodry), Paul Stewart (Mr. Kellerton), Ruth Roman (Mrs. Kellerton), Anthony Ross (Ross), Richard Benedict (Drunken Seaman Who Is murdered), Jim Nolan (Stranger on Street), Ken Terrell (Man), Lee Phelps, Eric Mack, Charles Flynn, Budd Fine, Carl Faulkner, Lloyd Dawson, Carl Saxe (Police Officers), Lee Kass (Reporter), Tex Swan (Milkman).

A tense, nail-biting thriller set in the tenement section of New York's Lower East Side, about a young boy, Driscoll, who has a habit of "crying wolf." One day, however, while playing around on the fire escape, he climbs up to the next floor and witnesses Stewart and Roman murdering a drunken seaman, Benedict. Of course, no one believes Driscoll, falsely assuming that this is just another one of the boy's tales. The frightened, frustrated boy goes, instead, to the police, who send a detective disguised as a building inspector to the apartment. When the boy's parents, Kennedy and Hale, learn what he has done, they think he has gone too far with his storytelling and force him to apologize to the murderers, thereby revealing to them that he witnessed the crime. Driscoll's plan to run away is thwarted by Kennedy, who proceeds to imprison the boy in his room, nailing the windows shut to ensure that he cannot leave. Later, when Driscoll is left alone in the apartment, he is confronted by Stewart, who tries to convince the boy that he wants to go to the police and confess his crime. Driscoll tries to run away, but loses consciousness after a chase into a subway station, and is brought back home by Stewart, who leaves him out on the fire escape with the hope that the boy will fall to his death. When Driscoll comes to, he makes his escape, taking refuge in a nearby abandoned building. Following him, however, is Stewart, who is now fully intent on ridding himself of the nuisance that the boy presents. Kennedy comes home and, concerned about his boy's safety, alerts the police. Meantime, Driscoll is pursued across the rafters of the abandoned building by Stewart who eventually falls to his death. When the police arrive, Driscoll's story is confirmed, Roman is arrested, and the boy is reunited with his parents, having promised to never again "cry wolf." Based on a story by Cornell Woolrich, whose writing was also the basis for REAR WINDOW, a movie in which a murder is also witnessed through a window, THE WINDOW presents a frightening vision of helplessness which clearly illustrates the habit that adults have of too easily dismissing or ignoring their children. Director and one-time cameraman Tetzlaff adroitly injects a maximum of suspense into the film, enabling the audience to identify with the child's predicament and, interestingly, view his parents as being evil, almost as evil as the murderers themselves. Tetzlaff had, without a doubt, learned something of his suspense-building craft from the master, himself, Alfred Hitchcock (as did just about every working director), having photographed NOTORIOUS just three years before. By casting the 12-year-old Driscoll, a star of such heart-warming Disney pictures as SONG OF THE SOUTH and SO DEAR TO MY HEART, Tetzlaff was able to twist the idyllic Disney image that the boy had into a nightmare world of death and violence where his parents and neighbors are his worst fears come true. Adding to the film's effect is the on-location photography and the dark quality given to the tenements, where evil and death seem to lurk in every shadow, where the drunken seaman's corpse is found, and where the pursued boy is nearly killed. In a perverse twist of fate, it was in an abandoned, crumbling, New York City tenement that Driscoll was found dead some 20 years later, the victim of an apparent drug overdose. THE WINDOW, which cost only $210,000 to produce and made many times that at the box office, was voted the best mystery film of the year by the Mystery Writers of America. Editor Knudtson was nominated for an Academy Award, while Driscoll was named Outstanding Juvenile Actor and given a miniature statuette.

p, Frederic Ullman, Jr.; d, Ted Tetzlaff; w, Mel Dinelli (based on the novelette The Boy Cried Murder by Cornell Woolrich); ph, William Steiner;

m, Roy Webb; ed, Frederic Knudtson; md, Constantin Bakaleinikoff; art d, Walter E. Keller, Sam Corso; set d, Darrell Silvera, Harley Miller; spec eff, Russell A. Cully; makeup, Gene Romer.

Crime   **Cas.**   **(PR:C   MPAA:NR)**

WINDOW IN LONDON, A   (SEE: LADY IN DISTRESS, 1942, Brit.)

WINDOW TO THE SKY, A   (SEE: OTHER SIDE OF THE
                                       MOUNTAIN, THE, 1975)

WINDOWS*   (1980) 96m UA c

Talia Shire (Emily Hollander), Joseph Cortese (Bob Luffrono), Elizabeth Ashley (Andrea Glassen), Kay Medford (Ida Marx), Michael Gorrin (Sam Marx), Russell Horton (Steven Hollander), Michael Lipton (Dr. Marin), Rick Petrucelli (Obecny), Ron Ryan (Detective Swid), Linda Gillin (Policewoman), Tony Di Benedetto (Nick), Bryce Bond (Voiceover), Ken Chapin (Renting Agent), Marty Greene (Ira), Bill Handy (Desk Officer), Robert Hodge (Desk Sergeant), Kyle Scott Jackson (Detective), Pat McNamara (Doorman), Gerry Vichi (Ben), Oliver (Jennifer the Cat).

The directorial debut of photographer Gordon Willis, who's best known for making Woody Allen's neuroses a joy to watch. As with the superbly picturesque MANHATTAN, Willis captures the feeling of the city, but receives no support from Siegel's script–a psychotic thriller with sexual overtones that lacks any sort of cohesiveness. Shire is the subject of a perverse obsession by a lesbian neighbor, Ashley, who not only is in lust with her but hires a rapist in order to get audio tapes of her moaning. Ashley turns Peeping Tom and watches Shire with a telescope as she begins a relationship with detective Cortese. Even Shire's decision to move cannot deter Ashley. Nothing ever gels here because of the lack of logic and motivation; only the camera work and score (by Morricone) stand out. Perhaps with a better script...

p, Michael Lobell; d, Gordon Willis; w, Barry Siegel; ph, Willis (Technicolor); m, Ennio Morricone; ed, Barry Malkin; prod d, Melvin Bourne; art d, Richard Fuhrman; set d, Les Bloom; cos, Clifford Capone.

Drama   **(PR:O   MPAA:R)**

WINDOWS OF TIME, THE*   (1969, Hung.) 85m Studio 4-Mafilm bw
                                              (AZ IDOE ABLAKAJ)

Beata Tyszkiewicz (Eva), Ian Andonov (Avram), Krystina Mikolajewska (Maguy), Heidemarie Wenzel, (Beryl), Miklos Gabor (Sinis).

A stale attempt at accepting responsibility in post-holocaust days in which there are only five survivors, including the man who ordered the quark bombs dropped that destroyed the world. They awake from a deep-freeze, all of different Eastern European nationalities, and are forced to accept the catastrophe that they created. A rare Hungarian science-fiction film without much to recommend it except its impressive photography.

d, Tamar Fejer; w, Peter Kuczka; ph, Miklos Herczenik.

Science-Fiction   **(PR:A   MPAA:NR)**

WINDS OF THE WASTELAND½**   (1936) 57m REP bw

John Wayne (John Blair), Phyllis Fraser (Barbara Forsythe), Yakima Canutt (Smoky), Douglas Cosgrove (Cal Drake), Lane Chandler (Larry Adams), Sam Flint (Dr. William Forsythe), Lew Kelly (Rocky O'Brien), Bob Kortman (Cherokee Joe), Ed Cassidy (Dodge), Merrill McCormick (Pete), Charles Locher [Jon Hall] (Jim, Pony Express Rider), Joe Yrigoyen (Pike), Chris Franke (Grahame), Bud McClure, Jack Ingram (Guards), Art Mix, Jack Rockwell, Arthur Millett, Tracy Layne, Lloyd Ingraham.

Wayne and Chandler buy a dilapidated stagecoach and compete for a chance at a $25,000 mail contract by racing a rival coach line. Canutt tries to sabotage Wayne's attempt, but to no avail. A fine western entry which firmly established Wayne as star material.

p, Nat Levine; d, Mack V. Wright; w, Joseph Poland; ph, William Nobles; ed, Murray Seldeen, Robert Jahne; md, Harry Grey.

Western   **Cas.**   **(PR:A   MPAA:NR)**

WINDSPLITTER, THE zero   (1971) 95m Pop Films c

Jim McMullan (Bobby Joe), I. Van Charles (Louis), Joyce Taylor (Jenny), Paul Lambert (Buford Jenkins), Richard Everett (R.T.), Jim Sedlow (Mr. Smith), Chris Wilson (Mrs. Smith), Anne Layne (Annie Smith), John Martin, Carter Smith, Ray O'Leary, Ruth Roberts, Greg Ford, Lee Ryan, Mahlon Foreman, Tobe Hooper, John Barten.

McMullan is a respectable small town kid who heads to Hollywood, makes it big as an actor, and returns home to Houston to crown the homecoming queen. The townspeople are repulsed when they find him to be a longhaired motorcyclist and a threat to their old-fashioned ways, and they use vigilante-type methods to make him leave. Actor Tobe Hooper was later to direct THE TEXAS CHAINSAW MASSACRE and POLTERGEIST. Filmed in Houston, and written, financed, produced, and directed by Houstonians.

p, David L. Ford; d&w, Julius D. Feigelson; m, Jackie Mills, Al Capps. m/l. "The Road Home," Joyce Taylor.

Drama   **(PR:C   MPAA:GP)**

WINDWALKER½**   (1980) 108m Windwalker/Pacific International c

Trevor Howard (Windwalker), Nick Ramus (Smiling Wolf/Twin Brother/ Narrator), James Remar (Windwalker As a Young Man), Serene Hedin (Tashina), Dusty Iron Wing McCrea (Dancing Moon), Silvana Gallardo (Little Feather), Billy Drago (Crow Scout), Rudy Diaz (Crow Eyes), Harold Goss-Coyote (Crow Hair), Roy J. Cohoe (Wounded Crow), Emerson John (Spotted Deer), Jason Stevens (Horse that Follows), Roberta Deherrera (Happy Wind), Curtis Powers (Renegade Crow), Ivan Naranjo (Crooked Leg), Chief Tug Smith (Tashina's Father), Fredelia Smith (Tashina's Mother), Dominique Gallegos (Tashina at 5), Marvin Takes Horse (Young Crow Eyes), Wamni-Omni-Ska-Romideau (Windwalker at 5), Jason Tahbo (Twin at 5), Benjamin Huber (Smiling Wolf at 2), David Huber (Twin Brother at 2).

Howard is unfortunately miscast in this western oddity which was filmed in the Cheyenne and Crow Indian languages. An admirable authenticity is achieved on all fronts except for Howard's role as an aging Indian chief who, on his deathbed, retells his story (his voice dubbed by Ramus). As a young Cheyenne his wife (Hedin) was killed by the Crow and one of his twin sons kidnaped. When old Howard dies family order is restored by his returning from the grave, only to rejoin his wife in the afterlife. A beautifully photographed attempt at representing Indian life in the Americas. (In Cheyenne and Crow Indian Languages; subtitled in English.)

p, Arthur R. Dubs, Thomas E. Ballard; d, Keith Merrill; w, Ray Goldrup (based on the novel by Blaine M. Yorgason); ph, Reed Smott (CFI Color); m, Merrill Jensen; ed, Stephen L. Johnson, Janice Hampton, Peter L. McCrea; prod d, Thomas Pratt.

Western   **Cas.**   **(PR:C   MPAA:PG)**

WINE AND THE MUSIC, THE   (SEE: PIECES OF DREAMS, 1970)

WINE, WOMEN AND HORSES*   (1937) 64m WB bw

Barton MacLane (Jim Turner), Ann Sheridan (Valerie), Dick Purcell (George Mayhew), Peggy Bates (Marjorie Mayhew), Walter Cassell (Pres Barrow), Lottie Williams (Mrs. Mayhew), Kenneth Harlan (Jed Bright), Eugene Jackson (Eight Ball), Charles Foy (Broadway), James Robbins (Joe), Nita (Lady Luck), Addison Richards (Bit).

MacLane stars in this shoddy programmer about a former gambler who settles down with a self-righteous wife but soon finds himself drawn to the horse races once again. She leaves him and he remarries his former flame, versatile, good-natured Sheridan. A remake of the Edward G. Robinson picture DARK HAZARD (1934).

p, Bryan Foy; d, Louis King; w, Roy Chanslor (based on the story "Dark Hazard" by W.R. Burnett); ph, James Van Trees, Sr.; ed, Jack Saper; art d, Esdras Hartley; cos, Howard Shoup.

Drama   **(PR:A   MPAA:NR)**

WINE, WOMEN, AND SONG**   (1934) 70m Chadwick bw

Lilyan Tashman (Frankie Arnette), Lew Cody (Morgan Andrews), Marjorie Moore (Marilyn Arnette), Matty Kemp (Ray Joyce), Paul Gregory (Don), Gertrude Astor (Jennie Tilson), Bobbe Arnst (Imogene), Esther Muir (Lolly), Jesse Divorsky (Irving), Bobby Watson (Lawrence).

Backstage life is brought to the screen again in this tightly knit but sometimes vulgar little entertainment, with Cody taking the role of a tyrannical theatrical magnate who pushes chorine Tashman to the edge. Along the way she promises Cody her daughter if the magnate takes her from the chorus line to stardom, as offensive a bargain as any movie has ever made. However, Tashman atones for it by poisoning Cody's champagne, and the daughter and her real boy friend are in a till-death-do-us-part clinch at the end.

d, Herbert Brenon; w, Leon D'Usseau (based on a play by D'Usseau); ph, Alvin Wyckoff; ed, Carl Pierson; m/l, Con Conrad, Archie Gottler, Sidney D. Mitchell; ch, Beatrice Gollenette.

Drama   **(PR:A   MPAA:NR)**

WING AND A PRAYER**   (1944) 97m FOX bw

Don Ameche (Flight Comdr. Bingo Harper), Dana Andrews (Sqdn. Comdr. Edward Moulton), William Eythe (Oscar Scott), Charles Bickford (Capt. Waddell), Sir Cedric Hardwicke (Adm.), Kevin O'Shea (Cookie Cunningham), Richard Jaeckel (Beezy Bessemer), Henry [Harry] Morgan (Malcolm Brainard), Richard Crane (Ens. Gus Chisholm), Glenn Langan (Executive Officer), Renny McEvoy (Ens. Cliff Hale), Robert Bailey (Paducah Holloway), Reed Hadley (Comdr. O'Donnell), George Mathews (Dooley), B. S. Pully (Flat Top), Dave Willock (Hans Jacobson), Murray Alper (Benny O'Neill), Charles Lang (Ens. Chuck White), John Miles (Ens. "Lovebug"

Markham), Joseph Haworth (*Murphy*), Charles B. Smith (*Alfalfa*), Ray Teal (*Exec. Officer*), Charles Trowbridge (*Medical Officer*), John Kelly (*Lew*), Larry Thompson (*Sam Cooper*), Billy Lechner (*Anti-Aircraft Gunner*), Jerry Shane (*Foley*), Carl Knowles (*Marine Orderly*), John Kellogg (*Assistant Air Officer*), Raymond Roe (*Gunner*), Stanley Andrews (*Marine General*), Robert Condon, Frank Ferry, William Manning, Mel Schubert, Blake Edwards, Mike Kilian (*Pilots*), Eddie Acuff, Eddie Friedman, Frank Marlowe, Irving Bacon (*Sailors*), Terry Ray, Chet Brandenburg, Jimmy Dodd, Robin Short, Jay Ward (*Mail Orderlies*), Selmer Jackson, Edward Van Sloan, Charles Waldron, Pierre Watkin, Crane Whitley, Frederick Worlock, Jack Mower, Van Antwerp, Frank McLure (*Admirals*), Matt McHugh.

An energetic WW II tale which highlights the daring and courageous escapades of a Navy aircraft carrier on a mission in the Pacific. Ameche stars as the gutsy flight officer who leads squadron commander Andrews and his men against the Japanese. The film builds to an exciting climax at the battle of Midway. Well-researched (director Hathaway spent a great deal of time on board a carrier in preparation) and authentically photographed.

p, William A. Bacher, Walter Morosco; d, Henry Hathaway; w, Jerome Cady (Mortimer Braus, uncredited); ph, Glen MacWilliams; m, Hugo W. Friedhofer; ed, J. Watson Webb; md, Emil Newman; art d, Lyle Wheeler, Lewis Creber; spec eff, Fred Sersen

War Drama   (PR:A   MPAA:NR)

WINGED DEVILS   (SEE: ABOVE THE CLOUDS, 1933)

WINGED SERPENT   (SEE: STARSHIP INVASIONS, 1978, Can.)

WINGED SERPENT, THE   (SEE: Q, 1982)

WINGED VICTORY****   (1944) 130m FOX bw

Pvt. Lon McCallister (*Frankie Davis*), Jeanne Crain (*Helen*), Sgt. Edmond O'Brien (*Irving Miller*), Jane Ball (*Jane Preston*), Sgt. Mark Daniels (*Alan Ross*), Jo-Carroll Dennison (*Dorothy Ross*), Cpl. Don Taylor (*Danny "Pinky" Scariano*), Cpl. Lee J. Cobb (*Doctor*), Judy Holliday (*Ruth Miller*), T/Sgt. Peter Lind Hayes (*O'Brian*), Cpl. Alan Baxter (*Maj. Halper*), Geraldine Wall (*Mrs. Ross*), Cpl. Red Buttons (*Whitey*), George Humbert (*Mr. Scariano*), Cpl. Barry Nelson (*Bobby Crills*), Sgt. Rune Hultman (*Dave Anderson*), Cpl. Richard Hogan (*Jimmy Gardner*), Cpl. Phillip Bourneuf (*Col. Gibney*), Cpl. Gary Merrill (*Capt. McIntyre*), Cpl. Damian O'Flynn (*Col. Ross*), Sgt. George Reeves (*Lt. Thompson*), Pfc. George Petrie (*Barker*), Pfc. Alfred Ryder (*Milhauser*), Cpl. Karl Malden (*Adams*), Pfc. Martin Ritt (*Gleason*), Cpl. Harry Lewis (*Cadet Peter Clark*), Capt. Ray Bidwell (*Officer*), Cpl. Henry Rowland (*Flight Surgeon*), Lt. Carroll Riddle (*Capt. Speer*), S/Sgt. Sascha Branstoff (*Carmen Miranda*), Cpl. Archie Robbins (*Master of Ceremonies*), Cpl. Jack Slate, Cpl. Red Buttons, Pfc. Henry Slate (*Andrews Sisters*), Timmy Hawkins (*Irving, Jr.*), Moyna MacGill (*Mrs. Gardner*), Don Beddoe 'AAF' (*Man*), Frances Gladwin (*WAC*), Sally Yarnell (*Cigarette Girl*), Sgt. Kevin McCarthy (*Ronny Meade*).

A paean to the Army Air Force training program, this film was adapted from the smash hit Broadway play by Moss Hart. Much of the same cast, most of them actual members of the AAF, is also carried over from the play. The plot, what there is of it, follows McCallister through his flight training, along with his friends and comrades from all over the country, O'Brien, Daniels, Taylor, and others. Their trials and tests on the way to getting their wings is contrasted with the worries of their wives, mothers, and girl friends, including Holliday, Crain, Dennison, and Ball. One of the wives is pregnant, but after the baby is born she doesn't tell her husband because she wants him to concentrate on his flying in an upcoming solo flight. During that flight he crashes and dies, never knowing that he had a son. Eventually the men graduate, get their wings, and, with their women watching from the windows of a San Francisco hotel, they fly their planes out over the Pacific to the war. The men frequently break out in patriotic song and today those sentiments seem embarrasing, but it must be remembered that all these men, although actors, were also real members of the AAF who had lived through this training and who were only temporarily on detached duty. Soon they would all be going back to the war, and a surprising number would go on to be some of the better character actors and second leads of the following couple of decades. This film marked the first meeting of director George Cukor with Judy Holliday, who would later become one of his favorite actresses, appearing in such films as ADAM'S RIB (1949), THE MARRYING KIND (1952), and IT SHOULD HAPPEN TO YOU (1953) for the director. Her performance here is excellent, making the other women look stiff and artificial by comparison. The profits from this film, like those of the stage production, went to assorted Army charities, and the film made a lot of money for those coffers.

p, Darryl F. Zanuck; d, George Cukor; w, Moss Hart (based on his play); ph, Glen MacWilliams; m, David Rose; art d, Lyle Wheeler, Lewis Creber; spec eff, Fred Sersen; m/l, "The Whiffenpoof Song," Tod B. Galloway, Meade, Minnigerode, George S. Pomeroy.

War Drama   (PR:A   MPAA:NR)

WINGS AND THE WOMAN**½   (1942, Brit.) 96m Imperator/RKO bw
                                        (GB: THEY FLEW ALONE)

Anna Neagle (*Amy Johnson*), Robert Newton (*Jim Mollison*), Edward Chapman (*Mr. Johnson*), Nora Swinburne (*ATA Commandant*), Joan Kemp-Welch (*Mrs. Johnson*), Charles Carson (*Lord Wakefield*), Brefni O'Rorke (*Mac*), Muriel George (*Housekeeper*), Martita Hunt (*Schoolmistress*), Eliot Makeham (*Mayor*), Ronald Shiner (*Mechanic, Stag Lane*), David Horne (*Solicitor*), Charles Victor (*Postmaster*), Miles Malleson (*Salesman*), Ian Fleming (*Lord Wakefield's Secretary*), Anthony Shaw (*Official, Stag Lane*), George Merritt (*Journalist*), Arthur Hambling (*Policeman*), Aubrey Mallalieu (*Barber*), Hay Petrie (*Retired General*), Charles Maxwell (*BBC Commentator*), Anne Crawford, Leslie Dwyer, Billy [William] Hartnell, John Slater, Perry Parsons, Cyril Smith, MacDonald Park, Ted Andrews, Peter Gawthorne, Margaret Halston.

The biography of ill-starred husband-and-wife fliers Jim Mollison and Amy Johnson, both renowned pilots before and during WW II. The film concentrates both on their aerial feats and their domestic problems–a marriage that despite its celebrity status failed to provide happiness and ended in divorce. The finale has Neagle going down in the English Channel in 1941 while ferrying a fighter plane from the factory to an airfield for the RAF. Her former husband drowned similarly because of a crippled airplane when he bailed out over the Thames estuary in 1959.

p&d, Herbert Wilcox; w, Miles Malleson (based on the story by Lord Castlerosse); ph, Mutz Greenbaum, Frederick A. Young; art d, David Rawnsley; spec eff, Alan Jaggs, Douglas Woolsey, Desmond Dickenson.

War/Biography   (PR:A   MPAA:NR)

WINGS FOR THE EAGLE**   (1942) 85m WB bw

Ann Sheridan (*Roma Maple*), Dennis Morgan (*Corky Jones*), Jack Carson (*Brad Maple*), George Tobias (*Jake Hanso, Factory Foreman*), Russell Arms (*Pete Hanso*), Don DeFore (*Gil Borden*), Tom Fadden (*Tom "Cyclone" Shaw*), John Ridgely (*Johnson*), Frank Wilcox (*Stark*), George Meeker (*Personnel Man*), Fay Helm (*Miss Baxter*), Billy Curtis (*Midget*), Emory Parnell (*Policeman*), Edgar Dearing (*Motorcycle Officer*).

An enjoyable and informative melodrama that glorifies the work of those who made the planes that flew during WW II. Morgan is a young mechanic at Lockheed Aircraft who, despite being an out-and-out draft dodger, becomes one of the top servicemen after the Pearl Harbor attack. The plot's romantic angle comes when Morgan and coworker Carson find themselves in competition for the wise cracking, down-to-earth Sheridan. The kind of film that makes one want to work in an airplane factory.

p, Robert Lord; d, Lloyd Bacon; w, Byron Morgan, B.H. Orkow, Richard Macaulay (based on the story "Shadow of Their Wings" by Morgan, Orkow); ph, Tony Gaudio; m, Frederick Hollander; ed, Owen Marks; md, Leo F. Forbstein; art d, Max Parker; spec eff, Byron Haskin, H.F. Koenekamp.

War/Drama   (PR:A   MPAA:NR)

WINGS IN THE DARK**½   (1935) 75m PAR bw

Myrna Loy (*Sheila Mason*), Cary Grant (*Ken Gordon*), Roscoe Karns (*Nick Williams*), Hobart Cavanaugh (*Mac*), Dean Jagger (*Tops Harmon*), Bert Hanlon (*Yipp Morgan*), James Burtis (*Joy Burns*), Russell Hopton (*Jake Brashear*), Samuel S. Hinds (*Kennel Club Secretary*), Arnold Korff (*The Doctor*), Matt McHugh (*Sheila's 1st Mechanic*), Graham McNamee (*Radio Announcer*), Alfred Delcambre (*Cameraman*), Lee Phelps (*Ken's Mechanic*), Henry Roquemore (*Air Show Chief Kelly*), Sam Flint (*George Rockwell*), Stanley Andrews (*Jack, an Official*), Phil Tead (*Reporter*), Perry Ivins (*Radioman*), Virgil Simons (*Boy at Coney Island*), Esther Michelson (*Boy's Mother*), Tola Nesmith (*Housekeeper*), Allen Fox, Ben Sharpe, Charles Hines (*Reporters in Ken's Hangar*), Peter Hancock, Antrim Short (*Radio Announcers at Field*), Phil Tead, Gene Morgan (*Reporters*), Hyman Fink, J.B. Scott, Herb Watson (*Photographers at Last Flight*), Charley Hines, Duke York, Allen Fox (*Reporters at Last Flight*), Arthur S. Byron (*Guard*), Julian Madison (*Jerome*), Rita Owin (*Nurse*), Mabel Forrest (*Secretary*), George Reed (*Waring*), Hanley Andrews (*Landers*), Charles Morris (*Wallace*), George MacQuarrie (*Banker Crawford*).

MGM loaned Loy to Paramount for this romantic adventure, her first film with Grant. Years later, they were to team up far more successfully in RKO's THE BACHELOR AND THE BOBBY SOXER and MR. BLANDINGS BUILDS HIS DREAM HOUSE. Grant is a pilot who thinks that too many lives have been lost due to flying in bad weather and fog so he is busily working on instruments that will help cut down the death toll. Loy is an aviatrix who ekes out a living writing messages in the sky and doing various death- defying stunts under the management of Karns. Grant and Loy meet, and she falls hard for him, but he is quite aloof to her affection. He's terribly involved in his work on the flying machinery and it appears as though he's made a final breakthrough when it all falls apart as he is hurt in a gas explosion and loses his sight. He is depressed by this turn of events and moves to the country, accompanied by Cavanaugh, his long-time mechanic and best pal. With Cavanaugh and his seeing-eye dog as his only companions, Grant attempts to become a writer and sends item after item to the magazines. His only rewards are a raft of rejections, but he doesn't know that. Loy is working furiously at several different high-flying tasks and she is sending checks to Grant. The checks are cashed and he never is aware that the money is coming from her risking her neck. Because she's sending so much money to Grant, Loy can't afford to keep up the payments on her plane and it is to be taken back by the manufacturer. She's in Russia planning a spectacular solo flight and Karns wants her home right away so she starts on her return and manages to make it across the Atlantic as far as Newfoundland before she is unable to continue due to the heavy fog. Using her radio, she calls several cities trying to get some help. News and sportscaster Graham McNamee gives a panting world the account of her perilous voyage and Grant is listening all the way. He decides that he's in love with her and, with Cavanaugh as his seeing-eye man, they break into a hangar, take up a plane, and Grant contacts Loy on the radio. The two talk over the air, fall even more deeply in love, and then Grant uses new equipment to talk Loy down to a safe landing. Karns gets whatever laughs he can in his role as Loy's manager and Cavanaugh, using his thick Scottish accent, chimes in with a good turn as Grant's aide-de- vision. The picture was produced by the man who later became Loy's first husband. She was not thrilled with the stipend MGM was paying so she moved to England right after this and waited until the studio management people came to their senses and gave her the kind of money she demanded and deserved. A good editing job by Shea, especially in all the flying sequences which provided the visual excitement in the film. Note a very young Dean Jagger, appearing high-billed in only his third movie, after YOU BELONG TO ME (1934) and THE WOMAN FROM HELL (1929).

p, Arthur Hornblow, Jr.; d, James Flood; w, Jack Kirkland, Frank Partos, Dale Van Every, E.H. Robinson, (based on a story by Neil Shipman, Philip D. Hurn); ph, William C. Mellor, Dewey Wrigley; ed, William Shea; art d, Hans Dreier, Earl Hendrick; spec eff, Wrigley.

Adventure/Romance   **(PR:A   MPAA:NR)**

WINGS OF ADVENTURE*   (1930) 53m TIF bw

Rex Lease (*Dave Kent*), Armida (*Maria*), Clyde Cook (*Skeets Smith*), Fred Malatesta (*La Panthera*), Nick De Ruiz (*Manuel*), Eddie Boland (*Viva*).

Lease is a flier who is downed in Mexico and captured by guerrilla fighters. He is befriended by Armida, helps her avoid an unwanted marriage to the guerrilla leader, and then receives help in his rescue attempt from the U.S. Calvary. Talentless Armida gains enough composure at one point to sing a song.

d, Richard Thorpe; w, Harry Frazer, Zella Young (based on the story by Frazer); ph, Arthur Reeves; ed, Clarence Kolster.

Adventure/Western   **(PR:A   MPAA:NR)**

WINGS OF CHANCE**   (1961, Can.) 76m Tiger/UNIV c

James Brown (*Steve Kirby*), Frances Rafferty (*Arlene Baker*), Richard Tretter (*Johnny Summers*), Patrick Whyte (*Mike Farrel*).

A pair of Canadian bush pilots in business together become rivals over the hand of Rafferty. Brown flies a mission without the usual maintenance check and winds up crash-landing in the wilds with little chance of discovery or survival. After weeks of loneliness he hits on the idea of tagging geese with his name and whereabouts, is rescued, and succeeds in winning the girl. A hair-raiser in parts.

p, Larry Matanski; d, Edward Dew; w, Patrick Whyte (based on the story "Kirby's Gander" by John Patrick Gillese); ph, Leonard Claremont (Eastmancolor); m, Michael Andersen; ed, Walter Hannemann, Monty Pearce; spec eff, Meredith Evans; makeup, Richard Cobos.

Adventure/Drama   **(PR:A   MPAA:NR)**

WINGS OF DANGER   (SEE: DEAD ON COURSE, 1952, Brit.)

WINGS OF EAGLES, THE***½   (1957) 110m MGM c

John Wayne (*Frank W. "Spig" Wead*), Maureen O'Hara (*Minnie Wead*), Dan Dailey (*"Jughead" Carson*), Ward Bond (*John Dodge*), Ken Curtis (*John Dale Price*), Edmund Lowe (*Adm. Moffett*), Kenneth Tobey (*Capt. Herbert Allen Hazard*), James Todd (*Jack Travis*), Barry Kelley (*Capt. Jock Clark*), Sig Rumann (*Party Manager*), Henry O'Neill (*Capt. Spear*), Willis Bouchey (*Barton*), Dorothy Jordan (*Rose Brentmann*), Peter Ortiz (*Lt. Charles Dexter*), Louis Jean Heydt (*Dr. John Keye*), Tige Andrews (*"Arizona" Pincus*), Dan Borzage (*Pete*), William Tracy (*Air Force Officer*), Harlan Warde (*Executive Officer*), Jack Pennick (*Joe McGuffey*), Bill Henry (*Naval Aide*), Alberto Morin (*2nd Manager*), Mimi Gibson (*Lila Wead*), Evelyn Rudie (*Doris Wead*), Charles Trowbridge (*Adm. Crown*), Mae Marsh (*Nurse Crumley*), Janet Lake (*Nurse*), Fred Graham (*Officer in Brawl*), Stuart Holmes (*Producer*), Olive Carey (*Bridy O'Faolain*), Maj. Sam Harris (*Patient*), May McEvoy (*Nurse*), William Paul Lowery (*"Commodore Wead's Baby*), Chuck Roberson (*Officer*), James Flavin (*M.P. at Garden Party*), Cliff Lyons, Veda Ann Borg, Christopher James.

An intensely personal and little seen Ford film that serves as a biography of his close personal friend Frank W. "Spig" Wead, a career Navy man and writer who was one of the pioneers of naval aviation (Wead had written the screenplays to such aviation classics as Frank Capra's DIRIGIBLE, Howard

Hawks' CEILING ZERO, Victor Fleming's TEST PILOT, King Vidor's THE CITADEL, and two Ford pictures, AIR MAIL and THEY WERE EXPENDABLE). Wayne turns in one of his best performances as the naval man whose obsession with military life destroys his marriage, family, and health. The film begins just after WW I as Wayne and his men try to prove to the Navy the value of seaplanes in warfare. To gain attention for his ideas, Wayne and his team win several prestigious air races and endurance records. Unfortunately, Wayne's all- consuming efforts to impress the Navy begin to erode his home life with O'Hara. When their infant son dies he finds himself unable to comfort his wife. He is a stranger to his two young daughters. O'Hara secretly hopes that Wayne's increasingly insane antics--which include landing a plane in the swimming pool of an admiral during a tea party--will get him canned, but in the long run they pay off and he is assigned to command a fighter squadron. The night he receives the news he accidentally falls down the steps in his home and is paralyzed. Consumed with self- pity, he rejects O'Hara's efforts to comfort him and tells her to leave him and start her life over. After dispatching his family, Wayne does accept the help of Navy buddies Dailey and Curtis and it is they who force him to rehabilitate. Urged by his friends, Wayne begins to write thrilling tales of aviation and eventually pens successful stage plays and scripts for hit movies. His close collaboration with director Bond (who does an amazing imitation of director Ford) on two films earns the pair critical kudos (a clip from the 1932 HELL DIVERS, directed by George Hill and starring Clark Gable and Wallace Beery, is seen in a screening room scene). By 1941 Wayne and O'Hara (who has now become a successful, independent businesswoman) are on the verge of patching up their marriage when the Japanese bomb Pearl Harbor. Realizing that Wayne will once again heed the call of the Navy, O'Hara finally gives up on him. Wayne manages to convince the Navy to put him back on active duty and he hits on the idea of supplying small "jeep" carriers that will take new planes into battle to replace the ones lost by the combat aircraft carriers. His idea works beautifully at the battle for Kwajalein, but Dailey is severely wounded during the skirmish when he saves the crippled Wayne from enemy strafing. Though Wayne survives the battle, the strain proves to be too much and he suffers a heart attack. This latest brush with death brings home the painful loneliness of his life and Wayne knows full well that it is now too late to make amends. Practically destroyed physically and emotionally, Wayne is slowly transferred from one ship to another via a cage attached to a cable hanging precariously over the ocean-very alone. As in Ford's western THE SEARCHERS, Wayne's character is a man so driven by his personal obsessions that he is unable to participate in normal society. In THE WINGS OF EAGLES Wayne cannot accept the love and help of those not in the military (he even insists on being taken to a Navy hospital after his crippling fall). Instead, he hides out in the company of men similar to himself and will only accept help from his peers (Dailey and Curtis) and not his family. Wayne's character seems almost adolescent in his pursuits-as demonstrated by a scene that ends in a sprawling, rowdy cake fight and one where he becomes absorbed with a toy airplane while his son lies ill-and is unwilling or unable to accept adult emotional responsibility. It is not that he chooses the Navy over his family; it is simply that Wayne finds the Navy-even with all its danger and violence-easier to handle than the love of his wife and children. By Ford's own admission THE WINGS OF EAGLES was a difficult, very personal film for him to make. In his interview with Peter Bogdanovich he said: "I didn't want to do the picture because Spig was a great pal of mine. But I didn't want anyone *else* to make it either." The director also denied any involvement in the delightful portrayal of himself enacted by Ward Bond as the character named "John Dodge." Sporting Ford's trademark hat, sunglasses, and pipe, Bond does an uncanny impersonation of the director-right down to his walk and speech patterns. Considering that several of Ford's personal effects (including his Oscars) are scattered around the set, it is hard to believe Ford's contention that the whole thing was actor Bond's idea. Bond's portrayal of Ford notwithstanding, the film really belongs to Wayne. Once again under Ford's direction, Wayne turns in a superior, multifaceted performance that explores the emotional depths of his character. Spanning nearly 30 years, Wayne gives the film his all and even sheds his toupee in the scenes when Wead is middle-aged. THE WINGS OF EAGLES is a powerful, deeply emotional film and Ford again shows us the strength of the human spirit and the tragedy of loneliness that sometimes go hand in hand.

p, Charles Schnee; d, John Ford; w, Frank Fenton, William Wister Haines (based on the life and writings of Comdr. Frank W. Wead, U.S.N., and the biography *Wings of Men*); ph, Paul C. Vogel (Metrocolor); m, Jeff Alexander; ed, Gene Ruggerio; art d, William A. Horning, Malcolm Brown; set d, Edwin B. Willis, Keogh Gleason; cos, Walter Plunkett; spec eff, Arnold Gillespie, Warren Newcombe; makeup, William Tuttle; aerial stunts, Paul Mantz; tech adv, Adm. John Dale Price, Dr. John Keye.

Biography   **(PR:A   MPAA:NR)**

WINGS OF MYSTERY**   (1963, Brit.) 55m Rayant/Children's Film
                                                             Foundation bw

Judy Geeson (*Jane*), Hennis Scott (*Don*), Patrick Jordan (*McCarthy*), Francesca Bertorelli (*Yvette*), Graham Aza (*Antoine*), Anthony Jacobs (*Agent*), John Gabriel (*Father*), Richard Carpenter (*Ted*), Arnold Ridley (*Mr. Bell*).

An entertaining children's film with a group of British youngsters flying to

Belgium in pursuit of some stolen steel alloy plans. A fast-moving story and some nice location photography of Belgium.

p, Anthony Gilkison; d&w, Gilbert Gunn (based on a story by H.K. Lewenhak).

Children's Film							(PR:AAA MPAA:NR)

## WINGS OF THE HAWK**						(1953) 80m UNIV c

Van Heflin (*Irish Gallager*), Julia Adams (*Raquel*), Abbe Lane (*Elena*), George Dolenz (*Col. Ruiz*), Antonio Moreno (*Father Perez*), Noah Beery, Jr (*Orozco*), Pedro Gonzales-Gonzales (*Tomas*), Paul Fierro (*Carlos*), Mario Siletti (*Marco*), Rico Alaniz (*Capt. Gomez*), John Daheim (*Capt. Rivera*), Rodolfo Acosta (*Arturo*), Ricardo Alba (*Ramon*), Nancy Westbrook (*Lita*).

A pleasing western which casts Heflin as a hard-edged mining engineer who loses his property in Mexico to a Mexican Federales colonel, Dolenz. Heflin joins a group of Pancho Villa's rebels, reclaims his mine, and falls in love with Adams, a female bandit who is as tough as she is pretty. Originally photographed in 3-D, WINGS OF THE HAWK fortunately doesn't resort to the usual 3-D technique of throwing everything but the kitchen sink at the audience. Shown "straight" it retains a lively likableness, with plenty of action and some striking touches by director Boetticher.

p, Aaron Rosenberg; d, Budd Boetticher; w, James E. Moser, Kay Lenard (based on the novel by Gerald Drayson Adams); ph, Clifford Stine (3-D, Technicolor); m, Frank Skinner; ed, Russell Schoengarth; art d, Bernard Herzbrun, Robert Clatworthy; cos, Bill Thomas.

Western							(PR:A MPAA:NR)

## WINGS OF THE MORNING***					(1937, Brit.) 88m NW/FOX c

Prolog: Annabella (*Marie*), Leslie Banks (*Lord Clontarf*), D. J. Williams (*Marik*), Philip Sydney Frost (*Valentine*), Modern Story: Annabella (*Maria*), Henry Fonda (*Kerry*), Stewart Rome (*Sir Valentine*), Irene Vanbrugh (*Marie*), Harry Tate (*Paddy*), Helen Haye (*Jenepher*), Teddy Underdown (*Don Diego*), Mark Daly (*Jimmy*), Sam Livesey (*Angelo*), E. V. H. Emmett, Capt. R. C. Lyle (*Racing Commentators*), John McCormack, Steve Donoghue (*Themselves*), Hermione Darnborough, Pat Noonan, Emmanuelo, Nicholas Nadejine, Evelyn Ankers.

Banks is a member of the Irish gentry, circa 1889, who falls in love with Annabella, a beautiful Spanish gypsy. In spite of pressure applied by Banks' uppercrust family and peers, the two are wed. Their marriage ends tragically when Banks dies after being thrown from a horse. Annabella goes back to Spain, where she is once more accepted into the gypsy fold. Three generations pass and the woman (now played by Vanbrugh) returns to Ireland, bringing with her a horse she plans to enter in the famed Epsom Downs Derby. Also joining Vanbrugh is her granddaughter, played by Annabella in a dual role. Annabella disguises herself as a boy, hoping to ride her grandmother's horse in the Derby. She meets Fonda, a Canadian horse trainer, who quickly learns the girl's secret. At a party Fonda sees Annabella dressed in a lovely evening dress, and is immediately smitten. Despite Annabella's engagement to Underdown, the two fall in love and work together at winning the Derby. Their efforts, despite some trials and tribulations, pay off when Vanbrugh's horse wins the race. Underdown realizes Annabella loves Fonda, so he breaks their engagement leaving his ex-fiancee free to marry. This was the first British film shot in Technicolor, and the process was utilized to its fullest extent. WINGS OF THE MORNING is subtle in color, using soft tones to capture the English and Irish countrysides. Compared with the often garish use of Technicolor by American filmmakers, the effect is marvelous, creating a genuinely beautiful film that never overpowers the eye with brilliant hues. (Oddly, Fonda had starred in the first outdoor all-Technicolor feature, TRAIL OF THE LONESOME PINE, made in the U.S. the previous year.) The simple story doesn't ask much of its players but their combined talents make for a pleasant movie. This was Annabella's first English language film. The French actress-best known for American and British audiences for her work in Rene Clair's LE MILLION—handles her dual role well, though there are moments where her French accent is difficult to decipher. Fonda is affable in an easygoing role which doesn't require much work on his part. The actor agreed to make this film simply because it gave him an excuse to take his first trip abroad. He enjoyed working on screen with Annabella but when the actress tried to extend their *amour* to private life as well, Fonda took to leaving the set immediately after the day's shootin was completed. Annabella was a married woman and Fonda had no desire to get involved in a sticky extramarital affair. He successfully dodged the actress, but one day was confronted by Annabella's husband. The man had received a letter from his wife claiming she and Fonda were now lovers. Fonda was able to convince the man no such affair was taking place, and the production continued with no further incidents between the costars. However, Fonda did find romance during the film's shooting in a most unexpected manner. A group of Americans touring England paid a visit to the set after asking permission to see a film in production. Among the visitors was socialite Frances Seymour Brokaw. She and Fonda were taken with one another and were eventually married.

p, Robert T. Kane; d, Harold Schuster; w, Tom Geraghty (based on stories by Donn Byrne); ph, Ray Rennahan, Henry Imus, Jack Cardiff (Technicol-

or); m, Arthur Benjamin; ed, James Clark; md, Benjamin; art d, Ralph Brinton; cos, Irene Hubert.

Drama/Romance						(PR:A MPAA:NR)

## WINGS OF THE NAVY**						(1939) 88m COS/WB bw

George Brent (*Cass Harrington*), Olivia de Havilland (*Irene Dale*), John Payne (*Jerry Harrington*), Frank McHugh (*Scat Allen*), John Litel (*Comdr. Clark*), Victor Jory (*Lt. Parsons*), Henry O'Neill (*Prolog Speaker*), John Ridgely (*Dan Morrison*), John Gallaudet (*Lt. Harry White*), Donald Briggs (*Instructor*), Edgar Edwards (*Ted Parsons*), Regis Toomey (*1st Flight Instructor*), Albert Morin (*Armando Costa*), Jonathan Hale (*Commandant*), Pierre Watkin (*Capt. March*), Don Douglas (*Officer of the Day*), Max Hoffman (*Drilling Officer*), Alan Davis (*Check Pilot*), Larry Williams (*Aviator*), Renie Riano (*Woman*), Lee Phelps (*Conductor*), Selmer Jackson (*Doctor*), Ed Keane (*Psychology Examiner*), Fred Hamilton (*Cadet*), Walter Miller (*Henry*), Max Wagner (*Boss Mechanic*), Carlyle Moore, Jr, Ed Parker, Larry Williams (*Navy Men*), Mary Gordon (*Housekeeper*), Joseph Crehan (*Doctor*), William B. Davidson (*Brown*), Howard Hickman (*Capt. Dreen*), Jack Gardner (*Mechanic*), Emmett Vogan (*Flight Commander*), Morgan Conway (*Duty Officer*).

More of a government training film (the Navy was more than generous in providing assistance) than a drama, WINGS OF THE NAVY takes a detailed look at pilot training and aviation technicalities, with the Pensacola Naval Air Training Station as the background. Against this is a romance with de Havilland as the object of two brothers' affections–veteran flier Brent and the younger rookie pilot, Payne, who transfers from submarine service to the air arm. By the finale it's Payne who gets the girl. De Havilland's role was not much in this unabashed call to arms, and she was beginning to fear that her career was in a nosedive.

p, Lou Edelman; d, Lloyd Bacon; w, Michael Fessier; ph, Arthur Edeson Elmer Dyer; ed, William Holmes; md, Leo F. Forbstein; m/l, "Wings Over the Navy," Harry Warren, Johnny Mercer; cos, Orry-Kelly.

War/Romance							(PR:A MPAA:NR)

## WINGS OF VICTORY**			(1941, USSR) 97m Artkino bw (VALERI CHKALOV)

Vladimir Belokurov (*Valeri Chkalov*), Mikhail Gelovani (*Joseph Stalin*), Semyon Nedhinsky (*Sergo Ordzhonikidze*), Zenia Tarasova (*Olga*), Vasili Vanin (*Pasha Palich*), Piotr Berezov (*Georgi Baldukov*), Sergi Yarov (*Alexander Belyakov*), Boris Zhukovsky (*Comdr. Alioshin*), Fyodor Bogdanov (*Grandpa*).

Valeri Chkalov, a Soviet hero of the air, is shown here flying as both a fighter pilot and a test pilot, with his Moscow-to-Seattle flight being the picture's high point. The subplot has Belokurov (as Chkalov) in a strained relationship with Tarasova, a wife who has trouble sharing the man she loves with the planes he flies. Director Kalatozov went on to direct the renowned THE CRANES ARE FLYING in 1957. (In Russian; English subtitles.)

d, Mikhail Kalatozov; w, Georgi Baidukov, D. Tarasov, B. Chirskov; ph, A. Ginsburg; m, V. Pushkov.

Drama/Biography						(PR:A MPAA:NR)

## WINGS OVER AFRICA*½			(1939) 62m Premier-Stafford/Merit bw

Joan Gardner (*Carol Reade*), Ian Collin (*Tony Cooper*), James Harcourt (*Wilkins*), James Carew (*Norton*), James Craven (*John Trevor*), Alan Napier (*Redfern*), Charles Oliver (*Collins*), Phil Thomas (*Quincey*), Ferrule.

Set in Africa, WINGS OVER AFRICA follows the adventures of a small group of Britons as they try to locate a buried diamond treasure. Rivalry soon turns to violence, and after one member is killed and another is wounded, the guilty party is disposed of, leaving the others to share the fortune.

p, John Stafford; d, Ladislaus Vajda; w, Akos Tolnay; ph, James Dunlin; m, Jack Beaver.

Adventure							(PR:A MPAA:NR)

## WINGS OVER HONOLULU**					(1937) 78m UNIV bw

Wendy Barrie (*Lauralee Curtis*), Ray Milland (*Lt. "Stony" Samuel Gilchrist*), Kent Taylor (*Greg Chandler*), William Gargan (*Lt. Jack Furness*), Polly Rowles (*Rosalind Furness*), Samuel S. Hinds (*Adm. Furness*), Mary Philips (*Mrs. Hattie Penletter*), Margaret McWade (*Nellie Curtis*), Robert Spencer (*Wayne*), Clara Blandick (*Evie Curtis*), John Kelly (*Gob*), Louise Beavers (*Mamie*), Jonathan Hale (*Judge Advocate*), Granville Bates (*Grocery Clerk*), Robert Gleckler (*Lieutenant Commander of Squadron*), Joyce Compton (*Caroline, Blonde on Telephone*), Charles Irwin (*Al's Friend the Drunk*), Maude Turner Gordon (*Mrs. MacEwen*), Maynard Holmes (*Tommy*), Ivan Miller, Jack Mulhall (*Officers*), Ruth Robinson (*Mrs. MacEwen's Friend*), Franklyn Ardell (*Al the Drunk*), Milburn Stone (*Telephone Operator*), George Offerman, Jr, John Bruce, Buddy Messinger (*Boys*), Rudolph Chavers (*Black Boy*), Frank Melton (*Budge*), Mildred Gover (*Cook*), George

H. Reed (*Fauntleroy*), Max Wagner, Sherry Hall, Frank Marlowe, Jack Egan, Arthur Singley, Marion "Bud" Wolfe (*Marines*), Virginia Rogan (*Hawaiian Dancer*), Billy Wayne (*Orderly*), Capt. P.N.L. Bellinger (*Officer on U.S.S. Ranger*), Phillip "Lucky" Hurlic (*Robert Lee*), Mabelle Palmer, Hazel Langton (*Women in Beauty Shop*), Louise Latimer (*Woman*), Isabel La Mal (*Woman Shopper*), Grace Cunard (*Mrs. Strange*), Al Kikume (*Hawaiian*), Martin Turner (*Porter*), Bernard Kikume (*Hawaiian Policeman*), Loretta Sayers (*Woman with Baby*), Michael Loring, Robert Anderson (*Naval Officers*), Ray Turner (*Waiter*), Eddie Fetherston (*Radio Enlisted Man*), Edith Penn (*Woman at Car*), Lucia Lusca (*Woman Washing Dishes*).

Barrie naturally becomes unraveled when her Navy pilot husband, Milland, is transferred to Pearl Harbor on the day of their wedding. She follows and gets an unexpected surprise in the form of an old boy friend, Taylor, who makes his way around the Pacific in his spiffy yacht. When her husband pays more attention to his maneuvers than he does to her, she goes sailing with Taylor. Milland learns of her extracurriculars and crashes his plane in the harbor, winding up court-martialed. Barrie, who sees the error of her ways, defends her husband, clears his name, and remains devoted to him. A handsome production with handsome leading players in one of the handsomest settings on the globe.

p, Charles R. Rogers; d, H.C. Potter; w, Isabel Dawn, Boyce De Gaw (based on a story by Mildred Cram); ph, Joseph Valentine; ed, Maurice Wright; md, Charles Previn.

War Drama   **(PR:A   MPAA:NR)**

WINGS OVER THE PACIFIC*   (1943) 59m MON bw

Inez Cooper (*Nona Butler*), Edward Norris (*Allan, U. S. Navy Aviator*), Montagu Love (*Jim Butler*), Robert Armstrong (*Pieter, Dutch Trader*), Henry Guttman (*Kurt, Nazi Fighter Pilot*), Ernie Adams (*Harry, Butler-Handyman*), Santini Pauiloa (*Island Chief*), John Roth (*Taro*), Alex Havier (*Japanese Officer*), James Lono, George Kamel, Hawksha Paia (*Natives*).

Love is an American WW I veteran who enjoys the peace and quiet that surrounds him and his daughter, Cooper, on a quiet Pacific island. The silence is broken, however, when a pair of pilots–the American Norris and the Nazi Guttman, who is an advance scout for the Japanese–crash-land on the island after a dogfight. The Nazi discovers that the island is soaked in oil and radios the Japanese to invade, but Norris nixes that plan and also ends up with the girl. Pure baloney in spite of a generally excellent cast and a generous budget. Veteran character actor Love died just before the film's release.

p, Lindsley Parsons; d, Phil Rosen; w, George Wallace Sayre; ph, Mack Stengler; ed, Carl Pierson; md, Edward J. Kay.

War/Drama   **(PR:A   MPAA:NR)**

WINGS OVER WYOMING   (SEE: HOLLYWOOD COWBOY, 1937)

WINK OF AN EYE*   (1958) 72m UA bw

Jonathan Kidd (*Mr. Alvin Atterbury*), Doris Dowling (*Myrna Duchane*), Barbara Turner (*Judy Carlton*), Irene Seldner (*Mrs. Lazlow*), Jaclynne Greene (*Mrs. Atterbury*), Wally Brown (*Sheriff Cantrick*), Taylor Holmes (*Vanryzin*), Max Rich (*Max*), Paul Smith (*Ben Lazlow*), Jack Grinnage (*Delivery Boy*), Lucien Littlefield (*Old Man*), Rodney Bell (*Rand*), Dick Nelson (*Butler*), Sam Levin (*Trumpet Player*), Howard Roberts (*Guitar Player*), Henry Slate (*Attendant*), Tom Browne Henry (*Mr. Hix*).

Chemist Kidd conceives a far-fetched scheme to murder his wife so that he can flee to South America with his lab assistant, Dowling. But his inventiveness is so confusing it becomes hard to follow. Meant to be a horror laugh riot but all it has finally is a snappy ending that takes an awful long time getting to.

p, Fernando Carrere; d, Winston Jones; w, Robert Radnitz, Robert Presnell, Jr., James Edmiston (based on the story by Chester Davis, Jones); ph, Jones; m, Ernest Gold; ed, Chester Shaeffer.

Comedy/Mystery   **(PR:A   MPAA:NR)**

WINNER, THE   (SEE: PIT STOP, 1969)

WINNER TAKE ALL*½   (1932) 68m WB bw

James Cagney (*Jim Kane*), Marian Nixon (*Peggy Harmon*), Virginia Bruce (*Joan Gibson*), Guy Kibbee (*Pop Slavin*), Clarence Muse (*Rosebud the Trainer*), Dickie Moore (*Dickie Harmon*), Allan Lane (*Monty*), John Roche (*Roger Elliott*), Ralf Harolde (*Legs Davis*), Alan Mowbray (*Forbes*), Clarence Wilson (*Ben Isaacs*), Charles Coleman (*Butler*), Esther Howard (*Ann*), Renee Whitney (*Lois*), Harvey Perry (*Al West*), Julian Rivero (*Pice*), Selmer Jackson (*Ring Announcer*), Chris-Pin Martin (*Manager*), George Hayes (*Intern*), Bob Perry (*Referee*), Billy West (*Second*), Phil Tead (*Reporter*), Jay Eaton (*Society Man*), Charlotte Merriam (*Blonde*), Lee Phelps (*Ring Announcer for Championship Bout*), John Kelly (*Boxing Spectator*), Rolfe Sedan (*Waiter*).

For his first boxing picture, Cagney plays a fighter on the mend in a New

Mexico health resort. He's been sent there courtesy of fans' donations, after having spent most of his money on alcohol and women. At the resort he meets Nixon and her small son Moore, who are about to be kicked out because she can't pay her bill. Cagney agrees to help out by entering the ring once more. He wins the prize money, but gets his nose smashed for his efforts. Cagney goes back to New York City, determined to take the town by storm. He meets Bruce, a society woman, and Cagney falls for her. After getting his nose fixed to impress her, Cagney takes care to protect his new snooter in the ring. His skills as a fighter suffer as a result, and the fans turn on him. Bruce also grows bored with the pug. The inevitable happens when Cagney finally takes another punch square on the proboscis. Bruce dumps the broken-nosed fighter, and Cagney ends up returning to Nixon. Though the story is simplistic, this is a strong drama, delivered with gusto by the cast. Cagney is at his best, creating a realistic portrait of a fighter who lets his ego balloon out of proportion. Del Ruth's direction wisely concentrates on the characters, allowing the fine ensemble to give the drama its strength. Seen briefly is a clip from the 1929 film QUEEN OF THE NIGHT CLUBS, featuring Texas Guinan and George Raft. Cagney approached his role with the utmost seriousness and was determined to make his characterization realistic. He trained with Harvey Perry, an ex-welterweight who also has a bit part in the film. The sparring sessions paid off, for Cagney's moves look like the real thing and it's obvious he's in the thick of things in both closeups and long shots. In his autobiography *Cagney by Cagney*, the actor remembered: "While we were shooting...a professional fighter who had been watching me in the ring at the studio came up to me and said, 'So you know how to use your dukes, that's possible for an amateur to do. But where'd you get your footwork?...' I said '...I'm a *dancer*. Moving around is no problem.' 'Oh,' he said. 'I get it. When I first saw you doing your stuff, I said this son-of-a-bitch has been at it. Now I get it.' " Cagney's skills in the film were so impressive that the rumor circulated for some time that the actor was a former prizefighter. Both critical and public receptions were excellent as WINNER TAKE ALL turned a tidy profit for Warner Bros. On the basis of this success Cagney demanded a raise, which was subsequently denied. Cagney was suspended by the studio in April of 1932 but arbitration settled the issue and the actor was back at work by October.

p, Roy Del Ruth; w, Wilson Mizner, Robert Lord (based on the story "133 at 3" by Gerald Beaumont); ph, Robert Kurrle; m, W. Franke Harling; ed, Thomas Pratt; md, Leo F. Forbstein; art d, Robert Haas; cos, Orry-Kelly; makeup, Perc Westmore.

Sports   **(PR:A   MPAA:NR)**

WINNER TAKE ALL**   (1939) 62m FOX bw

Tony Martin (*Steve Bishop*), Gloria Stuart (*Julie Harrison*), Henry Armetta (*Papa Gambini*), Slim Summerville (*Muldoon*), Kane Richmond (*Paulie Mitchell*), Robert Allen (*Tom Walker*), Inez Palange (*Mama Gambini*), Johnnie Pirrone, Jr (*Tony Gambini*), Pedro de Cordova (*Pantrelli*), Betty Greco (*Maria Gambini*), Eleanor Virzle (*Rosa Gambini*).

A prizefight picture with an interesting twist finds Martin as a waiter who scores a knockout in a benefit match. He goes on to fame and fortune through a series of fights fixed by gamblers who are counting on him, without his knowing, to give them a big score. His success goes to his head, something that does not set well with girl sportswriter Stuart, who likes him and believes he needs a comeuppance to set him straight. She arranges for Richmond to beat him to a pulp, which he does, after which she persuades Martin to go into serious training. A rare nonsinging role for Martin.

p, Jerry Hoffman; d, Otto Brower; w, Frances Hyland, Albert Ray (based on a story by Jerry Cady); ph, Edward Cronjager; ed, Nick DeMaggio; md, Samuel Kaylin.

Sports Drama/Comedy   **(PR:A   MPAA:NR)**

WINNER TAKE ALL, 1948   (SEE: JOE PALOOKA IN WINNER
                                                   TAKE ALL, 1948)

WINNERS, THE   (SEE: MY WAY, 1974, South Africa)

WINNER'S CIRCLE, THE**   (1948) 70m FOX bw

Johnny Longden, Morgan Farley, Robert S. Howard, William Gould, John Berardino, Russ Conway, Frank Dae, Jean Willes, Champion Horses: Man O'War, Seabiscuit, Whirlaway, Alsab, Assault, Gallant Fox, Bold Venture, Stymie, Phar Lap, Bull Lea, Discovery, War Admiral, Sir Barton, Equipoise.

A neatly contrived horse race story, told from the viewpoint of the horse. The picture follows the thoroughbred from the time of its birth on a Kentucky farm, its training, its first setbacks, the loyalty and devotion of its owner, Willes, to its first victory at Santa Anita, with famous jockey Longden on top. A moving inside look at a universal pastime.

p, Richard K. Polimer; d, Felix E. Feist; w, Howard J. Green, Leonard Praskins; ph, Elmer Dyer; m, Lucien Caillet; ed, Richard G. Wray; md, Caillet; equestrian manager, John Eppers.

Drama   **(PR:A   MPAA:NR)**

WINNETOU, PART I   (SEE: APACHE GOLD, 1965, Fr./Ital./Ger.)

WINNETOU, PART II   (SEE: LAST OF THE RENEGADES, 1966, Fr./Ital./Ger.)

WINNETOU, PART III   (SEE: DESPERADO TRAIL, THE, 1967, Ger./Yugo.)

WINNING***   (1969) 123m Newman-Foreman/UNIV c

Paul Newman (*Frank*), Joanne Woodward (*Elora*), Robert Wagner (*Luther Erding*), Richard Thomas (*Charley*), David Sheiner (*Lee Crawford*), Clu Gulager (*Larry Morechek*), Barry Ford (*Les Bottineau*), Toni Clayton (*The Girl*), Maxine Stuart (*Miss Redburne's Mother*), Karen Arthur (*Miss Dairy Queen*), Eileen Wesson (*Miss Redburne*), Robert Quarry (*Sam Jagin*), Pauline Myers (*Cleaning Woman*), Ray Ballard (*Trombone Player*), Charles Seel (*Eshovo*), Alma Platt (*Mrs. Eshovo*), Harry Basch (*The Stranger*), Allen Emerson (*Desk Clerk*), Marianna Case (*Motorcycle Girl*), Carolyn McNichol (*Party Girl*), Bobby Unser, Tony Hulman (*Themselves*), George Mason (*Indianapolis Policeman*), Mimi Littlejohn (*Indianapolis Queen*), Pat Vidan (*Starter*), Bruce Walkup (*Driver No. 1*), Timothy Galbraith (*Driver No. 2*), Lou Palmer, Jay Reynolds (*Indianapolis Interviewers*), Dan Gurney, Roger McCluskey, Bobby Grim.

Paul Newman has three loves, Joanne Woodward and family, acting, and automobile racing. In this film, he was able to have all three surrounding him and the result is a fast-moving drama that starts quickly, sags a bit in the middle, but winds up at 150 miles per hour. Newman is a bit tipsy after having won a 200-mile auto race. He meets Woodward, who works in a car rental store, and talks her into having a drive with him. The two are soon in love with each other and he takes her home with him to California. They marry and he adopts her son, 13-year-old Thomas, the offspring of her previous marriage. The moment Newman marries, his sweet luck begins to turn sour as he loses race after race to his No. 1 competitor, Wagner. They race at Riverside and Newman's car turns over. Another race at Minneapolis finds Wagner repeating his win. In northern California, Newman's engine blows and in a New Jersey race Wagner takes the checkered flag again when Newman's car is disabled due to a damaged minor part. Newman is nonplussed to figure out why he has hit such a bad streak. He thinks that he might be neglecting his work so he plunges himself even more deeply into it and the result is that he pays scant attention to Woodward. Desperate for affection, she has a one-night stand with Wagner at their motel in Indianapolis on the eve of the 500. Newman finds them in bed together. He accepts the fact in an understated fashion, shrugs, and moves out of the abode. Both Newman and Wagner drive for the same owner, Sheiner, and he has noticed Newman's want of winning so he hands the better of his two cars to Wagner for the Indy 500. Thomas hitchhikes across the country to try to put Newman's and Woodward's marriage back together. Thomas adores Newman and roots for him to vanquish Wagner in the race. The Indy 500 begins with a huge 17-car crash (actually shot at an earlier race). Wagner's car suffers engine problems and Newman wins. Later, Newman journeys to meet Woodward and they patch up their marriage. Thomas was excellent as the teenager in this, his first film. All of the other cameo performances were well-drawn and special note should be made for Sheiner and Gulager. There have been many car racing films, some worse, but only a few better. The major problem with most of the auto films was that they concentrated on cars careening and crashing and neglected the human side to the lives of the men and women in that milieu. This was supposed to be a TV movie for NBC but it was soon expanded for the big screen with the addition of Newman (who was also an uncredited producer) and the others. It grossed almost $7 million on the first go-around and did well in Europe, where racing is even more important to the sports fan. Several real racers appear, to lend credibility to the tale. Newman did his own race driving (the studio insured him for $3 million), something he continued to do well into the 1980s, after he'd turned 60 years of age. There was one sex scene that took the picture out of the general audience category. The footage seen in the Indy race is from the awesome crackup that began the 1968 festivities. By interpolating that, the picture seemed even more authentic although the film stock used in the actual race scenes appears to be slightly different from the stock used in the rest of the movie. The moments between Woodward and Newman are among the best ever shot with the husband-wife team and one particular scene, with both drinking beer out of cans and just talking, would appear to be as close to the way they are in real life as anyone could dream. Newman's passion for beer was widely known and his love for his wife was just as famous so the scene reeks with authenticity. Director Goldstone, who has misfired many times since (THE GANG THAT COULDN'T SHOOT STRAIGHT, SWASHBUCKLER, ROLLERCOASTER) did a fairly good job of keeping the action and the drama both moving quickly enough to generally sustain interest in the otherwise overlong movie. The locations were done at Indianapolis and in Wisconsin at Elkhart Lake.

p, John Foreman; d, James Goldstone; w, Howard Rodman; ph, Richard Moore (Panavision, Technicolor); m, Dave Grusin; ed, Edward A. Biery, Richard C. Meyer; art d, Alexander Golitzen, John J. Lloyd, Joe Alves; set d, John McCarthy, George Milo; cos, Edith Head; spec eff, Frank Brendel; makeup, Bud Westmore.

Sports Drama/Romance   Cas.   (PR:AC   MPAA:G/M)

WINNING OF THE WEST**   (1953) 57m COL bw

Gene Autry (*Himself*), Smiley Burnette (*Himself*), Gail Davis (*Ann Randolph*), Richard Crane (*Jack Austin*), Robert Livingston (*Art Selby*), House Peters, Jr (*Marshal Hackett*), Gregg Barton (*Clint Raybold*), William Forrest (*John Randolph*), Ewing Mitchell (*Ranger Capt. Hickson*), Rodd Redwing (*Pete Littlewolf*), George Chesebro (*Boone*), Frank Jaquet (*Manager*), Charles Delaney (*Jules Brent*), Charles Soldani, Eddie Parker, Terry Frost, James Kirkwood, Boyd Morgan, Bob Woodward, Champion, Jr. the Horse.

Singing cowboy Autry discovers that his kid brother is part of a gang that has been using hoodlum tactics in the Old West, forcing ranchers to pay for protection or else. Autry at length succeeds in persuading his brother to fight for justice, and together they round up and dispose of the gross ones. Autry sings: "Cowboy Blues," "Find Me My 45," "Cowpoke Poking Along."

p, Armand Schaefer; d, George Archainbaud; w, Norman S. Hall; ph, William Bradford; ed, James Sweeney; art d, George S. Brooks.

Western   Cas.   (PR:A   MPAA:NR)

WINNING POSITION   (SEE: NOBODY'S PERFECT, 1968)

WINNING TEAM, THE***½   (1952) 98m WB bw

Doris Day (*Aimee Alexander*), Ronald Reagan (*Grover Cleveland Alexander*), Frank Lovejoy (*Rogers Hornsby*), Eve Miller (*Margaret*), James Millican (*Bill Killefer*), Rusty Tamblyn (*Willie Alexander*), Gordon Jones (*Glasheen*), Hugh Sanders (*McCarthy*), Frank Ferguson (*Sam Arrants*), Walter Baldwin (*Pa Alexander*), Dorothy Adams (*Ma Alexander*), Bonnie Kay Eddie (*Sister*), James Dodd (*Fred*), Fred Millican (*Catcher*), Pat Flaherty (*Bill Klem*), Tom Greenway (*Foreman*), Frank MacFarland (*Johnson*), Arthur Page (*Preacher*), Tom Browne Henry (*Lecturer*), Larry Blake (*Detective*), Frank Marlowe (*Taxi Driver*), Kenneth Patterson (*Dr. Conant*), Bob Lemon, Jerry Priddy, George Metkovich, Hank Sauer, Peanuts Lowrey, Irving Noren, Al Zarilla, Gene Mauch (*Ball Players*), Glen Turnbull, John Hedloe (*Reporters*), Henry Blair (*Bat Boy*), Gordon Clark (*Pianist*), John Kennedy (*Announcer*), Allan Wood (*Usher*), Alan Foster (*Customer*), Alex Sharp (*1st Baseman*), William Kalvino (*Batter*), Robert Orrell (*Catcher*), Russ Clark (*Umpire*).

This biography of baseball legend Grover Cleveland Alexander is an entertaining sports film, though the story glosses over some of the more controversial parts of his life. Reagan begins the film working as a telephone lineman in Nebraska. He pitches in amateur leagues, but his skills are incredible and within a few years he has become a star player with the Philadelphia Phillies. His career takes a bad turn when he is hit in the head, which causes dizzy spells. Serving in WW I, his condition worsens after he is exposed to battlefield explosions. Soon he begins seeing double, so Reagan begins drinking to stave off pain. Alcohol takes an inevitable toll on his career, reducing the once great pitcher to bush league games. His bouts with double vision are mistaken as public inebriation by others, and Reagan finally leaves the game he loves. Desperate for money, the former star takes a job working in a sideshow at a two-bit circus. Throughout these trials and tribulations, his wife, Day, continues to believe in her husband. She, along with pitcher Millican, talk to Lovejoy (playing the famed Rogers Hornsby) and persuade him to give Reagan another shot at the big leagues. Lovejoy agrees, and Reagan makes a spectacular comeback. Pitching for the St. Louis Cardinals, he leads the team on to victory in the 1926 World Series against the New York Yankees. This was one of Reagan's favorite roles, and he gives it some real grit, portraying Alexander as an incredible talent beset by all-too-human problems. Day is fine as the wife who stands by through thick and thin, and the film is directed with empathy for its subject. Reagan, who had formerly been a radio announcer for the Chicago Cubs, trained with Arnold "Jigger" Statz, a contemporary of Alexander's, and Jerry Priddy, second baseman for the Detroit Tigers, before beginning the film. The actor would spend two hours every day for three solid weeks, working on his pitching, with Priddy coaching him in fundamentals. In actuality, Alexander suffered from epilepsy and had a much more involved alcohol problem than presented here. Reagan was angered by studio avoidance of a very real problem in the man's life, later stating: "I've always regretted that the studio insisted we not use the word (epilepsy), although we tried to get the idea across. The trouble was that a frank naming of the illness would have the ring of truth, whereas ducking it made some critics accuse us of inventing something to whitewash his alcoholism." Alexander's widow served as a story consultant, and Reagan was pleased that their real life romance was accurately portrayed in the film. This was Reagan's last film for Warner Bros., his 40th with the studio in 15 years. Producer Foy had also produced many of Reagan's early B films, and this was their last collaboration. This was no musical, but surprisingly was packed with a number of well-known songs. They include: "Take Me Out to the Ball Game" (Albert von Tilzer, Jack Norworth), "I'll String Along with You" (Al Dubin, Harry Warren), "Lucky Day" (B.G. De Sylva, Lew Brown, Ray Henderson), "Ain't We Got Fun" (Gus Kahn, Richard Whiting), "Old St. Nicholas."

p, Bryan Foy; d, Lewis Seiler; w, Ted Sherdeman, Seelag Lester, Merwin Gerard (based on the story by Lester, Gerard); ph, Sid Hickox; m, David Buttolph; ed, Alan Crosland, Jr.; art d, Douglas Bacon; set d, William Kuehl;

cos, Leah Rhodes; spec eff, H.F. Koenekamp; makeup, Gordon Bau.

Biography   (PR:A MPAA:NR)

WINNING TICKET, THE*½   (1935) 70m MGM bw

Leo Carrillo (*Joe Tomasello*), Louise Fazenda (*Nora Tomasello*), Ted Healy (*Eddie Dugan*), Irene Hervey (*Mary Tomasello*), James Ellison (*Jimmy Powers*), Luis Alberni (*Tony, Attorney*), Purnell Pratt (*Mr. Powers*), Akim Tamiroff (*Giuseppe*), Betty Jane Graham (*Noreen Tomasello*), Billy Watson (*Joe Tomasello, Jr.*), Johnny Indrisano (*Lefty Costello*), Ronald Fitzpatrick (*Mickey Tomasello*).

An Italian barber wins the Irish sweepstakes, and the fun begins. First the ticket cannot be found; then it is suspected that the baby hid it. A baleful of laughs results when the adults try to get the baby to remember what it did with the valuable piece of paper. At the end, it is found in Carrillo's guitar, so the song is played after all. A lot of fun from very little substance.

p, Jack Cummings, Charles Riesner; d, Riesner w, Ralph Spence, Richard Schayer (based on the story by Robert Pirosh, George Seaton); ph, Charles Clarke; ed, Hugh Wynn.

Comedy   (PR:A MPAA:NR)

WINNING WAY, THE   (SEE: ALL-AMERICAN, THE, 1953)

WINSLOW BOY, THE***½ (1950) 97m Anatole de Grunwald-LFP/EL
                                                                    bw

Robert Donat (*Sir Robert Morton*), Margaret Leighton (*Catherine Winslow*), Cedric Hardwicke (*Arthur Winslow*), Basil Radford (*Esmond Curry*), Kathleen Harrison (*Violet*), Francis L. Sullivan (*Attorney General*), Marie Lohr (*Grace Winslow*), Jack Watling (*Dickie Winslow*), Frank Lawton (*John Watherstone*), Neil North (*Ronnie Winslow*), Walter Fitzgerald (*1st Lord*), Wilfrid Hyde-White (*Wilkinson*), Kynaston Reeves (*Lord Chief Justice*), Ernest Thesiger (*Mr. Ridgeley-Pearce*), Lewis Casson (*Adm. Springfield*), Stanley Holloway, Cyril Richard (*Comedians*), Nicholas Hannen (*Col. Watherstone*), Evelyn Roberts (*Hamilton*), Billy Shine (*Fred*), Anthony Bird (*1st Lord's P.P.S.*), Barry Briggs (*Sir Robert's P.P.S.*), Cecil Bevan (*Speaker*), Wilfred Caithness (*Minister*), Lambert Enson (*Mr. Williams*), Hugh Dempster (*Agricultural Member*), Philip Ray (*1st Speaking Member*), Archibald Batty, Edward Lexy, Gordon McLeod (*Elderly Members*), W.A. Kelley (*Brian O'Rourke*), George Bishop (*Usher*), Charles Groves (*Clerk of the Court*), Ian Colin (*Mr. Saunders*), Ivan Samson (*Comdr. Flower*), Dandy Nichols (*Miss Hawkins*), Vera Cook (*Violet's Friend*), Jane Gill Davies (*Mrs. Curry*), Frank Tickle (*Mr. Gunn*), Honor Blake (*Edwina Gunn*), Margaret Withers (*Mrs. Jordan*), Noel Howlett (*Mr. Williams*), Aubrey Mallalieu (*Mr. Roberts*), Mary Hinton (*Mrs. Elliott*), Nicholas Hawtrey (*Charles Elliott, Jr.*), Beatrice Marsden (*Cook*), Hilary Pritchard (*Dr. Anstruther*), Mona Washbourne (*Miss Barnes*).

In 1912 in London, Hardwicke is a retired bank official whose 14- year-old son, North, is expelled from naval college when he is accused of stealing a five-shilling postal order from another cadet. Hardwicke is convinced of his son's innocence but he is prevented by British law and unconcerned bureaucrats from fighting for his son's honor. Stymied at every turn, he hires the most famous attorney in Britain, Donat. Donat makes an impassioned speech in the House of Commons that results in a Petition of Right that allows Hardwicke to sue the Admiralty and make them prove in the courts that his son stole the postal order. The case is making headlines now and Hardwicke's family is facing the consequences: Hardwicke's daughter, suffragette Leighton, is left by her fiance; son Watling is forced to leave Oxford; and various legal fees are bringing Hardwicke almost to bankruptcy. In a courtroom trial, Donat finally gets North to admit the truth about what he was doing when the postal order was stolen: sneaking a cigarette in the locker room. The court finds in favor of North and Donat makes clear that he intends to see a great deal more of Leighton. The story may seem rather dry, but the performances of Hardwicke, as the father prepared to face ruin to restore his son's honor, and of Donat, as the brilliant lawyer who finally breaks through the boy's own personal code of honor to exonerate him, keep the movie an engrossing experience. Based on the true Archer-Shee case of 1912.

p, Anatole de Grunwald; d, Anthony Asquith; w, Terence Rattigan, Asquith, de Grunwald (based on the play by Rattigan); ph, Freddie Young, Osmond Borradaile; m, William Alwyn; ed, Gerald Turney- Smith; prod d, Andre Andrejew; md, Dr. Hubert Clifford; cos, William Chappell.

Drama   **Cas.**   (PR:A MPAA:NR)

WINSTANLEY**½   (1979, Brit.) 96m British Film Institute bw

Miles Halliwell (*Winstanley*), Jerome Willis (*Gen. Lord Fairfax*), Terry Higgins (*Tom*), Phil Oliver (*Will*), David Bramley (*Parson*), Alison Halliwell (*Mrs. Platt*), Dawson France (*Capt. Gladman*), Bill Petch (*Henry*), Barry Shaw (*Col. Rich*), Sid Rawle (*Ranter*), George Hawkins (*Coulton*), Stanley Reed (*Recorder*), Philip Stearns (*Drake*), Flora Skrine (*Mrs. Drake*).

Originally released in 1975, WINSTANLEY is a historical drama detailing the rise of a religious sect known as the Diggers following the beginnings

of the Protestant Reformation. Halliwell plays Winstanley, the leader of the movement and an advocate of nonviolence, who organizes his people to work farm land that the rich are not using. The landowners, however, force the Diggers from their makeshift homes with violence and destruction. Brownlow and Mollo, who collaborated on 1964's IT HAPPENED HERE, take great care in re-creating 17th-Century England, both in costuming and design and historical accuracy. The film also shares its visual style with the pictures of the silent era, which is no surprise considering Brownlow's interest in that time. Brownlow wrote the fine film book *The Parade's Gone By* and was responsible for the restoration of Abel Gance's 1927 silent classic NAPOLEON, which resurfaced in 1981.

d&w, Kevin Brownlow, Andrew Mollo (based on the novel Comrade Jacob by David Caute); ph, Ernest Vincze; m, Sergei Prokofiev; ed, Sarah Ellis; art d, Andrew Mollo; cos, Carmen Mollo.

Historical Drama   (PR:C MPAA:NR)

WINSTON AFFAIR, THE   (SEE: MAN IN THE MIDDLE, 1964, U.S.,
                                                                    Brit.)

WINTER A GO-GO*   (1965) 87m COL c

James Stacy (*Danny Frazer*), William Wellman, Jr (*Jeff Forrester*), Beverly Adams (*Jo Ann Wallace*), Anthony Hayes (*Burt*), Jill Donahue (*Janine*), Tom Nardini (*Frankie*), Duke Hobbie (*Bob*), Julie Parrish (*Dee Dee*), Nancy Czar (*Jonesy*), Linda Rogers (*Penny*), Judy Parker (*Dori*), Bob Kanter (*Roger*), Walter Maslow (*Jordan*), H.T. Tsiang (*Cholly*), Buck Holland (*Will*), Cherie Foster, Carey Foster, Arlene Charles, Cheryl Hurley (*Winter A-Go-Go Girls*), Nooney Rickett Four, Joni Lyman, The Reflections (*Themselves*).

It's the old unsophisticated story of teens trying to get a place where they can play their music, done in an ordinary and predictable fashion. This time it's a ski lodge that Wellman (the untalented son of the director of PUBLIC ENEMY and A STAR IS BORN) has inherited and wants to turn into a hot spot, but first he must overcome the setbacks provided by Maslow. Songs include: "King of the Mountain" (Howard Greenfield, sung by Joni Lyman, Nooney Rickett Four), "Winter A-Go-Go," "Ski City" (Greenfield), "Hip Square Dance" (Steve Venet, Tommy Boyce, Bobby Hart, Harry Betts, sung by James Stacy), "I'm Sweet On You" (Boyce, Hart, Venet, sung by The Reflections), "Do the Ski (with Me)" (Venet, Boyce, Hart, Toni Wine).

p&w, Reno Carell; d, Richard Benedict; w, Bob Kanter (based on the story by Carell); ph, Jacques Marquette (Pathe Color); m, Harry Betts; ed, Irving Berlin; art d, Walter Holscher; set d, Morris Hoffman; cos, Joseph Dimmitt, Angela Alexander; ch, Kay Carson; makeup, Dan Greenway.

Musical   (PR:A MPAA:NR)

WINTER CARNIVAL*   (1939) 105m UA bw

Ann Sheridan (*Jill Baxter*), Richard Carlson (*John Welden*), Helen Parrish (*Ann Baxter*), James Corner (*Mickey Allen*), Robert Armstrong (*Tiger Reynolds*), Alan Baldwin (*Don Reynolds*), Joan Brodel [Leslie] (*Betsy Phillips*), Virginia Gilmore (*Margie Stafford*), Cecil Cunningham (*Miss Ainsley*), Robert Allen (*Rocky Morgan*), Marsha Hunt (*Lucy Morgan*), Morton Lowry (*Count Von Lundborg*), Jimmy Butler (*Larry Grey*), Kenneth Stevens (*Male Soloist*), Benny Drohan (*Bartender*), Martin Turner (*Pullman Porter*), Susan and Molly McCash (*The Twins*), Robert E. Homans (*Conductor*), John Wray (*Poultry Truck Driver*), Emory Parnell (*New York Mercury Editor Williams*), Al Hill, George Magrill (*Mercury Reporters*), Robert Walker (*Wes*), Cyril Ring, John Berkes (*Reporters at Terminal*).

Beautiful Sheridan has just divorced the oily count she married, and in an attempt to find surcease from a barrage of reporters she takes refuge at Dartmouth College during carnival time. At one time queen of the carnival, she now watches her sister try to win the same honor and she also flirts with an old flame, unexciting professor Carlson. The background is the thing in this handsome production, and no wonder–scripters Schulberg and Rapf both were Dartmouth alumni. The great American novelist F. Scott Fitzgerald was personally hired by producer Wanger but, after writing only a few lyrical scenes, Fitzgerald went on a toot and Wanger fired him. This was one of the author's last scriptwriting assignments before his untimely death the following year.

p, Walter Wanger; d, Charles F. Reisner; w, Lester Cole, Budd Schulberg, Maurice Rapf, (uncredited) F. Scott Fitzgerald (based on the story "Echoes That Old Refrain" by Corey Ford); ph, Merritt Gerstad; m, Werner Janssen; ed, Dorothy Spencer; md, Janssen; m/l, L. Wolfe Gilbert, Janssen.

Drama   (PR:A MPAA:NR)

WINTER KEPT US WARM*½ (1968, Can.) 81m Varsity/Film-Makers'
                                                                    bw

John Labow (*Doug*), Henry Tarvainen (*Peter*), Joy Tepperman (*Bev*), Janet Amos (*Sandra*), Iain Ewing (*Artie*), Jack Messinger (*Nick*), Larry Greenspan (*Larry*), Sol Mandelsohn (*Hall Porter*), George R. Appleby (*House Don*).

Student film from the University of Toronto about an older student who takes an awkward freshman under his wing, only to become enraged when the youngster shows that he's able to act on his own. Trials and tribulations of student life revealed in both plot and film techniques.

p&d, David Secter; w, Secter, Ian Porter, John Clute; ph, Bob Fresco, Ernest Meershoek; m, Paul Hoffert; ed, Michael Foytenyi.

Drama **(PR:C MPAA:NR)**

WINTER KILLS***½ (1979) 97m AE c

Jeff Bridges *(Nick Kegan)*, John Huston *(Pa Kegan)*, Anthony Perkins *(John Ceruti)*, Sterling Hayden *(Z.K. Dawson)*, Eli Wallach *(Joe Diamond)*, Dorothy Malone *(Emma Kegan)*, Tomas Milian *(Frank Mayo)*, Belinda Bauer *(Yyvette Malone)*, Ralph Meeker *(Gameboy Baker)*, Toshiro Mifune *(Keith)*, Richard Boone *(Keifitz)*, Elizabeth Taylor *(Lola Comante)*, Donald Moffat *(Captain)*, David Spielberg *(Miles)*, Brad Dexter *(Capt. Heller)*, Peter Brandon *(Doctor)*, Michael Thoma *(Ray)*, Ed Madsen *(Capt. Heller Two)*, Irving Selbert *(Irving Mentor)*, Chris Soldo *(Jeffreys)*, Robert Courleigh *(1st Mate of T.K.)*, Joe Spinell *(Arthur Fletcher)*, Ira Rosenstein *(Orderly on T.K.)*, Kyle Morris *(John Kullens)*, Phil Lito *(Police Driver)*, Barbara Richert *(Woman Cyclist)*, Jake Hughes *(Child on Cycle)*, Patrice Bough *(Secretary One)*, Eloise Hardt *(Secretary Two)*, Gladys Hill *(Rosemary)*, Kim O'Brien *(1st Blonde)*, Candice Rialson *(2nd Blonde Girl)*, Bill P. Wilson *(Admiral)*, Loyd Catlett *(Z.K. Dawson, Guard)*, Michael Bond *(Flight Engineer)*, Helene Fagan *(Stewardess)*, Peter Kilman *(Pilot)*, Gianni Russo *(Copilot)*, Peter Koshel *(Cop/Casino Latino)*, Lissette *(Cuban Singer)*, Robert Boyle *(Desk Clerk)*, Sidney Lanier *(Raymond the Butler)*, Helen Curry *(Black Maid)*, Rick Lynn-Thomas *(Maitre d')*, Jesse Veliz *(Cuban Man in Havana)*, Robert Wolcott *(Shoeshine Boy)*, Robert Moresco *(Intern)*, Agneta Eckmyr *(Nurse One)*, Tisa Farrow *(Nurse Two)*, Billie Allen *(Receptionist)*, Joe Ragno *(Doorman)*, Loutz Gage *(Butler)*, Camillia Sparv, Andrea Claudio, Erin Gray, Susan Walden, Rebecca Grimes, Jennifer Keith, Amanda Jones *(Beautiful Women)*, Berry Berenson *(Morgue Attendant)*, Tim Culbertson *(Security Guard)*, Regis Mull *(Cop with Keifetz)*.

In an age where most American films have willingly abandoned the thinking adult audience in favor of the more financially lucrative mindlessness of roller-coaster adventure films, a witty, intelligent, and thought-provoking movie like William Richert's WINTER KILLS becomes all the more precious. Unfortunately, when one of these rare filmmaking gems surfaces amid the mire of teenage fantasy, play-it-safe studios simply dump the film on the market in order to hold screens for their next insipid blockbuster. The world portrayed in WINTER KILLS is no less ludicrous. Based on a novel by Richard Condon (Who also wrote The Manchurian Candidate and Prizzi's Honor), the film stars Bridges as the youngest son of a Kennedyesque family run by the powerful and eccentric tycoon Huston. Not wanting to follow in the footsteps of his older brother who became president and then was later assassinated, Bridges has drifted through life trying to avoid the influence of his father. Content to simply work on one of his father's oil rigs, Bridges tries to maintain a relationship with a sexy magazine editor, Bauer, but only seems to be able to talk to her via her answering machine. One day Boone, the family watchdog, brings Bridges a dying man who claims to have been the "2nd rifle" at the president's assassination 19 years before. This sets into motion a bizarre series of events which sees Bridges dig deeper and deeper into the past to find out who is truly responsible for his brother's assassination. As he lurches from clue to clue, several seemingly concrete solutions to the murder are offered by a variety of witnesses. One arrow seems to point to Huston's rival business interests. Another confirms that mobsters Meeker and Wallach contracted for the president's assassination to regain control of gambling interests in Cuba. Strangest of all, facts seem to suggest that Hollywood power brokers wanted revenge after the president broke off an affair with one of their hot young starlets who later killed herself, an event which cost the studios $50 million. After Bridges uncovers these odd tidbits, each person he talks with is murdered. It even seems that Bauer, who is murdered during the investigation, played a part in the conspiracy. Eventually the trail leads back to Huston's own Chief of Information, Perkins. The unassuming bureaucrat ushers Bridges into his top-secret inner sanctum and shows the heir apparent the masses of information stored there. Massive towers of contracts, audio-video recordings, satellite surveillance and other eavesdropping materials are all under Perkins' command. Perkins controls every piece of information pertaining to Huston's world-wide business affairs. Under duress, the crypt keeper tells Bridges that it was Huston who had the president killed after his son refused to cover up a bad campaign debt that would cause his father scandal and ruin. When Bridges goes back to Manhattan and confronts his father, Huston turns the tables and claims that Perkins was actually responsible for the assassination. Over the years the information gatherer had become all powerful over Huston and ordered the murder of the president to gain complete control of the company. "Damndest part...he don't even give himself a raise. Lives in Brooklyn in a rabbit hole," Huston muses. On Huston's orders, Boone bursts in to kill Bridges. In the ensuing gunfight, Boone is killed and Huston runs to the terrace of his high-rise office building. Giving chase, Bridges discovers that his father has slipped over the side of the building and is clinging to a giant American flag. Before he falls, Huston gives his son a business tip ("Put my money in South America"), and slides to his doom, ripping the flag in half. Bridges, stunned and more than a little confused, wanders off muttering to his father's secretary that he's still "part of the family." The film ends just as it begins, with Bridges listening to Bauer's voice on her answering machine. To describe WINTER KILLS in words is to do the film a grave disservice. Richert turned Condon's novel about the insanity of the American power structure into a wickedly funny black comedy. Members of the incredible cast (Taylor appears unbilled) are allowed to play their parts in a slightly exaggerated manner, but the acting style seems to fit because all of the characters are big and powerful forces. Bridges is the smallest person (authority and influence) in the film and it is he who unwittingly destroys the balance of power in America. In the end he weakly accepts the throne, but all he really ever wanted to do was talk with the woman he loved. Huston is magnificent and if the film had ever found a decent release or popular favor, it would have earned him an Oscar. The man he plays seemingly owns everything, and the world is his playground. He is a vulgar man who is never afraid to say what he thinks, and thinks nothing of walking around his mansion wearing nothing but an open robe and red bikini underwear. By the time the film has taken all it's bizarre twists and turns one is left wondering whether or not the whole thing was just a scheme by Huston to test his youngest son. Richert's observations of the perversity and lunacy of the American power structure are relevant, gripping, and ultimately disturbing. The fact that Richert got the project off the ground at all is a miracle. To be taken seriously by the studio, this first-time director went out and got written commitments from such acting notables as Huston, Bridges, Taylor, and Perkins. Filling out his cast with Mifune, Malone, Hayden, Wallach, and Boone, Richert began production and acquired Alfred Hitchcock's favorite production designer, Robert Boyle (who also makes a hysterically funny cameo as a hotel desk clerk) to execute the lush, detailed look of the film. About a week before the $6.5 million production was completed, the studio pulled the financial plug (rumors that the Kennedy family was responsible seem unfounded). Determined to finish his film, Richert immediately launched into another, smaller budget picture, THE AMERICAN SUCCESS COMPANY, and shot it in Munich. He had planned to use the revenues from the second film to finish the first, but American studios thought the product too strange and refused to release it. Fortunately, a group of investors was impressed with THE AMERICAN SUCCESS COMPANY, and they fronted Richert the money to finish WINTER KILLS. The film was released by Avco Embassy with little fanfare and disappeared from screens in a week only to be replaced by their big summer movie, GOLDENGIRL, which starred Susan Anton. Finally Richert formed his own company and struck complicated financial deals with Avco Embassy in an effort to resurrect his films and distribute them on his own. The effort was valiant, and WINTER KILLS garnered some attention, but few people went to see it. Luckily, it is available on video cassette, where it has found a whole new audience.

p, Fred Caruso; d&w, William Richert (based on the novel by Richard Condon); ph, Vilmos Zsigmond; m, Maurice Jarre; ed, David Bretherton; prod d, Robert Boyle; art d, Norman Newberry; set d, Arthur Seph Parker.

Comedy/Drama **Cas.** **(PR:O MPAA:R)**

WINTER LIGHT, THE** (1963, Swed.) 79m Svensk Filmindustri bw (NATTVARDSGAESTERNA)

Ingrid Thulin *(Marta Lundberg)*, Gunnar Bjornstrand *(Tomas Ericsson)*, Max von Sydow *(Jonas Persson)*, Gunnel Lindblom *(Karin Persson)*, Allan Edwall *(Algot Frovik)*, Kolbjorn Knudsen *(Knut Aronsson)*, Olof Thunberg *(Fredrik Blom)*, Elsa Ebbesen *(Magdalena Ledfors)*, Tor Borong *(Johann Akerblom)*, Bertha Sannell *(Hanna Appelblad)*, Helena Palmgren *(Doris Appelblad)*, Eddie Axberg *(Johan Strand)*, Lars-Owe Carlberg *(Police Inspector)*, Johan Olafs *(Gentleman)*, Ingmarie Hjort *(Persson's Daughter)*, Stefan Larsson *(Persson's Son)*, Lars-Olof Andersson *(Frederiksson's Boy I)*, Christer Ohman *(Fredriksson's boy II)*.

Second in a trilogy that also includes THROUGH A GLASS DARKLY and THE SILENCE, all centering on man's metaphysical state and his place in God's scheme of things. An extremely personal theme for Bergman which many people feel is something the cinema should not be subjected to and is incapable of properly handling, while others think it is boring. A minority are captivated by such indulgences and consider Bergman an extremely insightful expressionist of questions lurking in the dark recesses of the human mind. THE WINTER LIGHT takes place in rural Sweden where pastor Bjornstrand finds the members of his congregation dwindling until there are only a few people left, including a woman who is blindly in love with him. Still he goes through the rituals of his office, less out of faith but more out of his own inability to answer the ultimate question, "Why is God silent?" His doubts come out in the open when he hears the confession of von Sydow, a fisherman obsessed with the thought of the Chinese using the atom bomb, who has come to the pastor not only to vent his confusion but for guidance. Instead, all he receives from the pastor is uncertainty, and shortly after his confession he kills himself. The pastor visits the scene of the suicide, then von Sydow's wife. Back at the church for vespers, he finds the rows of seats empty except for the woman who loves him, and he proceeds to begin the service with the by now hollow words, "The earth is full of the Glory of God." A philosophical and moral puzzlement without any definite answers, THE WINTER LIGHT remains one of Bergman's most finished works and the one freest of his usual theatricalities.

p,d&wm Ingmar Bergman; ph, Sven Nykvist ed, Ulla Ryghe; set d, P.A. Lundgren; cos, Mago; makeup, Borje Lundh.

Drama **Cas.** **(PR:C MPAA:NR)**

WINTER MEETING**   (1948) 104m WB-FN bw

Bette Davis (Susan Grieve), Janis Paige (Peggy Markham), James Davis (Slick Novak), John Hoyt (Stacey Grant), Florence Bates (Mrs. Castle), Walter Baldwin (Mr. Castle), Ransom Sherman (Mr. Moran), Hugh Charles (Headwaiter), George Taylor, Mike Lally, Doug Carter, Harry McKee, Joe Minitello (Waiters), Harry Lewis (Juvenile), Ezelle Poule, Russ Clarke (Cafe Couple), Laura Treadwell (Gray Lady), Lois Austin (Marcia), Robert Riordan (Marcia's Escort).

This one has more talk than a senate filibuster and is only a tenth as interesting. Bette Davis is one of the great "sufferers" of the silver screen and she does it again here but the audience suffers just as much in this overblown drama. Davis is a spinster living alone in a swank New York City flat. She is the daughter of a stern New England man of the cloth and that has colored her life gray so it seems her only role is to work at various charities and spend her off-hours writing poetry. She has a few friends and when one of them, Hoyt, invites her to a partly in honor of James Davis–a recent Navy hero of WW II–her heart goes fluttering when she dances with Davis. She is not accustomed to having a man in her arms and feels uncomfortable. James Davis has come to the party with busty beauty Paige, but he only has eyes for the dowdy Bette. At the end of the evening, he takes Davis home, and she innocently asks him in for a last drink. She prepares the nightcaps and then discovers that he's off in dreamland. Later, he awakens and says he feels awful about what's happened. She bids him good night but he is not eager to leave her apartment until she responds to his amorous advances. She tries to keep him at arm's length and eventually gives in when he showers her with kisses. The following morning, they take a long drive up to Connecticut where she owns a country home. She doesn't want to go into the house but he presses her and they arrive to be greeted by Bates and Baldwin, the couple who watch the property. Later, Bette Davis admits why she stays away from the house. It was here that her father took his own life after her mother ran away with another, a more interesting man. James Davis chooses this time to tell her that he had intended becoming a Catholic priest but changed his mind after all the battles in the war and now questions his ability to don the cloth. In the morning, she is surprised to learn that he has departed. Back in New York, Bette Davis finds out that her mother is ill in a local hospital. Hoyt calls her for a friendly dinner date and they run into James Davis and Paige, who makes some snide remarks about Bette Davis. The next day, he arrives at her residence to say that he only went out with Paige to keep himself from falling in love with Davis. She tells him that he has to follow his dream of becoming a priest as she thinks that's what he really wants to do. He is still wavering between his love of the church and his affection for her but she persuades him to wear the collar in the end by showing him the letter from her mother. She has forgiven her parent for what she did to her other parent and is now planning to be at the woman's side to help her through her illness. Davis exits, now sure of his vocation in life. James Davis later used the first name of "Jim" when he began appearing in westerns. He eventually had his greatest success on the "Dallas" TV series in a role he was playing successfully at the time of his death. A dull movie made palatable by Bette Davis, who never seemed to give a bad performance in the 1930s and 1940s.

p, Henry Blanke; d, Bretaigne Windust; w, Catherine Turney (based on the novel by Ethel Vance); ph, Ernest Haller; m, Max Steiner; ed, Owen Marks; md, Leo F. Forbstein; art d, Edward Carrere; set d, Fred MacLean; spec eff, H.F. Koenekamp, Harry Barrdollar; makeup, Perc Westmore.

Drama   (PR:A   MPAA:NR)

WINTER OF OUR DREAMS**½   (1982, Aus.) 89m
                                        Vega/Enterprises-Satori c

Judy Davis (Lou), Bryan Brown (Rob), Cathy Downes (Fretel), Baz Luhrmann (Pete), Peter Mochrie (Tim), Mervyn Drak (Mick), Margie McCrae (Lisa), Mercie Deane-Johns (Angela), Joy Hruby, Kim Deacon, Caz Lederman, Jenny Ludlam, Virginia Duigan, Rosemary Lenzo, Alex Pinder.

Davis plays a Sidney prostitute trapped in a vicious circle of meanness and dope from which she is desperately trying to escape. A slow introspective pace is developed to portray her inner turmoil, which she does in a superb performance.

p, Richard Mason; d&w, John Duigen; ph, Tom Cowan (Eastmancolor); m, Sharon Calcraft; ed, Henry Dangar; prod d, Lee Whitmore.

Drama   Cas.   (PR:O   MPAA:NR)

WINTER RATES   (SEE: OUT OF SEASON, 1975, Brit.)

WINTER WIND***   (1970, Fr./Hung.) 80m Marquise-Mafilm/ Grove
        Press c (SIROKKO; SIROCCO D'HIVER; TELI SIROKKO)

Jacques Charrier (Lazar Marko), Marina Vlady (Maria), Eva Swann (Ilona), Jozsef Madaras (Markovics), Istvan Bujtor (Tarro), Gyorgy Banffy (Ante), Philippe March (Capt. Kovacs), Andras Kozak (Farkas), Pascal Aubier (Tihomir), Miklos Csanyi, Tihamer Vujicsics, Laszlo Horvath, Geza Polgar, Tibor Orban, Gyorgy Pinter, Lajos Fazekas (Serbian Anarchists), Laszlo Szabo (Allied translator), Philippe Haudiquet, Jozsef Pecsenke (Allied Officers), Gaborne Jakab, Ida Simenfalvy (Old Women), Francoise Prevost, Barna Basilides, Claude Beausoleil, Gyorgy Bordas, Michel Delahaye,

Gaspar Ferdinandy, Geza Ferdinandy, Peter Fodor, Levente Hidvegi, Vilmos Izsof, Jozsef Konrad, Balazs Kosztolanyi, Zoltan Kovacs, Marton Kulinyi, Mihaly Papp, Denes Szunyogh, Tibor Toth, Gyozo Varga, D. Sztojan Vujicsics.

One of the leading spokesmen of Hungarian cinema, Jancso, created this bleak and revealing look at the ironies of politics. Taking place in 1930s Hungary, Charrier plays an anarchist sought by the government, yet feared by his leftist comrades because of his violence and his fiery temper. When they learn of Charrier's situation with the government, they kill him. Oddly, these same people look upon his death as the perfect means of creating a martyr. Jancso's style is extremely harsh, consisting of a minimum of shots that can be hard to watch, yet are powerful in making a point.

p, Jacques Charrier; d, Miklos Jancso; w, Gyula Hernadi, Jancso, Jacques Rouffio, Francis Girod (based on the story by Hernadi); ph, Janos Kende (AgfaScope, Eastmancolor); m, Tihamer Vujicsics; ed, Zoltan Farkas; art d, Tamas Banovich; cos, Zuzsa Vicze.

Historical Drama   (PR:C   MPAA:NR)

WINTER WONDERLAND**   (1947) 71m REP bw

Lynne Roberts (Nancy Wheeler), Charles Drake (Steve Kirk), Roman Bohnen (Timothy Wheeler), Eric Blore (Luddington), Mary Eleanore Donahue (Betty Wheeler), Renee Godfrey (Phyllis Simpson), Janet Warren (Marge), Harry Tyler (Seth), Renie Riano (Mrs. Schuyler-Riggs), Diana Mumby (Telephone Operator), Alvin Hammer (Bellboy).

The boiling romance between farm girl Roberts and ski instructor Drake is set against a cold but stunning snow-filled background. When the pair aren't busy romancing, they do a spectacular job of racing down the slopes. A pleasant interlude at any time.

p, Walter Colmes, Henry Sokal; d, Bernard Vorhaus; w, Peter Goldbaum, David Chandler, Arthur Marx, Gertrude Purcell (based on the idea by Fred Schiller); ph, John Alton; m Paul Dessau; ed, Robert Jahns; md, Cy Feuer; set d, Glenn T. Thompson.

Drama   (PR:A   MPAA:NR)

WINTERHAWK*½   (1976) 98m Howco International c

Michael Dante (Chief Winterhawk), Woody Strode (Big Rude), Leif Erickson (Elkhorn Guthrie), Denver Pyle (Arkansas), L.Q. Jones (Gates), Elisha Cook, Jr (Rev. Will Finley), Seamon Glass (Big Smith), Dennis Fimple (Scobie), Arthur Hunnicut (Trader McCluskey), Dawn Wells (Clayanna), Chuck Pierce, Jr (Cotton), Jimmy Clem (Littlesmith), Sacheen Littlefeather (Paleflower), Ace Powell (Red Calf), Gilbert Lucero (Crow).

An Indian, Dante, kidnaps a white girl with whom he falls in love. Erickson heads a search party which tracks Dante across the beauty of the Northwest mountains and woods. A choice cast, particularly Strode and Erickson, as well as stunning backgrounds are misused through the inexperienced direction of Pierce. His attempts at trying to make Dante appear to possess mystic and spiritual powers, as he thinks all Indians must, are extremely shallow and more laughable than dramatic.

p&d, Charles B. Pierce; w, Pierce, Earl E. Smith; ph. Jim Roberson (Techniscope, Technicolor); m, Lee Holdridge; ed, Tom Boutrouss; art d, Charles Hughes, David Powell; spec eff, Conrad Rothman; m/l, "Winterhawk," Holdridge, Smith; stunts, Bud Botham.

Western   (PR:C   MPAA:PG)

WINTER'S TALE, THE**   (1968, Brit.) 151m WB-Seven Arts/WB c

Laurence Harvey (King Leontes), Jane Asher (Perdita), Diana Churchill (Paulina), Moira Redmond (Hermione), Jim Dale (Autolycus), Esmond Knight (Camillo), Richard Gale (Polixenes), David Weston (Florizel/Archidamas), John Gray (Clown), Edward Dewsbury (Shepherd/Gailer), Allan Foss (Antigonus), Monica Maughan (Lady).

Filmed rendition of Shakespeare's latter period tragicomedy lensed directly from the stage in London, where it had traveled after bowing at the 1966 Edinburgh festival. No compensation was made for the screen version except for some clever mixing by photographer Morris and editor Pilkington to suggest gaps in time. A brisk look at a lighthearted yet serious romance.

p, Peter Snell; d, Frank Dunlop; w, William Shakespeare; ph, Oswald Morris (Eastmancolor); m, Jim Dale; ed, Gordon Pilkington; prod d, Carl Toms; m/l, Dale.

Drama   (PR:A   MPAA:NR)

WINTERSET***½   (1936) 78m RKO bw

Burgess Meredith (Mio), Margo (Miriamne), Eduardo Ciannelli (Trock), Paul Guilfoyle (Garth), John Carradine (Romagna), Edward Ellis (Judge Gaunt), Stanley Ridges (Shadow), Maurice Moscovich (Esdras), Myron McCormick (Carr), Willard Robertson (Policeman), Mischa Auer (Radical), Barbara Pepper, Lucille Ball (Girls), Alec Craig (Hobo), Helen Jerome Eddy (Maria Romagna), Fernanda Eliscu (Piny), George Humbert (Lucia),

Murray Alper (Louie), Paul Fix (Joe), Alan Curtis (Sailor), Arthur Loft (District Attorney), Otto Hoffman (Elderly Man), Grace Hayle (Woman), Al Hill (Gangster), Bobby Caldwell (Mio as a Boy).

Loosely based on the trial of Nicola Sacco and Bartolomeo Vanzetti, this adaptation of Maxwell Anderson's Broadway play featured Meredith (in his film debut), Ciannelli, and Margo recreating the roles they had originated on stage. Meredith is the son of Carradine, a radical Italian immigrant who had been executed for murder on flimsy evidence. It is now 15 years later, and Burgess wants to prove his father's innocence. The film begins with a prolog explaining how Carradine came to be executed. In the 1920s Ciannelli, accompanied by his sidekick Ridges, and Guilfoyle, a most unwilling young man, steal a car that is used in a payroll robbery. The paymaster is murdered and the automobile is abandoned. When the car is found by police, they discover some of Carradine's writings inside and wrongfully pin the murder on him. Meredith learns that Guilfoyle, who was identified by many as the getaway driver, was never called before the court to testify on Carradine's behalf. Burgess gets involved with Guilfoyle's sister Margo, and through his diligent efforts is able to clear Carradine's name. Though somewhat stagy, WINTERSET is a strong and powerful drama. Burgess is excellent in his role, matched by the fine talents of the rest of the ensemble. Margo and Guilfoyle look amazingly similar, as though they were real life brother and sister. Of course they were not, but the resemblance is uncanny. The film unfortunately did poorly at the box office, as audiences seemed intimidated by its weighty topic. RKO executives were pleased with the film and its dramatic power, however.

p, Pandro S. Berman; d, Alfred Santell; w, Anthony Veiler (based on the play by Maxwell Anderson); ph, Peverell Marley; m, Roy Webb; ed, Wm. Hamilton; md, Nathaniel Shilkret; ed, William Hamilton; spec eff, Vernon Walker.

Drama   **Cas.**   **(PR:A-C   MPAA:NR)**

WINTERTIME*½   (1943) 82m FOX bw

Sonja Henie (Nora), Jack Oakie (Skip Hutton), Cesar Romero (Brad Barton), Carole Landis (Flossie Fouchere), S.Z. Sakall (Hjalmar Ostgaard), Cornel Wilde (Freddy Austin), Woody Herman and His Band (Themselves), Helene Reynolds (Mrs. Daly), Don Douglas (Jay Rogers), Geary Steffen (Jimmy the Skating Partner), Matt Briggs (Russell Carter), Georges Renavent (Bodreau), Jean Del Val (Constable), Arthur Loft (Advertising Man), Charles Irwin (Drunk), Eugene Borden, Muni Seroff (Working Men), Kay Linaker (Wife), Dick Elliott (Husband), Charles Trowbridge (Mr. Prentice), Nella Walker (Mrs. Prentice), Claire Whitney, Betty Roadman, Leila McIntyre, Kate Harrington (Bridge Players).

Another light, sugar-coated excuse to show off Norwegian skating star Henie's showy form has her traveling in Canada with her rich uncle, and saving an old, run-down hotel by her charming presence. Dark-haired Romero and Wilde complement her blonde good looks and keep her dimples much in evidence. It was Henie's last big musical and surely the most mindless. Musical numbers include: "Wintertime," "Later Tonight," "Dancing in the Dawn," "I'm All A-Twitter Over You," "We Always Get Our Girl," "I Like It Here," (Nacio Herb Brown, Leo Robin).

p, William Le Baron; d, John Brahm; w, E. Edwin Moran, Jack Jevne, Lynn Starling (based on a story by Arthur Kober); ph, Joe MacDonald, Glen MacWilliams; ed, Louis Loeffler; md, Alfred Newman Charles Henderson; art d, James Basevi, Maurice Ransford; set d, Thomas Little; cos, Rene Hubert; spec eff, Fred Sersen; ch, James Gonzalles, Carlos Romero.

Musical   **(PR:A   MPAA:NR)**

WIRE SERVICE**   (1942) 67m MON bw

Mal Burton (Harry Stewart), Rex Romer (Sid Beck), Valerie Cox (Lucille Charles), Burt Gervis (Willie Gavin), Chuck Sedacca (Marv Alvin), Blanche Turer (Michele), Ruth Baron (Sarah), Matt Hyman (Irving Zane), Moe Richards (Andy Lavin).

Sort of a DETECTIVE STORY set in the small offices of a local wire service in Los Angeles. Everything takes place in one eight-hour shift. Burton is the city editor, the man in charge of seeing what goes out over the wires. He is noisy, dyspeptic, and given to popping ulcer pills as he rattles off assignments to his reporters. Romer hears about a "jumper" who is about to leap eight stories from the downtown building in which the wire service has its offices. They can't allow any of the local papers to get the "beat" (which is the real name newshawks apply to what used to be called "a scoop"). Romer goes up three flights and does his best to talk the jumper into coming off the ledge. While he's using psychology on the distraught man, Cox, other things are happening. Cox is the food and restaurant features writer and she hears that a neighborhood dining establishment is having its liquor license revoked for having served a minor under 21. She goes out to investigate and learns that it was a setup and that rival restaurateur Sedacca was trying to put the more successful Hyman out of business so he could get the prime location. The person who ordered the drink, Baron, had been wearing heavy makeup to look older than her 20 years and 10 months, then she squealed to the local liquor board. (She was in the employ of Sedacca as well as being his daughter-in-law.) Richards is a madman who comes into the wire service with bombs attached to his body, fully intending to blow up editor Burton

and the rest of the staff because a story about him appeared in the paper that had been reported by the service. Richard's wife left him because of the report that he'd been seen with other women at a local hangout and he went mentally over the edge. He is about to pull the strings that will set the place ablaze when his wife, Turer, arrives and says she'll take him back. The picture ends with all three stories (plus a few sidebar items) all being concluded and the employees of the wire service go out for a well-earned drink as the next shift comes on. It looked like a play that hadn't been able to find a stage and had been transformed into a movie and that's exactly what it was. Still, within the confines of the one major set, they managed to get lots of action, some good characterizations, and more than a bit of humor. Another plus was the score by Stein, who only did this movie and then went into music teaching at a small New Jersey college.

p, Martin Rabb; d, Paul De Luca; w, Tony Ryan, Kenneth Pfeffer (based on an unproduced play by Gericho Falcon); ph, Hilton Hall; m, S. Bernard Stein; ed, Don Stern; art d, Bernard Krosinksy; set d, Robin Lindsay; cos, Vincent Petrosino; stunts, Lewis Arbogast; makeup, Burke Lipson.

Drama   **(PR:A   MPAA:NR)**

WIRETAPPERS*   (1956) 80m Great Commission/EM-Continental bw
                                        (AKA: THE JIM VAUS STORY)

Bill Williams (Jim Vaus), Georgia Lee (Vaus' Wife), Douglas Kennedy, Phil Tead, Stanley Clements, Ric Roman, Richard Benedict, Paul Picerni, Steve Conte, Melinda Plowman, Art Gilmore, Howard Wendell, Dorothy Kennedy, Barbara Hudson, Evangeline Carmichael.

Based on the life story of a petty chiseler, cheat, and mafia hood who turned from his life of crime after a spiritual conversion brought about by evangelist Billy Graham. A shallow treatment of an engaging story, which fails utterly to catch the force and power and sincerity of the book.

p, Jim Vaus; d, Dick Ross; w, John O'Day (based on the book Why I Quit Syndicated Crime by Vaus); ph, Ralph Woolsey; m, Ralph Carmichael; ed, Eugene Pendleton; art d, Bill Powers.

Crime/Drama   **(PR:A   MPAA:NR)**

WISE BLOOD***   (1979, U.S./Ger.) 108m Ithaca-Anthea/New Line c

Brad Dourif (Hazel Motes), Ned Beatty (Hoover Shoates), Harry Dean Stanton (Asa Hawks), Daniel Shor (Enoch Emery), Amy Wright (Sabbath Lilly), Mary Nell Santacroce (Landlady), John Huston (Grandfather).

The later films of John Huston's career often are called obscure, many of them being adaptations from books which are not good material themselves for film treatment. WISE BLOOD easily could have been such a failure, but instead it is a disturbing story of religious phonies in the South which is saved from its inbuilt dangers by its maniac characters. Dourif plays a soldier home from the war who changes his uniform for the garb of a preacher, although he has little belief or faith in religion. He hooks up with a blind preacher who turns out not to be blind, but who nevertheless persuades Dourif to blind himself so he can learn the truth. Truth turns out to be illusionary, however, as his landlady, who wants to care for him, virtually makes him a prisoner. A totally downbeat story and decidedly kinky here and there, yet a kind of affecting tenderness enshrouds these lonely and pathetic people.

p, Michael Fitzgerald, Kathy Fitzgerald: d, John Huston; w, Benedict Fitzgerald (based on the novel by Flannery O'Connor); ph, Gerald Fisher; m, Alex North; ed, Roberto Silvi; set d, Sally Fitzgerald; cos, Sally Fitzgerald.

Drama   **Cas.**   **(PR:O   MPAA:PG)**

WISE GIRL*½   (1937) 70m RKO bw

Miriam Hopkins (Susan Fletcher), Ray Milland (John O'Halloran), Walter Abel (Karl), Henry Stephenson (Mr. Fletcher), Alec Craig (Dermont O'Neil), Guinn ["Big Boy"] Williams (Mike), Betty Philson (Joan), Marianna Strebly (Katie), Margaret Dumont (Mrs. Bell-Rivington), Jean de Briac (George), Ivan Lebedeff (Prince Michael), Rafael Storm (Prince Ivan), Gregory Gaye (Prince Leopold), Richard Lane, Tom Kennedy (Detectives), James Finlayson (Jailer).

Socialite heiress Hopkins poses as a poor Greenwich Village artist to seek custody of her sister's two children, who are living a hand-to-mouth existence with their destitute artist father, Milland. Only Milland's performance and the antics of the wacky bohemian types he lives among add spice to this moronic little tale.

p, Edward Kaufman; d, Leigh Jason; w, Allan Scott (based on the story by Scott, Charles Norman); ph, Peverell Marley; ed, Jack Hively.

Drama   **(PR:A   MPAA:NR)**

WISE GIRLS**   (1930) 97m MGM bw (AKA: KEMPY)

Elliott Nugent (Kempy), Norma Lee (Kate Bence), Roland Young (Duke Merrill), J.C. Nugent (Dad Bence), Clara Blandick (Ma Bence), Marion Shilling (Ruth Bence), Leora Spellman (Jane Wade), James Donlan (Ben Wade).

Nugent is a sheepish plumber who gets conned into marrying Lee, the eldest daughter of the man who hired him out. But Lee only married him in order to get her real love jealous. When Nugent learns the truth he gets the marriage annulled and marries Lee's younger sister, Shilling. With the help of a shrewd lawyer, Nugent also manages to get ownership of Lee's house.

d, E. Mason Hopper; w, J.C. Nugent, Elliott Nugent (based on their play "Kempy"); ph, William Daniels; ed, Margaret Booth; art d, Cedric Gibbons; cos, David Cox; m/l, "I Love You Truly," Carrie Jacobs Bond.

Comedy (PR:A MPAA:NR)

WISE GUYS**   (1937, Brit.) 67m FOX bw

Charlie Naughton (Charlie), Jimmy Gold (Jimmy), Audrene Brier (Flo), Robert Nainby (Phineas McNaughton), Walter Roy (Drake), Sydney Keith (Eddie), David Kier (Lawyer), Peter Popp.

A disappointing comedy directed by American silent comedian Langdon which stars Naughton and Gold as a pair of vagabonds who learn that they can purchase their uncle's loan company if they can raise the necessary cash. The duo attempt to win big at the horse races, but there they cross the path of the vampish Brier and her boy friend who overhear the plan and decide to buy into the business themselves. Brier winds up being the big winner at the track and she buys the company, leaving Naughton and Gold in the cold. Director Langdon at one time was ranked among silent comedic geniuses Chaplin, Lloyd, and Keaton, for his sensitive (now some say smarmy) portrayal of a naive, baby-like character who represented the innocent, wide-eyed child in all of us. Unfortunately, his real-life personality was similar to his screen persona and he became a pathetic case by the time sound had arrived due to his bratty egotistical ravings and unreasonable demands. Rejecting directors Frank Capra and Harry Edwards, who had guided him successfully in the past, Langdon insisted on directing himself in three films. Each was a disaster. In 1931 Langdon left the movies and returned to vaudeville, but failed there as well. He declared bankruptcy and sank out of sight only to make token cameo appearances in forgettable features. When he died of a cerebral hemorrhage in 1944 he was nearly penniless. WISE GUYS is an extremely obscure film that was made in a period of Langdon's life that is not well documented and therefore all the more fascinating.

p, Ivor McLaren; d, Harry Langdon; w, David Evans (based on a story by Alison Booth); ph, Stanley Grant.

Comedy (PR:A MPAA:NR)

WISE GUYS**   (1969, Fr./Ital.) 100m Belles Rives-S.N.C.-Alexandra Produzione/UNIV c (LES GRANDES GUEULES; AKA: THE WISE GUYS)

Bourvil (Hector Valentin), Lino Ventura (Laurent), Marie Dubois (Jackie), Jean-Claude Rolland (Mick), Jess Hahn (Nenesse), Nick Stephanini (Therraz), Paul Grauchet (Pelissier), Roger Jacquet (Capester), Henia Suchar (Christiane), Reine Courtois (Yvonne), Pierre Frag (Fanfan), Marc Eyraud (L'Educateur), Jean Constantin (Skida).

Sawmill owner Bourvil tries to revive his sagging business by adopting the plan of ex-con Ventura to employ convicts from a prison-work program. This plan backfires when the men start a brawl with the workers from a competing mill. One man is left dead and the prisoners are no longer allowed to work at the mill. But a touching friendship develops between Bourvil and Ventura, whose plan was mainly a ploy to gain vengeance on a prisoner who was responsible for sending him to jail, but whose involvement with the struggling mill succeeds in changing his attitude.

p, Michel Ardan; d, Robert Enrico; w, Enrico, Jose Giovanni (based on the novel Le Haut Fer by Giovanni); ph, Jean Boffety (Techniscope, Technicolor); m, Francois de Roubaix; ed, Jacqueline Meppiel, Michel Lewin, Nicole Courtois; art d, Jean Saussac; spec eff, Marcel Ravel; makeup, Louis Dor.

Drama (PR:A MPAA:G)

WISER AGE*½   (1962, Jap.) 111m Toho bw (ONNA NO ZA; AKA: A WOMAN'S PLACE, WOMAN'S STATUS)

Hideko Takamine, Tatsuya Mihashi, Akira Takarada, Yoko Tsukasa, Reiko Dan, Yuriko Hoshi, Chishu Ryu, Haruko Sugimura, Keiju Kobayashi, Yosuke Natsuki, Mitsuko Kusabue, Keiko Awaji, Aiko Mimasu, Daisuke Kato.

The trials of five sisters are revealed as they struggle in their Tokyo suburb to pursue careers or find love and happiness in marriage. An interesting assortment of characters is gathered together to add life to this expose of the problems women face in modern-day Japan.

p, Sanezumi Fujimoto, Hidehisa Suga; d, Mikio Naruse; w, Toshiro Ide, Zenzo Matsuyama; ph, Atsushi Yasumoto.

Drama (PR:C MPAA:NR)

WISER SEX, THE*   (1932) 76m PAR bw

Claudette Colbert (Margaret Hughes), Melvyn Douglas (David Rolfe), Lilyan Tashman (Claire Foster), William Boyd (Harry Evans), Ross Alexander (Jimmie O'Neill), Franchot Tone (Phil Long), Effie Shannon (Mrs. Hughes), Paul Harvey (Blaney), Granville Bates (City Editor), Victor Kilian (Ed), Robert Fischer (Fritz), Douglas Dumbrille (Chauffeur).

Dreadfully conceived film in which Colbert resorts to a number of unbelievable escapades in order to clear the name of her beau. One of the worst, if not the worst, roles she ever attempted finds her as well as the rest of the cast hampered by idiotic situations and witless dialog.

d, Berthold Viertel; w, Harry Hervey, Caroline Francke (based on the play "Her Confessions" by Clyde Fitch); ph, George Folsey.

Drama (PR:A MPAA:NR)

WISHBONE, THE*½   (1933, Brit.) 78m Sound City/MGM bw

Nellie Wallace (Mrs. Beasley), Davy Burnaby (Peters), A. Bromley Davenport (Harry Stammer), Jane Wood (Mrs. Stammer), Renee Macready (Grace Elliott), Geoffrey King (Fred Elliott), Fred Schwartz (Jeweler), Hugh Lethbridge (Lord Westland), Joselyn Sparks, Bettina Montahners, Reggie de Beer.

Nonsensical little comedy starring Wallace as a poor charwoman whose life is changed briefly by an inheritance. Feeling guilty after a short shopping spree, Wallace uses what is left of the money to help out a street performer in need of a big break. Heartwarming, but the material is a bit slim to convey any memorable moments.

p, Ivar Campbell; d, Arthur Maude; w, N.W. Baring Pemberton (based on the short story "One Crowded Hour" by W. Townend).

Comedy (PR:A MPAA:NR)

WISHBONE CUTTER*½   (1978) 90m Fairwinds/Howco International c (AKA: SHADOW OF CHIKARA)

Joe Don Baker, Sondra Locke, Ted Neeley, Slim Pickens, Joy Houck, Jr, Dennis Fimple, John Chandler, Linda Dano.

The film starts well, but begins disintegrating after the first 15 minutes. Baker and Houck come across the dying Pickens, who tells them of a treasure of diamonds he buried deep in a mountain wilderness. On their journey to find the treasure, Houck, who plays an Irish-Indian named Half Moon O'Brien, senses that he and his partner are being followed. Houck's uneasiness is accounted for when, during the middle of the search, it is discovered that the diamonds are under a curse, which is why the search party is disappearing one by one for no explainable reason. Large gaps in credibility and lack of imagination make one hope the missing never return. The only real highlight is the Band's classic song "The Night They Drove Ol' Dixie Down" playing behind images of the South being ravaged by Northern troops during the Civil War.

p, Earl E. Smith, Barbara Pryor; d&w, Smith; ph, Jim Roberson, (Panavision, Technicolor); m, Jaime Mendoza-Nava; ed, Tom Boutross.

Western (PR:C MPAA:PG)

WISHING MACHINE**   (1971, Czech.) 75m Studio Gottwaldow/Xerox c (AUTOMAT NA PRANI)

Vit Weingaertner, Milan Zerman, Frantisek Filipovsky, Josef Hlinomaz, Miloslav Holub, Rudolf Deyl, Jr, Karel Effa, Jana Rendlova, Marketa Rauschgoldova.

Two boys have their fantasies come true when they encounter a wishing machine at a carnival. They build a similar machine, only their overactive imaginations take them on a perilous journey to the moon. Unmindful of the risks involved, such as how they will return home, they are given a good lesson in discovering the limitations of their dreams. The children are presented in a realistic and winning fashion, without the romantic notions of most Hollywood depictions. Likewise, their journey is a moral lesson designed to draw differences between fantasy and reality. English dubbing is outstanding.

d, Josef Pinkava; w, Pinkava, Jiri Blazek; ph, Jiri Kolin; m, William Bukovy; set d, Zdenek Rozkopal; m/l, Arthur De Cenzo, Robert Braverman.

Fantasy (PR:AAA MPAA:G)

WISTFUL WIDOW, THE   (SEE: WISTFUL WIDOW OF WAGON GAP, THE, 1947)

WISTFUL WIDOW OF WAGON GAP, THE**
(1947) 78m UNIV bw (GB: THE WISTFUL WIDOW)

Bud Abbott (Duke Eagan), Lou Costello (Chester Wooley), Marjorie Main (Widow Hawkins), Audrey Young (Juanita Hawkins), George Cleveland (Judge Benbow), Gordon Jones (Jake Frame), William Ching (Jim Simpson), Peter Thompson (Phil), Olin Howland [Howlin] (Undertaker), Bill Clauson (Matt Hawkins), Billy O'Leary (Billy Hawkins), Pamela Wells (Sarah

Hawkins), Paul Dunn (Lincoln Hawkins), Diane Florentine (Sally Hawkins), Jimmie Bates (Jefferson Hawkins), Rex Lease (Hank), Glenn Strange (Lefty), Edmund Cobb (Lem), Dewey Robinson (Miner), Emmett Lynn (Old Codger), Iris Adrian (Dance Hall Hostess), Charles King (Gunman), Ed Peil (Townsman), Lee "Lasses" White (Shot Gun Rider), Gilda Feldrais (Hostess), Billy Engle (Undertaker's Helper), Dave Sharpe (Man Thrown by Widow), Frank Hagney (Barfly), Harry Evans (Card Dealer), Frank Marlow, Ethan Laidlaw, Jerry Jerome, Zon Murray (Cowboys), Wade Crosby (Squint), Murray Leonard (Bartender), George Lewis (Cow Puncher), Jack Shutta (Tough Miner), Mickey Simpson (Big Miner), Forbes Murray.

A fairly inventive idea had the comedy team poking fun at the western hero with Costello cast as a traveling salesman who accidentally becomes involved in killing a man. According to the law of the land, if someone kills another man, he is responsible for the welfare of the surviving family. In this case the widow placed under Costello's care is pretty distasteful, with a whole slew of kids to boot. Naturally, this makes the little comedian untouchable in the eyes of the rest of the men in town, since they want no part of the widow and her brood. Costello lets this new-found power quickly go to his head, allowing himself to be appointed sheriff, and even cleaning the town of its lower elements. Plot is good, though B&L relied too often on their usual antics. (See ABBOTT AND COSTELLO series, Index.)

p, Robert Arthur; d, Charles T. Barton; w, Robert Lees, Frederic I. Rinaldo, John Grant (based on the story by D.D. Beauchamp, William Bowers); ph, Charles Van Enger; m, Walter Schumann; ed, Frank Gross; art d, Bernard Herzbrun, Gabriel Scognamillo; set d, Russell A. Gausman, Charles Wyrick; cos, Rosemary Odell; makeup, Bud Westmore.

Comedy   **(PR:A   MPAA:NR)**

WITCH, THE*   (1969, Ital.) 103m Arco Film/G.G. Productions bw (LA STREGA IN AMORE; AKA: AURA)

Rosanna Schiaffino (Aura), Richard Johnson (Sergio), Sarah Ferrati (Consuelo), Gian Maria Volonte (Fabrizio), Margherita Guzzinati (Lorna).

Johnson is hired by a wealthy widow to help assemble some erotic papers of her late husband, a general, but first he must help the widow and her daughter get rid of Fabrizio, who currently holds the position of historian in the household. Johnson at once is struck by the beauty of the daughter, Schiaffino, and they fall in love, awakening a jealous rage in Fabrizio, her lover. Johnson accidentally kills his rival and the two women help him dispose of the body; it is then that Schiaffino's passion for Johnson dies out and he discovers she is a witch who has already hired another man to replace him. Before he meets the same fate as Fabrizio, he destroys Schiaffino by fire.

p, Alfredo Bini; d, Damiano Damiani; w, Ugo Liberatore, Damiani (based on the novel Aura by Carlos Fuentes); ph, Leonida Barboni; m, Luis Enriquez Bacalov; ed, Nino Baragli; art d, Luigi Scaccianoce; cos, Pier Luigi Pizzi; ch, Robert Curtis.

Horror   **(PR:C   MPAA:R)**

WITCH BENEATH THE SEA, THE   (SEE: MARIZINIA, 1962, U.S./Braz.)

WITCH DOCTOR   (SEE: KISENGA, MAN OF AFRICA, 1952, Brit.)

WITCH WITHOUT A BROOM, A*½   (1967, U.S./Span.) 86m Westside International-L.M. Cinemagic-Lacy International/PRC c (UNA BRUJA SIN ESCOBA)

Jeffrey Hunter (Garver Logan), Maria Perschy (Marianna), Gustavo Rojo (Cayo), Perla Cristal (Octavia), Reginald Gilliam (Don Ignacio), Al Mulock (Wurlitz the Wizard), Katherine Ellison (Yolanda), Felix Dafauce (Necio), Esperanza Roy (Valeria), John Clarke (Chariot Master), Carl Rapp (Proprietor), Susan Talbot, Lewis Gordon, May Johnson, Gillian Simpson, Hercules Cortes.

An American professor in Spain takes a tour through the ages when he ignites the desires of a 15th Century witch. Taking him from modern times to her times, Perschy, as the girl just learning the secrets of black magic, can't figure out how to return to the 20th Century. The two hop around from prehistoric times to ancient Rome, and even into the future, and are not saved until Perschy's father comes to the rescue.

p, Sidney Pink; d, Joe Lacy [Jose E. Lorietta]; w, Howard Berk [Jose Luis Navarro Basso] (based on a story by Basso, Jose Maria E. Lorrieta); ph, Alfonso Nieva (Eastmancolor); m, Fernando Garcia Morcillo; ed, John Horvath; art d, Teddy Villaba; spec eff, Luis Castro.

Fantasy   **(PR:C   MPAA:NR)**

WITCHCRAFT**   (1964, Brit.) 80m Lippert/FOX bw

Lon Chaney, Jr (Morgan Whitlock), Jack Hedley (Bill Lanier), Jill Dixon (Tracy Lanier), Viola Keats (Helen Lanier), Marie Ney (Malvina Lanier), David Weston (Todd Lanier), Diane Clare (Amy Whitlock), Yvette Rees (Vanessa Whitlock), Barry Linehan (Myles Forrester), Victor Brooks (Inspec-

tor Baldwin), Marianne Stone (Forrester's Secretary), John Dunbar (Doctor), Hilda Fenemore (Nurse).

Decent horror film has Chaney, a witch, trying to protect the family cemetery from being dug up by archenemy, Hedley. The cemetery is filled with witches burned at the stake 300 years earlier, and initial bulldozing causes them to be revived from their deep slumber. A number of mysterious happenings occur, mainly directed at the family of Hedley, but the discovery of Chaney's true identity soon puts an end to the hokum. Production maintains proper atmosphere of eeriness, which theater owners tried to heighten during WITCHCRAFT's initial release by issuing witch deflectors to patrons. One of the last roles in which Chaney was called upon to actually act, he appeared to be a bit rusty.

p, Robert Lippert, Jack Parsons; d, Don Sharp; w, Harry Spalding; ph, Arthur Lavis; m, Carlo Martelli; ed, Robert Winter; art d, George Provis; makeup, Harold Fletcher.

Horror   **(PR:A   MPAA:NR)**

WITCHES, THE   (SEE: DEVIL'S OWN, THE, 1967, Brit.)

WITCHES, THE*½   (1969, Fr./Ital.) 100m DD-Les Productions Artistes Associes/Lo pert Films c (LE STREGHE; LES SORCIERES)

"The Witch Burned Alive": Silvana Mangano (Gloria), Annie Girardot (Valeria), Francisco Rabal (Valeria's Husband), Massimo Girotti (Sportsman), Elsa Albani (Gossip), Helmut Steinberger [Berger] (Waiter), Veronique Vendell (Young Girl Friend), Bruno Filippini (Singer), Leslie French (Industrialist), Dino Mele (Waiter), Marilu Tolo, Clara Clamai, Nora Ricci; "Civic Sense": Silvano Mangano (Lady), Alberto Sordi (Truckdriver), "A Night Like Any Other: Silvana Mangano (Giovanna), Clint Eastwood (Her Husband), Armando Bottin (Nembo Kid), Gianni Gori (Diabolik), Paolo Gozlino (Mandrake), Angelo Santi (Flash Gordon), Piero Torrisi (Batman), Valentino Macchi (Man at stadium), Franco Moruzzi (Sadik), Toto (Ciancicato Miao), Ninetto Davoli (Baciu Miao), Laura Betti (A Tourist), Luigi Leoni (Her Husband), Mario Cipriani (Priest), Pietro Tordi (Father).

Some of Italy's most talented directors were gathered together to make this monstrosity of short segments, none well developed nor worth a glance, with the possible exception of Visconti's effort. In "The Witch Burned Alive," Mangano plays a famous film star staying at a resort in the Alps where she is the center of attention. The men eye her because they adore her, and the women because all they can think about is scratching her eyes out. Beyond all the attention, Mangano in a lonely and isolated woman, pregnant by a husband who does not want her to have a child. The other segments are not worth mentioning.

"The Witch Burned Alive; " d, Luchino Visconti, w, Giuseppe Patroni Griffi, Cesare Zavattini; ed, Mario Serandrei; "Civic Sense"; d, Mauro Bolognini; w, Agenore Incrocci, Furio Scarpelli, Bernardino Zapponi; ed, Nino Baragli; "The Earth As Seen from the Moon"; d&w, Pier Paolo Pasolini; ed, Baragli; "The Girl from Sicily"; d, Franco Rossi; w, Rossi, Luigi Mann; ed, Giorgio Serralonga; "A Night Like Any Other"; d, Vittorio De Sica; w, Zavattini, Fabio Carpi, Enzio Muzii; ed, Adriana Novelli. Overall: p, Dino de Laurentiis; ph, Giuseppe Rotunno (Technicolor); m, Piero Piccioni; art d, Mario Garbuglia, Piero Poletto; cos, Piero Tosi; spec eff, Joseph Nathanson; makeup, Goffredo Rocchetti.

Drama   **(PR:C   MPAA:NR)**

WITCHES CURSE, THE   (SEE: WITCH'S CURSE, THE, 1963, Ital.)

WITCHES--VIOLATED AND TORTURED TO DEATH
                          (SEE: MARK OF THE DEVIL II, 1975,

WITCHFINDER GENERAL   (SEE: CONQUEROR WORM, THE, 1968, Brit.)

WITCHING, THE   (SEE: NECROMANCY, 1972)

WITCHING HOUR, THE**   (1934) 69m PAR bw

Sir Guy Standing (Martin Prentice), John Halliday (Jack Brookfield), Judith allen (Nancy Brookfield), Tom Brown (Clay Thorne), Olive Tell (Mrs. Thorne), William Frawley (Foreman of Jury), Richard Carle (Lew Ellinger), Ralf Harolde (Frank Hardmuth), Purnell Pratt (District Attorney), Frank Sheridan (Chief of Police), Gertrude Michael (Margaret Price), Ferdinand Gottschalk (Dr. Meiklejohn), John Larkin, Selmer Jackson, Howard Lang, George Webb, Robert Littlefield.

Halliday, a clairvoyant gifted also with mesmeric powers, runs a gambling den. He inadvertently hypnotizes his daughter's (Allen) young suitor, Brown, while threatening to kill a rascally politician. Mesmerized, Brown actually does the dirty deed. Retired attorney Standing, learning that other lawyers have refused to take Brown's case because of their disbelief in his hypnotic motivation, undertakes the young man's defense. Audiences similarly inclined to suspend disbelief will enjoy this well-paced, well-acted courtroom thriller.

p, Bayard Veiller; d, Henry Hathaway; w, Salisbury Field, Anthony Veiller (based on the play by Augustus Thomas); ph, Ben Reynolds; ed, Jack Dennis; art d, Earl Hedrick.

Drama   **(PR:A   MPAA:NR)**

WITCHMAKER, THE*½   (1969) 97m Las Cruces-Arrow
Films/Excelsior c (AKA: LEGEND OF WITCH HOLLOW)

John Lodge (*Luther the Beserk*), Alvy Moore (*Dr. Ralph Hayes*), Thordis Brandt (*Anastasia/"Tasha"*), Anthony Eisley (*Victor Gordon*), Shelby Grant (*Maggie*), Robyn Millan (*Sharon the Students*), Tony Benson (*Owen, the Student*), Helen Winston (*Jessie One, Old Witch*), Warrene Ott (*Jessie Two, Young Witch*), Burt Mustin (*Boatman*), Kathy Lynn (*Patty Ann*), Sue Bernard (*Felicity Johnson*), Howard Viet (*San Blas*), Nancy Crawford (*Goody Hale*), Patricia Wymer (*Hag of Devon*), Carolyn Rhodimer (*Marta*), Diane Webber (*Nautch of Tangier*), Larry Vincent (*Amos Coffin*), Del Kaye (*Le Singe*), Gwen Lipscomb (*Fong Quai*), Valya Garanda (*El A Haish Ma*).

A group of witch hunters led by parapsychology professor Moore journeys into the swamps of Louisiana to seek the cause behind the murders of eight young woman, all apparently the victims of witchcraft. They encounter a devious warlock who sets his aims on Brandt, a member of the group with an ancestor who was a witch, and who thus possesses a few secret powers of her own. Numbered among the members of the called-up coven is Webber, whose still pictures were said to have been the inspiration behind *Playboy* magazine, and a couple of centerfolds from that publication. Actor Moore was associate producer; horror-film *auteur* and actor L. Q. Jones was executive producer. Location scenes filmed in the Louisiana swamps.

p,d&w, William O. Brown; ph, John Arthur Morrill (Techniscope, Technicolor); m, Jaime Mendoza-Nava.

Horror   **(PR:C   MPAA:M)**

WITCH'S CURSE, THE*½   (1963, Ital.) 78m Panda-L'Industria
Cinematografica Italiana/Medallion c (MACISTE ALL'INFERNO; AKA: THE WITCHES CURSE)

Kirk Morris (*Maciste*), Helene Chanel (*Matha Gunt*), Vira Silenti (*Young Martha Gunt*), Andrea Bosic (*Parris*), Angelo Zanolli (*Charley Law*), John Karlsen (*Burgermaster*), John Francis Lane (*Coachman*), Howard Nelson Rubien (*Old Villager*), Neil Robinson (*Villager*), Charles Fawcett (*Doctor*), Mauro Donatella, Gina Mascetti, Antonella Della Porta, Antonio Cianci, Remo De Angelis, Evaristo Maran.

Body builder Morris plays a 17th-Century Scottish shepherd given the job of combatting the curse set upon a small town by a witch burned at the stake. To accomplish his feat he descends the steps of hell for a direct confrontation with the wicked lady.

p, Ermanno Donati, Luigi Carpentieri; d, Riccardo Freda; w, Oreste Biancoli, Piero Pierotti, Ennio De Concini (based on the story by Eddy H. Given from the film "Maciste al, Inferno" by Guido Brignone); ph, Riccardo Pallottini (CinemaScope, Eastmancolor); m, Carlo Franci; ed, Ornella Micheli; art d, Andrea Crisanti; set d, Luciano Spadoni; spec eff, Serse Urbisaglia.

Horror   **(PR:A   MPAA:NR)**

WITCH'S MIRROR, THE*   (1960, Mex.) 75m Cinematografica
A.B.S.A./K. Gordon Murray-Trans International bw (EL ESPEJO DE LA BRUJA)

Armando Calvo (*Husband*), Rosita Arenas (*Wife*), Isabela Corona (*Witch*), Dina de Marco.

Weird tale of love from beyond the grave, only here it's the dead person, godchild to a witch, that's jealous of her husband's new wife. So much so that the witch conjures up her ghost to come back and haunt the couple, causing the husband to mar the face of his pretty wife. To try to regain her old features, he goes about taking skin from corpses and grafting it to his wife's face.

p, Abel Salazar; d, Chano Urueta; w, Alfredo Ruanova, Carlos Enrique Taboada, Urueta; ph, Jorge Stahl, Jr.; m, Gustavo Cesar Carrion; ed, Alfredo Rosas Priego; art d, Javier Torres Torija.

Horror   **(PR:C   MPAA:NR)**

WITH A SMILE***   (1939, Fr.) 80m Pathe bw (AVEC LE SOURIRE)

Maurice Chevalier (*Victor Larnois*), Marie Glory (*Gisele*), Andre Lefaur (*Mons. Villary*), Paule Andral (*Mme. Villary*), Marcel Vallee (*Pascaud*), Marcel Simon (*Opera Superintendent*), Milly Mathis (*Cachier*).

Charming scoundrel Chevalier, lacking so much as a sou, falls for the glories of Glory, a music-hall chorine. To be near his inamorata, he arranges for the theater's doorman to be dismissed, then charms his way into the job. Chevalier's *bonhomie* is such that he wins the hand of Glory, then is given the post of secretary to the theater's proprietor, Lefaur. Since he controls the books in this position, he is soon able to arrange a quarrel between Lefaur and the latter's business partner, thereby gaining a partnership. Then, with the help of his bride, he gulls his partner out of his share of the

theater. Chevalier's further ambition is realized when he blackmails his way into the directorship of the Paris Opera House. Encountering his former employer Lefaur–now destitute–Chevalier magnanimously offers him the job of secretary, never realizing that he has now put his nemesis into a position to topple him, using his own means. (In French; English subtitles.)

p&d, Maurice Tourneur; w, Louis Verneuil (based on his play "Avec le Sourire"); ph, Thiraud and Nee; art d&set d, Carre and Cartingny; m/l, Marcel Lattes, Borrell Clerc; English titles, Herman G. Weinberg.

Drama/Comedy   **(PR:A   MPAA:NR)**

WITH A SONG IN MY HEART***½   (1952) 116m FOX c

Susan Hayward (*Jane Froman*), Rory Calhoun (*John Burns*), David Wayne (*Don Ross*), Thelma Ritter (*Clancy*), Robert Wagner (*GI Paratrooper*), Helen Westcott (*Jennifer March*), Una Merkel (*Sister Marie*), Richard Allan (*Dancer*), Max Showalter (*Guild*), Lyle Talbot (*Radio Director*), Leif Erickson (*General*), Stanley Logan (*Diplomat*), Jane Froman (*Singing Voice of Jane Froman*), Frank Sully (*Texas*), George Offerman (*Muleface*), Ernest Newton (*Specialty*), William Baldwin (*Announcer*), Carlos Molina, Nestor Paiva, Emmett Vogan (*Doctors*), Maude Wallace (*Sister Margaret*), Dick Ryan (*Officer*), Douglas Evans (*Colonel*), Beverly Thompson (*USO Girl*), Eddie Firestone (*USO Man*).

So many film biographies about musical stars have been just so much hogwash, contrived stories that have only been written to serve the music. In many cases, such liberties have been taken that even the person being lionized would not have recognized their own lives. In this film, there were some bent facts but, by and large, it hewed closely to singer Jane Froman's life and is an excellent movie about what happened regarding her exciting career and tragic accident. Hayward is Froman and the picture begins as she's being given an award at a ball tossed by the Newspapermen of New York. The award is handed her for her courage. Calhoun and Ritter are seated in the audience and, as Hayward sings, they reminisce about her life and times. It's 1936 and Hayward is a young singer on the brink of stardom. She walks into a Cincinnati radio station to audition and meets Wayne, whom she believes to be the man in charge. She sings a tune for him and he thinks she should take it down a bit, be more understated. Wayne is not the director and when the real man in charge enters, Talbot, he listens to Hayward and suggests that she turn on her charm and be a bit more dramatic. Hayward and Wayne get together, have a chuckle, and she is signed to a deal on the show. Her radio appearances shoot her into instant recognition. She plays Radio City, the New York Paramount, and becomes an important performer across the country. All the while, Wayne is at her side and asking for her hand in marriage. Hayward can't make up her mind about Wayne but eventually succumbs and they are wed. No sooner has she been taken across the threshhold when problems arise. He's not having any success and is terribly jealous of her talent. World War II breaks out and Hayward, who needs to get away from Wayne, volunteers to entertain the troops. She's on her way to Portugal, a neutral country, where she will then go off to wherever she is to be assigned. On the plane, she meets Calhoun, the pilot, and he presses her into service to show the other passengers how to use the life vests, just in case anything might happen and they have to go down in the sea. The plane is getting close to the Portuguese coast when it is forced to land in the Atlantic. Hayward barely survives the crash and is taken to a Lisbon hospital after Calhoun rescues her from a watery grave. Her nurse is Ritter (a fictional character) and the tough bird and Hayward become fast friends. (Both women were nominated for Oscars. Alfred Newman won for his musical direction.) It looks as though Hayward's mobility will be gone forever. Her right leg was nearly cut off and her left knee is a mass of bone chips. Calhoun has fallen in love with Hayward and tells her that, but she, realizing that she's a married woman, holds back her own passion toward him. At one point, the doctors are considering amputating her right leg, then they decide that U.S. medicos might be able to save it so Wayne comes to Portugal and returns with Hayward to the U.S. where she must undergo a series of painful operations. Ritter comes back to the States and to Hayward's side and, in between surgeries, Wayne engages a piano player so her voice will stay in shape. Wearing a huge cast up to her hip, Hayward attempts a comeback in "Artists and Models" on Broadway and the public welcomes her back with applause and ovations. But the physical woes are still with her and Hayward must go to the hospital again for further surgery. Once on her shaky feet, Hayward accepts a booking at a New York nightclub and both Calhoun and Wayne are there. Wayne now knows about Calhoun and there is a confrontation between the two. Hayward can't handle the loves in her life so she goes back to working in front of the servicemen in Europe. She's hobbled by crutches but her magnificent voice has not been affected. Ritter accompanies her on her trip, which is a great success. She's about ready to come back and Wayne calls to tell her that she won't be coming home to him. He's had it and she can do whatever she wants to do now. She arrives back in the U.S. where Calhoun is waiting to take her into his life. Jane Froman's voice was used and Hayward mimed to the glorious sounds as she sang a host of tunes from various writers. They include: "California, Here I Come" (Buddy De Sylva, Al Jolson, Joseph Meyer), "Alabamy Bound" (De Sylva, Jolson, Meyer, Bud Green), "Blue Moon" (Richard Rodgers, Lorenz Hart), "With a Song in My Heart" (Rodgers, Hart), "Dixie" (Daniel D. Emmett), "Tea for Two" (Irving Caesar, Vincent Youmans), "That Old Feeling" (Sammy Fain, Lew Brown), "I've Got a Feelin' You're Foolin'" (Nacio Herb Brown, Arthur Freed), "It's a Good Day" (Dave Barbour, Peggy Lee), "I'll Walk Alone" (Sammy Cahn, Jule Styne), "They're Either Too Young or Too Old" (Frank Loesser, Arthur Schwartz), "Chicago" (Fred Fisher), "America, the Beautiful" (Samuel Ward, Katherine Lee Bates), "I'm Through with Love" (Gus Kahn, Matty Malneck, Fud Livingston), "On the Gay White Way" (Ralph Rainger, Leo Robin), "Embraceable You" (George, Ira Gershwin), "Jim's Toasted Peanuts," "Wonderful Home Sweet Home" (Ken Darby), "Get Happy" (Ted Koehler, Harold Arlen), "Carry Me Back to Old Virginny" (James Bland), "Give My Regards to Broadway" (George M. Cohan), "Deep in the Heart of Texas" (Don Swander, June Hershey), "The Right Kind of Love" (Charles Henderson, Don George), "Maine Stein Song" (Lincoln Colcord, E.A. Fenstad), "Montparnasse" (Eliot Daniel, Alfred Newman), "Hoe that Corn" (Jack Woodford, Max Showalter), "Back Home Again in Indiana" (James F. Hanley, Ballard MacDonald) plus snippets of more tunes. As you can see by the list of music, this is almost a singalog as well as being a biography. Look for Robert Wagner as a shell-shocked serviceman (his fifth movie) and Una Merkel doing an amusing cameo as a nun. Jeanne Crain wanted to play the role but Froman had something to say and chose Hayward, a smart decision. One of the reasons the looping was so good is that Hayward actually sang the songs (with no recording) so her neck muscles and mouth were right on the money. An expensive wardrobe by LeMaire featured more than 40 costumes, in keeping with Froman's reputation as a clotheshorse that won her a mention on the "Ten Best Dressed Women" list. Uncredited background singing in the film was done by "The Skylarks," "The Modernaires," "The Melody Men," "The King's Men," "The Starlighters," and "The Four Girlfriends." A most satisfying film on all levels starring a woman who always gave her best, Brooklynite Edythe Marrener, who was nominated five times for the coveted Oscar under her screen name of Susan Hayward.

p, Lamar Trotti; d, Walter Lang; w, Trotti; ph, Leon Shamroy (Technicolor); ed, J. Watson Webb; md, Alfred Newman; art d, Lyle Wheeler, Joseph C. Wright, Earle Hagen; set d, Thomas Little, Walter M. Scott; cos, Charles LeMaire; spec eff, Fred Sersen, Ray Kellog; ch, Billy Daniel; makeup, Ben Nye.

Musical/Biography   (PR:A   MPAA:NR)

WITH FIRE AND SWORD   (SEE: INVASION 1700, 1965,
                                                                Fr./Ital./Yugo.)

WITH GUNILLA MONDAY EVENING AND TUESDAY
                                                    (SEE: GUILT, 1967, Swed.)

WITH JOYOUS HEART (SEE: TWO WEEKS IN SEPTEMBER, 1967,
                                                                Fr./Brit.)

WITH LOVE AND KISSES*   (1937) 67m Melody bw

Kane Richmond (*Don Gray*), Russell Hopton (*Flash Henderson*), Peters Sisters (*Themselves*), Arthur Housman (*Gilbert Holbrook*), Fuzzy Knight (*Butch*), Jerry Bergen and Billy Gray (*Themselves*), G. Pat Collins (*Joe*), Olaf Hytten (*Dickson*), Bunny Bronson (*Jane*), Bob McKenzie (*Mayor Jones*), Eva McKenzie (*Mrs. Higgins*), Bruce Mitchell (*Desk Sergeant*), Kernan Kripps (*Turnkey*), Si Jenks (*Sheriff Wade*), Chelito and Gabriel, Pinky Tomlin, Toby Wing.

An awful film in which a bunch of people get all excited about several horrible songs Tomlin creates while milking his cows. Songs include "Don't Ever Lose It," I'm Right Back Where I Started" (Coy Poe, Pinky Tomlin), "The Trouble with Me is You" (Harry Tobias, Tomlin), "Sweet" (Buddy LeRoux, Tomlin, Al Heath), "With Love and Kisses" (Connie Lee), "Sittin' on the Edge of My Chair" (Paul Parks, Poe, Tomlin).

p, Maurice Conn; d, Les Goodwins; w, Sherman L. Lowe (based on a story by Al Martin, Lowe); ph, Arthur Reed; ed, Martin G. Cohn; md, Eddie Kay.

Musical   (PR:A   MPAA:NR)

WITH LOVE AND TENDERNESS½   (1978, Bulgaria) 100m
Bulgarofilm-Meadost Creative Group c (S LYUBOV I NEZHNOST)

Alexander Dyakov (*Sasho*), Tsvetana Eneva (*Lotte*), Gergana Gerassimova (*Patricia*), Yossif Surchadijev (*The Architect*), Theodor Youroukov (*The Artist*).

Sculptor Dyakov, an artistic recluse living in a Black Sea resort area, is besieged by sycophantic well-wishers. Isolated for years, supported by donations from local fishermen and village folk, he and his German-born wife are interrupted by a visit from an architect and an artist from the big city, who inform him that the sculpture on which he has devoted his energies for many years has been singled out for exhibit. He will be paid a large sum of money--the price established by the Communist government-- for the long-awaited work. The destitute sculptor agrees to accept the substantial sum, but he has gnawing doubts about the sculpture, believing it to be unfinished. Following a night's celebration at which he drunkenly quarrels with his friends and neighbors, he decides that the answer is suicide. At dawn, he puts out to sea in his boat, intending to drown himself. His discovery of the architect's small, charming daughter as a stowaway finishes this plan. A late work by one of the most influential post-WW II

Bulgarian directors, Vulchanov, with his frequent collaborater, scripter Petrov. The latter is one of the most respected Eastern European writers, responsible also for translating many of Shakespeare's works into his own tongue.

d, Rangel Vulchanov; w, Valeri Petrov; ph, Dimko Minov; m, Kiril Donchev; art d, Maria Ivanova.

Drama   (PR:A   MPAA:NR)

WITH SIX YOU GET EGGROLL***   (1968) 95m Arwin-Cinema
                    Center/NGP c (AKA: A MAN IN MOMMY'S BED)

Doris Day (*Abby McClure*), Brian Keith (*Jake Iverson*), Pat Carroll (*Maxine Scott*), Barbara Hershey [Seagull] (*Stacey Iverson*), George Carlin (*Herbie Flack*), Alice Ghostley (*Housekeeper*), John Findlater (*Flip McClure*), Jimmy Brachen (*Mitch McClure*), Richard Steele (*Jason McClure*), Herbert Voland (*Harry Scott*), Allan Melvin (*Desk Sergeant*), Elaine Devry (*Cleo*), Peter Leeds (*Police Officer Joelson*), Victor [Vic] Tayback (*Chicken Truck Driver*), Jamie Farr (*JoJo*), William Christopher (*Zip*), Pearl Shear (*Laughing Lady*), Mickey Deems (*Sam Bates*), Milton Frome (*Bud Young*), John Copage (*Lumberyard Employee*), Lord Nelson (*Calico the Dog*), The Grass Roots, Jackie Joseph.

The perennial virgin's last picture before going on to her successful TV series. Day is a widow with three sons and a sheepdog, the successful proprietress of a lumberyard; Keith is a widower with a daughter and a French poodle. Brought together at a party by inveterate matchmaker Carroll, Day's sister, Keith and Day are embarrassed by the forced encounter. Meeting again by accident at an all-night market, the two fall in love and elope. On their return, they find that their respective offspring are constantly at odds, and that even their dogs hate one another. Keith buys a recreational vehicle so that he and his bride can have some privacy, but their families' disputes provoke an argument between them and she drives off, inadvertently dumping Keith from the vehicle clad only in his underwear and clutching a teddy bear. When she discovers Keith's loss, Day attempts to find him, assisted by a group of hippies led by Farr. Meanwhile, Keith looks for her. After a series of misadventures, both end up in a police station. Hearing of their parents' misfortune, all the children race to their defense, united at last. This was one of six unsuccessful scripts selected for Day by her ailing husband, producer Melcher, in the last years of his life (he died before the film's release). Melcher was widely reported to have done no work at all on these films, save for collecting his customary fee of $150,000 and selecting the scripts (toward the end he had chronic diarrhea, a condition that may lead readers to an appropriate analogy). The beaded, bearded, charismatic hippie leader played by Farr, joyfully joining Day in the chase, appears to have portended something truly sinister. A year after this picture's release, members of the Charles Manson "family" murdered actress Sharon Tate and four other people in the Bel-Air house recently vacated by Day's son Terrence Jordan and his live-in girl friend Candice Bergen. Jordan, a record producer, had auditioned would-be songwriter Manson and had rejected his tunes. Day suspected that Manson, a Farr character lookalike, might have been after her son.

p, Martin Melcher; d, Howard Morris; w, Gwen Bagni, Paul Dubov, Harvey Bullock, R. S. Allen (based on the story by Bagni, Dubov); ph, Ellsworth Fredricks, Harry Stradling, Jr. (Panavision, DeLuxe Color); ed, Adrienne Fazan; art d, Cary Odell; set d, James Berkey; cos, Glenn Connelly; spec eff, David Lee; makeup, Harry Maret, Emile LaVigne; m/l, "You Make Me Want You," Robert Mesey, Robert Hilliard.

Comedy   **Cas.**   (PR:A   MPAA:G)

WITHIN THE LAW   (SEE: PAID, 1930)

WITHIN THE LAW**   (1939) 65m MGM bw

Ruth Hussey (*Mary Turner*), Tom Neal (*Richard Gilder*), Paul Kelly (*Joe Garson*), William Gargan (*Cassidy*), Paul Cavanagh ("*English Eddie*"), Rita Johnson (*Agnes*), Samuel S. Hinds (*Mr. Gilder*), Lynne Carver (*June*), Sidney Blackmer (*George Demarest*), Jo Ann Sayers (*Helen Morris*), James Burke ("*Red*"), Ann Morriss (*Saleswoman*), Donald Douglas (*Inspector Burke*), Cliff Clark (*McGuire*), Claude King (*Art Dealer*).

When a guilty coworker plants stolen goods in her locker, innocent store clerk Hussey is accused of the crime and sent to prison, even though Neal, the son of store owner Hinds, knows of her innocence. The embittered Hussey spends her three years in prison studying law, finding unethical ways of making money through legal loopholes without risking conviction. Released after serving time for three years, the vengeful Hussey puts her studies to work for her while simultaneously vamping Neal. She finds, at the picture's conclusion, that even near crime doesn't pay. This is the fourth version of Veiller's 1912 Broadway hit. Two silents appeared in 1917 and 1923 and a sound version, PAID, starred Joan Crawford. Czech director Machaty's first feature film in the U.S. (he was well known as the director of 1933's ECSTASY which first brought Hedy Lamarr--in her entirety--to the attention of Hollywood). The screenplay is updated with modern touches. The department store owned by Hinds sells private airplanes, anticipating Dallas's Neiman Marcus store by some years. Neal thus becomes a dashing pilot, demonstrating an aircraft to the unrecognized Hussey after her release.

p, Lou Ostrow; d, Gustav Machaty; w, Charles Lederer, Edith Fitzgerald (based on the play by Bayard Veiller); ph, Charles Lawton; m, Dr, William Axt; ed, George Boemler.

Crime/Drama   **(PR:A MPAA:NR)**

WITHIN THESE WALLS**   (1945) 71m FOX bw

Thomas Mitchell (*Michael Howland*), Mary Anderson (*Anne Howland*), Edward Ryan (*Tommie Howland*), Mark Stevens (*Steve Russel*), B.S. Pully (*Harry Bowser*), Roy Roberts (*Martin Deutsch*), John Russell (*Rogers*), Norman Lloyd (*Peter Moran*), Edward Kelly (*Tommy Callahan*), Harry Shannon (*McCaffrey, Assistant Warden*), Rex Williams (*Hobey Jenkins*), Ralph Dunn (*Pearson*), Dick Rush (*Station Agent*), William Halligan (*Collins*), Freddie Graham (*Stunt Guard*), Joseph Bernard, Jack Daley, Louis Bacigalupi, Otto Reichow, Charles Wagenheim, Frank Scannell, Lennie Bremen, Steve Olsen, Harry Strang, Bob Perry, Paul Newlan, James Flavin, Eddie Hart, Dick Rich, Max Wagner.

Mitchell, a hanging judge who is as iron-handed at home as he is in his courtroom, accepts a proferred assignment as warden of a riot-plagued prison. He imposes the strictest of discipline on the institution. His two children, daughter Anderson and son Ryan, on whom the rod has not been spared, take different paths. The compassionate Anderson becomes romantically involved with Stevens, a model prisoner–wrongfully convicted–who has become Mitchell's chauffeur. Delinquent son Ryan turns to serious crime, turning up in his own father's prison as a result. Joining other prisoners in a jailbreak scheme, Ryan sees his father threatened, and tries to save him. The boy dies in the process, causing the enraged Mitchell himself to shoot it out with his son's convict killer. His son's redemption and death brings Mitchell to a newly empathic view of his charges and he begins a program of prison reforms.

p, Ben Silvey; d, H. Bruce Humberstone; w, Eugene Ling, Wanda Tuchock (based on the story by Coles Trapnell, James B. Fisher); ph, Glen MacWilliams, Clyde DeVinna; m, David Buttolph; ed, Harry Reynolds; md, Emil Newman; art d, Lyle Wheeler; Richard Irvine; set d, Thomas Little, Ernest Lansing; spec eff, Fred Sersen.

Drama   **(PR:A MPAA:NR)**

WITHOUT A HOME**½   (1939, Pol.) 90m Foreign Cinema Arts bw

Adam Domb (*Jacob Elchonon*), Alexander Marten (*Awrejmel*), Ida Kaminska (*Bas Shewe*), Ben Zuker (*Henoch*), Sz. Dzigan (*Motel*), J. Shumacher (*Fishel*), Vera Gran (*Bessie*), Dora Fakiel (*Lina*).

Marten, a Polish Jew, migrates to the land of gold-paved streets leaving his wife, Kaminska, and his children behind in the old country. Once in America, Marten falls hard for cafe singer Gran, who is selflessly attempting to help his family to join him. When Kaminska arrives with their only surviving child–another son drowned–Marten subdues his unconfessed passion for Gran. When the surviving son is also thought to have been drowned, Kaminska's mind is affected. Saved by elderly fisherman Domb, the boy is returned and Kaminska recovers her senses; life goes on. Directed by its star Marten, the Polish-made drama features the entire cast of the Warsaw Art Theater. (In Yiddish; English subtitles.)

p, Adolph Mann; d, Alexander Marten; w, based on the play "Ahn a Heim" by Jacob Gordin; ph, Jonilowicz; m/l, Sajewiez; English titles, George Roland, Leonora Fleischer.

Drama   **(PR:A MPAA:NR)**

WITHOUT A TRACE**   (1983) 121m FOX c

Kate Nelligan (*Susan Selky*), Judd Hirsch (*Al Menetti*), David Dukes (*Graham Selky*), Stockard Channing (*Jocelyn Norris*), Jacqueline Brookes (*Margaret Mayo*), Keith McDermott (*Phillippe*), Kathleen Widdoes (*Ms. Hauser*), Daniel Bryan Corkill (*Alex Selky*), Cheryl Giannini (*Pat Menetti*), David Simon (*Eugene Menetti*), William Duell (*Polygraph Operator*), Joan McMonagle (*Vivienne Grant*), Louise Stubbs (*Malvina Robbins*), Deborah Carlson (*Naomi Blum*), Charles Brown (*Sachs*), Sheila M. Coonan (*Anna*), Peter Brash (*Mr. Garrett*), L. Scott Caldwell (*Janet Smith*), Ellen Barber (*Martina*), Theodore Sorel (*Dr. Mandlebaum*), Sam J. Coppola (*Schoyer*), Elaine Bromka (*Production Assistant*), Roger Kozol (*Makeup Man*), Caroline Aaron (*Makeup Woman*), Lee Sandman (*Coffee Shop Owner*), Fred Coffin (*Officer Coffin*), Marissa Ryan (*Justine Norris*), Dan Lauria (*Baker*), Donny Burke (*Ward*), Stephanie Ann Levy (*Marcia Menetti*), Peggy Woody, Kathrin King Segal (*Girls on Movie Line*), Marcella Lowery (*Sgt. Rocco*), Luke Sickle (*Hank*), Jane Cecil (*Mrs. Applegate*), Todd Winters (*Technician*), Timothy Minor (*Soundman*), Lynn Cohen (*Woman with Dog*), Kymbra Callaghan (*Hairdresser*), Ronald Barber (*Guard*), Carolotta A. DeVaughn (*Correction Officer*), Robert Ott Boyle, Joseph M. Costa, Richmond Hoxie, Elizabeth Lathram, Terrance K. O'Quinn, Angela Pietropinto, Tory Wood, (*Parents*), Don Amendolia, Tony Devon, Thomas Kopache, Lou Leccese, Mark McGovern, Steve Mendillo, Bob Scarantino, Martin Shakar, Bill Smitrovich (*Police*), Ashby Adams, Hy R. Agens, MacKenzie Allen, Peter Burnell, Bruce Carr, Maria Cellario, Gregory Chase, Paul Collins, Ken Cory, William Fowler, Edmund Genest, Roxanne Gregory, Gracie Harrison,

Richmond Hoxie, W. H. Macy, Freda Foh Shen, James Storm, Brenda Thomas, Allan Weeks, Hattie Winston (*Reporters*).

In its time, an intensely topical picture. Young mother Nelligan, whose husband recently left her for a younger woman, loses her 6-year-old son as well when he disappears while walking to school. Her upper lip staying stiff throughout her ordeal, she contacts the police–notably detective Hirsch–and traces all possible leads to try to regain her lost boy. Intimations of physical mutilation and sexual abuse abound. The major suspect in the boy's disappearance is a homosexual youth who has a record of child molestation, but he turns out to be a false lead. The mother's story is told with uncharacteristic restraint. In a welcome deviation from cinematic convention, Nelligan and her husband do not get together again, united by their grief, nor do Nelligan and Hirsch form a romantic attachment to one another. At the film's happy conclusion, the boy proves to have been abducted by an old woman, who wanted him to help her with her chores. Mother and son are reunited. Based on an actual case which had a less sugary ending, the picture raised public consciousness, as did its made-for-TV counterpart ADAM. Snapshots of missing children began appearing on milk cartons, in buses, and on TV news programs.

p&d, Stanley R. Jaffe; w, Beth Gutcheon (based on her novel *Still Missing*); ph, John Bailey (DeLuxe Color); m, Jack Nitzsche; ed, Cynthia Scheider; prod d, Paul Sylbert; art d, Gregory Bolton; set, Alan Hicks; cos, Gloria Gresham.

Drama   **Cas.**   **(PR:A MPAA:PG)**

WITHOUT APPARENT MOTIVE***   (1972, Fr.) 102m
                President-Cineteleuro/FOX c (SANS MOBILE APPARENT)

Jean-Louis Trintignant (*Stephane Carella*), Dominique Sanda (*Sandra Forest*), Sacha Distel (*Julien Sabirnou*), Carla Gravina (*Jocelyne Rocca*), Paul Crauchet (*Francis Palombo*), Laura Antonelli (*Juliette Vaudreuil*), Jean-Pierre Marielle (*Perry Rupert-Foote*), Stephane Audran (*Helene Vallee*), Pierre Dominique (*Di Bozzo*), Erich Segal (*Hans Kleinberg*), Jean-Jacques Delbo (*Commissioner*), Gilles Segal (*Bozzo*), Andre Falcon (*Mayor*), Alexis Sellan (*Pierre Barroyer*), Esmeralda Ruspoli (*Mme. Forest*), Michel Bardinet (*Tony Forest*).

A deft thriller in the hardboiled tradition of Raymond Chandler and Dashiell Hammett, this story of murderous revenge opens with Bardinet, a wealthy Frenchman, being gunned down in broad daylight. Trintignant is the detective assigned to the case but he can find no motive behind the slaying. Soon Erich Segal, an astrologer, and Sellan, a roguish older man, are killed in the same mysterious way. Trintignant is convinced a link exists between the three deaths, yet has nothing to go on. A slim thread of hope comes when Sanda, Bardinet's stepdaughter, gives the detective a pocket diary that had belonged to the dead man. The diary contains, among other things, a list of Bardinet's lovers. One woman on this role call is Gravina, a former passion of Trintignant's as well. Gravina meets the detective at his flat, hoping to rekindle their affair. After it's revealed that she had known all three of the murdered men Gravina leaves, disappointed this liaison was for business reasons rather than a sexual encounter. Before Trintignant can catch up with her, a shot rings out, adding Gravina to the list of mysterious sniper killings. Trintignant goes with Sanda to a local university, acting on a tip from her boy friend, television personality Distel. There they recover a theater program from a play performed some eight years earlier. Trintignant sees that the first four names on the cast list have all been victims of the mysterious sniper. Distel is the next name in the cast. Trintignant rushes to an outdoor location where Distel is shooting his television program and manages to save him just as the sniper's gun goes off. Audran, another member of the play's cast, goes to the police. She tells about a long-ago cast party which had gotten out of hand, turning into an all-out orgy. During it the male cast members gang-raped Antonelli, a shy actress also appearing in the play. Trintignant goes to Antonelli's apartment but is met by her husband Marielle, who shoots at the detective with a high-powered rifle. Trintignant fires back, killing the man. Antonelli is taken away by authorities and her secret is exposed. As a result of the gang rape Antonelli had gone mad and her husband decided to assassinate those responsible in his quest for revenge. Trintignant, beaten by the horrors he has experienced in this case, decides that the time has come for him to leave police work. Though the plot, adapted from a pulp novel by Ed McBain, clearly takes its cue from *film noir*, director Labro takes some interesting chances with his adaptation. Rather than use the classic darkened settings of a 1940s crime film, Labro shoots in the sun-drenched streets of the French Riviera city of Nice. Despite the antithetical settings, the mood is just as dark here as in a good Humphrey Bogart crime story. Labro slowly but surely builds up a feeling of impending doom, holding the mystery's solution until the very end and maintaining a consistent mood. The background music enhances the atmosphere, a pulsating rhythm that adds to these feelings. Labro also understands the essentials of creating a thriller, building suspense before letting out the short bursts of violence. As the lone detective Trintignant also owes a great deal to his cinematic forerunner. His performance, filled with suppressed emotions, shows the influence of Bogart but wisely avoids parodying him. A real surprise in the cast is Segal, better known for his novel *Love Story*. In his cameo role the author shows a genuine flair for acting and handles his French dialog with ease. Released both in an English-dubbed version and in French with English subtitles.

p, Jacques-Eric Strauss; d, Philippe Labro; w, Labro, Jacques Lanzmann (based on the novel *Ten Plus One* by Ed McBain); ph, Jean Penzer (Eastmancolor); m, Ennio Morricone; ed, Claude Barrois, Nicole Saunier; prod d, Andre Hoss; set d, Louis Le Barbenchon; makeup, Georges Bouban.

Crime   **(PR:O MPAA:PG)**

WITHOUT CHILDREN   (SEE: PENTHOUSE PARTY, 1936)

WITHOUT EACH OTHER**½   (1962) 90m Allen Klein c

Tony Anthony *(Boy)*, Ann Hergira *(Mother)*, Michael Dunn *(Dwarf)*, Ann Harris *(Girl)*, Brud Talbot *(Boy Friend)*.

Following the death of his father, young circus performer Anthony seeks out the mother he has never seen, Hergira. The eccentric woman has turned reclusive, dwelling alone in a large house in a small town, her only companion her caretaker, dwarf Dunn. A powerful local resident covets her crumbling old house, believing it to be a suitable gift for his pampered son. The house is about to be auctioned off in payment of back taxes when Anthony arrives and strives to make good the debt. He incurs the wrath of the covetous local residents, battling the town tough. When a group of drunken youths converge on the house, the once-cloistered Hergira has a heart attack. When she dies, Anthony puts her cold body in his circus truck and begins a slow march to the local burial ground, the whole town following. An ambitious first feature film by a group of young Florida filmmakers with a fine score by Hollywood's Tiomkin. Shown at the Cannes film festival in 1962 (but not entered in competition), the picture–which, apart from the talented Dunn, has no name players–was not theatrically released.

p, Allen Klein; d, Saul Swimmer; w, Swimmer, Tony Anthony, Ted Apstein, William Herman; ph, Arthur Ornitz (Pathecolor); m, Dimitri Tiomkin; ed, Ralph Rosenblum.

Drama   **(PR:A MPAA:NR)**

WITHOUT HONOR*½   (1949) 69m UA bw

Laraine Day *(Jane Bandle)*, Dane Clark *(Bill Bandle)*, Franchot Tone *(Dennis Williams)*, Agnes Moorehead *(Katherine Williams)*, Bruce Bennett *(Fred Bandle)*, Frank Marlowe *(Radio Man)*, Harry Lauter, Peter Virgo *(Ambulance Attendants)*, Margie Stapp *(Neighbor's Wife)*, Patricia Ann Ewing, Joan Dupius *(Girl Scouts)*, Lester Dorr *(Neighbor)*, Harrison Hearne *(2nd Radio Man)*.

Housewife Day receives a visit from her ex-lover, cad Tone, who gets a barbecue skewer in his chest for his presumptuousness. Dragging the "corpse" into her laundry room, Day spends the remainder of the preposterous picture looking alternately terrified and distraught as her nasty brother-in-law Clark (who had been rejected in his own amorous advances prior to her marriage to his brother Bennett) discloses her affair to her husband and to Tone's wife Moorehead. Overwhelmed by her fragmentation of two out of ten biblical commandments, Day confesses her "murder" of Tone and attempts to commit suicide. Rushed to a nearby hospital by the survivors, Day discovers that the tenacious Tone has clung to life, and Phoenix-like has been brought to the self-same hospital after wandering, wounded, out into the street. Day is reconciled with the magnanimous Bennett, who then reads the riot act to his rotten brother, Clark. Fine actors can't save this poorly paced, humorless picture. Top-billed Tone's briefest featured appearance, as he is consigned to the laundry room a few minutes into the film.

p, Robert Hakim, Raymond Hakim; d, Irving Pichel; w, James Poe; ph, Lionel Lindon; m, Max Steiner; ed, Gregg Tallas; md, Steiner; art d, Perry Ferguson; set d, Robert Priestley; makeup, Harry Ray.

Drama   **(PR:A MPAA:NR)**

WITHOUT HONORS**   (1932) 65m Supreme/Artclass bw

Harry Carey, Mae Busch, Gibson Gowland, George ["Gabby"] Hayes, Lafe McKee, Mary Jane Irving, Tom London, Ed Brady, Jack Richardson, Partner Jones, Lee Sage.

Better than average early oater in which Carey is set on redeeming the reputation of his dead brother, accused of being a thief and murderer. To do so, Carey repudiates his own gambling habits and joins the Texas Rangers, quickly bringing the actual culprits–who also are responsible for his brother's murder–to justice. Exceptional and detailed photography lifts this out of the abyss of being just another western.

p, Louis Weiss; d, William Nigh; w, Harry P. Christ [Harry Fraser], Lee Sage (based on a story by Sage); ph, Edward Linden.

Western   **(PR:A MPAA:NR)**

WITHOUT LOVE**½   (1945) 111m MGM bw

Spencer Tracy *(Pat Jamieson)*, Katharine Hepburn *(Jamie Rowan)*, Lucille Ball *(Kitty Trimble)*, Keenan Wynn *(Quentin Ladd)*, Carl Esmond *(Paul Carrell)*, Patricia Morison *(Edwina Collins)*, Felix Bressart *(Prof. Grinza)*,

Emily Massey *(Anna)*, Gloria Grahame *(Flower Girl)*, George Davis *(Caretaker)*, George Chandler *(Elevator Boy)*, Clancy Cooper *(Sergeant)*, Wallis Clark *(Prof. Thompson)*, Donald Curtis *(Prof. Ellis)*, Charles Arnt *(Col Braden)*, Eddie Acuff *(Driver)*, Clarence Muse *(Porter)*, Franco Corsaro *(Headwaiter)*, Ralph Brooks *(Pageboy)*, William Forrest *(Doctor)*, Garry Owen, Joe Devlin, William Newell *(Soldiers)*, James Flavin *(Sergeant)*, Hazel Brooks *(Girl on Elevator)*.

Not one of the team's best, but enough fun flowed from the combined pens of Barry (who wrote the play) and Stewart (who wrote the screenplay) to make it a pleasant comedy. Hepburn, who did the role on stage, is a widow living in Washington, D.C., where accommodations are scarcer than an honest politician. She has a large house with plenty of room. Tracy is a scientist who is trying to convince the government that his new invention should be adapted by the Air Force. It's a pilot's helmet that would have oxygen pumped into it, thereby eliminating the need for a separate oxygen mask. Tracy shares a cab with tipsy Wynn, who is Hepburn's cousin. When Wynn learns that Tracy needs a place to conduct his experiments, he suggests Tracy contact Hepburn. The two meet and, after some sparring, Hepburn says that she just can't have a man living in her house–what would the neighbors think? She suggests that they just might try a platonic marriage, for the sake of society. Tracy hates women but he needs a place to do his work so he agrees. The two are married, without love, and she becomes his lab assistant. Well, is there anyone who doesn't know the end of this? Right. Despite their attempts at keeping their relationship aboveboard, love happens and the two eventually find that it is possible for the twain to meet. Some cute bits include Tracy's sleepwalking and a dog that has been specially trained to stop him, good wisecracks from Ball as a real estate woman with an eye for men, and Wynn, who is shnockered most of the film and plays the drunk with flair. The entire reason for seeing this is to watch Tracy and Hepburn deliver the witty lines, because the plot was as frothy as a bubble bath. Stewart had earlier adapted another Barry play with better results. That was THE PHILADELPHIA STORY, for which Stewart won an Oscar.

p, Lawrence A. Weingarten; d, Harold S. Bucquet; w, Donald Ogden Stewart (based on the play by Philip Barry); ph, Karl Freund; m, Bronislau Kaper; ed, Frank Sullivan; art d, Cedric Gibbons, Harry McAfee; set d, Edwin B. Willis, McLean Nisbet; cos. Irene, Marion Herwood Keyes; spec eff, A. Arnold Gillespie, Danny Hall; makeup, Jack Dawn.

Comedy   **(PR:A MPAA:NR)**

WITHOUT ORDERS*½   (1936) 64m RKO bw

Sally Eilers *(Kay Armstrong)*, Robert Armstrong *(Wad Madison)*, Frances Sage *(Penny Armstrong)*, Charley Grapewin *(J.P. Kendrick)*, Vinton Haworth *(Len Kendrick)*, Ward Bond *(Tim Casey)*, Frank M. Thomas *(Trueman)*, Arthur Loft *(Calkins)*, Walter Miller *(Commerce Official)*, May Boley.

Flashy playboy pilot Haworth vies with nice-but-dull pilot Armstrong for the affections of saucy stewardess Eilers in this airline drama. The rotter wins the girl over the objections of her sister, Sage, whose skull he fractures because of her interference. During some bad weather, Haworth bails out of an erratically moving aircraft, leaving a planeload of passengers and his sweetheart Eilers abandoned to the air. Eilers takes the controls and–guided by radio by her true love, the stable, sturdy Armstrong–brings the craft safely to the ground. The villain's parachute, fortuitously, fails to open. One of the worst of the spate of aerial melodramas of the mid-1930s, borrowing heavily from Howard Hawks' CEILING ZERO of the previous year.

p, Cliff Reid; d, Lew Landers; w, J. Robert Bren, Edmund L. Hartmann (based on a story by Peter B. Kyne); ph, J. Roy Hunt, Vernon Walker; ed, Desmond Marquette.

Drama   **(PR:A MPAA:NR)**

WITHOUT PITY*½   (1949, Ital.) 95m Lux bw (SENZA PIETA)

Carla Del Poggio *(Angela)*, John Kitzmiller *(Jerry)*, Pierre Claude *(Pierre Luigi)*, Giulietta Masina *(Marcella)*, Folco Lulli *(Giacomo)*, Lando Muzio *(South American Captain)*, Enza Giovine *(Sister Gertrude)*, Daniel Jones *(Richard)*, Otello Fava *(Dumb Man)*.

Occupied Italy in the aftermath of WW II, where women sell themselves for C-rations and black-market barter is the order of the day. The struggle for survival brutalizes the inhabitants of Livorno, site of a large American Army base which serves as the nucleus for a flourishing array of satellite entrepreneurs. Beautiful blonde Del Poggio, searching for her missing brother, is recruited for prostitution by the most powerful of the gangs–which also engages in smuggling and stealing–headed by Claude. When black U.S. soldier Kitzmiller is set upon by thieves and wounded, he is helped by the compassionate Del Poggio. First grateful, then amorous, Kitzmiller hopes to keep his helper from the sordid life she faces, and to get her out of Italy. To this end, he deserts his military unit, which results in his blackmail by the vicious Claude. He steals some money from the gang and escapes in a truck with Del Poggio. She is killed by their pursuers, and Kitzmiller suicidally drives the truck into a cliff. A stark and bitter exposition, well photographed by the talented Tonti and coscripted by Fellini, who was later to codirect with director Lattuada. Not very kind to the occupying Americans, the film was banned in the American and British occupation zones in Germany. (In Italian and English; English subtitles.)

d, Alberto Lattuada; w, Federico Fellini, Tullio Pinelli (based on an idea by Ettore M. Margadonna); ph, Aldo Tonti; m, Nino Rota; English titles, Clare Catlano.

Drama   (PR:C   MPAA:NR)

WITHOUT REGRET**½   (1935) 74m PAR w

Elissa Landi (*Jennifer Gage*), Paul Cavanagh (*Sir Robert Godfrey*), Frances Drake (*Mona Gould*), Kent Taylor (*Steven Paradine*), Gilbert Emery (*Inspector Hayes*), David Niven (*Bill Gage*), Betty Holt (*Godfrey's Baby*), Marina Schubert (*Given*), Joseph North (*Jessup*), Colin Tapley (*Cleaver*), Mrs. Wong Wing (*Fat Chinese Woman*), Virginia Bassett (*Sour Faced Old Dame*), Eddie Lee (*Chinese Officer*), Victor Wong (*Soldier*), Henry Roquemore (*Stout Man*), Tom Gubbins, Gino Corrado (*Men*), Tetsu Komai (*Gen. Wu Chen*), Luke Chan (*Wing*), Peter Hobbes (*Fred*), Doris Stone (*Girl*), Clive Morgan (*Boy*), Stuart Hall (*Drunk*), Reginald Sheffield (*Reporter*), Forrester Harvey (*Doctor*), Alex Pollard (*Waiter*).

A bizzare adventure melodrama which is a loose remake of a 1928 film entitled INTERFERENCE. Landi stars as a young woman who is kidnaped by bandits while traveling in China. One of the hoodlums is Taylor, an independent pilot who has hired himself out to the bandits for a quick buck. Taylor dumps his current girl friend, Drake, and falls in love with Landi, protecting her from the lascivious attentions of her captors. Eventually Landi marries him. Years later she manages to escape her strange adventure when Taylor is killed in a plane crash. Back in London, the widowed Landi marries a brilliant heart specialist, Cavanagh, and settles down to a life of gentility. This is not to be, however, because none other than Drake and the very much alive Taylor show up at her doorstep. Faced with a possible bigamy case by a supposedly deceased husband still very much in love with her, Landi is beside herself with anguish. Drake, angry because Taylor still loves his wife, attempts to blackmail Landi. Trying to help, Taylor poisons Drake, but Landi winds up the prime suspect. Nobly, Taylor confesses to the crime and exits from Landi's life. There is not much special about WITHOUT REGRET except a sense of heightened melodrama which carries the film from one highly unlikely event to another. The film works on that level if the viewer doesn't take things too seriously. WITHOUT REGRET also marks young David Niven's first important role in his third film appearance.

p, B.P. Fineman; d, Harold Young; w, Doris Anderson, Charles Brackett (based on a story by Roland Pertwee, Harold Dearden); ph, William C. Mellor.

Drama   (PR:A   MPAA:NR)

WITHOUT RESERVATIONS**½   (1946) 107m LAS-RKO/RKO bw

Claudette Colbert (*Christopher "Kit" Madden*), John Wayne (*Rusty Thomas*), Don DeFore (*Dink Watson*), Anne Triola (*Consuela "Connie" Callaghan*), Phil Brown (*Soldier*), Frank Puglia (*Oraga*), Thurston Hall (*Baldwin*), Dona Drake (*Dolores*), Fernando Alvarado, Michael Economides, Jose Alvarado, Miguel Tapia, Rosemary Lopez, Henry Mirelez, Herbert Espinosa (*Mexican Youths*), Charles Arnt (*Salesman*), Louella Parsons, Jack Benny, Cary Grant (*Themselves*), Charles Evans (*Jerome*), Harry Hayden (*Mr. Harry Randall*), Lela Bliss (*Mrs. Randall*), Houseley Stevenson (*Turnkey*), Junius Matthews (*Porter*), Griff Barnett (*Train Conductor*), Will Wright (*Pullman Conductor*), Thelma Gyath (*WAC*), J. Louis Johnson (*Car Porter*), Frank Dae (*Man with Book*), Ian Wolfe (*Charlie Gibbs*), Grace Hampton (*Lois*), Minerva Urecal (*Sue*), Esther Howard (*Sarah*), Dick Dickerson (*Young Sailor*), Joel Fluellen (*Waiter in Club Car*), Jack Parker, John Crawford, Henry Vroom, Lee Bennett (*Soldiers*), Oscar O'Shea (*Conductor*), Ruth Roman (*Girl in Negligee*), William Challee (*Corporal*), Sam McDaniel (*Freddy*), Henry Hastings (*Waiter*), Ralph Hubbard, Russ Whiteman (*Sailors*), Tay Dunn (*Navy Ensign*), Harold Davis, Tom Hubbard, Bob Wallace, Sid Davies, Charles Elmergreen, Fleet White, Bill Shannon, Roger Creed, Peter Michael, Joe Haworth (*Marines*), Brock Hunt, Bruce Brewster (*Army Lieutenants*), John Gilbreath, Bill Udell (*Navy N.C.s*), Bill O'Leary (*Candy Butcher*), Chef Milani (*Diner Captain*), Ernest Anderson (*Waiter*), Harry Evans, Paul Gustine (*Travelers*), Art Miles (*Truck Driver*), Charles Hall (*Window Washer*), John Bleifer (*Coal Heaver*), Jan Wiley (*Manicurist*), June Glory (*Girl*), Bob Pepper (*Man*), Wallace Scott, Harry Holman (*Gas Station Attendants*), Warren Smith, Eric Alden (*Chauffeurs*), Leona Maricle (*Baldwin's Secretary*), Jean Koehler (*Western Union Operator*), William Benedict (*Western Union Boy*), Lorin Raker (*Mr. Klotch*), Tom Chatterton (*Pullman Conductor*), Cy Kendall (*Bail Bondsman*), Jesse Graves (*Porter*), Al Rosen (*Train Mechanic*), Raymond Burr (*Paul Gill*), Fred Coby (*French Officer*), Verne Richards (*Brakeman*), George Economides (*Mexican Boy*), Marilyn Buford (*WAC*), Harry Strang (*Policeman*), Dudley Dickerson (*Red Cap*), Erskine Sanford (*Tim*), Dolores Moran (*Herself*), Charles Williams (*Louis Burt*), Charles Evans (*Philip Jerome the Publisher*), Robert "Bob" Anderson (*Radio Announcer*), Charlie Moore (*Redcap*), Lois Austin (*Congresswoman*), Blanca Vischer (*Mexican Beauty*), Lisa Golm (*Alma*), Marvin Miller (*Announcer*), John Kellogg, Robin Short, Nanette Vallon, Jean Wong (*Reporters*), Mervyn LeRoy (*Diner*).

In this reworking of IT HAPPENED ONE NIGHT, Colbert plays the author of a best-selling novel, traveling incognito to Hollywood where she plans to

work on the film version of the book. On the train she meets Wayne and DeFore, two Marine fliers who dislike Colbert's book and don't realize they are striking up a friendship with the novel's author. Colbert is convinced Wayne is the right man to star in her story, and sends a telegram to the film's producer. The trio arrives in Chicago, where Colbert learns Wayne and DeFore are taking another train. Leaving her baggage hastily behind, Colbert boards the two Marines' train. The three get a little inebriated in the club car, then Wayne and DeFore decide to teach Colbert the art of flying. After they create a mock airplane from furniture, Colbert is discovered by railroad officials and tossed off the train. Wayne and DeFore join her, then buy a used car to continue the journey westward. One night, as DeFore is working on the car's engine, Wayne and Colbert find some idyllic moments in a haystack. They confess a growing love for one another, though Colbert worries that Wayne will discover she has lied to him about her identity. Colbert cashes a check with her real name when the trio arrives in New Mexico, and the local population is thrilled to find the famous author in their midst. A story then leaks out of Hollywood that Colbert has arrived in Tinsel Town, so Colbert ends up in jail for passing forged checks. Wayne and DeFore sell their car to raise bail, but Colbert's producer comes to town to help out the writer. With her identity revealed, Wayne goes to the Marine base in San Diego, convinced Colbert was merely using him for some fun. Meanwhile, Colbert becomes embroiled in the filming of her novel. Parsons (playing herself), in a radio broadcast, hints that Colbert may be romantically involved with the film's intended leading man. Wayne hears the broadcast, which further angers him. DeFore, in the meantime, has been in touch with Colbert and is determined to see true love conquer. Eventually he succeeds, as Colbert and Wayne are reunited. As Wayne walks to his beloved, Colbert repeats the prayer aviators use after getting out of a tight jam: "Thanks, God, I'll take it from here." This is an atypical film for the Duke, and Wayne isn't helped much by the tired script. Every conceivable situation crops up as the three make their cross-country trek, with laughs petering out long before the film's end. Wayne and Colbert do play well off one another, though Colbert seems a bit old for her part. In no way does she equal her marvelous Oscar-winning performance in IT HAPPENED ONE NIGHT. LeRoy tries to give this some energy with his direction, but at best the film is only mildly amusing. In addition to Parsons' cameo, there are quick appearances by Benny as an autograph seeker, and Grant, who briefly dances with Colbert. LeRoy also takes a bit part, as a man eating dinner with Colbert. The production cost $1,683,000 and proved to be a popular box-office attraction.

p, Jesse L. Lasky; d, Mervyn LeRoy; w, Andrew Solt (based on the novel *Thanks, God] I'll Take It From Here* by Jane Allen, Mae Livingston); ph, Milton Krasner; m, Roy Webb; ed, Jack Ruggiero; md, C. Bakaleinikoff; art d, Albert S. D'Agostino, Ralph Berger; set d, Darrell Silvera, James Altwies; spec eff, Vernon L. Walker, Russell A. Cully, Clifford Stine.

Comedy   **Cas.**   (PR:A   MPAA:NR)

WITHOUT RISK   (SEE: PECOS RIVER, 1951)

WITHOUT WARNING**   (1952) 75m UA bw (AKA: THE STORY
                                                                    WITHOUT A NAME)

Adam Williams (*Carl Martin*), Meg Randall (*Jane*), Edward Binns (*Pete*), Harlan Warde (*Don*), John Maxwell (*Fred Saunders*), Angela Stevens (*Blonde*), Byron Kane (*Charlie*), Charles Tannen (*Wolf*), Marilee Phelps (*Virginia*), Robert Foulk (*Wilson*), Connie Vera (*Carmelita*), Robert Shayne (*Psychiatrist*).

There's a documentary feel to this low-budget film about the pursuit of maniacal killer Williams, who–his beautiful blonde wife having deserted him–picks up look alikes and murders them with garden shears. Policemen Binns and Warde attempt to entrap the madman, staking out blonde policewomen in likely Los Angeles bars, but to no avail. Dogged forensic work finally pinpoints Williams as the guilty party. A capable first feature by the production team, with talented unknowns as actors. Producer Sol Lesser (best known for his TARZAN series) acquired an interest in the picture following its filming and arranged for its release through a major distributing company.

p, Arthur Gardner, Jules Levy; d, Arnold Laven; w, Bill Raynor; ph, Joseph F. Biroc; m, Herschel Burke Gilbert; ed, Arthur H. Nadel.

Crime/Thriller   (PR:C   MPAA:NR)

WITHOUT WARNING zero   (1980) 89m Filmways c (AKA: IT
                                                          CAME... WITHOUT WARNING)

Jack Palance (*Taylor*), Martin Landau (*Fred*), Tarah Nutter (*Sandy*), Christopher S. Nelson (*Greg*), Cameron Mitchell (*Hunter*), Neville Brand (*Leo*), Sue Ann Langdon (*Aggie*), Larry Storch (*Scoutmaster*), Ralph Meeker (*Dave*), Lynn Theel (*Beth*), David Caruso (*Tom*), Darby Hinton (*Randy*).

Aging stars play crazy old coots in cameo roles in this science-fiction horror throwback to the 1950s which has teenaged Nutter and Nelson heading for a remote lake to join their camping friends Theel and Caruso. Stopping at a service station, they are abjured by Palance to avoid the lake, where something evil lurks. Sure enough, hunter Mitchell and son Hinton become fair game for an evil alien which flings carnivorous flapjacks at them. The flapjacks adhere to their victims, extruding mouthparts that messily penetrate flesh as they undaintily devour their target humans. Scoutmaster Storch, camping at the lake with his Cub Scout troop, is the next victim of the ferocious flapjacks. Nutter and Nelson, arriving at the lake, find their friends and the other victims hanging from meathooks in a shed, partially devoured. Under flapjack attack, the two seek shelter in a saloon occupied by crazy coots Landau, Brand, and Meeker, accompanied by Langdon. Following a talky interval of crazy cootery, the kids venture forth with Landau and Palance and find a way to neutralize the flapjacks. The ending reminds the audience that more maniacal aliens may be out there, paving the way for an equally idiotic sequel.

p&d, Greydon Clark; w, Lyn Freeman, Daniel Grodnik, Ben Nett, Steve Mathis; ph, Dean Cundy (Movielab Color); m, Dan Wyman; ed, Curtis Burch; prod d, Jack DeWolf.

Horror   **(PR:O   M PAA:R)**

WITHOUT YOU*½   (1934, Brit.) 66m BL/FOX bw

Henry Kendall (Tony Bannister), Wendy Barrie (Molly Bannister), Margot Grahame (Margot Gilbey), Fred Duprez (Baron von Steinmeyer), Georgie Harris (Harrigan), Joe Hayman (Blodgett), Billy Mayerl (Fink).

Seeking life as a playwright, would-be writer Barrie leaves husband Kendall, a composer. Six months go by and Barrie finds herself the subject of baron Duprez's amorous attentions. The wily baron hires Kendall to serve as a co-respondent in his own divorce, but Kendall gets to the bottom of things. All ends happily and Barrie's first play is a hit. Another minor British programmer with a heavy dose of sap.

p, Herbert Smith; d, John Daumery; w, Michael Barringer (based on a story by W. Scott Darling); ph, Alex Bryce.

Comedy   **(PR:A   MPAA:NR)**

WITNESS, THE**   (1959, Brit.) 58m Merton Park/Anglo Amagamated bw

Dermot Walsh (Richard Brinton), Greta Gynt (May), Russell Napier (Inspector Rosewarne), Martin Stephens (Peter Brindon), John Chandos (Lodden), Derek Sydney (Manny), Hedger Wallace (Manbre), Tom Bowman, Geoffrey Denton, Ronald Wood, Rupert Osborne, Stewart Guidotti, Malcolm Knight.

After Walsh is imprisoned his 10-year-old son Stephens is teased no end by his peers. The lad then witnesses a crime committed by others for which is father is suspect. The cops use the boy as bait to catch the real crooks. Though there is some dangerous moments for the boy the plan works and Walsh is reunited with Stephens. Stephen's natural performance is okay and covers the fact that this isn't much of a story.

p, Jack Greenwood; d, Geoffrey Muller; w, Julian Bond (based on a story by John Salt); ph, John Wiles.

Crime   **(PR:AA   MPAA:NR)**

WITNESS, THE**½   (1982, Hung.) 108m Mafilm/Cinegate-Libra c
                                         (AKA: WITHOUT A TRACE)

Ferenc Kallai (Jozsef Pelika), Lili Monori (Gizi, His Daughter), Zoltan Fabri (Zoltan), Lajos Oze (Comrade Virag), Bela Both (Gen. Bastya), Georgette Metzradt, Robert Rathonyi, Karoly Bicskei, Laszlo Yamos, Ida Yersenyi, Gyorgy Balint, Pal Bano, Tibor Feher, Jozsef Ivanyi, Pal Jako, Gyorgy Kezdi, Peter Korbuly, Lajos Mezei, Istvan Nemeth, Istvan Novak, Gyorgy Palffy, Jozsef Pecsenke, Tibor Sipeki, Lajos Tandor, Masok Es.

This Franz Kafka-like stark comedy dealing with the serpentin pathways in which the mazes of the bureaucracy must be threaded in Stalinist Hungary was made in 1969, but was withheld from release in its native land until 1978. One of many pictures dealing with the events leading up to the political unrest of 1965, which saw Soviet tanks patroling the streets of Budapest, the film is the product of the imagination of one of the older Hungarian "New Wave" writer-directors.

p, Lajos Gulyas; d&W, Peter Bacso; ph, Janos Zsombolyai (CinemaScope, Eastmancolor); m, Gyuorgy Yukan; ed, Sandor Boronkay; art d, Laszlo Blaho.

Satire   **(PR:C   MPAA:NR)**

WITNESS CHAIR, THE*   (1936) 64m RKO bw

Ann Harding (Paula Young), Walter Abel (Jim Trent), Douglas Dumbrille (Stanley Whittaker), Frances Sage (Connie Trent), Moroni Olsen (Lt. Poole), Margaret Hamilton (Grace Franklin), Maxine Jennings (Tillie Jones), William ["Billy"] Benedict (Benny Ryan), Paul Harvey (Martin), Murray Kinnell (Conrick), Charles Arnt (Henshaw), Frank Jenks (Levino), Edward LeSaint (Judge McKenzie), Hilda Vaughn (Anna Yifnick), Barlowe Borland (O'Neil).

A conventional courtroom drama with flashbacks, illustrating the trauma faced by Harding when her sweetheart Abel comes close to being convicted

(on damning circumstantial evidence) of a murder she herself committed. The deed was done in righteous anger over embezzler Dumbrille's plan to elope with innocent Sage, daughter of the accused Abel. When suspicion shifts to Sage on the witness stand, Harding cries out her courtroom confession that she herself did Dumbrille in. The unhappy Harding, once a major star for the studio, was pushed into this film following conflicts over her contact. She left the studio after this financial and artistic failure.

p, Cliff Reid; d, George Nicholls, Jr.; w, Rian James, Gertrude Purcell based on the story by Rita Weiman); ph, Robert de Grasse; ed, William Morgan.

Mystery   **(PR:A   MPAA:NR)**

WITNESS FOR THE PROSECUTION***½
                                     (1957) 114m Theme/UA bw

Tyrone Power (Leonard Stephen Vole), Marlene Dietrich (Christine 'Helm' Vole), Charles Laughton (Sir Wilfrid Robarts), Elsa Lanchester (Miss Plimsoll), John Williams (Brogan-Moore), Henry Daniell (Mayhew), Ian Wolfe (Carter), Una O'Connor (Janet MacKenzie), Torin Thatcher (Mr. Meyers), Francis Compton (Judge), Norma Varden (Mrs. Emily French), Philip Tonge (Inspector Hearne), Ruta Lee (Diana), Molly Roden (Miss McHugh), Ottola Nesmith (Miss Johnson), Marjorie Eaton (Miss O'Brien), J. Pat O'Malley (Shorts Salesman).

A terse adaptation of the Agatha Christie hit play which is brought to the screen with ingenuity and vitality by Billy Wilder. Laughton stars as a sickly barrister who is told by his doctors, and forced by his pesty nurse Lanchester, to keep his wig in moth balls and retire from criminal cases. When his solicitor, Daniell, arrives at his home with murder suspect Power, Laughton cannot resist, at least, giving some advice. Interrogating the client in his office, the barrister learns that Power is the prime suspect in the murder of a rich old widow, Varden. Power, a drifter with little money, tells Laughton how he met Varden at a hat store, giving her advice on a purchase. After meeting her again at a movie house, he was invited back to her luxurious home. After some time they became very close, raising the suspicions of O'Connor, Varden's partly deaf and wholly inconsiderate housekeeper. Hearing Power's story, Laughton becomes convinced of the man's innocence, but because his only alibi is his wife, Dietrich, prospects for an acquittal look dim. Before their meeting ends, word is received that Power has inherited 80,000 pounds sterling from Varden's estate. Because of the apparent clarity of Power's motive, Scotland Yard soon arrives and places him under arrest. Rather than risk his health, and the wrath of Lanchester, Laughton hands the case over to his junior partner, Williams. Williams, however, is not convinced of Power's innocence and sees the case as a difficult one to win. As Laughton is about to retire to his room, Dietrich arrives and plainly states that she is Power's alibi only because he wants her to be, and not because it is the truth. Her position piques Laughton's interest and, unable to resist any longer, he takes the case. Although she does not sound sincere, Dietrich upholds Power's claim that he was indeed home with her when the murder took place. She also admits that she is not really Power's wife--that their marriage in Germany during the war was not legal since she was already married to another man named Otto Ludwig Helm. Later, as Laughton briefs his imprisoned client, he learns that Power met singer Dietrich in a crumbling German cabaret. The pair fell in love and Power arranged for her to leave her miserable life behind and accompany him to England. The trial soon starts with Laughton being poked, prodded, and pampered by Lanchester and his doctors while trying to defeat the prosecuting attorney, Thatcher, in a battle of legal wits and courtroom eloquence. After much questioning, Thatcher pulls a surprise move and calls Dietrich to the witness box, arguing that since she is not legally married to Power she can testify against him. And testify against him is exactly what she does, admitting to her previous marriage and telling the judge and jury that she was forced into providing Power with an alibi. Dietrich then tells the courtroom that Power admitted to the murder. Meantime, Power, standing in the court dock, is physically and mentally breaking apart at her "lies," loudly protesting his innocence. Laughton counters by trying to make Dietrich appear as a bigamist and compulsive liar. Both barristers rest their cases and retire for the evening, awaiting the jury's verdict on the following morning. That evening, however, Laughton receives a phone call from a vulgar young cockney woman who offers to sell him some evidence. He and Daniell meet with her and purchase some incriminating love letters that Dietrich wrote to a mysterious lover named Max. The following day, Laughton requests that the case be reopened. He calls Dietrich back to the witness box and confronts her with the new evidence, proving to the jury that she planned to lie in court and put Power away, in order to be with Max. In light of this, the jury returns a verdict of "not guilty." Everyone is thrilled at Laughton's brilliance, except for Laughton himself. A series of twists and turns then follows, which the moviegoing audience (and film critics) was asked not to reveal. With the trial over, Laughton sits alone in the courtroom. Dietrich then walks in and informs him, in a cockney accent, that she was the mysterious informer who supplied him with the letters. She explains that the only way she could insure her husband's acquittal was to falsely testify against him and be discredited by Laughton, thereby "proving" Power's innocence. The catch, however, is that Power actually did commit the murder, as he admits when he enters the courtroom. Knowing that he cannot be retried for the same crime, Power admits his guilt to the dumbfounded Laughton, and then promises to secure the top barrister for Dietrich's perjury defense. Power, however, is more ruthless than even

Dietrich had imagined. He pushes her aside and tells her that he is leaving her for another woman. An enraged Dietrich grabs a nearby knife and plunges it into Power, killing, or as Laughton says "executing" him. Rather than put his judge's wig back in moth balls, Laughton agrees to defend Dietrich. Improving on Christie's play, Wilder has rid WITNESS FOR THE PROSECUTION of much of the usual static courtroom scenes and filled the film with an active, visual excitement. Whether it be the fluidity of the camera, the use of an occasional flashback, or the diversion of Laughton's constant medical attention, Wilder succeeds in finding a way to relieve the boredom that typically accompanies the courtroom. Wilder even introduces Lanchester's nurse character into Christie's scenario to add some life and a comic angle to Laughton's character. At the film's halfway point Wilder flashes back to wartime Germany for the standard Dietrich-as-cabaret-singer scene, giving her a chance to show off one of her attractive legs, play the accordian, and deliver "I Never Go There Anymore" (Ralph Arthur Roberts, Jack Brooks). The part, one of her finest, was pure Dietrich, casting her as a woman who throws away everything–her homeland, her reputation, and her life–for a man who then throws her away. Of Dietrich's chance to play the cockney woman, Lanchester said: "Marlene was forever up at our house, trying on scarves, shawls, and various wigs, and taking lessons in cockney from Charles 'Laughton, Lanchester's husband'. She was obsessed with this impersonation. I never saw anyone work so hard." On the screen one has difficulty even telling that it is Dietrich and, in fact, rumors soon spread that it was another actress altogether. This is highly unlikely, knowing that Dietrich would probably never consent to such a thing, and because production stills exist of Dietrich rehearsing the scene without makeup. Unfortunately, however, Dietrich was overlooked at Oscar time because word of her dual role had to be suppressed to keep from revealing the ending. While Dietrich was slighted, others in the cast were not. In addition to receiving a Best Picture nomination, WITNESS FOR THE PROSECUTION gave the husband and wife acting team of Laughton and Lanchester nominations for Best Actor and Best Supporting Actress. Though, another dubious omission was Power, who in his final role before his fatal heart attack the following year, turned in a superb performance as the murderer who deceives everyone with his supposed innocence. Other Oscar nominations included Best Director, Wilder, Best Sound, Gordon Sawyer and the Goldwyn Studio Sound Department, and Best Editing, Daniel Mandell. Although the Academy didn't commend art director Alexandre Trauner for his work, it definitely was worthy of such attention. Trauner, who so brilliantly designed the sets of such French classics as QUAI DES BRUMES (1938), LE JOUR SE LEVE (1939), THE DEVIL'S ENVOYS (1942), and CHILDREN OF PARADISE (1944), again showed his talents in his re-creation of England's Old Bailey courtroom. After making detailed sketches (he was not allowed to take photographs), Trauner had the set built for $75,000, complete with 60 removable Austrian oak panels and a sectioned floor which could be rearranged as needed. Although WITNESS FOR THE PROSECUTION is not top-drawer Billy Wilder a la DOUBLE INDEMNITY (1944) or SUNSET BOULEVARD (1950), it is a superbly directed picture which is one of the top courtroom suspensers to hit the screen.

p, Arthur Hornblow, Jr.; d, Billy Wilder; w, Wilder, Harry Kurnitz, Larry Marcus (based on the novel and the play by Agatha Christie); ph, Russell Harlan; m, Matty Malnick; ed, Daniel Mandell; md, Ernest Gold; art d, Alexandre Trauner; set d, Howard Bristol; cos, Edith Head, Joseph King; m/l, "I May Never Go Home Anymore," Ralph Arthur Roberts, Jack Brooks; makeup, Ray Sebastian, Harry Ray, Gustaf Norin.

Courtroom Drama   Cas.   (PR:A MPAA:NR)

WITNESS IN THE DARK**   (1959, Brit.) 62m Ethiro-Alliance/Rank
                                                                          bw

Patricia Dainton (Jane Pringle), Conrad Phillips (Inspector Coates), Madge Ryan (Mrs. Finch), Nigel Green (Intruder), Enid Lorimer (Mrs. Temple), Richard O'Sullivan (Don Theobold), Stuart Saunders (Mr. Finch), Ian Colin (Supt. Thompson), Noel Trevarthen, Maureen O Reilly, Larry Burns, Ann Wrigg, Frazer Hines.

Dainton Plays a blind woman employed as a switchboard operator. When a neighbor is killed she inherits the victim's valuable brooch. However, the murderer had accidentally brushed against the blind woman and now fears that her sense of touch will do him in. He is determined to get her as well, but thanks to Dainton's work with the police the killer is captured when he returns to the murder site. Standard and predictable though Dainton gives a nice performance.

p, Norman Williams; d, Wolf Rilla; w, Vance, John Lemont; ph, Brendan Stafford.

Crime   (PR:A MPAA:NR)

WITNESS OUT OF HELL***   (1967, Ger./Yugo.) 83m
CCC-Filmproducktion-Avala/RANK bw (ZEUGIN AUS DER HOELLE)

Irene Papas (Lea Weiss), Heinz Drache (Hoffman), Danile Gelin (Petrovid), Werner Peters (Von Walden), Jean Claudio (Carlo Bianchi), Alice Treff (Frau von Keller), Hans Zesch-Ballot (Dr. Berger), Branco Tatic, Radmilla Gutesa, Petar Banicevic.

Yugoslav journalist Gelin is enlisted by German policeman Drache to help

locate Papas, sole surviving ex-inmate of a concentration camp, whom police believe to be an important witness in the trial for wartime atrocities of the camp's physician. Gelin, a friend of Papas in prewar times, traces her whereabouts. Police and prosecutors try to convince her to testify at the trial, but the persecuted Papas refuses. Her tormentors persist in their entreaties to the point where Papas, once again pursued, commits suicide rather than exist in a world which offers her no respite. Papas' performance as the haunted concentration camp alumna is superb, with the rest of the international cast strictly secondary. Director Mitrovic, a seminal figure in Serbian cinema, made many war-related action films which reflected his experiences as a partisan fighter and a documentarist. (In German.)

d, Zita Mitrovic; w, Frieda Filipovic, Michael Mansfield (based on an idea by Filipovic; ph, Milored Markovic; ed, Katarina Stagarovic, Ursula Karlband.

WITNESS TO MURDER***   (1954) 81m UA bw

Barbara Stanwyck (Cheryl Draper), George Sanders (Albert Richter), Gary Merrill (Lawrence Matthews), Jesse White (Eddie Vincent), Harry Shannon (Capt. Donnelly), Clare Carleton (The Blonde), Lewis Martin (Psychiatrist), Dick Elliott (Apartment Manager), Harry Tyler (Charlie), Juanita Moore (Woman), Joy Hallward (Woman's Coworker), Gertrude Graner (Policewoman), Adeline DeWalt Reynolds (Old Lady), Brad Trumbull, Hugh Sheraton, Fred Graham, Sam Edwards, Jean Fenwick, Helen Kleeb, Ted Thorpe, Lyn Thomas.

On a hot, windy Los Angeles night, Stanwyck wakes up to close her window and across the way she sees Sanders murder a woman. She calls the police, but by the time they arrive Sanders has hidden the body in the apartment next door and cleaned up any evidence of his crime. Police detective Merrill tells Stanwyck that she must have been mistaken and Sanders finds out it was she who reported him. He is a writer of historical novels and the victim was his mistress, who was standing in the way of his marriage to a wealthy woman. He pays a visit to Stanwyck and as he leaves he tampers with the lock so that he can get back into the apartment later. When Stanwyck goes out, he enters, and on her typewriter writes somes letters threatening himself. He mails them to his address, then later shows them to the police as evidence that Stanwyck is mentally disturbed and is persecuting him. She is taken to an asylum where she is repulsed by the lunacy around her, and when she is released she sees Sanders reading the newspapers telling of the discovery of the body of his mistress. She figures out what he has been doing to her and confronts him. Sanders feels he has nothing to fear from this officially labeled "disturbed woman" and tells her his own semi-Nazi beliefs that call for the elimination of the mediocre. He tells her he intends to write a suicide note on her typewriter and murder her, but she runs away, fleeing to a rooftop. Sanders pursues her and they struggle on a rickety scaffold. As the police close in, Sanders falls to his death and Stanwyck is left dangling when the scaffold collapses, but she is rescued just before she loses her grip. Interesting melodrama has good performances by Sanders and Stanwyck, who gets to go through much of the same hysteria she handled so well in SORRY, WRONG NUMBER. The cinematography is very good, conveying the claustrophobic apartments and asylum and the hot wind blowing over everything. Stanwyck and Sanders were both on the long slide from stardom, but they still make this one worth watching.

p, Chester Erskine; d, Roy Rowland; w, Erskine; ph, John Alton; m, Herschel Burke Gilbert; ed, Robert Swink; art d, William Ferrari; set d, Alfred E. Spencer; cos, Jack Masters, Irene Caine, Dave Berman, Kay Nelson; m/l, Gilbert, Sylvia Fine.

Crime Drama   (PR:C MPAA:NR)

WITNESS VANISHES, THE*½   (1939) 66m UNIV bw

Edmund Lowe (Peters), Wendy Barrie (Joan Marplay), Bruce Lester (Lord Noel Stretton), Walter Kingsford (Amos Craven), Forrester Harvey (Allistair MacNab), Barlowe Borland (Lucius Marplay), J.M. Kerrigan (Flinters), Vernon Steele (Nigel Partridge), Robert Noble (Inspector Wren), Reginald Barlow (Digby), Leyland Hodgson (Dade), Denis Green (Leets), Boyd Irwin (Ellis).

A publishing takeover plot is initiated when newspaper executive Lowe, with three of his publishing peers, has Borland–owner of the prestigious paper the London Sun–committed to an insane asylum. Borland soon escapes his white-coated captors and the conspiratorial quartet begins to dwindle. Obituaries of the soon-to-be deceased appear in a rival paper prior to their demises as the four become three, then two, and finally Lowe alone, anxious about his continuing existence. Spooky music heralds the discovery of each fresh corpse in this newspaper necrology, the fifth and final film in Universal's CRIME CLUB series (see Index). This picture is probably the best of the series, and–with THE MYSTERY OF THE WHITE ROOM in the same year–the best of B-picture director Garrett's limited output.

p, Irving Starr; d, Otis Garrett; w, Robertson White (based on the story "You Can't Hang Me" by James Ronald); ph, Arthur Martinelli; ed, Harry Keller.

Crime/Mystery   (PR:A MPAA:NR)

WIVES AND LOVERS**   (1963) 103m PAR bw

Janet Leigh (*Bertie Austin*), Van Johnson (*Bill Austin*), Shelley Winters (*Fran Cabrell*), Martha Hyer (*Lucinda Ford*), Ray Walston (*Wylie Driberg*), Jeremy Slate (*Gar Aldrich*), Claire Wilcox (*Julie Austin*), Lee Patrick (*Mrs. Swanson*), Dick Wessel (*Mr. Liberti*), Dave Willock (*Dr. Partridge*).

A witty, deftly penned farce about working wife Leigh, whose cold water flat existence with husband Johnson, an unemployed novelist, becomes less than idyllic when his first novel scores a great success. The *nouveau riche* writer has his once-happy wife resign her job, and they move from New York City to a fashionable Connecticut exurb. With his sexy agent, Hyer, he goes to the Great White Way to adapt his novel to the stage while Leigh idles her time away with the bibulous Winters and her weird boy friend, Walston, her new neighbors. As Johnson spends more and more time with Hyer, his jealous, disaffected wife encourages the amorous advances of actor Slate. Johnson's play opens on Broadway to critical raves, but Leigh fails to attend the opening. Johnson drives home to tell Leigh that their marriage is over, and he runs into the ardent actor. Like bucks in rut, the two males lock horns. Having cleaned the Slate, Johnson turns to Leigh and confesses fidelity. When she, in turn, confirms her purity, the two are reunited. If you can forget the traditional Hollywood fudging in the belated denial of the adultery that has been obvious throughout the film, this is an enjoyable picture with a fine cast, good pacing by director Rich in his first feature film assignment following his shift from TV, and superior production values. Star Leigh had paired with costar Johnson in her first feature film, THE ROMANCE OF ROSY RIDGE, 16 years previously.

p, Hal B. Wallis; d, John Rich; w, Edward Anhalt (based on the play "The First Wife" by Jay Presson Allen); ph, Lucien Ballard; m, Lyn Murray; ed, Warren Low; art d, Walter Tyler, Hal Pereira; set d, Arthur Krams, Sam Comer; cos, Edith Head; makeup, Gary Morris.

Comedy   (PR:A   MPAA:NR)

WIVES BEWARE*   (1933, Brit.) 63m Cinema House/Regent bw (GB: TWO WHITE ARMS)

Adolphe Menjou (*Maj. Carey Liston*), Margaret Bannerman (*Lydia Charrington*), Claud Allister (*Dr. Biggash*), Jane Baxter (*Alison Drury*), Kenneth Kove (*Bob Russell*), Ellis Jeffreys (*Lady Ellerslie*), Rene Ray (*Trixie*), Jean Cadell (*Mrs. Drury*), Henry Wenman (*Mears*), Spencer Trevor (*Sir George*), Melville Cooper (*Mack*), Peter English, Archibald Batty, Arthur Stratton.

Menjou, having married unwisely, feigns amnesia with the help of physician Allister and finds a new identity as a car saleman. The philandering faker flirts with a number of women, but is finally found by a friend of his deserted wife. The friend, herself long enamored of the miscreant Menjou, persuades him to return to his wife, whose pregnancy was unknown to him. An unpleasant little comedy, despite a strong cast.

p, Eric Hakim; d, Fred Niblo; w, Harold Dearden (based on his play); ph, Harry Gerrard; ed, Helen Lewis.

Comedy   (PR:A   MPAA:NR)

WIVES NEVER KNOW**   (1936) 75m PAR bw

Charles Ruggles (*Homer Bigelow*), Mary Boland (*Marcia Bigelow*), Adolphe Menjou (*J. Hugh Ramsay*), Vivienne Osborne (*Renee La Journee*), Claude Gillingwater (*Mr. Gossamer*), Fay Holden (*Mrs. Gossamer*), Louise Beavers (*Florabelle*), Constance Bergen (*Miss Giddings*), Purnell Pratt (*Higgins*).

Menjou is a writer who pens polemics against the institution of marriage, citing the benefits of single bliss. He persuades his friend Ruggles that the only meaningful relationships are those that include interludes of strife, suggesting that the latter find a way to make wife Boland jealous. Ruggles spends a night with aging actress Osborne–a French floozy with whom Menjou himself is taken–expecting to reap the joys of anguished forgiveness upon his return home to Boland. Instead, he finds raging rancor, not only on Boland's part, but from the jealous Menjou as well. The latter is brought to the altar with Osborne, ending the arguing in this pleasant, predictable bedroom farce.

p, Harlan Thompson; d, Eliott Nugent; w, Frederick Hazlett Brennan (based on a story by Keene Thompson); ph, George Clemens; ed, Richard Currier.

Comedy   (PR:A   MPAA:NR)

WIVES UNDER SUSPICION**   (1938) 75m UNIV bw

Warren William (*District Atty. Jim Stowell*), Gail Patrick (*Lucy Stowell*), Ralph Morgan (*Prof. Shaw McAllen*), William Lundigan (*Phil*), Constance Moore (*Elizabeth*), Cecil Cunningham (*Sharpy, Stowell's Secretary*), Samuel S. Hinds (*Dave Marrow*), Jonathan Hale (*Dan Allison*), Lillian Yarbo (*Creola, Maid*), Milburn Stone (*Kirk*), Anthony Hughes (*Murphy*), Edward Stanley (*The Judge*), James Flavin (*Jenks*), Minerva Urecal, David Oliver.

William is a dedicated district attorney, immersed in his work, carrying absolute certitude about his conviction that those who kill–no matter what the circumstances–should be executed. He employs the very latest scientific techniques–sound recording apparatus, for one–to covertly obtain confessions from those he prosecutes. During the course of one of his cases–

Morgan, a professor who, in a paroxysm of jealousy, murdered his wife–William experiences a sense of foreboding. In his rare moments at home with his neglected wife, Patrick, *deja vu* occurs; William has heard his own life, and Patrick's, recounted in the courtroom. Lundigan is the young man on whom the lonely Patrick has riveted her attention. William's own home life closely matches that of the prosecuted professor, as does his enraged reaction to Patrick's apparent betrayal. The realization of his own culpability brings compassion to him; he appreciates Morgan's temporary derangement and re-orients his prosecution, no longer seeking a first-degree murder charge. Director Whale, best known for FRANKENSTEIN (1931), here remade his earlier THE KISS BEFORE THE MIRROR (1933).

p, Edmund Grainger; d, James Whale; w, Myles Connolly (based on the story "Suspicion" by Ladislaus Fodor); ph, George Robinson; ed, Charles Maynard; md, Charles Previn; art d, Jack Otterson.

Drama   (PR:A   MPAA:NR)

WIZ, THE½   (1978) 133m Motown/UNIV c

Diana Ross (*Dorothy*), Michael Jackson (*Scarecrow*), Nipsey Russell (*Tinman*), Ted Ross (*Lion*), Mabel King (*Evillene*), Theresa Merritt (*Aunt Em*), Thelma Carpenter (*Miss One*), Lena Horne (*Glinda the Good*), Richard Pryor (*The Wiz*), Stanley Greene (*Uncle Henry*), Clyde J. Barrett (*Subway Peddler*), Carlton Johnson (*Head Winkie*), Harry Madsen (*Cheetah*), Glory Van Scott (*Rolls Royce Lady*), Vicki Baltimore (*Green Lady*), Derrick Bell, Roderick Spencer Sibert, Kashka Banjoko, Ronald Smokey Stevens (*Crows*), Tony Brealond, Joe Lynn (*Gold Footmen*), Clinton Jackson, Charles Rodriguez (*Green Footmen*), Ted Williams, Mabel Robinson, Damon Pearce, Donna Patrice Ingram (*Munchkins*), Carlos Cleveland, Mariann Aalda, Aaron Boddie, Gay Faulkner, Ted Butler, T.B. Skinner, Jamie Perry, Daphene McWilliams, Douglas Berring, James Shaw, Johnny Brown, Gyle Waddy, Dorothy Fox, Francis Salisbury, Beatrice Dunmore, Traci Core, Donald King, Claude Brooks, Billie Allen, Willie Carpenter, Denise DeJon, Kevin Stockton, Alvin Alexis.

This disappointing remake of THE WIZARD OF OZ has none of the sparkle and shine that made this all-black musical such a success on Broadway. Diana Ross plays a 24-year-old Harlem schoolteacher who's at her aunt's home for Thanksgiving dinner. She walks out into a snowstorm, which magically whisks her away from Harlem to the Emerald City (an easily recognizable Manhattan). The story follows the same lines as the original, with Jackson, Russell, and Ted Ross as Diana Ross' three comrades. Eventually they find the Wiz, leading to a happy conclusion. This film takes some marvelous talents and a terrific premise, then promptly turns into a bungled mess. Lumet's direction is overblown, stripping the story of its magic. Though Diana Ross tries her best, she is too old for the part and never successfully projects the innocence her character needs. Pryor is once again wasted in a film that ill suits his talents, though Jackson does give some enjoyable moments as the Scarecrow. King rises above the dross with her marvelous portrayal of the witch, and the whole mess might be worth sitting through just to hear Lena Horne's fine number. Walton's imaginative sets are another wasted attraction. Universal sank $24 million into the project, which grossed only $13 million at the box office. This $11 million loss effectively killed off what little interest major studios had in doing black-oriented films for some time to come. Interiors were shot at the recently refurbished Astoria Studios. The many musical numbers tended toward the garish, with 206 studio musicians, a 36-voice children's choir, and a 73-voice adult choir (which included well-known vocalist Roberta Flack); major theaters tended to go full-volume with the Dolby Stereo, to the annoyance of some audience members. Songs include: "The Feeling That We Have" (Charles Smalls, sung by Theresa Merritt), "Can I Go On Not Knowing?" (Quincy Jones, Nick Ashford, Valerie Simpson, sung by D. Ross), "Glinda's Theme" (Jones, sung by chorus), "He's the Wizard" (Smalls, sung by Thelma Carpenter), "Soon as I Get Home" (Smalls, sung by D. Ross), "You Can't Win" (Smalls, sung by Jackson), "Ease On Down the Road" (Smalls, sung by D. Ross, Jackson, Russell, T. Ross), "What Would I Do If I Could Feel?" "Slide Some Oil to Me" (Smalls, sung by Russell), "I'm a Mean Old Lion" (Smalls, sung by T. Ross), "Poppy Girls" (Jones, Anthony Jackson), "Be a Lion" (Smalls, sung by D. Ross, Jackson, Russell, T. Ross), "Emerald City Ballet" (Jones, Smalls, sung by chorus), "Is This What Feeling Gets?" (Jones, Ashford, Simpson, sung by D. Ross), "Don't Nobody Bring Me No Bad News" (Smalls, sung by King), "Everybody Rejoice" (Luther Vandross, sung by cast), "Believe in Yourself" (Smalls, sung by Lena Horne, D. Ross). Other songs and musical numbers are: "Brand New Day," "So You Wanted to See the Wizard," "He's the Wizard" (Smalls), "Liberation Agitato," "The Wiz," "March of the Munchkins," "Now Watch Me Dance," "End of the Yellow Brick Road," "A Sorry Phoney" (Jones).

p, Rob Cohen; d, Sidney Lumet; w, Joel Schumacher (based on the book *The Wonderful Wizard of Oz* by L. Frank Baum, and the musical "The Wiz" by William F. Brown, Charlie Smalls); ph, Oswald Morris (Technicolor); m, Quincy Jones; ed, Dede Allen; prod d, Tony Walton; art d, Philip Rosenberg; cos, Walton; spec eff, Albert Whitlock, Al Griswold; ch, Louis Johnson; makeup, Stan Winston.

Musical   **Cas.**   (PR:C   MPAA:G)

WIZARD OF BAGHDAD, THE*½   (1960) 92m FOX c

Dick Shawn (Genii-Ali Mahmud), Diane Baker (Princess Yasmin), Barry Coe (Prince Husan), John Van Dreelen (Sultan Jullnar), Robert F. Simon (Shmadin), Vaughn Taylor (Norodeen), Michael David (Meroki), Stanley Adams (Kvetch), William Edmonson (Asmodeus, King of the Genii), Leslie Wenner (Princess Yasmin as a Child), Michael Burns (Young Prince Husan), Don Beddoe (Raschid), Kim Hamilton (Teegra), "Tiny Tim" Baskin (Desert Chieftain), Hortense Peters (Barmaid).

Cafe comedian Shawn, who made his first starring feature film appearance earlier the same year in WAKE ME WHEN IT'S OVER, is a bumbling genie who should have stayed bottled in this "Arabian Nights" spoof. Reprimanded by the genie king, Edmonson, for failing to fulfill his geniacal missions (a result of his passion for women and wine, forget the song), Shawn is offered one final assignment; failure will result in his conversion to mere mortality (a fate not worse than death, but certainly culminating in it). In human form, but little wishing to sustain that condition, Shawn sets off, riding a singularly humorless talking horse. His assignment: to become THE WIZARD OF BAGHDAD, in which guise he must fulfill a prophecy requiring the marriage of a princess, Baker, and a prince, Coe, who are to jointly rule the city-state upon the demise of the elderly incumbent. Van Dreelen is the sinister sultan who attempts to circumvent the prophecy. The many gags are mostly topical, so the film doesn't wear well. The wires suspending the magic carpets are all too apparent.

p, Sam Katzman; d, George Sherman; w, Jesse L. Lasky, Jr., Pat Silver (based on a story by Samuel Newman); ph, Ellis W. Carter (CinemaScope, DeLuxe Color); m, Irving Gertz; ed, Saul A. Goodkind; art d, Duncan Cramer, Theobold Holsopple; spec eff, L.B. Abbott, Emil Kosa, Jr.; m/l, "Enie Menie Geni," Diane Lampert, Peter Farrow, David Saxon (sung by Dick Shawn).

Fantasy/Comedy   (PR:A   MPAA:NR)

WIZARD OF GORE, THE zero   (1970) 96m Mayflower c

Ray Sager (Montag the Magnificent), Judy Cler (Sherry Carson), Wayne Ratay (Jack), Phil Laurenson (Greg), Jim Rau (Steve), John Elliot (Detective Harlan), Don Alexander (Detective Kramer), Monika Blackwell, Corinne Kirkin, Karin Alexana, Sally Brody, Karen Burke (Girls), Jack Gilbreth (Maitre d'Hotel), Alex Ameripoor (Man on Stage).

Witnessing a spectacular stage appearance of Montag the Magician (Sager), TV show hostess Cler and her journalist boy friend Ratay are impressed, little realizing the implications of his act. Having sawn one audience member in half and driven a steel spike through the head of another, both victims returning unharmed to their theater seats, Sager has retired to the acclaim of the audience. Hours later, both "butchered" women die horribly, their wounds reflecting their theatrical experiences. Unaware, Cler calls the clever magician, inviting him to make a guest appearance on her talk show. As he hypnotizes the entire studio audience, viewer Ratay realizes the danger. Rushing to the studio, he kills the mad magician. In a surrealistic aftermath, in Cler's apartment, Ratay removes his face and reveals that he is Sager. He chops Cler into mincemeat. She proves to possess the power herself, and transmutes time, bringing the entire affair back to its theatrical beginning. A surrealistic splatter film.

p&d, Herschell Gordon Lewis; w, Allen Kahn; ph, Alex Ameripoor, Dan Krogh (Eastmancolor); m, Larry Wellington; ed, Eskandar Ameripoor; makeup, Frank Morelli.

Horror   Cas.   (PR:O   MPAA:R)

WIZARD OF MARS*   (1964) 81m Borealis Enterprises/American General c

John Carradine (Wizard of Mars), Roger Gentry, Vic McGee, Jerry Rannow, Eve Bernhardt.

In his dotage, despite his painful arthritis, charismatic actor Carradine bent his considerable talents to many such silly scripts and low-budget independent productions. Loosely following the story line of L. Frank Baum's Wonderful Wizard of Oz, four astronauts crash on the red planet and find the remnants of a lost civilization. The sole survivor is the wizard, Carradine. Judy Garland groupies will consider this to be sacrilege.

p,d&w, David L. Hewitt.

Fantasy   Cas.   (PR:A   MPAA:NR)

WIZARD OF OZ, THE*****   (1939) 101m MGM c/bw

Judy Garland (Dorothy), Ray Bolger (Hunk/The Scarecrow), Bert Lahr (Zeke/The Cowardly Lion), Jack Haley (Hickory/The Tin Woodsman), Billie Burke (Glinda), Margaret Hamilton (Miss Gulch/The Wicked Witch), Charles Grapewin (Uncle Henry), Clara Blandick (Auntie Em), Pat Walsh (Nikko), Frank Morgan (Prof. Marvel/The Wizard/Guard/Coachman), The Singer Midgets (Munchkins), Mitchell Lewis (Monkey Officer), Terry the Dog (Toto).

One of the world's most beloved films, THE WIZARD OF OZ presents an eye-dazzling fantasy-musical, a treat for young and old. This film is so beautifully directed and acted that is has rightly remained a classic since its initial release in the spectacular year of 1939 when GONE WITH THE WIND, STAGECOACH, and a host of other classics appeared as magically as those fabulous ruby slippers clinging to Garland's feet. Garland is a 14-year-old schoolgirl living on a Kansas farm whose little dog, Toto, gets her into trouble with Hamilton, a mean spinster living in the area, one bitten by the mutt. Garland, at this time, sings her classic "Somewhere Over the Rainbow." Hamilton shows up on the farm and orders Garland's aunt and uncle, Blandick and Grapewin, to turn over the dog to her, saying that she has an order to take the animal which will be put to sleep as a vicious creature. Despite Garland's pleas, the helpless farm couple comply with the law and wicked Hamilton takes the dog away in a basket affixed to her bicycle. But the dog gets loose and runs back to Garland's farm where the girl, fearful that Hamilton will return for the animal, runs away. She meets Morgan, a down-and-out carnival actor and so-called professor of magic whose horse-drawn wagon has broken down along the roadway. Morgan fascinates Garland with his ability to perform great feats of magic but he talks about his abilities rather than showing them. After learning that she is a runaway, Morgan subtly persuades Garland to return home. Just as she and her dog get back to the farm, a huge tornado is seen at great distance across the flat plains, grinding its way toward the farm. The farmhands, Lahr, Haley, and Bolger, go running with Grapewin and Blandick into a storm cellar, closing and locking the doors before Garland, unseen by them, can join them. She runs into the house as wind fiercely engulfs the area and is knocked unconscious by a window screen torn off a window and sent flying through her room. Garland, in her unconscious state, envisions her farmhouse uprooted by the twister and sent skyward. She stands up and looks, astonished, as the house spins upward inside the eye of the tornado. On its whirling periphery she can see farm animals, and even an old woman sitting quietly knitting in her rocking chair, and then, cycling madly, is the image of Hamilton who soon changes into a hideous-looking witch riding a broomstick and wearing a peaked cap. Then the farmhouse begins to descend, spinning toward earth and landing with a crash. Garland apprehensively steps to the door of the farmhouse and opens it to a beautiful, dazzling world of color (the beginning of the film being shot in black and white by LeRoy to heighten the image of Garland's fantasy when she steps into a Technicolor Oz). She is in Munchkin Land and the little people are free of her tyrannical rule. They laud her and sing songs to her and then Burke, the good witch of of the North, appears to tell the bewildered Garland that she is now a national hero for deposing the despot. A red cloud of smoke, however, heralds the arrival of Hamilton, the wicked witch of the West, who threatens Garland, but she has no real power in Munchkin Land, as Burke points out. The feet of the dead witch protrude from beneath Garland's house and she wears the magic ruby slippers. Before Hamilton can retrieve these powerful ruby slippers from her sister's corpse, Burke waves her wand and they appear on Garland's feet. Hamilton demands she be given the slippers but when she reaches for them, they give off electric waves that drive her back. She declares that she will seek vengeance, leaning her pointed face toward the terrified Garland to squeal, "I'll get you, my pretty, and your little dog, too!" She vanishes in a puff of red smoke. Garland tells Burke that all she wants is to go home to Kansas and Burke tells her that "only the great and all-powerful Wizard of Oz" has the ability to return her to her native state and that she must seek his help in the Emerald City where his palace resides. Burke points Garland toward the Yellow Brick Road, telling her to follow it to Emerald City. Waving goodbye to the Munchkins, Garland sets down the road where she meets a trio of strange characters who all decide to accompany her to Emerald City: Bolger, a witless scarecrow searching for a brain, Haley, a tin woodsman searching for a heart, and Lahr, a cowardly lion looking for courage. As the four dance, scurry, and saunter apprehensively down the road, with Toto at their side, they are beset by dangers and hazards that wicked witch Hamilton puts in their path. Just when they have Emerald City in sight, Hamilton has them run through a field of poppies that puts them to sleep but Burke, also looking over Garland and her friends, sends down a light shower of snow that revives them and sends them on their way to the gates of the resplendent city. After they are admitted to the city by Morgan, playing a gate guard, they are driven by coach to the Wizard's palace by a coachman, also played by Morgan, whose carriage is pulled by "A Horse of a Different Color," a marvelous horse that changes from one bright color to another as they move along. A flustered palace guard, also played by Morgan (he's everywhere), finally admits the four travelers after they have been suitably cleaned up by the industrious citizens of Emerald City and shows them into the august presence of the Wizard. They stand before a huge image of a floating skull-like face that booms down on them and sends terror into their bodies so that Garland and her friends quiver in fright. The Wizard tells them that he will grant their wishes but they must obtain the broomstick of the wicked witch of the West. They glumly go off to accomplish their impossible chore. As the foursome walk through a dark forest, Hamilton sends a horde of her winged-monkeys to swoop down on them; they capture Garland and her dog and fly them to Hamilton's remote mountaintop castle where the witch tries to get the ruby slippers through persuasion and threat. One of the most terrifying moments of the film occurs when the witch leaves Garland alone for a while and she peers into the witch's crystal ball to see the homey image of her aunt, kindly Blandick. She cries out, "Auntie Em! Auntie Em!" And then the image changes to the green-faced ugly countenance of Hamilton, mimicking Garland's cry before dissolving. Meanwhile, Garland's three companions, led by Bolger, find enough courage to climb the mountain to the castle and they knock out three of the witch's guards, dressing up in their uniforms and entering the castle. They find Garland just before Hamilton is about to do away with her and then race about the castle with the girl and her dog until Hamilton and her green-faced guards corner them. The vicious witch tells them they are all doomed and lights a fire at the end of her broomstick, jutting this forth so that she sets Bolger's straw arm on fire. Garland grabs a pail of water and tosses it onto Bolger's arm but it also douses Hamilton. The witch screams that she is melting, the water, her ancient enemy, destroying her. Garland and her friends watch in amazement as Hamilton shrinks into nothingness, with only her peaked cap and black gown remaining on the stone floor of the castle room. "You've killed her," says one of the astonished guards in a bassy voice, and the guards kneel before Garland, who is now *their* liberator. Returning with the witch's broom to the Wizard, having accomplished their herculean task, they are rebuffed by the fierce image on the wall and are told to go away. But Garland sees a man behind a drape frantically working the levers of an elaborate machine and pulls the drape back. It's Morgan, who has created the image of the Wizard on the screen. Garland angrily calls him a fraud and he tells her that he is "a very good man but a very bad wizard." He nevertheless says he will grant all the wishes of the travelers. He gives Bolger a diploma, making him a professor of "Thinkology." To the Tin Man Morgan awards a red metallic heart, and to the Cowardly Lion he gives a medal for courage. Garland, he says, can accompany him back to Kansas in his balloon which is leaving momentarily. But when Garland is saying goodbye to her friends later the balloon slips away with Morgan on it and he cannot return for Garland, no matter how hard he tries, shouting down to her, "I don't know how it works!" Garland is tearful and heartbroken. "Now I'll never get back home," she weeps. Bolger holds her and tells her that she can stay with him, Lahr, and Haley, who love her, but she cannot be consoled. Just then Burke arrives in her white bubble from on high and tells Garland that she's always had the power to return to Kansas. She tells her to click her ruby slippers three times and repeat the line, "There's no place like home." She does and in a flash Garland is back in Kansas (and the film goes to black and white), in her bed with Blandick, Grapewin, the three farmhands who have been her traveling companions in Oz, and the kindly sideshow man, Morgan, all looking down on her. She excitedly tells them that she's been to a strange and beautiful land but that "there's no place like home!" The film ends with a closeup of Garland, bright face smiling, an image that would hearten generations of viewers to come who watched this great classic. This film has probably been seen by more people (and more times in repeated viewership) than any other motion picture ever made, including GONE WITH THE WIND. The special effects help to make this fairy tale fantasy come alive with flying monkeys, apple trees with arms that throw their own fruit at passersby, witches good and bad, and a host of little Munchkins (their voices altered by speeding up and slowing down the recorded soundtrack) to delight everyone. The songs are also terrific and they include: "Munchkinland" (Arlen, Harburg, sung by the Munchkins), "Ding Dong the Witch is Dead" (Arlen, Harburg, sung by Garland, Burke, the Munchkins), "Follow the Yellow Brick Road" (Arlen, Harburg, sung by Garland, the Munchkins), "If I Only Had a Brain/a Heart/the Nerve" (Arlen, Harburg, sung by Bolger, Lahr, Haley), "If I Were the King of the Forest" (Arlen, Harburg, sung by Lahr), "The Merry Old Land of Oz" (Arlen, Harburg, sung by chorus), "Threatening Witch," "Into the Forest of the Wild Beast," "The City Gates Are Open," "At the Gates of the Emerald City," "Magic Smoke Chords," "Toto's Chase," "On the Castle Wall," "Delirious Escape" (Herbert Stothart), "The Cornfields" (Stothart, George Stall, George Bassman), "Poppies" (Stothart), "Optimistic Voices" (Arlen, Stothart, Harburg), "The Witch's Castle" (Stothart, Felix Mendelssohn), "March of the Winkies" (Stothart, Roger Edens), "Dorothy's Rescue" (based on Modest Petrovich Mussorgsky's "Night on Bald Mountain," arranged by Edens), "In the Shade of the Old Apple Tree" (Van Alstyne), "Come Out, Come Out Wherever You Are" (sung by Burke), "It Really Was No Miracle" (sung by Garland), "Lions and Tigers and Bears" (sung by Lahr), "You're Out of the Woods" (sung by the chorus). Several directors had a hand in the creation of this astounding film, including George Cukor, Richard Thorpe, and Norman Taurog, with Fleming finally brought in to direct. He only accepted the assignment because his little girl asked him to do it, or so he later said. To think that Fleming directed GONE WITH THE WIND *and* THE WIZARD OF OZ in the same year (or years that led up to their 1939 releases), the two most popular films ever made, is astounding. Garland, who has been forever identified as the wide-eyed Dorothy Gale and is magical in the role, was not the first choice for this part. Producer LeRoy thought to cast Shirley Temple or Deanna Durbin in the role but neither was available and the 16-year-old Garland was finally selected. Wallace Beery coveted the role of the Wizard but MGM boss Louis B. Mayer did not want to put up with the big man's antics. Beery had slipped considerably and was drunk half the time and starting fights and knocking over scenery when he reported for duty at the studio. "Get him in and get him out," was the motto Mayer gave for Beery. W.C. Fields was offered the part but he insisted upon getting $100,000 and that was too much, according to LeRoy. The Wizard's part was too small, said Ed Wynn when he was offered the role and Morgan, who begged for the part, finally got it, but only after he made a screen test, even though he was one of the most experienced and best character actors in the business. Bolger also coveted a role in the film, the part of the Scarecrow, but that role went to Buddy Ebsen and Bolger got the role of the Tin Man. Ebsen took ill, however, and Bolger was given the part which gave him screen immortality. Haley then took over the role of the Tin Man and had to suffer through the most arduous makeup of all the players, later complaining that his "costume was agony. I couldn't bend in that Tin Man thing. When I wasn't working, I was on a reclining board. The only chance I had all day to get out of that costume was when Judy was at school." Lahr was the one and only choice for the Cowardly Lion and he reveled in the role, adding all kinds of little pieces of business from his many years in burlesque and the Broadway stage. Morgan took Lahr aside before shooting began and told him, "You're going to be a great hit in this picture, but it's not going to do you a damned bit of good– you're playing an *animal!*" For the insidious and hateful Wicked Witch, the producers had originally chosen Edna May Oliver and later thought to cast Gale Sondergaard in the role but Hamilton, with her hatchet face, won the role and it became the most important of her life, although it was not without its hazards. She was severely burned several times by the explosive powder that engulfed her when she arrived and departed scenes and had to receive medical attention for these burns throughout the film. She grew wary of the special effects department and refused to mount her broomstick for one scene that was supposed to shoot her through the air, even though she was assured that the broomstick was safe. Her stand-in, Betty Danko, took her place and was promptly blown almost through the sound stage roof; she spent almost two weeks in the hospital and the witch's hat and broomstick were found months later embedded in the roof of the sound stage. Helen Gilbert was to have played the part of the Good Witch but Burke was assigned that part after Gilbert vanished on a romantic vacation. Burke was perfect for the delicate and shining Glinda, although her vocals were dubbed by Lorraine Bridges. The Munchkins were made up of 124 midgets from the famed Singer's Midgets group, a wild lot of people who had no respect whatsoever for Hollywood moguls. Neither LeRoy nor Fleming could control them and several of these irascible characters destroyed their hotel rooms because the furniture was not fitted to their size. They drank booze on the set, told dirty stories, threw knives at each other and the crew members, especially those technicians who were very tall, and the male midgets were constantly crawling under the dresses of showgirls or chasing them about shouting obscenities. One of the leading midget players was so drunk one day that he fell into a toilet, according to Lahr, and had to be rescued just before an important scene. Fleming was called off the production when it was almost complete and King Vidor, his close friend, came in to complete the film, never getting credit, but reportedly directing the sepiatone beginning and the ending of the film, including the tornado sequence and Garland singing "Somewhere Over the Rainbow" (Harold Arlen, E.Y. Harburg), a song which became her unstated theme song and would be identified with her for the rest of her traumatic career. Garland, at the time of this film, was a healthy teenager, a normal schoolgirl whose fame became worldwide when THE WIZARD OF OZ was released. MGM realized it had a great star on its hands. The studio would make that star work ceaselessly to retain that fame until the sweet and innocent Dorothy Gale was no more. When released, the film was a smash at the box office and gleaned more than $3 million; Garland would win a special Academy Award for "Best Juvenile Performance of the Year." The film would go on to make many more millions of dollars, becoming one of the all-time box office champions and each year, beginning in 1976, CBS-TV paid MGM $800,000 to show it. The film since its release has touched just about every child in the world (although the more impressionable may become alarmed at some of the scenes dealing with the Wicked Witch), and during WW II, the tune "We're Off to See the Wizard" (Arlen, Harburg) became the official marching song of the Australian army. MGM later produced a spinoff film, the animated JOURNEY BACK TO OZ, where the animation was flat and uninspiring, but the voices of the characters–Mickey Rooney, Liza Minnelli, Margaret Hamilton (reprising her role), Ethel Merman, Danny Thomas, and Rise Stevens–were effective. The film was poorly and dim- wittedly remade as a vehicle for Diana Ross in 1978, THE WIZ, a mistake that proved to be an insult to the original sound classic. A silent version was made in 1925, and in 1985 Frank Baum's novel was faithfully adapted in the interesting, though commercially unsuccessful, RETURN TO OZ.

p, Mervyn LeRoy; d, Victor Fleming, (uncredited) King Vidor; w, Noel Langley, Florence Ryerson, Edgar Allen Woolf (based on the novel by L. Frank Baum); ph, Harold Rosson (Technicolor); m, Herbert Stothart; ed, Blanche Sewell; art d, Cedric Gibbons; set d, Edwin B. Willis; cos, Adrian; spec eff, Arnold Gillespie; ch, Bobby Connolly; makeup, Jack Dawn.

Fantasy/Musical Cas. (PR:AAA MPAA:NR)

WIZARDS½** (1977) 80m Bakshi/FOX c

Voices: Bob Holt *(Avatar)*, Jesse Wells *(Elinor)*, Richard Romanus *(Weehawk)*, David Proval *(Peace/Necron 99)*, James Connell *(President)*, Steve Gravers *(Blackwolf)*, Barbara Sloane *(Fairy)*, Angelo Grisante *(Frog)*, Hyman Wien *(Priest)*, Christopher Tayback *(Peewhittle)*, Mark Hamil *(Sean)*, Peter Hobbs *(General)*, Tina Bowman *(Prostitute)*.

Bakshi, the man who put genitalia on anthropomorphic cartoon characters in FRITZ THE CAT (1972), the first X-rated cartoon feature, turns to fairies in this futuristic PG-rated parable of good and evil. In an effective mix of animation, stock footage, and rear projection, the post-nuclear millenium vision of Bakshi is revealed to be without shades of gray. In a world of mutants, a fairy queen is magically impregnated and gives birth to twins, one good, the other bad. The good twin eschews all technology (the very thing that brought the world to this sorry state); the bad one espouses it. The latter digs up an ancient movie projector and some newsreels which reveal to him the way in which Adolf Hitler's panzers overran Europe. Using these as a model, he launches an attack against his good brother, who has only magic with which to defend himself. After heavy losses, the good brother– with other survivors, an elf and a sexy princess– captures the bad brother's general, Necron 99, converts him, and renames him Peace. The four run into a bunch of fairies, whose help they solicit. After a few more reverses, good wins over evil. Visually striking, but flawed by poor scripting.

p,d&w, Ralph Bakshi; ph, Ted C. Bemiller (DeLuxe Color); animation ph, Jack Hooper; m, Andrew Belling; ed, Donald W. Ernst; md, Belling; prod d, Ian Miller (backgrounds); animators, Brenda Banks, Irven Spence, Martin B. Taras, Robert Taylor, Arthur Vitello (sequence animation by Spence).

Animated Fantasy   **(PR:C MPAA:PG)**

WOLF CALL*½   (1939) 61m MON bw

John Carroll (*Michael Vance*), Movita (*Towanah*), Peter George Lynn (*Father Devlin*), Guy Usher (*Vance, Sr.*), Holmes Herbert (*Winton*), Polly Ann Young (*Natalie*), George Cleveland (*Dr. MacTavish*), John Kelly (*Bull Nelson*), Wheeler Oakman (*Carson*), John Sheehan (*Grogan*), Charles Irwin (*Police Sergeant*), Grey Shadow (*Smokey the Dog*), Roger Williams, Pat O' Malley.

One of many dog sagas based on Jack London themes, this has the canine running wild with wolves between bouts of helping Carroll fulfill the assignment given him by his father. Carroll heads to the North Country with his faithful pooch to discover whether a pitchblende mine is worth keeping in the family holdings. Once there, the city-bred dog finds some she-wolves in heat, and Carroll discovers Indian girl Movita, who seems somewhat seasonal herself. Mine manager Oakman proves to have been concealing the true richness of the deposit when Carroll flies some samples out for independent assay. Grey Shadow and his vulpine friends do some vocalizing, as do Carroll and Movita.

p, Paul R. Malvern; d, George Waggner; w, Joseph West (based on the novel by Jack London); ph, Fred Jackman, Jr.; m, Edward J. Kay; ed, Carl Pierson; art d, E.R. Hickson; m/l, "Song of Sixpence," "Love Call," Fleming Allen (Sung by John Carroll, Movita).

Western   **(PR:A MPAA:NR)**

WOLF DOG*   (1958, Can.) 61m RF/FOX bw

Jim Davis (*Jim Hughes*), Allison Hayes (*Ellen Hughes*), Tony Brown (*Paul Hughes*), Austin Willis (*Krivak*), Don Garrard (*Trent*), Juan Root (*Hawkins*), B. Braithwaite (*Mrs. Bates*), Lloyd Chester (*Slim*), Syd Brown, Daryl Masters, Les Rubie, Jay MacDonald, John Nevette, John Paris, Ed Holmes, Chuck Kehoe, Glen Momott, Prince the Dog.

It's the old story of war between ranchers and farmers as a group of men get greedy for some land in the Canadian farm lands and a dog comes to the fore with some intelligent antics. Pretty insipid stuff without any originality, except on the part of Prince.

p&d, Sam Newfield; w, Louis Stevens; ph, Frederick Ford (Regalscope); m, John Bath; ed, Douglas Robertson; art d, Tom Kemp.

Adventure/Western   **(PR:AA MPAA:NR)**

WOLF HUNTERS, THE*½   (1949) 70m MON bw

Kirby Grant (*Rod*), Jan Clayton (*Greta*), Chinook (*Chinook, the Dog*), Edward Norris (*Henri*), Helen Parrish (*Marcia*), Charles Lang (*McTavish*), Ted Hecht (*Muskoka*), Luther Crockett (*Cameron*), Elizabeth Root (*Minnetaki*).

This canine caper of the far North has parallel romances, one happy, the other tragic. Royal Canadian Mounted Police constable Grant, with his faithful dog Chinook, seeks the slayers of fur traders who rob them for their goods. He meets a jolly trapper, Norris, who successfully romances a local village maiden. Chinook the dog is not so fortunate; in his one fling, he gets aced out by a wolf. The rest of the film is all action, with the killers finally brought to bay. An early low-budget effort from director Boetticher, who handled the crime genre well in THE RISE AND FALL OF LEGS DIAMOND (1960).

p, Lindsley Parsons; d, Oscar[Budd[Boetticher; w, W. Scott Darling (based on the novel by James Oliver Curwood); ph, William Sickner; m, Edward J. Kay; ed, Ace Herman; md, Kay; art d, Dave Milton.

Western   **(PR:A MPAA:NR)**

WOLF LARSEN**   (1958) 83m AA bw

Barry Sullivan (*Wolf Larsen*), Peter Graves (*Van Weyden*), Gita Hall (*Kristina*), Thayer David (*Mugridge*), John Alderson (*Johnson*), Rico Alaniz (*Louis*), Robert Gist (*Matthews*), Jack Grinnage (*Leach*), Jack Orrison (*Haskins*), Henry Rowland (*Henderson*).

One of a number of screen adaptations of Jack London's famed novel "The Sea Wolf," the best known being the 1920 silent featuring Noah Beery, Sr. and the 1941 version with Edward G. Robinson. Sullivan is the crazed, cruel

captain who totally tyrannizes over his fiefdom, his ship; Graves is the young, well-to-do shipwreck victim who, rescued by Sullivan, serves as one of his crew. Sullivan carries on a litany of abuses against the men under his command; the latter finally rebel against his cruelties and kill him. Well acted and well paced, with a fine musical score.

p, Lindsley Parsons; d, Harmon Jones; w, Jack DeWitt, Turnley Walker (based on t he novel *The Sea Wolf* by Jack London); ph, Floyd Crosby; m, Paul Dunlap; ed, Maurice Wright, John Blunk; art d, William Ross.

Adventure/Drama   **(PR:A MPAA:NR)**

WOLF LARSEN**   (1978, Ital.) 92m Cougar c (AKA: THE LEGEND OF SEA WOLF)

Chuck Connors, Barbara Bach, Giuseppi Pambieri.

Connors is the sadistic sea captain of a mysterious ship in this lesser version of the Jack London story. Pretty dull despite Connors' pell-mell acting.

p, Mino Loy; d, Joseph Green [Giuseppi Vari]; ph, (Gerry Color).

Adventure   **(PR:A MPAA:PG)**

WOLF MAN, THE**   (1941) 71m UNIV bw

Claude Rains (*Sir John Talbot*), Lon Chaney, Jr. (*Larry Talbot*), Evelyn Ankers (*Gwen Conliffe*), Ralph Bellamy (*Capt. Paul Montford*), Warren William (*Dr. Lloyd*), Patric Knowles (*Frank Andrews*), Maria Ouspenskaya (*Maleva*), Bela Lugosi (*Bela*), Fay Helm (*Jenny Williams*), Leyland Hodgson (*Kendall*), Forrester Harvey (*Victor Twiddle*), J.M. Kerrigan (*Charles Conliffe*), Kurt Katch (*Gypsy with Bear*), Doris Lloyd (*Mrs. Williams*), Olaf Hytten (*Villager*), Harry Stubbs (*Rev. Norman*), Tom Stevenson (*Richardson the Graveyard Digger*), Eric Wilton (*Chauffeur*), Harry Cording (*Wykes*), Ernie Stanton (*Phillips*), Ottola Nesmith (*Mrs. Bally*), Connie Leon (*Mrs. Wykes*), La Riana (*Gypsy Dancer*), Caroline Cooke (*1st Woman*), Margaret Fealy (*2nd Woman*), Jessie Arnold (*Gypsy Woman*), Eddie Polo (*Churchgoer*), Gibson Gowland (*Villager*), Martha Vickers.

Seeking to keep the second great sound horror boom going strong at the box office, Universal Studios decided to resurrect the forgotten monster from their 1935 THE WEREWOLF OF LONDON and transform him into THE WOLF MAN. Bearing no resemblance to the previous film, THE WOLF MAN was given a whole new look and treatment by the studio. Chaney stars as a young British heir who returns to the mansion of his father, Rains, after getting a college education in America. While exploring the tiny shops of the town, Chaney wanders into an antique store where he meets Ankers, the daughter of the owner. He flirts with the pretty young woman and then buys an old walking cane with a silver handle formed in the shape of a wolf's head with a pentagram (a five pointed star) engraved on it. Ankers informs Chaney that the pentagram is the sign of the werewolf and recites an old gypsy folk rhyme: "Even a man who is pure in heart/And says his prayers at night/May become a wolf when the wolf-bane blooms/And the autumn moon is bright." Chaney laughs off the rhyme as silly superstition and invites Ankers to join him at a carnival that has recently come to town. Ankers agrees, but she brings along her best friend, Helm, as a chaperone. At the carnival the trio meets a gypsy fortune teller, Ouspenskaya, and her son, Lugosi. While Chaney and Ankers go for a walk in the fog- shrouded moors, Helm has her fortune read by Lugosi. Lugosi looks into Helm's hand and sees the sign of the pentagram. Knowing that this means she will be killed by a werewolf, Lugosi quickly ends the session and tells the woman to leave. In the moors, Chaney and Ankers hear a bone-chilling wolf's howl followed by a scream. Chaney rushes to the source of the hideous noises and is attacked by a vicious beast. Before beating it to death with the heavy silver handle of his cane, Chaney is bitten on the chest by the hairy animal. Chaney passes out from the pain, and when the police arrive the dead bodies of Helm and Lugosi are found–but no animal. Lugosi's corpse has had its head smashed in and his feet are bare. Helm appears to have had her throat ripped out by a wild animal. Despite Helm's wound the police, headed by inspector Bellamy, doubt Chaney's story and when he is examined his chest wound has vanished. Seeking answers, Chaney goes back to the gypsy camp to see Ouspenskaya. She tells him that her son was a werewolf and because he was bitten, Chaney will become one as well. Chaney dismisses her explanation as nonsense, but when she asks to see his wound, the pentagram appears on his chest. She tells him that he will turn into a wolf when the moon is full and that a werewolf can only be killed by silver–be it a bullet, knife, or cane. That night the moon is full and Chaney transforms into a werewolf. His nose becomes a wet snout, his hands and feet paws, and his body is covered with thick fur. Now an animal trapped in a bedroom, the wolf man crashes through the window and runs off into the night in search of prey. The next morning police find the mangled body of a gravedigger and trace the paw prints back to Rains' mansion. Since it is daytime, Chaney has turned back into his normal self and the police leave. Tortured by guilt, Chaney asks his father if he believes in the werewolf legend. Rains dismisses it as nonsense and states that men's minds can play strange tricks. Rains attributes his son's agitated state to the shock of Helm's murder. Determined to capture the mysterious beast, Bellamy has his men set bear traps on the moors. That night the moon is full once again and Chaney undergoes his hideous transformation. While stalking the moors, Chaney steps into one of the traps and is unable to free himself. Morning arrives before the police find him and he turns back into human form. Ouspenskaya happens by and she frees Chaney. Growing more and more desperate, Chaney tries to convince Ankers that he is a werewolf, but she refuses to believe him. When he spots the sign of the pentagram in the palm of her hand, Chaney realizes that she is to be his next victim. Horrified, Chaney flees back to his father's castle and tries to convince Rains he is a werewolf. Rains worries about the mental anguish his son is suffering and to prove that his ideas are hogwash, ties Chaney to a chair and locks him in a room to prevent the "werewolf" in him from escaping. That night Rains joins in the search for the vicious beast that has been terrorizing the community and he brings Chaney's cane along with him. At the castle Chaney once again transforms into a werewolf. He easily breaks free of his bonds and escapes the castle. In the dense fog and among the twisted shapes Chaney finds Ankers and attacks her. Rains hears the girl's screams for help and comes to the rescue. He beats the hairy beast about the head with the silver-tipped cane until it moves no more. Then–before Rains' eyes–the dead werewolf turns back into the lifeless form of his son. The rest of the hunting party arrives and assumes Chaney was killed while trying to save Ankers. Ouspenskaya makes her way through the crowd and recites a final prayer for Chaney declaring that his suffering is now over. Fearing comparison with his famous father, Lon Chaney, Sr., who starred in such horror classics as THE HUNCHBACK OF NOTRE DAME (1923) and THE PHANTOM OF THE OPERA (1925), Chaney, Jr. avoided appearing in horror films and eventually made a name for himself with his superior portrayal of the slow-witted Lennie in stage and screen versions of John Steinbeck's novel *Of Mice and Men*. Gaining new confidence in his abilities, Chaney agreed to try the horror genre and created a character with whom he would always be identified–the wolf man. Though actor Henry Hull refused to let Universal makeup artist Jack Pierce apply any heavy makeup to him in the 1935 THE WEREWOLF OF LONDON, Chaney had no such fears. Pierce was able to create a memorable monster using a rubber snout, fangs, claws, and lots of yak hair. The process took nearly five hours to complete, and shooting the transformation scenes–where Chaney's head was braced still while Pierce applied small parts of the makeup so the camera could record the actor actually becoming the werewolf–took as much as 20 hours. Despite the fact that THE WOLF MAN was released only two days after the bombing of Pearl Harbor, the film was a smash hit at the box office–the studio's biggest grosser of the season–and catapulted Chaney to horror film stardom. The wolf man gave Universal enough hit monsters to form a basketball team, the others being Frankenstein's monster, The Invisible Man, The Mummy, and the inimitable Dracula. Universal gave the film good production values and a superior cast. Screenwriter Siodmak patched together the legend of the werewolf by combining elements from lycanthropic folklore, witchcraft, and Bram Stoker's *Dracula*, creating a new monster for the screen. All elements combined to make a thrilling, scary, and ultimately tragic horror classic. Ankers' first horror outing (she'd appeared in a number of more sedate British films) shot her to B film stardom, ultimately earning her the sobriquets "The Screamer" and "Queen of the Horror Pictures," and–in Hollywood, at least–"the poor man's Fay Wray." Ankers had recounted that her first meeting with Chaney during the filming was none too cordial. The actor was being reprimanded by the studio for vandalizing the posh dressing room he shared with Broderick Crawford during playful drinking bouts. The studio gave the dressing room to Ankers to share with another contract player. "So you're the gal who swiped my dressing room," said the angry Chaney. During the scenes in the gypsy encampment, the original story line had Chaney wrestling with a trained bear (the sequence–and actor Kurt Katch, listed in the credits as playing the bear's keeper–was eliminated from the final cut). Ankers recounts that the 600-pound bear became fascinated by her, pulled its chain from the keeper's hand, and loped toward her. Ankers raced up a ladder into the gaffers' rigging where an electrician pulled her onto the platform, then frightened off the enamored animal by shining a spotlight into its eyes. Art director Otterson's English-countryside sets were exceptional, made more haunting by the enormous amounts of low-hanging fake fog that pervaded them. The actors played in a veritable sea of "fog," their nether extremities only rarely visible during the moorland scenes. Ankers recalls that when the wolf man pursued her through the "forest," after screaming–a specialty she handled most adroitly throughout her horror-film career–she feigned a faint and literally disappeared into the shroud of low-flying "fog." Inhaling vapors, Ankers really did pass out in the chemical mist. The set was being struck by the crew when one of the technicians tripped over her near-lifeless form in the mist, salvaging her for future frightenings. Chaney essayed the role of the werewolf six times, the next appearance being in FRANKENSTEIN MEETS THE WOLFMAN (1943). HOUSE OF FRANKENSTEIN (1944), HOUSE OF DRACULA (1945), ABBOTT AND COSTELLO MEET FRANKENSTEIN (1948), and a guest appearance on the television show "Route 66" followed. Chaney soon found himself picking up where the likes of Lugosi and Karloff left off by playing monsters they had created. Chaney played the Frankenstein monster in THE GHOST OF FRANKENSTEIN (1942)–he also filled in for Glenn Strange (who was playing Frankenstein's monster) in two scenes when the actor injured his leg in ABBOTT AND COSTELLO MEET FRANKENSTEIN–the mummy in THE MUMMY'S TOMB (1942), THE MUMMY'S GHOST (1944), and THE MUMMY'S CURSE (1945) and a vampire in SON OF DRACULA (1943). THE WOLF MAN, however, remained Chaney's favorite achievement because it was he who originated the role and remains to this day the definitive wolf man. Rains does his usual fine work in a role that perhaps is beneath him in its limited scope, as does Lugosi, whose character dies early in the movie. Ankers was later to meet

a cultured, rather shy European gentleman who stated that he enjoyed working with her. She failed to recognize Lugosi–with whom she'd played in two pictures (the other was THE GHOST OF FRANKENSTEIN)–without his makeup, and only later figured out who he was. Moscow Art Theater actress Ouspenskaya is marvelous in her restrained portrayal as the wise old gypsy who foretells the tradegy that is to befall the innocent Chaney and the other victims of capricious fate (the original title of the picture was "Destiny"). A talented supporting cast helped to propel the picture to its now-classic status

p&d, George Waggner; w, Curt Siodmak; ph, Joseph Valentine; m, Charles Previn; ed, Ted Kent; art d, Jack Otterson; makeup, Jack P. Pierce.

Horror   Cas.   **(PR:C MPAA:NR)**

WOLF OF NEW YORK*½   (1940) 69m REP bw

Edmund Lowe (*Chris Faulkner*), Rose Hobart (*Peggy Nolan*), James Stephenson (*Hiram Rogers*), Jerome Cowan (*Cosgrave*), William Demarest (*Bill Ennis*), Maurice Murphy (*Frankie Mason*), Charles D. Brown (*Constable Nolan*), Edward Gargan (*Upshaw*), Andrew Tombes (*Duncan*), Ben Welden (*McGill*), Ann Baldwin (*Gladys*), Roy Gordon (*Governor*).

Brilliant, flamboyant criminal attorney Lowe, who has made his mark–a nd his fortune–successfully defending the wicked against their just deserts, finally loses a case. The one truly innocent man he has ever defended is executed for the murder of Brown, a policeman, after an important witness has been executed. The experience is cathartic for Lowe, who proceeds to turn his talents to the pursuit of true justice. At the urging of inamorata Hobart, the governor, Gordon, appoints the reborn Lowe to the position of district attorney. Newly zealous in his pursuit of criminals, Lowe prosecutes the big brain behind a mob of racketeers–Stephenson, his one-time client. Justice triumphs over art in this stereotyped story with unclever dialog.

p, Robert North; d, William McGann; w, Gordon Kahn, Lionel Hauser (based on a story by Leslie Turner White, Arnold Belgard); ph, Reggie Lanning; ed, Ernest Nims; md, Cy Feuer.

Crime Drama   **(PR:A MPAA:NR)**

WOLF OF WALL STREET THE**   (1929) 74m PAR bw

George Bancroft (*Jim Bradford*), Olga Baclanova (*Olga Bradford*), Nancy Carroll (*Gert the Maid*), Paul Lukas (*David Tyler*), Arthur Rankin (*Frank*), Brand on Hurst (*Sturges*), Paul Guertzman (*Office Boy*), Crauford Kent (*Jessup*), J ack Luden.

Like a time bomb, a ticker-tape telegraph plays a major role in this suspense-filled saga. Rough, rowdy Bancroft plays a market manipulator who heads a pool of investors. Jeering at the "suckers" who lose their patrimony through his machinations, Bancroft little suspects that he may lose at love. When Bancroft succeeds in cornering the copper market,–where his partner in the financial pool, Lukas, failed in the attempt,–Bancroft taunts his proud partner. Angered, Lukas plots vengeance. He seduces Baclanova, Bancroft's social-striving immigrant wife, a one-time trapeze performer. Carroll, Baclanova's maid, observes the adulterous affair with distaste. Privy to the secrets of the business, Carroll feeds financial information to her boy friend, Rankin, who invests his savings in copper and wins heavily. Reinvesting his winnings in the same market, Rankin loses everything and more when Bancroft's manipulations force the market down, his pool having sold short. When his margin is called, Rankin embezzles from his firm, but he is caught and jailed. The angry Carroll confronts Bancroft, blaming him for her lover's troubles. When the vulpine Bancroft laughs at her, Carroll discloses his wife's affair with Lukas. Bancroft exacts revenge in a characteristic fashion: he buys out his other partners, then once again manipulates the market. As Lukas and Baclanova register mounting alarm, Bancroft calmly waits until the market peaks, then announces to the perfidious pair that they are all penniless. Walking on Wall Street, he meets Carroll and Rankin. Bancroft's vengeful manipulations have inadvertently made Rankin a fortune, and the two intend to wed. THE WOLF OF WALL STREET quietly sees the happy couple depart. Bancroft, who usually played gangster roles, here has his meatiest part; he does the role full justice in what is generally regarded as his finest film performance. Baclanova–who often used only her surname in her film credits–here has her first speaking part. The Russian-born actress was again to play a trapeze performer in her best-known role, that of the mercenary circus girl who marries a midget for his money in Tod Browning's classic horror film FREAKS (1932).

d, Rowland V. Lee; w, Doris Anderson; ph, Victor Milner; ed, Robert Bassler; m/l, "Love Take My Heart," Harold Cristy, Joseph Meyer.

Drama   **(PR:C MPAA:NR)**

WOLF SONG***   (1929) 93m PAR bw

Gary Cooper (*Sam Lash*), Lupe Velez (*Lola Salazar*), Louis Wolheim (*Gullion*), Constantine Romanoff (*Rube Thatcher*), Michael Vavitch (*Don Solomon Salazar*), Ann Brody (*Duenna*), Russell "Russ" Columbo (*Ambrosia Guiterrez*), Augustina Lopez (*Louisa*), George Rigas (*Black Wolf*), Leona Lane (*Dance Hall Girl*).

Set in the 1840s in the trapper country of California and Canada, WOLF SONG was billed by Paramount as the "first musical film romance." Cooper stars as a disheveled Kentucky trapper who rides the trails with his friends Wolheim and Romanoff until he meets and falls in love with Velez. Her father, Vavitch, a Mexican don, is opposed to their romance, but rather than give up Cooper elopes with the girl and takes her off to the mountains. They marry and Cooper settles into a life of domesticity. Before long, however, he yearns to be back in the wilderness with his trapper friends. One day he leaves Velez and sets out to find Wolheim and Romanoff, but before he does so he has a change of heart and heads back. Along the way, he is ambushed by a band of Indians led by Rigas. Badly wounded, Cooper makes his way back to Velez who, although she hates him for abandoning her, accepts him back. While performing okay at the box office, WOLF SONG received a great deal of attention for the torrid love affair that had erupted off-screen between Cooper and Velez, and a rumored nude swimming scene that had been included in the picture. The swimming scene proved to be too far in the distance to be revealing, but rumors of the stars' romance were indeed a reason to gossip. Cooper and Velez had fallen in love during the production and talk of marriage was in the air. Hoping to discourage such a union, Paramount reportedly threatened to take action if Cooper and Velez wed. After being a gossip column item for two years, Cooper and Velez, without ever hearing the ring of wedding bells, went their separate ways. The film includes two Mexican love songs delivered by Velez: "Mi Amado" and "Yo Te Amo Means I Love You" (Richard Whiting, Alfred Bryan). Acting as assistant director was Henry Hathaway, who would eventually direct Cooper in seven pictures including the fine 1935 film THE LIVES OF A BENGAL LANCER.

p&d, Victor Fleming; w, John Farrow, Keene Thompson (based on the story by Harvey Ferguson); ph, Allen Siegler; ed, Eda Warren; md, Irvin Talbot.

Romance   (PR:A-C MPAA:NR)

WOLFEN***½   (1981) 115m Orion/WB c

Albert Finney *(Dewey Wilson)*, Diane Venora *(Rebecca Neff)*, Edward James Olmos *(Eddie Holt)*, Gregory Hines *(Whittington)*, Tom Noonan *(Ferguson)*, Dick O'Neill *(Warren)*, Dehl Berti *(Old Indian)*, Peter Michael Goetz *(Ross)*, Sam Gray *(Mayor)*, Ralph Bell *(Commissioner)*, Max. M. Brown *(Christopher Vanderveer)*, Anne Marie Photamo *(Pauline Vanderveer)*, Sarah Felder *(Cicely Rensselaer)*, Reginald Vel Johnson *(Morgue Attendant)*, James Tolkan *(Baldy)*, John McCurry *(Sayad Alve)*, Chris Manor *(Janitor)*, Donald Symington *(Lawyer)*, Jeffery Ware *(Interrogation Operator)*, E. Brian Dean *(Fouchek)*, Jeffery Thompson *(Harrison)*, Victor Arnold *(Roundenbush)*, Frank Adonis *(Scola)*, Richard Minchenberg *(Policeman)*, Raymond Serra, Thomas Ryan *(Detectives)*, Tony Latham, David Connell, Jery Hewitt *(Victims)*, Ray Brocksmith *(Fat Jogger)*, Michael Wadleigh *(Terrorist Informer)*, Joaquin Rainbow, John Ferraro, Rino Thunder, Glenn Benoit, Eddy Navas, Ricky Hawkeye, Pete Dyer, Paul Skyhorse, Gordon Eagle, Javier First-Day-of-Light, George Stonefish, Julie Evening Lilly *(Native Americans)*, Jane Lind, Annie Gagen, Cullen Johnson, Robert Moberly, Tony Stratta, Max Goff, Robert L. King, Caitlin O'Heaney, William Sheridan *(ESS Operators)*, Linda Gary, Burr DeBenning, Mel Welles, Pat Parris, Dan Sturkie, Andre Stolka, Charles Howerton, Corey Burton *(ESS Voices)*.

Between the years 1981 and 1982, Hollywood released no less than four horror films dealing with werewolves. Three of them, AN AMERICAN WEREWOLF IN LONDON, FULL MOON HIGH, and THE HOWLING, approached the legendary subject matter with a disarming sense of humor and gruesome special effects. The other film, WOLFEN, is told in a straightforward, intelligent manner and became one of the most engrossing movies of the year. Boasting a strong performance by Finney, WOLFEN begins as a young, very rich industrialist and his wife (Brown and Photamo) are driven back to Manhattan in their stretch limousine after breaking ground for a new, multi-million dollar development project in the most decimated area of the South Bronx slums. Still celebrating his new endeavor, Brown has his driver-bodyguard McCurry stop in Manhattan's Battery Park so he and his wife can cavort among the sculptures. Suddenly, the point of view shifts and the viewer is looking up at the trio from only a few feet above the ground. The colors change radically and the people leave strange, ghost-like images behind them that linger for a moment and then disappear. The camera floats along behind Brown, his wife, and the bodyguard, slowly moving in. McCurry senses something is wrong and quietly draws his pistol. Suddenly the camera angle seems to lunge at the man, a vicious roar is heard, and the bodyguard's severed hand–still clutching the pistol–sails through the air. The screen explodes with several of these oddly colored lunges and soon all three people are dead, their throats ripped out. The next morning Finney, a New York homicide detective, is assigned to the case and it is decided by the police that the murders must have been the work of terrorists. To help Finney's investigation, the police assign Venora, a young female criminal psychologist specializing in the study of terrorism, to the case as well. To determine the cause of death, Finney visits the morgue and discusses the case with Hines, a hip black coroner with a disarming sense of graveyard humor. Most of Hines' employees possess the same sense of humor and during one scene when an orderly pushes a corpse-laden gurney over the foot of another orderly the line, "Oh man, you just rolled that dude over my foot" can be heard in the backround. Hines comes to the conclusion that the victims'

throats were ripped out by some sort of animal, perhaps a wolf. Finney then connects these killings with several murders that have occurred in the South Bronx where the bodies of winos, drug addicts, and bums have been found with their throats ripped out. Hines steers Finney to Ferguson, a naturalist and expert with wolves who works at the Central Park Zoo. All three come to the conclusion that there must be a pack of urban wolves who feed only at night and are mistaken for wild dogs. Meanwhile, the "Wolfen," who are extremely intelligent, sense that Finney's investigation is getting too close. Ferguson is killed by the wolves, as is Hines, during a stake out in an abandoned South Bronx church that seems to be their lair. Eventually Finney learns from a group of American Indian construction workers that the Wolfen are a race of super-intelligent wolves that once roamed the land that is now New York City. Learning how to survive in an urban environment, the Wolfen inhabit only the slum areas and feed off those members of society who will not be missed. The Wolfen are very sensitive and have great compassion for those they kill, choosing only those who are dying or ready to give up life. Since the Indians and wolves shared the same fate at the hands of white settlers (being nearly wiped out in the name of progress) they understand each other and the Indians surmise that the industrialist was killed by the Wolfen to prevent the new development project from once again pushing them off their land. Eventually there is a showdown between the Wolfen and police which takes place, ironically, on Wall Street. The previously unseen Wolfen suddenly appear on the steps of the New York Stock Exchange and confront Finney, Venora, and Finney's disbelieving boss, O'Neill. The Wolfen reveal themselves to be magnificently beautiful black wolves led by another gorgeous wolf with light fur. They all have piercing eyes that seem to glow. When the panicky O'Neill pulls his service revolver, the Wolfen attack and decapitate the man in a swift orgy of bloody special effects. Finney and Venora escape to dead industrialist Brown's office building and hide in the rich man's office several floors above the street. Thinking they are safe, Finney and Venora are suddenly surprised when the pack of Wolfen comes crashing through the windows. As the beasts stare at the couple, Finney tries to make mental contact with the lead Wolfen. To prove to the Wolfen that he is sympathetic to their existence (and he is), Finney smashes the scale model of Brown's development project. Sensing that he is sincere, the Wolfen allow Finney and Venora to live and then disappear. Directed by Wadleigh, whose only other feature was the famous rock documentary WOODSTOCK (1970), WOLFEN is an intelligent, insightful, and visually creative twist on the werewolf legend. Though at times the film borders on the pretentious with its preachy approach to the problems of urban decay, the homeless, Indians, ecology, and big business, Wadleigh also spins a fascinating horror tale that is as engrossing as it is thrilling. Finney is superb as the rumpled cop searching for clues and Hines is terrific in his film debut as the wisecracking medical examiner (the film was also Venora's first feature). The "Wolfen Vision" effects are sensational and really bring a previously unseen vision to the screen. Using a variety of optical printing techniques, the "Wolfen Vision" conveys the wolves' heightened sense of heat, smell, movement, and texture. The gore effects by Carl Fullerton are effective, if somewhat gratuitous. Perhaps the most incredible aspect of WOLFEN are the wolves. Having heightened the viewers' expectations of what the beasts look like by leaving them unseen through much of the film, Wadleigh took the risk of disappointing today's special-effects-engorged audiences by using real wolves. However, when the animals finally reveal themselves, the effect is stunning and exhilarating because the wolves are so magnificent. These are beautiful and noble creatures and the viewer is immediately awed by them. Budgeted at $15 million and plagued with production difficulties, WOLFEN turned out to be a commercial disaster (probably due to the publicity department, which didn't know what to do with it–the posters and advertising were simply awful) despite the fact that it was one of the most unique and thought-provoking horror films in years.

p, Rupert Hitzig; d, Michael Wadleigh; w, David Eyre, Wadleigh (based on the novel by Whitley Strieber); ph, Gerry Fisher (Panavision, Technicolor); m, James Horner; ed, Chris Lebenzon, Dennis Dolan, Martin Bram, Marshall M. Borden; prod d, Paul Sylbert; art d, David Chapman; cos, John Boxer; spec eff, Robert Blalack, Betz Bromberg; makeup, Carl Fullerton.

Horror   Cas.   (PR:O MPAA:R)

WOLFMAN*½   (1979) 101m E. D. Corp./Omni c (AKA: THE WOLFMAN)

Earl Owensby *(Colin Glasgow)*, Ed L. Grady *(Rev. Leonard)*, Julian Morton *(Edwin Glasgow)*, Kristine Reynolds *(Lynn Randolph)*, Richard Dedmon *(Uncle Clement)*, Maggie Lauterer *(Aunt Elizabeth)*, Sid Rancer *(Dr. Tate)*, Victor Smith *(Luthor)*, Helen Tryon *(Grandmother)*, Brownlee Davis.

Poor DeLuxe Color drive-in trash from one of the sub-Mason-Dixon line moguls of movies, starring himself. Near the turn of the century, the scion of southern wealth is slain by sinister preacher Grady, who is responsible for maintaining a curse on his family instituted when a long-dead relative reneged on a Faustian pact with Satan. Owensby, the son of the murdered Morton, inherits the lycanthropic mantle and proceeds to lope through the night biting out throats. Preacher Grady finally finishes off Owensby, using an appropriate silver weapon, but dies in the process himself. Never noticed in the North, the picture made money.

p, Earl Owensby; d&w, Worth Keeter; ph, Darrell Cathcart (DeLuxe Color)

; m, Arthur Smith, David Floyd; ed, Richard Aldridge; art d, David Cadell; spec eff, Al Yehoe; makeup, Sandy Barber, Keeter.

Horror   **Cas.**   **(PR:O   MPAA:R)**

WOLFPACK   (SEE: McKENZIE BREAK, THE, 1970)

WOLFPEN PRINCIPLE, THE*½   (1974, Can.) 96m Image Flow c

Vladimir Valenta (*Henry Manufort*), Doris Chillcot (*His Wife*), Alica Ammon (*Her Mother*), Tom Snelgrove (*Her Father*), Lawrence Brown (*Indian Smith*), Janet Wright (*Miss Mervin*), Lee Taylor (*Sailor*), Ivor Harries (*Watchman*), Bullus Hutton (*Clergyman*).

Fine comedy-drama has Valenta playing a middle-aged man looking for something to do with his life. He and his wife, Chillcot, are supported by her parents and the little money Valenta makes at his job. Valenta begins spending his evenings at the local zoo, endlessly watching the wolves. He meets Brown, a Northern Indian, who shares a similar fascination for the animals. Together they concoct a plan to free the wolf pack, but ultimately are defeated by the animals themselves who don't care to leave the security of their cage. This is a film that delivers its message with grace and subtlety. The story is told with genuine feeling for its characters (including the wolf pack) while showing a nice comic touch by the director. Another fine example of what is possible by a low budget filmmaker with sensibility and imagination.

p, Werner Aellen; d&w, Jack Darcus; ph, Hans Klardie; m, Don Druick; ed, Raymond Hall; art d, Hagen Beggs.

Comedy/Drama   **(PR:AA   MPAA:NR)**

WOLF'S CLOTHING**   (1936, Brit.) 80m Wainwright/UNIV bw

Claude Hulbert (*Ambrose Girling*), Gordon Harker (*Prosser*), Lilli Palmer (*Lydia*), George Graves (*Sir Roger Balmayne*), Peter Gawthorne (*Sir Hector*), Helen Haye (*Mildred Girling*), Joan Swinstead (*Mary Laming*), Frank Birch (*Rev. John Laming*), Ernest Sefton (*Finden Charvet*), George Hayes (*Yassiov*), Shayle Gardner (*Babo*), Mme. Von Major (*Babo's Mother*), Violet Gould (*Kiosk Proprietress*).

A pleasant lighthearted farce in which Hulbert unwittingly becomes the target of a group of spies when they take him for a trained assassin. The young man is such a clod it's hard to see how such a mistake in identity could be made, but it is and the comic talent of Hulbert takes full advantage of the situation for some splendidly humorous moments. One of Palmer's earliest starring roles, made in the same year as her far more successful appearance in Alfred Hitchcock's SECRET AGENT.

p, Richard Wainwright; d, Andrew Marton; w, Evadne Price, Brock Williams (based on their play "The Emancipation of Ambrose").

Comedy   **(PR:A   MPAA:NR)**

WOLVES zero   (1930, Brit.) 57m British and Dominions/Wardour bw

Charles Laughton (*Capt. Job*), Dorothy Gish (*Leila McDonald*), Malcolm Keen (*Pierre*), Jack Osterman (*Hank*), Arthur Margetson (*Mark*), Franklyn Bellamy (*Pablo*), Griffith Humphreys (*Semyon*), Andrews Englemann (*Pfeiffer*), Betty Bolton (*Naroutcha*).

Gish is reduced to mediocrity in this film where she plays a woman trapped in an arctic cabin with a band of outlaws. While she is suffering from weather-induced illness, the gang members draw lots to see who will possess her. Things look dismal for her until gang leader Laughton takes pity on her, undergoes a change of heart, and helps her escape, only to be killed himself in the attempt. Gish's stylized gestures served her better in the silent days. Production values are bad, with the sound of a wind machine often drowning out the dialog. Six years later the film showed up as a 35-minute short under the title WANTED MEN and was shown on a bill with MR. DEEDS GOES TO TOWN. Both Gish and Laughton ignored the American "premiere" of WANTED MEN but Osterman, a secondary character in the film, did not. He had acquired a name on Broadway as a comedian and didn't want this ghost from his past coming back to haunt him. Upon learning that the film was going to be shown, he raised $50 to buy it, thus making sure it wouldn't resurface. Alas, on his way to the theater on the night before WANTED MEN opened, Osterman was mugged and thus the show went on.

p, Herbert Wilcox; d, Albert de Courville; w, Reginald Berkeley (based on the play by Georges Toudouze); ph, Roy Overbaugh, Dave Keesan.

Drama   **(PR:A   MPAA:NR)**

WOLVES OF THE RANGE*½   (1943) 60m PRC bw

Bob Livingston (*Rocky Cameron*), Al "Fuzzy" St. John (*Fuzzy Jones*), Frances Gladwin (*Ann*), I. Stanford Jolley (*Dorn*), Karl Hackett (*Corrigan*), Ed Cassidy (*Brady*), Jack Ingram (*Hammond*), Kenne Duncan (*Adams*), Budd Buster (*Foster*), Bob Hill (*Judge Brandon*), Slim Whitaker, Jack Holmes, Roy Bucko.

Standard oater fare has Livingston and St. John riding to the rescue of helpless ranchers being victimized by gunmen trying to drive them off their

land. The mastermind behind the operation has designs on creating an irrigation project, with only the ranchers standing in his way. (See LONE RIDER series, Index.)

p, Sigmund Neufeld; d, Sam Newfield; w, Joe O'Donnell; ph, Robert Cline; ed, Holbrook N. Todd.

Western   **(PR:A   MPAA:NR)**

WOLVES OF THE SEA*   (1938) 65m Guaranteed Pictures bw (GB: JUNGLE ISLAND)

Hobart Bosworth (*Capt. Wolf Hansen*), Jeanne Carmen (*Nadine Miller*), Dirk Thane (*William Rand*), Pat West (*Jim Lane*), Warner Richmond (*Snoden*), John Merton (*Mitchell*), Edward Kaye (*Frankie*).

With a title and a leading-role name strongly redolent of the popular (and many-times-filmed) Jack London novel *The Sea Wolf*, this low-budget thriller mixes genres in an abortive attempt to please every taste. Bosworth is the diamond-dotty captain of a salvage ship who hopes to recover a hoard of jewels from an ocean liner sunk in tropical waters. Carmen is a child of wealth, the only human survivor of the sinking, stranded on an island with a shipload of wild animals which had been bound for a zoo. She staves off an attack by a stuffed leopard and observes some stock jungle shots of cute monkeys until, finally, she is rescued by the treasure salvors. A mutinous crew headed by villain Richmond compounds the plot, but second officer Thane manages to straighten things out. Initially repulsed by Carmen's riches, Thane ultimately succumbs to her charms. Badly directed and edited and ludicrously acted.

p, J. D. Kendis; d&w, Elmer Clifton; ph, Eddie Linden; ed, Duke Goldstone.

Adventure   **(PR:A   MPAA:NR)**

WOLVES OF THE UNDERWORLD*   (1935, Brit.) 57m REA/Regal bw (GB: PUPPETS OF FATE)

Godfrey Tearle (*Richard Sabine*), Isla Bevan (*Joan Harding*), Russell Thorndike (*Dr. Orton Munroe*), Fred Groves (*Arthur Brandon*), Michael Hogan (*Gilbert Heath*), Kynaston Reeves (*John Heath*), Roland Culver (*Billy Oakhurst*), John Turnbull (*Supt. deSabine*), Ben Welden, S. Victor Stanley.

Beautiful blonde Bevan, beset by problems, solicits the assistance of attorney Tearle, who turns detective to help her resolve her difficulties. Bevan's uncle, Thorndike, a diabolical doctor, has been blackmailed by escaped convict Welden into helping his gang of criminals. Tearle's deductive powers bring the bad men to bay. Low-key lighting and a sincere, humorless screenplay make this picture as soporific as a sleeping draught despite a strong cast and some action in the form of a train crash.

p, Julius Hagen; d, George A. Cooper; w, H. Fowler Mear (based on the play "Puppets of Fate" by Arthur Rigby and R. H. Douglas).

Crime   **(PR:A   MPAA:NR)**

WOMAN ACCUSED**½   (1933) 70m PAR bw

Nancy Carroll (*Glenda O'Brien*), Cary Grant (*Jeffrey Baxter*), John Halliday (*Stephen Bessemer*), Irving Pichel (*District Attorney Clark*), Louis Calhern (*Leo Young*), Norma Mitchell (*Martha*), Jack LaRue (*Little Maxie*), Frank Sheridan (*Inspector Swope*), John Lodge (*Dr. Simpson*), William J. Kelly (*Captain of Boat*), Harry Holman (*Judge Osgood*), Jay Belasco (*Tony Graham*), Gertrude Messinger (*Evelyn Craig*), Lona Andre (*Cora Matthews*), Donald Stuart (*The Steward*), Gregory Golubeff (*The Band Leader*), Robert Quirk (*Cheerleader*), Amo Ingraham (*3rd Girl*), Dennis Beaufort (*2nd Boy*), Gaylord Pendleton (*3rd Boy*).

Not very good but rather interesting crime drama has Carroll about to marry Grant during a three-day pleasure cruise on which they are to embark. While Carroll packs, Calhern, her former lover, who lives upstairs, calls and asks her to come up. She takes the fire escape and Calhern begs her not to marry Grant and to return to him. She refuses and Calhern threatens to have his killer friend, LaRue, murder his rival. He calls up LaRue, but before he can order the murder, Carroll comes up behind him and bashes in his head with a small statue, killing him. Hysterical, she goes back down the fire escape, her dress covered in blood, and her housekeeper, Mitchell, cleans her up and helps hide any evidence connecting Carroll to the crime. The murderer goes on her cruise and marries Grant. Also on the ship is Halliday, a friend of Calhern's who suspects Carroll. He tries to trap her into confessing a number of times during the cruise, but constantly fails. Finally, on the last night out, there is a costume party and the guests settle down to play a game where they stage a mock murder trial. Carroll ends up the defendant and Halliday the prosecutor. While the other guests enjoy what they see as lighthearted play-acting, Carroll and Halliday are dueling with their wits. Finally Halliday opens a suitcase and pulls out the blood-spattered dress. Carroll breaks down and confesses and all the guests applaud her magnificent acting. While Halliday makes preparations to have Carroll arrested when the ship docks, Carroll confesses to Grant that she did, indeed, kill Calhern. When the ship docks Halliday produces more damaging testimony in the person of LaRue, who tells police that Carroll was the voice he heard in the room the night of Calhern's murder. Grant, though, is not prepared to let his love go to jail and he goes to LaRue and beats him with a belt until the gunman agrees to recant his testimony. LaRue's evidence gone, the district attorney has no choice but to release Carroll. About as silly as it sounds, with the odd twist of the guilty person actually getting away with it because the victim deserved killing. The story originated as a series in *Liberty Magazine*, written in 10 chapters, each by a different famous author (although few of the names are familiar today), without any consultation between them. The series was a great success but the film less so. Some of the performances are pretty good, but the whole thing falls flat because it is simply not believable.

d, Paul Sloane; w, Bayard Veiller (based on a story by Polan Banks from a *Libery Magazine* serial by Rupert Hughes, Vicki Baum, Zane Grey, Vina Delmar, Irvin S. Cobb, Gertrude Atherton, J.P. McEvoy, Ursula Parrott, Banks, Sophie Kerr); ph, Karl Struss.

Crime Drama   (PR:A-C MPAA:NR)

WOMAN AGAINST THE WORLD*   (1938) 66m COL bw

Ralph Forbes (*Larry Steele*), Alice Moore (*Anna Masters*), Edgar Edwards (*Johnny Masters*), Collette Lyons (*Patsy*), Sylvia Welsh (*Betty Jane*), Ethel Reese-Burns (*Aunt Frieda*), George Hallett (*Mr. Plummer*), James McGrath (*Detective Flavin*), Grant MacDonald (*Jimmy*), Fred Bass (*Prosecutor*), Harry Hay (*Mr. Martin*), Enid Cole (*Mrs. Martin*), Reginald Hincks (*The Judge*).

Moore (in her first big role) plays a long-suffering lass to whom virtually every possible tragedy migrates in this melange of mixed themes. Widowed by the death of Edwards, Moore's fatherless baby is taken from her by her aunt, Reese-Burns, whom Moore accidentally kills. Convicted of murder, Moore is imprisoned, but is pardoned through the intervention of likable lawyer Forbes. Trying to find her missing tyke, Moore gets involved with a swindling private detective. Trapped in a speakeasy nightclub, Moore is jailed following a police raid. Meanwhile, her missing infant–finally located– is abducted by criminals. There's a courtroom scene in which Moore is exonerated through the offices of the friendly Forbes. Too much too soon characterizes this chock-full screenplay by Edwards, who plays the husband who dies, like the picture, in the first reel.

p, Lew Golder; d, David Selman; w, Edgar Edwards; ph, Harry Forbes, William Beckway; ed, William Austin.

Drama   (PR:A MPAA:NR)

WOMAN AGAINST WOMAN**½   (1938) 60m MGM bw

Herbert Marshall (*Stephen Holland*), Virginia Bruce (*Maris Kent*), Mary Astor (*Cynthia Holland*), Janet Beecher (*Mrs. Holland*), Marjorie Rambeau (*Mrs. Kingsley*), Juanita Quigley (*Ellen*), Zeffie Tilbury (*Grandma*), Sarah Padden (*Dora*), Betty Ross Clarke (*Alice*), Dorothy Christy (*Mrs. Morton*), Morgan Wallace (*Morton*), Joseph Crehan (*Sen. Kingsley*).

The distaff-bedeviled Marshall is hectored mercilessly by his coven of crones in this clever high-society divorce drama. Bride Bruce and ex-wife Astor squabble over the hapless husband like two dogs battling over a bone while neighboring harridans gossip about the prospective outcome of the verbal duel. Finding that his stoical forbearance gains him no respite from his tormentors, Marshall finally puts his foot down and gains a measure of self-respect in this epic of male liberation. Essentially stagy, the dialog-heavy drama was the directorial debut (in film) of theatrical director Sinclair.

p, Edward Chodorov; d, Robert B. Sinclair; w, Chodorov (based on the story "Enemy Territory" by Margaret Culkin Banning); ph, Ray June; m, Dr. William Axt; ed, George Boemler; art d, Cedric Gibbons; cos, Dolly Tree.

Comedy   (PR:A MPAA:NR)

WOMAN ALONE, A   (SEE: TWO WHO DARED, 1937, Brit.)

WOMAN ALONE, THE   (SEE: SECRET AGENT, THE, 1937)

WOMAN AND THE HUNTER, THE*   (1957) 78m
Gross-Krasne-Phoenix bw (GB: TRIANGLE ON SAFARI)

Ann Sheridan, David Farrar, John Loder, Jan Merlin.

While off in the jungles of Kenya a love triangle develops which causes problems for all, except late night television viewers trying to combat insomnia . Sheridan tries her best with her cutting delivery and her still lovely 1940s glamor but can only do so much with the turgid material.

d, George Breakston.

Drama   (PR:A MPAA:NR)

WOMAN AT HER WINDOW, A**½   (1978, Fr./Ital./Ger.) 110m
Albina Productions-Rizz oli Film-Cinema 77/Cinema Shares c (UNE FEMME A SA FENTRE)

Romy Schneider (*Margot*), Philippe Noiret (*Raoul*), Victor Lanoux (*Michel*), Umberto Orsini (*Rico*), Delia Boccardo (*Dora*), Gastone Moschin (*Primou-*

kis), Carl Mohner (*Von Pahlen*).

Classes and cultures clash as well-to-do beauty Schneider is pursued by three suitors of disparate backgrounds. Orsini, a dissolute aristocrat of diminished means, has married Schneider for her wealth but loves her after his cynical fashion. Noiret is all establishment, a successful capitalist, upright, up tight, and desperate for the damsel. Lanoux is a Greek Communist evading the secret police of dictator Johannes Metaxas (the time is 1936). Rich, jaded Schneider finds fleeting romance with idealistic rebel Lanoux and a daughter is born of their brief union. Lanoux is killed; Schneider disappears during WW II. Years later, the daughter–now a woman– makes a pilgrimage to Greece to reprise her parents' chronicle. Orsini and Noiret meet again and discuss the events of the past. Essentially a love story within a political setting, the film is stunningly photographed. Author La Rochelle committed suicide during WW II, apparently as a result of his fling with fascism.

p, Albina de Boisrouvray; d, Pierre Granier-Deferre; w, Granier-Deferre, Jorge Semprun (based on the novel by Pierre Drieu La Rochelle); ph, Aldo Toni (Eastmancolor); ed, Jean Ravel.

Drama   (PR:O MPAA:NR)

WOMAN BETWEEN, THE, 1931   (SEE: WOMAN DECIDES, THE, 1931, Brit.)

WOMAN BETWEEN*   (1931) 81m RKO bw (GB: MADAME JULIE)

Lily Damita (*Mme. Julie*), O. P. Heggie (*John Whitcomb*), Lester Vail (*Victor Whitcomb*), Miriam Seegar (*Doris Whitcomb*), Anita Louise (*Helen Weston*), Ruth Weston (*Mrs. Black*), Halliwell Hobbes (*Barton*), Lincoln Stedman (*Buddy*), Blanche Frederici (*Mrs. Weston*), William Morris.

In the mannish style of Marlene Dietrich, Damita plays a French woman newly married to the wealthy Heggie, but who finds the attractions of his son Vail more appealing. A rather daring theme for the early 1930s failed to ignite much of a spark.

p, William LeBaron; d, Victor Schertzinger; w, Howard Estabrook (based the play "Madame Julie" by Irving Kaye Davis); ph, J. Roy Hunt; ed, William Hamilton; m/l, "Close to Me," Schertzinger.

Drama   (PR:C MPAA:NR)

WOMAN BETWEEN, THE, 1937 (SEE: WOMAN I LOVE, THE, 1937)

WOMAN CHASES MAN*½   (1937) 71m UA bw

Miriam Hopkins (*Virginia Travis*), Joel McCrea (*Kenneth Nolan*), Charles Winninger (*B. J. Nolan*), Erik Rhodes (*Henri Saffron*), Ella Logan (*Judy Williams*), Leona Maricle (*Nina Tennyson*), Broderick Crawford (*Hunk Williams*), Charles Halton (*Mr. Judd*), William Jaffrey (*Doctor*), George Chandler (*Taxi Driver*), Alan Bridge, Monte Vandrgrift, Jack Baxley, Walter Soderling (*Process Servers*), Al K. Hall, Dick Cramer (*Men in Subway*).

Hopkins is an ambitious career woman, a promising architect, who feels that her career is threatened by gender discrimination. Winninger, a scatter-brained old land developer, becomes her target for success. She brings him a set of plans and convinces the old codger that his latest failing suburban development venture can be turned into a winner with her help. The bottleneck to the plan is that the carefree Winninger is deeply in debt, and must pay off his creditors before the project can begin. His stodgy, stingy son McCrea has millions, but has refused to invest in Winninger's erratic schemes. Determined to succeed, Hopkins recruits movie theater doorman Crawford (in his screen debut) and usherette Logan to pose as Winninger's servants so that son McCrea will think the old man has accumulated some money from his ventures. She then has to overcome the obstacle of fortune-hunter Maricle, who has set her cap for McCrea. Discovering that McCrea's Achilles' heel is a weakness for champagne, Hopkins proceeds to get him besotted. The bibulous boy loosens up and signs the contract that will bail out the housing project, and he and Hopkins discover love. Fine comic performances and producer Goldwyn's traditionally lavish production don't quite save a fundamentally defective script. Goldwyn had long sought another comic vehicle for his romantic pairing of Hopkins and McCrea (this is their fifth and final such film). His search turned into a producer's nightmare, running through a whole legion of screenwriters and directors. Reportedly, the project began with Ben Hecht–the highest-paid scripter of his time–two years pre viously. Goldwyn, unhappy with Hecht, hired Sam and Bella Spewack to doctor his product; they determined that their patient, Hecht's script, was dead. Instead, the Spewacks decided to adapt a story by putative authors Root and Fenton that Goldwyn had previously purchased. Goldwyn didn't like that script either, so he hired Dorothy Parker and her husband Alan Campbell who, joined by Joe Bigelow, doctored the doctored script. A production schedule was established and director Edward Ludwig was called in. He wisely made himself unavailable before the cameras rolled, and the sorry script–already much patched and mended–was sent to a bat tery of studio hacks for more surgery. Director William Wyler was next called in. After reading the latest script, he returned the money he had been paid by Goldwyn–and paid more–to be taken off the project. Star Ho pkins next tried to get out of the picture but decided to stay with it when Goldwyn threatened not to pick up her contract option (this was the last film she made for Goldwyn). Hopkins and Goldwyn compromised, with the star consenting to play her role if Gregory LaCava would direct. Like his predecessors in this parade, LaCava took a walk after he read the much maligned script. Goldwyn finally lined up Blystone to direct. Production had finally begun when contract player Andrea Leeds, signed to play the part of the fortune-hunting female, resigned the role. The producer put her on suspension and borrowed Maricle from Columbia at the last moment. The picture was made; Goldwyn's tenacity became the stuff of legend.

p, Samuel Goldwyn; d, John Blystone; w, Joseph Anthony, Mannie Seff, David Hertz (based on the story "The Princess and the Pauper" by Lynn Root, Frank Fenton); ph, Gregg Toland; m, Alfred Newman; ed, Daniel Mandell; md, Newman; art d, Richard Day; cos, Omar Kiam.

Comedy   (PR:A MPAA:NR)

WOMAN COMMANDS, A**   (1932) 83m RKO bw

Pola Negri (Mme. Maria Draga), Roland Young (King Alexander), Basil Rathbone (Capt. Alex Pasitsch), H. B. Warner (Col. Stradimirovitsch), Anthony Bushell (Iwan), Reginald Owen (The Prime Minister), May Boley (Mascha), Frank Reicher (The General), George Baxter (Chedo), Cleo Louise Borden (Crown Prince Milan), David Newell (Adjutant).

Sultry silent screen vamp Negri's first talking picture was her final film in the U.S. until her brief cameo reappearance in 1943 in HI DIDDLE DIDDLE. This lavish period production has Negri as a beautiful cabaret performer who wins the heart of a Balkan king (Young) while simultaneously bringing officer Rathbone nearly to ruin with her excessive demands for costly gifts. Finally forced to accept an assignment at a distant outpost, Rathbone temporarily disappears from Negri's life; she weds carefree king Young. The marriage galvanizes his enemies into action, and Young is killed by a bomb. Negri, newly selfless and nonmercenary, reunites with Rathbone. The studio spared no expense in this production which, executives hoped, would make a talking star of a valuable silent-screen property. The film was well chosen; Negri's heavy Russian accent and rather guttural contralto delivery were assets rather than liabilities in this Balkan-based picture. Promotional efforts were substantial; Negri personally attended the New York City premiere, as did flashy mayor Jimmy Walker. The gala opening was so well attended that several notable cinema lights of the time--including Edmund Lowe and Lilyan Tashman--were forced to sit in gallery seats with the plebians. Director Stein had worked with Negri before; he had directed one of her first silents in Berlin. Laurence Olivier had originally been cast in Rathbone's role as the impecunious young captain, but an illness forced the studio to replace him. Rathbone, cast against type, was an unfortunate choice; his wooden performance was one of his worst. Despite all efforts, the picture lost more than a quarter of a million dollars for the studio. Negri, held to be largely responsible, never worked for RKO again; the executives elected to cut their losses. Their decision was probably ill-advised, since Negri's performance was effective, including her husky rendition of a cabaret song. The fault lay with the script, which vacillated wildly between lighthearted farce and heavy tragedy, a mix that was difficult for audiences to accept.

p, Charles R. Rogers; d, Paul L. Stein; w, Horace Jackson (based on a story by Thilde Forster); ph, Hal Mohr; m, Nacio Herb Brown; ed, Dan Mandell; art d, Carroll Clark; cos, Gwen Wakeling; m/l, "Promise You'll Remember Me For I'll Remember You," Brown, Gordon Clifford.

Drama   (PR:A MPAA:NR)

WOMAN DECIDES, THE*½   (1932, Brit.) 70m BIP/Powers bw (GB: THE WOMAN BETWEEN)

Owen Nares (Tom Smith), Adrianne Allen (Lady Pamela), C.M. Hallard (Earl Bellingdon), Barbara Hoffe (Mrs. Tremayne), Margaret Yarde (Mrs. Robinson), Winifred Oughton (Mrs. Jones), C. Disney Roebuck (Daniels), Netta Westcott.

A Behind-the-scenes romance during a Parliament election provides the premise for this mild piece of entertainment. Allen plays the mistress of the Conservative candidate, but finds herself drawn to the Labor candidate, whose past includes stealing money from a diner. When Allen's relationship to the Labor candidate is discovered, the Conservative member threatens to use his opponent's spotty past against him. Direction is a bit shaky in attempting to make the simplistic theme seem more prominent through the misuse of camera and cutting techniques.;

p, John Maxwell; d&w, Miles Mander, Frank Launder (based on the story by Miles Malleson); ph, Henry Gartner; ed, J.W. Stokvis.

Drama   (PR:A MPAA:NR)

WOMAN DESTROYED, A   (SEE: SMASH-UP, THE STORY OF A WOMAN, 1947)

WOMAN DOCTOR*½   (1939) 65m REP bw

Frieda Inescort (Judith), Henry Wilcoxon (Allan), Claire Dodd (Gail), Sybil Jason (Elsa), Cora Witherspoon (Fanny, Nurse), Frank Reicher (Dr. Mathews), Gus Glassmire (Dr. Martin), Dickie Jones (Johnny), Joan Howard (Louise), Spencer Charters (Veterinarian), Virginia Brissac (Miss Crenshaw), Rex (Moxie, the Dog.).

In the late 1930s the major studios turned out a succession of pictures--many of them light comedies--dedicated to the premise that a woman's place is in the home, rather than in the business world in competition with men. Republic, ever eager to grow to the stature of its larger competitors, was quick to imitate. This heavy-handed effort is the result of one such emulation. Summoned to a hospital on her wedding anniversary, female physician Inescort deserts husband Wicoxon and daughter Jason to practice her considerable surgical skills. The disgruntled Wilcoxon attends a party given by the delectable Dodd, and finds himself greatly drawn to his attentive hostess. As demands on Inescort's professional services increase, her alienated husband turns more and more to the company of Dodd until, finally, he decides on divorce. Polarized into action by her family's absence, Inescort eschews her life-saving skills and devotes herself to winning Wilcoxon back. When daughter Jason is injured in a fall from a horse while riding with Dodd, Wilcoxon pilots a plane to get her to a medical facility. Inescort does ambulatory surgery on her daughter up in the air. The near-tragedy reunites the family.

p, Sol. C. Siegel; d, Sidney Salkow; w, Joseph Moncure March (based on a story by Alice Altschuler, Miriam Geiger); ph, Ernest Miller; ed, Ernest Nims, Murray Seldeen; md, Cy Feuer; art d, John Victor Mackay; cos, Irene Saltern.

Drama   (PR:A MPAA:NR)

WOMAN EATER, THE*   (1959, Brit.) 70m Fortress/COL bw (GB: WOMANEATER)

George Coulouris (Dr. James Moran), Vera Day (Sally), Joy Webster (Judy Ryan), Peter Wayn (Jack Venner), Jimmy Vaughan (Tanga), Sara Leighton (Susan Curtis), Joyce Gregg (Margaret Santor), Maxwell Foster (Detective Inspector Brownlow), Edward Higgins (Sgt. Bolton), Robert MacKenzie (Lewis Carling), Marpessa Dawn (Native Girl), Roger Avon (Constable), Norman Claridge (Dr. Patterson), Stanley Platts (Steward), Peter Lewiston (Detective Freeman), Susan Neil (Coffee Girl), Harry Ross (Bristow), Alexander Field (Rifle Range Attendant), Shief Ashanti (Witch Doctor), John Grant (Rescue Party Leader), John Tinn (The Lascar), David Lawton (Man at Pub).

Nubile maidens make meals for the tentacled title vegetable when the human residents of the Amazon jungles practice their ritual sacrifices. Mad scientist Coulouris, observing the strange rites, develops the idea that sap oozing from the cutie-gobbling carnivore might confer immortality on humankind, so he transports the tree to his London laboratory. In order to persuade the plant to exude its marvelous sap, Coulouris must lure lots of lissome ladies to his lair at feeding time. Curvaceous blonde Day, an employee of the dotty doctor, is the chief incipient meal. Another employee, housekeeper Gregg, is murdered by Coulouris, who then brings her back to life with a serum made from the plant's exudations. The revivified Gregg proves to be a mindless zombie, so the disappointed doctor attempts to destroy the vegetable by fire. He perishes in the attempt. Performances are as good as the script will allow; screenwriter Fleming is not a particularly cunning linguist.

p, Guido Coen; d, Charles Saunders; w, Brandon Fleming; ph, Ernest Palmer; m, Edwin Astley; ed, Seymour Logie; md, Astley; art d, Herbert Smith.

Horror   (PR:C MPAA:NR)

WOMAN FOR CHARLEY, A   (SEE: COCKEYED COWBOYS OF CALICO COUNTY, 1970)

WOMAN FOR JOE, THE*½   (1955, Brit.) 91m Rank bw

Diane Cilento (Mary), George Baker (Joe Harrao), Jimmy Karoubi (George Wilson), David Kossoff (Max), Violet Farebrother, Earl Cameron (Lemmie), Sydney Tafler (Butch), A. J. "Man Mountain" Dean (Vendini), Patrick Westwood (Freddie the Kid), Derek Sydney (Harry the Spice), Verna Gilmore (Princess Circassy), Martin Miller (Iggy Pulitzer), Meier Tzelniker (Sol Goldstein), Miriam Karlin (Gladys), Frank Paulo (Stephan), Philip-Stainton (Sullivan), David Gabriel (Jack Evans), Dennis Rosaire (Franz), Douglas Hurn (Doctor), Amy Veness (Landlady), Edwin Ellis (Manager), Joan Hickson (Manager's Wife), Majorie Stewart (Saleswoman), Terence Longdon (Doctor at the Circus), Jill Ireland, Arthur Lowe.

A circus serves as the background for this trying love story in which midget Karoubi falls head-over-heels for Cilento, going so far as to use his influence with the circus to land her a job singing to lions. Though she likes the little man, her heart is pointed more in the direction of circus owner Baker, causing considerable tension in the operation of the circus. The highlight of this picture is the elaborate circus set, but this does little to benefit the unfolding of the plot, which has a predictable format.

p, Leslie Parkyn; d, George More O'Ferrall; w, Neil Paterson (based on his story "And Delilah"); ph, Georges Perinal (VistaVision, Technicolor); m, Malcolm Arnold; ed, Alfred Broome; m/l, "A Fool and His Heart," Jack Fishman.

Drama   **(PR:A   MPAA:NR)**

WOMAN FROM HEADQUARTERS*
(1950) 60m REP bw (AKA: WOMEN FROM HEADQUARTERS)

Virginia Huston (Joyce), Robert Rockwell (Gates), Barbra Fuller (Ruby), Norman Budd (Max Taylor), Frances Charles (Ann Rogers), K. Elmo Lowe (Capt. Parr), Otto Waldis (Joe Calla), Grandon Rhodes (Richard Cott), Jack Kruschen (Sam), Bert Conway (Leo Pawley), Marlo Dwyer (Bessie Collier), Sid Marion (Customer/Drunk), John DeSimone (Drunk), Gil Herman (Capt. Brady), Leonard Penn (Officer Allen).

Farfetched depiction of the life of a woman police officer, with Huston playing the super heroine in such a manner that it's hard to understand how crime can exist on the streets of America with such gutsy and tough people working to keep the cities safe. And she's pretty, too. A bottom-of-the drawer effort whose extravagant situations are unforgiveable.

p, Stephen Auer; d, George Blair; w, Gene Lewis; ph, John MacBurnie; m, R. Dale Butts; ed, Harold Minter.

Crime   **(PR:A   MPAA:NR)**

WOMAN FROM MONTE CARLO, THE**   (1932) 65m FN-WB bw

Lil Dagover (Lottie Corlaix), Walter Huston (Capt. Corlaix), Warren William (Lt. D'Ortelles), John Wray (Comdr. Brambourg), George E. Stone (Le Duc), Robert Warwick (Morbraz), Matt McHugh (Chief Petty Officer Vincent), Maude Eburne (Dowager Sister), Dewey Robinson (Cook), Robert Rose (Lt. Rosseau), Reginald Barlow (Defense Attorney), Frederick Burton (President of the Courtmartial), John Rutherford (Verguson), Frank Leigh (Pilot), Jack Kennedy (Admiral), Ben Hendricks, Jr (Chief Engineer), Francis McDonald (Karkuff), Oscar Apfel, Clarence Muse, Warner Richmond, Paul Porcasi, Elinor Wesselhoeft.

Huston is the commander of the French cruiser Lafayette which is attacked by German submarines and sunk. The few survivors are rescued and Huston undergoes a formal hearing to determine whether his negligence was responsible for the loss of the ship. Unbeknownst to Huston, his much younger wife, Dagover, was aboard the naval vessel at the time of the tragedy; dallying with handsome young lieutenant William, she was inadvertently trapped in the latter's cabin when the ship put to sea. Also rescued (strangely, the principal players appear to be the sole survivors of the sinking), Dagover is forced to reveal her adulterous indescretion in order to save husband Huston from court-martial proceedings. A remake of Alexander Korda's 1928 silent THE NIGHT WATCH, this film differed substantially both from that picture and from its precursor play. This was the Dutch-born Dagover's one and only role in a U.S.-made film; she scooted back to continuing stardom in Germany after this failure. Oddly, the actress' personal life paralleled that of the character she played in some respects. At the age of 20, she had married a German actor old enough to be her father. Huston's performance in the film is one of the worst of his long and honorable career. Only William, as the dashing young lieutenant, here boosted his career.

d, Michael Curtiz; w, Harvey Thew (based on the play "The Night Watch by Claude Ferrere, Lucien Nepoty); ph, Ernest Haller; ed, Harold McLernon.

Drama   **(PR:A   MPAA:NR)**

WOMAN FROM TANGIER, THE**   (1948) 66m COL bw

Adele Jergens (Nylon), Stephen Dunne (Ray Shapley), Michael Duane (Ned Rankin), Denis Green (Capt. Graves), Ivan Triesault (Rocheau), Curt Bois (Parquit), Ian MacDonald (Paul Moreice), Donna Demario (Flo-Flo), Anton Kosta (LeDeux), Maurice Marsac (Martino).

Various modes of transport figure largely in this crime drama wherein a ship at harbor is the scene of one murder and an in-flight aircraft that of another. Insurance investigator Dunne arrives in the torrid title town to investigate the theft of 50,000 pounds sterling from the unsafe-havened ship which his company had underwritten. With the help of cafe entertainer Jergens, she of the plastic role name, Dunne solves the mystery of the dual slayings and recovers the loot.

p, Martin Mooney; d, Harold Daniels; w, Irwin Franklyn; ph, Henry Freulich; ed, Richard Fantl; md, Mischa Bakaleinikoff; art d, Walter Holscher; set d, James Crowe; makeup, Gordon Hubbard.

Crime   **(PR:A   MPAA:NR)**

WOMAN HATER*½   (1949, Brit.) 69m RANK-TC/UNIV bw

Stewart Granger (Lord Terence Datchett), Edwige Feuillere (Colette Marly), Ronald Squire (Jameson, Butler), Jeanne de Casalis (Claire, Maid), Mary Jerrold (Dowager Lady Datchett), David Hutcheson (Robert), W. A. Kelly (Patrick), Georgina Cookson (Julia), Henry Edwards (Major), Stewart Rome (Col. Weston), Valentine Dyall (George Spencer), Richard Hearne, Cyril Ritchard (Revellers), Graham Moffatt (Fat Boy), Miles Malleson (Vicar), Dino Galvani (Charles), Vernon Greeves (Wedding Usher), Vida Hope (Girl Fan), H. G. Stoker (Old Boy), Michael Medwin (Harris), Jeremy Annett, Peter Cotten (Pageboys), John Stevens, Anne Holland (Publicity Assistants), Rosemary Treston Diana Chandler, Margaret Thorburn, Barbara Gurnhill, Diana Hope, Doreen Lawrence (Bridesmaids).

Misogynist Granger meets misanthrope Feuillere with predictable results in this lighthearted farce. French film star Feuillere emulates Greta Garbo, announcing that she wishes only to be alone. Disbelieving her public pronouncement, the titled Granger sets out to prove that all women are alike. He offers her the haven of his immense estate in the countryside, hoping to find her desire for solitude a sham. Posing as the real estate agent of his own property, he encounters Feuillere frequently, learning that her reclusive leanings are real. In the course of time, Feuillere discovers Granger's deception and decides to teach him a lesson, which ends with their marriage. Released in England at 105 minutes, the picture was cut to a more satisfactory length for its U.S. screenings.

p, William Sistrom; d, Terence Young; w, Robert Westerby, Nicholas Phipps (based on a story by Alec Coppel); ph, Andre Thomas; ed, Vera Campbell; md, Muir Mathieson; art d, Carmen Dillon; cos, Eleanor Abbey; makeup, Tony Sforzini.

Comedy   **(PR:A   MPAA:NR)**

WOMAN HE SCORNED, THE*   (1930, Brit.) 105m WB bw

Pola Negri (Louise), Warwick Ward (Maxim), Cameron Carr (Magistrate), Hans Rehmann (John), Margaret Rawlings (Woman).

Released as a silent in 1929 and later with partial dubbed sound, this ridiculous picture deals with the travails of Rehmann who, breaking one of the lenses in the French lighthouse he tends, is forced to row ashore for a replacement. Pausing in town for a pick-me-up, the innocent lad is beset by prostitutes. Reluctantly wayward Negri is slapped about by vicious pander-er Ward, and Rehmann leaps to her defense. The grateful girl, hoping to find respite from her shameful life, follows him seaward. Unwilling to assume responsibility for Negri, Rehmann pushes off alone, only to founder in a sudden storm. Seeking heavenly intervention in his plight, the lad pledges that he will succour hapless reject Negri in return for salvation from the elemental forces. Saved from the storm, Rehmann redeems his pledge by wedding Negri. Their marriage is marred by the reintroduction of rotter Ward who, wanted for murder, seeks sanctuary with his former floozy, Negri. Divine intervention might have made something of this picture; the acting, directing, and scripting sorely needed it. Some of the dubbed sound appears to have been borrowed from a completely different picture. Negri's fluttering waif is execrable; the role ruined her chances in British films just as her A WOMAN COMMANDS wrecked her U.S. career two years later.

p, Charles Whittaker; d, Paul Czinner; w, Whittaker (based on a story by Czinner).

Drama   **(PR:A   MPAA:NR)**

WOMAN HUNGRY*½   (1931) 65m FN-WB c (GB: THE CHALLENGE)

Sidney Blackmer (Geoffrey Brand), Lila Lee (Judith Temple), Raymond Hatton (Joac), Fred Kohler, Sr (Kampen), Kenneth Thomson (Leonard Temple), Olive Tell (Betty Temple), David Newell (Dr. Neil Cranford), Tom Dugan (Same Beeman), Blanche Frederici (Mrs. Temple), J. Farrell Mac-Donald (Buzzard).

Three rowdy western lads – Blackmer, Hatton, and Kohler – ride back to the hills after terrorizing the local town and happen upon the hapless Lee, a visiting Easterner, alone at her brother's home. The libidinous three prepare to ravish the unfortunate girl, but she has the wit to set them against one another. Promising Blackmer that she will offer him any reward he wishes if he will save her from his salacious sidekicks, she manages to elicit his aid. He pays one companion money in return for his one-third interest in Lee and wounds the other in a duel. Lee honors the bargain and marries Blackmer, who then tries his best to gain her affection. Ultimately, East and West manage to reach an accord. Filmed in two-color Technicolor in the Mount Whitney region of California. The lovely Lee reportedly had a nervous breakdown following the filming – and small wonder, considering her character's plight. An earlier adaptation of author Moody's play was filmed as THE GREAT DIVIDE in 1929.

d, Clarence Badger; w, Howard Estabrook (based on the play "The Great Divide" by William Vaughn Moody); ph, Sol Polito, Charles Schoenbaum (Technicolor); ed, Al Hall; cos, Edward Stevenson.

Western/Drama   **(PR:C   MPAA:NR)**

WOMAN HUNT** (1962) 60m AP/FOX bw

Steven Piccaro (*Hal Weston*), Lisa Lu (*Li Sheng*), Berry Kroeger (*Petrie/ Osgood*), Bob Okazaki (*Dr. Sheng*), Ann Carroll (*Janet Oberon*), Tom Daly (*Mr. Davalos*), Ivan Bonar (*Jacobs*), Harold Bostwick, William O'Connell, Norman Burton, Dal McKennon, Lloyd Kino, Lee Frederick, Paule Lakis, Hideo Imamura, George Riley.

Seeking his ex-wife – who divorced him to marry his one-time partner, Kroeger (in his role as Petrie) – Piccaro comes to Los Angeles, where he recruits Lu to help in the search, as well as the duplicitous Kroeger (in hisrole as Osgood). Told that his former partner has died, Piccaro ultimately discovers that Kroeger (as Petrie) actually murdered the missing woman, then persuaded Lu's father, surgeon Okazaki, to fake a death certificate for him, and had the woman buried in "his" coffin. Kroeger (Petrie) then collected on his own life insurance with the assistance of his mistress, Carroll, who posed as his bereaved widow. Kroeger (as Osgood) discovers that Kroeger (as Petrie) has had Pkazaki surgically modify his appearance so that the two Kroeger became look-alikes. Suspecting that Kroeger (Petrie) plans to murder Kroeger (Osgood) and assume the latter's identity, the latter kills the former and is, in turn, killed by Piccaro. Less confusing on the screen than on the printed page.

p&d, Maury Dexter; w, Edward J. Lakso, Russ Bender (based on a story by Harry Spalding); ph, Floyd Crosby (CinemaScope); m, Henry Vars; ed, Jodie Copelan, Carl Pierson; md, Vars; set d, Harry Reif; makeup, Harry Thomas.

Mystery   **(PR:C   MPAA:NR)**

WOMAN HUNT, THE zero (1975, U.S./Phil.) 80m Four Associates/New World c (AKA: THE HIGHEST BIDDER)

John Ashley, Pat Woodell, Laurie Rose, Charlene Jones, Lisa Todd, Sid Haig, Eddie Garcia, Ken Metcalfe.

American garbage king Roger Corman's New World Pictures coproduced this piece of trash from that Filipino master of sleaze, Eddie Romero (not to be confused with Pittsburgh's own George Romero). THE WOMAN HUNT is basically a crummy, exploitative remake of the classic THE MOST DANGEROUS GAME (1933) which sees a bevy of captured women in various stages of undress used as prey for the psychotic hunter who likes to kill humans. Stick to Joel McCrea and Fay Wray.

p, Eddie Romero, John Ashley; d, Romero.

Adventure   **(PR:O   MPAA:R)**

WOMAN I LOVE, THE**½ (1937) 85m RKO bw (GB: THE WOMAN BETWEEN)

Paul Muni (*Lt. Claude Maury*), Miriam Hopkins (*Mme. Helene Maury*), Louis Hayward (*Lt. Jean Herbillion*), Colin Clive (*Capt. Thelis*), Minor Watson (*Deschamps*), Elizabeth Risdon (*Mme. Herbillion*), Paul Guilfoyle (*Berthier*), Wally Albright (*Georges*), Mady Christians (*Florence*), Alec Craig (*Doctor*), Owen Davis, Jr. (*Mezziores*), Sterling Holloway (*Duprez*), Vince Barnett (*Mathieu*), Adrian Morris (*Marbot*), Donald Barry (*Michel*), Joe Twerp (*Narbonne*), William Stelling (*Pianist*), Doodles Weaver (*Flyer*).

During WW I, Muni is a French pilot with a reputation for getting his observers and gunners killed. Other members of the squadron refuse to fly with him but along comes Hayward. The two men become fast friends and successful flying partners and for a time it looks as though Muni's jinx is broken. Complications arise, though, when Hayward falls in love with nurse Hopkins, not knowing that she is Muni's wife. Eventually the truth comes out, but before the men can settle their differences, they are called into the air once more. They become embroiled in a desperate air battle and when the plane limps back to the aerodrome, Hayward is dead and Muni badly injured. He is taken to the hospital where Hopkins nurses him back to health and asks his forgiveness. Routine romantic triangle stuff but there are some good aerial sequences and above-average performances. The film is a remake of a 1928 French effort, L'EQUIPAGE, and the Muni role was originally offered to Charles Boyer. When he turned it down, Muni stepped forward and said that he was interested. Although he does a good job, the picture is something of an anomaly in Muni's career, bracketed by his fine performances in historical roles in THE LIFE OF EMILE ZOLA just before and JUAREZ just after this hackneyed melodrama. Director Litvak, who had directed L'EQUIPAGE in France, made his American debut here, and he later married Hopkins. Clive, as the squadron commander, gives a very good performance which is surprising because he was drinking heavily all through the production and all his scenes had to be shot before noon because he was uselessly bombed by lunch time. For the over-the-shoulder shots someone had to hold him up. Less than three months after the release of THE WOMAN I LOVE, Clive had drank himself to death.

p, Albert Lewis; d, Anatole Litvak; w, Mary Borden (based on the novel *L'Equipage* by Joseph Kessel); ph, Charles Rosher; m, Arthur Honneger, Maurice Thiriet; ed, Henri Rust; md, Roy Webb; art d, Van Nest Polglase; spec eff, Vernon Walker.

Drama   **(PR:A   MPAA:NR)**

WOMAN I STOLE, THE** (1933) 69M COL bw

Jack Holt (*Jim Bradler*), Fay Wray (*Vida Corew*), Noah Berry, Sr (*Gen. Rayon*), Raquel Torres (*Teresita*), Donald Cook (*Corew*), Edwin Maxwell (*Lentz*), Charles Browne (*Deleker*), Ferdinand Munier (*Sixto*), Lee Phelps (*Murdock*).

Hero Holt races across the windswept dunes of an oil-rich sheikdom and wins the heart of Wray, the wife of his best friend, oil company manage r Cook. Angered by the apparent perfidy of Holt when the latter seemingly attempts to ruin his business, Cook later learns the truth. Holt has actually played undercover agent, subverting the plans of villainous desert bandits to take over the company under the leadership of another official. His mission completed, Holt disavows the faithless Wray to go his cocksure way on his own. A well-made action film in almost every respect.

d, Irving Cummings; w. Jo Swerling (based on a story by Joseph Herge-sheimer); ph, Benjamin Kline; ed, Gene Havlick.

Adventure   **(PR:A   MPAA:NR)**

WOMEN IN A DRESSING GOWN*** (1957, Brit.) 93m Godwin-Willis/WB bw

Yvonne Mitchell (*Amy Preston*), Anthony Quayle (*Jim Preston*), Sylvia Syms (*Georgie Harlow*), Andrew Ray (*Brian Preston*), Carole Lesley (*Hilda*), Michael Ripper (*Pawnbroker*), Nora Gordon (*Mrs. Williams*), Marianne Stone (*Hairdresser*), Olga Lindo (*Manageress*), Harry Locke (*Wine Merchant*), Max Butterfield (*Harold*), Roberta Woolley (*Christine*), Melvyn Hayes (*Newsboy*), Cordelia Mitchell (*Hilda's Baby*).

In a performance that won her the Best Actress Award at the Berlin Film Festival, Mitchell plays a blowzy housewife approaching middle age whose unsuccessful attempts to create a homelike atmosphere for her husband, Quayle, results in him having an affair with a younger girl from the office, Syms. No surprise, considering that Mitchell is anything but the ideal housewife, seldom able to prepare an eatable dinner or to greet her husband in anything but a soiled dressing gown. With divorce on his mind, when it comes to the final wire Quayle, the husband, can't make a break with his family. A realistic portrayal of married life, with Mitchell giving a pointedly humane performance as a woman who can't overcome her own handicaps, regardless of the effort she puts forth.

p, Frank Godwin, J. Lee Thompson; d, Lee Thompson; w, Ted Willis; ph, Gilbert Taylor; m, Louis Levy; ed, Richard Best.

Drama   **(PR:A   MPAA:NR)**

WOMAN IN BONDAGE, 1932 (SEE: WOMAN IN CHAINS, 1932, Brit.)

WOMAN IN BONDAGE, 1943 (SEE: WOMEN IN BONDAGE, 1943)

WOMAN IN BROWN (SEE: VICIOUS CIRCLE, THE, 1948)

WOMAN IN CHAINS**½ (1932, Brit.) 69m Associated Talking Pictures-RKO/Harold Auten b w (GB: THE IMPASSIVE FOOTMAN; AKA: WOMAN IN BONDAGE)

Owen Nares (*Bryan Daventry*), Betty Stockfeld (*Grace Marwood*), Allan Jeayes (*John Marwood*), George Curzon (*Simpson*), Aubrey Mather (*Dr. Bartlett*), Frances Ross-Campbell (*Mrs. Angers*), Florence Harwood (*Mrs. Hoggs*).

Cranky hypochondriac Jeayes, who has turned his home into a virtual hospital suite, attempts to refashion his bright, vivacious wife Stockfeld into a nurse. On a sea trip with her constantly ailing husband, Stockfeld meets young surgeon Nares. Home again, she seeks respite from the tyranny of her husband's health problems with Nares, attending conc erts with him and having long talks in public places. Ironically, Jeayes develops a real illnes – a serious spinal disease – and selects Nares as the surgeon who will operate to effect a cure. Jeayes has discovered what he incorrectly believes to be his wife's infidelity with Nares, and tells the young doctor that if he should die from the operation, he has left a letter accusing the surgeon of murder. The horrible hypochondriac's footman, Curzon, floats impassively through the frames of the production, reacting with raised eyebrow to the goings-on. The operation is successful, and the jubilant Jeayes confronts his unwilling wife with the prospect of more unbearable bondage. During the course of his treatment, Nares has discovered that Jeayes has another real health problem, a weak heart. Footman Curzon hears his master being told of the condition, and warned that any sudden shock might prove fatal to Jeayes. Curzon, who has waited many yars to avenge himself on his irritable master, provides the necessary shock. Overacted stagily, this quota film – financed by RKO to fulfill the British mandate that a certain percentage of the films shown on its turf had to be home-grown – has its moments, most notably a surrealistic scene showing Jeayes' dreams as he sinks into unconsciousness under the operating room anesthetic. The exploitive American release title of the picture appears calculated to draw the droolers.

p&d, Basil Dean; w, John Farrow, John Paddy Carstairs, Harold Dearden (based on the play "The Impassive Footman" by "Sapper" [H. C. McNeile]);

ph, Robert Martin.

Drama   **(PR:A   MPAA:NR)**

WOMAN IN COMMAND, THE*   (1934 Brit.) 71m Gainsborough/GAU
bw (GB: SO LDIERS OF THE KING)

Cicely Courtneidge (*Jenny/Maisie Marvello*), Edward Everett Horton (*Sebastian Marvello*), Anthony Bushell (*Lt. Ronald Jamieson*), Dorothy Hyson (*Judy Marvello*), Frank Cellier (*Col. Markham*), Leslie Sarony (*Wally*), Bransby Williams (*Dan Marvello*), [Albert] Rebla (*Albert Marvello*), Herschel Henlere (*Mozart Marvello*), Ivor McLaren (*Harry Marvello*), Olive Sloane (*Sarah Marvello*), Arty Ash (*Doug*), O. B. Clarence (*Tom*), David Deveen, Andre Rolet, Betty Sempsey, William Pardue.

Courtneidge, in a dual role, plays both the reigning queen and the retired queen mother of a family troupe of traveling music-hall performers. The matriarch's word is law in this family, and Courtneidge the younger had been forbidden by Courtneidge the elder to marry a young Guards officer 15 years earlier, a marriage which would have finished his career in the stuffy, upper-class soldiery. A similar situation arises when ingenue Hyson falls in love with Guardsman Bushell. The latter's commanding officer proves to be the very soldier who had been denied the hand of Courtneidge the younger years before. She importunes him to let the young people wed without harassment, and the sentimental soldier complies with her wish. Inspired by the romantic atmosphere, stage manager Horton, a fumbling fool, screws up his courage and proposes to Courtneidge the younger. These romantic activities occur in the context of a struggle to mount a new show. In masculine attire, Courtneidge sings "There's Something About a Soldier" and a number of other songs. Although Courtneidge is hardly ever offscreen, Horton makes the most of his diminished role.

p, Michael Balcon; d, Maurice Elvey; w, Jack Hulbert, W. P. Lipscomb, J.O.C. Orton (based on a story by Douglas Furber); ph, Leslie Rowson, Percy Strong; ed, Ian Dalrymple; md, Louis Levy; art d, Alex Vetchinsky; m/l, Noel Gay, Clifford Grey, Furber.

Musical/Drama   **(PR:A   MPAA:NR)**

WOMAN IN DISTRESS*½   (1937) 68m COL bw

May Robson (*Phoebe Tuttle*), Irene Hervey (*Irene Donovan*), Dean Jagger (*Fred Stevens*), Douglas Dumbrille (*Jerome Culver*), George McKay (*Sgt. Casey*), Gene Morgan ("*Slug" Bemis*), Paul Fix (*Joe Emery*), Frank Sheridan (*Inspector Roderick*), Charles Wilson (*Herbert Glaxton*), Arthur Loft (*Stew Sadler*), Wallis Clark (*Seymour*).

Reportorial romance flourishes as ace wordsmith Jagger and sob sister Hervey learn of the existence of a valuable Rembrandt painting believed to have been destroyed years before. The competing scriveners race to the rescue of erratic old spinster Robson, owner of the masterpiece, which has been purloined by a band of thieves. Unable to fence the Dutch delight because of some symbols on the back of the canvas – otherwise known only to the scatterbrained spinster – the crooks decide to kill Robson. Hervey has moved in with the imperiled old lady, so is similarly threatened when the thieves set fire to Robson's house. Jagger arrives in time to warn the women and drap the thieves.

d, Lynn Shores; w, Albert DeMond (based on a story by Edwin Olmstead); ph, Allen G. Siegler; ed, Byron Robinson; cos, Robert Kalloch.

Crime   **(PR:A   MPAA:NR)**

WOMAN IN GREEN, THE**   (1945) 68m UNIV bw

Basil Rathbone (*Sherlock Holmes*), Nigel Bruce (*Dr. John H. Watson*), Hillary Brooke (*Lydia Marlow, Hypnotist*), Henry Daniell (*Prof. Moriarty*), Pa ul Cavanagh (*Sir George Fenwick*), Matthew Boulton (*Inspector Gregson*), Eve Amber (*Maude Fenwick*), Frederick Worlock (*Onslow*), Tom Bryson (*Williams*), Sally Shepherd (*Crandon*), Mary Gordon (*Mrs. Hudson, Holmes' Housekeeper*), Percival Vivian (*Dr. Simnell*), Olaf Hytten (*Norris*), Harold De Becker (*Shabby Man*), Tommy Hughes (*Newsman*), Billy Bevan (*Street Peddler*).

A series of mutilation murders of young women in London brings puzzled Scotland Yard inspector Boulton to the Baker Street rooms of Rathbone, in his oft-portrayed role as the great detective. Each corpse has been found with a single finger missing from the right hand. Rathbone agrees to use his great deductive powers to try to solve the apparently motiveless crimes. Dissolve to wealthy knighted clubman Cavanagh entering the flat of the beautiful but brittle Brooke, who proceeds to hypnotize the old lecher. Cavanagh awakens in a seedy room in another part of London with no memory of the previous evening. Although he never has ladyfingers with his tea, the terrified man finds a severed digit in his pocket. Back in Baker Street, the attractive Amber, Cavanagh's daughter, consults Rathbone. She has witnessed her father burying the incriminating digit in their garden. With Amber in tow, Rathbone rushes to his home to question her frightened father, only to find him murdered. Rathbone rightly deduces that Cavanagh was killed to prevent the disclosure that the digit-severing deaths, rather than the work of a madman, are part of a blackmail plot. The mastermind behind the scheme? Who but the infamous Moriarty (Daniell, in his only appearance in the role, was thought by Rathbone to have been the last and

best at the characterization), the great sleuth's long-time nemesis, believed long dead. Bruce, Rathbone's bumbling physician friend and flatmate, is called from the Baker Street rooms to handle a medical emergency. As the detective bows his violin – an arpeggio appears to enhance his thought processes – an unbidden guest arrives. It is Daniell, the arch-criminal, who engages his enemy in riposte-filled repartee, concluding with a warning that Rathbone had best not interfere with his plans. Departing, Daniell surreptitiously shifts the sleuth's favorite chair nearer a window. Later, from the opposite side of Baker Street, a sniper shoots through the shaded window at what appears to be Rathbone's silhouette. The shot shatters a bust of Julius Ceasar, cleverly substituted for his person by the perspective detective. The war-veteran sniper, who had been mesmerized like Cavanagh, is murdered like Cavanagh to prevent further disclosures. With Bruce, Rathbone repairs to the Mesmer Club (the detective's much-admired brother Mycroft is a member), a gathering place of hypnotists. There, he encounters Brooke. Apparently enamored of the lady, Rathbone accompanies her to her flat, where she "hypnotizes" him, after he accepts an apparently harmless drug from her (in one of the few filmic references to the narcotics habit, made plain in author Conan Doyle's stories). As the mesmerized sleuth stares off into space, Daniell appears to test his trance, having a helper jab a scalpel into him. when Rathbone has no reaction, Daniell decides he is truly under hypnosis. He instructs the insensitive detective to write a suicide note, and then to walk over a parapet to fall to his death in the street below. Bruce and Boulton arrive just as Rathbone strides the high ledge. Never fear: the detective had faked his apparent hypnosis. His ability to withstand the pain of the scalpel test without reaction stemmed from his having substituted a painkilling narcotic for the drug Brooke had offered him (apparently never without cocaine, the hideous habit here worked to the sleuth's advantage). Not one of the best of the series, this tired effort was the last to be scripted by screenwriter Millhauser. The regulars in the cast gave lackluster performances, although they knew one another well enough to play on the set betwwen takes. Brooke reported that she and Rathbone did an impromptu drunk act at the bar of the Mesmer Club set for the benefit of the cast and crew, the only unamused member being the punctilious Daniell, always professionally pretentious. Brooke had appeared in two of the previous films in the series, as had Daniell (though not in the role of Moriarty). The one regular who was missing from the cast was Dennis Hoey, the slow-witted Inspector Lestrade of private entries. His place was filled by a new characterization, that of the far smarter Inspector Gregson–a worthier foil for the prowess of the private detective–played by Boulton. (See SHERLOCK HOLMES series, Index.)

p&d, Roy William Neill; w, Bertram Millhauser (based on characters created by Sir Arthur Conan Doyle); ph, Virgil Miller; ed, Edward Curtiss; md, Mark Levant; art d, John B. Goodman, Martin Obzina; set d, Russell A. Gausman, Ted Von Hemert; cos, Vera West; spec eff, John P. Fulton.

Mystery   **Cas.**   **(PR:A   MPAA:NR)**

WOMAN IN HER THIRTIES, A   (SEE: SIDE STREETS, 1934)

WOMAN IN HIDING***   (1949) 92m UNIV bw

Ida Lupino (*Deborah Chandler Clark*), Howard Duff (*Keith Ramsey*), Stephen McNally (*Seldon Clark*), John Litel (*John Chandler*), Peggy Dow (*Patricia Monahan*), Taylor Holmes (*Lucius Maury*), Irving Bacon (*Link*), Joe Besser (*Fat Salesman*), Don Beddoe (*Salesman*), Peggy Castle (*Waitress*).

Suspenseful film with the inimitable Lupino opens with a bang as she drives a car at breakneck speed and crashes through a guardrail, falling into the river below. From there the film moves back in time to show Lupino, the daughter of a rich mill owner in a small southern town, marrying McNally, scion of the clan that gave the town its name but which has lately fallen on hard times. He wants the mill to restore his family fortunes, and in short order he has murdered Lupino's father and is going after her. He tampers with the brakes on her car, which is why it crashes off the bridge. She is not killed in the accident, but when McNally comes along to check on his handiwork, she pretends to be dead. Soon, though, McNally discovers that he was duped and sets out in pursuit of his bride. She narrowly escapes his clutches a number of times before being rescued by Duff, an ex-soldier just returned home. Lupino is very good here, conveying the terror of a woman threatened by the man she thought loved her, and the other roles are similarly well done, especially Duff, who was working with Lupino for the first time. They would later marry and work together many more times.

p, Michel Kraike; d, Michael Gordon; w, Oscar Saul, Roy Huggins (based on the magazine serial "Fugitive from Terror" by James R. Webb); ph, William Daniels; m, Frank Skinner; ed, Milton Carruth; md, Milton Schwarzwald; art d, Bernard Herzbrun, Robert Clatworthy; set d, Russell A. Gausman, Ruby R. Levitt; spec eff, David S. Horsley; makeup, Bud Westmore, Del Armstrong, John Holden.

Crime   **(PR:A-C   MPAA:NR)**

WOMAN IN HIDING*½   (1953, Brit.) 79m Exclusive-Hammer/UA bw
(GB: MANTRAP; AKA: MAN IN HIDING)

Paul Henreid (*Hugo Bishop*), Lois Maxwell (*Thelma Tasman*), Kieron
Moore (*Mervyn Speight*), Hugh Sinclair (*Maurice Jerrard*), Lloyd Lamble
(*Frisnay*), Anthony Forwood (*Rex*), Bill Travers (*Victor Tasman*), Mary
Laura Wood (*Susie*), Kay Kendall (*Vera*), Bishop's Secretary, John Penrose
(*du Vancet*), Barbara Kowan [*Shelley*], Liam Gaffney, Conrad Phillips, John
Stuart, Anna Turner, Christina Forrest, Arnold Diamond, Jane Welsh,
Geoffrey Murphy, Terry Carney, Sally Newland.

A ludicrous thriller starring Maxwell as the wife of an insane killer found
guilty of murder and jailed. Maxwell assumes a new identity and remarries.
Her new identity is only known to her boss, Sinclair. Soon after beginning
her new life, her ex-husband, Moore, escapes prison. Detective Henreid is
hot on his trail but to his surprise discovers that the fugitive is not insane
after all and has escaped to seek the man who framed him. In the end it is
revealed that Sinclair is the real culprit; he manages to get himself killed
in the climactic chase. An early effort from the newly formed Hammer
Studios and its premier director Terence Fisher. Both the studio and Fisher
would soon start a new, more bloody revival of the horror film with THE
CURSE OF FRANKENSTEIN (1957) and HORROR OF DRACULA (1958).

p, Michael Carreras, Alexander Paal; d, Terence Fisher; w, Fisher, Paul
Tabori (based on the novel *Queen in Danger*   by Elleston Trevo r); ph,
Reginald Wyer; ed, Jim Needs; art d, Elder Wills.

Crime   (PR:A   MPAA:NR)

WOMAN IN HIS HOUSE, THE   (SEE: ANIMAL KINGDOM, THE,
1932)

WOMAN IN QUESTION, THE   (SEE: FIVE ANGLES ON MURDER,
1950, Brit.)

WOMAN IN RED, THE***   (1935) 68m WB-FN bw

Barbara Stanwyck (*Shelby Barrett*), Gene Raymond (*Johnnie Wyatt*),
Genevieve Tobin (*Mrs. "Nicko" Nicholas*), John Eldredge (*Gene Fairchild*),
Dorothy Tree (*Olga Goodyear*), Phillip Reed (*Dan McCall*), Arthur Treacher
(*Maj. Casserly*), Doris Lloyd (*Mrs. Casserly*), Hale Hamilton (*Wyatt Furness*),
Ann Shoemaker (*Cora Furness*), Nella Walker (*Aunt Bettina*), Claude
Gillingwater, Sr. (*Grandpa Furness*), Brandon Hurst (*Uncle Emlen*), Jan
Buckingham (*Estella*), Gordon "Bill" Elliott (*Stuart Wyatt*), Edward Keane,
Marcoretta Hellman (*Ringmasters*), Jack Mulhall (*Mr. Crozier*), Evelyn
Wynans (*Woman*), Edward Van Sloan (*Foxall*), Fredrik Vogeding (*Erick-
son*), George Chandler, Olive Jones, Franklin Parker (*Reporters*), William B.
Davidson (*Goodyard*), Edward Le Saint (*Judge*), Russell Hicks (*Prosecuting
Attorney*), Harry Seymour (*Clerk*), Arthur Aylesworth (*Village Grocer*),
Robert Homans (*Guard*), Ross Allen Castlen (*2nd Debutante*), Nan Grey,
Dave O'Brien, Eleanor Wesselhoeft, Gunnis Davis.

Stanwyck stars as a horsewoman who is forced to take a stable job working
for an uppity society matron, Tobin. It's not long before she meets the
impoverished Raymond, a polo player who works at the stables and is a
favorite of Tobin's. Because of the growing closeness between Stanwyck and
Raymond, Tobin becomes quite jealous, as does Eldredge who wants
Stanwyck for himself. Raymond risks falling from the grace of his
high-society family by eloping with Stanwyck, but their love for each other
helps them survive the turbulent times. Later, while at a yacht party, a
drunken showgirl falls overboard and drowns, causing one of the ship's
officers to place blame on Eldredge. The future looks dim for Eldredge when
he is placed on trial, but Stanwyck clears his name by admitting she was the
mysterious "woman in red" who was seen leaving the yacht that night. By
making public her whereabouts, Stanwyck risks alienating herself from
Raymond's family. Instead, they firmly support her stand, solidly bonding
her marriage. Filmed from a dangerously weak screenplay, THE WOMAN
IN RED is a success only because Stanwyck is a success. It's her picture all
the way (originally it was planned as a Bette Davis vehicle), so fans of hers
will love it while her detractors will find it woefully impossible.

p, Harry Joe Brown; d, Robert Florey; w, Mary McCall, Jr., Peter Milne
(based on the novel *North Shore* by Wallace Irwin); ph, Sol Polito; ed, Terry
Morse; art d, Esdras Hartley; cos, Orry-Kelly; m/l, "So Close to the Forest,"
J. Young, L. Reginald; tech adv, Marcoreta Hellman.

Drama   (PR:A   MPAA:NR)

WOMAN IN ROOM 13, THE*   (1932) 67m FOX bw

Elissa Landi (*Laura Ramsey*), Ralph Bellamy (*John Bruce*), Neil Hamilton
(*Paul Ramsey*), Myrna Loy (*Sari Loder*), Gilbert Roland (*Victor Legrand*),
Walter Walker (*Howard Ramsey*), Luis Alberni (*Tonelli*), Charley Grapewin
(*Andy*).

Landi, a composer, spends much of her time with the womenizing Roland,
a concert singer. His suspicions aroused, Walker–her father-in-law– hires
unscrupulous detective Bellamy to find evidence of a presumed affair.
Bellamy conceals a dictating machine microphone in the singer's room and,
two floors below, listens to their conversations. When the sex-obsessed
singer is murdered, Bellamy fabricates evidence pointing to Landi as the

culprit. His motive? She is Bellamy's ex-wife; he seeks revenge. Landi's
current husband Hamilton shields his wife from the charge by assuming the
blame for the crime. Although Hamilton's attorney believes that the
unwritten law will get his client exonerated, Hamilton is convicted and
imprisoned. Landi befriends ex-husband Bellamy, inviting him to her home.
Using his own weapon against him, she has concealed a microphone, and the
real murderer is revealed. An interesting portent of things to come, this
feature opened a field that culminated in Francis Coppola's THE CONVER-
SATION (1974). A well-mounted production, with fine players and a talented
director, but flawed by a lack of suspense; every turning is readily
anticipated. A change of pace for Bellamy, who had in previous roles been
the personification of stability. In a small part, Loy once again played a
half-caste with her standard ethnic accent. On loan from MGM, this was a
regression for her; she had progressed beyond such roles. Speculation is that
her contract studio was punishing her for some infraction.

d, Henry King; w, Guy Bolton (based on the play by Sam Shipman, Max
Marcin, Percival Wilde); ph, John F. Seitz; ed, Al DeGaetano; cos, David Cox.

Mystery   (PR:A   MPAA:NR)

WOMAN IN THE CASE, 1935   (SEE: HEADLINE WOMAN, THE,
1935)

WOMAN IN THE CASE, THE, 1945   (SEE: ALLOTMENT WIVES, 1945)

WOMAN IN THE DARK**   (1934) 68m Select/RKO bw

Fay Wray (*Louise Lorimer*), Ralph Bellamy (*Bradley*), Melvyn Douglas
(*Robson*), Roscoe Ates (*Tommy Logan*), Reed Brown, Jr (*Conroy*), Ruth
Gillette (*Lil Logan*), Nell O'Day (*Helen Grant*), Granville Bates (*Sheriff
Grant*), Frank Otto (*Kraus*), Clifford Dunstan (*Doctor*), Charlie Williams
(*Clerk*).

This film adaptation of a lesser Dashiell Hammett story centers around the
efforts of Bellamy to lead a straight and quiet life after serving a three-year
stretch in prison. His biggest problem is his hot temper and his quickness
to turn to his fists when his anger is aroused. This is what put him behind
bars in the first place, when he accidentally killed a man in a fight over a
girl, and it forces him to go on the run. Wray is the girl who walks into his
life trying to escape the clutches of the no-good Douglas, a man who-not
willing to give up his pretty dependent all that easily – comes searching for
her. His bursting into Bellamy's cabin forces the young man to set his fists
in motion, giving a pal of Douglas a knock on the head that leads Douglas
to secure a warrant for Bellamy's arrest. A romance begins to develop
between Wray and Bellamy as they try to evade the law. Performances were
sufficient to deliver the drama, with Ates giving an interesting peformance
as a prison buddy of Bellamy.

p, Burt Kelly; d, Phil Rosen; w, Sada Cowan, Marcy Klauber, Charles
Williams (based on the story by Dashiell Hammett); ph, Joseph Ruttenberg.

Drama   (PA:A   MPAA:NR)

WOMAN IN THE DARK*   (1952) 60m REP bw

Penny Edwards (*Anna Reichardt*), Ross Elliott (*Father Tony Morello*), Rick
Vallin (*Phil Morello*), Richard Benedict (*Gino Morello*), Argentina Brunetti
(*Mama Morello*), Martin Garralaga (*Papa Morello*), Edit Angold (*Tante
Maria*), Peter Brocco (*Nick Petzick*), Barbara Billingsley (*Evelyn*), John
Doucette (*Dutch Bender*), Richard Irving (*Slats Hylan*), Luther Crockett
(*Inspector Johnson*), Carl Thompson (*Mickey*), Charles Sullivan (*Bartender*).

A dreadfully conceived family drama in which Benedict plays the black
sheep in a family that also includes a lawyer and a priest, who both prove
their binding love for their brother when he walks into a jam. As the lawyer,
Vallin goes so far as to take on the mob when Benedict is gunned down. The
script is at fault here, relying on cliches and highly contrived situations to
evoke unwarranted molodrama.

p, Stephen Auer; d. George Blair; w, Albert DeMond (based on the play by
Nicholas Cosentino); ph, John MacBurnie; m, Stanley Wilson; ed, John Rich;
art d, Frank Hotaling; set d, John McCarthy, Jr., George Milo; cos, Adele
Palmer.

Drama/Crime   (PR:A   MPAA:NR)

WOMAN IN THE DUNES*****   (1964, Jap.) 123m Teshigahara/Pathe
bw (SUNA NO ONNA; AKA: WOMAN OF THE DUNES)

Eiji Okada (*Niki Jumpei*), Kyoko Kishida (*Woman*), Koji Mitsui, Hiroko Ito,
Sen Yano, Ginzo Sekigushi, Kiyohiko Ichiha, Tamutsu Tamura, Hiroyuki
Nishimo.

A profoundly moving parable of man's search for meaning in life and love
told in a deceptively simple manner. Okada, a reserved entomologist,
collects specimens along a Japanese beach. He is met by some villagers who
offer him both a place to sleep and a woman. He is led to a shack located
at the bottom of a sand pit, climbing down a rope ladder to greet the woman,
Kishida. The next morning he notces that the ladder has been removed. A

panicky urge to climb out of the pit is followed with a futile attempt to scale the sand walls, which cascade beneath his feet. Helpless, he watches Kishida endlessly shovel the sand into buckets which are then hoisted by the villagers above. In return, food and water are sent down – no shoveling, no food. Okada soon realizes the necessity of the woman's work. He becomes accustomed to his new life style and takes the woman as his lover. Soon, she learns that she has become pregnant. His urge to escape, however, never ceases and he finally gets his freedom. It is short-lived as the villagers track him down and return him to the pit. He resigns himself to his existence, offering no more resistance to his surroundings. While digging a hole in the pit one day, he discovers fresh water which slowly rises. Again he seizes an opportunity to escape. He ventures to the sea, but decides to turn back and reenter the pit with the desire to contine his search for a water supply that will aid the woman and the villagers. Beautifully photographed and confined almost exclusively to a single set, WOMAN IN THE DUNES is a poetic affirmation of life. As frustrating and claustrophobic as the man's situation may first appear, the film becomes increasingly seductive as it lulls the audience into the woman's sandpit existence. By the time we reach the finale, Okada's decision to remain seems a wholly logical act of responsibility to life and nature. An emotionally draining picture which was nominated for Best Foreign Film at the 1964 Academy Awards and the following year earned Teshigahara a nomination for Best Director – the only Japanese director to receive such acclaim from the Academy.

p, Kiichi Ichikawa, Tadashi Ohono; d, Hiroshi Teshigahara; w, Kobo Abe (based on his novel *Suna no Onna*) ph, Hiroshi Segawa; m, Toru Takemitsu; ed, F. Susui.

Drama   **Cas.**   **(PR:O   MPAA:NR)**

WOMAN IN THE HALL, THE**   (1949, Brit.) 93m
RANK-Wessex/GFD-EL bw

Ursula Jeans (*Lorna Blake*), Jean Simmons (*Jay Blake*), Cecil Parker (*Sir Halmar Barnard*), Joan Miller (*Susan*), Jill Raymond (*Molly Blake*), Edward Underdown (*Neil Inglefield*), Nigel Buchanan (*Toby*), Ruth Dunning (*Shirley*), Russell Waters (*Alfred*), Terry Randal (*Ann*), Lily Kann (*Baroness*), Barbara Shaw (*Mrs. Maddox*), Dorothy [Totti] Truman Taylor (*Miss Gardiner*), Martin Walker (*The Judge*), Hugh Pryse (*Counsel for the Defense*), Everly Gregg (*Lady Cloy*), Alexis France (*Miss Mounce*), Hugh Miller (*Mr. Walker*), Susan Hampshire (*Young Jay*), Tania Tipping (*Young Molly*).

A very unpretty, though realistic, look at the negative effects a mother's misconduct can have on her daughter, with Simmons growing up under the domain of Jeans, a leech living off the charity of other people instead of working for a living. Jeans is pretty good at convincing others of her need, though deep down she's scheming. She eventually bags herself a wealthy husband in Parker, but by this time Simmons has decided to strike an honest living. Portions of her mother still remain in her as she forges a check, and although her objective is a charitable one she still must face the consequences when caught. Performances were not up to the quality of the script or originality of the idea.

p, Ian Dalrymple; d, Jack Lee; w, G. B. Stern, Lee, Dalrymple (based on the novel by Stern); ph, C. Pennington Richards, H. E. Fowle; m, Temple Abady; ed, John Krish; md, Muir Mathieson; prod d, Peter Proud; makeup, John Wilcox.

Drama   **(PR:A   MPAA:NR)**

WOMAN IN THE WINDOW, THE*½   (1945) 99m
Christie-International Pictures/RKO bw

Edward G. Robinson (*Prof. Richard Wanley*), Joan Bennett (*Alice Reed*), Raymond Massey (*Frank Lalor*), Edmond Breon (*Dr. Michael Barkstone*), Dan Duryea (*Heidt/Doorman*), Thomas E. Jackson (*Inspector Jackson*), Arthur Loft (*Claude Mazard 'ulias Frank Howard' the Club Checkroom Clerk*), Dorothy Peterson (*Mrs. Wanley*), Frank Dawson (*Collins the Steward*), Carol Cameron (*Elsie Wanley*), Bobby Blake (*Dickie Wanley*), Frank Melton, Don Brodie (*Men in Front of Art Gallery*), Alec Craig (*Garageman*), Ralph Dunn (*Traffic Cop*), Frank Mills (*Garage Helper*), Lane Watson (*Man by Taxi*), James Beasley (*Man in Taxi*), Joe Devlin (*Toll Collector Sergeant*), Fred Graham (*Motorcycle Cop*), Tom Hanlon (*Radio Announcer*), Calvin Emery (*Newsreel Cameraman*), Spanky McFarland (*Boy Scout with Glasses in Newsreel*), Harry Hayden (*Druggist*), Jack Gardner (*Fred, Lalor's Chauffeur*), Arthur Space (*Capt. Kennedy*), Harold McNulty, Joel McGinnis, Donald Kerr, Frank McClure (*Elevator Operators*), Ann O'Neal (*Woman at Elevator*), Fred Chapman (*Child at Elevator*), Eddy Chandler (*Police Driver*), Thomas P. Dillon (*Officer Flynn*), Iris Adrian (*Streetwalker*), Ruth Valmy (*Magazine Glamour Model*), Hal Craig (*News Vendor*), Fred Rapport (*Club Manager*), Alex Pollard (*William the Head Waiter*), James Harrison, Jack Gargan (*Stewards*), Lawrence Lathrop, William Dyer (*Page Boys*), Brandon Beach, Austin Bedell, Al Bensalt, Paul Bradley, James Carlisle, William Holmes, Fred Hueston, Sheldon Jett, J. W. Johnston, Charles Meakin, Harold Minjer, Ralph Norwood, Wedgewood Nowell, Louis Payne, David Pepper, Roy Saeger, Scott Seaton, Wyndham Standing, Larry Steers (*Club Members*), Bess Flowers (*Bar Extra*), Anne Loos, Frances Morris (*Stenographers*).

A gripping psychological thriller which stars Robinson as a fortyish,

intellectual college professor who, with his friends, discusses the dangers of becoming too adventurous at their age. Robinson has a wife and children (who are away on vacation) and sees no reason to wander from his staid, secure path. He soon does, however, when admiring a portrait of a beautiful model in a gallery window. He then notices the model, Bennett, standing beside him. Bennett asks if Robinson would like to come up to her apartment under honest pretenses: "I'm not married. I have no designs on you," she assures him. Once in her apartment, this fantasy girl of Robinson's brings about his downfall, though unintentionally. Her boy friend, wealthy financier Loft, arrives unexpectedly and, thinking that the two are having an affair, begins to slap his mistress around. He then lunges at Robinson, who grabs a nearby scissors and, in self-defense, stabs his attacker in the back. Frightened both of the police and of the disgrace he will cause his family, Robinson plots, with Bennett, to dispose of the body. Battling countless obstacles and nearly getting caught a number of times, they take the corpse, sitting up in the back seat of a car with open, glazed eyes, to a secluded woody area. They manage to carry out their plan without getting caught. Robinson, however, is still subject to mental torture, especially by his friend, Massey, a district attorney who continually talks about the case, unaware that Robinson is the man he's after. Through Massey, Robinson learns all the most intricate details of the investigation and is able to follow the progress of the police. He also learns his mistakes, which mount by the day. Making matters worse is a blackmail scheme engineered by Loft's bodyguard, Duryea, who has discovered Robinson's guilt. Robinson's change of character is made clear when he plans the murder of Duryea–a cold, calculated murder which is a step worse than his earlier act of self-defense. When his plan fails, however, and it appears as if the police are hot on his trail, Robinson opts for an easy way out. Sitting in his apartment he prepares a poison for himself. In the meantime, Duryea visits Bennett and collects $5,000 in blackmail money and a watch that used to belong to Loft. On his way out of the apartment, he is surprised by the police and begins shooting, only to be killed in the exchange. Bennett rushes to the phone to tell Robinson the good news–that Duryea is dead and the police have attributed the murder to him–but there is no answer. Robinson, having swallowed his fatal mixture, slumps forward in his chair. The camera dollies forward into the darkness of the chair back, and then dollies back out to reveal a slumped-over Robinson in his club (where we earlier saw him talking to his friends). A barkeep shakes Robinson awake and we learn that the entire film was a dream–its players visible as bar patrons, Loft as the checkroom clerk, and Duryea as the doorman. On his way home, Robinson approaches the window where he first saw Bennett's portrait. When he is approached by a streetwalker who wants a match, Robinson quickly leaves and avoids the possibility of an adventure like the one he just dreamed. With its terse pacing and elegant camerawork, THE WOMAN IN THE WINDOW was a great box office success and one of the most praised *films noir* of its time. Robinson, in a role different from his standard gangster, shines and holds the film's credibility together by turning in a convincing portrayal of a good man who is caught off guard just once (to paraphrase the title of the novel, *Once Off Guard*, on which the film is based). Bennett, in her second Lang film after 1941's MAN HUNT, is dazzlingly alluring as the fantasy girl who comes to life (though in a dream) for Robinson. The collaboration between Bennett and Lang was so amiable that they would work together two more times, in SCARLET STREET with Robinson again as costar, and in SECRET BEYOND THE DOOR, both produced by her and husband Walter Wanger's own Diana Productions. Perhaps the most memorable aspect of THE WOMAN IN THE WINDOW is the transition shot from Robinson's dream to real life. This spectacular shot was not a product of trick editing and flashy dissolves, but was one continuous take. According to producer-writer Nunnally Johnson: "The shot which involved a complete change of wardrobe and set was done without a cut. It was done so perfectly that it had to be explained to me. Robinson was wearing a break-away suit of clothes and in the few seconds of the head shot an assistant crept up under the camera and snapped it off, leaving him in the suit he was wearing when he fell asleep, and in the same few seconds the crew has substituted the club set for the room in which he had taken the poison. It was that sort of ingenuity that helped make Fritz the great director he was." Although Lang has often defended his "it was only a dream" ending, one can't help but feel cheated at the outcome. The dream ending almost always seems a cop-out and makes the audience feel like rubes for believing what it just saw. (The dream ending does work in certain, more stylish films such as the silent classic, THE CABINET OF DR. CALIGARI, the ending of which, not without coincidence, was written by Lang and, in fact, the entire film was to have been directed by him.) Because Lang felt he could not kill Robinson off at the end, and because Hollywood production codes would not allow a murderer to go unpunished, the dream was, according to Lang, the only way out. The studio was not happy, nor was Johnson and, in Lang's words: "a hell of a big fight" broke out. Johnson later relented and allowed Lang to have it his way, mainly because of Lang's known cinematic brilliance: "Eddie 'Robinson' played it so beautifully," Johnson commented of the film's end, "that you accepted the fact that he had a dream and that it had embodied people that he knew. The audience accepted the fact that they'd been taken, because it was all in such good humor by then... The comedy end really saved it, because I hate dream pictures unless you let them know in the beginning. I think it's a cheat otherwise. I didn't want to do it that way, but there it was."

p, Nunnally Johnson; d, Fritz Lang; w, Johnson (based on the novel *Once Off Guard* by J. H. Wallis); ph, Milton Krasner; m, Arthur Lange; ed, Marjorie

Johnson, Gene Fowler, Jr.; art d, Duncan Cramer; set d, Julia Heron; cos, Muriel King; spec eff, Vernon Walker.

Crime Drama   **Cas.**   **(PR:C   MPAA:NR)**

WOMAN IN WHITE, THE***   (1948) 109m WB bw

Eleanor Parker (*Laura Fairlie/Anne Catherick*), Alexis Smith (*Marian Halcombe*), Sydney Greenstreet (*Count Fosco*), Gig Young (*Walter Hartright*), Agners Moorehead (*Countess Fosco*), John Abbott (*Frederick Fairlie*), John Emery (*Sir Percival Glyde*), Curt Bois (*Louis*), Emma Dunn (*Mrs. Vesey*), Matthew Boulton (*Dr. Nevin*), Anita Sharp-Bolster (*Mrs. Todd*), Clifford Brooke (*Jepson*), Barry Bernard (*Dimmock*).

This eerie mood piece features Greenstreet as an unscrupulous count bent on wresting a fortune away from Parker. After plotting to marry her off to his partner in crime, Emery, Greenstreet works on the woman's twin sister (Parker in a dual role) by having the sibling committed to an insane asylum. The sister escapes and appears in white garb, a seeming ghostly apparition, trying to warn Parker of the evil doings. Young is an artist who also helps rescue Parker from Greenstreet's clutches. After his plans are foiled, Greenstreet's mad wife Moorehead goes completely over the edge and murders her portly spouse. Based on an 1860 gothic novel, this works well thanks to Greenstreet's ultra villainous histrionics. He is the quintessential blackguard, comical in this portrait, yet never reducing his characterization into shameless self-parody. Emery provides good support with his evil sidekick role, while Parker handles her two parts adequately. The mysterious ambiance of the film is further enhanced by an appropriate set design and Max Steiner's excellent background music. The directional pace, however, could have been a little tighter as a whole, though many individual scenes are particularly striking, riveting the viewer to the screen. Though only a minor horror film, THE WOMAN IN WHITE is an effective entertaiment, drawing out suspense and scares from its beginning to its deadly conclu sion. Wilkie Collins' novel served as a basis not only for this 1948 venture, but also for no less than four silent film versions in 1912, 1914 (as THE DREAM WOMAN), 1917 (as TANGLED LIVES), and 1929.

p, Henry Blanke; d, Peter Godfrey; w, Stephen Morehouse Avery (based on a novel by Wilkie Collins); ph, Carl Guthrie; m, Max Steiner; ed, Clarence Kolster; md, Leo F. Forbstein; art d, Stanley Fleischer; cos, Bernard Newman.

Horror/Mystery   **(PR:C   MPAA:NR)**

WOMAN INSIDE, THE*½   (1981) 94m FOX c

Gloria Manon (*Holly/Hollis*), Dane Clark (*Dr. Rassner*), Joan Blondell (*Aunt Coll*), Michael Champion (*Nolan*), Marlene Tracy (*Dr. Parris*), Michael Mancini (*Marco*), Luce Morgan (*Maggie*), Terri Haven (*Agnes*).

A film about a sex change by its nature alone is more apt than not to turn off a large portion of the filmgoing public. But this film handles the risque theme in such a mature manner that it has quite a few merits. Prime among these is the final film appearance of Joan Blondell as the aunt baffled by the desire of her wounded-veteran nephew to dress like a woman. Even though a workmanlike effort is made to get behind the motivation of its lead character, this too often takes the form of saccharine treatment, thus defeating its own objective intent. When compared with Rainer Werner Fassbinder's IN A YEAR OF THIRTEEN MOONS (1978), a subtly comic and tragic look at a man trying to maintain self respect as a transsexual, THE WOMAN INSIDE lacks both compassion and a humane understanding of its characters. Independently made on a very low budget in 1979, the picture was – surprisingly – purchased by a major studio for release. For a truly campy glance at the same object, see GLEN or GLENDA? (1953), with Bela Lugosi.;

p, Sidney H. Levine; d&w, Joseph Van Winkle; ph, Ron Johnson (CFI Color); Eddy Lawrence Manson; ed, John Duffy.

Drama   **(PR:O   MPAA:R)**

WOMAN IS A WOMAN, A***½   (1961, Fr./Ital.) 80m Rome-Paris Pathe Contemporary c (UNE FEMME EST UNE FEMME; LA DONNA E DONNA)

Anna Karina (*Angela*), Jean-Claude Brialy (*Emile Recamier, Bookseller*), Jean-Paul Belmondo (*Alfred Lubitsch*), Nicole Paquin (*Suzanne*), Marie Dubois (*1st Prostitute*), Marion Sarraut (*2nd Prostitute*), Jeanne Moreau (*Woman in Bar*), Catherine Demongeot.

Godard's third feature film, his first one in color, following LE PETIT SOLDAT is perhaps the most enjoyable of all of this master's films, tak ing an extremely lighthearted tone that is bursting with a passion so in love with the medium of film that every single shot expresses this. The plot is very simple and could almost be taken for homage to Hollywood musical comedy, but homage seems much too tacky a term to express the fascination Godard had and the playful manner in which he approached this film. Karina (Godard's wife at the time) plays a stripp er in a club, living with boy friend Brialy, who refuses to marry her upon her expressed desire to have a child.

Using an old feminine ploy, Karina starts to turn her attentions toward Belmondo, easily making him fall in love with her. Sure enough, it works, with Brialy breaking down when faced with the prospect of losing the girl he loves. Every moment of this picture is filled with charm, from Brialy riding a bicycle around their apartment in a strange mating dance to the buffoonish manner in which Belmondo tries to declare his love for Karina. The loose style almost seems to state that Godard just placed the camera down and then told his three stars to play; they look like children who have not yet outgrown the play lot and are unwilling to accept responsibility. The way Karina announces that she wants to have a baby is totally whimsical, a thing to do because that is what couples do then they are in love. Next to Godard's nonstylish stylishne ss, the most outstanding feature is the mere presence of Karina; her subtle glance and loftiness coincident with little mistakes in technical performance that most directors would not tolerate, but which actually serve to make her that much more human and irresistible. In fact, the picture appears almost to be a private photograph album showcasing the charming Karina in many moods. This is the first of Godard's films to be shot largely in a studio, under tightly controlled conditions. The director insisted on using sets with ceilings in the interest of naturalism; the unusual technique mitigated against the use of overhead lighting. This was also Godard's first experience with direct synchronous sound; his previous films had been dubbed. Elements of some of the director's earlier short subjects – most notably the 10-minute UNE FEMME COQUETTE – can be seen in the plot and the characterizations. (In French; English subtitles.)

p, Carlo Ponti, Georges de Beauregard; d&w, Jean-Luc Godard (based on an idea by Genevieve Cluny); ph, Raoul Coutard (FranScope, Eastmancolor); m, Michel Legrand; ed, Agners Guillemot, Lila Herman; art d, Bernard Evein; cos, Evein; m/l, "Chanson d'Angela," Legrand, Godard, "Tu te Laisses Aller," Charles Aznavour.

Drama/Comedy   **(PR:A   MPAA:NR)**

WOMAN IS THE JUDGE, A**   (1939) 62m COL bw

Frieda Inescort (*Mary Cabot*), Otto Kruger (*Steven Graham*), Rochelle Hudson (*Justine West*), Mayo Methot (*Gertie*), Gordon Oliver (*Robert Langley*), Arthur Loft (*Tim Ryan*), Walter Fenner (*Harper*), John Dilson (*Ramsey*), Bentley Hewlett (*Wolf*), Beryl Mercer (*Mrs. Butler*).

Inescort plays a lady judge who suddenly finds herself presiding over a case in which her long-lost daughter, Hudson, is on trial for murder. The lady barrister quickly switches to the other side of the bench to act as the defending counsel for Hudson. Well-paced direction and decent performances help overcome much of the story's predictability and heavy sentiment, including a romance between Inescort and Kruger as the opposing lawyer.

d, Nick Grinde; w, Karl Brown; ph, Benjamin Kline; ed, Byron Robingson; md, M. W. Stoloff.

Drama   **(PR:A   MPAA:NR)**

WOMAN NEXT DOOR, THE***   (1981, Fr.) 106m Les Films du Carrosse-TFI/UA c (LA FEMME D'A COTE)

Gerard Depardieu (*Bernard Coudray*), Fanny Ardant (*Mathilde Bauchard*), Henri Garcin (*Philippe Bauchard*), Michele Baumgartner (*Arlette Coudray*), Veronique Silver (*Mme. Jouve*), Philippe Morier-Genoud (*Doctor*), Roger Van Hool (*Roland Duguet*), Olivier Becquaert, Nicole Vauthier, Muriel Combe.

A dark entry from Truffaut which stars Depardieu and Ardant as former flames whose relationship ended many years previously. Since then they have both married others and, by chance, end up living next door to each other. Their love for one another reaches an obsessive level and quite quickly they are lovers again. Opposing the romance, however, is a hateful, violent side which emerges when Ardant tries to break off the affair. A loud public shouting match at a sports club follows but the affair continues. Depardieu is the next to throw in the towel, sending Ardant into a deep depression. Her husband decides to relocate, bringing the emotionally clouded Ardant with him. She is compelled to return to her lover and they have one final, fatal meeting at Depardieu's house. They make love and the relationship is capped by Ardant sending a bullet into Depardieu and then into herself. Truffaut once again displays his interest in obsessive love and the pain and destruction it causes as he did in JULES AND JIM (1961) and THE STORY OF ADELE H (1975). Ardant makes a stunning starring debut as the woman obsessed, appearing again in Truffaut's final film (she lived with him until his death in 1984) CONFIDENTIALLY YOURS.

d, Francois Truffaut; w, Truffaut, Suzanne Schiffman, Jean Aurel; ph, William Lubtchansky (Fujicolor); m, Georges Delerue; ed, Martine Barraque; art d, Jean-Pierre Kohut-Svelko; cos, Michele Cerf.

Drama   **Cas.**   **(PR:O   MPAA:R)**

WOMAN OBSESSED**½ (1959) 102m FOX c

Susan Hayward (*Mary Sharron*), Stephen Boyd (*Fred Carter*), Barbara Nichols (*Mayme Radzevitch*), Dennis Holmes (*Robbie Sharron*), Theodore Bikel (*Dr. Gibbs*), Ken Scott (*Sgt. Le Moyne*), Arthur Franz (*Tom Sharron*), James Philbrook (*Henri*), Florence MacMichael (*Mrs. Gibbs*), Jack Raine (*Ian Campbell*), Mary Carroll (*Mrs. Campbell*), Fred Graham (*Officer Follette*), Mike Lally (*Ticket Taker*), Richard Monahan (*Store Clerk*), Dainty Doris (*Fat Woman*), Harry "Duke" Johnson (*Juggler*), Lou Manley (*Fire Eater*), Tommy Farrell, Freeman Morse, Jimmy Ames (*Carnival Spielers*), Al Hustin (*Fire Warden*).

A generally satisfying outdoor adventure cum love story that was aided greatly by Hathaway's vigorous direction. Hayward is the widow of Franz, who dies early when a forest fire takes his life in the wilds of Canada. Hayward is left with son Holmes, precious little money, and a farm she can't handle alone. She hires Boyd, a rough-hewn handyman, to help her run the place. Holmes and Boyd get along well (not unlike Alan Ladd and Brandon de Wilde in SHANE). He is a dour man with a history that seems to have been one rotten break after another. Everything is going along fine but people in the nearby town are beginning to talk about the widow woman and her handsome lout. The fortunes of life have tossed them together and Boyd asks for Hayward's troth. Holmes likes Boyd but is not sure he'll like him as a father. Hayward tells Holmes that everything will be just the same as before except that she and Boyd will be sleeping in the same bed. As soon as the marriage vows have been spoken, a subtle alteration begins. Life isn't easy in the woods and Boyd doesn't make it any easier for Holmes, who resents the way he's treated. Boyd, who has been around a while, knows how tough life can be and thinks it's better not to coddle Holmes but to equip him for what he'll face later in his adulthood. Boyd is not always able to express himself in words and when that happens, he is quick to hit both Hayward and Holmes. Hayward learns that she's pregnant just as Holmes and Boyd get into a violent hassle. Later, Boyd goes into town, has a fistfight with a local, and is thrown into jail for 30 days to cool off. When he is released and returns to the farm, Hayward has put all of his gear in the barn. There's a rainstorm and Hayward is caught in it, miscarries, and almost dies. Boyd finds her and totes her to Bikel, a local doctor, through the wind and the rain, then he takes off to search for Holmes. In the woods, Holmes sees Boyd and thinks he may have killed Hayward so he entices Boyd into a pool of quicksand. It looks as though Boyd will die but Holmes has a change of mind and saves him. Meanwhile, Bikel tells Hayward, who has just come around after having fainted, that Boyd is the reason why she's alive. It turns out there's a psychological reason why Boyd is so tough on Holmes. He'd been married before and his kid brother fell apart in a desperate situation that called for action. Boyd's wife perished in a fire and could have been saved if his brother would have acted quickly and coolly. Hayward returns home after her recovery and Boyd is about to move on. She prevails on him to stay and the family unit is saved to begin anew. Cinematographer Mellor took ill during the shoot and was replaced by Leon Shamroy, although the latter received no screen credit. All of the predictable disasters expected in an outdoor film are here, plus some fine acting on the part of the three principals. Barbara Nichols has a few good moments as a townie. It was shot in the same general area in which Henry Hathaway lensed THE TRAIL OF THE LONESOME PINE more than 20 years before.

p, Sydney Boehm; d, Henry Hathaway; w, Boehm (based on the novel *The Snow Birch* by John Mantley); ph, William C. Mellor, (uncredited) Leon Shamroy (CinemaScope, DeLuxe Color); m, Hugo Friedhofer; ed, Robert Simpson; md, Lionel Newman; art d, Lyle R. Wheeler, Jack Martin Smith; set d, Walter M. Scott, Stuart A. Reiss; cos, Charles Le Maire; spec eff, L.B. Abbott; makeup, Ben Nye.

Adventure/Romance (PR:A-C MPAA:NR)

WOMAN OF ANTWERP (SEE: DEDEE, 1949, Fr.)

WOMAN OF DARKNESS** (1968, Swed.) 112m Svensk Filmindustri/Freena Films bw (YNGSJOMORDET)

Gunnel Lindblom (*Anna Mansdotter*), Gosta Ekman, Jr (*Per Nilsson*), Christina Schollin (*Hanna Johansdotter*), Rune Lindstrom (*Wahlbom*), Heinz Hopf (*Helmertz*), Elsa Prawitz (*Hilda Persdotter*), Isa Quensel (*Grave-Karna*).

Near the turn of the 19th Century, Lindblom languishes in a prison cell, awaiting execution. In flashback, she recalls the events of her trial, which have outlined her violation of a social taboo. She and her son, co-defendant Ekman, have been indicted for murder and incest. Ekman had married Schollin to quell community misgivings about his relationship with his mother. When Schollin attempted to force the impotent Ekman to consummate the marriage, he beat her unconscious, and his mother strangled her. Ekman is tricked into confessing the murder Lindblom actually committed, and she confesses in order to save her son. A dark and forbidding drama from Sweden's most prolific director, Mattsson, who helmed that country's greatest box-office attraction, ONE SUMMER OF HAPPINESS (1955), before segueing into crassly commercial crime pictures. This film brought him back to the critical acclaim he had managed to avoid for a decade.

p, Lorens Marmstedt; d, Arne Mattsson; w, Eva Dahlbeck (based on the novel *Yngsjomordet* by Yngve Lyttkens); ph, Lars Bjorne; m, Georg Riedel; ed, Carl-Olov Skeppstedt.

Drama (PR:O MPAA:NR)

WOMAN OF DISTINCTION, A** (1950) 85m COL bw

Ray Milland (*Alec Stevenson*), Rosalind Russell (*Susan Middlecott*), Edmund Gwenn (*Mark Middlecott*), Janis Carter (*Teddy Evans*), Mary Jane Saunders (*Louisa*), Francis Lederer (*Paul Simone*), Jerome Courtland (*Jerome*), Alex Gerry (*Herman Pomeroy*), Charlotte Wynters (*Miss Withers*), Charles Evans (*Dr. McFall*), Clifton Young (*Chet*), Gale Gordon (*Station Clerk*), Jean Willes (*Pearl*), Wanda McKay (*Merle*), Elizabeth Flournoy (*Laura*), Harry Tyler (*Charlie*), Robert Malcolm, William E. Green (*Conductors*), Harry Cheshire (*Stewart*), Dudley Dickerson (*Waiter*), Gail Bonney (*Woman*), Charles Trowbridge (*Jewelry Salesman*), John Smith (*Boy*), Billy Newell (*Bartender*), Myron Healey (*Cameraman*), Harry Strang, Richard Bartell, Charles Jordan, Larry Barton, Donald Kerr, Ted Jordan (*Reporters*), Lucille Ball (*Guest*), Harry Harvey, Jr (*Joe*), Maxine Gates (*Goldie*), Lucille Brown (*Manicurist*), Walter Sande (*Officer*), Marie Blake (*Wax Operator*), Ed Keane (*Sergeant*), Lois Hall (*Stewardess*), Mira McKinney, Lelah Tyler (*Members*), Napoleon Whiting, Wilda Biber, Kathryn Moore, Patricia Reynolds, Ethel Sway, Elaine Towne.

Only the likes of Russell and Gwenn could save this rather inane slapstick concept to create such lively and fun-loving merriment. Russell plays the stuffy dean of a women's college with a serious attitude that leaves her with little time to pursue romance. That is until a malicious reporter decides to start some nasty rumors regarding her and visiting astronomy professor Milland, for which Russell holds the baffled Milland responsible. As the dean's father, Gwenn steps in and decides that it's time his daughter devoted herself to something other than books and teaching, seeing Milland as the perfect catalyst for his plan. Russell was perhaps the one actress with the skill to approach such a role and still maintain her dignity while doing so. She had a charming complement in Gwenn, who was just as tender and loving as ever.

p, Buddy Adler; d, Edward Buzzell; w, Charles Hoffman, Frank Tashlin (based on the story by Hugo Butler, Ian McClellan Hunter); ph, Joseph Walker; m, Werner R. Heymann; ed, Charles Nelson; md, Morris Stoloff; art d, Robert Peterson; cos, Jean Louis.

Comedy (PR:A MPAA:NR)

WOMAN OF DOLWYN (SEE: LAST DAYS OF DOLWYN, THE, 1949, Brit.)

WOMAN OF EXPERIENCE, A*½ (1931) 65m RKO bw

Helen Twelvetrees (*Elsa*), William Bakewell (*Karl*), Lew Cody (*Capt. Otto von Lichstein*), ZaSu Pitts (*Katie*), H. B. Warner (*Maj. Hugh Schmidt*), C. Henry Gordon (*Capt. Muller*), Franklin Pangborn (*Hans*), Nance O'Neil (*Countess Runyi*), George Fawcett (*A General*), Bertha Mann (*Red Cross Nurse*), Edward Earle (*Capt. Kurt von Hausen*), Max Waizman (*Brunck*), William Tooker, Alfred Hickman (*Colonels*).

Twelvetrees is a lady with a shady past who is recruited by Austrian intelligence agents to get involved with officer Cody, suspected of being a German spy. Bakewell is a young naval officer who truly has her affections, which she subordinates for the good of her country. Cody commits suicide to avoid exposure, and Twelvetrees is wounded in the process. Knowing she has only months to live, Bakewell makes her his bride over the objections of his knowing family, who are apparently concerned about the prospect of a venereal disease. Lightened by Pitts' comic deliveries, the picture's formula plot was ancient even in its own time.

p, Charles R. Rogers; d, Harry Joe Brown; w, John Farrow, Ralph Murphy (based on the play "The Registered Woman" by Farrow); ph, Hal Mohr; ed, Fred Allen.

Drama (PR:A MPAA:NR)

WOMAN OF MYSTERY, A*½ (1957, Brit.) 71m Danzigers/UA bw

Dermot Walsh (*Ray Savage*), Hazel Court (*Joy Grant*), Jennifer Jayne (*Ruby Ames*), Ferdy Mayne (*Andre*), Ernest Clark (*Harvey*), Diana Chesney (*Mrs. Bassett*), Paul Dickson (*Winter*), David Lander, Gordon Tanner, Robert Hunter.

When reporter Walsh begins investigating the facts behind a young girl's suicide he discovers that she was murdered. As he digs for the identity of the killer Walsh uncovers a vicious counterfeiting ring and causes their downfall. Wooden direction kills whatever chance the film had for any genuine thrills.

p, Edward and Harry Lee Danziger; d, Ernest Morris; w, Brian Clemens, Eldon Howard; ph, Jimmy Wilson.

Crime (PR:A MPAA:NR)

WOMAN OF ROME½   (1956, Ital.) 93m Ponti-DD/DCA bw (LA ROMANA)

Gina Lollobrigida (*Adriana*), Daniel Gelin (*Mino*), Franco Fabrizi (*Gino*), Raymond Pellegrin (*Astarita*), Pina Piovani (*The Mother*), Xenia Valderi (*Gisella*), Renato Tontini (*Sonzongno*), Mariano Bottino (*Padre Elia*).

Starting with nude modeling at the behest of her mother, Piovani, Lollobrigida rapidly rises to become a cynical, sought-after courtesan. Of her many lovers-for-pay, she desires only the rejecting Gelin, who commits suicide. Left with a baby, the adaptable lady elects to start a new life. Author Moravia's novel linked his hooker heroine's fall from virtue with the contrapuntal rise of fascism in the Italy of the time; the picture fails to bring in that interesting background, becoming little more than a case history of a prostitute.

d, Luigi Zampa; w, Zampa, Alberto Moravia, Giorgio Bassani, Ennio Flainao (based on the novel by Moravia), ph, Enzo Serafini; ed, Eraldo De Roma; art d, Flavio Mogherini.

Drama   (PR:O   MPAA:NR)

WOMAN OF SIN**   (1961, Fr.) 93m Films Marius Bouchet-Films Artistiques Francais/Ellis bw (LA MOUCHARDE)

Dany Carrel (*Betty*), Pierre Vaneck (*Frederic*), Yves Deniaud (*Parola*), Noel Roquevert (*Lawyer*), Andre Weber (*Jeannot*), Albert Dinan (*Betty's father*), Serge Sauvion, Henri Cremieux, Paul Crauchet, Georges Chamarat, Yvonne Clech, Fernand Sardou, Paul Vandenberghe, Jean Morel.

Mildly interesting thriller about a young girl who turns police informer while her Father is locked up in prison for his part in a jewel theft. The girl's greed gets the better part of her as she attempts to compete with more experienced crooks seeking the jewels her father has stashed away. Her efforts lead to her own arrest and the killing of her lover.

p, Paul de Saint-Andre; d, Guy Lefranc; w, Lefranc, Jacques Severac, Georges Tabet, Andre Tabet (based on the novel La Fille de Proie by Christian Coffinet); ph, Maurice Barry; ed, Armand Psenny; art d, Claude Bouxin; makeup, Gisele Jacquin .

Crime/Drama   (PR:A MPAA:NR)

WOMAN OF STRAW**½   (1964, Brit.) 120m Novus/UA c

Gina Lollobrigida (*Maria*), Sean Connery (*Anthony Richmond*), Ralph Richardson (*Charles Richmond*), Alexander Knox (*Lomer*), Johnny Sekka (*Thomas*), Laurence Hardy (*Baines*), Danny Daniels (*Fenton*), Peter Madden (*Yacht Captain*), Joseph Wise (*Peters*), Ronald Hatton (*Mate of Yacht*), George Zenios (*Boy at Island Hotel*), Michael Goodliffe (*Penfield*), A.J. Brown, Edward Underdown, George Curzon (*Executives*), Douglas Wilmer (*Dr. Murray*), Andre Morell (*Judge*), Georgina Cookson, Gilda Dahlberg (*Guests at Villa Salon*), Robert Bruce (*John the Chauffeur*), Michael Corcoran (*Cook*), Peggy Marshall (*Wardress*).

Connery is a man whose rich and crippled uncle, Richardson, has dictated that his entire fortune go to charity after his death, a fortune that Connery thinks should go to him. He hires nurse Lollobrigida to care for Richardson, enlisting her in his scheme to have Richardson marry her and change his will. She is then to cut Connery in for $3 million when the old man dies. Things go according to plan and Lollobrigida marries Richardson, but then she finds that she is actually rather fond of the old codger. Richardson dies suddenly on his yacht and Connery tells Lollobrigida that she will be accused of murder if she doesn't help him get the body back to the house. She believes him and helps get the corpse ashore, but when they arrive at the house the police are waiting and Lollobrigida is taken off to jail. Another servant in the household, however, comes up with a tape recording of Connery committing the murder and in a struggle for the tape, Connery tumbles down the stairs and is killed. Hardly a feather in the cap of anyone involved, the film starts out well enough, but the last half degenerates into complete implausibility. The ending is about as believable as the worst Victorian melodrama and Richardson is the only actor to come out of it undamaged, perhaps because he dies before the film gets too ridiculous. Lollobrigida was reportedly rather difficult to work with and when she walked onto the set for the first day of shooting she immediately began giving the director directions on how she was to be shot. Connery quickly stepped forward and told the imperious Italian: "Either he is directing the picture or you are directing it. If it's you I may not be in it." Lollobrigida simmered down and accepted the situation, but in light of the final result, letting Lollobrigida direct might not have been such a bad idea, and Connery certainly couldn't have done his career much harm by walking out on this one.

p, Michael Relph; d, Basil Dearden; w, Robert Muller, Stanley Mann, Relph (based on the novel La Femme de Paille by Catherine Arley); ph, Otto Heller (Eastmancolor); m, Ludwig van Beethoven, Hector Berlioz, Wolfgang Amadeus Mozart, Nikolai Andreevich Rimski-Korsakov; ed, John D. Guthridge; prod d, Ken Adam; md, Muir Mathieson; art d, Peter Murton; set d, Freda Pearson; cos, Beatrice Dawson, Christian Dior; m/l, "Woman of Straw," Norman Percival; makeup, Basil Newall, Paul Rabiger.

Crime   (PR:C MPAA:NR)

WOMAN OF THE DUNES   (SEE: WOMAN IN THE DUNES, 1964, Jap.)

WOMAN OF THE NORTH COUNTRY**   (1952) 90m REP c

Ruth Hussey (*Christine Powell*), Rod Cameron (*Kyle Ramlo*), John Agar (*David Powell*), Gale Storm (*Cathy Nordlund*), J. Carroll Naish (*Mulholland*), Jim Davis (*Steve Powell*), Jay C. Flippen (*Axel Nordlund*), Taylor Holmes (*Dawson*), Barry Kelley (*O'Hara*), Grant Withers (*Chapman*), Stephen Bekassy (*Andre Duclos*), Howard Petrie (*Rick Barton*), Hank Worden (*Tom Gordon*), Virginia Brissac (*Mrs. Dawson*).

A satisfying outdoor picture which has Cameron starting an iron-ore mine in Minnesota over the objections of Hussey's family, who are already entrenched in the area and don't want any competition. When he can't be bullied off his property, Hussey tries to charm him into marriage. Blindly Cameron falls for her trick, jilting his true love, Storm. He finally wakes up long enough to see that Hussey is just digging her claws into his wealth. Banker Naish shoots Hussey, paving the way for an embrace between Cameron and Storm. Two traditional folk songs, "Blue-Tail Fly" and "Erie Canal."

p&d, Joseph Kane; w, Norman Reilly Raine (based on a story by Charles Marquis Warren, Prescott Chaplin); ph, Jack Marta (Trucolor); m, R. Dale Butts; ed, Richard L. Van Enger; art d, Frank Arrigo; set d, John McCarthy, Jr., Charles Thompson; cos, Adele Palmer.

Action/Drama   (PR:A   MPAA:NR)

WOMAN OF THE RIVER**   (1954, Fr./Ital.) 92m EX-Les Films de Centaur/COL c (LA DONNA DEL FIUME)

Sophia Loren (*Nives Mongolini*), Gerard Oury (*Enzo Cinti*), Lise Bourdin (*Tosca*), Rik Battaglia (*Gino Lodi*), Enrico Olivieri (*Oscar*).

After Loren made her first big splash in GOLD OF NAPLES, Carlo Ponti rushed her into this film, a loose remake of BITTER RICE, which had shot Silvana Mangano, the wife of Ponti's partner, Dino De Laurentiis, to stardom five years before. Loren is the sexiest girl at the eel cannery and she is loved by Oury, the local constable. She, however, is in love with fisherman Battaglia, who works as a smuggler to make ends meet. Battaglia leaves town and Loren follows him, telling him she is pregnant and the police are after him. He thinks she is simply trying to force him to marry her and he rudely sends her away. Angry and brokenhearted, she turns stool pigeon and tells Oury where to find Battaglia. Some years later, Battaglia escapes from prison and goes looking for the woman who betrayed him. Oury finds her first, working in the cane fields on the banks of the Po River to support herself and her son. When Battaglia finally tracks her down, he finds that his son has just drowned accidentally. He is watching the funeral procession when the police arrest him. Loren looks her best in the short shorts and hip boots she gets to wear, and she does display some talent here, although all told, the film is just another Italian potboiler of little interest to most, though it was the first screenwriting job for Pasolini, who would later go on to direct his own films. It was just after the conclusion of shooting that Ponti gave Loren an engagement ring, although he was still married, and, in fact, had never kissed his young discovery or even spoken to her of his feelings. (Dubbed in English.)

p, Basilio Franchina; d, Mario Soldati; w, Franchina, Giorgio Bassani, Pier Paolo Pasolini, Florestano Vancini, Antonio Altoviti, Soldati, (English dialog) Ben Zavin (based on an idea by Ennio Flaiano, Alberto Moravia); ph, Otello Martelli (Technicolor); m, Angelo F. Lavagnino, Armando Trovaioli; ed, Leo Cattozzo; art d, Flavio Mogherini; ch, Leo Coleman.

Drama   (PR:O   MPAA:NR)

WOMAN OF THE TOWN, THE**½   (1943) 90m UA bw

Claire Trevor (*Dora Hand*), Albert Dekker ("*Bat*" *Masterson*), Barry Sullivan (*King Kennedy*), Henry Hull (*Inky Wilkinson*), Marion Martin (*Daisy Davenport*), Porter Hall (*Dog Kelly*), Percy Kilbride (*Rev. Samuel Small*), Beryl Wallace (*Louella Parsons*), Arthur Hohl (*Robert Wright*), Clem Bevans (*Buffalo Burns*), Teddi Sherman (*Fanny Garretson*), George Cleveland (*Judge Blackburn*), Russell Hicks (*The Publisher*), Herb Rawlinson (*Doc Sears*), Marlene Mains (*Annie Logan*), Dorothy Grainger (*Belle*), Wade Crosby (*Crockett*), Hal Taliaferro [*Wally Wales*] (*Wagner*), Glenn Strange (*Walker*), Charley Foy (*Eddie Foy, Sr.*), Claire Whitney (*Mrs. Wright*), Russell Simpson (*Sime*), Eula Guy (*Mrs. Brown*), Frances Morris (*Mrs. Logan*), Tom London (*Cowboy*), Garry Owen (*Dealer*), Joseph Crehan.

Decent part-fact, part-fiction depiction of the life of reporter/gunfighter Bartholomew "Bat" Masterson, centering on the period he spent as marshal of Dodge City, a job he took when unable to find work on a newspaper. Dekker makes a convincing lawman who doesn't undertake the pursuit of his true goal until the woman he loves, social worker-cum-dance hall girl Trevor, is shot down by local cattle baron Sullivan. The marshal has been the only man willing to stand up against the ruthlessness that has made Sullivan such a success, to which he responds by kidnaping Trevor in a last-ditch effort to get Dekker off his back. The woman dies scorned by the "decent" people of the town who could not begin to understand the efforts she put forth in trying to make their lives better, singing only to put bread on the table. A good combination of fiction and fact that gets most of its strength through the portrayal of historical legends as common people with goals quite similar to those of most people.

p, Harry Sherman; d, George Archainbaud; w, Aeneas MacKenzie (based on a story by Norman Houston); ph, Russell Harlan; ed, Carrol Lewis; art d, Ralph Berger.

Western   **Cas.**   **(PR:A   MPAA:NR)**

WOMAN OF THE WORLD, A   (SEE: OUTCAST LADY, 1934)

WOMAN OF THE YEAR****   (1942) 112m MGM bw

Spencer Tracy (Sam Craig), Katharine Hepburn (Tess Harding), Fay Bainter (Ellen Whitcomb), Reginald Owen (Clayton), Minor Watson (William Harding), William Bendix (Pinkie Peters), Gladys Blake (Flo Peters), Dan Tobin (Gerald), Roscoe Karns (Phil Whittaker), William Tannen (Ellis), Ludwig Stossel (Dr. Martin Lubbeck), Sara Haden (Matron at Refugee Home), Edith Evanson (Alma), George Kezas (Chris), Henry Roquemore (Justice of the Peace), Cyril Ring (Harding's Chauffeur), Ben Lessy (Punchy), Johnny Berkes (Pal), Duke York (Football Player), Winifred Harris (Chairlady), Joe Yule (Building Superintendent), Edward McWade (Adolph), William Holmes (Man at Banquet), Jimmy Conlin, Ray Teal (Reporters), Michael Visaroff (Guest), Gerald Mohr (Voice of Radio M.C.), Connie Gilchrist, Grant Withers.

This was the first on-screen pairing of Tracy and Hepburn, a team that would last 25 years until Tracy's death in 1967. He plays a rough-edged sportswriter for a New York newpaper who becomes angry after hearing Hepburn on a radio broadcast boldly stating that baseball should be eliminated until WW II comes to an end. Hepburn, the daughter of diplomat Watson and an important international affairs writer, works on the same paper as Tracy, and her remarks begin a battle waged in their respective columns. Once they meet in person, a definite attraction occurs, much to the surprise of their friends and colleagues. Eventually Tracy and Hepburn wed, but their marriage rests on shaky grounds. Hepburn's attempts as a homemaker are an outright disaster, as she feels her job must come before anything else. Tracy is angered by her lack of commitment to the marriage, and ends up getting too drunk to write his column. Hepburn, whose knowledge of sports isn't much better than her abilities as a housewife, pens Tracy's column and the results are catastrophic. Hepburn is voted "Woman of the Year," ironically hearing the news while she is contemplating whether to remain with Tracy. When her father remarries, Hepburn listens closely as the marriage vows are read. The words strike a deep chord in her, and Hepburn decides to go back to Tracy with renewed zeal for married life. This is a marvelous comedy, brimming with wit, style, and sophistication. Hepburn is strong and assured, a woman fueled by intense pride along with a good-sized ego. Tracy is her male opposite, just as opinionated and just as stubborn. Their chemistry is engaging, a solid teaming that enhances the accomplished script. The film was an original idea of Garson Kanin's, who created the story. He was inspired by the internationally renowned columnist Dorothy Thompson, and wrote his idea with Hepburn in mind. Because of Kanin's other commitments, he was unable to develop the story further, instead giving the project to his brother Michael and Ring Lardner, Jr. The writers concocted a 30,000-word treatment, and Hepburn immediately fell in love with the property. It was decided that Hepburn would talk MGM into buying the script. Hepburn, at 5 feet 7 inches, was already considered to be tall among the actresses on the MGM lot. For her meeting with studio head Louis B. Mayer, Hepburn donned four-inch heels, thus increasing her height to an even more imposing stature. Mayer, who was not a tall man to begin with, listened to her every demand. Though Hepburn was convinced she had not succeeded, the strong-minded actress was shocked when she learned Mayer had given her everything she wanted on WOMAN OF THE YEAR. In addition to her own salary of $100,000, Hepburn received a $11,000 commission as a script agent, plus her choice of director and costar. Kanin and Lardner each received $50,000 for their efforts, far beyond the $200 to $300 a week salaries they were used to as unknown writers. For her leading man, Hepburn had only one choice. She wanted Tracy, but at the time he was on location in Florida, working on MGM's production of THE YEARLING. However, various problems on the set caused that project to be halted (Gregory Peck would eventually play Tracy's role), leaving Tracy free for WOMAN OF THE YEAR. The two were introduced in the studio commissary by producer Mankiewicz. Hepburn, decked out in her four-inch heels, said to her costar, "I'm afraid I'm a little tall for you, Mr. Tracy." "Don't worry, Miss Hepburn," Tracy shot back. "I'll cut you down to my size." (In years to follow, Mankiewicz took credit for the clever retort whenever he told the story.) After a few days of shooting, Tracy and Hepburn dropped the formalities, addressing each other as Kate and Spence. In addition to marking the beginnings of their famous screen partnership, Tracy and Hepburn developed a close friendship working on this film, one that would last throughout their lives. Undoubtedly the two would have married, but Tracy's Catholic upbringing prevented him from divorcing his wife. The Tracy-Hepburn chemistry was generated with astonishing ease during the shooting. During one scene, Hepburn recalled: "I accidentally knocked over a glass. Spencer handed me a handkerchief, and I took his handkerchief and I thought, 'Oh, you old so-and-so, you're going to make me mop it up right in the middle of a scene.' So I started to mop it, and the water started to go down through the table. I decided to throw him by going down under the table, and he just stood there watching me. I mopped and mopped, and George Stevens kept the camera running. Spencer just smiled. He wasn't thrown at all." (Quoted from Kate by Charles Higham.) The picture was an instant success, popular with both the public and critics. WOMAN OF THE YEAR received Academy Award nominations for Best Actress and Best Original Screenplay. Though Hepburn lost that year, Kanin and Lardner won Oscars for their wonderful script. Tracy was billed over Hepburn in the film's advertising and credits, something Garson Kanin scolded the actor for: "...She's a lady. You're the man. Ladies first?" he asked. Tracy's response was a classic. "This is a movie, Chowderhead," he replied, "not a lifeboat."

p, Joseph L. Mankiewicz; d, George Stevens; w, Ring Lardner, Jr., Michael Kanin; ph, Joseph Ruttenberg; m, Franz Waxman; ed, Frank Sullivan; art d, Cedric Gibbons, Randall Duell; set d, Edwin B. Willis; cos, Adrian; makeup, Jack Dawn.

Comedy   **Cas.**   **(PR:AA   MPAA:NR)**

WOMAN ON FIRE, A*½   (1970, Ital.) 93m Ferti/Commonwealth United/Ellman c (BRUCIA, RAGAZZO, BRUCIA)

Francoise Prevost (Clara), Gianni Macchia (Giancarlo), Michel Bardinet (Silvio), Monica Strebel (Marina), Anna Pagano (Monica), Danika (Aunt Bice), Franca Sciutto, Miriam Alex, Maria Luisa Sala, Marco Veliante, Ettore Geri.

Tepid drama about a woman, Prevost, who finally discovers the pleasure of sex while on a vacation with her husband and young daughter. The problem is that the pleasure she has found is with a lifeguard, not her husband. To complicate matters, Prevost makes life miserable for herself by telling her husband about her new discoveries, then takes an overdose of barbiturates and dies. Seamy, not naughty, and certainly not nice.

p, Tiziano Longo; d, Fernando Di Leo; w, Di Leo, Antonio Racioppi; ph, Franco Villa (Telecolor); m, Gino Peguri; ed, Mario Morra; art d, Pietro Liberati; m/l, Peguri, Di Leo.

Drama   **(PR:O   MPAA:R)**

WOMAN ON PIER 13, THE*½   (1950) 73m RKO bw (I MARRIED A COMMUNIST)

Laraine Day (Nan Collins), Robert Ryan (Brad Collins), John Agar (Don Lowry), Thomas Gomez (Vanning), Janis Carter (Christine), Richard Rober (Jim Travis), William Talman (Bailey), Paul E. Burns (Arnold), Paul Guilfoyle (Ralston), G. Pat Collins (Charles Dover), Fred Graham (Grip Wilson), Harry Cheshire (Mr. Cornwall), Jack Stoney (Garth), Lester Mathews (Dr. Dixon), Marlo Dyer (Evelyn), Erskine Sanford (Clerk), Bess Flowers (Secretary), Charles Cane (Hagen), Dick Ryan (Waiter at Cocktail Bar), Barry Brooks (Burke), William Haade (Cahill), Iris Adrian (Waitress), Don Brodie (Drunk), Al Murphy (Jeb), Evelyn Ceder (Girl Friend), Marie Voe (Striptease Dancer), George Magrill (Tough), Allan Ray (Man), Louise Lane (Girl), Jim Nolan (Cop), John Duncan (Bellhop).

Ryan is the vice-president of a San Francisco shipping company who, when he was younger, was involved with the Communist Party. Gomez, a Communist leader, wants Ryan to help the party again by causing a strike. He blackmails him by threatening to reveal a murder Ryan had committed when he was in the party. Ryan's wife, Day, and her brother, Agar, are also harassed by the Communist and Agar is killed when he finds out what the Commies are doing. Ryan decides to take care of the Reds and he knocks them off in a blazing gun battle. The title is ridiculous but the film is a well-paced action melodrama.

p, Jack J. Gross; d, Robert Stevenson; w, Charles Grayson, Robert Hardy Andrews (based on a story by George W. George, George F. Slavin); ph, Nicholas Musuraca; m, Leigh Harline; ed, Roland Gross; md, Constantin Bakaleinikoff; art d, Albert D'Agostino, Walter E. Keller; set d, Darrell Silvera, James Altwies; cos, Michael Woulfe; makeup, W. H. Phillips.

Crime Drama   **(PR:A   MPAA:NR)**

WOMAN ON THE BEACH, THE***   (1947) 71m RKO bw

Joan Bennett (Peggy Butler), Robert Ryan (Lt. Scott Burnett), Charles Bickford (Ted Butler), Nan Leslie (Eve Geddes), Walter Sande (Otto Wernecke), Irene Ryan (Mrs. Wernecke), Frank Darien (Lars), Jay Norris (Jimmy), Glenn Vernon (Kirk), Hugh Chapman (Young Fisherman), Carl Faulkner (Old Fisherman), Marie Dodd (Nurse), Harry Harvey (Dr. Smith), Charles Pawley (Barton), Robert Anderson, Drew Miller, Robert Manning (Coast Guardsmen), Bill Shannon (Blacksmith), Harry Tyler (Carter), Donald Gordon (Donnie), Jackie Jackson (Johnnie), Carl Armstrong (Lenny), John Elliott (Old Workman), Bonnie Blair, Carol Donell, Kay Christopher, Nancy Saunders (Girls at Party), Martha Hyers (Mrs. Barton), Nan Leslie (Alice).

The fifth and final American film for France's most brilliant director, Jean Renoir, THE WOMAN ON THE BEACH is an accomplished piece of filmmaking which probes into the interrelationships of three characters—their past, present, and future together—and how they find themselves entangled in a film noir atmosphere, though without any of them having committed a crime. Ryan, a veteran Coast Guard lieutenant haunted by torturous combat nightmares, happens on Bennett one day while walking along the beach. Initially Ryan is antagonistic towards Bennett, insulting her for collecting broken pieces of wood which have drifted ashore from a wrecked ship. Although he is married to the loving Leslie, he becomes attracted to Bennett. Since Ryan lives nearby, he is eventually introduced to Bennett's husband, Bickford, a crotchety, aging, blind painter who lives a nasty, unhappy existence with his wife and his paintings, which he no longer can see. The more Ryan falls in love with Bennett, the more he learns about her past. Something of a gold digger, Bennett married Ryan when he was a wealthy, promising artist. One day, in a rage, Bennett threw a glass at her husband, blinding him and thereby simultaneously ruining his career and her dreams for a champagne and caviar life as a socialite. Ryan grows increasingly paranoid that Bickford suspects him of romancing his wife. The paranoia then reaches the point where Ryan is no longer convinced that Bickford is blind. To test the painter's sight, Ryan leads him toward a cliff and lets him walk over the edge. Bickford miraculously survives, but by now Ryan is sure of his blindness. His emotions in disarray, Ryan returns to his wife and the safety of the boat-building yard run by her father. Later, however, he gets a phone call from a panicked Bennett who begs him to come to her house. He arrives to find it in flames, and Bickford destroying his past by throwing his paintings into the pyre. Bennett helps Bickford to safety, while Ryan realizes that his chances to love Bennett are over, causing him to return to Leslie. Not surprisingly, American audiences in 1947 were less than responsive to THE WOMAN ON THE BEACH, unable (or unwilling) to grasp the subtleties and complex characterizations of Ryan, Bennett, and Bickford. What appears initially to be a *film noir* involving a romantic triangle and the murder of the woman's husband, turns out completely opposite. Rather than being a *femme fatale*, Bennett is an unhappy but devoted wife, Bickford is not an evil man but one crippled emotionally by his inability to paint, and Ryan is too confused to decipher the truth from his murderous fantasies and paranoia. The film's theme is a dark one as Jean Renoir writes in his autobiography *My Life and My Films*: "The actions of all three principal characters were wholly without glamor; they occurred against empty backgrounds and in a perfectly abstract style. It was a story quite opposite to everything I had hitherto attempted. In all my previous films I had tried to depict the bonds uniting the individual to his background. The older I grew, the more I had proclaimed the consoling truth that the world is one; and now 'with THE WOMAN ON THE BEACH' I was embarked on a study of persons whose sole idea was to close the door on the absolutely concrete phenomenon which we call life." Originally to have been produced by Val Lewton, THE WOMAN ON THE BEACH was directed by Renoir at the request of Joan Bennett who had wanted to work with the great French director. When Lewton became involved in other projects, Jack Gross, an RKO contract producer, took the project under his wing. What was initially to have been a low-budget feature became a major production, but before its completion Gross died, leaving Renoir in charge. According to Renoir, "I made it and was very happy," but, to others, the finished film posed some problems. "We arranged some previews. It was very badly received and we returned to the studios pretty depressed....I was the first to advise cuts and changes. I asked for a writer as collaborator so as not to be alone." Again, as with the director's masterpiece RULES OF THE GAME, Renoir found himself recutting the film on the basis of audience response, failing to believe in the strength of his own vision. Bennett's husband, Walter Wanger, suggested changes, especially in the scenes between Bennett and Ryan. After reshooting one-third of the film, Renoir correctly noted, in retrospect: "I'm afraid I was too far ahead of the public's mentality." As with so many films of the great directors, THE WOMAN ON THE BEACH has, after re-evaluation, proven to be a far better film than originally perceived.

p, Jack Gross; d, Jean Renoir; w, Renoir, Frank Davis, Michael Hogan (based on the novel *None So Blind* by Mitchell Wilson); ph, Leo Tover, Harry Wild; m, Hanns Eisler; ed, Roland Gross, Lyle Boyer; md, Constantine Bakaleinikoff; art d, Albert S. D'Agostino, Walter E. Keller; set d, Darrell Silvera, John Sturtevant; spec eff, Russell A. Cully; tech adv, Lt. Comdr. Charles H. Gardiner, U.S. Coast Guard Reserve.

Drama (PR:A MPAA:NR)

WOMAN ON THE RUN*½ (1950) 77m Fidelity/UNIV bw

Ann Sheridan (*Eleanor Johnson*), Dennis O'Keefe (*Danny Leggett*), Robert Keith (*Inspector Ferris*), Frank Jenks (*Detective Shaw*), Ross Elliott (*Frank Johnson*), John Qualen (*Mailbus*), J. Farrell MacDonald (*Sea Captain*), Thomas P. Dillon (*Joe Gordon*), Joan Shawlee (*Blonde*), Steven Geray (*Dr. Hohler*), Reiko Sato (*Suzie*), Victor Sen Yung (*Sammy*).

Elliott is an artist who accidentally witnesses a mob killing. Fearing retaliatiion he goes into hiding. His wife Sheridan shows little concern. Their marriage has been an unhappy one, and Elliott's absence seems like a blessing. Sheridan is soon confronted by the police, who desperately want to find her husband. Though initially reluctant, Sheridan learns her missing spouse has a potentially life-threatening heart condition that he is unaware of. In spite of their marital difficulties, Sheridan comes to realize that she does love Elliott, and finally agrees to help police inspector Keith with the hunt. O'Keefe, a reporter, offers Sheridan assistance, During their search O'Keefe becomes attracted to the woman, but it gradually dawns on Sheridan that this journalist is actually the killer Elliott is running from.

O'Keefe catches on to her suspicions, and plans to kill both her and Elliott, but the police arrive in time and arrest the murderer. Tension takes some dramatic turns within this well-crafted film, switching character relationships with frightening results. Each time Sheridan finds comfort and security, her character is forced into an opposite change of loyalties by unexpected circumstances which inevitably crop up. Sheridan is strong in the part, heading a cast that infuses the tricky plotting with believability and life. WOMAN ON THE RUN was shot on location in San Francisco, and the city is smartly utilized. Like people and the developments within the story, these streets seem to offer Sheriddan a haven from danger, yet prove to be the very ground from which she must escape. Under director Foster's tight control, the various elements are woven together for an intelligent and always fascinating entertainment. This movie was the subject of a brief legal controversy when two writers sued the production company, claiming a story of theirs had been plagiarized for this motion picture. An out-of-court settlement was finally agreed upon, ending the troubles.

p, Howard Welsch; d, Norman Foster; w, Alan Campbell, Foster (based on a story by Sylvia Tate); ph, Hal Mohr; m, Emil Newman, Arthur Lange; ed, Otto Ludwig; art d, Boris Levin; set d, Jacques Mapes; cos, Martha Bunch, William Travilla.

Crime (PR:A MPAA:NR)

WOMAN POSSESSED,A** (1958, Brit.) 68m Danzigers/UA bw

Margaretta Scott (*Katherine Winthrop*), Francis Matthews (*Dr. John Winthrop*), Kay Callard (*Ann Winthrop*), Alison Leggatt (*Emma*), Ian Fleming (*Walter*), Jan Holden (*Mary*), Denis Shaw (*Bishop*), Totti Truman Taylor (*Miss Frobisher*), Tony Thawnton, Edith Saville.

Matthews, an English doctor, returns from a trip to the U.S. with Callard, his fiancee. Scott, his domineering mother, takes an immediate dislike to the proposed nuptials and lets everyone know it. Since Callard has a heart condition Scott insists they live with her. When Callard's condition takes a bad turn, her mother-in-law gives her the wrong pills. Matthews saves his beloved's life and accuses his mother of trying to kill Callard. However, it turns out that Leggatt, the family maid, had switched the pills. With the crisis out of the way, the three protagonists realize it's time to settle all differences. Despite some good performances from the cast, this isn't a very engaging drama. Even Ralph Kramden had more interesting mother-in-law confrontations.

p, Edward J. and Harry Lee Danziger; d, Max Varnel; w, Brian Clemens, Eldon Howard; ph, Jimmy Wilson.

Drama (PR:A MPAA:NR)

WOMAN RACKET, THE*½ (1930) 60m MGM bw (GB:LIGHTS AND SHADOWS)

Tom Moore (*Tom, Policeman*), Blanche Sweet (*Julia Barnes*), Sally Starr (*Buddy*), Bobby Agnew (*Rags*), John Miljan (*Chris*), Tenen Holtz (*Ben*), Lew Kelly (*Tish*), Tom London (*Hennessy*), Eugene Borden (*Lefty*), John Byron (*Duke*), Nita Martan (*Rita*), Richard Travers (*Wardell*).

Police officer Moore marries nightclub hostess Sweet, only to have her leave him for the night life and a gangster when life in a squalid apartment begins to take its toll. Sweet becomes mixed up in a murder which forces the gangster boy friend to look for a convenient manner to get her out of the way, and giving Moore a chance to play the hero and rescue his wife. Strictly routine.

d, Robert Ober, Albert Kelley; w, Albert Shelby Le Vino (based on the play "Night Hostess" by Philip Dunning, Frances Dunning); ph, Peverell Marley; ed, Basil Wrangell; art d, Cedric Gibbons; cos, David Cox; ch, Sammy Lee.

Crime/Drama (PR:A MPAA:NR)

WOMAN REBELS, A** (1936) 86m RKO bw

Katharine Hepburn (*Pamela Thistlewaite*), Herbert Marshall (*Thomas Lane*), Elizabeth Allan (*Flora Thistlewaite*), Donald Crisp (*Judge Thistlewaite*), Doris Dudley (*Young Flora*), David Manners (*Alan*), Lucile Watson (*Betty Bumble*), Van Heflin (*Gerald*), Eily Malyon (*Piper*), Margaret Seddon (*Aunt Serena*), Molly Lamont (*Young Girl*), Lionel Pape (*Mr. White*), Constance Lupino (*Lady Gaythorne*), Lillian Kemble- Cooper (*Lady Rinlake*), Nick Thompson (*Signor Grassi*), Inez Palange (*Signora Grassi*), Tony Romero (*Italian Boy*), Joe Mack (*Italian Bit*), Marilyn French (*Flora as an Infant*), Bonnie June McNamara (*Flora at Age 5*), Marilyn Knowlden (*Flora at Age 10*).

A modestly budgeted movie that, it was hoped, would bring Hepburn back from a few disasters she'd had earlier. It didn't, and the film lost about a quarter of a million dollars. Once again, Hepburn is a strong, rebellious type. She's living in the prudish Victorian society and the film covers about 25 years of that repressed era as she becomes an early fighter for female equality. Her father is Crisp, a stern disciplinarian under whose parentage Hepburn feels stifled. He's a judge and in that capacity judges his own daughter. She lashes out by having an affair and conceiving a child--without benefit of clergy or a justice of the peace--through the auspices of Heflin.

Meanwhile, Marshall has been her long-time suitor and waiting in the wings for the right moment to marry her. He decides this may be her most vulnerable moment, but she fools him and stays single through a series of sufferings that would do Bette Davis justice. She winds up editing a women's magazine, the turn-of-the-century version of *Cosmopolitan.* Marshall sticks close by and familiarity finally breeds affection so she marries him. Hepburn's daughter is played by Dudley, daughter of a Broadway star of the era, Bide Dudley. Marshall is a bit stiff but the role calls for him to be a good deal less than flamboyant and he carries that off. The movie was originally titled "Portrait of a Rebel" but that was altered for reasons known only to the studio. Both Heflin and Dudley were making their screen debuts after having been discovered by Hepburn in the stage play "End of Summer" by Ina Claire. Dudley's career did not take off and Heflin's did as he began to appear in larger roles, won an Oscar for Best Supporting Actor in JOHNNY EAGER, and continued his excellent work until his death in 1971. He was having his daily swim at his hotel apartment on Alta Loma in West Hollywood when he succumbed to a heart attack.

p, Pandro S. Berman; d, Mark Sandrich; w, Anthony Veiller, Ernest Vajda (based on the novel *Portrait of a Rebel* by Netta Syrett); ph, Robert De Grasse; m, Roy Webb; ed, Jane Loring; md, Nathaniel Shilkret; art d, Van Nest Polglase, Perry Ferguson; set d, Darrell Silvera; cos, Walter Plunkett; ch, Hermes Pan; makeup, Mel Burns.

Historical Drama **Cas.** **(PR:A-C MPAA:NR)**

WOMAN TAMER (SEE: SHE COULDN'T TAKE IT, 1935)

WOMAN THEY ALMOST LYNCHED, THE** (1953) 90m REP bw

John Lund *(Lance Horton),* Brian Donlevy *(William Quantrill),* Audrey Totter *(Kate Quantrill),* Joan Leslie *(Sally Maris),* Ben Cooper *(Jesse James),* Nina Varela *(Mayor Delilah Courtney),* James Brown *(Frank James),* Ellen Corby *(1st Woman),* Fern Hall *(2nd Woman),* Minerva Urecal *(Mrs. Stewart),* Jim Davis *(Cole Younger),* Reed Hadley *(Bitterroot Bill Maris),* Ann Savage *(Glenda),* Virginia Christine *(Jenny),* Marilyn Lindsey *(Rose),* Nacho Galindo *(John Pablo),* Richard Simmons *(Captain),* Gordon Jones *(Sergeant),* Frank Ferguson *(Bartender),* Post Park *(Driver),* Tom McDonough *(Quantrill's Henchman),* Ted Ryan *(Soldier),* Richard Crane *(Lieutenant),* Carl Pitti *(Hangman),* Joe Yrigoyen *(Guard),* Jimmie Hawkins *(Boy),* James Kirkwood *(Old Man),* Paul Livermore *(Bill Anderson).*

There is not much of a plot to this offbeat western by the prolific director Dwan (with over 400 pictures to his credit), and that which does exist is extremely hard to follow. The action takes place in the heat of the Civil War in a small town on the Arkansas-Missouri border, which supposedly is not involved in the conflict. This proves to be a fallacy when Leslie is about to be hanged as a Confederate spy, something she isn't, but is accused of being because she is an easterner who wandered into town and is tough enough to run a saloon and even tote a gun. The real spy is her beau, Lund, who goes about his business without being bothered by anyone. Also thrown into the mix are the head of a gang of outlaws and a town drunk who can't get over the loss of his beloved wife. An oddity in the male-dominated western genre is a scene in which two women, Totter and Leslie, face each other in a gun duel. A must-see for any fan of oater legends.

p&d, Allan Dwan; w, Steve Fisher (based on the story by Michael Fessier); ph, Reggie Lanning; m, Stanley Wilson; ed, Fred Allen; art d, James Sullivan; cos, Adele Palmer; m/l, Victor Young, Peggy Lee, Sam Stept, Sidney Mitchell.

Western **(PR:A MPAA:NR)**

WOMAN TIMES SEVEN** (1967, U.S./Fr./Ital.) 99m EM-FOX-Societe Nouvelle des Films Cormoran/EM c (SEPT FOIS FEMME; SETTE VOLTE DONNA)

"Funeral Procession": Shirley MacLaine *(Paulette),* Peter Sellers *(Jean),* Elspeth March *(Annette),* Rossano Brazzi *(Giorgio),* Catherine Samie *(Jeannine),* Judith Magre *(2nd Prostitute),* Vittorio Gassman *(Cenci),* Clinton Greyn *(MacCormick),* Lex Barker *(Rik),* Elsa Martinelli *(Woman in Market),* Robert Morley *(Dr. Xavier),* Patrick Wymark *(Henri Minou),* Adrienne Corri *(Mlle. Lisiere),* Alan Arkin *(Fred),* Michael Caine *(Handsome Stranger),* Anita Ekberg *(Claudie),* Philippe Noiret *(Victor).*

It's difficult enough doing one role well. Playing several parts in the same movie, though each of the septet of sequences is different, is almost impossible and requires the talents of an Alec Guinness or a Sellers to make it work. MacLaine had not yet achieved the maturity nor did she have the acting ability to bring this off and the result is MacLaine Times Seven, which means it's just ol' Shirl' in a host of different costumes, hairstyles, and makeup, but still the essential redhead. In the first segment, she's a widow accompanying the coffin of her late husband to the cemetery. Her close pal is Sellers who is offering her balm and solace. As they move slowly along the road, Sellers admits that he loves her and always has. She is delighted by his confession and her tears dry and a smile curves her lips as the couple begin to talk about the good times they are going to have. They approach a crossroad and are so enraptured by their conversation that they miss the turn. The hearse goes right and they go left. Black humor, but not very funny except for Sellers' amorous ogling. The second segment has MacLaine returning to her home to find her husband, Brazzi, cavorting in the sack with another woman. MacLaine is incensed, exits, and swears that she will exact revenge by making love to the very first man who talks to her. She meets a group of hookers (if one were to use a collective noun for these ladies of the evening, it might be "a blare of strumpets") lead by Samie and Magre. They teach her some things about walking the streets and when push comes to shove, MacLaine can't come across. A local pimp gives her a lift home. They arrive and Brazzi showers them both with invective. The pimp decks Brazzi with a right cross, then turns, expecting MacLaine to come with him. Instead, she berates him and races to kneel by the semiconscious Brazzi. Little more than an extended joke. The third section gets a bit sexy as MacLaine is seen as an interpreter, a hippie type, who is working at a convention of cybernetics experts. She has an off- stage lover who she thinks is a bore. She is complaining of this to Gassman, an Italian, and Greyn, a Scot. Both men find her attractive, if a bit dippy. She takes them to her apartment where she doffs her clothes and begins to read the collected works of T.S. Eliot. The sight of the nude woman fans the passions of the men and when an advance is made, MacLaine responds by saying that they are animals, little better than cavemen. She reads them the riot act and the two men begin to hit each other to prove that they have been properly chastised. MacLaine watches this new behavior with delight and responds by throwing her lover's photo away and promptly unites with Gassman and Greyn in a *menage a trois.* This piece is satirical and takes shots at the prattle one hears so often at vacant cocktail soirees. No.4 is a good one as MacLaine is seen to be a grumpy housewife married to Barker, a successful author of trashy novels which feature a mythical heroine named "Simone." The creation is the type of hoyden who drives men mad with her passionate ways and wild ideas. MacLaine thinks there is no way she can compete with her husband's mental fantasies but she is determined to try so she begins to act in a weird way and Barker has no recourse other than to bring Morley, a psychiatrist, back to the house to see what's brought on this insane behavior. After a while, MacLaine understands that they think she's totally bananas and she has to rectify the situation before she is committed so she runs onto the roof of their apartment building and shouts aloud to whoever can hear her that she's not crazy, she's simply in love with her own husband. Morley does his usual delicious work in this one and Barker shows that he's not just a handsome face. The fifth episode has MacLaine as a rich Parisian matron married to Wymark. The opera is about to open the new season and MacLaine intends to wear a spectacular new gown to cause oohs and aahs but she is disgruntled to discover that her chief social competitor, Corri, will be wearing the same dress to the festivities. Determined to be the belle of the ball, MacLaine prevails upon Wymark to sabotage Corri by having a trio of Wymark's assistants plant an explosive in Corri's limo. When MacLaine gets to the opera first, she is chagrined to learn that yet a third woman has arrived wearing the same dress. This woman is rotund and older and MacLaine is angered enough to run from the theater when she sees the heavy-set socialite. As she exits the opera, MacLaine sees Corri, now in tatters and with a blackened face from the explosion, walking into the opera, undaunted, and still about to make her grand appearance. MacLaine laughs when she sees Corri and wonders how the woman will respond to seeing the fat lady in the same gown. A silly piece, mean-spirited and dumb. No.6 examines another subject. MacLaine and Arkin are lovers married to other people. They are depressed that their love will never be permanent and since they can't be united in life, they plan to be wed in death. They don bride and groom costumes and conspire to take their own lives in a seedy hotel room. Their calm determination begins to rock when they can't agree on the means to their deaths. An argument breaks out and MacLaine takes refuge in the tacky bathroom. Arkin sits there by himself, begins to pace, and then thinks that maybe life is better than death so he makes a move toward the door and begins to open it quietly when he hears the window break in the bathroom. He looks outside and sees MacLaine scamper down the fire escape. She's already made the decision to live and is exiting quickly. The final section of the film has MacLaine out shopping with her best pal, Ekberg. MacLaine is a woman married to Noiret and deeply in love with him but when the two comely wives spot handsome Caine watching them, they are thrilled that such a good-looking man would find these old married ladies sensuous. Ekberg departs and Caine continues to follow MacLaine. She arrives home, is met by Noiret, then looks out the window and sees Caine is still there. She smiles happily with the knowledge that she is still attractive to other men, never dreaming that Caine is there as a hired "shadow" who has been employed to keep an eye on her by her jealous husband. All of the segments, save the first, run between 14 and 16 minutes. The Funeral episode goes about eight minutes, which is all it's worth. Ortolani's music is second-rate but the rest of the technical credits are all excellent. Special note should be taken of Alex Archambault's hairstyles and the makeup work done by Alberto De Rossi and Georges Bouban. Although Marcel Escoffier gets credit for the well-planned costumes, it was Pierre Cardin who designed MacLaine's gowns. The picture takes place in France but MacLaine is so typically American that it's not easy to accept her as Gallic. Shot on location in Paris with interiors at the Boulogne Studios, it features production people and actors from many countries, including the U.S., Britain, Italy, France, and Sweden. What might have been a *tour de force* turns out to be only a *tour de France.*

p, Arthur Cohn; d, Vittorio De Sica; w, Cesare Zavattini; ph, Christian Matras (Pathe Color); m, Riz Ortolani; ed, Teddy Darvas, Victoria Mercanton; md, Ortolani; art d, Bernard Evein; set d, Georges Glon; cos, Marcel Escoffier; makeup, Alberto De Rossi, Georges Bouban.

Comedy/Drama   Cas.   (PR:C-O MPAA:NR)

WOMAN TO WOMAN** (1929) 90m TIF bw

Betty Compson (Lola), George Barraud (David), Juliette Compton (Vesta), Margaret Chambers (Florence), Reginald Sharland (Hal), Georgie Billings (Davey), Winter Hall (Dr. Gavrin).

Betty Compson plays a French ballerina who has a brief affair with Englishman Barraud during WW I. He leaves her pregnant, promising to come back after his stint in the front lines. He doesn't, the heavy shelling causing him to lose his memory, and instead returns to London to marry the wealthy Juliette Compton. Years pass before Betty Compson finds herself making an appearance on the London stage, and once again running into her old flame. Emotions start to fly, with Barraud realizing that he has fathered a child, something he is happy about because his wife is barren. In her moment of extreme sacrifice, Betty Compson gives up her boy to Barraud and Juliette Compton, while she goes on to die. The object in this tearjerker seemed to be to try to put as many lumps as possible in the patrons' throats but the hardboiled ruled the day and stayed away.

p, Michael Balcon, Victor Saville; d, Saville; w, Saville, Nicholas Fodor (based on the play by Michael Morton); ph, Benjamin Kline; cos, Rahvis.

Drama   (PR:A MPAA:NR)

WOMAN TO WOMAN** (1946, Brit.) 99m BN/Anglo-American bw

Douglas Montgomery (David Anson), Joyce Howard (Nicolette Bonnet), Adele Dixon (Sylvia Anson), Yvonne Arnaud (Henriette), Paul Collins (David Junior), Eugene Deckers (De Rillac), John Warwick (Dr. Gavron), Ballet Rambert (Dancers), Kay Young (Pauline), Gerard Kempinski (Cafe Proprietor), Lilly Kann (Concierge), Martin Miller (Postman), Marcel De Haes (Hotel Clerk), Agnes Bernelle (Lolo, the Chorus Girl), Therese Carroll (Bookst all Woman), Rene Poirier (Music Hall Attendant), Alan Sedgwick (John Meredith), Eric Lindsay (Hotel Page), H.G. Guinle (Gaston), George Carney (Taxi Driver), Keith Lloyd (Page Boy), Manushka (French Chorus Girl), Daphne Day, Molly Rayner (Sylvia's Friends), Carole Coombe (Sylvia's Secretary), Griffiths Moss (Sylvia's Butler), Ralph Truman (Colonel), Willi Werder (Junk Shop Keeper), Carol Lawton (Sylvia's Maid), Charles Victor (Stage Manager), Harry Fine (Observer), Melville Crawford (Pilot), Finlay Currie (Theater Manager), Charles Paton (Stage Door Keeper), Ernie Priest (Theater Guard), Fajni Amand (Neighbour's Child), Robert Ross (Page Boy), Lydia Donovan, Maxie Taylor, Francis Adams, Daisy Burrell (Stage Box Committee), Brenda Hamlyn, Suzanne Stracey, Lulu Dukes (Joyce Howard's Dancing Doubles).

This same picture had been made twice before, once as a silent in 1924, and again in a dreadful early talkie in 1929 starring Betty Compson and George Barraud. A few of the angles are here twisted about. It is a WW II setting instead of a WW I. Montgomery is already married and is Canadian instead of single and English, and the script is tightened to make for a smoother and more believable effort. Montgomery plays the Canadian officer accepting a dangerous mission, mainly to escape a bitchy wife, which sets him behind enemy lines. In Paris he has an affair with dancer Howard, and leaves her pregnant before he continues with his mission. Years later Montgomery searches for the woman who brought him so much happiness, and finds her a successful star in London and also suffering a heart condition with only a short time to live. As in the earlier version, the main objective is heavy melodramatics, but this is more readily conceived here through more adept handling.

p, Louis H. Jackson; d, Maclean Rogers; w, James Seymour, Marjorie Dean (based on the play by Michael Morton); ph, James Wilson; m, George Melachrino; ed, Dan Birt; md, Hans May; art d, R. Holmes Paul; cos, Rahvis; ch, Andree Howard; makeup, Harry Hayward.

Drama   (PR:A MPAA:NR)

WOMAN TRAP*½ (1929) 82m PAR bw

Hal Skelly (Dan Malone), Chester Morris (Ray Malone), Evelyn Brent (Kitty Evans), William B. Davidson (Watts), Effie Ellsler (Mrs. Malone), Guy Oliver (Mr. Evans), Leslie Fenton (Eddie Evans), Charles Giblyn (Smith), Joseph L. Mankiewicz (Reporter), Wilson Hummell (Detective Captain), William "Sailor Billy" Vincent (Himself, a Boxer), Virginia Bruce (Nurse).

Confusingly portrayed effort in which Skelly plays a tough police sergeant with a mission to get the gangs cleaned up, and finds his brother is a criminal big shot. Nothing out of the ordinary, the most prominent feature being the appearance of Joseph Mankiewicz (future director of GUYS AND DOLLS and THE BAREFOOT CONTESSA, to name just a couple of his many successful ventures) in a bit role as a reporter.

d, William A. Wellman; w, Louise Long, Bartlett Cormack (based on the play by Edwin Burke); ph, Henry Gerrard; ed, Allison Shaffer.

Crime   (PR:A MPAA:NR)

WOMAN TRAP*½ (1936) 63m PAR bw

Gertrude Michael (Barbara Andrews), George Murphy (Kent Shevlin), Akim Tamiroff (Ramirez), Sidney Blackmer (Riley Ferguson), Samuel S. Hinds (Sen. Andrews), Dean Jagger ("Honey" Hogan), Roscoe Karns (Mopsy), David Haines (Jimmy Emerson), Julian Rivero (Pancho), Ed Brophy (George), Bradley Page (Flint), Ralph Malone (Brace), Arthur Aylesworth (City Editor), Hayden Stephenson (Sheriff), John Martin (Boy Radio Operator).

Murphy plays a reporter investigating a murder, and suddenly findng himself helping out the FBI. Tamiroff is the most interesting one to watch in this film that quickly collapses under the burden of its script. He's a Mexican bandido who turns out to be a secret policeman, and his dialect is totally scene-stealing.

p, Harold Hurley; d, Harold Young; w, Brian Marlowe, Eugene Walter (based on the story by Charles Brackett); ph, William C. Mellor; ed, Richard Currier.

Crime   (PR:A MPAA:NR)

WOMAN UNAFRAID* (1934) 68m Goldsmith bw

Lucille Gleason (Officer Winthrop), Skeets Gallagher (Anthony), Lona Andre (Peggy), Warren Hymer (John), Barbara Weeks (Mary), Laura Treadwell (Mrs. Worthington), Eddie Phillips (Mack), Jason Robards, Sr (Big Bill Lewis).

Tough cop lady Gleason pushes the meanest thugs around while doing other good deeds that make her a great asset to the improvement of the neighborhood. She is one cop so tough and good at her job that she's able to bring the hood to justice whom everyone else wanted a shot at but couldn't seem to manage. Poor and careless effort which leaves it with no importance whatsoever.

d, William J. Cowen; w, Mary E. McCarthy; ph, Gilbert Warrenton.

Crime   (PR:A MPAA:NR)

WOMAN UNDER THE INFLUENCE, A***½ (1974) 155m Faces International c

Peter Falk (Nick Longhetti), Gena Rowlands (Mabel Longhetti), Matthew Cassel (Tony Longhetti), Matthew Laborteaux (Angelo Longhetti), Christina Grisantii (Maria Longhetti), Katherine Cassavetes (Mama Longhetti), Lady Rowlands (Martha Mortensen), Fred Draper (George Mortensen), O.G. Dunn (Garson Cross), Mario Gallo (Harold Jensen), Eddie Shaw (Dr. Zepp), Angelo Grisanti (Vito Grimaldi), James Joyce (Bowman), John Finnegan (Clancy), Cliff Carnell (Aldo), Joanne Moore Jordan (Muriel), Hugh Hurd (Willie Johnson), Leon Wagner (Billy Tidrow), John Hawker (Joseph Morton), Sil Words (James Turner), Elizabeth Deering (Angela), Jacki Peters (Tina), Elsie Ames (Principal), Nick Cassavetes (Adolph), Dominique Davalos (Dominique Jenson), Xan Cassavetes (Adrienne Jensen), Pancho Meisenheimer (John Jensen), Charles Horvath (Eddie the Indian), Sonny Aprile (Aldo), Vince Barbi (Gino), Frank Richards (Adolph), Ellen Davalos (Nancy).

Movies about mad, or even semi-mad, housewives have been done often, though seldom with as much detail as this too-long picture that fell into the same trap Cassavetes has fallen into before. A brief synopsis can't do it justice because the joy is in the performance by Rowlands and the sum of all the parts adds up to more than the whole. She's a lower middle-class wife and mother. Falk is her faithful husband, and Laborteaux, Grisanti, and Cassel are their children. She is an unfulfilled woman who only lives through Falk and the kids. Mental breakdowns are no longer the sole property of bored Park Avenue or Beverly Hills dowagers and Rowlands is soon a victim of her own convoluted brain. All of her actions, while making perfect sense to her, are looked upon as insane by almost everyone else. She tells the kids that they should dance in the nude, she flits in and out of reality like a fly buzzing around a room, and lashes out physically when she finds that she can't express herself in words. Her behavior becomes increasingly more erratic and Falk finds that he must commit her to an institution for a half year in order to get her mind in balance. His mother, Katherine Cassavetes, has been pushing for that and they believe she will come out cured. That's not the case and when Rowlands does finally emerge, she is shaky, still off-kilter, just as loving toward her husband and children, and the audience realizes that nothing has changed. It takes more than two-and-a-half hours to tell the story and 40 minutes could have been easily cut. Both Rowlands and Cassavetes were nominated for Oscars (his for direction) for this unexpected minor hit that grossed well over $6 million the first time around. It began as a theatrical piece for Rowlands but she balked at having to play such a demanding role nightly and the suggestion was made to transform it into a movie. Cassavetes took out a mortgage on his home, contacted pals and relatives for financing, and that began a two year shooting schedule that was dictated by the money they had in the bank. She has a one-night affair with a stranger that was not needed in the film as the important things were how she dealt with those around her who loved her and who could see how her mind had been shattered by the pressures of being a wife-mother. A very complex and confounding film that one wishes could have been more focused. Cassavetes has an infuriating habit of allowing his scenes to go on far too long after the point of the scene has been made. Nevertheless, it's one of the best from Cassavetes, who has always stood solidly outside the mainstream of movies and doggedly waited for the picture-going public to rise to his level, rather than allow himself to be dragged down to theirs. Perhaps it's this elitist attitude that has caused him to have very few commercial successes. Note the names of the cast and you'll see three people named Cassavetes, two Rowlands, one Shaw, and one Cassel. Seymour Cassel is a pal of the director and appeared in several movies for him, including FACES (nominated for Best Supporting Actor Oscar), MINNIE AND MOSKOWITZ and THE KILLING OF A CHINESE BOOKIE. We can only assume that Matthew Cassel is related. But when people are making a movie for love, not money, nepotism must come into the situation. In this case, the acting was so good that it didn't matter that the actors were related.

p, Sam Shaw; d&w, John Cassavetes; ph, Mitch Breif (MGM Color); m, Bo Harwood; ed, David Armstrong, Elizabeth Bergeron, Sheila Viseltear, Tom Cornwell; art d, Phedon Papamichael.

Drama   (PR:C MPAA:R)

WOMAN WANTED*½   (1935) 70m MGM bw

Maureen O'Sullivan (Ann), Joel McCrea (Tony), Lewis Stone (District Attorney), Louis Calhern (Smiley), Edgar Kennedy (Sweeney), House Detective, Adrienne Ames (Betty), Robert Grieg (Peedles, Butler), Noel Madison (Joe Metz), Granville Bates (Casey), William B. Davidson (Collins), Richard Powell (Lee), Erville Alderson (Constable), Gertrude Short (Gertie).

McCrea plays a well-meaning lawyer who unknowingly takes in a girl fleeing from the law and a murder charge. When he discovers O'Sullivan's plight, instead of turning her in he falls in love with her, then helps get the goods on the real murderer. A few good moments and caricatures, but generally dull.

d, George B. Seitz; w, Leonard Fields, Dave Silverstein (based on the story by Wilson Collison); ph, Charles Clarke; ed, Ben Lewis.

Crime/Drama   (PR:A MPAA:NR)

WOMAN WHO CAME BACK**   (1945) 68m REP bw

John Loder (Dr. Matt Adams), Nancy Kelly (Lorna Webster), Otto Kruger (Rev. Stevens), Ruth Ford (Ruth Gibson), Harry Tyler (Noah), Jeanne Gail (Peggy Gibson), Almira Sessions (Bessie), J. Farrell MacDonald (Sheriff), Emmett Vogan (Dr. Peters).

A New England setting serves for this effective and engrossing tale of witchraft, with Kelly playing a young woman who thinks she is bewitched returning to the small town where her family has resided for centuries. A few skeletons come out of the closet as the townsfolk become convinced that the girl is possessed of a curse passed down to her from three centuries earlier. The extremes to which people are driven before everything is cleared up are frightening, one such being Kelly's attempted suicide and another the threat of mob violence that runs through the story.

p&d, Walter Colmes; w, Dennis Cooper, Les Willis (based on the story by John Kafka and an idea by Phillip Yordan); ph, Henry Sharp; m, Edward Plump; ed, John Link; md, Walter Scharf; set d, Jacques Mapes.

Horror/Drama   (PR:A MPAA:NR)

WOMAN WHO DARED*   (1949, Fr.) 102m Siritzsky International bw
                                          (LA CIEL EST A VOU S)

Madeleine Renaud (Therese Gauthier), Charles Vanel (Pierre Gauthier), Jean Debucourt (Piano Teacher).

It's love in the air and on the ground for aviators Renaud and Vanel, as the pair's passion for flying is not allowed to interfere with their marriage. Never gets off the ground. (In French; English subtitles.)

p&d, Jean Gremillon; w, Charles Spaak.

Drama   (PR:A MPAA:NR)

WOMAN WHO WOULDN'T DIE, THE**   (1965, Brit.) 84m
                             Parroch-McCallum AP/WB bw (GB: CATACOMBS)

Gary Merrill (Raymond Garth), Jane Merrow (Alice Taylor), Georgina Cookson (Ellen Garth), Neil McCallum (Dick Corbett), Rachel Thomas (Christine), Jack Train (Solicitor), Frederick Piper (Police Inspector).

Eerie tale in which Merrill and McCallum create a complicated scheme to get the domineering and crippled Cookson out of the way. Merrill becomes involved because Cookson is an unloving wife, while her niece offers a much more pleasant relationship; McCallum, because he is being forced by blackmail to work as her secretary. They stash her away all right, but find they didn't do a good job because a terrible presence soon emanates from the tool shed where they buried her. Neat little thriller that combines a tight script with great foreboding atmosphere.

p, Neil McCallum, Jack Parsons; d, Gordon Hessler; w, Daniel Mainwaring (based on the novel Catacombs by Jay Bennett); ph, Arthur Lavis; m, Carlo Martelli; ed, Robert Winter; art d, George Provis; makeup, Wally Schneiderman.

Horror/Drama   (PR:A MPAA:NR)

WOMAN-WISE**   (1937) 71m FOX bw

Rochelle Hudson (Alice Fuller), Michael Whalen (Tracey Browne), Thomas Beck (Clint De Witt), Alan Dinehart (Richards), Douglas Fowley (Stevens), George Hassell (John De Witt), Astrid Allwyn ("Bubbles" Carson), Chick Chandler (Bob Benton), Pat Flaherty (Duke Fuller).

A lighthearted romp through the dusty halls of fixed prize fights, which is not above making a few moral comments as well. Whalen plays a newspaper sports editor who wants to clean up the dirty racket. He sets his sights on shyster promoter Dinehart and takes on one of his ex-champs himself, knocking out the pug and showing how easy it is. This annoys the champ's daughter, Hudson, but they come together, fall in love, and together clean up the game. Thoroughly enjoyable, and hats off to Hudson, who not only performs like a trouper but sings a number surprisingly well.

p, Sol M. Wurtzel; d, Allan Dwan; w, Ben Markson; ph, Robert Planck; ed, Al DeGaetano; cos, Herschel; m/l, "You're a Knockout," Sidney Clare, Harry Akst (sung by Rochelle Hudson and uncredited male singer).

Drama/Comedy   (PR:A MPAA:NR)

WOMAN WITH NO NAME, THE
                          (SEE: HER PANELLED DOOR, 1951, Brit.)

WOMAN WITH RED BOOTS, THE**   (1977, Fr./Span.) 92m
        Procinex-Serafino Garcia True ba-Gerico-Claude Jaeger-Daniel Carrilo/
                     Gamma III c (LA FEMME AUX BOTTES ROUGES)

Catherine Deneuve (Francoise), Fernando Rey (Perrot), Adalberto Maria Merli (Man), Jacques Weber (Painter), Laura Betti (Leonore), Jose Sacristan (Valet).

A highly symbolic film from the son of celebrated filmmaker Luis Bunuel takes some not always clear or effective stabs at the relationship between art and reality, namely at which affects which. Deneuve is a writer who plays some seemingly nasty tricks on the sadistic Rey that wind up with him being killed by a man angered at his wife's death. Hard to fully understand, but fascinating to watch if for no other reason than as a product of the offspring of Bunuel.

d&w, Juan Bunuel; ph, L. Vilasenor (Eastmancolor).

Drama   (PR:O MPAA:NR)

WOMAN WITHOUT A FACE   (SEE: MISTER BUDDWING, 1966)

WOMAN WITHOUT CAMELLIAS, THE
                          (SEE: LADY WITHOUT CAMELIAS, 1953, Ital.)

WOMANEATER   (SEE: WOMAN EATER, THE, 1951, Brit.)

WOMANHOOD**   (1934, Brit.) 62m BUT bw

Eve Gray (Leila Mason), Leslie Perrins (Richard Brent), Esmond Knight (Jack Gordon), Christine Adrian (Ann Gordon), MacArthur Gordon (Bolton), Charles Castella (Klein).

Perrins is a jewel thief who is put in prison for three years due to reporter Knight's fine investigating. Perrins is released and vows to get revenge, but before he carries out his threat he is killed by his former mistress Gray.

p, Louis London; d, Harry Hughes; w, Brandon Fleming.

Crime   (PR:A MPAA:NR)

WOMANLIGHT**   (1979, Fr./Ger./Ital.) 105m Cibc-Corona Parva
       Cinematografica-Film Produktion Janus/GAU c (CLAIR DE FEMME)

Romy Schneider (Lydia), Yves Montand (Michel), Romolo Valli (Galba), Lila Kedrova (Sonia), Heinz Bennent (Georges).

For once Costa-Gavras left politics alone to concentrate on personal relations and proved that he is unaware of how people behave toward one another. His characters, as in Z or STATE OF SIEGE, are usually people forced into extreme conditions by political oppression, and thus isolated from others as they try to cope with physical or emotional intrusions. Seldom are these characters (usually portrayed by Yves Montand) allowed to show any real emotions toward living people. It comes as no surprise how ill-at-ease WOMANLIGHT appears as Montand and Schneider attempt to strike up a relationship after both have recently suffered extreme losses, he his wife, she her daughter. The oppressive camera angles that added a sense of power to the earlier works are not appropriate here, nor is the approach in other aspects of production. Overall a dismal effort.

p, Georges-Alain Vuille; d&w, Constantine Costa-Gavras (based on the novel by Romain Gary); ph, Ricardo Aranovich; m, Jean Musy; ed, Francoise Bonnot; art d, Mario Chiari, Eric Simon.

Drama   (PR:C MPAA:NR)

WOMAN'S ANGLE, THE*   (1954, Brit.) 86m Bow Bells/Stratford bw

Ernest Thesiger (*Judge*), Lois Maxwell (*Enid Mansell*), Anthony Nicholls (*Dr. Nigel Jarvis*), Peter Reynolds (*Brian Mansell*), Isabel Dean (*Isobel Mansell*), John Bentley (*Renfro Mansell*), Marjorie Fielding (*Mrs. Mansell*), Edward Underdown (*Robert Mansell*), Olaf Pooley (*Rudolph Mansell*), Eric Pohlmann (*Steffano*), Claude Farell (*Disya Veronova*), Geoffrey Toone (*Count Cambia*), Peter Illing (*Sergai*), Cathy O'Donnell (*Nina Van Rhyne*), Joan Collins (*Marina*), Dagmar[Dana] Wynter (*Elaine*), Anton Diffring (*Peasant*), Miles Malleson (*Secrett*), Malcolm Knight, Frederick Berger, Leslie Weston, Lea Seidl, Thelma D'Aquiar, Sylvia Langova, Bill Shine, Nora Gordon, Wensley Pithey, Rufus Cruikshank, Fred Griffiths.

Trite romantic drama about a musician's many loves, none of which reaches fulfillment until he meets young music critic O'Donnell. Sure makings for an uninspired song–or movie.

p, Walter C. Mycroft; d, Leslie Arliss; w, Arliss, Mabbie Poole (based on the play "Three Cups of Coffee" by Ruth Feiner); ph, Erwin Hiller; m, Robert Gill.

Drama   **(PR:A MPAA:NR)**

WOMAN'S DEVOTION, A**   (1956) 88m REP bw (GB: WAR SHOCK; AKA: BATTLESHOCK)

Ralph Meeker (*Trevor Stevenson*), Janice Rule (*Stella Stevenson*), Paul Henreid (*Capt. Henrique Monteros*), Rosenda Monteros (*Maria*), Fanny Schiller (*Senora Reidl*), Jose Torvay (*Gomez*), Yerye Beirute (*Amigo Herrera*), Tony Carbajal (*Sergeant*), Jamie Gonzalez (*Roberto*), Carlos Requelme (*Chief of Police*).

Meeker plays a WW II veteran and artist, still mentally disturbed from his war experiences, on a honeymoon with Rule in Acapulco, where he becomes involved in the murder of two women, one a model, the other a maid. Meeker is believed to be innocent by the local police so they give him permission to leave the country, but then change their minds and arrest him at the airport. This unhinges him and, believing he is back in the war, he tries to gun down the police but is killed instead, without the audience knowing whether or not he did murder the two women. Engrossing and quite disturbing.

p, John Bash; d, Paul Henreid; w, Robert Hill; ph, Jorge Stahl, Jr. (Trucolor); m, Lex Baxter; ed, Richard L. Van Enger; art d, Ramon Rodriguez; cos, Adele Palmer; m/l, Gwen Davis, Baxter.

Mystery/Drama   **(PR:A MPAA:NR)**

WOMAN'S FACE, A***   (1939, Swed.) 100m Svenskfilmindustri bw (EN KVINNAS ANSIKTE)

Ingrid Bergman (*Anna Holm*), Anders Henrikson (*Dr. Wegert*), Karin Carlsson-Kavil (*Fru Wegert*), Georg Rydeberg (*Torsten Barring*), Goran Bernhard (*Lars-Erik*), Tore Svennberg (*Consul Magnus Barring*), Magnus Kesster, Gosta Cederlund, Gunnar Sjoberg, Hilda Borgstrom, John Ericsson, Sigurd Wallen, Bror Bugler, Erik Berglund.

Bergman is exquisite as a young woman with a hideous scar on her face that she received in an accident as a child, and which has made her emotionally deadened, deeply bitter, and a criminal. A miraculous change in her personality takes place when plastic surgeon Henrikson successfully operates on her and her beauty becomes visible. But she is in love with Rydeberg, an aristocrat without a conscience, who wants to use her in a scheme of his to murder his nephew, Bernhard, so that she will be the sole heir to the fortune of his father. Bergman is repelled by the idea, but, still in love with him, she takes a position as governess in the father's household to carry out the scheme. Her change of personality and character from an ugly, bitter woman to a woman of great beauty and nobility corresponding to her new physical features issuperbly portrayed as Bergman refuses to carry out the plan and at the end shoots Rydeberg. Unusual story is first class from top to bottom.

d, Gustaf Molander; w, Gosta Stevens (based on the play "Il Etait Une Fois" by Francois de Croisset); ph, Ake Dahlquist.

Drama   **(PR:A MPAA:NR)**

WOMAN'S FACE, A***½   (1941) 105m MGM bw

Joan Crawford (*Anna Holm*), Melvyn Douglas (*Dr. Gustav Segert*), Conrad Veidt (*Torsten Barring*), Reginald Owen (*Bernard Dalvik*), Albert Basserman (*Consul Barring*), Marjorie Main (*Emma*), Donald Meek (*Herman*), Connie Gilchrist (*Christine Dalvik*), Richard Nichols (*Lars Erik*), Osa Massen (*Vera Segert*), Charles Quigley (*Eric*), Henry Kolker (*Judge*), George Zucco (*Defense Attorney*), Henry Daniell (*Public Prosecutor*), Robert Warwick, Gilbert Emery (*Associate Judges*), William Farnum, Rex Evans (*Notaries*), Sarah Padden (*Police Matron*), Gwili Andre (*Gusta*), Manart Kippen (*Olaf*), Lionel Pape (*Einer*), Doris Day, Mary Ellen Popel (*Party Girls*), Clifford Brooke (*Wickman*), Cecil Stewart (*Pianist*), Veda Buckland, Lilian Kemble-Cooper (*Nurses*), Alexander Leftwich, George Pauncefort (*Guests*), Robert C. Flasher (*Court Attendant*), Catherine Proctor (*Mrs. Segerblum*).

A superior remake of the 1937 Ingrid Bergman Swedish film EN KVINNAS ANSIKTE which was based on the French drama "Il Etait Une Fois" by Francis de Croisset. Crawford is a wow in this atypical story and should have been nominated for an Oscar but this was the year of Joan Fontaine in SUSPICION plus some excellent films by Greer Garson, Olivia de Havilland, Bette Davis, and Barbara Stanwyck. They kept the Swedish background to the story although it could work just as well with a U.S. setting. Crawford lives in Stockholm. She is angry and totally alone by her own choice. As a child, half her face had been disfigured and the resultant damage to her psyche has caused her to seek a life of retribution for the bad cards she's been dealt. She becomes a part of a blackmail ring. That leads her to meet Veidt, a mean scion of society who needs money. They get together in her cafe outside of the city and the scheming Veidt spots her for what she is right away, a woman who seems to be stronger than steel but who is needy beneath that veneer. Veidt is a charmer and uses his wit, plus a soupcon of flattery, to cause her to fall in love with him. Veidt is in line for the fortune of his father, Basserman, but Veidt's nephew, Nichols, is the fly in the ointment. Veidt wants to see Nichols dead and has devised a plan to use Crawford in the murder of his nephew. Crawford is mad for Veidt and talks herself into thinking he feels the same way about her. Not neglecting her blackmailing business, Crawford gets her hands on some letters written by Massen, who is married to plastic surgeon Douglas. Massen plays around on Douglas and he is totally unaware of it. When Crawford gets these steamy love letters she's written to another man, she decides to raise some money by using them against Massen. She goes to the Massen-Douglas home and is about to put the arm on Massen when Douglas comes home early. His office is in his house and she hides in his examining room, then hurts her foot when she tries to make her way out. Douglas is told by Massen that Crawford is a burglar and when Douglas wants to call the cops, Massen prevails on him to forget about it. Douglas can't help but notice Crawford's face and suggests that he operate on her. She is, at first, reluctant, but finally agrees. She knows the surgery can be dangerous but her situation is desperate and the operation has a successful conclusion. Douglas is delighted with his own work although he soon sees that his scalpel may have healed the exterior but the interior of Crawford is still scarred. Crawford rushes to Veidt and enters, proudly showing off her new look. Veidt is happy to see her looking so splendid, then changes the subject to get back to his plan to murder Nichols. Veidt gets Crawford a position in Basserman's mansion as the nanny to Nichols. No sooner does she go to work in that capacity when she realizes Nichols is a sweet young lad and the new Crawford softens and begins to enjoy Nichols' company, becoming as close as a mother could be to the youth. The plot calls for Crawford to disengage a safety coupling on a cable car that spans a mountain pass. She is to do it when the boy is in the car and the murder will look like an accident. As Crawford becomes even closer to Nichols, she finds that she cannot carry out the crime. It all takes place during a festive weekend at Basserman's home and one of the guests is Douglas, who has his own theories about Crawford and why she's there. Through powerful binoculars, Douglas watches the cable car, although there is no "accident." Veidt is angry that she has disobeyed him and now understands that Crawford is no longer in his Svengali influence. Evidently, the operation has gone much deeper than skin and she has become beautiful from within. In desperation, Veidt attempts to kill Nichols that evening during a snowy sleigh ride. Crawford is aware of Veidt's motivations and shoots the man to death. There is a murder trial and Crawford is acquitted when the defense produces a letter she'd written earlier to Basserman that detailed Veidt's plot. Douglas, who is finally wise to Massen's promiscuity, falls in love with Crawford and the two are united at the conclusion. The picture begins at the trial and is rolled in flashback and the victim's identity in the trial is not revealed until the end. It's almost, but not quite, *film noir*, perhaps due to Cukor's attempt to put gloss and glamor to the story, rather than shoot it with any sort of dark style. This was Veidt's second U.S. picture after ESCAPE and he was properly evil. Basserman, a well-known actor from Germany, did not speak English and learned his role phonetically, a tribute to the man's sensitivity because there was not one wrong inflection in any of his speeches as the Swedish consul. The picture was not a hit when it was first released because of the ad campaign. Then they began thumping the tub by calling her "a female monster" and audiences flocked in. In between all of the criminal machinations, there are some good romantic moments, such as the scene where the female criminal shows that she has a sensitive side by playing a Chopin piece for Veidt. There is also one lovely sequence as Crawford, having just emerged from the operation, finally realizes that she no long has to tug her hat down over the side of her face to hide the scar. She removes her hat, lets the breeze waft through her mane, and strides down the street with joy in her step. Impeccably produced, sharply edited, and, most of all, tastefully acted, A WOMAN'S FACE goes well beyond being "a woman's picture" and takes its place as one of Crawford's best.

p, Victor Saville; d, George Cukor; w, Donald Ogden Stewart, Elliott Paul (based on the play *Il Etait Une Fois* by Francis de Croisset); ph, Robert Planck; m, Bronsilau Kaper; ed, Frank Sullivan; art d, Wade B. Rubottom; cos, Adrian.

Crime   **(PR:A-C MPAA:NR)**

WOMAN'S LIFE, A** (1964, Jap.) 120m Toho bw (ONNA NO REKISHI; AKA: A WOMAN'S STORY)

Hideko Takamine (Nobuko), Tatsuya Nakadai (Akimoto), Akira Takarada (Koichi), Yuriko Hoshio (Hostess), Tsutomu Yamazaki.

A beautiful story of transcendence about a woman who loses her husband in the war and her son in an automobile accident soon after he had married over her objections. She finds peace at last by accepting her daughter-in-law when she finds out the girl is pregrant, outwitting fate with a kind of quietude many Japanese films are known for.

d, Mikio Naruse; w, Ryozo Kasahara; ph, Asaichi Nakai (Tohoscope).

Drama   (PR:A MPAA:NR)

WOMAN'S PLACE, A   (SEE: WISER AGE, 1962, Jap.)

WOMAN'S REVENGE, A   (SEE: MAN FROM SUNDOWN, THE, 1939)

WOMAN'S SECRET, A** (1949) 85m RKO bw

Maureen O'Hara (Marian Washburn), Melvyn Douglas (Luke Jordan), Gloria Grahame (Susan Caldwell), Bill Williams (Lee), Victor Jory (Brook Matthews), Mary Phillips (Mrs. Fowler), Jay C. Flippen (Police Detective Fowler), Robert Warwick (Roberts), Curt Conway (Doctor), Ann Shoemaker (Mrs. Matthews), Virginia Farmer (Millie), Ellen Corby (Nurse), Emory Parnell (Desk Sergeant), Dan Foster (Stage Manager), Alphonse Martel, Eddie Borden (Waiters), Charles Wagenheim (Piano Player), Marcelle De LaBrosse (Baker), Lynne Whitney (Actress), Rory Mallinson (Benson), George Douglas, Lee Phelps, Mickey Simpson, Guy Beach, Tom Coleman (Policemen), Raymond Bond (Dr. Ferris), Bill Purington (Intern), Bernice Young (Nurse), Loreli Vitek (Waitress), John Goldsworthy (Harold), Frederick Nay (Master of Ceremonies), Forbes Murray (Mr. Emory), Donna Gibson, Evelyn Underwood (Girls), John Parrish (Prof. Camelli), Oliver Blake (Mr. Pierson), Paul Guilfoyle (Moderator), Jack Rourke, Norman Nesbitt (Announcers), Conrad Binyon (Messenger Boy), Ralph Stein (Mr. Harris), Robert Malcolm (Bit).

It is hard to believe that a film directed by Ray and written by Mankiewicz could be anything less than brilliant. But RKO lost a whopping $760,000 on this convoluted mess of pottage. In flashback, O'Hara tells how she shot her young protege, the hellcat Grahame, whom she had groomed for fame as a singer when her own voice began to give out. Criss-cross flashbacks follow, telling how Grahame rebelled against O'Hara's attempts to make her a lady as well as a thrush. And then the whole flimsy structure topples when Grahame, coming briefly out of a coma, reveals who actually shot her, and it was not O'Hara. Why O'Hara confessed in the first place is never explained, further compounding the mystery of why this story by Vicki Baum was handled in such a preposterous way.

p, Herman J. Mankiewicz; d, Nicholas Ray; w, Mankiewicz (based on the novel Mortgage on Life by Vicki Baum); ph, George Diskant; m, Frederick Hollander; ed, Sherman Todd; md, C. Bakaleinikoff; art d, Albert S. D'Agostino, Carroll Clark; set d, Darrell Silvera, Harley Miller; cos, Edward Stevenson; spec eff, Russell A. Cully; m/l, "Estrellita," Manuel Ponce, "Paradise," Nacio Herb Brown, Gordon Clifford; makeup, Gordon Bau.

Drama   (PR:A MPAA:NR)

WOMAN'S TEMPTATION, A** (1959, Brit.) 60m Danzigers/BL bw

Patricia Driscoll (Betty), Robert Ayres (Mike), John Pike (Jimmy), Neil Hallett (Glyn), John Longdon (Inspector Syms), Kenneth J. Warren (Warner), Robert Raglan (Police Constable), Gordon Needham, Frazer Hines, Ross Yeo, Michael Saunders, Malcolm Ranson, Howard Lang, Ian Wilson, Joey White, Christopher Cooke, Claude Kingston, Carl Conway, Raymond Hodge.

Driscoll is a likable widow who is struggling to raise her son on her meager savings. When she stumbles across some stolen money she hides it away for her son's education. The crooks come after their booty, but are fought off by her friend Ayres. Driscoll turns the money over to the police but still fares okay at the finale.

p, Edward J. Danziger, Harry Lee Danziger; d, Geoffrey Grayson; w, Brian Clements, Eldon Howard; ph, Jimmy Wilson.

Crime Drama   (PR:A MPAA:NR)

WOMAN'S VENGEANCE, A, 1939
                    (SEE: MAN FROM SUNDOWN, THE, 1939)

WOMAN'S VENGEANCE, A**½ (1947) 96m UNIV bw

Charles Boyer (Henry Maurier), Ann Blyth (Doris), Jessica Tandy (Janet Spence), Sir Cedric Hardwicke (Dr. Libbard), Mildred Natwick (Nurse Braddock), Cecil Humphreys (Gen. Spence), Rachel Kempson (Emily Maurier), Hugh French (Robert Lester), Valerie Cardew (Clara), Carl Harbord (Coroner), John Williams (Prosecuting Counsel), Leyland Hodgson (1st Ward), Ola Lorraine (Maisey), Harry Cording (McNabb), Frederick Worlock

(Bit).

One of a handful of screenplays the celebrated author of Brave New World made for Hollywood. Boyer is accused of murdering his invalid wife because of the affair he has had with a younger and prettier woman, whom he married soon after his wife's death. All the evidence points to his guilt until the real killer, Tandy, confesses in a last-minute breakdown. A love-starved spinster, Tandy murdered Boyer's wife to get back at Boyer for not reciprocating her affections. The best scene in this film is the one where Hardwicke and Tandy are sitting in a living room as he works on her to admit her guilt in the murder of Boyer's wife, as the hour of Boyer's execution approaches. When she leaves the room for a minute, Hardwicke quickly turns the mantel clock forward one hour. The tension continues as the "supposed" time comes and goes as she admits her guilt. After finally getting the truth out of Tandy, Hardwicke phones the prison to save Boyer's life. Definitely one of Hardwicke's finest acting parts. An intriguing tale, classily produced, and boasting a stellar performance by Boyer and a strong script and dialog by Huxley.

p&d, Zoltan Korda; w, Aldous Huxley (based on his short story "The Gioconda Smile"); ph, Russell Metty; m, Miklos Rozsa; ed, Jack Wheeler; art d, Bernard Herzbrun, Eugene Lourie; set d, Russell A. Gausman, T. F. Offenbecker; cos, Orry-Kelly.

Drama   (PR:A MPAA:NR)

WOMAN'S WORLD*** (1954) 94m FOX c

Clifton Webb (Gifford), June Allyson (Katie), Van Heflin (Jerry), Lauren Bacall (Elizabeth), Fred MacMurray (Sid), Arlene Dahl (Carol), Cornel Wilde (Bill Baxter), Elliott Reid (Tony), Margalo Gillmore (Evelyn), Alan Reed (Tomaso), David Hoffman (Jarecki), George Melford (Worker at Auto Plant), Eric Wilton (Butler), Conrad Feia (Bellhop), George E. Stone, George Eldredge, Paul Power, William Tannen, Jonathan Hole, Rodney Bell, Carleton Young (Executives), Beverly Thompson, Eileen Maxwell (Models), Melinda Markey (Daughter), Maude Prickett (Mother), Kathryn Card, Ann Kunde, Jean Walters, Janet Stewart, Billie Bird, Jarma Lewis (Women in Bargain Basement), George Spalding (Ship's Captain), Edward Astran (Cab Driver), Marc Snow (Waiter), Bert Stevens (Doorman).

In 1954, long before it was fashionable to stand up for women's equality and make the point that the distaff members of humanity were just as important as men, this movie quietly pushed that fact to the forefront. Those were the days when Lucy was trying to finagle a new way to get more household money out of Desi so she could buy a new dress and the nature of America's viewing habits was such that some of the subtleties of this movie may have gone unnoticed. Macho men might have sneered at the nature of WOMAN'S WORLD but anyone with any sense saw that women were as productive as men and far more than merely curvaceous serfs whose only jobs were to iron shirts, tend the children, and make sure dinner was ready at seven. Webb is the head of a large automobile manufacturing company. His sales manager has just left the company by way of death and Webb needs someone strong and polished to take over the important assignment. He imports a trio of his vice presidents and district managers to company headquarters in New York to get a closer look at them. The three are equally competent and Webb is at a loss to decide which to choose so he opts to let his selection be determined by which has the best wife for the job of being wife to a top executive. Heflin is married to Dahl, an ambitious and cunning woman who wants her husband to have the job at any cost. Heflin is surely able to handle it but he doesn't have the ambition to go along with his abilities. MacMurray is married to Bacall. He is totally devoted to the company and Bacall knows that if he gets the job their marriage is all but finished as he would double his already Herculean efforts and never see her at all. Wilde is married to Allyson, essentially a small town woman from the Middle West. She is faithful and devoted to her husband and will help in any way to achieve Wilde's goal but she knows she would be far happier in Kansas City than in New York City. The wives become the focus of attention and take it upon themselves to help their husbands. Allyson is adorable, sweet, and terribly clumsy as she attempts to win over Webb. There is not one iota of sham in her and he appreciates her reality as she mistakenly locks herself in the ladies room and spills martinis all over the place. Bacall fits right in with the glitz and glamor of New York City and she tries to remain as outwardly loyal as she can to MacMurray, all the while hoping that the job goes somewhere else. Dahl is on the make and uses her wiles in a smarmy fashion. She comes on strongly to certain men, thinking she can persuade them to help make the decision to give the job to "them" (as she feels she is as much a part of the executive staff as Heflin). She errs and chooses the wrong man to ply her wares upon and Heflin's name is taken off Webb's list right away, thus leaving Wilde and MacMurray in the running. Heflin finds out about Dahl's behavior, goes to Webb, and explains that her activities were strictly her own. He apologizes for what she's done and explains to Webb that he would have liked the job, but surely not enough to send his wife on a sexual foray to get it. Webb is impressed by Heflin's integrity and pencils his name back on the list. Heflin winds up getting the job, which is the best for all concerned. Bacall and MacMurray will have the opportunity to revive their flagging marriage and Wilde and Allyson can happily return to their Kansas City lifestyle. Heflin walks out on Dahl and she doesn't get her chance to shine in the aeries of Manhattan society. There are similarities to EXECUTIVE SUITE, issued earlier, and

PATTERNS, made a few years later with Heflin in a similar role. The difference is that the posit is made that women are as important as men in the halls of executivedom. Good acting, good story, and a nostalgic look at New York in the 1950s all combine to make this worth viewing. Lots of shots of Macy's, Fifth Avenue, The UN, Park Avenue, and the long-gone Stork Club which was owned by Sherman Billingsley, a man who did his best to keep blacks out of his night spot. Beautiful costumes, witty dialog from five writers, and intelligent direction from Negulesco. The title song by Sammy Cahn and Cyril Mockridge became a hit as done by "The Four Aces."

p, Charles Brackett; d, Jean Negulesco; w, Claude Binyon, Mary Loos, Richard Sale, Howard Lindsay, Russel Crouse (based on a story by Mona Williams); ph, Joe MacDonald (CinemaScope, Technicolor); m, Cyril J. Mockridge; ed, Louis Loeffler; art d, Lyle Wheeler; cos, Charles Le Maire; m/l, "It's a Woman's World" Mockridge, Sammy Cahn (sung by The Four Aces).

Drama (PR:A-C MPAA:NR)

WOMBLING FREE* (1977, Brit.) 96m Rank c

David Tomlinson, Frances De La Tour, Bonnie Langford, Bernard Spear.

Beneath Wimbledon Common dwells a race of furry little individuals who want to meet some people from up above. Unfortunately they do, and they spend the next hour and a half inducing your child to ask for more popcorn and trips to the bathroom. This was based on a popular British television show which was broadcast in five-minute episodes. When expanded to the longer requirements of feature films the results are slow, plodding, and too ridiculous for anyone in its intended juvenile audience.

p, Ian Shand; d&w, Lionel Jeffries (based on characters created by Elizabeth Beresford); ph, Alan Hume (Eastmancolor); m, Mike Batt.

Children (PR:AAA MPAA:NR)

WOMEN, THE** (1939) 132m MGM bw-c

Norma Shearer (*Mary Haines*), Joan Crawford (*Chrystal Allen*), Rosalind Russell (*Sylvia Fowler*), Mary Boland (*Countess DeLave*), Paulette Goddard (*Miriam Aarons*), Joan Fontaine (*Peggy Day*), Lucile Watson (*Mrs. Moorehead*), Phyllis Povah (*Edith Potter*), Florence Nash (*Nancy Blake*), Virginia Weidler (*Little Mary*), Ruth Hussey (*Miss Watts*), Muriel Hutchison (*Jane*), Margaret Dumont (*Mrs. Wagstaff*), Dennie Moore (*Olga*), Mary Cecil (*Maggie*), Marjorie Main (*Lucy*), Esther Dale (*Ingrid*), Hedda Hopper (*Dolly Dupuyster*), Mildred Shay (*Helene the French Maid*), Priscilla Lawson, Estelle Etterre (*Hairdressers*), Ann Morriss (*Exercise Instructor*), Mary Beth Hughes (*Miss Trimmerback*), Marjorie Wood (*Sadie, Old Maid in Powder Room*), Virginia Grey (*Pat*), Cora Witherspoon (*Mrs. Van Adams*), Veda Buckland (*Woman*), Charlotte Treadway (*Her Companion*), Theresa Harris (*Olive*), Virginia Howell, Vera Vague 'Barbara Jo Allen' (*Receptionists*), May Beatty (*Fat Woman*), May Hale (*Mud Mask*), Ruth Findlay (*Pediatrist*), Charlotte Wynters (*Miss Batchelor*), Aileen Pringle (*Miss Carter*), Florence Shirley (*Miss Archer*), Judith Allen (*Model*), Florence O'Brien (*Euphie*), Hilda Plowright (*Miss Fordyce*), Mariska Aldrich (*Singing Teacher*), Leila McIntyre (*Woman with Bundles*), Dot Farley (*Large Woman*), Flora Finch (*Woman Window Tapper*), Dorothy Sebastian, Renie Riano (*Saleswomen*), Grace Goodall (*Head Saleswoman*), Lilian Bond (*Mrs. Erskine*), Winifred Harris (*Mrs. North*), Gertrude Astor, Nell Craig (*Nurses*), Grace Hayle, Maude Allen (*Cyclists*), Natalie Moorhead (*Woman in Modiste Salon*), Jo Ann Sayers (*Debutante*), Carole Lee Kilby (*Theatrical Child*), Lita Chevret, Dora Clemant, Ruth Alder (*Women Under Sunlamps*), Marie Blake (*Stock Room Girl*), Dorothy Adams (*Miss Atkinson*), Carol Hughes (*Salesgirl at Modiste Salon*), Peggy Shannon (*Mrs. Jones*), Josephine Whittell (*Mrs. Spencer*), Rita Gould (*Dietician*), Gertrude Simpson (*Stage Mother*), Betty Blythe.

Another in the superb roster of movies issued in 1939, THE WOMEN took no Oscars, mainly due to the competition that included some of the very best movies Hollywood ever made, including GONE WITH THE WIND, GOOD-BYE, MR CHIPS, WUTHERING HEIGHTS, THE WIZARD OF OZ, STAGECOACH, and many more. Based on the smash hit play by Clare Boothe (who was also Mrs. Luce, by dint of marriage to the man who began *Time* magazine), as produced by Max Gordon on Broadway, the movie is rightly titled THE WOMEN because there are more than 130 roles and no dialog in a bass or a baritone or even a tenor. Shearer is a wealthy and loving woman married to an adoring husband and the mother of a sweet daughter, Weidler. She has no idea that her mate is enthralled and having it on with shopgirl Crawford, a redheaded wench with the morals of an alley cat. Crawford sells perfume and the affair is a secret only to Shearer, whose bitchy girl friends learn about it from gossip Moore, a manicurist at their beauty salon. Russell and Povah (who was only one of two members from the Broadway cast to make it into the movie) are thrilled to hear the news, but they can't tell Shearer themselves, so they set up a nail appointment between Shearer and Moore, correctly figuring that big-mouth Moore will tell Shearer of her husband's affair. And that is exactly what happens. Shearer is destroyed by this news and tells her mother, Watson, who advises her to not confront her husband with the knowledge of his perfidy. Shearer beards the lioness, Crawford, in her den, the dressing room at the salon where Crawford works. Shearer leaves New York to race to Reno for a six-week divorce and meets Boland, an aging countess and former showgirl

who has been married several times. She also encounters younger chorine Goddard, who is having an affair with Russell's husband. Shearer and the others check into a ranch owned by Main (the other Broadway holdover), a funny and talkative woman who caters to the divorcing crowd. Russell arrives and when she realizes that it was Goddard who stole her husband, a battle ensues between the two women that has Shearer and everyone else in stitches. Her laughter is soon tempered as she learns that her former mate has married Crawford. Later, when she gets home to New York, she discovers that her ex is unhappily married to Crawford, who has taken to spending money with a passion and is now having an affair with a radio singing cowboy who was once married to Boland. She buys some new finery and goes to a party where Crawford's current boy friend tells everyone assembled (off-stage) that he's having a liaison with Crawford. Shearer's ex is at the party and is hurt by the confession. Crawford tells the assemblage that she is planning to dump Shearer's ex and marry the singing cowboy. However, his radio show is sponsored by wealthy Boland, as she is the only person who would put up money for the singularly untalented man. If Crawford marries the cowboy, Boland will withdraw her sponsorship. Crawford realizes that she's defeated and announces that she is planning to return to selling perfume, but not before she states to the other women, "There's a word for you ladies, but it is seldom used in high society, outside of a kennel." With Crawford out of the way, Shearer runs back to her ex-husband, who has realized the folly of his ways and will take up the marriage with renewed dedication. A "back fence" movie filled with witty lines, vicious gossip, and a chance to see women without men, wearing all sorts of scanty lingerie and letting their carefully coiffed hair down in a series of scenes in bathtubs, parties, a health spa-gym and, of course, a ladies' room. In the midst of the black-and-white footage, time is taken out for a Technicolor fashion show staged by Adrian that lasts five minutes and has nothing to do with the story line. A nasty movie that is also a delightful one, THE WOMEN opened on Broadway in December, 1936, with a cast that included Povah, Main, Margalo Gillmore, Ilka Chase, and Audrey Christie. It ran two years, then was scheduled to be a Claudette Colbert vehicle with Greg LaCava directing until MGM took over the reins. Although there are only the two female screenplay credits, it is rumored that F. Scott Fitzgerald did an early adaptation, then was joined by Donald Ogden Stewart and Sidney Franklin. It was later given to Murfin, then was rewritten by Loos. Goddard was on loan from Selznick. Russell campaigned actively for her part, having to overturn the wishes of Cukor, who had told Chase she could play the role she did on the stage. A very interesting credits sequence has the women being shown as animals before the screen dissolves to a shot of each actress. Russell was a panther, Main a donkey, Weidler a doe, Povah a cow, Goddard a fox, Fontaine a lamb, Boland a chimpanzee, Watson an owl, Crawford a leopard, and Shearer, who was top-billed, a fawn. There was backstage tension because Shearer and Crawford didn't like each other and Crawford was jealous of the affection given Shearer, who was married to the studio chief Irving Thalberg who had died a few years before. Still, all of the studio people liked Shearer and danced attention on her. The problems were there right through the end of shooting and beyond, when Crawford and her friend Goddard snubbed the closing party hosted by Shearer. The picture was remade terribly as THE OPPOSITE SEX with Joan Collins, June Allyson, Ann Miller, Joan Blondell, Charlotte Greenwood, Ann Sheridan, Dolores Gray, and, tsk, tsk, tsk, several men! The whole idea of doing a show without men was lost on the makers of the second film, producer Joe Pasternak and director David Miller. The original play script was much harder than the screenplay and many of the lines couldn't get past the censors. The screenwriters solved that by writing funnier (and cleaner) jokes for the movie and the result was that this film was better than the play. Shearer is super; so are Russell and Crawford, who plays her part with such an edge that audiences cheered when she lost out at the end. In the early 1970s, a revival of the play was seen on Broadway with Kim Hunter, Rhonda Fleming, Alexis Smith, Myrna Loy, and Dorothy Loudon heading a superb cast. It closed within two months, despite the players. Many of the lines are memorable, but play better than they read, such as Moore's dialog when she says, "I'd like to do Mrs. Fowler's (Russell) nails, right down to the wrist, with a nice big buzz saw." Good fun, terrific acting, some lapses in Cukor's direction (pacing, not performances) and a general feeling of "I'm glad *I'm* not like that!"

p, Hunt Stromberg; d, George Cukor; w, Anita Loos, Jane Murfin (based on the play by Clare Boothe); ph, Oliver T. Marsh, Joseph Ruttenberg (Part Technicolor); m, Edward Ward, David Snell; ed, Robert J. Kerns; art d, Cedric Gibbons, Wade B. Rubottom; set d, Edwin B. Willis; cos, Adrian; m/l, "Forever More," Chet Forrest, Bob Wright, Ed Ward.

Comedy Cas. (PR:C MPAA:NR)

WOMEN, THE, 1969 (SEE: VIXENS, THE, 1969)

WOMEN AND BLOODY TERROR zero
(1970) 97m Joy-Oke/Howco c (AKA: HIS WIFE'S HABIT; WOMEN OF BLOODY TERROR)

Georgine Darcy (*Lauren Worthington*), Marcus J. Grapes (*Jerry*), Christa Hart (*Karen Worthington*), David Gelpi (*Danny*), Michael Anthony (*Zool*), Gerald McRaney (*Terrance Bradford*), Len Swanson (*Mr. Worthington*), Cheryl Rodrigue (*Missie*), Buddy Lewis (*Paul Chase*), David Krippner (*Johnny*), Evelyn Hendricks (*Party Hostess*), Jed Wheeler, Michael Oglesbee

(Boys in Dream Sequence), Lance Gordon (Hustler), Jim Egan (Bartender), C.S. Fontelieu (Father in Dream Sequence), Augie Lapara (Bar Manager), Michael Byrd (Carhop), Nita Wilson (Woman at Motel), Dale G. Thompson (Man at Motel), The Armadillo (Rock Band), John Rigol (Policeman), Waddy Jones (Holiday Inn Manager), Ken Addington, Everett Addington, Bill Stillwell, Cathy Campbell, Renita Hamsher, Alice LeBlanc, Sandy Macera, Rita Gonsouline (Karen's Party Guests).

A wretched piece about a promiscuous woman, Darcy, who has affairs with every man she meets, including her daughter's boy friend. She is terrorized by a motel parking attendant, Grapes, who chases her and one of her lovers on his motorcycle. The lover is killed but Darcy lives. Grapes and his psychotic friend Anthony continue harassing Darcy and her daughter, Hart. The two women are attacked but the police arrive and kill Grapes and Anthony. This one flushes morality right down the toilet, where the film itself should be tossed.

p, Albert J. Saltzer; d, Joy N. Houck, Jr.; w, Houck, J.J. Milane, Robert A. Weaver, J. Saltzer (based on a story by Joy N. Houck, Sr., Milane); ph, Robert A. Weaver (Eastmancolor); ed, Weaver, John H. Post; m/l, "Lady in the Early Morning," Jim Helms, Gary LeMel, Norma Green (sung by LeMel), "Come on In," "Mr. Funky," Helms, LeMel, Green (sung by Sonny Geraci).

Drama/Crime   **(PR:O   MPAA:R)**

WOMEN AND WAR*   (1965, Fr.) 100m Films A. de la Bourdonnaye-Compagnie Lyonnaise de Cinema/Parade Releasing bw (ARRETEZ LES TAMBOURS; AKA: WOMEN IN WAR)

Bernard Blier (Mayor Leproux), Lucile Saint-Simon (Catherine Leproux), Lutz Gabor (Maj. Frantz), Anne Doat (Dany), Beatrice Bretty (Germaine), Daniel Sorano (Toulousain), Paulette Dubost (Widow), Henri Virlojeux (Drummer), Jacques Marin (Grocer), Jacques Chabassol, Guy Dakar, Christian Melsen, Catherine Le Couey.

Ironic story about a doctor who becomes a marked man to both the Nazis occupying France and the French Resistance because of his humanistic attitudes. As a doctor and small-town mayor, Blier saves the life of an Englishman, for which he is arrested by the Nazis. But the commanding officer, also a humane individual, falls in love with Saint-Simon. Encouraged by the doctor, the two elope. Frantz flees from the army, and Blier is condemned to death by the Resistance fighters who don't condone marriages between French women and German soldiers. A Nazi firing squad finally kills him. An effective look at how war can stifle values normally deemed commendable.

p&d, Georges Lautner; w, Pierre Laroche, Lautner (based on the story by Richard Prentout); ph, Maurice Fellous; m, Georges Delerue; ed, Michele David; art d, Louis Le Barbenchon.

War/Drama   **(PR:C   MPAA:NR)**

WOMEN ARE LIKE THAT*   (1938) 78m FN-WB bw

Kay Francis (Claire Landin), Pat O'Brien (Bill Landin), Ralph Forbes (Martin Brush), Melville Cooper (Mainwaring), Thurston Hall (Claudius King), Grant Mitchell (Mr. Snell), Gordon Oliver (Howard Johns), John Eldredge (Charles Braden), Herbert Rawlinson (Avery Flicker), Hugh O'Connell (George Dunlap), Georgia Caine (Mrs. Amelia Brush), Joyce Compton (Miss Hall), Sarah Edwards (Mrs. Snell), Josephine Whittell (Miss Douglas), Loia Cheaney (Miss Perkins), Edward Broadley (Holliwell), Sam McDaniel (Porter).

Dreadfully dull story of marital strife evolving from Francis' desire to see her husband's business get off the ground. O'Brien, as the husband, is much too proud to let her interfere with his conception of a man's and woman's place in the scheme of things. Capable cast comes out flat through inane dialog and lifeless direction.

p, Robert Lord; d, Stanley Logan; w, Horace Jackson (based on the story "Return From Limbo" by Albert Z. Carr); ph, Sid Hickox; ed, Thomas Richards; md, Leo F. Forbstein; art d, Max Parker; cos, Orry-Kelly.

Drama   **(PR:A   MPAA:NR)**

WOMEN ARE TROUBLE*   (1936) 60m MGM bw

Stuart Erwin (Casey), Paul Kelly (Blaine, City Editor), Florence Rice (Ruth), Margaret Irving (Frances), Cy Kendall (Inspector Matson), John Harrington (Gleason), Harold Huber ("Pusher"), Kitty McHugh (Mrs. Murty), Raymond Hatton (Murty).

Decent cheapie in which Erwin and Rice play reporters from different newspapers with the same goal in mind, that of seeing the local thugs brought to justice for their interference in the running of legitimate businesses, in this case liquor establishments which have been making things tough for racketeers to continue their profiteering. Comedy and action are effectively combined to create a fair level of entertainment, with a clever portrayal of an honest cop by Kendall, who is at odds with the corruption in the police department.

p, Lucien Hubbard; d, Errol Taggart; w, Michael Fessier (based on the story

by George Harmon Coxe); ph, Oliver T. Marsh; m, Edward Ward; ed, Conrad Nervig.

Crime/Drama   **(PR:A   MPAA:NR)**

WOMEN AREN'T ANGELS½**   (1942, Brit.) 85m ABF/Pathe bw

Robertson Hare (Wilmer Popday), Alfred Drayton (Alfred Bandle), Polly Ward (Frankie Delane), Joyce Heron (Karen), Mary Hinton (Thelma Bandle), Peggy Novack (Elizabeth Popday), Ethel Coleridge (Mrs. Featherstone), Charles Murray (Bertie), Ralph Michael (Jack), John Stuart (Maj. Gaunt), Leslie Perrins (Schaffer), George Merritt, Michael Shepley, Peter Gawthorne, Sydney Monckton.

Hare and Drayton run a music publishing business, but find themselves passing their time in a far more ridiculous way when their wives go off with the ATS (Auxiliary Territorial Service) during WW II. The men dress in their wives' uniforms and capture a group of fifth columnists. Good, clean wartime fun which once again gives British comedians an excuse to dress in women's clothing.

p, Warwick Ward; d, Lawrence Huntington; w, Vernon Sylvaine, Barnard Mainwaring, Huntington (based on the play by Sylvaine); ph, Gunther Krampf.

Comedy   **(PR:A   MPAA:NR)**

WOMEN EVERYWHERE*   (1930) 83m FOX bw

J. Harold Murray (Charles Jackson), Fifi D'Orsay (Lili La Fleur), George Grossmith (Aristide Brown), Clyde Cook (Sam Jones), Ralph Kellard (Michel Kopulos), Rose Dione (Zephyrine), Walter McGrail (Legionnaire).

One of Korda's last Hollywood ventures before taking off to make pictures in Europe shows that he had matured in his handling of actors and in his ability to combine settings with action. Morocco serves as the background (in sets only) for this tale in which Murray tries to escape the grip of the French Foreign Legion by seeking refuge in the nightclub where D'Orsay is the sexy singer. Numerous songs slow the action but all are top drawer. They include: "Women Everywhere," "Beware of Love," "One Day," "Good Time Fifi," "Bon Jour," "Marching Song" (William Kernell), "All in the Family" (Kernell, George Grossmith), and "Smile, Legionnaire" (Kernell, Charles Wakefield Cadman).

p, Ned Marin; d, Alexander Korda; w, Harlan Thompson, Lajos Biro (based on a story by George Grossmith, Zoltan Korda); ph, Ernest Palmer; ed, Harold Schuster; set d, William Darling; cos, Sophie Wachner.

Musical/Drama   **(PR:A   MPAA:NR)**

WOMEN FROM HEADQUARTERS
              (SEE: WOMAN FROM HEADQUARTERS, 1950)

WOMEN GO ON FOREVER*   (1931) 64m TIF bw

Clara Kimball Young (Daisy Bowman), Marian Nixon (Betty), Paul Page (Eddie), Thomas Jackson (Detective), Yola D'Avril (Pearl), Eddie Lambert (Elmer Givner), Nellie V. Nichols (Mrs. Givner), Wallace Morgan (Jake), Maurice Black (Pete), Maurice Murphy (Tommy).

A routine gang picture with the central figure a tenderhearted landlady of a rooming house whose roving eyes take in any and all males who darken her door. Mainly of interest because it features a siren from the Theda Bara silent days, Young, whose popularity as a screen beauty was legendary, making a stab at talkies as a character actress which, quite simply, did not work out, then or ever after.

p, James Cruze; d, Walter Lang; w, Daniel N. Rubin; ph, Charles Schoenbaum.

Drama   **(PR:A   MPAA:NR)**

WOMEN IN BONDAGE*   (1943) 72m MON bw (AKA: HITLER'S WOMEN)

Gail Patrick (Margot Bracken), Nancy Kelly (Toni Hall), Gertrude Michael (Gertrude Schneider), Anne Nagel (Deputy), Tala Birell (Ruth Bracken), Mary Forbes (Gladys Bracken), Maris Wrixon (Grete Ziegler), Gisela Werbiseck (Herta's Grandmother), Rita Quigley (Herta Rumann), Francine Bordeaux (Litzl), Una Franks (Blonde), H.B. Warner (Pastor Renz), Alan Baxter (Otto Bracken), Felix Basch (Dr. Mensch), Roland Varno (Ernest Bracken), Ralph Lynn (Cpl. Mueller), Frederic Brunn (District Leader).

Title refers to women working under the Hitler regime, one of whom, Patrick, an officer in the German youth movement, becomes disillusioned when she is required to start helping repopulate Germany with blonde blue-eyed supermen. The trouble is, her husband has been wounded and is unable to help her produce offspring. Patrick sees the light in time to help Allied forces in their invasion of Germany. Though heavy on the propaganda, this is a well-executed effort.

p, Herman Millakowsky; d, Steve Sekely; w, Houston Branch (based on the story by Frank Bentick Wisbar); ph, Mack Stengler; ed, Richard Currier.

War/Drama   (PR:A   MPAA:NR)

WOMEN IN CELL BLOCK 7 zero   (1977, Ital./U.S.) 90m
Aquarius-Overseas/Aquarius c (DIARIO SEGRETO DI UN CARCERE
FEMMINELE)

Anita Strinberg *(Hilda)*, Eva Czemeys *(Daniela)*, Olga Bisera *(Chief Matron)*, Jane Avril *(Gisa)*, Valeria Fabrizi *(Napolitana)*, Paola Senatore *(Musumeci)*, Roger Browne *(Inspector Weil)*, Jenny Tamburi *(Gerda)*, Cristina Gaioni *(Mamma S)*.

The ever-popular women's prison and all that that implies for fans of bad movies are to be found in abundance in this mindless exploitation film. The poorly constructed story involves some troubles in the mob, and life inside an all-female prison. The two stories are held together by a strange narration, suggesting that this was probably two movies stitched together. Inside the pen are to be found the innocent woman wrongly accused; lesbian guards who foist themselves with clockwork regularity on the inmates; and, of course, the genre's speciality: cat fights. The film relies on skin and foul language in place of anything resembling a plot. Lock it up and throw away the key.

p, Terry Levene; d&w, Rino Di Silvestro; ph, (Eastmancolor); m, George Craig; ed, Simon Nuchtern.

Prison Drama   **Cas.**   **(PR:O   MPAA:R)**

WOMEN IN HIS LIFE, THE*   (1934) 74m MGM bw

Otto Kruger *(Kent Barringer)*, Una Merkel *(Miss Simmons)*, Ben Lyon *(Roger Kane)*, Isabel Jewell *(Catherine Watson)*, Roscoe Karns *(Lester)*, Irene Hervey *(Doris Worthing)*, C. Henry Gordon *(Tony Perez)*, Samuel S. Hinds *(Worthing)*, Irene Franklin *(Mrs. Steele)*, Muriel Evans *(Molly)*, Raymond Hatton *(Curly)*, Jean Howard, Paul Hurst.

Dismal story of a celebrated criminal lawyer with a predilection for whiskey and women as a way of forgetting his failed marriage. But the past comes back to haunt him when he is given a case in which his ex-wife is the victim in a murder. The lawyer gets his wits together in time to keep an innocent man from being convicted while pinning the goods on a notorious gangster, the man who stole his wife. Only the performance of Kruger as the drunken lawyer is worth a nickel.

p, Lucien Hubbard; d, George B. Seitz; w, F. Hugh Herbert; ph, Ray June; ed, Conrad Nervig; cos, Adrian.

Crime/Drama   **(PR:A   MPAA:NR)**

WOMEN IN LIMBO   (SEE: LIMBO, 1972)

WOMEN IN LOVE**   (1969, Brit.) 130m Brandywine/UA c

Alan Bates *(Rupert Birkin)*, Oliver Reed *(Gerald Crich)*, Glenda Jackson *(Gudrun Brangwen)*, Jennie Linden *(Ursula Brangwen)*, Eleanor Bron *(Hermione Roddice)*, Alan Webb *(Thomas Crich)*, Vladek Sheybal *(Loerke)*, Catherine Willmer *(Mrs. Crich)*, Sarah Nicholls *(Winifred Crich)*, Sharon Gurney *(Laura Crich)*, Christopher Gable *(Tibby Lupton)*, Michael Gough *(Tom Brangwen)*, Norma Shebbeare *(Anna Brangwen)*, Nike Arrighi *(Contessa)*, James Laurenson *(Minister)*, Michael Graham Cox *(Palmer)*, Richard Heffer *(Leitner)*, Michael Garratt *(Maestro)*, Leslie Anderson *(Barber)*, Charles Workman *(Gittens)*, Barrie Fletcher, Brian Osborne *(Miners)*, Christopher Ferguson *(Basis Crich)*, Richard Fitzgerald *(Salsie)*.

This adaptation of D.H. Lawrence's classic novel has some of the interesting visual sequences that mark director Russell's style, but the overall film is an unsatisfying, ponderous work. It is 1920s England. Jackson is a free-thinking artist who, along with her schoolteacher sister, Linden, watches from a graveyard as Gurney and Gable are married. Later, at an outdoor luncheon given for the couple, the two women meet Reed and Bates. Bates, a school inspector, constantly ruminates on the topic of love, and begins a fledgling relationship with Linden. At a picnic at the plush home of Gurney's wealthy family, the newlyweds are lost beneath the dark waters of the estate's lake. The water is drained from the lake, revealing the two drowned bodies entwined together in the muddy lake bed. That night Bates and Reed, in a discussion on friendship, strip before a fireplace and engage in a nude wrestling match. After Bates and Linden marry, they go, with Reed and Jackson, for a honeymoon in Switzerland. Jackson meets Sheybal, a sculptor like herself, and engages in an affair with the bisexual man, while her sister and brother-in-law leave Switzerland. Reed is enraged at Sheybal's intrusion and attacks the man, then tries to choke Jackson. Reed then flees into the snow, wandering until he dies. Bates, stunned by the death, still questions the mystery of relations between men and women. Russell, as usual, shows an excellent sense for visual style but his images are strangely cold and distant. There are moments of sheer visual poetry, such as Bates and Linden running into each others arms, naked in a wheatfield. The camera is turned horizontally and the bodies seem to defy gravity, moving up and down within the frame through the golden vegatation. In another, much heralded piece of editing, Russell cuts from the intertwined bodies of Bates and Linden after a lovemaking session to the cold, stiff corpses of Gurney and Gable as they lie dead on the bottom of the emptied lake. Russell did some of his own camerawork (though Williams received

credit as cinematographer), and showed an excellent eye for shot composition and editing rhythms. But his abilities as storyteller are much less satisfactory. Despite the passion of the topic and the beauty of the images, this is curiously lifeless. The story plods from one set piece to the next, remaining unsatisfyingly dry throughout. Even the film's most controversial moment, the nude wrestling match between Reed and Bates, barely contains any of the charged emotions it promises. When a film version of Lawrence's novel was proposed in the 1920s, the author had no objections, but the project never saw fruition. Some 40 years later producer-writer Kramer obtained the rights, and the project was set to be directed by Silvio Narrizano, who had helmed the popular film GEORGY GIRL (1966). Executives at United Artists turned down this choice, instead pushing Russell as the right man for the project. Russell incorporated many dance images into the film, sensing what he considered to be dance elements in the source material. Russell later stated that he "should have turned the whole thing into a musical; it wasn't far off in some ways." He received an Oscar nomination for Best Director, with nominations also going to Kramer for his script, and Williams' lovely cinematography. Jackson, in a restrained, distant performance won an Oscar that year for Best Actress.

p, Larry Kramer; d, Ken Russell; w, Kramer (based on the novel by D.H. Lawrence); ph, Billy Williams (DeLuxe Color); m, Georges Delerue, Petr Ilich Tchaikovsky; ed, Michael Bradsell; md, Delerue; art d, Ken Jones; set d, Luciana Arrighi; cos, Shirley Russell; ch, Terry Gilbert; makeup, Charles Parker.

Drama   **Cas.**   **(PR:O   MPAA:R)**

WOMEN IN PRISON   (SEE: LADIES THEY TALK ABOUT, 1933)

WOMEN IN PRISON**   (1938) 59m COL bw

Wyn Cahoon *(Ann Wilson)*, Scott Colton *(Bob Wayne)*, Arthur Loft *(Barney Morse)*, Mayo Methot *(Daisy Saunders)*, Ann Doran *(Maggie)*, Sarah Padden *(Martha Wilson)*, Margaret Armstrong *(Mrs. Tatum)*, John Tyrrell *(Jerry Banks)*, Bess Flowers *(Florence)*, Dick Curtis *(Mac)*, Eddie Fetherston *(Manny)*, John Dilson *(Henry Russell)*, Lee Prather *(District Attorney)*.

Methot goes to jail after taking part in a robbery in which she is the only gang member to know where the loot is buried. One of the men she was in cahoots with goes to extremes to get her free, even making the warden's innocent daughter look as though she were part of a murder plot. But it doesn't take. Decent portrayals of roles women were seldom depicted in 1930s Hollywood.

d, Lambert Hillyer; w, Saul Elkins (based on the story by Mortimer Braus); ph, Benjamin Kline; ed, Dick Fantl; cos, Robert Kalloch.

Crime   **(PR:A   MPAA:NR)**

WOMEN IN PRISON**   (1957, Jap.) 102m Tokyo Eiga/Toho bw

Setsuko Hara, Kinuyo Tanaka, Michiyo Kogure, Kyoko Kagawa, Yoshiko Kuga, Mariko Okada, Kyoko Anzai, Keiko Awaji, Chieko Naniwa.

A probing look at life in Japan's prisons for women which is given a semi-documentary feel. The main story is that of a young mother who has killed her child and seems reluctant to reform. A prison guard makes numerous attempts to bring her around and is rewarded when the girl gives a blood transfusion which saves the guard's life. Surprisingly the film makes no attempt to cover up the existence of lesbianism in the prison.

d, Seiji Hisamatsu; w, Sumie Tanaka; ph, Joji Ohara; m, Ichiro Saito.

Prison Drama   **(PR:O   MPAA:NR)**

WOMEN IN THE NIGHT*½   (1948) 90m Southern California
Pictures/Fil m Classi cs bw (AKA: WHEN MEN ARE BEASTS)

Tala Birell *(Yvette Aubert)*, William Henry *(Maj. Van Arnheim)*, Virginia Christine *(Claire Adams)*, Richard Loo *(Col. Noyama)*, Gordon Richards *(Col. Von Meyer)*, Bernadene Hayes *(Frau Thaler)*, Benson Fong *(Chang)*, Frances Chung *(Li Ling)*, Kathy Frye *(Helen James)*, Helen Mowery *(Sheila Hallett)*, Philip Ahn *(Prof. Kunioshi)*, Iris Flores *(Maria Gonzales)*.

A group of women from Allied nations is rounded up and taken prisoner i n Shanghhai by the Nazis looking for the murderer of a German officer. While being detained, they are used as informants and for "entertainment" of the Germans and Japanese, and furtively work for the Chinese underground. They are finally freed when American OSS man Henry flies in to break up a "cosmic ray" plot between the Axis partners. Supposedly based on United Nations files on crimes against women in WW II.

p, Louis K. Ansell; d, William Rowland; w, Robert St. Clair, Edwin Westrate (based on a story by Rowland and on case histories from United Nations Information Office); ph, Eugen Shuftan; m, Raul Lavista; ed, Dan Milner; art d, Shuftan; set d, Shuftan; makeup, Enrique Hutchinson.

War Drama   **(PR:A   MPAA:NR)**

WOMEN IN THE WIND½   (1939) 65m WB bw

Kay Francis (Janet Steele), William Gargan (Ace Boreman), Victor Jory (Doc), Maxie Rosenbloom (Stuffy McInnes), Sheila Bromley (Frieda Boreman), Eve Arden (Kit Campbell), Eddie Foy, Jr (Denny Carson), Charles Anthony Hughes (Bill Steele), Frankie Burke (Johnnie), John Dilson (Sloan), Spencer Charters (Farmer), Vera Lewis (Farmer's Wife), Sally Sage, Alice Connors, Marian Alden, Iris Gabrielle, Diana Hughes (Aviatrixes), John Harron (Process Server), Nat Carr, Richard Bond, Jack Mower, Frank Mayo (Salesmen), Lucille Denver, Marie Astaire (Women), Steven Darrell, David Kerman (Photographers), Emmett Vogan (Radio Announcer), Frank Faylen (Mechanic), George O'Hanlon (Bellboy), Eddie Graham (Microphone Man), Milton Kibbee (Bartender), William Gould (Palmer), Gordon Hart (Air Races Official), Ila Rhodes (Joan), Rosella Towne (Phyllis), Wilfred Lucas (Official).

Francis stars in this fluffy drama about a women's air race which she enters in order to win enough cash for her brother's operation. She gets some help from top flier Gargan who arranges for her to use his plane. That plan is foiled by Gargan's former wife, Bromley, who hops in the cockpit first. Gargan then manages to get Francis Foy's plane, which carries her across the finish line first. Arden was another woman who took to the air in this enjoyable flying drama. Francis announced this as her final film, choosing to live the life of a wife, but in three years she was back on the screen.

p, Mark Hellinger; d, John Farrow; w, Lee Katz, Albert De Mond (based on the novel by Francis Walton); ph, Sid Hickox; ed, Thomas Pratt; md, Leo F. Forbstein; art d, Carl Jules Weyl; cos, Orry-Kelly.

Drama   (PR:A   MPAA:NR)

WOMEN IN WAR½   (1940) 71m REP bw

Elsie Janis (O'Neil), Wendy Barrie (Pamela Starr), Patric Knowles (Lt. Larry Hall), Mae Clarke (Gail Halliday), Dennie Moore (Ginger), Dorothy Peterson (Frances Phelps), Billy Gilbert (Pierre), Colin Tapley (Capt. Tedford), Stanley Logan (Col. Starr), Barbara Pepper (Millie), Pamela Randell (Phyllis Grant), Lawrence Grant (Gordon), Lester Matthews (Sir Humphrey, King's Counsel), Marion Martin (Starr's Date), Holmes Herbert (Chief Justice), Vera Lewis (Pierre's Wife), Charles D. Brown (Freddie), Peter Cushing (Capt. Evans).

Janis is the head of a wartime nursing unit in this standard programmer which is one of the earliest to use the U.S. involvement in the war as a backdrop. Barrie is a nurse who is pulled from her high-society life style and put through a demanding training period and eventually risks danger helping soldiers during a bombing raid. The usual romance has Barrie falling for air corps lieutenant Knowles, which gives the audience and the characters a break from daily duties. The film marked the brief return to the screen for silent star Janis, the "Sweetheart of the AEF" in WW I.

p, Sol C. Siegel; d, John H. Auer; w, F. Hugh Herbert, Doris Anderson; ph, Jack Marta; ed, Edward Mann; md, Cy Feuer; art d, John Victor Mackay; cos, Adele Palmer; spec eff, Howard Lydecker.

War Drama   (PR:A   MPAA:NR)

WOMEN IN WAR, 1965   (SEE: WOMEN AND WAR, 1965, Fr.)

WOMEN LOVE ONCE½   (1931) 71m PAR bw

Paul Lukas (Julien Fields), Eleanor Boardman (Helen Fields), Juliette Compton (Hester Dahlgren), Geoffrey Kerr (Allen Greenough), Judith Wood (Olga), Marilyn Knowlden (Janet Fields), Claude King (Theodore Stewart), Mischa Auer (Oscar), Helen Johnson.

Melodramatic fare which stars Lukas as an aspiring artist who is married and has a young daughter. He gets an offer to study in Paris for a year and after some encouragement from his wife, packs his bags. When he returns his new bohemian outlook on life leads him to separate from his wife. The death of his daughter in an auto accident shocks him back to his senses, however, and closes the film in a decidedly unpleasant manner. Very poor amusement fare.

d, Edward Goodman; w, Zoe Akins (based on her play "Daddy's Gone-A-Hunting"); ph, Karl Struss.

Drama   (PR:A   MPAA:NR)

WOMEN MEN MARRY zero   (1931) 76m Headline Pictures bw

Natalie Moorhead, Sally Blane, Randolph Scott, Kenneth Harlan, Crauford Kent, Jean Del Val, James Aubrey.

A worthless, poorly written drama which would have been better off had it come in the silent days. A naive husband and wife move to the big city and get mixed up with an undesirable couple, ending with a multiple shooting that straightens out the lives of everyone involved.

d, Charles Hutchinson; John Francis Natteford; ph, Leon Shamroy; ed, B.B. Ray.

Drama   (PR:A   MPAA:NR)

WOMEN MEN MARRY, THE   (1937) 60m MGM bw

George Murphy (Bill Raeburn), Josephine Hutchinson (Jane Carson), Claire Dodd (Claire Raeburn), Sidney Blackmer (Walter Wiley), Cliff Edwards (Jerry Little), John Wray (Brother Namelcez), Peggy Ryan (Mary Jane), Helen Jerome Eddy (Sister Martin), Rollo Lloyd (Peter Martin), Edward McWade (Brother Lam), Toby Wing (Sugar), Leonard Penn.

A witty newspaper tale with Murphy starring as a reporter who uncovers a scam run by a religious cult, but fails to realise that his wife is carrying on with his managing editor. He leaves her to her new love and begins a romance with fellow reporter Hutchinson, the girl he should have married to begin with. A minor programmer which is blessed with some refreshing dialog.

p, Michael Fessier; d, Errol Taggart; w, Harry Ruskin, Donald Henderson Clarke, James E. Grant (based on a story by Matt Taylor); ph, Lester White; m, Edward Ward; ed, George Boemler.

Drama   (PR:A   MPAA:NR)

WOMEN MUST DRESS*   (1935) 76m MON bw

Minna Gombell (Linda), Gavin Gordon (Philip), Hardie Albright (David), Suzanne Kaaren (Janet), Lenita Lane (Eve), Robert Light (Brand Whitney), Zeffie Tilbury (Peg), Alan Edwards (Jerry Benson), Paul Ellis (Mendoza), Gerald Young (Jim Daniels), Anne Johnston (Miss Peterson), Arthur Lake.

Plain but good wife Gombell teaches her philandering husband a thing or two by donning makeup and walking out on him, taking their daughter along, and going modern with a vengeance. The daughter begins an affair with a dull young doctor, then attaches herself to some undesirables, and finally returns to the doctor. Gombell tires of the charade and goes back to her husband and in no time at all the family peace is restored. Shallow mixture badly told and acted.

p, Mrs. Wallace Reid; d, Reginald Barker; w, Dorothy Reid, Edmund Joseph (based on a story by Frank Farnsworth); ph, Milton Krasner; ed, Jack Ogilvie.

Drama   (PR:A   MPAA:NR)

WOMEN OF ALL NATIONS½   (1931) 72m FOX bw

Victor McLaglen (Sgt. Flagg), Edmund Lowe (Sgt. Quirt), Greta Nissen (Elsa), El Brendel (Olsen), Fifi D'Orsay (Fifi), Marjorie White (Pee Wee), T. Roy Barnes (Captain of Marines), Bela Lugosi (Prince Hassan), Humphrey Bogart (Stone), Joyce Compton (Kiki), Jesse De Vorska (Izzie), Charles Judels (Leon), Marion Lessing (Gretchen), Ruth Warren (Ruth).

Disappointing third installment in the Flagg and Quirt series (WHAT PRICE GLORY and THE COCKEYED WORLD were the first two) that remains fascinating nonetheless for Lugosi's first appearance since DRACULA and an early nonperformance from Bogart whose bit part was cut out by a studio desperate to salvage what they considered to be a dog. Several years after WW I rollicking rivals McLaglen and Lowe find themselves back in their beloved Brooklyn. McLaglen now works as a Marine recruiting officer and Lowe, who has had enough of the military, runs a Turkish bathhouse for women. When Lowe's establishment is raided by the police, McLaglen offers to help him escape–but only if he re-enlists. Desperate, Lowe rejoins the Marines and soon finds himself on another crazy adventure. Hooking up with their Marine buddy Brendel, Lowe and McLaglen make their way to Sweden where they all fall in love with cafe singer Nissen. The three Marines pull their usual mischief on one another while vying for the affections of the sexy Miss Nissen, but they find themselves outclassed when Nissen's huge boy friend arrives on the scene and tosses them out. The crazed, lovesick Swedish giant then proceeds to tear apart the entire building as the three Marines quickly head for the next port. After a brief stop in Nicaragua where the Marines are sent to help the locals recover from an earthquake, the boys find themselves in Turkey where they once again run into Swedish songbird Nissen. Anxious to resume their romantic rivalry, the Marines are dismayed to discover that Nissen is now among the many wives of prince Lugosi's vast harem. Taking a chance while Lugosi is away, the Marines sneak into the harem and entertain the wives with tall tales of their military escapades. Unfortunately, Lugosi returns and catches the making advances on his wives. The outraged Lugosi orders the Marines castrated, but before the deed can be done, McLaglen, Lowe, and Brendel ship out for their next port. A lackluster effort for all involved, WOMEN OF ALL NATIONS does deliver a few solid laughs, but the series was running out of gas. Director Walsh himself remarked in his autobiography that the film was "...a turkey because it could not be anything else." Elaborating his point, the director continued, "A third McLaglen-Lowe film was too much for the public; I had been afraid of this from the start. It should have been called the League of Nations because it flopped just as hard." Walsh was right, the film garnered bad reviews and little box office. McLaglen, Lowe, and Brendel did just fine in roles that were becoming so familiar they could have performed them in their sleep, and Lugosi is effective in his brief role as the crazed prince, though it must have been a disappointment to fans awaiting another DRACULA. Considering the fate of this film, perhaps Bogart was lucky that his face was left on the cutting room floor.

d, Raoul Walsh; w, Barry Connors (based on characters created by Laurence Stallings, Maxwell Anderson); ph, Lucien Andriot; m, Reginald H. Bassett; ed, Jack Dennis; md, Carli D. Elinor; art d, David Hall.

Comedy Adventure (PR:A-C MPAA:NR)

WOMEN OF DESIRE zero (1968) 71m Boxoffice bw

Tiffany James, Harold Lasko, Bonny Allison, Nancy Brent, Jeanette Mason, Nick Sanicandro, Cindy Stewart, Angela Towers, Ronald Edwards.

After being awakened by the cops who tell him that his wife was killed by a truck, a man reaches the bizarre conclusion that she was not on her job as a nurse but instead was working as a hooker. In flashback we see that that bizarre instinct was true. Upset and drinking over her losses at the racetrack, she's approached by a smooth talking individual who convinces her where the real money is. After working a motel for a while, she meets a neighbor and fears the truth will finally be exposed. She tells the pimp she's quitting and promptly runs off. Unfortunately for her, it's into the path of an oncoming truck. A film for which the concept "garbage" is too dignified a word.

p, Roger Scott; d, Vincent L. Sinclair; w, Carl Baker; ph, Allan Jansen; cos, Pat Hoffman.

Drama (PR:O MPAA:NR)

WOMEN OF GLAMOUR★★ (1937) 68m COL bw

Virginia Bruce (Gloria Hudson), Melvyn Douglas (Richard Stark), Reginald Denny (Frederick Eagan), Pert Kelton (Nan LaRoque), Leona Maricle (Carol Coulter), Thurston Hall (Mr. Stark), Mary Forbes (Mrs. Stark), John Spacey (Winkler), Maurice Cass (Caldwell), Miki Morita (Kito), Clarissa Selwynne, Bess Flowers, Addie McPhail, Mary Jane Temple, Leona Valde, Nadine Dore (Women), Thomas Pogue (Travis), Harvey Clark (Roger), Henry Roquemore (Travis' Friend), Virginia Carroll, Ann Roth (Girls), Paul Power, Bruce Sidney, Eric Alden, Richard Kipling (Men), Stanley Mack (Waiter), Douglas Gordon (Steward).

Bruce stars as a showgirl-gold digger who competes with socialite Maricle for the love of Douglas. She has a tough time of it but finally proves that her hard-boiled heart is warmer and truer than the rich girl's. A remake of the Barbara Stanwyck vehicle LADIES OF LEISURE.

d, Gordon Wiles; w, Lynn Starling, Mary McCall, Jr. (based on the story by Milton Herbert Gropper); ph, Peverell Marley, Henry Freulich; ed, Otto Meyer; cos, Robert Kalloch.

Drama/Comedy (PR:A MPAA:NR)

WOMEN OF NAZI GERMANY (SEE: HITLER, 1962)

WOMEN OF PITCAIRN ISLAND, THE★ (1957) 72m FOX bw

James Craig (Page), Lynn Bari (Maimitia), John Smith (Thursday), Arleen Whelan (Hutia), Sue England (Nanai), Rico Alaniz (Spanisher), John Stevens (Charles Quintelle), Carol Thurston (Balhadi), Sonia Sorel (Tuarua), Charlita (Susannah), Lorna Thayer (Mortua), Roxanne Reed (Jenny), Millicent Patrick (Prudence), Harry Lauter (Fish), Pierce Lyden (Scruggs), Henry Rowland (Muskie), Paul Sorenson (Allard), House Peters, Jr (Coggins), Richard Devin (Miahiti), Rad Fulton (Alfred), Michael Miller (Tom McCoy), Robert Cabal (Moani), Robert Kendall (John Martin), Joel Collin (Robert Brown), Tim Johnson (Henry Smith).

A mindless tale of what may have happened to the survivors of the HMS Bounty after the mutiny. Having made it to Pitcairn Island, the women and children are the only survivors, burying the last of the men at the film's opening. They are terrorized by a crew of pirate survivors of a shipwreck who are looking not only for women to abuse, but pearls stolen by an escaped crewman. The pirates end up killing themselves off over the pearls, with the islanders getting rid of whomever is left standing.

p, Jean Yarbrough, Aubrey Wisberg; d, Yarbrough; w, Wisberg (based on the novel by Wisberg); ph, Harry Neumann (RegalScope); m, Paul Dunlap; ed, William Austin.

Drama (PR:A MPAA:NR)

WOMEN OF THE NORTH COUNTRY
(SEE: WOMAN OF THE NORTH COUNTRY, 1952)

WOMEN OF THE PREHISTORIC PLANET★
(1966) 90m Standard Club of California/REA c

Wendell Corey (Adm. King), Keith Larsen (Comdr. Scott), John Agar (Dr. Farrell), Irene Tsu (Linda), Paul Gilbert (Lt. Bradley), Merry Anders (Karen), Communications Officer, Stuart Lasswell (Charles), Robert Ito (Tang), Adam Roarke (Centurion), Suzie Kaye (Crew Member), Stuart Margolin (Chief), Gavin McLeod (Radio Operator), Lyle Waggoner.

A cheaply made science-fiction entry which has a ship crash-land on an unidentified planet with the only survivor being a young boy. Three months later a reconnaissance craft comes to the ship's rescue, only to find that 18

years have passed on the planet. The surviving member takes one of the rescue mission's women for his companion, and during a volcanic eruption the ship is forced to leave the couple behind. As the ship leaves, the admiral decides to name the planet Earth, and presumably that is how it all started, the begetting, begetting, begetting...

p, George Edwards; d&w, Arthur C. Pierce; ph, Arch R. Dalzell (DeLuxe Color); ed, George White; art d, Paul Sylos; set d, Harry Reif; spec eff, Howard A. Anderson.

Science-Fiction Cas. (PR:A MPAA:NR)

WOMEN OF TWILIGHT (SEE: TWILIGHT WOMEN, 1953, Brit.)

WOMEN THEY TALK ABOUT★★ (1928) 60m WB bw

Irene Rich (Irene Mervin Hughes), Audrey Ferris (Audrey Hughes), William Collier, Jr (Steve Harrison), Anders Randolph (John Harrison), Claude Gillingwater (Grandfather Mervin), Jack Santoro (Frame-Up Man), John Miljan (Officer).

When rich girl Ferris and mayor's son Collier fall in love their relationship is met with opposition by their widow and widower parents (Rich and Randolph) and the crotchety Gillingwater. Before long the youngsters' love is blooming as well as their parents'. A partial talkie, WOMEN THEY TALK ABOUT has only 25 percent dialog.

d, Lloyd Bacon; w, Robert Lord (based on a story by Anthony Coldeway); ph, Frank Kesson; ed, Tommy Pratt.

Comedy (PR:A MPAA:NR)

WOMEN WHO PLAY★★½ (1932, Brit.) 78m PAR British bw

Mary Newcomb (Mona), Benita Hume (Margaret Sones), George Barraud (Richard Sones), Joan Barry (Fay), Barry Jones (Ernest Steele), Edmond Breon (Rachie Wells), Gerald Lyley (Bobby), Sylvia Lesley (Lady Jane), Peter Evan Thomas (Willie), Mary Hamilton, Frank Lacy.

Hume is a playful wife who surrounds herself with phony socialites and a philanderer who is out to get her, until her husband, Barraud, makes her pay for her foolish actions. Barraud hires Newcomb, an actress, to pose as a prostitute and come to a high-society party and make Hume jealous. Newcomb plays her part well and Barraud gets his wife back, a little wiser and soberer.

p, Walter Morosco; d, Arthur Rosson; w, Gilbert Wakefield, Basil Mason (based on the play "Spring Cleaning" by Frederick Lonsdale).

Comedy (PR:A MPAA:NR)

WOMEN WITHOUT MEN (SEE: BLOND BAIT, 1956, Brit.)

WOMEN WITHOUT NAMES★★ (1940) 62m PAR bw

Ellen Drew (Joyce King), Robert Paige (Fred MacNeil), Judith Barrett (Peggy Athens), John Miljan (Assistant District Atty. John Marlin), Fay Helm (Millie), John McGuire (Walter Ferris), Louise Beavers (Ivory), James Seay (O'Grane), Esther Dale (Head Matron Inglis), Marjorie Main (Mrs. Lowry), Audrey Maynard (Maggie), Kitty Kelly (Countess), Virginia Dabney (Ruffles), Helen Lynch (Susie), Mae Busch (Rose), Thomas E. Jackson (Detective Sgt. Reardon), Joseph Sawyer (Principal Keeper Grimley), Eddie Saint (Priest), Wilfred Lucas, Dick Elliott, Ruth Warren (Roomers), Harry Worth (Trailer Salesman), Lillian Elliott (Mrs. Anthony), George Anderson, Henry Roquemore, John Harmon, Arthur Aylesworth, Leila McIntyre, Helen MacKellar, Mary Gordon (Jurors), Eddie Fetherston, Allen Fox, Ralph McCullough, Allen Conner, Jack Egan, Paul Kruger (Reporters), Blanche Rose (Jail Matron), Douglas Kennedy (Secretary), James Flavin (Guard).

A minor league programmer about two lovebirds, Drew and Paige, who are convicted of the murder of a policeman when an overeager district attorney railroads the case. Paige goes to Death Row and Drew to life in prison, and the rest of the picture concentrates on her trials and tribulations there. At the last minute a confession comes in from an eyewitness to the killing that the wife found in her cell block, clearing the lovebirds.

p, Eugene Zukor; d, Robert Florey; w, William R. Lipman, Horace McCoy (based on a play by Ernest Booth); ph, Charles Lang; ed, Anne Bauchens; art d, Hans Dreier, William Flannery.

Crime Drama (PR:A MPAA:NR)

WOMEN WON'T TELL★ (1933) 66m Bacheller/CHES bw

Sarah Padden, Otis Harlan, Gloria Shea, Larry Kent, Edmund Breese, Mae Busch, Walter Long, William V. Mong, Robert Ellis, Tom Ricketts, Isobel Withers, John Hyams, Jane Darwell, Dewey Robinson, Donald Kirke, June Bennett, Charles Hill Mailes, Betty Mack.

A slow-mover about a woman living a meager existence in the city garbage dump and trying to prove that her daughter is the rightful heir to a tycoon's fortune. Everyone believes the girl is illegitimate but Mom proves she was fathered by the tycoon during a legal marriage.

d, Richard Thorpe; w, Lela E. Rogers; ph, M.A. Anderson.

Drama   **(PR:A   MPAA:NR)**

WOMEN'S PRISON**   (1955) 80m COL bw

Ida Lupino (*Amelia Van Zant*), Jan Sterling (*Brenda Martin*), Cleo Moore (*Mae*), Audrey Totter (*Joan Burton*), Phyllis Thaxter (*Helene Jensen*), Howard Duff (*Dr. Clark*), Warren Stevens (*Glen Burton*), Barry Kelley (*Warden Brock*), Gertrude Michael (*Sturgess*), Vivian Marshall (*Dottie*), Mae Clarke (*Saunders*), Ross Elliott (*Don Jensen*), Adelle August (*Grace*), Don C. Harvey (*Capt. Tierney*), Juanita Moore (*"Polyclinic" Jones*), Edna Holland (*Sarah*), Lynne Millan (*Carol*), Mira McKinney (*Burke*), Mary Newton (*Enright*), Diane DeLaire (*Head Nurse*), Francis Morris (*Miss Whittier*), Jana Mason (*Josie*), Lorna Thayer (*Woman Deputy*), Murray Alper (*Mug*), Ruth Vann, Mary Lou Devore (*Girl Patients*), Eddie Foy III (*Warden's Secretary*).

Lupino is a psychopathic prison warden who takes out her lack of sexuality on her women inmates. She's challenged by Duff, a caring doctor, who tries to improve the hostile atmosphere of the jail. Sterling and Moore take reform into their own hands and start a riot which ends in Lupino's breakdown. WOMEN'S PRISON is just what one would expect from a B priso n movie.

p, Bryan Foy; d, Lewis Seiler; w, Crane Wilbur, Jack DeWitt; ph, Lester H. White; m, Mischa Bakaleinikoff; ed, Henry Batista; art d, Cary Odell; set d, Louis Diage.

Prison Drama   **(PR:A-C   MPAA:NR)**

WON TON TON, THE DOG WHO SAVED HOLLYWOOD*
                                             (1976) 92m PAR c

Bruce Dern (*Grayson Potchuck*), Madeline Kahn (*Estie Del Ruth*), Art Carney (*J.J. Fromberg*), Phil Silvers (*Murray Fromberg*), Teri Garr (*Fluffy Peters*), Ron Leibman (*Rudy Montague*), Dennis Morgan (*Tour Guide*), Shecky Greene (*Tourist*), Phil Leeds, Cliff Norton (*Dog Catchers*), Romo Vincent (*Short Order Cook*), Sterling Holloway (*Old Man on Bus*), William Demarest (*Studio Gatekeeper*), Virginia Mayo (*Miss Battley*), Henny Youngman (*Manny Farber*), Rory Calhoun (*Philip Hart*), Billy Barty (*Assistant Director*), Henry Wilcoxon (*Silent Film Director*), Ricardo Montalban (*Silent Film Star*), Jackie Coogan (*Stagehand 1*), Aldo Ray (*Stubby Stebbins*), Ethel Merman (*Hedda Parsons*), Yvonne De Carlo (*Cleaning Woman*), Joan Blondell (*Landlady*), Andy Devine (*Priest in Dog Pound*), Broderick Crawford (*Special Effects Man*), Richard Arlen (*Silent Film Star 2*), Jack LaRue (*Silent Film Villain*), Dorothy Lamour (*Visiting Film Star*), Nancy Walker (*Mrs. Fromberg*), Gloria DeHaven (*President's Girl 1*), Louis Nye (*Radio Interviewer*), Johnny Weissmuller-Gonzales (*Stagehand 2*), Stepin Fetchit (*Dancing Butler*), Ken Murray (*Souvenir Salesman*), Rudy Vallee (*Autograph Hound*), George Jessel (*Awards Announcer*), Rhonda Fleming (*Rhoda Flaming*), Ann Miller (*President's Girl 2*), Dean Stockwell (*Paul Lavell*), Dick Haymes (*James Crawford*), Tab Hunter (*David Hamilton*), Robert Alda (*Richard Entwhistle*), Fritz Feld (*Rudy's Butler*), Janet Blair (*President's Girl 3*), Dennis Day (*Singing Telegraph Man*), Mike Mazurki (*Studio Guard*), The Ritz Brothers (*Cleaning Women*), Jesse White (*Rudy's Agent*), Carmel Myers (*Woman Journalist*), Jack Carter (*Male Journalist*), Victor Mature (*Nick*), Barbara Nichols (*Nick's Girl*), Army Archerd (*Premiere M.C.*), Fernando Lamas (*Premiere Male Star*), Zsa Zsa Gabor (*Premiere Female Star*), Cyd Charisse (*President's Girl 4*), Huntz Hall (*Moving Man*), Doodles Weaver (*Man in Mexican Film*), Edgar Bergen (*Prof. Quicksand*), Morey Amsterdam, Eddie Foy, J r (*Custard Pie Stars*), Peter Lawford (*Slapstick Star*), Patricia Morison, Guy Madison (*Stars at Screening*), Regis Toomey (*Burlesque Stagehand*), Alice Faye (*Secretary at Gate*), Ann Rutherford (*Grayson's Studio Secretary*), Milton Berle (*Blind Man*), John Carradine (*Drunk*), Keye Luke (*Cook in Kitchen*), Walter Pidgeon (*Grayson's Butler*), William Benedict (*Man on Bus*), Dorothy Gulliver (*Old Woman on Bus*), Eli Mintz (*Tailor*), Edward Ashley (*2nd Butler*), Kres Mersky (*Girl in Arab Film*), Jane Connell (*Waitress*), Jack Bernardi (*Fluffy's Escort*), Pedro Gonzales-Gonzales (*Mexican Projectionist*), Eddie Le Veque (*Prostitute's Customer*), Ronny Graham (*Mark Bennett*), James E. Brodhead (*Priest*), Augustus Von Schumacher (*Won Ton Ton*).

A treacherously unfunny comedy about the escapades of the title pooch in the mid-1920s and how he saves Carney's New Era Studios from going down the drain. The dog becomes a star, Carney's studio becomes the most prosperous, and Dern is promoted from tour bus driver to producer. Later, a movie they produce bombs, and they lose their jobs, but by the finale everyone is cheerfully reunited. Somewhere along the line someone told director Winner that quantity was more important than quality, so WON TON TON is filled with cameo appearances, from Johnny Weissmuller to Billy Barty and from Tab Hunter to Dennis Day, and the cast list is more fun to read than the movie is to watch. Songs include: "Paramount on Parade" (J. King, E. Janis), "Love Theme" from THE GODFATHER (Nino Rota), "Happy Birthday To You" (M.J. Hill, P.S. Hill), "Dagger-Dance" from NATOMA (Victor Herbert).

p, David V. Picker, Arnold Schulman, Michael Winner; d, Winner; w, Schulman, Cy Howard; ph, Richard H. Kline (Technicolor); m, Neal Hefti;

ed, Bernard Gribble; art d, Ward Preston; set d, Ned Parsons; makeup, Philip Rhodes.

Comedy   **(PR:A   MPAA:PG)**

WONDER BAR***   (1934) 84m WB-FN bw

Al Jolson (*Al Wonder*), Dolores Del Rio (*Inez*), Ricards Cortez (*Harry*), Kay Francis (*Liane Renaud*), Dick Powell (*Tommy*), Guy B. Kibbee (*Henry Simpson*), Hugh Herbert (*Corey Pratt*), Robert Barrat (*Capt. Von Ferring*), Ruth Donnelly (*Ella Simpson*), Louise Fazenda (*Pansy Pratt*), Fifi D'Orsay (*Mitzi*), Merna Kennedy (*Claire*), Henry Kolker (*Mr. Renaud*), Henry O'Neill (*Richards*), Kathryn Sergava (*Ilka*), Gordon De Main (*1st Detective*), Harry Woods (*2nd Detective*), Marie Moreau (*Maid*), George Irving (*Broker*), Emile Chautard (*Concierge*), Pauline Garon (*Operator*), Mahlon Norvell (*Artist*), Alphonse Martel (*Doorman*), Mia Ichioka (*Gee-Gee*), William Granger (*Bartender*), Rolfe Sedan (*Waiter*), Eddie Kane (*Frank*), Edward Keane (*Captain*), Jane Darwell (*Baroness*), Demetrius Alexis (*1st Young Man*), John Marlow (*2nd Young Man*), Billy Anderson (*Call Boy*), Bud Jamison (*Bartender*), Hobart Cavanaugh (*Drunk*), Dave O'Brien (*Chorus Boy*), Dennis O'Keefe (*Extra at Bar*), Gino Corrado (*Waiter*), Grace Hayle (*Fat Dowager*), Gordon 'Bill' Elliott (*Norman*), Paul Power (*Chester*), Dick Good (*Page Boy*), Michael Dalmatoff (*Count*), Renee Whitney (*1st Chorus Girl*), Amo Ingraham (*2nd Chorus Girl*), Rosalie Roy (*3rd Chorus Girl*), Lottie Williams (*Wardrobe Woman*), Clay Clement (*1st Businessman*), William Stack (*2nd Businessman*), Spencer Charters (*Pete*), Gene Perry (*Gendarme*), Louis Ardizoni (*Cook*), Robert Graves (*Police Officer*), Alfred P. James (*Night Watchman*), Hal LeRoy (*Himself*).

You can't help comparing this musical (from a play that opened in Vienna and was based in that city) to GRAND HOTEL because of the number of characters, plots, and subplots. It didn't make it on Broadway when Jolson played it on the roof of the 44th Street Theater but the screen version fared better. Jolson is the owner- singer of his own nightspot. His star attraction is Del Rio and both he and band singer Powell are in love with her, but she is moon-eyed over Cortez, her partner in dancing. Tourist Kibbee is married to Donnelly and his pal Herbert is wed to Fazenda. That doesn't stop these aging butter-and-egg men from flirting with D'Orsay and Kennedy, two of the hostesses at the "Wonder Bar." (Kennedy was married, in real life, to the movie's choreographer, Berkeley.) At the same time Jolson and Powell are competing for Del Rio, her amour, Cortez, is the eye-apple of wealthy socialite Francis, who is also married. One of the secondary stories includes Barrat as a suicidal soldier who is in deep financial trouble and having a final fling before doing himself in. With that much story, it's amazing there was any room for songs and production numbers, but there they are, and plenty of them. Most of the Harry Warren-Al Dubin songs are only serviceable, but push the several plots along. One terribly tasteless production sequence has Jolson in his standard blackface singing "I'm going to Heaven on a Mule," which takes him into a scene filled with hundreds of small black children. On his visit to Heaven, he finds that all the angels look like "Uncle Tom." An oddity is that Francis' character is named "Liane Renaud" and, in later years, that was close to the real name of famed French chanteuse Line Renaud, who had a very successful career in Las Vegas. Dancer Hal LeRoy makes his film debut and taps his way into the audience's hearts. The lapse in taste in the all-black number was almost overcome by the "Don't Say Goodnight" section as Berkeley made use of his infinity of mirrors filled with handsome young men and gorgeous young women. Although set in Paris, it could have taken place anywhere, and will probably eventually be taken up by some smart Broadway producer for a musical in years to come. Jolson's contract called for him to have a percentage of the gross receipts and he added to his overflowing coffers with the money that flowed in.

p, Robert Lord; d, Lloyd Bacon; w, Earl Baldwin (based on the play by Geza Herczeg, Karl Farkas, Robert Katscher); ph, Sol Polito; ed, George Amy; md, Leo F. Forbstein; art d, Jack Okey; cos, Orry-Kelly; ch, Busby Berkeley; m/l, "At the Wonder Bar," "I'm Going to Heaven on a Mule," "Why Do I Dream Those Dreams?" "Don't Say Goodnight," "Vive la France," "Fairer on the Riviera," "Tango Del Rio," "Dark Eyes," Harry Warren, Al Dubin.

Musical Comedy/Drama   Cas.   (PR:A   MPAA:NR)

WONDER BOY**   (1951, Brit./Aust.) 86m LFP/Snader bw
(ENTFUHRUNG INS GLUCK; AKA: WONDER CHILD; THE WONDER KID)

Bobby Henrey (*Sebastian Giro*), Robert Schackleton (*Rocks Cooley*), Christa Winter (*Anni*), Muriel Aked (*Miss Frisbie*), Elwyn Brook-Jones (*Mr. Gorik*), Paul Hardtmuth (*Prof. Bindl*), Oskar Werner (*Rudi*), Sebastian Cabot (*Pozzo*), Klaus Hirsch (*Nik*), June Elvin (*Miss Kirsch*), Hugo Gottschlieh, Frank Boeheim (*Gendarmes*), Lowe the Dog.

Henrey is a child piano prodigy exploited by his manager who has plans of becoming the boy's legal guardian. When the boy's governess learns of this she arranges to have Henrey taken away for a while, but her plan gets out of hand when he is held for ransom. Eventually he returns, a stronger and less vulnerable youngster who puts the manager in his place and secures a fair contract.

p&d, Karl Hartl; w, Gene Markey (based on a story by Hartl); ph, Robert Krasker, Gunther Anders; m, Willy Schmidt-Gentner; ed, Reginald Beck;

md, Dr. Hubert Clifford; prod d, Joseph Bato, Werner Schlighting.

Drama   (PR:A   MPAA:NR)

WONDER CHILD   (SEE: WONDER BOY, 1951, Brit.)

WONDER KID   (SEE: WONDER BOY, 1951, Brit.)

WONDER MAN***   (1945) 98m Goldwyn/RKO c

Danny Kaye (*Buzzy Bellew/Edwin Dingle*), Virginia Mayo (*Ellen Shanley*), Vera-Ellen (*Midge Mallon*), Donald Woods (*Monte Rossen*), S.Z. Sakall (*Schmidt*), Allen Jenkins (*Chimp*), Edward S. Brophy (*Torso*), Steve Cochran (*Ten-Grand Jackson*), Otto Kruger (*District Attorney R. J. O'Brien*), Richard Land (*Assistant District Attorney Grosset*), Natalie Schafer (*Mrs. Leland Hume*), Huntz Hall (*Mike, Sailor*), Virginia Gilmore (*Girl Friend*), Edward Gargan (*Cop in Park*), Grant Mitchell (*Mrs. Wagonseller*), Gisela Werbiseck (*Mrs. Schmidt*), Alice Mock (*Prima Donna*), Mary Field (*Stenographer*), Aldo Franchetti (*Opera Conductor*), Maurice Cass (*Stage Manager*), Luis Aberni (*Prompter*), Noel Cravat, Nick Thompson, Nino Pipitone, Baldo Minuti (*Opera Singers*), James Flavin (*Bus Driver*), Jack Norton (*Drunk in Club*), Frank Orth (*Bartender*), Charles Irwin (*Drunk at Bar*), Cecil Cunningham (*Barker*), Eddie Dunn (*Cop*), Byron Foulger (*Customer*), Margie Stewart (*Page Girl*), Frank Melton (*Waiter*), Barbara La Rene (*Acrobatic Dancer*), Al Ruiz, Willard Van Simons (*Specialty Dancers*), Chester Clute (*Man on Bus*), Eddie Kane (*Headwaiter*), Ray Teal (*Ticket Taker*), Leon Belasco (*Pianist*), Carol Haney (*Dancer*), Ruth Valmy, Margie Stewart, Alma Carroll, Georgia Lange, Karen Gaylord, Mary Moore, Gloria Delson, Deannie Best, Mary Meade, Martha Montgomery, Ellen Hall, Phyllis Forbes, Mary Jane Woods, Katherine 'Karin' Booth, Chili Williams (*Goldwyn Girls*), Maureen Cunningham, Georganne Smith, Janet Lavis, Dorothy Jean, Betty Marion, Jane Allen, Doris Toddings, Jean Marley, Helen McAllister, Virginia Kepler, Helen McCowan, Charles Teske, Ray Nyles, Walter Pietila, Bob Mascagno, Eddie Cutler, Allen Pinson (*Dancers*), Grace Johnson, Dorothy Koster, Loretta Daye, Susan Scott, Alice Stansfield, Betty Lane, Mickey Maloy, Alice Kersten (*Entertainers*), Billy Wayne, Ralph Dunn, Eddie Acuff, Harry Depp, John Kelly, Sarah Selby, William Newell, James Farley.

In his second film for producer Goldwyn, Kaye plays a dual role and is on screen for just about every frame of the movie. After the profitable public acceptance of UP IN ARMS, Goldwyn must have reckoned that two Kayes are better than one, hence the following plot which will use the name "Danny" for one character and "Kaye" for the other, so as not to confuse you (or us). Danny is a famous nightclub performer about to marry Vera-Ellen, his partner in their singing-dancing act. Earlier, Danny had seen a mobster rubbed out by gang lord Cochran (in his movie debut, as was Vera-Ellen in hers). To keep him from blabbing to district attorney Kruger, Danny is killed by Cochran's hoods Brophy and Jenkins. His corpse is tossed into Brooklyn's Prospect Park lake (not far from where Kaye himself was born and raised). Danny has a twin brother, Kaye, an intellectual with whom he lost touch a long time ago, as they were in different worlds. Kaye is having a bite in a delicatessen with Mayo, a sweet librarian, and suddenly he finds himself mysteriously drawn to the lake where Danny has been dumped. Kaye is approached by Danny's ghost at the park site. Danny prevails upon his shy and ineffectual brother to wreak revenge on Cochran and bring the information about both killings to D.A. Kruger. Kaye doesn't want to do it as he is a fearful type and doesn't believe he can bring it off. Danny solves that by placing himself *inside* his brother and causing him to be more like the dead half of the twins, flamboyant and bold and slightly wacky. Kaye finally agrees and, from time to time, whenever the bookish Kaye is in trouble, Danny enters his body and gets him off the book with bravado and bravura. All sorts of problems crop up when Vera-Ellen, who is ready to get married, pounces on Kaye. At the same time, Kaye is in love with Mayo (in their first of four movies, after she'd been elevated from her status as one of the "Goldwyn Girls") and he has to juggle both gorgeous women. When Cochran spots Kaye, he thinks his hoods have botched the job so he orders another put on right away. Danny gets drunk (hard to believe a ghost could succumb to alcohol) inside Kaye as he sits opposite villain Cochran at a nightclub. When Kaye finally gets to the office of Kruger and his aide, Lane, he awaits the appearance of Danny to divulge the information, but Danny is nowhere to be found (hungover somewhere). Kaye leaves and is immediately chased through Manhattan by Jenkins and Brophy. He races to the venerable Metropolitan Opera House (the old one on Broadway), gets backstage, then runs on-stage, pretending to be a famous opera singer. Kruger is in the audience and Kaye *sings* the entire story of the murders. The criminals are caught, Danny's ghost is happy at last and can retire, Kaye can marry Mayo, and Vera-Ellen winds up with Woods, the nightclub boniface who has been pursuing her all along. Lots of familiar situations have been slightly altered to fit Kaye's abilities and he does well by them, adding his own kind of zeal and verve. The opera number is brilliant as Kaye gets involved in a shoving match with Mock, the well-endowed prima donna. Vera-Ellen was only 19 at the time and had been discovered after early successes that included a tour of duty with the Rockettes and appearances in several Broadway shows. She was an accomplished dancer and a pretty good singer so it was a surprise that her tunes were sung by June Hutton and she pantomimed to Hutton's voice. The song by Leo Robin and David Rose was "So in Love" (sung by Vera-Ellen

'Hutton' and danced by Cecil Cunningham 'a female' and the Goldwyn Girls). Mrs. Kaye (Sylvia Fine) had always written her husband's material and contributed "Bali Boogie" (Kaye, Vera-Ellen), "Ortchi Chornya" (Kaye as a Russian singer having a fit of sneezing), and the "Opera Number" (Kaye, Alice Mock). "So in Love" was Oscar-nominated and the Special Effects department (John Fulton, sound by A. W. Johns) won the coveted statuette. One of the Goldwyn dancers was Carol Haney, who would become a Broadway star in "The Pajama Game" before hurting herself and having her understudy take over, a move that made Shirley MacLaine a star. Lots of laughs, although Kaye was yet to hit his full stride.

p, Samuel Goldwyn; d, Bruce Humberstone; w, Don Hartman, Melville Shavelson, Philip Rapp, Jack Jevne, Eddie Moran (based on a story by Arthur Sheekman); ph, Victor Milner, William Snyder (Technicolor); m, Ray Heindorf; ed, Daniel Mandell; md, Louis Forbes; art d, Ernst Fegte, McClure Capps; set d, Howard Bristol; spec eff, John Fulton; ch, John Wray.

Comedy/Musical   (PR:AA   MPAA:NR)

WONDER OF WOMEN*   (1929) 95m MGM bw

Lewis Stone (*Stephen Tromolt*), Peggy Wood (*Brigitte*), Leila Hyams (*Karen*), Harry Myers (*Bruno Heim*), Sarah Padden (*Anna*), Blanche Frederici (*Tromolt's Housekeeper*), Wally Albright, Jr (*Wulle-Wulle*), Carmencita Johnson (*Lottie*), George Fawcett (*Doctor*), Dietrich Haupt (*Kurt*), Ullrich Haupt (*Kurt*), Anita Fremault [Anita Louise] (*Lottie*).

Stone is a concert pianist who marries Wood after barely knowing her, and before long starts looking around for another gal. He spends some time with Hyams and plans to call it quits with his wife when he is told that she is seriously ill and has only hours to live. An incredibly maudlin part-talkie.

d, Clarence Brown; w, Bess Meredyth, Marion Ainslee (based on the novel *Die Frau des Steffan Tromholt* by Hermann Sudermann); ph, Merritt B. Gerstad; ed, William LeVanway; art d, Cedric Gibbons; cos, David Cox, Howard Greer.

Drama   (PR:A   MPAA:NR)

WONDER PLANE   (SEE: MERCY PLANE, 1940)

WONDER WOMEN zero   (1973, Phil.) 82m GEN c

Nancy Kwan (*Dr. Tsu*), Ross Hagen (*Mike Harber*), Maria De Aragon (*Linda*), Roberta Collins (*Laura*), Tony Lorea (*Paulson/Lorenzo*), Sid Haig (*Gregorius*), Vic Diaz (*Lapu-Lapu*), Claire Hagen (*Vera*), Shirley Washington (*Maggie*), Gail Hansen (*Gail*), Eleanor Siron (*Mei-Ling*), Bruno Punzalan (*Nono, Fisherman*), Joonee Gamboa (*Won Ton Charlie*), Rick Reveke (*Paulson's Attendant*), Rudy De Jesus (*Boy*), Wendy Greene (*Swimmer*), Leila Benitez (*Lillian Taylor*), Ross Rival (*Ramon Jai A'Lai, Player*).

A ridiculous horror picture which stars Kwan as a crazed lady who sells the body parts of famous kidnaped athletes to decaying old millionaires. Her unlikely plan is foiled by insurance investigator Hagen who not only prevents her from committing more murders, but saves world sport.

p, Ross Hagen; d, Robert O'Neil; w, Lou Whitehill, O'Neil; ph, Ricardo M. David; m, Carson Whitsett; ed, Richard Greer; art d, Ben Otico.

Horror   (PR:C   MPAA:PG)

WONDERFUL COUNTRY, THE*** (1959) 96m DRM/UA c

Robert Mitchum (*Martin Brady*), Julie London (*Ellen Colton*), Gary Merrill (*Maj. Stark Colton*), Pedro Armendariz (*Gov. Cipriano Castro*), Jack O akie (*Travis Hight*), Albert Dekker (*Capt. Rucker*), Victor Mendoza (*Gen. Castro*), Charles McGraw (*Doc Stovall*), John Banner (*Ben Turner*), LeRoy "Satchel" Paige (*Sgt. Tobe Sutton*), Tom Lea (*Peebles*), Jay Novello (*Diego Casas*), Mike Kellin (*Pancho Gil*), Joe Haworth (*Stoker*), Chuck Roberson (*Gallup*), Chester Hayes (*Rascon*), Mike Luna (*Capt. Verdugo*), Anthony Caruso (*Ludwig "Chico" Turner*), Claudio Brook (*Ruelle*), Judy Marsh (*Entertainer at Fiesta*), Max Slaten.

Mitchum stars in this atmospheric western as a gunrunner hired by the local "dictator," Armendariz, and his brother Mendoza. He crosses the border into Texas to carry out the mission but breaks his leg and is forced to remain among the gringos, receiving care from London, the unsatisfied wife of Merrill. Mitchum soon learns that Merrill is working for Armendariz, attempting to rid the area of Apaches for the sake of the railroad. Mitchum loses the guns he was sent for and is forced to flee south of the border on a murder charge. He runs into Merrill, who has been badly beaten by the Indians, and helps him and his troops to safety. Armendariz sends a gunman to kill Mitchum, but in a showdown, Mitchum is the one left standing. His horse is killed, he lays down his gun, and he returns to Texas and his beloved London in the hope of starting anew. A beautifully photographed, gritty western which is heavy on the closeups (a blessing when there's a face like Mitchum's to fill the screen). Produced by Mitchum's own company. Legendary baseball pitcher Leroy "Satchel" Paige appears here as a cavalry sergeant.

p, Chester Erskine; d, Robert Parrish; w, Robert Ardrey (based on the novel by Tom Lea); ph, Floyd Crosby, Alec Phillips (Technicolor); m, Alex North;

ed, Michael Luciano; md, North; art d, Harry Horner; cos, Mary Wills.

Western   (PR:A MPAA:NR)

WONDERFUL DAY   (SEE: I'VE GOTTA HORSE, 1965, Brit.)

WONDERFUL LAND OF OZ, THE**   (1969) 72m Cinetron/Childhood
c

Joy Webb, Channy Mahon.

An unnoticed version of *The Marvelous Land Of Oz*, owing more to the novel 4than to the 1939 film classic, but the comparison is inevitable. Another more-publicized attempt was made in 1985 with RETURN TO OZ, which not surprisingly went over like a lead balloon. This one includes a couple of tolerable tunes. Songs include: "Did You Come to See the Wizard?" "How Do I Brew This Stew?" "I Lost My Heart," "Open Your Eyes," "The Wonderful Land Of Oz" (Loonis McGlohon, Alec Wilder), "I Would Like to Have a Brain," "I'm a Scaredy Cat," "Wail of the Witch" (McGlohon).

p,d&w, Barry Mahon (based on the novel *The Marvelous Land Of Oz* by Lyman Frank Baum); ph, (Movielab Color).

Children's Film   (PR:AAA MPAA:NR)

WONDERFUL LIFE   (SEE: SWINGER'S PARADISE, 1965, Brit.)

WONDERFUL STORY, THE**   (1932, Brit.) 72m Fogwell/Sterling bw

Wyn Clare (*Mary Richards*), John Batten (*John Martin*), Eric Bransby Williams (*Bob Martin*), Moore Marriott (*Zacky Richards*), J. Fisher White (*Parson*), Sam Livesey (*Doctor*), Ernest Lester (*Amos*).

This dark tale of romance set in the Devon countryside concerns two brothers who are in love with the same farm girl, Clare. When one brother becomes a cripple, she weds the other. The first learns to accept the situation and is even pleased when she and his brother have a child together. It is a story but it's not especially wonderful.

p&d, Reginald Fogwell; w, Fogwell (based on the novel by I.A.R. Wylie).

Romance   (PR:A MPAA:NR)

WONDERFUL THINGS!**½   (1958, Brit.) 84m Everest/Associated
British-Pathe bw

Frankie Vaughan (*Carmello*), Jeremy Spenser (*Mario*), Jackie Lane (*Pepita*), Wilfrid Hyde-White (*Sir Bertram*), Jean Dawnay (*Anne*), Eddie Byrne (*Harry*), Harold Kasket (*Poppa*), Christopher Rhodes (*Codger*), Nancy Nevinson (*Mamma*), Cyril Chamberlain (*Butler*), Barbara Goalen (*Herself*), Elizabeth [Liz] Fraser, Ronnie Barker.

This engaging romance follows a pair of brothers, Vaughan and Spenser, who devote more time to Lane than to earning their living as fishermen. Vaughan sets off for London planning on bringing Lane later. Spenser helps her raise enough money for the trip by selling his boat, an act of kindness which causes Lane to fall in love with him. Vaughan handles the news without any hard feelings, however, since he's fallen in love with blonde socialite Dawnay. Produced by British actress Anna Neagle.

p, Anna Neagle; d, Herbert Wilcox; w, Jack Trevor Story; ph, Gordon Dines; m, Harold Rome; ed, Basil Warren.

Romance   (PR:A MPAA:NR)

WONDERFUL TO BE YOUNG!**   (1962, Brit.) 92m Associated British
Picture/PAR c (GB: THE YOUNG ONES)

Cliff Richard (*Nicky Black*), Robert Morley (*Hamilton Black*), Carole Gray (*Toni*), Richard O'Sullivan (*Ernest*), Melvyn Hayes (*Jimmy*), Teddy Green (*Chris*), Annette Robertson (*Barbara*), Sonya Cordeau (*Dorinda*), Sean Sullivan (*Eddie*), Harold Scott (*Dench*), Gerald Harper (*Watts*), Rita Webb (*Woman in Market*), Robertson Hare (*Chauffeur*), The Shadows (*Themselves*).

Richard, the son of a millionaire land tycoon, organizes his friends and puts on a musical in the hope of raising enough cash to buy a chunk of land before his father can. Morley, the father, foils their plan, angering one of the youngsters enough to kidnap the tycoon. Richard comes to dad's aid, gaining his respect, and in return getting control of the property and the youth club that goes with it. Includes the songs: "Wonderful To Be Young!" (Burt Bacharach, Hal David), "What D'You Know We've Got a Show," "Nothing's Impossible," "All for One," (Ronald Cass, Peter Myers), "When the Boy in Your Arms is the Boy in Your Heart," "When the Girl in Your Arms is the Girl in Your Heart," (Sid Tepper, Roy C. Bennett), "Peace Pipe," "The Savage" (Norrie Paramor), "Got a Funny Feeling" (Bruce Welch, Hank B. Marvin), "We Say Yeah" (Welch, Marvin, Peter Gormley), "Lessons In Love" (Sy Soloway, Shirley Wolfe).

p, Kenneth Harper; d, Sidney J. Furie; w, Ronald Cass, Peter Myers; ph, Douglas Slocombe (CinemaScope, Technicolor); m, Stanley Black; ed, Jack Slade; art d, John Howell; ch, Herbert Ross; cos, Alan Sievewright.

Comedy/Musical   (PR:A MPAA:NR)

WONDERFUL WORLD OF THE BROTHERS GRIMM, THE**
(1962) 135m MGM-Cinerama/MGM c

Laurence Harvey (*Wilhelm Grimm*), Karl Boehm (*Jacob Grimm*), Claire Bloom (*Dorothea Grimm*), Walter Slezak (*Stossel*), Barbara Eden (*Greta Heinrich*), Oscar Homolka (*The Duke*), Arnold Stang (*Rumpelstiltskin*), Martita Hunt (*Story Teller*), Betty Garde (*Miss Bettenhausen*), Bryan Russell (*Friedrich Grim*), Ian Wolfe (*Gruber*), Tammy Marihugh (*Pauline Grimm*), Cheerio Meredith (*Mrs. von Dittersdorf*), Walter Rilla (*Priest*), Regensburg Domspatzen Choir, "The Dancing Princess": Yvette Mimieux (*The Princess*), Russ Tamblyn (*The Woodsman*), Jim Backus (*The King*), Beulah Bondi (*The Gypsy*), Clinton Sundberg (*The Prime Minister*), "The Cobbler and the Elves": Laurence Harvey (*The Cobbler*), Walter Brooke (*The Mayor*), Sandra Gale Bettin (*The Ballerina*), Robert Foulk (*The Hunter*), The Puppetoons, "The Singing Bone": Terry-Thomas (*Ludwig*), Buddy Hackett (*Hans*), Otto Kruger (*The King*), Robert Crawford, Jr. (*The Shepherd*), Sydney Smith (*The Spokesman*).

THE WONDERFUL WORLD OF THE BROTHERS GRIMM was not all that wonderful. Matter of fact, when one considers that this was the second Cinerama-process film that had a story to it, that famed producer-director George Pal had a hand in it, and that the film had an all-star cast, it was downright disappointing. Three of the Grimm tales are used but they are not the right ones. The stories are shown along with a highly fictionalized bit of the lives of the two brothers, played by Boehm and Harvey. It's early in the 1800s and Harvey and Boehm have been asked by the authorities to write a tale of the local squire's family in the Bavarian area in which they reside. The duke, Homolka, wants a laudatory piece but Harvey finds himself distracted and spends most of his time telling his wife, Bloom, and his brother some of the folk tales he has compiled. The first of them is "The Dancing Princess" and he sits down one night to relate the story to his children, Russell and Marihugh. Backus is the king in this tale. His daughter is Mimieux and he can't understand why she wears out a pair of slippers every single day. To learn the answer to this, Backus offers her hand in marriage to the first man who can uncover the reason. Tamblyn is a young woodsman. He puts on a "cloak of invisibility" and trails Mimieux into the forest one night where she joins with a pack of gypsies, lead by Bondi. She dances with the gypsies and Tamblyn joins in. The two fall in love. Later, Tamblyn goes to Backus and gives him the answer to his question. Backus must keep his bargain so he tells Mimieux that she must marry Tamblyn. She, of course, is thrilled. Cut back to what's happening and we see Harvey trying to convince the local bookseller, Slezak, that there is a market for his kind of fairy tales. Slezak is not convinced so Harvey tells his next story to some children in order to prove his point. It's "The Cobbler and the Elves." Harvey is an aged shoemaker who is not keeping his customers happy because he neglects their shoes in favor of carving elves for orphans who have no presents for Christmas. Bone-tired, Harvey falls asleep and his creations come to life and take care of his shoe business so that when he awakens, the work has been done. Back into the present and Homolka, who is getting rankled, wants some action on his family history. He dispatches Harvey to a nearby town to do some research on another section of the family. Harvey encounters Hunt, a witch, or so it is thought, who lives in the forest. All she is, though, is a storyteller and the children of the nearby town love her. Harvey sits in as she tells them the story of "The Singing Bone." Hackett is a humble servant who kills a mean dragon. Then he is murdered by his boss, Terry-Thomas, who takes all of the applause for having slain the dragon. One of Hackett's bones becomes a musical instrument and it tells of Terry-Thomas' lies and the fact that Hackett is the true hero. When Terry-Thomas admits the truth, Hackett comes back to life and becomes Terry-Thomas' boss. Harvey leaves the forest and loses all of the material he's gathered for Homolka, who fires him. Boehm has been seeing Eden and decides to marry her and work without his brother. Harvey becomes very sick and is near death when all of his mental creations "arrive" and plead with him to recover so their tales can be told. Harvey recovers, Boehm postpones his wedding in order to help support Harvey's family while he gets better, and the brothers unite again, finally achieving recognition from the Academy in Berlin, although Harvey is irked that Boehm's writings were apparently more appreciated than his own fairy tales. When they get to the German capital, Harvey's spirits are raised as he finds hundreds of children there awaiting his arrival so he cantell them one of his stories. Bob Merrill wrote several tunes for the film including: "The Theme from the Wonderful World of the Brothers Grimm," "Gypsy Rhapsody," "Christmas Land," "Ah-Oom," "Above the Stars," "Dee-Are-A-Gee-O-En (Dragon)," and he collaborated with coscreenwriter Beaumont on "Singing Bone." Many local people from the Rhine River Valley as well as residents of Rothenburg and Dinkelsbuhl help lend a feeling of authenticity. The picture was premiered for prospective exhibitors and members of the Fourth Estate in Denver, at the Cooper Theatre, which was designed specifically for the Cinerama process of the time. The hemispherical building accommodated the curved screens to which three separate films were projected in synchronization, virtually surrounding the audience with imagery. The very first story film made in the process, HOW THE WEST WAS WON (1962), used the original Cinerama technique: three cameras on the same platform recorded the action, the cameras being fanned out to catch a wide panorama. This second story film used an entirely different technique, resembling the other systems widely used in decades to come. A single camera using 70mm film was employed; this eliminated some of the objections raised by viewers of the older process, such as image overlaps and asynchronous flutterings. The curved screens were still used in the newer technique.

p, George Pal; d, Henry Levin, (fairy tales sequence, Pal); w, David P. Harmon, Charles Beaumont, William Roberts (based on *Die Bruder Grimm* by Herman Gerstner, screen story by Harmon); ph, Paul C. Vogel (Cinerama, Metrocolor); m, Leigh Harline; ed, Walter Thompson; art d, George W. Davis, Edward Carfagno; set d, Henry Grace, Dick Pefferle; cos, Mary Wills; spec eff, Gene Warren, Wah Chang, Tim Barr, Robert R. Hoag; ch, Alex Romero; makeup, William Tuttle.

Musical/Fantasy   **Cas.**   **(PR:A-C MPAA:NR)**

WONDERFUL YEARS, THE   (SEE: RESTLESS YEARS, THE, 1958)

WONDERS OF ALADDIN, THE*½   (1961, Fr./Ital.) 93m Lux Film-C.C.F. Lux/MGM c (LES MILLE ET UNE NUITS; LE MERAVIGLIE DI ALADINO)

Donald O'Connor (*Aladdin*), Noelle Adam (*Djalma*), Vittorio De Sica (*Genie*), Aldo Fabrizi (*Sultan*), Michele Mercier (*Princess Zaina*), Milton Reid (*Omar*), Mario Girotti (*Prince Moluk*), Fausto Tozzi (*Grand Vizier*), Marco Tulli (*Fakir*), Raymond Bussieres (*Magician*), Alberto Farnese (*Bandit Chieftain*), Franco Ressel (*Vizier's Lieutenant*), Vittorio Bonos (*Lamp Merchant*), Adriana Facchetti (*Aladdin's Mother Benhai*), Giovanna Galletti (*Midwife*), Luigi Tosi.

O'Connor stars in this childish retelling of the Aladdin's lamp tale, casting De Sica as the genie. O'Connor uses his three wishes to get out of a jam when he robs some merchants; to avoid death at the hands of a murderous Amazon; and finally to save his city from destruction. Schlock horror director Mario Bava acted as second unit director. The kids might buy this hunk of gibberish, but it's not likely.

p, Joseph E. Levine; d, Henry Levin; w, Luther Davis, Silvano Reina, Franco Prosperi, Pierre Very, Marc Vicario (based on a story by Stefano Strucchi, Duccio Tessari); ph, Tonino Delli Colli (CinemaScope, Technicolor); m, Angelo Francesco Lavagnino; ed, Gene Ruggiero; md, Mario Ammonini; art d, Flavio Mogherini; cos, Giorgio Desideri, Rosine Delamare; ch, Secondino Cavallo.

Fantasy/Adventure   **(PR:AA MPAA:NR)**

WONDERWALL*½   (1969, Brit.) 92m Cinecenta c

Jack MacGowran (*Oscar Collins*), Jane Birkin (*Penny*), Irene Handl (*Mrs. Peurofoy*), Richard Wattis (*Perkins*), Iain Quarrier (*Young Man*), Beatrix Lehmann (*Mother*), Brian Walsh (*Photographer*), Sean Lynch (*Riley*), Bea Duffell (*Mrs. Charmer*).

MacGowran stars as a butterfly collector who discovers one day that he can watch his neighbor Birkin, a model, through a crack in his wall. As he becomes obsessed with his voyeurism, his psychedelic fantasies provide the occasion for some bizarre camerawork. Written by long-time Polanski collaborator Brach and produced by Braunsberg (both of whom worked on Polanski's THE TENANT), WONDERWALL features a score by then-Beatle George Harrison.

p, Andrew Braunsberg; d, Joe Massot; w, G. Cain (based on a story by Gerard Brach); ph, Harry Waxman (Eastmancolor); m, George Harrison; ed, Rusty Coppleman; art d, Assheton Gorton; cos, Jocelyn Rickards.

Drama   **(PR:O MPAA:NR)**

WOODEN HORSE, THE***½   (1951) 101m BL-Wessex/BL-Snader bw

Leo Genn (*Peter*), David Tomlinson (*Phil*), Anthony Steel (*John*), David Greene (*Bennett*), Peter Burton (*Nigel*), Patrick Waddington (*Senior British Officer*), Michael Goodliffe (*Robbie*), Anthony Dawson (*Pomfret*), Bryan Forbes (*Paul*), Franz Schaftheitlein (*Commandant*), Hans Meyer (*Charles*), Jacques Brunius (*Andre*), Peter Finch (*The Australian*), Dan Cunningham (*David*), Russell Waters (*"Wings" Cameron*), Ralph Ward (*Adjutant*), Herbert Kilitz (*Camp Guard*), Lis Lovert (*Kamma*), Helge Ericksen (*Sigmund*), Walter Hertner (*German Policeman*), Meinhart Maur (*Hotel Proprietor*), Walter Gotell (*The Follower*), Philip Dale, Bill Travers, Johannes Johanson.

Probably the cleverest escape of WW II was pulled off by British prisoners at Stalag Luft III in 1943. Deciding that the distance to tunnel from the barracks to the outside is too great, Genn, Steel, and Tomlinson hit on a brilliant scheme. They construct a boxlike vaulting horse and daily have it carried out to the yard for a few hours of exercise. Inside, though, are one and sometimes two men who start a tunnel from underneath the horse, then cover it over at the end of each day's vaulting. After months of digging and several near detections by the Germans, the tunnel is ready. Three men remain in the tunnel after the vaulting and when it becomes dark, they break through the last few feet of ground to the surface, safely beyond the fence. Genn and Steel travel together, making contact with the French and Danish underground and eventually are spirited to Sweden by sympathetic Danes. In Stockholm they meet Tomlinson, who has also been successful in his escape. This was the first of the British prisoner-of-war films, and set the style for all to come. As one British writer has pointed out, the camps are

"the nearest thing to their public schools the officer heroes of these films have experienced. Both school and camp are alike—in the absence of women, the spartan conditions, the rigorous discipline, and a hierarchic system in which the Jerries function as rather nasty prefects, who exist simply to be tricked and humiliated." THE WOODEN HORSE suffers from this same trivialization of what was really a horrible and degrading experience, but as an adventure drama it is more than successful. All the leads are well done in the stiff-upper-lip style of British war heroes, and the film is suspenseful and fast-moving. One of the best of this subgenre.

p, Ian Dalrymple; d, Jack Lee; w, Eric Williams (based on the book by Williams); ph, G. Pennington-Richards; m, Clifton Parker; ed, John Seabourne, Sr., Peter Seabourne; prod d, William Kellner; md, Muir Mathieson.

War/Prison Drama   **(PR:A MPAA:NR)**

WOORUZHYON I OCHEN OPASEN   (SEE: ARMED AND DANGEROUS, 1977, USSR)

WORD, THE   (SEE: ORDET, 1957, Den.)

WORDS AND MUSIC**   (1929) 72m FOX bw

Lois Moran (*Mary Brown*), David Percy (*Phil Denning*), Helen Twelvetrees (*Dorothy Bracey*), Elizabeth Patterson (*Dean Crockett*), William Orlamond (*Pop Evans*), Duke Morrison [John Wayne] (*Pete Donahue*), Frank Albertson (*Skeet Mulroy*), Tom Patricola (*Hannibal*), Ward Bond (*Ward*), Richard Keene (*Singer in "Stepping Along"*), Dorothy Ward (*Girl*), Bubbles Crowell (*Bubbles*), Collier Sisters (*Dancers*), Eddie Bush, Paul Gibbons, Bill Seckler, Ches Kirkpatrick (*Biltmore Quartet*), Vina Gale, Arthur Springer, Harriet Griffith, John Griffith, Helen Hunt, Charles Huff (*Adagio Dancers*), Sugar Adair, Iris Ashton, Lita Chevret, Marie Cooper, Blanche Fisher, Katherine Irving, Lucile Jacques, Jean Lorraine, Marion Mills, Sue Rainey, Betty Recklaw (*Showgirls*), Harry Albers, Sayre Dearing, Carl Dial, Tom Gentry, Kenneth Gibson, Dick Gordon, Earl Hughes, Earl McCarthy, William Miller, Paul Power, Maurice Salvage, John Sylvester, M. Troubetsky (*Chorus Men*), Darline Addison, Julie Blake, Raymonda Brown, Adele Cutler, Diana Dare, Dot Darling, Lucille Day, June Glory, Charlotte Hagaler, Kathryne Hankin, Billy Kittridge, Paula Langlen, Mildred Laube, Mildred Livingston, Helen Louise, Mae Madison, Peggy Malloy, Mavis May, Emily Renard, Bobby Renee, Thelma Roberts, Bernice Snell, Darleen Ver Jean, Marion Waldon, Wilma Wray (*Young Ladies of the Ensemble*), Muriel Gardner, Dorothy Jordan, Helen Parrish, David Percy, Jack Wade (*Song and Dance Principalss*).

John Wayne (here billed as Duke Morrison) took sixth billing in this standard musical exercise as a composer in competition with Percy to take a $1,500 college prize for the best show tune. Moran agrees to sing for both of them but chooses Percy as her beau; Percy's also is the winning tune. The story, as usual in this sort of pic, is negligible with concentration on Moran's musical talent. Her numbers were reportedly outtakes from MOVIETONE FOLLIES OF 1929 that had to be used somehow. Songs include: "Too Wonderful for Words" (William Kernell, Dave Stamper, Paul Gerard Smith, Edmund Joseph), "Stepping Alo ng" (Kernell), "Shadows" (Con Conrad, Sidney Mitchell, Archie Gottler).

d, James Tinling; w, Andrew Bennison (based on a story by Frederick Hazlitt Brennan, Jack McEdwards); ph, Charles Clarke, Charles Van Enger, Don Anderson; ed, Ralph Dixon; md, Arthur Kay; ch, Frank Merlin, Edward Royce; cos, Sophie Wachner.

Musical   **(PR:A MPAA:NR)**

WORDS AND MUSIC**½   (1948) 119m MGM c

Perry Como (*Eddie Lorrison Anders*), Mickey Rooney (*Lorenz "Larry" Hart*), Ann Sothern (*Joyce Harmon*), Tom Drake (*Richard "Dick" Rodgers*), Betty Garrett (*Peggy Lorgan McNeil*), Janet Leigh (*Dorothy Feiner*), Marshall Thompson (*Herbert Fields*), Jeanette Nolan (*Mrs. Hart*), Richard Quine (*Ben Feiner, Jr.*), Clinton Sundberg (*Shoe Clerk*), Harry Antrim (*Dr. Rodgers*), Ilka Gruning (*Mrs. Rodgers*), Emory Parnell (*Mr. Feiner*), Helen Spring (*Mrs. Feiner*), Edward Earle (*James Fernby Kelly*), Cyd Charisse (*Margo Grant*), Judy Garland, June Allyson, The Blackburn Twins, Gene Kelly, Vera-Ellen, Mel Torme (*Guest Stars*), Allyn Ann McLerie, John Butler, Dee Turnell, Sid Frohlich.

Film biographies of composers are usually short on fact and long on wonderful musical numbers. This is no exception. Lorenz Hart and Richard Rodgers led relatively unexceptional professional lives, turning out hit after hit, with rarely an ill word between the two. Hart never married because of his homosexuality, but since such a topic was unheard of for 1940s Hollywood productions, a largely fabricated story was concocted. Hart (Rooney) meets Rodgers (Drake) in the 1920s. The two decide to compose songs together, and before long are successful. Drake meets Leigh, and love blossoms. They marry while Rooney, the more colorful of the pair, tries to woo Garrett. Garrett rejects Rooney, but he continues to pine for her. Loneliness combined with alcohol wears down Rooney despite his overwhelming successes with Drake. Rooney finally succumbs to his self-induced physical punishment and passes away at the height of his creativity. The story, as expected, is simplistic and not very well played. Rooney is all ham, throwing about a good deal of energy with no central focus. Drake, on the other hand, is as boring as his character is supposed to be, yet without any of the marvelous talent. There is no insight into the relationship between the pair, or into the creative process. The fictionalized Rodgers and Hart story is simply an unimaginative soap opera, taking predictable twist after twist. What gives this film its strength is the wonderful music. Plenty of Rodgers and Hart tunes fill in the story, performed by some of the best talents MGM had in its stock company. Garland's rendition of "Johnny One Note" is a showstopper, as the singer gives the number everything she's got. Garland was on suspension from the studio at the time for a variety of infractions caused by her growing addiction to drugs, and related illnesses. Still, she was highly regarded by studio chief Louis B. Mayer, who offered her $50,000 if she could do the number. Garland, who was being fed glucose intravenously, took up the offer. Despite her condition, Garland's performance was phenomenal. Mayer was highly impressed, and though the singer was on still on suspension, he offered her another $50,000 for an encore number. Garland, buoyed by success, regained her health and put on 20 pounds for her duet with Rooney: "I Wish I Were in Love Again." Leigh, in her book *There Really Was a Hollywood*, recalled: "Around eleven o'clock Mr. (Arthur) Freed escorted Miss Garland to the stage, where she was greeted like royalty....My God, she was pure magic. I was hypnotized. When she and Mickey sang and danced they lit up that sound stage like exploding rockets." Another of the highlights in WORDS AND MUSIC is Kelly's re-creation of "Slaughter on Tenth Avenue," originally choreographed on Broadway by George Balanchine (and danced by Ray Bolger) in the 1937 show "On Your Toes." Kelly cut the piece from eleven to seven minutes, putting emphasis on the dance's dramatic moments. After four weeks of rehearsals, the sequence was filmed in three days. The reception was tremendous, and the piece set new standards in cinematic dancing. Both Kelly and his partner, Vera-Ellen, are marvelous. Vera-Ellen, one of Kelly's favorite dance partners, considered this the best work of her career. Other Rodgers and Hart songs include: "The Lady Is a Tramp," "Where or When" (sung by Lena Horne), "Thou Swell" (sung by June Allyson and The Blackburn Twins), "This Can't Be Love" (sung by Cyd Charisse, Dee Turnell), "Blue Room," "With a Song in My Heart" (sung by Perry Como), "Spring Is Here Again," "Manhattan" (sung by Rooney), "Way Out West on West End Avenue," "There's a Small Hotel" (sung by Garrett), "Where's that Rainbow" (sung by Ann Sothern), "Blue Moon" (sung by Mel Torme), "Mountain Greenery" (sung by Como, Allyn McLerie), "Lover," "A Tree in the Park," "On Your Toes," "You Took Advantage of Me," "Someone Should Tell Them," "I Didn't Know What Time It Was," "I Married an Angel," "Spring Is Here," "My Romance," "We'll Be the Same," "Here in My Arms," "Yours Sincerely," "The Girl Friend," "Ship Without a Sail," "March of the Knights," "Nothing But You," "Hollywood Party," "Dancing on the Ceiling."

p, Arthur Freed; d, Norman Taurog; w, Fred Finklehoffe, Ben Feiner, Jr. (based on a story by Guy Bolton, Jean Holloway, adapted by Feiner, Holloway, Bolton, Isabel Lennart, Jack Mintz); ph, Charles Rosher, Harry Stradling (Technicolor); ed, Albert Akst, Ferris Webster; md, Lennie Hayton; art d, Cedric Gibbons, Jack Martin Smith; set d, Edwin B. Willis, Richard A. Pefferle; cos, Helen Rose, Valles; spec eff, Warren Newcombe; ch, Robert Alton; makeup, Jack Dawn.

Musical/Biography   (PR:A   MPAA:NR)

WORK IS A FOUR LETTER WORD**   (1968, Brit.) 93m
                                                      Cavalcade/UNIV c

David Warner (*Val Brose*), Cilla Black (*Betty Dorrick*), Elizabeth Spriggs (*Mrs. Murray*), Zia Mohyeddin (*Dr. Narayana*), Joe Gladwyn (*Pa Brose*), Julie May (*Mrs. Dorrick*), Alan Howard (*The Reverend Mort*), Jan Holden (*Mrs. Price*), John Steiner (*Anthony*), Roger Booth (*Pincher*), Tony Church (*Arkwright*), Derek Royle (*Briggs*), David Waller (*Mr. Price*), Cyril Cross (*Commissionaire*), Gladys Dawson (*Gran*), Donegal (*Gramps*), Royston Tickner (*Train Guard*), Clifford Rose, Paul Dawkins, Tommy Godfrey, Peter Hutchins, Gordon Craig.

Offbeat comedy has its roots in some fantasy world of the future where man is pitted against machinery and automation. Warner is an eccentric fellow more concerned with cultivating mushrooms than working or paying attention to his wife-to-be Black. He takes a job in a power plant, knocks out the entire city's power, and feeds the authorities his mushrooms, sending them into hallucinogenic bliss. He then is able to escape with Black and a baby carriage loaded with mushrooms. Occasionally hilarious but without much direction or purpose.

p, Thomas Clyde; d, Peter Hall; w, Jeremy Brooks (based on the play "Eh?" by Henry Livings); ph, Gilbert Taylor (Technicolor) m, Guy Woolfenden; ed, KeithGreen; art d, Philip Harrison; spec eff, Michael Stainer-Hutchins; cos, Ruth Myers; m/l, "Work Is a Four Letter Word" Woolfenden, Don Black (sung by Cilla Black).

Comedy/Fantasy   (PR:C   MPAA:PG)

WORKING GIRLS**   (1931) 80m PAR bw

Paul Lukas, Frances Dee, Judith Wood, Charles Rogers, Dorothy Hall, Stuart Erwin, Alberta Vaughn, Dorothy Stickney, Mary Forbes, Frances Moffett, Claire Dodd.

A typical "woman's picture" boasted the adroit hand of director Dorothy Arzner as well as the writing talents of Zoe Akins and Vera Caspary (on whose novel LAURA, 1941, was based). The plot is similar to other Akins-penned pictures and tells the story of two country girls, Dee and Wood, who head to the big city. After some misadventures they find themselves jobs and husbands. Pictures like WORKING GIRLS served their purpose back when films were separated into "men's pictures" (gangster and western genres) and "women's pictures" (weepy melodramas and films like this one), and might now fit with movies like NINE TO FIVE, but their obsession with finding guys for the gals makes them seem hopelessly out of date.

d, Dorothy Arzner; w, Zoe Akins (based on the story "Blind Mice" by Vera Caspary, Winifred Lenihan); ph, Harry Fischbeck.

Drama   (PR:A   MPAA:NR)

WORKING GIRLS, THE**   (1973) 81m Dimension c

Sarah Kennedy (*Honey*), Mary Beth Hughes (*Mrs. Borden*), Laurie Rose (*Denise*), Mark Thomas (*Nick*), Lynne Guthrie (*Jill*), Ken Del Conte (*Mike*), Solomon Sturges (*Vernon*), Gene Elman (*Sidney*), Cassandra Peterson (*Stripper*), Lou Tiano, Bob Schott.

Three women living together in Los Angeles are hard up for cash. This trio will do just about any and everything for money, which leads to some predictable though mildly amusing hijinks. Peterson later became popular on television with her "Elvira" character, while Sturges is the son of the great comedy director Preston Sturges. Apparently not everything of his father's was passed through the genes.

p, Charles S. Swartz; d&w, Stephanie Rothman; ph, (Metrocolor).

Comedy   **Cas.**   (PR:O   MPAA:R)

WORKING MAN, THE**½   (1933) 77m WB bw (AKA: THE
                                                    ADOPTED FATHER)

George Arliss (*John Reeves*), Bette Davis (*Jenny Hartland*), Hardie Albright (*Benjamin Burnett*), Theodore Newton (*Tommy Hartland*), Gordon West-cott (*Freddie Pettison*), J. Farrell MacDonald (*Hank Davidson*), Charles Evans (*Haslitt*), Frederick Burton (*Judge Larson*), Pat Wing (*Secretary*), Edward Van Sloan (*Briggs*), Claire McDowell (*Stenographer*), Ruthelma Stevens (*Mrs. Price*), Edward Cooper (*Butler*), Harold Minjur (*Tommy's Bridge Partner*), Gertrude Sutton (*Maid*), Douglas Dumbrille (*Lawyer Hammersmith*), Richard Tucker (*Board Member*), James Bush (*Bridge Player*), Selmer Jackson, Clay Clement, James Donlan (*Company Men*), Wallis Clark.

Arliss is a millionaire shoe manufacturer who is bored. His chief rival, the head of Hartland Shoes, dies leaving his own company on the brink of bankruptcy and Arliss without adequate competition to spur him on. Arliss takes off on a vacation, putting his eager nephew, Albright, in charge of the firm. While on holiday he meets Davis and Newton, a fun-loving brother and sister who are actually heirs to the Hartland company. Arliss pretends to be a destitute bum and is offered work in the shoe factory by the Hartlands. In no time at all he turns a profit and begins competing with his know-it-all nephew. He also teaches Davis and Newton a thing or two about life, forcing them to take jobs in the factory after becoming their legal guardian. By the finale he reveals his true identity and gives his blessings to the blossoming romance of Davis and the now-wiser nephew Albright. A thoroughly enjoyable piece of entertainment which serves no other purpose than to put a smile on your face.

p, Jack L. Warner; d, John G. Adolfi; w, Charles Kenyon, Maude T. Howell (based on the story "The Adopted Father" by Edgar Franklin); ph, Sol Polito; ed, Owen Marks; art d, Jack Okey; cos, Orry-Kelly.

Drama/Comedy   (PR:A   MPAA:NR)

WORKING WIVES   (SEE: WEEK-END MARRIAGE, 1932)

WORLD ACCORDING TO GARP, THE***½
                                            (1982) 136m Pan Arts/WB c

Robin Williams (*T.S. Garp*), Mary Beth Hurt (*Helen Holm*), Glenn Close (*Jenny Fields*), John Lithgow (*Roberta Muldoon*), Hume Cronyn (*Mr. Fields*), Jessica Tandy (*Mrs. Fields*), Swoosie Kurtz (*Hooker*), James McCall (*Young Garp*), Peter Michael Goetz (*John Wolfe*), George Ede (*Dean Bodger*), Mark Soper (*Michael Milton*), Nathan Babcock (*Duncan*), Ian MacGregor (*Walt*), Warren Berlinger (*Stew Percy*), Susan Browning (*Midge Percy*), Brandon Maggart (*Ernie Holm*), Jenny Wright (*Cushie*), Brenda Currin (*Pooh*), Jillian Ross (*Young Cushie*), Laurie Robyn (*Young Pooh*), Victor Magnotta (*1st Coach*), Dominic A. Cecere (*Opposing Coach*), John Irving (*Referee*), Dan Goldman (*Wrestler*), Christopher Farr (*Bosworth*), Brett Littman (*Zipper Boy*), Brendon Roth (*Infant Garp*), Steven Krey (*Baby Sitter*), Al Cerullo, Jr. (*Helicopter*), Matthew C. Materazo, Deborah Watkins (*Roof Stunt*), Mark Sutton (*Car Stunt*), Amanda Plummer (*Ellen James*), Bette Henritze (*Candidate*), Jeanne DeBaer (*Speaker*), Ron Frazier (*Stephen*), Katherine Borowitz (*Rachel*), Isabell Monk (*Woman with Book*), Edgard L. Mourino (*Piano Stunt*), John S. Corcoran (*Man in Tree*), Tim

Gallin (Freman), Kate McGregor-Stewart (Real Estate Lady), Sabrina Lee Moore (Baby Sitter), James Appleby (Stunt Pilot), Matthew Cowles (Speeding Plumber), Eve Gordon (Marge), David Fields (Infant Duncan), Ryan David (Duncan at Age 2), Kaiulani Lee (Chief Ellen Jamesian), Harris Laskawy (Randy), Lori Shelle (Laurel), Kath Reiter (Alice), Thomas Peter Daikos (Flying Baby Garp), Laura Kaye.

It's often unfair to compare a movie to the novel from whence it sprung because they are, after all, two different kinds of writing and what works on the printed page often falls flat on the screen. Still, from time to time, that comparison must be made. In Tesich's screenplay of Irving's most successful novel, there had to be cuts made and the casting of Williams in the leading role was a surprise to those who'd only thought of him comedically, so what was expected was "The World According to Mork," but that's not what was delivered. It's a bittersweet tale of a man's growth from birth to adulthood and how he deals with the vices of lust and fanaticism that whirl around him. Williams is almost a solo creation of his mother, Close (who was breathtaking in the part). It's 1944 and Close wants a child but not a husband. A soldier lies dying in the hospital and Close has sex with him as his last act on earth. She becomes pregnant, thus shocking her conservative parents, Tandy and Cronyn, by her renegade act. Close is a nurse and well able to take care of herself and her love child (played by Daikos, Roth, and McCall, before maturing into Williams). Close and McCall move into a preppie boys' boarding school and the young lad grows up wanting a father, wanting to fly, and fearing death. McCall is interested in sex and that curiosity almost kills him when his neighbor (Robyn) sics a dog on him as he is moving in on Robyn's equally curious and pre-pubescent sister. He also almost dies when he climbs to the top of the main building. McCall gives way to Williams (looking a bit old to be a teenager) who wants to be a writer and loves wrestling at the school. (Look for author Irving in a cameo appearance as a referee in a wrestling match scene.) The young lad is bubbling with lust and eager to have some hands-on experiences so he can write about them, rather than fantasize. Williams meets Hurt, daughter of wrestling coach Maggart, and he attempts to impress her with his writing. It doesn't work so he turns to the flame of his youth for sex and when the bete noire sister tells that to a hurt Hurt, the woman ignores Williams' first short story. Williams is about ready to leave the school and go to college just as Close is finishing her autobiography "A Sexual Suspect," and preparing to take it to New York to have it published. Dissolve and Williams returns from college as a real author about to have his first novel published. He is now engaged to Hurt, who helped him on his book. But it is Close who becomes the literary lioness as her book is a smash hit and the feminist movement embraces her. Williams is somewhat envious of his mother's success but he surprises that as he continues writing and raising the two sons Hurt has borne him. Close's book inspires a movement, known as the "Ellen Jamesians," which is inspired by the rape and tongue removal of a young woman named Ellen James. In order to be part of this movement, many young women have their tongues removed (no jokes here!). Close throws open her huge home as a haven for the "Ellen Jamesians" so Williams and family are surrounded by a horde of mute and militant women. Lithgow arrives. He is a former football player who has elected to become transsexual and is part of the covey who inhabit Close's home. Williams stays at his nearby home with his wife and two sons, Babcock and MacGregor. And while he enjoys being a father, he doesn't much like getting older. He tries his best to teach the boys about life and its undertow (which the youths call the "undertoad") and he is limited by his own inability to fathom mortality. Hurt has begun her own career as a teacher as he continues to write and publish but their relationship rapidly fills with ennui. He has a fling with Moore, an 18-year-old baby sitter, and Hurt takes Soper, one of her students, as her lover. She is in need of love and open to Soper's advances but she maintains that discretion is of the utmost importance. Williams finds out about Hurt's affair and is devastated. His own dalliance is minor by comparison (to him, although Hurt may not share that opinion) and he orders her to cease seeing Soper, then leaves. Soper continues attempting to date her and she decides to meet with him one more time. They are seated in the front of a large Buick and Soper pleads with her for sexual pleasure. She agrees and is in the process of performing an act when Williams arrives in his old Volvo, with the children in the car. They have a little game they play whereby he cuts off his lights and drives in the darkness into their driveway. Because he doesn't have his lights on and he surely doesn't expect a car to be where he usually puts his car, the Volvo smashes into the rear of the Buick and Soper is turned into capon by Hurt's teeth. MacGregor is killed, Babcock loses an eye, and both Hurt and Williams are seriously injured. They take time off to heal at Close's home where Williams and Lithgow become friendly. Close becomes politically involved and is speaking at a rally on behalf of a feminist candidate when she is assassinated. The world is shocked and the "Ellen Jamesians" are madder than ever (though not any more vocal). Williams eventually meets Plummer (the real "Ellen James") who thanks him for writing a book about her (even though he has never understood the rage); she kisses him and that is his absolution. Williams appears to be happy now and returns to his old school to become the wrestling coach. He wants to rest, to spend more time with what remains of his family, and to have some days to ruminate on his life. Currin, the mature version of the woman who had been his nemesis from the time the young Garp trifled with her sister, walks into the wrestling room and shoots Williams. We are glad to learn that Williams will live and, at the conclusion, he's flown away with Hurt in a helicopter. The music of "When I'm Sixty-Four" (John Lennon, Paul McCartney) plays over

the end credits, as it did over the opening. Excellent performances from all and a special kudos for the children, who show none of the cutesiness that so often occurs when youngsters work. The movie was not a huge success, despite its excellence. Williams was a tower and showed more in this movie than in most of his other films. The picture was long at 136 minutes, but there was so much story to tell that it's understandable. A bit less adherence to the original might have benefited the production. All in all, a tasteful adaptation of something that could have been tasteless in another director's hands.

p, George Roy Hill, Robert L. Crawford; d, Hill; w, Steve Tesich (based on the novel by John Irving); ph, Miroslav Ondricek (Technicolor); ed, Ronald Roose, Stephen A. Rotter; prod d, Henry Bumstead; art d, Woods Mackintosh; set d, Robert Drumheller, Justin Scoppa, Jr.; cos, Ann Roth; animation, John Canemaker.

Drama   Cas.   (PR:C-O   MPAA:R)

WORLD ACCUSES, THE*½   (1935) 62m CHES bw

Vivian Tobin, Dickie Moore, Russell Hopton, Cora Sue Collins, Mary Carr, Robert Elliott, Jameson Thomas, Barbara Bedford, Paul Fix, Harold Huber, Bryant Washburn, Jane Keckley, Robert Frazer, Sarah Edwards, Lloyd Ingraham, Broderick O'Farrell.

Tobin loses custody of her son, Moore, after her wealthy husband dies. She takes a job at the nursery her son attends, unaware, however, that the child is her own. A further unbelievable twist occurs when Tobin's former love, Huber, escapes from prison and hides out in her attic, taking Moore and young friend Collins hostage. The police arrive, guns are fired, the children are saved, Huber is shot, but in the end it all works out for the best.

p, Lon Young; d, Charles Lamont; w, Charles Belden; ph, M.A. Anderson; ed, Roland Reed.

Drama   (PR:A   MPAA:NR)

WORLD AND HIS WIFE, THE (SEE: STATE OF THE UNION, 1948)

WORLD AND THE FLESH, THE*½   (1932) 75m PAR bw

George Bancroft (Kylenko), Miriam Hopkins (Maria Yaskaya), Alan Mowbray (Duke Dimitri), George E. Stone (Rutchkin), Emmett Corrigan (Gen. Spiro), Mitchell Lewis (Sukhanov), Oscar Apfel (Banker), Harry Cording (Ivan Ivanovitch), Max Wagner (Vorobiov), Reginald Barlow (Markov), Ferike Boros (Sasha, Maria's Maid), Francis McDonald, Michael Mark, Henry Victor, Bob Kortman (Reds), Lucien Prival (Cossack).

Bancroft, a mercenary sea captain, sticks out his neck in order to save Russian emigre dancer Hopkins, who also happens to be involved with Mowbray, a grand duke. Bancroft proves that he is a better lover than a fighter when, in the finale, Hopkins is the only one of the fleeing Russians to make it successfully to safety in France.

d, John Cromwell; w, Oliver H.P. Garrett (based on a play by Philip Zeska, Ernst Spitz); ph, Karl Struss.

Drama   (PR:A   MPAA:NR)

WORLD CHANGES, THE***   (1933) 90m WB-FN bw

Paul Muni (Orin Nordholm, Jr.), Aline MacMahon (Anna Nordholm), Mary Astor (Virginia), Donald Cook (Richard Nordholm), Patricia Ellis (Natalie), Jean Muir (Selma Peterson), Margaret Lindsay (Jennifer), Guy Kibbee (Claflin), Theodore Newton (Paul), Alan Dinehart (Ogden Jarrett), Henry O'Neill (Orin Nordholm, Sr.), Anna Q. Nilsson (Mrs. Peterson), Douglas Dumbrille (Buffalo Bill), Clay Clement (Capt. Custer), Gordon Westcott (John), Alan Mowbray (Sir Phillip), William Janney (Orin II), Marjorie Gateson (Mrs. Clinton), Arthur Hohl, Philip Faversham, Sidney Toler, George Meeker, Mickey Rooney, Jackie Searle, Marjorie Gateson, Oscar Apfel, William Burress, Wallis Clark, Willard Robertson.

The "world" of the title is America's Midwest and the "change" takes place from 1852 until the stock market crash of 1929. The film centers on the Nordholm family, a group of pioneers who have called the Dakotas their home. Young Muni decides to leave the home of his parents–MacMahon and O'Neill – and head for Texas with a herd of cattle. Eventually he meets Kibbee, the owner of a Chicago slaughterhouse, and forms a partnership with him. Soon Muni has fallen in love with Kibbee's daughter, Astor, and the pair marry, settling down to a posh life style. By now, Muni has made a fortune by devising a way to ship beef in refrigerated train cars. After the birth of two sons and the death of Kibbee, Muni's future appears to be a solid and prosperous one. As the years pass, Astor grows discontented with her standard of living and views her husband's occupation as a "butcher" socially unacceptable. She tries to pressure him into selling his company and investing in a stock brokerage firm for their now-grown son, Cook, who has recently married Lindsay, the daughter of a New York high-society family. Astor continues her manipulative attempts to get Muni to sell, but fails and is reduced to lunacy and, eventually, death. As time progresses to 1929, the world has changed even more. Muni, now a grandfather, has sold his meat business and invested in his son's brokerage business. When the market crashes, Cook turns to embezzlement to cushion his fall, but instead winds up facing a prison sentence. In the hope of keeping the family name of Nordholm honorable, Muni offers the remainder of his personal fortune to his son. However, when Cook discovers that his wife is having an affair with a business associate, he turns to suicide. Devastated by the loss of his son, Muni, now 77 years of age, dies of a stroke. A picture of great scope, THE WORLD CHANGES benefits greatly from Muni's superb performance. At the age of 38 Muni convincingly portrayed a young man in his twenties and a grandfather in his late seventies, displaying an ability to capture the essence of both. (His very first acting performance, at the age of 12, actually proved to be early training for THE WORLD CHANGES–he hid behind a beard and played a man of 60.) This was Muni's second outing for Warner's, following I AM A FUGITIVE FROM A CHAIN GANG, also directed by LeRoy and written by Gibney.

p, Robert Lord; d, Mervyn Leroy; w, Edward Chodorov (based on the story "America Kneels" by Sheridan Gibney); ph, Tony Gaudio; ed, William Holmes; m, Leo Forbstein; art d, Jack Okey, Robert Haas; cos, Earl Luick.

Drama   **(PR:A MPAA:NR)**

WORLD FOR RANSOM***   (1954) 82m Plaza/AA bw

Dan Duryea (*Mike Callahan*), Gene Lockhart (*Alexis Pederas*), Patric Knowles (*Julian March*), Reginald Denny (*Maj. Bone*), Nigel Bruce (*Gov. Coutts*), Marian Carr (*Frennessey March*), Douglas Dumbrille (*Inspector McCollum*), Keye Luke (*Wong*), Clarence Lung (*Chan*), Lou Nova (*Guzik*), Arthur Shields (*Sean O'Connor*), Carmen D'Antonio (*Dancer*).

Expanding their television show "China Smith" into a feature film, director Aldrich and star Duryea turned in a taut, exciting, and ultimately grim little *film noir*. Duryea plays a WW II veteran turned private eye who is based in mysterious Singapore. One day a former lover, Carr, hires Duryea to extricate her husband from the criminal activities he has become ensnared in. The husband, Knowles, has fallen in with Lockhart, a powerful black marketeer who wants to kidnap a prominent nuclear physicist, Shields, and hold him for ransom to the highest bidder, be it capitalist or communist. Knowles poses as an Army officer and meets Shields at the airport. The scientist, believing Knowles to be his escort, falls into the trap and is abducted. One of Duryea's informants spots the kidnaping and takes a picture of Knowles and Shields together. The next day the informant turns up dead and incriminating evidence is found in Duryea's hotel room. When police inspector Dumbrille confronts Duryea with the evidence, the private eye knocks the cop cold and hides out at Carr's place. Duryea surmises that the scientist has been brought to a deserted jungle island and goes there to find out. British Intelligence agent Denny follows Duryea to the island and the two eventually team up to find Lockhart, Knowles, and Shields. The men find the hideout and decide to take action. In the ensuing battle, Denny is wounded and Duryea finds himself in a room alone with the villains. With Shields safely outside, Duryea tosses two grenades and ducks for cover. The explosion kills both Lockhart and Knowles, enabling Duryea to escape with Shields. Duryea regretfully informs Carr that he was unable to save her husband from the consequences of his criminal life, but hopes he can renew his relationship with her. In a shockingly vicious attack on Duryea, Carr slaps his face and informs him that she hates all men, finds them repellent, and that she only put up with Knowles because the relationship was purely platonic. Stunned by her rejection of him both emotionally and physically, Duryea leaves Carr and wanders the streets of Singapore. WORLD FOR RANSOM was shot in merely 10 days on a budget of $90,000, with director Aldrich halting production to shoot TV commercials needed to raise money for post-production. In the film, Aldrich creates a bleak world where nothing is what it seems and everyone is trapped. The rather sensational lesbian overtones in Carr's character were even more explicit in the original version of the film, which opened with a lesbian kiss. This, of course, was cut by the censors. Stylistically, Aldrich's visuals are superbly crafted, with the emphasis on enclosure. The camera set-ups and editing serve to trap the characters in their scenes, refusing to give them room to maneuver. Another fascinating, skillful film from Aldrich, a master of the film genre that would come to be known as *film noir*.

p, Robert Aldrich, Bernard Tabakin; d, Aldrich; w, Lindsay Hardy, (uncredited, Hugo Butler); ph, Joseph F. Biroc; m, Frank DeVol; ed, Michael Luciano; art d, William Glasgow; set d, Ted Offenbacher; m/l, "Too Soon," Walter Samuels.

Crime   **(PR:C-O MPAA:NR)**

WORLD GONE MAD, THE**   (1933) 80m Majestic bw (GB: THE
                              PUBLIC BE HANGED; AKA: PUBLIC BE DAMNED)

Pat O'Brien (*Andy Terrell*), Evelyn Brent (*Carlotta Lamont*), Neil Hamilton (*Lionel Houston*), Mary Brian (*Diane Cromwell*), Louis Calhern (*Christopher Bruno*), J. Carroll Naish (*Ramon Salvadore*), Buster Phelps (*Ralph Henderson*), Richard Tucker (*Graham Gaines*), John St. Polis (*Grover Cromwell*), Geneva Mitchell (*Evelyn Henderson*), Wallis Clark (*District Attorney Avery Henderson*), Huntley Gordon (*Osborne*), Max Davidson (*Cohen*), Joseph Girard (*Nichols*), Lloyd Ingraham (*Baird*), Inez Courtney (*Susan Bibens*).

The usual tough reporter (O'Brien) takes on the usual disgusting crook (Tucker) when he discovers that the former district attorney was the victim of a murder plot. Present district attorney Hamilton is in for the same

treatment, until O'Brien exposes the whole disgusting mess.

p, Philip Goldstone; d, Christy Cabanne; w, Edward T. Lowe; ph, Ira Morgan; ed, Otis Garrett; art d, Daniel Hall.

Crime   **Cas.**   **(PR:A MPAA:NR)**

WORLD IN HIS ARMS, THE***   (1952) 104m UNIV c

Gregory Peck (*Jonathan Clark*), Ann Blyth (*Countess Marina Selanova*), Anthony Quinn (*Portugee*), John McIntire (*Deacon Greathouse*), Andrea King (*Mamie*), Carl Esmond (*Prince Semyon*), Eugenie Leontovich (*Anna Selanova*), Sig Rumann (*Gen. Ivan Vorashilov*), Hans Conreid (*Eustace*), Bryan Forbes (*William Cleggett*), Rhys Williams (*Eben Cleggett*), Bill Radovich (*Ogeechuk*), Gregory Gay (*Paul Shushaldin*), Henry Kulky (*Peter*), Gregg Barton, Gregg Martell, Carl Andre, George Scanlon, Carl Harbaugh, Frank Chase (*Seamen*), Eve Whitney (*Lilly*), Millicent Patrick (*Lena*), Syl Lamont (*Jose*), Leo Mostovoy (*Nicholas*), Wee Willie Davis (*Shanghai Kelley*).

A strong period adventure film set in Alaska that marked the first of three films in which Peck and Quinn appeared together. Lots of action, a good story, and better acting from Peck than usual in this modest hit (budgeted at about $3 million) that began shooting around October, 1951. Peck is the captain of a vessel that illegally hunts seals. He returns to San Francisco's Barbary Coast after a good voyage and checks into a hotel with his crew. Also in that hotel is Blyth, a Russian countess, and her coterie of servants. Blyth is fleeing an arranged marriage with Esmond, a Czarist peer. She thinks she can get away and find safety in Sitka, Alaska, under the aegis of her uncle, Rumann, who is the governor general of the area. She approaches Quinn, another seal hunter, and says she'll pay well to be taken north, but Quinn can't raise a crew to make the voyage. Quinn and Peck are competitors and there is no love lost between the New Englander and the Portuguese. When Blyth discovers that Peck has a ship and a crew, she asks him to take her to Alaska. Peck finds her most attractive and doesn't know that royal blood pumps in her veins when he takes her around the city at night for a tour of Baghdad by the Bay. The two become close by the time the morning sun dawns and he proposes marriage, which she accepts. They are about to be wed when Esmond, at the helm of a Russian boat, comes into San Francisco harbor, steals Blyth and her entourage, and sets sail for Alaska, promising to kill Rumann if Blyth doesn't fulfill her marriage obligation to the Russian. Peck finds that Blyth is gone, drinks himself into a stupor, and winds up broke after he's had a huge fist fight with Quinn. To raise money, Peck proposes a bet with Quinn. The men will race to Sitka and the winner will get the other captain's seal catch as well as his boat. Quinn agrees and the race begins. Peck's boat arrives slightly ahead of Quinn's but then both ships are captured by the Russians who impound the vessels, the catches, and the crews. Both Peck and Quinn are seal poachers and are arrested as such and tossed into jail. Blyth saves them when she agrees to marry Esmond if he will order the release of the duo. This he does and, under guard, Quinn and Peck are taken back to their ships. Later, they stealthily make their ways to Rumann's residence, where the wedding is about to commence, and join forces to snatch Blyth away from the cunning Esmond. Then, to insure their safe arrival back in the U.S., Quinn oversees the wrecking of the Russian gunboat. Peck and Blyth sail south, happily planning the rest of their lives together. Superb sea footage, socko action, and a robust relationship between Peck and Quinn help make this a terrific way to spend slightly more than an hour and a half. Every so often, overtones of anti-communism creep in (remember, this was the time of the "witch hunts" in the movie industry and the studio must have been covering its backside). Since that time, seal hunters have been reviled for the cruel way in which they kill their prey and it would be difficult to paint a modern-day sealer as a hero. The hunting sequences are minimalized and anyone who hates the practice will not be insulted as producer Rosenberg and director Walsh must have anticipated the outcry and reduced those scenes to almost nil. In his first U.S. film as an actor (he'd done two in the U.K.), note Bryan Forbes, who later abandoned emoting for writing, producing, and directing. A good-looking film with excellent special effects of a storm at sea.

p, Aaron Rosenberg; d, Raoul Walsh; w, Borden Chase, Horace McCoy (based on the novel by Rex Beach); ph, Russell Metty (Technicolor); m, Frank Skinner; ed, Frank Gross; art d, Bernard Herzbrun, Alexander Golitzen; cos, Bill Thomas; ch, Harold Belfer.

Historical Drama/Adventure   **(PR:A-C MPAA:NR)**

WORLD IN MY CORNER**½   (1956) 82m UNIV bw

Audie Murphy (*Tommy Shea*), Barbara Rush (*Dorothy Mallinson*), Jeff Morrow (*Robert Mallinson*), John McIntire (*Dave Bernstein, Trainer*), Tommy Rall (*Ray Kacsmerek*), Howard St. John (*Harry Cram, Fight Promoter*), Chico Vejar (*Steve Carelli, Welterweight Champion*), Cisco Andrade (*Parker*), Baby Ike (*Bailey*), Sheila Bromley (*Mrs. Mallinson*), Dani Crayne (*Doris*), H. Tommy Hart (*Stretch Caplow*), James F. Lennon (*Ring Announcer*), Steve Ellis (*TV Announcer*), Art Aragon, Freddie Herman, Sammy Shack (*Fighters*), Pat Miller.

Murphy takes his hero's stance to the boxing ring this time out as a poor kid from the ghetto who quickly rises in the ranks of welterweight competition, but never gets a chance at a title fight. Anxious to wed Rush and get her away from her overbearing father, Murphy agrees to throw a bout against the champ in exchange for a hefty amount of cash. He can't bring himself to take a fall, however, gets beaten senseless, and hangs up his gloves forever.

p, Aaron Rosenberg; d, Jesse Hibbs; w, Jack Sher (based on a story by Sher, Joseph Stone); ph, Maury Gertsman; ed, Milton Carruth; md, Joseph Gershenson; art d, Alexander Golitzen, Bill Newberry; cos, Bill Thomas.

Sports Drama   **(PR:A   MPAA:NR)**

WORLD IN MY POCKET, THE**   (1962, Fr./Ital./Ger.) 93m Corona Filmproduktion-Crit erion-Erredi-Panta Cinematografica-CCC-Filmkunst/ MGM bw (VENDREDI 13 HEURES; PAS DE MENTALITE; IL MONDO NELLA MIA TASCA; AN EINEM FREITAG UM HALB ZWOLF; AKA: ON FRIDAY AT ELEVEN)

Rod Steiger (Frank Morgan), Nadja Tiller (Ginny), Peter Van Eyck (Bleck), Ian Bannen (Kitson), Jean Servais (Gypo), Marisa Merlini (Frau Mandini), Memmo Carotenuto (Herr Mandini), Edoardo Venola (Carlo Mandini), Carlo Giustini (Pierre).

Taut thriller featuring Tiller as a mysterious German woman who convinces a gang of thieves led by Steiger to plan and execute a daring payroll robbery. Since the money is being transported in an armored car, Steiger and company decide to fake a car crash to lure the guard out of the truck, which will give the other robbers a chance to capture the vehicle. From there the gang will drive the truck to a carnival ground and work on opening the vault unnoticed. Unfortunately the plan goes awry almost immediately when the guard refuses to leave his truck. This leads to gunplay and the guard is injured, but he manages to kill a gang member in the process. This forces the remaining members to hurriedly flee with the truck and in the confusion more fatal mistakes are made which seal the gang's doom. The villainous vehicle resists all efforts to open it, resulting in frustration almost to the point of madness. The fears and phobias of the principal characters emerge gradually. The final scene is a surrealistic love dance in which Steiger and Tiller—never, until then, a romantic duo—clasp hands and leap to their death from the cliff where their pursuers have trapped them. Well done and exciting.

p, Alexander Gruter; d, Alvin Rakoff; w, Frank Harvey (based on the novel by James Hadley Chase); ph, Vaclav Vich; m, Claude Bolling; ed, Alice Ludwig-Rasch, E.B. Jarvis; md, Bolling; art d, Hanns Kuhnert, Wilhelm Vorwerg; makeup, Gerda Scholz-Grosse, Gunther Frank.

Crime   **(PR:A   MPAA:NR)**

WORLD IS FULL OF MARRIED MEN, THE*
            (1980, Brit.) 106m New Realm-Married Men/New Line c

Anthony Franciosa, Carroll Baker, Gareth Hunt, Georgina Hale, Anthony Steel, Sherrie Lee Cronin, Paul Nicholas, Jean Gilpin, John Nolan, Hot Gossip.

The immoral jet-setting crowd is once again brought to the screen thanks to another Jackie Collins novel, whose trashy writings were also filmed as THE STUD (1978) starring sister Joan, and the made-for-TV HOLLYWOOD WIVES. Franciosa plays an advertising executive whose infidelity sends his wife into a flurry of vengeance and promiscuity. The kind of film that gives British cinema a bad name, it features a title tune by the gruff-voiced, once popular Bonnie Tyler and some pathetic dancing by Hot Gossip.

p, Malcolm Fancey, Oscar S. Lerman; d, Robert Young; w, Jackie Collins (based on her novel); ph, Ray Parslow (Eastmancolor); m, Frank Musker, Dominic Bugatti.

Drama   **Cas.**   **(PR:O   MPAA:R)**

WORLD IS JUST A 'B' MOVIE, THE zero   (1971) 90m Robinson c

James Christopher (Jonathan Peru), Robert Lincoln Robb (Harry Greene), Riki Ferguson (Gandalf), Georgina Clegg (Alice Weatherspoon), Willie Harris (The Speaker), Walter Jones (Mitch-the-Match), Jerry Charburn, Pigeon Darbo, Uschi Digaid, Eleanor Dixson, Monica Gayle, Mike Hall, Hans Ludermilk, Nadra McClain, Carl MacIntre, Colin MacKenzie, Patti Newby, Joe Saunders, Alan Slecker, Don Vandergriff, Linda York.

Despite its promising title, this film is crippled by atrocious performances, an awful script, and a minuscule $20,000 budget. Christopher and Robb pull off a bank robbery and the former decides to spend his cash living it up in topless nightclubs. The filmmakers deserve some credit for actually getting this low-budget 16mm picture off the ground, but good intentions and hard work do not a movie make.

p&d, R.D. Robinson, Alan Steckery; w, Robinson; ph, Robinson, Steckery, Denny Clairmont (Eastmancolor); m, Bob Lind; ed&set d, Robinson, Steckery; m/l, "The World Is Just a 'B' Movie," Lind.

Drama   **(PR:O   MPAA:NR)**

WORLD MOVES ON, THE**   (1934) 104m FOX bw

Madeleine Carroll (Mrs. Warburton, 1824/Mary Warburton, 1914), Franchot Tone (Richard Girard), Lumsden Hare (Gabriel Warburton, 1824/Sir John Warburton, 1914), Raul Roulien (Carlos Girard, 1824/Henri Girard, 1914), Reginald Denny (Erik Von Gerhardt), Siegfried [Sig] Rumann (Baron Von Gerhardt), Louise Dresser (Baroness Von Gerhardt), Stepin Fetchit (Dixie), Dudley Digges (Mr. Manning), Frank Melton (John Girard, 1824), Brenda Fowler (Mrs. Agnes Girard, 1824), Russell Simpson (Notary Public, 1924), Marcelle Corday (Miss Girard, 1824), Walter McGrail (French Duelist, 1824), Charles Bastin (Jacques Girard, 1914), Barry Norton (Jacques Girard, 1929), George Irving (Charles Girard, 1914), Ferdinand Schumann-Heink (Fritz Von Gerhardt, 1914), Georgette Rhodes (Jeanne Girard, 1914), Claude King (Braithwaite), Ivan Simpson (Clumber), Frank Moran (Culbert), Jack Pennick, Francis Ford (Legionnaires), Torben Meyer (German Chamberlain, 1914).

A will read in the 1800s links the fortunes of two prominent New Orleans families represented by Carroll and Tone. Their wealth grows, leading to expansion in both France and Germany, but WW I and the market plunge of the 1920s destroy the families' empire. However, Carroll and Tone survive the debacle and begin anew. A strong anti-war statement, this includes some striking battle footage culled from an earlier French feature, CROSSES OF WOOD. Dramatic war scenes of this sort would become a staple of John Ford's latter films. THE WORLD MOVES ON also included the first performance by Carroll in a U.S. production.

p, Winfield R. Sheehan; d, John Ford; w, Reginald C. Berkeley; ph, George Schneiderman; m, Max Steiner, Louis De Francesco, R.H. Bassett, David Buttolph, Hugo Friedhofer, George Gershwin; md, Arthur Lange; art d, William Darling; set d, Thomas Little; cos, Rita Kaufman; m/l, "Should She Desire Me Not," De Francesco, "Ave Maria," Charles Gounod.

Drama   **(PR:A   MPAA:NR)**

WORLD OF APU, THE***½   (1960, India) 103m Satyajit Ray/Edward Harrison bw (APUR SANSAR)

Soumitra Chatterjee (Apurba Kumar Roy), Sharmila Tagore (Aparna), Shapan Mukerji (Pulu), S. Alke Chakravarty (Kajal).

The third and final installment of The Apu Trilogy, the most famous group of films to come out of India and directed by India's most famous director Satyajit Ray. After following the young character of Apu from his early years (PATHER PANCHALI [1955]) to his school are year (APARAJITO [1956]), the trilogy picks up with Chatterjee in the role of Apu as finances force him to abandon his university studies. His desire is to become a writer, but his life changes when he is reacquaints himself with an old friend, Mukerji. Together they travel to the wedding of Mukerji's cousin, Tagore. The bridegroom turns out to be insane and the wedding is canceled But to prevent the life of spinsterhood for Tagore that custom demands, Chatterjee marries her and they return to his Calcutta apartment to set up housekeeping. Tagore becomes pregnant and dies during childbirth, though her newborn son lives. Chatterjee, who grew to love Tagore, enters a deep depression, destroys his unfinished novel, and wanders around central India before taking a job in a coal mine. Mukerji eventually discovers him and convinces him to return to his son, who is now 5 years old. Father and son grow to love each other and start life anew. A wonderfully insightful picture which, despite cultural differences, strikes a universal chord of humanism.

p,d&w, Satyajit Ray (based on the novel Aparajito by Bibhutibhusan Bandopadhaya); ph, Subrata Mitra; m, Ravi Shankar; ed, Dulal Dutta; art d, Banshi Chandra Gupta; English subtitles, Norman R. Clare.

Drama   **Cas.**   **(PR:A   MPAA:NR)**

WORLD OF HANS CHRISTIAN ANDERSEN, THE**½
            (1971, Jap.) 75m Toei-Sean/UA c (HANSU KURISHITAN ANDERU-
                                              SAN NO SEKAI)

Voices of: Chuck McCann (Uncle Oley), Hetty Galen (Hans Christian Andersen), Corinne Orr (Elisa/Kitty Kat/Little Boy/Match Girl/Mouse), Sidney Filson (Karen), Jim MacGeorge (Kaspar Kat/Governor/Hans' Father), Lionel Wilson (Hannibal Mouse/Mayor/Watchdog), Ruth Ballew (Elisa's Grandmother), Frances Russell, Jim Yoham (Mice), Earl Hammond (Ducks/Theater Manager).

A beautifully animated tale (Americanized for U.S. release) that combines Andersen's tales "The Red Shoes" and "The Poor Little Match Girl." Little Hans is depressed because he cannot go to the opera. He is visited by Uncle Oley the Sandman who, sympathetic to his situation, provides Hans' father with some magic red leather to use to make a pair of shoes for a contest. The shoes take first prize but the shifty mayor cheats the shoemaker out of his winnings. Refusing to give up, Hans takes a number of odd jobs and earns enough money to buy an opera ticket. But before he pays for it, Hans sees his friend Elisa who has been forced by poverty to sell matches outside of the theater. Instead of seeing the performance, Hans spends all his money on her matches and passes the evening spinning yarns for the crowd outside the theater. The governor overhears his stories and is so impressed that he makes Hans his ward. A great heartwarmer for the kids.

p, Hiroshi Okawa; d&w, Al Kilgore, Chuck McCann; ph, (CinemaScope,

DeLuxe Color); m, Ron Frangiapane, Seiichiro Uno; art d, Tadashi Koyama; m/l, Frangiapane, Kilgore (sung by Linda November, Ron Dante); animation director, Koyama.

Animated Children's Film (PR:AAA MPAA:G)

WORLD OF HENRY ORIENT, THE*** (1964) 115m UA c

Peter Sellers (*Henry Orient*), Paula Prentiss (*Stella*), Tippy Walker (*Valerie Boyd*), Merrie Spaeth (*Marian "Gil" Gilbert*), Angela Lansbury (*Isabel Boyd*), Tom Bosley (*Frank Boyd*), Phyllis Thaxter (*Mrs. Gilbert*), Bibi Osterwald (*Boothy*), Peter Duchin (*Joe Byrd*), John Fiedler (*Sidney*), Al Lewis (*Store Owner*), Fred Stewart (*Doctor*), Philippa Bevans (*Emma*), Jane Buchanan (*Kafritz*).

A charming comedy about the adolescent agony of infatuation. Whether the object of the teen's affections is a teacher, a movie star, or even a best friend's older sibling, the experience can be delightfully gut-wrenching if handled properly by the filmmakers. Walker and Spaeth are boarding school chums pursuing an egotistical concert pianist, Sellers. Walker is the daughter of wealthy parents who trot the globe constantly, thereby leaving her with lots of time to exercise her healthy imagination. Spaeth lives with her divorced mother, Thaxter, who is more protective than she should be. The girls, just 14 or so, believe that they are in love with Sellers, whose opinion of his talents far exceeds his actual abilities. Sellers is a Casanova and his latest conquest is Prentiss, a married woman. When she spots Walker and Spaeth several times, Prentiss is convinced they are a pair of teenage detectives who are tailing her on behalf of her jealous husband. Walker and Spaeth begin collecting newspaper items and compile a scrapbook about Sellers. When Walker's mother, Lansbury, finds the scrapbook, she reads things the wrong way and believes that Sellers must have taken advantage of her daughter. Lansbury visits Sellers' apartment and angrily accuses him. Ever the suave *roue*, Sellers turns it on and winds up having an affair with Lansbury, who is boringly married to Bosley. When Walker finds out that her mother has strayed, she is shattered. Lansbury then informs Walker that she must break up her deep friendship with Spaeth. Bosley decides that he cannot continue being married to Lansbury now that she is an adulteress, so he talks to Walker and takes her with him on a trip abroad. Upon their return, Walker and Spaeth resume their friendship and have now found a new interest, boys, to replace their infatuation with Sellers. This was one of the rare films in which someone has "stolen" the film away from the comedic Englishman. Walker and Spaeth are a joy to behold, with none of the professional cloying sweetness so often seen in younger thespians. Lansbury does her usual good work and Bosley again plays the father everyone would like to have. He repeated this successfully in the long-running TV series "Happy Days." The script was a father-daughter creation by Nora and Nunnally Johnson, based on the daughter's novel. Prentiss overacted a bit and Sellers seemed to be walking through the job, which may have contributed to the fact that the youngsters are what one remembers about this movie. Filmed on location in New York City, the plot made a fine book for a musical, and so it was as "Henry, Sweet Henry" a few years later. One of the young girls in that production was a teenager named Pia Zadora. The best part of this movie is the depiction of the young girls. It never strays from truth, even when they are on wild flights of fancy, and anyone who has ever been a teenager will recognize the believability of it, which means that *everyone* will. Walker and Spaeth were making their debuts and neither was heard from much after this auspicious start. The dialog is sharp, the satire of marriage and broken homes is accurate, and Hill's direction, though a trifle slow at times, is mostly on the money. As one of Thaxter's pals, Bibi Osterwald chimes in with a few good moments. Note society pianist Peter Duchin in a small role. He's the son of Eddy Duchin, the famed pianist whose life was filmed as THE EDDY DUCHIN STORY with Tyrone Power in the title role. Location scenes were done in New York City and all interiors shot on Long Island at the Meyerberg Studios. Good score from Elmer Bernstein, who is known as "Bernstein West" to distinguish him from Leonard Bernstein, who is quartered in New York, and is aptly known as "Bernstein East." The good-natured film did excellent business when it opened at Radio City Music Hall as the Easter attraction, but it didn't capture as much interest across the country as the producers had hoped.

p, Jerome Hellman; d, George Roy Hill; w, Nora Johnson, Nunnally Johnson (based on the novel by Nora Johnson); ph, Boris Kaufman, Arthur J. Ornitz (Panavision, DeLuxe Color); m, Elmer Bernstein, "Henry Orient Concerto," Ken Lauber; ed, Stuart Gilmore; prod d, James Sullivan; art d, Jan Scott; set d, Kenneth Krausgill; cos, Ann Roth; makeup, Dick Smith.

Comedy Cas. (PR:C MPAA:NR)

WORLD OF SPACE, THE (SEE: BATTLE IN OUTER SPACE, 1960, Jap.)

WORLD OF SUZIE WONG, THE** (1960) 129m PAR c

William Holden (*Robert Lomax*), Nancy Kwan (*Suzie Wong*), Sylvia Syms (*Kay O'Neill*), Michael Wilding (*Ben*), Laurence Naismith (*Mr. O'Neill*), Jacqueline Chan (*Gwenny Lee*), Andy Ho (*Ah Tong*), Bernard Cribbins (*Otis*), Yvonne Shima (*Minnie Ho*), Lier Hwang (*Wednesday Lu*), Lionel Blair (*Dancing Sailor*), Robert Lee (*Barman*), Ronald Eng (*Waiter*), Calvin Hsai

(*Suzie's Baby*).

This unrealistic soap opera has Holden playing an American architect who decides to spend a year in Hong Kong, trying to become a painter. He meets Kwan, who tells Holden that she is a wealthy heiress, innocent in the ways of the world. Holden is naturally surprised when he walks into a bar and finds Kwan drinking with sailors. She pretends not to recognize him, but eventually the truth comes out. Kwan is a prostitute, and offers to become Holden's "steady girl friend." Holden will have nothing to do with this offer, and instead uses Kwan as a model. Kwan then repeats her offer to playboy Wilding, who accepts with alacrity. Holden meets Syms, the daughter of an English banker. She helps Holden sell his work and wants to marry him. However, Holden's relationship with Kwan is more than she can bear, so Syms breaks off with him. Kwan, in the meantime, has been dumped by playboy Wilding and continues to walk the streets. Holden realizes his feelings for her, and becomes her lover. After she disappears for many hours, Holden learns that Kwan has a baby whom she has kept secret. With his money running out, Kwan suggests to Holden that she go back to prostitution. Holden throws her out, then later discovers her baby was killed in a landslide. Holden finds Kwan giving her dead child a traditional Chinese funeral and proposes marriage to her as the story ends. THE WORLD OF SUZIE WONG is rife with problems. Quine's direction is too slow, dragging out scenes well beyond their dramatic potency. The script is pockmarked with a variety of implausible situations and unbelievable circumstances. The portrait of Hong Kong's prostitutes is grossly sugar-coated, showing none of the hardships, disease, and death that are everyday facts of life. On the plus side is Unsworth's fine photography, which captures Hong Kong's lively atmosphere. Holden is tolerable in the lead, though he looks too old for the part. Kwan, despite the simplicity of her character, is surprisingly natural. Her role was to have been taken by France Nuyen, who originated the part on Broadway. Arriving at the Hong Kong location, Nuyen was distressed at reports that her lover, Marlon Brando, was carrying on with another woman (actress Barbara Luna). Nuyen drowned her sorrows in food, gaining so much weight that she was fired from the part. Kwan, who had played the role in road companies of the play, was then hired as a replacement. Direction was begun by Jean Negulesco, who also was dismissed from production. Quine, who had known Holden at Columbia, and briefly worked with producer Stark on an early version of FUNNY GIRL, was hired almost immediately to take over.

p, Ray Stark; d, Richard Quine; w, John Patrick (based on the novel by Richard Mason and the play by Paul Osborn); ph, Geoffrey Unsworth (Technicolor); m, George Duning; ed, Bert Bates; art d, John Box; m/l, title song, James Van Heusen, Sammy Cahn.

Drama (PR:O MPAA:NR)

WORLD OWES ME A LIVING, THE** (1944, Brit.) 91m BN/Anglo American bw

David Farrar (*Paul Collyer*), Judy Campbell (*Moira Barrett*), Sonia Dresdel (*Eve Heatherley*), Jack Livesey (*Jack Graves*), Jack Barker (*Chuck Rockley*), John Laurie (*Matthews*), Anthony Hawtrey (*Jerry*), Wylie Watson (*Conductor*), Roy Minear, Alan Keith, Howard Douglas, Humphrey Kent, Amy Veness, MacKenzie Ward, Stewart Rome, Ian MacLean, Max Melford, Richard Clarke, Terence O'Brien, Joss Ambler.

A hokey melodrama about a pilot, Farrar, who loses his memory when his plane crashes. Campbell helps bring back his past, sparking his recollection of the troop transport plane they designed together. Still confined to the hospital, he works up the courage to ask for Campbell's hand in marriage, only to learn that they are already married.

p, Louis H. Jackson; d, Vernon Sewell; w, Sewell, Erwin Reiner (based on a novel by John Llewellyn-Rhys); ph, Gerald Gibbs, Geoffrey Faithfull.

War/Romance (PR:A MPAA:NR)

WORLD PREMIERE**½ (1941) 70m PAR bw

John Barrymore (*Duncan DeGrasse*), Frances Farmer (*Kitty Carr*), Eugene Pallette (*Gregory Martin*), Virginia Dale (*Lee Morrison*), Ricardo Cortez (*Mark Saunders*), Sig Rumann (*Franz von Bushmaster*), Don Castle (*Joe Bemis*), William Wright (*Luther Skinkley*), Fritz Feld (*Muller*), Luis Alberni (*Signor Scaletti*), Cliff Nazarro (*Peters*), Andrew Tombes (*Nixon*).

A silly and occasionally uproarious comedy which stars Barrymore as a film producer who is preparing to have his picture, "The Earth in Flames," premiered in Washington, D.C. To heighten word-of-mouth about his anti-Axis film, Barrymore and his publicity agent, Castle, hire three "spies" to deliver threatening messages which promise to disrupt the premiere. What confuses the matter, however, is that three actual spies--Rumann, Feld, and Alberni--plan to show a propaganda film in place of Barrymore's much-awaited epic. The spies, in the Keystone Kops tradition, supply the picture with fast-paced confusion, endless bungling, and a series of side-splitting routines. Their main obstacle in switching the film is getting into the cage of a Bengal tiger--the company mascot of Bengal Pictures--where the film is being kept as yet another publicity stunt. The trip from Hollywood to Washington is spiced with romance when the film's star, Cortez, finds himself explaining to traveling companion Farmer his attraction for bit player Dale. Meantime, Farmer's annoyance at his crush on Dale is magnified by gossipmonger Wright, who plays her against Cortez in order to get juicy material for his column. By the time the entourage reaches Washington, Rumann's plan of espionage has been succesfully carried out and, when the curtain rises, the propaganda picture begins to roll. It takes Barrymore a few moments to realize the ruse, but before long everything is straightened out and the world premiere goes on without any further hitches. As masterful as Barrymore can be, WORLD PREMIERE, is a success chiefly because of the comic scene-stealing by Rumann, Feld, and Alberni. Rumann, who two years previously had gained fame in both NINOTCHKA and ONLY ANGELS HAVE WINGS, was here given license to bring the house down with laughter, and would do so again brilliantly in TO BE OR NOT TO BE (1942). WORLD PREMIERE was the directorial debut for Tetzlaff, who had previously gained recognition as a top Hollywood cameraman photographing a number of early Frank Capra pictures (THE POWER OF THE PRESS, 1928, THE YOUNGER GENERATION, and THE DONOVAN AFFAIR, both 1929) as well as MY MAN GODFREY (1936). After a stint in WW II, Tetzlaff returned to Hollywood for a short time as cameraman on two masterpieces, THE ENCHANTED COTTAGE (1945) and NOTORIOUS (1946), before resuming his directorial status.

p, Sol C. Siegel; d, Ted Tetzlaff; w, Earl Felton (based on a story by Felton, Gordon Kahn); ph, Dan Flapp; ed, Archie Marshek.

Comedy   **(PR:A   MPAA:NR)**

WORLD TEN TIMES OVER, THE   (SEE: PUSSYCAT ALLEY, 1965, Brit.)

WORLD, THE FLESH, AND THE DEVIL, THE**
(1932, Brit.) 53m REA/RKO bw

Harold Huth (*Nicholas Brophy*), Isla Bevan (*Beatrice Elton*), S. Victor Stanley (*Jim Stanger*), Sara Allgood (*Emme Stanger*), James Raglan (*Robert Hall*), Fred Groves (*Dick Morgan*), Frederick Leister (*Sir James Hall*), Felix Aylmer (*Sir Henderson Trent*), Barbara Everest (*Mrs. Brophy*).

An uninvolving story about a power-hungry lawyer who is the illegitimate son of a baronet. He schemes to dispose of the rightful heir and take the title himself, but he is caught and dealt with justly.

p, Julius Hagen; d, George A. Cooper; w, H. Fowler Mear (based on the play by Lawrence Cowen).

Drama   **(Pr:A   MPAA:NR)**

WORLD, THE FLESH, AND THE DEVIL, THE½**
(1959) 95m Sol C. Siegel-HarBel/MGM b w

Harry Belafonte (*Ralph Burton*), Inger Stevens (*Sarah Crandall*), Mel Ferrer (*Benson Thacker*).

An intersting but ultimately unfulfilling and unconvincing post-holocaust allegory which is really more concerned with the problem of racism than with surviving a nuclear attack. Belafonte is a coal miner who represents the moral stance of the "world," while Stevens is meant to be the "flesh." After wandering around alone for the first half of the picture, Belafonte encounters his first survivor in an otherwise deserted New York City–Stevens. At first she is hostile toward him because he is black, but she soon grows attached to him. Belafonte resists, conscious that in the days before the holocaust she would have gone nowhere near him. Enter a third survivor, Ferrer, a bigoted seaman who eventually takes up arms against Belafonte. A chase through deserted New York streets adds the final climactic cap, ending with the hope that all three can live in peace. The performances all express the urgency of the situation, but the film soon gets bogged down in its own traps and plot holes.

p, George Englund; d, Ranald MacDougall; w, MacDougall, Ferdinand Reyher (based on the story "The End of The Wall" and the novel *The Purple Cloud* by Matthews Phipps Shiel); ph, Harold J. Marzorati (CinemaScope); m, Miklos Rozsa; ed, Harold F. Kress; art d, William A. Horning, Paul Groesse; spec eff, Lee LeBlanc.

Science Fiction   **Cas.**   **(PR:A   MPAA:NR)**

WORLD WAR III BREAKS OUT   (SEE: FINAL WAR, THE, 1962, Jap.)

WORLD WAS HIS JURY, THE**   (1958) 82m Clover/COL bw

Edmund O'Brien (*David Carson*), Mona Freeman (*Robin Carson*), Karin Booth (*Polly Barrett*), Robert McQueeney (*Capt. Jerry Barrett*), Paul Birch (*Martin Ranker, 2nd officer*), John Berardino (*Tony Armand*), Dick [Richard H.[Cutting (*District Attorney Wendell*), Harvey Stephens (*Judge Arthur Farrell*), Carlos Romero (*1st Mate Johnson*), Hortense Petra (*Pretty Girl*), Kelly Junge, Jr (*Jimmy Barrett*), Gay Goodwin (*Jane Barrett*).

O'Brien is a defense attorney who's never lost a case. In this courtroom drama he defends a ship captain who is almost certainly guilty of criminal negligence when his ship sinks, killing 162 passengers. Everyone, including O'Brien's wife, Freeman, becomes disillusioned and abandons the lawyer,

but by the finale O'Brien has pinned the guilt on a ship's mate who had it in for the captain. Bogged down by the usual courtroom melodrama but generally watchable.

p, Sam Katzman; d, Fred F. Sears; w, Herbert Abbott Spiro; ph, Benjamin H. Kline; ed, Edwin Bryant; md, Mischa Bakaleinikoff; art d, Paul Palmentola.

Drama   **(PR:A   MPAA:NR)**

WORLD WITHOUT A MASK, THE**   (1934, Ger.) 109m Ariel bw
(DIE WELT OHNE MASKE)

Harry Piel, Kurt Vespermann, Annie Markart, Olga Tschechowa, Rudolf Klein-Rogge, Hubert von Meyerinck, Philipp Manning, Hermann Picha, Gerhard Dammann, Ernst Behmer.

A pulp thriller about a comic pair who invent a television that can see through walls and transfer the images to the screen. They, of course, are pursued by any number of cheats and gangsters who want the invention for themselves. Directed by and starring Piel, Germany's answer to Douglas Fairbanks.

d, Harry Piel; w, Hans Rameau; ph, Ewald Daub.

Science Fiction/Comedy   **(PR:A   MPAA:NR)**

WORLD WITHOUT END**   (1956) 80m AA c

Hugh Marlowe (*John Borden*), Nancy Gates (*Garnet*), Nelson Leigh (*Dr. Galbraithe*), Rod Taylor (*Herbert Ellis*), Shawn Smith (*Elaine*), Lisa Montell (*Deena*), Christopher Dark (*Henry Jaffe*), Booth Colman (*Mories*), Everett Glass (*Timmek*), Intellectual Leader, Stanley Fraser (*Elda*), William Vedder (*James*), Rankin Mansfield (*Beryl*), Paul Brinegar (*Vida*), Mickey Simpson (*Naga*).

Marlowe and three other astronauts get zapped into the future during a test flight and land on Earth in the year 2508. The world has experienced nuclear destruction and its surface is overrun by mutant cyclopes. The only real connection to civilization is an underground community of elfish beings who befriend the spacemen. Together they battle the cyclopes and destroy giant spiders that roam the decaying planet. The astronauts, destined to live in the future, make no attempt to leave and instead help the dying race rebuild. The costumes of the underground dwellers were designed by Vargas, the famed pin-up illustrator for *Esquire*.

p, Richard Heermance; d&w, Edward Bernds; ph, Ellsworth Fredricks (CinemaScope, Technicolor); m, Leith Stevens; ed, Eda Warren; md, Stevens; cos, Vargas; spec eff, Milton Rice, Irving Block, Jack Rabin.

Science Fiction   **Cas.**   **(PR:A   MPAA:NR)**

WORLDLY GOODS*½   (1930) 71m Continental Talking Pictures bw

James Kirkwood (*John C. Tullock*), Merna Kennedy (*Mary Thurston*), Shannon Day (*Cassie*), Ferdinand Schumann-Heink (*Jeff*), Eddie Featherston (*Jimmy*), Thomas Curran (*Secretary*).

Schumann-Heink loses his sight in a plane crash and vows to get back at the man who owns the company that built the plane, Kirkwood. Schumann-Heink pretends to be dead, refusing to tell even his sweetheart Kennedy that he survived the crash. He gets a job with Kirkwood and accepts his employer's offer to pay for his eye surgery. In the meantime, Kennedy agrees to marry Kirkwood. When Kirkwood discovers that his new wife is still in love with Schumann-Heink (who is able to see again), he kills himself by jumping from a plane. A depressing melodrama that doesn't amount to much.

p, Trem Carr; d, Phil Rosen; w, John Grey, Scott Littleton (based on a story by Andrew Soutar); ph, Herbert Kirkpatrick; ed, Carl Himm.

Drama   **(PR:A   MPAA:NR)**

WORLDS APART**   (1980, U.S., Israel) 94 K.E.R.K. c

Amos Kollek (*Assaf*), Shelby Leverington (*Lee*), Joseph Cortese (*Ram*), Joseph Yadin (*Father*), Shraga Harpaz (*Mustafaa*), Joseph Pollak (*Rotman*), Lia Konig (*Mother*), Gidi Gov (*Mickey*), Avi Luzia (*Muhammed*), Lee Orsher (*Ruthi*), Esti Zebka (*Nomi*).

Occasionally interesting film from his novel loosely based on his own life (his father was mayor of Jerusalem) stars Kollek as the son of a prominent Jerusalem family. He serves in the reserves, fighting Arabs a couple of days a week, then returning home and dating an American woman (Leverington) who lives in the Arab quarter. This makes him uncomfortable, naturally, and then one day he spots a wanted terrorist and the film resolves itself into a more or less conventional chase movie. Some insights into the Israeli character are to be found here, but as an entertainment vehicle it's mediocre at best.

p, Amos Kollek, Rafi Reibenbach; d, Barbara Noble; w, Kollek (based on his novel, *Don't Ask Me If I Love*); ph, David Gurfinkel; m, Nurit Hirsh; ed, Alain Jakubowicz.

Drama   **(PR:C   MPAA:NR)**

WORLD'S GREATEST ATHLETE, THE*** (1973) 93m Disney/BV c

Tim Conway *(Milo Jackson)*, Jan-Michael Vincent *(Nanu)*, John Amos *(Coach Sam Archer)*, Roscoe Lee Browne *(Gazenga)*, Dayle Haddon *(Jane Douglas)*, Billy DeWolfe *(Maxwell)*, Nancy Walker *(Mrs. Petersen)*, Danny Goldman *(Leopold Maxwell)*, Vito Scotti *(Sports Fan)*, Don Pedro Colley *(Morumba)*, Clarence Muse *(Gazenga's Assistant)*, Liam Dunn *(Dr. Winslow)*, Leon Askin *(Dr. Gottlieb)*, Ivor Francis *(Dean Bellamy)*, Bill Toomey *(TV Spotter)*, Joe Kapp *(Buzzer Kozak)*, Howard Cosell, Frank Gifford, Jim McKay, Bud Palmer *(Announcers)*, Virginia Capers, John Lupton, Russ Conway, Dick Wilson, Jack Griffin, Leigh Christian, Philip Ahn, Sarah Selby, Al Checco, Dorothy Shay, David Manzy.

Coaches Amos and Conway discover jungle boy Vincent showing off his amazing super-physical abilities in the wilds of Africa. They bring him back to their college and transform him into a track star, saving their team from once again becoming the laughing stock of the league. There's also some witch doctoring which shrinks Conway down to a rambling miniature for a spell. Howard Cosell appears as himself, doing a better parody of his sportscaster role than any comedian. Sports announcers Bud Palmer, Frank Gifford, and Jim McKay also are featured. A snappy family entry which was the ninth largest grosser of 1973, bringing in a shade more green than AMERICAN GRAFFITI. The Amos role was initially essayed by Godfrey Cambridge, but he was forced to leave the project after a week due to physical exhaustion.

p, Bill Walsh; d, Richard Scheerer; w, Gerald Gardner, Dee Caruso; ph, Frank Phillips (Technicolor); m, Marvin Hamlisch; ed, Cotton Warburton; art d, John B. Mansbridge, Walter Tyler; set d, Hal Gausman; cos, Chuck Keehne, Emily Sundby; spec eff, Eustace Lycett, Art Cruickshank, Danny Lee; makeup, Robert J. Schiffer.

Comedy   (PR:AAA   MPAA:G)

WORLD'S GREATEST LOVER, THE** (1977) 89m FOX c

Gene Wilder *(Rudy Valentine)*, Carol Kane *(Annie)*, Dom DeLuise *(Zitz)*, Fritz Feld *(Hotel Manager)*, Cousin Buddy *(Himself)*, Hannah Dean *(Maid)*, Candice Azzara *(Anne Calassandro)*, Carl Ballantine *(Uncle Harry)*, Matt Collins *(Rudolph Valentino)*, Lou Cutell *(Mr. Kipper)*, James Gleason *(Room Clerk)*, Ronny Graham *(Director)*, Michael Huddleston *(Barber)*, Florence Sundstrom *(Aunt Tillie)*, Robert E. Ball, Carol Arthur, Stanley Brock, Warren Burton, Danny DeVito, Richard Dimitri, Josip Elic, Melissa Fellen, Ricky Fellen, James Hong, David Huddleston, Richard Karron, Michael McManus, Art Mendelli, Sidney Miller, Jorge Moreno, Jack Riley, Billy Sands, Rolfe Sedan, Sal Viscuso, Randolph Dobbs, Sandy Rovetta, Rita Conde, Lupe Ontiveros, Teda Bracci, Elaine Everett, Gustaf Unger, Harry Gold, Poncie Ponce, Frank O'Brien, Marya Small, Harriet Gibson, Richard A. Roth, Norbert Schiller, Peter Elbing, Federico Roberto, Charles Knapp, George Memmoli, Pat Ast, Tracey Cohn.

There's no question that Gene Wilder has a big head, but it's not quite big enough to wear all of the hats he attempts to don here as he writes, directs, produces, and stars in this up-and-down satire of moviemaking in the silent era. DeLuise is the crazed head of production at a studio. He is searching for an actor to rival Rudolph Valentino, then the reigning king of romance. De Luise, overplaying as usual, has a cordon of yes-men around him and wreaks havoc on their insincerity. His barber is Michael Huddleston and when he doesn't join in agreeing with DeLuise, Huddleston is soon raised to the level of studio executive. Wilder is married to Kane and hopes to win the talent search. He gets off the train from the East wearing an all-white outfit and thinking he is the cat's pajamas; then he is chagrined to see that every other man de-training is dressed in the exact same costume. Graham is the director in charge of finding the right person for the role and he teeters on the brink of madness, because every single one of the actors is the same as the actor before, including Dimitri as the other major Valentino pretender. Kane truly loves Wilder but she is infatuated with Valentino and when she comes to the studio to meet him, Wilder pretends to be the great Italian star by dressing as a sheik and seducing his own wife. Several set pieces fall flat, including Wilder swimming in a sunken living room that is flooded, Wilder working on the assembly line of a bakery owned by David Huddleston, and one or two others. It's not easy to make a comedy when it is cast with some of the least funny people on screen. DeLuise adds another manic characterization to a career of overemoting; David Huddleston gets about as many laughs as watching a baby seal being clubbed; and Wilder, in a vain attempt to emulate Mel Brooks, falls back on his patented yelling rages that have long since palled. A few standouts in comedy include Dimitri, Jack Riley as a smart aleck studio projectionist, the always-enjoyable Carl Ballantine as Wilder's uncle, and Candy Azzara as a studio contract actress. Ballantine, who became nationally famous on TV's "McHale's Navy," had another career as a comedy magician in the 1940s and 1950s, when he played major nightclubs and theaters in a brief and hysterical act. His 10-minute act had more belly laughs in it than this entire movie, which was an amalgam of styles, blurred attitudes, and no focus. Any of the few jokes that played were either smarmy or concerning bodily functions, such as the one that featured Elya Baskin as an actor whose breath was so foul that it shrank the film. Good production design from Marsh, who was also credited as coproducer, and sharp editing from the razor of supervisor Chris Greenbury, another coproducer. This was Wilder's second attempt at being Orson Welles, the premier effort being THE

ADVENTURE OF SHERLOCK HOLMES' SMARTER BROTHER–which he wrote, directed, and starred in–a far better film, perhaps because he had a producer, Richard A. Roth (who appears in this movie), to oversee his excesses.

p,d&w, Gene Wilder; ph, Gerald Hirschfeld (DeLuxe Color); m, John Morris; ed, Chris Greenbury, Anthony A. Pellegrino; prod d, Terence Marsh; art d, Steve Sardanis; set d, Craig Edgar, John Franco, Jr.; cos, Ruth Myers, Ed Wynigear, Phyllis Garr, Darryl Athons, Carolina Ewart; m/l, "Ain't It Kinda Wonderful," Gene Wilder (sung by Harry Nilsson), "I'm Bringing a Red, Red Rose," Walter Donaldson, Gus Kahn; stunts, Mickey Gilbert.

Historical   **Cas.**   (PR:A-C   MPAA:PG)

WORLD'S GREATEST SINNER, THE* (1962) 82m Frenzy bw/c

Timothy Carey *(Clarence Hilliard)*, Gil Baretto *(Alonzo)*, Betty Rowland *(Edna Hilliard)*, James Farley *(Devil)*, Gail Griffen *(Betty Hilliard)*, Grace De Carolis *(Mother)*, Gitta Maynard *(Elderly Woman)*, Gene Pollock *(Priest)*, Whitey Jent *(Guitar Player)*, Carolina Samario *(Nate)*, Victor Floming *(Office Boss)*, Ann Josephs *(Secretary)*, Jenny Sanches *(Old Lady in Church)*, Tyde Rule, Gene Koziol, Dana Madison, Titus Moede, Betty Sturm, Marty Prisco, George F. Carey, Duana Dedda, Doris Carey, Eleanor Enderle, Jerry Mobley, George Seemer, Ben Avila, Joe Powell, Bob Divorsney, Victor Corey, Don Mozee *(Followers)*.

An curious experimental film which predates the spirituality and rock'n' roll messiah mumbo-jumbo of TOMMY by over a decade. Carey is an insurance salesman who refuses to believe that a deity rules the universe and thereby proclaims himself to be God. With guitar in hand, he gathers followers and is financially supported by a wealthy old woman. His reign is cut short by a miracle (the film's only color sequence) which proves the insignificance of man. Dopey, poorly acted, scripted with a dull pencil, and outdated, but still a little bit of fun. Music by rock experimentalist Frank Zappa.

p,d&w, Timothy Carey; ph, Ove H. Sehested, Robert Shelfow, Frank Grande, Raymond Steckler (Technicolor); m, Frank Zappa; ed, Carl Mahakian.

Drama   (PR:O   MPAA:NR)

WORLD'S GREATEST SWINDLES
        (SEE: BEAUTIFUL SWINDLERS, 1967, Fr./Ital./Jap.)

WORLDS OF GULLIVER, THE   (SEE: THREE WORLDS OF GULLIVER, THE, 1960, Brit.)

WORM EATERS, THE zero (1981) 94m Cinema Features-Genini/New American c

Herb Robins, *(Hermann Umgar)*, Lindsay Armstrong Black, Joseph Sacket, Robert Garrison, Muriel Cooper, Mike Garrison, Barry Hostetler, Carla.

A worm breeder (?!) is the victim of developers who want to construct condominiums on his property, but his squirmy wormies don't like the idea. His enemies then turn into "worm people"–half man, half worm wriggly things. The worm breeder has (what else but) worms in his mouth much of the time and then gets mushed by a truck. A godawful piece of annelid waste which was filmed in 1977.

p, Ted V. Mikels; d&w, Herb Robins (based on a story by Nancy Kapner); ph, Willis Hawkins (Eastmancolor); m, Theodore Stern; ed, Soly Bina; prod d, Jack DeWolf.

Horror/Comedy   (PR:O   MPAA:NR)

WORM'S EYE VIEW** (1951, Brit.) 77m Byron/ABF bw

Ronald Shiner *(Sam Porter)*, Garry Marsh *(Pop Brownlow)*, Diana Dors *(Thelma)*, John Blythe *(Duke)*, Bruce Seton *(Squadron Leader Briarly)*, Digby Wolfe *(Cpl. Mark Trelawney)*, Eric Davies *(Taffy)*, Everley Gregg *(Mrs. Bounty)*, Christina Forrest *(Bella Bounty)*, William Percy, Jonathan Field.

Five members of the Royal Air Force, headed up by Shiner, are billeted in a family home during WW II. Gregg is the landlady whose sour personality doesn't jibe with that of her new guests. In on the antics are Gregg's henpecked spouse, nasty stepson, and beautiful daughter. Dors is the maid who provides a bit of spice. Some mild amusement is to be found here, particularly in the dialog, though all in all this is nothing special. British filmgoer's thought otherwise, though, making both the film and Shiner big successes.

p, Henry Halstead; d, Jack Raymond; w, R.F. Delderfield, Jack Marks (based on the play by Delderfield); ph, James Wilson.

Comedy   (PR:A   MPAA:NR)

WORST SECRET AGENTS   (SEE: OO-2 MOST SECRET AGENTS, 1965, Ital.)

WORST WOMAN IN PARIS**½   (1933) 78m LAS/FOX bw

Benita Hume (*Peggy Vane*), Adolphe Menjou (*Adolphe Ballou*), Harvey Stephens (*John Strong*), Helen Chandler (*Mary Dunbar*), Margaret Seddon (*Mrs. Strong*), Adele St. Maur (*Jeanine*), Leonard Carey (*Chumley*), Maidel Turner (*Mrs. Jensen*), George Irving (*Doctor*).

Hume, an American art student living abroad, earns the title tag by associating with wealthy shipping magnate Menjou, becoming the subject of endless gossip. She soon departs Paris, bound for her hometown. En route, she is hailed as a heroine for her actions during a Kansas train wreck and passes an eventful stay in the Jayhawker State. Upon learning that Menjou has lost his fortune, she returns to France, returning some jewels that Menjou had given her and allowing him to recoup his loses.

p, Jesse L. Lasky; d, Monta Bell; w, Martin Brown, Marion Dix, Bell (based on a story by Bell); ph, Hal Mohr; m, Louis de Francesco; cos, Rita Kaufman.

Romance   (PR:A MPAA:NR)

WORTHY DECEIVER   (SEE: BIG BLUFF, THE, 1933)

WOULD YOU BELIEVE IT!**   (1930, Brit.) 56m Nettlefold/Big Four bw

Walter Forde (*Walter*), Pauline Johnson (*Pauline*), Arthur Stratton (*Cuthbert*), Albert Brouett (*Spy*), Anita O'Day (*Farmer's Wife*), Anita Sharp Bolster (*Presbyterian*).

Forde is an inventor who creates a tank operated by remote control. Of course, things don't quite go as planned and the tank loses control. It smashes everything in its path, incuding a gang of spies. Originally released as a silent film in England, sound was added in October of 1929 and it opened as a talkie in February 1930 in the U.S.

p, Archibald Nettlefold; d, Walter Forde; w, Forde, Harry Fowler Mear; ph, Geoffrey Faithfull.

Comedy   (PR:AAA MPAA:NR)

WOULD-BE GENTLEMAN, THE*½   (1960, Fr.) 95m Productions Cinematographiques/King sley-Union c

Jean Meyer (*Covielle*), Louis Seigner (*Mr. Jourdain*), Jacques Charon (*Dance Master*), Robert Manuel (*Music Master*), George Chamarat (*Philosopher*), Jean Piat (*Cleonte*), Jacques Eyser (*Fencing Master*), George Descrieres (*Dorante*), Jean-Louis Jemma (*Master Tailor*), Andree De Chauveron (*Mme. Jourdain*), Micheline Boudet (*Nicole*), Marie Sabouret (*Dorimene*), Michelle Grellier (*Lucille*), Henri Tisot (*Tailor's Assistant*), Rene Camoin (*1st Lackey*).

The upper rung of the social ladder is satirized in this piece of filmed theater based on a play by Moliere. It marks the first film appearance for the famed Comedie Francaise, who normally would only allow one member at a time to appear in a film. The performances are all top notch, as is the writing and the adaptation of the original. As a film, however, it offers nothing. The purpose, while intelligent and admirable, seems solely to preserve the Comedie Francaise for future generations to enjoy. (In French; English subtitles.)

p, Pierre Gerin; d, Jean Meyer (based on the play "Le Bourgeois Gentilhomme" by Moliere); ph, Henri Alekan (Eastmancolor); m, Jean Baptiste Lully; cos&set d, Suzanne Lalique; ch, Leone Mail.

Drama   (PR:A MPAA:NR)

WOZZECK*½   (1962, E. Ger.) 81m DEFA/Brandon bw

Kurt Meisel (*Wozzeck*), Helga Zulch (*Marie*), Arno Paulsen (*Captain*), Richard Haussler (*Sergeant-Major*), Paul Henkels (*Doctor*), Max Eckard (*Georg Buchner*), Wolfgang Kuhne (*Barker*), Willi Rose (*Andreas*).

Released in East Germany in 1947, WOZZECK tells the story of a soldier who allows himself to be subjected to a series of experiments by army doctors. His only time of pleasure is with his girl friend. Eventually he is taunted into killing her and is hung for the murder. (In German: English titles.)

p, Kurt Halme; d&w, Georg Klaren; (based on the play by Georg Buchner); ph, Bruno Mondi; m, Herbert Trantow; ed, Lena Neumann; set d, Hermann Warm, Bruno Monden; English subtitles, Charles Clement.

Drama   (PR:A MPAA:NR)

WRANGLER'S ROOST**   (1941) 57m MON bw

Ray Corrigan (*Crash*), John King (*Dusty*), Max Terhune (*Alibi Joslin*), Forrest Taylor (*The Deacon*), Gwen Gaze (*Molly*), George Chesebro (*Miller*), Frank Ellis (*Brady*), Jack Holmes (*Collins*), Walter Shumway (*Grover*), Frank McCarroll, Carl Mathews, Hank Bell, Tex Palmer, Jim Corey, Al Haskell, Ray Jones, Horace B. Carpenter, Tex Cooper, Herman Hack, Chick

Hannon.

An decent oater entry which has Taylor cast as a deacon interested in building a church on a piece of property donated by the town drunk. In the meantime, Corrigan, King, and Terhune are trying to crack a string of robberies performed in a gentlemanly fashion by the notorious Black Bart. Turns out that Taylor was the original Bart, but he's hung up his unloaded gun, paving the way for saloon owner Ellis to take his place. King sings a pair of tunes "Wrangler's Roost" and "Joggin'." (See RANGE BUSTERS series, Index.)

p, George W. Weeks; d, S. Roy Luby; w, John Vlahos, Robert Finkle (based on a story by Earle Snell); ph, Robert Cline; ed, Roy Claire; md, Frank Sanucci.

Western   (PR:A MPAA:NR)

WRATH OF GOD, THE**½   (1972) 111m Rainbow-Cineman/MGM c

Robert Mitchum (*Van Horne*), Frank Langella (*Tomas De La Plata*), Rita Hayworth (*Senora De La Plata*), John Colicos (*Col. Santilla*), Victor Buono ((*Jennings*), Ken Hutchinson (*Emmet Keogh*), Paula Pritchett (*Chela, Indian Girl*), Gregory Sierra (*Jurado, One-eyed Rebel*), Enrique Lucero (*Nacho, Chela's Father*), Jorge Russek (*Cordona*), Frank Ramirez (*Moreno, Cantina Operator*), Chano Urueta (*Antonio*), Jose Luis Parades (*Pablito*), Aurora Clavel (*Senora Moreno*), Victor Eberg (*Delgado*), Pancho Cordova (*Tacho*), Guillermo Hernandez (*Diaz*), Ralph Nelson (*Executed Prisoner*).

A western satire not unlike BEAT THE DEVIL in that it was misread by most people who thought it was just another violent oater. It's the Roaring Twenties in an unnamed Central American country (the kind of place O. Henry wrote about in his lesser-known works). Hutchinson (in a spoof on the role he did in STRAW DOGS) is an Irish citizen who has been caught in this country that bubbles with revolution. He meets Buono, a bootlegger-con man from England. Buono, who would have been the next Sidney Greenstreet-Laird Cregar if his obesity hadn't taken his life, talks Hutchinson into a whiskey smuggling run. Before he can take his profits, Hutchinson saves the life of Pritchett, a mute Indian maiden, when bandits are about to have their way with her. For his efforts, Hutchinson is about to be killed when his life is saved by Mitchum, who is apparently a defrocked priest. Mitchum, satirizing his own laconic persona, carries a knife in his crucifix and a shooting iron in his New Testament. Buono is captured by the local revolutionary leader, Colicos, and the same fate befalls Mitchum and Hutchinson. Colicos makes the trio an offer. If they are willing to kill Langella, who governs the area, Colicos will give them freedom and safe passage to the U.S. Langella is supposedly nuts and, even worse, a confirmed atheist! This all took place because of some of Colicos' men murdered Langella's father, raped his mother, and played sexual games with his sister until she finally went mad and took her own life. Posing as engineers, Mitchum and Buono go to the village where Langella rules. Mitchum shifts his collar around and arrives in the village as a man of the cloth. Despite Langella's turning away from God, the villagers still retain their piety and are immediately at Mitchum's side when he reopens the local church. Operating undercover, Buono, Hutchinson, and Mitchum try their best to undermine Langella but it's no go, even with the help of several locals and Pritchett's Indian tribe. Langella is angered by Mitchum's interference, has the man arrested and put up on a stone cross, held there by rusting barbed wire. Langella's mother is Hayworth and she has been watching the increasing madness of her boy. Just before Langella goes hurtling off the deep end, Hayworth shoots him and he lands at the feet of Mitchum, who is struggling on the cross. Mitchum causes himself to fall on top of Langella, killing the despot and himself. There's a huge battle and Buono dies and it looks as though Hutchinson will go the way of his pal's flesh when Pritchett, miraculously recovering her power of speech, shouts a warning to the Irishman and he is able to avoid a bullet with his name on it. There are many movie cliches which come under Nelson's script and direction. (Nelson got a solo credit on the screenplay but there were two writers who had been announced for the job shortly before and one never knows if they had a hand in it.) Anyone who took this seriously was making an error as it was made with tongue firmly in cheek. All of the actors were playing parts that had originally been played by other actors. Langella was doing "Caligula" out of THE ROBE, Buono was Kasper Gutman in THE MALTESE FALCON, and Mitchum was having a ball poking fun at himself. It has his third time around as a cleric, having donned the cloth in NIGHT OF THE HUNTER and FIVE CARD STUD. Bloody, but lots of fun.

p,d&w, Ralph Nelson (based on the novel by James Graham); ph, Alex Phillips, Jr. (Panavision, Metrocolor); m, Lalo Schifrin, excerpts from "Misa Criolla," Ariel Ramirez; ed, J. Terry Williams, Richard Bracken, Albert Wilson; prod d, John S. Poplin, Jr.; set d, William Kiernan; spec eff, Federico Farfan; stunts, Everett Creach; makeup, Del Armstrong.

Western/Satire   (PR:C-O PR:PG)

WRATH OF JEALOUSY**   (1936, Brit.) 70m FOX British bw (GB: WEDDING GROUP)

Fay Compton (*Florence Nightingale*), Patric Knowles (*Robert Smith*), Barbara Greene (*Janet Graham*), Alastair Sim (*Angus Graham*), Bruce Seton (*Dr. Jock Carnegie*), Ethel Glendinning (*Margaret Graham*), David Hutcheson (*George Harkness*), Arthur Young (*Dr. Granger*), Derek Blomfield, Billy Dear, Michael Wilding, Naomi Plaskitt.

Greene, a minister's daughter from Scotland, meets army officer Knowles in the year 1853. The two fall in love, but the romance is broken up by Greene's covetous sister Glendinning. Later Greene becomes a nurse and goes to the Crimean War to serve with Compton (playing the famed nurse Florence Nightingale). There she meets up with her beloved once more as she ends up saving his life.

p, Leslie Landau; d, Alex Bryce, Campbell Gullan; w, Selwyn Jepson, Hugh Brooke (based on the radio play by Philip Wade); ph, Roy Kellino; cos, Elizabeth Haffenden.

Romance   **(PR:A   MPAA:NR)**

WRECK OF THE MARY DEARE, THE***½   (1959) 105m MGM c

Gary Cooper (Gideon Patch), Charlton Heston (John Sands), Michael Redgrave (Mr. Hyland), Emlyn Williams (Sir Wilfred Falcett), Cecil Parker (The Chairman), Alexander Knox (Petrie), Virginia McKenna (Janet Taggart), Richard Harris (Higgins), Ben Wright (Mike Duncan), Peter Illing (Gunderson), Terence De Marney (Frank), Ashley Cowan (Burrows), Charles Davis (Yules), Alexander Archdale (Lloyd's Counsel), John Le Mesurier (M.O.A. Lawyer), Louis Mercier (Commander of Police), Albert Carrier (Ambulance Attendant), Lilyan Chauvin (Nun), Paul Bryar (Port Official), Lomax Study (Photographer), Jean Del Val (Javot), Kalu K. Sonkur (Lascar), Noel Drayton (Bell), Charles Lamb (Court Clerk), John Dearth (Reporter), George Dee (French Captain).

In this unusual sea drama, Heston plays a ship salvager who comes upon a seemingly empty vessel one stormy night. He boards the smoldering ship, which apparently had been set afire before being abandoned. While exploring this ship, dubbed the Mary Deare, Heston comes upon Cooper, the only crew member aboard, who demands that Heston leave, exclaiming that the ship is not abandoned. Heston is unable to reboard his tugboat, the Sea Witch, and nearly falls into the rough water below. Cooper saves him, and allows Heston to remain aboard. Heston learns that Cooper intends to drive his ship straight into some reefs along the English Channel. This angers Heston, who then asks Cooper for contract rights to refloat the Mary Deare. Cooper refuses to give him a definite answer, then asks Heston to keep this incident quiet. Heston reluctantly agrees after being reminded that Cooper had saved his life. Knox, an investigator for the Mary Deare's owner, begins to look into the matter. Heston skirts around Knox's questions, though the investigator sees through him. Cooper then asks Heston not to reveal where the ship is grounded. The Mary Deare is found by a French salvager, ruining Heston's plans for the ship, as well as Cooper's attempts at secrecy. Cooper finally tells a court of inquiry the truth. The ship had been carrying a cargo, but this was dropped off in Rangoon. A fire had then been set and the crew abandoned ship. The ship's owners now intend to collect an insurance settlement worth millions for the long gone cargo. Only Cooper stands in the way of their illegal intentions. The French salvage company is working hand in hand with the owners, hoping to sink the ship once it is back at sea. Cooper and Heston take scuba equipment and sneak back to the Mary Deare, where they catch the salvage crew (led by Harris, in an early role) in the act. Cooper is cleared and shares with Heston the reward money paid out by the insurance company. This film originally was to be directed by Alfred Hitchcock, who turned down the project to do NORTH BY NORTHWEST. Anderson took over and did a good job with the material. Though the script has a few gaps, Anderson pulls together the suspense elements in an intelligent manner. Heston and Cooper work well together. Cooper's performance is slightly distant, giving the character a rugged edge. Heston was thrilled to work with Cooper, though at first he resented the fact that the film was more Cooper's than his. Heston later realized how foolish this was. In his book The Actor's Life Heston wrote: "...of course it was Cooper's film...I was lucky to be in it. The experience of working with him and the friendship it created is one of the most valuble I've had in film."

p, Julian Blaustein; d, Michael Anderson; w, Eric Ambler (based on the novel by Hammond Innes); ph, Joseph Ruttenberg (CinemaScope, Metrocolor); m, George Duning; ed, Eda Warren; art d, Hans Peters, Paul Groesse; set d, Henry Grace, Hugh Hunt; spec eff, A. Arnold Gillespie, Lee Le Blanc; makeup, William Tuttle.

Adventure/Drama   **(PR:A   MPAA:NR)**

WRECKER, THE*   (1933) 72m COL bw

Jack Holt (Chuck Regan), Genevieve Tobin (Mary Regan), George E. Stone (Sam Shapiro), Sidney Blackmer (Tom Cummings), Ward Bond (Cramer), Irene White (Sarah), Russell Waddle, (Chuck Regan, Jr.), P.H. Levy (Hyam), Ed Le Saint (Doctor), Clarence Muse (Chauffeur), Wallie Albright.

A lame melodrama about a love triangle in which Holt, a building demolisher, has his marriage to Tobin wrecked by Blackmer. Instead of beating Blackmer to a pulp, Holt disappears on a drunk. But he reappears when an earthquake traps the cuckolding couple under a heap of threatening debris. Holt contemplates burying them himself but Stone dissuades him. Fate, however, exacts his revenge for him. Hokey.

d, Albert Rogell; w, Jo Swerling (based on a story by Rogell); ph, Benjamin Kline; ed, Richard Cahoon; cos, Robert Kalloch.

Drama   **(PR:A   MPAA:NR)**

WRECKERS, THE   (SEE: FURY AT SMUGGLER'S BAY, 1963, Brit.)

WRECKING CREW**   (1942) 73m PAR bw

Richard Arlen (Matt Carney), Chester Morris (Duke Mason), Jean Parker (Peggy Starr), Joseph Sawyer (Fred Bunce), Esther Dale (Mike O'Glendy), Alexander Granach (Joe Poska), Billy Nelson (Tom Kemp), Evelyn Brent (Martha Poska), Ralph Sanford (A Worker), Frank Melton (Pete), William Hall (Red), Fred Sherman (Emil), Alec Craig (Charlie), Nigel de Brulier (Priest), Byron Foulger (Mission Worker).

A well-crafted actioner which employs the wrecking trade as its gimmick and stars Arlen and Morris as competitive coworkers who get paid to reduce skyscrapers to a pile of dust and bricks. Their rivalry takes a romantic turn when they both become interested in Parker, but work comes first. They gain each other's respect as the both face death atop a building which is on the verge of collapse.

p, William Pine, William Thomas; d, Frank McDonald; w, Maxwell Shane, Richard Murphy (based on a story by Robert T. Shannon, Mauri Grashin); ph, Fred Jackman, Jr.; ed, William Ziegler; art d, F. Paul Sylos.

Action/Drama   **(PR:A   MPAA:NR)**

WRECKING CREW, THE**   (1968) 105m Meadway-Claude 4/COL c

Dean Martin (Matt Helm), Elke Sommer (Linka Karensky), Sharon Tate (Freya Carlson), Nancy Kwan (Yu-Rang), Nigel Green (Count Massimo Contini), Tina Louise (Lola Medina), John Larch (MacDonald), John Brascia (Karl), Weaver Levy (Kim), Wilhelm von Homburg (Gregor), Bill Saito (Ching), Fuji (Toki), Ted H. Jordan (Guard), Pepper Martin (Frankie), Whitney Chase (Miss Natural Gas), Bill Ryusaki (Henri), Chuck Norris (Garth), David Chow (Bartender), Jon Kowal (Kelly), Allen Pinson (Page), James Lloyd (Desk Clerk), James Daris, Tony Giorgio, Brick Huston, Josephine James, Harry Fleer, Vincent Van Lynn, Dick Winslow, Harry Geldard, Noel Drayton, Rex Holman, J.B. Peck.

Martin stars in the fourth and final "Matt Helm" entry as the debonair secret agent who again saves the world from doom. This time he and Tate prevent the world's economy from a catastrophe as a crime ring headed by Green hijacks $1 billion in gold. Green's plan is eventually foiled, but only after countless fights, chases, and murders. Tate, in a straightforward comedy role as a bumbling assistant agent, turns in the film's finest performance, though her career would come to an abrupt end in muder just a few months after the picture's release. To aid her with the kung-fu scenes that the script emphasized, Columbia hired Bruce Lee to train her. Also appearing in the picture was young karate star Chuck Norris, who would soon become quite a box-office name himself.

p, Irving Allen; d, Phil Karlson; w, William P. McGivern (based on the novel by Donald Hamilton); ph, Sam Leavitt, Frank Tallman (Technicolor); m, Hugo Montenegro; ed, Maury Winetrobe; md, Montenegro; art d, Joe Wright; set d, Frank Tuttle; cos, Moss Mabry, Sy Devore; makeup, Ben Lane, Hank Edds; spec eff, Paul Stewart; m/1, "House of 7 Joys," Mack David, DeVol; karate advisor, Bruce Lee.

Action/Drama/Comedy   **Cas.**   **(PR:C   MPAA:M)**

WRECKING YARD, THE   (SEE: ROTTEN APPLE, 1963)

WRESTLER, THE*   (1974) 95m Gagne-Frank/Entertainment Ventures c

Billy Robinson (Billy Taylor), Edward Asner (Frank Bass), Elaine Giftos (Debbie), Verne Gagne (Mike Bullard), Sarah Miller (Betty Bullard), Harold Sakata (Odd Job), Sam Menecker (Mobster), Hardboiled Haggerty (Bartender), Dusty Rhodes, Dick Murdoch, The Crusher, The Bruiser, Lord James Blears, Superstar Billy Graham (Themselves).

For once we get to see wrestling matches as they should be seen–in a fictional framework instead of under the misleading banner of sports. All the theatrical elements of the drop-kicking, full nelsoning monsters of the mats are tossed onto the screen in THE WRESTLER. The story is simple, as expected, and pits the wrestlers against a criminal faction who want a piece of the action–and the profits. Gagne appropriately plays an aging champ (his real-life role) as well as acting as the film's executive producer. Also in the cast is announcer Sam Menecker, and the granddaddies of wrestling–Dick the Bruiser and The Crusher. Aaargh! Enjoy the campiness of this movie or have your head crushed and bruised!

p, W.R. Frank; d, Jim Westman; w, Eugene Gump; ph, Gil Hubbs; m, William Loose, William Allen Castleman; ed, Neal Chastain; m/1, "I See Them," Howard Arthur (sung by Mona Brandt, Pat McKee).

Action/Crime Drama   **(PR:C   MPAA:PG)**

WRITTEN LAW, THE*½   (1931, Brit.) 79m Fogwell/Ideal bw

Madeleine Carroll (*Lady Margaret Rochester*), Percy Marmont (*Sir John Rochester*), Henry Hewitt (*Harry Carlisle*), James Fenton (*Dr. Rawlinson*), Barbara Barlowe (*Celia*), Ernest Lester.

Carroll is about to leave her husband Marmont (a doctor) for another man, when Marmont is blinded in an automobile accident. Eventually he regains his sight but conceals this fact, using his seeming disability to win back Carroll's love. An early effort for Carroll, who later achieved stardom in her work with Alfred Hitchcock.

p, Reginald Fogwell, Mansfield Markham; d&w, Fogwell.

Drama   **(PR:A   MPAA:NR)**

WRITTEN ON THE SAND   (SEE: PLAY DIRTY, 1969, Brit.)

WRITTEN ON THE WIND***   (1956) 99M UNIV c

Rock Hudson (*Mitch Wayne*), Lauren Bacall (*Lucy Moore Hadley*), Robert Stack (*Kyle Hadley*), Dorothy Malone (*Marylee Hadley*), Robert Keith (*Jasper Hadley*), Grant Williams (*Biff Miley*), Robert J. Wilke (*Dan Willis*), Edward C. Platt (*Dr. Paul Cochrane*), Harry Shannon (*Hoak Wayne*), John Larch (*Roy Carter*), Joseph Granby (*R.J. Courtney*), Roy Glenn (*Sam*), Maidie Norman (*Bertha*), William Schallert (*Reporter*), Joanne Jordan (*Brunette*), Dani Crayne (*Blonde*), Dorothy Porter (*Secretary*), Jane Howard, Floyd Simmons (*Beer Drinkers*), Cynthia Patrick (*Waitress*), Glen Kramer, Phil Harvey, Coleen McClatchey, Carlene King Johnson (*College Students*), Carl Christian (*Bartender*), Gail Bonney (*Hotel Floorlady*), Paul Bradley (*Maitre d'*), Robert Brubaker (*Hotel Manager*), Bert Holland (*Court Clerk*), Don C. Harvey (*Taxi Starter*), Robert Malcolm (*Hotel Proprietor*), Robert Lyden (*Kyle as a Boy*), Robert Wilson (*Mitch as a Boy*), Susan Odin (*Marylee as a Girl*), Kevin Corcoran (*Boy in Drugstore*), June Valentine, Hedi Duval, George DeNormand.

The ultimate in melodrama, WRITTEN ON THE WIND is not only the finest directorial effort from Sirk but also one of the most notable films on the subject of the American family. The family is the Hadley-a wealthy clan of Texas oil barons (the town they live in is even named Hadley) which includes patriarch Keith, a freewheeling alcoholic son, Stack, and a nymphomaniac daughter, Malone. While not blood kin, Hudson, a friend of the family's since childhood, has practically been adopted by Keith, who shows more faith in him than in Stack. While passing through New York, Hudson, who is employed by Hadley Oil as a geologist, meets a young advertising executive, Bacall, to whom he is immediately attracted. He makes the mistake, however, of introducing her to Stack, who refers to Hudson as "my sidekick-he's eccentric, he's poor." While poor financially, Hudson is rich in morality and integrity. Although Bacall initially resists Stack's charms and riches (he offers to buy her the advertising firm), she gradually is taken in by him. Stack tries to get rid of Hudson, but to no avail. A whirlwind romance, which includes Hudson as a third party, begins on a private flight to Florida. When they land, Bacall is shocked to find that Stack has not only booked her a hotel suite but filled it with expensive dresses and perfumes. Bacall is speechless, while Stack humorously states, "a great invention-the telephone," referring to the ease with which he ordered the gifts. Still apprehensive, Bacall sneaks away. Stack finds her at the airport, ready to return to New York. He persuades her to stay with him. They secretly marry-a society-page event that the newspapers pounce on. After five weeks of globetrotting, Keith has yet to meet his new daughter-in-law. All the talk of marriage gets Keith thinking about the possibility of Hudson and Malone marrying, an idea which Hudson dislikes because of his brotherly feelings towards her. Just then stack and Bacall arrive at the office. Thoroughly impressed with Bacall, Keith welcomes her to Hadley, "the town and the family." He then has a private conversation with her, questioning her about Stack's two vices-drinking and keeping a gun under his pillow-both of which stack has kicked since meeting Bacall. After a year of living in Texas, Stack and Bacall are still happily married, but tensions soon rise. It is Malone who is the root of everyone's problems. Her loose sexual attitudes get her in trouble at the local bar when she comes onto Larch. The bartender calls Hudson to the scene. Stack accompanies him and a fight breaks out with Larch, after which Hudson drives off with Malone in her sporty red convertible. Malone is straightforward with Hudson. She has a passionate desire for him and is determined to hook him into marriage. Hudson's interest, however, lies with Bacall, although both respect her marriage. Later that evening Malone is brought home by the police (the town name of Hadley also graces the side of their squad car) who have apprehended a young man found in a motel with her. The young man makes it clear that Malone did the seducing and that everyone in town-except her father-knows that she is a tramp. Keith's temper blows and he grabs a gun, but is prevented from firing it. Meanwhile, Malone has retreated to her room. Listening to some deafening rumba music, Malone orgasmically dances around her room in a flowing red nightgown. While climbing the long staircase to her bedroom, Keith's heart gives way and he tumbles down the stairs to his death. Absorbed in her music, Malone is completely oblivious to the fact that her promiscuity has just killed her father. The combination of Keith's death and the news that he is sterile, drives Stack to resume his drinking. He becomes irrational and when confronted by his sister with the possibility that Hudson and Bacall are having an affair, he lashes out against her. "You're a filthy liar," he

attacks. "I'm filthy, period," she responds. Fearing that she will lose Hudson to Bacall, Malone continues to play on Stack's fears until she completely convinces him of his wife's infidelity. Later Hudson offers Bacall a ride into town. Bacall has an appointment with a doctor, while Hudson is visiting his father, a rugged individual who lives in a small house and spends his time cleaning his guns. When Hudson picks Bacall up from the doctor's, he announces his intention to leave for Iran to work with a foreign oil interest. He also confesses his love for her, but she responds by telling him that she is pregnant with Stack's baby. According to Bacall, the diagnosis of Stack as sterile was "a medical opinion, not a fact." When Bacall tells the drunken Stack the good news, he immediately becomes suspicious. He jumps to the paranoid conclusion that Hudson is the father. "You shouldn't have done that to me," he moans before viciously, knocking Bacall to the ground. Hudson comes to Bacall's aid and delivers a couple of punches to Stack. As Stack staggers out of the house, Hudson shouts that he'll kill him next time. The entire confrontation is witnessed by the Hadley's maid. Stack runs off to the bar where he unsuccessfully attempts to buy a gun, complaining to the bartender that his "best friend" tried to kill him. Stack returns to the house, tearing apart his father's study searching for the gun he kept hidden there. He finds it and tears into Hudson: "You lousy trash. You no-count, two-faced dog. I'm gonna watch you cringe, then I'm gonna put a bullet in your belly." Hudson tries to convince Stack of his innocence. He tells him that nothing ever happened between him and Bacall. Stack's tirade continues, however: "You made me small in my father's eyes. You made my sister spit at me. Then, you stole my wife." Hudson then breaks the news that Bacall just had a miscarriage and that the child would have been Stack's. In the meantime, Malone has walked into the room and has stopped behind Stack, without him noticing. She tries to wrestle the gun away. A shot is accidentally fired into Stack, who stumbles out the front door and collapses. The death makes the headlines and a court case follows. Being the only witness, Malone threatens to place the blame on Hudson unless he marries her. Hudson's future looks dim as a collection of people are called to the stand-each of them attesting to the fact that Hudson threatened to kill Stack. While on the stand, Malone initially blames Hudson, but has a change of heart and tells the truth. Back at the Hadley estate, Bacall and Hudson are seen driving off. A broken Malone sits at her father's desk, clutching a miniature oil well as a portrait of her father in the same pose looks down at her. In WRITTEN ON THE WIND, Sirk manages to successfully combine all the elements of the melodrama-which his name has become synonymous with-into one picture. While melodrama existed in many forms before Sirk, it is he who began using it as a tool to depict truly American ideals. Sirk's melodramas are America-in the large, stereotypical, capitalistic sense. The men are strong; the women are sexy; the cars are fast; the houses are magnificent. Sirk's America has guns, liquor, dancing, oil wells, private planes. The film is filled with tremendous emotional upheavals and intimate secrets which suggest a dark side of life. It is paced in a lightning-fast style with sports cars and frantic music, and photographed in a vibrant technicolor with a heavy use of shadows to capture mood and personality. The common belief that WRITTEN ON THE WIND is merely a soap opera couldn't be farther from the truth. It is a scathing social indictment of the American family. In the midst of the 1950s' era of good feeling, Sirk was busy shaking the skeletons out of the closet. As the Hadleys discovered, a family may be hiding a variety of secrets: alcoholism, sexual promiscuity, incest, sterility, blackmail, and murder. Instead of limiting himself to only one of these skeletons, Sirk chooses to find a place for all of them in this film. The effect is an exaggerated and unrealistic-or melodramatic-one, which while not documenting American family life, does offer an intellectual and highly cinematic comment on it. In WRITTEN ON THE WIND the supposed American Dream of great prosperity is actually nothing but a thin disguise which is easily blown away to reveal the nightmare underneath.

p, Albert Zugsmith; d, Douglas Sirk; w, George Zuckerman (based on the novel by Robert Wilder); ph, Russell Metty (Technicolor); m, Frank Skinner; ed, Russell F. Schoengarth; md, Joseph Gershenson; art d, Alexander Golitzen, Robert Clatworthy; set d, Russell A. Gausman, Julia Heron; cos, Bill Thomas, Jay Morley, Jr.; spec eff, Clifford Stine; on the Wind," Victor Young, Sammy Cahn (sung by The Four Aces).

Drama   **(PR:C   MPAA:NR)**

WRONG ARM OF THE LAW, THE*   (1963, Brit.) 91m Romulus/CD   bw

Peter Sellers (*Pearly Gate/"Mons. Jules"*), Lionel Jeffries (*Inspector Parker*), Bernard Cribbins (*Nervous O'Toole*), Davy Kaye (*Trainer King*), Nanette Newman (*Valerie*), Bill Kerr (*Jack Coombes*), Ed Devereaux (*Bluey Max*), Reg Lye (*Reg Danton*), John Le Mesurier (*Assistant Commissioner*), Graham Stark (*Sid Cooper*), Martin Boddey (*Supt. Forest*), Irene Browne (*Dowager*), Arthur Mullard (*Brassknuckles*), Dermot Kelly (*Misery Martin*), Vanda Godsell (*Annette*), Tutte Lemkow (*Siggy Schmultz*), Barry Keegan (*Alf*), John Junkin (*Maurice*), Dennis Price (*Educated Ernest*), Dick Emery (*Man in Apartment*), John Harvey, Michael Caine.

A very amusing comedy, the kind of cops and robbers antics that only the British seemed capable of making in the 1950s and 1960s. Sellers pretends to be the owner of a posh dress shop in the upper-crust area of Bond Street. It's just a front, though. His real occupation is leading a pack of London thieves. The burglary business is well organized and the various crooks have made a vow not to tread in one another's territories. That all blows up when a trio of felons from down under arrives impersonating police officers. They grab off the loot and Sellers is in a quandary. Up until now, everything has been running smoothly and Sellers has been running his "business" like a benevolent Henry Ford, with free lunches, paid vacations in Spain, and even showing his cohorts films like RIFIFI as part of their continuing education. Sellers catches on that he's been had but he doesn't realize that the men raided his place after having been informed of the location by Sellers' amour, Newman. Sellers calls for a general confab with all of the other honest crooks in London and they make a deal with Scotland Yard for a one-day truce so they can join forces and nab these Aussies who are ruining matters for all concerned. To do this, they fake a gold robbery and Yardman Jeffries is assigned to be one of crooks. Jeffries is an incompetent and the whole thing goes up for grabs so they have to set a second snare involving an armored car at the airport. Sellers steals the money but Jeffries is handcuffed to the money box. All of the gangs are apprehended save Sellers and his group. They get away on a plane and Newman's also aboard, having stowed away. When they arrive on a tropical island, they are shocked to see that the money in the strongbox is bogus. Shrugging that off, the gang settles down in the sunny paradise and goes into business manufacturing grass skirts for the local denizens. Fast-moving, very witty, and filled with excellent character bits by a host of actors whose faces you'll recognize.

p, Aubrey Baring; d, Cliff Owen; w, John Warren, Len Heath, Ray Galton, Alan Simpson, John Antrobus (based on a story by Ivor Jay, William Whistance Smith); ph, Ernest Steward; m, Richard Rodney Bennett; ed, Tristam Cones; md, John Hollingsworth; art d, Harry White.

Crime/Comedy   **(PR:A   MPAA:NR)**

WRONG BOX, THE*   (1966, Brit.) 107m Salamander/COL c

John Mills (*Masterman Finsbury*), Ralph Richardson (*Joseph Finsbury*), Michael Caine (*Michael Finsbury*), Peter Cook (*Morris Finsbury*), Dudley Moore (*John Finsbury*), Nanette Newman (*Julia Finsbury*), Tony Hancock (*Detective*), Peter Sellers (*Dr. Pratt*), Cicely Courtneidge (*Maj. Martha*), Wilfrid Lawson (*Peacock*), Thorley Walters (*Lawyer Patience*), Gerald Sim (*1st Undertaker*), Peter Graves (*Military Officer on Train*), Irene Handl (*Mrs. Hackett*), Norman Bird (*Clergyman*), John Le Mesurier (*Dr. Slattery*), Hilton Edwards (*Lawyer*), Norman Rossington (*1st Rough*), Diane Clare (*Mercy, Salvation Army Girl*), Tutte Lemkow (*Bournemouth Strangler*), Charles Bird (*Bonn's Vanman*), Joseph Behrman (*Vanman's Mate*), Marianne Stone (*Spinster on Train*), Michael Bird (*Countryman*), Thomas Gallagher (*2nd Rough*), Timothy Bateson (*Clerk*), Reg Lye (*3rd Undertaker*), John Junkin (*1st Engine Driver*), Roy Murray (*1st Stoker*), Tony Thawnton (*2nd Undertaker*), George Selway (*Railway Vanman*), Gwendolyn Watts (*Maid*), Vanda Godsell (*Mrs. Goodge, Bournemouth Landlady*), Donald Tandy (*Ticket Collector*), Lionel Gamlin (*2nd Engine Driver*), Martin Terry (*2nd Stoker*), George Spence (*Workman in Road*), Jeremy Lloyd (*Brian Allen Harvey, Artillery Officer*), James Villiers (*Sydney Whitcombe Sykes, Falconer*), Graham Stark (*Ian Scott Fife, Mountaineer*), Dick Gregory (*Leicester Young Fielding*), Nicholas Parsons (*Alan Fraser Scrope*), Willoughby Goddard (*James White Wragg, Mine Owner*), Valentine Dyall (*Oliver Pike Harmsworth*), Leonard Rossiter (*Vyvyan Alastair Montague, Duel Umpire*), Hamilton Dyce (*Derek Lloyd Peter Digby*), Donald Oliver (*Gunner Sergeant*), Totti Truman-Taylor (*Lady at Launching*), Jeremy Roughton (*Bugler*), Frank Singuineau (*Native Bearer*), Michael Lees (*Young Digby, Bathchair Pusher*), Andre Morell (*Club Butler*), Avis Bunnage (*Queen Victoria*), Penny Brahms, Maria Kazan (*Twittering Females on Moors*), Freddy Clark, George Hillsden (*Constables*), Alf Mangun, Norman Morris (*Gravediggers*), Arthur Sandiford, Louise Noland (*Mourners*), John Tateham (*Verger*), Sarah Harrison (*Governess*), Peggy Ray (*Child with Governess*), John Parker, John Fitch, Norman Hibbert, Jimmy Scott, Alistair Dick (*Undertaker's Assistants*), Dan Cressey (*Judas*), Lindsay Hooper (*Matthew*), Dorothy Ford, Unity Greenwood (*Salvation Army Girls*), John Morris, (*Sotheby's Assistant*), The Temperance Seven (*Themselves*), Denis Cowles (*Sotheby's Partner*), Patsy Snell, Andrea Allen (*Girls on Train*), Phillip Stewart (*Elderly Man on Train*), Rita Tobin (*Elderly Woman on Train*).

Often funny period comedy based on a story co-authored by Robert Louis Stevenson and Lloyd Osbourne in the last century. Americans Gelbart and Shevelove expanded on the tale, added a great deal of comedy, and wrote the script for this packed-with- sight-gags farce. Mills and Richardson are brothers in Victorian London. They haven't seen each other for four decades and for good reason. When they were young lads, they were part of a multi-youth "tontine" and they are the last survivors of the odd pact. Years before, several parents had tossed about $2,800 each into a pool. As the calendar pages were ripped off, the money began to mount through good investments and it is now a bundle. Little by little, in a series of gags, we see how the other members of the strange lottery have gone to their final rewards. The brothers are each awaiting the news that the other has died so the remaining one can have all the money. Mills is dying and can't bear the thought that Richardson will outlive him so he attempts to have Richardson killed but that is botched. Mills wants the money to go to Caine, his grandson, a moon-eyed medical student. Mills continues to engineer plots on Richardson's life to no avail. Richardson is an addled man, given to collecting odd bits of information which mean nothing to anyone but him. At one point, when told he's going to London, he mentions that if numbers

were assigned to the letters in the alphabet ("A" equals one, "B" equals two), that the word "London" would add up to 74, which is his precise age. Richardson has no children but he does have two avaricious nephews, Cook and Moore, who know about the treasure trove and want it for themselves. Cook and Moore erroneously think that Mills has died and that Caine is not telling the truth about the old man's demise. Richardson has supposedly been killed in a train wreck and they don't want that fact to be publicized so they put Richardson's body (or so they mistakenly believe) into a wooden box and ship it back home in the hopes that the corpse won't be discovered. It's the wrong body, though. This one belongs to a notorious murderer known as the "Bournemouth Strangler." It's taken in error to Mills' house where Caine has no idea of what's transpired. All he knows is that he has a dead body on his doorstep and had better get rid of it. As this transpires, Cook and Moore pay a bribe to a disreputable physician, Sellers, to sign a death certificate for Richardson that is post-dated. When the police find that the body of the killer is missing, they begin a frantic search for it. There's a mad chase and, following that, it turns out that both Mills and Richardson are alive. Cook and Moore are sent to Coventry and Caine is the beneficiary of the money when it is learned that he is in love with Richardson's ward, Newman. Sellers is on screen only a few minutes but registers quite well, as does Lawson as the butler. It's shot, in part, like a British version of a Mack Sennett film, replete with subtitles. All of the smaller roles are deliciously cast with several of the best comic actors England had to offer in that decade, a heyday of British humor. The picture gets flabby from time to time and comes alive when the old masters, Mills and Richardson, are on screen. The plot works but there are so many sight gags that fall flat that it begins to pall occasionally. The score is by John Barry and The Temperance Seven perform funeral and military airs.

p&d, Bryan Forbes; w, Larry Gelbart, Burt Shevelove (based on the novel by Robert Louis Stevenson, Lloyd Osbourne); ph, Gerry Turpin (Eastmancolor); m, John Barry; ed, Alan Osbiston; md, Barry; art d, Ray Simm; set d, Peter James; cos, Julie Harris; m/l, "Light of Head," Clifford Bevan; makeup, Paul Rabiger, Basil Newall.

Historical Comedy   **Cas.**   **(PR:A   MPAA:NR)**

WRONG DAMN FILM, THE zero   (1975) 84m c

Barry Bostwick (*Alex Rounder*), Barbara Dana (*Donna Compere*), Keene Curtis (*Agent Bradfort/Businessman Wilton/Saleman Hughes*).

This sophomoric satire on politics came out in the wake of Watergate. Badly bungled from beginning to end, the film received only a few showings before mercifully disappearing without a trace.

p,d&w, Carson Davidson; ph, Richard Francis; m, Arnold Eldus; ed, Davidson.

Comedy   **(PR:C-O   MPAA:NR)**

WRONG IS RIGHT**   (1982) 117m Rastar COL c (GB: THE MAN WITH THE DEADLY LENS)

Sean Connery (*Patrick Hale*), George Grizzard (*President Lockwood*), Robert Conrad (*Gen. Wombat*), Katharine Ross (*Sally Blake*), G.D. Spradlin (*Philindros*), John Saxon (*Homer Hubbard*), Henry Silva (*Rafeeq*), Leslie Nielsen (*Mallory*), Robert Webber (*Harvey*), Rosalind Cash (*Mrs. Ford, Vice President*), Hardy Kruger (*Helmut Unger*), Dean Stockwell (*Hacker*), Ron Moody (*King Awad*), Cherie Michan (*Erika*), Tony March (*Abu*), Marianne Marks (*Suzy*), Jeffrey Wheat (*Mike*), Joseph Whipp (*John Brown*), Tom McFadden (*Billy Bob Harper*), Ivy Bethune (*Housewife*), Jennifer Jason Leigh (*Young Girl*), Kiva Lawrence (*Receptionist*), Barry Cahill (*Husband*), Angelo Bertolini (*Cardinal*), Keith MacConnell (*Smythe*), Alexander Zale (*Faheem*), Donald Bishop (*Congressman*), Dianne Lynn Wilson (*Woman with Dog*), George Skaff (*Qadee*), Denis Hoppe (*Hagreb Officer*), Milt Jamin (*Hagreb Doctor*), Edward L. Moskowitz (*Technician*), Myron Natwick (*Admiral*), Paul Lambert (*Defense Secretary*), Suzanne Reynolds (*TV Reporter*), David Frankham (*British Reporter*), Ed Pennybacker (*U.S. Reporter*), Ken Bibeau (*Marcus*), Art Evans, Mio Polo (*Guards*), Charles Hutchins (*Cabbie*), Robert Alan Browne (*Motorist*), Mickey Jones (*Gunman*), Dawna O'Brien (*President's Secretary*), Pamela V. Kobbe (*Hale's Secretary*), Claire Grenville (*Campaigner*), Merrill M. Mazuer, Ken Gale, Kerry Sullivan, Melanie Stensland, Ray Conners, Melinda Ann Casey, Don Dunwell, Don Worsham (*News Staff*).

Connery stars as a TV reporter with a global beat in this satiric look at the increasingly negative American image abroad. He finds himself up against A-bomb armed revolutionaries from the Middle East, the CIA, the FBI, and even the President of the U.S. It's all rather haphazard in its visual style and plotting, tallying up to a confused condemnation of our lack of morality.

p,d&w, Richard Brooks (based on the novel *The Better Angels* by Charles McCarry); ph, Fred J. Koenekamp (Panavision, Metrocolor); m, Artie Kane; ed, George Grenville; prod d, Edward Carfagno; art d, Karl Heuglin; set d, Arthur Jeph; cos, Ray Summers.

Satire/Drama   **Cas.**   **(PR:O   MPAA:R)**

## WRONG KIND OF GIRL, THE						(SEE: BUS STOP, 1956)

## WRONG MAN, THE****								(1956) 105m WB bw

Henry Fonda (Christopher Emmanuel "Manny" Balestrero), Vera Miles (Rose Balestrero), Anthony Quayle (Frank O'Connor), Harold J. Stone (Lt. Bowers), Esther Minciotti (Mrs. Balestrero), Charles Cooper (Detective Matthews), Nehemiah Persoff (Gene Conforti), Laurinda Barrett (Constance Willis), Norma Connolly (Betty Todd), Doreen Lang (Ann James), Frances Reid (Mrs. O'Connor), Lola D'Annunzio (Olga Conforti), Robert Essen (Gregory Balestrero), Kippy Campbell (Robert Balestrero), Dayton Lummis (Judge Groat), John Heldabrand (Tomasini), Richard Robbins (Daniell), John Vivyan (Detective Holman), Will Hare (McKaba), Werner Klemperer (Dr. Banay), Mel Dowd (Nurse), Peggy Webber (Miss Dennerly), Anna Karen (Miss Duffield), Michael Ann Barrett (Miss Daly), Alexander Lockwood (Emmerton), Emerson Treacy (Mr. Wendon), Bill Hudson (Police Lieutenant, 110th Precinct), Marc May (Tomasini's Assistant), William Le Massena (Sang), Josef Draper, William Crane (Jurors), Leonard Capone (Court Clerk), Charles J. Guiotta, Thomas J. Murphy (Court Officers), Harold Berman (Court Stenographer), John Caler (Soldier), Silvio Minciotti (Mr. Balestrero), Barry Atwater (Mr. Bishop), Dino Terranova (Mr. Ferrero), Rossana San Marco (Mrs. Ferrero), Daniel Ocko (Felony Court Judge), Olga Fabian (Mrs. Mank), Otto Simanek (Mr. Mank), Dave Kelly (Policeman), Maurice Manbson (District Atty. John Hall), John McKee, Gordon Clark (Police Attendants), Paul Bryar (Interrogation Officer), Sammy Armaro, Allan Ray, John Truax (Suspects), Ray Bennett, Clarence Straight (Policemen), Don Turner (Detective), Penny Santon (Spanish Woman), Bonnie Franklin, Pat Morrow (Young Girls), Charles Aidman (Jail Medical Attendant), Richard Durham, Harry 'Dean' Stanton, Mike Keene, Frank Schofield, Chris Gampel, Maurice Wells (Department of Correction Officers), Helen Shields (Receptionist), Don McGovern (Waving Man), Cherry Hardy, Elizabeth Scott (Waving Women), Walter Kohler (Manny's Attorney, Felony Court), Spencer Davis (Prisoner's Lawyer), Ed Bryce (Court Officer), Harry Beckman (Prisoner), Maria Reid (Spanish Woman), Paul Carr (Young Man), Tuesday Weld, Barbara Karen (Giggly Girls), Dallas Midgette (Customer at Bickford's), Donald May (Arresting Patrolman), John C. Becher (Liquor Store Proprietor), Earl George (Delicatessen Proprietor), Mary Boylan (Curious Customer), Natalie Priest (Delicatessen Proprietor's Wife), Rhodelle Heller, Olive Stacey, John Stephen (Stork Club Customers), John Stephen (Man in Stork Club).

The bleakest of Hitchcock's films, this stark, deliberate probing of an innocent man accused is almost wholly based on fact, creating its drama from real-life incidents which occurred, in a celebrated New York City case, to Christopher Emmanuel Balestrero. Fonda plays Balestrero, known to everyone as Manny, a family man who plays standup bass at a Queens nightspot called the Stork Club. He seems content enough with his job, devoting himself to music, and even finding the time to teach his two young sons how to play. Although he doesn't have much money, he manages to keep his life together with the help of his wife, Miles, a devoted woman he cares deeply for. When she complains of dental pains, Fonda decides to borrow on her life insurance policy–the last place they can borrow money since their debts have already piled too high. Although Fonda makes a practice of picking horses in the race section of the newspaper, he never dares bet on them, lacking the desire to take such a gamble even though it could get him out of debt. The following morning, Fonda goes to the insurance office where, in a wicked twist of fate, he is identified by the office girls as the man who previously robbed them. Later that night, Fonda is arrested at the Stork Club. After being identified by a number of witnesses, he is interrogated at the police station. When he makes a nervous mistake in a handwriting test (misspelling the word "drawer" as "draw"–the same mistake made on the robber's ransom note), Fonda is fingerprinted, photographed, and imprisoned. When he is finally released on bail, Fonda, who is joyfully reunited with Miles, retains lawyer Quayle to help him prove his innocence. When Fonda is unable to find any witnesses to provide his alibi, the prospect of an acquittal looks dim. Meantime, Miles begins to crack under the pressure, retreating into her own mental imprisonment, no longer able to deal with her husband's trial and defense. She is committed to a sanatorium for treatment while Fonda's proceedings move on. During the trial, his case hits a snag and a retrial is declared after a juror, who has already presumed his guilt, asks if all the questioning is really necessary. Back in his cell, Fonda, who has no other choice, begins to pray. While doing so, the real criminal is miraculously discovered, as his face is superimposed over the innocent Fonda's. A free man, Fonda visits his wife in the sanatorium and tells her the good news. "That's fine for you," she coldly states in a distant, troubled tone. Having become accustomed to the lighter, more commercial tone of such films as TO CATCH A THIEF, THE TROUBLE WITH HARRY, and THE MAN WHO KNEW TOO MUCH, the public was then shaken back into reality with the unexpectedly bleak, hopeless, Kafka-esque style (more frightening than Orson Welles' THE TRIAL), of THE WRONG MAN. Basing the film on the life and incidents of this real-life Queens bass player which began with his arrest on January 13, 1953 (Hitchcock learned of the case through a Life magazine article), Hitchcock takes us to the actual locations–the Stork Club, a Long Island Prudential insurance office, Balestrero's Seventy-fourth Street Queens home, the asylum where his wife was committed, the actual police station, and Balestrero's prison cell–with the intent of representing the case in all its authenticity. Hitchcock spares us nothing in procedural terms. The

questioning of the suspect, for example, is done in necessary tedium, wearing the audience down as much as Fonda's character. We see him fingerprinted–the ink being applied to his fingertips, the printing, the paper he is given to clean his hands. We are forced to sit through the entirety of his handwriting analysis, comparing the actual holdup note to Fonda's handwritten version of it. As the police officer reads him the note, Fonda writes, the police officers examine and compare it to the original copy, the task is then repeated, the officer rereads the note, Fonda rewrites the note, the officer reexamines and recompares the two versions, and then, finally, after this unbearable wait, tells us that it doesn't look good for Fonda. Hitchcock in THE WRONG MAN has succeeded in finding, in the real world, a story which is truly Hitchcockian–that idea of the wrong man accused–and has brought it to the screen, as if to present evidence to any critics or viewers who thought the director's films were not credible. Paradoxically, it is THE WRONG MAN which is one of Hitchcock's least believable films. Incidents are constantly occurring that frustrate and baffle the viewer, doubting that what happened to the clearly innocent Fonda could actually happen in real life. Though the film is based almost entirely on fact (Hitchcock made special efforts to contact everyone involved, including the Balestreros and attorney O'Connor), it seems less real than Hitchcock's fiction, which benefits from his creative license and his careful attention to making everything seem credible. To add legitimacy to the story's events, Hitchcock even tacked on a prolog in which he introduced himself and then verified that the story about to be shown was based in fact. While the film is based chiefly on Fonda's trauma, Hitchcock doesn't ignore the mental torture Miles is put through, temporarily departing from the story of Fonda's conviction to delve further into her problems. It was Miles' first of two appearances in a Hitchcock film (PSYCHO was the second), although she did act in the first episode of the director's television series "Alfred Hitchcock Presents..." (Titled "Revenge," this episode, the second one filmed but the first to be broadcast, was one of the handful to be directed by Hitchcock himself.) Using Miles' television spot as a testing ground for THE WRONG MAN, Hitchcock then planned to cast her in VERTIGO, but had to cast Kim Novak instead when the newly wed actress became pregnant. (Hitchcock took her pregnancy personally and commented "Vera, instead of leaping at the chance of her life, got pregnant!. She was going to be a real star with this film 'VERTIGO', but she couldn't resist her Tarzan of a husband, Gordon Scott. She should have taken a jungle pill!") Don't look too hard for Hitchcock's usual cameo in this picture– he originally intended to be seen as a customer walking into the Stork Club, but edited himself out of the final print. There are a few other interesting cameos, however–Harry Dean Stanton in one of his countless minor roles, and two giggling girls who later found fame, Bonnie Franklin and Tuesday Weld.

p&d, Alfred Hitchcock; w, Maxwell Anderson, Angus MacPhail (based on "The True Story of Christopher Emmanuel Balestrero" by Anderson); ph, Robert Burks; m, Bernard Herrmann; ed, George Tomasini; art d, Paul Sylbert, William L. Kuehl; tech adv, Frank O'Connor.

**Crime Drama						Cas.						(PR:A MPAA:NR)**

## WRONG NUMBER**						(1959, Brit.) 60m Merlin/Anglo Amalgamated
														bw

Peter Reynolds (Angelo), Lisa Gastoni (Maria), Peter Elliot (Dr. Pole), Olive Sloane (Miss Crystal), Paul Whitsun-Jones (Cyril), Barry Keegan (Max), John Horsley (Supt. Blake), Harold Goodwin (Bates), Arthur Lovegrove, Catherine Ferraz, Christopher Trace.

Sloane is a sweet old lady who finds herself mixed up in murder. Seems she's dialed a wrong number and heard part of a conversation involving Reynolds, who killed a man in a mail truck heist. Thanks to Sloane, the law is able to close in on and arrest the killer and his henchmen. Pretty ridiculous plot development, but Sloane is fun as the little old lady.

p, Jack Greenwood; d, Vernon Sewell; w, James Eastwood (based on the play by Norman Edwards); ph, Josef Ambor.

**Crime														(PR:A MPAA:NR)**

## WRONG ROAD, THE*½						(1937) 62m REP bw

Richard Cromwell (Jimmy Caldwell), Helen Mack (Ruth Holden), Lionel Atwill (Mike Roberts), Horace MacMahon (Blackie Clayton), Russ Powell (Chief Ira Foster), Billy Bevan (McLean), Marjorie Main (Martha Foster), Rex Evans (Victor J. Holbrook), Joseph Crehan (District Attorney), Arthur Hoyt (Beamish the Banker), Syd Saylor (Big Hobo), Selmer Jackson (Judge), Chester Clute (Dan O'Fearna), Gordon Hart (Headwaiter), Sidney Bracey (Waiter), Gladden James (Bank Official), Harry Wilson (Convict), Forbes Murray (Chairman of Parole Board), James Marcus (Parole Board Member), Jack Perrin (Policeman), Ferris Taylor (Bidder), FRank O'Connor, Larry Steers (Men at Auction).

The road chosen is one of crime and those traveling toward trouble are Cromwell and Mack, a boy friend-girl friend team who decide to steal $100,000 from the bank where Mack works as a teller. They hide the loot in a music box, get caught, and do a few years in the pen. They get out, thinking they'll be in the money, but can't seem to find the music box. The antique dealer with whom they left it has since died. In the end, they turn the money over to the authorities in exchange for clear consciences.

p, Colbert Clark; d, James Cruze; w, Gordon Rigby, Eric Taylor (based on a story by Rigby); ph, Ernest Miller; ed, William Morgan, Murray Seldeen; md, Alberto Colombo; cos, Eloise.

Crime   (PR:A MPAA:NR)

WRONGLY ACCUSED   (SEE: BAD MEN OF THE HILLS, 1942)

WU-HOU   (SEE: EMPRESS WU, 1965, Hong Kong)

WUSA**   (1970) 115m Coleytown-Mirror-Stuart Rosenberg/PAR c

Paul Newman (Rheinhardt), Joanne Woodward (Geraldine), Anthony Perkins (Rainey), Laurence Harvey (Farley), Pat Hingle (Bingamon), Cloris Leachman (Philomene), Don Gordon (Bogdanovich), Michael Anderson, Jr. (Marvin), Leigh French (Girl), Moses Gunn (Clotho), Bruce Cabot (King Wolyoe), B.J. Mason (Roosevelt Berry), Robert Quarry (Noonan), Wayne Rogers (Calvin Minter), Hal Baylor (Shorty), Jim Boles (Hot Dog Vendor), Diane Ladd (Barmaid at Railroad Station), Sahdji (Hollywood), Skip Young (Jimmy Snipe), Geoff Edwards (Irving), Clifton James (Speed), Tol Avery (Senator), Paul Hampton (Rusty Fargo), Jerry Catron (Sidewinder Bates), Geraldine West, Lucille Benson (Matrons), Susan Batson (Teenaged Girl), Zara Cully (White-Haired Woman), The Preservation Hall Jazz Band of New Orleans (Themselves), David Huddleston (Heavy Man).

Lest you mistake the title as being some word in an obscure Serbo-Croatian dialect, be aware that it refers to the call letters of a super-patriotic and near-Nazi radio station in the Deep South. Newman is a roamer with a background in radio. He comes to New Orleans with barely beer money in his jeans, contacts Harvey, a former con man turned phony fundamentalist minister, and prevails upon Harvey to repay an old debt. More importantly, Harvey tells Newman that there's an announcing job open at WUSA, a local radio station owned by Hingle. Newman talks his way into a job at the station and finds that he has to distribute the right wing diatribe ordered by Hingle. Quarry is the manager of the station which is devoted to exposing welfare fraud and other things that Hingle thinks are all inspired by godless Communists. Just prior to getting the job, Newman's in a sleazy bar down near the docks and meets Woodward, a semi-pro who is attempting to talk a sailor into buying her a meal. Newman has a few bucks now that Harvey has come across and buys Woodward her first decent meal in a while. She rewards him by taking him back to her tacky rooming house where they spend a passionate night. After Hingle explains what Newman's duties are at the station, Newman encounters Perkins, a liberal bleeding-heart social worker. Perkins is quite naive and Hingle is using him to create a white riot against the blacks. Newman moves in with Woodward and continues his job at the station; then, when he finds out what a heel Hingle is, he gets drunk, battles with Perkins, and leaves Woodward. Perkins finally learns how he's being marionetted by Hingle when local newsman Mason explains the facts of life to him. The station backs a big concert that is actually a hate rally cloaked in music. Hingle hires Cabot, an old western star, gospel singers, and a full show. Outside the arena, there's a full demonstration taking place by a militant group of blacks. Perkins, who has been mild-mannered up until now, becomes almost like Carl Weiss (who killed Huey Long) and tries to assassinate Hingle but misses and hits Quarry, one of Hingle's sycophants. The crowd panics upon hearing the gunshots and begins running helter-skelter, crushing Perkins to death in the melee. The gospel group are all neighbors of Woodward and they're worried that they might be discovered to be marijuana users so they plant their stuff on Woodward. The cops arrest her and find the pot. She is taken to jail where she is despondent and commits suicide in her cell by hanging. Leachman is Woodward's best friend, a cripple who lives on the edge of reality. She tells Newman what's happened to Woodward and he feels he must leave the Crescent City now. He pays his last respects to Woodward at the site of her grave, returns home to pack his meager gear, and departs. He leaves the same way he entered, with little money and no future. An expensive movie (almost $9 million) but what was missing was someone to root for. Newman is soon established as a sellout, as is Harvey. Perkins is half mad, and the only person with a modicum of sincerity is a partial hooker, Woodward, and when she dies, the movie becomes a vacuum. The dialog was often unintentionally funny (the worst kind of laughs) and Rosenberg's pacing is snail-like. It could have made a statement without jamming it down the audience's throats. Instead, it's a misfire that erred when it became self-conscious instead of socially conscious. Jazz fans will appreciate the inclusion of the venerable Preservation Hall Jazz Band and the score by Lalo Schifrin which also used a bit of "Maple Leaf Rag" by Scott Joplin. The phenomenon of the ultra right and its side-by-side hand-clasp with evangelism has still not been plumbed.

p, Paul Newman, John Foreman; d, Stuart Rosenberg; w, Robert Stone (based on his novel A Hall of Mirrors); ph, Richard Moore (Panavision, Technicolor); m, Lalo Schifrin; ed, Robert Wyman; md, Schifrin; art d, Philip Jefferies; set d, William Kiernan; cos, Travilla; m/l, "Glory Road," Neil Diamond (sung by Diamond); makeup, Lynn Reynolds, Jack Wilson.

Drama   (PR:C MPAA:GP)

WUTHERING HEIGHTS***   (1939) 103m Goldwyn/UA bw

Merle Oberon (Cathy Linton), Laurence Olivier (Heathcliff), David Niven (Edgar Linton), Donald Crisp (Dr. Kenneth), Flora Robson (Ellen Dean), Hugh Williams (Hindley Earnshaw), Geraldine Fitzgerald (Isabella Linton), Leo G. Carroll (Joseph), Cecil Humphreys (Judge Linton), Miles Mander (Lockwood), Sarita Wooton (Cathy as a Child), Rex Downing (Heathcliff as a Child), Douglas Scott (Hindley as a Child), Cecil Kellaway (Mr. Earnshaw), Romaine Callender (Robert, the Butler), Helena Grant (Miss Hudkins), Susanne Leach (Guest), Tommy Martin, Schuyler Standish (Little Boys), William Stelling (Dancer), Harold Entwistle (Beadle), Mme. Alice Ahlers (Frau Johann, the Harpsichordist), Vernon Downing (Giles), Frank Benson (Heathcliffe Servant), Eric Wilton (Linton Servant), Major Sam Harris (Wedding Guest).

1939 was Hollywood's golden year. Such varied classics as STAGECOACH, THE WIZARD OF OZ, MR. SMITH GOES TO WASHINGTON, and GONE WITH THE WIND were released that year to receptive audiences across the nation. WUTHERING HEIGHTS, the film version of Emily Bronte's tragic novel, was another of the masterworks from 1939, a haunting and beautiful love story that remains timeless. The year is 1841 and Mander is caught in a terrible snowstorm. He takes refuge in Wuthering Heights, a mysterious old house where his landlord, Olivier, lives with his wife, Fitzgerald, and Carroll, who is the caretaker of the house. Mander is given a cold reception, but Robson, Olivier's housekeeper, remains friendly. Later Mander hears a strange woman's voice outside his window, calling out: "Heathcliff!" A cold hand then mysteriously grabs at Mander. Mander tells Olivier, who runs out into the raging storm. Robson sits down with Mander, and in flashback relates to him the tragic story of Olivier and Oberon. Forty years before, Olivier (played as a child by Downing) had been brought to Wuthering Heights. Downing is a gypsy who has been found playing in the streets of Liverpool. Kellaway has brought Downing to the manor so he might have a better life. Though Williams (played as a child by Scott), Kellaway's son, takes an immediate dislike to Downing, Wooton (Oberon as a child) falls in love with the boy. She and Downing play in a make-believe castle. After Kellaway's death, Scott becomes master of the house. Still hating Downing with undying passion, he forces his rival to leave the house and become a stable boy. Within a few years, as the children become adults, Williams has become an alcoholic, while Olivier and Oberon continue to meet at their castle. Oberon wants to move into affluent society though, and begins seeing Niven, a wealthy young man. This angers Olivier, who thought Oberon had pledged her undying love to him. After a misunderstanding, Olivier decides to leave, riding off in a terrible storm. Oberon grows despondent over this, but ends up marrying Niven. Eventually, after acquiring great wealth, Olivier returns. He takes over Wuthering Heights and pays off Williams' debts. Olivier allows Williams to remain, but behaves cruelly towards his former tormentor. Olivier remains cold to Oberon as well, and marries Niven's sister Fitzgerald. He knows that Oberon still loves him and that to marry Fitzgerald will crush his former amour. Olivier is spiteful to Fitzgerald, and she begins hoping Oberon will die so her husband will forget about his past love. Oberon slowly begins to succumb, the victim of her own will to die. Before she passes on, Olivier sneaks into her bedroom. The two pledge a love for one another that even death will not sever. Olivier carries Oberon to a window and together they look at the site where they played as children. Oberon tells Olivier that she will wait there for him, while Olivier insists that she haunt him forever, even if means driving him mad. As Robson winds up her story, Crisp, a doctor, enters the room. He says that he saw Olivier walking through the storm with a strange woman, then found the man lying dead on Oberon's grave. Robson explains that Olivier and Oberon are together at last, and the film closes with the two eternal lovers walking towards their childhood castle. WUTHERING HEIGHTS is a beautifully told story with impeccable talent both in front of and behind the camera. Wyler had been interested in Bronte's story as a vehicle for Charles Boyer and Sylvia Sidney who had starred in his 1937 film DEAD END. Hecht and MacArthur were assigned to write the film, and they headed for the island home of drama critic Alexander Woolcott to work on their script. Situated off the Vermont coast, Hecht and MacArthur worked hard to create a script faithful to the novel, though Woolcott was convinced the two writers would destroy Bronte's beautiful story. The portly eccentric took to spying on the pair, so to divert Woolcott, Hecht and MacArthur came up with a phony script. "We dramatized a line in the book," MacArthur recalled, "that said Heathcliff spent a year among the Indians of the New World. We wrote it in 'Ugh, ugh, heap big pow-wow' dialog between Heathcliff and Chief Crooked Head. Woolcott wouldn't speak to us for three days." Wyler eventually got Goldwyn to back the script, though Boyer was no longer being considered for the lead. The next choice was Olivier, a relative unknown to American audiences at the time. Hecht, who was an uncredited writer on QUEEN CHRISTINA (1933), remembered Olivier from that film. He had originally been hired to play opposite Greta Garbo in QUEEN CHRISTINA, but was removed from the production in favor of John Gilbert. Olivier was furious, and had harbored ill feelings towards Hollywood ever since. He was interested in the part of Heathcliff however, and agreed to portray the doomed lover only if his wife, Vivien Leigh, could be his Cathy. Oberon had already been signed for the role, however, and Goldwyn would not consider firing her. Leigh was offered the role of Olivier's unloved wife instead, but she turned this down, saying she felt more akin to the tragic lead character. Besides, Leigh had already been featured as the lead in several British films and was simply unwilling to step down for Hollywood. Eventually Olivier agreed to take the role, and Leigh ended up playing Scarlett O'Hara in GONE WITH THE WIND that year. As things turned out Olivier and Oberon were perfectly cast (they had previously appeared together in THE DIVORCE OF LADY X, a 1938 British film), an unforgettable romantic duo that brought the tragic story an undeniably human factor. Niven reportedly hated his part and at first refused to appear in the film, which nearly earned him a suspension from the studio. He thought the part to be a bad one for any actor, and furthermore, had no desire to work for Wyler, a man he considered dictatorial behind the camera. Eventually Niven acquiesced, though his fears about Wyler proved to be correct. Wyler often asked for as many as 40 takes, something that angered both Niven and Olivier. Though the film understandably condenses Bronte's lengthy novel (which she had originally published under a male pseudonym, fearing the book would never be printed if people thought a woman wrote it), Goldwyn spared no expense in creating the right atmosphere for the picture. 450 acres of land in California's Conejo Hills were transformed into authentic-looking English moors, as the area was completely relandscaped. No less than 1,000 heather plants were transplanted, and Goldwyn completed his re-creation by building a period manor on the site. However, Goldwyn did switch the novel's period from the original Regency to the Georgian era. His reasoning was simple. The Georgian period was marked by fancier dresses for women, and Goldwyn was eager to show off Oberon in beautiful costumes. Goldwyn considered the picture his own and once, when a reporter asked him about "...Wyler's WUTHERING HEIGHTS," Goldwyn retorted, "*I* made WUTHERING HEIGHTS; Wyler only directed it!" Goldwyn reportedly was unhappy with the film's tragic ending, and demanded the ghostly images of Olivier and Oberon walking off in the end. Wyler disagreed with his producer, and completely disowned the scene. Olivier was pleased with the film, however, and realized that his QUEEN CHRISTINA experience was not the end-all of Hollywood professionalism. "...Wyler gave me the simple thought," Oliver later stated, "if you do it right, you can do anything. And if he hadn't said that, I think I wouldn't have done HENRY V five years later." WUTHERING HEIGHTS earned several well-deserved Oscar nominations, including Best Picture, Best Actor, Best Screenplay, and Best Director. The competition that year was strong, but Toland did win an Academy Award for his brilliant photography, a moody black-and-white that often gave the story an ethereal quality. Surprisingly, WUTHERING HEIGHTS was unpopular with filmgoers, and it was not until a 1950 re-release that Goldwyn finally saw a profit from his film. Bronte's novel was adapted for the screen in several remakes, including Luis Bunuel's 1954 ABISMOS DE PASION, a 1955 Egyptian version (in *Arabic*), as well as the 1970 British film featuring Timothy Dalton and Anna Calder-Marshall. None approached the brilliance of this version though, a definitive and classic work that is unsurpassable in its tragic beauty.

p, Samuel Goldwyn; d, William Wyler; w, Ben Hecht, Charles MacArthur (based on the novel by Emily Bronte); ph, Gregg Toland; ed, Daniel Mandell; md, Alfred Newman; art d, James Vasevi; set d, Julia Heron; cos, Omar Kiam; makeup, Blagoe Stephanoff.

Romance/Drama   **Cas.**   **(PR:C   MPAA:NR)**

WUTHERING HEIGHTS★★   (1970, Brit.) 105m AIP c

Anna Calder-Marshall (*Catherine Earnshaw*), Timothy Dalton (*Heathcliff*), Harry Andrews (*Mr. Earnshaw*), Pamela Brown (*Mrs. Linton*), Judy Cornwell (*Nellie*), James Cossins (*Mr. Linton*), Rosalie Crutchley (*Mrs. Earnshaw*), Hilary Dwyer (*Isabella Linton*), Julian Glover (*Hindley Earnshaw*), Hugh Griffith (*Dr. Kenneth*), Morag Hood (*Frances*), Ian Ogilvy (*Edgar Linton*), Peter Sallis (*Mr. Shielders*), Aubrey Woods (*Joseph*), Wendy Allnutt, John Comer, Dudley Foster, Gordon Gostelow, Lois Daine, Keith Buckley, James Berwick, Patricia Doyle, Mark Wilding, Sandra Bryant, Bruce Beeby, Jonathan Brewster, Gillian Hayes, Libby Granger, Gertan Klauber.

When it comes to adaptations of classic writings AIP should stick to Poe (their version of THE RAVEN is the most enjoyable Poe yet) instead of attempting "respectibility" by bringing Bronte's Wuthering Heights to the screen. It is moderately faithful to the original–a tale of two lovers separated by the woman's marriage into wealth and the dejected lover's departure–though out of the running when compared to the 1939 classic. While this version is beautifully photographed and admirably acted, there is never any real feeling of romance or sadness. It is all treated in a matter-of-fact approach, which doesn't make for a great film.

p, Samuel Z. Arkoff, James H. Nicholson; d, Robert Fuest; w, Patrick Tilley (based on the novel by Emily Bronte); ph, John Coquillon (Movielab Color); m, Michel Legrand; ed, Ann Chegwidden; art d, Philip Harrison; set d, Josie MacAvin; cos, Evelyn Gibbs; makeup, Bill Lodge.

Romance   **Cas.**   **(PR:A   MPAA:G)**

WYLIE   (SEE: EYE OF THE CAT, 1969)

WYOMING★★½   (1940) 89m MGM bw (AKA: BAD MAN OF WYOMING)

Wallace Beery (*Reb Harkness*), Leo Carrillo (*Pete Marillo*), Ann Rutherford (*Lucy Kincaid*), Lee Bowman (*Sgt. Connolly*), Joseph Calleia (*John Buckley*), Bobs Watson (*Jimmy Kincaid*), Marjorie Main (*Mehitabel*), Henry Travers (*Sheriff*), Paul Kelly (*Gen. George Armstrong Custer*), Stanley Fields (*Curley*), William Tannen (*Reynolds*), Chill Wills (*Lafe*), Donald MacBride (*Bart*), Clem Bevans (*Pa McKinley*), Russell Simpson (*Bronson*), Addison Richards (*Kincaid*), Dick Curtis (*Corky*), Dick Alexander (*Gus*), Chief Thundercloud (*Lightfoot*), Ethel Wales (*Mrs. Bronson*), Dick Botiller (*Rusty*), Glenn Lucas (*Smokey*), Francis McDonald (*Dawson*), Edgar Dearing (*Officer*), Archie Butler, Harley Chambers (*Cavalrymen*), Glenn Strange (*Bill Smalley*), Lee Phebs (*Man*), Ted Adams (*Brother*), Betty Jean Nichols (*Child*), Howard Mitchell (*Conductor*).

Army veteran Beery leaves Missouri and heads for Wyoming where he takes care of a dead rancher's children and cleans up a town by ridding it of a cattle rustling gang. He then heads out in pursuit of his former outlaw partner, Carrillo, to teach him a thing or two about his new-found respect for law and order. WYOMING was the first picture to pair Beery and Main, who would soon become one of the screen's popular couplings.

p, Milton Bren; d, Richard Thorpe; w, Jack Jevne, Hugo Butler (based on a story by Jevne); ph, Clyde DeVinna; ed, Robert J. Kern; cos, Vera Tree, Valles.

Western   **(PR:A   MPAA:NR)**

WYOMING★★½   (1947) 84m REP bw

William Elliott (*Charles Alderson*), Vera Ralston (*Karen Alderson*), John Carroll (*Glenn Forrester*), George "Gabby" Hayes (*Windy*), Albert Dekker (*Lassiter*), Virginia Grey (*Lila Regan*), Mme. Maria Ouspenskaya (*Maria*), Grant Withers (*Joe Sublette*), Harry Woods (*Ben Jackson*), Minna Gombell (*Queenie*), Dick Curtis (*Ed Lassiter*), Roy Barcroft (*Sheriff Niles*), Trevor Bardette (*Timmons*), Paul Harvey (*Judge Sheridan*), Louise Kane (*Karen at Age 12*), Linda Green (*Karen at Age 3*), Tom London (*Jennings*), George Chesebro (*Wolff*), Jack O'Shea (*Bartender*), Charles Middleton (*Doctor*), Eddy Waller (*Grub Liner*), Olin Howland, Charles King, Glenn Strange (*Cowboys*), Eddie Acuff (*Homesteader*), Marshall Reed (*Man*), Rex Lease (*Clerk*), Charles Morton (*Settler*), Tex Terry (*Morrison*), Dale Fink (*Boy*), Ed Peil, Sr (*Nester*), Roque Ybarra, James Archuletta (*Indian Boys*), David Williams (*Hotel Clerk*), Lee Shumway (*Rancher*).

Elliott's rise to power from pioneer to Wyoming's top cattle rancher is the central plot of this expertly photographed oater. When the Homestead Act is introduced in the U.S., the villainous Dekker rallies the incoming farmers against Elliott. Elliott's patience is pushed to the limit when Dekker, after rustling all of the rancher's herd, tries to take hotel owner Grey. The rancher also loses his daughter, Ralston, to Dekker, but when his wicked ways are revealed she returns to her father's side. Appearing as the young Ralston is Louise Kane, the daughter of producer-director Joseph Kane.

p&d, Joseph Kane; w, Lawrence Hazard, Gerald Geraghty; ph, John Alton; m, Nathan G. Scott, Ernest Gold; ed, Arthur Roberts; md, Cy Feuer; art d, Frank Hotaling; set d, John McCarthy, Jr., George Suhr; spec eff, Howard Lydecker, Theodore Lydecker; cos, Adele Palmer.

Western   **(PR:A   MPAA:NR)**

WYOMING BANDIT, THE★★   (1949) 60m REP bw

Allan "Rocky" Lane (*Himself*), Eddy Waller (*Nugget Clark*), Trevor Bardette (*Wyoming Dan*), Victor Kilian (*Ross Tyler*), Rand Brooks (*Jim Howard*), William Haade (*Lonnegan*), Howard Goodwin (*Sheriff*), Lane Bradford (*Buck*), Bob Wilke (*Sam*), John Hamilton (*Head Marshal*), Edmund Cobb (*Deputy Marshal*), Reed Hadley, Black Jack the Horse.

Lane is a U.S. marshal on the trail of a gang of outlaws who gets assistance in his search from former outlaw Bardette. After learning that his son has been shot, Bardette takes up with the law, and he and Lane go undercover to battle the guilty ones.

p, Gordon Kay; d, Philip Ford; w, M. Coates Webster; ph, John MacBurnie; m, Stanley Wilson; ed, Harold Minter; md, Morton Scott; art d, Frank Arrigo; set d, John McCarthy, Jr., Charles Thompson; makeup, Whitey Lawrence.

Western   **(PR:A   MPAA:NR)**

WYOMING KID, THE   **(SEE: CHEYENNE, 1947)**

WYOMING MAIL★★   (1950) 87m UNIV c

Stephen McNally (*Steve Davis*), Alexis Smith (*Mary Williams*), Howard Da Silva (*Cavanaugh*), Ed Begley (*Haynes*), Dan Riss (*George Armstrong*), Roy Roberts (*Charles DeHaven*), Whit Bissell (*Sam Wallace*), Armando Silvestre (*Indian Joe*), James Arness (*Russell*), Richard Jaeckel (*Nafe*), Frankie Darro (*Rufe*), Felipe Turich (*Pete*), Richard Egan (*Beale*), Gene Evans (*shep*), Frank Fenton (*Gilson*), Emerson Treacy (*Ben*).

This competent but uneventful western has postal inspector McNally going undercover to prevent a gang from robbing mail trains. He stages a prison break to get in good with the outlaws and then, when the time is right, reveals his true identity and lets justice take its course. Smith is the saloon singer who gets information from the robbers and passes it along to the authorities, naturally falling in love with McNally in the process. You'd think with all the postal inspectors and U.S. marshals posing as outlaws that gang leaders would be a little more choosy in whom they work with–maybe forcing their employees to take a polygraph test or something. Songs: "Endlessly" and "Take Me To Town" (Dan Shapiro, Lester Lee).

p, Aubrey Schenck; d, Reginald LeBorg; w, Harry Essex, Leonard Lee (based on a story by Robert Hardy Andrews); ph, Russell Metty (Technicolor); ed, Edward Curtiss; md, Joseph Gershenson; art d, Bernard Herzbrun, Hilyard Brown; cos, Bill Thomas.

Western   (PR:A   MPAA:NR)

WYOMING OUTLAW**   (1939) 62m REP bw

John Wayne (Stony Brooke), Ray Corrigan (Tucson Smith), Raymond Hatton (Rusty Joslin), Donald "Red" Barry (Will Parker), Adele Pearce [Pamela Blake] (Irene Parker), LeRoy Mason (Balsinger), Charles Middleton (Luke Parker), Katherine Kenworthy (Mrs. Parker), Elmo Lincoln (U.S. Marshal), Jack Ingram (Sheriff), David Sharpe (Newt), Jack Kenney (Amos), Yakima Canutt (Ed Sims), Dave O'Brien, Curley Dresden, Tommy Coats, Ralph Peters, Jack Kirk, Al Taylor, Bud McTaggert, Budd Buster, Ed Payson.

Wayne, Corrigan, and Hatton (replacing Max Terhune) star as the Three Mesquiteers in this series entry based on a true-life incident about a small town man who kills an outlaw who has been tearing up the territory. Barry, in the outlaw role, is forced to turn to crime after his involvement with a corrupt politician who demands campaign money in exchange for employment. The role launched Barry into a red hot career as an oater star. Also featured in a supporting role is the screen's first Tarzan, Elmo Lincoln. (See THREE MESQUITEERS series, Index.)

p, William Berke; d, George Sherman; w, Betty Burbridge, Jack Natteford (based on a story by Natteford and characters created by William Colt MacDonald); ph, Reggie Lanning; m, William Lava; ed, Tony Martinelli.

Western   (PR:A   MPAA:NR)

WYOMING RENEGADES**½   (1955) 73m COL c

Phil Carey (Brady Sutton), Gene Evans (Butch Cassidy), Martha Hyer (Nancy Warren), William Bishop (Sundance Kid), Douglas Kennedy (Charlie Veer), Roy Roberts (Sheriff McVey), Don Beddoe (Horace Warren), Aaron Spelling (Petie Carver), George Keymas (George Curry), Harry Harvey (Medford), Mel Welles (Whiskey Pearson), Henry Rowland (Elza Lay), Boyd Stockman (Tom McCarthy), A. Guy Teague (Black Jack Ketchum), Bob Woodward (Matt Garner), Don C. Harvey (Ben Kilpatrick), John [Bob] Cason (O.C. Hanks), Don Carlos (Bob Meeks).

Carey is a former outlaw who tries to go straight but when he starts hanging around Evans he gets drawn back into the six-gunnin', bank-robbin' way of life, much to the chagrin of Hyer, his gal. Carey really is hoping to clear his name by bringing in Evans and his gang. However, in a strange and delightful twist, it's Hyer and the town's women who successfully stage the ambush that finishes the gang. And Zoe Tamerlis, the avenging femme killer in MS. 45, thought she was tough!

p, Wallace MacDonald; d, Fred F. Sears; w, David Lang; ph, Lester White (Technicolor); m, Mischa Bakaleinikoff; ed, Edwin Bryant; art d, Cary Odell.

Western   (PR:A   MPAA:NR)

WYOMING WILDCAT**   (1941) 56m REP bw

Don "Red" Barry, Julie Duncan, Syd Saylor, Frank M. Thomas, Dick Botiller, Edmund Cobb, Ed Brady, Edward Cassidy, George Sherwood, Ethan Laidlaw, Al Haskell, Frank Ellis, Curley Dresden, Art Dillard, Cactus Mack, Kermit Maynard, Frank O'Connor, Fred Burns.

Trouble looms ahead when a guard on the Wells Fargo line turns out to be a nefarious outlaw. One of the many westerns Barry made during this period. He was quite a successful cowboy hero and was voted one of the Top Ten Money-Making Western Stars by the Motion Picture Herald in 1942, 1943, and 1944.

p&d, George Sherman; w, Bennett Cohen, Anthony Coldeway (based on a story by Cohen); ph, William Nobles; ed, Lester Orlebeck; md, Cy Feuer.

Western   (PR:A   MPAA:NR)

X

X   (SEE: "X"–THE MAN WITH X-RAY EYES, 1963)

X-15**   (1961) 107m Essex-EC/UA c**

Charles Bronson (*Lt. Col. Lee Brandon*), Brad Dexter (*Maj. Anthony Rinaldi*), James Gregory (*Torn Deparma*), Lisabeth Hush (*Diane Wilde*), David McLean (*Matt Powell*), Mary Tyler Moore (*Pamela Stewart*), Patricia Owens (*Margaret Brandon*), Kenneth Tobey (*Col. Craig Brewster*), Ralph Taeger (*Maj. Ernest Wilde*), Stanley Livingston (*Mike Brandon*), Lauren Gilbert (*Col. Jessup*), Phil Dean (*Maj. McCully*), Chuck Stanford (*Lt. Comdr. Joe Lacrosse*), Patty McDonald (*Susan Brandon*), Mike MacKane (*B-52 Pilot*), Robert Dornam (*Test Engineer*), Frank Watkins (*Security Policeman*), Barbara Kelley (*Secretary*), Darlene Hendricks (*Nurse*), Ed Fleming, Lee Giroux, Grant Holcomb, Lew Irwin (*Themselves*), Ric Applewhite, Pat Renella (*Engineers*), Jerry Lawrence, Richard Norris (*Operators*), James Stewart (*Narrator*).

Bronson, McLean, and Taeger are test pilots in California preparing the X-15 rocket plane for a scheduled launch. During the test run Bronson is killed, but in the process saves the lives of his copilots. The tensions of the fliers are paralleled with their home lives, while special attention, in an almost documentary style, is paid to technological and aeronautic explanations. Jimmy Stewart narrates X-15, the directorial movie debut of Richard Donner. Donner, who began his career in television, took to the skies again in his comic-book adventure SUPERMAN.

p, Henry Sanicola, Tony Lazzarino; d, Richard D. Donner; w, Lazzarino, James Warner Bellah (based on a story by Lazzarino); ph, Carl Guthrie (Panavision, Technicolor); aerial ph, Jack Freeman; ed, Stanley E. Rabjohn; art d, Rolland M. Brooks; set d, Kenneth Schwartz; spec eff, Paul Pollard; spec ph eff, Howard Anderson; makeup, Beans Ponedel, Jack Wilson.

Drama   (PR:A MPAA:NR)

X MARKS THE SPOT**   (1931) 68m TIF bw**

Lew Cody (*George Howe*), Sally Blane (*Sue*), Fred Kohler (*Riggs*), Wallace Ford (*Ted Lloyd*), Mary Nolan (*Vivyan Parker*), Virginia Lee Corbin (*Hortense*), Helen Parrish (*Gloria*), as a Child, Joyce Coad (*Gloria*).

Newspaper drama has Broadway columnist Ford embroiled in a murder case. A showgirl, who had been suing his paper for libel, is found murdered shortly after Ford had interviewed her in her apartment. Of course Ford is accused but he quickly discovers the real killer to be a man he had previously met. All comes to a head in a courtroom battle and a final climactic scene in which Ford is forced to engage in a gun battle when he's locked in a room with the killer. The drama tries hard to have a realistic newspaper look with busy city rooms but instead looks like the Hollywood B picture it is. The script was cowritten by an ex-New York newspaperman and the producers originally wanted Walter Winchell for an added touch of realism. However, his paper refused to give him time off for filmmaking, and thus Ford was cast.

p, Samuel Bischoff; d, Erle C. Kenton; w, Warren Duff, Gordon Kahn, F. Hugh Herbert.

Crime   (PR:A MPAA:NR)

X MARKS THE SPOT**   (1942) 55m REP bw**

Damian O'Flynn (*Eddie Delaney*), Helen Parrish (*Linda Ward*), Dick Purcell (*Lt. Decker*), Jack LaRue (*Marty Clark*), Neil Hamilton (*John Underwood*), Robert E. Homans (*Sgt. Delaney*), Anne Jeffreys (*Lulu*), Dick Wessel (*Dizzy*), Esther Muir (*Bonnie*), Joseph Kirk (*Jerry*), Edna Harris (*Billie*), Fred Kelsey (*Riley*), Vince Barnett (*George*).

Police sergeant Homans is killed by ex-bootleggers now engaged in black-market dealings with rubber, a scarce item in the WW II era. The dead man's son O'Flynn is a private eye who takes up the investigation. Along the way he hooks up with Parrish, his token B movie love interest, and zeros in on the man behind the murder. Characteristic of such films, the plot follows its trail hitting all the standard benchmarks before winding up. Things move quickly enough, though, to make this mildy entertaining.

p&d, George Sherman; w, Stuart Palmer, Richard Murphy (based on a story by Mauri Grashin, Robert T. Shannon); ph, Jack Marta; ed, Arthur Roberts; md, Morton Scott; art d, Russell Kimball.

Crime   (PR:A MPAA:NR)

"X"--THE MAN WITH THE X-RAY EYES***½**
  (1963) Alta Vista/AIP c (AKA: THE MAN WITH THE X-RAY EYES; X)

Ray Milland (*Dr. James Xavier*), Diana Van Der Vlis (*Dr. Diane Fairfax*), Harold J. Stone (*Dr. Sam Brant*), John Hoyt (*Dr. Willard Benson*), Don Rickles (*Crane*), Carnival Owner, Lorie Summers (*Party Dancer*), Vicki Lee

(*Young Girl Patient*), Kathryn Hart (*Mrs. Mart*), Carol Irey (*Woman Patient*), Morris Ankrum (*Foundation Head*), Richard Miller (*John Trask/Heckler*), Jonathan Haze.

A superb science fiction picture which stars Milland in one of his most memorable roles as a scientist who takes a serum that allows him to see with X-ray vision. He is able to see through paper (no problem), clothes (no problem and great fun at parties), and skin (a valuable asset to have around the operating room). His powers get stronger and after being dismissed from his job, Milland hooks up with sideshow moneymaker Rickles as a mindreader. He can no longer stand his condition, which now causes him pain so severe he has to wear lead glasses. His headaches grow more intense (maybe it's just from listening to Rickles all day long?) until he flees, ending up at a revivalist meeting after smashing his car. When he hears the preacher say, "If thine eye offend thee, pluck it out!" he does just that. Corman, in one of his finest films (it took top honors at the Trieste Science Fiction Film Festival), explores an idea which has captivated scientists as well as drunken practical jokers for years and comes up with an intelligent, compelling, and downright enjoyable movie.

p&d, Roger Corman; w, Robert Dillon, Ray Russell based on the story by Russell); ph, Floyd Crosby (Spectarama, Eastmancolor); m, Les Baxter; ed, Anthony Carras; md, Al Simms; art d, Daniel Haller; set d, Harry Reif; cos, Marjorie Corso; spec eff, Butler-Glouner, Inc.; makeup, Ted Coodley.

Science Fiction   Cas.   (PR:C MPAA:NR)

X THE UNKNOWN**½   (1957, Brit.) 80m Hammer/WB bw**

Dean Jagger (*Dr. Adam Royston*), Edward Chapman (*Elliott*), Director of Atomic Research, Leo McKern (*McGill*), Marianne Brauns (*Zena, Nurse*), William Lucas (*Peter Elliott*), John Harvey (*Maj. Cartwright*), Peter Hammond (*Lt. Bannerman*), Michael Ripper (*Sgt. Grimsdyke*), Anthony Newley (*Pvt. Spider Webb*), Ian MacNaughton (*Haggis*), Kenneth Cope (*Pvt. Lancing*), Edwin Richfield (*Old Soldier*), Jameson Clark (*Jack Harding*), Jane Aird (*Vi Harding*), Michael Brook (*Willie Harding*), Fraser Hines (*Ian*), Neil Hallett (*Unwin*), Norman Macowan (*Old Tom*), Neil Wilson (*Russell*), John Stone (*Gerry*), Archie Duncan (*Sgt. Yeardye*), Edward Judd.

A smartly directed and inventive science fiction picture about a living mud glob that feeds on radioactivity and bursts out of the Earth's crust every 50 years or so. This time, however, it has to deal with Jagger, brilliant scientist and mud globologist, who "kills" it with electronic waves. Similar to the British series of Quatermass pictures, which also contained some creeping unknown terrors.

p, Anthony Hinds; d, Leslie Norman; w, Jimmy Sangster; ph, Gerald Gibbs; m, James Bernard; ed, James Needs; md, John Hollingsworth; spec eff, Les Bowie, Jack Curtis; makeup, Philip Leakey.

Science Fiction   (PR:A-C MPAA:NR)

X Y & ZEE**½ (1972, Brit.) 110m Zee/COL c (GB: ZEE & CO.)**

Elizabeth Taylor (*Zee Blakeley*), Michael Caine (*Robert Blakeley*), Susannah York (*Stella*), Margaret Leighton (*Gladys*), John Standing (*Gordon*), Mary Larkin (*Rita*), Michael Cashman (*Gavin*), Gino Melvazzi (*Headwaiter*), Julian West (*Oscar*), Hilary West (*Shaun*).

Caine, an architect, is married to Taylor, a brash, obnoxious woman. At a party he is introduced to York and is immediately taken by this widowed mother of two. York is the proprietor of a boutique and has a personality that is the polar opposite of Taylor's. She and Caine soon become involved, which sets Taylor off on a jealous rampage. First she confronts York at her shop, making nasty remarks about her rival's slimmer figure. Caine and York try to escape Taylor's wrath by taking a vacation but their idyll is brief: Taylor deliberately totals her husband's car, then telephones the lovers, claiming the damage to be the result of an accident. Returning from Scotland to London, Caine and York remain intent on pursuing their affair. One night, as they make love, an inebriated Taylor rages below York's window, screaming obscenities and flinging garbage cans. Caine is undaunted and determined to start a new life with York, free from the shrewish Taylor forever. Taylor, devastated by Caine's decision, cuts her wrists while taking a bath, a final attempt to win back her husband. The suicide attempt makes no difference to Caine, so upon recovery the spurned woman decides to go after York. Taylor invites her rival over for a visit, pretending to be cordial while probing the younger woman for any exploitable flaw. Taylor hits pay dirt when York confides she had once been tossed out of school for a lesbian attraction to a nun. At a party she throws for Caine, Taylor gets her husband raging drunk, then cons him into staying with her overnight. The next morning Taylor claims Caine made violent love to her. York is angered by Caine's drunken behavior, but the architect is disgusted with both women. He storms out and has a quick afternoon affair with his secretary. When Caine returns to the new apartment he has rented with York, he is shocked by what he sees. Taylor is in bed with a weeping York, claiming victory and daring Caine to join them. Decked out in gaudy eye makeup, outrageous costumes, and excessive jewelry, Taylor chews up scenery left and right in a volcanic performance. She goes beyond her role in WHO'S AFRAID OF VIRGINIA WOOLF? making vulgarity and drunken rages an art form all their own. Given free rein by the director, Taylor is clearly having fun with the part and the extremes it allows her to go to. The story alone isn't much, but, inflated by the Taylor hurricane, the movie works as an incredible portrait of a marriage on the rocks. Though the closing implies that Caine will give up York, screenwriter O'Brien's original ending was given a much harsher twist. Published in England under the film's alternate title, the original screenplay ends with Caine accepting Taylor's challenge. He joins the women: "the last we see are their three bodies–arms, heads, torsos, all meeting for a consummation." For a brief nude scene Taylor used a body double, though the figure shown is decidedly slimmer than the actress' form.

p, Jay Kanter, Alan Ladd, Jr.; d, Brian G. Hutton; w, Edna O'Brien; ph, Billy Williams; m, Stanley Myers; ed, Jim Clark; art d, Peter Mullins; set d, Arthur Taksen; cos, Beatrice Dawson; m/l, "Going in Circles," Ted Myers, Jaiananda; "Whirlwind," "Coat of Many Colours," Rick Wakeman, Dave Lambert (played by Iroko), "Revolution," "Granny's Got a Painted Leg" (played by The Roy Young Band), "Glady's Party," John Mayer; makeup, Alex Garfath.

Drama   (PR:O   MPAA:R)

XANADU*   (1980) 93m UNIV c

Olivia Newton-John (Kira), Gene Kelly (Danny McGuire), Michael Beck (Sonny Malone), James Sloyan (Simpson), Dimitra Arliss (Helen), Katie Hanley (Sandra), Fred McCarren (Richie), Ren Woods (Jo), Sandahl Bergman, Lynn Latham, Melinda Phelps, Cherise Bate, Juliette Marshall, Marilyn Tokuda, Yvette Van Voorhees, Teri Beckerman (Muses).

With XANADU, Gene Kelly put himself into a unique position in the annals of Hollywood musical history. Not only could he claim honor for appearing in the greatest musical of all time (SINGIN' IN THE RAIN)–he now had the dubious distinction of being cast in one of the genre's most gaudy and utterly mindless ventures. In a sort of remake of 1947's DOWN TO EARTH, Beck plays an artist engaged in an ongoing struggle with his work. All he needs is a muse, which comes in the form of Newton-John. She and her sisters exist as paintings on a wall, but faster than you can say "let's put on a show!" the figures come alive to sing, roller skate, and get the plot moving. Newton-John tries to inspire Beck with his work, The Kelly is introduced; he plays a wealthy construction executive who had been a clarinet player in the 1940's. Kelly, it is revealed in flashback, had also been taken by the Newton-John muse (who at that time sported an Andrews Sisters-tupe outfit). Though Kelly claims that he still longs for her, he doesn't recognize Newton-John in her modern day incarnation. Kelly hopes to open a small nightclub, while Beck prefers to use his talents to create a rock 'n' roll hall. With the influence of their mutual muse, the two men combine their ideas to create Xanadu, a schizophrenic nightclub that combines 1940s and 1980s music in a sea of rollerskates and neon. Beck has now fallen in love with Newton-John, something she hadn't counted on while helping the man out. She skates her way back into her painting but Beck is right behind her. After magically joining her, Beck convinces Newton-John to come back. Eventually she does, returning to Xanadu where she puts on a show. After singing several numbers, Newton-John vanishes again, this time for good. Beck feels sad, thinking he's lost the love of his life. Happiness does come his way, though, for in the end Beck meets a waitress whose looks are a carbon copy of Newton-John's. XANADU clearly takes its cue from the old-style Hollywood musicals, but has replaced style and substance with flash and glitz. Packed with color and music, there is no charm to this at all. Kelly (using the same character name from his 1944 film COVER GIRL) is more like a warhorse than a performer, giving the film its only link to the past, a link it so desperately wants to invoke. One number tries to combine a 1940s female trio with a 1980s New Wave band, and the results are disastrous. In trying to appeal to all audiences this movie ends up shooting itself in the foot, holding little interest for anyone. An animated sequence by Don Bluth (creator of the fine animated feature, THE SECRET OF N.I.M.H.) is really the only imaginative moment in this mess. The soundtrack yielded several hits for Newton-John on the pop charts. Songs include: "I'm Alive," "The Fall," "Don't Walk Away," "All Over the World" (Jeff Lynne, performed by the Electric Light Orchestra), "Xanadu" (Lynne, performed by Newton-John), "Magic" (John Farrar, performed by Newton-John), "Suddenly"

(Farrar, performed by Newton-John and Cliff Richard), "Dancing" (Farrar, performed by Newton-John and The Tubes), "Suspended In Time" (Farrar, performed by Newton-John), "Whenever You're Away from Me" (Farrar, performed by Newton-John and Kelly).

p, Lawrence Gordon; d, Robert Greenwald; w, Richard Christian Danus, Marc Reid Rubel, Michael Kane; ph, Victor J. Kemper (Technicolor); m, Barry DeVorzon; ed, Dennis Virkler; prod d, John W. Corso; cos, Bobbie Mannix; spec eff, Richard Greenberg; ch, Kenny Ortega, Jerry Trent; m/l, Jeff Lynne, John Farrar, DeVorzon; animation, Don Bluth.

Musical   **Cas.**   (PR:C   MPAA:PG)

XICA*   (1982, Braz.) 117m Jarbas Barbosa-Distrifilmes-Embrafilme/Embrafilme-Unifilm c (AKA: XICA DA SILVA)

Zeze Motta (Xica da Silva), Walmor Chagas (Joao), Altair Lima (Theodoro), Elke Maravilha (Hortensia), Stepan Nercessian (Jose), Rodolfo Arena (Sargento-Mor), Jose Wilker (Conde), Marcus Vinicius (Teodoro), Joao Felicio dos Santos (Paroco), Dara Kocy (Zefina), Adalberto Silva (Cabeca), Julio Mackenzie (Raimundo), Luis Mota (Taverneiro), Beto Leao (Mathias), Paulo Padilha (Ourives), Baby Conceicao (Figena), Iara Jati (Tonha), Luis Felipe (Major).

Released in Brazil in 1976, this country's sensation was not released in the U.S. until some six years later. It tells an erotic tale of sexual corruption as Motta takes the role of a Brazilian slave from the 18th Century who turns her countrymen on their heads with her nondescript sexual bravura. By using her body she rises out of the lower class and controls Chagas, the powerful governor of a diamond-mining town, becoming Brazil's unofficial empress. Reportedly based on a real-life character, a black slave of Brazilian legend who is referred to as that country's "Joan of Arc," XICA is one of the most compelling works to come out of Brazil in recent years. (In Portuguese; English subtitles.)

p, Jarbas Barbosa; d, Carlos Diegues; w, Diegues, Joao Felicio dos Santos; ph, Jose Medeiros (Eastmancolor); m, Roberto Menescal, Jorge Ben; ed, Mair Tavares; ch, Marlene Silva.

Drama   (PR:O   MPAA:NR)

XICA DA SILVA   (SEE: XICA, 1982, Braz.)

XOCHIMILCO   (SEE: PORTRAIT OF MARIA, 1945, Mex.)

X-RAY   (SEE: HOSPITAL MASSACRE, 1982)

XTRO zero (1983, Brit.) 80m Amalgamated Film Enterprises/New Line c

Philip Sayer (Sam Phillips), Bernice Stegers (Rachel Phillips), Danny Brainin (Joe Daniels), Simon Nash (Tony Phillips), Maryam D'Abo (Analise), David Cardy (Michael), Anna Wing (Miss Goodman), Peter Mandell (Clown), Robert Fyfe (Doctor), Arthur Whybrow (Knight-Porter), Anna Mottram (Teacher), Katherine Best (Jane), Robert Pereno (Ben), Tik (Monster), Vanya Seager (Paula), Tok (Commando).

A vile exercise in grotesque special effects in which the wretched sexual splatterings are more important than the family unit that is created. Dad Sayer is kidnaped by aliens one day and returns to his family three years later in the form of a four-legged crablike monster. He assaults a gorgeous blonde and the next day explodes from her womb, a full-grown human. He then infects his son with the same bug that's inside him. It combines all the perverse morbid anatomical atrocities that one associates with David Cronenberg with the sterile home life that pervades the outwardly stable Spielbergian family. Not only is it disgusting, but structurally the picture is unsound and lacks anything that remotely resembles suspense. The preproduction title was JUDAS GOAT, which no doubt has some significance not worth figuring out.

p, Mark Forstater; d, Harry Bromley Davenport; w, Iain Cassie, Robert Smith, Jo Ann Kaplan (based on a screenplay by Michel Parry, Davenport); ph, John Metcalfe, John Simmons (Kay Color); m, Davenport, Shelton Leigh Palmer; ed, Nick Gaster, Kaplan; art d, Andrew Mollo, Peter Body; spec eff, Tom Harris; makeup eff, Robin Grantham, John Webber; creature eff, Francis Coates.

Science Fiction   **Cas.**   (PR:O   MPAA:R)

Y

...Y EL DEMONIO CREO A LOS HOMBRES
(SEE: HEAT, 1970, Arg.)

YA KUPIL PAPU (SEE: DIMKA, 1964, USSR)

YA SHAGAYU PO MOSKVE (SEE: MEET ME IN MOSCOW, 1966, USSR)

YABU NO NAKA NO KURONEKO (SEE: KURONEKO, 1968, Jap.)

YABUNIRAMI NIPPON (SEE: WALL-EYED NIPPON, 1963, Jap.)

YAGYU BUGEICHO (SEE: SECRET SCROLLS, PART I, 1968, Jap.)

YAGYU SECRET SCROLLS (SEE: SECRET SCROLLS, PART II, 1968, Jap.)

YAKUZA, THE*½** (1975, U.S./Jap.) 112m WB-Toei c (AKA: BROTHERHOOD OF THE YAKUZA)

Robert Mitchum (*Harry Kilmer*), Takakura Ken (*Tanaka Ken*), Brian Keith (*George Tanner*), Herb Edelman (*Oliver Wheat*), Richard Jordan (*Dusty*), Kishi Keiko (*Tanaka Eiko*), Okada Eiji (*Tono Toshiro*), James Shigeta (*Goro*), Kyosuke Mashida (*Kato Jiro*), Christina Kokubo (*Hanako*), Go Eiji (*Spider*), Lee Chirillo (*Louise Tanner*), M. Hisaka (*Boy Friend*), William Ross (*Tanner's Bodyguard*), Akiyama (*Tono's Bodyguard*), Harada (*Goro's Doorman*).

A fascinating crime drama that mixes action, intrigue, honor, romance, and a clash of cultures to great effect. *Yakuza* is the name of the Japanese organized crime community–the Eastern equivalent of American-Italian Mafia–which has been in existence for over 350 years. Made up of gamblers and confidence men, the *Yakuza* conform to a code of honor as strict as that of the samurai. The film opens as Keith, a powerful shipping magnate, learns that his daughter, Chirillo, has been kidnaped by Okada Eiji, a *Yakuza* clan leader. Keith had been paid a handsome sum by Eiji to purchase and ship arms to the *Yakuza*. The American failed to deliver the goods and now Eiji has kidnaped Keith's daughter to force shipment. Desperate, Keith calls his old Army buddy Mitchum and asks him to help rescue Chirillo. Mitchum is hesitant because he has left some painful memories in Japan (where he was an MP during WW II) and helping Keith requires opening up old wounds. Keith sends his young bodyguard Jordan, a somewhat arrogant and cocky punk, along with Mitchum, with plans to join them in Japan later. In Japan, Mitchum is greeted by Edelman, another Army buddy, who decided to stay behind in Japan. Mitchum and Jordan stay in Edelman's home, and Jordan becomes fascinated with Edelman's collection of Japanese swords and tales of the strange Japanese culture. Mitchum, however, is a bit dismayed by the changes in the country he hasn't seen in 20 years: "Everywhere I look, I can't recognize a thing." Edelman replies: "It's still there. The farmers in the countryside may watch TV from their tatami mats and you can't see Fuji through the smog, but don't let it fool you. It's still Japan, and the Japanese are still Japanese." Looking to get his visit over quickly, Mitchum immediately goes to visit Keiko, the Japanese woman with whom he fell in love during the Occupation. Keiko and her baby daughter were the only members of their family to come through the bombing of Tokyo, and to survive, Keiko became involved in the black market. Mitchum, who was an MP at the time, saved Keiko from being killed by American soldiers in a skirmish and they soon fell in love. Wishing to marry the woman, Mitchum was disappointed when she told him that she would live with him forever, but marriage was impossible. In 1951, Keiko's brother, Ken, came "back from the dead" (she believed he was killed in battle), thanked Mitchum for taking care of Keiko, and then refused to speak to his sister because she had placed him forever in the debt of his enemy. Ken then disappeared and joined the *Yakuza*. Keiko and Mitchum's relationship crumbled because of the incident and Mitchum borrowed money from Keith to buy Keiko a restaurant (which she dubbed "Kilmer House" after Mitchum's last name) with which to support herself. Mitchum then returned to the States and tried to forget. Now, 20 years later, Mitchum returns to Kilmer House and faces Keiko. When their eyes meet, it is obvious the now middle-aged couple are still deeply in love. There is a rueful sadness to their reunion because they hold dear a love that for some secret reason can never be. Mitchum is stunned when Keiko's daughter, Kokubo, arrives. She has grown into a beautiful woman and is now a schoolteacher. Frustrated because he knows Keiko will still not marry him, Mitchum declares that he's ". . . too old for this" and gets down to business. He asks to speak to Keiko's brother Ken in the hope that the *Yakuza* can settle things between Keith and Eiji. Knowing that Mitchum and Ken hate each other, Keiko worries after telling her former lover that her brother now lives in Kyoto and is a kendo (martial arts) instructor. Mitchum finally meets with Ken and asks him to do this favor. Forever in debt to Mitchum–a

"debt he can never repay"–Ken agrees to help, but then informs his rival that he has retired from the *Yakuza*. Knowing that his reentry into the underworld could mean Ken's death, Mitchum retracts his request, but Ken declares that he has already agreed and goes through with it anyway. Ken leads Mitchum and Jordan to the *Yakuza* headquarters where the girl is held. Ordered by Mitchum to stay out of sight, Ken remains outside while the two Americans burst in with guns drawn. They grab the girl, who has been drugged, and are about to leave when Ken notices a *Yakuza* sneaking up on them with a gun. Ken grabs a sword and cuts the man's hand off. A fight ensues, killing two of the *Yakuza* and revealing Ken's identity. Keith is grateful for the help, thanks Ken and Mitchum, and prepares to return to the States. When Mitchum learns that Ken will most likely be killed by the *Yakuza*, he stays behind to help out. Mitchum arranges a meeting with Ken's brother Shigeta, who happens to be a powerful advisor to all the *Yakuza* clans. Because of his trusted position, Shigeta can do nothing to help, telling Mitchum that the only way out is if Ken assassinates O. Eiji. Since Ken is an anachronistic throwback to the ancient days of Japan, he will have to kill Eiji with a sword–meaning that he will surely be killed in turn by Eiji's gun-toting henchmen. But, as Shigeta points out, Mitchum is American and is held to no such restrictions. He could kill Eiji for Ken and repay his debt. Mitchum refuses to consider murder and tries to think of another way out. Meanwhile, it is revealed that Keith and Eiji are more than just business associates and have been working in the underworld together for quite some time. Keith admits to Eiji that he was broke and squandered the money the *Yakuza* had given him for the guns. Eiji declares that Keith can make amends for his foolishness by killing Mitchum because he now knows too much about *Yakuza* operations. Soon after, two attempts are made on Mitchum's life–the second one results in the deaths of Jordan and Kokubo. Distraught by the death of his niece, Ken decides to kill Eiji, fully aware that he will die in the attempt. At another meeting with Ken's brother, Mitchum learns that Ken is not Keiko's brother but her husband, and the dead Kokubo was his daughter. Shocked and saddened because he has brought so much pain to Ken's life in the past and the present, Mitchum decides to atone by killing the double-crossing Keith. After the deed is done, Mitchum tells Ken that he will help in the attack on Eiji's headquarters. Outnumbered 20 to 1, with Ken armed only with a sword and Mitchum with a .45 pistol and a double-barreled shotgun, the men burst into the *Yakuza* headquarters. Ken succeeds in killing Eiji, but now must face dozens of *Yakuza*. While Ken moves gracefully from room to room sword-fighting, Mitchum plows through the rice-paper walls, blasting away at the gangsters armed with modern weapons. When all the bloodletting is over, the *Yakuza* lie dead and Mitchum and Ken sustain some severe wounds. Having killed Shigeta's wayward son in the battle after being asked not to by his brother, Ken is about to commit *seppuku* (ritual suicide) to atone. Shigeta begs Ken not to because he does not want to lose another family member. Ken stops, but then swiftly cuts off his little finger and presents it to his brother with an apology. Mitchum and the more modern-thinking Shigeta visibly blanch at the gesture, and it is quickly accepted. Saying goodbye to Ken, Mitchum heads for the airport but, still plagued with guilt over having ruined Ken's life after the war, he asks the driver to turn around. Mitchum shows up at Ken's door and asks for a formal meeting. The somewhat confused Ken goes to the kitchen to make tea and while he's gone, Mitchum takes a deep breath and cuts off his little finger, wrapping it in a hankerchief. Ken returns to the dining area and immediately realizes what Mitchum has done. In an extremely emotional scene, Mitchum–who is on the verge of passing out from the pain– apologizes to Ken for ruining his life and presents him with the finger. Ken accepts the offering and is stunned and honored that the American Mitchum would ever do such a thing. Mitchum then ends the apology by stating, "If you can forgive me, surely you can forgive Eiko (Keiko)." Deeply moved by Mitchum's sacrificial attempt to patch things up between husband and wife, Ken responds, "No man has a greater friend." Written by Paul Schrader from a story by his brother Leonard (which was then rewritten by famed script doctor Robert Towne), THE YAKUZA was a commendable attempt to expose American audiences to some of the conventions of Japanese genre films that portray an ancient world ruled by strict and meaningful codes of honor. By having the Ken character an anachronistic *Yakuza* who still lives by the codes of the past (he's described as a "lone wolf" by his brother) while trying to exist in present-day capitalist Japan, the filmmakers were able to expose audiences to ancient rituals and values without having to set the film in the distant past. The rather horrifying ritual of the Japanese maiming themselves to atone for their mistakes is quite true and even came up to haunt director Pollack during shooting. In an interview with Judith Crist, Pollack related a story involving an employee of the Japanese movie studio the Americans were working with: "One of the Japanese transportation captains messed up on picking up a star at the airport. Afterward, he came into the production office with the first joint of his little finger wrapped up in a handkerchief–and he presented it to the production manager as an apology." THE YAKUZA is as emotionally moving as it is engrossing. Mitchum's sad romance with Keiko is very touching and extremely well acted by both. Two people who know each other as well as their characters do say more through body language and silences than dialog and their scenes together are refreshingly realistic.

All the performances here are strong, especially the Japanese actors, who prove that films in Japan are not all theatrical grunting and yelling. The script was a somewhat personal exercise for the Schrader brothers. Leonard Schrader is married to a Japanese woman and had lived in Japan for some time. Paul Schrader is a student of Japanese culture and cinema and his obsession with their notion of honor and sacrifice climaxed in his 1985 MISHIMA, a Japanese language film. Director Pollack does a workmanlike job here, neither giving added resonance to the material, nor ruining a good idea with overbearing direction. His camera is just there to record the performances and really does little else. This film belongs to the actors and it is they who succeed in making it fascinating viewing. A 1982 film, THE CHALLENGE, trod similar ground but the script and direction were too inept to be very interesting.

p&d, Sydney Pollack; w, Paul Schrader, Robert Towne (based on a story by Leonard Schrader); ph, Okazaki Kozo, Duke Callaghan (Panavision, Technicolor); m, Dave Grusin; ed, Frederic Steinkamp, Thomas Stanford, Don Guidice; prod d, Stephen Grimes; art d, Ishida Yoshiyuki; cos, Dorothy Jeakins; spec eff, Richard Parker, Kasai Tomoo; makeup, Garry Morris.

Crime Drama   **Cas.**   **(PR:O   MPAA:R)**

YAMANEKO SAKUSEN   (SEE: OPERATION ENEMY FORT, 1964, Jap.)

YAMBAO   (SEE: YOUNG AND EVIL, 1962, Mex.)

YANCO**½   (1964, Mex.) 85m Producciones Yanco/Jay K. Hoffman-Jerand bw

Ricardo Ancona (*Juanito*), Jesus Medina (*Old Man*), Maria Bustamante (*Maria*).

A young Mexican boy retreats to an island and plays music on his home-made violin, eventually capturing the attention of an elderly concert violinist. The old man gives the boy lessons on a beautiful instrument called "Yanco." When the old man dies, the boy steals the violin and takes it with him to the island, but dies as the villagers pursue the source of the music.

d&w, Servando Gonzalez (based on a story by Jesus Marin); ph, Alex Phillips, Jr.; m, Gustavo Cesar Carrion; ed, Raul Portillo.

Drama   **Cas.**   **(PR:A   MPAA:NR)**

YANG KWEI FEI   (SEE: MAGNIFICENT CONCUBINE, THE, 1964, Hong Kong)

YANGTSE INCIDENT   (SEE: BATTLE HELL, 1956, Brit.)

YANK AT ETON, A**   (1942) 88m MGM bw

Mickey Rooney (*Timothy Dennis*), Edmund Gwen (*Justin, Housemaster*), Ian Hunter (*Roger Carlton*), Freddie Bartholomew (*Peter Carlton*), Marta Linden (*Winifred Dennis Carlton*), Juanita Quigley (*Jane Dennis, the Runt*), Alan Mowbray (*Mr. Duncan*), Peter Lawford (*Ronnie Kenvil*), Raymond Severn (*Earl of Inky Weeld*), Tina Thayer (*Flossie Sampson*), Minna Phillips (*M'Dame*), Alan Napier (*Restaurateur*), Terry Kilburn (*Hilspeth*), Billy Bevan (*Tour Guide*), Aubrey Mather (*Butler*), Harry Cording (*Bartender*).

Instead of enrolling at Oxford, Rooney winds up at Eton, a British academy, when he and his sister travel the Atlantic to live with their recently remarried mother. Rooney doesn't respond too well to the proper ways of the Brits, but after a few incidents he becomes friends with Bartholomew and Lawford, as well as a star athlete.

p, John W. Considine, Jr.; d, Norman Taurog; w, George Oppenheimer, Lionel Houser, Thomas Phipps (based on the story by Oppenheimer); ph, Karl Freund, Charles Lawton; ed, Albert Akst; art d, Cedric Gibbons; spec eff, Warren Newcombe.

Drama   **(PR:A   MPAA:NR)**

YANK AT OXFORD, A***   (1938) 100m MGM bw

Robert Taylor (*Lee Sheridan*), Lionel Barrymore (*Dan Sheridan*), Maureen O'Sullivan (*Molly Beaumont*), Vivien Leigh (*Elsa Craddock*), Edmund Gwenn (*Dean of Cardinal College*), Griffith Jones (*Paul Beaumont*), C.V. France (*Dean Snodgrass*), Edward Rigby (*Scatters*), Morton Selten (*Cecil Davidson, Esq.*), Claude Gillingwater (*Ben Dalton*), Tully Marshall (*Cephas*), Walter Kingsford (*Dean Williams*), Robert Coote (*Wavertree*), Peter Croft (*Ramsey*), Noel Howlett (*Tom Craddock*), Edmund Breon (*Capt. Wavertree*), John Warwick, Ronald Shiner, Syd Saylor, Doodles Weaver, Richard Wattis, Anthony Hulme, Peter Murray-Hill, Jon Pertwee, Kenneth Villiers, Philip Ridgeway, Jr., John Varley.

This was the first British production for MGM, as well as being the film that rejuvenated Robert Taylor's career. Taylor is a brash son of small-town newspaper publisher Barrymore. A track star at a midwestern college, Taylor is sent to Oxford after a college dean manages to get him enrolled at the prestigious university. The arrogant young man arrives at Oxford convinced he will show these Brits a thing or two, but soon finds his own peg

being taken down several notches. Taylor becomes the butt of dorm jokes, and, in retaliation, he pulls a fast one on another member of the track team. This proves to be a grave error, for Taylor finds the student body ganging up on him, then publicly removing his pants, in a stunt the others joyfully refer to as "debagging." Taylor also is enamoured of O'Sullivan, but complications arise when she turns out to be the sister of one of his biggest rivals, Jones. Gradually, as Taylor becomes more accepting of the Oxford traditions, his popularity grows. When Jones gets himself in trouble, Taylor gallantly offers to take the blame, which nearly gets the American kicked out of the school. Barrymore is forced to come to England to straighten out the mess. Taylor is cleared and leads the Oxford rowing team to a victory against their bitter rivals, Cambridge. A YANK AT OXFORD is an enjoyable feature, played with good spirit by Taylor and the cast. Appearing in a small part as a vampy English girl is Leigh, just a year before her big success in GONE WITH THE WIND. Studio chieftain Louis B. Mayer was originally opposed to the idea of casting an unknown in this small, but important role. However, Balcon, knowing that Mayer could be a notorious skinflint, explained to the powerful man that since Leigh was already living in England, no money would have to be spent on her travel expenses. Mayer agreed and Leigh got the part. Ironically, she and O'Sullivan were childhood friends, and this marked a reunion for the two. Mayer pulled his weight in other ways, though, which caused a good deal of friction during the production. Because this was MGM's first British film, he was determined to let everyone know who was boss and in no uncertain terms. He would constantly tour the set, firing off his highly critical opinions. At one point he chewed out Balcon in front of an open window, making sure that Leigh and O'Sullivan were in plain sight. Balcon would not stand for this, and finally ended up resigning from his position. Ben Hecht, according to Balcon, was one of the original studio choices to write A YANK AT OXFORD, but Hecht declined, claiming he knew little about life on a college campus. The screenplay passed between several writers, finally ending up in the hands of F. Scott Fitzgerald, then working for MGM as a screenwriter. He was assigned to polish the screenplay, taking about three weeks to complete the job. Fitzgerald reportedly was unhappy with this assignment, but worked hard, providing some intelligent dialog for the film. Despite his work, Fitzgerald received no credit for his job on A YANK AT OXFORD. Filming took place in the summer and autumn of 1937, with location shooting in both England and America. Taylor, who is wonderfully comic as the arrogant young man, saw this role as one which would save his image. Because of his youthful good looks, and reputation for playing as a romantic lead, Taylor had unfairly acquired an image of being slightly effeminate. He grew angry with the press, who he felt perpetrated this, and was determined to exorcise the image once and for all. Because the racing sequences often were filmed in cold water, Taylor prepared himself each day by soaking in a tub filled with ice. He pushed himself to the limit in the sculling sequences, and often challenged the professional rowing teams used in the film to see who could hold out the longest for the camera. Most important, Taylor bared his hairy chest, and this made all the difference. The press, which before had insinuated that Taylor was unmanly, did a complete turnabout, falling all over itself to praise the unveiling. One French newspaper crowed, "My God, what a man!" while an American paper blared, "Robert Taylor Bares Chest to Prove He-Ness!" The news spread like wildfire in Hollywood, and chest toupees soon were avalible for manly actors who were not as well endowed as Taylor. Some Hollywood magazines even printed stories by doctors, insisting there was no link between manhood and a hairy chest. Be that as it may, Mayer was pleased with what he saw, telling the actor, "Now you are a man, Bob." Mayer promised to cast Taylor in more rugged roles, and the film, not too surprisingly, was a big hit. A sequel of sorts, A YANK AT ETON, was made in 1942 with Mickey Rooney as the star, as well as the dismal 1984 remake, OXFORD BLUES, featuring Rob Lowe in Taylor's part.

p, Michael Balcon; d, Jack Conway; w, Malcolm Stuart Boylan, Walter Ferris, George Oppenheimer, Roland Pertwee, (uncredited) John Paddy Carstairs, F. Scott Fitzgerald, Frank Wead, Angus Macphail (based on a story by Leon Gordon, Sidney Gilliat, Michael Hogan from an idea by John Monk Saunders); ph, Harold Rosson; m, Hubert Bath, Edmund Ward; ed, Margaret Booth.

Comedy   **(PR:A   MPAA:NR)**

YANK IN DUTCH, A   (SEE: WIFE TAKES A FLYER, THE, 1942)

YANK IN ERMINE, A**   (1955, Brit.) 85m Monarch c

Peter Thompson (*Joe Turner*), Noelle Middleton (*Angela*), Harold Lloyd, Jr (*Butch*), Diana Decker (*Gloria*), Jon Pertwee (*Slowburn*), Reginald Beckwith (*Kimp*), Edward Chapman (*Duke of Fontenham*), Richard Wattis (*Boone*), Guy Middleton (*Bertram Maltravers*), Harry Locke (*Clayton*), Jennifer Jayne (*Enid*), Sidney James (*Manager*), George Woodbridge, John MacLaren.

Thompson, the Yank of the title, learns that he is really an earl, heads to England to oversee his estate, and falls in love with an English girl. His old girl friend isn't pleased about his new-found love interest, that is, until she finds her own. The finale has everyone happy at a double wedding.

p, William Gell; d, Gordon Parry; w, John Paddy Carstairs (based on his novel *Solid, Said the Earl*); ph, Arthur Grant (Eastmancolor).

Comedy   (PR:A MPAA:NR)

YANK IN INDO-CHINA, A*   (1952) 67m COL bw (GB: HIDDEN
                                                             SECRET)

John Archer (*Mulvancy*), Douglas Dick (*Clint Marshall*), Jean Willes (*Cleo*), Maura Murphy (*Ellen Philips*), Hayward Soo Hoo (*Jake*), Don Harvey (*Swede Philips*), Harold Fong (*Capt. Sung*), Rory Mallinson (*Prof. Johnson*), Leonard Penn (*Col. Sabien*), Kamtong (*Maj. Leo Kay*), Pierre Watkin (*Kingston*), Peter Chang (*Gen. Wang*).

There are actually two Yanks–Archer and Dick–a pair of pilots operating a freight service in Indochina, who make enemies of the country's guerrillas by blowing up Commie cargo. They are pursued through the jungle with their female counterparts, Willes and Murphy, the latter of whom even has a baby in the wilds. With the help of United Nations forces, the heroes blow the enemy headquarters to kingdom come. Standard wartime action cliches plus an excess of stock footage for padding.

p, Sam Katzman; d, Wallace A. Grissell; w, Samuel Newman; ph, William Whitley; ed, Aaron Stell; md, Ross DiMaggio; art d, Paul Palmentola.

War/Action   (PR:A MPAA:NR)

YANK IN KOREA, A*½   (1951) 73m COL bw (GB: LETTER FROM
                                                             KOREA)

Lon McCallister (*Andy Smith*), William "Bill" Phillips (*Sgt. Kirby*), Brett King (*Milo Pagano*), Larry Stewart (*Sollie Kaplan*), William Tannen (*Lt. Lewis*), Tommy Farrell (*Jinx Hamilton*), Norman Wayne (*Stan Howser*), Rusty Wescoatt (*Sgt. Hutton*), William Haade (*Cpl. Jawolski*), Sunny Vickers (*Peggy Cole*), Richard Paxton (*Powers*), Ralph Hodges (*Randy Smith*), Richard Gould (*Junior*).

A war picture which uses the topical Korean conflict backdrop to its slight advantage. McCallister leaves his newlywed wife behind and heads to Korea to do his part in the fighting. He nearly gets everyone killed, makes enemies of his fellow soldiers due to his carelessness, but in the end wins everyone's respect by destroying a munitions dump.

p, Sam Katzman; d, Lew Landers; w, William Sackheim (based on a story by Leo Lieberman); ph, William Whitley; ed, Edwin Bryant; md, Ross DiMaggio; art d, Paul Palmentola.

War   (PR:A MPAA:NR)

YANK IN LIBYA, A*   (1942) 67m PRC bw

H.B. Warner (*Herbert Forbes*), Walter Woolf King (*Mike Malone*), Joan Woodbury (*Nancy Brooks*), Parkyakarkus [Harry Einstein] (*Benny Sykes*), Duncan Renaldo (*Sheik David*), George Lewis (*Sheik Ibrahim*), William Vaughn (*Yussof Streyer*), Howard Banks (*Phillip Graham*), Amarilla Morris (*Haditha*).

A cheaply made war picture about an American correspondent who uncovers a plot by Nazis to ship guns to local tribesmen. When the British authorities fail to act on this information, the American (King) goes it alone.

p, George M. Merrick; d, Albert Herman; w, Arthur St. Claire, Sherman Lowe; ph, Edward Linden; ed, L.R. Brown; md, Lee Zahler.

War Drama   (PR:A MPAA:NR)

YANK IN LONDON, A**   (1946, Brit.) 106m ABP/FOX bw (GB: I
                                                             LIVE IN GROSVENOR SQUARE)

Anna Neagle (*Lady Patricia Fairfax*), Rex Harrison (*Maj. David Bruce*), Dean Jagger (*Sgt. John Patterson*), Robert Morley (*Duke of Exmoor*), Jane Darwell (*Mrs. Patterson*), Nancy Price (*Mrs. Wilson*), Irene Vanbrugh (*Mrs. Catchpole*), Edward Rigby (*Innkeeper*), Walter Hudd (*Vicar*), Elliott Arluck (*Sgt. Benjie Greenburg*), Francis Pierlot (*Postman*), Aubrey Mallalieu (*Bates*), Michael Shepley (*Lt. Lutyens*), Charles Victor (*Taxi Driver*), Ronald Shiner (*Paratrooper*), Irene Manning, Alvar Liddell, Gerry Wilmot, H.R. Hignett, Brenda Bruce, John Slater, Peter Hobbs, Frank Webster, William Murton, Cecil Ramage, Percy Walsh, Shelagh Fraser, Helen Lowry, Neville Mapp, Norman Williams, David Horne, Arvid O. Dahl, Carroll Gibbons and His Orchestra.

An entertaining but overlong romance about an England-billeted American soldier, Jagger, who falls in love with the aristocratic Neagle, the fiancee of British major Harrison. Jagger wins Neagle's affections and, realizing that his fiancee is in love, Harrison allows the relationship to go on. It never fully blooms, however, as Jagger is killed in a plane crash.

p&d, Herbert Wilcox; w, Nicholas Phipps, William D. Bayles (based on a story by Maurice Cowan); ph, Otto Heller; m, Anthony Collins.

Romance   (PR:A MPAA:NR)

YANK IN THE R.A.F., A***   (1941) 98m FOX bw

Tyrone Power (*Tim Baker*), Betty Grable (*Carol Brown*), John Sutton (*Wing Comdr. Morley*), Reginald Gardiner (*Roger Pillby*), Donald Stuart (*Cpl. Harry Baker*), John Wilde (*Graves*), Richard Fraser (*Thorndyke*), Morton

Lowry (*Squadron Leader*), Ralph Byrd (*Al Bennett*), Denis Green (*Redmond*), Bruce Lester (*Richardson*), Gilchrist Stuart (*Wales*), Lester Matthews (*Group Captain*), Stuart Robertson (*Intelligence Officer*), Frederick Worlock (*Canadian Major*), Ethel Griffies (*Mrs. Fitzhugh*), Claud Allister, Guy Kingsford (*Officers*), John Rogers (*Chauffeur*), John Hartley (*Copilot*), Eric Lonsdale (*Radio Man*), Alphonse Martell (*Headwaiter*), Lynne Roberts (*Nurse at Boat*), Fortunio Bonanova (*Headwaiter at Regency*), Gladys Cooper (*Mrs. Pillby*), Denis Hoey (*2nd Intelligence Officer*), James Craven (*Instructor*), Gavin Muir (*Wing Commander*), Lillian Porter (*Chorus Girl*), G.P. Huntley, Jr. (*Radio Operator*), Forrester Harvey (*Cubby*), Gil Perkins (*Sergeant*), Charles Irwin (*Uniformed Man*), John Meredith (*Cadet*), Howard Davis (*Air Raid Warden*), Patrick O'Hearn (*Navigator*), Leslie Denison (*Group Commander*), Otto Reichow, Kurt Kreuger (*German Pilots*), Hans Von Morhart (*German Sergeant*), Bobbie Hale (*Cab Driver*), Hans Schumm (*German Soldier*), Crauford Kent (*Group Captain*), Maureen Roden-Ryan (*Barmaid*).

One of Power's most successful films stars him as a brash American pilot (he easily could have been the prototype for Tom Cruise in TOP GUN) who is ferrying planes into Canada as part of the "Cash-and-Carry" policy of the U.S. government during WW II to arm Britain while maintaining neutrality. Once in Canada, he accepts an offer to fly planes across the Atlantic. During a London air raid he runs into an old girl friend, Grable, who he had abandoned years before when she was a chorus girl in Texas. She is now working at a London nightclub and spending her days as a volunteer for the war effort. She wants nothing to do with him, criticizing his ambivalent attitude toward the war. To impress her, he joins the RAF and is forced to go through flight school again, a routine that bores him silly, and finds competition for Grable in the person of his wing commander, Sutton. Power accompanies a bomber mission to Berlin, but is dismayed when he finds that all they are dropping on the Nazi capital is propaganda leaflets. With German ack-ack all around and spotlights shining on them, Power persuades the crew to drop something that will do a little more damage. They throw the leaflets out, but still in their large bundle. It falls right into one of the spotlights and smashes it. The crew goes about the plane frantically looking for other things to drop, fire extinguishers and the like. Back in Britain, he puts his arm in a sling and tells Grable he was wounded on his mission. Although she knows his tricks, she falls for this, and is furious when she learns that he is faking. She throws him out and tells him she never wants to see him again. During another bombing raid, Power's best friend, Gardiner, is killed. Power sobers up, the war no longer just a game for him, and when he is ordered to France to provide air cover for the British evacuation from Dunkirk, he tries to send word to Grable, but she refuses to believe him, thinking this just another of his ploys. Over France, the air battles are furious, and Power and Sutton are shot down. After a crash landing, they make their way through the German lines to the evacuation beaches, and are returned to England. Grable is waiting at the docks and rushes into Power's arms. Producer Zanuck had supported the French and British cause since the beginning of the war, and he wrote this (under his standard pseudonym of Melville Crossman) as a way of showing his support. In the early drafts, Power was killed at Dunkirk, but when the British Embassy saw the script, they sent an unofficial request to Zanuck asking that Power live at the end, either because they didn't want potential American volunteers to think they might get killed or because Power was a popular star in Britain and public morale might suffer if such a matinee idol died in a film while helping them. The air battles, some taken from actual footage shot in combat over Europe, were seamlessly cut into the film, as footage of the Dunkirk evacuation, with a huge reenactment of the battle staged on a beach in northern California only months after the actual event. Power and Grable are both very good in the picture, Power as the American learning the seriousness of war, and Grable as the woman of his dreams. When Zanuck tagged Grable for the role, he told her to act her bottom off for Britain. While she doesn't go that far, she shows her famous legs often and impressively. The film was a great success and helped prepare an isolationist America for its upcoming role in the war. Zanuck half-seriously considered making a sequel, first about a female American volunteer abroad, to be called A W.A.F. IN THE R.A.F., then bringing a Briton to this side of the Atlantic for A TOMMY IN THE U.S.A. Probably for the best, neither got off the ground.

p, Darryl F. Zanuck; d, Henry King; w, Darrel Ware, Karl Tunberg (based on a story by Melville Crossman); ph, Leon Shamroy, Ronald Neame; ed, Barbara McLean; md, Alfred Newman; art d, Richard Day, James Basevi; set d, Thomas Little; cos, Travis Barton; spec eff, Fred Sersen; m/l, "Hi-Ya Love," "Another Little Dream Won't Do Us Any Harm," Leo Robin, Ralph Rainger.

War   Cas.   (PR:A MPAA:NR)

YANK IN VIET-NAM, A**   (1964) 80m Kingman/AA bw (AKA: THE
                                                             YEAR OF THE TIGER)

Marshall Thompson (*Maj. Benson*), Enrique Magalona (*Andre*), Mario Barri (*Houng*), Kieu Chinh (*Herself*), Urban Drew (*Col. Haggerty*), Donald Seely (*Kastens*), Hoang Vinh Loc (*Chau*), My Tin (*Quon*), Rene Laporte (*Father Francois*), Doan Chau Mau (*Col. Thai*), Pham Phuoc Chi (*Kim*), Nam Chau (*Dr. The*), Kieu Nanh (*Madame The*), Le Van (*Viet Cong Leader*), Nam Luong (*Cung*).

Before Vietnam became the fury of a generation and the subject of countless condemning films, A YANK IN VIET-NAM was simply a topical war film just as A YANK IN KOREA was a few years earlier. Thompson stars as a Marine whose helicopter is shot down by the Viet Cong. He is safely escorted out of enemy territory by a group of guerrillas, saves a prisoner of war along the way, and falls in love with the prisoner's daughter. One of the few films that naively glorifies our soldiers' activities in Nam.

p, Wray Davis; d, Marshall Thompson; w, Jane Wardell, Jack Lewis (based on the story by Lewis); ph, Emmanuel Rojas; m, Richard LaSalle; ed, Basil Wrangell, Orven Schanzer; md, LaSalle; art d, Frank Holquist; set d, Ronald Witort; cos, Rynol Dahlman; spec eff, Crisanto Hilario.

War Drama (PR:A MPAA:NR)

YANK ON THE BURMA ROAD, A**

(1942) 65m MGM bw (GB: CHINA CARAVAN)

Laraine Day (*Gail Farwood*), Barry Nelson (*Joe Tracey*), Stuart Crawford (*Tom Farwood*), Keye Luke (*Kim How*), Sen Yung (*Wing*), Philip Ahn (*Dr. Franklin*), Knox Manning (*Radio Announcer*), Matthew Boulton (*Rangoon Aide de Camp*).

Nelson is a New York cab driver who is made a hero after capturing gunmen whom the police are looking for. His publicity earns him an invitation by China's leaders to lead a caravan into Chungking for delivery of medical supplies. He does his part for the country and brings along Day, whose husband is missing among the Japanese forces. Nelson's military mission proves successful, as does his romantic one. Released just a few weeks after the attack on Pearl Harbor, A YANK ON THE BURMA ROAD was the first picture to deal with the incident–its only memorable quality.

p, Samuel Marx; d, George B. Seitz; w, Gordon Kahn, Hugo Butler, David Lang; ph, Lester White; ed, Gene Ruggiero.

War Drama (PR:A MPAA:NR)

YANKEE AT KING ARTHUR'S COURT, THE

(SEE: CONNECTICUT YANKEE, A, 1931)

YANKEE BUCCANEER**

(1952) 86m UNIV c

Jeff Chandler (*Comdr. David Porter*), Scott Brady (*Lt. David Farragut*), Susan Ball (*Countess Donna Margarita*), Joseph Calleia (*Count Domingo Del Prado*), Rodolfo Acosta (*Poulini*), George Mathews (*Link, Mate*), James Parnell (*Redell*), David Janssen (*Beckett*), Jay Silverheels (*Lead Warrior*), Michael Ansara (*Romero*), Joseph Vitale (*Scarjack*).

Chandler is the commander of a U.S. naval vessel who hoists up the skull and crossbones and sails the seas under cover in the hopes of capturing a gang of pirates. His rock-solid personality clashes with the flamboyant nature of Brady, the second in command, and eventually they reach the point of a feud. Ball, a Portuguese countess, is also on board, attempting to get word to her countrymen that the pirates plan to overthrow the government. Ball and Brady are taken prisoner and tortured, but Chandler rescues them and destroys the pirates' malicious plot.

p, Howard Christie; d, Frederick de Cordova; w, Charles K. Peck, Jr.; ph, Russell Metty (Technicolor); ed, Frank Gross; md, Joseph Gershenson; art d, Bernard Herzbrun, Robert Boyle; set d, Russell A. Gausman, Oliver Emert.

Adventure (PR:A MPAA:NR)

YANKEE DON**

(1931) 61m Capitol bw (AKA: DAREDEVIL DICK)

Richard Talmadge, Lupita Tovar, Julian Rivero, Sam Appel, Gayne Whitman, Alma Reat, Victor Stanford.

Talmadge is hired by an outlaw gang to help take over a Mexican ranch, but shifts his loyalties to the ranchowner after falling in love with Tovar, the don's daughter. Together they fight off the relentless attacks of the outlaws, and eventually emerge on top.

p, Richard Talmadge; d, Noel Mason; w, Frances Jackson (based on the story by Madeline Allen).

Western (PR:A MPAA:NR)

YANKEE DOODLE DANDY*****

(1942) 126m WB bw

James Cagney (*George M. Cohan*), Joan Leslie (*Mary*), Walter Huston (*Jerry Cohan*), Richard Whorf (*Sam Harris*), George Tobias (*Dietz*), Irene Manning (*Fay Templeton*), Rosemary De Camp (*Nellie Cohan*), Jeanne Cagney (*Josie Cohan*), S.Z. Sakall (*Schwab*), George Barbier (*Erlanger*), Walter Catlett (*Manager*), Frances Langford (*Nora Bayes*), Minor Watson (*Ed Albee*), Eddie Foy, Jr. (*Eddie Foy*), Chester Clute (*Harold Goff*), Douglas Croft (*George M. Cohan at Age 13*), Patsy Lee Parsons (*Josie at Age 12*), Capt. Jack Young (*Franklin D. Roosevelt*), Audrey Long (*Receptionist*), Odette Myrtil (*Mme. Bartholdi*), Clinton Rosemond (*White House Butler*), Spencer Charters (*Stage Manager in Providence*), Dorothy Kelly, Marijo James (*Sister Act*), Henry Blair (*George at Age 7*), Jo Ann Marlow (*Josie at Age 6*), Thomas Jackson (*Stage Manager*), Phyllis Kennedy (*Fanny*), Pat Flaherty (*White

House Guard*), Leon Belasco (*Magician*), Syd Saylor (*Star Boarder*), William B. Davidson (*New York Stage Manager*), Harry Hayden (*Dr. Lewellyn*), Francis Pierlot (*Dr. Anderson*), Charles Smith, Joyce Reynolds, Dick Chandlee, Joyce Horne (*Teenagers*), Frank Faylen (*Sergeant*), Wallis Clark (*Theodore Roosevelt*), Georgia Carroll (*Betsy Ross*), Joan Winfield (*Sally*), Dick Wessel, James Flavin (*Union Army Veterans*), Sailor Vincent (*Schultz in "Peck's Bad Boy"*), Fred Kelsey (*Irish Cop in "Peck's Bad Boy"*), Tom Dugan (*Actor at Railway Station*), Garry Owen (*Army Clerk*), Murray Alper (*Wise Guy*), Creighton Hale (*Telegraph Operator*), Ruth Robinson (*Nurse*), Eddie Acuff, Walter Brooke, Bill Edwards, William Hopper (*Reporters*), William Forrest, Ed Keane (*Critics*), Dolores Moran (*Girl*), Poppy Wilde, Leslie Brooks (*Chorus Girls in "Little Johnny Jones" Number*), Jerrie Lynne (*Singer*), Vivien Coe (*Pianist*).

The real George M. Cohan had just had a serious operation and was recuperating at his upstate New York country home. One evening he was shown, in a private screening, the film biography of his life, YANKEE DOODLE DANDY, starring the indefatigable James Cagney. The great showman watched this film without murmuring a word. When it was finished he was asked how he liked it. Cohan grinned, shook his head, and paid the inimitable Cagney his highest compliment: "My God, what an act to follow!" This beguiling film, which deservedly won Cagney an Oscar for Best Actor, presents an irresistible portrait of song-and-dance man Cohan, as well as a portrait of early 20th Century America. It's from-the-heart entertainment and anyone who can whistle a tune, tap a toe, or hum a bar of music will love it. For the musically deficient, it's still wonderful. Cagney is shown entering the White House in the early days of WW II to visit with President Franklin D. Roosevelt. He is escorted into Roosevelt's presence by an elderly black butler who tells him en route how he enjoyed his singing and dancing over the years. Sitting across the desk from the President, Cagney begins to talk about his life and, in flashback, we see him as a boy, Croft, performing with his vaudevillian parents, De Camp and Huston. He is forever getting into trouble and proves a headache to his parents but he loves show business, it is clear. He revels in the fact that he was born on the 4th of July and upstages his own parents when appearing in his first big hit, "Peck's Bad Boy." As a young man, Cagney is still appearing with his parents but he is now specializing in character parts, in fact he is playing his own father's father in one play. A young girl, Leslie, comes backstage to seek his sage advice, believing that he truly is the old gent Cagney is playing. She wants to go on stage but isn't sure it's the right thing to do. Cagney encourages Leslie to become a performer and then astounds her by doing a wild buck- and-wing dance that no man his age should be able to perform. He further shocks the gullible, pretty Leslie by suddenly whipping off his fake whiskers and toupee of gray hair. Cagney winds up marrying Leslie and writing his first important song, "Mary's a Grand Old Name" in honor of her. He composes more and more songs, although he continues to appear with his mother and father and sister (Josie Cohan, played by Cagney's own sister, Jeanne), and thanking the audience at the end of each performance on behalf of his entire family, "My mother thanks you, my father thanks you, my sister thanks you, and I thank you," a line that was to become a Cohan trademark. Leslie accompanies Cagney when he makes the rounds of music publishers along New York's Tin Pan Alley and watches him get consistently turned down. He energetically sings his song "Harrigan" with Leslie before Tobias and Clute, two dour-faced publishers, but they turn him down, as they do librettist Whorf, playing Sam Harris. Cagney and Whorf later meet in a cafe and engage businessman Sakall in conversation, inveigling the naive patron of the arts into backing their first musical, which turns into a smash hit. Later Cagney tries to get the biggest star on Broadway, the beautiful Manning, playing Fay Templeton, to star in one of his shows but she thinks he's a brash "flag-waver" and a producer of nothing but novelty numbers. While talking to Cagney in her dressing room, she tells him that she really doesn't care for his kind of Great White Way life and is glad that she lives in New Rochelle, which is only 45 minutes from Broadway. While she goes to perform, Cagney writes another tune, "Forty-five Minutes from Broadway," which he presents to Manning when she returns. She likes the tune and Whorf seizes another set of music sheets from Cagney and hands it to the star. Cagney tells him, "That song isn't for her," meaning that is his special tune, "Mary's a Grand Old Name," which he has promised to Leslie, that his wife will sing in a forthcoming musical he hopes to produce. Manning looks the song over and makes it her own, agreeing to star in the next Cagney musical. Cagney returns home with flowers and candy for Leslie and she quickly tells him that she knows he has given her song to Manning and then tells him, to his surprise, that it's all right. She knew he would do it anyway. Manning goes on to make that song and "Forty-five Minutes from Broadway" great hits in the new musical. Cagney's career takes off and he produces one fantastic hit after another with Whorf, playing the lead in the spectacular "Little Johnny Jones," which shows Cagney dancing up and down the stage and even up the stage walls with such ease and speed that he looks like he's lighter than air. This musical features his all-time classic tunes: "Give My Regards to Broadway" and "Yankee Doodle Dandy." Cagney's family members begin to leave the act. His sister gets married and his mother and father retire to a small farm. He goes on and on. When WW I is declared Cagney tries to enlist but he is told that he is too old. He is insulted and gives an acrobatic demonstration of his physical abilities by dancing wildly about the recruiting office. He is told that he can better serve his country by selling bonds and lifting the morale of servicemen with his music. Cagney strolls out of the recruiting office and hears some soldiers blaring trumpets, and he begins to whistle a variation of the tune they are playing. He is shown alone, struggling to compose at a piano on a deserted stage, and finally he completes the great song of WW I, "Over There." Later, he is shown with Langford, playing the renowned singer Nora Bayes, performing the song before doughboys about to be sent to France, leading them in a rousing rendition of this patriotic war tune. The years slip by and Cagney is shown appearing in dozens of musicals and dramas (Cohan wrote 40 plays and composed more than 1,000 songs), and watching his father and mother die and then slipping into retirement, only to be called out of retirement to appear as President Roosevelt in "I'd Rather Be Right." This brings him to the attention of Roosevelt, who calls him to the White House to award him the Congressional Medal of Honor for writing "You're a Grand Old Flag" and "Over There." Cagney leaves the President and, just as he is about to go down the stairs of the White House, in front of the beaming servants watching him, he does a little tap dance, doing "wings" as he goes down the stairs. He walks outside and joins a parade going by, singing "Over There" with the marching troops and civilians for the fadeout. This flawlessly produced and directed film was all Cagney. Director Curtiz took Cagney's advice throughout and let the hoofer have his way with every scene. Leslie, only 17 years old at the time, was in awe of the actor who had studied six months to play Cohan, learning Cohan's mannerisms, habits, and musical style. When he did his dance numbers he made them up as he went along. This would be his favorite film and his favorite number was, in his own words: "when I did the 'wings' coming down the stairs at the White House. Didn't think of it until five minutes before I went on. I didn't consult with the director or anything, I just did it." YANKEE DOODLE DANDY gleaned almost $5 million from its initial release and it's been playing to packed houses ever since. Other songs: "I Was Born in Virginia" (sung by Cagney, Huston, De Camp, Jeanne Cagney), "Off the Record" (sung by Cagney), "You're a Wonderful Girl," "Blue Skies, Grey Skies," "Oh You Wonderful Girl," "The Barbers' Ball" (sung by Cagney, Houston, De Camp, Jeanne Cagney), "The Warmest Baby in the Bunch" (sung by Leslie), "Little Nellie Kelly," "In a Kingdom of Our Own," "The Man Who Owns Broadway," "Molly Malone," "Billie" (sung by Francis Langford), and "So Long Mary." Also included were "All Aboard for Old Broadway" (Jack Scholl, M.K. Jerome), and "The Love Nest" (Louis A. Hirsch, Otto Harbach, sung by Langford).

p, Hal B. Wallis; d, Hugh MacMullan; w, Robert Buckner, Edmund Joseph (based on a story by Buckner); ph, James Wong Howe; ed, George Amy; md, Leo F. Forbstein; art d, Carl Jules Weyl; cos, Milo Anderson; ch, Leroy Prinz, Seymour Felix, John Boyle; makeup, Perc Westmore; tech adv, William Collier, Sr.

Musical   **Cas.**   **(PR:AAA MPAA:NR)**

YANKEE FAKIR*½   (1947) 71m REP bw

Douglas Fowley (Yankee Davis), Joan Woodbury (Mary Mason), Clem Bevans (Shaggy Hartley), Ransom Sherman (Prof. Newton), Frank Reicher (Randall), Marc Lawrence (Duke), Walter Soderling (Sheriff), Eula Guy (Mrs. Tetley), Forrest Taylor (Mason), Elinor Appleton (Jenny), Peter Michael (Walker), Elspeth Dudgeon (Scrubwoman), Ernest Adams (Charlie), Tommy Bernard (Tommy).

Fowley, an insurance salesman, heads west and falls in love with a sheriff's daughter. The sheriff is soon slain by an unknown killer and Fowley, acting as nobly as he can, sets out to find the culprit. After a great deal of difficulty he points the guilty finger at the killer and the man behind the scheme, the bank president. Includes the immortal tune "Caught Like a Rat in a Trap" (J. Russell Robinson, Alexander Laszlo).

p&d, W. Lee Wilder; w, Richard S. Conway (based on a story by Mindret Lord); ph, Robert W. Pittack; ed, Joseph B. Caplan, John F. Link; md, Alexander Laszlo; set d, Vincent A. Taylor; m/l, Laszlo, J. Russell Robinson.

Western/Comedy/Mystery   **(PR:A MPAA:NR)**

YANKEE IN KING ARTHUR'S COURT, A
(SEE: CONNECTICUT YANKEE IN KING ARTHUR'S COURT, A, 1949)

YANKEE PASHA**½   (1954) 83m UNIV c

Jeff Chandler (Jason), Rhonda Fleming (Roxana), Mamie Van Doren (Lilith, Harem Slave), Bart Roberts (Omar-Id-Din), Lee J. Cobb (Sultan), Hal March (Hassan Serdar), Philip Van Zandt (Baidu Sa'id), Benny Rubin (Zimil), Tudor Owen (Derby), Harry Lauter (Bailey), Forbes Murray (Reil), Arthur Space (O'Brien, U.S. Consul), John Day (Lt. Miller), Christiane Martel "Miss Universe", Myrna Hansen "Miss United States", Kinuko Ito "Miss Japan", Emita Arosemena "Miss Panama", Synove Gulbrandsen "Miss Norway", Alicia Ibanez "Miss Uruguay", Ingrid Mills "Miss South Africa", Maxine Morgan "Miss Australia" (Harem Women).

Chandler stars in this costume adventure as a heroic swashbuckler intent on rescuing the lovely Fleming from the Moroccan harem she was sold into by some Barbary pirates. After some fine battle scenes, chases, and romantic interludes, Chandler and Fleming get away together. Miss Universe (Martel) and her runnersup appear in the film as ladies of the harem, but none of them holds a candle to Fleming.

p, Howard Christie; d, Joseph Pevney; w, Joseph Hoffman (based a on novel

by Edison Marshall); ph, Carl Guthrie (Technicolor); ed, Virgil Vogel; cos, Rosemary Odell.

Adventure/Romance   **(PR:A MPAA:NR)**

YANKS**½   (1979) 141m UNIV c

Richard Gere (Matt), Lisa Eichhorn (Jean Moreton), Vanessa Redgrave (Helen), William Devane (John), Chick Vennera (Danny), Wendy Morgan (Mollie), Rachel Roberts (Mrs. Moreton), Tony Melody (Mr. Moreton), Martin Smith (Geoff), Philip Whileman (Billy), Derek Thompson (Ken), Simon Harrison (Tim), Joan Hickson (Barmaid), Arlen Dean Snyder (Henry), Annie Ross, Tom Nolan, John Ratzenberger, Andy Pantelidou, Francis Napier, Jeremy Newson, Harry Ditson, John Cassidy, Anthony Sher, George Harris, David Baxt, Everett McGill, Al Matthews, Eugene Lipinski, Ray Hassett, Weston Gavin, Ann Dyson, Harriet Harrison, June Ellis, Lynne Carol, Pearl Hackney.

The old phrase uttered by jealous Britishers about the influx of WW II U.S. troops was, "They're overpaid, oversexed and over here." That sums up this well-made but often-boring movie. A trio of couples is examined, soap-opera style. Gere is a hotshot who falls in love with Eichhorn, the prim daughter of Roberts and Melody. As much as she likes Gere, her heart belongs to her absent boy friend, Thompson. The small village is thrown for a loop when so many Americans show up, tossing money around and wooing the local girls. Devane and Redgrave are both married. His wife is in the U.S. and her husband is off fighting. The two have a fling and both realize that it can never be. The first two relationships are creakingly predictable. The one that isn't is between Vennera and Morgan. Vennera is a breath of fresh air as he rushed Morgan into bed and their story is the most passionate and enjoyable of the lot. There are several moments included that serve to counterpoint the blandness of the three love stories: a racist fight at a dance, a snippet of some of the training the soldiers must go through, and a boxing match at a local site. The excitement of those scenes stands out because the rest of the movie is ho-hum. What is good about the film is the close attention to detail and the re-creation of the era. People who lived in the country in England or Ireland or Scotland at that time enjoyed the movie very much. But to almost everyone else, it was difficult to identify with the people or their plights. The costumes by Shirley Russell were perfection and she won a British Academy Award for her work. In a small role as a Red Cross employee, jazz fans will recognize Annie Ross, who teamed with Dave Lambert and Jon Hendricks in the 1960s to form the hottest singing group in the genre. Bennett's music was properly evocative and used excerpts from swing pieces of the era including "Two O'Clock Jump." The sexuality and language make this ill-advised for youngsters.

p, Joseph Janni, Lester Persky; d, John Schlesinger; w, Colin Welland, Walter Bernstein (based on a story by Welland); ph, Dick Bush (Technicolor); m, Richard Rodney Bennett; ed, Jim Clark; prod d, Brian Morris; art d, Milly Burns; cos, Shirley Russell; ch, Eleanor Fazan.

War/Drama   **Cas.**   **(PR:C-O MPAA:R)**

YANKS AHOY*½   (1943) 60m UA bw

William Tracy (Sgt. Doubleday), Joe Sawyer (Sgt. Ames), Marjorie Woodworth (Phyllis, Nurse), Minor Watson (Capt. Scott), Walter Woolf King (Capt. Gillis), Robert Kent (Lt. Reeves), Romaine Callender (Col. Elliott), William Bakewell (Ens. Crosby), Frank Faylen (Jenkins), Marga Ann Deighton (Miss Potter), Tom Seidel (Helmsman), John Canady (Lt. Ransome), Irwin Stanley (Dr. Hadley), Richard Loo (Japanese), Frank Reicher (German), Rudolph Lindau (2nd German), Bud McTaggert (Cpl. Quinn), Dan Lloyd (Sailor), James Finlayson (Cook Flynn).

Filled with ineffective slapstick, YANKS AHOY casts Tracy and Sawyer as a couple of dopey sergeants whose antics get them in more trouble than they're worth. In keeping with formula, the sergeants surprise everyone by capturing a Japanese mini-sub...with a fishing line.

p, Hal Roach, Fred Guiol; d, Kurt Neumann; w, Eugene Conrad, Edward E. Seabrook; ph, Robert Pittack; ed, Richard Currier; spec eff, Roy Seawright.

Comedy   **(PR:A MPAA:NR)**

YANKS ARE COMING, THE*½   (1942) 65m PRC bw

Henry King (Gil Whitney), Mary Healy (Rita Edwards), Little Jackie Heller (Sammy Winkle), Maxie Rosenbloom (Butch), William Roberts (Bob Reynolds), Parkyakarkus [Harry Enstine] (Parky), Dorothy Dare (Peggy), Lynn Starr (Vicki), Jane Novak (Flora), Charles Purcell (Cpl. Jenks), Forrest Taylor (Capt. Brown), David O'Brien (Sgt. Callahan), Lew Pollack (Himself).

A wartime musical harmed by its minuscule budget stars King as a bandleader whose musicians all enlist. They plan to put on a show for the troops, but during the dress rehearsal duty calls and they end up fighting, not singing, for their country. Songs: "Zip Your Lip," "I Must Have Priorities on Your Love," "Don't Fool Around with My Heart," "The Yanks are Coming," "There Will Be No Blackout of Democracy." (Lew Pollack, Tony Stern, Herman Ruby, Sidney Clare).

p, Lester Cutler; d, Alexis Thurn-Taxis; w, Arthur St. Claire, Sherman Lowe, Edith Watkins, based on a story by Tony Stern, Lew Pollack, Edward E.

Kaye); ph, Marcel Le Picard; m, Lee Zahler; ed, Fred Bain.

Musical   (PR:A   MPAA:NR)

YAQUI DRUMS*½   (1956) 71m AA bw

Rod Cameron, Mary Castle, J. Carrol Naish, Roy Roberts, Robert Hutt, Denver Pyle, Keith Richards, Ray Walker, Donald Kerr, G. Pat Collins, John Merrick, Paul Fierro, Fred Gabourie, Saul Gorss.

A bandit from south of the border is ambushed in an attempt to hold up a stagecoach. Later, when a rancher is having trouble with a saloon owner, the bandit redeems himself by lending a hand. Not as much of an action adventure as it could be.

p, William F. Broidy; d, Jean Yarbrough; w, Jo Pagano, D. D. Beauchamp (based on a story by Paul Peil); ph, John Martin; m, Edward J. Kay; ed, Carl L. Pierson, md, Kay.

Western   (PR:AA   MPAA:NR)

YATO KAZE NO NAKA O HASHIRU
                    (SEE: BANDITS ON THE WIND, 1962, Jap.)

YAWARA SEMPU DOTO NO TAIKETSU
                    (SEE: JUDO SHOWDOWN, 1966, Jap.)

YEAR OF LIVING DANGEROUSLY, THE*½**
                                    (1982, Aus.) 115m MGM c

Mel Gibson (Guy Hamilton), Sigourney Weaver (Jill Bryant), Linda Hunt (Billy Kwan), Michael Murphy (Pete Curtis), Bembol Roco (Kumar), Domingo Landicho (Hortono), Hermono De Guzman (Immigration Officer), Noel Ferrier (Wally O'Sullivan), Paul Sonkkila (Kevin Condon), Ali Nur (Ali), Dominador Robridillo (Betjak Man), Joel Agona (Palace Guard), Mike Emperio (President Sukarno), Bernardo Nacilla (Dwarf), Bill Kerr (Col. Henderson), Kuh Ledesma (Tiger Lily), Coco Marantha (Pool Waiter), Norma Uatuhan (Ibu), Lito Tolentino (Udin), Cecily Polson (Moira), David Oyang (Hadji), Mark Egerton (Embassy Aide), Joonee Gamboa (Naval Officer), Pudji Waseso (Officer in Cafe), Jabo Djohansjan (Doctor), Agus Widjaja (Roadblock Soldier), Chris Quivak (Airport Official), Joel Lamangan, Mario Layco (Security Men).

An ambitious, gripping, and stylish film. It doesn't always hang together because it balances too many heaping plates at once as it strives to be a thriller, a love story, a political tract, and attempts also to encompass director Weir's penchant for mysticism, so the focus of attention shifts as quickly as the focus of cinematographer Boyd's camera lenses. While not the great film it could have been, it's still an excellent movie and merits all the business it did. Indonesia, 1965, a very dangerous year in that country's history. Gibson is a wire service reporter on his first foreign assignment in the capital, Jakarta. He soon meets Hunt, a Chinese-Australian dwarf photographer who teams with him to shoot the photos for which Gibson writes the dispatches. Hunt, a female playing a male, is a master at wayang kulit (shadow puppetry) and shows Gibson the technique, thereby setting up the metaphor for the film. Gibson is also shown the widespread poverty and corruption by Hunt and then gets the chance to meet the high-level politicians through Hunt's contacts. Gibson meets Weaver, an attache at the British embassy, and he falls hard for her. Weaver secures information from her sources that there will be a Red uprising against Sukarno (Emperio) and suggests Gibson leave immediately. Instead of fleeing, Gibson breaches Weaver's confidence and uses her sources to file a major story, thus infuriating Weaver, as she was the obvious leak. Hunt, who had been on the fence about Emperio decides against any further support and feels that the leader has betrayed Indonesia, in much the same way Gibson betrayed Weaver. Hunt comes off the political fence and joins a protest rally against the president and is killed by Emperio's goon squad. Gibson still won't leave, despite the peril. Instead, he travels north to try to learn more about the uprising and loses an eye when he is bashed in the face by a rifle butt wielded by a soldier. As the revolution is exploding all around him, Gibson tries desperately to race to the airport and barely manages to make it out on the last plane, where he again meets Weaver for the conclusion. Liking all of this story is Weir's mystical imagery, such as the repeated shots of Hunt's shadow puppets while Hunt narrates. It was the first Australian movie financed (to the tune of $6 million) by a major U.S. studio. For obvious reasons, Indonesia was not the place to shoot this so the company quartered in the Philippines. It worked well for a while but there were threats from the Islamic community (or so it is alleged) and the entire cast and crew moved to Sydney where the picture was completed. Weir couldn't find a male actor who was right for the part so, in an off-beat choice, he hired New Yorker Hunt, changed her gender, and the result was an Oscar for Best Supporting Actress (she could have won for Best Supporting Actor if the Academy had any sense of humor) and the new York Film Critic's Award. The ambience of the film is such that one can almost feel the heat and humidity pour off the screen. It has some of the same nervousness as the later film THE KILLING FIELDS and there is more than a little similarity between the two, though both were based on true incidents in different countries. A fascinating movie that gives us the picture of the way it must have been during that terrifying year in the Far East. The violence will

frighten youngsters.

p, James McElroy; d, Peter Weir; w, David Williamson, Weir, C.J. Koch (based on the novel by Koch); ph, Russell Boyd (Panavision, Metrocolor); m, Maurice Jarre; ed, Bill Anderson; art d, Herbert Pinter; cos, Terry Ryan; makeup, Judy Lovell.

Adventure/Romance   **Cas.**   (PR:C   MPAA:PG)

YEAR OF THE CRICKET   (SEE: KENNER, 1969)

YEAR OF THE HORSE, THE**   (1966) 58m Myriad/Noel Meadow
                                                Associates c

Gabriel Mason (Michael Farrow), Bradley Joe (Richard Han, Jr.), Alvin Lum (Richard Han, Sr.), Mary Mon Toy (Mrs. Richard Han, Sr.), Lorraine Wong (Tina Han), Mr. Thom, Mrs. Thom (Han Grandparents), Mary Hui (Stewardess), Peter Wong (Bachelor), Dick Hanover (Veterinarian), Burt Harris (Policeman), Mark Hubley (Narrator).

A charming children's tale about a 7-year-old Chinese boy (Joe) who is befriended by an elderly carriage driver (Mason) and becomes especially fond of the horse that pulls the carriage. When the horse dies, the old man slips into a depression and loses his will to continue. The youngster rallies his family and friends to chip in enough cash to buy another horse. Filmed in and around New York's Chinatown and Central Park, THE YEAR OF THE HORSE has an amateurish quality to it (as well as some keen animation sequences), but still conveys a pleasant story.

p, Mildred Dienstag, Therese Orkin; d, Irving Sunasky; w, Sunasky, Faith Hubley (based on the story by Sunasky, Thomas Miller); ph, Morton L. Heilig (Eastmancolor); ed, Peggy Lawson; animation, John Hubley.

Children's Drama   (PR:AA   MPAA:NR)

YEAR OF THE HORSE   (SEE: HORSE IN THE GRAY FLANNEL
                                        SUIT, THE, 1968)

YEAR OF THE TIGER, THE   (SEE: YANK IN VIET-NAM, A, 1964)

YEAR OF THE YAHOO zero   (1971) 90m International Arts c

Claude King (Hank Jackson), Ray Sager (Sid Angelo), Ronna Riddle (Tammy Parker), Robert Jolly (Chet Stoner), Terrell Cass (Ed Varnett), Jeffrey Allen (Gov. Baxter), Tom Lytel (Art Farnsworth), Leslie Slater (Carole), Robert Swain (Sen. Fred Burwell).

Swain is a senator in an unnamed Southwestern state running for re-election. Governor Allen, his political foe, enlists help from the White House to defeat Swain. The entire campaign takes an unexpected twist when some New York ad men led by movie producer Sager take popular country singer King and make a candidate out of him. King is forced to go against his conscience in his attempt to win but eventually becomes drunk with the possibility of power. His fiancee Riddle leaves him to join a strike King now opposes and is raped during a demonstration. King is urged by Sager to use the sympathy factor to gain votes but this unsavory suggestion proves to be too much for King and he fires the advisors. The remainder of the campaign is run his way and is, of course, a failure. Without any Madison Avenue gloss, King is shown to be a boring individual. Swain is re-elected and King is relieved that his ordeal is over. Allen decides that the voters have taken their stand against political commercialization, and Sager sees the outcome as a mere blip on the screen of the political future. The commercialization and packaging of political hopefuls is an interesting theme, dealt with in such movies as THE CANDIDATE (1972) and POWER (1986). This production, however, is a product of the infamous Herschell Gordon Lewis, the shclockmeister of such cinematic garbage as BLOOD-BATH and THE GORE GORE GIRLS. Though this is a departure from his usual violence-for-profit's-sake style, it shows not an iota of intelligence or insight into the subject.

p&d, Herschell Gordon Lewis; w, Allen Kahn; ph, Alex Ameri, Daniel P. Krough (Eastmancolor); m, Sheldon Seymour [Lewis]; ed, Eskandar Ameripoor.

Drama   (PR:O   MPAA:R)

YEAR ONE*   (1974, Ital.) 123m Rusconi Film/Italnoleggio c (ANNO
                                                                UNO)

Luigi Vannucchi (Alcide De Gasperi), Dominique Darel (Romanoa De Gasperi), Rita Calderoni (Giornalista), Valeria Sabel (Francesca De Gasperi), Ennio Balbo (Ninni).

In the midst of a string of historical pictures made for Italian television, Rossellini directed this biography of political leader De Gasperi for the cinema. Vannucchi coldly portrays the leader who in the postwar years headed the Christian Democratic Party. Dialog is held to a bare minimum, Rossellini relying on historical documents rather than invention. Gregory Peck was rumored to have been considered for the lead, which at the very least would have made the picture more appealing to American viewers.

d, Roberto Rossellini; w, Rossellini, Luciano Scaffa, Marcello Mariani; ph,

Mario Montuori (Eastmancolor); m, Mario Nascimbene; ed, Iolanda Ben-venuto.

Historical Drama/Biography   (PR:A MPAA:NR)

YEAR 2889   (SEE: IN THE YEAR 2889, 1966)

YEARLING, THE**   (1946) 134m MGM c

Gregory Peck (*Pa Baxter*), Jane Wyman (*Ma Baxter*), Claude Jarman, Jr. (*Jody Baxter*), Chill Wills (*Buck Forrester*), Clem Bevans (*Pa Forrester*), Margaret Wycherly (*Ma Forrester*), Henry Travers (*Mr. Boyles*), Forrest Tucker (*Lem Forrester*), Donn Gift (*Fodderwing*), Daniel White (*Millwheel*), Matt Willis (*Gabby*), George Mann (*Pack*), Arthur Hohl (*Arch*), June Lockhart (*Twink Weatherby*), Joan Wells (*Eulalie*), Jeff York (*Oliver*), B.M. Chick York (*Doc Wilson*), Houseley Stevenson (*Mr. Ranger*), Jane Green (*Mrs. Saunders*), Victor Kilian (*Captain*), Robert Porterfield (*Mate*), Frank Eldredge (*Deckhand*).

A splendid family film with a history of problems behind it and nothing but applause and big box-office receipts in front of it. Just after the war between the states in the wilds of southern Florida, Peck, Wyman, and their son, Jarman, are having a tough time ekeing out a living on their small farm. Peck's ambition is to earn enough money from his next crop to be able to sink a well nearer the house so Wyman won't have to tote water. They've had four children but Jarman is the only survivor. As an only child living in the wilderness, Jarman needs some company and asks his parents if he might have a pet. Wyman turns thumbs down. Not that she doesn't like animals, but they are living such a sparse existence that they can't afford another mouth to feed. Peck is bitten by a rattlesnake and in danger of dying. To save his life, he is forced to kill a doe and utilize the dead animal's liver and heart to get the poison out. The doe has left behind an orphaned fawn and when Jarman begs his parents to allow him to raise the baby, they give him permission. Time passes and the bond between boy and animal deepens, but as it grows it begins eating some of the crops, the very stuff upon which they live. Peck has no choice in the matter and tells Jarman that the youth must kill his beloved companion. Jarman thinks hard about what he is called upon to do and, in the end, can't bear it so he releases his "yearling" into the thickets surrounding the house. This is of no use because the grown up fawn comes back again to the only home it has ever known. Wyman takes matters into her own hands and shoots the animal but she is a poor shot and only wounds it. The task of finishing off the pained animal now falls under Jarman's aegis and, with tears in his eyes, he kills the animal. Next, he runs away from home and spends three days alone. He's hungry, bitter, and can't live off the soil so he eventually returns to the family house. In those three days Jarman has himself grown up and is no longer the "yearling" he was. He finally realizes that what was done had to be done or the animal would have eaten them out of existence and that his parents were not being cruel, they were being pragmatic. Based on the 1938 prize-winning novel by Rawlings, the studio had originally intended it as a vehicle for Spencer Tracy, Anne Revere, and newcomer Gene Eckman as the boy. They went to Florida in 1941 but there were many problems. Tracy and director Victor Fleming didn't see eye to eye, hordes of insects attacked the area, the weather was rotten, the fawn grew too quickly, and so did Eckman. In the end, the idea was shelved with a loss of half a million dollars. Producer Franklin never gave up on the story and next considered Roddy McDowall for the part but it was again tabled until 1946 when Brown took over the direction and the John Lee Mahin script which had been written for the Tracy version was tossed aside in favor of the new adaptation by Osborn. Jarman was chosen after a nationwide talent hunt that saw thousands of youths interviewed and/or tested. The movie was a huge success for the studio, one of its top moneymakers. It was nominated for Best Film (losing to THE BEST YEARS OF OUR LIVES), for Peck's performance as Best Actor (he lost to Fredric March for the above Goldwyn classic), and for Best Actress (Wyman lost to de Havilland in THE HEIRESS). Jarman won a special Oscar for his beautifully etched performance and statuettes were also handed to Gibbons, Groesse, and Willis for their set decorations (color), and Rosher, Smith, and Arling for their color cinematography. A remarkable film that is truly for the entire family. In a small role, note Forrest Tucker, a much underrated actor. Tucker was about to get his own star on Hollywood Boulevard in August, 1986, when he collapsed and was taken to the hospital. He died in October after a long career that began with his 1940 debut in THE WESTERNER.

p, Sidney Franklin; d, Clarence Brown; w, Paul Osborn (based on the novel by Marjorie Kinnan Rawlings); ph, Charles Rosher, Leonard Smith, Arthur Arling (Technicolor); m, Herbert Stothart, themes from Frederick Delius; ed, Harold F. Kress; art d, Cedric Gibbons, Paul Groesse; set d, Edwin B. Willis; spec eff, Warren Newcombe, Chester Franklin.

Historical Drama   Cas.   (PR:AA MPAA:NR)

YEARNING**   (1964, Jap.) 98m Toho bw (MIDARERU)

Hideko Takamine (*Reiko Morita*), Yuzo Kayama (*Koji*), Mitsuko Kusabue (*Hisako*), Yumi Shirikawa, Mie Hama, Aiko Mimasu, Yu Fujiki, Kazuo Kitamura, Hisao Soga, Kan Yanagiya, Chieko Nakakita, Kumeko Urabe.

This depressing picture concerns a widowed grocery store owner who operates the business for years after her husband's suicide. Her brother-in-

law is romantically interested in her and after some time she gives in to his advances. With little warning she jilts him, preferring to live with her husband's memory. Depressed, the man commits suicide. As with many of Naruse's pictures, the penalty for hope and yearning for something better is bitter disappointment.

p, Sanezumi Fujimoto, Mikio Naruse; d, Naruse; w, Zenzo Matsuyama; ph, Jun Yasumoto (CinemaScope); m, Saito; art d, Ichiro saito.

Drama   (PR:C MPAA:NR)

YEARS BETWEEN, THE*½   (1947, Brit.) 88 Sydney Box/GFD-UNIV bw

Michael Redgrave (*Col. Michael Wentworth*), Valerie Hobson (*Diana Wentworth*), Flora Robson (*Nanny, Housekeeper*), James McKechnie (*Richard Llewellyn*), Felix Aylmer (*Sir Ernest Foster*), Dulcie Gray (*Jill*), John Gilpin (*Robin Wentworth*), Edward Rigby (*Postman*), Esma Cannon (*Effie*), Lyn Evans (*Ames*), Wylie Watson (*Venning*), Yvonne Owen (*Alice*), Muriel George (*Mrs. May*), Joss Ambler (*Atherton*), Ernest Butcher (*Old Man*), Katie Johnson (*His Wife*), Maxwell Reed, Michael Hordern, Gwen Clark.

A promising enough idea is offered in THE YEARS BETWEEN but a weak script results in nothing more than a third-rate melodrama. Parliament member Redgrave is reportedly killed during the war so his wife, Hobson, takes over his seat. She falls in love with McKechnie, a local farmer, and is about to marry him when Redgrave returns. He has trouble adjusting to her new fondness for a career, but learns to accept it. He takes over his old seat and she gets herself elected to another. It's all based on a play by Daphne Du Maurier.

p, Sydney Box; d, Compton Bennett; w, Sydney Box, Muriel Box (based on the play by Daphne Du Maurier); ph, Reginald H. Wyer, Bert Mason.

Drama   (PR:A MPAA:NR)

YEARS WITHOUT DAYS   (SEE: CASTLE ON THE HUDSON, 1940)

YELLOW BALLOON, THE½**   (1953, Brit.) 80m ABF-Marble Arch/AA bw

Andrew Ray (*Frankie*), Kathleen Ryan (*Em*), Kenneth More (*Ted*), Bernard Lee (*Constable Chapman*), Stephen Fenemore (*Ron*), William Sylvester (*Len*), Marjorie Rhodes (*Mrs. Stokes*), Peter Jones (*Spiv*), Elliot Makeham (*Pawnbroker*), Sydney James (*Barrow Boy*), Veronica Hurst (*Sunday School Teacher*), Sandra Dorne (*Iris*), Campbell Singer (*Potter*), Laurie Main (*Bibulous Customer*), Hy Hazell.

This fairly effective thriller follows a crook, Sylvester, who tells a schoolboy, Ray, that he witnessed a struggle the boy had with another youngster over a balloon which resulted in the other kid's death. With that information, Sylvester forces the boy to steal items from his parents' house, then involves him in a bigger crime, setting him up as a decoy. The plan is foiled and after a hair-raising chase the crook meets his maker.

p, Victor Skutezky; d, J. Lee Thompson; w, Anne Burnaby, Thompson (based on the story by Burnaby); ph, Gilbert Taylor; m, Philip Green; ed, Richard Best; art d, Robert Jones.

Crime   (PR:A MPAA:NR)

YELLOW CAB MAN, THE½**   (1950) 85m MGM bw

Red Skleton (*Augustus "Red" Pirdy*), Gloria DeHaven (*Ellen Goodrich*), Walter Slezak (*Dr. Byron Dokstedder*), Edward Arnold (*Martin Creavy*), James Gleason (*Mickey Corkins*), Jay C. Flippen (*Hugo*), Paul Harvey (*Pearson Hendricks*), Guy [Herbert] Anderson (*Willis Tomlin*), John Butler (*Gimpy*), John Indrisano (*Danny*), Polly Moran (*Bride's Mother*).

Slapstick adventure abounds in this enjoyable and often hilarious comedy which stars Skelton as a Yellow Cab driver who invents, among other gadgets, an unbreakable elastic glass. Thugs try to get the invaluable formula out of his possession leading to an almost nonstop romp which has him escaping by the skin of his teeth. His bizarre inventions are worth a laugh apiece, as is the dream sequence Skelton experiences after being drugged.

p, Richard Goldstone; d, Jack Donohue; w, Devery Freeman, Albert Beich (based on a story by Freeman); ph, Harry Stradling; m, Scott Bradley; ed, Albert Akst; art d, Cedric Gibbons, Eddieu Imazu.

Comedy   (PR:A MPAA:NR)

YELLOW CANARY, THE**   (1944, Brit.) 84m Imperator/RKO bw

Anna Neagle (*Sally Maitland*), Richard Greene (*Jim Garrick*), Nova Pilbeam (*Betty Maitland*), Lucie Mannheim (*Mme. Orlock*), Albert Lieven (*Jan Orlock*), Cyril Fletcher (*Himself*), Margaret Rutherford (*Mrs. Towcester*), Claude Bailey (*Maj. Fothergill*), Patric Curwen (*Sir William Maitland*), Marjorie Fieldding (*Lady Maitland*), Aubrey Mallalieu (*Reynolds*), David Horne (*Admiral*), Franklin Dyall (*Captain*), George Thorpe (*Col. Hargreaves*), Valentine Dyall (*German Commander*), Gordon McLeod, John Longden, Hedley Goodall, Winifred Oughton, David Ward, Eliot Makeham,

Ian Fleming, MacDonald Parke, John Kannowin, Gerry Wilmott, Clifford Buckton, Grace Allardyce, Anthony Eustrel, Tatiana Lieven, Leslie Dwyer, Edgar Driver, Grizelda Hervey.

A WW II spy picture stars Neagle as an accused Nazi spy on a ship bound for Nova Scotia, though she's really a British agent. With the help of her assistant Greene, who pretends to be following her, Neagle exposes a plot to blow up a Halifax shipping harbor. One of countless espionage films that cluttered up screens on both sides of the Atlantic, THE YELLOW CANARY was a hopelessly muddled attempt to fuse art and patriotism from the husband and wife team of Wilcox and Neagle.

p&d, Herbert Wilcox; w, Miles Malleson, DeWitt Bodeen (based on a story by D.M. [Pamela] Bower); ph, Max Green [Mutz Greenbaum]; m, Clifford Parker; ed, Vera Campbell; art d, W.C. Andrews.

Spy Drama   **(PR:A   MPAA:NR)**

YELLOW CANARY, THE*   (1963) 93m Cooga Mooga/FOX bw

Pat Boone (Andy Paxton), Barbara Eden (Lissa), Steve Forrest (Hub Wiley), Jack Klugman (Lt. Bonner), Jesse White (Ed Thornburg), Steve Harris (Bake), Milton Selzer (Vecchio), John Banner (Sam Skolman), Jeff Corey (Joe), Jo Helton (Rene Pyle), Vici Raaf (Crystal Towers), Harold Gould (Ponelli), Joseph Turkel (Policeman), Charles Keane (Reporter).

Boone is thoroughly unpleasant as a pop star with an attitude, a fed-up wife (Eden), and a kidnaped son. Boone finally takes action after a trio of murders occur, though he refuses to cooperate with the police. He attempts to pay a $200,000 ransom, but no kidnapers come to meet him. Eventually he heroically shoots the culprit, a deranged bodyguard played by Forrest, abd becomes a likable fellow...at least compared with what he was like at the beginning of the picture. Written by TWILIGHT ZONE creator Rod Serling, making for a rather odd combination of talents.

p, Maury Dexter; d, Buzz Kulik; w, Rod Serling (based on the novel Evil Come, Evil Go by Whit Masterson); ph, Floyd Crosby (CinemaScope); m, Kenyon Hopkins; ed, Jodie Copelan; art d, Walter Simonds; set d, Don Greenwood; cos, Charles James, Sy Devore; makeup, Bob Mark, Lynn Reynolds.

Crime Drama   **(PR:A   MPAA:NR)**

YELLOW CARGO½**   (1936) 70m GN bw

Conrad Nagel (Alan O'Connor), Eleanor Hunt (Bobbie Reynolds), Vince Barnett ("Bulb" Callahan), Jack LaRue (Al Perrelli), Claudia Dell (Fay Temple), Henry Strange (Joe Beeze), John Ivan (District Commissioner), Vance Carroll (Burke Darrell), Lillian Wessner.

YELLOW CARGO should receive some sort of special mention for sporting one of the most ingenious plots in B-movie history. Nagel and Hunt are government agents who uncloak a tricky smuggling team operating under the guise of a Hollywood movie crew. Pretending to be shooting a film, the smugglers dress the "actors" to look like Chinese extras and ship them to Catalina Island for "filming." They then strip off their makeup and send back real Chinese in their place. Nagel and Hunt, the dynamic agent duo, pose as extras and infiltrate the ring, not revealing their true identities until the finale. It's a silly way to kill an hour.

p, George A. Hirliman; d&w, Crane Wilbur; ph, Mack Stengler; ed, Tony Martinelli.

Crime   **(PR:A   MPAA:NR)**

YELLOW DOG*   (1973, Brit.) 101m Scotia-Barber/Akari c

Jiro Tamiya, Robert Hardy, Carolyn Seymour, Joseph O'Conor.

Muddled spy drama set in London has Tamiya tailing a top scientist. Pretty silly, and no one concerned with the production seems to have cared what they were doing. If this were the last movie on earth, it would still be a waste of time.

p&d, Terence Donovan; w, Shinobu Hashimoto; ph, David Watkin (Eastmancolor); m, Ron Grainer.

Spy Drama   **(PR:A-C   MPAA:NR)**

YELLOW DUST*   (1936) 68m RKO bw

Richard Dix (Bob), Leila Hyams (Nellie), Moroni Olsen (Missouri), Jessie Ralph (Mrs. Brian), Andy Clyde (Solitaire), Onslow Stevens (Hanway), Victor Potel (Jugger), Ethan Laidlaw (Bogan), Ted Oliver (McLearney), Art Mix.

Dix is a gold miner who strikes a rich vein but must clear his name of a string of stagecoach robberies before he can carry on. He goes under cover, saves Hyams from a certain demise, and deals Stevens all the justice he can handle. An empty vein is struck when it comes to action, making the film seem twice as long as it is, though it's already twice as long as it should be.

p, Cliff Reid; d, Wallace Fox; w, Cyril Hume, John Twist (based on the play "Mother Lode" by Dan Totheroh, George O'Neil); ph, Earl A. Wolcott; ed, James Morley; md, Alberto Columbo.

Western   **(PR:A   MPAA:NR)**

YELLOW FIN½**   (1951) 74m MON bw

Wayne Morris (Mike), Adrian Booth (Jean), Gloria Henry (Nina), Damian O'Flynn (John), Gordon Jones (Breck), Paul Fierro (Mano), Nacho Galindo (Murica), Warren Douglas (Steve), Guy Zanette (Larson).

Morris stars in this rewarding father-and-son drama set against the backdrop of deep-sea tuna fishing. After a series of bad luck incidents culminates with Morris' father being thrown from the boat and hospitalized for shock, Morris makes plans to sell the craft. He is talked into taking the ship out just once more, this time with his father on board, in the hope that it will cure him of his shock. Of course dad comes around, the fishing trip is a success, the debts they've amassed are paid off, and Morris takes his childhood sweetheart in his arms.

p, Lindsley Parsons; d, Frank McDonald; w, Warren D. Wandberg, Clint Johnson; ph, William Sickner; ed, Ace Herman; md, Edward J. Kay; art d, Dave Milton.

Adventure Drama   **(PR:A   MPAA:NR)**

YELLOW GOLLIWOG, THE   (SEE: GUTTER GIRLS, 1964, Brit.)

YELLOW HAT, THE** 1966, Brit. 77m Margot Dagmar/Monarch c

Valentine Palmer (Tony), Frances Barlow (Sally), Toni Palmer (Christine), Tommy Bruce (Harry), Eleanor Summerfield (Lady Xenia), Pierre Dduan (Raoul), John Slater (Slack), Salina Jones (Patsy), Derek Nimmo (Douglas), Canna Kendal (Hortense), Elspeth Duxbury (Customer), Fugere, Centre De Danse Classique Dancers, Harlequin Ballet Trust.

This musical film traces the path of the title chapeau after it's borrowed by an assistant to a milliner. Cute idea.

p, David Henley; d, Honoria Plesch; w, Dai Noel, M.A.F. Stevens, Plesch (based on a story by Noel); cos, Plesch.

Musical   **(PR:A   MPAA:NR)**

YELLOW JACK*½   (1938) 83m MGM bw

Robert Montgomery (John O'Hara), Virginia Bruce (Frances Blake), Lewis Stone (Maj. Walter Reed), Andy Devine (Charlie Spell), Henry Hull (Dr. Jesse Lazear), Charles Coburn (Dr. Finlay), Buddy Ebsen (Jellybeans), Henry O'Neill (William Gorgas), Janet Beecher (Miss MacDade), William Henry (Breen), Alan Curtis (Brinkerhof), Sam Levene (Busch), Stanley Ridges (Dr. James Carroll), Phillip Terry (Ferguson), Jonathan Hale (Maj. Gen. Leonard Wood), C. Henry Gordon (Col. Wiggins), Frank O'Connor, Billy Arnold, Larry Steers (Officers), Harry Strang (Aide), Roger Converse (Lieutenant), Dutch Schlickenmeyer (Corporal), Francisco Maran (Interpreter), Brick Sullivan (Sergeant), Hudson Shotwell, Brent Sargent, Dick Wessel, Ted Oliver, John Patterson, Charlie Sullivan, George Magrill (Cavalrymen), Rosina Galli (Spanish Woman), Lucio Villegas (Old Man in Bed), Inez Palange (Dr. Finlay's Housekeeper), Joseph Dominguez (Interpreter), Harry Semels (Cuban Carriage Driver), William "Billy" Newell (Soldier), Douglas McPhail (Joey).

This intelligent drama follows a group of medical scientists as they attempt to find the cause behind the dreaded yellow fever. It is just after the Spanish-American War, and Stone (playing Maj. Walter Reed) is head of a medical staff stationed in Cuba. Convinced he has found the carrier of yellow fever (nicknamed "yellow jack" by the men), Stone needs five volunteers from the U.S. Army to serve as human guinea pigs. Montgomery heads up the enlisted volunteers, understanding well the unknown dangers of what he is about to undergo. " 'O'Hara,' I said to myself, 'suppose you do give your life. It'll be a noble thing–but will you be able to say so?' " he tells some gravediggers. Montgomery is bitten by some mosquitos carrying the yellow fever; three others stay in a "dirty room"; the fifth must sleep in a bed of a dead yellow fever victim. The film wisely concentrates on the ordeals of the five volunteers. This is a story filled with tension and suspense, backed by an underlying humanity. Montgomery (taking the role created on Broadway by James Stewart) is excellent as the lead volunteer, projecting a stoic image as he submits to an unknown agent. The film is slightly marred by an unneeded romance between Montgomery and camp nurse Bruce. Their scenes together, though well played, seem out of place and detract from the already strong drama. The ensemble is a good one, with Stone, Devine, and Ebsen particular standouts.

p, Jack Cummings; d, George B. Seitz; w, Edward Chodorov (based on the play by Sidney Howard, Paul de Kruif); ph, Lester White; m, William Axt; ed, Blanche Sewell.

Drama   **(PR:A   MPAA:NR)**

YELLOW MASK, THE*   (1930, Brit.) 76m BIP/Wardour bw

Dorothy Seacombe (Mary Trayne), Warwick Ward (Li San), Wilfred Temple (John Carn), Winnie Collins (Molly), Haddon Mason (Ralph Carn), Frank Cochrane (Ah-Song), William Shine (Sunshine), Wallace Lupino (Steward), Lupino Lane (Sam Slipper).

An easily forgotten musical melodrama with a dose of slapstick concerns a Chinese nobleman who steals the crown jewels from the Tower of London. For his getaway he brings along a gal who is subsequently rescued by her courageous boy friend. He also succeeds in getting the jewels back to London, but by the end you couldn't care less.

p, John Maxwell; d, Harry Lachman; w, Val Valentine, Miles Malleson, George Arthurs, Walter C. Mycroft, W. David (based on the play "The Traitor's Gate" by Edgar Wallace); ph, Claude Friese-Greene; ed, E.B. Jarvis, Emile de Ruelle.

Musical Drama   **(PR:A MPAA:NR)**

YELLOW MOUNTAIN, THE*   (1954) 77m UNIV c

Lex Barker (*Andy Martin*), Mala Powers (*Nevada Wray*), Howard Duff (*Pete Menlo*), William Demarest (*Jackpot Wray*), John McIntire (*Bannon*), Leo Gordon (*Drake*), Dayton Lummis (*Geraghty*), Hal K. Dawson (*Sam Torrence*), William Fawcett (*Old Prospector*), James Parnell (*Joe*).

Barker and Duff are gold-mining partners who become enemies in a dispute over a claim, as well as battling over the affections of Powers. When McIntire attempts to cheat Powers' father, Demarest, Barker and Duff work together and patch up their friendship. Standard plot from top to bottom.

p, Ross Hunter; d, Jesse Hibbs; w, George Zuckerman, Russell Hughes, Robert Blees (based on the story by Harold Channing Wire); ph, George Robinson (Technicolor); ed, Edward Curtiss; md, Joseph Gershenson; cos, Bill Thomas.

Western   **(PR:A MPAA:NR)**

YELLOW PASSPORT, THE   (SEE: YELLOW TICKET, THE, 1931)

YELLOW ROBE, THE**   (1954, Brit.) 51m Danzigers/ABF-Pathe bw

Tony Penderell (*Frank*), Honor Blackman, Ron Randell, Robert Raglan, Iris Russell, Peter Neil, Mona Washbourne, Nicholas Hill, Clifford Evans, Martin Boddey.

This is a two-story film. In the first tale, Penderell is a down-and-out man who becomes the prime suspect in a murder case because the victim had possessed evidence that would have prevented Penderell from inheriting a fortune. However, he is cleared when a solicitor is discovered to have had an even greater motive for the murder. The second story–much the better of the two–features Blackman as a widow who captures the two men who did her husband in when he stood in the way of their money-making plans.

p, Edward J. Danziger, Harry Lee Danziger; d, David MacDonald; w, George St. George, James Eastwood; ph, Jimmy Wilson.

Crime   **(PR:A MPAA:NR)**

YELLOW ROLLS-ROYCE, THE**½   (1965, Brit.) 122m MGM c

First Episode–England: Rex Harrison (*Marquess of Frinton*), Jeanne Moreau (*Marchioness Eloise of Frinton*), Edmund Purdom (*John Fane*), Michael Hordern (*Harmsworth*), Lance Percival (*Assistant Car Salesman*), Roland Culver (*Norwood*), Moira Lister (*Lady Angela St. Simeon*), Harold Scott (*Taylor*), Richard Pearson (*Osborn*), Isa Miranda (*Duchesse d'Angouleme*), Gregoire Aslan (*Albanian Ambassador*), Jacques Brunius (*Duc d'Angouleme*), Richard Vernon, Reginald Beckwith, Tom Gill, Dermot Kelly, Second Episode–Italy: Shirley MacLaine (*Mae Jenkins*), George C. Scott (*Paolo Maltese*), Alain Delon (*Stefano*), Art Carney (*Joey Friedlander*), Riccardo Garrone (*Bomba*), Third Episode–Yugoslavia: Ingrid Bergman (*Gerda Millett*), Omar Sharif (*Davich*), Joyce Grenfell (*Hortense Astor*), Wally Cox (*Ferguson*), Carlo Croccolo (*Mrs. Millett's Chauffeur*), Guy Deghy (*Mayor*), Martin Miller (*Headwaiter*), Andreas Malandrinos (*Hotel Manager*).

A three-episode film loosely tied together through the ownership of "the world's best automobile," or so the makers of Rolls- Royce claim. Literate, but essentially empty, it features an all- star cast that seems to be playing the wrong roles. French Moreau is a British aristocrat, American Scott plays an Italian, Middle Easterner Sharif is a Yugoslav, Swedish Bergman is an American, and Gallic Delan essays an Italian. The car in the title is Phantom II, rare and exotic and bright yellow, definitely not a color favored by the conservatives who usually want anonymity in their automobiles. In the first segment, Moreau, Harrison, Purdom, and the others are featured. Harrison is a peer of the realm who purchases the vehicle for his spouse, Moreau, and gives her the keys at an elegant dinner party celebrating their wedding anniversary. He doesn't know that she is having an affair with his assistant, Purdom. At the Ascot races, Lister, a pal of the couple, learns about the lovers and tells Harrison. He catches them in the rear of the Rolls and is terribly hurt by the situation. But he blames the vehicle rather than Moreau and keeps his wife while he sells the car. (He might have been better off doing it the other way around.) The second section finds Scott, a big-time mobster, touring the old country (Italy) with his lover, MacLaine, and his No. 1 henchman, Carney (in his movie debut). They encounter photographer Delon who makes a pass a MacLaine. Scott returns to the U.S. on business (he has to kill someone) and MacLaine and Delon begin an affair. Carney knows all about it and realizes that it's dangerous but he also knows that

MacLaine is a needy woman and this fling might be good for her, so he invokes the code of *omerta* on himself and keeps mum. When Scott's work is over, he comes back to Italy. He is immediately jealous of the way Delon and MacLaine appear to be and MacLaine loves Delon so much that she understands he'll die at Scott's hands if she doesn't take steps. To that end, she pretends she no longer cares for Delon, sends him away, and moves back into Scott's embrace and good graces. The Harrison-Moreau episode begins when the car is new, in the late 1920s. The MacLaine-Scott section takes place before the war in the gangster heyday of the 1930s. The last of the trio occurs just before WW II engulfs the world. Bergman now owns the world. She's a rich U.S. widow in Trieste and is about to visit the Yugoslavian capitol to attend a royal party. She is traveling with her frumpy companion, Grenfell, when she buys the car, intending to show it off when she gets to the party. The Nazis are in the area and searching for Sharif, a patriotic Yugoslav. He wants to get across the border to safety and he pleads with Bergman to help him. Bergman is, at first, reluctant, but finally agrees. The Nazis attack the hotel where Bergman is staying and the formerly passive woman decides that she can tolerate them no longer. She had been a totally neutral person but now commits herself to the cause and she and her auto are enlisted into the fray. Bergman aids the guerrillas and Sharif. The pair has a night of lovemaking in the car; then Sharif tells her she must go home and inform the U.S. of exactly what's going on in Europe. They part company and Bergman returns to the U.S. with Grenfell and a host of passionate memories. A pleasant bit of entertainment, but the material that's supposed to be hilarious is only faintly amusing and the dramatic sections don't grab the viewers beyond a surface level. It was heavy on the production values and directed at a medium-brisk pace by Asquith, who was to die after this movie. Carney's debut, after he had been asked to appear in several movies, was cut but not anything special. Delon was a huge star in Europe and wanted to establish himself in the U.S. so he took far less of a fee to work in the movie than he usually received. His steamy scenes with MacLaine were excellent and Delon hoped they would make him a U.S. favorite, but that didn't happen. Rolls-Royce's ad man, David Ogilvy, once wrote a piece of copy that said, "The loudest noise one can hear in a Rolls at 60 miles per hour is the ticking of the clock." It may be apocryphal but it is alleged that when the company's president read the ad, he commented, "We're just going to have to do something about that noisy clock!" The movie was shot on location in Italy, Austria, and England, boasted superior production credits, and a cast that today would cost millions. Producer de Grunwald had earlier made another star-studded movie, THE V.I.P.S, which did somewhat better at the box office. A quartet of hairdressers had to be signed on for the movie. Sidney Guilaroff did MacLaine's tresses, Carita handled Moreau's mane, Bergman's locks were fondled by Giorgia di Roma, and Joan Johnstone took care of everyone else.

p, Anatole De Grunwald; d, Anthony Asquith; w, Terence Rattigan; ph, Jack Hildyard (Panavision, Metrocolor); m, Riz Ortolani; ed, Frank Clarke; art d, Elliot Scott, Vincent Korda, William Kellner; set d, John Jarvis, Pamela Cornell; cos, Castillo, Edith Head, Pierre Cardin, Gene Coffin, Anthony Mendleson; spec eff, Tom Howard; m/l, "Forget Domani," Ortolani, Norman Newell (sung by Katyna Ranieri); makeup, Tom Smith, John O'Gorman.

Comedy/Romance   **(PR:C MPAA:NR)**

YELLOW ROSE OF TEXAS, THE**   (1944) 69m REP bw

Roy Rogers (*Roy*), Dale Evans (*Betty Weston*), Grant Withers (*Lukas*), Harry Shannon (*Sam Weston*), George Cleveland (*Capt. Joe*), William Haade (*Buster*), Weldon Heyburn (*Charlie Goss*), Hal Taliaferro (*Ferguson*), Tom London (*Sheriff Allen*), Dick Botiller (*Indian Pete*), Janet Martin (*Specialty Singer*), Brown Jug Reynolds (*Pinto*), Bob Wilke, Jack O'Shea, Rex Lease, Emmett Vogan, John Dilson, Bob Nolan and the Sons of the Pioneers, Trigger the Horse.

Rogers is hired by an insurance company to recover some lost funds, so he gets a gig as a singer on the title showboat. He gets the cash back and clears the name of Evans' father, who was wrongly convicted of the crime. (See ROY ROGERS series, Index.)

p, Harry Grey; d, Joseph Kane; w, Jack Townley; ph, Jack Marta; ed, Tony Martinelli; md, Morton Scott; art d, Fred A. Ritter; ch, Larry Ceballos.

Western   **Cas.**   **(PR:A MPAA:NR)**

YELLOW SANDS***   (1938, Brit.) 68m ABF bw

Marie Tempest (*Jennifer Varwell*), Belle Chrystal (*Lydia Blake*), Wilfrid Lawson (*Richard Varwell*), Robert Newton (*Joe Varwell*), Patrick Barr (*Arthur Varwell*), Amy Veness (*Mary Varwell*), Coral Browne (*Emma Copplestone*), Drusilla Wills (*Minnie Masters*), Muriel Johnston (*Nellie Masters*), Edward Rigby (*Tom Major*), Roddy McDowall.

Tempest is an elderly spinster who leaves $20,000 to Newton, her Communist nephew. He's always been opposed to her capitalistic ways, but now that he has her money, things change. In keeping with his ideology, he plans on evenly distributing the money to the nation's unemployed, but when he realises they'll only get a penny apiece, he questions his beliefs. Charming and witty.

p, Walter C. Mycroft; d, Herbert Brenon; w, Michael Barringer, Rodney Ackland (based on a play by Eden and Adelaide Philpotts); ph, Walter

Harvey.

Comedy   (PR:A   MPAA:NR)

YELLOW SKY***   (1948) 98m FOX bw**

Gregory Peck (*Stretch*), Anne Baxter (*Mike*), Richard Widmark (*Dude*), Robert Arthur (*Bull Run*), John Russell (*Lengthy*), Henry 'Harry' Morgan (*Half Pint*), James Barton (*Grandpa*), Charles Kemper (*Walrus*), Robert Adler (*Jed*), Victor Kilian (*Bartender*), Paul Hurst (*Drunk*), William Gould (*Banker*), Norman Leavitt (*Bank Teller*), Chief Yowlachie (*Colorado*), Eula Guy (*Woman in Bank*), Harry Carter (*Lieutenant*), Hank Worden (*Rancher*), Jay Silverheels (*Indian*).

The old West, just post-Civil War, filled with drifters abandoning the battles. Peck leads his outlaw band of seven kerchief-faced desperadoes in a bank robbery. Loading the bullion into their saddlebags, the robbers gallop off, the U.S. Cavalry in hot pursuit. Their travels take them to the edge of an enormous salt flat, the outlaws' only conceivable avenue of escape. Shrugging, Peck leads the band into the arid, sun- blistered area. Reining up their horses, the pursuing troopers abort the chase, believing the gang to be as good as dead. The bandits' transit of the waterless sea of salt is a painful, difficult one. The outlaws walk their parched, weary steeds; Peck pours a little precious water from his nearly empty canteen onto his neckerchief and wipes the saline rime from his mount's mouth. Their water gone, the dehydrated desperadoes chance upon a ghost town, heralded by a sign that reads "YELLOW SKY . . . fastest growing town in the territory." The town is completely deserted, save for dotty old prospector Barton and his tomboy granddaughter Baxter. Greed for both the gold and the girl causes dissension among the men, a situation further exacerbated when Barton hides the outlaws' loot. Villain Widmark makes a try at wresting the role of leader from Peck, and poses a threat to both beautiful Baxter and her grandfather. In a showdown, Widmark and one of his partisans are gunned down by the quick-drawing Peck. Driven by a desire to reform through his association with the small family, Peck returns to the bank and sticks it up again, this time to return the gold he and his band had stolen. An unlikely ending doesn't injure this brilliantly filmed and directed western, which qualifies as one of the best of the genre. The high- contrast black-and-white photography of MacDonald is stunning; the salt-flat scenes made audiences run to the theater lobby water fountain. Dialog was all the more telling for being sparse; the story is carried visually. As actor Peck pointed out about director Wellman, who had started his career with silent films, he was ". . . another master of the art of telling a story with pictures. Words are important but of secondary importance to these pioneer directors." Wellman directs his fine cast to tell the tale in delicate nuances. The musical score by Newman is fine, starting the action out scene by scene, then fading to muteness as stark realism takes hold and only natural sounds are heard. Peck is thoroughly believable in a part which contrasts so greatly with many of his others. Tanned and lined, etched with fatigue and thirst, his usually pallid countenance completely altered by makeup artist Nye's fine simulation of the ravages of weather, the leadership qualities of Peck's strong, short-of- speech badman are never in doubt. This was the actor's third film for the studio. Basically a formula western, the film was transmuted into a movie of major impact by the talents of its production staff and its cast. Baxter–an Oscar winner two years previously for her Best Supporting role in THE RAZOR'S EDGE–had begun her screen career at the age of 17 in a western, TWENTY MULE TEAM (1940). Her naively hoydenish tomboy characterization here is wonderful. In his first of the genre, Widmark plays again the sort of smiling psychopath that had originally brought him fame in his screen debut, KISS OF DEATH. The supporting cast members all do a fine job. Screenwriter Trotti and author Burnette received an award from the Writers Guild of America for this "Best Written American Western" of the year. Versatile director Wellman, helmer of such cinematic masterpieces as PUBLIC ENEMY (1931) and A STAR IS BORN (1937)–which he also wrote– demonstrates motion picture alchemy here as he takes basic western dross and turns it into gold. A less-than-successful remake with a South African setting, THE JACKALS, starring Vincent Price and Dana Ivarson, was made in 1967.

p, Lamar Trotti; d, William A. Wellman; w, Trotti (based on the novel by W.R. Burnett); ph, Joe MacDonald; m, Alfred Newman; ed, Harmon Jones; md, Newman; art d, Lyle R. Wheeler, Albert Hogsett; set d, Thomas Little, Ernest Lansing; spec eff, Fred Sersen; makeup Ben Nye.

Western   Cas.   (PR:A   MPAA:NR)

YELLOW SLIPPERS, THE   (1965, Pol.) 83m Iluzjon/Film Polski c**
(HISTORIA ZOLTEJ CIZEMKI)

Gustaw Holoubek (*Wit Stwosz*), Andrzej Szczepkowski (*Rafal*), Marek Kondrad (*Wawrzek*), Bronislaw Pawlik (*Gregorius*), Tadeusz Bialoszczynski (*The King*), Bogumil Kobiela (*Fracek*), Bogdan Niewinowski, Mieczyslaw Czechowicz, Bohdan Baer, Eugeniusz Szewczyk, Beata Barszczewska, Hanna Bedrynska, Aleksander Fogiel, Maria Kieszkowa, Wlodzimiers Kwaskowski, Ignacy Machowski, Zygmunt Malawski, Marian Wojtczak, Zygmund Zintel, Antoni Zukowski.

An orphaned youngster in 16th-Century Poland helps capture a thief, receiving a pair of yellow slippers as a reward. He becomes a sculptor's apprentice but is later abducted by the vengeful criminal. The boy is rescued, however, just as the sculptor unveils his new work–the Altar of St. Mary's Church. Released in Poland in 1961.

d, Sylwester Checinski; w, Zdzislaw Skowronski, Wanda Zolkiewska (based on a story by Antonina Domanska); ph, Kazimierz Konrad; m, Zbigniew Turski; ed, Janina Niedzwiecka.

Drama   (PR:A   MPAA:NR)

YELLOW STOCKINGS*   (1930, Brit.) 87m Welsh-Pearson-Elder/LAS**
                                                                       bw

Percy Marmont (*Gavin Sinclair*), Marjorie Mars (*Iris Selton*), Georges Gaili (*Richard Trevor*), Enid Stamp-Taylor (*Nellie Jackson*), Marie Ault (*Countess*), J. R. Tozer (*Tom Jackson*), Franklin Bellamy (*Menelos*), Lydia Sherwood (*Erica*), May Calvin (*Mona*), Elizabeth Kerr (*Mrs. Higgins*).

A man with a great deal of pluck is after a woman, though he doesn't know that she is about to inherit a fortune. Considering that this was supposed to be a romantic piece, it's pretty gloomy. Originally filmed as a silent, the picture was given some dialog after the advent of sound and released as a part-talkie.

p, George Pearson; d, Theodor Komisarjevsky; w, Fred Paul, Alicia Ramsay (based on the novel by Wilson McArthur).

Romance   (PR:AA   MPAA:NR)

YELLOW SUBMARINE**   (1958, Brit.) 85m King**
                                                        Features-Subafilms/UA c

Voices of: John Clive (*John*), Geoffrey Hughes (*Paul*), Peter Batten (*George*), Paul Angelus (*Ringo/Chief Blue Meanie*), Dick Emery (*Lord Mayor/ Nowhere Man/Max*), Lance Percival (*Old Fred*).

A zesty, satisfying celebration of animation, fantasy, love, and the Beatles which pleases the eyes as much as the ears. It tells the glorious tale of a make-believe world inhabited by Blue Meanies, a wicked little bunch who suck the color out of people and bop them on the heads with apples. The Beatles and Old Fred are called in to stop the Blue Meanies' rage. The singing heroes hop in their yellow submarine and sail the seas–of green, of science, of time, of monsters, and, best of all, of holes–until they finally reach Pepperland and straighten out the villains by overpowering them with love, love, love. The animation is superb, filled with exciting and unexpected transformations that are thoughtfully complimented by the music. The endless stream of Beatles songs includes: "Yellow Submarine," "All You Need Is Love," "Hey, Bulldog," "When I'm Sixty-Four," "Nowhere Man," "Lucy in the Sky with Diamonds," "Sgt. Pepper's Lonely Hearts Club Band," "A Day in the Life," "All Together Now," "Eleanor Rigby" (John Lennon, Paul McCartney), "Only a Northern Song," "It's All Too Much" (George Harrison), "March of the Meanies," Pepperland," "Pepperland Laid Waste," "Sea of Holes," "Sea of Monsters," "Sea of Time" (George Martin).

p, Al Brodax; d, George Dunning; w, Lee Minoff, Brodax, Erich Segal, Jack Mendelsohn (based on a story by Minoff, from the song by John Lennon, Paul McCartney); ph, John Williams (DeLuxe Color); ed, Brian J. Bishop; md, George Martin; art d, Heinz Edelmann; spec eff, Charles Jenkins; animation d, Jack Stokes, Robert Balser; animation, Eldrick Radage, Alan Ball, Reg Lodge, Tom Halley, Dave Livesey, Diane Crowther, Rich Cox, Pam Ford, Mike Pocock, Jeff Loynes, Mike Stewart, Malcolm Draper, Ted Percival, Lawrence Moorcroft, John Challis, Diane Jackson, Dennis Hunt, Arthur Humberstone, Anne Jolliffe, Tony Cuthbert, Paul Driessen, Hester Coblentz, Dick Horn, Jeff Collins, Jerry Potterton, Jim Hiltz, Terry Moesker.

Animated Musical   (PR:A   MPAA:G)

YELLOW TEDDYBEARS, THE   (SEE: GUTTER GIRLS, 1964, Brit.)

YELLOW TICKET, THE**   (1931) 78m FOX bw (GB: THE YELLOW
                                                      PASSPORT)

Elissa Landi (*Marya Kalish*), Lionel Barrymore (*Baron Igor Andrey*), Laurence Olivier (*Julian Rolfe*), Walter Byron (*Count Nikolai*), Sarah Padden (*Mother Kalish*), Arnold Korff (*Grandfather Kalish*), Mischa Auer (*Melchoir*), Rita LaRoy (*Fania*), Boris Karloff (*Orderly*), Edwin Maxwell, Alex Melesh.

Landi, a Jewish girl, attempts to travel through her native Russia in 1913 to see her father who is dying in a St. Petersburg prison. The only way she can get permission to travel is with a "yellow ticket," which identifies her as a prostitute. In St. Petersburg she learns that her father has died, but while in the city, she falls in love with Olivier, a British journalist. After hearing her story, he writes a number of articles for British and American newspapers that expose the oppressed condition of the Russian people under the Czar's rule. When Barrymore, the chief of the Czar's secret police, becomes aware of Olivier's articles, he tries to imprison the scribe. Barrymore's primary objective, however, is to get Landi in bed, and when he tries, she kills him. As Austria invades the country, the lovers escape to England. The Lionel Barrymore role had been performed by his brother John in the stage play that provided the basis for this film and the 1918 Pathe silent of the same name, which starred Milton Sills and Fanny Ward.

Though Giacomo Puccini doesn't figure in the writing credits, the plot owes more than a little to his opera "La Tosca."

d, Raoul Walsh; w, Jules Furthman, Guy Bolton (based on the play by Michael Morton); ph, James Wong Howe; ed, Jack Murray.

Drama   **(PR:A   MPAA:NR)**

YELLOW TOMAHAWK, THE** (1954) 82m Schenck-Koch-Bel-Air/UA
c

Rory Calhoun (*Adam*), Peggie Castle (*Katherine*), Noah Beery, Jr (*Tonio*), Warner Anderson (*Maj. Ives*), Peter Graves (*Sawyer*), Lee Van Cleef (*Fireknife*), Rita Moreno (*Honey Bear*), Walter Reed (*Keats*), Dan Riss (*Sgt. Bandini*), Adam Williams (*Cpl. Maddock*), Ned Glass (*Willy*).

Calhoun is an Indian scout who gets caught in the middle of a rivalry between Indian chief Van Cleef and Cavalry officer Anderson. The Indian warriors deal a fatal blow to Anderson's troops and the only way Calhoun can rescue the major and what's left of his force is to kill his friend Van Cleef. Heavy on the action, but everything else is weak.

p, Howard W. Koch; d, Lesley Selander; w, Richard Alan Simmons (based on a story by Harold Jack Bloom); ph, Gordon Avil (Color Corp. of America); m, Les Baxter; ed, John F. Schreyer.

War   **(PR:A   MPAA:NR)**

YELLOWBEARD** (1983) 101m Seagoat/Orion c

Graham Chapman (*Yellowbeard*), Peter Boyle (*Moon*), Richard "Cheech" Marin (*El Segundo*), Tommy Chong (*El Nebuloso*), Peter Cook (*Lord Lambourn*), Marty Feldman (*Gilbert*), Martin Hewitt (*Dan*), Michael Hordern (*Dr. Gilpin*), Eric Idle (*Comdr. Clement*), Madeline Kahn (*Betty*), James Mason (*Capt. Hughes*), John Cleese (*Blind Pew*), Kenneth Mars (*Crisp/Verdugo*), Spike Milligan (*Flunkie*), Stacey Nelkin (*Triola*), Nigel Planer (*Mansell*), Susannah York (*Lady Churchill*), Beryl Reid (*Lady Lambourn*), Ferdinand [Ferdy] Mayne (*Beamish*), John Francis (*Chaplain*), Peter Bull (*Queen Anne*), Bernard Fox (*Tarbuck*), Ronald Lacey (*Man with Parrot*), Greta Blackburn (*Mr. Prostitute*), Nigel Stock (*Admiral*), Kenneth Danziger (*Mr. Martin*), Monte Landis (*Prison Guard*), Richard Wren (*Pirate*), Gillian Eaton (*Rosie*), Bernard McKenna (*Askey*), John Diar (*Big John*), Carlos Romano (*Priest*), Alvaro Carcano (*Beggar*), Leopoldo Frances (*Helmsman*), Ava Harela (*Flower Girl*), Garry O'Neill (*Sergeant of the Marines*), David Bowie (*Henson*).

A directionless jumble of comedy skits–some that work, most that don't–which has to do with the efforts of a villainous pirate (Chapman) to locate a treasure he buried years earlier. The map, however, is tattooed on the head of his pansy of a son (Hewitt), who has a pretty face but lacks the pirate savvy of his adventurous father. After a series of comic obstacles, they unearth the jewels but Hewitt, accepting his role as a mean ol' pirate, kills Chapman, which actually pleases the dying buccaneer. Unfortunately for the makers of YELLOWBEARD, there are about as many laughs in the film's 101 minutes as in a three-minute sketch by the Monty Python troupe, from which much of the cast hails. The credits read like a "Who's Who" of British comedy, as well as including U.S. countercultural jokers Cheech and Chong (in completely unfunny roles), Boyle (in a role originally set for rock drummer Keith Moon, who is reputed to have come up with the idea for the film, hence the character name "Moon"), Mason (in a wonderfully restrained performance), and rock personality and part-time actor David Bowie (in an uncredited role as a "shark"). Appearing in his final film is Marty Feldman (to whom the picture is dedicated), who died during production. A disappointment, but then again any Python-related picture since MONTY PYTHON AND THE HOLY GRAIL is a disappointment.

p, Carter De Haven; d, Mel Damski; w, Graham Chapman, Peter Cook, Bernard McKenna; ph, Gerry Fisher (DeLuxe Color); m, John Morris; ed, William Reynolds; prod d, Joseph R. Jennings; art d, Jack Shampan; set d, Tim Hutchinson, Peter James, Teresa Pecanins; cos, T. Stephen Miles, Gilly Hebden; spec eff, Andy Evans, Arthur Beavis; stunts, B. Van Horn.

Comedy/Adventure   **Cas.**   **(PR:C-O   MPAA:PG)**

YELLOWNECK** (1955) 83m Empire/REP c

Lin McCarthy (*The Sergeant*), Stephen Courtleigh (*The Colonel*), Berry Kroeger (*Plunkett*), Harold Gordon (*Cockney*), Bill Mason (*The Kid*).

The struggle of five Confederate Army deserters (tagged "Yellownecks") is depicted here as they make their way through the Florida Everglades in the hope of reaching Cuba. The muggy, buggy swamps take their toll, however, devouring the deserters who must also fend off Indian attacks. When the sole survivor makes it to the coast, he finds that the boat that was supposed to be awaiting his arrival is not there. Photographed on location, YELLOW-NECK has a great atmosphere, but not much else.

p, Harlow G. Frederick; d, R. John Hugh; w, Nat S. Linden, Hugh (based on a story by Hugh); ph, Charles O'Rork (Trucolor); m, Laurence Rosenthal; ed, William A. Slade; art d, Larry Lossing.

Adventure   **(PR:A   MPAA:NR)**

YELLOWSTONE* (1936) 63m UNIV bw

Henry Hunter (*Dick Sherwood*), Judith Barrett (*Ruth Foster*), Ralph Morgan (*James Foster*), Alan Hale (*Hardigan*), Andy Devine (*Pay Day*), Monroe Owsley (*Marty Ryan*), Michael Loring (*Merritt Billing*), Paul Fix (*Dynamite*), Rollo Lloyd (*Franklin Ross*), Paul Harvey (*Raddle*), Raymond Hatton (*Pete*), Diana Gibson, Mary Gordon, Claude Allister.

A group of ex-cons come together in Yellowstone National Park to recover a hidden bundle of loot worth $90,000. A decent cast and some excellent locales can't save this weak programmer from insignificance.

p, Val Paul; d, Arthur Lubin; w, Jefferson Parker, Stuart Palmer, Houston Branch (based on a story by Arthur Phillips); ph, Milton Krasner; ed, Maurice Wright; cos, Vera West.

Crime/Mystery   **Cas.**   **(PR:A   MPAA:NR)**

YELLOWSTONE KELLY** (1959) 91m WB c

Clint Walker (*Kelly*), Edward [Edd] Byrnes (*Anse Harper*), John Russell (*Gall*), Ray Danton (*Sayapi*), Claude Akins (*Sergeant*), Rhodes [Rex] Reason (*Maj. Towns*), Andra Martin (*Wahleeah*), Gary Vinson (*Lieutenant*), Warren Oates (*Corporal*), Harry Shannon (*Riverboat Captain*).

Walker is a rugged fur-trapper who survives by staying on good terms with the Sioux Indians, but eventually has to lend a hand to the U.S. Cavalry when they get pulverized by the tribe. He also offers his help to an Arapaho Indian girl, Martin, who is being held captive by the Sioux. Features television stars Walker of "Cheyenne," John Russell of "Lawman," Edd "Kookie" Byrnes of "77 Sunset Strip," and an early Warren Oates appearance.

d, Gordon Douglas; w, Burt Kennedy (based on the book by Clay Fisher); ph, Carl Guthrie (Technicolor); ed, William Ziegler; md, Howard Jackson; art d, Stanley Fleischer; cos, Marjorie Best; makeup, Gordon Bau.

Western   **(PR:A   MPAA:NR)**

YENTL* (1983) 134m Ladbroke-Barwood/MGM-UA c

Barbra Streisand (*Yentl*), Mandy Patinkin (*Avigdor*), Amy Irving (*Hadass*), Nehemiah Persoff (*Papa*), Steven Hill (*Reb Alter Vishkower*), Allan Corduner (*Shimmele*), Ruth Goring (*Esther Rachel*), David DeKeyser (*Rabbi Zalman*), Bernard Spear (*Tailor*), Doreen Mantle (*Mrs. Shaemen*), Lynda Barron (*Peshe*), Jack Lynn (*Bookseller*), Anna Tzelniker (*Mrs. Kovner*), Miriam Margolyes (*Sarah*), Mary Henry (*Mrs. Jacobs*), Robbie Barnett (*Tailor's Assistant*), Ian Sears (*David*), Renata Buser (*Mrs. Shaemen's Daughter*), Frank Baker, Anthony Rubes (*Village Students*), Kerry Shale, Gary Brown, Peter Whitman, Danny Brainin, Jonathan Tafler, Teddy Kempner (*Students*).

Isaac Bashevis Singer's beautiful short story is turned into a musical ego trip in Barbra Streisand's directorial debut. It is 1904 in a small Eastern European village. Streisand prefers to study the Torah with her father (Persoff), rather than do the woman's work expected of her. Such studies are prohibited to women by Jewish law, but Streisand refuses to give into community pressure. When Persoff dies, Streisand leaves the village, disguising herself as a young man. This way she hopes to be accepted into a yeshiva, where she can study to her heart's content. Eventually she meets Patinkin, a yeshiva student who takes a liking to Streisand. The two become study partners, Patinkin never realizing this young man is actually a woman. Patinkin introduces Streisand to his fiancee, Irving, but eventually this engagement is broken. It is revealed Patinkin's brother had committed suicide, and Irving's parents do not want this to infect their family. Streisand, in the meantime, has fallen in love with Patinkin and is torn because she cannot reveal her true identity. Patinkin, distraught at being separated from Irving, persuades Streisand to marry his former fiancee. Patinkin figures this will at least put him a little closer to the woman he loves. Streisand reluctantly agrees, then continually puts off consummation of the marriage once she and Irving are wed. Streisand begins to teach Irving the Torah, but finds her bride's increasing desires more than she can bear. She and Patinkin go off on a holiday, and there Streisand reveals her secret. At first Patinkin is shocked beyond belief, then accepts Streisand for what she is. He returns to Irving, while Streisand leaves for America, hoping to resume her studies in the New World. A potentially interesting drama, this film quickly turns into Streisand's homage to her own talents. Director Streisand is fascinated with star Streisand (influenced, no doubt, by co-producer and cowriter Streisand). However, she lacks the skills needed to tell a story visually, instead using songs to link the story's episodes and reveal the thoughts of nearly every character. There are nine tunes (with a few reprises as well), all sung by Streisand, and usually in closeup. To no one's surprise, this quickly grows tedious as important characters get tossed aside so Streisand can belt out another tune. Her ending is almost a re-creation of the final moments of her 1968 debut film, FUNNY GIRL. Patinkin and Irving are both good in their roles, but are, more often than not, overpowered by Streisand's relentless control. Streisand had owned the rights to Singer's story for 14 years, fighting long and hard to bring it to the screen her way. Major studios were reluctant to take on the project but Streisand (who had spent 10 years working on the film's design), with typical determination finally saw the project come to light. Singer was appalled by what she had done to his story, and spoke bitterly about it. Gone were

Singer's intricate subtleties and understatements, replaced by Streisand's overblown vanity. The songs, penned by Michel Legrand with lyrics by Alan and Marilyn Bergman, include: "A Piece of Sky," "No Matter What Happens," "This Is One of Those Moments," "Tomorrow Night," "Where Is It Written," "No Wonder," "The Way He Makes Me Feel," "Papa, Can You Hear Me," "Will Someone Ever Look at Me That Way?"

p, Barbra Streisand, Rusty Lemorande; d, Streisand; w, Streisand, Jack Rosenthal (based on the short story "Yentl, the Yeshiva Boy" by Isaac Bashevis Singer); ph, David Watkin (Technicolor); m, Michel Legrand; ed, Terry Rawlings; prod d, Roy Walker; art d, Leslie Tomkins; set d, Tessa Davies; cos, Judy Moorcroft; spec eff, Alan Whibley; ch, Gillian Lynne.

Drama/Musical   Cas.   (PR:C MPAA:PG)

YES, GIORGIO½   (1982) 110m MGM/UA c

Luciano Pavarotti (*Giorgio Fini*), Kathryn Harrold (*Pamela Taylor*), Eddie Albert (*Henry Pollack*), Paola Borboni (*Sister Teresa*), James Hong (*Kwan*), Beulah Quo (*Mei Ling*), Norman Steinberg (*Dr. Barmen*), Rod Colbin (*Ted Mullane*), Kathryn Fuller (*Faye Kennedy*), Joseph Mascolo (*Dominic Giordano*), Karen Kondazian (*Francesca Giordano*), Leona Mitchell, Kurt Adler, Emerson Buckley (*Themselves*).

This ridiculous attempt to update romantic comedy formulas of the 1930s and 1940s features Pavarotti, the famed opera tenor, in his film debut. He more or less plays a caricature of himself, a world famous tenor who's touring the U.S. Before an outdoor concert in Boston, Pavarotti inexplicably loses his voice. His manager, Albert, sends the portly tenor to Harrold, a beautiful throat specialist. The two dislike each other from the start, but only someone in a comatose state couldn't figure out what happens next. Harrold falls for the big lug, despite Pavarotti's male chauvinist attitudes and overwhelming ego. She ends up following him all the way to San Francisco. Never mind that Pavarotti has a wife and child back in Italy; true love conquers all. Eventually Pavarotti is asked to sing at the Metropolitan Opera of New York, but the tenor is hesitant. Years before he had encountered disaster at the Met, and now has a sort of "Met- a-phobia." Of course, his lady love talks him into accepting, and the film ends with Pavarotti wowing the audience in a colorful production of Puccini's "Turandot." YES, GIORGIO suffers from a terminal case of the cutes. Reviving the simplistic formula of an earlier era simply doesn't achieve the same effect with audiences who have grown to expect more realism in romance, with such films as ANNIE HALL redefining the genre. Scenes such as Pavarotti singing a love song while floating over vineyards in a hot air balloon play more like unintentional self- parody than anything else. Schaffner, who seemed a long way from his success with THE PLANET OF THE APES and PATTON, kept his direction simple and anonymous, which was probably the best thing to do with this material. Still, any film that features Pavarotti's wonderful voice can't be all bad. The opera sequences, as expected, are lavish and very entertaining. For the Boston concert scene, Pavarotti gave a free performance at the city's outdoor Hatch Shell. Over 100,000 people watched, serving as extras while they enjoyed the show. YES, GIORGIO cost some $19 million to produce, but proved to be a box-office catastrophe, returning only $1 million in ticket sales. Songs: "If We Were in Love" (John Williams, Allan and Marilyn Bergman, sung by Pavarotti), "I Left My Heart in San Francisco" (George Cory, Douglas Cross), selections from "Turandot" (Giacomo Puccini).

p, Peter Fetterman; d, Franklin J. Schaffner; w, Norman Steinberg (based on the novel by Anne Piper); ph, Fred J. Koenekamp (Metrocolor); m, John Williams; ed, Michael F. Anderson; prod d, William J. Creber; set d, William Durrell, Jr., Perry Gray; cos, Rita Riggs.

Romance   Cas.   (PR:C MPAA:PG)

YES, MADAM?   (1938, Brit.) 77m ABF bw

Bobby Howes (*Bill Quinton*), Diana Churchill (*Sally Gault*), Wylie Watson Albert Peabody, Bertha Belmore (*Emily Peabody*), Vera Peace (*Pansy Beresford*), Billy Milton (*Tony Tolliver*), Fred Emney (*Sir Charles Drake-Drake*), Cameron Hall (*Catlett*).

Howes and Churchill are told that they will inherit a fortune if they work as servants for a month without getting fired. If they fail the money will go to Milton, who tries to get Howes canned, but by the finale, everything is squared away. This passable musical comedy was a remake of a 1933 feature which starred Frank Pettingell and Kay Hammond.

p, Walter C. Mycroft; d, Norman Lee; w, Clifford Grey, Bert Lee, William Freshman (based on the novel by K.R.G. Browne); ph, Walter Harvey; m/l, Jack Waller, Joseph Tunbridge, Harris Weston, R.P. Weston, Grey, Bert Lee.

Musical/Comedy   (PR:A MPAA:NR)

YES, MR. BROWN½ (1933, Brit.) 94m British and Dominions/Wolfe and Freedman-G AU bw

Jack Buchanan (*Nicholas Baumann*), Elsie Randolph (*Anne Webber*), Margot Grahame (*Clary Baumann*), Hartley Power (*Mr. Brown*), Vera Pearce (*Franzi*), Clifford Heatherley (*Carlos*), Anna Lee.

Based on a German play that was produced in London under the title "Business With America," this disappointing musical comedy was co-directed by its star, suave song-and-dance man Buchanan. The ambitious Vienna representative of a U.S.-based company, Buchanan hopes the visit of his American boss, Power, will lead to an offer of partnership. A tiff with wife Grahame leads to her untimely departure, so Buchanan recruits his secretary, Randolph, to pose as his wife. The ruse blows up in his face, but all's well that ends well, as Power and Randolph fall for each other and Buchanan's "old secretary" returns to the U.S. with his "new partner."

p, Herbert Wilcox; d, Wilcox, Jack Buchanan; w, Douglas Furber (based on the play "Geschaft Mit Amerika" by Paul Frank, Ludwig Hershfield); ph, F.A. Young; lyrics, Furber.

Musical Comedy   (PR:A MPAA:NR)

YES, MY DARLING DAUGHTER½   (1939) 86m WB-FN bw

Priscilla Lane (*Ellen Murray*), Jeffrey Lynn (*Douglas Hall*), Roland Young (*Titus Jaywood*), Fay Bainter (*Ann Murray*), May Robson ('Granny' Whitman), Genevieve Tobin (*Connie Nevins*), Ian Hunter (*Lewis Murray*), Robert E. Homans (*Sgt. Murphy*), Edward Gargan (*Police Officer*), Spencer Charters (*Angus Dibble*), Lottie Williams (*Martha*).

A skillfully scripted comedy about a young woman, Lane, who is determined to spend a weekend with boy friend Lynn before he leaves for a new job in Europe. Lane's mother, Bainter, an outspoken feminist (who, unbeknowst to her daughter, had her own "free-love" adventure with poet Young years before) doesn't approve of the proposed excursion. She gives in, however, when Lane confronts her with her failure to live up to her own pronouncements. The lovebirds spend an uneventful weekend but their return is greeted by an uproar. Taking the advice of granny Robson, Lane accompanies Lynn on a transatlantic voyage that includes a shipboard tying of the knot. Not surprisingly, the Board of Censors demanded a few cuts before the picture could hit the screens, fearing that the audience would hit the ceiling. The publicity that followed only helped the film's box-office showing.

p, Jack L. Warner, Hal B. Wallis; d, William Keighley; w, Casey Robinson (based on the play by Mark Reed); ph, Charles Rosher; ed, Ralph Dawson.

Comedy   (PR:A MPAA:NR)

YES SIR, MR. BONES½   (1951) 60m Spartan/Lippert bw

Cotton and Chick Watts, Ches Davis, F.E. Miller, Billy Green, Elliott Carpenter, The Hobnobbers, Ellen Sutton, Sally Anglim, Gary Jackson, Phil Arnold, Slim Williams, Emmett Miller, Ned Haverly, Brother Bones, Scatman Crothers, Monette Moore, Jimmy O'Brien, Archie Twitchell, Cliff Taylor, Boyce and Evans, Pete Daily and His Chicagoans, Jester Hairston Singers.

A young boy pays a visit to a home for elderly minstrels and gets a feel for what it was like in their heyday via a flashback. On board an old showboat the minstrels deliver a heavy dose of entertainment. Musical numbers include: "I Want to Be a Minstrel Man," "Stay Out of the Kitchen," "Is Your Rent Paid Up In Heaven," "Flying Saucers," "Memphis Bill," "Southland."

p,d&w, Ron Ormond; ph, Jack Greenhalgh; m, Walter Greene; ed, Hugh Winn; art d, F. Paul Sylos.

Musical   (PR:A MPAA:NR)

YES SIR, THAT'S MY BABY   (1949) 82m UNIV c

Donald O'Connor (*William Waldo Winfield*), Charles Coburn (*Prof. Jason Hartley*), Gloria DeHaven (*Sarah Jane Winfield*), Joshua Shelley (*Arnold Schultze*), Barbara Brown (*Prof. Boland*), Jim Davis (*Joe Tascarelli*), James Brown (*Tony Cresnovitch*), Michael Dugan (*Eddie Koslowski*), Hal Fieberling (*Pudge Flugeldorfer*), Patricia Alphin (*Mrs. Tascarelli*), June Fulton (*Mrs. Koslowski*), Joan Vohs (*Girl*).

O'Connor and DeHaven are husband and wife in this postwar musical about veterans who return to campus life in order to finish that college education. De Haven and her fellow wives are subject to the speeches given by professor Brown who thinks the husbands should stay at home instead of starting up a football team. Coburn, a biology professor, is determined to hit the gridiron, however. When Coburn's job is jeopardized, the husbands and wives see eye to eye, as do Brown and Coburn, who, it turns out, had a relationship years before. The songs penned by Jack Brooks and Walter Scharf include: "Men Are Little Children" (sung by DeHaven), "They've Never Figured Out a Woman" (O'Connor), "All Look at Me" (DeHaven, O'Connor). The memorable title tune written by Gus Kahn and Walter Donaldson, and sung here by DeHaven and O'Connor, played a big part in A THOUSAND CLOWNS, 16 years later.

p, Leonard Goldstein; d, George Sherman; w, Oscar Brodney; ph, Irving Glassberg (Technicolor); ed, Ted J. Kent; art d, Bernard Herzbrun, John F. De Cuir; cos, Rosemary Odell; ch, Louis Da Pron.

Musical/Comedy   (PR:A MPAA:NR)

YESTERDAY*   (1980, Can.) 97m Dal/Cinepix c

Claire Pimpare (*Gabrielle Daneault*), Vince Van Patten (*Matt Kramer*), Eddie Albert (*Bart Kramer*), Nicholas Campbell (*Tony*), Daniel Gadouas (*Claude Daneault*), Jacques Godin (*Mons. Daneault*), Gerald Parkes (*Prof. Saunders*), Cloris Leachman (*Mrs. Kramer*).

A sappy, predictable piece about a romance between French-Canadian art student Pimpare and Van Patten, an American who is studying in Montreal and trying to decide if he should fight in Vietnam. She gets pregnant; he goes to war and dies. But–surprise–he's really not dead and a tearful reunion follows. This story has already been told a thousand times, usually better than it has been here.

p, John Dunning, Andre Link; d, Larry Kent; w, Bill Lamond, Dunning (based on an idea by Dunning); ph, Richard Ciupka; ed, Debra Karen; art d, Roy Forge Smith.

Drama/Romance   (PR:C MPAA:NR)

YESTERDAY, TODAY, AND TOMORROW***
(1964, Ital./Fr.) 119m C.C. Champion-Les Films Concordia/EMB c (IERI, OGGI E DOMANI; GB: SHE GOT WHAT SHE ASKED FOR)

"Adelina–Naples": Sophia Loren (*Adelina*), Marcello Mastroianni (*Carmine*), Aldo Giuffre (*Pasquale Nardella*), Agostino Salvietti (*Lawyer Verace*), Lino Mattera (*Amadeo Scapece*), Tecla Scarano (*Bianchina Verace*), Silvia Monelli (*Elvira Nardella*), Carlo Croccolo (*Auctioneer*), Pasquale Cennamo (*Police Captian*), "Anna–Milan": Sophia Loren (*Anna*), Marcello Mastroianni (*Renzo*), Armando Trovajoli (*Other Man*), "Mara–Rome": Sophie Loren (*Mara*), Marcello Mastroianni (*Augusto Rusconi*), Tina Pica (*Grandmother*), Giovanni Ridolfi (*Umberto*), Gennaro Di Gregario (*Grandfather*).

A saucy Italian sex trilogy which stars that country's two most bankable names–Sophia Loren and Marcello Mastroianni–both favorites of American audiences as well as those in Europe. Adding to the film's respectability is the direction of De Sica who, while faltering often in his later years, still could boast such fine credits as THE BICYCLE THIEF and UMBERTO D. The first and most interesting episode, "Adelina," takes place in Naples and stars Loren as a woman about to be imprisoned for selling contraband cigarettes when her husband, Mastroianni, learns of a legal loophole. In Italy, women cannot be imprisoned if they are pregnant until six months after the child's birth, thereby allowing for ample nursing time. To avoid prison, Loren gets pregnant, and after her six-month grace period, gets pregnant again, keeping this up for some time, until Mastroianni can no longer tolerate it. The police try to imprison Loren, but her case causes such a stir that her sentence is commuted by the President. In the second episode, "Anna," the location switches to the north in Milan, where Loren is the swanky wife of industrialist Mastroianni. When her husband accidentally wrecks his sports car while trying to avoid hitting a child, Loren angrily takes off with another man. Lastly, in "Mara," which takes place in Rome, Loren titillates not only the audience but a young seminarian, Ridolfi, as well. Playing a prostitute, Loren becomes the object of desire for the young man, while her lover and best client, Mastroianni, is away on business. Unsure of his ability to take a vow of chastity, Ridolfi struggles with his calling, and finally decides to give it up upon seeing Loren perform an erotic strip tease down to only her bra and panties. When Loren is told that Ridolfi is planning to enter the French Foreign Legion instead of the priesthood, the prostitute decides to talk to him. She convinces him that his calling is genuine, and even takes a one-week vow of chastity herself, turning the sex-crazed Mastroianni into a wreck. Winning the Academy Award for Best Foreign Film, YESTERDAY, TODAY AND TOMORROW is another clear-cut example that moviegoers of the early 1960s easily mistook films about big-breasted women and ogling men as being artistic, just because there were subtitles running along the bottom of the frame. YESTERDAY, TODAY AND TOMORROW is an enjoyable romp with a certain amount of importance in its underlying themes, but it is Loren's practicallybare breasts and Mastroianni's sex appeal that sell the film–all of which is sold under the pretense of being "art." Unfortunately the 1964 Academy Award judges overlooked two finer films (as they always do)–a delightfully peculiar musical from France called THE UMBRELLAS OF CHERBOURG and a masterpiece of Japanese existentialism entitled WOMAN IN THE DUNES. An interesting footnote occured in Italy during the production of YESTERDAY, TODAY AND TOMORROW when a Neopolitan woman named Concetta "Black Market Connie" Musscardo complained that it was her story being told in "Adelina." Threatened with a 70 day prison term for selling contraband cigarettes, Musscardo, who was once again pregnant, made sure that she received compensation from the film's producers. Loren, who had just suffered a miscarriage and identified with the pregnant woman, arranged for her to be paid $4,000, a somewhat different ending from the fictionalized episode. For the curious, the title YESTERDAY, TODAY AND TOMORROW means absolutely nothing since everything in the film seems to take place in the present. Ponti's original title was "Three Women," but that was apparently too complex for Hollywood executives to figure out. (In Italian, with English subtitles, later dubbed in English.)

p, Carlo Ponti; d, Vittorio De Sica; w, "Adelina," Eduardo De Filippo, Isabella Quarantotti, "Anna," Cesare Zavattini, Billa Billa Zanuso (based on the story "Troppo Ricca" by Alberto Moravia), "Mara," Zavattini; ph,

Giuseppe Rotunno (Techniscope, Technicolor); m, Armando Trovajoli; ed, Adriana Novelli; art d, Ezio Frigerio; set d, Ezio Altieri; cos, Piero Tosi, Christian Dior, Annamode, Jean Barthet; ch, Jacques Ruet.

Comedy/Drama   (PR:O MPAA:NR)

YESTERDAY'S ENEMY****   (1959, Brit.) 95m Hammer/COL bw

Stanley Baker (*Capt. Langford*), Guy Rolfe (*Padre*), Leo McKern (*Max*), Gordon Jackson (*Sgt. MacKenzie*), David Oxley (*Doctor*), Richard Pasco (*2nd Lt. Hastings*), Russell Waters (*Brigadier*), Philip Ahn (*Yamazaki*), Bryan Forbes (*Dawson*), Wolf 'Wolfe' Morris (*Informer*), David Lodge (*Perkins*), Percy Herbert (*Wilson*), Edwina Carroll (*Suni*), Barry Lowe (*Turner*), Alan Keith (*Bendish*), Howard Williams (*Davies*), Timothy Bateson (*Simpson*), Arthur Lovegrove (*Patrick*), Donald Churchill (*Elliott*), Nicholas Brady (*Orderly*), Barry Steele (*Brown*).

This disturbing WW II film focuses on the survivors of a battle-decimated British brigade trying to make their way through the Burmese jungle to rejoin the main British force. Led by Baker, they come upon a village where they surprise a small Japanese detachment. Found on a dead Japanese colonel is a coded map that details future battle strategy against the British. Baker interrogates a captured Burmese agent, demanding an explanation of the code. The prisoner refuses to talk, so Baker carries through a threat to shoot two innocent villagers. This extreme action breaks the prisoner, who confesses all. Rolfe and McKern, a priest and reporter who travel with the unit, are appalled by Baker's sadistic actions. Baker tries to get the information to divisional headquarters, but he and his men are captured by Japanese troops. Now Baker is on the receiving end of similar torture. He refuses to talk, so the Japanese kill Baker and the surviving men. YESTERDAY'S ENEMY takes a hard, unflinching look at the effects war plays on a man's psyche. Rolfe and McKern, who try to be the voices of reason, cannot understand why Baker does what he does, applying their own set of standards to a wholly different situation. There is no right and wrong in Baker's act. Instead, the brutality is depicted as an evil necessity for that specific moment. It is the perverse irony of war that ends up reversing the entire situation. Guest's direction is excellent, building tensions, then snapping them with sudden violence. Though shot in the studio, the film is highly realistic, putting the viewer in the midst of the Burmese jungle. The performances rivet attention, with an ensemble that works well together. The small cast is uncanny in its portrait of a platoon, creating an honest feeling of men under the pressure of incredible circumstances.

p, Michael Carreras; d, Val Guest; w, Peter R. Newman (based on his television play); ph, Arthur Grant (MegaScope); ed, James Needs, Alfred Cox; art d, Bernard Robinson, Don Mingaye.

War   (PR:O MPAA:NR)

YESTERDAY'S HERO, 1937   (SEE: HOOSIER SCHOOLBOY, THE, 1937)

YESTERDAY'S HERO*½   (1979, Brit.) 95m Cinema Seven/EMI c

Ian McShane (*Rod Turner*), Suzanne Somers (*Cloudy Martin*), Adam Faith (*Jake*), Paul Nicholas (*Clint*), Sam Kydd (*Sam Turner*), Glynis Barber (*Susan*), Trevor Thomas (*Speed*), Sandy Ratcliffe (*Rita*), Alan Lake (*Georgie Moore*), Matthew Long (*Mack Gill*), John Motson (*TV Interviewer/Commentator*), Paul Medford (*Marek*).

Scripted by Jackie Collins (sister of Joan, author of such trashy high-society novels as *Hollywood Wives*, and the source for numerous prime time TV mini-series), YESTERDAY'S HERO tells the story of a has-been soccer player who again rises in the ranks. Somers, one of television's resident dippy blondes ("Three's Company"), is second-billed as the woman who gets herself hooked up with the soccer player, McShane. Nicholas is cast as a pop star who owns the team, giving the filmmakers a feeble excuse to toss in some equally feeble music.

p, Oscar S. Lerman, Ken Regan; d, Neil Leifer; w, Jackie Collins; ph, Brian West; ed, Anthony Gibbs; prod d, Keith Wilson; md, Stanley Myers; m/l, Dominic Bugatti, Frank Musker.

Sports/Drama   (PR:C-O MPAA:NR)

YESTERDAY'S HEROES**   (1940) 65m FOX bw

Jean Rogers (*Lee*), Robert Sterling (*Wyman*), Ted North (*Hammond*), Katharine Aldridge (*Janice*), Russell Gleason (*Garrett*), Richard Lane (*Slater*), Edmund MacDonald (*Jones*), George Irving (*Stovall*), Emma Dunn (*Winnie*), Harry Hayden (*Kellogg*), Isabel Randolph (*Mrs. Kellogg*), Pierre Watkin (*Mason*), Frank Sully (*Walsh*), Mike Frankovitch, Don Forbes (*Announcers*), Bert Roach, Matt McHugh, Truman Bradley, George Meeker.

Sterling is one of the title-variety heroes, a doctor recalling how his college gridiron heroics nearly sabotaged his studies and love life. Persuaded to join the football team, he was, in no time at all, abandoning his schoolwork for the sport, as well as deserting his true love, Rogers, for college hussy Aldridge. Thanks to helpful chum Gleason, Sterling got back on the right track and what could have been a disaster became only a painful memory–the stuff movies are made of.

p, Sol M. Wurtzel; d, Herbert I. Leeds; w, Irving Cummings, Jr., William Counselman, Jr. (based on the serialized novel by William Brent); ph, Charles Clarke; ed, Al De Gaetano; md, Emil Newman; art d, Richard Day, Lewis Creber.

Sports Drama (PR:A MPAA:NR)

YETI zero (1977, Ital.) 105m Stefano c

Mimmo Crau *(Yeti)*, Phoenix Grant *(Jane)*, Jim Sullivan *(Herbie)*, John Stacey *(Prof. Wassermann)*, Eddie Faye *(Hunnicut)*, Tony Kendall *(Cliff)*.

A lifeless Bigfoot picture in which the creature (Crau, hidden under an abominable makeup job) is befriended by a young girl, a deaf-mute boy, and a cuddly collie. The kids might be fooled by the atrocious special effects and false motivations, but only if they are not very bright.

p, Nicolo Pomilia, Wolfranco Coccia Mario, Di Nardo, Gianfranco Parolini; d, Frank Kramer [Gianfranco Parolini]; w, Di Nardo, Kramer; ph, Sandro Mancori (Technicolor); m, Santa Maria Romitelli; art d, Claudio De Santis; spec eff, Ermanno Biamonte.

Science Fiction/Adventure Cas. (PR:A MPAA:NR)

YIDDLE WITH HIS FIDDLE* (1937, Pol.) 92m Warsaw/Sphinx bw

Molly Picon *(Yiddle)*, S. Fostel *(Arye)*, M. Bozyk *(Isaac Kalamutker)*, L. Liebgold *(Efraim)*, D. Fakiel *(Teibele)*, B. Liebgold *(Liebskierowa)*, S. Landau *(Gold)*, M. Brin *(Marshelik)*, Ch. Lewin *(Widow)*, S. Nathan *(Director)*, A. Kure *(Restaurateur)*.

This Polish-produced, Yiddish-language vehicle for vaudeville star Picon lacks anything substantial in terms of script, direction, and technical know-how, but does present its star in as likable a manner as possible. Picon dresses as a boy fiddle-player in order to travel and find work, but when she falls for a fellow, she reveals her female identity. Includes stagy vaudeville routines and a few tunes: "Yiddle With His Fiddle" and "Arye With His Bass." (In Yiddish; English subtitles.)

p, Joseph Green; d, Green, Jan Nowina-Przybylski; w, Konrad Tom; ph, J. Jonilowicz; m, Abraham Ellstein; art d, Jacob Kalich; set d, J. Weinrajeh; m/l, Ellstein, I. Manger.

Musical/Romance (PR:A MPAA:NR)

YIELD TO THE NIGHT (SEE: BLONDE SINNER, 1956)

YNGSJOMORDET (SEE: WOMAN OF DARKNESS, 1968, Swed.)

YO YO*** (1967, Fr.) 92m C.A.P.A.C./Magna bw

Pierre Etaix *(The Millionaire/ Yo Yo)*, Philippe Dionnet *(Yo Yo as a Child)*, Luce Klein *(The Equestrienne)*, Claudine Auger *(Isolina)*, Siam, Pipo, Dario, Mimile.

Etaix displays his brand of silent comedy in YO YO, his finest work in a mediocre career as a filmmaker. The story begins in the mid-1920s. Etaix is a millionaire living the good life in a magnificent castle but carrying a torch for a circus performer long since departed. By coincidence, he encounters her again, and when the stock market crash devours his fortune, he joins her circus troupe. Their son, who performs as a child clown, later becomes a stage-and-screen mega-star, amassing enough wealth to buy back the castle for his parents. They, however, prefer to continue to travel with the big top, and when he finds life in the castle to be as empty as his father did, he rejoins the circus. Etaix's debt to Jacques Tati (for whom he worked on MON ONCLE) and Buster Keaton is clear in YO YO with his use of visual gags that occur without dialog but that rely greatly on an innovative use of sound. Co-scripted by Carriere, who also worked with Bunuel in his later years and received an Oscar nomination for THAT OBSCURE OBJECT OF DESIRE.

p, Paul Claudon; d, Pierre Etaix; w, Etaix, Jean-Claude Carriere; ph, Jean Boffety; m, Jean Paillaud; ed, Henri Lanoe; art d, Raymond Gabutti, Raymond Tournon; cos, Jacqueline Guyot.

Comedy (PR:A MPAA:NR)

YODELIN' KID FROM PINE RIDGE*½
(1937) 62m REP bw (GB: THE HERO OF PINE RIDGE)

Gene Autry *(Gene)*, Smiley Burnette *(Frog)*, Betty Bronson *(Milly Baynum)*, LeRoy Mason *(Len Parker)*, Charles Middleton *(Autry Sr.)*, Russell Simpson *(Bayliss Baynum)*, Jack Dougherty *(Jeff Galloway)*, Guy Wilkerson *(Clem)*, Frankie Marvin *(Luke)*, Henry Hall *(Sheriff)*, Snowflake [Fred Toones] *(Sam)*, The Tennesse Ramblers [Dick Hartman, W.J. Blair, Elmer Warren, Happy Morris, Pappy Wolf] *(Themselves)*, Jack Kirk, Bob Burns, Al Taylor, George Morrell, Lew Meehan, Jim Corey, Jack Ingram, Art Dillard, Art Mix, Bud Osborne, Oscar Gahan, Champion the Horse.

Autry stars in this oater which has been relocated in the South where the Singing Cowboy tries to break up the Georgia equivalent of a range war. He

enlists the help of his Wild West show and the ever-reliable Burnette to defeat the baddies. Includes stock footage from ANNIE OAKLEY as well as a couple of tunes: "Sing Me a Song of the Saddle" and "The Millhouse Wild West Show."

p, Armand Schaefer; d, Joseph Kane; w, Dorrell and Stuart McGowan, Jack Natteford (based on a story by Natteford); ph, William Nobles; ed, Lester Orlebeck; m/l, Gene Autry, Smiley Burnette, Frank Harford, Jack Stanley, William Lava.

Western Cas. (Pr:A MPAA:NR)

YOG-MONSTER FROM SPACE* (1970, Jap.) 84m Toho/AIP c (AKA: SPACE AMOEBA)

Akira Kubo *(Taro Dudo)*, Atsuko Takahashi *(Ayako Hoshino)*, Yoshio Tsuchiya *(Kyoichi Miya)*, Kenji Sahara *(Makoto Obata)*, Noritake Saito *(Rico)*, Yukiko Kobayashi *(Saki)*, Satoshi Nakamura *(Ombo, Supplicator)*, Chotaro Togin *(Yokoyama, Engineer)*, Wataru Omae *(Sakura)*, Sachio Sakai *(Magazine Editor)*, Yu Fujiki *(Promotion Division Manager)*, Yuko Sugihara *(Stewardess)*.

A typical Japanese monster picture dubbed into English (poorly, of course) that sees a giant octopus, crab, and turtle made into unstoppable killing machines when their carcasses are taken over by an alien force. Promoters scouting a Pacific island for a tourist site are threatened by the gigantic inhabitants, causing one of the more unscrupulous of the promoters to sabotage the others' efforts to kill the creatures. He thinks it would be a marvellous tourist trap, but in the end he gives up his life as punishment. It's the high-pitched screech of the island's bats that over powers the giant monsters, whipping them into a state of panic which causes their death.

p, Tomoyuki Tanaka, Fumio Tanaka; d, Ishiro Honda; w, Ei Ogawa; ph, Taaichi Kankura (Tohoscope, Movielab Color); m, Akira Ifukube; ed, Masahisa Himi; art d, Takeo Kita; set d, Yasuyuki Inoue; spec eff, Sadamasa Arikawa; spec eff ph, Yoichi Manoda, Yoshiyuki Tokumasa

Science Fiction (PR:A MPAA:GP)

YOICKS!**½ (1932, Brit.) 62m B&D bw

Ron Hodges *(Sir Percy Roper)*, Caroline Morton *(Lady Evelyn)*, Miles Madison *(Lord Cleves)*, Ellen Drury *(Lady Cleves)*, Shel Rowlands *(Binky)*, Janet Stuart *(Leslie)*, Carl Hemingway *(Farr)*, Hester Ellingsworth *(Betty)*, Karen Doe *(Belle)*, Reginald Carter *(Constable Arnold)*.

Oscar Wilde once wrote a description of fox hunting which was "The English country gentleman galloping after a fox – the unspeakable in full pursuit of the uneatable." Such is the basis for this early British comedy that satirized the inanities and silliness of the red-coated tradition. Hodges and Morton are hosting a fox hunting weekend at their country estate, Bransbury Court. Their best friends are Madison and Drury and there are several other weak-chinned Colonel Blimp-types and their mates. Rowlands is the house butler and oversees a staff of Hemingway, Ellingsworth, Stuart, and Doe. All five have recently been hired and what the owners of the house don't realize is that they are a pack of thieves. The night before the fox hunt, there's a drunken party tossed for the guests and most of them pass out. Under cover of darkness, the servants steal the jewelry from the guests. Early in the morning, the thefts are discovered and policeman Carter is called in. Not wanting to ruin a perfectly good day of hunting, Hodges suggests to his guests that the case be left in the hands of Carter and they can all go out and chase the animal. Rowlands, realizing that they can't get caught with the goods, puts the baubles in a bag and ties it around the neck of the fox to be hunted, then releases it. Two sequences intercut. The hunt (very funny as the peers and peeresses are terribly inadequate horsepeople and every sight gag that one might imagine would happen happens–falling into the stream, getting knocked off the horse by a low branch, etc.). In the house, Carter (who has been reading too many Sherlock Holmes stories) is interrogating the staff and since they are far smarter than he is, the dialog is quite amusing at times. Carter is attracted to Stuart (who was a reluctant member of the gang anyhow). She'd just been released from jail for shoplifting and wanted to go straight and she finds his innocent bumpkin ways appealing. The picture comes to a happy conclusion when the fox is caught and not killed (Morton thinks he's "darling" and wants to make it a household pet), the jewels are recovered and no one can explain how they got on the back of the fox, Carter and Stuart fall in love, and the members of the jewel-robbers have second thoughts and wonder about living a criminal life. Rowlands tells the others: "Look, we all want a nice home, good food, lots of fresh air, and to live like millionaires. These people only come to the country home once a month and the rest of the time it's *ours* and we're not only living well, we're actually getting *paid* for it." The others see the sense in that and they all decide to stay on as domestic servants and enjoy their good fortune. A dated comedy in that fox hunting is, today, a dim memory. Good characterizations, typically convoluted situations, and more than a dollop of social comment.

p, Kirby Grey; d, Lloyd Brinder; w, Thomas Talbot, Abbe Holt; m, Winston Berry; ed, Robert L. Peters; md, Berry; art d, Richard Bowser; set d, Melinda James; cos, Clair MacMahon.

Comedy (PR:AA MPAA:NR)

YOJIMBO* ½**   (1961, Jap.) 110m Toho Co.-Kurosawa/Seneca International bw

Toshiro Mifune (*Sanjuro Kuwabatake*), Eijiro Tono (*Gonji the Sake Seller*), Seizaburo Kawazu (*Seibei, Tazaemon's Henchman*), Isuzu Yamada (*Orin, His Wife*), Hiroshi Tachikawa (*Yoichiro, Their Son*), Kyu Sazanka (*Ushitora*), Daisuke Kato (*Inokichi*), Tatsuya Nakadai (*Unosuke*), Kamatari Fujiwara (*Tazaemon the Silk Merchant*), Takashi Shimura (*Tokuemon the Sake Merchant*), Ikio Sawamura (*Hansuke*), Atsushi Watanabe (*Coffin Maker*), Yoshio Tsuchiya (*Kohei the Farmer*), Yoko Tsukasa (*Nui, His Wife*), Akira Nishimura (*Kuma*), Susumu Fujita (*Homma*), Yosuke Natsuki (*Farmer's Son*), Jerry Fujio (*Roku*).

A spirited, strangely moralistic tale of a samurai (Mifune) who wanders into a town which is in the midst of a civil war. On one side stands silk merchant Fujiwara and on the other sake merchant Shimura, both of them equally evil. Mifune sees their strife as an opportunity to make himself some money as well as secure food and lodging. He is hired by Fujiwara as a "yojimbo," or bodyguard, but has a devious plan of his own. He pretends to hire himself out to Shimura and secretly kills off some of his men. Mifune is caught, brutally beaten, and tossed in prison. He escapes, however, in time to witness a momentous battle between the two factions. Both sides suffer extreme losses as swords cut down any obstacle in their path. When the warring is over, Mifune glances over the mounds of corpses and displays a sense of accomplishment in finally bringing peace to the village. Superbly photographed by Miyagawa (who also shot UGETSU and RASHOMON), YOJIMBO once again proves Kurosawa's influence on Western filmmaking. As THE SEVEN SAMURAI would lay the path for THE MAGNIFICENT SEVEN so YOJIMBO would breed A FISTFUL OF DOLLARS.

d, Akira Kurosawa; w, Kurosawa, Ryuzo Kikushima, Hideo Oguni; ph, Kazuo Miyagawa (Tohoscope); m, Masaru Sato; art d, Yoshiro Muraki.

Drama/Action   **Cas.**   **(PR:O   MPAA:NR)**

YOKEL BOY **   (1942) 69m REP bw (GB: HITTING THE HEADLINES)

Joan Davis (*Molly Malone*), Albert Dekker (*Bugsie Malone*), Eddie Foy, Jr (*Joe Ruddy*), Alan Mowbray (*R.B. Harris*), Roscoe Karns (*Al Devers*), Mikhail Rasumny (*Amatoff*), Lynne Carver (*Vera Valaize*), Tom Dugan (*Professor*), Marc Lawrence (*Trigger*), Florence Wright (*Receptionist*), Pierre Watkin (*Johnson*), Charles Lane (*Cynic*), Cyril Ring (*Reporter*), Betty Blythe (*Woman Reporter*), Lois Collier (*Stewardess*), Tim Ryan (*Waiter*), Harry Hayden (*Bank President*), Anne Jeffreys, Mady Lawrence (*Witnesses at Wedding*), Rod Bacon (*1st Assistant Director*), Arthur O'Connell (*2nd Assistant Director*), Emmett Vogan (*Doctor*), Charles Quigley (*Policeman*), James C. Morton (*Painter*), Marilyn Hare (*Stenographer*).

Foy is cast as a country boy who has seen so many movies that he can accurately foresee how much money any given film will bring in. Karns, an employee of a failing Hollywood studio, brings Foy back to Hollywood with him, where he only gets into trouble. He convinces the studio to cast gangster Dekker in the role of a gangster, while messing around with the thug's sister. Dekker can't act worth a dime and Foy, of course, is blamed. The finale has Foy getting out of his mess, but not until we hear a few songs: "Comes Love," "It's Me Again," "Let's Make Memories Tonight," "I Can't Afford to Dream" (Lew Brown, Charles Tobias, Sammy Stapt), "Jim" (Caesar Petrillo, Nelson Shawn, Edward Ross). YOKEL BOY, based on a stage play of the same name (though it bears little resemblance), was originally planned as a vehicle for Judy Canova who starred in the stage version, but with no harm to her career she was dropped.

p, Robert North; d, Joseph Santley; w, Isabel Dawn (based on the story by Russell Crouse, from the play by Lew Brown); ph, Ernest Miller; ed, Edward Mann; md, Cy Feuer.

Musical   **(PR:A   MPAA:NR)**

YOL* ½**   (1982, Turkey) 111m Guney-Cactus/Triumph-Artificial Eye c

Tarik Akan (*Seyit Ali*), Halil Ergun (*Mehmet Salih*), Necmettin Cobanoglu (*Omer*), Serif Sezer (*Zine*), Meral Orhousoy (*Emine*), Semra Ucar (*Gulbahar*), Hikmet Celik (*Mevlut*), Sevda Aktolga (*Meral*), Tuncay Akca (*Yusuf*).

An extraordinarily painful drama about five Turkish convicts given a week leave from prison to visit their loved ones. What promises to be an emotionally uplifting period of freedom instead takes a bitter turn when each of the men discovers tragedy–one returns home to find that his brother has been murdered by police, while another hears of hiw wife's infidelity. A visually intense probing into Turkish ways and customs (the scene of the prisoner dragging his unfaithful wife into a snowy wasteland is striking yet foreign to Western audiences) written by Guney while he was behind bars. YOL shared the top prize at Cannes with Costa-Gavras' MISSING, an equally powerful study of charged emotions. (In Turkish; English subtitles.)

p, Edi Hubschmid, K.L. Puldi; d, Serif Goren; w, Yilmaz Guney; ph, Erdogan Engin (Fujicolor); m, Sebastian Argol, Kendal; ed, Guney, Elisabeth Waelchli.

Drama   **Cas.**   **(PR:O   MPAA:PG)**

YOLANDA AND THE THIEF***   (1945) 108m MGM c

Fred Astaire (*Johnny Parkson Riggs*), Lucille Bremer (*Yolanda*), Frank Morgan (*Victor Budlow Trout*), Mildred Natwick (*Aunt Amarilla*), Mary Nash (*Duenna*), Leon Ames (*Mr. Candle*), Ludwig Stossel (*Schoolteacher*), Jane Green (*Mother Superior*), Remo Bufano (*Puppeteer*), Francis Pierlot (*Padre*), Leon Belasco (*Taxi Driver*), Ghislaine 'Gigi' Perreau (*Gigi*), Charles La Torre (*Police Lieutenant*), Michael Visaroff (*Major-domo*), Andre Charlot (*Dilettante*).

In this stylish, rarely seen musical Astaire and Morgan play a pair of con men who head down to South America to hide out from the law. On arrival, the two learn about Bremer, an innocent young woman who's heiress to enormous wealth, and Astaire decides to fleece her for some money. Bremer returns from the convent she has grown up in to find everyone around her wants a piece of her fortune. One evening, as Astaire is trying to get into her home, Bremer prays to her guardian angel. Astaire overhears Bremer, then appears in her room, pretending to be her guardian angel in the flesh. Slowly he works his way into her life, preparing to nab the fortune. However, things go awry when Morgan suggests Astaire has actually fallen in love with Bremer. Also messing with Astaire's plans is Ames, a mysterious figure who comes and goes without warning. Eventually Ames reveals himself to be Bremer's real guardian angel. Astaire admits his love for the girl, and, with Ames' blessings, they are wed. Under Minnelli's stylized direction YOLANDA AND THE THIEF becomes something unique. Producer Freed had read a short story by Bemelmans and Thery, and was convinced that the unusual tale would make an excellent film. In his autobiography *I Remember It Well* Minnelli wrote: "I tried to get the quality of Bemelman's books and illustrations, a curious mixture of worldliness in high places and a primitive naivete, using his sometimes crude prism colors right out of a child's paint box and combining them with beautifully subtle monotones." Astaire was eager to create some unusual dances for the film and confronted choreographer Loring before shooting began. Astaire presented Loring with five hours worth of dance clips from his previous films, telling the choreographer: "Look at this first, and then we'll go to work. I don't like to repeat myself." The film's highlight is a beautiful, dream-like ballet in which Astaire imagines himself choosing between his chosen life or his love for Bremer. This marvelous work encompasses 16 minutes, marking the first time a ballet had been used to advance a film's story. Unfortunately, all the care and attention was lost on both filmgoers and critics of the day, as the film lost $1.6 million for MGM. Minnelli was convinced that YOLANDA AND THE THIEF was a film ahead of its time, which may have accounted for its unfortunate and undeserved failure. Bremer had been a discovery of Freed, who envisioned a great film career for her. Though her dancing was excellent, Bremer never caught on with the public. The songs here by Arthur Freed and Harry Warren include: "This is the Day for Love" (performed by Bremer), "Angel" (performed by Bremer), "Yolanda" (performed by Astaire), "Coffee Time," "Will You Marry Me."

p, Arthur Freed; d, Vincente Minnelli; w, Irving Brecher (based on a story by Jacques Thery, Ludwig Bemelmans); ph, Charles Rosher (Technicolor); ed, George White; md, Lennie Hayton; art d, Cedric Gibbons, Jack Martin Smith; set d, Edwin B. Willis, Richard Pefferle; cos, Irene, Irene Sharaff; spec eff, A. Arnold Gillespie, Warren Newcombe; ch, Eugene Loring; m/l, Freed, Harry Warren; makeup, Jack Dawn.

Musical   **(PR:A   MPAA:NR)**

YOLANTA**   (1964, USSR) 82m Riga Film Studio/Artkino c

Natalya Rudnaya (*Yolanta*), sung by Galina Oleinichenko, Fyodor Nikitin (*King Rene*), sung by Ivan Petrov, Yuri Perov (*Vaudemont*), sung by Zurab Andjaparidze, Alexander Belyavsky (*Duke Robert*), sung by Pavel Lisitsian, Pyotr Glebov (*Eon-Hakkia*), sung by V. Valaitis, Valentina Ushajova (*Martha*), sung by Y. Verbitskaya, Valdis Sandberg (*Bertrand*), sung by V. Yaroslavtsev, Ya. Filipson (*Almerik*), sung by V. Vlasov, V. Sharykina (*Brigitta*), sung by M. Miglau, O. Amalina (*Laura*), sung by K. Leonova, T. Starova (*Matilda*), A. Milbret (*Jester*).

An opera film based on Tchaikovsky's tale of a young woman who is unaware that she is blind because of her father's fears that Robert, the Duke of Burgundy (Belyavsky), betrothed to her since childhood, will refuse to marry her. He does betray her but his friend Vaudemont (Perov), a brave knight, tells her the truth and reveals the world's beauties to her. They fall in love and in the end her sight is restored.

d, Vladimir Gorikker; ph, Vadim Mass (Magicolor); m, Peter Ilich Tchaikovsky (performed by the Bolshoi Theater Orchestra); ed, M. Chardynini; cos, U. Pauzer; spec eff, E. August, V. Shildknekht; makeup, V. Kuznetsova.

Opera   **(PR:A   MPAA:NR)**

YONGKARI MONSTER FROM THE DEEP*
          (1967 S.K.) 100m Kuk Dong bw (DAI KOESU YONGKARI; AKA: MONSTER YONGKARI; GREAT MONSTER YONGKARI)

Yungil Oh, Chungim Nam, Soonjai Lee, Moon Kang, Kwang Ho Lee.

A Godzilla-like critter terrorizes Seoul, for once sparing the constantly monster-plagued citizens of Tokyo. An earthquake wakes up the monster, he leaves a trail of destruction in his path, and is destroyed by an ammonia substance. Nothing special except for some effective shots of the Korean landscape.

d, Kiduck Kim; w, Yunsung Suh; ph, Kenichi Nakagawa, Inchib Byon.

Science Fiction (PR:A MPAA:NR)

YOR, THE HUNTER FROM THE FUTURE zero
(1983, Ital.) 88m Diamant COL c (IL MONDO DI YOR; AKA: THE WORLD OF YOR)

Reb Brown (Yor), Corinne Clery (Ka-Laa), John Steiner (Overlord), Carole Andre (Ena), Alan Collins (Pag), Ayshe Gul (Roa), Aytekin Akkaya (Ukan), Marina Rocchi (Tarita), Sergio Nicolai (Kay), Ludovico Dello Joio, Adnan Akdemir, Herent Akdemir, Zeynip Selgur, Nurdan Asar, Yadigar Ajder, Nilgun Bubikoglu, Tevfik Sen, Yasemin Celenk, Levent Cakir, Ali Selgur.

A brainless outing set in the future but with a cast full of loin-clothed Hercules types. Nuclear destruction has wiped out modern civilization as tough guy Brown arms himself with some modern destructo-nology enabling him to blow dinosaurs into oblivion. The monsters are awful, the dialog worse, and the dubbing evokes some unintentional chuckles from the audience.

p, Michele Marsala; d, Anthony M. Dawson [Antonio Margheriti]; w, Dawson, Robert Bailey (based on the novel by Juan Zanotto, Ray Collins); ph, Marcello Masciocchi (Eastmancolor); m, John Scott, Guido De Angelis, Maurizio De Angelis; ed, Alberto Moriani; art d, Walter Patriarca; cos, Enrico Luzzi; spec eff, Antonio Margheriti, Antonella Margheriti, Eduardo Margheriti; makeup, M. Scutti.

Science Fiction/Adventure Cas. (PR:A MPAA:PG)

YOSAKOI JOURNEY*½ (1970, Jap.) 91m Shochiku Co./Shochiku Films of America c (YOSAKOI RYOKO)

Frankie Sakai (Ryota Sakamoto), Chieko Baisho (Machiko), Chocho Miyako (Sei Ueda), Junzaburo Ban (Kichigoro Yamashita), Aiko Nagayama (Takako), Shin-ichi Yanagizawa (Rikizo), Takuya Fujioka (Ryotei Katsurai), Kensaku Morita (Shinsuke), Yasushi Koga (Sanpei Koga), Yasushi Suzuki, Toshie Kusunoki, Chiharu Kuri, Hiroshi Tatehara, Pinky and the Killers.

A Japanese melodrama about a railway employee who is unfaithful to his independent wife. He finds a girl to have an affair with, discovers that she is already engaged, then returns to his wife, who has just learned that she is pregnant and is now dependent on him.

p, Kiyoshi Shimazu; d, Shoji Segawa; w, Kazuo Funabashi; ph, Sozaburo Shinomura; m, Taku Izumi; art d, Masao Kumagi.

Drama (PR:C MPAA:NR)

YOSAKOI RYOKO (SEE: YOSAKOI JOURNEY, 1970, Jap.)

YOSEI GORASU (SEE: GORATH, 1964, Jap.)

YOSIE GORATH (SEE: GORATH, 1964, Jap.)

YOTSUYA KAIDAN (SEE: ILLUSION OF BLOOD, 1966, Jap.)

YOU AND ME* (1938) 90m PAR bw

Sylvia Sidney (Helen Dennis), George Raft (Joe Dennis), Harry Carey (Mr. Morris), Barton MacLane (Mickey), Warren Hymer (Gimpy), Roscoe Karns (Cuffy), Robert Cummings (Jim), George E. Stone (Patsy), Adrian Morris (Knucks), Roger Gray (Bathhouse), Cecil Cunningham (Mrs. Morris), Vera Gordon (Mrs. Levine), Egon Brecher (Mr. Levine), Willard Robertson (Dayton), Guinn "Big Boy" Williams (Taxi), Bernadene Hayes (Nellie), Joyce Compton (Curly Blonde), Carol Paige (Torch Singer), Harlan Briggs (McTavish), William B. Davidson (N.G. Martin), Oscar G. Hendrian (Lucky), Edward J. Pawley (Dutch), Joe Gray (Red), Jack Pennick, Kit Guard (Gangsters), Paul Newlan (Bouncer), Hal K. Dawson (Information Clerk), Herta Lynd (Swedish Waitress), Matt McHugh (Newcomer), Jimmie Dundee (Bus Driver), Jack Mulhall, Sam Ash (Floorwalkers), Julia Faye (Secretary), Arthur Hoyt (Mr. Klein), Max Barwyn (German Waiter), Harry Tenbrook (Bartender), Ernie Adams (Nick the Waiter), Paula de Cardo, Harriette Haddon (Cigarette Girls), Blanca Vischer (Flower Girl), Gwen Kenyon, Louise Seidel (Hat Check Girls), Greta Granstedt, Juanita Quigley, Helaine Moler, Marie Burton, Lola Jensen, Cheryl Walker, Yvonne Duval, Dorothy Dayton, Carol Parker (Girls), Ethel Clayton (Woman), Ellen Drew (Cashier), Sheila Darcy (Perfume Clerk), Margaret Randall (Shoplifter), Ruth Rogers (Salesgirl), Barbara Salisbury, Marion Weldon, Barbara Jackson (Demonstrators), Richard Denning, Archie Twitchell, Jack Hubbard, Ray Middleton (Men), Phillip Warren (Secretary), Jane Dewey, Joyce Mathews (Clerks), John McCafferty (Policeman), Fern Emmett (Mother), James McNamara (Big Shot).

Deemed an artistic failure at the time of its release, Fritz Lang's YOU AND ME is, nonetheless, an interesting misfire with enough creativity and imagination to warrant viewing. Attempting a mixture of romance, drama, social observation, comedy, and music, the film has a distracting schizoph-renic quality that can be frustrating at times. Raft stars as an ex-con now in the employ of department store owner Carey, who staffs his establishment with a good number of ex-cons as a humanitarian gesture to those who have paid their debt to society. At the store Raft meets and falls in love with Sidney, another employee. The two begin a romance, but Sidney hides the fact that she is an ex-con as well. Raft proposes marriage and Sidney accepts, but worries because she is still on parole and the rules forbid parolees to wed. When Raft finally learns that Sidney is an ex-con on parole and their wedding was illegal, the news sinks him into a depression that sends him back into the underworld. Raft organizes a gang to rob Carey's store. Sidney learns of the plan and convinces the amazingly patient and benevolent Carey to let her talk the gang out of the robbery. Sidney waits for the gang to invade the store and then sits them down in front of a chalkboard and calculates that each gang member would only garner $133.33 from the robbery—a sum not worth risking a jail term over—thus proving that crime really does not pay (the scene is supposed to be played for laughs but doesn't quite work). Embarrassed and angered by his wife's intervention, Raft leaves the gang and disappears. He returns months later, however, upon receiving news that Sidney is about to give birth to their child. Joined by his gang, the proud father gazes at his baby and proposes again to Sidney, whose parole is finally up. The film ends with Raft, Sidney, and the baby at the altar. YOU AND ME was originally supposed to be directed by the author of the story, Krasna, and was to star Carole Lombard and George Raft. Lombard left the picture and Sidney was chosen to replace her. Neither Raft nor Sidney had any confidence in Krasna as a director and they wanted him out. Sidney requested Lang whom she had worked with in FURY and YOU ONLY LIVE ONCE. The German director was hired and shooting began. Lang saw in the material an opportunity to create a Brechtian drama that would continue the series of socially relevant films he had made in America with Sidney—but in a different vein. The director called in fellow German expatriate Kurt Weill to pen songs for the film that would reflect the themes Lang was dealing with. Unfortunately, Weill became disillusioned with the project and left after writing only three songs. While the musical numbers are well done in and of themselves, they are badly integrated into the narrative and seem as if they have been inserted from another film. While certainly not noted for his comedic flair (there is little humor in any of his films), Lang does a reasonably good job with the light moments and delivers some big laughs. Perhaps best is the scene where Raft seriously intones, "I'm telling you this is a good racket, and there isn't a racket I haven't tried." Only then does Lang's camera reveal that the ex-crook is in the department store talking to a customer while holding a tennis racket. When Lang finally delivered the film, the bewildered studio didn't know what to make of it and tried to sell it in the same vein as Lang's ultra-serious dramas FURY and YOU ONLY LIVE ONCE. The ads showed a sullen Sidney with her back against a very official looking document detailing the rules of the State Parole Board with rule number one, "You May Not Marry," in bigger type and boldface. A large quote of dialog appears to the right of the ad screaming, "I've done my time...now I want my man!" The tag line proclaims: "Two great dramatic stars bring you the searing story of love on parole!" The ads were a bit misleading to say the least, but they are indicative of the critical and popular confusion over this strange hybrid of a film.

p&d, Fritz Lang; w, Virginia Van Upp (based on a story by Norman Krasna); ph, Charles Lang, Jr.; m, Kurt Weill, Boris Morros; ed, Paul Weatherwax; md, Morros; art d, Hans Dreier, Ernst Fegte; set d, A.E. Freudeman; m/l, title song, Ralph Freed, Frederick Hollander, "The Right Guy for Me," Weill, Morros.

Drama (PR:A-C MPAA:NR)

YOU ARE THE WORLD FOR ME** (1964, Aust.) 107m Erma/Ring Film Corp. bw (DU BIST DIE WELT FUR MICH; AKA: THE RICHARD TAUBER STORY)

Rudolf Schock (Richard Tauber), Annemarie Duringer (Christine), Richard Romanowsky (Prof. Beines), Fritz Imhoff (Director Stapler), Dagny Servaes (His Wife), Helli Servi, Anni Korin, Gerda Scheyrer, Joachim Brennecke.

A straightforward biography of composer-singer Richard Tauber who rises in the opera world, ignoring the ballerina with whom he is in love. He achieves great fame, but in the end loses his love. Recordings of Tauber are used to dub in actor Schock's singing voice. Released in Austria in 1953.

p, Karl Ehrlich; d&w, Ernst Marischka; ph, Sepp Ketterer; md, Anton Profes, set d, Fritz Juptner-Jonstorff.

Biography/Musical (PR:A MPAA:NR)

YOU BELONG TO ME** (1934) 67m PAR bw

Lee Tracy (Bud Hannigan), Helen Mack (Florette Faxon), Helen Morgan (Mme. Alva), Lynne Overman (Theater Manager), David Holt (Jimmy Faxon), Arthur Pierson (Hap Stanley), Edwin Stanley (School Principal), Dean Jagger (Instructor), Irene Ware (Lila Lacey), Lou Cass (Joe Mandel), Max Mack (Jack Mandel), Mary Owen (Maizie Kelly), Rev. Neal Dodd (Minister), Irving Bacon (Stage Manager).

A sturdy tearjerker with 8-year-old Holt being put into a military academy when his father dies and his vaudevillian mother remarries. The boy is at odds with his new stepdad, who also has become his mother's stage partner.

He's not much of a husband, however, and soon packs his bags to romance another. The finale has the boy's mother dying during her act after an argument with her philandering mate.

p, Louis D. Lighton; d, Alfred Werker; w, Walter DeLeon, Grover Jones, William Slavens McNutt (based on a story by Elizabeth Alexander); ph, Leo Tover; cos, Edith Head; m/l, Sam Coslow.

Drama   (PR:A MPAA:NR)

YOU BELONG TO ME*   (1941) 94m COL bw (GB: GOOD MORNING DOCTOR)

Barbara Stanwyck (Helen Hunt), Henry Fonda (Peter Kirk), Edgar Buchanan (Billings), Roger Clark (Vandemer), Ruth Donnelly (Emma), Melville Cooper (Moody), Ralph Peters (Joseph), Maude Eburne (Ella), Renie Riano (Minnie), Ellen Lowe (Eva), Mary Treen (Doris), Gordon Jones (Robert Andrews), Fritz Feld (Desk Clerk), Paul Harvey (Barrows), Harold Waldridge (Smithers), Stanley Brown, Lloyd Bridges (Ski Patrol), George Meader (Doctor), Byron Foulger (Delaney), Charles Smith (Boy), Sarah Edwards (Mrs. Snyder), Arthur Loft (Reporter), Lester Dorr (Photographer), William "Billy" Newell (Parking Attendant), Roger Gray (Caretaker), Eloise Hardt (Blondie), Sidney Bracy (Butler), Barbara Brown (Woman), Georgia Backus (Attendant), Howard Hickman (Superintendent), Sam McDaniel (Porter), Jack Norton (Keckel), Larry Parks (Blemish), Grady Sutton (Clerk), Mira McKinney (Lipstick Woman), George Lessey (Marshall), Georgia Caine (Necktie Woman), Jeff Corey.

Fonda, a bored multimillionaire playboy, goes on a skiing trip and finds himself enamored of Stanwyck, a beautiful woman he spots on the slopes. Trying to get a better look at her, he steers himself into a snowdrift and suffers an injury to his rear end. He is taken to the local doctor, who turns out to be Stanwyck. The serious professional woman and the charming playboy soon fall in love and are married, but the relationship quickly shows signs of strain when Stanwyck discovers that Fonda, who needs no job and therefore has nothing much else to do, spends all his time working himself up into a jealous frenzy while she treats handsome male patients. Stanwyck expresses doubt about being able to continue with the marriage unless Fonda finds something to do so he can stop pestering her. She suddenly hits upon the idea of finding him a job. Willing to try to salvage the marriage, Fonda reluctantly looks for work and finds himself working as a lowly clerk in a department store because he has no qualifications for anything else. Stanwyck is quite pleased with Fonda's success, but he soon loses the job because the other employees find out he's a millionaire and complain that he's robbing an unemployed person of a good position. Fonda finally ends his frustrations when he decides to use all his money to buy a bankrupt hospital and install Stanwyck as the chief of staff while he runs the business end. YOU BELONG TO ME was a weak attempt to recreate the success of the previous Fonda-Stanwyck coupling, THE LADY EVE. Whereas THE LADY EVE had inimitable Preston Sturges at the helm, YOU BELONG TO ME only had the competent Ruggles to direct a so-so screenplay by Binyon from a story by Trumbo. The material was quite cliched by 1941 and it is only through the strength of performers Stanwyck and Fonda that the film works at all. A pleasant and amusing comedy, but really nothing more.

p&d, Wesley Ruggles; w, Claude Binyon (based on a story by Dalton Trumbo); ph, Joseph Walker; m, Frederick Hollander; ed, Viola Lawrence; md, M.W. Stoloff; art d, Lionel Banks; cos, Edith Head.

Romantic Comedy   (PR:A MPAA:NR)

YOU BELONG TO MY HEART   (SEE: MR. IMPERIUM, 1951)

YOU BETTER WATCH OUT**   (1980) 100m Pressman c (AKA: CHRISTMAS EVIL)

Brandon Maggart (Harry Stadling), Dianne Hull (Jackie Stadling), Scott McKay (Fletcher), Joe Jamrog (Frank Stoller), Peter Friedman (Grosch), Ray Barry (Gleason), Bobby Lesser (Gottleib), Sam Gray (Grilla), Ellen McElduff (Harry's Mother), Patty Richardson (Moss' Mother).

An exploitable horror picture which takes its title from the Christmas carol "Santa Claus Is Coming to Town." This time we find out that Santa's definitely naughty, not nice, and is, in fact, a murdering lunatic. It should go without saying, but YOU BETTER WATCH OUT is not for kids.

p, Burt Kleiner, Pete Kameron; d&w, Lewis Jackson; ph, Ricardo Aronovich; ed, Corky O'Hara, Linda Leeds; prod d, Lorenzo Jodie Harris; cos, Dierdre Williams.

Horror   (PR:O MPAA:R)

YOU CAME ALONG½   (1945) 103m PAR bw

Robert Cummings (Maj. Bob Collins), Lizabeth Scott (Ivy Hotchkiss), Don DeFore (Capt. Shakespeare Anders), Charles Drake (Handsome Janoshek), Julie Bishop (Joyce Heath), Kim Hunter (Frances Hotchkiss), Robert Sully (Bill Allen), Helen Forrest (Herself), Rhys Williams (Col. Stubbs), Franklin Pangborn (Hotel Clerk), Minor Watson (Uncle Jack), Howard Freeman (Drunk Middle-Aged Man), Andrew Tombes (2nd Drunk Man), Lewis L. Russell (Chairman), Frank Faylen (Bellboy), Will Wright (Col. Armstrong),

Cindy Garner (Gertrude), Marjorie Woodworth (Carol Dix), Ruth Roman (Gloria Revere), Crane Whitley (Capt. Taylor), Charles La Torre (Orchestra Leader), Hugh Beaumont (Army Chaplain at Funeral), Louis Jean Heydt (Navy Man), Robert Emmett Keane (Real Estate Agent), William B. Davidson.

YOU CAME ALONG tugs at the old heartstrings as three fliers–Cummings, the fun-loving major; DeFore, the intellect; and Drake, the guy with the looks–embark on a promotional tour for bonds with Scott as their guide. Cummings falls in love with Scott, though he keeps her in the dark about his battle with leukemia. They wed, but Scott is soon widowed, and is consoled by Cummings' fellow fliers. Songs: "You Came Along (From Out of Nowhere)" (Edward Heyman, John Green), "Kiss the Boys Goodbye" (Frank Loesser, Victor Schertzinger). One of three screenplays written by the polemical writer and espouser of "rational selfishness," Ayn Rand, whose influential supermanlike novel The Fountainhead had appeared only two years before YOU CAME ALONG. Scott's second featured role in films won her raves from the critics for her "sonorous speaking voice" and "an intriguing manner." One critic went so far as to say she suggests a "young Garbo."

p, Hal B. Wallis; d, John Farrow; w, Robert Smith, Ayn Rand (based on the story by Smith); ph, Daniel L. Fapp; m, Victor Young; ed, Eda Warren; art d, Hans Dreier, Hal Pereira; spec eff ph, Farciot Edouart; cos, Edith Head.

Drama   (PR:A MPAA:NR)

YOU CAME TOO LATE*½   (1962, Gr.) 75m Mirma Films/Hellenic Films bw

Helen Hatziagyri (Girl), Andrew Barkoulis (Boy), Dino Papagianopoulos (Father), Theo Karousos (Uncle).

A minor version of the classic Alexandre Dumas (the younger) play about two young lovers who must battle their parents' opposition to their relationship. The finale has the girl contracting a disease and dying in a bed of camellias, though this reference is lost in this version's second-rate title. La Dame Aux Camelias was one of the playwright's most popular works.

d, D. Kapsakis; w, Giannis Maris (based on the novel and play by Alexandre Dumas fils La Dame Aux Camelias).

Drama   (PR:A MPAA:NR)

YOU CAN'T BEAT LOVE*½   (1937) 82m RKO bw

Preston Foster (Jimmy Hughes), Joan Fontaine (Trudy Olson), Herbert Mundin (Jasper), William Brisbane (Clem Bruner), Alan Bruce (Scoop Gallagher), Paul Hurst (Butch Mehaffey), Bradley Page (Dwight Parsons), Berton Churchill (Chief Brennan), Frank M. Thomas (Mayor Olson), Harold Huber (Pretty Boy Jones), Paul Guilfoyle (Louie the Weasel), Barbara Pepper (May Smith), Milburn Stone (Reporter), Fred Kelsey (Cop).

Foster is a wealthy playboy who accepts a dare to run for mayor, falling in love with the incumbent's daughter, Fontaine. Some run-of-the-mill laughs are had as he exposes a gang of crooked politicians who are exploiting the mayor's power. Fontaine's third featured role (she was then 20 years old) was designed to give her some experience before the camera during a build-up campaign set in motion by RKO. And that's about all she got from this turkey, for it certainly did not win her any attention except from one critic who said she had a lot to learn.

p, Robert Sisk; d, Christy Cabanne; w, David Silverstein, Maxwell Shane (based on the story "Quintuplets to You" by Olga Moore); ph, Russell Metty; ed, Ted Cheesman; cos, Edward Stevenson.

Comedy   (PR:A MPAA:NR)

YOU CAN'T BEAT THE IRISH**   (1952, Brit.) 73m ABF/Stratford Pictures bw (GB: TALK OF A MILLION)

Jack Warner (Bartley Murnahan), Barbara Mullen (Bessie Murnahan), Joan Kenny (Sally Murnahan), Elizabeth Erskine (Norah Murnahan), Ronan O'Casey (Derry Murnahan), Vincent Ball (Jack Murnahan), Noel Purcell (Matty McGrath), Paul Connell (Joe McGrath), Michael Dolan (Tubridy), Niall McGinnis (Tom Cassidy), Alfie Bass (Lorcan), Sidney James (John C. Moody), Anita Bolster (Miss Rafferty), Tony Quinn (Sacristan), John McDarby (Porter), Milo O'Shea (Signwriter), Fred Johnson, E.J. Kennedy, John Kelley, Joe Linnane, Gordon Tanner, Bill Shine, Christie Humphrey.

Warner is a lovably lazy Irishman who poses as a royal heir and proves a thing or two to his presumptuous neighbors. They believe him to be of royal blood after he meets with an American attorney, allowing him to ring up a fortune in credit. He buys up half the town before the truth comes out. Pleasantly whimsical, as expected from the title.

p, Alex Boyd; d, John Paddy Carstairs; w, Frederic Gotfurt (based on the play "They Got What They Wanted" by Louis d'Alton); ph, Jack Hildyard; m, Leighton Lucas; ed, E.H. Jarvis

Comedy   (PR:A MPAA:NR)

YOU CAN'T BEAT THE LAW   (SEE: SMART GUY, 1943)

YOU CAN'T BUY EVERYTHING**   (1934) 80m MGM bw

May Robson (*Hannah Bell*), Jean Parker (*Elizabeth Burton*), Lewis Stone (*John Burton*), Mary Forbes (*Kate Farley*), Reginald Mason (*Dr. Lorimer*), William Bakewell (*Donny Bell as a Man*), Tad Alexander (*Donny Bell as a Boy*), Walter Walker (*Josiah Flagg*), Reginald Barlow (*Tom Sparks*), Claude Gillingwater (*Asa Cabot*).

Robson stars as a woman driven to a psychotic state after being jilted by Stone. Though years have passed, Robson still holds a grudge against Stone, even to the point where she withdraws her money from the bank when her former love becomes an officer. Her head is sent spinning when her son, Bakewell, falls in love with Stone's daughter, Parker, but by the finale she has had a change of heart. YOU CAN'T BUY EVERYTHING was originally scheduled for Marie Dressler but her death left a vacancy which needed filling. Robson, who had just hit big in Frank Capra's LADY FOR A DAY, was chosen for the part of Henrietta Howland, known as Hetty Green, who amassed a fortune on Wall Street around the turn of the century by both investment and manipulation and became reputedly the richest woman in America. Known as the "witch of Wall Street," legend abounds with stories of her miserliness, some of them noted in this film, such as waiting on a train until one of the passengers is sleeping before she steals his newspaper, and sending her son to a charity clinic when he was injured.

d, Charles F. Riesner; w, Zelda Sears, Eve Green (based on the story by Dudley Nichols, Lamar Trotti); ph, Len Smith; ed, Ben Lewis.

Drama   **(PR:A   MPAA:NR)**

YOU CAN'T BUY LUCK*½   (1937) 61m RKO bw

Onslow Stevens (*Joe Baldwin*), Helen Mack (*Betty*), Vinton Haworth (*Paul*), Maxine Jennings (*Jean*), Paul Guilfoyle (*Frank Brent*), Frank M. Thomas (*Bond*), Richard Lane (*McGrath*), Murray Alper (*Spike*), Hedda Hopper (*Mrs. White*), Dudley Clements (*Ben*), Margaret Fielding (*Alice*), George Irving (*Mr. White*), Barbara Pepper (*Clerk*), Edgar Norton (*Rivers*), Eddie Gribbon (*Chuck*), John Kelly (*Puggy*), Edward Gargan (*Butch*).

A slow-moving crime drama about a racehorse owner who believes that luck is all-important. He becomes extremely charitable, turning good deeds and buying things for anyone he comes in contact with. His logic is that he is buying himself well-wishers and with all those people rooting for him his horse can't possibly lose. A racetrack murder occurs and he is brought to trial, though before he is put away he brings in the real culprit. Harmed by preachiness about sincerity and honest-to-goodness charity, this is a wild concoction of blarney no greener than an Irish turnip.

d, Lew Landers; w, Martin Mooney, Arthur T. Horman (based on the story by Mooney); ph, J. Roy Hunt; ed, Jack Hively; cos, Edward Stevenson.

Drama/Crime   **(PR:A   MPAA:NR)**

YOU CAN'T CHEAT AN HONEST MAN***½   (1939) 76m UNIV bw

W.C. Fields (*Larson E. Whipsnade*), Edgar Bergen (*Himself*), Charlie McCarthy (*Himself*), Mortimer Snerd (*Himself*), Constance Moore (*Vicky Whipsnade*), Mary Forbes (*Mrs. Bel-Goodie*), Thurston Hall (*Archibald Bel-Goodie*), Princess Baba 'Valerie Brooke/Valerie Gregory' f2 (*Herself*), John Arledge (*Phineas Whipsnade*), Charles Coleman, Leyland Hodgson (*Butlers*), Edward Brophy (*Corbett*), Arthur Hohl (*Burr, Bill Collector*), 'Pietro' Blacaman (*Himself*), Eddie "Rochester" Anderson (*Cheerful*), Grady Sutton (*Chester Dalrymple*), Ferris Taylor (*Deputy Sheriff*), James Bush (*Roger Bel-Goodie III*), Ivan Lebedeff (*Ronnie*), Irving Bacon (*Jailer*), Eddie Dunn, Frank O'Connor (*Cops*), Jan Duggan (*Mrs. Sludge*), James C. Morton (*Judge*), Walter Tetley (*Boy with Candy Cane*), Evelyn Del Rio (*Little Girl Who Cries*), Delmar Watson (*Boy in Bleachers*), Lloyd Ingraham (*Mayor*), David Oliver (*Man at Window*), Edward Woolf (*Thin Man*), Lee Phelps (*Sheriff*), Ethelreda Leopold (*Blonde at Party*), Frank Jenks (*Jerry, Assistant*), Don Terry, Byron Munson (*Ping Pong Players*), Ed Thomas (*Butler With Phone*), Charles Murphy (*Lon*), Ted Hardy (*Russian Circus Performer*), Dorothy Arnold (*Debutante*), Si Jenks (*Hillbilly*), Joe King (*Policeman*), Frank Melton (*Yokel*), Ralph Sanford (*Truck Driver*), Eddie Chandler (*Highway Patrol Officer*), Dora Clemant (*Woman*), Leyla Tyler f2 (*Society Woman*), Jack Clifford (*Riding Master*), Otto Hoffman (*Mayor*), Ray Moyer (*Fire Eater*), George Offerman, Jr. (*Western Union Messenger*), Grace Goodall, Minerva Urecal (*Spinsters*), Dick Dickinson (*Contortionist*), Bill Wolfe, Bill Worth (*Hillbilly Twins*), Kay Marlowe, Jennifer Gray (*Debs*), George Ovey, Billy Engle, Lewis Morphy, Bobby Hare (*Circus Attendants*), Beryl Wallace (*Girl*), Jack Gardner (*Ticket Seller*), Duke York (*Man*), Art Yeoman, Ernie Adams, James Lucas, Jack Kenny, Drew Demarest (*Barkers*), Maj. Sam Harris, Russell Wade, Ralph Brooks, Dale Van Sickel (*Wedding Guests*).

Universal Studios waved big money under comedian Fields' legendary proboscis and wooed him away from Paramount. In his first film for Universal, Fields returned to the kind of character he loved best–a terminally broke and nomadic huckster who must live by his wits to stay one step ahead of the law. Owner of "Larson E. Whipsnade's Circus Giganticus," Fields is first seen hustling his caravan of wagons over the county line to

escape the police he had angered at his previous stop. While setting up tents in a new town, Fields is confronted by ventriloquist Bergen and his smart-aleck dummy Charlie McCarthy. The two are the bane of Fields' existence, but he cannot fire them because of a strange clause in their contract. Luckily for Fields, Bergen has decided to quit because he hasn't been paid in months. The ventriloquist quickly changes his mind, however, when he meets Fields' beautiful daughter, Moore. Charlie voices loud protests over Bergen's change of heart but is silenced when informed that Moore has a younger sister. Moore goes off to find her father, who is busy selling tickets out of a wagon. Fields seems to move in a dozen directions at once, passing out tickets, bilking customers, trying to avoid the heavy wooden flap that hangs above him from hitting his head, keeping his assistants out of his "lunch" (a bottle), battling a nasty little dog, getting his foot stuck in a bucket–all the while mumbling insults under his breath. Moore finally catches up with Fields and during their talk he is forced to grab a piece of rope, stick it under his nose, and adopt a phony German accent to disguise his identity from a creditor. Feeling sorry for her father, Moore tells him that a rich boy she has been dating, Bush, has proposed marriage. Fields sees this as an opportunity to bail out his financially ailing circus and urges his daughter to marry Bush. Moore doesn't really love Bush, but to help her father she decides to accept the proposal. Also enthusiastic about the marriage is Arledge, Fields' son, who has rejected his father's lifestyle and yearns for a higher station in life. The date for the wedding is soon set and it will take place at Bush's parents' mansion. Meanwhile, Moore has fallen in love with Bergen and the couple meet frequently in a moored hot-air balloon so that they can be alone. Moore hasn't the heart to tell Bergen she is going to marry Bush, so on the day of the wedding she asks her father to go to their meeting place and tell the ventriloquist for her. Always willing to take a dig at Bergen, Fields goes to the balloon for a chat with the ventriloquist and his dummy. Armed with a knife with which he pretends to whittle during the conversation, Fields takes swipes at the balloon's mooring rope when Bergen and Charlie aren't looking. Eventually the rope snaps and the pair soon find themselves floating into space. Asleep under some blankets in the corner of the basket is another ventriloquist's dummy, Mortimer Snerd, a dull-witted farm boy. As the trio float above, Moore drives to her wedding beneath them. Meanwhile, Fields dresses up in tie, top hat, and tails for his daughter's nuptials. Fields has Sutton drive him to the mansion in the circus chariot. Up in the balloon Bergen, Charlie, and Mortimer decide to parachute and they land in the car with Moore. The parachute covers the whole car and because Moore can't see she crashes the car into a gas pump. All four wind up in jail. Because Moore is about to marry the son of the town's most prestigious family, she is released. Eventually Bergen–who is heartbroken by Moore's impending marriage–and his dummies are set free and they ride off on a bicycle. Back at the mansion, Fields wanders through the stuffy, upper-crust crowd insulting everyone he meets. His son trails along behind begging Fields to behave himself. When Fields launches into a lengthy story about a snake who befriended him on the shore of Lake Titicaca, the groom's mother, Forbes, who has an aversion to snakes, faints at the mere mention of the reptile. Every time the woman comes to, Fields manages to work the word "snake" back into his story and Forbes passes out again. The worried wedding guests give Forbes sips of whiskey to revive her, and when another asks Fields what is wrong with the woman he replies, "Evidently she's had too much to drink." Fields then wanders into the mansion's game room where a young woman asks him, "How's your ping-pong?" Not missing a beat, Fields responds, "Fine, how's yours?" He soon enters a game of ping-pong with the woman's male companion. The contest is heated and other guests gather around to watch. Both men make incredible shots, but Fields is driven farther and farther away from the table in order to hit the ball. Eventually he is worked from the game room, through the dining room, and out to the patio. Fields takes one last vicious swat at the ping-pong ball and it shoots right into the mouth of one of the local dowagers. Fields extracts the ball with a smart swat of the bat to the back of the woman's neck, which makes the offending sphere shoot out of her mouth like a rocket. Meanwhile, Moore finally arrives at the wedding only to engage in a fight with her stuck-up groom who is deeply offended by her tardiness and her father. Moore tells Bush off and defends Fields. Arledge also rises to Fields' defense and the wedding is called off. The sheriff arrives on the scene, which is Fields, Moore, and Arledge's cue to mount the circus chariot and make a hasty escape. As in most of Fields' films, YOU CAN'T CHEAT AN HONEST MAN is a virtually plotless array of hilarious verbal and visual gags designed to make the most of the comedian's prodigious talents. The script was actually a reworking of two previous projects, a rejected screenplay titled "Grease Paint" written by H. M. Walker in 1933 with added plot lines from Fields' silent movie TWO FLAMING YOUTHS. Once again Fields wrote the story under the pseudonym of "Charles Bogle," but Universal and director Marshall removed several important scenes that Fields felt were essential to his character development. In the film, Fields seems to be an entirely unlikable character with little or no compassion for his workers or family. In the script, Fields began the film with a tender scene where his wife, a trapeze artist who has suffered a fall, dies in his arms. Another scene meant to show the tender, vulnerable side of Fields' character was to have occurred toward the end of the film outside the mansion where Fields bares his soul to his children and confirms his deep love for them–thus motivating them to rise to his defense. Fields was very upset about the changes and wrote several letters to producer Cowan demanding that the scenes be shot. Unfortunately, his complaints did no good and the film remained as it was. So disappointed was Fields that he refused to go on the road to promote what he felt was an "...embarrassment and humiliation." There was trouble from the start on the set of YOU CAN'T CHEAT AN HONEST MAN. Director Marshall–who admitted he didn't find Fields' brand of humor funny–couldn't get along with his star. In a scene where Anderson and Fields had to leave one of the circus wagons and walk down three steps to go to the shower (a trained elephant named Queenie who sprays water on the command of: "Give, Queenie!"), director Marshall made them take the walk down the steps eight times. On the ninth take, Fields finally had had enough and locked himself and Anderson inside the wagon and drank martinis–refusing to come out for several hours. Despite pleading and yelling, Marshall was eventually forced to cancel the day's shooting, leaving Fields and Anderson alone on the deserted set. To solve the problems between star and director, Universal brought in director Eddie Cline–whom Fields liked–to direct Fields' scenes while Marshall handled everything else. YOU CAN'T CHEAT AN HONEST MAN also gave moviegoers a chance to *see* Fields and Bergen's wooden pal Charlie square off instead of just *listening* to them on the radio. Fields and Charlie had developed a quite popular and funny "feud" on Bergen's radio show and Universal was delighted at the chance to pull in Bergen's large and loyal audience at the box office. Fields and Bergen's feud was comedy only and the two were great friends, each respecting the talents of the other. Fields was also outraged by the haphazard presentation of Bergen's scenes in the film and again complained to the studio that, "Edgar Bergen doesn't have to be whisked around in a basket to be funny." Despite all of Fields' disgust, YOU CAN'T CHEAT AN HONEST MAN is an extremely funny film which contains several classic moments of the Great One's brand of comic genius.

p, Lester Cowan; d, George Marshall, (uncredited) Eddie Cline; w, George Marion, Jr., Richard Mack, Everett Freeman (based on a story by Charles Bogle 'W.C. Fields'); ph, Milton Krasner; ed, Otto Ludwig (uncredited); md, Charles Previn; art d, Jack Otterson; set d, R.A. Gausman; cos, Vera West; m/l, "Camptown Races," Stephen Collins Foster, "Hi, Charlie McCarthy."

Comedy   **(PR:A   MPAA:NR)**

YOU CAN'T DO THAT TO ME   (SEE: MAISIE GOES TO RENO, 1944)

YOU CAN'T DO WITHOUT LOVE**   (1946, Brit.) 74m COL bw

Vera Lynn (*Vera Baker*), Donald Stewart (*Michael Thorne*), Mary Clare (*Mrs. Trout*), Frederick Leister (*Hampton*), Richard Murdoch (*Illusionist*), Phyllis Stanley (*Lucille*), Cyril Smith (*Joe*), Mavis Villiers (*Mabel*), Peggy Anne, Jeannette Redgrave, Patricia Owens.

Decent song farce in which Lynn plays a would-be singer desperate at having a shot to impress producer Stewart with her abilities. Her chance comes at a benefit concert that is also the scene of an attempted kidnap of Stewart by a gang after a priceless Rembrandt, when she thwarts the rascals and wins over the audience with her thrushing.

p, Ben Henry, Culley Forde; d, Walter Forde; w, Howard Irving Young, Peter Fraser, Margaret Kennedy, Emery Bonnet (based on the story by Fraser); ph, Otto Heller; md, Harry Bidgood; art d, George Provis.

Musical/Comedy   **(PR:A   MPAA:NR)**

YOU CAN'T ESCAPE*   (1955, Brit.) 77m Forth/ABF-Pathe bw

Noelle Middleton (*Kay March*), Guy Rolfe (*David Anstruther*), Robert Urquhart (*Peter Darwin*), Peter Reynolds (*Rodney Nixon*), Elizabeth Kentish (*Claire Segar*), Barbara Cavan (*Aunt Sue*), Martin Boddey (*Inspector Crane*), Thorley Walters (*Chadwick*), Jacqueline Mackenzie (*Mrs. Baggerley*), Llewellyn Rees, Paddy Brannigan, Hal Osmond, Sam Kydd, Barbara Leake, Oliver Johnston, Wensley Pithey, Edward Forsyth, Alec Finter, Walter Horsbrugh, Gerald Andersen.

A novelist goes beserk in this stilted attempt at a suspense thriller in which Urquhart leaves his typewriter long enough to kill an old lover and then a blackmailer. His fiancee, Middleton, originally agrees to help him get rid of the bodies, but when Urquhart starts to incriminate innocent people, she turns back and is in danger of becoming his next victim. Nothing much to get excited about.

p, Robert Hall; d, Wilfred Eades; w, Hall, Doreen Montgomery (based on the novel *She Died Young* by Alan Kennington); ph, Norman Warwick.

Crime/Drama   **(PR:A   MPAA:NR)**

YOU CAN'T ESCAPE FOREVER*½   (1942) 77m WB bw

George Brent (*Steve "Mitch" Mitchell*), Brenda Marshall (*Laurie Abbott*), Gene Lockhart (*Carl Robelink*), Roscoe Karns (*"Mac" McTurk*), Edward Ciannelli (*Boss Greer*), Paul Harvey (*Maj. Turner*), Edith Barrett (*Lucille*), Harry Hayden (*Judge Hardaker*), Charles Halton (*Charley Gates*), Don DeFore (*Reporter Davis*), George Meeker (*Cummings*), Joseph Downing (*Varney*), Erville Alderson (*Mr. Crowder*), Fay Helm (*Kirsty Lundstrom*), Bill Edwards (*Radcliffe*), Dick Elliott (*Meeker*), Joseph Crehan (*Warden*), Dick Wessel (*Moxie*), Paul Newlan (*Louie*), John Dilson (*Pop*), Edward McWade (*Jimmy*).

Demoted newspaperman Brent teams up with fellow reporter and girl friend Marshall to take a stab at exposing the biggest crime chief in the city. This was the third time this exact story had been brought to the screen, beginning with HI NELLIE (1934), and it's amazing to see how little this one differs from its predecessors. Possible exceptions are a few comic touches, like Brent being forced to write a "broken hearts" column when he messes up.

p, Mark Hellinger; d, Jo Graham; w, Fred Niblo, Jr., Hector Chevigny (based on the story by Roy Chanslor); ph, James Van Trees, Tony Gaudio; ed, Frank Magee; art d, Stanley Fleischer; cos, Milo Anderson.

Crime/Drama   **(PR:A   MPAA:NR)**

YOU CAN'T FOOL AN IRISHMAN*   (1950, Ireland) 67m Vandyke/Bell Pictures bw (GB: THE STRANGERS CAME)

Tommy Duggan (*Stefan Wurlitz*), Shirl Conway (*Jane McDonald*), Shamus Locke (*Tom O'Flaherty*), Tony Quinn (*Hotelier*), Reed de Rouen (*Manager*), Eve Eacott (*Dona del Monte*), Josephine Fitzgerald (*Widow McDermott*), Sheila Martin (*Mary Laffey*), Geoffrey Goodheart (*Joe Bantham*), Seamus Harty, Gabriel Fallon, Robert Mooney, Ivan Craig.

The only recommendation for this sorry excuse for a film is that it was made in Ireland and so has plenty of a flavorful Irish background and even a couple of refreshing performances from Dublin talent. Otherwise the plight of an American producer coming to Ireland to make a picture about the life of St. Patrick is pretty lame. As the filmmaker, Duggan arrives in Dublin to discover himself without the backing to go on with production until a waiter agrees to put up the money in exchange for a starring role. Most of the comedy borders too close to slapstick to be very effective.

p, Roger Proudlock, Michael Healy; d, Alfred Travers; w, Healy, Travers, Tommy Duggan; ph, Cyril Aradoff; m, Eamonn O'Galehur.

Comedy   **(PR:A   MPAA:NR)**

YOU CAN'T FOOL YOUR WIFE*½   (1940) 68m RKO bw

Lucille Ball (*Clara Hinklin/Mercedes Vasquez*), James Ellison (*Andrew Hinklin*), Robert Coote (*Battincourt*), Virginia Vale (*Sally*), Emma Dunn (*Mom Fields*), Elaine Shepard (*Peggy*), William Halligan (*J.R. Gillespie*), Oscar O'Shea (*Chaplain*), Rosina Galli (*Mama Brentoni*), Charles Lane (*Salesman*), Norman Mayes (*Porter*), Patsy O'Byrne (*Hotel Maid*), Charlie Hall (*Bellhop*), Del Henderson (*Hotel Manager*), Minerva Urecal (*Mrs. Doolittle*), Leo Cleary (*Mr. Doolittle*), Harrison Green (*Sullivan*), Max Wagner (*Burglar*), Hobart Cavanaugh (*Potts*), Walter Sande (*Young Gillespie*), Walter Fenner (*Walker*), Irving Bacon (*Lippincott*).

It's the old story of the mother-in-law getting in the way of an otherwise successful marriage. This time it's Dunn putting her nose in the affairs of Ball and Ellison once too often, forcing the two to separate only to have them seek each other out at a masquerade party. Decent performances and a good line here and there were at the mercy of an uneventful script.

p, Cliff Reid; d, Ray McCarey; w, Jerry Cady (based on the story "The Romantic Mr. Hinklin" by McCarey, Richard Carroll); ph, J. Roy Hunt; m, Roy Webb; ed, Theron Warth; art d, Van Nest Polglase; cos, Edward Stevenson.

Comedy   **(PR:A   MPAA:NR)**

YOU CAN'T GET AWAY WITH MURDER***   (1939) 78m WB-FN bw

Humphrey Bogart (*Frank Wilson*), Billy Halop (*Johnnie Stone*), Gale Page (*Madge Stone*), John Litel (*Attorney Carey*), Henry Travers (*Pop*), Harvey Stephens (*Fred Burke*), Harold Huber (*Scappa*), Joseph Sawyer (*Red*), Joseph Downing (*Smitty*), George E. Stone (*Toad*), Joseph King (*Principal Keeper*), Joseph Crehan (*Warden*), John Ridgely (*Gas Station Attendant*), Herbert Rawlinson (*District Attorney*), Lane Chandler, Robert E. Homans (*Guards*), Eddy Chandler (*Keeper*), Frank Faylen (*Spieler*), Robert Strange, Robert Emmett O'Connor (*Detectives*), Tom Dugan, Eddic "Rochester" Anderson (*Convicts*), Emory Parnell (*Cop*).

In three years, between DEAD END in 1937, and HIGH SIERRA, in 1940, Bogart made 18 films; in 11 he played a gangster and in nine he died at the end. This film qualifies on both counts, giving us a forgettable 1939 gangster picture in which Bogart ends up going to the electric chair. He plays a hardened criminal who takes on young Halop as his apprentice in stealing. They start with the robbery of a gas station which goes according to plan. Halop is ecstatic over the thrills and rewards of his new career, and objects little when Bogart orders him to go out and steal a pistol for their next job. Halop takes the gun belonging to Stephens, his sister's fiance. The duo stick up a pawnshop, and when things don't go as planned, Bogart shoots the proprietor. The bullets are traced and Stephens is arrested and quickly convicted and sentenced to death. Halop wants to confess, but Bogart terrorizes him into silence. Later, Halop and Bogart are arrested when they try to steal a car, and they are sent to Sing Sing. In prison, Halop is befriended by Travers, the kindly old prison librarian, who tries to persuade the boy to confess. When Bogart learns of this, he forces Halop to accompany him and two other convicts, Downing and Huber, in an escape attempt. Bogart plans to murder the boy first chance he gets. As they begin their move, Halop drops a piece of paper with a full confession in Travers' cell.

The breakout fails, the other two men are killed, and Bogart and Halop are cornered in a boxcar. Bogart confronts Halop with the confession he recovered from Travers' cell, and, after hiding it, he shoots the boy down while the police outside shoot at the boxcar. Bogart then walks out of the boxcar hands over head and tells the police that they killed Halop. Halop isn't quite dead, though. He recovers the confession and tells the whole story to the warden before dying. Stephens is pardoned and Bogart is sent to the chair instead. Hardly the most memorable role of Bogart's career, but well-done in the usual craftsmanlike manner of Warner Bros. films. Halop is good, too, in another of the juvenile-delinquent-with-a-heart- of-gold roles he first played in DEAD END and which he was forced to repeat through innumerable Dead End Kids and Bowery Boys movies. The usual cast of Warner contract players are in evidence, as well as a number of good perfomances, particularly Stone and Travers. Most importantly, though, Bogart does his usual tough gangster in his usual tough manner, and that is always worth watching.

p, Samuel Bischoff; d, Lewis Seiler; w, Robert Buckner, Don Ryan, Kenneth Gamet (based on the play "Chalked Out" by Warden Lewis E. Lawes, Jonathan Finn); ph, Sol Polito; m, Heinz Roemheld; ed, James Gibbon; art d, Hugo Reticker; cos, Milo Anderson.

Crime   **(PR:A-C MPAA:NR)**

YOU CAN'T HAVE EVERYTHING***   (1937) 99m FOX bw

Alice Faye (Judith Poe Wells), Harry Ritz, Al Ritz, Jimmy Ritz (The Ritz Brothers, Themselves), Don Ameche (George Macrea), Charles Winninger (Sam Gordon), Louise Hovick 'Gypsy Rose Lee' (Lulu Riley), David Rubinoff (Himself), Tony Martin (Bobby Walker), Arthur Treacher (Bevins), Phyllis Brooks (Evelyn Moore), Louis Prima (Orchestra Leader), Tip, Tap, Toe 'Samuel Green, Ted Fraser, Ray Winfield' (Specialty Dancers), George Humbert (Romano), Wally Vernon (Jerry), Jed Prouty (Mr. Whiteman), George Davis, Frank Puglia (Waiters), Paul Hurst (Truck Driver), Frank Yaconelli (Accordion Player), Nick Moro (Guitar Player), Dorothy Christy (Blonde), Gordon "Bill" Elliott (Lulu's Bathing Companion), Margaret Fielding (Miss Barkow), Robert Murphy (Alderman Barney Callahan), Inez Palange (Mrs. Romano), Joan Davis (Dance Bit), Si Jenks (Janitor), Jane Kerr, Mary Gordon, Bonita Weber (Scrubwomen), Clara Blandick (Townswoman), Robert Lowery (Copilot), June Gale (Girl in YWCA), Hank Mann (Cab Driver), Jayne Regan (Stewardess), Lynne Berkeley (Joan), William Mathieson (Bagpiper), Thomas Pogue (Standee), Claudia Coleman (Matron in YWCA), Sam Ash (Publicity Agent), Howard Cantonwine (Tony).

Faye and Ameche made six films together, and this enjoyable, lighthearted musical was the first. Faye, a struggling writer and direct descendant of Edgar Allan Poe, goes out for dinner, ordering more food than she can pay for. She tries to sing for her supper, but this will not do and Faye must carry a sandwich board advertising the restaurant. Gallant Ameche, inebriated, offers to pay her check but Faye will not allow this. Faye confides in him that she has tried to sell her play to an important producer (Winninger) but has yet to hear anything. Ameche, who knows Winninger, goes back to his apartment where he is met by Hovick (famed stripper Gypsy Rose Lee's real name, making her film debut). Hovick is furious, as Ameche forgot all about their date for the evening. The next day, Ameche has Winninger look at Faye's opus entitled "North Wind." The play is wretched, but Ameche is able to talk Winninger into paying Faye $250 for "North Wind's" rights. With hopes of romancing the writer, Ameche has Hovick take a vacation while he gives Faye a part in the new production. Hovick returns after the musical's opening, telling Faye to stay away from her man. Though Faye is in love with Ameche, she leaves town. Ameche finally breaks up with Hovick, then tries to find Faye. Ameche turns her play into a musical, hoping somehow this will lure her back. Faye has taken back her old job clerking at a music store, and is surprised to find sheet music bearing her name. She puts two and two together and returns to New York, where her work is the toast of Broadway and Ameche lovingly welcomes her back. This is an enjoyable musical, filled out with a zany subplot involving the Ritz Brothers (in their third film with Faye), as comic performers who get into more than their share of trouble. Faye and Ameche make a good team, playing out the simple plot with grace and style. Faye's voice is in excellent form, and she sings with verve. Hovick/Lee plays her nasty role with a good sense of fun, giving her well-known gusto to the supporting role. Studio officials were worried that Lee's former profession might prejudice potential audiences for YOU CAN'T HAVE EVERYTHING, thus the use of her real name (which fooled no one). A very young Martin makes an early film appearance as a nightclub singer. Shortly after the production was finished he and Faye were married, though the marriage broke up in 1940. The songs include: "Danger, Love at Work," "Please Pardon Us We're In Love" (Mack Gordon, Harry Revel, sung by Faye), "The Loveliness of You" (Gordon, Revel, sung by Martin), "You Can't Have Everything," "Afraid to Dream," "Long Underwear" (Gordon, Revel), "It's a Southern Holiday" (Louis Prima, Jack Loman, Dave Franklin, performed by Prima and His Band), "Rhythm on the Radio" (Prima, performed by Prima and His Band).

p, Darryl F. Zanuck; d, Norman Taurog; w, Harry Tugend, Jack Yellen, Karl Tunberg (based on a story by Gregory Ratoff); ph, Lucien Andriot; ed, Hansen Fritch; md, David Buttolph; art d, Duncan Cramer; set d, Thomas Little; cos, Royer; ch, Harry Losee.

Musical   **Cas.**   **(PR:A MPAA:NR)**

YOU CAN'T HAVE EVERYTHING, 1972
(SEE: CACTUS IN THE SNOW, 1972)

YOU CAN'T RATION LOVE*   (1944) 78m PAR bw

Betty Rhodes (Betty), Johnnie Johnston (John "Two-Point" Simpson), Bill Edwards (Pete), Marjorie Weaver (Marian), Marie Wilson (Bubbles), Johnnie "Scat" Davis (Kewpie), Mabel Paige (Miss Hawks), Jean Wallace (Madge), Roland Dupree (Pickles), Christine Forsythe (Christine), D'Artega All-Girl Orchestra.

The inane basis for this weak musical was having college girls being forced to ration their dates because of the unavailability of eligible men in wartime America. Suddenly the biggest wimp on campus becomes a stud when Rhodes decides to date him as part of a joke. She helps to bring out the ladies man lurking underneath Johnston's nerdish exterior, and the first thing you know, every girl on campus starts to fall for him. Songs and musical numbers include: "Love Is This" (Jerry Seelen, Lester Lee, sung by Johnston, Lee), "Ooh-Ah-Oh," "Look What You Did to Me" (Seelen, Lee, sung by Johnston), "How Did It Happen?" (Seelen, Lee, sung by Wilson, Davis, with acrobatic dancing by Dupree and Forsythe), "Louise" (Leo Robin, Richard A. Whiting, sung by Rhodes, Johnston), "Nothing Can Replace a Man," (sung by Rhodes). The D'Artega All-Girl Orchestra performs a medley of three numbers: "I Don't Want to Walk Without You" (Frank Loesser, Jule Styne), "Oodles of Noodles" (Jimmy Dorsey), and "One O'Clock Jump" (Count Basie, Harry James).

p, Michel Kraike; d, Lester Fuller; w, Val Burton, Hal Fimberg (based on the story by Muriel Roy Bolton); ph, Stuart Thompson; ed, Tom Neff; md, Irvin Talbot; art d, Hans Dreier, Walter Tyler.

Musical   **(PR:A MPAA:NR)**

YOU CAN'T RUN AWAY FROM IT**   (1956) 95m COL c

June Allyson (Ellie Andrews), Jack Lemmon (Peter Warne), Charles Bickford (A.A. Andrews), Paul Gilbert (George Shapely), Jim Backus (Danker), Stubby Kaye (Fred Toten), Henny Youngman (1st Driver), Allyn Joslyn (Gordon), Jacques Scott (Ballarino), Walter Baldwin (1st Proprietor), Byron Foulger (Billings), Richard Cutting (Hotel Manager), Howard McNear, Elvia Allman (2nd Proprietor and Wife), Louise Beavers (Maid), Raymond Greenleaf (Minister), Edwin Chandler (TV Announcer), Jack Albertson (3rd Proprietor), Queenie Smith (Elderly Lady), William Forrest (Captain), Frank Sully (Red), Dub Taylor (Joe), Steve Benton (2nd Driver), Bill Walker (Norville), Herb Vigran, Larry Blake (Detectives).

Remaking classic films as musicals seems to be a hit-and-miss affair. SILK STOCKINGS was a fine adaptation of NINOTCHKA, but YOU CAN'T RUN AWAY FROM IT is another story. This reworking of Frank Capra's IT HAPPENED ONE NIGHT is an unsuccessful attempt that never approaches the original film in humor or charm. The plot is essentially unchanged. Lemmon takes the Clark Gable role, as a reporter who accidentally falls onto the story of the year. He meets Allyson (in Claudette Colbert's part), a runaway heiress who's trying to escape from her father Bickford's grasp. Allyson wants to marry Scott, so Lemmon promises to help her if she'll give him exclusive rights to her story. Just about every scene is reprised from IT HAPPENED ONE NIGHT as Lemmon and Allyson come to fall in love in the course of their travels. Bickford takes a liking to Lemmon, realizing that the man wants no part of the reward for delivering Allyson. Finally Allyson takes her father's advice, and runs away from the altar to marry the man she really loves: Lemmon. YOU CAN'T RUN AWAY FROM IT seems to reverse everything that made IT HAPPENED ONE NIGHT such a wonderful film. The simple black-and-white Depression-era look has been tossed aside for big-screen Technicolor, updating the story to 1956. The results clearly show why new and bigger doesn't always mean better. This is a light story that the additions of color and song simply can't improve. Rather than add to plot development, the songs slow the pace, sapping the film of a much needed energetic flow. Powell's direction doesn't help much either; a heavy-handed job where a light touch was necessary. Lemmon actually fares well in the part, wisely avoiding any imitation of Gable's original performance. He gives the role some good comic flair, playing well off Allyson, though it's just not enough to make the film work. The Gene DePaul and Johnny Mercer-penned songs include: "You Can't Run Away from It" (sung by The Four Aces), "Howdy, Friends and Neighbors!" (sung by Stubby Kaye, Allyson, Lemmon, ensemble), "Temporarily" (sung by Lemmon, Allyson), "Thumbin' a Ride" (sung by Lemmon, Allyson), "Scarecrow Ballet" (sung by Allyson), "Old Reporters Never Die" (sung by Lemmon), "Finale" (sung by chorus).

p&d, Dick Powell; w, Claude Binyon, Robert Riskin (based on the screenplay "It Happened One Night" by Riskin, from a short story, "Night Bus," by Samuel Hopkins Adams); ph, Charles Lawton, Jr. (CinemaScope, Technicolor); m, George Duning; ed, Al Clark; md, Morris Stoloff; art d, Robert Peterson; set d, William Kiernan, Robert Priestly; cos, Jean Louis; ch, Robert Sidney.

Musical   **(PR:A MPAA:NR)**

YOU CAN'T RUN FAR   (SEE: WHEN THE CLOCK STRIKES, 1961)

YOU CAN'T SEE 'ROUND CORNERS**   (1969, Aus.) 93m UNIV c

Ken Shorter (*Frankie McCoy*), Rowena Wallace (*Margie Harris*), Carmen Duncan (*Myra Neilson*), Judith Fisher (*Peg Clancy*), Lyndall Barbour (*Mrs. McCoy*), Slim DeGrey (*Mick "Patto" Patterson*).

Young misanthrope Shorter is on the make for the pure and wholesome Wallace, who is glad to receive the man's advances until he becomes an army deserter. Originally a bookie, shorter is inducted into the Viet Nam War, involved in a big brawl, and soon left disillusioned and in search of his former life. But the bookie trade isn't too rewarding, and neither are his renewed attempts at romancing Wallace. He robs a butcher and seeks a life of fast pleasure, sinking quickly into a dark abyss that leaves him with a carved-up face after another brawl. Though a valiant attempt is made at creating a powerful urban drama, the narrowly developed characters and cliches of plot and dialog make it a superficial film.

p, Peter Summerton; d, David Cahill; w, Richard Lane (based on the novel by Jon Cleary); m, Thomas Tycho.

Drama   (PR:A   MPAA:NR)

YOU CAN'T SLEEP HERE   (SEE: I WAS A MALE WAR BRIDE, 1949)

YOU CAN'T STEAL LOVE   (SEE: MURPH THE SURF, 1974)

YOU CAN'T TAKE IT WITH YOU****   (1938) 126m COL bw

Jean Arthur (*Alice Sycamore*), Lionel Barrymore (*Martin Vanderhof*), James Stewart (*Tony Kirby*), Edward Arnold (*Anthony P. Kirby*), Mischa Auer (*Kolenkhov*), Ann Miller (*Essie Carmichael*), Spring Byington (*Penny Sycamore*), Samuel S. Hinds (*Paul Sycamore*), Donald Meek (*Poppins*), H.B. Warner (*Ramsey*), Halliwell Hobbes (*DePinna*), Dub Taylor (*Ed Carmichael*), Mary Forbes (*Mrs. Anthony Kirby*), Lillian Yarbo (*Rheba*), Eddie Anderson (*Donald*), Clarence Wilson (*John Blakely*), Joseph Swickard (*Professor*), Ann Doran (*Maggie O'Neill*), Christian Rub (*Schmidt*), Bodil Rosing (*Mrs. Schmidt*), Charles Lane (*Henderson*), Harry Davenport (*Judge*), Pierre Watkin, Edwin Maxwell, Russell Hicks (*Attorneys*), Byron Foulger (*Kirby's Assistant*), James Flavin (*Jailer*), Ian Wolfe (*Kirby's Secretary*), Irving Bacon (*Henry*), Chester Clute (*Hammond*), Pert Kelton, Kit Guard (*Inmates*), James Burke, Ward Bond (*Detectives*), Edward Hearn (*Court Attendant*), Edward Keane (*Board Member*), John Ince, Edward Peil (*Neighbors*), Dick Curtis (*Strong Arm Man*), Wallis Clark (*Hughes*), Paul Irving (*Office Manager*), Eddie Kane (*Kirby's Attorney*), Gene Morgan, Lou Davis, Lester Dorr, William Arnold, Jack Gardner, Bill Dill, William Lally (*Reporters*), Stanley Andrews (*Attorney*), Walter Walker (*Mr. Leach*), Robert Greig (*Lord Melville*), Gladys Blake (*Mary*), Eddy Chandler (*G-Man*), Edwin Stanley (*Executive*), Edward Earle (*Bank Manager*), Boyd Irwin (*Attorney*), Pat West (*Expressman*), Frank Shannon (*Mac*), John Hamilton (*Capt. Drake*), Laura Treadwell (*Mrs. Drake*), Doris Rankin (*Mrs. Leach*), Hilda Plowright (*Lady Melville*), Blanche Payson (*Matron*), James Farley (*Police Sergeant*), Eddie Fetherston, Bess Flowers, Beatrice Curtis, Beatrice Blinn, Bessie Wade, Eva McKenzie, Dorothy Vernon, Tina Marshall, Betty Farrington, Howard Davies, Charles Brinley, George Pearce, Eddie Randolph, Frank Austin, Harry Bailey, Fred Parker, Bert Starkey, Frankie Raymond, Stella LeSaint, Belle Johnstone, Joe Bernard, Gale Ronn, Margaret Mann (*Neighbors*), John Tyrrell (*Dopey*), Lee Phelps (*Bailiff*), James Millican, Bid Wiser, Jack Grant, Bruce Mitchell (*Policemen*), Vernon Dent (*Expressman*), Roland Dupree, Dorothy Babb, Joe Geil, Gloria Browne, Patty Thomas, Will Wolfstone (*Dancers*), Ann Cornwall (*Blakely's Secretary*), Larry Wheat (*Secretary*), Eugene Anderson, Jr. (*Bobby*), Charles Hamilton, Charles MacMurphy (*Guards*), Frank Mills, Sid D'Albrook (*Trustees*), Nick Copeland (*Barber*), Clarence L. Sherwood (*Drunk*), Alex Woloshin (*Russian General in Jail*), Dick Rush (*Bank Guard*), Harry Hollingsworth (*Doorman*), Jimmy Anderson (*Bank Porter*), Dick French, Carlton Griffin, Carlie Taylor Bruce Sidney, Harry Stafford (*Bank Clerks*), Arthur Murray (*Elevator Boy*), Joe Bordeaux (*Taxi Driver*), Mario Rotolo (*Accordion Player*), Dutch Hendrian (*Ice Man*), Oliver Eckhardt, Homer Dickinson, Ralph McCullough, Harry Semels, Cy Schindell, Kit Guard, Robert Kortman, Lou King, Ernie Shields, Jessie Graves, Clive Morgan, Colonel Starrett Ford, Victor Travers, Wedgewood Nowell (*Men*), Alice Keating, Nell Craig, Nell Roy, Florence Dudley, Kitty Lanahan, Pearl Varvell, Gertrude Weber, Kay Desleys, Jane Talent, Georgia O'Dell, Rosemary Theby, Dagmar Oakland, Almeda Fowler, Hilda Rhodes (*Women*).

Director Frank Capra took the phenomenally successful Kaufman-Hart stage play *You Can't Take It With You* and turned it into a phenomenally successful film—it garnered Capra his third Oscar for Best Director and the film won Best Picture that year as well (it was also nominated for Best Supporting Actress (Byington), Screenplay, Cinematography, Editing, and Sound Recording). Barrymore is the eccentric patriach of a clan of frustrated artists who had decided to retire from the rat-race 30 years before and use his fortune to encourage friends and family to pursue vocations that really interest them. He has taken up painting, which he does badly, but at least he enjoys himself. His daughter, Byington, has taken up writing mystery novels, which she was inspired to do when a typewriter was left on

the doorstep one day. Byington's husband Hinds tinkers with explosives in the basement working towards perfecting the Roman Candle and the rocket. Their daughter Miller desires to be a ballet dancer and her cynical Russian teacher, Auer, follows her around barking instructions. Miller's husband Taylor practices playing the xylophone, while Barrymore's friend Meek invents new toys and party masks. The huge house is a frenzy of bizarre activities and in the center of hit all is Barrymore's other granddaughter, Arthur, who is pursuing a relatively normal life by working as a receptionist in the offices of Arnold, a powerful, very dour businessman who has been known to make shady deals and wants to have Barrymore's mansion torn down so he can build on the property. Arthur is in love with Arnold's son Stewart, and while Stewart is amused at her family's eccentricities, he fears that his father will never approve of a girl from such a family. The couple decide to arrange a dinner between the families to be held at Arthur's house, and Barrymore commands the clan to tone down their normal antics as to make a good impression on Arnold and his stuffy wife Forbes. Unfortunately, there is confusion over what night the dinner date is to be and Stewart shows up with his parents a day early. As Arthur and her family rush around to prepare a decent dinner for their guests, Arnold and Forbes become mortified at the strange goings-on. Before the guests can leave, Hinds accidentally sets off a flurry of fireworks in the basement and the whole neighborhood is treated to the show. The police arrive and cart everyone off to jail–including an outraged Arnold and Forbes. Luckily, everyone is eventually released by a bemused judge, but Stewart's parents force him to break up with Arthur. Worried that she will never have a normal life if she stays in the house, Arthur decides to leave, but she is dissuaded by Barrymore who tells her he's decided to sell the mansion to Arnold and move the clan to the country. Meanwhile, Stewart who is angry with his father because of the situation with Arthur, and the fact that he has discovered his father's shady business dealings, lets loose with a tirade of insults at Arnold and concludes that his father has become a heartless monster. Stewart then leaves to join Arthur as her family is being moved out of the mansion. As Barrymore sits on a box and surveys his empty home, Arnold arrives for a heartfelt chat with his nemesis. Stewart's harangue struck a cord in Arnold and he has decided to give up the pursuit of money and live again. He turns the house back over to Barrymore and the former enemies celebrate by staging a delightful harmonica duel that attracts the whole family and the film ends happily as they all share a laugh together. YOU CAN'T TAKE IT WITH YOU is a hysterically funny and entertaining film packed with so much loony activity that there is literally a laugh-a-minute. Capra assembled a superb cast of players and each scores solidly in their roles. Perhaps the most amusing character in the film is Meek, a milquetoast of a man who enjoys sneaking up on family members and scaring them with his latest Halloween mask. YOU CAN'T TAKE IT WITH YOU was the first film veteran actor Barrymore was in where the crippling arthritis which would soon put him in a wheelchair became evident. Barrymore, at this time 60 years old, needed crutches to move around. To remedy the situation, Capra had a fake leg cast put on the actor and explained it by having him state that he broke his leg while sliding down a bannister–just the kind of reckless, carefree act one would expect from his character. Fans of character actor Dub Taylor, who has appeared in hundreds of films and television shows, made his acting debut in this film. Out of work and his wife expecting a baby, Taylor saw the casting call for a xylophone player in the trade papers and auditioned for the part. Capra hired the young musician, and though he already knew how to play the xylophone, put him on salary a few months before shooting started to take "lessons" so that Taylor would have enough money when the baby arrived. Capra knew he had a big hit on his hands and eagerly awaited the gala premiere. Tragically, on the very night of the big event Capra was called from the theater and rushed to the hospital where his young son Johnny had just had his tonsils removed. During his recovery the boy had developed a massive blood clot in his brain and died–all the subsequent acclaim and awards paled by comparison.

p&d, Frank Capra; w, Robert Riskin (based on the play by George S. Kaufman, Moss Hart); ph, Joseph Walker; m, Dimitri Tiomkin; ed, Gene Havlick; md, Morris Stoloff; art d, Stephen Goosson; cos, Bernard Newman, Irene.

Comedy   **Cas.**   (PR:A   MPAA:NR)

YOU CAN'T TAKE MONEY   (SEE: INTERNES CAN'T TAKE MONEY, 1937)

YOU CAN'T WIN 'EM ALL   (SEE: ONCE YOU KISS A STRANGER, 1969)

YOU CAN'T WIN 'EM ALL*½   (1970, Brit.) 97m COL c

Tony Curtis (*Adam Dyer*), Charles Bronson (*Josh Corey*), Michele Mercier (*Aila*), Gregoire Aslan (*Osman Bey*), Fikret Hakan (*Col. Elci*), Salih Guney (*Capt. Enver*), Patrick Magee (*General*), Tony Bonner (*Reese*), John Acheson (*Davis*), John Alderson (*U.S. Army Major*), Horst Janson (*Woller*), Leo Gordon (*Bolek*), Reed De Rouen (*U.S. Navy Chief Petty Officer*), Paul Stassino (*Gunner Major*), Suna Keskin (*Girl in Cafe*), Yuskel Gozen (*Papadopoulos*), Henia Halil (*Madam*), Howard Goorney, Erol Koskin, Ken Buckle, Terry Yorke, Mumtaz Alpaslan, Manny Michael.

Another in the long list of unexciting Bronson outings. Here he is teamed with Curtis as a couple of would-be soldiers of fortune in 1920 Turkey, during the demise of the Ottoman Empire. They agree to escort three girls of important parentage and a shipment of gold to safety, but their greed gets the better of them. However, they are such bunglers that they lose some of their loot and get robbed of the rest, meanwhile losing the woman both had their eyes on. Surprisingly, they play well off each other, with Curtis the clown to Bronson's hardened man of action, but this is not enough to keep the script from residing in Dullsville.

p, Gene Corman, Harold Buck; d, Peter Collinson; w, Leo V. Gordon; ph, Kenneth Higgins (Panavision, Technicolor); m, Bert Kaempfert; ed, Raymond Foulton; md, Muir Matheson; art d, Seamus Flannery, cos, Dinah Greet, Leyla Suren; m/l, title song, Kaempfert, Herbert Rehbein; makeup, Freddie Williamson.

Adventure   **(PR:C   MPAA:PG)**

YOU DON'T NEED PAJAMAS AT ROSIE'S
                          (SEE: FIRST TIME, THE, 1969)

YOU FOR ME½   (1952) 71m MGM bw

Peter Lawford (*Tony Brown*), Jane Greer (*Katie McDermad*), Gig Young (*Dr. Jeff Chadwick*), Paula Corday (*Lucille Brown*), Howard Wendell (*Oliver Wherry*), Otto Hulett (*Hugo McDermad*), Barbara Brown (*Edna McDermad*), Barbara Ruick (*Ann Elcott*), Kathryn Card (*Nurse Vogel*), Tommy Farrell (*Rollie Cobb*), Paul Smith (*Frank Elcott*), Helen Winston (*Flora Adams*), Elaine Stewart (*Girl in Club Car*), Perry Sheehan (*Nurse*), Stephan Chase (*Bretherton*), Ned Glass (*Harlow Douglas*), Nikki Justin (*Maid*), Martha Wentworth (*Lucille's Mother*), Jerry Hausner (*Patient*), John Rosser (*Brill*), John Close, Robert Smiley (*Cops*), Ivan Browning (*Pullman Porter*), Hal Smith (*Malcolm*), Alvy Moore (*Friend*), Ralph Grosh (*Photographer*), Joann Arnold, Diann James, Marjorie Jackson, Kathy Qualen (*Nurses*), Tommy Walker (*Elevator Operator*), Alan Harris (*Court Clerk*), Julia Dean (*Aunt Clara*).

Lawford once again, as in JUST THIS ONCE, plays the suave millionaire playboy with the seemingly sole interest of having fun and pursuing women. Here he is placed in a hospital that his donations have kept running, after having his seat filled with buckshot in a hunting accident. But his reception from nurse Greer is far from that given to a VIP as Lawford expected. To keep his money coming in, head doctor Young has Greer turn on her charms, which she does though her sights are set on Young. Nothing pretentious intended, but director Weis kept things moving in a fast and lighthearted pace for an amiable entertainment.

p, Henry Berman; d, Don Weis; w, William Roberts; ph, Paul C. Vogel; ed, Newell P. Kimlin; md, Alberto Colombo; art d, Cedric Gibbons, Eddie Imazu; set d, Edwin B. Willis, Alfred A. Spencer.

Comedy   **(PR:A   MPAA:NR)**

YOU GOTTA STAY HAPPY***   (1948) 100m Rampart-William
                                                    Dozier/UNIV bw

Joan Fontaine (*Dee Dee Dillwood*), James Stewart (*Marvin Payne*), Eddie Albert (*Bullets Booker*), Roland Young (*Ralph Tutwiler*), Willard Parker (*Henry Benson*), Halliwell Hobbes (*Martin*), Stanley Prager (*Jack Samuels*), Mary Forbes (*Aunt Martha*), Edith Evanson (*Mrs. Racknell*), Peter Roman (*Barnabas*), Porter Hall (*Mr. Caslon*), Marcy McGuire (*Georgia Goodrich*), Percy Kilbride (*Mr. Hacknell*), William Bakewell (*Dick Hebert*), Houseley Stevenson (*Jud Travis*), Emory Parnell (*Bank Watchman*), Don Kohler (*Ted*), Bert Conway (*Neil*), Hal K. Dawson (*Night Clerk*), Vera Marshe (*Mae*), Jimmy Dodd (*Curly*), Robert Rockwell (*Eddie*), Joe (*Himself*), Arthur Walsh (*Milton Goodrich*), Paul Cavanagh (*Dr. Blucher*), Bill Clauson (*Simon*), Eddie Ehrhart (*Thaddeus*), Joe Cook, Jr., Don Garner (*Bellhops*), Hal Melone, Frank White (*Elevator Operators*), Beatrice Roberts (*Maid*), Fritz Feld (*Small Man*), Arthur Hohl (*Cemetery Man*), Frank Jenks (*Man In Checkered Suit*), Frank Darien (*Old Man*), Edward Gargan (*Detective*), Don Shelton (*Minister*), George Carleton (*Portly Man*), Chief Yowlachie (*Indian*), Isabell Withers (*Maid*), Al Murphy (*Mechanic*), Myron Healey (*Day Clerk*), Harland Tucker (*Mr. Thrush*), David Sharpe (*Motorcycle Rider*), Donald Dewar (*Boy*), Tiny Jones (*Pedestrian*), William H. O'Brien (*Waiter*).

A lightweight charmer which works its way into your heart by starring Fontaine and Stewart as a delightful pair falling in love. Fontaine plays a wealthy heiress who has gotten herself into a marriage to Parker that she quickly regrets. On the night of her New York honeymoon she realizes her mistake, and, instead of entering her husband's hotel bedroom, she takes refuge down the hall in Stewart's. Stewart, whose airplane cargo company is on the verge of bankruptcy, is left to care for Fontaine. Assuming that she is a poor and helpless girl, he feels an obligation towards her. When she takes an overdose of sleeping pills and is unable to be awakened, Stewart is forced to take her with him to California. The plane ride, however, is practically a circus. In addition to copilot Albert, there is an escaped criminal, Hall, a love-stricken pair of newlyweds, Walsh and McGuire, a trained chimp that smokes cigars, a corpse lying in a coffin, and a shipment of lobsters. Amidst all the confusion, Stewart and Fontaine fall in love. After

a crash landing in a farm field, Stewart declares his love for Fontaine and discovers, much to his delight, that he has fallen for an extremely wealthy girl. While not top-drawer Stewart or Fontaine, both turn in commendable performances, aided by the zany, haphazard style that director Potter employed in his 1941 picture HELLZAPOPPIN'.

p, Karl Tunberg; d, H.C. Potter; w, Tunberg (based on the *Saturday Evening Post* serial by Robert Carson); ph, Russell Metty; m, Daniele Amfitheatrof; ed, Paul Weatherwax; md, Milton Schwarzwald; prod d, Alexander Golitzen; set d, Russell A. Gausman, Ruby R. Levitt; cos, Jean Louis; spec eff, David S. Horsley; makeup, Bud Westmore, Leo LaCava, V. Curtis.

Comedy/Romance   **(PR:A   MPAA:NR)**

YOU HAVE TO RUN FAST**   (1961) 73m UA bw (AKA: MAN
                                                            MISSING)

Graig Hill (*Dr. Roger Condon/Frank Harlow*), Elaine Edwards (*Laurie Maitland*), Grant Richards (*Big Jim Craven*), Shepherd Sanders (*Bert Klee*), John Apone (*Toothpick Stan*), Brad Trumbull (*Deputy*), Ken Kayer (*Injun George*), Willis Bouchey (*Col. Maitland*), Max Melinger (*Doc Rayburn*), Jack Mann (*Lt. Dan Corbo*), John Clarke (*Chuck*), Claudia Barrett (*Fran*), Ric Marlow (*Jay Rocco*), Jack Kenny (*Lou Miles*), Joel Lewinson (*Small Boy*).

Decent B gangster picture in which Hill plays a doctor on the run from the mob because he identified two hoods involved in a murder. He takes to the backwoods, getting a job as a sales clerk and falling in love with Edwards, daughter of a former Army colonel who is now confined to a wheelchair. It is this old colonel who saves Hill's life when the gangsters sniff him out, by sharpshooting his way over the crooks. Though obviously done on a limited budget, this is a thorough and workmanlike job whose faults are easily overlooked.

p, Robert E. Kent; d, Edward L. Cahn; w, Orville H. Hampton; ph, Gilbert Warrenton; m, Richard La Salle; ed, Robert Carlisle; set d, Harry Reif; cos, Einar Bourman, Barbara Maxwell; makeup, Harry Thomas.

Crime/Drama   **(PR:A   MPAA:NR)**

YOU JUST KILL ME   (SEE: ARRIVEDERCI, BABY!, 1966, Brit.)

YOU KNOW WHAT SAILORS ARE**
                          (1954, Brit.) 89m PC Group/UA c

Akim Tamiroff (*President of Agraria*), Donald Sinden (*Lt. Sylvester Green*), Sarah Lawson (*Betty*), Naunton Wayne (*Capt. Owbridge*), Bill Kerr (*Lt. Smart*), Dora Bryan (*Gladys*), Martin Miller (*Prof. Pfumbaum*), Michael Shepley (*Admiral*), Michael Hordern (*Capt. Hamilton*), Ferdy Mayne (*Stanislaus Voritz*), Bryan Coleman (*Lt. Comdr. Voles*), Cyril Chamberlain (*Stores Officer*), Hal Osmond (*Petty Officer*), Peter Arne (*Ahmed*), Shirley Lorrimer (*Jasmin*), Janet Richards (*Almyra*), Eileen Sands (*Hepzibah*), Marianne Stone (*Elsie*), Peter Dyneley (*Lt. Andrews*), Peter Martyn (*Lt. Ross*), Shirley Eaton, Lisa Gastoni, Jan Miller.

Pleasant naval farce in which three officers cause general havoc during a drunken spree by placing a pawnbroker's sign welded to an old perambulator on the deck of a visiting naval vessel. Sinden eases the immediate problem by stating that the object is a sophisticated radar detector. But then he is given the job of teaching other naval men how to use it, and the British navy bras make plans to install the device on one of their ships. Beautiful women fill the screen at frequent intervals in this amiable comedy.

p, Julian Wintle, Peter Rogers; d, Ken Annakin; w, Rogers (based on the novel *Sylvester* by Edward Hyams); ph, Reginald Wyer (Technicolor); m, Malcolm Arnold; ed, Alfred Roome; cos, Julie Harris; ch, David Paltenghi.

Comedy   **(PR:A   MPAA:NR)**

YOU LIGHT UP MY LIFE*   (1977) 90m COL c

Didi Conn (*Lauri Robinson*), Joe Silver (*Si Robinson*), Michael Zaslow (*Cris Nolan*), Stephen Nathan (*Ken Rothenberg*), Melanie Mayron (*Annie Gerrard*), Jerry Keller (*Conductor*), Lisa Reeves (*Carla Wright*), John Gowans (*Charley Nelson*), Simmy Bow (*Mr. Granek*), Bernice Nicholson (*Mrs. Granek*), Ed Morgan (*Account Executive*), Joe Brooks (*Creative Director*), Amy Letterman (*Lauri as a Child*), Marty Zagon (*Mr. Nussbaum*), Martin Gish (*Harold Nussbaum*), Brian Byers (*Singer*), Tom Gerrard (*Best Man*), Ruth Manning (*Mrs. Rothenberg*), Jeffrey Kramer (*Background Singer*), Frank Conn (*Stage Manager*), Sparky Watts (*Uncle Fritz*), Robin O'Hara (*Aunt Emma*), Aurora Roland (*Gail Gerard*), Thelma Pelish (*Rachel*), John Millerburg (*Studio Musician*), Nancy Chadwick (*Producer*), Bob Manahan (*Assistant Engineer*), Rosemary Lovell, Judy Novgrad (*Receptionists*), Ken Olfson, Richmond Shepard (*Commercial Directors*), Matt Hyde, Jerry Barnes (*Engineers*), Arnold Weiss, Terry Brannen, Barry Godwin, John Miller, Stephan Tice (*Ushers*), Eileen Dietz, Lindsey Jones, Greta Ronnegun, Lisa Nicholson, Kasey Ciszk (*Bridesmaids*), Mary Kwan, Edward Steefe, Cynthia Szigeti (*Cousins*).

Dreadfully sentimentalized version of a daughter of an entertainer trying to make it herself as an entertainer when she grows up. In typically telegraphed form that never overcomes its shallow emotional intent, Conn meets with both professional and romantic failure as she keeps on plucking away. An unfitting upbeat ending has the girl racking one up for experience. The title song by Joseph Brooks and sung by Kasey Ciszk was a hit over the air waves, though its content was on the same level as the film.

p,d&w, Joseph Brooks; ph, Eric Saarinen (Technicolor); m, Brooks; ed, Lynzee Klingman; art d, Tom Rasmussen; set d, Rasmussen; cos, John Patton, Nancy Chadwick.

Musical Drama   **Cas.**   **(PR:C   MPAA:PG)**

YOU LIVE AND LEARN**   (1937, Brit.) 80m WB-FN-Teddington bw

Glenda Farrell (Mamie Wallis), Claude Hulbert (Peter Millett), Glen Alyn (Dot Harris), John Carol (George), James Stephenson (Sam Brooks), George Galleon (Lord Haverstock), Arthur Finn (Joseph P. Munro), Wallace Evenett (Amos Biddle), Margaret Yarde (Mrs. Biddle), Charlotte Leigh (Miss Tanner), Pat Fitzpatrick (Jimmy Millet), Anna Murrell (Anne Millet), Gibb McLaughlin (Mons. Duval).

When American showgirl Farrell is about to be stranded in Paris while traveling with a shoddy revue, she takes up an offer of marriage by Hulbert, thinking him to be a man of wealth when actually he's a lowly farmer with three children and a rundown shack on his land. Though incredibly let down, Farrell has a chance to show her stuff by contending with her situation, including catty gossiping of a jealous schoolteacher who hates the ex-showgirl. As the strait-laced teacher, Leigh gives a delightful performance and is the begetter of most of the film's laughs.

p, Irving Asher; d, Arthur Woods; w, Brock Williams, Tom Phipps (based on the novel Have You Come for Me by Norma Patterson), ph, Basil Emmott.

Comedy   **(PR:A   MPAA:NR)**

YOU LUCKY PEOPLE*½   (1955, Brit.) 79m Advance/Adelphi bw

Tommy Trinder (Tommy Smart), Mary Parker (Pvt. Sally Briggs), Dora Bryan (Sgt. Hortense Tipp), RSM Brittain (Himself), James Copeland (Pvt. Jim Campbell), Michael Kelly (Sgt. Manners), Mark Singleton (Lt. Robson), Charles Rolfe (Hooky), Rolf Harris (Pvt. Proudfoot), Rufus Cruickshank (Sgt.-Maj. Thickpenny), Michael Trubshawe (Col. Barkstone-Gadsby), Derek Prentice, Mignon O'Doherty, Harold Goodwin.

Other than an occasional laugh here and there it's hard to find much worth recommending in this farce on British army life, which has Trinder playing an army surplus salesman doing his two-week reserve stint. In slapstick fashion Trinder makes the most of obvious situations, before proving his wit by outsmarting his archenemy, sergeant-major Cruickshank.

p, David Dent; d, Maurice Elvey; w, Anthony Verney, Tommy Trinder (based on the story by Maurice Harrison, Sidney Wilson); ph, Gordon Dines (CameraScope).

Comedy   **(PR:A   MPAA:NR)**

YOU MADE ME LOVE YOU*½   (1934, Brit.) 63m BIP/Majestic bw

Stanley Lupino (Tom Daly), Thelma Todd (Pamela Berne), John Loder (Harry Berne), Gerald Rawlinson (Jerry), James Carew (Oliver Berne), Charles Mortimer (Mr. Daly), Hugh E. Wright (Father), Charlotte Parry (Mother), Arthur Rigby, Jr (Brother), Syd Crossley (Bleak), Monty Banks (Taxi Driver).

The trouble with this film is that it would have made a decent short, but when extended to feature length it sags like a hammock holding a 200-pound weight. Lupino plays a decent composer gent who is inspired to write a hit song upon sighting gorgeous Todd at a traffic light. Predictably, that is not grounds enough for marriage, and so our two instant lovers spend the rest of the film quarreling, and practically demolish their house at one point during a violent quarrel. A musical comedy takeoff on Shakespeare's "The Taming of the Shrew."

p, John Maxwell; d, Monty Banks; w, Frank Launder (based on an idea by Stanley Lupino); ph, John J. Cox; ed, A.S. Bates; md, Harry Acres; m/l, "Miss What's Her Name," "Why Can't We?" Lupino, Noel Gay, Clifford Grey.

Comedy   **(PR:A   MPAA:NR)**

YOU MAY BE NEXT*½   (1936) 67m COL bw (GB: PANIC ON THE AIR; AKA: CALLING ALL G-MEN; TRAPPED BY WIRELESS)

Ann Sothern (Fay Stevens), Lloyd Nolan (Neil Bennett), Douglas Dumbrille (Beau Gardner), John Arledge (Eddie House), Berton Churchill (J.J. Held), Nana Bryant (Miss Abbott), Robert Middlemass (Dan McMahon), George McKay (Mitch Cook), Gene Morgan (Ted Lane), Clyde Dilson (Nick Barrow).

It seems that the gangsters of the 1930s were willing to take a crack at anything in order to make a buck–here it's using a high frequency radio transmitter in order to jam the frequency of a radio station. A nifty blackmail scheme is created by Dumbrille, proceeding until the Navy steps in to interfere with his game. Though basically a good idea, its handling did little to expand upon the situations. Performances are all walk-throughs.

d, Albert S. Rogell; w, Fred Niblo, Jr., Ferdinand Reyher (based on the story

by Henry Wales and Reyher); ph Allen G. Seigler; ed, John Rawlins; cos, Samuel Lange.

Crime   **(PR:A   MPAA:NR)**

YOU MUST BE JOKING!**½   (1965, Brit.) 99m Ameran/COL bw

Michael Callan (Lt. Tim Morton), Lionel Jeffries (Sgt.-Maj. McGregor), Denholm Elliott (Capt. Tabasco), Wilfrid Hyde-White (Gen. Lockwood), Bernard Cribbins (Sgt. Clegg), James Robertson Justice (Librarian), Leslie Phillips (Young Husband), Gabriella Licudi (Annabelle Nash), Patricia Viterbo (Sylvie Tarnet), Terry Thomas (Maj. Foskett), Lee Montague (Staff Sgt. Mansfield), Irene Hand (Elderly Woman), Richard Wattis (Parkins), Norman Vaughn (Norman Stone), Miles Malleson (Salesman), Clive Dunn (Doorman), Tracy Reed (Poppy Penington), James Villiers (Bill Simpson), Gwendolyn Watts (Young Wife), Ronald Howard (Cecil), David Jacobs (Himself, a Disc Jockey), Peter Bull (Ferocious Man in library), Lance Percival (Young Man), Graham Stark, Arthur Lowe, Jon Pertwee, Jill Mai Meredith, Stanley Meadows, Richard Caldicott, Marianne Stone, Peter Gilmore, Peter Barkworth.

A modern rendition of the "feats of Hercules" has five British soldiers ordered to undertake a 48 hour test of their endurance. Among the feats that must be accomplished in this time are getting out of a maze, obtaining a rare rose and the hood ornament off a Rolls-Royce, and securing a lock of hair from a popular singer. American Callan is the only one of the five men to accomplish all the tasks. He turns down the prize after coming in contact with the beautiful singer, when he decides to quit the service and marry the girl. Cribbins plays the bumbling member unable to pass the first obstacle, getting out of the maze, and Elliott contributes his specialty, adding a little mannered decay to his role of captain. Lunacy and laughs galore, with director Winner's gimmicky style much in evidence.

p, Charles H. Schneer; d, Michael Winner; w, Alan Hackney (based on the story by Winner, Hackney); ph, Geoffrey Unsworth; m, Laurie Johnson; ed, Bernard Gribble; art d, Maurice Carter; cos, Tony Armstrong; m/l, "I'm With You," "I'll Be True to You, Baby," Buddy Bregman, Hal Shaper.

Comedy   **(PR:A   MPAA:NR)**

YOU MUST GET MARRIED*½   (1936, Brit.) 68m City/GFD bw

Frances Day (Fenella Dane), Neil Hamilton (Michael Brown), Robertson Hare (Percy Phut), Wally Patch (Chief Blow), Gus McNaughton (Bosun), Fred Duprez (Cyrus P. Hankin), Dennis Wyndham (Albert Gull), C. Denier Warren (Mr. Wurtsell), James Carew (Mr. Schillinger), Bryan Powley, Hilary Pritchard.

Day plays an American film star who marries steamer captain Hamilton for the purpose of obtaining British citizenship, after which she plans to leave him. Hamilton kidnaps her after the ceremony and sails away with her on his steamer, attempting to tame her at sea. In port, she slips away from him and finds a big contract awaiting her, but Hamilton sweeps her away again and true love at last blooms. Frivolous but entertaining.

p, Basil Humphreys; d, Leslie Pearce; w, F. McGrew Willis, Richard Fisher (based on the novel by David Evans); ph, Claude Friese-Greene.

Comedy   **(PR:A   MPAA:NR)**

YOU NEVER CAN TELL**   (1951) 78m UNIV bw (GB: YOU NEVER KNOW)

Dick Powell (Rex Shepherd), Peggy Dow (Ellen Hathaway), Charles Drake (Perry Collins), Joyce Holden (Goldie), Albert Sharpe (Grandpa Hathaway), Sara Taft (Mrs. Bowers), Will Vedder (Nicholas), Watson Downs (Slott), Lou Polan (Lt. Gilpin), Anthony George (Detective), Henry Kulky (Large Prisoner), Frank Nelson (Policeman), Olan Soule (Salesman), King and Tillie the Dogs, Boots the Cat.

In spite of the unbelievability of the plot–a poisoned dog comes back to Earth to find its killer–YOU NEVER CAN TELL turns out to be a cleverly handled and well thought out romp worth seeing. A dog is left the estate of its master and soon after is poisoned. In the "Beastatory" upstairs, it pleads to be allowed to return to Earth to find its murderer and the plea is granted. The dog, in the form of Powell now, accompanied by a former champion filly in the form of Holden, goes amusingly through his capers as a private investigator and finally finds the culprit. Lots of word play, plenty of fire hydrants, and a slew of dog biscuits and hamburger grace this distinguished little comedy and you never can tell, it might have happened.

p, Leonard Goldstein; d, Lou Breslow; w, Breslow, David Chandler (based on the story by Breslow); ph, Maury Gertsman; m, Hans J. Salter; ed, Frank Gross, art d, Bernard Herzbrun, Alexander Golitzen; cos, Bill Thomas.

Comedy   **(PR:A   MPAA:NR)**

YOU NEVER KNOW   (SEE: YOU NEVER CAN TELL, 1951)

YOU ONLY LIVE ONCE**   (1937) 86m UA bw

Sylvia Sidney (*Joan Graham*), Henry Fonda (*Eddie Taylor*), Barton Ma-cLane (*Stephen Whitney*), Jean Dixon (*Bonnie Graham*), William Gargan (*Father Dolan*), Warren Hymer (*Muggsy*), Charles "Chic" Sale (*Ethan*), Margaret Hamilton (*Hester*), Guinn "Big Boy" Williams (*Rogers*), Jerome Cowan (*Dr. Hill*), John Wray (*Warden*), Jonathan Hale (*District Attorney*), Ward Bond (*Guard*), Ben Hall (*Messenger*), Jean Stoddard (*Stenographer*), Wade Boteler (*Policeman*), Henry Taylor (*Kozderonas*), Walter De Palma (*Bit*), Jack Carson (*Gas Station Attendant*).

This brooding and powerful tale, which suggests the story of Bonnie and Clyde, is one of Lang's best efforts in Hollywood. Fonda and Sidney are excellent as the average Depression-era couple made into criminals through circumstances and just plain bad luck. Fonda is not the average law-abiding citizen, however, having committed many robberies in the past and served three prison terms. He is a four-time loser (the fourth conviction carrying with it an automatic life term). He vows, however, that he is going straight and he gets a job, working hard and then marrying his patient, long-time sweetheart, Sidney. But his past catches up with him and his landlord turns him and his wife out of their room after finding out he has a record. His employer at the trucking firm where he works fires him when he learns that Fonda is an ex-con. There seems to be no hope and there isn't. Fonda's hat is found at the scene of a bank holdup where a guard has been killed. He is quickly tried and sentenced to death. Once in prison, Fonda resolves to fight back against a system that offers him no way of surviving. He pretends to be ill and is sent to the prison hospital. There he obtains a gun and uses the prison doctor as a shield to get to the prison yard. The prison chaplain runs to him to say that he has been pardoned but by then Fonda will believe nothing any authority figure tells him. He thinks the chaplain is trying to hoodwink him into surrendering and, when the priest makes the wrong move, Fonda fires, killing the chaplain. He manages to escape the prison and rejoin wife Sidney. Together they drive toward the Canadian border, trying to get out of a country that has persecuted and hounded them. They do manage to reach the border but their joy is only momentary. A sharpshoot-ing member of the New York State Police raises his rifle and spots the fugitives through his telescopic sights. He fires several rounds which mortally wound both Fonda and Sidney. Sidney is first hit and Fonda takes her in his arms, carrying her the last few steps into Canada, freedom, and death in which he joins her. This tragedy is distinguished by Lang's meticulous direction and carefully constructed scenes. Fonda gives a terrific performance as the social pariah fighting for his mere existence. Sidney is poignant and beautiful. It was once stated that this superb actress had "The face of the Great Depression," and this film is undoubtedly the reason for the sobriquet. There is little mirth in this film, one with permanent steel-gray skies, and the director's murky, diffused shots suggest a kind of futility to life that is sometimes unbearable. His figures, especially in the prison escape scenes, are hazy, almost transparent, as mist covers the yard and searchlights reach out for Fonda who moves like a ghost before them. Fonda held Lang in high regard as a director but he felt that Lang pushed his actors too hard in his quest to attain perfection, causing, in the 46-day shooting schedule of this film, his cast and crew to go without sleep and physically exhaust themselves to achieve the effect he desired to have on film. There is a grimness to this film that is often overwhelming and though it is technically flawless, it offers little hope to the viewer for satisfaction. Justice is not served here, only irony.

p, Walter Wanger; d, Fritz Lang; w, Gene Towne, Graham Baker (based on a story by Towne); ph, Leon Shamroy; m, Alfred Newman; ed, Daniel Mandell; md, Newman; art d, Alexander Toluboff; m/l, "A Thousand Dreams of You," Louis Alter, Paul Francis Webster.

Crime Drama   Cas.   (PR:C   MPAA:NR)

YOU ONLY LIVE ONCE**   (1969, Fr.) 95m Euro Images-Les Films Modernes/Sigma III c (TU SERAS TERRIBLEMENT GENTILLE)

Karen Blanguernon (*Clara Verly*), Leslie Bedos (*Julie Verly*), Frederic de Pasquale (*Patrice Verly*), Jean Moussy (*Roger*), Victor Lanoux (*Rene*), Rene Goliard (*Charles*), Jean-Paul Moulinot, Tony Kinna, Tessa Sanders, Made-leine Lambert.

De Pasquale plays a struggling photographer who decides to move to Paris in hopes of getting a start, forcing his daughter, Bedoes and wife, Blanguernon, to remain behind. Three years pass and Blanguerон, bored with her provincial life, also moves to Paris, but becomes a model instead of reuniting with her husband, though a reconciliation of the small family does finally occur. Whimsical nonsense.

p, Emile Natan; d, Dirk Sanders; w, Paul Soreze, Sanders; ph, Roger Duculot (Eastmancolor); m, Jacques Loussier; ed, Philippe Murcier; cos, Pierre Car-din, Christian Dior.

Drama   (PR:A   MPAA:G)

YOU ONLY LIVE TWICE½   (1967, Brit.) 117m Eon/UA c

Sean Connery (*James Bond*), Akiko Wakabayashi (*Aki*), Tetsuro Tamba (*Tiger Tanaka*), Mie Hama (*Kissy Suzuki*), Teru Shimada (*Osato*), Karin Dor (*Helga Brandt*), Lois Maxwell (*Miss Moneypenny*), Desmond Llewelyn ("Q"), Charles Gray (*Henderson*), Tsai Chin (*Chinese Girl*), Bernard Lee ("M"),

Donald Pleasence (*Ernst Stavro Blofeld*), Alexander Knox (*American President*), Robert Hutton (*President's Aide*), Burt Kwouk (*SPECTRE No. 3*), Michael Chow (*SPECTRE No. 4*), Diane Cilento (*Double*).

The fifth entry of the Bond series with Connery as the amazing spy; his contract expiring after this film, the actor would take a long recess from this part, returning several years later in NEVER SAY NEVER AGAIN. At a cost of $10 million, a staggering sum in the mid-1960s, the crew went to Japan and several other points around the world to do its filming. A large portion of this money, however, can be attributed to the construction of the volcano headquarters of SPECTRE agent Pleasence, a man set on taking control of the world by instigating World War III. Using a spacecraft that defies detection, he has captured an American spaceship by literally gobbling it up. The Americans blame the Soviets, who in turn think the Americans are just trying to foment trouble. Such are the circumstances as Connery embarks on an attempt to save the world. He sails to Japan where an elaborate ploy has been developed to make Pleasence think he has died, his body riddled with bullets and buried at sea. Connery is freed from his tomb in the ocean by a frogman and starts his journey to halt Pleasence. The spy makes his way into the villain's volcano headquarters by assuming the identify of a peasant fisherman, even getting married to make it appear more convincing. Aided by machine-gunning Ninja soldiers, he accomplishes his task and the world is once again free from the possibility of a holocaust. The script and situations are all highly contrived, writers Dahl and Bloom being forced to incorporate certain specifications to enhance the Bond character which did nothing to move the story along—one of these being the need to have Bond involved with at least three women. Another serious problem in casting was the use of Pleasence as the villain. The original choice for the role, Czech actor Jan Werich, having been taken ill, Pleasence was a last-minute replacement. The attempts to alter his looks—a hump, then a limp, then a beard and a lame hand, all failed to make him sinister looking enough. So a simple scar was settled on. Despite the obvious shortcomings of the picture, it turned out to be a tremendous commercial success. (See JAMES BOND series, Index).

p, Albert R. Broccoli, Harry Saltzman; d, Lewis Gilbert; w, Roald Dahl, Harry Jack Bloom (based on the novel by Ian Fleming); ph, Freddie Young (Panavision, Technicolor); m, John Barry; ed, Peter Hunt; prod d, Ken Adam; art d, Harry Pottle; set d, David Ffolkes; cos, Eileen Sullivan; spec eff, John Stears; m/l, "You Only Live Twice," Barry Leslie Bricusse (sung by Nancy Sinatra); makeup, Basil Newall, Paul Rabiger.

Spy Drama/Fantasy   Cas.   (PR:C   MPAA:NR)

YOU PAY YOUR MONEY*½   (1957, Brit.) 68m BUT bw

Hugh McDermott (*Bob Westlake*), Jane Hylton (*Rosemary Delgardo*), Honor Blackman (*Susie Westlake*), Hugh Moxey (*Tom Cookson*), Ivan Samson (*Steve Mordaunt*), Ferdy Mayne (*Delal*), Shirley Deane (*Doris Squire*), Gerard Heinz (*Dr. Burger*), Peter Swanwick (*Hall Porter*), Basil Dignam (*Currie*), Fred Griffiths (*Fred the Driver*), Ben Williams (*Seymour*), Elsie Wagstaff (*Ada Seymour*), Vincent Holman (*Briggs*), Mark Daly (*Goodwin*), Jack Taylor (*1st Thug*), Larry Taylor (*2nd Thug*), Don Qureshi (*Arab*), Lucette Marimar (*Telephonist*), Amando Guinlee (*Belgian Seaman*), Myles Rudge (*Estate Agent*), Shayn Bahadur (*Said*), Shripad Pai (*Man*), George Roderick (*Oley Jackson*).

Despite capable handling there was little that could be done to overcome this inane plot in which Arabs kidnap Blackman as hostage for a couple of rare books. A turn of events allows McDermott, as Blackman's husband and an assistant to a smuggler of valuable books, to get his wife back without having to forfeit the rare volumes. Again, execution top notch, but the witlessness of the story rankles.

p, W.G. Chalmers; d&w, Maclean Rogers (based on the novel by Michael Cronin); ph, Jimmy Harvey.

Crime   (PR:A   MPAA:NR)

YOU SAID A MOUTHFUL*½   (1932) 75m FN-WB bw

Joe E. Brown (*Joe Holt, a Clerk*), Ginger Rogers (*Alice Brandon*), Sheila Terry (*Cora*), Guinn "Big Boy" Williams (*Joe Holt, a Swim Champ*), Harry Gribbon (*Harry Daniels*), Oscar Apfel (*Armstrong*), Edwin Maxwell (*Dr. Vorse*), Frank Hagney (*Holt's Manager*), Selmer Jackson (*Jones*), Mia Marvin (*Armstrong's Secretary*), William Burress (*Colby*), Harry Seymour (*Announcer*), Arthur S. Byron (*Elliott*), Anthony Lord (*Bookkeeper*), Bert Morehouse (*Office Manager*), Farina (*Sam*), Preston Foster (*Edward Dover, a Swimmer*), Walter Walker (*Tom Brandon*), Don Brodie (*Judge's Assist-ant*), Wilfred Lucas (*Official*), James Eagles (*Messenger*).

Browbeaten Brown, the butt of many jokes in his business office, invents an unsinkable swim suit. Testing his lifesaving livery, he meets heiress Rogers, who mistakes him for a swimming champion. Through a series of wild mishaps, Brown—hydrophobic to the core; he doesn't even like to drink water—becomes a contestant in a marathon swimming race. Still sillier incidents—an accidental tow by a speedboat, for instance—conspire to bring his race to a successful conclusion despite the conniving of his rivals, Williams and Foster. The first of the cavern-mouthed comedian's pictures to feature the word "mouth" in the title was his second with Rogers (who, said a reviewer, was "made for a bathing suit"). In a role for which Gloria

Shea had originally been signed, Rogers played well against Brown's slapstick style. Director Bacon thought well enough of her to give her a show-stopping, scene-stealing part in his next picture, FORTY-SECOND STREET (1933).

p, Ray Griffith; d, Lloyd Bacon; w, Robert Lord, Bolton Mallory (based the story by William B. Dover); ph, Richard Towers; ed, Owen Marks; art d, Jack Okey; makeup, Perc Westmore; tech d, Harold Kruger.

Comedy   (PR:A MPAA:NR)

YOU WERE MEANT FOR ME**   (1948) 92m FOX bw

Jeanne Crain (Peggy Mayhew), Dan Dailey (Chuck Arnold, Bandleader), Oscar Levant (Oscar Hoffman, Band Manager), Barbara Lawrence (Louise Crane), Selena Royle (Mrs. Cora Mayhew), Percy Kilbride (Mr. Andrew Mayhew, Brickyard Owner), Herbert Anderson (Eddie), Lee MacGregor (Roy), Charles Tannen (Harry Jarvis), John Fontaine (Boy in Drugstore), Morgan Farley (Ticket Taker), Janet King (Flapper), Charles Flickinger (Western Union Boy), Dick Ryan (Ticket Seller), Erskine Sanford (Dr. Sanford), Kenny Williams, Harry Barris, Les Clark, William Sheehan, Dick Winslow, Barney Elmore, "Tiny" Timbrell, Robert McCord, Maurice Kelly, Michael Towne, Billy Snyder, Perc Launders (Members of the Band), Kenneth Niles (Narrator), Charles Owens, Ann Fredrick, Otto Forrest, Milton Gowman, Ben Pollock, John C (Kay), Marion Marshall.

Small-town flapper Crain marries bandleader Dailey and their honeymoon comprises a series of one-night stands, musically speaking. Tiring of the trauma of constant travel, Crain goes home. His bookings ruined by the onset of the Great Depression, Dailey joins her there, along with his cynical, world-weary manager, Levant. Having difficulty with the hicks, Dailey takes off alone, determined to conquer the big city. When he lands permanent employment with a hotel band, wife Crain joins him for a happy finish; the urbane Levant elects to continue rusticating. Pert Crain is charismatic, Dailey sings and dances well, and Levant gives his usual delightful characterization. The picture is a much-altered remake of the studio's ORCHESTRA WIVES (1941). Dailey's alto sax solos were dubbed by Russ Cheever. Songs and musical numbers included: "Crazy Rhythm" (Irving Caesar, Roger Wolfe Kahn, Joseph Meyer), "You Were Meant for Me" (Arthur Freed, Nacio Herb Brown), "Goodnight Sweetheart" (James Campbell, Reginald Connolly, Ray Noble), "If I Had You" (Campbell, Connolly, Ted Shapiro), "Ain't She Sweet" (Jack Yellen, Milton Ager), "Ain't Misbehavin" (Andy Razaf, Fats Waller), "I'll Get By" (Roy Turk, Fred Ahlert), "Concerto in F" (George Gershwin, played by Levant), "Sweet Georgia Brown" (Ben Bernie, Maceo Pinkard, Kenneth Casey), "What Can I Say After I Say I'm Sorry" (Walter Donaldson, Abe Lyman), the latter two done by Eddie Miller on the soundtrack.

p, Fred Kohlmar; d, Lloyd Bacon; w, Elick Moll, Valentine Davies; ph, Victor Milner; ed, William Reynolds; md, Lionel Newman; art d, Lyle Wheeler, Richard Irvine; ch, Lee Clark, Kenny Williams.

Musical   (PR:A MPAA:NR)

YOU WERE NEVER LOVELIER***½   (1942) 97m COL bw

Fred Astaire (Robert Davis), Rita Hayworth (Maria Acuna), Adolphe Menjou (Edwardo Acuna), Leslie Brooks (Cecy Acuna), Adele Mara (Lita Acuna), Isobel Elsom (Mrs. Maria Castro), Gus Schilling (Fernando), Barbara Brown (Mrs. Delfina Acuna), Douglas Leavitt (Juan Castro), Catherine Craig (Julia Acuna), Kathleen Howard (Grandmother Acuna), Mary Field (Louise), Larry Parks (Tony), Stanley Brown (Roddy), Xavier Cugat and His Orchestra (Themselves), Kirk Alyn (Groom), George Bunny (Flower Man), Ralph Peters (Chauffeur), Lina Romay (Singer).

A followup to their successful YOU'LL NEVER GET RICH (1941), this equally enjoyable musical was the second and last screen pairing of Astaire and Hayworth. Astaire plays an American dancer who loses all his money betting on ponies, thus stranding him in Buenos Aires. Desperate for funds, he goes to Menjou, the owner of a posh hotel, in hopes of finding some work. The current feature artist at the hotel is Cugat and his Orchestra, along with singer Romay. The bad tempered Menjou wants nothing to do with Astaire; he has much more troubling matters on his mind. It seems the oldest of his four daughters is about to marry, and his two youngest daughters want to, but his second child, Hayworth, is ruining everyone's plans. Menjou has a strict rule for his children: they must marry in order of their age. Hayworth fosters romantic ideals of love that no man can possibly live up to. Menjou has been secretly sending her flowers and love notes, hoping to put a dent into her fantasies. Astaire, who is still lingering about the hotel, is mistaken for a messenger and sent to deliver Hayworth's latest bunch of flowers. Naturally Hayworth thinks that Astaire is her mystery man, which gladdens Menjou's weary disposition. He hires Astaire, not as a dancer, but to fill the role of Hayworth's secret admirer. Astaire takes the job, and under a direct order from Menjou, offers to marry Hayworth. Hayworth refutes every argument for marriage that Astaire has been supplied with by his prospective father-in-law. Other complications arise when Menjou's jealous wife wonders who her husband has been sending secret love notes to, but, as expected, all works out happily in the end. A remake of an earlier Argentinian film THE GAY SENORITA, YOU WERE NEVER LOVELIER exudes an effervescent charm with every frame. Hayworth is an excellent counterpart to Astaire in the dance numbers, gliding about the floor with

natural ease. They work well as a romantic couple, adding flavor to the slimness of the story. Hayworth, decked out in beautiful costumes that flatter her much-admired figure, had her singing dubbed for the film by Nan Wynn. During the making of YOU WERE NEVER LOVELIER, the Columbia lots were busy with various productions, making rehearsal space scarce. To practice their dance numbers, Astaire and Hayworth were forced to locate any place that could accommodate them. A good rehearsal space was a premium commodity, and the two finally found room in the most unlikely of spots: an empty hall above a funeral parlor. In his autobiography Steps in Time Astaire recalled: "Every time a funeral came through the gates we could see it from the windows and naturally we'd have to stop until it moved well on past. One of the men from the office downstairs would come running up half whispering, 'Hold it a minute, folks, they're bringing one in.' " Astaire remained convinced that some of the film's best routines came out of these sessions at the funeral parlor, despite the rather ominous atmosphere that permeated the rehearsal space. One dance sequence called for Astaire to tap Menjou on the head with a cane. Menjou told Astaire not to be afraid to give some gusto to the move, because, he explained, "I've got a hard head." "I carried out (Menjou's) wishes," Astaire wrote, "...he told me afterward, 'I wish I had kept my big mouth shut–I didn't know that cane was a baseball bat!' " When asked by Astaire why nothing was said at the time, Menjou replied "I couldn't. I was unconscious." YOU WERE NEVER LOVELIER was well received by the public, and garnished three Oscar nominations for Best Sound Recording, Best Score, and Best Scoring for Harline's musical direction. The numbers in Kern and Mercer's resplendent bundle of songs include: "Dearly Beloved" (sung by Hayworth, dubbed by Wynn, danced by Astaire, Hayworth), "Audition Dance" (performed by Astaire, Cugat and Orchestra), "Wedding in the Spring" (performed by Lina Romay, Cugat and Orchestra), "I'm Old Fashioned" (performed by Astaire, Hayworth),"You Were Never Lovelier" (sung by Astaire, danced by Astaire, Hayworth), "The Shorty George" (performed by Astaire, Hayworth), "These Orchids" (performed by The Delivery Boys), "Chiu Chiu" (Alan Surgal, Nicanor Molinare, performed by Romay, Cugat and Orchestra), "Ding Dong Bell", "On the Beam" (Kern, Mercer).

p, Louis F. Edelman; d, William A. Seiter; w, Michael Fessier, Ernest Pagano, Delmer Daves (based on the story and screenplay "The Gay Senorita" by Carlos Olivari, Sixto Pondal Rios); ph, Ted Tetzlaff; m, Jerome Kern; ed, William Lyon; md, Leigh Harline; art d, Lionel Banks, Rudolph Sternad; set d, Frank Tuttle; cos, Irene; ch, Val Raset.

Musical   **Cas.**   (PR:A MPAA:NR)

YOU WILL REMEMBER*½   (1941, Brit.) 87m BL bw

Robert Morley (Tom Barrett/Leslie Stuart), Emlyn Williams (Bob Slater), Dorothy Hyson (Ellaline Terriss), Tom E. Finglass (Eugene Stratton), Nicholas Phipps (Earl of Potter), Gertrude Musgrove (Polly), Charles Lefeaux (Mr. Carr), Allan Jeayes (Signor Foli), Charles Victor (Pat Barrett), Maire O'Neill (Mrs. Barrett), Maurice Kelly (Young Tom Barrett), Roddy McDowall (Young Bob Slater), Marie Ault, Muriel George, Mary Merrall, Band of HM Grenadier Guards.

An initially slow-paced fictionalized biography of poor boy Kelly, who changes his name and grows up to be famed music-hall songwriter Morley, playing Leslie Stuart. With the aid of his lifelong friend Williams, Morley makes it big with his catchy numbers, but then falls victim to the rise of the Jazz Age. In debtor's prison, Morley is saved by the friends and well-wishers of better times. Production numbers featuring the singing of music-hall performer Finglass are well done, overcoming the weaknesses of the sentimental screenplay. Morley and Williams both went on to better things in the George Bernard Shaw classic MAJOR BARBARA. Songs include "Lily of Laguna," "Little Dolly Daydream," "Soldiers of the King," and "Sue" (Leslie Stuart).

p, Charles Q. Steele; d, Jack Raymond; w, Lydia Hayward, Christopher Morley, Sewell Stokes; ph, Henry Harris

Musical Biography   (PR:A MPAA:NR)

YOU'D BE SURPRISED!*½   (1930, Brit.) 64m Nettlefold/BUT bw

Walter Forde (Walter), Joy Windsor (Maisie Vane), Frank Stanmore (Frankie), Frank Perfitt (Major), Douglas Payne (Convict 99), Donald Russell, Sidney Gilliat.

Unsuccessful singer-songwriter Forde makes a desperate last-ditch effort to gain the accolades of the public. In evening dress, he is mistaken for an escaped convict who stole some clothing. An unsuccessful transition from silent films for its director-star Forde, surprising in view of his successful vaudeville career as a singer and pianist. Forde was England's major silent-screen comedian. A talent director, he went on to helm dozens of pictures, finally forming his own company, Holbein Films. In a rare screen appearance, look for director-screenwriter-producer Gilliat in a small part. With his partner Frank Launder, Gilliat went on to greater things, as well.

p, Archibald Nettlefold; d, Walter Forde; w, Forde, H. Fowler Mear; ph, Geoffrey Faithfull.

Comedy   (PR:A MPAA:NR)

YOU'LL FIND OUT**   (1940) 97m RKO bw

Kay Kyser (*Himself*), Peter Lorre (*Prof. Fenninger*), Boris Karloff (*Judge Mainwaring*), Bela Lugosi (*Prince Saliano*), Helen Parrish (*Janis Bellacrest*), Dennis O'Keefe (*Chuck Deems*), Alma Kruger (*Aunt Margo*), Joseph Eggenton (*Jurgen*), Leonard Mudie (*The Real Fenninger*), Ginny Simms, Harry Babbitt, Sully Mason, Ish Kabibble (*Themselves*), Kay Kyser's Band.

Concluding their regular weekly radio show, "Kay Kyser's Kollege of Musical Knowledge" heads for Bellacrest Manor to perform for the 21st birthday party of pretty young Parrish, beloved of O'Keefe, the program's manager. Arriving at the forbidding dwelling during a lightning-punctuated rainstorm, the radio performers are isolated there when the drawbridge at the entryway is destroyed by a lightning bolt. The eerie mansion is inhabited by strange artifacts collected by its deceased owner, an explorer, Parrish's father. It also contains Parrish's silly aunt, Kruger, and her guest, Saliano (Lugosi), a sinister medium Kruger has employed in hopes of contacting the spirit of her late brother. They also meet retired judge Karloff, the family's attorney, and newly arrived Lorre, purportedly a psychologist and spiritualist-debunker recruited by Karloff to expose Lugosi. When band singer Simms dons a dress of Parrish's and is nearly pinked by a poisoned dart, it becomes apparent that someone is attempting to prevent Parrish from reaching 21 years (the age when she will inherit the estate). That evening, at one of Lugosi's phony seances, Parrish is nearly killed by a falling chandelier. Between musical numbers, Kyser and his crew explore the secret passages of the gloomy mansion and discover the mechanisms used by Lugosi to lend credibility to his act. They also learn that Karloff, Lugosi, and Lorre are coconspirators in a scheme to take over the fortune which would otherwise go to Parrish. During the next seance, Kyser exposes the trickery, which includes a voiced theremin making spooky musical pronouncements. The sinister trio retreat, inadvertently blowing themselves to bits with the dynamite they intended to use on the other guests. This happy-go-lucky melange of genres could hardly go wrong with the menacing talents of its sinister threesome combined with the pleasant performances of Kyser and his popular radio ensemble. RKO-Radio did not belie the latter half of its name in taking advantage of the weekly audience exposure of such airwave names, and other studios—notably Republic—followed suit. This was Kyser's second feature; he had invested his own money in his first, THAT'S RIGHT-YOU'RE WRONG (1939), which netted him—and RKO—a healthy profit. The cast mingled pleasantly on the set, enjoying the ludicrous occurrences of the story, prompting producer-director Butler to later reminisce, "The picture was one of the happiest I ever did. Everyone simply had fun making it". The film was a benchmark in that it was Lorre's first exposure as a horror star (Karloff and Lugosi were already fixtures in the genre). Simms and Babbitt sing pleasantly, and the Beatle-banged Kabibble is outstanding with the comic number "The Bad Humor." Other songs and musical numbers (also penned by Jimmy McHugh and Johnny Mercer) include "I'd know You Anywhere," "You've Got Me This Way," "Like the Fella Once Said," I've Got a One-Track Mind," "Don't Think it Ain't Been Charming."

p&d, David Butler; w, James V. Kern, Monte Brice, Andrew Bennison, R. T. M. Scott (based on the story by Butler, Kern); ph, Frank Redmond; ed, Irene Morra; md, Roy Webb; art d, Van Nest Polglase; cos, Edward Stevenson; spec eff, Vernon L. Walker

Musical/Thriller   Cas.   (PR:A MPAA:NR)

YOU'LL LIKE MY MOTHER***   (1972) 92m BCP/UNIV c

Patty Duke (*Francesca Kinsolving*), Rosemary Murphy (*Mrs. Kinsolving*), Richard Thomas (*Kenny*), Sian Barbara Allen (*Kathleen Kinsolving*), Dennis Rucker (*Red Cooper, Bus Driver*), Harold Congdon (*Man*), James Glazman (*Breadman*), James Neumann (*Joey*).

An intriguing and tautly directed thriller in which Duke plays an expectant mother who journeys to the colds of Minnesota to visit the family of her recently deceased Army husband. What she discovers awaiting her arrival after a treacherous journey through a snowstorm is hardly what had been suggested by her husband's descriptions. As the mother-in-law, Murphy is cold and distant, refusing to acknowledge that her son made any mention of his being married. There is also a mentally retarded younger sister (Allen) whom the husband never mentioned. Forced to stay the night because of the snowstorm, Duke begins to uncover more mysteries about the family. Prompted by Allen, she discovers that the woman posing as her mother-in-law is in fact her husband's aunt, who has cooked up this masquerade in order to inherit the magnificent mansion. Duke also discovers the presence of Murphy's son (played by Thomas, "John Boy" of TV's "The Waltons"), a homicidal maniac wanted for rape and murder, and residing in the basement of the mansion. The trauma pushes Duke into labor; Murphy delivers the child but claims it was stillborn. But Allen leads Duke to the attic where the child is being cradled, at which point she attempts to leave the mansion and return to California, only to encounter Thomas as her chauffeur to the bus station. Surprisingly, a high level of terror and tension are maintained without resorting to any visual violence, unusual in a period of commercial filmmaking so heavily dependent on visual impact. It was a refreshing bit of casting to have Thomas out of the pure-boy image created for him on the television series, and playing the exact opposite type of character. Much of the impact in this thriller derives from the atmosphere provided, particularly that of the snowstorm. The performances and direction were also essential

in overcoming a script that could be criticized for being too dependent upon contrivances. Shot entirely in Minnesota using a mansion constructed on the shore of Lake Superior in 1903 at a cost of $1.3 million, the picture is characterized by excellent use of a moving camera. Actress Duke's fifth starring feature, her third under the helm of talented director Johnson. The menacing Murphy, a stage actress, made the transition to cinema extremely well.

p, Mort Briskin; d, Lamont Johnson; w, Jo Heims (based on the novel by Naomi A. Hintze); ph, Jack A. Marta (Technicolor); m. Gil Melle; ed, Edward M. Abroms; art d, William D. De Cinces.

Thriller   (PR:C MPAA:PG)

YOU'LL NEVER GET RICH***   (1941) 88m COL bw

Fred Astaire (*Robert Curtis*), Rita Hayworth (*Sheila Winthrop*), John Hubbard (*Tom Barton*), Robert Benchley (*Martin Cortland*), Osa Massen (*Sonya*), Frieda Inescort (*Mrs. Cortland*), Guinn "Big Boy" Williams (*Kewpie Blain*), Donald MacBride (*Top Sergeant*), Cliff Nazarro (*Swivel Tongue*), Marjorie Gateson (*Aunt Louise*), Ann Shoemaker (*Mrs. Barton*), Boyd Davis (*Col. Shiller*), Mary Currier (*Costume Designer*), Robert E. Homans (*Stage Doorman*), Sunnie O'Dea (*Marjorie*), Martha Tilton, Gwen Kenyon (*Singers*), Frank Ferguson (*Justice of Peace*), Emmett Vogan (*Jenkins*), Jack Rice (*Jewelry Clerk*), Hal K. Dawson (*Information*), Harry Burns (*Foreigner*), Patti McCarty (*Young Girl*), Edward McWade (*Army Doctor*), Lester Dorr (*Photographer*), Tim Ryan (*Policeman*), Frank Sully, Garry Owen (*Robert's Guards*), Paul Irving (*Gen. Trafscott*), Harry Strang (*Colonel's Orderly*), Eddie Laughton (*Lieutenant*), Dorothy Vernon (*Kewpie's Mother*), Stanley Brown (*Draftee*), Monty Collins (*Sleeper*), Paul Philips (*Capt. Nolan*), Harold Goodwin (*Capt. Williams*), Jack O'Malley (*Sentry*), Eddie Coke (*Chauffeur*), Larry Williams, James Millican (*Privates*), Forrest Prince (*Soloist*), Frank Wayne, Tony Hughes (*Prisoners*), Rudolph Hunter, John Porter, Lucius Brooks, Leon Buck (*The Four Tones*).

This was the first of two pairings for Astaire and Hayworth, and the combination was a marvelous moment for screen dance. Astaire plays a Broadway choreographer working up a new routine with a group of chorus girls. The newest of the chorines, Hayworth, is constantly out of step, so the much-annoyed Astaire takes her from the line to show her a few fancy moves. To his surprise, Hayworth picks up on Astaire's routine with ease, matching his every step. The other girls in line try to discourage any thoughts of partnership from entering Hayworth's mind, but a meeting at a rooftop restaurant quickly puts their suggestions in the ash can. Astaire and Hayworth do an impressive number, but their future as dance partners is diverted when Astaire is drafted. The new inductee's antics make him a well-known visitor to the guardhouse, though this is hardly enough to stop Astaire from continually practicing his steps. By sheer coincidence (as it only happens in the movies) Hayworth just happens to be the girl friend of a captain assigned to the base. A few quick mishaps later, and Hayworth jettisons her captain in favor of Astaire's charms. The plot is full of far-fetched occurrences, but whipped up with such happy frivolity that they really don't matter. The script is full of clever bon mots between Astaire and Hayworth that transcend the film's surface simplicity. Directed with a good sense of style, this is enjoyable, though not a stellar musical. The dance sequences between Astaire and Hayworth are marvelous. Her footwork is tops, complementing Astaire's skills without playing second fiddle to him. After Ginger Rogers, Hayworth was probably Astaire's best dance partner and the two would team up once more in YOU WERE NEVER LOVELIER the following year. Astaire was pleased to work with Hayworth, particularly because she was the daughter of Eduardo Cansino, a dancer-choreographer who was an old friend of Astaire. Hayworth was understandably nervous about dancing opposite a talent of Astaire's caliber but the ever-playful dancer did everything he could to put her at ease, teasing her with cold hands dipped in ice water before taking her in his arms during rehearsals. Astaire always remained disappointed that this and the follow-up film weren't Technicolor productions, but wartime considerations made the expensive process an unrealistic budget item. Porter's wonderful songs include the Oscar nominated tune "Since I Kissed My Baby Goodbye." None, however, became the big hit that other Porter numbers did because of a then ongoing ASCAP radio strike. No ASCAP songs received any air play during this lengthy battle, and the tunes from YOU'LL NEVER GET RICH consequently never got the attention they deserved. Writing the score for a military- themed musical was hardly Porter's forte, and he had a few problems in adapting his style from romantic love songs to patriotic ditties. Studio boss Harry Cohn insisted that Porter's songs be heard by secretaries and other office workers before final approval, convinced that these ordinary people would be a good measuring stick for public tastes. Porter took this unusual practice in stride, though he was somewhat annoyed by it. The other songs include: "The A-stairable Rag" (performed by the Delta Rhythm Boys, danced by Astaire), "Shootin' the Works for Uncle Sam" (sung by Astaire, chorus), "Wedding Cake Walk," "Dream Dancing," "Boogie Barcarolle," "So Near and Yet So Far."

p, Samuel Bischoff; d, Sidney Lanfield; w, Michael Fessier, Ernest Pagano; ph, Phil Tannura; ed, Otto Meyer; md, Morris Stoloff; art d, Lionel Banks, Rudolph Sternad; cos, Robert Kalloch; ch, Robert Alton; m/l, Cole Porter; makeup, Clay Campbell.

Musical   Cas.   (PR:A MPAA:NR)

YOUNG AMERICA½   (1932) 70m FOX bw

Spencer Tracy (*Jack Doray*), Doris Kenyon (*Edith Doray*), Tommy Conlon (*Arthur Simpson*), Ralph Bellamy (*Judge Blake*), Beryl Mercer (*Grandma Beamish*), Sarah Padden (*Mrs. Taylor*), Robert E. Homans (*Patrolman Weems*), Raymond Borzage (*Nutty*), Dawn O'Day 'Anne Shirley' (*Mabel Saunders*), Betty Jane Graham (*Cassie Taylor*), Louise Beavers (*Maid*), Spec O'Donnell (*Bull Butler*), William Pawley, Eddie Sturgis.

A mediocre melodrama which is raised from obscurity only by the fine performances of Tracy and Bellamy as their lives are affected by a young delinquent, Conlon. The youngster and his friend, Borzage (the nephew of the director), are paroled by judge Bellamy into the custody of Conlon's stodgy aunt, Graham, only to find that life under her roof is unbearable. They decide to take refuge with Borzage's grandmother, Mercer. When the boys discover that she has taken ill they try to awaken druggist Tracy but have no success. Instead they break into his store in the hope of finding medicine, but are apprehended by police. Conlon again faces the judge when Kenyon, Tracy's sympathetic wife, agrees to take the boy into her custody. Tracy, however, is violently opposed to her act of kindness. Later, when Conlon overhears an argument between Tracy and Kenyon, he sees himself as an obstacle coming between their marriage. He decides to run off, but before he can leave for good he witnesses a robbery in the drugstore. Conlon intervenes and is taken hostage by the criminals. The quick-thinking lad causes an accident in the getaway car, enabling the police to capture the lawbreakers. Tracy is moved by Conlon's heroic actions and is now convinced that he should adopt the boy. This was the first pairing of Tracy and director Borzage (they would work together again the following year in MAN'S CASTLE), though Tracy had nearly appeared in Borzage's Oscar-winning BAD GIRL. Tracy, who had been friends with Borzage since arriving in Hollywood, had been looking forward to working with the director who, after winning an Oscar in 1927 for SEVENTH HEAVEN, was being highly touted. However, the studio chief at Fox, Winfield Sheehan, was pressured by investors to cast the up-and-coming James Dunn in the role. Although YOUNG AMERICA got none of the same praise as BAD GIRL, Tracy received a handsome share of laudatory reviews. While his next film, SOCIETY GIRL, had him second-billed to Dunn, Tracy would soon come into his own as one of Hollywood's favorite faces.

d, Frank Borzage; w, William Conselman (based on a play by John Frederick Ballard); ph, George Schneiderman; ed, Margaret Clancey; md, George Lipschultz; art d, Duncan Cramer.

Drama   (PR:AA MPAA:NR)

YOUNG AMERICA**   (1942) 73m FOX bw (GB: WE HUMANS)

Jane Withers, Jane Darwell, Lynne Roberts, William Tracy, Robert Cornell, Roman Bohnen, Irving Bacon, Ben Carter, Louise Beavers, Darryl Hickman, Sally Harper, Carmencita Johnson, Daphne Ogden, Charles Arnt, Myra Marsh, Hamilton McFadden.

Basically a vehicle with which to promote the ventures of the 4-H Club, with Withers journeying from her spoiled city existence to a midwestern farm. She becomes so involved in the work on the farm that not only does her personality take a sharp turnabout, but when her sojourn is up she decides to stick it out on the farm. Propaganda even finds a place to take a couple of digs against WW II draft dodgers in the form of the no-good kid Tracy refused to report when his time came up. The 15-year-old Withers, too big for the bratty child roles she had so successfully essayed in the past, didn't quite possess the appearance necessary for the romantic adolescent roles she had played in her three previous pictures; here she reverted to brat-dom, albeit the on-screen conversion to responsible farm girl. Her contract studio, 20th Century-Fox, apparently questioned her continued value; she signed with a lesser light, Republic, the year of this picture's release.

p, Sol M. Wurtzel; d, Louis King; w, Samuel G. Engel; ph, Glen MacWilliams; ed. Louis Loeffler; md, Cyril J. Mockridge.

Drama   (PR:AA MPAA:NR)

YOUNG AND BEAUTIFUL½   (1934) 63m Mascot bw

William Haines (*Bob Preston*), Judith Allen (*June Dale*), Joseph M. Cawthorn (*Herman Cline*), John Miljan (*Gordon Douglas*), Shaw and Lee (*The Piano Movers*), James Bush (*Dick*), Vincent Barnett (*Sammy*), Warren Hymer (*The Champion*), Franklin Pangborn (*Radio Announcer*), James Burtis (*Farrell*), Syd Saylor (*Hansen*), Greta Myers (*Mrs. Kline*), Fred Kelsey (*Hennessy*), Andre Beranger (*Henry Briand*), Ray Mayer (*Song Writer*), Roy Russell (*Don Raymond*), Edward Hearn (*The Director*), Ted Fio Rito, The Wampas Baby Stars: Hazel Hayes, Jean Carmen, Katherine Williams, Judith Arlen, Lu Annie Meredith, Lucille Lund, Jean Gale, Betty Bryson, Dorothy Drake, Ann Hovey, Neoma Judge, Lenore Keef.

Haines is a youthful, exuberant, hyperactive public relations man for a Hollywood movie studio who attempts to show his affection for his sweetheart, Allen, by turning her into a star. So busy is he in this quest that he neglects to demonstrate his feelings in more meaningful ways. The neglected lady turns to Miljan for comfort and finally succeeds in evoking enough jealousy in Haines to get him back together with her. A number of capable character actors fill in the comedy in this inside-the-industry picture, most notably Cawthorn as an irascible, Yiddish-accented studio

magnate. The film is basically a vehicle to showcase the talents of the Wampas Baby Stars of 1934, the first year in which all 12 of the starlets annually selected as "stars of the future" by the Western Association of Motion Picture Advertisers were brought together in a feature film. Executives at low-budget Mascot took advantage of the considerable promotional efforts of the trade association which had first brought to public notice such stars-to-be as Janet Gaynor, Clara Bow, and Joan Crawford.

d, Joseph Santley; w, Santley, Milton Krims, Dore Schary, Al Martin, Colbert Clark; ph, John Stumar ed, Thomas Scott; cos, Claire Julianne; m/l, Ted Fio Rito, Neil Moret, J. Bernard Grossman, Ted Snyder, Jay Kern Brennan, Jack Sterns, Henry Tobias.

Comedy   (PR:A MPAA:NR)

YOUNG AND DANGEROUS½   (1957) 78m Regal/FOX bw

Mark Damon (*Tommy Price*), Lili Gentle (*Rosemary Clinton*), Eddie [Edward] Binns (*Dr. Price*), Frances Mercer (*Mrs. Price*), Dabbs Greer (*Mr. John Clinton*), Ann Doran (*Mrs. Clara Clinton*), George Brenlin (*Weasel Martin*), Jerry Barclay (*Stretch Grass*), William Stevens (*Rock*), Connie Stevens (*Candy*), Danny Welton (*Bones*), Shirley Falls (*Rock's Girl*), Ronald Foster, Bill Shannon (*Rock's Buddies*), Marilyn Carrol (*LR, Girl 1*), Joan Bradshaw, Marion Collier, June Burt (*Carhops*), James Canino (*Other Boy*), X Brands (*Motorcycle Cop*), Bill [William] Boyett (*Pier Cop*), Don Devlin (*Tough Teenager*), Paul Bryar (*Desk Sergeant*), Buddy Mason (*Station House Cop*), Judy Bember, Kim Scala (*Party Girls*), Doris Kemper (*Juvenile Hall Mother*), Brandy Bryan (*Juvenile Hall Girl*), Roy Darmour (*Arresting Officer*), Ron Barbanell (*Drive-In Worker*), Clancy Herne.

This no-name flaming-youth film of the 1950s deals with the coming-of-age of one-time delinquent Damon. Interested only in souped-up cars, juvenile scraps, and scoring with girls, Damon's life style is modified when he puts the make on the aptly named Gentle. Their first date lands them both in a police station, a circumstance that causes her parents, Greer and Doran, to forbid her to see the lusty lad again. This injunction, naturally, spurs their youthful resolve to meet secretly. As the teenage terror discusses his problems with the empathic Gentle, his character changes.

p&d, William F. Claxton; w, James Landis; ph, John M. Nickolaus, Jr. (Regalscope); m, Paul Dunlap; ed. Frank Baldridge; md, Dunlap; art d, Ernst Fegte.

Drama   (PR:A MPAA:NR)

YOUNG AND EAGER   (SEE: CLAUDELLE INGLISH, 1961)

YOUNG AND EVIL**   (1962, Mex.) 79m Domino/John Alexander c
                                  (YAMBAO; AKA: CRY OF THE BEWITCHED)

Ninon Sevilla (*Yambao*), Ramon Gay (*Jorge*), Rosa Elena Durgel (*Beatriz*), Ricardo Roman, Luis Lopez Puente, Olga Guillot.

The presence of Sevilla on a sugar plantation during an extremely bad pestilence has everyone pointing to her as the cause behind the tragedy. That is, everyone except the owner, who saves the girl's life, finding himself trapped into a romance despite the fact that his wife is pregnant. Weird tale of superstition and romance, aimed only at a naive audience.

p, Ruben A. Calderon; d, Alfredo B. Crevenna; w, Julio Alejandro de Castro (based on a story by Julio Albo); ph, Raul Martinez Solares (Eastmancolor); m, Lan Adomian; ed, Gloria Schoemann; art d, Salvador Lozano Mena; ch, Rodney.

Drama   (PR:C MPAA:NR)

YOUNG AND IMMORAL, THE   (SEE: SINISTER URGE, THE, 1961)

YOUNG AND INNOCENT*½   (1938, Brit.) 84m GAU-G.B.
                                  Productions bw (THE GIRL WAS YOUNG)

Nova Pilbeam (*Erica Burgoyne*), Derrick de Marney (*Robert Tisdall*), Percy Marmont (*Col. Burgoyne*), Edward Rigby (*Old Will*), Mary Clare (*Aunt Margaret*), John Longden (*Inspector Kent*), George Curzon (*Guy*), Basil Radford (*Uncle Basil*), Pamela Carme (*Christine Clay*), George Merritt (*Sgt. Miller*), J.H. Roberts (*Henry Briggs*), Jerry Verno (*Driver*), H.F. Maltby (*Sergeant*), Gerry Fitzgerald (*Singer*), Alfred Hitchcock (*Clumsy Photographer*), John Miller, Torin Thatcher, Peggy Simpson, Anna Konstam, Beatrice Varley, William Fazan, Frank Atkinson, Fred O'Donovan, Albert Chevalier, Richard George, Jack Vyvian, Clive Baxter, Pamela Bevan, Humbertson Wright, Syd Crossley, Frederick Piper, Billy Shine.

One of Hitchcock's more charming efforts, this thriller stars the endearing 18-year-old Pilbeam, who had previously been seen as the kidnaped daughter from 1935's THE 39 STEPS. Pilbeam is the daughter of police constable Marmount, who is heading an investigation into the strangulation death of an actress whose body was washed ashore, along with the murder weapon-the belt of a raincoat. The prime, and in fact only, suspect is de Marney who maintains his innocence, despite the fact that everything is against him-he was friendly with the dead woman, he was included in her will, and his raincoat is missing. On learning of his supposed guilt, de

Marney faints and is revived by Pilbeam, who has had some nurses training. De Marney is brought to trial, but dons a disguise and slips out of the courtroom. He later meets up with Pilbeam while escaping through the countryside, getting a ride as far as a deserted farmhouse. Fearing the repercussions of Marmount and his office, Pilbeam resists the temptation to help de Marney, with whom she is falling in love. De Marney charmingly tries to convince her to return later that evening and drive him to the tavern where he lost his raincoat. That evening at dinner with Marmount and her precocious brothers, Pilbeam is torn trying to decide whether or not to slip away. Everyone around the table begins to discuss the case and Pilbeam learns that De Marney has no money and very little hope at escaping. She sneaks away unnoticed and brings de Marney food and money. When De Marney carelessly throws some paper out an open window, he is spotted by a couple of fumbling constables. De Marney and Pilbeam are pursued but manage to escape to the tavern where the raincoat was lost. De Marney learns, after a scuffle, that an old hobo, Rigby, has the coat. To provide herself with an alibi which explains her lengthy absence, Pilbeam plans a quick visit to her aunt, Clare. The visit doesn't go as planned, however, when Pilbeam realizes that it is her young cousin's birthday party. Pilbeam and de Marney are forced into staying for a while, while the suspicious Clare grows increasingly nosey. The young and innocent fugitives make their getaway when Clare is blind-folded in a game of "blind-man's bluff." Clare calls Marmount to inform him that Pilbeam has just left, allowing Marmount the chance to leave a message for her at the next town along the way. When the town police inform Pilbeam of her father's call, de Marney is recognized and again they are pursued. De Marney finally finds Rigby at a homeless shelter and explains his situation. He is overheard, however, and the police are called. Along the way Rigby gives him the raincoat, but de Marney is still in trouble since the belt is missing. Rigby does provide the pair with an important clue, describing the man he got the coat from as having a nervous eye twitch. The police catch up and this time the chase leads to a coal mine. The weight of their car leads to a cave-in and Pilbeam is nearly swallowed up in the process, being saved at the last possible second by de Marney's outstretched hand (a rescue scene that would be duplicated over twenty years later in NORTH BY NORTHWEST). Pilbeam is apprehended, but de Marney eludes the police. Pilbeam is reunited with her father, who plans to resign from his post out of humiliation for his daughter's criminal involvement. Later that evening, Pilbeam is rustled from her bedroom by de Marney and Rigby. Another clue leads them to a hotel where they suspect the murderer with the eye twitch is staying. De Marney stays out of sight while Pilbeam and Rigby scope the crowded grand ballroom, searching among the hundreds of dancers for someone with a twitch. As the band plays the singer sings, "Who's the man you seldom think of when you think of a band?" From across the ballroom, the camera begins moving towards the bandstand through the crowd, while the song continues, "When it comes to doing tricks with a pair of hickory sticks, I'm right here to tell you, mister, no one can like the drummer man." The camera continues its long, sweeping, suspenseful dolly to a group of musicians in blackface, finally, coming to rest just inches away from the drummer's twitching eyes. Noticing the police who have surrounded the ballroom (the police looking for de Marney), and spotting Rigby in the crowd, the drummer's paranoia sets in, thinking that he is about to be caught. He loses the beat, his eyes twitch uncontrollably, he bangs cymbals with no regard to rhythm. It seems to be too late, however, as De Marney has been caught, and the police have just begun taking Pilbeam and Rigby away. Just then the drummer collapses, prompting Pilbeam, with her nursing skill, to come to his aid. His twitching eyes give him away, and when he is identified by Rigby, he confesses laughing maniacally and described how he killed the actress. De Marney's name is cleared, Marmont can return to his post as Chief Constable, and the contented Pilbeam shines proudly as she stands between them. While not generally considered one of Hitchcock's finer films, YOUNG AND INNOCENT, because of its simplicity (or innocence, in keeping with the title), is often overlooked, especially in light of the director's oher British successes, THE MAN WHO KNEW TOO MUCH, THE 39 STEPS, or THE LADY VANISHES. Although its plot is simply a reworking of THE 39 STEPS without the spy angle, YOUNG AND INNOCENT has a certain delightful charm to it, due entirely to the young Pilbeam, with her glowing Sylvia Sydney-type face. The film also boasts some of Hitchcock's most memorable visual effects, namely the coal mine collapse and the dolly shot into the drummer. For the coal mine, Hitchcock had constructed in the studio a platform which stood 18 feet off the ground. The coal set was created atop that and, when the car and Pilbeam began to slip into the crumbling hole, it was actually slowly falling to the floor of the sound stage. The dolly shot in the hotel is a prime example of Hitchcock's marvelous command of the technical aspects of filmmaking. The shot begins 145 feet away and swoops down and across the ballroom, through the band, and ends up only four inches from the drummer's face–a shot which pushes suspense to the limit as we wonder where, and on whose eyes, it will stop. The British release of this film ran 84 minutes, but when released in the U.S. (under its less popular title THE GIRL WAS YOUNG) it was chopped down to 70 minutes, completely omitting the birthday party scene. To the U.S. distributors, the "blind- man's bluff" scene slowed down the suspense of the chase, but Hitchcock said it was a pivotal one which illustrated the futility of the police's chase, adding "When the film was released in this country, that one scene they cut out. It was absurd, that was the essence of the film!" Another scene that never made it into the film (in both the U.S. and British prints) was a finale which saw de Marney sitting at the dinner table beside

Pilbeam and opposite Marmount, with the the girl's mouthy brothers in between. YOUNG AND INNOCENT also marks one of Hitchcock's most memorable, and lengthiest, cameos–as a photographer outside the courthouse fumbling absent-mindedly with his camera.

p, Edward Black; d, Alfred Hitchcock; w, Charles Bennett, Alma Reville, Antony Armstrong, Edwin Greenwood, Gerald Savory (based on the novel *A Schilling for Candles* by Josephine Tey); ph, Bernard Knowles; m, Louis Levy; ed, Charles Frend; art d, Alfred Junge; spec ph eff, Jack Whitehead.

Crime   **Cas.**   **(PR:A   MPAA:NR)**

YOUNG AND THE BRAVE, THE**   (1963) 84m MGM bw

Rory Calhoun *(Sgt. Ed Brent)*, William Bendix *(Staff Sgt. Peter L. Kane)*, Richard Jaeckel *(Cpl. John Estway)*, Manuel Padilla *(Han)*, Richard Arlen *(Col. Ralph Holbein)*, John Agar *(Intelligence Officer)*, Robert Ivers *(Pvt. Kirk Wilson)*, Weaver Levy *(Communist Soldier)*, Dennis Richards *(Stretcher Bearer)*, Robert Goshen *(Lt. Ulysses Nero)*, Willard Lee *(Han's Father)*, Beirne Lay, Jr *(Army Major)*, Flame the Dog.

During the Korean Conflict Calhoun, Bendix, and Ivers escape their captors to flee across enemy lines to freedom, a feat that is made possible only through the efforts of a young boy and his German Shepherd dog. The boy's parents were earlier killed by the Communists for harboring the American soldiers. Ivers is killed and the brainwashed Jaeckel joins the survivors. Nearing their rescue helicopter, Calhoun and Bendix refuse to board until they are sure that the Korean lad who helped them is safe. Though they will have to face a possible court-martial, they bring the youth back to America with them, Calhoun acting as his adopted father. Though a good cast was assembled for this routine feature, it was virtually wasted with material laden with sappy cliches and overly talk.

p, A. C. Lyles; d, Frances D. Lyon; w, Beirne Lay, Jr. (based on a story by Ronald Davidson, Harry M. Slott); ph, Emmett Bergholz; m, Ronald Stein; ed, Robert Leo; art d, Paul Sylos, Jr.; spec eff, Roger George; makeup, Ted Coodley.

War   **(PR:A   MPAA:NR)**

YOUNG AND THE COOL, THE   (See: TWIST ALL NIGHT, 1961)

YOUNG AND THE DAMNED, THE   (SEE: LOS OLVIDADOS, 1950, Mex.)

YOUNG AND THE GUILTY, THE**   (1958, Brit.) 65m
Welwyn/Associated British-Pathe bw

Phyllis Calvert *(Mrs. Connor)*, Andrew Ray *(Eddie Marshall)*, Edward Chapman *(Mr. Connor)*, Janet Munro *(Sue Connor)*, Campbell Singer *(Mr. Marshall)*, Hilda Fenemore *(Mrs. Marshall)*, Jean St. Clair *(Mrs. Humbolt)*, Sonia Rees *(Brenda)*.

The budding romance between two above-average high-school students is given a temporary setback when their parents come across one of their love letters and begin making a mountain out of a molehill. When the two are told they cannot see each other, more secretive meetings take place, which gives their innocent affair a touch of passion. Eventually the ice breaks and the kids are allowed to pursue their friendship in the open. Given validity by the touching performances of the two lead youngsters, Ray and Munro.

p, Warwick Ward; d, Peter Cotes; w, Ted Willis (based on his TV play); ph, Norman Warwick; m, Sydney John Kay; ed, Seymour Logie.

Drama   **(PR:A   MPAA:NR)**

YOUNG AND THE IMMORAL, THE
(SEE: THE SINISTER URGE, 1961)

YOUNG AND THE PASSIONATE, THE   (SEE: VITELLONI, 1956, Ital./Fr.)

YOUNG AND WILD**   (1958) 69m Esla/REP bw

Gene Evans *(Detective Sgt. Fred Janusz)*, SCott Marlowe *(Rick Braden)*, Carolyn Kearney *(Valerie Whitman)*, Robert Arthur *(Jerry Coltrin)*, James Kevin *("Allie" Allison)*, Tom Gilson *("Beejay" Phillips)*, Ken Lynch *(David Whitman)*, Emlen Davies *(Mrs. Whitman)*, Morris Ankrum *(Capt. Egan)*, Wendell Holmes *(Uncle Lew)*, John Zaremba *(Sgt. Larsen)*.

Marlowe leads a group of thrill-seeking young punks as they drive down the California highways, sideswiping one couple and then becoming involved in a hit-and-run accident which leaves the passengers in the other car dead. As the only people capable of identifying the youngsters, Arthur and Kearney find themselves the victims of intense harassment, forcing the pair of lovers to resort to their wits in order to hold off the hoodlums until the law can arrive. Fast, furious, and frightening. Kearney is effective in her first feature film.

p, Sidney Picker; d, William Witney; w, Arthur T. Horman; ph, Jack Marta (Naturama); m, Gerald Roberts; ed, Joseph Harrison; md, Roberts; art d,

Ralph Oberg; cos, Alexis Davidoff.

Crime/Drama   (PR:A MPAA:NR)

YOUNG AND WILLING**½   (1943) 83m Cinema Guild/UA bw

William Holden (*Norman Reese*), Eddie Bracken (*George Bodell*), Robert Benchley (*Arthur Kenny*), Susan Hayward (*Kate Benson*), Martha O'Driscoll (*Dottie Coburn*), Barbara Britton (*Marge Benson*), Mabel Paige (*Mrs. Garnet*), Florence MacMichael (*Muriel Foster*), James Brown (*Tony Dennison*), Jay Fassett (*Mr. Coburn*), Paul Hurst, Olin Howlin 'Howland' (*Cops*), Billy Bevan (*Phillips*), Barbara Slater, Laurie Douglas, Blanche Grady, Lynda Grey, Louise LaPlanche, Judith Gibson, Cheryl Walker, Kenneth Griffith (*Performers*), Fay Helm (*Miss Harris*), Kenny's Secretary, William Cabanne (*Soda Jerk*), Betty Farrington (*Woman*).

A fluffy film adaptation of an equally fluffy Broadway play about three struggling actors who share a Greenwich Village apartment with three struggling actresses. The young men–Holden, Bracken, and Brown–sleep in one bedroom while the ladies–Hayward, O'Driscoll, and Britton–share another. While trying to strike it rich on the stage the group must figure out a way to pay past- due rent to landlady Paige. They get a break when they learn that their downstairs neighbor is Benchley, a highly regarded playwright. Naturally, the close confines of the six lead to an entanglement of romances. O'Driscoll has fallen for Holden, but he seems not to take notice; Hayward is in love with Bracken; and Britton and Brown have secretly married. To further complicate matters, Britton is pregnant and Brown is about to enter the service. One day Paige, who is still demanding her rent, hands the young hopefuls an unsigned play that she has found. They enthusiastically begin rehearsals in the apartment. Benchley soon discovers that they are rehearsing his long-lost first play–one he wrote when he lived in the apartment years ago as a struggling playwright. Holden and the gang con Benchley into watching their rehearsal by telling him the play has been lost, but that they have memorized it. Eventually their young talent is recognized and, with Benchley's assistance, they are given the chance to bring their version of the play to the stage. While the source material isn't particularly strong, the enthusiasm of the young actors (Holden was 24; Hayward 23) is enough to recommend the picture. Hayward discovered that playwright Swann had based his work on the true adventures of his sister (on whom Hayward's character was based). With characteristic preparatory fervor, Hayward made contact with Swann's sister, who was in Hollywood at the time, and based her characterization on the resulting experience. Produced by Paramount in 1942, YOUNG AND WILLING was one of a handful of films that were sold to United Artists (I MARRIED A WITCH and THE CRYSTAL BALL were also included) and thereby saw a delayed release. Unfortunately for Holden, this less-than-memorable picture did not have the public waiting in anticipation for his follow-up. Holden would fall further from memory until 1947, the date that marked his return to the screen after a stint in the service.

p&d, Edward H. Griffith; w, Virginia Van Upp (based on the play "Out of the Frying Pan" by Francis Swann); ph, Leo Tover; ed, Eda Warren; art d, Hans Dreier, Ernst Fegte; cos, Edith Head; makeup, Wally Westmore.

Comedy   **Cas.**   (PR:A MPAA:NR)

YOUNG AND WILLING**½   (1964, Brit.) 113m Rank/UNIV bw (GB: THE WILD AND THE WILLING; AKA: THE YOUNG AND THE WILLING)

Virginia Maskell (*Virginia Chown*), Paul Rogers (*Prof. Chown*), Ian McShane (*Harry Brown*), Samantha Eggar (*Josie*), John Hurt (*Phil*), Catherine Woodville (*Sarah*), David Summer (*John*), John Standing (*Arthur*), Johnny Briggs (*Dai*), Johnny Sekka (*reggie*), Jeremy Brett (*Gilby*), Charles Kay (*Tibbs*), John Barrie (*Mr. Corbett*), Victor Brooks (*Fire Chief*), Ernest Clark (*Vice Chancellor*), Denise Coffey (*Jane*), George A. Cooper (*1st Customer*), Harry Locke (*2nd Customer*), Megs Jenkins (*Mrs. Corbett*), Richard Leech (*Police Inspector*), Marianne Stone (*Clara*), Richard Warner (*Coroner*), John Welsh (*Publican*), Jeremy Young (*Policeman*).

McShane is a student from a poor family who is going to a university on scholarship. He is well aware of his background and finds the class consciousness of his professors to be repugnant. He rebels against everything, getting drunk and fooling around with his girl friend Eggar. Rogers is a professor who likes McShane for his academic brilliance though he is unimpressed with the hell-raising. He takes on McShane as a sort of protege and helps him with his studies. Rogers and his younger wife Maskell have a troubled marriage. They constantly argue and she has an occasional romantic fling with a student. He puts up with this as well as with her drinking. Maskell and McShane have a brief affair but when he wants her to run off with him to start a new life she leaves him. He and his roommate Hurt (excellent in an early role) go off to climb a university tower. Hurt, a shy young man who is much taken with his brash roommate, slips and falls to his death. McShane leaves school in disgrace. This is a well-played drama with an excellent cast. McShane gives a fine portrayal and is well supported by Maskell. However, the drama is hackneyed. Youth in rebellion is a theme older than movies and this film brings nothing new to the idea. Despite the excellent characterizations these are people any filmgoer has seen before and will doubtless see again. Worth seeing simply for the strong performances. In addition to Paramor's score, music includes "Rhapsody on a

Theme by Paganini" (Sergei Rachmaninoff, played by Edward Rubach) and a jazz sequence performed by Mike Cotton and his Jazzmen.

p, Betty E. Box; d, Ralph Thomas; w, Nicholas Phipps, Mordecai Richler (based on the play "The Tinker" by Laurence Dobie, Robert Sloman); ph, Ernest Steward; m, Norrie Paramor; ed, Alfred Roome; md, Paramor; art d, Alex Vetchinsky; set d, Arthur Taksen; cos, Yvonne Caffin; makeup, W. T. Partleton.

Drama   (PR:C MPAA:NR)

YOUNG ANIMALS, THE   (SEE: BORN WILD, 1968)

YOUNG APHRODITES**   (1966, Gr.) 89m Minos Anzervos/Janus bw (MIKRES APHRODITES)

Takis Emmanouel (*Tsakalos*), Eleni Prokopiou (*Arta*), Vangelis Joannides (*Skymnos*), Cleopatra Rota (*Chloe*), Anestis Vlachos (*Erster Hirte*), Yannis Jeannino (*Molassas*), Kostas Papakonstantinou (*Stummer Hirte*).

Tragic tale of a young shepherd's disastrous attempt to find affection from an older village girl with whom he has fallen in love. As she mimics what she has seen adults doing, the boy catches her making love to another youth. A hard-to-swallow ending has the shepherd committing suicide as a result.

p, George Zervos, Nikos Koundouros; d, Koundouros; w, Vassilis Vassilikos, Kostas Sphikas; ph, Giovanni Variano; m, Yannis Markopoulos; ed, George Tsaoulis.

Drama   **Cas.**   (PR:C MPAA:NR)

YOUNG AS YOU FEEL**½   (1931) 78m FOX bw

Will Rogers (*Lemuel Morehouse*), Fifi D'Orsay (*Fleurette*), Lucien Littlefield (*Marley*), Donald Dillaway (*Billy Morehouse*), Terrance Ray (*Tom Morehouse*), Lucille Browne (*Dorothy Gregson*), Rosalie Roy (*Rose Gregson*), John T. Murray (*Col. Stanhope*), C. Henry Gordon (*Lamson*), Marcia Harris (*Mrs. Denton*), Joan Standing (*Lemuel's Secretary*), Gregory Gaye (*Pierre*).

Owner of a successful meatpacking business, Rogers adheres to a rigid schedule, sensing that to deviate in any respect from his rigid habits will bring ruin. His two sons, Dillaway and Ray, are playboys: one a womanizing cafe-goer, the other a Greenwich Village dilettante with arty pretensions. The punctilious Rogers bursts out of his self-imposed confinement when he meets saucy D'Orsay. Now nattily attired, he spends his afternoons at the racetrack with the Gallic girl. He is spotted by his boys at their favorite haunts; his hilarious criticisms at a gallery opening highlight his performance. During the course of his revivification, Rogers even turns heroic, helping D'Orsay escape the ruinous financial scheming of swindler Stanhope. His astonished sons are shocked into assuming responsibility for their lives and livelihoods by these paternal peccadilloes. Rogers' relationship with D'Orsay proves to have been platonic as, finally, he helps her to return to her husband.

d, Frank Borzage, w, Edwin Burke (based on the play "Father and the Boys" by George Ade); ph, Chester Lyons; ed, Margaret V. Clancey; art d, Jack Schultze; m/l, "The Cute Little Things You Do," James F. Hanley.

Comedy   (PR:AAA MPAA:NR)

YOUNG AS YOU FEEL**½   (1940) 59m FOX bw

Jed Prouty (*John Jones*), Spring Byington (*Mrs. Jones*), Joan Valerie (*Bonnie*), Russell Gleason (*Herbert Thompson*), Kenneth Howell (*Jack Jones*), George Ernest (*Roger Jones*), June Carlson (*Luey Jones*), Florence Roberts (*Granny Jones*), William Mahan (*Bobby Jones*), Helen Ericson (*Sandra*), George Givot (*Boris Mousilvitch*), Marvin Stephens (*Tommy McGuire*), Harlan Briggs (*Dr. Ainsley*), Harry Shannon (*Gillespie*), Jack Carson (*Norcross*), Guy Repp (*Baron Gonzales de Corbana*), Esther Brodelet (*Polly Marshall*), Gladys Blake (*Ann Benton*), Irma Wilson (*Brenda Walters*), John Sheehan (*Fire Chief*), Lee Shumway (*New York Policeman*), John H. Elliott (*Ambulance Doctor*), Bruce Warren (*Norcross Representative*), Joan Leslie, Constance Keane [Veronica Lake] (*Girls*), Billy Lechner (*Boy*).

This was the final entry in the JONES FAMILY series (see Index), the sixteenth adventure of the clan designed for family audiences of the 1930s. The father (Prouty) decides it's time they led a more sophisticated life style so he sells the family drugstore and leads his pack off to New York City. There they find sophistication is not all it's cracked up to be as various confidence artists and shady ladies try to bilk the bumpkins for everything they have. Tired of "sophistication," the family packs up and heads back to the small town where they truly belong. Though the comedy is slight, the simple plot is told in an entertaining manner and given a good production. The cast is fine for the fare. The fourth-billed Gleason was, with his parents James and Lucille, a staple of Republic's concurrently competititve family series, THE HIGGINS FAMILY (see Index). Such intercasting amity among competitors was rare at the time, but the producer of Republic's series had died, and the product was temporarily shelved. When it was renewed the following year, the elder Gleasons were not part of it.

p, John Stone; d, Malcolm St. clair; w, Joseph Hoffman, Stanley Rauh (based on the play "Merry Andrew" by Lewis Beach, and on characters created by

Katharine Kavanaugh); ph, Charles Clarke; ed, Harry Reynolds; md, Samuel Kaylin; cos, Helen A. Myron.

Comedy (PR:AAA MPAA:NR)

YOUNG AT HEART*** (1955) 117m Arwin/WB c

Doris Day (*Laurie Tuttle*), Frank Sinatra (*Barney Sloan*), Gig Young (*Alex Burke*), Ethel Barrymore (*Aunt Jessie*), Dorothy Malone (*Fran Tuttle*), Robert Keith (*Gregory Tuttle*), Elisabeth Fraser (*Amy Tuttle*), Alan Hale, Jr. (*Robert Neary*), Lonny Chapman (*Ernest Nichols*), Frank Ferguson (*Bartell, Bar Owner*), Marjorie Bennett (*Mrs. Ridgefield, Neighbor with Dogs*), John Maxwell (*Doctor*), William McLean (*Husband*), Barbara Pepper (*Wife*), Robin Raymond (*Girl*), Tito Vuolo (*Fat Man in Car*), Grazia Narciso (*Fat Man's Wife*), Ivan Browning (*Porter*), Joe Forte (*Minister*), Cliff Ferre (*Bartender*), Harte Wayne (*Conductor*), Celeste Bryant (*Little Girl*).

A slick but empty remake of 1938's FOUR DAUGHTERS, sans one daughter. Day and sisters Malone and Fraser live with their father (Keith) and aunt (Barrymore). Into their lives comes Young, a composer working on a musical comedy. Day quickly falls in love with him, as does Malone. Young calls in a friend of his to arrange the musical score, embittered pianist and composer Sinatra. Sinatra falls in love with Day, although she and Young plan to marry. On the eve of their wedding, Day learns of her sister's feelings and leaves to go to the city with Sinatra. They are married, and in time she comes to love him totally, though he is unconvinced of the sincerity of her emotion. Bad luck strikes again and again, and Sinatra decides to end it all with a car crash. He survives, though, and accepts that Day loves him and they start a new and happy life together. All the talents of the studio were behind this film, but to no avail. It simply fails to generate much interest. Day is relaxed and reasonably convincing and Sinatra is also good, though rather limited. The rest of the cast do little to distinguish themselves and the production values, while full of the usual studio polish, don't pull this one off. The songs are nice, though, including "Young at Heart" (Johnny Richards, Carolyn Leigh), "Someone to Watch Over Me" (George Gershwin, Ira Gershwin), "Just One of Those Things" (Cole Porter), "One for My Baby" (Harold Arlen, Johnny Mercer), all sung by Frank Sinatra, "Hold Me in Your Arms" (Ray Heindorf, Charles Henderson, Don Pippin), "Ready, Willing, and Able" (Floyd Huddeston, Al Rinker), "Till My Love Comes Back to Me" (Paul Francis Webster to Felix Mendelssohn's "On Wings of Song"), "There's a Rising Moon for Every Falling Star" (Webster, Sammy Fain), sung by Day. Day and Sinatra sing a duet on "You, My Love" (Mack Gordon, James Van Heusen).

p, Henry Blanke; d, Gordon Douglas; w, Liam O'Brien (based on the screenplay for the film FOUR DAUGHTERS by Julius J. Epstein, Lenore Coffee from the story "Sister Act" by Fanny Hurst); ph, Ted McCord (Warner Color); ed, William Ziegler; md, Ray Heindorf; art d, John Beckman; set d, William Wallace; cos, Howard Shoup; spec eff, H.F. Koenekamp; makeup, Gordon Bau; piano solos played by Andre Previn.

Musical Cas. (PR:A MPAA:NR)

YOUNG BESS***½ (1953) 112m MGM c

Jean Simmons (*Young Bess*), Stewart Granger (*Thomas Seymour*), Deborah Kerr (*Catherine Parr*), Charles Laughton (*King Henry VIII*), Kay Walsh (*Mrs. Ashley*), Guy Rolfe (*Ned Seymour*), Kathleen Byron (*Anne Seymour*), Cecil Kellaway (*Mr. Parry*), Rex Thompson (*Edward*), Robert Arthur (*Barnaby*), Leo G. Carroll (*Mr. Mums*), Norma Varden (*Lady Tyrwhitt*), Alan Napier (*Robert Tyrwhitt*), Noreen Corcoran (*Young Bess at age 6*), Ivan Triesault (*Danish Envoy*), Elaine Stewart (*Anne Boleyn*), Dawn Addams (*Kate Howard*), Doris Lloyd (*Mother Jack*), Lumsden Hare (*Archbishop Thomas Cranmer*), Lester Matthews (*Sir William Paget*), Fay Wall (*Woman*), Patrick Whyte (*Officer*), Frank Eldridge, John Sheffield (*English Officers*), Carl Saxe (*Executioner*), Ann Tyrrell (*Mary*), Maj. Sam Harris, Raymond Lawrence, David Cavendish (*Council Men*), Clive Morgan, Charles Keane (*Halberdiers*), Ian Wolfe (*Stranger*), Reginald Sheffield (*Court Recorder*), John Trueman (*Yeoman*).

Good costume drama has Simmons the title princess, on her way to becoming Elizabeth I. Starting out showing Elizabeth as queen, the film moves to flashback as two old, loyal retainers recall when, as a young girl, she is sent away by her father, Henry VIII (Laughton), when her mother, Anne Boleyn, goes to the headsman's block. Laughton goes through a series of wives until he marries Kerr, and Simmons finally is allowed to move back into the palace, finding some measure of love with her new stepmother. Laughton dies not long after and sickly Thompson, Simmons' younger half-brother, becomes regent. Simmons loves Granger, the First Lord Admiral of the Navy, but she arranges to have her brother order Granger to marry Kerr. Granger is devoted to his wife, but when she dies he tells Simmons that he has always loved her. Granger's brother, Rolfe, is a court schemer, and when he finds out about his brother's infatuation, he accuses him of seducing Simmons and Granger goes to the block even as Thompson is writing out a pardon. Although playing fast and loose with a lot of facts, the film is dramatically very sound and the flashback structure is remarkably smooth. All the performances by the almost entirely British cast are excellent, with Thompson, Rolfe, and Laughton (redoing his most famous role) standouts. Rosher's color photography is masterful, conveying the feeling of old paintings from the period, and the score by Rozsa is very good.

p, Sidney Franklin; d, George Sidney; w, Jan Lustig, Arthur Wimperis (based on the novel by Margaret Irwin); ph, Charles Rosher (Technicolor); m, Miklos Rozsa; ed, Arthur E. Winters; art d, Cedric Gibbons, Urie McCleary.

Historical Drama (PR:A MPAA:NR)

YOUNG BILL HICKOK** (1940) 59m REP bw

Roy Rogers (*Bill Hickok*), George "Gabby" Hayes (*"Gabby"*), Jacqueline Wells [Julie Bishop] (*Louise Mason*), John Miljan (*Nicholas Tower*), Sally Payne (*Calamity Jane*), Archie Twitchell (*Phillip*), Monte Blue (*Marshal Evans*), Hal Taliaferro [Wally Wales] (*Morrell*), Ethel Wales (*Mrs. Stout*), Jack Ingram (*Red*), Monte Montague (*Majors*), Iron Eyes Cody, Fred Burns, Frank Ellis, Slim Whitaker, Jack Kirk, Hank Bell, Henry Wills, Dick Elliott, William Desmond, John Elliott, Jack Rockwell, Bill Wolfe, Tom Smith, Trigger the Horse.

Western history a la Roy Rogers. He plays the famed gunslinger in a wholly fictionalized story, complete with cowboy songs, that bears absolutely no resemblance to the actual Bill Hickok. Just after the Civil War Taliaferro and Blue lead a guerrilla band that is plotting–with foreign agent Miljan–to build a mighty and evil empire in the American Southwest. Rogers defeats them in the usual style with Payne (as another maltreated historical figure, "Calamity Jane") giving some assistance. A routine, efficiently told Western with the usual chases, fighting, and musical interludes.

p&d, Joseph Kane; w, Norton S. Parker, Olive Cooper; ph, William Nobles; ed, Lester Orlebeck; md, Cy Feuer.

Western (PR:A MPAA:NR)

YOUNG BILLY YOUNG**½ (1969) 88m Talbot-Youngstein/UA c
(AKA: WHO RIDES WITH KANE)

Robert Mitchum (*Ben Kane*), Angie Dickinson (*Lily Beloit*), Robert Walker, Jr (*Billy Young*), David Carradine (*Jesse Boone*), Jack Kelly (*John Behan*), John Anderson (*Frank Boone*), Deana Martin (*Evvie Cushman*), Paul Fix (*Charlie*), Willis Bouchey (*Doc Cushman*), Parley Baer (*Bell*), Bob Anderson (*Gambler*), Rodolfo Acosta (*Mexican Officer*), Chris Mitchum (*Kane's son*).

After killing a Mexican general, hired killers Walker and Carradine ride off with a posse close behind. Walker's horse falls and he is left stranded by his partner. Ex-sheriff Mitchum, who is hunting for his son's killer, comes upon Walker and takes him along. Mitchum becomes the marshal of Lordsburg in hopes of catching murderer John Anderson. There he meets and falls for Dickinson, a dance hall girl who warns the new marshal about Kelly. He and his sidekick, who just happens to be Carradine, are out to get Mitchum. After Carradine tries to do in the Marshal, Walker changes his mind and accepts Mitchum's offer of a deputy job. Mitchum arrests Carradine, not knowing he's the son of his own son's killer. After learning this, Mitchum decides to use the jailed Carradine as bait in catching Anderson. Walker frees Carradine to prevent a confrontation, but Anderson and Kelly are killed in a violent shoot-out and Carradine is recaptured. Mitchum leaves town with Dickinson and Walker is left in charge as deputy marshal. Direction is effective (though Kennedy had clearly proved he could do much more with the genre the previous year with SUPPORT YOUR LOCAL SHERIFF). Good performances from Mitchum and particularly Dickinson. Considering that this plot is steeped in father-son relationship, the casting was appropriate. Carradine is the son of John; Walker is Jennifer Jones' son; Deana Martin (in a minor role) is Dean's daughter; and Chis Mitchum played Robert's film son in flashback sequences. The elder Mitchum sings the title song!

p, Max E. Youngstein; d&w, Burt Kennedy (based on the novel *Who Rides with Wyatt?* by Will Henry); ph, Harry Stradling, Jr. (DeLuxe Color); m, Shelly Manne; ed, Otho Lovering; art d, Stan Jolley; set d, Richard Friedman; m/1, title song, Manne, Ernie Sheldon.

Western (PR:A MPAA:G)

YOUNG BLOOD*½ (1932) 59m MON bw (GB: LOLA)

Bob Steele, Charles King, Helen Foster, Harry Semels, Neoma Judge, Hank Bell, Henry Roquemore, Lafe McKee, Art Mix, Perry Murdock, Roy Bucko.

An offbeat western with the diminutive Steele as a Robin Hood of the plains who gets his adrenaline rushes from robbing the rich and helping the poor. He also helps a stigmatized foreign actress who is being ostracized by the townswomen. Gunfights and fisticuffs galore in an unusual adult western from the low-budget studio. This is one of eight Steele westerns made at Monogram just after producer Carr joined forces with the studio following the demise of World Wide, his former releasing company. Mon ogram's two major western stars, Bill Cody and Tom Tyler, were released from the studio shortly thereafter. This was the only picture of the eight to be directed by Rosen.

p, Trem Carr; d, Phil Rosen; w, Wellyn Totman.

Western (PR:A MPAA:NR)

YOUNG BRIDE½   (1932) 80m RKO bw (AKA: LOVE STARVED)

Helen Twelvetrees *(Allie Smith)*, Eric Linden *(Charlie Riggs)*, Arline Judge *(Maisie)*, Cliff Edwards *(Pete)*, Roscoe Ates *(Mike)*, Polly Walters *(Patsy)*, Blanche Frederici *(Miss Gordon)*, Allan Fox *(Skeets)*.

Love among the tenements of the big city as the fantasizing Twelvetrees finds the man of her dreams in streetwise Linden, a loudmouthed pool-hall hustler who flaunts his manhood among the taxi-dancing floozies of the local public terpsichorium. When dreamy Twelvetrees learns the nature of the man she married–not too difficult within the confines of a one-room boarding-house domicile–she contemplates suicide. Linden wins some money at pool, but loses it to the mercenary Judge. When he attempts to recover the money, Linden gets overly meretricious, and is beaten for his pains. His lesson learned, the contrite lad creeps back to his bride a changed man. Early kitchen-sink drama with restrained performances and excellent support.

p, David O. Selznick, Harry Joe Brown; d, William A. Seiter; w, Garrett Fort, Ralph Murphy, Jane Murfin (based on the play "Veneer" by Hugh Stanislaus Stange); ph, Arthur Miller; ed, Joseph Kane.

Drama   (PR:C MPAA:NR)

YOUNG BUFFALO BILL**½   (1940) 59m REP bw

Roy Rogers *(Buffalo Bill)*, George "Gabby" Hayes *("Gabby")*, Pauline Moore *(Tonia Regas)*, Hugh Sothern *(Don Regas)*, Chief Thundercloud *(Akuna)*, Julian Rivero *(Pancho)*, Trevor Bardette *(Montez)*, Gaylord Pendleton *(Jerry)*, Wade Boteler *(Col. Calhoun)*, Anna Demetrio *(Elena)*, Estelita Zarco *(Dolores)*, Hank Bell, William Kellogg, Iron Eyes Cody, Jack O'Shea, George Chesebro, Trigger the Horse.

Another pseudo-historical film finds Rogers as the famed western hero, remolded to fit the movie cowboy's persona. The standard, though entertaining, plot finds Rogers helping out the cavalry as they fight off an Indian attack on a Spanish ranch. Hayes plays Rogers' assistant, his usual part, even further bungling any historical accuracy. Even so, the direction builds some excitement in an otherwise standard western outing. The film's only musical number, "Blow, Breeze, Blow", is a better-than-usual cowboy ballad.

p&d, Joseph Kane; w, Harrison Jacobs, Robert Yost, Gerald Geraghty, (based on an original story by Norman Houston); ph, William Nobles; ed, Tony Martinelli; md, Cy Feuer.

Western   (PR:AAA MPAA:NR)

YOUNG CAPTIVES, THE**½   (1959) 61m PAR bw

Steven Marlo *(Jamie Forbes)*, Luana Patten *(Ann Howel)*, Tom Selden *(Benjie Whitney)*, James Chandler *(Tony)*, Ed Nelson *(Norm Britt)*, Dan Sheridan *(Dave)*, Marjorie Stapp *(Blonde Woman)*, Miles Stephens *(Rusty Webster)*, Edward Schaaf *(Gas Station Attendant)*, William C. Shaw *(American Officer)*, Carlo Fiore *(Mexican Officer)*, Lawrence J. Gelbmann *(Sheriff Parker)*, Dan Blocker *(Oil Field Roughneck)*, Allen Kramer *(Shorty)*, Phillip A. Mansour *(Patrolman)*, Joan Granville *(Mrs. Howell)*, Lenore Kingston *(Other Woman)*, Raymond Guth *(Mr. Kingston)*, Carol Nelson *(Waitress)*, Herb Armstrong *(Mr. Howel)*.

A wonderfully lurid low-budget film features Selden and Patten as two starry-eyed teenagers who head to Mexico with elopement in mind. They pick up Marlo, a hitchhiker, and their plans are radically changed, to say the least. He's just killed an oil field worker and now wants to give Selden the same treatment so he can have Patten for himself. To add to their problems, Selden and Patten don't want to contact the law, lest it interfere with their intended marriage! When will these kids learn? A good jazz soundtrack and a pseudo-documentary camera style help out. Look for an appearance by Blocker, soon to move to TV's western hit "Bonanza." An early directorial effort for Kershner, who went on to do the excellent THE EMPIRE STRIKES BACK for George Lucas' STAR WARS series (see Index). The story line bears a strong resemblance to Ida Lupino's THE HITCH-HIKER (1953).

p, Andrew J. Fenady; d, Irvin Kershner; w, Fenady (based on a story by Gordon Hunt, Al Burton); ph, Wallace Kelley; m, Richard Markowitz; ed, Terry Morse; art d, Hal Pereira, Al Y. Roelofs; spec eff, Farciot Edouart.

Drama   (PR:O MPAA:NR)

YOUNG CASSIDY***   (1965, U.S./Brit.) 108m Sextant/MGM c

Rod Taylor *(John Cassidy)*, Flora Robson *(Mrs. Cassidy)*, Jack MacGowran *(Archie)*, Sian Phillips *(Ella)*, T.P. McKenna *(Tom)*, Julie Ross *(Sara)*, Robin Sumner *(Michael)*, Philip O'Flynn *(Mick Mullen)*, Maggie Smith *(Nora)*, Julie Christie *(Daisy Battles)*, Pauline Delaney *(Bessie Ballynoy)*, Edith Evans *(Lady Gregory)*, Michael Redgrave *(William Butler Yeats)*, Arthur O'Sullivan *(Foreman)*, Joe Lynch, Vincent Dowling *(Hurlers)*, Tom Irwin *(Constable)*, John Cowley *(Barman at Cat & Cage)*, Bill Foley *(Publisher's Clerk)*, John Franklin *(Bank Teller)*, Harry Brogan *(Murphy)*, Anne Dalton *(Neighbor)*, Donal Donnelly, Martin Crosbie *(Hearsemen)*, Fred Johnson *(Cab Driver)*, Eddie Golden *(Capt. White)*, Chris Curran *(Man in Phoenix Park)*, James Fitzgerald *(Charlie Ballynoy)*, Shivaun O'Casey *(Lady Gregory's Maid)*, Harold Goldblatt *(Abbey Theatre Manager)*, Ronald Ibbs *(Theat-*

er Attendant), May Craig, May Cluskey *(Women in Foyer)*, Members of the Abbey Theatre Company.

The massive 13-volume autobiography of Irish playwright and rebel Sean O'Casey serves as the source material for this film. Taylor is a young Irishman from a poor family. He spends his days digging ditches as a laborer, and his nights at political meetings and reading books. He eventually turns his attention away from fighting the British to writing pamphlets against them. When a riot breaks out, sparked by a Taylor pamphlet, he meets Christie, a music hall dancer, and they enter into an affair. After a time he leaves her and takes up with Smith, the owner of a small bookshop Taylor frequents. His plays are produced at the Abbey Theatre and he comes to the attention of the literary world. Constantly, though, he is struggling against his own background in poverty and trying to keep from being co-opted by the literary establishment. When his play "The Plough and the Stars" is produced, the audience riots, but later it is hailed as a work of brilliance. As the film ends, Taylor is leaving his home for England and international acclaim. Although the film carries a title at the beginning claiming this as "A John Ford Film,"the great director's contributions are small, totaling less than 10 minutes of screen time. Although he was not in great health and was thoroughly occupied with making CHEYENNE AUTUMN, Ford jumped at the chance to direct this film, offering to forego his usual fee for a mere $50,000. When the shooting of that film was complete, Ford went to Ireland to look over locations. He drank steadily on the flight to Dublin, and when he got off the airplane, the producers of the film, Robert Ginna and Robert Graff, whom Ford came to call "The Bobs," had trouble believing that the drunken, unshaven man who stumbled off the airplane was really Ford. Ford had only a week to spend in Dublin before returning to California for the premiere of CHEYENNE AUTUMN. When the Bobs expressed their dismay over the little time Ford could give them, the crusty director replied, "What do you expect for a lousy 50 grand?" When he returned to Ireland after the disastrous reception of CHEYENNE AUTUMN, he worked only 13 days on the film before falling ill. The Bobs, who had never had much faith in Ford after that initial meeting, were just as happy when they replaced him with Jack Cardiff. The film is unsuccessful on a number of counts, mainly because it lacks a focal point for the story. The performances are good, though, especially Taylor and Christie. The scenes between them were mostly shot by Ford and his idea for the ending, not in the final film, was told to Peter Bogdanovich 'after the disastrous opening of "The Plough and the Stars"': "I wanted Julie Christie, by now a streetwalker, to come over to him and say, 'Oh, Sean, I loved it–it was wonderful–you ought to be proud of yourself. God bless you.' It took this poor little tart to appreciate what he'd done. And she walks away, disappears in the rain, leaving him there. The producers told me why it shouldn't be done that way, but I argued with them, and they promised to do it after I got sick and left. But they didn't. It would have kicked the damn story up."

p, Robert O. Graff, Robert Emmett Ginna; d, Jack Cardiff, John Ford; w, John Whiting (based on the autobiography *Mirror in My House* by Sean O'Casey); ph, Ted Scaife (Metrocolor); m, Sean O'Riada; ed, Anne V. Coates; md, Marcus Dods; art d, Michael Stringer; cos, Margaret Furse; makeup, Ernest Gasser.

Biography/Drama   (PR:C MPAA:NR)

YOUNG CYCLE GIRLS, THE zero   (1979) 80m Peter Perry c

Loraine Ferris, Daphne Lawrence, Deborah Marcus, Lonnie Pense, Kevin O'Neill, Bee Lechat, Billy Bullet.

The odyssey of three nubile girls who set out on their cycles from their Colorado town thinking, like Balboa, to see the Pacific Ocean. On the road, the three undergo numerous adventures involving dancing, drugs, bondage, and violation. On their journey, they are offended by the driver of a pickup truck that has a skull painted on its door. They excoriate the driver. When at last the ladies motorbike over a final dune and see the sea, someone unseen blows their brains out. As the catsup flows, we observe once more the sinister skull on the door of the truck. EASY RIDER (1969) it isn't. Trashy, odoriferous garbage it is.

p&d, Peter Perry; w, John Arnoldy; ph, Ron Garcia; ed, Marco Perri.

Action   (PR:O MPAA:R)

YOUNG DANIEL BOONE**½   (1950) 71m MON c

David Bruce *(Daniel Boone)*, Kristine Miller *(Rebecca Bryan)*, Damian O'Flynn *(Capt. Fraser)*, Don Beddoe *(Charlie Bryan)*, Mary Treen *(Helen Bryan)*, John Mylong *(Col. von Arnheim)*, William Roy *(Little Hawk)*, Stanley Logan *(Col. Benson)*, Herbert Naish *(Pvt. Haslet)*, Nipo T. Strongheart *(Walking Eagle)*, Richard Foote *(Lt. Perkins)*, Stephen S. Harrison *(Sentry)*.

A good film for action though the story isn't much. Bruce plays the frontier hero who must rescue two women who've been kidnaped by Indians. He ends up marrying Miller, one of the hapless victims. O'Flynn is a French spy who could damage the American forces until Bruce unmasks him. The action runs at a high level, which is good, since the cast is little more than adequate. Some nice color camera work adds to the film's quality; all in all, an entertaining picture that children will probably enjoy.

p, James S. Burkett; d, Reginald LeBorg; w, Clint Johnston, LeBorg (based on a story by Johnston); ph, Gilbert Warrenton (Cinecolor); m, Edward J. Jay; ed, Charles Craft

Adventure   (PR:AAA MPAA:NR)

YOUNG DESIRE**   (1930) 68m UNI bw

Mary Nolan (*Helen Herbert*), William Janney (*Bobby Spencer*), Ralf Harolde (*Blackie*), Mae Busch (*May*), George Irving (*Mr. Spencer*), Claire McDowall (*Mrs. Spencer*), Alice Lake, Gretchen Thomas.

Carnival kootch dancer Nolan falls madly in love with Janney, a handsome young man of higher social status. The romance, set against the backdrop of the carnival's hubbub, is ultimately doomed and Nolan ends up killing herself. The production values aren't bad and despite the hackneyed plot, the story holds some interest. However, both leads are terribly miscast, which makes the film as hopeless as the story it tells.

d, Lew Collins; w, Matt Taylor, Winifred Reeve (based on the play "Carnival Girl" by William R. Doyle); ph, Roy Overbaugh.

Drama   (PR:C MPAA:NR)

YOUNG DILLINGER**½   (1965) 102m Zimbalist/AA bw

Nick Adams (*John Dillinger*), Robert Conrad (*Pretty Boy Floyd*), John Ashley (*Baby Face Nelson*), Mary Ann Mobley (*Elaine*), Victor Buono (*Prof. Hoffman*), Dan Terranova (*Homer Van Meter*), John Hoyt (*Dr. Wilson*), Reed Hadley (*Federal Agent Parker*), Robert Osterloh (*Federal Agent Baum*), Anthony Caruso (*Rocco*), Art Baker (*Warden*), Gene Roth (*Justice of Peace*), Ayllene Gibbons (*Justice of Peace's Wife*), Frank Gerstle (*Watchman*), Emile Meyer (*Detective Jergins*), Beverly Hills (*Floyd's Girl*), Harvey Gardner (*Mills*), Helen Kay Stephens (*Van Meter's Girl*), Patty Joy Harmon (*Nelson's Girl*), Sol Gorse, Wally Rose (*Guards*), Walter Sande (*Judge*), Ted Knight (*Johnsyn*), Mike Masters (*Driver*), Robin Raymond, Charles Sloan.

A mildly entertaining, though wholly inaccurate account of the infamous John Dillinger's early days opens when the soon-to-be famous outlaw (played by Adams), along with his girl, Mobley, decide to rob her father's safe. The pair are caught by Mobley's father (Knight, who would achieve great fame on TV's "Mary Tyler Moore Show"), and Adams takes the rap. He goes to prison and there links up with Pretty Boy Floyd (Conrad), Baby Face Nelson (Ashley), and Homer Van Meter (Terranova). After escaping from prison, Adams manages to get his friends out as well. Along with their respective molls and the help of Buono, Adams and his thugs become the most wanted men in America. Adams goes through plastic surgery to change his looks, but kills the doctor (Hoyt) after he tries to rape Mobley. Eventually Mobley gets fed up with Adams and this hard life. Pregnant, she demands marriage but Adams refuses. The FBI later closes in on Adams' hideout after Mobley has revealed their whereabouts to the feds. She is hit by a gunshot and tells Adams to flee for his life. He does manage to get away, the only member of the gang who manages to escape. Though Dillinger did link up with the other infamous criminals portrayed in this film at one time in his career, their outlaw partnership bore no resemblence to the events of this film. Adams predicted this low-budget feature would make a fortune at the box office, though the movie-going public quickly cut this boast down to size. As exploitation features go, this isn't bad and the ending is fairly effective. No one seemed to notice though that despite the 1930s setting, the actors are often seen in 1965 era garb, the year this film was made. A few years later, YOUNG DILLINGER occasionally wound up on a double bill with another film chronicling famous 1930s gangsters, BONNIE AND CLYDE.

p, Alfred Zimbalist; d, Terry O. Morse; w, Donald Zimbalist, Arthur Hoerl (based on a story by Zimbalist); ph, Stanley Cortez; m, Shorty Rogers; ed, Morse; art d, Don Ament.

Crime Drama   **Cas.**   (PR:O MPAA:NR)

YOUNG DR. KILDARE***½   (1938) 81 MGM bw

Lew Ayres (*Dr. James Kildare*), Lionel Barrymore (*Dr. Leonard Gillespie*), Lynne Carver (*Alice Raymond*), Nat Pendleton (*Joe Wayman*), Jo Ann Sayers (*Barbara Chanler*), Samuel S. Hinds (*Dr. Stephen Kildare*), Emma Dunn (*Mrs. Martha Kildare*), Walter Kingsford (*Dr. Walter Carew*), Nella Walker (*Mrs. Chanler*), Pierre Watkin (*Mr. Chanler*), Truman Bradley (*John Hamilton*), Monty Woolley (*Dr. Lane Porteus*), Don Castle (*Bates*), Phillip Terry (*Vickery*), Roger Converse (*Joiner*), Donald (*Don "Red"*), James Mason (*1st Lodger*), Murray Alper (*Waiter*), Marie Blake (*Sally the Switchboard Operator*), Leonard Penn (*Stuart Walden*), Virginia Brissac (*Landlady*), Clinton Rosemond (*Conover*), Nell Craig, Barbara Bedford (*Nurses*), Grace Hayle (*Stout Lady*), Emmett Vogan (*Detective Heerman*), Jack Murphy, Cyril Ring (*Interns*), Howard Hickman (*Dr. Harris*).

Newly graduated from medical school, Ayres returns to his home town and the prospect of joining his father's medical practice. To the disappointment of his parents and his sweetheart, Carver, Ayres elects to accept a proffered internship in a large New York City hospital. There, he attains adverse publicity in the newspapers when a powerful politician dies while under his care. He is exonerated of blame when it is discovered that an ambulance attendant failed to follow Ayres' orders to administer oxygen to the alcoholic politician. Crusty old wheelchair-bound diagnostician Barrymore takes the young man under his abrasive wing, to Ayres' discomfiture. (Ayres has yet to learn that Barrymore's bark is directed mostly at those in whom he sees some potential). One of Ayres' patients is Sayers, daughter of wealthy Watkin and Walker. Sayers has attempted suicide, and eminent psychiatrist Woolley has adjudged her mentally unbalanced, decreeing that she be institutionalized. Ayres diagrees with the opinion and countermands the decision on his own authority. As the youthful physician is about to be discharged for insubordination, the ever-irascible Barrymore–who agrees with his diagnosis–appoints Ayres as his new assistant. The first of MGM's DR. KILDARE series (see Index), this was not the first filmed adaptation of author Brand's characters. That honor belongs to INTERNES CAN'T TAKE MONEY (1937), starring Joel McCrea and Barbara Stanwyck. MGM had recently started its HARDY FAMILY series to considerable acclaim, and Louis B. Mayer wanted another profitable series vehicle. He assigned the HARDY staff to search for something suitable and settled on a hospital theme partly because of the nearly infinite plot variations it appeared to afford and partly because it offered a continuing role for is favorite actor, Barrymore (who had only recently suffered the crippling hip injury that required him to use a wheelchair). Ayres, with his gentle manner, was a fortuitous selection as Kildare; his career had been in decline. Ayres was none too pleased with the series at the outset; he has been quoted as saying of this initial entry, "Frankly, I thought it was terrible." Ayres and Barrymore were to work together in eight more films in the series (Barrymore continued on with other actors assuming the young-doctor characterization). Players Pendleton, Hinds, Dunn, and Kingsford were to become regulars on the series; actress Laraine Day joined the group in the next picture in the series, CALLING DR. KILDARE (1939). When Barrymore was asked how long he wanted to continue in the profitable series, he answered, "...until Hell freezes over." The studio's feature-release series ended in 1947 with DARK DELUSION, but the young doctor and his mentor were to be rejuvenated on TV.

p, Lou Ostrow; d, Harold S. Bucquet; w, Harry Ruskin, Willis Goldbeck (based on characters created by Max Brand); ph, John F. Seitz; m, David Snell; ed, Elmo Veron; art d, Cedric Gibbons, Malcolm Brown; set d, Edwin B. Willis

Drama   (PR:A MPAA:NR)

YOUNG DOCTORS, THE**½   (1961) 100m Drexel-Miller-Turman/UA bw

Fredric March (*Dr. Joseph Pearson*), Ben Gazzara (*Dr. David Coleman*), Dick Clark (*Dr. Alexander*), Ina Balin (*Cathy Hunt*), Eddie Albert (*Dr. Charles Dornberger*), Phyllis Love (*Mrs. Alexander*), Edward Andrews (*Bannister*), Aline MacMahon (*Dr. Lucy Grainger*), Arthur Hill (*Tomaselli*), Rosemary Murphy (*Miss Graves*), Barnard Hughes (*Dr. Kent O'Donnell*), Joseph Bova (*Dr. Shawcross*), George Segal (*Dr. Howard*), Matt Crowley (*Dr. Rufus*), Dick Button (*Operating Intern*), William Hansen (*X-Ray Technician*), Addison Powell (*Board Physician*), Ronald Reagan (*Narrator*), Dolph Sweet, Ella Smith, Nora Helen Spens, Bob Dahdah (*Physicians*), Gloria Vanderbilt (*Elizabeth Alexander*), James Broderick (*Dr. Alexander*).

March is an aging doctor who runs the pathology department at a major hospital. When young doctor Gazzara is hired to work in the same department, March takes it as a personal affront. The two battle over a number of medical issues, once when Gazzara orders three blood tests to see if an expectant mother, Love, has sensitized blood that would endanger her child. March thinks three tests unnecessary and forbids the third. Meanwhile, Gazzara begins an affair with student nurse Balin but when she develops a tumor on her knee, March finds that it is malignant and has the limb amputated. Gazzara doesn't accept March's decision, but submits to the older doctor's authority. The blood-test decision comes back to haunt March, though, when Love's baby is born seriously ill. Doctor Albert is Love's personal physician and he verbally attacks March for his professional carelessness before going off to save the infant's life with a total blood transfusion. March decides that he is indeed too old and resigns. Gazzara, whose respect for March has grown since his discovery that the doctor's diagnosis of Balin was correct, asks March to reconsider but the doctor's mind is made up, and he leaves the department in Gazzara's hands. Soap-opera treatment harks back to the days of the Dr. Kildare series and the writing is mostly ridiculous. The performances, by an amazing conglomeration of talented and talentless actors and actresses, are mostly indifferent, but March is at the height of his art and makes his aging doctor facing the fact that his knowledge is obsolete an impressively believable character. The film is slick but moves quickly enough to cover up the worst of its script problems and keeps the actors moving on and off before the audience can catch on to the degree of their incompetence.

p, Stuart Millar, Lawrence Turman; d, Phil Karlson; w, Joseph Hayes (based on the novel *The Final Diagnosis* by Arthur Hailey); ph, Arthur J. Ornitz; m, Elmer Bernstein; ed, Robert Swink; prod d, Richard Sylbert; art d, Angelo Laiacona, Jimmy Di Gangi; cos, Ruth Morley; tech adv, Dr. Charles F. Begg.

Drama   (PR:A-C MPAA:NR)

YOUNG DOCTORS IN LOVE*   (1982) 95m ABC/FOX c

Michael McKean (*Dr. Simon August*), Sean Young (*Dr. Stephanie Brody*), Harry Dean Stanton (*Dr. Oliver Ludwig*), Patrick MacNee (*Dr. Jacobs*), Hector Elizondo (*Angelo/Angela*), Dabney Coleman (*Dr. Joseph Prang*), Pamela Reed (*Norine Sprockett*), Taylor Negron (*Dr. Phil Burns*), Saul Rubinek (*Dr. Floyd Kurtzman*), Patrick Collins (*Dr. Walter Rist*), Ted McGinley (*Dr. Bucky DeVol*), Rick Overton (*Dr. Thurman Flicker*), Michael Richards (*Malamud*), Titos Vandis (*Sal Bonafetti*), Kyle T. Heffner (*Dr. Charles Litto*), Crystal Bernard (*Julie*), Gary Friedkin (*Dr. Milton Chamberlain*), Haunani Minn (*Nurse Chang*), Becky Gonzales (*Nurse Perez*), Lynne Marie Stewart (*Nurse Thatcher*), Esther Sutherland (*Nurse Willa Mae*), Ann Washington (*Nurse Annie*), Hillary Horan (*Nurse Theresa*), Coleen Maloney (*Nurse Jones*), Claudia Crown (*Nurse Sanchez*), Sonia Jennings (*Nurse Nina*), Kelly Moran (*Nurse Skateboard*), John Beradino, Emily McLaughlin, Michael Damian, Steven Ford, Chris Robinson, Stuart Damon, Jamie Lyn Bauer, Tom Ligon, Kin Shriner, Janine Turner, Jackie Zeman, Mr. T (*Cameos*).

With the success of the one-joke comedy feature AIRPLANE] (1980), it appeared that every studio wanted a scattershot-humor production to capitalize on that sleeper's success. The most notable was YOUNG DOCTORS IN LOVE, a particularly unfunny comedy that cashed in on the topical success of the TV soap opera "General Hospital." The ABC television network financed the production, but giving successful TV situation-comedy director Marshall his first shot at the big screen. The simple story line revolves around a group of interns and the year they spend at a big-city hospital. Romance, intrigue, and bad jokes abound, as well as cameo appearances by the "General Hospital" TV cast. It's a hit-and-mostly-miss comedy with none of the gleeful fun that permeated AIRPLANE. Not much done with the conventions of hospital drama other than the most perfunctory of jokes. There's also some genuine cruelty, with jokes about a midget doctor who can't reach anything. One line heard over the hospital public address system is, "Attention, E.T.: Phone home." The gag hastily added shortly before this film's release to get a quick laugh from 1982's big summer hit.

p, Jerry Bruckheimer; d, Garry Marshall; w, Michael Elias, Rich Eustis; ph, Don Peterman (Metrocolor); m, Maurice Jarre; ed, Dov Hoening; prod d, Polly Platt; art d, Tracy Bousman.

Comedy   Cas.   (PR:O   MPAA:R)

YOUNG DONOVAN'S KID*   (1931) 76m RKO bw (GB: DONOVAN'S KID)

Richard Dix (*Jim Donovan*), Jackie Cooper (*Midge Murray*), Marion Shilling (*Kitty Costello*), Frank Sheridan (*Father Dan*), Boris Karloff (*Cokey Joe*), Dick Rush (*Burke*), Fred Kelsey (*Collins*), Richard Alexander (*Ben Murray*), Harry Tenbrook (*Spike Doyle*), Wilfred Lucas (*Duryea*), hil Sleeman (*Mike Novarro*), Charles Sullivan, Jack Perry, Frank Beal.

Dix is a major crime figure who adopts Cooper, the young brother of a fellow ganster who was killed in a police raid. A child-care inspector removes the boy from his care, claiming Dix is a bad influence. This enrages the gangster, and he goes on a rampage. Shilling, the daughter of a local minister, persuades Dix to make an honest man of himself and gets him a job at the ironworks where she's employed. All appears well but when the payroll is stolen Dix is the first to be blamed. His former cronies have taken the cash and Dix recovers the money, getting wounded in the process. In the end he recovers and is once more reunited with Cooper. Overly sentimental, and a story only to be found in the movies. Cooper held up well, playing his role naturally rather than making the character too cute. Karloff, whose roles were steadily slipping in stature at RKO at the time (FRANKENSTEIN and good fortune were still two years away), played a dope pusher who tries to hook Cooper.

p, Louis Sarecky; d, Fred Niblo; w, J. Walter Ruben (based on the novel *Big Brother* by Rex Beach); ph, Edward Cronjager.

Drama   (PR:A   MPAA:NR)

YOUNG DON'T CRY, THE*   (1957) 89m COL bw

Sal Mineo (*Leslie Henderson*), James Whitmore (*Rudy Krist*), J. Carrol Naish (*Plug*), Gene Lyons (*Max Cole*), Paul Carr (*Bradley*), Thomas Carlin (*Clancy*), Leigh Whipper (*Doosy*), Stefan Gierasch (*Billy*), Victor Thorley (*Whittaker*), Roxanne (*Maureen Cole*), James Reese (*Mr. Gwinn*), Ruth Attaway (*Philomena*), Leland Mayforth (*Allan*), Dick Wigginton (*Jimmy*), Stanley Martin (*Stanley*), Josephine Smith (*Mrs. Gwinn*), Joseph Killorin (*Solomon*), Phillips Hamilton (*Whigs*), Victor Johnson (*Hardhead*).

Mineo is a maturing young man trying to discover who he is while about to matriculate from a Georgia orphanage. When convicted murderer Whitmore escapes from a local prison, the unwitting teenager is used by the convict to aid in his getaway. The Savannah locations were nicely rendered with some fine photography. Columbia advertised Mineo as "the screen's most dynamic teen-age star."

p, Philip A. Waxman; d, Alfred L. Werker; w, Richard Jessup (based on his novel *The Cunning and the Haunted*); ph, Ernest Haller; m, George Antheil; ed, Maurice wright; md, Ernest Gold.

Drama   (PR:C   MPAA:NR)

YOUNG DRACULA   (SEE: SON OF DRACULA, 1974, Brit.)

YOUNG DYNAMITE*   (1937) 57m Ambassador/SYN-Conn bw

Frankie Darro (*Freddie*), Kane Richmond (*Tom*), Charlotte Henry (*Jane*), David Sharpe (*John*), William Costello (*Flash Slavin*), Carlton Young (*Spike*), Pat Gleason (*Butch*), Frank Austin (*Endeberry*), Frank Sarasino (*Peddler*).

When Sharpe, a new deputized state trooper, is killed his first day on the job his kid brother Darro – who also wants to be a trooper – swears revenge. His sister Henry's fiance Richmond joins him in the search for the gangsters responsible. The pair finally lures the gang to a boarding house with the promise of gold but it turns out Austin, a crippled boarder, is really head of the outfit. The law comes in at the end to save the day and all is resolved. This was the final pairing of diminutive Darro (who often played jockeys) and the handsome Richmond who did a series of low-budget action films together in 1936 and 1937. The perfunctory plot is told with each genre element firmly in place with acting production values to match the format.

p, William Berke; d, Lee Goodwins; w, Arthur Durlam, Joseph O'Donnell, Stanley Roberts (based on a story by Peter B. Kyne); ph, John Kline; ed, Martin G. Cohn.

Crime   (PR:A   MPAA:NR)

YOUNG EAGLES½   (1930) 70m PAR bw

Charles "Buddy" Rogers (*Lt. Robert Banks*), Jean Arthur (*Mary Gordon*), Paul Lukas (*Von Baden*), Stuart Erwin (*Lt. Pudge Higgins*), Virginia Bruce (*Florence Welford*), Gordon De Main (*Maj. Lewis*), James Finlayson (*Scotty*), Frank Ross (*Lt. Graham*), Jack Luden (*Lt. Barker*), Freeman Wood (*Lt. Mason*), George Irving (*Col. Wilder*), Stanley Blystone (*Capt. Deming*), Newell Chase, Lloyd Whitlock.

While on leave in Paris during WW I, American pilot Rogers meets Arthur, another American in the city. After falling in love, Rogers returns, to action and captures Lukas, a German flying ace known as "The Grey Eagle." Rogers brings his prisoner to American intelligence headquarters in Paris but Rogers is drugged there by none other than his seeming lover, Arthur. Lukas escapes with the lady and Rogers believes Arthur to be a German spy. Later he discovers she is actually a counterspy on the American side. Though the story occasionally steps over the line of believability it is told with a good sense of excitement. Wellman's direction does the material justice. Some good aerial camera work as well. The author of the stories on which the picture is based was an air ace during the war. He later attained greater fame when, after assuming control of his family textile firm, he wrote a series of risque magazine advertisements, including one showing an Indian girl departing from a hammock occupied by an exhausted Indian man, captioned "A Buck Well Spent on a Springmaid Sheet."

d, William A. Wellman; w, Grover Jones, William Slavens McNutt (based on the short stories "The One Who Was Clever" and "Sky-High" by Elliott White Springs); ph, Archie J. Stout; ed, Allyson Schaffer; m/l, Ross Adrian, Lee Silesu, Arthur A. Penn.

War/Action   (PR:AA MPAA:NR)

YOUNG FRANKENSTEIN**   (1974) 108m FOX bw

Gene Wilder (*Dr. Frederick Frankenstein*), Peter Boyle (*Monster*), Marty Feldman (*Igor*), Madeline Kahn (*Elizabeth*), Cloris Leachman (*Frau Blucher*), Teri Garr (*Inga*), Kenneth Mars (*Inspector Kemp*), Gene Hackman (*Blind Hermit*), Richard Haydn (*Herr Falkstein*), Liam Dunn (*Mr. Hilltop*), Danny Goldman (*Medical Student*), Leon Askin (*Herr Waldman*), Oscar Beregi (*Sadistic Jailer*), Lou Cutell (*Frightened Villager*), Arthur Malet (*Village Elder*), Richard Roth (*Kemp's Aide*), Monte Landis, Rusty Blitz (*Gravediggers*), Anne Beesley (*Little Girl*), Terrence Pushman, Ian Abercrombie, Randolph Dobbs (*Villagers*), John Dennis, Lidia Kristen, Michael Fox, Patrick O'Hara, John Madison, Rick Norman, Rolfe Sedan, Norbert Schiller, Anatol Winogradoff.

Brooks' followup to his enormously successful western spoof BLAZING SADDLES tackles another genre, the Frankenstein film, but this time tones down much of the broad humor to create a work that is both an affectionate parody and an homage to its cinematic forebears. Wilder is a teacher at an American medical school, instructing his students on the central nervous system. One student, Goldman, asks him about the work of his grandfather, Victor Frankenstein. Angered, Wilder insists his own name is pronounced "Fronk-en-steen," and dismisses his grandfather's work as "doo-doo." A man arrives, bearing the late baron's will, which endows Wilder with his entire Transylvanian estate. Wilder bids farewell to his fiancee Kahn, and goes to Transylvania to claim the inheritance. On arrival he is greeted by Feldman, a pop-eyed hunchback. Feldman tells Wilder that his own grandfather used to work for Victor Frankenstein, "although the rates have gone up." Surprised at Wilder's pronunciation of the family name, Feldman insists on being called "Eye-gore." They ride to the Frankenstein castle, accompanied by Garr, a young girl who will assist Wilder, and they are greeted at the castle by Leachman, a hideous looking old woman who causes horses to whinny in fright at the mention of her name. In the middle of the night, Wilder hears strange music. Accompanied by Garr and Feldman, he follows the music to its source. Eventually he finds his grandfather's private library, with a copy of his book *How I Did It* lying in the open. Wilder, though initially skeptical, reads through the book (which quotes actual passages from Mary Shelley's novel *Frankenstein*) and realizes the plan could work. After a body is fetched, Feldman is dispatched to get the brain of the recently departed Hans Delbruck, a scientist and saint. Feldman does as he's told, but is frightened by his own reflection in the mirror. He drops Delbruck's brain, destroying the gray matter, and decides to replace it with a brain sitting in a jar marked "abnormal." Wilder assembles the creature, and, employing much of the original laboratory equipment used in James Whale's 1931 FRANKENSTEIN, attempts to bring his monster to life. The experiment is a failure, but the local townspeople are upset by the presence of a new Frankenstein in their midst. Mars, in a brilliant parody of Lionel Atwill in SON OF FRANKENSTEIN (1939), is a local inspector outfitted with a wooden arm and a monocle worn over his eye patch. He goes to the castle just as the creature comes to life. Wilder frantically humors Mars, and eventually is rid of him. Going to the laboratory, he is attacked by the creature (Boyle) and, through a game of charades, tells Garr and Feldman to sedate the monster. He confronts Feldman, asking him about the brain. Feldman tells Wilder it formerly belonged to "Abby Normal," which enrages the scientist. Leachman reveals that she set up Wilder to recreate his grandfather's experiments. Wilder presses her further, and Leachman triumphantly confesses that Victor Frankenstein was "my boy friend!" Boyle escapes and goes wandering through the countryside. He happens upon a little girl, a la the original FRANKENSTEIN, and helps her toss flowers into a well. The girl's parents find her missing and grow frightened that she might be in the monster's clutches. They rush to her bedroom, hoping she is there. Meanwhile, the girl tries to get Boyle to play with her on a teeter-totter. The humongous creature ends up catapulting the girl right into her bedroom, her parents none the wiser. Next, Boyle comes to a little cottage, inhabited by Hackman, a blind man. The sequence, spoofing the famed blind man sequence in BRIDE OF FRANKENSTEIN (1935), is one of the film's best, as Hackman accidentally pours soup on Boyle, then lights the creature's thumb instead of a cigar. Boyle flees in terror, and is eventually recaptured by Wilder and his assistants. Wilder, though frightened, confronts the locked-up Boyle, and, with a soothing tone, tells the creature what a good boy he is. Through a wooden door Garr shouts: "Dr. Fronk-en-steen! Are you all right?" Replies Wilder, "My name is *Frankenstein!*" Now it is time for the monster's big debut at the local science academy. Wilder and Boyle perform a buck and wing to Irving Berlin's "Puttin' on the Ritz," and are a big hit with the audience. A stage light explodes, frightening Boyle. Wilder tries to go on with the routine, but the crowd boos and throws rotten vegtables. Boyle is angered and fights back, but is captured by authorities. A guard teases Boyle, and once more Boyle escapes to roam the countryside. Kahn, who has come to the castle for a surprise visit, is combing out her hair before going to bed. Boyle bursts into the room, and in the best of Frankenstein movie traditions, takes her off to his lair. He starts to make love to her, which Kahn initially protests. But the monster's sexual prowess is so great that Kahn is enraptured, crooning "Ah, Sweet Mystery of Life." Later, in a post-coital embrace, Boyle offers her a cigarette. He hears a mysterious violin, and leaves the now angered Kahn, who screams, "You men are all alike!" Boyle ends up back at the castle where Wilder has been playing the violin, hoping to lure back his creation. Wilder now conducts an experiment, hoping to transfer part of his brain to Boyle's in an attempt to make the creature"as right as rain." Meanwhile, the townspeople are enraged. Mars leads them to storm the castle, interrupting the experiment moments before its completion. Boyle awakens, and demands the still sleeping Wilder be left alone. The newly reformed monster tells the rioters how Wilder has risked his life for him, and everyone makes peace. Later, Kahn and Boyle are married. As Boyle lies in bed reading *The Wall Street Journal*, Kahn enters the room, wearing a hairdo similar to Elsa Lanchester's in BRIDE OF FRANKENSTEIN. Boyle shoots an amused look to the camera, as Kahn prances towards the marriage bed. Meanwhile, Wilder has married Garr. She hums the tune that haunted Boyle, and Wilder goes into a trance. When Garr asks Wilder what happened to him during the brain transference with Boyle, he attacks her with animal-like passion. Garr sings "Ah Sweet Mystery of Life," and the film comes to a happy conclusion. YOUNG FRANKENSTEIN is Brooks' most accomplished work, combining his well-known brand of comedy with stylish direction. The cast is uniformally excellent. Wilder gives one of his best performances as the doctor, and Boyle makes a fine creature. However, Garr, with her charming German accent, and the irrepressible Feldman end up stealing the film, glowing in their priceless characterizations. The key to this ensemble is the sensitivity they bring to the material, giving the story some humanistic feelings as well as their fine comic acting. Brooks' direction achieves a seemingly impossible task, balancing out off-the-wall humor within the framework of a classic Universal Studio-styled Frankenstein film. "It's a salute to James Whale, and the wonderful directors of the past, and that beautiful black-and-white look," Brooks later told an interviewer. "I want it to be a spectacular and rich (visually and philosophically) entertainment that would house the comedy. It should be funny, thrilling, moving, and touching." Brooks' use of light and shadow, along with the set design and Morris' fine score, gives this the look of the past films without sacrificing an iota of the comedy. The film was shot at a 1:85 frame ratio, as were FRANKENSTEIN, BRIDE OF FRANKENSTEIN, and SON OF FRANKENSTEIN. This ratio, which was long gone from filmmaking by 1974, helps create the film's classic look, as do the old time linking devices of iris outs, spins, and wipes. The Frankenstein castle, with its cobwebs, dust, skulls, and strange goings-on could easily have been inhabited by Boris Karloff or Bela Lugosi. Using the original laboratory equipment proved to be a real coup for Brooks. Kenneth Strickfaden, who had created the unusual machinery for FRANKENSTEIN in 1931, had the equipment stored in his garage and happily provided Brooks with the pieces, creating some new devices to go with the old. When Wilder stumbles onto his grandfather's dusty lab, the soundtrack, like a ghost from the past, has the creation scene from FRANKENSTEIN–Colin Clive shouting instructions–echo within the room. The black-and-white photography is the best touch, creating the proper atmosphere for horror. Brooks fills the comic story with numerous throwaway gags, subtle touches, and outright belly laughs. Boyle's head is held on firmly with a zipper rather than bolts, while Feldman's hunchback switches from left to right, then back again without the slightest explanation. The script is crammed with witty lines, double entendres, puns, and a few well-placed bits of slapstick. Brooks' worst moments in his films usually arise from his hammy performances, but he wisely stays behind the camera in YOUNG FRANKENSTEIN, making a brief cameo as an off-screen cat yowl when Wilder and Mars play darts. Wilder came up with the original concept for the film while starring in BLAZING SADDLES, and approached Brooks with his idea. The two worked on the script, filling in each other's weaknesses with their respective strengths. "My job was to make him more subtle. His job was to make me more broad," Wilder told an interviewer. "I would say, 'I don't want this to be BLAZING FRANKENSTEIN,' and he'd answer, 'I don't want an art film that only 14 people see.' " For their efforts, the two received an Oscar nomination for Best Adapted Screenplay (the film credits Mary Wollstonecraft Shelley as their original source). Brooks took the project to Columbia studios, but was rejected on the claims his budget of $2.2 million was excessive. He then took his script to 20th Century-Fox, which granted him a budget of $2.8 million as well as complete control over the film's final cut. YOUNG FRANKENSTEIN was enormously popular with filmgoers, grossing some $38,825,000 at the box office, and made Brooks, along with Woody Allen, one of America's foremost comedy directors. Unfortunately his later films bogged down in comic mire, with Brooks parading his face all over the screen. Wilder attempted to branch out as a comedy director with his own movie parodies, but never achieved the success he had with this marvelous piece of work.

p, Michael Gruskoff; d, Mel Brooks; w, Gene Wilder, Brooks (based on the characters from the novel *Frankenstein* by Mary Wollstonecraft Shelley); ph, Gerald Hirschfield; m, John Morris; ed, John Howard; md, Morris; art d, Dale Hennesy; set d, Robert DeVestel; cos, Dorothy Jeakins; spec eff, Hal Millar, Henry Miller, Jr.; makeup, William Tuttle.

Comedy/Horror **Cas.** **(PR:C MPAA:PG)**

YOUNG FUGITIVES½** (1938) 67m UNIV bw

Harry Davenport *(Joel Bentham)*, Robert Wilcox *(Ray)*, Dorothea Kent *(Meg)*, Clem Bevans *(Benjie)*, Larry Blake *(Sam)*, Mary Treen *(Kathy)*, Tom Ricketts *(Tom Riggins)*, Mira McKinney *(Letty)*, Henry Roquemore *(Scudder)*, Ferris Taylor *(Seth)*, George Guhl *(Fred)*, Eddie Acuff *(Loafer)*, Edward Hearn *(Commander)*, William [Billy] Benedict *(Judd)*, Bob McKenzie *(Zeke)*, Douglas Evans *(Announcer)*, Eddy Chandler *(Alfred)*, George Douglas *(Dressy)*, Victor Adams *(Nick)*, George Ovey *(Gas Station Attendant)*, Thomas Carr *(Telegraph Clerk)*.

Two aging Civil War veterans (Davenport and Bevans) have saved $50,000 between them. When Bevans passes away Davenport goes looking for his late friend's son Wilcox. He has promised to treat the boy as his own but soon discovers that Wilcox would rather cheat him of his money. However, Davenport grows wise to him and under the older man's influence Wilcox finally changes his ways. Though direction is rudimentary and the material below the actor's abilities, this is a fairly entertaining mix of comedy and drama. Kent is Wilcox's love interest.

p, Barney Sarecky; d, John Rawlins; w, Ben Grauman Kohn, Charles Grayson (based on the story "Afraid to Talk" by Edward James); ph, George Robinson; ed, Frank Gross; md, Charles Previn; art d, Ralph DeLacy.

Drama/Comedy **(PR:A MPAA:NR)**

YOUNG FURY** (1965) 80m PAR c

Rory Calhoun *(Clint McCoy)*, Virginia Mayo *(Sara McCoy)*, Lon Chaney, Jr *(Bartender)*, Richard Arlen *(Sheriff Jenkins)*, John Agar *(Dawson)*, Preston Pierce *(Tige McCoy)*, Linda Foster *(Sally Miller)*, Bob Biheller *(Biff)*, Merry Anders *(Alice)*, Joan Huntington *(Kathy)*, Marc Cavell *(Pancho)*, Jody McCrea *(Stone)*, Rex Bell, Jr *(Farmer)*, William Wellman, Jr *(Peters)*, Reg Parton *(Jeb)*, Jay Ripley *(Slim)*, Kevin O'Neal *(Curly)*, Jerry Summers *(Gabbo)*, Fred Alexander *(Pony)*, Dal Jenkins *(Sam)*, William Bendix *(Blacksmith)*, Steve Condit, Sailor Vincent, Jorge Moreno, Bill Clark, Dave Dunlop, Jesse Wayne, Robert Miles, Eddie Hice, Fred Krone, Joe Finnegan, Kent Hays.

Years after abandoning his wife (Mayo) and infant son, Calhoun returns to town as he flees from the notorious Dawson gang. The baby has now grown up to be a young hell-raiser (Pierce) who believes his mother dead and who despises his deserter father. Mayo is now a saloonkeeper, though Pierce doesn't recognize her. He meets his father in a showdown and is humiliated by the older man. The Dawsons finally catch up with Calhoun and Pierce intends to watch as they kill the man. But when Mayo is gunned down she tells the boy the truth before dying. He learns that she had been unfaithful to Calhoun, which caused him to abandon the family. Father and son unite in the end for the climactic gun battle. The combination of younger and older actors in the cast was a good idea, but unfortunately the production doesn't work with them as it should have. The film is a string of Western cliches with some more modern "youth film" stereotypes tossed in for good measure. Bendix, in a cameo part, died before the picture was released.

p, A. C. Lyles; d, Christian Nyby; w, Steve Fisher (based on a story by Lyles, Fisher); ph, Haskell Boggs (Techniscope, Technicolor); m, Paul Dunlap; ed, Marvin Coil; art d, Hal Pereira, Arthur Lonergan; set d, Sam Comer, Ralph S. Hurst; cos, Hazel Hegarty, Buddy Clark; makeup, Wally Westmore, Jack Stone.

Western   **(PR:C   MPAA:NR)**

YOUNG GIANTS*½   (1983) 97m Entertainment Enterprises/Miracle c

John Huston, Pele, Peter Fox, Lisa Wills, F. William Parker, David Ruprecht, Severn Darden, Richard Grant, Mark Schneider, Pamela McKee, Christopher Bringard, Erik Bringard, Varney Fahnbulleh, Brian Jay Frederick, Donte I. Henry, Michael David Kafka, German Laverde, Kenneth McMurphy, Rene Portugal, Brian John Stankiewicz, Aldo Tassara, Jay Louden, E. Hampton Beagle, Alan Miller, Jeannetta Arnette, Robert Barron, Stan Yale, Calvin Greenfield, Shawn Nelson.

Even the mighty need a fast dollar now and again as Huston proves by starring in this sticky-sweet nonsense. He's a dying priest who runs an orphanage. The home is threatened by possible closing but a soccer match (the sport permeates the film throughout) saves the day for all. The great soccer legend Pele, whom Huston had directed in VICTORY (1981), is featured.

p, Tom Moyer, Megan Moyer; d, Terrell Tannen; w, T. Moyer, Tannen, Mike Lammers; ph, Raoul Lomas (Panavision, DeLuxe Color); m, Rick Patterson; ed, Denine Rowan, Marion W. Cronin, Daniel Gross; art d, Daniel R. Webster.

Drama   **(PR:A   MPAA:NR)**

YOUNG GIRLS OF ROCHEFORT, THE½**   (1968, Fr.) 125m Parc-Madeleine/WB-Seven Arts c (LES DEMOISELLES DE RO-CHEFORT)

Catherine Deneuve (Delphine Garnier--role sung by Anne Germain), Francoise Dorleac (Solange Garnier--sung by Claude Parent), George Chakiris (Etienne--sung by Romuald), Grover Dale (Bill--sung by Jose Bartel), Gene Kelly (Andy Miller--sung by Donald Burke), Danielle Darrieux (Yvonne), Jacques Perrin (Maxence--sung by Jacques Revaux), Michel Piccoli (Simon Dame--sung by George Blaness), Pamela Hart (Judith--sung by Christiane Legrand), Leslie North (Esther--sung by Claudine Meunier), Jacques Riberolles (Guillaume Lancien--sung by Jean Stout), Henri Cremieux (Dutrouz), Patrick Jeantet (Boubou--sung by Olivier Bonnett), Genevieve Thenier (Josette--sung by Alice Gerald), Rene Bazart (Pepe), Dorothee Blank (Passerby), Agnes Varda (Nun), Daniel Mocquay (Sailor), Peter Ardran, Wendy Barry, Sarah Butler, Ann Chapman, Jane Darling, Tudor Davies, Lindsay Dolan, John MacDonald, Keith Drummond, Maureen Evans, Tara Fernando, Sara Flemington, Johnny Greenland, Leo Guerard, David Hepburn, Bob Howe, Alix Kirsta, Jerry Manley, Tony Manning, Tom Merrifield, Connel Miles, Albin Pahernik, Nicky Temperton, Barrie Wilkinson, Maureen Willsher (Dancers), Sue Allen, George E. Becker, W. Earl Brown, Ronald D. Hicklin, Frank Allen Howren, Thomas D. Kenny, Judith E. Lawler, Bill Lee, Diana K. Lee, Gilda Maiken, Gene Merlino, Joseph A. Pryor, Ronald T. Reeve, Sally Stevens, Sara Jane Tallman, Robert Tebow, Jackie Ward (Singers), Bernard Fradet, Remy Brozeck, Daniel Gall, Veronique Duval, Pierre Caden.

Another lively musical from Demy in the same vein as his previous THE UMBRELLAS OF CHERBOURG. Again Demy collaborated with composer Legrand and set designer Evein to create a world which owes its genesis to the Hollywood musicals of the early 1950s (AN AMERICAN IN PARIS, SINGIN' IN THE RAIN, THE BAND WAGON). The "girls" of the title are twin sisters, Deneuve and Dorleac (sisters in real life, though not twins), who run a ballet school-music shop in Rochefort-sur-Mer, an endearing town along the northwest coast of France. When boat salesmen Chakiris and Dale arrive in town to pitch their products in a carnival, they find that their girl friends have left the company for a couple of sailors. Chakiris and Dale scout the town for new talent and discover Deneuve and Dorleac. Meantime, the twins' mother, Darrieux, runs a cafe while dreaming of her long-lost love Piccoli, who resides nearby and runs a music shop. The twins dream as well of romance and these dreams finally materialize as Perrin and Kelly. Perrin is an artistic sailor who paints his dream girl one day only to find that he has painted Dorleac's picture. He meets Dorleac and falls instantly in love. Kelly, an American in Rochefort, is a concert pianist who has found a masterfully written score which, by a fateful romantic coincidence, turns out to have been written by Deneuve. When Chakiris and Dale leave town, Dorleac and Deneuve decide to stay behind with their newly found loves.

Harmony even comes to the life of Darrieux as she finally connects with Piccoli. Demy, a master at creating idyllic worlds, has given each of his characters a storybook existence in which they can safely live, love, dance, and sing. (In an odd connection with reality, Demy has also included a character who brutally murders the women who spurn his advances.) As he did with the small town of Cherbourg, Demy has taken a real-life town and turned it into a backlot fantasy. With the cooperation of Rochefort residents and officials, Demy took his crew into the town, repainted their Colbert Square with a wide pallette of pastel colors, and peopled it with dancing and singing extras. (After the film's release, Rochefort, like Cherbourg, gained the attention of numerous tourists.) Where THE YOUNG GIRLS OF ROCHEFORT fails, however, is in its inability to provide a story line which captures an audience as gracefully as THE UMBRELLAS OF CHERBOURG. Another plus for CHERBOURG over ROCHEFORT is a tighter, more haunting score which managed to provide the hit songs that this film desperately needed. Included are the following Legrand-Demy musical collaborations: "Arrivee des Camionneurs," "Le Pont Transbordeur," "Chanson de Maxence," "Chanson de Delphine a Lancien," "Marins, Amis, Amants ou Maris," "Chanson de Simon," "La Femme Coupee en Morceaux," "Chanson d'un Jour d'ete," "Andy Amoureux," "Chanson des Jumelles," "Chanson d'Andy," "Chanson de Solange," "Chanson de Delphine," "Nous Voyageons de Ville en Ville," "Chanson d'Yvonne," "De Hambourg a Rochefort," "Dans le Port de Hambourg," "Les Recontres," "Toujours Jamais," "Kermesse," "Depart des Camionneurs" (Legrand, Demy). Although both French and English versions exist try to see the French one--Kelly aptly handles the language and the lettering of the subtitles are a treat.

p, Gilbert de Goldschmidt; d&w, Jacques Demy; ph, Ghislain Cloquet (Franscope, Technicolor); m, Michel Legrand; ed, Jean Hamon; set d, Bernard Evein; cos, Jacqueline Moreau, Marie-Claude Fouquet, Jean-Marie Armand, Jean Barthet; ch, Norman Maen; m/l, Legrand, Demy; makeup, Aida Carange, Janine Jarreau, Lud Durand, Christiane Sauvage.

Musical   **(PR:A   MPAA:NR)**

YOUNG GIRLS OF WILKO, THE*½**   (1979, Pol./Fr.) 116m Polish Corporation for Film Production-Zespody Filmowe Unit X-Pierson-Films Moliere/Artificial Eye c (PANNY Z WILKA; AKA: THE GIRLS FROM WILKO; GB: THE YOUNG LADIES OF WILKO)

Daniel Olbrychski (Wiktor), Krystyna Zechwatowicz (Kazia), Anna Senluk (Julia), Maja Komorowska (Yola), Christine Pascal (Tunia), Stanislawa Celinska (Zosla), Zofia Jaroszewska (Wiktor's Aunt), Tadeusz Bialoszczynski (Wiktor's Uncle), Zbegniew Zapasiewicz, Andrzej Lapicki, Joanna Poraska, Paul Dutron, K. Brodzikowski, A. Rostkowska, K. Orzechowski, H. Michelaska, Krystyna Wolanska, J. Kozak-Sutowicz, Andrzej Szenajch, Witold Kaluski, Barbara Stepniakowna, Andrzej Grzybowski, F. Jasinski, A. Wachnickie, M. Wachnickie.

In the late 1920s a gentleman approaching his middle years goes to visit a quintet of sisters with whom he had spent a wonderful summer in the year before the outbreak of WW I. He fondly remembers how they all tried to attract him, in ways both comical and tragic. The flashback story reveals the women to be either foolishly infatuated or shockingly passionate. This is a sensitive, well-told story recalling a more innocent time. The use of color is marvelous, adding a sad, nostalgic feel.

d, Andrzej Wajda; w, Zbigniew Kaminski (based on the novella Panny Z Wilka by Jaroslav Iwaszkiewicz; ph, Edward Klosinski (Eastmancolor); m, Karol Szymanowski; ed, Halina Prugar; art d, Allan Starski.

Drama   **(PR:C   MPAA:NR)**

YOUNG GO WILD, THE½**   (1962, Ger.) 88m Ultra/Manson-Paul Mart bw (VERBRECHEN NACH SCHULSCHLUSS)

Peter Van Eyck (Dr. Knittel), Christian Wolff (Fabian Konig), Heidi Bruhl (Tonia Anders), Corny Collins (Florence Eikelberg), Hans Nielsen (Dr. Senftenberg), Erica Beer (Erna Kallies), Walter Clemens (Jules Bregulla), Richard Munch (Mr. Konig), Alice Treff (Mrs. Konig), Wolfgang Koch (Joachim Eikelberg), Claus Wilcke (Gunther Steppe), Jorg Holmer (Roger Richter), Bum Kruger, Joseph Offenbach.

Wolff tries to break into a coal yard after his teacher asks him to save a mistreated dog. The lad is caught climbing the fence and charged with theft. The teacher refuses to admit his part in the incident and Wolff's parents believe the boy is guilty. He's expelled from school and gets involved in the underworld. He gets in touch with Clemens, a fence for stolen goods. At Clemens' apartment building Wolff meets Bruhl, a young orphan to whom the boy is attracted. Later Wolff catches Clemens trying to rape the girl. She escapes and Clemens is found dead. Wolff is arrested again but cannot find Bruhl to help prove his innocence. Van Eyck is a prison doctor who believes Wolff to be innocent and after investigating finds that Bruhl's girl friend Beer is the actual killer. Bruhl comes out of hiding and waits for Wolff to finish a one-year sentence for robbery.

p, Herbert Sennewald; d, Alfred Vohrer; w, Harald G. Petersson (based on the novel Verbrechen nach Schulschluss by Walter Ebert); ph, Kurt Hasse; m, Ernst Simon; ed, Ira Oberberg; art d, Mathias Matthies, Ellen Schmidt.

Drama   **(PR:C   MPAA:NR)**

YOUNG GRADUATES, THE zero   (1971) 100m Tempo/Crown c

Patricia Wymer (Mindy Evans), Steven Stewart (Jack Thompson), Gary Rist (Bill), B. Kirby, Jr (Les), Jennifer Ritt (Gretchen Thompson), Dennis Christopher (Pan), Marly Holiday (Sandy), Anthony Mannino (Stud), Robert Almanza (Danny), Joe Pepi (Sgt. Doyle), Max Manning (Bartender), Frances Tremaine (Mrs. Dorth, Teacher), Tom Benko (Reporter), Victor Lamb (Principal), Pat Russell and the Spare Change.

Wymer is a high school senior with a taste for the wild life. In the course of this film she seduces a high school teacher (Stewart) while stoned, then – fearing she's pregnant – heads off into the mountains with her pal Holiday and hippie Christopher. They encounter a vicious motorcycle gang, members of which mash the hippie and try to rape the girls The two escape on one of the gang's bikes and are eventually arrested for selling drugs. They end up cleared of the charges, Wymer isn't pregnant, and her pedant lover goes back to his wife. Just as well, for Wymer's met a new teacher at a school dance by the film's end. Wymer, who clearly is well past the 18 years of her character, is a typical "teeniebopper" for this trash epic. She's smarter than all the adults and has the derring-do of a test pilot. The adults in this film, have the IQs of the average jelly doughnut. Of course, there aren't many adults to be found here, for this film takes place in that special land where just about everyone is a teenager: California. Christopher, in his pre-BREAKING AWAY (1979) days, is the hapless hippie, and he gives the film's best performance, though this certainly isn't a difficult feat. Though rated GP on initial release, this is hardly a film for children. For that matter, it's no film for adults, or for any life form with a smattering of intelligence.

p, Robert Anderson, Terry Anderson; d, R. Anderson; w, David Dixon (based on a story by R. Anderson, T. Anderson); ph, J. Barry Herron, John Toll (DeLuxe Color); m, Ray Martin; ed, Bill Anderson, cos, Irene Langer

Drama   (PR:O   MPAA:GP)

YOUNG GUNS, THE**   (1956) 84m AA bw

Russ Tamblyn (Tully), Gloria Talbott (Nora), Perry Lopez (San Antone), Scott Marlowe (Knox Cutler), Wright King (Jonesy), Walter Coy (Peyton), Chubby Johnson (Grandpa), Myron Healey (Deputy Nix), James Goodwin (Georgie), Rayford Barnes (Kid Cutler), I. Stanford Jolley (Felix Briggs).

In an outlaws' roost–a safe community for fugitives from the law–young Tamblyn must decide whether to go into the family business (his late father was a famous gunfighter) or to turn peaceable. He faces down a few young roughnecks, and becomes regarded as their leader, but still can't make a decision. When the other members of his gang decide to rob a bank without his knowledge, he is pressed into making a choice; he opts for the lawful life and prevents the others from committing the crime. Relatively little action in this coming-of-age story.

p, Richard Heermance; d, Albert Band; w, Louis Garfinkle; ph, Ellsworth Fredricks; m, Marlin Skiles; ed, George White; art d, Dave Milton; m/l, "Song of the Young Guns," Imogen Carpenter, Lenny Adelson (sung by Guy Mitchell).

Western   (PR:A-C   MPAA:NR)

YOUNG GUNS OF TEXAS**   (1963) 78m AP/FOX c

James Mitchum (Morgan Coe), Alana Ladd (Lily Glendenning), Jody McCrea (Jeff Shelby), Chill Wills (Preacher Sam Shelby), Gary Conway (Tyler Duane), Barbara Mansell (Martha Jane Canary), Robert Lowery (Jesse Glendenning), Troy Melton (Luke), Fred Krone (Pike), Alex Sharp (Red), Robert Hinkle (Sheriff Hubbard), Will Wills (Cowhand).

A minor and forgettable western, This might be worth a look simply for its filial cast. When Conway is expelled from West Point he goes looking for a brother accused of stealing some money from the Union Army. He becomes friends with McCrea (real-life son of Joel). At a church dance he meets Ladd (Alan's real-life daughter). A fight breaks out, some bullets fly, and the trio flees. Mitchum, the third actor-scion (the son of Robert), a young man brought up by Comanches, joins them outside town and marries Ladd. The search continues for Conway's brother, and the group is joined by Mansell, a cattle rustler. Ladd's father is pursuing the group and Conway's brother is finally found murdered, killed by soldiers in a fight over the stolen money. The story comes to a bloody climax as greed, Indians, and the trailing band of ranchers catch up with the group in a melee. Mitchum is killed and Conway recovers the money. He is ready to clear his name and settle down with Ladd. The trio of second-generation actors shows that talent isn't necessarily transmitted through one's genes.

p&d, Maury Dexter; w, Henry Cross [Harry Spalding]; ph, John Nickolaus, Jr. CinemaScope, DeLuxe Color), m, Paul Sawtell, Bert Shefter; ed, Jodie Copelan, Richard Einfeld; set d, Harry Reif; cos, Wesley Sherrard; m/l, Sawtell, Shefter, John Herring (sung by Kenny Miller); makeup, Bob Mark.

Western   (PR:C   MPAA:NR)

YOUNG GUY GRADUATES** ½   (1969, Jap.) 90m Toho c
(FURESSHUMAN WAKADAISHO)

Yuzo Kayama (Yuichi Tanuma), Wakako Sakai (Setsuko), Kunie Tanaka (Ishiyama), Keiko Cho (Midori), Choko Iida, Ichiro Arishima, Machiko Naka, Tatsuyoshi Ebara.

Kayama is tardy on the first day of his new job at an automobile company. He explains that he had to help an old man and his daughter (Sakai) find a cab, which suffices as an excuse. Later he meets Sakai and finds her with Tanaka, who works for a rival company. When an important customer for Kayama's firm cancels his contract, Kayama is sent out to investigate the complaint of defective motors. Tanaka also goes to the man's home. There Kayama meets Cho, the customer's daughter. He isn't attracted to her realizes that through this woman he can get to the customer. Sakai hears about this plot and grows jealous. Finally the stories of engine defects prove to be untrue and both men return to their respective companies. Sakai meets with them both and finally decides to choose Kayama as her man.

d, Jun Fukuda; w, Yasuo Tanami; ph, Yuzuri Aizawa (Eastmancolor); m, Kenjiro Hirose; art d, Yoshibumi Honda.

Drama   (PR:C   MPAA:NR)

YOUNG GUY ON MT. COOK** ½   (1969, Jap.) 86m Toho c
(NVUIIRANDO NO WAKADAISHO)

Yuzo Kayama (Yuichi Tanuma), Wakako Sakai (Setsuko), Kunie Tanaka (Ishiyama), Tatsuyoshi Ebara (Enguchi), Jessica Peters (Elizabeth), Choko Iida (Riki), Ichiro Arishima (Kyutaro), Midori Utsumi (Saeko), Machiko Naka (Teruko), Mari Nakayama.

In this sequel to YOUNG GUY GRADUATES Kayama is now a sales engineer for a Japanese automobile firm living in Sydney, Australia. When Tanaka, a schoolmate from his homeland, comes for a visit he's too busy to show him the sights. He asks Peters, a colleague, to show Tanaka around. Tanaka falls for his escort, though she loves Kayama. When Kayama is sent back to Japan he is reunited with his family. His father Arishima is trying to open a restaurant. Business suffers, though, as he is trying to romance, Utsumi, the owner of a boutique. Kayama meets Sakai, who works for a company promoting development in New Zealand. He falls madly in love, but along comes Peters. Sakai no longer will have anything to do with Kayama with the appearance of the Australian. Sent to Auckland to arrange a parade of new cars, Kayama is reluctantly joined by Sakai. There the pair kiss and make up, stating their undying love for one another on Mt. Cook.

d, Jun Fukuda; w, Yasuo Tanami; ph, Shinsaku Uno (Eastmancolor); m, Kenjiro Hirose; art d, Juichi Ikuno.

Drama   (PR:A   MPAA:NR)

YOUNG HELLIONS   (SEE: HIGH SCHOOL CONFIDENTIAL, 1958)

YOUNG HUSBANDS***   (1958, Ital./Fr.) 101m Nepi-Silver-Film Zodiaque/Lux bw (GIOVANI MARITI)

Sylva Koscina (Mara), Antonella Lualdi (Lucia), Gerard Blain (Marcello), Franco Interlinghi (Antonio), Antonio Ciffariello (Ettore), Isabelle Corey (Laura), Raf Mattioli (Giulio), Anna Maria Guarnieri, Enio Girolami.

In a small Italian town, the local youngsters realize that their youth is coming to an end and marriage will soon follow. They gather together for one last time in an attempt to revive their younger days but this comes to a dismal conclusion. Gradually it dawns on the group that childhood is over and their next stage in human growth must be faced. Intelligent and done with style, YOUNG HUSBANDS is a beautiful look at a most difficult time for maturing youngsters. The film shows a real sense of humanity with many jeweled moments. The cast is guided well under thoughtful direction. The good photography captures the dismal atmosphere of the small village. Redolent of Federico Fellini's I VITELLONI (1953).

d, Mauro Bolognini; w, Bologini, Flaiano, Cureli, Pier Paolo Pasolini, Martino (based on a story by P. F. Campanile, Massimo Franciosa); ph, Armando Nannuzzi; m, Marie Zafred; ed, Roberta Cinquini.

Drama   (PR:A   MPAA:NR)

YOUNG IDEAS** ½   (1943) 77m MGM bw

Susan Peters (Susan Evans), Herbert Marshall (Michael Kingsley), Mary Astor (Jo Evans), Elliott Reid (Jeff Evans), Richard Carlson (Tom Farrell), Allyn Joslyn (Adam), Dorothy Morris, Frances Rafferty (Co-Eds), George Dolenz (Pepe), Emory Parnell (Judge Kelly), Ava Gardner (Girl).

A light, frothy comedy with Reid and Peters as a sibling pair of midwestern college students. Their mother Astor is a writer and lecturer (ironically, something Astor herself would later become). Astor is newly married to Marshall, a fellow professor, and the two kids do their best to split up the marriage. They don't have much success and the whole plan goes out the window when Peters falls for Carlson, her dramatics teacher. This is an amusing little film, lacking in any real weight but entertaining nevertheless. It has several clever moments and the players take it in the intended spirit. The script was a real Hollywood rarity. It had been sent in over the transom by a college undergraduate and accepted for production with the author (Noble) hired for the rewrite. This picture also marked the beginning of a five-year contract with MGM for Astor.

p, Robert Sisk; d, Jules Dassin; w, William Noble, Ian McLellan Hunter; ph, Charles Lawton, m, George Bassman; ed, Ralph E. Winters; md, David Snell; art d, Cedric Gibbons, Leonid Vassian; set d, Edwin B. Willis, Mac Alper.

Comedy (PR:A MPAA:NR)

YOUNG IN HEART, THE***½ (1938) 90m UA bw

Janet Gaynor (*George-Ann Carleton*), Roland Young (*Col. Anthony ["Sahib"] Carleton*), Billie Burke (*Marmy Carleton*), Douglas Fairbanks, Jr (*Richard Carleton*), Richard Carlson (*Duncan McCrea*), Minnie Dupree (*Miss Ellen Fortune*), Paulette Goddard (*Leslie Saunders*), Henry Stephenson (*Felix Anstruther*), Miss Fortune's Lawyer, Eily Malyon (*Sarah, Servant*), Tom Ricketts (*Andrew, Servant*), Irvin S. Cobb (*Mr. Jennings*), Margaret Early (*Adela Jennings*), Lucile Watson (*Mrs. Jennings*), Ian McLaren (*Doctor*), Billy Bevan (*Kennel Man*), Lawrence Grant (*Mr. Hutchins*), Walter Kingsford (*Prefect of Police*), Lionel Pape (*Customer*), Charles Halton (*Mr. Jennings*), Lya Lys (*Lucille*), George Sorrell, Georges Renevant (*Detectives*).

A marvelous, beautifully told story has Dupree playing an elderly woman who is painfully lonely. While traveling on a European train she meets a rather unusual family of charming connivers. They've just been kicked out of the Riviera and see this rich, lonely old woman as their next meal ticket. However, Dupree proves to be not so easy a mark, teaching Young and Burke, along with their children Gaynor and Fairbanks, Jr., a thing or two about life. The family even learns about something called "work." Young gets a job as a car salesman in an art deco showroom demonstrating "Flying Wombat" cars (a very low-slung fast modernistic model). The story is told with sensitivity and the right amount of humor with a loving, warm-hearted result. The photography and music, both excellent, received Oscar nominations. In the film's preview the end had Dupree dying but this proved unpopular with test audiences. The cast and crew were called back and a new, happier ending was shot.

p, David O. Selznick; d, Richard Wallace; w, Paul Osborn, Charles Bennett (based on the novel *The Gay Banditti* by I. A. R. Wylie); ph, Leon Shamroy; m, Franz Waxman; ed, Hal C. Kern; art d, Lyle Wheeler; spec eff, Jack Cosgrove.

Drama/Comedy (PR:A MPAA:NR)

YOUNG INVADERS (SEE: DARBY'S RANGERS, 1958)

YOUNG JESSE JAMES*½ (1960) 73m AP/FOX bw

Ray Stricklyn (*Jesse James*), Willard Parker (*Cole Younger*), Merry Anders (*Belle Starr*), Robert Dix (*Frank James*), 0Emile Meyer (*William Quantrill*), Jacklyn O'Donnell (*Zerelda Mimms*), Rayford Barnes (*Pitts*), Rex Holman (*Zack*), Bob Palmer (*Bob Younger*), Sheila Bromley (*Mrs. Samuels*), Johnny O'Neill (*Jim Younger*), Leslie Bradley, Norman Leavitt (*Folsom*), Lee Kendall (*Jennison*).

This is one of the lesser re-tellings of the famous outlaw's adventures, filmed without much imagination or freshness. Stricklyn is the title character who can't adjust to life after the Civil War. Together with brother Dix, he joins Meyer in the famous Quantrill's Raiders after seeing his father hanged. Later on Parker and Anders (as the historical characters Cole Younger and Belle Starr) make their appearances as Stricklyn moves his way up in the annals of crime with a series of bank robberies. Stricklyn is just a mixed-up kid at heart for he really wants to settle down and become a farmer. The film is uninspired, packed with easy motivations and with flat, uneven direction. Stricklyn is not helped by a largely ineffectual supporting cast. Production credits are well below average with a poor editing job and occasional out-of-focus shots.

p, Jack Leewood; d, William F. Claxton; w, Orville H. Hampton, Jerry Sackheim; ph, Carl Berger (CinemaScope); m, Irving Gertz; ed, Richard C. Meyer; art d, Lyle Wheeler, John B. Mansbridge; m/l, Gertz, Hal Levy (sung by Johnny O'Neill).

Western (PR:C MPAA:NR)

YOUNG LAND, THE** (1959) 89m C. V. Whitney/COL c

Pat Wayne (*Jim Ellison*), Yvonne Craig (*Elena de la madrid*), Dennis Hopper (*Hatfield Carnes*), Dan O'Herlihy (*Judge Isham*), Roberto de la Madrid (*Don Roberto de la madrid*), Cliff Ketchum (*Ben Stroud*), Ken Curtis (*Lee Hearn*), Pedro Gonzalez Gonzalez (*Santiago*), Edward Sweeney (*Sully*), John Quijada (*Vaquero*), Miguel Camacho (*Miguel*), Tom Tiner (*Court Clerk*), Carlos Romero (*Quiroga*), Edward Jaurequi (*Drifter*), Cliff Lyons (*Jury Foreman*), Mario Arteaga, Charles Heard.

Hopper plays a young malcontent who has goaded a respected Hispanic into a fatal gun battle in the new state of California in the year 1848. His jury trial is watched with great interest by the largely Spanish-speaking citizens of the new state, who consider it to be a test of the Anglo system of justice. When a guilty verdict is reached, the judge (O'Herlihy) faces a difficult

sentencing task. He gives the gunman a 20-year suspended sentence, provided that Hopper agree never to wear a weapon again. The disgruntled youth then grabs a gun from deputy marshal Ketchum and challenges the sheriff, Wayne, to an equivalent duel. Wayne kills Hopper, rendering the entire test case moot. Two scions of cinematic institutions--producer Ford, the son of director John, and actor Wayne, the son of actor John--here demonstrate the futility of eugenics, at least as applied to pictures. Hopper is fine in an early starring role much hindered by screenplay redundancies and inept direction. Young Wayne's love interest, Craig, a budding ballet dancer, was spotted by producer Ford in a restaurant in traditional Hollywood style, according to publicists. This film is the third in a series of period dramas purportedly recounting truth in American history from financier Cornelius Vanderbilt Whitney, whose inherited wealth permitted him such self-indulgences. The first of the three, THE SEARCHERS (1956), was directed by producer Ford's father, John, and starred star Wayne's progenitor, John. The second of the series was THE MISSOURI TRAVELER (1958). The films were not made in chronological order of release; THE YOUNG LAND had been scheduled for release by Walt Disney's Buena Vista in 1957, but was shelved for two years before Columbia picked it up. Production costs were high for what is essentially a courtroom drama; art director Okey and his staff constructed an entire Mexican pueblo just for the film, complete with a plaza, a church, houses, a cantina, and a jail. The director took full advantage of the constructions; the film has hardly any close-ups.

p, Patrick Ford; d, Ted Tetzlaff; w, Norman Shannon Hall (based on the story "Frontier Frenzy" by John Reese); ph, Winton C. Hoch, Henry Sharp (Technicolor); m, Dimitri Tiomkin; ed, Tom McAdoo; md, Tiomkin; art d, Jack Okey; cos, Frank Beetson, Ann Peck; m/l, "Strange Are the Ways of Love," Tiomkin, Ned Washington (sung by Randy Sparks).

Western (PR:A MPAA:NR)

YOUNG LIONS, THE**** (1958) 167m FOX bw

Marlon Brando (*Christian Diestl*), Montgomery Clift (*Noah Ackerman*), Dean Martin (*Michael Whiteacre*), Hope Lange (*Hope Plowman*), Barbara Rush (*Margaret Freemantle*), May Britt (*Gretchen Hardenberg*), Maximilian Schell (*Capt. Hardenberg*), Dora Doll (*Simone*), Lee Van Cleef (*Sgt. Rickett*), Liliane Montevecchi (*Francoise*), Parley Baer (*Brant*), Arthur Franz (*Lt. Green*), Hal Baylor (*Pvt. Burnecker*), Richard Gardner (*Pvt. Cowley*), Herbert Rudley (*Capt. Colclough*), John Alderson (*Cpl. Kraus*), Sam Gilman (*Pvt. Faber*), L.Q. Jones (*Pvt. Donnelly*), Julian Burton (*Pvt. Brailsford*), Vaughn Taylor (*John Plowman*), Gene Roth (*Cafe Manager*), Stephen Bekassy (*German Major*), Ivan Triesault (*German Colonel*), Clive Morgan (*British Colonel*), Ashley Cowan (*Maier*), Paul Comi (*Pvt. Abbott*), Michael Pataki (*Pvt. Hagstrom*), John Gabriel (*Burn*), Kendall Scott (*Emerson*), Stan Kamber (*Acaro*), Robert Ellenstein (*Rabbi*), Jeffrey Sayre (*Drunk*), Kurt Katch (*Camp Commandant*), Milton Frome (*Physician*), Otto Reichow (*Bavarian*), Robert Burton (*Col. Mead*), Harvey Stephens (*Gen. Rockland*), Anne Stebbins (*Brunette*), Mary Pierce (*Young French Girl*), Ann Codee (*French Woman*), Christian Pasques (*French Boy*), Doris Wiss (*Nurse*), Alfred Tonkel (*German Waiter*), John Banner (*Burgermeister*), Norbert Schiller (*Civilian*), Henry Rowland (*Sergeant*), Art Reichle, David Dabov (*Soldiers*), Wade Cagle (*Lt. Emerson*), Lee Winter (*PFC*), Nicholas King (*Medic*), Harry Ellerbe (*Draft Board Chairman*), Craig Karr (*Draft Board Secretary*), Michael Smith (*Draft Board Member*), Voltaire Perkins (*Druggist*), Ann Daniels (*Hatcheck Girl*), Alberto Morin (*Bartender*), George Meader (*Milkman*), Joan Douglas (*Maid*), Ed Rickard (*Mailman*), Joe Brooks, Hubert Kerns, Ann Paige.

A fascinating and intelligent look at the men who fought WW II, THE YOUNG LIONS follows three soldiers through the war, up to the point where their lives cross and one of them dies. The film opens in 1938, as American tourist Rush is taking skiing lessons from Brando, who tells her about his belief in Naziism as a cure for the ills plaguing Germany. Rush returns to America and her boy friend, Martin, a Broadway playboy. Meanwhile, Clift, a Jew, visits his estranged father and watches him die in a cheap motel room. As the war gets underway, Brando joins the German army and marches into Paris with it and his superior officer, Schell. Martin and Clift are drafted and become friends. Martin invites Clift to a party where he meets Lange, whom he later marries. In North Africa, Brando is now an officer of the Afrika Korps, and he is becoming increasingly disillusioned with the war and the brutality of his comrades, especially Schell. During basic training, Clift withstands the anti-Semitism of the other soldiers, and when four of them take him on in a fist fight, he is brutally beaten, but he does gain their respect with his endurance. He deserts, but when he learns that Lange is pregnant, he turns himself in. Back in North Africa, the tide of war has turned and Schell and Brando are fleeing for their lives on a motorcycle. They hit a mine and Schell is badly injured, although Brando escapes almost unscathed. When Brando goes to visit Schell, whose face is entirely covered in bandages, Schell asks Brando to bring him a bayonet so that he can put the horribly burned man next to him out of his misery. Later, when Brando goes to visit Schell's wife, Britt, with whom he has had something of an affair, she coldly tells him that her husband has killed himself with a bayonet. Brando is so repulsed by her indifference that he flees her embraces. Back at the front, in France now, Brando sees his entire command wiped out. Later, near the German border, he wanders aimlessly until he comes to a concentration camp. The commander there takes him in and feeds him, complaining about the burden of trying to kill 6,000 people a day with a staff of only 12. All his beliefs shattered now, Brando roams the countryside, tossing aside his submachine gun. Eventually he comes across Martin and Clift, who have also just come from the concentration camp, having helped liberate it. Both men are sickened and angry. Brando pulls out his pistol, then decides to surrender. He fires his gun into the air. Martin and Clift quickly turn and Martin shoots Brando dead. Great changes were made in the script from Irwin Shaw's original story, mostly in the way of Brando's character. In the book, he is an unredeemed Nazi to the last, and when the final confrontation comes, he kills the Jewish soldier and is killed by the other American. It was largely Brando's work in making the German a sympathetic character, his argument for it being that Shaw had written his book in the immediate aftermath of the war, when tempers were still hot, although Shaw later told the actor that he wouldn't have changed his opinions even if he had written the book 10 years later. The shooting of the film was far from smooth. First of all, the script had to go through three rewrites before the Pentagon would give its support. Brando and Clift were constantly at odds. Brando used to come and watch Clift work, hiding behind a camera. Clift almost never went to see Brando work, though. When the time came to shoot the death scene, Brando wanted to die Christlike, arms outstretched on a coil of barbed wire. Clift exploded, "If Marlon's allowed to do that, I'll walk off the picture." This led a bystander on the set to comment, "When Monty's around, there's only room for one Jesus Christ." Clift had torn a picture of Franz Kafka from a magazine and tried to conform himself to his likeness for the film. He dropped his weight from 150 to 139 pounds and altered his features with putty behind his ears to make them stick out and a false nose. At one point in the shooting, while the crew was filming on the site of an actual concentration camp in Alsace-Lorraine, the French crew members refused to work. Asked why, they explained that they didn't feel the Americans, who had stripped to the waist in the hot sun, were showing the proper respect for those who had died there. Grudgingly, the Americans put their sweaty shirts back on. Brando was happy with his performance, even naming his first child Christian, after his character. Clift, who was usually not happy with himself on the screen, was also pleased with his work here. Brando made a number of public statements about his role and about people living in peace and brotherhood and the like, leading one German reporter to comment, "Brando speaks more like a statesman than a movie actor."

p, Al Lichtman; d, Edward Dmytryk; w, Edward Anhalt (based on the novel by Irwin Shaw); ph, Joe MacDonald (CinemaScope); m, Hugo Freidhofer; ed, Dorothy Spencer; md, Lionel Newman; art d, Lyle R. Wheeler, Addison Hehr; set d, Walter M. Scott, Stuart A. Reiss; cos, Adele Balkan, Charles LeMaire; spec eff, L.B. Abbott; makeup, Ben Nye.

War Drama   Cas.   (PR:C-O   MPAA:NR)

YOUNG LORD, THE***   (1970, Ger.) 137m Beta-United/International
                                        Television Trading c (DER JUNGE LORD)

Edith Mathis (*Luise*), Donald Grobe (*Wilhelm*), Loren Driscoll (*Barrat*), Barry McDaniel (*Secretary*), Otto Graf (*Sir Edgar*), Vera Little (*Begonia*), Lisa Otto (*Frau Hasentraffer*), Margrette Ast (*Baroness*), Gita Mikes (*Frau von Hufnagel*), Bella Jaspers (*Ida*), Manfred Rohri (*Mayor*), Ivan Sardi (*Hasentreffer*), Ernst Krubowski (*Scharf*), Helmut Krebs (*Professor*), Gunther Treptow (*LaRocca*), Fritz Hoppe (*Lamplighter*), Marina Tuerke (*Chambermaid*), Leopold Clam (*Meadows*).

This is an adaptation of the Henze-Bachmann opera "Der Jungle Lord." It is 1830 and Graf, an elderly English nobleman, arrives in a German town bringing along an entourage of servants and animals. The town shows great awe for the man but Graf feels nothing but contempt for the simple people. He ultimately shows his feelings by creating a mythical "young lord" and convincing the people that this fictional man truly exists.

d, Gustav Rudolf Sellner; w, Ingeborg Bachmann (based on the opera "Der Junge Lord" by Hans Werner Henze and Bachmann, and "Der Junge Englander", a fable by Wilhelm Hauff); ph, Ernst Wild (Eastmancolor); m, Hans Werner Henze; md, Christoph von Dohnanyi; cos, Filippo Sanjust; m/l, Henze, Bachmann(sung and played by the Deutsch Opera Berlin Chorus and Orchestra).

Opera   (PR:A   MPAA:NR)

YOUNG LOVERS, THE, 1950   (SEE: NEVER FEAR, 1950)

YOUNG LOVERS, THE, 1954   (SEE: CHANCE MEETING, 1954, Brit.)

YOUNG LOVERS, THE**½   (1964) 110m MGM-Tigertail/MGM bw

Peter Fonda (*Eddie Slocum*), Sharon Hugueny (*Pam Burns*), Nick Adams (*Tarragoo*), Deborah Walley (*Debbie*), Beatrice Straight (*Mrs. Burns*), Malachi Throne (*Prof. Schwartz*), Joseph Campanella (*Prof. Reese*), Nancy Rennick (*Mary Resse*), Kent Smith (*Dr. Shoemaker*), Jennifer Billingsley (*Karen*).

At a college campus a relationship grows between Fonda, an art student, and Hugueny, a teacher trainee. The friends become lovers and finally Hugueny becomes pregnant. Fonda, with no source of money, thinks marrying her would damage his future, so Hugueny decides to get an abortion and forget

about Fonda. She can't bring herself to go through with it, though. With the help of her mother Straight, Hugueny leaves town but Fonda,–gaining some maturity,–realizes that he must be responsible for his actions and follows her. This "youth in trouble" film is hardly fresh in story content and is lacking in production values. However the young cast, particularly Fonda, gives the picture a much-needed boost. The direction is choppy, with a somewhat confusing time frame, but the cast proves able to overcome the problems and inherent soap-opera qualities of the script. Fonda was not the only second-generation Hollywood brat associated with the film; it was produced and directed by Samuel Goldwyn, Jr. in his directorial debut.

p&d, Samuel Goldwyn, Jr.; w, George Garrett (based on the novel *The Young Lovers* by Julian Halevy); ph, Joseph Biroc, Ellsworth Fredricks; m, Sol Kaplan; ed, William A. Lyon; md, Kaplan; prod d, Fernando Carrere; set d, Frank Wade; makeup, Mark Reedall.

Drama   (PR:C-O   MPAA:NR)

YOUNG MAN OF MANHATTAN**½   (1930) 75m PAR bw

Claudette Colbert (*Ann Vaughn*), Norman Foster (*Toby McLean*), Ginger Rogers (*Puff Randolph*), Charles Ruggles (*Shorty Ross*), Leslie Austin (*Dwight Knowles*), H. Dudley Hawley (*Doctor*), Lorraine Aalbu, Aileen Aalbu, Fern Aalbu, Harriet Aalbu (*Sherman Sisters*), Tommy Reilly (*Referee*), John MacDowell.

Foster is a sports reporter who meets fellow reporter Colbert during the Gene Tunney-Jack Dempsey fight. They fall in love and marry in short order, living in a small New York apartment. When he travels to St. Louis to cover the World Series, he is introduced to socialite Rogers, but he is still too much in love with Colbert to pay attention. Soon, though, Colbert becomes a well-known magazine writer and, jealous of her success, Foster throws himself into an affair. Later, when Foster comes home after a late-night drinking binge, Colbert throws him out. She tries to drown her sorrows with some of the bootleg Scotch Foster left in the apartment and she temporarily goes blind from the bad booze. Foster is horror-stricken and he abandons Rogers and devotes himself to his work, and soon friend Ruggles engineers a reconciliation. Adequate romance has more historic than filmic interest, being Roger's first feature and one of Colbert's last dues-paying pictures before becoming a major star. The writing is melodramatic and the direction uninspired, as are the performances, likable though they are. The film had little else going for it, though, except perhaps some glimpses of major sporting events like the above-mentioned fight, the Army-Navy football game, the World Series, a six-day bicycle race, and others. Perhaps the most significant thing about this film is that it made Rogers' come-on phrase "Cigarette me, big boy." one of the most popular catch-phrases of the 1930s. d, Monta Bell; w, Robert Presnell, Daniel Reed (based on a novel by Katherine Brush); ph, Larry Williams; ed, Emma Hill; md, David Mendoza; art d, William Saulter; cos, Caroline Putnam; m/l, "I've Got 'It' but 'It' Don't Do Me No Good," "I'll Bob Up with the Bob-O-Link," "Good 'n' Plenty," "If You Can Just Forgive and Forget" (Irving Kahal, Pierre Norman, Sammy Fain).

Drama   (PR:A   MPAA:NR)

YOUNG MAN OF MUSIC   (SEE: YOUNG MAN WITH A HORN,
                                                            1950)

YOUNG MAN WITH A HORN****   (1950) 111m WB bw

Kirk Douglas (*Rick Martin*), Lauren Bacall (*Amy North*), Doris Day (*Jo Jordan*), Hoagy Carmichael (*Smoke Willoughby*), Juano Hernandez (*Art Hazzard*), Jerome Cowan (*Phil Morrison*), Mary Beth Hughes (*Margo Martin*), Nestor Paiva (*Louis Galba*), Orley Lindgren *Rick as a Boy*), Walter Reed (*Jack Chandler*), Jack Kruschen (*Cab Driver*), Alex Gerry (*Dr. Weaver*), Jack Shea (*Male Nurse*), James Griffith (*Walt*), Dean Reisner (*Joe*), Everett Glass (*Man Leading Song*), Dave Dunbar (*Alcoholic Bum*), Robert O'Neill (*Bum*), Paul E. Burns (*Pawnbroker*), Julius Wechter (*Boy Drummer*), Ivor James (*Boy Banjoist*), Larry Rio (*Owner*), Hugh Charles, Sid Kane (*Men*), Vivian Mallah, Lorna Jordan, Lewell Enge (*Molls*), Bridget Brown (*Girl*), Dan Seymour (*Mike*), Paul Dubov (*Maxie*), Keye Luke (*Ramundo*), Frank Cady (*Hotel Clerk*), Murray Leonard (*Bartender*), Hugh Murray (*Doctor*), Dick Cogan (*Interne*), Katharine Kurasch (*Miss Carson*), Burk Symon (*Pawnbroker*), Bill Walker (*Black Minister*), Helene Heigh (*Tweedy Woman*), Ted Eckelberry (*Elevator Boy*).

Inspired by the brilliant but tragic life of jazz coronet player Leon Bismark "Bix" Beiderbecke who died in 1931 at the age of 28 after a long battle with chronic alcoholism, YOUNG MAN WITH A HORN stars Douglas as the fictional counterpart of the great jazz musician. The film begins as a piano player, Carmichael, reminisces about the fabulously talented trumpet player Douglas. In flashback we see Douglas as a child (played by Lindgren). He is an introspective young boy with a fascination for music. At night he combs the streets of Skid Row listening to the jazz music drifting out the bars. Lindgren becomes entralled with one player in particular, Hernandez, a black jazz musican who leads a five-piece band. Inspired by his idol, Lindgren takes a job as a pin boy in a bowling alley and earns enough money to buy a second-hand trumpet. Lindgren becomes Hernandez's protege and the musician teaches the eager youngster everything he knows. By the time he is twenty (now played by Douglas) the young horn player is good enough

3979 YOUNG MAN WITH IDEAS-

to get a job playing with a dance band. There he becomes close friends with piano player Carmichael and torch singer Day. Douglas soon becomes frustrated by the dull sound of the big band and he runs into trouble with the band leader for trying to improvise on the horn instead of playing the song as written. Together with Carmichael, Douglas tries to jazz up an arrangement one night and both are fired. From there it is a string of cheap dives for the musicians, and while the money is poor the music is more expressive. Carmichael grows frustrated and decides to go back home to Indiana, while Douglas heads off to see if he can get a good gig in New York City. There he finds Day, singing with a new band. Douglas and Day go to hear good jazz in a small cafe, and Douglas is shocked to find his mentor, Hernandez, old, sick and frail not playing half as well as he used to. Douglas mounts the stage and helps out. His brilliant playing lands him a job with a popular dance band and he soon rises to stardom. With his stardom comes trouble in the form of a rich, beautiful diletante, Bacall, who sets out to make Douglas her own. His passionate affair with Bacall engulfs his desire to play jazz and he begins drinking heavily. The couple are married, but the union turns into a nightmare when Bacall, who is extremely jealous of Douglas' talent, stifles his creativity and subjects him to dozens of boring parties where the guests are snobby rich folks who can't relate to Douglas' creative passion. When Hernandez is killed by a hit-and-run driver, Douglas skips one of Bacall's parties to attend the funeral. When he returns he finds his wife in a rage and she destroys all his jazz records. The marriage is over and Douglas finds bitter solace in the bottle. The drinking makes him unreliable and he loses his job with the band. Once again he works cheap dives, and when he must be roused out of a drunken stupor to make a recording session, he becomes frustrated with his inability to play well and smashes his trumpet. He soon winds up in the gutter–a pathetic alcoholic. Eventually Carmichael and Day take him to a hospital to dry out, and there is an indication that he will try and make a comeback. While it suffers at times from being a bit too melodramatic, YOUNG MAN WITH A HORN boasts several fine performances, and most importantly of all–plenty of jazz. Douglas studied for three months under studio orchestra trumpeter Larry Sullivan and he learned how to play the trumpet convincingly. Unfortunately, his constant practicing in his dressing room began to annoy the cast and crew and director Curtiz was forced to ask the actor to stop. It really didn't matter what Douglas sounded like because all his trumpet playing was dubbed by Harry James (some of Carmichael's piano playing was dubbed by Buddy Cole, and Jimmy Zito handled actor Hernandez's playing). James was an odd choice to recreate the music because Beiderbecke was a coronet player, a instrument with a superior sound–the true jazzman's instrument. Bacall turns in a fabulous performance as the bored, hollow rich girl who sucks the life out of Douglas as if she were a vampire. It was a surprisingly unsympathetic role for the actress to choose and she handled it with aplomb proving she had a wider range than anyone suspected. Although the drama may be hackneyed and cliched when it comes to the portrayal of a jazz musician, the music is what counts and there is plenty of it. Songs include: "The Very Thought of You" (Ray Noble), "I May Be Wrong" (Henry Sullivan, Harry Ruskin), "The Man I Love" (George and Ira Gershwin); "Too Marvelous for Words" (Johnny Mercer, Richard A. Whiting), "With a Song in My Heart" (Richard Rogers, Lorenz Hart), "Pretty Baby" (Egbert Van Alstyne, Tony Jackson), "I Only Have Eyes for You" (Harry Warren, Al Dubin), "Limehouse Blues" (Philip Braham, Douglas Furber), "Melancholy Rhapsody" (Sammy Cahn, Ray Heindorf), "Lullaby of Broadway" (Harry Warren, Al Dubin), "Get Happy" (Harold Arlen, Ted Koehler).

p, Jerry Wald; d, Michael Curtiz; w, Carl Foreman, Edmund H. North (based on the novel by Dorothy Baker); ph, Ted McCord; ed, Alan Crosland, Jr.; md, Ray Heindorf; art d, Edward Carrere; set d, William Wallace; cos, Milo Anderson; makeup, Perc Westmore.

Musical/Drama   **(PR:C MPAA:NR)**

YOUNG MAN WITH IDEAS***   (1952) 85m MGM bw

Glenn Ford (*Maxwell Webster*), Ruth Roman (*Julie Webster*), Denise Darcel (*Dorianne Gray*), Nina Foch (*Joyce Laramie*), Donna Corcoran (*Caroline Webster*), Ray Collins (*Edmund Jethrow*), Mary Wickes (*Mrs. Gilpin*), Bobby Diamond (*Willis Gilpin*), Sheldon Leonard (*Brick Davis*), Dick Wessel (*Eddie Tasling*), Carl Milletaire (*Tux Cullery*), Curtis Cooksey (*Judge Jennings*), Karl Davis (*Punchy*), Fay Roope (*Kyle Thornhill*), John Call (*Bushy-Haired Man*), Nadene Ashdown (*Susan Webster*), Barry Rado, Norman Rado (*Max, Jr.*), Wilton Graff (*Mr. Cardy*), Martha Wentworth (*Mrs. Hammerty*), Selmer Jackson.

Ford plays an overworked, underpaid legal researcher who–determined to make a success of his life–moves to the coast with wife Roman and their children. Studying for the California bar examination, Ford meets fellow student Foch, who is enormously attracted to him. He also runs into French chanteuse Darcel, who appears tempted to give up a prospective career in pictures on his behalf. Other troubles arrive in the form of a string of telephone calls from people seeking to place bets on horse races; Ford's phone number had previously been assigned to a bookmaker. When Roman jokingly accepts a winning bet, Ford is threatened by hoodlums attempting to collect the payoff. Ultimately, Ford, bookie Leonard, and the hoodlums are all arrested on charges of illegal gambling. Ford's successful defense of his own case kicks off his new California career nicely. Ford's first try at light domestic comedy demonstrates that he has the touch in director Leisen's first film for MGM (with writer Sheekman, he had worked at

Paramount).

p, Gottfried Reinhardt, William H. Wright; d, Mitchell Leisen; w, Arthur Sheekman; ph, Joseph Ruttenberg; m, David Rose; ed, Fredrick Y. Smith; art d, Cedric Gibbons, Arthur Lonergan; set d, Edwin B. Willis, Hugh Hunt; spec eff, Sidney Guilaroff.

Comedy   **(PR:A MPAA:NR)**

YOUNG MAN'S FANCY***   (1943, Brit.) 77m EAL/ABF bw

Griffith Jones (*Lord Alban*), Anna Lee (*Ada Gray*), Seymour Hicks (*Duke of Beaumont*), Billy Bennett (*Capt. Boumphrey*), Edward Rigby (*Gray*), Ada's Father, Francis L. Sullivan (*Blackbeard*), Martita Hunt (*Duchess of Beaumont*), Meriel Forbes (*Miss Crowther*), Felix Aymler (*Sir Caleb Crowther*), Aimos (*Tramp*), Phyllis Monkman (*Esme*), Morton Selten (*Fothergill*), George Carney (*Chairman*), Allan Aynesworth (*Mr. Trubshaw*), Athene Seyler (*Milliner*), George Benson (*Booking Clerk*), Violet Vanbrugh, Irene Eisinger, Peter Bull, Aubrey Dexter, Harry Terry.

A wonderful light comedy has Jones playing an English nobleman unhappily betrothed to a rich brewery heiress. Life takes a complete turnaround for him one day when he attends a circus. Lee, the human cannonball, is fired right into his lap and it's love at first sight. The two elope to Paris and presumably live happily ever after. The amiable cast makes this marvelous little comedy work. Jones and Lee have wonderful chemistry, backed by good direction and nice attention to Victorian period detail. Reportedly Lee was quite unhappy that a stunt double was fired out of the cannon rather than herself!

p, S. C. Balcon; d, Robert Stevenson; w, Roland Pertwee, E. V. H. Emmett, Rodney Ackland (based on a story by Stevenson); ph, Ronald Neame; m, Ernest Irving; ed, Charles Saunders, Ralph Kemplen; art d, Wilfred Shingleton.

Comedy   **(PR:A MPAA:NR)**

YOUNG MR. LINCOLN****   (1939) 100m FOX-COS bw

Henry Fonda (*Abraham Lincoln*), Alice Brady (*Abigail Clay*), Marjorie Weaver (*Mary Todd*), Arleen Whelan (*Hannah Clay*), Eddie Collins (*Efe Turner*), Pauline Moore (*Ann Rutledge*), Richard Cromwell (*Matt Clay*), Ward Bond (*John Palmer Cass*), Donald Meek (*John Felder*), Spencer Charters (*Judge Herbert A. Bell*), Eddie Quillan (*Adam Clay*), Dorris Bowdon (*Carrie Sue*), Milburn Stone (*Stephen A. Douglas*), Cliff Clark (*Sheriff Billings*), Robert Lowery (*Juror*), Charles Tannen (*Ninian Edwards*), Francis Ford (*Sam Boone*), Fred Kohler, Jr. (*Scrub White*), Kay Linaker (*Mrs. Edwards*), Russell Simpson (*Woodridge*), Edwin Maxwell (*John T. Stuart*), Charles Halton (*Hawthorne*), Robert Homans (*Mr. Clay*), Steven Randall (*Juror*), Jack Kelly (*Matt Clay as a Boy*), Dickie Jones (*Adam Clay as a Boy*), Harry Tyler (*Barber*), Jack Pennick (*Big Buck*), Louis Mason (*Court Clerk*), Paul Burns, Frank Orth, George Chandler, Dave Morris (*Loafers*), Ivar McFadden (*Juror*), Sylvia McClure (*Baby*), Herbert Heywood (*Official*), Arthur Aylesworth, Harold Goodwin (*Men*), Dorothy Vaughan, Virginia Brissac (*Women*), Clarence Wilson, Elizabeth Jones.

The early days of Abraham Lincoln get the full Ford treatment here, simultaneously making him human and making him a myth. The film opens with a poem familiar to most: "If Nancy Hanks/came back as a ghost/seeking news/of what she loved most/She'd ask first/'Where's my son?/What's happened to Abe?/What's he done?'" This sets the tone for the rest of the film, in which these questions are answered, but only in the context of what Lincoln (played by Fonda) had done by 1837. The film's scene has Fonda making a speech to a convention of the Whig party in 1832, in which the first words from his mouth are "You all know me." In that same year he talks with his girl friend, Moore, by a riverside, which dissolves to the same riverside five years later, covered with ice. Moore is dead, and her grave is on the same spot where they had spoken. Fonda speaks to it and asks her to help him decide his fututre. He stands a stick up on the grave, holding it with his finger at the top, and tells her that if it falls on her grave, he'll go into the legal profession. It falls for the law and soon we see Fonda practicing his first case, a dispute between two men. Fonda listens to both of them, then proposes a compromise. They both refuse that solution, so he threatens them: "Did you fellas ever hear 'bout the time I butted two heads together?" They acquiesce, and it is with great satisfaction that Fonda collects his fee. Following a fair in which Fonda serves as the pie judge, there is a murder during a fight involving the two sons of an old friend, Brady, and two local roughnecks, of whom the survivor is Bond. Fonda takes on the boys' defense, first by stopping a lynch mob from killing the pair on the spot. He tries to learn from Brady which of her sons killed the victim, but she can't say. Bond indicates that it was the bigger of the two, though neither is especially larger than the other. The judge tries to convince Fonda that he is too inexperienced for a case of this importance and suggests that he let an established lawyer take on the defense, namely Stone, a noted trial lawyer and Fonda's rival for the hand of socialite Weaver. Fonda refuses, and in court he manages to uses the *Farmer's Almanac* to trap Bond into confessing to the crime himself. Fonda is triumphant and Stone comes up to him and says he'll never underestimate him again. Fonda walks away, in a rainstorm that just happened to come up that day of shooting, and as he is lost in the rain, the film dissolves to a picture of the statue in the Lincoln Memorial, to Lincoln the myth, whom we all know. Ford was originally reluctant to take on the film. He had just made STAGECOACH and was in a position to pick and choose his work. Two plays had recently been on Broadway on the subject of Lincoln's early years, and Ford felt that the subject had been "worked to death." But when he read the Lamar Trotti script he changed his mind. Executive Producer Darryl F. Zanuck wanted rising actor Fonda to take on the title role, but Fonda was too much in awe of the character, and he turned it down. Some time later he was called into John Ford's office. "What's all this b...s... about you not wanting to play Abraham Lincoln?" Ford exploded. " You're not playing the Great Emancipator. You're playing a jacklegged lawyer from Springfield, Illinois, a gawky kid still wet behind the ears who rides a mule because he can't afford a horse!" (A number of variations of this statement exist, most of them with more expletives.) Fonda immediately changed his mind and took the part, turning in a marvelous performance that simultaneously captures the awkwardness of the young man, yet hints at the glory to come. Unlike most of Ford's films after STAGECOACH, this was very much a studio project, and Ford knew he was going to move on to his next film almost immediately after finishing work on this, leaving control of the editing to others. Since Ford had already argued with Zanuck over the slow, elegiac pace Ford was taking with the material, he ensured that the film would be cut the way he wanted by editing in the camera, setting up slow dissolves, and destroying the negatives of all the takes except the ones he wanted. Robert Parrish, who later became a director in his own right, cut the sound effects for this film, and recalled later that "We just cut the slates off and spliced it together." Throughout the film Zanuck gave Ford a lot of input about how he thought the film should go, mostly wanting it to move faster, and he did manage to cut one scene that Ford described for Peter Bogdanovich: "They cut some nice things out of it. For example, I had a lovely scene in which Lincoln rode into town on a mule, passed by a theatre and stopped to see what was playing, and it was the Booth family doing "Hamlet"; we had a typical old-fashioned poster up. Here was a poor shabby country lawyer wishing he had enough money to go see "Hamlet" when a very handsome young boy with dark hair–you knew he was a member of the Booth family–fresh, snobbish kid, all beautifully dressed– just walked out to the edge of the plank walk and looked at Lincoln. He looked at this funny, incongruous man in a tall hat riding a mule, and you knew there was some connection there. They cut it out–too bad." The story of the murder in the film was taken from Trotti's own experiences as a reporter in the South. There he had reported on a murder case in which one of two brothers was accused of killing a man. Their mother refused to tell which of them did it, so both were hanged. A superb motion picture, and one in which Ford's obsession with Americana and the forces and emotions that made this country what it is are plainly on view.

p, Kenneth Macgowan; d, John Ford; w, Lamar Trotti; ph,Bert Glennon, Arthur Miller; m, Alfred Newman; ed, Walter Thompson; md, Louis Silvers; art d, Richard Day, Mark-Lee Kirk; set d, Thomas Little; cos, Royer.

Biography   (PR:A MPAA:NR)

YOUNG MR. PITT, THE*½**   (1942, Brit.) 118m FOX bw

Robert Morley (Charles James Fox), Robert Donat (William Pitt/Earl of Chatham), Phyllis Calvert (Eleanor Eden), Raymond Lovell (George III), Max Adrian (Richard Brinsley Sheridan), Felix Aylmer (Lord North), Albert Lieven (Talleyrand), Stephen Haggard (Lord Horatio Nelson), Geoffrey Atkins (Pitt as a Child), Jean Cadell (Mrs. Sparry), Agnes Laughlan (Queen Charlotte), A. Bromley Davenport (Sir Evan Nepean), Frank Pettingell (Coachman), Leslie Bradley (Gentleman Jackson, Boxer), Roy Emerton (Dan Mendoza, Boxer), Hugh McDermott (Mr. Melvill), John Mills (William Wilberforce), Herbert Lom (Napoleon), Ian MacLean (Henry Dundas), John Salew (Smith), Stuart Lindsell (Earl Spencer), Henry Hewitt (Henry Addington), Frederick Culley (Sir William Farquhar), Alfred Sangster (Lord Grenville), Austin Trevor (French Registrar), Kathleen Byron, Jack Watling, Ronald Shiner, John Slater, Leslie Dwyer, Hugh Ardele, Frederick Leister, Esma Cannon, Merle Tottenham, Aubrey Mallalieu, Margaret Vyner, Leo Genn, James Harcourt, Muriel George, Dalla Black, Louis Diswarte, Townsend Whitling, Kynaston Reeves, Johnnie Schofield, Ann Stephens, Bruce Winston, Owen Reynolds, Billy Holland, Gerald Cooper, Ralph Roberts, Edgar Vosper, Edmund Willard, Alf Goddard, Frederick Valk, J.H. Roberts, Esme Percy, Gibb McLaughlin, D.J. Williams, Morland Graham, Lloyd Pearson, W.E. Holloway, Charles Paton, Neal Arden, Gordon James, Stanley Escane, Leslie Harcourt, James Kenney, Sydney Tafler.

Good biographical feature stars Donat as the famous English politician and statesman. He rises to prominence early and becomes prime minister at age 24. Morley is his political nemesis who eventually comes to respect the youthful leader. When war with France comes in 1793, Donat's career is imperiled, but he leads his country against Napoleon until his health begins to fail and he resigns after the British suffer a string of battlefield defeats in 1801. In 1804 he returns to power as the tide turns against Napoleon after the Battle of Trafalgar, although he dies in 1806 before the final defeat of the French. Mostly an exercise in wartime propaganda as Britain faced another threatened invasion from the continent. Donat is marvelous, as always, but Morley nearly steals the picture as his rival. Mills is fine in a smaller role that he took on with only four hours notice after the actor originally cast for the part died following the last rehearsal. The direction by Reed is restrained and the film may move too slowly for the impatient, but it does have its rewards, among them excellent costumes and sets and

intelligent scripting.

p, Edward Black; d, Carol Reed; w, Frank Launder, Sidney Gilliat, Viscount Castlerosse; ph, Frederick A. Young; ed, R.E. Dearing; md, Louis Levy; art d, Alex Vetchinsky.

Biography   (PA:A MPAA:NR)

YOUNG MONK, THE   (1978, Ger.) 84m Achternbush (DER JUNGE MOENCH)

Herbert Achternbush, Karolina Herbig, Brank Samarovski, Heinz Braun, Barbara Grass, Luisa Francia.

Off-the-wall, utterly mad comedy that takes place after an unnamed global disaster. The Earth is now a giant desert with only a few survivors left. One man is in search of God, another tries to remember what the word "nation" means. Between the two they become a pope and cardinal, choosing an Easter bunny found in a cemetery to serve as their Lord. Taking the floppy-eared deity with them in a boat, the religious figures go off with a female survivor to Italy only to discover that the country has sunk into the ocean. This is a film laced with strange and wonderful comic turns, wholly unexpected and wildly original. Achternbush, who wrote, directed, and produced the film in addition to taking a featured role, is known for his outrageous sense of humor, much in the same vein as the Monty Python crew. Like that group's biblical epic THE LIFE OF BRIAN (1979), his own New Testament parody DAS GESPENST inflamed authorities. He must have been doing it well for authorities shut down the film's production before its completion.

p,d&w, Herbert Achternbush; ph, Joerg Jeshel.

Comedy   (PR:O MPAA:NR)

YOUNG NOWHERES*   (1929) 65m FN-WB bw

Richard Barthelmess (Albert [Binky[Whalen), Marion Nixon (Annie Jackson), Bert Roach (Mr. Jesse), Anders Randolf (Cleaver), Raymond Turner (George), Jocelyn Lee (Brunette).

An unusual and well-done drama told within the simplest of forms. Barthelmess, playing an atypical role, is an elevator operator for a large hotel. He and Nixon, a hotel chambermaid, are found together in a guest's suite and charged with breaking and entering. As it turns out, they were there for an important reason which gives the film a clever, O. Henry-style ending. This works like a cinematic version of a short story, told with excellent style and some fine performances by the leads. The small production never goes beyond its boundaries, making a fine tale about genuinely human characters told with heart.

d, Frank Lloyd; w, Bradley King Wray (based on the story by Ida Alexa Ross Wylie); ph, Ernest Haller; ed, Ray Curtiss.

Drama   (PR:A MPAA:NR)

YOUNG NURSES, THE   (1973) 77m New World c (AKA: NIGHTINGALE)

Jean Manson (Kitty), Ashley Porter (Joanne), Angela Gibbs (Michelle), Zack Taylor (Donahue), Richard Miller (Policeman), Jack La Rue, Jr (Ken), William Joyce (Fairbanks), Sally Kirkland (Patient), Allan Arbus (Krebs), Mary Doyle (Nurse), Don Keefer (Chemist), Nan Martin (Reporter), Jay Burton (Manager), Linda Towne (Chris), John Thompson (Chicken), Kimberly Hyde (Peppermint), James Anthony (Nurse), Jeff Young (Anesthetist), Tom Baker (Floyd), Caro Kenyatta (Lester), Mantan Moreland, Sam Fuller.

Another in the Nurse films that made so much money for New World in the early 1970s (THE CANDY STRIPE NURSES followed). This time the title hospital workers run into a drug ring supervised by film director Sam Fuller in a cameo. The usual Roger Corman formula is in evidence here, a little nudity, a lot of violence, and a vague social message. Fans of exploitation should enjoy it. This was character actor Mantan Moreland's ("Birminghan" Brown, Charlie Chan's chauffeur in the later films of that series) last film as he died the same year.

p, Julie Corman; d, Clinton Kimbro; w, Howard R. Cohen; ph, Sam Clement (Metrocolor); m, Greg Prestopino; ed, Karen Johnson; prod d, Tim Kincaid; art d, Barbara Peters.

Crime   **Cas.**   (PR:O MPAA:R)

YOUNG ONE, THE½**   (1961, Mex.) 94m Producciones Olmeca/Valiant-Vitalite bw (LA JOVEN)

Zachary Scott (Miller, Game Warden), Kay Meersman (Evalyn), Bernie Hamilton (Traver), Claudio Brook (Reverend Fleetwood), Crahan Denton (Jackson).

Hamilton is a black jazz clarinetist who's wrongly accused of raping a white woman. He runs from his small southern town and heads to a small island which serves as a private hunting ground for some wealthy sportsmen. There he meets Meersman, a young adolescent whose grandfather, the island handyman, has just died. The two become friends and he gives her some money for needed supplies. Scott, the racist island gamekeeper, hears about this and becomes angry. However, he allows Hamilton to remain as the new handyman, then forces himself on the sexually maturing Meersman. He swears her to secrecy when Brook and his boatman Denton come to fetch the girl to a welfare home. Hamilton is accused of rape once more and is captured. The girl reveals that Scott is the real culprit. Finally, in fear of the consequences, Scott helps Hamilton escape and convinces Brook he really wants to marry the girl. The story is straightforward enough but Bunuel's little touches here and there don't quite work. Some of the racist elements are too heavy-handed and well below the great director's caliber for satire. Though the film has a handsome look and some good moments, this is one of Bunuel's lesser efforts.

p, George P. Werker; d, Luis Bunuel; w, Bunuel, H. B. Addis [Hugo Butler[(based on the short story "Travelin' Man" by Peter Matthiessen); ph, Gabriel Figueroa; m, Jesus Zarzosa; ed, Carlos Savage; art d, Jesus Bracho; m/l, "Sinner Man" (sung by Leon Gibb).

Drama   (PR:O MPAA:NR)

YOUNG ONES, THE   (SEE: WONDERFUL TO BE YOUNG, 1962, Brit.)

YOUNG PAUL BARONI   (SEE: KID MONK BARONI, 1952)

YOUNG PEOPLE*   (1940) 78m FOX bw

Shirley Temple (Wendy), Jack Oakie (Joe Ballantine), Charlotte Greenwood (Kit Ballantine), Arleen Whelan (Judith), George Montgomery (Mike Shea), Kathleen Howard (Hester Appleby), Minor Watson (Dakin), Frank Swann (Fred Willard), Frank Sully (Jeb), Sarah Edwards (Mrs. Stinchfield), Mae Marsh (Marie Liggett), Irving Bacon (Otis), Charles Halton (Moderator), Arthur Aylesworth (Doorman), Olin Howland (Station Master), Billy Wayne (Stage Manager), Harry Tyler (Dave), Darryl Hickman (Tommy), Shirley Mills (Mary Ann), Diane Fisher (Susie), Bobby Anderson (Jerry Dakin), Robert Shaw (Usher), Syd Saylor (Vaudevillian), Del Henderson (Eddie's Father), Ted North (Eddie), Evelyn Beresford (English Woman), Billy Benedict (Boy).

At 12 years of age, Temple's career as moviedom's cutest-ever child actress was just about over. In the last film on her 20th-Century Fox contract she's once more an orphan (didn't that poor girl ever have movie parents?) adopted by Oakie and Greenwood. They're a couple retiring from the song-and-dance life to a more sedate existence in a small town. No one in town really likes the new family but when a big storm hits Oakie becomes a hero and the family gives a fantastic show that ends all bitter feelings. It's not much but Temple, as usual, carries the film with her customary sincerity overcoming the story's inherent treacle. There's a fun use of clips from Temple's earlier films to show her character's past, making this a sort of full-circle picture for the young actress. Fans and anyone under the age of 10 will enjoy it thoroughly. Songs and musical numbers include "Tra-La-La," "Fifth Avenue," "I Wouldn't Take a Million," "The Mason-Dixon Line," "Young People" (Mack Gordon, Harry Warren), and, from the early clips of Temple singing and dancing, "On the Beach at Waikiki" and "Baby Take a Bow".

p, Harry Joe Brown; d, Allan Dwan; w, Edwin Blum, Don Ettlinger; ph, Edward Cronjager; ed, James H. Clark; md, Alfred Newman; art d, Richard Day, Rudolph Sternad; cos, Gwen Wakeling; ch, Nicholas Castle, Geneva Sawyer; m/l Mack Gordon, Harry Warren.

Musical   (PR:AAA MPAA:NR)

YOUNG PHILADELPHIANS, THE*   (1959) 136m WB bw (GB: THE CITY JUNGLE)

Paul Newman (Tony Lawrence), Barbara Rush (Joan Dickinson), Alexis Smith (Carol Wharton), Brian Keith (Mike Flannagan), Diane Brewster (Kate Judson), Billie Burke (Mrs. J.A. Allen), John Williams (Gil Dickinson), Robert Vaughn (Chet Gwynn), Otto Kruger (John M. Wharton), Paul Picerni (Louis Donetti), Robert Douglas (Morton Stearnes), Frank Conroy (Dr. Shippen Stearnes), Adam West (William Lawrence), Fred Eisley (Carter Henry), Richard Deacon (George Archibald), Isobel Elsom (Mrs. Lawrence).

A genuine 1950s soap-opera melodrama set among the upper-crust of Philadelphia society complete with infidelities, suicides, seductions, ambition, and plenty of skeletons in closets. Newman once again essays the wholly confident, ambitious, and seductive young man role and it is his performance that saves an otherwise average sudser. The film opens with a prolog set in 1924 where we see Brewster, a pretty and ambitious girl from the wrong side of the tracks, jilt her lover Keith to marry rich socialite West. Much to the newlyweds' dismay, West proves impotent during the honeymoon. Embarrassed, ashamed, and humiliated, the young millionaire kills himself, leaving Brewster a widow. Brewster immediately flies back into the arms of Keith and conceives his child. Declaring that her baby was fathered by West, Brewster ensures that the child will retain West's name and status. The move does not fool West's mother and though she cannot prove the child was not her son's she disinherits both mother and child. Brewster maintains that her son, Newman, is West's child and raises him as if he were part of the wealthy family--much to Keith's annoyance. Eventually Newman grows to manhood (thinking Keith is just a friend of the family) and attends

Princeton law school where he does quite well. Newman falls in love with Rush, the daughter of prominent lawyer Williams, but Williams does not like Newman much and offers him a job in his law office if he will stay away from his daughter. The success-driven Newman immediately accepts the offer and the shocked Rush marries another man, Eisley, on the rebound. Soon after the wedding, Eisley is drafted and killed in the Korean Conflict. When Newman sees a chance to get a good position with powerful lawyer Kruger, he launches into a subtle seduction of the attorney's frustrated wife, Smith, so that she will ensure his success. His rise to prominence is put on hold when Newman is drafted and goes off to Korea with his school chum Vaughn. Vaughn loses an arm in battle and both men eventually return to Philadelphia where Newman picks up where he left off working for Kruger's firm. Newman attempts to rekindle his romance with Rush--now a widow--and further stretches his influence by gaining the confidence of Burke, one of the richest women in the country. Eventually politics calls Newman and he gives the thought serious consideration. His political ambitions are sidetracked, however, when he learns that his pal Vaughn has been arrested for murdering his rich uncle. Rising to Vaughn's defense, Newman launches into the case with his usual zeal. Conroy, a doctor and relative of the dead man, who does not want to see Vaughn set free, threatens to reveal the true nature of Newman's parentage. Rather than have the truth revealed by a stranger, Brewster and Keith finally tell Newman that they are his parents. Unfazed, Newman continues his defense of Vaughn, despite the chance that the revelation could ruin his political career. At the trial, Newman introduces evidence that proves Vaughn's uncle had committed suicide and the case is closed. Impressed by Newman's willingness to risk his future to save a friend, Rush decides to forgive the young lawyer and start their relationship anew. Well over two hours long, THE YOUNG PHILADELPHIANS moves fairly quickly through the variety of melodramatic situations that clash and intertwine. Based on a very popular novel, the film is a competent but undistinguished effort that breathes only through the presence of its dynamic star. The supporting players are solid, but are never given much to do by the script or veteran director Sherman. In the hands of a master-dramatist like director Douglas Sirk, THE YOUNG PHILADELPHIANS could have been imbued with more insight, intelligence, and passion, propelling the soap-opera material into the realm of film art.

d, Vincent Sherman; w, James Gunn (based on the novel The Philadelphian by Richard Powell); ph, Harry Stradling, Sr.; m, Ernest Gold; ed, William Ziegler; md, Ray Heindorf; art d, Malcolm Bert; set d, John P. Austin; cos, Howard Shoup; makeup, Gordon Bau.

Drama   **Cas.**   (PR:C MPAA:NR)

YOUNG RACERS, THE**   (1963) 82m Alta Vista/AIP c

Mark Damon (Stephen Children), William Campbell (Joe Machin), Luana Anders (Henny), Robert Campbell (Robert Machin), Patrick Magee (Sir William Dragonet), Bruce McLaren (Lotus Team Manager), Milo Quesada (Italian Driver), Anthony Marsh (Announcer), Marie Versini (Sesia Machin), Beatrice Altariba (Monique), Margaret Robsahm (Lea), Christina Gregg (Daphne).

William Campbell is a womanizing Grand Prix race driver who does the European racing circuit, deceiving wife Versini at every pit stop. Damon plays a one-time racing driver, now a writer, who travels to Monte Carlo at race time to meet his fiancee, Altariba. Piqued to discover her engaged in an apparent affair with W. Campbell, the disgruntled Damon decides to write a book exposing the daredevil as a dirty driver. Damon and W. Campbell travel the race circuit together and Damon's planned penning is revealed to W. Campbell. The two decide on a driving duel. When Damon's car goes out of control, W. Campbell spins out to avoid hitting him, sustaining severe injuries in the process. During his recovery, Damon discovers that the demon driver is actually sensitive and misunderstood, and the two become fast friends. Ever able to take advantage of ready sets and available locations, low-budget producer-director Corman made this picture while on a European vacation, touring the racetracks in England, France, Belgium, and Monaco. Young Francis Ford Coppola, who served as sound man on the production, picked up some pointers from Corman; he used the major cast members in his forthcoming directorial effort, DEMENTIA 13 (1963), saving money in the process. Another fast learner on the set was prop man Menachem Golan, who was later to form the exploitation film production company Cannon Films with his partner, Yoram Globus. THE YOUNG RACERS has thrills and spills, but more important, it has some very attractive young actresses (billed in publicity handouts as "The International Playgirls"). "A Little Death Each Day...a Lot of Love Every Night!...They Treated Beautiful Women as if They Were Fast Cars...Rough!" So read the posters.

p&d, Roger Corman; w, R. Wright Campbell; ph, Floyd Crosby (Eastmancolor); m, Les Baxter; ed, Ronald Sinclair; art d, Albert Locatelli; makeup, Rachel Golan.

Action/Drama   (PR:C MPAA:NR)

YOUNG REBEL, THE**   (1969, Fr./Ital./Span.) 111m
Prisma-Protor-Procinex/AIP-Comm onwealth United c (LES AVEN-
TURES EXTRAORDINAIRES DE CERVANTES; CERVANTES; LE AV-
VENTURE E GLI AMOIR DI MIGUEL CERVANTES)

Horst Buchholz (*Miguel de Cervantes*), Gina Lollobrigida (*Giulia*), Jose
Ferrer (*Hassam Bey, Arab Envoy*), Louis Jourdan (*Cardinal Acquaviva*),
Francisco Rabal (*Rodrigo de Cervantes*), Fernando Rey (*King Philip II of
Spain*), Soledad Miranda (*Nessa*), Maurice de Canonge, Antonio Casa, Angel
Del Pozo, Jose Jaspe, Ricardo Palacios, Claudine Dalmas, Jose Nieto, Enzo
Curcio, Guadenzio Di Pietro, Andres Mejuto, Vidal Molina, Fernando
Hilbeck, Concha Humbria, Jorge Rigaud.

Uninspired epic about the great Spanish novelist, dramatist, and poet as a
young man. Buchholz is the 16th-Century hero who leaves his homeland,
Spain, for Italy, where he becomes a soldier for the Pope and helps the
Pope's emissary, Jourdan, in the church's war against the Moors in Spain.
Gradually Buchholz wins prestige and concurrently falls in love with
courtesan Lollobrigida, but they are separated when the Pope orders the
banishment of all prostitutes. Disillusioned, Buchholz endures the famous
sea battle of Lepanto, in which he acquitted himself with distinction, then
a later capture and imprisonment by Barbary pirates, and his ransom by the
Trinitarian friars. Overblown and overlong, but an interesting look at the
author of Don Quixote before he settled down to write.

p, Miguel Salkind, Pier Luigi Torri; d, Vincent Sherman; w, David Karp,
Enrique Llovet, Enrico Bomba (based on the book CERVANTES by Bruno
Frank); ph, Edmond Richard (Totalscope); m, Jean Ledrut, Angel Arteaga;
ed, Margarita Ochoa; art d, Enrique Alarcon, Luciano De Nardi; cos, Luis
Arguello.

Historical Epic   **(PR:C MPAA:M)**

YOUNG REBELS, THE   (SEE: TEENAGE DOLL, 1957)

YOUNG RUNAWAYS, THE**   (1968) 91m Four Leaf/MGM c

Brooke Bundy (*Shelly Allen*), Kevin Coughlin (*Dewey Norson*), Lloyd
Bochner (*Raymond Marquis Allen*), Patty McCormack (*Deanie Donford*),
Lynn Bari (*Mrs. Donford*), Norman Fell (*Mr. Donford*), Quentin Dean
(*Joanne*), Richard Dreyfuss (*Terry*), Dick Sargent (*Freddie*), James Edwards
(*Sgt. Joe Collyer*), Hortense Petra (*Mrs. Morse*), Isabell Sanford (*Sarah*),
Stacey Maxwell (*Alicia*), Cynthia Hull (*Carol Mae*), Ken Del Conte (*Loch
Riccano*), Lance Le Gault (*Curly*), Angus Duncan (*Dan Clark*), Romo
Vincent (*Club Manager*), Nicholas Georgiade (*Driver*), Steve Mitchell
(*Marty*), Ted Gehring (*Charley*), Cully Richards (*Police Sergeant*), Edwin
Cook (*Guru*), Keith Taylor (*Claude Bradville*), The Gordian Knot (*Them-
selves*), Army Archerd (*Himself*).

Unrealistic nonsense that tries to explain the turbulent youth of the 1960s
but results in an overdramatized and preposterous story. Bundy, Coughlin,
and McCormack run off from their homes around the country and head for
Chicago to see what that city will offer. There they discover the usual perils
of dope dealing, prostitution, and poverty which all lead to the conclusion
presented long ago in THE WIZARD OF OZ: there's no place like home.
There are some occasional good moments. Best of the bunch is Dreyfuss in
an early appearance as a cocky little draft dodger who steals a car whenever
he feels like it. Look for an appearance by columnist Archerd.

p, Sam Katzman; d, Arthur Dreifuss; w, Orville H. Hampton; ph, John F.
Warren (Panavision, Metrocolor); m, Fred Karger; ed, Ben Lewis; art d,
George W. Davis, Merrill Pye; set d, Henry Grace, Keogh Gleason; m/l, "The
Young Runaways," Karger, Kevin Coughlin (sung by Arthur Prysock),
"Ophelia's Dream," "Couldn't We?" James D. Weatherly, John D. Lobue,
Leland Russell (sung by The Gordian Knot); makeup, William Tuttle.

Drama   **(PR:O MPAA:R)**

YOUNG SAVAGES, THE***   (1961) 103m UA bw

Burt Lancaster (*Hank Bell*), Dina Merrill (*Karin Bell*), Shelley Winters
(*Mary di Pace*), Edward Andrews (*Dan Cole*), Vivian Nathan (*Mrs. Es-
calante*), Larry Gates (*Randolph*), Telly Savalas (*Lt. Richard Gunnison*),
Pilar Seurat (*Louisa Escalante*), Jody Fair (*Angela Rugiello*), Roberta Shore
(*Jenny Bell*), Milton Selzer (*Walsh*), Robert Burton (*Judge*), David Stewart
(*Barton*), Stanley Kristien (*Danny di Pace*), John Davis Chandler (*Arthur
Reardon*), Neil Nephew (*Anthony Aposto*), Luis Arroyo (*Zorro*), Jose Perez
(*Roberto Escalante*), Richard Velez (*Gargantua*), William Sargent (*Soames*),
Chris Robinson (*Pretty Boy*), Stanley Adams (*Lt. Hardy*), William Quinn
(*Capt. Larsen*), Linda Danzil (*Maria Amora*), Raphael Lopez (*Jose*), Henry
Norell (*Pierce*), Jon Carlo (*McNally*), Bob Biheller (*Turtleneck*), Mario
Roccuzzo (*Diavolo*), Harry Holcombe (*Doctor*), Helen Kleeb (*Mrs. Patton*),
Thom Conroy (*Mr. Abbeney*), John Walsh (*Lonnie*), Irving Steinberg (*Officer
Wohlman*), Clegg Hoyt (*Whitey*), Joel Fluellen (*Clerk of the Court*), Robert
Cleaves (*Sullivan*).

In a brilliant credit sequence, three leather-jacketed hoodlums stride across
a scarred slum, until, just after director Frankenheimer's name crosses the
screen, they arrive at the front steps of a brownstone where a group of
Puerto Rican youths sit chatting. The three pull out switchblades and stab
one of the youths, an individual wearing dark glasses. They take off running

back across the slum area but are quickly captured by police. The victim of
this vicious gang murder was blind and the arrested gang members,
Chandler, Nephew, and Kristien, refuse to talk to police, even to explain
how their victim was selected, and the politically ambitious district
attorney, Andrews, wants to go after the death penalty for the lads. Andrews
assigns his assistant, Lancaster, to the case, and Lancaster tries to learn the
boys' motives. Lancaster is from the same Italian ghetto as the boys, and the
mother of Kristien, Winters, is an old flame of his. He interrogates various
members of Italian and Puerto Rican gangs and eventually learns that the
slain boy, although blind, was an active gang member with whom the other
gang members would deposit their weapons whenever the police came
around, as well as serving as pimp for his own sister. He was hardly the
innocent, helpless victim police thought and his murder was far from the
random act they supposed. A Puerto Rican gang leader tells Lancaster that
it's a war out there, and that no one is exempt from fighting for his people.
Later, Merrill is threatened by gang members as a warning to her husband
and Lancaster is beaten up on the subway. Angry, he wants revenge against
the gangs, then realizes his anger is the same thing that motivates these
slum youths. In court he manages to get Kristien to admit he didn't do any
of the actual stabbing, and proves that Nephew is retarded and not
responsible for his actions. Chandler gets 20 years, Nephew is sent to a
mental hospital, and Kristien is acquitted. Lancaster has ruined his boss'
political ambitions (and consequently his own) but his principles are intact.
Frankenheimer's second feature and first of five associations with Lancaster (including THE BIRDMAN OF ALCATRAZ, 1962, and SEVEN DAYS IN
MAY, 1964,) shows a great deal of influence from the television dramas
where the director first made his name in the late 1950s, especially in the
attention-grabbing opening sequence. Audiences are hooked after that
heart-pounding assassination, although nothing in the rest of the film lives
up to that promise. Lancaster gives a strong performance, and the gang
members, especially the sleepy-eyed Chandler, ring frighteningly true, but
the rest of the cast members seem only to be devices to state various points
of view on juvenile delinquency. Technically the film is quite competent and
the look and feel of the mean streets of New York comes through well (the
film was largely shot on location) and the music of Amram is discordant and
perfectly suited to the action.

p, Pat Duggan; d, John Frankenheimer; w, Edward Anhalt, J.P. Miller
(based on the novel *A Matter of Conviction* by Evan Hunter); ph, Lionel
Linden; m, David Amram; ed, Eda Warren; art d, Burr Smidt; set d, James
Crowe; cos, Jack Angel, Roselle Novello; makeup, Robert Schiffer.

Drama   **(PR:C MPAA:NR)**

YOUNG SCARFACE   (SEE: BRIGHTON ROCK, 1947, Brit.)

YOUNG SINNER, THE**½   (1965) 81m T.C. Frank/United Screen
                                       Artists bw (AKA: AMONG THE THORNS)

Tom Laughlin (*Chris Wotan*), Stefanie Powers (*Ginny Miller*), William
Wellman, Jr (*John*), Robert Angelo (*Priest*), Linda March (*Tury Martin*),
Julia Paul (*Mrs. Martin*), Clint Gunkel (*Mr. Martin*), Dorothy Downey (*Mrs.
Wotan*), Charles Heard (*Mr. Wotan*), Roxanne Heard (*Joan Meyers*), John
Burns (*Head Coach Ferguson*), Jack Starrett (*Football Coach Jennings*), Ed
Cook (*Assistant Coach Webster*), Jane Taylor (*Tury's Friend*), Harry
Zumach (*Principal*), A.C. Pagenkoff (*Teacher*), Conny Van Dyke (*Joan's
Friend*), Richard A. Colla (*Ginny's Date*), James Stacy (*Art*), Chris Robinson
(*Bobby*), Dennis O'Flaherty (*Marty*), Bob Colonna (*Harry*), Chuck Siebert
(*Lee*), Marlene Kelly, Charles Stobert, Terry Thompson.

An early effort from the creator of BILLY JACK and not a bad outing at
all. He's a high school athlete who is confessing the story of his life to a
priest. At first he is a top football player with hopes of getting a scholarship.
His home life, with an alcoholic father and a working mother, is a shambles.
One day he gets into trouble by using the school pool after hours and is put
on probation. Though in love with Powers, he dates March, the daughter of
wealthy parents who Laughlin hopes will get him a scholarship. However,
her parents catch the two in bed. Next he's wrongly accused of taking part
in a robbery and expelled from school. With no one to turn to, he
accompanies Heard, a 14-year-old sexpot, to a secret place in the church in
hopes of making love. However, he is disgusted with himself and goes to
confession, where the priest will try to help him reshape his life. Despite his
quadruple credits of star-producer-director-writer, Laughlin keeps his ego
in check to produce a surprisingly interesting story of teenage angst. The sex
is never exploitative, and Laughlin wisely filled his cast with some good
character actors, resulting in believable people who make the story work.
This was originally released in 1961 under the preview title AMONG THE
THORNS but was withdrawn for four years before it's final release. It was
to be the first part of Laughlin's trilogy entitled We Are All Christ, but
neither of the other two works ever came through.

p,d&w, Tom Laughlin; ph, Ed Martin, Sven Walnum, James A. Crabe; m,
Shelly Manne; ed, Donald Henderson.

Drama   **(PR:C MPAA:NR)**

YOUNG SINNERS**   (1931) 78m FOX bw

Thomas Meighan (Tom McGuire), Hardie Albright (Gene Gibson), Dorothy Jordan (Constance Sinclair), Cecelia Loftus (Mrs. Sinclair), James Kirkwood (John Gibson), Edmund Breeze (Trent), Lucien Prival (Baron von Konitz), Arnold Lucy (Butler), Nora Lane (Maggie McGuire), Joan Castle (Sue), John Arledge (Jimmy), Eddie Nugent (Bud), Yvonne Pelletier (Madge), Gaylord Pendleton (Reggie), Billy Butts (Tim).

A wild youth is set up with a man who specializes in calming down juvenile delinquents. The two engage in cat and mouse games, both psychological and physical. When the man attempts to isolate the youth in a mountain cabin the boy is surprised and pleased to receive a secret visit from a girl friend. The story is for the most part unbelievable with much more dialog than required and the pacing is too slow for story development. Albright is okay as the boy and Meighan does a good job as the man in charge, though the best performance is Jordan as the girl.

d, John Blystone; w, William Conselman (based on a play by Elmer Harris); ph, John Seitz; ed, Ralph Dixon.

Drama   (PR:A MPAA:NR)

YOUNG STRANGER, THE**   (1957) 84m RKO/UNIV bw

James MacArthur (Hal Ditmar), Kim Hunter (Helen Ditmar), James Daly (Tom Ditmar), James Gregory (Sgt. Shipley), Whit Bissell (Grubbs, Theater Manager), Jeff Silver (Jerry), Jack Mullaney (Confused Boy), Eddie Ryder (Man in Theater), Jean Corbett (Girl in Theater), Gary Vinson (Boy in Courtroom), Charles Davis (Detective), Marian Seldes (Mrs. Morse), Terry Kelman (Donald Morse), Edith Evanson (Lotte), Tom Pittman (Lynn), Howard Price (Doorman).

MacArthur, in a promising screen debut, is the misunderstood 16-year-old son of film executive Daly. He goes to the movies and gets himself kicked out, but not before being provoked into hitting the house manager, Bissell. MacArthur is arrested and insolent to the police, and loses any sympathy he had gained from arresting officer Gregory. Daly uses his influence to get the charges dropped, though he won't listen to his son's side of the story. MacArthur tries to get Bissell to tell his father the truth but he refuses and tries to toss the teenager out of his office. MacArthur hits the man once more and is again arrested. However, this time Gregory believes the boy was really provoked and finally gets the truth out of Bissell. Daly begins to make an attempt to get closer to the son he doesn't know and Gregory begins thinking the same thing about his own boy. The film is a marvelous story of father-son bonds, told with gritty honesty. The cast brings truth to their characterizations under Frankenheimer's controlled direction. This was Frankenheimer's theatrical debut, adapting a TV play, DEAL A BLOW, he had directed in 1955. This earlier work had the same writer and also featured MacArthur in the lead. Frankenheimer had nothing but anxiety on the set, besieged by deadline problems and an open lack of confidence by his crew. The results were not what he had intended, but it still plays as strong stuff and is fine for a first film. THE YOUNG STRANGER was one of RKO studio's last features and was turned over to Universal for distribution.

p, Stuart Millar; d, John Frankenheimer; w, Robert Dozier (based on his television play "Deal A Blow"); ph, Robert Planck; m, Leonard Rosenman; ed, Robert Swink, Edward Biery, Jr.; art d, Albert D'Agostino, John B. Mansbridge.

Drama   (PR:C MPAA:NR)

YOUNG SWINGERS, THE*   (1963) 71m FOX bw

Rod Lauren (Mel Hudson), Molly Bee (Vicki Crawford), Gene McDaniels (Fred Lewis), Jack Larson (Pete Mundy), Jo Helton (Roberta Crawford), Justin Smith (Bruce Webster), Jerry Summers (Roger Kelly), Jack Younger (Irving Bird), Karen Gunderson (Judi Sherwood), John Merritt (Ken Sherwood), Ray Dannis, Dodie Warren, Elizabeth Thompson, Rusty Westcoatt, The Sherwood Singers.

Laughable trash has ruthless real estate lady Helton trying to remove a teenie-bopper club so she can put up a new high rise. Her niece, Bee, goes to the club with Summers, a snotty, rich boy friend. There she meets Lauren, the club's singer, who won't knuckle under to Helton's pressure. Of course bee is taken with the young man and leaves her aunt's camp to join the enemy. When the club burns down Helton is accused of torching it, but faulty wiring is the real culprit. Helton does a wild turnabout, offering to help build a new club, and she tosses a huge birthday bash for Bee. A film that is exactly what it sets out to be with no pretensions whatsoever. Musical numbers include: "Come to the Party," ("By" Dunham, Hank Levine), "Mad, Mad, Mad" (Susan Quickel, Bill Baker), "Elijah," "Come A-Runnin'," "Watutsi Surfer" (Dunham), "Voice on the Mountain" (Dunham, Henry Vars), "Greenback Dollar" (Hoyt Axton, Ken Ramsey), "I Can't Get You Out of My Heart" (Robert Marcucci, Russell Faith), "You Pass Me By" (Rod McKuen).

p&d, Maury Dexter; w, Harry Spalding; ph, Jack Marquette; m, Hank Levine; ed, Jodie Copelan; set d, Harry Reif; makeup, Ray Sebastian.

Comedy/Drama   (PR:AA MPAA:NR)

YOUNG SWORDSMAN*½   (1964, Jap.) 108m Toho bw (HIKEN)

Somegoro Ichikawa (Tenzen Hayakawa), Hiroyuki Nagato (Chojuro), Nami Tamura (Fiancee), Junko Ikeuchi (Hill Woman), Ryunosuke Tsukigata.

When swordplay of all forms is banned in 17th Century Japan, Ichikawa becomes angry. A fine swordsman, he thinks the law is unfair. His brother, Nagato, is less vocal about it and keeps his thoughts to himself. In frustration, Ichikawa takes to cutting off opponents' thumbs. His family is angered by this and he is banished from the home. Ichikawa then takes to theft, so Nagato is forced to defend the family honor by meeting his brother in a duel.

p, Tomoyuki Tanaka; d, Hiroshi Inagaki; w, Inagaki, Takeshi Kimura.

Drama/Action   (PR:C MPAA:NR)

YOUNG, THE EVIL AND THE SAVAGE, THE*½
                    (1968, Ital.) 82m Super International-B.G.A./AIP c (NUDE...SI
                                                                        MUORE)

Michael Rennie (Inspector Duran), Mark Damon (Richard), Eleanora Brown (Lucille), Sally Smith (Jill), Pat Valturri (Denise), Ludmilla Lvova (Miss Clay), Alan Collins (DeBrazzi), Franco De Rosa (Detective Gabon), Vivian Stapleton (Miss Tranfield), Esther Masing (Miss Martin), Valentino Macchi (Policeman), Aldo De Carellis (Professor), Sylvia Dionisio, Kathleen Parker, Paola Natale, Marisa Longo (Girls), Umberto Papiri, John Hawkwood.

When a student of a private school for girls finds a body in a trunk, the young lady is mysteriously strangled. Another strangling and one missing body later, enter Rennie (speaking English in an otherwise all-dubbed feature) to check out the trouble. First he suspects the gardener, but when he is strangled Rennie must look elsewhere. He goes through a few more suspects and a hint at who or who may not be the culprit until a student's distant cousin reveals himself to be the real murderer, who had actually been after Brown and was murdering people one by one until he could get at the intended victim. This way the young man had hoped to gain her inheritance. Poorly produced and badly dubbed, the title itself is a quick ripoff of the popular THE GOOD, THE BAD, AND THE UGLY. The cast sleepwalks through their roles but the film's camera work is not bad. This was originally released on a double bill with the immortal THE CONQUEROR WORM.

p, Lawrence Woolner, Giuseppe De Blasio; d, Anthony Dawson [Antonio Margheriti]; w, Dawson, Frank Bottar [Franco Bottari] (based on a story by John [Giovanni] Simonelli); ph, Frank [Fausto] Zuccoli (Cromoscope, Perfect Color); m, Carlo Savina; ed, Otello Colangeli; art d, Antonio Visone; makeup, Piero Mecacci.

Horror   (PR:O MPAA:NR)

YOUNG TOM EDISON*   (1940) 85m MGM bw

Mickey Rooney (Tom Edison), Fay Bainter (Mrs. Samuel Edison), George Bancroft (Samuel Edison), Virginia Weidler (Tannie Edison), Eugene Pallette (Mr. Nelson), Victor Kilian (Mr. Dingle), Bobbie Jordan (Joe Dingle), J.M. Kerrigan (Mr. McCarney), Lloyd Corrigan (Dr. Pender), John Kellogg (Bill Edison), Clem Bevans (Mr. Waddell), Eily Malyon (Schoolteacher), Harry Shannon (Capt. Brackett).

Good biographical story about two years in the life of Edison as a youth. Rooney gives warmth and vitality to the title role as he goes about upsetting the lives of those around him with his experiments. He is branded crazy by his parents, teachers, and peers, but when his mother falls ill his inquisitive mind comes up with the very trick the doctor needs to perform a delicate operation. Well-directed with enthusiasm, this is a fine film for children who are used to historical figures being cardboard cutouts. Made in tandem with EDISON, THE MAN, both scripted by the same team.

p, John W. Considine, Jr.; d, Norman Taurog; w, Bradbury Foote, Dore Schary, Hugo Butler (based on material gathered by H. Alan Dunn); ph, Sidney Wagner; m, Edward Ward; ed, Elmo Veron; art d, Cedric Gibbons; cos, Dolly Tree, Gile Steele.

Drama   (PR:AAA MPAA:NR)

YOUNG TORLESS*½   (1968, Fr./Ger.) 90m Nouvelles
        Editions/Kanawha bw (DER JUNGE TORLESS; LES DESARROIS DE
                            L'ELEVE TORLESS; AKA: YOUNG TOERLESS)

Mathieu Carrier (Torless), Marian Seidowsky (Basini), Bernd Tischer (Beineberg), Alfred Dietz (Reiting), Barbara Steele (Bozena), Jean Launay (Mathematics Teache r), Hanne Axmann-Rezzori (Frau Torless), Herbert Asmodi (Herr Torless), Lotte Ledl Innkeeper, Fritz Gehlen (School Director).

Carriere goes off to boarding school to finish out his senior year. This expensive academy is located on the eastern border of the Austro-Hungarian Empire. Upon joining his friends Dietz and Tischer, the trio go to visit Steele, a local waitress who engages in sexual initiation of the schoolboys. When another student (Seidowsky) is caught stealing money from Tischer's locker, Dietz promises not to turn him in on condition Seidowsky become his personal slave. Seidowsky is subjected to constant abuse from his masters Tischer and Dietz, who get a sadistic joy from their physical and psychological tortures. Carriere becomes fascinated with the process as well, though he doesn't engage in the brutality. When the sadism becomes more than Carriere can bear, he threatens to tell authorities, prompting Tischer and Dietz to blame their schoolmate if he dares to report their actions. When the two masters hang their slave by his heels in a gymnasium full of students Carriere is horrified. The school authorities investigate this incident and call in Carriere. He fully owns up to participating in the torture, yet cannot explain his actions. The film ends with Carriere leaving school on the recommendation of the headmasters. The film is based on a novel originally published in 1906 that proved strangely prophetic as an allegory. Director Schlondorff (in what was his first feature) turns the suitable aspect of the tale into an allegory of what happened to the German people during WW II. The story is filmed in stark black and white, with a deliberately muted aura around the unfolding events. The boys themselves are clad in uniforms devoid of any personality. In many ways YOUNG TORLESS recalls the pre-Hitler era German film MADCHEN IN UNIFORM with its theme and tone. Though not the classic that the previous film is, this is certainly powerful in its own right. Schlondorff would later deal with the German people under Hitler's rule in his film version of THE TIN DRUM.

p, Franz Seitz; d&w, Volker Schlondorff (based on the novel *Die Verwirrungen des Zoglings Torless* by Robert Musil); ph, Franz Rath; m, Hans Werner Henze; ed, Claus Von Boro; art d, Maleen Pacha.

Drama (PR:C MPAA:NR)

YOUNG WARRIORS, THE**   (1967) 93m UNIV c

James Drury (*Sgt. Cooley*), Steve Carlson (*Hacker*), Jonathan Daly (*Guthrie*), Robert Pine (*Foley*), Jeff Scott (*Lippincott*), Michael Stanwood (*Riley*), Johnny Alladin (*Harris*), Hank Jones (*Fairchild*), Tom Nolan (*Tremont*), Norman Fell (*Sgt. Wadley*), Buck Young (*Schumacher*), Kent McWhirter (*The Lieutenant*), George Sawaya, Morgan Jones, Noam Pitlik, Jon Drury, Buck Kartalian.

A group of naive young men goes off to fight in this trivial war picture, each reacting to the horrors they encounter in their own way. Carlson is at first stunned by it all, but soon turns into a sadistic killer. He's rebuked by sergeant Drury (giving the film's best performance) for gunning down a surrendering German. Later Carlson redeems himself by rescuing the sergeant under dangerous circumstances and the two become postwar friends. The direction is perfunctory but the camera work is surprisingly good, giving the film a fine look and feel that occasionally disguises it's weaker elements.

p, Gordon Kay; d, John Peyser; w, Richard Matheson (based on his novel *The Beardless Warriors*); ph, Loyal Griggs (Panavision, Technicolor); ed, Russell F. Schoengarth; art d, Alexander Golitzen, Alfred Ybarra; set d, John McCarthy, Ralph Sylos; makeup, Bud Westmore.

War (PR:C MPAA:NR)

YOUNG WARRIORS**   (1983) 105m Star Cinema/Cannon c

Ernest Borgnine (*Lt. Bob Carrigan*), Richard Roundtree (*Sgt. John Austin*), Lynda Day George (*Beverly Carrigan*), James Van Patten (*Kevin Carrigan*), Anne Lockhart (*Lucy*), Tom Reilly (*Scott*), Ed De Stefane (*Stan*), Mike Norris (*Fred*), Dick Shawn (*Prof. Hoover*), Linnea Quigley (*Ginger*), John Alden (*Jorge*), Britt Helfer (*Heather*), Don Hepner (*Animation Instructor*), April Dawn (*Tiffany Carrigan*), Nels Van Patten (*Roger*), Rick Easton (*Bartender*), Paul Tanashian (*Doctor*), Jimmy Patterson, Bernard Bloomer, Darlene D'Angelo, George O'Mara Mason, Gregory Bennett, Michelle Rossi, Randy Woltz.

When police officer Borgnine's daughter is raped and killed by a gang of youths, he does what is expected of him and cooperates with the police. However, the dead girl's brother, James Van Patten, decides to bypass frustrating legal methods and organizes his college fraternity pals into a vigilante squad. They cruise the streets in search of the killers, taking on any criminals they encounter. This DEATH WISH-inspired comic book approach to reality ends with the obligatory "justice prevails" bloodbath. It's not so much that this is a bad film, it's just that YOUNG WARRIORS (and similar films) is so predictable in its preachiness and its outcome. Nothing new here. YOUNG WARRIORS is just a quick way to make a buck.

p, Victoria Paige Meyerink; d, Lawrence D. Foldes; w, Foldes, Russell W. Colgin; ph, Mac Ahlberg; m, Rob Walsh; ed, Ted Nicolaou; prod d, Karl Pogany; art d, Richard S. Bylin; cos, Nicolaou, Laura Cogin; spec eff, John Eggett; animation sequences, Adam Slater.

Crime Cas. (PR:O MPAA:R)

YOUNG WIDOW**   (1946) 100m UA bw

Jane Russell (*Joan Kenwood*), Louis Hayward (*Jim Cameron*), Faith Domergue (*Gerry Taylor*), Marie Wilson (*Mac*), Kent Taylor (*Peter Waring*), Penny Singleton (*Peg Martin*), Connie Gilchrist (*Aunt Cissie*), Cora Witherspoon (*Aunt Emeline*), Steve Brodie (*Willie*), Norman Lloyd (*Sammy*), Richard Bailey (*Bill Martin*), Robert Holton (*Bob Johnson*), Peter Garey (*Navy Lieutenant*), Bill Moss (*Marine Lieutenant*), Bill "Red" Murphy

(*Army Lieutenant*), James Burke (*Motorcycle Cop*), Jimmie Dodd (*Officer Friend*), Harry Barris (*Officer's Club Pianist*), Dick Wessel (*Cabby*), George Meader (*Photographer*), George Lloyd (*Man on Platform*), James Flavin (*Conductor*), Walter Baldwin (*Miller*), William ["Billy"] Newell, Gerald Mohr.

Break out the pocket tissues as Russell plays a war widow turned journalist. She meets Hayward, a cocky young pilot, who proceeds to romance the beautiful woman. But will the memory of her late husband overwhelm any chance he might have? The film is told in a choppy style, poorly weaving together the various plot elements. Russell is wrong for the part but she gives a fair performance that's heavy on facial gestures. The support, including Singleton of the BLONDIE series, is ordinary.

p, Hunt Stromberg; d, Edwin L. Marin; w, Richard Macaulay, Margaret Buell Wilder (based on the novel by Clarissa Fairchild Cushman); ph, Lee Garmes; m, Carmen Dragon; ed, James Newcom; prod d, Nikolai Remisoff; art d, Remisoff.

Drama (PR:A MPAA:NR)

YOUNG, WILLING AND EAGER**½   (1962, Brit.) 77m Brenner Associates-Manson bw (GB: RAG DOLL)

Jess Conrad (*Joe Shane*), Hermione Baddeley (*Princess Sophia*), Kenneth Griffith (*Mort Wilson*), Christina Gregg (*Carol Flynn*), Patrick Magee (*Flynn*), Patrick Jordan (*Wills*), Michael Wynne (*Bellamy*), Frank Forsyth (*Superintendent*), Marie Devereux (*Ann*), Eve Eden (*Daphne*), David Gregory (*1st Youth*), Leon Garcia (*2nd Youth*), Frank Hawkins (*Taxi Driver*), Linda Castle (*Girl in Cellar*), John Line (*Guitarist*).

Seventeen-year old Gregg runs away from a horrid home life and hitchhikes to Soho in London. With the help of Baddeley, a carnival fortune teller who takes a liking to the girl, she gets a job waiting on tables. Griffith, her employer, makes a pass at her, which she rebuffs. She turns her attentions to Conrad, a fledgling singer, and the two marry when she finds she's carrying his child. To finance a move to a new life in Canada, Conrad burglarizes Griffith's home. However, Griffith awakens and shoots Conrad. The latter is wounded and flees after killing the older man. Conrad steals a car and heads off with Gregg. As the police close in Conrad tries to fight them off but drops dead from loss of blood, leaving Gregg in tears next to his body.

p, Tom Blakeley; d, Lance Comfort; w, Brock Williams, Derry Quinn (based on a story by Williams); ph, Basil Emmott; m, Martin Slavin; ed, Peter Pitt; art d, John Earl; m/l, "Why Am I Living?" Martin Slavin, Abbe Gail (performed by Mike Sammes Singers, Jess Conrad.)

Drama (PR:C MPAA:NR)

YOUNG WINSTON**½   (1972, Brit.) 145m Highroad-Hugh French/COL c

Simon Ward (*Winston Churchill/Sir Winston Churchill's Voice*), Peter Cellier (*Captain 35th Sikhs*), Ronald Hines (*Adjutant 35th Sikhs*), Dino Shafeek (*Sikh Soldier*), John Mills (*Gen. Herbert Kitchener*), Anne Bancroft (*Lady Jennie Churchill*), Russell Lewis (*Winston at Age 7*), Pat Heywood (*Mrs. Everest*), Robert Shaw (*Lord Randolph Churchill*), Laurence Naismith (*Lord Salisbury*), William Dexter (*Arthur Balfour*), Basil Dignam (*Joseph Chamberlain*), Robert Hardy (*Prep School Headmaster*), Edward Burnham (*Henry Labouchere*), John Stuart (*Speaker Viscount Peel*), Colin Blakely (*Butcher*), Noel Davis (*Interviewer*), Michael Audreson (*Winston at Age 13*), Jack Hawkins (*Dr. James Welldon*), Ian Holm (*George Buckle*), Richard Leech (*Mr. Moore*), Clive Morton (*Dr. Roose*), Robert Flemyng (*Dr. Buzzard*), Reginald Marsh (*Edward, Prince of Wales*), Patrick Magee (*Gen. Bindon Blood*), Jeremy Child (*Austen Chamberlain*), Robert Lankesheer (*Sympathetic M.P.*), Jane Seymour (*Pamela Plowden*), Dinsdale Landen (*Capt. Weaver*), Julian Holloway (*Capt. Baker*), Thorley Walters (*Maj. Finn*), Patrick Holt (*Col. Martin*), Norman Bird (*Party Chairman*), Edward Woodward (*Capt. Haldane*), Gerald Sim (*Engineer*), Ron Pember (*Fireman*), James Cosmo (*Officer on Train*), Andrew Faulds (*Mounted Boer*), Maurice Roeves (*Brockie*), Richard Beale, Nigel Hawthorne (*Boer Sentries*), James Cossins (*Barnsby*), John Woodvine (*Howard*), Norman Rossington (*Dewsnap*), Raymond Mason (*Man in Theater Gallery*), Brenda Cowling (*Mrs. Dewsnap*), Anthony Hopkins (*David Lloyd George*), Pippa Steel (*Clementine Hozier*), Norman Gay (*Sir Charles Dilke*), Robert Harris (*Speaker Gully*), Sanders Watney (*Sir Winston*), George Mikell (*Field Cornet*), Raymond Huntley, Willoughby Gray.

Winston Churchill was one of the titanic figures of the 20th Century, as well as a talented and erudite writer of history and memoirs. It was after viewing Carl Foreman's production of THE GUNS OF NAVARONE that Churchill himself decided that Foreman was just the man to adapt and produce Churchill's memoirs of his adventures as a young man, *My Early Life: A Roving Commission*, as a motion picture. As it happened, Foreman was busy and Churchill died in 1965 before the film could be shot. It was in 1972 that the film was finally completed with a script by Foreman and direction by the current master (or at least the most frequent practitioner) of the historical epic, Richard Attenborough. The film opens with Churchill (Ward) a junior officer in India out to make a name for himself. One of his superiors suggests that becoming a war correspondent is a good way to get in the newspapers.

There is a native uprising that Ward helps suppress, and that provides the material for his first dispatches from the field and eventually a book which angers many of the top brass with its outspoken opinions. Back in England, Ward's father, Shaw, resigns his post as Chancellor of the Exchequer over his disagreement with the ruling party over new arms expenditures. His career goes downhill quickly after that, particularly when he contracts syphilis. Ward and mother Bancroft can only watch horror-stricken from the gallery as Shaw babbles incoherently while trying to make a speech before the House of Commons. After Shaw's death, Ward returns to the army and goes to the Sudan to put down the Dervish uprising. The Arabs fight with all the fury that Allah can give them, but the British have machine guns and the Dervish army is destroyed at Omdurman. On the strength of his record in that war, Ward returns to England and runs for Parliament, but loses. He goes off to the Boer War as a correspondent and has a number of adventures not quite in keeping with his status as a noncombatant. After helping to foil a Boer ambush of an armored train, Ward is captured and put into a Boer concentration camp (the term originates from this war). Along with Woodward, he escapes and makes his way back to the British lines. (Woodward would later return to the Boer War in the film that made him something of an international star, BREAKER MORANT). Once he returns to England, his adventures have made him a household name and he easily wins election to Parliament at the age of 26. In his first speech before the House of Commons, Ward repeats and drives home the lessons of his father's beliefs as his mother proudly sits watching from the gallery. (A scene cut from most prints ends the film, with Churchill 'Watney', now an old man, sleeping in front of one of his unfinished landscapes, dreaming of his father coming to him and telling his son he doesn't understand his actions.) The film works as an action-packed adventure, with lots of rousing battle scenes and hairbreadth escapes, but when it tries to penetrate the motivations of its hero with the profundity of a high school psychology text, the film falls flat. Ward is convincing as the figure everyone today knows, and the other performances, particularly that of Shaw, are of a high order. The direction by Attenborough is smooth and the film doesn't dally over the slow parts, though it is almost two- and-a-half hours long. One can only wonder what Churchill would have thought.

p, Carl Foreman; d, Richard Attenborough; w, Foreman (based on *My Early Life: A Roving Commission* by Sir Winston Churchill); ph, Gerry Turpin (Panavision, Eastmancolor) m, Alfred Ralston, Sir Edward Elgar; ed, Kevin Connor; prod d, Geoffrey Drake, Don Ashton; md, Ralston; art d, John Graysmark, William Hutchinson; set d, Peter James; cos, Anthony Mendleson; spec eff, Cliff Richardson, Tom Howard, Charles Staffel; makeup, Stuart Freeborn.

Biography/Adventure   **Cas.**   **(PR:A-C   MPAA:PG)**

YOUNG WIVES' TALE***   (1954, Brit.) 78m Associated British Pictures/AA bw

Joan Greenwood (*Sabina Pennant*), Nigel Patrick (*Rodney Pennant*), Derek Farr (*Bruce Banning*), Guy Middleton (*Victor Manifold*), Athene Seyler (*Nanny Gallop*), Helen Cherry (*Mary Banning*), Audrey Hepburn (*Eve Lester*), Fabia Drake (*Nurse Blott*), Irene Handl, Joan Sanderson (*Nurses--Regents Park*), Selma Vaz Dias (*Ayah*), Jack McNaughton (*Taxi Driver*), Brian Oulton (*Man in Pub*), Carol James (*Elizabeth*).

Cute slapstick has playwright Patrick and wife Greenwood sharing a house with an assorted cast of loonies. Cherry and Farr are another married couple and Hepburn is a boarder. The major conflict is between the two married couples: the former is often harried while the latter is hopelessly efficient. But nothing in this house seems to go right, from the constant flow of nannies to the dinner-stealing pooch. The zaniness builds and builds as the spouses fight and angry mixups constantly occur. The story is told in a wild, free-wheeling style that works well considering the thin plot line. Broad humor is the order of the day.

p, Victor Skutetzky; d, Henry Cass; w, Ann Burnaby (based on the play by Ronald Jeans); ph, Erwin Hillier; m, Philip Green; ed, E. Jarvis; md, Louis Levy; art d, Terence Verity; makeup, Bob Clark.

Comedy   **(PR:A   MPAA:NR)**

YOUNG WOODLEY**½   (1930, Brit.) 71m BIP bw

Madeleine Carroll (*Laura Simmons*), Frank Lawton (*Woodley*), Sam Livesey (*Mr. Simmons*), Gerald Rawlinson (*Milner*), Billy Milton (*Vining*), Aubrey Mather (*Mr. Woodley*), John Teed (*Ainger*), Tony Halfpenny (*Cope*), Rene Ray (*Kitty*).

While studying in his final school term 18-year-old Lawton meets Carroll (24 years old at the time), the young wife of an elderly, pompous schoolmaster (Livesey). The two fall in love, which, of course, leads to a host of problems. Adapted from a popular stage play, the story is well handled with some genuine sensitivity toward the subject. However, there are problems with the style, which can't quite overcome its theatrical lineage. Still, it's not bad for an early talkie. For its day, the theme was considered risque.

d, Thomas Bentley; w, John Van Druten, Victor Kendall (based on the play by Van Druten); ph, A.F. Birch.

Drama   **(PR:C   MPAA:NR)**

YOUNG WORLD, A*   (1966, Fr./Ital.) 83m Terra-Les Productions Artistes-Sol Produzioni-Montoro/Lopert bw (UN MONDE NOUVEAU; UN MONDO NUOVO)

Christine Delaroche (*Anne*), Nino Castelnuovo (*Carlo*), Tanya Lopert (*Mary*), Madeleine Robinson (*Woman*), Georges Wilson (*Doctor*), Pierre Brasseur (*Boss*), Nadiege Ragoo (*Judith*), Isa Miranda, Jeanne Aubert, Jean-Pierre Darras, Francoise Brion, Franco Bucceri, Arlette Gilbert, Paul Mercey, Charles Millot, Laure Paillette, Antoine de Rudder, Jacques Masson.

Pretentious little effort by De Sica features Delaroche and Castelnuovo as, respectively, a Paris medical student and an Italian freelance photographer. They meet at a ball and it's love at first sight. They retire to a secluded alcove and when they emerge, she is pregnant. Castelnuovo is in a quandary, torn between making a commitment to this woman or keeping his free life style. He allows himself to be seduced by an older woman to get money for an abortion, but Delaroche refuses to go through with it. In the end they go to a movie and the film ends unresolved. A sad effort by De Sica, occasionally one of the best directors in the world. Here, though, he seems intent on imitating the French New Wave and the whole thing is rife with freeze frames, odd cuts, and the like. (In French; English subtitles.)

p, Raymond Froment; d, Vittorio De Sica; w, Cesare Zavattini; ph, Jean Boffety; m, Michel Colombier; ed, Paul Cayatte; art d, Max Douy (English titles, Noelle Gillmor).

Drama   **(PR:C   MPAA:NR)**

YOUNGBLOOD***   (1978) 90m Aion/AIP c

Lawrence-Hilton Jacobs (*Rommel*), Bryan O'Dell (*Youngblood*), Ren Woods (*Sybil*), Tony Allen (*Hustler*), Vince Cannon (*Corelli*), Art Evans (*Junkie*), Jeff Hollis (*Pusher*), Dave Pendleton (*Reggie*), Ron Trice (*Bummie*), Sheila Wills (*Joan*), Ralph Farquhar (*Geronimo*), Herbert Rice (*Durango*), Lionel Smith (*Chaka*), Maurice Sneed (*Skeeter-Jeeter*), Ann Weldon (*Mrs. Gordon*), Isabel Cooley (*School Principal*), Bernie Weissman (*Bodyguard*).

Jacobs returns from Vietnam to the world of the Los Angeles ghettos he knows so well. Back on the street, he educates the younger O'Dell in the ways of gang life. When a member of their gang, the Kingsmen, dies of a drug overdose, they go after the neighborhood pushers: Cannon, the white bankroller, and Pendleton, who, ironically, is O'Dell's older brother. Unlike many cheap black exploitation films of the 1970s, YOUNGBLOOD takes a serious look at its subject. It is rarely anything but honest, benefitting from gutsy performances by the leads, and tight, tension-filled direction. Both the music (by the rock group War) and the Los Angeles street locations are used for maximum effect. The result is a well-made, intelligent portrayal of black streetlife.

p, Nick Grillo, Alan Riche; d, Noel Nosseck; w, Paul Carter Harrison; ph, Robbie Greenberg (CFI Color); m, War: ed, Frank Morriss; art d, James Dultz; stunts, Eddie Smith.

Drama   **(PR:O   MPAA:R)**

YOUNGBLOOD HAWKE**½   (1964) 137m WB bw

James Franciscus (*Youngblood Hawke*), Suzanne Pleshette (*Jeanne Green*), Genevieve Page (*Frieda Winter*), Eva Gabor (*Fannie Prince*), Mary Astor (*Irene Perry*), Lee Bowman (*Jason Prince*), Edward Andrews (*Quentin Judd*), Don Porter (*Ferdie Lax*), Mildred Dunnock (*Mrs. Sarah Hawke*), Kent Smith (*Paul Winter, Sr.*), John Dehner (*Scotty Hawke*), John Emery (*Georges Feydal*), Mark Miller (*Ross Hodge*), Hayden Rorke (*Mr. Givney*), Werner Klemperer (*Mr. Leffer*), Berry Kroeger (*Jock Maas*), Rusty Lane (*Gus Adam*).

After moving from Kentucky to New York City, trucker-cum-novelist Franciscus finds his world changing with amazing speed. Pleshette is the editor who helps guide the naive young man, falling in love with him in the process. This causes him more than a little anguish, for with his new-found fame, Franciscus discovers he's wanted by other women. He gets involved with Page, a wealthy socialite, and the jealous Pleshette takes a job with a different publishing house. His first novel is greeted by only middling reviews though it's picked up as a Broadway vehicle for Astor, an aging actress. Franciscus' next book (again with Pleshette as editor) is a big hit but Page's husband finds out about the affair and sets out to ruin the writer. His third book flops, his business ventures go under, and Page's son, who idolizes Franciscus, kills himself after finding out about the affair. Franciscus heads off to a Kentucky cabin for some solitude to work on his next book but comes down with pneumonia. While recovering, he finally realizes that his future is with Pleshette. As a drama this isn't much, but with the soapy Hollywood treatment given here, it's a minor field day for fans of lurid pulp. It rarely fails to entertain, under a controlled, high-gloss direction. Franciscus is unexceptional as the title character but Page turns in an excellent performance.

p,d&w, Delmer Daves (based on the novel *Youngblood Hawke* by Herman Wouk); ph, Charles Lawton, Jr; m, Max Steiner; ed, Sam O'Steen; art d, Leo K. Kuter; set d, John P. Austin; cos, Howard Shoup; makeup, Gordon Bau.

Drama   **(PR:O   MPAA:NR)**

YOUNGER BROTHERS, THE**½ (1949) 77m WB c

Wayne Morris (Cole Younger), Janis Paige (Kate), Bruce Bennett (Jim Younger), Geraldine Brooks (Mary Hathaway), Robert Hutton (Johnny Younger), Alan Hale (Sheriff Knudson), Fred Clark (Ryckman), James Brown (Bob Younger), Monte Blue (Joe), Tom Tyler (Hatch), William Forrest (Hendricks), Ian Wolfe (Chairman).

The often-filmed story of the western-outlaw Younger clan gets an okay telling with this film. Morris, Bennett, Hutton, and Brown are the four siblings who have to stay out of trouble for the final two weeks of their parole so they can obtain a pardon. Using the seductive Paige to do his dirty work, Clark maneuvers the boys into the incriminating middle of a bank holdup, but the Youngers turn the tables, abort the robbery, and are rewarded with pardons. The direction is effective but not much more than that, creating a standard western with nothing new to add to the Younger legend. The title quartet aren't bad, playing off one another with aplomb. This was Morris' second time around as one of the nefarious brothers. He had previously been a member of that clan in 1941's BAD MEN OF MISSOURI. But where are the James boys?

p, Saul Elkins; d, Edwin L. Marin; w, Edna Anhalt (based on the story "Three Bad Men" by Morton Grant); ph, William Snyder (Technicolor); m, William Lava; ed, Frederick Richards; art d, Charles Clarke.

Western (PR:A MPAA:NR)

YOUNGER GENERATION* (1929) 75m COL bw

Jean Hersholt (Julius Goldfish), Lina Basquette (Birdie Goldfish), Rosa Rosanova (Tildie Goldfish), Ricardo Cortez (Morris Goldfish/Morris Fish), Rex Lease (Eddie Lesser), Martha Franklin (Mrs. Lesser), Julia Swayne Gordon (Mrs. Striker), Julanne Johnston (Irma Striker), Jack Raymond (Pinsky), Syd Crossley (Butler), Otto Fries (Tradesman), Donald Hall.

An early effort from director Capra that proved that he still had plenty to learn about making movies. Cortez, the son of a Jewish pushcart-vendor, works his way up the ladder of success and moves his family to a classy Fifth-Avenue address. Ashamed of his humble background, he introduces his mother and father as his domestics when the wealthy parents of the woman he hopes to marry stop by for a visit. Hersholt, his father, is understandably crushed. Adding insult to injury, Cortez sends his sister packing when she remains loyal to her struggling-tunesmith sweetheart even though he has been arrested for his role in a robbery. In the end, though, the family is reunited and Hersholt dies with all of his loved ones gathered around him. The production is chock-full of cheap sentiment and heavy on implausibility. The characters don't get much beyond classic Jewish stereotypes, which doesn't help things any. Consequently, Capra shows none of the humanity and wisdom that would be the hallmark of his work later in his career. This was partially silent, using subtitles at some moments and badly synched sound at others.

p, Jack Cohn; d, Frank Capra; w, Sonya Levien, Howard J. Green (based on the play "It Is to Laugh" by Fannie Hurst); ph, Ted Tetzlaff; ed, Arthur Roberts ; art d, Harrison Wiley.

Drama (PR:A MPAA:NR)

YOUNGEST PROFESSION, THE**½ (1943) 81m MGM bw

Virginia Weidler (Joan Lyons), Edward Arnold (Mr. Lawrence Lyons), John Carroll (Hercules), Jean Porter (Patricia Drew), Marta Linden (Edith Lyons), Dick Simmons (Douglas Sutton), Ann Ayars (Susan Thayer), Agnes Moorehead (Miss Featherstone), Marcia Mae Jones (Vera Bailey), Raymond Roe (Schuyler), Scotty Beckett (Junior Lyons), Jessie Grayson (Lilybud), Greer Garson, William Powell, Lana Turner, Walter Pidgeon, Robert Taylor (Guest Stars), Beverly Tyler (Thyra Winters), Patricia Roe (Polly), Marjorie Gateson (Mrs. Drew), Thurston Hall (Mr. Drew), Aileen Pringle (Miss Farwood), Nora Lane (Hilda), Dorothy Christy (Sally), Mary Vallee (Mary), Gloria Tucker (Gladys), Jane Isbell (Jane), Hazel Dawn (Hazel), Beverly Boyd (Beverly), Randa Allen (Randa), Ann MacLean (Ann), Gloria Mackey (Gloria), Bobby Stebbins (Richard), Shirley Coates, Mary McCarty (Girls), Mark Daniels (Les Peterson), William Tannen (Hotel Clerk), Ann Codee (Sandra's Maid), Eddie Buzzell (Man in Theater), George Noisom (Delivery Boy), Leonard Carey (Valet), Harry Barris (Man), Herberta Williams (Hortense), Sara Haden (Salvation Army Lass), Leigh De Lacey, Vangie Beilby, Ruth Cherrington, Claire McDowell, Sandra Morgan, Leota Lorraine (Montage Bits), Ray Teal (Taxi Driver), Polly Bailey, Margaret Bert, Violet Seton, Alice Keating, Hazel Dohlman (Governesses), Dorothy Morris (Secretary), Roland Dupree, Robert Winkler (Mail Room Boys).

An innocuous little juvenile comedy starring Weidler, formerly MGM's resident imp now struggling to make it in adolescent territory. Weidler, the president of her high school's movie star fan club, is a teenager possessed with a passion for collecting the autographs of major stars. Leading her pack of equally zealous girl friends on excursions resembling a big game safari, Weidler stalks New York City train stations and hotels in search of the elusive autograph. Weidler and her girls waylay Lana Turner in her dressing room–she is already swimming in tons of fan mail–and come away with the valued prize. During this collection frenzy, Weidler and her governess, Moorehead, visit her father, Arnold, at his business office. Moorehead spies Arnold showing his sexy secretary some lingerie and

immediately assumes he is having an affair with the woman (the lingerie is actually for his wife). Moorehead fills Weidler's head with her suspicions and the movie-clouded teenager believes every word. While pondering what to do about her father, Weidler manages to corner the unflappable Greer Garson in her hotel room. Garson calmly invites the autograph hounds in for tea, and the girls get doubly excited when Walter Pidgeon arrives to join them. Seeking his paternalistic knowledge, Weidler asks Pidgeon what he would do if he had a daughter who knew he was having an affair with his secretary and so on and so on. Pidgeon immediately replies that he would probably kill the child–a response totally unlike Pidgeon's screen persona and, therefore, it garners the biggest laugh in the film. Despite Pidgeon's rather disarming "advice," Weidler decides to sell one of her valuable autograph books and hire a handsome muscle man, Carroll, to pose as a foreign diplomat at a charity ball attended by her mother, Linden, and her father. At the ball Carroll tries to seduce Linden–a move Weidler hopes will make her father jealous enough to abandon his floozy secretary. The plan works too well and soon Arnold and Carroll are thrashing it out in the middle of the dance floor. Panic-striken by this disaster, Weidler runs away from home and joins the Salvation Army. Eventually her parents sort out what has happened, dismiss the nosey Moorehead, and find Weidler and bring her home. A silly and episodic comedy, THE YOUNGEST PROFESSION is a typical MGM tribute to the popularity of its stable of stars disguised as a vehicle for a new young rising star. In addition to Turner, Garson, and Pidgeon, Robert Taylor and finally William Powell make guest shots in the expected manner. Weidler never caught on with the public after she "grew up" and made only one other film, BEST FOOT FOREWARD (1943), before retiring from the movies. Tragically, she died in 1968 of a heart attack. She was only 40 years old.

p, B.F. Ziedman; d, Edward Buzzell; w, George Oppenheimer, Charles Lederer, Leonard Spigelgass (based on the book by Lillian Day); ph, Charles Lawton; m, David Snell; ed, Ralph Winters; art d, Cedric Gibbons, Edward Carfagno; set d, Edwin B. Willis, Helen Conway; cos, Irene, Howard Shoup.

Comedy (PR:A MPAA:NR)

YOUNGEST SPY, THE (SEE: MY NAME IS IVAN, 1963, USSR)

YOUR CHEATIN' HEART*** (1964) 100m Four Leaf/MGM bw

George Hamilton (Hank Williams), Susan Oliver (Audrey Williams), Red Buttons (Shorty Younger), Arthur O'Connell (Fred Rose, Music Publisher), Shary Marshall (Ann Younger), Rex Ingram (Teetot), Chris Crosby (Sam Priddy), Rex Holman (Charley Bybee), Hortense Petra (Wilma the Cashier), Roy Engel (Joe Rauch), Donald Losby (Young Hank Williams), Kevin Tate (Boy Fishing).

Hamilton chalks up one of his best screen performances as the legendary country-and-western singer Hank Williams in this small but enjoyable musical biography. After learning to play the guitar as a boy, Hamilton joins up with a traveling medicine show and meets Oliver. She is mightily impressed by his song "Your Cheatin' Heart" and secretly sends it off to a publisher. They marry and he auditions for and is a great success on the famous "Louisiana Hayride" radio show. Later he joins the Grand Ole Opry and becomes a C&W hit-maker. His fame, however, brings with it a drinking problem that disrupts his career and personal life. After plenty of help and support from life-long buddy Buttons, he gets his life together and returns to performing but dies from heart failure at the shockingly tender age of 29. Though it's told in the classic rise-and-fall show-business style, YOUR CHEATIN' HEART is a marvelous showcase for its cast and it is the performances which make this film interesting–particula rly those by Hamilton and Buttons. The early scenes with Losby as the 14-year-old Williams learning to play the guitar from Ingram are especially rewarding. Hank Williams, Jr. (whose own life story was told in a TV movie) dubbed his voice for Hamilton's on the songs his father made famous. Those songs include: "Long Gone Lonesome Blues," "I Saw the Light," "I Can't Help It," "Jambalaya," "Cold, Cold Heart," "I'm So Lonesome I Could Cry," "Hey Good Lookin," "Ramblin' Man," "Kaw-Liga," "You Win Again."

p, Sam Katzman; d, Gene Nelson; w, Stanford Whitmore; ph, Ellis W. Carter (Panavision); m, Fred Karger; ed, Ben Lewis; md, Karger; art d, George W. Davis, Merrill Pye; set d, Henry Grace, Don Greenwood, Jr.; makeup, William Tuttle, Don Cash.

Biography (PR:A MPAA:NR)

YOUR MONEY OR YOUR WIFE*½ (1965, Brit.) 91m Ethiro-Alliance/Ellis bw

Donald Sinden (Pelham Butterworth), Peggy Cummins (Gay Butterworth), Richard Wattis (Hubert Fry), Peter Reynolds (Theodore Malek), Georgina Cookson (Thelma Cressingdon), Gladys Boot (Mrs. Compton-Chamberlain), Barbara Steele (Juliet Frost), Betty Baskcombe (Janet Fry), Olive Sloane (Mrs. Withers), Ian Fleming (Judge), Candy Scott (Maid), Noel Trevarthen (Chauffeur).

Unfunny farce has Cummins a woman due to inherit a large sum only if she is widowed or divorced. Hoping to find another way to make ends meet, Cummins and her husband, Sinden, take in a host of zany boarders. When none of these lodgers is able to come up with any scratch, the couple opt for divorce. They plan to remarry as soon as the money comes through, but complications arise, and though Sinden returns to the house, he does so as a rent-paying boarder. The one-joke plot is helped little by an overabundance of slapstick, humorless performances, and sledgehammer direction.

p, Norman Williams; d, Anthony Simmons; w, Ronald Jeans; ph, Brendan J. Stafford; m, Philip Green; ed, Bernard Gribble; art d, Tony Inglis.

Comedy (PR:A MPAA:NR)

YOUR NUMBER'S UP**½ (1931) 72m INVINCIBLE bw

Theodore Newton (*Harold Carmichael*), Greta Nissen (*Janet Carmichael*), Robert Warwick (*Dr. Jim Haley*), Paul Kilfoyle (*Wilson*), Wilma Harvey (*Vera*), Irwin Charles (*Sedacca*).

Taut mystery with an unusual twist. Newton hasn't been feeling well lately. He's fatigued, depressed, and not up to snuff. He sees his doctor, Warwick, who prescribes some medicine but it doesn't seem to help. Warwick gives Newton the results of his various tests and tells Newton that he only has a few months to live. Newton is devastated. He loves his wife, Nissen, and has everything to live for but he feels he must provide for his wife so he increases his insurance to $500,000, with his insurance man, Charles. Now Newton contacts some people he knows in the mob and asks for the name of a good assassin. He is put in contact with Kilfoyle, who appears to be anything but a professional killer. Kilfoyle raises horses in the suburbs, and lives in a trailer. Newton explains that he wants Kilfoyle to murder him! He has instructed his lawyer to pay Kilfoyle $10,000 as part of his will. Kilfoyle has never had that kind of assignment before but agrees and says he'll get to the job in two weeks. Newton will never know what hit him. The two men shake hands on the deal and part. When Newton goes back to see Warwick, he gets the pills and is about to leave. The nurse, Harvey, asks to see the pills and is shocked. She tells Newton that they must meet away from the office. That night, Harvey tells Newton that those pills will make anyone feel fatigued and depressed. Further, she has gone into his files and the so-called tests the doctor ran were all bogus. Newton is in excellent health and it is only the pills that have made him feel badly. But why? Now, Newton and Harvey join forces and do some hawkshawing and discover that Nissen and Warwick are lovers and have conspired to make Newton think he's dying, knowing full well that he would take his own life in order to leave his "beloved wife" a legacy. But how to confront them? Meanwhile, Kilfoyle has attached a car bomb onto Newton's car but Nissen takes the car that day for a tryst at a hotel with Warwick. There's a time detonator and, after the matinee performance by the lovers, they are leaving the hotel. Warwick gets into his car, Nissen gets into hers, and blows up. Warwick races away. The newspapers are filled with the incident. Kilfoyle shrugs; he's made a mistake but that's all right, killers often do that. Newton tells Harvey what he's done and how he must now get in touch with Kilfoyle and call him off. The two of them frantically attempt to find Kilfoyle but he's moved his trailer and no one knows where he is. Warwick and Newton have a confrontation in the office and Newton kills his doctor, blaming him for everything. Harvey can't believe what's happened to Newton and leaves him. In the final scene, Newton is approached by Kilfoyle on a lonely street and explains that the deal is off. He'll be willing to pay the man the $10,000 for his time but there's no need to murder him. Kilfoyle thinks differently. What's to keep Newton from reneging? Kilfoyle knows that his name is in the will and that's a *fait accompli*. As Newton begs for his life, Kilfoyle calmly plugs him saying, "A deal is a deal" and walks away into the night. It's a mean little movie, one of the first of the film *noir genre*. The only problem is that there's no one to root for except Harvey, an innocent nurse who uncovered the plot. This story was done before the Motion Picture Code made it mandatory to have retribution for the villains.

p&w, Benjamin Glazer; d, John Francis Dillon; ph, Henry Kohler; m, Marvin Flavin; ed, Dick Post; art d, Gloria Nelson; set d, Irving Zane; stunts, Mickey Douglas.

Crime/Mystery (PR:C MPAA:NR)

YOUR PAST IS SHOWING*** (1958, Brit.) 87m
RANK-Anglofilm/RANK bw (GB: THE NAKED TRUTH)

Terry-Thomas (*Lord Mayley*), Peter Sellers (*Sonny MacGregor*), Peggy Mount (*Flora Ransom*), Shirley Eaton (*Belinda Right*), Dennis Price (*Michael Dennis*), Georgina Cookson (*Lady Mayley*), Joan Sims (*Ethel Ransom*), Miles Malleson (*Rev. Bastable*), Kenneth Griffith (*Porter*), Moultrie Kelsall (*Mactavish*), Wally Patch (*Fred*), Henry Hewitt (*Gunsmith*), Wilfrid Lawson (*Sgt. Rumbold*), Bill Edwards (*Bill*), John Stuart (*Inspector*), George Benson (*Photographer*), Peter Noble (*TV Announcer*), David Lodge (*Policeman*), Joan Hurley (*Authoress*), Victor Rietti (*Doctor*), Jerrold Wells.

Price is a journalist who runs a scandal sheet entitled "The Naked Truth," in which the public can read all they want to know about the lives of celebrities. He tries to squeeze $28,000 each out of Terry-Thomas, a peer and an insurance racketeer; Mount, a writer; Eaton, a model; and Sellers, a popular TV personality. They each try to have Price killed but fail. Eventually, after breaking him from jail, they get rid of him, fearful that he will tell their stories as part of his trial. A hard-hitting laugh riot, which only occasionally fizzles.

p&d, Mario Zampi; w, Michael Pertwee; ph, Stanley Pavey; m, Stanley

Black; ed, Bill Lewthwaite, art d, Ivan King.

Comedy **Cas.** (PR:A MPAA:NR)

YOUR SHADOW IS MINE**½ (1963, Fr./Ital.) 90m Precitel-Da.
Ma.-Cathay-Keris-Co films/CD c (TON OMBRE EST LA MIENNE)

Jill Haworth (*Sylvie "Devi" Bergerat*), Michel Ruhl (*Phillippe Bergerat*), Ruos Vanny (*Rahit*), Marcel Pagliero (*Dr. Rouvier*), Clotilde Joano (*Anne Bergerat*), Catherine Zago (*Mme. Moniveau*), Mme. Pung-Peng-Cheng (*Mate*), Philippe Forquet (*Young Man at Party*).

In Cambodia, Haworth is a French girl who has been raised by a native family that found her wandering in the forest. Now she is readying to marry Vanny, her foster brother, but this dream is dashed when the government tells her that her real brother, Ruhl, has been searching for her all these years. The Japanese had attacked their family's plantation in 1943, which led to her sojourn in the woods. Ruhl wants nothing but his sister's love, a desire he sacrifices his entire life for. Soon this need grows into a physical passion that frightens the girl. Vanny comes to help her and together they run off, with Ruhl pursuing in his car. The two young people hide in the forest and Ruhl is killed when his car skids and goes off the road in a fiery crash.

p, Pierre Courau; d, Andre Michel; w, Jean-Rene Huguenin, Diego Fabbri, Madeleine Courau, Han Suyin (based on an idea by Michel); ph, Edmond Sechan; m, Maurice Jarre; ed, Jean-Michel Gautier; md, Jarre; art d, Jacques Paris.

Drama (PR:O MPAA:NR)

YOUR TEETH IN MY NECK (SEE: FEARLESS VAMPIRE KILLERS, OR PARDON ME BUT YOUR TEETH ARE IN MY NECK, THE)

YOUR THREE MINUTES ARE UP***½
(1973) 93m Minutes/Cinerama c

Beau Bridges (*Charlie*), Ron Leibman (*Mike*), Janet Margolin (*Betty*), Kathleen Freeman (*Mrs. Wilk*), David Ketchum (*Mr. Kellogg*), Stu Nisbet (*Dr. Claymore*), Read Morgan (*Eddie Abruzzi*), Jennifer Ashley (*Teenage Driver*), Sherry Bain (*Sugar*), Paul Barselou (*Gas Station Man*), Kitty Carl (*Susan*), Rhodie Cogan (*Operator's Wife*), James Dixon (*Howard*), Ronda Copland (*Sherry*), James Driskill (*Pickup Truck Driver*), Barbara Douglas (*Bun Warmer Girl*), June Fairchild (*Sandi*), Lester Fletcher (*Clothing Salesman*), Robert Funk (*Policeman*), Don Gazzaniga (*Repossession Man*), Larry Gelman (*Mr. Roberts*), Suzi Goei (*Massage Receptionist*), Elizabeth Harding (*Josie*), Sylvia Hayes (*Elsie*), Leigh Heine (*Pharmacist*), Pat Houtchens (*Mr. Catto*), Candace Howerton (*1st Nurse*), Sharon Johanson (*Ilsa*), Raymond Kark (*Western Union Messenger*), Carol Kristy (*Bank Teller*), Myrna La Bow (*2nd Nurse*), Paul Lichtman (*Chef*), Sherry Miles (*Debbie*), Tom Moses (*Gas Station Attendent*), Sam Nudell (*Tailor*), Michael Perrotta (*Waiter*), Barbara Sammeth (*Cindy*), Patti Shayne (*Waitress*), Orville Sherman (*Mr. Sherman*), Lynne Marie Stewart (*Ibis Lady*), Nedra Volz (*Free Press Lady*), Patricia Walker (*Unemployment Clerk*).

Well-made "buddy" film has Bridges and Leibman playing a truly odd couple. Bridges is a successful, though easily intimidated, insurance clerk engaged to Margolin. His pal Leibman, a con man, talks Bridges into taking off a day from work to drive him to the airport. They end up on a freewheeling adventure involving young girls and a few confidence schemes as the pair drive up the California Coast. Leibman's devil-may-care attitude perfectly complements Bridges' mild-mannered characterization. The chemistry between the two actors grows naturally; their friendship is as believable as they come. Schwartz' direction gives the ambling plot fine steady guidance and injects humor without disrupting the dramatic flow.

p, Jerry Gershwin, Mark C. Levy; d, Douglas N. Schwartz; w, James Dixon; ph, Stephen M. Katz (DeLuxe Color); m, Perry Botkin, Jr; ed, Aaron Stell; art d, Joseph Crowingham; cos, Jac McAnelly; m/1, "It's Only Me," Dennis Lambert, Brian Potter, Botkin, Jr. (sung by Mark Lindsay).

Comedy-Drama (PR:O MPAA:R)

YOUR TURN, DARLING**½ (1963, Fr.) 93m Prodis bw (A TOI DE
FAIRE, MIGNONNE)

Eddie Constantine (*Lemmy Caution*), Christian Minazzoli (*Carletta*), Gaia Germani (*Geraldine*), Elga Andersen (*Valerie*), Noel Roquevert (*Welmer*), Philippe Lemaire (*Gront*), Henry Cogan.

When an American lady spy is killed and an important scientist is kidnaped, it's up to Constantine, a secret agent with one of the greatest character names in film history (Lemmy Caution), to find out what's up. He heads off to Europe, chases a few skirts, and finally discovers that the scientist is really the head of a spy ring. Constantine would play Caution again in Godard's noted film ALPHAVILLE.

d, Bernard Borderie; w, Borderie, Marc-Gilbert Sauvajon (based on the novel by Peter Cheyney); ph, Henri Perrin; m, Paul Misraki; ed, Christian Gaudin.

Spy Drama (PR:C MPAA:NR)

YOUR UNCLE DUDLEY½   (1935) 70m FOX bw

Edward Everett Horton (*Dudley Dixon*), Lois Wilson (*Christine Saunders*), John McGuire (*Robert Kirby*), Rosina Lawrence (*Ethel Church*), Alan Dinehart (*Charlie Post*), Marjorie Gateson (*Mabel Dixon*), William ["Billy"] Benedict (*Cyril Church*), Florence Roberts (*Janet Dixon*), Jane Barnes (*Marjorie Baxter*).

Horton is a civic-minded businessman in a small town. He so loves his community that he ends up deep in debt by constantly making sacrifices for the good of the town. This nets him plenty of awards but also plenty of trouble. Finally, Horton reorganizes his priorities and gets his business back in shape. Though the film is a bit slow and overwritten, Horton works nicely in the lead, giving this a nice, light comic touch.

p, Edward T. Lowe; d, James Tinling, Eugene Forde; w, Dore Schary, Joseph Hoffman, Allen Birkin (based on the play by Howard Lindsay, Bertrand Robinson); ph, Harry Jackson; ed, Louis Loeffler; md, Samuel Kaylin; cos, Alberto Luza.

Comedy   (PR:A MPAA:NR)

YOUR WITNESS   (SEE: EYE WITNESS, 1950, Brit.)

YOU'RE A BIG BOY NOW***   (1966) 96m Seven Arts c

Elizabeth Hartman (*Barbara Darling*), Geraldine Page (*Margery Chanticleer*), Julie Harris (*Miss Thing*), Peter Kastner (*Bernard Chanticleer*), Rip Torn (*I.H. Chanticleer*), Michael Dunn (*Richard Mudd*), Tony Bill (*Raef*), Karen Black (*Amy*), Dolph Sweet (*Policeman Francis Graf*), Michael O'Sullivan (*Kurt Doughty*), Ronald Colby, Rufus Harley, Frank Simpson, Nina Verella, Len De Carl.

YOU'RE A BIG BOY NOW is significant as an early example of the developing talent of one of the most important (if not the most important) American directors of the 1970s and 1980s. Coppola scripted and directed this whimsical look at coming of age in the 1960s as his part of his graduate thesis at U.C.L.A. Though not his first film, it revealed a willingness to experiment with technique and themes that would continue throughout his career. As in both RUMBLE FISH and THE OUTSIDERS, made by Coppola nearly two decades later, his subject here is a teenager's passage into manhood. The tone in this film is much less serious, though, more appropriate for the 1960s, when a laid-back attitude toward drama in general was prevalent and deep messages lurked beneath surfaces. But unlike the work of either Jean-Luc Godard or Richard Lester (both obvious influences on Coppola at this point in his career), YOU'RE A BIG BOY NOW fails to have much impact beyond its lightheartedness. It is as if Coppola were too concerned with creating a style to put much effort into the implications of his material. Kastner plays a young Long Islander given his first taste of what it's like to be on his own. His move to New York City has come at the behest of Torn, his father, who wants to get him away from his security-blanket existence with doting mother Page. Kastner moves into a boarding house run by Harris and discovers sex and drugs under the guidance of older and wiser Bill, with whom he works at the New York Public Library. Kastner is obsessed with discotheque dancer and actress Hartman in a big way, but his pursuit of her leaves him with an extremely bitter taste of romance. He eventually does discover something about love through his relationship with Black, the woman who has been waiting on the sidelines all along, acting as his friend while harboring a gigantic crush. Though YOU'RE A BIG BOY NOW has been criticized for being too whimsical, it offers a wide range of fascinating characters and situations that makes for great entertainment. The soundtrack by The Lovin' Spoonful is also a delight. Like much of Coppola's early work, however, it presents his themes in a cliched manner, almost as if he has learned about human experience and emotions through the cinema instead of real life. That Coppola, an unknown just embarking on his career, was able to persuade so many established performers to appear in the film, is indicative of the organization skills and the ability to gain people's trust and respect that have made him such an outstanding director.

p, Phil Feldman; d&w, Francis Ford Coppola (based on the novel by David Benedictius); ph, Andrew Laszlo (Pathe Color); m, Robert Prince; ed, Aram Avakian; md, Arthur Schroeck; art d, Vassele Fotopoulos; set d, Marvin March; cos, Theoni V. Aldredge; ch, Robert Tucker; makeup, Bob Philippe.

Comedy/Drama   **Cas.**   (PR:C MPAA:NR)

YOU'RE A LUCKY FELLOW, MR. SMITH*½   (1943) 63m UNIV bw

Allan Jones (*Tony*), Evelyn Ankers (*Lynn*), Billie Burke (*Aunt Harriet*), David Bruce (*Harvey*), Patsy O'Connor (*Peggy*), Stanley Clements (*Squirt*), Luis Alberni (*Goreni, Painter*), Francis Pierlot (*Doc Webster*), Harry Hayden (*Judge*), Mantan Moreland (*Porter*), Mary Gordon (*Woman*), William Haade (*Soldier*), Wallis Clark (*Travers*), John Dilson (*Head of Board*), Emmett Vogan (*Spokesman*), Lorin Raker (*Little Man*), John Elliott (*Lawyer*), Clarence Straight (*Soldier*), Dorothy Shearer, Robert Cherry (*Artists*), The King's Men.

Ankers knows she can receive a vast inheritance if she marries by her twenty-fourth birthday, which is exactly what she plans to do as she heads to Chicago to wed Bruce. On the train, however, Miss O'Connor plays

matchmaker and tricks her big sister Ankers into marrying Jones. The newlywed's pursuit of her unloved spouse to get his signature on her checks creates most of the humor in this romantic comedy. High points come mostly from supporting cast, including Moreland, Burke, and O'Connor (Donald's cousin). Songs and musical numbers include: "Your Eyes Have Told Me So" (Gus Kahn, Walter Blaufuss, Egbert Van Alstyne), "When You're Smiling" (Joe Goodwin, Mark Fisher, Larry Shay), "What is This Thing Called Love" (Cole Porter), "On the Crest of a Rainbow" (Al Sherman, Harry Tobias), "You're a Lucky Fellow Mr. Smith," (Don Raye, Hughie Prince, Sonny Burke), "Soldier Specialty" (Inez James, Buddy Pepper).

p, Edward Lilley; d, Felix Feist; w, Lawrence Riley, Ben Barzman, Louis Lantz (based on the story by Oscar Brodney); ph, Paul Ivano; ed, Ray Snyder; md, Charles Previn; art d, John Goodman.

Musical   (PR:A MPAA:NR)

YOU'RE A SWEETHEART½   (1937) 96m UNIV bw

Alice Faye (*Betty Bradley*), George Murphy (*Hal Adam*), Ken Murray (*Don King*), Oswald (*Himself*), William Gargan (*Fred Edwards*), Frances Hunt (*Penny*), Frank Jenks (*Harry Howe*), Andy Devine (*Daisy Day*), Caspar Reardon (*Cousin Caspar*), Charles Winninger (*Cherokee Charlie*), Donald Meek (*Conway Jeeters*), David Oliver (*Yes-Man*), Andrew A. Trimble (*Will Rogers*), Edna Sedgwick (*Ballet Dancer*), Bob Murphy (*Bailiff*), Renie Riano (*Mrs. Hepplethwaite*), Bobby Watson (*Defense Attorney*), Norville Brothers, The Four Playboys, Malda and Ray (*Specialties*), Ben Lewis (*Man*).

Faye's only film for Universal Studios has her playing the star of a show bound for Broadway. Producer Murray discovers their opening night on the Great White Way conflicts with a big charity event for the Milk Fund. The show's success seems doomed until Murphy, a waiter, suggests making tickets impossible to get, thus stirring interest in the production. Murray loves the idea, and has Murphy pose as a wealthy oilman who has bought all the tickets for opening week out of love for Faye. The scheme appears to be working when Meek enters the scene, suggesting to Faye that Murphy be signed to an advertising contract. To complicate matters, Murray has missed some payments for costumes and sets, threatening the show's opening. Faye forges Murphy's name on a contract to get some much needed cash from Meek. Murray gives Meek a 50 per cent interest in the show, but things come to a head when he learns Murphy's signature is fake. Meek threatens Murray and Murphy with legal action, but finally agrees to wait and see what an important critic has to say about the show. Devine and Oswald manage to get the critic to applaud, making the show a hit. Meek gets back his money, while Murphy and Faye are wed. This is a slight musical, with a largely unbelievable plot. There's also a "tribute" to the late Will Rogers in the film, one that is more maudlin than reverent. The script is stale, and Butler's direction is uninspired. In spite of the weaknesses, Faye gives it everything she's got, and dances some dandy numbers with Murphy. The music helps as well, with some enjoyable tunes. They include "You're a Sweetheart," "Broadway Jamboree," "My Fine Feathered Friend," "Who Killed Maggie?" "Oh, Oh Oklahoma" (Harold Adamson, Jimmy McHugh), "Scraping the Toast" (Murray Mencher, Charles Tobias), "So It's Love" (Mickey Bloom, Arthur Quenzer, Lou Bring). A remake, COWBOY IN MANHATTAN, followed in 1943.

p, B.G. De Sylva; d, David Butler; w, Monte Brice, Charles Grayson (based on an original story by Warren Wilson, Maxwell Shane, William Thomas); ph, George H. Robinson; ed, Bernard W. Burton; md, Charles Previn; art d, Jack Otterson; ch, Carl Randall.

Musical   (PR:A MPAA:NR)

YOU'RE DEAD RIGHT   (SEE: ARRIVEDERCI, BABY!, 1966, Brit.)

YOU'RE IN THE ARMY NOW**   (1937, Brit.) 71m GAU bw (GB: O.H.M.S.)

Wallace Ford (*Jim Tracey*), John Mills (*Cpl. Bert Dawson*), Anna Lee (*Sally Bridges*), Grace Bradley (*Jean Burdett*), Frank Cellier (*Sgt.-Maj. Briggs*), Frederick Leister (*Vice Consul*), Lawrence Anderson (*Trader*), Athol Fleming (*Schoolmaster*), Peter Evan Thomas (*General*), Cyril Smith (*Steward*), Arnold Bell (*Matthews*), Peter Croft (*Student*), Arthur Chesney (*Sugar Daddy*), Leslie Roberts (*Dance Instructor*), Robertson Hare, Leon von Porkorny, Arthur Seaton, Ernest Jay, Richard Gray, Henry Hallat, Pat Vyvyvan, Donald Gadd, Denis Cowles.

One of only a few films director Walsh made for British studios. Yarn centers around the efforts of a New York hood, Ford, to flee a murder rap by hightailing it to England, where he joins the Army by posing as a Canadian. Once there he joins up with Mills, and the two fall for their sergeant-major's daughter, Lee. Ford is wildly distracted when old girl friend Bradley shows up from the States and threatens to blow his cover. To avoid embarrassment, the soldier mistakenly stows away on a ship heading for China with his regiment and heart-throb aboard. Once there, he proves his worth by saving the woman he loves from plundering Chinese bandits. Of note: impressive battle scenes in China and humorous byplay from Ford's response to British Army discipline.

p, Geoffrey Barkas; d, Raoul Walsh; w, Bryan Edgar Wallace, Austin Melford, A.R. Rawlinson (based on the story by Lesser Samuels, Ralph

Gilbert Bettinson); ph, Roy Kellino; ed, Charles Saunders.

War/Comedy (PR:A MPAA:NR)

YOU'RE IN THE ARMY NOW**½ (1941) 79m WB bw

Jimmy Durante (*Jeeper Smith*), Phil Silvers (*Breezy Jones*), Jane Wyman (*Bliss Dobson*), Regis Toomey (*Joe Radcliffe*), Donald MacBride (*Col. Dobson*), Joe Sawyer (*Sgt. Madden*), Clarence Kolb (*Gen. Winthrop*), Paul Harvey (*Gen. Philpott*), George Meeker (*Capt. Austin*), Paul Stanton (*Col. Rogers*), William Haade (*Sgt. Thorpe*), Etta McDaniel (*Della*), Marguerite Chapman, Georgia Carroll, Peggy Diggins, Alice Talton, Kay Aldridge, Leslie Brooks (*Navy Blues Sextette*), Matty Malneck and His Orchestra (*Themselves*), Murray Alper (*Supply Sergeant*), Charles Drake, Harry Lewis (*Recruits*), Gig Young, Jack Gardner, Arthur Gardner (*Men*), Dick French (*Capt. Plant*), Sally Loomis (*Drum Majorette*), Armando & Lita (*Dance Team*), David Newell (*Staff Sergeant*), Weldon Heyburn (*Sergeant of the Guard*).

This madcap farce features Durante and Silvers as a pair of vacuum cleaner salesmen eager to make a fast buck. They go to the local Army recruiting station in hopes of making a sale, but inadvertently end up as inductees. The two buck privates need more than Uncle Sam to stop their zany antics, as Durante and Silvers become well acquainted with the guardhouse as a result of various schemes. The film ends as Durante and Silvers, now old men engaged in a game of chess, discuss the good old days in the Army. Sitting on a nearby piano are two grandchildren, also played by Durante and Silvers. The slapstick flies thick and furious throughout this comic spree, and consequently keep the gags don't always work. There are enough amusing episodes to keep this one entertaining, though, as the two comic actors make a nice duo. There's also a big production number, "I'm Glad My Number Was Called." One of many films designed to relieve a war-minded America from its troubles, YOU'RE IN THE ARMY NOW was released only days before the bombing of Pearl Harbor.

p, Ben Stoloff; d, Lewis Seiler; w, Paul Gerard Smith, George Beatty; ph, Arthur Todd; ed, Frank Magee.

Comedy (PR:A MPAA:NR)

YOU'RE IN THE NAVY NOW*** (1951) 93m FOX bw (AKA: U.S.S. TEAKETTLE)

Gary Cooper (*Lt. John Harkness*), Jane Greer (*Ellie*), Millard Mitchell (*Larrabee*), Eddie Albert (*Lt. Bill Barron*), John McIntire (*Comdr. Reynolds*), Ray Collins (*Adm. Tennant*), Harry Von Zell (*Capt. Eliot*), Jack Webb (*Ens. Anthony Barbo*), Richard Erdman (*Ens. Chuck Dorrance*), Harvey Lembeck (*Norelli*), Henry Slate (*Ryan, Chief Engineer*), Ed Begley (*Commander*), Fay Roope (*Battleship Admiral*), Charles Tannen (*Houlihan*), Charles Buchinsky 'Bronson' (*Wascylewski*), Jack Warden (*Morse*), Ken Harvey, Lee Marvin, Jerry Hausner, Charles Smith (*Crew Members*), James Cornell (*New Sailor*), Glen Gordon, Laurence Hugo (*Shore Patrolmen*), Damian O'Flynn (*Doctor*), Biff McGuire (*Sailor Messenger*), Norman McKay (*Admiral's Aide*), John McGuire (*Naval Commander*), Elsa Peterson (*Admiral's Wife*), Herman Cantor (*Naval Captain*), Joel Fluellen (*Mess Boy*), William Leicester (*C.P.O.*), Ted Stanhope (*Naval Officer*), Rory Mallinson (*Lieutenant Commander*), Bernard Kates (*Tugboat Sailor*).

A lightweight naval comedy which casts Cooper as an inexperienced Navy officer, or "90-day wonder," who is placed in charge of an experimental patrol vessel which is equipped with a steam engine, instead of the usual diesel. To no one's surprise, Cooper is over his head in problems, especially since his entire crew, with one exception, is made up of other "90-day wonders." That one exception, Mitchell, does his best to keep order but the obstacles prove too numerous. Cooper's troubles come to a head when the Admiral's Board announces that the steam-powered vessel, now dubbed the "U.S.S. Teakettle," will take part in a series of tests. The engines jam and the ship goes haywire, but Cooper and the crew come out of the mess with a commendation from naval captain Von Zell for their dedication and hard work. Although this sixth Cooper-Hathaway teaming received a number of glowing reviews, it failed to find an audience, chiefly because of its nondescript original title, U.S.S. TEAKETTLE. The film was temporarily reshelved until it received its new title–YOU'RE IN THE NAVY NOW–the title which brought the film greater box office results, and the one by which it is best known today. Cooper hadn't worked at 20th Century-Fox for 25 years, when he was an extra in a Tom Mix cowboy vehicle, the silent THE LUCKY HORSESHOE (1925). The film served as a stepping stone for not one, but two aspiring actors–Charles Bronson and Lee Marvin–both of whom made their film debuts here and would later gain fame in a number of "tough guy" roles. Bronson, a married, 29-year-old first- year student at the Pasadena Playhouse, was sent by the theater school to audition for his first role in films after the school received a casting request calling for an actor who was "a cross between Humphrey Bogart and John Garfield." Since the two latter stars couldn't be crossbred due to a want of pollen, the studio opted for Bronson. He got favorable reviews and other small parts, and liked the business enough to move to Hollywood, where he made a total of 16 pictures using the name Buchinsky (also spelled Buchinski).

p, Fred Kohlmar; d, Henry Hathaway; w, Richard Murphy (based on the *New Yorker* magazine article by John W. Hazard); ph, Joe MacDonald; m, Cyril Mockridge; ed, James B. Clark; md, Lionel Newman; art d, Lyle

Wheeler, J. Russell Spencer; set d, Thomas Little, Fred J. Rode; cos, Charles Le Maire; spec eff, Fred Sersen, Ray Kellogg; makeup, Ben Nye; technical advisor, Joseph Warren Lomax, U.S.N.

Comedy (PR:A MPAA:NR)

YOU'RE MY EVERYTHING**½ (1949) 94m FOX c

Dan Dailey (*Timothy O'Connor*), Anne Baxter (*Hannah Adams*), Anne Revere (*Aunt Jane*), Stanley Ridges (*Mr. Mercer, Producer*), Shari Robinson (*Jane O'Connor*), Henry O'Neill (*Prof. Adams*), Selena Royle (*Mrs. Adams*), Alan Mowbray (*Joe Blanton, Film Director*), Robert Arthur (*College Boy*), Mack Gordon (*Song Writer*), Buster Keaton (*Himself*), Phyllis Kennedy (*Elizabeth*), Chester Jones (*Butler*), Hal K. Dawson (*Ticket Seller*), Charles Lane (*Mr. Pflum*), Robert Emmett Keane (*Architect*), Ruth Clifford (*Nurse*), J. Farrell MacDonald (*Doorman*), Charles Tannen (*Director*), Rita LeRoy (*Fashion Editor*), Patricia Weil (*Jane, Age 3*), Sherry Jackson (*Jane, Age 6*), Sammy McKim (*Messenger Boy*), George Nokes (*Mark*), Jack Mulhall (*Leading Man*), John Hiestand, Joe Haworth, Libby Taylor, Geraldine Harris, Vincent Graeff, Nyas Berry, Warren Berry.

It's backstage fare with Dailey and Baxter playing the married couple who struggle with separate careers in pictures at the dawn of talkies. Baxter makes the big time but Dailey settles for being a song-and-dance man. He prefers the peace of their newly acquired ranch. The picture features some memorable musical numbers with excellent choreography by Castle. Musical numbers include: "You're My Everything" (Harry Warren, Mort Dixon, Joe Young, sung by Dailey), "Varsity Drag" (B.G. DeSylva, Lew Brown, Ray Henderson), "I May Be Wrong" (Harry Ruskin, Henry Sullivan, sung by Dailey), "Chattanooga Choo Choo," "Serenade in Blue" (Mack Gordon, Warren), "I Can't Begin to Tell You" (James V. Monaco, Gordon), "Would You Like to Take a Walk?" (Warren, Dixon, Billy Rose), and "On the Good Ship Lollipop" (Sidney Clare, Richard Whiting, sung by Shari Robinson).

p, Lamar Trotti; d, Walter Lang; w, Trotti, Will H. Hays, Jr. (based on a story by George Jessel); ph, Arthur E. Arling (Technicolor); m, Leonard Doss; ed, J. Watson Webb, Jr.; md, Alfred Newman; art d, Lyle Wheeler, Leland Fuller; set d, Thomas Little, Ernest Lansing; cos, Bonnie Cashin, Charles LeMaire; spec eff, Fred Sersen; ch, Nick Castle; makeup, Ben Nye, Frank Prehoda, Ernie Parks.

Musical (PR:A MPAA:NR)

YOU'RE NEVER TOO YOUNG**½ (1955) 102m PAR c

Jerry Lewis (*Wilbur Hoolick*), Dean Martin (*Bob Miles*), Diana Lynn (*Nancy Collins*), Nina Foch (*Gretchen Brendan*), Raymond Burr (*Noonan*), Mitzi McCall (*Skeets*), Veda Ann Borg (*Mrs. Noonan*), Margery Maude (*Mrs. Ella Brendan*), Romo Vincent (*Ticket Agent*), Nancy Culp (*Marty's Mother*), Milton Frome (*Lt. O'Malley*), Donna Percy (*Girl*), Emory Parnell (*Conductor*), James Burke (*Pullman Conductor*), Tommy Ivo (*Marty*), Whitey Haupt (*Mike Brendan*), Mickey Finn (*Sgt. Brown*), Peggy Moffitt (*Agnes*), Johnstone White, Richard Simmons (*Professors*), Louise Lorimer, Isabel Randolph (*Faculty Members*), Robert Carson (*Tailor*), Hans Conried (*Francois*), Stanley Blystone (*Passenger*), Bobby Barber (*Newsboy*), Donna Jo Gribble, Irene Walpole, Gloria Penny Moore (*School Girls*), Bob Morgan (*Texan*), Marty Newton (*Faculty Member*), Dick [Richard] Cutting (*Hotel Guard*).

One of the less cohesive Lewis and Martin vehicles with Lewis playing a barber's apprentice who unwittingly comes into the possession of stolen diamonds. From here it's pure hokum as Jerry, attempting to avoid the grasp of thief Burr, dresses up like an 11-year-old in a sailor suit and takes refuge in the all-girls' school where Martin is a teacher. Plenty of slapstick antics to delight the Lewis fans. This is a remake of THE MAJOR AND THE MINOR (1942).

p, Paul Jones; d, Norman Taurog; w, Sidney Sheldon (based on the story by Edward Childs Carpenter, Fannie Kilbourne); ph, Daniel L. Fapp (Vistavision, Technicolor); m, Walter Scharf; ed, Archie Marshek; art d, Hal Pereira, Earl Hedrick; cos, Edith Head.

Comedy (PR:A MPAA:NR)

YOU'RE NOT SO TOUGH** (1940) 71m UNIV bw

Billy Halop (*Tommy Abraham Lincoln*), Huntz Hall (*Pig/Albert*), Bobby Jordan (*Rap*), Gabriel Dell (*String*), Bernard Punsley (*Ape*), Nan Grey (*Millie*), Henry Armetta (*Salvatore*), Rosina Galli (*Mama "Lisa" Posita*), Cliff Clark (*Griswold*), Joe King (*Collins*), Arthur Loft (*Marshall*), Harry Hayden (*Lacey*), Eddy Waller (*Les*), Evelyn Selbie (*Bianca*), Joe Whitehead (*Brakeman*), Harry Humphrey (*1st Picker*), Don Rowan (*Conley*), Hally Chester (*2nd Newsboy*), Harris Berger (*Jake*), David Gorcey (*1st Worker*), Ralph Dunn (*Valley Truck Driver*), Kernan Cripps (*Guard*), Eddie Phillips (*Jorgenson*), Ralph LaPere (*3rd Picker*), Marty Faust (*2nd Picker*), Frank Bischell (*3rd Worker*), Heinie Conklin (*Store Proprietor*), Harry Strang (*Truck Driver*), Ed Piel, Sr (*Carstens*).

The Dead End Kids are out of the slums of New York's East Side and running around the sunny valleys of California looking for a way to make a quick buck. The idea of working never enters their minds until Halop is egged on by Grey to show his capabilities. Before long he and Hall are working on the ranch of Galli, an elderly Italian woman who treats her workers like human beings instead of animals. Galli lost her son who disappeared as an infant, and Halop tries to convince her that he is that long lost son, thus possibly sharing in her wealth. But Galli is much too good a person, and Halop, soon motivated by respect instead of greed, devises a plan to help her when truckers and a labor organization band together to keep her crops from making it to market. Unlike other "Bowery" entries the emphasis is not placed upon comedy, but on the character development of Halop as he becomes a well-meaning young man. There is also an attack against a social problem, the unfair treatment of laborers and migrant workers during the late 1930s and early 1940s. (See BOWERY BOYS series, Index.)

p, Ken Goldsmith; d, Joe May; w, Arthur T. Horman (based on the story "Son of Mama Posita" by Maxwell Aley); ph, Elwood Bredell; ed, Frank Gross; md, Hans J. Salter; art d, Jack Otterson.

Drama (PR:A MPAA:NR)

YOU'RE ONLY YOUNG ONCE**½ (1938) 78m MGM bw

Lewis Stone (Judge Hardy), Mickey Rooney (Andy Hardy), Cecilia Parker (Marian Hardy), Fay Holden (Mrs. Hardy), Frank Craven (Frank Redmond), Ann Rutherford (Polly Benedict), Eleanor Lynn (Jerry Lane), Ted Pearson (Bill Rand), Sara Haden (Aunt Milly), Selmer Jackson (Hoyt Wells), Charles Judels (Capt. Swenson), Oscar O'Shea (Sheriff).

The second in the long line of Andy Hardy features that usually depicted Mickey Rooney's affairs of the heart. But here it's more of a family venture, with Stone taking his family to Catalina for a summer vacation. The judge's main desire is to try his hand at catching a large fish, at which he is not too successful, while Rooney has a go at Lynn while Sis flirts with the handsome lifeguard, who turns out to be already married. Stone and Holden were given their first shot at playing the judge and his wife, Lionel Barrymore and Spring Byington having had the honors in A FAMILY AFFAIR. They would become permanent fixtures and part of the image of all that was good in small town American family life. (See ANDY HARDY series, Index.)

d, George B. Seitz; w, Kay Van Riper (based on the story by Aurania Rouverol); ph, Lester White; m, David Snell; ed, Adrienne Fazan.

Drama/Comedy (PR:A MPAA:NR)

YOU'RE ONLY YOUNG TWICE* (1952, Brit.) 81m Group 3/ABF bw

Duncan Macrae (Prof. Hayman), Joseph Tomelty (Dan McEntee), Patrick Barr (Sir Archibald Asher), Charles Hawtrey (Adolphus Hayman), Diane Hart (Ada Shore), Robert Urquhart (Sheltie), Edward Lexy (Lord Carshennie), Jacqueline Mackenzie (Nellie), Eric Woodburn (The Bedellus), Molly Urquhart (Lady Duffy), Reginald Beckwith (BBC Commentator), Moultrie Kelsall, Roddy MacMillan, Wendy Noel, Archie Duncan, Alistair Hunter, Andrew Downie, Russell Waters.

A far-fetched farce in which Tomelty is a famous Irish rebel poet whose true identity is kept secret while he resides at a Scottish university. His position as gatekeeper allows him to run a bookmaking business on the side, but his niece comes along and spoils everything while searching for him. Very nonsensical piece of make-believe more tiring than most failed film efforts.

p, John Grierson, John Baxter, Barbara K. Emary; d, Terry Bishop; w, Bishop, Reginald Beckwith, Lindsay Galloway (based on the play "What Say They" by James Bridie); Ph, Jo Jago.

Comedy (PR:A MPAA:NR)

YOU'RE OUT OF LUCK* (1941) 60m MON bw

Frankie Darro (Frankie), Mantan Moreland (Jeff), Kay Sutton (Margie), Billy Snyder (Cameraman), Tristram Coffin (Whitney), Richard Bond (Tom), Ralph Peters (Mulligan), Gene O'Donell (Pete), Vicki Lester (Sonya), Janet Shaw (Joyce), William Costello (Burke).

An elevator boy and this detective brother try to solve a number of gangland murders in his lame-brained crime story. The mobsters are dull, the policemen ridiculous, the newspaper reporters brash, and the molls dumb, all of which lead to a bottom-of-the-drawer picture.

p, Lindsley Parsons; d, Howard Bretherton; w, Ed Kelso; ph, Fred Jackman, Jr.; ed, Jack Ogilvie.

Crime (PR:A MPAA:NR)

YOU'RE TELLING ME**** (1934) 67m PAR bw

W.C. Fields (Sam Bisbee), Joan Marsh (Pauline Bisbee), Larry "Buster" Crabbe (Bob Murchison), Adrienne Ames (H.R.H. Princess Lescaboura), Louise Carter (Mrs. Bessie Bisbee), Kathleen Howard (Mrs. Murchison), James B. "Pop" Kenton (Doc Beebe), Robert McKenzie (Charlie Bogle), George Irving (President of the Tire Company), Jerry Stewart (Frobisher), Del Henderson (Mayer Brown), Nora Cecil (Mrs. Price), George MacQuarrie (Crabbe), John M. Sullivan (Gray), Vernon Dent (Fat Man in Train), Tammany Young (Caddy), Lee Phelps (1st Cop), Dorothy Vernon Bay (Mrs. Kendall), Edward Le Saint (Conductor), Elise Cavanna (Mrs. Smith, Gossip), Eddie Baker (Motorcycle Police Escort), James C. Morton (George Smith,

Gossip), Billy Engle (1st Lounger), George Ovey (2nd Lounger), Al Hart (3rd Lounger), Alfred Del Cambre (Phil Cummings), Frederic Sullivan (Mr. Murchison), William Robyns (Postman), Harold Berquist (Doorman), Frank O'Connor (2nd Cop), Florence Enright (Mrs. Kelly), Isabelle La Mal (Rosita), Hal Craig (Motor Cop), Josephine Whittell (Bit).

A virtual duplicate of Fields' popular 1926 silent feature SO'S YOUR OLD MAN, YOU'RE TELLING ME explores new heights of hilarity with the addition of sound–an essential ingredient to Fields' comedy. Fields plays a struggling inventor who is having trouble scraping up enough money to support his family. Having turned to drink to drown his frustration, we first see Fields as he stumbles home long after midnight. When the discombobulated Fields finally makes it to his front door, his blurred vision prevents him from getting his key in the lock. Luckily he has invented a device to assist him. He produces a special funnel which he inserts into the keyhole allowing a clear guide path for his shaky hand. Once inside he finds his wife, Carter, awake and waiting. Much to his relief he learns that it is their daughter, Marsh, she is waiting for and not him. Once again Marsh has been out with Crabbe, the son of local millionaires. Soon the daughter arrives home and she happily announces her engagement to Crabbe. The news does not thrill her parents, however, because their financial state is an embarrassment. Hoping to strike it rich so he can impress Crabbe's family, Fields invents a puncture-proof tire that will revolutionize the auto industry. He is invited by a tire company to come and demonstrate his invention and he parks his car–fitted with four of the super- tires–in a no parking zone in front of the company office building. After a brief introduction, Fields ushers the executives outside for a demonstration. He produces a handgun and a baseball mitt with which he will shoot the tires and then catch the ricocheted bullet. Fields takes aim and fires. The tire deflates. Confused, he shoots another. It also deflates. All four tires collapse under fire. What he failed to notice was that a police car–identical to his own–had pushed his car out of the no parking zone and then parked there. Embarrassed and extremely depressed, Fields takes a train home. On board he decides to spare his daughter the shock of his failure by committing suicide. Finding a bottle of iodine, Fields carefully pours a lethal dose into a spoon. Unfortunately, the utensil he chooses happens to be a collapsible spoon of his own invention and, of course, it collapses before he can bring it to his lips. This, however, shakes Fields into realizing that he wants to live and he abandons the suicide attempt. Soon after, Fields spots a beautiful woman, Ames, in another compartment about to use a bottle of iodine. He rushes up to her, smashes the bottle, and gives her a heartfelt lecture against committing suicide. Little does Fields know that the woman was simply trying to use the iodine on a small scratch on her finger. Amused and touched by this stranger, Ames, who is a princess, decides to help Fields gain new social standing by staying in his home. At the same time, the tire executives have discovered that Fields' tires really are puncture-proof and they try to find him. The town is so thrilled with Fields because of Ames that they invite him to open the community's new golf course. As a crowd of people watch, including Marsh and Crabbe, Fields tries to tee off and the ensuing madness is the comedian's famed golf routine (seen in SO'S YOUR OLD MAN and in the sound short THE GOLF SPECIALIST in 1930). The tire executives finally catch up with Fields on the golf course and award him with a million dollar check for his invention. Whereas most of Fields' films were virtually plotless, YOU'RE TELLING ME has a complex, linear story line that gives Fields plenty of room for comedy and a surprising number of opportunities to show off his talents as a serious actor. Fields demonstrates a till then untapped sensitivity in several scenes– especially in his anti-suicide speech to Ames. It is a side of his character little seen. He is no less than brilliant in the suicide scene, intertwining pathos and comedy so gently that one feels like crying and laughing at the same time (critics at the time praised the scene and one writer declared that even Chaplin couldn't have done it as skillfully as Fields). YOU'RE TELLING ME is also a superior Fields vehicle because the comedian is on screen throughout most of the film–unlike many of his other films where his appearances are infrequent and sometimes almost incidental to the other plot lines which are padded out with boring romances or musical numbers. YOU'RE TELLING ME has no time for such nonsense. Held to a taut 67 minutes, the film concentrates wholly on Fields and allows him to develop a full, emotionally complex, and fascinating character. The stronger the characterization, the better the film and YOU'RE TELLING ME is a great testament to Fields' skills as a comedian and an actor. An interesting sidenote: it is in YOU'RE TELLING ME that Fields picked up his pseudonym "Charles Bogle" from a character in the film named "Charlie Bogle." The comedian used the name several times on stories and screenplays he had written as well as the more exotic pseudonyms "Mahatma Kane Jeeves" and "Otis J. Criblecoblis" much later in his career. The great compiler of outlandish proper nouns (the town of Lompoc was one of his favorite victims), explaining why he selected the less-than- lampoon names of Doc Beebe and Charlie Bogle for his cronies, pointed out that these two real individuals were instrumental in procuring him some much-needed snakebite medicine during a vaudeville tour in Prohibition times. Part of the picture was filmed in the town of Sierra Madre, where some of the local people extorted money from the studio by such means as loud radio playing and noisy children, elements which, if continued, would have interfered with sound takes. The studio was forced to blacklist the town for future production work. Sam Coslow is credited with writing the lyrics for the picture's songs. However, what songs had been planned were apparently left on the floor of the cutting room; none are in the movie.

p, William Le Baron; d, Erle C. Kenton; w, J.P. McEvoy, Walter De Leon, Paul M. Jones (based on the short story "Mr. Bisbee's Princess" by Julian Leonard Street); ph, Alfred Gilks; m, Arthur Johnston; ed, Otho Lovering; art d, Hans Dreier, Robert Odell.

Comedy   (PR:A   MPAA:NR)

YOU'RE TELLING ME**   (1942) 60m UNIV bw

Hugh Herbert (Hubert), Anne Gwynne (Kit), Robert Paige (Burnsy), Edward Ashley (Glen), Esther Dale (Aunt Fanny), Eily Malyon (Aunt Appleby), Ernest Truex (Handley), Helen Lynd (Miss Ames), Charles Smith (Bill), Romaine Callender (Dorsett), Boyd David (Driscoll), Harry Hayden (Judge), Jan Wiley (Girl Announcer), Jack Arnold (Announcer), Phil Tead (Chauffeur), Grace Stafford (Switchboard Operator), Olaf Hytten (Fielding), Vicki Lester (Miss Parks), Emmett Lynn (Scientist), Jane Cowan (Freckled Kid), Linda Brent (Chee Chee), Wilson Benge (Butler), Heinie Conklin (Scooter Man), Pat Maier (Girl Reporter), Wilbur Mack (Gallant Reporter), Gene O'Donnell, Jack Gardner (Reporters), Ralph Dunn, William Haade (Doormen), Eddy Chandler, Charles Sullivan, Charles McMurphy, Frank O'Connor (Policeman), Ralph Brooks, Kernan Cripps, Charles Sherlock (Men), Fritzi Burnette, Vera Burnette, Gertrude Mack (Women), Marie MacDonald, Susan Miller, Elaine Morley, Nell O'Day, Kathryn Adams (Girls).

A slightly daffy young man gets a job with his family's advertising agency. His first duty is to hire a big-game hunter for a radio show but problems arise when the hunter proves to be a fraud.

p, Ken Goldsmith; d, Charles Lamont; w, Frances Hyland, Brenda Weisberg (based on a story by Charles O'Neil, Duane Decker); ph, Jerome Ash; ed, Philip Kahn.

Comedy   (PR:A   MPAA:NR)

YOU'RE THE DOCTOR*½   (1938, Brit.) 78m New Georgian/British
                                                    Independent bw

Barry K. Barnes (John Meriden), Googie Withers (Helen Firmstone), Norma Varden (Lady Beatrice), Joan White (Jane), Gus McNaughton (Kemp), Paul Blake (Reggie Bissett), James Harcourt (William Firmstone), Margaret Yarde (Mrs. Taggart), Aubrey Mallalieu (Vicar), Bruce Seton (Appleby), Eliot Makeham (Prout), Bryan Powley, Jack Vyvyan, Billy Shine, Julian Vedey, Michael Ripper.

Withers uses scientist Barnes as a ploy to keep her from having to travel with her parents and the young suitor she finds nauseating, getting him to pose as a doctor and say she is ill. Before long the two are racing across the countryside to avoid the parents, eventually falling in love and marrying. Strained idea cleverly carried off.

p, A. George Smith; d, Roy Lockwood; w, Beaufoy Milton, H.F. Maltby p, A. George Smith; d, Roy Lockwood; w, Beaufoy Milton, H.F. Maltby (based on the story by Guy Beauchamp); ph, Geoffrey Faithfull.

Comedy   (PR:A   MPAA:NR)

YOU'RE THE ONE*   (1941) 83m PAR bw

Orrin Tucker (Himself), Bonnie Baker (Herself), Albert Dekker (Luke Laramie), Jerry Colonna (Dr. Colonna), Edward Everett Horton (Joe Frink), Lillian Cornell (Miss Jones), Walter Catlett (Program Director), Don Castle (Tony Delmar), Teddy Hart (Julius), Renie Riano (Aunt Emma), Eddie Conrad (Mr. Ziffnidyiff), Tom Dugan (Edgar Crump), Clarence Wilson (Mr. Miggles), Mariska Aldrich (Mme. Ziffnidyiff), Charles Lane (Announcer), Orrin Tucker's Orchestra.

Only the songs are worth mention in this farce where Horton plays an agent trying to push the talents of his young star, Baker. After a number of inane and contrived situations she gets her chance to chirp a few tunes with Orrin Tucker's Orchestra. Even Horton, a highly talented comedian, was at the mercy of a totally inadequate script. Songs included: "Strawberry Lane," "I Could Kiss You for That," "My Resistance is Low," "The Yogi Who Lost His Will Power," "Gee I Wish I'd Listened to My Mother" (Johnny Mercer, Jimmy McHugh), "Oh, Johnny, Oh" (Abe Olman, Ed Rose).

p, Gene Markey; d, Ralph Murphy; w, Markey; ph, Ted Tetzlaff; ed, Archie Marshek.

Musical   (PR:A   MPAA:NR)

YOURS FOR THE ASKING½**   (1936) 68m PAR bw

George Raft (Johnny Lamb), Dolores Costello Barrymore (Lucille Sutton), Ida Lupino (Gert Malloy), Reginald Owen (Dictionary McKinney/Col. Evelyn Carstairs), James Gleason (Saratoga), Edgar Kennedy (Bicarbonate), Lynne Overman (Honeysuckle), Richard "Skeets" Gallagher (Perry Barnes), Walter Walker (Mr. Crenshaw), Robert Gleckler (Slick Doran), Richard Powell (Benedict), Louis Natheaux (Dealer), Keith Daniels (Henchman), Florence Wix, Bess Flowers, Olive Tell, Rosemary Theby, Jean Fowler (Women), Dennis O'Keefe, Tom Curran, Edmund Mortimer, Phillips Smalley, William Arnold, Fred Minter (Men), Sally West, Marie Wells (Girls), Harry C. Bradley (Art Dealer), Jack 'John' Byron (Chauffeur), Arthur Stuart Hull (Deaf and Dumb Man), Henry Roquemore (Pot-bellied Man),

Betty Blythe (May), Albert Pollet (Head Waiter), Max Barwyn, Francis Sayles, Edward Peil, Sr. (Waiters), Charles Requa (Mr. Ames), Huntley Gordon (Clark Bering), Ralph Remley (O'Rorke), Groucho Marx, Charles Ruggles (Sunbathers on Beach).

An entertaining but flimsy Raft vehicle which mixes his gangster image with comedy in an unsatisfactory combination. Raft, a streetwise hood, hooks up with impoverished Miami socialite Costello Barrymore and they decide to form a partnership, converting her old family mansion into a hideaway gambling casino. Raft feels that her good looks will draw in a crowd and with the profits she'll be able to cover her debts. However, Raft's henchmen–Gleason, Kennedy, and Overman–are more suited to society's dregs than to its upper crust and concoct a scheme to ruin the partnership, fearing that Raft has forgotten his roots. The comic trio hire a pair of cons–Owen and Lupino–to pose as a British colonel and his niece and hopefully persuade Raft this high-society woman isn't his type. When Lupino sets her sights for Raft, he falls for her and forgets about his initial interest in Barrymore. Gleason, Kennedy, and Overman soon realize that Lupino has overstretched her limits and is actually trying to snare Raft for her own financial gain. Raft is soon clued in on Lupino, causing him to realize that it is Barrymore who he has loved all along. While YOURS FOR THE ASKING may benefit from Raft's gangster stylings, it surely is crippled by his lame attempt at comedy–a critique that goes ditto for Barrymore. Neither of the leads is capable of carrying the weight, leaving the chore to a solid supporting cast. It is that list of players–the henchman trio of Gleason, Kennedy, and Overman, and the con duo of Owen and Lupino–that not only makes the film watchable, but also comprises most of the screen time.

p, Lewis E. Gensler; d, Alexander Hall; w, Eve Green, Harlan Ware, Philip MacDonald (based on a story by William R. Lipman, William H. Wright); ph, Theodor Sparkuhl; art d, Hans Dreier, Roland Anderson.

Crime   (PR:A   MPAA:NR)

YOURS, MINE AND OURS**   (1968) 111m Desilu-Walden/UA c

Lucille Ball (Helen North), Henry Fonda (Frank Beardsley), Van Johnson (Darrell Harrison), Tom Bosley (Doctor), Louise Troy (Frank's Date), Ben Murphy (Larry), Jennifer Leak (Colleen North), Kevin Burchett (Nicky North), Kimberly Beck (Janette North), Mitch Vogel (Tommy North), Margot Jane (Jean North), Eric Shea (Phillip North), Gregory Atkins (Gerald North), Lynnell Atkins (Teresa North), Tim Matthieson [Matheson] (Mike Beardsley), Gil Rogers (Rusty Beardsley), Nancy Roth (Rosemary Beardsley), Gary Goetzman (Greg Beardsley), Suzanne Cupito [Morgan Brittany] (Louise Beardsley), Holly O'Brien (Susan Beardsley), Michele Tobin (Veronica Beardsley), Maralee Foster (Mary Beardsley), Tracy Nelson (Germaine Beardsley), Stephanie Oliver (Joan Beardsley).

Fonda, a widowed Navy officer with 10 children, meets Ball, herself a widowed nurse with eight children. With the encouragement of Van Johnson the two begin dating and finally marry despite the unhappy prospect of raising 18 children under one roof. The expected problems of food, privacy, and bathroom rights abound as do inherent jealousies between the children. However, Ball's son Shea begins a sort of hero-worshiping of Fonda's eldest son, Matthieson, which breaks the family barriers. This is further strengthened when Ball announces that she's pregnant. With the baby's birth the children decide they want a formal adoption so they can all be one family. In the end Matthieson must go to war and Leak falls in love, two events which bring the large family even closer together. The potential for "Brady Bunch" saccharine was enormous for a film of this nature, but happily YOURS MINE, AND OURS never condescends to overdramatize the true story it was based on. The direction manages to place the enormous cast of children in believable situations that ring with truthful clarity. Ball, whose Desilu production company was behind the film, is surprisingly good. Fonda also holds up well (he had been Ball's second choice when Fred MacMurray proved to be unavailable) with a warm performance. It was premiered at a Fonda Film Festival at Syracuse University and delighted the college audience. Fine fare for family viewing.

p, Robert F. Blumofe; d, Melville Shavelson; w, Shavelson, Mort Lachman (based on the story by Madelyn Davis, Bob Carroll, Jr. from the book Who Gets the Drumstick? by Helen Beardsley); ph, Charles Wheeler (DeLuxe Color); m, Fred Karlin; ed, Stuart Gilmore; md, Karlin; art d, Arthur Lonergan; set d, James Payne; cos, Renita Reachi, Frank Cardinale; makeup, Bill Phillips.

Comedy/Drama   (PR:AAA   MPAA:NR)

YOUTH AFLAME zero   (1945) 61m CD bw

Joy Reese (Katy), Warren Burr (Frank), Kay Morley (Lafot), Michael Owen (Al), Rod Rogers (Lester), Edwin Brian (Harry), Julie Duncan (Peggy), Shelila Roberts (Helen), Edward Cassidy (Father), Mary Arden (Mrs. Clark), Duke Johnson (Tom).

Boring, ineptly created "youth in trouble" film. The gist of the story is its heavy-handed message that parents are to blame for problem kids. Delivered up with poor dialog, wooden performances, and a crude theme.

p, J.D. Kendis; d&w, Elmer Clifton (based on a story by Helen Kiedy); ph, Jack Greenhalgh; ed, George Merrick.

Drama   (PR:A   MPAA:NR)

YOUTH AND HIS AMULET, THE**½   (1963, Jap.) 111m Toho bw-c
(GEN TO FUDO-MYOH)

Toru Koyanagi (Gen), Hisako Sakabe (His Sister), Toshiro Mifune (Fudo-Myoh), Chishu Ryu, Yosuke Natsuki, Minoru Chiaki, Nobuko Otowa, Mie Hama.

Ten-year-old Koyanagi lives in the Japanese countryside with his sister, Sakabe, and his father, a widowed Buddhist priest. When the father decides to remarry, Koyanagi's world falls apart. His father places him with a parishioner in a different village so there will be no problems with the new marriage. The boy's new home is run by an old woman who despises children and is constantly correcting the boy. Tired of her and the menial tasks he must perform, Koyanagi takes an idol he finds and talks with it about the troubles in his life. However, the idol has come from a village shrine and Koyanagi is arrested for theft. He is returned to his father, who is having troubles of his own with his new wife. She tosses the boy's prized amulet away and leaves when he accuses her of stealing it. Later he and his sister go in search of their stepmother. However, this is taken to mean something larger than their innocent intent and Koyanagi is placed for adoption.

p&d, Hiroshi Inagaki; w, Toshiro Ide, Zenzo Matsuyama (based on the story by Shizue Miyaguchi); ph, Kazuo Yamada; m, Ikuma Dan; spec eff, Eiji Tsuburaya.

Drama   (PR:C   MPAA:NR)

YOUTH IN FURY**   (1961, Jap.) 89m Shochiku./Shochiku Films of
America c (KAWAITA MIZUMMI)

Shin-ichiro Mikami (Takuya Shimojo), Shima Iwashita (Yoko Katsura), Hizuru Takachiho (Fumie Sono), Kayoko Honoo (Setsuko Kitamura), Jun-ichiro Yamashita (Michihiko Kihara), Kazuya Kosaka (Seiichi Mizushima), Yunosuke Ito (Oseto), Yachiyo Otori (Shizue), Shinji Takano (Fujimori), Eiko Kujo (Miyoko Edamura), Yuki Tominaga (Sakiko Ota), Keiko Kuni (Takako Shinoyama), Teiko Sawamura.

Mikami is a student radical with heroes ranging from Adolf Hitler to Leon Trotsky to Fidel Castro. He, too, wishes to achieve dictatorial power as these men did. At summer's end he and girl friend Honoo are invited by Yamashita, heir to a fortune, to a seashore estate for sailing and a party. Iwashita, one of the partygoers, hears that her father killed himself after being caught in a business scandal with political ramifications. Mikami meets Ito at a bar and in a political discussion announces he would like to kill the wealthy classes and take over their place. He proposes that Ito should pay money to a college girl for sexual favors only to learn that Takachiho, the bartender, already is Ito's mistress. After failing to help his fellow political comrade Kosaka get a job with Yamashita, Mikami becomes attracted to Iwashita. She has been humiliated by the scandal, which had come as a result of her host's family. Mikami has a boxer friend attack the caddish fiance of Iwashita's sister. Later Mikami is expelled from his political group for his too radical beliefs, so he drowns his sorrows at various parties thrown by rich friends. As protests over U.S. and Japanese security pacts mount, Mikami decides that these demonstrations are pointless and decides to take direct action. He buys material to make dynamite and tells the now pregnant Honoo he's too busy for her. When leaving his apartment, though, Mikami is met by the police who charge him for the assault he arranged and thus thwart his plans to use the explosives. A close retelling of director Shinoda's PUNISHMENT ISLAND, where the hero is stripped of one illusion after another, leaving him with nothing to take their place.

d, Masahiro Shinoda; w, Shuji Terayama (based on a story by Eiji Shimba); ph, Masao Kosugi (Shochiku GrandScope, Eastmancolor); m, Toru Takemitsu; ed, Keiichi Uraoka; art d, Kiminobu Sato

Drama   (PR:O   MPAA:NR)

YOUTH ON PARADE**½   (1943) 72m REP bw

John Hubbard (Prof. Gerald Payne), Martha O'Driscoll (Sally Carlyle), Bruce Langley (Himself), Ruth Terry (Patty Flynn/Betty Reilly), Charles Smith (Willie Webster), Nana Bryant (Agatha Frost), Ivan Simpson (Dean Wharton), Chick Chandler (Eddie Reilly), Paul Fix (Nick Cramer), Lynn Merrick (Emmy Lou Piper), John Boyle, Jr (The Character), Marlyn Schild (Marlyn), Eddie Acuff, Bud Jamison (Cops), Sue Robin (Bouncy), Ruth Daye (Butch), Edward Earle (Major), Betty Atkinson (Drum Majorette), Harry Hayden (Dr. Witherspoon), Walter Soderling, Boyd Irwin, Walter Fenner, Alfred Hall, Elmer Jerome (Professors), Maurice Cass (Prof. Bowilowicz), Barbara Slater (Curvy Coed), Ric Vallin (Customer), Ben Lessy (Piano Player), Warren Ashe (Clerk), Frank Coghlan, Jr (Student), Yvonne De Carlo (Girl), Jack Boyle, Ivan Miller.

A group of collegians decide to create a fictional student, giving her the finest qualites any university could possibly dream of. When the psychology professor (Hubbard) becomes interested in meeting this whiz kid, the precocious students suddenly find themselves facing expulsion unless they can produce her. Terry is the New York actress hired for the job and the scam ends happily. This college musical is ridiculous and one of the more far-fetched films of its type. However, the production has charm and Terry's

good comic performance. This marked the first film pairing for the song writing team of Sammy Cahn and Jule Styne. The number "I've Heard that Song Before" was later recorded by Harry James and proved to be a big hit. Other songs: "You're So Good to Me," "If It's Love," "Man," "Gotcha Too Ta Mee," "You Got to Study, Buddy."

p, Albert J. Cohen; d, Albert S. Rogell; w, George Carleton Brown; ph, Ernest Miller; ed, Howard O'Neill; md, Cy Feuer; art d, Russell Kimball.

Musical   (PR:AAA   MPAA:NR)

YOUTH ON PAROLE*½   (1937) 60m REP bw

Marian Marsh (Bonnie Blair), Gordon Oliver (Phillip Henderson), Margaret Dumont (Landlady), Peggy Shannon (Peggy), Miles Mander (Sparkler), Sarah Padden (Mrs. Blair), Wade Boteler (Mr. Blair), Joe Caits (Fingle), Mary Kornman (Mae Blair), Milburn Stone (Ratty), Harry Tyler (Danny), Ranny Weeks (Michael), Theodore Von Eltz (Lawyer), Ula Love (Maizie), Paul Stanton (Inspector).

After being paroled from jail Marsh and Oliver meet and a romance blooms. When it seems the two are guilty of a new crime, Oliver proves they are being framed and all ends happily. An average programmer with a poorly developed story line, though the two leads are okay. Dumont appears lost without the Marx Brothers after her many films as the good-looking foil for their zany antics.

p&d, Phil Rosen; w, Hershel Rebuas, Henry Blankfort, Jr.; ph, Edward Snyder; ed, Ernest Nims; cos, Eloise.

Drama   (PR:A   MPAA:NR)

YOUTH ON TRIAL**   (1945) 59m COL bw

Cora Sue Collins (Cam Chandler), David Reed (Tom Lowry), Eric Sinclair (Denny Moore), Georgia Bayes (Meg Chandler), Robert Williams (Officer Ken Moore), Mary Currier (Judge Chandler), John Calvert (Jud Lowry), Boyd Bennett (Stacey), William Forrest (Robert Reynolds), Muni Seroff (Mario), Florence Auer (Maude McGregor), Boyd Davis (Mayor Townsend), Joseph Crehan (Commissioner Ryan), Edwin Stanley (Commissioner Collins).

In youth court, Currier is a tough judge. When she has a well-known roadhouse raided for serving teens, she's shocked to find her daughter Collins among the customers. Collins escapes with local bad boy Reed but the other teens gladly snitch on them. Currier realizes that in her zealousness she's neglected her home life. Some good performances in a contrived story, directed with nice pacing.

p, Ted Richmond; d, Oscar [Budd] Boetticher, Jr.; w, Michel Jacoby; ph, George Meehan; ed, Gene Havlick; art d, Jerome Pycha, Jr.

Drama   (PR:A   MPAA:NR)

YOUTH RUNS WILD*½   (1944) 67m RKO bw

Bonita Granville (Toddy), Kent Smith (Danny), Jean Brooks (Mary), Glenn Vernon (Frank), Tessa Brind (Sarah Taylor), Ben Bard (Mr. Taylor), Mary Servoss (Mrs. Hauser), Arthur Shields (Mr. Dunlop), Lawrence Tierney (Duncan), Dickie Moore (Georgie Dunlop), Johnny Walsh (Herb Vigero), Rod Rodgers (Rocky), Elizabeth Russell (Mrs. Taylor), Juanita Alvarez (Lucy), Gloria Donovan (Nancy Taylor), Jack Carrington (Bart), Ida Shoemaker (Card Player), Claire Carleton (Taxi Driver), Art Smith (Mr. Hauser), Harold Barnitz (Stevie), Frank O'Connor (Cop), Rosemary La Planche, Joan Barclay (Women), Margaret Landry (Hysterical Girl), Harry Clay (Good Humor Man), George De Normand (Fireman), Danny Desmond (Eddie Wilson), Fritz Lieber (Judge), Robert Strong (Juvenile Officer), Tom Burton (Soldier with Sarah), Russell Hopton (Dickens), Chris Drake (Usher), Edmund Glover (Lineman), Lee Phelps (Fireman), Gordon Jones (Truck Driver), Harry Harvey (Watchman), Maxwell Hayes (Priest), Bud Wiser (Motor Cop).

While the cat's away the mouse will play and so do bad little teenagers, as this film so obviously states. While their parents are either at war or working in the local defense plant, the working class kids in a small town go crazy. A boy gets run over by a car thief, a while runaway girl falls in with "a bad crowd." Fortunately a soldier, returning to civilian life after being wounded overseas, opens up a center for the kids to hang out in and helps the boys with job training. This turgid drama was one of the few nonhorror films produced by Val Lewton, creator of THE CURSE OF THE CAT PEOPLE. He had set out to create a socially important drama but studio chiefs insisted on re-cutting the picture with some new scenes shot as well. The result was far from what Lewton intended and he angrily demanded his name be removed from the film. This request was denied. The result was a string of cliches and stock situations with only occasional moments of spark. Ruth Clifton, a teenager from Moline, Illinois, who had helped create the Illinois Plan for Youth Guidance, was brought in to serve as technical adviser, another sign of the simplicity demanded by the studio. Look at the movie house in the mythical town portrayed: it's plastered with advertisements for other Lewton films.

p, Val Lewton; d, Mark Robson; w, John Fante, Ardel Wray (based on a story by Fante, Herbert Kline); ph, John J. Mescall; m, Paul Sawtell; ed, John

Lockert; md, C. Bakaleinikoff; art d, Albert S. D'Agostino, Carroll Clark; set d, Darrell Silvera, Ross Dowd; cos, Edward Stevenson; spec eff, Vernon L. Walker.

Drama   (PR:C   MPAA:NR)

YOUTH TAKES A FLING**   (1938) 77m UNIV bw

Joel McCrea (Joe Meadows), Andrea Leeds (Helen Brown), Frank Jenks (Frank Munson), Dorothea Kent (Jean), Isabel Jeans (Mrs. Merrivale), Virginia Grey (Madge), Grant Mitchell (Mr. Duke), Brandon Tynan (Tad), Oscar O'Shea (Capt. Walters), Catherine Proctor (Mrs. Aspitt), Granville Bates (Mr. Judd), Marion Martin (Girl on Bench), Willie Best (George), Roger Davis (Floorwalker), Olaf Hytten.

After coming from Kansas to New York City McCrea discovers there are few jobs open for a sea-minded young man like himself. He's forced to find other work and takes a job as a department store truck driver. Salesgirl Leeds takes one look at McCrea, decides he's the man for her, and forces her attentions on the unwilling Midwesterner. A naive comedy without many laughs, this is hampered by slow development. Kent and Jenks in supporting roles steal most of the show.

p, Joseph Pasternak; d, Archie Mayo; w, Myles Connolly; ph, Rudolph Mate; ed, Philip Cahn; md, Charles Previn; art d, Jack Otterson; cos, Vera West; m/l, Jimmy McHugh, Harold Adamson.

Comedy   (PR:AA   MPAA:NR)

YOUTH TAKES A HAND   (SEE: BEHIND PRISON WALLS, 1943)

YOUTH WILL BE SERVED**   (1940) 66m FOX bw

Jane Withers (Eadie-May), Jane Darwell (Supervisor Stormer), Robert Conway (Dr. Bob), Elyse Knox (Pamela), Joe Brown, Jr (Benjy), John Qualen (Clem Howie), Charles Holland (Ephraim), Lillian Porter (Lisbeth), Clara Blandick (Miss Bradshaw), Tully Marshall (Rufus Britt), Edwin Stanley (CCC Camp Major), Mildred Gover (Lily), Richard Lane (Mr. Hewitt), Cy Kendall (Sheriff), James Flavin (Buck Miller), Eddie Marr (Dan McKay), Claire Du Brey (Henrietta McNutt).

After her father is arrested for moonshining, young Withers goes off to a National Youth Administration camp. Marshall is a local rich man who wants to buy up the camp's land, but Withers puts together a camp show that wins over the ornery old man. When Marshall's payroll is stolen, her father escapes from prison and captures the fiends responsible. That's all Marshall needs to decide that the camp is worth keeping. Typical programmer for kid wonder Withers with standard production values. In addition to plugging the government's Depression-era NYA program the Civilian Conservation Corps also got a plug in the film.

p, Lucien Hubbard; d, Otto Brower; w, Wanda Tuchock (based on a story by Ruth Fasken, Hilda Vincent); ph, Edward Cronjager; ed, Nick De Maggi; md, Emil Newman; ch, Nicholas Castle; m/l, Frank Loesser, Louis Alter (sung by Charles Holland).

Musical   (PR:A   MPAA:NR)

YOUTHFUL FOLLY**   (1934, Brit.) 72m Sound City/COL bw

Irene Vanbrugh (Lady Wilmington), Jane Carr (Ursula Wilmington), Mary Lawson (Susan Grierson), Grey Blake (Larry Wilmington), Arthur Chesney (Lord Wilmington), Eric Maturin (Tim Grierson), Fanny Wright (Mrs. Grierson), Betty Ann Davies, Merle Tottenham, Belle Chrystal, Kenneth Kove.

When a musician from a working class background meets a society girl, he gives up his city love to pursue this new romance. His sister tries to persuade her to forget about him but in the end he overcomes his caddish ways and the pair reunite. Unconvincing mash of romance embarrassing for all concerned.

p, Norman Loudon; d, Miles Mander; w, Heinrich Frankel (based on a play by Gordon Daviot).

Romance   (PR:A   MPAA:NR)

YOU'VE GOT TO BE SMART*   (1967) 88m World-Cine Associates-Stage 19/PRC c

Tom Stern (Nick Sloane), Roger Perry (Jerry Harper), Gloria Castillo (Connie Jackson), Mamie Van Doren (Miss Hathaway), Preston Foster (D.O. Griggs), Jeff Bantam (Methuselah Jones), Mike Bantam, Fritz Bantam (Methuselah's Brothers).

A frighteningly bad picture in which Stern plays a no-good promoter trying to take advantage of a backwoods singing preacher and his two brothers. His antics deceive Castillo long enough to get her aid in helping him to find backing. She finally sees through the promoter, leaving him alone with the beautiful but dumb Van Doren. This was the untalented Van Doren's final try at film acting. Songs: "Him Who Loves Ain't Got Time to Hate," "Time Will Tell," "Restin' Time," "Look Before You Leap," and "Don't Look in Other Pastures," all sung by the Bantams.

d&w, Ellis Kadison; m&md, Stan Worth, Gerald Alters.

Drama   (PR:A   MPAA:NR)

YOU'VE GOT TO WALK IT LIKE YOU TALK IT OR YOU'LL LOSE THAT BEAT*½   (1971) 85m J.E.R. c

Zalman King (Carter Fields), Allen Garfield [Goorwitz] (Herby Moss), Suzette Green (Susan), Richard Pryor (Wino), Bob Downey (Head of Ad Agency), Liz Torres (Singer in Men's Room), Roz Kelly (Girl in Park), Karen Ludwi (Erica), Billy Cunningham (Fat Lady), Ruth Locke (Carter's Mother), Daisy Locke (Old Woman), Stan Gottlieb (Fellestrio), Peter Locke (Shoe Thief/Purse Snatcher), Chick Kozloff (Mooner), Michael Sullivan (Man on Toilet), Steve Landisberg (Men's Room Attendant), Tommy Cerafice (Boy in Men's Room), Erick Krupnik (Hood-Group Therapy), Stephen Berke (Food Eater on Park Bench), Ann Taylor, Karen Smith (Pickpockets), St. Louis (Gynecologist), George Schultz (Judge), Jan Smith (Garbage Eater), Walter Klusner (Father), Tony Middleton (Stranger), Paula Frankle (Corinna), John Fodor (Revolutionary), Elaine Everett (Anita Lorraine Teitlebaum), Roger Parsons (Narrator).

King is an idealistic young man who is seeking the meaning of life among the inanities and absurdities of New York. In Central Park he is set upon by a fat black woman and he watches incredulously as a young man exposes his behind to an old woman shouting obscenities at him. After many such ridiculous adventures, he finally marries an understanding girl, becomes a father, gets a job and, seemingly in a jiffy, he loses the job, his wife leaves him with the baby, and he is back in Central Park still seeking the "meaning" of it all. A mishmash of intent and execution and too annoyingly clumsy to watch.

p,d&w, Peter Locke; ph, Stephen Bower (Eastmancolor); m, Walter Becker, Donald Fagin, Billy Cunningham; ed, Wes Craven, David Finfar, Lana Jokel, Locke; art d, Linda Sampson.

Drama/Comedy   (PR:O   MPAA:R)

YOYO   (SEE: YO YO, 1967, Fr.)

YUKIGUMI   (SEE: SNOW COUNTRY, 1969, Jap.)

YUKON FLIGHT**½   (1940) 57m Criterion/MON bw

James Newill (Renfrew), Louise Stanley (Louise), Warren Hull (Shipley), William Pawley (Yuke), Dave O'Brien (Kelly), George Humbert (Nick), Karl Hackett (Raymond), Jack Clifford (Smith), Roy Barcroft (Lodin), Bob Terry (DeLong), Earl Douglas (Smoky).

An enjoyable entry in the "Renfrew" series finds the Mountie hero checking out some illegal gold operations in the Yukon. Pawley and Hackett are running an air freight service for miners and aren't above helping themselves to the cargo. They occasionally kill a client or two as well, but Newill saves the day with a good amount of action. Newill and his love interest, Stanley, are a handsome pair who add to the film's quality. Good fun. (See RENFREW series, Index.)

d, Ralph Staub; w, Edward Halperin (based on the story "Renfrew Rides North" by Laurie York Erskine); ph, Mack Stengler; ed, Martin G. Cohn.

Adventure   (PR:A   MPAA:NR)

YUKON GOLD**   (1952) 62M MON bw

Kirby Grant, Martha Hyer, Harry Lauter, Philip Van Zandt, Frances Charles, Mauritz Hugo, James Farnell, Sam Flint, I. Stanford Jolley, Chinook the Dog.

There's a murder in a gold mine settlement in the far north. A Mountie goes off to investigate and there meets a lady gambler before the bullet-filled climax. Michigan-born author Curwood was a master in this genre, with most of his writings laid in the American Northwest and the Yukon.

p, William F. Broidy; d, Frank McDonald; w, William Raynor (based on a story "Gold Hunters" by James Oliver Curwood); ph, John Martin; art d, David Milton.

Adventure   (PR:A   MPAA:NR)

YUKON MANHUNT**   (1951) 63M MON bw

Kirby Grant, Gail Davis, Margaret Field, Rand Brooks, Nelson Leigh, John Doucette, Paul McGuire, Dick Barron, Chinook the Dog.

When there are a series of robberies, the Mounties come in to solve the problem. The truth is that payroll messengers are being held up by people in their own organization and Chinook gets another chance to shine.

p, Lindsley Parsons; d, Frank McDonald; w, William Raynor (based on a short story by James Oliver Curwood) ph, William Sickner; ed, Ace Herman; md, Ed Jay; art d, David Milton.

Adventure   (PR:A   MPAA:NR)

YUKON VENGEANCE*½   (1954) 68m AA bw

Kirby Grant, Monte Hale, Mary Ellen Kay, Henry Kulky, Carol Thurston, Park MacGregor, Fred Gabourie, Billy Wilkerson, Marshall Bradford.

The Yukon territory is the background for this tale of a Mountie who tracks down the killer of three mail carriers. A standard vengeance plot with some picturesque settings.

p, William F. Broidy; d, William Beaudine; w, Bill Raynor (based on the story by James Oliver Curwood).

Western   **(PR:A   MPAA:NR)**

YUSHA NOMI   (SEE: NONE BUT THE BRAVE, 1965)

YUSHU HEIYA   (SEE: MADAME AKI, 1963, Jap.)

Z

Z****　　(1969, Fr./Algeria) 127m Reggane-Office National Pour Le Commerce Et L'Industrie Cinematographique/Cinema V c

Yves Montand *(The Deputy)*, Jean-Louis Trintignant *(The Examining Magistrate)*, Irene Pappas *(Helene the Deputy's Wife)*, Jacques Perrin *(Photojournalist)*, Charles Denner *(Manuel)*, Francois Perier *(Public Prosecutor)*, Pierre Dux *(The General)*, Julien Guiomar *(The Colonel)*, Bernard Fresson *(Matt)*, Renato Salvatori *(Yago)*, Marcel Bozzufi *(Vago)*, Jean Bouise *(Deputy Georges Pirou)*, Georges Geret *(Nick)*, Magali Noel *(Nick's Sister)*, Jean Daste *(Coste)*, Jean-Pierre Miquel *(Pierre)*, Guy Mairesse *(Dumas)*, Clotilde Joano *(Shoula)*, Maurice Baquet *(The Bald Man)*, Gerard Darrieu *(Baron)*, Jose Artur *(The Newspaper Editor)*, Van Doude *(The Hospital Director)*, Eva Simonet *(Niki)*, Hassan Hassani *(The General's Chauffeur)*, Gabriel Jabbour *(Bozzini)*, Jean-Francois Gobbi *(Jimmy the Boxer)*, Andree Tainsy *(Nick's Mother)*, Steve Gadler *(English Photographer)*, Bob de Bragelonne *(Undersecretary of State)*, Sid Ahmed Agoumi, Allel El Mouhib, Habib Reda, Georges Rouquier.

Originally subtitled "The Anatomy of a Political Assassination," this intense political thriller is based on the real-life 1963 killing of Gregorios Lambrakis, a Greek liberal whose extreme popularity and advocacy of peace shook the stability of the government in power. Starring is Montand who, although referred to only as "the Deputy," is clearly Lambrakis. After his liberal organization, the Friends of Peace, loses a large meeting hall at the last moment, Montand is forced to find another venue. He appeals to the general in charge, Dux, and is given a permit to hold the meeting in a small 200-seat auditorium. Because they are expected to draw over 4,000 supporters, Montand applies for permission to install a public address system which would broadcast his speech to those standing outside. Later that evening during the meeting (which coincides with the premiere of the Bolshoi Ballet–the evening's high- society event) Montand's supporters are taunted by a violent right-wing faction while the supposed police protection stands by. One agitator sneaks up behind Montand and clubs him in the head. Shaken, he is able to go on with his speech, but before long the speakers are shut off. When Montand goes into the crowd to question the general's reasons for sabotaging his speech, he is approached by a speeding truck and clubbed in the head by one of its passengers. Unconscious, he is taken to the hospital where his wife, Pappas, comes to be near him. In order to give the appearance of an investigation, the general appoints as the examining magistrate Trintignant, who is believed to be a pawn of the government. Trintignant questions the official report that calls the assassination attempt a hit-and-run accident and begins probing deeper. He does not believe that the driver of the truck was drunk, nor does he believe that Montand was injured when his head hit the pavement. Despite the efforts of the doctors, Montand dies. An autopsy which follows proves, without a doubt, that he was struck on the head. With the help of a sensationalistic photojournalist, Perrin, and a brave informant, Geret, Trintignant learns that the assassination was engineered by a secret fascist organization, C.R.O.C. (Royalist Fighters of the Christian West), which has ties with the upper echelon of the government. Pressured to drop his investigation, Trintignant fights back with both barrels, indicting numerous top officials, including the general who appointed him, in a conspiracy plot. A television news report says that after the indictments a military coup d'etat took place and a fascist military regime took control. What followed was the suspicious death of a number of witnesses, a pardoning of the indicted officials, and a ban on such things as long hair, the Beatles, Peace Movements, and the letter "Z," which came to represent the assassinated deputy and means, in Greek, "He is Alive." As with so many political films, the history of the production is nearly as interesting as the film itself. Costa-Gavras, the son of a Greek Resistance fighter, left his home country after being refused university admission, as were most other politically oppressed persons and their families. After taking up residence in Paris and completing two well-received features– THE SLEEPING CAR MURDERS (1965) and SHOCK TROOPS (1967)– Costa-Gavras went to work on bringing Vassilikos' powerful novel to the screen. His hope was to bring to the rest of the world a knowledge of the Lambrakis affair, which began on the night of the assassination, May 22, 1963. Rather than basing his film on rumor, Costa-Gavras took the incidents in his film from the actual trial. He has stated, "By sticking absolutely to what was proved at the trial, we have made it all but impossible for people to say, 'How do you know? That isn't true. That's a rumor.'" He took as his central character the examining magistrate (a parallel of sorts to Costa-Gavras' role as director) who in real life was one Christos Sartzetakis. After uncovering the conspiracy, Sartzetakis found himself a target of the new regime. After the fascists took power in April, 1967, Sartzetakis was arrested, tortured, and disbarred. Because of the controversial and political nature of the film, Costa-Gavras had great difficulty raising money. Having signed box office names Montand, Trintignant, and Pappas, the director had some leverage to convince investors of its moneymaking potential. Unable to attract production companies in Europe or the U.S., Costa-Gavras finally got Perrin, the photojournalist in the film, to become a coproducer. On a budget of less than $1 million, the film was completed, with the actors receiving a small salary and the promise of a percentage. Costa- Gavras was lucky enough to be collaborating with two of Europe's top names–

screenwriter Semprun, who had previously scripted LE GUERRE EST FINIE, a political drama from Alain Resnais, which also starred Montand, and cameraman Coutard, who had gained fame by shooting for both Jean-Luc Godard and Francois Truffaut. Also involved in the project was composer Mikis Theodorakis, who, because he was under house-arrest in Greece, was unable to complete the film's score. He did, however, manage to smuggle out an original song which was incorporated, along with earlier works of his, into the picture. Instead of appealing only to a politically minded audience, Z found a great deal of enthusiastic support from almost everyone who saw it. At the Cannes Film Festival it received a unanimous vote for the Jury Prize, with Trintignant receiving Best Actor honors. The New York Film Critics and the National Society of Film Critics chose it as their Best Picture. The Academy Awards also bestowed a number of honors: Oscars for Best Foreign Film and Best Editing, and nominations for Best Picture, Best Director, Best Adapted Screenplay. It wasn't just the critics that responded, however. Audiences came out in droves, making Z the 14th largest grosser of the year with $6,750,000. Z succeeded where so many other political pictures failed because of Costa-Gavras' and Semprun's concentration on the thriller aspects. Borrowing heavily from American thrillers and *film noir* conventions, Z contains many action-packed, high-tension scenes which help speed along the sometimes confusing politics. Rather than worrying about which right-wing general did what, the audience becomes wrapped up in whether or not a character will survive a beating, or be run down by a speeding car. There are even some added comic touches, especially in Geret's informer character and in the indictment montage, which make the film entertaining rather than intellectually or politically torturous. Detractors complained that the film commercialized and simplified the Lambrakis incident and politics in general. Costa-Gavras responded: "That's the way it is in Greece. Black and White. No Nuances." It is this "black and white" which probably appealed to most American viewers who were looking for clear answers to recent assassinations (John F. Kennedy, Robert Kennedy, and Martin Luther King) rather than the convoluted reports that Washington was passing along. Instead of serving only as a statement about Greece from 1963 to 1967, Z offers insight into the politics of all nations. Costa-Gavras commented on the universality of his film by stating, "Z is the just man underhandedly murdered within an oppressive climate of official hypocrisy." Not surprisingly, Z was banned in Greece (as well as other fascist countries) until the military government was finally disposed of in 1974. (In French; dubbed in English.)

p, Jacques Perrin, Hamed Rachedi; d, Costa-Gavras; w, Costa- Gavras, Jorge Semprun (based on the novel by Vassili Vassilikos); ph, Raoul Coutard (Technicolor); m, Mikis Theodorakis; ed, Francoise Bonnot; md, Bernard Gerard; art d, Jacques d'Ovidio.

Political Drama　　　　　　　　**Cas.**　　　　　　　　**(PR:C-O　MPAA:M)**

Z.P.G.*½　　(1972) 95m Sagittarius/PAR c (AKA: ZERO POPULATION GROWTH)

Oliver Reed *(Russ McNeil)*, Geraldine Chaplin *(Carole McNeil)*, Don Gordon *(George Borden)*, Diane Cilento *(Edna Borden)*, David Markham *(Dr. Herrick)*, Sheila Reid *(Dr. Mary Herrick)*, Aubrey Woods *(Dr. Mallory)*, Bill Nagy *(President)*, Lotte Tholander *(Telescreen Nurse)*, Wayne John Rhodda *(Metromart Salesman)*, Ditte Maria *(Telescreen Operator)*, Birgitte Federspiel *(Psychiatrist)*, Lone Lindorff *(Mother)*, Belinda Donkin *(Daughter)*, Claus Nissen, Jeff Slocombe *(Guards)*, Dale Robinson *(1st Guide)*, Victor Lipari *(Headwaiter)*, Michel Hildsheim *(Thief)*, Tour Guide *(Paul Secon)*, Carlotta Magnoff *(Informer)*, Eugene Blau, Bent Christensen *(Baby Shop Salesmen)*, Sam Maisel, Anne-Lise Gabold *(Baby Shop Father and Mother)*, Torben Hundahl *(Presidential Aide)*, Peter Ronild *(Edict Doctor)*, Birthe Tove, Birgitte Frigast *(Nurses)*, Brian Keifer, Vladimir Kandell *(Edict Examiners)*, Lene Vesegaard *(Edict Mother)*, Peter Hohnen *(Edict Boy)*, Theis Ib Husfelt *(Jessie)*.

A potentially intriguing idea for a science fiction film unfortunately is dealt with in a shallow manner here. Z.P.G. means Zero Population Growth, which is the law of the land in the 21st Century. No one is allowed to have children for the next 30 years under penalty of death. In this world one must wear a gas mask to get around because of the pollution caused by previous generations. Chaplin and Reed are a married couple who work at the State Museum of Nature (artificial grass being a popular attraction there) who decide to have a baby in secret. Gordon and Cilento are their neighbors who discover the secret. Tired of the robot doll they must use in place of a child, the pair grow jealous and blackmail their friends into sharing the child. When Gordon and Cilento become too possessive, Reed and Chaplin refuse to let them see the baby again. Their angered friends report them to the authorities and the couple, along with the child, are set to be executed. However, Reed has planned ahead and runs with wife and child through the sewers until they come upon a boat and supplies he's stowed away. Together they travel by sea to a pollution-free island, ready to live a life of peace. Visually this is a wonderful film, presenting an interesting futuristic society. However, the story, which starts with an interesting premise, quickly wears down into utter tripe about the meaning of family and motherhood. Both direction and script go for easy answers and the result is a predictable, boring mess. The film is too somber for it's own good, as a strong sense of satire would have helped immensely. Real Z.P.G. groups strongly denounced the film as contrary to their goals and a complete misrepresentation. The acting is bad, with one of the more over-maudlin casts science fiction had seen in some time.

p, Thomas F. Madigan; d, Michael Campus; w, Max Ehrlich, Frank De Felitta; ph, Michael Reed, Michael Salmon (Eastmancolor); m, Jonathan Hodge; ed, Dennis Lanning; prod d, Tony Masters; art d, Harry Lange, Peter Hojmark,; set d, Erling Jorgensen; cos, Margit Brandt; spec eff, Derek Meddings; makeup, Lena Henriksen.

Science Fiction (PR:C MPAA:PG)

ZA DVUNMYA ZAYTSAMI (SEE: KIEV COMEDY, 1963, USSR)

ZABRISKIE POINT** (1970) 112m MGM-Trianon/MGM c

Mark Frechette (Mark), Daria Halprin (Daria), Rod Taylor (Lee Allen), Paul Fix (Cafe Owner), G.D.Spradlin (Lee Allen's Associate), Bill Garaway (Morty), Kathleen Cleaver (Kathleen), The Open Theater of Joe Chaikin (Lovemakers in Death Valley).

The first American film for Antonioni, ZABRISKIE POINT was his follow-up to the successful but uncharacteristically lightweight BLOW-UP (1966, his first English-speaking film). With BLOW-UP, Antonioni made an attempt to understand the English youth movement of the 1960s. Here, in ZABRISKIE POINT, Antonioni continues his search for answers in America. Unfortunately, with this picture the director has fallen into two traps--employing endless "anti-Establishment" cliches and saddling himself with Frechette, an actor who is even less compelling than BLOW-UP star David Hemmings. The picture opens in a documentary style with a meeting of college radicals discussing the meaning of revolution. Frechette, disgusted with the students' stagnant ideals, declares that he is ready to die, but not of boredom, and walks out. He soon finds himself in the midst of a campus riot and is about to shoot a policeman when the officer is gunned down by another student. Frechette runs but is identified as the killer. He takes refuge in an airfield and steals a small private plane. Flying through California's Death Valley, he spots a beat-up old Buick being driven by Halprin, a pretty, pot-smoking, meditative secretary who is traveling to Phoenix to meet with her boss (and lover?), Taylor. He rather obnoxiously decides to buzz the car with the plane, but the free-spirited Halprin doesn't seem to object. Later, Halprin and Frechette again cross paths, but by now his plane has run out of gas. She offers him a ride and before long they are holding hands at Zabriskie Point--a tourist spot marked by a small plaque which explains that a man named Zabriskie discovered mineral matter there. Halprin offers Frechette a chance to "turn on" (smoke marijuana), but he explains that he is on a "reality trip." She then tries to get him to play "death games"--they each start at opposite ends of the desert and kill everything they can; whoever kills the most things is the winner and gets to kill the loser--but he doesn't seem interested. They finally decide to make love on the ground, covering themselves with dust and sand. They, however, are not the only ones with carnal ideas--countless other couples (and trios, and quartets) have appeared in the desert and in a lengthy, psychedelic romantic interlude everyone makes love. Afterwards, Frechette and Halprin (once again alone in the desert) have a confrontation with a police officer. While Frechette hides, the officer questions Halprin who is able to satisfy his curiosity with vague answers. As the officer is leaving, however, Frechette points a gun at him. Halprin, notices the gun and stands between Frechette and the policeman. After the policeman leaves, Halprin realizes that Frechette is the one that is wanted for killing the officer at the riot. Denying the charge, Frechette tells her that he is going to return the plane and risk being captured by the police. He goes back to the plane (which has now been repainted in a psychedelic camouflage style) and heads home. Halprin heads for Phoenix. While listening to the radio she hears the news that Frechette was gunned down on the airport runway by police. She finally arrives at Taylor's modernistic desert home while he is embroiled with fellow businessmen in a land development deal. Instead of staying, Halprin gets in her car and imagines a series of devastating explosions which rock Taylor's home to the ground. Based on Antonioni's "art house" following in America and his success with 1966's BLOW-UP, MGM decided to jump on the bandwagon and gave the director carte blanche. Greatly enthralled by college radicals (as was the equally influential director Jean-Luc Godard) and the billboard culture of California, Antonioni descended upon America and delivered ZABRISKIE POINT with the help of four screenwriters (two of whom were Americans), one of which was American-icon-to-be playwright Sam Shepard. The result is a critical but relatively accurate portrait of America in the late 1960s, though the film now seems horribly dated. Antonioni concentrates chiefly on the gap between student radicals and the establishment; naturalism and plasticity; free-spirited individualism and the restraints of modern life. While Antonioni's visual sense is once again in top form (the largeness of the billboards imposes on the characters much like the landscapes of his L'AVVENTURA, 1960, and THE RED DESERT, 1964), his dialog doesn't wear well with age, suffering from an excess of "mind-expanding" hippie cliches. Had Antonioni chosen two more competent leads then perhaps these cliches would have been more tolerable. Instead, he chose two unknowns--Frechette, a listless, wholly uncharismatic actor who stumbles through his dialog (according to the

pressbook, he was cast when the director saw him "standing at a bus stop in Cambridge, Massachusetts, swearing at a man who had thrown a geranium pot at a quarreling couple"); and Halprin, a Berkeley student who dropped out of school to appear in the film (reportedly Antonioni had seen her in an unbilled part in the 1968 documentary REVOLUTION). MGM hoped that a combination of the "art house" crowd and the hippie audience would help return their $7 million investment. Their hopes went unrealized, however, when the film grossed only $892,000. MGM understandably panicked and changed the direction of the advertising campaign, gearing it strictly to a younger audience. For the first time in Antonioni's celebrated career he had a film on his hands which promised to "Blow Your Mind." After a five-year absence (not including a 1972 documentary) Antonioni returned to the screen with his finest film since L'AVVENTURA, the Jack Nicholson vehicle THE PASSENGER. As for unknowns Frechette and Halprin, they soon became romantically involved and lived together in a Boston-area commune. By 1972, Halprin had married EASY RIDER star Dennis Hopper while Frechette (after appearing in two minor foreign films, MAN AGAINST and MANY YEARS AGO) had taken a strong anti-Nixon stance. With a couple of cohorts, Frechette staged a bank robbery of a New England bank. Frechette insisted that he had robbed the federally insured bank as "a way of robbing Richard Nixon without hurting anybody." Frechette may not have gotten hurt, but he did find himself serving six to 15 years in prison. One morning in 1975, Frechette was found dead in the prison's exercise room with a barbell crushing his throat. Songs include: "Heart Beat, Pig Meat," "Come in Number 51, Your Time Is Up," "Crumbling Land" (Pink Floyd, performed by Pink Floyd), "Brother Mary" (Jerry Garcia, Robert Hunter, performed by Kaleidoscope), "Dark Star"-(Hunter, Garcia, performed by The Grateful Dead), "Mickey's Tune" (David Lindley, performed by Kaleidoscope), "Love Scene" (Garcia, performed by Garcia), "You've Got the Silver" (Mick Jagger, Keith Richard, performed by The Rolling Stones), "Sugar Babe" (Jesse Colin Young, performed by The Youngbloods), "Dance of Death" (John Fahey, performed by Fahey), "I Wish I Was a Single Girl Again" (performed by Roscoe Holcomb), "Tennessee Waltz" (Pee Wee King, Redd Stewart, sung by Patti Page).

p, Carlo Ponti; d, Michelangelo Antonioni; w, Antonioni, Fred Gardner, Sam Shepard, Tonino Guerra, Clare Peploe (based on a story by Antonioni); ph, Alfio Contini (Panavision, Metrocolor); ed, Franco Arcalli; prod d, Dean Tavoularis; set d, George R. Nelson; cos, Ray Summers; spec eff, Earl McCoy; makeup, Joe McKenney.

Drama Cas. (PR:O MPAA:R)

ZACHARIAH** (1971) 92m ABC Pictures/Cinerama Releasing c

John Rubinstein (Zachariah), Pat Quinn (Belle Starr), Don Johnson (Matthew), Country Joe and the Fish (The Cracker Band), Elvin Jones (Job Cain), Doug Kershaw (The Fiddler), William Challee (The Old Man), Robert Ball (Stage Manager), Dick Van Patten (The Dude), The James Gang (Job Cain's Band), White Lightnin' (Old Man's Band), The New York Rock Ensemble (Belle Starr's Band), Lawrence Kubik (Man in Bar).

After receiving a mail order gun (the time is the 1870s) Rubinstein and his pal, Johnson, (later of TV's "Miami Vice") get themselves in trouble and kill a man. They join up with Country Joe and the Fish, playing a group of traveling musicians who also indulge in bank robbery. Rubinstein decides he wants to be the fastest gun in the West so he takes on outlaw king Jones, an infamous black man. However, after seeing Jones and his gang, Rubinstein changes his mind. Johnson hitches up with Jones' gang while Rubinstein heads out on his own, taking up with a lonely old man (Challee). Later he heads out again and meets Quinn, taking her to bed. He realizes the city is not for him and returns to Challee. The old man dies but not before convincing the kid that violence is not the way to go in this world. Johnson, having killed Jones, comes gunning for Rubinstein but quickly sees that peace is the only way to exist and the two friends are once again united. Billed as the first "electric western" for it's abundance of rock tunes, ZACHARIAH is ridiculous without being funny. The rock format simply doesn't fit a western and the story itself is a sledgehammer morality play. The direction doesn't do much with the material, trying for myth and falling short of the goal. The script was by Austin, Bergman, Ossman, and Procter, the four zanies behind the Firesign Theater. One look at the finished film and they disowned the work.

p, George Englund, Lawrence Kubik; d, Englund; w, Joe Massot, Philip Austin, Pet er Bergman, David Ossman, Philip Proctor; ph, Jorge Stahl (Metrocolor); m, Jimmie Haskell; ed, Gary Griffen; prod d, Asheton Gordon; cos, Nino Novarese; songs, Joe McDonald, Barry Melton, The James Gang, Doug Kershaw, White Lightnin'

Western Cas. (PR:C MPAA:GP)

ZAMBA*½ (1949) 75m EL bw (GB: ZAMBA THE GORILLA)

June Vincent (Jenny), Jane Nigh (Carol), Jon Hall (Steve), Beau Bridges (Tommy), George Cooper (Doug), George O'Hanlon (Marvin), Harry Lauter (Jim), Darby Jones (Keega), Theron Jackson (Kayla), Pierre Watkin (Benton), Alphonse Martel (Gaston), Ray Corrigan (Zamba).

Minor, poorly made jungle adventure has Vincent and her 8-year-old young son Bridges (who would go on to become a fairly good adult actor) parachuting from a doomed plane into a jungle. Bridges is found by a gorilla who takes him as its own. Vincent employs the use of safari hunters, led by Hall, to find him for a tearful reunion. In between there's plenty of stock jungle footage, impossibly hokey dialog, and Corrigan in a cheap gorilla suit.

p, Maurice H. Conn; d, William Berke; w, Barbara Worth (based on a story by Conn); ph, James S. Brown; m, Raoul Kraushaar; ed, Martin G. Cohn; art d, Fred Preble.

Adventure   (PR:A MPAA:NR)

ZAMBA THE GORILLA   (SEE: ZAMBA, 1949)

ZANDY'S BRIDE**½   (1974) 116m WB c

Gene Hackman (Zandy Allan), Liv Ullmann (Hannah Lund), Eileen Heckart (Ma Allan), Harry Dean Stanton (Songer), Joe Santos (Frank Gallo), Frank Cady (Pa Allan), Sam Bottoms (Mel Allan), Susan Tyrrell (Maria Cordova), Bob Simpson (Bill Pincus), Fabian Gregory Cordova (Paco), Don Wilbanks (Farraday), Vivian Gordon (Street Girl), Alf Kjellin.

A beautifully photographed, intimate little western shot in the Big Sur area of California that boasts some fine acting but really nothing more. Hackman stars as an ill-tempered rancher who decides to end his loneliness by sending off for a mail-order bride (Ullmann). When the woman arrives she is shocked by Hackman's apparent cruelty and heartlessness toward her as he treats her like a slave. Eventually Ullmann decides to fight back against his tyranny and the shock of someone standing up to him begins to arouse long-repressed feelings of tenderness and compassion in Hackman. By the end of the film, Hackman accepts Ullmann as an equal and demonstates his ability to be a loving father when she bears his child. Despite the gorgeous scenery and strong performances, ZANDY'S BRIDE is a rather hollow film that suffers from lackadaisical scripting. There is not much plot here--and there is nothing wrong with that if the characters are interesting--but the people and their actions are cliched and predictable. There is no spontaneity and it all seems very cold and mannered. Hackman and Ullmann (with able support from Heckart, Stanton, and Bottoms) struggle to wring some life and meaning out of the material and it is through their efforts that ZANDY'S BRIDE works at all. Directed by celebrated Swedish helmsman Troell, whose films THE EMIGRANTS and THE NEW LAND were magnificent period pieces about Swedes settling in America during the 19th Century, ZANDY'S BRIDE suffered because of his inability to adjust to American production methods. In Sweden, Troell worked with a close-knit crew of 15 and had complete access to the camera--even shooting scenes himself if he chose to. Warner Bros. gave the Swedish director a union crew that numbered 100. The sheer number of these strangers intimidated the director and made him extremely nervous and self-conscious. He was also not allowed anywhere near the camera--union rules. In her book Changing Liv Ullmann relates how Troell and his actors sneaked a camera into the cabin and "rehearsed" while the director photographed the whole scene hand-holding the camera-- finally able to feel as if he controlled the set. Problems aside, ZANDY'S BRIDE is beautiful to look at, and at times an interesting look into frontier life.

p, Harvey Matofsky; d, Jan Troell; w, Marc Norman (based on the novel The Stranger by Lillian Bos Ross); ph, Jordan Cronenweth (Panavision, Technicolor); m, Michael Franks; ed, Gordon Scott; prod d, Al Brenner; set d, George Gaines; cos, Pat Norris.

Western   (PR:A MPAA:PG)

ZANZIBAR**½   (1940) 69m UNIV bw

Lola Lane (Jan Browning), James Craig (Steve Marland), Eduardo Ciannelli (Koski), Tom Fadden (Rhad Ramsey), Robert C. Fischer (The Sultan), Henry Victor (Mate Simpson), Clarence Muse (Bino), Samuel S. Hinds (Dale), Oscar O'Shea (Capt. Craig), Abner Biberman (Aba), Lionel Pape (Michael Drayton), Everett Brown (Umboga), Harry Stubbs (Alf), Ray Mala (Mayla).

A quintessential Saturday afternoon picture, designed for maximum thrills demanded by young audiences. The ancient skull of an African sultan will bring its possessor total control of the native population. It's up to the British team, led by intrepid exlorers Lane and Craig, to return the skull to its rightful jungle owners. Meanwhile, they've got to outwit some Nazis, who also want the skull, and outrun a belching volcano. Great fun with some nonsense about the Versailles Treaty tossed in for good measure. It's directed with vigor and a sense of humor and happily the action never lets up. This is the sort of film that inspired RAIDERS OF THE LOST ARK.

p, Warren Douglas; d, Harold Schuster; w, Maurice Tombragel, Maurice Wright (based on the stories "Rigadoon" by Tombragel and "River of Missing Men" by Wright); ph, Milton Krasner; ed, Milton Carruth.

Action-Adventure   (PR:A MPAA:NR)

ZAPPED!*   (1982) 96m EM c

Scott Baio (Barney), Willie Aames (Peyton), Robert Mandan (Walter Johnson), Felice Schachter (Bernadette), Scatman Crothers (Dexter Jones), Roger Bowen (Mr. Springboro), Marya Small (Mrs. Springboro), Greg Bradford (Robert), Hilary Beane (Corrine), Sue Ane Langdon (Rose), Heather Thomas (Jane), Hardy Keith (Roscoe), Curt Ayers (Art), Merritt Butrick (Cary),

Jennifer Chaplin (Melissa), Irwin Keyes ("Too Mean"), Henry Ford Robinson (Umpire), Dick Balduzzi (Waiter), Bennett Liss (Croupier), Ron Deutsch (Larry), Ed Deezen (Sheldon), Bryan O'Byrne (Father Murray), Ed Bakey (Father Gallagher), Jan Leighton (Einstein), Lawanda Page (Mrs. Jones), Rosanne Katon (Donna), Sandy Serrano (Amy), Susan Ursitti (Debby), Corine Borher (Cindy), Michael Wainwright, Jason Hickman, Phil Gilbreth, Fred Grabert, Richard Paine, Holly Rutherford, Lisa LeCover, P.J. Martin, Kym Fisher, Mieke Lanter, Hyde Anderson, James Loren, Dale Lott, Lynn Seibel, Randy Patrick, Demetre Phillips, Joshua Daniel, Daniel Dayan.

After a high school chemistry experiment explodes, teenage genius Baio discovers he has telekinetic powers. Should he use them to solve world peace? Why bother, it's more fun to magically remove dresses off girls. Utterly stupid and sexist trash, delivered up for a teen audience. As so often in teen exploitation features, the kids are hip to just about everything while adults are mindless buffoons. Surprisingly, the special effects aren't bad but they were wasted in a film that features a vomiting contest as a highlight. Skip this one.

p, Jeffrey D. Apple; d, Robert J. Rosenthal; w, Rosenthal, Bruce Rubin; ph, Daniel Pearl (CFI Color); m, Charles Fox; ed, Bob Bring, Robert Ferretti; art d, Boyd Willat; spec eff, Robert Blalack, Dick Albain, Ron Nary; m/l, Steve Geyer.

Comedy   Cas.   (PR:O MPAA:R)

ZARAK**½   (1956, Brit.) 94m COL c

Victor Mature (Zarak Khan), Michael Wilding (Maj. Ingram), Anita Ekberg (Salma), Bonar Colleano (Biri), Finlay Currie (The Mullah), Bernard Miles (Hassu), Frederick Valk (Haji Khan), Eunice Gayson (Cathy Ingram), Peter Illing (Ahmad), Eddie Byrne (Kasim), Patrick McGoohan (Moor Larkin), Harold Goodwin (Sgt. Higgins), Andre Morell (Atherton), Alec Mango (Akbar), Oscar Quitak (Youssuff), George Margo (Chief Jailor), Arnold Marle (Flower Seller), Conrad Phillips (Young Officer).

This routine desert saga, produced by the team that would soon bring the James Bond series to the screen (coproducer Broccoli and director Young), is enlivened up somewhat by the outstanding action scenes handled by associate directors Yakima Canutt and John Gilling. Mature stars as the title character, a bandit chief whose outlaw gang roams India's northwest frontier raping and pillaging. Wilding, a British major, is sent to capture the unruly bandits and succeeds. His victory over the outlaws is short-lived, however, when Mature manages to escape with the help of Illing, a sadistic nomad hell-bent on slaughtering the British. When Mature and Illing's men attack the British garrison, there is much bloodshed and Illing captures Wilding and tortures him. Mature, who, like Wilding, has developed a mutual sense of respect for his adversary during his pursuit and capture, is outraged by Illing's treatment of the Britisher and gives his life to save him. Gorgeous Technicolor and CinemaScope photography shows off the picturesque locations.

p, Irving Allen, Albert J. Broccoli; d, Terence Young; w, Richard Maibaum (based on the novel Story of Zarak Khan); ph, John Wilcox, Ted Moore, Cyril Knowles (CinemaScope, Technicolor); ed, Alan Osbiston, Bert Rule; md, Muir Mathieson; art d, John Box; m/l, "Climb Up the Wall" Hosseini, Norman Gimbel, sung by Yana.

Adventure   (PR:C MPAA:NR)

ZARDOZ*   (1974, Brit.) 104m FOX c

Sean Connery (Zed), Charlotte Rampling (Consuella), Sara Kestelman (May), Sally Anne Newton (Avalow), John Alderton (Friend), Niall Buggy (Zardoz/Arthur Frayn), Bosco Hogan (George Saden), Jessica Swift (Apathetic), Bairbre Dowling (Star), Christopher Casson (Old Scientist), Reginald Jarman (Death).

Frequently brilliant director Boorman--always an interesting visual stylist--falls flat on his face with this pretentious piece of banal science fiction claptrap which presents its dull ideas in such a confused and annoying fashion as to anger even the most devoted fan of the genre. The year is 2293 and the Earth has been divided into two distinct camps. The Brutals are a race of crude and violent people who live in a desolated area known as the Outlands. Their population is kept under control by an elite group of killers known as the Exterminators. The Exterminators worship a pagan god called Zardoz who comes to them in the form of a giant stone head which floats into their domain and spews guns and ammunition out of its mouth. One of the Exterminators, Connery, begins to question his faith in Zardoz and stows away inside the mouth of the giant head to see where it will take him. Before it lands he spies a man inside the head with him, Buggy, and immediately shoots him. Buggy falls to his death from the mouth of the flying stone head. The ship lands in an area called the Vortex which is populated by a group known as the Eternals. The Eternals are the sons and daughters of a scientist who had figured out how to sustain life forever. Because they will live forever there is no need for procreation, therefore all the men are impotent. The scientists also developed a super-computer, known as the Tabernacle, that controls all life-control systems in the Vortex, including a force field that keeps the Brutals out of the Vortex. Among the Eternals, however, are two other subgroups: the Apathetics, people who cannot deal with the boredom of their immortality and have reverted to a catatonic state; and the Renegades, Eternals who have been made old and senile. The Eternals have been using the Exterminators to make slaves of the Brutals so that enough wheat can be grown to feed those in the Vortex. When Connery is discovered in the Vortex, his presence causes chaos. A genetic engineer, Kestelman, wants to study him, while Rampling sees him as a threat and wants him destroyed. Kestelman manages to win some time and discovers that Connery is genetically superior to all Eternals. Meanwhile, another Eternal who has befriended the brute-man, Alderton (cleverly named "Friend"), shows him to a group of Apathetics who immediately become aroused by his presence. During what seems like an eternity of screen time, Connery manages to totally destroy life in the Vortex by figuring out the computer and then destroying it. A group of Eternal women who are pregnant by Connery, including Kestelmen, ride off into the Outlands under his protection, while he wins over Rampling and they run off together and live in a cave. During Connery and Rampling's escape, the now mortal Eternals beg the marauding Exterminators (who have invaded the Vortex because the force field is no longer operative) to kill them. In the cave, Connery and Rampling produce a son, grow old, and die. ZARDOZ (the word is a contraction of *The Wizard of Oz*, the book which inspired those clever Eternals to trick the Exterminators) is a mess. The first five minutes of the film–where the giant stone head floats into the Outland and spews guns at the Exterminators–are visually stunning. The image of the stone head is the most haunting and successful aspect of the film. From the moment Connery lands in the Vortex, the film collapses into a frustrating mess of pompous dialog, bad costuming, dull performances, and just plain lousy narrative storytelling. The structure of the scenes where plot points are developed and revealed seems haphazard and unnecessarily obtuse. Director Boorman has made some brilliant films where he toys with a genre in order to recreate it. ZARDOZ is pretentious sludge with some memorable visuals. By the end of this insufferable film the viewer is left to ponder the deep philosophical notion that it is better to die than to live forever. Big deal. Frankly, it is better to die than to sit through ZARDOZ more than once.

p,d&w, John Boorman; ph, Geoffrey Unsworth (Panavision, DeLuxe Color); m, David Munrow; ed, John Merritt; prod d, Anthony Pratt; set d, John Hoesli, Martin Atkinson; cos, Christel Kruse Boorman; spec eff, Gerry Johnston; makeup, Charles Staffell, Basil Newall.

Science Fiction   **Cas.**   **(PR:O   MPAA:R)**

ZARTE HAUT IN SCHWARZER SEIDE
(SEE: DANIELLA BY NIGHT, 1962, Fr./Ger.)

ZATO ICHI CHIKEMURI KAIDO (SEE: ZATOICHI CHALLENGED, 1970, Jap.)

ZATO ICHI KENKATABI (SEE: ZATOICHI, 1968, Jap.)

ZATO ICHI TO YONJINBO (SEE: ZATOICHI MEETS YOJIMBO, 1970, Jap.)

ZATOICHI**½ (1968, Jap.) 90m Daiei c (ZATOICHI KENKATABI; AKA: ZATOICHI AND THE SCOUNDRELS; ZATOICHI ON THE ROAD)

Shintaro Katsu (*Zatoichi*), Shiho Fujimura (*Omitsu*), Ryuzo Shimada (*Jingoro*), Reiko Fujiwara (*Ohisa*), Matasaburo Niwa (*Yamada*), Yoshio Yoshida (*Tomegoro*), Sonosuke Sawamura (*Tobei*), Shosaku Sugiyama (*Hikozo*), Yutaka Nakamura (*Matsu*).

Katsu, a blind swordsman and masseur in feudal Japan, is talked into selling his services to Sugiyama, who is preparing to battle Sawamura. En route to Sugiyama, Katsu and a companion are attacked by three of Sawamura's men. Though his friend is murdered, Katsu manages to fight back and kill the three. Next, he honors a dying man's request and accompanies Fujimura, a young woman, to her parents' home. She is kidnaped but Katsu, who has developed supersensory powers to overcome his blindness, manages to find and rescue her. Upon being returned home the girl is once more taken by Shimada. Fujimura is brought to Sawamura as Katsu fights off more members of Sawamura's family. He learns that a plot has been hatched for his murder by members of both Sawamura's and his own family. Katsu fights all off handily and finally gets Fujimura home safely.

p, Ikuro Kubokawa; d, Kimiyoshi Yasuda; w, Minoru Inuzuka (based on a story by Kan Shimozawa); ph, Shozo Honda (Daiei Scope,Eastmancolor); m, Akira Ifukube; art d, Yoshinobu Nishioka; fights staged by, Shohei Miyauchi.

Action   **(PR:A   MPAA:NR)**

ZATOICHI CHALLENGED** (1970, Jap.) 87m Daiei c (ZATOICHI CHIKEMURI KAIDO)

Shintaro Katsu (*Zatoichi*), Jushiro Konoe, Miwa Takada, Yukiji Asaoka, Mie Nakao, Mikiko Tsubouchi, Tomoo Koike.

While escorting a young boy home to his father, blind samurai Katsu is attacked by five assassins. Katsu kills the attackers and then is joined by a mysterious samurai who helps fight off a second gang. Upon arriving in the

boy's home town, they learn the father is being held by a gang of black marketers. The second samurai reveals himself to be an agent as signed to destroy the gang. Katsu agrees to help if the man will aid in freeing the boy's father, but the man cannot stray from his mission, so he and Katsu fight the predictable duel, Japanese customs sometimes make for American confusion.

d, Kenji Misumi; w, Ryozo Kasahara (based on a story by Kan Shimozawa); ph, Chishi Makiura (Daiei Scope, Eastmancolor); m, Akira Ifukube; art d, Shigenori Shimoishizaka.

Action   **(PR:A   MPAA:NR)**

ZATOICHI JOGKUTABI (SEE: SHOWDOWN FOR ZATOICHI, 1968, Jap.)

ZATOICHI MEETS YOJIMBO**½ (1970, Jap.) 90m Katsu/Daiei-Bijou of Japan c (ZATO ICHI TO YOJIMBO)

Shintari Katsu (*Zatoichi*), Toshiro Mifune (*Yojimbo*), Mori Kirshida (*Kuzuryu*), Kanjuro Arashi (*Hyoroku*), Osamu Takizawa (*Eboshiya the Elder*), Ayako Wakao (*Umeno the Courtesan*), Masakane Yonekura (*Boss Masagoro*), Shigeru Kamiyama, Toshiyuki Hosokaw.

Katsu, the blind samurai, grows tired of his violent life and returns to his home village, finding its been taken over by gangster Yonekura. Yonekura orders his bodyguard, Mifune, to attack Katsu. In the battle, Mifune gains respect for the blind man's powers, but the two remain enemies. Katsu is taken in by Takizawa, Yonekura's father, and it turns out Mifune is a spy seeking gold belonging to Takizawa. When Takizawa's younger son shows up demanding the gold, Takizawa refuses to cooperate and the son kills him. Katsu finds the gold hidden in a statue, but a gust of wind blows it all away before anyone can claim it.

d, Kihachi Okamoto; w, Tetsuro Yoshida, Okamoto (based on a story by Kan Shimozawa); ph, Kazuo Miyagawa (Daiei Scope, Eastmancolor); m, Akira Ifukube; art d, Yoshinobu Nishioka.

Action   **(PR:C   MPAA:NR)**

ZATOICHI'S CONSPIRACY**½ (1974, Jap.) 90m Toho c

Shintaro Katsu (*Zatoichi*), Eiji Okada (*Shinbei*), Kei Sato (*Bailiff*), Takashi Shimura (*Sakubei*), Yukie Toake (*Omiyo*).

Katsu repeats his role as the blind swordsman for the 25th time or so in this adventure. After years of fighting and wandering he passes through his birthplace and finds that his childhood friend, Okada, is now the gang chief in the area, stealing all the peasants have. With his mastery of the sword and his unnaturally sharp hearing, Katsu slices up Okada and his lackeys with little difficulty and restores peace, only to hit the road again for the next sequel. (In Japanese; English subtitles.)

p, Shintaro Katsu, Nishioica Kozen; d, Kimoyoshi Yasuda; w, Kan Shimozawa; ph, Shozo Honda; m, Akira Ifukube.

Adventure   **(PR:A   MPAA:NR)**

ZAZA** (1939) 83m PAR bw

Claudette Colbert (*Zaza*), Herbert Marshall (*Dufresne*), Bert Lahr (*Cascart*), Helen Westley (*Anais*), Constance Collier (*Nathalie*), Genevieve Tobin (*Florianne*), Walter Catlett (*Marlardot*), Ann Todd (*Toto*), Rex O'Malley (*Bussey*), Ernest Cossart (*Marchand*), Rex Evans (*Michelin*), Robert C. Fischer (*Pierre*), Janet Waldo (*Simone*), Dorothy Tree (*Mme. Dufresne*), Duncan Renaldo (*Animal Trainer*), Olive Tell (*Jeanne Liseron*), John Sutton, Michael Brooke, Philip Warren (*Dandies*), Alexander Leftwich (*Larou*), Frederika Brown (*Pierre's Wife*), Clarence Harvey, John Power (*Conductors*), Maude Hume (*Woman*), Olaf Hytten (*Waiter*), Tom Ricketts (*Old Gentleman*), Frank Puglia (*Rug Merchant*), Monty Woolley (*Fouget/ Interviewer*), Dorothy Dayton (*Dancer*), Billie Beurne, Darlyn Heckley, Virginia Larsen, Grace Richey, Virginia Rooney, Lillian Ross, Peggy Russell (*Tiller Girls*), Harriette Haddon, Helaine Moler, Dorothy White, Louise Seidel (*Dancers*), Dorothy Hamburg, Emily La Rue, Mae Packer, Colleen Ward, Jeanne Blanche, Penny Gill, Jacqueline Dax (*French Girls*), Alice Keating (*Maid*).

This is a lesser version of a popular play (and later opera) which casts Colbert in the title role as a featured cabaret girl. She meets Marshall, a married man, and the two enter into a torrid affair. This could have been a moving drama but unfortunately the restrictions imposed by the Hays office drain the tempestuous life needed for the material to succeed. The cabaret numbers are also lackluster and don't help to flesh out the film. Lahr, a wonderful burlesque comedian, is never given a chance to show his stuff, and Colbert projects too much wholesomeness for the part. A disappointment from director Cukor, who clearly was capable of a better showing with such material. Previous versions include a 1909 Italian silent, a 1915 silent, and a 1923 Gloria Swanson vehicle.

p, Albert Lewin; d, George Cukor; w, Zoe Akins (based on the play by Pierre Breton, Charles Simon); ph, Charles Lang, Jr.; m, Frederick Hollander, Frank Loesser; ed, Edward Dmytryk; art d, Hans Dreier, Robert Usher; ch,

LeRoy Prinz; m/l, "Hello My Darling," Frederick Hollander, Loesser (sung by Claudette Colbert), "Zaza," Hollander, Loesser (sung by Colbert, Bert Lahr).

Drama (PR:C MPAA:NR)

ZAZIE***½ (1961, Fr.) 86m Nouvelles Editions de Films/Astor c
(ZAZIE DANS LE METRO; AKA: ZAZIE IN THE UNDERGROUND; ZAZIE IN THE SUBWAY)

Catherine Demongeot (Zazie), Philippe Noiret (Uncle Gabriel), Hubert Deschamps (Turnadot), Antoine Roblot (Charles), Annie Fratellini (Mado), Carla Marlier (Albertine), Vittorio Caprioli (Trouscaillon), Yvonne Clech (Mme. Mouaque), Nicholas Bataille (Fedor), Jacques Dufilho (Gridoux), Odette Picquet (Mme. Lalochere), Marc Doelnitz (Mons. Coquetti), Jacques Gheusi, Louis Lalanne, Little Bara, Georges Faye, Sylvine Delannoy, Jean-Marie DeConinck, Paul Vally, Jean-Yves Bouvier, Jean-Pierre Posier, Jeanne Allard, Jacqueline Doyen, Arlette Balkiss, Alegrina, Virginie Merlin, Irene Chabrier, Christine Howard.

Demongeot is an 11-year-old nuisance who must spend a few days with her uncle Noiret in Paris after her mother goes off with a new lover. She wants nothing more than to ride the subway but a strike by the Paris Metro workers prevents this. The foul-mouthed girl blames it on grownups but decides to have fun in spite of this setback. She takes Noiret on a mad chase through the great town and at one point he's forced to leap from the Eiffel Tower using a balloon as a parachute! Finally she is granted her wish when the strike ends, but Demongeot is tuckered out from all the loony goings on and ends up falling asleep on the way home. This is a great romp with some wonderfully wild moments. A fine early effort from the director of ATLANTIC CITY and MURMUR OF THE HEART.

p&d, Louis Malle; w, Malle, Jean-Paul Rappeneau (based on the book Zazie dans le Metro by Raymond Queneau); ph, Henri Raichi (Eastmancolor); m, Andre Pontin, Fiorenzo Carpi; ed, Kenout Peltier; art d, Bernard Evein; cos, Marc Doelnitz; spec eff, Locafilms; makeup, Aida Carange.

Comedy (PR:A MPAA:NR)

ZAZIE DANS LE METRO (SEE: ZAZIE, 1961, Fr.)

ZBEHOVIA A PUTNICI (SEE: DESERTER AND THE NOMADS, THE, 1969, Czech.)

ZEBRA IN THE KITCHEN**½ (1965) 92m MGM c

Jay North (Chris Carlyle), Martin Milner (Dr. Del Hartwood), Andy Devine (Branch Hawksbill), Joyce Meadows (Isobel Moon), Jim Davis (Adam Carlyle), Dorothy Green (Anne Carlyle), Karen Green (Wilma Carlyle), Vaughn Taylor (Councilman Pew), John Milford (Sgt. Freebee), Tris Coffin (Councilman Lawrence), Merritt Bohn (Chief of Police), Robert Clarke (Sheriff), Percy Helton (Mr. Richardson), Jimmy Stiles (Tim), Dal Jenkins (Kookie), Gordon Westcourt (Ribs), Gary Judis (Greenie), Robert Lowery (Preston Heston), Wayne Thomas (Newscaster), Doodles Weaver (Nearsighted Man), Jon Lormer (Judge), Vince Barnett (Man in Man-hole), Phil Arnold (Man in Tub).

Pleasant family fare has North forced to give up his pet puma when his family moves to a small town. The animal hides out in a trailer and the clan unwittingly brings it with them to the new home. North's father, Davis, has the boy give the pet to the local zoo, run by Milner. Though accommodations are nice, North feels sad that the animals must be locked in cages. When he has a chance, he steals Milner's keys and lets all the beasts loose, and mayhem results with hippos, lions, elephants, zebras, monkeys, and also the beloved puma running amok. Finally, the beasts are herded up and the town votes on some much needed new funding to improve zoo conditions. It's all rather silly for adult viewers but then that wasn't the intended audience. Directed by the creator of TV's "Flipper."

p&d, Ivan Tors; w, Art Arthur (based on a story by Elgin Ciampi); ph, Lamar Boren (Metrocolor); m, Warren Barker; ed, Warren Adams; art d, George W. Davis, Addison Hehr; set d, Henry Grace, Jack Mills; m/l, title song, Hal Hopper (sung by the Standells); makeup, William Tuttle; animals, supplied by Africa U.S.A.

Children's Comedy (PR:AAA MPAA:G)

ZEE & CO. (SEE: X, Y & ZEE, 1972, Brit.)

ZELIG** (1983) 80m Orion/WB bw-c

Woody Allen (Leonard Zelig), Mia Farrow (Dr. Eudora Fletcher), John Buckwalter (Dr. Sindell), Marvin Chatinover (Glandular Diagnosis Doctor), Stanley Swerdlow (Mexican Food Doctor), Paul Nevens (Dr. Birsky), Howard Erskine (Hypodermic Doctor), George Hamlin (Experimental Drugs Doctor), Ralph Bell, Richard Whiting, Will Hussong (Other Doctors), Robert Iglesia (Man in Barber Chair), Eli Resnick (Man in Park), Edward McPhillips (Scotsman), Gale Hansen (Freshman No. 1), Michael Jeeter (Freshman No. 2), Peter McRobbie (Workers Rally Speaker), Sol Lomita (Martin Geist), Mary Louise Wilson (Sister Ruth), Alice Beardsley (Telephone Operator),

Paula Trueman (Woman at Telephone), Charles Denney (Actor Doctor), Michael Kell (Actor Koslow), Garrett Brown (Actor Zelig), Sharon Ferrol (Miss Baker), Richard Litt (Charles Koslow), Dimitri Vassiloupoulos (Martinez), John Rothman (Paul Deghuee), Stephanie Farrow (Sister Meryl), Francis Beggins (City Hall Speaker), Jean Trowbridge (Dr. Fletcher's Mother), Ken Chapin (On- Camera Interviewer), Gerald Klein, Vincent Jerosa (Hearst Guests), Deborah Rush (Lita Fox), Stanley Simmonds (Lita's Lawyer), Robert Berger (Zelig's Lawyer), Jeanine Jackson (Helen Gray), Erma Campbell (Zelig's Wife), Anton Marco (Wrist Victim), Louise Deitch (House Painting Victim), Bernice Dowis (Vilification Woman), John Doumanian (Greek Waiter), Ed Lane (Man on Telephone), Marianne Tatum (Actress Fletcher), Will Holt (Rally Chancellor), Cole Palen (Zelig's Stunt Double), Pam Barber (Fletcher's Stunt Double), Bernie Herold (Carter Dean), Marshall Coles, Sr. (Calvin Turner), Ellen Garrison (Older Doctor Fletcher), Jack Cannon (Mike Geibell), Theodore R. Smits (Ted Bierbauer), Sherman Loud (Older Paul), Elizabeth Rothschild (Older Sister Meryl), Kuno Spunholz (Oswald), Susan Sontag, Irving Howe, Saul Bellow, Bricktop, Dr. Bruno Bettelheim, Prof. John Morton Blum, Ed Herlihy, Dwight Weist, Gordon Gould, Windy Craig, Jurgen Kuehn (Themselves).

Easily Allen's worst film, ZELIG relies on gimmick filmmaking to deliver a simple, heavy-handed message. The premise is an interesting one, telling in documentary fashion the story of Leonard Zelig (Allen), a minor celebrity of the Depression era, whose abilities as a "human chameleon" astounded the world. Using pseudo-documentary footage, Allen's story unfolds. He is a man desperate to be accepted by others, who goes to extraordinary lengths to become one of the crowd. Footage is seen of Allen waiting in the on-deck circle as Babe Ruth is batting, and other clips show him as an Oriental, a black, and growing a beard as he turns into a Hassidic rabbi. His case captures the imagination of America, as well as the attentions of Farrow, a psychiatrist. She hypnotizes Allen and learns that he only wants to be loved, thus the reason behind his uncanny transformations. Songs are written about Allen, his life inspires a Warner Bros. picture, and a new dance, "The Chameleon," sweeps the country. Interspersed within this black and white cinematic collage are color sequences of such social commentators as Sontag, Bettleheim, and Howe giving their own interpretations of Allen's unusual condition and what it means. Farrow falls in love with Allen, but he marries another woman. After some legal troubles Allen mysteriously disappears, but Farrow later discovers he has become a Nazi. She goes to Germany and attends a Nazi rally, where Allen spots her from a podium. Eventually they make a daring escape from the Nazis and finally marry. Allen passes away, content that he has finally developed his own personality. In such films as ANNIE HALL and MANHATTAN, Allen showed an excellent gift for making statements with comic subtlety. In ZELIG, he tosses this aside and lets every seam show. He states his theme often, and at one point pathetically moans to Farrow, "I want to be liked." As if this weren't enough, the social critics' intellectual ponderings drive home Allen's message like a jackhammer. Allen's other films take audience intelligence as a given; ZELIG lectures as though viewers aren't clever enough to figure things out for themselves. His recreation of period material is fine but his gimmick of appearing in found footage of the 1920s and 1930s grows wearisome. Though this is his shortest work, at times it feels like his longest. Some throwaway gags, such as an all-Hassidic version of "A Midsummer Night's Dream," or a drug that causes Allen to walk on walls, recall the filmmaker's earlier work in his other pseudo- documentary TAKE THE MONEY AND RUN (1969). The differences between the two are obvious, and remind viewers how clever Allen can be when he isn't mired in attempts to provide deep philosophical meaning. His recreation of a 1930s programmer here (titled THE CHANGING MAN) points towards the direction he would take in 1985 with his much more graceful THE PURPLE ROSE OF CAIRO. Hyman's songs for the film, all of which capture the sound of 1930s pop music nicely, include: "Leonard the Lizard," "Doin' the Chameleon," "Chameleon Days," "You May Be Six People, but I Love You," "Reptile Eyes," "The Changing Man Concerto."

p, Robert Greenhut; d&w, Woody Allen; ph, Gordon Willis; m, Dick Hyman; ed, Susan E. Morse; prod d, Mel Bourne; art d, Speed Hopkins; set d, Les Bloom, Janet Rosenbloom; cos, Santo Loquasto; spec eff, Joel Hynick, Stuart Robinson, R. Greenberg Associates; ch, Danny Daniels; makeup, John Caglione; animation, Steven Plastrik.

Comedy Cas. (PR:A MPAA:PG)

ZENOBIA** (1939) 71m UA bw (AKA: ELEPHANTS NEVER FORGET)

Oliver Hardy (Dr. Tibbitt), Harry Langdon (Prof. McCrackle), Billie Burke (Mrs. Tibbitt), Alice Brady (Mrs. Carter), James Ellison (Jeff Carter), Jean Parker (Mary Tibbitt), June Lang (Virginia), Olin Howland (Atty. Culpepper), J. Farrell MacDonald (Judge), Stepin Fetchit (Zero), Hattie McDaniel (Dehlia), Phillip Hurlie (Zeke), Hobart Cavanaugh (Mr. Dover), Clem Bevans (Sheriff), Chester Conklin (Farmer), Tommy Mack (Butcher), Robert Dudley (Court Clerk), The Hall Johnson Choir.

Hardy without Laurel is like popcorn without salt, not quite satisfying. Here the rotund comic is teamed with former silent clown Langdon (a much overlooked artist in his own right). The latter is a carnival man who owns the title character, a loving pachyderm. When the elephant comes down with illness it's doctor Hardy who brings her back to health. The beast falls for the new man and Langdon takes him to court for "alienation of affections." It all works out in the end; the elephant returns to Langdon just b efore she gives birth. As a comedy this is fair but the duo doesn't really click. Hardy clearly needed his regular partner and Langdon, his famed baby face now aged, was well past his prime. Still worth a look as an oddity for comedy buffs.

p, Hal Roach; d, Gordon Douglas; w, Corey Ford (based on a story by Walter DeLeon, Arnold Belgard); ph, Karl Struss; m, Marvin Hatley; ed, Bert Jordan; art d, Charles D. Hall; cos. Omar Kiam; spec eff, Roy Seawright.

Comedy (PR:A MPAA:NR)

ZEPPELIN**½ (1971, Brit.) 97m WB c

Michael York (*Geoffrey Richter-Douglas*), Elke Sommer (*Erika Altschul*), Peter Carsten (*Maj. Alfred Tauntler*), Marius Goring (*Prof. Christian Altschul*), Anton Diffring (*Col. Johann Hirsch*), Andrew Keir (*Lt. Comdr. Horst von Gorian*), Rupert Davies (*Capt. Whitney, R.N.*), Alexandra Stewart (*Stephanie Ross*), William Marlow (*Lt. Comdr. Colin Anderson*), Alan Rothwell (*Bradner*), Richard Hurndall (*Rear Admiral*), John Gill (*Meier*), Michael Robbins (*Scot's Sergeant*), Ben Howard (*Jamie Fergusson*), George Mikell (*German Officer*), Arnold Diamond (*Maj. Proudfoot*), Clive Morton (*Lord Delford*), Bryan Coleman (*Col. Whippen*), Gary Waldhorn (*Harlich*), Ronald Adam (*Prime Minister*), Frazer Hines (*Radio Operator*), Ruth Kettlewell (*Mrs. Parker*), Ray Lonnen (*Sgt. Grant*), John Clark (*Naval Captain*), Peter Frazer (*Marine*), Matthew Long (*Naval Gunner*).

Mediocre WW I adventure has York a Scotch-German lad persuaded by the British Admiralty to pretend to defect to the Germans in order to steal the secret plans to Germany's latest super-dirigible. In Germany he quickly reestablishes his long-standing friendship with Goring, designer of the zeppelin in question, as well as Goring's wife, Sommer. Sommer quickly deduces that York is a spy, but she says nothing in order to protect her husband. Although he suffers from vertigo, York agrees to go on a test flight of the craft, but once aloft it is announced that the airship is going on a secret mission–first to Norway to pick up mustard gas, bombs, and soldiers, then to Scotland to break into the secret archives where the British have moved all their national treasures for the duration. The big prize they seek is the Magna Carta, and they believe British morale will crumble if this document is stolen. York kills the radio operator aboard and tries to contact the British, but fails. The ship lands near the Scottish castle and the Germans pull off their well- choreographed assault. York breaks away and reaches the guardhouse, but the men there refuse to believe him (he's still in his German uniform). Eventually he convinces them and they call London. Soon reinforcements arrive and the Germans retreat back to the ship with heavy losses. Most of them don't make it aboard, including Goring, who kills himself over his horror at the misuse of his great invention. York and Sommer make it aboard, though, and start back to Germany with the remainder of the crew. The British dispatch fighter planes after the airship and it continues to lose altitude over the North Sea. Finally York and Sommer jump into the water as the craft explodes and they swim ashore in neutral Holland to sit out the rest of the war. Certainly not a good film, ZEPPELIN fails on nearly every count. The script is ludicrous, the acting mediocre, and the direction indifferent. On the plus side, though, the battle scenes are well done and the real star of the film, the dirigible itself, is quite impressive. Tragedy struck during the production when a plane and a helicopter collided, killing four persons, including second unit cameraman Skeets Kelly, a veteran of such films as CHITTY CHITTY BANG BANG and THE BATTLE OF BRITAIN. Perhaps the most interesting thing about ZEPPELIN is the fact that its executive producer, J. Ronald Getty, is the son of oil billionaire J. Paul Getty.

p, Owen Crump; d, Etienne Perier; w, Arthur Rowe, Donald Churchill (based on a story by Crump); ph, Alan Hume (Panavision, Technicolor); m, Roy Budd; ed, John Shirley; prod d, Fernando Carrere; art d, Bert Davey; set d, Arthur Taksen; cos, Sue Yelland; spec eff, Cliff Richardson; makeup, Neville Smallwood; tech adv, Dr. Friedrich Sturm.

War Drama (PR:A MPAA:G)

ZERO HOUR, THE* (1939) 62m REP bw

Frieda Inescort (*Linda Marsh*), Otto Kruger (*Julian Forbes*), Adrienne Ames (*Susan*), Don Douglas (*Brewster*), Jane Darwell (*Sophie*), J.M. Kerrigan (*Timothy*), Ann Todd (*Beth*), Leonard Carey (*Butler*), Sarah Padden (*Sister Theodosia*), Ferris Taylor (*Weber*), Willard Parker (*Lansdowne*), Landers Stevens (*Doctor*).

Insipid, poorly filmed story about a young girl (Inescort) who, nurtured by producer Kruger, has become a Broadway star. Now they want to marry so they head off to the country to find a justice of the peace. The car runs out of gas and while flagging down help Kruger is hit by another vehicle. He's paralyzed but Inescort marries him anyway. Nine years later Inescort wants to adopt a child. Douglas, a widower, has a previous claim to the child she wants. During their visits to the child, the two meet and soon begin an affair. Kruger, observing this turn of events, commits suicide, feeling that he is in the way of his wife's happiness. Unusually morbid tearjerker.

p, Sol C. Siegel; d, Sidney Salkow; w, Garrett Fort (based on a story by Fort); ph, Ernest Miller; ed, William Morgan; md, Cy Feuer; art d, John Victor

Mackay; cos, Adele Palmer.

Drama (PR:C MPAA:NR)

ZERO HOUR!*** (1957) 81m PAR bw

Dana Andrews (*Ted Stryker*), Linda Darnell (*Ellen Stryker*), Sterling Hayden (*Treleaven*), Elroy "Crazylegs" Hirsch (*Capt. Wilson*), Geoffrey Toone (*Dr. Baird*), Jerry Paris (*Tony Decker*), Peggy King (*Stewardess*), Carole Eden (*Mrs. Wilson*), Charles Quinlivan (*Burdick*), Raymond Ferrell (*Joey Stryker*), David Thursby (*Whitmond*), Russell Thorson (*Flight Dispatcher*), Joanne Wade (*Baby Sitter*), Richard Keith (*Station Manager*), Steve London (*Copilot Stewart*), John Ashley (*TV Singer*), Willis Bouchey (*RCAF Doctor*), Maxine Cooper, Noel Drayton, Fintan Meyler, Larry Thor, Robert Stevenson, Mary Newton, Willard Sage, Will White, Hope Summers, Arthur Hanson, Roy Gordon.

The crew of a Canadian passenger plane comes down with food poisoning and cannot finish the flight. WW II fighter pilot Andrews must take the controls and land the plane. Can he overcome his neurosis about flying? Can he rekindle wife Darnell's love for him? Can ground controller Hayden bring it all to a happy ending? Great fun, based on a TV drama written by Hailey, who would go on to pen the novel and film AIRPORT, ZERO HOUR! also served as the basis for the wild comedy AIRPLANE!

p, John Champion; d, Hall Bartlett; w, Arthur Hailey, Bartlett, Champion (based on a story by Hailey from his television play); ph, John F. Warren; m, Ted Dale; ed, John C. Fuller.

Drama (PR:A MPAA:NR)

ZERO IN THE UNIVERSE zero (1966) 85m Jock Livingston bw

Jock Livingston (*Zero*), George Bartenieff (*Steinmetz*), Pamela Badyk (*Vivian*), George Moorse (*Peep*), Rob Du Mee (*Dubois*), Henke Raaf (*Gillomovitch Mullendorf*), Louis Lehmans (*The Major*).

Two men and a secretary are constantly getting in one another's way in improbable places, and in strange situations and guises. So much for the story. This poses as avante-gardefilmmaking but like so many "art" films the result is a confusing mess, laden with symbolism understood only by the filmmakers. A worthless piece, though the actors take it all with the utmost seriousness. One consolation – it is well photographed.

p, Jock Livingstom; d, George Moorse; w, Livingston, Moorse; ph, Gerard Vandenberg; m, Donald Cherry, ed. Moorse.

Drama (PR:O MPAA:NR)

ZERO POPULATION GROWTH (SEE: Z.P.G., 1972)

ZERO TO SIXTY* (1978) 96m First Artists c (AKA: REPO)

Darren McGavin (*Mike*), Denise Nickerson (*Larry*), Joan Collins (*Gloria*), Dick Martin (*Attorney*), Sylvia Miles (*Flo*), Hudson Brothers (*Repo Crew*).

A divorced man and a 16 year-old girl work together repossessing cars from their owners. McGavin is fun to watch, but the rest of the cast quickly gets on one's nerves. The same idea was done much better in 1984's REPOMAN.

p, Katherine Brown; d, Don Weis; w, W. Lyle Richardson (based on a story by Peg Shirley, Judith Bustany); ph, Don Birnkrant; art d, Jim Newport.

Comedy Cas. (PR:C MPAA:PG)

00-2 MOST SECRET AGENTS*½ (1965, Ital.) 83m Mega/Sherpix-AA c (AGENTI SEGRETISSIMI; AKA: OH! THOSE MOST SECRET AGENTS; WORST SECRET AGENTS)

Franco Franchi (*Franco*), Ciccio Ingrassia (*Ciccio*), Ingrid Schoeller, Aroldo Tieri, Annie Gorassini, Carla Calo, Poldo Bendandi, Luca Sportelli, Enzo Andronico, Nando Angelini, Connie Jorgenson, Francesco Torrisi.

Franchi and Ingrassia are two would-be thieves who get trapped by some foreign spies when they break into a villa. One of the spies plants a phony formula for a secret weapon in the teeth of one of the bumblers and a madcap chase ensues. The spies let the enemy know that the two have the "real" formula. As it turns out, they do have it and the chase intensifies. Finally, Americans help the pair out by taking the encoded teeth and the two fools go back to their life of petty crime. Inane and boring comedy.

p, Antonio Colantuoni; d, Lucio Fulci; w, Fulci, Vittorio Metz, Amedeo Sollazzo, Mario Guerra, Vittorio Vighi (based on a story by Metz); ph, Adalberto Albertini (Eastmancolor); m, Piero Umiliani; ed, Ornella Micheli; art d, Giuseppe Ranieri; spec eff, Sergio Canevari.

Comedy (PR:A MPAA:NR)

ZHENITBA BALZAMINOVA (SEE: MARRIAGE OF BALZAMINOV, THE, 1966, USSR)

ZHENITBA BALZAMINOVA
        (SEE: MARRIAGE OF BALZAMINOVA, THE, 1966, USSR)

ZHILI-BYLI STARIK SO STARUKHOY
        (SEE: THERE WAS AN OLD COUPLE, 1967, USSR)

ZIEGFELD FOLLIES***   (1945) 110m MGM c

William Powell (*The Great Ziegfeld*), "ZIEGFELD DAYS:" Fred Astaire, Bunin's Puppets, "MEET THE LADIES:" Astaire, Lucille Ball, "LOVE:" Lena Horne, "THIS HEART OF MINE:" Astaire (*The Imposter*), Lucille Bremer (*The Princess*), Count Stenfenelli (*The Duke*), Naomi Childers (*The Duchess*), Helen Boice (*The Countess*), Robert Wayne (*Retired Dyspeptic*), Charles Coleman (*The Major*), Feodor Chaliapin (*The Lieutenant*), Sam Flint (*The Flunky*), Shirlee Howard, Natalie Draper, Noreen Roth, Dorothy Van Nuys, Katherine Booth, Lucille Casey, Eve Whitney, Elaine Shepard, Frances Donelan, Helen O'Hara, Aina Constant, Aileen Haley (*Showgirls*), "WE WILL MEET AGAIN:" Esther Williams, James Melton, "THE INTERVIEW:" Judy Garland (*Herself*), Rex Evans (*The Butler*), "WHEN TELEVISION COMES:" Red Skelton, "THE BABBIT AND THE BRO-MIDE:" Astaire, Gene Kelly, "TRAVIATA:" James Melton, Marion Bell, Lena Horne, Avon Long, "THE SWEEPSTAKES TICKET:" Fannie Brice (*Norma*), Hume Cronyn (*Monty*), William Frawley (*Martin*), Arthur Walsh (*Telegraph Boy*), "PAY THE TWO DOLLARS:" Victor Moore, Edward Arnold (*Themselves*), Ray Teal (*Special Officer*), Joseph Crehan (*Judge*), William B. Davidson (*Presiding Judge*), Eddie Dunn, Garry Owens (*Officers*), Harry Hayden (*Warden*), "LIMEHOUSE BLUES:" Astaire (*Tai Long*), Bremer (*Moy Ling*), Captain George Hill, Jack Deery (*Men*), Charles Lunard, Robert Ames, Jack Regas, Sid Gordon (*Four Men with Masks*), Cyd Charisse (*Chicken*), James King (*Rooster*), Eugene Loring (*Costermonger*), Harriet Lee (*Singer in Dive*), "NUMBER PLEASE:" Keenan Wynn, Kay Williams (*On Phone*), Peter Lawford (*Phone Voice*), Audrey Totter (*Voice of Telephone Operator*), "BEAUTY:" Kathryn Grayson, The Ziegfeld Girls.

On his deathbed, Florenz Ziegfeld, in the throes of a delirium, reportedly cried out: "Curtain! Fast music! Lights! Ready for the last finale! Great! The show looks good! The show looks good!" ZIEGFELD FOLLIES takes its cue from there. The film opens with the great showman (played by Powell, reprising his role in THE GREAT ZIEGFELD, 1936) up in heaven, sitting in his swanky apartment (the real Ziegfeld died broke, but in heaven or Hollywood, anything is possible). Powell dreams about putting on a new show, then a group of puppets (featuring caricatures of some of the original Ziegfeld's Follies stars) entertains him. Astaire appears to pay tribute to the great showman, and then begins a grand review. The following twelve sequences, a variety of sketches and musical numbers, are all in the Ziegfeld tradition. The first number features Ball and O'Brien on a carousel, singing their tribute to that glorious gender: the handsome and virile male. Their song, titled "Bring on Those Wonderful Men," is a parody of an opening song performed by Ball, Astaire, and Charisse called "Bring on Those Beautiful Girls" (Earl Brent, Roger Edens). The next number features Williams in–what else?–an exotic water-laden location. Bell and Merton next sing "The Drinking Song," from Giuseppe Verdi's opera "La Traviata," which is followed in turn by Moore and Arnold in a comic bit about a man jailed for spitting in the subway. Astaire and Bremer then dance a number called "This Heart is Mine." Next is another sketch, involving Wynn and a telephone operator. Horne follows with the torch song "Love" (Ralph Blane, Hugh Martin), and then Skelton performs a marvelous comedy routine, "When Television Comes." Imagining what liquor commercials will be like in the age of the orthicon tube, Skelton essays a televison announcer who gets progressively more drunk as he tries to sell gin on the airwaves. "Limehouse Blues" is a ballet between Astaire and Bremer, involving the infatuation of a Chinese coolie for a beautiful prostitute. Garland performs next, a clever bit lampooning Greer Garson, as she plays an actress preparing for her next role (a role originally offered to Garson herself). The next number, a little-known composition by George and Ira Gershwin called "The Babbit and the Bromide," features an historic moment in screen dance. This number marks the first time the cinema's greatest dancers, Astaire and Kelly, ever teamed up for a number. (They would dance together once again as the co-hosts for the entertainment documentary THAT'S ENTERTAIN-MENT, PART 2 in 1976.) Finally, amidst a sea of bubbles, Grayson sings "There's Beauty Everywhere" (Arthur Freed, Brent). This was the third and last of MGM's films about Ziegfeld. In 1944 studio head sanctioned a musical extravaganza to celebrate MGM's 20th year in the picture business. After acquiring the rights to the title ZIEGFELD FOLLIES for $100,000 from the showman's widow Billie Burke and stage impressario Lee Shubert, producer Freed was given $3 million to create the film, a budget Freed was able to stick with in spite of a host of production troubles. Sidney began direction, but he was later replaced by Minnelli, MGM's best musical director. Minnelli was well qualified for the project as he had worked on some of the Broadway Ziegfeld revues in the early 1930s. (Robert Lewis, Charles Walters, Roy Del Ruth and Lemuel Ayres also directed some sequences for the film, though they received no screen credit.) Because the film used so many of the studio's biggest names, the film was shot bit by bit, calling off actors from their other productions to shoot their sequences for ZIEGFELD FOLLIES. Writers were called in from other projects (enough to field no less than *four* baseball teams) to help contribute bits to the script. Grayson's big bubble sequence was to have originally included Astaire but his footage was edited out. Astaire had been preparing for a USO tour, and consequently had to receive five vaccinations. These shots affected the actor's health, and he went into the sequence with a temperature of 102 degrees. "The setting for this thing was a massive formation of rocklike scenery," Astaire wrote in his autobiography *Steps in Time*. "...Beautiful girls were spotted up high on the rocks at different points like great sea gulls. Several of them fainted from the chemical fumes used to make the bubbles. All this for an effect which did not come off...because most of it was deleted from the final released picture." Astaire's sequence with Kelly was much more successful. The song had originally been a number of Astaire's and his sister Adele, in the 1927 Broadway show "Funny Face." After a week of rehearsal, the number, telling the story of two polite but boring gentlemen, was filmed in just a few days. "There was no rivalry at all," Freed said of the two dancers. "Each is a genuine admirer of the other. My only problem was their deference for each other. Each was willing to do whichever dance the other wanted." Astaire and Bremer's "Limehouse Blues" was shot on a revamped set left over from THE PICTURE OF DORIAN GRAY (1945). Elaborate in scope, the number required 18 rehearsal days, followed by a ten day shoot. It cost over $200,000, one of the most expensive numbers in the film. Because of the film's elaborate, grandiose nature, ZIEGFELD FOLLIES took much longer than expected to finish. The film premiered with 19 sequences, clocking in at 273 minutes. Of course this was too long for any sensible release and several cuts were made to bring the film in at a more reasonable length. Among the numbers excised were some tunes between Garland and her old screen partner, Mickey Rooney, as well as some comedy numbers. One comic bit featuring Fanny Brice was cut from the American release though it remained in the European version of the film. Long and Horne's rendition of the Gershwin song "Liza" was also cut, but Minnelli remained fond of the number, and ended up naming his daughter in honor of the song. ZIEGFELD FOLLIES was finally released in 1946, and was met with great response. Freed amazingly had only gone a little over $200,000 past his budget. He recouped the production costs and then some, as the film brought in over $5 million in box office receipts. It was a well deserved honor. Despite the problems and delays, ZIEGFELD FOLLIES is a marvel of music and dance as only MGM could do it.

p, Arthur Freed; d, Vincente Minnelli, (uncredited) George Sidney, Robert Lewis, Charles Walters, Roy Del Ruth, Lemuel Ayres; w, E.Y. Harburg, Jack McGowan, Guy Bolton, Frank Sullivan, John Murray Anderson, Lemuel Ayers, Don Loper, Kay Thompson, Roger Edens, Hugh Martin, Ralph Blane, William Noble, Wilkie Mahoney, Cal Howard, Erick Charell, Max Liebman, Bill Schorr, Harry Crane, Lou Holtz, Eddie Cantor, Allen Boretz, Edgar Allan Woolf, Phil Rapp, Al Lewis, Joseph Schrank, Robert Alton, Eugene Loring, Robert Lewis, Charles Walters, James O'Hanlon, David Freedman, Joseph Erons, Irving Brecher, Samson Raphaelson, Everett Freeman, Devery Freeman; ph, George Folsey, Charles Rosbher, William Ferrari (Technicolor); ed, Albert Akst; md, Lenny Hayton; art d, Cedric Gibbons, Jack Martin Smith, Merrill Pye, Lemuel Ayers; set d, Edwin B. Willis, Mac Alper; cos, Florence Bunin, Irene; ch, Robert Alton; makeup, Jack Dawn.

Musical   **Cas.**   **(PR:AA MPAA:NR)**

ZIEGFELD GIRL*½   (1941) 131m MGM bw

James Stewart (*Gilbert Young*), Judy Garland (*Susan Gallagher*), Hedy Lamarr (*Sandra Kolter*), Lana Turner (*Sheila Regan*), Tony Martin (*Frank Merton*), Jackie Cooper (*Jerry Regan*), Ian Hunter (*Geoffrey Collis*), Charles Winninger (*Pop Gallagher*), Edward Everett Horton (*Noble Sage*), Paul Kelly (*John Slayton*), Eve Arden (*Patsy Dixon*), Dan Dailey, Jr. (*Jimmy Walters*), Al Shean (*Himself*), Fay Holden (*Mrs. Regan*), Felix Bressart (*Mischa*), Rose Hobart (*Mrs. Merton*), Bernard Nedell (*Nick Capalini*), Ed McNamara (*Mr. Regan*), Mae Busch (*Jenny*), Josephine Whittell (*Perkins*), Renie Riano (*Annie*), Six Hits and a Miss (*Singers*), Elliott Sullivan, James Flavin (*Truckers*), Joyce Compton (*Miss Sawyer*), Ruth Tobey (*Beth Regan*), Bess Flowers (*Palm Beach Casino Patron*), Jean Wallace, Myrna Dell, Georgia Carroll, Louise La Planche, Virginia Cruzon, Alaine Brandeis, Patricia Dana, Irma Wilson, Lorraine Gettman 'Leslie Brooks', Madeleine Martin, Vivien Mason, Harriet Bennett, Nina Bissell, Frances Gladwin Anya Taranda (*Ziegfeld Girls*), Antonio and Rosario (*Specialty Dancers*), Fred Santley (*Floorwalker*), Claire James (*Hopeful*), Sergio Orta (*Native Dancer*), Reed Hadley (*Geoffrey's Friend*), Armand Kaliz (*Pierre*), Joan Barclay (*Actress in Slayton's Office*), Donald Kirke (*Playboy*), Ray Teal (*Pawnbroker*), Al Hill (*Truck Driver*), Roscoe Ates (*Theater Worker*), George Lloyd (*Bartender*), Ginger Pearson (*Salesgirl*), Philip Dorn (*Franz Kolter*).

An MGM musical extravaganza which tells of the rise of three aspiring showgirls–Garland, Lamarr, and Turner–and how they handle their subsequent success as Ziegfeld girls. When Garland is discovered, she makes the painful decision to leave the vaudeville act run by her father, Winninger. Before long she falls in love with Cooper, the brother of another new Ziegfeld girl, Turner. Turner is discovered when she is spotted working as an elevator operator. She quickly gives up that job and becomes absorbed in the glamor of footlights and evening gowns. She begins to hobnob with the high-society crowd and becomes enamored with Park Avenue socialite, Hunter. Left behind is Stewart, a truck driver still hopeful of winning back his love. To compete with Hunter, Stewart tries to make some extra money by entering the bootlegging business. He soon runs into trouble with the law and winds up in prison. The third Ziegfeld girl is Lamarr, who finds life on the stage more eventful than life with Dorn, her penniless, aspiring violinist husband. When she finally comes to her senses, she realizes that Dorn means more to her than show business. She returns to his side and he goes on to find fame in the musical world. Garland uses her success to renew interest in her father's career, bringing him together with Shean for an audience-pleasing vaudeville act. Turner is the one who cannot handle her success. She becomes an alcoholic and at the premiere of a new Ziegfeld show, while watching from the balcony, experiences delusions that she is the star. As she descends the staircase of the theater lobby, she tumbles to the bottom and dies of a heart attack. As beautiful as Turner, Lamarr, and Garland are, the true star of the show is the lavish, spectacular dance numbers which, in the tradition of Florenz Ziegfeld, employ hundreds of dancing girls outfitted in glittery costumes. This was Pandro S. Berman's first production at the MGM lot after years of work at RKO. Without wasting time, he proved that he could splash the screen with eye-popping musical opulence just as good as anyone had before. Five years earlier, in 1936, THE GREAT ZIEGFELD was released, based on the story by William Anthony McGuire. In the hope of cashing in on that film's Oscar-winning success, MGM hired him to pen ZIEGFELD GIRL. Originally slated in 1938 as a vehicle for the talents of Joan Crawford, Eleanor Powell, Virginia Bruce, and Walter Pidgeon, the film was delayed by the death of McGuire. By October, 1940, Berman got the production rolling and, though it in no way matched THE GREAT ZIEGFELD, it did serve as an entertaining musical with the exceptional production numbers staged by Busby Berkeley, splendid art direction by Gibbons and Cathcart, colossal sets by Willis, and sleek, revealing gowns by Adrian. Garland delivered four numbers: "Minnie from Trinidad" (Roger Edens), "I'm Always Chasing Rainbows" (Joseph McCarthy, Harry Carroll), "You Never Looked So Beautiful Before" (Walter Donaldson, Harold Adamson, from THE GREAT ZIEGFELD), "Laugh! I Thought I'd Split My Side" with Tony Martin, "Ziegfeld Girls" (Edens), and one deleted number with Martin "We Must Have Music" (which was released as a short subject film the following year). Other numbers include: "Caribbean Love Song" (Edens, Ralph Freed; performed by Martin), "Whispering" (John Schonberger, Richard Coburn, Vincent Rose), "Mr. Gallagher and Mr. Shean" (Ed Gallagher, Al Shean; performed by Winninger and Shean), "You Stepped Out of a Dream" (Gus Kahn, Nacio Herb Brown; performed by Martin), "You Gotta Pull Strings" (Harold Adamson, Walter Donaldson, from THE GREAT ZIEGFELD).

p, Pandro S. Berman; d, Robert Z. Leonard; w, Marguerite Roberts, Sonya Levien (based on a story by William Anthony McGuire); ph, Ray June; m, Herbert Stothart; ed, Blanche Sewell; md, George Stoll; art d, Cedric Gibbons, Daniel B. Cathcart; set d, Edwin B. Willis; cos, Adrian; ch, Busby Berkeley; makeup, Jack Dawn.

Musical (PR:A MPAA:NR)

ZIGZAG* (1970) 105m MGM c (GB: FALSE WITNESS)

George Kennedy (*Paul R. Cameron*), Anne Jackson (*Jean Cameron*), Eli Wallach (*Mario Gambretti*), Steve Ihnat (*Assistant District Atty. Gates*), William Marshall (*Morrie Bronson*), Joe Maross (*Lt. Max Hines*), Dana Elcar (*Harold Tracey*), Walter Brooke (*Adam Mercer*), Anita O'Day (*Sheila Mangan*), Joan Tompkins (*Judge Beth Weaver*), Robert Sampson (*Burt Stennis*), Leonard Stone (*Jim Barris*), Stewart Moss (*Edgar Courtland*), Charlene Holt (*Sara Raymond*), Robert Donner (*Sgt. Mason Weber*), Pamela Murphy (*Elaine Mercer*), Abigail Shelton (*Muriel*), Douglas Henderson (*Dr. Leonard*), Robert Patten (*John Raymond*), Richard McMurray (*Dr. Sean Thompson*), Elizabeth Colla (*Camerons' Daughter*).

After discovering he is dying from a fatal brain tumor, insurance investigator Kennedy decides to confess to an unsolved murder so his family will be provided for with the reward money. He carefully constructs a case against himself and after his trial he collapses. He's given a new laser beam surgery and fully recovers. He escapes from the hospital and with help of his attorney, Wallach, discovers that Murphy, daughter of the dead man's associate, was the mistress of the victim. Her father Brooke, the real killer, shoots Kennedy before being gunned down himself by the police. A quirky story but it is neatly handled and has some unusual twists. Good stuff for a low-budget thriller.

p, Robert Enders, Everett Freeman; d, Richard A. Colla; w, John T. Kelley (based on a story by Enders); ph, James A. Crabe (Panavision, Metrocolor,); m, Oliver Nelson; ed, Ferris Webster; art d, George W. Davis, Marvin Summerfield; set d, Robert R. Benton, Chuck Pierce; cos, Gene Ostler; m/l, title song, Mike Curb, Enders, Guy Hemric, sung by Roy Orbison.

Thriller (PR:C MPAA:GP)

ZIG-ZAG½** (1975, Fr./Ital.) 90m Renn-Les Films de la Citrouille-FRAL/ Peppercorn-Wormser c

Catherine Deneuve (*Marie*), Bernadette Lafont (*Pauline*), Hubert Deschamps (*Jean*), Walter Chiari (*Tramp*), Stephane Shandor (*Bruyere*), Jean-Pierre Kalfon (*Guitarist*), Georgette Anys (*Singer*), Jean-Pierre Maud (*Edelweiss*), Paola Senatore (*Mme. Bruyer*), Tino Carraco (*Aldo Minnelli*), Yves Alfonse (*Cafe Owner*), Georges Adet, Gonz Curtis, Michel Berto.

Life on the sleazy side in Paris' disreputable Pigalle sector is portrayed in this unusual production. Deneuve and Lafont live a free and easy life as song and dance partners in a nightclub, and hookers on the side, until Lafont gets caught up in a kidnaping which finally ends in her death. Deneuve and

Lafont are wonderful, both to look at and to listen to, but the badness of the story and filming make this one decidedly hard to take.

d&w, Laszlo Szabo; ph, Jean Pierre Baux (Eastmancolor); m, Carl Hans Sachafer; ed, Jacques Witta; art d, Jean-Pierre Kohut-Sweko; cos, Son Zalone.

Drama (PR:O MPAA:R)

ZIS BOOM BAH** (1941) 62m MON bw

Grace Hayes, Peter Lind Hayes, Mary Healy, Huntz Hall, Jan Wiley, Frank Elliot, Lois Landon, Skeets Gallagher, Benny Rubin, Ed Kane, Leonard Sues, Roland Dupree.

Good college programmer has Hayes playing a musical comedy star. After a separation of 20 years she becomes reacquainted with her college son Hayes (Hayes' real life son as well) and is so overjoyed she buys him a cafe. He and his pals transform the place into a restaurant-theater and you know how the film is going to wind up. Despite the simple story line the cast is exuberant enough to make this work. Songs include: "Annabella," "It Makes No Difference When You're in the Army," Johnny Lange, Lew Porter, "Put Your Trust in the Moon," June Baldwin, Charles Callender, "Zis Boom Bah," Elaine Cannon, "Good News Tomorrow," "I've Learned to Smile Again," Neville Fleeson.

p, Sam Katzman; d, William Nigh; w, Harvey Gates, Jack Henley (based on a story by Connie Lee, Gates); ph, Marcel Le Picard; ed, Robert Golden; md, Johnny Lange, Lew Porter; ch, George King.

Musical Cas. (PR:A MPAA:NR)

ZITA½** (1968, Fr.) 92m S.N.C./Regional c (TANTE ZITA)

Joanna Shimkus (*Annie*), Katina Paxinou (*Aunt Zita*), Suzanne Flon (*Yvette*), Jose Maria Flotats (*Simon*), Paul Crauchet (*Dr. Bernard*), Bernard Fresson (*Boni*), Med Hondo (*James*), Roger Ibanez (*The Spaniard*), Jacques Rispal (*The Sergeant*), Odette Piquet (*The Day Watchman*), Solange Certain (*The Night Watchman*), Jean-Gabriel Nordmann (*Manuel*), Paul Pavel, Claude Leveque, Bernard Klein, Corinne Armand, Jean Darle, Lydie Murguet, Marie Pascale Daveau.

After Paxinou has a stroke her teenage niece, Shimkus, faces the prospect of death for the first time in her life. Unable to cope, she leaves home and her job of caring for Paxinou and wanders aimlessly about the city. She comes under the influence of a variety of Parisian underground characters at a nightclub, but soon grows bored with them and leaves. She runs into a poor Spaniard, Ibanez, killing a cat to eat, and is arrested with him, but Crauchet, the family doctor, wins her release. Trying to distract her, he drives her around the city and happens to collide with a van driven by Fresson and Hondo, two men she had met at the club. All go back to the club together where Crauchet learns that Paxinou has died, and he leaves without telling the girl. Meanwhile, Fresson proposes to her but she rejects him and later encounters Flotats, a jazzman she had also met, and while they make love she recalls her childhood with Paxinou. The next morning, fortified by her experiences, she is ready to face the fact of her aunt's death.

p, Gerard Beytout; d, Robert Enrico; w, Lucienne Hamon, Pierre Pelegri, Enrico (based on a story by Hamon); ph, Jean Boffety (Eastmancolor, print by Technicolor); m, Francois de Roubaix; ed, Michel Lewin; art d, Jacques Saulnier.

Drama (PR:O MPAA:NR)

ZOKU MIYAMOTO MUSHASHI (SEE: SAMURAI PART II, 1967, Jap.)

ZOKU NINGEN NO JOKEN (SEE: ROAD TO ETERNITY, 1962, Jap.)

ZOLTAN, HOUND OF DRACULA (SEE: DRACULA'S DOG, 1978)

ZOMBIE, 1971 (SEE: I EAT YOUR SKIN, 1971)

ZOMBIE zero (1980, Ital.) 91m Variety/Jerry Gross Organization c (AKA: ZOMBIE 2; ZOMBIE FLESH EATERS)

Tisa Farrow (*Anne*), Ian McCulloch (*Peter*), Richard Johnson (*Dr. Menard*), Al Cliver (*Brian*), Arnetta Gay (*Susan*), Olga Karlatos (*Mrs. Menard*), Stefania D'Amario (*Nurse*).

Disgusting ripoff of Romero's excellent satire DAWN OF THE DEAD has Mia's lesser known sister Tisa Farrow going off with McCulloch to a strange island where zombies do their thing. The action then is just a series of monster cliches backed by some of the goriest special effects ever created. Audiences on the West Coast were given ZOMBIE barf bags before going into the theater. In Europe this was known as ZOMBIE 2 in an effort to cash in on DAWN OF THE DEAD's European title, ZOMBIE.

p, Ugo Tucci, Fabrizio de Angelis; d, Lucio Fulci; w, Elsia Briganti; ph, Sergio Salvati (Technicolor); m, Fabio Frizzi, Giorgio Tucci; ed, Vincenzo Tomassi;

spec eff, Giannetto De Rossi.

Horror   Cas.   (PR:O MPAA:NR)

ZOMBIE CREEPING FLESH* (1981, Ital./Span.) 99m Beatrice/Films
Dara c (INFERNO DEI MORTI-VIVENTI)

Margit Evelyn Newton, Frank Garfield, Selan Karay, Robert O'Neil, Gaby
Renom.

At the HOPE research center in New Guinea the staff appears to be working
for the good of underdeveloped countries. In actuality the place is run by a
bunch of madmen who are trying to create a substance that will cause local
populations to become cannibals, thus killing the overpopulation and
hunger problems at the same time. However, a gas leak causes the workers
to turn into flesh-eating zombies and the doctors have to cover up the
problem before it's discovered. Gradually the problem increases and the
world is seemingly doomed. This zombie film attempts to create an illusion
that it carries a much deeper meaning. The use of Third World troubles is
nothing more than an excuse for some genuinely gory moments that exist
to shock rather than satirize. Disgusting.

p, Sergio Cortona; d, Vincent Dawn [Bruno Mattei]; w, Claudio Fragasso,
J.M. Cunilles; ph, John Cabrera; spec eff, Giuseppe Ferranti.

Horror   (PR:O MPAA:NR)

ZOMBIES OF MORA TAU* (1957) 70m COL bw

Gregg Palmer (Jeff Clark), Allison Hayes (Mona Harrison), Autumn Russell
(Jan Peters), Joel Ashley (George Harrison), Morris Ankrum (Jonathan
Eggert), Marjorie Eaton (Mrs. Peters), Gene Roth (Sam), Leonard Geer
(Johnny), Lewis Webb (Art), Ray "Crash" Corrigan (Sailor), Mel Curtis
(Johnson), Frank Hagney (Capt. Jeremy Peters), Karl Davis, William Baskin
(Zombies).

Good cheap zombie picture has Palmer and Ashley off in search of diamonds
under the sea off the coast of Africa. Little do they know that zombies guard
the treasure and won't let anyone who tries to take it get out alive. Palmer
escapes in the end, scattering the diamonds so no one can get at them, thus
giving the creatures the first period of peace they have had in eons.
Standard horror quality for grade B films.

p, Sam Katzman; d, Edward L. Cahn; w, Raymond T. Marcus (based on a
story by George Plympton); ph, Benjamin H. Kline; ed, Jack Ogilvie; art d,
Paul Palmentola.

Horror   Cas.   (PR:O MPAA:NR)

ZOMBIES OF SUGAR HILL   (SEE: SUGAR HILL, 1974)

ZOMBIES OF THE STRATOSPHERE (SEE: SATAN'S SATELLITES,
1958)

ZOMBIES ON BROADWAY½** (1945) 68m RKO bw (GB: LOONIES
ON BROADWAY)

Wally Brown (Jerry Miles), Alan Carney (Mike Strager), Bela Lugosi (Prof.
Richard Renault), Anne Jeffreys (Jean La Dance), Sheldon Leonard (Ace
Miller), Frank Jenks (Gus, His Henchman), Russell Hopton (Benny), Joseph
Vitale (Joseph), Ian Wolfe (Prof. Hopkins), Louis Jean Heydt (Douglas
Walker), Darby Jones (Kolaga), Sir Lancelot.

Press agents Brown and Carney, RKO's answer to Bud Abbott and Lou
Costello, are sent to the Caribbean by a nightclub owner to find some
zombies for a new act. They meet Lugosi who helps out by providing living
dead through eerie experiments. With the success of I WALKED WITH A
ZOMBIE studio executives figured a comedy zombie film would be another
hit. Jones and Sir Lancelot, a calypso singer, repeat their roles from the
original film without much success. It's all pretty predictable and very flat.
The set was from the RKO Sol Lesser "Tarzan" film.

p, Ben Stoloff; d, Gordon Dines; w, Lawrence Kimble (based on a story by
Robert Farber, Charles Newman); ph Jack Mackenzie; m, Roy Webb; ed,
Philip Martin, Jr.; md, C. Bakaleinikoff; art d, Albert S. D'Agostino, Walter
E. Keller; makeup, Maurice Seiderman.

Horror/Comedy   (PR:A MPAA:NR)

ZONTAR, THE THING FROM VENUS½** (1966) 80m Azalea c

John Agar (Dr. Curt Taylor), Susan Bjorman (Martha), Anthony Houston
(Deith), Neil Fletcher (Sheriff), Patricia Delaney, Warren Hammack, Bill
Thurman.

A special effects bat-like creature invades Agar's mind in an effort to take
over the world. Poor Agar then tries to shut off all the world's power sources
while tiny crowds (pretending to be teeming masses) shriek at the sight of
the monster. Unintentionally funny with some wonderfully campy scenes.
This uncredited remake of IT CONQUERED THE WORLD comes to us from
the director of MARS NEEDS WOMEN.

p&d, Larry Buchanan; w, Buchanan, H. Taylor; ph, Robert B. Alcott

Science Fiction   Cas.   (PR:A MPAA:NR)

ZOO BABY*   (1957, Brit.) 59m Pennington-Eady/RANK bw

Angela Baddeley (Mrs. Ramsey), Gerard Lohan (Pip), Maurice Kaufmann
(Steve), Dorothy Bromiley (Sarah), Bruce Seton (Zoo Superintendent),
Ronald Leigh-Hunt (Supt. Copton), Peter Sinclair (Benham), Doreen Keogh,
Erik Chitty, Peter Allenby, June Clarke, Alan Penn, Garard Green, Robert
Raglan, Michael Peake.

Lohan is a young boy and son of a big game hunter. He loves all sorts of
animals and wants a coatimundi for his very own. When one of these
ring-tailed animals with long flexible snouts disappears from the local zoo
a newsreel cameraman is thought to be the guilty party but Lohan confesses
to the crime. Kids and animal lovers will be charmed by this simple tale well
told of a boy and the South American raccoon-like creature.

p, Jon Pennington; d, David Eady; w, Jan Read; ph, Ernest Palmer.

Children's Drama   (PR:AAA MPAA:NR)

ZOO IN BUDAPEST**½**   (1933) 85m LAS/FOX bw

Loretta Young (Eve), Gene Raymond (Zani), O.P. Heggie (Dr. Grunbaum),
Wally Albright (Paul Vandor), Paul Fix (Heinie), Murray Kinnell (Garbosh),
Ruth Warren (Katrina), Roy Stewart (Karl), Frances Rich (Elsie), Niles
Welch (Mr. Vandor), Lucille Ward (Miss Murst), Russ Powell (Toski),
Dorothy Libaire (Rosita).

Long considered lost, this film proves, on rediscovery, to be a delightful
romantic fantasy full of dreamlike sets and misty photography. Young is an
orphan on the verge of being apprenticed out to harsh, almost slave-like
conditions until she reaches legal adulthood. Rather than face this fate, she
takes advantage of a trip to the zoo to run away from her class and hide.
Raymond is a keeper who is getting in trouble with kindly zoo supervisor
Heggie because he is outspokenly kind to the animals. A rich woman wants
to buy one of the animals so she can kill it and make a coat from its fur.
Raymond steals her fur and hides in the zoo, where he soon meets the lovely
orphan girl. While the police look for Raymond, another keeper, the cruel
Fix, assaults Young and she is saved in the nick of time by Raymond.
Eventually chaos breaks out at the zoo as a child becomes trapped in the
tiger's cage, and more animals escape, some of them fighting among
themselves. Raymond emerges from hiding to rescue the boy with the help
of an elephant, and the boy's grateful father agrees to hire the keeper as the
gamekeeper of his estate and to adopt Young. The two lovers decide to
marry as soon as they can. Many of the early prints of this film were tinted.
The film's simple sets are highly stylized. Photographer Garmes recalled
how much simple potted plants and fog suggested a magical environment.
Director Lee proved here that he had a great deal of talent that was
generally submerged in his long years as a competent hack for the studios.
Performances by Young and Raymond are breezy and enjoyable, and
Heggie, as a good guy, and Fix, as a bad guy, are similarly fine. Only in its
too- neat finish is the film weak, but this is not too annoying as it seems in
keeping with the air of fantasy that pervades the picture. The simple, lovely
sets were used in other films from the studio, most notably HOOPLA (1933),
a picture with a traveling-carnival background; Clara Bow took a nude swim
in the flamingo pool that had been crafted for the zoo. This was producer
Lasky's first effort for 20th Century-Fox; the film was sufficiently successful
to warrant a similarly simple romance from the same team (this one with
musical numbers), I AM SUZANNE (1934).

p, Jesse L. Lasky; d, Rowland V. Lee; w, Dan Totheroh, Louise Long, Lee
(based on a story by Melville Baker, John Kirkland); ph, Lee Garmes; ed,
Harold Schuster.

Romance   (PR:A MPAA:NR)

ZOOT SUIT*   (1981) 103m UNIV c

Daniel Valdez (Henry Reyna), Edward James Olmos (El Pachuco), Charles
Aidman (George), Tyne Daly (Alice), John Anderson (Judge), Abel Franco
(Enrique), Mike Gomez (Joey), Alma Rose Martinez (Lupe), Frank McCarthy
(Press), Lupe Ontiveros (Dolores), Ed Peck (Lt. Edwards), Robert Phalen
(D.A.), Tony Plana (Rudy), Rose Portillo (Della), Marco Rodriguez (Smiley),
Kelly Ward (Tommy), Helena Andreyko (Blondie), Bob Basso (Baliff),
Darlene Bryan (Little Blue), Bernadette Cologne (Legs), Miguel Delagado
(Rafas), Roberta Delgado (Tillie), Anacani Echeverria, Bertha E. Oropeza,
Candice L. Silva (Pachuca Vocalists), Carlos Garcia (Budda), Honey Garcia
(Chola), James Hogan (Shore Patrol), Laura Leyva (Elena), Sal Lopez
(Hobo), Luis Manuel (Cholo), Kim Miyori (Manchuka), Angela Moya
(Bertha), Jeff Reynolds (P-Coat), Juan Rios (Crow), Greg Rosatti (Leather-
neck), Nancy Salis (Bonita), Geno Silva (Galindo), Kurtwood Smith (Sgt.
Smith), Dennis Stewart (Swabbie), Duke Stroud (Guard), Judy Susman
(Sugarfoot), Jon Thomas (Ragman), Lewis Whitlock (Zooter), Antonette
Yuskis (Guera), Robert Beltran (Lowrider), Alma Beltran (His Mother),
Julio Medina (His Father), Socorro Valdez (His Girl/Friend), Diane
Rodriguez (Stenographer).

An interesting film both for the final product as well as the story behind the
film. This is a filmed version of the play "Zoot Suit" which was based on the
1942 Sleepy Lagoon murder mystery in Los Angeles in which several

Hispanics were sent to jail on a trumped up murder charge. Attempts were made to free the group, but to no avail. Valdez, who adapted his play for the screen, keeps the story moving and uses good camera motion. The film was shot in 11 days on a tiny budget (by 1980s standards) of $2 ½ million. It proved to be a good showcase for the talents of several Hispanic-American actors.

p, Peter Burrell, Kenneth Brecher, William P. Wingate; d&w, Luis Valdez (based on his play); ph, David Myers (Technicolor); m, Daniel Valdez, Shorty Rogers; ed, Jacqueline Cambas; prod d, Tom H. John; cos, Yvonne Wood; ch, Patricia Birch.

Drama (PR:O MPAA:R)

ZORBA THE GREEK***½ (1964, U.S./Gr.) 142m FOX-Cacoyannis-Rochley/International Classics bw (ZORMBA)

Anthony Quinn (*Alexis Zorba*), Alan Bates (*Basil*), Irene Papas (*The Widow*), Lila Kedrova (*Mme. Hortense*), George Foundas (*Mavrandoni*), Eleni Anousaki (*Lola*), Sotiris Moustakas (*Mimithos*), Takis Emmanuel (*Manolakas*), George 'Yorgo' Voyadjis (*Pavlo*), Anna Kyriakou (*Soul*).

Though Quinn has often played lively, exuberant characters, his title role in ZORBA THE GREEK was a career performance, a role loved by both critics and audiences. The film opens with Bates, a young English writer, arriving in Greece to collect his thoughts and discover his own identity. He then goes to Crete to work at a lignite mine, an inheritance from his father, a native Greek. He is joined by Quinn, a lusty Greek peasant who also wants to work at the mine. The unusual duo move into a hotel run by Kedrova, an aging French prostitute, former lover to four different admirals, and ex-cabaret dancer. Quinn begins wooing her, and encourages Bates to show some affection towards Papas, a beautiful widow desired by all the local males. The mine is in need of some repairs, so the irrepressible Quinn cons a group of monks into letting him remove some lumber from a forest located on a nearby mountain. Quinn comes up with a scheme to transport the lumber to the mine, but must first obtain some necessary equipment. When Quinn ventures into the city, Kedrova helps Bates overcome his bashful demeanor and the Englishman gathers up the courage to visit Papas. They make love, and rumors begin spreading about the island after Bates is seen leaving the house. Voyadjis, one of Papas' many admirers, is crushed by this, and kills himself in despair. Quinn returns, but arrives too late to help Papas as the angry villagers stone her to death. He and Bates witness this terrible act, but are helpless to do anything about it. When Kedrova grows seriously ill, the big-hearted Quinn agrees to marry her. While working at the mine, Quinn hears Kedrova has taken a turn for the worse. He hurries to the hotel, and Kedrova dies in his loving arms. Meanwhile, the old women of the town, dressed in black, come to Kedrova's home and strip the deathbed of everything before Kedrova's body is even cold. Though Bates is shocked by this, Quinn explains that this is a customary way of dealing with life and death on the island. Quinn's system of transporting lumber makes its debut, but an important link breaks, destroying the entire system. In the aftermath, Bates looks at the ruins with Quinn. Broken, both emotionally and financially, Bates is comforted by his friend. He comes to realize, while learning a happy Greek dance, that Quinn's continually positive philosophy towards life and all its riches may be crazy, but is beautiful none the less. Quinn brings magic to his part, crazy, happy, and overflowing with energy. It's a larger-than-life role that easily could have turned into a caricature, but Quinn's portrait makes Alexis Zorba a unique and special individual. It was a part he would play again on Broadway, when ZORBA THE GREEK was adapted into a spirited musical, "Zorba," for the 1968-1969 Broadway season. Bates, as the inhibited Englishman, is a good contrast, never overshadowed by the enormity of Quinn's character as he learns about the forces in life. This is far from a happy film, though, as Quinn's philosophies are tested time and time again by overwhelming circumstances that could easily break a man. Cacoyannis' direction understands this dichotomy, and weaves the opposing elements together skillfully. The story is loosely structured and consequently the film runs a little longer than it should, though ZORBA THE GREEK is still a marvelous entertainment. The film itself was somewhat revolutionary in its language and irreverent sense of humor, though these controversial elements of 1964 have since become commonplace. Quinn deservedly won an Oscar nomination, but lost that year to Rex Harrison for MY FAIR LADY. The latter film also beat ZORBA THE GREEK for Best Picture, but Kedrova received an Oscar as Best Supporting Actress. The film also won Oscars for art direction and cinematography (in the now defunct black and white category), which prompted a change in ZORBA THE GREEK's distribution. It was originally released to the art house circuit through 20th Century-Fox's International Classics, but after these Oscar successes, the parent company took over for a general distribution.

p,d&w, Michael Cacoyannis (based on the novel by Nikos Kazantzakis); ph, Walter Lassally; m, Mikis Theodorakis; ed, Cacoyannis; md, Theodorakis; art d, Vassele Fotopoulos; cos, Anna Stavropoulou; makeup, Monique Archambault.

Drama Cas. (PR:A MPAA:NR)

ZORRO CONTRO MACISTE (SEE: SAMSON AND THE SLAVE QUEEN, 1963, Ital.)

ZORRO, THE GAY BLADE*½ (1981) 93m Melvin Simon/FOX c

George Hamilton (*Don Diego Vega/Bunny Wigglesworth*), Lauren Hutton (*Charlotte*), Brenda Vaccaro (*Florinda*), Ron Leibman (*Esteban*), Donovan Scott (*Paco*), James Booth (*Velasquez*), Helen Burns (*Consuela*), Clive Revill (*Garcia*), Carolyn Seymour (*Dolores*), Eduardo Noriega (*Don Francisco*), Jorge Russek (*Don Fernando*), Eduardo Alcaraz (*Don Jose*), Carlos Bravo (*Luis*), Roberto Dumont (*Ferraro*), Jorge Bolio (*Pablito*), Dick Balduzzi (*Old Man*), Ana Eliza Perez Bolanos (*Granddaughter*), Francisco Mauri (*Guard*), Julian Colman (*Martinez*), Francisco Morayta (*Ramirez*), Pilar Pellicer (*Francisco's Wife*), Owen Lee (*Sergeant*), Gustavo Ganem (*Barman*), Armando Duarte (*Soldier*), Norm Blankenship (*Whipping Master*), Frank Welker (*Narrator*).

Hamilton's follow-up film to the spoof LOVE AT FIRST BITE again parodies a famous movie legend, but the results are less successful. This time Hamilton takes on Zorro, playing a dual role of the dashing masked swordsman and his flamboyant twin brother, Bunny Wigglesworth. Hamilton, as Zorro, is called to defend innocent villagers when Leibman, a cruel dictator, begins an oppressive reign. In an accident, Hamilton renders himself incapable of any nimble-footed heroics so a new hero must be found. Enter the twin brother, a gay (in every sense of the word) blade with a wardrobe that rivals Liberace's. Eventually Leibman is defeated, and Hamilton (as his Zorro incarnation) ends up with Hutton. This is a one-joke film that beats the punch line into a lifeless pulp. Everything is played for big laughs, with the bulk of the humor resting on Hamilton's gay stereotype. Though there are a few amusing moments, most of the film is predictable, brash, and boring. Hamilton (who coproduced) chews up scenery like a hungry dog attacking a bone. The supporting cast is bland, giving way to Hamilton's campy performance. Though he's clearly having a good time with himself, Hamilton fails to understand there was always a subtle element of self-parody within the best of the Zorro films, such as Douglas Fairbanks, 1920 silent film THE MARK OF ZORRO. The gay stereotype humor is more offensive than comical.

p, George Hamilton, C.O. Erickson; d, Peter Medak; w, Hal Dresner (based on a story by Dresner, Greg Alt, Don Moriarty, Bob Randall); ph, John A. Alonzo (DeLuxe Color); m, Ian Frazer; ed, Hillary Jane Kranze; md, Frazer; prod d, Herman A. Blumenthal; art d, Adrian Gorton; cos, Gloria Gresham; ch, Alex Romero.

Comedy Cas. (PR:A-C MPAA:PG)

ZOTZ!** (1962) 85m COL bw

Tom Poston (*Prof. Jonathan Jones*), Julia Meade (*Prof. Virginia Fenster*), Jim Backus (*Horatio Kellgore*), Fred Clark (*Gen. Bulliver*), Cecil Kellaway (*Dean Updike*), Zeme North (*Cynthia Jones*), Margaret Dumont (*Persephone Updike*), James Millhollin (*Dr. Kroner*), Carl Don (*Josh Bates*), Mike Mazurki (*Igor*), Jimmy Hawkins (*Jimmy Kellgore*), Bart Patton (*Mr. Crane*), Judee Morton (*Miss Blakiston*), Michael Westfield (*Capt. Byron*), Russ Whiteman (*Maj. Folger*), George Moorman (*Lt. John G. Stefanski*), Elaine Martone (*Secretary*), Susan Dorn (*Nurse*), Albert Glasser (*"Khrushchev"*), Louis Nye.

Moronic comedy has Poston playing a professor who comes across an ancient coin that gives him unusual powers. Pointing his index finger inflicts pain, shouting the title word "Zotz!" makes things move in slow motion, and combining the two causes instant death. He tries to convince his colleagues of his new abilities but they all think he's crazy. So Poston goes to the Pentagon and offers himself as a new secret weapon. The Army brass is just as convinced as the college board of Poston's wavering sanity, but leave it to the Russians to catch on to the idea. They attempt to kidnap him. Poston uses the coin's power to defend himself and then loses it in a sewer, after which he returns to the academic, and much more sedate, lifestyle. This is a lesser effort from Castle. The insipid screenplay doesn't give him much to work with. There are some humorous moments but mostly it's pointless fluff. Theaters gave away Zotz coins at the initial release of the film. This marked one of the final screen appearances for Dumont, long-time leading lady in Marx Brothers films.

p&d, William Castle; w, Ray Russell (based on the novel by Walter Karig); ph, Gordan Avil; m, Bernard Green; ed, Edwin Bryant; art d, Robert Peterson; set d, James M. Crowe; makeup, Joseph Di Bella.

Comedy (PR:A MPAA:NR)

ZULU***** (1964, Brit.) 135m Diamond/EM c

Stanley Baker (*Lt. John Chard*), Jack Hawkins (*Rev. Otto Witt*), Ulla Jacobsson (*Margareta Witt*), James Booth (*Pvt. Henry Hook*), Michael Caine (*Lt. Gonville Bromhead*), Nigel Green (*Color Sgt. Bourne*), Ivor Emmanuel (*Pvt. Owen*), Paul Daneman (*Sgt. Maxfield*), Glynn Edwards (*Cpl. Allen*), Neil McCarthy (*Pvt. Thomas*), David Kernan (*Pvt. Hitch*), Gary Bond (*Pvt. Cole*), Peter Gill (*Pvt. 612 Williams*), Tom Gerrard (*Lance-Corporal*), Patrick Magee (*Surgeon Reynolds*), Richard Davies (*Pvt. 593 Jones*), Dafydd Havard (*Gunner Howarth*), Denys Graham (*Pvt. 716 Jones*), Dickie Owen (*Cpl. Schiess*), Larry Taylor (*Hughes*), Joe Powell (*Sgt. Windridge*), John Sullivan

(Stephenson), Harvey Hall (Sick Man), Gert Van Den Bergh (Adendorf), Dennis Folbigge (Commissary Dalton), Kerry Jordan (Company Cook), Ronald Hill (Bugler), Chief Buthelezi (Cetewayo), Daniel Tshabalala (Jacob), Ephraim Mbhele (Red Garters), Simon Sabelo (Dance Leader), Richard Burton (Narrator).

Heroism of a gritty and determined kind is shown with magnificence in this historically accurate tale of one of Britain's finest hours, on January 22, 1879, in the defense of the tiny outpost, Rorke's Drift, Natal. The film opens with missionaries Hawkins and his daughter Jacobsson watching a mass wedding ceremony take place in a Zulu encampment. Word comes that other Zulu warriors have attacked a large contingent of British troops and destroyed it, taking their equipment and rifles. Hawkins and Jacobsson make a dash in their carriage out of the camp and head for Rorke's Drift to alert the small garrison there. They arrive and tell commander Baker to flee, but Baker decides that it's his duty to defend the post. His second-in-command, Caine, an effete young officer, tries to persuade Baker to abandon the post. Baker won't hear of turning tail and orders barricades put up to repel the Zulus coming against him. Hawkins rants on about the immorality of battle and tries to persuade the soldier's to desert their posts. He has to be locked up and somehow he finds a bottle, gets drunk, and then raves on at the soldier's who are now preparing for battle. Caine bristles as he obeys Baker's command, since he feels he should be in charge, his entire ancestry having been distinguished by a long line of famous military leaders. The resolute Baker, however, an engineer, goes about his defense preparations methodically, unconcerned about shedding Caine's blue blood. Then the approach of the Zulus is heard, a long, deep chant that sounds like the chugging of a train. The defenders look up to a ridge to see it turn black with thousands of Zulu warriors, 4,000 of them. The British reel back in their ranks from the sheer size of the enemy force, realizing that they are doomed. Baker orders Hawkins and Jacobsson put into a carriage and sent from the post so they will be out of harm's way. As their carriage races along, the Zulu chief recognizes the missionaries and instructs his warriors not to molest them. Then the Zulus attack in waves, coming first against one wall, then another, the chief actually testing the firepower of the British with the lives of his men. As the Zulus press against the fortress, the British soldiers die but the British casualties are minimal compared to the hundreds of Zulus mowed down by the fire from the post. The Zulus later break through a weak spot, the small medical clinic, but they are driven back as the place catches fire. A herd of cattle is accidentally let loose and this, too, helps the defenders, as the cattle stampede over a charging line of Zulus. Still the Zulus bring the attack to the British, charging into the crumbling barricades night and day, winnowing down the ranks of the soldiers. In the end, the British muster every man who can hobble to a position, the wounded, even the dying, to turn back the waves of Zulus pounding at them. Baker covers several breaches in the walls by having a flying squad plug up areas where the Zulus momentarily break through. He also orders a secret barricade built during the night and, when the Zulus make their final attack, he faces them with three ranks of solid fire that decimates the warriors. The Zulus are finally beaten, having lost hundreds of men. they stand atop ridges chanting at the British, saluting them for their courage, before turning away and going back to their villages. This amazing film is devastatingly accurate in its depiction of the Rorke's Drift action and it is superbly directed and acted. Baker, however, had a difficult time getting the Zulus to cooperate with him when making the film on location in Natal. None had ever seen a motion picture and he couldn't make the chiefs understand what he intended to do. He finally had an old western starring Gene Autry flown into the remote area and he showed this to the Zulus who fell to the ground laughing at it, before they understood what Baker, Caine, and all the others wanted them to do. Then they did it magnificently. The film is dramatically narrated by Richard Burton who points out that of the 1,344 Victoria Crosses awarded since 1856, 11 were given to the defenders at Rorke's Drift, an all-time record for one engagement.

p, Stanley Baker, Cy Endfield; d, Endfield; w, John Prebble, Endfield (based on a story by Prebble); ph, Stephen Dade (Technirama, Technicolor); m,

John Barry; ed, John Jympson; art d, Ernest Archer; cos, Arthur Newman; makeup, Charles Parker; stunts, John Sullivan.

War Drama   **Cas.**   **(PR:C MPAA:NR)**

ZULU DAWN***   (1980, Brit.) 117m Samarkand-Lamitas/WB c

Burt Lancaster (Col. Durnford), Peter O'Toole (Lord Chelmsford), Simon Ward (William Vereker), John Mills (Sir Bartle Frere), Nigel Davenport (Col. Hamilton-Brown), Michael Jayston (Col. Crealock), Ronald Lacey (Norris Newman), Denholm Elliott (Lt. Col. Pulleine), Freddie Jones (Bishop Colenso), Christopher Cazenove (Lt. Coghill), Ronald Pickup (Lt. Harford), Donald Pickering (Maj. Russell), Anna Calder-Marshall (Fanny Colenso), James Faulkner (Lt. Melvill), Peter Vaughan (Quartermaster Sergeant), Graham Armitage (Capt. Shepstone), Bob Hoskins (Sgt. Maj. Williams), Dai Bradley (Pvt. Williams), Paul Copley (Pvt. Storey), Chris Chittell (Lt. Milne, Royal Navy), Nicholas Clay (Lt. Raw), Patrick Mynhardt (Maj. Harness), Brian O'Shaughnessy (Maj. Smith), Simon Sabela (Cetshwayo), Midge Carter (Lt. Cavaye), Phil Daniels (Boy Soldier Pullen), Raymond Davies (Sgt. Murphy), Ken Gampu (C.S.M. Kambula).

Fifteen years after ZULU documented the heroic stand of a hundred British soldiers against thousands of Zulu warriors under King Cetshwayo, ZULU DAWN documents the precursor to that battle, the increasing tensions between the British colonial officials and the Zulus, and the eventual extermination of 1500 British soldiers at the battle of Isandhlwana. O'Toole is the overall commander of British forces in the area and Lancaster the one-armed hero who leads his men to their deaths. There are a number of impressive scenes as the British column marches into Zulu territory and the Zulus group for the attack. The attack, when it finally swoops down on the British, is spectacular, and though the British fight with courage, they are outnumbered 16 to 1 and are wiped out in fairly short order. Lancaster manages to get to a gully where a warrior kills him with a spear. The film was written by Cy Endfield, who wrote and directed the original ZULU, but this film is a far cry from that classic, lacking the interpersonal conflicts that made the first film so fascinating. Although the battle scenes are well done, they simply don't capture the imagination the way similar scenes did in ZULU. The film proved a box-office failure in the U.S. despite its high-powered cast. Lancaster, who had turned down THE WILD GEESE earlier that year bacause it wasn't truthful about Africa, took this role and told reporters: "This is an honest film, full of action and courage. It is very realistic with an almost documentary approach that follows the course of history accurately." The British have long had a way of turning their military disasters into gallant tales of brave Englishmen, from the Charge of the Light Brigade at Balaklava, to the bloody and mismanaged Somme Offensive, to the evacuation at Dunkirk. ZULU DAWN is yet another installment in the mythology of the British Army, despite the fact that it was a humiliating defeat.

p, Nate Kohn; d, Douglas Hickox; w, Cy Endfield, Anthony Storey (based on a story by Endfield); ph, Ousama Rawi (Panavision, Technicolor); m, Elmer Bernstein; ed, Malcolm Cooke; prod d, John Rosewarne; art d, Peter Williams; stunts, Bob Simmons.

Historical Drama   **(PR:C-O MPAA:PG)**

ZVEROLOVY   (SEE: HUNTING IN SIBERIA, 1962, USSR)

ZVONYAT, OTKROYTE DVER   (SEE: GIRL AND THE BUGLER, THE, 1967, USSR)

ZVYODY I SOLDATY   (SEE: RED AND THE WHITE, THE, 1969, Hung./USSR)

ZWEI SARGE AUF BESTELLUNG
          (SEE: WE STILL KILL THE OLD WAY, 1968, Ital.)

1984

A NOS AMOURS**½ (1984, Fr.) 102m Les Films du Livradois-GAU-FR3/Triumph c (GB: TO OUR LOVES)

Sandrine Bonnaire (*Suzanne*), Dominique Besnehard (*Robert*), Maurice Pialat (*The Father*), Evelyne Ker (*The Mother*), Anne-Sophie Maille (*Anne*), Christophe Odent (*Michel*), Cyr Boitard (*Luc*), Maite Maille (*Martine*), Pierre-Loup Rajot (*Bernard*), Cyril Collard (*Jean-Pierre*), Nathalie Gureghian (*Nathalie*), Guenole Pascal (*Instructor*), Caroline Cibot (*Charline*), Jacques Fieschi (*Jacques*), Valerie Schlumberger (*Marie-France*), Tom Stevens (*American*), Tsilka Theodorou (*Fanny*), Vanghel Theodorou (*Claude*), Herve Austen (*Freddy*), Eric Viellard (*Henri*), Pierre Novion (*Adrien*), Isabelle Prades (*Solange*), Alexandre De Dardel (*Alex*), Alexis Quentin (*Richard*).

A NOS AMOURS is the story of an amoral teenage heroine, Bonnaire, who is only happy when she is with a guy. After an unromantic night with an American, Bonnaire becomes increasingly interested in the opposite sex. Her promiscuity makes her a popular item among the boys, as well as an object of jealousy among her girl friends. Her consistent late hours cause dissension in her family, especially with her stern father, played by director Pialat. Her sexual awakening confuses her, as does her inability to feel love. This lack is further illustrated when her father moves out of the house. None of it ever really rings true, however, seeming more like a parody of teenage behavior. Bonnaire's actions seem dishonest in light of films such as Francois Truffaut's THE 400 BLOWS. Instead of being emotionally drawn into Bonnaire's character as we are with Truffaut's Antoine Doinel, we can only laugh at the hopeless melodrama of the situations. (In French; English Subtitles.)

p&d, Maurice Pialat; w, Pialat, Arlette Langmann; ph, Jacques Loiseleux; m, Klaus Nomy; ed, Yann Dedet, Sophie Coussein, Valerie Condroyer, Corinne Lazare, Jean Gargonne, Nathalie Letrosne, Catherine Legault; art d, Jean-Paul Camail; cos, Valerie Schlumberger, Martha de Villalonga; m/l, Henry Purcell's "The Cold Song" (performed by Nomi).

Drama   Cas.   (PR:O MPAA:R)

ACT, THE** (1984) 94m Film Ventures c (AKA: BLESS 'EM ALL)

Robert Ginty (*Don*), Sarah Langenfeld (*Leslie*), Nick Surovy (*Julian*), John Aprea (*Ron*), John Tripp (*Dixie*), Eddie Albert (*Harry*), James Andronica (*Mickey*), John Cullum (*President*), Roger Davis (*Police Chief*), Pat Hingle (*Frank*), David Huddleston (*Corky*), Jill St. John (*Elise*), Arika Wells (*Hooker*), Tom Hunter (*The John*).

A greedy lawyer gets involved with union politics when he accepts a $2 million payment to defend a crooked union leader and keep him out of prison. Once the lawyer receives his payment he finds that the union is determined to get back its money. Instead of buckling under pressure, he puts up a fight and must now defend himself against their dirty methods.

p, David Greene, Sig Shore; d, Shore; w, Robert Lipsyte; ph, Benjamin Davis; m, John Sebastian, Phil Goldston; ed, Ron Kalish; prod d, Steve Wilson.

Crime   (PR:O MPAA:R)

ADERYN PAPUR**½ (1984, Brit.) 75m Red Rooster c (AKA:...AND PIGS MIGHT FLY)

Richard Love (*Alun Owen*), Iola Gregory (*Aunty Catrin*), John Ogwen (*Gwyn Owen*), Robert E. Roberts (*Idris Owen*), Llewelyn Jones (*Gareth*), Stewart Jones (*Granddad*), Tasaki Noguchi (*Kazuo*), Yoshio Kawahara (*Naoyuki*).

One of a small number of Welsh-language films, this is the story of a small, economically depressed Welsh village which rallies itself when a pair of Japanese men rent a house. Everyone immediately assumes that they are there to scout a location for business and so they put on their best faces. Finally they realize that the pair are only tourists, but their morale has substantially improved and hope grows again in the village. The film shows the restrictions of a tiny budget, but it has enough style and content to compare with any major film.

p, Linda James; d, Stephen Bayly; w, Ruth Carter; ph, Richard Greatrex; m, Trevor Jones; ed, Scott Thomas; art d, Hildegard Bechtler.

Comedy/Drama   (PR:A-C MPAA:NR)

ADVENTURES OF BUCKAROO BANZAI: ACROSS THE 8TH DIMENSION, THE*** (1984) 103m Sherwood/FOX c

Peter Weller (*Buckaroo Banzai*), John Lithgow (*Dr. Emilio Lizardo/Lord John Whorfin*), Ellen Barkin (*Penny Priddy*), Jeff Goldblum (*New Jersey*), Christopher Lloyd (*John Bigboote*), Lewis Smith (*Perfect Tommy*), Rosalind Cash (*John Emdall*), Robert Ito (*Prof. Hikita*), Pepe Serna (*Reno Nevada*), Ronald Lacey (*President Widmark*), Matt Clark (*Secretary of Defense*), Clancy Brown (*Rawhide*), William Traylor (*Gen. Catburd*), Carl Lumbly (*John Parker*), Vincent Schiavelli (*John O'Connor*), Dan Hedaya (*John Gomez*), Mariclare Costello (*Sen. Cunningham*), Bill Henderson (*Casper Lindley*), Damon Hines (*Scooter Lindley*), Billy Vera (*Pinky Carruthers*), Laura Harrington (*Mrs. Johnson*), Michael Santoro (*Billy Travers*), Kent Perkins (*Mission Control*), Jonathan Banks (*Lizardo Hospital Guard*), Robert Gray (*First Radar Blaze*), Gary Bisig (*Second Radar Blaze*), Kenneth Magee (*Duck Hunter Burt*), James Keane (*Duck Hunter Bubba*), John Ashton (*Highway Patrolman*), Yakov Smirnoff (*National Security Advisor*), Leonard Gaines (*Artie Duncan*), James Saito (*Dr. Masado Banzai*), Leonard Gaines (*Artie Duncan*), Jamie Lee Curtis (*Dr. Sandra Banzai*), Francine Lembi (*TV Anchorwoman*), John Walter Davis (*Star Surgeon*), Read Morgan (*Exhibitor*), James Rosin (*John Yaya*), Raye Birk (*1st Reporter*), Jane Marla Robbins (*2nd Reporter*), Kevin Sullivan (*John Gant*), Jessie Lawrence Ferguson (*Black Lectroid*), Radford Polinsky (*Marine Lieutenant*), Sam Minsky, Robert Hummer (*Kolodny Brothers*), Gerald Peterson (*Rug Sucker*), Greg Mires, Matthew Mires (*Young Buckaroos*).

A strange film that just tries to do too much in too short a time. Weller is a nuclear physicist, brain surgeon, and rock'n'roll singer who manages to save the world from the domination of aliens from a distant galaxy. As the film opens, Weller is trying to drive his superpowered car through a mountain in an attempt to test the "oscillation overthruster" he has invented. This device is also needed by the aliens to return to their own world. Lithgow is a mad scientist (literally, for when we first see him he is an inmate at an asylum) who had worked on the same research decades before, when he had driven a rocket sled through a wall and into the 8th dimension. When he hears of Weller's success, he breaks out of the asylum and sets up shop again, making plans for world domination with the aliens, the Red Lectroids, who have been on Earth since Halloween, 1939, when Orson Welles broadcast the invasion, then was hypnotized into claiming that it was all a hoax (Weller and his crew figure this out when they notice that all the suspicious characters they've been dealing with have social security numbers issued on November 1 of that year. Weller leads his cohorts into the enemy camp and saves the day, though. At least that's what may be going on in this movie. Never has a film been seen in which it is as obvious that so much has been cut out. Punch lines appear without set- ups and set-ups without punch lines. Characters come and go with such bewildering speed that it is all but impossible to keep track of the story, which also jumps around so much as to induce motion sickness. Weller is perhaps a little too relaxed as the jack-of-all-trades hero, but Goldblum, as the latest addition to his rock'n'rolling scientist followers, is as good as usual, and Lithgow, whose star has been much on the rise of late, is superb as the mad scientist, a role that lets him adopt a ludicrous Italian accent, roll his eyes, and foam at the mouth while speaking some of the silliest lines ever put on paper.

p, Neil Canton, W.D. Richter; d, Richter; w, Earl Mac Rauch; ph, Fred J. Koenekamp (Panavision, Metrocolor); m, Michael Boddicker; ed, Richard Marks, George Bowers; prod d, J. Michael Riva; art d, Richard Carter, Stephen Dane; set d, Linda De Scenna; cos, Aggie Guerrard Rodgers; spec eff, Michael Fink; stunts, James Arnett.

Science Fiction/Comedy   Cas.   (PR:C-O MPAA:PG)

AFTER THE FALL OF NEW YORK* (1984, Ital./Fr.) 95m Nuova Dania-Medusa Les Films du Griffon/Almi c

Michael Sopkiw (*Parsifal*), Valentine Monnier (*Giaiada*), Anna Kanakis (*Ania*), Roman Geer (*Rachet*), Vincent Scalondro (*Bronx*), George Eastman (*Big Ape*), Edmund Purdom (*President of PAC*), Louis Ecclesia (*Shorty*).

European imitation of successful American films like RAIDERS OF THE LOST ARK, BLADE RUNNER, and, especially, ESCAPE FROM NEW YORK. In the year 2019, World War III has been over for 20 years, what's left of the U.S. is grouped in Alaska, and none of the women who survive is fertile. Sopkiw is sent out to New York, deep in enemy territory, to retrieve a woman believed to be the last chance at propagation of the species, largely because her father, a scientist, kept her frozen all through the nuclear wars. Silly at best, with a ludicrous plot filled with cliches and holes, bad acting, and laughable special effects.

p, Luciano Martino; d, Martin Dolman, Sergio Martino; w, Julian Berry, Gabriel Rossini, Dolman (based on a story by Barry, Dolman); ph, Giancarlo Ferrando (Telecolor); m, Oliver Onions; ed, Eugenio Alabiso; prod d, Sergio Borelli; art d, Antonello Geleng; spec eff, Paolo Ricci; makeup, Fabrizio Sforza, Gino Tamagnini; stunts, Nazzareno Cardinali.

Science Fiction   (PR:O MPAA:R)

AFTER THE REHEARSAL** (1984, Swed.) 72m Cinematograph-Personafilm/Triumph c

Erland Josephson (*Henrik Vogler*), Ingrid Thulin (*Rakel*), Lena Olin (*Anna Egerman*), Nadja Palmstjerna-Weiss (*Anna at age 12*), Bertil Guve (*Henrik at age 12*).

Filmed for Swedish television, AFTER THE REHEARSAL was announced as Ingmar Bergman's farewell to cinema (a claim which was also made upon FANNY AND ALEXANDER's release in 1983). Partly autobiographical in nature, the film concerns an aging theater director, Josephson, who looks back on the pain and suffering he caused those around him. Somewhat of a rogue, Josephson prided himself on the actresses he became involved with during the production of his plays. After the rehearsal of his fifth production of August Strindberg's "Dream Play" the aging director rests his weary self on a couch which is part of the stage set. He is visited by a young actress, Olin, who has returned to the theater in search of a bracelet she supposedly left behind. She is attracted to Josephson, and he to her. They sit on the couch and discuss esoterica like life and theater. It is revealed that Josephson once had an affair with Olin's mother. Their discussion is interrupted by the arrival of Thulin, a has-been actress whose fondness for drinking has destroyed her ability to act. Thulin fails to notice Olin and attacks Josephson for abandoning her. She does her best to make a fool of him and then to further annoy him she details an affair she is having with her doctor. He promises to have dinner with her and she finally leaves. Olin and Josephson then resume their talk, imagining the course of their affair–should they choose to have one. After having lived out their future together in words, they decide not to bother with having an affair. Though AFTER THE REHEARSAL is blessed with three superb performances, it is trapped in its staginess. One wonders why Bergman ever decided to bring this story to the screen. For those who bow at the throne of Bergman, AFTER THE REHEARSAL will be judged a masterpiece. Others, however, will see this film as one that neatly and safely fits into the already defined "art film" mold. (In Swedish; English subtitles.)

p, Jorn Donner; d&w, Ingmar Bergman; ph, Sven Nykvist; ed, Sylvia Ingemarsson; art d, Anna Asp; cos, Inger Pehrsson.

Drama   **Cas.**   **(PR:C-O   MPAA:R)**

AGAINST ALL ODDS*   (1984) 128m New Visions/COL c

Rachel Ward (*Jessie Wyler*), Jeff Bridges (*Terry Brogan*), James Woods (*Jake Wise*), Alex Karras (*Hank Sully*), Jane Greer (*Mrs. Wyler*), Richard Widmark (*Ben Caxton*), Dorian Harewood (*Tommy*), Swoosie Kurtz (*Edie*), Saul Rubinek (*Steve Kirsch*), Pat Corley (*Ed Phillips*), Bill McKinney (*Head Coach*), Allen Williams (*Bob Soames*), Sam Scarber (*Assistant Coach*), John St. Elwood (*Ahmad Cooper*), Tamara Stafford (*Kirsch's Girl Friend*), Jonathan Terry (*Ryskind*), Paul Valentine (*Councilman Weinberg*), Ted White (*Guard with Dog*), Stone Bower (*Security Guard*), Mel Scott-Thomas (*Quarterback*), Barnetta McCarthy, Ginger LaBrie (*Receptionists*), David Dayan (*Car Valet*), Tom Kelly (*Football Announcer*), August Darnell (*Kid Creole*), Adriana Kaegi, Cheryl Poirier, Taryn Hagey (*Coconuts*), Gary Davis (*Porsche Stunt Driver*), Carey Loftin (*Ferrari Stunt Driver*), Carl Ciarfalio (*Sully Stunt Double*), Jophery Brown, Bill Burton, David Burton, Bud Davis, Buddy Joe Hooker, Charles Picerni, Ronnie Rondell, Dennis Scott, Glen Wilder, Dick Ziker (*Stunts*).

Disappointing remake of OUT OF THE PAST, generally regarded to be one of the best *film noir* pieces of the 1940s. When are producers going to realize that to redo a classic, in whatever genre, is an error? No matter how good the new version, they will always be jousting with shadows and so it was with this. Bridges is a professional football player who has been injured in his shoulder and is desperately trying to hang on in the NFL. Woods is a shady nightclub owner and sometime bookie. The two men are in love with Ward, a spoiled woman who is the daughter of Greer, the mean owner of the team that is about to cut Bridges. (knowledgeable football fans will recognize her character.) Ward has always been taken care of by Greer (who played the Ward role in the 1947 Jacques Tourneur movie) but resents the fact that she has also been controlled. So what we have are three not very sympathetic characters, especially once it's learned that Bridges shaved points in a game. He needed money and made a deal with Woods to do the scam but, in order to make us feel something for Bridges, we are told that he is somewhat guilty about it. Ward and Woods have a battle and she cuts out for Mexico, taking lots of money after she stabs him in a violent disagreement. Woods sends Bridges down to Mexico to find Ward. (They shot in the jungles of Yucatan as well as at some Mayan ruins, the first time the Mexican government had allowed that to occur. One wonders if the powers in the government had read the script or if liberal doses of "la mordida" 'the bite' had been spread in the right palms. No accusations, just a question.) Bridges is cut from the team and needs money so he takes the job of traveling south of the border. Once they meet, Ward and Bridges find much to like about each other and spend a few glorious weeks in the sun and have a number of luke-hot scenes together that give this an "R" rating. Bridges calls Woods and says that he has been unable to find Ward and needs a bit more time. Woods doesn't believe him and sends Karras, a football buddy of Bridges', to see what's happening. Ward knows that Bridges was sent by Woods but she doesn't care because she has fallen hard for him. This may be due to the incestuous fact that he reminds her of his late brother. Meanwhile, Greer and new husband Widmark, a real-estate shark and an attorney (are those two professions aligned or what?) are biding their time. Ward and Bridges run out of money as Karras arrives. Bridges trusts the man and doesn't know that his buddy's first allegiance is to Woods, the man who is paying him. Karras finds Ward and Bridges making love in an ancient temple, the two men fight, and Karras is about ready to throttle Bridges when Ward picks up Karras' gun and fatally shoots him in the chest. Ward flees and Bridges is left behind to dispose of the body.

Later, Bridges comes back to Los Angeles and tells Woods that he never did find Ward. Ward walks into the room and Woods smiles, as everyone there has something on everyone else. Now it's the moment for the subplot to rear its head in this complex, labyrinthian, pale imitation of CHINATOWN. At the start of the film, we learned that Greer and Widmark owned some valuable West Los Angeles property that was to be developed. Ecologists and environmentalists were against this. Some grease was laid on to make the deal go through; heavy bribes were handed over, and if the truth were ever bared, it might mean the end of the career of some important people. Files on all of this are in the hands of Rubinek, who is the former agent and attorney for Bridges. These files are dynamite and both Woods and Widmark want them. But it's Bridges who manages to get the goods, with the help of Rubinek's secretary, Kurtz, as they make their way through an alarm system almost as elaborate as the one in RIFIFI. Bridges now has the goods on everyone but he can't use the information as he is "dirty" as well, because it was his throwing of the game which caused one of the environmentalists to win money and...are you confused yet? Now everyone is after Bridges and they finally catch up to him, after a chase on Sunset Boulevard, high on a hill overlooking Los Angeles at night. Bridges has the papers but Woods has a gun. Widmark and Ward are there as well. Ward eventually shoots the villainous Woods and the picture ends as Widmark can return to running his real-estate empire, Bridges can have his old job back with the team, and Ward can continue acting as though she were in a coma. Phil Collins wrote and sang the Oscar-winning "Against All Odds" as the end credits rolled. This has more twists than a licorice stick and all the empty calories and general decay that go with it. It's not much more than an awful film contrivance that afforded the cast and crew the opportunity to hang out in Cancun, which is an entirely manufactured resort community with as much charm as a plastic bath mat. Hackford, who had done so well with AN OFFICER AND A GENTLEMAN, falls into the remake hole with this and one hopes he'll spend his talents on something original next time. Woods' nightclub was "The Palace" on Vine Street and it is used well for the music scenes, especially one with "Kid Creole and the Coconuts." If you don't think much of Los Angeles, this film fuels the fire that L.A. is a totally corrupt city filled with amoral citizens and no police officers. The original film starred Robert Mitchum, Kirk Douglas, and Greer. Bringing Greer back to play the mother of the role she did 37 years before was a bit of "stunt" casting which added nothing and sullied the image she'd created back then.

p, Taylor Hackford, William S. Gilmore; d, Hackford; w, Eric Hughes (based on the screenplay OUT OF THE PAST by Daniel Mainwaring and the novel $fBuild My Gallows High by William Morrow); ph, Donald Thorin (MetroColor); m, Michel Colombier, Larry Carlton; ed, Frederic Steinkamp, William Steinkamp; art d, Richard James Lawrence; set d, Garrett Lewis; cos, Michael Kaplan; m/l, "Against All Odds," Phil Collins.

Crime Drama   **Cas.**   **(PR:C-O   MPAA:R)**

AH YING*   (1984, Hong Kong) 110m Feng Huang/Museum of
                                                          Modern Art c

Hui So-ying (*Ah Ying*), Peter Wang (*Cheung Chung-pac*), Hui Pui (*Ah Ying's Father*), Yao Lin-shum (*Ah Ying's Mother*), Cheng Chi-hung (*Ah-Ying's Boy Friend*), Hui Wai-hon (*The Married Brother*), Hui So-lin (*Ah Lin*), Hui So-Kei (*Ah Kei*), Hui So-Kam (*Ah Kam*), Hui So-lam (*Ah Lam*), Lau Ka-chun (*Ah Shan*), Cheung Ka-yan (*Ah Lin's Boy Friend*).

A compelling tale of a 22-year-old girl who lives in Hong Kong with her parents and seven brothers and sisters. She works at the family fish market but has hopes of breaking away from traditional family expectations. She has much more modern ideas, as well as an undying devotion to David Bowie, American music (she sings a moving version of Jim Croce's "Time in a Bottle" in English), and movies. She answers an ad for a position at the Film Culture Center in Hong Kong and soon enrolls in an acting class. Her instructor takes a platonic interest in her and their relationship blossoms– she hoping to gain notoriety as an actress and he hoping to find success as a filmmaker. Director Fong said that this film was based on two things–the real-life experiences and aspirations of Hui So-ying, his young actress, and his friendship with a director named Koh Wu, who died in 1982 before he was able to begin production on a new film. Having studied at the University of Georgia and the University of Southern California, Fong is similar to his actress–an Asian exposed to and fascinated with Western culture. (In Cantonese, Mandarin, and English; English subtitles.)

d, Allen Fong [Fong Yuk-Ping]; w, Sze Yeun-ping, Peter Wang; ph, Chang Lok-yee; m, Violet Lam; ed, Chow Muk-leung, Ng Kam-wah.

Drama   **(PR:A   MPAA:NR)**

ALIEN FACTOR, THE*   (1984) 80m Cinemagic c

Don Leifert (*Ben*), Tom Griffith (*Sheriff*), Richard Dyszel (*Mayor*), Mary Martens (*Edie*), Richard Geiwitz (*Pete*), George Stover (*Steven*), Eleanor Herman (*Mary Jane*), Anne Frith (*Dr. Sherman*), Christopher Gummer (*Clay*), Don Dohler (*Ernie*), Dave Ellis (*Rich*), Johnny Walker (*Rex*), Tony Malnowski (*Ed*).

A spaceship crash-lands near a rural community and three scary monsters climb out and begin to terrorize the populace. Silly low-budget effort that was produced five years earlier and went unreleased until it was sold to television. Only the undiscriminating will be able to sit through this one.

d&w, Donald M. Dohler; ph, Britt McDonough (Quality Color); m, Kenneth Walker; ed, Dohler, Dave Ellis; spec eff, Larry Schlechter.

Science Fiction   Cas.   (PR:C MPAA:NR)

ALL OF ME***   (1984) 93m Kings Road/UNIV c

Steve Martin (*Roger Cobb*), Lily Tomlin (*Edwina Cutwater*), Victoria Tennant (*Terry Hoskins*), Madolyn Smith (*Peggy Schuyler*), Richard Libertini (*Prahka Lasa*), Dana Elcar (*Burton Schuyler*), Jason Bernard (*Tyrone Wattell*), Selma Diamond (*Margo*), Eric Christmas (*Fred Hoskins*), Gailard Sartain (*Fulton Norris*), Neva Patterson (*Gretchen*), Michael Ensign (*Mr. Mifflin*), Peggy Feury (*Dr. Betty Ahrens*), Nan Martin (*Divorce Lawyer*), Basil Hoffman (*Court Clerk*), Hedley Mattingly (*Grayson*), Harvey Vernon (*Judge*), Stu Black (*Police Officer*), Marilyn Tokuda (*Receptionist*), David Byrd (*Minister*), Nick Shields (*Hard Hat*), Bill Saito (*Security Guard*), Neil Elliott (*Cabbie*), Jillian Scott (*Courtroom Spectator*), Judy Nagy (*Nurse*), Ronn Wright (*Cook*), Jim Welch (*James Welch IV*).

Carl Reiner has, more or less, directed all of this before. From WHERE'S POPPA? to OH, GOD! to THE JERK, Reiner has comedically depicted the shlemiel trying to make his life work. This time, it's Martin again as a man who is frustrated romantically, personally, and professionally. He is a music-loving, guitar-playing attorney semi-engaged to Smith, who is the daughter of his boss at a large law firm. His wisecracking secretary is Diamond (in a Thelma Ritter role) and the firm's most important client is a very wealthy, very ill Tomlin. Tomlin realizes that she hasn't much more time to live and wants to amend her will to allow Tennant, who is the daughter of Christmas, Tomlin's stable master, to inherit her soul in exchange for Tennant's healthy body. If you can accept this as true, read on. If not, forget this film. The switch of soul for body will be accomplished through the auspices and intervention of Tomlin's personal guru, Libertini (who adds one more hysterical portrait in his gallery of excellent characterizations through the years). Martin is on the brink of turning 38 and not certain whether he wants to marry Smith or not. He can't even bring himself to say the "M" word. He enjoys playing guitar in a small group led by blind jazz sax player Bernard, a good pal, but is harassed by boss Elcar, a skirt-chaser, to forget about such musical nonsense and concentrate on legal matters. Martin is confused about what to do as he doesn't like the law nearly as well as he enjoys music. Martin is given the Tomlin last will and testament to oversee. The first third of the movie is very funny, almost breakneck in pace. It ends when Tomlin dies and, through a silly turn of events, her soul is not transferred into Tennant's body, it's injected into...guess who? Right, Martin now has his own personality and that of Tomlin fighting for control of his being. This causes several excellent comic moments as Martin, a fine physical funnyman, tries to operate the left side of his body in his usual goofy fashion while Tomlin's cynical and unhappy persona is handling the right side. The predictable gags of shaving, urinating, walking, and the like begin to wear thin after a brief while. Tomlin continues making the attempt to crawl out of Martin's body and into Tennant's. Meanwhile, Tennant is angry because she'd looked forward to spending all of Tomlin's money. Tennant tries to find Libertini to effect this operation but he has dropped out of sight. At the same time, Martin would like very much to enter Tennant's body (in a different fashion), but with Tomlin still controlling half of him, that will never happen. The conclusion is confusing as Tomlin and Martin opt for life together, doing all the things that both of them wanted to do. With her money and his body, they can have lots of fun. In the course of the film, Tomlin's grating personality softens and by the time the picture is over, Martin and Tomlin have become two friends occupying the same space. Their reward (and ours) is a scene in which they dance to the voice of Joe Williams singing "All of Me" in a Billy May arrangement. It was the best scene in the movie because the joy on the faces of both stars (don't ask how that happened) was evident. Martin does some of his best acting in this film, which stretches him far beyond what had been seen before. He steals the movie from Tomlin, whose character was, at best, a one-note creation. If you're a Martin fan, you'll love ALL OF ME and even if you aren't, there's enough fun in spots to make it worth your precious time, something which this movie tells us not to waste. It bears some resemblance to films such as HEAVEN CAN WAIT, HERE COMES MR. JORDAN, and the TOPPER films with an overlay of TOOTSIE.

p, Stephen Friedman; d, Carl Reiner; w, Phil Alden Robinson, Henry Olek (based on the novel *Me Too* by Ed Davis); ph, Richard H. Kline (Technicolor); m, Patrick Williams; ed, Bud Molin; prod d, Edward Carfagno; set d, Jerry Wunderlich; cos, Ray Summers; spec eff, Bruce Steinhemmer.

Comedy   Cas.   (PR:A-C MPAA:PG)

ALLEY CAT*½   (1984) 82m Dragonfly/Film Ventures International c

Karin Mani (*Billie*), Robert Torti (*Johnny*), Britt Helfer (*Hooker*), Michael Wayne (*Scarface*), Jon Greene (*Boyle*), Jay Fisher (*Charles*), Claudia Decea (*Rose*), Tim Cutt (*Thomas*), Jay Walker (*Judge Taylor*), Moriah Shannon (*Sam*), Marla Stone (*Karen Stride*), Kevin Velligan (*Gouger*), Tony Oliver (*Bob Mertel*), Victoria Shea (*Police Lady*), Bob Baisa (*Capt. Smith*), Tom Bismark (*Thug*), Robert Dennis (*Strickland*), Peter Furman (*Grossman*), Mark Zaslove (*Bailiff*), Mark Defrain, Dennis Keep (*Toughs*), Gino Valenti (*Sergeant*), Mark Bradford (*Switchboard Operator*), Bois Elwell (*Stage

Director), John Cardona (*Bondsman*), Rose Dreifus (*Kate Clark*), Rosemary Patterson (*Admitting Clerk*), Edward Archer (*Accompanist*), Dolores Waggoner (*Prison Matron*), Adolfo Lopez (*Gonzales*), Robert Noonoo, Ashok Mukhey (*Attorneys*), Barry Jamesby (*Doctor*), Patricia Heald (*Nurse*), Suzan Stadner, Charon Heuer, Beth Staeheli (*Guards*), Cynthia Helferstay, Roxanne Duvall, Vanessa McCabe, Tracy O'Brien, Irene Waters, Diane Stroebel (*Prisoners*), Tony R. Martinez (*Storeowner*), Craig Dinkel, Adrian Barnes, Eben McCabe (*Car Strippers*).

Mani is terrorized by a gang in her neighborhood, but when she gets them arrested the judge releases them on a technicality and locks her up. She manages to survive a vicious women's prison, and when she's released she goes out for vengeance on the thugs responsible. Enough violence and nakedness to keep exploitation audiences happy, but the acting and writing are laughably bad. Directed by three men under one pseudonym.

p, Robert E. Waters, Victor Ordonez; d, Edward Victor [Eduardo Palmos, Al Valletta, Ordonez]; w, Waters; ph, Howard Anderson III (United Color); m, Quito Colayco; ed, Robert Ernst; prod d, Robert Lee; set d, Mannie Lee; stunts, Lita Vasquez; makeup, Melanie Kay.

Crime   Cas.   (PR:O MPAA:R)

ALMOST YOU½**   (1984) 96m Wescom/FOX-TLC c

Brooke Adams (*Erica Boyer*), Griffin Dunne (*Alex Boyer*), Karen Young (*Lisa Willoughby*), Marty Watt (*Kevin Danzig*), Christine Estabrook (*Maggie*), Josh Mostel (*David*), Laura Dean (*Jeannie*), Dana Delany (*Susan McCall*), Miguel Pinero (*Ralph*), Joe Silver (*Uncle Stu*), Joe Leon (*Uncle Mel*), Daryl Edwards (*Sal*), Suzzy Roche (*Receptionist*), Spalding Gray (*Travel Agent*), Stephen Strimpell (*Lecturer*), Suzanne Hughes (*Bartender*), Wendy Creed (*Waitress*), Harvey Waldman (*Director*), Karsen Lee Gould (*Assistant*), Mark Metcalf (*Andrews*), Steve DeLuca, Jim Phelan (*Policemen*), Seth Allen (*Frank Rose*), Will Hussung (*Doorman*), Harry Madsen (*Taxi Driver/Stunt Coordinator*).

Dunne is a young man dissatisfied with his life and his wife (Adams). When she is badly hurt in a car accident, they hire nurse Young to care for her and soon Dunne is having an affair with her. In addition, he strikes up a friendship with Watt, Young's boy friend. Mostly boring and laden with characters totally without appeal (with the possible exception of Dunne).

p, Mark Lipson; d, Adam Brooks; w, Mark Horowitz (based on a story by Brooks); ph, Alexander Gruszynski; m, Jonathan Elias; ed, Mark Burns; art d, Nora Chavoosian; set d, Leslie Pope; cos, Eugenie Del Greco; makeup, James Sarzotti.

Drama   (PR:C MPAA:R)

ALPHABET CITY*   (1984) 85m Atlantic c

Vincent Spano (*Johnny*), Michael Winslow (*Lippy*), Kate Vernon (*Angie*), Jami Gertz (*Sophia*), Zohra Lampert (*Mama*), Ray Serra (*Gino*), Kenny Marino (*Tony*), Daniel Jordano (*Juani*), Tom Mardirosian (*Benny*), Christina Maire Denihan (*Baby Renee*), Amy Gootenberg (*Suicide Squeeze Customer*), Miguel Pinero (*Dealer*), Barry Mitchell (*Water Pistol Man*), Bob Fuchs (*Bouncer*), Martine Malle (*Karen*), Lauren Hamilton (*Linda*), James Cox Chambers (*Ronnie*), Cintia Cruz (*La Tropicana Girl No. 1*), Nandrea Lin (*La Tropicana Girl No. 2*), Tom Wright (*Cahuffeur*), Bruno Damon (*Mamma's Friend*), Clifton Powell (*Ramon*), Richard Bassett (*Preppie*), John McCurry (*Junkie/Guard No. 1*), George Kyle (*Junkie/Guard No. 2*), Gary Tacon (*Junkie/Guard No. 3*), Luther Rucker (*Junkie/Guard No. 4*), Harry Madsen (*Hitman No. 1*), Alex Stevens (*Hitman No. 2*), Bill Anagnos, Jery Hewitt, Lisa Loving, Popcorn, Webster Whinery, Tom Wright (*Stunt People*).

Set in the seedy milieu of Manhattan's Lower East Side between avenues A through D (hence the title), this confused, pretentious exercise in meaningless visual style stars Spano as a small-time neighborhood drug kingpin who lives in a so-so chic loft with his wife, Vernon, and their baby. Aided by his drug-addicted friend Winslow, Spano makes the rounds of the hot night spots in the area selling dope and collecting extortion money for his bosses. A moral dilemma actually intrudes upon Spano's hip-but-vapid existence when the upper echelon of the mob, Serra, orders him to torch the apartment building where his mother, Lampert, and sister, Gertz, live. Though Spano definitely shows promise as an up-and-coming mobster, and he knows how to live well (fancy clothes, a Porsche and a motorcycle, the loft), the young hood decides to give it all up for the love of his family. Grabbing the wife and kid, Spano zooms off into the night, leaving the filth behind. ALPHABET CITY was the first Hollywood-produced feature to be directed by famed 8mm and 16mm independent filmmaker Amos Poe. While Poe is able to convey a very slick visual style that celebrates wet streets, drifting smoke, neon lights, and blue-steel night, his plot and characters are dull and observations of them insipid. The audience is given no reason whatsoever to even watch these people, let alone care about them. Spano, a talented young actor who has made a good showing in films as diverse as John Sayles' BABY, IT'S YOU (1982), Francis Coppola's RUMBLE FISH (1983), and Andre Konchalovsky's MARIA'S LOVERS (1984), struggles mightily to wrest some meaning from his role, but there isn't any. ALPHABET CITY is nothing more than a feature length, high-tech commercial for a product that is never shown.

p, Andrew Braunsberg; d, Amos Poe; w, Gregory K. Heller, Poe, Robert

Seidman (based on a novel by Heller); ph, Oliver Wood; m, Nile Rodgers; ed, Grahame Weinbren, Lois Freeman; prod d, Nord Haggerty; art d, Stephen J. Lineweaver, Terence McCorry; cos, Anna Taylor; spec eff, Lineweaver; makeup, Ed French; stunts, Harry Madsen.

Crime/Drama   **Cas.**   **(PR:O   MPAA:R)**

AMADEUS*****   (1984) 158m Orion c

F. Murray Abraham (*Antonio Salieri*), Tom Hulce (*Wolfgang Amadeus Mozart*), Elizabeth Berridge (*Constanze Mozart*), Simon Callow (*Emanuel Schikaneder*), Roy Dotrice (*Leopold Mozart*), Christine Ebersole (*Katerina Cavalieri*), Jeffrey Jones (*Emperor Joseph II*), Charles Kay (*Count Orsini-Rosenberg*), Kenny Baker (*Parody Commendatore*), Lisabeth Bartlett (*Papagena*), Barbara Bryne (*Frau Weber*), Martin Cavani (*Young Salieri*), Roderick Cook (*Count Von Strack*), Milan Demjanenko (*Karl Mozart*), Peter DiGesu (*Francesco Salieri*), Richard Frank (*Father Vogler*), Patrick Hines (*Kappelmeister Bonno*), Nicholas Kepros (*Archbishop Colloredo*), Philip Lenkowsky (*Salieri's Servant*), Herman Meckler (*Priest*), Jonathan Moore (*Baron Van Swieten*), Cynthia Nixon (*Lorl*), Brian Pettifer (*Hospital Attendant*), Vincent Schiavelli (*Salieri's Valet*), Douglas Seale (*Count Arco*), Miroslav Sekera (*Young Mozart*), John Strauss (*Conductor*), Karl-Heinz Teuber (*Wig Salesman*).

To fully comprehend the genius of director Milos Forman, one need only speculate as to what might have happened to Shaffer's play in the hands of someone like Ken Russell, who had already tossed several musical geniuses on the rubbish heap of his own cinematic ego. Rather than stylize, Forman chose to naturalize and therein lay the success of the movie, which won many accolades, including Best Picture from the Motion Picture Academy. Filmed mostly on location in Prague (which hasn't changed much for centuries), Shaffer did his own adaptation under Forman's sure hand and the result was a movie that was better than the play. It begins in the 1820s as an aging Abraham (as Antonio Salieri) is seated in an asylum awaiting his death. He is confessing to a young priest, Frank, all of his transgressions and we are flashed back to a time, 30 years before, when Abraham was the official composer of the Austrian court. He meets Hulce, a 26-year-old genius, and cannot reckon the coarse vulgarian he encounters with the brilliant music that flows from Hulce's pen, with nary an erasure. Hulce is a giggling lout, almost an *idiot savant* (which is the way the play portrayed him) and it galls Abraham because he realizes that the boy's talent comes from a higher source, a source that has obviously overlooked the scholastically trained Abraham. Hulce's father is Dotrice (so brilliant in his stage protrayal of "Brief Lives" in London's West End) and his fiancee is Berridge. Abraham recognizes Hulce's talent but is determined to never allow that talent to be applauded by those who matter, so he attempts to sabotage the young composer at every turn and keep Hulce from any fame and-or fortune. Hulce is offensive to the cultured Abraham and the older man feels he has been betrayed by God, who bestowed a gift upon this obscene creature and overlooked himself. Austria is a place where good music is appreciated, *if* it is looked upon with favor by the royal court. With Abraham in charge of the king's listening habits, it is certain that Hulce will never rise in the hierarchy. The Emperor is Jones (in a superb cameo) who realizes that he doesn't really know music so he relies on Abraham to tell him what's good and what's not. Hulce composes "The Magic Flute," "The Marriage of Figaro," and we have the opportunity to watch a re-creation of "Don Giovanni" staged in the same theater, the Tyl, where Mozart conducted the orchestra two centuries before. The "Don Giovanni" sequence is a bit off- base in that it's almost a parody of what is supposed to have happened but this falls under the imprimatur of artistic license, as does much of the film. Mozartists may fault the fact that their hero is seen to be a *l'enfant terrible* in so many ways but that is Shaffer's interpretation, after much research, and the result may even be more interesting than the truth. At the conclusion, Hulce is laboring feverishly to finish his "Requiem" and dies. That he may have been poisoned by Abraham is never fully indicated. That he was tossed into a pauper's grave is clearly seen. Abraham won an Oscar for his characterization of a man who was half Machiavelli and half Mephistopheles. Oddly, Salieri was not an untalented man. Some of his works are played today. In another time and another place, he might have had some lasting success, but having been born in the same era as Mozart was the bane of his existence. His presence on earth may have been a boon to music lovers as it is postulated that Salieri was behind Mozart's completion of the "Requiem," if only for his own pleasure at hearing the work of the dying composer. On stage, Paul Scofield played Salieri in London and Ian McKellen did it in New York. All three interpretations were unique, differing greatly from one another, and Abraham presented the most subtle characterization of the trio, with considerably more shading but less power. Seeing it on screen is an entirely refreshing experience, even for those who attended either the British or U.S. play. The cinematography by Ondricek is spectacular, the costumes by Pistek are flawless, and all technical credits are excellent. Ondricek's camera work and the editing team of Chandler and Danevic were nominated for Oscars but lost. In addition to the aforementioned Oscar winners, Forman took a statuette for his direction, Shaffer for his adaptation of material based on another medium, Pistek for his costumes, Dick Smith for his makeup, Chris Newman for sound, the art direction of Karel Cerny (who handled the Czech locations) and Francesco Chianese (who did the Italian art direction). In addition to Neville Marriner's musical direction (using the Academy of St. Martin-in-

the-Fields, Academy Chorus, Ambrosian Opera Chorus, and the Westminster Abbey Choristers), music of Mozart, Salieri, Pergolesi, and many others is heard. The picture's music was recorded in Dolby Stereo and should be heard on that type of equipment in order to have full impact. Mozart died December 5, 1791, and the official cause of death was listed as typhoid fever. It was in this year that his "Concerto No. 27 for Pianoforte and Orchestra in B Flat Major" was performed in Vienna on March 4. Working feverishly, as though he knew he would not last out the year, Mozart also wrote the motet "Ave Verum Corpus," as well as "A Quintet for Strings in E Flat," "A Concerto for Clarinet and Orchestra in A Major," and several other pieces. He wrote a trio of works in 1788, in less than two months. They were the unperformed X symphonies known as "Number 39 in E Flat Major," "Number 40 in G Minor" and "Number 41 in C Major." Since there was no way to indicate everything he wrote, Forman concentrated on the more popular works, but the point about Mozart's prodigious output was more than made. AMADEUS is a must for any music lover, any film lover, and anyone who reveres excellence.

p, Saul Zaentz; d, Milos Forman; w, Peter Shaffer (based on his stage play); ph, Miroslav Ondricek (Panavision, Technicolor); m, Wolfgang Amadeus Mozart, Antonio Salieri, Giovanni Battista Pergolesi, and others; ed, Nena Danevic, Michael Chandler; md, Neville Marriner; prod d, Patrizia Von Brandenstein; art d&set d, Karel Cerny, Francesco Chianese (opera sets, Josef Svoboda); cos, Theodor Pistek; ch, Twyla Tharp; makeup, Dick Smith; music coordinator, John Strauss.

Musical Biography   **Cas.**   **(PR:C   MPAA:PG)**

AMBASSADOR, THE***   (1984) 90m Northbrook/Cannon c (AKA: PEACEMAKER)

Robert Mitchum (*Peter Hacker*), Ellen Burstyn (*Alex Hacker*), Rock Hudson (*Frank Stevenson*), Fabio Testi (*Mustapha Hashimi*), Donald Pleasence (*Minister Eretz*), Heli Goldenberg (*Rachel*), Michael Bat-Adam (*Tova*), Ori Levy (*Abe*), Uri Gavriel (*Assad*), Zachi Noy, Joseph Shiloah, Shmulik Kraus, Yossi Virginsky, Iftah Katzur, Shai Scwartz, Ran Vered, Assi Abaiov, Yaacov Banai, Avi Kleinberger, Peter Freistadt, Danny Noiman, Rachel Steiner, Dana Ben Yehuda, Zehava Kailos, Esther Zabco, Avi Pnini, Yosef Bee.

Mitchum is the U.S. ambassador to Israel who goes about bringing the sides of the Middle East conflict together despite the objections of security advisor Hudson, and the story also deals with wife Burstyn's affair with a Palestine Liberation Organization official. Well-constructed political drama, with Mitchum's always welcome world-weary face giving weight to a role that few other actors could bring. Just what all this has to do with its alleged source material–Elmore Leonard's novel, *52 Pick-Up*, which concerns a Detroit factory owner who goes about eliminating the thugs who framed him for the murder of his mistress and are blackmailing him–is something of a mystery.

p, Menahem Golan, Yoram Globus, Issac Kol; d, J. Lee Thompson; w, Max Jack (based on the novel *52 Pick-Up* by Elmore Leonard); ph, Adam Greenberg (TVC Color); m, Dov Seltzer; ed, Mark Goldblatt; prod d, Yoram Barzilai.

Drama   **(PR:C   MPAA:R)**

AMERICAN DREAMER**   (1984) 105m CBS Theatrical Films/WB c

JoBeth Williams (*Cathy Palmer*), Tom Conti (*Alan McMann*), Giancarlo Giannini (*Victor Marchand*), Coral Browne (*Margaret McMann*), James Staley (*Kevin Palmer*), C.B. Barnes (*Kevin Palmer, Jr.*), Huckleberry Fox (*Karl Palmer*), Jean Rougerie (*Don Carlos Dominguez*), Pierre Santini (*Inspector Klaus*), Leon Zitrone (*Russian Ambassador*), Alain Flick, Yassan Khan, Christian De Tiliere (*Train Passengers*), Andre Valardy (*Dimitri*), Robin Coleman, Jeffrey Cramer, Alan Haufrect (*Golf Buddies*), Jean-Claude Montalban (*Bellman*), Fernand Guiot (*Limo Driver*), Frank Olivier Bonnet (*Thief on Bike/Man with Matchbook*), Pierre Gerard (*Thief on Bike*), Yanou Collart (*Marguerite Lasueur*), Anna Gaylor (*Woman at Bookstore*), Brian Eatwell (*Malcolm*), Ginette Garcin (*Nurse*), Annick Alane (*Givenchy Saleswoman*), Serge Berry (*Givenchy Manager*), Michel Melki (*Crillon Desk Clerk*), Jacques Maury (*Crillon Manager*), Helene Hily (*Miss Bonner*), Michel Bardinet (*Rafael Lesueur*), Vlodek Press (*Russian Diplomat*), Jerzy Rogulski (*Russian Diplomat*), Beatrice Camaraut, Gilberte Geniat, Alain Janey, Alexandra Lorska, Katia Tchenko, Genevieve Omni (*Embassy Guests*), Francois Viaur (*Crillon Night Doorman*), Nancy Stephens (*Jacqueline*), Murray Gronwalk (*Gendarme*), Pierre Olaf (*Priest*), Hubert Noel (*Doctor at Nightclub*), Eleanore Heutschy (*American Tourist*), Janine Darcey (*Lady on Train*), Micheline Bourdax (*Doctor*), Albert Augier (*Customs Inspector*), Guy Montagni (*Cab Driver*), Eugenivze Priwizencew, Jerzy Pujszo (*Russian Diplomats*), Vic Heutschy (*American Tourist*).

Williams is a housewife from Ohio who takes refuge from her boring life and boring husband by reading trashy romance novels about a woman named "Rebecca Ryan." When the publishers of the books hold a contest to see who can write the best outline for one of the novels, Williams wins it and a trip to Paris to meet the writer of the series. Husband Staley opposes the trip and refuses to go, so Williams goes by herself. Soon after arriving, she suffers a blow to the head and becomes convinced that she is the "Rebecca

Ryan" character. She mistakes Conti for her personal secretary, although he's really the son of Browne, who writes the Ryan novels with Conti ghostwriting for her. Williams somehow gets involved in some real-life intrigue, with Conti falling in love with her despite his knowing that she's obviously out of her gourd. Incredibly shallow, in fact it's hard to find anything here at all except for pretty scenery and one nice instant when Williams regains her memory and realizes that she has to give up the adventure of the last days and return to her stifling suburban life.

p, Doug Chapin; d, Rick Rosenthal; w, Jim Kouf, David Greenwalt (based on a story by Ann Biderman); ph, Giuseppe Rotunno (Technicolor); m, Lewis Furey; ed, Anne Gousaud; prod d, Brian Eatwell; art d, Marc Frederix, Jeff Goldstein; set d, Juan-Carlos Conti, Gregory Garrison; cos, Michael Kaplan; m/l, "Dreamer," Furey.

Comedy   **Cas.**   **(PR:A-C MPAA:PG)**

AMERICAN NIGHTMARE zero   (1984) 87m Mano c

Lawrence S. Day (*Eric*), Lora Staley (*Louise*), Neil Dainard (*Tony*), Lenore Zann (*Tina*), Michael Ironside (*Skylar*), Paul Bradley (*Manager*), Claudia Udy (*Andrea*), Larry Aubrey (*Dolly*), Mike Copeman (*Fixer*), Alexandra Paul (*Isabel*).

Day delves into the seamy side of American city life searching for his missing sister among the prostitutes and dope peddlers. Worthless exploitation of the cities-are-dirtier-than-ever theme without illumination or regrets.

p, Ray Sager; d, Don McBrearty; w, John Sheppard (based on a story by John Gault, Steven Blake); ph, Daniel Hainey; m, Paul Zaza; ed, Ian McBride; art d, Andrew Deskin.

Crime   **(PR:O MPAA:NR)**

AMERICAN TABOO**   (1984) 87m Lustgarten c

Jay Horenstein (*Paul Wunderlich*), Nicole Harrison (*Lisa*), Mark Rabiner (*Michael*), Katherine King (*Maggie*), Ki Skinner (*1st Model*), Suzette Taylor (*2nd Model*), Dorothy Anton (*Lisa's Mother*).

Horenstein is a loser who allows himself to be seduced by nymphet-next-door Harrison in this tedious, amateurish film. Dull, with two-dimensional characters and overlong gratuitous sex scenes. The film was the winner of the 1983 Student Film Academy Award, a fact that does not bode well for the future, and was written by its two leads, Horenstein and Harrison, and producer Lustgarten.

p, Sali Borchman, Steve Lustgarten, Ron Schmidt; d, Lustgarten; w, Lustgarten, Jay Horenstein, Nicolle Harrison; ph, Lustgarten, Eric Edwards, Mark Whitney, Lee Nesbit; m, Dana Libonati, Dan Brandt; ed, Schmidt, Lustgarten.

Drama   **(PR:O MPAA:NR)**

...AND PIGS MIGHT FLY   (SEE: ADERYN PAPUR, Brit.)

ANGEL**   (1984) 92m Adams Apple-Sandy Howard/New World c

Cliff Gorman (*Lt. Andrews*), Susan Tyrrell (*Mosler*), Dick Shawn (*Mae*), Rory Calhoun (*Kit Carson*), John Diehl (*Billy Boy*), Donna Wilkes (*Angel/Molly*), Robert Acey (*Driver/John*), David Anthony (*Howie*), Ronnie Barron (*Blind Eddie*), Josh Cadman (*Spike*), Joseph Cala (*Usher*), Mel Carter (*Jenkins*), Jackie De Rouen (*Tanya*), Donna Fuller (*Jesus Peddler*), Elaine Giftos (*Patricia Allen*), Bob Gorman (*Zigmand*), Ross Hagen (*Urban Cowboy*), Marc Hayashi (*Young Cop*), Todd Hoffman (*Punker*), Vincent Isaac (*Pimp*), Peter Jason (*Middle-Aged Man*), Dennis Kort (*Wayne*), Greg Lewis (*Themopolis*), Chuck Lyles (*Blind Eddie's Friend*), Donna McDaniel (*Crystal*), Graem McGavin (*Lana*), Ken Olfson (*Mr. Saunders*), Karyn Parker (*Diana*), Steven Porter (*Yo Yo Charlie*), Gene Ross (*Driver/Vice Cop*), Laura Sorrenson (*Roxie*), David Underwood (*Ric Sawyer*), Dick Valentine (*Older Cop*).

For a film where the ads promised "High School Honor Student By Day, Hollywood Hooker By Night," ANGEL is a surprisingly tame little crime melodrama which shows no flesh or sex while it wallows in the seedy streets of Hollywood. Filled with eccentric characters, the film stars Wilkes, a 15-year-old high school student at an exclusive prep school who harbors a deep, dark secret from her classmates. On her own from the age of 12 (no father, mother ran off with a lover), Wilkes is determined to survive and improve her station in life. She does this by turning tricks in Hollywood to pay the rent on the apartment she and mother used to share. Wilkes pretends her mother still lives with her so the landlady, a strange bull-dyke type played with flair by Tyrrell, won't get suspicious and notify the juvenile authorities. The child-hooker also funnels some of her nightly earnings to pay the tuition for an exclusive prep school she attends during the day, while coyly fending off the advances of amorous jock-types who want to date her. Though the film is about a teen-age hooker, never do we see the sweet-faced Wilkes plying her trade (thankfully). There are a few scenes where she just talks with potential customers, but that's as far as it goes. Since a 15 year old working the mean streets of Hollywood is fair game for any sicko, Wilkes surrounds herself with a surrogate family of friendly street people. Her two guardian angels are Calhoun, a washed-up cowboy star who still wanders

around in costume packing six-shooters (sans bullets), and Shawn, a burly transvestite with a great sense of humor who can easily intimidate anyone who crosses him. These character vignettes are loosely strung together with a "plot" that follows a young TAXI DRIVER-type psychopathic killer, Diehl, who picks up hookers and murders them. Wilkes and her street friends become determined to find the fiend and stop the killings, but are extremely distrustful of nosy police detective Gorman. The leads are scant, however, and finally most of Wilkes' hooker friends are dead, leaving her a likely target. The killer does come calling then, but Shawn flies to the rescue. The ensuing battle between psycho-killer and the wise-cracking transvestite (in his-her full-dress glory) is one of the most bizarre fight scenes ever committed to film. Shawn loses his life in the struggle, but Diehl is hunted down and peace returns to seedy Hollywood. Though extremely silly and distasteful, ANGEL does manage to throw some interesting curves on standard exploitation material. The characters are fully developed with Calhoun, Tyrrell, and especially Shawn, turning in some genuinely fine performances. Wilkes is really nothing special (and she didn't return for the sequel, AVENGING ANGEL, 1985), but she has a vaguely likable quality. The maniac, Diehl, is memorably threatening, but the script provides nothing more than cliche mother-problems as motivation for his vile deeds. Readers will recognize Diehl from his regular supporting role as a wacked-out detective on television's "Miami Vice."

p, Roy Watts, Donald P. Borchers; d, Robert Vincent O'Neil; w, O'Neil, Joseph Cala; ph, Andy Davis (CFI color); m, Craig Safan; ed, Charles Bornstein, Wilt Henderson; art d, Stephen Marsh; set d, Christopher Amy.

Crime   **Cas.**   **(PR:O MPAA:R)**

ANNE DEVLIN**   (1984, Ireland) 120m Aeon c

Brid Brennan (*Anne Devlin*), Bosco Hogan (*Robert Emmett*), Des McAleer, Gillian Hackett.

Historical drama based on the diaries of Anne Devlin, a farm girl who played a minor part in an abortive Irish revolution in the early 19th Century and who spent several years in prison. Slow-moving and terribly earnest, although the second half, in which Brennan defies her captors in a variety of ways, is somewhat better.

p, Pat Murphy, Tom Hayes; d&w, Murphy; ph, Thaddeus O'Sullivan; m, Robert Boyle; ed, Arthur Keating; prod d, John Lucas; cos, Consolata Boyle.

Historical Drama   **(PR:C MPAA:NR)**

ANOTHER COUNTRY**   (1984, Brit.) 90m Goldcrest-National Film Finance Corp./Orion Classics c

Rupert Everett (*Guy Bennett*), Colin Firth (*Tommy Judd*), Michael Jenn (*Barclay*), Robert Addie (*Delahay*), Anna Massey (*Imogen Bennett*), Betsy Brantley (*Julie Schofield*), Rupert Wainwright (*Devenish*), Tristan Oliver (*Fowler*), Cary Elwes (*Harcourt*), Frederick Alexander (*Menzies*), Adrian Ross-Magenty (*Wharton*), Geoffrey Bateman (*Yevgeni*), Philip Dupuy (*Martineau*), Guy Henry (*Head Boy*), Jeffrey Wickham (*Arthur*), John Line (*Best Man*), Gideon Boulting (*Trafford*), Llewelyn Rees (*Senior Chaplain*), Arthur Howard (*Waiter*), Ivor Roberts (*Chief Judge*), Crispin Redman (*Prefect*), Nick Rowe (*Spungin*), Kathleen St. John (*Ivy*), Martin Wenner, Christopher Milburn (*Batsmen*), Tristram Jellinek (*Nicholson*), Tristram Wymark (*Henderson*), Ralph Perry-Robinson (*Robbins*).

A fiction loosely based on the lives of Burgess and Maclean, the two upper-crust Englishmen who renounced their country, became spies for the Soviet Union, and eventually fled there to avoid prosecution. If we are to believe Mitchell's screenplay of his stage play, the reason for it all was the sense of repression both men felt while attending their boarding school in the 1930s. If that were truly the case, half the men who run Great Britain today would be gay and the other half would be spies. It begins as Everett (playing the Burgess-type) is ensconced in Moscow, allowing himself to be interviewed, for the first time in years, by a woman from the U.S., Brantley. The film flashes back to the 1930s and Everett is seen to be an Oscar Wilde type at school, tart-tongued and professionally outrageous. He falls hard for Elwes but keeps it secret so he will be eligible to join a group of upperclassmen known as "The Gods" who make certain their members are taken care of in the business and government world upon graduation, sort of a young "Old Boys" network. When his romantic penchant--more especially, his inability to be discreet about it--is discovered by the members of "The Gods," they will no longer consider him a candidate for membership and he begins his lifelong attempt at revenge against "Authority." How this translates into treachery against his country is the implausible leap of cinematic faith. At the same time, Firth is Everett's only pal. While still almost beardless, Firth is already a hardened Marxist, although it appears, at first, to be the kind of schoolboy infatuation that so many students have. The college seen is hardly that at all as it appears that the students do no studying, only posturing and dallying. British public schools (they are called "public" but are, in fact, private) have been seen often and with better results in several movies such as CHARIOTS OF FIRE and IF...and the fact that they espouse a rigid form of education is well known. Indicating that it was the treatment at the hands of his fellows that caused Burgess (Everett) to scheme and plan to bring down the Empire is foolish. The man was a flamboyant homosexual and, at best, slightly mentally awry. In any school, at any time, such a personality was liable to crack. For a look at the real-life character of Burgess, may we refer you to a one-hour British TV program, directed by John Schlesinger, written by Alan Bennett, starring Alan Bates as Burgess and Coral Browne as herself. It was titled "An Englishman Abroad" and was based on a true encounter Browne had with Burgess while she was appearing as an actress in Moscow. In 60 minutes or so, it made all the points attempted by this film and then some. Watch for it only on Public Television as the language is too rough for commercial airing. Burgess and Maclean fled England in 1951 when they were warned of their impending investigation by Kim Philby, the master spy who'd recruited them. Philby himself disappeared behind the Iron Curtain on July 30, 1963. The best part of this otherwise inconsequential movie is the cinematography of Peter Biziou, which won a prize in 1984 at the Cannes Film Festival. Director Kanievska, in his feature-picture debut, gets good results from the unwieldy cast.

p, Alan Marshall; d, Marek Kanievska; w, Julian Mitchell (based on his novel); ph, Peter Biziou; m, Michael Storey; ed, Gerry Hambling; prod d, Brian Morris; art d, Clinton Cavers; cos, Penny Rose.

Historical Drama   **Cas.**   **(PR:C   MPAA:PG)**

ANOTHER TIME, ANOTHER PLACE*½   (1984, Brit.) 101m
Umbrella-Rediffusion/Goldwyn c

Phyllis Logan (Janie), Giovanni Mauriello (Luigi), Gian Luca Favilla (Umberto), Claudio Rosini (Paolo), Paul Young (Dougal), Gregor Fisher (Beel), Tom Watson (Finlay), Jennifer Piercey (Kirsty), Denise Coffey (Meg), Yvonne Gilan (Jess), Carol Ann Crawford (Else), R · Jeffries (Alick), Scott Johnston (Jeems), Corrado Sfogli (Raffaello), Nadio Fortune (Antonio), Peter Finlay (Officer), David Mowat (Randy Bob), Stephen Gressieux (POW).

In World War II Scotland, bored housewife Logan embarks on an affair with Italian prisoner-of-war Mauriello, assigned to work on her farm. He fills her head with visions of sunny Naples, far from the bleak highlands, though clearly all he is interested in is sex. Mediocre drama lacks any real appeal.

p, Simon Perry; d&w, Michael Radford (based on the novel by Jessie Kesson); m, John McLeod; ed, Tom Priestley; art d, Hayden Pearce; cos, Louise Frogley.

Drama   **(PR:O   MPAA:R)**

ANTARCTICA*   (1984, Jap.) 112m Fuji
Telecasting-Gakken-Kurahara/TLC-FOX c

Ken Takakura (Ushioda), Tsunehiko Watase (Ochi), Masako Natsume (Wife), Keiko Oginome (Dog Owner), Eiji Okada, Takeshi Kusaka, Shigeru Koyuma, So Yamamura.

Interesting dog story, narrated in English, concerns a team of sled dogs left chained to posts at an antarctic research station by a Japanese team which expects to be replaced immediately. Bad weather delays the relief team and the dogs are forced on their own resources for survival. Eight of the 15 manage to slip their collars. The rest die where they're chained. The freed dogs search for food, attacking a walrus, catching fish through the ice, and one by one meet a variety of sad ends. One falls through a crevasse on the ice shelf and drowns, another gets caught on a small floe and heartbreakingly drifts away. Yet another is injured in a fall and crawls into a whale skeleton to die. When a team finally does return to the research station, only two dogs have survived and there is a joyous, tearful reunion with the dog handlers. Amazing cinematography of locations in Canada, the Arctic, and Antarctica, and the direction makes each dog a distinct character in the same way the old Walt Disney "True-Life" adventures did. Good score by Vangelis (CHARIOTS OF FIRE) contributes to the effect. The harrowing deaths of some of the dogs may be too much for some smaller children. Based on a true story from 1958, the film became the second most successful film in Japanese history, after Steven Spielberg's E.T. (1982).

p, Masaru Katutani, Koreyoshi Kurahara; d, Kurahara; w, Tatsuo Nogami, Kan Saji, Toshiro Ishido, Kurahara; ph, Akira Shiizuka (Fuji Color); m, Vangelis; ed, Akira Susuki; prod d, Hiroshi Tokuda.

Adventure   **Cas.**   **(PR:A   MPAA:G)**

AT   (SEE: HORSE, THE, Turk.)

AVE MARIA**   (1984, Fr.) 104m Films Galaxie/AAA c

Feodor Atkine (Adolphe Eloi), Anna Karina (Berthe Granjeux), Isabelle Pasco (Ursula), Pascale Ogier (Angelique), Dora Doll (Constance), Bernard Freyd (Mathieu).

Defrocked priest Atkine and his mistress Karina venture to the French countryside and con a group of villagers into thinking that they are messengers of God. Going by the names "Holy Father" and "Holy Mother," Atkine and Karina swindle the people out of their land and money by feeding on their religious fervor. When a farmer's daughter taunts the villagers with devil worship she is beaten to death after an evening of exorcism. Atkine and Karina then engineer a scheme which places blame on the girl's father. Contrasting the evil which Atkine and Karina embody is Ogier, a saintly nun who receives prophecies from heaven while in a trance.

Some controversy surrounded the film's initial release when the courts banned a poster which sported a bare-breasted woman on a cross. This was the final film appearance for the 24-year-old Ogier (daughter of Bulle Ogier) who received much acclaim for her role in Eric Rohmer's FULL MOON IN PARIS before her untimely death in 1984 and it was also the last film for scripter Gegauff who died late in 1983.

p, Irene Silberman; d, Jacques Richard; w, Richard, Paul Gegauff; ph, Dominique Brenguier (Cinemascope/Panavision); m, Jorge Arriagada; ed, Luc Barnier; art d, Dominique Barouh, Gilles Lacombe.

Drama   **(PR:O   MPAA:NR)**

BACHELOR PARTY zero   (1984) 106m Aspect Ratio-Twin
Continental-Bachelor Party/FOX c

Tom Hanks (Rick Gassko), Tawny Kitaen (Debbie Thompson), Adrian Zmed (Jay O'Neill), George Grizzard (Mr. Thompson), Robert Prescott (Cole Whittier), William Tepper (Dr. Stan Gassko), Wendie Jo Sperber (Dr. Tina Gassko), Barry Diamond (Rudy), Gary Grossman (Gary), Michael Dudikoff (Ryko), Bradford Bancroft (Brad), Martina Finch (Phoebe), Deborah Harmon (Ilene), Tracy Smith (Bobbi), Florence Schauffler (Sister Mary Francis), Sumant (Rajah), John Bloom (Milt), Kenneth Kimmins (Hotel Manager), Gerard Prendergast (Michael), Brett Clark (Nick), Ji-Tu Cumbuka (Alley Pimp), Katie Mitchell (Kelley), Christopher Morley (She/Tim), Toni Alessandrini (Desiree), Monique Gabrielle (Tracey), Angela Aames (Mrs. Klupner), Richard Lorenzo Hernandez (Raul), Jonathan Tyler Trevillya (Skip), Cynthia Kania (Sue), Hugh McPhillips (Father O'Donall), Michael Yama (Japanese Businessman), Sheri Short, Peaches Johnson (Hookers), Dorothy Bartlett (Candy Counter Lady), Annie Gaybis (Stunts), Elizabeth Arlen (Garage Customer), Rebecca Perle (Screaming Woman), Pat Proft (Screaming Man), Marcelino Razo, Gregory Brown, Donald Thompson (Schoolboys), Arlee Reed, Coleen Maloney (Jean Store Customers), Milt Kogan, Gregory Norberg (Restaurant Customers), Ben Slack (Suitcase Man), Dean Dittman (Elkshead Executive), Jim Hudson (Neighbor), Billy Beck (Patient), Dani Douthette, Rosanne Katon (Bridal Shower Hookers), Michele Stark, Renee Breault, Kim Robinson, Elizabeth Carter, Lisa Purcell, Paul Angelo, Bruce Block, William T. Yamadera, Tad Horino, George Sasaki, Angel and the Reruns: 'Angel, Lovey, Julia, Ginger'.

A smash hit teeny-bopper movie that proves again there is no accounting for taste. If Tom Hanks had not starred, it's doubtful anyone would have gone to see this trash. He is as talented, bright, and funny as this movie is inane, time-wasting, and foolish. In 1986, Hanks proved that he was a major actor in Garry Marshall's NOTHING IN COMMON, which had a far superior script by two young comics, Rick Podell and Mike Preminger. Hanks is a lower middle-class school bus driver, a carefree type who enjoys his work, his hobby (metal sculpture), and his life. He meets and falls for wealthy Kitaen and they decide to marry, over and above the wishes of her snobbish parents, Grizzard and Stuart. The night before the nuptials, the traditional rite of the bachelor party is to take place. Hanks has several friends, each more playful than the next, and they decide that this is going to be a bachelor party to end all bachelor parties, with hookers, plenty of drinks, etc. On the same evening, Kitaen's girl friends have planned to take her out to a male strip show like the ones made famous at "Chippendale's" club in California. It seems like a good idea but Kitaen thinks she has a better one. She wants to make sure that Hanks does not betray his fidelity to her so she and her pals dress up as prostitutes in order to attend the party for Hanks. While both the males and females are making their plans for the big night before the big day, Grizzard has something else in store. He hires Kitaen's ex-boy friend, Prescott, to attempt winning Kitaen away from Hanks and put her back on the right track with "the right people." This, of course, backfires as the ineffectual Prescott is no match for the charismatic Hanks. The party is held at a swank hotel and fire and brimstone break loose right from the start. It turns into a raucous nightmare, not so much for the actors on screen, but for the audience. Meatballs are cooked with a blowtorch, there's a suicide try with an electric razor, and a hired donkey is forced to sniff cocaine. Add that to bestiality, transvestism, hostility to women, and sadomasochism and you come away feeling disgusted, as well as exhausted, due to the lightning pace of the cutting. Despite the success of the movie, we have to turn thumbs way down as it is a melange of cheap thrills and flat jokes, saved only by the performance of Hanks and some good work by pal Zmed. Hanks is a younger Bill Murray and his comedy technique allows him to get away with more than most actors in the same situation. He is the only oasis in this Sahara of smut. Zmed, Stuart, and Sperber (who costarred with Hanks in the TV show "Bosom Buddies") give the film a few familiar faces but the donkey had the right idea. The only way to enjoy this trash may be in a drug-induced stupor. In addition to the music by Folk, contributions to the score were made by Barry Schleifer and Tom Jenkins. Poor technical credits, too much scatology, and a witless script by Neal Israel and Pat Proft (who makes a cameo appearance as a screaming man).

p, Ron Moler, Bob Israel; d, Neal Israel; w, Neal Israel, Pat Proft (based on a story by Bob Israel); ph, Hal Trussel (DeLuxe Color); m, Robert Folk, Tom Jenkins, Barry Schleifer; ed, Tom Walls; md, Folk; art d, Kevin Conlin, Martin Price; cos, Nina Padovano, Jeanne Mascia, Buddy R.Cone; spec eff, Martin Becker, Frank Inez, Ken Sher; ch, Kathleen Knapp.

Comedy   **Cas.**   **(PR:O   MPAA:R)**

BAD MANNERS*½   (1984) 85m New World c (AKA: GROWING PAINS)

Karen Black (*Gladys Fitzpatrick*), Martin Mull (*Warren Fitzpatrick*), Anne De Salvo (*Sister Serena*), Murphy Dunne (*Kurtz*), Pamela Segall (*Girl Joey*), Georg Olden (*Piper*), Michael Hentz (*Mouse*), Joey Coleman (*Whitey*), Christopher Brown (*Blackie*), Steve Stucker (*Dr. Bender*), Kimmy Robertson (*Sarah*), John Paul Lussier (*Garth*), Edy Williams (*Mrs. Slatt*), Hy Pike (*Slatt*), Gertrude Flynn (*Mother Celestina*), Lark Hackshaw (*Nurse Bates*), Bill Quinones (*Pepe*), Seth Wagerman (*Professor*), Thomas Stokes (*Chubby*), Michelle Cundey (*Suzy*), Marshall Effron (*Cabbie*), Susan Ruttan (*Biker*), Richard Deacon (*Ticket Salesman*), Bridget Sienna (*Carnation*), Barry Cutler (*Pizza Man*), Steve Lalande (*Gay Guy*), Rex Ryon (*Cop*), Bobby Houston (*Retard*), Drew Davis (*Teenage Samurai*).

Sort of a modern-day version of *Oliver Twist*, BAD MANNERS was an independently made movie that might have made noise at the box office if more attention were paid to detail and less to overplaying. Several orphans are incarcerated in a Catholic home known as the Bleeding Heart Orphanage. It ranks only behind Devil's Island for being tough, and just ahead of Stalag 17. Run by a tyrannical nun, De Salvo, and her aide, Dunne, who wields an electrified cattle prod, it appears to be a Kiddies' Koncentration Kamp. But these are not sweet-faced moppets who have been tossed in there by twists of Dickensian fate. Rather, they are scruffy toughs, mini-gangsters, and there's hardly an Oliver in the lot. Black and Mull are *nouveau riche* types who think that a new adopted child might go well with their decor in Santa Barbara. They take Hentz home with them to their posh living quarters but it's like sending Francois Truffaut's "Wild Child" to stay at the White House. Hentz hates his new life, and his pals at the orphanage think that they might be better off than he is so they decide to get him back. A quartet of the children break out and raid the Mull-Black home with results that you can see coming for at least a reel ahead. Mull and Black are seen to be just this side of nuts and the kids are portrayed as bright raccoons. Lots of whacks at "The Establishment" and the shame of it is that this might have been a good film. Redoing classics by another name is a tradition in the movie business and as recently as 1986, one could see the antecedent of RUTHLESS PEOPLE in O. Henry's "The Ransom of Red Chief." So the idea of attempting a modern-day *Oliver Twist* was meritorious. It just fell into the wrong hands. Some nice comedy cameos from Steve Stucker, Marshall Effron, and Richard Deacon. Tiny Pamela Segall scores as Girl Joey. A graduate of Beverly Hills High School, Segall became one of the busiest teenage actresses around in the 1980s. Her father, Don Segall, is a producer and writer and served as the basis for the Bob Hoskins character in SWEET LIBERTY.

p, Kim Jorgensen; d, Bobby Houston; w, Houston, Joseph Kwong; ph, Jan De Bont (Metrocolor); m, Sparks 'Ron and Russell Mael', Michael Lewis; ed, Barry Zetlin; art d, Jim Dulz; set d, David Glazer; cos, Linda Bass, Jack Buehler.

Comedy   Cas.   (PR:C MPAA:R)

BALLAD OF NARAYAMA, THE****   (1984, Jap.) 130m Toei/Shochiku c

Ken Ogata (*Tatsuhei*), Sumiko Sakamoto (*Orin, His Mother*), Takejo Aki (*Tamayan, His Wife*), Tonpei Hidari (*Risuke, His Brother*), Shoichi Ozawa (*Katsuzo*), Seiji Kurasaki (*Kesakichi, Older Son*), Kaoru Shimamori (*Tomekichi, Younger Son*), Ryutaro Tatsumi (*Matayan*), Junko Takada (*Matsu*), Nijiko Kiyokawa (*Old Widow Okane*), Mitsuko Baisho (*Young Widow Oei*), Mitsuaki Fukamizu (*Tadayan*), Norihei Miki (*Old Salt Dealer*), Akio Yokoyama (*Amaya*), Sachie Shimura (*Amaya's Wife*), Masami Okamoto (*Amaya's Son*), Fugio Tsumeda (*Jinsaku*), Taiji Tonoyama (*Teruyan*), Keishi Takamine (*Arayashiki*), Yukie Shimura, Rytaro Shimamori, Kan Eto, Fusako Iwasaki, Hideo Hasegawa, Kenji Murase, Sayuka Nakamaru, Azumi Tanba, Kosei Sato.

A remarkable picture based on the award winning stories by Fakazawa and previously filmed in 1958 under the same title. The story takes place in a Japanese village of 100 years ago–a village plagued by famine. In accord with their methods of rationing food, newborn males are left to die in the rice paddies while newborn females are given the chance to live, in hopes they'll someday bear children. It is customary for the elderly (anyone who lives to age seventy) to be carried to the top of Mount Narayama by their eldest son and left to die of starvation. This self-enforced polulation control is heartily greeted by Sakamoto, a 69-year-old woman who is healthier than most men half her age. Because it is an age-old custom, however, she willingly looks forward to her trip to the mountain. She has lived a long life, finding wives for both her sons and preparing her family for her absence. The villagers begin to doubt the custom when they realize it means losing Sakamoto. To calm them, Sakamoto purposely wears herself down, even going so far as to knock out her strong teeth on a rock. Ogata reluctantly begins the trip up the mountain, carrying his bundled mother on his back. After a seemingly endless ascent he reaches the ancient grounds scattered with the bones of those who came before to die. With great difficulty he leaves his mother there to die and returns to the village. In this picture director Imamura has gone to great effort to equate man with the nature that surrounds him. THE BALLAD OF NARAYAMA is splendidly photographed with an eye that evokes a great love of grass, trees, insects, and animals. The characters in this village are born of the earth, live out their lives in the earth, and ultimately return to the earth. While seemingly morbid on a surface level, the film is filled with life-affirming signs and is one of the most beautiful and peaceful films to come from Japan in some time. Winner of 1983's Palm D'Or at the Cannes Film Festival. (In Japanese: English Subtitles).

p, Goro Kusakaba, Jiro Tomoda; d&w, Shohei Imamura (based on the stories "Narayama Bushi-ko" and "Tohoku No Zunmatachi" by Scichiro Fakazawa); ph, Masao Tochizaqa; m, Shin'ichiro Ikebe; ed, Hajime Okayasu; art d, Nobutaka Yoshino; m/l "Song of Risuke," Hitoshi Machida.

Drama   (PR:C MPAA:NR)

BASILEUS QUARTET***   (1984, Ital.) 118m RAI-C.E.P./Libra-Cinema 5-Almi c

Hector Alterio (*Alvaro*), Omero Antonutti (*Diego*), Pierre Malet (*Edo*), Francois Simon (*Oscar Guarneri*), Michel Vitold (*Guglielmo*), Alain Cuny (*Finkel*), Gabriele Ferzetti (*Mario Cantone*), Veronique Genest (*Sophia*), Lisa Kreuzer (*Lotte*), Euro Bulfoni, Francesco Carnelutti, Mimsy Farmer, Alessandro Haber, Jose Quaglio, Rado Rossimov, Alessandra Romano, Alessandra Story, Catherine Jarrett, Lidia Koslovich, Laura Lenzi, Antonio Orlando, Sergia Pieri.

Fascinating film explores the lives of three aging musicians, members of a world-famous string quartet, who suddenly find themselves adrift when the lead violinist dies. They try to go their separate ways but are drawn back together by youthful prodigy Malet, who persuades them to re-form with him as lead violin. The others are amazed at his playing, and even more amazed at the life he leads off-stage, bedding groupies, smoking marijuana, and more. The others, who have denied themselves these pleasures for years, find their sacrifices made pointless. The nagging notion even creeps into their heads that he plays so brilliantly because he indulges in earthly delights. Finally, the tensions he creates are too great. One member who has been denying his homosexuality cracks, another tries to keep up with Malet in the womanizing department and suffers a heart attack. Only one of the original members survives, still drawn to the charismatic newcomer. Carefully paced and beautifully acted, the film raises any number of issues about aging and art. Well worth seeing. (In Italian; English subtitles.)

p, Arturo La Pegna; d&w, Fabio Carpi; ph, Dante Spinotti; m, Franz Schubert, Ludwig Von Beethoven, Bedrich Smetana, Nicolo Paganini, Achille Claude Debussy, Franz Joseph Haydn; ed, Massimo Latini; set d, Franco Vanorio; cos, Corrado Colabucci.

Drama   (PR:O MPAA:NR)

BAY BOY**½   (1984, Can.) 107m Hachette Fox-Antenne 2-Films A2-CTV-Telefilm Canada-HBO/ORION c

Liv Ullmann (*Jennie Campbell*), Kiefer Sutherland (*Donald Campbell*), Alan Scarfe (*Sgt. Tom Coldwell*), Mathieu Carriere (*Father Chaisson*), Peter Donat (*Will Campbell*), Isabelle Mejias (*Mary McNeil*), Leah Pinsent (*Saxon Coldwell*), Jane McKinnon (*Dianna Coldwell*), Peter Spence (*Joe Campbell*), Chris Wiggins (*Chief Charles McInnes*), Thomas Peacocke (*Father McKinnon*), Josephine Chaplin (*Marie Chaisson*), Stephane Audran (*Blanche*), David Ferry (*Walt Roach*), Pauline Lafont (*Janine Chaisson*), Roy McMullin (*Paul Ratchford*), Kathy McGuire (*Sister Roberta*), Robbie Gallivan (*Frank Carrey*), Robert Rose (*Danny McIssac*), Darren Arsenault (*Malcolm Broderick*), Betty MacDonald (*Nurse*), Fannie Shore (*Mrs. Silver*), Sander Zilbert (*Mr. Silver*), Tom Rack (*Sol Silver*), Robert Taylor (*Paddy O'Neil*), Joe MacPherson (*Rory McInnes*), Kevin McKenzie (*Mr. Rankin*), Iris Currie (*Mrs. Carrey*), Francis MacNeil (*Terry O'Shea*), Michael Egyes (*Basil Broderick*), Mary MacKinnon (*Aunt Coldwell*).

Director Dan Petrie (SYBIL; FORT APACHE, THE BRONX; THE DOLLMAKER; LIFEGUARD) went back to his Canadian upbringing as he wrote and produced this nostalgic look at life in Glace Bay, on Cape Breton Island in Nova Scotia. It wanders a bit, as most remembrances do, and shoots off in many directions, as life does, and the result is a modest achievement at best. Sutherland (son of actor Donald, and a dead ringer for his dad) is the "Bay Boy" of the title. The time is 1937 and the Depression has engulfed the area. Sutherland is the son of Ullmann and Donat. They are a poor family, barely able to eke out a living in the harsh area. The parents would like their son to join the priesthood but he finds the thought of celibacy a difficult one, especially since he is attracted to a nun, McGuire, then has to fend off a homosexual advance from his local priest, Carriere. Further, he also likes the two young sisters who live across the road, Pinsent and McKinnon. That is made even more difficult when he sees the girls' father, Scarfe, kill an aged Jewish couple. Since Scarfe is the local police officer and renowned in the area as a sadist, Sutherland doesn't know how to handle matters. He tells the police that he didn't see the killing and this gnaws at his conscience. The finale neatly takes care of the problem. Ullmann is top-billed as Sutherland's mother but she is more a re-actress than an actress in this and never gets the chance to strut her stuff. Her role could have been played by anyone. Donat, a superior actor who has never received his due, does well as the father and Spence contributes as the brother who is suffering from a disease. Despite running in several directions at once, the film was obviously made with love by Petrie and won a number of Genie Awards in Canada. The weakest link in the presentation was the vapid performance by Sutherland, who may yet have a career as he does project the same sort of charisma as his father, as long as he doesn't have to speak. It's sort of a modern equivalent of HOW GREEN WAS MY VALLEY, in that it deals with the hardships of the miners, the miserable climate, and the coming of age of a young man. One of Charlie Chaplin's daughters, Josephine, makes an appearance.

p, John Kemeny, Denis Heroux; d&w, Daniel Petrie; ph, Claude Agostini; m, Claude Bolling; ed, Susan Shanks, Petrie, Peter Wintonick; prod d, Wolf Kroeger; art d, Richard Harrison; cos, Renee April; spec eff, Martin Malivoire, Michael Kavanaugh; makeup, Josianne Deschamps.

Drama   (PR:C MPAA:R)

BE MY VALENTINE, OR ELSE...   (SEE: HOSPITAL MASSACRE)

BEAR, THE**½   (1984) 110m EM c

Gary Busey (*Paul "Bear" Bryant*), Cynthia Leake (*Mary Harmon Bryant*), Carmen Thomas (*Mae Martin Bryant*), Cary Guffey (*Grandson Marc*), Harry Dean Stanton (*Coach Thomas*), Jon-Erik Hexum (*Pat Trammell*), Pat Greenstein (*Joe Namath*), Michael McGrady (*Gene Stallings*), William Wesley Neighbors, Jr (*Billy Neighbors*), Brett Rice (*Don Hutson*), Buddy Farmer (*Herman Ball*), Owen E. Orr (*Ermal Allen*), Charles Gabrielson (*Steve Meilinger*), D'Urville Martin (*Billy*), Ken Taylor (*Jimbo*), Muriel Moore (*Miss Vernon*), Ivan Green (*Mr. Gallagher*), Scott Campbell (*Dennis Goehring*), Robert Craighead (*Jack Pardee*), Damon Sarafian (*Don Watson*), Tod Spangler (*Bobby Keith*), Michael Prokopuk (*Bob Lockett*), Jeff Tyler (*Dee Powell*), Mike M. Elias (*Lloyd Hale*), Walter Edmiston (*Dr. Rose*), Terry Beaver (*Walter Kuhen*), John J. York (*Manning*), Rhett Evers (*Mr. Jackson*), Inman Banks (*Larry*), Joe Rainer (*Dr. Thomas*), Glenn Montgomery (*Phillips*), Bobby Butler (*Wilbur Jackson*), Gordon E. "Chet" Chessher (*Timothy Gallagher*), Eric Hipple (*Illinois Quarterback Tony Eason*).

A reverential biography of the colorful Alabama college football coach Paul "Bear" Bryant, faithfully portrayed by Gary Busey. The film covers his playing days at Alabama under a coaching staff led by Stanton to his fiery 1982 Liberty Bowl win. The film's chief fault is that it merely presents the audience with the Bear's life story, without drama or conflict in the presentation. Busey is clearly the star of the show, and the only real reason to watch for anyone who is not a Bryant devotee. His performance covers a 50-year span from his college days to his death in 1983. Busey has already proven his ability to transmute into a character in THE BUDDY HOLLY STORY, when he lost a great deal of weight to get down to Holly's scrawny size. Busey then went on to play another sports figure, Joe DiMaggio, in the 1985 film INSIGNIFICANCE. Making an appearance in THE BEAR is Detroit Lions quarterback Eric Hipple, who is cast as Illini quarterback Tony Eason in the Liberty Bowl victory.

p, Larry G. Spangler; d, Richard Sarafian; w, Michael Kane; ph, Laszlo George (DeLuxe Color); m, Bill Conti; ed, Robert Florio; prod d, George Costello; set d, Maria Rebman Caso; cos, Ron Talsky; m/l, "I'll Be Home Again," Conti, Dennis Lambert.

Sports Drama/Biography   (PR:C MPAA:PG)

BEAT STREET**½   (1984) 105m Orion c

Rae Dawn Chong (*Tracy*), Guy Davis (*Kenny*), Jon Chardiet (*Ramon*), Leon W. Grant (*Chollie*), Saundra Santiago (*Carmen*), Mary Alice (*Cora*), Shawn Elliot (*Domingo*), Jim Borrelli (*Monte*), Dean Elliott (*Henry*), Franc Reyes (*Luis*), Tonya Pinkins (*Angela*), Lee Chamberlin (*Alicia*), Antonia Rey (*Flora*), Duane Jones (*Robert*), Hope Clarke (*Dancing Instructor*), Kool Herc (*Himself*), Gina Belafonte (*Elizabeth*), Kimry Smith (*Erika*), Roxy D.J. (*Jazzy Jay*), Douglas Davis (*Douggie Fresh*), Richard Thomsen (*Paul*), Leon Stephenson (*Monte's Bouncer*), Robert Taylor (*Lee*), Kadeem Hardson (*High School Student*), Lorenzo Soto (*Bronx Rocker*), Dadi Pinero (*Young Writer*), Pedro B. Serrano (*Pedro*), Mervyn E. Griffith (*Student*), Joseph Verhauz (*Transit Policeman*), Vic Magnotta, Erick Mourino, Renier Mourino, Tom Wright, Bret Smrz, Bill Anagnos (*Stunts*), Susan Roffer (*Monte's Assistant*), Us Girls, Treacherous Three, Grand Master Melle Mel and the Furious Five, Afrika Bambaataa/Soul Sonic Force/Shango, The New York City Breakers, Rock Steady Crew, The Magnificent Force.

Another attempt to cash in on the rap and break dancing scenes that commenced in the South Bronx. This film is little more than a group of large musical numbers supplemented by a cliched plot but it does capture a sense of the craze and is more entertaining than most of the films that tried to coin money on the short- lived trend. Guy Davis (the real-life son of actors Ossie Davis and Ruby Dee) is a rap music disc jockey and Taylor, his younger brother, a dancer. They meet Chong (daughter of Tommy Chong of Cheech and Chong), a music major at college, who takes an interest in both boys for different reasons. While this is developing, Davis plays his music and scores of break dancers do their things in spectacular numbers on streets, in clubs, and just about anywhere else they can. The various groups seen include Grand Master Melle Mel and The Furious Five, Afrika Bambaataa/Soul Sonic Force/Shango, and many more. Davis and Chong fall in love for a short romance and that's juxtaposed against a subplot featuring Chardiet, a Puerto Rican graffiti artist who is trying to find subway cars to paint and how to handle problems with his girl friend and their infant. The film winds up in a grand melange of all the ingredients as there is a benefit at the Roxy

in Manhattan to help out the family of a character who died spraying a train car. Thus the combination of art, music, dancing, etc., is all realized simultaneously. There's little to actually think about in BEAT STREET and the final arbitration must be put to the test of whether or not a person enjoys seeing the amazing moves of the many break dancers who inhabit the film. Produced by Harry Belafonte and studio veteran Harry V. Picker, both men spent lots of time and money making the movie and promoting it once it was done. The original cowriter-director, Andy Davis, was released during the shooting and Lathan was engaged to replace him. In an all-out try at making this authentic, the producers also hired famed music mavin Arthur Baker to supervise the sounds and hire the rap groups to play in the picture. Lots of time was spent making this and that gave Cannon Films the opportunity to rush out BREAKIN' at a price equivalent to one tenth of BEAT STREET's budget. BREAKIN' was in the theater a few months before BEAT STREET, which made the latter look like a copy-cat film when it was not that at all. By the time this was released, the public had already seen the other and this may have been one too many films on the subject so it would end up a loser, even though it was superior. BEAT STREET issued three excellent record albums but they were also whipped at the record stores by the music from BREAKIN'. BREAKIN' 2: ELECTRIC BOOGALOO came out and was lost in the shuffle that included a few other attempts at capturing the fad on film, none of which was notable. Too bad that they allowed some vulgar language to creep into a film that otherwise would have been a perfect family picture. Technical credits were all terrific, as befits a picture that cost a reported $10 million. Songs include: "Beat Street Breakdown" (Melvin Glover, Reggie Griffin), "Baptize the Beat" (Michael Murphy, David Frank), "Stranger in a Strange Land" (Jack Holmes), "Beat Street Strut" (Eumir Deodato, Alan Palanker, Milton G. Barnes, Katreese Barnes), "Us Girls" (Ross Levinson, Debora Hooper), "This Could be the Night" (Arthur Baker, Tina B. Evan Rogers, Carl Sturken, Chris Lord-Alge), "Breakers Revenge" (Arthur Baker), "Tu Carino (Carmen's Theme)" (Carlos Franzetti, Ruben Blades), "Frantic Situation" (Arthur Baker, Leroi Evans, Ray Serrano, William Henderson, Ellis Williams, Afrika Bambaataa Aasim, Wilford Fowler, John Miller, Robert Allen).

p, David V. Picker, Harry Belafonte; d, Stan Lathan; w, Andy Davis, David Gilbert, Paul Golding (based on a story by Steven Hager); ph, Tom Priestley, Jr. (DeLuxe Color); m, Belafonte, Arthur Baker; ed, Dov Hoenig; prod d, Patrizia Von Brandenstein; art d, Wynn Thomas; set d, George DeTitta, Jr.; cos, Kristi Zea, Bernard Johnson; spec eff, Al Griswold; ch, Lester Wilson.

Musical   **Cas.**   (PR:A-C MPAA:PG)

BEDROOM EYES*½   (1984, Can.) 95m RSL-Pan Canadian c

Kenneth Gilman (*Harry Ross*), Dayle Haddon (*Alixe Barnes*), Barbara Law (*Jobeth*), Christine Cattell (*Caroline*), Jane Catling (*Marry Kittricke*).

Gilman is a stockbroker who takes time out of his eventful day for a nighttime jog around the neighborhood. While passing one house he notices some sexual goings-on involving fiery redhead Law. He makes a habit of returning to the house and gets increasingly involved with its inhabitants. Of course, he is emotionally distraught and flees to his nearest psychiatrist, Haddon, in the hopes of getting to the roots of his obsessive voyeurism. One night he sees a murder and becomes targeted by an unknown killer. None of this amounts to anything more than third-rate wanderings into REAR WINDOW territory accompanied by feeble psychological explanations.

p, Robert Lantos, Stephen Roth; d, William Fruet; w, Michael Alan Eddy; ph, Miklos Lente; m, John Tucker, Paul Hoffert; ed, Tony Lower; art d, Lindsey Goddard; cos, Julie Ganton.

Crime   (PR:O MPAA:NR)

BEST DEFENSE zero   (1984) 94m PAR c

Dudley Moore (*Wylie Cooper*), Eddie Murphy (*Landry*), Kate Capshaw (*Laura*), George Dzundza (*Loparino*), Helen Shaver (*Claire Lewis*), Mark Arnott (*Brank*), Peter Michael Goetz (*Frank Joyner*), Tom Noonan (*Holtzman*), David Rasche (*Jeff, Spy*), Paul Comi (*Chief Agent*), Darryl Henriques (*Col. Zayas*), Joel Polis (*1st Agent*), John A. Zee (*Col. McGuinn*), Matthew Laurance (*Ali*), Christopher Mahar (*Sayyid*), Lorry Goldman (*Rupp*), Stoney Richards (*Mugger*), Tyler Tyhurst (*American Captain*), Eduardo Ricard (*Garcia Vega*), William Marquez (*Padilla*), Deborah Fallender (*Toni*), Raye Birk (*Sonny*), Ellen Crawford (*Sonya*), Gene Dynarski (*Gil*), John Hostettner (*Quirk*), David Paymer (*Kurly*), Dennis Redfield (*Specs*), Jerry Hyman (*Col. Kleinman*), Hugo L. Stanger (*Blevin*), Tracey Ross (*Arab Girl*), Michael Scalera (*Morgan*), Rob Wininger (*Lt. Chapin*), Gary Bayer (*Lubell*), Ronald Salley (*Transportation Captain*), Paul Eiding (*Tourist*), Stephen Bradley (*Deputy Director*), Sanford Jensen, Gerald Jann (*Engineers*), Jennifer Wallace (*Waitress*), Renny Temple (*Coffee Machine Mover*), Ziporah Tzabari (*Ancient Kuwaiti Woman*), Gabi Amrani (*Old Villager*), Rozsika Halmos (*Seamstress*), Diane Carter (*Technician*), Jake Dengel (*Doorman*), Billy Ray Sharkey (*Radio Man*), Burton Collins (*Cameraman*), Bill Geisslinger (*Walkie-Talkie Agent*), Itzhak Bbi Neeman (*Refugee*), Jim Jansen (*Lieutenant*), Javier Grajeda (*Freddie Gomez*), Patricia Pivaar (*Newscaster*), Julie Ellis (*Waitress*), Yulis Ruval (*French Singer*), Pamela Stonebrook (*Singer*), Elizabeth Kubota (*Japanese Singer*).

The best defense a viewer can take against total boredom is to avoid this sad attempt at comedy. It boggles the mind that the writers of INDIANA

JONES AND THE TEMPLE OF DOOM and AMERICAN GRAFFITI could have teamed up with luminaries like Moore, Murphy, and others to make such a poor offering. Moore and Murphy are a beleaguered engineer and an Army officer, respectively (but not respectfully). In 1982, Moore is struggling to perfect a gyro which will be the core component in the missile system for a new tank. Flash ahead to 1984 and Murphy is on duty in an Arabian desert vainly attempting to keep his new tank under control, but the gyro is not functioning. These scenes are played one after the other and the picture cuts back and forth from 1982 to 1984 so the audience wonders if they are watching flashbacks or premonitions of things to come. In addition to having a tough time with his invention, Moore is also having woes with wife Capshaw and is rapidly falling under the influence of vampish fellow worker Shaver. When Moore accidentally comes upon the plans for a gyro that will work, he is in danger of death from Rasche, the nutso industrial spy who has also been seeking the plans. Flash ahead to see Murphy suffering through the results of all the above with a tank that is functioning improperly, crashing into things, and acting in a generally recalcitrant manner. The film continues to cut back and forth as Moore is busy straightening out the mistake in order to save the project while, in the other time frame, Murphy finds himself involved in a situation that calls for a reliable weapon. It's confusing and it is not funny. Try as they might, this stellar cast couldn't cover up the fact that this movie, like the gyro Moore tried to create, was a dud. There is no rhyme or reason for the cross-cutting and this picture should be laid to rest next to another film the husband and wife team of Katz and Huyck did, LUCKY LADY. Also, shooting a movie with Moore and Murphy would have been just fine and sparks might have flown, except for the fact that the two *never* appear together in a scene! The humor, such as it is, is capped when war breaks out between Iraq and Kuwait, always a funny subject for a film. The only genuine fun comes from Rasche, a newcomer, as the wacky spy. He carried some of this characterization into his 1986 TV series "Sledge Hammer," which was not quite as funny as this movie, which was not funny at all. Moore's scenes were shot in the local Los Angeles area, while Murphy's work was lensed in Israel. And never the twain met. Superfluous foul language and some violence remove any possibility of children seeing this film, much less appreciating it.

p, Gloria Katz; d, Willard Huyck; w, Katz, Huyck (based on the novel *Easy and Hard Ways Out* by Robert Grossbach); ph, Don Peterman (Movielab Color); m, Patrick Williams; ed, Sidney Wolinsky, Michael A. Stevenson; prod d, Peter Jamison; art d, Robert W. Welch III, Ariel Roshko; set d, R. Chris Westlund, Giora Porter; cos, Kristi Zea, Gordon Brockway, Jennifer Parsons; spec eff, Richard E. Johnson, John R. Elliott; stunts, Rick Dees, Chuck Street, Everett Creach.

Comedy   **Cas.**   **(PR:O   MPAA:R)**

BETRAYAL, THE   (SEE: KAMILLA, Norway)

BETRAYAL: THE STORY OF KAMILLA (SEE: KAMILLA, Norway)

BEVERLY HILLS COP***   (1984) 105m PAR c

Eddie Murphy (*Axel Foley*), Judge Reinhold (*Detective Billy Rosewood*), John Ashton (*Sgt. Taggart*), Lisa Eilbacher (*Jenny Summers*), Ronny Cox (*Lt. Bogomil*), Steven Berkoff (*Victor Maitland*), James Russo (*Mikey Tandino*), Jonathan Banks (*Zack*), Stephen Elliott (*Chief Hubbard*), Gilbert R. Hill (*Inspector Todd*), Art Kimbro (*Detective Foster*), Joel Bailey (*Detective McCabe*), Bronson Pinchot (*Serge*), Paul Reiser (*Jeffrey*), Michael Champion (*Casey*), Frank Pesce (*Cigarette Buyer*), Gene Borkan (*Truck Driver*), Michael Gregory (*Hotel Manager*), Alice Cadogan (*Hotel Clerk*), Philip Levien (*Donny*), Karen Mayo-Chandler (*Maitland Receptionist*), Gerald Berns (*Beverly Hills Cop*), William Wallace (*2nd Beverly Hills Cop*), Israel Juarbe (*Room Service Waiter*), Randy Gallion (*Bell Hop*), Damon Wayans (*Banana Man*), Chuck Adamson, Chip Heller (*Crate Openers*), Rick Overton (*Bonded Warehouse Night Superintendant*), Rex Ryon (*Bonded Warehouse Security Guard*), Michael Pniewski, Douglas Warhit (*Bonded Warehouse Clerks*), Paul Drake, Tom Everett (*Holdup Men*), Sally Kishbaugh (*Waitress*), Barry Shade (*Valet*), Jack Heller (*Maitre d'*), Michael Harrington (*Arresting Officer*), David Wells (*Dispatcher*), Scott Murphy (*Detective Owenby*), Dennis Madden, John Achorn, John Pettis, Nick Shields, Carl Weintraub, Darwyn Carson, Anthony De Fonte (*Detroit Cops*), Darwyn Carson (*Barmaid*), Mark E. Corry (*Pool Player*), Thomas J. Hageboeck (*Maitland Body Guard*).

Young black comedian Eddie Murphy's third film (48 HOURS and TRADING PLACES came first) was a phenomenally successful smash at the box office, grossing more money than any comedy in history. Aided substantially by a soundtrack filled with songs that became massive hits in their own right, BEVERLY HILLS COP is a fun, if empty-headed, cop film which sees street-smart Detroit detective Murphy out to avenge the murder of a close friend. After a harrowing chase scene involving an 18-wheel truck which destroys thousands of dollars of private property and wipes out half a neighborhood, Murphy is sent on vaction by his superior. Murphy uses the time off to trace the killers of his friend to Beverly Hills. Dressed in old bluejeans and a sweatshirt, Murphy travels to California in his beat-up Chevy Nova. The sight of Murphy causes a bit of a stir in the exclusive white-bread society of Beverly Hills and he is refused a room in one of the swankiest hotels in town. Quick-thinking Murphy drops the name of Michael Jackson, and the easily intimidated clerk immediately gives the brash black man a suite. His connection in the art gallery scene, Eilbacher, a girl he knew in Detroit, steers him toward the villain, Berkoff, an evil British crime kingpin whose Beverly Hills mansion is a veritable fortress. Though the arrogant Beverly Hills Police, led by Cox, try their best to keep the irrepressible Murphy from destroying their town, the black cop manages to win over a young detective, Reinhold, and his middle- aged partner Ashton, by bringing excitment back to their jobs. The climax sees a huge shoot-out at Berkoff's mansion, where Murphy handles most of the gunplay while Reinhold and Ashton stumble around like Laurel and Hardy trying to back up Murphy. In the end the villains are dispatched and Murphy redeems himself in the eyes of both the Beverly Hills Police Department and his own department back in Detroit. BEVERLY HILLS COP is really nothing more than a star vehicle designed to show off the talents of Murphy--at which it succeeds admirably. The comedy is deftly balanced with the stunningly staged action scenes and surprisingly most of the laughs are given to Reinhold and Ashton. Originally intended as a vehicle for the muscle-bound Sylvester Stallone (where the only laughter would have been unintentional), Murphy and director Brest transformed what would have been an ultra-violent, routine cop film into something a bit different and a lot more fun. The language is too raw for children and the violence is excessive. Former Eagles band member Glen Frey scored big with the film's theme song, "The Heat Is On" (Harold Faltermeyer, Keith Forsey), as did most of the other tunes heard in the movie, including contributions by The Pointer Sisters and Patti LaBelle.

p, Don Simpson, Jerry Bruckheimer; d, Martin Brest; w, Daniel Petrie, Jr. (based on a by story Petrie, Danilo Bach); ph, Bruce Surtees (Technicolor); m, Harold Faltermeyer; ed, Billy Weber, Arthur Coburn; prod d, Angelo Graham; art d, James J. Murakami; set d, Jeff Haley, John M. Dwyer; cos, Tom Bronson; spec eff, Kenneth D. Pepiot.

Comedy   **Cas.**   **(PR:O   MPAA:R)**

BEYOND GOOD AND EVIL*   (1984, Ital./Fr./Ger.) 106m Silvio
                                Clementelli/Films Inc. c (OLTRE IL BENE E IL MALE)

Dominique Sanda (*Lou Andreas-Salome*), Erland Josephson (*Friedrich "Fritz" Nietzsche*), Robert Powell (*Paul Ree*), Virna Lisi (*Elisabeth Nietzsche*), Philippe Leroy (*Peter Gast*), Elisa Cegani (*Franziska Nietzsche*), Umberto Orsini (*Bernard Forster*), Michael Degen (*Karl Andreas*), Amedeo Amodio (*Dr. Dulcamara*), Carmen Scarpitta (*Malvida*), Nicolette Macchiavelli (*Amanda*).

An intellectual exercise in the politics of sexual game-playing with Sanda starring as the socialist free-love poet, Josephson as philosopher Nietzsche, and Powell as the intellectual physician Ree. The three lives enter into a *menage a trois*, devoting as much of their lives to bedroom antics as to psychological insights--neither of which is worth much. Before long it all becomes rather absurd and will no doubt pass over the heads of many a movie goer. Josephson is enjoyable as Nietzsche, rivaling his performance in Ingmar Bergman's AFTER THE REHEARSAL released the same year. Poorly dubbed into English.

p, Robert Gordon Edwards; d, Liliana Cavani; w, Cavani, Franco Arcalli, Italo Moscati (based on a story by Cavani); ph, Armando Nannuzzi; m, Daniele Paris; ed, Arcalli, Robert Jose Pomper; art d, Lorenzo Mongiardino.

Drama   **(PR:O   MPAA:NR)**

BIG MEAT EATER**½   (1984, Can.) 82m BCD/New Line Cinema c

George Dawson (*Bob*), Andrew Gillies (*Jan*), Big Miller (*Abdulla*), Stephen Dimopoulous (*Josef*), Georgina Hegedos (*Rosa*), Ida Carnevali (*Babushka*), Howard Taylor (*Mayor*), Heather Smith-Harper (*Secretary*), Peter Anderson (*Alderman*), Gillian Neumann (*Mrs. Campbell*), Sharon Wahl (*Nina*), Jon Bryden (*Ace*), Shannon Keane (*Kid*), Kim Stebner (*1st Heavy*), Jay Samwald, Neil MacDonald (*Meat Carriers*), Scott Swansom (*Announcer*), Helen Le Counte, Bente Friemel, Elaine Thompson.

A frequently flawed but occasionally hilarious parody of science fiction films. Aliens arrive to gather radioactive meat waste that forms in the septic tank below the shop of butcher Dawson. They revive the corpse of the mayor (Taylor) and he uses corrupt techniques to buy the land and put up a processing plant for the invaders. Gillies is the hero, the son of the crooked contractor Taylor hires, who takes some of the radioactive lunchmeat and converts his car into a spaceship in which he blasts into orbit and destroys the alien mother ship in a low budget special effects battle. The highlight comes when Miller (whose first name, Big, is not undeserved) murders Dawson and performs the "Baghdad Boogie" complete with belly dancers who appear from nowhere before he shoves the body into the incinerator. Not everyone's cup of tea, but worth a look for those who appreciate a strange sense of humor.

p, Laurence Keane; d, Chris Windsor; w, Keane, Windsor, Phil Savath; ph, Doug McKay; m, J. Douglas Dodd; ed, Keane, Windsor, Lilla Pederson; spec eff, Michael Dorsey, Iain Best, Jim Bridge; ch, Helen LeCounte.

Science Fiction/Comedy   **(PR:O   MPAA:NR)**

BIGGER SPLASH, A-**   (1984) 105m Buzzy Enterprises c

David Hockney (*Painter*), Peter Schlesinger (*Painter's Friend*), Ossie Clark (*Dress Designer*), Celia Birtwell (*Designer's Wife*), Mo McDermott (*Friend*), Henry Geldzahler (*Collector*), Kasmin (*Dealer*).

Three years in the making and 10 years in the releasing, A BIGGER SPLASH was first shown at the New York Film Festival in 1974, but waited on the shelf until 1984 before getting a minor art house release. Essentially a fiction film in which all the characters play themselves, the picture has painter Hockney a painter whose male lover (Schlesinger) leaves him. Hockney mopes around and is unable to finish a painting, much to the consternation of his friends. Occasionally interesting as a time capsule of the early 1970s art scene, the film is too serious in its treatment, as if none of the people it concerns ever laughs. Hazan and Mingay later brought their semi-documentary technique to RUDE BOY.

p&d, Jack Hazan; w, Hazan, David Mingay; ph, Hazan; m, Patrick Gowers, Greg Bailey; ed, Mingay.

Drama   (PR:O   MPAA:NR)

BIRDY****   (1984) 120m Malton/Tri-Star c

Matthew Modine (*Birdy*), Nicolas Cage (*Al Columbato*), John Harkins (*Dr. Weiss*), Sandy Baron (*Mr. Columbato*), Karen Young (*Hannah Rourke*), Bruno Kirby (*Renaldi*), Nancy Fish (*Mrs. Prevost*), George Buck (*Birdy's Father*), Delores Sage (*Birdy's Mother*), Robert L. Ryan (*Joe Sagessa*), James Santini (*Mario Columbato*), Maude Winchester (*Doris Robinson*), Marshall Bell (*Ronsky*), Elizabeth Whitcraft (*Rosanne*), Sandra Beall (*Shirley*), Victoria Nekko (*Claire*), Crystal Field (*Mrs. Columbato*), John Brumfield (*Mr. Kohler*), Joe Lerer (*Military Doctor*), Alice Truscott (*Mother on Train*), Ed Taylor (*Zimmy the Human Fish*), Irving Selbst (*Fairground Announcer*), Steve Lippe (*Junkyard Proprietor*), William Clark (*Policeman on Beach*), James Pruett (*Emergency Doctor*), Priscilla Alden (*Waiting Room Lady*), Howard Kinsley (*Mr. Tate*), Robert Diamond (*Maloney*), Bud Seese (*Drunk in Jail*), Ray Pili, Lawrence J. McKenna, David W. Kuhn, Kevin P. Kuhn, Ronald Distefano, Larry Hochman (*High School Band*), Guy Jones, Erskine Morgan (*Hospital Orderlies*), Ramona Bajema (*Girl on Train*), Maurice Frizzell, Jr. (*Nuts and Bolts Patient*), Richard Mason (*Injured Soldier*), Charles A. Tamburro, Rick Holley, Harry Hauss (*Helicopter Pilots*), Mark Simpson, Clark Taylor (*Helicopter Soldiers*), Michael Runyard, Reid Rondell, Mic Rodgers (*Stuntmen*).

A rare movie that successfully brings a psychological novel to the screen without omitting one salient point or complex image as it flows and flies along. Director Parker, whose films include MIDNIGHT EXPRESS, FAME, and BUGSY MALONE, has never been satisfied doing the same thing twice. He always seems to strive for something new, something he can stretch to achieve. BIRDY puts him in the forefront of the best directors of the 1980s. It's the story of a deep friendship between Modine and Cage, a pair of young men whose lives have been scarred by the Vietnam experience. Modine has had an obsessive affinity for birds since he was a lad. We are shown this in flashbacks and flash-forwards surrounding the main setting, a military hospital for the insane where Modine is currently "recovering." Modine has been little more than a vegetable, almost in a coma for the last year. Cage is his best friend and is himself a veteran of the war. But Cage's wounds were physical and he has since recovered from them and is now bound and determined to bring Modine out of his stupor. To that end, he visits Modine regularly and tries vainly to get some sort of reaction. Modine has spent the better part of a year sitting naked in his hospital room, staring at a high window above his head. He is acting like a caged bird, moving like a parakeet, and refusing to respond to any of Cage's entreaties. While this is happening, the film flashes back to see the boys as they grew up, their hassles with their parents (Buck and Sage are Modine's, Baron and Field are Cage's) and their exploits with young women. A pattern begins to emerge and Modine's lack of mental balance is established. Cage is a suave type, finding no problem with women, while Modine is extraordinarily shy and tongue-tied around anyone whose voice is higher than his. He finds his release in flying, without an airplane. Several times he believes he can really fly and makes a pair of wings out of pigeon feathers which he thinks will take him, like Icarus, up, up, and away. Modine is forever in trouble and Cage is the friend who races after him, trying to extricate the youth from his various problems. At one point in their teens, Modine leaps from a high place, totally convinced that he will be able to fly. Cage arrives a second too late to help him and the result is that Modine is taken to a hospital. Cage is ridden with guilt about having been too late to help his buddy. Modine's obsession continues. It's not enough to fly like a bird, he really wants to *be* a bird and his bedroom is soon a monument to his passion. It becomes an aviary and his life is now a twisted tribute to John James Audubon. The boys go to war and Modine goes totally over the edge and lands in the mental hospital where the doctors despair of ever breaking through his chirps. Cage has now recovered from his own wounds and is spending as much time as he can with Modine. He is strangled by all the red tape and the bureaucracy and begs the consulting doctor, Harkins, to try to understand why Modine is the way he is. Modine finally comes out of his stupor and the film ends happily, and comically, as the two boys stand on a rooftop. Modine leaps off the roof and Cage thinks he's lost his pal forever. Cage runs to the roof ledge and sees that Modine has jumped from the high roof to the roof of a building right next to it, perhaps eight feet lower. Modine is cured and the boys are

united. Cage and Modine offer outstanding performances and why the film was not recognized by the movie academy is a bewilderment although it did receive the Special Grand Jury Prize at the 1985 Cannes Film Festival. Modine's sensitive portrayal of the young man who transcends species boundaries is spellbinding. Cage is, at once, affable, then concerned, then frustrated and shows that he is much more than just Francis Coppola's relative; he is an actor to be reckoned with. Parker's direction is forthright and never intrusive, even when lesser lights might have been. The scene where Modine thinks he is flying is a wonder. All of the acting is first quality and the score by rocker Peter Gabriel is on the money. Parker has always known the importance of music to heighten moods (just look at his credits) and the choice of Gabriel was an excellent one. One-time nightclub comic Baron impresses as the blue collar father of Cage. Baron played "Lenny" in the stage show about comic Lenny Bruce (an early pal of Baron's) and has been seen in several movies since, including BROADWAY DANNY ROSE. Englishman Parker is at home with the U.S. and his foreign background gives him the ability to look at America with a fresh eye–in much the same way directors like Michael Apted have been able to do. The movie cost $12 million and may not have made that back but it will probably be a cult movie in years to come. A most unusual picture about a most unusual subject, BIRDY will haunt your memory for a long time. Not for children.

p, Alan Marshall; d, Alan Parker; w, Sandy Kroopf, Jack Behr (based on the novel by William Wharton); ph, Michael Seresin (Metrocolor); m, Peter Gabriel; ed, Gerry Hambling; prod d, Geoffrey Kirkland; art d, Armin Ganz, Stu Campbell; set d, George R. Nelson; cos, Kristi Zea.

Drama   **Cas.**   (PR:O   MPAA:R)

BIZET'S CARMEN****   (1984, Fr./Ital.) 152m GAU-Production Marcel Dassault- Opera Film Produzione/Triumph c (AKA: CARMEN)

Julia Migenes- Johnson (*Carmen*), Placido Domingo (*Don Jose*), Ruggero Raimondi (*Escamillo*), Faith Esham (*Micaela*), Jean-Philippe Lafont (*Dancairo*), Gerard Garino (*Remendado*), Susan Daniel (*Mercedes*), Lilian Watson (*Frasquita*), Jean Paul Bogart (*Zuniga*), Francois Le Roux (*Morales*), Julien Guiomar (*Lillas Pastia*), Accursio Di Leo (*Guide*), Maria Campano (*Manuelita*), Christina Hoyos, Juan Antonio Jimenez (*Court Dancers*), Enrique El Cojo (*Old Dancer/Innkeeper*), Santiago Lopez (*Escamillo's Double*), Aurora Vargas, Carmen Vargas, Concha Vargas, Esperanza Fernandez, Lourdes Garcia, Maria Gomez, Pilar Becerra (*Carmen's Friends*), Virgilio Daddi (*Stunts*), Antonio Gades Dance Company.

With any luck, this should be the last of the many adaptations of Merimee's story and Bizet's opera. Why the last? Because, so far, it's the best. It's been done so many times that the plot should be as familiar as the Bill of Rights by now. Migenes-Johnson is the flamboyant cigarette worker at the tobacco factory, Domingo is her foil as the wooden soldier. (There were those who thought Domingo was too wooden but the truth is he was perfect as the role calls for him to be a stiff.) Where this version stands out is that director Rosi (THE MATTEI AFFAIR, CHRIST STOPPED AT EBOLI) took a bold step when he decided to return to the basics of the Merimee-Bizet tale and present this as realistically as possible. Heads snapped at that decision because the story of Carmen had been depicted in every possible fashion by this time. It had been done as a Flamenco film, with an all-black cast, and in numerous stylistic incarnations. Filmed operas can be as exciting as watching dogs sleep, if the job of directing them is given to a lesser talent than Rosi. This one is a knockout, a smasher, and will even thrill people who hate opera. Rosi and cinematographer De Santis have taken their actors and their cameras all through the Andalusian landscapes of Spain and given the warhorse of a story a different look. Carmen was the first true feminist who would not tolerate being under the thumb of men. She's independence personified and will not brook any interference in her quest for realization. She uses her wiles to entrap Don Jose and get him tossed in jail and is finally given her comeuppance in the last act when she is stabbed to death. Migenes-Johnson is surely the sexiest Carmen to come along in years. A Puerto Rican background and strict operatic training also help as she manages to make every note of Bizet's ring to the rafters. Winner of an award from NOSOTROS (the Hispanic show business group headed by Ricardo Montalban) in 1986, Migenes- Johnson's career should be a long and healthy one, if her performance in this picture is any indication. Domingo is a joy to listen to. Playing his records next to those of past tenors will prove that he deserves to be listed with Caruso and other masters as a voice for the ages. Esham shows her versatility in the thankless role of the dippy Micaela and all other parts are equally well-cast. Why is this version the best, though? Given the fact that there have been other great voices in the roles of Carmen and Don Jose, we have to cite Rosi for the film's success because it is his vision and energy that keep this from becoming placid and tame. He's chosen to examine the story in much the same way as he did his SALVATORE GIULIANO and his other works, with a similar neo-realistic eye as Fellini and De Sica used when making their earlier works. It's almost a documentary with music as we go inside the cigarette factory and see the sweatshop it is, as we see the poor, ragged children who roam the streets instead of the traditional well-scrubbed kids one usually sees in this story. Rosi also handles crowds well, almost like a King Vidor or a John Ford, except that this time the people are singing, not calling for some outlaw to be guest of honor at a necktie party. At 152 minutes, it's true to the length of the opera but it might have been trimmed a bit in spots. There are a few holes in the story that belong to Merimee and Bizet, not to Rosi, who hewed closely to the original and must be applauded for that. Opera has always been thought of as too histrionic or stylized or fake for film audiences. That's because the operas seen before were probably just that. By using actual locations and shooting this more as a dramatic tragedy, Rosi has forever lifted the veil of artificiality and brought a new dimension to the medium. (In French; English subtitles.)

p, Patrice Ledoux; d, Francesco Rosi; w, Rosi, Tonino Guerra (based on the story by Prosper Merimee and the opera "Carmen" by Georges Bizet); ph, Pasqualino De Santis (Panavision, Eastmancolor); m, Bizet; ed, Ruggero Mastroianni, Colette Semprun; prod d, Enrico Job; md, Lorin Maazel; set d, Gianni Giovagnonni, Pierre Thevenet, Enrico Job; cos, Job; ch, Antonio Gades.

Opera   Cas.   (PR:A-C MPAA:PG)

BLACK CAT, THE*½   (1984, Ital./Brit.) 91m Selenia/World Northal c

Patrick Magee (Mr. Miles), Mimsy Farmer (Jill Travers), David Warbeck (Inspector Gorley), Al Cliver (Policeman), Dagmar Lassander (Mrs. Grayson), Geoffrey Copleston (Inspector Flynn), Daniela Dorio (Maureen).

Ridiculous horror film has Farmer a reporter investigating the mysterious deaths of some villagers. The trail leads to the cat owned by Magee, a researcher trying to contact the dead. Hilarious scenes where Magee and his pet each try to dominate the other, but otherwise a film to avoid like the plague.

p, Giulio Sbarigia; d, Lucio Fulci; w, Biagio Proietti, Fulci (based on a story by Proietti from a story by Edgar Allan Poe); ph, Sergia Salvati (Technovision, Eastmancolor); m, Pino Donaggio; ed, Vincenzo Tomassi; spec eff, Paolo Ricci; makeup, Franco de Girolama; stunts, Nazzareno Cardinali.

Horror   (PR:O   MPAA:R)

BLACK ROOM, THE zero   (1984) 87m CI Films c

Stephen Knight (Jason), Cassandra Gaviola (Bridget), Jim Stathis (Larry), Clara Perryman (Robin), Geanne Frank (Sandy), Charlie Young (Lisa), Christopher McDonald (Terry), Linnea Quigley (Milly).

A brother and sister invite passing strangers to their castle for sexual fun and games, where a variety of nasty fates await them. Total trash with nothing to redeem it. Not to be confused with the superb horror feature with the same title starring Boris Karloff, made nearly half a century earlier.

p, Aaron C. Butler; d, Elly Kenner, Norman Thaddeus Vane; w, Vane; ph, Robert Harmon; m, Art Podell, James Achley; ed, David Kern; prod d, Yoram Barzilai.

Horror   (PR:O   MPAA:R)

BLAME IT ON RIO zero   (1984) 110m Sherwood/FOX c

Michael Caine (Matthew Hollis), Joseph Bologna (Victor Lyons), Valerie Harper (Karen Hollis), Michelle Johnson (Jennifer Lyons), Demi Moore (Nicole Hollis), Jose Lewgoy (Eduardo Marques), Lupe Gigliotti (Signora Botega), Michael Menaugh (Peter), Tessy Callado (Helaine), Ana Lucia Lima (1st Macumba Lady), Maria Helena Velasco (2nd Macumba Lady), Zeni Pereira (Mother of the Bride), Eduardo Conde (Singer in the Dance Club), Betty Von Wien (Isabella), Nelson Dantas (Doctor), Thomas Lee Mahon (Lorenzo), Victor Haim (Bernardo), Jane Duboc (Singer in Cafe), Romulo Arantes (Diego), Giovanna Sodre (Astrid), Grupo Senzala (Capoeirista), Angelo Mattos (Dancer).

This fulsome comedy involves the story of two men (Caine and Bologna) who go off for a month to Rio with their two teenage daughters (Moore and Johnson). Caine's wife Harper pulls out of the trip at the last minute, saying she wants time to think about the marriage, then heads off to Club Med for a month. Once in Rio, Bologna, who is going through a messy divorce, heads off for the city's nightlife to chase women. Caine is less enthusiastic about this, but soon finds he is being seduced by none other than his best friend's daughter, Johnson. The nubile lass has always had a crush on Caine and won't stop until she gets him into bed. At this point BLAME IT ON RIO turns into a most uncomfortable film, watching the development of the affair with the unsettling gaze of gapers at an auto wreck. In between the gratuitous nudity (mostly by Johnson, and, of course, never of any men) and the catalog of lame songs, there's plenty of travelog shots to pad out the thin plot line. Eventually Bologna finds out that Johnson has been sleeping with an older man, and begs Caine to help him find his daughter's lover so he can beat the man to a pulp. Of course Caine can't tell Bologna his secret, but eventually the conflict is resolved as the film winds up its perverse story. Woody Allen explored a similar affair in MANHATTAN (1979), but did it with taste and sensitivity. BLAME IT ON RIO takes an easier route, simply exploiting the situation for cheap laughs. Caine looks embarrassed through the entire film, as well he should be. A remake of Claude Berri's 1977 French film ONE WILD MOMENT, BLAME IT ON RIO has some considerable talents behind the cameras with Donen as director and Gelbart as cowriter. Knowing what these two men were capable of makes the film all the more reprehensible. Songs include: "Nothing to Say," "Time Out," "Strong is the Urge," "Afterthoughts" (Ken Wannberg, Dennis Spiegel), "Programa Carioca," "Grumari," "Cartoes Postais," "Un, Deux, Trois, Samba" (Oscar

Castro-Neves, Aldir Blanc), "Blame It on Rio," "I Must Be Doing Something Right," (Cy Coleman, Sheldon Harnick).

p&d, Stanley Donen; w, Charlie Peters, Larry Gelbart (based on the screenplay "Un Moment d'Egarement" by Claude Berri); ph, Reynaldo Villalobos (Metrocolor); m, Ken Wannberg; ed, George Hively, Richard Marden; art d, Marcos Flaksman; set d, Yeda De Mellow Lewinsohn; cos, Helena Gastal.

Comedy   Cas.   (PR:O   MPAA:R)

BLAME IT ON THE NIGHT*   (1984) 85m Pentimento/Tri-Star c

Nick Mancuso (Chris Dalton), Byron Thames (Job Dalton), Leslie Ackerman (Shelly), Dick Bakalyan (Manzini), Leeyan Granger (Melanie), Rex Ludwick (Animal), Michael Wilding (Terry), Dennis Tufano (Leland), Stephen John Hunter (S. G.), Gary Chase (Buster), Melissa Prophet (Charlotte), Joe Mantell (Attorney), Sandy Kenyon (Colonel), Linda Blais (Stewardess), James Bem Sobieski (Cadet), Ida Martin, Lily Martin (Baby Nicholas), Anthony T. Mazzucchi (Mazzucchi), Shepard Sanders (Bob Ritz), Robert O. Michaels (Peter Styne), Judith Marx (Yvonne), Marissa Ravelli, Wendy Brainard (Daughters), Nina Franciosa (Girl in Audience), Andrew Lauer (Boy in Audience), Richard Caruso (Sax Player), Susan MacDonald (Gloria Aaron), Marla Phillips (Woman in Bar), Merry Clayton (Herself), Billy Preston (Himself), Ollie E. Brown (Himself).

Tiresome story of rock 'n' roller Mancuso forced to take the son he's never seen (Thames) on the road with him when the latter's mother dies. The boy, a product of a long-ago one-night-stand, has been in a military academy, so the sudden immersion in the world of groupies and the wild life is something of a jolt, but gradually--and predictably--father and son grow together. Based on a story cooked up between producer-director Taft and Rolling Stones vocalist Mick Jagger, the movie is little more than a string of maudlin cliches unimaginatively carried off. The most annoying feature however, is the score, written and performed by Ted Neeley, and dubbed by Neeley over Mancuso's lip-synching. Neeley, the annoying, whiny Jesus from JESUS CHRIST, SUPERSTAR hasn't improved his singing since and would have been little missed if he had vanished after it. Uninvolving at every level, though mercifully brief.

p&d, Gene Taft; w, Len Jenkin (Based on a story by Taft, Michael Philip [Mick] Jagger); ph, Alex Phillips (Technicolor); m, Ted Neeley; ed, Tony Lombardo; prod d, Ted Haworth; set d, Jo-Ann Chorney; m/l, "Lost in The Light," "Old Grinnin' Moon," Ted Neeley; "Blame It On The Night," "Another One Night Stand," "Takin' Care of Each Other," Neeley, Tom Scott; "One By One," Neeley, Judith Myers-Mark, "Stone Me," Neeley, Scott, Taft, "A Man Without a Woman," Neeley, Taft.

Drama   Cas.   (PR:C MPAA:PG-13)

BLESS 'EM ALL   (SEE: ACT, THE)

BLESS THEIR LITTLE HEARTS***   (1984) 80m Black Independent Features bw

Nate Hardman (Charlie Banks), Kaycee Moore (Andais Banks), Angela Burnett, Ronald Burnett, Kimberly Burnett (Banks Children), Eugene Cherry, Lawrence Pierott, Ernest Knight, Ellis Griffin.

Impressive low-budget feature shot around the Watts community of Los Angeles an unemployed black family man who drifts into an affair with a welfare mother. Sensitively written and excellently acted, the film deserved a much wider release than it got.

p&d, Billy Woodberry; w&ph, Charles Burnett; m, Archie Shepp, Little Esther Phillips; ed, Woodberry.

Drama   (PR:O   MPAA:NR)

BLIND ALLEY   (SEE: PERFECT STRANGERS)

BLIND DATE*   (1984) 99m Omega-Westcom/New Line c

Joseph Bottoms (Jonathon Ratcliffe), Kirstie Alley (Claire Parker), James Daughton (David), Lana Clarkson (Rachel), Keir Dullea (Dr. Steiger), Charles Nicklin, Michael Howe, Gerald Kelly, Jerry Sandquist, Marina Sirtis, Kathy Hill, Louis Sheldon, Danos Lygizos, Spyros Papafrantzis, Antigone Amanitis, Ankie Grelson, Noelle Simpson, Agatha Visviki, Chris Paps, Brian Walker, Mirella Vardi, Charol Shideler, Beatrice Vetterly, Jan Geneen, Christy Keenan.

Stupid slasher film set in Athens has Bottoms a blind advertising man who has been fitted up with a special computerized camera that allows him to "see," though not much. He sees a murder in progress and eventually manages to track down the killer, despite his handicap. Gaping holes in credibility and a lot of obvious filler material doomed this one to a brief run at the theater and then straight to the video store.

p&d, Nico Mastorakis; w, Mastorakis, Fred C. Perry; ph, Andrew Bellis (Technicolor); m, Stanley Myers; ed, George Rosenburg; prod d,set d&cos, Anne Marie Papadelis; m/l, John Kongos.

Crime   Cas.   (PR:O MPAA:R)

BLOOD SIMPLE**   (1984) 97m River Road/Circle c

John Getz (Ray), Frances McDormand (Abby), Dan Hedaya (Julian Marty), M. Emmet Walsh (Private Detective Visser), Samm-Art Williams (Maurice), Deborah Neumann (Debra), Raquel Gavia (Landlady), Van Brooks (Man from Lubbock), Senor Marco (Mr. Garcia), William Creamer (Old Cracker), Loren Bivens (Strip Bar Exhorter), Bob McAdams (Strip Bar Senator), Shannon Sedwick (Stripper), Nancy Ginger (Girl on Overlook), Rev. William Preston Robertson (Radio Evangelist).

A stylish but frightfully empty film noir thriller which stars Walsh as a sleazy private eye who is hired by Texas strip bar owner Hedaya to kill his wife, McDormand, and her lover, Getz, a worker at the bar. Hedaya, who plans to pay Walsh with bar money, plans to cover things by making it appear as though the money was stolen from the safe (a crime he could easily blame on one of his employees). However, Walsh, whose morality originates from his wallet, has plans of his own. He finds McDormand and Getz tucked away in bed one evening and snaps some photographs of them. The pictures are then doctored to make it appear that McDormand and Getz have been murdered. Hedaya is satisfied when he learns that the job is done. The greedy Walsh takes his cash and then promptly plugs Hedaya full of holes, leaving him to die in a back room at the bar. Later Getz arrives on the scene and notices two things–a pool of blood that has drained from Hedaya's limp body and a gun of McDormand's lying nearby. Getz immediately draws the wrong conclusion–that McDormand has killed her husband in a crime of passion–and goes "simple" at the sight of the "blood." He foolishly begins to clean up after the murder, a murder he didn't commit, to protect the woman he loves. He loads the body into the back seat of his car with the intention of burying it somewhere desolate. While on the road, however, he hears a cryptic sound coming from the back seat. What he finds is Hedaya–alive, but barely. Getz, who has now gone completely blood simple, is determined to finish off the murder. He digs a grave in an open field and drags the groaning, vomiting Hedaya into it, in order to assure that the "dead" man stays dead. In a marvelously disturbing scene, Getz shovels dirt onto his victim, as Hedaya makes a pathetic effort to shoot Getz. He is too weak to even pull the trigger and Getz calmly takes the gun away before resuming his shoveling. He then delivers a coup-de-grace by pounding the shovel down onto Hedaya's dirt-covered face. The following morning, having regained his composure, Getz calls on McDormand. He tells her that he took care of everything and that they just need to remain calm. Not surprisingly, McDormand looks at him as though he's lost his mind. Meantime, Walsh has discovered that the doctored photo he showed to Hedaya is missing and he tries, unsuccessfully, to break into the safe at the bar to find it (which inadvertently adds substance to Hedaya's original claim of a robbery). Naturally, he is puzzled at the disappearance of Hedaya's body. Assuming McDormand and Getz are intending blackmail with the photos, Walsh telephones them, but remains silent when McDormand answers. McDormand, still unaware that Hedaya is dead, assumes it is her husband and tells Getz so, confusing him even further. He thinks that McDormand is involved with someone else (the person who called) and leaves. Believing that someone broke into the safe and stole some money, Getz checks for himself. He doesn't find any cash, but does notice the missing photo which shows him lying dead with McDormand. McDormand chases after Getz, who is packing his things, and persuades him to stay. Later, at McDormand's apartment, Getz stands in the dark and peers out the window, hoping to get a glimpse of whoever is tormenting him. McDormand mistakenly turns on the light, thereby, allowing Walsh to see in. A shotgun blast shatters the window and mortally wounds Getz. Walsh, whom McDormand wrongly believes is Hedaya (she has yet to see his face or get the complete story from Getz), pursues and she retreats to the bathroom where she sneaks out the window into a neighboring apartment. In the phenomenal finale Walsh reaches his hand into the neighboring window, only to have it pinned to the sill by the knife-wielding McDormand. Stretched halfway outside the window, Walsh struggles to free himself, but to no avail. He begins shooting through the wall at McDormand (causing brilliant shafts of light to pierce into the darkened room in which she hides) and eventually punches his way through in order to free himself. McDormand comes back around through the apartment (via the front door) and grabs her gun. As Walsh nears the closed bathroom door McDormand fires, dropping him to the floor. "I'm not afraid of you no more, Marty (Hedaya)" she sighs defiantly. Walsh, who is lying flat on his back, bleeding from the stomach and hand, lets out a roar of laughter at her total incomprehension of the entire situation. "Well ma'am, if I see him I'll sure give him the message." After which he dies. BLOOD SIMPLE purposely approaches the style of James M. Cain's crime novels–The Postman Always Rings Twice, Double Indemnity–two lovers tangled in a web of murder which involves the woman's husband. In fact, one could almost be convinced that BLOOD SIMPLE was based on a Cain story, except for one element it lacks–characters with dimension. BLOOD SIMPLE is brimming with characters who simply exist as chess pieces to further Joel and Ethan Coen's flashy stylistics. The Coens' concern isn't with emotional drama and intensity, but with camera moves and chic lighting. Flashy techniques consistently interrupt scenes which would otherwise be emotionally intense, practically nullifying the cast's superb performances. McDormand is wonderfully naturalistic as the not-too-bright girl with a homey sensuality, and Hedaya somehow manages to be vile yet sympathetic, but the film-schoolish

technical exercises overshadow their characters and refuse to allow them breathing room. In the end, BLOOD SIMPLE is only a half of a movie, style without content. If the Coens' had devoted as much energy to creating electric relationships (like the fires which consume Frank and Cora in The Postman Always Rings Twice, or Walter and Phyllis in Double Indemnity) as they had in creating their superb plot twists, then perhaps their film would not be so emotionally crippled. Hailed by some critics as the finest American independent film to hit the screens (a ridiculous overstatement that proves how hungry they are for a good film), BLOOD SIMPLE was completed on an astonishingly small budget of less than $1.5 million and looks as if it cost 10 times as much. But that can't hide the film's faults. Justifying BLOOD SIMPLE'S stylish look, Ethan Coen said, "We wanted to trick people into thinking we'd made a real movie." In BLOOD SIMPLE the Coen Brothers have made a real movie, a real average movie. The biggest disappointment, however, is that they could have made a great movie. Songs include: "I'm a Believer" (Neil Diamond, sung by Diamond), "Louie, Louie" (Richard Berry, performed by Toots and the Maytals), "Nada Mucho" (Jim Roberge), "He'll Have to Go" (Joe Allison, Audrey Allison, sung by Joan Black), "El Sueno" (Camilio Namen, performed by Johnny Ventura and His Combo), "Amalia" (Marin Luisa Buchino), "Rogucinno."

p, Ethan Coen; d, Joel Coen; w, Ethan Coen, Joel Coen; ph, Barry Sonnenfeld (DuArt Color); m, Carter Burwell; ed, Roderick Jaynes, Don Wiegmann, Peggy Connolly; prod d, Jane Musky; set d, Steve Roll; cos, Sara Medina-Pape; spec eff, Loren Bivens; makeup, Jean Ann Black, Paul R. Smith.

CRIME   Cas.   (PR:O MPAA:NR)

BLOODBATH AT THE HOUSE OF DEATH zero
(1984, Brit.) Wildwood/EMI c

Kenny Everett, Pamela Stephenson, Vincent Price, Gareth Hunt, Don Warrington, John Fortune, Sheila Steafel, John Stephen Hill, Cleo Rocos, Graham Stark, Pat Ashton, David Lodge, Davilia David, Debbie Linden, Tim Barrett, Oscar Quitak, Ellis Dale, Barry Cryer, Ray Cameron, Anna Dawson, Gordon Rollings, Jack Le White.

A team of supernatural investigators led by Everett spend the night in a scary old house with a history of murder. There's not so much as a smile raised by the old, obvious jokes and even Price, usually a welcome face in a horror parody, is bad here. Steer clear.

p,d&w, Ray Cameron; ph, Brian West, Dusty Miller; m, Mike Moran, Mark London; ed, Brian Tagg; art d, John Sunderland.

Comedy   (PR:C-O MPAA:NR)

BODY DOUBLE zero   (1984) 109m COL-Delphi II COL c

Craig Wasson (Jake), Melanie Griffith (Holly), Gregg Henry (Sam), Deborah Shelton (Gloria), Guy Boyd (Jim McLean), Dennis Franz (Rubin), David Haskell (Drama Teacher), Rebecca Stanley (Kimberly), Al Israel (Corso), Douglas Warhit (Video Salesman), B.J. Jones (Douglas), Russ Marin (Frank), Lane Davies (Billy), Barbara Crampton (Carol), Larry "Flash" Jenkins (Assistant Director), Monte Landis (Sid Goldberg), Linda Shaw (Herself), Mindi Miller (Tina), Denise Loveday (Actress/Vampire Movie), Gela Jacobson (Corso's Secretary), Ray Hassett, Rick Gunderson, Jerry Brutsche (Police Officers), Michael Kearns (Male Porno Star), Rob Paulsen (Cameraman), Jeremy Lawrence (Theater Director), Rod Loomis (TV Director), Gary F. Griffith (Auditioning Actor), Michael White (Security Guard), Emmett Brown (Studio Guard), H. David Fletcher (Security Guard at Bellini's), Marcia Del Mar (Production Assistant), Phil Redrow (Naked Man), Slavitza Jovan (Saleslady), Jack Mayhall (Jake's Replacement), Alexandra Day, Pamela Weston, Brinke Stevens, Melissa Christian (Girls in Bathroom), Patty Lotz, Barbara Peckinpaugh (Girls in Holly Does Hollywood), David Ursin, Casey Sanders, Wes Edwards (Men in Holly Does Hollywood), Chuck Waters (Jogger), Paul Calabria (Man with Dog), Nanci Rogers, Richard Warlock, Jerry Wills, Ted Grossman (Stuntpeople).

De Palma has done it again. Not content with having ripped off Hitchcock for several of his other films, he comes back to loot REAR WINDOW and VERTIGO in the same fashion Colin Higgins lifted THE MAN WHO KNEW TOO MUCH for FOUL PLAY. One would think that after all of the critical barbs he's taken, De Palma would have learned something. He tried another genre with SCARFACE which he shamefully dedicated to Ben Hecht and Howard Hawks) but has now returned to Hitchcock, the source of whatever success he's had. Wasson is a second-rate actor who has just been released from his latest opus, a sleazy horror movie. His problem is that he can't bear to be encased in the coffin he must lie in to play a vampire. After discovering his girl friend cheating on him, he storms out of his place before he realizes that he has nowhere to sleep that night. Henry is a fellow worker who is off to do a job in Washington and offers Wasson a place to stay. It's a huge circular home atop a Hollywood mountain and if Wasson is willing to house-sit, he can stay. Wasson accepts the task and Henry shows Wasson some of the benefits of the plush abode. One of them is a powerful telescope and Henry gleefully demonstrates what's happening in the house across the way. A beautiful woman undresses nightly in front of an unshaded window and puts on a strip, probably knowing that everyone in the neighborhood is watching. Wasson watches her every night and is soon in love with her. This is Shelton, a battered wife. He begins to follow her and notes that she is also being followed by a huge, ugly Indian. Wasson tails Shelton on her day's hegira to the Rodeo Collection (an elegant shopping area on Rodeo Drive in Beverly Hills), to several other stops, and finally to the Santa Monica beach where her purse is stolen. They finally meet and the entire sequence is not only reminiscent of VERTIGO, De Palma has stolen from his own earlier DRESSED TO KILL. Shelton is murdered in such a hideous fashion (Wasson is watching from across the street and tries to save her but can't) that it could cause retching. Then Wasson's story is not believed by policeman Boyd (the best actor in the film) because there is no evidence of the murder. Wasson meets Griffith, a punky porno actress who has been hired by an unknown someone to play the role of the woman doing the strip in the window. It's a body double for Shelton, but why? The truth comes out when Henry is unmasked as the real villain.... It's all so improbable and so laughable that you'd be better advised to forget the whole thing. While De Palma knows how to use his camera to great advantage, he is not nearly as adroit with the words he and co-author Avrech have written. Matter of fact, the dialog is so dull that your ears may fall asleep. Griffith, the daughter of Tippie Hedren (one of Hitch's favorites), is quite good and has a big career looming in front of her if she stays away from movies like this mean, shallow, and voyeuristic picture that shows De Palma hasn't lost his touch.

p&d, Brian De Palma; w, De Palma, Robert J. Avrech (based on a story by De Palma); ph, Stephen H. Burum (Metrocolor); m, Pino Donaggio; ed, Jerry Greenberg, Bill Pankow; prod d, Ida Random; set d, Cloudia; cos, Gloria Gresham; m/l "Relax," Frankie Goes to Hollywood (Group); stunts, Jerry Brutsche.

Terror/Murder   Cas.   (PR:O MPAA:R)

BODY ROCK*½   (1984) 93m Angeles Entertainment
                                  Group-Inverness/New World c

Lorenzo Lamas (Chilly D), Vicki Frederick (Claire), Cameron Dye (E-Z), Michelle Nicastro (Darlene), Ray Sharkey (Terrence), Grace Zabriskie (Chilly's Mother), Carole Ita White (Carolyn), Joseph Whipp (Donald), Oz Rock (Ricky Riccardo), La Ron A. Smith (Magick), Rene Elizondo (Snake), Seth Kaufman (Jama), Russell Clark (Jay), Robin Menken (Jodie), Tony Ganios (Big Mac), Shashawnee Hall (Theo), Barbara Beaman (Cashier), Mimi Kinkade (Little Freak), Ellen Gerstein (Secretary), Mark Sellers (D.J.), Theresa Belle, Carol Mosner, Jeannine Bisignano, Julie Sperow (Girls), Shawn Patrick Whittington (Dwayne), Ken Powell (Fred), Gino Garcia (Kid), Dark Hoffman, James Greene (Chilly's Friends), David Andrews, Robert L. Ghiblieri (Middle-Aged Men), Philip Granger (Young Man), Jeff Dollison (Teammate), Robert Kessler (Doctor), Gil Gex (20-Year-Old Man), Allison Suzanne (Girl in Crowd), Margit Haut (Sex Rap Dancer).

Just one more in a horde of "break-dance" movies that were released around the same time. Lamas is part of a group of New Yorkers who spend their time dancing and doing elaborate graffiti art. Smith is the best dancer in the group and shows Lamas the ropes. They are doing their act when seen by entrepreneur Sharkey (in another role like the one he did in THE IDOLMAKER) who talks Lamas into quitting the group and going to work at Sharkey's neon disco. Lamas is living with his mother, Zabriskie, and leaves the shabby flat as well as his long-time girl friend Nicastro, in favor of a flashier apartment and a new relationship with Frederick. After awhile, Sharkey and his pals find Lamas a bore and dump him but he is again surrounded by his old pals and the ending is happy. A pale imitation of SATURDAY NIGHT FEVER, BREAKIN', and BEAT STREET. The usual elements of every teen movie are seen: dancin', romancin', a bit of prancin', and a large yawn. The music is nonstop, heavy-beat rock and roll and the visions on screen would have benefited had they the same vitality as the score by Levay and the many tunes that were bought for the film. Songs include: "Body Rock" (Sylvester Levay, sung by Maria Vidal), "Team Work" (Ruth Roberts, Andy Goldmark, sung by David Lasley), "Why Do You Want to Break My Heart?" (Dwight Twilley, sung by Twilley), "One Thing Leads to Another" (Roberta Flack, Phil Galdston, Andy Goldmark, sung by Flack), "Let Your Body Rock" (Ralph MacDonald, sung by MacDonald), "Vanishing Point" (Baxter Robertson, sung by Robertson), "Sharpshooter" (Mark Biatte, Larry Gottlieb, sung by Laura Branigan), "The Jungle" (Ashford and Simpson, sung by Ashford and Simpson), "Deliver" (Martin Briley, Galdston, sung by Briley, Galdston), "The Closest to Love" (Ashford and Simpson, sung by Ashford and Simpson). Lamas doesn't have the charisma or the dance ability of Travolta and would be better served in a more sedate role. The fact that he becomes a star is hard to swallow as his dancing and rapping and singing are nothing much at all. The same thing happened when Kris Kristofferson was supposedly a huge singing star in A STAR IS BORN (Streisand's version) and the tune he sang over and over was as boring as listening to a dental drill. Even the usually reliable Sharkey offers nothing much to his role here. Break-dancing was an idea whose time had come and gone. This may have been an "R" film that was re-edited to give it the "PG-13" designation. In one spot, Nicastro's lips clearly indicate a well-known four-letter word and the soundtrack has her saying something else.

p, Jeffrey Schechtman; d, Marcelo Epstein; w, Desmond Nakano; ph, Robby Muller (CFI color); m, Sylvester Levay; ed, Richard Halsey; prod d, Guy Comtois; art d, Craig Stearns; set d, Cricket Rowland; cos, Marlene Stewart; ch, Susan Scanlan.

Musical Drama   Cas.   (PR:C MPAA:PG-13)

BOLERO zero   (1984) 106m Golan-Globus/Cannon c (AKA: BOLERO:
                                        AN ADVENTURE IN ECSTASY)

Bo Derek (Ayre McGillvary), George Kennedy (Cotton Grey), Andrea Occhipinti (Angel Contreras), Ana Obregon (Catalina Terry), Olivia d'Abo (Paloma), Greg Bensen (The Sheik), Ian Cochran (Robert Stewart), Mirta Miller (Evita), Mickey Knox (Sleazy Moroccan Guide), Paul Stacy, James Stacey (Young Valentinos).

Subtitled "An Adventure in Ecstasy," this movie must rank as one of the worst major movies ever made. Only two films in recent history come close to rivaling this junk for stupidity and ineptitude and both of them just happen to have been directed by Derek. They were TARZAN, THE APE MAN and A BOY...A GIRL. Derek could open his own turkey farm. Many awful movies are, at least, funny in a campy sort of way, so something like Edward Wood's BRIDE OF THE MONSTER (AKA: BRIDE OF THE ATOM) or his PLAN 9 FROM OUTER SPACE do have the redeeming value of humor. The Dereks, however, make films that are so sincerely bad that they offer nothing extra at all. BOLERO is abominable and the curvaceous Bo Derek comes off as erotically as a Dresden doll. The only desire aroused is one that involves leaving the theater and going home to sleep. She's a rich girl who graduates from an exclusive British boarding school and is now determined to lose her virginity. She flashes her body at the graduation ceremony (just so we know what's going to happen later) and tells one and all that she wants to experience "extasy" (which is the way she spells it, a tribute to the education she's received) with anyone who reminds her of her favorite movie star, Rudolph Valentino. She and best friend Obregon go off to Arabia, accompanied by her chauffeur-bodyguard, Kennedy (and how he ever got involved in this is the greatest mystery of them all). She meets the sheik of her dreams who offers to deflower her. This is Bensen. Milk and honey are lathered on Derek's comely torso but Bensen falls asleep after he has licked the goo off and before he gets to the flesh. (When the actors fall asleep in the movie, you know the production is in trouble.) When she has failed to have her wish granted in Arabia, she moves on to Spain where she meets bullfighter Occhipinti (who was replacing Fabio Testi when the young man had a cold sore develop on his lip. Ms. Derek couldn't bear the thought of kissing such a yucchy lip so Testi was tossed aside. He should consider himself fortunate). Occhipinti is reluctant to do the deed but who can say no to Derek when she stands there, nude, and softly whispers..."Do everything to me. Show me how I can do everything to you.?" Hey, that's tough to resist and the young torero finally capitulates. What happens next is a long and painfully boring series of soft-focus soft-porn shots of Bo and her beau making love to some original music written expressly for this scene by Elmer Bernstein. (He received credit as having scored the love scenes, while the music composer listed for the other sharps and flats was Peter Bernstein.) Elmer also wrote the music for another, even more ludicrous love scene later in the film. Unfortunately for the couple and the audience, the action takes a pointed turn for the worse when the matador is gored in the exact spot that renders him, sob, impotent. To add to her woes, Bo is menaced by Miller, Occhipinti's gypsy girl friend, who comes at the star with a knife. In between this heavy drama, Bo rides a gorgeous blonde horse that she somehow acquired and spends a good deal of time galloping along the ocean for no other reason than to give John Derek some good shots. After that, she returns to her gored lover to vow "That thing is going to work, I guarantee it!" Since Bo is the star, she's right and this gives Elmer Bernstein the chance to score some more heavy breathing. The fantasy scene is loaded with clouds of dry ice vapor and a neon sign that reads "Extasy" just in case anyone forgot her spelling problem. In the end, Occhipinti and Bo marry and will live the rest of their lives fighting for space at the bathroom mirror. BOLERO was the subject of undeserved controversy when John Derek screamed after MGM/UA made him cut six seconds from his TARZAN epic. He couldn't fathom why the Burroughs estate thought the sight of Bo naked on her hands and knees was distasteful to the image of the Ape Man. The Dereks, having felt their 112-minute film was "ruined" by the six-second snip, decided to go "indy" and make the film with Golan and Globus. Then, when the two Israeli mini-moguls made a distribution deal with Derek's archenemy, MGM/UA, feathers flew as the studio thought it would earn an "X" rating from the MPAA and refused to release it. Cannon took it back and released it with a self-imposed "X" rating, and without much success, either. The film bombed and put an end to the Dereks' next venture, "Eve and That Damned Apple." BOLERO had several titles early in the game. They ranged from "Extasy," "Bo in Extasy," "Bo-Bolero" every other permutation of "Bo" and "Extasy" they could dream up. A rose by any other name would smell the same, and so did this stinker. Since there was no Editor credit, we can only assume that John Derek did that also but didn't want the movie to look like a vanity production with too many credits in his name. Derek, who was also married to Ursula Andress and Linda Evans, knows how to make blonde women happy, but he doesn't know how to make movies.

p, Bo Derek; d,w&ph, John Derek; m, Peter Bernstein, Elmer Bernstein; prod d, Alan Roderick-Jones; set d, Juan Jesus Escudero.

Drama   Cas.   (PR:O MPAA:R)

BONA* ½   (1984, Phil.) 90m Film Forum c

Nora Aunor *(Bona)*, Philip Salvador *(Gardo)*, Rustica Carpio *(Bona's Mother)*, Venchito Galvez *(Bona's Father)*, Marissa Delgado *(Katrina)*.

A fascinating Filipino film by one of that country's best directors. Aunor is a schoolgirl from a middle-class family who falls in love with Salvador, a seedy gigolo and part-time movie extra. She moves into his shanty in a Manila slum and takes care of him, performing menial tasks and patiently standing by while he carries on with other women. When he plans to leave her to go to America, though, she gets violent. Although Brocka is perhaps the best-known Filipino filmmaker (in Europe, at least), his works were frequently banned under the Ferdinand Marcos regime. Much of BONA was shot in 1980 in the slums of Manila, one of the last films to be made in the area. Filipino First Lady Imelda Marcos called most of the power structure of Filipino filmmaking into her office and reportedly announced, "American films make everyone want to be American. Filipino films should make us all pleased to be Filipinos, and must only reflect the good, the true, the beautiful." (In Tagalog; English subtitles).

p, Nora Villamayor; d, Lino Brocka; w, Cenen Ramones; ph, Conrado Balthazar.

Drama   (PR:O   MPAA:NR)

BOSTONIANS, THE*   (1984) 120m Merchant Ivory/Almi c

Christopher Reeve *(Basil Ransom)*, Vanessa Redgrave *(Olive Chancellor)*, Madeleine Potter *(Verena Tarrant)*, Jessica Tandy *(Miss Birdseye)*, Nancy Marchand *(Mrs. Burrage)*, Wesley Addy *(Dr. Tarrant)*, Barbara Bryne *(Mrs. Tarrant)*, Linda Hunt *(Dr. Prance)*, Nancy New *(Adeline Luna)*, John Van Ness Philip *(Henry Burrage)*, Wallace Shawn *(Mr. Pardon)*, Maura Moynihan *(Henrietta Stackpole)*, Martha Farrar *(Mrs. Farrinder)*, Peter Bogyo *(Mr. Gracie)*, Dusty Maxwell *(Newton)*, Charles McCaughan *(Music Hall Policeman)*, J. Lee Morgan *(Music Hall Official)*, Lee Doyle *(Mr. Filer)*, De French *(Patient)*, Jane Manners *(Maid)*, Janet Cicchese *(Irish Washerwoman)*, Scott Kradolfer *(Tough Boy)*, June Mitchell *(Party Guest)*.

An elegant, stylish, and ultimately boring adaptation of the Henry James novel starring "Superman" Reeve (who must love costume pieces of any kind, having already appeared in the 19th- Century SOMEWHERE IN TIME), and Redgrave, who puts her subtle form of acting to the test here and comes up wanting. Reeve and Redgrave are encountered in the midst of a conversation that is, at once, uncomfortable and sluggish. On the surface, she is dry, humorless, and downright desiccated, and her only passion is political (neat bit of casting when one reads the newspapers, eh?). Reeve is a charming sophisticate with a streak of stifled anger beneath his veneer. Through the auspices of Potter, Redgrave and Reeve meet. Potter is a sweet, talented, and attractive woman with a gift for public speaking. Redgrave has no ability for that and would like to use Potter to help further her female suffrage cause. At the same time, Reeve is thinking he'd like to use Potter for quite another reason. He's falling in love with her and so the triangle is put into position; a man and a woman vying for the same woman. It is this geometric design that is the focus of the leisurely, well-shot film. Potter is sought by a poor but honest Boston attorney who chases her through the movie until she catches him. Reeve and Redgrave give good performances, and Reeve, especially, is a surprise because he'd been so lacerated for MONSIGNOR. Hunt, as the short but witty doctor, fits right into the setting of James' work. The transition from novel to screenplay was well-handled by author Jhabvala (who has been teamed with Merchant and Ivory for many years) but it is Ivory's tedious direction which makes this a fine movie to watch on cassette late at night when one is suffering from incurable insomnia. Youngsters should not watch THE BOSTONIANS because it will give them the wrong idea about classic literature and turn them on to tripe like BACHELOR PARTY. In a small role, note actor-writer Wallace Shawn, who will not best be forgotten for his own exercise in tedium, MY DINNER WITH ANDRE.

p, Ismail Merchant; d, James Ivory; w, Ruth Prawer Jhabvala (based on the novel by Henry James); ph, Walter Lassally; m, Richard Robbins; ed, Katherine Wenning, Mark Potter; prod d, Leo Austin; art d, Tom Walden, Don Carpentier; set d, Richard Elton; cos, Jenny Beavan, John Bright.

Historical Drama   **Cas.**   (PR:A-C MPAA:PG)

BOUNTY, THE*   (1984) 132m Bounty/Orion c

Mel Gibson *(Fletcher Christian)*, Anthony Hopkins *(Lt. William Bligh)*, Sir Laurence Olivier *(Adm. Hood)*, Edward Fox *(Capt. Greetham)*, Daniel Day-Lewis *(Fryer)*, Bernard Hill *(Cole)*, Philip Davis *(Young)*, Liam Neeson *(Churchill)*, Wi Kuki Kaa *(King Tynah)*, Tevaite Vernette *(Mauatua)*, Philip Martin Brown *(Adams)*, Simon Chandler *(Nelson)*, Malcolm Terris *(Dr. Huggan)*, Simon Adams *(Heywood)*, John Sessions *(Smith)*, Andrew Wilde *(McCoy)*, Neil Morrissey *(Quintal)*, Richard Graham *(Mills)*, Dexter Fletcher *(Ellison)*, Pete Lee-Wilson *(Purcell)*, Jon Gadsby *(Norton)*, Brendan Conroy *(Lamb)*, Barry Dransfield *(Blind Fiddler)*, Steve Fletcher *(Valentine)*, Jack May *(Prosecuting Captain)*, Mary Kauila *(Queen Tynah)*, Sharon Bower *(Mrs. Bligh)*, Tavana *(King Tynah's Councillor)*.

At least the fourth film version of the real incident that occurred in 1789, when sailors of the British Royal Navy seized control of their ship from Capt. Bligh, setting him and a few loyal crewmen adrift in an open boat

which Bligh managed to sail 4,000 miles in 40 days to land. The mutineers eventually stumbled across obscure Pitcairn Island; and, noticing that on their official Royal map, it was several thousand miles from where it was supposed to be, they built a settlement there that was not discovered for years and years and which is inhabited to this day by the descendants of those mutineers and the Polynesian women they married. Earlier films on the subject include an obscure Australian film, IN THE WAKE OF THE BOUNTY (1933), in which Errol Flynn made his film debut, the 1935 Hollywood production with Clark Gable as Christian and Charles Laughton as Bligh, and the 1962 version with Marlon Brando and Trevor Howard in the same roles. The film opens as Hopkins sits in front of a naval board back in London, chaired by Olivier. As the film unrolls in flashback, Hopkins and first-mate Gibson start off on a new voyage to the South Seas to bring back some examples of breadfruit for study of its suitability as food for slaves in the West Indies. The voyage is long and harrowing, with the men battling storms around Cape Horn before getting to their destination. On Tahiti, the crew has a long layover during which they grow indolent while carrying on with the sexually uninhibited women of the island. Gibson, in particular, falls in love with one beautiful native girl. When the time comes to sail for home, the men are none too happy, and Gibson, mooning over his lost love, is no help in trying to get the crew whipped back into shape. Hopkins grows increasingly more harsh in his attempts to restore discipline, having three men flogged for desertion. Finally the crew has had enough, and they revolt, with a slightly delirious Gibson their ostensible leader. Hopkins and his followers are put in the small boat, and Hopkins is shown as a fine navigator and seaman as he guides the boat to safety. The men on the *Bounty* head back for Tahiti, but the local king doesn't want the inevitable British gunboat that will come looking for the ship to blame him, so he orders them to move on. Eventually they arrive at Pitcairn, where the ship is burned and the mutineers settle. This is the first time that a reasonably balanced version of this story has reached the screen, portraying Bligh as a competent sailor and commander with some personality flaws that make the conflict between himself and his crew inevitable. Gibson, one of the most exciting actors in film today, is surprisingly bland and wishy-washy here, and he is simply blown off the screen by Hopkins' fascinating and complex Bligh. The direction seems haphazard and not very concerned with the real issues of the film, but the production design and values are excellent, as is the score by Vangelis (CHARIOTS OF FIRE). This project was originally conceived as two films to be directed by David Lean, and to be entitled THE LAW-BREAKERS and THE LONG ARM, but that project collapsed and this film was put together from scraps of the two previous scripts.

p, Bernard Williams; d, Roger Donaldson; w, Robert Bolt (based on the novel *Captain Bligh and Mr. Christian* by Richard Hough); ph, Arthur Ibbetson (Technicolor); m, Vangelis; ed, Tony Lawson; prod d, John Graysmark; art d, Tony Reading; set d, Bob Cartwright, Louise Carrigan; cos, John Bloomfield; spec eff, John Stears; ch, Terry Gilbert.

Drama   **Cas.**   (PR:O   MPAA:PG)

BRADY'S ESCAPE½   (1984, U.S./Hung.) 96m Robert Halmi-Brady's
                              Run Associates/ Satori c (GB: THE LONG RIDE)

John Savage *(Brady)*, Kelly Reno *(Miki)*, Ildiko Bansagi *(Klara)*, Laszlo Mensaros *(Dr. Dussek)*, Ferenc Bacs *(Wortman)*, Dzsoko Rosic *(Csorba)*, Laszlo Horvath *(Moro)*, Matyas Usztics *(Sweede)*, Zoltan Sarkozy, Sandor Halmagyi, Istvan Jeney, Tibor Kenderesi, Zotland Vadasz, Janos Garai, Istvan Molnar, Istvan Novak, Anna Muszte, John Turner Jones II, David Morgan, Pat Elliott.

Savage is a U.S. bomber pilot in WW II forced to bail out over Nazi-occupied Hungary. He and his wounded navigator, Usztics, are found by Csikos, hard-riding, hard-living nomads who at first want to kill Savage for bombing their country, then decide to hide him from the Germans. Usztics dies of his wounds; Savage falls in love with Bansagi, who is teaching him Hungarian, and little orphan Reno begins following Savage everywhere. Eventually the flier makes a break for freedom, riding fast across the Hortobagy plain for Yugoslavia, where he can join up with Tito's partisans. The kind of war film no one makes anymore, mostly for good reason, BRADY'S ESCAPE is surprisingly good–an exciting story well told. Only the villains, cardboard Nazis indistinguishable from the thousands of other Nazi villains throughout film history, are weak enough to damage the picture, but the camera work, the quick pace, and the competent performances by Savage and the others make the film well worth checking out for simple entertainment.

p, Robert Halmi, Jr.; d, Pal Gabor; w, William W. Lewis (based on a story by Gabor); ph, Elemer Ragayli; m, Charles Gross; ed, Norman Gay, Eva Karmento; art d, Jozsef Romvari; cos, Gay.

War   **Cas.**   (PR:C   MPAA:NR)

BREAKIN'½   (1984) 87m Golan-Globus/Cannon/MGM/UA c (GB:
                                                        BREAKDANCE)

Lucinda Dickey *(Kelly)*, Adolfo "Shabba- Doo" Quinones *(Ozone)*, Michael "Boogaloo Shrimp" Chambers *(Turbo)*, Phineas Newborn III *(Adam)*, Christopher McDonald *(James)*, Ben Lokey *(Franco)*, Bruno "Pop N' Taco" Falcon *(Electro Rock No. l)*, Timothy "Poppin' Pete" Solomon *(Electro Rock No. 2)*, Anna "Lollipop" Sanchez *(Electro Rock No. 3)*, Tracey "Ice-T" Morrow *(Rap Talker)*, Peter Bromilow, Eleanor Zee, Scott Cooper *(Judges)*,

Eb Lottimer (Judge's Assistant), T.C. Laughlin II (Vickey), Ric Mancini (Joe the Cook), Lyla Grahm (Caroline Divine), Bea Silvern (Jennifer Sweet), Gwendolyn Brown (Sophie Cunningham), Andre Landzaat (Waiter), Dalton Cathey, Larry Newburg (Producers), Lisa Freeman (Waitress).

The main problem with doing a movie based on a trend is that the picture usually comes out after the trend is over. Such was not the case with BREAKIN', which began shooting in February and was already in the theaters by early May. Directed by Israeli Silberg (who took over the helming chores from David Wheeler), it's a nonstop celebration of break dancing that owes much to the original movie of this genre, FLASHDANCE. That an Israeli director could manage to handle such an American phenomenon is a tribute to the fact that film knows no national barriers. Dickey is a serious dance student taking lessons from Lokey, a tough and almost distasteful taskmaster. She's working as a waitress and hates her life and her studies. When she meets a group of street dancers, her life is altered. Her pal is Newborn (son of the famed jazz pianist and another of the graduates of Beverly Hills High School who has made out well in movies), a gentle gay who introduces her to Chambers and Quinones, two dancers who are well-known in Los Angeles for their abilities. They join forces, dance their way through the sun-splattered L.A. streets, then get the chance to audition for a New York show and convince all of their detractors that they have what it takes to make it on the Great White Way. That's about it for the story. Dickey and the others handle their sparse lines well enough but the real star is the dancing, as choreographed by Jaime Rogers. It did well at the box office because it was ingenuous, happy-go-lucky, and didn't stretch the mind one millimeter. BREAKIN' is about dancing and little else. It was made for a pittance and in a great hurry and that shows. But if dancing is what you want to see, you need look no further than this. Songs include: "Tibetan Jam," "Reckless" (David Storrs, Tracey "Ice-T" Morrow), "Heart of the Beat" (Dan Hartman, Charlie Midnight), "Breakin'...There's No Stopping Us." "Street People" (Ollie E. Brown, Jerry Knight), "Showdown" (Brown, Joe Curiale), "99½" (Joe Footman, Maxi Anderson). Some unnecessary foul language takes this out of the realm of a true family film.

p, Allen DeBevoise, David Zito; d, Joel Silberg; w, Charles Parker, DeBevoise, Gerald Scaife (based on a story by Parker, DeBevoise); ph, Hanania Baer (Metrocolor); m, Gary Remal, Michael Boyd; ed, Larry Bock, Gib Jaffe, Vincent Sklena; prod d, Ivo G. Christante; set d, Julia Kaye Towery; cos, Dana Lyman; ch, Jaime Rogers.

Musical Drama   **Cas.**   **(PR:A-C MPAA:PG)**

BREAKIN' 2: ELECTRIC BOOGALOO***½

(1984) 94m Cannon/Tri-Star c (GB: BREAKDANCE 2 - ELECTRIC BOOGALOO; AKA: ELECTRIC BOOGALOO 'BREAKIN' 2')

Lucinda Dickey (Kelly), Adolfo "Shabba-Doo" Quinones (Ozone), Michael "Boogaloo Shrimp" Chambers (Turbo), Susie Bono (Rhonda), Harry Caesar (Byron), Jo de Winter (Mrs. Bennett), John Christy Ewing (Mr. Bennett), Steve "Sugarfoot" Notario (Strobe), Sabrina Garcia (Lucia), Lu Leonard (Head Nurse), Ken Olfson (Randall), Peter MacLean (Mr. Douglas), Herb Mitchell (Stanley), Sandy Lipton (Mrs. Snyder), William Cort (Howard Howard), Don Lewis (Magician), Vidal "Coco" Rodriquez (Coco), Tracey "Ice-T" Morrow (Radiotron Rapper), Jay "Suave" Sands (Rapper), Nicholas Segal (Derek), Tim Wise (Doctor), Alicia Bond (Nurse), Jerry Lazarus (Paris Director), Sam Livneh (Dancer), John LaMotta (Policeman), Jay Rasumny (Hardhat), Daniel Riordan (Surveyor), Alberta Sanchez (Rosa), Richard Gross (Juggler), Frankie Crocker (Emcee), Kimberly McCullough (Kimberly), Jim W. Jones (Bulldozer Driver), Fred Asparagus (Hispanic Man), Carol Lynn Townes (Singer), Toi Overton, Paulette McWilliams (Firefoxes), Edie Marie Rubio, Cyd Glover (Little Girls), Marta Marrero, Kimberly Ann Miller (Girls), Branden Williams, Jay Bautista, Jason Fan, Kamie Harper, Beto Lovato, Jimmy E. Keegan, Joshua Mott, Vajra Ky Barzaghi, Roy Mansano (Kids), Vince Deadrick, Sr. (Stunts Coordinator).

One of the fastest sequels on record (both the original and this were released the same year, within seven months), this has all the spirit of the original in an old-fashioned, newfangled way. The story is right out of the 1930s and could have come off the MGM shelf of scripts that Garland and Rooney didn't get the chance to do. The only difference is, of course, the music and the dancing. If you recall, Dickey, Quionones, and Chambers had just won an audition to a New York show in BREAKIN' and everything was terrific. This movie begins as we learn that their act didn't charm the worms in The Big Apple and the trio have returned to The Big Orange. Dickey is taking a few dumb dance jobs to keep her superb body (and soul) together and the two boys have returned to East Los Angeles where they are happily teaching the gang youths how to dance and have a good time without shooting at each other. Dickey's parents, the snooty Ewing and de Winter, hope that she'll stop seeing her low-class pals and go off to an Ivy League college. Dickey keeps in touch with Chambers and Quinones and comes to their aid once it's learned that the community center where the boys work is in danger of being torn down in favor of another shopping mall. The real estate man is MacLean and he's in cahoots with bent politico Olfson, both of whom can make a bundle if they can clear the tacky center out of the area. The place is run-down and needs repairs and if they can bring it up to safety standards, there is no way MacLean and Olfson can get the land. But to do that, they need to raise $200,000. Now, if Mickey and Judy were faced with this problem, what would they have done? You guessed it, they put on a

show. Only this time, it's not in a barn; it's all over the streets of East Los Angeles and across the rooftops. Quinones does a dance high above the city that's a marvel, and the beat goes on...and on. Need we tell you that the money is raised and the community center (named "Miracles") has been saved by a miracle? Early in the film, Dickey dances into the streets with all the local gentry, from cops to kids, from mailmen to old folks, and the number is as good as anything seen in FAME, be it the movie or the TV show. There's another scene in a hospital that gets doctors, nurses, and even dead patients to come to life under the insistent beat of the music. Included are the songs "Electric Boogaloo" (Ollie E. Brown, Attala Z. Giles, Russ Regan), "Radiotron," "Action," "When I.C.U." (Brown, Giles, Jerry Knight), "Go Off" (David Storrs, Tracey "Ice-T" Morrow). This was one of those "sleepers" that proved you didn't need high- priced stars or egocentric directors to make a movie that was enjoyed by almost everyone who saw it. Golan and Globus, the men who were behind the film, went on to make several small blockbusters and several large duds. BREAKIN' and BREAKIN' 2 are not movies that will live on in time. Since they were both about a short-lived trend, they had to be seen at the right moment in order to have impact. And yet, just as WW II stories about the "Lindy" or movies about the folk music craze of the 1950s will be looked at in later years sociologically, both of the BREAKIN' movies are moments frozen in time and are worthwhile if for that alone.

p, Menahem Golan, Yoram Globus; d, Sam Firstenberg; w, Jan Ventura, Julia Reichert (based on characters created by Charles Parker, Allen DeBevoise); ph, Hanania Baer (TVC color); m, Russ Regan; ed, Sally Allen, Bert Glatstein, Bob Jenkis, Barry Zetlin; prod d, Joseph T. Garrity; art d, Patrick E. Tagliaferro; set d, Jerie Kelter; cos, Dorothy Baca, David Baca; ch, Bill Goodson.

Musical   **Cas.**   **(PR:A-C MPAA:PG)**

BREAKOUT***

(1984, Brit.) 61m Eyeline/Children's Film and Television Foundation c

David Jackson (Donny the Bull), Ian Bartholomew (Keith), Simon Nash (David), John Hasler (Stephen), John Bowler (Phil).

Nash and Hasler are a pair of youngsters who go out on a birdwatching expedition. However their intended afternoon of simple fun turns into a genuine adventure when two escaped prisoners (Jackson and Bartholomew) come onto the scene. The convicts are looking for some stolen money they had previously buried and then want to take a boat to Australia. The two boys get themselves in the thick of it, helping out the older men and trying to stop them from being caught at the film's end. Unlike so many children's adventures, this film relies on its characters and not a lot of "gee-whiz" special effects to carry the story. It tells its tale on a child's level without taking a condescending tone towards its audience. Nash and Hasler are fine as the two boys but Jackson runs away with the film. He's wonderful as a hard-drinking runaway, imposing in size but with enough charm to win the two lads over.

p&d, Frank Godwin; w, Ranald Graham (based on the novel A Place To Hide by Bill Gillham); ph, Ray Orton; m, Harry Robertson; ed, Gordon Grimward; art d, Michael Rickwood, Richard Hornsby.

Children's Adventure   **(PR:AA MPAA:NR)**

BREED APART, A*½

(1984) 101m Hemdale-Sagittarius/Orion c

Rutger Hauer (Jim Malden), Powers Boothe (Michael Walker), Kathleen Turner (Stella Clayton), Donald Pleasence (J.P. Whittier), John Dennis Johnston (Charlie Peyton), Brion James (Huey Miller), Adam Fenwick (Adam Clayton), Jayne Bentzen (Amy Rollings).

An international cast and crew went into the backwoods of North Carolina to film this good-looking but diffused story that never fully involved an audience. Hauer is a self-styled conservationist in the wild who resents the fact that people have been trying to steal the rare eggs of that rarest of birds, the bald eagle. A new breed of bald eagle has been discovered and Pleasence, who is more a collector than anything else, wants the shells for himself. To that end, he hires Boothe, a mountain climber, to masquerade as a latter-day Ansel Adams and pretend to be a nature photographer. Boothe arrives at the small village near where the birds are nesting and meets Hauer and Turner (who runs a shop and is raising her small son, Fenwick). Hauer and Turner are very close but there is no overt evidence of any passion between them at the start. Hauer suspects that Boothe is not what he claims and keeps him away from the area where the birds are until Boothe gets close enough to inspire Hauer's trust. There's some action when a group of hunters want to kill Hauer but Boothe intercedes and saves Hauer's life. A few scenes to spice matters up but nothing much else except Boothe's abrupt change of allegiance. The big question is: What were they trying to do when they made this film? A great deal of the script must have been trimmed (or footage edited) because much of it makes no sense and one can hardly believe that such intelligent actors as Hauer, Turner, Boothe, and Pleasence would have taken their jobs without knowing exactly what the movie touched upon. Stephenson's cinematography was excellent and it's too bad that the backgrounds were far more intriguing than the actors standing in the foreground. Some scenes seemed to be out of place and could have been edited into the movie at any time so there was no sense of real narrative here, which was surprising, since it was directed by a man who should have known better, Mora, who has a background that belies this final product. Even Bee Gee Maurice Gibb's music fell far from his usual standard.

p, John Daly, Derek Gibson; d, Philippe Mora; w, Paul Wheeler; ph, Geoffrey Stephenson (Metrocolor); m, Maurice Gibb; ed, Chris Lebenzon; art d, Bill Barclay.

Drama   **(PR:A-C   MPAA:R)**

BROADWAY DANNY ROSE**   (1984) 86m Jack Rollins & Charles
                                                          H. Joffe/Orion bw

Woody Allen (Danny Rose), Mia Farrow (Tina Vitale), Nick Apollo Forte (Lou Canova), Sandy Baron Corbett Monica, Jackie Gayle, Morty Gunty, Will Jordan, Howard Storm, Jack Rollins, Joe Franklin, Howard Cosell, Milton Berle (Themselves), Craig Vandenburgh (Ray Webb), Herb Reynolds (Barney Dunn), Paul Greco (Vito Rispoli), Frank Renzulli (Joe Rispoli), Edwin Bordo (Johnny Rispoli), Gina Deangelis (Johnny's Mother), Peter Castellotti (Hood at Warehouse), Sandy Richman (Theresa), Gerald Schoenfeld (Sid Bacharach), Olga Barbato (Angelina), David I. Kissel (Phil Chomsky), Gloria Parker (Water Galss Virtuoso), Bob & Etta Rollins (Balloon Act), Bob Weil (Herbie Jayson), David Kieserman (Ralph, Club Owner), Mark Hardwick (Blind Xylophonist), Alba Ballard (Bird Lady), Maurice Shrog (Hypnotist), Belle Berger (Lady in Trance), Herschel Rosen (Lady's Husband), Cecilia Amerling (Fan in Dressing Room), Maggie Ranone (Lou's Daughter), Charles D'Amodio (Lou's Son), Joie Gallo (Angelina Assistant), Carl Pistilli (Tommy's Brother), Lucy Iacono (Tommy's Mother), Julia Barbuto (Tropical Fish Lady), Anna Sceusa (Lady at Angelina's), Nicholas Pantano, Rocco Pantano (Greeters at Party), Tony Turco (Rocco), Gilda Torterello (Annie), Ronald Maccone (Vincent), Antoinette Raffone $2 (Vincent's Wife), Michael Badalucco, Richard Lanzano (Money Rippers), Dom Matteo (Carmine), Leo Steiner, George Axler, William Paulson, Diane Zolten, Sid Winter, Gary Reynolds, John Doumanian, Betty Rosotti, Sheila Bond, Camille Saviola.

After winning the hearts of America with ANNIE HALL and MANHATTAN, Allen decided to become experimental and had far less success with the Bergman-inspired A MIDSUMMER NIGHT'S SEX COMEDY, the Fellini-inspired STARDUST MEMORIES, and the who-knows-who-inspired ZELIG. Allen comes back to what he knows best with BROADWAY DANNY ROSE and offers a charming comedy that blends gangsters with backstage show business. It begins as a group of Broadway types (more about them later) are seated at the Carnegie Delicatessen in New York and reminiscing about the career of Allen, a two-bit agent who specializes in all of the offbeat acts that can't find any other representative to handle them. (There are only a few of these types of agents left, but anyone who has ever been around show business will recognize the characters.) He has clients that include a blind xylophonist (Hardwick), a Bird Lady (Ballard), a hypnotist (Shrog) and others. His one straight client is Forte, a lounge singer who drinks too much, weighs too much, and cheats on his wife too much, and uses Allen to cover for him when he's off with his girl friend, Farrow. Farrow wears dark glasses for the first fourth of the picture and is almost unrecognizable in the role of a mob girl (not unlike Angelica Huston in PRIZZI'S HONOR). As an agent, Allen has to do many things, not the least of which is being to be Farrow's boy friend when Forte gets a chance to perform at a better place than the upholstered sewers where he's been working. That gets him into trouble because Farrow is due to marry a gangland figure and the other members of the gang think that their pal has been cuckolded, thereby starting a chase that begins at the mafia mansion and going along the various turnpikes and into the city of New York. That's about it for the story except to say that Forte turns out to be a real ingrate, signing with another agent the moment he can smell big money. Farrow and Allen sort of wind up together and it is assumed that the agent will continue with his work, once he gets straightened out with the Mafia. Lots of huge verbal jokes (Allen's forte) but the visual comedy falls short. One hole in the story has Allen and Farrow being surrounded by the gangsters at the mansion and it looks as though he will be crushed. Then the next cut has them driving away, with no answer as to how they escaped. Comedians Sandy Baron, Jackie Gayle, Corbett Monica, and Will Jordan play themselves. The last member of the men who tell "Broadway Danny Rose" stories while eating corned beef was Morty Gunty, an excellent club date comic who gave up a career as a high school teacher to follow a life on the stage. Gunty died soon after the movie was made and, for anyone who saw him in his Catskill Mountains heyday, he will be missed. Director Howard Storm ("Laverne and Shirley" and many others) plays a comic, which he used to be. Milton Berle does a short bit that he claims took all day to shoot. He didn't know how deeply Allen likes to cut his films and was surprised when it wound up to be a cameo. Joe Franklin, who has been running a TV show more than 30 years on WOR-TV in New York, plays himself, as does Howard Cosell, whom Allen used in BANANAS. In a small role, look for Beverly Hills High School graduate Joie Gallo (daughter of Joey Gallo), a sensational stage performer. BROADWAY DANNY ROSE just misses the status of MANHATTAN in that the laughs are grins and chuckles rather than guffaws. But even less-than-classic Woody Allen is better than no Woody Allen at all. Allen's co-manager, Jack Rollins, does a short bit. Rollins and executive producer Charles Joffe take turns overseeing Allen's output and have done so since the beginning.

p, Robert Greenhut; d&w, Woody Allen; ph, Gordon Willis; ed, Susan E. Morse; prod d, Mel Bourne; set d, Les Bloom; cos, Jeffrey Kurland; m/l, "Agita," "My Bambina," Nick Apollo Forte (sung by Forte).

Comedy   **Cas.**   **(PR:A-C   MPAA:PG)**

BROTHER FROM ANOTHER PLANET, THE½
                                                     (1984) 110m A-Train/Cinecom c

Joe Morton (The Brother), Darryl Edwards (Fly), Steve James (Odell), Leonard Jackson (Smokey), Bill Cobbs (Walter), Maggie Renzi (Noreen), Tom Wright (Sam), Ren Woods (Bernice), Reggie Rock Bythewood (Rickey), David Strathairn, John Sayles (Men In Black), Rosetta Le Noire (Mama), Fisher Stevens (Card Trickster), Josh Mostel (Casio Vendor), Michael Albert Mantel (Mr. Love), Jaime Tirelli (Hector), Edward Baran (Mr. Vance), Caroline Aaron (Randy Sue), Herbert Newsome (Little Earl), Dee Dee Bridgewater (Malverne), Sidney Sheriff, Jr (Virgil), Rosanna Carter (West Indian Woman), Ray Ramirez (Hispanic Man), Yves Rene (Haitian Man), Peter Richardson (Islamic Man), Ginny Yang (Korean Shopkeeper), Liane Curtis (Ace), Chip Mitchell (Ed), David Babcock (Phil), Copper Cunningham (Black Hooker), Marisa Smith (White Hooker), Ishmael Houston-Jones (Dancer), Kim Staunton (Teacher), Dwania Kyles (Waitress), Carl Gordon (Mr. Price), Leon W. GRant, Anthony Thomas (Basketball Players), Andre Robinson, Jr (Pusher), John Griesemer (White Cop), Ellis Williams (Watcher), Deborah Taylor (Vance's Receptionist), Herb Downer (Floor Buffer), Olga Merediz (Noreen's Client), Minnie Gentry (Mrs. Brown), Alvin Alexis (Willis), Randy Frazer (Bouncer).

Though filled with enormous promise, this is a film that just never quite delivers what it could. Morton is an escaped slave from an unnamed planet who crash-lands his space capsule off Ellis Island. Though he has lost one of his three-toed feet in the crash, it regenerates overnight and Morton goes walking. His ragged clothing and the shoes he takes from a garbage can make him look like any street bum. Morton, who cannot speak, makes his way into Harlem and ends up in a local bar. The regular patrons find him odd, to say the least, but set him up with a social worker after it's discovered Morton can repair video games with just a touch of his hand. The film turns into a series of vignettes, following the mute alien as he discovers the new world that surrounds him. Hot on the black man's trail are Strathairn and Sayles (the latter the film's writer/director), a pair of white aliens dressed in black who aim to recapture the escapee. Bridgewater is a jazz singer whom Morton falls for with the two ending up having a brief affair. The basic problem with the film is that, like its protagonist, it never stops wandering around the environment. Situations and characters are introduced and then played out before exiting completely from the picture. It becomes a bit frustrating after awhile, particularly when a situation (such as when two Midwestern college students accidentally end up in Harlem) seems to be nothing more than filler. At other moments things become too heavyhanded for their own good, particularly Morton's pursuit of a decidedly lethargic businessman who deals heroin to poor black kids. Sayles may have a reputation as one of the best independent American directors for his time but he shows little ability here. His screenplay is imaginative at moments but he has a real feeling for his setting. Harlem is neither romanticized nor pitied, but instead is presented as a not-at-all unusual place with its own share of joy and pain. But the vignette construction simply is not enough to hold its own weight. Eventually the film succumbs to this, culminating in a somewhat confusing and altogether unsatisfying conclusion. What makes this film work is Morton's wonderful performance. His mute portrayal, reacting and adapting to the new environment, reminds one of Buster Keaton. Morton becomes the common thread that holds the film together, making this his picture much more than the director's. THE BROTHER FROM ANOTHER PLANET was something of a step forward for black filmmakers. Though Sayles is white (causing many critics to argue that this was merely another white liberal's view of blacks) he chose an interracial crew, many fresh out of film school. It also gave an opportunity for a good number of black actors to work at their craft. Apart from THE COTTON CLUB, A SOLDIER'S STORY, and THE COLOR PURPLE–three major studio productions–this isone of the few American films of its time to feature a largely black cast.

p, Peggy Rajski, Maggie Renzi; d&w, John Sayles; ph, Ernest Dickerson (Movielab Color); m, Mason Daring; ed, Sayles; prod d, Nora Chavooshian; art d, Stephen J. Lineweaver; set d, Gina R. Alfano, Thom De Jesu, Lin Wilson; cos, Karen Perry; m/l, "Burning My Heart Out," "Boss Of The Block," "Getaway," "You Can't Get to Heaven from Here," "Mason Daring; "Homeboy," Daring, Sayles; "Dinero," Frank London, Daring, Efrain Salgado; "El Calle," London; "Promised Land," Daring, Sayles.

Fantasy   **Cas.**   **(PR:O   MPAA:NR)**

BROTHERS**   (1984, Aus.) 99m Areflex c

Chard Hayward (Adam Wild), Ivar Kants (Kevin Wild), Margaret Laurence (Lani Aveson), Jennifer Cluff (Allison Levis), Alyson Best (Jenine Williams), Joan Bruce (Mrs. Williams), Les Foxcroft (Jim Williams), Ricky May (Bill Mason), Ken Wayne (Bureau Chief), Desmond Tester (Journalist), Roger Ward (Cameraman).

Based on a true incident in which a number of Australian journalists were killed in 1975, this picture stars Hayward as an unpleasant brute who survives the bloodletting, along with his brother (hence the title) Kants. Years later Kants, having settled down in a homey New Zealand town, is visited by Hayward who is upset with his brother's domestic ways. While trying to convince Kants to uproot, Hayward gets involved with a prostitute, Laurence, who attempts suicide when he walks out on her in favor of Cluff, an attractive woman from the city. His philandering attitude finally catches up with him when Cluff is killed in an auto wreck. Although some moments are genuinely suspenseful, BROTHERS is hampered by the audience's strong dislike for Hayward's character–one incapable of soliciting sympathy from anyone. BROTHERS never received a theatrical release and was marketed directly on videocassette.

p,d&w, Terry Bourke (based on the book *Reflex* by Roger Ward); ph, Ray Henman (Eastmancolor); m, Bob Young; ed, Ron Williams; art d, Paul Tolley.

Drama   **Cas.**   **(PR:O   MPAA:NR)**

BUCKAROO BANZAI   (SEE: ADVENTURES OF BUCAKAROO
                          BANZAI: ACROSS THE 8TH DIMENSION, THE)

BUDDY SYSTEM, THE***   (1984) 110m FOX c

Richard Dreyfuss *(Joe)*, Susan Sarandon *(Emily)*, Nancy Allen *(Carrie)*, Jean Stapleton *(Mrs. Price)*, Wil Wheaton *(Tim)*, Edward Winter *(Jim Parks)*, Keene Curtis *(Dr. Knitz)*, Tom Lacy *(The Man Who Gives Emily the Test)*, Lee Weaver *(Ray)*, Carolyn Coates *(Teacher)*, Milton Selzer *(Landlord)*, Todd Everett *(Frank)*, F. William Parker *(Lawyer)*, Bianca Ferguson *(Woman Customer)*, Lew Horn *(Pet Shop Owner)*, Frank Coppola *(Mr. Fleeze)*, Brent Price *(Man Customer)*, Jason Hervey *(Potato)*, Scott Crow, Josh Schulman *(Indians)*, Mike Lawrence *(Pilgrim)*, Adam Carl *(Corn)*, Jason Castellano, Jimmy E. Keegan *(Trees)*.

Dreyfuss had so much success with THE GOODBYE GIRL (he won an Oscar) that the studio thought it might be able to catch lightning in a bottle again with this one. It didn't, but it's a neat little comedy that makes a few telling points about life and love in a contemporary urban world. Dreyfuss is a struggling author who lives in a ramshackle house by a canal in Venice, California. Since he can't make a living with his typewriter, he has a day job as a security guard at a public school. Sarandon is the single mother of Wheaton, a bright 11 year old. She's raised the child alone since her husband departed and she now lives with her domineering mother, Stapleton, who is over-protective of her daughter and grandson. Dreyfuss is seeing Allen, a singularly selfish young woman who is not only out to lunch, she is out to all other meals as well. At the same time, Sarandon is dating avaricious attorney Winter, who is every bit as self-centered as Allen. Sarandon is trying to discern what kind of work she's cut out for and takes a series of tests administered by Lacey (in a funny scene). Wheaton and Dreyfuss hit it off and the boy wants his mother to meet his friend. She is short with Dreyfuss and there is obvious friction at the start. Later, Wheaton invites Dreyfuss to attend a Thanksgiving pageant at school and when Sarandon meets him again, they begin to like each other. Dreyfuss tosses Allen aside and Sarandon does the same with Winter, and Dreyfuss becomes part of Sarandon's life. Then Allen comes back into Dreyfuss' life once more and the couple break up. Time passes and both Dreyfuss and Sarandon are unhappy without each other but both are too proud to admit it. On the anniversary of the Thanksgiving show, they are united once more and, one may assume, will remain that way for the rest of their lives. A pleasant comedy with a few sharp lines of dialog; winning performances, and the feeling that it's a TV movie with feature picture names. In an attempt to get out of the "Edith Bunker" rut, Stapleton plays a shrew and is the one discordant note in an otherwise melodious picture, metaphorically speaking, of course. The first film for screenwriter Donoghue as well as the first American production for former Warner Bros. European production chief Chammas.

p, Alain Chammas; d, Glenn Jordan; w, Mary Agnes Donoghue; ph, Matthew F. Leonetti (DeLuxe Color); m, Patrick Williams; ed, Arthur Schmidt; prod d, Rodger Maus; set d, Robert Checchi; cos, Joseph G. Aulisi; spec eff, Garr J. Elmendorf; m/l, "Here's That Sunny Day," Williams, Will Jennings.

Comedy/Drama   **Cas.**   **(PR:A-C   MPAA:PG)**

BURIED ALIVE zero   (1984, Ital.) 94m D. R. Mass
                                   Communications/Aquarius c

Kieran Canter, Cinzia Monreale, Franca Stoppi, Sam Modesto, Ana Cardini, Mario Pizzin, Klaus Rainer.

Confusing and boring Italian gore film about a strange young man who exhumes his wife's corpse and mounts it for display at the house he shares with an older woman who may or may not be a relative, but with whom he certainly has more than a platonic relationship. Bloody murders take place until the near-twin sister of the stuffed woman shows up but what it all means is a mystery. Styleless and irritatingly explicit and not worth any attention at all. Badly dubbed in English.

d, Joe D'Amato [Aristide Massaccesi]; w, Ottavio Fabbri; ph, Massaccesi (Telecolor); m, The Goblins; ed, Ornella Micheli; art d, Donatella Donati; set d, Ennio Michittoni; makeup, Cesare Bisco.

Horror   **(PR:O   MPAA:NR)**

C.H.U.D.**   (1984) 110m New World c

Laure Mattos *(Flora Bosch)*, John Heard *(George Cooper)*, Kim Geist *(Lauren Daniels)*, Brenda Currin *(Francine)*, Christopher Curry *(Capt. Bosch)*, Justin Hall *(Justine)*, Michael O'Hare *(Fuller)*, Cordis Heard *(Sanderson)*, Vic Polizos *(Hays)*, Eddie Jones *(Chief O'Brien)*, Sam McMurray *(Crespi)*, Frank Adu *(Interrogation Cop)*, J.C. Quinn *(Murphy)*, Patricia Richardson *(Ad Woman)*, Raymond Baker *(Ad Man)*, Beverly Bentley *(Doris)*, Daniel Stern *(The Reverend)*, Graham Beckel *(Val)*, Gene O'Neill *(Jackson)*, Rocco Siclari *(Hugo)*, William Joseph Raymond *(Victor)*, Peter Michael Goetz *(Gramps)*, Shanan Lee Farrell *(Cindy)*, John Ramsey *(Commissioner)*, George Martin *(Wilson)*, John Bradford-Lloyd *(Shadow)*, Henry Yuk *(Coroner)*, Robert Toupin *(Benson)*, Ivar Brogger *(Goonery NRC Man)*, Parnell Hall *(Judson)*, John Goodman, Jay Thomas *(Cops in Diner)*, Hallie Foote *(Waitress)*, Jon Polito *(Newscaster)*, Mark Mikulski *(Cop at Wrecked Diner)*, Lou Leccese, Sanford Clark, James Dudley, Carey Eidel *(CHUDs)*, Frankie R. Faison *(Parker)*.

The title stands for "Cannibalistic Humanoid Underground Dwelling" and that about sums up what this enjoyable low-budget picture is about. At the start, an innocent woman and her dog are walking along a city street when they are suddenly clutched by some creature that rises out of the sewer. It doesn't look like a human and we are not certain if it's an animal or what. Heard and Geist are the leads, a pair of young lovers, though their romance has almost nothing to do with the rest of this ecological horror story that tells of toxic wastes being dumped down into the city's sewers (and being covered up by government bureaucrats). The next thing you know, the foul chemicals affect all the city's homeless who have been living underground to stay warm. The hoboes and tramps turn into grotesque monsters and begin to wreak havoc on the topside world that made them the way they now are. The first inclination that something is awry happens when preacher Stern's regular soup kitchen feeding is sparsely attended and many of his regulars have not shown up. That's because they are now eating human beings instead and the heck with vegetable soup. A good story and some good effects but it's a subject that could stand a better, more defined script and more attention paid to the issues involved, rather than the easy way out. Stern, who was so funny in HANNAH AND HER SISTERS as the rock star, graduated to bigger roles after this and starred in THE BOSS'S WIFE for Tri-Star in 1986-87. This was an independently produced film later sold for distribution to New World. The special effects are often gamey and children may have bad dreams about the subject, or they just may never want to go down into a city sewer, which isn't a bad idea. John Heard had been confused with John Hurt and William Hurt when they were all getting started and before each had developed a particular screen personality.

p, Andrew Bonime; d, Douglas Cheek; w, Parnell Hall; ph, Peter Stein (TVC Color); m, Cooper Hughes; ed, Dennis O'Connor; prod d, William Bilowit; art d, Jorge Luis Toro; cos, Susan Money; makeup, John Caglione, Jr.

Horror   **Cas.**   **(PR:O   MPAA:R)**

CAGED FURY*   (1984, Phil.) 84m LEA/Saturn International-Shapiro c

Bernadette Williams *(Denise)*, Jennifer Laine *(Linda)*, Taffy O'Connell, Catherine March, S. P. Victoria, Mari Karen Ryan, Ken Metcalf.

Dull women-in-prison film has a number of American women held captive by the Vietnamese after the war and brainwashed into human bombs who wear explosives and set them off near important figures. The women attempt to escape a number of times until the Army comes to the rescue, guns blazing. A pale imitation of the memorable films of this sub-genre like RENEGADE GIRLS and TERMINAL ISLAND; This one is flat, tiresome, and technically inept.

p, Emily Blas; d, Cirio H. Santiago; w, Bobby Greenwood; ph, (Imperious Color); m, Ernani Cuenco.

Crime   **(PR:O   MPAA:R)**

CAGED WOMEN* (1984, Ital./Fr.) 96m Beatrice-Imp. Ex. Ci.-Les Films
                          Jacques Leitienne/Motion Picture Marketing c

Laura Gemser *(Emanuelle/Laura)*, Gabriele Tinti *(Dr. Moran)*, Lorraine de Selle *(Warden)*, Marie Romano, Ursula Flores, Raul Cabrera.

More women-in-prison action, this time with Gemser reprising her "Emanuelle" role from better than a dozen R-rated bedhopping adventures (not to be confused with the generally more explicit "Emanuelle" films with Silvia Kristel, of which there are only four). Here she's a reporter who impersonates a prostitute in order to get the inside story on what goes on at a women's prison. What goes on, of course, is sadistic beatings by the guards, swarms of rats, and a good dose of soft-focus sex scenes. Fans of bad exploitation films won't be disappointed, but the majority will not be amused.

p, Jacques Leitienne; d, Vincent Dawn [Bruno Mattei]; w, P. Molteni, Oliver LeMat; ph, Luigi Ciccarese (Telecolor); m, Luigi Ceccarelli; ed, Mattei; art d, Maurizio Mammi; makeup, Marcello di Paolo.

Crime   **Cas.**   **(PR:O   MPAA:R)**

CAL***   (1984, Ireland) 102m Enigma/WB c

Helen Mirren (*Marcella*), John Lynch (*Cal*), Donald McCann (*Shamie*), John Kavanagh (*Skeffington*), Ray McAnally (*Cyril Dunlop*), Stevan Rimkus (*Crilly*), Kitty Gibson (*Mrs. Morton*), Louis Rolston (*Dermot Ryan*), Tom Hickey (*Preacher*), Gerard Mannix Flynn (*Arty*), Seamus Ford (*Old Man Morton*), Edward Byrne (*Skeffington Senior*), J.J. Murphy (*Man In Library*), Audrey Johnston (*Lucy*), Brian Munn (*Robert Morton*), Daragh O'Malley (*Scar-Faced Policeman*), George Shane (*Second Policeman*), Julia Dearden (*Shop Assistant*), Yvonne Adams (*Neighbor*), Lawrence Foster (*Soldier at Roadblock*), Scott Frederick, Gerard O'Hagan (*Soldiers At Farm*).

A bleak but beautiful love story set amidst the hotbed of Northern Ireland's Catholic-Protestant conflict. The picture opens with Lynch, a confused 19-year-old Catholic who is more interested in blues music than joining the Irish Republican Army working as a driver for an IRA terrorist who has just murdered a Protestant policeman. A year passes. Lynch, who lives at home with his genteel widowed father McCann in a quiet all-Protestant neighborhood, spots the policeman's young widow, Mirren, working at a library and is drawn to her. He learns where she lives and takes a load of wood to her farmhouse, where she lives with her in-laws. Before long he gets himself a job there as a field hand. Back at home Lynch discovers, under the front door, a Protestant threat to burn down the house he shares with McCann. He and his father arm themselves and sit up all night in defense of their house, but the promised attack doesn't come. The bond between them grows stronger, but Lynch still cannot inform his father of his part in the murder. Lynch is continually hounded by friends who are loyal to the IRA's cause. Against his father's wishes and his own better judgment, Lynch continues to work as an IRA driver, without expressing any loyalty at all to either side. Lynch and his father cannot escape the conflict, however, and their house is finally burned to a cinder. Neither is injured, but all their belongings are destroyed. McCann takes refuge with a friend, but Lynch has other ideas. He manages to get an invitation from Mirren and her mother-in-law to stay in the farmhouse. The attraction between them builds until they finally sleep together. He keeps his secret about the murder to himself. His guilt increases, even though Mirren admits that she didn't love her husband. Lynch's friends in the IRA continue to pressure him into joining. He still expresses no interest, being concerned more with Mirren than the conflict that rages around him. His friends are captured by British guards and he narrowly escapes. He heads for the safety of Mirren's farmhouse. Tortured with the guilt that he has been trying to suppress, Lynch admits his part in the murder to Mirren. He professes his love for her, telling her that he would die for her. A police siren is heard and Lynch flees to a shed, but is easily tracked down, thanks to Mirren. Lynch is treated brutally and thrown into a police truck. A lonely Mirren stares on with an empty look as Lynch is carted away. Although the end is tragic, it is a realistic one. Of his debut film, director O'Connor said: "What I would like is to allow people to see Northern Ireland for the tragedy it is, through the love affair in which these two people are trapped by what goes on around them." CAL succeeds in painting a realistic picture of the Catholic-Protestant conflict because it avoids simplification. The reasons for love and war in CAL are presented as full of complications and contradictions, just as in the real-life conflict. The day-to-day struggle that these characters encounter has taken away their incentive, yet they're still expected to go on. Heavily dependent on characterization, CAL wouldn't have worked without the superb performances of Mirren, Lynch, and McCann (as well as the rest of the entire cast). Lynch is mesmerizing as the lad who refuses to die for his Catholic heritage, but willingly vows to die for love. McCann's performance as the steadily weakening father is touching, especially after the fire has destroyed his desire to live. It is Mirren, however, who is the film's most complex character. She is expected to mourn for the death of a man she never loved and remain loyal to in-laws from whom she wants to run away. She then finds herself torn between her love for Cal and her inability to forgive him for what he did. For this beautiful piece of acting, Mirren was named Best Actress at the 1984 Cannes Film Festival, where CAL was Ireland's official entry. Another plus is the haunting musical soundtrack by Mark Knopfler (guitarist for the popular rock band Dire Straits), who also scored Bill Forsythe's LOCAL HERO (1983). CAL is the brightest spot in this year's Irish film industry and points to O'Connor–in his feature-film debut- as a directorial force with a great deal of promise.

p, Stuart Craig, David Puttnam; d, Pat O'Connor; w, Bernard McLaverty (based on his novel); ph, Jerzy Zielinski (Rank Color); m, Mark Knopfler; ed, Michael Bradsell; prod d, Craig; art d, Josie MacAvin; cos, Penny Rose; m/l, "Freak," Bruce Foxton.

Drama   **Cas.**   **(PR:O   MPAA:R)**

CALIFORNIA GIRLS*   (1984) 83m Westwind c

Al Music (*Mad Man Jack*), Lantz Douglas (*Mike*), Mary McKinley (*Jackie*), Alicia Allen (*Joyce*), Barbara Parks (*Chrissie*), Jim Benny (*Don*).

Music is a Southern California disc jockey running a contest to find the most exciting girl in the state. Mostly an excuse for scenes of pretty girls windsurfing, aerobic dancing, and hang gliding while a collection of popular songs play. The film was shot in 1981 and sat on the shelf until released exclusively on videocassette. Inoffensive, but utterly superficial. Background music includes song hits by such groups as The Police, Kool & The Gang, Blondie, and Queen.

p, Wiliam Webb, Monica Webb; d&w, William Webb (Additional material, Al Music, Michael Sherman); ph, Eric Anderson; ed, Michael J. Duthie.

Comedy   **Cas.**   **(PR:O   MPAA:NR)**

CAMEL BOY, THE***   (1984, Aus.) 72m Yoram Gross c

Voices of: Barbara Frawley, Ron Haddrick, John Meillon, Robyn Moore, Michael Pate.

A technically superb children's film which combines animated characters with actual Australian backgrounds. Beginning in the 1920s, THE CAMEL BOY tells the story of Ali, a young Arab lad who ventures across the Great Victoria Desert with his camel-driver grandfather. They are subjected to radical shifts in weather–first a torrential downpour, then a dangerous dry spell. They also have to fend off an attack by wild dogs before they are forced to turn back. Twenty years pass, grandfather dies, and Ali becomes a police officer in his native land. He catches a suspected spy, another young camel boy–an Australian–who gets himself on a ship carrying camels to the Arabic nation. Ali shows some compassion and, instead of arresting the boy, he lets him go free. A choice pick for youngsters, who'll marvel at the visuals and empathize with the delightful characters.

p&d, Yoram Gross; w, Gross, John Palmer; ph, Graham Sharpe; m, Bob Young; ed, Christopher Plowright; animation director, Ray Nowland.

Animation/Children's Film   **Cas.**   **(PR:AAA   MPAA:NR)**

CANICULE   (SEE: DOG DAY, Fr.)

CANNIBALISTIC HUMANOID UNDERGROUND DWELLING
(SEE: C.H.U.D.)

CANNONBALL RUN II zero   (1984) 108m WB c

Burt Reynolds (*J. J. McClure*), Dom Deluise (*Victor/Chaos*), Shirley MacLaine (*Veronica*), Marilu Henner (*Betty*), Dean Martin (*Blake*), Sammy Davis, Jr (*Fenderbaum*), Susan Anton (*Jill*), Catherine Bach (*Marcie*), Ricardo Montalban (*King*), Jim Nabors (*Homer*), Charles Nelson Reilly (*Don Don*), Telly Savalas (*Hymie*), Jamie Farr (*Sheik*), Jack Elam (*Doc*), Richard Kiel (*Arnold*), Don Knotts, Tim Conway (*CHP Officers*), Henry Silva (*Slim*), Frank Sinatra (*Himself*), Sid Caesar, Foster Brooks, Louis Nye (*Fishermen*), Jackie Chan (*Jackie*), Michael V. Gazzo (*Sonny*), Alex Rocco (*Tony*), Joe Theisman (*Mac*), Doug McClure (*The Slapper*), Dub Taylor (*Sheriff*), Tony Danza (*Terry*), Molly Picon (*Mrs. Goldfarb*), Mel Tillis (*Mel*), Abe Vigoda (*Caesar*), Fred Dreyer (*CHP Officer No. 3*), Dale Ishimoto (*Japanese Father*), Arte Johnson (*Pilot*), Linda Lei (*Beautiful Girl*), Christopher Lemmon (*Young Cop*), George Lindsey (*Cal*), Jilly Rizzo (*Jilly*), Jack Smith (*Announcer*), Lee Kolima (*Nicky*), Shawn Whetherly (*Dean's Girl*), John Worthington Stuart (*Bartender*), Debi Greco (*Sheik's Girl*), John A. Zee (*Sheldon*), Bob Sheldon (*Policeman at Lake*), Fred S. Ronnow (*Pilot*), Kai Joseph Wong (*Japanese Executive*), Sandy Hackett (*Official*), Sean Alexander (*Gas Station Attendant*), Marty Allen, Avery Schreiber, C. James Lewis, Harry Gant, Hal Needham, Robert B. Chandler, Frank O. Hill, Alan R. Gibbs, Regina Parton, Kathleen M. Shea, Mario Roberts, Patricia Bolt, Jim Cassett Anderson, Beverly Budinger, Marian Issacks, Suzynn Herzog, Caroline Reed, Ralph S. Salcido, Budd Stout, Frieda Smith.

This offensive sequel to the mindless CANNONBALL RUN stars Reynolds and a cast of washed-up has-beens who would probably have been more comfortable on TV's "The Love Boat." Once again we get a story of a group of auto enthusiasts engaged in a cross-country race. The race is merely an excuse for director Needham to put his friends on screen in some poorly written, insipid "comedy" sketches. If the overall cinematic ineptitude fails to put you to sleep, maybe the cast from Screen Actors Guild Hell will. After all, were it not for Needham, where–other than game shows–could one see such notables as Foster Brooks, Charles Nelson Reilly, Jamie Farr, Marty Allen, Avery Schreiber...the list goes on and on. Like its puerile precursor, this picture made a lot of money; foreign rentals and videocassette distributors were pre-sold on the strength of the prior pap. The film actually premiered in Japan in 1983, demonstrating the international character of the lowest common denominator.

p, Albert S. Ruddy; d, Hal Needham; w, Needham, Ruddy, Harvey Miller (based on the characters created by Brock Yates); ph, Nick McLean (Technicolor); m, Al Capps; ed, William Gordean, Carl Kress; art d, Tho. E. Azzari; set d, Charles M. Graffeo; cos, Norman Salling, Don Vargas, Kathy O'Rear; spec eff, Philip Cory; animated sequence, Ralph Bakshi; m/l, "Like A Cannonball," Milton Brown, Steve Dorff, Snuff Garrett.

Sports Drama   **Cas.**   **(PR:O   MPAA:PG)**

CAREFUL, HE MIGHT HEAR YOU**½   (1984, Aus.) 116m
Syme-N.S.W./T.L.C.- FOX c

Nicholas Gledhill (*P.S. [Bill]*), Wendy Hughes (*Vanessa*), Robyn Nevin (*Lila*), Peter Whitford (*George*), John Hargreaves (*Logan*), Isabelle Anderson (*Agnes*), Geraldine Turner (*Vere*), Colleen Clifford (*Ettie*), Julie Nihill (*Diana*), Beth Child (*Mrs. Grindel*), Pega Williams (*Winnie Grindel*), Steven

Fyfield *(Chauffeur)*, Jacqueline Kott *(Miss Pile)*, Kylie Burgess *(Cynthia)*, Toby Blanchard *(Ian)*, Virginia Portingale *(Miss Golden)*, Michael Long *(Mr. Hood)*, Edward Howell *(Judge)*, Len London *(Mr. Gentle)*, Colin Croft *(Magician)*.

Wallowing in second-rate melodrama, CAREFUL, HE MIGHT HEAR YOU is, unfortunately, a half-superb film. The successful half features 6-year-old Gledhill, a wide-eyed lad who lives in the depression-era home of Nevin and Whitford. Gledhill is really the son of Nevin's sister, who died during childbirth and is referred to only as "Dear One" by the boy and his caring but stifling guardians. Gledhill too is given a nickname–"P.S."–because because he was a postscript to his mother's life. The dreaded day finally arrives when a third sister, Hughes, arrives from a global vacation and requests custody of Gledhill. An extremely wealthy and beautiful woman, Hughes picks Gledhill up in a chauffeur-driven limousine, signs him up for music lesons, and showers him with material gestures of love. Hughes is everything Gledhill imagines as a dream come true, offering love, beauty, and luxury. Nevin agrees to allow Hughes partial custody but eventually a court battle ensues. In the meantime, Gledhill grows increasingly disillusioned and hostile towards Hughes, who proves to be mentally unstable and unnaturally frightened of such phenomena as thunderstorms. Matters are only further complicated by the arrival of Gledhill's long-absent father, Hargreaves, a drinker who takes a genuine liking to the boy but can't commit himself to raising him. Melodrama runs rampant towards the film's end when an inexplicable ship accident occurs. By the film's finale Gledhill comes to an understanding with his guardians by discovering who he really is–Bill, not "P.S.," not a postscript to somebody else's life. Gledhill is the film's saving grace. A joy to watch, he prevents the film from drowning in its tangled plot and melodramatic leanings. It is his naturalness that offsets the counterproductive plasticity of the other characters. The performances are all noteworthy, especially Hughes (the winner of Australia's Best Actress Award) who would make Joan Crawford proud with her demented idea of love, but they are trapped in a script which would have handcuffed Douglas Sirk. The fact that CAREFUL, HE MIGHT HEAR YOU garnished a handful of awards and much acclaim in Australia is proof not of its greatness, but of the weakness of Australian films during this year.

p, Jill Robb; d, Carl Schultz; w, Michael Jenkins (based on the novel by Sumner Locke Elliott; ph, John Seale (Panavision, Eastmancolor); m, Ray Cook; ed, Richard Francis-Bruce; prod d, John Stoddart; art d, John Carroll, John Wingrove; cos, Bruce Finlayson.

Drama   **Cas.**   **(PR:A-C MPAA:PG)**

CARMEN   (SEE: BIZET'S CARMEN, Fr.)

CENSUS TAKER, THE**   (1984) 95m Argentum/Seymour Borde c

Garrett Morris *(Harvey McGraw)*, Greg Mullavey *(George)*, Meredith MacRae *(Martha)*, Austen Taylor *(Eva)*, Timothy Bottoms *(Pete)*.

Occasionally funny black comedy has Morris a census taker who comes to the home of Mullavey and MacRae and asks a lot of nosy questions. The couple put up with him for a while, but when they finally lose their collective tempers they shoot him in the head. The rest of the film concerns their efforts to hide the corpse from weird detective Bottoms. The end finds Mullavey and Bottoms joining Morris as corpses and the wives collecting their insurance money. The opening parts, with Morris intruding into Mullavey and MacRae's private life, are the best.

p, Robart Bealmer; d, Bruce Cook; w, Cook, Gordon Smith; ph, Tom Jewett; m, Jay Seagrave; ed, Cook.

Comedy   **(PR:O MPAA:NR)**

CHAMPIONS***   (1984) 115m United British Artists/EMB c

John Hurt *(Bob Champion)*, Gregory Jones *(Peter)*, Mick Dillon *(Snowy)*, Ann Bell *(Valda Embiricos)*, Jan Francis *(Jo)*, Peter Barkworth *(Nick Embiricos)*, Edward Woodward *(Josh Gifford)*, Ben Johnson *(Burly Cocks)*, Kirstie Alley *(Barbara)*, Alison Steadman *(Mary Hussey)*, Jonathan Newth *(Mr. Griffith Jones)*, Ceri Jackson, Francesca Brill *(Nurses)*, Andrew Wilde *(Graham)*, Judy Parfitt *(Dr. Merrow)*, Carolyn Pickles *(Sally)*, Andrew Fell *(Doctor)*, Fiona Victory *(Helen)*, Julie Adams *(Emma Hussey)*, Michael Byrne *(Richard Hussey)*, Anthony Carrick *(Ken)*, Frank Mills *(Charles)*, Hubert Rees *(Bill/Hiawatha)*, Richard Adams *(Nicky Hussey)*, Stephen Jenn *(Bald Patient)*, Edwin Richfield *(Ashton)*, Les Conrad *(Masseur)*, Noel Dyson *(Mrs. Champion)*, John Woodnutt *(Mr. Champion)*, Richard Leech *(Beck)*, Anthony Dawes *(Fred)*, Wendy Gifford *(Althea)*, Trevor Clarke *(Phil)*, John Buckingham *(Valet)*, Mark Burns *(Thorne)*, Mark Lambert *(Sean)*, Graham Welcome *(Clerk of the Scales)*, Leonard Trolley *(Steward)*, John Guise *(Starter)*.

If any screenwriter had submitted this idea to a studio, he (or she) might have been laughed out by the management because it appears so improbable, so pat. It is also true. In 1979, Bob Champion was one of England's most successful jockeys. Then he was diagnosed as having cancer and given only eight more months of life. He survived the disease, made a victorious comeback and, in November of 1983, sired a son, despite the removal of one of his testicles. Hurt is on top of the world, winning races, traveling the world, and having an affair with Alley, a veterinarian. After coming home

from a trip to the blue grass state, Kentucky, Hurt learns of his ailment. For the next hour or so, we see his difficulties, emotional and physical, as he deals with the dread malady and the treatment he must undergo. The effects of chemotherapy are hideous: nausea, hair loss, emaciation, bleak conversations with doctors, and deep despair. His already depressing life is sent reeling downward when his favorite horse is injured and in danger of being "put down" (destroyed). Hurt's lungs are damaged, his hands and feet have little feeling, and it's apparent that his career is over. Hurt won't accept that and spends the next years building his ravaged body into condition once the chemotherapy thankfully ends. Hurt's one goal is to ride the grueling four-and-one-half-mile-long Grand National, a race that has 30 jumps and has spelled the end for many healthy riders. Hurt may be bloody, but he is unbowed. His spirit soars as his body aches and his determination is evident in every frame of the film. What one might imagine to be the conclusion is exactly that. Hurt gets the chance to ride in the 1981 Grand National Steeplechase and gloriously wins. The movie resembles several fictional films like NATIONAL VELVET and so it is predictable but that can be forgiven once one is aware that it is all true and did happen. The race footage is bumpy and a good indication of how it must feel for the horse and rider. Hurt is excellent as the jockey while Francis, a woman who appears mysteriously at Hurt's side in the hospital and remains faithful to him, comes across as a champion in her own right. The horse that Champion rode, Aldaniti, plays itself and a few of the actors are real-life track people too. Although moviegoers have been saturated with true to life sagas since film began, it's always interesting to eavesdrop on someone else's life, even when it is rife with tragedy and misfortune. In this case the conclusion was a happy one and the audiences who saw it enjoyed the ultimate success of the man who came back from the brink. It could have done with a bit less of the standard slow-motion shots of horses galloping (has anyone ever made a horse movie that *didn't* have that? Of course they have, and those pictures were better off for the lack of cinematic technique). The score by Davis was monotonous and too loud, just in case we should have missed the inherent drama of any of the situations. For once, medicine gets a positive nod from filmmakers. In real life, Champion retired after the race to open his own training facilities.

p, Peter Shaw; d, John Irvin; w, Evan Jones (based on the book *Champion's Story* by Bob Champion, Jonathan Powell); ph, Ronnie Taylor (Rank Color); m, Carl Davis; ed, Peter Honess; art d, Roy Stannard; set d, Ninkey Dalton.

Biography   **Cas.**   **(PR:C MPAA:PG)**

CHATTANOOGA CHOO CHOO*   (1984) 102m April Fools c

Barbara Eden *(Maggie)*, George Kennedy *(Bert)*, Melissa Sue Anderson *(Jenny)*, Joe Namath *(Newt)*, Bridget Hanley *(Estelle)*, Christopher McDonald *(Paul)*, Clu Gulager *(Sam)*, Tony Azito *(Lucky Pierre)*, Davis Roberts *(Woodrow)*, Professor Toru Tanaka *(Hashimoto)*, James Horan *(Mason)*, Curtis Taylor *(Jim Bob)*, Cliff Frazier *(Ulysses)*, Joe Ciasulli *(1st Biker)*, Paul Brinegar *(Pee Wee)*, John Steadman *(Norman)*, Parley Baer *(Alonzo)*, Jineane Ford *(Mary Lou)*, Candi Brough *(Terri)*, Randi Brough *(Susie)*, Ellen Sweeney *(Heather)*, Jimmy Weldon *(Reverend Norbert Puckett)*, Bill Zuckert *(Owen Meredith)*, Jack Stauffer *(Rex Richardson)*, Joe Tornatore *(2nd Biker)*, John J. York *(Mickey)*, Leonard Ross *(Vendor)*, Wehman Caldwell *(Farmer)*, Lyle Byrum *(Ultra Lite Pilot)*, Jenifer Taurins *(Lady in Club Car)*, Kelcie Blades *(Rube)*, Charlie Holliday *(Hector)*.

Football team owner Kennedy inherits one million dollars, but in order to collect, he must restore a vintage train and drive it from Tennessee to New York City in twenty-four hours. A decent cast does the best it can, but the silly script dooms the whole thing.

p, George Edwards, Jill Griffith; d, Bruce Bilson; w, Robert Mundy, Stephen Phillip Smith; ph, Gary Graver; m, Nelson Riddle; ed, Bud S. Isaacs; art d, Philip Thomas; set d, Jerie Kelter; cos, Jef Bilings.

Comedy   **Cas.**   **(PR:A-C MPAA:PG)**

CHEECH AND CHONG'S THE CORSICAN BROTHERS zero
          (1984) 90m Cheech and Chong's The Corisican Brothers/Orion c

Richard "Cheech" Marin, Thomas Chong *(Corsican Brothers)*, Roy Dotrice *(Evil Fuckaire/Ye Old Jailer)*, Shelby Fiddis *(Princess No. 1)*, Rikki Marin *(Princess No. 2)*, Edie McClurg *(The Queen)*, Robbi Chong *(Princess No. 3)*, Rae Dawn Chong *(The Gypsy)*, Simono *(The Waiter)*, Kay Dotrice *(The Midwife)*, Jennie C. Kos *(The Pregnant Mother)*, Martin Pepper *(Martin)*, Yvan Chiffre, Dan Schwartz *(Tax Collectors)*, Jean-Claude Dreyfus *(Marquis Du Hickey)*, Serge Fedoroff *(Nostrodamus)*, Bernard Szabo *(Spanish Hairdresser)*, David Gabison *(Doctor)*, Leslie Rain *(Gypsy Dancer)*, Claude Aufaure *(Villager)*, Dominique Degeorge *(Villager's Wife)*, Johns Rajohnson *(Dancer)*, Michael Dahan, Joel Dobart *(Musicians)*, Anna Gaylor, Jacques Cancellier, Gilles Tamiz *(Store Owners)*, Oliver Achard *(Mime Actor)*, Claude Meyer *(Drummer)*, Marc Andreoni *(Travesti)*, Cristel Couchane-Lehman *(Pretty Girl)*, Marie-Christine Robert *(Nurse)*, Marina Defosse, Elizabeth Grosz *(Pretty Servants)*, Rebecca Potok, Claire Magnin *(Female Courtiers)*, Andre Penvern, Pierre Olaf, Andre Chaumeau *(Male Courtiers)*, Famille Lopez, Guila Salama *(Acrobats)*, Roxanne Nouban, Sophie Favier, Murielle Dabrule, Alexandra Pandev *(Lovelies)*, Georgette Awys, Josine Comellas, Germaine Delbat *(Knitting Ladies)*.

The drug addled duo of Cheech and Chong dropped all their chemical-inspired jokes for this film, but there's enough scatalogical jokes, homophobic humor, and perverse sexual gags to fill in that gap. In this outing, they reenact Alexandre Dumas' famous story of the two brothers in revolutionary France who each can feel the pain of the other. The story, simply put, has them separated at birth, only to reunite as adults to help fight in the people's cause. Chong directs from the script he wrote with Marin, two tasks he proves to be totally inept at. The film is a poorly structured mess, an unfunny jumble of gutter humor.

p, Peter MacGregor-Scott; d, Thomas Chong; w, Richard "Cheech" Marin, Chong; ph, Harvey Harrison (DeLuxe Color); m, Geo; ed, Tom Avildsen; art d, Daniel Budin; set d, Pierre Jannic; cos, Catherine Corne.

Comedy   **Cas.**   **(PR:O   MPAA:R)**

CHILDREN OF THE CORN*½   (1984) 93m Gatlin-Angeles Group-Inverness/New World c

Peter Horton (*Dr. Burt Stanton*), Linda Hamilton (*Vicky Baxter*), R.G. Armstrong (*Diehl*), John Franklin (*Isaac*), Courtney Gains (*Malachai*), Robby Kiger (*Job*), Annemarie McEvoy (*Sarah*), Julie Maddalena (*Rachel*), Jonas Marlowe (*Joseph*), John Philbin (*Amos*), Dan Snook (*Boy*), David Cowan (*Dad*), Suzy Southam (*Mom*), D.G. Johnson (*Mr. Hansen*), Patrick Boylan, Elmer Soderstrom, Teresa Toigo (*Hansen Customers*).

As a short story, this made for interesting reading. Light, but interesting. Although not one of King's best works, there was enough to fill the scant pages. Not so 93 tedious minutes. King addicts will watch anything based on his works but this is a disappointment to even the most devout Kingfish. Horton and Hamilton are a white-bread couple driving cross-country. Horton is a newly minted physician about to begin his period of internship in Seattle. They are somewhere in flattest Nebraska when they find themselves on a deserted highway. Thunk! Horton accidentally drives over a child. He leaps out of the car to administer his freshly learned skills and discovers that he didn't kill the boy at all. The child had been dead before the car hit him. Horton looks around and sees nothing but miles of corn fields. He marches into the fields and finds a small suitcase stained with blood. Surmising that the lad was running away from someone or something, Horton and Hamilton head for the nearest town where the local gas station attendant tells them they would be much safer if they got out of this area. That is easier suggested than completed and, after driving around in a huge circle, they find themselves right back where they started in the deserted town. What they don't know (and are soon to learn) is that the children of the area murdered all the adults in the once-thriving town and have now set themselves up as a religious cult of the strangest sort. Franklin leads the group, which worships a deity of the corn fields. Franklin wants to kill the couple rather than allow them to spread the word. Hamilton is captured and incarcerated in a deserted house where she is finally rescued by Horton and two dissidents, Kiger and McEvoy, just before she is to be crucified on a cross of corn. A slow movie with no high points. In the King tradition, there are a few gory scenes, a mild scare now and then, but nowhere near the frights he's given us before. Franklin is excellent as the malevolent child and the two holdout moppets are also worth noting. Too many cooks must have spoiled the witch's broth here as it was produced by Gatlin Productions, Inverness Productions, and the Angeles Group, then presented by New World in conjunction with Hal Roach Studios and an outfit called Cinema Group Venture. It will only scare the youngest children but it will bore anyone old enough to shave. The premise of the movie was okay (a mini- Manson mob marauding) but somewhere between the story and the screenplay, someone went out for popcorn and didn't come back.

p, Donald P. Borchers, Terence Kirby; d, Fritz Kiersch; w, George Goldsmith (based on the short story "Night Shift" by Stephen King); ph, Raoul Lomas (CFI Color); m, Jonathan Elias; ed, Harry Keramidas; art d, Craig Stearns; set d, Cricket Rowland; cos, Barbara Scott; spec eff, Max W. Anderson; stunts, Bruce Paul Barbour.

Horror   **Cas.**   **(PR:C-O   MPAA:R)**

CHINESE BOXES***   (1984, Ger./Brit.) 87m Road Movies/Palace c

Will Patton (*Lang Marsh*), Gottfried John (*Zwemmer*), Adelheid Arndt (*Sarah*), Robbie Coltrane (*Harwood*), Beate Jensen (*Donna Johnson*), Susanne Meierhofer (*Eva*), Jonathan Kinsler (*Alan*), L. M. Kit Carson (*Crewcut*), Chris Sievernich (*Snake*), Christopher Petit (*Gunsel*), Martin Muller, Jochen von Vietinghoff, Ben De Jong, Michael Buttner, Michael Maichle, Edgar Hinz.

An engrossing–though convoluted–crime thriller which turns standard cinematic conventions inside out. Patton is an innocent American living in a less-than-respectable section of West Berlin who gets himself mixed up with a murderous drug kingpin's operations. The night before he is to depart for Amsterdam for a rendezvous with his girl friend, Patton has a tete-a-tete with the nymphish Jensen. The following morning Jensen turns up dead in his bathroom, having overdosed on heroin. If that isn't enough to hang Patton, the fact that she is an American diplomat's 15-year-old daughter almost is. From that point on, Patton is on the run, eluding a strange array of ominous characters while trying to find a safe way home. Somewhat reminiscent of Wim Wender's AN AMERICAN FRIEND (1977), which is perhaps more than a coincidence. The producer of CHINESE BOXES, Chris Sievernich, also produced Wender's PARIS, TEXAS (as well as director

Petit's previous film, FLIGHT TO BERLIN, also released this year), and L. M. Kit Carson wrote the story on which PARIS, TEXAS is based. Director Petit appears in a brief scene as a murderous "gunsel" (the often misused term author Dashiell Hammett slipped over on his puritanical publisher in his novel *The Maltese Falcon*; the term actually refers to a catamite–which Hammett's character, Wilmer, certainly was–and not to a pistol-packing hit man), and screenwriter Carson also appears in a minor role.

p, Chris Sievernich; d, Christopher Petit; w, L. M. Kit Carson, Petit; ph, Peter Harvey; m, Gunther Fischer; ed, Fred Srp; art d, Edgar Hinz, Klaus Beiser; cos, Ulrike Schutte.

Crime   **Cas.**   **(PR:O   MPAA:NR)**

CHOOSE ME***   (1984) 114m Island Alive c

Keith Carradine (*Mickey*), Lesley Ann Warren (*Eve*), Genevieve Bujold (*Ann/"Dr. Nancy Love"*), Patrick Bauchau (*Zack Antoine*), Rae Dawn Chong (*Pearl Antoine*), John Larroquette (*Billy Ace*), Edward Ruscha (*Ralph Chomsky*), Gailard Sartain (*Mueller*), Robert Gould (*Lou*), John Considine (*Dr. Ernest Greene*), Jodi Buss (*Babs*), Sandra Will (*Ida*), Mike E. Kaplan (*Harve*), Russell Parr (*Bradshaw*), Teresa Valarde (*Studio Secretary*), Henry G. Sanders (*Hospital Administrator*), Margery Bond (*Cousin*), Debra Dusay (*Nurse La Mer*), Minnie Lindsay (*Woman on Bus*), Richard Marion (*Gilda*), Albert Stanislaus (*Max*), Karyn Isaacs (*Farrah*), Elizabeth Lloyd Shaw (*Miss Muffin*), Edward C. Lawson (*Chrome*), Chase Holiday (*Champagne*), Patrick McFadden (*Rudy*), Greg Walker (*Stuntman*).

A most interesting love story-comedy-drama where the characterizations outweigh and eventually overwhelm the plot. Bujold is a radio psychologist who dispenses advice but is hopelessly maladjusted herself. She masquerades under the *nom de radio* of "Dr. Love" and keeps her anonymity protected. Warren is the owner of a small bar she bought only because it had already been owned by a woman with the same name, Eve, and there's no need to change the sign. She's blessed and cursed with the ability to attract and capture any man she pleases. Warren is fascinating in that she is not what she seems. Instead, she is a frightened woman living on the edge of a breakdown and not the supremely self-confident person she appears to be. Carradine, a wayward genius, or the world's greatest liar, walks into the bar. He's dated the former owner and is surprised to meet yet another "Eve" running the tavern. In passing, he casually talks about his life and mentions that he's been a jet pilot, a poetry professor at Yale, and a spy for the CIA. Ironically, the man with the wildest stories turns out to be the only person in the film who is not living a lie. Warren spends a lot of time calling Bujold on the phone. Bujold seems to be the pillar of mental stability but she is actually a mouse and hides behind her radio microphone. Warren is lonely and advertises for a roommate. That ad is answered by Bujold, who tells Warren that she runs an "answering service." The women get along well but there are other factors arising. Chong is a regular at Warren's bar. She is married to charmer Bauchau and only comes to the bar to keep an eye on him because she suspects that he and Warren have been having an affair. She's right, but she can't think of what to do about it. Carradine is suspected of being nuts but he is so witty and so much fun that everyone decides to accept him as he is. He is also quite sensuous and, at one time or another, asks Bujold, Warren, and Chong to be his wife. The women are all jealous of his affections toward the others and it even causes Bauchau to get crazy. The picture is made up of many moments and many wonderful verbal insights, such as when Warren is asked why she never married and replies, "I've ruined too many marriages to ever have one of my own." Carradine admits that he is a recent patient at a mental hospital, thus strengthening the beliefs of the others that not one word of his can be accepted. But Carradine, who is the spine of the movie, tells nothing but the truth, which is all the more infuriating because everyone else in the movie is sailing under false flags and they just assume he is doing the same. The players walk the fine line between madness and obsession, each searching for an elusive "something" that they hope will make them happy and contented. We never find out why they do what they do and every time we think we have a handle on them, Rudolph's script makes an abrupt turn. This is his best work, although it doesn't have a beginning, middle, and end, the way stories are supposed to. The score, by various composers, the songs performed by Pendergrass, and the cinematography by Kiesser go far in capturing the mood of the people and the places. Carradine is a standout and the picture would have been far less effective with anyone else in the role. Bujold, who had a great resurgence in her career in the 1980s, shows that she is capable of many looks and moods. Lest you think this is some somber Ibsenian story, forget that. This is also very funny at times, never taking itself too seriously and, in the end, is an intriguing piece of work. Recommended for audiences who like to think.

p, Carolyn Pfeiffer, David Blocker; d&w, Alan Rudolph; ph, Jan Kiesser (Movielab Color); ed, Mia Goldman; prod d, Steven Legler; art d, Legler; set d, K.C. Scheibel; cos, Tracy Tynan; m/l "Choose Me," Luther Vandross, Marcus Miller, Michael Masser, Cynthia Weil (sung by Teddy Pendergrass).

Comedy/Drama   **Cas.**   **(PR:O   MPAA:R)**

CITY GIRL, THE**½   (1984) 85m Moon c

Laura Harrington (Anne), Joe Mastroianni (Joey), Carole McGill (Gracie), Peter Riegert (Tim), Jim Carrington (Steve), Lawrence Phillips (The Stripper), Geraldine Baron (Monica), Colleen Camp (Rose), Janice Green (Sugar), Rosanne Katon (Ira).

This interesting drama actually marked the feature-film debut of director Coolidge, although it sat on the shelf until her subsequent VALLEY GIRL became a hit. Harrington is a young woman trying to make it in the modern world as a photographer and an independent person. Freeing herself from her attachment to her long-time boy friend Mastroianni, she plays the field. Disappointed by the outcome, she's terrified when a pimp she's been secretly photographing comes and wrecks her apartment. Harrington gives an excellent three-dimensional performance; her character has obvious faults like selfishness and simply being wrong a lot of the time. Production on the film began in 1981, but the producers ran out of money before it could be completed. It was a year before Peter Bogdanovich took on the role of executive producer and raised the money to finish it.

p&d, Martha Coolidge; w, Judith Thompson, Leonard-John Gates (based on a story by John MacDonald, Coolidge); ph, Daniel Hainey (DeLuxe Color); m, Scott Wilk, Marc Levinthal; ed, Linda Leeds, Eva Gardos; art d, Ninkey Dalton; set d, Elise Rowland.

Drama   (PR:O   MPAA:NR)

CITY HEAT*½   (1984) 97m Malpaso-Deliverance/WB c

Clint Eastwood (Lt. Speer), Burt Reynolds (Mike Murphy), Jane Alexander (Addy), Madeline Kahn (Caroline Howley), Rip Torn (Primo Pitt), Irene Cara (Ginny Lee), Richard Roundtree (Dehl Swift), Tony Lo Bianco (Leon Coll), William Sanderson (Lonnie Ash), Nicholas Worth (Troy Roker), Robert Davi (Nino), Jude Farese (Dub Slack), John Hancock (Fat Freddie), Tab Thacker (Tuck), Gerald S. O'Loughlin (Counterman Louie), Bruce M. Fisher, Art La Fleur (Bruisers), Jack Nance (Aram Strossell), Dallas Cole (Redhead Sherry), Lou Filippo (Referee), Michael Maurer (Vint Diestock), Preston Sparks (Keith Stoddard), Ernie Sabella (Ballistics Expert), Christopher Michael Moore (Roxy Cop), Carey Loftin (Roxy Driver), Harry Caesar (Locker Room Attendant), Charles Parks (Dr. Breslin), Hamilton Camp (Garage Attendant), Jack Thibeau, Gene LeBell, Nick Dimitri, George Fisher, Bob Herron, Bill Hart (Garage Soldiers), Arthur Malet (Doc Loomis), Fred Lerner (Pitt Roof Sniper), George Orrison (Pitt Doorway Thug), Beau Starr (Pitt Lookout), Anthony Charnota, Walter Robles, Richard Foronjy (Poker Players), Joan Shawlee (Peggy Barker), Minnie Lindsey (Bordello Maid), Darwyn Swalve (Bordello Bouncer), Wiley Harker, Bob Maxwell ("Mr. Smiths"), Tom Spratley (Chauffeur), Bob Terhune (Billiard Soldier), Holgie Forrester (Little Red), Harry Demopoulos, M.D. (Roman Orgy Patron), Jim Lewis (Roxy Patron), Edwin Prevost (Butler), Alfie Wise (Short Guy), Hank Calia (Shorter Friend), Alex Plasschaert (Shortest Friend), Daphne Eckler (Agnes), Lonna Montrose (Didi), Michael Cassidy, Vincent Deadrick, Jr., Richard Drown, Bud Ekins, Allan Graf, Chuck Hicks, Julius Le Flore, Fritz Manes, Debby Porter, James Hooks Reynolds, Mic Rodgers, Sharon Schaffer, Wayne Van Horn, Chuck Waters, George Wilbur, Glenn Wilder (Stunts).

What could have been an interesting and funny period piece under the helm of original screenwriter-director Blake Edwards (under the title "Kansas City Blues") is turned into a tedious, infantile mess by Benjamin. Because of disagreements between the director and his stars, Edwards walked off the film and had his name removed from the screenwriting credits by substituting a pseudonym–"Sam O. Brown"–which stands for "S.O.B." the title of one of his previous films which dealt with the insanity of the movie business. Benjamin, who had scored memorably with MY FAVORITE YEAR and RACING WITH THE MOON, had proved himself quite adept at evoking times gone by (the 1950s in the former and the 1940s in the latter) and was hired to take over the picture. CITY HEAT is set in Kansas City in 1933. Eastwood is a police detective now on bad terms with his former partner Reynolds who has turned in his badge for the trenchcoat of a private eye. Business is lousy however, and when his partner, Roundtree (whom he doesn't like much either), shows up with a huge wad of cash, Reynolds suspects things aren't quite on the up-and-up. Roundtree has acquired the books for local mobster Lo Bianco's outfit and has sold them to local mobster Torn. Roundtree pulls a double-cross, however, and turns around and offers to sell the books back to Lo Bianco for twice the price. Torn gets mad and has Roundtree killed. Roundtree's girl friend, Cara, a torch singer at a nightclub, must go into hiding, while Reynolds is left holding the bag with both mob chieftains. Driven by the same motivation that sent Sam Spade into the mysteries of THE MALTESE FALCON ("It doesn't make any difference what you thought of him. He was your partner and you're supposed to do something about it."), Reynolds sets out to avenge his partner. Eastwood, meanwhile, tails Reynolds in hopes of ruining both Lo Bianco and Torn. To ensure that Reynolds turns over the books, Torn has his men kidnap the private eye's girl friend, Kahn, a rich, ditzy nymphomaniac. Eastwood initially stays uninvolved as he observes Reynolds trapped between Lo Bianco's men and Torn's men in a shootout, but when the windshield of his car gets shot, the stoic Eastwood finally gets mad and he grabs a shotgun and calmly walks down the center of the street blowing up cars and shooting gunmen. This leads to a showdown with Torn and his boys and Eastwood mops them up in short order. They then find the place

where Kahn is being held (a bordello) and they rescue her. At the same time Reynolds' secretary, Alexander, (Eastwood's nominal sweetheart) is kidnaped by Lo Bianco and the lawmen are faced with the same dilemma they've just solved. Reynolds turns the suitcase full of books over to Lo Bianco and the gangster turns Alexander over to Eastwood. The mobster and his goons drive off and a few seconds later the car is blown to bits. Reynolds had rigged it with dynamite. Half the reason CITY HEAT isn't as funny as it should be is the extreme and sadistic violence that Benjamin tries to pass off as humor. In one sequence Eastwood shoots a huge gangster at least 12 times before he falls and it's played for laughs. There is another scene where Eastwood and Reynolds pour rubbing alcohol on the exposed rear-end of a gangster and then drop a match on it–funny stuff right? The body count in CITY HEAT is somewhere on the far side of one of Eastwood's Sergio Leone westerns and the supposedly humorous violent scenes are obviously inserted to make up for the totally flat and unfunny dialog that a 10-year-old would find stupid. Most shocking off all are the lazy performances from both Reynolds and Eastwood. Reynolds acts as if he's in another mindless Hal Needam epic and Eastwood glides through the movie as if hoping no one will notice him. Eastwood does get credit for providing a few of the mild chuckles by playing off his well- established screen persona–though this is easily Eastwood's worst film. Surprisingly, the best performances come from Lo Bianco and Torn who look as if they're actually enjoying themselves, and Alexander scores nicely in a Rosalind Russell homage. The only thing that works in this disaster is the costume and set designs which are really quite impressive and once again it looks as if Benjamin was more interested in the period detail (as was the case with RUNNING WITH THE MOON) than his characters. Despite serious flaws and negative reviews, the film was a hit with the public based solely on the names on the marquee–which was really the only reason why this dog was produced in the first place.

p, Fritz Manes; d, Richard Benjamin; w, Sam O. Brown 'Blake Edwards', Joseph C. Stinson (based on a story by Brown); ph, Nick McLean (Technicolor); m, Lennie Niehaus; ed, Jacqueline Cambas; prod d, Edward Carfagno; set d, George Gaines; cos, Norman Salling; spec eff, Joe Unsinn; stunts, Wayne Van Horn; makeup, Tom Ellingwood, Dan Striepeke; m/l, "City Heat" (Irene Cara, Bruce Roberts, sung by Joe Williams), "Million Dollar Baby" (Billy Rose, Mort Dixon, Harry Warren, sung by Al Jarreau), "Between the Devil and the Deep Blue Sea" (Ted Koehler, Harold Arlen, sung by Eloise Laws), "Get Happy" (Koehler, Arlen, sung by Cara), "Embraceable You" (George and Ira Gershwin, sung by Cara), "Let's Do It" (Cole Porter, sung by Rudy Vallee), "Montage Blues" (Lennie Niehaus, performed by Mike Lang, Pete Jolly, Clint Eastwood).

Comedy   Cas.   (PR:O   MPAA:PG)

CLASS ENEMY**   (1984, Ger.) 125m Teleculture c

Greger Hansen (Angel), Stefan Reck (Pickel), Jean-Paul Raths (Koloss), Udo Samel (Vollmond), Ernst Stoetzner (Fetzer), Tayfun Bademsoy (Kebab).

A one-set drama moved from its original London slum setting to Berlin. Six toughs sit in a classroom waiting for a new teacher to arrive. They argue, lecture each other, fight, and fret that no teacher is ever going to come. A bit too strident in making its obvious points, the film at least keeps its technique unobtrusive, letting the strength of the stage production come through. (In German; English subtitles).

p, Regina Ziegler; d, Peter Stein; w, Stein, Juergen Klose (based on the play by Nigel Williams); ph, Robby Mueller; ed, Inge Behrens; prod d, Karl-Ernst Herrmann; cos, Dorothea Katzer.

Drama   (PR:O   MPAA:NR)

CLOAK AND DAGGER***   (1984) 101m UNIV c

Henry Thomas (Davey Osborne), Dabney Coleman (Jack Flack/Hal Osborne), Michael Murphy (Rice), Christina Nigra (Kim Gardener), John McIntire (George MacCready), Jeanette Nolan (Eunice MacCready), Eloy Casados (Alvarez), Tim Rossovich (Haverman), Bill Forsythe (Morris), Robert DoQui (Lt. Fleming), Shelby Leverington (Marilyn Gardener), Linden Chiles (Airport Security Chief), Robert Curtin (Murdoch), William Marquez, Wendell Wright (Airport Security Guards), Doris Hargrave (Woman in Cafe), Gary Moody (Man in Cafe), Eleese Lester (Woman on Boat), John P. Edson, Jr., Steve Fromholtz (Men on Boat), Charles Beall, Stuart MacGregor (Alamo Guards), Norman Bennett (Texan), Corey Rand (Building Security Guard), Nicolas Guest, Louis Anderson (Taxi Drivers), Karen Leigh Hopkins (Receptionist), Tammy Hyler (Check-In Clerk), Alvaro Rojas, Jr. (Boat Captain), Robert Traynor (Ticket Agent), Berkley Garrett, Gene Ross (Bus Drivers), Earl Houston Bullock (Navigator), Al Gomez (Ground Crewman).

Producer Carr took some time off from making musicals to oversee this surprisingly good thriller. Thomas is a young child with a great imagination and his own computer. Nobody believes Thomas and his tall tales because they're all going on in his head. So when he accidentally uncovers a plot to smuggle top secret information out of the U.S., his fear is again perceived to be part of his active fantasy world. He runs to his father, Coleman, who, it should go without saying, doesn't believe a word of it. Thomas has been playing a game called "Cloak and Dagger" on his computer and Coleman thinks his son may have confused reality with fantasy. Thomas has conjured up a character in his mind named "Jack Flack" (also played by Coleman) who pops up and helps Thomas whenever the lad gets into a pickle. Meanwhile, Thomas and his young girl friend, Nigra, find themselves clamped in the jowls of the malfeasants who are perpetrating the real- life plot. Thomas' creation of "Flack" can't help him here as the boy is plunged into a morass of mayhem and is sought by the criminals for execution. Thomas must use his native intelligence to extricate himself and Nigra from the clutches of the villains, led by Murphy as the chief spy, a rotten person who eats kids for breakfast (figuratively). Without the aid of his mental superhero, it falls on Thomas' slim shoulders to save his country. The film races through San Antonio, Texas, a place that has not been over-shot in the movies of late, so the backgrounds are new and interesting for the audience. The bad guys chase the kids but, as you can gather, it all ends happily. Tight direction and good humor from the Holland script. Aussie helmer Franklin had obviously seen a few Alfred Hitchcock pictures in his day (he had already collaborated with Holland once before in the making of PSYCHO II) although he doesn't rip off the master, only using some of his tried-and-true techniques. What separates this from most of the "boy who cried wolf" stories is the addition of the dual role for Coleman which serves to examine the relationship between father and son, thus supplementing the yarn with another dimension and almost making the spy plot a diversion rather than the core element of the story. If the plot seems familiar, be aware that it was based loosely on the 1949 Bobby Driscoll- starrer known as THE WINDOW, a first-rate second feature. That was the story of a slum boy in the 1940s, but since this movie was made in the 1980s, the addition of a computer was introduced to indicate the boy's passion for mental adventure. Murphy is properly heinous as the heavy and there are good cameos by veterans John McIntyre and Jeanette Nolan as a kindly old tourist couple who turn out to be anything but kindly. Coleman is excellent in both his roles. Thomas, who was the star of E.T. THE EXTRA-TERRESTRIAL, is remarkably natural in a role that might have had other child actors reeling. An ingratiating film with much to recommend it, CLOAK AND DAGGER feels like a Hitchcock movie produced by Walt Disney.

p, Allan Carr; d, Richard B. Franklin; w, Tom Holland (based on the short story "The Boy Cried Murder," by Cornell Woolrich); ph, Victor J. Kemper (Technicolor); m, Brian May; ed, Andrew London; prod d, William Tuntke; art d, Todd Hallowell; set d, Hal Gausman; cos, John Casey, Nancy McArdle.

Adventure   Cas.   (PR:C MPAA:PG)

COLD FEET* **   (1984) 96m Cinecom International c

Griffin Dunne (*Tom Christo*), Marissa Chibas (*Marty Fenton*), Blanche Baker (*Leslie Christo*), Mark Cronogue (*Bill*), Kurt Knudson (*Louis*), Joseph Leon (*Harold Fenton*), Marcia Jean Kurtz (*Psychiatrist*), Peter Boyden (*Dr. Birbrower*), Dan Strickler, John Jellison (*Executives*), Mary Fogarty (*Susan*).

Dunne and Chibas, each recently freed from a bad relationship, find each other. They engage in long, semi-witty conversations about their bad relationships and their desires, and finally before the fadeout–feeling their strong new relationship can take it–they go to bed. Oddly depressing for a comedy with two people as likable as Dunne and Chibas, but well worth seeing.

p, Charles Wessler; d&w, Bruce van Dusen; ph, Benjamin Blake; m, Todd Rundgren; ed, Sally Joe Menke.

Comedy   Cas.   (PR:C MPAA:PG)

COMFORT AND JOY* **   (1984, Brit.) 106m Kings Road/UNIV c

Bill Paterson (*Alan "Dickie" Bird*), Eleanor David (*Maddy*), C.P. Grogan (*Charlotte*), Alex Norton (*Trevor*), Patrick Malahide (*Colin*), Rikki Fulton (*Hilary*), Roberto Bernardi (*Mr. McCool*), George Rossi (*Bruno*), Peter Rossi (*Paolo*), Billy McElhaney (*Renato*), Gilly Gilchrist (*Rufus*), Caroline Guthrie (*Gloria*), Ona McCracken (*Nancy*), Elizabeth Sinclair (*Fiona*), Katy Black (*Sarah*), Robin Black (*Lily*), Ron Donachie (*George*), Arnold Brown (*Psychiatrist*), Iain McColl (*Archie*), Billy Johnstone (*Amos*), Douglas Sannachan, Alan Tall, Bob Starrett, Billy Greenless, Robert Buchanan (*Trevor's Workmen*), David O'Hara (*Engineer*), Allan Wylie (*Newsreader*), Alistair Campbell (*Keith*), Charles Kearney (*All-Night Deejay*), Elspet Cameron (*Mrs. Wilson*), Teri Lally (*Shop Assistant*), Pearl Deans (*Maria*), Ray Jeffries, Patrick Lewsley (*Removal Men*), Ronald McCleod Veitch (*Dentist*), Johnny Irving (*Bob Hope Look-alike*), Johnny Mac (*Fred Astaire Look- alike*), Alan Stuart (*Fight Arranger*), Ray Alon (*Stunts*).

Although technically listed as a British film, COMFORT AND JOY is actually Scottish, and another one of a string of first-rate comedies directed and written by home-grown Bill Forsyth. For fans of GREGORY'S GIRL and LOCAL HERO, this one may be a bit under par but it's got plenty of laughs, more than a few insights, and several offbeat characters. The movie commences as David, an attractive woman wearing a large coat, is blithely making her way through a Glasgow department store, stuffing items under her coat, without benefit of paying. She is followed closely by Paterson, who we suspect is a store detective ready to pounce the moment she exits the store. Instead, he simply follows her outside and they get into a car together. It turns out that they are live-in lovers and she is a klepto. As she gleefully totals up the goods she's purloined (none of which are of any use to them–they include items like mis-sized clothing, ugly cigarette lighters, stuff

like that), Paterson drives them to their apartment. She's a kooky type, given to saying things that one wouldn't expect, and the dialog between them is fresh and always surprising. After they enjoy a lovely Christmas Eve dinner and make love (off screen), David begins removing items and places them in suitcases, as though she were planning a round-the-world cruise. When the items begin to include pictures and other heavy gear, Paterson wonders what it's all about and David blithely announces that she's leaving him and has been planning it for quite some time. He wonders why she never mentioned it before and she shrugs and answers that she just forgot. And with that, David walks out of Paterson's life, leaving him somewhere beyond depression. Paterson is a disc jockey in Glasgow and a popular one at that. He is known as "Dickie" Bird (even though his name is Alan) and his voice is heard throughout the city. Paterson has been living a very placid life until now, but that's all thrown away when he becomes mired in the midst of a gang war between two rival Mafioso families who are seeking to control the Glasgow ice cream business. Actually, the two families are branches of one but bad blood has arisen among the members and heads are being cracked, ice cream trucks are being torched, and lives are in danger of being lost. The two companies are known as "Mr. Bunny" and "Mr. McCool," and Paterson, unwilling to see chaos erupt and innocent people hurt, uses his radio show to relay messages between the warring factions. This puts him at risk of losing his job at the station and wins him the anger of the ice cream combatants. In the end, Paterson's beloved BMW car is ruined but he does manage to effect a truce between the ice cream groups and cuts himself in for a share of the profits of the merger he has caused to happen. As you can readily tell from the synopsis, this is a unique idea for a film and while some of the potentially hilarious situations don't always garner as many laughs as they could have, there are several funny moments and the picture is always seeming to throw curve balls at the audience. Forsyth's work is almost always joyous and this would have to be the least of the lot, although there is more here than has been seen in British comedies since the dear days of the Ealing Studios. Anyone who has ever been to Scotland will argue that the average American's beliefs about the Scots is totally wrong. Far from being dour or cheap, they are a happy breed, dedicated and devoted to good food, good drink, and having a good time. Forsyth is the best of the directors in the area and his work has been consistently superior. He's still young and there's lots more to come. Keep an eye on Forsyth, laddie (or lassie), as he is one of the best comedy directors around from any country.

p, Davina Belling, Clive Parsons; d&w, Bill Forsyth; ph, Chris Menges (Technicolor); m, Mark Knopfler; ed, Michael Ellis; prod d, Adrienne Atkinson; art d, Andy Harris; cos, Mary Jane Reyner, Lindy Hemming.

Comedy   Cas.   (PR:A-C MPAA:PG)

CONAN THE DESTROYER* **   (1984) 103m UNIV c

Arnold Schwarzenegger (*Conan*), Grace Jones (*Zula*), Wilt Chamberlain (*Bombaara*), Mako (*Akjiro "The Wizard"*), Tracey Walter (*Malak*), Sarah Douglas (*Queen Taramis*), Olivia D'Abo (*Princess Jehnna*), Pat Roach (*Man Ape/Thoth-Amon*), Jeff Corey (*Grand Vizier*), Sven Ole Thorsen (*Togra*), Bruce Fleischer (*Village Heckler*), Ferdinand [Ferdy] Mayne (*The Leader*).

Superior sequel to John Milius' plodding CONAN THE BARBARIAN (1982) is directed by veteran helmsman Fleischer with much more speed, skill, and ingenuity than its predecessor. Schwarzenegger is hired by evil queen Douglas to escort her virgin niece, D'Abo, along with her massive bodyguard, Chamberlain, on a mystical quest to find a magic gem. Unfortunately, what Schwarzenegger doesn't know is that Douglas has instructed Chamberlain to kill the big lug after they find the gem, and then bring the virginal D'Abo back to be sacrificed. Also along for the ride are an eccentric old wizard, Mako, and Schwarzenegger's cowardly toady, Walter. A short time into their journey, Schwarzenegger and company come across a wild woman, Jones, who has been captured by a group of primordial grunts. The noble strongman helps free the grateful Jones and she joins their troupe. Together the band battles all manner of creatures, mortal and supernatural, eventually completing their mission. During the return to Douglas' castle, Schwarzenegger learns of the queen's plan and persuades Chamberlain to help him overthrow her tyrannical rule. This, of course, leads to the climactic battle with a horrid monster called Dagoth, but in the end the good guys win. Fleischer succeeds here where Milius failed. instead of the ponderous seriousness of the first film, Fleischer injects a sense of humor into the proceedings and lets Schwarzenegger relax and have fun with the role. The rest of the cast has a good time as well. Chamberlain, who looks hilariously out of place riding a horse (he's twice as big as the animal), is fine as the noble guardsman. Douglas looks stunning as a seductively evil villain, and Walter adds another zonked-out persona to his repertoire (for others see RUMBLE FISH, REPO MAN, and AT CLOSE RANGE). Jones, however, steals the show from her comrades and provides the most crowd-pleasing moments in her wild woman role, which she portrays with wonderful abandon. Good fun.

p, Raffaella De Laurentiis; d, Richard Fleischer; w, Stanley Mann (story by Roy Thomas, Gerry Conway, based on the character created by Robert E. Howard); ph, Jack Cardiff (JDC Widescreen, Technicolor); m, Basil Poledouris; ed, Frank J. Urioste; prod d, Pier Luigi Basile; art d, Kevin Phipps, Jose Maria Alarcon; set d, Giorgio Desideri; cos, John Bloomfield; stunts, Vic Armstrong; makeup, Giannetto De Rossi.

Adventure/Fantasy   Cas.   (PR:C MPAA:PG)

CONQUEST*   (1984, Ital./Span./Mex.) 89m Clemi
Cinematographia-Golden Sun-Esme/UFDC c

Jorge Rivero (*Max*), Andrea Occhipinti (*Ilias*), Sabrina Siani (*Ocron*), Conrado San Martin, Violeta Cela, Jose Gras Palau, Maria Scola.

A simple-minded sword-and-sorcery "epic" which is set somewhere off in fantasyland. Siani is an omnipotent demon who makes life difficult for a pair of warriors by sending forth a number of obstacles. These include the usual fantasy creatures that are half-man half-beast and can readily transform themselves into whatever they choose. Battle after battle fills the screen, paving the way for an excess of gory violence. Siani, who shows both her strength and her flesh, is finally killed but conveniently changes into a wolf and scurries away to safety. Music is a synthesized rock score by Simonetti, whose former band, Goblin, was credited with scoring DAWN OF THE DEAD (1983). Definitely not a film for the kids, though it would probably impress diehard surrealists.

p, Giovanni Di Clemente; d, Lucio Fulci; w, Gino Capone, Jose Antonio de la Loma, Sr., Carlos Vasallo (based on a story by Di Clemente); ph, Alejandro Alonso Garcia (Telecolor); m, Claudio Simonetti; ed, Emilio Rodriguez Oses; art d, Massimo Lentini; makeup, Franco Rufini.

Fantasy/Adventure   (PR:O MPAA:R)

CONSTANCE* (1984, New Zealand) 103m Mirage-New Zealand Film Commission-Miramax-Enterprise c

Donogh Rees, Shane Bryant, Judie Douglass, Martin Vaughan, Donald McDonald, Mark Wignall, Graham Harvey, Hester Joyce, Dana Purkis, Lee Grant, Don Kjestrup, Susan Trainer, Jules Regal, Miranda Pritchard, Roman Watkins, Beryl Te Wiata, Elric Hooper, Lenore Truscott, Stephen Taylor, Mark Hadlow.

A picturesque period piece set in post-WW II Auckland concerning Rees, a young woman deeply affected by Hollywood. Rees makes every attempt to surround herself with the plush style and passion that is associated with Hollywood, but discovers that her surroundings don't quite permit it. Although it borders on ineffective melodrama, the gorgeous Rees single-handedly makes the picture watchable.

p, Larry Parr; d, Bruce Morrison; w, Jonathan Hardy, Morrison; ph, Kevin Hayward; m, Dave Fraser; ed, Phillip Howe; prod d, Richard Jeziorny, Judith Crozier; art d, Ric Kafoed.

Drama   (PR:O MPAA:NR)

CORRUPT* (1984, Ital.) 99m Jean Vigo-Radiotelevision Italia/New Line Cinema c (AKA: ORDER OF DEATH)

Harvey Keitel (*Lt. Fred O'Connor*), John Lydon (*Leo Smith*), Sylvia Sidney (*Margaret Smith*), Nicole Garcia (*Lenore Carvo*), Leonard Mann (*Bob Carvo*), Carla Romanelli, Bob Kelly, Tony Mayer, Harriet Kurland, Paul Ragonese, Al Sheppard, Mike Tremont.

A perverse and offbeat film which pits cop Keitel against the demented Lydon in a sado-masochistic psychological battle. Lydon is supposedly a cop killer who lives with his mother Sidney in a plush mansion. One day, however, Keitel pulls Lydon off the street and drags him back to his apartment where he viciously beats him. Lydon refuses to supply Keitel with the information he wants, taunting his abductor to further abuse him. For days Keitel keeps him locked in his apartment and eventually Lydon gets a chance to escape but doesn't do so. Though Keitel continues to beat him, he becomes increasingly tortured by Lydon's attitude and his refusal to defend himself against the violence. A memorable film which is interesting not for its plot, but for the strange tension between the characters. CORRUPT delves into the darkest side of the law and its criminal element presenting the audience with an eerie reality. The perversions and violence displayed in CORRUPT are, in many ways, comparable to those that can be seen in *film noir*. Keitel's mind twists and turns in the name of the law much in the same way as Ralph Meeker's in 1955's KISS ME DEADLY, while Lydon's role as a manipulative psychological oppressor has roots in the Ann Savage character of DETOUR (1945). Keitel turns in a commendable performance, but it's the charismatic Lydon who steals the film. For those who may not be up on rock-and-roll history, Johnny Lydon came to fame as "Johnny Rotten," the hate-spewing purveyor of destruction who was the idolized lead singer of the punk rock band The Sex Pistols.

p, Elda Ferri; d, Roberto Faenza; w, Ennio de Concini, Hugh Fleetwood, Faenza (based on the novel *The Order of Death* by Fleetwood); ph, Giuseppe Pinori; m, Ennio Morricone; ed, Nino Baragli; art d, Giantito Burchiellaro.

Crime/Drama   Cas.   (PR:O MPAA:R)

COTTON CLUB, THE*½**   (1984) 127m Zoetrope/Orion c

Richard Gere (*Dixie Dwyer*), Gregory Hines (*Sandman Williams*), Diane Lane (*Vera Cicero*), Lonette McKee (*Lila Rose Oliver*), James Remar (*Dutch Schultz*), Nicolas Cage (*Vincent Dwyer*), Allen Garfield (*Abbadabba Ber-*

man), Bob Hoskins (*Owney Madden*), Fred Gwynne (*Frenchy Demange*), Gwen Verdon (*Tish Dwyer*), Lisa Jane Persky (*Frances Flegenheimer*), Maurice Hines (*Clay Williams*), Julian Beck (*Sol Weinstein*), Novella Nelson (*Mme. St. Clair*), Larry Fishburne (*Bumpy Rhodes*), John Ryan (*Joe Flynn*), Tom Waits (*Irving Stark*), Ron Karabatsos (*Mike Best*), Glen Witherow (*Ed Popke*), Jennifer Grey (*Patsy Dwyer*), Wynonna Smith (*Winnie Williams*), Thelma Carpenter (*Norma Williams*), Charles "Honi" Coles (*Sugar Coates*), Larry Marshall (*Cab Calloway*), Joe Dallesandro (*Charles "Lucky" Luciano*), Ed O'Ross (*Monk*), Frederick Downs, Jr. (*Sullen Man*), Diane Venora (*Gloria Swanson*), Tucker Smallwood (*Kid Griffin*), Woody Strode (*Holmes*), Bill Graham (*J.W.*), Dayton Allen (*Solly*), Kim Chan (*Ling*), Ed Rowan (*Messiah*), Leonard Termo (*Danny*), George Cantero (*Vince Hood*), Brian Tarantina (*Vince Hood*), Rony Clanton (*Caspar Holstein*), Damien Leake (*Bub Jewett*), Bill Cobbs (*Bib Joe Ison*), Joe Lynn (*Marcial Flores*), Oscar Barnes (*Spanish Henry*), Sandra Beall (*Myrtle Fay*), Zane Mark (*Duke Ellington*), Tom Signorelli (*Butch Murdock*), Steve Vignari (*Trigger Mike Coppola*), Susan Meschner (*Gypsy*), Gregory Rozakis (*Charlie Chaplin*), Marc Coppola (*Ted Husing*), Norma Jean Darden (*Elida Webb*), Robert Earl Jones (*Stage Door Joe*), Vincent Jerosa (*James Cagney*), Rosalind Harris (*Fanny Brice*), Bruce MacVittie, James Russo (*Vince Hoods*), Giancarlo Esposito, Bruce Hubbard (*Bumpy Hoods*), Edward Zang (*Clerk*), Paul Herman, Randle Mell (*Cops*).

Considering its troubled production history (reportedly $47 million was spent) and the fact that director Coppola was brought in by producer Evans at the last minute to salvage his dream project (inspired by a book of photographs of the famed Cotton Club in Harlem), THE COTTON CLUB is surprisingly good. Returning to the genre that had made him a force in Hollywood with THE GODFATHER and THE GODFATHER II, Coppola presents a vivid, exciting, wholly entertaining musical gangster film. Although at times the film suffers from an uneven script (Coppola did considerable tinkering with Kennedy's screenplay), its strengths outweigh its weaknesses. A melange of history and fiction, THE COTTON CLUB follows Gere, a jazz cornet player trying for a big break. One night, while playing in a small club, he attracts the attention of local gangster Dutch Schultz (Remar)–the warlord of Harlem. Schultz calls Gere over to the table and the horn player is introduced to a young girl, Lane, who enjoys hanging around gangsters. During the conversation an attempt is made on Remar's life and Gere saves the mobster. Grateful, Remar decides to make Gere a pet favorite and entrusts the musician with escorting Lane to and from wherever she wants to go. Remar also hires Gere's ambitious brother Cage as a bodyguard. Though Gere tries hard to ignore her advances, he finally succumbs to Lane's charms and the two indulge in a quiet affair. Now most of the action swirls around famed Harlem nightspot the Cotton Club, owned by gangster Owney Madeen (Hoskins). Hoskins and his right-hand man Gwynne seem to be the center of the gangland universe and are looked upon to settle disputes among mob factions. Meanwhile, another story develops. The Cotton Club is owned by whites and whites only are allowed to enter–but all the entertainers are black. Duke Ellington's band plays there, Cab Calloway (Marshall turns in an amazing impersonation) is a regular feature, and a score of singers and dancers. The Hines brothers (Gregory and Maurice) try out for a dancing job at the Cotton Club and are hired. Gregory immediately spots a singer, McKee, and falls in love. She won't have much to do with him because she's looking for bigger things. A light-skinned black, McKee can pass for white and has been doing so with several rich white men. During the course of the film, McKee's defenses break down and she starts an affair with Gregory, but she knows it can't last. Meanwhile, Gregory begins to pull away from his brother in the popularity contest and he breaks up their act to go solo. This crushes Maurice, he disowns Gregory, refuses to talk to him, and quits the club. In the meantime, things have gone from bad to worse on the mob front. Remar has become too big for his britches and has made too many enemies among the rest of the underworld. Gere gets fed up with Remar and Lane and he goes off to Hollywood where he becomes a big movie star in gangster pictures (his character is obviously patterned after George Raft). Gere's brother Cage gets a bit too ambitious and tries to start his own gang. Because of his violence and the accidental murder of two children during a hit, he is dubbed "Mad Dog" by the press (Cage's character is obviously based on Vincent "Mad Dog" Coll). Hiding out from both the mob and the law, Cage makes a desperate move and has his boys kidnap Gwynne. This sends Hoskins into a rage and he asks Gere to come back and negotiate with his brother. Cage eventually releases Gwynne, but he has ensured his own death and dies in a hail of bullets. Remar's days are numbered as well. The Italian mob, represented by "Lucky" Luciano (Dallesandro) wants Remar out and Hoskins gives his approval for the hit. Meanwhile, after a long separation and being urged on by McKee, Gregory Hines finds his brother Maurice dancing in a small club and, in a very emotional scene, the brothers make amends and dance a stunning number together. Later, back at the Cotton Club, Hines performs a scorching solo tap dance routine. Intercut with this is the murder of Remar, which then dovetails into a scene at the train station where Lane and Gere reunite and go back to Hollywood. Gwynne bids his buddy Hoskins farewell as the gangster goes off to jail to serve a brief term, and Gregory Hines and McKee go off together. The final scene is an exhilarating, very romantic sendoff that serves as a loving homage to the films of the 1930s. THE COTTON CLUB is a sumptuously produced film that captures the flavor and look of the period in the perfectly flashy Hollywood manner. Though not handled as deftly as the multi-layered plots of the GODFATHER movies, Coppola does spin an entertaining web of stories with considerable flair. Unfortunately, great performances from the Hines brothers, McKee, Cage, Beck (as Remar's creepy enforcer), and especially Hoskins and Gwynne are nearly unbalanced by Remar's over-the-top histrionics as Schultz, Gere's lackluster portrayal, and Lane, who is just plain miscast. The film seems unbalanced by giving us too much of the fairly mundane romance between Gere and Lane and not enough of the Hines brothers' relationship, McKee's relationship with Gregory Hines, Hoskins and Gwynne's incredibly funny friendship, or, perhaps the most interesting–the forming of the black underworld which is only alluded to in a few fascinating scenes. These are all minor annoyances, for in an age where American films seem to be about nothing, THE COTTON CLUB is so jam-packed with interesting characters and situations it is like sitting down to a feast (the film was obviously trimmed heavily to fit into the standard two- hour running time. Have producers forgotten that THE GODFATHER ran three hours and THE GODFATHER II nearly four hours and they made more money than most films ever made?). The musical numbers in the film are incredible. Mostly derived from the Duke Ellington tunes made famous at the Cotton Club, the score is nonstop jazz. As stated above, Marshall turns in an amazing imitation of Cab Calloway performing "Minnie the Moocher," but the real showstopper is McKee's rendition of "Ill Wind," (Ted Kohler, Harold Arlen), her performance coupled with Coppola's sweeping camera moves makes for one breathtaking sequence. Though most certainly too flawed to approach the status of Coppola's best works, THE COTTON CLUB is a vastly entertaining film that will hold up to several viewings. A sad footnote: one of the highlights of the film is a beautifully executed montage sequence that harkens back to the terrific montage "passing of time" sequences in the films of the 1930s. The montage was directed by Francis Coppola's son Giancarlo and it was definitely a sign of things to come. Tragically, Giancarlo was killed in a boating accident in 1986. Songs include: "The Mooch," "Ring 'Dem Bells" (Duke Ellington, Irving Mills), "Drop Me Off in Harlem" (Ellington, Nick Kenny), "Cotton Club Stomp "Cotton Club Stomp " "Creole Love Call" (Ellington), "East St. Louis Toodle-Do" (Ellington, Bubber Miley), "Truckin'" (Ted Koehler, Rube Bloom), "Minnie the Mooch- er" (Koehler, Harold Arlen), "Mood Indigo" (Ellington, Mills, Albany "Barney" Bigard), "Copper Colored Gal" (Benny Davis, J. Fred Coots).

p, Robert Evans; d, Francis Coppola; w, William Kennedy, Coppola (based on a story by Kennedy, Coppola, Mario Puzo, inspired by a pictorial history by James Haskins); ph, Stephen Goldblatt (Technicolor); m, John Barry; ed, Barry Malkin, Robert Q. Lovett; prod d, Richard Sylbert; art d, David Chapman, Gregory Bolton; set d, George Gaines, Les Bloom; cos, Milena Canonero; spec eff, Conrad Brink; ch, Michael Smuin, Henry LeTang, Gregory Hines, Claudia Asbury, George Faison, Arthur Mitchell, Michael Meachum.

Crime/Musical   **Cas.**   **(PR:O   MPAA:R)**

COUNTRY**   (1984) 105m BV c

Jessica Lange (*Jewell Ivy*), Sam Shepard (*Gil Ivy*), Wilford Brimley (*Otis*), Matt Clark (*Tom McMullen*), Therese Graham (*Marlene Ivy*), Levi L. Knebel (*Carlisle Ivy*), Jim Haynie (*Arlon Brewer*), Sandra Seacat (*Louise Brewer*), Alex Harvey (*Fordyce*), Stephanie-Stacie Poyner (*Missy Ivy*), Jim Ostercamp (*Cowboy*), Robert Somers (*Grain Elevator Operator*), Frank Noel, Jr. (*Semi Operator*), Warren Duit (*Preacher*), Conrad Doan (*Auctioneer*), James Harrell (*Bank Officer*), Dean French (*Bartender*), Betty Smith (*Secretary*), Vern Porter (*Longley*), Sandra J. Hughes (*Mrs. McAdams*), Rudy Newoff, Ambrose Knebel, Bernard Larimer, Norbert W. Bruns, Albert B. Schmitt, Norman Bennett, Roy Rechkemmer, Roland F. Miller, Ralph E. Deuhr (*Farmers*), Curtis Siemens, Donna Manbeck, Edwin Manbeck, Robert Growney, John Jones (*Band*).

William Wittliff wrote the script, coproduced with Lange and Beaudine, and began directing the movie until some basic differences emerged and Pearce, a director-cinematographer (HEARTS AND MINDS, HEARTLAND) took over the reins while Lange's boy friend, Shepard, did some further work on the script. All those backstage woes notwithstanding, this is a terrific movie that details the plight of the 1980s farmer in such a fashion that modern Iowa may well have been Oklahoma in the 1930s. Lange and Shepard are married with three children, Graham, Knebel, and Poyner. They live on their small Iowa farm with Lange's father, Brimley. Hard times are evident and they have had many ups and downs but they seem to be making it through when a huge tornado hits the area. It's early in the movie and one wonders if this is the major cataclysm the family must face. It's minor compared to what's in store. The local Farmers Home Administration is about to relieve the farmers of their land and gives them 30 days before the mortgages will be called in. It's this time frame that book-ends the picture as the family and friends must band together to avoid the "voluntary liquidation" they all face. Their farm has been in the family for a century and the prospect of losing it turns Shepard into jelly and forges Lange into tensile steel. As in the 1920s, when stockbrokers leaped from windows rather than go bankrupt, one of the local farmers takes his own life. At first, the children are blissfully unaware of the situation but soon have an inkling when they hear their normally placid parents arguing late into the night. Brimley suffers at the thought of losing the farm while Shepard takes to liquid solace from any bottle handy. As his drinking bouts become more frequent, he starts to beat up Lange and Knebel and she responds by tossing him off their land. Lange becomes increasingly forceful, not unlike Spacek in THE RIVER and Field in PLACES IN THE HEART (it was a big year for

strong women, weak men, and farm problems). The auctioneers arrive to get rid of the land and the accoutrements but they are forced to leave when a large crowd shows up and there is absolutely not one bid. In between her own ills, Lange is seen as a gutsy woman who helps out her neighbors. When a pal's sheep have been foreclosed upon, she goes to the area with her dog and herds the animals away from the men who've come to collect them. It's too bad that this movie was released at the same time as the others mentioned above, otherwise any of them might have found a larger audience. Lange was the creative force behind the movie and her excellent acting was on a par with her production abilities. Many of the people associated with the movie have rural backgrounds. Wittliff is from a small village in Texas; Lange is from an even smaller area in Minnesota; Brimley had been an Idaho rancher before his place was foreclosed upon and he took to acting to make a living. Pulitzer prize-winner Shepard's history is well known to anyone who has seen or read his plays (he's also a farm boy), and even Knebel, a local Iowan who auditioned for the role when the company moved to location, comes off a farm. Some wonderful moments of humanity in the film are what will be recalled long after the major plot points are forgotten. The dull routine of the farmer's life is depicted with affection, never affectation, and the lovely moments include a sequence with the two female children playing with mama's makeup, and the opening scene when Lange stands at her grill, frying up burgers for the men in the fields. The acting is so un-actory that it feels more like a PBS documentary than a staged, rehearsed film, and that's the supreme compliment. Perhaps a bit more drama could have been squeezed in to heighten the emotions but the creators felt it was enough to show the truth, without adding any editorial comment. COUNTRY is a film that will open many eyes, and probably moisten a few. Lange was nominated for Best Actress by the Academy as was Spacek, but both lost to Sally Field for PLACES IN THE HEART.

p, William D. Wittliff, Jessica Lange, William Beaudine, Jr.; d, Richard Pearce; w, Wittliff; ph, David M. Walsh, Roger Shearman (Technicolor); m, Charles Gross; ed, Bill Yahraus; prod d, Ron Hobbs; art d, John B. Mansbridge; set d, John Franco, Jr.; cos, Tommy Welsh, Rita Salazar; stunts, Whitey Hughes.

Drama   **Cas.**   **(PR:C   MPAA:PG)**

COURAGE   (SEE: RAW COURAGE)

COVERGIRL*   (1984, Can.) 93m Filmplan/New World c (AKA: DREAMWORLD)

Jeff Conaway (*T.C. Sloane*), Irena Ferris (*Kit Paget*), Cathie Shirriff (*Tessa*), Roberta Leighton (*Dee*), Deborah Wakeham (*Avril*), Kenneth Welsh (*Harri- son*), William Hutt (*Cockridge*), Charles Dennis (*Blitzstein*), Paulle Clark (*Eva Randall*), Tiiu Leek (*Zara*), August Schellenberg (*Joel*), Samantha Logan (*Topsy*), Ian White (*Walter*), Philip Akin (*Cairo*), Almaini (*Raoul*), Caroline Yeager (*Bunny*), Charles Jolliffe (*Owen*), Christopher Newton (*Paul*), Sandi Ross (*Dessie*), Stephanie Daniels (*Joyce*), Henry Ramer (*Klaus*), Bronwen Mantel (*Claire*), Arnie Achtman (*Taddy*), Bernard Hop- kins (*Priest*), Michelle Scarabelli (*Snow Queen*), Les Rubie (*Cabbie*), Colin Fox (*Maitre d'*).

A dislikable entry produced with the participation of the Canadian Film Development Corporation in 1981 under the title DREAMWORLD, but released regionally in the U.S. this year. Conaway (the aspiring actor from TV's "Taxi" series) is an enterprising millionaire who has made a fortune in the high-tech industry. He surrounds himself with electronic gadgets and robots, but soon finds another interest when he is introduced to the gorgeous Ferris through a traffic accident. She's trying to find fame and fortune in the glamorous world of modeling, but so far has had no luck. Moneybags Conaway, however, buys the modeling agency she works for and then sets his sights on turning her into a star–"The Dreamworld Girl–the face of the 80's." The road to stardom is paved with money-grabbing freaks, sexual misfits, unscrupulous fashion photographers, and a deceitful business partner. The latter comes in the form of Welsh, an associate of Conaway's who tries to tumble his empire. By the less-than-spectacular finale the only thing that tumbles is the film itself. It resorts to every cliche known to man, insults most creatures with an intelligence level higher than that of a newt, and bores its audience to tears. Other than that, however, COVERGIRL is okay. The only saving grace is the hint of a romance between Conaway (normally an impressive actor) and Ferris, but nothing ever develops past the embryonic stage. COVERGIRL is as shallow as its high-gloss title and will hopefully do nothing but gather dust on the shelves of video stores.

p, Claude Heroux; d, Jean-Claude Lord; w, Charles Dennis; ph, Rene Verzier (Film House Color); m, Christopher L. Stone; ed, Christopher Holmes; art d, Michel Proulx; cos, Paul Andre Guerin, Jean-Claude Poitras.

Drama   **Cas.**   **(PR:O   MPAA:R)**

CRACKERS zero   (1984) 92m UNIV c

Donald Sutherland (*Weslake*), Jack Warden (*Garvey*), Sean Penn (*Dillard*), Wallace Shawn (*Turtle*), Larry Riley (*Boardwalk*), Trinidad Silva (*Ramon*), Christine Baranski (*Maxine*), Charlaine Woodard (*Jasmine*), Tasia Valenza (*Maria*), Irwin Corey (*Lazzarelli*), Edouard DeSoto (*Don Fernando*), Anna Maria Horsford (*Slam Dunk*), Mitchell Lichtenstein (*Artiste*), Marjorie Eaton (*Mrs. O'Malley*), Edward Call (*Officer Darney*), Joseph Hindy (*Officer*

Ronnie), Charles Bouvier *(Cable Man)*, Richard Bright, Paul Drake *(Guys)*, Ed Corbett *(Kurnitz)*, James Edward Bryan *(Tyrone)*, Darryl Henriques *(Irate Motorist)*, Joe Bellan, Gary Ross *(Immigration Officers)*, Maria Alcorcha *(Mama)*, Sally Schaub *(Cosmetic Lady)*, Elba Montes *(Market Woman)*, Raymond Rios *(Painter)*.

A deplorable attempt at comedy that falls flat most of the time. Bad as it is, the movie is even more infuriating when one realizes that it was based on the delightful BIG DEAL ON MADONNA STREET (1956). Sutherland is an unemployed security guard who pals with a cadre of assorted misfits in the Mission District of San Francisco. They include Penn, a sometime thief and often guitar player (whom Penn claims he modeled after Texan Charlie Sexton); Silva, an illegal alien; Riley, a black pimp whose girl has left him with their baby (his tenderness to the child provides whatever warmth is in the film); hard-bitten meter maid Baranski; hooker Woodard; and safe-cracker Corey. In the original film, the conspirators were lovable, while here they are totally unsympathetic. Warden owns a pawnshop and knows everyone in the group but that doesn't stop them from planning to rob his safe while he is off visiting his mother. As in BIG DEAL ON MADONNA STREET, the criminals are as inept as this script and their plans (and the movie) begin to fall apart. They finally do manage to open the safe just as Warden returns to his store and shows them that there was no money in the safe in the first place. Despite the predictability of the story, there might have been moments of mirth, but Malle can't sustain a narrative and since we don't care a whit for anyone in the movie, the picture implodes in its own cynicism. It drags on and on and when the robbery is finally done we begin to breathe more easily because we sense that the end of the 92 minutes must be near. Once again, they've attempted to remake a good film and failed. Coproducer Lewis vied for the rights for more than two decades but was stymied by various copyrights. Shooting in San Francisco caused various local officials to carp due to the racial stereotypes and there had to be alterations on the script (but evidently not enough). In 1986, producer-director-writer-choreographer and sometimes-genius Bob Fosse tried to do the same story in blackface with his Broadway presentation of "Big Deal," using hit songs from the 1930s. It failed and lost about $5 million. When are hungry producers and directors going to realize how foolish their efforts are when it comes to redoing classics or even near-classics?

p, Edward Lewis, Robert Cortes; d, Louis Malle; w, Jeffrey Fiskin (based on the movie BIG DEAL ON MADONNA STREET by Suso Cecchi D'Amico, Mario Monicelli, Agenore Incrocci, Furio Scarpelli); ph, Laszlo Kovacs (Technicolor); m, Paul Chihara; ed, Suzanne Baron; prod d, John J. Lloyd; set d, Hal Gausman; cos, Deborah Nadoolman; spec eff, Larry Roberts; m/l, "We Got More Than We Need," Michael McDonald, Ed Sandford.

Comedy   Cas.   **(PR:A-C MPAA:PG)**

CREEPS   (SEE: SHIVERS, Pol.)

CRIMES OF PASSION zero   (1984) 102m China Blue/New World c

Kathleen Turner *(Joanna Crane/China Blue)*, Anthony Perkins *(Rev. Peter Shayne)*, John Laughlin *(Bobby Grady)*, Annie Potts *(Amy Grady)*, Bruce Davison *(Hopper)*, Norman Burton *(Bateman)*, James Crittenden *(Tom)*, Peggy Feury *(Adrian)*, Dan Gerrity, Vince McKewin *(Men)*, Lisa Hayslip *(Hooker)*, Terry Hoyos, Deanna Oliver, Patricia Stevens *(Women)*, Gordon Hunt *(Group Leader)*, Janice Kent *(Patty)*, Christina Lange *(Lisa)*, Stephen Lee *(Jerry)*, Roxanne Mayweather *(Hooker)*, Yvonne McCord *(Sheila)*, Pat McNamara *(Frank)*, Thomas Murphy *(Chambers)*, Gerald S. O'Loughlin *(Ben)*, Ian Petrella *(Jimmy's Friend)*, Janice Renny *(Stripper)*, John Rose *(Arthur)*, John G. Scanlon *(Carl)*, Louise Sorel *(Claudia)*, Seth Wagerman *(Jimmy)*.

Just when you thought it was safe to go see a Ken Russell movie and that he'd gotten over his excesses, his indulgences, and his ego, along comes CRIMES OF PASSION to prove you wrong. This is one of the most offensive films Russell, or anyone, has ever made, and plumbs new depths. It's technically brilliant, as are most of Russell's movies, but his subject matter is so bizarre that it almost induces nausea. The first time around for the movie it received an "X" rating. After considerable editing, that was softened to an "R," although it still is something no child should be allowed to see, under *any* circumstances. Turner is a prim clothes designer by day and lives a double life by night. When darkness falls, she doffs her conservative togs, dons a cheap blonde wig, and garish attire, and becomes a $50 streetwalker, sort of a *Belle De Nuit*. Perkins is, once again, a deranged person. This time, he's a fanatic minister who claims he wants to save her. He is given to practicing voyeurism on nude dancers, then shouting his sermons to anyone who will listen in the local vice area of the city. Turner's motivation is that she is basically a sexual person, but can't give vent to those lusts in her daytime capacity, so she has taken this second personality in order to satisfy her passions. Perkins is, deep down, a man who would like to be a woman, and that comes out in a few of his speeches. In a subplot, Laughlin and Potts are a married couple with no sex in their union after a dozen years. She doesn't want him at all, no matter how much he pleads. Laughlin is an electronics repair person and when Turner's boss thinks that she may be pirating designs and taking them elsewhere, Laughlin gets a side job of shadowing her. To that end, he becomes one of her customers, when he sees what she is up to. The picture winds up as Perkins seems about to murder Turner in a violent takeoff of Sadie Thompson and her minister, but

that's switched as Perkins drops the knife he has in his hand and sits down at the piano to play and sing "Get Happy." The picture is often funny, perhaps deliberately, but we can't always be certain with Russell. Perkins has been making a living for more than two decades by playing madmen or, at least, misunderstood men. It's about time he assumes a role more in keeping with the real Perkins, a father and happily married husband. There is so much psycho babble in the film that it begins to resemble one of those afternoon telephone talk shows which feature analysts giving thumbnail advice to patients on the edge of reality. Turner is a terrific actress, as proven by BODY HEAT, ROMANCING THE STONE, and, in 1986, PEGGY SUE GOT MARRIED. As the clothing designer, she is perfection. When she becomes the hooker, she goes over the top (perhaps that was Russell again exercising his excess). The jokes are smarmy, lower than high school in their aim, and elicits moans from anyone with taste. Whether Perkins is an accredited reverend or a lay minister (no pun intended) is never totally established. Sandler's screenplay is mean-spirited and seems to come from the typewriter of a man who doesn't like women. He is the man who also wrote another apparently anti-feminine movie, MAKING LOVE, which was the story of a married man who gives up his wife for another man. 'Nuf said on *that* subject. At best, the picture satirizes America's morality. At worst, which is most of the time, it becomes a self-parody. The technique, the camerawork, and half of Turner's performance are the only elements which merit attention. Otherwise, pass on this. Brian De Palma-like effort to rip off Luis Bunuel's much more interesting BELLE DE JOUR (1968).

p, Barry Sandler, Donald P. Borchers; d, Ken Russell; w, Sandler; ph, Dick Bush; m, Rick Wakeman; ed, Brian Tagg; prod d, Richard Macdonald; art d, Stephen Marsh; set d, Christopher Amy, Gregory Melton; cos, Ruth Myers; m/l, "It's a Lovely Life," Wakeman, Norman Gimbel.

Drama   Cas.   **(PR:O MPAA:R)**

DADDY'S DEADLY DARLING zero   (1984) 83m Safia S.A./Aquarius c (AKA: DADDY'S GIRL; THE PIGS) c

Toni Lawrence *(Lynn Webster)*, Marc Lawrence *(Zambrini)*, Jesse Vint *(Sheriff Dan Cole)*, Walter Barnes *(Doctor)*, Katherine Ross *(Miss Macy)*, Jim Antonio, Erik Holland, Paul Hickey, Iris Korn, William Michael.

Garbage comes in many forms, but they had to scrape the bottom of the pigpen to find this one. Marc Lawrence is a geek who runs a roadside cafe connected to a pigpen. Instead of feeding his animals the usual slop, Lawrence kills passersby and uses them as feed. When traumatized Toni Lawrence–an escapee from a mental hospital–takes a job at the cafe she lends a helping hand to the owner...after all, slaughtering humans is a tough job. Their game is exposed by neighbor Ross (not the Katharine Ross of GRADUATE fame) who informs the local sheriff, Vint, a redneck dolt who doesn't believe her story. Shot in 1972 as THE PIGS, DADDY'S DEADLY DARLING is not only reprehensible, but boring and poorly executed. This is the kind of film that makes you want to go home and eat sausage in revenge.

p&d, Marc Lawrence; w, F. A. Foss [Lawrence]; ph, Glenn Roland, Jr. (CFI Color); m, Charles Bernstein; ed, Irvin Goodnoff; set d, Boris Michael.

Horror   **(PR:O MPAA:R)**

DADDY'S GIRL   (SEE: DADDY'S DEADLY DARLING)

DARK ENEMY **   (1984, Brit.) 82m Children's Film Foundation c

Rory Macfarquhar *(Aron)*, Martin Laing *(Barnaby)*, Chris Chescoe *(Garth)*, David Haig *(Ash)*, Douglas Storm *(Ezra)*, Jennifer Harrison *(Ruth)*, Helen Mason *(Rosemary)*, Cerian Van Doorninck *(Beth)*, James Guest, Isobel Mason, Oliver Hicks, Bethan Van Doorninck, James Mills, Philip Dragoumis, Mark Wallace, Elissa Phipps, Alan Chapman.

A children's film set in a post-nuclear holocaust age when most adults have died out and the young are left in control. Macfarquhar is a farm boy who searches for answers to the questions he has about the past. By the finale his worst nightmares are realized as he discovers the truth: that greed caused the holocaust. A surprisingly depressing film which informs children that the world isn't all sugarplum fairies and wooden soldiers...but is that really necessary?

d, Colin Finbow; w, Finbow, The Children's Film Unit; ph, Amos Richardson; m, David Hewson; cos, Griselda Wallace; makeup, Wallace.

Children's   **(PR:A MPAA:NR)**

DE STILTE ROND CHRISTINE M...
       (SEE: QUESTION OF SILENCE, A, Neth.)

DEATHSTALKER, THE*½   (1984) 80m Palo Alto/New World c

Richard Hill *(Deathstalker)*, Richard Brooker *(Oghris)*, Victor Bo *(Kang)*, August Larreta *(Salmaron)*, Marcos Woinsky *(Gargit)*, George Sorvic *(King Tulak)*, Horace Marassi *(Creature Leader)*, Maria Fournery *(Anella)*, Sebastian Larreta *(Talan)*, Claude Petty, Rudy Kumze *(Guards)*, Barbi Benton *(Codille)*, Lana Clarkson *(Kaira)*, Bernard Erhard *(Munkar)*, Lilliam Ker *(Toralva)*, Adrian De Perio *(Nicor)*, Boy Olmi *(Young Man)*, Patrick

Duggan (Colobri), Gabriela Rubinstein (Tarra), Amalia Marty (Zaptiah).

Shot in Argentina, this low-budget fantasy tried to take advantage of the public's brief love affair with sword-and-sorcery movies that was occurring at the time. The special effects were tacky, the acting ordinary, and the script almost nonexistent, but there were a passel of semi-clad beauties and a number of clanging sword battles. Hill is a man who roams the world like an early-day Charles Bronson, Chuck Norris, or Sylvester Stallone (as Rambo), He is a warrior looking for new lands to conquer, new women to ravage, and new excitement to stir his blood. Benton is a princess, daughter of king Sorvic. She's currently in the slimy hands of Erhard, a Telly Savalas-type bald wizard. Hill has no particular love for Benton or anyone else but he has heard that Erhard possesses an amulet that can give him magical powers. Next thing you know, Hill is headed for Erhard's castle. On his way there for the inevitable conclusion, Hill meets and vanquishes animal creatures, humans, and even has a brief association with Clarkson, a topless fencer whose skill with the sabre is second only to her jiggling. Meanwhile, back at Erhard's castle, he is no paragon of virtue and there are several moments of orgiastic proceedings as well as a brief interlude of mud wrestling. The climactic scene is a grand tournament of jousting and other deadly athletic games between Hill and everyone else, with the winner getting Erhard's position as local wizard as well as the pick of all the lasses who live in Erhard's harem. The movie looks as though it was shot on a budget somewhat smaller than the local six o'clock newscast. Benton's body was, as always, gorgeous to look at and anyone who has followed her career has seen that she's become a better actress with each job. Her acting took a brief respite when she called time out to have her first child in 1986. She and her husband, real estate tycoon George Gradow, live in a Pasadena mansion know as "PegFair" that is far more attractive than Erhard's castle in the film. "Pegfair" was built to outshine "PickFair," (the home of Mary Pickford and Douglas Fairbanks) when the builder couldn't get an invitation to that Beverly Hills address. He erected a fabulous house on spectacular grounds and it was eventually acquired by Benton and Gradow in the 1970s.

p, James Sbardellati, Hector Olivera, Alex Sessai; d, John Watson; w, Howard Cohen; ph, Leonardo Rodriguez Solis, m, Oscar Cardozo Ocampo; ed, John Adams, Silvia Ripoll; art d, Emilio Basaldua; set d, Mary Spargarino; cos, Maria Julia Bertott; spec eff, John Buechler.

Historial Adventure   Cas.   (PR:O   MPAA:R)

DELIVERY BOYS*   (1984) 94m New World/Pegasus c

Joss Marcano (Max), Tom Sierchio (Joey), Jim Soriero (Conrad), Nelson Vasquez (Izzie), Victor Colicchio (Tony), Naylon Mitchell (Jazz Mace), Ralph Cole, Jr. (Wild Man), Jody Oliver (Angelina), Deckard Fontanes (Paulie), Lisa Vidal (Tina), Kelly Nichols (Elizabeth Belmont), Jerome Bynder (Septimus Belmont), Kuno Sponholz (Dr. Schmidt), Frank Canzano (Elmer Goodale), Craig Horrall (Young Intern), Taija Rae (Stripper No. 1), Suzanne Remey Lawrence (Stripper No. 2), Deborah Quayle (Beautiful Girl), Yvette Edelhart (Mama Ciucaferri), Anthony Matteo (Spiro), Geralynn Gerard (Buxom Lady), Joey Faye (Baggy Pants Comic), Carolyn Green (Deborah), Veronica Hart (Feiffer Woman), Annabelle Gurwitch (Woman with Big Hat), Jeff Nielsen (Man with Beret), Mario Van Peebles (Spider), Samantha Fox (Woman in Tuxedo), Joseph Maldonado (Miguel), Rob Roy (Macho Policeman), Jo-Ann Marshall (Passenger), Naima Eriksen (Librarian), Scott Baker (Snooty Man), Carlos Jiminez (D.J.), John Debello (Policeman), Crist Swann (Babcock), Sammy Luquis (Sike), Rodney Harvey (Fast Action), Frank Lynn (Funky Frankie), Alex Wood (Mighty Whitie), George Ovalle (Sailor), Richie Pinero (Sir Fresh), Jose Roman (Thunder), Angel Valentin (Tiny), Eddie Gonzalez (Scandal), Pablo Vasquez (Mr. Spin), Israel Crespo (Kid Swipe), Eddie Roman (Fast Frost), Marilyn Randall (Judge), Galli Horacio (Bus Driver), Kenji Takabayashi (Danceman), Paul Vargas (Big Shot No. 1), Jorge Gonzalez (Big Shot No. 2), Andre De Lise (Big Shot No. 3), Kevin Rogers (Boy with Radio), Elizabeth Stern (Old Lady), Susan Mitchell, Linda Ipanema, John Eitel, Michael Masone (Statues).

An inane film about three pizza delivery boys who want to enter a breakdancing contest for the $10,000 prize. Before they can get to the contest, the young men must deliver pizzas and, as expected, it leads to some rather strange hijinks. One lad gets caught up with a Nazi doctor; one encounters a bizarre sculptor; and the third gets the obligatory sexy woman. Finally the kids end up in the big breakdance contest against their rivals and the results are predictable. Though the story is silly and worthless, this is a somewhat unique film in that writer/director Handler was a youth counselor who used many former street gang members in DELIVERY BOYS.

p, Craig Horrall, Per Sjostedt; d&w, Ken Handler; ph, Larry Revene; ed, Gary Karr; art d, George Brown; cos, The Bob Pusilo Studio; ch, Nelso Vasquez; makeup, Laurie Aiello.

Comedy   Cas.   (PR:O   MPAA:R)

DELUSION   (SEE: HOUSE WHERE DEATH LIVES, THE)

DEMONIOS EN EL JARDIN   (SEE: DEMONS IN THE GARDEN, Span.)

DEMONS IN THE GARDEN**   (1984, Span.) 100m Producciones Cinematograficas/International Spectrafilm c (DEMONIOS EN EL JARDIN)

Angela Molina (Angela), Ana Belen (Ana), Encarna Paso (Gloria), Imanol Arias (Juan), Eusebio Lazaro (Oscar), Alvaro Sanchez-Prieto (Juanito), Francisco Merino (Traveling Salesman), Rafael Diaz (Osorio), Pedro Del Rio (Projectionist), Eduardo McGregor (Family Doctor), Luis Lemos (Clerk), Francisco Catala (Street Vendor), Pedro Basanta (Specialist), Amparo Climent (Maid), Jorge Roelas (Tono).

An emotionally packed look at Spain in the 1950s, centering on one bourgeois family and its members' ability to manipulate each other. The family is made up of two brothers, a sister, a domineering grandmother, an adopted sister–who marries the older brother while making love to the younger one–and a son who results from her extramarital, intra-Familial affairs. The story begins in 1942 but jumps ahead 10 years to postguerra Spain where Molina, the adopted sister, struggles with the factions of her family in the raising of her son. Heavy on symbolism, the film contrasts the brothers–the younger is a sexual dynamo who despises commerce, adores feudal society, and eventually becomes a servant of El Caudillo, Francisco Franco, while the older brother is presented as an impotent bourgeois. The young boy (Sanchez-Prieto in a startling show of naturalism) is the synthesis of the two–a melding of both the sexual and social opposites of the family. A lesser director would break under the weight of such themes, but Manuel Gutierrez Aragon handles it all with adroit grace. He even tackles a scene of an enormous bull (a powerful macho symbol) thundering through a wedding party. The uninvited guest is nearly shot, but the younger brother protests in favor of the animal, exclaiming that he "just wants to play." DEMONS IN THE GARDEN is an effective and poetic film, and one of a handful of such memorable Spanish pictures this year, including Carlos Saura's CARMEN, Victor Erice's EL SUR, and the Academy Award-winning TO BEGIN AGAIN. (In Spanish; English subtitles.)

p, Luis Megino; d, Manuel Gutierrez Aragon; w, Gutierrez Aragon, Megino; ph, Jose Luis Alcaine; m, Javier Iturralde; ed, Jose Salcedo; prod d, Andrea D'Odorico; cos, Flora Salamero.

Drama   (PR:O   MPAA:R)

DESIREE½**   (1984, Neth.) 96m Cosmic Illusion/The Movies c

Marian Rolle (Desiree), Dan Strayhorn (Freddy), Cynthia Belgrave (Mother), Joanne Jacobson (Mrs. Resnick), Maxwell Glanville (Father Siego), Askina Touree (Desiree, as a Child).

A compelling though stagey Dutch film shot in New York with English-speaking actors. Based on a real-life 1980 incident, DESIREE tells the story of a black woman who loses her mind and believes her infant child to be possessed, causing her to burn it alive in her oven. As the woman, Rolle wanders around town taking care of an imaginary baby. Only through flashbacks do we learn of the incidents that led up to this horrific act. Mothered by a domineering woman and "uncled" by any number of men, Rolle eventually turned to a religious sect known as the True Confessors. The sect's rules are rigid and when Rolle becomes pregnant she is excommunicated. Her life takes a downhill slide until the pressure finally causes her rationality to give way. A jarring performance by Rolle (who also sings quite well in the film) is the film's biggest plus, for without her abilities the drama wouldn't play at all. It's all rather stiff, however, and never seems to successfully shed its origins as a play.

p, Norman de Palm; d, Felix de Rooy; w, de Palm (based on his play); ph, Ernest Dickenson; m, Ronald Snijders; ed, Edgar Burcksen, Jacques Marcus; m/l, Marian Rolle.

Drama   (PR:O   MPAA:NR)

DIARY FOR MY CHILDREN**   (1984, Hung.) 106m Mafilm-Hungarofilm/New Yorker bw (N APLO GYERMEKEIMNEK)

Zsuzsa Czinkoczi (Juli), Anna Polony (Magda), Jan Nowicki (Janos/Juli's Father), Tamas Toth (Janos' Son), Pal Zolnay (Grandpa), Mari Szemes (Grandma).

A sobering tale of Stalinist purges in Hungary during the period of 1943 to 1956 starring Czinkoczi as a teenaged Hungarian girl whose father disappears in the Soviet Union after being arrested without explanation. When Czinkoczi's mother dies, she returns to Hungary to live with Polony, a former revolutionary and now a deeply political newspaper editor. Polony's strong political convictions turn Czinkoczi away. The young girl retreats to afternoons in movie houses with Polony's friend, Nowicki, a factory worker who eventually ends up in prison for his beliefs. Czinkoczi's only choice is to pay regular visits to Nowicki's cell. The reason behind Czinkoczi's devotion is that Nowicki reminds her of her father, and in fact is played by the same actor in flashbacks. DIARY FOR MY CHILDREN is a profoundly moving and political picture, mainly because director Meszaros has brought her own experiences to the screen. She, like the young heroine in the movie, was separated from her father (sculptor Laszlo

Meszaros) in 1938 and returned to Hungary in 1946. Surprisingly honest politically (Meszaros makes use of actual newsreel footage intercut with the drama), DIARY FOR MY CHILDREN is a film which probably would have resulted in the director's imprisonment, if it had been able to be made at all, in more oppressive times. Awarded the Special Jury Prize at the 1984 Cannes Film Festival as well as winning the Grand Prize at the National Film Festival, in Hungary. (In Hungarian: English subtitles.)

d&w, Marta Meszaros; ph, Miklos Jancso, Jr.; m, Zsolt Dome; ed, Eva Karmento; prod d, Eva Martin.

Drama   **(PR:O   MPAA:NR)**

DIE FLAMBIERTE FRAU   (SEE: WOMAN IN FLAMES, A, Ger.)

DIE UNENDLICHE GESCHICHTE
                          (SEE: THE NEVERENDING STORY)

DOG DAY zero   (1984, Fr.) 101m Swanie-TopI-TFI-Cinetele/UGC c
                                                        (CANICULE)

Lee Marvin (*Jimmy Cobb*), Miou-Miou (*Jessica*), Jean Carmet (*Socrate*), Victor Lanoux (*Horace*), David Bennent (*Chim*), Bernadette Lafont (*Segolene*), Jean-Pierre Kalfon (*Torontopoulos*), Grace de Capitani (*Lily*), Henri Guybet (*Marceau*), Pierre Clementi (*Snake*), Tina Louise (*Noemie Blue*), Jean-Claude Dreyfus (*Le Barrec*).

What a piece of junk! Marvin should have known better than to become involved in such a scurrilous attempt at cadging money from his fans. Marvin is a gunman on the run with his girl friend, Louise. He begins in an area filled with pigs (the nicest characters in this sleazy movie), after having arranged to have some of his French compatriots arrested by the cops. He manages to get away with a valise filled with francs taken from a bank in a small French city. The cops are trailing him in cars, with copters, with dogs, and it just doesn't seem possible or logical that he can get away. He then goes from the frying pan into the fire as he takes refuge at the home of a family that makes the Borgias look like a Disney cartoon. The patron is Lanoux, a farmer with penchants for drinking, wearing women's clothing, and posing as a scarecrow so he can watch schoolgirl nymphets who sun bathe in the nearby woods to avoid the summer temperatures. (Lanoux winds up beating these girls to death.) The farmer's meek, oppressed wife is Miou-Miou, who wants to help Marvin get away once he becomes a prisoner. She's no better than Lanoux and needs Marvin to aid her in killing the lout. Their son is Bennent (the little tyke in THE TIN DRUM), a half-nuts child who acts as though he were the illegitimate son of Cagney in WHITE HEAT and who thrives on gangster dialog. Lafont is Lanoux's maimed and oversexed sister. She sleeps with most of the workers on the farm and casts her eyes lewdly on Marvin when he appears on the scene. Lanoux's brother is the equally avaricious Carmet and he plans to steal Marvin's money. Lafont dies after trying to sleep with Marvin and he gets away, then commits suicide and Bennent stands over the body and holds Marvin's hair to the delight of the press which has been following the story. There is absolutely no redeeming value whatsoever in this story. Lots of blood, little motivation, no subtlety; a movie that died a quick and well- earned death.

p, Norbert Saada; d, Yves Boisset; w, Boisset, Michel Audiard, Dominique Roulet, Serge Korber, Jean Herman (based on the novel by Jean Vautrin 'Herman'); ph, Jean Boffety (Fujicolor); m, Francis Lai; ed, Albert Jurgenson; art d, Jacques Dugied; cos, Rosine Lan; makeup, Joel Lavau.

Crime   **Cas.**   **(PR:O   MPAA:NR)**

DOGS OF HELL   (SEE: ROTWEILER: DOGS OF HELL)

DON'T OPEN TILL CHRISTMAS zero   (1984, Brit.) 86m Spectacular
                          (Trading) International/21st Century c

Edmund Purdom (*Inspector Harris*), Alan Lake (*Giles*), Belinda Mayne (*Kate*), Gerry Sundquist (*Cliff*), Mark Jones (*Sgt. Powell*), Caroline Munro (*Herself*), Kevin Lloyd (*Gerry*), Kelly Baker (*Experience Girl*), Pat Astley (*Sharon*), Des Dolan (*Detective Constable*).

Dull, dismal, and tasteless is about the best one can say for this movie, although it's still not as offensive as a similar U.S. film, SILENT NIGHT, DEADLY NIGHT, which trod on some of the same territory. It took a year for the film to be released (or did it escape?) after shooting in London was completed. Purdom, who once was on the brink of a large Hollywood career, directed as well as starred. It seems there is a madman murdering all of the men who play Santa Claus during the holiday season. (In England, Santa is referred to as "Father Christmas.") Purdom is the Scotland Yard man assigned to track down this crazy killer and bring him to justice. Try as he might, Purdom can't make any headway and is then replaced by his underling, Jones, who takes to the assignment with relish. The Santas are seen as drunks and tramps who have accepted the temporary jobs and are now paying for them with their lives and-or horrible dismemberment, including a brutal scene where one of them is in a public restroom and is emasculated. There are several suspects, including Lake, a newsman who always seems to be present at the scene of the crime just after it happens, and Sundquist, who is in love with Mayne, the daughter of one of the slain

Santas. At one point, even Purdom is thought to be a suspect. In the end, the killer is unmasked as Lake and the psychononsense offered as the reason is that he was shocked one Christmas when he was a wee lad and has carried a hatred for the holiday ever since. The only decent performance is by Lake, who was married to Diana Dors for many years until she died of cancer. He took his own life shortly thereafter. Munro, herself a star in the genre, stops by for a cameo to sing and dance in a rock 'n' roll production number that only seems to have been inserted to relieve the tedium. Children would be well advised to stay away as it portrays the famous folk hero in a tawdry fashion and any child who might mistakenly see this film will never believe in St. Nick again.

p, Dick Randall, Steve Minasian; d, Edmund Purdom; w, Derek Ford, Al McGoohan; ph, Alan Pudney; m, Des Dolan; ed, Ray Selfe; spec eff, Coast to Coast Ltd.; makeup, Pino Ferranti.

Horror   **Cas.**   **(PR:O   MPAA:NR)**

DOOR TO DOOR**   (1984) 88m Shapiro c

Ron Liebman (*Larry Price*), Arliss Howard (*Leon Spencer*), Jane Kaczmarek (*Katherine Holloway*), Alan Austin (*Jimmy Lupus*).

A standard comedy which offers nothing more than an hour-and-a-half of mindless entertainment. Liebman is a slick salesman who travels cross country selling vacuum cleaners. He seems harmless enough, but that's all part of his gag. He's really a confidence man who is being blackmailed by Austin, a detective for the vacuum cleaner company. Along the way, Liebman meets Howard and teaches him the tricks of the swindling game. They try every trick in the book, hoodwinking car dealers and a defenseless widow before finally coming out on top of this mess. What little romance the film offers comes in the form of the pleasant Kaczmarek as the widow's swift niece.

p, Ken Wales; d, Patrick Bailey; w, Peter Baloff, Dave Wollert.

Comedy   **Cas.**   **(PR:C   MPAA:PG)**

DREAM ONE**½**   (1984, Brit./Fr.) 97m NEF Diffusion-Christel-Films
                          A2-Channel 4/COL c (AKA: NEMO)

Jason Connery (*Nemo, as a Teen*), Seth Kibel (*Nemo, as a Child*), Mathilda May (*Alice*), Nipsey Russell (*Mr. Rip/Benjamin*), Harvey Keitel (*Mr. Legend*), Carole Bouquet (*Rals-Akrai*), Michel Blanc (*Boris/Nemo's Father*), Katrine Boorman (*Duchka/Nemo's Mother*), Charley Boorman (*Cunegond*), Dominique Pinon (*Monkey*), Gaetan Bloom (*Pushkin*).

A visually stunning fantasy about the teenage son, Connery, of New York socialite parents, Blanc and Katrine Boorman (producer John Boorman's daughter). One evening after his parents have gone out on the town he lets his imagination run wild. Before you can say "20,000 Leagues Under the Sea" Connery is whisked away (via an elevator that burrows through the earth) to another planet which is heavily influenced by Jules Verne's novel. Connery (whose character name is conveniently Nemo, as in Captain Nemo) soon discovers Captain Nemo's submarine, the *Nautilusall*, and his man-monkey assistant Pinon. They embark on a number of breathtaking adventures and meet some memorable storybook characters. Keitel stiffly plays a fellow named Mr. Legend, a romantic masked avenger who has designs on May, a charming princess from "Yonderland." There's also Russell as Mr. Rip, a lover of fantasy and Connery's guide. Even Connery's jet-set parents show up in this magical land as Arctic explorers. By the finale, Connery is piloting the *Nautilus* with Pinon at his side, bravely searching for his lost love May. The film has excellent production values–dreamy and magical set design, superb camera work (by Rousselot of DIVA fame), and convincing special effects. Unfortunately, however, director Selignac's attention is focused on detail and fantasy instead of story and acting. This aside, it is still surprising that Columbia, the film's U.S. distributor, chose not to release the film. With the recent interest in fantasy and magical lands–STAR WARS, RAIDERS OF THE LOST ARK, and their clones, RETURN TO OZ (1985), THE NEVERENDING STORY (1984)– one would think that DREAM ONE would stand a chance. Produced by John Boorman, DREAM ONE employs a few of his family members–son Charley who starred in 1985's THE EMERALD FOREST, and daughters Katrine and Telshe, the latter of whom receives co-screenwriting credit. Another familial note: Jason Connery is the son of Sean Connery.

p, John Boorman, Claude Nedjar; d, Arnaud Selignac; w, Selignac, Jean-Pierre Esquenazi, Telshe Boorman (based on the novel *Vingt Mille Lieues Sous les Mers* by Jules Verne); ph, Philippe Rousselot; m, Gabriel Yared; ed, Tom Priestley; prod d, Les Productions de l'Ordinaire, Gilles Lacombe, Nikos Meletopoulos; cos, Michele Hamel; spec eff, Les Productiones de l'Ordinaire, Lacombe, Meletopoulos.

Fantasy   **(PR:A   MPAA:NR)**

DREAMSCAPE**   (1984) 95m Zupnick-Curtis/FOX c

Dennis Quaid (*Alex Gardner*), Max Von Sydow (*Paul Novotny*), Christopher Plummer (*Bob Blair*), Eddie Albert (*The President*), Kate Capshaw (*Jane Devries*), David Patrick Kelly (*Tommy Ray Glatman*), George Wendt (*Charlie Prince*), Larry Gelman (*Mr. Webber*), Cory "Bumper" Yothers (*Buddy*), Redmond Gleeson (*Snead*), Peter Jason (*Babcock*), Chris Mulkey

(Finch), Jana Taylor (Mrs. Webber), Madison Mason (Fred Schoenstein), Kendall Carly Brown (Mr. Matusik), Kate Charleson (President's Daughter), Carl Strano (Edward Simms), Brian Libby (McClaren), Bob Terhune (Dobbs), Fred M. Waugh (Bill Hardy), Timothy Blake (Mrs. Blair), Carey Fox, Marii Mak, Claudia Lowe (Tech Aides), Anna Chavez (Newswoman), Ben Kronen (Train Conductor), John Malone (Trolley Conductor), Mindi Iden (Waitress), Betty Kean (Grandma), Trent Dolan (Desk Guard), Andrew Boyer (Webber's Brother), George Caldwell (Buddy's Father), Ernest Harada (Gardener), Tina Greenberg (Nurse), Alan Buchdahl (Track Announcer), Larry Cedar (The Snakeman).

DREAMSCAPE is a perfect B movie for the 1980s. Light, fun, trashy, with political overtones and a blend of science fiction and paranoia, all calculated to keep the audience from not taking matters too seriously. Quaid is a psychic who has been using his ESPowers to pick winners at the horse races. Von Sydow is a scientist working with Capshaw. They operate a hospital research clinic for patients who have been suffering from nightmares and can't seem to free themselves of their nightly pain. Von Sydow's solution is to have gifted psychics walk inside the dreams of his tortured patients, find their fears, and alter the finales of the dreams so the patients can overcome their woes. The money for the project comes from the government and the purse strings are pulled by Plummer, a somewhat overzealous martinet who works for the intelligence department. One of the patients is Albert, the President of the U.S., a man understandably hounded by nightmares of a nuclear war. Quaid is recruited to be part of the project. He is against the whole idea but the government agents convince him. Also recruited is Kelly, who is a psychotic psychic Plummer takes a liking to. Quaid begins his work by entering the dreams of a young boy whose brain is plagued by monsters. In a sequence not unlike THE CABINET OF DR. CALIGARI or some other early German expressionist films, Quaid gets inside the boy's head and heroically slays the snake man who has been tormenting the youth. Quaid finds Capshaw attractive but she keeps him at arm's length so he decides to get to her while she's asleep on a train. Once in her dreams, Quaid makes love to Capshaw, causing her to change her conscious mind about her attraction for Quaid. This continues until she catches on to what he's doing. Albert has been so racked by his dreams that he relents on his strong stance and decides to open nuclear reduction talks with the Russians. This thought is not appealing to the right-wing Plummer, who feels that the U.S. must have a strong nuclear arsenal for defense and that any sign of weakness on the part of the country will be an indication to the USSR that we are ready to be destroyed. While doing his research, Von Sydow has discovered that if the dreamer dies while asleep, he (or she) will also die in real life. Armed with that information, Plummer sends Kelly into Albert's dream to kill him. By doing it that way, the world will think the President died peacefully in his sleep. Quaid has made friends with newsman Wendt who has learned what's about to take place. Wendt informs Quaid and is then slain by Plummer's minions for having had the information. Thus, the stage is set for the ultimate battle inside Albert's head. Quaid and Kelly will joust and the winner will then have control of the President. They slug it out in a corpse-strewn subway car after the bombs have destroyed almost everything. To win the fight, both men have to alter their physical bodies into those of monsters. Quaid manages to kill Kelly in the dream (thereby killing him in real life), saves the world from nuclear war by saving Albert, wins Capshaw's love, and eventually wreaks revenge on Plummer by slipping inside one of the zealot's dreams and knocking him off. An interesting and original idea that doesn't quite live up to the promise of the premise. Made on a tight budget, the special effects are never very convincing but the performances are all good and if you are willing to allow the suspension of disbelief to enter into your consciousness, this is a neat thriller that's enjoyable from start to finish.

p, Bruce Cohn Curtis, Jerry Tokofsky; d, Joseph Ruben; w, David Loughery, Chuck Russell, Ruben (based on a story by Loughery); ph, Brian Tufano (CFI Color); m, Maurice Jarre; ed, Richard Halsey; art d, Jeff Staggs; cos, Linda M. Bass; spec eff, Craig Reardon, Peter Kuran, Richard Taylor; animation, Edward Manning.

Science Fiction   **Cas.**   **(PR:C-O   MPAA:PG-13)**

DREAMWORLD   (SEE: COVERGIRL, Can.)

DRIFTING***   (1984, Israel) 80m Kislev/Nu-Image c (NAGOOA)

Jonathan Sagalle (Robi), Ami Traub (Han), Ben Levin (Exri), Dita Arel (Rachel), Boaz Torjemann (Baba), Mark Hassman (Robi's Father).

An impressive debut feature from one of Israel's brightest young directors, Guttman. The film, which played the festival circuit, stars Sagalle as a fearful homosexual living with his eccentric grandmother and working in her grocery store. At night, Sagalle cruises local parks, finds companions, and brings them home with him. In the meantime, Sagalle struggles with a desire to make films. Although a young man living in Israel, Sagalle cares nothing for politics or societal change. His gravest need is for love and filmmaking. Semi-autobiographical, DRIFTING has a production history which is as involved as its personal history. Guttman applied for a $100,000 production grant from the Israel Film Fund, an organization known as for the time for its bureaucratic red tape. After an initial okay from the Fund, production was postponed and halted and, amidst fund member resignations, Guttman completed the film himself within the original $100,000

budget. Considering its limiting subject matter, DRIFTING found a surprisingly large audience in Israel and has found favorable response at the Montreal and Chicago Film Festivals. (In Hebrew; English subtitles.)

d, Amos Guttman; w, Guttman, Edna Mazia; ph, Yossi Wein; m, Arik Rudich; ed, Anna Finkelstein; art d, Eitan Levi.

Drama   **(PR:O   MPAA:NR)**

DUBEAT-E-O*½   (1984) 85m duBEAT-e-o/H-Z-H c

Ray Sharkey (duBEAT-e-o), Joan Jett (Herself), Derf Scratch (Benny), Nora Gaye (Sharon), Len Lesser (Hendricks), Johanna Went (Benny's Nightmare), Linda "Texas" Jones (duBEAT-e-o's Nightmare), Zachary (Singing Telegram), El Duce (El Duce), Joseph Herrera (Wolfgang), Chuck E. Weiss (Hendricks' Sidekick).

The silliness of the Los Angeles punk rock scene is brought into full light in DUBEAT-E-O, an odd audio-visual attack which has some interesting technique but zero content. Sharkey (star of 1980's THE IDOLMAKER) is a filmmaker working on a rockumentary about real-life rock songstress Joan Jett (who long ago shed her punk rock roots in the form of an all-femme band called "The Runaways"). Sharkey, under the crunch of deadlines, is given 31 hours to complete his film by his wheelchaired financier Lesser. Sharkey then hunts down his editor, Scratch (a member of the band "Fear"), and chains him to the editing bench. Vulgarity runs rampant and nothing insightful comes out of these characters' editing room chats. If you've got an undying interest in the L.A. punk rock scene then DUBEAT-E-O may prove entertaining. Otherwise the film is a self-serving expose of a narcissistic fad. Producer-director Alan Sacks was the creator of TV's "Welcome Back Kotter." That should tell you something.

p&d, Alan Sacks; w, Mark Sheffler, El Duce, Alan & Friends (based on an idea by Sacks); ph, Robert Primes (United Color Lab Color); ed, Linda Folk, Joe Zappala; md, Doug Moody, Phillip Raves; art d, George DiCaprio; set d, Ned Parsons, Virginia Parsons; cos, Sunny Chayes; still photography, Ed Colver; "The Mentors" film by Gary Pressman.

Drama/Musical/Comedy   **(PR:O   MPAA:NR)**

DUNE**   (1984) 140m DD/UNIV c

Kyle MacLachlan (Paul Atreides), Francesca Annis (Lady Jessica), Leonardo Cimino (the Baron's Doctor), Brad Dourif (Piter De Vries), Jose Ferrer (Padishah Emperor Shaddam IV), Linda Hunt (Shadout Mapes), Freddie Jones (Thufir Hawat), Richard Jordan (Duncan Idaho), Virginia Madsen (Princess Irulan), Silvana Magnano (Reverend Mother Ramallo), Everett McGill (Baron Vladimir Harkonnen), Jack Nance (Nefud), Sian Phillips (Reverend Mother Gaius Helen Mohiam), Jurgen Prochnow (Duke Leto Atreides), Paul Smith (The Beast Rabban), Patrick Stewart (Gurney Halleck), Sting (Feyd Rautha), Dean Stockwell (Dr. Wellington Yueh), Max von Sydow (Dr. Kynes), Alicia Raonne Witt (Alia), Sean Young (Chani), Danny Corkill (Honorato Magalone), Judd Omen (Molly Wyrn).

An overwhelming $52 million science-fiction visual feast which, like a black hole, swallowed up everything that came near it including the visionary talents of director David Lynch, and emerged as one of Hollywood's biggest bombs in memory, grossing about 32 cents at the box office. Based on Frank Herbert's multi-million selling epic novel, which first appeared in magazine form in 1963, DUNE remains faithful to the writings, but in doing so gorges itself with an infinitesimal amount of facts, figures, and general information about this imaginary, futuristic science-fiction universe. At 140 minutes, DUNE is about two hours shorter than it should be to accommodate all its information (Lynch's original script, in fact, ran 200 pages and would have run four hours), thereby practically necessitating the use of a computer to translate and spew back the facts. In the opening prolog alone, there is so much background about the four planets in DUNE, that it becomes comical to attempt to absorb it. If one pays close attention (or is a devout fan of the novel), then they learn that the story takes place in the year 10,991 on four planets–"Giedi Prime," the home of the evil Harkonnens, "Kaitain," the home of the malevolent Emperor of the Universe Ferrer, "Caladan," home of the anointed savior MacLachlan, and "Arrakis," the desert planet which is best known as Dune. It turns out that Dune is the only planet in the Universe which produces "melange," a life-prolonging spice which the Harkonnens, under the leadership of the vile and disgusting leader MacMillan, have taken control of and mine for their own personal strength. Mining, however, is not easy since the planet is infested with gargantuan Sandworms which are many miles long, and are attracted to the steady, pulsating rhythms of the mining machinery. After proving his skills as a warrior and a being of supreme mental capacity, MacLachlan begins to train the subterranean people of Dune, the Fremens, his method of fighting, one based on the power of telepathy and the destructive powers of certain thoughts. Before long, an army of fighters is trained of which the best are chosen to aide MacLachlan in the toppling of Harkonnen MacMillan and emperor Ferrer. The battle is waged and MacLachlan's forces emerge victorious, MacMillan and Ferrer see the end of their reigns, and a spiritual cleansing of the planet Dune takes place with the resulting arrival of the Messiah. Even in its barest synopsis, the plot of DUNE is a difficult thing to follow, unless it is approached in its most simple terms–a blessed hero defeating the forces of evil–those which are no different than FLASH GORDON serials or of the STAR WARS trilogy (one of which–RETURN OF

THE JEDI–Lynch was asked to direct before deciding on DUNE). Herbert's novel was so complex that it was complete with appendices and lists to explain this new universe which he created. What Lynch has created is an extremely faithful adaptation of a novel, but unfortunately for him and his audience, that doesn't make for a good film (a multi- film structure, such as the STAR WARS series, may have proven more successful). Lynch, who began his career with the nightmarish ERASERHEAD on a $20,000 budget (he could have remade ERASERHEAD approximately 270 times for was spent on DUNE), had been best known in underground circles for his ability to bring aural and visual textures to life. DUNE if viewed only as an extention of Lynch's career (which includes an impressive short titled THE GRANDMOTHER, the Oscar-nominated picture THE ELEPHANT MAN, and the scheduled 1986 release of BLUE VELVET) is an interesting addition–interesting though only in a few select scenes where the director's talents show best. (The sounds designed for DUNE by long-time Lynch collaborator Alan Splet, deserve special mention since they add as much to the director's work as do the visuals.) Otherwise, however, it is just downright silly and a shameful waste of money. Lynch, who has since admitted his dislike for the science-fiction genre, is completely drowned by the enormity of the project–a project which is of such scale that it would threaten even such great epic directors as D.W. Griffith, Abel Gance, Cecil B. DeMille, or David Lean (had any of them been dumb enough to try). Lynch seems merely like a kid having fun at someone else's expense while learning his trade as best as he can, which is to be expected if someone like Dino De Laurentiis agrees to throw upwards of $50 million your way. The genesis of DUNE goes back much further than 1984 to 1973 when Arthur P. Jacobs, the producer of the PLANET OF THE APES series bought the rights to Herbert's novel. With Jacob's death, however, the project switched hands and bizarre Chilean director Alejandro Jodorowsky of EL TOPO (a cult film with a following that equals ERASERHEAD) was brought in to direct. He managed to assemble one of the most phenomenal groups of science-fiction minds that could possibly exist–French illustrator Jean "Moebius" Giraud, Swiss designer H.R. Giger, British science-fiction Chris Foss, special effects creator Dan O'Bannon, and celebrity surrealist Salvador Dali (cast in the Ferrer role of Emperor at a reported fee of $100,000 per hour). This production soon fell apart and, in 1979, wound up in the hands of De Laurentiis who hired Ridley Scott (having just completed ALIEN with the help of Moebius, Giger, and Foss) to direct, Giger to design the production, and Rudolph Wurlitzer (screenwriter of PAT GARRETT AND BILLY THE KID and TWO-LANE BLACKTOP) to write the script. De Laurentiis said, in a television interview, "To make DUNE you must be crazy, and I believe I am crazy enough, and I have the courage enough to do DUNE." He persisted and finally found Lynch, at the insistence of daughter Raffaella, the film's on-line producer, who had seen the wonderful job he had done with THE ELEPHANT MAN. Lynch and Raffaella then assembled a crew which consisted of practically everyone, everywhere who was involved with special effects and production design, including Tony Masters, the Oscar-winning art director of LAWRENCE OF ARABIA (a desert film) and 2001: A SPACE ODYSSEY (a space film), thereby qualifying him perfectly. (Among those who were involved was the company of special effects headed by John Dykstra, of STAR WARS fame, who left the DUNE after production disagreements.) Carlo Rimbaldi, a standard De Laurentiis collaborator who designed the giant mechanical ape for the remake of KING KONG was responsible for designing the Sandworms of this film. Filmed in Mexico's famous Churubusco Studios, using all eight sound stages, DUNE was some of the most magnificent sets ever committed to celluloid, including the Great Hall of Arrakeen with its hand-inlaid tile floor (which took two months to complete) and the Golden Lion Throne Room on Kaitain which is gilded in real gold. One of the most staggering feats of special effects appeared in DUNE, concerning the spice-induced bright blue eyes of the inhabitants of the planet Dune. Rather than force the actors to wear uncomfortable blue contact lenses to achieve this effect, the filmmakers decided to employ an animation technique known as rotoscoping. The result was a gargantuan task which involved coloring character's eyes in 48,000 frames, or 30 minutes of film. If the statistics and facts of the plot aren't enough, there are even more behind the scenes–some 20,000 Mexican extras, a production crew of 1,000, 75 total sets, over 10,000 total costumes, 4,000 unique specially designed costumes, 24,000 styrofoam stalactites, 100 specially constructed models, over 400 special visual effects, and 12 tons of sand. Lynch also managed to assemble a jaw-dropping international cast which ranged from such veterans as Ferrer and von Sydow to recent Oscar winner Hunt (THE YEAR OF LIVING DANGEROUSLY) to Dino's wife and Raffaella's mother Magnano to ERASERHEAD star Nance to, finally, MacLachlan, in a superb film debut.

p, Rafaella De Laurentiis; d, David Lynch, w, Lynch, (uncredited) Eric Bergren, (uncredited) Christopher De Vore (based on the novel by Frank Herbert); ph, Freddie Francis (Todd AO, Technicolor); m, Toto, Marty Paich, Brian Eno, Roger Eno, Daniel Lanois; ed, Antony Gibbs; prod d, Anthony Masters; art d, Pierluigi Basila, Benjamin Fernandez; set d, Giorgio Desideri; cos, Bob Ringwood; makeup, Gianetto DeRossi, Luigi Rochetti, Mario Scutti; spec ph eff, Barry Nolan; mechanical spec eff, Kit West, mechanical creatures, Carlo Rambaldi; models, Brian Smithies.

Science-Fiction   **Cas.**   **(PR:C-O   MPAA:PG-13)**

EDITH AND MARCEL**½   (1984, Fr.) 140m Film
13-Parafrance/Miramax c (EDITH ET MARCEL)

Evelyne Bouix *(Edith Piaf/Margot de Villedieu)*, Marcel Cerdan, Jr *(Marcel Cerdan)*, Charles Aznavour *(Himself)*, Jacques Villeret *(Barbier)*, Francis Huster *(Francis)*, Jean-Claude Brialy *(Loulou)*, Jean Bouise *(Lucien)*, Charles Gerard *(Charlot)*, Charlotte de Turkheim *(Ginou)*, Micky Sebastian *(Marinette)*, Maurice Garrel *(Margot's Father)*, Ginette Garcin *(Guite)*, Philippe Khorsand *(Jo)*, Jany Gastaldi *(Momone)*, Candice Patou *(Margot's Sister)*, Tanya Lopert *(English Teacher)*, Jean Rougerie *(Theater Director)*, Beata Tyszkiewicz.

A sentimental tale about the real-life romance between legendary French chanteuse Edith Piaf and world middleweight boxing champion Marcel Cerdan. After meeting once, the two are reintroduced in 1948 in New Jersey where Cerdan has just defeated former champion Tony Zale. Their passion for one another burns until the following year when Cerdan dies in a trans atlantic plane crash. Intercut with their headline-making romance is an everyday love story about two young Parisians who admire Piaf and Cerdan. Director Lelouch never allows the romance to rise above a level of slush and much of the film feels overly sweet. It's worth it, however, just to see postwar Paris, hear Piaf's delicate songs, and watch Cerdan Jr. capture the spirit of his father. (In French; English subtitles.)

p, Tania Zazulinsky; d, Claude Lelouch; w, Pierre Uytterhoeven, Gilles Durieux, Lelouch; ph, Jean Boffety; m, Francis Lai; ed, Hugues Darmois, Sandrine Pery; art d, Jacques Bufnoir; cos, Adrienne Ghenassia; m/l, Lai, Charles Aznavour.

Biography/Romance   **Cas.**   **(PR:A   MPAA:NR)**

EINE LIEBE IN DEUTSCHLAND   (SEE: LOVE IN GERMANY, A, Fr./Ger.)

EL NORTE****   (1984) 139m Independent Productions/Cinecom-Island Alive c

Zaide Silvia Gutierrez *(Rosa Xuncax)*, David Villalpando *(Enrique Xuncax)*, Ernesto Gomez Cruz *(Arturo Xuncax)*, Alicia Del Lago *(Lupe Xuncax)*, Eraclio Zepeda *(Pedro)*, Stella Quan *(Josefita)*, Emilio del Haro *(Truck Driver)*, Rodolfo Alejandre *(Ramon)*, Rodrigo Puebla *(Puma)*, Trinidad Silva *(Monty)*, Abel Franco *(Raimundo)*, Mike Gomez *(Jaime)*, Lupe Ontiveros *(Nacha)*, John Martin *(Ed)*, Ron Joseph *(Joel)*, Larry Cedar *(Bruce)*, Sheryl Bernstein *(Karen)*, Gregory Enton *(Len)*, Tony Plana *(Carlos)*, Enrique Castillo *(Jorge)*, Diane Civita *(Alice)*, Jorge Moreno *(Man in Bus)*.

Produced by independent filmmakers in association with the PBS TV series "American Playhouse," EL NORTE is an effective and moving drama about the strength of the human spirit and the will to survive. Villalpando and Gutierrez are brother and sister, Gautemalan Indians, who are forced to flee their village when their politically active father is murdered and their mother is taken away by authorities. They decide to go to "el norte" (the north) where–across the border in America–the siblings feel their future lies. They manage to make their way to Tijuana in hopes of finding a "coyote," a person who smuggles immigrants across the border from Mexico into California. After nearly being robbed by a hustler, Villalpando finds a man who had been recommended by a friend back in Guatemala. He directs the pair to an unused sewer pipe that serves as a tunnel between the borders. Forced to crawl on their hands and knees, their trip is a living hell as Villalpando and Gutierrez must endure the stench and a harrowing attack by rats. After making it through, they are met on the other side by their coyote. He sets them up in a cheap motel with other illegal immigrants and their search for work begins. Since there is more of a demand for women, Gutierrez is able to get a factory job right away. This soon ends when the immigration authorities raid the factory, but fortunately Gutierrez is taken under the wing of Ontiveros. She suggests that the two of them become housekeepers for the wealthy of Los Angeles. Villalpando finally gets a job as well when he's hired as a waiter's assistant for a fancy restaurant. Both work hard at their jobs, and also on learning English, determined to make good. When Villalpando receives a promotion at the restaurant a jealous Chicano calls immigration. Villalpando must flee and is now out of work. He considers an offer by a businesswoman to take a factory foreman's job in Chicago but cannot be parted from his sister. Eventually he decides to take the job, little knowing that Gutierrez has fallen sick, having contracted typhus from the rat bites. As Villalpando prepares to leave, Ontiveros arrives, pleading with him to come to the hospital. Though initially hesitant to turn down his new job, Villalpando goes to the hospital, missing his flight to Chicago. Gutierrez dies, leaving her brother alone and unemployed. Back at the motel he stands with a group of other unemployed illegals waiting for a truck that will take the men to temporary jobs. The truck arrives and Villalpando joins the other men with the cry "I have strong arms!" He is hired to do some digging on a construction site and there is haunted by images of his father who had earlier told Villalpando that unless he fought for his rights all he would ever amount to would be "a pair of strong arms" for employers. What makes the film succeed on all levels is the simplicity of its telling. Villalpando and Gutierrez are excellent in their roles, giving this real heart and substance. There is a certain naivete to their portrayals but there is never a loss of dignity by either. Though their jobs be menial, the two never lose an ounce of pride, taking great care in what they do. The cinematic style alternates between straightforward storytelling and moments of surreal imagery in the dreams of the characters. Though there certainly is a subtle political message throughout the film, this wisely is never made overt. Rather, situations are allowed to speak for themselves, carefully avoiding any obvious, heavyhanded messages. Compared by some critics to a cinematic poem, EL NORTE stands as one of the best films of 1984. Without big-name actors or an expensive budget, it delivers a powerful and a beautiful testament to the human spirit. (In English and Spanish; English subtitles.)

p, Anna Thomas; d, Gregory Nava; w, Thomas, Nava; ph, James Glennon; m, Gustav Mahler, Samuel Barber, Giuseppe Verdi, The Folkloristas, Melecio Martinez, Emil Richards, Linda O'Brien; ed, Betsy Blankett; set d, David Wasco.

Drama   Cas.   (PR:O MPAA:R)

ELECTRIC BOOGALOO: BREAKIN' 2
(SEE: BREAKIN' 2 ELECTRIC BOOGALOO)

ELECTRIC DREAMS***   (1984) 95m Virgin/MGM-UA c

Lenny Von Dohlen (*Miles*), Virginia Madsen (*Madeline*), Maxwell Caulfield (*Bill*), Bud Cort (*Edgar*), Don Fellows (*Ryley*), Alan Polonsky (*Frank*), Wendy Miller (*Computer Clerk*), Harry Rabinowitz (*Conductor*), Mariam Margolyes (*Ticket Girl*), Holly De Jon (*Ryley's Receptionist*), Stella Maris (*Woman at Airport*), Mary Doran (*Millie*), Diana Choy (*Checkout Girl*), Jim Steck, Gary Pettinger, Bob Coffey, Mac McDonald (*Removal Men*), Regina Walden, Howland Chamberlin (*Neighbors*), Patsy Smart (*Lady in Ticket Line*), Madeleine Christie (*Lady at Concert*), Preston Lockwood (*Man at Concert*), Shermaine Michaels (*Girl Outside Concert*), Lisa Vogel (*Tour Guide*), Koo Stark (*Girl in Soap Opera*), Gina Francis (*Sales Girl/Aerobic Instructor*), Giorgio Moroder (*Radio Producer*), Dr. Ruth Westheimer (*Talk Show Host*), Frazer Smith (*Deejay*).

A modern day retelling of "Cyrano" story with one major switch: this time, instead of a long-nosed romantic, the rival for the sweetie's affections is a computer. Von Dohlen is a nerdy northern California architect who is in love with his neighbor, Madsen. She lives above him in a San Francisco apartment house and he wishes he could get to know this cello-playing comely lass. Von Dohlen buys himself a microcomputer and drops it as he's bringing it to his walkup. It doesn't hurt the electronic device beyond sending it slightly awry and putting it into a realm of thought that goes past the usual computer's limitations. He unpacks the unit the way Stan Laurel might, dropping things, getting confused. Once he assembles the unit, the fun begins. Madsen's cello can be heard through the ventilation duct and the computer (using the voice of Bud Cort) falls in love with her and begins writing songs on her behalf. Von Dohlen pretends that these musical messages have been written by him, something that endears Madsen to Von Dohlen. The computer's name is Edgar and it is able to do many more things than the average machine (due to having been dropped, or so we are led to believe). It can reproduce the sound of a cello in order to play duets with Madsen, it can turn on all the appliances, it can speak well enough to convince an airlines reservation clerk that it's human, and using that voice it can (and does) call Dr. Ruth Westheimer for advice. The computer beginning to meddle in Von Dohlen's apartment (and thus finding out the true source of his creativity) is what occupies much of the second half of the film, thereby giving this a feeling of having been a Neil Simon-type play that author Lemorande couldn't get staged, so he turned it into a screenplay. ELECTRIC DREAMS relies heavily on graphics, state-of-the art video tricks, and lots of electronic music (well done by Giorgio Moroder, who also plays the role of a radio show producer), and the direction is a bit frantic, as might be expected from a first-time feature helmer. Barron is veteran of many videos for various music channels and his expertise in that field stands him in good (and sometimes bad) stead with this movie. Style seldom triumphs over substance and there is a bit of a struggle between the two. Other than the pop songs listed in the credits at the end of this review, there is some classical music by J.S. Bach and P.I. Tchaikowsky. The story gets silly from time to time and credibility must be stretched to the breaking point, but the final result is an old-fashioned love triangle made new by the fact that the third party is made of semiconductors, steel, plastic, and microchips (or whatever it is they use to make computers). Barron's previous most important credit was the Michael Jackson video for "Billie Jean." In a small role, look for the former royal sweetheart, Koo Stark, who caused a furor when she dated Prince Andrew of the British reigning family.

p, Rusty Lemorande, Larry De Waay; d, Steve Barron; w, Lemorande; ph, Alex Thomson (Metrocolor); m, Giorgio Moroder; ed, Peter Honess; prod d, Richard MacDonald; art d, Richard Dawking; set d, Peter Young; cos, Ruth Myers; m/l, "Electric Dreams," George O'Dowd, Phil Pickett, "Now You're Mine," Moroder, Helen St. John, Lemorande, "Video," "Let It Run," Jeff Lynne, "Love is Love," "The Dream," Moroder, Phil Oakey, "Together in Electric Dreams," "Chaserunner," Ian Craig Marsh, Martyn Ware, Glen Gregory.

Romance   Cas.   (PR:A-C MPAA:PG)

ELEMENT OF CRIME, THE**   (1984, Den.) 100m Per Holst Filmproduktion-Danish Film Institute c (FORBRYDELSENS ELEMENT)

Michael Elphick (*Fisher*), Esmond Knight (*Osborne*), Me Me Lei (*Kim*), Gerald Wells (*Kramer*), Ahmed el Shenawi (*Therapist*), Astrid Henning Jensen (*Housekeeper*), Janos Hersko (*Coroner*), Stig Larsson (*His Assistant*), Camilla Overbye (*1st Lotto Girl*), Maria Behrendt (*2nd Lotto Girl*), Lars von Trier (*Schmuck of Ages*), Harry Harper, Roman Moszkowicz, Frederik Casby, Duke Addabayo, Jon Bang-Carlsen, Leif Magnusson, Preben Leerdorff-Rye.

Vaguely impressive but amazingly pretentious, this Danish film shot with English dialog features Elphick (QUADROPHENIA, GORKY PARK) as a retired policeman living in Cairo who undergoes hypnosis to help him recall the details of the "Lotto Murders"--killings of little girls. He travels through a ravaged Europe (exactly what happened is never made clear, but it looks like a nuclear war). Following the advice of criminologist Knight, he begins thinking like the killer, and eventually becomes the killer himself. Shot with a great deal of visual style, the film looks terrific, but makes almost no sense, save for its insider references to various *films noir*, to Jean-Luc Godard's ALPHAVILLE, and to Fritz Lang's M, among other works. The picture also owes a debt to the surrealistic imageries of Luis Bunuel. Although it's a Danish production, director von Trier refused to let the film be dubbed into that language even for domestic showings.

p&d, Lars von Trier; w, von Trier, Niels Voersel (English translation, Steven Wakelam, William Quarshie); ph, Tom Elling (Eastmancolor); m, Bo Holten; ed, Tomas Gislason; prod d, Peter Hoimark; cos, Manon Rasmussen; m/l, "Der Letzte Tourist in Europa," Mogens Dam, Henrik Blichman, performed by Sonja Kehler.

Science Fiction   (PR:O MPAA:NR)

ELLIE zero   (1984) 88m Film Ventures c

Sheila Kennedy (*Ellie*), Shelley Winters (*Cora*), Edward Albert (*Tom*), Pat Paulsen (*Sheriff*), George Gobel (*Preacher*).

Appallingly stupid redneck comedy with a painfully inept cast. Winters, a widow with three sons, marries a rich old widower. At a picnic she pushes his wheelchair down a hill into a pond. When she orders her sons to go down and hold him under, they refuse, saying they had to kill her last two husbands. Winters herself, chicken leg in hand, sits on the old man until he drowns. Kennedy, the old man's voluptuous daughter whom Winters' sons have been lusting after, suspects what happened and vows on her father's grave to get revenge. She teases them all to their dooms, one falling off a cliff, another out of the hayloft, the third bitten by a snake in her bed. Sheriff Paulsen, though in love with Winters, finds evidence of her guilt in the old man's death and arrests her while she and Kennedy fight in the mud. Rather than send her to jail, Kennedy uses the evidence to blackmail her stepmother into marrying Paulsen. Slow and unfunny.

p, Francine Roudine; d, Peter Wittman; w, Glenn Allen Smith; ph, George Tirl (Eastmancolor); m, Bob Pickering; ed, John Davis.

Comedy   (PR:O MPAA:NR)

ERENDIRA½**   (1984, Mex./Fr./Ger.) 103m Cine Qua-Non-Les Films du Triangle-Atlas Saskia/Miramax c

Irene Papas (*The Grandmother*), Claudia Ohana (*Erendira*), Michael Lonsdale (*The Senator*), Oliver Wehe (*Ulysses*), Ernesto Gomez Cruz (*The Grocer*), Pierre Vaneck (*Ulysses' Father*), Carlos Cardan (*The Smuggler*), Humberton Elizondo (*Blacaman*), Jorge Fegan (*The Commandant*), Francisco Mauri (*The Postman*), Sergio Calderon (*The Truck Driver*), Martin Palomares (*The Messenger*), Salvador Garcini (*The Juggler*), Felix Bussio Madrigal (*The Fiance*), Juan Antonio Ortiz Torres (*The Musician*), Delia Casanova (*The Narrator*), Rufus (*The Photographer*), Blanca Guerra (*Ulysses' Mother*), Carlos Calderon (*The Missionary*), Rene Barrera (*Indian Chief*), Gaspar Humberto Mena Escobar (*Guard*).

A hallucinatory picture which brings to the screen the surrealistic images of famed South American writer Gabriel Garcia Marquez (*One Hundred Years Of Solitude*). The story is of a 14-year-old girl, Ohana, who lives in luxury with her intense grandmother, Papas. One day, however, Ohana's carelessness in extinguishing a candelabra leads to a fire which completely destroys everything Papas owns. Papas simply informs Ohana: "My poor darling, you will not be able to live long enough to pay me back." Papas sets off across the country with Ohana in tow. She first sells the girl's virginity and then continues prostituting the girl. The lengths of the lines which stretch to Ohana's tent are astonishing, as is the girl's physical and mental stamina. Ohana soon meets Wehe, an angelic customer who offers to take Ohana away from the sentence she is serving. Wehe and Ohana flee, but Papas heartily pursues and finally catches up with them. She comes between the young lovers, but by the finale they overcome her and are reunited. A bizarre picture which will appeal to those familiar with Garcia Marquez and satisfy the desire to see his writings come to the screen in a faithful manner.

p, Alain Queffelean; d, Ruy Guerra; w, Gabriel Garcia Marquez; ph, Denys Clerval; m, Maurice Lecoeur; ed, Kenout Peltier; art d, Pierre Cadiou, Rainer Chaper; cos, Albert Negron; spec eff, Sergio Jara, Ruben Rodriquez.

Drama/Fantasy   Cas.   (PR:O MPAA:NR)

ESCAPE FROM SEGOVIA***   (1984, Span.) 98m Grange Communications c

Xabier Elorriaga (Ion), Virginia Mataix (Pxuno), Klara Badiola (Maruja).

Bearded, intellectual Basque separatists escape from a Spanish prison through an elaborate scheme, then flee for France, only to be caught near the border. Excellent prison-break film filled with scenes detailing their preparations. Based on a true story that occurred in 1976. (In Spanish and Basque; English subtitles.)

p, Angel Amigo; d, Imanol Uribe; w, Amigo, Uribe; ph, Jabler Agirresarobe; m, Amaia Zubiria, Xavier Lasa; ed, Julio Pena.

Crime   **(PR:C MPAA:NR)**

EVERY PICTURE TELLS A STORY**½   (1984, Brit.) 82m Falmingo-Every Picture Ltd. c

Phyllis Logan (Agnes Scott), Alex Norton (William Scott, Sr.), Leonard O'Malley (William, Age 15-18), John Docherty (William, Age 11-14), Mark Airlie (William, Age 5-8), Paul Wilson (Tocher), Willie Joss (Grandfather), Natasha Richardson (Miss Bridle), Jack McQuoid (Mr. Trimble).

Norton returns from WW I and moves his family to Northern Ireland. He takes work as a sign painter and encourages his son's talent for painting. When Norton is killed helping to put out a fire in a shop, the townsfolk save their money to send the boy off to art school. Eventually he becomes a respected painter who incidentally was the father of the director of the film. An affectionate film (as any film dealing with one's father and grandfather must be), the film looks better than its budget should allow, but it still suffers from poor structuring of scenes and an anticlimactic conclusion after the death of Norton.

p, Christine Oestreicher; d, James Scott; w, Shane Connaughton; ph, Adam Barker-Mill (Technicolor); m, Michael Storey; ed, Chris Kelly; prod d, Louise Stjernsward.

Drama   **(PR:C MPAA:NR)**

EVIL THAT MEN DO, THE*   (1984) 90m ITC/Tri-Star c

Charles Bronson (Holland), Theresa Saldana (Rhiana), Joseph Maher (Mulloch), Jose Ferrer (Lomelin), Rene Enriquez (Max), John Glover (Briggs), Raymond St. Jacques (Randolph), Antoinette Bower (Claire), Enrique Lucero (Aristos), Jorge Luke (Cillero), Mischa Hausserman (Karl), Roger Cudney (Cannell), Constanza Hool (Isabel), Joe Seneca (Santiago), Jorge Zepeda (Victim), Alan Conrad (Fugitive), Ernesto Gomez Cruz (Cafe Owner), Angelica Aragon (Maria), Rodrigo Puebla (Farmer), Nicole Thomas (Sarah), Anais De Mello (Dominique), Eduardo Lopez Rojas (Bartender), Carlos Romano (Cripple), Miguel Angel Fuentes (Latino), Richard Brodie (Driver Gunman), Alfredo Gutierrez (Gunman), Jorge Humberto Robles (Jorge), Fernando Saenz (Assael), Ken Fritz (Stuntman).

Charles Bronson is a true aberration among actors today. While most of them are constantly bemoaning the lack of range of parts they are offered, Bronson seems to revel in limiting his range to one role, the vengeance-obsessed vigilante. Here he's a retired killer who is called out of retirement to go down to Guatemala to kill a British doctor, Maher, who is a torture expert working for the repressive regime there and protected by some sinister U.S. agency. Car chases, multiple deaths, and big guns are all seen in abundance before the finale, which has Bronson entering Maher's compound, killing scads of guards, and finally coming face to face with the villain himself, who in the end is literally torn to shreds by a swarm of his enraged and mutilated victims. To explain to Bronson the wider implications of his mission is Saldana, whose husband dies at Maher's hands gruesomely in the opening moments of the film, having been hooked up to electrodes and fried. Bronson certainly knows his way around this kind of story, and his performance is simple and direct, but although he is in impressive shape for a man of 63, he is just too old to be galivanting around the jungles of Central America with a submachine gun. Under a lot of bad or indifferent performances, though, the film does succeed in its primary goal, to provide 90 minutes of fast-moving and fairly exciting action, and as Bronson shoots up Central American fascists, he shows that his heart is in the right place, as is his trigger finger.

p, Pancho Kohner; d, J. Lee Thompson; w, David Lee Henry, John Crowther (based on the novel by R. Lance Hill); ph, Javier Ruvalcaba Cruz (CFI Color); m, Ken Thorne; ed, Peter Lee-Thompson; art d, Enrique Estevez; cos, Poppy Cannon; spec eff, Laurencio Cordero; stunts, Ernie Orsatti.

Action/Drama   **Cas.**   **(PR:O MPAA:R)**

EXECUTIONER PART II, THE zero   (1984) 85m 21st Century c

Christopher Mitchum (Lt. O'Malley), Aldo Ray (Police Commissioner), Antoine John Mottet (Mike), Renee Harmon (Celia Amherst), Dan Bradley, Jim Draftfield.

The sequel to a film that never existed, THE EXECUTIONER PART II was apparently shot some years before release and held on the shelf. Mitchum is a cop looking for the man who is killing groups of street criminals by lobbing grenades in their midst. He finds out that the killer is an old friend,

Mottet, who had saved Mitchum's life in a Vietnam flashback. No production values, unbearably bad acting, and heaps of gratuitous violence make this a film to miss.

p, Renee Harmon; d, James Bryant; ph, (Pacific Color).

Crime   **(PR:O MPAA:R)**

EXTERMINATOR 2 zero   (1984) 89m Cannon c

Robert Ginty (Johnny Eastland), Mario Van Peebles ("X"), Deborah Geffner (Caroline), Frankie Faison (Be Gee), Scott Randolf (Eyes), Reggie Rock Bythewood (Spider), Bruce Smolanoff (Red Rat), David Buntzman (Head Mafioso), Kenny Martino (Tony), Derek Evans (Squealer), Irwin Keyes (Monster), Robert Louis King (Philo), Ayre Gross (Turbo), Janet Rotblatt (Mom), Stefen Zacharias (Pop), Jennifer Brandon (Lisa), Deanna Crowe (Newscaster), Thomas Calabro (Larry), Jesse Aragon (Crackers), Marc Vahanian (Stitch), Jayne Kell (Tina), Jack Meeks (Norman Strate), Edgard Mourino (Guard), Kashka (Gang Member), Stanley Brock (Man), L. Scott Caldwell (Patron), Tom Wright (Youth), Ron Taylor (Dude), Bob Watt (Policeman No. 1), Al Sheppard (Policeman No. 2), Herb Downer (Dr. Turner), Diane Ketterling (Policewoman), Kim Kahana (Bartender), John Turturro (Guy No. 1), Paul Bates (Guy No. 2).

A very bad sequel to the equally bad THE EXTERMINATOR (1980) sees Ginty return as the ultra-violent Vietnam veteran who has gotten fed up with the sickos in society (although he doesn't notice that he's one of them himself). The "plot" sees a gang leader with delusions of grandeur, Van Peebles (son of director Melvin Van Peebles), leading his sadistic bunch of followers through the streets of New York City torturing and murdering anything in their path. When one of the victims turns out to be Ginty's girl friend, Geffner, the vet reaches for his welding mask and flame thrower and hits the bricks in hot pursuit. Whereas Ginty worked alone in the first film, for EXTERMINATOR 2 he employs his buddy, Faison, a black Vietnam vet who drives a garbage truck, to assist in cleaning the streets of vermin like Van Peebles. When the gang leader and his followers hatch a plan to steal $500,000 from the city to buy drugs from the mob, Ginty closes in. Having outfitted Faison's garbage truck with armor plating and machine-gun turrets, Ginty and his buddy do battle with the evildoers. After much graphic bloodletting the film comes fitfully to a close. A totally repugnant film which parades acts of mindless violence on top of more mindless violence to illustrate some sort of moral dilemma of our time. EXTERMINA-TOR 2 continues to propagate the myth that Vietnam veterans are trained killers with short fuses who won't hesitate to blow people's heads off on the slightest provocation. The only significant aspect of EXTERMINATOR 2 is that many video-rental patrons have confused it with the vastly superior Arnold Schwarzenegger action picture THE TERMINATOR and rented it by mistake. Believe it or not, there are songs that are supposed to be tongue-in-cheek funny, but they are just as repulsive as the rest of the film. "Return to Cinder" (Peter Bernstein), "Shake It to Bake It" (Jim Covell), "Under Fire" (Benny Harrison), "Rally 'Round the Moon" (David Webster). Stay away.

p,d&w, Mark Buntzman, William Sachs; ph, Bob Baldwin, Joseph Mangine (TVC Color); m, David Spear; ed, George Norris, Marcus Manton; art d, Mischa Petrow, Virginia Field; set d, Nell Stifel, Doree Jones, Randy Ser, Escott Norton; cos, Kristin McNiff, Toyce Anderson; makeup, Ed French.

Crime   **Cas.**   **(PR:O MPAA:R)**

EYES OF FIRE*½   (1984) 106m Elysian c

Dennis Lipscomb (Will Smythe), Guy Boyd (Mr. Dalton), Rebecca Stanley (Eloise Dalton), Sally Klein (Fay Dalton).

A technically superior independent horror picture which offers little in terms of story or character. Lipscomb is a preacher in the mid-1700s who is nearly hanged as a witch. With the help of black magic (or so it seems) Lipscomb manages to escape with his followers, taking refuge in a Shawnee Indian valley. Strange occurrences begin to frighten them and apparitions appear. Lipscomb then discovers that, in Shawnee folklore, the valley is the home of "the hunted ones" and the Devil. EYES OF FIRE is chock full of showy special effects and makeup but it's all gratuitously wasted on an empty script.

p, Philip J. Spinelli; d&w, Avery Crounse; ph, Wade Hanks (CFI Color); m, Brad Fiedel; ed, Michael Barnard; art d, Greg Fonseca; set d, John Stadelman; cos, Bernadette O'Brien; makeup, Annie Mansicalco.

Horror   **(PR:O MPAA:R)**

FALLING IN LOVE**   (1984) 107m PAR c

Robert DeNiro (Frank Raftis), Meryl Streep (Molly Gilmore), Harvey Keitel (Ed Lasky), Jane Kaczmarek (Ann Raftis), George Martin (John Trainer), David Clennon (Brian Gilmore), Dianne Wiest (Isabelle), Victor Argo (Victor Rawlins), Wiley Earl (Mike Raftis), Jesse Bradford (Joe Raftis), Chevi Colton (Elevator Woman), Richard Giza (Salesman), Frances Conroy (Waitress), James Ryan (Cashier), Sonny Abagnale (Tow Truck Driver), George Barry, L.P. McGlynn (Conductors), Paul Herman (Engineer), Kenneth Welsh (Doctor), John H. Reese, Clem Caserta (Taxi Drivers), Yanni Sfinias (Hot Dog Vendor), Rev. Donald Goodness (Priest), Florence Anglin

(Saleslady), Gerald M. Kline *(1st Man)*, Barry R. Smith *(Usher)*, John Ottavino *(Construction Worker)*.

The eagerly awaited reunion of DeNiro and Streep, whose tender relationship in THE DEER HUNTER (1978) proved to be one of the highlights of that superb film, was a heartbreaking disappointment. FALLING IN LOVE is a distinctly passionless film where deep emotions are only hinted at and all character development takes place off screen. DeNiro is a successful architect who travels from Westchester County to Manhattan every day on the same commuter train. Streep is a freelance graphic artist who also lives in Westchester County and she rides the same train to visit her ailing father in Manhattan. DeNiro is married and has two little boys. Streep is also married. The Christmas season has arrived in Manhattan and the streets are filled with shoppers laden down with packages. One evening both DeNiro and Streep are shopping in Rizzoli's bookstore on Fifth Avenue. On the way out they collide and dump their packages. Nervous and embarrassed apologies follow as they scramble to sort out the various gifts they have dropped. There is an immediate attraction between them, but they both go their separate ways. When the packages are unwrapped on Christmas morning however, each winds up giving the other's book purchase to their respective spouses. Weeks later the pair bump into each other at the train station and laugh over the accidental exchange of gifts. Their mutual attraction begins to pull harder and DeNiro suggest they ride home together. The next day they ride into Manhattan together and meet for lunch. Thus far the relationship is purely open and platonic, but DeNiro seems ready for more while Streep is still hesitant. When DeNiro is offered a job that will take him to Houston, Texas for a year, he looks to Streep instead of his wife to help him decide. Streep meanwhile, has been unable to disguise her mixed feelings regarding DeNiro and the guilt begins to show. Her husband suspects something and the marriage becomes unstable. DeNiro decides to take the initiative and he rents an apartment in Greenwich Village that he and Streep can use. Streep finally decides to take the plunge and make love to DeNiro, but when they get to the apartment she can't go through with it. They return to Westchester County in silence, and Streep watches as DeNiro is met at the station by his wife and children. When she arrives home her husband informs her that her father has died and the feelings of guilt from the affair and having not been at her father's side collide and she has an emotional breakdown. She avoids contact with DeNiro and he decides to take the job in Houston. DeNiro's wife, Kaczmarek, suspects something is wrong and in an angry confrontation he confesses his affair. Kaczmarek informs him that their marriage is over and that he will be going to Houston by himself. Now without anyone to turn to, DeNiro calls Streep's house several times, only to hear her husband answer the phone. Streep's husband finally has tangible proof of his suspicions and he too wants an end to their marriage. Streep tries to see DeNiro before he leaves for Houston, but she is too late. A year later they bump into each other at Rizzoli's. For what was supposed to be a bittersweet, forbidden romance in the tradition of BRIEF ENCOUNTER, FALLING IN LOVE presents two dull, unappealing, and unsympathetic people and tries to make us understand and appreciate their dilemma. Their characters are both fairly young and financially successful; they have nice houses and pleasant spouses. Whereas Streep's marriage appears to have some problems (complicated by the annoying screenwriter's device of the ill father), DeNiro seems devoted to his family and they to him. When the couple collide outside of Rizzoli's there is little spark between them that would warrant such an angst-filled affair. DeNiro and Streep are great actors, but at times their distinct "method" mannerisms overpower any kind of naturalness in their characterizations and they become acting machines instead of people. None of the relationships in the film is presented with any detail or reality and both DeNiro and Streep are saddled with two of the most intolerant spouses ever to hit the screen. When they learn of the affair, neither offers to work things out, forgive, understand, or even discuss it–they both simply walk out. The basic flaw in FALLING IN LOVE is the fact that no one in the film–including the lovers–seems to be in love.

p, Marvin Worth; d, Ulu Grosbard; w, Michael Cristofer; ph, Peter Suschitzky (Technicolor); m, Dave Grusin; ed, Michael Kahn; prod d, Santo Loquasto; art d, Speed Hopkins; set d, Steven Jordan; cos, Richard Bruno; makeup, Mickey Scott.

Drama   **Cas.**   **(PR:C   MPAA:PG-13)**

FAMILY GAME, THE*** (1984, Jap.) 107m Art Theater of Japan-New Century-Nikkatsu /Film Society c

Yusaku Matsuda *(Yoshimoto)*, Juzo Itami *(Mumata)*, Saori Yuki *(Mother)*, Junichi Tsujita *(Older Brother)*, Ichirota Miyagawa *(Shigeyuki)*.

A fresh and energetic domestic drama about the effects of modernism on a middle-class family. Miyagawa is a teenaged boy who lives in a crowded, prefab house with his older brother and parents. Their confines are so small that the parents must retreat to their Toyota to have private conversations. Because of Miyagawa's failing grades a tutor, Matsuda, is hired. Matsuda, a determined humanist, is, at times, patient with Miyagawa but he also resorts to slapping the teen around. Not only does he help him with his school studies, but he offers advice on growing up. On one occasion he even teaches Miyagawa self-defense. It's not until the end of the film that the normally calm Matsuda lashes out at the family and expresses his true opinions of the household. One can't help thinking, while watching THE

FAMILY GAME, that the screen has come alive. The characters almost always do the unexpected, the photography and art direction are vibrant and colorful, and young director Morita seems fully in control of the entire picture. (In Japanese; English subtitles.)

p, Shiro Sasaki, Yu Okada; d&w, Yoshimitsu Morita (based on the novel by Yohei Honma); ph, Yoneo Maeda; ed, Akimasa Kawashima; art d, Tatsumi Nakazawa.

Drama/Comedy   **(PR:C   MPAA:NR)**

FANATIC, THE   (SEE: LAST HORROR FILM, THE)

FANTASY MAN*   (1984, Aus.) 79m Centaur c

Harold Hopkins *(Nick Bailey)*, Jeanie Drynan *(Liz Bailey)*, Kerry Mack *(Donna)*, Kate Fitzpatrick *(Neighbor)*, John Howitt *(Howard)*, Colin Croft *(Art Teacher)*.

A drab story about a disenchanted Sydney, Australia, office worker, Hopkins. He is bored with his desk job, he is bored with his wife, Drynan, and she is bored with him. He retreats to Hallmark Card-ish fantasies involving the pleasant-looking Mack, who owns a nearby hamburger stand. His wife contemplates an affair with a past love, but nothing ever happens and the movie is just as boring as the characters it presents.

p, Basil Appleby, Darrell Lass; d&w, John Meagher; ph, Lesnie; m, Adrian Payne; ed, Rod Hibberd; prod d, Lass.

Drama   **(PR:C   MPAA:NR)**

FAR FROM POLAND**   (1984) 106m Film Forum bw-c

Ruth Maleczech *(Anna Walentynowicz)*, Mark Margolis *(Adam Zarewski)*, John Perkins *(Gen. Jaruzelski)*, William Raymond *(K-62)*, David Warrilow *(Voice of Gen. Jaruzelski)*.

What began as a straightforward documentary on Poland's Solidarity fight gradually developed into this pseudo-documentary which employs footage from Poland, interviews with Polish Americans, and re-enacts speeches. While in Poland in August, 1980, Godmilow found herself in the midst of a strike in the Lenin Shipyards at Gdansk. She returned to New York, raised $20,000, hired a crew of five, and intended to return to Gdansk. Martial law was quickly called, however, and she was unable to return. Even an appeal from famed Polish director Andrzej Wajda (who would soon leave his country) failed to sway the Russian-backed government. Receiving film footage from the Solidarity Film Agency in Poland, Godmilow began constructing her documentary. It was not long before the agency was disbanded and the film stopped coming. Rather than abandon the project or resort to a cliched "open" ending, Godmilow cast actors from the Mabou Mines company to portray famed Poles–Anna Walentynowicz, a 55-year-old crane operator whose firing began the strikes in Gdansk, and "K-62," a "bureaucrat's bureaucrat–and recite their published speeches. An insightful look at the situation in Poland, FAR FROM POLAND is not only highly informative (an expectation of any documentary), but manages to stretch the boundaries of fiction and documentary further than they've been stretched in quite some time.

p&d, Jill Godmilow, Susan Delson, Mark Magill, Andrzej Tymowski; ph, Jacek Laskus; m, Michael Sahl.

Docu-drama   **(PR:C   MPAA:NR)**

FEAR CITY**½   (1984) Zupnick-Curtis Enterprises/Chevy Chase Distribution c

Tom Berenger *(Matt Rossi)*, Billy Dee Williams *(Al Wheeler)*, Jack Scalia *(Nicky Piacenza)*, Melanie Griffith *(Loretta)*, Rossano Brazzi *(Carmine)*, Rae Dawn Chong *(Liela)*, Michael V. Gazzo *(Mike)*, Joe Santos *(Frank)*, Jan Murray *(Goldstein)*, Ola Ray *(Honey)*, Janet Julian *(Ruby)*, Daniel Faraldo *(Sanchez)*, Maria Conchita *(Silver)*, Nina Jones *(Dixie)*, John Foster *(Pazzo)*, Emilia Lesniak *(Bibi)*, Frank Roznio *(Harry)*, Juan Fernandez *(Jorge)*, Jim Boeke *(Architect)*, Vinny Argiro *(Bruno)*, Carl Strano *(Priest)*, Ben Kronen *(Club Announcer)*, Madison Mason *(Leila's Doctor)*, Bill Henderson *(Nicky's Doctor)*, Victor Rivers *(Jimmy)*, Joe Palese *(Tony)*, Joe Shea *(Solvi)*, Bob Yothers *(Sergeant)*, John Roselius *(Rossi's Manager)*, Tracy Griffith *(Sandra Cook)*, Lori Eastside *(Goldy's Girl)*, Barbara Andrews *(Waitress)*, James Brewer *(Referee)*, Alvaro Lopez *(Rio's Manager)*, Eddie Ruffal *(Cameraman)*, Jay Michael, Linda Lee *(Metropolis Dancers)*, Peter Mele, Robert Miano, Rafael Berko *(Hitmen)*, Anthony Ponizine, Frank Sivero *(Mobsters)*, Brent Jennings, William Kennedy *(Hawkers)*, Robert Giarratano, Peter Gumeny *(Customers)*, Justin Derosa, Adrian McKnight, John Barons *(Policemen)*, Kendal Carey Brown, Nancy Mott *(Nurses)*, Christine Greenberg *(Medical Technician)*, Pat Banta, Arnaldo L. Diaz, Sidney Filson, Daryle Ann Lindley *(Stunt Players)*.

A gritty probe into the seedy nighttime world of sex clubs and the perverts who populate them, starring Berenger as a seemingly callous manager of topless dancers. With his partner, Scalia, he runs a small-time booking agency which is in competition with Murray and his girls. The city scum rises to the top one night in the form of a demented killer who practices martial arts and keeps a diary filled with his hatred of "dirty" girls. Fear grows in the girls after a rash of vicious, perverse attacks. Berenger has reason to believe that Murray is behind the attacks in order to scare away business. But soon Murray's girls also fall victim to the madman. In the meantime, Williams, a nasty, foul-mouthed cop, threatens everyone involved–except for the killer. Most of the girls refuse to dance and the sex clubs are forced to hire unappealing types, which causes customers to head for the exit. Berenger and Murray make a pact between them to safely escort their girls to and from the clubs. The killer, however, manages to zero in on those who stray from the fold, continuing his killing spree. Berenger fears for the safety of his former girl friend, Griffith, who has left him in favor of a lesbian relationship with Chong. He also has an increasing number of flashbacks to his days as a championship boxer when he killed an opponent in the ring. Dejected by the murder of Chong, Griffith returns to her drug habit and calls on a former supplier in his dingy back-alley apartment. She is turned away when she can't come up with the necessary cash. She later returns, only to find her supplier hanging from the fire escape and the killer standing in the shadows. She is slashed, but retaliates with a shot of Mace. Berenger arrives and a fight breaks out. The killer's martial arts expertise is no match for Berenger's boxing training, however, and Berenger once again kills a man with his fists–this time in self-defense instead of sport. Berenger and Griffith manage to survive the ordeal with their love intact. Directed by Abel Ferrara (the director of MS. 45, a 1981 film which garnered much favorable criticism and a loyal following), FEAR CITY does not, like most slasher films, cater to the sexual desires of men in the audience. In less commendable films, sex and nudity are followed by a graphic murder scene. The result is a scene which is gratifying both sexually (the audience gets to see some flesh) and in terms of violence (the audience gets to see some blood). Although the killer in FEAR CITY is driven by sex, the murders are not sexually gratuitous. The only nudity (and there is a great deal of it) is seen during the dance sequences in the clubs– satisfying the audience, but not accompanying this tittilation with the mutilation of the women. Sacrificing a sugar-coating for a harsh, sleazy city portrait, FEAR CITY is definitely not a film for all tastes. With FEAR CITY there is some hope that films of this genre can exist without being entirely devoid of morality. Songs include: "New York Dolls," "Sucker City" (David Johanson, Joe Dylio, sung by Johanson), "Funn," "Two-Timer," "You're the One," "Method to Your Sadness," "Feels Like It's Going to be Good," "Rotation," "You'll Never Know," "Cowgirl Blues," "Liar on the Wire," "Get Tough," "Keep On," "Walking Slow," "Povero Amico Mio."

p, Bruce Cohn Curtis, Jerry Tokofsky; d, Abel Ferrara; w, Nicholas St. John; ph, James Lemmo (DeLuxe Color); m, Dick Halligan; ed, Jack Holmes, Anthony Redman; set d, Cricket Rowland; cos, Linda M. Bass.

Crime   Cas.   (PR:O MPAA:R)

FINDERS KEEPERS½   (1984) 96m CBS/WB c

Michael O'Keefe (*Michael Rangeloff*), Beverly D'Angelo (*Standish Logan*), Louis Gossett, Jr. (*Century*), Pamela Stephenson (*Georgiana Latimer*), Ed Lauter (*Josef Sirola*), David Wayne (*Stapleton*), Brian Dennehy (*Mayor Frizzoli*), Jack Riley (*Ormond*), John Schuck (*Police Chief Norris*), Timothy Blake (*Estelle Norris*), Jim Carrey (*Lane Biddlecoff*), Robert Clothier (*Art Bumbalee*), Jayne Eastwood (*Anna-Marie Biddlecoff*), Alf Humphreys (*Mulholland*), Barbara Kermode (*Isadora Frizzoli*), Paul Jolicoeur (*Deputy Police Chief Dunaway*), Blu Mankuma (*Wade Eichorn*), Richard Newman (*Pawnbroker*), Nadine Gardner (*Frances Flanagan*), Campbell Lane (*Stanton Gilmore*), Wayne Robson (*Zev Tyndale*), Margaret Martin (*Flo Humberside*), Judy Leigh-Johnson (*Harriet Frizzoli*), Kevin Cork (*Hotel Night Clerk*), John Stocker (*UBS Editor*), Harvey Atkin (*Salesman in Train*), J.C. Roberts (*Pilkington Man*), Peter Haworth (*Weld*), Kymm Dungy, Margaret Hertlein (*Unholy Rollers*).

A crazy, quirky comedy from Richard Lester that starts slow and warms up to provide some funny moments. One of the few films from the abortive attempt by CBS to establish a theatrical division (which ended in early 1986), FINDERS KEEPERS failed to find much of an audience, despite a cast of box office favorites, or so it seemed. Set in 1973, which makes it almost, but not quite, a period comedy, Lester takes advantage of 11 years of hindsight to poke fun at that moment in time and demonstrate some of the differences in the decades. Lauter and Stephenson (dressed in widow's weeds) get past the security system of a large estate and loot the safe of $5 million, and all of it belongs to Stephenson's father. Cutaway to meet O'Keefe, the manager of a femme "Roller Derby" team. He has fallen upon hard times with his skaters and when they learn that he's failed to get them any more bookings, they come after him with blood in their eyes. He races away from them, hides in a used clothing store, then buys himself a soldier's uniform and plans to board a train from Oakland, California, to New York. It's at the station where he meets Stephenson and where an Army officer also begins to grill him on his status (he's thought to be a Vietnam defector), he grabs for an American flag and drapes it over a nearby coffin, saying that the corpse inside the coffin is his slain buddy and he is escorting the body back home to the dead youth's parents. (Actually, inside the coffin is the purloined five mil.) At first Lauter and Stephenson are brought up short by what O'Keefe tells the Army officer, then they realize that they'll go along with the gag as it will insure the safekeeping of the money. O'Keefe steps on the train. Lauter follows and Stephenson will cross the country by bus. Aboard the train, O'Keefe meets D'Angelo, an aspiring actress with a Las Vegas background and a foul mouth. D'Angelo complains about the lack of

warmth in show people and says that her agent even tried to take his percentage of her unemployment check. Also on the train is FBI man Riley, who is trying to uncover the riddle of who stole the money and, in a delightful cameo, Wayne, as the world's oldest and most senile train conductor. O'Keefe continues his charade of being a saddened soldier and when Wayne asks the name of his dead comrade, O'Keefe chooses a name he sees in the newspaper obituaries, "Lane Biddlecoff" of Nebraska. Wayne thinks it's only fitting and proper that the train make an unscheduled stop in Nebraska, instead of going all the way to New York, so the late "Lane Biddlecoff" can be laid to rest more quickly. To do that, heavy strings must be pulled and Wayne calls then-President Richard Nixon (whom he continues to refer to as "Nickerson") to have the AMTRAK schedule altered and make the stop. He tells the Prez that if he is refused, he will go over Nixon's head and take it directly to Walter Cronkite. While this is happening, O'Keefe peeks into the coffin and sees the money and decides that he wants it all for himself. Now he finds Gossett, his former partner in con games from years ago. The two conspire to find some way they can get the money off the train. Meanwhile, Stephenson, still in widow's clothes, is stuck on the bus with a covey of nuns who insist on singing interminable choruses of "Row, Row, Row Your Boat." She's fretting about the money and can't do a thing about it. Wayne tells the passengers that the train is about to stop in Nebraska (in real life, Alberta, Canada, doubled for Nebraska) and Gossett, O'Keefe, and Lauter are all worried about what will happen to the coffin and the cash. In the Nebraska town, the mayor, Dennehy, learns about the special treatment for "Lane Biddlecoff" and this throws him for a loop because there really is a Lane Biddlecoff and he is Dennehy's draft-dodging nephew, Carrey. Dennehy had planted a phony obituary to keep the kid out of the clutches of the law. Dennehy and his entire family fear they are to be exposed for aiding and abetting Carrey. The service begins and a gay bandleader plays "Wild About Boys" at the wake. When Carrey is spotted by someone, a relative shouts, "Cousin Lane has risen!" O'Keefe is messing about with police chief Schuck's nympho wife, Blake, and has to run when chased by Dennehy and family who are also after Gossett and Lauter. The action winds up in a two-story farmhouse with O'Keefe, Gossett, and D'Angelo happily ensconced with the money. They don't realize that the house is being transported on a huge flatbed truck and the final chases and battles are humorously complicated by the fact that the quarry is in a moving home. It's far too frantic and the audience doesn't have any time to rest its eyes. Lots of irreverence, perhaps too much so, because it takes pot shots at government (always okay), homosexuals (not so okay), and Jews as a group (not okay at all). The latter two whacks were totally uncalled for and detracted, rather than added, to the movie. Some very funny dialog by Graham, Marsh, and Dennis (who wrote the novel from whence this sprang) including a scene between FBI man Riley and O'Keefe featuring a confusing array of redundant names and actions which cause D'Angelo to inquire, "Who's writing this dialog? Kafka?" Riley keeps talking, then does a double take, narrows his eyes and asks, "Wait! Who's Kafka?" Wayne gets his share of laughs with malapropisms when he says that he likes all dogs, but especially "English Settlers and Labrador Repeaters." The movie contains elements of many films, such as SILVER STREAK, IT'S A MAD, MAD, MAD, MAD WORLD and several others. Several moments of questionable taste but good performances on the part of the actors and a chance to see Lauter, who always plays a heavy, do some comedy under a silly black wig. Coscreenwriter Graham is the same man who appeared on TV as "Mr. Dirt" and who starred in "New Faces Of 1952" with Robert Clary, Paul Lynde, Eartha Kitt, and others.

p, Sandra Marsh, Terence Marsh; d, Richard Lester; w, Ronny Graham, Terence Marsh, Charles Dennis (based on the novel *The Next to Last Train Ride* by Dennis); ph, Brian West (Technicolor); m, Ken Thorne; ed, John Victor Smith; prod d, Terence Marsh; art d, J. Dennis Washington; set d, Michael Seirton; cos, Yvonne Blake.

Comedy   Cas.   (PR:C-O MPAA:R)

FIRESTARTER½   (1984) 116m DD/UNIV c

David Keith (*Andrew McGee*), Drew Barrymore (*Charlie McGee*), Freddie Jones (*Dr. Joseph Wanless*), Heather Locklear (*Vicky McGee*), Martin Sheen (*Capt. Hollister*), George C. Scott (*John Rainbird*), Louise Fletcher (*Norma Manders*), Moses Gunn (*Dr. Pynchot*), Art Carney (*Irv Manders*), Antonio Gargas (*Taxi Driver*), Drew Synder (*Orville Jamieson*), Curtis Credel (*Bates*), Keith Colbert (*Mayo*), Richard Warlock (*Knowles*), Jeff Ramsey (*Steinowitz*), Jack Magner (*Young Serviceman*), Lisa Anne Barnes (*Serviceman's Girl Friend*), Larry Sprinkle (*Security Guard*), Cassandra Ward-Freeman (*Woman in Stall*), Scott R. Davis (*Bearded Student*), Nina Jones (*Grad Assistant*), William Alspaugh (*Proprietor*), Laurens Moore (*Old Man*), Anne Fitzgibbon (*Old Lady*), Steve Boles (*Mailman*), Stanley Mann (*Motel Owner*), Robert Miano, Leon Rippy (*Blinded Agents*), Carole Francisco (*Joan Dugan*), Wendy Womble (*Josie*), Etan Boritzer, Joan Foley (*DSI Technicians*), John Sanderford (*Albright*), Orwin Harvey, George Wilbur (*DSI Orderlies*), Carey Fox (*Agent Hunt*).

Fans of Stephen King (and they number in the millions) will enjoy this pyromaniacal suspenser more than anyone else. Cute little Barrymore can start a blaze by just willing it to happen and, for that alone, she would make a valuable asset on any camping trip. The picture begins with a flashback as Barrymore's parents, Locklear and Keith, are presented as collegians who subject themselves to a drug experiment under what they believe to be controlled circumstances. There are no apparent side effects for them but when they have a child, things start to happen as the baby exhibits signs of a rare ability at an early age. Later, we learn that the experiments had been overseen by the DSI (Department of Scientific Intelligence), a CIA-type agency which is referred to as "The Shop" in much the same way that the CIA is referred to as "The Company." When the powers at DSI learn about Barrymore's unusual powers, they decide that they would like to nab her for further tests. Locklear leaves the film early when her daughter's powers get the best of her and cause her demise, leaving Keith and Barrymore remaining. The DSI not only wants to take Barrymore in for a closer look, they want to eventually dispose of her and Keith as they are the only remaining proof of the heinous drug experimentation which took place earlier. Once Keith learns that he and his offspring are being sought, a chase begins that is the structural spine of the movie. Along the way, as in so many Hitchcock films, interesting characters are encountered. These include farm couple Carney and Fletcher. The two Oscar-winners suspect that Keith and Barrymore are no ordinary father and daughter and, once they learn the truth, they seek to protect their guests. As a result they almost have their property burned when Barrymore has to protect herself and Keith from agents of DSI and has to torch them for self-protection. Their freedom is short-lived as they are captured and taken to DSI's palatial headquarters where they are immediately separated. Barrymore misses her daddy and is told that she can join him only if she agrees to submit to experiments which will confirm her abilities. Enter Scott, a pig-tailed, one-eyed man whose job it is to befriend Barrymore, then kill her after the information has been gleaned. Scott masquerades as the janitor for the elegant Virginia estate where DSI is located. (It was actually shot on the Orton Plantation in North Carolina, 12,000 acres in size and more than 250 years in operation.) Naive Barrymore is so needy of an ally that she doesn't see through Scott's charade. Barrymore and Keith are united near the end of the film and attempt to flee but the whole thing literally goes up in flames. Keith is killed, so is Scott, and Barrymore wreaks her revenge by setting fire to the house and lighting up the sky. Everyone within range of the licking flames is barbecued, cars are reduced to molten metal, and buildings explode. The final scene occurs when the sweet, young orphan approaches the farmhouse where Carney and Fletcher live. She's taken in by them and lives happily ever after. The movie stays close to King's novel and the casting of Scott (also an Oscar winner) and Sheen as the head of dastardly DSI are excellent. The special effects for the $15 million movie are also good. Where the movie falls is in Lester's direction of the actors. He's always been good with effects, hardware, and anything that doesn't require too much depth of character. The movie wilts when Lester attempts to evoke any humanity. The picture was much like THE FURY, a Brian De Palma film. It was also De Palma who directed CARRIE, based on another King novel, which had a similar plot. A good, insistent score by "Tangerine Dream" helped perk up the sagging scenes.

p, Frank Capra. Jr.; d, Mark L. Lester; w, Stanley Mann (based on the novel *Firestarter* by Stephen King; ph, Guiseppe Ruzzolini (Technicolor); m, Tangerine Dream; ed, David Rawlins, Ron Sanders; art d, Giorgio Postiglione; set d, Lynn Wolverton; cos, Wes Eckhardt, Jennifer Butler; spec eff, Mike Wood, Jeff Jarvis.

Fantasy/Suspense   **Cas.**   **(PR:O   MPAA:R)**

FIRST NAME: CARMEN*½   (1984, Fr.) Sara-Jean Luc Godard-Film A2/ International Spectrafilm c (PRENOM: CARMEN)

Maruschka Detmers *(Carmen X)*, Jacques Bonnaffe *(Joseph Bonnaffe)*, Myriem Roussel *(Claire)*, Christophe Odent *(The Boss)*, Jean-Luc Godard *(Uncle Jean)*, Hyppolite Girardot *(Fred)*, Bertrand Liebert *(Carmen's Bodyguard)*, Alain Bastien-Thiry *(Hotel Worker)*, Pierre-Alain Chapuis, Odile Roire, Valerie Dreville, Christine Pignet, Jean-Michael Denis, Jacques Villeret.

As a director Godard has always seemed like the type who would paint a mustache on the "Mona Lisa" and this time out he has taken a broad stroke, with his camera as a brush, at Bizet's famed opera "Carmen." Filmed twice within a year–by Francesco Rosi in 1984 and Carlos Saura in 1983, both titled CARMEN–the story was given a reverent treatment by both directors. Godard, however, chose to greatly depart from the original Merimee novel and, to the horror of Bizet fans, replaced Bizet's score with Beethoven violin concertos and a ballad called "Ruby's Arms" by the gruff-voiced Tom Waits. The entrancing Detmers stars as Carmen, a *femme fatale* who concocts a daring plan of robbing a bank while pretending to shoot a movie. Luckily she has an uncle who once was a brilliant movie director and is now a resident loon at the local mental hospital. Godard casts himself in this role and turns in one of the finest comic performances in memory. Looking disheveled in his long coat, messy hair, and half-chewed cigar, Godard makes an impassioned attempt to the nurses to allow him to stay in the hospital. Convinced that he is in perfect health, they try to dismiss him. He, in turn, promises that he'll have a fever by Friday. He is also upset at the difficulty he has in creating (the only line he can write that day is "Badly seen, badly said"), which is why he jumps at the chance to "direct" Detmer's film of the robbery. While staging the robbery Detmers is nearly apprehended by policeman Bonnaffe, but they fall in love instead and decide to escape to Godard's vacant seaside house. Detmers is in complete control of the relationship and even warns Bonnafe, "If I love you, that is the end of you." By the finale, however, it is her life that comes to an end. As she lies dying,

looking out a window, she asks a waiter nearby, "What is the name of that moment when all the damned are drawn up on one side and all the innocents on the other?" The waiter, naturally, is unable to answer her question. She persists and finally gets an answer. "That's called the dawn," he responds. It is with that response that Godard closes his most optimistic film–after the movie has ended and the heroine dies, there is still a dawn; there is still hope. Not only is FIRST NAME: CARMEN optimistic, it is also relatively linear in its narrative structure, making it perhaps Godard's most most accessible film. More importantly, FIRST NAME: CARMEN is Godard's first comedy. He has always had his funny moments, but this film is his first real step in the direction of the great comedians. Godard, in one of the film's most hysterical scenes, even carries a Buster Keaton book under his arm. Although it may seem strange to think of the intellectual Godard performing slapstick comedy, it seems to be his calling. In an interview with Gideon Bachmann, Godard claims, "I was doing it because I want to prepare myself to play a principle part in a film, something like Harry Langdon did or a bit like Jerry Lewis." FIRST NAME: CARMEN is not a comedy in the usual way, but neither are Godard's gangster films nor his dramas. It is spiced with passion, philosophy, eroticism, and technical innovations, and while it is relatively accessible it is still not "easy" viewing. Interestingly, the film was intended as a vehicle for Isabelle Adjani but after some disagreements she walked off the project. Reports conflict–Adjani says too much nudity was required of her; Godard says Adjani was fearful of being photographed in natural light and thereby looking less beautiful than in an artificially lit scene. The latter explanation seems rather feeble considering Adjani isn't known for doing nude scenes and has already appeared looking extremely frumpy in parts of both THE TENANT and THE STORY OF ADELE H. Thankfully, Godard's choice of Detmers was an excellent one. He also cast, in a lesser role, Myriem Roussel, who went on to appear in Godard's controversial HAIL, MARY (1985)–a film which is actually something of an extension of FIRST NAME: CARMEN. Godard found support for his film at the Venice Film Festival, which showered him with three major awards–Best Film, Best Cinematography (Raoul Coutard), and Best Sound (Francois Musy). In accepting his award, the Golden Lion, Godard Commented that he "probably only deserved the mane, and maybe the tail. Everything in the middle should go to all the others who work on the picture: the paws to the director of photography, the face to the editor, the body to the actors." At the close of the festival, Godard found himself in an argument with a hotel clerk and, feeling that he too deserved part of the award, reportedly threw the Golden Lion at him. (In French; English subtitles.)

p, Alain Sarde; d, Jean-Luc Godard; w, Anne Marie Mieville (based on the novel *Carmen* by Prosper Merimee); ph, Raoul Coutard (Eastmancolor); m, Ludwig von Beethoven; ed, Suzanne Lang-Willar; cos, Renee Renard; m/l, "Ruby's Arms," Tom Waits.

Drama   **(PR:O   MPAA:NR)**

FIRST TURN-ON!, THE zero   (1984) 90m Troma c

Georgia Harrell *(Michelle Farmer)*, Michael Sanville *(Mitch)*, Googy Gress *(Henry)*, John Flood *(Danny Anderson)*, Heidi Miller *(Annie Goldberg)*, Al Pia *(Alfred)*, Betty Pia *(Mrs. Anderson)*, Gilda Gumbo *(Mme. Gumbo)*, Lara Grills *(Lucy the Hooker)*, Kristina Marie Wetzel *(Barbara Billingham)*, Frank Trent Saladino *(Jeff)*, Davida Berardi *(Johnny)*, Ted Henning *(Ted)*, Donna Winter *(Mona)*, Sheila Kennedy *(Dreamgirl)*, Mark Torgl *(Dwayne)*, Donna Barnes *(Jane)*, Sioban Fergus *(Cathy)*, Steve Hollander *(Stinky)*, Vincent D'Onofrio *(Lobotomy)*, Russel Matthews *(Pissing Johnnie)*, Mitchell Whitfield *(Micky)*, Nick Pannone *(Bozo)*, Michael Schoffel *(Melvin)*, Randy Matthews *(Snake)*, Gretchen Weiner *(Mrs. Richards)*, Ebb Miller *(Richards)*, William Kirksey *(Announcer)*.

A wretched teen sex comedy about four campers who spend the summer at Camp Big Tee-Pee, under the guidance of chesty counselor Harrell. They set off on a cave exploration and wind up trapped inside. Since they are isolated in a dark, damp cave it is only natural (at least in teen sex comedies) for the subject to turn to sex. They all relate experiences about their "first turn-on"–all of which are so infantile and embarrassing that they sound more like turnoffs. Everyone in the cast is manipulative or cowardly and the end result is 82 minutes of repulsive sexual memories. In cases like THE FIRST TURN-ON it is the ad campaign that sells the film. This time, however, the poster is so unappealing it's amazing that anyone ever saw the film.

p, Lloyd Kaufman, Michael Herz; d, Herz, Samuel Weil; w, Stuart Strutin, Mark Torgl, Georgia Harrell, Kaufman, Hertz; ph, Kaufman; ed, Richard Haines, Adam Fredericks, Richard King; art d, Ellen Christiansen; cos, Danielle Brunon; spec eff, Less Lar Larraine

Comedy   **(PR:O   MPAA:R)**

FIRSTBORN*   (1984) 103m Jaffe-Lansing/PAR c

Teri Garr *(Wendy)*, Peter Weller *(Sam)*, Christopher Collet *(Jake)*, Corey Haim *(Brian)*, Sarah Jessica Parker *(Lisa)*, Robert Downey *(Lee)*, Christopher Gartin *(Adam)*, James Harper *(Mr. Rader)*, Richard Brandon *(Dad)*, Gayle Harbor *(Joanne)*, Ellen Barber *(Wendy's Girl Friend)*, Richard E. Szlasa *(Coach Gant)*, Beverly W. May *(Mrs. Mercer)*, Brian Lima *(Robby)*, J.D. Roth *(Ken)*, Larry Atlas *(Stranger)*, Vebe Borge *(Friend)*, Sarah Inglis

(Jill), Christopher Russo *(Beckman)*, Josh Hamilton *(Brad)*, Joseph M. Costa *(Headman)*, Jason Berger *(Jeffrey)*, Thomas Daggett *(Boy in Pizza Shop)*, Frank Ferrara *(Driver of Car)*, Nole R. Cohen *(Party Man)*, Christina Swing *(Party Woman)*, Scott Wilder, Leslie Arnett, Linda Lee Arvidson, Bill Anagnos, Jery Hewitt.

Former Fox studio president Sherry Lansing teamed with Stanley R. Jaffe and TV veterans Witt and Thomas ("Benson," and "Soap") to present this flawed but interesting children's rights drama that spent about 70 minutes making points and the last 30 minutes losing them. Garr is a divorcee with two sons, Haim and Collet. Being a single parent is never easy but Garr has a good relationship with her boys and they are making the best out of the difficulty. When Garr learns that her ex-husband is about to marry once more, the tranquility alters. Almost out of revenge, Garr takes Weller as her lover. He is an interloper, a villain who insinuates himself into the Garr household and proceeds to turn the family members against each other. At first he attempts to be "one of the guys" and does everything to curry favor with the two boys. They see through him and he continues his campaign by trying to buy their affection with expensive gifts. Garr doesn't realize what kind of a man Weller is because she is so insecure that she needs someone, anyone, to make her feel fulfilled. She begins to argue about Weller with her boys as she is dumb to his faults. The arguments become intense and she finds the rift widening. Weller is a man with no mission in life, a late 30s drifter who fancies himself an entrepreneur but doesn't have the brains to back up his dream of owning a restaurant. Collet is only about 16 but wise beyond his years and he can see Weller for the leech he is. The two boys commence rebelling. They get into trouble at school and the house is becoming an unarmed camp. It comes to a head when Collet wakes up one morning to find Garr and Weller stupefied on the couch, the result of too much booze and too many drugs at what is becoming a continuous party at the once-peaceful home. Garr and Weller take off for a few days, leaving the boys to fend for themselves. Collet begins to search through Weller's personal gear and finds a stash of cocaine. Rightly assuming that Weller is now dealing in the white powder (he will do anything to raise the stake he wants for his restaurant), Collet removes it from the house and hides it. When Weller returns, the first thing he looks for are his drugs. He had been verbally abusive of Collet before but now becomes physically abusive when Collet will not tell him the whereabouts of the narcotics. He drags the teenager out of the house to look for the drugs and here's where the solid, intelligent domestic drama falls apart. We are now treated to a typical TV movie chase, with Weller in a pickup truck tailing Collet on his motorbike. There's a locomotive, a dog, and all of the cliches we've seen for so long in chases. When there is a final violent confrontation, Garr's dim eyes are thankfully opened and she understands how destructive her relationship with Weller has been. The family tosses the bum out and reconciles as the film concludes. A sage once stated that children eventually are their parents' parents. Such was the case with Collet as he convincingly took over and assumed the parental responsibility of his temporarily love-blinded mother. He cared for himself and his younger brother and managed to solve a problem that never should have been there at all. Weller was excellent as the sleazy visitor and Garr's portrayal of the most insecure woman in her neighborhood was equally good. The realistic portrayal of this family's *angst* almost overturns the sappy reconciliation and the *de rigeur* chase which mar an otherwise thoughtful movie. It was hardly seen by audiences and dropped out of sight quickly.

p, Paul Junger Witt, Tony Thomas, Ron Koslow; d, Michael Apted; w, Koslow; ph, Ralf D. Bode (Technicolor); m, Michael Small; ed, Arthur Schmidt, Angelo Corrao; prod d, Paul Sylbert; set d, Alan Hicks; cos, Colleen C. Atwood.

Drama **Cas.** **(PR:C MPAA:PG)**

FLAMINGO KID, THE*½** (1984) 100m Mercury Entertainment-ABC/FOX c

Matt Dillon *(Jeffrey Willis)*, Hector Elizondo *(Arthur Willis)*, Molly McCarthy *(Ruth Willis)*, Martha Gehman *(Nikki Willis)*, Richard Crenna *(Phil Brody)*, Jessica Walter *(Phyllis Brody)*, Carole R. Davis *(Joyce Brody)*, Janet Jones *(Carla Samson)*, Brian McNamara *(Steve Dawkins)*, Fisher Stevens *(Hawk Ganz)*, Leon Robinson *(Fortune Smith)*, Bronson Pinchot *(Alfred Schultz)*, Frank Campanella *(Col. Cal Eastland)*, Richard Stahl *(Charlie Cooper)*, Joe Grifasi *(Mario Minetta)*, Ron McLarty *(Pat McCarty)*, Seth Allen *(Jerry Berlin)*, Irving Metzman *(Big Sid)*, Adam Klugman *(Lewis Madrone)*, Ray Roderick *(Danny Walsh)*, Googy Gress *(Freddy)*, Sharon Thomas *(Mrs. Unger)*, The Barbarian Brothers *(Turk and Dirk)*, Christopher Chadman *(Dance Instructor)*, Martin Chatinover *(Dr. Gold)*, Lisa Beth Ross, Laurie Stratford *(Bimbettes)*, Steven Weber *(Paul Hirsch)*, Eric Douglas *(Donny)*, Marisa Tomei *(Mandy)*, Tracy Reiner *(Polly)*, Kristina Kossi *(Kristina)*, Bobbie Jo Burke *(Bobbie Jo)*, Leslie S. Sachs *(Big Sid's Girl)*, Michael Mahon *(Lifeguard)*, Lee Morey *(Mrs. Bakalentnikoff)*, Jillian Scharf *(Waitress)*, Carol Williard *(Mrs. Rifkin)*, Richard Buck *(Man on Lounge)*, Bradley Kane *(Mitch)*, Lauren Costa *(Lauren McCarty)*, Linda Costa *(Peter's Mother)*, Peter Costa *(Peter)*, Scott Marshall *(Stickball Player)*, Blake Brocksmith *(Shel)*, Steve Whitting *(Frank)*, Freddy Frogs *(Hot Dog Man)*, Lee Steele *(Furniture Store Owner)*, Beth Noreen Einhorn *(Bridgette, Contortionist)*, Bo Sabato *(Uncle Jack)*, Frances Peach *(Aunt Frances)*, Jack Danny Foster *(Pete from Pinky's)*, John Turturro *(Ted from Pinky's)*, Mark Strait *(Bocko from Pinky's)*, Mike Markowitz *(Nervous Man)*, Kathi Marshall *(Adventurer's Inn Hostess)*, Novella Nelson *(Lizzy the Housekeeper)*, David Berry *(Steve's Father)*, Mark Kaplan *(Ron, Car Salesman)*, George Blumenthal *(Hawk's Father)*, Mel Allen *(Himself)*.

THE FLAMINGO KID, unlike countless coming-of-age films in which guzzling beer and ogling girls represents initiation into manhood, is an honest and often touching account of one young man's introduction to a more sophisticated life. Dillon is an 18-year-old Brooklyn kid, the son of Elizondo, a plumber, and McCarthy. One summer day he joins some friends on a jaunt to "El Flamingo," a ritzy beachside club for affluent Long Islanders. There he observes Crenna, a wealthy auto dealer and the club's champion gin player, effectively demolish any competition at the card table. Dillon is hired by the club for the summer, and slowly gets involved with Crenna's niece, Jones. Crenna takes a liking to Dillon as well, admiring the boy's determination, as well as his skill at gin. With Crenna's help, Dillon receives a quick promotion and begins dreaming of a better future. After a talk with his mentor, Dillon decides he wants to become a car salesman. Elizondo, who has dreamed of his son going to college, is dead set against the idea. Dillon argues with his father and decides to move out. He asks Crenna about a previously offered job at one of Crenna's car dealerships, but is shocked when he is only offered a position as a stockboy. Later, after his hero has deflated all his previously held illusions, Dillon discovers that Crenna has been cheating all summer long at the card table. When Crenna's shill becomes ill from being in the sun too long, Dillon challenges the older man at cards. He soundly defeats Crenna, winning a large chunk of money. Crenna, stunned by this, tries to buy off Dillon by offering him a good job, but Dillon refuses. Instead he goes to his father's favorite restaurant, where his family is dining. Father and son reconcile and Dillon contemplates what he has learned from his summer experiences. There's not a single bad performance in this film, with each role cast to perfection. Dillon's metamorphosis from a Brooklyn street punk to a determined young man is a marvelous portrait. Relationships between Dillon and adults are carefully drawn in the film as his feelings for Crenna and Elizondo go through a variety of changes. There is a special chemistry between Dillon and each of these men, created with care by the three actors and director Marshall. Marshall builds his film on small moments, a wise choice that gives this comedy empathy and intelligence. The differences in the social stratas between Dillon and the members of the El Flamingo are obvious, but never overstated. Dillon explores their world slowly, gradually becoming more entrenched in the life style. In one of THE FLAMINGO KID's best moments, Dillon is shocked to find cherry-shaped soap in the bathroom at Crenna's home. He is amazed by this, but as he places another unusually shaped piece of soap in his pocket to use at his Brooklyn home, Dillon hears Crenna's bigoted wife complaining that the uncouth young man might steal soap from the bathroom. Marshall took care in creating an early 1960s atmosphere for the film with costumes, set design, and period automobiles. At one point, as Crenna watches television, a rerun of "The Real McCoys"–a popular show from 1957 to 1963–flashes on the sceen. The clip briefly shows a much younger Crenna, who played Luke on that series. Neal Marshall (who is no relation to the director) wrote the original script for THE FLAMINGO KID in the early 1970s. Producer Philips first heard of it in 1973 while playing cards with Cass Elliott ("Mama Cass" from the group the Mamas and the Papas). "We played cards and talked about playing cards until the sun came up," said Philips. "Cass said, 'You've got to read this script that a friend of mine wrote about playing gin rummy.' " Philips liked what he saw and took out an option on the work, though it would be another 10 years before the script finally went before the cameras. One of the best reasons for the successful period re-creation is the marvelous background music used in the film. A virtual catalog of the era's greatest hits, these songs include: "Breakaway" (Bennett Salvay, Snuffy Walden, Arlene Matza, performed by Jesse Frederick), "Just One Look" (Doris Payne, Gregory Carroll, performed by Doris Troy), "It's All Right" (Curtis Mayfield, performed by The Impressions), "Finger Poppin' Time" (Hank Ballard, performed by Ballard and the Midnighters), "Chain Gang" (Sam Cooke, C. Cooke, performed by Sam Cooke), "Get a Job" (Horton, Lewis, Edward, Beal, performed by The Silhouettes), "Walk Right In" (Gus Cannon, H. Woods, performed by The Rooftop Singers), "Theme from 'A Summer Place' " (Max Steiner), "Money (That's What I Want)" (Berry Gordy, Jr., Janie Bradford, performed by Barrett Strong), "Stand By Me" (Ben E. King, Glick, Jerry Lieber, Mike Stoller, performed by King), "Good Golly Miss Molly" (J. Marachlco, Bumps Blackwell, performed by Little Richard), "South Street" (Kal Mann, David Appell, performed by The Orlons), "Runaround Sue" (Ernest Maresca, Dion DiMucci, performed by Dion), "Da Doo Ron Ron" (Phil Spector, Ellie Greenwich, Jeff Barry, performed by The Crystals), "Stranger on the Shore" (Acker Bilk, Robert Mellin, performed by Bilk), "Heat Wave (Love Is Like A)" (Eddie Holland, Lamont Dozier, Brian Holland, performed by Martha Reeves and the Vandellas), "Yes, Indeed" (Sy Oliver, performed by Ray Charles), "He's So Fine" (Ronald Mack, performed by The Chiffons), "Green Onions" (Booker T. Jones, Steve Crooper, Lewis Steinberg, Al Jackson, Jr., perfromed by Booker T. and the M.G.'s), "One Fine Day" (performed by Carole King, Gerry Goffin, performed by the Chiffons), "Cha Cha Dinero" (The Roper Band, performed by the Roper Band).

p, Michael Phillips; d, Garry Marshall; w, Garry Marshall, Neal Marshall (based on a story by Neal Marshall); ph, James A. Contner (Panavision, DeLuxe Color); ed, Priscilla Nedd; prod d, Lawrence Miller; art d, Duke Durfee; set d, Fred Weiler; cos, Ellen Mirojnick; stunts, Harry Madsen; makeup, Mickey Scott, Irving Buchman.

Comedy/Drama Cas. (PR:C MPAA:PG-13)

FLASH OF GREEN, A***½ (1984) 131m Spectrafilm c

Ed Harris (*Jimmy Wing*), Blair Brown (*Kate Hubble*), Richard Jordan (*Elmo Bliss*), George Coe (*Brian Haas*), Joan Goodfellow (*Mitchie*), Jean De Baer (*Jackie Halley*), Helen Stenborg (*Aunt Middie*), William Mooney (*Leroy Shannard*), Isa Thomas (*Doris Rohl*), John Glover (*Ross Halley*), Bob Murch (*Dial Sinnat*), Joan MacIntosh (*Nan Haas*), Bob Harris (*Borklund*), Nancy Griggs (*Nat Sinnat*), Linda Lee Larsen (*Sally Ann Lesser*), Michael Doyle (*Burt Lesser*), Joe Carioth (*Tom Jennings*), Maggie Beistle (*Dellie Bliss*), Maggie Klekas (*Trailer Lady*), Charles Kahlenberg (*Ernie Willihan*), Phil Hunt (*Barlow*), Gregory Jones (*Walker*), Brad Wallace (*Martin Cable*), Margaret Bachus (*Eloise Cable*), Gene Densmore (*Photographer*), Bill Schaaf (*Van Hubble*), Jerry Clark (*Major*), Carly Asse (*Roy Hubble*), Kelly O'Brien (*Alicia Hubble*), Jim Hooks, David Shelton (*Commissioners*), Herbert Childs (*Nightwatchman*), Tiel Rey (*Gloria Wing*).

An intelligent, well-shot, beautifully acted adaptation of the MacDonald book that came and went faster than the flash of green it takes its title from. People who live in Florida know what the flash of green is. On the west coast, overlooking the Gulf of Mexico, if the air is clear and the temperature correct, there is an incredible phenomenon which takes place at sunset, when the sun dips down into the Gulf and there is an explosion of light. Written and directed by Nunez, this movie is a sure-handed look at corruption in Florida, with all the attendant complex characterizations that can usually be found in a MacDonald novel. Set in the mythical town of Palm City, we first meet Harris, a likable reporter for the local paper. Harris doesn't betray the pressure he's under but it's heavy. His wife is brain-damaged in a local hospital and there is no chance for her recovery. At the same time he is deeply in love with Brown, the widow of his best friend, but he can't bring himself to declare that love. Jordan is the local county commissioner and a pal of Harris' since they were in school years before. Jordan is very ambitious and comes to Harris with a bribe offer. There's a group of do-gooders known as the "S.O.B.s" (Save Our Bay) who are against a potential real estate development. The land is owned by the public and Jordan and his buddies want to gain control of it but are stymied by the ecological "S.O.B.s" and mean to get that opposition out of the way. A few years before, some out-of-towners wanted to get their hands on the property but the newspaper and Brown combined to fend them off. Now that the property is wanted by locals, not carpetbaggers, the press is taking another stance. Harris doesn't feel right about finding blackmail material to discredit the conservationists but he is too weak to say no and he thinks that it might all work out for the best, or so he hopes. Jordan believes that what he's doing will, in the end, be important. Not only will he get enough publicity to make himself well-known enough to run for governor, building the real estate development will bring new jobs and lots of money to the area. Harris begins muckraking and finds out some things about various members of the ecology group. He feeds the information to Jordan, who has promised to hold the dirt in reserve and only use it if absolutely necessary. Jordan breaks his word as he enlists a local right-wing Christian fundamentalist cult known as "The Army of God" who are no better than the KKK. When the group kidnaps the conservationist leader, De Baer, and beats her, Harris' boiling point is finally reached and he joins with the group to outwit Jordan and his minions. A complex story with no easy answers, A FLASH OF GREEN is one of the few adaptations of a MacDonald novel that sticks closely to the intent of the original. Where it falls apart is in failing to provide a sustained story line for an audience to grasp. There are many sidebar moments that detract from the narrative and the uncertain editing doesn't help. It's moody, steamy, and provocative enough to merit your attention, if you can overlook the flaws. Several new faces make the film all the more believable and Harris turns in a crackling, convincingly understated performance. It was released only briefly and later seen on PBS as part of the "American Playhouse" series.

p, Richard Jordan; d&w, Victor Nunez (based on the novel by John D. MacDonald); ph, Nunez; m, Charles Engstrom; ed, Nunez; art d, Carlos Asse; set d, Melissa Sykes, Art Alvarez; cos, Marilyn Wall-Asse, Dana Moser.

Drama Cas. (PR:A-C MPAA:NR)

FLASHPOINT*½ (1984) 94m Tri-Star c

Kris Kristofferson (*Bob Logan*), Treat Williams (*Ernie Wiatt*), Rip Torn (*Sheriff*), Kevin Conway (*Brook*), Kurtwood Smith (*Carson*), Miguell Ferrer (*Roget*), Jean Smart (*Doris*), Guy Boyd (*Lambasmino*), Mark Slade (*Hawthorne*), Roberts Blossom (*Amarillo*), Tess Harper (*Ellen*), Terry Alexander (*Peterson*).

Producers are always looking for new occupations they can make films about. For a while, it was the U.S. Border Patrol and a couple of pictures about those men were released. In this, Kristofferson and Williams are a pair of south Texas members of that unit. They are pals as well as coworkers although there is little indication of what they have in common. Williams is a redneck, blue-collar drinker who adheres to the letter of the law, while Kristofferson is a West Point graduate and a one-time Green Beret in Vietnam who has since walked away from his history. They are on patrol and discover the remains of a Jeep that has been buried in the sand for what looks like decades. They also find almost $1 million in cash. Williams is the law-abiding type and suggests that they had better find out whose money

it is. Kristofferson is from the people who say possession is nine-tenths of the law and he's all for bolting with the money. They look at the serial numbers and reckon that the money is circa the early 1960s. Next, they begin looking for the rightful owner, after first hiding the loot. Their search is soon noticed by other people and it's not long before their lives are in danger from a multitude of sources, not the least of which are agents from the Federal Bureau of Investigation. Evidently the money is the result of some long-ago cabal and the powers-that-be would like to keep the whole thing under cover. Along the way, there are a couple of interesting characters, including Blossom as a cantankerous curmudgeon who lives in a trailer, Torn as a thick-accented Texas sheriff who helps Kristofferson (Torn really is from Texas and loves nothing better than retreating to the accent he grew up using), and the team of Harper and Smart, two sweet young things in a stalled car. The writers use these women as false leads because it seems that they might be part of the overall conspiracy, but that's just a device to give them some screen time. The money is actually from 1963 and anyone who recalls what happened in November of that year, in Dallas, will have a clue as to why it was supposed to be there and where it came from. We won't give you any more of a hint than that. The picture is far too langorous in pace to be deemed a true action-adventure. It promises more than it delivers and when one considers that it didn't promise all that much, you can understand the disappointment of the denouement. Williams emotes most of the time but doesn't get into too much over-the-top playing this time. Kristofferson seems to be acting as though someone just woke him up and he'd like to go back to sleep right away, something many in the audience found themselves doing.

p, Skip Short; d, William Tannen; w, Dennis Shyrack, Michael Butler (based on a book by George La Fountaine); ph, Peter Moss (Metrocolor); m, Tangerine Dream; ed, David Garfield; prod d, Paul Greimann.

Action/Adventure Cas. (PR:O MPAA:R)

FLESHBURN zero (1984) 90m Fear/Crown c

Steve Kanaly (*Sam MacKenzie*), Karen Carlson (*Shirley Pinter*), Macon McCalman (*Earl Dana*), Robert Chimento (*Jay Pinter*), Sonny Landham (*Calvin Duggai*), Robert Alan Browne (*Jim Brody*), Duke Stroud (*Smyley*), Larry Vigus (*Marine Sergeant*), Newton John Skinner (*Chris*), Jack Dunlap, Ed Adams, Will Morton, John Pearce (*Stunts*).

The ever-handy movie stereotype of a deranged Vietnam veteran rears its ugly head once again for this insipid trash. Landham is that man who's also a Navajo Indian. He's escaped from the mental hospital and is now after the four psychiatrists who sent him there. (Considering the rate of psychos escaping from institutions in American films, one can only wonder what psychiatrists are telling their Hollywood clientele.) Landham catches up with his quartet of shrinks, Carlson, Chimento, Kanaly, and McCalman, and strands them in the desert to prove that his own brand of medicine is more powerful than the white man's. It's a well known fact that the desert heat is grueling, but that would seem like a picnic compared to this. The premise is ridiculous to start with, with a cast that more or less suits the quality of the screenplay. Landham is best remembered as the psychotic killer in 48 HOURS. With this he tries to continue making a career playing maniacal Indians and ends up wallowing in cliches. Outside of animal life or cacti growing, there are few exciting moments to be found on the desert. This film, to say the least, is not one of them.

p, Beth Gage; d, George Gage; w, B. Gage, G. Gage (based on the novel *Fear in a Handful of Dust* by Brian Garfield); ph, Bill Pecchi (DeLuxe Color); m, Arthur Kempel, Don Felder; ed, Sonya Sones; cos, Annie Hayes; spec eff, Jim Hoagland.

Drama Cas. (PR:O MPAA:R)

FLETCH*** (1984) 98m UNIV c

Chevy Chase (*Fletch*), Joe Don Baker (*Chief Karlin*), Dana Wheeler-Nicholson (*Gail Stanwyk*), Richard Libertini (*Walker*), Tim Matheson (*Alan Stanwyk*), M. Emmet Walsh (*Dr. Dolan*), George Wendt (*Fat Sam*), Kenneth Mars (*Stanton Boyd*), Geena Davis (*Larry*), Bill Henderson (*Speaker*), William Traylor (*Mr. Underhill*), George Wyner (*Gillet*), Tony Longo, James Avery (*Detectives*), Larry Flash Jenkins (*Gummy*), Ralph Seymour (*Creasy*), Kareem Abdul-Jabbar (*Himself*), Reid Cruickshanks (*Sergeant*), Bruce French (*Pathologist*), Burton Gilliam (*Bud*), David Harper (*Teenager*), Chick Hearn (*Himself*), Alison LaPlaca (*Pan Am Clerk*), Joe Praml (*Watchman*), William Sanderson (*Swarthout*), Penny Santon (*Velma Stanwyk*), Robert Sorrels (*Marvin Stanwyk*), Beau Starr (*Willy*), Nico DeSilva, Rick Garcia (*Waiters*), Peggy Doyle (*Identification Nurse*), Grace Gaynor (*Mrs. Underhill*), Freeman King, Roger Ammann (*Cops*), Loraine Shields (*Records Nurse*), Bill Sorrells, Henry 'Hank' Bleeker (*Surfer Cops*), Arnold Turner, Darren Dublin (*Reporters*), Mary Battilana (*Madeline Turner*), Donald Chaffin (*Banquet Guest*), Kristine M. Grossman (*Secretary*), Irene Olga Lopez (*Maid*), Merv Maruyama (*Chinese Busboy*).

Based on the successful book by Gregory McDonald, this film afforded Chase the chance to be funny again without going too far. The sure hand of Ritchie's direction is evident as Chase cavorts through this mystery-comedy playing the role of an investigative reporter who will stop at nothing to get his story, including using such aliases as Harry Truman, Don Corleone, and G. Gordon Liddy. He's trying to get a handle on some drug dealing at the local beach so he poses as a beach bum and tries to go under cover to garner the information. Chase is approached by successful aviation executive Matheson who apparently thinks that Chase is a real bum. Matheson is married to the company founder's daughter, Wheeler-Nicholson. He tells Chase that he's willing to pay him $50,000 to commit a murder and the plan is foolproof. Further, he has even provided Chase with a perfect escape plan. The target of the murder is Matheson himself. He explains that he is suffering from a terminal illness and would rather die than suffer through the final months of his life. The company has taken out a huge insurance policy on his life and since suicide would negate the large sum to be awarded to his beneficiary, he believes murder would be the proper solution. Chase sees right through the slickness of Matheson and decides to uncover the truth. The mystery begins to unravel as Chase works himself through a web of entanglements, unanswered questions, intrigue, etc., and he uses the various aliases to discover the information. He learns that Matheson is involved in the drug dealing at the beach and his partner-in-crime is the local police chief, sadistic Baker. A confrontation between Matheson and Chase occurs and the plan appears to have been that Matheson meant to kill Chase, burn the body, have him identified as the executive, then run off with his mistress. The picture ends with one person dead, one in jail, and the rest going off to Rio. Good acting from all concerned, including the solid Walsh as a nutso doctor, Wendt as a beach person involved with drugs, and Baker as the mean cop. This is Chase's best solo venture to date. We don't include FOUL PLAY as he costarred in that with Goldie Hawn. It's amusing, fast-paced, witty, and will hold almost anyone's attention for the well-edited 98 minutes. McDonald thought Chase would make a perfect "Fletch" and he was correct. The movie darts from a posh tennis club to a small Utah town to a pig farm to a huge banquet scene where Chase, in a scene reminiscent of Robert Donat's pickle in THE 39 STEPS, leaps on the dais at a Legionnaire's reunion to escape the goons chasing him. Locations were many, including Rio and Pearblossom, California, and no expense was spared to give this a glossy sheen. The use of the various aliases was seen before in CHARADE and Chase appeared to be attempting to emulate Cary Grant in a hip, updated fashion. Special note should be made of Libertini who plays Chase's editor. Libertini is one of those second bananas who always turns in a good performance, as in UNFAITHFULLY YOURS (the Dudley Moore version), THE IN-LAWS, SHARKEY'S MACHINE, BEST FRIENDS, and many others. Ritchie has done some very special films in the past such as SMILE, THE CANDIDATE, and THE BAD NEWS BEARS. He's also done some sloppy ones like THE SURVIVORS. This time, he was on his game and the movie made a big score at the box office. Coproduced by Kirk Douglas' son, Peter, who also produced THE FINAL COUNTDOWN and SOMETHING WICKED THIS WAY COMES.

p, Alan Greisman, Peter Douglas; d, Michael Ritchie; w, Andrew Bergman (based on the novel by Gregory McDonald); ph, Fred Schuler (Panavision, Technicolor); m, Harold Faltermeier; ed, Richard A. Harris; prod d, Boris Leven; art d, Todd Hallowell; set d, Marvin March; cos, Gloria Gresham, Francine Jamison, Jim Tyson; spec eff, Cliff Wenger; m/l, "Bit by Bit" (theme from "Fletch"), Faltermeier, Franie Golde (performed by Stephanie Mills), "Fletch, Get Outa Town," Dan Hartman (performed by Hartman), "Letter to Both Sides," The Fixx (performed by The Fixx); stunts, Dean Jeffries; makeup, Ken Chase.

Comedy/Crime   **Cas.**   **(PR:C   MPAA:PG)**

FLIGHT TO BERLIN**½   (1984, Ger./Brit.) 90m Road Movies-BFI
Productions/Channel 4 c

Tusse Silberg, Paul Freeman, Lisa Kreuzer, Eddie Constantine, Jean-Francois Stevenin, Ewan Stewart, Jonathan Kinsler, Gisela Gluck, Bogdan Faluta, Larry Lamb, Sema Poyraz, Udo Helland, Tatjana Blacher, Ellen Umlauf, Sonja Warnke, Claus D. Streuber.

A mysterious atmospheric thriller about a woman caught up in a web of strange doings in Europe. The importance of detail and plot are diminished in favor of creating a mood and heightening the mystery of the woman going among her European friends in attempting to escape from herself. Director Petit, who works here with Wim Wenders' producer and editor, achieves the same sort of feel and pacing as Wenders' THE AMERICAN FRIEND (1977), and PARIS, TEXAS (1984). Petit's followup, also released this year and shown at the Director's Fortnight at the Cannes Film Festival, is CHINESE BOXES.

P, Chris Sievernich; d, Christopher Petit; w, Petit, Hugo Williams (based on the novel *Strange Days* by Jennifer Potter); ph, Martin Schafer; m, Irmin Schmidt; ed, Peter Przygodda; art d, Rainer Schaper.

Crime Drama   **(PR:O   MPAA:NR)**

FOOTLOOSE**½   (1984) 107m PAR c

Kevin Bacon (*Ren*), Lori Singer (*Ariel*), John Lithgow (*Rev. Shaw Moore*), Dianne Wiest (*Vi Moore*), Christopher Penn (*Willard*), Sarah Jessica Parker (*Rusty*), John Laughlin (*Woody*), Elizabeth Gorcey (*Wendy Jo*), Frances Lee McCain (*Ethel McCormick*), Jim Youngs (*Chuck*), Douglas Dirkson (*Burlington Cranston*), Lynne Marta (*Lulu*), Arthur Rosenberg (*Wes*), Timothy Scott (*Andy Beamis*), Alan Haufrect (*Roger Dunbar*), Linda MacEwen (*Eleanor Dunbar*), Kim Jensen (*Edna*), Michael Telmont (*Travis*), Leo Geter

(*Rich*), Ken Kemp (*Jeff*), Russ McGinn (*Herb*), Sam Dalton (*Mr. Gurntz*), H.E.D. Redford (*Widdoes*), Jay Bernard (*Harvey*), David Valenza (*Team Member*), Meghan Broadhead (*Sarah*), Mimi Broadhead (*Amy*), Gene Pack (*Bernie*), Marcia Yvette Reider (*Virginia*), John Perryman (*Fat Cowboy*), Mary Ethel Gregory (*Mrs. Allyson*), Oscar Rowland (*Mr. Walsh*), J. Paul Broadhead (*Mayor Dooley*), John Bishop (*Elvis*), Carmen Trevino, Melissa Renee Graehl, Monica M. da Silva, Terri Gay Ulmer (*Girls*), Peter Tramm (*Stunt Dancer*), Robert Allen, Wayne Brown, J. Suzanne Fish, Donna Garrett, Paul Godwin, Norman Howell, Clair E. Leucart, Daniel K. Moore, Lane Parrish, Carol L. Rees, John-Clay Scott.

Basically a 1950s movie in 1980s clothing, FOOTLOOSE was a gigantic smash at the box office and one of the rare instances where style did triumph over substance. FOOTLOOSE joined FLASHDANCE and several other MTV-type musicals scored with pop songs by big name artists. It's not really a musical because the actors don't sing and most of the songs were composed *after* the film was done. Bacon is a young Chicagoan who moves to a smaller Midwest town with his mother, McCain. Bacon has a new wave hair style and he likes to dance so he's immediately looked upon as a crazed big city boy who will drive the morals of the small towners straight to Hades. Nobody is allowed to dance in this burg because the leader of the place, Lithgow, is a fundamentalist minister who thinks that dancing can lead to other, more sinful pursuits. Bacon now has a cause and he is determined to see it through with no compromise and to bring the community around to his way of thinking: that dancing is fun and evil is in the eyes of the beholder. Lithgow's daughter, Singer, is Bacon's classmate. She's dating redneck Youngs and he and Bacon have a "chicken" match on tractors in a variation of the scene in REBEL WITHOUT A CAUSE. Bacon wins the match, Singer's love, dull-witted oaf Penn's admiration, and total acceptance by his school chums. He rallies the other students and asks Lithgow for permission to hold a dance, but that's denied. Bacon arranges the dance just beyond the city limits and Lithgow finally relents when he sees the folly of his ways. That's it for the story, no more or less than a hundred Sam Katzman or AIP-type pictures. It's ludicrous and says that the only thing these Moral Majority students are worrying about is dancing, with no mention of the more serious problems of the age. No rebellion, no caring, just the fact that these kids feel as though they're going to be left out if they don't have a prom. The soundtrack album was also a hit and two of the songs, "Footloose" (Kenny Loggins, Dean Pitchford) and "Let's Hear it for the Boy" (Tom Snow, Pitchford) were Oscar nominated. Other songs: "The Girl Gets Around" (Sammy Hager, Pitchford) "Dancing in the Sheets" (Bill Wolfer, Pitchford) "Somebody's Eyes" (Snow, Pitchford) "Almost Paradise" (Eric Carmen, Pitchford) "I'm Free" (Loggins, Pitchford), "Never" (Michael Gore, Pitchford) "Holding Out for a Hero" (Jim Steinman, Pitchford). Good dancing, although not nearly enough, and a fine performance by Lithgow in a role that could have been a comic-strip character but was given flesh and blood by his intelligent attack and grasp of the part.

p, Lewis J. Rachmil, Craig Zadan; d, Herbert Ross; w, Dean Pitchford; ph, Ric Waite (Movielab Color); m, Miles Goodman, Becky Shargo; ed, Paul Hirsch; prod d, Ron Hobbs; set d, Mary Olivia Swanson; cos, Gloria Gresham, Kendall Errair, Barton K. James; spec eff, James W. Beauchamp; ch, Lynne Taylor-Corbett.

Musical   **Cas.**   **(PR:A-C   MPAA:PG)**

FORBRYDELSENS ELEMENT   (SEE: ELEMENT OF CRIME, THE, Den.)

FOREVER YOUNG*½   (1984, Brit.) 84m Enigma-Goldcrest-Channel
4/FOX c-bw

James Aubrey (*James*), Nicholas Gecks (*Father Michael*), Alec McGowen (*Father Vincent*), Karen Archer (*Mary*), Joseph Wright (*John*), Liam Holt (*Paul*), Jane Forster (*Cathy*), Jason Carter (*Young Michael*), Oona Kirsch (*Maureen*), Eileen Fletcher (*Alison*), Carol MacReady (*Brenda*), Julian Firth (*Young James*), Pamela Miles, Martin Duncan, Robin Wentworth, Shelley Borkum, Kate Percival, James Wynn, Joseph Wright, Jimmy Mac, Stanley Lloyd, Philip McGough, Anje Byer, Ruth Davies, Peter Scott Harrison, Kathy Burke, Michael Sundin.

Aubrey is a rock musician who reunites with Gecks, his partner some 20 years before. Gecks is now a priest, having taken up the collar after leaving the promising musical duo. Their reunion sets off some still deep-seated emotional wounds that become intensified. Aubrey further complicates issues when he makes eyes at the mother of a boy Gecks has taken under his wing. Though there are a few glimmers of intelligence in some black and white flashbacks of Aubrey and Gecks' younger days, on the whole this is a rather tedious bit of melodrama. The central conflict between the two leads is never fully explored, with the plot relying more on extraneous characters to develop the story. McGowen as an elder priest who looks down on his younger colleague's interest in rock n roll is a wholly unnecessary character, played like the stereotype he is. The two leads aren't able to provide the needed spark that should be snapping between them which sufficiently damages any potential the film could have had. This was the first film in a projected bargain-basement British series called "First Love."

p, Chris Griffin; d, David Drury; w, Ray Connolly; ph, Norman Langley; m, Peter Maxwell-Davies; ed, Max Lemon; art d, Jeffrey Woodbridge; cos, Tudor George.

Drama   (PR:C   MPAA:NR)

FOUR DAYS IN JULY½   (1984) 99m BBC c

Brid Brennan (*Colette*), Des McAleer (*Eugene*), Charles Lawson (*Billy*), Paula Hamilton (*Lorraine*), Shane Connaughton (*Brendan*), Eileen Pollock (*Carmel*), Stephen Rea (*Dixie*).

War-torn Belfast is the setting for this absorbing drama involving two couples who are about to become parents for the first time. McAleer is a disabled Catholic man who has come to rely on his wife for many of his needs after being shot. Though the two have a rocky life they look forward to their forth coming child. Lawson represents an opposite viewpoint as an oft-drunken member of the Ulster Defense League who shows an occasional glimmer of tenderness in his infrequent sober moments. In the end he and McAleer strike up a friendship of the moment as they sit in the waiting room outside the maternity ward where their respective wives are in labor. The women also end up friends as they sit in their adjacent beds holding their newborns. The story and dialog were largely improvised by the cast during workshop sessions rather than being scripted, and the results are extremely personal, giving an honest feeling to the quartet and the people who surround them. The actual Belfast locations help this along; in fact, the film may be a little too realistic. While filled with moments of charm and pathos, there are also dull stretches. Overall, though, these are not sufficient to mar an otherwise enjoyable feature an d its fresh approach.

p, Kenith Trodd; d, Mike Leigh; ph, Remi Adefarasin; m, Rachel Portman; ed, Robin Sales; prod d, Jim Clay.

Drama   (PR:C-O   MPAA:NR)

FOURTH MAN, THE½   (1984, Neth.) 104m De Verenigde
                                        Nederlandsche/International Spectrafilm c

Jeroen Krabbe (*Gerard Reve*), Renee Soutendijk (*Christine Halsslag*), Thom Hoffman (*Herman*), Dolf DeVries (*Dr. DeVries*), Geert De Jong (*Ria the Lady in Blue*), Hans Veerman (*Funeral Director*), Hero Muller (*Josefs*), Caroline De Beus (*Adrienne*), Reinout Bussemaker (*1st Husband*), Erik J. Meijer (*2nd Husband*), Ursul DeGeer (*3rd Husband*), Filip Bolluyt (*Surfer*), Hedda Lornie (*Sales Clerk in Bookstore*), Paul Nygaard (*Gerard's Boy Friend*), Guus van der Made (*Waiter on Train*), Pamela Teves (*Nurse*), Hella Faassen (*Woman at Lecture*), Helen Hedy (*AKO Sales Clerk*).

A cryptic and intense thriller-black comedy about a bisexual hard-drinking fatalistic writer, Krabbe, who travels out of town for a speaking engagement. Along the way he has a number of hallucinations which predict his demise, including seeing a funeral wreath which bears what appears to be his name. During his lecture he notices Soutendijk paying him a great deal of attention and filming him with a movie camera. Their relationship develops quickly and Krabbe learns that Soutendijk has gone through three husbands, each of whom has died in a freak accident. Krabbe's imagination begins to run wild. He has a nightmare that he is being castrated, imagines that he is seeing a mysterious woman whom he believes is Mary, the mother of God, and has frightening visions of the dead men in Soutendijk's life. Krabbe's interest in Soutendijk grows when he learns that she is involved with Hoffman, a handsome young man to whom Krabbe is deeply attracted. While in a cemetery, Hoffman and Krabbe are caught in a rainstorm and flee to the shelter of a nearby crypt. Krabbe attempts to seduce Hoffman, but then realizes that they are in the crypt of Soutendijk's dead husbands. By now Krabbe is convinced that Soutendijk is an evil witch who, like the symbolic spider that opens and closes the movie, devours the men who love her. Krabbe warns Hoffman that he will be her next victim, and on the drive back from the cemetery he notices a funeral wreath bearing Hoffman's name. Hoffman loses control of his car and crashes into a construction site. A steel pipe crashes through the front windshield and is driven through Hoffman's head, impaling him into the car seat. Krabbe is taken to a hospital where his bizarre accusation of Soutendijk gets him sent to the psycho ward. Meanwhile, Soutendijk has quickly recovered from the death of Hoffman and has found herself a new victim, substantiating Krabbe's claims. Directed by veteran Dutch director Verhoeven, THE FOURTH MAN delivers a heavy dose of religious and sexual symbolism, a bit of gore, and a sharp-edged offering of perversity. While definitely not a film for everyone, those who like their films on the fringe will revel in this one's ideas. (In Dutch; English subtitles.)

p, Rob Houwer; d, Paul Verhoeven; w, Gerard Soeteman (based on the novel by Gerard Reve); ph, Jan De Bont; m, Loek Dikker; ed, Ine Schenkkan; prod d, Roland De Groot; set d, Harry Ammerlaan; cos, Elly Claus.

Drama   Cas.   (PR:O   MPAA:NR)

FRIDAY THE 13TH--THE FINAL CHAPTER zero

                                                            (1984) 91m PAR c

E. Erich Anderson (*Rob*), Judie Aronson (*Samantha*), Peter Barton (*Doug*), Kimberly Beck (*Trish*), Tom Everett (*Flashlight Man*), Corey Feldman (*Tommy*), Joan Freeman (*Mrs. Jarvis*), Lisa Freeman (*Nurse Morgan*), Thad Geer (*Running Man*), Crispin Glover (*Jimmy*), Wayne Grace (*Officer Jamison*), Alan Hayes (*Paul*), Bonnie Hellman (*Hitchhiker*), Frankie Hill (*Lainie*), Barbara Howard (*Sara*), William Irby (*Helicopter Pilot*), Paul Lukather (*Doctor*), Bruce Mahler (*Axel*), Lawrence Monoson (*Ted*), Arnie

Moore (*Medic*), Camilla More (*Tina*), Carey More (*Terri*), Robert Perault (*Medic*), Antony Ponzini (*Vincent*), Gene Ross (*Cop*), Abigail Shelton (*Woman*), John Walsh (*TV Newscaster*), Robyn Woods (*Girl in Shower*), Kristen Baker, Richard Brooker, Peter Brouwer, Ronn Carroll, Steve Daskawisz, Marta Kober, Jack Marks, Tom McBride, Betsy Palmer, Jaime Perry, Rex Everhart, John Furey, Walt Gorney, Dana Kimmell, Adrienne King, Jeffrey Rogers, Nick Savage, Amy Steel, Lauren-Marie Taylor, Russell Todd.

Just because the title said this was the "Final Chapter" didn't mean that Paramount Studios was ready to dismantle their bloody money-making machine just yet. The first three mindless exercises in graphic bloodletting grossed a total of over $42 million with very little money spent on production. Considering all that is really needed for these films is an endless supply of teenagers willing to disrobe for some on-screen hanky-panky, and then submit themselves to the special effects crew whose job it is to devise dozens of gory ways to slice them up, the overhead is low. The studio certainly doesn't have to hire any brilliant writers, since the plot of the first film has been repeated in every sequel. The plot, as if it mattered, sees the crazed Jason once again stomping through the woods of a lonely summer camp carving up all the nubile young camp counselors. As usual, the open ending prepared blood-lusting viewers craving for another sequel, FRIDAY THE 13th–A NEW BEGINNING, which is a rather laughable title considering the previous four films came out of a Xerox machine. If there were only some way to sue Paramount for breach of promise after the "Final Chapter," perhaps these insults to humanity could be incinerated before they have a chance to pollute the nation's screens. This is as about as vile as it gets.

p, Frank Mancuso, Jr., Tony Bishop; d, Joseph Zito; w, Barney Cohen (story by Bruce Hidemi Sakow, based on characters created by Victor Miller, Ron Kurz, Martin Kitrosser, Carol Watson); ph, Joao Fernandes (Movielab Color); m, Henry Manfredini; ed, Joel Goodman, Daniel Loewenthal; prod d, Shelton H. Bishop III; art d, Joe Hoffman; spec eff, Martin Becker; m/l, "Love is a Lie," Cal Swan; makeup, Tom Savini.

Horror   Cas.   (PR:O   MPAA:R)

FULL MOON IN PARIS*½   (1984, Fr.) 101m Les Films du
Losange-Les Films Ariane/Orion Classics c (LES NUITS DE LA PLEINE
                                                                    LUNE)

Pascale Ogier (*Louise*), Fabrice Luchini (*Octave*), Tcheky Karyo (*Remi*), Christian Vadim (*Bastien*), Virginia Thevenet (*Camille*), Anne-Severine Liotard (*Marianne*), Laszlo Szabo, Lisa Garneri, Mathieu Schiffman, Herve Grandsart, Noel Coffman.

The fourth entry in Rohmer's "Comedies and Proverbs" series (THE AVIATOR'S WIFE, 1980, LE BEAU MARRIAGE, 1982, and PAULINE AT THE BEACH, 1983), FULL MOON IN PARIS offers the same enlightening conversations on youth and romance as the other. Ogier stars as the quintessential Rohmer woman, loved and admired by the men around her but desperately confused by the meaning of romance. A trainee at an interior design firm, Ogier lives with her architect-tennis player lover, Karyo, in a plastic suburb outside of Paris. He wants to marry Ogier and settle down, but she is still young and enjoys dancing at parties until dawn. Karyo's pressure proves too much for Ogier and she takes an apartment in Paris in order "to experience loneliness." Ideally, Ogier will spend her late party nights in Paris, sleep in her new apartment, and return to Karyo the following afternoon. While in Paris she spends a great deal of time with Luchini (whose character Octave is comparable to the Jean Renoir character of the same name in RULES OF THE GAME), a likable writer who is tortured by the fact that Ogier won't sleep with him. Ogier and Karyo begin to drift apart. She becomes suspicious of a possible affair he may be having, while he grows less concerned with her Parisian life. At one fateful party, Ogier meets Vadim (the real-life son of Roger Vadim and Catherine Deneuve) and takes him back to her apartment. The following morning she realizes her mistake and returns to Karyo with a newfound affection. Karyo, however, has fallen in love with another. While its subject matter is simple, FULL MOON IN PARIS is anything but a superficial meandering on the philosophies of love. What Rohmer has done in this film, and has done so successfully in the past, is to take a brief, intelligent, comic look at a young Frenchwoman and her ideas of love. It's not that the ideas are revelatory, but that they are presented in such a fresh tone. This is due mainly to his choice of superb, unknown actresses in the lead roles. Ogier (the 24-year-old daughter of renowned actress Bulle Ogier) delivers her lines with an animated energy that is rarely captured on the screen. Her performance earned her a Best Actress award at the Venice Film Festival (a prize also garnered by Beatrice Romand two years earlier for her role in LE BEAU MARRIAGE), although her career was tragically cut short after a fatal heart attack. As has become tradition with Rohmer's films, FULL MOON IN PARIS begins with a French proverb: "He who has two women loses his soul. He who has two houses loses his mind." (In French; English subtitles.)

p, Margaret Menegoz; d&w, Eric Rohmer; ph, Renato Berta; m, Elli Jacno; ed, Cecile Decujis; art d, Pascale Ogier; cos, Ogier.

Drama   Cas.   (PR:O   MPAA:R)

GABRIELA**   (1984, Braz.) 102m MGM/UA Classics c

Sonia Braga *(Gabriela)*, Marcello Mastroianni *(Nacib)*, Antonio Cantafora *(Tonico Bastos)*, Paulo Goulart *(Colonel)*, Nelson Xavier *(Capitao)*, Nuno Leal Maia *(Engineer)*, Fernando Ramos *(Tuisca)*, Nicole Puzzi *(Malvina)*, Tania Boscoli *(Gloria)*, Jofre Soares *(Ramiro)*, Paulo Pilla *(Prince)*, Claudia Gimenez *(Dona Olga)*, Ricardo Petraglia *(Prof. Josue)*, Antonio Pedro *(Doctor)*, Ivan Mesquita *(Col. Melk)*, Zeni Pereira *(Dona Arminda)*, Flavio Galvao *(Mundinho)*, Miriam Pires *(Mae De Malvina)*, Iris Nascimento *(Empregada De Malvina)*, Mauricio do Vale *(Capitao)*, Luthero Luiz *(Capitao)*.

A sexy, sultry, and close-to-erotic film based on the 1925 novel by Amado which also served as the basis for a long-running soap opera, also starring Braga, which has been playing on Spanish and Portuguese-language TV for years. Mastroianni (looking bloated and ancient) owns a bar. Braga is hired to be his cook and the fact that the hip-swinging Braga finds Mastroianni attractive is the first lie in the story. It's 1925 in the Bahian village of Parati, where a great drought has come upon the land. Braga and some of her thirsty compadres come to town from the country. The moment she meets Mastroianni, it's evident that she will be doing lots for the proprietor, in several departments. Once the mud is cleaned off her face, Braga begins to appear attractive to many of the other men in the village and Mastroianni decides to put a stop to that by marrying her. He insists that she doff her old sexy clothing and wear more conservative togs. He also feels that it would be wrong for them to sleep with each other until they are married. Naturally, the pneumatic Braga pays little attention to his "Henry Higgins" attempts at making her into a dark-haired "Eliza Doolittle." They marry but his attempts at changing her soon wear thin and she takes lovers. Despite that, Mastroianni can't give her up and soon is the change*e*, rather than the change*r*. It's close to being a porno movie and just stops short. The novel was a comic look at life in the town of Ilheus. It was rich with interesting characters, satire, and politics, This version seems to have only concentrated on the sex, with a bit of comedy, and omitted the other elements which made the Amado book a classic sociological work. Braga is not that seductive, if one examines her dispassionately. But she *thinks* she's sexy and that inner confidence pours off the screen in the same way it worked for Anna Magnani and Silvana Mangano. Barreto, who also directed Braga in DONA FLOR AND HER TWO HUSBANDS, attempts to introduce a secondary story between some of the village's bluenoses and the powers who rule the town but that falls apart and the only reason to see this is to watch Braga, reeking sensuality at all times, and having a good time as she plays the "Sadie Thompson" to Mastroianni's reverend.

p, Harold Nebenzal, Ibrahim Moussa; d, Bruno Barreto; w, Leopaldo Serran, Barreto (based on the novel *Gabriela, Clove and Cinnamon* by Jorge Amado); ph, Carlo Di Palma (Technicolor); m, Antonio Carlos Jobim, Gal Costa; ed, Emmanuelle Castro; art d, Helio Eichbauer; cos, Diana Eichbauer.

Drama   **Cas.**   **(PR:O MPAA:R)**

GARBO TALKS***   (1984) 103m MGM/UA c

Anne Bancroft *(Estelle Rolfe)*, Ron Silver *(Gilbert Rolfe)*, Carrie Fisher *(Lisa Rolfe)*, Catherine Hicks *(Jane Mortimer)*, Steven Hill *(Walter Rolfe)*, Howard Da Silva *(Angelo Dokakis)*, Dorothy Loudon *(Sonya Apollinar)*, Harvey Fierstein *(Bernie Whitlock)*, Hermione Gingold *(Elizabeth Rennick)*, Richard B. Shull *(Shepard Plotkin)*, Michael Lombard *(Mr. Morganelli)*, Ed Crowley *(Mr. Goldhammer)*, Alice Spivak *(Claire Rolfe)*, Maurice Sterman *(Dr. Cohen)*, Antonia Rey *(Puerto Rican Nurse)*, Court Miller *("Romeo & Juliet" Director)*, Denny Dillon *(Elaine)*, Karen Shallo *(Harriet)*, Maxwell Alexander *(Roger Kellerman)*, Peter Gumeny *(Arresting Officer)*, Stephen Burks *(Black Officer)*, Tony DiBenedetto, Burtt Harris *(Construction Workers)*, Mervyn Nelson *(Movie Shop Owner)*, John Ring *(Garbo Doorman)*, Anne Gartlan *(Garbo Maid)*, Jose Santana *(Sanchez/Orderly)*, Jennifer M. Ogden *(Nurse)*, David Hammil *(Ferry Conductor)*, Roderick Cook *(Von Klammer)*, Mary McDonnell *(Lady Capulet)*, Leila Danette *(Augusta)*, Nadine Darling, Joan de Marrais *(Flea Market Salesladies)*, Ethel Beatty *(Lady in Jail)*, Adolph Green *(Himself)*, Arthur Schlesinger, Jr. *(Himself)*, Didi D'Errico *(Actors Equity Receptionist)*, Harry Madsen *(Delivery Man)*, Betty Comden, Nina Zoe *(Garbo)*.

A sweet, often endearing movie with rich characters and a fanciful premise. Bancroft is a woman who has adored Garbo ever since she was a child. She watches CAMILLE with regularity and cries every time she sees it. Bancroft is divorced from Hill, who couldn't take her various obsessions. She's the kind of woman who talks to amorous construction workers in their own gutter tongue, wears space shoes, and doesn't know of a liberal cause she hasn't backed. The result of her flag-waving and demonstrating has placed her in the hoosegow once too often for conservative Hill and he divorced her for the same reason he married her; she is unique. Bancroft and Hill have a son, Silver, who is married to the ultimate Jewish Princess, Fisher, a young woman who is bilingual; she speaks English and Gucci. Fisher misses the joys and sunshine of California and lets Silver know that often. For many years, Greta Garbo has lived as a recluse in New York and Bancroft's one desire is to meet her idol. When it's learned that Bancroft is dying, she makes one request of her son and Silver attempts to fulfill it. Bancroft wants to meet Garbo. But how does Silver get to find Garbo when, for so many years, so many people have failed? He begins to stalk Garbo (played in some scenes by Nina Zoe, in others by famed author-lyricist Betty Comden), a

chore that takes him all over New York. To do that, he gives up his job and when Fisher finds out about that she leaves him and returns to California. The moment she learns that they are actually living on savings, she says that's tantamount to "spitting on God!." Silver's quest takes him outside Garbo's East Side apartment house where he meets old, tired photographer Da Silva, who exists on the proceeds from snapshots of celebrities. Da Silva and Silver have a superb scene as they shudder in the Manhattan cold while drinking stale coffee from paper cups. Later, Silver goes to Fire Island where he doesn't come in contact with Garbo but does meet Fierstein, a resident of the island who lends Silver a pair of pants. (Fierstein, in case you don't recognize the name, is the author of the Broadway musical "La Cage Aux Folles" as well as the play which brought him national fame, "Torch Song Trilogy.") Silver continues searching for Garbo, encountering Gingold, an ancient actress currently appearing in "Romeo and Juliet," the Joseph Papp production for "Shakespeare in the Park." Gingold is an addled woman who shakes from side to side when her director, Dillon, pleads with her to stand still. He also meets Loudon (overplaying somewhat) who is Da Silva's agent. When Fisher departs for the West Coast, Silver takes up with Hicks, an actress who is far more sympathetic to Silver's desire than Fisher. In the end, Silver manages to get to Garbo and persuade her to come to the hospital room where Bancroft lies dying. Bancroft's character is summed up in a line she speaks early in the film to the effect that she knows everyone has to die but thought she'd be the exception. (A nice line, except that it may have first been spoken by William Saroyan.) The museum party sequence was actually filmed at a Museum of Modern Art reception so some of the attendees were seen in the movie. They included Pat Kennedy Lawford, Francesco Scavullo (the photographer), George Plimpton, Arthur Schlesinger, Jr., and Comden's lifetime writing partner, Adolph Green. This was Silver's first starring role after excellent work as a second banana in SILKWOOD, LOVESICK, and a particularly good performance as a promoter in "Murder at the Mardi Gras," a CBS-TV movie. Fisher shows that she is far better than the wooden princess seen in STAR WARS but it is Bancroft's picture to recall, though she is actually on screen far less than one might think. But just as "Lefty" and "Godot" never appear in the plays where people were waiting for them, Bancroft's character is constantly referred to and thought about so one is left with the impression that she has been on screen for the entire film. Some very funny lines from first-timer Grusin are mixed in with sadness at watching Bancroft ebb. The blend worked well enough in James Brooks' TERMS OF ENDEARMENT which, in some ways, was not as good as this movie, although it made mincemeat of the other contenders at the Oscars that year.

p, Burtt Harris, Elliott Kastner; d, Sidney Lumet; w, Larry Grusin; ph, Andrzej Bartkowiak (Technicolor); m, Cy Coleman; ed, Andrew Mondshein; prod d, Philip Rosenberg; set d, Philip Smith, John Godfrey; cos, Anna Hill Johnstone.

Comedy/Drama   **Cas.**   **(PR:C MPAA:PG-13)**

GERMANY PALE MOTHER*½**   (1984, Ger.) 145m New Yorker c

Eva Mattes *(Lene)*, Ernst Jacobi *(Hans)*, Elisabeth Stepanek *(Hanne)*, Angelika Thomas *(Lydia)*, Rainer Friedrichsen *(Ulrich)*, Gisela Stein *(Aunt Imchen)*, Fritz Lichtenhahn *(Uncle Bertrand)*, Anna Sanders *(Anna)*.

The whys and hows behind the horrors of Nazi Germany are subjects often explored by filmmakers. This fine film differs from others in that it takes a look at the subject through the eyes of a civilian German woman, Mattes, a Berlin housewife newly married to Jacobi. Though she is not a party member, she tolerates the actions of Adolf Hitler's government, believing they will make for a stronger Germany. Eventually the Reich crumbles and with it Mattes' life. During an air raid she goes into labor, giving birth to a daughter under the most harrowing of circumstances. Later she is raped by the Americans overrunning the country and is accused of infidelity by Jacobi. As life grows to unbearable levels Mattes contemplates suicide but ultimately decides to continue to live, emerging as a brave, determined woman. Originally released in Germany in 1980, this is a film of tremendous pain and em otional power. Mattes is stunning in the lead, portraying a character whose real life horrors become our own. Director Sanders-Brahms has created a nightmare vision out of genuine tragedy, basing the film on wartime events in her mother's life. She effectively tells the story of the average German, who likewise was a victim of Hitler's madness, with a special insight that permeates the filmand in a viewpoint unabashedly feminist, dedicating the work "for my mother, for thousands of women." The ravages of war and ideology of the Nazi party could only have been conceived by men, a point continually put forth through the course of the story. GERMANY PALE MOTHER is not an easy film to sit through considering its deeply disturbing ideas and situations, but the daring of its vision makes this an important film on a much-ignored subject. In an interesting production note, the director cast her daughter as herself in the role of Mattes' child. (In German; English subtitles.)

p, Ursula Ludwig; d&w, Helma Sanders-Brahms; ph, Jurgen Jurges; m, Jurgen Knieper; ed, Elfi Tillack, Ute Periginelli; cos, Janken Janssen.

Drama   **(PR:O MPAA:NR)**

GHARE BAIRE   (SEE: HOME AND THE WORLD, THE, India)

GHOST DANCE*½   (1984, Brit.) 100m Looseyard/Other c

Pascale Ogier (*Pascale*), Leonie Mellinger (*Marianne*), Jacques Derrida (*Himself*), Stuart Brisley, Robbie Coltrane, Dominique Pinon.

"The idea of my idea is that I don't have an idea." "I see. We'll talk again tomorrow." Dialog exchanges such as these can be baffling, pretentious, or just plain silly but this film manages to be all three simultaneously. Ogier and Mellinger are off on a journey, searching for the ghosts of the past that continually haunt the present dream-like world they dwell in. They flit between London and Paris with a sort of casual incoherence that never really gels. The film has some fine moments, including good characterizations by Coltrane and Pinon, along with the cameo appearance by French philosopher Jacques Derrida. There's a good flair for comedy and moments of visual delight as well, but ultimately the film is brought down by the weight of its own intentions. McMullen shows a heavy influence of Godard with the unusual construction but can't muster what he attempts. Like Godard at his worst moments, he tries to pack in too much, attempting to incorporate ideas on politics, psychology, philosophy, and sexual identity along with the nature of film itself. It results in McMullen trying to say everything and conveying little. (In English and French; English subtitles.)

p,d&w, Ken McMullen; ph, Peter Harvey; m, David Cunningham, Michael Giles, Janie Muir; ed, Robert Hargreaves.

Fantasy   **(PR:O MPAA:R)**

GHOSTBUSTERS***½   (1984) 107m COL c

Bill Murray (*Dr. Peter Venkman*), Dan Aykroyd (*Dr. Raymond Stantz*), Sigourney Weaver (*Dana Barrett*), Harold Ramis (*Dr. Egon Spenler*), Rick Moranis (*Louis Tully*), Annie Potts (*Janine Melnitz*), William Atherton (*Walter Peck*), Ernie Hudson (*Winston Zeddmore*), David Margulies (*Mayor*), Steven Tash Jennifer Runyon (*Students*), Slavitza Jovan (*Gozer*), Michael Ensign (*Hotel Manager*), Alice Drummond (*Librarian*), Jordan Charney (*Dean Yeager*), Timothy Carhart (*Violinist*), John Rothman (*Library Administrator*), Roger Grimsby, Larry King, Joe Franklin, Casey Kasem (*Themselves*), Norman Matlock (*Fire Commissioner*), Joe Cirillo (*Police Captain*), Joe Schmieg (*Police Sergeant*), Reggie Vel Johnson (*Jail Guard*), Rhoda Gemignani (*Real Estate Woman*), Murray Rubin (*Man at Elevator*), Larry Dilg (*Con Edison Man*), Danny Stone (*Coachman*), Patty Dworkin (*Woman at Party*), Jean Kasem (*Tall Woman at Party*), Lenny Del Genio (*Doorman*), Frances E. Nealy (*Chambermaid*), Sam Moses (*Hot Dog Vendor*), Christopher Wynkoop (*TV Reporter*), Winston May (*Businessman in Cab*), Tommy Hollis (*Mayor's Aide*), Eda Reiss Merin (*Louis' Neighbor*), Ric Mancini (*Cop at Apartment*), Kathryn Janssen (*Mrs. Van Hoffman*), Paul Trafas (*Ted Fleming*), Cheryl Birchfield (*Annette Fleming*), Ruth Oliver (*Library Ghost*), Kym Herrin (*Dream Ghost*), Nancy Kelly, Frantz Turner, James Hardie, Carol Ann Henry, Stanley Grover (*Reporters*).

An enormously successful movie that owes much to many less successful movies that preceded it, GHOSTBUSTERS will remind older readers of SPOOK CHASERS (1957), THE SENTINEL (1977), SPOOK BUSTERS (1946), SCARED STIFF (1953), THE GHOST BREAKERS (1940), GHOST CATCHERS (1944), and countless others. The difference between those and this is that GHOSTBUSTERS had a huge special effects budget and the presence of Bill Murray, who personally makes the whole thing work. With the total cost of production estimated at around $32 million, it had to earn a great deal of money to show a profit and it did. Murray and Aykroyd are Columbia University teachers in New York. Murray is a psychologist and Aykroyd a metallurgist-physicist and general all-around scientific Renaissance Man. Both are interested in parapsychology and are excellent in their fields. Just as they are about to make what they feel is an important discovery, they are fired from their teaching assignments and barred from their laboratory when their reserch grant runs out. Together with Ramis, an expert in electronics, they set up their own investigatory shop in a downtown building with Potts as their bored secretary. They claim that for a fee they can rid your residence of whatever spirits move you. Weaver is a cellist with a symphony and lives in a spectacular apartment above Central Park. (How she does it on the salary of a cellist is never explained.) "Things" have been happening in her apartment and Murray, a lecher, offers to help. He puts a move on Weaver but she holds back, more concerned with what's transpiring in her apartment than in her love life, or lack of one. When a large gooey green ghost is found in a hotel ballroom, the three ghost chasers move in with high-tech equipment and catch the ghost, then bring it back to their offices, located in an old firehouse. Once the ghost is placed in their basement, all the other ghosts infesting the city of New York team up with it and the entire city is suddenly swept by a heretofore unheard-of attack of wraiths. After their first success, they become well known and Weaver finally says she'll go out with Murray. When he gets to her apartment, he finds the attractive Weaver has been possessed by a Babylonian spirit and she calls herself "Zool." Weaver's normally shy character has been turned into a sexual, sensual creature right out of a teenager's fantasies. In the end, the city is attacked by a creature that's a cross between the Pillsbury Doughboy and the balloon-like Michelin Man and the creature has to be destroyed in a burlesque of the RODAN, MOTHRA, and GODZILLA-type movies out of Japan. The movie was to have been an Aykroyd and John Belushi picture but when Belushi died at the Chateau Marmont on Sunset

Boulevard in 1982, the picture was switched to accommodate the new stars. Moranis gets his share of laughs as a yutz accountant who lives in the same building as Weaver, and Atherton is briefly seen as an EPA man who is a comedy foil for Murray's irreverent insults. This is sort of a modern blend between "The Three Stooges" and "The Three Musketeers" and it makes no sense whatsoever but there are so many good lines and such excellent effects that it's best not to question the logic, just sit back and laugh. Murray does a few lines to the camera, a la Oliver Hardy, and they work. At first he didn't want to do the film but agreed when the studio gave its nod to finance his film THE RAZOR'S EDGE, which was as much of a disaster as this was a hit. Aykroyd and Ramis wrote the script but they wisely gave the best jokes to Murray and took a back seat themselves. When Weaver's refrigerator begins to rumble and perk and look as though it's the "Frigidaire from Hell," Murray quips, "Usually, you don't see this sort of behavior in a major appliance." And when Weaver begins to exhibit certain animalistic tendencies, Murray's comment is, "I think we can get her a guest shot on 'The Wild Kingdom.' " Lots of fun, slightly tasteless. Broadcasters Roger Grimsby, Casey Kasem, Joe Franklin, and Larry King play themselves, as only they can.

p&d, Ivan Reitman; w, Dan Aykroyd, Harold Ramis; ph, Laszlo Kovacs, Herb Wagreitch (Panavision, Metrocolor); m, Elmer Bernstein; ed, Sheldon Kahn, David Blewitt; prod d, John DeCuir; art d, John DeCuir, Jr., John Moore; set d, Marvin March, Robert Drumheller; cos, Theoni V. Aldredge; spec eff, Richard Edlund, John Bruno, Mark Vargo, Chuck Gaspar; m/l, "Ghostbusters," Ray Parker, Jr., "Cleanin' Up the Town," Kevin O'Neal, Brian O'Neal; stunts, Bill Couch.

Comedy/Science Fiction   **Cas.**   **(PR:A-C MPAA:PG)**

GIMME AN 'F' zero   (1984) 100m Poll/FOX c

Stephen Shellen (*Tom Hamilton*), Mark Keyloun (*Roscoe*), Jennifer C. Cooke (*Pam*), Beth Miller (*Mary Ann*), Daphne Ashbrook (*Phoebe*), Karen Kelly (*Lead Demon*), Sarah M. Miles (*Eileen*), John Karlen (*Bucky Berkshire/"Dr. Spirit"*).

Like pollutants spewed out daily by steel mills, idiotic teenaged sex films are endlessly churned out, causing wear and tear on projector bulbs and adding nothing of merit to society. This one involves a cheerleaders' training camp with the misogynist moniker "Camp Beaver View." The place is run by Karlen, an actor with no shame, playing an unexpendable bundle of energy with the nickname of "Dr. Spirit." The plot has him betting one of his cheerleading instructors (Shellen) $10,000 that an underdog squad won't be able to withstand the competition of a popular team. If he loses Shellen must work for "Dr. Spirit" another five years. A subplot involves Karlen's attempt to finance a chain of boutiques with some Japanese investors, but the real point of the film is to watch a group of well-scrubbed high schoolers prance about in a series of decidedly unerotic sexual antics. What makes this film different from most of its ilk is the relative lack of female nudity. In a sort of reversal of PORKY'S, a group of cheerleaders peek through the showers to watch Shellen dance about under the streaming water clad in underwear, making him perhaps the only man in America who showers in his shorts. It's 100 minutes of time one could spend engaging in far more enjoyable activities, like chewing on tinfoil.

p, Martin Poll; d, Paul Justman; w, Jim Hart; ph, Mario Di Leo (CFI Color); m, Jan Hammer; ed, Tom Walls: prod d, Kim Colefax; art d, Tom Randol; ch, Steve Merritt; stunts, Cindy "Toad" Wills.

Comedy   **Cas.**   **(PR:O MPAA:R)**

GIRLS NIGHT OUT zero   (1984) 96m GK/Aries c (AKA: THE SCAREMAKER)

Julie Montgomery, James Carroll, Suzanne Barnes, Rutanya Alda, Hal Holbrook, David Holbrook, Lauren-Marie Taylor, Al McGuire, Matthew Dunn, Paul Christie, Richard Bright.

A night of fun for some sorority girls and an escaped mental patient killer of a sorority girl who jilted him years before can only add up to one thing: an hour and a half of tedious mad slasher movie cliches. It seems the killer had done his ex-girl friend in on the evening of a scavenger hunt. This night he makes things a bit different by stealing the school's bear mascot costume and attaching several knives to one of the paws. The girls start dropping and the cops investigate. Like most local mad slasher police forces, the law is composed of a bunch of incompetents, so Holbrook, in a major career low point as the original victim's father and head of campus security, goes after the slasher. The ending tries for a surprise twist but scarcely succeeds. The point of films like this is to watch women in danger, an entertainment form that continues to hold its own despite its repellent nature. Most of the college kids are played by actors old enough to be teaching higher education. Holbrook's son begins his own acting career with this picture, though it's certainly not an auspicious beginning.

p, Anthony N. Gurvis; d, Robert Deubel; w, Gil Spencer, Jr., Joe Bolster, Kevin Kurgis, Gurvis; ph, Joe Rivers (TVC Color); ed, Arthur Ginsberg; prod d, Howard Cummings; makeup, Tom Brumberger.

Horror   **(PR:O MPAA:R)**

GIVE MY REGARDS TO BROAD STREET**

(1984, Brit.) 108m FOX c

Paul McCartney (Paul), Bryan Brown (Steve), Ringo Starr (Ringo), Barbara Bach (Journalist), Linda McCartney (Linda), Tracey Ullman (Sandra), Ralph Richardson (Jim), John Burgess (Chauffeur), Philip Jackson (Alan), Ian Hastings (Harry), Marie Collett (Valerie), Graham Dene (Disc Jockey Voice), Anthony Bates (City Banker), Leonard Fenton (Company Accountant), Jeremy Child, Richard Kane (Record Company Executives), Anthony Brown (Police Inspector), Donald Douglas (Police Detective), Alison McGuire, Rosina Stewart (Blue-Rinsed Ladies), John Salthouse (Tom the Roadie), Amanda Redman (Office Receptionist), Mr. Bennett (Mr. Rath), Christopher Ellison (Rath's Minder), Clive Ellis (2nd Chauffeur), George Martin (Producer), Geoff Emerick (Engineer), Jon Jacobs, Roland Jaquarello (Studio Assistants), Robert Longden (Tape Operator), Leslie Sarony (Gatekeeper), James Wynn (Assistant Director), Nicholas Askew (Teacup Child), Desmond Askew, Sian Pinder, Jason Savage (Magic Carpet Children), David Easter, Gary Shail (Apache Dancers), Isobel Hurl, Peter Jessup (Ballroom Dance Couple), Les Pendergast, Tana Pendergast (Leading Rock 'n' Roll Couple), Gordon Rollings (Monster), Luke "Giant Haystacks" McMasters (Big Bob), John Hammel, Trevor Jones (Roadies), John Harding (Ernest), Mark Kingston (Terry), Frank Duncan (William), John Murphy (Wino), Ruby Buchanan (Bag Lady).

An excessive "star vehicle" that took two years and about $9 million to make with a screenplay and music by McCartney. He plays himself, a musician, composer, and recording company executive whose company has misplaced the only copy of a tape of his latest works. Bennett is a gangster-type who has been quietly buying up stock in the record firm and tells McCartney that he has just 14 hours to find the missing master tape...or else. McCartney can't imagine where the tape has gone but everyone around him thinks that is may have been stolen by Hastings, an ex-con McCartney hired a few years ago and still maintains faith in. Brown is McCartney's manager and ineffective in suggesting an answer to the tape's disappearance. Hastings is missing and even his wife, weepy Ullman, can't help as she doesn't know where her hubby has gone. That's the premise. The denouement occurs when, just after the deadline imposed by Bennett, Hastings and the tape are found. He'd been accidentally locked in a shed at the Broad Street station of London's underground (subway). That's about it for the story but the songs come thick and fast, with scarcely a bit of motivation. The acting is weaker than the slim story but people went to see this to hear music by the "Prince of Lightness" and they got to hear plenty of it. There were both old tunes and new ones and each set piece looked like a music video for MTV. Directed by Peter Webb, whose background is mostly in commercials, nothing moves or connects and the only reason to see the movie is to hear the music and notice how old McCartney seems to have become. The best tunes were "Eleanor Rigby" in a Victorian dream sequence featuring McCartney, wife Linda, Ringo Starr, and his wife, Barbara Bach, and "Ballroom Dancing," a conceptual piece which featured two sets of dancers, the usual type and punkers. Other tunes include: "Good Day, Sunshine," "Silly Love Songs" (done in a pretentious and silly fashion), "No Values," "No More Lonely Nights," "Yesterday," "Not Such A Bad Boy," and "The Long and Winding Road." All the music was produced by veteran George Martin. The picture, despite the swiftness of the pacing and editing, creaked along like a senior citizens' home movie. One of the great shames of this is that it marked the last performance of Sir Ralph Richardson, in a strange scene with a monkey in a dockside pub. This is a far cry from HELP! or A HARD DAY'S NIGHT, although both of those movies shared the manic pace of this and had many disjointed scenes. The worst part of this is that the missing tape turns out to be a nightmare on McCartney's part (that cliche about the whole thing being a dream). The most memorable scene is one of McCartney standing outside the Leicester Square station of the subway. He plays his guitar, with the case lying open at his feet, trying to cadge a few bob from the passersby. It is an actual candid sequence and a few unsuspecting Londoners get a chance to see and hear an egoless McCartney living out what must have been another nightmare he must have once had. A large budget, excellent costumes by Milena Canonero (she did CHARIOTS OF FIRE), and some inventive choreography by David Toguri cannot make up for the lack of depth in the story.

p, Andros Epaminondas; d, Peter Webb; w, Paul McCartney; ph, Ian McMillan (Rank Color); m, McCartney; ed, Peter Beston; md, George Martin; prod d, Anthony Pratt; art d, Adrian Smith; set d, Stephenie McMillan; cos, Milena Canonero; ch, David Toguri; m/l, McCartney.

Musical   **Cas.**   (PR:A-C MPAA:PG)

GO TELL IT ON THE MOUNTAIN***

(1984) 96m Learning In Focus c

Paul Winfield (Gabriel Grimes), Rosalind Cash (Aunt Florence), James Bond III (John Grimes), Roderic Wimberly (Roy Grimes), Olivia Cole (Elizabeth Grimes), Ving Rhames (Young Gabriel), Alfre Woodard (Esther), C.C.H. Pounder (Deborah), Linda Hopkins (Sister McCandless).

Baldwin's important novel gets a fine adaptation in this condensed version of the sprawling tale. It was made with money from three grants, rather than with movie studio involvement. The money came from TV's American Playhouse (PBS), The National Endowment for the Humanities, and the National Endowment for the Arts. Anyone who read the book or knows

anything of Baldwin's background will recognize the essential honesty with which the film was made. It begins in 1935 although a series of flashbacks are included that return the story to other eras. Winfield is a young Southerner who can't stand the shackles of the area, runs North, and assumes the role of a preacher in the Baptist denomination. He marries Pounder but their union is childless and unsatisfying. Flashing back, we see the young man (played by Rhames) as he has an affair with older Woodard and when she gives birth, the child is raised by his mother. When the boy dies early, the older Winfield goes to Harlem and begins anew. He has to work as a day laborer to make ends meet while trying to raise his status in the church. He marries Cole and they have two sons, Bond and Wimberly. Also living in the Harlem home is Winfield's sister, spinster Cash. Winfield becomes an angry man and takes it out on those closest to him. The boys are not allowed to partake in city pleasures like stickball and hanging out. Instead, they are forced to read the Bible regularly. Further, Winfield is a man who hates anyone white and when Bond wins a prize for writing, Winfield forces him to return it because it was bestowed by whites. The boys grow up and are totally different. Wimberly looks as though he'll end up in jail because of the company he keeps. The worst thing that Bond does is sneak downtown to see OF HUMAN BONDAGE, although little is made of that incident and it only serves as a discovery interlude because it's the first movie the boy has ever seen. Bond is paralleling Baldwin's own life. He is shown to be just a little odd and so it rings falsely at the conclusion when he accepts Jesus (under Winfield's incessant prodding) at a prayer meeting. Perhaps it's unfair to compare the long, rich-with-anecdotes novel with this pared-down movie. As a film, it surely stands on its own. The acting is all first-rate, with a special nod to Winfield in an unsympathetic role, Cole as his long-suffering wife, and Woodard as a steamy siren.

p, Calvin Skaggs; d, Stan Lathan; w, Gus Edwards, Leslie Lee (based on the novel by James Baldwin); ph, Hiro Narita (TVC Color); m, Webster Lewis; ed, Jay Freund; prod d, Charles Bennett; set d, Joe Rainey; cos, Bernard Johnson.

Historical   (PR:A MPAA:NR)

GODS MUST BE CRAZY, THE****

(1984, Botswana) 109m Mimosa/FOX-TLC c

Marius Weyers (Andrew Steyn), Sandra Prinsloo (Kate Thompson), Louw Verwey (Sam Boga), Nixau (Xi), Jamie Uys (The Reverend), Michael Thys (Mpudi), Nic De Jager (Jack Hind), Fanyana Sidumo (1st Card Player), Joe Seakatsie (2nd Card Player), Ken Gampu (President), Brian O'Shaughnessy (Mr. Thompson), Vera Blacker (Mrs. Thompson), Paddy O'Byrne (Narrator).

A surprisingly fresh comedy, this South African film is a brilliantly funny throwback to the days of slapstick silent comedy. It begins as a "National Geographic" sort of documentary about the Kalahari Bushmen, an uncivilized African tribe which knows no violence, is thoroughly self-contained, and holds no material possessions. One day, however, a small plane flies overhead and drops a Coke bottle at their feet. Assuming that the bottle is a gift from the gods, the tribe begins to make use of it. They discover that it has not one, but many uses--mashing meal, flattening skins, playing music, making patterns. Since it is such a valuable tool, the tribe soon becomes possessive of it. This leads to greed, greed leads to anger, and anger leads to violence. It's not long before they are bopping each other over the head with the bottle. Nixau (an actual Bushman), being the tribal leader, is elected to dismiss the bottle by taking it to the end of the earth and throwing it off. Little does Nixau know that it is a long walk to "the end of the earth." He comes across a number of situations that are new to him, and meets a variety of people, some of them being white men that he mistakes for gods. He is befriended by Weyers, a bumbling microbiologist, and Prinsloo, a flighty schoolteacher who is new to the region. While Weyers and Prinsloo make disastrously funny attempts to start up a romance, Nixau makes equally funny attempts to understand modern life. Mixed in with their everyday problems is the threat of a military coup led by the crazed Verwey, who eventually takes Prinsloo and her schoolchildren hostage. However, Nixau comes to the rescue with his unique driving skills and saves the day. He then continues along on his journey until he finds a breathtaking, fog-enveloped chasm which could easily pass for the end of the earth, and tosses the Coke bottle away. Uys, who has directed 22 features in 34 years, resurrects a familiar, long-forgotten style of sight-gags and traditional comic techniques in THE GODS MUST BE CRAZY. He gets a great deal of use, for example, out of fast-motion--a technique which brings to mind the films of comedic greats like Charlie Chaplin and Buster Keaton. Nixau is not that far off from the Chaplin character of "The Little Tramp"--he is an innocent fellow who emits his feelings through the art of pantomime. The seemingly helpless Bushman is caught in a world where everything is foreign to him. He speaks a tribal language of clucks and pops which the white man doesn't understand, dresses in primitive skins, and has no concept of technology and machinery. As different as he is from his audience, Nixau is able to elicit a great deal of sympathy and identification from the viewer. The audience feels for Nixau because he is essentially an alien lost in a strange land, in much the same way as the stranded extraterrestrial in E.T. Unfortunately, THE GODS MUST BE CRAZY received a disturbing number of unenthusiastic reviews in the U.S. from knee-jerk liberals who felt it necessary to fault the film because of South Africa's system of apartheid. Far more than being a racist picture, THE GODS MUST BE CRAZY is a commentary on American imperialism, the evils of consumerism and modernism, and the effects of greed and power within a society. It is easiest to judge the film's intention by examining the filmmakers, and here Uys claimed a "deep respect" for the Bushmen. One cannot imagine how he could even complete such a picture (which took three years of filming in the Kalahari) without having a great love for the people. Whatever its political leanings, THE GODS MUST BE CRAZY is a delightfully pleasing comedy which succeeds as both entertainment and a nostalgic homage to the earliest days of comedy.

p,d&w, Jamie Uys; ph, Buster Reynolds, Robert Lewis, Uys; m, John Boshoff: ed, Uys; art d. Caroline Burls; cos, Gail Grobbelaar, Mij Reynolds.

Comedy   **(PR:C MPAA:PG)**

GOODBYE PEOPLE, THE***   (1984) 104m EM c

Judd Hirsch (*Arthur Korman*), Martin Balsam (*Max Silverman*), Pamela Reed (*Nancie Scot*), Ron Silver (*Eddie Bergson*), Michael Tucker (*Michael Silverman*), Gene Saks (*Marcus Soloway*), Sammy Smith (*George Mooney*), James Trotman (*Velasquez*), Sid Winter (*The Jogger*), Vincent Gugleotti (*Irwin Abrams*), Louis Bufano, Nicky Deems, David Follander, Raymond Gardner, Gabe Manarino, Morris Morrison, Paul Navarro, Sam Rubinsky, Vito Sansone (*"Dixie Land Devils"*).

A charming, talky flop, THE GOODBYE PEOPLE was the movie based on Gardner's reminiscences of his Coney Island family life. His play had been staged 15 years before and he struggled to get it to the screen with himself at the directorial helm. The stage origins are very evident as most of the action takes place at a beach-front location. Balsam is a jaunty man in his 70s who has just recovered from heart surgery and is thrilled to be alive. Many of his friends have retired and promptly passed away and Balsam feels he cannot allow himself to be put out to vegetate. When he was 50, he had closed his hot dog stand, "Max's Original Hawaiian Ecstasies," and now he dreams of reopening in the same location. Balsam meets Hirsch, a man who yearns to sculpt heroic statues that would be placed in the city's parks. However, life being what it is, Hirsch's current job (he's had it for 18 years) is designing elves and pixies for a display firm. Hirsch keeps promising himself that he'll quit his job but he hasn't the guts to tell his boss goodbye so he just ambles along, saving money and being very unhappy. His best means of allaying his frustration is to come to Coney Island very late at night and wait for the sun to rise. Unfortunately, he always falls asleep and misses the occasion. When Balsam tells Hirsch about his desire to open again, the younger man is drawn into the plan. Balsam's long-missing daughter, Reed, shows up. She's changed her name and she's changed her nose and her hair color. She was always Balsam's favorite child and affectionately recalled by him as "Crazy Shirley." She left her husband, a used car dealer, more than a year ago to seek a new life and when she heard of Balsam's heart problems, she's come back. Both Reed and Balsam are dreamers and cut from the same bolt of cloth. He dreams of the hot dog stand, she dreams of changing her life and becoming a fulfilled woman. Reed's ex-to-be is Silver, a decent enough guy who truly wants her to come home but is not so certain that he likes the new woman she's become. Still, he's willing to put that aside and take her back in whatever shape she's in (and with whatever nose she sniffs through) but Reed and Hirsch discover each other and triumph over Balsam's stuffed shirt lawyer son, Tucker, who is against the whole plan from the start. It's a gentle comedy with many sharp lines (what else would one expect from the man who wrote A THOUSAND CLOWNS and won the 1985 Tony Award for "I'm Not Rappaport"?) and good acting from all involved. Gardner didn't open up the play enough and the result is a slightly claustrophobic feeling, even though it takes place outdoors. The play began in 1968 and has since run all over the world with Tucker having been in four separate productions. Saks, who was also in A THOUSAND CLOWNS and has since become one of the most respected Broadway directors around, plays Balsam's old pal. Saks had played the Hirsch role in Elaine May's version of the play done in 1971. Balsam had also appeared in A THOUSAND CLOWNS as Jason Robards' brother. The movie was made in 43 days under terrible weather conditions and it's a marvel that it was finished at all. Gardner is another graduate of Lincoln High School in Coney Island, the same school that turned out two score writers in film, television, the stage, and literature. The Coney Island of Garner's youth no longer exists but he thanked all the people who ever lived there in the credits and dedicated the movie to Paddy Chayefsky. The musical score consisted of songs as noted: "Is It True What They Say About Dixie?" (Irving Caesar, Sammy Lerner, Gerald Marks, performed by the Dixie Land Devils), "California Here I Come" (B.G. De Sylva, Al Jolson, Joseph Meyer, sung by Jolson), "Careless Love," "Over the Waves" (standards, performed by Pete Fountain), "South Rampart Street Parade" (Ray Bauduc, Bob Haggart, played by Fountain), "Down Yonder" (L. Wolfe "Wolfy" Gilbert), "Moonlight Becomes You" (James Van Heusen, Johnny Burke), "Don't Anybody Waltz Anymore?" (Shel Silverstein), "Toot Toot Tootsie, Goodbye" (Gus Kahn, Ted Fiorito, Ernie Erdman), and "Happy Birthday To You" (written by...are you ready? Bet you didn't know it was actually written by Mildred J. Hill and Patty S. Hill and was published by Summy-Birchard Music Division of the Birch Tree Music Group. See how much you can learn by reading the MPG?) Also, "Over the Waves," "Under the Double Eagle," "After the Ball," "Pony Boy," "Tic Toc Polka," "The Billboard (March)," "American Patrol," "The Thunderer," "The Battle of the Bird," "Manhattan Beach," "El Capitan," "Washington Post."

p, David V. Picker; d&w, Herb Gardner (based on his stage play); ph, John Lindley (DeLuxe Color); ed, Rick Shane; prod d, Tony Walton; cos, Walton, Dona Granata; set d, Chris Kelly; makeup, Aaron Quarles.

Comedy   **Cas.**   **(PR:A-C MPAA:PG)**

GRACE QUIGLEY   (SEE: THE ULTIMATE SOLUTION OF GRACE QUIGLEY)

GRANDVIEW, U.S.A.**½   (1984) 97m CBS/WB c

Jamie Lee Curtis (*Michelle "Mike" Cody*), C. Thomas Howell (*Tim Pearson*), Patrick Swayze (*Ernie "Slam" Webster*), Troy Donahue (*Donny Vinton*), Jennifer Jason Leigh (*Candy Webster*), William Windom (*Bob Cody*), Carole Cook (*Betty Welles*), M. Emmet Walsh (*Mr. Clark*), Ramon Bieri (*Mr. Pearson*), Elizabeth Gorcey (*Bonnie Clark*), John Philbin (*Cowboy*), John Cusack (*Johnny Maine*), Joan Cusack (*Mary*), Camilla Hawk (*Mrs. Pearson*), Melissa Domke (*Susan Pearson*), Jason Court (*Benny*), Tim Gamble (*Larry Hurlbuck*), Fred Lerner (*Tucker Smith*), Larry Brandenburg (*Mickey*), Taylor Williams (*Mr. Fleming*), Kathryn Joosten (*Mrs. Clark*), Fern Persons (*Teacher*), Bruno Aclin (*Foreman*), Steve Dahl (*Moose Shook*), Tony Lincoln (*Mr. Kutch*), George Womack (*Mr. Whitewood*), Frank T. Panno (*Mr. Pettiman*), Bob Swan (*Fire Chief*), Michael Winslow (*Spencer*), Donald Bernardi (*Randy*), Gene Hartline (*Fred*).

In a summer filled with ax murderers, obnoxious teenagers, feature-length rock videos, and homicidal robots from the future, GRANDVIEW U.S.A., though no great shakes as art, was a pleasant surprise. Set in a fictitious small midwestern town (it was shot in southern Illinois), the film follows Howell, a recent high school graduate itching to flee his boring community. During the summer he meets Curtis, a 27-year-old woman who is trying to keep the demolition derby she inherited from her father. At the track is Swayze, a likable blue-collar type who went to high school with Curtis and still harbors deep feelings for her as his marriage to the bubble-headed Leigh collapses. To vent his small-town frustrations, Swayze becomes king of the demolition derby by winning every match. Despite his renewed interest in Curtis, she is drawn to teenager Howell and begins an affair with him in an effort to recapture the days when she wasn't saddled with so much responsibility. Howell tells her of his desire to leave Grandview in the dust, and is shocked when Curtis relates that she once felt the same way and fled to California. When asked why she returned to Grandview, Curtis replies that everyone in California had come there from someplace else, so she decided to return home where people knew each other and had roots. Howell sees her logic, but still wants to learn for himself. His departure is delayed, however, when he learns that his father, Bieri, has been trying to close Curtis' demolition derby so that he can buy the land and turn it into a golf course and condo development. Howell confronts his father and together with Curtis and Swayze he battles with the town council in an attempt to save the track. While GRANDVIEW U.S.A. suffers from some misguided humor (there are two fantasy sequences shot as parodies of rock videos and they don't really work) and scant scripting, the performances of Curtis and Howell are engaging. It is a small film, with small, and at times cliched, ideas about rural life, but there is a pleasant sweetness about it that is an appealing and refreshing change from the usual roller-coaster films that bombard audiences in the summer.

p, William Warren Blaylock, Peter W. Rea; d, Randal Kleiser; w, Ken Hixon; ph, Reynaldo Villalobos (Astro Color); m, Thomas Newman; ed, Robert Gordon; prod d, Jan Scott; set d, Bill Harp; cos, Wayne A. Finkelman; ch, Lisa Niemi, Patrick Swayze; spec eff, Chuck Dolan, Kevin Quibel.

Drama   **Cas.**   **(PR:O MPAA:R)**

GRASS IS SINGING, THE   (SEE: KILLING HEAT)

GREMLINS*   (1984) 111m WB c

Zach Galligan (*Billy*), Phoebe Cates (*Kate*), Hoyt Axton (*Rand Peltzer*), Frances Lee McCain (*Lynn Peltzer*), Polly Holiday (*Mrs. Deagle*), Keye Luke (*Grandfather*), John Louie (*Chinese Boy*), Dick Miller (*Mr. Futterman*), Jackie Joseph (*Mrs. Futterman*), Scott Brady (*Sheriff Frank*), Harry Carey, Jr (*Mr. Anderson*), Don Steele (*Rockin' Ricky Rialto*), Corey Feldman (*Pete*), Arnie Moore (*Pete's Father*), Glynn Turman (*Roy Hanson*), Belinda Balaski (*Mrs. Harris*), Judge Reinhold (*Gerald*), Jonathan Banks (*Deputy Brent*), Joe Brooks (*Santa*), Edward Andrews (*Mr. Corben*), Chuck Jones (*Mr. Jones*), Kenny Davis (*Dorry*), Jim McKrell (*Lew Landers*), Susan Burgess (*Little Girl*), Don Elson (*Man on Street*), Daniel Llewelyn (*Hungry Child*), Lois Foraker (*Bank Teller*), Nick Katt, Tracy Wells (*School Children*), John C. Becher (*Dr. Molinaro*), Gwen Willson (*Mrs. Molinaro*).

One of the biggest box-office hits of 1984 was also one of the most distressing examples of crass commercial cynicism ever perpetrated in the name of family entertainment. Presented with executive producer Steven Spielberg's name prominent in the advertising, GREMLINS was sold to the parents of unsuspecting pre-pubescents as a delightfully scary little film suitable for youngsters and given standard "PG" rating. What the kiddies got, however, was an alarmingly violent and cynical film which glorified gore, death, and murder while manipulating the audience to laugh at the mayhem. Set during the Christmas season in a small town, director Dante and executive producer Spielberg work overtime trying to evoke memories of such true family classics as Frank Capra's IT'S A WONDERFUL LIFE. Axton, an eccentric would-be inventor and father of our young hero, Galligan, buys an unusual gift for his son while on business in San Francisco. In a seedy area of Chinatown, Axton tries to purchase a cute little furry creature called a mogwai. Although the old shopkeeper, Luke, refuses to sell the animal, the old man's grandson secretly hands it over to Axton. There are three warnings concerning the care of the creature: never get it wet, never let it into the sunlight, and never feed it after midnight no matter how much it whines. Axton presents the creature to his excited son, and in the next few hours the loyal family dog is ignored while everyone marvels at the unusual little mogwai. Of course, the rules are soon broken and the cute creature gives birth to dozens of little mogwais, which then evolve into totally repugnant, evil, lizard-like creatures which set about destroying the town. The first batch wanders into the family kitchen where they attack Galligan's mother, McCain. She retaliates by decapitating one with a knife, blending another's head in the food processor, and for the grand finale, exploding one in the microwave. These gory scenes of violence are presented in a humorous fashion that may amuse some adults, but children in the audience were horrified. Eventually the mischievous gremlins have taken over the town, murdered several people (including an invalid), and destroyed thousands of dollars worth of property. Hiding out with his girl friend Cates, Galligan and the original mogwai (which has somehow escaped becoming evil) ponder how to stop the gremlins. During this breather, Cates, who has always hated Christmas, finally tells Galligan why. When she was a little girl, she and her mother waited up one Christmas Eve for her father to come home. It got very late and after several phone calls, dad was nowhere to be found. Christmas day came and went with no sign of her father. Weeks went by and he remained missing. "That's when we noticed the smell," states Cates. The odor was coming from the fireplace. Workmen were called to investigate and that's when they found her father. He had dressed up as Santa Claus and had gotten stuck and died while climbing down the chimney to surprise his little girl. The foul smell was her father's rotting flesh. "That is how I found out there is no Santa Claus," she concludes. For a film aimed at young children, with the name of the director of E.T. prominently displayed in the ads, this scene is one of the most thoughtless, disgusting, and reprehensible moments ever committed to film. The movie continues on and we are made to laugh when the evil gremlins are blown up by Galligan while he watches SNOW WHITE AND THE SEVEN DWARFS. Finally the gremlins are defeated, leaving the survivors of the decimated town to rebuild. Even if this film was marketed for adults, rated "R", and made even more terrifying (in the original script the gremlins eat Galligan's dog), it still would be a sloppily made movie. The characters are cardboard cutouts that only serve as fodder for the special effects. The narrative drive is so scattershot and ill-conceived that the film is only made up of clever moments and has no real dimension. Yes, the special effects by Chris Walas are amazing, but good effects are not an excuse to make a hollow film. GREMLINS has no uplifting facets to justify the violent action. It has no moral consciousness whatsoever (the invalid woman is shown to be a modern-day version of Lionel Barrymore's Mr. Potter in IT'S A WONDERFUL LIFE, but that is no justification for her brutal murder) and only seems concerned with showing off the skills of the technicians. The fact that GREMLINS was consciously marketed as a vehicle with which to sell toys to unsuspecting children makes this film a moral outrage. Dante and Spielberg suck the audience in during the first half-hour by showing us this pleasant small town at Christmas and then introducing the undeniably cute little mogwai. Then the tables are turned and GREMLINS descends into this insane orgy of mayhem that is supposed to be scary and amusing. These men demonstrate no sensitivity for the minds of small children, nor do they seem to care. Adult audiences may be able to appreciate Dante and Spielburg's aren't-we-clever humor and self-congratulating in-jokes, but the small children the film was aimed at don't care. All they know is that the cute mogwais have turned into the gremlins of their nightmares and there is no Santa Claus because daddy is decomposing in the chimney. The MPAA, which rated the film "PG" because Spielberg's name was on it, also should share the blame. The justifiable outrage over this film and Spielberg's INDIANA JONES AND THE TEMPLE OF DOOM forced the MPAA to create the PG-13 rating. Steven Spielberg is sold to the public as the Walt Disney of the 1980s and with E.T. it looked as if that claim might be true. But there is a disturbing trend in his work that indicates his appreciation of the intricacies children's imaginations is less than wholesome. In Spielberg's universe adults are ineffectual failures who must be tolerated by their knowing and clever children. The height of this youthful arrogance was demonstrated in the Spielberg-produced BACK TO THE FUTURE where Michael J. Fox travels back in time to "fix" his parents so they will turn out better. This may make for some glitzy, technically superior entertainment, but the overall effect on young audiences is a negative one. These films pander to underdeveloped, frustrated minds and offer no insight or alternatives to that frustration except those to be found in the fantasy world of the movies. Songs include: "Out, Out" (Peter Gabriel, performed by Gabriel), "Mega-Madness" (Michael Sembello, Mark Hudson, Don Freeman, performed by Sembello), "Christmas" (performed by Darlene Love), "Make It Shine" (performed by Quarterflash), "Do You Hear What I Hear" (sung by Johnny Mathis).

p, Michael Finnell; d, Joe Dante; w, Chris Columbus; ph, John Hora (Technicolor); m, Jerry Goldsmith; ed, Tina Hirsch; prod d, James H. Spencer; set d, Jackie Carr; cos, Norman Burza, Linda Matthews; spec eff,

Chris Walas.

Horror   Cas.   (PR:O   MPAA:PG)

GREYSTOKE: THE LEGEND OF TARZAN
(SEE: GREYSTOKE: THE LEGEND OF TARZAN, LORD OF THE APES)

GREYSTOKE: THE LEGEND OF TARZAN, LORD OF THE APES****
(1984) 129m WB c

Ralph Richardson (The 6th Lord of Greystoke), Ian Holm (Capt. Phillippe D'Arnot), Christopher Lambert (John Clayton/Tarzan), Andie MacDowell (Jane Porter), James Fox (Lord Esker), Ian Charleson (Jeffson Brown), Nigel Davenport (Maj. Jack Downing), Paul Geoffrey (Lord Jack Clayton), Cheryl Campbell (Lady Alice Clayton), Nicholas Farrell (Sir Hugh Belcher), Colin Charles (Olly), Elaine Collins (Ruby), David Endene (Boat Captain), Richard Griffiths (Capt. Billings), Tristam Jellineck (White), Roddy Maude-Roxby (Olivestone), Hilton McRae (Willy), John Wells (Sir Eveylyn Blount), Eric Langlois (Tarzan at Age 12), Tali McGregor (Baby Tarzan), Daniel Potts (Tarzan at Age 5), Ravinder (Dean), Harriet Thorpe (Iris), David Suchet (Buller/Prince Max Von Hesse), Philemon Blake Andhoua (Aloo), Paul Brooke (Rev. Stimson), Sheila Latimer (Duchess), Andrea Miller (Governess), Jacobin Yarro (Riverbank Chief), Elliot W. Cane (Silverbeard, Primate Father), Ailsa Berk (Kala, Primate Mother), John Alexander (White Eyes, Primate Leader), Christopher Beck (Droopy Ears, Tarzan's Childhood Friend), Mak Wilson (Figs, Tarzan's Follower), Alison Macrae, Bridget Biargi, Emile Abossolo.

Certainly the most intelligent and probably the best filmic treatment of Edgar Rice Burroughs' classic pulp novels about Tarzan, the white child of noble blood raised by apes in the jungle. Although there are literally scores of movies based on the character, they have all been simple kiddie fare, ignoring the serious themes that underlie the familiar tale. The film opens with the shipwreck that casts Geoffrey and wife Campbell, three months pregnant, on the wild coast of Africa. They build a hut in the jungle, she bears a son, and shortly thereafter they both die. The infant is adopted by a clan of apes, and there, with surrogate parents Kala and Silverbeard (played with remarkable emotion and skill–through elaborate Rick Baker costumes and makeup–by Berk and Cane, respectively), he grows to manhood, eventually becoming the leader of the group. His ape mother is killed by pygmies, who shortly thereafter wipe out the first white men Lambert (playing Tarzan as a young man) has ever seen, a party of white hunters. He saves one of them, a wounded Belgian, Holm, whom Lambert nurses back to health and who teaches him the speak English (with a French accent). Eventually Lambert returns to civilization with Holm, and goes to his ancestral home in Scotland, Greystoke Manor. There, his grandfather, Richardson, is thrilled to see him and tries to integrate his heir into upper-crust society. At a posh dinner party, Lambert picks up his soup bowl and begins loudly slurping. While the rest of the guests look on in horror, Richardson tosses his spoon away and starts to slurp his soup the same way. Another of Richardson's eccentricities is his fondness for sliding down the grand staircase of the manor sitting on a silver tray. Lambert meets MacDowell, his grandfather's American ward, and the attraction is instant and mutual, despite the fact that she is engaged to Fox. Most of the people Lambert meets are shocked that Richardson would consider passing his title on to this uncivilized savage, and they actively plot against him. When Richardson tries his stair-sliding stunt again, he suffers a terrible accident and dies, after a touching deathbed speech (this was Richardson's last role; he himself died shortly after filming). Not long after, Lambert roams the halls of the Natural History Museum in London and is horrified to see a gorilla on a dissecting table, its chest pulled open. Then he sees Silverbeard (Cane), his ape father, in a cage. In a tremendously touching moment, they reach out for each other and embrace. Lambert frees him and the two tear through a London park. Lambert realizes that he cannot live in Britain with Richardson gone, and has little desire to, so he goes back to his jungle home, accompanied by Cane and MacDowell. Beautifully photographed and marvelously acted, the film is the first to deal with the issue of how a child could be raised by apes, and how civilzation would treat him if he returned to it (some of the same ground was covered in Francois Truffaut's THE WILD CHILD). His lack of social graces outrages the stodgy gentry he is forced into contact with, while his open and natural manner shows them for the prejudiced boors they are. All the performances are fine, with Lambert showing remarkable subtlety and emotion as he tries to fit in, then rejects civilized life. Richardson is equally good, and his good humor carries much of the second half of the film, when the tale starts to slow up. Fox is properly despicable in his first film role in 14 years. (Supposedly, during the production of PERFORMANCE for director Nicolas Roeg, star Mick Jagger and Roeg helped the very controlled, disciplined actor get into his role by slipping him hallucinogens and playing various psychologically manipulative games with him. So disturbed was Fox by this that he gave up acting and became something of a mystic for years.) This project had been around Hollywood for years, mostly in the hands of Robert Towne, who cowrote the script under the pseudonym of P.H. Vazak. The special effects costuming by Rick Baker is superb, and his apes are so expressive and natural that it is almost impossible to tell them from the real apes that appear in the scenes with them. The talented group of actors who donned the suits and learned to move and behave like apes also deserve a great deal of credit. Since Elmo

Lincoln first brought Tarzan to the screen in 1918, no film of his exploits has ever been so lovingly based on the fictional character created by Burroughs, and it is unlikely that any film about him after this will reach the same heights achieved in this thinking man's adventure movie.

p, Hugh Hudson, Stanley S. Canter; d, Hudson; w, P.H. Vazak 'Robert Towne', Michael Austin (based on the novel *Tarzan of the Apes* by Edgar Rice Burroughs); ph, John Alcott (Super Techniscope, Eastmancolor); m, John Scott; ed, Anne V. Coates; prod d, Stuart Craig; md, John Warrack; art d, Simon Holland, Norman Dorme; set d, Ann Mollo; cos, John Mollo, Shirley Russell; spec eff, Albert J. Whitlock; ch, Peter Elliot; primate costume design and creation, Rick Baker.

Adventure   Cas.   **(PR:C MPAA:PG)**

GROWING PAINS   (SEE: BAD MANNERS)

GUEST, THE****   (1984, Brit.) 114m RM Productions c

Athol Fugard *(Eugene Marais)*, Marius Weyers *(Dr. A.G. Visser)*, Gordon Vorster *(Oom Doors)*, Wilma Stockenstrom *(Tante Corrie)*, James Borthwick *(Doorsie)*, Emile Aucamp *(Louis)*, Susan MacLennan *(Little Corrie)*, Trix Plenaar *(Brenda)*, Dan Poho *(Stuurie)*.

Fugard, best known for his strong political dramas on the apartheid system in South Africa, takes the lead in this fine biography of that country's well-known poet Eugene Marais. Fugard plays the writer, who was also a naturalist, at a particularly disturbing point in his life: one of his many attempts to kick an all-consuming morphine habit. He visits the country home of friend Weyers, a doctor who is trying to get him off drugs. As Fugard goes through withdrawal he undergoes bouts of screaming and hunger and he finally enters a catatonic state. When he does overcome the drug habit he emerges from his room and gets to know the native population, all the while trying to understand his addiction. "I hurt, therefore I am," he states, an overriding theme in the film. Once back in the world of the unaddicted, Fugard must cope with new problems in what he sees as an empty life. Eventually he ends up back on morphine with a closing title which states Marais killed himself some 10 years later in the throes of withdrawal anxiety. This is a powerful film on the nature of pain and how it is staved off, explored with intelligence. The cast is, without exception, excellent in support of Fugard's dynamic performance.

p, Gerald Berman; d, Ross Devenish; w, Athol Fugard; ph, Rod Stewart; ed, Lionel Selwyn; prod d, Jeni Halliday.

Drama   **(PR:O MPAA:NR)**

GWENDOLINE   (SEE: PERILS OF GWENDOLINE, THE, Fr.)

HADLEY'S REBELLION**   (1984) 96m The East India Company/ADI c

Griffin O'Neal *(Hadley Hickman)*, William Devane *(Coach Ball)*, Charles Durning *(Sam Crawford)*, Adam Baldwin *(Bobo McKenzie)*, Lisa Lucas *(Linda Johnson)*, Eric Boles *(Mr. Stevens)*, Dennis Hauge *(Joe Forster)*, Israel Juarbe *(Manuel Hernandez)*, Chas McQueen *(Rick Stanton)*.

O'Neal is a high schooler who transfers from the Deep South to a snooty prep school in Southern California. Besides the usual teenage problems that plague him, he is labeled a yahoo by the other students, so he takes to wrestling to prove his worth. Predictable stuff, somewhat redeemed by Devane as the coach. Durning is awful as an old professional wrestler-turned-drunk whom O'Neal Looks up to.

p, Steve Feke; d&w, Fred Walton; ph, David Golia (CFI Color); m, Mike Post; ed, Sam Vitale; prod d, Diane Campbell; art d, Martin Price; cos, Erica Phillips.

Drama   **(PR:C MPAA:PG)**

HAMBONE AND HILLIE**   (1984) 89m Adams Apple-Cineamerica-VTC/New World c

Lillian Gish *(Hillie)*, Timothy Bottoms *(Michael)*, Candy Clark *(Nancy)*, O.J. Simpson *(Tucker)*, Robert Walker *(Wanderer)*, Jack Carter *(Lester)*, Alan Hale *(McVicker)*, Anne Lockhart *(Roberta)*, William Jordan *(Bert)*, Paul Koslo *(Jere)*, Nancy Morgan *(Ellen)*, Arnie Moore *(Dognapper)*, Sidney Robin Greenbush *(Amy)*, Maureen Quinn *(Edna)*, Mark Bentley *(Danny)*, Nicole Eggert *(Marci)*.

"First Lady of the Silent Screen" Gish and her beloved pooch are separated in an airport and each criss crosses the country looking for the other. Cutesy and nauseatingly maudlin, although thoroughly safe for children. A rare chance to see Gish, at 86 years of age, still performing.

p, Gary Gillingham, Sandy Howard; d, Roy Watts; w, Sandra K. Bailey, Michael Murphey, Joel Soisson (based on a story by Ken Barnett); ph, Jon Kranhouse (Astral Bellevue Pathe Color); m, George Garavarentz; ed, Robert J. Kizer; prod d, Helena Reif; art d, Helena Rubinstein; cos, Kathy Estocin.

Comedy-Drama   Cas.   **(PR:A MPAA:PG)**

HARD CHOICES***   (1984) 90m Screenland-Breakout c

Margaret Klenck *(Laura Stephens)*, Gary McCleery *(Bobby Lipscomb)*, John Seitz *(Sheriff Mavis Johnson)*, John Sayles *(Don)*, John Snyder *(Ben)*, Martin Donovan *(Josh)*, Larry Golden *(Carl)*, Judson Camp *(Jimmy)*, Wiley Reynolds III *(Horton)*, Liane Curtis *(Maureen)*, J.T. Walsh *(Deputy Anderson)*, Spalding Gray *(Terry Norfolk)*, John Connolly *(Preach)*, Ruth Miller *(Mrs. Lipscomb)*, Thom McCleister *(Blinky)*.

An interesting film that passed virtually unnoticed; the tale concerns Klenck, a social worker whose job is to get juveniles out of adult jails. She begins working to help 15-year-old McCleery, who had accompanied his two older brothers on a holdup that ended with death of a cop. When funds for her program are cut off, Klenck goes to her old college friend, drug dealer Sayles. He gives her the money to hire McCleery a good lawyer because he feels that kids need to stay out of jail so they can buy drugs from him. When legal recourses fail and it looks like McCleery is penitentiary-bound, Klenck takes a gun and helps him break out of jail. They travel to Florida and she seduces him, but ultimately the law closes in on the pair. Good performances and a story that twists and turns unpredictably make this one a good bet.

p, Robert Mickelson; d&w, Rick King (based on a story by King, Mickelson); ph, Tom Hurwitz (DuArt Color); m, Jay Chattaway; ed, Dan Loewenthal; prod d, Ruth Ammon; cos, Jeffrey Ullman.

Crime   **(PR:O MPAA:NR)**

HARD TO HOLD*   (1984) 93m UNIV c

Rick Springfield *(James Roberts)*, Janet Eilber *(Diana Lawson)*, Patti Hansen *(Nicky Nides)*, Albert Salmi *(Johnny Lawson)*, Gregory Itzen *(Owen)*, Peter Van Norden *(Casserole)*, Tracy Brooks Swope *(Toby)*, Heather Devore-Haase *(Cal Mussetter)*, Carole Tru Foster *(Mrs. Mussetter)*, Garry Goodrow *(Maitre d')*, Frank Ronzio *(Flower Vendor)*, Charles Sweigart *(Punk Leader)*, Selma Archerd *(Mrs. Adilman)*, Paul Jenkins *(Hawker)*, Warren Miller, Lew Gallo *(Cab Drivers)*, John Blyth Barrymore *(Recording Engineer)*, Laura Summer, Tiffany Helm *(Fans)*, Al Hansen *(Jack)*, Jack Stryker *(Phil)*, Brass Adams, Gino Ardito *(Longshoremen)*, Don Hepner *(Johnny's Friend)*, Larry Daugherty, Harry Northup *(Limo Drivers)*, Stu Charno *(Techie)*, Johnathan Findlater *(Ambulance Driver)*, Michael V. Murphy *(Doug)*, Cindy Pearlman *(Ethel)*, Eddie Hice *(Waiter)*, Dale Townsend *(Airline Clerk)*, Frank Pisani *(Himself)*, Monique Gabrielle, Sharon Hughes, Charlene Jones *(Wives)*.

Pretentious claptrap clothed in a 1984 rock music love story that never goes beyond the superficial. Director Peerce has made some boring films (A SEPARATE PEACE, THE OTHER SIDE OF THE MOUNTAIN 'PARTS ONE AND TWO', and THE BELL JAR) but he outdoes those with this. Springfield plays a highly successful rock songwriter- performer. He works with Patti Hansen on the song composition and she is a strong influence on him. Springfield is driving in his car and bangs into Eilber, a tense psychologist who specializes in helping children. They meet, fall in love very quickly, and he pursues her around the city of San Francisco until he catches her. Interspersed with the insipid love story is a subplot of Springfield having a creative problem and being unable to write. A couple of nice scenes but no motivation whatsoever for the couple's coupling early in the film with no apparent reason other than animal desire. (Eilber's role as a stiff-backed woman is quickly established so it's hard to believe that she would leap into the sack with such alacrity.) Eilber's father, Salmi, dies and she is depressed. She alternates between anger, ire, annoyance, or iciness and Springfield is presented as a knight of such spirituality that he would make Lancelot feel impure. He's a lousy actor, she's a boring actress, Peerce is an overrated director, and this picture has little more than Scott's music to recommend it. It's a teeny-bopper picture that is even too juvenile for them. Scuttlebutt around the industry is that there were several salacious scenes which had to be trimmed to escape the dreaded "R" rating which would have kept the youngsters out of the theaters. They stayed away of their own accord once the word got out.

p, D. Constantine Conte; d, Larry Peerce; w, Tom Hedley (based on a story by Hedley, Richard Rothstein); ph, Richard H. Kline (Technicolor); m, Tom Scott, Rick Springfield; ed, Bob Wyman; prod d, Peter Wooley; set d, Philip Abramson; cos, Rosanna Norton.

Musical Drama   Cas.   **(PR:A-C MPAA:PG)**

HARDBODIES*   (1984) 88m Chroma III/COL c

Grant Cramer *(Scotty)*, Teal Roberts *(Kristi)*, Gary Wood *(Hunter)*, Michael Rapport *(Rounder)*, Sorrels Pickard *(Ashby)*, Roberta Collins *(Lana)*, Cindy Silver *(Kimberly)*, Courtney Gaines *(Rag)*, Kristi Somers *(Michelle)*, Crystal Shaw *(Candy)*, Darcy DeMoss *(Dede)*, Antony Ponzini *(Rocco)*, Marvin Katzoff *(Dorky Geek)*, Kip Waldo *(Head Geek)*, Michael Miller *(Landlord)*, Chuck Hart *(Young Geek)*, Kane Hodder *(Old Geek)*, Kit Hamilton, Ericka Dockery *(Hardbodies in Car)*, Karen Lee Kelly *(Hardbody on Bike)*, Karen LaVoie *(Jogging Hardbody)*, Kathleen Kinmont *(Pretty Skater)*, Steve Workman *(Hair Stylist)*, Jackie Easton *(Girl in Dressing Room)*, Janet Gardner *(Vixen Lead Vocalist)*, Jan Kuehnemund *(Lead Guitar)*, Pia Miacco *(Bass)*, Laurie Hedlund *(Drums)*, Tamara Ivanov *(Rhythm Guitar)*, Juli Lawrence *(Nicki)*, Steve Gold *(Fransey)*, Joyce Jameson *(Rounder's Mom)*.

Dumb sex comedy centers on the efforts of three middle-aged men to score with the beautiful beach girls known as hardbodies. Their first attempts are laughably bad, so they go to a pro, Cramer, and he gives them pointers. All goes well until one of the men starts after Cramer's girl friend and gets his comeuppance. Not much here except loads of beautiful women in swimsuits, but sometimes that's enough.

p, Jeff Begun, Ken Dalton; d, Mark Griffiths; w, Steve Greene, Eric Alter, Griffiths (based on a story by Greene, Alter); ph, Tom Richmond (DeLuxe Color); ed, Andy Blumenthal; md, Vic Caesar; prod d, Greg Fonseca; set d, Anne Huntley; cos, Bernadette Brady; ch, Randy DiGrazio.

comedy-Drama   **(PR:O   MPAA:R)**

HARRY AND SON½**   (1984) 117m Orion c

Paul Newman (*Harry*), Robby Benson (*Howard*), Ellen Barkin (*Katie*), Wilford Brimley (*Tom*), Judith Ivey (*Sally*), Ossie Davis (*Raymond*), Morgan Freeman (*Siemanowski*), Katherine Borowitz (*Nina*), Maury Chaykin (*Lawrence*), Joanne Woodward (*Lilly*), Michael Brockman (*Al*), Cathy Cahill (*Waitress*), Robert Goodman (*Andy*), Tom Nowicki (*Jimmy*), Claudia Robinson (*Nurse*), Russ Wheeler (*Doctor*), Joseph Alva, Joe Sikorra (*Young Men*), Jerry Barrett (*Cop*), David Mungenast (*Max*), Don Moody (*1st Construction Worker*), Leroy Dukes (*2nd Construction Worker*), Joseph Hess (*1st Worker*), Harold Bergman (*Night Watchman*), Al Nesor (*Taxi Driver*), Jill Selkowitz (*1st Factory Girl*), Patricia A. Frye (*2nd Factory Girl*), Dennis W. Edwards (*Iron Construction Worker*), Jan Siegel (*Woman Driver*), Suzanne M. Brierley (*Beauty Parlor Woman*), Will Knickerbocker (*Willie*), Terry Miller (*Surplus Clerk*), Mark Anthony Wade (*Delivery Man*), George E. Warren (*Superintendent*), Fred M. Wilkins (*Concrete Mixer Operator*), Bunny Yeager (*Marina Bar Waitress*), Gilberto Costa Nunes (*Spanish Parrot*), Jack Kassewitz (*Parrot*), Jeffrey Finn (*Motorcyclist*), Michael Brockman (*Stunt Driver*).

Newman returns the the director's chair for the first time in 12 years (not counting a made-for-TV film, "The Shadow Box," in 1980). He also coproduced and cowrote the script, and plays the lead. As a middle-aged construction worker, he is laid off when he temporarily loses his sight, leaving him more time to sit around his house feeling bitter and sorry for himself and hassling his son, Benson, who dreams of being a writer but generally lacks real ambition, at least in Newman's eyes. Most of the film is taken up by their confrontations. Benson takes a couple of jobs, none of which he likes, and tries to get back together with his old girl friend, Barkin, even though she's carrying another man's child. The film never takes on any real direction and leaves the audience nowhere, with nothing resolved. What strength the film does have is from Newman's performance in the first half, before the film starts to follow Benson more, and leaves Newman wallowing in self-pity. Benson is as annoyingly untalented as ever and the film is definitely overlong and bordering on dull. Newman is one of the biggest stars around today, but HARRY AND SON came and went with barely a whimper.

p, Paul Newman, Ronald L. Buck; d, Newman; w, Newman, Buck (based on the novel *A Lost King* by Don Capite); ph, Don McAlpine (DeLuxe Color); m, Henry Mancini; ed, Dede Allen; prod d, Henry Bumstead; set d, Don K. Ivey; stunts, Stan Barrett.

Drama   **Cas.**   **(PR:C   MPAA:PG)**

HEART OF THE STAG**½   (1984, New Zealand) 91m Southern
                                                          Light/NW c

Bruno Lawrence (*Peter Daly*), Terence Cooper (*Robert Jackson*), Mary Regan (*Cathy Jackson*), Anne Flannery (*Mary Jackson*), Michael Wilson (*Jack Bostwick*), Susanne Cowie (*Young Cathy*), John Bach, Tim Lee, Greg Naughton, Tania Bristowe (*Shearing Gang*).

On an isolated New Zealand farm Regan is forced to endure a living hell as her brutal father, Cooper, forcibly has sexual relations with her. Lawrence is a drifter, unaware of the incestuous situation, who is hired by Cooper to help out during the annual sheep roundup. An uneasy chemistry builds up between the two as Cooper informs his new employee never to go after the wild stags that graze his land. Lawrence also is informed by another farmhand (Wilson) never to touch anything that belongs to their employer, but he doesn't realize that this includes Regan. He tries warming up to the girl and is puzzled by her avoidance of him. After the sheep shearing is finished, Lawrence is told by Cooper that he will have to leave, and at a drunken party Cooper kisses another woman, causing Regan to flee in tears. Lawrence follows her and coaxes her into spilling out her terrible secret. He tries to help her escape from the farm, but the two are followed by an enraged Cooper, whom they evade for a night, but he finds them the next morning up in the mountains. After Lawrence manages to dodge his pursuer he cries out a stag call. A prize beast comes charging from the woods and Cooper, unable to move quickly enough, is gored on its antlers. Incest is a difficult topic for any filmmaker but has been handled well on several occasions in such intelligent films as MURMUR OF THE HEART, FORBIDDEN RELATIONS, and the made-for-television feature SOMETHING ABOUT AMELIA. Here, this taboo is merely part of a story. Though it serves as a motivational factor behind Cooper's and Regan's behavior, there is nothing new or dramatic about the situation. This essentially is what is wrong with the film. Its strength lies in the cast. Regan is particularly good as the abused girl, adding edges to the character where the script falters.

Lawrence and Cooper also manage to rise above the simplicity of their characters.

p, Don Reynolds, Michael Firth; d, Firth; w, Neil Illingsworth, Firth, Martyn Sanderson, Bruno Lawrence (based on a story by Firth); ph, James Bartle; m, Leonard Rosenman; ed, Michael Horton; prod d, Gary Hansen.

Drama   **Cas.**   **(PR:O   MPAA:R)**

HEARTBREAKERS**   (1984) 98m ORION c

Peter Coyote (*Blue*), Nick Mancuso (*Eli*), Carole Laure (*Liliane*), Max Gail (*King*), James Laurenson (*Terry Ray*), Carol Wayne (*Candy*), Jamie Rose (*Libby*), Kathryn Harrold (*Cyd*), George Morfogen (*Max*), Jerry Hardin (*Warren Williams*), Henry G. Sanders (*Reuben*), Walter Olkewicz (*Marvin*), Terry Wills (*Mortician*), Annie O'Neill (*Dukes Waitress*), Michelle Davison (*Fatburger Waitress*), Claire Malis (*Marilyn*), Carmen Argenziano (*Ron Bell*), Adele Corey (*Eli's Mother*), Tina Chappel (*Punk Girl*), Justin Leir, Scott Wade (*Gallery Assistants*), Alfonse Ruggiero, Howard Shatsky (*Gym Assistants*).

An incisive look at male friendship and the contemporary Los Angeles art scene and a scanning of sociology that often goes beneath the surface, HEARTBREAKERS is the fourth film by Roth and he is a moviemaker who will eventually take his place in the higher echelon if he ever gets the script and marketing to match his originality. Mancuso and Coyote are best friends in their middle 30s. Coyote is a bohemian loft artist specializing in sado-masochistic works of women with whips, chains, wearing garter belts, high-heeled spiked shoes, and like that. As the film opens, Harrold, Coyote's live-in lover of five years, is leaving. She feels that his art is more important to him than she is and that hurts her enough to cause her to depart. Her exit forces Coyote to reassess himself and his occupation so he plunges even deeper into his art, as there is an upcoming exhibition. Harrold moves off and finds herself toying with Coyote's No. 1 competitor, Gail (a good actor attempting to break the image he maintained for so long on TV's "Barney Miller"). As close as Mancuso is to Coyote, that's how opposite the two men are. Mancuso is the Jewish heir to a garment manufacturing company and his main ambition appears to be an avoidance of any female relationships beyond breakfast the morning after. One-night stands are all he yearns for...until he meets art gallery employee Laure, whose philosophy about attachments is just as tenuous as his, which puts him into a complete turnaround and makes him fall hard for her. Meanwhile, Coyote's diversion becomes Wayne, a dizzy model who poses for his S&M pictures. At one point, Coyote shares her with Mancuso in a *menage a trois*. Mancuso's father dies and he learns that the prospering business wasn't nearly as successful as he thought it was. This happens as Coyote's star is rising and as Mancuso is trying to crack Laure's tough veneer. There is a confrontation over Laure between the two men and their friendship is tested to the limits. Authentically filmed in L.A. with all the trendy spots like Spago, Fatburger, The Sports Connection, etc., HEARTBREAKERS has excellent technical work (with cinematography by Rainer Werner Fassbinder's camera collaborator Ballhaus), good performances from all (and a dandy one from Wayne, who drowned in a freak accident after the picture was completed). Roth had made INDEPENDENCE DAY, CIRCLE OF POWER, and THE BOSS' SON prior to this, all small independently produced pictures that showed promise, as did this one. The fine score was by the European group "Tangerine Dream" which also did the music for THIEF. The art was actually painted by L.A. artist Robert Blue and Coyote's character was named "Blue" as well, probably in tribute to the painter. Not a great movie but worth seeing for anyone interested in relationships and a real depiction of Los Angeles in the 1980s.

p, Bob Weis, Bobby Roth; d&w, Roth; ph, Michael Ballhaus (DeLuxe Color); m, Tangerine Dream; ed, John Carnochan; prod d, David Nichols; set d, Florence Fellman; cos, Betsy Jones; m/l, "The Blues Don't Care," Etta James, Brian Ray, "You Want More," James, Ray, Steve Le Gassick, Leo Nocentelli.

Romantic Drama   **Cas.**   **(PR:C-O   MPAA:R)**

HEAT OF DESIRE**   (1984, Fr.) 89m Cineproduction-GAU-Films
                                        Dara/Triumph c (PLEIN SUD)

Patrick Dewaere (*Serge Laine*), Clio Goldsmith (*Carol*), Jeanne Moreau (*Helene*), Guy Marchand (*Max*), Pierre Duxx (*Rognon*), Jose-Luis Lopez Vasquez (*Martinez*), Nicole Jamet (*Serge's Wife*), Roland Amstut (*Jeannot*), Beatrice Camurat (*Pepita*).

A feeble attempt at bringing passion to the screen, HEAT OF DESIRE (released in France in 1980) stars Dewaere as a foolish lecturer who is on his way to Barcelona with his wife for a speaking engagement. By accident, he becomes the subject of Goldsmith's desires. The bored mistress of a politician, Goldsmith (she starred as the gift in 1983's THE GIFT), decides to have a steamy affair with the first man who walks by her window. Dewaere is that unlucky sod. He begins devoting all his time and money to Goldsmith, who enjoys nothing more than playing sex games in posh hotel rooms. Dewaere steadily deteriorates and finds himself penniless, having to steal in order to satisfy his desire to see Goldsmith. The flame burns out, however, and a beaten Dewaere returns home to his sorrowful wife. What starts off as a promising picture ends up as a meaningless moral about passion and its consequences. Dewaere, one of the top French actors along with Gerard Depardieu, Yves Montand, Jean-Paul Belmondo, and Michel Piccoli, committed suicide in 1982, shortly after this film was completed. (In French; English subtitles.)

p, Lise Fayolle, Giorgio Silvagni; d, Luc Beraud; w, Beraud, Claude Miller; ph, Bernard Lutic; m, Eric Demarsen; ed, Joelle Van Effenterre.

Drama   Cas.   (PR:O MPAA:R)

HERE COMES SANTA CLAUS**½ (1984) 78m New World Pictures c

Emeric Chapuis (Simon), Armand Meffre (Santa Claus), Karen Cheryl (Teacher/Magic Fairy), Alexia (Elodie), Dominique Hulin (The Ogre), Jeanne Herviale (Simon's Grandmother), Helene Zidi (Simon's Mother), Jean-Louis Foulquier (Simon's Father), Bouake (Baye- Fall).

Chapuis is a 7-year-old boy whose parents (Zidi and Foulquier) have mysteriously disappeared somewhere in Africa. After telling his teacher, Cheryl, he heads to the North Pole with his friend Alexia, in hopes of enlisting Santa Claus (Meffre) to help him out. En route Chapuis must pass through the forest of an evil ogre (Hulin), but eventually he makes it to St. Nick's home. Of course the jolly fat man is more than willing to help. Meffre takes Chapuis and Alexia on a tour of his toy shop. Cheryl also plays a fairy who runs the shop, and, with Meffre, goes off to find Chapuis' parents. Meffre and Cheryl find Zidi and Foulquier held by hostile natives, while Chapuis and Alexia end up back in the Hulin's clutches. After freeing Chapuis' parents, Meffre and Cheryl rescue the boy and his friend as all ends happily. Fine for the kids. The special effects were created by George Lucas' Industrial Light & Magic company.

p&d, Christian Gion; w, Gion, Didier Kaminka; ph, Jacques Assueurs; m, Francis Lai; ed, Pauline Leroy; md, Roland Romanelli; set d, Patrice Renault, Pascal Schouteeten; cos, Olga Pelletier; spec eff, Industrial Light and Magic; makeup, Monique Granier, Maryse Felix.

Children's Feature   Cas.   (PR:AAA MPAA:G)

HEY BABE!* (1984, Can.) 105m Rafal c

Buddy Hackett (Sammy Cohen), Yasmine Bleeth (Theresa), Marushka Stankova (Miss Wolf), Vlasta Vrana (Roy), Denise Proulx (Miss Dolores).

With Shirley Temple grown up, the singing-and-dancing orphan movie appeared to be a genre left only to filmgoers' memories and the late-late show. Unfortunately, someone decided to revive the concept, which results in the mess presented here. Bleeth is a precocious 12-year-old determined to make it big in show business. She crashes professional drama schools, invades television studios, and, in general, lies, cheats, and steals in her efforts to get to the top. Eventually she's taken in by Hackett, a former entertainer whose career plummeted as his alcohol intake rose. He shows her the ropes of the business which proceeds to the stock happy ending. In between the wafer-thin plot segments are a series of predictable and wholly unrealistic scenes that unashamedly cross the saccharine line. Nothing is a surprise, including the puffed-up musical numbers. The only realistic thing in the film is Bleeth. Though not even a teenager, she comes on like a herd of thundering horses, giving everything she can to her role. Her energy grows on the viewer, causing one to ponder just how far from the truth this film really is.

p, Rafal Zielinski, Arthur Voronka; d, Zielinski; w, Edith Rey (based on a story by Zielinski, Rey); ph, Peter Czerski; m, Gino Soccio, Roger Pilon, Mature Adults; ed, Scott Conrad, Afte Chiriaeff; ch, Lynn Taylor.

Musical   (PR:A MPAA:NR)

HIGHPOINT** (1984, Can.) 88m New World c

Richard Harris (Louis Kinney), Christopher Plummer (James Hatcher), Beverly D'Angelo (Lise Hatcher), Kate Reid (Mrs. Rachel Hatcher), Peter Donat (Don Maranzella), Robin Gammell (Banner), Maury Chaykin (Falco), Saul Rubinek (Centino), George Buza (Alex), Louis Negin (Molotov), Bill Lynn (Deitrich), David Calderisi (Prisoner/Agent), Eric House (Henchman), Lynda Mason Green (Model), Ken James (Briefcase Man), Frank Gibbs, Trent Dolan (Guards), Ardon Bess, Steve Pernie (Freightmen), Bill Starr, Jack Van Evera (Patrolmen), Susan Connors (Dancer), Roger Periard (Dr. Dumont), Devon Britton, Kathy Deckard, Sallianne Spence, Margaret Doty (Girls at Pool).

It took five years for this film to come out although we can't see why, as it's a fair thriller with enough leavening humor to provide a pleasant 88 minutes of entertainment. Plummer is an industrialist who has stolen $10 million by double-dealing both the mob and the cops. Donat is the head hood and sends his hit men, Chaykin and Rubinek, after Plummer. At the same time, the local CIA agent is Gammell, and he is also after Plummer. Plummer's idea is to make believe he's dead and scoot with the loot. Enter Harris, an accountant who can't hold a job. He somehow gets the job of guarding the body of Plummer's sister, D'Angelo, and tending to Plummer's wheelchair-ridden mother, Reid. Then Plummer makes it look as though Harris is a murderer and Harris' task becomes locating Plummer so he can get the cops off his back. Although there are a couple of high points in the film, the title refers to the conclusion, a lofty battle atop the CN tower in Toronto. There are so many near-misses and hair-raising scrapes that there

is little time for actual characterizations and the result is that we don't know enough about any of the good guys to care about them. The mistake made by the creators was that they confused style and speed for content and the result was a breakneck pace but not much else. It was made at a time when there was quite a bit of money around if the producers could satisfy the "Canadian content" rule, so many of the actors are natives of The Great White North, most notably Plummer, Reid, and Rubinek, who starred in many Canadian movies before coming south to Hollywood and scoring in Alan Alda's SWEET LIBERTY.

p, Daniel Fine; d, Peter Carter; w, Richard A. Guttman; ph, Bert Dunk (Eastmancolor); m, John Addison; ed, Eric Wrate; prod d, Seamus Flannery; art d, Rose Marie McSherry; cos, Patti Unger; spec eff, Cliff Wenger, Jr.; stunts, Carey Loftin.

Thriller   Cas.   (PR:C MPAA:PG)

HIGHWAY TO HELL* (1984) 95m Lucky 13-Highbroad/Anglo-American c

Monica Carrico, Eric Stoltz, Stuart Margolin, Richard Bradford, Joe George, Virgil Frye, Louise Baker, Laurel Patrick, Sorrells Pickard, Ben Hammer, Juliette Cummins, Bob Carroll, Lesley Woods, Clark Howat, Geno Havens, Seth Kaufman, Richard Walsh, Matt Boston.

A hooker runs into an escaped murderer and the two hit the road. The killer, being just a teenager, is innocent of the charge but that doesn't stop more deaths from occurring during the film's running time. The body count is high, with occasional dashes of imagination (one victim is electrocuted when his water bed is torn by some high-wired equipment) though the overall production differs little from any one of many similar exploitation pictures. Stoltz would show much better acting abilities in 1985 as the deformed teenager of MASK.

p, David Calloway; d&w, Mark Griffiths; ph, Tom Richmond; m, Al Capps; ed, Andy Blumenthal; prod d, Katherine Vallin; art d, Anthony Cowley.

Crime   (PR:O MPAA:NR)

HOLLYWOOD HIGH PART II zero (1984) 85m Lone Star c

April May (Bunny), Brad Cowgill (Rocky), Donna Lynn (Kiki), Drew Davis (Jock), Bruce Dobos (Skip), Camille Warner (Ginger), Alisa Ann Hull (Chessie), Angela Field, Anne Morris.

A film that again asks the eternal moviegoer's question: Why did I pay good money to see this garbage? The story vaguely deals with some beach-going teenagers who never seem to go to school. Instead, they take some photos of a local policeman having sex with Hull, the one (and seemingly only) class prude. Later the officer finds the boys have been cheating on their girl friends with none other than their teachers. What else are the teachers going to do, seeing as no one's ever in class? There are threats of blackmail, bad impersonations of Mae West and Fonzie (even though the famed greaser of the long-gone television comedy show "Happy Days" was strictly passe in 1984), and plenty of fairly tame sex. There's not an iota of intelligence or value to be found anywhere in this trash. For the record, this film is not an "official" sequel to the original HOLLYWOOD HIGH.

p, Cotton Whittington, Colleen Meeker; d, Lee Thornburg, Caruth C. Byrd; w, Whittington, Meeker, Thornburg, Byrd; ph, Gary Graver (CFI Color); m, Doug Goodwin; ed, Warren Chadwick; m/l, Goodwin.

Comedy   Cas.   (PR:O MPAA:R)

HOLLYWOOD HOT TUBS zero (1984) 102m Seymour Borde and Associates/Manson c

Donna McDaniel (Leslie Maynard), Michael Andrew (Jeff), Paul Gunning (Eddie), Katt Shea (Dee Dee), Edy Williams (Desire), Jewal Shepard (Crystal).

A mindless clinker about a Hollywood teenager who gets into the hot-tub repair business. The usual teen-sex-comedy pattern is followed by putting the star in situations that audiences would love to be in. Filled with necessary flashes of flesh and stupid dialog, HOLLYWOOD HOT TUBS is a real time-waster.

p, Mark Borde; d, Chuck Vincent; w, Borde, Craig McDonnell; ph, Larry Revene; m, Joel Goldsmith; ed, Michael Hoggan; art d, Loma Lee Brookbank; cos, Lesley Levin.

Comedy   Cas.   (PR:O MPAA:R)

HOLY INNOCENTS, THE*** (1984, Span.) 108m Ganesh/Samuel Goldwyn c (LOS SANTOS INOCENTES)

Alfredo Landa (Paco), Francisco Rabal (Azarias), Terele Pavez (Regula), Belen Ballesteros (Nieves), Juan Sanchez (Quirce), Juan Diego (Master Ivan), Agustin Gonzalez (Don Pedro), Susana Sanchez (Little One), Agata Lys (Dona Purita), Mary Carillo (Marchioness), Maribel Martin (Miriam), Jose Guardiola (Senorito de la Jara), Manuel Zarzo (Physician).

A socially relevant tale of a peasant struggle in Franco-era Spain which is grounded in realism. Landa is a devoted laborer who, with his wife Pavez and his mute crippled daughter, S. Sanchez, works the land and displays a special talent for tracking birds. Diego, a vile bird hunter from the upper class, enlists Landa's help on his hunt. He is less than compassionate, however; when Landa breaks his foot, he is forced to continue on by Diego. It is this relationship between the ruling class and the peasant class that is most indicative of the film's sentiments. The peasants are degraded by the rich, but the rich cannot function without the peasants' knowledge of nature and their working of the land. According to director Camus, the film's title refers not only to the peasant class but to all classes. "It also offers something very welcome," Camus continues "and that is that the poor people are happy people because they are vital human beings, and manifest themselves in more spontaneous ways. They have nothing more than that world, and it fills them." The Cannes Film Festival in 1984 rewarded THE HOLY INNOCENTS with a shared Best Actor award–going to both Landa and Rabal (a veteran of Luis Bunuel films) as Landa's eccentric older brother. (In Spanish; English subtitles.)

p, Julian Mateos; d, Mario Camus; w, Camus, Antonio Larreta, Manuel Matji (based on the novel by Miguel Delibes); ph, Hans Burmann (Eastmancolor); m, Anton Garcia Abril; ed, Jose Maria Biurrun; art d, Rafael Palmero.

Drama (PR:O MPAA:PG)

HOME AND THE WORLD, THE* (1984, India) 140m National Film Development Corp. of India/European Classics c (GHARE BAIRE)

Soumitra Chatterjee (Sandip Mukherjee), Victor Bannerjee (Nikhilesh Choudhury), Swatilekha Chatterjee (Bimala Choudhury), Gopa Aich (Sister-in-Law), Jennifer Kapoor [M. Kendal] (Miss Gilby), Manoj Mitra (Headmaster), Indrapramit Roy (Amulya), Bimala Chatterjee (Kulada).

A graceful film which is as much a tragic love story as it is an examination of India's political turmoil in 1908. Bannerjee stars as a highly educated Hindu who lives with his wife, Swatilekha Chatterjee, in colonialized East Bengal. Political tension rises when Lord Curzon, the British governor-general of India, puts into action a plan of "divide and rule," driving a wedge between the Hindus and Muslims. Because of the unrest, Soumitra Chatterjee, a fiery rebel and friend of Bannerjee's, pays a visit to the town. Bannerjee encourages his wife to come out of purdah (orthodox seclusion) and meet some men other than himself, namely his rebellious friend; Bannerjee is not convinced that she truly loves him, because she has met no other men. He will be convinced of her love only if she remains faithful to him after having met others. His plan backfires, however, and she falls in love with the rebel. Political differences arise in the men as well. Soumitra Chatterjee favors a ban on British goods, while Bannerjee opposes a ban which will hurt the poor people worse than the rebellious middle-class intelligencia. Bannerjee soon sees his friend's true nature as a man more concerned with his own political power than with the people of India. After some time, his wife also sees this side of him. By then, however, it is too late. The political wedge has been driven too deep and riots have broken out amongst the Hindus and Muslims. The rebel, who must be held responsible, flees the town, leaving Bannerjee and his wife facing a mob which firmly believes that Bannerjee, since he was a friend of Soumitra Chatterjee, must also be in favor of the ban. Based on a novel by Nobel Prize-winning author Rabindranath Tagore, THE HOME AND THE WORLD was initially to be filmed 30 years previously as Satyajit Ray's first film. Tagore, a friend of Ray's family, had published his book in 1919, and received much acclaim. Ray, who had only a passing interest in film at the time, read the book and wrote a screenplay based on it. A producer became interested and signed a contract with Ray as screenwriter and a friend of Ray's as director. The deal soon fell through in what Ray calls his "greatest good fortune." It wasn't until 1980 that Ray returned to the project. Ray explains, "The fact that 30 years intervened between desire and fulfillment has, I think, helped the film because of the experience I have gained in the meantime, not only of my craft but of human nature." (In Bengali and English; English subtitles.)

d&w, Satyajit Ray (based on the novel by Rabindranath Tagore); ph, Soumandu Roy (Eastmancolor); m, Ray; ed, Dulal Dutt; art d, Ashoke Bose; makeup, Ananta Das.

Drama **Cas.** (PR:C MPAA:NR)

HOME FREE ALL*½ (1984) 93m Almi c

Allan Nichols (Barry), Roland Caccavo (Roland), Maura Ellyn (Cathy), Shelly Wyant (Rita), Lucille Rivin (Lynn), Lorry Goldman (Marvin), Janet Burnham (Chastity), Jose Ramon Rosario (Carlos), Daniel Benzalli (Therapist), Melanie Bradshaw (Melanie), Francesca Valerio (Samantha), Joyce Sozen (Mildred), Elizabeth Burkland (Cathy's Friend), John Hallow (Investor), Mark Urman (Edmonds), Sam Rubinsky (Cabbie), Mike Alpert (Picketer), Steve Powers (Reporter), Chazz Palminteri (Hijacker), Tom Kopache (Truck Driver), Harve Soto, Mario Todisco, Joe Lisi (Thugs), Geoffrey Ewing, Pura Bobe (Tenants at Meeting), Jimmy Adler (Clown), Rose Geffen (Customer).

An unpleasant look at a group of people from New York's Greenwich Village and their struggles with their past as radicals from the late 1950s and early 1960s. They grow increasingly more dependent on each other, turn to dishonorable jobs (arson-for-hire seems to be a popular one), and wind up in empty relationships with other failed radicals. It may be realistic, but the characters on the screen are so unlikable that the film is torturous to sit

through.

p, Stewart Bird, Peter Belsito; d&w, Bird; ph, Robert Levi; m, Jay Chattaway; ed, Daniel Loewenthal; prod d, Mischa Petrow.

Drama **Cas.** (PR:O MPAA:NR)

HORSE, THE* (1984, Turk.) 116m Asaya/Kentel c (AKA: HORSE, MY HORSE)

Genco Erkal (Father), Harum Yesilyurt (Son), Ayberk Colok (Merchant), Yaman Okay (Remzi), Guler Okten (Foolish Woman), Erol Demiroz (Hamu), Macit Koper (Selim).

A powerful film (released in Turkey in 1982) about the sorry state of Turkish life which centers on the relationship between a father, Erkal, and his son, Yesilyurt. After characteristically leaving behind his wife, Erkal heads for the city with his son in tow, and then struggles to find work in the hopes of raising enough money to send the boy to school. Meantime, he fantisizes about his son's future, envisioning him behind the wheel of a luxurious automobile. Erkal is able to buy himself a pushcart, but cannot afford the necessary permit and is pursued by the police. To further his troubles, his dreams of a free education for his son are complicated when he learns that the only children who get free schooling are those whose fathers have died. The only way then that Yesilyurt can become educated is with the death of his father. A dark, brutally realistic portrait of Turkish life which is not dissimilar to 1983's YOL, directed by Yilmez Guney. Like Guney (with whom he worked as an assistant), director Ali Ozgenturk served a prison term for his disapproval of the Turkish inhumane practices and his supposedly political statements. THE HORSE, however, is far less concerned with political systems than with the treatment of humankind. (In Turkish; English subtitles.)

d, Ali Ozgenturk; w, Isil Ozgenturk; ph, Kenan Ormanlar (Fuji Color); m, Okay Temiz.

Drama (PR:O MPAA:NR)

HORSE, MY HORSE (SEE: HORSE, THE, Turk.)

HOSPITAL MASSACRE zero (1984) 88m CANNON c

Barbi Benton (Susan Jeremy), Chip Lucia (Harry), Jon Van Ness (Jack), John Warner Williams (Dr. Saxon), Den Surles (Dr. Beam), Gay Austin (Dr. Jacobs), Gloria Morrison (Nurse Dora), Karyn Smith (Nurse Kitty), Lanny Duncan (Hal).

It took four years for this wretched film to graduate from the cutting room to the theaters. Made under the title "Be My Valentine, or Else," they had to change that moniker when the film MY BLOODY VALENTINE surfaced. Then it was altered to X-RAY, but that was tossed aside in favor of the final title when VISITING HOURS came out first. Lucia is a psychotic killer who sent a valentine to Benton and was embarrassed when she and her brother laughed at his attempt to move closer to her. This all happened 19 years ago but Lucia knows how to hold a grudge so he killed the brother and waited almost two decades to exact his revenge on the comely Benton. It's now the present. Benton has just received a job promotion for which she had to take a physical. It's the week before February 14 and Benton arrives at a local hospital to pick up the results of the routine examination. Austin is Benton's doctor and she is killed by Lucia, who is wearing medical garb. He takes her X-rays, which show nothing amiss, and switches them. Another doctor, Williams sees the X-rays and thinks they belong to Benton. He concludes that she is quite sick and orders her to stay in the hospital for observation and eventual cutting to cure whatever ails her. Benton dutifully submits and Lucia begins to terrorize the sparsely occupied hospital, leaving a bloody trail of bodies strewn about. Since so many people think doctors are butchers anyhow, there didn't have to be that much of a suspension of disbelief here. The movie stinks. Benton, who has improved in her acting since the movie was made, has trouble conveying fear. Lucia, as a psychotic degenerate, is just fine as far as psychotic degenerates go. The movie is not a total waste, though, as there seems to be an audience for just about anything these days, no matter how gory, yucky, or tasteless. There is also some inadvertent satire of the medical field which any patient, who has been slaughtered by enormous hospital bills, will appreciate. It seems that just about all the holidays have been covered by horror films with this, HALLOWEEN (all of them), SILENT NIGHT, DEADLY NIGHT and so forth. The only one missing is Arbor Day.

p, Menahem Golan, Yoram Globus; d, Boaz Davidson; w, Marc Behm; ph, Nicholas von Sternberg (TVC Color); m, Arlon Ober; ed, Jon Koslowsky; art d&set d, J. Rae Fox; makeup, Alan Apone, Kathy Shorkey.

Horror **Cas.** (PR:O MPAA:R)

HOT AND DEADLY* (1984) 90m Saturn International-Arista c (AKA: THE RETRIEVERS)

Max Thayer (Tom), Shawn Hoskins (Janice), Randy Anderson (Trigger), Lenard Miller (Danny), Bud Cramer (Philip).

A woefully inept action picture made in 1981, which saw a video release as THE RETRIEVERS, and finally made it to the theaters. Thayer stars as a new recruit in a CIA-like organization–his first assignment involving Miller, a former agent who is threatening to publish a scathing expose on the organization's inner workings. Thayer soon grows impatient with the methods his fellow agents use, usually resulting in the death of innocnent bystanders. His tactics become subversive and he goes on the run with Hoskins, the sister of Miller, in order to get the expose published, and their mission leads to a steamy romance. The script never really gels, and all that remains are some poorly photographed martial arts fight scenes.

p, Elliot Hong, Larry Stamper; d, Hong; ph, Stephen Kim (United Color); m, Ted Ashford, Paul Fontana; ed, Rob "Smitty" Smith.

Crime/Drama   Cas.   (PR:O   MPAA:R)

HOT DOG...THE MOVIE*   (1984) 96m Hot Dog Partnership/MGM-UA c

David Naughton (Dan), Patrick Houser (Harkin), Tracy N. Smith (Sunny), John Patrick Reger (Rudi), Frank Koppola (Squirrel), James Saito (Kendo), Shannon Tweed (Sylvia Fonda), George Theobold (Slasher), Marc Vance (Heinz), Erik Watson (Fergy), Lynn Wieland (Michelle), Sandy Hackett (Lester the Molester), Crystal Smith (Motel Receptionist), Peter Vogt (Fader Black), Robert Fuhrmann (Rick Lauter), Mark Costello (Competition Starter), Deborah Dutton, Anders Stenstedt Daniel K. Moore, Michael Moore, Linda Briggs McCulloch (Rudettes), Ami Julius (Georgette), Victoria Rae Walker (Girl In Gondola), Gregory Beck (Referee), M. Lisa Cooper, Lauri Price, Robin Rael (Girls At Party), Mike Marvin (Downhill Starter), Jim Clark (Cowboy at Bar), Ronald Hurley (Gas Station Attendant), Robin Haynes (Announcer).

An odious sexploitationer which sets a sophomoric script against a background of skiing at Lake Tahoe–specifically a skiing technique called "hotdogging," which is highly choreographed. Outside of that, however, it resorts to the standard methods of boys trying to bed the girls who tease them. Naughton is a Manhattan brat who shows a streetwise sensibility as well as an ability to gracefully handle the slopes. He becomes friends with a country boy, Houser, who falls for the comely Smith when he picks her up, hitchhiking, on the way to the World Freestyle Championship. What little conflict the movie has to offer comes in the form of a brash group of Australian skiers, led by Reger. One would think that to become a championship skier one's social life would suffer. But not these youngsters–all they ever seem to do is hop from bed to bed, dress in new ski outfits, and then quickly shed them at the first sign of the opposite sex. Former Playboy Playmate of 1982, Shannon Tweed, is especially good at this. The film's only plus (other than Miss Tweed's aforementioned talent) is some superb ski photography by Paul G. Ryan. If some of the ski sequences look familiar it's because they were designed by producer-writer Mike Marvin, who also worked on the brilliant ski sequences of THE SPY WHO LOVED ME (1977).

p, Edward S. Feldman, Mike Marvin; d, Peter Markle; w, Marvin; ph, Paul G. Ryan (CFI Color); m, Peter Bernstein; ed, Stephen Rivkin; art d, Don DeFina; set d, Carl Arena; cos, Shari Feldman; stunts, Max Kleven; m/l, "Top of the Hill," "Hold On," Peter Bernstein, Mark Goldenberg, "Dreamers on the Rise," "Bringing Down the Moon," John Stewart, "Rudi's Victory Song," John Patrick Reger.

Comedy   Cas.   (PR:O   MPAA:R)

HOT MOVES*   (1984) 86m Spectrum/Cardinal c

Michael Zorek (Barry), Adam Silbar (Mike), Jill Schoelen (Julie Ann), Jeff Fishman, Johnny Timko, Debi Richter, Virgil Frye, Tami Holbrook, Monique Gabrielle, David Christopher.

HOT MOVES exists for one reason only–to excite virginal teenage boys who think about nothing but watching blondes undress on the beach. Nothing else happens in this film. Voluptuous girls sun themselves, oil their bodies, run and splash in the water (in slowmotion), with only the barest thread of plot. Chubby Zorek wants nothing more in life than a girl friend and he obsessively peeps at the beaches with his father's telescope. His friend, Silbar, has the same high hopes. He sets his sights on Schoelen and grows to care about her as a person instead of a sexual plaything. HOT MOVES is merely an outlet for non-California or non-Florida youngsters who don't live near beaches and can't find their own girls to spy on.

p&d, Jim Sotos; w, Larry Anderson, Peter Foldy; ph, Eugene Shugleit (CFI Color); m, Louis Forestieri; ed, Drake P. Silliman; art d, George Costello; set d, Maria Caso; cos, Phillip Herzog Richards; ch, Andrea Muller.

Comedy   Cas.   (PR:O   MPAA:R)

HOTEL NEW HAMPSHIRE, THE½**   (1984) 110m ORION c

Rob Lowe (John), Jodie Foster (Franny), Paul McCrane (Frank), Beau Bridges (Father), Lisa Banes (Mother), Jennie Dundas (Lilly), Seth Green (Egg), Wally Aspell (Hotel Manager), Joely Richardson (Waitress), Wallace Shawn (Freud), Jobst Oriwal (German Man), Linda Clark (German Woman), Nicholas Podbrey (Boy with Rifle), Norris Domingue (High School Band Conductor), Matthew Modine (Chip Dove/Ernst), Wilford Brimley (Iowa Bob), Cali Timmins (Bitty Tuck), Dorsey Wright (Junior Jones), Richard Jutras (Lenny Metz), Johnny O'Neil (Chester Pulaski), Colin Irving, Anthony Ulc, Nick Mardi (Chip Dove Gang Members), Charles Fournier

(Howard Tuck), Anita Morris (Ronda Ray), Fred Doederlein (Finnish Doc), Walter Massey (Texan), Jerome Tiberghien (Stunts), Young Sup Chung, Emma Chung (Oriental Couple), Ada Fuoco (New Jersey Woman), Joan Heney (Connecticut Woman), Robert Thomas (Harold Swallow), Robert Harrison (Skinny Weightlifter), Gayle Garfinkle (Doris Wales/Screaming Annie), Jonelle Allen (Sabrina), Elie Oren (King of Mice), Nastassja Kinski (Susie the Bear), Roger Blay (Arbeiter), Timothy Webber (Wrench), Janine Manatis (Schwanger), Jean-Louis Roux (Old Billie), Amanda Plummer (Miss Miscarriage), Sharon Noble (Babette), Lorena Gale (Dark Inge), Jade Bari (Jolanta), Adrian Aron (American Woman), Arthur Grosser (American Husband), Tara O'Donnell (American Daughter), Louis Di Bianco (Bartender), Jyana Honey (Bar Patron), Michele Scarabelli (Chip Dove's Girl Friend), Jeffrey Cohen (New York Journalist), Benoit Laberge (Bookstore Man), Jon Hutman, James V. Mathews (Reporters), Prudence Emery (Mean Female Reporter).

Englishman Richardson has constructed a complex screenplay based on an even more convoluted novel. It's a fairy tale about everything and, as such, will not satisfy everybody. There is hardly a topic left untouched as it is laced with black humor on the subjects of homosexuality, heterosexuality, incest, abandonment, Nazis, masochism, and other "fun things" to do! Despite all of the woes and ills which befall most of the characters, Richardson attempts to keep it as light as though he were handling a Noel Coward drawing-room comedy. Bridges and Banes are the parents of a remarkable family in New England. Their children include Lowe, a high school student who is the center of much of the action, Foster, the eldest daughter and the victim of a gang rape at the hands of Modine and his pals, McCrane, the gay brother, and Dundas, the little sister who stays little because she has stopped growing. (This pays off when Dundas writes her autobiography, "Trying to Grow," and becomes a world-famous, though short, author.) The family has only one major rule to live by which consists of always passing by open windows. The family patriarch is grandpa Brimley, a wonderfully vital character, and when he dies of a heart attack early, it's stunning. The family also has a black Labrador named "Sorrow" which has a problem with his digestion (always an easy laugh, as proven by the flatulent dog in 10). Shawn is a wise youth named "Freud" who is a pal to Bridges and Banes and he brings them his pet bear to watch while he goes off to Europe. This is before WW II and at a time when people could keep bears the way they now keep poodles. After the war, when Shawn is again found in Europe, he's been blinded by the Nazis and is running a hotel in Vienna named, you guessed it, the "Hotel New Hampshire." Shawn owns the hotel and Bridges and family join him to help oversee it. Living there is Kinski, who wears a bear costume the entire time and calls herself "Susie the Bear" and doesn't have enough confidence in herself to come out of the skin. Foster has now met Wright, a jock, who helps her get over being raped by Modine and his friends. Modine plays two roles in the picture and in the second half he is seen as a pornographer. What this means and why only Modine played two parts is never explained. The hotel is filled with pimps, hookers, and terrorists, and those are the nice guests. One of the prostitutes is Morris, an older woman who helps the family get on its feet when she isn't on her back. She and Lowe have a fling and he matures quickly under her tutelage. The last child of Bridges and Banes is Green, and when he and Banes die in a plane crash, the rest of the family want to go back to the U.S. but Foster has something she wants to finish with Modine. Now the shenanigans really begin when Foster sleeps with Kinski (right), then Lowe and the others in the family foil Modine's radical plot to bomb the Vienna Opera House, Bridges is blinded in an explosion, Dundas' book comes out and is a success, Foster takes revenge on Modine with the help of McCrane, then Foster, who will sleep with anyone, sleeps with her brother, Lowe, and the longing they have had for each other is finally quenched. If that's not enough, Foster finally goes straight and marries Wright, leaving the way clear for Lowe and Kinski. Dundas commits suicide and the picture wraps up quickly after having been through more shifts than the 500-mile Indy track requires of a car. Filmed in and around Montreal, this is a hard picture to fathom because it sounds grim and glum and dreary and smarmy and yet it manages to keep up the interest. Not for children and not for too many adults, either, THE HOTEL NEW HAMPSHIRE was not a great success. Author Irving has always been fascinated by Vienna and bears and much of the same feeling as this novel had can be found in his short story within the novel The World According to Garp, which was also made into a less-than-successful movie.

p, Neil Hartley, James Beach; d&w, Tony Richardson (based on the novel by John Irving); ph, David Watkin (DeLuxe Color); m, Jacques Offenbach; ed, Robert K. Lambert; prod d, Jocelyn Herbert; art d, John Meighen; cos, Herbert.

Drama   Cas.   (PR:C-O   MPAA:R)

HOUSE BY THE CEMETERY, THE zero
                    (1984, Ital.) 78m Fulvia/Almi c (QUELLA VILLA ACCANTO AL CIMITERO)

Catriona MacColl (Lucy Boyle), Paolo Malco (Norman Boyle), Ania Peironi (Ann), Giovanni Frezza (Bob Boyle), Dagmar Lassander (Mrs. Gittelson), Giovanni de Nari (Dr. Freudstein).

An Italian gore-fest by prolific, wholly untalented director Fulci. This one is set outside Boston where researcher Malco, his wife, MacColl, and his child, Frezza, move into a new house. As the title suggests, the house is next to a cemetery. What the title doesn't say is that a deranged killer lives in the basement and has a penchant for bloodletting. De Nari is the killer–a crazed scientist who has been alive for more than 100 years, thanks to his advances in cellular regeneration. The only catch is that he gets his cells from his victims. Fans of this sort of excess will enjoy THE HOUSE BY THE CEMETERY, but these people are out of touch with reality and should probably be yanked from the movie theaters and put in padded cells. Strongly objectionable for children.

p, Fabrizio De Angelis; d, Lucio Fulci; w, Fulci, Dardano Saccheti, Giorgio Mariuzzo (based on a story by Elisa Livia Briganti); ph, Sergio Salvati (Luciano Vittori Color); m, Walter Rizzati; ed, Vincenzo Tomassi; cos, Tomassi; stunts, Mazzeno Cardinale; makeup, Gianette De Rossi, Maurizio Trani.

Horror   **Cas.**   **(PR:O   MPAA:R)**

HOUSE OF GOD, THE**   (1984) 108m UA c

Tim Matheson (*Dr. Basch*), Charles Haid (*Fats*), Michael Sacks (*Dr. Potts*), Lisa Pelikan (*Jo*), Bess Armstrong (*Dr. Worthington*), George Coe (*Dr. Leggo*), James Cromwell (*Officer Quick*), Ossie Davis (*Dr. Sanders*), Howard Rollins, Jr (*Chuck*).

Filmed in 1979, THE HOUSE OF GOD is one of those special cases which did not see a theatrical release until a number of its stars began hitting it big. The film is a black comedy about a group of young interns and their daily dilemmas in trying to survive in their high-pressure hospital jobs. All the performances are topnotch but there wasn't much of a reason to watch in 1979, except for Matheson, who made a name for himself in NATIONAL LAMPOON'S ANIMAL HOUSE (1978). Charles Haid went on to television fame as "Renko" in "Hill Street Blues;" Bess Armstrong costarred with Tom Selleck in HIGH ROAD TO CHINA (1983); and Howard Rollins, Jr. received an Academy Award nomination for his role in RAGTIME (1981), and turned in a startling performance in A SOLDIER'S STORY (1984). Producer Joffe should be a familiar name to fans of Woody Allen, since he's produced much of that comedian's work.

p, Charles H. Joffe, Harold Schneider; d&w, Donald Wrye (based on a novel by Samuel Shem); ph, Gerald Hirschfeld (Technicolor); m, Basil Poledouris; ed, Bob Wyman, Billy Weber; prod d, Bill Malley.

Drama/Comedy   **(PR:O   MPAA:R)**

HOUSE WHERE DEATH LIVES, THE*
                (1984) 82m Trauma/New American c (AKA: DELUSION)

Patricia Pearcy (*Meredith Stone*), David Hayward (*Jeffrey Fraser*), John Dukakis (*Gabriel*), Joseph Cotten (*Ivar Langrock*), Leon Charles (*Phillip*), Alice Nunn (*Duffy*), Patrick Pankhurst (*Wilfred*), Simone Griffeth (*Pamela*).

This was made in 1980 as DELUSION and kicked around the country for a few years before surfacing in 1984. Cotten finds himself trapped in this uneventful gothic horror as an invalid being cared for by a new nurse, Pearcy. Before long the cast members start dying off as a mysterious killer pounds their heads in with a wooden table leg. A number of hints are made that the house is supernaturally possessed, but the explanation turns out to be quite earthly. Nothing exciting here as THE HOUSE WHERE DEATH LIVES is completely bankrupt in originality.

p, Alan Beattie, Peter Shanaberg; d, Beattie; w, Jack Viertel (based on a story by Beattie, Viertel); ph, Stephen Posey (Metrocolor); m, Don Peake; ed, Robert Leighton; art d, Steven Legler.

Horror   **Cas.**   **(PR:O   MPAA:R)**

HUNDRA**   (1984, Ital.) 109m Continental/GTO c

Laurene Landon, John Ghaffari, Marissa Casel, Romiro Oliveros, Luis Lorenzo.

With the popularity of Arnold Schwarzenegger's CONAN films, it was only a matter of time before someone decided to do a gender switch to liven up the genre. Landon is an Amazon who survives a slaughter of her all-women tribe. She reluctantly must take up the task of finding a man suitable for her needs in order to save her people. It's definitely no film for misogynists unless they want to rupture a blood vessel. Landon's quest involves some episodes that are the precise opposite of the Playboy philosophy. Despite the far-fetched plot, this has a good sense of energetic fun to it that just might be well taking a look at.

p, John Ghaffari; d, Matt Cimber; w, Cimber, John Goff; ph, John Cabrera; m, Ennio Morricone; ed, Claudio Cutry.

Fantasy/Adventure   **(PR:C   MPAA:NR)**

HUNTER OF THE APOCALYPSE
                                        (SEE: LAST HUNTER, THE, Ital.)

HUNTERS OF THE GOLDEN COBRA, THE**   (1984, Ital.) 94m
                                          Gico-Regal/World Northal c

David Warbeck (*Bob Jackson*), Almanta Suska (*June/April*), John Steiner (*Capt. David Bracken*), Alan Collins (*Uncle*), Protacio Dee (*Yamato*).

The mega-budgeted RAIDERS OF THE LOST ARK, inspired by the inexpensive adventure serials of the 1940s, itself served as inspiration for numerous producers who churned out adventure stories hoping to cash in on that success. This one has Warbeck playing an Englishman in search of "The Golden Cobra," an idol stolen a year previously. He heads out to the jungle along with Suska and her uncle, Collins. Suska is searching through the jungle as well, looking for her long-missing twin sister, played by the actress in a dual role. The sister is found and the idol taken from the drugged natives who worship it like a god, but not without the prerequisite amount of danger and peril. There are snakes, dungeons, exploding volcanos, natives with poisonous blowguns, and Suska gets kidnaped as well. It turns out that her sister is the queen of the natives, but Warbeck and Suska manage to get out intact with the idol. This WW II-era adventure isn't bad, considering its background. The miniature sets look realistic and there are some fairly accomplished special effects, such as the volcano explosion. The dubbing could be better, for Warbeck's voice wavers between his British accent and that of the American actor who dubbed his lines. Fans of the genre should find some worthwhile enjoyment here.

p, Gianfranco Couyoumdjian; d, Anthony M. Dawson [Antonio Margheriti]; w, Tito Carpi (based on a story by Couyoumdjian); ph, Sandro Mancori (Eastmancolor); m, Carlo Savina; ed, Alberto Moriani; spec eff, Appollonio Abadesa.

Adventure   **(PR:A   MPAA:NR)**

I NUOVI BARBARI (SEE: WARRIORS OF THE WASTELAND, Ital.)

ICE PIRATES, THE**   (1984) 96m MGM/UA c

Robert Urich (*Jason*), Mary Crosby (*Princess Karina*), Michael D. Roberts (*Rosoe*), Anjelica Huston (*Maida*), John Matuszak (*Killjoy*), Ron Perlman (*Zeno*), John Carradine (*Supreme Commander*), Natalie Core (*Nanny*), Jeremy West (*Zorn*), Bruce Vilanch (*Wendon*), Alan Caillou (*Count Paisley*), Marcia Lewis (*Frog Lady*), Daryl Roach (*Fitzcairn*), Robert Symonds (*Lanky Nibs*), Gary Brockette (*Percy the Robot*), Rockne Tarkington (*Patch*), Ian Abercrombie (*Hymie*), Dolores Albin (*Old Karina*), Hank Worden (*Elderly Jason*), Bonnie Campbell-Britton (*Dara*), Carmen Filpi (*Vendor*), John Gillespie (*Dogbite*), Patty Maloney (*Waitress*), Shane McCamey, Ralph Meyerling, Jr. (*Templar Crewmen*), Myron Natwick (*Karina'a Father*), Daryl Roach (*Prisoner*), Raymond Skipp (*Doper*), Debra Troyer (*Blonde Girl*), Diana Webster (*Seamstress*), Ric Young (*Debs*), Sander Johnson (*Political Prisoner*), Steffen Zacharias (*Prisoner*), Todd Allen, Johnny Atkinson, Billy Bates, Monty Cox, Jimmy Davis, Gary DePew, Gardner Doolittle, Jonathan Epstein, Kenny Endoso, Dean Ferrandini, Alan R. Gibbs, Al Jones, Lane Leavitt, Ken Maurer, Bob Ozman, Eddie Paul, Larry Charles White, Jonathan Yarborough (*Stunts*).

An amiable spoof of science-fiction pictures cowritten by long- time "Batman" writer Sherman, THE ICE PIRATES suffers from a tiny budget that caused the special effects to be anything but special. They tried to capture the same audiences that went to see STAR WARS but failed because the level of humor was so low that it became ludicrous. Urich leads the pirates, a band of brigands in the future, and Crosby is a princess who has misplaced her explorer father who may, or may not, have found a new water supply for this particular galaxy, which is rapidly running out. Urich's merry men spend their time in a futuristic "Robin Hood" fashion by robbing the wealthy and distributing to the impoverished. Urich's best pal is Roberts and whenever they get into one of the contrived pickles, they just seem to escape without any motivation and only by dint of a fast cutaway. Most of the derring-do is derring-don't in that it's forced, the bravura is false, and the whole feeling is on a par with "Buck Rogers of the 25th Century." Mindless fun, though, if you don't look too hard at the effects and are willing to accept the wooden Urich as Errol Flynn or Louis Hayward. It would be a few months after this that Huston would make the movie that would make her a star, PRIZZI'S HONOR. The big guy in the picture is former football player John Matuszak, also known as "The Tooz" when he was crashing heads in the National Football League. The picture borrows heavily from STAR WARS in a barroom scene as well as from SOYLENT GREEN in the use of an environmental chamber with soft music and dreamy scenes.

p, John Foreman; d, Stewart Raffill; w, Raffill, Stanford Sherman; ph, Matthew F. Leonetti (Metrocolor); m, Bruce Broughton; art d, David M. Haber, Ronald Kent Foreman; set d, John M. Dwyer; cos, Daniel Paredes, Dennis Fill, Barbara Lee Maccarone; spec eff, Max W. Anderson.

Science   **Cas.**   **(PR:A-C   MPAA:PG)**

ICEMAN**½   (1984) 101m Huron/UNIV c

Timothy Hutton (*Dr. Stanley Shephard*), Lindsay Crouse (*Dr. Diane Brady*), John Lone (*Charlie*), Josef Sommer (*Whitman*), David Strathairn (*Dr. Singe*), Philip Akin (*Dr. Vermeil*), Danny Glover (*Loomis*), Amelia Hall (*Mabel*), Richard Monette (*Hogan*), James Tolkan (*Maynard*), Stephen E. Miller (*Temp Doc*), David Petersen (*Scatem Doc*), Judy Berlin (*E.K.G. Doc*),

Paul Batten (Technician), Lovie Eli (Nurse), Stephen Nemeth, Real Andrews (Lab Techs), Bob Reimer (Helicopter Pilot), Blair Anderson (Powell), Dave Ryder (Powell's Assistant), Herb "Kneecap" Nikal (Indian Guide), Elizabeth Aulajut (Inuit Storyteller), Dennis Letkeman (Air Traffic Controller), Paul Stanley (Canuck).

An ambitious movie that both fails and succeeds in its telling of the story of a caveman brought back to life after having been cryogenically frozen eons before. Hutton is a scientist with an angelic disposition. He is working with others on a frozen tundra somewhere near the North Pole. Hutton and his cohorts discover a man frozen in the ice for thousands of years. The man wears nothing but an animal skin so it's clear to see he wasn't dressed for his flash freezing when it happened. The body is brought back to the lab via a helicopter (not unlike the opening scene of LA DOLCE VITA where a huge statue of Christ is flown over the city of Rome) and a series of tense scenes commence as the Iceman is thawed, then revived. The technology involved seems logical as envisioned by art director Murray but it has not yet come to pass in actuality. These high-tech moments are among the best and most suspenseful in the film as the scientists wait anxiously to see what the Iceman is about. They are shocked when he begins to respond to stimuli and comes back to life. The Iceman, played by Asian actor Lone, returns to the world of warm bloodedness and is placed in a huge habitat, replete with animals and insects and everything the scientists feel must have been around him when he lived in another age. Lone and Hutton begin a relationship as the scientist tries to teach Lone the language of today rather than attempt to learn the cave dweller's language (which would have been more intriguing). The other scientists are all for dissecting Lone to see what makes him tick and why he survived the rigors he did. (This is the biggest flaw in the story. A dead cave man is just meat on a gurney, while a live one can provide fantastic insights.) Hutton protects Lone from the others, feeling that the Neanderthal has rights that must be observed. One of Hutton's colleagues is Crouse and she helps Hutton in his quest for knowledge. As Hutton spends more time with Lone, while being observed by the others, he is becoming the student and Lone the teacher. It is in these scenes that Hutton appears most natural and least actorish. Lone begins to get bored with the habitat they've built for him in what appears to be a huge warehouse structure. He would like to get back to the outside world and continue his search for whatever it is he was looking for when he was caught in the ice so many years before. Lone finally gets out, with Hutton's help, and races happily back into the world he once knew. Because they are in the Pole area of the earth where time has stood almost still and nothing seems to have changed, Lone is able to make his way happily. The movie is a good idea, sort of a variation on THE THING, but a good idea is not always a good movie. On paper, it must have appeared to be a winner. The picture was miscast. Hutton just isn't believable as a man of science, although they must have felt they could take the edge off his youth by adding a beard to his face. He was at least 10 years too young to play this role. Crouse is very glamorous, perhaps too much so, to convince anyone that she'd spent the last dozen years studying cryobiology and other assorted ologies. Lone, who was a New York actor with no film experience, is the best actor of the bunch. To see what he looks like without the beard and broken teeth and scraggly hair, catch him as the Asian villain in YEAR OF THE DRAGON. A fine actor with a big future. Although Lone plays the least believable character in the movie, he is the most captivating and honest of them all. ICEMAN's idea had been seen before many times in all the TARZAN movies, QUEST FOR FIRE, and the "fish out of water" theory is often used in TV so what must be done to make any of these films successful is to apply some brilliant execution and a unique script. Schepisi's direction was better than the story and screenplay. The interiors were done in Vancouver, British Columbia, at a bus warehouse that had been converted at a cost of more than half a million dollars. The exteriors were shot in the province of Manitoba, Canada, around a small town named Churchill, and the teeth chattering and the shivering were all real as the movie company suffered in subzero temperatures.

p, Patrick Palmer, Norman Jewison; d, Fred Schepisi; w, Chip Proser, John Drimmer (based on a story by Drimmer); ph, Ian Baker (Panavision, Technicolor); m, Bruce Smeaton; ed, Billy Weber; art d, Leon Ericksen, Josan Russo, Graeme Murray; set d, Thomas L. Roysden, Kimberley Richardson; cos, Rondi Johnson; makeup, Michael Westmore, Michele Burke.

Drama/Fantasy   **Cas.**   **(PR:A-C MPAA:PG)**

IMPULSE**½   (1984) 91m ABC/FOX c

Tim Matheson (Stuart), Meg Tilly (Jennifer), Hume Cronyn (Dr. Carr), John Karlen (Bob Russell), Bill Paxton (Eddie Russell), Amy Stryker (Margo), Claude Earl Jones (Sheriff), Robert Wightman (Howard), Lorinne Vozoff (Mrs. Russell), Peter Jason (Man in Truck), Adam Baumgarten (Boy with Danny), Abigail Booraem (Mrs. Ashley), Leonard Burns (Pissing Man), Mary Celio (Mary Woodson), Jack T. Collis (Mr. Anson), Christian Crane (Shawn), Dan Danforth (Guard), Chuck Dorsett (Reverend), Holgie Forrester (Teller), Christian Giannini (Jimmy), Allan Graf (Deputy), Anne Haney (Mrs. Piersall), Gary Kirk (Plant Manager), Bernard Kuby (Mr. Bidemeyer), Darren Muir (Mr. Harrison), Richard E. Norlie (Mary's Brother-in-Law), Svi Peter (Danny), Thomas J. Sauber (Band Leader), Dawn Eisler Smith (Mary's Sister), Hugo L. Stanger (Old Geezer), Sherri Stoner (Young Girl), S. Angelece Dunaway (Body Double for Meg Tilly), Janet Sassoon (Ballet

Mistress).

A strange chiller that an audience will watch halfheartedly, wonder about what's going on, sit through until the end, and then feel disappointed because it felt like a cheat. There is something compelling about it that keeps one's interest up to a point but it's hard to fathom exactly what it is. The small town of Sutcliffe is the setting. The locals are milling around on Main Street when the area feels a mild earthquake. A few windows break, some merchandise falls off a store's shelf, a typical quake in which nobody is hurt. The people shrug it off and go about their business. Former resident Tilly lives in a big city where she is pursuing a career as a dancer. She's coupled with Matheson, a bright young doctor. Tilly has a good relationship with her mom, Vozoff, so it comes as a shock when her maternal parent calls her on the phone and starts to abuse her verbally. It's totally out of character for the normally placid Vozoff and the call ends as Mom puts a gun to her head and pulls the trigger! Matheson and Tilly race to the tiny town and run to the local hospital where, miraculously, Vozoff is alive, but barely. The gunshot did terrible things to her but didn't kill her and the woman is on life support under the aegis of benevolent doctor Cronyn, a man right out of the Dr. Kildare-Ben Casey mold. Tilly's father, Karlen, and her brother, Paxton, can't understand what got into Vozoff. A brief foray around the town and Matheson and Tilly see that things aren't as peaceful or as normal in the area as appear on the surface. The weirdness starts slowly but any viewer with sensitivity soon observes the off-center attitude of the residents. Tilly and Matheson meet her pal, Stryker, at the local tavern to hoist a brew or two and Tilly notices that the woman seems to have changed, subtly, but there is a definite alteration in her personality. It's the same sort of personality shift that Karlen and Paxton are undergoing, an undercurrent of rage, sniping, and open hostility. Matters boil when Tilly's old beau walks up to their table at the bar and gives them all a demonstration of what pain is really like as he breaks two of his own fingers (with the sound effective CRUNCH to punctuate the action). Now all hell breaks loose. The townspeople raid the bank and steal the money, Cronyn's eyes light up when he decides to have some "fun" as he blocks Vozoff's air hose in the hospital, just to watch her struggle, and more. There is no explanation for all this behavior for most of the movie. It continues unabated and even Matheson is now subject to the madness of the town. Matheson kills Paxton, Cronyn kills Vozoff, and just about the only person in the town who is not a candidate for an asylum is Tilly. Why is this happening? Even Matheson can't explain his actions. The truth finally emerges when we learn that the earthquake caused the ground to shift and some toxic chemicals were sent dripping into the water supply. The water was slurped up by the dairy cows in the area. The cows gave milk, the milk was ingested by the townsfolk, and they all went nuts. The American Dairy Association would have been happy to know that so many people drink milk but the process of pasteurization is such that it should have effectively killed any danger in the fluid. The pacing is slow and the narrative often muddy but there is no faulting the major performers, all of whom respectfully act their scenes as though Shakespeare had written them. Cronyn is excellent as the kindly doctor toying with his patient like a pussycat with a ball of yarn. IMPULSE reminds one of many movies, especially some of the early sci-fi pictures of the 1950s like INVASION OF THE BODY SNATCHERS (the one with Kevin McCarthy). It's not a terrible movie, but it isn't terribly good, either. If you have nothing else to watch and the movie comes on TV late at night, give it a look, but don't treat yourself to a glass of warm milk at the same time. And don't let children see it because it does get bloody and the child will never want to drink milk again.

p, Tim Zinnemann; d, Graham Baker; w, Bart Davis, Don Carlos Dunaway; ph, Thomas Del Ruth (Panavision, DeLuxe Color); m, Paul Chihara; ed, David Holden; prod d, Jack T. Collis; set d, Jim Duffy; cos, Bill Flores, Llandys Williams.

Suspense   **Cas.**   **(PR:O MPAA:R)**

INDIANA JONES AND THE TEMPLE OF DOOM***½
                              (1984) 118m Lucasfilm/PAR c

Harrison Ford (Indiana Jones), Kate Capshaw (Willie Scott), Ke Huy Quan (Short Round), Amrish Puri (Mola Ram), Roshan Seth (Chattar Lal), Philip Stone (Capt. Blumburtt), Roy Chiao (Lao Che), David Yip (Wu Han), Ric Young (Kao Kan), Chua Kah Joo (Chen), Rex Ngui (Maitre d'), Philip Tann (Chief Henchman), Dan Ackroyd (Weber), Akio Mitamura (Chinese Pilot), Michael Yama (Chinese Copilot), D.R. Nanayakkara (Shaman), Dharmasdasa Kuruppu (Chieftain), Stany De Silva (Sanju), Ruby DeMiel, D.M. Denawake, I. Serasinghe (Village Women), Darshana Panangala (Village Child), Raj Singh (Little Maharaja), Frank Olegario, Ahmed El-Shenawi (Merchants), Art Repola (Eel Eater), Nizwar Karanj (Sacrifice Victim), Pat Roach (Chief Guard), Moti Mokan (Guard), Mellan Mitchell, Bhasker Patel (Temple Guards), Arjun Pandher, Zia Gelani (Boys in Cell).

After the 1981 release of Spielberg's RAIDERS OF THE LOST ARK, the question on almost everyone's lips was, "How can he top this?" The answer won't be found in that film's $25 million sequel INDIANA JONES AND THE TEMPLE OF DOOM, a breakneck adventure which moves at twice the pace of the original but has only half the creative strength. The film opens with one of the most purely entertaining scenes in many years as a Busby Berkeley-style dance number to Cole Porter's jumpy "Anything Goes" gives a clue to the line of logic the filmmakers will follow for the remainder of the story. The setting is a swanky Shanghai nightclub in 1935. A dazzling gold chorus line of girls kick their legs while ditzy blonde Capshaw belts out her song. In the crowd is Ford, the heroic archaeologist last seen saving the Lost Ark from Nazis. Murder and mayhem soon fill the air as Ford tries to retrieve a valuable vial which is being kicked around the dance floor by unaware dancers. When a Capshaw diamond also winds up on the floor, blending in with a load of ice cubes, confusion breaks out and everyone is on hands and knees trying to get the vial and the diamond. Ford is forced to make his getaway, taking Capshaw along, and moments later meeting up with a scrawny 12-year-old named Short Round (a character name stolen from Sam Fuller's 1951 film STEEL HELMET) played by Quan, who sports a baseball cap. Without wasting much time, Spielberg gets his characters into a small cargo plane high above the Himalayas. Since the plane has no parachutes, they improvise and use an inflatable rubber raft, which safely carries them to the ground, but slides uncontrollably down the mountainside, over a cliff, and into a river's violent rapids–a brilliant action sequence which manages to cover air, land, and water in one clean sweep. The trio comes to rest in a primitive East Indian village where Ford is beckoned to capture a prized gem from a heavily guarded fortress. The gem, along with all of the village's children, has mysteriously disappeared. After an elephant ride which turns into an embarrassing fiasco for the air-headed, wholly urban Capshaw, the trio arrives at a palace. Before long, however, they are in danger of winding up dead, or at least violently turned off by the palace cuisine. At a grand dinner sequence, the finest East Indian dishes are served–an order of wriggling baby snakes, unshelled beetles, chilled monkey brains (fresh from the skull)–bringing grimaces of disgust to the trio's faces, while everyone else seems ready to dig right in. When Quan disappears without a clue, Ford and Capshaw set out to find him, discovering a secret passageway which leads through an insect-infected tunnel and into an infernal underground ritual meeting place, as well as a secret mine where the missing village children are enslaved and forced to work until they collapse. Capshaw eventually gets captured as well, ending up tied to a torture device for a ritual sacrifice in which she is to be lowered into a flaming pit. Ford heroically tries to rescue her, battling guards while trying to prevent the sacrifice leader from tearing his heart out with his bare hands, a feat he has already tried on another poor victim. All the while Capshaw gets nearer and nearer to death in the red-hot pit. Ford, of course, saves her and they hightail it to the mines to rescue Quan. This does not prove an easy task, even for Ford, who can ingeniously overcome any obstacle. A spectacular rollercoaster ride takes place in the railed mining cars with Ford, Capshaw, and Quan being chased by guards in other cars. Traveling at unbearable speeds, the cars goes up slopes, make quick turns, switch rails, go under and over each other, even fly off one set of tracks onto another–none of it in the least believable, as if believablilty is even an issue. By the end, Ford has deposed the evil leader, destroyed the palace, and emancipated the village children, including a brave young prince. INDIANA JONES AND THE TEMPLE OF DOOM doesn't hide what it's about, concerning itself only with providing nonstop entertainment on the level of an amusement park ride. Spielberg has crammed an endless barrage of effects, chases, and gross-outs into the film's nearly two hours–never allowing the pace to relax. It's as if you were on the world's largest, fastest, and most dangerous rollercoaster. This film differs, however, from RAIDERS OF THE LOST ARK. The thrills in the original were paced further apart, allowing the audience a few minutes of recuperation in between, whereas in INDIANA JONES the nonstop pace soon produces a numbing effect after which one cannot even feel or enjoy the thrills anymore. The INDIANA JONES action whirlpool swirls its audience around for two hours straight, suffocating viewers by refusing to let them come up for air. Spielberg, following the mold set by the early serials, had successfully integrated that structure (originally a 15-minute episode every week for a few months) into RAIDERS OF THE LOST ARK by separating the chases with character interactions allowing the audience time to think to themselves, "What's going to happen next?" (the same question serial viewers were left asking themselves for an entire week). With INDIANA JONES, however, audiences never get the time to ask themselves that question. While a great deal of criticism has been leveled at Spielberg for the political and social underpinnings of the film–the subordinate role of women, the stereotypically evil portrayal of the East Indians, the need for foreign problems to be solved by a white outsider–none of this holds any bearing. Spielberg's detractors insist on judging this picture's morality in terms of present situations, without realizing that he is copying an earlier genre–its situations, its locale, its characters, and much of its morality. Spielberg must also be congratulated for bringing the classical hero back into Hollywood in Ford, a handsome, brawny, brainy tough guy who always finds a way out of a life-threatening dilemma. What Spielberg must be attacked for, however, is his increasingly graphic depictions of gore. Having imposed on children a number of gruesome, nightmarish horrors in films he has produced, though not directed–POLTERGEIST and the vile GREMLINS, both astonishingly rated PG–Spielberg seems to revel in sneaking such scenes into his films. While the dinner sequence in INDIANA JONES is disgusting, it is presented in a childish "gross-out" manner, which children will most likely laugh at (it was adults, not children, who found this scene most disturbing) rather than be bothered by. The horrific ritual scene of the sacrifice getting his heart ripped out–blood oozing from the globulous red mass that the high priest holds in his hand–is unforgivable, however, and seems only to take away from the old-style Hollywood fun of the film, a comic book style of fun where blood doesn't exist and people don't really get

hurt. Again, as with POLTERGEIST and GREMLINS, the gore has been pushed through the unreliable MPAA rating system, thereby exposing millions of impressionable and easily frightened children to violent and bloody assaults in exchange for the almighty box- office dollar.

p, Robert Watts; d, Steven Spielberg; w, Willard Huyck, Gloria Katz (based on a story by George Lucas and on characters from the movie RAIDERS OF THE LOST ARK by Lawrence Kasdan); ph, Douglas Slocombe (Panavision, DeLuxe Color); m, John Williams; ed, Michael Kahn; prod d, Elliot Scott; art d, Allan Cassie, Roger Cain, Joe Johnston, Errol Kelly; set d, Peter Howitt; cos, Anthony Powell; spec eff, Dennis Muren; ch, Dany Daniels m/l, "Anything Goes," Cole Porter.

Adventure   **Cas.**   **(PR:C-O   MPAA:PG)**

INITIATION, THE*½   (1984) 97m Initiation Associates/NW c

Vera Miles *(Frances Fairchild)*, Clu Gulager *(Dwight Fairchild)*, Daphne Zuniga *(Kelly Terry)*, James Read *(Peter)*, Marilyn Kagan *(Marcia)*, Patti Heider *(Nurse)*, Robert Dowdell *(Jason Randall)*, Frances Peterson *(Megan)*, Deborah Morehart *(Alison)*, Robert Stroud *(Ralph)*, Peter Malof *(Andy)*, Christopher Bradley *(Chad)*, Joy Jones *(Heidi)*, Mary Davis Duncan *(Gwen)*, Rusty Meyers *(Night Watchman)*, Christi Michelle Allen *(Kelly at Age 9)*, Dan Dickerson *(Detective)*, Ronald M. Hubner *(Cop)*, Jerry L. Clark *(Orderly)*, Kathy Lee Kennedy *(Nurse)*, Cheryl Foster, Diane Page, Traci Odom, Melissa Toomin, Jennifer Suttles *(Sorority Girls)*, Lance Funston, Andrea Vaccarello *(Students)*, Trey Strood *(Ralph)*, Paula Knowles *(Beth)*.

Boring slasher stuff has Zuniga a pledge at the Delta Rho Chi sorority with amnesia since age nine. She is also troubled with disturbing dreams involving her parents, Gulager and Miles. Read is a teaching assistant doing research on dreams who studies Zuniga and helps her recover, though not before someone gets to run amok in the sorority house with a knife. Miles is barely in the film, and Gulager is present even less. Conventional ending dissipates all the mystery but it isn't the least bit credible. Shot in 1983, the film received only a small release before emerging on an unsuspecting world in videocassette form.

p, Scott Winant; d, Larry Stewart; w, Charles Pratt, Jr.; ph, George Tirl (Movielab Color); m, Gabriel Black; ed, Ronald LaVine; set d, Ellen Freund; spec eff, Jack Bennett.

Horror   **Cas.**   **(PR:O   MPAA:R)**

INVISIBLE STRANGLER*½   (1984) Jordan Lyon-New Century/Seymour Borde c

Robert Foxworth *(Lt. Charles Barrett)*, Stefanie Powers *(Candy Barrett)*, Elke Sommer *(Chris)*, Sue Lyon *(Miss DeLong)*, Leslie Parrish *(Coleen Hudson)*, Mariana Hill *(Bambi)*, Mark Slade, Frank Ashmore, Alex Dreier, Percy Rodriguez, Jo Anne Meredith, Cesare Danova, John Hart.

Ridiculous cheapy horror film about a young lad who strangles his mother when she tells him that she wishes she had aborted him. Locked away in an asylum, he studies books on the occult (what kind of mental hospital would let a disturbed inmate have books like this is a question left unanswered) until he learns an ancient Buddhist technique for becoming invisible. He escapes his rubber padded room and goes on a murder spree, invisibly strangling his mother's old friends in their posh homes. These scenes are pretty funny, as women suddenly start choking and their eyes roll up in their heads, although no one is in the room, at least that the audience can see. Foxworth is the detective assigned to the case, and he finally gets rid of the unseen assailant by hooking a metal handrail up to an electrical outlet and frying the fellow. Sue Lyon makes a tiny appearance with no dialog, and Elke Sommer has a slightly larger role as a cocktail waitress. Shot in 1976 under the title of THE ASTRAL FACTOR, the film languished on the shelf for eight years before being sprung on an unwanting world.

p, Earle Lyon; d, John Florea; w, Arthur C. Pierce (based on a story by Lyon, Pierce); ph, Alan Stensvold; m, Richard Hieronymous, Alan Oldfield; ed, Bud S. Isaacs; spec eff, Roger George.

Horror   **Cas.**   **(PR:C-O   MPAA:PG)**

IRRECONCILABLE DIFFERENCES***   (1984) 114m Lantana/WB c

Ryan O'Neal *(Albert Brodsky)*, Shelley Long *(Lucy Van Patten Brodsky)*, Drew Barrymore *(Casey Brodsky)*, Sam Wanamaker *(David Kessler)*, Allen Garfield 'Goorwitz' *(Phil Hanner)*, Sharon Stone *(Blake Chandler)*, Hortensia Colorado *(Maria Hernandez)*, Kim Marriner, Wendy Gordon, Ken Gale, Deborah Cody, Mark May, Steven K. Miller *(Reporters)*, Annie Meyers-Shyer *(Little Girl in Crowd)*, Lauren Hartman *(Woman on the Street)*, David Paymer *(Alan Sluiser)*, Larry Margo *(Court Clerk)*, Lorinne Vozoff *(Judge Shalack)*, David Graf *(Bink)*, Ida Random *(Woman at Party)*, Steffen Zacharias *(Man at Party)*, Laura Campbell *(Uptight Woman)*, Jenny Gago *(Tracy)*, Verna Cornelius *(Englishwoman at Party)*, Johna Stewart *(Little Casey)*, David D'Arnal *(Waiter)*, Don Benjamin *(Whispering Man)*, Ildiko Jaid *(Whispering Woman)*, Kelly Lange *(Anchorperson)*, Rex Reed *(Entertainment Editor)*, Irv Meyers *(Man in Bar)*, William A. Fraker *(Cinematographer)*, Beverlee Reed *(Dotty Chandler)*, Eloise Hardt *(Elaine Kessler)*, Art Bradley *(Handsome Party Guest)*, Stuart Pankin *(Ronnie)*, Laura Winitsky *(Amy)*, Gregory Hodal *(Atlanta Preacher)*, Carl Byrd

(Sound Man), Luana Anders *(Atlanta Widow)*, Richard Minchenberg *(Howard Kay)*, Charlotte Stewart *(Sally)*, Dana Kaminsky *(Woman in Dress Shop)*, Arlin Miller *(Radio Newscaster)*, Ken Lerner *(Doctor)*, Minnie Lindsey *(Inez)*.

A good human comedy that suffered at the turnstiles because it may have been marketed incorrectly and in the 1980s, movies have come and gone with great speed and if they don't make it over the first week or so, they have been pulled from the theaters. It was billed as the story of a 9-year-old, Barrymore, who is the daughter of O'Neal and Long. She sues her parents for divorce and that's what was seen in the trailers and the TV spots. However, the picture is far more than that. It's about how Long and O'Neal met, worked together, succeeded together, and then fell into Hollywood's velvet snare, the trappings of success. Their relationship begins to crumble and that's when Barrymore seeks an attorney's help as she wants to find a more loving set of parents. Flash back to 1973 when O'Neal hitchhiked from New York to teach at UCLA. Traveling across Indiana, he is picked up by Pittsburgher Long, who is driving her Navy boy friend's car across country. The moment she arrives in L.A., she and her sailor are to be wed, although we can tell very soon that the thought of being a Navy wife doesn't appeal to her. In the three days it takes to get from Indiana to California, O'Neal and Long fall for each other and are caught making love by Graf, her fiance. He's no fool and walks away when he sees the happiness on Long's face as she cuddles O'Neal. Flash forward and the couple now have a young daughter when O'Neal is offered a film writing job by producer Wanamaker. O'Neal's encyclopedic knowledge of film is what brings him to Wanamaker, who needs O'Neal to help repair a crumbling project. O'Neal accepts the screenplay assignment and when he runs into a block, he calls on Long for help. She doesn't much like Wanamaker and the phony life he and his friends lead and she is determined that it won't happen to her and O'Neal. She is an excellent writer and the movie they pen turns out to be ironically named "An American Romance." It's a smash hit and O'Neal, who gets solo credit, becomes the latest Hollywood darling, while Long is just another Hollywood wife. All the while, Barrymore is growing up in Los Angeles *nuevo rico* style, which means that she spends more time with her *Latina* housekeeper, Colorado, than she does with her parents. O'Neal is becoming a man who wraps his ego around him every morning just after his shower. Long resents the fact that O'Neal has become such a *wunderkind* and is terribly involved with himself. The marriage starts to slip. In an attempt to keep it together, the two collaborate on another script. O'Neal begins searching for the right face to play the lead role and comes across Stone, a yo-yo with a face that could cause grown men to cry. O'Neal convinces Long that they should take Stone into their home so he can work with the lass and help her with the character he wants her to play. The predictable happens as O'Neal falls for Stone and Long is squeezed out, after a nine- year marriage. She takes Barrymore with her and tries to be brave, but it's to no avail. She begins to fall apart, gets depressed, and can no longer write. O'Neal continues on his egocentric spiral as he becomes insufferable to everyone around him, except the nubile Stone. (There were those who felt there was a parallel here between a well-known boy wonder director and the incredibly beautiful woman he loved who was eventually killed by her estranged husband.) As O'Neal soars higher in his career, his sympathetic nature disintegrates. Long finally emerges from her funk and starts to write again, while O'Neal is busily preparing to direct a musical version of GONE WITH THE WIND to be titled "Atlanta." It becomes the greatest flop in the history of film (and anyone who knew that there really had been an attempt at a musical version of GWTW done in England could have told them that it would flop, as that musical did) and O'Neal's star falls as he had placed his fragile reputation on the film's success by casting the untalented Stone in the lead (shades of CITIZEN KANE and his talentless opera-singing wife). Long has written a novel and it is released to critical acclaim and best- seller status. As O'Neal's star falls, hers rises. In no time, she becomes almost as obnoxiously egotistical as O'Neal. Meanwhile, Barrymore lives a Ping-Pong existence as she goes from Long to O'Neal and back again. He's now bankrupt, jobless, and hoping to reconnect with Long. They do spend one night with each other and the coldness seen earlier seems to be warmed by the glow of their love for each other. That continues until O'Neal casually asks if they've yet picked the director to handle the filming of her novel, *He Said it Was Going to Be Forever*. She does it! She tosses him out and says that he only came back to use his sex appeal on her to get a job . . .and she may be right. Cut to the courtroom where Barrymore tells judge Vozoff that she wants out of her relationship with her parents and would prefer to stay with the housekeeper and her family. Barrymore is granted her wish and Long and O'Neal realize the folly of their ways. They receive visitation rights to Barrymore and finally pay attention to the young girl and the film ends as there is a glimmer of hope that the family may yet get together. O'Neal and Long are excellent comic actors and demonstrate several changes of character. Barrymore is good as the Hollywood child but her story goes much further than the movie business, as she represents any child who is caught in a marital chess match. The screenwriters knew the movie business and filled the picture with inside jokes and insights about movies that went right over the heads of most of the public. They must have drawn on their own collaboration, as the scenes between Long and O'Neal while they write smack of the truth. O'Neal and Long are "bonded" for life; they just can't live with each other and that's a sad conclusion to an otherwise lovely and sharp-witted comedy. The song "We Wanted it All" became a hit as Frank Sinatra sang it. It was written by Peter Allen and Carol Bayer Sager. Shyer's direction was on the money most of the time and just a little

flabby at other times, perhaps due to the fact that he cowrote the script with Meyers and hated to lose a precious word. This should have been a bigger hit than it was but teenagers couldn't identify with it and flocked to see the break dancing pictures instead.

p, Arlene Sellers, Alex Winitsky; d, Charles Shyer; w, Nancy Meyers, Shyer; ph, William A. Fraker (Technicolor); m, Paul De Senneville, Olivier Toussaint; ed, John F. Burnett; prod d, Ida Random; art d, Jane Bogart; cos, Joe I. Tompkins, Mort Schwartz, Anne Marie Thomas.

Comedy/Drama   Cas.   (PR:A-C MPAA:PG)

ISAAC LITTLEFEATHERS*½   (1984, Can.) 94m
King-Alberta-Allarcom-Telefilm Canada-Canadian Broadcasting-Cinema Concepts/Lauron c

Lou Jacobi *(Abe Kapp)*, William Korbut *(Isaac Littlefeathers)*, Scott Hylands *(Jesse Armstrong)*, Lorrain Behnan *(Golda Hersh)*, George Clutesi *(Moses Ankewat)*, Thomas Heaton *(Mike Varco)*.

Korbut, the half-breed son of a neer-do-well hockey player and a Canadian Indian woman, is taken in by Jacobi, a Jewish storekeeper who wants to raise the boy in his faith. Korbut is confused between cultures and grows rebellious as a result. He finds himself getting into trouble and is in a constant battle with a neighboring family of bullies. Korbut and one of that clan get into a boxing match which the Indian boy wins handily, but the opposing family, furious, sets fire to Jacobi's store in retaliation. In anger, Korbut gets a rifle and takes Heaton hostage, leading to an eventual reuniting of the boy and his real father in an emotional climax. The film's technical qualities are professional but each character is a stereotype and despite the volatile nature of some of the plot points there's little excitement. There are attempts at making some statements about prejudice but these are so simplistic that their effect is practically nil.

p, Barry Pearson, Bill Johnston; d, Les Rose; w, Rose, Pearson; ph, Ed Higginson; m, Paul Zaza; art d, Richard Hudolin; cos, Mairin Wilkinson.

Drama   (PR:C MPAA:NR)

IT'S NEVER TOO LATE***   (1984, Span.) 98m Incline and Impala/Films Inc. c

Jose Luis Gomez *(Antonio)*, Angela Molina *(Teresa)*, Madeleine Christie *(Ursula)*, Maria Silva, Maite Blasco, Eduardo Calvo, Chus Lampreave, Julia Trujillo, Josefina del Cid, Julia Lorente.

A strange and unusual film from Spain, this drama features Christie as an amiable 73-year-old spinster obsessed with a newlywed couple whose apartment window faces her own. She gets to know the couple, continually making excuses to drop over, particularly when the wife (Molina), is away. On one visit she steals a wedding picture of Molina and her husband, Gomez, replacing Molina's face with a photograph of herself. After watching the couple make love Christie believes herself to be pregnant. A visit to an extremely surprised doctor proves this to be true, a fact which stuns Christie's family. Meanwhile, Molina is convinced that her betrothed is seeing another woman, never realizing that the affair is only in the mind of their odd drop-in guest. Originally made in 1977, the film develops it's offbeat story in a straightforward, conventional style that doesn't always jibe with the strange plot developments. However, the story is engaging with a cast that handles the material nicely. (In Spanish; English subtitles.)

p, Francisco Hueva; d, Jaime De Arminan; w, De Arminan, Juan Carlos Eguillor (based on an idea by Concha Gregori); ph, Teo Escamilia; m, Jose Nieto; ed, Jose Luis Matesanz.

Drama   (PR:O MPAA:NR)

JAZZMAN*½ (1984, USSR) 80m Mosfilm/International Film Exchange c

Igor Sklyar *(Konstantine)*, Alexander Chorny *(Stefan)*, Nikolai Averyuskin *(George)*, Pyotr Shcherbakov *(Ivan)*, Elena Tsiplakova *(Katie)*, Larissa Dolina *(Clementine)*.

Despite wavering "official" attitudes toward jazz in the Soviet Union, this has been a musical form that has always enjoyed popularity with the Russian people. This film pretends to be a story of a dzhez band in 1930, but, because of not-too-subtle government influence, it never quite develops into the charming period piece it could have been. It is the first year of the Five Year Plan. Sklyar, Chorny, Averyuskin, and Shcherbakov are jazz street entertainers. They are noticed and hired to play a party for some seemingly important people, only to learn that their employers are Jewish gangsters, which puts the group in a quandary: Do they keep their ill-gotten gains (which the threadbare band members clearly need) or is the money to be turned over to the government? There are no surprises here nor is the story engaging. Each character is a symbol for various political viewpoints, with a czarist loyalist being the band's least talented member. There are also some slams at the U.S. as one character explains, that dzhez is music born from the blues tunes of oppressed Negro Americans. Had this film been made from a populist point of view it might well have been a charming portrait of a people and an era. Such is not the case and the results are enormously disappointing. (In Russian; English subtitles.)

d, Karen Shakhnazarov; w, Shakhnazarov, Alexander Borodyansky; ph, Vladimir Shevtsik; m, Anatoly Kroll; art d, Konstantin Forostenko.

Drama/Comedy (PR:C MPAA:NR)

JIGSAW MAN, THE** (1984, Brit.) 91m Evangrove/United Film Distribution c

Michael Caine (Sir Philip Kimberly), Laurence Olivier (Adm. Sir Gerald Scaith), Susan George (Penny), Robert Powell (Jamie), Charles Gray (Sir James Charley), Michael Medwin (Milroy), Anthony Shaw (Matthews), Maureen Bennett (Susan), Patrick Dawson (Ginger), Juliet Nissen (Miss Fortescue), David Kelly (Cameron), Peter Burton (Douglas), Maggie Rennie (Pauline), Peggy Marshall (Polly), David Allister (Sgt. Lloyd), P.G. Stephens (Driver), Richard Borthwick (Plainclothesman), Matthew Scurfield (Hepner, KGB Man), Robert Austin (Daa, KGB Man).

Mediocre spy drama has Caine an aging British spy for the Russians who has long ago defected and is living in Moscow. (His character is loosely based on British traitor Kim Philby, note the similarity between his name and Caine's character's name.) For some reason the Russians don't want him around anymore, embarrassing them, so they give him plastic surgery which makes him look years younger (more like the Michael Caine we all know) and send him off to Britain to retrieve a dangerous list of Soviet agents in London. Under the identity of a Russian, he defects to the British, then escapes the men assigned to protect him while he goes off to find the list. Olivier is the head of British intelligence and Caine's old rival, and he assigns Powell, an agent who lives with Caine's daughter, to find the escaped defector. There's more nonsense about a highly placed "mole" in the British government, his identity easily guessed, and the running battle of wits between Caine and Olivier, but the whole thing is so uninvolving that it almost evaporates in the distance between the eyes and the brain. Caine and Olivier, who were so marvelous together in SLEUTH, seem only concerned with getting their scenes over with quickly and getting their check.. If Olivier isn't more careful about the roles he picks, someone should look into taking away his lordship. Apparently the film had a troubled production history, with money running out in the middle of shooting and the whole project lying dormant for some time before someone came up with the moeny to finish it. Pity.

p, Ben Fisz; d, Terence Young; w, Jo Eisinger (based on the novel by Dorothea Bennet); ph, Freddie Francis (Eastmancolor); m, John Cameron; ed, Derek Trigg; prod d, Cameron; art d, John Roberts.

Spy Drama Cas. (PR:C MPAA:PG)

JOB LAZADASA (SEE: REVOLT OF JOB, THE, Hung./Ger.)

JOHNNY DANGEROUSLY**½ (1984) 89m FOX c

Michael Keaton (Johnny Dangerously), Joe Piscopo (Vermin), Marilu Henner (Lil), Maureen Stapleton (Mom), Peter Boyle (Dundee), Griffin Dunne (Tommy), Glynnis O'Connor (Sally), Dom DeLuise (The Pope), Richard Dimitri (Maroni), Danny DeVito (Burr), Ron Carey (Pat), Ray Walston (Vendor), Dick Butkus (Arthur), Byron Thames (Young Johnny), Alan Hale ', Jr.' (Desk Sergeant), Scott Thomson (Charley), Sudie Bond (Cleaning Lady), Mark Jantzen (Dutch), Gary Watkins (Manny), Mike Bacarella (Vito), Hank Garrett (Mayor), Leonard Termo (Tony Scarano), Troy W. Slaten (Young Tommy), Alexander Herzberg (Boy in Suit), Georg Olden (Young Vermin), Cynthia Szigeti (Mrs. Capone), Elizabeth Arlen (Girl on Steps), Doris Grossman (Woman), Richard Warwick, Mike Finneran, Paul B. Price (Prisoners), Katie La Bourdette (Blond Girl), Norman Steinberg (Reporter Duffy), Frank Slaten (Henchman), Dean R. Miller (Photographer), Neal Israel (Dr. Zillman), Edward C. Short (Porter), Shelley Pogoda (Woman), Jerome Michaels (Reporter Diering), Russell Forte (Hood), Jack Nance (Priest), Joy Michael (Chorus Girl), Richard L. Rosenthal (Judge), Carl A. Gottlieb (Dr. Magnus), Paula Dell (Mrs. Zimmer), Harvey Parry (Policeman), Jeffrey Weissman (T-Shirt Vendor), Richard A. Roth (Prisoner Rabbi), Chuck Hicks (Governor), Bob Eubanks (Emcee), Gordon Zimmerman, Dick Dalduzzi, Mert Rich, Will Seltzer, Hal Riddle, Trisha Long, Claudia Kim.

A bomb at the box office despite the presence of Keaton, it nevertheless merits your attention, for some of the funniest scenes of the year appear in this film. The picture has several lapses of taste, gets downright dumb in spots, and goes beyond satire into burlesque and parody as it spoofs the Warner Bros. crime movies of the 1930s and 1940s. Thames is the young "Johnny Dangerously," a goodhearted boy who is forced into a life of crime to help pay for the medical bills of his mother, Stapleton, a walking "Gray's Anatomy" of ailments. His kid brother is Dunne, and Thames keeps his criminal activities a secret from the lad as he pays for the boy's legal education until the younger brother grows up and becomes part of the district attorney's office, under the helm of DeVito, a criminal district attorney who is on the take. Since he was a child, Thames/Keaton has been rivals with Piscopo and the two men grow up as enemies, both working for Boyle, the local benevolent Godfather. When Boyle leaves the business as a result of a running feud with Dimitri, a rival boss, Keaton takes over and Piscopo vows to get him. Keaton is eventually framed and sent to jail through Piscopo's evildoing and, while inside, Keaton learns that his brother and mother are to be killed. He hears this through the prison grapevine in

a hysterical sequence as the message is passed by the prisoners while they are at the mess table. By the time it gets to Keaton, it bears no resemblance at all to the original sentence but he manages to understand it anyhow. He breaks out, saves the day, and eventually quits crime to settle down with Henner, his long- time moll. The movie is told in flashback as Keaton is running a pet shop and stops a young boy from stealing a puppy, then launches into his life story and how crime doesn't pay. The picture is played out and winds up back in the pet shop. The young boy decides that Keaton is right, then exits. Keaton leaves and gets into a limousine and is obviously a living example that crime *does* pay. Ray Walston does a bit as a street-corner newsdealer who is blind until he gets hit with a paper bundle, then regains his sight. The next time he's hit, he goes deaf and when he's hit the final time, he gets his hearing back but forgets who and where he is. Swarthy Dimitri, who is also a writer, is hysterical as a foreigner whose heritage is never revealed, but he claims to be Swedish. He speaks in a combination of Italian, Greek, and several other dialects and mangles the English language as he attempts to use four-letter words to make his points but they always come out slightly awry. They spoof just about every known crime movie cliche and when the jokes work, they are sensational, as in the opening shot when we see the date supered on screen in front of the pet shop. But it isn't superimposed at all, it's actual huge block letters that are banged out of frame as a car pulls up in front of the pet store and knocks the numbers away. Co-author Steinberg (who also wrote YES, GIORGIO, and co-created "When Things Were Rotten" for TV), does a cameo, as do writers Neal Israel and Carl Gottlieb (JAWS, etc.). The title song was sung by "Weird Al" Yankovic and sets a proper tone. With more attention paid to making the gags pay off and not stooping to toilet humor, this could have been terrific. Even with all its flaws, JOHNNY DANGEROUSLY has many genuinely funny moments and if you're in the mood for silliness, you won't stop laughing at jokes like when Mrs. Capone (Szigeti) comes to Keaton and Henner's apartment and asks if she can borrow a cup of bullets. Keaton is obviously doing a takeoff on Cagney, right down to the jerky, quirky mannerisms (but not the voice) and the only thing missing is screwing a grapefruit into a blonde's face.

p, Michael Hertzberg; d, Amy Heckerling; w, Norman Steinberg, Bernie Kukoff, Harry Colomby, Jeff Harris; ph, David M. Walsh (DeLuxe Color); m, John Morris; ed, Pem Herring; prod d, Joseph R. Jennings; set d, Rick Simpson; cos, Patricia Norris; m/l, "Dangerously," Morris, Norman Gimbel, (sung by "Weird Al" Yankovic).

Comedy/Crime Cas. (PR:C MPAA:PG-13)

JOKE OF DESTINY, A (SEE: JOKE OF DESTINY LYING IN WAIT AROUND THE CORNER LIKE A STREET BANDIT, A, Ital.)

JOKE OF DESTINY LYING IN WAIT AROUND THE CORNER LIKE A STREET BANDIT, A* (1984, Ital.) 105m Radiovideo/Samuel Goldwyn c (AKA: A JOKE OF DESTINY)

Ugo Tognazzi (Vincenzo De Andreiis), Piera Degli Esposti (Maria Theresa De Andreiis), Gastone Moschin (Minister of the Interior), Roberto Herlitzka (Minister's Assistant), Renzo Montagnani (Pautasso, Captain of the Digos), Enzo Jannacci (Gigi Pedrinelli, Terrorist), Valeria Golino (Adalgisa), Massimo Wertmuller (Beniamino, Carabiniere), Livia Cerini (Pot-Smoking Grandmother), Antonella D'Agostino (Wife of Minister), Pina Cei (Maria's Sister), Pierluigi Misasi (Driver).

Lina Wertmuller, who seems to specialize in long-titled films, disappointed audiences and critics alike with this work, continuing a decline from the quality for which her work had been lauded in the 1970s. Moschin is the Italian Minister of the Interior, out for a drive with his chauffeur when the limousine they are in stalls. Because the car is a specially designed anti-terrorist vehicle, the two are locked in tight, unable to escape the elaborate systems which are now unintentionally holding them hostage (the very condition the vehicle was to have prevented). Tognazzi, a member of the Italian parliament and Moschin's political rival, is out for a stroll and finds the two hapless victims. He manages to get the car into the garage of his nearby estate and summons help, which leads to a parade of various shenanigans. Tognazi and Moschin already have personal grudges against one another, which are further complicated by the situation. Esposti, Tognazzi's wife, shares Moschin's loathing for her husband and engages in an affair with a Red Brigade terrorist. Their daughter Golino takes a pair of handcuffs, then shackles herself to an unwitting policeman, pleading for the man to "deflower" her. Calls for help repeatedly end up going to a local pizza parlor. Wertmuller develops the comedy along predictable lines but with few of the satirical elements so desperately needed to make the film work. The situation serves as a one-joke idea on which to hang numerous subplots, but nothing is developed to any great extent. Though the ensemble gives it their all Wertmuller's dismal (and occasionally heavy handed) script never gives the cast much direction, resulting in a most uneven and not very funny comedy. The film, Wertmuller stated in an interview, "is just my reaction to the enormous impact that technology and science are having on mankind. It is an ironic, outrageous approach to comedy." This may have been her intent, but the results are anything but. Wertmuller had slipped into sincerity with her two previous films, A NIGHT FULL OF RAIN (1977) and BLOOD FEUD (1978); after a lengthy hiatus from pictures, she returned to her comedic roots with this entry, a further celebration of humankind in chaos. As in Rene Clair's A NOUS LA LIBERTE (1931) and Charles

Chaplin's MODERN TIMES (1936), the theme is Mary Shelley's: man victimized by a monster of his own creation. Where Clair and Chaplin–accustomed to the two-reeler format–held their man-eaten-by-machine segments down to a reasonable limit, Wertmuller made the mistake of stretching the story too thin. (In Italian, English subtitles.)

p, Giuseppe Giovannini; d, Lina Wertmuller; w, Wertmuller, Age (based on a story by Wertmuller, Silvia D'Amico Bendico); ph, Camillio Bazzoni; m, Paolo Conte; ed, Franco Fraticelli; art d, Enrico Job.

Comedy   Cas.   (PR:C   MPAA:PG)

JOY OF SEX zero   (1984) 93m PAR c

Cameron Dye (*Alan Holt*), Michelle Meyrink (*Leslie Hindenberg*), Colleen Camp (*Liz Sampson*), Ernie Hudson (*Mr. Porter*), Lisa Langlois (*Melanie*), Charles Van Eman (*Max Holt*), Joanne Baron (*Miss Post*), Darren Dalton (*Ed Ingalls*), Heidi Holicker (*Candy*), Cristen Kauffman (*Sharon*), David H. MacDonald (*Ernie Carpenter*), Paul Tulley (*Ted*), Joe Unger (*Mr. Ranada*), Christopher Lloyd (*Coach Hindenberg*), Conni Marie Brazelton (*Allison*), D. W. Brown (*Dinko*), Randolph Dreyfuss (*Mushroom*), Ellen Gerstein (*Nurse*), Eugene Robert Glazer (*Dr. Fox*), Sharee Gregory Laura Harrington (*Pretty Girls*), Peter MacPherson (*Earl*), DeVera Marcus (*Mrs. Fish*), Nancy Neumann (*Inga*), Miguel A. Nunez Jr, Jason Planco (*Jocks*), Robert Prescott (*Tom Pittman/Richard*), Danton Stone (*Farouk*), Jan Stration (*Miss Bismark*), Sherry Unger (*Mrs. Holt*), Perry Van Soest (*Student*), Terry Wagner-Otis (*Jenny Hindenberg*), Carole Ita White (*Roberta*), Marlon Whitefield (*Punk Student*).

A shockingly awful teenage sex comedy which couldn't be more inappropriately titled. It concerns a group of high schoolers at Richard Nixon High (though a few letters on the sign are missing, resulting in a sophomoric joke). Naturally, the only thing on these kids' minds is sex. The boys "ooh" and "ah" over all the shapely girls, while the girls do their best to turn on their admirers. Dye is an energetic youngster who will try almost anything to lose his virginity, even resort to phone ads for Swedish "nurses." He is attracted to Meyrink, the daughter of the most-feared physical education teacher ever to walk the earth, Lloyd in a fine performance. Lloyd has made it perfectly clear that anyone who touches his daughter will swiftly be emasculated. Dye is duly intimidated, but finds himself risking his life in order to win Meyrink over. In the meantime, Richard Nixon High is up for grabs. A glue phantom is vandalizing the school by affixing the most unlikely objects in the most unlikely places. A foreign exchange student, Stone, is getting more attention from the girls than all the other guys combined – especially when they discover he is extremely wealthy and owns four Mercedes Benz's. To further complicate matters, Camp (the mother in VALLEY GIRL, 1983) is an undercover narcotics agent who is preparing a massive drug bust. While some of these characters may sound humorous, nothing in JOY OF SEX is funny. Nothing. Every single line of dialog, every gag, and every scene is dependent upon sex for its laugh. The humor is crude and must rely on such crass subjects as gastric explosions, frigidity, and vile language. The film was plagued with problems from its inception. Originally to be titled NATIONAL LAMPOON'S JOY OF SEX, the script was such a dog that the National Lampoon people backed out, taking their name with them. Another setback occurred with the death of John Belushi, who was working on the script at the time of his death. Responsibility was then thrown on the shoulders of talented director Coolidge, who had previously delivered VALLEY GIRL, a much-heralded teen picture which treated its young audience as intelligent people instead of pandering to them. Not surprisingly, Coolidge came up empty with JOY OF SEX, especially since the script is such offensive drivel. The only thing worthwhile is the final two minutes as Dye and Meyrink finally get their chance to get under the covers. For the first time in the film the characters become real as they decide, instead, to talk. With this scene one can cling to the belief that VALLEY GIRL wasn't a fluke, and that Coolidge does indeed have promise.

p, Frank Konigsberg; d, Martha Coolidge; w, Kathleen Rowell, J. J. Salter (based on the book by Alex Comfort); ph, Charles Correll (Movielab Color); m, Bishop Holiday, Scott Lipsker, Harold Payne; ed, Alan Jacobs, William Elias, Ned Humphreys, Eva Gardos; art d, Jim Murakami; set d, Bob Gould; spec eff, John R. Elliott.

Comedy   Cas.   (PR:O   MPAA:R)

JUNGLE WARRIORS**   (1984, U.S./Ger./Mex.) 93m TAT-Jungle
                          Warriors-International Screen-Araiz-Condoy-Popular/Aquarius c

Nina Van Pallandt (*Joanna*), Paul L. Smith (*Cesar*), John Vernon (*Vito*), Alex Cord (*Nicky*), Sybil Danning (*Angel*), Woody Strode (*Luther*), Kai Wulff (*Ben*), Dana Elcar (*Michael*), Suzi Horne (*Pam*), Mindy Iden (*Marci*), Kari Lloyd (*Brie*), Ava Cadell (*Didi*), Myra Chason (*Cindy*), Angela Robinson (*Monique*), Louisa Moritz (*Laura*), Marjoe Gortner (*Larry*).

In some unnamed South American cocaine republic, producer Gortner, photographer Van Pallandt, and a bevy of leggy models arrive for a fashion shoot. Simultaneously arriving is American mafioso Vernon and his contingent, there to make a big deal with hefty heavy Smith, whose relationshiop to half-sister Danning is more than sibling. When a small plane carrying the models strays too far into Smith's territory, he orders it shot down. Led by the pilot, the survivors try to make their way to safety, pursued by some of Smith's private army led by Strode (still looking mean

at age seventy). Gortner manages to kill two of the men and is about to shoot Strode when he is impaled on a booby trap. The rest are quickly captured and taken to Smith, who promptly has the pilot decapitated and locks the women in his dungeon. Danning tortures the models, then gives them to the soldiers for a gang-rape. As Smith and Vernon are exchanging politenesses before getting down to business, the women escape from their cell and a three-way running gun battle erupts between the ladies, Smith's troops, and Vernon's men. Danning is killed and Smith shrugs it off with "She was only my half-sister." When Vernon tries to escape in a helicopter, Smith pulls him out and holds him up into the blades. Smith then tries to flee in the chopper but is shot out of the sky by Van Pallandt as helicopters from the Pan-American Drug Enforcement Agency fly in to the rescue. With an amazingly prominent cast for an exploitation item and some clever writing, this obscure film is almost the quintessence of mindless entertainment, although there's not enough naked flesh or spraying blood to please genre aficionados. The performances are nearly all unremittingly silly, and one is glad when Gortner gets killed just as he starts to act like a hero so no one won't have to listen to his amateurish line readings any more. Smith is the exception here, never raising his voice or breaking out in a sweat as he twists necks, orders executions, and gives his half-sister back rubs. Certainly nothing special here, but an inoffensive and sometimes amusing way to kill an hour and a half.

p&d, Ernst R. von Theumer; w, von Theumer, Robert Collector; ph, Nicholas von Sternberg (CFI Color); m, Roland Baumgartner; ed, Juan Jose Marino, Warren Chadwick; art d, Richard McGuire; stunts, Roberto Messina.

Crime   (PR:O   MPAA:R)

JUST THE WAY YOU ARE*   (1984) 94m MGM/UA c

Kristy McNichol (*Susan Berlanger*), Michael Ontkean (*Peter Nichols*), Kaki Hunter (*Lisa*), Andre Dussollier (*Francois*), Catherine Salviat (*Nicole*), Robert Carradine (*Sam Carpenter*), Alexandra Paul (*Bobbie*), Lance Guest (*Jack*), Timothy Daly (*Frank*), Patrick Cassidy (*Steve*), Gerard Jugnot (*Desk Clerk*), Andre Oumansky (*Doctor*), Billy Kearns (*Earl*), Joyce Gordon (*Answering Service Lady*), Wayne Robson (*Assistant Manager*), Jean-Claude Ostrander (*Ski Instructor*), Garrick Dowhen (*Bill Holland*), Paul Soles (*Arthur*), Joanna Noyes (*Doris*), Gisella Witkowsky (*Prima Ballerina*), Robert Scott (*Waiter*), Jefferson Mappin (*Cabbie*), Jim Fusco (*Conductor*), Madeleine Ganne (*Spectator*), Frank Emmanuel (*Porter*), Caroline Beaune (*Sophie*), Beatrice Masson (*Coat Check Girl*).

A dumb premise, a vapid script, and uncertain direction all contribute to making this a must-miss. McNichol has a game leg, the result of a childhood affliction, and she also has a bubbling attraction to men. She's a talented flutist and constantly surrounded by males, which is a flaw in the picture at the start because she's just not that comely and it's hard to believe that so many guys would find her irresistible. Guest works at McNichol's answering service and is enthralled by her voice, Carradine is a wolf she encounters in a restaurant, and even Daly, a gay stockbroker, wants to marry her. She can't handle all of the attention and hies herself off to a French ski resort to meditate on matters. She wears a leg brace most of the time and wants to avoid the usual conversation that comes with it so she has her leg encased in a cast in order to appear like a skier who schussed when she should have slalomed. At the resort, she meets three more men who can't take their eyes off her. They are Ontkean, a photographer, Dussollier, a French businessman, and Cassidy, a skier. Dussollier eventually goes for her roommate, Salviat, and the ending is a phony contrived one with Ontkean, who may be the dullest suitor she's had in the interminable 94-minute running time. Hunter does a few good lines as McNichol's ballerina friend but the rest of the movie just lies there. The idea of having her go off to Europe is motivated by the ballet company for which she blows getting a European tour, after which she repairs to the resort. Originally called "I Won't Dance," it was halted temporarily when McNichol was discovered to have been suffering from a "chemical imbalance" and what that means can be interpreted in many ways. JUST THE WAY YOU ARE was shot in Toronto to resemble an unnamed U.S. industrial city. Molinaro, who had directed LA CAGE AUX FOLLES, was out of his element with this, although he had little to work with in Burns' script. Nice European travelog shots and something of a social conscience when it comes to dealing with the handicapped are all that rescue this from total obscurity.

p, Leo L. Fuchs; d, Edouard Molinaro; w, Allan Burns; ph, Claude Lecomte (Eastmancolor); m, Vladimir Cosma; ed, Claudio Ventura, Georges Klotz; art d, Francois De Lamothe; set d, Anthony Greco, David Harbonn; cos, Jean Zay.

Romantic Comedy   Cas.   (PR:C   MPAA:PG)

KAMILLA*½**   (1984, Norway) 100m AS/New Line c
                    (LOPERJENTEN; THE BETRAYAL; BETRAYAL: THE STORY OF
                                                                    KAMILLA)

Nina Knapskog (*Kamilla*), Vibeke Lokkeberg (*Kamilla's Mother*), Helge Jordal (*Kamilla's Father*), Kenneth Johansen (*Svein*), Karin Zetlitz Haerem, Renie Kleivdal, Thorleifsson, Klaus Hagerup, Marie Takvam, Johnny Bergh, Per Jansen, Kjell Pettersen.

A realistic look at growing up in post-war Norway, KAMILLA tells the story of two 7-year-old children who are deeply affected by decisions made by their parents. Knapskog is a glowing young girl caught in the turmoil of her parents' failing marriage. Her father, Jordal, has taken up with his opportunistic blonde shop assistant and dreams of finding a new life in America. Knapskog is left with her mother, Lokkeberg, who is living on some money that Jordal had stashed away. Knapskog, unable to find the attention she needs among adults, becomes best friends with a neighboring boy, Johansen, who also lives alone with his mother. Together they begin unraveling the little mysteries that occupy children's imaginations, but before long Johansen is sent away to an orphanage. KAMILLA is a lyrical and gritty picture, beautifully acted by its two young stars and by Lokkeberg, as the mother who dearly loves her daughter but is unable to express it. Lokkeberg also acted as the film's director, writing the screenplay with her husband, producer Kristiansen. (In Norwegian; English subtitles.)

p, Terje Kristiansen; d, Vibeke Lokkeberg; w, Kristiansen, Lokkeberg; ph, Paul Rene Roestad; ed, Edith Toreg.

Drama   (PR:A-C MPAA:NR)

KARATE KID, THE*½**   (1984) 126m COL c

Ralph Macchio (Daniel), Noriyuki "Pat" Morita (Miyagi), Elisabeth Shue (Ali), Martin Kove (Kreese), Randee Heller (Lucille), William Zabka (Johnny), Ron Thomas (Bobby), Rob Garrison (Tommy), Chad McQueen (Dutch), Tony O'Dell (Jimmy), Israel Juarbe (Freddy), William H. Bassett (Mr. Mills), Larry B. Scott (Jerry), Juli Fields (Susan), Dana Andersen (Barbara), Frank Burt Avalon (Chucky), Jeff Fishman (Billy), Ken Daly (Chris), Tom Fridley (Alan), Pat E. Johnson (Referee), Bruce Malmuth (Ring Announcer), Darryl Vidal (Karate Semi-Finalist), Frances Bay (Lady with Dog), Christopher Kriesa (Official), Bernard Kuby (Mr. Harris), Joan Lemmo (Restaurant Manager), Helen J. Siff (Cashier), Molly Basler (Cheerleading Coach), Larry Drake, David Abbott (Yahoos), Brian Davis (Boy in Bathroom), David De Lange (Waiter), Erik Felix (Karate Student), Peter Jason (Soccer Coach), Todd Lookinland (Chicken Boy), Clarence McGee, Jr., Sam Scarber (Referees), William Norren (Doctor), Scott Strader (Eddie).

This is ROCKY by another name. It's incredibly manipulative and totally irresistible, treading the same path as Sylvester Stallone's star-making movie, and with good reason, as it was directed by John Avildsen, the same man who helmed ROCKY. Macchio and his mother, Heller, move from Newark, New Jersey, to Southern California, where the whole world seems to be blond and brutal. Macchio is immediately bullied by his schoolmates, lead by Zabka. Shue is Zabka's ex-girl friend and when she begins to have a relationship with Macchio, the young lad is in for trouble from Zabka and his motorcycle-riding pals. Macchio must learn to defend himself against the bigger Zabka and when he meets Morita, a janitor, his life changes. Morita (who uses his real name of Noriyuki in the credits, rather than Pat, which is how he was known for many years when he toured the nitery circuit as a comic) is sensational in his offbeat role and was nominated for an Oscar for his work. He takes Macchio under his wing and begins to teach the boy about life and about karate. The scenes between the two are warm and diverting, even when Morita gets drunk and talks about his past, then reveals that he was a Congressional Medal of Honor winner. (In real life, Morita was one of the many West Coast Japanese interned in the concentration camp at Manzanar in central California during WW II). Zabka is also learning karate under the tutelage of ex-veteran Kove, a man who has the charm and personality of an East German border guard. Macchio continues his relationship with Shue as they go out on dates, with Heller acting as chaperone (a foolish addition and not motivated). While Morita is training Macchio in the ways of the Orient, Kove is forcing his charges to go through all sorts of regimens and instructing them how to fight dirty. You just know, right from the start, that it's going to come down to a karate battle between Zabka and Macchio and the only question about the film is how long will it take to get to that "Rocky versus Apollo Creed" scene? With no father in his life, Morita becomes Macchio's dad and he listens to everything the wise old Asian has to say, forgoing the usual kicks and yells to engage in a series of house chores like waxing, sanding, painting, all carefully calculated to get Macchio in the right frame of mind, which, evidently, is just as important for karate as serious training. The karate battle is for the Valley Karate Championship (presumably the San Fernando Valley) and Macchio defeats Zabka, gets the girl, and the audience leaves the theater with a good, warm feeling, the same way they left after Stallone went the distance with his tormentor. Made for a pittance the way the first ROCKY was (less than a million for that Oscar winner), THE KARATE KID reaped a bonanza at the box office, perhaps because it was one of the few teenage movies of the year that didn't feature gratuitous sex gropings among the leads, did not have the usual food fights or car chases, and did have some genuine moments of warmth, humor, and excitement. Morita has one sequence where he karate-chops all of Macchio's bullies and shows that he can handle himself in physical scenes as well as in his comedy and drama. Naturally, the movie gave birth to a sequel and, naturally as well, the sequel wasn't as good as the original. The music by Conti (who also did ROCKY) was similar and noisy. It was augmented by several pop tunes including: "(Bop Bop) On the Beach" (written by Mike Love of "The Beach Boys"), "(It Takes) Two to Tango" (written by Peter Beckett, Dennis Lambert), "No Shelter" and "Please Answer Me" (both written by Richard Fenton, John Mark), "Desire" (written by Andy Gill, Jon King), and three tunes with

music by Conti: "Feel the Night" (lyrics by Baxter Robertson), "You're the Best" (lyrics by Allee Willis), "The Moment of Truth" (lyrics by Beckett, Lambert). The executive producer was Jerry Weintraub who later took over as production boss at UA for a brief time until he decided that he liked being an independent even more than running a studio.

p, Jerry Weintraub; d, John G. Avildsen; w, Robert Mark Kamen; ph, James Crabe (Metrocolor); m, Bill Conti; ed, Bud Smith, Walt Mulconery, Avildsen; prod d, William J. Cassidy; set d, John Anderson; cos, Richard Bruno, Aida Swinson; spec eff, Frank Toro; ch, Pat E. Johnson.

Sports Drama   **Cas.**   (PR:A-C MPAA:PG)

KIDCO½**   (1984) 104m FOX c

Scott Schwartz (Dickie Cessna), Cinnamon Idles (Nene Cessna), Tristine Skyler (Bette Cessna), Elizabeth Gorcey (June Cessna), Charles Hallahan (Richard Cessna), Maggie Blye (Joan Cessna).

An entertaining comedy about a group of youngsters who decide to form their own company. Led by Schwartz, a lad with posters of mega-buck American companies adorning his bedroom walls, the kids battle their parents' financial domination. The film is filled with flag-waving and business talk, but it's all in good fun. The videotape is close-captioned, making it accessible to hearing-impaired children, as well.

p, Frank Yablans, David Niven, Jr.; d, Ronald F. Maxwell; w, Bennett Trainer; ph, Paul Lohmann (DeLuxe Color); m, Michael Small; ed, David McKenna; prod d, Fred Price; set d, Jacqueline Martin; cos, William Ware Theiss.

Children's Film   **Cas.**   (PR:C MPAA:PG)

KILLERS, THE½**   (1984) 60m Patrick Roth Film c

Jack Kehoe (Harry), Raymond Mayo (Bill), Allan Magicovsky (Husband), Susanne Reed (Wife), Anne Ramsey (1st Ragpicker), Susan Tyrrell (Susu, 2nd Ragpicker), Charles Bukowski (The Author).

A strange, independent film shot on 16mm, and based on a story by Charles Bukowksi, a sort of disgusting Boswell of the underbelly of society. Kehoe is a former insurance man who has dropped off the edge of society. One night, in an all-night cafe, he meets Mayo, a small time robber who tells Kehoe about an easy score to be made on a mansion in Beverly Hills. They shake hands on the deal and Kehoe begins his life of crime. They break into the house without difficulty, but the noise they make awakes the people who live there, Magicovsky and Reed. Magicovsky comes to investigate, and is overpowered by Mayo, who taunts him for a while, then murders him. Kehoe, his baser instincts rising, rapes Reed. Later Mayo slits her throat, as well. The two men leave, taking nothing, as Kehoe wonders why he doesn't feel anything. Shot in a minimal, low-key manner, the film is rather effective, thanks to excellent, disturbing performances by Kehoe and Mayo. Bukowski himself makes an appearance at the beginning of the film to give a prolog. Shot in 1981, the film has only been seen in various festivals.

p,d&w, Patrick Roth; (based on "Short Story" by Charles Bukowski); ph, Patrick Prince; m, Doug Lynner, Bill Boydstun; ed, Daniel Gross.

Crime   (PR:O MPAA:NR)

KILLING FIELDS, THE*½**   (1984, Brit.) 141m
                                    Enigma-Goldcrest/WB c

Sam Waterston (Sydney Schanberg), Haing S. Ngor (Dith Pran), John Malkovich (Al Rockoff), Julian Sands (Jon Swain), Craig T. Nelson (Military Attache), Spalding Gray (U.S. Consul), Bill Paterson (Dr. Macentire), Athol Fugard (Dr. Sundesval), Graham Kennedy (Dougal), Katherine Krapum Chey (Ser Moeun, Pran's Wife), Oliver Pierpaoli (Titonel, Pran's Son), Edward Entero Chey (Sarun), Tom Bird (U.S. Military Advisor), Monirak Sisowath (Phat, KR Leader, 2nd Village), Lambool Dtangpaibool (Phat's Son), Ira Wheeler (Ambassador Wade), David Henry (France), Patrick Malahide (Morgan), Nell Cambell (Beth), Joan Harris (TV Interviewer), Joanna Merlin (Schanberg's Sister), Jay Barney (Schanberg's Father), Mark Long (Noaks), Sayo Inaba (Mrs. Noaks), Mow Leng (Sirik Matak), Chinsaure Sar (Arresting Officer), Hout Ming Tran (KR Cadre, 1st Village), Thach Suon (Sahn), Neevy Pal (Rosa).

A deeply moving, though flawed film, THE KILLING FIELD is the somewhat fictionalized story of New York Times reporter Sidney Schanberg (Waterston) and his efforts to find his friend Dith Pran (Ngor) after the Cambodian translator is taken into the brutal hands of the Khmer Rouge. The film opens in the closing days of U.S. involvement in Vietnam. Waterston is covering the situation for his paper, and is completely dependent on Ngor to help him get around the country. With Ngor's help, Waterston files several important stories, including the hushed up U.S. bombing of an innocent village. However Waterston callously puts Ngor's loyalty to the test when the U.S. army evacuates Cambodian citizens for an airlift to the U.S. Waterston has arranged for Ngor's family to leave, but insists he needs Ngor to help him continue covering the unfolding situation. Though the choice is left up to Ngor, Waterston strongly implies that he wants the man to stay despite the great personal risk. Ngor watches his family leave in a helicopter, agreeing to help Waterston with his work.

When Waterston, his photographer Malkovich, and some other reporters are taken hostage by the Khmer Rouge, Ngor pleads for the journalists' lives, explaining to the soldiers that these men are not Americans, but French. This works, but later Waterston is unable to help when Ngor's life is endangered. Holing up in the French embassy, the journalists learn that all Cambodian citizens must be turned out before the embassy is evacuated. Waterston and his colleagues frantically put together a phony passport for Ngor, hoping authorities will believe he is a British citizen. Fighting against time, Malkovich is able to photograph Ngor for the phony passport, but because of the primitive conditions he has been forced to work with, Malkovich's picture of Ngor clouds up by the time authorities check the Cambodian's passport. Ngor must leave the embassy, knowing he will soon be taken in by the Khmer Rouge. Back in New York, Waterston begins an endless search for Ngor. He sends pictures of his friend to all relief camps along the Thailand border, and tries to assure Ngor's wife Moeun that her husband will survive. When Waterston wins the Pulitzer Prize for his Cambodian stories, he accepts it on behalf of Ngor. Malkovich confronts him later that evening, damning Waterston for keeping Ngor in Cambodia when he had the chance to escape. In the meantime, Ngor is being held in one of the Khmer Rouge's reeducation camps. The government has declared it to be "The Year Zero" and is forcing people to give up all notions of loyalty to anything but the Khmer Rouge. Children are taught to sever ties with family, and many of the camp's guards are gun- toting youngsters. In order to survive, Ngor pretends to be a common laborer, and this has saved him from extermination. Prisoners are treated as slaves, given small rations of food, and killed for the slightest indiscretion. Ngor does what it takes to survive, sneaking into a cattle pen to suck blood from camp oxen. He is caught in the act however, and Ngor is severely beaten. Authorities decide to let him live though, and Ngor takes this chance as an opportunity to escape. While returning from the rice fields, Ngor jumps into a stream and silently swims out of the camp. Later, in a harrowing sequence, Ngor walks silently among literally thousands of human bones, the remains of his fellow Cambodians who have been exterminated by the Khmer Rouge. Eventually Ngor makes it to the border, and he is finally reunited with Waterston. THE KILLING FIELDS wisely emphasizes the human factor of the story, concentrating more on Waterston's friendship with Ngor and Ngor's will to survive than on political situations. Ngor, a former Cambodian doctor chosen to play Dith Pran, went through a similar experience as the one he reenacts. His emotions are real, and thus all the more heartrendering. Waterston is less effective, a bland portrait that should have had more intensity. Malkovich makes an impressive film debut as the photographer, an energetic performance that often overshadows Waterston's dispassionate characterization. Joffe's directorial debut is an impressive one. Sequences unfold with precision, as Joffe effectively heightens the already heartfelt emotions within his story. Ngor's farewell to his family is a good example of Joffe's directorial work, as helicopters float eerily in and out of the smoke-filled frame, the soundtrack blaring with the confused cries of refugees and Oldfield's haunting electronic score. Though Joffe's standards remain taut throughout the gripping story, he inexplicably allows the film to fall apart at its conclusion. When Waterston and Ngor are reunited–a sequence charged with already inherent emotions–Joffe chooses to play John Lennon's song "Imagine" at an overbearing level, a trite and patronizing ending to a story that deserves much more. Schanberg, after seeing the unflattering portrait of himself on screen, wrote: "It...depicts me as a real person, warts and all–which was one of my conditions before agreeing to make the film....The story of this film...is more important than one's fantasy wish to appear heroic and perfect." Dith Pran's real life journey out of Cambodia was not exactly like the events presented in the film. After escaping, he served for a time as mayor of his home town in Vietnam, and was able to get word to Schanberg that he was alive. Appearing in a small role as a U.S. official is Spalding Gray, a noted monologist who created a much praised one-man theater piece titled "Swimming to Cambodia," which was based, in part, on his experiences making the film.

p, David Puttnam; d, Roland Joffe; w, Bruce Robinson (based on the magazine article "The Death and Life of Dith Pran," by Sidney Schanberg); ph, Chris Menges; m, Mike Oldfield; ed, Jim Clark; prod d, Roy Walker; art d, Roger Murray Leach, Steve Spence; set d, Tessa Davies; cos, Judy Moorcroft; spec eff, Fred Cramer; stunts, Terry Forrestal; makeup, Tommie Manderson.

Drama   Cas.   (PR:O MPAA:R)

KILLING HEAT**   (1984) 104M Satori c (AKA: THE GRASS IS SINGING)

Karen Black (*Mary Turner*), John Thaw (*Dick Turner*), John Kani (*Moses*), John Moulder-Brown (*Tony Marston*), Patrick Mynhardt (*Charlie*), Bjorn Gedda (*Sgt. Denham*), Ian Nygren (*Doctor*).

Black stars in this occasionally moving drama as a career woman working in South Africa who falls in love with a jungle farmer. The film shows her struggling through her adaptation from city life to surviving in a primitive region. If you can stand Black's overblown acting style then you'll like KILLING HEAT; otherwise, steer clear.

p, Mark Forstater; d&w Michael Raeburn (based on the novel *The Grass Is Singing* by Doris Lessing); ph, Billie August, Fritz Schroder; m, Bjorn Isfalt,

Temba Tana; ed, Thomas Schwalm; prod d, Disley Jones.

Drama   Cas.   (PR:O MPAA:R)

KILLPOINT zero   (1984) 89m Killpoint/Crown c

Leo Fong (*Lt. James Long*), Richard Roundtree (*Agent Bill Bryant*), Cameron Mitchell (*Joe Marks*), Stack Pierce (*Nighthawk*), Hope Holiday (*Anita*), Diana Leigh (*Candy*), Bernie Nelson (*Pawnbroker*), Danene Pyant (*Chauffeurette*), Marlene McCormick (*Cafe Waitress*), James P. Parker (*Dan the Bartender*), James Lew, Steve "Nasty" Anderson, Ray Dalke, Ed Otis (*Nighthawk's Gunmen*), Wardell Campbell (*Sylvester*), Richard L. Johnson (*R. J.*), Lee Wagner (*Lee*), Anthony Rivera (*Sanchez*), Ronnie A. Lopez, Larry Garcia, Anthony Moreno (*Sanchez' Gang*), Michael Farrell (*Capt. Skidmore*), Larry Lunsford (*Agent Crawford*), William Ryle (*Watch Commander*), Ed Michelotti (*Joe De Julio*), Alvin Cunningham (*Snake*), Carl Smith (*Coroner*), Joey Greenwood (*Brad*), Jesse Lee hunter (*Jess*), Laverne Lucille Brown (*Hooker In Bar*), Jacquelyn Sawyer (*Grocery Shopper*), Troy Zuccolotto (*Muscleman*), Ronn Kipp, Mike Smith, Gary Barnes (*Police Officers*), Steve Adams (*Truck Driver*).

A documentary-styled actioner starring Fong as a martial arts expert-police lieutenant who is out to avenge the rape-murder of his wife. With the help of government agent Roundtree, Fong tracks down the killers – a gang of gunrunners led by the sadistic Mitchell. Producer-director-writer-cameraman-editor Frank Harris must have been too busy to realize that KILLPOINT is incredibly boring. The martial arts sequences are so poorly photographed that they are worse than is usual, and there is so much violence that the picture becomes laughable.

p, Frank Harris, Diane Stevenett; d,w&ph, Harris (Metrocolor); m, Herman Jeffreys, Daryl Stevenett; ed, Harris; art d, Larry Westover; set d, Jennifer Chung; spec eff, Ron Adams; ch, Leo Fong; stunts, Rick Avery, Gene Lehfeldt; m/l, "I'm Getting Old," "Truck Drivin' Man," "Cheatin' On Yer Daddy," "Good Men Die Young," Daryl Stevenett; "Livin' On the Inside," Herman Jeffreys.

Crime   Cas.   (PR:O MPAA:R)

KINGS AND DESPERATE MEN** (1984, Brit.) 118m Kineversal/Blue Dolphin c

Patrick McGoohan (*John Kingsley*), Alexis Kanner (*Lucas Miller*), Andrea Marcovicci (*The Girl*), Margaret Trudeau (*Elizabeth Kingsley*), John-Pierre Brown (*Kingsley Child*), Robin Spry (*Harry Gibson*), Frank Moore (*Herrera*), Budd Knapp (*Judge McManus*), Kevin Fenlon, Peter McNeil (*Judge Captors*), David Patrick (*Grant Gillespie*), August Schellenberg (*Aldini*), Neil Vipond (*Henry Sutton*), Kate Nash (*Mrs. MacPherson*), Frederic Smith-Bolton, Jane Hooper.

A slow-moving drama about a political extremist, Kanner, who takes over a radio station by gunpoint. Before long the talk show host is taking telephone callers and staging a phone-in "trial". The premise may sound interesting but it doesn't ever reach any depth. Stuck on the shelves for some time, KINGS AND DESPERATE MEN reunited former "Prisoner" TV stars McGoohan and Kanner. Trudeau, the jet-set ex-wife of one-time Canadian Prime Minister Pierre Trudeau, also makes an appearance.

p&d, Alexis Kanner; w, Kanner, Edmund Ward; ph, Henry Lucas [Kanner], Paul van der Linden; m, Michael Robidoux, Pierre F. Brault; ed, Lucas [Kanner]; prod d&cos, Will McGow.

Drama   (PR:C MPAA:NR)

KIPPERBANG***   (1984, Brit.) 85m Enigma-Goldcrest-Channel 4/MGM-UA Classics c (GB: P'TANG, YANG, KIPPERBANG)

John Albasiny (*Alan "Quack Quack" Duckworth*), Abigail Cruttenden (*Ann*), Maurice Dee (*Geoffrey*), Alison Steadman (*Miss Land*), Garry Cooper (*Tommy*), Robert Urquhart (*Headmaster*), Mark Brailsford (*Abbo*), Chris Karallis (*Shaz*), Frances Ruffelle (*Eunice*), Nicola Prince (*Maureen*), Richenda Carey (*Botany Teacher*), Tim Seeley (*French Master*), Maurice O'Connell (*Gym Teacher*), Peter Dean (*Policeman*), Dave Atkins (*Fish and Chips Shop Owner*), Eric Richard, Arthur Whybrow (*Workmen*), Philip Edkins (*School Boy*), John Arlott.

An enchanting and nostalgic look at adolescent life in 1948 in England starring Albasiny as an oft-ignored schoolby nicknamed "Quack Quack" because of his surname, Duckworth. One day Albasiny decides that he is going to get his first kiss. He sets his sights on Cruttenden, an attractive schoolmate who doesn't even notice him. In fact, most girls in his class fail to notice him, forgetting ever to include him among the "dishiest" boys. His big chance comes when he is picked to star in a school play as the romantic lead. Luckily for him, his costar is Cruttenden. Better yet is the play's finale, which has the characters kissing each other. Intercut with the scenes of the adolescents are the lives of their teachers, mainly English teacher Steadman, who is pregnant by groundskeeper Cooper. With David Puttnam (CHARIOTS OF FIRE) acting as an executive producer, KIPPERBANG, which was produced for British television, came in on a budget of a meager $700,000 and in only 18 days. Although some portions of KIPPERBANG fall flat (the boy's inner voice which narrates in the style of a cricket-match announcer, and some preachy dialog exchanges), much of the picture accurately captures the awkwardness of growing up. The ability to capture this quality no doubt comes from director Apted's experience with British youth. His documentary 28UP was filmed over a period of 21 years, following a group of children from age 7 and through 28 and recording their development. Many of the personalities of the children in 28UP can easily be transferred to the fiction in KIPPERBANG, adding a remarkably truthful element to the film. For the curious, the title refers to a nonsensical grade school saying – "P'tang, Yang, Kipperbang" – which sounds more like an inaudible grunt when the youngsters blurt it out.

p, Chris Griffin; d, Michael Apted; w, Jack Rosenthal; ph, Tony Pierce-Roberts (Kay Color); m, David Earl; ed, John Shirley; art d, Jeff Wood-bridge; cos, Sue Yelland.

Romance/Comedy   **Cas.**   **(PR:A-C   MPAA:PG)**

LA FEMME DE MON POTE   (SEE: MY BEST FRIEND'S GIRL, Fr.)

LA FLUTE A SIX SCHTROUMPFS
                    (SEE: THE SMURFS AND THE MAGIC FLUTE)

LA LINEA DEL CIELO   (SEE: SKYLINE, Span.)

LA PETIT SIRENE***   (1984, Fr.) 104m Hamster-GAU-Stand Art
                                    FR3-Elefilm/World Artists c

Laura Alexis (*Isabelle*), Philippe Leotard (*Georges*), Evelyne Dress (*Nelly*), Marie Dubois (*Benedicte*), Marianne Winquist (*Veronique*), Diane Sorelle (*Claire*).

An enchanting tale of obsession which stars Alexis as a 14-year-old schoolgirl who sets her sights on Leotard, a 40-year-old mechanic, after he whistles at her prettier cousin. Alexis thinks she is the one he whistled at, and begins to follow him around Paris. Patterning her obsession on both Hans Christian Andersen's story "The Little Mermaid" and Francois Truffaut's 1975 film THE STORY OF ADELE H., Alexis retreats into a fantasy world. Eventually, however, Leotard is drawn into her world and the two begin a sexual relationship. Released in France in 1980, LA PETIT SIRENE succeeds chiefly because of the alluring performance of Alexis, an American girl living in France. (In French; English subtitles.)

p,d&w, Roger Andrieux (based on the novel *Les Petites Sirenes* by Yves Dangerfield); ph, Robert Alazraki; m, Alain Maline; ed, Kenout Peltier; art d, Jean-Baptiste Poirot.

Romance   **(PR:C   MPAA:PG)**

LA VIE EST UN ROMAN   (SEE: LIFE IS A BED OF ROSES, Fr.)

L'AMOUR PAR TERRE   (SEE: LOVE ON THE GROUND, Fr.)

L'ARGENT*****   (1984, Fr./Switz.) 90m Marion's Films-FR 3-EOS
                                    Films/Cinecom International c

Christian Patey (*Yvon Targe*), Sylvie van den Elsen (*Old Woman*), Michel Briguet (*The Woman's Father*), Caroline Lang (*Elise Targe*), Vincent Risterucci (*Lucien*), Beatrice Tabourin (*Woman Photographer*), Didier Baussy (*Man Photographer*), Marc Ernest Fourneau (*Norbert*), Brune Lapeyre (*Martial*), Andre Cler (*Norbert's Father*), Claude Cler (*Norbert's Mother*), Jeanne Aptekman (*Yvette*), Francois Barrier, Alain Aptekman, Dominique Mullier, Jacques Behr, Gilles Durieux, Alain Bourguignon, Anne de Kervazdoue, Bernard Lamarche Vadel, Pierre Tessier, Eric Franklin, Jean-Louis Berdot, Yves Martin, Luc Solente, Valerie Mercier, Alexandre Pasche, Jean-Michel Coletti, Stephane Villette.

Bresson's 13th film in 40 years, L'ARGENT (which translates as "Money") is, like so many of his other films, a work of true cinematic genius which stands heads above most other pictures and seems to defy critical judgment. A new Bresson film is an event (comparable to 1977's release of THAT OBSCURE OBJECT OF DESIRE from Luis Bunuel, or 1985's release of RAN from Akira Kurosawa) which celebrates the director's seeming infallibility and longevity and confirms his place in the pantheon of great directors. L'ARGENT is such a film. It begins with a young schoolboy, Fourneau, trying to get money from his parents. His father won't pay attention to him, while his mother cavalierly refuses. An enterprising classmate gives him some counterfeit bills which Fourneau passes on to a worker in a photographic shop. Baussy, the shop owner, is determined to get rid of the phony bills. He passes them off to an unsuspecting deliveryman, Patey, who innocently pays a cafe bill with the forged notes and is promptly arrested. Protecting himself, the counterfeit-passing shop owner bribes his assistant, Risterucci, to keep his mouth shut when the authorities come snooping. The schoolboy's mother pays the shop owner to keep silent about her son's involvement. Patey is brought to trial and acquitted. The scandal, however, causes him to lose his job. Patey becomes desperate and gets involved with a robbery in order to support his wife, Lang, and his child. Patey's job is to drive the getaway car, but the heist is foiled and he is sentenced to three years behind bars. Life grows progressively bleaker for Patey. He receives news that his child has fallen victim to diphtheria and died. Patey, trapped in this viciously tangled web of predetermination, goes

berserk and is sentenced to solitary confinement. A prison warden who has witnessed Patey's outburst makes the prophetic comment: "A man who never killed may be more dangerous than a murderer." As Patey is returned to the prison population he meets Risterucci, who is beginning a sentence for his complicity in a racket involving theft from cash deposit machines. Risterucci was also stealing from the photo shop in order to give donations to the local poor people. In the meantime, Patey has learned that his wife has decided to leave him. Risterucci makes a futile attempt to atone for his part in Patey's dilemma, offering to help him escape, but Patey rejects Risterucci's proffered conscience-salving sop. Patey finally is released–into a world which has nothing for him. He has no wife, no child, and no job. Worst of all, Patey has no money. He stops at a little hotel, kills the owner and his wife, and steals a paltry sum of money. He meets friendly old woman van den Elsen who takes him in. She passes no judgment on him when he confesses to his two murders and allows him to stay under her roof. Patey observes her long-suffered slave labors on her family's behalf; he then takes an axe and proceeds to kill her, her two sisters, her father, her nephew, and her brother-in-law. He pockets whatever money he can find and then turns himself over to the police. Like the character in "The False Note" by Leo Tolstoy, on which this film is loosely based, Patey is led by his fate. Patey exists for one purpose – not to be the deliveryman that he is at the film's start, but to be a killer. Bresson describes his character. (from ANGELS OF THE STREETS to this film) this way: "My heroes seem like shipwrecked men, leaving to discover an unknown island, even as early as the creation of Adam." Patey, an Adam of sorts whose idyllic life is destroyed, finds that his "island" is inhabited by the casually vicious. In the director's vision, petty rudenesses point inexorably to major malfeasances; a want of ingrained politesse signifies a person's liability to commit truly terrible acts. The randomly rude are incipient rapists; mere maledictions are portents of murders. The cardinal sin is *imposition*. There is another leading player in L'ARGENT – one that isn't listed in any cast list, but in the title – money. Throughout the first half-hour of the film (before we are certain that Patey is the leading player, money is the central character. It changes hands from one person to another in extreme close ups and carries us from one scene to the next, one location to the next. The bills are recognizable, while the people passing them are not. We see only their hands, their feet, their pockets, or their wallets (not unlike the director's earlier PICKPOCKET, 1959). Money is the active performer in L'ARGENT, Patey only a poor sod who falls victim to its use and misuse. Bresson won acclaim from the Cannes Film Festival which voted him Best Director (an award he shared with Andrei Tarkovsky for NOSTALGHIA), but he also received boos. The negative response stemmed not from the film's artistic merits, but from a political situation which surrounded the film's production. The French critics – at their silliest and least credible at times like this – were unhappy with Bresson's choice of Caroline Lang in a leading role. She's the daughter of French Minister of Culture Jack Lang, a Socialist. Naturally the right wing felt it necessary to attack Bresson via his association with Lang, even though the right has long supported Bresson's devout Catholicism. (In French; English subtitles.)

p, Jean-Marc Henchoz; d&w, Robert Bresson (based on the story "The False Note" by Leo Tolstoy); ph, Emmanuel Machuel, Pasqualino De Santis; m, Johann Sebastian Bach ("Chromatic Fantasy"); ed, Jean-Francois Naudon; art d, Pierre set d, Pierr Lefait; cos, Monique Dury; makeup, Thi Loan Nguyen.

Crime   **(PR:O   MPAA:NR)**

LASSITER**½   (1984) 100m Golden Harvest/WB c

Tom Selleck (*Lassiter*), Jane Seymour (*Sara*), Lauren Hutton (*Kari*), Bob Hoskins (*Becker*), Joe Regalbuto (*Breeze*), Ed Lauter (*Smoke*), Warren Clarke (*Max Hofer*), Edward Peel (*Allyce*), Paul Antrim (*Askew*), Christopher Malcolm (*Quaid*), Barrie Houghton (*Eddie Lee*), Peter Skellern (*Pianist*), Harry Towb (*Roger Boardman*), Belinda Mayne (*Helen Boardman*), Morgan Sheppard (*Sweeny*), Brian Coburn (*Bruno Gunz*), Jane Wood (*Mary Becker*), Tristram Jellinek (*Phipps*), David Warbeck (*Agent*), Michael Howarth (*Commander*), Nicholas Bond-Owen (*Boy*), Eleanor Fazan (*Choreographer*), George Malpas (*Old Man*), Fanny Carby (*Old Lady*), Desmond Barritt, Terence Mountain (*Cops*), Jurgen Andersen, Richard Ridings, Peter McNamara, Bill Leadbitter (*German Guards*), Elliott Johnston, Scott Johnson (*Becker's Sons*), Clive Curtis, George Cooper (*Boxers*), Dinny Powell (*Referee*), Chryss Healey, Debbie Estell, Christine Cartwright, Carol Beddington, Gayna Martine (*Dancers*).

Popular television actor Selleck's follow-up to his disappointing HIGH ROAD TO CHINA was a wholehearted attempt at evoking the suave and charming rogues played by such actors as David Niven and Cary Grant during the heyday's of Hollywood. Unfortunately, while Selleck tries hard and does reasonably well, the script doesn't provide much in the way of rapport between characters to prove very memorable. Set in London in 1934, Selleck plays an American jewel thief who is forced by the British and American governments to enter into a dangerous mission where he will have to steal $10,000,000 worth of diamonds about to be shipped from the German Embassy to help the mounting Nazi war threat. Rather than go to prison, Selleck agrees to the plan and the bulldog- like British cop Hoskins is going to be watching him every moment. Selleck learns that the diamonds are to be transported by Hutton, a sadistic German agent who derives sexual pleasure from inflicting pain on her partners. Selleck tries to ingratiate himself with Hutton by attending black tie parties and eventually becoming another one of her lovers, but she is too smart for him and he must make several attempts at the diamonds with lots of help from his pal Lauter and his girl friend Seymour. LASSITER successfully evokes the look and flavor of London in the 1930s and the set and costume design are superior. Selleck has a definite screen prescence and Hoskins nearly steals the movie with a delightfully hammy performance. Hutton however, is almost laughable with her thick German accent sounding like a Marlene Dietrich impersonation done by Rich Little. Most of what goes wrong here can be blamed on the script, which provides little in the way of the kind of smart and snappy dialog needed to pull off a film like this. Parents note: there is a graphic sex scene where Hutton kills off an enemy agent while making love to him that is certainly not for children.

p, Albert S. Ruddy; d, Roger Young; w, David Taylor; ph, Gil Taylor (Technicolor); m, Ken Thorne; ed, Benjamin A. Weissman, Richard Hiscott; prod d, Peter Mullins; art d, Alan Tomkins, Brian Ackland-Snow; set d, Jack Stephens; cos, Barbara Lane; ch, Eleanor Fazan; stunts, Marc Boyle.

Drama   **Cas.**   **(PR:O   MPAA:R)**

LAST BATTLE, THE   (SEE: LE DERNIER COMBAT, Fr.)

LAST HORROR FILM, THE zero (1984) 87m Shere Productions/Twin Continental Films c (AKA: THE FANATIC)

Caroline Munro (*Jana Bates*), Joe Spinell (*Vinny Durand*), Judd Hamilton (*Alan Cunningham*), Devin Goldenberg (*Marty Bernstein*), David Winters (*Stanley Kline*), Stanley Susanne Benton (*Susan Archer*), Mary Spinell (*Vinny's Mother*), Glenn Jacobson (*Bret Bates*), J'len Winters (*Girl in Jacuzzi*), Sharon Hughes (*Stripper*), Sean Casey (*Jonathan*), Don Talley (*Cowboy*), June Chadwick (*Reporter*).

Inferior slasher film has cult favorite Munro an actress with a cult following visiting Cannes for the film festival. Also visiting the Riviera is Spinell, a New York taxi driver and her most devoted fan, who feels that she can be a great actress under his direction. When he invades her hotel room while she is taking a shower and makes his offer, she tries to toss him out. He smashes the bottle of champagne he brought with him and holds the jagged edge up to her throat. She manages to escape and runs through the crowded lobby wrapped only in a towel, with Spinell in pursuit. The festival crowd thinks it's a publicity stunt and applauds and Spinell, taken off guard, stops and makes a hesitant bow. His psychotic pursuit of his idol claims more victims (including one unfortunate chased by Spinell and decapitated with a chainsaw) before he himself meets a messy end. Nonsensical conclusion reveals that the whole thing is a film Spinell is showing to his mother (played by his real mother). Shot at the 1981 Cannes Festival, the film includes scenes with stars like Kris Kristofferson, Karen Black, and Marcello Mastroianni making unwitting appearances. Munro, who had been previously harassed by Spinell in the despicable MANIAC (1981) and producer Hamilton (her real-life husband) were unable to come to New York for dubbing sessions, so their voices were replaced by Americans. Sleazy fun for fans of blood and bad acting.

p, Judd Hamilton, David Winters; d, Winters; w, Hamilton, Winters, Tom Clasen; ph, Tom DeNove (Technicolor); m, Jesse Frederick; Jeff Koz; ed, Chris Barnes, Edward Salier; prod d, Jeff Sharpe; art d, Brian Savagar; spec eff, Peter McKenzie.

Horror   **(PR:O   MPAA:R)**

LAST HUNTER, THE*   (1984, Ital.) 95m Flora-Gico Cinematografica/World Northal c (AKA: HUNTER OF THE APOCA-LYPSE)

David Warbeck (*Capt. Harry Morris*), Tisa Farrow (*Jane Foster*), Tony King (*Sgt. George Washington*), Bobby Rhodes (*Carlos*), Margit Evelyn Newton (*Carol*), John Steiner (*Maj. Cash*), Alan Collins (*Bartender*), Massimo Vanni, Dino Conti, Gianfranco Moroni.

Italian rip off of American Vietnam films (the alternate title betrays its two most obvious sources) has Warbeck an officer sent out on a dangerous mission behind enemy lines to destroy the transmitter that is broadcasting propanganda a la Tokyo Rose. Along with him are pretty correspondent Farrow, token minority soldiers King and Rhodes, and a psychotic major (Steiner) reminiscent of Robert Duvall in APOCALYPSE NOW. When they arrive at their target, Warbeck learns that the woman behind the micro-phone is none other than his best friend's girl. Buckets of blood and loads of guts, lots of pyrotechnics and some decent model work are the only attractions here. The Italians can make westerns, the Italians can make gangster movies, the Italians can occasionally make a decent horror movie, but if this film and Dawson's followup, TORNADO (1985) are any indication, they should steer clear of war movies.

p, Gianfranco Couyoumdjian; d, Anthony M. Dawson [Antonio Margheriti]; w, Dardano Sacchetti; ph, Riccardo Pallottini (Technicolor); m, Franco Micalizzi; ed, Alberto Moriani; prod d&cos, Bartolomeo Scavia; makeup, Massimo Giustini.

War   **(PR:O   MPAA:NR)**

LAST NIGHT AT THE ALAMO*   (1984) 80m Alamo/Cinecom bw/c

Sonny Carl Davis (*Cowboy*), Louis Perryman (*Claude*), Steven Matilla (*Ichabod*), Tina-Bess Hubbard (*Mary*), Amanda LaMar (*Lisa*), Peggy Pinnell (*Ginger*), Doris Hargrave (*Janice*), J. Michael Hammond (*Steve*), Henry Wideman (*Willie*), George Pheneger (*Skipper*), Ernest Huerta, Jr (*Hector*), David Schied (*Poke*), John Heaner (*Wayne*), Sarah Louise Hudgins (*Darla*), Kim Henkel (*Lionel*), Jeanette Wiggins (*Lois*), Judie Stephens (*Mavis*), Hi Bice (*Slim*), Oscar James (*Dub*), Henry Kana (*Ray*), Pam Feight (*Connie*), Eagle Pennell (*Bo*), Eric A. Edwards (*Charlie*), Arnold Cavasos (*Armando*).

Interesting feature set in a Houston bar about to be torn down to make room for a high-rise office building. The regulars gather for one last blowout, fight among themselves, swear a lot, talk about their ambitions and failures, and one of them, Davis, tries to call his old college roommate, now a state representative, to try to save the old watering hole. The incessant cursing and whining of the patrons gets on the nerves after a while and some of the writing is clumsy, but the film is still effective, giving a look at Texas good-ol'-boys caught in the transition as their familiar life is lost to them forever.

p, Kim Henkel, Eagle Pennell; d, Pennell; w, Henkel; ph, Brian Huberman, Eric A. Edwards; m, Chuck Pennell, Wayne Bell; ed, Eagle Pennell art d, Fletcher Mackey; m/l, "Apocalypso," "Tear It Down," "Tall Dark Stranger," "Long Road Out of Here," John Sargent, "Little Bit Crazy," "Temporary Feeling," Paul Cox.

Drama   **Cas.**   **(PR:O   MPAA:NR)**

LAST STARFIGHTER, THE*½**   (1984) 101m Lorimar/UNIV c

Lance Guest (*Alex Rogan*), Dan O'Herlihy (*Grig*), Catherine Mary Stewart (*Maggie Gordon*), Barbara Bosson (*Jane Rogan*), Norman Snow (*Xur*), Robert Preston (*Centauri*), Kay E. Kuter (*Enduran*), Chris Hebert (*Louis Rogan*), Dan Mason (*Lord Kril*), John O'Leary (*Rylan Bursar*), George McDaniel (*Kodan Officer*), Charlene Nelson (*Rylan Technician*), John Maio (*Friendly Alien*), Robert Starr (*Underling*), Al Berry (*Rylan Spy*), Maggie Cooper, Bruce Abbott (*Rylan Sergeants*), Scott Dunlop (*Tentacled Alien*), Vernon Washington (*Otis*), Peter Nelson (*Jack Blake*), Peggy Pope (*Elvira*), Meg Wyllie (*Granny Gordon*), Ellen Blake (*Clara Potter*), Britt Leach (*Mr. Potter*), Bunny Summers (*Mrs. Boone*), Owen Bush (*Mr. Boone*), Marc Alaimo (*Hitchhiker*), Cameron Dye (*Andy*), Geoffrey Blake (*Gary*), Kimberly Ross (*Cheerleader*), Wil Wheaton (*Louis' Friend*), Bob Kenaston (*Uncle Bob*), Ed Berke (*Cop No. 1*).

Very good science fiction film has Guest living in a trailer park in California with mother Bosson and little brother Hebert, and longing to leave, taking girl friend Stewart with him. Responsibilities at the trailer park and the refusal of his student loan seem to doom him to remain forever in a mobile home that never goes anywhere. His only solace is a video game, "Starfighter," on which he breaks the record one evening. Later that night Preston drives up in an odd-looking car. He tells Guest that he is the inventor of the game and asks him to climb into the car to talk about a business proposition. Within minutes the bewildered youth finds himself hurtling through space at the speed of light and landing on a strange planet, where he's given a uniform and put in a room with a lot of strange-looking aliens for a briefing on the evil Kodan forces under the traitor Xur who are attacking the Star League. It dawns on Guest that he's being asked to be a real starfighter, and his immediate reaction is to demand to be taken home. It comes out that Preston shouldn't have been recruiting on a planet not yet "mature" enough to be asked to join the Star League, so Preston flies him home but leaves him with a pager that can call him back if Guest changes his mind, and a robot duplicate of himself, who is having trouble relating to Stewart. Meanwhile, back in space, sabotage destroys the defenses of the starfighter base and all the starfighters are killed, but the Kodan learn that one starfighter (Guest) escaped and they send an alien hit beast to Earth to kill him. Between the attempt on his life and the guilt his robot double is laying on him for deserting the universe in its time of need, Guest returns to the fighting and is teamed with the last surviving navigator, O'Herlihy, who Guest describes at one point as "a gung-ho iguana." They hide their ship in the caves of an asteroid while the invasion fleet passes overhead, then zip out and the destroy the communication system of the enemy mother ship, rendering the Kodan fighters directionless. Guest then proceeds to blow them out of the sky with video game skill. Hailed as a hero and the savior of the universe, he is asked to help rebuild the starfighter corps, an offer he accepts, setting up the sequel. Then he flies back to Earth and lands at the trailer park, greatly amazing and impressing his mother and his neighbors. He asks Stewart to leave with him, but she can't because she has to take care of her grandmother. The old woman tells her to go, though, and they blast off to further adventures. Clever, exciting, and fun, THE LAST STAR-FIGHTER boasts good performances by Guest and Preston and a literate, funny script that understands the story here is not the space war that only Guest can win, but the difficulty of leaving home and family and security for a totally new life when the opportunity presents itself. The special effects, computer-generated rather than STAR WARS-type models, work quite well, giving the film an odd but effective look. Marred only by the clumsy way it sets up the sequel, the film is excellent family fare but was a disappointment at the box office. However, it became a very successful videocassette, topping those charts for some time.

p, Gary Adelson, Edward O. DeNault; d, Nick Castle; w, Jonathan Betuel; ph, King Baggot (Panavison, Technicolor); m, Craig Safan; ed, C. Timothy O'Meara; " prod d, Ron Cobb; art d, James D. Bissell; set d, Linda Speeris; cos, Robert Fletcher; spec eff, Kevin Pike.

Science Fiction   **Cas.**   **(PR:C MPAA:PG)**

LAUGHTER HOUSE** (1984, Brit.) 93m Green Point/Film Four International (AKA: SINGLETON'S PLUCK)

Ian Holm (*Ben Singleton*), Penelope Wilton (*Alice Singleton*), Stephanie Tague (*Emma Singleton*), Bill Owen (*Amos Lintott*), Richard Hope (*Hubert*), Aran Bell (*Tristram*), Rosemary Martin (*Sylvia*), Stephen Moore (*Howard*), Patrick Drury (*David Wolmer*), C. J. Allen, Aran Bell, Norman Fisher, Clare Laine, Denise Summers, Kenneth MacDonald, Barbara Burgess, Ben Wright, Tim Seely, Johnny Golde, Stephen Phillips, Gillian Barge.

When a strike by his workers cripples Holm's goose farm, he sets out on a hundred-mile goose drive to the slaughterhouse in London. The television news people get hold of the story and turn Holm into a folk hero. More quietly amusing than funny; Holm is quite good while everyone else seems flat.

p, Ann Scott; d, Richard Eyre; w, Brian Glover; ph, Clive Tickner; m, Dominic Meldowney; ed, David Martin; art d, Jamie Leonard.

Comedy   **Cas.**   **(PR:C MPAA:NR)**

LE BAL**½ (1984, Fr./Ital./Algeria) 112m Cineproduction-Film A2-Massfilm-O.N. C.I.C./Almi Classics c

Etienne Guichard, Regis Bouquet, Francesco de Rosa, Arnault Lecarpentier, Liliane Delval, Martine Chauvin, Danielle Rochard, Nani Noel, Azis Arbia, Marc Berman, Genevieve Rey-Penchenat, Michel Van Speybroeck, Rossana Di Lorenzo, Michel Toty, Raymonde Heudeline, Anita Picchiarini, Olivier Loiseau, Monica Scattini, Christophe Allwright, Francois Pick, Chantal Capron, Jean-Francois Perrier, Jean-Claude Penchenat.

One of the most unique European films to play American screens in quite some time, LE BAL is set entirely in a French ballroom, spans the last 50 years, and contains not a word of dialog. The result is a fabulously photographed tableaux history of France through the music and dance of the day – in 1936 during the Popular Front society, the German Occupation of the early 1940s, the Liberation, Saint-Germain-des-Pres, the carefree 1950s, the rebellious atmosphere in May 1968, and the present day. The actors play an assortment of unrealistic characters throughout the decades, with their movements choreographed and exaggerated in a most ridiculous way. The most memorable of these is Perrier with his greased back hair and flagrant swishiness. Others include Bouquet, a hefty tough guy reminiscent of both Jackie Gleason and Charles Durning; the elegant Delval and her scientist-like partner Guichard; the mousey Scattini; the fiery Chauvin; and de Rosa as the ever-present barkeep who's seen it all. Based on a play which was a smash success in France, LE BAL cannot reproduce the same experience on the screen as on the stage. The stage is more physically representative of a ballroom and allows the audience to watch any dancers they choose. The film, however, is selective and can highlight a particular character that it finds interesting–an impossibility on the stage. LE BAL is sometimes boring (but never for long), sometimes frustrating (why can't these characters just say a few words?), and sometimes outrageously funny (as in the scene when the swinging Acapulco Boys play "Brazil"). Not surprisingly, LE BAL includes a plethora of musical numbers from Edith Piaf ("La Vie en Rose" by Piaf and Louiguy) to The Glenn Miller Orchestra ("In The Mood" by Joe Garland, Andy Razaf) to The Beatles ("Michelle"). Other arrangements include "Top Hat White Tie and Tails," "Let's Face The Music And Dance" (Irving Berlin), "Harlem Nocturne" (Earle Hagen), Count Basie's "Shuffle Blues," Cliff Richard's rendition of the rock-and-roll classic "Tutti Frutti" (Richard Penniman, D. La Bostrie, Joe Lubin), The Platters' "Only You" (Buck Ram, Ande Rand) Maurice Chevalier's "Fleur de Paris," and Django Reinhardt's version of "La Marseillaise."

p, Giorgio Silvagni; d, Ettore Scola; w, Scola, Ruggero Maccari, Jean-Claude Penchenat, Furio Scarpelli (based on the stage production of the Theatre du Campagnol from an original idea by Penchenat); ph, Ricardo Aronovich (Fujicolor); m, Vladimir Cosma; ed, Raimondo Crociani; md, Cosma; prod d, Luciano Ricceri; cos, Ezio Altieri, Francoise Tournafond; ch, D'Dee, Jacques Bense; makeup, Otelli Sisi.

Musical   **Cas.**   **(PR:A MPAA:NR)**

LE BON PLAISIR**½ (1984, Fr.) 108m MK2-S.F.P.C.-Films A2/MK2 c

Catherine Deneuve (*Claire*), Jean-Louis Trintignant (*The President*), Michel Serrault (*Minister of the Interior*), Michel Auclair (*Herbert*), Hippolyte Girardot (*Pierre*), Claude Winter (*The First Lady*), Matthew Pillsbury (*Mike*), Alexandra Stewart (*Julie*).

A French political comedy written by a woman who ought to know, as she used to be a minister in the government after first having been a screenwriter (ANTOINE AND ANTOINETTE, 1947). Girardot is a young purse-snatcher who steals the purse of Deneuve. It might just be an ordinary street crime except that Deneuve has a letter in her purse that was written to her, many years before, by the man who is now the president of the

Republic and married to Winter. Deneuve and the president, Trintignant, had been lovers. When she became pregnant, she left for the U.S. and had a son, a fact that Trintignant doesn't discover until now, when the boy is 10 years old. Trintignant is in a bad marriage with Winter and she admits that she wouldn't stay with him if he ever lost his post as the country's leader. Deneuve comes to Trintignant to tell him what's happened and introduces him to their son. The effect is both frightening and happy for the president who takes the boy and Deneuve to his Versailles palace by copter, and tries to keep them hidden until the purloined letter can be located. Meanwhile, Girardot has a relationship with Auclair, a gay journalist who specializes in Palais-watching and would love to get the "beat" (which is what they call it, not "scoop") on the other news hacks. Some funny and touching moments occur when Trintignant admits that he doesn't even know where the kitchen is in his own house. Another nice scene takes place when the boy loses his pet cat and the entire security force at the estate is forced to rake the grounds for the pussy. In the end, the letter is found and Trintignant is allowed to continue as president without having been compromised. The major woe of this film is that it just isn't funny. Manners and morals take the place of real laughs and everyone postures and struts and it may just be that French viewers might have enjoyed it more as they might have found the similarities between the actors' roles and real-life politicians amusing. Without knowing who it was who was being satirized, the comedy was not evident. Politicians are not too funny (deliberately, that is!) and if Trintignant, minister Serrault, and the others are any example of the Gallic sense of humor, that country is in for dour times.

p, Marin Karmitz; d, Francis Girod; w, Girod, Francoise Giroud (based on a novel by Francoise Giroud); ph, Jean Penzer (Eastmancolor); m, Georges Delerue; ed, Genevieve Winding; art d, Francois de Lamothe.

Romantic Comedy   **(PR:A-C MPAA:NR)**

LE CRABE TAMBOUR*** (1984, Fr.) 120m Bela-AMLF-Lira/Interama c

Jean Rochefort (*Captain*), Claude Rich (*Doctor*), Jacques Dufilho (*Chief Engineer*), Jacques Perrin (*Willsdorff, "Le Crabe Tambour"*), Odile Versois (*Bar Hostess*), Aurore Clement (*Francine*), Morgan-Jones (*Lieutenant*), Hubert Laurent (*Fishing Fleet Officer*), Joseph Momo (*Bongo-Ba*), Pierre Rousseau (*Babourg*), Fred Personne (*Bar Owner/Gendarme*), Francois Landoit (*Bochau*), Bernard Lajarrige (*Rector*).

An offbeat militaristic film which won three French Cesars in 1977 but didn't get a U.S. release until 1984. Directed by Schoendoerffer, whose THE ANDERSON PLATOON won an Oscar for feature-length documentary in 1967, LE CRABE TAMBOUR stars Perrin as the title character, a commander who is only seen in flashback. Fighting in the French-Indochina War and in Algeria, Perrin earned his nickname, "The Crab Drum," by his habit of beating his stomach after eating crabs. Years afterward, army captain Rochefort, doctor Rich, and engineer Dufilho are traveling on a Newfoundland-bound ship exchanging stories about "le Crabe Tambour" and their involvement with him. Rich is still displeased with himself for not standing by Perrin in Indochina, and returning to France instead to marry. Rochefort is also agonized by his failure to follow Perrin into Algeria in 1962. Rochefort, who reveals that he has terminal lung cancer, is determined to find Perrin, who reportedly runs a cod-fishing boat with other war veterans. Essentially a character study, LE CRABE TAMBOUR succeeds in creating honest characters who ring true in their reminiscences and their devotion to former war mates. (In French; English subtitles.)

p, Georges de Beauregard; d, Pierre Schoendoerffer; w, Schoendoerffer, Jean-Francois Chauvel (based on the novel by Schoendoerffer); ph, Raoul Coutard; m, Philippe Sarde; ed, Nguyen Long.

Drama   **(PR:O MPAA:NR)**

LE DERNIER COMBAT*** (1984, Fr.) 92m Les Films du Loup/Triumph by (AKA: THE LAST BATTLE)

Pierre Jolivet (*The Man*), Jean Bouise (*The Doctor*), Fritz Wepper (*The Captain*), Jean Reno (*The Brute*), Maurice Lamy (*The Dwarf*), Petra Muller (*The Woman in the Cell*), Pierre Carrive, Bernard Havet, Jean-Michel Castanie, Michel Doset, Marcel Berthomier, Garry Jode (*Captain's Men*), Christiane Kruger (*Captain's Concubine*).

The setting is the post-apocalyptic future where few humans remain and none of those can speak. One of these is Jolivet, who lives in a half-buried skyscraper and spends his spare time building an airplane. Nearby is a compound ruled over by Wepper, whose subjects are in his thrall because he has a slave dwarf kept in the trunk of an old car who scurries down a hole at the end of a rope to fill canteens from one of the last sources of water. One night Jolivet sneaks into Wepper's compound to steal a battery and when Wepper awakes, Jolivet spears him and cuts off one of his fingers as a trophy. Chased by Wepper's lackeys he narrowly escapes by flying his airplane to safety. After flying over a huge desert, he crashes in the ruins of Paris and eats fish that inexplicably fall from the sky. He observes a huge man (Reno) trying to get into a hospital in which doctor Bouise has barricaded himself. Reno then attacks Jolivet and severely wounds him. Bouise takes Jolivet into the hospital and in time the men come to a level of trust and communication. Bouise tells him that the reason Reno wants in, is because of a woman he has locked up. One day falling rubble kills Bouise, and Jolivet, looking for the woman's room, encounters Reno and they fight, Jolivet walking away triumphant only to find that Reno has already killed the woman. Jolivet returns to his original skyscraper home, deposes Wepper, and becomes the new boss of all that remains of civilization. An excellent debut effort by director Besson, the film is a witty, exciting, and frightening all at once. Its creation of a blasted, blighted landscape of half-recognizable, half-buried buildings is an amazing feat, which helped win it prizes at science fiction festivals throughout Europe and to become successful in its U.S. release. A definite candidate for cult status. (In French; English subtitles.)

p, Luc Besson, Pierre Jolivet; d, Besson; w, Besson, Jolivet; ph, Carlo Varini (Panavision); m, Eric Serra; ed, Sophie Schmit; art d, Christian Grosrichard; Thierry Flamand, Patrick Leberre; cos, Martine Rapin, Marie Beau.

Science Fiction   **Cas.**   **(PR:O   MPAA:R)**

LES COMPERES*½   (1984, Fr.) 92m Fideline-Efve-D.D./European
                                                                     International c

Pierre Richard (*Francois Pignon*), Gerard Depardieu (*Jean Lucas*), Anne Duperey (*Christine Martin*), Michel Aumont (*Paul Martin*), Stephane Bierry (*Tristan Martin*), Jean-Jacques Scheffer (*Ralph*), Philippe Khorsand (*Milan*), Roland Blanche (*Jeannot*), Jacques Frantz (*Verdier*), Maurice Barrier (*Raffart*), Charlotte Maury (*Mme. Raffart*), Gisella Pascal (*Louise*), Patrick Blondel (*Stephane*), Florence Moreau (*Michele Raffart*), Bruno Allain, Francois Bernheim, Philippe Brigaud, Pulchier Castan, Robert Dalban, Luc-Antoine Duquiero, Natacha Guinaudeau, Sonia Laroze, Patrick Laurent, Jean-Claude Martin, Guy Matchoro, Charlotte Maury, Jacques Maury, Patrick Melennec, Jacqueline Noelle, Christian Bianchi, Gerard Camp, Patrick Le Barz, Philippe Ribes, Claude Rossignol.

Bierry is a 16-year-old runaway who leaves his middle-class Paris parents and hitchhikes to Nice with Moreau, a tough young girl who hangs out with a degenerate gang of bikers. His parents, Duperey and Aumont, inform the authorites but receive only the feeble assurance that their son will turn up sooner or later, "like a stolen car." Duperey decides to question Moreau's father, Barrier, at the hotel he owns in Nice, but receives nothing but insults from the man, who prefers not to get involved. They return to Paris, whereupon Duperey hits on an idea. She calls up newspaperman Depardieu, an old flame of 17 years ago, and convinces him that he is the actual father of her son, hoping that he will offer to find Bierry. When he refuses, citing his job as a reporter as more important, she pulls the same scheme on another lover from her past. Richard, a suicidal manic depressive, is thrilled by the request and agrees to help. In the meantime, Depardieu has reconsidered. Both men travel separately to Barrier's hotel, each unaware of the other's existence. Barrier retains his close-lipped attitude to the situation, but a beating from Depardieu starts him talking. Depardieu is given a clue to Bierry's whereabouts and soon meets Richard, who is trying to find out the same information. They discover that they have a mutual interest – finding their missing sons – but it takes them a while to realize that they are both looking for the *same* son. Naturally, the question of the boy's real parentage is raised, with both men claiming to be the father. In addition to searching for Bierry, Depardieu is also spending time in Nice gathering evidence for a news story about a corrupt politico named Rossi who is protecting a killer. Shadowing Depardieu are a pair of Rossi's thugs who are unaware that he is actually spending all his time looking for Bierry. As they become more involved in the search, Depardieu and Richard become friends who share their new-found feelings of fatherhood. They each project their own ideas of what Bierry is like – Depardieu is convinced he is tough and aggressive, while Richard believes he is sensitive and poetic – based on their own perceptions of themselves. They finally find Bierry, passed out drunk, at a club where the bikers hang out. Moreau informs the two "fathers" that she no longer cares about Bierry and that she and her friends would prefer it if he were gone. Depardieu and Richard attempt to take Bierry back to Paris, but he adamantly refuses and returns to Moreau. Before they can continue their pursuit, Depardieu receives a telephone call from one of his informants, Blanche, who arranges a meeting. Depardieu is actually being set up by Rossi's thugs and a chase ensues. Meanwhile, Richard makes contact with Blanche, unaware of Depardieu's situation. Richard extends an offer of friendship to Blanche, whose visible fear of Rossi's thugs is mistaken to be a case of manic depression by Richard. Depardieu reaches safety and he and Richard make another attempt to get to Bierry. After a brutal fistfight with Moreau's new boy friend, Bierry breaks his arm and is taken to the hospital by his two "fathers." While the threesome rest in a hotel room, Richard gets a phone call from a desperate Blanche. Richard assumes that her depression is at its peak, but in reality she has been shot by Rossi's thugs and is hiding out. When Richard arrives, a dying Blanche hands him an incriminating photo of Rossi. Acting on Depardieu's advice to not get involved, Richard throws the photo in an alley garbage can, not realizing its importance. When Depardieu learns that Blanche has been killed he puts the pieces together and, with Richard and Bierry, begins rummaging through garbage cans to find the photo. Tensions stretch to the breaking point when all three characters threaten to go their separate ways. Bierry finally lets down his guard and accepts his two new "fathers." Bierry finds the photo, gaining the respect of Depardieu. The threesome retreat to the country until the heat dies down, but Rossi's thugs try to kidnap the boy. Gunfire is exchanged and the thugs are killed. Having come to terms with his real father, Aumont, Bierry plans to return home.

Realizing what he means to Depardieu and Richard, however, he tells them both, secretly, that each is his real father. Both men are thrilled at the reality of having a son, and the three leave together arm-in-arm. A delightful film, LES COMPERES combines a level dose of comedy, drama, and crime with three superbly sketched characters. One quickly becomes fascinated at the ways in which Depardieu and Richard react to the possibility of fatherhood, and the way they interact with each other. LES COMPERES is a film which depends on actor chemistry and thankfully there is not a moment where it fails. Depardieu and Richard are both superb, evoking memories of Laurel and Hardy – the hulkish Depardieu playing the Hardy role to Richard's wimpering Laurel – in their affectionate dislike for each other. The result is a thoroughly enjoyable film which celebrates fatherhood in an entertaining, funny, and touching way.

d&w, Francis Veber (based on his story); ph, Claude Agostini; m, Vladimir Cosma; ed, Marie Sophie Dubus; prod d, Gerard Daoudal; cos, Corinne Jorry; makeup, Thi Loan N'Guyen.

Comedy/Drama   **Cas.**   **(PR:A   MPAA:PG)**

LES NUITS DE LA PLEINE LUNE
                                                              (SEE: FULL MOON IN PARIS, Fr.)

LES RIPOUX   (SEE: MY NEW PARTNER, Fr.)

LES TROIS COURONNES DU MATELOT
                                                     (SEE: THREE CROWNS OF THE SAILOR, Fr.)

L'ETE MEURTRIER   (SEE: ONE DEADLY SUMMER, Fr.)

LIES*   (1984, Brit.) 102m New Empire-Westcom/Alpha c

Ann Dusenberry, Gail Strickland, Bruce Davison, Clu Gulager, Terence Knox, Bert Remsen, Stacy Keach, Sr, Douglas Leonard, Patience Cleveland, Julie Philips, Ann Gibbs, Dick Miller, Walter Wood, Jerry Vaughn, Guy Remsen, Tony Miller, Jean Howell, B. J. Davis, Eddie Braun, Jane Lillig, Miriam Byrd Douglas Manes, Omar Paxson.

Dusenberry is an actress hired by some mysterious men to impersonate a crazy heiress. Next thing she knows she's locked in a rubber room unable to convince anybody of two she is. Starts out promisingly enough, but it quickly gets predictable and dull.

p, Ken Wheat, Jim Wheat, Shelley Hermann; d&w, K. Wheat, J. Wheat; ph, Robert Ebinger (DeLuxe Color); m, Marc Donahue; ed, Michael Ornstein, Dennis Hill; prod d, Christopher Henry; art d, Deborah Moreland.

Drama   **(PR:C   MPAA:R)**

LIFE IS A BED OF ROSES*   (1984, Fr.) 111m
                     Soprofilm-A2-Fideline-Ariane-Filmedis/SpectraFilm c (LA VIE EST UN
                                                                                                          ROMAN)

Vittorio Gassman (*Walter*), Ruggero Raimondi (*Count Michel Forbek*), Geraldine Chaplin (*Nora*), Fanny Ardant (*Livia*), Pierre Arditi (*Robert*), Sabine Azema (*Elizabeth*), Robert Manuel (*Georges*), Martine Kelly (*Claudine*), Samson Fainsilber (*Zoltan*), Nathalie Holberg (*Veronique*), Raoul Vandamme (*Andre*), Andre Dussolier, Fabienne Guyon, Guillaume Boisseau, Sabine Thomas, Rodolphe Schacher, Jean-Claude Corbel, Jean-Michel Dupuis, Flavie Ducorps, Cathy Berberian.

A unique and fun film from intellectual French director Resnais which combines a three-part narrative structure with fantasy, comedy, and musical elements. Raimondi is a wealthy turn-of-the-century eccentric who designs a "temple of happiness" in which people who revert back to a state of infancy. To create a Utopian aura, Raimondi's guests are exposed to only positive sensations – strains of harmonious music fill the air and blindfolds keep out unpleasant sights – while lying blissfully in oversized cribs. Raimondi's plan goes awry when Ardant, who never drank the assigned potion, discovers that one of her friends accidentally died due to negligence. The arrival of WW I, however, puts an end to the temple of happiness and to Raimondi's dreams. Intercut with this episode is a present-day symposium on the methods of Raimondi and the possibility of achieving Utopia, attended by teachers, philosophers, anthropologists, and city planners. The gist of the symposium is that the imagination must be nurtured and developed in order for lives to improve. This theory quickly leads to a difference of opinion among those in attendance and results in a flurry of heated arguments. The third tale, which is intercut with the others and related through the imaginations of a group of children in a forest, is a medieval one in which a warrior must battle a diabolical king. As usual with Resnais, there is a certain portion of the film which the audience can comprehend and another (usually greater) portion which seems completely out of reach. Instead of simply filming a story, Resnais films a puzzle. It is the choice of the viewer whether or not to unravel Resnais' tightly woven structure. Unless one possesses a genius level I.Q. it is probably best (for sanity's sake) to just sit back and be bewildered by LIFE IS A BED OF ROSES. (In French; English subtitles.)

p, Philippe Dussart; d, Alain Resnais; w, Jean Gruault; ph, Bruno Nuytten (Eastmancolor, Fujicolor); m, M . Philippe-Gerard; ed, Albert Jurgenson,

Jean-Pierre Besnard; art d, Jacques Saulnier, Enki Bilal; cos, Catherine Leterrier.

Fantasy   (PR:C MPAA:PG)

LISTEN TO THE CITY*½   (1984, Can.) 87m Sphinx/International SpectraFilm c

P.J. Soles (*Sophia*), Michael Glassbourg (*Goodman*), Sandy Horne (*Arete*), Jim Carroll (*Hupar*), Barry Callaghan (*Arete's Father*), Sky Gilbert (*Shadow*), Mary Hawkins (*White*), Real Andrews (*Green*), Gary Augustynek (*Black*), Peter Wintonick (*Peter*), Bill Lord (*Preston Sturrock*), Gigi Guthrie (*Christie Hines*), Pete Griffin (*Mayor*), Geets Romo (*Data Base*).

Soles is a television journalist investigating a large corporation that is threatening a shutdown. Pretentiously written, with loads of digressions and heavy symbolism, and a scene with Martin Sheen that was cut out of the final print. Director Mann is a talented documentary filmmaker, and it appears that be should stick with that.

p&d, Ron Mann; w, Mann, Bill Schroeder (based on a story by Schroeder); ph, Rene Ohashi (Eastmancolor); m, Gordon Deppe; ed, Elaine Foreman; art d, Barbara Dunphy.

Drama   (PR:O MPAA:NR)

LITTLE DRUMMER GIRL, THE*½   (1984) 130m Pan Arts/WB c

Diane Keaton (*Charlie*), Yorgo Voyagis (*Joseph*), Klaus Kinski (*Kurtz*), Sami Frey (*Khalil*), David Suchet (*Mesterbein*), Eli Danker (*Litvak*), Ben Levine (*Dimitri*), Jonathan Sagalle (*Teddy*), Shlomit Hagoel (*Rose*), Juliano Mer (*Julio*), Danni Roth (*Oded*), Sabi Dorr (*Ben*), Doron Nesher (*David*), Smadar Brener (*Toby*), Shoshi Marciano (*Rachel*), Philipp Moog (*Aaron*), Avi Keiddar (*Raoul*), David Shalit (*Zev*), Dor Zweigenbom (*Udi*), Anna Massey (*Chairlady*), Thorley Walters (*Ned Quilley*), Julian Firth (*Young Man*), Simon Osman (*Ezra*), Albert Moses (*Green Grocer*), Ben Robertson (*Policeman*), David Cornwell (*Commander*), Sebastian Graham Jones (*Director*), Gwen Grainger (*Actor*), Michael Graham Cox (*Donald/Soldier*), Illona Linthwaite (*Lucy*), Irene Marot (*Pam*), Bill Nighy (*Al*), Dee Sadler (*Diana*), Melanie Kilburn (*Heloise*), Rowena Cooper (*Miss Bach*), Peter Capell (*Schwili*), Sasi Saad (*Leon*), Heinz Weiss, Rolf Becker (*Red Cross*), Ori Levy (*Lenny*), Moti Shirin (*Michel*), Robert Pereno (*Rossino*), Kerstin De Ahna (*Helga*), Yasein Shawaf (*Cadre*), Suhiel Haddad (*Danny*), Dana Wheeler- Nicholson (*Katrin*), Rene Kolldehoff (*Inspector*), Shimon Finkel (*Prof. Minkel*), Elisabeth Neumann-Viertel (*Mrs. Minkel*), Yossi Werzansky (*Ben Ami*), Aviva Joel (*Mrs. Ben Ami*), Michael Cristofer (*Tayeh*), Max Schillinger, Dieter Augustin, Noam Almaz, Paul Prosper, Jeff Lester, Mahmoud Abu Elkhair, Ali Badarni, Adib Jashan, Mohammed Ali Badarni, Johnny Arbid, Mohammed Kassas.

Take 500 or so pages of a complex novel, boil it down to 130 minutes, and what do you have? Boiled novel. Le Carre's *Tinker, Tailor, Soldier, Spy* took British TV many hours to tell and it worked. Here, the multi-charactered and well- motivated book has been pruned to a point where they have attempted to cram so much into it that there is no time for motivation and, instead, we are regaled with a flat, confusing and boring espionage tale that is a major disappointment from Hill. It begins, as most of these films begin, with a title card designating the time and place. So far, so good. But the action exists in so many times and places (London, Munich, Beirut, Mykonos, The Acropolis and more and more) that these titles eventually become funny (although that's not what's intended), sort of like the gag titles in START THE REVOLUTION WITHOUT ME. Keaton is a direct copy of Vanessa Redgrave, an actress who makes no bones about her fervent pro-Palestinian stance. The fact that she's an American acting in Shakespearean roles is totally unconvincing. While shooting a wine commercial in sun baked Greece, she falls in love with Voyagis, whom she believes is a PLO terrorist. She then learns that the commercial and Voyagis are fakes and both have been set up by Kinski, a heavyweight in Israeli intelligence. Since her views have been trumpeted all over the world in the press, Kinski and company think that she is the perfect person to be converted into a double agent. She is brainwashed by the Israelis and, after an impassioned plea by Kinski, she changes her views on matters. The flaw here is that the scene with Kinski and Keaton is so badly written that nobody in the audience can swallow what he's saying so it's hard to believe that Keaton does. She goes along with the plan but it is never convincing, nor is her romance with Voyagis. She goes to a Palestinian training camp and informs Frey, their leader, that she wants to enlist her mind and body in the cause, (her real job is to kill Frey). They fall for the ploy which is also unconvincing since she is traipsing around the desert in an outfit that would make ANNIE HALL toss her cookies. The locales change quickly, jumping from place to place as Kinski and his minions search out terrorists and stop them before too much terror can take place. All the while, Keaton is worming her way into Frey's confidence and he is soon in love with her. Just as he realizes he's been set up by Keaton, Israeli agents rush in and slay him, then raze the Palestinian camp and kill all the members of the band. Right here, THE LITTLE DRUMMER GIRL runs into real problems because, while it purports to take no sides in the continuing struggle between the PLO-types and the Israelis, the massacre scenes have been deliberately staged to cause an audience to stand up and cheer when the Arabs are knocked off, which is hardly "taking no sides." Matter of fact, one murder of a Palestinian is even staged to evoke

mirth and murder and is no laughing matter. This kind of slaughter is offensive enough in any film but when a movie supposedly has no ax to grind, it is even more offensive. When the deed has been done, Keaton returns to London and her former career. Voyagis has fallen in love with her and would like to keep that love alive but it's too late. Keaton is now a burnt-out case (see Graham Greene) and can't handle anything. This confusion and its effects on Keaton's psyche could have been an interesting theme for a film but the picture stops there, and none too soon. Her performance is flat, not even close to the fire she's shown before, and there is no humor at all in what might have been a role with a few chuckles, especially since everyone knew who was being satirized. She was miscast, the script was devoid of any wit, and the actors were hamstrung by a muddy narrative. Perhaps Hill was trying to make a "fun" adventure picture, but that doesn't come across, as the subject matter is right out of the newspapers and too serious to be toyed with. Kinski is a standout as the Israeli and it's a far cry from some of his weird roles and shows that he can do other things beyond suck necks and drink blood. Lots of suspense and action but it appears to be happening in the wrong places and to the wrong people. 1984 was definitely not Keaton's year and it was during the same 12 months when she appeared in yet another stinker, MRS. SOFFEL. Perhaps she should take up with Woody Allen again.

p, Robert L. Crawford; d, George Roy Hill; w, Loring Mandel (based on the novel by John Le Carre); ph, Wolfgang Treu (Technicolor); m, Dave Grusin; ed, William Reynolds; prod d, Henry Bumstead; art d, Helmut Gassner, Mikis Karapiperis, Ariel Roshko, Geoffrey Tozer; cos, Ille Sievers, Kristi Zea; m/l, "Always in Love," "Eyes of Fire," Grusin, Sylvester Levay.

Espionage Drama   Cas.   (PR:C-O MPAA:R)

LONELY GUY, THE*½   (1984) 90m UNIV c

Steve Martin (*Larry Hubbard*), Charles Grodin (*Warren Evans*), Judith Ivey (*Iris*), Steve Lawrence (*Jack Fenwick*), Robyn Douglass (*Danielle*), Merv Griffin (*Himself*), Dr. Joyce Brothers (*Herself*), Candi Brough, Randi Brough (*Anita and Chelsea, the Schneider Twins*), Julie Payne (*Rental Agent*), Madison Arnold (*Lonely Cop*), Roger Robinson (*Greeting Card Supervisor*), Joan Sweeney (*Girl in Blood Bank*), Daniel P. Hannafin (*Park Guard*), Nicholas Mele (*Maitre d'*), Leon Jones (*Traffic Cop*), Richard Delmonte (*Raul*), Leslie Wing (*Brenda, Girl in Bar*), Helen Verbit (*Woman in Window*), Kenneth O'Brien (*Holdup Man*), Erica Hiller (*Carol*), Girl in Bank, Karyn Harrison, Hunt Block (*Couple in Bar*), Alan Leach (*Bookstore Man*), Ed Beheler (*Jimmy Carter Look-alike*), Jerry Grayson (*Man Who Gets Shot*), Michael Greer (*Counterman*), George Saurel (*Waiter*), Erik Holland (*Ship's Officer*), Hugh Douglas (*Narrator*), Sarah Abrell (*Bride*), Ken Hixon (*Guest in Church*), Rance Howard (*Minister*), Billy James (*Bridge Jumper*), Jose Martinez (*Gang Member*), Jade Bari (*Cabbie*), Gloria Irizarry (*Woman at Elevated*), Beau Starr (*Cop No. 2*), Dominic Barto (*Holdup Man No. 2*), Charles De Vries (*Ship's Maitre d'*), Santos Morales (*Janitor*), Jolina Collins (*Verna*), Lena Pousette (*Frieda*), Charlie Laiken, Steve Hurwitz, Hardy Rawls, Doug Smith, Tom Kubiak (*Men on Roof*), Joanne Dalsass (*Model at Party*), Robina Suwol (*Girl at Party*), Stephanie Segel (*Agent at Party*).

A mindless comedy which is about as funny as a life-long sentence in solitary confinement, THE LONELY GUY stars perennial buffoon Martin as a New York greeting card writer who comes home from work one day to find his nymphomanic girl friend, Douglass, in bed with a beefcake dancer named Raul (Delmonte). Dejected Martin wanders around town until he meets Grodin on a park bench. Grodin, a whining dufus who talks to ferns and lives in an apartment peopled by life-size carboard cut-outs of Dolly Parton and the like, informs Martin that he is a "lonely guy." Martin soon meets countless others like himself, everyone from policemen to former presidents (namely a pathetic look-alike for Jimmy Carter). Determined to find a girl by becoming a jogger, he meets Ivey, a likeable girl who has been married to a half-dozen lonely guys. She gives him her phone number, but being the moron that he is he smears the writing. A frantic search begins, looking through phone books, dialing at random, shouting from his rooftop, until he finally finds her, but loses her again. A little while later he finds her again. In the meantime, Grodin prepares to jump to his death from the Brooklyn Bridge, as are countless other lonely guys. Ivey later realizes that Martin is too good for her, and inexplicably runs off to marry Steve Lawrence (yes, the Steve Lawrence of wretched television and Las Vegas variety show fame). Distressed, and fearing that he will be a lonely guy forever, he heads for the Brooklyn Bridge. He stands at the edge and prepares to jump when Ivey, unhappy with her marriage and also leaping to her death, falls into his arms from above. They declare their love and go off together, running into Grodin, who introduces him to his new sweetheart, Dr. Joyce Brothers. Even worse than it sounds, THE LONELY GUY is a dumb idea from start to finish, better suited for the pages of the juvenile humor publication *Mad Magazine*, than for the "R-rated" audience it is supposedly aimed at. The romance between Martin and Ivey is occassionally charming (though their bedroom sneezing scene should be obliterated), and Grodin's brand of sad-sack humor is potentially funny, but the film drags on endlessly, overplaying jokes ad infinitum. Director Hiller and his editors couldn't have paced this worse if they tried, resulting in a viewing experience on par with trying to run through chest-high water. The film includes appearances by Lawrence, Dr. Joyce Brothers, Merv Griffin and very briefly, Loni Anderson, leaving one to only wonder why.

p&d, Arthur Hiller; w, Ed Weinberger, Stan Daniels, Neil Simon (based on the novel *The Lonely Guy's Book of Life* by Bruce Jay Friedman); ph, Victor J. Kemper (Technicolor); m, Jerry Goldsmith; ed, William Reynolds, Raja Gosnell; prod d, James D. Vance; set d, Linda DeScenna; cos, Betsy Cox; spec eff, Albert J. Whitlock; m/l, "The Lonely Guy," Glenn Frey, Jack Tempchin, "Love Comes without Warning," Jerry Goldsmith, John Bettis.

Comedy   Cas.   (PR:O   MPAA:R)

LONG RIDE, THE   (SEE: BRADY'S ESCAPE, U.S./Hung.)

LOOSE CONNECTIONS**   (1984, Brit.) 96m
Umbrella-Greenpoint-NFFC-Virgin/FOX c

Lindsay Duncan, Stephen Rea, Carole Harrison, Frances Low, Andrew De La Tour, David Purcell, Keith Allen, Robbie Coltrane, Ruth Bruck, Gary Olsen, Ingrid Domann, Jan Niklas, Henry Reinheimer, Anneliese Dobbertin, Eberhard Melzer, Ken Jones, Nevzat Yuceyildez, Uwe-Karsten Koch, Joachim Regelien, Otto Bleidner, Benjamin Kramer.

A likable class comedy about a righteous city girl who travels from London to Munich with an enthusiastic football fan. A pleasant old-fashioned pairing between Duncan and Rea makes this one watchable, not to mention some picturesque European settings.

p, Simon Perry; d, Richard Eyre; w, Maggie Brooks; ph, Clive Tickner (Eastmancolor); m, Dominic Muldowney; art d, Jamie Leonard.

Comedy   (PR:C   MPAA:PG)

LOPERJENTEN   (SEE: KAMILLA, Norway)

LOS SANTOS INOCENTES   (SEE: HOLY INNOCENTS, THE, Span.)

LOUISIANE**   (1984, Fr./Can.) I.C.C.-Filmax-Antenne 2-Films A2-
R.A.I.II/Parafrance c

Margot Kidder (*Virginia Tregan*), Ian Charleson (*Clarence Dandridge*), Victor Lanoux (*Charles de Vigors*), Andrea Ferreol (*Mignette*), Lloyd Bochner (*Adrien de Danvilliers*), Len Cariou (*Oswald*), Larry Lewis (*Adrien Junior*), Raymond Pellegrin (*Morley*).

At slightly more than three hours, this movie version is just half of what the consortium shot for the television market. It was made by several companies in Canada and France and purported to be a history of Louisiana as seen through the eyes of a doughty heroine, Kidder, who married three men and kept her promise to maintain her family manse, known as "Bagatelle." Now, if the story of a tough woman in the Deep South in the 1800s sounds familiar, you're absolutely right. Forty years go by and we see Kidder age gracefully as she marries, has affairs, gives birth, battles, and winds up with the one man who has stuck with her through thick, thicker and thickest, Charleson, the steward at the plantation who can satisfy her intellectual needs (such as they are) but is a total washout in the bedroom. After having her early sexual flings, Kidder finally realizes how fleeting they are and how much she cares about Charleson. By the time the movie has ended, Kidder has been involved with Parisian socialite Lanoux and cotton man Pellegrin as well as a few others who are hinted at. Pellegrin eventually rapes, then murders Kidder's daughter. The period costumes and settings all have the look of money-saving to them. Again, this is a "Canadian Content" movie that took advantage of the liberal monies handed out by the Canadian government which depended on the number of Canadians involved. the picture could have used any of several U.S. actresses in the lead but Kidder, a Canadian, was chosen and she left much to be desired. The usual cliches in the script and a painful feeling that we've seen it all before, and better. De Broca had previously made a few fine comedies such as THAT MAN FROM RIO, KING OF HEARTS, and DEAR INSPECTOR. Directing this movie did nothing for his reputation but it did do something for his personal life when he married Kidder. Two other fine French directors had previously been selected to captain the miniseries- movie, Etienne Perier and Jacques Demy, but both had second thoughts after seeing the script.

p, Denis Heroux, John Kemeny; d, Philippe de Broca; w, Dominique Fabre, Etienne Perier, Chuck Israel (based on the stories "Louisiane" and "Fausse-Riviere," by Maurice Denuziere); ph, Michel Brault; m, Claude Bolling; ed, Hanri Lanoe; prod d, Jack Macadam; cos, John Hay; makeup, Joan Isaacson, Josiane Deschamps.

Historical Epic   (PR:A-C   MPAA:NR)

LOVE IN GERMANY, A**½   (1984, Fr./Ger.) 110m CCC
Filmkunst-GAU-TF 1 F.P. Stand Art/Triumph c (UN AMOUR EN AL-
LEMAGNE; EINE LIEBE IN DEUTSCHLAND)

Hanna Schygulla (*Paulina Kropp*), Marie-Christine Barrault (*Maria Wyler*), Armin Mueller-Stahl (*Mayer*), Elisabeth Trissenaar (*Elsbeth Schnittgens*), Daniel Olbrychski (*Wiktorczyk*), Piotr Lysak (*Stanislaw Zasada*), Gerard Desarthe (*Karl Wyler*), Bernhard Wicki (*Dr. Borg*), Ralf Wolter (*Schultze*), Otto Sander (*Narrator*), Ben Becker (*Klaus*), Thomas Ringelmann (*Herbert, Paulina's Son*), Friedrich G. Beckhaus (*Zinngruber the Mayor*), Gernot Duda (*Stackmann*), Sigfrit Steiner (*Melchior*), Erika Wackernagel (*Mrs.*

Melchior), Serge Merlin (*Alker*), Rainer Basedow (*Stackmann's Son*), Jutta Kloppel (*Stepdaughter*), Heidi Joschko (*Mrs. Zinngruber*), Jurgen Von Alten (*Old Zinngruber*), Ilse Bahrs (*Old Schnittgens*), Hannes Kaetner (*Klages*), Jurgen Born, Dieter Kursawe (*Policemen*), Dietrich Mattausch (*Counsel*), Gerd Holtenau (*Chief Physician*), Dorothea Moritz (*Martha*), Dieter Kirchlechner (*Mari De Paulina*), Gundula Petrovska (*Postal Employee*), Herbert Weissbach (*Pharmacist*), Evelyn Meyka (*Nurse*), Christoph Beyertt (*Old Patient*), Ellen Esser (*Prison Guard*).

Schygulla is a German shopkeeper in the village of Brombach during WW II. With her husband away at war, she falls in love with Lysak, a Polish laborer, disregarding the law which strictly forbids relationships between Germans and prisoners of war. They go to great lengths to keep their romance a secret but a snoopy neighbor, Barrault, who wants to take over Schygulla's shop, discovers them. To escape the gossipmongers and the threat of discovery by the Nazis, Schygulla tries to visit her husband in Bavaria. When the Nazi's finally learn of the affair, after intercepting one of Schygulla's letters to Lysak, they apprehend the Pole. Out of respect for Schygulla, the Nazi officials in Brombach attempt to Aryanize Lysak, thereby saving Schygulla from criminal misconduct. Lysak, however, refuses to deny his Polish blood and is sentenced to death, while Schygulla is shipped off to a concentration camp. Intercut with the wartime story is the modern-day search by a mysterious stranger who, with his 16-year-old son in tow, tries to discover what really happened between Schygulla and Lysak. Based on a nonfiction best-seller by Hochhuth which documents this actual case (including the Nazi's embarrasing failure to Aryanize the Pole and their botched attempt to execute him in a stone quarry), A LOVE IN GERMANY seems less concerned with the "love" of the title than with the political climate and the anti-Nazi message. Wajda, who has turned out some of cinema's most provocative political statements (MAN OF IRON, 1981), has againdone so. The problem, however, is that the politics (which always seem heavy-handed to American audiences) seem to get in the way of the love which Wajda undoubtedly intended. Schygulla, who is normally superbly naturalistic, seems to fall back on tried-and-true acting techniques and comes off as a caricature of her of her familiar Fassbinder persona. A must for those interested in Wajda or political history, though others will find themselves lost in a sea of political references. (English subtitles.)

p, Arthur Brauner; d Andrzej Wajda; w, Wajda, Boleslaw Michalek, Agnieszka Holland (based on the book by Rolf Hochhuth); ph, Igor Luther; m, Michel Legrand; ed, Halina Prugar-Ketling; art d, Allan Starski, Gotz Heymann, Jurgen Henze; cos, Ingrid Zore, Krystyna Zachwatowicz-Wajda.

Drama   Cas.   (PR:O   MPAA:R)

LOVE ON THE GROUND*   (1984,Fr.) 129m La Cecilia-French
Ministry of Culture/Spectrafilm-Cannon-Gala c (L'AMOUR PAR TERRE)

Jane Birkin (*Emily*), Geraldine Chaplin (*Charlotte*), Andre Dussollier (*Paul*), Jean-Pierre Kalfon (*Clement*), Facundo Bo (*Silvano*), Laszlo Szabo (*Virgile*), Sandra Montaigu (*Eleonore*), Eva Roelens (*Adriana*), Isabelle Linnartz (*Beatrice*).

The title means nothing and the picture means even less, except if you are one of those people who likes directorial conceits. Rivette, who had made the far superior CELINE AND JULIE GO BOATING (1974) re-examines similar ground as he strives to seal the gap between what is life and what is theater. Birkin and Chaplin are two actresses doing what appears to be a domestic scene with Bo in an apartment but it turns out to be a performance of a play they have adapted, without benefit of an okay from pompous playwright Kalfon. He sees it and is amused so he asks them to come to his huge estate where they will do the show again and learn how the unfinished work ends. At the mansion are Szabo, an oily butler and handyman who translates the play, Kalfon's lover, Montaigu, who walks around grumpily annoyed at all of these people who've come to the house, and Dussollier, a magician who can do some truly frightening things. The play is rehearsed over and over (it's a bore concerning Kalfon's *menage a trois* with a woman who has disappeared, Linnartz, and Dussollier) until one wonders why. Since the story has no end–as it is actually happening–Kalfon calls on Birkin, Chaplin, and Bo to finish the plot with their improvisations so he'll know what to write. The last act of the play will be provided by the actors but so what? There are several special effects sequences including an eerie room that emits eerier sounds. Chaplin and Birkin see themselves in dreams and nothing is what it seems. The improvisations are dull, the camera work is self-indulgent, and the actors are mechanical. It's all a game by the playwright and by the film's director and the net result is a long ho-hum that looks like a French version of a latter-day Robert Altman film. Rivette is another one of the former 1950s film critics for *Cahiers du Cinema* magazine who thought he could do better behind the camera than behind the typewriter. His previous films, CELINE AND JULIE GO BOATING and L'AMOUR FOU, were somewhat better but no less pretentious.

p, Martine Marignac; d, Jacques Rivette; w, Rivette, Pascal Bonitzer, Marilu Parolini, Suzanne Schiffman; ph, William Lubtchantsky (Kodak Color); ed, Nicole Lubtchansky, Louise de Champfleury; set d, Roberto Plate; cos, Renee Renard.

Drama   (PR:C   MPAA:NR)

LOVE STREAMS*½ (1984) 141m MGM/UA c

Gena Rowlands (Sarah Lawson), John Cassavetes (Robert Harmon), Dianne Abbott (Susan), Seymour Cassel (Jack Lawson), Margaret Abbott (Margarita), Jakob Shaw (Albie Swanson), Michele Conway (Agnes Swanson), Eddy Donno (Stepfather Swanson), Joan Foley (Judge Dunbar), Al Ruban (Milton Kravitz), Tom Badal (Sam the Lawyer), Risa Martha Blewitt (Debbie Lawson), David Rowlands (Psychiatrist), Robert Fieldsteel (Dr. Williams), Raphael DeNiro (Billy), Tony Brubaker (Frank), John Roselius (Ken), Jessica St. John (Dottie), Frank Beetson (Cashier), John Finnegan, Gregg Berger, John Qualls, Phedon Papamichael, Jim W. Jones (Taxi Drivers), Christopher O'Neal (Phyllis George Delano), Susan Wolf (Jade Meadows Swift), Doe Avedon (Mrs. Kiner), Alexandra Cassavetes, Dominique Davalos (Backup Singers), Julie Allan (Charlene), Renee Le Flore (Renee), Leslie Hope (Joanie), Joan Dykman (Phyllis), Browyn Bober (Jeanine), Victoria Morgan (Laurie), Barbara DiFrenza (Mary), Cindy Davidson (Annette), Hugo Napton (Ben the Bartender), Jamie Horton, Francois Duhamel, William Thompson, Avram Leibman, Michael Stein (Porters), Leonard P. Geer (Lenny), Neil Bell (The Dog Man), George Endoso (House Man), Kelly Lawrence, Logan Carter, Christopher Morley (Female Impersonators), Joe LeFlore, Michael Gallant, Dean Shindel, Al Lopez.

With Israeli filmmakers Golan and Globus watching over him, Cassavetes was guilty of less self-indulgence than ever before and the result is one of his best movies in a career that can only be described as roller coaster. Appearing for the first time in a movie of his own direction, Cassavetes teams with real- life spouse Rowlands as a brother and sister, two sides of the parental coin. Their intensity oozes off the screen and though they are meant to have different personalities, there is a oneness of spirit that is hard to refute. Cassavetes is a well- known author, not unlike Gay Talese or George Plimpton, two men who get to the core of their work by actually engaging in whatever they write about. He is researching a book on prostitution and becomes the den mother to a flock of lively ladies of the evening. His research takes him on nightly forays to the underbelly of the town, into nightclubs, bistros, cafes, and he will, from time to time, end the evening drunk or bloodied at the hands of another drunk. Rowlands is a delicate creature who is in the throes of a divorce and custody case against her husband Cassel. The two stories are intercut and the tawdriness of Cassavetes' life is seen in contrast to Rowlands' existence. She claims to be a happy person, has a heart for people less fortunate than she is, and is known to be a Florence Nightingale, visiting relatives, sick people, and trying to spread joy. It doesn't help her and she has recently landed in a mental institution. For half the movie we see their separate lives and wonder when and if they will get together (not unlike the two leads in AND NOW MY LOVE). Rowlands finally comes to see Cassavetes and the script leads one to believe they might have once been lovers. The revelation that they are siblings is uncovered. There is an immediate closeness as they reawaken all the affection they had for each other when children. Cassavetes has an 8-year-old son, Shaw, whom he hasn't seen since the child's birth. Shaw pays an unexpected visit to Cassavetes and just about the same time, Cassel appears. Rowlands loses the custody battle, then flies to Europe on a whim. Cassavetes departs with Shaw for Las Vegas and a chance to get to know the son he didn't know before. It is only then that we understand what Cassavetes may have been attempting to show; that two people from the same parents could have different and yet similar ways of handling matters. Rowlands is wonderful and is given many opportunities for unusual scenes to play, such as the one where she bowls alone, in full evening dress, to prove to herself that she can function on her own and is a happy human being. She pulls this off with total believability. Cassavetes also has his moments, such as the scene when Rowlands has decided that he needs something to love so she packs a cab with a dog, chickens, a duck, a parrot, a goat, and a pair of miniature horses. There are many terrific bits and pieces of the movie, rather than a real story. Like so many of Cassavetes' works, it goes on too long but this time it all seems to work. LOVE STREAMS won a Silver Bear at the Berlin Film Festival and was much respected by everyone who saw it. The main trouble is that not many people saw it. In a rare dual assignment, cinematographer Ruban also served as the executive producer. We don't recommend it for children. Not that there is bad language or even violent scenes, it's merely that the movie has so many layers, twists, and turns that it will be outside a young person's ken. The supposed theme is that "love is a stream, it's continuous and it doesn't stop." It could very well be true.

p, Menahem Golan, Yoram Globus; d, John Cassavetes; w, Ted Allan, Cassavetes (based on the play by Allan); ph, Al Ruban (Metrocolor); m, Bo Harwood; ed, George C. Villasenor; art d, Phedon Papamichael; cos, Jennifer Smith-Ashley.

Drama Cas. (PR:C MPAA:PG-13)

LOVELINES zero (1984) 93m Taines-Lloyd-Tri Star-Delphi II/Tri-Star c

Greg Bradford (Rick Johnson), Mary Beth Evans (Piper), Michael Winslow (J.D.), Don Michael Paul (Jeff), Tammy Taylor (Priscilla), Stacey Toten (Cynthia), Robert Delapp, Frank Zagarino (Godzilla), Todd Bryant (Hammer), Jonna Lee (Lisa), Robin Watkins (Theresa), Claudia Cowan (Brigit), Lynn Cartwright (Mrs. Woodson), Albert Szabo (Prof. Framowitz), David Jolliffe (Tongue), Miguel Ferrer (Dragon), Sherri Stoner (Suzy), Sarah

Buxtom (Cathy), Joyce Jamison (Mary Asquith), Shecky Greene (Emcee), Gary Morgan (Cafeteria Attendant), Marguerite Kimberley (Bathtub Girl), Kelley Jean Browser (Ventriloquist), Michael Lloyd (Lloyd Sidewalk), Paul Valentine (Mr. Vandermeer), Conrad E. Palmisano, Robert Fiacco (Motorcycle Officers), James Davis Trenton (Disk Jockey), Ernest Robinson (Porno Spectator), Aimee Eccles (Nisei).

A flaccid teen sex comedy set in Los Angeles concerning a battle-of-the-bands between two rival high schools (Malibu High and Coldwater Canyon High, if anyone cares). There's also a plot line about a teen telephone service, hence the title. LOVELINES offers absolutely nothing at all but bad rock-and-roll music, some unnecessary breakdancing, sophomoric sex jokes, glimpses of female flesh, and Michael Winslow doing the tiresome sound effects routine he made popular in POLICE ACADEMY (1984). Another big time-waster from Tri-Star Pictures.

p, Hal Taines, Michael Lloyd; d, Rod Amateau: w, Chip Hand, William Hillman (based on a story by Hand, Hillman, Lloyd); ph, Duke Callaghan (Metrocolor); ed, David Bretherton, Fred A. Chulack; art d, Robert K. Kinoshita; set d, A.C. Montenaro.

Comedy Cas. (PR:O MPAA:R)

LUCKY 13 (SEE: RUNNING HOT)

MAJDHAR*½ (1984, Brit.) 74m Retake Film & Video Collective c

Rita Wolf (Fauzia khan), Tony Wredden (Afzal Khan), Feroza Syal (Rehana), Andrew Johnson (Arun), Sudha Bhuchar (Gulshan), Daniel Foley (David), Julianne Mason (Sandra).

Wolf stars as a Pakistani girl who arrives in England in order to marry Wredden, who has been living there for several years. Wredden long ago assimilated to Western ways and soon finds her tiresome. He leaves her for a white woman, assuming that Wolf will return home. Her friends encourage her to stay, which she does. She begins to adopt Western ways herself. She follows the new fashions, has an abortion, becomes involved with an Englishman, and basically enjoys her new-found freedom. Wolf plays the role with a certain charm that makes the film watchable despite its simplistic script.

p, Mahmood Jamal; d&w, Ahmed A. Jamal; ph, Philip Chavannes; m, Ustad Imrat Khan; ed, John Dinwoodie; art d, Fay Rodrigues.

Drama (PR:C MPAA:NR)

MAKING THE GRADE* (1984) 105m Golan-Globus/MGM-Cannon-UA c (AKA: PREPPIES)

Judd Nelson (Eddie Keaton), Joanna Lee (Tracey Hoover), Gordon Jump (Mr. Harriman), Walter Olkewicz (Coach Wordman), Ronald Lacey (Nicky), Dana Olsen (Palmer Woodrow), Carey Scott (Rand), Scott McGinnis (Bif), Andrew Clay (Dice), John Dye (Skip), Daniel Schneider (Blimp), John Stevens (Mr. Hoover), Lucille Ewing (Mrs. Hoover), Patrice Watson (Muffy), Moses Peace (Regis), Robert Meltzer (Mr. Townsend), Ray Hill (Dr. Mueller), Mattie Grayson (Maid), Tim Fall (Caddy), Jeri Boyle, Waldo Zimmerman (Elders), Vince Lemorocco, Ronald Gordon (Henchmen), Christopher Thomas (Thomas), Jack Ray (Chauffeur), Marc G. Wilson (Scared Freshman), Steve Wilkerson (Passing Senior), Edgar Orman (Old Chauffeur), Treat McDonald (Reggie), Pam Shirley, Gail Stone-Stanton, Teresa Nix (Dicettes), Mike Crews, The Revolving Band.

Nelson is a tough street kid from New Jersey who is fleeing his bookie's thugs when he crosses a golf course and runs into Olsen, a wealthy young man about to go unwillingly to a prep school in order to qualify for his trust fund. He wants to travel, though, so he offers Nelson $10,000 to take his place for the year. Nelson does well in his new environment, shedding the red polyester suit he arrives in for logotyped polo shirts, and he quickly becomes the Big Man On Campus. Predictable complications arise and are dealt with in predictable ways, and much of the humor seems lifted out of successful teenage comedies of the last several years. Slightly better than most of its ilk, but still an insult to the intelligence.

p, Gene Quintano; d, Dorian Walker; w, Quintano (based on a story by Quintano, Charles Gale); ph, Jacques Haitkin (TVC Color); m, Basil Poledouris; ed, Dan Wetherbee; art d, Joseph T. Garrity; set d, Leslie Morales; cos, Emily Draper; m/l, "Living On the Edge," "Double Trouble" Jerry Lee, Shandi Sinnamon.

Comedy Cas. (PR:O MPAA:R)

MAN OF FLOWERS*½ (1984, Aus.) 91m Flowers International/International Spectrafilm c

Norman Kaye (Charles Bremer), Alyson Best (Lisa), Chris Haywood (David), Sarah Walker (Jane), Julia Blake (Art Teacher), Bob Ellis (Psychiatrist), Barry Dickins (Postman), Patrick Cook (Coppershop Man), Victoria Eagger (Angela), Werner Herzog (Father), Hilary Kelly (Mother), James Stratford (Young Charles), Eileen Joyce, Marianne Baillieu (Aunts), Lirit Bilu (Florist), Juliet Bacskai (Florist), Dawn Klingberg (Cleaning Lady), Tony Llewellyn-Jones (Church Warden).

Kaye is a sexually repressed, middle-aged painter who sublimates his desires into paintings of flowers and impassioned organ playing. He hires artist's model Best for $100 a week to come to his house and take off her clothes for him on a makeshift altar while he plays "The Love Duet" from Donizetti's "Lucia Di Lammermoor," after which he rushes to church and vents his emotion in a pipe organ. Kaye finally goes to a psychiatrist, who, in the tradition of movie shrinks, is kinkier than his patients. An interesting, sometimes funny film about loneliness and emotional isolation. It has a literate script, a lush, sensual texture, and, best of all, a silent cameo by German director Werner Herzog as Kaye's domineering father in a flashback.

p, Jane Ballantyne, Paul Cox; d, Cox; w, Cox, Bob Ellis; ph, Yuri Sokol (Fujicolor); m, Gaetano Donizetti; ed, Tim Lewis; art d, Asher Bilu; set d, Luba Bilu, Lirit Bilu; cos, Lirit Bilu.

Drama   (PR:O   MPAA:NR)

MARIANNE   (SEE: MIRRORS)

MARIGOLDS IN AUGUST*½**   (1984, S. Africa) 87m RM
                                                                    Productions

Winston Ntshona (Daan), John Kani (Melton), Athol Fugard (Paulus Olifant).

South African author Athol Fugard wrote and costarred in this, the final work in his socially conscious trilogy. Playwright Fugard has been responsible for awakening the world to the apartheid policies of South Africa with such works as "The Island" and "Sizwe Banzi Is Dead" and his first two pieces for this trilogy were "Boesman and Lena" and "The Guest," both of which were made into films. Ntshona is a black South African who ekes out an existence working as a gardener and general jack-of-all-trades in a white town near the seaside village of Port Elizabeth. He is proud to do what he does and, more or less, has the handyman market cornered. When another young black (Kani) arrives, Ntshoni is livid at the thought that someone would tread on his turf and he attempts to force Kani out of town by threats and eventually by chasing him to the outskirts. Enter Fugard, a "colored," a man of mixed racial heritage. He works at an odd occupation earning his keep by trapping snakes like puff adders and cobras and selling them to panting buyers in the town. Kani is desperate for work as one of his children has just died due to malnutrition and he is in danger of losing his remaining child unless food and medicine can be purchased. Fugard attempts to intervene on behalf of Kani and questions Ntshona about how he would respond if he were in the same position. Ntshona shrugs and answers "I'm not!" and that's that for the moral issue involved. Fugard keeps trying and finally gets the two men together and the effect is that these two men represent all of the various black factions in South Africa and that this first step may be the answer to unifying the many tribes and clans in South Africa in a last-ditch try at defeating the racial policies of the country. Fugard is essentially a playwright rather than a screenwriter and it's evident in the wise, witty, and literate script that feels stage-bound, even though the backgrounds are varied and we get a chance to see the town, the sea, and the national park. A movie with only three people in it feels like a play, and this does more than most. Fugard, Kani, and Ntshona are all superb and the two blacks have had a running relationship with Fugard as both have appeared in plays he's written.

p, Jonathan Cohen, Mark Forstater; d, Ross Devenish; w, Athol Fugard; ph, Michael Davis; ed, Lionel Selwyn.

Drama   (PR:A   MPAA:NR)

MASS APPEAL***   (1984) 100m Operation Cork/UNIV c

Jack Lemmon (Father Farley), Zeljko Ivanek (Mark Dolson), Charles Durning (Msgr. Burke), Louise Latham (Margaret), Alice Hirson (Mrs. Hart), Helene Heigh (Mrs. Hart's Mother), Sharee Gregory (Marion Hart), James Ray (Father De Nicola), Lois De Banzie (Mrs. Dolson), Talia Balsam (Liz Dolson), Jerry Hardin (Mr. Dolson), R.J. Williams (Boy), Noni White (Mother), Gloria Stuart (Mrs. Curry), Maggie Gwinn (Mrs. Quinn), F. William Parker (Mr. Hartigan), John Vargas (Scott Alvarez), Fran Robinson (Robin), Richard Doyle (Faculty Member), Terry Wills (Bill Kelly), Suzanne Kent (Mickey Kelly), Christopher Carroll (Salvatore Fitzgerald), John Devlin (Choir Leader), Ann Nelson (Miss Barber), John C. Becher (Mr. Jennings).

Jack Lemmon extended his streak of good pictures with this adaptation of a successful and award-winning Broadway play. Here he plays a priest in an affluent suburb of Los Angeles, something of a clown and immensely popular with the parishioners. Into his life comes Ivanek, a bright, devout, and dedicated seminarian who is on the verge of being expelled because of the controversial stand he takes on various issues. Lemmon takes him under his wing, despite Ivanek accusing him of being a "Father Bojangles" who conducts "song-and-dance theology." Lemmon teaches him that the way of absolute truth and perfect moral behavior is frequently not the best, and certainly not the easiest, and he explains that "the collection plate is the Nielsen rating after the sermon." The two men argue loudly and frequently, and each comes, in time, to respect the other's opinions. When a controversy involving the church arises, Ivanek influences Lemmon to take the side of

right, against the orders of his superiors. The film expanded on what was a two-person drama on the stage, adding the characters of Durning, as the monsignor of the seminary, and Latham, as Lemmon's housekeeper. Their performances, along with those of Lemmon and Ivanek, make MASS APPEAL one of the most honest and well-acted films of the year, though it was not a big money maker. The film was produced by Operation Cork, an anti-alcoholism organization run by Joan Kroc, the widow of McDonald's hamburger empire founder Ray Kroc.

p, Lawrence Turman, David Foster; d, Glenn Jordan; w, Bill C. Davis (based on his stage play); ph, Don Peterman (Technicolor); m, Bill Conti; ed, John Wright; prod d, Philip Jeffries; set d, Robert Checchi; cos, Shari Feldman, Bruce Walkup.

Drama   **Cas.**   (PR:C   MPAA:PG)

MASSIVE RETALIATION*   (1984) 90m One Pass-Hammermark c

Tom Bower (Kirk Fredericks), Karlene Crockett (Marianne Briscoe), Peter Donat (Lee Briscoe), Marilyn Hassett (Louis Fredericks), Susan O'Connell (Jackie Tolliver), Michael Pritchard (Harry Tolliver), Jason Gedrick (Eric Briscoe), Mimi Farina (Susie Barker).

When word comes over the airwaves of nuclear war in the Middle East, three families leave their homes in the city and head out to the survivalist outpost they have stocked with provisions for just such an event. Their children, following in a van, have engine trouble and there is some concern as to whether they'll make it. Donat, the nominal leader and most gung-ho of the novice survivalists, starts on the inevitable power-mad slide into paranoia and lunacy and the film simultaneously begins on its own slide into cliche-ridden tedium.

p&d, Thomas A. Cohen; w, Larry Wittnebert, Richard Beban; ph, Richard Lerner; m, Harn Soper, Paul Potyen; ed, B.J. Sears.

Drama   **Cas.**   (PR:O   MPAA:NR)

MEATBALLS PART II*   (1984) 95m Space/Tri-Star c

Archie Hahn (Jamie), John Mengatti (Flash), Tammy Taylor (Nancy), Kim Richards (Cheryl), Ralph Seymour (Eddie), Richard Mulligan (Giddy), Hamilton Camp (Hershey), John Larroquette (Meathead), Paul Reubens (Albert), Nick Ryan (Cop), David Hollander (Tommy), Misty Rowe (Fanny), Vivi Lorre (Tula), Joanne Giudici (Sally), Elayne Boosler (Mother), Nancy Glass (Daughter), Patti Kirkpatrick (Dibble Mother), Paul Stout (Larry), Scott Stout (Barry), Jonna King (Susie), Tim Bartell (Damien), Chad Sheets (Ted), Scott Nemes (Butterball), Jason Hervey (Steve), Felix Silla (Foxglove), Vic Martinez (Indian Chief), Blackie Dammett (Palladin), Christian Brackett (Wild Eyes), Donald Gibb (Mad Dog), Vic Dunlop (Rene), Joe Nipote (Boomer).

Another sequel that has absolutely nothing to do with the original film other than tacking PART II onto the title. Mengatti is a tough city youth sent to Camp Sasquatch to act as a counselor as part of his probation. There, he meets sweet, sheltered Richards, a naive girl for whom the outing represents her first time on her own. Camp (was he hired on the basis of his last name?) plays the evil head of a rival recreation spot, aided by a homosexual assistant, Larroquette. The film comes to a conclusion when Mengatti takes to a boxing ring to defend his camp's honor. Mixed into this slight story are the usual amount of anatomy gags and camp hijinks, along with a subplot involving the cheapest looking movie alien this side of ROBOT MONSTER. The difference between this film and the original MEATBALLS is Bill Murray, whose charm gave the first film its best moments, lifting the mediocre plot into something mindless but sweet. Here the characters are stereotypes. Perhaps the only reason to see the film is for Reubens, who has a relatively minor part. The ad campaign for the film promoted him as a leading player based on the success of his cult character "Pee Wee Herman," though Reubens doesn't portray that oddball creation here.

p, Tony Bishop, Stephen Poe; d, Ken Wiederhorn; w, Bruce Singer (based on a story by Martin Kitrosser, Carol Watson); ph, Donald M. Morgan (Movielab Color); m, Ken Harrison; ed, George Berndt; prod d, James William Newport; art d, Peg Cummings; set d, Lou Mann; cos, Sandi Love; spec eff, Barry Nolan; m/l, "We've Been Waiting for the Summer" Harrison, Hermine Hilton.

Comedy   **Cas.**   (PR:C   MPAA:PG)

MELVIN, SON OF ALVIN*½   (1984, Aus.) 85m Roadshow c

Gerry Sont (Melvin Simpson), Lenita Psillakis (Gloria Giannis), Graeme Blundell (Alvin Purple), Jon Finlayson (Burnbaum), Tina Bursill (Dee Tanner), Colin McEwan (Mr. Simpson), Abigail (Mrs. Simpson), David Argue (Cameraman), Ariathe Galani (Mrs. Giannis), Greg Stroud (Ferret), David Beresh (Streaky), Katy Manning (Estelle), Marian Callopy (miss Fosdyke).

Following 1973's Australian features ALVIN PURPLE (the largest grossing Aussie film of the time) and ALVIN RIDES AGAIN (1974), this sequel is even less funny than its predecessors. The 18-year-old son of Alvin is played by Sont, a lad who's inherited his dad's animal magnetism but is scared of women. He does, however, find himself at ease with Psillakis, a lovely usherette at the local movie theater. A weak subplot has television journalist Bursill and cameraman Argue doing a news story on the reunion between Sont and his father. A stale and unfunny film which should have died back in 1974 along with ALVIN RIDES AGAIN.

p, James McElroy; d, John Eastway; w, Morris Gleitzman; ph, Ross Berryman; m, Colin Stead; ed, John Hollands; prod d, Jon Dowding.

Comedy   **Cas.**   **(PR:O   MPAA:NR)**

MEMED MY HAWK**   (1984, Brit.) 110m Peter Ustinov-Jadran/Focus c

Peter Ustinov, Herbert Lom, Denis Quilley, Michael Elphick, Simon Dutton, Leonie Mellinger, Relja Basic, Edward Burnham, Ernest Clarke, Rosalie Crutchley, Barry Dennen, Walter Gotell, Michael Gough, Marne Maitland, Siobhan McKenna, T. P. McKenna, Phil Rose, Vladek Sheybal, Clive Swift, Eileen Way, Jeffrey Wickham, Bozidar Alic, Petre Arsovski, Mara Isaja, Mirce Donevski, Venco Kapural, Dzemal Maksut, Igor Galo, Fahro Konjhodzic, Boris Bakal.

A pet project of Peter Ustinov's, who acted as writer and director as well as star, MEMED MY HAWK tells the story of a tyrant whose involvement in the feudal Turkey of the 1950s leads to his death. Turkish peasant life is given a well-meaning but stereotypical treatment that never really rings true. There are also a number of familiar British thespians who seem as if they'd rather be somewhere else.

p, Fuad Kavur; d&w, Peter Ustinov (based on the novel by Yashar Kemal); ph, Freddie Francis; m, Manos Hadjidakis; ed, Peter Honess; art d, Veljko Despotovic.

Drama   **(PR:C   MPAA:NR)**

MEMOIRS*   (1984, Can.) 91m Les Productions Chbib c

Philip Baylaucq (Johnny Daze), Norma Jean Sanders (Ida Rage), Julia Gilmore (Lotta Lov), Rotwang.

A dark, artsy story of Baylaucq, a young man who ventures to a big city and finds himself deep in the perverse inner recesses of the punk rock community. He moves in with Sanders, a strange femme who calls herself "Ida Rage" and likes to collect art which looks more like refuse than anything else. Sanders becomes attracted to a weirdo performance artist, Gilmore, who then moves in, pushing Baylaucq into the street. A bizarre look at a bizarre subculture, but not much of a movie. Filmed in 16mm, a first feature for its producer-director, Chbib.

p&d, Bachar Chbib; w, John Beckett Wimbs, Chbib (based on the play "Memoirs of Johnny Daze" by Wimbs); ph, Christian Duguay, Bill Kerrigan; m, Julia Gilmore, Edward Straviak, Philip Vezina; ed, Chbib, Amy Webb.

Drama   **(PR:O   MPAA:NR)**

MEMOIRS OF PRISON**   (1984, Braz.) 135m International Home Cinema c (MEMORIAS DO CARCERE; AKA: MEMORIES OF PRISON)

Carlos Vereza (Graciliano Ramos), Gloria Pires (Heloisa Ramos), Paulo Porto (Dr. Cabral), David Pinheiro (Capt. Lobo), Jofre Soares (Soares), Nildo Parente (Manoel), Joseh Dumont (Mario Pinto), Wilson Grey (Gaucho), Waldyr Onofre (Cubano), Jackson De Souza (Arruda), Tonico Pereira (Desiderio), Jorge Cherques (Goldberg), Antonio Almeijeiras (Leonardo).

An insufferably long Brazilian picture based on a semi-autobiographical novel by Graciliano Ramos. Set during the Getulio Vargas dictatorship of the 1930s, MEMOIRS OF PRISON shows its audience the horrors of the Brazilian penal system through the eyes of Vereza, who stars as the imprisoned Ramos. Arrested with no explanation (though it is obviously for his Marxist leanings), Vereza is allowed to continue his writing. Initially he has some difficulty acquiring a pen and paper. By the finale, however, Vereza has garnered so much publicity from his writings that the government decides to set him free rather than execute him by brutal, sustained mistreatment. Unfortunately, the film soon becomes tedious in its lack of drama and is unable to rely solely on Vereza's fine performance. Awarded the International Critics' Prize at the 1984 Cannes Film Festival. (In Portuguese; English subtitles.)

p, Luiz Carlos Barreto, Lucy Barreto; d&w, Nelson Pereira dos Santos; (based on the novel MEMORIAS DO CARCERE By Graciliano Ramos); ph, Jose Medeiros, Antonio L. Soares; ed, Carlos Alberto Camuyrano; art d, Irenio Maia; cos, Ligia Medeiros.

Drama   **(PR:O   MPAA:NR)**

MEMORIAS DO CARCERE   (SEE: MEMOIRS OF PRIZON, Braz.)

MICKI AND MAUDE***½   (1984) 118m COL-Delphi III-Blake Edwards Entertainment/COL c

Dudley Moore (Rob Salinger), Amy Irving (Maude Salinger), Ann Reinking (Micki Salinger), Richard Mulligan (Leo Brody), George Gaynes (Dr. Eugene Glztzski), Wallace Shawn (Dr. Elliot Fibel), John Pleshette (Hap Ludlow), H.B. Haggerty (Barkhas Guillory), Lu Leonard (Nurse Verbeck), Priscilla

Pointer (Diana Hutchison), Robert Symonds (Ezra Hutchison), George Coe (Gov. Lanford), Gustav Vintas (Dr. Kondoleon), Ken Olfson (Interior Decorator), Phillippe Denham (TV Cameraman), Emma Walton (Maude's Nurse), Ruth Silveira (Micki's Nurse), Richard Drown (Stunt Double), Jack "Wildman" Armstrong (Wrestler), Andre Rousimmoff (Andre the Giant), John Minton (Big John Stud), Joe Scarpa (Chief Jay Strongbow), John J. Flynn, Jr. (Madman O'Rourke), Gene Le Bell (Wrestling Referee), Wiley Harker (Oliver Cushing III), Tina Theberge (Maid of Honor), Jim Giggins, Roger Rose, Tiiu Leek (Newscasters), Jamie Abbott (Frank Lanford), Christa Denton (Alice Lanford), Robby Kiger (Ehren Lanford), Paul Bright (Teenager on Bike), Robert Nadder (Geologist), Hanna Hertelendy (Admissions Clerk), Billy Beck (Finn), Lou Felder (Sales Clerk), Virginia Kiser (Mrs. Lanford), Jerry Martin (Security Guard), Gerry Gibson (Ben Sitkowitz), Edith Fields (Valerie Sitkowitz), Arthur Lessac (Bailiff), Edward Call (Campaign Manager), Aphasia Peters (7-Year-Old Girl), Jessica Rubin (7-Year-Old Girl), Jaime McEnnan (5-Year-Old Boy), Hailey McAfee (5-Year-Old Boy), Mark Harris (3-Year-Old Boy), Avianka Guzman (3-Year-Old Girl), Patrick Sean Murphy, Nick Coddington, Doug Donatelli, Peter Nicholas, Joe Davis, Sam Cupae (Male Models), Cambodian Art Preservation Group (Themselves).

The recipe is as follows: take one happily married man, add an extramarital affair, stir in a dash of pregnancy, saute lightly, and serve with heaping spoonfuls of irony and slapdash action, and what do you have? The story line of a hilarious comedy. Moore is the Los Angeles-based host of a typically inane TV talk show who does nothing more controversial than review the comestibles served at the election eve party of a candidate. He's married to a busy and competent attorney, Reinking, and he yearns to be a father but her breakneck schedule keeps them from having enough time to even try for a child, other than the occasional quick coupling in a car that is hardly satisfying. Moore meets Irving, a seductive cellist who finds him fascinating. She sets her sights for him, and he is easy prey for her wiles. She has no idea that he's married and he manages to carry off the deception until she announces that she's pregnant. Moore meets Irving's father, the behemoth Haggerty, who is an ex-footballer and wrestler and is now thinking about becoming an interior decorator. Being a kind gentleman, Moore does the proper thing and marries Irving, believing that bigamy is the only answer to his problem. Once he is ensconced in his double life, the fun heats up. Both women are consulting the same gynecologist team (Shawn and Gaynes) and Moore almost has a heart attack when he accompanies one wife to their office and finds the other one there. All of this turns up the nose of the attending nurse, Leonard, who is hilarious in a brief but telling cameo. The two women are quite different. Reinking is ambitious and in line to be a judge, but she foregoes that for the joys of motherhood. Irving is happy to be the dutiful wife, crocheting, cooking, doing all the things Moore wished Reinking would have done at the start. When both women go into labor at the same time, Moore races from room to room in order to look like the harassed husband, which he is in spades. There's no question that a morality lapse is at the core of the movie but Moore is so engaging in the role that he can't be faulted because he has been tapped by Fate and, loving both women, he does his best to make them happy. The denouement is less than satisfying, but it does come as a mild surprise and we won't reveal it except to say that the movie peters out rather than ends with a bang. Some very funny scenes and excellent acting from all the performers. It begins a bit slowly but builds well and winds up in a comic celebration. Mulligan is superior as Moore's best friend and confidante. In the past, Mulligan has appeared for Edwards and was usually guilty of a bit of overemoting. Not so here, as his is a wonderfully understated turn. As mentioned, Leonard is hysterical and the script throws a curve when this heavyset, hard-nosed woman is discovered to have been conducting an affair with nebbish Shawn. The scene where they rendezvous for their tryst is uproarious. Blake Edwards has his ups and downs. When he is up, as in A SHOT IN THE DARK, VICTOR/VICTORIA, and 10, he is terrific. When he is down, as in THE CAREY TREATMENT, DARLING LILI, and THE TAMARIND SEED, he is dull. In MICKI AND MAUDE, he is up, up, and away. Moore and Edwards should make more films together, as when the little Englishman works for other directors he makes bombs like ROMANTIC COMEDY, LOVESICK, BEST DEFENSE, and SIX WEEKS. The incisive script for this film was by a fledgling screenwriter whose only other notable credit was the off-Broadway show "Geniuses," which was based on his experiences in the Philippines with Francis Ford Coppola during the making of APOCALYPSE NOW.

p, Tony Adams; d, Blake Edwards; w, Jonathan Reynolds; ph, Harry Stradling, Jr. (Panavision, Metrocolor); m, Lee Holdridge; ed, Ralph E. Winters; prod d, Rodger Maus; art d, Jack Senter; set d, Stuart A. Reiss; cos, Patricia Norris; spec eff, Roy L. Downey; m/l, "Something New in My Life," Michel Legrand, Alan and Marilyn Bergman (performed by Stephen Bishop); stunts, Joe Dunne; makeup, Rich Sharp, Gary D. Liddiard.

Comedy   **Cas.**   **(PR:C   MPAA:PG-13)**

MIDSUMMER NIGHT'S DREAM, A**½   (1984, Brit./Span.) 80m Cabochon-Television Espanola SA c (SUENO DE NOCHE DE VERANO)

Lindsay Kemp (Puck), Manuela Vargas (Hippolyta), The Incredible Orlando [Jack Birkett] (Titania), Michael Matou (Oberon), Francois Testory (Changeling), David Meyer (Lysander), Neil Caplan (Theseus/The Beast), David Haughton (Demetrius), Annie Huckle (Hermia), Cheryl Heazelwood

(Helena), Atilio Lopez *(Romeo/Bottom)*, Christian Michaelson *(Juliet/Flute)*, Javier Sanz *(Starveling/Moon)*.

Another Shakespearean oddity from the director who gave us the equally outlandish HAMLET in 1976. This time the text has been all but abandoned in favor of mime and song and dance numbers performed by the Lindsay Kemp stage company. The characters are truly absurd, dressing in wild costumes and wearing bizarre makeup, and display a perverse sexual aura. This low-budget film, like the 1976 HAMLET, must be seen by Shakespeare lovers for the sake of comparison.

p, Miguel Angel Perez Campos; d&w, Celestino Coronado (based on the stage production by Lindsay Kemp, David Haughton from the play by William Shakespeare); ph, Peter Middleton; m, Carlos Miranda; prod d, Kemp, Haughton; art d, Carlos Dorremochea; cos, Kemp, Haughton.

Drama   **(PR:O   MPAA:NR)**

MIKE'S MURDER**   (1984) 97m WB c

Debra Winger *(Betty Parrish)*, Mark Keyloun *(Mike)*, Paul Winfield *(Phillip)*, Darrell Larson *(Pete)*, Brooke Alderson *(Patty)*, Robert Crosson *(Sam)*, Daniel Shor *(Richard)*, William Ostrander *(Randy)*, Gregory Hormel *(Kid Drug Buyer)*, John Michael Stewart, Victor Perez *(Tough Guys)*, Mark High *(Ben)*, Ken Y. Namba *(Sushi Chef)*, Ruth Winger *(Betty's Mother)*, April Ferry *(Boss Lady)*, Randy White *(Boss Man)*, Robert Kincaid *(Bodyguard)*, Kym Malin, Lori Butler, Dawn Abraham *(Beautiful Girls)*, Freeman King, Alphonse Walter *(Killers)*, James Carrington *(Jim)*, Rebecca Marder, Bruce Marder *(Cafe Workers)*, Sarah Zinsser *(Girl in Video Tape)*, James Dale Ryan, Robert Johnstreet, Gordon Hoban *(Police Technicians)*, Javier Jose Gonzalez *(Bus Stop Boarder)*, Cliff Jenkins *(Bus Boarder)*, Aurelia Gallardo *(Pancho's Waitress)*, Frank Cavestani *(Charles)*, Spazz Attack *(Himself)*, Johnny B. Frank, MariSol Garcia *(Blonde Punkers)*, Jennifer Dixon, Steve Solberg, Annie Jones, Michael Uhlenkot *(Party Goers)*.

Alan Ladd, Jr. was the man behind this film although he took no credit other than his corporate logo. A small, intense movie with a disappointing premise and a host of unlikable people as they make their ways through a Los Angeles that can only be described as seamy. It took two years from the time the movie was completed until, after recutting, it was released. Winger is a bank teller having an affair with Keyloun, a tennis teacher who lives far above any earnings he could gather teaching tennis. The way he can afford his nice house and all the other accoutrements is by dealing drugs on the side. Their affair is, at best, erratic. He seems to call her only when he can't call anyone else and he needs some sex. She doesn't really know much about him other than he is a will-of-the-wisp who comes into her life for short but passionate periods. Keyloun and drug-dealer pal Larson take a batch of white powder from a big-shot dealer and the moment they burn him, their fates are sealed. Keyloun is killed and Larson is a marked man. Larson is a user as well as a dealer and he and Winger get together to solve the crime (Larson knows fully well who did it). There are endless shots of driving around Los Angeles late at night, a few good moments for Winfield as a gay and lonely record producer, and Shor as Winger's sometime boy friend, but otherwise this picture is a washout. Bridges attempts to make up for the lack of any meat to give us potatoes in the form of cute scenes, such as the one where Winger waits patiently for Keyloun to show up (he never does) and spends her time playing with a video game and on her piano. To show that Crosson, a photographer with a penchant for peeping, is a sophisticate, Bridges has him listening to classical music. Then, to contrast the lack of class Keyloun possesses, Bridges comes in close so we can see all the details of the cheap, greasy burger the doomed man has ordered. In the end, Larson goes nuts and is about to kill Winger but, by that time, it's almost a relief. Winger is good with what she is given but no actor or actress can overcome an empty script and that is the fault of this film. To its credit, there is very little violence, but that is also the detriment to commercial success. The actors keep talking about mayhem but little of it is seen. A failure with intentions beyond its abilities.

p, Kim Kurumada, Jack Larson; d&w, James Bridges; ph, Reynaldo Villalobos (Technicolor); m, John Barry, Joe Jackson; ed, Jeff Gourson, Dede Allen; prod d, Peter Jamison; art d, Hub Braden; set d, R. Chris Westlund; cos, April Ferry; spec eff, Bruce Mattox.

Murder Mystery   **Cas.**   **(PR:O   MPAA:R)**

MIRRORS*   (1984) 88m First American c (AKA: MARIANNE)

Kitty Winn *(Marianne)*, Peter Donat *(Dr. Godard)*, William Swetland *(Charbonnet)*, Mary-Robin Redd *(Helene)*, William Burns *(Gary)*, Lou Wagner *(Chet)*, Don Keefer *(Peter)*, Vanessa Hutchinson *(Marie)*.

Dreams can have a nasty effect on someone, particularly when those dreams start encroaching on others. In this minor horror feature, one woman's dreams do just that with murder being the end result. New Orleans is never the same when it's over.

p, John T. Parker, Stirling W. Smith; d, Noel Black; w, Sidney L. Stebel; ph, Michael D. Murphy (CFI Color); m, Stephen Lawrence; ed, Robert Estrin; prod d, Ronald Weinberg; art d, Ray Kutos.

Horror/Crime   **(PR:O   MPAA:PG)**

MISSING IN ACTION**   (1984) 101m Cannon c

Chuck Norris *(Braddock)*, M. Emmet Walsh *(Tuck)*, David Tress *(Sen. Porter)*, Lenore Kasdorf *(Ann)*, James Hong *(Gen. Tran)*, Ernie Ortega *(Vinh)*, Pierrino Mascarino *(Jacques)*, E. Erich Anderson *(Masucci)*, Joseph Carberry *(Carter)*, Avi Kleinberger *(Dalton)*, Willy Williams *(Randall)*, Ric Segreto *(GI)*, Bella Flores *(Mme. Pearl)*, Gil Arceo, Roger Dantes *(Vietnamese Businessmen)*, Sabatini Fernandez *(Dinh)*, Renato Morado *(Mike)*, Jim Crumrine *(Gibson)*, Jeff Mason *(Barnes)*, Stephen Barbers *(Moore)*, Nam Moore *(Translator)*, Kim Marriner, Deanna Crowe *(Newscasters)*, Jesse Cuneta *(Street Hawker)*, Juliet Lee *(Bar Girl)*, Joonee Gamboa *(Bartender)*, Augusto Victa *(Tran's Aide)*, Protacio Dee *(Yang)*, Omar Camar, Jack Perez *(Bouncers)*.

Norris is an American officer who spent seven years in a Vietnamese prisoner-of-war camp before escaping. Later he accompanies a government investigation team that travels to Ho Chi Minh City to check out reports of Americans still held prisoner. He gets the evidence he needs, then travels to Thailand where he meets Walsh, an old Army buddy turned black market kingpin, and together they launch a mission deep into the jungle to free the POW's and shoot up a lot of Communists. This is the film that opened the floodgates of Viet Nam revisionism that was carried to its macho extreme in RAMBO: FIRST BLOOD PART II (1985). If America couldn't win the war, they can make films in which we can get even. As an action picture it works fairly well–Norris is a worthy hero, shooting and kicking oriental enemies right and left and the film is blessed with production values that make it quite watchable. A major success at the box office, the film spawned an equally successful prequel, MISSING IN ACTION 2; THE BEGINNING (1985), shot at the same time and released only four months after MISSING IN ACTION.

p, Menahem Golan, Yoram Globus; d, Joseph Zito; w, James Bruner (based on a story by John Crowther, Lance Hool, from characters created by Arthur Silver, Larry Levinson, Steve Bing); ph, Joao Fernandes (Metrocolor); m, Jay Chattaway; ed, Joel Goodman, Daniel Loewenthal; art d, Ladi Wilhelm, Toto Castillo; set d, Celso dela Cruz; cos, Nancy Cone.

War   **Cas.**   **(PR:O   MPAA:R)**

MISSION, THE***   (1984) 108m New Film Group-Aria/New Line c

Parviz Sayyad *(Colonel)*, Mary Apick *(Maliheh)*, Houshang Touzie, Saeed Rajai *(Agents from Teheran)*, Kamran Nozad *(Ghaffar)*, Mohammad B. Ghaffari *(His Eminence)*, Hatam Anvar *(Maziar)*, Hedyeh Anvar *(Farzaneh)*, Soraya Shayesteh *(Woman)*, Richard Mansfield, David Filinni *(Muggers)*, Liz Jones, John Neil *(Passersby)*, Frank Oddo *(Cabbie)*, Murie Alcid *(Cleaning Lady)*, Aaron Moss, Susan Sands *(Couple)*, Helen Nitsiog *(Fabric Seller)*, James Deenen *(Cop)*, Dalton Alexander *(Morgue Attendant)*.

An offbeat and thoroughly engaging film has Touzie playing a hit man from Iran, sent by the Khomeini regime to eliminate enemies of the state and former allies of the deposed Shah. In New York, his new assignment is to bump off Sayyad, a former colonel in the Shah's SAVAK secret police. As a devout Muslim in the Babylon of New York City, Touzie goes through numerous culture shocks to which he cannot adjust such as a lightly clad Marilyn Monroe displayed openly on television. Eventually he closes in on his victim but before Touzie can strike, he inadvertently saves his target from being mugged. Sayyad, grateful for what his fellow countryman has done, takes his would-be killer into his home and treats him as a member of the family. Not realizing Touzie's true intent, Sayyad introduces him to his wife and children who have all assimilated American culture. Sayyad, who also directed and wrote the film, gives a wonderful performance as the amiable colonel; Touzie is an excellent counterpart with his confused character. Never heavyhanded about a subject that requires great care, Sayyad creates a story that is at once both funny and thrilling. The political and religious satires are woven into the film with skill, making a point while never ceasing to entertain. Sayyad at one time had been a popular Iranian filmmaker with a string of successful comedies and his own television series, the latter often being yanked off the air for political content. During the Iranian revolution he had been out of the country; his Teheran movie theater was destroyed in the violent street riots that followed. Sayyad fled to New York, where he worked for a P.D. before helming this film. With THE MISSION he has created a fair portrait of the Iranian people and both sides of the conflict without showing extreme prejudice towards either viewpoint. Barry Rosen, one of the American hostages during the 444-day embassy crisis, felt that the film was a fair portrait of the revolutionaries he had gotten to know while in Iran, portraying them as actual human beings with their own problems rather than mindless zealots. (In Farsi; English subtitles.)

p, Parviz Sayyad, Reza Aria; d&w, Sayyad (based on a story by Hesam Kowsar); ph, Aria; ed, Sayyad.

Comedy/Thriller   **(PR:O   MPAA:NR)**

MR. HOT SHOT   (SEE: FLAMINGO KID, THE)

MRS. SOFFEL**½   (1984) 110m MGM/MGM-UA c

Diane Keaton (*Kate Soffel*), Mel Gibson (*Ed Biddle*), Matthew Modine (*Jack Biddle*), Edward Herrmann (*Peter Soffell*), Trini Alvarado (*Irene Soffel*), Jennie Dundas (*Margaret Soffel*), Danny Corkill (*Eddie Soffel*), Harley Cross (*Clarence Soffel*), Terry O'Quinn (*Buck McGovern*), Pippa Pearthree (*Maggie*), William Youmans (*Guard Koslow*), Maury Chaykin (*Guard Reynolds*), Joyce Ebert (*Matron Garvey*), John W. Carroll (*Guard McGarey*), Dana Wheeler-Nicholson (*Jessie Bodyne*), Wayne Robson (*Halliday*), Les Rubie (*Mr. Stevenson*), Paula Trueman (*Mrs. Stevenson*), David Huckvale, Douglas Huckvale (*Russian Twins*), Ralph Zeldin (*Russian*), Nancy Chesney (*Mrs. Fitzgerald*), Samantha Follows (*Becky Knotts*), Katie McCombs (*Rachel Garvey*), Linda Gabler (*Leota Yoeders*), Eric Hebert (*Paperboy*), Alar Aedma (*Guard*), Tom Harvey (*Atty. Rose*), Jack Jessop (*Atty. Watson*), Lou Pitoscia (*Prisoner*), John Dee (*Old Prisoner*), William Duell (*Lenny*), Len Doncheff (*Polish Guard*), David Fox (*McNeil*), Fred Booker (*Trustee*), Valerie Buhagiar (*Alice*), Jane Foster (*Elsie*), Phillip Craig (*Sketch Artist*), John Innes, Norma Dell'Agnese, Al Kozlik, Derek Keurvorst, Don McManus (*Reporters*), Kay Hawtrey (*Peter's Secretary*), Brian Young (*McNeil's Secretary*), Frank Adamson (*Swinehart*), Don Granberry (*Roach*), Gerald Tucker (*Policeman*), Heather Graham, Linda Carola (*Factory Girls*), George Belsky (*Mr. Bodyne*), Marushka Stankove (*Mrs. Bodyne*), James Bradford (*Minister*), Charles Jolliffe (*Sheriff Hoon*), Rodger Barton (*Deputy Hoon*), Jack Mather (*Mr. Watson*), Lee-Max Walton (*Harry*), Sean Sullivan, Warren Van Evera, Clay Follett (*Farmers*), Chris Cummings (*Boy*), Dan Lett (*Young Man*), Dorothy Phelan (*Old Aunt*), Walter Massey (*Mr. Robinson*), Victoria Vanderkloot, Chuck Waters.

Based on a scandalous true story which unfolded in turn-of-the-century Pittsburgh, MRS. SOFFEL was a multimillion dollar bust at the box office, despite the presence of two box-office leaders in Gibson and Keaton. She's the often-ill wife of prison warden Herrmann, a bit of a martinet who runs his jail with a tough attitude. They are the parents of four children who spend a great deal of time ministering to Keaton's ailments. The children are Cross, Corkill, Alvarado, and Dundas. Keaton spends a great deal of her time walking around the jail (they actually used the jail built in 1883 that was the site of the real occurrences depicted in the film) and reading the Bible to the various prisoners. (Many real-life prisoners were used in the making of the film, as the jail is still in use and home to several hundred felons.) Keaton and Herrmann and family live in the prison which consists of two buildings connected by a replica of Venice's Bridge of Sighs. Awaiting execution for the murder of a grocer are two brothers, Gibson and Modine, who have become media favorites because of the letters Gibson has been writing to the newspapers. Gibson, like Charles Manson in later years, is the idol of teenage girls who find him attractive and dangerous. Keaton meets Gibson and Modine when the brothers are battling some guards and there is instant magnetism. Keaton begins visiting Gibson, who maintains that he is sorry about what he's done and wishes he could get another chance. Ever so subtly, Keaton is enraptured by Gibson and she helps him and Modine escape. Suddenly, this pillar of the community is a fugitive. Once on the outside, Gibson, who had intended on dumping Keaton, finds that he loves her and cannot abandon her. Meanwhile, Herrmann (and everyone else) is shocked by her behavior. In real life, the warden said that he had been "basely betrayed by the person who was nearest and dearest to him." The three steal a sled and attempt to make their way to Canada but they never do find freedom. Both men are killed and Keaton attempts suicide but fails when the bullet she's aimed toward her heart misses. The two men were so famous in their day that a short film was made about them by Edwin S. Porter. MRS. SOFFEL was shot on location in Pittsburgh and had interiors done in Canada where they matched some of the interiors at Toronto International Studios in Kleinberg, Ontario. There is an exciting chase sequence with the trio in a sled, and they moved inside a refrigerated warehouse for the closeups. The reason why they had to do it there was so the actors' breath would show on screen. The direction was slow (Gillian Armstrong in her first American feature after successes in Australia with MY BRILLIANT CAREER and STARSTRUCK) and the cinematography was murky. In real life, the bodies of the two men were on display in the town of Butler and people paid a fee to see them. The actual escape was done when Soffel smuggled nun's robes to the men and they left dressed as Sisters of Mercy. Their plan was to go to some isolated place in Canada, work the mines, and live in peace. It didn't work out and neither did this picture. Keaton (who was born Diane Hall) also made LITTLE DRUMMER GIRL in 1984, a year she would just as soon forget.

p, Edgar J. Scherick, Scott Rudin, David A. Nicksay; d, Gillian Armstrong; w, Ron Nyswaner; ph, Russell Boyd (Metrocolor); m, Mark Isham; ed, Nicholas Beauman; prod d, Luciana Arrighi; art d, Roy Forge Smith; set d, Jacques Bradette, Hilton Rosemarin, Dan Conley; cos, Arrighi, Arthur Rowsell, Patty Unger; spec eff, Neil Trifunovich; stunts, Glenn H. Randall, Jr.; makeup, Linda Gill.

Historical Drama   Cas.   (PR:C   MPAA:PG-13)

MISUNDERSTOOD**   (1984) 91m MGM-UA c

Gene Hackman (*Ned*), Henry Thomas (*Andrew*), Rip Torn (*Will*), Huckleberry Fox (*Miles*), Maureen Kerwin (*Kate*), Susan Anspach (*Lilly*), June Brown (*Mrs. Paley*), Helen Ryan (*Lucy*), Nadim Sawalha (*Ahmed*), Nidal Ashkar (*Mrs. Jallouli*), Khaled Akrout (*Electronics Shop Clerk*), Rajah Gafsi

(*Ali-Baroutta, Cafe Owner*), Moheddine Mrad (*Kassir*), James R. Cope (*Mr. Grace*), Halima Daoud (*Aisha*), Raad Rawi (*Doctor*), Habiba (*Girl on Donkey*), Fathia Boudabous (*Woman in Red Light District*), Nabil Massad (*Mr. Jallouli*), Anick Allieres (*Marie*), Mohamed Ben Othman (*Chocolate Merchant*), Abdellatif Hamrouni (*Holy Man*), Salah Rahmouni (*Rachid*), Mohamed Dous (*Judo Instructor*), Tarak Sancho (*Ned's Driver*), Noureddine Kasbaoui, Moncef Dhouib (*Servants*), Zoubeir Bornaz (*Kassir's Assistant*), Hattah Dhib (*Kassir's Driver*), Mohamed Sghaier Ftouhi (*Baroutta Spring Owner*), Hella Boulila (*Secretary at Ned's Office*), Habib Chaari (*Injured Man*), Neal Anderson (*Andrew's Opponent*), Andre Valiquette (*Bob*), Dirk Holzapfel (*Lucien*).

The title may have been prophetic for this movie which was allegedly made in 1982 but did not find a release for two years. Written by the same woman who gave us SLOW DANCING IN THE BIG CITY, it is another story cut from the same bar of soap. Based on a novel more than 90 years old as well as a 1967 Italian film INCOMPRESO, the place and the time have been changed but the essentials remain similar. Hackman and Anspach had a reasonably happy marriage until she died of a malady that is never totally explained. She is seen only in flashbacks as the relationship between Hackman and his two sons, Thomas and Fox, is examined. Hackman is a former black marketeer who made millions after the war, then turned to legit interests and made more millions in shipping. He and his young sons live in a mansion in Tunisia. Anspach has only just passed away and Hackman has to explain this to the boys. Fox is too young to comprehend the loss but Thomas, at 8, is not. After he does this, Hackman finds that he cannot relate to his young sons. Hackman is the rough-hewn, self-made type and, to quench his grief, plunges himself even more deeply into his business and neglects the boys, who only have each other to play with. Torn is Anspach's brother and he thinks Hackman might get closer to Thomas if he treats him in a more adult fashion, which Hackman attempts. But Thomas is not an adult and communications between them break down. Thomas runs away and finds himself deep in the desert where he is taken in by some Arab nomads. Hackman is frantic with worry and begins a search. When Hackman finds Thomas, the boy has been hurt in an accident and it is this occurrence which brings the father and son back together. INCOMPRESO had the boy pass away but they hedge the bet here and end on a freeze frame so we're not sure if he survives, we can only hope. One wonders why this movie was made until we discover that the country of Tunisia made it easy for filmmakers to come in and shoot, perhaps even sweetening the pot with concessions. The actors try vainly to overcome a script that only tickles the surface of emotions. The Hackman house is so plush and breathtaking (and hardly referred to by the actors) that it was more attention-getting than the story and when the background overpowers the foreground you know the picture has problems. Hackman is, as always, believable and Thomas and Fox are terrific.

p, Tarak Ben Amar; d, Jerry Schatzberg; w, Barra Grant (based on the novel by Florence Montgomery and the screenplay for INCOMPRESO by Leo Benvenuti, Piero De Bernardi, m, Luci Drudi Demby, Guiseppe Mangione); ph, Pasqualino DeSantis (Technicolor); m, Michael Hoppe; ed, Marc Laub; prod d, Joel Schiller; set d, Franco Fumagalli; cos, Jo Ynocencio.

Drama   Cas.   (PR:C   MPAA:PG)

MIXED BLOOD***½   (1984) 98m Sef Satellite/Sara-Cinevista c

Marilia Pera (*Rita La Punta*), Richard Ulacia (*Thiago*), Linda Kerridge (*Carol*), Geraldine Smith (*Toni*), Angel David (*Juan the Bullet*), Ulrich Berr (*The German*), Marcelino Rivera (*Hector*), Rodney Harvey (*Jose*), Pedro Sanchez (*Commanche*), Carol Jean Lewis (*Woman Cop*), Yuko Yamamoto (*Capt. Kenzo*), Susan Blond (*Caterer*).

An engaging mix of off-the-wall black humor and obdurate violence features Pera as a Brazilian woman running a drug pushing outfit in New York City's Lower East Side. Her gang consists of neighborhood teenagers living in a squalid apartment whom she sincerely loves as her own. When her gang intercepts a shipment intended for a rival group, a 14-year-old is tossed off a rooftop in retaliation. Instead of intimidating Pera, the action results in an all-out war between her gang and rival David's group. The film juxtaposes opposing and often unlikely elements to create an honest feeling to the proceedings. Pera, who has a penchant for some strange outfits, constantly bullies her charges with the loving despotism of a Jewish mother. Her performance is wacky and believable—a determined businesswoman who takes each ensuing problem with a sigh and much grit. Ulacia is her dimwitted son, the gang's leader who dates Kerridge, a rich brat who hangs out with the gang for reverse chic but she's ultimately shot in the head during the film's bloody climax. This is a story steeped in violence, which comes as casual and frequently as spitting on a sidewalk. Unlike Morrissey's films for Andy Warhol or some of his 1970s underground work, this is not a comic gore fest. Despite the often hysterical proceedings the work is steadfastly rooted to realism. It captures the heart and soul of a neighborhood in one of the more unique slice/of/life pictures in a long time. Because this was shot along New York's avenues A, B, and C the original title was to be ALPHABET CITY, the area's nickname. However this title was taken by Amos Poe for his much inferior work of a similar nature, forcing Morrissey to choose another title.

p, Antoine Gannage, Teven Fierberg; d, Paul Morrissey; w, Morrissey, Alan Browne; ph, Stefan Zapasnik (Eastmancolor); m, Andy "Sugarcoated"

Hernandez; ed, Scott Vickerey; art d, Stephen McCabe.

Drama   **Cas.**   **(PR:O   MPAA:NR)**

MOHAN JOSHI HAAZIR HO*½ (1984, India) 123m Mirza c (AKA: SUMMONS FOR MOHAN JOSHI)

Bhisham Sahni, Dina Pathak, Naseeruddin Shah, Deepti Naval, Rohini Hattangady, Mohan Gokhale, Satish Shah, Amjad Khan.

According to the *Guinness Book of Records*, the longest lawsuit in history was a property dispute in India which took 761 years to decide. Knowing that, the plot of this excellent film makes a great deal of sense. Bombay is, perhaps, the most teeming city in the world and a dichotomy in every way. The rich are very rich and the poor are beyond poverty. It's a beautiful city, if one wears blinders to the human degradation around every corner. The Indian movie industry was, for many years, the most censored business in the sub-continent. The typical Indian movie, and there were more made there than in the U.S., had the same plot: boy meets girl, boy loses girl, boy gets girl, but boy doesn't ever get the chance to kiss girl–not on screen anyhow. This feature is indicative of the new wave of Indian movies because it tackles different subject matter and does it with unusual candor. Sahni is an aged man who lives in a slum tenement that is as bad as anything one might find in Harlem or East Los Angeles. He is a proud man, a decent man, and his one desire is to get the slumlord to make the needed alterations in the building and bring it up to livable standards. The landlord has other ideas. He's trying to force the tenants out so he can tear down the apartments and use the valuable land in a more profitable enterprise. Sahni tries to gather the other tenants around him in a strike against the landlord but they are frightened people and will not rock their leaking boat. Sahni will not be cowed and engages an attorney, Shah, to represent him. The lawsuit goes on for what feels like a lifetime and Sahni's savings are wiped out by the endless motions introduced by the opposition. It finally reaches the court and the judge feels that he must go to the tenement and see the conditions for himself. When that happens, the other tenants realize that Sahni has done what he promised and flock to his side. Sahni believes in the law and that belief is shattered when he sees how the legal fraternity in India are just that, a fraternity, and that he cannot afford to keep the case going. The judge won't make a decision and the case will eventually take forever. Essentially an indictment of the Indian legal system, it never takes a stance, but the subtle way in which the points are made more than indicates the feelings of the creators of this fine movie. Made for under $200,000, it was shot in 16 millimeter, then blown up to 35 millimeter, thus making some of the scenes grainy. However, that less-than-slick look also makes it appear more real than if it had been made on a large budget with an all-pro cast. Instead, only the leading actors were from Bombay's thespian community and all of the smaller roles were done by non-pros. (In Hindi.)

p&d, Saeed Akhtar Mirza; w, Yusuf Mehta, Mirza; ph, Virendra Saini; m, Vanraj Bhatia; ed, Renu Saluja.

Drama   **(PR:A   MPAA:NR)**

MOSCOW ON THE HUDSON*   (1984) 115m COL c

Robin Williams (*Vladimir Ivanoff*), Maria Conchita Alonso (*Lucia Lombardo*), Cleavant Derricks (*Lionel Witherspoon*), Alejandro Rey (*Orlando Ramirez*), Savely Kramarov (*Boris*), Elya Baskin (*Anatoly*), Oleg Rudnik (*Yury*), Alexander Beniaminov (*Vladimir's Grandfather*), Ludmila Kramarevsky (*Vladimir's Mother*), Ivo Vrzal (*Vladimir's Father*), Natalie Iwanow (*Sasha*), Tiger Haynes (*Lionel's Grandfather*), Edye Byrde (*Lionel's Mother*), Robert Macbeth (*Lionel's Stepfather*), Donna Ingram-Young (*Lelanne*), Olga Talyn (*Svetlana*), Alexander Narodetzky (*Leonid*), Pierre Orcel (*Young Frenchman*), Stephanie Cotsirilos (*Veronica Cohen*), Fred Strother (*Bill*), Anthony Cortino (*Male Clerk*), Betsy Mazursky (*Bloomingdale's Manager*), Kaity Tong (*Herself*), Royce Rich (*Bloomingdale's Cop*), Christopher Wynkoop (*Agent Ross*), Lyman Ward (*Agent Williams*), Joe Lynn (*Mean Man on Subway*), Joy Todd (*Blanche*), Paul Mazursky (*Dave*), Thomas Ikeda (*Korean Cab Driver*), Barbara Montgomery (*Mrs. Marlowe*), Dana Lorge (*Wanda*), Adalberto Santiago (*Latin Band Leader*), Sam Moses (*Dr. Reddy*), Yakov Smirnoff (*Lev*), Sam Stoneburger (*Panama Hat*), Michael Greene (*Texan*), Rosetta Le Noire (*The Judge*), Sal Carollo (*Uncle Sal*), Filomena Spanguolo (*Uncle Sal's Mother*), Annabella Turco (*Uncle Sal's Wife*), George Kelly (*Wild Bill Hawthorne*), Yury Olshansky (*Blozonov*), Jacques Sandulescu (*Truck Driver*), Emil Feist (*Circus Performer*), Vladimir Tukan (*Strong Man*), Mark Rutenberg (*Animal Trainer*), Yury Belov, Igor Panich (*Circus Clowns*), Jurij Gotowtschikow (*Russian Officer*), Sina Kasper, Ken Fitch, Murray Grand, Ann E. Wile, Michael T. Laide, Linda Kerns, Armand Dahan, Jose Rabelo, Jim Goodfriend, Antonia Rey, James Prendergast, Brandon Rey, Paul Davidovsky, Andrei Kramarevsky, Arkady Shabashev, Donald King, David Median, Juanita Mahone, Robert Kasel, Kikue Tashiro, Joyce R. Korbin, Luis Ramos, Kim Chan.

A loving, dramatic comedy that resembles early Frank Capra in the patriotic and sentimental sense. This movie just misses on several levels but there is enough humor to make you smile and enough corn to warm anyone's heart cockles. Williams is a saxophonist with a Russian circus visiting the U.S. on a tour. All of the members of the circus are carefully watched by the KGB agents attached to the troupe, just in case they might

have the feeling that the U.S. would welcome them. Just before leaving New York, Williams is in Manhattan's trendiest department store, Bloomingdale's, when he makes the decision to defect. He races around the store, chased by the KGB men, and hides under a counter womaned by Alonso. After the cops come in and Williams tells them he's defecting, he is taken to Harlem by security guard Derricks and welcomed by his black family. It isn't long before Williams and Alonso are an item and she tries to help him get official status in the U.S. through immigration attorney Rey (he's excellent in this role and should get several other parts due to his portrayal). Just as Williams saw the U.S. with "new eyes" when he played an alien in the TV show "Mork and Mindy," the same holds true here, but since we saw it all before in the TV show, much of the freshness is lost. There is the expected comparison between life in these United States and life in Russia, and Williams is believable as he actually speaks Russian in the film. In the end, he winds up playing saxophone at the International Club in Brighton Beach, a Russian enclave in New York. That scene was actually shot at the International, which is on Brighton Beach Avenue. There is no great story to speak or write of, just the adjustments Williams has to make to become an American. Williams has yet to have his energy accurately captured on screen. He's made a series of bombs (as of 1986), although this may have been the best of the lot because he didn't have to play a cartoon character and could show his acting range. Another problem is that there are several times when gratuitous four-letter words are used and this removes many of Williams' fans from the theaters because of the "R" rating. Director Mazursky makes a cameo appearance, as he usually does, in the role of Dave. Russian comedian Yakov Smirnoff does a small bit. Smirnoff was one of the thousands who were made citizens in the Statue of Liberty ceremonies of July, 1986. The depiction of the Russians is a bit grotesque in keeping with the nature of the country's sentiments in 1984, when millions were flocking to see pro-American action films.

p&d, Paul Mazursky; w, Mazursky, Leon Capetanos; ph, Don McAlpine (Metrocolor); m, David McHugh; ed, Richard Halsey; prod d, Pato Guzman; art d, Michael Molly, Peter Rothe; set d, Steven Jordan; cos, Albert Wolsky; m/l, "People Up in Texas," Waylon Jennings; "Suenos," "Long Day," "Freedom," McHugh.

Comedy/Drama   **Cas.**   **(PR:C-O   MPAA:R)**

MUPPETS TAKE MANHATTAN, THE*½   (1984) 94m Tri-Star c

Steve Burnett, Mary Lou Harris (*College Students*), Cheryl McFadden (*Mr. Price's Secretary*), Joanne Hamlin (*Woman in Price's Office*), Hector Troy, Norman Bush (*Cops*), Nancy Kirsch (*Screaming Woman*), Alice Spivak (*Customer in Pete's*), John Bentley (*Train Conductor*), Dorothy Baxter, Stephen Sherrard Hicks, Susan Miller-Kovens, John Maguire, Sinead MaGuire, Trish Noel (*Elevator Passengers*), Ron Foster, Michael Hirsch (*Men in Winesop's Office*), Vic Polizos, Kenneth MacGregor, Chet Washington (*Construction Workers*), Graham Brown (*Mr. Wrightson*), James Bryson, Chico Kasinoir (*Customers in Pete's*), Viola Borden (*Bingo Caller*), Paul Stolarsky (*Aquacade Announcer*), Maree Dow (*Woman in Bleachers*), Don Quigley (*Man in Bleachers*), Michael Connolly (*Maitre d' at Sardi's*), Wade Barnes (*Customer at Sardi's*), Ruth Button, Lee-Ann Carr, Richard DuBois, Diana Hayes, Jane Hunt, Harriet Rawlings, Milton Seaman (*Customers*), Jacqueline Page (*Stunts*), Gary Tacon (*Thief in Central Park*), Christa Tomasulo, Cheryl Blackman, Denise Lucadamo (*Miss Piggy Stunt Doubles*), Joe Jamrog (*Cop in Central Park*), Mark Marrone (*Chauffeur*), Cyril Jenkins (*The Minister*), Jim Henson (*Kermit/Rowlf/Dr. Teeth/Swedish Chef, Waldorf*), Frank Oz (*Miss Piggy/Fozzie/Animal*), Dave Goelz (*Gonzo/Chester/Rat/Bill/Zoot*), Steve Whitmire (*Rizzo the Rat/Gil*), Richard Hunt (*Scooter/Janice/Statler*), Jerry Nelson (*Camilla/Lew Zealand/Floyd*), Karen Prell (*Yolanda*), Kathryn Mullen (*Jill*), Brian Muehl (*Tatooey Rat*), Bruce Edward Hall (*Masterson/Beth*), Juliana Donald (*Jenny*), Lonny Price (*Ronnie*), Louis Zorich (*Pete*), Art Carney, James Coco, Dabney Coleman, Gregory Hines, Linda Lavin, Joan Rivers, Elliott Gould, Liza Minnelli, Brooke Shields, Francis Bergen, Mayor Edward I. Koch, John Landis, Vincent Sardi.

The third time was not the charm for the Muppets. Following the successes of THE MUPPET MOVIE and THE GREAT MUPPET CAPER, this was something of a disappointment, mostly due to the script by director Oz and TV veterans Patchett and Tarses. The premise was hoary years ago and is essentially "let's find a barn, get some kids together, and put on a show." Except that this time the kids are a frog, a chicken, a pig, and other assorted creations by executive producer and Muppet master Henson. The barn is Broadway and the story is just what one might expect. Kermit (voiced by Henson) and the gang are presenting a senior show called "Manhattan Melodies" at Danhurst College and they feel that the show is good enough to take to New York. The entire cast moves off to conquer the Big Apple. The doors of all the reputable producers are sealed tightly, and they wind up in the office of Coleman, an offensive, nasty producer who says that he'll be happy to take the Muppets under his protective wing if they are willing to kick in $300 each. They are downtrodden and break up, with several cliched situations taking place, like Kermit's amnesia. They all go off in different directions to raise money for their show and Kermit gets a job at an ad agency run by frogs with rhyming names (judging by some of the commercials coming out of Madison Avenue, this may be truer than we realize). A few funny scenes dot the dullness such as the one where Miss Piggy (voiced by Oz) meets cosmetic salesperson Rivers who gives her a set of eyebrows. Eventually, they meet Price, a young producer with talent and taste, and they get to put on their show. Along the way they meet Minnelli, Gould, Carney, Hines, Coco, and even Mayor Koch. In for a brief cameo is director John Landis, who was charged with negligence in the deaths of Vic Morrow and two youngsters while filming TWILIGHT ZONE THE MOVIE (1983). Whereas the charm of the Muppets had always been the adult fashion in which these creatures treated life, this script aims for the preteen market and falls below it. Gone is the hipness, the wit, the joy. Instead, we have effects and trite words in the mouths of the Muppets. Poking fun at show business has to be handled with extra care because so many in the audience cannot identify with the satire. Such was the situation here. The most fun to be had was in seeing all the large stars who make small appearances. Also included in that cadre were Linda Lavin, Brooke Shields, famed restaurateur Vincent Sardi, and Edgar's widow, Frances Bergen. The movie owes much to BABES ON BROADWAY and BABES IN ARMS, but if they were going to take the plots of those they should have paid more attention to motivation. Director Oz has talent and will show it as soon as he gets a better script with which to work, although he is one- third guilty for this one. The songs by Jeff Moss were mostly forgettable except for "Together Again" (sung by Kermit- Henson).

p, David Lazer; d, Frank Oz; w, Oz, Tom Patchett, Jay Tarses (based on a story by Patchett, Tarses); ph, Robert Paynter (Technicolor, Metrocolor); m, Ralph Burns; ed, Evan Lottman; prod d, Stephen Hendrickson; art d, W. Stephen Graham, Paul Eds; set d, Robert Drumheller, Justin Scoppa, Jr.; cos, Karen Roston, Calista Henrickson, Polly Smith; spec eff, Ed Drohan; ch, Chris Chadman; m/l, Jeff Moss; muppet d, Caroly Wilcox.

Comedy   **Cas.**   **(PR:AAA MPAA:G)**

MY BEST FRIEND'S GIRL**   (1984, Fr.) 99m Renn-Sara/European International c (LA FEMME DE MON POTE)

Coluche (Micky), Isabelle Huppert (Vivane), Thierry Lhermitte (Pascal), Farid Chopel (Hoodlum), Francois Perrot (Doctor), Daniel Colas (Flirt), Frederique Michot.

An unimpressive French sex comedy which stars Huppert in the title role--a perky woman who hops from bed to bed with little regard for morality. She enters the lives of Coluche and Lhermitte, old friends who work together at a ski resort in Courcheval. Huppert doesn't play favorites and willingly sleeps with both men, nearly destroying the friendship. While all three performances are enchanting, especially Huppert's daring portrayal, the film is never much more than a burlesque. (In French; English subtitles.)

p, Alain Sarde; d, Bertrand Blier; w, Blier, Gerard Brach; ph, Jean Penzer (Eastmancolor); m, J.J. Cale; ed, Claudine Merlin; set d, Theo Meurisse; cos, Michele Cerf.

Comedy   **(PR:O MPAA:NR)**

MY KIND OF TOWN**½**   (1984, Can.) 76m Milltown/Petra c

Peter Smith (Peter Hall), John Cooper (Sam the Mayor), Martina Schleisser (Astrid Heim), Michael Paul (Michael Hall), Michael Marks (Brad), Roy Evarts (Uncle Roy), Frank Irvine (Frank Hall), Haida Paul (Margaret Hall).

In a small Vancouver Island town the local population suffers from an unemployment problem due to a lengthy economic recession. Smith plays a young man confused by the frustrations of both his unemployed father and his own hopes. Schleisser is a West German photojournnalist who comes to the island town and engages in an affair with Smith. When the young man is caught committing vandalism he is arrested and assigned to do compulsory work for the community. An often-charming film, this is an accurate portrait of small-town life that rarely lags. The script accurately captures the rhythms and day-to-day life of a Canadian province town. Director Wilkinson had previously shot a documentary, THE LITTLE TOWN THAT DID, in the same area and shows a good feel for the people he is dealing with. The characters and their relationships are believable, shot in a semi-documentary style that heightens the realism. Shot in 16mm, but well photographed and edited.

d&w, Charles Wilkinson; ph, David Geddes; m, Wilkinson; ed, Frank Irvine.

Drama   **(PR:A MPAA:NR)**

MY NEW PARTNER**½**   (1984, Fr.) 107m Film 7/Orion c (LES RIPOUX)

Philippe Noiret (Rene), Thierry Lhermitte (Francois), Regine (Simone), Grace de Capitani (Natacha), Julien Guiomar (Commissioner Bloret), Claude Brosset (Inspector Vidal), Albert Simono (Inspector Leblanc), Bernard Bilaoul (Camoun), Pierre Frag (Pierrot), Jacques Santi (Inspector del'I.G.S.).

A standard police comedy-drama which was such a crowd-pleaser in France that it walked away with the Cesar for Best Picture and Best Director. All the awards in the world, however, won't save MY NEW PARTNER from being anything but run-of-the-mill. The story concerns Noiret, a disheveled plainclothes policeman who has long ago thrown away the rule book. With the majority of his income from bribes, he lives comfortably with a former prostitute and relaxes by playing the horses. A wrench is thrown into

Noiret's game when he is assigned a new partner–Lhermitte, a rookie cop who knows all the rules. It's not long before Noiret has corrupted his partner by fixing him up with a lovely callgirl who quickly depletes his pocketbook with her expensive tastes. When Lhermitte's meager police salary can no longer satisfy his sweetheart's desire, he begins to follow in Noiret's bribing, freeloading footsteps. Lhermitte's morals now totally twisted, he comes up with a scheme to pocket the profits of a $1 million drug bust. The success of MY NEW PARTNER comes not from the story but from the chemistry between Noiret and Lhermitte. Noiret, who has proven his talents in such films as the excellent COUP DE TORCHON (1981), again makes it clear that he is one of France's finest actors. This otherwise unchallenging, hackneyed comedy must be seen solely for his performance. (In French; English subtitles.)

p&d, Claude Zidi; w, Zidi, Didier Kaminka (based on a story idea by Simon Mickael); ph, Jean-Jacques Tarbes (Eastmancolor); m, Francis Lai; ed, Nicole Saulnier; art d, Francoise de Leu; cos, Olga Pelletier; makeup, Jean-Eric Pierre.

Comedy/Crime Drama   **Cas.**   **(PR:O MPAA:R)**

MYSTERY MANSION**   (1984) 95m Pacific International c

Dallas McKennon (Sam), Greg Wynne (Gene), Jane Ferguson (Mary), Randi Brown (Susan), Lindsay Bishop (Billy), David Wagner (Johnny), Barry Hostetler (Fred), Joseph D. Savery (Willy).

Three plucky kids get involved with a one hundred-year-old mystery that leads them to a search for a cache of gold. Adventure that's strictly for juvenile audiences.

p, Arthur R. Dubs; d, David E. Jackson; w, Jack Duggan, Arn Wihtol, Jackson; ph, Milas C. Hinshaw (CFI Color); m, William Loose, Jack K. Tillar, Marty Wereski; ed, Stephen Johnson.

Children   **(PR:C MPAA:PG)**

NADIA**   (1984, U.S./Yugo.) 100m Dave Bell-Tribune-Jadran/Tribune-Cori c

Talia Balsam, Jonathan Banks, Joe Bennett, Simone Blue, Johann Carlo, Conchata Ferrell, Carrie Snodgress, Carl Strano, Karrie Ullman, Leslie Weiner, Sonja Kereskenji, Pat Starr, Gregory Cooke, Geza Poszar, Vjenceslav Kapural, Tom Vukusic, Bozo Smiljanic, Gheorghe Berechet.

With the world's eyes focused on the Olympics every four years, one can only wonder what goes through the minds of the teenaged competitors who dominate the women's gymnastics events. To reach one's peak at age 14 is an overwhelming emotional feeling that can be severely damaging as the years pass. In 1976, Nadia Comaneci astounded the world with her perfect Olympic scores of 10 points, the first time this had ever happened. This film tells her post-Olympic story and it is not a happy one. Nadia's international fame causes several domestic problems leading her mother (Snodgress) to dissolve her marriage in fights over how to raise Rumania's heroine. Further problems arise when the Communist Party decides to change her coach, then her gymnastic partner leaves in her jealousy over Nadia's success. As these events begin taking their toll on the girl's psyche the gold medalist escapes through overeating. She puts on weight, which of course affects her abilities, then in a moment of loneliness drinks some bleach. Eventually Nadia is able to overcome her personal burdens to make a near-perfect comeback in a Fort Worth, Texas, competition, then retires before reaching her 22nd birthday. This real-life drama certainly has enough potential to say a few things about the nature of hero-worship in the modern era but unfortunately is told in a simplistic, straightforward manner. The story is reduced to formula filmmaking complete with a pat happy ending. Despite good performances by the cast, this is no better than the average made-for-television movie. Despite its Rumanian setting, the picture was shot in Yugoslavia.

p, James E. Thompson; d, Alan Cooke; w, Jim McGinn (based on a story by McGinn); ph, Frank Beascoechea (Foto-Kem Color); m, Christopher L. Stone (performed by Zagreb Studio Orchestra); ed, Raymond Bridgers; prod d, George Becket; art d, Zeljko Senecic.

Drama   **Cas.**   **(PR:C MPAA:NR)**

NAGOOA   (SEE: DRIFTING, Israel)

NAKED FACE, THE**½**   (1984) 103m Cannon c

Roger Moore (Dr. Judd Stevens), Rod Steiger (Lt. McGreavy), Elliott Gould (Angeli), Art Carney (Morgens), Anne Archer (Ann Blake), David Hedison (Dr. Hadley), Deanna Dunagan (Mrs. Hadley), Ron Parady (Cortini).

When Oscar-winning screenwriter Sidney Sheldon turned to writing novels, he became immensely wealthy and successful. Sheldon took his statuette at the age of 30 for THE BACHELOR AND THE BOBBY- SOXER, then turned his attentions to TV and created "I Dream of Jeannie." This film was from the first novel he wrote, though not the first one released. Moore, in a deliberate attempt to move away from the James Bond image, is a mild-mannered Chicago psychiatrist. (We know his manners are mild because he wears eyeglasses and underplays.) His wife has just died and he is mourning her loss, making regular visits to pay his respects at the cemetery. One of his patients is Archer, an attractive matron, but her problems are vague and Moore doesn't seem able to understand why she's coming to see him. Archer is, in reality, the wife of crime boss Parady and she can't handle being a Mafia Princess. Then Moore begins having other problems. One of his patients is murdered, his secretary is killed, and there have been threats on his life. Policeman Steiger doesn't believe Moore about the threats and thinks the doctor may be behind the murders and the threats. The reason for Steiger's disbelief is that Moore had once testified in a court case concerning the death of a colleague of Steiger's and when the criminal was not sent to execution, Steiger never forgave the psychiatrist's "expert" testimony. Steiger is seething most of the time, as contrasted with his new partner, Gould, who seems like a regular guy with more than a little compassion. Steiger is taken off the case and Gould gets the assignment, doing his best to help discover the truth of the situation. The answer comes when we learn that Archer's husband, Parady, fears that she has been telling "family" secrets to the analyst. She hasn't been doing that but Parady doesn't believe it. Gould is in the employ of the mobster and delivers Moore to the palatial suburban home where Parady and his hoods interrogate Moore. Not satisfied with his innocent answers, they decide to kill him and take him to Parady's garbage processing plant where he will be crushed, mangled, and turned into fill. Naturally, it doesn't work out that way. Parady beats Moore to a pulp, then turns on Gould, whose usefulness is now over. Gould is tossed into the mangler to die and Moore's life is saved when Steiger arrives with a cadre of police. Along the way, there is a neat cameo by Carney, an eccentric private eye who surrounds himself with all sorts of timepieces. Carney is engaged by Moore to protect him but what he mostly does is provide whatever humor there is in the picture. Moore goes to visit his wife's grave in the final scene and is joined by Archer. Her husband is now in jail and she is, at last, safe. Then, an unknown sniper's bullet cracks across the tranquility and Archer is killed in the final scene. A rare movie for director-screenwriter Forbes, who had been doing this for a quarter of a century, in that he could not find a part for his wife, Nannette Newman, who usually appears in his pictures. Lots of talk, little action, and a very cliched depiction of the Mafia chieftain. Policeman Steiger's tense rage was reminiscent of Kirk Douglas in DETECTIVE STORY.

p, Menahem Golan, Yoram Globus; d, Bryan Forbes; w, Forbes (based on the novel by Sidney Sheldon); ph, David Gurfinkel (Metrocolor); m, Michael J. Lewis; ed, Philip Shaw; prod d, William Fosser.

Crime Drama   Cas.   (PR:C MPAA:R)

NAPLO GYERMEKEIMNEK   (SEE: DIARY FOR MY CHILDREN, Hung.)

NATURAL, THE***   (1984) 134m Natural/Tri-Star c

Robert Redford (Roy Hobbs), Robert Duvall (Max Mercy), Glenn Close (Iris), Kim Basinger (Memo Paris), Wilford Brimley (Pop Fisher), Barbara Hershey (Harriet Bird), Robert Prosky (The Judge), Darren McGavin (Unbilled Role), Richard Farnsworth (Red Blow), Joe Don Baker (The Whammer), John Finnegan (Sam Simpson), Alan Fudge (Ed Hobbs), Paul Sullivan (Young Roy), Rachel Hall (Young Iris), Robert Rich III (Teb Hobbs), Michael Madsen (Bump Bailey), Jon Van Ness (John Olsen), Mickey Treanor (Doc Dizzy), George Wilkosz (Bobby Savoy), Anthony J. Ferrera (Coach Wilson), Philip Mankowski (Hank Benz), Danny Aiello III (Emil LaJong), Joe Castellano (Allie Stubbs), Eddie Cipot (Gabby Laslow), Ken Grassano (Al Fowler), Robert Kalaf (Cal Baker), Barry Kivel (Pat McGee), Steven Kronovet (Tommy Hinkle), James Meyer (Dutch Schultz), Michael Starr (Boone), Sam Green (Murphy), Martin Grey, Joseph Mosso, Richard Oliveri, Lawrence Couzens, Duke McGuire, Stephen Poliachik, Kevin Lester, Joseph Charboneau, Robert Rudnick, Ken Kamholz (Knights), Sibby Sisti (Pirates Manager), Phillip D. Rosenberg (Pitcher Youngberry), Christopher B. Rehbaum (Pitcher John Rhoades), Nicholas Koleff (Umpire Augie), Jerry Stockman (Umpire Babe), James Quamo (Memorial Game Umpire), Joseph Strand (Home Plate Umpire at Final Game), Buffalo Swing (Night Club Band).

This is one of the few sports films which projects with understanding the mythical qualities that Americans associate with baseball, yet paradoxically carries this imagery beyond reasonable boundaries. The film opens as Redford is about to try out for the major leagues, a 19-year-old hotshot, "the best that ever was." He surprises sportswriter Duvall by his ability to strike out Baker, a Babe Ruth type, on three straight pitches, with blazing throws unprecedented in the game. Redford seems headed for a great career but his dreams are destroyed when Hershey–a beautiful, enigmatic woman–shoots him in his hotel room. Fifteen years pass, and Redford shows up at the clubhouse of the New York Knights, a major league team with one of the worst win-loss records in all baseball. Brimley, the Knights' curmudgeonly manager, is initially reluctant to take on a 34- year-old rookie, but Redford is finally given a chance when another player kills himself by running into a wall. Redford surprises everyone by literally knocking the cover off the ball his first time at bat, and is soon rallying his team toward a victorious season. Prosky, the team's shady owner, stands to make a lot of money if the Knights lose, so he sends Basinger, a classic femme-fatale, to get her hooks into Redford. She begins an affair with the star player, and Redford soon goes into a slump. The Knights fall in the standings, but while playing in Chicago, Redford spies Close, his old girl friend from childhood, sitting in

the stands. Soon he is back on track and Prosky must seek another way to destroy the team. Eventually he has Redford poisoned at a party, which puts the star in the hospital right before a crucial game. Redford's old gunshot wound begins affecting him, and doctors tell him if he plays, it could kill him. Despite this danger, Redford suits up. When the game is in the final inning, Redford takes his turn at the plate, determined to hit a game-winning home run. His stomach is bleeding through his uniform, and he is in great pain. Redford hits a foul ball, breaking "Wonderboy," the only bat he has owned since childhood. The batboy gives Redford a new bat, one the star player had made especially for the boy. With this in hand, Redford slams the next pitch into the stadium lights, setting off an enormous fireworks display that triumphantly heralds the greatest home run in the history of the game. Redford does not die, and is reunited with Close and their illegitimate son, whom he had fathered years before. THE NATURAL is at its best when portraying action on the field. Director Levinson accurately captures the tension between each pitch, using closeups of pitcher, ball, and batter, editing shots with precision to draw out suspense. In doing so, he captures the poetry inherent in baseball, a game that, unlike any other sport, is deeply embedded in the American consciousness. Redford's preeminent home run–a dazzling display of light, backed by Newman's wonderfully evocative score–is a gem of a sequence, the dream long-ball that every baseball fan envisions his favorite player smacking. THE NATURAL, unfortunately, is not nearly as good when it leaves the ball park. Though Redford gives a solid performance, he is too old for the part, and completely unbelievable as a 19-year-old whiz kid. Levinson tries too hard to canonize his star, constantly lighting his head with a distracting halo. Redford brings enough to the role without needing any fancy cinematic effects to enhance his characterization. The dreamy ending, with Redford tossing a ball back and forth with his son, is anticlimactic and too treacly for its own good. The scene has the impossible task of topping the greatest home run ever hit by any man, and stylized sentiment is not the answer. (Malamud's original novel had a more honest ending, with Roy Neary dying after his home run.) Though Close and Hershey unfortunately aren't given much to do other than serve as plot motivations, the rest of the supporting cast is fine, particularly Brimley's wonderful characterization. The baseball sequences were shot in the Buffalo, New York, War Memorial Stadium, a minor league park built in the 1930s, perfect for THE NATURAL's 1939 setting. Though the uniforms and gloves were designed from period photographs, the production ran into some difficulty filling the stadium with 10,000 extras all dressed in 1930s garb. To field a team of actors who looked like professional ballplayers, the filmmakers ran drills testing the hitting, pitching, and fielding skills of all auditionees. Strangely, though McGavin had a major role in the feature, he received no billing in either the film's credits or press material.

p, Mark Johnson; d, Barry Levinson; w, Roger Towne, Phil Dusenberry (based on the novel by Bernard Malamud); ph, Caleb Deschanel (Technicolor); m, Randy Newman; ed, Stu Linder; prod d, Angelo Graham, Mel Bourne; art d, James J. Murakami, Speed Hopkins; set d, Bruce Weintraub; cos, Bernie Pollack, Gloria Gresham; spec eff, Roger Hensen; tech adv, Gene Kirby.

Sports   Cas.   (PR:C MPAA:PG)

NEMO   (SEE: DREAM ONE, Brit./Fr.)

NEVERENDING STORY, THE***½   (1984, Ger.) 94m Neve Constantin Filmproduktion- Bavaria-WDR/WB c

Barret Oliver (Bastian), Gerald McRaney (Bastian's Father), Drum Garrett, Darryl Cooksey, Nicholas Gilbert (Bullies), Thomas Hill (Koreander), Deep Roy (Teeny Weeny), Tilo Pruckner (Night Hob), Moses Gunn (Cairon), Noah Hathaway (Atreyu), Alan Oppenheimer (Folkor's Voice), Sydney Bromley (Engywook), Patricia Hayes (Urgl), Tami Stronach (The Childlike Empress).

Only a certified grump could dislike this engaging fantasy that wends its way into the imagination and is a delight on most levels. The phrase "nothing can harm you" takes on new meaning in the film because "nothing" is exactly what is feared in the story. Oliver is a young lad who has just lost his mother. He lives in an unnamed town in the U.S. (it was actually shot in Canada) with his father, McRaney, who likes to lecture Oliver about the boy's penchant for daydreaming. McRaney feels that Oliver has to bone up on his school work and make his way into the real world, rather than spending too much time woolgathering. The boy is troubled, has to fend off school bullies, and is having difficulty adjusting to being motherless. One day, instead of going to school, he wanders into a weird bookstore, borrows a volume, and goes up to the school's attic to read it. The book is called The Neverending Story (which was the title of the book from whence the film was drawn). As Oliver turns the book's pages, the story comes to life. Stronach is a childlike empress who is young and not physically well. She lives in a land called "Fantasia" (was this a tribute to Disney?) and fears that it will be taken over if she dies. So she sends Hathaway, a young warrior, off on a hegira to find a cure for her lingering illness. What menaces Fantasia is a plague of "nothing" which is generated by the dreams and imaginations of all the people on Earth. When the inhabitants of Earth lose hope and forget their aspirations, Fantasia is due to crumble as a direct result. Hathaway's voyage is fraught with peril. The tranquility of Fantasia (where there is a

"Sea of Possibilities," a "Swamp of Sadness," and the princess lives in an "Ivory Tower") is nothing like what he must face. He meets a cast of fantastic characters like the "Flying Luck Dragon" (the cuddliest creature to come along in years), he must pass through forbidding gates guarded by mammoth stone sphinxes, he has to deal with a swamp-dwelling turtlelike creature, and encounters a little man who spends his time riding the shell of a "racing snail." Oliver is so enthralled by the story that he is plunged into it as a character. Hathaway comes home from his journey realizing that the only way Fantasia can be saved from the destruction is if an Earth child can step forward and rename the kingdom. Oliver fills that bill perfectly. The film ends as the entire kingdom is reduced to a single grain of sand in Stronach's hand and Oliver is given unlimited wishes and the ability to recreate Fantasia from his own imagination. Made on a huge budget of more than $27 million, it was shot mostly in Germany at studios in Munich. The special effects were by some of the same people who worked on THE EMPIRE STRIKES BACK, ALIEN, RAIDERS OF THE LOST ARK, and other films and they are all state- of-the-art examples of puppetry, animation, opticals, and makeup. Adding the human actors and using them against the animation, through the diligent work of the people who manned the mattes and blue screens, was a marvel and made the fantasy all the more believable. THE NEVERENDING STORY far surpasses earlier attempts to this genre like OZ, THE BLACK CAULDRON, and THE DARK CRYSTAL. It owes much to ALICE IN WONDERLAND and THE DAY THE EARTH STOOD STILL in some of the sequences, but director Petersen (who was responsible for DAS BOOT) showed that he knew how to combine all the elements into a charming film that is excellent for children and won't put any adults to sleep. It's rated "PG" because some of the sequences might be frightening to very small ones. The picture was a hit in Europe but not nearly as popular in the U.S., perhaps due to improper marketing.

p, Bernd Eichinger, Dieter Geissler; d, Wolfgang Petersen; w, Petersen, Herman Weigel (based on the novel by Michael Ende); ph, Jost Vacano (Technivision, Technicolor); m, Klaus Doldinger, Giorgio Moroder; ed, Jane Seitz; prod d, Rolf Zehetbauer; art d, Gotz Weidner, Herbert Strabel, Johann Iwan Kot; set d, Zehetbauer; cos, Diemut Remy; spec eff, Brian Johnson; m/l "The Neverending Story," Moroder, Keith Forsey; stunts, Tony Smart; makeup Colin Arthur; animation, Steve Archer.

Fantasy   Cas.   (PR:C MPAA:PG)

NEW YORK NIGHTS*   (1984) 102m International Talent Marketing/Bedford Entertainment c

Corinne Alphen (Brooke the Debutante), George Ayer (Jesse the Rock Star), Bobbi Burns (Leonora Woolf the author), Peter Matthey (Werner Richards the Photographer), Missy O'Shea (Christina, Model/Wife), Nicholas Cortland (Harris the Husband), Marcia McBroom (Nicki the Prostitute), Cynthia Lee (Margo the Porno Star), William Dysart (Owen the Financier), Tamara Jones (Young Model), Thomas Happer (Gigolo), Michael Medeiros (Foster the Porno Director), Willem Dafoe (Punk Boy friend), Gordon Press (Chauffeur).

Spawned from the same play (Arthur Schnitzler's "Reigen") as Max Ophul's cunningly witty and gracefully charming LA RONDE (1950), Vanderbes and Nuchtern threw away all the substance to create this wretched, boring depiction of the seedy side of Manhattan night life. The film has a similar episodic structure as LA RONDE- a chain of sexual liaisons is created with one character from each episode moving onto a new affair that eventually evolves into an overlapping chain. There are nine such episodes, each as trite and uninteresting as its predecessor. The one bright spot in this picture is the appearance of McBroom as a compromising prostitute. Hers is the only performance which could even slightly be considered as acting. NEW YORK NIGHTS was made in 1981, but legal problems delayed its release for three years–a delay which wasn't nearly long enough.

p, Romano Vanderbes; d, Simon Nuchtern; w, Vanderbes (based on the play "Reigen" by Arthur Schnitzler, uncredited); ph, Alan Doberman (Technicolor);

m, Linda Schreyer; ed, Victor Zimet; art d, Frank Boros, Patrick Mann; m, Linda Schreyer; ed, Victor Zimet; art d, Frank Boros, Patrick Mann; cos, Donna Williams; m/l, Schreyer, Rod Stewart, Peter Newland, Dave Immer, Tom Bernfield.

Drama   Cas.   (PR:O MPAA:R)

NIGHT OF THE COMET*½**   (1984) 95m Atlantic 9000/Atlantic c

Robert Beltran (Hector), Catherine Mary Stewart (Regina), Kelli Maroney (Samantha), Sharon Farrell (Doris), Mary Woronov (Audrey), Geoffrey Lewis (Carter), John Achorn (Oscar), Michael Bowen (Larry), Ivan Roth (Willy), Raymond Lynch (Chuck), Janice Kawaye (Sarah), Chance Boyer (Brian), Bob Perlow (News Reporter), Peter Fox (Wilson), Devon Erickson (Minder), Lissa Layng (Davenport), Andrew Boyer (Rogers), Stanley Brock (Mel), Marc Poppel (DMK), John Stuart West (Monster Cop), Alex Brown (Monster in Alley), Dick Rude, Chris Pederson (Stock Boys), Karl Johnson (Guard No. 1), Joel Levine (Guard No. 2), Wilson Camp Anna Mathias, Tim

Hannon (Party Guests), Bobby Porter (Monster Kid), Steve LeBeau (Voice of Deejay), Michael Hanks (Narrator), Chris Chesser (Radio Spot Announcer), Dale House (Helicopter Pilot).

A comet is approaching the Earth and all over California people are celebrating, even though, as the narrator points out, the last time the comet passed was coincidental with the overnight extinction of the dinosaurs. Sisters Stewart and Maroney for different reasons spend the night in steel-lined rooms and when they come out in the morning all they can find of humanity are piles of empty clothes and some fine red dust. It takes them a while to find each other and realize what has happened, which, in addition to the evaporation of those taking the full effects of the comet's rays, includes turning into flesh-eating zombies those only partly exposed. Together they make their way to a radio station that is still on the air, but when they arrive all they find is an automated tape. They soon discover another survivor, Beltran, likewise attracted to the radio station, and the sisters squabble over him, Maroney accusing Stewart of stealing every boy friend she ever had and of now stealing the last boy on Earth. Beltran leaves to search for his family while the girls go down to the local armory to pick up some submachine guns (their father, a Green Beret training soldiers in Central America, taught them how to use them). Armed to the teeth they realize what awaits them in the abandoned city--the ultimate shopping spree. They joyously ransack the department stores and boutiques until they are captured by punked-out zombie stockboys. Soldiers from a secret government agency rescue the girls and kidnap Maroney, planning to drain her immune blood to save their own lives (they had anticipated the comet's effects and locked themselves in an underground base, but someone left a vent open so all are slowly succumbing to the comet's effects). Stewart finds Beltran and together they rescue Maroney from the desert research base to which she's been taken. As the film ends, Beltran, Stewart, Maroney, and two children they found are dressed and acting like a respectable middle-class family, though Maroney is still unhappy over losing Beltran. Suddenly a Mercedes convertible with a handsome young man roars up to the group and stops. He asks Maroney if she wants to go for a ride and she happily hops in. A terrifically witty, refreshingly unpretentious science fiction film with the least likely and most likable heroines in memory, conspicuously consuming Valley girls who know how to handle a submachine gun (when they practice by shooting up a Cadillac, Maroney's gun jams. "That's the problem with these things," she says in disgust. "Daddy would have gotten us Uzis.") All the performers are excellent, especially Maroney, who can veer from petulant to heroic in the blink of an eye. Cult movie heroine Woronov, as a scientist who decides it's wrong to steal Maroney's blood, has a relatively small role, but she's always a joy to find in any film. Lost in the shuffle of bloated big, budget science fiction epics released at the same time (DUNE, 2010), the film received almost universally favorable reviews but failed to find an audience.

p, Andrew Lane, Wayne Crawford; d&w, Thom Eberhardt; ph, Arthur Albert; m, David Campbell; ed, Fred Stafford; md, Don Perry; prod d, John Muto; set d, David Wasco; spec eff, Court Wizard; makeup, David B. Miller.

Science Fiction   Cas.   (PR:C-O MPAA:PG-13)

NIGHT PATROL zero   (1984) 82 m NW c

Linda Blair (Sue), Pat Paulsen (Kent), Jaye P. Morgan (Kate), Jack Riely (Dr. Ziegler), Billy Barty (Capt. Lewis), Murray Langston (Melvin/Unknown Comic), Pat Morita (Rape Victim), Sidney Lassick (Peeping Tom), Kent Perkins (Tex), Lori Sutton (Edith), Roxanne Cybelle (Kicking Girl), Joe Battaglia (Bum), Mik One (Press Agent), Alex Polks (Leroy's Bartender), Patrie Allen (Officer Judie), Bob Biggert ("Motherforking" Cop), Brad Biggart (Punk Busboy), Frances Natividad (Big Bust), Michael Crabtree (Attorney), John Hazelwood (Santa/Big Prisoner), Vic Dunlap (Crazy Man), Kip Waldo (Gross Waiter), Dan Taylor (Bar Owner), Greg Wolf (Hippie), Jody Miller (Waitress), Robert Kline (Bombing Comic).

This police comedy does the impossible. It makes POLICE ACADEMY look like a piece of sophisticated humor. With the success of that previous witless outing, it was only a matter of time before the cheap imitations were churned out. New World Pictures wasted no time tossing out this slapdash job, a homage to bad taste and has-been/never-ere talents. For what it's worth (and that's not saying much) the "plot" has Langston playing a meek-mannered cop bullied by his captain, Barty, everybody's favorite movie midget. Langston isn't satisfied being a lawman, he also wants to be a stand-up comedian. In order to keep his identity a secret Langston puts a paper bag over his head when he performs and gets Morgan as his manager. This marks a cinematic reuniting of the two, for the pair had previously worked together on the utterly jejune television program "The Gong Show." Morgan had been a "judge" for the strangely gifted performers on the show while Langston achieved a sort of cult status wearing the paper bag on his head as "The Unknown Comic." The switch to a larger medium is a success for both: they still display an unbelievable amount of chutzpah that substitutes for talent. Eventually a crook discovers Langston's dual identity and takes to committing crimes wearing a similar paper bag. Strung onto this clothesline plot are scattershot gags, most of which are beyond the realm of sheer stupidity. NIGHT PATROL resorts to racist and homophobic humor, along with plenty of bodily function jokes. Blair, whose film career can be divided between THE EXORCIST and garbage, displays her to-heavy physical attributes as Langston's love interest, along with her decidedly limited acting ability. "Laugh-In" refugee Paulsen also sticks in his basset eyes every now and then as Langston's patrol partner. It's not enough that this film is idiotic, for it's a complete technical disaster to boot. Following the opening credits (in French. Pretty funny, eh?) this shows every sign of incompetence. The photography is awful with a soundtrack that is often inaudible. Of course the argument could always be raised that such problems might actually be the film's only attributes.

p, Bill Osco; Jackie Kong; d, Kong; w, Osco, Kong, Murray Langston, Bill Levey; ph, Jurg Walthers, Hanania Baer; ed, Kong; art d, Jay Burkhardt, Bob Danyla; set d, Barbara Benz, Debbie Madalina; cos, Terry Roop; makeup, Debbie Figuley.

Comedy   **Cas.**   **(PR:O MPAA:R)**

NIGHT SHADOWS*½   (1984) 99m Laurelwood/Film Ventures c (AKA: MUTANT)

Wings Hauser (*Josh*), Bo Hopkins (*Sheriff Will Stewart*), Lee [Harcourt] Montgomery (*Mike*), Jennifer Warren (*Dr. Myra Tate*), Jody Medford (*Holly*), Marc Clement (*Albert*), Cary Guffey (*Billy*), Danny Nelson (*Jack*), Mary Nell Santacroce (*Mrs. Mapes*).

For mavens of the truly silly horror film genre comes this enjoyable item. Hauser and Montgomery are two brothers from the North who find themselves up to their armpits in zombies and rednecks (and sometimes a combination of the two) when they take a trip to rural Georgia. When Montgomery disappears under weird circumstances Hauser enlists the help of local lawman Hopkins and schoolteacher Medford to find his brother. The trail leads them to a group of monsters in bad makeup, walking with the classic movie zombie gait as they terrorize the populace. It's great trashy fun with the cast taking it all quite seriously, which of course only adds to the film's chock-filled unintentional humor. Fans of bygone child stars should note that Montgomery had convincingly emoted to a rat in BEN some 12 years previously. Also in the cast is Guffey, the little boy from CLOSE ENCOUNTERS OF THE THIRD KIND. This originally had been helmed by Mark Rosman but he ha d quickly been replaced by Cardos, who knows how to direct a fight scene with good effect. Not much overall, but enjoyable on its own campy level.

p, Igo Kantor; d, John "Bud" Cardos; w, Peter Z. Orton, Michael Jones, John C. Kruize (based on a story by Jones, Kruize); ph, Al Taylor (TVC Color); m, Richard Band; ed, Michael J. Duthie; spec eff, Paul Stewart; makeup, Eric Fiedler, Louis Lazzara; stunts, Lonnie R. Smith, Jr.

Horror   **Cas.**   **(PR:O MPAA:R)**

NIGHTMARE ON ELM STREET, A*½**
                 (1984) 91M New Line Cinema c

John Saxon (*Lt. Thompson*), Ronee Blakley (*Marge Thompson*), Heather Langenkamp (*Nancy Thompson*), Amanda Wyss (*Tina Gray*), Nick Corri (*Rod Lane*), Johnny Depp (*Glen Lantz*), Charles Fleischer (*Dr. King*), Joseph Whipp (*Sgt. Parker*), Robert Englund (*Fred Krueger*), Lin Shaye (*Teacher*), Joe Unger (*Sgt. Garcia*), Mimi Meyer-Craven (*Nurse*), Jack Shea (*Minister*), Edward Call (*Mr. Lantz*), Sandy Lipton (*Mrs. Lantz*), David Andrews (*Foreman*), Jeffrey Levine (*Coroner*), Donna Woodrum (*Tina's Mom*), Shashawnee Hall, Carol Pritikin, Brian Reise (*Cops*), Jason Adam, Don Hannah (*Surfers*), Leslie Hoffman (*Hallguard*), Paul Grenier (*Tina's Mom's Boy Friend*).

"One, two, Freddy's comin' for you; three, four, better lock your door; five, six, grab your crucifix; seven, eight, gonna stay up late; nine, ten, never sleep again." A NIGHTMARE ON ELM STREET, one of the most intelligent and terrifying horror films in recent years, begins and ends with this haunting children's song. The film opens as a teenage girl, Wyss, clad only in a nightgown, wanders around a maze of leaky pipes in a dark boiler room. A horribly scarred man wearing a ragged slouch hat and a dirty red and green striped sweater stalks her. On his hands he wears crude gloves outfitted with knives at the fingers. He scrapes his metal fingers on the pipes to make a spine tingling screech. Just as we think she may have lost him, the man pops up behind Wyss and grabs her. She wakes up screaming in her bed. It was just a dream. The next morning Wyss learns that her friends Langenkamp and Corri have had the same dream. Afraid to sleep alone the next night, Wyss invites Langenkamp and her boy friend, Depp, to stay over (her mother has gone to Las Vegas with a lover). Corri drops by as well and he and Wyss go to her mother's room to make love. After falling asleep, Wyss has another dream where she is being chased by the man in the hat (Englund). Suddenly Corri wakes up in bed to hear Wyss screaming next to him. He looks under the covers and sees Englund attacking his girl friend. Before he can fight, Corri is knocked clear across the room. Dazed, he watches as Wyss is pulled from the bed by invisible hands and tossed around the room. She finally falls to the bed in a pool of blood. She has been murdered and this time it's no dream. Corri is arrested for the crime and jailed by Langenkamp's father, Saxon, who is the local sheriff. Soon Langenkamp's dream are being invaded by Englund. In a dream she burns her arm on a boiler pipe. When she awakes, her arm has a burn mark on it. Terrified by her nightmares, Langenkamp becomes determined not to fall asleep. That night, Corri's bedsheet wraps around his neck and hangs him. The police assume Corri committed suicide, but Langenkamp begins to suspect that the man in her dreams is real. Still refusing to sleep, she is

taken to dream specialists by her mother, Blakley. During the testing, Langenkamp has a violent nightmare that even shocks the specialists. When they awaken her the doctors are amazed to find her clutching a ragged old hat. She has pulled the killer's hat out of her dream and inside the brim is the name "Fred Krueger." Now convinced that the man in her dreams is real, Langenkamp tries to find out who he is. When confronted by her daughter, Blakley tells her that Fred Krueger (Englund) was a man who had killed nearly 20 children in the neighborhood when Langenkamp was just a child. He took them to a boiler room where he committed his heinous acts. Though he was eventually caught by police, he was freed on a technicality. Seeking justice, Blakley and a group of angry parents tracked Englund to his boiler room hideout and set it ablaze. Englund was burned to death in the fire. After this revelation, Langenkamp becomes convinced that Englund has returned to enact his revenge on the children of the people who killed him by attacking them through their dreams. Soon after, her friend Depp is also attacked and killed in his sleep. Determined to catch the killer and bring him out of her dream, she then phones her father and asks him to come to the house in 20 minutes so that he can capture the killer. Saxon, aware that his daughter has not slept for weeks, humors the girl and tells her to go to sleep. She does and Englund attacks her. After a terrifying chase, she manages to grab the killer just as her alarm clock goes off. When she awakes, Englund is in the room with her. She runs through the house screaming as Englund gives chase. In the basement, Lagenkamp sets Englund on fire and the horrified killer, forced to relive his death, runs upstairs to Blakley's bedroom. By now Saxon has seen the smoke coming from his house and with the help of some of his men, he breaks the door down. Following the flaming footsteps upstairs, Saxon and Langenkamp watch as Englund, engulfed in flames, takes Blakley with him. The pair slowly sink into the bed and disappear into a blue glow. A stunned Saxon leaves Lagenkamp alone in the room for a moment and while he is gone, Englund reappears. Lagenkamp turns her back on Englund and tells him that she wants her friends and mother back. She created him in her dreams and now she has decided to take back all the energy she had given him. Englund disappears. In the morning, all seems normal. Blakley is alive as are Lagenkamp's friends who pull up in a red Cadillac convertible to take her to school. Once she gets inside the car, the windows suddenly roll up and the doors lock them in. The top of the car slams shut. It is painted red and green, just like Englund's sweater. The car cruises away with the screaming teenagers trapped inside. As Blakley stands outside waving goodbye, the gloved hand of Englund breaks through the window and pulls her inside. At the house next door three little girls in white are skipping rope and singing their chilling song. In an era where the horror film has become little more than a mindless exercise in gratuitous high-tech bloodletting, the films of director Wes Craven have brought some hope to those concerned about the fate of the genre. A NIGHTMARE ON ELM STREET intelligently probes into the audiences' fear of nightmares and combines them with another horrific element, the very real fear of killers in one's own neighborhood. Craven understands that prayers ("If I die before I wake") and songs children sing ("Ring Around the Rosy" is a ditty about the Black Plague) are rooted in some terrifying realities. By making Freddy Krueger the result of a deep, dark secret in the neighborhood, the motivation for mayhem is much deeper than in the average slasher film. Though Krueger is a truly horrible villain, his crimes existed in the past. The teenagers' parents are responsible for the resurrection of the terror because they committed an act just as heinous. The teenagers in A NIGHTMARE ON ELM STREET are paying for the sins of their parents; they are not simply fodder for the special effects crew, but have distinct personalities and are independent and intelligent. Langenkamp is not about to cower in the corner and let herself be killed. She fights back. Craven's nightmare world is rooted in reality. He understands that it is the psychological that scares us the most, not simple gore. Half the time the viewer is not sure whether the characters are dreaming, therefore the unease is constant. When the line between nightmare and reality becomes blurred, the terror is almost nonstop. This is a truly scary and disturbing film. Craven manages to tap our fears of being trapped in a nightmare we can't escape from, and manipulates it for all its worth. He knows how to pace a horror film properly by letting the terror build. He pulls the classic Hitchcock trick from PSYCHO by killing off the one the audience assumed was the main character early on. He fills the film with so many imaginative, unexpected ways to terrify, that the viewer is afraid to relax during the lulls in the action. All these savvy technical tricks, combined with the intelligent, thought-provoking premise, resulted in one of the best and most financially successful horror films of the 1980s. See it at your own peril. A sequel, A NIGHTMARE ON ELM STREET PART II – Freddy's REVENGE (1986), while inferior, had some interesting elements as well. Not for children.

p, Robert Shaye, Sara Risher; d&w, Wes Craven; ph, Jacques Haitkin (DeLuxe Color); m, Charles Bernstein; ed, Rick Shaine; prod d, Greg Fonseca; set d, Anne Huntley; cos, Dana Lyman; spec eff, Jim Doyle; makeup, David Miller; m/l, "Nightmare," Martin Kent, Steve Karshner, Michael Schurig.

Horror   **Cas.**   **(PR:O MPAA:R)**

NIGHTSONGS**½   (1984) 116m FN Films c

Mabel Kwong *(Chinese/Vietnamese Woman)*, David Lee *(Fung Tak Men)*, Victor Wong *(Fung Leung)*, Ida F. O. Chung *(Fung Lai Ping)*, Rose Lee *(Fung Mei Fun)*, Roger Chang *(Fung Tak Sing)*, Geoff Lee *(Gang Recruiter)*.

A labor of love for Iranian director Nabili, NIGHTSONGS tells the story of a young Chinese Vietnamese refugee who leaves her family back home to stay with relatives in the U.S. She struggles through a period of adjustment and is barely able to communicate, resorting to a favorite book, "Women Poets Of China," as a means of connecting with people. Filmed largely with Chinese dialog, the film hits home with its targeted audience, but serves only as a cultural reference tool for others. (In Chinese; English subtitles.)

p, Thomas A. Fucci; d&w, Marva Nabili; ph, Ben Davis; m, R. I. P. Hayman; ed, Fritz Liepe.

Drama   **(PR:C   MPAA:NR)**

1984***   (1984, Brit.) 117m Umbrella-Rosenblum-Virgin/Atlantic
                                                          Releasingc

John Hurt *(Winston Smith)*, Richard Burton *(O'Brien)*, Suzanna Hamilton *(Julia)*, Cyril Cusack *(Charrington)*, Gregory Fisher *(Parsons)*, James Walker *(Syme)*, Andrew Wilde *(Tillotson)*, David Trevena *(Tillotson's Friend)*, David Cann *(Martin)*, Anthony Benson *(Jones)*, Peter Frye *(Rutherford)*, Roger Lloyd Pack *(Waiter)*, Rupert Baderman *(Winston as a Boy)*, Corinna Seddon *(Winston's Mother)*, Martha Parsey *(Winston's Sister)*, Merelina Kendall *(Mrs. Parsons)*, P.J. Nicholas *(William Parsons)*, Lynne Radford *(Susan Parsons)*, Pip Donaghy *(Inner Party Speaker)*, Shirley Stelfox *(Whore)*, Janet Key *(Instructress)*, Hugh Walters *(Artsem Lecturer)*, John Hughes *(Man in White Coat)*, Robert Putt *(Shouting Prole)*, Christine Hargreaves *(Soup Lady)*, Garry Cooper, Matthew Scurfield *(Guards)*, John Golightly, Rolf Saxon *(Patrolmen)*, Ole Oldendorp *(Eurasian Soldier)*, Eddie Stacey *(Executioner)*, Norman Bacon *(Man on Station)*, John Foss *(Youth Leader)*, Carey Wilson, Mitzi McKenzie *(Party Members)*, Phyllis Logan *(Telescreen Announcer)*, Pam Gems *(Washerwoman)*, Joscik Barbarossa *(Aaronson)*, John Boswall *(Goldstein)*, Bob Flag *(Big Brother)*.

An admirable attempt at bringing George Orwell's classic novel to the screen, director Radford's film is incredibly faithful to its source material–perhaps too faithful. This is the well-known story of Winston Smith (effectively played by Hurt) a citizen of Oceania whose job it is to rewrite history for Big Brother, the autocratic symbol of a repressive regime which has forbidden such things as freedom of thought and expression–including sex. Hurt becomes involved in an illict love affair with Hamilton, a young woman who works in the Ministry of Truth. Unfortunately for Hurt, a high-ranking member of the government, Burton, who has looked upon him as a protege discovers the rebellion and after a brutal torture session manages to sap any resistance out of Hurt and bring him back to the fold. Orwell wrote his novel in 1948 and his vision of the future is unrelentingly bleak. Because audiences in 1984 would be looking at a film that was a prophecy of the very year they were living in–a prophecy that had yet to be realized–director Radford chose to present a view of the future as it might have looked to Orwell in 1948. Oceania resembles the bombed out look of London immediately after WW II. While communication technology has advanced considerably, the devices with which Big Brother communicates with the citizens have the familiar look of old telephones and television sets. This is not a future made up of colorful blinking lights and high-tech manufacturing; it is a gray, dull, stark, depressing world possessed of little color or visual stimulation. Though shot in color, Radford's 1984 looks as if it is in black and white. Even the complexions of the actors have a gray pallor. The performances in the film are excellent. Hurt is superb as Winston, and Burton, in his very last role, is bone-chilling as the cynical tormentor. The appearance and feel of the film is entirely appropriate and fascinating to look at–but only for a while. The basic flaw in 1984 is that it is just too painful, too depressing, and too slow to watch. While Orwell's vision is an extremely important prophecy that has become a cornerstone of discussion regarding totalitarianism and whose language has entered the dictionary of political thought (such terms as "doublespeak" and "unperson" sprang from the novel), his presentation of this world is much more suited to literature than the cinema. The very next year another British director, Terry Gilliam (actually an American expatriate), would tread much the same ground with his amazing film BRAZIL. While BRAZIL presents the same bleak view of a future dominated by a Big Brother-type of totalitarian regime, the film itself is wildly creative and, shall we dare say it–entertaining–as it hurtles to the same unbearably bleak conclusion. BRAZIL is a much more clever film, while 1984 almost seems too reverent in its execution. It seems as if Radford must have realized this, for at one point the post- punk pop duo Eurythmics was hired to add songs and a very modern- sounding score to the film. After the work was done the music was deemed wholly inappropriate (as it must have been) and only one song was retained to play on a black screen before the film begins. The score Radford finally went with composed by Muldowney works well. Jonathan Gems, who had a hand in the screenplay and wrote lyrics for three of the songs that were used, is the son of British playwright Pam Gems ("Dusa, Fish, Stas and Vi"), who appears briefly in the film as a washerwoman.

p, Simon Perry; d, Michael Radford; w, Radford, Jonathan Gems (based on the novel by George Orwell); ph, Roger Deakins (Eastmancolor); m, The

Eurythmics, Dominic Muldowney; ed, Tom Priestley; prod d, Allan Cameron; art d, Martin Hebert, Grant Hicks; set d, Mark Raggett; cos, Emma Porteous; m/l, "Oceania, 'Tis for Thee," "The Washerwoman's Song" (Muldowney, Gems, Orwell), "The Hiking Song" (Muldowney, Gems).

Drama   **Cas.**   **(PR:O   MPAA:R)**

1919***   (1984, Brit.) 99m British Film Institute-Channel 4 c

Paul Scofield *(Alexander Scherbatov)*, Maria Schell *(Sophie Rubin)*, Frank Finlay *(The Voice of Sigmund Freud)*, Diana Quick *(Anna)*, Clare Higgins *(Young Sophie)*, Colin Firth *(Young Alexander)*, Sandra Berkin *(Nina)*, Alan Tilvern *(Sophie's Father)*.

Made by Channel 4 in Great Britain and the British Film Institute, this retrospective drama looks and feels as though it may have been a play that was later adapted for television, then released in the remainder of the world as a feature film. Schell and Scofield are two older people who were both patients of Sigmund Freud back in 1919, 65 years before. She's been living in the U.S. for many years and when she sees Scofield interviewed on television and talking of his days with the Viennese master, she decides that she has to meet Scofield and discuss how the process of psychiatry worked for him. She flies to Vienna to meet Scofield and the two of them recall their sessions on Freud's couch as they sit in Scofield's kitschy flat. The picture cuts between the present and the past and when it flashes back, Scofield's character is played by Firth, while Schell is played by Higgins. Her problems are more complex than his, as she is having difficulty with a domineering father, Tilvern, and, at the same time, is trying to squash her sexual attraction for Quick, an older woman who was six months pregnant when the two women slept together. Firth is shy, almost reclusive, and consults Freud (voiced by Frank Finlay) in order to come out of his shell. In between the cuts of today and yesterday, newsreel footage of what was transpiring at the time is intercut so the audience gets a feeling of the period. In the end, nothing much has happened beyond the two older people being united and deciding that Dr. Freud wasn't so terrific after all. The acting by Scofield and Schell is superb and they do the best with what they have been given but it's a conceit and serves to poke some fun at Freud, something that was also done in LOVESICK and a few other movies. The director was making his feature debut after having established himself as a documentarian with an Eskimo film called PEOPLE OF THE ISLANDS. It might have been better as a play because the exterior scenes appear tacked-on rather than organic to the story. Youngsters will not understand much of the subtlety and should be sound asleep within minutes.

p, Nita Amy; d, Hugh Brody; w, Michael Ignatieff, Brody; ph, Ivan Strasburg; m, Brian Gascoigne; ed, David Gladwell; art d, Caroline Amies; cos, Jane Robinson.

Period Drama   **Cas.**   **(PR:C   MPAA:NR)**

NINJA III--THE DOMINATION*½   (1984) 95M
                                            Golan-Globus/MGM-UA-Cannon c

Sho Kosugi *(Yamada)*, Lucinda Dickey *(Christie)*, Jordan Bennett *(Secord)*, David Chung *(Black Ninja)*, Dale Ishimoto *(Okuda)*, James Hong *(Miyashima)*, Bob Craig *(Netherland)*, Pamela Ness *(Alana)*, Roy Padilla *(Winslow)*, Moe Mosley *(Pickwick)*, John LaMotta *(Case)*, Ron Foster *(Jimenez)*, Alan Amiel *(Black Ninja Double)*, Steven Lambert *(Pilot)*, Earl Smith *(Jefferson)*, Carver Barnes *(Nicholson)*, Karen Petty *(Tracy)*, Randy Mulkey *(Thug)*, James Maher *(Frankel)*, Judy Starr *(Doctor)*, Cheryl Van Cleve *(Stacy)*, Suzanne Collins *(Patty)*, Rosemary Ono *(Megumi)*, Janet Marie Heil *(Lucy)*, Charly Harroway *(Chang)*, John Perryman *(Tom)*, Chris Micelli *(Pulley)*, Lem Cook *(Helicopter Pilot)*, Howard Dean *(Policeman)*, Tom Catronova *(Sgt. Cone)*, Jay Rasumny *(1st Morgue Attendant)*, Terence O. Goodman *(2nd Morgue Attendant)*, Bill Helmintoller *(Minister)*.

An evil ninja (a highly trained oriental assassin) arrives from Japan and wreaks havoc on a golf course until the police pump him full of bullets in a sandtrap. With his last energy, he throws a smoke bomb and under its cover crawls into pretty telephone lineperson and aerobics instructor Dickey's phone company van. Dying there, his soul possesses her body, much to the consternation of her boy friend, cop Bennett. She periodically uses exotic Eastern skills to slaughter the evil ninja's foes until good ninja Kosugi comes to her rescue, exorcising the spirit. Enjoyable in a foolish way as Dickey performs amazing acrobatic feats while slicing up dozens of people with her sword. More slick exploitation from schlockmeisters Golan and Globus.

p, Menahem Golan, Yoram Globus; d, Sam Firstenberg; w, James R. Silke; ph, Hanania Baer (Metrocolor); m, Udi Harpaz, Misha Segal, Arthur Kempel; ed, Michael J. Duthie; art d, Elliott Ellentuck; set d, Dian Perryman; cos, Nancy Cone; ch, Sho Kosugi; m/l, "Body Shop," "Starting Out Right," "Obsession," "What Kind of Boy is This," "Welcome to the Party" by Dave Powell, "Love Bites" by Powell, Margaret Harris, Sall Zapulla; stunts, Steve Lambert.

Martial Arts   **Cas.**   **(PR:O   MPAA:R)**

NO SMALL AFFAIR** (1984) 102m COL-Delphi II/COL c

Jon Cryer (*Charles Cummings*), Demi Moore (*Laura Victor*), George Wendt (*Jake*), Peter Frechette (*Leonard*), Elizabeth Daily (*Susan*), Anne Wedgeworth (*Joan Cummings*), Jeffrey Tambor (*Ken*), Judy Baldwin (*Stephanie*), Jennifer Tilly (*Mona*), Scott Getlin (*Scott*), Hamilton Camp (*Gus Sosnowski*), Tim Robbins (*Nelson*), Kene Holliday (*Walt Cronin*), Thomas Adams (*Waiter*), Steven James Brown (*Boy at Stag Party*), Myles Berkowitz (*John*), Joe Cappatta, James Guidera (*Cafe Patrons*), Jack R. Clinton (*Bartender*), Joseph Darling (*Elderly Man*), Tate Donovan (*Bob*), Rick Ducommun (*Groom*), Jan Dunn (*Lady with Dog*), Joseph Geneva (*Cabbie*), Ashley Woodman Hall (*Band Leader at Jake's*), Rupert Holmes (*Band Leader at Wedding*), Mia Kelly (*Waitress at Jake's*), Lori Kruger (*Woman in Crowd*), Joe Lerer (*French Teacher*), Katherine Lyons (*Wedding Cocktail Waitress*), Steve Monarque (*Larry*), Shermaine Michaels (*Bride*), George Pentecost (*Minister*), Maureen Ann Schatzberg (*Prostitute*), Mischa Schwartzmann (*Bum*), Ramona Scott (*Grace*), Sally Schaub (*Museum Employee*), Helen Swee (*Elderly Woman*), Arthur Taxier (*Bouncer*), Morgan Upton (*News Vendor*), Michael Vaughn (*Nelson's Friend*), E. F. Valderrama (*Biker*), Joan Valderrama (*Biker's Girl*), Michael David Wright (*Jim*).

A standard teen romantic comedy which is saved by a pair of well-written, three-dimensional characters – Cryer and Moore. Set against a picturesque San Francisco backdrop, NO SMALL AFFAIR tells the exploits of a likable teen photographer, Cryer, who knows how to capture girls on film better than in real life. Along the water's edge he randomly snaps a photo of the stunning Moore who's a few years his senior (making her a whopping 22). Later, while wandering through a rather sleazy nightclub, Cryer spots her again and has her pose for a session. Absolutely fascinated with her, Cryer makes it his mission to help her find success. He drains his bank account and has her picture plastered on top of a fleet of San Francisco taxis. Moore is at first reluctant, but when a record executive in Los Angeles shows interest she displays nothing but gratitude to her benefactor. NO SMALL AFFAIR, while nothing special, at least doesn't resort to the usual teen sex-fantasy cliches, and gains more points for what it isn't (sophomoric) than what it is (occasionally touching). This is one of those films that has kicked around Hollywood for a while. It was originally scheduled to go into production in 1981 with Matthew Broderick (before his WARGAMES, 1981, rise to stardom) and Sally Field in the leads and Martin Ritt at the helm. Ritt's ill health caused a shutdown after a week and a half until producer Sackheim reassembled the production two years later.

p, William Sackheim; d, Jerry Schatzberg; w, Charles Bolt, Terence Mulcahy (based on a story by Bolt); ph, Vilmos Zsigmond (MGM Color); m, Rupert Holmes; ed, Priscilla Nedd, Eve Newman, Melvin Shapiro; prod d, Robert Boyle; art d, Frank Richwood; set d, Arthur Jeph Parker; cos, Jo Ynocencio; m/l, "No Small Affair," "Hot Headed," "Double Barrels," "Itchin' for a Fight," "Otherwise Fine" Holmes.

Comedy/Romance   Cas.   (PR:O   MPAA:R)

NOSTALGHIA**** (1984, USSR/Ital.) 120m Sovin-RAI Rete 2-Opera/Grange bw/c

Oleg Yankovsky (*Andre Gortchakov*), Domiziana Giordano (*Eugenia*), Erland Josephson (*Domenico*), Patrizia Terreno (*Gortchakov's Wife*), Delia Boccardo (*Domenico's Wife*), Laura DeMarchi (*Chambermaid*), Milena Vukotic (*Civil Servant*), Alberto Canepa (*Farmer*).

A meditative film by visionary Soviet filmmaker Tarkovsky which lures viewers into its mysterious, mystical world and completely envelops them for a two hour stretch. Yankovsky is a Soviet architecture professor who travels to Northern Italy's Tuscan Hills to research an exiled 18th Century Russian composer who committed suicide there. Away from his homeland, Yankovsky becomes nostalgic – suffering with his unfulfilled desire to return to a home which is out of reach. The melancholy Yankovsky becomes involved with Giordano, his volatile, strong-minded interpreter. Their relationship, however, is never consummated and gradually deteriorates. Their romance is strained even further by Yankovsky's growing friendship with Josephson, a batty Italian professor who years ago locked his family inside their house and awaited Armageddon – for seven years. Josephson proves too much for Giordano, who makes plans to return to her lover in Rome. Yankovsky finds Josephson living amongst the rain-soaked ruins of a 16th Century spa. In this ancient crumbling structure is a large, placid mineral bath which Josephson unsuccessfully tries to wade across (its waters are chest high) while holding a lit candle. His crazy belief is that to save mankind he must cross the bath without letting the candle flame extinguish. Having once again failed, Josephson makes a public proclamation. He climbs atop Michelangelo's statue of Marcus Aurelius in Rome, plays Beethoven's "Ode to Joy" on a portable turntable, and shouts prophetic doomsday messages to those who'll listen. At the same time, Yankovsky has taken up Josephson's plight to cross the bath. His first two attempts fail, each time the candle flame flickering out in the swirling drafts of hot air. Back atop the statue, Josephson soaks himself with kerosene and sets himself ablaze. As he burns to death, Yankovsky completes a successful trip across the waters. The candle burns, but Yankovsky's energy is extinguished. Struggling at the water's edge to stay alive, Yankovsky envisions his homeland as the snow covers its grassy hills. The final sequence of NOSTALGHIA is one of the most captivating ever put on film. The viewer becomes completely swept away by Tarkovsky's world where

the elements reign supreme – fire and water are everywhere. The atmosphere Tarkovsky creates is one of constantly dripping water, unsettling mists, and dew which seeps through the eternally damp walls. Coupled with these memorable visuals is a remarkable highlighting of sounds (a job admirably performed by Remo Ugolinelli), i.e., the echoing drip of water or the swirling of the drafts. NOSTALGHIA is not a film for everyone – if it is fast-paced action you desire then you will quickly be snoring. Instead of excitement, the feeling one gets after seeing NOSTALGHIA is one of utter relaxation; one which completely calms both the audio and visual senses; one which brings out nostalgic feelings for the world left behind in the theater. (In Italian; English substitles.)

d, Andrei Tarkovsky; w, Tarkovsky, Tonino Guerra; ph, Giuseppe Lanci (Technicolor); m, Ludwig von Beethoven; ed, Amedeo Salfa, Erminia Marani; md, Gino Peguri; prod d, Andrea Grisanti; cos, Lina Nerli Taviani; spec eff, Paolo Ricci; m/l, Guiseppe Verdi, Ludwig von Beethoven, Russian folk songs.

Drama   (PR:O   MPAA:NR)

NOT FOR PUBLICATION**½ (1984) 88m Goldwyn/Thorn EMI c

Nancy Allen (*Lois Thorndyke*), David Naughton (*Barry*), Laurence Luckenbill (*Mayor Claude Franklyn*), Alice Ghostley (*Doris*), Richard Paul (*Troppogrosso*), Barry Dennen (*Senor Woparico*), Cork Hubbert (*Odo*), Richard Blackburn (*Jim*), Robert Ahola (*Signore Scoppi*), Jeanne Evan (*Helen*), J. David Moeller (*Duffy*), Michael O'Sullivan (*Eddie*), Hart Sprager (*Gene*).

If Paul Bartel ever allows himself to get out of the mire of bad taste, he will be a director with whom to contend. The maker of the trashy EATING RAOUL steps up in class considerably with this but forgets that tastelessness is not enough to make something funny. Allen works for a sleazy New York newspaper once edited by her late daddy. The current editor is Paul and he is determined to uncover all of the scandals in the city. In that capacity, he assigns Allen to go on regular raids. It takes place in the 1950s, when magazines like *Confidential* were making millions while printing dubious stories. Allen is living a double life (as in a 1930s Capra-type or Hawks-type comedy) and working as assistant to the mayor, Luckenbill, a slick "Silk Stocking" district man. Allen hires Naughton to work for Luckenbill. Naughton is a photographer and Allen suspects the mayor may be up to no good so she wants to get the drop on him with actual photos. Luckenbill is up for election again and means to shutter all the pornography stores in the city, but Allen warns him against doing that as he may lose the 21-30 age vote. The story wends its way through several interesting places, including the incredible apartment of pimp Dennen, where a huge orgy takes place, a large Long Island estate, where Allen discovers that Luckenbill is, indeed, a villain, and, in what is the best scene, a song sung by Allen and Naughton ("You Bring Out the Beast in Me" by coscreenwriter John Meyer) at a sado- masochistic sex club known as the "Bestiary," which looks like a satire on shuttered sex club "Plato's Retreat." Coming back to the city aboard a plane piloted by Luckenbill, Allen and Naughton are stunned when the mayor takes a swan dive out the window, leaving them to bring in the airplane. Since neither knows how to handle a plane, Naughton's psychic mother, Ghostley, brings them and the plane safely crash-lands in the Hudson River. It's all wildly improbable and sometimes hilariously funny. The dialog is inventive, the characters bizarre, and it all smacks of being one of those cult movies that will have a long life in the Saturday Night Midnight Shows around the country. Bartel will eventually make his mark in the movie business and this picture proved that he wasn't just another ugly face behind the camera.

p, Ann Kimmel; d, Paul Bartel; w, John Meyer, Bartel; ph, George Tirl (uncredited color); m, Meyer; ed, Alan Toomayan; prod d, Robert Schulenberg; art d, Michael O'Sullivan; cos, Rondi Hilstrom-Davis; ch, Utah Ground; m/l "You Bring Out the Beast in Me," Meyer.

Comedy   Cas.   (PR:C-O   MPAA:R)

NOTHING LASTS FOREVER** (1984) 82m Broadway/MGM-UA c

Zach Galligan (*Adam Beckett*), Apollonia van Ravenstein (*Mara Hofmeier*), Lauren Tom (*Ely*), Dan Aykroyd (*Buck Heller*), Imogene Coca (*Daisy Schackman*), Anita Ellis (*Aunt Anita*), Eddie Fisher (*Himself*), Sam Jaffe (*Father Knickerbocker*), Paul Rogers (*Hugo*), Mort Sahl (*Uncle Mort*), Jan Triska (*Swedish Architect*), Rosemary De Angelis (*Helen Flagella*), Clarice Taylor (*Lu*), Bill Murray (*Lunar Cruise Director*).

A strange, offbeat piece of filmmaking that doesn't quite gel in its absurd intentions. Galligan is an artist in a New York City of the future, ruled by the Port Authority that now regulates those who possess the creative muse. Galligan is turned down in his artistic pursuits and is instead assigned to the Holland Tunnel as a traffic director. His boss is Aykroyd, in one of the many cameos that dot the proceedings. Later he meets van Ravenstein (who would drop her last name entirely with her appearance in PURPLE RAIN) who engages in a brief affair with him, then introduces Galligan to the real art world of the New York underground. He later boards a bus, not knowing that the vehicle is a lunar transport that takes consumers for shopping trips on the moon. There -- in the craft's lounge -- he listens to Fisher singing "Oh! My PaPa" (Paul Burkhard, John Turner, Geoffrey Parsons) while he suffers under the gaze of Murray, the ship's cruise director. Eventually the hapless Galligan ends up back on Earth where he makes a triumphant return to

Carnegie Hall, a place at which he had previously embarrassed himself. He also meets Tom, the woman he really loves, and the strange cinematic excursion comes to a conclusion. The film's unusual storyline is further enhanced (depending on one's tolerance levels) by a liberal mix of old newsreel footage and scenes from such classics as INTOLERANCE. The results are a strange fantasy that could be taken as either an absurdist journey or a real waste of time. The film succeeds on some points, then loses interest on others. The cameo performances by some of the most talented comic actors of the last thirty years (Coca, Sahl, Aykroyd, Murray) are surprisingly not all that funny. The film marks the directorial debut for Schiller, who had created the short "Schiller's Reel" for TV's "Saturday Night Live." Producer Michaels was the original producer of that show; he too here makes his first feature-film bow. In another cameo, singer Ellis does a fine job with "It's Only a Paper Moon" (Harold Arlen, Billy Rose, E.Y. Harburg). It's certainly not a film for all tastes, but worth taking a look at by fans of the way-out.

p, Lorne Michaels, John Head; d&w, Tom Schiller; ph, Fred Schuler (Technicolor); ed, Kathleen Dougherty, Margot Francis; art d, Woods MacKintosh.

Comedy   (PR:C   MPAA:PG)

NUMBER ONE**½   (1984, Brit.) 105m Videoform/Stageforum c

Bob Geldof (Harry [Flash] Gordon), Mel Smith (Billy Evans), Alison Steadman (Doreen), P. H. Moriarty (Mike the Throat), Phil Daniels (Terry the Boxer), Alfred Molina (D-C Rogers), James Marcus (D-C Fleming), David Howey (Brad Bookie), Ian Dury (Teddy Bryant), Ron Cook (The Wasp), David Squire, Alun Armstrong, Tony Scott, Kate Hardie, Ray Winstone, Albie Woodington, Jack Eden, A. J. Clark, Harry Scott, Eric Richard, Jimmy Tippet.

Geldof is a snooker hustler (the British equivalent of pool) who makes his living winning games in seedy London joints. Eventually promoter Smith persuades him to get himself out of these low-life halls (and out of trouble) and compete in a professional snooker match. The bets are heavily against him and Geldof is pressured to throw the match. Reminiscent of the sort of dramas produced in Britain during the late 1950s and early 1960s, this film works chiefly due to its cast. The ensemble is a tight one, actors playing well off one another to give this a good sense of realism. Geldof, lead singer of The Boomtown Rats and contemporaneously known for his fund-raising efforts for Ethiopia, gives a nice performance as a hustler who ultimately refuses to sell out. the script, however, is a formula piece which holds few surprises as it goes through its paces. The result is a well-acted and well-meaning piece that never manages to hit its intended mark.

p, Mark Forstater, Raymond Day; d, Les Blair; w, G.F. Newman; ph, Bahram Manocheri (Technicolor); m, David Mackay; ed, John Gregory; prod d, Martin Johnson.

Drama   (PR:C   MPAA:NR)

OASIS, THE*   (1984) 92m Titan c

Chris Makepeace (Matt), Scott Hylands (Jake), Richard Cox (Paul), Dori Brenner (Jill), Rick Podell (Alex), Mark Metcalf (Eric), Ben Slack (Louis), Anne Lockhart (Anna), Suzanne Snyder (Jennifer).

A standard tale of survival set deep in the desert after a plane crashes. There are nine survivors but that number rapidly diminshes as the film goes on. THE OASIS borrows from every known survival film including SANDS OF THE KALAHARI (1959), FLIGHT OF THE PHOENIX (1965), SURVIVE] (1976), and the made-for-TV picture HEY, I'M ALIVE (1975). Makepeace may be remembered for his admirable performance in MY BODYGUARD (1980).

p, Myron Meisel, Sparky Greene; d, Greene; w, Tom Klassen (based on a story by Meisel, Greene); ph, Alexander Gruszynski; m, Chris Young; ed, Mary Bauer; prod d, Woodward Romine.

Drama   (PR:O   MPAA:NR)

OH GOD! YOU DEVIL***   (1984) 96m WB c

John Doolittle (Arthur Shelton), Julie Lloyd (Bea Shelton), Ian Giatti (Young Bobby), George Burns (God), Ted Wass (Bobby Shelton), Janet Brandt (Mrs. K.), Roxanne Hart (Wendy Shelton), Belita Moreno (Mrs. Vega), Danny Ponce (Joey Vega), Jason Wingreen (Hotel Manager), Danny Mora (Bellhop), Eugene Roche (Charlie Gray), Henry Reiss, Joseph Samperi, Donald Cadette (Wedding Party), Jane Dulo (Widow), Steven Dunaway (Waiter), Susan Peretz (Louise), Robert Desiderio (Billy Wayne), Mitchell Group (Cap), Anthony Sgueglia (Bodyguard), Cynthia Tarr (Receptionist), Robert Picardo (Joe Ortiz), Ron Silver (Gary Frantz), Kent DeMarche, Trey Thompson, Charles Button, Dave Morgan, John Wolff, Jack Kelly (Billy's Band), Christie Mellor (Groupie), Arthur Malet (Houseman), Crawford Binion, Tracy Bogart (Couple in Restaurant), James Cromwell (Priest), Martin Garner (Shamus), Arnold Johnson (Preacher), Patricia Springer (Reporter), Dom Angelo, Red McIlvaine, Betty Bunch, Roger Rhu (Poker Players), Buddy Powell (Stage Manager), Jim Hodge (Doctor), Brandy Gold (Bobby's Daughter), Chere Bryson, George Fisher, Ted Grossman, Tom Rosales, Jr., Victoria Vanderkloot (Stunts).

In the Betty Comden-Adolph Green script for THE BAND WAGON, Jack Buchanan stated, "The Faust legend always works" and that was never more accurate than in this umpteenth reworking of the "I would sell my soul to the Devil" tale. It reminds one of DAMN YANKEES, ALIAS NICK BEAL, THE DEVIL AND DANIEL WEBSTER, and several other well-known stories as it treads the same exact path except that this time, Burns gets to play God as well as the Devil. Burns is best when he's playing Burns and he has the chance to play Burns often here. Struggling musician Wass (who had been the recipient of some lousy scripts in the past, namely SHEENA and CURSE OF THE PINK PANTHER) is married to Hart and they have a little one on the way. He is having a tough time making ends meet and when he states aloud the familiar plea that he would sell his soul to the Devil, those words are heard by Devil Burns, who is at the wheel of a sports car bearing vanity license plate that reads "Hot." A deal is struck between the two and Wass is transformed into the persona of Desiderio, a famous rock musician who also made a deal with Burns but whose contract ran out. Desiderio becomes Wass and vice versa and Desiderio also inherits Hart and the unborn child. Wass now owns a mansion, limo, jet, is surrounded by countless nubile groupies, and has everything a man would want, but he remains unhappy as he comes to realize that what he had with Hart was more valuable than all the trappings of wealth and fame. Wass wants out of the deal and manages to do that in a poker game with Burns when the Devil shows a sense of fair play. Some of Burns' lines are priceless, as when he bemoans the fact that he hardly has to compete for souls with God anymore as Heaven is only half full and they had to close down the main dining hall. God, in the person of Burns, shows Wass how to outsmart the Devil and it ends happily, as everyone knew it would. It's a hoary story but Burns lends a new twist with his slick portrayal. Wass, Hart, and Desiderio give good, if shallow, performances, but they are handcuffed by the words they were handed. Silver is excellent as a fast-talking record company executive (he's played that kind of part often) and Roche chimes in with a neat cameo as Wass' agent. It's light, mostly amusing, and better than the second Burns-God film, but not as good as the first. The executive producer was Burns' lifetime associate, Irving Fein, and if that's not enough nepotism, one of the assistant directors was Peter Bogart, whom we can only assume must have been related to director Paul Bogart, a TV veteran who did some of the best "All in the Family" shows.

p, Robert M. Sherman; d, Paul Bogart; w, Andrew Bergman; ph, King Baggot (Technicolor); m, David Shire; ed, Andy Zall; prod d, Peter Wooley; set d, Gary Moreno; cos, Bill Tiegs, Jean Rosone- Puckett; spec eff, Ray Klein; m/l "If It Was Only Up to Me," "Dangerous Eyes," Mike Post, John Bettis.

Comedy   **Cas.**   (PR:A-C   MPAA:PG)

OLD ENOUGH***   (1984) 91m Silverfilm/Orion Classics c

Sarah Boyd (Lonnie Sloan), Rainbow Harvest (Karen Bruckner), Neill Barry (Johnny Bruckner), Danny Aiello (Mr. Bruckner), Susan Kingsley (Mrs. Bruckner), Roxanne Hart (Carla), Fran Brill (Mrs. Sloan), Gerry Bamman (Mr. Sloan), Alyssa Milano (Diane Sloan), Anne Pitoniak (Katherine), Charlie Willinger (Danny), Michael Monetti (Mikey), Manny Jacobs (Jimmy), Gina Batiste (Marlene), Tristine Skyler (Sarah), Al Israel (Bodega Owner), Paul Butler (Guard), Primy Rivera (Spanish Boy), Nance Kass.

Boyd is a 12-year-old rich kid living in New York City. She meets Harvest, a slightly older girl from a less affluent nearby neighborhood, and a charming friendship blossoms. Together the girls face the heartbreaks and joys of early adolescence and learn about the class divisions that separate them. When Boyd begins a romance with Harvest's brother Barry, some tension builds in the friendship but together the girls learn about themselves as a result. The plot is just a series of vignettes involving the two girls but it is a sensitive and often marvelous film. Boyd and Harvest are a genuine pair, giving a real portrait of friendship at a special and crucial time in life. There are some problems with plot contrivances but the overall effect isn't marred by them, resulting in a unique and serious film. Produced in association with the Sundance Institute in Utah, the film was produced by Dina Silver with her sister Marisa writing and directing. The two are daughters of Joan Micklin and Ralph Silver, talented filmmakers in their own right.

p, Dina Silver; d&w, Marisa Silver; ph, Michael Ballhaus; m, Julian Marshall; ed, Mark Burns; prod d, Jeffrey Townsend; cos, Teri Kane.

Drama   **Cas.**   (PR:C   MPAA:PG)

OLTRE IL BENE E IL MALE   (SEE: BEYOND GOOD AND EVIL, Ital./Fr./Ger.)

ON THE LINE***   (1984, Span.) 95m El Iman-Amber c (RIO ABAJO)

David Carradine (Bryant), Scott Wilson (Mitch), Victoria Abril (Engracia), Jeff Delgar (Chuck), Sam Jaffe (Gabacho), Paul Richardson, Jesse Vint, Mitch Pileggi, Christopher Saylors, David Estuardo, Anne Galvin.

An engrossing, emotionally charged tale of romance and vengeance which takes place entirely along the U.S.-Mexican border. Abril is a gorgeous illiterate prostitute who becomes involved with border guards Wilson and Delgar, as well as with her guide Carradine. Although there are some extraneous border-jumping affairs (one Mexican is killed and an investigation follows), the main concentration is on Abril's desire to "cross the line." (In English.)

d&w, Jose Luis Borau (based on a treatment by Borau, Barbara Probst Solomon); ph, Teo Escamilla, Steven Posey, Mikhail Suslov, Joan Gelpi, Nicholas von Sternberg (Eastmancolor); m, George Michalski, Armando Manzanero, Munuel Munoz, Pam Savage; ed, Curtiss Clayton, Cary Caughlin; set d, Philip Thomas; cos, Sawnie Ruth Baldridge.

Drama **(PR:O MPAA:NR)**

ONCE UPON A TIME IN AMERICA**** (1984) 227m Ladd/WB c

Robert DeNiro *(Noodles)*, James Woods *(Max)*, Elizabeth McGovern *(Deborah)*, Treat Williams *(Jimmy O'Donnell)*, Tuesday Weld *(Carol)*, Burt Young *(Joe)*, Joe Pesci *(Frankie)*, Danny Aiello *(Police Chief Aiello)*, Bill Forsythe *(Cockeye)*, James Hayden *(Patsy)*, Darlanne Fleugel *(Eve)*, Larry Rapp *(Fat Moe)*, Dutch Miller *(Van Linden)*, Robert Harper *(Sharkey)*, Dick 'Richard' Bright *(Chicken Joe)*, Gerard Murphy *(Crowning)*, Amy Ryder *(Peggy)*, Olga Karlatos *(Woman in the Puppet Theater)*, Mario Brega *(Mandy)*, Ray Dittrich *(Trigger)*, Frank Gio *(Beefy)*, Karen Shallo *(Mrs. Aiello)*, Angelo Florio *(Willie the Ape)*, Scott Tiler *(Young Noodles)*, Rusty Jacobs *(Young Max/David)*, Brian Bloom *(Young Patsy)*, Adrian Curran *(Young Cockeye)*, Mike Monezzi *(Young Fat Moe)*, Jennifer Donnelly *(Young Deborah)*, Noah Moazezi *(Dominic)*, James Russo *(Bugsy)*, Frankie Caserta, Joey Marzella *(Bugsy's Gang)*, Clem Caserta *(Al Capuano)*, Frank Sisto *(Fred Capuano)*, Jerry Strivelli *(Johnny Capuano)*, Julie Cohen *(Young Peggy)*, Marvin Scott *(Interviewer)*, Mike Gendel *(Irving Gold)*, Paul Herman *(Monkey)*, Ann Neville *(Girl in Coffin)*, Joey Faye *(Adorable Old Man)*, Linda Ipanema *(Nurse Thompson)*, Tandy Cronin, Richard Zobel, Baxter Harris *(Reporters)*, Arnon Milchan *(Chauffeur)*, Bruno Iannone *(Thug)*, Marty Licata *(Cemetary Caretaker)*, Marica Jean Kurtz *(Max's Mother)*, Estelle Harris *(Peggy's Mother)*, Richard Foronjy *(Whitey)*, Gerritt Debeer *(Drunk)*, Sergio Leone *(Ticket Agent)*, Margherita Pace, Alexander Godfrey, Cliff Cudney, Paul Farentino, Bruce Bahrenburg, Mort Freeman, Sandra Solberg, Massimo Liti.

Italian director Sergio Leone returned to the screen after a 12- year absence and the result is this ambitious, sprawling, insightful, frustrating, and ultimately challenging gangster film. The desire to make ONCE UPON A TIME IN AMERICA had been a passion for Leone for over a decade. Always seen as a companion piece to his western masterpiece ONCE UPON A TIME IN THE WEST– which chronicled the rise of the businessman and the death of the outlaw–Leone chose to explore the amalgamation of the outlaw and business: the roots of organized crime. But ONCE UPON A TIME IN AMERICA is much more than that–it is also a cinematic exploration of time. Time, how it passes, how it is remembered, and perhaps, how we see the future. The film's structure is so incredibly complex that any detailed synopsis of it (and the all- important transitions between the three periods of time it covers, 1923, 1933, and 1968) would take dozens of pages. The basic plot outline follows a group of young Jewish boys who grow up together on Manhattan's Lower East Side, eventually becoming small-time crime lords. The film opens in 1933 as the gang falls apart. Vicious hoods from another gang kill DeNiro's girl and try to find him. He hides out in an opium den and indulges in the dreamy smoke. From there he goes to a train station and heads out of town. As he walks through the doorway leading to the trains, the music slowly shifts until the Beatles' tune "Yesterday" is heard. DeNiro reenters the scene 35 years older. It is 1968. He visits one of the old gang, Rapp, who now runs his family restaurant. A strange letter has brought DeNiro back from his self-imposed exile and he spends the film trying to sort out the events of the past and how they have shaped the situation he finds himself in at the present time. From there the film flashes back to 1923 and we see how the gang was formed. The youngsters (Tiler, Jacobs, Monezzi, Curran, and Bloom) hook up with some Italian gangsters and run into trouble with the local Irish toughs who resent the sudden competition. While these adolescent power plays act themselves out, Tiler (the DeNiro character in his youth) actively pursues Connelly, the beautiful sister of one of his friends. She wants to be a dancer and an actress and though she likes Tiler, she knows he will never be any good. Connelly has a strong, independent maturity that both fascinates and intimidates Tiler and he spends the rest of his life trying to capture her. Eventually the boys grow up and get more involved with the Italian mobsters. A local chieftain, Young, pays the boys to rob a diamond vault. Through Woods, the ambitious second-in-command and DeNiro's best friend, the gang becomes involved with in a dangerous power play which sees Young's brother Pesci order him killed to gain control of the mob. Woods kills Young, much to DeNiro's surprise, and takes over control of their group, while Pesci gives the Jewish boys a higher rank in the organization. After being assigned the task of quashing labor organizer Williams, and forcing police chief Aiello to see things their way, Woods gets a big head and decides to rob the Federal Reserve Bank. DeNiro thinks the plan insane and that they'll all be killed, but Woods won't listen and declares that they'll do it without him. In order to save his friends, DeNiro commits an act that will haunt him for the rest of his life–he calls the police and informs them of the robbery. Instead of saving their lives, his friends are killed in a fiery car wreck while being pursued by the police (before the robbery even takes place). Woods is burned beyond recognition. The action at the beginning of the film is then repeated (the hoods' pursuit of DeNiro, the opium den) and we are eventually transported back to 1968. DeNiro discovers that Woods is alive and has taken a new identity and become a respected senator. He has also become rich and taken DeNiro's life-long heartthrob (now played by McGovern) as his wife. Scandal has rocked Woods' empire, however (labor leader Williams has come back to haunt him), and he now summons DeNiro and begs to be murdered. Though Woods has lived well and has stolen his girl while DeNiro remained in hiding for 35 years, DeNiro doesn't hate Woods enough to enact revenge. He simply walks away leaving Woods to do it himself. In the most frustratingly ambiguous sequences of this frequently ambiguous movie, we get the *impression* that Woods ends up a suicide in the crusher of a garbage truck as DeNiro walks off into the night. The film then shifts back to the opium den in 1933. DeNiro is stoned, lost in dreamlike reverie. We see an upside-down closeup of his face and a slight, enigmatic smile sweeps across it. The film ends. The strange structure and last shot of the film have stirred much debate. Some look at the plot as a literal, standard movie story line. Leone seems to be hinting however, that DeNiro–guilt-ridden from informing on his friends–has gone to the opium den to escape, only to fantasize how Woods would someday get his revenge. Everything in 1968 is a dope-clouded, guilt-projected dream. There is much to support this view of the film–some of the more confusing passages make more sense when viewed with this in mind–but again, it doesn't hold up very well when subjected to intense scrutiny. The debate is merely an interesting diversion in a film filled with rich and valuable moments. The performances in the film are uniformly excellent with DeNiro taking top honors. The performances Leone gets from his cast of young actors who play the gangsters in their adolescence are phenomenal. Jennifer Connelly as the young girl turns in a remarkably confident performance which totally outclasses her adult incarnation McGovern. The film is worth seeing for this young actress' performance alone–her passages with Tiler (young DeNiro) are some of the best in the movie. ONCE UPON A TIME IN AMERICA's best moments take place in the 1923 segments and in a film filled with graphic depictions of sex and violence, the most memorable, best-directed moment is in a scene where one of the boys brings a delicious-looking cupcake to the local good-time girl who will accept it in exchange for brief sexual favors. As the boy sits on the tenement steps outside her door and waits for her to come out, the lure of the cupcake slowly overtakes his sexual desires. Tentatively he unwraps the package and scoops out a tiny bit of icing. He then covers his indiscretion and continues to wait. Once again the sweet promise of the cupcake calls and the boy scoops off more icing. Finally he gives in to his hunger and eats the whole cupcake. The door to the apartment opens suddenly and the girl steps out. The boy quickly hides the wrapper, wipes his mouth, mumbles an excuse, and leaves. In this one scene Leone shows the boy struggling to be a man–with the childhood pleasures winning out over the adult carnal ones. In one scene we see the essence of these men who spend their lives playing a dangerous kids' game of cops and robbers. ONCE UPON A TIME IN AMERICA is filled with such poetic and insightful moments. The production is simply gorgeous. Mostly shot on location in New York City, the 1923 section evokes the look and feel of Francis Coppola's GODFATHER films with their attention to historical accuracy. The film juggles dozens of characters and seemingly thousands of extras through its 45-year expanse, giving it an epic feel. Ennio Morricone, who scored all of Leone's westerns, turns in one of his most haunting, beautiful scores, which heightens the most intimate and spectacular moments. The main theme is heard throughout, a haunting little tune played on a wooden flute which echoes memories of things past. Leone's monumental gangster film was looked on in horror by its American distributor who thought it too confused and too long for U.S. audiences. They took the film and pared it down by an incredible 83 minutes, reducing the running time to 143 minutes (shades of the fate suffered by Leone's ONCE UPON A TIME IN THE WEST). The reedited version stripped all of Leone's marvelous, delicate time transitions–the very heart of the film–and turned the story into a linear film which starts in 1923, moves to 1933, and then concludes in 1968. All the exploration of time, memory, and dream was gone. The reedited version justifiably bombed at the box office, and the original version was released to major markets months later, doing respectable business. The uncut version of the film is what is available on videotape, and that may be the best place to view the film, for it is a multi-faceted jewel, albeit with flaws, that must be looked at again and again for the viewer to see all its wonderful secrets.

p, Arnon Milchan; d, Sergio Leone; w, Leonardo Benvenuti, Piero De Bernardi, Enrico Medioli, Franco Arcalli, Franco Ferrini, Leone, Stuart Kaminsky (based on the novel *The Hoods* by Harry Grey); ph, Tonio Delli Colli (Technicolor); m, Ennio Morricone; ed, Nino Baragli; art d, Carlo Simi, James Singelis; set d, Giovanni Natalucci, Gretchen Rau; cos, Gabriella Pescucci, Baragli.

Crime **Cas.** **(PR:O MPAA:R)**

ONE DEADLY SUMMER** (1984, Fr.) 130m SNC-CAPAC-TFI/UNIV c (L'ETE MEURTRIER)

Isabelle Adjani *(Elaine/Elle)*, Alain Souchon *(Pin Pon)*, Suzanne Flon *(Cognata)*, Jenny Cleve *(Pin Pon's Mother)*, Francois Cluzet *(Mickey)*, Manuel Gelin *(Boubou)*, Michel Galabru *(Gabriel)*, Maria Machado *(Elle's Mother)*, Roger Carel *(Henry IV)*, Jean Gaven *(Leballech)*, Max Morel *(Touret)*, Cecile Vassort *(Josette)*, Martin LaMotte *(Georges)*, Jacques Nolot *(Fiero)*, Raymond Meunier *(Brochard)*, Jacques Dynam *(Ferraldo)*, Evelyne Didi *(Calamite)*, Yves Alfonso *(Rostollan)*, Edith Scob *(Lady Doctor)*, Daniel

Langlet (*Maitre*), Catherine Le-Gouey (*Mrs. Brochard*), Maiwen Lebesco (*Elle*), as a Child, Marie-Pierre Casey, Virginie Vignon, Patrice Melennec, Pierre Gallon, Renaud Bossert.

Once again the French Cesars–the equivalent of the U.S. Oscars–prove to be a kiss of death for a picture on American shores. ONE DEADLY SUMMER received a handful of Cesars, but amounts to little more than a convoluted thriller about a rather deranged young woman, Adjani, who searches for the three men (her father included) who years ago battered and raped her mother. In order to execute her plan Adjani ensnares a helpless volunteer fireman, Souchon, who is entranced by her alluring quality. (For some flimsy reason–Everywoman, perhaps–Adjani is referred to throughout the film as "Elle" which is short for Elaine and translates as "she.") A Directed by Jean Becker (son of the legendary (son of the legendary Jacques), ONE DEADLY SUMMER has little to recommend it except for Adjani's beauty and Delerue's haunting score. (In French; English subtitles.)

p, Christine Beytout; d, Jean Becker; w, Becker, Sebastien Japrisot (based on the novel by Japrisot); ph, Etienne Becker (Panavision, Eastmancolor); m, Georges Delerue; ed, Jacques Witta; art d, Jean-Claude Gallouin; cos, Therese Ripaud.

Crime Drama   (PR:O   MPAA:R)

ORDEAL BY INNOCENCE**   (1984, Brit.) 88m Cannon/MGM/UA c

Donald Sutherland (*Dr. Arthur Calgary*), Faye Dunaway (*Rachel Calgary*), Christopher Plummer (*Leo Argyle*), Sarah Miles (*Mary Durrant*), Ian McShane (*Philip Durrant*), Diana Quick (*Gwenda Vaughan*), Annette Crosbie (*Kirsten Lindstrom*), Michael Elphick (*Inspector Huish*), George Innes (*Archie Leach*), Valerie Whittington (*Hester Argyle*), Phoebe Nichols (*Tina Argyle*), Michael Maloney (*Micky Argyle*), Cassie Stuart (*Maureen Clegg*), Anita Carey (*Martha Jessup*), Ron Pember (*Ferryman*), Kevin Stoney (*Solicitor*), John Bardon (*Night Porter*), Brian Glover (*Executioner*), Billy McColl (*Jacko Argyle*), Rex Holdsworth (*Police Doctor*), Martyn Townsend (*Detective*), Doel Luscombe (*Prison Governor*), Alex Porwal (*Young Policeman*), Roberta McBain (*Hotel Manager*).

Produced by the Cannon Group, which later went into some larger though not necessarily better movies, this creaky adaptation of an Agatha Christie mystery is set in the 1950s, for no apparent reason, and seems mired there when compared with the mysteries of the 1980s. Sutherland is a scientist who has been doing research in the frozen Antarctic for the last two years. He comes back to Britain and seeks to return an address book that was the property of a man he's met before going to the very deep south of this Earth. Sutherland had provided the man with transportation back then and is shocked to learn that the fellow had been accused, tried, convicted, and executed for murder while Sutherland was away. Further, the murder took place the night Sutherland met the man and he could have provided the innocent guy with an alibi. Sutherland feels awful about what's happened and wants to get to the bottom of things, if only to assuage his own guilt for the man's execution. Sutherland begins to investigate and is surprised because the family of the innocent man doesn't seem to much care about reopening the case and clearing the accused name. The victim was Dunaway (seen in flashback), who was the mother of the executed youth, and it appears that she wasn't at all beloved by her husband, Plummer, who'd been having an affair with his aide, Quick. Dunaway apparently was about to cut everyone in the house out of her will and there was also a cabal involving blackmail. As in many Christie mysteries, it seems that everyone (with the exception of the upstairs maid) had a motive for killing the victim. Sutherland's peregrinations brings him into contact with policeman Elphick, suspects Miles and McShane, Dunaway's near and dear relatives, Nichols and Maloney, and he finally solves the case. Burbeck's music was not up to par and the direction was snail-like.

p, Jenny Craven; d, Desmond Davis; w, Alexander Stuart (based on the novel by Agatha Christie); ph, Billy Williams (Eastmancolor); m, Dave Brubeck, Timothy Gee; prod d, Ken Bridgeman; art d, Richard Hornsby; cos, Gwenda Evans; makeup Wally Schneiderman.

Mystery   **Cas.**   (PR:C   MPAA:PG-13)

ORDER OF DEATH   (SEE: CORRUPT, Ital.)

OVER THE BROOKLYN BRIDGE**½   (1984) 106m MGM/UA c

Elliott Gould (*Alby Sherman*), Margaux Hemingway (*Elizabeth Anderson*), Sid Caesar (*Uncle Benjamin*), Burt Young (*Phil Romano*), Shelly Winters (*Becky Sherman*), Carol Kane (*Cheryl Goodman*), Robert Gosset (*Eddie*), Karen Shallo (*Mariena*), Jerry Lazarus, Francine Beers, Leo Postrel, Rose Arrick, Matt Fischel, Lynnie Greene, Amy S. Ryder, Sal Richards, Leib Lensky, Lou David, Tom McDermott, Zvee Schooler, Mort Freeman, Mary Gutzi, Jean Elliott, Aki Aleong, Kim Chan, Claude Vincent, Manuel Santiago, Jackie James, Linda Kerns, Christopher Wyncoop, Barbara Rucker.

Pleasant if old-fashioned update of "Abie's Irish Rose" that looks as though it may have been written in the 1960s by late screenwriter Somkin, who passed away before the picture was made and in whose name the film is dedicated. Produced by *shlockmeisters* Golan and Globus, and directed by Golan, it's elevated by the presence of a fine cast that knows how to handle

the dated material. Gould is a hustling restaurateur who owns a small coffee shop-luncheonette in Brooklyn. He has plans to buy a Manhattan restaurant on the fashionable East Side but he needs money and the only wealthy person in the family is his uncle, Caesar, a man in women's underwear (not that he is actually *in* women's underwear, he just makes scads of money manufacturing the stuff). Gould's girl friend is Hemingway, the ultimate *shicksa* (gentile). She is Catholic, from a wealthy family in Philadelphia, and he loves her dearly. Caesar would like to see Gould marry within the Jewish faith so he agrees to lend Gould the money on the proviso that Gould marry Kane, a distant cousin who appears to be innocent and virginal but who is traveling under a false flag, as she is, in fact, a wild and kinky woman who is given to spiked heels, whips, and all sorts of sexual gear that would shock Caesar if he knew about it. Winters is Gould's corpulent mother and Young is his best friend. Good laughs for anyone who knows the milieu but it will be lost on most people who live west of Newark. There is a very emotional scene between Caesar and Gould at a family dinner in a restaurant where Gould makes it clear that he cannot and will not give up Hemingway for anything, even if it means not getting the money to realize his dream of moving uptown. Caesar is wonderful in his role, one of the best he's ever done on the large screen. Gould plays his schlepp part the way he's always played his schlepp parts, with total believability. The Kane sequence feels anachronistic not only in time but in place. She does well enough with a hapless characterization. New York is seen in a good light for a change and the ethnic types are on the nose. In a small role, note Aki Aleong, who was, for years, a singer of surfing tunes in Los Angeles. The language and some of the sexuality makes this a bad set for youngsters.

p, Menahem Golan, Yoram Globus; d, Golan; w, Arnold Somkin; ph, Adam Greenberg (Metrocolor); m, Pino Donaggio; ed, Mark Goldblatt; art d, John Lawless.

Romantic Comedy   **Cas.**   (PR:O   MPAA:R)

OXFORD BLUES*   (1984) 93m Baltic/MGM-UA c

Rob Lowe (*Nick Di Angelo*), Ally Sheedy (*Rona*), Amanda Pays (*Lady Victoria*), Julian Sands (*Colin*), Julian Firth (*Geordie*), Alan Howard (*Simon*), Gail Strickland (*Las Vegas Lady*), Michael Gough (*Dr. Ambrose*), Aubrey Morris (*Dr. Boggs*), Cary Elwes (*Lionel*), Bruce Payne (*Peter*), Anthony Calf (*Gareth*), Pip Torrens (*Ian*), Richard Hunt (*Larry*), Peter Jason (*Father*), Peter-Hugo Daly (*Malcolm*), Carrie Jones (*Sandra*), Sonia Smyles (*Rita*), Richard Pescud (*Male Secretary No.1*), Jeffrey Perry (*Male Secretary*), Charles Grant (*Student Photographer*), Laura Francis (*Girl in T-Shirt*), Aimee Delamain (*Lady Belmore*), Hugh Morton (*Butler*).

This film is a compendium of just about every banal element to be found in the teen-oriented films of 1984. Sex, rock videos, jingoism, a climactic athletic event, and plenty of free-spirited, beautiful looking young people. Lowe is a dropout from a college in Nevada, working as a car parker for a Las Vegas hotel. Within the first 10 minutes of the film he's been picked up by Strickland, a wealthy recent divorcee. They go to bed, win a lot of money at the gaming tables, then she gives him her car as a token of appreciation. So much for the reality factor. With the money, Lowe is able to pay off a computer hacker who can illegally get him into Oxford. Does this egotistical young man want to go to the noted university to get ahead in life? No, Lowe's intentions are a little more base. He's got a mad crush on Pays, a famous and pretty member of British royalty, and he's determined to make her his girl. Off he goes to Oxford, where he immediately makes an impression by smashing his car into some important architecture. He decides to major in that subject since that's what his would-be love is studying. He manages to infuriate every Englishman with his attitude, but Sheedy, an American student also in Oxford, befriends the anarchistic Lowe. He gets involved with the sculling team, insults Pays' boy friend and, in general, flaunts authority at every turn. He's finally tossed out of an elite rowing society because of his obnoxious behavior but redeems himself in the end. During the course of events Lowe gets Pays to sleep with him, though he ends up in Sheedy's arms during the final frames. This is a sort of remake of A YANK AT OXFORD without any of that film's charm or humor. Lowe is his own rebel without a cause (complete with James Dean's portrait on his wall for anyone who doesn't catch on) passing off arrogance as a cute personality quirk. One wishes that the proper Englishmen would drop all decorum and give Lowe what's really coming to him, rather than the occasional punches the oaf periodically staves off. For all the prestige of Oxford, the institution portrayed here might well be a correspondence school. Talk, drinking, rowing, and sexual dalliances precede studying at every turn. For what it's worth, the rowing sequences all pull together well. The psychology of a rowing team could have been an interesting subject but OXFORD BLUES is permeated with predictability from the first frame to the last, going for the obvious at every moment.

p, Cassian Elwes, Elliott Kastner; d&w, Robert Boris; ph, John Stanier (Technicolor); m, John DuPrez; ed, Patrick Moore, James Symons; prod d, Terry Pritchard; cos, Pip Newberry; m/l, "Oxford Blues," "I've Got What You Want," Paul Jabara, Harold Wheeler.

Drama   **Cas.**   (PR:O   MPAA:PG-13)

PALLET ON THE FLOOR*½ (1984, New Zealand) 90m Mirage c

Bruce Spence *(Basil Beaumont-Foster)*, Peter McCauley *(Sam Jamieson)*, Jillian O'Brien *(Sue Jamieson)*, Shirley Gruar *(Miriam Breen)*, Alistair Douglas *(Stanley Breen)*, Tony Barry *(Larkman)*, John Bach *(Jack Voot)*, Marshall Napier *(Joe Voot)*, Terence Cooper *(Brendon O'Keefe)*.

Set in a small New Zealand coastal village in 1966, PALLET ON THE FLOOR concerns a trio of married couples, a hushed-up murder, and the arrival of a British aristocrat who solves their problems in a rather unorthodox manner. O'Brien, the Maori wife of McCauley, was once lustfully assailed (while pregnant) by truck driver Bach. Fists began to fly and when the dust cleared Bach was dead. His brother, Napier, makes an equally unsuccessful attempt to disrupt McCauley and O'Brien to average his brother's death, ending up dead like Bach. The police, who cannot be accused of being too intelligent, assume that the brothers' deaths are accidental. Gruar and Douglas, however, know the real, untold story so they blackmail McCauley and O'Brien. Spence arrives on the scene, takes Gruar and Douglas out for a ride in his car, and drives them and himself into a deep ravine. Problem solved. Spence is a martyr. The movie's over, and everyone is repeating one question, "Why?"

p, Larry Parr; d, Lynton Butler; w, Martyn Sanderson, Robert Rising, Butler (based on the novel by Ronald Hugh Morrieson); ph, Kevin Hayward; m, Bruno Lawrence, Jonathan Crayford; ed, Patrick Monaghan; prod d, Lyn Bergquist; cos, Christine West.

Crime/Drama **(PR:O MPAA:NR)**

PAR OU T'ES RENTRE? ON T'A PAS VUE SORTIR zero (1984, Fr./Tunisia) 91m Carthago /GAU c

Jerry Lewis, Philippe Clair, Marthe Villalonga, Jakie Sardou, Philippe Castelli.

France has given the world some of the cinema's greatest artists including such revered names as Jean Renoir, Abel Gance, and the great directors of the New Wave era. The list of French film masterpieces is staggering. Yet for some inexplicable reason they revere Jerry Lewis as a genius from the same mold as Charlie Chaplin. Both "Cahiers Du Cinema" and "Positif," the two leading and oft opposed film journals of France, drop any argument when it comes to singing praises of "Le Roi Du Crazy," as Lewis is affectionately known. Lewis has been enrolled as a Commander of Arts and Letters by France's cultural minister and has been inducted into the "Legion D'honneur," an exclusive academy formed by Napoleon in 1802 as an order of chivalry for those who make "outstanding services in times of war and peace." Seeing as to how his films were "unappreaciated" (for lack of a better term) by American audiences in recent years, Lewis made a wise career move by beginning to appear in French films. This is his second and like his recent American comedies SMORGASBORD and HARDLY WORKING explores the forbidden territory of the impossibly inane. Lewis plays a private detective hired by a woman to catch her husband (Clair, the film's director as well) in one of his dalliances out of the bonds of wedlock. Instead, Lewis and Clair become friends. When Clair gets in trouble because of larceny the duo must flee to Tunisia (a handy location considering that the film's producer hails from there) where they get involved in intrigue between rival factions in the international hotbed of fast food chains. It doesn't take much for one to realize that a French Lewis film is no different from an American one. Among the "zany" gags include an aerobics class of portly women who cause a building to shake as they go through their routines. Clair's direction is just as incompetent as Lewis' later work, showing no talent for comedy. As if that weren't enough, the Frenchman takes every chance he can get to top Lewis in mugging and pratfalls. Lewis himself is uninspired, merely going through the motions in his performance. Some French critics have suggested that Lewis represents something unique about the U.S. that is beyond the comprehension of most Americans. This film makes a strong case for saying that there is something about the French that most Americans do not want to comprehend. (In French.)

p, Tarak Ben Ammar; d, Philippe Clair; w, Clair, Daniel Saint-Hamon, Bruno Tardon; ph, Andre Domage; ed, Francoise Javet Frederix; art d, Jean-Michael Hugon.

Comedy **(PR:A MPAA:NR)**

PARIS, TEXAS****** (1984, Ger./Fr.) 150m Road Movies-Argos-Westdeutscher Rundfunk-Channel 4-Pro-Ject/FOX c

Harry Dean Stanton *(Travis Clay Henderson)*, Nastassja Kinski *(Jane)*, Dean Stockwell *(Walt Henderson)*, Aurore Clement *(Anne)*, Hunter Carson *(Hunter)*, Bernhard Wicki *(Dr. Ulmer)*, Viva Auder *(Woman on TV)*, Socorro Valdez *(Carmelita)*, Tom Farrell *(Screaming Man)*, John Lurie *(Slater)*, Jeni Vici *(Stretch)*, Sally Norvell *(Nurse Bibs)*, Sam Berry *(Gas Station Attendant)*, Claresie Mobley *(Car Rental Clerk)*, Justin Hogg *(Hunter At Age 3)*, Edward Fayton *(Hunter's Friend, Edward)*, Sharon Menzel *(Comedienne)*, The Mydolls *(Rehearsing Band)*.

An intimate epic which combines the European sentiments of German director Wenders with the expansive locations of America's west. Against the rocky desert and brilliant blue sky of Big Bend, Texas, a catatonic Stanton aimlessly wanders under the boiling sun wearing a dusty suit and a bright red baseball cap. Having run out of water, he makes a pit stop in a remote adobe tavern, swallows a handful of crushed ice, and promptly collapses. He awakes in the care of a shifty German doctor, Wicki, who pokes and probes Stanton but cannot get him to speak. Assuming his patient is a mute, Wicki calls a phone number that is buried in Stanton's wallet. Stanton's brother, Stockwell, is contacted at his billboard painting business in Los Angeles where he lives with Clement, his French wife, and Carson, the 7-year-old son of Stanton and his estranged wife Kinski. The news comes as a complete shock to Stockwell, since Stanton has been missing for four years and was assumed dead. Stockwell immediately travels to Wicki's clinic, only to find that Stanton left early that morning. Stockwell drives through the desert until he finds the dazed Stanton. Stanton still refuses to talk and barely even recognizes Stockwell. Stockwell talks his brother into getting into the car. Stanton experiences an anxiety attack while waiting for a Los Angeles-bound airplane to take off, so Stockwell is forced to drive the entire distance home. Along the way, Stanton finally begins to talk. Instead of explaining his four-year absence, he asks his brother if they can drive to Paris, Texas. As it turns out, Stnaton owns a small plot of desert land there – where their parents made love for the first time and possibly where Stanton was conceived. Once in Los Angeles, in Stockwell's picturesque hilltop home, Stanton and Carson meet again. It is an awkward and childlike meeting in which father and son say nothing more than "Hi" to each other. Stanton does his best to act like a model father, but Carson remains distant. One morning Stanton offers to walk Carson home from school, but the boy violently refuses and insists "Nobody walks. Everybody drives." When Stanton arrives at the schoolyard, Carson ignores him and accepts a ride home from a friend's mother. Later that evening, Stockwell suggests that they watch some old Super-8 films of a family vacation that includes Stanton, Kinski, and a 3-year-old Carson (played by Hogg) in happier times. The films impress upon Stanton and Carson that they are father and son, and that Kinski is also part of their family. Stanton makes a conscious effort to look and act like a father. The following day, with the help of Stockwell's Spanish cleaning lady, Valdez, he dresses up in a fashionable white three-piece suit and cowboy hat – what he perceives as proper father attire – and meets Carson at school. This time instead of ignoring him Carson decides to walk home with him. Meantime, Clement feels like she is losing Carson and becomes increasingly depressed. She is aware that Carson is the stabilizing factor in her marriage and without him her relationship with Stockwell may collapse. To save her "family," Clement tells Stanton that she knows where Kinski is, hoping that he will leave town on a trek to find her. On the fifth of every month, Kinski deposits money for Carson at a Houston bank. Stanton gets himself a beatup Ford Ranchero and makes plans to drive to Houston. He informs his son of his planned trip only to have Carson insist on accompanying him. They arrive in Houston on the fifth and station themselves at strategic points outside the bank, armed with walkie-talkies to report the first sighting of Kinski. The day passes and both Stanton and Carson fall asleep. As fate would have it, Carson wakes up just as Kinski's little red car is pulling away. Stanton awakens just on time. They give Kinski chase onto a highway. After losing sight of her car, they spot it again. They also spot a second, identical car which is about to exit the highway. By chance, they follow the correct car to an alley parking lot. Carson stays in the car while Stanton goes into a nearby building. Stanton soon realizes that Kinski works in a sex club where customers, seated in a private booth, can talk to girls via a one-way mirror. Stanton manages to summon Kinski. He talks briefly to her, though she cannot see him and doesn't seem to recognize his voice. Realizing that the family life he envisioned will never be possible, Stanton takes Carson to a downtown hotel and leaves him. A tape-recorded message to Carson explains that, even though he loves him, he can no longer stay and that Carson and Kinski belong together. Stanton then returns to the club and talks, in the booth, with Kinski. He tells here his feelings in the form of a story about two lovers who "turned everything into an adventure," eventually revealing that their idyllic romance turned sour when he quit his job to be with her. He began to drink and grow suspicious. Later he began to beat her. One night, he awoke to find himself and the trailer he lived in on fire. Running through the flames to save his wife and child, he discovers that they had left in the middle of the night. Stanton then tells Kinski that he brought Carson with him, giving her the name of the hotel and the room number. Later, in the hotel room, Carson and Kinski are reunited, while on the street below Stanton gets into his Ranchero and drives off into the night. While most filmmakers today continue to confuse "long" with "epic," Wenders has delivered in PARIS, TEXAS A film which, at 150 minutes, doesn't seem to be nearly *long* enough. Separating this film from the usual epics is a surprisingly warm and genuine intimacy. In the forefront of PARIS, TEXAS are not epic themes, or grandiose sets, or a cast of thousands, but five very average characters who are searching for family and identity. From the opening shots one can feel this epic quality, but in an altered form. The expansive landscapes seem an homage to those of John Ford, but instead of the typical Ford hero wandering across the fame we see Stanton in a suit and tie – a modern American father – displaced, aimless, and emotionally dead. On foot (a car crash is what killed his father), Stanton continues an odyssey to find himself. He not only knows where he began (on that lot in Paris, Texas), but has purchased the place, and carries a snapshot of it in his packet. What he must find out now is who he is and where he is going. It is by finding his family – his brother, sister-in-law, wife, and son – that he finds himself. At the film's end, he is no longer the mute without emotions that we saw at the beginning. While his greatest hope goes unrealized – that of resuming family life with Kinski – he does, at least, confirm some sort of identity; being a father. Based on Shepard's stories

"Motel Chronicles," PARIS, TEXAS was written over a period of a year and a half, during which Shepard was on and off the set of COUNTRY, in which he had a starring role. As much as one can sense Shepard's presence (the film's talky last half-hour, for example), the feeling of Americana that is captured in the film is wholly Wenders'. Wenders, a German director deeply fascinated by American culture, spent three months scouting western locations hoping to find those which would best illustrate his ideal of America. Like the title implies, however, Wenders' perception of America is a European one. Wenders' America is not purely American, but a by-product of foreign cultures – the doctor is German, Stockwell's wife is French, his and Stanton's mother was Spanish but constantly introduced by their father as "the girl he met in Paris," and much of the film takes place near the Mexican-American border. Having a superb script would mean nothing if PARIS, TEXAS had not been graced with equally superb performances. Stanton, after years of playing thankless supporting roles, shines, as does the oddly cast Stockwell. Clement, a leading French actress, succeeds in making her character perhaps the most complex in the film – a temporary mother who is losing her child and, as a result, possibly her husband and who breaks down in the process. Kinski successfully convinces with a Texas accent and blonde hair. The most pleasant surprise is Carson's debut performance. The son of Karen Black and this film's adapter, L. M. Kit Carson (he also wrote the script to DAVID HOLZMAN'S DIARY, 1968), the blond-haired Carson has a screen presence that won't quit and a keen sense of naturalism in his "acting," which hardly seems like acting at all. What is equally rare in a film with such emphasis on script and character is the brilliant cinematography by Muller, one of the finest cameramen in the world. A major contributing factor in PARIS, TEXAS's walkaway victory at the 1984 Cannes Film Festival, Muller's photography perfectly captures the notion of "America." PARIS, TEXAS marked a return, after a several year hiatus, for Muller as Wenders' cameraman (during which time Muller photographed Peter Bogdanovich's THEY ALL LAUGHED, 1981, and Alex Cox's REPO MAN, 1984, which also starred Stanton). Muller, a nontechnical cameraman and a strong proponent of using only natural light to illuminate a scene, delivers a simple, down-to-earth America, one which parallels the simple, down-to-earth characters. A final factor to PARIS, TEXAS's atmosphere is a remarkably haunting score by bluesy guitarist Ry Cooder, whose work on Walter Hill's films (notably THE LONG RIDERS, 1980) and Tony Richardson's THE BORDER (1982) is equally commendable.

p, Don Guest; d, Wim Wenders; w, Sam Shepard (based on a story adapted by L.M. Kit Carson); ph, Robby Muller; m, Ry Cooder (performed by Cooder, David Lindley, Jim Dickinson); ed, Peter Pryzgodda; art d, Kate Altman; cos, Birgitta Bjerke; makeup, Charles Balazs.

Drama   **Cas.**   **(PR:C-O   MPAA:R)**

PASSAGE TO INDIA, A*½**   (1984, Brit.) 163m John Heyman-Edward Sands-Home Box Office/COL c

Judy Davis (Adela Quested), Victor Banerjee (Dr. Aziz), Peggy Ashcroft (Mrs. Moore), James Fox (Richard Fielding), Alec Guinness (Godbole), Nigel Havers (Ronny Heaslop), Richard Wilson (Turton), Antonia Pemberton (Mrs. Turton), Michael Culver (McBryde), Art Malik (Mahmoud Ali), Saeed Jaffrey (Hamidullah), Clive Swift (Maj. Callendar), Anne Firbank (Mrs. Callendar), Roshan Seth (Amritrao), Sandra Hotz (Stella), Rashid Karapiet (Mr. Das), H.S. Krishnamurthy (Hassen), Ishaq Bux (Selim), Moti Makan (Guide), Mohammed Ashiq (Haq), Phyllis Bose (Mrs. Leslie), Sally Kinghorne (Ingenue), Paul Anil (Clerk of the Court), Z.H. Khan (Dr. Pana Lal), Ashok Mandanna (Anthony), Dina Pathak (Begum Hamidullah), Adam Blackwood (Mr. Hadley), Mellan Mitchell (Indian Businessman), Peter Hughes (P.& O. Manager).

Fourteen years after RYAN'S DAUGHTER, David Lean, the 75-year-old director of three of the most visually astounding epics of all- time–THE BRIDGE ON THE RIVER KWAI, LAWRENCE OF ARABIA, and DOCTOR ZHIVAGO (which together have won 19 Oscars)–has returned to the screen with this adaptation of the well-known novel about sexual repression and racial prejudice in 1924 India. Set in the fictional town of Chandrapore, the story concerns a young, well- trained British woman, Davis, who settles into her Indian surroundings with the desire to discover the "real India." She is taken there by her elderly companion, Ashcroft, to find a husband in the old woman's son, Havers, the town magistrate. Before long, however, she grows tired of the stodginess of the tea-and-crumpet crowd and yearns to see more of the country. Banerjee, a well-educated Indian who socializes with the British but still suffers the stigma of his race, offers to take her to the Marabar caves. She readily agrees, but her excursion takes a violent twist. At Marabar, she suddenly and inexplicably emerges from the caves battered and bloodied. Banerjee is then shocked to learn that Davis has accused him of raping her. The English ruling class jumps to Davis' defense, as if it had been waiting all along for an incident like this to occur. Banerjee's friendship with English scholars is severed, though good friend Fox tries to stand by him. The case comes to trial and in the end Banerjee is acquitted, but both his and Davis' lives are ruined in India, and the tensions between the two races are stretched even thinner than before. In keeping with the Forster novel, Lean chose to keep the incident in the caves mysterious. So important was this mystery (which represents the mystery the entire country of India holds to foreigners) to Lean that when the film's producer Brabourne contacted the director after purchasing the rights to the novel, the director immediately asked, "What happened in the caves?" Whatever happened in

the caves, Davis emerges from the incident with an awakened sexuality, one which comes in response to the repressions of the British society from which she tries so hard to free herself. Davis, an Australian actress, plays the part superbly, convincingly portraying a woman who initially seems very plain and asexual, but then showing the discovery of a certain sexual desire. Also a marvel is the performance of Ashcroft (who is remembered as far back as 1935 in Alfred Hitchcock's THE 39 STEPS, as well as for her lengthy career on the British stage), who deservedly won a Best Supporting Actress award for this role. Director Lean deserves much credit for taking Forster's difficult novel and somehow pulling a cohesive narrative line out of it, thereby giving his actors a path to follow, as opposed to the tangents for which Forster has a preference. As usual, Lean's visuals are the highlight of the picture, bringing the beauty of the country (the majority of the film was shot in Bangalore) to the screen with the help of photographer Day and production designer Box, both of whom worked on LAWRENCE OF ARABIA and DR. ZHIVAGO, with Box winning Oscars on both occasions.

p, John Brabourne, Richard Goodwin; d&w, David Lean (based on the play by Santha Rama Rau and the novel by E.M. Forster); ph, Ernest Day (Metrocolor); m, Maurice Jarre; ed, Lean; prod d, John Box; art d, Leslie Tomkins, Clifford Robinson, Ram Yedekar, Herbert Westbrook; set d, Hugh Scaife; cos, Judy Moorcroft; m/l, "Freely Maisie," John Dolby; makeup, Jill Carpenter, Eric Allwright.

Drama   **Cas.**   **(PR:C   MPAA:PG)**

PEACEMAKER   (SEE: THE AMBASSADOR)

PERFECT STRANGERS**   (1984) 94m Helmdale/New Line c (AKA: BLIND ALLEY)

Anne Carlisle (Sally), Brad Rijn (Johnny), John Woehrle (Fred), Matthew Stockley (Matthew), Stephen Lack (Lt. Burns), Ann Magnuson (Feminist), Zachary Hains (Maletti), Otto von Wernherr (Private Eye).

An effective little suspenser which doubles as a romance and stars Carlisle (LIQUID SKY) as a divorced mother living in New York's East Village with her 2-year-old son. The boy witnesses a murder, but since he is unable to speak yet he cannot identify the killer. The killer begins following Carlisle and her son around, wondering if the boy can recognize him. Carlisle is attracted to the killer and the two soon become romantically involved. In the meantime, Carlisle's ex-husband fights to get custody of the youngster, while the killer is under pressure from his criminal cohorts to bump off the boy. The gripping finale has the audience wondering if the husband will be able to kidnap the child before the killer reaches him. Cohen adroitly handles the intriguing plot which bears some similarity to Peter Weir's superior WITNESS (1985).

p, Paul Kurta; d&w, Larry Cohen; ph, Paul Glickman; m, Dwight Dixon; ed, Armond Lebowitz; m/1, Michael Minard.

Crime   **Cas.**   **(PR:O   MPAA:R)**

PERILS OF GWENDOLINE, THE*½   (1984, Fr.) 102m Parafrance-Alma-G.F.P.I/Goldwyn c (GWENDOLINE; AKA: THE PERILS OF GWENDOLINE IN THE LAND OF THE YIK-YAK)

Tawny Kitaen (Gwendoline), Brent Huff (Willard), Zabou (Beth), Bernadette Lafont (The Queen), Jean Rougerie (D'Arcy), Roland Amstutz, Vernon Dobtcheff, Kristopher Kum, Jim Adhi Lima, Roger Paschy, Jean Stanislas Capoul, Andre Julien, Loi Lam Duc, Georges Lycan, Chen Chang Ching, Takashi Kawahara, Maurice Lamy, Dominique Marcas, Hua Quach.

After her father disappears during an expedition to the mysterious East to gather a specimen of a semi-legendary butterfly, Kitaen leaves the French convent where she has been educated in order to look for him. She and best friend Zabou stow away on a ship, but as soon as they arrive in Asia she is captured by white slavers who sell her to a brothel. Handsome smuggler Huff rescues her and she persuades him to accompany her to the land of Yik-Yak, from which no man has has ever returned. Surviving pirates, cannibals, and a desert, they find the underground city of Yik-Yak, an amazon society ruled by Lafont. After winning a gladiatorial contest to see which of the warrior women will get Huff, Kitaen takes advantage of an earthquake to escape with him and Zabou. A silly adventure with a lot of exposed breasts (though nothing more explicit), and some sense of style (to be expected from the director of EMMANUELLE), the film is mostly boring–frequently promising but never delivering action, sex, or even a decent line reading. Based on a notorious erotic comic strip of the 1930s, the color film doesn't titillate or entertain nearly as well as the black and white line drawings of its source. Allegedly the most expensive production in French film history, one can't help but wonder where the money went.

p, Jean-Claude Fleury, Serge Laski; d&w, Just Jaeckin (based on a comic strip by John Wilie); ph, Andre Domage; m, Pierre Bachelet; ed, Michele Boehm; prod d, Francoise Deleu; art d, Andrew Guerin; makeup, Reiko Kruk, Dominique Collandant; cos, Daniel Elis.

Adventure   **Cas.**   **(PR:O   MPAA:R)**

**PERILS OF GWENDOLINE IN THE LAND OF THE YIK-YAK,
THE**   (SEE: PERILS OF GWENDOLINE, THE, Fr.)

PHAR LAP*½** (1984, Aus.) FOX c (AKA:PHAR LAP–HEART OF A
NATION)

Tom Burlinson (*Tommy Woodcock*), Ron Leibman (*Dave Davis*), Martin
Vaughan (*Harry Telford*), Judy Morris (*Bea Davis*), Celia De Burgh (*Vi
Telford*), Richard Morgan (*"Cashy" Martin*), Robert Grubb (*William
Neilsen*), Georgia Carr (*Emma*), James Steele (*Jim Pike*), Vincent Ball
(*Lachlan McKinnon*), Peter Whitford (*Bert Wolfe*), John Stanton (*Eric
Connolly*), Roger Newcombe (*James Crofton*), Len Kaserman (*Baron Long*),
Tom Woodcock (*Trainer*), Steven Bannister, Richard Terrill, Warwick Moss,
Henry Duvall, Pat Thompson, Redmond Phillips, Maggie Miller, Anthony
Hawkins, Brian Anderson, Paul Riley, Brian Adams, Alan Wilson.

Another story of a boy and his horse, this time set in Australia in the early
1930s. The film opens as the horse lays dying in a stable in Mexico after
winning the biggest race of its career, the Agua Caliente in April of 1932.
The cause of the horse's death goes unexplained, as it is to this day, though
the blame is clearly pointed toward the Australian gamblers who had
consistently lost money as the horse consistently won race after race. From
this point the narrative moves backward, showing how the young horse was
purchased in New Zealand by Vaughan, a trainer whose experienced eye
spots potential in the animal, despite its lack of pedigree. His partner in the
purchase is Leibman, a fast-talking American Jew who suffers greatly at the
hands of anti-semites in Australia as his horse triumphs over their horses.
The horse is extremely skittish, though, and loses its first four races, even
as Vaughan tries even more brutal methods of snapping it into line. It is
finally Burlinson, a stable boy, who establishes a bond with the horse
through kindness, and from that time on it wins every race. Bookies in
Sydney are all but wiped out as everyone bets the horse. More weight is
added on the horse's back to try to even out the odds, but still he wins.
Finally Vaughan and Leibman take him to Mexico, where he wins the big
race, then dies under mysterious circumstances. Phar Lap today is remembered in the same way as Man O' War is in the U.S. or Red Rum in Britain,
the greatest horse of its day, and a symbol of national pride. While the film
plays a little too heavily on this patriotic theme, it still works on the simple
level of a story about a horse and a boy (incidentally, the child Burlinson
plays is still alive today, and at age 78 appears in the film as a trainer, in
addition to acting as a technical advisor). The film is impressively done, with
some of the same feeling as CHARIOTS OF FIRE (right down to slow-motion
scenes of the horse running along a beach). The performances are all good,
with Leibman excellent. One of the most expensive films in Australian
history, it was also one of the most successful.

p, John Sexton; d, Simon Wincer; w, David Williamson (based on the book
The Phar Lap Story by Michael Wilkinson); ph, Russell Boyd (Panavision);
m, Bruce Rowland; ed, Tony Paterson; prod d, Laurence Eastwood; art d,
David Bowden; set d, Sally Campbell; cos, Anna Senior.

Sports Drama   Cas.   (PR:C MPAA:PG)

PHILADELPHIA EXPERIMENT, THE½**
(1984) 102M New World c

Michael Pare (*David Herdeg*), Nancy Allen (*Allison*), Eric Christmas
(*Longstreet*), Bobby Di Cicco (*Jim Parker*), Kene Holliday (*Maj. Clark*),
Louise Latham (*Pamela*), Joe Dorsey (*Sheriff Bates*), Michael Currie
(*Magnusson*), Stephen Tobolowsky (*Barney*), Gary Brockette (*Adjutant/
Andrews*), Debra Troyer (*Young Pamela*), Miles McNamara (*Young Long-
street*), Ralph Manza (*Older Jim*), Jim Edgecomb (*Officer Boyer*), Glenn
Morshower (*Mechanic*), Rodney Saulsberry (*Doctor*), Vivian Brown (*Ma
Willis*), Ed Bakey (*Pa Willis*), Stephanie Faulkner (*Newscaster No.1*),
Michael Villani (*Newcaster No.2*), Vaughn Armstrong (*Cowboy*), Bill Smillie
(*Evangelist*), Lawrence Lott (*Technician*), Stephen O'Reilly (*Punk Rocker*),
Clayton Wilcox (*Transvestite*), Pat Dasko (*Dry Wells Newscaster*), Pamela
Brull (*Doris*), Pamela Doucette (*Nurse*), Richard Jewkes (*Technician*),
Michael Rudd (*Truck Driver*), Deborah E. Dixon (*Nurse*), Mary Lois
Grantham (*Mrs. Waite*), Rick Schrand (*Mandell*), Brent E. Laing (*Radar
Tecnician*), Patrick De Santis (*Jim, Jr.*), Andrew McCartney (*Technician*),
Robin Krieger (*X-Ray Technician*), Andrew R. Nuzzo (*Generator Techni-
cian*), Charles Hall (*Commander*), Joe Moore (*Commander's Buddy*), Ray-
mond Kowalski (*Radio Technician*), Don Dolan (*Driver*), Jeffrey S. Smith
(*Sailor*), Tony Farrell (*Bandleader*), Andrew Bracken (*Crazed Sailor*), Rudy
Daniels, Gilbert Girion (*Policemen*), Sharon Doss (*Violet*), Jay Bernard
(*Engineer*), Steve Sachs (*1st Sailor*), Harry Beer (*2nd Sailor*), Bo Parkam,
Kerry Lee Maher (*Radio Operators*), Lawrence Doll (*Helicopter Pilot*).

A fascinating but thoroughly unbelievable science fiction film about a 1943
military experiment that goes awry. Pare and Di Cicco are young sailors on
board a battleship which a scientist is trying to render invisible to the
enemy's radar. The experiment fails and the entire ship disappears from its
Philadelphia port. Pare and Di Cicco try to jump ship but instead fall
through an electromagnetic time zone and land in the middle of a Nevada
test sight in 1984. It seems that scientist Christmas, now 40 years older, is
still trying to perfect his experiment. This time, however, he has made an
entire city disappear. The confused sailors are shocked to find out that
they've jumped ahead 40 years. Everything has changed – television,
aluminum cans, vans, video games – leaving Pare and Di Cicco practically

helpless. While at a small town diner, Di Cicco inadvertently finds that he
is a sparking, zapping conductor of electric energy. The sailors are forced to
make a getaway, kidnaping Allen and stealing her car, which they cannot
drive because of its automatic transmission. Di Cicco's condition worsens
until he dies in a hospital and disappears. Pare and Allen plan to get to the
Nevada military base, but not before Pare can pay a visit to his California
home town. They stop at the gas station his father once owned, and meet
with Di Cicco's widow who lives, to Pare's amazement, with an aged Di Cicco
(played by Manza). After being chased down by the military, Pare finally
manages to penetrate the base where Christmas is trying to right his wrong.
As a result of his experimentation, the immediate area is being destroyed
by high winds caused by a "hole" in the sky – the same hole that Pare fell
through. The only way to prevent doomsday is for Pare to return to the hole,
climb aboard his battleship (which is stranded in limbo alongside the town)
and shut down its generators. Pare is torn between his duty as a sailor and
his growing affection for Allen, but agrees to help Christmas. He succeeds
on his mission and even returns to Allen for a romantic finale. THE
PHILADELPHIA EXPERIMENT, while loaded down with pseudo-scientific
mummbo-jumbo, still manges to be entertaining. One can't help but watch
in awe as Pare rediscovers the things and people that he once knew. One
particularly humorous scene has Ronald Reagan, whom Pare knows only as
an actor in B pictures, delivering a Presidential speech on television.
Another fascinating moment has Pare trying to comprehend the outcome of
WW II, and the fact that the U.S. became allies with the Germans and
Japanese when they were previously enemies. Fortunately, THE PHILA-
DELPHIA EXPERIMENT has enough such moments to make the film
watchable, instead of merely being an exercise in baffling the audience with
incomprehensible scientific ramblings.

p, Douglas Curtis, Joel B. Michaels; d, Stewart Raffill; w, William Gray,
Michael Janover (based on a story by Wallace Bennett, Don Jakoby from the
book by William I. Moore, Charles Berlitz); ph, Dick Bush (CFI Color), m,
Ken Wannberg; ed Neil Travis; art d, Chris Campbell; set d, Diane Campbell;
cos, Joanne Palace; spec eff, Max Anderson; m/1, "In the Mood," Joe
Garland, "Memories of You," Eubie Blake, Andy Razaf, "I'll Never Be the
Same Again," Ruth Lowe, "The Runner," Ian Thomas (performed by
Manfred Mann).

Science Fiction   Cas.   (PR:C MPAA:PG)

PIGS**   (1984, Ireland) 78m Irish Film Board/Samson c

Jimmy Brennan (*Jimmy*), George Shane (*George*), Maurice O'Donoghue
(*Tom*), Liam Halligan (*Ronnie*), Kwesi Kay (*Orwell*), Joan Harpur (*Mary*).

A character study of a group of outcasts living in a slum section of Dublin.
The film centers mainly around Brennan, a homosexual ex-convict who
takes refuge in an abandoned house. Before long others have moved in –
pimps, prostitutes, a con man, and a mental patient. Well-photographed and
occasionally poignant, but too short to reach any real depth.

p, David Collins; d, Cathal Black; w, Jimmy Brennan; ph, Thaddeus
O'Sullivan; m, Roger Doyle; ed, Se Merry; art d, Frank Conway.

Drama   (PR:C MPAA:NR)

PIGS, THE   (SEE: DADDY'S DEADLY DARLING)

PLACES IN THE HEART*½**   (1984) 112m Tri-Star c

Sally Field (*Edna Spalding*), Lindsay Crouse (*Margaret Lomax*), Ed Harris
(*Wayne Lomax*), Amy Madigan (*Viola Kelsey*), John Malkovich (*Mr. Will*),
Danny Glover (*Moze*), Yankton Hatten (*Frank*), Gennie James (*Possum*),
Lane Smith (*Albert Denby*), Terry O'Quinn (*Buddy Kelsey*), Bert Remsen
(*Tee Tot Hightower*), Raymond Baker (*Royce Spalding*), Jay Patterson (*W.E.
Simmons*), Toni Hudson (*Ermine*), DeVoreaux White (*Wylie*), Jerry Haynes
(*Deputy Jack Driscoll*), Lou Hancock (*Dispossessed Lady*), Shelby Brammer
(*Ruby*), Norma Young (*Beauty Shop Customer*), Bill Thurman, Jim Gough,
Cliff Brunner (*Lone Star Syrup Boys*), Arthur Pugh (*Dove Haslip*), Matthew
Posey (*Eugene*), Greg Brazzell, Lynn Covey, Randy Fife, Vernon Grote, Ned
Dowd, Paul Nuckles (*KKK Men*), Lynn D. Lasswell, Jr. (*Preacher*), J.C.
Quinn, Robert Schenkkan, Trey Wilson (*Texas Voices*), Bascom Newman
(*Farmhouse Dance Voice*), Paul Goodwin (*Mr. Cheeves*), Connie Grandell
(*Mrs. Cheeves*), William J. Welch (*Narrator, "Trent's Last Case"*), Bobby
Porter, Sharon Schaffer (*Stunt Doubles*), Shanna Shrum.

Fields won another Oscar for this role, which bore more than a passing
resemblance to NORMA RAE insofar as it was a rural tale about a woman
who fought back against the fat cats of authority. Director-writer Benton
(who made KRAMER VS. KRAMER) went back to his own memories of life
in the dreary Texas town where his family had been for numerous
generations. It's 1930 in Waxahachie and Field is the newly widowed wife
of the local lawman, Spalding, who is shot to death in the first few minutes
by a bullet accidentally fired from the gun of a local black drunk. It's not
minutes before Field learns that her mortgage of $240 is to be foreclosed by
the bank if she doesn't come up with the cash. She has no money to speak
of and is in danger of losing the property soon unless she can think of some
sort of plan. Her property totals 40 acres and she reckons she might be able
to plant and harvest a cotton crop in time to make the payment but she
knows as much about raising cotton as Butterfly McQueen knew about

"birthin' babies" in another southern-based story. One day, salvation comes in the form of Glover, a black laborer who ambles up to the house and asks if she needs anyone to help around the property. The fact that Glover knows as much about cotton as Eli Whitney helps a great deal and the two combine to plant, cultivate, pick, and sell the crop. To keep body and soul together, Field takes in a blind boarder, Malkovich, who gives a first-rate performance as the blind man and is so convincing that one wonders how much research he did to get that good. There are other characters, such as Field's sister, Crouse, and the neighborhood adulterers, Harris and Madigan, but they seem to be in the movie as counterpoint rather than melody. Field does an excellent job in the film although it seems as though we've seen it before in a few of her other movies and it was hardly worth the Oscar she received. You may recall her surprise at winning the award and her gushing speech which said "You really *like* me," as though anyone could not like such a sweet woman whose reputation as a person and as an actress has always been untarnished, even when she was flying around the sky in a nun's habit. Since breaking away from TV, Field has made her mark in movies, a rare occurrence for someone who came out of the tube. Benton's script is intelligent, spare, and authentic, and his direction equally meritorious. The characters are all real, the background believable, and the story, thankfully, has none of the forced melodrama of COUNTRY or THE RIVER, two films rooted in the same area, if not the same generation. The music by Kander and Shore is a great help to the movie and feels exactly right. Harris does a good job in a smaller role than he usually plays.

p, Arlene Donovan; d&w, Robert Benton; ph, Nestor Almendros (Technicolor); m, John Kander, Howard Shore; ed, Carol Littleton; prod d, Gene Callahan; art d, Sydney Z. Litwack; set d, Lee Poll, Derek Hill; cos, Ann Roth; spec eff, Bran Ferren; stunts, Sharon Schaffer, Bobby Porter.

Drama   Cas.   (PR:A-C MPAA:PG)

PLAGUE DOGS, THE**   (1984, U.S./Brit.) 103m Nepenthe/United
International c

Voices: John Hurt, Christopher Benjamin, James Bolam, Nigel Hawthorne, Warren Mitchell, Bernard Hepton, Brian Stirner, Penelope Lee, Geoffrey Mathews, Barbara Leigh-Hunt, John Bennet, John Franklyn-Robbins, Bill Maynard, Malcolm Terris, Judy Geeson, Philip Locke, Brian Spink, Tony Church, Anthony Valentine, William Lucas, Dandy Nichols, Rosemary Leach, Patrick Stewart.

Distasteful animated film from the same bunch that brought Adams' novel WATERSHIP DOWN to the screen, dealing with the issue of animal experimentation none too tactfully. Two dogs escape from a scientific research center and forage around England looking for food and shelter. Unfortunately, the government is hot on their heels because one had been infected with bubonic plague. Thinking there is an island they can escape to, the dogs plunge into the sea and make a desperate swim for it, only to find that the island was just an illusion (a symbol perhaps?). The animation is better than average but not outstanding, and the script is overly simplistic in its examination of the thematic content.

pd&w, Martin Rosen (based on a novel by Richard Adams); ph, James Farrell, Marlyn O'Connor, Ron Jackson, Ted Bemiller, Jr., Bill Bemiller, Robert Velguth, Thane Berti (Technicolor); m, Patrick Gleeson, Alan Price; prod d, Gordon Harrison; animation director, Tony Guy, Colin White.

Drama   Cas.   (PR:C-O MPAA:NR)

PLEIN SUD   (SEE: HEAT OF DESIRE, Fr.)

PLOUGHMAN'S LUNCH, THE****   (1984, Brit.) 107m
Greenpoint/Samuel Goldwyn c

Jonathan Pryce (*James Penfield*), Tim Curry (*Jeremy Hancock*), Rosemary Harris (*Ann Barrington*), Frank Finlay (*Matthew Fox*), Charlie Dore (*Susan Barrington*), David De Keyser (*Gold*), Nat Jackley (*Mr. Penfield*), Bill Paterson (*Lecturer*), William Maxwell, Paul Jesson, Andy Rashleigh (*Journalists*), Christopher Fulford (*Young Journalist*), David Lyon (*Newsreader*), Polly Abbott (*Gold's Assistant*), Peter Walmsley (*Bob Tuckett*), Bob Cartland (*Editor*), Pearl Hackney (*Mrs. Penfield*), Simon Stokes (*Edward*), Anna Wing (*Woman at Poetry Reading*), Ken Drury (*Young Man at Poetry Reading*), Richard Cottan (*Student at Poetry Reading*), Peter Birch (*Barman*), Ken Shorter (*Squash Coach*), Orlando Wells (*Tom Fox*), Witold Schejbal (*Jacek*), Libba Davies (*Betty*), Sandra Voe (*Carmen*), Andrew Norton (*Pete*), Cecily Hobbs (*Carol*), Clare Sutcliffe (*Jill*), Robert McIntosh (*Dad in Commercial*), Vivienne Chandler (*Mum in Commercial*), Nicole Kleeman (*Daughter in Commercial*), Allan Mitchell (*Junior Minister*), Bernard Mullins (*Son in Commercial*).

This gripping episodic tale set against the backdrop of the Falklands War explores the relationship between the politics and morality of individuals and those of governments. It follows the fortunes of BBC radio journalist Pryce as he pursues career success and the girl of his dreams with the same determined self-interest. A would-be historian and unbridled opportunist, he burns the midnight oil patriotically reinterpreting the British role in the 1956 Suez crisis in the light of events in the South Atlantic. Assuring his conservative publisher that he is *not* a socialist, Pryce tailors his work-in-progress to suit the spirit of the times. The object of his affections is Dore,

a TV documentary researcher and, more important, the daughter of eminent left-wing historian Harris, an impassioned expert on Suez. Pryce wangles an invitation to Harris' home in picturesque Norfolk, as much to advance his conquest of Dore as to pick her mother's brain. Harris is captivated by Pryce. He assures her that the *is* a socialist, and she sees him as a young idealist ready to take over the torch. She invites him to return the following weekend for a more extensive visit. Back in London, Pryce continues to woo Dore, consulting the friend who had arranged his introduction to her, Curry, a tabloid hack with oily Oxbridge self-confidence. Pryce returns to Norfolk. Dore is there but unable (or unwilling) to find any time for him; not so for Harris, who comes to Pryce at night and seduces him. Meanwhile, Pryce's own mother lies dying, ignored by her son who, seeking to hide his lower-class origins, has said that his parents are dead. In London again, Pryce is besieged by phone calls from Harris, and though he brushes her off, her husband asks to meet with him. Instead of the confrontation Pryce expects, Finlay tells him that he knows the journalist has slept with his wife and that it's fine by him. Over a meal, Finlay explains the origins of the Ploughman's Lunch (speciously, some have said). He avers that while the familiar pub grub is popularly thought to be a traditional meal it is, in fact, a marketing gimmick of recent origin, "a completely successful fabrication of the past. Time passes and Pryce and Dore become an item. With Curry along for the ride, they drive to Brighton to report on the Conservative Party conference. In amazing footage reminiscent of Haskell Wexler's MEDIUM COOL (which was shot in and around the 1968 Democratic Convention), the trio roam the actual 1982 conference. Prime Minister Margaret Thatcher preaches patriotism and Victorian rectitude (her own fabrication of the past) and Pryce meets his personal Suez when he discovers that Curry and Dore, "old allies," are having an affair. Angry but resolute, Pryce completes his book. In the film's chilling final scene, the camera pans across a cemetery, coming to rest on Pryce as he stands graveside at his mother's burial. He glances at his watch. The frame freezes. Novelist McEwan's script is airtight; stage director Eyre's first cinematic foray is stunning if not seamless; and Pryce's performance is outstanding amidst a cast full of find portrayals. He wrenches audience empathy for a most unsympathetic character, setting the stage for his triumph as the more likable lead in BRAZIL (1985). His yuppie-ish James is to 1980s Britain what Dustin Hoffman's Benjamin (THE GRADUATE) was to the U.S. in the 1960s: where Benjamin was aimless and confused, James is directed, a chameleon-like pragmatist to Benjamin's idealistic innocent. Parallels between these two films abound and in many ways Eyre has taken Mike Nichols' classic and stood it on its head. THE PLOUGHMAN'S LUNCH is also an example of an important development in the resurgence of the British cinema in the 1980s, the bankrolling of independent productions by Channel Four, the U.K.'s fourth and newest TV network. Coming into existence in the early 1980s and striving for innovative programming, Channel Four eschewed in-house made-for-TV films and instead put up the money for independent projects. The resulting films – which also numbered among their early successes THE DRAUGHTSMAN'S CONTRACT and MOONLIGHTING – were in some cases given theatrical release even before appearing on "telly." This was true of Eyre's film, which played the theaters, was shown on TV, and then returned to the movie houses. Interestingly, McEwan's original screenplay was completed before the onset of the Falklands conflict and he and Eyre incorporated those events into their story to great advantage. While some of the politics and the inevitable influence of social class may be unfamiliar to U.S. audiences, no one should let that prevent them from watching this masterful example of British filmmaking.

p, Simon Relph, Ann Scott; d, Richard Eyre; w, Ian McEwan; ph, Clive Tickner; m, Dominic Muldowney; ed, David Martin; prod d, Luciana Arrighi; art d, Michael Pickwoad; cos, Arrighi; makeup, Elaine Carew.

Drama   Cas.   (PR:O MPAA:R)

POLICE ACADEMY*   (1984) 95m Ladd/WB c

Steve Guttenberg (*Carey Mahoney*), G.W. Bailey (*Lt. Harris*), George Gaynes (*Commandant Lassard*), Michael Winslow (*Larvell Jones*), Kim Cattrall (*Karen Thompson*), Bubba Smith (*Moses Hightower*), Andrew Rubin (*George Martin*), Donovan Scott (*Leslie Barbara*), Leslie Easterbrook (*Sgt. Callahan*), David Graff (*Tackleberry*), Marion Ramsey (*Laverne Hooks*), Scott Thompson (*Chad Copeland*), Brant Van Hoffman (*Kyle Blankes*), Georgina Spelvin (*Hooker*), Debralee Scott (*Mrs. Fackler*), Bruce Mahler (*Doug Fackler*), Ted Ross (*Capt. Reed*), Brant Van Hoffman (*Kyle*), Doug Lennox (*Bad Guy*), George R. Robertson (*Chief Hurnst*), Don Lake (*Mr. Wig*), Bill Lynn (*Parking Lot Manager*), Michael J. Reynolds (*Office Executive*), Joyce Gordon (*Mrs. Thompson*), Don Payne (*Barber*), Bruce McFee (*Supply Clerk*), Beth Amos (*Old Lady*), Araby Lockhart (*Mrs. Lassard*), Barry Greene (*Cadet*), Gary Farmer (*Sidewalk Store Owner*), Josef Field, Gary Colwell (*Dancers*), Jim Bearden (*Driver*), Fred Brigham (*Punk*), Marco Bianco, Ted Hanlan, Braun McAsh, Rob Watson (*Toughs*), Roger Dunn (*Booking Sergeant*), Wally Bondarenko, J. Winston Carroll, David Clement, George Zeeman (*Officers*), Gino Marrocco (*Arresting Cop*), Gene Mack (*Thug*), Bob Collins (*Drill Instructor*), Danny Pawlick (*Pool Hall Man*), Ruth Sisberg (*Mayor*), Peter Cox, Danny Lima, Dwayne McLean, Brent Meyers, Carole Alderson, Suzanne Barker, Kimberley Foorman, Jayne Broughton, Julie McLeod, Karen Robyn, Joe Dunne.

With the success of AIRPLANE! in 1980 the scattershot-joke, madcap adventure became *the* hot property for just about any studio putting out a low-budget comedy. POLICE ACADEMY was one of the most successful (spawning sequels and a few lookalike projects) but only as far as the box office was concerned. As a screen comedy it's about as funny as dirty jokes told by third graders. Sisberg is elected mayor to an unnamed city. In one of her first actions she decides to overhaul the police force, allowing anyone regardless of race, creed, or physical condition to join up. A police academy for the misfits who apply is set up, run by cops who naturally disapprove strongly of Sisberg's actions. Guttenberg is a hotshot parking attendant assigned to the academy in lieu of parole when he gets into trouble. He's determined to get out at any cost until he meets Cattrall, a pretty cadet. Other recruits include Smith, the ex-football player portraying a florist who wants to be a lawman. Winslow is Guttenberg's pal in the academy and one of the strangest movie talents ever put on celluloid: His uncanny ability is to imitate innumerable sounds ranging from doors to tommyguns, all with surprising accuracy. (Winslow did his sound effects bit in one of the strangest presentations at the 1985 Academy Awards ceremony.) Also appearing, in what might be called a "legitimate" film role, is Spelvin, a noted actress in such pornographic films as THE DEVIL IN MISS JONES. Appropriately enough, she plays a cheap hooker but manages to keep her clothes on during her brief appearance. Eventually the hapless cops quell a riot downtown in predictable manic fashion and graduate from the academy so they can go on to the sequel POLICE ACADEMY II: THEIR FIRST ASSIGNMENT. The characterizations in this film are stereotypes, leading to obvious conclusions. One female cop (Ramsey) has a shy and quiet voice at the film's beginning but is able to stop bad guys with her big booming shout during the climax. And yes, the film comes complete with some naked female flesh and naughty gags. Helmed and cowritten by Wilson, an ex-TV sitcom director, the film looks very much like a television comedy both in visual style and writing.

p, Paul Maslansky; d, Hugh Wilson; w, Neal Israel, Pat Proft, Wilson (based on a story by Israel and Proft); ph, Michael D. Margulies (Technicolor); m, Robert Folk; ed, Robert Brown, Zack Staenberg; prod d, Trevor Williams; set d, Steve Shewchuk; cos, Christopher Ryan.

Comedy   Cas.   (PR:O   MPAA:R)

POPE OF GREENWICH VILLAGE, THE½**   (1984) 120m
Koch-Kirkwood/MGM-UA c

Eric Roberts (*Paulie*), Mickey Rourke (*Charlie*), Daryl Hannah (*Diane*), Geraldine Page (*Mrs. Ritter*), Kenneth McMillan (*Bed Bug Eddie*), Tony Musante (*Pete*), M. Emmet Walsh (*Burns*), Burt Young (*Bed Bug Eddie*), Jack Kehoe (*Bunky*), Philip Bosco (*Paulie's Father*), Val Avery (*Nunzi*), Joe Grifasi (*Jimmy the Cheese Man*), Tony DiBenedetto (*Ronnie*), Ronald Maccone (*Nicky*), Betty Miller (*Nora*), Thomas A. Carlin (*Walsh*), Leonard Termo (*Fat Waldo*), Marty Brill (*Mel*), John Bentley (*Summons Man*), Ed Setrakian (*Inspector*), Rik Colitti (*Barber*), John Finn (*Ginty*), Kevin Breslin (*Tommy Botondo*), Gerard Murphy (*Garber*), Ed O'Ross (*Bartender at Sal's*), Peter Conti (*Waiter at Sal's*), Tony Lip (*Frankie*), Clem Caserta (*Eating Man at Sal's*), Frank Vincent (*1st Crew Chief*), Claude Vincent (*Bartender at Limehouse*), Anna Levine (*Waitress at Country Inn*), Randall Edwards (*Hat Check Girl*), Bo Smith (*Terry the Groom*), Jacques Sandulescu (*Chef*), Ed DeLeo (*Anthony*), Jose Santana (*Bus Boy*), Samuel G. Laken (*Vinny*), Linda Ipanema (*Cooky*), Tina Vaughn (*Dancer*), Paul Herman (*Stickball Player*), Joan Shangold (*Policewoman*), Henry Yuk (*Assistant Cook*), Felix Pitre (*Restaurant Helper*), James Bulleit (*Cashier*), Paul Austin, William Duell (*Toll Booth Attendants*).

They tried to make a Martin Scorsese film and forgot one essential ingredient–Martin Scorsese. Scorsese has made an art of portraying the seedy side of New York City in such dramas as WHO'S THAT KNOCKING?, MEAN STREETS, TAXI DRIVER, and RAGING BULL. THE POPE OF GREENWICH VILLAGE treads much the same ground as it chronicles the lives of two cousins, Rourke, a guy desperately trying to escape the neighborhood, and Roberts, his dim-witted cousin always looking for another get-rich-quick scheme. Rourke works as a supervisor in a swanky restaurant and Roberts is a waiter. Because of another screw-up by Roberts, both are fired and Rourke must go home to his girl friend, Hannah, with the bad news. Hannah (who seems to be in various stages of undress every time we see her) is a bit upset at the news because she has just learned she is pregnant. This forces Rourke to listen to his crazy cousin's next get-rich-quick scheme which is borrowing money from the local mob to buy a $15,000 racehorse sure to be a champion because it was sired through artificial insemination using sperm stolen from this year's Belmont winner. When asked how he proposes to pay the mob back (their uncle, Musante, is part of the mob), Roberts says he knows an old safecracker, McMillan, who'll get them the dough if they help him on his next job. Against his better judgment, Rourke agrees and the robbery is a success–unfortunately, the money robbed belongs to the local Mafia chieftan, Young, and he wants it back. Young's goons eventually catch up with Roberts and cut his thumb off to remind him to return the money. Rourke tries to cut a deal with Young, but when Young won't listen, crazy Roberts slips lye into the mobster's coffee and as Young thrashes on the floor screaming in pain, the cousins take off with hopes of escaping to California. Considering the screenplay was written by the author of the novel on which it was based, THE POPE OF GREENWICH VILLAGE is a surprising mess. Strong performances from Rourke, McMillan, Musante, and Young are totally offset by Hannah's

vapid appearance and Roberts' over-the-top histrionics. Roberts in this film makes Jack Nicholson's scenery-chewing performance in Kubrick's THE SHINING look restrained. When Roberts reveals to Rourke that the mob has cut off his thumb, the potentially dramatic and heart-wrenching scene is turned into one of uncontrollable laughter as he screams and sobs at the top of his lungs: "He took my thumb!!!" The film tries hard to capture the Keitel-DeNiro relationship in Scorsese's MEAN STREETS but the actors' performances are so out of sync that the effort quickly becomes hopeless. Rourke looks as if he'd rather run the other direction everytime Roberts enters a scene. Hannah's character is never developed and the viewer doesn't buy it that a blonde, yuppie, Waspish girl would be hanging around a seedy character like Rourke. THE POPE OF GREENWICH VILLAGE is filled with such frustrations and the bad aspects of the film simply outweigh the good. Stick to Scorsese.

p, Gene Kirkwood; d, Stuart Rosenberg; w, Vincent Patrick (based on his novel); ph, John Bailey (Metrocolor); m, Dave Grusin; ed, Robert Brown; prod d, Paul Sylbert; set d, George DeTitta, Sr.; cos, Joseph G. Aulisi; m/l, "Summer Wind," (sung by Frank Sinatra); stunts, Bill Anagnos.

Drama   Cas.   (PR:O   MPAA:R)

POWER, THE*   (1984) 84m Jeffrey Obrow Productions/Artists
Releasing-Film Ventures International c

Susan Stokey (*Sandy*), Warren Lincoln (*Jerry*), Lisa Erickson (*Julie*), Chad Christian (*Tommy*), Ben Gilbert (*Matt*), Chris Morrill (*Ron Prince*), Rod Mays (*Lee McKennah*), J. Dinan Mytrelus (*Francis Lott*), Jay Fisher (*Raphael*), Costy Basile (*Jorge*), Juan Del Valle (*Jeep Driver*), Alice Champlin (*Roxanne*), Gabe Cohen (*Marty*), Milton Robinson (*Jack*), Steve Nagle (*Driver*), Barbara Murray (*Tommy's Mother*), Joseph Scott (*Doctor*), Richard Cowgill (*Cemetery Guard*).

Three high school students come into possession of a cursed Aztec idol and use it to try to contact the head. When they become frightened by the power they have unleashed, they contact reporter Stokey. Her boy friend, Lincoln, steals the figurine and is possessed by the demon and transformed into an ugly monster. Finally it occurs to someone to smash the statuette. The monster dies and the day is saved. Low budget, low intelligence horror story offers nothing not already familiar to fans of the genre.

p, Jeffrey Obrow; d&w Obrow, Stephen Carpenter (based on a story by Obrow, Carpenter, John Penny, John Hopkins); ph, Carpenter (Getty Color); m, Chris Young; ed, Obrow, Carpenter; prod d, Chris Hopkins; makeup, Matthew Mungle.

Horror   (PR:O   MPAA:R)

PRENON: CARMEN   (SEE: FIRST NAME: CARMEN, Fr.)

PREPPIES**   (1984) 83m Platinum/Playboy c

Dennis Drake (*Robert "Chip" Thurston*), Steven Holt (*Bayard*), Peter Brady Reardon (*Marc*), Nitchie Barrett (*Roxanne*), Cindy Manion (*Jo*), Katie Stelletello (*Tip*), Katt Shea (*Margot*), Lynda Wiesmeier (*Trini*), Jo Ann Marshall (*Suzy*), Paul Sutton (*Dick Foster*), Leonard Haas (*Blackwel*), Anthony Matteo (*Louie*), Leslie Barrett (*Dean Flossmore*), Wayne Franson (*Binki*), Myra Chasen (*Corki*), Lara Berk (*Kiki*), William Hardy (*Boobie*), William Soso (*Mickey*), Robert Poletick (*Terry*), Mark Cronogue (*Bosco*), Jack Mead (*Mechanic*), Virgil Roberson (*Foreman*), Beverly Brown (*Tanya*), Lynette Sheldon (*Saleswoman*), Jack Burkhard (*Roxanne's Father*), Perry Rosen (*Mike*), Dayton Callie, Bruce Smolanoff (*Break Dancers*), Jerry Winsett (*Waiter*), Joe Geschwind (*Cop*), Craig Horrall (*Barman*), Samuelle Easton (*Waitress*), Jim Bonney (*Guard*), Phil LoPresti (*Singer*), James Louis Fleming (*Snob*).

A reworking of several teenage plots replete with the usual sex jokes, low comedy, and lower budget. Produced in collaboration with the Playboy Channel, PREPPIES suffers from the basic flaw of making the leads unsympathetic and if you have no one to root for, why bother making the movie? Reardon, Drake, and Holt are a trio of snobbish Ivy Leaguers at a mythical college in New York state. They are planning for careers in the law but their grades are so poor that they are close to being tossed out of school. Drake is in line for a huge trust fund if he finishes school but if he doesn't all of those millions will go to his nefarious cousin, Haas, who proceeds to hire a trio of local wenches, Stelletello, Barrett, and Manion, to keep the boys away from the books over a critical weekend. There's an important test coming up and the boys have to hit the books and cram for the exam and Haas reckons that they will be diverted enough by the girls to ensure their failure. Shea is Drake's love, a tight-lipped parody of the upper-crust type made famous in AUNTIE MAME when "Gloria Upson" became real in the portrayal by Joanna Barnes. Lots of pulchritude, as you might expect from anything made for Playboy, including Playmate Lynda Weismeier who plays a sort of cliched innocent friend of Shea's. In a subplot, Marshall, another of the "townie" girls, has a thing for Sutton, who might be recognized by viewers under the other name he uses, "Jerry Butler," when he makes adult films. A wordy script with too many gags that fail to deliver the punch needed. Some good physical comedy and a general feeling that director Vincent is a man to be watched, when and if he gets a script of higher caliber. If you wouldn't let a child watch the Playboy Channel, you'd do well to keep the tot away from this as there is a lot of flesh and smarminess in almost every reel.

p&d, Chuck Vincent; w, Rick Marx, Vincent (based on the story by Todd Kessler); ph, Larry Revene; m, Ian Shaw; ed, Clement Barclay; art d, George C. Brown; cos, Robert Pusilo; stunts, Jerry Hewitt; m/l, Shaw, Vincent, Jonathan Hannah, Shannon MacLoughlin.

Comedy   Cas.   (PR:O   MPAA:R)

PREPPIES   (SEE: MAKING THE GRADE)

PREY, THE*   (1984) 80m Essex International/New World c

Debbie Thureson (Nancy), Steve Bond (Joel), Lori Lethin (Bobbie), Robert Wald (Skip), Gayle Gannes (Gail), Philip Wenckus (Greg), Carl Struycken (The Giant), Jackson Bostwick (Mark), Jackie Coogan (Lester), Ted Hayden (Frank), Connie Hunter (Mary), Garry Goodrow (Cop).

A big critter of some sort is looking for a mate in the woods but finds a bunch of camping youths instead. Most interesting thing about this slight teenagers-in-peril film is the game the audience can play picking out who will be the victims and who will be the survivors.

p, Summer Brown, Randy Rovins; d, Edwin Scott Brown; w, Summer Brown, Edwin Scott Brown; ph, Teru Hayashi; m, Don Peake; ed, Michael Barnard; art d, Roger Holzberg; cos, Julie Dresner.

Horror   (PR:O   MPAA:R)

PRIVATES ON PARADE*   (1984, Brit.) 96m HandMade/Orion
                                                          Classics c

John Cleese (Maj. Giles Flack), Dennis Quilley (Acting Capt. Terri Dennis), Michael Elphick (Sgt. Maj. Reg Drummond), Nicola Pagett (Acting Lt. Sylvia Morgan), Bruce Payne (Flight Sgt. Kevin Artwright), Joe Melia (Sgt. Len Bonny), David Bamber (Sgt. Charles Bishop), Simon Jones (Sgt. Eric Young-Love), Patrick Pearson (Sgt. Steven Flowers), Phil Tan (Lee), Vincent Wong (Cheng), Neil Pearson (Band Pianist), John Standing (Capt. Sholto Savory), Talat Hussain (Armoury Indian), John Quayle (Capt. Henry Cox), Brigitte Kahn (Mrs. Reg), Ishaq Bux (Sikh Doorman), Robin Langford (Electrician), Tim Barlow (Commanding Officer), William Parker, Mark Elliot, Tim Sinclair (Armed Escorts), David Griffin (Infantry Officer in the Bush), Julian Sands (Sailor).

Backed by ex-Beatle George Harrison, PRIVATES ON PARADE is a good example of why the sun has set on the British Empire. The play by Peter Nichols was a big success in the West End seven years before and won Quilley the British equivalent of the "Tony" award, but time and tide passed it by and this movie is a sniggering homosexual farce that spends most of its time in predictable low comedy with only the occasional reach for excellence. Cleese is a silly leader of a morale-boosting group of entertainers in the area of Singapore just after WW II. The British troops posted to the Far East are in need of something to break the ennui and boredom and Cleese's group (named SADUSEA– or "sad, you see"–it stands for "Song And Dance Unit, Southeast Asia) has been sent to perk up their spirits. The picture spends most of its time doing "drag" jokes as most of the entertainers apparently like their vice versa. They are all terribly inept until it comes time to don the dress and makeup and then they leap to life as they prance and sing like talented female impersonators. Quilley is the unit's director, a man who is as gay as he can be and still speak in a baritone. There is one female member of the troupe, Pagett, a supposed half-caste Indian-Anglo. She becomes pregnant by villain Elphick, a sergeant-major who would make Hume Cronyn's "Captain Munsey" look like Grandpa Walton by comparison. He sells the local recalcitrants ammunition and classified information and turns out to be an erstwhile London cop. Rather than accept what he's done to Pagett, he palms her off on a young, straight, and virginal soldier and, when she objects, hits her (which is a good indication about how women are treated in this movie). The troupe sings and dances for staring soldiers and yawning locals and the picture then switches to an adventure as the performers are shipped into a dangerous area to divert the Chinese Communist guerrillas while some real spying is taking place. It's then that bullets fly and several people are killed and any comedic edge is taken off the film. Lots of gay jokes, a plea for an end to racism, a demonstration of the difference between lisping gays and macho gays, and a sense that nobody knew what this movie was about. The 1977 Royal Shakespeare Company version of the play won King an award for writing the Best Musical Score of the season, which is a good indication of what a dreadful musical season 1977 must have been. The title may or may not have been a sendup of flashers. Hard to believe that director Blakemore, who was responsible for staging one of the funniest farces ever ("Noises Off") could have been responsible for such tripe, although if your sense of comedy leans toward the burlesque stage, you might have three or four laughs out of this.

p, Simon Relph; d, Michael Blakemore; w, Peter Nichols (based on his play); ph, Ian Wilson; m, Dennis King; ed, Jim Clark; prod d, Luciana Arrighi; ed, Jim Clark; art d, Michael White, Andrew Sanders; cos, Arrighi, Jane Bond; spec eff, Peter Hutchinson; ch, Gillian Gregory; m/l, "Privates on Parade," "Sadusea," King, Nichols.

Comedy   Cas.   (PR:O   MPAA:R)

PRODIGAL, THE**   (1984) 105M World Wide c

John Hammond (Greg Stuart), Hope Lange (Anne Stewart), John Cullum (Elton Stuart), Morgan Brittany (Sheila Holt-Browning), Ian Bannen (Riley Wyndham), Joey Travolta (Tony), Arliss Howard (Scott Stuart), Sarah Rush (Laura), Gerry Gibson Rev, Wharton, Johanna Briem (Ursula), Lee Adams III (Ollie), Tamu Gray (Doreen), Anne Whitfield (Mrs. Wharton), Bob Ashmun (Jack Hilgard), Alexandra Powers (Nancy Pringle), Mark Dempsey (Doyle Fredericks), Clayton Corzatte (Ray Cooley), Shelley Henning (Janis Ritchie), Walt Brotherton (George Marler), Jane Wilbur (S.S. Teacher), Lee Corrigan (Boat Captain), Pamela Mitchell (Agnes Spielman), John Boylan (Alex Thornhill), Bill Ontiveros (Landlord), Richard Willis (Mr. Holt-Browning), Susan Ludlow (Martha), Ken Wales (Crusade Chairman), Donald W. Kiehl (Greek Professor), Ashley Bystrom (Girl Student), Maggie Savage (Madge), Jim Smith (Tennis Referee), Rod Pilloud (Glen Basker), Jahanna Beecham (Young Mother), Jeanette Deering (Woman Tenant), Terry Johnson (Log Stacker), Darrell DeRoche (Boy Student), Billy Graham.

A right-wing message film about the effect of church traditions on a deteriorating family. It's the temptations of everyday life that pressure the clan and nearly cause the members to abandon their own faith. A clean-cut picture for those who aren't in the mood for the latest FRIDAY THE 13TH sequel.

p, Ken Wales; d&w, James F. Collier; ph, Frank Stanley; m, Bruce Broughton; ed, Bill Brame; prod d, Bill Creber; set d, Jim Payne; cos, Michael Butler; m/l, "I Have Today," Broughton, Dennis Spiegel.

Drama   (PR:A   MPAA:PG)

PROTOCOL**   (1984) 96m Hawn-Sylbert/WB c

Goldie Hawn (Sunny), Chris Sarandon (Michael Ransome), Richard Romanus (Emir), Andre Gregory (Nawaf Al Kabeer), Gail Stickland (Mrs. St. John), Cliff De Young (Hilley), Keith Szarabajka (Crowe), Ed Begley, Jr. (Hassler), James Staley (Vice President Merck), Kenneth Mars (Lou), Jean Smart (Ella), Maria O'Brien (Donna), Joel Brooks (Ben), Grainger Hines (Jerry), Kenneth McMillan (Sen. Norris), Richard Hamilton (Mr. Davis), Mary Carver (Mrs. Davis), Jack Ross Obney (Jimmy), Kathleen York (Charmaine), Georganne LaPiere (Bobbie), Pamela Myers (Gloria), Joe George (Bartender), Tom Spratley (Grandpa), Dortha Duckworth (Grandma), Sally Thorner, Jeanne Mori, Elizabeth Anderson (TV Newspersons), Archie Hahn, George D. Wallace, Julie Hampton, Thom Sharp, Paul Willson, Holly Roberts (TV Commentators), Lyman Ward (Sen. Kenworthy), Joe Lambie (Doctor), Daphne Maxwell (Helene), Michael Zand (Assissin), Cece Cole (Jimmy's Girl), Roger Til (Belgium Ambassador), Marcella Saint Amant (Belgium Ambassador's Wife), Ellen Tobie (Mrs. St. John's Secretary), Alice O'Connor (Mother of America), A.S. Csaky (Sunny's Cousin), Ken Gibbel (Husky Biker), Ken Hill (Man in Green Jacket), Albert Leong, Peter Pan (Cooks), Robert Donovan, Amanda Bearse (Soap Opera Actors), Marcie Barkin, Deborah Dutch, Lorraine Fields (Safari Girls).

Executive producer/star Hawn wasn't about to allow any of the other 280 speaking roles in the film upstage her (and there were more than 4000 extras) so it's her picture from start to finish. A minor league comedy that smacks of MR. SMITH GOES TO WASHINGTON, this has a few funny moments and some good Buck Henry jokes but it is nothing special and is mostly noted for the fact that nobody can play Goldie Hawn as well as she can. Hawn works for Mars in a tacky Washington D.C. cocktail lounge. He's a typical bar owner who wants his waitresses to wear silly costumes. She balks at getting dressed in a chicken outfit even though Mars does his best to convince her that it's not a chicken, it's an emu, and that makes all the difference in the world. Hawn, who was born just outside Washington, is her usual vulnerable, sweet self who is ditsy and out to lunch, but has a strong sense of truth and is as patriotic as John Wayne. There's an assassination attempt on oil-rich Romanus and Hawn foils it and gets a bullet in her backside for her heroism. This plunged her into national media attention and her refreshing interview on TV endears her to the nation. She is offered a position as a protocol officer in the government although her qualifications are few and the gushing newscaster has to struggle to mention the fact that she "graduated in the top 75 percent of her class and was a member of the high school's hairdressing club," which are hardly credentials for her position. Once in her new job, Hawn finds that the infighting in Washington is far more violent than anyone had imagined. She is hated by Strickland, her boss (who was the only person in the film who was not costumed by Finkelman. Instead, she was clad by James Galanos.). Hawn never had a political thought to speak of before her appointment and now she finds she has to adhere to correct etiquette in serving the foreign dignitaries. This tosses her into comedic situations as she is totally out of place in the world of diplomacy. Despite her bumbling (though always endearing) ways, she captures the eye of blonde-loving Romanus. Strickland would like to get Hawn out of her hair so she attempts to arrange a deal between Romanus and the U.S. government. Hawn will become his bride if the U.S. can build military bases. All well and good except that Hawn doesn't know a thing about it. She is told to go to his country and show him a good time and does just that until she learns that she is to become his wife. Dressed in veils, Hawn is told that the following day will mark the end of her singleness. She manages to get out of the deal when Romanus' men trigger a revolt against the U.S. bases which, in turn, causes a great deal of trouble on Capitol Hill and becomes a cause celebre known as "SunnyGate." When Hawn learns how she's been marionetted, she delivers a stinging monologue in front of a senatorial committee chaired by McMillan. Her lengthy speech quotes freely from several documents in U.S. history and is as unbelievable as most of the rest of the movie. Hawn had the original idea for the film and turned it over to Shyer, Miller, and Meyers (who wrote the screenplay for her enormously successful PRIVATE BENJAMIN). Buck Henry then wrote the final script and his touch is evident in several spots including one delicious moment when Romanus and his entourage are joined by a cadre of Japanese businessmen, a group of heavy leather motorcyclists, and a corps of homosexuals at a party. When a fracas occurs and the entire hassle spills out onto the street, the government people are called in to break up matters and wonder what the make-up of the cocktail lounge is. The nearby cop answers: "Looks like one of those gay Arab biker sushi bars." Gregory, who co-wrote and co-starred in the movie about himself, MY DINNER WITH ANDRE (1981), gets about the best part here as a cross-eyes Arab who loves western ways and western women. Strickland plays the heavy well and most of the other performances are up to par although, as stated earlier, the other roles are shallow. Sarandon is supposed to be the male romantic lead but he doesn't have enough to do to make much of an impression. Ross was coming off having directed the youth-oriented FOOTLOOSE, which was a bigger hit than this was, despite the presence of the potent Hawn. The movie was shot in several locations and cost a great deal of money. Made in Washington D.C., Auburn California, Grass Valley California, and various locations in Southern California including the Wrigley Mansion (Pasadena), College of the Canyons, Los Angeles City Hall, Burbank airport, Pasadena Post Office, and various Hollywood streets. PROTOCOL was better than Hawn's SWING SHIFT, but so was just about everything else that was released that year. Several pop songs used include "I Love You, Suzanne" (sung by Lou Reed), "I Feel For You" (sung by Chaka Khan, "I'm So Excited" (sung by The Pointer Sisters), "Dynamite" (sung by Jermaine Jackson), "The Glamorous Life" (sung by Sheila E.), "Hopeless Love" (sung by Phil Marsh and the Hopeless Lovers), "Don't Stop" (sung by Jeffrey Osborne) and "Strut" (sung by Sheena Easton).

ex p, Goldie Hawn; p, Anthea Sylbert; d, Herbert Ross; w, Buck Henry (based on a story by Charles Shyer, Nancy Meyers, Harvey Miller); ph, William A. Fraker (Panavision, Technicolor); m, Basil Poledouris; ed, Paul Hirsch; prod d, Bill Malley; art d, Tracy Bousman, Enrico Fiorentini; set d, Chuck Pierce, Mary Olivia Swanson; cos, Wayne A. Finkelman, Galanos; spec eff, Phil Cory; ch, Charlene Painter; makeup, Thomas Case, Frank Griffin; stunts, Max Kleven.

Comedy   **Cas.**   **(PR:A-C   MPAA:PG)**

P'TANG, YANG, KIPPERBANG   (SEE: KIPPERBANG, Brit.)

PURPLE HEARTS**   (1984) 115m Ladd/WB c

Ken Wahl (*Don Jardian*), Cheryl Ladd (*Deborah Solomon*), Stephen Lee (*Wizard*), Annie McEnroe (*Hallaway*), Paul McCrane (*Brenner*), Cyril O'Reilly (*Zuma*), David Harris (*Hanes*), Hillary Bailey (*Jill*), Lee Ermey (*Gunny*), Drew Snyder (*Lt. Col. Larimore*), Lane Smith (*Comdr. Markel*), James Whitmore, Jr. (*Bwana*), Kevin Elders (*CIA Driver*), Sydney Squire (*Nurse*), David Bass (*Lt. Grayson*), Bruce Guilchard (*Jackson*), Rod Birch, Joel Escamilla (*Patients*), Helen McNeely (*Chief of Nursing*), Steve Rosenbaum (*Schoenblum*), Steven Rodgers (*August*), Adam Rice (*Mail Clerk*), Rudy Nash (*Hartman*), John Smith (*Dr. Altman*), Paul Williams (*MP-Jeep*), Koko Trinidad (*Black Marketeer*), Paul Anderson (*Marine Captain*), Chuck Dougherty (*Comdr. Norbitt*), Ted Thomas (*R & R Sergeant*), Claude Wilson (*CIA Man*), Richard Bean (*Recon Sergeant*), Rick Natkin (*Hospital MP*), Don Tamuty (*Kevin's Father*), Art Thompson (*Soldier in Warehouse*), Hugh Gilliam (*Dr. Weymuth*).

It took a few years, but British-born director Furie finally rid himself of his visual excesses and started concentrating on story. This time, the tale told is not up to his abilities as a director, but he must take some of the blame as he coauthored the screenplay with associate producer Natkin, who also does a cameo as a soldier. Wahl is a handsome devil, not unlike Richard Gere in demeanor and style. He's a young doctor in Vietnam and just counting the moments until he can flee the Far East and hustle back to the U.S. where he can open an office and make lots of money. He meets Ladd, a nurse who believes in the war and in what she's doing. Wahl falls in love with Ladd but she keeps him at arm's length because she can't bear the thought that anyone would become a doctor for any other reason than to heal. (Little does she know that many physicians' *real* specialty is apartment building tax shelters.) Her devotion to duty soon inspires him, and their love affair flourishes amid the horror of war. They swear undying love and plan to return to the U.S. together and use their medical knowledge to help people. Then he's killed, or so it seems. Next, it appears that she is dead, but she isn't. True love never runs smoothly, nor does this war, though there is so little made of the actual Vietnam skirmish that this story could have been set in the Spanish-American war or any of the other conflicts the U.S. has entered. The leads are engaging but not compelling and the picture is stolen by Harris as a black corpsman who has to use what little medical knowledge he has, plus a lot of common sense and guts, to suddenly perform some delicate surgery when there is nobody else around who can do it. His character is far more interesting than the main thrust.

p&d, Sidney J. Furie; w, Rick Natkin, Furie; ph, Jan Kiesser (Panavision,

Technicolor); m, Robert Folk; ed, George Grenville; art d, Francisco Balangue; set d, Ramon Nicdao; spec eff, Danilo Dominguez.

War Drama   **Cas.**   **(PR:C-O   MPAA:R)**

PURPLE RAIN**   (1984) 111m Purple/WB c

Prince (*The Kid*), Apollonia Kotero (*Apollonia*), Morris Day (*Morris*), Olga Karlatos (*Mother*), Clarence Williams III (*Father*), Jerome Benton (*Jerome*), Billy Sparks (*Billy*), Jill Jones (*Jill*), Charles Huntsberry (*Chick*), Dez Dickerson (*Dez*), Brenda Bennett (*Brenda*), Susan Moonsie (*Susan*), Sandra Claire Gershman (*Beautiful Babe*), Kim Upshur (*Kim*), Alan Leeds (*Stage Hand*), Israel Gordon (*Taste Emcee*), Gil Jacobson (*Cop in Basement*), Joseph F. Ferraro (*First Avenue Emcee*), James French (*Cabbie*), Wendy (*Wendy*), Lisa Coleman (*Lisa*), Bobby Z (*Bobby Z.*), Matt Fink (*Matt Fink*), Brown Mark, Jelly Bean Johnson, Mark Cardenas, Gerald E. Hubbard, Jr., Paul Peterson, Jesse Johnson, Al Jones (*Stunts*).

There should be a special rating system for movies that would warn anyone who doesn't like pop music to stay away. For Prince fans and others who appreciate rock 'n' roll, this movie is one that will be purchased on videocassette and watched weekly. But even those fans will have to deal with a basic flaw in the movie and that is the disgusting and demeaning way women are treated by all the male characters, including Prince. His royal purpleness plays "The Kid," a temperamental singer trying to make waves in Minneapolis' music scene. He likes Apollonia, a young woman who also wants to be a star. Prince's rival for her affections is Day, lead singer in his own group, The Time. Day fancies himself a ladies' man and wants Apollonia for his own. He's a bit of a fool but wise enough to give her the chance to showcase her own act, something Prince is reluctant to do. She's a newcomer to Minnesota, having recently arrived from New Orleans, and she is torn between her attraction to Prince and Day's offer to provide her with a stairway to stardom. Both Prince and Day toy with her ambitions and though she is sexually hip enough to take care of herself, her ego gets in the way of her good sense. Prince's desire for her is set against his terrible home life where his father, Williams, spends his spare time beating up his mother, Karlatos. Even though he is an alleged adult, Prince still lives at home and is plagued by mixed feelings regarding his parents—a crazed father and a professional victim mother. Prince tries to stop Williams from hitting Karlatos and gets pounded for his efforts and the theme of woman being the property of man, to be handled any which way man desires, is grotesquely repeated throughout the movie. There is no development of Williams or Karlatos other than to learn that Williams had once been a musician. Prince channels all of his pent-up rage into his music so the stage becomes his creative world. At the club where he works, Prince is trying to win Apollonia's hand and sings "Baby, Baby, Baby, do you want him?" in "The Beautiful Ones" (which he wrote) and it's as provocative a song as rock can be. He seduces her with his music and when the two physically get together away from the club, the bedroom scene becomes tawdry in comparison to the subtlety of the wooing as he sang. She agrees to sing with Day's group and this hurts Prince's feelings. He goes from a sympathetic moment when he gives her his earring to responding in the manner in which he was raised by knocking her around. The drama is enough, so why all the violence? It was not needed and lent a seamy touch to the proceedings. Club manager Sparks tells Prince that he now has four groups to work the joint and he only needs three so Prince will be the one to go. Prince sings "Darling Nikki" (which he also wrote) to Apollonia and his performance stops the show. She finally gets the chance to sing and does "Sex Shooter" (written by Apollonia and The Starr Company), a tune that's as subtle as its title. Prince and Apollonia can't deny their passion for each other and are united once more until she throws his earring at him after some more slapping around. (It's as though Prince takes women out for "dinner and a beating.") He rides off on his beloved motorcycle and gets home in time to see Williams attempt to blow his brains out. He saves Williams from suicide but begins to freak out and starts to destroy the house. Then he finds some sheet music of his father's. Somehow moved, he goes on stage to sing "Purple Rain" (written by him) and dedicates the tune to his dad. Everyone at the club feels the difference in Prince as he has now stepped outside himself and his anger. The applause is deafening and he is brought back on stage for an encore and kicks into "I Would Die 4 U" (written by Prince), and his manic-depressive character has now been redeemed by music and love. There have been comparisons of Prince to Jimi Hendrix, James Brown, Little Richard, and others, and they are valid. The concert scenes, photographed by Donald Thorin and brilliantly lit by Leroy Bennett, are among the best in the film and will stand as the rock footage of the 1980s. How much of the story is autobiographical and how much was concocted by rookie writer Magnoli and TV veteran Blinn ("The Rookies," "Fame," and many more) is open to conjecture although Prince's background has been widely publicized and there appear to be similarities between reality and fiction. The dialog is authentic and reflects the way young people speak. Many of the actors are non-pros and convince you that they aren't. There is very little humor in the movie other than a "Who's on First?"-type routine done by Day and partner Benton. It will only be funny to anyone who hasn't seen Abbott and Costello's classic sketch. The movie was a huge success and the young patrons were literally dancing in the theater aisles. In 1984, the soundtrack album was *Billboard's* top choice and "When Doves Cry" was that year's No. 1 single. That the film's success was based on the dynamics of Prince, the musician, and not Prince, the storyteller, is proven by the awful thud heard when his next movie UNDER THE CHERRY MOON was released. The club seen in the film was the same one where Prince played as a young man (although he was only 24 or so when this was made). He's sort of a cross between Liberace and Johnny Mathis and is now probably as wealthy as both of them put together. Other songs in the film written by Prince include : "Take me with U," "Let's Go Crazy," "Baby I'm a Star." Other songs by other writers were: "Jungle Love" (Morris Day, Jesse Johnson), "Modernaire" (Dez Dickerson), and "The Bird" (Day, Johnson). The background scoring was by Michel Colombier. Almost everyone involved with this movie was doing it for the first time and they made it look easier than it is. The bottom line is that if you like rock 'n' roll, and particularly Prince, you'll love this movie. If you couldn't care less about the music or the pint-size dynamo, stay away. The sex and the language make this something to keep children away from.

p, Robert Cavallo, Joseph Ruffalo, Steven Fargnoli; d, Albert Magnoli; w, Magnoli, William Blinn; ph, Donald Thorin (Metrocolor); m, Michel Colombier; ed, Magnoli, Ken Robinson; prod d, Ward Preston; set d, Ann McCulley; cos, Marie-France, Sonja Berlovitz, Jimmell Mardorne, Lewis & Vaughn; makeup, Richard Amington, Susan Wensel, Jayson Jeffried, Lee Romanoff.

Musical   **Cas.**   **(PR:O   MPAA:R)**

QUELLA VILLA ACCANTO AL CIMITERO
(SEE: HOUSE BY THE CEMETERY, THE, Ital.)

QUESTION OF SILENCE***½   (1984, Neth.) 92m
Sigma/Quartet-Films Inc. c (DE STILTE ROND CHRISTINE M...)

Cox Habbema (Dr. Janine Van Den Bos), Edda Barends (Christine M.), Nelly Frijda (Waitress), Henriette Tol (Secretary), Eddy Brugman (Rudd), Dolf de Vries (Boutique Manager), Kees Coolen (Police Inspector), Onno Molenkamp (Pathologist), Hans Croiset (Judge), Eric Plooyer, Anna van Beers, Eric Besseling, Noa Cohen, Edgar Danz, Diana Dobbelman, Miranda Frijda, Frederik de Groot, Noortje Jansen, Rene Lobo, Sally Loswijk, Win de Meijer, Jan Simon Minkema, Carl van der Plas, John Smit, Herman Vinck, Bram van der Vlugt, Erzsebeth Weber.

A peculiar film about three women – housewife Barends, Waitress Frijda, and secretary Tol – who, though unacquainted, spontaneously kill a male boutique owner when he catches one of them shoplifting. They are arrested and assigned a female psychiatrist, Habbema, who prepares a plea of insanity. As she talks with the women, however, she begins to have her doubts. The murder begins to make more sense in her eyes. The women, who had never met before the incident, were each dealing with their own frustrations in their relationships with men. Barends was a slave to her housekeeping duties and victim of a thoughtless husband; Frijda was subjected to the rude comments of her male customers on a daily basis; and Tol was constantly treated as a subordinate at the executive office where she worked. Instead of confirming the expected insanity pleas Habbema tells the courtroom that the women are fully responsible for the crime against the patronizing shopkeeper. To the surprise of the males in the courtroom, all the women present unite and the crowd erupts into one grand show of female solidarity. Writer-director Gorris' first screenplay – suggested by an article about a working-class woman's arrest for shoplifting – was so enthusiastically viewed by the Dutch Film Finance Corporation that its officials not only fronted the money for the production, but also offered her the helm. The result exceeded their expectations. a superb, funny feminist film which, thankfully, achieved a release outside of the usual feminist circles, enabling it to reach a male audience. (In Dutch; English subtitles.)

p, Matthijs van Heijningen; d&w, Marleen Gorris; ph, Frans Bromet; m, Lodewijk De Boer, Martijn Hasebos; ed, Hans van Dongen; prod d, Harry Ammerlaan.

Crime/Drama   **(PR:O   MPAA:R)**

RACE FOR THE YANKEE ZEPHYR
(SEE: TREASURE OF THE YANKEE ZEPHYR)

RACING WITH THE MOON**½   (1984) 108m PAR c

Sean Penn (Henry "Hopper" Nash), Elizabeth McGovern (Caddie Winger), Nicolas Cage (Nicky), John Karlen (Mr. Nash), Rutanya Alda (Mrs. Nash), Max Showalter (Mr. Arthur), Crispin Glover (Gatsby Boy), Barbara Howard (Gatsby Girl), Bob Maroff (Al), Dominic Nardini (Soldier with Annie), John Brandon (Mr. Kaiser), Eve Brent Ashe (Mrs. Kaiser), Suzanne Adkinson (Sally Kaiser), Shawn Schepps (Gretchen), Charles Miller (Arnie), Patricia Allison (Mrs. Spangler), Al Hopson (Elmer), Ted Grossman (Skating Soldier), Scott McGinnis (Michael), Brian Trumbull (Kid in Skating Rink), Kate Williamson (Mrs. Winger), Julie Philips (Alice Donnelly), Fielding Greaves (Mr. Donnelly), Arnold Johnson (Tattoo Artist), Kevin Fraser (Marine), Gerry Gibson (High School Principal), Shane Kerwin (R.D.), Page Hannah (High School Girl), Jonathan Charles Fox (Arnold Billings), Michael Madsen (Frank), Dana Carvey (Baby Face), Victor Rendina (Mr. Luzzato), Rebecca Pollack (Girl in Bowling Alley), Victor Paul (Pool Hall Barman), Lou Butera (Pool Player), Michael Talbott (Bill), Philip Adams, Charles Picerni, Jr., Phillip Romano (Bill's Shipmates), Arlen Miller (Voice of the Minister), Carol Kane (Annie), Jan Rabson, Walter Matthews (Voice

of Sailors), Sue Allen, Katherine L. Brown, Peggy Clark (Singers), Steven Lambert, Patrick McGaughy, Patrick Green, Richard Calkins.

Bad boy Penn and good girl McGovern refused to do any promotion for this movie and it sunk out of sight quickly, a fate it didn't deserve. It's a slight film about two boys about to be drafted into WW II and takes place in the same year as SUMMER OF '42 and even resembles the picture in many ways, none the least of which is the backdrop, which was shot in northern California. Everyone tries hard but the movie is essentially superficial and has difficulty sustaining audience interest. Penn and Cage have six weeks before they are due to be Marines and the movie concerns that period, thus making it similar in parts to THE LAST PICTURE SHOW. The script, by 24-year-old tyro Kloves, has Penn meeting McGovern and thinking she is wealthy. She is new in town and lives in a mansion and Penn just assumes it's hers. She resists his advances for a while, then succumbs, and they fall in love. Cage is a street youth who gets his girl friend, Adkinson, pregnant, and has to raise the needed $150 for her abortion, a sum that is not going to be easy on the money he earns pin-setting at the local bowling alley. He and Penn try to hustle some sailors into a pool game at a bar but they are discovered and flee the bar with their lives. Cage asks Penn to ask McGovern for the money and he does, only to learn that her parents are the servants in the mansion, not the owners. Cage leaves Adkinson and Penn is angered at the move. McGovern and Penn begin arguing and she wonders if she was attractive to him because she was supposedly rich. McGovern and Penn unite to help Adkinson out of her plight and the film ends as Penn and Cage engage in their favorite pastime, jumping on moving trains, or "Racing with the Moon." Good period evocation, excellent costumes by Norris (who was an Oscar nominee for VICTOR/VICTORIA), and a few funny scenes which include the already-mentioned pool hall sequence and a roller skating bit by Penn. Cage is far too urbane to be believed and his accent smacks more of "Little Italy" than Mendocino. The executives in charge of the production were Stanley Jaffe and Chicagoan Sherry Lansing, the glamour girl who had run Fox for years after having had a brief acting career. A nice little movie, perhaps too nice, with none of the edge that is apparently needed to sell tickets in the 1980s.

p, Alain Bernheim, John Kohn; d, Richard Benjamin; w, Steven Kloves, ph, John Bailey (Movielab Color); m, Dave Grusin; ed, Jacqueline Cambas; prod d, David L. Snyder; set d, Jerry Wunderlich; cos, Patricia Norris; spec eff, Garry J. Elmendorf; stunts, Steven Lambert, Patrick McGaughy, Patrick Green, Richard Calkins.

Comedy/Drama   **Cas.**   **(PR:C   MPAA:PG)**

RARE BREED**   (1984) 94m New World c

George Kennedy (Nathan Hill), Forrest Tucker (Jess Cutler), Tom Hallick (Lou Nelson), Don Defore (Frank Nelson), Tracy Vaccaro (Anne Cutler).

A harmless tale of a young girl and her love for a horse. The animal is sent to Europe for training but is kidnaped along the way. With some help the girl and her horse are reunited in time for the big competition.

p, Jack Cox; d, David Nelson; w, Gardner Simmons; ph, Darryl Cathcart.

Drama   **(PR:A   MPAA:PG)**

RAW COURAGE zero   (1984) 90m Sandy Howard-Adams Apple
VTV/New World c (AKA: COURAGE)

Ronny Cox (Pete Canfield), Lois Chiles (Ruth), Art Hindle (Roger Bower), M. Emmet Walsh (Colonel Crouse), Tim Maier (Craig Jensen), William Russ (Sonny), Lisa Sutton (Stephanie), Noel Conlon (Clay Matthews), Anthony Palmer (Herb Jensen).

Utterly void of logic, RAW COURAGE tells the story of three marathon runners who are passing through a New Mexico desert on a 72-mile run. They are stopped by a wacked-out group of survivalists who are training for war. In order to propel the mindless plot further, the runners manage to escape and are chased through both the desert and the mountains...treating us to a wide variety of picturesque expanses. A few unnecessary deaths occur, including one of the runners, though the other two manage to retreat to safety... and cross the finish line as well. A ridiculous waste of time, the only thing worthwhile about RAW COURAGE is Walsh who, once again, does his best to breathe life into an expired picture.

p, Ronny Cox, Robert Rosen; d, Robert L. Rosen; w, Ronny Cox, Mary Cox; ph, F. Pershing Flynn; ed, Steven Polivka; art d, Don Nunley.

Drama   **Cas.**   **(PR:O   MPAA:R)**

RAZORBACK**½   (1984, Aus.) 95m UAA/WB c

Gregory Harrison (Carl Winters), Arkie Whiteley (Sarah Cameron), Bill Kerr (Jake Cullen), Chris Haywood (Benny Baker), Judy Morris (Beth Winters), John Howard (Danny), John Ewart (Turner), Don Smith (Wallace), Mervyn Drake (Andy), Redmond Phillips (Magistrate), Alan Beecher (Counsel), Peter Schwartz (Lawyer), Beth Child (Louise Cullen), Rick Kennedy (Farmer), Chris Hession (TV Cowboy), Brian Adams (Male Newscaster), Jinx Lootens (Female Newscaster), Angus Malone (Scotty), Peter Boswell (Wagstaff), Don Lane (Himself), David Argue.

American journalist Morris travels to Australia to do a story on the illegal hunting of kangaroos. She meets hostility from the outback locals and that night her car is run off the road. She pulls herself to safety but is attacked by an enormous wild pig and killed. Husband Harrison goes to find out just what happened and meets up with Kerr, whose baby grandson had earlier been carried off by the mutant porker, and who has dedicated his life to hunting it down. Harrison isn't convinced until he barely escapes the monster, then he helps Kerr track it to a dog-food factory run by a couple of sleazy types who actually feed the thing. The pig is finally killed, though at the cost of Kerr's life. A stylish horror film with one of the most unusual monsters in memory, the film nonetheless suffers from some clumsy scripting and poorly motivated characters. Still, horror fans won't be disappointed.

p, Hal McElroy; d, Russell Mulcahy; w, Everett DeRoche (based on the novel by Peter Brennan); ph, Dean Semler (Panavision); m, Iva Davies; ed, William Anderson; prod d, Bryce Walmsley; art d, Neil Angwin, Nick McCallum; cos, Helen Hooper.

Horror   **Cas.**   **(PR:O MPAA:R)**

RAZOR'S EDGE, THE**½   (1984) 128m Colgems/COL c

Bill Murray (Larry Darrell), Theresa Russell (Sophie), Catherine Hicks (Isabel), Denholm Elliott (Elliott Templeton), James Keach (Gray Maturin), Peter Vaughan (MacKenzie), Brian Doyle-Murray (Piedmont), Stephen Davies (Malcolm), Saeed Jaffrey (Raaz), Faith Brook (Louisa Bradley), Andre Maranne (Joseph), Bruce Boa (Henry Maturin), Serge Feuillard (Coco), Joris Stuyck (Bob), Helen Horton (Red Cross Lady), Michael Fitzpatrick (Tyler), Robert Manuel (Albert), Sam Douglas (Man at Kissing Booth), Nora Connolly (Governess), Jeff Harding (Brian Ryan), Richard Oldfield (Doug Van Allen), Gordon Sterne (Doctor), Mary Larkin (Nun), Christopher Muncke (Kevin), Russell Sommers (Party Guest), John Moreno, Hugo Bower (French Detectives), Abbie Shilling (Priscilla Maturin), Cassie Shilling (Joan Maturin), Jean- Francois Soubielle (Communist Vendor), Claude Le Sache (Morgue Attendant), Caroline John (Mrs. MacKenzie), Daniel Chatto, Louis Sheldon (Wounded French Soldiers), Kunchuck Tharching (Lama).

Remaking a classic Hollywood film is always risky business because invariably the new version is miles below par, ridiculed by critics, and ignored at the box office, especially if, like THE RAZOR'S EDGE, it is based on a classic novel as well. The only reason this remake was ever filmed in the first place was because of Bill Murray, a superb comic actor with intentions of getting his pet project off the ground. His selling point to Columbia executives was simple–if they let him do THE RAZOR'S EDGE then he would star in their upcoming blockbuster GHOSTBUSTERS. Murray takes the lead role (played by Tyrone Power in the 1946 original), a wealthy upperclass lad from Lake Forest, Illinois, who isn't ready to settle into marriage, home, and job. Instead he wants to travel, read, and learn about life–to find the path to redemption. He breaks off his engagement to Hicks and says farewell to friends Keach and Russell, shortly thereafter finding himself in the trenches of WW I. After the death of a fellow soldier, Doyle-Murray (Murray's real-life brother) in a powerful, hard-edged performance, Murray moves on to India in search of religious enlightenment. Living life atop the Himalayas and discovering his own spirituality from Jaffrey, Murray continues to grow. It is in India that he is warned: "The path to salvation is narrow, and it's as difficult to walk as the razor's edge." From there he travels to Paris where he is reunited with Hicks and Keach, who have since married. While inside a seedy nightclub, they find Russell, a drug-addicted, drunken prostitute sporting a Louise Brooks haircut. Murray convinces her to leave that lifestyle behind, trying to save her life as he is trying to save his own. They are soon making wedding plans–plans that Hicks cannot cope with because she is still in love with Russell. Later, the malicious Hicks gets Russell drinking again, prompting her to return to her former ways. Murray again tries to rescue her from the arms of her pimp, but is beaten by a gang of thugs. Soon afterwards, he is informed that Russell has been murdered–her throat slit by a razor's edge. Murray then bids farewell to Europe and returns to America. THE RAZOR'S EDGE is clearly Murray's movie and that, unfortunately, is where the fault lies. The success or failure of THE RAZOR'S EDGE rested directly on his shoulders. As fine a comic actor as he is, he simply does not have the ability (at least not yet) or, more importantly, the direction to pull off this performance. Vacillating between a solid dramatic performance and being a goof-off, Murray never seems to have a handle on the character, snickering more often than showing real emotion. One never gets close enough to Murray's character to understand why he continues his search, and what, if anything, he is learning. The entire tone of his character is gray, as if acting without any sense of direction, fluctuating from scene to scene. Never does THE RAZOR'S EDGE come close to showing an enlightened Murray. Instead of trying to discover himself while in the trenches, in the Himalayas, or in Paris, he simply wanders around, pausing occasionally to read a book. The clearest illustration of the direction the film takes is in a card-playing scene between Murray and Jaffrey while in India. Discussing spirituality and salvation, Jaffrey asks Murray for his thoughts. Holding his cards in his hand, Murray seriously says, "I believe...," followed by a pause which seems to indicate that he is truly searching for what he believes in, then his answer, "that you are saving nines." That's it–Murray doesn't believe anything, nor has he seemed to learn anything while in India. Anyone who has read the book will know he learns something, but Murray sure doesn't show it in his

performance. Nevertheless, Murray is watchable. A commanding, likeable, charismatic personality, Murray easily charms the viewer into smiling along with him, but unfortunately that's not enough. The only truly noteworthy performances in the picture belong to Russell, who is marvelously captivating as the self-degrading, suffering prostitute (a role neglected by the Oscar voters), and the always-impressive Elliott, as the wealthy uncle who, in his own way, searches for salvation, but here is written off as a supporting character. Director Byrum seems more concerned with showing off the lavishness of his sets and costumes, than he is with any sort of authenticity. Millions of dollars were spent on this picture, much of it for location photography, but the result could have probably been more effectively achieved on a back lot. Most deplorable is the WW I battle footage which is more suited for a television sitcom than for the tragic, soul-shaking event that it was to Murray's character. Underneath the surface of THE RAZOR'S EDGE lies a fine movie (which, as a matter of fact, was made some forty years ago) and a potentially interesting dramatic performance from Murray, but the Hollywood sugar-coating that has been added onto this picture, pandering to the illiteracy of the viewing audiience, is its biggest drawback.

p, Robert P. Marcucci, Harry Benn; d, John Byrum; w, Byrum, Bill Murray (based on the novel by W. Somerset Maugham); ph, Peter Hannan; m, Jack Nitzsche; ed, Peter Boyle; prod d, Philip Harrison; art d, Malcolm Middleton; set d, Ian Whittaker, Stuart Rose, Sabi Zaidi; cos, Shirley Russell.

Drama   **Cas.**   **(PR:C-O MPAA:PG-13)**

REAL LIFE**   (1984, Brit.) 92m Bedford c

Rupert Everett (Tim), Christina Raines (Laurel), Catherine Rabett (Kate), James Faulkner (Robin), Isla Blair (Anna), Norman Beaton (Leon), Warren Clarke (Gerry), Lynsey Baxter (Jackie), Annabel Leventon (Carla), Michael Cochrane (Lipton).

Everett is a mischievous lad from London who spices up his daily routine by creating a story about a theft of a Rembrandt and giving it to a local newspaper. His fictitious crime has a gang of guttersnipes working under the hand of a big-shot leader in support of South African guerrillas. Everett runs into a problem, however, when he finds out that there is a real-life Rembrandt thief he has to contend with. Before the thief can catch Everett, the police catch the thief and save the national art collection. Besides Rembrandt, Everett also has an interest in Rabett, a lovely girl who turns up in his fantasies, and Raines, an older lawyer who is on the run from her estranged husband. Rabett jilts Everett, but by the finale the two end up in each other's arms. Everett turns in a fine performance and, with his performance in ANOTHER COUNTRY this year, is definitely becoming a name to remember.

p, Mike Dineen; d, Francis Megahy; w, Megahy, Bernie Cooper; ph, Peter Jessop; m, David Mindel; ed, Peter Delfgou; prod d, John White.

Drama/Crime   **(PR:C MPAA:NR)**

RECKLESS**   (1984) 90m MGM-UA c

Aidan Quinn (Johnny Rourke), Daryl Hannah (Tracey Prescott), Kenneth McMillan (John Rourke, Sr.), Cliff De Young (Phil Barton), Lois Smith (Mrs. Prescott), Adam Baldwin (Randy Daniels), Dan Hedaya (Peter Daniels), Bill Jacoby (David Prescott), Toni Kalem (Donna), Jennifer Grey (Cathy Bennario), Haviland Morris (Mary Pat Sykes), Pamlea Springsteen (Karen Sybern), Susan Kingsley (Eileen), Adam LeFevre (Officer Haskell), Ellen Mirojnick (Physics Teacher), Robert F. Colesberry (Marine Recruiter), Charles R. Cronin (Mr. Johnson), Tom Timcho (Gus Ulensky), Jon Erwin (Scott Metcalf), Janet LaRue (Career Day Student), Teri Brown (Pinky), Joseph Tenaglio (Career Day Student), Judy Sullivan (Student Announcer), Bernard Orbovich (Man in Locker Room), Thaddeus Grondalski (Priest).

Quinn, a boy with a bad reputation and a drunkard father (McMillan), falls in love with Hannah, a good girl from a good family. Society, of course, disapproves of the pairing, but Hannah sees it as a chance to break free of her boring life so she happily goes off with him, riding on the back of his motorcycle, having sex in the school boiler room, and generally raising hell. Boring, cliche-ridden teen drama looks nice and features Quinn, who is fairly impressive in his debut. Hannah looks nice but seems completely without depth, as do all the other characters in this routine bad-boy-loves-good-girl drama.

p, Edgar J. Scherick, Scott Rudin; d, James Foley; w, Chris Columbus; ph, Michael Ballhaus (Metrocolor); m, Thomas Newman; ed, Albert Magnoli; prod d, Jeffrey Townsend; art d, Anamarie Michnevich; set d, Nora Chavoosian; cos, Ellen Mirojnick; m/l, "Understanding Gravity", Newman.

Drama   **Cas.**   **(PR:O MPAA:R)**

RED DAWN*   (1984) 100m MGM/UA c

Patrick Swayze (Jed), C. Thomas Howell (Robert), Lea Thompson (Erica), Charlie Sheen (Matt), Darren Dalton (Daryl), Jennifer Grey (Toni), Brad Savage (Danny), Doug Toby (Aardvark), Ben Johnson (Mason), Harry Dean Stanton (Mr. Eckert), Ron O'Neal (Bella), William Smith (Strelnikov), Vladek Sheybal (Bratchenko), Powers Boothe (Andy), Frank McRae (Mr. Teasdale), Roy Jenson (Mr. Morris), Pepe Serna (Aardvark's Father), Lane

Smith *(Mayor Bates)*, Judd Omen *(Nicaraguan Captain)*, Michael D'Agosta *(Boy in Classroom)*, Johelen Carleton *(Girl in Classroom)*, George Ganchev, Waldemar Kalinowski *(Soldiers)*, Sam Slovick *(Yuri)*, Radames Pera *(Stepan Gorsky)*, Lois Kimbrell *(Mrs. Mason)*, Elan Oberon *(Alicia)*, Harley Christensen *(Man on Pole)*, Fred Rexer *(Tank Survivor)*, Michael Meisner, Victor Meisner *(Russian Tankers)*, Phil Mead *(Mr. Barnes)*, Sam Dodge, Ben Zeller, Dan Sparks *(Men at Drive-In)*, Ben Schick *(Russian Sergeant)*, George Fisher *(KGB Major)*, Zitto Kazann *(Political Officer)*, Chuk Besher *(Door Gunner)*, Jay Dee Ruybal *(Cuban Crew Chief)*, Pacho Lane *(Firing Squad Officer)*, Julius L. Meyer *(Latin Soldier)*.

Yet another infantile right-wing fantasy sprung from the adolescent mind of middle-aged writer-director Milius. Definitely a film for the Reagan era, RED DAWN is one of those paranoid delusions spouted by militarists, survivalists, and television evangelists brought to life on the big screen. It's as if the clock has turned back to the mid-1950s when short subjects like RED NIGHTMARE (a man wakes up one morning and his small American town has been taken over by Communists) and COMMUNISM AT OUR DOOR were presented to scare the daylights out of the complacent public. After a rather lame and unsatisfying explanation of how the Americans and Soviets have launched into a conventional war, RED DAWN begins as students in a small Northwestern town watch in amazement as Russian/Cuban troops parachute into the area and open fire. A few clever kids (Swayze, Howell, Thompson, Sheen, Dalton, Grey, and Savage) jump in Swayze's pickup truck and hightail it to the general store where they stock up on food, weapons and ammo. They head for the mountains, where they begin launching guerilla operations on par with those currently being fought in Afghanistan. Meanwhile, after token resistance from the adults, the Commies take over and a temporary occupation government is installed. The Soviet commander, Smith, puts a Cuban, O'Neal, in charge. The male American adults are rounded up and put into a camp which used to be the local drive-in theater. There the poor Americans are forced to watch Russian director Sergei Eisenstein's classic 1938 film ALEXANDER NEVSKY by their sadistic Commie captors (needless to say this is unintentionally hilarious). Back in town Communist propaganda springs up everywhere you turn, and the dreaded breadlines begin to form. In the mountains, the teenagers are having some success at blowing up and ambushing armed columns of the invasion force, aided and abetted by Johnson, a reclusive type who lives in a cabin. One day an American jet is shot down over the area and the pilot, Boothe, lands nearby. The teenagers save him and he helps them in their fight. One of the girls, Thompson, develops a crush on the pilot, but Boothe is killed after a firefight with the Russians and he dies in her arms. The film winds down as several of the teenagers die bravely in battle and the film ends with the war dragging on and a crude stone is erected to the young guerrillas, memory. RED DAWN would be a lot more offensive if it wasn't just so darn silly. This is basically the rumination of an adolescent sensibility with no concern for plausibility, character development, or social observation. The film even fails as an action movie because it is badly paced and poorly executed. Unintentional laughter erupts in nearly every scene, and the characters are so cliched and broadly sketched that there are no surprises at all. The cast struggles to make the material believable, with Stanton scoring the only memorable moment as an imprisoned father of one of the boys. Boothe, always a strong screen presence, seems to be retreading his role from SOUTHERN COMFORT, and O'Neal and Smith are laughable as the invaders, the former being a man with a troubled conscience and the latter a hard-line militarist. RED DAWN is simply too inept to be taken seriously. When is Mr. Milius going to put his toy soldiers away and grow up?

p, Buzz Feitshand, Barry Beckerman; d, John Milius; w, Kevin Reynolds, Milius (based on the novel by Reynolds); ph, Ric Waite (Metrocolor); m, Basil Poledouris; ed, Thom Noble; prod d, Jackson de Govia; art d, Vincent Cresciman; set d, Lowell Chambers; cos, Dan Chichester, Julie Starr Dresner.

War   Cas.   (PR:O   MPAA:PG-13)

RED ON RED   (SEE: SCARRED)

REFLECTIONS** (1984, Brit.) 103m Courthouse-Film Four/Artificial Eye c

Gabriel Byrne *(William Masters)*, Donal McCann *(Edward Lawless)*, Harriet Walter *(Ottilie Granger)*, Fionnula Flanagan *(Charlotte Lawless)*, Gerard Cummins *(Michael Lawless)*, Niall Tobin, Paedar Lamb, Des Nealon, Margaret Wade, Larry O'Driscoll, Noel O'Flaherty.

An analytical film about a young researcher, Byrne, who is preparing a study on the life of Isaac Newton. He rents a summer cottage in Ireland where he plans to do his writing, but instead he becomes involved with the lives of the family with which he shares the estate--Flanagan, the hard-working wife of McCann, a lazy boozer, their quiet son Cummins, and attractive niece Walter. Byrne, who's normally as cold and scientific as Newton, becomes involved emotionally with the clan. He and Walter begin an affair, although he has his sights on Flanagan. The approach of the filmmakers, however, is just as analytical as Newton and Byrne, resulting in a film which defies emotional attachment. REFLECTIONS does contain some commendable performances, especially the permanently soused McCann. This fine Irish actor also appeared as the troubled father in this

year's excellent CAL.

p, David Deutsch, Kevin Billington; d, Billington; w, John Banville; ph, Mike Malloy (Kay Laboratories Color); m, Rachel Portman; ed, Chris Ridsdale; art d, Martin Johnson; cos, Jane Boyd.

Drama   (PR:C   MPAA:NR)

RENO AND THE DOC* (1984, Can.) 88m Rose & Ruby/New World c

Ken Welsh *(Reginald "Reno" Coltchinsky)*, Henry Ramer *(Hugo "Doc" Billings)*, Linda Griffiths *(Savannah Gates)*, Gene Mack *(Stan Kukamunga)*, Brian Grandbois, Michael van Joseph, Phillip Jack Gabriel *(Kukamungas)*, Cliff Welsh *(Cliff)*, Laura Dickson *(Agnes)*, Sean Ryerson *(Long Jack)*, Damien Lee *(Gunther Schloss)*, Rick Lewson *(Brian)*, Charles Denning *(Delgado)*, Al Safrata *(Starter)*, Paddy Macafee *(Reporter)*, Tony Avola *(Bodyguard)*, Simone Stevenson *(Orchid)*, John Prince *(Bartender)*, Woody Sidarous *(Orderly)*, Trish Bakker *(Nurse)*, David Mitchell, George Holtz *(Sportscasters)*, Linda Stephen *(Dr. Livingston)*, Joseph Rabinowitch *(Elderly Patient)*, Eric Donkin *(Norbert Hiline)*, Michele Scarabelli *(Ann Marie)*, Zoltan *(Edsel the Dog)*.

A senseless example of filmmaking ineptitude which calls itself "a heart-warming adventure about friendship, competition and two irascible 'old men' who refuse to grow up," yet uses a cartoon drawing of a hot tub overflowing with nude skiers as its advertising campaign. RENO AND THE DOC, however, manages to be none of the above, especially not heartwarming. Walsh is a fortyish mountain man who one day meets Ramer, a former con man a few years his senior. The two soon find out that they are telepathic, or as the say, "on the same wavelength," and become best of friends with Ramer trying to convince Walsh to enter a professional skiing competition. Walsh faces the obstacles that his age presents, especially from an obnoxious, bald, thick-accented champion named Gunther, played ridiculously by Lee. Of course, Welsh surprises everyone (accept the audience) by winning the big race. By the "exciting" finale, he has, apparently, proven something about middle-aged men, won a fortune for the gambling Ramer, and won over a likeable sports writer he has fallen in love with. While it may seem harmless and well-intentioned, RENO AND THE DOC is littered with some completely out-of-place scenes (mainly the crazed Kukamungas, a fun-loving, gun-toting gang of rednecks) and, with only minor exceptions, excruciatingly bad performances across the board, for which most of the fault belongs to director-writer Dennis who seems to adamantly refuse to give his actors anything intelligent to say or do. If Ramer and Welsh's telepathic abilities aren't enough to spice up the weak script, they soon discover that they can exchange feelings as well as thought. In one embarrassing scene, Ramer, while drinking at a bar, experiences the effects of Welsh's lovemaking, While another later scene has Welsh suffering from a hangover caused by Ramer's drinking. To top it all off, the ski footage is nothing more than the standard coverage, which is better done on television sports shows.

p, David Mitchell, Sean Ryerson; d&w, Charles Dennis (based on a story by Damien Lee); ph, Ludvik Bogner; m, Betty Lazebnik, Brian Bell; ed, Jim Lahti, Mairin Wilkison; prod d, Stephen Surjik; cos, Trysh Bakker; m/l, "A Little Piece of Forever," Lazebnik, Dennis, performed by Alan Soberman, "Reno's Song, (Lazebnik, Bell, David Mitchell).

Comedy/Drama   Cas.   (PR:O   MPAA:NR)

REPO MAN***½   (1984) 92m Edge City/UNIV c

Harry Dean Stanton *(Bud)*, Emilio Estevez *(Otto)*, Tracey Walter *(Miller)*, Olivia Barash *(Leila)*, Sy Richardson *(Lite)*, Susan Barnes *(Agent Rogers)*, Fox Harris *(J. Frank Parnell)*, Tom Finnegan *(Oly)*, Del Zamora *(Lagarto)*, Eddie Velez *(Napo)*, Zander Schloss *(Kevin)*, Jennifer Balgobin *(Debbi)*, Dick Rude *(Duke)*, Michael Sandoval *(Archie)*, Vonetta McGee *(Marlene)*, Richard Foronjy *(Plettschner)*, Bruce White *(Rev. Larry)*, Biff Yeager *(Agent B)*, Ed Pansullo *(Agent E)*, Steve Mattson *(Agent S)*, Thomas Boyd *(Agent T)*, Charles Hopkins *(Mr. Humphries)*, Helen Martin *(Mrs. Parks)*, Jon St. Elwood *(Miner)*, Kelitta Kelly *(Delilah)*, Varnum Honey *(Motorcycle Cop)*, David Chung *(Sheriff)*, Cynthia Czigeti *(UFO Lady)*, Dorothy Bartlett *(Old Lady)*, Jonathan Hugger *(Otto's Dad)*, Sharon Gregg *(Otto's Mom)*, Dale Reynolds *(Peason)*, Jac MacAnelly *(Pakman)*, Ship Wickham, Gregg Taylor, Jon Fondy, Keith Miley, Michael Bennett, Brad Jamison, Jimmy Buffet *(Blond Agents)*, Janet Chan *(Repo Wife No. 1)*, Angelique Pettyjohn *(Repo Wife No. 2)*, Logan Carter *(Repo Wife No. 3)*, Laura Sorenson *(Repo Wife No. 4)*, George Sawaya *(Repo Victim No. 1)*, Connie Ponce *(Repo Victim's Wife)*, Robert Ellis *(Soda Jerk)*, The Circle Jerks *(Nightclub Band)*, The Untouchables *(Scooter Boys)*, Sue Kiel, Quentin Gutierrez, Harry Hauss, Tom Musca, Terry Schwartz, Kim Williams, Michele Person, Wally Cronin, Monona Wali, Delores DeLuxe, Linda Jensen, Todd Darling, Erin Darling, Abbe Wool, Alex Cox, Peter Wacks, Cosmo Mata, Rodney Bingenheimer, Jorge Martinez.

Estevez is a disaffected youth in Los Angeles who loses his supermarket stock boy job as the film opens. He spends the night wandering through the punk underground before he encounters Stanton, who tells him that his wife left her car in a bad neighborhood and offers Estevez $25 to drive it out for him. Estevez accepts and follows Stanton to an auto yard. He is indignant when he learns that Stanton lied to him and that he has just helped repossess a car. He throws the money back at him at first, but later listens to offers of big money and sets off to learn the trade under the tutelage of Stanton, who is constantly muttering to his pupil about the "Repo Code" and saying things like: "Look at those people. I'll bet they all have bad debts. Someone should catch 'em and make 'em pay." When Estevez mentions that most of them are poor, Stanton accuses him of being a Communist. Meanwhile, a nuclear physicist (Harris) who has had himself lobotomized to stop the guilt feelings about his work on the neutron bomb, has stolen something dangerous and glowing and put it in the trunk of his 1964 Chevy Malibu. Variously it is a nuclear device of some sort, or the decomposing body of an alien with spectacular powers. When a motorcycle cop stops the car and opens the trunk, there is a flash of light and all that's left is a pair of smoking boots as the scientist drives away singing maniacally. Several government agencies are after the car, and they offer a $20,000 reward for whoever finds it, a prize that makes it the most sought-after car in the city. Estevez is walking down the street when he spots the auto, and after chasing it on foot for a long time it suddenly stops and he climbs in next to Harris, who babbles incoherently, then dies. Estevez takes the car, but it is stolen from him again, beginning a long series of moves for the car. In the end, though, it ends up in the auto yard, glowing brightly and resisting all efforts of the authorities to get near it. Walter, the yard weirdo, walks right up to it and climbs in, notwithstanding that he can't even drive. He invites Estevez to join him and as he does, the car begins to rise, then it zips off through the skies above the city. Estevez looks down in disbelief and says: "Wow, this is intense!" *The* youth cult film of 1984, REPO MAN marked the auspicious debut of Alex Cox, born in Britain, educated as a lawyer at Oxford, and living in Los Angeles. The film looks at that neon-lit, horizontal sprawl in a way that no one has before, and a great deal of credit for the film's look goes to German cinematographer Robby Muller. Cox's familiarity with the post-punk milieu is impressive, and he would continue in this vein for his followup, SID AND NANCY (1986). The performances vary wildly in their quality, with Stanton and Estevez taking top honors, and most of the other characters little more than cartoons. The film is filled with sight gags and running jokes, like the little pine tree air fresheners hanging on the rear view mirrors of every car in the film, and the suburban punks who "do crimes" like sticking up liquor stores and skipping out on the bill in sushi restaurants, although they really want to settle down and get a house. Los Angeles hardcore punk band The Circle Jerks do a weird parody of themselves as a lounge act as Estevez shakes his head and muses, "I can't believe I used to like these guys." Another Los Angeles band, the ska-oriented Untouchables, also appears, chasing Estevez when he takes the band's car. In the background constantly are strange radio broadcasts, mostly created by ex-Monkee and Liquid Paper heir Michael Nesmith, who also served as executive producer for the film. Despite rave reviews in most of the underground press, the film received only a limited release and had to wait until its release on videocassette to find most of its audience. One of the most original films of recent memory, with an edge of black humor and punk sensibility, wickedly funny, ceaselessly inventive, and never boring.

p, Jonathan Wacks, Peter McCarthy; d&w, Alex Cox; ph, Robby Muller (DeLuxe Color); m, Tito Larriva, Steven Hufsteter; ed, Dennis Dolan; art d, J. Rae Fox, Lynda Burbank; set d, Cheryl Cutler; cos, Theda Deramus; spec eff, Robby Knott, Roger George; m/l, title song, Iggy Pop 'James Jewel Osterburg', performed by Pop.

Science Fiction/Comedy   Cas.   (PR:O MPAA:R)

RETENEZ MOI...OU JE FAIS UN MALHEUR
                              (SEE: TO CATCH A COP, Fr.)

RETRIEVERS, THE   (SEE: HOT AND DEADLY)

REVENGE OF THE NERDS*½   (1984) 90m Interscope
                                    Communications/FOX c

Robert Carradine *(Lewis)*, Anthony Edwards *(Gilbert)*, Tim Busfield *(Poindexter)*, Andrew Cassese *(Wormser)*, Curtis Armstrong *(Booger)*, Larry B. Scott *(Lamar)*, Brian Tochi *(Takashi)*, Julie Montgomery *(Betty)*, Michelle Meyrink *(Judy)*, Ted McGinley *(Stan)*, Matt Salinger *(Burke)*, Donald Gibb *(Ogre)*, James Cromwell *(Mr. Skolnick)*, David Wohl *(Dean Ulich)*, John Goodman *(Coach Harris)*, Bernie Casey *(U.N. Jefferson)*, Alice Hirson *(Mrs. Lowe)*, F. William Parker *(Sergeant)*, Roger Carter *(U.N.'s Assistant)*, Kres Mersky *(Mrs. Wormser)*, Marianne Muellerliele *(Woman)*, Lisa Welch *(Suzy)*, Suzanne B. Hayes *(Michelle)*, Shawn Sigueiros *(Joanne)*, Sandra Katzel *(Connie)*, Henry M. Kendrick *(Trainer)*, Fumio Kodama *(Japanese Man)*, Lance Lombardo *(Lamar's Date)*, William B. Wilson *(Tough-Looking Guy)*, Carl Cherry *(Tri-Lamb)*, Adam Frank *(Blonde Nerd)*, Taylor Samuels, Bradley Grunberg *(Plaid Brothers)*, James Anklam *(Hooded Alpha Beta)*, Matthew M. Haugh, William C. Horning *(Alpha Betas)*, Angela C. Gardaphe, Lisa Kolasa, Kristen Kinderman, Kay Strunk *(Pi Members)*, Gamble Baffert, Brian Lover, Jerry Kurinsky, Tonja Sue Philbee, Monique Sorensen, Calon Blackledge *(Rho-Rhos)*, Scott Bird, Steven Duran, Theodore Kerpez, Vincent Lindsley *(Nerds)*.

Forget the title (even though it's accurate), this is one of the funniest movies of the year and about 10 rungs above the usual teenage-college capers film. Carradine and Edwards are friends who are going off to college. They are the essential nerds, in that Edwards is a computer genius who wears old man's glasses, carries his pens and pencils in one of those plastic breast-

pocket holders, and is very shy. Carradine is a boy possessed of an annoying laugh and a huge overbite. They arrive at Adams College and try to join fraternities but are turned aside as they are so nerdy. In desperation, they join with other nerds Busfield (a redhead violinist who can't see past his bow if you take his thick glasses off), Armstrong (a man who uses his fingers to explore his nostrils and thus has achieved the nickname of "Booger"), Scott (an effeminate black), Tochi (a Japanese electronics whiz who loves nothing more than taking pictures), and a few others. The nerds are forced to sleep in the gymnasium until they can get some sort of affiliation and since no decent frat will have them, they decide to start their own branch of Lambda Lambda Lambda, an all-black fraternity that is functioning on other campuses. They rent an old house that makes Norman Bates' place look like the Taj Mahal. With their combined efforts, they turn the house into a mini-palace. All the while, they are being closely watched by the jock contingent led by McGinley, who is also the chairman of the Greek council at the school and does not allow the nerds to start their own fraternity and even questions their alliance with Lambda (3). McGinley's girl friend is Montgomery, the cheerleader and general all-around bitch-on-wheels who goads the jocks into committing all sorts of mayhem on the nerds after the boys have rigged up a remote video camera in the sorority house that allows them to peek at will. The jocks begin to make life miserable for the nerds (including trashing the house) but revenge is on its way (as the title indicates). The nerds have their first frat party under the surveillance of Casey, who heads the national office of Lambda (3) and, although the nerds have invited every sorority on campus to come, the only ones who show up are the female equivalent of the boys, sort of nerdettes. But all of those young women are quite sexual and eager to have fun so it's not a total disaster. With Carradine and Edwards leading the nerds, they begin to exact vengeance. There's a campus festival and each of the houses is invited to set up their own booth. McGinley dresses up as Darth Vader, then Carradine switches clothes with him (without McGinley's knowledge) and approaches gorgeous Montgomery, takes her to a private place while still wearing the STAR WARS outfit, and makes passionate love to her, without saying a word. She is thrilled to the marrow as McGinley has never been able to do what Carradine has done. When she pulls off the mask and sees that it's not McGinley, she is, at first, repulsed; then she remembers how good it was and wonders aloud why it is that a nerd has such ability in that department. Carradine explains: "All the jocks think about is football. All we nerds think about is sex." There is to be a "Best House on Campus" contest and the nerds have worked long and hard on the show they are presenting. They do a wonderful presentation that is almost sabotaged by McGinley and his hulking blond brutes who appear to be the U.S. branch of Hitler's SS men. Just before total chaos breaks out, Casey and his huge Lambda men arrive (all of whom make Bubba Smith look like Gary Coleman) to protect the nerds. There is a large sequence at the end as the nerds explain their position to the entire campus crowd and say that everyone is a nerd at one time or another and that they are proud to be nerds. This sways the crowd into realizing that what is being said is true. The shout of "nerd, nerd, nerd!" goes up, Montgomery joins Carradine and tosses McGinley out of her life, and the nerds have had revenge and will now begin to welcome countless others to their ranks, young men who understand what it is to be insecure, to be laughed at, to be an outcast. They realize that "belonging" to a certain group is a fallacy and that nerds are unique in their eccentricities and just as worth belonging to as any of the other frats on campus. This picture is hipper than NATIONAL LAMPOON'S ANIMAL HOUSE, PORKY'S, and all of the other teenage films lumped together. It's engaging, hysterically funny at times, wildly satiric, and with fewer lapses of good taste than most. Screenwriters Zacharias and Buhai and director Kanew are filmmakers to be watched. Made on a reasonable budget, REVENGE OF THE NERDS cleaned up at the box office as it satisfied William Faulkner's theory of "appealing protagonists struggle against apparently insurmountable odds in quest of a worthwhile goal." While the protagonists were appealing in their vulnerability and the odds were certainly against them, the revenge motive may not have been worthwhile but it surely was satisfying to anyone in the audience who ever felt left out, and that includes just about everyone. See this sleeper but keep youngsters away as the sex and language do cast a slightly smarmy aura over it. Songs include: "Revenge of the Nerds" (Bobby Paine, Gerhard Helmut), "One Foot in Front of the Other" (Scott Wilk, Marc Levinthal), "Breakdown" (T.V. Dunbar, C. Judge), "All Night Party" (Les Bohem, David Kendrick), "They're So Incredible" (Ollie E. Brown, Jerry Knight, Thomas Newman).

p, Ted Field, Peter Samuelson; d, Jeff Kanew; w, Steve Zacharias, Jeff Buhai (based on a story by Tim Metcalf, Miguel Tejada-Flores, Zacharias, Buhai); ph, King Baggot (DeLuxe Color); m, Thomas Newman; ed, Alan Balsam; prod d, James Schoppe; set d, Frank Lombardo; cos, Richard Polinsky, Deborah Hopper; spec eff, Joe Unsinn; ch, Dorain Grusman.

Comedy   Cas.   (PR:C-O MPAA:R)

REVOLT OF JOB, THE*½   (1984, Hung./Ger.) 98m Mafilm
        Tarsulas-Starfilm-ZDF-Macropus-Hungarian Television/Teleculture c
                                            (JOB LAZADASA)

Ferenc Zenthe *(Job)*, Hedi Temessy *(Roza)*, Gabor Feher *(Lacko)*, Peter Rudolf *(Jani)*, Leticia Caro *(Ilka)*.

A powerfully emotional drama set in a small East Hungarian farming village in 1943. Zenthe and his wife Temessy are an elderly Jewish couple who have outlived all seven of their children. Hoping to preserve their heritage, the couple schemes with an adoption center to obtain custody of a 7-year-old boy, Feher, by trading two calves for him. The boy is rebellious, however, and cannot be reached by his loving "parents." He chooses instead to play with a scruffy dog he has befriended. Eventually Feher begins to trust Zenthe and Temessy, learning the customs of their culture and honing new farming skills. Feher also is exposed to a world of sex that he never before knew existed. While in the market one day he spots two dogs mating. They are separated only when someone throws a bucket of cold water on them. Later when Feher sees the family's servant couple–Rudolf and Caro–making love he tries the same technique. In the meantime, the safety of Jews in Hungary is being threatened by the onslaught of Nazi troops. Zenthe and Temessy prepare for the fate that they know awaits them. They peddle their belongings and purchase a house for Rudolf and Caro. They also make arrangements for a gentile family to take care of Feher. The soldiers finally come to haul Zenthe and Temessy away to the bewilderment of young Feher. For the child's own safety, Zenthe ignores the boy's cries of "Papa." Zenthe only tells the boy to search for the Messiah. Confused at his parents' rejection, Feher runs off across the road, determined to follow his father's wish. Told from the young boy's point-of-view, THE REVOLT OF JOB is totally dependent on Feher's performance. Thankfully, Feher is superb in his debut role, entrancing the audience with his bright expressions and his innate ability to charm. As fine as the script and direction are, it is Feher who makes the film so watchable, in much the same way as Nicholas Gledhill in CAREFUL, HE MIGHT HEAR YOU (1984) and Moreno's D'E Bartolli in WHEN FATHER WAS AWAY ON BUSINESS (1985). Feher was selected from over 4,000 children by directors Gyongyossy and Kabay, who desperately wanted him in the role. Feher, however, had his own priorities and being in a film was not one of them. It was only when he was told that he wouldn't have to attend school during the shooting that Feher agreed. (In Hungarian; English subtitles).

d, Imre Gyongyossy, Barna Kabay; w, Gyongyossy, Kabay, Katalin Petenyi; ph, Gabor Szabo (Eastmancolor); m, Zoltan Jeny; ed, Petenyi; m/l, "The Cock Crows Loudly," Isaac Taub.

Drama   **Cas.**   **(PR:O   MPAA:NR)**

RHINESTONE zero   (1984) 111m FOX c

Sylvester Stallone (*Nick*), Dolly Parton (*Jake*), Richard Farnsworth (*Noah*), Ron Liebman (*Freddie*), Tim Thomerson (*Barnett*), Steven Apostle Pec (*Father*), Penny Santon (*Mother*), Russell Buchanan (*Elgart*), Ritch Brinkley (*Luke*), Jerry Potter (*Walt*), Jesse Welles (*Billie Joe*), Phil Rubenstein (*Maurie*), Thomas Ikeda (*Japanese Father*), Christal Kim (*Japanese Grandmother*), Arline Miyazaki (*Japanese Mother*), Tony Munafo (*Tony*), Don Hammer (*Sid*), Dean Smith (*Cowboy Doorman*), David Cobb (*Countryman*), Speck Rhodes (*Mr. Polk*), Guy Fitch (*Wino*), Stan Yale (*Street Player*), Robert Cook (*Scary Jan*), Cindy Perlman (*Esther Jean*), Bobby Martini (*Bartender*), Michael Gene Adams, Dan Munson (*Bouncers*), Bobbie La Salle (*Woman*), Jordan Myers, Bill Dearth (*Doormen*), Julee Erdahl, Robin D. Adler (*Waitresses*), Shelley Pogoda (*Photographer*), Laura Kingsley (*The Snorer*), Rod Ball, Troy Evans (*Heckler/Bettors*), Tony Compton, Gary Compton, Dean Wein, Adrienne Hampton, Lonna Montrose, Ross St. Phillips, Jill Gordon, Douglas Buttleman, Leslie P. Morris, Stanley Wells, Chip Heller, Larry Weiss, Sandy Policare, Paul "Mousie" Garner (*Hecklers*).

This rhinestone doesn't sparkle. It's a tarnished, feeble attempt to team potent box-office stars Stallone and Parton in a dumb comedy and is close to being a total failure. Parton is working in New York and bets her loudmouth manager, Liebman, that she can turn anyone into a country singer in two weeks. She says she can do it with the first man she meets and that man is, of course, Stallone, a tough-talking Manhattan cabbie. She takes him back to Tennessee with her in the hopes that the "down home" atmosphere will rub off and aid his transformation. When Stallone first opens his mouth to sing, the result is awful enough for director Clark to cut to quick shots of crazed animals racing around a farmyard and then Farnsworth, Parton's pa and an old-timer in the small town, quips, "Well, that was a mite scary, son, and for a minute there we all thought we was goin' to explode." Parton's ex-beau is Thomerson (who is the only glimmer of comedy in the proceedings) and he is enraged at Stallone for having stolen his gal. There is a funny beer-drinking sequence between them that offers the few laughs in this alleged comedy. (Note the number of neon signs advertising Budweiser and the other Anheuser-Busch products. It's a tribute to the men who do product placement in movies, as this one is darn near a 111-minute commercial.) In the end, Parton Stallone return to the Big Apple where he has to sing in front of a tough audience and gain its approval if Parton is to win her bet with Liebman, whose comedic moment comes when he chases Parton around a bedroom. John Wayne once said, early in his career, that he wanted to try different types of roles, but a wise man told him that if he was accepted as a certain type of character, he should give the public what it wanted (this was related by Wayne's son Patrick, in a TV interview). That advice should have been taken by Stallone. Movies where he gets to punch or shoot are what his fans want to see and even the most diehard Stalloneophiles stayed away from this. Oddly, Parton seemed able to rise above the script and maintain her status as adorable. Both stars changed clothes about twice a reel, perhaps in an attempt to cloak the essential blandness of the story. "Pygmalion and Galatea" (the famous comedy about a sculptor and his statue written in 1871 by W.S. Gilbert, from which George Bernard Shaw got his "Pygmalion" story) usually works as entertainment but the narrative has to have some basis in reality and some good reason for wanting it to succeed. Not so here. It's rife with hayseed humor, has no message, runs too long, and is definitely not worth seeing unless one really feels the need for punishment. Clark took over directorial chores when the original helmer, Don Zimmerman, either quit or was fired (the execs at the studio remained mum on that). It has always been acknowledged that comedy is the most difficult of all acting to do. Stallone's limited range does not include it and he mistakes mugging for timing. As two of the hecklers, note "Mousie" Garner, a well-known cabaret comedian-pianist, and blonde Sandy Policare, wife of Paramount executive Mike Policare, who decided that she wanted to get into show business after the family had been raised and has since appeared in many films and TV shows, thus proving there is life after 35. This movie is billed as a musical comedy but the music is undistinguished and the comedy is unwatchable.

p, Howard Smith, Marvin Worth, Bill Blake, Richard M. Spitalny; d, Bob Clark; w, Phil Alden Robinson, Sylvester Stallone (based on the song "Rhinestone Cowboy" by Larry Weiss, story by Robinson); ph, Timothy Glafas (Panavision, DeLuxe Color); m, Mike Post; ed, Stan Cole, John Wheeler; prod d, Robert Boyle; art d, Frank Richwood; set d, Dianne Wager; cos, Ron Heilman, Theadora Van Runkle, Linda M. Henrikson; m/l, "Hope You're Never Happy," "Too Much Water," "Goin' Back to Heaven," Dolly Parton, "The Day My Baby Died," Post, Robinson, Clark.

Comedy/Musical   **Cas.**   **(PR:C   MPAA:PG)**

RIDDLE OF THE SANDS, THE**   (1984, Brit.) 102m RANK c

Michael York (*Charles Carruthers*), Jenny Agutter (*Clara Dollman*), Simon MacCorkindale (*Arthur Davies*), Alan Badel (*Dollmann*), Jurgen Andersen (*Von Bruning*), Olga Lowe (*Frau Dollman*), Hans Meyer (*Grimm*), Michael Sheard (*Bohme*), Wolf Kahler (*The Kaiser*), Ronald Markham (*Withers*).

A British yachtsman (MacCorkindale) is sailing along the coast of Germany, circa 1901. He has an encounter with fellow Englishman Badel, a renegade naval officer. From Badel, MacCorkindale learns of a secret plan by the Kaiser to invade England. MacCorkindale calls on his old college chum York, and together they work to upset the evil plan. This film is based on the Childers novel which many consider to be the forerunner of the modern espionage thriller. However, there are no thrills in this, merely tedium. It's full of implausible situations and long spots where nothing really seems to be happening. MacCorkindale and York are adequate but are really given very little to do-they merely go through the motions. The exceptional Agutter may be familiar to fans of Nicholas Roeg's WALKABOUT. However the film does have some fine photography and interesting visual compositions. Made in 1979, it escaped in 1984 to the U.S.

p, Drummond Challis; d, Tony Maylam; w, Maylam, John Bailey (based on the novel by Erskine Childers); ph, Christopher Challis (Panavision, Eastman Color); m, Howard Blake; ed, Peter Hollywood; art d, Terry Pritchard.

Spy Thriller   **Cas.**   **(PR:C   MPAA:NR)**

RIO ABAJO   (SEE: ON THE LINE, Span.)

RIVER, THE***   (1984) 122m UNIV c

Mel Gibson (*Tom Garvey*), Sissy Spacek (*Mae Garvey*), Shane Bailey (*Lewis Garvey*), Becky Jo Lynch (*Beth Garvey*), Scott Glenn (*Joe Wade*), Don Hood (*Sen. Neiswinder*), Billy Green Bush (*Harve Stanley*), James Tolkan (*Howard Simpson*), Bob W. Douglas (*Hal Richardson*), Andy Stahl (*Dave Birkin*), Lisa Sloan (*Judy Birkin*), Larry D. Ferrell (*Rod Tessley*), Susie Toomey (*Sally Tessley*), Kelly Toomey (*Lisa Tessley*), Frank Taylor (*Zemke*), Ivan Green (*Smoot*), Desmond Couch (*Wilderfoot*), Charles G. Riddle (*Youngdall*), Jim Antonio (*Dan Gaumer*), Samuel Scott Osborne (*Billy Gaumer*), Amy Rydell (*Betty Gaumer*), David Hart (*Harley*), Barry Primus (*Roy*), Mark Erickson (*Raines*), Jack Starrett (*Swick*), Charlie Robinson (*Truck*), Dean Whitworth (*Doctor*), Charles S. Hanson (*Fat Man*), Ira M. Quillen II (*TV Weatherman*), Matt Bearson, Timothy Shadden (*Employees*), Elizabeth Lane (*Secretary*), Gary Gershaw (*Drifter*).

A good film for the viewer who isn't interested in being entertained but is willing to be thrown into the muck of the problems facing hard-working U.S. farmers. Rydell left many seams showing, and there's a constant feeling of "it's always something," so if you can handle the dozen or so "somethings" that befall the protagonists every few minutes, you'll like it. Strong, stubborn Gibson has been working his family farm since his youth. It's property that's been in his family for generations. Spacek is his "stand by your man" wife and they are struggling to maintain their way of life against terrible odds. The elements are not on their side and neither is local kingpin Glenn, who wants to build a dam on the river that runs through the Gibson acreage. Glenn needs the water for his own land and he wields a great deal of political influence and seems to be able to dictate orders to the local bank. He intends to use his clout to buy out all the farmers who stand in his way, then flood their lands in order to make a reservoir for his own use. Gibson and Spacek and their children, Bailey and Lynch, overcome the damage wrought by a large flood. Gibson's tenacity and pride lead the way and they come up with enough money to plant another crop on their land, despite the fact that Tolkan, the local banker who is in Glenn's pocket, won't lend them a penny. There's a painful scene of a farm auction (this could have come right from the network news) and neighbors watch neighbors lose everything to falling land and crop prices. The farmers are powerless to do anything beyond offering sympathy to each other. The back story is that Gibson and Glenn had been friends and Glenn had also been Spacek's lover before she chose Gibson and the hard life she now leads. Glenn is wonderfully sleazy and he might be able to crush Gibson if he desires, but he decides to wait a while longer and see if he can persuade Gibson with money to sell. They had a long relationship and Glenn is not all villain in that respect. Gibson's finances hit bottom and he has to find a job to sustain the family until the next corn crop can be harvested. Through a cousin, he gets a job at a steel mill in Alabama only to learn that it's not a regular position at all, it's scab work. He leaves his wife and kids to travel to Alabama and there is an agonizing moment as he reluctantly crosses the picket line that shows the desperate steel workers angrily pounding on the equally desperate scabs, most of whom are victims who never would have dreamed of crossing a line in palmier days. Meanwhile, back on the farm, Spacek gets her arm caught in a tractor gear and is saved by the family bull (no kidding!), then is helped by Glenn, who takes care of her at the hospital. Glenn is unhappily married and wants Spacek back. He makes it clear that her life will be a bed of roses with no thorns if she returns to him, but the plucky Spacek sends him away. At the same time, Gibson is stuck in the factory with the other scabs and is a virtual prisoner. A few good scenes depicting the purgatory of factory life and one memorable moment when a frightened deer mistakenly wanders into the mill. The workers chase the deer as a lark and are struck by the fear in the animal's eyes. They recognize that the deer is trapped, and they empathize as they also feel trapped, so they release the animal rather than harm it. Rydell proves his ability to handle group scenes in this and many others as he lets the faces tell the story rather than having dialog narrate. Gibson comes home to his farm visibly altered by his mill experience. Prior to this, Gibson had been containing his rage and affecting a cool exterior, but all his frustrations boil when Glenn's company offers him less for his corn crop than it cost him to grow it. Gibson lets Glenn know his emotions in no uncertain terms. The river rises again, there's a flood, and his corn is doused (as we said before, "it's always something"). Spacek is tired of the battle and pleads with Gibson to acquiesce but he won't hear of it and will continue fighting on his own. Then his neighbors come to the rescue and help build the levees that will hold the river back and allow his crop to be harvested. It's a good sign of non-familial solidarity and there appears to be a glimmer of sun behind the rain clouds. Glenn, however, is not to be deterred, so he waves some greenbacks in the faces of local unemployables and pays them to destroy the levees. Gibson appeals to the poor folks and says they are playing right into Glenn's hands. He wants them to toss the money back in Glenn's face and show that they are one people, and not available to the highest bidder. It almost works; then a traitor sets off an explosive charge and the water rushes forward. Gibson is stunned when a hole appears in the levee and it looks as though the whole structure will give way. He rebounds quickly and, mustering all his strength, his historical sense of what this land means to him, and his determination, he moves forward, is joined by Spacek, and then the neighbors step forward as well and begin to stem the tide of water that's coming in. As Glenn watches, even his own "employees" move in to stop the water and Glenn's own jeep is used to staunch the flow coming through the main hole in the levee. Glenn realizes that he has lost the battle, so he indicates that by placing a sandbag down where it will keep back the water. He'll return. It may take him a few years but, like Germany, he will rise again and attempt to conquer. The chances are he'll fail again, though. There is no question that Gibson, Spacek, and the others are coming from a different place. While Glenn's motivation is profit, the farmers' motivation is the land that they all love. Filmed in Tennessee and Alabama and lovingly lensed by Zsigmond, the earth is golden when dry and black when wet and many of the shots look like Andrew Wyeth paintings. The script barely manages to keep the characters from being caricatures, as everyone is too on the nose and does, more or less, exactly what is expected. The John Williams score rises with every inch of rain and the studio made certain that some of their MCA/Universal artists were heard in the background, thereby according the sound track album a bit more importance in the record stores than usual. Good performances, with Glenn as "Mr. Greed" and Spacek as "Earth Mother" garnering the best nods from the audience. U.S.-born Gibson (who became a star first in Australia) is somewhat rigid, although his is not an easy role to portray. The Southern dialects are well handled and the special effects are excellent. What is missing is any attempt to show any political or organizational solutions to the farm problems and the woes farmers face. Instead, we are shown the strong individualist who goes deeper into himself in order to outwit the forces of profit. It posed an interesting dilemma; what would you do if you were out of money and had something worthwhile to hold onto? As seen in COUNTRY and PLACES IN THE HEART, others in the cycle of farmers'-plight pictures, it's a question that farmers across the U.S. are facing in increasing numbers. The like-titled documentary film made by pioneer American documentarist Pare Lorentz in 1937 under the aegis of the Farm Security Administration at least made a case for federal flood control and soil conservation with its powerful imagery. Rugged individualism didn't cut it then, either.

p, Edward Lewis, Robert Cortes; d, Mark Rydell; w, Robert Dillon, Julian Barry (based on a story by Dillon); ph, Vilmos Zsigmond (Technicolor); m, John Williams; ed, Sidney Levin; prod d, Charles Rosen; art d, Norman Newberry; set d, Jane Bogart; cos, Joe I. Tompkins; spec eff, Ken Pepiot, Stan Parks; stunts, Alan R. Gibbs.

Drama   **Cas.**   **(PR:AC   MPAA:PG-13)**

RIVER RAT, THE★★½   (1984) 93m Sundance Institute/PAR c

Tommy Lee Jones (*Billy*), Martha Plimpton (*Jonsy*), Brian Dennehy (*Doc*), Shawn Smith (*Wexel*), Nancy Lea Owen (*Vadie*), Norman Bennett (*Sheriff Cal*), Tony Frank (*Poley*), Angie Bolling (*Joyce*), Roger Copeland (*Young Billy*), Tommy Burlison (*Whitey*), Tamara Hartley (*Young Joyce*), Louise Anderson (*Wexel's Aunt*), Melissa Hart (*Peggy*), Mary Harper (*Old Woman*), James Hurt (*Motorist*), Michael Shepard (*Cajun Sheriff*), Pete Renaday (*Cajun Doctor*), Louis R. Plante (*Cajun Deputy*), Rod Britt (*Cajun Deputy*), Robert Le Blanc (*Cajun In Cemetery*), Craig Cruse (*Boy on Levee*), Bill O'Neal (*Stretcher Bearer*), Creston B. Parker (*Red Bandana*), Melissa Davis (*Alida Le Blanc*), Kenyatta Beasley (*Little Daddy*), Charles E. Beasley (*Dad*).

A delightful, fast-paced adventure tale set in the Deep South and on the Mississippi River. Jones is a likable character who is released from prison after serving a 13-year stretch for an accidental murder. When he returns home he is introduced to his tomboyish daughter, Plimpton, who he has never met. Their relationship is at first strained, but a raft ride on the river brings them closer. Jones' life goes awry when Dennehy, a crooked parole officer, demands a huge payoff. Jones and his daughter are forced to flee, barely escaping Dennehy's evil ways. It is through this hair-raising raft journey that father and daughter are finally brought together and learn to love one another. THE RIVER RAT at times suffers from a saccharine treatment, but it must be commended for evoking a rural southern feel reminiscent of Mark Twain's finest writings. Director Tom Rickman previously worked as the screenwriter on COAL MINER'S DAUGHTER (1980), which also starred Tommy Lee Jones and was directed by Michael Apted, this film's executive producer.

p, Bob Larson; d&w, Tom Rickman; ph, Jan Keisser (Technicolor); m, Mike Post; ed, Dennis Virkler; prod d, John J. Lloyd; set d, Joe Mitchell; cos, Peter Saldutti; m/1, "The River Song," "Rock on the Bayou," "Wherever You Are," "Maybe Next Time," Post, Stephen Geyer; "Halfway Right" Post, Deborah Allen, "Take No Prisoners," "In One Ear and Out the Other" Post, Steve Plunkett.

Adventure   **Cas.**   **(PR:A   MPAA:PG)**

ROADHOUSE 66★   (1984) 90m Atlantic c

Willem Dafoe (*Johnny Harte*), Judge Reinhold (*Beckman Hallsgood, Jr.*), Kaaren Lee (*Jesse Duran*), Kate Vernon (*Melissa Duran*), Stephen Elliott (*Sam*), Alan Autry (*Hoot*), Kevyn Major Howard (*Dink*), Peter Van Norden (*Moss*), Erica Yohn (*Thelma*).

A minor league entry about two trendy fellows whose car breaks down in Arizona during Labor Day weekend. While waiting for a new radiator they enter a local drag race and take first place. It should also go without saying that they find some female companionship. A truly amateur production. The overcrowded soundtrack contains some popular tunes by Dave Edmunds, The Pretenders, and Los Lobos.

p, Scott M. Rosenfelt, Mark Levinson; d, John Mark Robinson; w, Galen Lee, George Simpson (based on a story by Lee); ph, Tom Ackerman (United Color Lab Color); m, Gary Scott; ed, Jay Lash Cassidy; prod d, Chester Kaczenski; md, Art Fein.

Drama/Comedy   **Cas.**   **(PR:C   MPAA:R)**

ROMANCING THE STONE★★★½   (1984) 105m FOX c

Michael Douglas (*Jack Colton*), Kathleen Turner (*Joan Wilder*), Danny De Vito (*Ralph*), Zack Norman (*Ira*), Alfonso Arau (*Juan*), Manuel Ojeda (*Zolo*), Holland Taylor (*Gloria*), Mary Ellen Trainor (*Elaine*), Eve Smith (*Mrs. Irwin*), Joe Nesnow (*Super*), Jose Chavez (*Santos*), Chachita (*Hefty Woman*), Camillo Garcia (*Bus Driver*), Rodrigo Puebla (*Bad Hombre*), Poco Morayta (*Hotel Clerk*), Jorge Zamora (*Maitre D'*), Kym Herrin (*Angelina*), Bill Burton (*Jessie*), Ted White (*Grogan*), Manuel Santiago, Ron Silver (*Vendors*), Mike Cassidy, Vince Deadrick, Sr., Richard Drown, Joe Finnegan, Jimmy Medearis, Jeff Ramsey (*Zolo's Men*).

A rousing, good old-fashioned romantic adventure yarn starring Turner as an author of successful romantic fiction who sits in her New York City apartment banging out novel after novel. The film opens as Turner in embroiled in her latest literary fantasy, tears streaming down her face as the saga reaches its romantic conclusion. She is snapped out of her reverie by the arrival of a strange package that contains some sort of treasure map showing the way to a glorious green jewel. This is followed by a frantic phone call from her sister who is being held captive by an evil art dealer, Norman, and his snarling cousin, DeVito. Her sister's husband has disappeared in Colombia, South America, and it was he who sent Turner the map. Norman and DeVito threaten to kill Turner's sister unless the treasure map is turned over to DeVito in Colombia. Turner packs a suitcase and marches off to the jungles of Colombia, decked out in a fancy dress and high heels. Upon her arrival in Colombia, she slowly realizes that DeVito isn't the only one after the map. A local corrupt military offical, Ojeda, dispatches his private army after Turner. Luckily, she is rescued by a handsome, young

American soldier-of-fortune, Douglas, and together they go after the treasure, falling in love along the way. Several chases, mudslides, shootouts, and narrow escapes later, Douglas and Turner run into another threat, that of a mountain bandit chieftain, Arau, who also covets the priceless green jewel. Fortunately, Arau is a big fan of Turner's novels and has memorized every one of them. When he learns her identity, he becomes their ally and chatters enthusiastically about his favorite passages in her novels. Eventually the factions converge on the treasure and it is found. Then, of course, the jewel changes hands and lands in the fist of Ojeda. From there the stone ends up in the stomach of an alligator (in a rather gratuitously bloody manner involving the amputation of Ojeda's arm). Though Turner couldn't care less about the jewel at this point because she has finally found true romance, Douglas jumps in after the alligator and the two disappear from sight. Turner waits for what seems like an eternity, but Douglas does not return. Crushed, Turner goes back to New York where her only welcome home is a cold typewriter. One day she hears a commotion outside and when she goes out to investigate she finds Douglas on the street aboard a giant sailboat (which is hooked up to a trailer). He found the stone and came back for her. The two sail together down the streets of Manhattan very much in love and yearning for more adventure. ROMANCING THE STONE moves like lightning through its 105 minute running time, barely giving the audience a chance to catch its breath. Although comparisons with Steven Spielberg's RAIDERS OF THE LOST ARK are inevitable (director Zemeckis is a protege of Spielberg), it is the interplay between Turner and Douglas that gives the film its real charm. Turner is wonderful as the repressed author suddenly propelled into the kind of life she only dreams about, and Douglas is charming as the adventurer vulnerable to romance. Norman and DeVito score strongly in roles that would have been played by Sidney Greenstreet and Peter Lorre 30 years ago, and the whole film has the feel of a Warner Bros. thriller with broadly comic overtones. The film was a huge hit at the box office and the title song by Eddy Grant shot to the top of the charts. The "PG" rating on the film is a bit liberal considering the brief passages of gore and a marijuana smoking scene between Turner and Douglas. An inferior sequel, THE JEWEL OF THE NILE, was released in 1985.

p, Michael Douglas; d, Robert Zemeckis; w, Diane Thomas; ph, Dean Cundey (Panavision, DeLuxe Color); m, Alan Silvestri; ed, Donn Cambern, Frank Morriss; prod d, Lawrence G. Paull; art d, Augustin Ituarte; set d, Enrique Estevez; cos, Marilyn Vance; ch, Jeffery D. Hornaday; m/l, "Romancing the Stone" (Eddy Grant, performed by Grant); stunts, Terry Leonard.

Adventure/Romance   Cas.   (PR:C-O   MPAA:PG)

ROSEBUD BEACH HOTEL**   (1984) 105m Almi c

Colleen Camp (Tracy), Peter Scolari (Elliott), Christopher Lee (King), Fran Drescher (Linda), Eddie Deezen (Sydney), Chuck McCann (Dorfman), Hank Garrett (Kramer), Hamilton Camp (Matches), Jonathan Schmock (Dennis), Jim Vallely (Leonard), Marie Curie Lukather (Marie), Cherie Currie (Cherie).

A mediocre comedy about a young man who buckles under the pressure of his domineering girl friend and undertakes the chore of managing a dilapidated hotel. The script has some funny gags enriched by an accomplished cast, especially C. Camp, who made a name for herself in Martha Coolidge's VALLEY GIRL (1983) and JOY OF SEX (1984).

p, Irving Schwartz, Harry Hurwitz; d, Hurwitz; w, Harry Narunsky, Schwartz, Thomas Rudolph; ph, Joao Fernandes; m, Jay Chattaway; ed, Daniel Lowenthal.

Comedy   Cas.   (PR:C-O   MPAA:R)

ROTWEILER: DOGS OF HELL zero (1984) 90m E.O. c (AKA: DOGS OF HELL)

Earl Owensby, Bill Gribble, Jerry Rushing.

A low-budget horror film intended mostly for the drive-in circuit in the South, this picture centers on sheriff Owensby trying to deal with a pack of the title dogs that is attacking the populace of his community. Shot in 3-D, the film is boring and ridiculous, with a lousy lead performance by Owensby, who insists on starring in most of the films his North Carolina-based company produces.

p, Earl Owensby; d, Worth Keeter III; w, Tom McIntyre; ph, (3-D).

Horror   Cas.   (PR:O   MPAA:R)

RUE CASES NEGRES   (SEE: SUGAR CANE ALLEY, Fr.)

RUNAWAY½**   (1984) 100m Tri-Star-Delphi III/Tri-Star c

Tom Selleck (Sgt. Jack Ramsey), Cynthia Rhodes (Sgt. Karen Thompson), Gene Simmons (Luther), Kirstie Alley (Jackie), Stan Shaw (Marvin), G.W. Bailey (Chief), Joey Cramer (Bobby), Chris Mulkey (Johnson), Anne-Marie Martin (Hooker at Bar), Michael Paul Chan (Wilson), Elizabeth Norment (Miss Shields), Carol Teesdale (Sally), Jackson Davies (Inspector), Paul Batten (Harry), Babs Chulla (Construction Supervisor), Marilyn Schreffler (Lois' Voice), Cec Verrell (Hooker), Natino Bellentino (Headwaiter), Judith

Johns (Data Tech), Betty Phillips (Linda), Andrew Rhodes (Cameraman), Louise Johan (Waitress), Stephen Thorne (Tommy), Steve Wright (Pilot), Stephen Miller (Rudy), Bob Metcalfe (Tracer), David Longworth (Man), Todd Duckworth (Paramedic), Moira Walley (Jogger), Albert Eggen (Floater Cop), John Brydon, Rodney Gage, Murray Ord, Daryl Hayes, Wayne York, Frank Serio, Keith Gordey (Cops), Lloyd Berry (Passenger), Dennis Kelli (Driver).

A futuristic good guy versus bad guy picture which is stylistically born out of the pages of a comic book. Selleck is a charming, rugged policeman who is raising a young son with the help of a robot maid, while risking his life as a specialist in terminating "runaways"– robots that short-circuit and become killers. A sudden rash of runaways causes a panic and Selleck is placed in charge of the investigation. He even gets himself a new partner, Rhodes, who is as tough and intelligent as she is pretty. Together they begin their pursuit of Simmons, an evil genius who is programming the robots for his own devices. Simmons' master plan is to kill off his enemies with specially designed heat-seeking bullets that respond only to the target's specified body temperature. Naturally, Selleck is Simmons' biggest obstacle, so the mad genius devotes his energy to trying to kill him. Meantime, Simmons infiltrates the police surveillance system and, with the help of his girl friend Alley, steals some vital microchips. Simmons makes an attempt on Selleck's life when the cop gets close to apprehending him, but he succeeds only in wounding Rhodes. Selleck still persists and manages to intercept the microchips. Simmons retaliates by kidnaping Selleck's son. To insure the boy's safety, Selleck must bring the chips to a skycraper construction site where the boy is being held. The site is deserted except for a horde of runaways–this time in the form of ankle-high metallic techno-critters which are the 21st Century equivalent of giant metal spiders–each of them anxious to leap up and kill anything human. Selleck, who conveniently suffers from vertigo, must travel to the top of the building via an open-air construction elevator. He meets Simmons' demands but is double crossed. After a battle of muscle and wits, Simmons is killed by the robot critters he programmed while Selleck and his son safely reach the ground where Rhodes is waiting. Directed by Crichton, who is responsible for such technological suspensers as WESTWORLD (1973) and COMA (1978), RUNAWAY offers much of the same quirky enjoyment as those two films. There is a certain ingenious fantasy quality to Crichton's films which is best described simply as "neat." One can't help but wish there were robots like those in RUNAWAY, or a place as magical as WESTWORLD. The problem with RUNAWAY is that it never reaches deeper than this level of playful "neatness," amounting to nothing more than great but shallow entertainment. RUNAWAY is helped along by a thoughtful performance by Selleck who comes across as a real, feeling person (the scenes with his son are genuinely touching), instead of the expected Rambo-esque tough guy stereotype. Another surprise is the debut appearance of Simmons as the campy evil genius. Simmons previously made a name for himself under a coat of makeup as the tongue-wagging lead singer for the popular rock group KISS. Special mention must also be made of the camera work which includes some of the most amazing Steadicam (a camera support system that maintains a gyropscopic-like steadiness while the cinematographer moves) shots ever put in a film. For the curious, Selleck and Crichton previously "worked" together in Coma, which cast Selleck as one of the many corpses which hung from the hospital ceiling.

p, Michael Rachmil; d&w, Michael Crichton; ph, John A. Alonzo (Panavision, Metrocolor); m, Jerry Goldsmith; ed, Glenn Farr; prod d, Douglas Higgins; art d, Michael Bolton; set d, Jim Erickson; cos, Betsy Cox; special robotic effects, Special Effects Unlimited, Broggie Elliott Animation; robotic spiders, Robotic Systems Intl.; robot designs, David Durand.

Science-Fiction/Crime   Cas.   (PR:C-O   MPAA:PG-13)

RUNNING HOT*   (1984) 95m Highroad/New Line c (AKA: LUCKY 13)

Monica Carrico (Charlene Andrews), Eric Stoltz (Danny Hicks), Stuart Margolin (Officer Trent), Virgil Frye (Ross the Pimp), Richard Bradford (Tom Bond), Louise Baker (Shane), Joe George (Officer Berman), Laurel Patrick (Angie), Sorrells Pickard (Ex-con in Desert), Ben Hammer (Danny's Father), Juliette Cummins (Jenny), Lesley Woods (Charlene's Mother), Bob Carroll (Harry), Clark Howat (Judge), Geno Havens (Foreman), Seth Kaufman (Bailiff), Dickie Walsh (Dickie).

A ridiculous heap of bad writing, aimless direction, and empty performances which concerns a 17-year-old boy, Stoltz, who has been convicted of murdering his father. He is supposed to receive the death penalty, but manages to escape and hide out with Carrico, a prostitute nearly twice his age who had spent her time writing him love letters while he sat in prison. They take off across the country in a car stolen from her pimp, avoiding capture by police officer Margolin. But, surprise, Stoltz is really innocent. The ending, however, has him getting killed anyway. The script has holes big enough to drive a fleet of trucks through and the performances are desperately in need of direction. Stoltz's name may ring a bell to those folks who've seen MASK (1985), a film which contains a considerably better performance from that young actor.

p, David Calloway, Zachary Feuer; d&w, Mark Griffiths; ph, Tom Richmond; m, Al Capps; ed, Andy Blumenthal; prod d, Katherine Vallin; art d, Anthony Cowley; set d, Kathy Orrison; cos, Jane E. Anderson; spec eff,

Roger George.

Crime   Cas.   (PR:O   MPAA:R)

RUSH*   (1984, Ital.) 77m Biro/Cinema Shares c

Conrad Nichols (*Rush*), Gordon Mitchell (*The Ruler*), Laura Trotter, Rita Furlan, Bridgit Pelz, Richard Pizzuti, Osiride Pevarello, Paolo Celli, Luigi Filippo Lodoli, Daniel Stroppa.

A stupid Italian hybrid of THE ROAD WARRIOR (1982) and FIRST BLOOD (1982) which stars Nichols as a superhero who lives in a post-nuclear holocaust jungle and fights for the freedom of a group of workers enslaved by the wicked Mitchell. RUSH is filled with wretched special effects, obviously faked fight scenes, and a lead actor who has studied Sylvester Stallone's posings long and hard. Directed by an Italian with an anglicized name "Anthony Richmond," who shouldn't be confused with the British director-cinematographer of the same name.

p, Marcello Romeo; d, Anthony Richmond [Tonino Ricci]; w, Tito Carpi (based on his story); ph, Giovanni Bergmanini (Luciano Vittori Color); m, Francesco De Masi; ed, Vincenzo Tomassi.

Science Fiction/Adventure   (PR:C-O   MPAA:NR)

SACRED GROUND½**   (1984) 100m Pacific International c

Tim McIntire (*Matt*), Jack Elam (*Witcher*), L.Q. Jones (*Tolbert*), Mindi Miller (*Wannetta*), Eloy Phil Casados (*Prairie Fox*), Serene Hedin (*Little Doe*), Vernon Foster (*Wounded Leg*), Lefty Wild Eagle (*Medicine Man*), Larry Kenoras (*Brave Beaver*).

An intriguing picture set in an Indian burial ground in the mid-1800s and centering on the relationship between a trapper and his new wife after his first wife dies during childbirth. The film is not only interesting on a dramatic level but also serves as an educational tool on the customs and lives of both the Apache and Paiute Indian tribes.

p, Arthur R. Dubs; d,w&ph, Charles B. Pierce (CFI Color); m, Gene Kauer, Don Bagley; ed, David E. Jackson, Steven L. Johnson, Lynne Sutherland.

Drama   Cas.   (PR:C   MPAA:PG)

SACRED HEARTS½**   (1984, Brit.) 89m Reality-Film Four c

Anna Massey (*Sister Thomas*), Katrin Cartlidge (*Doris*), Oona Kirsh (*Maggie*), Fiona Shaw (*Sister Felicity*), Anne Dyson (*Sister Perpetua*), Annette Badland (*Sister Mercy*), Sadie Wearing (*Mary*), Ann-Marie Gwatkin (*Lizzie*), Kathy Burke (*Tillie*), Gerard Murphy (*Father Larkin*), Murray Melvin (*Father Power*), John Bett (*Dr. Taylor*).

Cartlidge stars as a young woman who enters an English convent school at the start of WW II even though she isn't Catholic. She tells this secret to her friend, Kirsh, who tries to give her a crash course in the religion. This leads to some close calls in Cartlidge's interactions with the nuns. It is finally revealed that Cartlidge is actually a German Jew who is avoiding persecution if and when the Nazis invade England. Some nice characters are developed by the girls, offsetting the stereotypes of the nuns.

p, Dee Dee Glass; d&w, Barbara Rennie; ph, Diane Tammes; m, Dirk Higgins; ed, Martin Walsh; art d, Hildegard Echtler; cos, Monica Howe.

Drama/Comedy   (PR:A   MPAA:NR)

SAHARA*   (1984) 104m Cannon/MGM-UA c

Brooke Shields (*Gordon Dale*), Lambert Wilson (*Jaffar*), John Rhys-Davies (*Rasoul*), Horst Buchholz (*Von Glessing*), Perry Lang (*Andy*), Cliff Potts (*String*), John Mills (*Cambridge*), Steve Forrest (*R.J. Gordon*), Ronald Lacey (*Beg*), Terrence Hardiman (*Browne*), Tuvia Tabi (*Bertocelli*), Ilan Zahavi (*De La Forge*), Dov Friedman (*Lindstrom*), Rolf Brin (*Curt*), Yehuda Elboy (*Dramn*), Yossi Shiloa (*Halef*), Shachar Cohen (*Abu*), Barry Langford (*Concierge*), Yacov Ben Sira (*Mayor*), Zehava Twena (*Yasmin*), Dina Ledani (*Ismene*), Dorit Seadia (*Lallah*), Sam Omani (*Douvain*), Gabi Amrani (*Omar*), Joseph Bee (*Browne Crewman*), Don Angelo Muggia (*Bertocelli Crewman*), Ran Vered (*De La Forge Crewman*), Ezra Kafry (*Lindstrom Crewman*), Rocky Taylor (*Kamal*), Greg Powell (*Abdullah*), Shaul Taron (*Mustapha*), Paul Maxwell (*Chase*), David Lodge (*Ewing*), Caro Henley (*Mistress*).

An unrelentingly idiotic adventure story which stars cover girl Shields as the daughter of Detroit car designer Forrest. When he dies during a test run, Shields agrees to take his place in a treacherous endurance race through the Sahara. It's the 1920s, however, and women aren't allowed behind the wheel so Shields dons a hat and mustache and passes herself off as a man (and a rather effeminate one at that). Complications arise when tribal wars make the Sahara dangerous and cause the course to be rerouted. Shields decides to run the shorter original course as a time-saver, but winds up instead as a prisoner of mad sheik Rhys-Davies. Another member of the tribe, the young and virile Wilson, falls in love with Shields and takes her as his wife to save her from the brutalities of the piggish Rhys-Davies. Shields has no intention of becoming a tribal bride and sneaks off in the night to finish the race. She is soon captured by rival sheik Lacey and thrown into a pit full

of hungry jungle cats. Wilson and his followers attack Lacey's compound and after a seemingly endless tribal battle, rescue Shields. Wilson displays his love for Shields by allowing her to finish the race. She manages to get right back into the heat of the competition and edges her way into first place by defeating arch rival Buchholz. One of the dumbest films in recent memory to worm its way into.theaters, SAHARA thankfully received such a lousy response in its test screenings that it was never released east of the Mississippi River. Shields, who hasn't been good in a film since her PRETTY BABY debut, is simply embarrassing, while the rest of the cast makes the best of an impossible situation. In all fairness, however, the blame lies not with Shields, but in the awful script and McLaglen's catatonic direction--no excitement is ever achieved, the laughs come at all the wrong places, the romance is cardboard. On top of all this, Morricone's score seems like a bad joke. Pre-teen girls who idolize Shields may find this film enthralling, but all others should agree that SAHARA pins the "stupid meter" all the way to the right.

p, Menahem Golan, Yoram Globus; d, Andrew V. McLaglen; w, James R. Silke (based on a story by Golan); ph, David Gurfinkel, Armando Nannuzzi (Metrocolor); m, Ennio Morricone; ed, Alan Strachan, Michael J. Duthie; prod d, Luciano Spadoni; art d, John Hoesli; set d, Enzo Eusepi; cos, Mario Carlini.

Adventure   Cas.   (PR:C   MPAA:PG)

SAM'S SON½**   (1984) 104m Worldvision/Invictus c

Eli Wallach (*Sam Orowitz*), Anne Jackson (*Harriet Orowitz*), Timothy Patrick Murphy (*Gene Orowitz*), Hallie Todd (*Cathy Stanton*), Alan Hayes (*Robert Woods*), Jonna Lee (*Bonnie Barnes*), Michael Landon (*Gene Orman*), Howard Witt (*Cy Martin*), William Boyett (*Coach Sutter*), John Walcutt (*Ronnie Morgan*), David Lloyd Nelson (*Lonnie Morgan*), William H. Bassett (*Mr. Turner*), Harvey Gold (*Jake Bellow*), James Karen (*Mr. Collins*), David Wakefield (*Buddy*), Martin Rudy (*Dr. Warren*), Montana Smoyer (*Maxine Wagner*), Gavin H. Mooney (*Police Officer*), Barbara Collentine (*Miss Bass*), Phil Proctor (*Art Fisher*), Buck Young (*Marv Gates*), Herb Mitchell (*Coach Diener*), Dave Morick (*Field Judge*), Robert Balderson, Kurt Smildsin (*Track Officials*), Andrew Ethier (*Competitor*), Kathleen Coyne (*Cathy Orman*), B.J. Turner, Mickey Morton (*Customers*), Michael Griswold (*Cathy Stanton's Father*), Dave Adams (*Truck Driver*), Casey Erickson (*Harold*), Laurie Blower (*Car Hop*), Randy Faustino (*Tony*).

Although it's a feature film, this could have been made for TV, if some dubious humor about the lead's bathroom habits were excised. That's not meant to be pejorative because, had it been made for the tube, it would have been excellent for that medium. As a big-screen offering it's just a little light to capture the admission price that theaters are asking. It's easy to see how autobiographical this is when one knows that the lead's character name is "Orowitz," which is writer-director Landon's real monicker. Murphy is a slight young man with the ability to throw the javelin. He's been doing some weight training to build his frail body and give his throws more thrust. At present, he's dating high school sweetie Lee, a blonde cheerleader type who would never go for the small, dark Murphy for very long. And that's exactly what happens when she suddenly notices the muscles of football player Hayes. Murphy's home life is almost right out of any Phillip Roth-Herbert Gold-Joe Heller book. His father is henpecked, his mother is a *yenta* who pays more attention to her son's toilet training than his grades. Wallach is Murphy's father, the manager of a local movie theater. Murphy goes to watch DeMille's SAMSON AND DELILAH and sees a parallel between the Hebrew hero and himself. Since his father's name is "Sam," and since he is "Sam's Son," then it's only fitting that he allow his hair to grow long, like the biblical giant. Since this is taking place in the 1950s, long hair--except on classical musicians--is definitely out, and that's a focal point in the boy's struggle for individuality. Wallach has dreams of becoming a writer, but supporting his nagging wife, Jackson (Wallach's real wife in real life), and paying all the bills keeps him at his regular job and he is forced to do his writing late at night, while everyone else snores. When Lee turns her affections toward Hayes, she is replaced by Todd, and Murphy gets the chance to show his new strength by decking bully Hayes with one shot to the jaw. Murphy's desire is to be a champion javelin thrower. Just before the big track meet, Wallach has a heart attack while schlepping a half-dozen cans of film up to the projection room. On his death bed, Wallach hands Murphy his completed manuscript. Murphy is inspired to great heights, goes to the track meet, and throws that spear like a modern-day David slinging his shot at Goliath. The result is a scholarship to a college he could never have afforded and a happy ending. In a cameo, Landon himself arrives, now a big star who has changed his name to Orman. He goes to his old house and cries at the sight of it as he pulls up in a limousine. There is to be a world premiere of his latest film in his hometown and that's what sets the flashback mode. Landon really did win the USC scholarship, then started doing small parts, which lead to his historic I WAS A TEENAGE WEREWOLF, GOD'S LITTLE ACRE, THE LEGEND OF TOM DOOLEY, and his eventual success on TV's "Bonanza," "Little House on the Prairie," and "Highway to Heaven." Landon is never ashamed to aim for the heart and the tear ducts, and anyone short of an old grump will find the eyes glistening a bit here. Good acting from all concerned in a film that must have been a tribute to his long- gone father, sort of a "thanks, dad" for his love and guidance and wisdom. Had this been made for TV, instead of getting a small release from the distributor, it would have been seen and appreciated by many millions more.

p, Kent McCray; d&w, Michael Landon; ph, Ted Voigtlander; m, David Rose; ed, John Loeffler; art d, George Renne; set d, Dennis Peeples; cos, Mike Termini, Linda Taylor.

Biographical Drama   **Cas.**   **(PR:A-C MPAA:PG)**

SAVAGE DAWN*
(1984) 102m Media Home Entertainment c

George Kennedy (*Tick Rand*), Lance Henriksen (*Ben Stryker*), Karen Black, Richard Lynch, Claudia Udy.

A subpar modern day western about a town terrorized by a gang of motorcyclists who call themselves the "Savages." Kennedy and the locals do all they can to stop the harassment but nothing works. Nothing, that is, until Henriksen, a Special Forces war veteran, pays a visit to his old pal Kennedy. Henriksen has seen his share of killing and has no intention of getting involved in the town's crisis. When he can no longer sit back and watch the destruction he decides to go on the rampage. It takes itself far too seriously, however, to be much fun.

d, Simon Nuchtern; w, William P. Milling.

Crime   **(PR:O MPAA:NR)**

SAVAGE STREETS*
(1984) 93m Savage Streets/Motion Picture Marketing c

Linda Blair (*Brenda*), John Vernon (*Principal Underwood*), Robert Dryer (*Jake*), Johnny Venocur (*Vince*), Sal Landi (*Fargo*), Scott Mayer (*Red*), Debra Blee (*Rachel*), Lisa Freeman (*Francine*), Linnea Quigley (*Heather*), Marcia Kerr (*Stevie*), Luisa Leschin (*Maria*), Ina Romeo, Jill Bunker, Mitch Carter, Richard DeHaven, Bob DeSimone, Susan Dean, Joe Hyler, Louis P. Zito, Brian Mann, Catherine McGoohan, Sean O'Grady, Rebecca Perle, Paula Shaw, Kristi Sommers, Troy Tompkins, Perle Walter, Judy Walton, Carol Ita White.

Blair stars in this typical vengeance picture as an angry young sweater girl who is a combination of Mamie Van Doren and Charles Bronson. She's a member of a Los Angeles high school gang called the "Satins" who is brought to the boiling point when her deaf-mute sister is raped by some degenerates who call themselves the "Scars." Blair dons her commando outfit (which shows an appropriate amount of flesh) and a crossbow and hits the streets. She then gives the "Scars" an overdose of their own medicine. Blair's best performance since THE EXORCIST, 11 years ago, but that's not saying much. The film was begun with Billy Fine as producer and Tom DeSimone as director, but less than two weeks into production both left. The production then ran out of money, only to be resurrected for some ungodly reason a few months later.

p, John C. Strong III; d, Danny Steinmann; w, Norman Yonemoto, Steinmann; ph, Stephen Posey (CFI Color); m, Michael Lloyd, John D'Andrea; ed, Bruce Stubblefield, John O'Conner; art d, Ninkey Dalton; set d, Nancy Arnold; Stunts, Al Jones, B.J. Davis.

Crime   **Cas.**   **(PR:O MPAA:R)**

SCANDALOUS**
(1984) 92m Lantana/Orion c

Robert Hays (*Frank Swedlin*), Pamela Stephenson (*Fiona Maxwell Sayle*), Ron Travis (*Porno Director*), M. Emmet Walsh (*Simon Reynolds*), John Gielgud (*Uncle Willie*), Ed Dolan (*Purser*), Paul Reeve (*Flight Coordinator*), Alita Kennedy (*Stewardess*), Nancy Wood (*Lindsay*), Kevin Elyot (*Matt*), Duncan Preston (*Hal*), Maureen Bennett (*Patti*), Peter Dennis (*Maitre d'*), Preston Lockwood (*Leslie*), Conover Kennard (*Francine Swedlin*), Jim Dale (*Inspector Anthony Crisp*), Jim Magill (*The Bobby*), Mike Walling (*Scotty*), Stuart Saunders (*Croft*), Albert Moses (*Vishnu*), Toby Robins (*Pamela Reynolds*), Maggie Flint (*Landlady*), Richard Hope (*Young Detective*), Elizabeth Richardson (*Shop Girl*), Zoot Money, Richard Ireson, Ron Cook (*Taxi Drivers*), Peter Whitman (*Sgt. Mac Williams*), Emil Wolk (*Greek Restaurant Owner*), Robert Styles (*Schoolboy*), Michael Drew (*Newscaster*), Hilary Ryan (*Girl Reporter*), Terry Kingley (*News Scoop*), Jonathan Barlow (*Police Inspector*), Joris Stuyck (*Mustaad*), Anthony Gardner (*Salesman*), Davina Williams (*Metermaid*), Bow Wow Wow (*Themselves*).

A rather nonsensical murder mystery about a news reporter, Hays, who gets framed for the murder of his wife. His idyllic life as the television station master's son-in-law quickly deteriorates when he discovers that he is the butt of a blackmail scheme engineered by con artists Stephenson and Gielgud. Before long Hays and Stephenson get entangled in a heated romance in spite of their mistrust of each other. The films highlight is Gielgud, who dons many a disguise including a Japanese businessman and a punk rock fan attending a Bow Wow Wow concert.

p, Arlene Sellers, Alex Winitsky; d, Rob Cohen; w, Cohen, John Byrum (based on a story by Byrum, Rob Cohen, Larry Cohen); ph, Jack Cardiff (Technicolor); m, Dave Grusin; ed, Michael Bradsell; prod d, Peter Mullins; art d, John Siddal, Brian Ackland-Snow; set d, Harry Cordwell; m/l, "It's Scandalous," Grusin, Don Block (sung by Amanda Homi).

Comedy/Mystery   **Cas.**   **(PR:C MPAA:PG)**

SCAREMAKER, THE
(SEE: GIRLS NIGHT OUT)

SCARRED**½
(1984) 85m Seymour Borde and Associates c (AKA: RED ON RED; STREET LOVE)

Jennifer Mayo (*Ruby Star*), Jackie Berryman (*Carla*), David Dean (*Easy*), Rico L. Richardson (*Jojo*), Debbie Dion (*Sandy*), Lili (*Rita*), Randolph Pitts, Walter Klenhard (*Tricks*), Haskell Anderson, Andre Walters (*Barber Shop Pimps*), Willie (*Barber*), Eddie Pansullo (*Porno Producer*).

A gritty story of a young girl, Mayo, forced to hit the streets and resort to prostitution to cover her rent and support her infant child. She is befriended by a seemingly decent pimp, Dean, but is soon caught in a whirlwind of seedy characters before finally separating herself from that crowd. If SCARRED had been shot in the typical exploitative style then it would easily be forgotten, but the *cinema-verite* style adds a certain frightening potency to the picture. Begun by director Turko while a student at UCLA and finished with the help of American Film Institute and National Endowments for the Arts grants. Alex Cox, director of REPOMAN (1984), served as assistant director.

p, Marie Turko, Mark Borde, Dan Halperine; d&w, Turko; ph, Michael Miner (DeLuxe Color); ed, Turko; art d, Cecilia Rodarte.

Drama   **(PR:O MPAA:R)**

SCREAM FOR HELP zero
(1984) 88m Videoform-Miracle/LORIMAR c

Rachel Kelly (*Christie Cromwell*), Marie Masters (*Karen Cromwell Fox*), David Brooks (*Paula Fox*), Lolita Lorre (*Brenda Bohle*), Rocco Sisto (*Lacey Bohle*), Corey Parker (*John Dealey*), Sandra Clark (*Janey*), Tony Sibbald (*Bob Dealey*), Stacey Hughes, David Baxt, Leslie Lowe, Michael Corby, Ronald Pernee, Richard Oldfield, Tony Cyrus, Joel Cutrara, Marlene Marcus, Jeff Harding, Brittain Saine Walker, Erick Ray Evans, William Roberts, Michael Fitzpatrick, Diana Ricardo, Burnell Tucker, Bruce Boa, Robyn Mandell, Morgan Deare, Sarah Brackett, Chuck Julian, Clare Burt, Matthew Peters.

SCREAM FOR HELP is what the audience will probably do after viewing this film, not out of abject fear, but out of the sheer misery of having to sit through 88 minutes of this inane attempt at blending intrigue and terror. Convinced that her stepfather (Brooks) is trying to murder her mother (Masters), Kelly sets out on the task of attempting to convince everyone of this dastardly plot. Naturally, no one but the audience believes her, even when a series of "accidents" begins to occur, ones that are clearly not happenstance. Masters gets into an automobile accident and survives, leaving her with a cast on her leg as a memory. Kelly's best friend is killed by a hit-and-run driver after she discovers Brooks in the sack with his mistress, Lorre. Kelly takes some revealing Polaroids of Lorre and Brooks en flagrante delicto and almost loses her life. It all culminates when Brooks, Lorre, and Lorre's "brother" (actually her husband, Sisto) take Kelly and Masters as hostages in their own home and attempt to do away with them. That situation is not believable because, early on in the hostage drama, it's clearly indicated that Kelly and Masters are smarter than their captors and could probably whip them at any time so the question becomes not who will survive, but how long the villains will stick around. The basic lure for blood movie fans is the amount of gore tossed in for show and there's plenty of that here. A meter man comes to the house and winds up as a sizzling carcass on the cellar floor. The villains are dispatched with equal violence as one is electrocuted and another is impaled on a kitchen knife. It's uncertain whether the actors knew if the screenplay was supposed to be funny or not. It might have come off tongue-in-cheek but Winner opted for a heavy musical score and one wonders what effect he was trying to achieve. The actors either received no direction or the wrong direction and what might have been a delicious satire of this genre comes off as just another slash and scream movie. Lorimar had hired long-time film distribution man Irwin Yablans (brother of Frank, who ran various studios) to head up their low-budget unit and this movie may be why he didn't stay there very long. Director Winner again comes up a loser here as he did with THE SENTINEL, WON TON TON, THE DOG WHO SAVED HOLLYWOOD, and his awful remake of THE BIG SLEEP.

p&d, Michael Winner; w, Tom Holland; ph, Robert Paynter; m, John Paul Jones; ed, Arnold Ross; art d, Tony Reading.

Terror/Mystery   **(PR:O MPAA:R)**

SCRUBBERS**½
(1984, Brit.) 90m HandMade/Orion Classics c

Amanda York (*Carol*), Chrissie Cotterill (*Annetta*), Elizabeth Edmonds (*Kathleen*), Kate Ingram (*Eddie*), Debbie Bishop (*Doreen*), Dana Gillespie (*Budd*), Camille Davis (*Sharon*), Amanda Symonds (*Mac*), Kathy Burke (*Glennis*), Eva Motley (*Pam*), Imogen Bain (*Sandy*), Honey Bane (*Molly*), Rachel Weaver (*Gwen*), Dawn Archibald (*Mary*), Faith Tingle (*Hilary*), Lillian Rostkowska (*Phyllis*), Anna Mackeown (*Eva*), Pauline Melville, Pam St. Clement, Miriam Margoyles, Jackie Holborough, Caroline Needs, Olwen Griffiths, Carol Gillies, Richard Butler, Brian Croucher, Tim Knightley, Robbie Coltrane, Maggie Wright, Yvonne D'Alpra, Jane Freeman, Steve Alder, Ken Shorter, Bradley Hardiman, Gemma Murphy, Val Lilley, Finola Keogh.

Life in an English girls' reform prison is examined in this brutal picture written by Roy Minton, the person responsible for SCUM, which tells the same story in a prison for boys. The film centers mainly on two girls–York, a girl who longs for some sort of security behind the prison walls, and Cotterill, a driven mother who desperately wants to be reunited with her child. Although the girls are from all walks of life, they learn to survive together fighting the system and often each other. Ex-Beatle George Harrison acted as executive producer. Released in Britain in 1982.

p, Don Boyd; d, Mai Zetterling; w, Zetterling, Roy Minton, Jeremy Watt; ph, Ernest Vincze (Eastmancolor); m, Michael Hurd, Ray Cooper; ed, Rodney Holland; art d, Celia Barnett; cos, Susannah Buxton.

Drama   (PR:O   MPAA:R)

SECOND TIME LUCKY*½   (1984, Aus./New Zealand) 98m
                                       Eadenrock-Galatia/United International c

Diane Franklin (Eve), Roger Wilson (Adam), Robert Helpmann (The Devil), Jon Gadsby (Gabriel), John-Michael Howson (The Devil's Assistant), Bill Ewens (Chuck), Robert Morley (God).

A mindless, cutesy comedy in which the Devil and God make a bet that if Adam and Eve were given a second chance they would still fail their test. Wilson and Franklin, as Adam and Eve respectively, are seen as a couple of intellectuals at a party who are quickly transported to the Garden of Eden. They pass their test and are then beamed into the Roman era where temptation must again be resisted. This silly game goes on in WW I, Prohibition, and in the present day (with Adam as a rock star). Anderson, who's directed some respectable pictures in the past (AROUND THE WORLD IN 80 DAYS), fails miserably with this one. Besides, why would anyone cast Morley as God? Isn't that role saved for George Burns?

p, Anthony I. Ginnane; d, Michael Anderson; w, Ross Dimsey, David Sigmund, Howard Grigsby (based on a story by Dimsey, Sigmund); ph, John McLean (Panavision, Eastmancolor); m, Garry McDonald, Laurie Stone; ed, Terry Paterson; prod d, David Copping; cos, Bruce Finlavson.

Comedy   **Cas.**   (PR:C   MPAA:NR)

SECRET DIARY OF SIGMUND FREUD, THE*
                            (1984) 99m Dalyn-Film 41st Avala/FOX-TLC c

Bud Cort (Sigmund Freud), Carol Kane (Martha Bernays), Klaus Kinski (Dr. Max Bauer), Marisa Berenson (Emma Herrmann), Carroll Baker (Mama Freud), Dick Shawn (The Ultimate Patient), Ferdinand [Ferdy] Mayne (Herr Herrmann), Nikola Simic (Papa Freud), Rade Markovic (Dr. Schtupmann).

A strange picture which fictionalizes the early years of famed pscyhoanalyst Sigmund Freud, here portrayed with an odd flavor by Cort. The jokes come mainly from the development of his ideas about the human psyche, portrayed by Shawn as "the ultimate patient." There's even some romance tossed in–Cort has an affair with a lisping nurse, Kane; Freud's mother, Baker, carries on with demented doctor Kinski. SECRET DIARY is nothing more than a rather sparse series of vignettes which never seem to comprise a whole. Shown at the Cannes marketplace where it was purchased by 20th Century-Fox's subsidiary TLC, after which it rightfully vanished from sight and memory.

p, Wendy Hyland, Peer Oppenheimer; d, Danford B. Greene; w, Roberto Mitrotti, Linda Howard; ph, George Nikolic (DeLuxe Color); m, V. Boris; art d, Miodrag Miric.

Biography/Comedy   (PR:O   MPAA:PG)

SECRET HONOR**   (1984) 90m Sandcastle 5/Cinecom c (AKA:
        SECRET HONOR: THE LAST TESTAMENT OF RICHARD M. NIXON;
                          SECRET HONOR: A POLITICAL MYTH)

Philip Baker Hall (President Richard M. Nixon).

Strangely, SECRET HONOR represents the very worst in filmmaking, yet the very best in acting. Hall, who resembles Richard M. Nixon only in the very slightest way, delivers a virtuoso performance in this fictional account of the former President's inner turmoil. Hall, the only cast member, wanders around his study (the film's sole set) fondly reminiscing and spouting angry attacks at those politicians he's interacted with over the years. He speaks fondly of his family (cursing the tuberculosis that killed two brothers), but fumes and shakes at the thought of Henry Kissinger ("They gave him a Nobel Prize and accused me of stealing silverware from the White House"), Eisenhower (he once referred to Nixon as Nick Dixon), and the entire Kennedy clan. In short, Hall gives one of the finest performances put on film in recent memory–he is simply mesmerizing. Altman's direction, however, leaves much to be desired. He has simply filmed another stage play (this time in conjunction with the University of Michigan and the Los Angeles Actors' Theater) as he has with COME BACK TO THE FIVE AND DIME JIMMY DEAN, JIMMY DEAN (1982) and STREAMERS (1983). In an unsuccessful attempt to make SECRET HONOR cinematic, he has simply installed four video monitors in Nixon's study which watch his every move. Whenever Altman feels the need to cut away, he takes a shot of the monitors. It's like clockwork–every few minutes there's another shot of Hall

on video. That's the extent of Altman's creativity in SECRET HONOR. Fortunately, Hall's performance makes Altman's tedium worthwhile.

p&d, Robert Altman; w, Donald Freed, Arnold M. Stone (based on their stage play "Secret Honor: The Last Will and Testament Of Richard M. Nixon"); ph, Pierre Mignot (Movielab Color); m, George Burt; ed, Juliet Weber; art d, Stephen Altman; cos, Philip Baker Hall.

Drama   (PR:C   MPAA:NR)

SECRET HONOR: A POLITICAL MYTH   (SEE: SECRET HONOR)

**SECRET HONOR: THE LAST TESTAMENT OF RICHARD M.
NIXON**   (SEE: SECRET HONOR)

SECRET PLACES**½   (1984, Brit.) Skreba-Virgin-National Film
                                       Finance-Rediffusion/FOX c

Marie-Theres Relin (Laura Meister), Tara MacGowran (Patience), Claudine Auger (Sophy Meister), Ann-Marie Gwatkin (Rose), Pippa Hinchley (Barbara), Klaus Barner (Wolfgang Meister), Jenny Agutter (Miss Lowrie), Sylvia Coleridge (Miss Trott), Rosemary Martin (Mrs. MacKenzie), Amanda Grinling (Miss Winterton), Veronica Clifford (Miss Mallard), Adam Richardson (Stephen), Zoe Caryl (Junior), Bill Ward (Mrs. Watts), Rosamund Greenwood (Hannah the Boots), Maurice O'Connell (Police Sergeant), Marissa Dunlop (Little Girl), Margaret Lacey (Mrs. Burgess), Mike Haywood, John Blundell (Soldiers on Train), Lesley Nightingale (Woman on Train), Andrew Byatt (Scots Soldier), Tony London (Cockney Soldier), Georgia Slowe (Cordelia), John Henson (Jack), Robert Kenly (Gerald), Paul Ambrose (David), Francisco Morales (Carlo), Stewart Guidotti (Alfredo), Mark Lewis (Dino), Jessica Walker, Sian Dunlop (Girls in Art Room), Alan Barry (Dr. Parrish), Lala Lloyd (Nurse), John Segal (Al).

This is the dramatic side of such comedy classics as THE BELLES OF ST. TRINIAN'S and the three sequels that followed it. Set in a prim and proper British girls' school at the start of WW II, it's too nice for its own good and so underplayed that there is little bite to the story. MacGowran (daughter of actor Jack MacGowran) is an ugly duckling at the school who will probably mature into a great beauty but, for the nonce, she is all legs and clunky and spends most of her time alone. Her home life is dull and the school provides what little excitement occurs in her bleak existence. Enter Relin (daughter of Maria Schell), a sophisticated refugee from Germany. Relin and her gentile parents, Auger and Barner, have come to England from Germany after their virulent Nazi son denounced them to the authorities. They are placed in an alien camp at first because Barner is a physicist and the Brits aren't sure if he's a spy or not. MacGowran and Relin become best friends and develop a minor schoolgirl crush on each other. Relin loves being at school because her home life is dreadful as Auger is a drug addict on morphine. The other girls at the school and some of the teachers think that it would be best if MacGowran and Relin don't see each other as they fear the two will become lesbians (or so it's understated). Nothing much happens but the period is evoked well and the life in a segregated school is well depicted. Agutter plays a young teacher and Coleridge is the retired gray-haired one who has seen it all and has returned to the school to help out for the duration. It was produced by Skreba-Virgin Films in association with the National Film Finance corporation and Rediffusion and it boasts a lyric by Alan Jay Lerner, one of the last written by the genius before his death. A pleasant movie with more story than drama as much of what transpires happens off the screen and we are only given hearsay, thus violating the essential cinematic rule of "show, don't tell." Partial nudity and some double entendres take this picture out of the realm of youngsters' fare.

p, Simon Relph, Ann Skinner; d, Zelda Barron; w, Barron (based on the novel by Janice Elliott); ph, Peter Macdonald (Eastmancolor); m, Michel Legrand; ed, Laurence Mery-Clark; prod d, Eileen Diss; art d, Bob Cartwright, Judith Lang; cos, Jane Robinson; m/l, "Secret Place," Legrand, Alan Jay Lerner; makeup, Robin Grantham.

Drama   (PR:C   MPAA:PG-13)

SECRETS**½   (1984, Brit.) 78m Enigma-Goldcrest/Samuel Goldwyn c

Helen Lindsay (Mother), John Horsley (Dr. Jefferies), Anna Campbell-Jones (Louise), Daisy Cockburn (Sydney), Rebecca Johnson (Trottie), Lucy Goode (Jane), Richard Tolan (Paul), Carol Gillies (Miss Quick), Jane Briers (Miss Strickland), Judith Fellows (Elderly Teacher), Georgine Anderson (Matron), Cynthia Grenville (Miss Johnson), Elizabeth Choice (Miss Jones Wallace), Matyelock Gibbs (Miss Lane), Nancy Manningham (Miss Lightfoot), Peter Scott Harrison, Craig Stokes, Robert Stagg, Paul Gamble (Boys on Train).

An enjoyable story of a 13-year-old girl, Campbell-Jones, who lives alone with her widowed mother, Lindsay. Campbell-Jones is sent off to a boarding school, but not before she discovers some secret documents kept hidden by her father. A curious look reveals that her father was a member of the secret order of Freemasons. When she finally gets to school she tries to explain to her friends– Cockburn, Johnson, and Goode–what the Freemasons are. Later Campbell-Jones' mother discovers a box of condoms in her daughter's room and wrongly presumes that the girl is sexually active. It all winds up innocently enough and mother and daughter are brought closer. Originally made for a British television series entitled "First Love" and produced by David Puttnam.

p, Chris Griffin; d, Gavin Millar; w, Noella Smith; ph, Christopher Challis (Kay Color); m, Guy Woolfenden; ed, Eric Boyd-Perkins; art d, Jeffrey Woolbridge.

Comedy/Drama (PR:A-C MPAA:R)

SHEENA**½ (1984) 117m COL-Delphi II/COL c

Tanya Roberts (Sheena), Ted Wass (Vic Casey), Donovan Scott (Fletcher), Elizabeth of Toro (Shaman), France Zobda (Countess Zanda), Trevor Thomas (Prince Otwani), Clifton Jones (King Jabalani), John Forgeham (Jorgenson), Errol John (Bolu), Sylvester Williams (Juka), Bob Sherman (Grizzard), Michael Shannon (Phillip Ames), Nancy Paul (Betsy Ames), Kathryn Gant (Child Sheena), Kirsty Lindsay (Young Sheena), Nick Brimble (Wadman), Paul Gee (Blau), Dave Cooper (Anders), Tim Ward-Booth (Helicopter Pilot), Wilbur Nyabongo (Pilot), Oliver Litondo (Haromba), Louis Mahoney, Shane Mwigereri (Elders), Tom Mwangi (African Native), Margarita Ndisi (Receptionist), Joseph Olita, Lenny Juma (Policemen), William Allot (Prison Sergeant), Lucy Wangiu Gishomo (Old Lady), Mick Ndisho (Mechanic).

The saddest words of tongue or pen are, of course, "what might have been." This might have been a terrific movie. Surely, it had all the right ingredients: a beautiful woman in an odd situation, a background as colorful as any movie ever made, a script by veterans Semple and Newman, and a historic comic strip. So what went wrong? It has to be laid squarely on the shoulders of Guillermin who directed the movie as if he weren't sure if it was adventure, comedy, or camp. Semple, who wrote the pilot of "Batman" and the screenplay of the KING KONG remake knew full well how to write camp and Guillermin, who directed the abortive KONG should have had an idea that there was some humor to be mined out of a premise where a gorgeous blonde girl (who must have invented some incredible sunscreen lotion in her tree house because she is pale as a whitefish) is part of an African tribe and doesn't ever notice that her brethren and sistren are 27 shades darker than she is. Gant, a sweet blonde child, is lost in the African jungle and adopted by the Zambouli tribe, lead by Elizabeth of Toro (a real African queen) who recalls the tribe's prophecy that a woman will protect them when things go sour. Gant grows up to be Lindsay and finally Roberts as time passes. The Zambouli are a fierce but fair people and stay in their distant region of Africa, away from the political turmoil of many of the Third World countries. Scott and Wass are U.S. TV newsmen who have come to the kingdom of Tigorda to film a story on Thomas, the prince of the country who is a rakehell and a rat. He is also well known in the U.S., having played on an American football team. The country is poverty-stricken but that doesn't stop Thomas from parading his wealth for the people in the form of what must be the one decent car in the whole country, a Mercedes convertible. When Wass sees Roberts from afar, he can't believe his eyes and makes a beeline for her. Roberts talks in a Tarzan-like accent, has difficulty with English, and is fascinated by Wass. The fact that she struggles with English strikes one oddly because her fellow Zambouli mostly talk as though they've been educated at Eton. Thomas wants to rule the country so he disposes of his brother, Jones, in order to take over the country's reins. He needs a scapegoat and Elizabeth of Toro is chosen and tossed into jail to await execution. Roberts and E of T have an ESP relationship going for them and so when Roberts gets the mental call from her adopted mother, she and Wass and her tribe and a score of animal pals (all superbly trained by Wells) help to rescue E of T and the picture ends happily, if not in profits. It cost more than $25 million to make and the returns were negligible. The studio had hoped to get some of the same people who flocked to see KING KONG and GREYSTOKE but the reviews, some of them unfair, kept audiences away in droves. Producer Aratow had been walking around with the rights for years and set it up at a few different studios before Columbia bit. Many scripts had been written on the subject and several actresses were considered before Roberts, whose main experience had been on TV's "Charlie's Angels," was tapped. She looked wonderful and showed more of her body than what is normally seen in a "PG" film. It was a few days after the release of SHEENA that the "PG-13" designation was instituted, a rating that was more in keeping with all the flesh shown. Oddly, many of the animals had to be exported to Africa by the studio because they were not able to find and/or train local beasts to do the tricks. Shot on location in Kenya with many locals participating in the proceedings. The score by Hartley had a vague reminiscence of CHARIOTS OF FIRE, which may have been intended as a burlesque. The screenplay also had a faint resemblance to other films such as SUPERMAN and even some of the earlier TARZAN pictures. Aratow, a former professor of comparative literature at UC-Berkeley, had the rights for eight years and said, "My vision was not realized by Guillermin's interpretation. I'd intended making Sheena a role model for teenage women, a movie everyone could see, but Semple's rewrite of Newman's script added an unneeded hard edge that took it out of the realm of family fare I'd intended." For the record, the name "W. Morgan Thomas" is a pseudonym for S. M. Eiger and Will Eisner, the men who created "The Spirit" comic which has experienced a resurgence in the 1980s.

p, Paul Aratow; d, John Guillermin; w, David Newman, Lorenzo Semple, Jr. (based on a story by Newman, Leslie Stevens from the comic strip "Sheena, Queen of the Jungle," by W. Morgan Thomas 'S. M. Eiger, Will Eisner'); ph, Pasqualino De Santis (Panavision, Metrocolor); m, Richard Hartley; ed, Ray Lovejoy; prod d, Peter Murton; art d, Malcolm Middleton; set d, Ian Watson; cos, Annalisa Nasalli-Rocca; spec eff, Peter Hutchinson, Bob Nugent; stunts, Roy Scammell; animal trainer, Hubert G. Wells.

Adventure **Cas.** (PR:C-O MPAA:PG)

SHIVERS***½ (1984, Pol.) 106m Film Polski/New Yorker c (AKA: CREEPS)

Tomasz Hudziec (Tomasz), Teresa Marczewska (Pathfinder Camp Counselor), Marek Kondrat (School Teacher), Zdzislaw Wardejn (Supervisor), Teresa Sawicka (Tomasz' Mother), Wladyslaw Kowalski (Tomasz' Father), Bogdan Koca (Tutor), Zygmunt Bielawski (School Director), Jerzy Binycki, Wiktor Gotowicz.

Hudziec plays a boy growing up in Poland during the Stalinist era. His father is arrested under mysterious circumstances and taken from their village. Hudziec is shaken further by the constant flow of "visitors" to his sister's bedroom, forcing him to defend her honor in a fight with schoolmates. Eventually, he is sent to a Pioneer camp where he is to be re-educated along party lines. Though he finds the camp's ideals repugnant, Hudziec follows the training he receives in order to impress Marczewska, a camp teacher he has a crush on. Hudziec soon becomes a loyal Pioneer, believing party lines to be Utopian ideals. Though the camp is rocked when one of the children commits suicide, Hudziec continues to believe in his lessons. When Stalin dies his father is released from prison but the son he takes home from the camp is not the son he had left behind. This semi-autobiographical work is a harsh condemnation of the Stalinist era, filmed in an unusual mix of styles. Hudziec's village is a series of stark, cold images while the camp is almost lyrical with its sweeping use of camera. Yet the director's viewpoint is always clear, creating a paradox between image and emotion. Marczewski based his film on childhood memories of his father's arrest and his own period in a youth camp. Like the film's subject, he was told to forget his own father, for Stalin was his real father. Marczewski made his film with government approval in 1980, premiering the work late in 1981. Just three weeks after the film opened martial law was declared in Poland and SHIVERS was banned. It was also withdrawn by Polish authorities as the country's official entry for the Academy Awards. Marczewski was able to get his film into several important festivals, including the New York Film Festival of 1984. It also received top honors at the Berlin Festival in 1982. (In Polish; English subtitles.)

d&w, Wojciech Marczewski; ph, Jerzy Zielinski; m, Andrzej Trzaskowski; ed, Irena Chorynska; prod d, Anna Jekielek; set d, Andrzej Howalcyzk.

Drama (PR:C MPAA:NR)

SIGNAL 7*** (1984) 92m Taylor-Myron c

Bill Ackridge (Speed), Dan Leegant (Marty), John Tidwell (Johnny), Herb Mills (Steve), Don Bajema (Roger), Phil Polakoff (Phil), Don Defina (Setts), Frank Triest (Tommy), Jack Tucker (Hank), David Schickele (Bert), Paul Prince (Paul), Paul West (Pump Man), Bob Elross (Director), Charles Webb (Producer), Burns Ellison (Writer), Jules Burstein (Dr. Berfman), Sara Morris (Mrs. Berman), Hagit Farber (Sophie), Michelle Marrus (Ellen).

A compelling look at a pair of San Francisco cab drivers, Ackridge and Leegant, and their reactions to the goings-on around them. Largely improvised by these two exceptional actors, SIGNAL 7 moves briskly through the conversations of the two cabbies as they talk about union disputes, the murder of a fellow worker, and their aspirations of becoming actors. Dedicated, predictably, to John Cassavetes, SIGNAL 7 was shot on videotape then transferred to film on a budget of less than $1 million. The result is a lively character study which will please anyone who likes improvisation.

d&w, Rob Nilsson; ph, Geoff Schaaf, Tomas Tucker; m, Andy Narrell; ed, Richard Harkness; art d, Hildy Burns, Steve Burns.

Drama (PR:O MPAA:NR)

SILENT MADNESS* (1984) 97m Selim-MAG-Earls/Almi c

Belinda Montgomery (Dr. Joan Gilmore), Viveca Lindfors (Mrs. Collins), Solly Marx (Howard Johns), David Greenan (Mark McGowan), Sydney Lassick (Sheriff Liggett), Roderick Cook (Dr. Kruger), Stanja Lowe (Dr. Anderson), Ed Van Nuys (Dr. Van Dyce).

More senseless violence hits the screen in SILENT MADNESS, a formula slasher movie about a mental patient who is accidentally released from the hospital due to a computer error. The killer, Marx, returns to his old slashing grounds, a small town named Barrington, and takes up where he left off. Montgomery, a gutsy woman doctor at the hospital, schemes to apprehend Marx by posing as a Delta Omega sorority girl–just like the ones Marx used to kill. Incredibly brainless, it can at least boast some exceptional 3-D camera effects from Gerald Feil, whose work on FRIDAY THE THIRTEENTH PART III proved to be the only bright spot in the recent rash of slasher films.

p, Simon Nuchtern, William P. Milling; d, Nuchtern; w, Milling, Robert Zimmerman, Nelson de Mille; ph, Gerald Feil (ArriVision 3-D, Precision Color); m, Barry Salmon; ed, Philip Stockton; art d, Brian Martin.

Horror   Cas.   (PR:O   MPAA:R)

SILENT NIGHT, DEADLY NIGHT*   (1984) 79m Tri-Star c

Lilyan Chauvin (*Mother Superior*), Gilmer McCormick (*Sister Margaret*), Toni Nero (*Pamela*), Robert Brian Wilson (*Billy at 18*), Britt Leach (*Mr. Sims*), Nancy Borgenicht (*Mrs. Randall*), H.E.D. Redford (*Capt. Richards*), Danny Wagner (*Billy at 8*), Linnea Quigley (*Denise*), Leo Geter (*Tommy*), Randy Stumpf (*Andy*), Will Hare (*Grandpa*), Tara Buckman (*Mother/Ellie*), Charles Dierkop (*Father/Jim*), Eric Hart (*Levitt*), Jonathon Best (*Billy at 5*), A. Madeline Smith (*Sister Ellen*), Amy Stuyvesant (*Cindy*), Max Robinson (*Barnes*), Oscar Rowland (*Dr. Conway*).

It's not a very Merry Christmas for anyone who gets a visit from Santa in this film. Wilson is a toy-store Santa Claus with qualifications for the job that are a mite shady. It seems that when he was a lad Wilson had witnessed his parents' yuletide murder at the hands of a killer in a Santa suit. This, along with a cruel upbringing in an orphanage, has given him a decidedly negative view of the holiday season. Unhappy with his new job, Wilson takes to frightening the children who sit upon his knee, then takes the scares a step further. He goes off on a murder spree dressed as St. Nick, committing a series of a gruesome slayings and beheadings before his holiday visits come to an end. As slasher films go, this is about average. The sets are cheap, with most of the film's budget seemingly going to the gore effects. Ironically it was directed by the same man who produced such wholesome fare as THE LIFE AND TIMES OF GRIZZLY ADAMS. When Tri-Star Pictures advertised the film on television an unexpected controversy was spawned. A group of mothers objected to the idea of a murdering Santa Claus and organized a boycott of the film which spread nationwide. Hordes jumped on the bandwagon (including the television duo Roger Ebert and Gene Siskel), demanding the picture be withdrawn. What none of the angered protesters realized was that the killer Santa Claus had already been portrayed in a handful of low-budget films, creating a unique cult genre. Ironically, Tri-Star released SANTA CLAUS–THE MOVIE the following holiday season.

p, Ira Richard Barmak; d, Charles E. Sellier; w, Michael Hickey (based on a story by Paul Caimi); ph, Henning Schellerup (Metrocolor); m, Perry Botkin; ed, Michael Spence; prod d, Dian Perryman; set d, Linda Kiffe; spec eff, Rich Josephson.

Horror   (PR:O   MPAA:R)

SILENT ONE, THE**½   (1984, New Zealand) 95m Gibson c

Telo Malese (*Jonasi*), George Henare (*Paul Te Po*), Pat Evison (*Luisa*), Anzac Wallace (*Tasiri*), Rongo Tupatea Kahu (*Taruga*), Jo Pahu (*Etika*), Reg Ruka (*Bulai*), Anthony Gilbert (*Aesake*).

A mysterious, mythical picture about a boy, Malese, who arrives in a small village after emerging from the sea as an infant. He is adopted by Evison and tagged "the silent one," because he does not speak nor hear. He is soon resented by the villagers who believe he possesses strange powers. Malese makes little attempt to adapt to village life, choosing instead to swim in the sea with a friendly albino turtle. The boy's entire being is shrouded in mystery, especially when it seems that he has transformed into a turtle at the film's end. Based on a children's novel, THE SILENT ONE will probably find a number of young fans, but many adults will be intrigued by the mythical elements of the child. Historically, THE SILENT ONE stands as the first New Zealand feature directed by a woman.

p, Dave Gibson; d, Yvonne Mackay; w, Ian Mune (based on the novel by Jan Crowley); ph, Ian Paul, Ron Taylor, Valerie Taylor; m, Jenny McLeod; ed, Jamie Selkirk; prod d, Tony Rabbitt.

Fantasy   (PR:A   MPAA:NR)

SINGLETON'S PLUCK   (SEE: LAUGHTER HOUSE, Brit.)

SIXTEEN CANDLES***   (1984) 93m Channel/UNIV c

Molly Ringwald (*Samantha*), Justin Henry (*Mike Baker*), Michael Schoeffling (*Jake*), Haviland Morris (*Caroline*), Gedde Watanabe (*Long Duk Dong*), Anthony Michael Hall (*Ted the Geek*), Paul Dooley (*Jim Baker*), Carlin Glynn (*Brenda Baker*), Blanche Baker (*Ginny*), Edward Andrews (*Howard*), Billie Bird (*Dorothy*), Carole Cook (*Helen*), Max Showalter (*Fred*), Liane Curtis (*Randy*), John Cusack (*Bryce*), Darren Harris (*Cliff*), Deborah Pollack (*Lumberjack*), Ross Berkson (*Ray Gun Geek No. 1*), Jonathan Chapin (*Jimmy Montrose*), Joan Cusack (*Geek Girl No. 1*), Brian Doyle-Murray (*Reverend*), Bekka Eaton (*Female D.J.*), Paula Elser (*Shower Double*), Steven Farber (*Ray Gun Geek No.2*), Jami Gertz (*Robin*), Frank Howard (*Freshman*), Cinnamon Idles (*Sara*), John Kapelos (*Rudy*), Marge Kotlisky (*Irene*), Tony Longo (*Rock*), Steve Monarque (*Jock*), Bill Orsi (*Bruno*), Beth Ringwald (*Patty*), Zelda Rubenstein (*Organist*), Dennis Vero (*Bus Driver*), Elaine Wilkes (*Tracy*), Rick LeFevour, Shannon Madill, Cheryl Ivy Sweeney, Kay Whipple, Mike Yuan (*Stunts*).

This funny and unpretentious film marked writer Hughes' first time out as a director. The premise is ordinary but the gags are funny and the film is distinguished by some excellent performances by Ringwald and Hall. She's a high school sophomore about to turn 16 and her life is dominated by her love for Schoeffling, a senior and the high school heartthrob. Nothing seems

to be going right for Ringwald and the minor problems kids have are magnified because Ringwald's older sister is about to be married and her parents, Dooley and Glynn, are overlooking her birthday, a major moment in her young life. When her grandparents move into her room and her relationship with her smart aleck brother, Henry, gets to be tense, Ringwald is constantly on edge. At the same time as she dotes on Schoeffling, she is followed around by Hall, a younger boy who is acknowledged to be a nerd (and whose nickname is "Geek" in the picture). Simultaneously, she has to be kind and caring to Watanabe, a Japanese exchange student staying at her home. He's close to loony, but in a sweet way. She watches Schoeffling from afar as Hall watches her from "anear." The situations are predictable but Hughes saves them from being cliches with his attention to detail. Hall's best friends wear jockstraps on their heads and pretend they are aliens. Watanabe spends a great deal of time in trees and falling out of them, the marriage- minded sister gets drugged before the wedding, and so on. Ringwald finally succumbs to Hall's pleas and they become friends. (This is not unlike the same relationship Ringwald had with Jon Cryer in PRETTY IN PINK). Hall sees that he has no chance with Ringwald but he cares so much about her that he promises to set her up with Schoeffling. The only catch is that he asks Ringwald for a pair of her underpants. She agrees to deliver the briefs and then Hall charges money for his classmates to examine said lingerie. Schoeffling has been seeing Baker, a blonde hussy if there ever was one, and he's beginning to tire of her. Eventually he notices Ringwald and they befriend each other. Baker arranges a wild party at Schoeffling's home while his parents are away. The house is almost destroyed. On the eve of her birthday, Ringwald stays home alone and depressed until Dooley suddenly remembers, comes to her room, and wishes her a happy birthday. At the wild party, Schoeffling finds Hall trapped under a glass table. The two boys talk over their problems as they down martinis and Schoeffling tells Hall how Baker is starting to bore and distract him. Then Hall informs Schoeffling how Ringwald feels about him. In the end, there is the inevitable happy ending. Schoeffling gives Hall the keys to his parents' Rolls Royce so the nerd can take the besotted Baker home. The next morning dawns and Ringwald's sister is to be wed. Schoeffling arrives to sweep Ringwald off her feet and give her a remembrance to go along with her 16th candle. Hall and Ringwald became part of the Hollywood "Brat Pack" with this film and Hughes emerged as a hot director and went on to do THE BREAKFAST CLUB, again with Ringwald, a few months later. John Cusack, who went on to star in Rob Reiner's THE SURE THING, has a small role as one of Hall's pals. Still in her teens, Ringwald already had a lifetime of performing behind her, having begun as a singer with her father's jazz band. When "Annie" played Los Angeles, she was one of the orphans, then segued into "The Facts of Life" on TV. Her big break came in THE TEMPEST where she played John Cassavetes' daughter in the script adaptation by Paul Mazursky and Leon Capetanos. Gifted actor Dooley, a Robert Altman favorite, will be best recalled as the father in BREAKING AWAY and may wish for everyone to forget that he also played Wimpy in Altman's awful version of POPEYE.

p, Hilton Green; d&w, John Hughes; ph, Bobby Byrne (Technicolor); m, Ira Newborn; ed, Edward Warschilka; prod d, John W. Corso; set d, Jennifer Polito; cos, Mark Peterson, Marla Denise Schlom; title song perfromed by The Stray Cats.

Comedy   Cas.   (PR:A-C   MPAA:PG)

SKYLINE***   (1984, Spain) 83m La Salamandre P.C./Kino International c (LA LINEA DEL CIELO)

Antonio Resines (*Gustavo Fernandez*), Beatriz Perez-Porro (*Pat*), Jaime Nos (*Jaime Bos*), Roy Hoffman (*Roy*), Patricia Cisarano (*Elizabeth*), Irene Stillman (*Irene*), Whit Stillman (*Thornton*).

A refreshing comedy about a Spanish photographer, Resines, who travels to Manhattan with dreams of becoming famous. He takes pictures of the city's famed skyline, but fame is still a long way away. As much as he loves the city he finds that he doesn't fit in, mainly because of the language barrier. He enrolls in language classes and learns nothing of real importance, though he can order in a restaurant. He begins frequenting the social circle of Greenwich Village's art crowd and meets Hoffman, a southern novelist, and Perez-Porro, a woman from Barcelona who he becomes infatuated with. It is in Resines' interaction with these people that SKYLINE is most successful. Resines perfectly conveys the image of a likable foreigner trying to adjust to the new world around him. It is not just his struggle that is so fascinating, but the strange "customs" of Americans that are taken for granted in daily life. Director Colomo displays the ability to tell a story honestly and with economy, factors essential to the success of SKYLINE. Resines' character is a very simple man overwhelmed by a complex metropolis, a person an audience can easily identify with. Shot on a microscopic budget with portable equipment, SKYLINE has a style which is as simple as its character; a style which allows the audience to feel the city that nearly envelops Resines. Colomo explains: "I did not go to New York with the intention of shooting a film. My idea was just to spend two or three months learning English while doing research for another screenplay. However, after living in New York for a few weeks and after a number of experiences, I realized that the story I had to tell about New York had nothing to do with my original plan. The story was right there in the people I was meeting." Fortunately it is that story and those people that he chose to put on the screen, resulting in a thoroughly delightful comedy. (In Spanish and English; English subtitles.)

d&w, Fernando Colombo; ph, Angel Luis Fernandez; m, Manzanita; ed, Miguel Angel Santamaria.

Comedy   **Cas.**   **(PR:C MPAA:R)**

SLAPSTICK OF ANOTHER KIND*   (1984) 87m S.
Paul-Serendipity/Entertainment Releasing Co- International Film Marketing c

Jerry Lewis (*Wilbur Swain/Caleb Swain*), Madeline Kahn (*Eliza Swain/Letitia Swain*), Marty Feldman (*Sylvester*), John Abbott (*Dr. Frankenstein*), Jim Backus (*U.S. President*), Samuel Fuller (*Col. Sharp*), Merv Griffin (*Anchorman*), Virginia Graham (*Gossip Specialist*), 'Noriyuki' Pat Morita (*Ambassador Ah Fong*), Orson Welles (*Voice of Alien Father*), Ben Frank, Cheire Harris, Robert Hackman, Eugene Choy, Ken Johnson, Peter Kwong, Richard Lee-Sung, Steve Aaron, Becca Edwards, Steven Paul, Patrick Wright.

There are some questions in life which may never be answered: Will there ever be a cure for AIDS? Are flying saucers real? And why is it that the French think Jerry Lewis is the funniest human being who ever lived? Surely, there is no indication of it in this dull adaptation of Vonnegut's least-read book. Lewis and Kahn are wealthy and well known and have a pair of twins who are ugly as sin. The twins (also played by Lewis and Kahn) are so hideous to look at that the parents keep them under wraps. The parents don't realize that these children are really aliens who have been sent to Earth to help us out of our woes. Although the kids are incredibly intelligent, they are also symbiotic and their I.Q.s don't kick into gear until the two are next to each other. They deliberately keep their brains to themselves, thinking that they must conceal their intelligence and play the fool, because that's what everyone thinks they are. Once their mission is discovered, a horde of midget Chinese tries to kidnap the twins so they can put that potent power to their own use. Feldman plays the twins' personal servant and is one of the few bright spots in an otherwise dismal movie. Director Sam Fuller does a cameo and shows that he can act well enough to give up his rangefinder. Orson Welles' mellifluous voice is heard as the alien father and comic Pat Morita (who would be cited for his excellent work in THE KARATE KID) makes his presence felt. Some stunt casting with Merv Griffin taking time away from his desk to play an anchorman and Virginia Graham chiming in with a cameo. Inside jokes include the naming of the Morita character as "Ah Fong," which is, in fact, the name of a successful Hollywood Chinese restaurant across the street from where the famed Schwab's Drug Store used to be. One asset to counter all the liabilities was the music of Morty Stevens, which was more lilting than the film.

p,d&w, Steven Paul (based on the novel *Slapstick* by Kurt Vonnegut); ph, Anthony Richmond (MGM Color); m, Morty Stevens; ed, Doug Jackson; prod d, Joel Schiller; set d, Albert Heintzelman; cos, Darryl Levine; spec eff, William D. Nipper, Tim O'Connell; m/l," Puttin Our Heads Together," Randy Bishop, "Lonesome No More," Michel Legrand, Vonnegut.

Comedy/Science   **Cas.**   **(PR:A-C MPAA:PG)**

SLAYGROUND*½   (1984, Brit.) 89m EMI/UNIV c

Peter Coyote (*Stone*), Mel Smith (*Terry Abbatt*), Billie Whitelaw (*Madge*), Philip Sayer (*Costello*), Bill Luhrs (*Joe Sheer*), Marie Masters (*Joni*), Clarence Felder (*Orxel*), Ned Eisenberg (*Lonzini*), David Hayward (*Laufman*), Michael Ryan (*Danard*), Barrett Mulligan (*Lucy*), Kelli Maroney (*Jolene*), Margareta Arvidssen (*Grete*), Rosemary Martin (*Dr. King*), Malcolm Terris (*Venner*), Jon Morrison (*Webb*), Cassie Stuart (*Fran*), Debby Bishop (*Beth*), Stephen Yardley (*Turner*), P.H. Moriarty (*Seeley*), Ziggy Byfield (*Sams*), Erick Ray Evans (*Malpas*), Bill Dean (*Compere*), Ozzie Yue (*Waiter*).

A robbery of an armored car is botched with a little girl getting killed in the process. Coyote, knowing that only trouble will arise if he remains in America, flees to England. There he takes up residence with Smith, an old friend, and his live-in girl friend, Whitelaw. What Coyote doesn't realize is that he is being stalked by Sayer, a cold-blooded and efficient hit man hired by the grieving father of the dead girl. The film quickly turns into a series of cat and mouse games as Coyote realizes what is going on. He eludes his pursuer in an abandoned carnival with Coyote eventually killing Sayer. Like BLOOD SIMPLE, this film is all style and little substance. Bedford, a former television and commercial director, gives it an atmospheric look using such gimmicks as blood-red filters over the camera lens and silhouettes to create an interesting visual style. However, his skills as a story teller don't come close to his abilities as a visual stylist. The script is poorly concocted, lurching from one set piece to another without any of the much-needed suspense that should be inherent within the material.

p, John Dark, Gower Frost; d, Terry Bedford; w, Trevor Preston (based on the novel by Richard Stark); ph, Stephen Smith, Herb Wagreitch (Technicolor); m, Colin Towns; ed, Nicolas Gaster; prod d, Keith Wilson; art d, Dennis Bosher, Edward Pisoni; set d, Simon Wakefield, Fred Weiler; cos, Joseph G. Aulisi; spec eff, John Richardson, John Morris, Al Griswald.

Crime Drama   **Cas.**   **(PR:O MPAA:R)**

SLOW MOVES**½   (1984) 93m Jon Jost Productions c

Roxanne Rogers, Marshall Gaddis, Debbie Krant, Barbara Hammes, Geoffrey Rotwein, Bebe Bright, Roger Ruffin.

This low-budget feature from independent filmmaker Jost is thoroughly intriguing despite technical shortcomings that would usually cause viewer disinterest. Rogers and Gaddis play complete strangers who meet, and almost instantly fall in love, on San Francisco's Golden Gate Bridge. As their affair develops, they are faced with a desperate money shortage. They attempt to escape by hopping in to a beat-up car and wandering across the country. Gaddis takes to stealing from stores on the backroads and is eventually killed when one store owner refuses to allow him a free hand in the cash register. Interestingly Jost kept the film's two stars from meeting before production began, hoping to capture their first meeting in front of the cameras. Unfortunately this falls flat and neither Gaddis nor Rogers shows enough interest in the other to be believable as lovers. With only Jost and one other person (Rick Schmidt) as the crew, SLOW MOVES only took four-and-a-half days to shoot. The total cost came to a meager $8,000, barely enough to cover footage and lab fees.

p,d,w,ph,m&ed, Jon Jost.;

Drama   **(PR:O MPAA:NR)**

SMURFS AND THE MAGIC FLUTE, THE*½
(1984, Fr./Belg.) 74m Studios Belvision-Editions Dupuis/Atlantic Releasing c (*La Flute A Six Schtroumpfs*)

Try as we might, we couldn't find the names of the actors who did the voices for this sub-par feature based on the European characters which took U.S. Saturday morning TV by storm. We can only assume that some of the same actors, namely Paul Winchell, Casey Kasem, and the other regulars who do the Saturday show at Hanna-Barbera, were on hand for the dubbing. The Smurfs are known as "Schtroumpfs" in Europe where the characters have been successful for years. This feature adds nothing to their reputation. It's a simple enough story with a crook in the Middle Ages trying to purloin a magic flute which has the uncanny ability to send people into fits of dancing whenever it is played. It is owned by a character named "Pee Wee" who lives in a castle and, when it's stolen, Pee Wee and his pal, Johan, have to get it back. The actual blue-tinted Smurfs don't come into the plot until well into the movie, which is sort of a cheat for any of the children who thought they'd have a chance to see their favorites for an entire film. Pee Wee and Johan meet a wizard who sends them, via hypnosis, to Smurfland. The blue creatures build a duplicate flute for Pee Wee and there is sort of a blow-off as Pee Wee battles the villain, named Oilycreep. The animation is about Saturday morning standard and one would have hoped that they might have done something better for a feature. Watching something like this only makes audiences yearn for Walt Disney's brand of movie and his attention to animation detail. Perhaps it was funnier in French or Flemish because it didn't mean much in English. Even the score by usually reliable Legrand seemed phoned in. The only benefit we can cite is that it is truly a G-rated picture so kids can see it, if they don't fall asleep first.

p, Jose Dutillieu; d, Dutillieu, (English version) John Rust; w, Peyo Culliford, Yvan Delporte, (English version) Rust (based on a book by Culliford); ph, Francois Leonard, Jacques Delfosse, Marcel van Steenhuyse; m, Michel Legrand; ed, Nebiha Ben Milad, Michele Neny; animation supervision, Eddie Lateste; principal animators, Nic Broca, Marcel Colbrant, Louis-Michel Carpentier; m/l, Delporte, Culliford.

Animated Adventure/Comedy Cas.   **(PR:AAA MPAA:G)**

SOLDIER'S STORY, A***½   (1984) 101m COL c

Howard E. Rollins, Jr. (*Capt. Davenport*), Adolph Caesar (*Sgt. Waters*), Art Evans (*Pvt. Wilkie*), David Alan Grier (*Cpl. Cobb*), David Harris (*Pvt. Smalls*), Dennis Lipscomb (*Capt. Taylor*), Larry Riley (*C.J. Memphis*), Robert Townsend (*Cpl. Ellis*), Denzel Washington (*Pfc. Peterson*), William Allen Young (*Pvt. Henson*), Patti LaBelle (*Big Mary*), Wings Hauser (*Lt. Byrd*), Scott Paulin (*Capt. Wilcox*), John Hancock (*Sgt. Washington*), Trey Wilson (*Col. Nivens*), Patricia Brandkamp (*Ida Evans*), Carl Dreher (*Bus Driver*), Vaughn Reeves (*Capt. Estes*), Robert Tyler (*Pvt. Seymour*), Pat Grabe, Terry Dodd (*White Lieutenants*), Warren Clements (*Sgt. Hooks*), James W. Bryant (*Chaplain*), John Valentine (*Umpire*), Ronald E. Greenfield (*MP Sergeant*), Anthony C. Sanders (*MP at Gate*), Traftin E. Thompson (*MP in Barracks*), Roy Wells (*Training Field Sergeant*), Tommy G. Liggins (*Soldier Painting*), Calvin Franklin, Kevin T. Mosley, Michael Williams, David Ashley, Thomas Howard, Bobby McGaughey, Rick Ramey, Lacarnist Hiriams (*Barrack Soldiers*).

Charles Fuller's powerful play, originally produced by the Negro Ensemble Company in 1981 (a Pulitzer Prize winner), is adapted by Fuller himself for the screen and the power of the stage presentation is not diminished. Shot at Fort Chaffee, Arkansas, director Jewison went back to the South, the scene of one of his best movies (IN THE HEAT OF THE NIGHT), for another look at black-white tensions. The difference is that he also explores black-black differences. Many of the same actors who had appeared in the play reprise their roles as the movie unfolds. The action takes place at Fort Neal, Louisiana, a holding area for black soldiers during WW II. Caesar is a tough topkick, manager of the baseball team on which Riley stars. Caesar is coming back to the base drunk one night when he is shot to death by a

.45-caliber weapon. That's the only clue to his death. Rollins is an Army attorney who is sent to investigate the murder. The white officers on the base, as well as the blacks, are astounded at the choice of this ramrod, sunglassed man. Rollins is tough–he's a captain–and he will take no nonsense from anyone. Rollins finds that he's not getting any help in his search for the truth. The Klan is blamed by some of the black troops. Another suggestion is that it might have been one of the white soldiers who rankled at Caesar's attitude. Wilson, the redneck who commands the fort, tells Rollins that he would be wise to pack his overnight bag, go back north, and forget about the whole thing. A series of flashbacks establishes Caesar and the relationship he had with all those around him as Rollins interrogates various soldiers individually. Red herrings abound as it seems many may have wanted to see Caesar meet his ides of March. Rollins talks to militant Washington, a black of the 1940s who has the idea that blacks should be equal, not merely separate, but equal. Evans was Caesar's sycophant, a man scorned by Washington because of his fawning. Evans made his peace with his skin tone long ago and has decided that it's easier to submit than fight. Riley, besides being an ace ballplayer, is also a country singer (is this based on Charlie Pride?) content with his lot, something that Caesar had been attempting to change. The mystery unravels and more suspects are presented. Hauser is a racist who is also believed to be the killer. The writing leads one to believe that various people may have been the culprit and for us to reveal the answer would do any viewer a disservice. What makes this such a good film is the multilayered complexity of the script. Fuller has taken a basic Agatha Christie-type plot and bathed it in social issues so it is more than a mystery, it is an historical drama of the way it was in that era as well as a totally engaging study of various characters. Riley sings several of his own uncredited tunes and Patti LaBelle does a song, "Pouring Whiskey Blues," which she wrote with James Ellison and Armstead Edwards. The picture does become a trifle wordy at times, thus betraying the stage origin, but Fuller's words are almost always interesting and powerful so they make worthwhile listening. Caesar's performance was a standout and he received an Oscar nomination. This performance capped the talented actor's career, as he died of a heart attack two years after the film's release.

p, Norman Jewison, Ronald L. Schwary, Patrick Palmer; d, Jewison; w, Charles Fuller (based on the stage play "A Soldier's Play" by Fuller); ph, Russell Boyd (Metrocolor); m, Herbie Hancock; ed, Mark Warner, Caroline Biggerstaff; prod d, Walter Scott Herndon; set d, Thomas L. Roysden; cos, Chuck Velasco, Robert Stewart; stunts, Greg Elam, Melvin Jones.

Mystery/Drama   **Cas.**   **(PR:C   MPAA:PG)**

SOLE SURVIVOR*   (1984) 90m Grand National/International c

Anita Skinner (Denise Watson), Caren Larae Larkey (Karla Davis), Robin Davidson (Kristy Cutler), Kurt Johnson (Brian Richardson).

An airliner crashes in a remote area and the only survivor, advertising executive Skinner, finds herself hunted by flesh-eating zombies. Dull horror film shows little of the talent director Eberhardt would display in NIGHT OF THE COMET later the same year.

p, Don Barkemeyer; d&w, Thom Eberhardt; ph, Russ Carpenter (CFI Color); m, David F. Anthony; ed, Eberhardt.

Horror   **Cas.**   **(PR:O   MPAA:R)**

SONGWRITER**   (1984) 94m Songwriter/TRI-STAR c

Willie Nelson (Doc Jenkins), Kris Kristofferson (Blackie Buck), Melinda Dillon (Honey Carder), Rip Torn (Dino McLeish), Lesley Ann Warren (Gilda), Mickey Raphael (Arly and Harmonica, Gilda's Band), Rhonda Dotson (Corkie), Richard C. Sarafian (Rodeo Rocky), Robert Gould (Ralph), Sage Parker (Pattie McLeish), Shannon Wilcox (Anita), Jeff MacKay (Hogan), Gailard Sartain (Mulreaux), Stephen Bruton (Sam and Roarers Band), Glen Clark (Paul), Cleve Dupin (Road Manager), B.C. Cooper (Cooper), Poodie Locke (Purvis), Joe Keyes (Eddie), Amanda Bishop, Kristin Renfro (Daughters), Sammy Allred (Disc Jockey), Bill Boyd (Blind Tommy's Brother), Steve Fromholtz (Engineer), Johnny Gimble (Fiddle Player), Eloise Schmitt (Girl on Bus), Kate Cadenhead (Groupie), Christi Carafano (Girl in Bed), Joe Gallien (Electronics Engineer), Gates Moore (1st Concert Hall Manager), Larry Gorham (2nd Concert Hall Manager), Jackie King (Guitar Player), Catherine Molloy (Doc's Girl Friend), Bobby Rambo (Party Guest), Michael Reesburg (Roarer Roadie), John Shaw (Cashier), Pete Stauber (Vacuum Cleaner Salesman), Larry Trader (Golf Roadie), Priscilla Dougherty (Incredulous Woman), Bobbie Nelson (Piano, Gilda's Band), Paul English (Drums, Gilda's Band), Bee Spears (Bass, Gilda's Band), Jody Payne (Guitar, Gilda's Band), Grady Martin (Guitar, Gilda's Band), Booker T. Jones (Keyboard, Gilda's Band), Billy Swann, Donnie Fritts, Sammy Creason, Tommy McClure, Glen Clark (Roarers Band).

Another attempt at showing the way it is in the country music field, SONGWRITER covers a lot of the same acreage as PAYDAY (the 1972 film starring Rip Torn) and HONEYSUCKLE ROSE (1980) starring Dyan Cannon and Nelson. This is a cut above most of them and is far more authentic than many films of the genre, including such biographies as THE HANK WILLIAMS STORY and SWEET DREAMS but not as powerful as the best of the bunch, COAL MINER'S DAUGHTER. Nelson and Kristofferson are performing pals in their younger days (and we get a chance to see

Nelson without his patented facial hair) who break apart to pursue solo careers. Nelson becomes famous and rich and is acknowledged as the dean of C&W music, which is just about the way it is in real life for the Austin, Texas singer. Nelson's music is handled by sleazeball publisher Sarafian (an excellent TV director whose movie career has included such diverse films as VANISHING POINT, SUNBURN, and THE MAN WHO LOVED CAT DANCING) but there is lots of money being hidden by Sarafian and Nelson's business problems are mounting (which is also a real-life situation as Nelson went through great difficulties with the IRS. Join the club). Nelson is estranged from wife Dillon and tries to reconcile with her and his daughter, Dotson, while simultaneously attempting to get out of his business woes. One touching moment occurs when Nelson walks into their comfortable home, a place he hasn't been for a while, and sings a duet with the young girl. Nelson has an eye for talent as well as pulchritude and his latest "discovery" is Warren, a talented but troubled singer who gets into trouble when she takes up alcohol and controlled substances. Most of the movie belongs to Nelson, who displays a natural charm on screen and could develop into a superior actor, although none of his films (including THE ELECTRIC HORSEMAN) have taken off at the box office. Kristofferson is seen from time to time as the rebel who hasn't buckled under the pressure of commercial music and continues to live his life in his fortress the way he did in his twenties, with lots of drinking and carousing. He's supposed to be a rakehell and a romantic lead but we've never seen his charm and none of his prior acting roles have displayed much beyond what's seen here. Torn turns in another of his superior performances, this time as a semi-villainous concert promoter who masquerades as a "good old boy" but really has the calculating mind of a southwest Medici. It's a good-looking movie and Rudolph's direction is solid. Rudolph took over after two weeks when the original helmer, Steve Rash, was replaced. As you might expect, there were many songs but, as you might not expect, they were not terribly memorable. They include: "How Do You Feel About Foolin' Around," "Songwriter," "Who'll Buy My Memories," "Write Your Own Songs," "Nobody Said It was Going to Be Easy," "Good Times" (sung by Nelson), "Eye of the Storm," "Crossing the Border," "Down to Her Socks," "Under the Gun," "Final Attraction" (sung by Kristofferson).

p, Sydney Pollack; d, Alan Rudolph; w, Bud Shrake; ph, Matthew F. Leonetti (Metrocolor); m, Larry Cansler; ed, Stephen Lovejoy, George A. Martin; prod d, Joel Schiller; set d, Barbara Paula Kreiger; cos, Ernest Misko, Kathleen Gore-Misko.

Musical Drama   **Cas.**   **(PR:C-O   MPAA:R)**

SPECIAL EFFECTS**   (1984) 93m Larco/New Line c

Zoe Tamerlis (Andrea/Elaine), Eric Bogosian (Neville), Brad Rijn (Keefe), Kevin O'Connor (Delroy), Bill Oland, Richard Greene.

A film director, desperate for a hit after the failure of his last movie, a big-budget special-effects epic, meets aspiring actress Tamerlis and murders her, filming the killing with a hidden camera. He then sets about making a movie around his footage: locating an actress who looks just like the victim (also Tamerlis), asking lots of questions of the detective investigating the case, even posting bail for the victim's husband (who is accused of the crime) and having him act out the murder. A strange and interesting film that barely got a release in the U.S., it was made on a miniscule budget while director Cohen was putting together the money to produce THE STUFF (1985).

p, Paul Kurta; d&w, Larry Cohen; ph, Paul Glickman (Eastmancolor); m, Michael Minard; ed, Armond Labowitz.

Crime   **(PR:O   MPAA:R)**

SPINAL TAP   (SEE: THIS IS SPINAL TAP)

SPLASH**½   (1984) 111m Touchstone/BV c

Tom Hanks (Allen Bauer), Daryl Hannah (Madison), Eugene Levy (Walter Kornbluth), John Candy (Freddie Bauer), Dody Goodman (Mrs. Stimler), Shecky Greene (Mr. Buyrite), Richard B. Shull (Dr. Ross), Bobby Di Cicco (Jerry), Howard Morris (Dr. Zidell), Tony DiBenedetto (Tim the Doorman), Patrick Cronin (Michaelson), Charles Walker (Michaelson's Partner), David Knell (Claude), Jeff Doucette (Junior), Royce D. Applegate (Buckwalter), Tony Longo (Augie), Nora Denney (Ms. Stein), Charles Macaulay (The President), Ronald F. Hoiseck (Dr. Johanssen), Lou Tiano (Bartender), Joe Grifasi (Manny), Rance Howard (McCullough), Corki Corman-Grazer (Wife), Fred Lerner (Husband), David Lloyd Nelson (Lt. Ingram), Al Chesney (Fat Jack), Lowell Ganz (Stan the Tour Guide), James Ritz (TV Department Manager), Maurice Rice (TV Salesman), Babaloo Mandel (Rudy), Pierre Epstein (Dr. Hess), Cheryl Howard, Louisa Marie (Girls at Wedding), Valerie Wildman, Christopher Thomas, Richard Dano, Clint Howard (Wedding Guests), Ron Kuhlman (Man with Date), Lori Kessler (Girl with Date), Joe Cirillo (Sgt. Munson), Tom Toner (Parilli), Lee Delano (Sgt. Lelandowski), Migdia Varela (Wanda), Jack Denton (Man by Elevator), Nick Cinardo (George), Fil Formicola (Policeman), Than Wyenn (Mr. Ambrose), Clare Peck (TV Reporter), Jason Late (Young Freddie), Shayla MacKarvich (Young Madison), Eileen Saki (Dr. Fujimoto), David Kreps (Young Allen), Bill Smitrovich, Jack Hallett, Nancy Raffa, Daryl Edwards, Amy Ingersoll, Jeffrey Dreisbach, Victoria Lucas, Jodi Long.

An"alien" picture from an alien source (Disney with a new moniker), SPLASH, for all the nudity and hip humor, is a throwback to pictures of days past such as Annette Kellerman's 1914 NEPTUNE'S DAUGHTER and MR. PEABODY AND THE MERMAID (1948), which was a takeoff of the superior MIRANDA (1948, British). Young viewers who never heard of any of the aforementioned thought that this was something wildly creative and thus flocked to the theaters, sending this $11 million movie into the profit column right away. The premise is simple: boy meets girl, boy falls for girl, but girl is not girl at all, she's a mermaid. Boy is now in serious trouble as there are laws forbidding men to love fish, except if they are oceanographers or guppy collectors. Mermaid Hannah meets Hanks, a young, bright man employed as a wholesale fruit and vegetable dealer in New York. Hanks' brother is Candy (which is harder to believe than the existence of mermaids), a smarmy playboy pudge who loves chasing women. The brothers are very close and toil together. Hanks is due to get married (we all know that's a red herring from the start) although once he meets Hannah, he tosses that idea into the drink and goes after her. Hannah is human when on dry land but the moment she is touched by salt water, she reverts to her half- woman, half-tiger shark form. (The top half is the woman and a wonderful variation to all of these mermaid films would be to have the *bottom* half be a woman and the top half look like THE BEAST FROM TWENTY THOUSAND FATHOMS. It wouldn't be romantic but it sure would be unique.) Levy is a scientist who thinks that Hannah is a mermaid so he tracks her and Hanks through several sight gags (which eventually put him in an arm and shoulder cast) and finally turns water on Hannah, which transforms her into her other form in front of hundreds on a New York street. The mermaid is taken to an official and secret government laboratory run by Shull where she is examined closely while being kept in a tank. Levy ultimately realizes the harm he's done and helps Candy and Hanks steal Hannah from under the noses of the Army men. In a touching conclusion, Hanks takes Hannah to a pier overlooking the river and dumps her in the murky depths as soldiers advance and helicopters hover overhead. She invites Hanks to join her. He thinks he'll drown but she reminds him that she saved his life when he was drowning off Cape Cod as a young boy, and the memory comes back to him in that instant. He trusts her that he can adapt to life below the waves, dives into the river, and the two of them swim away happily to spawn, or whatever it is mermaids do. The movie took four years to get off the ground and into the water as Howard couldn't convince a few studios to make it until Disney's new "adult" division ("PG" rather than"G") decided to swim along with him. Candy and Levy, both of TV's "Second City," are good foils although the normally subtler Levy goes a bit over the top in his portrayal of the obsessed scientist. Howard, doing his third theatrical feature film after NIGHT SHIFT, GRAND THEFT AUTO, and a few TV pictures, has a good sense of the whimsical and a good sense of the nepotistic, judging from the number of Howards in the cast (Rance, Clint, and Cheryl). Cowriters Ganz and Mandel do cameos and TV and film director Howard Morris has a chance at one of his increasingly rare acting chores. It's sweet, unpretentious, and somewhat ribald when one realizes the studio from whence it sprang. The funniest scene has Hannah and Hanks in a ritzy restaurant with her ordering lobster and proceeding to eat it, shell and all. Once again, the idea of "new eyes" looking at familiar situations works well, the same way it did in "My Favorite Martian" and "Mork and Mindy" on TV and countless movies on the big screen.

p, Brian Grazer; d, Ron Howard; w, Lowell Ganz, Babaloo Mandel, Bruce Jay Friedman (based on the story by Grazer, Friedman); ph, Don Peterman (Technicolor); m, Lee Holdridge; ed, Daniel P. Hanley, Michael Hill; prod d, Jack T. Collis; art d, John B. Mansbridge; set d, Norman Rockett; cos, May Routh, Charles De Muth, Jody Berke; spec eff, Mitch Suskin; swimming ch, Mike Nomad; m/l, "Love Came for Me," Holdridge, Will Jennings, sung by Rita Coolidge.

Fantasy/Comedy   **Cas.**   **(PR:A-C MPAA:PG)**

SPLATTER UNIVERSITY zero   (1984) 77m Aquifilm/Troma c

Francine Forbes (*Julie Parker*), Dick Biel (*Father Janson/Daniel Grayham*), Cathy Lacommare (*Cathy*), Ric Randig (*Mark*), Joanna Mihalakis, George Seminara, Don Eaton, Sal Lumetta, Denise Texeira, John Michaels, Richard W. Haines, Laura Gold, Mary Ellen David.

Forbes is a sociology teacher who arrives at a small private college to take over the teaching duties of an instructor murdered the semester before. More killings take place, further dwindling enrollment. Poor slasher film that stomps over the same familiar turf with a numbing lack of imagination. Lots of college kids bite the dust between poorly written dialog scenes that fail to advance the story. On the plus side, the picture is quite short.

p, Richard W. Haines, John Michaels; d, Haines; w, Haines, Michaels, Michael Cunningham; ph, Fred Cohen, Jim Grib; m, Chris Burke; ed, Haines; m/l, The Pedestrians; makeup, Ralph Cordero, Ron Darrier, Amodio Giordano.

Horror   **Cas.**   **(PR:O MPAA:R)**

SPLITZ zero   (1984) 83m Edward L. Montoro/Film Ventures c

Robin Johnson (*Gina*), Patti Lee (*Joan*), Chuck McQuary (*Chuck*), Barbara M. Bingham (*Susie*), Shirley Stoler (*Dean Hunta*), Raymond Serra (*Vito*), Martin Rosenblatt (*Louie*), Sal Carollo (*Tony*).

Dredged up from the bottom of this year's pile of entries, SPLITZ is a worthless excuse to show off some more female skin and pander to sexually developing teens. Johnson, Lee, and Bingham are part of an all-girl rock 'n' roll band who are trying desperately for success. There's also a subplot about an evil college dean (this time it's Hooter College), Stoler, who is trying to close a sorority house. The only way to keep the house open is for the girls to win a series of sporting events. Naturally the events are demeaning, consisting of "strip" basketball and wrestling matches in which the girls dress in slinky lingerie. It's all been toned down a bit, however, to rate a "PG-13" and find a wider audience. Includes music from Del Shannon, Blondie, The Clonetones, and Diane Scanlon.

p, Kelly Van Horn, Stephen Low; d, Domonic Paris; w, Paris, Bianca Littlebaum, Harry Azorin, Van Horn; ph, Ronnie Taylor; m, George Small; art d, Tom Allen; ch, Matthew Diamond.

Comedy   **Cas.**   **(PR:O MPAA:R/PG-13)**

SQUIZZY TAYLOR**   (1984, Aus.) 98m Satori c

David Atkins (*Squizzy Taylor*), Jacki Weaver (*Dolly*), Kim Lewis (*Ida*), Michael Long (*Inspector Piggot*), Fred Cullen (*Henry*), Alan Cassell (*Detective Brophy*), Steve Bisley (*Snowy*), Peter Paulsen (*Harry*), John Larking (*Superintendent*), Terry Trimble (*Grazier*), Peter Hosking (*Angus*), Paul Trahair (*Detective*), Ernie Bourne (*Barber*), Jenni Caffin (*Lorna*), Tony Rickards (*Dutch*), Simon Thorpe (*Paddy*).

Melbourne in the 1920s is brought to life in this story of real-life Australian gangster Squizzy Taylor, played by the short but tough Atkins. Attention is paid to period detail, capturing the lively atmosphere, and memorable music, but Atkin's character approaches a campy sadistic quality.

p, Roger LeMesurier; d, Kevin Dobson; w, Roger Simpson; ph, Dan Burstall; m, Bruce Smeaton; prod d, Logan Brewer; cos, Jane Hyland.

Crime   **Cas.**   **(PR:O MPAA:NR)**

STAR TREK III: THE SEARCH FOR SPOCK***   (1984) 105m PAR c

William Shatner (*Kirk*), Leonard Nimoy (*Spock*), DeForest Kelley (*McCoy*), James Doohan (*Scotty*), Walter Koenig (*Chekov*), George Takei (*Sulu*), Michelle Nichols (*Uhura*), Robin Curtis (*Saavik*), Merritt Butrick (*David*), Phil Morris (*Trainee Foster*), Scott McGinnis (*"Mr. Adventure"*), Robert Hooks (*Adm. Morrow*), Carl Steven (*Spock, Age 9*), Vadia Potenza (*Spock, Age 13*), Stephen Manley (*Spock, Age 17*), Joe W. Davis (*Spock, Age 25*), Paul Sorensen (*Captain, Merchantship*), Cathie Shirriff (*Valkris, Merchantship*), Christopher Lloyd (*Kurge, Klingon*), Stephen Liska (*Torg, Klingon*), John Larroquette (*Maltz, Klingon*), Dave Cadiente (*Sergeant, Klingon*), Bob Cummings (*Gunner No. 1*), Branscombe Richmond (*Gunner No. 2*), Phillip Richard Allen (*Capt. Esteban, USS Grissom*), Jeanne Mori (*Helmsman, USS Grissom*), Mario Marcelino (*Communications, USS Grissom*), Allan Miller (*Alien*), Sharon Thomas (*Waitress*), Conroy Gedeon (*Civilian Agent*), James B. Sikking (*Capt. Styles, USS Excelsior*), Miguel Ferrer (*1st Officer, USS Excelsior*), Mark Lenard (*Sarek*), Katherine Blum (*Child Vulcan*), Dame Judith Anderson (*High Priestess of Vulcans*), Gary Faga, Douglas Alan Shanklin (*Prison Guards*), Grace Lee Whitney (*Woman in Cafeteria*), Frank Welker (*Spock Screams*), Teresa E. Victor (*USS Enterprise Computer*), Harve Bennett (*Flight Recorder*), Judi Durand (*Space Dock Controller*), Frank Force (*Elevator Voice*), John Meier (*Shatner's Stunt Man*), Al Jones (*C. Lloyd's Stunt Man*), Steve Blalock, Don Charles McGovern, David Burton, Tom Morga, Phil Chong, Alan Oliney, Eddy Donno, Charles Picerni, Jr., Kenny Endoso, Jim Halty, Chuck Hicks, Jeff Jensen, Danny Rogers, Frank James Sparks, David Zelliti (*Stunts*).

The third STAR TREK film is not as ponderous and overly gimmicked as the first and not as intelligent and witty as Jack Sowards' script for the second. Producer Harve Bennett (who was known as Fishman when he was a "Quiz Kid" on radio) wrote the script for this. This time around, we are taken on a pleasant trip by first-time director Nimoy (who had indicated, according to industry scuttlebutt, that he wouldn't act in another STAR TREK unless he could direct). The picture begins where the last one ended. The crew of the Enterprise is coming home and learns that their vaunted ship is to be put into the futuristic equivalent of mothballs. Nimoy died in the last feature and then his father, Lenard (who also played that role in the TV series) informs them that he is being kept alive in spirit in one of the crewpeoples' heads. Shatner now must find Nimoy's body and bring it to the planet of Vulcan, along with the possessed crewperson, so that Lenard can bring the pointy-eared sage back to life. Shatner investigates and finds that Nimoy's spirit lives inside Kelley as, just before the Vulcan died, he apparently melded his mind with that of Kelley and gave him all his thoughts. (Hey, if you can believe there are such people as Vulcans, surely this is not a leap of faith.) But how is Shatner going to do that when his beloved space ship is ready for the junk heap? Shatner steals the Enterprise, gathers the crew, and off they go on a mission of their own. Nimoy's coffin rests on the planet Genesis so, over the objections of the Federation, Shatner takes matters into his own hands. (If you didn't see the last movie, the genesis of Genesis was that it was created after being hit with a bomb that had the ability to breathe new life into long-dead planets.) Once there, Shatner's son, Butrick, and Vulcan Science Officer Curtis (this role was played by Kirstie Alley in the prior movie) discover a young mute Vulcan lad whom they think may be Nimoy reborn. They also learn that the nature of the planet is unstable and that the Vulcan youth is growing with the planet at an alarming rate. Enter Lloyd (who was a star on TV's "Taxi" before hitting it big in BACK TO THE FUTURE and hitting it small in CLUE), a Klingon villain (Klingon always sounded like a product one should wrap fish in). He wants to steal the secret of the Genesis project for himself (i.e. how to bring life back to dead places). There is a peace treaty but Lloyd breaks it and attacks the ship carrying Curtis and Butrick. Lloyd kills Butrick and then Shatner arrives to battle it out with Lloyd on the vacillating planet. All this happens as the young Vulcan is growing from tothood and through puberty right before our eyes. The boy keeps growing and matures into...one guess. You're right, Nimoy. Shatner is thrilled at seeing his old colleague again and the two men plan to flee the planet and get back to the safety of the ship. But the scuzzy Klingons have other plans for them and the only way to escape is to destroy the Enterprise and steal the Klingon ship. This they do and Lloyd is left behind to expire on Genesis. Later, Shatner watches happily as Anderson (the famed actress was 85 at the time), the high priestess, oversees a transformation which brings Nimoy totally back to life and the picture ends with them on the planet Vulcan as these words are superimposed: "And the adventure continues...." (Would Trekkers have it any other way?) It paves the road for STAR TREK IV, also directed by Nimoy. After spending more than $40 million on the first STAR TREK, Paramount wisely pulled in their financial horns and kept the budget down. This one only cost $16 million and grossed more than that in the first three days of release, which must be some sort of box office record for the time. Real fans of the show call themselves "Trekkers" and not "Trekkies," which they feel denigrates their passion for the program and the people. Sequels have become important in the industry and one wonders if STAR TREK will have a 10th or 20th edition, the same way that Stallone plans to keep boxing as ROCKY and shooting communists as RAMBO. Not nearly as much in the special effects department this time but what was done (by George Lucas' Industrial Light And Magic, with Ken Ralston in charge) was excellent. The concept has had a long and amazing history when one realizes that NBC tried to cancel the TV show in 1968 but was flooded with so many letters that it allowed the show to play one more season, thereby making the creators very rich as they now had enough for strip syndication on TV. For people who never watched "Star Trek" on TV, much of this will be confusing as it asks that you have some sort of familiarity with the characters and the situations. Except for the expensive effects, this would have been a typical two-part episode for the TV series, no better and no worse than most of them. Bennett's script was serviceable but lacking in humor and just a bit too heavy on the philosophic side to make this true escapist fare. Still, even mediocre STAR TREK is better than no STAR TREK at all. Only the most dedicated Trekkers will know this trivia question... what famed ventriloquist co-wrote an episode on the show? No, it wasn't Paul Winchell (now a voice on "The Smurfs") or Edgar Bergen. It was Shari Lewis. You can win big money on that one.

p, Harve Bennett; d, Leonard Nimoy; w, Bennett (based on the television production "Star Trek" by Gene Roddenberry); ph, Charles Correll (Panavision, Movielab Color); m, James Horner; ed, Robert F. Shugrue; art d, John E. Chilberg II; set d, Tom Pedigo; cos, Robert Fletcher; spec eff, Rocky Gehr; stunts, Ron Stein, R. A. Rondell.

Science Fiction Cas. (PR:A-C MPAA:PG)

STARMAN*** (1984) 115m COL c

Jeff Bridges *(Starman)*, Karen Allen *(Jenny Hayden)*, Charles Martin Smith *(Mark Shermin)*, Richard Jaeckel *(George Fox)*, Robert Phalen *(Maj. Bell)*, Tony Edwards *(Sgt. Lemon)*, John Walter Davis *(Brad Heinmuller)*, Ted White *(Deer Hunter)*, Dirk Blocker, M.C. Gainey *(Cops)*, Sean Faro *(Hot Rodder)*, Buck Flower *(Cook)*, Russ Benning *(Scientist)*, Ralph Coshan *(Marine Lieutenant)*, David Wells *(Fox's Assistant)*, Anthony Grumbach *(NSA Officer)*, Jim Deeth *(S-61 Pilot)*, Alex Daniels *(Gas Station Attendant)*, Carol Rosenthal *(Gas Customer)*, Mickey Jones *(Trucker)*, Lu Leonard *(Roadhouse Waitress)*, Charlie Hughes *(Bus Driver)*, Byron Walls *(Police Sergeant)*, Betty Bunch *(Truck Stop Waitress)*, Victor McLemore *(Roadblock Lieutenant)*, Steven Brennan *(Roadblock Sergeant)*, Pat Lee *(Bracero Wife)*, Judith Kim *(Girl Barker)*, Ronald Colby *(Cafe Waiter)*, Robert Stein *(State Trooper)*, Kenny Call *(Donnie Bob)*, Jeff Ramsey, Jerry Gatlin *(Hunters)*, David Daniell, Randy Tutton *(Lettermen)*.

A pleasant surprise from director Carpenter who had churned out several disappointments since his mega-hit HALLOWEEN in 1978 (specifically THE FOG, ESCAPE FROM NEW YORK, THE THING, and CHRISTINE). Allen plays a young Wisconsin widow still grieving over the loss of her husband. She spends her evenings looking through photo albums and watching 8mm home movies of their brief time together before finally dragging herself to bed. One night, a bright blue light zooms from outer space and flies into Allen's home. It hovers over the photo album and runs the home movies until it has assimilated enough characteristics of Earthlings to take on the shape of one–unfortunately for Allen it is the form of her dead husband. Allen is shocked and confused when confronted with this man who looks just like her dead husband (Bridges). The alien, Bridges, seems to have trouble adjusting to this new shell and its body movements are hesitant and jerky. It quickly learns a few phrases of English and tries to communicate with Allen. Allen is understandably horrified by this intruder, for she is both attracted to and repelled by him. Bridges tells her that he has come with greetings in return for the message Earth had sent into space on Voyager I. His people have arranged for him to be picked up in the Nevada desert in a few days time and Bridges forces Allen to drive him there. Meanwhile, the government, represented by National Security Council agent Jaeckel, is out to capture Bridges in order to study him. Called in to help the effort is Smith, who, as the film progresses, comes to believe that the alien should be allowed to go home. Eventually Allen's fear of Bridges is overcome by her compassion for the vulnerable being who is almost childlike in his sense of wonder about Earth and its inhabitants. Simple things like the taste of Dutch Apple pie and the sight of a deer enthrall Bridges. Slowly, hesitantly, Allen and Bridges fall in love. Knowing that he must return to his planet or die, Allen decides to expose Bridges to one last human experience–she makes love to him. During their adventure Bridges has become sensitive to Allen's emotions and knows that she will be destroyed by his departure (effectively losing her "husband" again). Bridges uses his powers to ensure that Allen conceives during their lovemaking–he gives her a child. "It will be a human baby" he reassures her. But he will know who his father was. With the help of Smith, Bridges escapes the NSC and makes his rendevous with the mother ship, leaving Allen behind with her "gift." STARMAN is a wonderful film that combines science- fiction, road movies, and romance into an engaging, very entertaining whole. While the plot may have some holes and the story may be a bit hard to swallow, the film works due to the two central performances by Bridges and Allen. Allen is heartbreaking as the young widow still trying to get over the loss of a deeply loved husband. The emotional turmoil she feels upon the arrival of Bridges is well detailed and her eventual embracing of the alien is moving and wholly believable. The script gives her character time to make the emotional adjustments which allow her to accept this alien and the film takes its time building up to their lovemaking (handled with taste). Even better than Allen however, is Bridges. In a performance that earned an Oscar nomination, Bridges manages to look as if he doesn't belong in his own body. His struggles to figure out just how to operate his human shell are amazing and the performance is done entirely without benefit of makeup or special effects. Bridges' alien is a charming, endearing creature who savors his experiences on Earth. It is a magnificent performance. Carpenter directs the film in a straightforward manner and the brief forays into special effects and pyrotechnics are handled deftly without distracting the audience from the basic storyline. Carpenter succeeds here where most of his films have failed because he is finally dealing with intimate, human emotions instead of special effects or comic book characters. STARMAN is an enjoyable film filled with the kind sensitivity, love and humor little seen on today's screens.

p, Larry J. Franco; d, John Carpenter; w, Bruce A. Evans, Raynold Gideon; ph, Donald M. Morgan (Panavision, MGM color); m, Jack Nitzsche; ed, Marion Rothman; prod d, Daniel Lomino; set d, Robert Benton; cos, Andy Hylton, Robin Michel Bush; spec eff, Roy Arbogast, Bruce Nicholson, Michael McAlister; makeup, Peter Altobelli; stunts, Terry Leonard.

Science Fiction/Romance Cas. (PR:C MPAA:PG)

STONE BOY, THE*½** (1984) 93m FOX c

Robert Duvall *(Joe Hillerman)*, Frederic Forrest *(Andy Jansen)*, Glenn Close *(Ruth Hillerman)*, Wilford Brimley *(George Jansen)*, Jason Presson *(Arnold Hillerman)*, Gail Youngs *(Lu Jansen)*, Cindy Fisher *(Amalie)*, Susan Blackstone *(Nora Hillerman)*, Dean Cain *(Eugene Hillerman)*, Kenneth Anderson, John L. Strandell *(Sheriffs)*, Tom Duncan *(Sheriff McDuff)*, Dana Duffy *(Margaret Mathews)*, Quentin Rhoades *(Clint Mathews)*, Mark Melander *(Clancy Mathews)*, Ken Magee *(Sam Sullivan)*, Mary Ellen Trainor *(Doris Simms)*, Ron Presson *(Amalie's Uncle)*, Cody Harvey, Buck Dear *(Men)*, Mayf Nutter *(Gary Maddox)*, Sharon Thomas *(Casino Waitress)*, Timothy Phillips *(Chuck)*, Linda Hamilton *(Eva Crescent Mood Lady)*, Lynne Brimley *(Woman at Fair)*, Steve Tsigonoff *(Barker)*, Pat Hustis *(Man in Suit)*.

At first glance, the story for this quiet, sensitive film would seem to bear a resemblance to ORDINARY PEOPLE. That's an error because this is not about upper-middle class Chicagoans who can afford an expensive psychiatrist for their guilt-ridden son. This is really about ordinary people, Montana farmers who have to cope with tragedy using strength from within and sans help from a professional shrink. Cain, whose only other film was the urban skid row drama, SIXTH AND MAIN, shows enormous talent as he leads the actors through tricky territory. Presson and Cain (the director's son) are brothers living on a farm in Montana. They rise early to go duck hunting but their happy plans soon turn to tears as Cain is accidentally shot by Presson's gun and nobody's life will ever be the same again. Presson becomes quiet, doesn't know what to do. His brother is dead and he realizes he'll have to tell everyone what happened, but he can't face the fact so he spends a little time in a pea patch, slowly picking the vegetables, trying to gather his thoughts. His parents are Duvall and Close and when he finally does return home to break the terrible news, he is immediately left outside of their sorrow. Duvall is a strong, silent, and proud man and since Presson is not in tears or hysterical, Duvall misreads that as his not caring and comprehending the enormity of his dead, accidental though it was. Close also can't fathom Presson's tranquil behavior but, as a mother, she is not nearly so stern as Duvall. Blackstone is the sister and shares Duvall's feelings about Presson's behavior. Cain's girl friend is Fisher and she is totally adrift by the accident and vulnerable when Close's Don Juan brother, Forrest, put a move on her for a sexual purpose. This causes Forrest's wife, Youngs, to become totally unglued, though she is well aware of Forrest's penchant for females. As the whirlpool swims around him, Presson gets quieter and quieter, becoming a "stone boy" in that he cannot be part of the swirling madness of a family in chaos. His grandfather, Brimley, tries to bring Presson out of his shell. Brimley knows that no good can come of the way the boy is being treated and that Presson is suffering, albeit silently, but he is suffering nevertheless. Eventually, Presson manages to come back to the world and, in doing so, the family begins to melt its reserve and is finally united once more. An excellent screenplay debut for Berriault, who has a day job as a professor at San Francisco State and writes books on the side. This was her own adaptation of a short story she wrote in her book *The Infinite Passion of Expectation*. Shot in Great Falls, Montana, THE STONE BOY was a family affair. In addition to Cain and his son working together, Youngs is married to Duvall in real life and she is also the sister of actor John Savage. A langorous movie with little of the tear jerking and often obvious sequences one might have expected. Walter Gropius, the architect, once wrote that "less is more" and such is the case with THE STONE BOY. Screenwriters would be well-advised to watch this movie and the 1986 film, CHILDREN OF A LESSER GOD, to see how dialog can be kept to a minimum without losing an audience. It pulls no punches and makes very few statements. All it does is present the facts and lets the audience decide what's right and what's wrong. There are a couple of times when some psychobabble is used and that's out of character for the people who speak those lines. Otherwise it's a marvel of restrained intelligence.

p, Joe Roth, Ivan Bloch; d, Chris Cain; w, Gina Berriault (based on her short story); ph, Juan Ruiz-Anchia (DeLuxe Color); m, James Horner; ed, Paul Rubell; prod d, Joseph G. Pacelli; art d, Stephanie Wooley; cos, Gail Viola; m/l, "Baby, You're So Young," "Jamboree in The Hills," Mayf Nutter.

Drama   **Cas.**   **(PR:C MPAA:PG)**

STRANGER THAN PARADISE**½   (1984, U.S./Ger.) 95m
Grokenberger-ZDF-Cinesthesia/Goldwyn bw

John Lurie (*Willie*), Eszter Balint (*Eva*), Richard Edson (*Eddie*), Cecillia Stark (*Aunt Lottie*), Danny Rosen (*Billy*), Rammellzee (*Man with Money*), Tom Docillo (*Airline Agent*), Richard Boes (*Factory Worker*), Rockets Redglare, Harvey Perr, Brian J. Burchill (*Poker Players*), Sara Driver (*Girl with Hat*), Paul Sloane (*Motel Owner*).

One of the most stylistically interesting films of the year, STRANGER THAN PARADISE paints a bleak American landscape on its grainy black-and-white film stock. This America is populated with three aimless but content characters who quickly discover that "paradise" isn't such an easy place to find. Living in a lonely place in a stark, dreary section of New York is the gaunt Lurie who arrived in the city 10 years earlier from Budapest, Hungary. Lurie's day-to-day existence is interrupted when his relatives ask him to house his adorable cousin, Balint, upon her arrival from the old country. Lurie dutifully obliges but is less than hospitable, having disassociated himself from his Hungarian past. He has become totally American and isn't thrilled with the ideals that Balint represents. Balint, however, is anything but a helpless foreigner. She is intelligent, opinionated, and distant from Lurie. She also isn't impressed with Lurie's disgusting habit of eating TV dinners (a meal which thoroughly baffles her). For Lurie life goes on. He goes about his business without including Balint, until one day Lurie's friend Edson asks if Balint can come along with them. She, however, would rather wander the streets with her portable cassette deck, listening to the flipped-out song "I Put a Spell on You" by Screaming Jay Hawkins, her "main man." It's not long before the trio drag themselves into a car and takes off down the highway. Their destination is the Cleveland, Ohio, home of their Aunt Lottie, charmingly played by Stark (who is too authentic to possibly be a professional actor). After a short visit with Stark, who loves to play poker ("I am the winner," she exclaims in her heavy accent), the trio steer towards Florida. They travel across an America which is usually kept off the movie screens. Their America is not "paradise." It is a barren, grey, factory-lined wasteland which stretches in all directions as far as the eye can see. Even their much awaited visit to Lake Erie is a bitter disappointment. Instead of a lake, they find nothing but a frozen, snow-covered patch of land. Although a bond develops between the characters, their relationships grow more and more strained until Balint finally leaves. Lurie, thinking that she has hopped a plane back to Hungary, chases after her. He gets on the plane just as it is taking off and unexpectedly finds himself on his way back to Hungary. In the meantime, Balint has her feet firmly planted on American soil. Jarmusch on a miniscule budget of about $120,000, STRANGER THAN PARADISE was made possible by film directors Nicholas Ray and Wim Wenders. Jarmusch's film career began to skyrocket at New York University where he was lucky enough to work as a teaching assistant for Ray. He was then introduced to German director Wenders, who was making a documentary about Ray (LIGHTNING OVER WATER). Noticing Jarmusch's talent, Wenders gave him some left over film stock from another of his pictures, STATE OF THINGS (1983), with which Jarmusch shot the first third of STRANGER THAN PARADISE. He managed to raise the remaining sum and finish the film. The film was then entered in the Cannes Film Festival where Jarmusch won the "Camera D'or" for best direction of

a first feature (he had, however, previously made a full-length thesis film entitled PERMANENT VACATION). Also receiving an award that evening was Wenders for his PARIS, TEXAS (which cast Lurie in a small role). Unfortunately, for all the praise STRANGER THAN PARADISE has received, it is not much of a film. Jarmusch's style-each scene is shot in one long take and these scenes are separated by a few seconds of black--soon grows tedious. Most disturbing, however, is the feeling that the film is as empty and void of life as the characters it comments on. One can't help but feel that the film spends more time being "hip" than with actually creating compelling characters and situations. One also can't help but hope that Jarmusch, despite all this picture's weaknesses, will develop into a powerful force in "rebel" cinema and shake up Hollywood expectations with the same spirit as his mentor, Nicholas Ray.

p, Sara Driver; d&w, Jim Jarmusch; ph, Tom Dicillo; m, John Lurie, Aaron Picht; ed, Jarmusch, Melody London.

Drama   **Cas.**   **(PR:O MPAA:R)**

STRANGERS KISS****   (1984) 93m Kill/Orion Classics bw-c

Peter Coyote (*Stanley the Director*), Victoria Tennant (*Carol Redding/ Betty*), Blaine novak (*Stevie Blake/Billy*), Dan Shor (*Farris the Producer*), Richard Romanus (*Frank Silva*), Linda Kerridge (*Shirley*), Carlos Palomino (*Estoban*), Vincent Palmieri (*Scandelli*), Jay Rasumny (*Jimmy*), Jon Sloan (*Mikey*), Joe Nipote (*Tony the Rose*), Jeannette Joseph (*Miss Stein*), Cecil Hill (*Studio Manager*), Frank Moon (*Rich Man*), Larry Dilge (*Clapper Man*), Arthur Adams (*Hanratty*), Leo Impellizzeri, Joe Pompa, Alex Hendrie, Larry Maggart, Michael Haywood, Ken Gerson, Rob Petersen, Mark Wendell, Eric Bartsch, Brian Maguire, Will Schwalbe, John Bennett, Annely Uherek, Jack Dolan, Calvin Greenfield, Paul Duncan.

A stylish, charming, honest, romantic, and obsessive look at filmmaking during the B-movie days of the 1950s which transcends its period setting and speaks to filmmakers and audiences of all times. Coyote is a crazed, manipulative director who is driven to make his picture, "Strange And Dangerous" (a carbon-copy of Stanley Kubrick's KILLER'S KISS), at all costs. With his sheepish, boy wonder producer, Shor, at his side, Coyote meets with gangster Romanus about funding the film. The likable but dangerous Romanus agrees on one condition--that his girl friend, Tennant, get the lead role. Coyote, angered at his loss of control in choosing an actress, reluctantly agrees. Starring opposite Tennant is the dopey, insecure Novak, who fails to light an onscreen romantic spark with his pretty costar. Distressed at the lack of chemistry between Novak and Tennant, Coyote plots to have his stars fall in love, a scheme which dares to permanently sever his financial tie with Romanus. Novak begins to show interest in Tennant, but she ignores his advances. In the meantime, Coyote grows more and more maniacal, pushing his actors to the limit and often requiring them to stay late. Romanus, essentially a simple man who is insecure in his relationship with Tennant, begins to grow impatient with her devotion to the film. He becomes tortured by the suspicion that she is having an affair on the set and sends his henchmen to the studio to keep watch. Because of Romanus' constant grilling, a hurt and confused Tennant turns to Novak for comfort. A mutual affection builds, though both fight off the attraction that they know will not subside. Pushed to his limit, Romanus storms onto the set and accidentally sees "rushes" of a love scene between Tennant and Novak, driving him into a fury. Tensions rise and personal and professional relationships stretch to the breaking point--Coyote cruelly abuses the hard-working Shor, the studio threatens a shutdown, and the cast and crew lose patience with their director. Tennant and Novak, however, find themselves falling headlong in love. When Romanus spots Tennant and Novak making love on a dark deserted set, he puts them in his gunsight and prepares to kill them. Instead, he returns to his home and drowns his feelings in a frenzied drinking binge. When Tennant arrives home late that night, a now calm, tuxedo-clad Romanus proposes marriage to her. With the filming complete, Novak tries desperately to reach Tennant by phone. He then learns from Coyote and Shor that she has left town to get married. The production is finished, the cast and crew have all gone their separate ways, and "Strange And Dangerous" is "in the can." Photographed in cool, vibrant color, reminiscent of the 1950s (especially of Douglas Sirk and Nicholas Ray), and scored with a jazzy saxophone melody, STRANGERS KISS stuns with one fresh scene after another. The film shines on all levels, from technique to acting performances, and from the direction to the script. What is most apparent in STRANGERS KISS is the filmmaker's love for filmmaking. The viewer can readily sense an obsessive love of filmmaking coming from the screenwriter and director, not unlike the characters in Francois Truffaut's DAY FOR NIGHT (1973) and Jean-Luc Godard's CONTEMPT. STRANGERS KISS understands the relationships that spring up during the production of a film--those short, passionate, secretive flings in which real people strive to capture the same exciting drama as the movie's characters only to see them quickly come to a halt when the film is completed. What separates this film from Truffaut's and Godard's is its unique American feel, its ability to look at American filmmaking in a positive light as opposed to the cynical (though equally fascinating) treatments rendered in SUNSET BOULEVARD and REAL LIFE. For anyone who is enthralled by that strange species known as "filmmakers," or for those who just love well-made entertainment reminiscent of a bygone era STRANGERS KISS is highly recommended.

p, Douglas Dilge; d, Matthew Chapman; w, Blaine Novak, Chapman (based on a story by Novak); ph, Mikhail Suslov; m, Gato Barbieri; ed, William Carruth; art d, Ginny Randolph; cos, Tracy Tynan; m/l, "Sh Boom (Life Could be a Dream)," J. Keyes, Carl Feaster, Claude Feaster, F. McRae, J. Edwards.

Drama/Romance **Cas.** **(PR:C MPAA:R)**

STREETS OF FIRE**½ (1984) 94m UNIV-RKO c

Michael Pare *(Tom Cody)*, Diane Lane *(Ellen Aim)*, Rick Moranis *(Billy Fish)*, Amy Madigan *(McCoy)*, Willem Dafoe *(Raven)*, Deborah Van Valkenburgh *(Reva)*, Richard Lawson *(Ed Price)*, Rick Rossovich *(Officer Cooley)*, Bill Paxton *(Clyde)*, Lee Ving *(Greer)*, Stoney Jackson *(Bird)*, Grand L. Bush *(Reggie)*, Robert Townsend *(Lester)*, Mykel T. Williamson *(B.J.)*, Elizabeth Daily *(Baby Doll)*, Lynne Thigpen *(Motorwoman)*, Marine Jahan *("Torchie's" Dancer)*, Ed Begley, Jr *(Ben Gunn)*, John Dennis Johnston *(Pete)*, Harry Beer *(Squirt)*, Olivia Brown *(Addie)*, Kip Waldo *(Waldo)*, Peter Jason *(Harry)*, Matthew Laurance *(Ardmore Cop)*, Sarah Marten *(Woman in Diner)*, Tamu Blackwell, Ric Moreno, Antonie Becker, Elizabeth Jordan *(Richmond Citzens)*, Susan Cheung, Vicki McCarthy *(Bar Patrons)*, John Hateley, Rock Walker *(Poker Players)*, Phil Alvin, Dave Alvin, John Bazz, Bill Bateman, Gene Taylor, Lee Allen, Steve Berlin [The Blasters] *(Bar Band)*, Paul Mones, Vince Deadrick, Jr, Paul Lane, Bernie Pock, Spiro Razatos, Jeff Smolek *(The Roadmasters)*, William Beard II, Stuart Kimbell, John Ryder, Angelo *(The Attackers)*.

Something of a disappointment for fans of director Walter Hill (THE WARRIORS, THE LONG RIDERS, SOUTHERN COMFORT, 48 HRS.), STREETS OF FIRE marked the beginning of a slump for this fascinating filmmaker. Set in a strange world that appears to be a view of the future envisioned by an adolescent urban male who grew up in the 1950s (all the cars are from the 1940s and 1950s, the set design is postwar modern), the film stars Lane as a local gal who has become a rock-star sensation (her vocals are performed by Laurie Sargent). She has returned to her home town to perform a sold-out concert. During her performance, a dangerous looking motorcycle gang called the "Bombers" (they ride old Harley-Davidsons) enters the concert hall and kidnaps Lane. Desperate to get Lane back, her somewhat dorky manager, Moranis, turns to the singer's old boy friend, Pare, for help. Pare, who has left town to become an urban soldier-of-fortune, agrees to fetch Lane from the clutches of slimy gang leader Dafoe. Accompanying Pare on his quest are Moranis and a tough female soldier-of-fortune, Madigan. Eventually the heroes enter the motorcycle gang's turf, get the girl, and bring her back home. On the way back, the heroes pick up four black do-wop singers called the "Sorels" (Pare commandeers their bus), and a young girl groupie, Daily. Dafoe, however, gives chase and Pare is forced to fight the gang leader in a brutal sledgehammer fight. The good guys win, of course, and rock 'n' roll is returned to the faithful. Though STREETS OF FIRE caught some vicious criticism from fans of the director, who felt he had sold out to the MTV rock-video visual style, Hill cannot be faulted on that account because he practically invented the style with THE WARRIORS. Flashy neon-lit visuals cut rhythmically to music were staples of his earlier film, and there is no reason why he should have been expected to abandon the style because it had suddenly come into vogue. Hill called STREETS OF FIRE a "rock 'n' roll fable," and it is nothing more, nothing less. Unfortunately, the film's failings are in the script and characterizations. Though all the actors have the right look, none of their characters are particularly interesting. The songs are serviceable, if unmemorable (with the exception of Dan Hartman's "I Can Dream About You," which became something of a radio hit in the summer of 1984), and the film suffers from a certain lifelessness one would not expect from Hill. Problems aside, the set design, art direction, costumes, and cinematography are top-rate and succeed in creating a unique screen world. While some of the exteriors where shot under the elevated tracks in Chicago, the majority of the filming was done on Universal Studios' backlot. To simulate the black of night, when most of the film takes place, a giant four-and-a-half acre tarpaulin was stretched over the outdoor set. Though the film seemed to have all the elements necessary to ensure heavy teenage turnout at the box office, it sank like a stone. Songs include: "Nowhere Fast," "Tonight Is What It Means to Be Young" (Jim Steinman), "Get Out of Denver" (Bob Segar), "Hold That Snake," "You Got What You Wanted" (Ry Cooder, Jim Dickinson), "Never Be You" (Tom Petty, Benmont Tench), "One Bad Stud" (Leiber and Stoller), "Blue Shadows" (Dave Alvin), "Sorcerer" (Stevie Nicks), "Countdown to Love" (Kenny Vance, Marty Kuppersmith), "I Can Dream About You" (Dan Hartman), "First Love, First Tears" (Duane Eddy, Lee Hazlewood), "Rumble" (Link Wray, Milt Grant), "Deeper and Deeper" (Cy Curnin, Jamie West-Oran, Adam Woods).

p, Lawrence Gordon, Joel Silver; d, Walter Hill; w, Hill, Larry Gross; ph, Andrew Laszlo (Panavision, Technicolor); m, Ry Cooder; ed, Freeman Davies, Michael Ripps, James Coblentz, Michael Tronick; prod d, John Vallone; art d, James Allen, Tony Brockliss; set d, Richard C. Goddard; cos, Marilyn Vance; ch, Jeffrey Hornaday.

Fantasy/Drama **Cas.** **(PR:C MPAA:PG)**

STRIKEBOUND** (1984, Aus.) 100m TRM/Mainline c

Chris Haywood, Carol Burns, Hugh Keays-Byrne, Rob Steele, Nik Forster, David Kendall, Anthony Hawkins, Marion Edward, Lazar Rodic, Reg Evans, Rod Williams, Ian Shrives, Tiriel Mora, May Howlett, Declan Affley, Denzil Howson, Charles Gilroy, Ivor Bowyer, Kirsty Grant, Alice Lowenstein, Hardy Stow.

A well-crafted worker's picture set in the subterranean world of Australia's coal mines. The film's docu-drama stylings capture the usual strike conflicts--those who play by the union rules versus the "scabs," and the hardened veterans versus the greenhorns. It's beautifully shot in a gritty realism, but it all seems so familiar.

p, Miranda Bain, Timothy White; d&w, Richard Lowenstein (based on the novel *Dead Men Don't Dig Coal* by Wendy Lowenstein); ph, Andrew De Groot; m, Declan Affley; ed, Jill Bilcock; prod d, Tracy Watt.

Drama **(PR:C-O MPAA:NR)**

STUCK ON YOU* (1984) 90m Troma c

Prof. Irwin Corey *(Judge)*, Virginia Penta *(Carol)*, Mark Mikulski *(Bill)*, Albert Pia *(Artie)*, Norma Pratt *(Bill's Mother)*, Daniel Harris *(Napoleon)*, Denise Silbert *(Cavewoman)*, Eddie Brill *(Caveman)*, June Martin *(Eve)*, John Gibham *(Adam)*, Robin Burroughs *(Isabella)*, Carl Sturmer *(Columbus)*, Julie Newdow *(Pocahantas)*, Pat Tallman *(Guinevere)*, Mr. Kent *(King Arthur)*, Barbie Kiellan *(Josephine)*, Louis Homyak *(Lance)*, Ben Kellman *(Indian Chief)*.

A ridiculous offering about a dimwitted judge, Corey, who presides over a palimony case. Corey is up to his usual stupid antics, the script is mindless, the performances are dry, and it all amounts to a sad waste of time. There are enough writers on STUCK ON YOU to start a baseball team, and maybe that's what they should think of doing next time the get an idea like this one.

p, Lloyd Kaufman, Michael Herz; d Samuel Weil; w, Stuart Strutin, Warren Leight, Don Perman, Darren Kloomok, Melanie Mintz, Anthony Gittleson, Duffy Caesar Magesis, Kaufman, Herz; ed, Kloomok, Richard Haines.

Drama **Cas.** **(PR:O MPAA:R)**

SUBURBIA*** (1984) 99m Suburbia-Bert Dragin/New World c (AKA: THE WILD SIDE)

Timothy Eric O'Brien *(Tom)*, Grant Miner *(Keef)*, Michael Bayer *(Razzle)*, Bill Coyne *(Evan)*, Andrew Pece *(Ethan)*, Chris Pederson *(Jack)*, Wade Walston *(Joe Schmo)*, Dee Waldron *(De Generate)*, Jennifer Clay *(Sheila)*, Maggie Ehrig *(Mattie)*, Christina Beck *(Tiresa)*, Andre Boutilier *(Peg Leg)*, Robert Peyton *(Jim Triplett)*, Jeff Prettyman *(Bob Skokes)*, Donald V. Allen *(Officer Rennard)*, Joe Battenberg *(Officer Bates)*, Dorlinda Griffin *(Mother)*, Robert Griffin *(Baby)*, Donna La Manna *(Tina)*, Julie Winchester *(Blonde)*, John McCormack *(Bouncer)*, Gavin Courtney *(Joe's Father)*, Robert A. Van Senus *(Joe's Father's Friend)*, Larry Wiley *(Camper Buyer)*, Marlena Brause *(Mrs. Triplett)*, Ron Hugo *(Pastor Farrell)*, Barbara Doyle *(Heatherton Ave. Woman)*, Arvid Blomberg *(Procedures Man)*, Jerry Madison *(Mr. Dawson)*, Barbara Benham *(Mrs. Martin)*, James Harrison *(Repaint Store Man)*, Ed Mertens *(Cop)*, Ray Lawrence *(Elderly Man)*, Gil Christner *(Jerry 7-11)*, J. Dinan Myrtetus *(Sheila's Father)*, Ricky Jewitt *(Elderly Man's Wife)*, Irene Latter, Mike B the Flea, Anna Schoeller.

A band of punk rockers in Los Angeles, alienated from their families and society for various reasons (incest, homosexuality, etc.), take over a house in an abandoned subdivision slated for demolition and set up a more or less conventional family structure there. Their neighbors, though, are less than thrilled with the punks next door, so they organize into a sort of vigilante force to chase them out, a measure that meets with retaliation from the more imaginative punkers. Although hardly believable, the story is effective, making its rather unwholesome characters sympathetic. Given the environments they're fleeing, it's no wonder they call themselves "The Rejected." Director Spheeris made a critically acclaimed feature debut here, after she made the pioneering punk documentary THE DECLINE OF WESTERN CIVILIZATION and produced Albert Brooks' REAL LIFE.

p, Bert Dragin; d&w, Penelope Spheeris; ph, Tim Suhrstedt; m, Alex Gibson; ed, Ross Albert; art d, Randy Moore; set d, Nancy Arnold.

Drama **Cas.** **(PR:O MPAA:R)**

SUCCESS IS THE BEST REVENGE*** (1984, Brit.) 90m DeVere-GAU-Emerald Film Partnership/GAU c

Michael York *(Alex Rodak)*, Janna Szerzerbic *(Wife)*, Michael Lyndon *(Adam, Older Son)*, George Skolimowski *(David, Younger Son)*, Michel Piccoli *(French Official)*, Anouk Aimee *(Monique de Fontaine)*, John Hurt *(Dino Montecurva)*, Ric Young, Claude Le Sache, Malcolm Sinclair, Hilary Drake, Jane Asher, Adam French, Sam Smart, Tim Brown, Maribel Jones, Mike Sarne, Maureen Bennett, Martyn Whitby, Bill Monks, Rory Edward, Archie Pool, Robert Whelan, Suzan Crowley, Tristram Jellinek, Ralph Nossek, Colin Bennett, Felicity Dean, Guy Degny, Eugeniusz Hczkiewicz, Stella Maris, Luis Pinilla.

Polish-born director Skolimowski (MOONLIGHTING, DEEP END) approaches one of his most common themes, the plight of the exiled Pole, in an intensely complex barrage of spectacular images. York is an exiled playwright, living a moderately comfortable life with his wife and two sons in London, where he is in the process of producing an abstract political play concerning Poland and its exiles. Though struggling to pay rent on his fashionable apartment, York finagles his way through some touchy situations, taking advantage of people without the least bit of remorse. His position as a heralded artist, and a politically exiled one at that, places his above common modes of decorum–at least in York's eyes. When his landlady demands some money, York quiets her by impulsively seducing her. The play is also financially threatened unless York and Aimee, the theater manager who is staging the play, can perform a near miracle. As a last resort York appeals to sleazy businessman Hurt for the necessary funding. Hurt gladly accommodates the artist, though not without some selfish motivation that makes the political statements of York seem like a complete mockery. In contrast to York's self-absorbed exploits are those of his eldest son, Lyndon, a high-school student facing an indentity crisis spurred on by his alienation from his "true" home, Poland. As his father runs about making a fool of himself in the name of art, Lyndon becomes increasingly disgusted and secretly plots to return to Poland on his own. Lyndon pawns the video camera which York bought him as a birthday present and purchases a one-way ticket. His ultimate decision to leave the comfort of England for the uncertainty of Poland comes after his father loses his integrity and appeals to Hurt for money. As the costly play (buses escort viewers to its realistic stages) is being performed, Lyndon dyes his hair a fluorescent red and prepares to board a plane for an unknown destination. In a puzzlingly complicated narrative structure (it skips about with little warning or preparation, combining realism with fantasy sequences that are impossible to differentiate as such), SUCCESS IS THE BEST REVENGE is a bold and probing search into the forces that mold political idealism into hypercritical complacency. In addition, Skolimowski insightfully constructs the building conflict between father and son that erupts into total separation. When this film was first shown in London, audiences exhibited little patience for the flamboyant and experimental style, and were quite vocal in their disapproval. As a result, SUCCESS has had a very limited release; a shame considering all the good things it has to offer.

p&d, Jerzy Skolimowski; w, Michael Lyndon, Skolimowski; ph, Mike Fash (Eastmancolor); m, Stanley Myers, Hans Zimmer; ed, Barrie Vince; prod d, Voytek.

Drama (PR:O MPAA:NR)

SUENO DE NOCHE DE VERANO
(SEE: MIDSUMMER NIGHT'S DREAM, A, Brit./Span.)

SUGAR CANE ALLEY* (1984, Fr.) 103m Su Ma Fa-Orca-NEF Diffusion/Orion Classics-Artificial Eye c (RUE CASES NEGRES)

Garry Cadenat (Jose), Darling Legitimus (M'Man Tine), Douta Seck (Medouze), Joby Bernabe (Mons. Saint-Louis), Francisco Charles (Le Gereur), Marie-Jo Descas (La Mere de Leopold), Marie-Ange Farot (Mme. Sanit-Louis), Henri Melon (Mons. Roc), Eugene Mona (Douze Orteils), Joel Palcy (Carmen), Mathieu Crico, Virgine Delaunay-Belleville, Tania Hamel, Maite Marquet, Laurent Saint-Cyr, Dominique Arfi, Emilie Blameble, Norita Blameble, Leon de la Guignaraye, Andre Lehr, Roger Promard, Joseph Rene-Corail, Lucette Salibur.

Set in the French colony of Martinique in the 1930s, this stark and charming picture takes a look at life in "Rue Cases Negres" (literally "Black Shack Alley")–a section of wooden shacks isolated in the middle of a sugar plantation. While the adults are toiling in the fields, the children fill the "alley." For many of the children it will be their last summer at the plantation. Those with the brains will find better jobs or even schooling, while the less fortunate will assist their parents in the fields. Most prominently featured is an 11-year-old youngster, Cadenat, who plays and frolics with all his energy, and still manages to get a prestigious scholarship to a high school at Fort de France. This well-acted film is an unexpected delight, showing that a ray of hope can materialize amidst the despondency of shantytown. (In French; English subtitles.)

p, Michel Loulergue, Alix Regis; d&w, Euzhan Palcy (based on the novel "La Rue Cases Negres" by Joseph Zobel); ph, Dominique Chapius (Fujicolor); m, Groupe Malavoi; ed, Marie-Joseph Yoyotte; art d, Hoang Thanh At; set d, Geoffrey Larcher; cos, Isabelle Filleul.

Drama Cas. (PR:C MPAA:PG)

SUNDAY IN THE COUNTRY, A**
(1984, Fr.) 94m Sara-A2/MGM-UA c (UN DIMANCHE A LA CAMPAGNE)

Louis Ducreux (Mons. Ladmiral), Sabine Azema (Irene), Michel Aumont (Gonzague/(Edouard), Genevieve Mnich (Marie-Therese), Monique Chaumette (Mercedes), Claude Winter (Mme. Ladmiral), Thomas Duval (Emile), Quentin Ogier (Lucien), Katia Wostrikoff (Mireille), Valentine Suard, Erika Faivre (Little Girls), Marc Perrone (Accordionist), Pascale Vignal (Dance Hall Servant), Jacques Poitrenaud (Hector), Jean-Roger Milo.

A beautiful film which details a day in the life of an elderly painter, Ducreux,

who is a holdover from the days of the French Impressionists. On one average Sunday in 1912, Ducreux entertains his grown son, Aumont, and his family. They walk through the picturesque grounds of Ducreux's country estate, prepare dinner, and tell wonderful stories about life and art. Unexpectedly, Ducreux's daughter, Azema, pays a rare visit. Although Azema is the troubled outcast of the family, she is still Ducreux's favorite. She is the kind of lively woman who sees no problem in waking Ducreux from his afternoon nap, although her stuffy brother objects. Ducreux's Sunday becomes exciting and worthwhile with her arrival. Father and daughter take a spontaneous drive in her new car and end up in town dancing and drinking. A phone call from a lover sends Azema into an emotional tailspin and she quickly leaves her father's estate. The Sunday visit ends and Ducreux returns to his canvas, finding new life in his work. The story line of A SUNDAY IN THE COUNTRY is simple and without much drama, but it is in this simplicity that the film's beauty lies. Ducreux's Sunday is a serene one–he is an old man who has lived a quiet life and enjoys reminiscing, his family is warm and loving, though not without idiosyncrasies, his surroundings are bathed in a peaceful light, and his canvas quietly awaits his artistic touch. The sum of these parts is a slice of life. Tavernier, who took Best Director honors at the Cannes Film Festival for this picture, has successfully struck the core of French life in the early 20th Century. "I wanted to make a film that would be based entirely on feelings," Tavernier has said, "a film where emotions could reach a peak simply because a young woman leaves her father a bit early on a Sunday afternoon–that's the only dramatic moment in the film. I found it irresistible." In addition to this desire to film emotions, Tavernier made a conscious effort to attain, on film, the appearance of the French Impressionist's painting, owing much to rookie cinematographer, de Keyzer. A SUNDAY IN THE COUNTRY is nothing short of a painting come to life. While often compared (quite favorably) to the films of Jean Renoir and to Ingmar Bergman's WILD STRAWBERRIES (Ducreux made a brilliant screen debut at a late age), A SUNDAY IN THE COUNTRY is, according to Tavernier, inspired most by Leo McCarey's MAKE WAY FOR TOMORROW (1937). (In French, English subtitles.)

p, Alain Sarde; d, Bertrand Tavernier; w, Tavernier, Colo Tavernier (based on the novella Monsieur Ladmiral Va Bientot Mourir by Pierre Bost); ph, Bruno de Keyzer (Eastmancolor); m, Gabriel Faure, Louis Ducreux, Marc Perrone; ed, Armand Psenny; prod d, Patrice Mercier; set d, Michel Grimaud; cos, Yvonne Sassinot de Nesles; makeup, Eric Muller.

Drama (PR:A MPAA:G)

SUPERGIRL* (1984) 114m Pueblo Film AG/Tri-Star c

Faye Dunaway (Selena), Helen Slater (Supergirl/Linda Lee), Peter O'Toole (Zaltar), Mia Farrow (Alura), Brenda Vaccaro (Bianca), Peter Cook (Nigel), Simon Ward (Zor-El), Marc McClure (Jimmy Olsen), Hart Bochner (Ethan), Maureen Teefy (Lucy Lane), David Healy (Mr. Danvers), Robyn Mandell (Myra), Jenifer Landor (Muffy), Diana Ricardo (Mrs. Murray), Nancy Lippold (Billy-Jo), Sonya Leite (Betsy), Linsey Beauchamp (Ali), Michelle Taylor (Amy), Nancy Wood (Nancy), Virginia Greig (Jodie), Julia Lewis (Gloria), Matt Frewer, Bill McAllister (Truck Drivers), Sally Cranfield (Argonian Teacher), Martin Serene (Eddie), Keith Edwards, Bradley Lavelle (Lucy's Friends), Carole Charnow (Cashier), Shezwae Powell (Waitress), Glory Annen (Midvale Protestor), Sandra Martin (Selena's Astral Image), Sandra Dickinson, Martha Parsey, Kelly Hunter, Ter Battenburg, Richard Bidwell, Desire, Christian Fletcher, Karen Hale, Beulah Hughes, Lia, Mike Pearce, Kevin Scott, James Snell, Jane Sumner, Bailie Walsh, Elaine Ives-Cameron, Gay Baynes, Fred Lee Own, Edwin Van Wyk, Orla Pederson, Joe Cremona, April Orlich, Erick Ray Evans, Zoot Money, Ron Travis, Danique, Russell Sommers, Dulcie Huston, David Graham.

With the success of the three SUPERMAN films, it seemed only natural that a film about his comic book cousin Supergirl would follow. Unfortunately, SUPERGIRL, unlike the first two SUPERMAN films, is barely worth a glance. Slater lives on the planet Argo, where the refugees from the exploded planet of Krypton now live. O'Toole has gotten hold of a power source for the planet, a small glowing ball that he accidentally zaps into space. Slater quickly goes after it, chasing the small globe in a space pod O'Toole has built. Dunaway is a witch who–in the best villainous tradition–wants to rule the world. She gains possession of the ball when it lands on Earth, and soon realizes its strength. Slater is nearby, and decked out in a mini-skirted version of her famous cousin's togs. Taking the guise of a student at a private school, Slater ends up as Teefy's roommate. Teefy, by sheer Hollywood-style coincidence, is Lois Lane's sister, and we all know who she is. Teefy also has a big picture of Superman on her wall, though the face is shadowed, indicating that perhaps Christopher Reeve had something to say about the use of his image. Eventually Slater confronts the evil Dunaway, rescuing her pals, along with handsome love interest Bochner, from the witch's clutches. Dunaway, as expected, is handily defeated, and Slater goes flying off to her home planet. What made SUPERMAN and SUPERMAN II work so well was their reverence towards the Man of Steel, coupled with some good tongue-in-cheek humor. SUPERGIRL takes the opposite approach, playing the story for high camp, which just doesn't work. The film, relying heavily on special effects, quickly grows boring, with a cast that's simply dreadful. Dunaway is all gestures and histrionics, an embarrassing display right out of MOMMIE DEAREST. She isn't helped any by Vaccaro as Dunaway's wise cracking sidekick, an annoying character that one wishes Supergirl would dispose of simply to shut her up. O'Toole is wasted in his small role, while Farrow barely appears on-screen before she goes rushing off to a better job with Woody Allen. As the title superheroine, Slater is passable, though she really doesn't do much more than look pretty and fly around in a short skirt (at least Superman wore tights). Szwarc's direction is flat and uninspired, emphasizing the jokey elements without any sense at all for the material. Some severe problems in the plot's logic suggest this film may have had some of its weightier problems excised in the cutting room. Originally this was to be a summer release through Warner Bros., but once they saw the film the studio decided to drop distribution. Tri-Star resurrected SUPERGIRL, giving it a Christmas release. Though this should have been a good adventure for children, some gratuitous breast jokes make this questionable for smaller children. Ilya Salkind, the executive producer behind the SUPERMAN films, served in the same capacity for SUPER-GIRL. Somewhere in between he lost sight of the characters (and their importance in American pop mythology) for like SUPERMAN III, SUPER-GIRL is a disappointing waste of time.

p, Timothy Burrill; d, Jeannot Szwarc; w, David Odell (based on the comic book character); ph, Alan Hume (Panavision, Rank Film Color); m, Jerry Goldsmith; ed, Malcolm Cooke; prod d, Richard MacDonald; art d, Terry Ackland-Snow; set d, Peter Young; cos, Emma Porteous; spec eff, John Evans; m/l, "New Song," Howard Jones, "What is Love," Jones, Bryant; makeup, Ann Brodie, Lee Harman; stunts, Alf Joint.

Adventure   Cas.   (PR:C MPAA:PG)

SURF II zero   (1984) 91m Surfs Up/International Film Marketing c
                              (AKA: SURF II-THE END OF THE TRILOGY)

Morgan Paull (Dad), Ruth Buzzi (Chuck's Mother), Lyle Waggoner (Chief Boyardie), Cleavon Little (Daddy-O), Linda Kerridge (Sparkle), Carol Wayne (Mrs. O'Finlay), Eddie Deezen (Menlo Schwartzer), Peter Isacksen (Beaker), Biff Maynard (Bob's Father), Tom Villard (Jocko O'Finlay), Eric Stoltz (Chuck), Jeffrey Rodgers (Bob), Corinne Bohrer (Cindy Lou), Lucinda Dooling (Lindy Sue), Brandis Kemp (Bob's Mother), Terry Kiser (Mr. O'Finlay).

Imbecilic teen exploitation film has Deezen a nerd constantly made the butt of practical jokes by a gang of arrogant surfers. When they go too far, slipping female hormones in his soft drink, he grows a tiny pair of breasts. Completely unhinged by the new development, he goes to a hidden laboratory at the bottom of the ocean and creates a drink that turns whoever consumes it into his zombie slave. Once he gathers an army of zombie surf punks (about a half dozen), he sets out to win the big surfing competition and show everyone he can't be pushed around. Stoltz is the hero, who manages to defeat Deezen and destroy his undersea lab before going on to win the surfing competition. An abysmal movie from beginning to end, with juvenile writing, lots of gratuitous nudity, and a cast of forgotten television actors who should have stayed forgotten. Stoltz, who won acclaim the following year for MASK, is adequate, but no more. The funniest thing about SURF II is its title–there was no SURF I.

p, George G. Braunstein, Ron Hamady; d&w, Randall Badat; ph, Alex Phillips (DeLuxe Color); m, Peter Bernstein; ed, Jacqueline Cambas; prod d, Jeff Staggs; art d, Syd Smillie; set d, Robert Lowy; cos, Carin Berger.

Comedy   Cas.   (PR:O MPAA:R)

SURROGATE, THE zero   (1984, Can.) 99m
                                          Cinepix-Telemetropole/Cinepix c

Art Hindle (Frank Waite), Carole Laure (Anouk Van Derlin), Shannon Tweed (Lee Waite), Michael Ironside (George Kyber), Marilyn Lightstone (Dr. Harriet Forman), Jim Bailey (Eric), Jackie Burroughs (Fantasy Woman), Barbara Law (Maggie Simpson), Gary Reineke (John Manion), Jonathan Welsh (Brenner).

Sexually unsatisfied in their marriage, Hindle and Tweed decide to go to sex therapist Laure, who specializes in helping couples release their more extreme fantasies. A series of sexually related murders begins shortly after the couple starts the sessions. Their neighbor, Bailey, a transvestite, is a suspect. Soon friends are being killed left and right, causing Hindle and Tweed to believe Laure may be involved with the crimes. The film soon becomes all-too predictable. This was the first directorial effort for the producer of PORKY'S, and he wins no plaudits. There's not a believable character in the group and the action is completely lacking in suspense. Filmed in Montreal, though it's supposed to be set in New York City.

p, John Dunning, Don Carmody; d, Carmody; w, Carmody, Robert Geoffrian; ph, Francois Protat (Eastmancolor); m, Daniel Lanois; ed, Rit Wallace; art d, Charles Dunlop.

Thriller   (PR:O MPAA:NR)

SWANN IN LOVE½   (1984, Fr.Ger.) 110m ORION CLASSICS c (UN AMOUR DE SWANN)

Jeremy Irons (Charles Swann), Ornella Muti (Odette De Crecy), Alain Delon (Baron De Charlus), Fanny Ardant (Duchesse de Guermantes), Marie-Christine Barrault (Mme. Verdurin), Ann Bennent (Chloe), Nathalie Juvent (Mme. Cottard), Charlotte Kerr (Sous-Maitresse), Humbert Balsan (Head of

Protocol), Jean Aurenche (Mons. Vinteuil), Veronique Dietschy (Mlle. Vinteuil), Philippine Pascale (Mme. De Gallardon), Charlotte de Turckheim (Mme. de Cambremer), Jean-Francoise Balmer (Mons. Cottard), Jean-Louis Richard (Mons. Verdurin), Jacques Boudet (Duc De Guermantes), Bruno Thost (Saniette), Roland Toper (Biche), Nicolas Baby (Juif), Catherine Lachens (Mme. V.'s Guest), Jean-Pierre Kopf (Aime), Roland de Chaudenay (Forcheville), Vincent Martin, Marc Arian, Romain Bremond, Pierre Celeyron, Jacques Dalafontaine, Martin Droch, Geoffrey Tory, Pierre Coffe.

It took four writers, the participation of several companies (Gaumont, Les Films Du Losange, FR3, SFPC, Bioskop), and the French Ministry of Culture to make this adaptation from Proust's monumental book and it still didn't quite come together. What they said could not be done wasn't done. Irons is Swann, a wealthy Jewish art critic who has overcome the hidden anti-Semitism in 19th Century Paris and managed to become part of the inner circle of le haute monde. The story of his courtship and marriage to courtesan Muti is depicted in a 24-hour period. Using the first and second volumes of Proust's seven-volume tome, the writers have condensed it all into a day in the life of Irons as we see his love for Muti become a jealous obsession. She has the assets he most admires in the female figures painted by the masters. She is quick, mysterious, innocent, and possesses all the qualities he wants in a woman. What Irons doesn't understand is that he cannot own her and that she is far less enigmatic than he imagines. In a series of splintery flashbacks, he recalls their wooing and comes to realize that he married her without the benefit of loving her. They are total opposites from the start, as she is witty and he is dour, he is unresponsive and she is passionate, and the twain is hardly meeting. Irons has a best friend, Delon, a notorious homosexual (and anyone who knows Delon's true-life penchant for women will realize just how good he is in this role, which is the opposite of the way he is). Irons marries Muti, despite the protestations of Barrault, a domineering social hostess who sees Muti for what she is, a half- hooker who probably will begin cheating on Irons before the honeymoon sheets have cooled. Irons understands that this marriage will probably cause his ostracism from the aristocratic milieu in which he now functions but his obsession for Muti blinds him to any reason. Directed by the man who gave us THE TIN DRUM and the Dustin Hoffman version of "Death of a Salesman" on TV, this film bites off too much as it wavers in style from Proust to Schlondorff. Lots of money was spent on the re-creation of the period and there was no stinting on the actors' fees. The biggest surprise was Delon, who showed that he was more than just a swarthy face capable of violence in various cheap thrillers. There was a bit of "Swann in Love" and some of "Within a Budding Grove" used in the screenplay but anyone who wants to know the whole story would be advised to read all of set of books, Remembrance of Things Past. The picture was shot on location and looks quite authentic with such backdrops as the posh Chateau de Champs-Sir-Marne, but locations do not a picture make and the splayed nature of this movie causes it to be less than satisfying and not at all involving. Adapting classics has always been chancy because so many people have read the original and each person sees the characters in a different fashion. When it works, as in GONE WITH THE WIND or MUTINY ON THE BOUNTY (the first one), it works wonderfully. When it fails, it becomes SWANN IN LOVE. Still, there is enough here to merit a look-see, even if you haven't slogged through Proust. Not for children's eyes at all. (In French; English subtitles.)

p, Margaret Menegoz; d, Volker Schlondorff; w, Schlondorff, Peter Brook, Jean-Claude Carriere, Marie-Helene Estienne (based on the novel Un Amour de Swann by Marcel Proust); ph, Sven Nykvist; m, Hans-Werner Henze, David Graham, Gerd Kuhr, Marcel Wengler; ed, Francoise Bonnot; prod d, Jacques Saulnier; cos, Yvonne Sassinot de Nesle.

Drama   Cas.   (PR:C-O MPAA:R)

SWEET GINGER BROWN   (SEE: FLAMINGO KID, THE)

SWING SHIFT**   (1984) 113m WB c

Goldie Hawn (Kay Walsh), Kurt Russell (Lucky Lockhart), Christine Lahti (Hazel Zanussi), Fred Ward (Biscuits Toohey), Ed Harris (Jack Walsh), Sudie Bond (Annie), Holly Hunter (Jeannie Sherman), Patty Maloney (Laverne), Lisa Pelikan (Violet Mulligan), Susan Peretz (Edith Castle), Joey Aresco (Johnny Bonnano), Morris "Tex" Biggs (Clarence), Reid Cruikshanks (Spike), Daniel Dean Darst (Deacon), Dennis Fimple (Rupert George), Christopher Lemmon (Lt. O'Connor), Charles Napier (Moon Willens), Stephen Tobolowsky (Documentary Narrator/French de Mille), Laura Hawn (Ethel), Marvin Miller (Rollo), Susan Barnes (Skinny), Beth Henley (Bible Pusher), Gene Borkan (MP at Embarkation Point), Alana Stewart (Frankie Parker), Phillip Christon (Recruit at Egyptian), Penny Johnson (Genevieve), Isabell Monk (Rita), Maggie Renzi (1st Interviewer), Sandy McLeod (2nd Interviewer), George Schwartz (Cribman), Alan Toy (Assistant Cribman), Oceana Marr (Ladies Room Inspector), Richard K. Way (Factory Soldier), Harold Jackson (Piano Player at Sorrentino's), Don Carrara (Drunk Sailor), Todd Allen (Cpl. Bobby Danzig), Gary Goetzman ("Swing Shift" Bandleader), Belinda Carlisle (Jamboree Singer), Lissette LeCorn (Peggy at Age 3), Jessica Gaynes (Peggy at Age 7), Deena Marie (Paper Girl), Roger Rook (Bellhop), Joseph Hutton (Seaman Amtzis), Harry Northrup, David B. Carlton (New Year's Eve Marines), Lisa Chadwick (Vocalist at Kelly's), Eddie Smith (Waiter at Kelly's), Eugene Jackson (Bartender), Chino "Fats" Williams (Bouncer), Belita Moreno (Mabel Stoddard), Roger

Corman *(Mr. MacBride)*.

Patriotism takes one giant step backwards as "Rosie the Riveter" turns adultress. Hawn and Harris are a typical couple during WW II. When he is called into service to help protect the U.S. from the scourge of the Axis, she takes her patriotism seriously and becomes an employee at the local aircraft factory. Naturally, she is a bit of a flake and a bumbler (as she usually is in films) and her attitude soon attracts the attention of Russell, a 4-F with a barely explained heart problem that keeps him out of uniform. Their fast friendship soon turns romantic, though Hawn mildly protests that she is a married woman with a husband going off to fight for freedom. The next few years of the skirmish are seen in a condensed passionate haze with Hawn and Russell finding plenty of time for parties, long rides, and languishing in each other's arms. Hawn's neighbor is Lahti (the modern-day version of the heroine's "best friend" as personified by Ann Miller, Eve Arden, and several others while the war was actually raging) and she helps Hawn cloak the illicit affair. Harris gets a furlough and comes home unexpectedly. Upon arrival, he is confronted with Hawn's infidelity, has his heart broken, and goes back to the war in depressed spirits. While Harris is home, Russell spends the night with Lahti. That, in turn, breaks Hawn's spirits. Later, Harris returns safely from the conflict with the Nazis and the Japanese and he and Hawn are happily reunited with the justification for the earlier adultery being that "War Is Hell." Using WW II to explain adultery isn't very patriotic or very amusing, especially since Hawn is characterized early as having a fine relationship with Harris and seemingly in no need of a man in her life. Harris was sympathetic from the start and far more likable than Russell, who was, at best, benign. Hawn wasn't devious so the idea of a love triangle without a villain or a villainess didn't come to fruition. The war, the life style, and the characters on the "swing shift" were far more interesting than the story. As a fairly accurate depiction of life in the U.S. in the 1940s, the movie does have some merit. Otherwise, it's a melodrama that should have been a comedy, and it is about as shallow as a pie pan. Lahti, the best character in the film and far more believable than the leads, was nominated for the supporting actress Oscar for her work. Making her debut as a nightclub singer is Belinda Carlisle, formerly of the Go-Gos female singing group. Jack Lemmon's son, Chris, does a small bit and famed producer-director Roger Corman has a small role. Corman likes to work as an actor from time to time and will be recalled as "Senator Number Two" in THE GODFATHER, PART II. A good light comedy could have been made using many of the elements, but they chose to look at the dark side and the result was a bust at the box office. The co-author, Bo Goldman, had won Oscars for ONE FLEW OVER THE CUCKOO'S NEST and MELVIN AND HOWARD before getting into a more somber mood with this and SHOOT THE MOON, which was also shot down by the critics and public. SWING SHIFT was released at various lengths: 113 minutes, 100 minutes, 99 minutes. It might have been a good 45-minute picture.

p, Jerry Bick; d, Jonathan Demme; w, Rob Morton; ph, Tak Fujimoto (Technicolor); m, Patrick Williams; ed, Craig McKay; prod d, Peter Jamison; art d, Bo Welch; set d, R. Chris Westlund, Jeff Haley; cos, Joe I. Tompkins; m/l, "Someone Waits for You," Peter Allen, Will Jennings.

Drama   Cas.   (PR:A-C MPAA:PG)

SWORD OF THE VALIANT* (1984, Brit.) 101m Golan-Globus/Cannon c

Miles O'Keeffe *(Gawain)*, Cyrielle Claire *(Linet)*, Leigh Lawson *(Humphrey)*, Sean Connery *(Green Knight)*, Trevor Howard *(King Arthur)*, Peter Cushing *(Seneschal)*, Ronald Lacey *(Oswald)*, Lila Kedrova *(Lady of Lyonesse)*, John Rhys-Davies *(Baron Fortinbras)*, Wilfrid Brambell *(Porter)*, Brian Coburn *(Friar)*, Bruce Lidington *(Bertilak)*, David Rappaport *(Sage)*, Douglas Wilmer *(Black Knight)*, Emma Sutton *(Morgan La Fay)*, John Serret *(Priest)*, Thomas Heathcote *(Armourer)*, Mike Edmonds *(Tiny Man)*, John Pierce-Jones *(Sergeant)*, James Windsor, Ric Morgan, Peter MacKriel *(Recruits)*, Jerold Wells, Harry Jones *(Torturers)*, John J. Carney *(Messenger)*, Peter Coogan, Hillary Johnson *(Garcons a Table)*.

Muddled adaptation of the classic legend of Sir Gawain and the Green Knight by a director who had already tried his hand at the tale in 1973 (GAWAIN AND THE GREEN KNIGHT). At old king Howard's castle, all the knights are growing lazy and contented. Into a feast one day strides Connery, with an eerie green glow around him. He offers a challenge—anyone can take a blow at him with a sword, as long as he himself can return the blow. No takers come forth, to Howard's disgust, and he is on the verge of doing it himself when O'Keeffe accepts the challenge. With one mighty swing of his broadsword he lops off Connery's head, which rolls across the floor. Connery's body goes over, picks it up, and puts it back on his neck. Connery then gives O'Keeffe one year to solve a riddle or else he'll cut his head off. O'Keeffe then embarks on a series of adventures along with his squire (Lawson), involving rescuing princess Claire from a variety of perils and engaging in frequent rounds of combat. After the opening scene, which is quite well staged, the film degenerates quickly into typical sword-and-sorcery cliche that O'Keeffe just can't pull off by himself. His line readings were so bad, in fact, that another actor's voice was dubbed in, an expense not incurred in O'Keeffe's debut, the wretched TARZAN, THE APE MAN (1981), simply because he didn't have any lines to speak. Howard's brief part proved difficult as well because he was reportedly unable to remember more than two sentences at a time. The only thing that redeems the film from total

worthlessness is Connery's Green Knight, a frightening vision in armor as he picks up his head and roars with laughter. Connery, who sports his new hair implants, took time off from shooting NEVER SAY NEVER AGAIN (1984) to film this. Shooting began in Wales in 1982, but when they took that footage to the editing room, they found it completely useless and reshot all of it in France and Scotland.

p, Menahem Golan, Yoram Globus; d, Stephen Weeks; w, Weeks, Philip M. Breen, Howard C. Pen; ph, Freddie A. Young, Peter Hurst (J-D-C Widescreen, Fujicolor); m, Ron Geesin; ed, Richard Marden, Barry Peters; prod d, Maurice Fowler, Derek Nice; set d, Val Wolstenholme; cos, Shuna Harwood; spec eff, Nobby Clarke, Daniel Parker, Aaron Sherman, Cliff Culley, Niel Culley.

Adventure   Cas.   (PR:C MPAA:PG)

SWORDKILL*½   (1984) 80m Albert Band-Swordkill-Empire-Harkham/Empire c

Hiroshi Fujioka *(Yoshimitsa)*, John Calvin *(Dr. Alan Richards)*, Janet Julian *(Chris Welles)*, Charles Lampkin *(Willie Walsh)*, Frank Schuller *(Detective Berger)*, Bill Morey *(Dr. Carl Anderson)*, Andy Wood *(Dr. Pete Denza)*, Robert Kino *(Prof. Tagachi)*, Joan Foley *(Ellie West)*, Peter Liapis *(Johnny Tooth)*, Mieko Kobayashi *(Chidori)*.

Fujioka is a samurai warrior in 1552 Japan searching for his wife who has been kidnaped by enemies. Wounded, he falls into an icy crevasse and is frozen. Four hundred years later he's found by a party of skiers and the body is shipped to Los Angeles for study. To everyone's surprise, particularly Fujioka's, the samurai awakens. He believes himself still to be in Japan and the culture shock of 1980s L.A. is astounding, to say the least. Undaunted, Fujioka takes his sword in hand and continues his search. He escapes from the hospital and the chase begins. Nasty doctor Calvin wants the man for his own purposes but nice girl Julian cares about Fujioka and wants to help him. It's predictable, but imaginative enough at moments to be a fairly amusing diversion. The plot is similar to ICEMAN (1984) but rather than treating the subject as serious material, this movie has some fun with the idea. It's not quite as satirical as it could have been, but Fujioka's performance makes the film much better than might be expected.

p, Charles Band; d, J. Larry Carroll; w, Tim Curnen; ph, Mac Ahlberg (CFI Color); m, Richard Band; ed, Brad Arensman; prod d, Pamela B. Warner, Robert Howland.

Drama   (PR:C MPAA:R)

TAIL OF THE TIGER*½   (1984, Aus.) 82m Producer's Circle/Roadshow c

Grant Navin *(Orville Ryan)*, Gordon Poole *(Harry)*, Caz Lederman *(Lydia Ryan)*, Gayle Kennedy *(Beryl)*, Peter Feeley *(Spike)*, Dylan Lyle *(Rabbit)*, Walter Sullivan *(Stan)*, Basil Clarke *(Jack)*.

Ten-year-old Navin is a Sydney youngster whose abiding passion is old airplanes. The neighborhood gang won't let him join them when they fly their model airplanes, so he hangs around with cantankerous old Poole, who is restoring an ancient DeHavilland Tiger Moth in an abandoned warehouse. Three ghosts of pilots frequently turn up to encourage the pair and even help them fight off a gang of ruffians who want to wreck the biplane. When the restoration is complete the duo fly above Sydney in an exhilarating sequence. Good children's story that even adults will enjoy.

p, James M. Vernon; d&w, Rolf de Heer; ph, Richard Michalak; m, Steve Arnold, Graham Tardif; ed, Surresh Ayyar; prod d, Judi Russell.

Children   (PR:AA MPAA:NR)

TANK*½   (1984) 113m Lorimar/UNIV c

James Garner *(Zack)*, Shirley Jones *(LaDonna)*, C. Thomas Howell *(Billy)*, Mark Herrier *(Elliott)*, Sandy Ward *(Gen. Hubik)*, Jenilee Harrison *(Sarah)*, James Cromwell *(Deputy Euclid)*, Dorian Harewood *(Sgt. Tippet)*, G.D. Spradlin *(Sheriff Buelton)*, John Hancock *(Mess Sergeant)*, Guy Boyd *(Sgt. Wimofsky)*, Daniel Albright, Beth Smallwood, Mark McGee *(TV Reporters)*, Gerald A. Atkins *(Food Server)*, Ron Baskins, Wallace Merck *(Deputies)*, Keith Jerome Brown *(Tank Motor Pool Man)*, Robert Henry Bryant *(NCO Wenton)*, Frederick R. Clark, David J. Dominick, Doneal G. Gersh *(NCO's)*, Alan G. Cornett, James T. Newton, Thomas P. Wann *(Sergeant Majors)*, Bill Crabb *(Jackson)*, T. Renee Crutcher *(Gwen Tippet)*, Raymond D. Eckel *(Radio Operator)*, J. Don Ferguson *(Gov. Sims)*, Bill Fleet *(State Trooper Commander)*, Jeff Folger, Laura Whyte *(Reporters)*, Jim Jackson *(Cook)*, Bob Hannah *(School Principal)*, Mickey Yablans *(School Kid)*, Larry Jordan *(Harris)*, Bob Neal *(TV Announcer)*, Danny Nelson *(Gant)*, Kathy Payne *(Dianne Fleming)*, Don Young *(Avery)*, Joan Riordan *(Rhonda Wimofsky)*, Larry S. Raines, Richard Lewis Smith *(Bikers)*, Andy Still *(Anchorman)*, Roy Tatum *(Coach)*, Ben Walburn *(Chattahoochee Slim)*, Alan Walker *(MP)*, Johnny Watson *(Young Prisoner)*, Wallace Wilkinson *(Governor of Georgia)*, Kathleen L. Petro *(Barmaid)*.

Garner is an Army officer nearing retirement who arrives at his new post in Georgia with wife Jones, son Howell, and his hobby on a trailer, a restored Sherman tank he putters around with. When someone asks him why he has a Sherman tank he answers "Because the odds against accidentally shooting yourself while cleaning it are incredible." One evening, Garner goes into town where he strikes up a conversation with Harrison, a 17 year-old prostitute who works for the local crimelord, who also happens to be local law enforcement officer, sheriff Spradlin. When one of Spradlin's henchman slaps Harrison around a little in front of Garner, he jumps to his feet and decks the guy. Spradlin is angry now, so he arranges to have Howell set up for a drug bust, and he is convicted and sent to a harsh prison farm that looks like something out of COOL HAND LUKE. Legal methods are of no help to Garner as he tries to free his son, so he finally resorts to his tank, first driving it into town and forcing a deputy to strip out in the street and handcuff himself to a telephone pole after destroying the jail by driving through it. Next he goes out to the prison farm and frees his son, and the pair, along with Harrison, set out for the Tennesse border, with Spradlin and his cohorts in pursuit. The rest of the film is one long chase, similar to SMOKEY AND THE BANDIT, and Garner, of course, triumphs and is vindicated while Spradlin gets his just desserts. A poor script and lackluster direction keep this film from achieving anything noteworthy, but the sheer likability and easy charm of Garner carry the film, and Spradlin is a worthy villain. The rest of the performances are mediocre, as is just about everything else about this film.

p, Irwin Yablans; d, Marvin J. Chomsky; w, Dan Gordon; ph, Don Birnkrant (Metrocolor); m, Lalo Schifrin; ed, Donald R. Rode; prod d, Bill Kenney; set d, Rick Gentz; cos, James Tyson, Ann Lambert; m/l, "Saturday Girl," Lalo, Donna Schifrin.

Comedy/Drama   **Cas.**   **(PR:C   MPAA:PG)**

TEACHERS½   (1984) 106m MGM/UA c

Nick Nolte *(Alex)*, JoBeth Williams *(Lisa)*, Judd Hirsch *(Roger)*, Ralph Macchio *(Eddie)*, Allen Garfield *(Rosenberg)*, Lee Grant *(Dr. Burke)*, Richard Mulligan *(Herbert)*, Royal Dano *(Ditto)*, William Schallert *(Horn)*, Art Metrano *(Troy)*, Laura Dern *(Diane)*, Crispin Glover *(Danny)*, Morgan Freeman *(Lewis)*, Madeleine Sherwood *(Grace)*, Steven Hill *(Sloan)*, Zohra Lampert *(Mrs. Pilikian)*, Mary Alice *(Linda Ganz)*, Katharine Balfour *(Theresa)*, Virginia Bonnell *(Nurse)*, Virginia Capers *(Landlady)*, Ellen Crawford *(Social Worker)*, Terry Ellis *(Tim Hahn)*, Aaron Freeman *(Brinkman)*, Patricia Gaul *(Lowe)*, Anthony Heald *(Narc)*, Ronald Hunter *(Mr. Pilikian)*, Julia Jennings *(The Blonde)*, Stephen Mendillo *(Lecture Cop)*, Jeff Ware *(Malloy)*, Richard Zobel *(Propes)*, Da Nang McKay *(Wounded Kid)*, Virginia Smith *(Lee)*, Ray Noch *(Dan Hall)*, Maria D. Magisano *(Alvado)*, Bill Marinella *(Paller)*, Noerena Abookire *(Terry Davis)*, Andrew Ream *(Henson)*, Jennifer Quilty *(Sarah)*, Kimberly Pullins, David Caltrider, Marvin Morgan, Donte St. John, Ken Feil, Vicki Lynn Puzinas, Danny Levinson, Shantel R. Chappel *(Students)*, Tony Lincoln, Wilbert Bradley, Roy Dean, Jamie Newell, Ronald Merians *(Guards)*.

If there's a shred of truth in this dramatic comedy set in a modern high school, then education has reached a new low point. Nolte is a 15-year veteran of the educational wars. He works at the fictional John Fitzgerald Kennedy High School (actually shuttered Central High in Columbus, Ohio). His fellow workers include Dano, aptly named "Ditto" because he never actually teaches, just hands out mimeographed exams to his students; Garfield, a man who is petrified of his students; and several others. The most interesting teacher at JFK is Mulligan, an escapee from a mental hospital, who teaches history by becoming the character about whom he is lecturing. Thus, when it's time for the kids to memorize the Gettysburg Address, they hear it from the lips of Mulligan, dressed as the Great Emancipator. And to illustrate his point about the crossing of the Delaware River during the Revolutionary War, Mulligan dresses up like the Father of Our Country. It's bizarre but highly effective as the students begin to better understand what history means. The wimpy principal of the school is Schallert, who is so stunned by the chaos around him that all he can do is grin and nod. Hirsch is the school's vice-principal, a man dedicated to protecting the school's reputation, a martinet and a very tough cookie. When a recent graduate files suit against the school because they allowed him to leave as an illiterate, the plot heats up. Grant is the hard-nosed superintendent of schools and Williams is the attorney who is serving notice on the school. She is also a graduate of JFK and has been crazy about Nolte ever since she put on her first lipstick and sat in his classes. Nolte's rep is that he likes the students and they trust him as they trust no other teacher. Macchio is an illiterate, street-wise young man who skips classes, runs with a rough crowd, and has a terrible life at home. Nolte sees that the boy has something to offer and attempts to befriend him, earn his trust, and show him the folly of his ways. Several plots are happening at the same time, in a mini-GRAND HOTEL fashion, and one of them has to do with gym teacher Metrano impregnating Dern, a student. Lots of action as students are attacked, dope is dealt, and even Garfield gets bitten by one of his charges. Plots, subplots, counterplots are mixed with many comic moments and some serious, even preachy sequences. Black comedy emerges when Dano, who does his customary handing out of the mimeo papers and then takes a snooze, dies at his desk. But the students are so used to seeing him asleep on the job, they don't realize that he's croaked until the next day. Hirsch and Nolte are, at first, good friends. That comes to an end when Hirsch attempts to manipulate Nolte's testimony in the case. Nolte is an honest man and will not cover up so Hirsch tries to get him dismissed because he senses Nolte will tell the truth about several subjects, even the delicate one concerning

Dern's abortion. Williams, now an adult, is still having her schoolgirl crush on teacher Nolte and is hurt to find that his feet are clay. Upon discovering that, she leaves his apartment; then the two are reunited at the conclusion (to nobody's surprise). It is Williams who inspires Nolte back to the ideals of teaching after it appeared that he was a burnt-out case. Movies about U.S. high schools, or their equivalents in England, have always had a following. Some of the best ever include GOODBYE MR. CHIPS, THE BLACKBOARD JUNGLE, TO SIR WITH LOVE, and FAST TIMES AT RIDGEMONT HIGH. Most of those movies made money, but this very expensive picture failed to find an audience. Hiller had done this kind of thing before in HOSPITAL, where he kept several pots boiling, but the juxtapositioning of reality against some unbelievable fantasy did not help matters. The realistic moments are well done and the message is clearly stated that teachers are overworked and, in some cases, not qualified to do what they do. Private school enrollment probably rose after parents sat through this picture. The story came from the brother team of Irwin and Aaron Russo (Aaron was the manager of Bette Midler before getting into pictures) and the script was by a young man who was not many years out of high school so the actuality of it was still fresh in 27-year-old McKinney's mind. Like many movies, TEACHERS tries to be all things to all people and consequently falls between the stools, never sure if it's a drama with comedy or a comedy with drama. A knockout score done by several heavy rockers is an added plus. The "R" rating is mostly due to the harsh language, some of the student violence, and one scene where Nolte challenges Williams to walk naked down the hall (it's a metaphor for being honest) and she does just that. An admirable attempt at a fresh version of an old genre, TEACHERS falls short, but not by much.

p, Aaron Russo; d, Arthur Hiller; w, W.R. McKinney (based on a story by Aaron Russo, Irwin Russo); ph, David M. Walsh (Metrocolor); ed, Don Zimmerman; md, Sandy Gibson; prod d, Richard MacDonald; set d, John M. Dwyer; cos, Ruth Myers, Norman Burza, Michele Neely; spec eff, Chuck Schulthies, Jr.; m/l, ZZ Top, Bob Seger, Joe Cocker, Night Ranger, 38 Special, The Motels, Freddie Mercury, Ian Hunter, Roman Holliday, Eric Martin and Friends.

Comedy/Drama   **Cas.**   **(PR:C-O   MPAA:R)**

TERMINATOR, THE*   (1984) 108m Hemdale-Pacific Western/Orion
                                                                                                    c

Arnold Schwarzenegger *(Terminator)*, Michael Biehn *(Kyle Reese)*, Linda Hamilton *(Sarah Connor)*, Paul Winfield *(Traxler)*, Lance Henriksen *(Vukovich)*, Rick Rossovich *(Matt)*, Bess Mott *(Ginger)*, Earl Boen *(Silberman)*, Dick Miller *(Pawn Shop Clerk)*, Shawn Schepps *(Nancy)*, Bruce M. Kerner *(Desk Sergeant)*, Franco Columbu *(Future Terminator)*, Bill Paxton *(Punk Leader)*, Brad Reardon, Brian Thompson *(Punks)*, William Wisher, Jr, Ken Fritz, Tom Oberhaus *(Policemen)*, Ed Dogans *(Cop in Alley)*, Joe Farago *(TV Anchorman)*, Hettie Lynne Hurtes *(TV Anchorwoman)*, Tony Mirelez *(Station Attendant)*, Philip Gordan, Anthony T. Trujillio *(Mexican Boys)*, Stan Yale *(Derelict)*, Al Kahn, Leslie Morris, Hugh Farrington, Harriet Medin, Loree Frazier, James Ralston *(Customers)*, Norman Friedman *(Cleaning Man)*, Barbara Powers *(Ticket Taker)*, Wayne Stone *(Tanker Driver)*, David Pierce *(Tanker Partner)*, John E. Bristol *(Phone Booth Man)*, Webster Williams *(Reporter)*, Patrick Pinney *(Bar Customer)*, Bill W. Richmond *(Bartender)*, Chino "Fats" Williams *(Truck Driver)*, Gregory Robbins *(Motel Customer)*, Marianne Muellerleile *(Wrong Sarah)*, John Durban *(Sentry)*.

The sleeper hit of the fall of 1984, James Cameron's THE TERMINATOR is a well-crafted, imaginative, and stylish low-budget science fiction film which will please any fan of the genre. The film opens in the hellish Los Angeles of the year 2029. We see a world destroyed by nuclear war and run by sophisticated machines who have decided to obliterate the weak humans who created them. The action then shifts back to Los Angeles in 1984. In two separate locations, two naked men, Schwarzenegger and Biehn, materialize out of what appear to be small electrical storms. Both men acquire clothes and wander off into the night. The next day, after having stolen several deadly weapons (including a .45 automatic pistol with a laser beam sight and an Uzi submachine gun) and a car, Schwarzenegger looks up the name "Sarah Connor" in the phone book. There are three Sarah Connors listed. The stoical mystery man sets off to kill each of them. Later, at the police station, coffee-swilling, chain-smoking detective Winfield and his partner Henriksen are shocked to discover that two women named Sarah Connor have been murdered within hours of each other. Learning that there are three women with that name in the phone book, they try to contact the third, Hamilton, but she has gone out for the evening. Noticing she is being followed by Biehn, the nervous Hamilton ducks into a nightclub called "Tech Noir" and tries to disappear into the crowd. Schwarzenegger traces Hamilton to the nightclub, but just as he aims the red laser beam at her forehead, Biehn appears at the bar and shoots the big man with a shotgun. Unshaken, Schwarzenegger turns and takes aim at Biehn, who pumps several additional rounds into the killer. Schwarzenegger is knocked to the floor, but despite several fatal gunshot wounds, he gets up and begins firing his Uzi. Biehn again shoots Schwarzenegger, knocking him through a window. A confused Hamilton allows Biehn to spirit her out of the bar, but Schwarzenegger again gets up and gives chase. In a flurry of dialog spoken during the car chase, Biehn explains that Schwarzenegger is not human, but a cyborg. Made from a robotic frame with flesh and blood grown around it,

Schwarzenegger is a "Terminator" whose only purpose is to kill. He cannot be stopped. When Hamilton expresses doubt that science has advanced that far yet, Biehn informs her that he and Schwarzenegger are from the future. Explaining the situation in the year 2029, Biehn tells Hamilton that she will give birth to a man who will lead a successful revolution against the machines that rule the Earth. In an effort to change this victory, the machines sent Schwarzenegger back in time to kill her, thus preventing the existence of the revolutionary leader. Biehn managed to follow the Terminator into the past, and it is his job to protect her. The car chase ends in a vicious crash from which Schwarzenegger walks away. Hamilton and Biehn, however, are arrested and brought to jail. Thinking Biehn crazy (and maybe Hamilton too for believing him), the police prepare to ship him off to a mental ward. Soon after, Schwarzenegger arrives at the police station and asks to see Hamilton. When told he cannot, the Terminator replies, "I'll be back," and simply drives his car into the station. The killing machine then walks the halls of the police station killing every cop coming at him during his search for Hamilton. Luckily, Hamilton and Biehn escape the carnage and once again try to hide from Schwarzenegger. The Terminator, of course, follows them wherever they go. During the chase, Hamilton grows attracted to Biehn and they make love. In the climactic scene, Schwarzenegger commandeers a gasoline tanker and tries to run down Hamilton. A severly injured Biehn manages to blow the truck up and incinerate Schwarzenegger. Hamilton tries to get the wounded Biehn on his feet, as behind her the silver robotic skeleton of Schwarzenegger rises from the flames and continues its murderous mission. Hamilton and Biehn run into a nearby factory in an effort to escape the robot, but the metal monster easily follows. In last-ditch effort to kill the robot, Biehn shoves a pipe bomb into the monster's chest cavity and blows it to pieces. Hamilton goes to Biehn, but discovers he has been killed in the explosion. Crying over his body, she is startled when the damaged torso of the robot comes to life and continues to pursue her by dragging itself along. Crawling away (she had previously broken her ankle), Hamilton manages to lure the legless robot into a press and crush it into oblivion. We next see Hamilton months later, in Mexico. She is pregnant with Biehn's child. It is obvious that he is the father of the man whose life he traveled back in time to save. Hamilton drives away from the gathering nuclear clouds, determined to fulfill her part in the future of mankind. THE TERMINATOR is an amazingly effective film that almost becomes doubly impressive because of its small budget. Looking better than most big-budget efforts, it contains dozens of impressive visual effects, including some very good stop-motion animation. The film is the second directing effort of former art director-special effects man James Cameron, whose first film, PIRANHA II-THE SPAWNING, showed little promise for a directing future. Cameron and producer Hurd (who married after shooting THE TERMINATOR) met when working on BATTLE BEYOND THE STARS, he as art director, she as production manager. Determined to make their own film, the pair began to develop Cameron's idea for THE TERMINATOR. They sent the script to Schwarzenegger and he was impressed enough to lend his support. Not only is Schwarzenegger physically impressive as the unstoppable killing machine, but he brings into play a sly sense of humor which serves the film well. Part of the appeal of this violent film is the wit that surfaces when least expected. This combination of action and humor proved potent at the box-office and the film made millions. Trouble arose for Cameron, however, when science-fiction writer Harlan Ellison threatened to sue the production company for copyright infringement. Claiming that the writer-director borrowed liberally from several of his stories and teleplays (two episodes of "Outer Limits"–one entitled "Soldier," the other "Demon with a Glass Hand"–and an episode of "Star Trek" entitled "City on the Edge of Forever" were cited), Ellison agreed to an out-of-court cash settlement, and an on-screen acknowledgement of his works on all video releases and cable showings of THE TERMINATOR (some of the terms of the agreement were botched by the production company and the cash settlement escalated). Legal problems notwithstanding, THE TERMINATOR is a fresh, exciting and surprisingly witty science-fiction film that will thrill any adult audience.

p, Gale Anne Hurd; d, James Cameron; w, Cameron, Hurd, William Wisher, Jr.; ph, Adam Greenberg (CFI color); m, Brad Fiedel; ed, Mark Goldblatt; art d, George Costello; set d, Maria Rehman Caso; cos, Hilary Wright; spec eff, Stan Winston, Gene Warren, Jr., Peter Kleinow; m/l, "You Can't Do that" (Ricky Phillips), "Pictures of You" (Jay Ferguson), "Photoplay" (Tahnee Cain, Pug Baker, Jonathan Cain), "Intimacy" (Lynn Van Hek, Joe Dolce), "Burnin' in the Third Degree" (Cain, Mugs Cain, Dave Amato, Brett Tuggle, Phillips); makeup, Jefferson Dawn.

Science Fiction   Cas.   (PR:O   MPAA:R)

THEY'RE PLAYING WITH FIRE*

(1984) 96m Hickmar/New World c

Sybil Danning (Dianne Stevens), Eric Brown (Jay Richards), Andrew Prine (Michael Stevens), Paul Clemens (Martin "Bird" Johnson), K. T. Stevens (Lillian Stevens), Gene Bicknell (George Johnson), Curt Ayers (Bartender), Dominick Brascia (Glenn), Bill Conklin (The Preacher), Therese Hanses (Pub Singer), Greg Kaye (Dale), Suzanne Kennedy (Janice), Violet Manes (Jenny), Alvy Moore (Jimbo), Joe Portaro (Professor), Beth Schaffell (Cynthia), Marlene Schmidt (Gas Station Customer), Margaret Wheeler (Lettie Stevens).

Danning is an English professor who seduces one of her students, then enlists him in a scheme to help her and her husband (Prine) kill the latter's mother and grandmother to gain an enormous inheritance. Plans go awry when someone else in a mask starts killing off characters left and right. Annoying, vapid melodrama has nothing going for it except three nude scenes by the reigning queen of the "B"s, Danning. Thanks to a canny, if misleading, ad campaign, the film made a good amount of money.

p, Howard Avedis, Marlene Schmidt; d, Avedis; w, Avedis, Schmidt; ph, Gary Graver (Deluxe Color); m, John Cacavas; ed, Jack Tucker; art d, Rosemary Brandenburg.

Crime   Cas.   (PR:O   MPAA:R:)

THIEF OF HEARTS**

(1984) 100m PAR c

Steven Bauer (Scott Muller), Barbara Williams (Mickey Davis), John Getz (Ray Davis), David Caruso (Buddy Calamara), Christine Ebersole (Janie Pointer), George Wendt (Marty Morrison), Alan North (Sweeney), Romy Windsor (Nicole), Joe Nesnow (Security Guard), Gordon Pulliam (Parking Attendant), David McElhatton (Himself), Annette Sinclair, Alena Downs (College Girls), Jane Marla Robbins, Ray Hassett, Marcia Wolf, Brenda Currin, Cindy Lambert (Reception Guests), Rick Holly (Helicopter Pilot), Vince Deadrick, Jr., Irene Poitrowski (Stunts).

An interesting movie from first-time director Stewart (who had previously written BLUE LAGOON and AN OFFICER AND A GENTLEMAN) with the theme that "it's a horrible experience to be robbed, but to have someone steal one's innermost thoughts is the most horrifying experience of all." Williams and Getz are a well-to- do San Francisco couple on the town celebrating their sixth anniversary when Bauer, a professional thief with a sense of style and taste, is in their home stealing various items. While on his foray, Bauer comes across the personal diaries written by Williams after he has noticed a painting of her on the wall. He takes the journals home with him and when their loss is discovered by Williams, she is understandably worried as they reveal her innermost thoughts and sexual fantasies and read like a two-bit romance novel. The more Bauer reads of the woman's writing, the more enthralled he becomes. He tracks her down and begins to insinuate himself into her life. Since he is armed with the knowledge of what turns her on, she is easy prey as he keeps bumping into her in various places, starts to flirt and she, of course, responds. Getz is a writer of children's fiction and so busy with his latest work that he is neglecting her so this mild flirtation is stimulating for Williams. After bumping into each other several times (really bumping in one case), they meet in a grocery store and Bauer tells her that he is a wealthy businessman who needs someone to decorate his place. Since that is exactly what she does for a living, the bait is now in her mouth and he is slowly reeling in his catch. They have coffee together and make a date for him to see another site she's decorated. He shows up at the exhibit where her work is being displayed and follows that up with flowers and a note asking her to have lunch with him. They meet at the San Francisco marina, he takes her out for a sail, and hires her to do his residence. As if Bauer didn't know, the sailboat ride turns out to be the actual living out of one of her fantasies. Later, Getz sees a change in Williams and wonders if there might be something going on between her and the mysterious client she's spoken about. Jealousy rears and Getz sits down to have a heart-to-heart talk with Wendt, his publisher, who tells the writer that he has been taking Williams for granted and acting like a cad around the house. Meanwhile, Bauer has seduced Williams in an interesting scene as he was teaching her how to fire a gun at his practice range at home. The affair goes on but she is becoming a trifle frightened by the way he is able to have such intimate knowledge about her and is unwilling to reveal anything about himself, except for the superficial fabrication he has invented. Bauer's partner in crime is Caruso and tempers are flaring between the men. They pull off a job and Caruso kills a cop in the course of the robbery, thus making Bauer an accessory to murder. Williams begins to pull away from Bauer and the more she distances herself from him, the more possessive he becomes. What began as a lark is now an obsession for Bauer. Getz has become suspicious, trails Bauer, and learns his true vocation and identity. Getz follows Bauer to Caruso's residence and once inside, he spots one of his stolen paintings, then is nearly shot by Caruso. Wendt has been on the tail with Getz and manages to save the irate husband before he is killed. Getz goes right to the police and informs them of Caruso, then rushes to his wife's office to tell her what he's learned. Bauer has beaten Getz to her office and is about to reveal his identity and what he's done when Getz races in. The two men battle and Bauer beats a hasty retreat. Getz and Williams reconcile and the next evening, when they go out to dinner, Bauer again breaks into their residence for one last time so he can read the remainder of Williams' journal. Not long after he's arrived, Caruso shows up to rob the place again. The two partners get into a battle and one of them is stabbed but we can't tell which. Meanwhile, the cops have been alerted and Getz and Williams have come home to hear the noises upstairs. Before the boys in blue can respond, the couple is confronted on the stairway by one of the intruders. Since both are wearing masks, they don't know whose face is beneath the disguise. The man is pointing a gun and Williams is also armed. A brief stand- off occurs and then the robber is shot dead. Williams doesn't recall pulling the trigger and when the cops finally arrive, Williams goes upstairs to find a wounded Bauer about to make his escape into the night through her bedroom window. She then realizes that she didn't fire the gun at all but it was Bauer who shot Caruso, thereby saving her life and the life of Getz. In true "Zorro" style, Bauer slips away after a poignant last glance at Williams and disappears into the darkness. All of the performances are good and the picture has a great deal of suspense and is not unlike BODY HEAT, which preceded it, and THE JAGGED EDGE, which came later. A pretty good movie that could have taken a bit of trimming. There's no question that it's an original idea and it might have had more acceptance if the author had allowed someone else to direct it. Getz was earlier seen in a superb thriller, BLOOD SIMPLE, and Bauer was previously seen in the awful remake of SCARFACE, where he played the role originally done by George Raft. In that dreadful bloodletting, Bauer was one of the very rare actors who stood out. In June of 1986, Bauer, of Latino heritage, received the NOSOTROS award as the "Most Promising Newcomer." NOSOTROS is the group spearheaded by Ricardo Montalban that has just about every actor of Hispanic background as a member.

p, Don Simpson, Jerry Bruckheimer; d&w, Douglas Day Stewart; ph, Andrew Laszlo (Metrocolor); m, Harold Faltermeyer; ed, Tom Rolf; art d, Edward Richardson; set d, R. Chris Westlund; cos, Michael Kaplan; spec eff, Michael Lantieri.

Crime/Romance   Cas.   (PR:C-O   MPAA:R)

THIS IS SPINAL TAP*½   (1984) 82m Spinal Tap/EM c (AKA: SPINAL TAP)

Rob Reiner (*Marty DiBergi*), Michael McKean (*David St. Hubbins*), Christopher Guest (*Nigel Tufnel*), Harry Shearer (*Derek Smalls*), R.J. Parnell (*Mick Shrimpton*), David Kaff (*Viv Savage*), Tony Hendra (*Ian Faith*), Bruno Kirby (*Tommy Pischedda*), Kimberly Stringer, Chazz Dominguez, Shari Hall (*Heavy Metal Fans*), Jean Cromie (*Ethereal Fan*), Patrick Maher (*New York Emcee*), Ed Begley, Jr. (*John "Stumpy" Pepys*), Danny Kortchmar (*Ronnie Pudding*), Fran Drescher (*Bobbi Flekman*), Patrick MacNee (*Sir Denis Eton-Hogg*), Memo Vera (*Bartender*), Julie Payne, Dane Carvey (*Mime Waitresses*), Sandy Helberg (*Angelo DiMentibello*), Robin Mencken (*Antelo's Associate*), Zane Buzby (*Rolling Stone Reporter*), Billy Crystal (*Morty the Mime*), Jennifer Child (*Limo Groupie*), J. J. Barry (*Rack Jobber*), George McDaniel (*Southern Rock Promoter*), Paul Benedict (*Tucker "Smitty" Brown*), Anne Churchill (*Reba*), Howard Hesseman (*Terry Ladd*), Paul Shortino (*Duke Fame*), Cherie Darr, Lara Cody (*Fame Groupies*), Andrew J. Lederer (*Student Promoter*), Russ Kunkel (*Eric "Stumpy Joe" Childs*), Diana Duncan, Gina Marie Pitrello (*Jamboree Bop Dancers*), June Chadwick (*Jeanine Pettibone*), Vicki Blue (*Cindy*), Joyce Hyser (*Belinda*), Gloria Gifford (*Airport Security Official*), Paul Shaffer (*Artie Fufkin*), Archie Hahn (*Room Service Guy*), Charles Levin (*Disc & Dat Manager*), Wonderful Smith (*Janitor*), Anjelica Huston (*Polly Deutsch*), Chris Romano, Daniel Rodgers (*Little Druids*), Fred Willard (*Lt. Hookstratten*), Fred Asparagus (*Joe "Mama" Besser*), Rodney Kemerer, Robert Bauer.

A funny and sometimes flawed documentary spoof of a British rock group that is so on the nose sometimes that it goes beyond parody and swings around to be so realistic that many in the audience thought it was actual. "Spinal Tap" is a fictitious, aging, heavy metal British rock band who are limping their way across the U.S. while a "Rockumentary" film is being made about them by Reiner. Reiner is a Yank who has been following the group since they burst on the scene 17 years before and now that they are fading, he decides to do their story rather than make some commercials for Wheat Thins. Every disaster that can befall a rock group happens to Guest, McKean, and Shearer. Management woes, promotional difficulties, hotel accommodations that fall apart, phony business people, lousy props, and an album that hasn't yet been distributed in the stores, all add up to major problems. Their new album, "Smell the Glove," is deemed to have a "sexist" cover and they refuse to compromise, even after foul-mouthed promotion woman Drescher reads them the riot act at a party send-up, and the record company's owner, MacNee, gives them what for. The group is trying to hold on to their style, which attracted so many screaming teenagers years before but is somewhat old hat now. Their audience has faded and they are frustrated and the result is often hysterical, as their smarmy manager, Hendra, and the local Chicago promo man, Shaffer, get in their licks. (Hendra is also a well-known comedy writer and Shaffer is, of course, the band leader on David Letterman's TV show.) The satire is knowledgeable and anyone who has ever been associated with the rock music business (or even on the periphery) will appreciate this more than the average Joe or Jane. Although there is a script credit, it was a *cinema- verite* improvisation with just an idea of what was to be in each scene and Reiner filming the scenes until he got whatever it was he wanted. The best moments from each scene were edited into the final print and nothing was rehearsed except the tunes. Even the songs are on the money when it comes to poking fun, and although such tunes as "Hell Hole," "Tonight, I'm Gonna Rock You Tonight," and "Sex Farm Woman" won't top the charts, they'll make you laugh. In one of the songs, the following lyric is sung: "My baby fits me like a flesh tuxedo/I love to sink her with my pink torpedo/ Big bottom, drive me out of my mind/ How can I leave this behind?" The amazing part of the movie is that the leads are all from the U.S. but their British accents are sensational and they never step out of character. The look and feel of a heavy metal band is perfectly captured and any resemblance between "Spinal Tap" and known groups is surely intended. Lots of cameos to delight the eyes and they even issued an album, "The Best of Spinal Tap," which became a hit in Japan. Inventing a musical group had been done before on TV with "The Monkees," but whereas that was fantasy, this is burlesque and it's as delicious as it's going to get. Reiner also made THE SURE THING and

the 1986 hit STAND BY ME, proving his promise shown with this movie was more than just promise, it was for real. Reiner, at his young age, is already a better director than his father, Carl. The language and some raw scenes make this out of range for young eyes but the chances are that even if the dialog would be cleansed, youngsters wouldn't understand it as it requires the viewer to have foreknowledge of the type of musical groups being jabbed.

p, Karen Murphy; d, Rob Reiner; w, Christopher Guest, Michael McKean, Harry Shearer, Reiner; ph, Peter Smokler (CFI Color); m, Guest, McKean, Shearer, Reiner; ed, Kent Beyda, Kim Secrist, Robert Leighton; prod d, Bryan Jones; cos. Renee Johnston; m/1, "Tonight I'm Going to Rock You Tonight," "Hell Hole," Guest, McKean, Shearer, Reiner.

Comedy   Cas.   (PR:C-O   MPAA:R)

THREE CROWNS OF THE SAILOR* (1984, Fr.) 117m L'Institut National de l'Audiovi suel-Antenne 2 c-bw (LES TROIS COURONNES DU MATELOT)

Jean-Bernard Guillard (*The Sailor*), Philippe Deplanche (*The Student*), Jean Badin (*The Officer*), Nadege Clair (*Maria*), Lisa Lyon (*Mathilde*), Claude Derepp (*The Captain*), Frank Oger (*The Blindman*), Raoul Guillet, Hugo Santiago (*Voices*), Jose de Carvalho, Mostepha Djadjam, Andre Gomes, Adelaide Joao, Claudio Martinez, Marthe Reynolds, Oscar Tebar.

A strongly praised work of surrealism from expatriate Chilean director Ruiz –living and working in France since 1973–about a story-telling sailor, Guillard, who catches a student murdering his tutor and proceeds to regale the lad with tales of his bizarre adventures in South American ports visiting the seedy opium dens and frequenting the brothels. It's not what happens in THREE CROWNS OF THE SAILOR but how it happens. Following the tradition of surrealism set in the 1920s, Ruiz directs this film with no basis in logic or reality–dreamy locations are filled with macabre individuals who utter dialog that is mystical nonsense. As difficult as it is to pin down, THREE CROWNS OF THE SAILOR is thoroughly enjoyable just as long as you don't try to understand. (In French; English subtitles.)

p, Jean Lefaux, Maya Feuiette, Jose-Luis Vasconselos; d, Raul Ruiz; w, Ruiz, Emilio de Solar, Francois Ede; ph, Sacha Vierny; m, Jorge Arriagada; ed, Janine Verneau, Valeria Sarmiento, Jacqueline Simoni-Adamus, Pascale Sueur; set d, Bruno Beauge, Pierre Pitrou.

Fantasy   (PR:O   MPAA:NR)

TIGHTROPE½   (1984) 114m Malpaso/WB c

Clint Eastwood (*Wes Block*), Genevieve Bujold (*Beryl Thibodeaux*), Dan Hedaya (*Detective Molinari*), Alison Eastwood (*Amanda Block*), Jennifer Beck (*Penny Block*), Marco St. John (*Leander Wolfe*), Rebecca Perle (*Becky Jacklin*), Regina Richardson (*Sarita*), Randi Brooks (*Jamie Cory*), Margaret Howell (*Judy Harper*), Rebecca Clemons (*Girl With Whip*), Janet MacLachlan (*Dr. Yarlofsky*), Graham Paul (*Luther*), Donald Barber (*Shorty*), Jamie Rose (*Melanie Silber*), Bill Holliday (*Police Chief*), John Wilmot (*Medical Examiner*), Margie O'Dair (*Mrs. Holstein*), Joy N. Houck, Jr. (*Swap Meet Owner*), Stuart Baker-Bergen (*Blond Surfer*), Robert Harvey (*Lonesome Alice*), Ron Gural (*Coroner Dudley*), Layton Martens (*Sgt. Surtees*), Richard Charles Boyle (*Dr. Fitzpatrick*), Becki Davis (*Nurse*), Jonathan Sacher (*Gay Boy*), Valerie Thibodeaux (*Black Hooker*), Lionel Ferbos (*Plainclothes Gus*), Eliott Keener (*Sandoval*), David Valdes (*Manes*), James Borders (*Carfano*), Fritz Manes (*Valdes*), Jonathan Shaw (*Quono*), Don Lutenbacher (*Dixie President*), George Wood (*Conventioneer*), Kimberly Georgoulis (*Sam*), Glenda Byars (*Lucy Davis*), John Schluter, Jr. (*Piazza Cop*), Nick Krieger (*Rannigan*), Lloyd Nelson (*Patrolman Restic*), David Dahlgren (*Patrolman Julio*), Rod Masterson (*Patrolman Gallo*), Glenn Wright (*Patrolman Redfish*), Angela Hill (*Woman Reporter*), Ted Saari (*TV News Reporter*).

Eastwood is again on familiar ground as he plays a maverick police officer. Director Tuggle, who also wrote the script for this as well as for ESCAPE FROM ALCATRAZ, makes his feature film directorial debut here and shows that he's better behind the typewriter than behind the camera. Eastwood is a New Orleans police officer on the trail of a vicious killer who specializes in dispatching the prostitutes and massage parlor girls who work the picturesque French Quarter. We don't get a chance to see the killer's face, only his distinctive sneakers. The murderer and Eastwood have something in common. They both enjoy the working girls of New Orleans. Eastwood's wife deserted him some time before and he is raising his daughters by himself. The girls are bright, sharp, and adorable and he loves them deeply, which makes his forays into the seamy side of life all the more startling. As Eastwood begins to learn more about the killer, he realizes that there are similarities between himself and the man, a Louisiana version of "Jack the Ripper." Eastwood meets rape counselor Bujold and they are at odds with each other at once. The ice, of course, melts and a romantic interest is kindled, spurred by his daughters' interest in having a new mother around the house. The murderer is running rampant and Eastwood is suffering from nightmares about it. (One of his dreams is a cheat as Tuggle makes it seem real and appear that Eastwood himself is the killer.) During Mardi Gras, Eastwood and Bujold take the young girls out into the streets and we can see the sneakers of a heavily made-up clown and wonder if he will strike. He doesn't. Eastwood eventually tracks the man to a beer bottling plant and thinks he'll be able to identify him from his sneakers.

When he sees that everyone at the plant wears sneakers, he understands that it will be impossible to track the culprit that way. Further research uncovers the man's identity, a killer who has been released from jail after a long stint for a similar murder. Bujold and the girls are at Eastwood's house when the dark-masked man, St. John, comes to the home and almost succeeds in killing the three. The men Eastwood had outside to guard the house have all been murdered by St. John and the house is now vulnerable. Predictably, Eastwood arrives in the nick of time to save the women he loves. There's a lot of *noir* in this film, both thematically and cinematographically; the dank, dark streets of the Quarter are rendered at below-register apertures by photographer Surtees in some scenes, requiring audiences to resort to their own imaginations at times, just like radio. There are just a few surprises, otherwise it rocks along the way most of Eastwood's DIRTY HARRY movies do. Not a wonderful movie, not even one of Eastwood's best. It's a curiosity to see straight arrow Eastwood in a role so kinky. His real-life daughter, Alison, makes her debut and is excellent. Diehard Eastwoodians will watch this if there he's in it and the rest will watch it on cable TV because there isn't anything else on that's any better. Now that Eastwood's gone into politics, we can only hope it influences him to cease these blood-and-sex movies and try something a little better, something as good as his BRONCO BILLY, which won everyone's heart who saw it and did no business whatsoever.

p, Clint Eastwood, Fritz Manes; d&w, Richard Tuggle; ph, Bruce Surtees (Panavision, Technicolor); m, Lennie Niehaus; ed, Joel Cox; prod d, Edward Carfagno; set d, Ernie Bishop; cos, Glenn Wright, Deborah Hopper; stunts, Wayne Van Horn, George Orrison.

Murder Mystery Cas. (PR:C-O MPAA:R)

TO CATCH A COP zero   (1984, Fr.) 90m Imacite-Coline-TF/GAU c
(RETENEZ MOI...OU JE FAIS UN MALHEUR)

Jerry Lewis (*Jerry Logan*), Michel Blanc (*Laurent Martin*), Charlotte de Turckeim (*Marie-Christine*), Laura Betti (*Carlotta Battucelli*), Maurice Risch (*Farett*).

In his stunning performance with the 1983 film THE KING OF COMEDY, Jerry Lewis surprised many as a serious actor with considerable talent. It appeared he had taken a new turn in his career after a long period of increasingly inept and inane films. Instead, Lewis went to France where he is canonized as the real king of comedy, a clown who ranks with cinema's greatest names. Lewis has called the French "...the most enthusiastic and loving audience I'd ever played to." While American critics continue to castigate his work, the French have held a retrospective of his oeuvre at the illustrious Cinematheque Francaise. So perhaps it made sense for Lewis to go to the country that adored him rather than take a risky shot as a serious actor. In this, the first of his two French movies released in 1984, Lewis plays a cop from Las Vegas visiting his ex-wife (Turckeim). She is now remarried to Frenchman Blanc and the two men can't stand each other. Lewis, the tall and cocky American, is fond of pulling practical jokes on the shorter, meeker Blanc. Eventually Blanc gets fed up with Lewis and decides to get even. He's also a cop, working on cracking a gang of art smugglers, and he gets the unwitting Lewis in on the case. Though Lewis didn't write or direct, the film has the same feelings as his later directorial efforts. In other words, it stinks. The comedy is witless and there's something genuinely pathetic about seeing the 56-year-old Lewis running around with the same high-pitched squeal he'd been using for almost 30 years. The direction more or less gives him free reign to pull his schtick and the results are terrible. Lewis looks like a bad imitation of his younger self, merely going through the motions of this poorly written comedy. Director Gerard formerly was employed as a movie theater manager and one wishes he had remained at that job for all the skill he shows here. Lewis followed this with another French comedy later in the year, an equally witless effort. (In French.)

p, Pierre Kalfon, Michel Gerard; d, Gerard; w, Gerard, David Milhaud, Jean-Francois Navarre; ph, Jean Monsigny (Fujicolor); m, Vladimir Cosma; ed, Gerard Le Du; art d, Gerard Viard, Philippe Ancellin.

Comedy (PR:A MPAA:NR)

TO OUR LOVES   (SEE: A NOS AMOURS, Fr.)

TOP SECRET!*   (1984) 90m PAR c

Omar Sharif (*Cedric*), Jeremy Kemp (*Gen. Streck*), Warren Clarke (*Col. Von Horst*), Tristram Jellinek (*Maj. Crumpler*), Val Kilmer (*Nick Rivers*), Billy J. Mitchell (*Martin*), Major Wiley (*Porter*), Gertan Klauber (*Mayor*), Richard Mayes (*Biletnikov*), Vyvyan Lorrayne (*Mme. Bergerone*), Nancy Abrahams (*Pregnant Woman*), Ian McNeice (*Blindman*), John Sharp (*Maitre D'*), Lucy Gutteridge (*Hillary Flammond*), Michael Burlington (*Waiter*), Marcus Powell (*Little German*), Louise Yaffe, Charlotte Zucker, Susan Breslau (*Cafe Diners*), Burton Zucker (*Chef*), Richard Pescud (*Priest*), John Carney (*Klaus*), O.T. (*Bruno*), Russell Sommers (*Student*), Michael Gough (*Dr. Flammond*), Sara Montague (*Crying Girl*), Peter Cushing (*Bookstore Proprietor*), Mandy Nunn (*Young Hillary*), Lee Sheward (*Young Nigel*), Janos

Kurucz (*Wagon Driver*), Sydney Arnold (*Albert Potato*), Harry Ditson (*Du Quois*), Christopher Villiers (*Nigel*), Jim Carter (*Deja Vu*), Eddie Tagoe (*Chocolate Mousse*), Dimitri Andreas (*Latrine*), Michelle Martin, Nicola Wright, Lisa Gruenberg (*Pizzahaus Girls*), Andrew Hawkins (*Pilot*), Richard Bonehill (*Scarecrow*), Gerry Paris, David Adams, Geoff Wayne, Steve Ubels, Chas Bryer, Mac MacDonald, Daisy the Cow.

A generally overlooked comedy that doesn't quite measure up to the movie made by the same authors, AIRPLANE, this is, nevertheless, very funny as it lampoons two separate genres: the spy movie and the teenage musical. Abrahams, Zucker, and Zucker began their careers with KENTUCKY FRIED MOVIE, a mixed satirical bag. From there, they took shots at airplane disaster movies and then went on to this. It's a strange mix that doesn't always work but when it does, your sides will hurt. Kilmer is a rock star who is sent to East Germany (we never know why) where he becomes embroiled in a Communist plot that involves taking over West Germany. Kilmer meets Gutteridge, the daughter of scientist Gough, who is held in captivity by the East Germans. She is involved with the underground who are trying to keep the Communist plan from happening. Gough is being forced by the Reds to design a super weapon which will insure that their plans will be a success and make them unbeatable. Sharif is a spy and he is uproarious in what amounts to a cameo appearance, even though he gets top billing. The scene where Sharif is crushed in a car-crunching machine, along with his Mercedes, and lives, and tells Kilmer to reach into his "glove compartment" will have you on the floor. The plot is not easy to describe as it is deliberately so convoluted that it parodies pictures like THE SPY WHO CAME IN FROM THE COLD and other John Le Carre works. When the addition of music and the Elvis Presley-like character are put in, plot goes out the window at times to allow Kilmer to sing various tunes. There is no reason why these songs are there; they just seem to happen whenever they feel like happening, but the picture is so high-spirited and so nonsensical that logic must be set aside from the opening credits. Kilmer teams with Gutteridge and they run into an ex-beau of hers, Villiers, and he seems to be helping but turns out to be one of the bad guys behind the whole ploy (a takeoff on Alfred Hitchcock's standard story: "innocent person is accused of crime he 'or she' didn't commit; person meets person of the opposite sex who doesn't believe innocence; they must get to third party who will clear first party of crime but third party turns out to be the brains behind the plot--we've just described about eight Hitchcock movies). Villiers professes to be part of the Resistance and takes the hero and heroine to meet a group of men (all named after various French words, see cast list) and then tries to crush their rebellion. A terrific ending that is pulse-pounding caps the action and tickles the funny bone at the same time. One joke after another and wildly inventive sight gags that have nothing to do with the plot. There is more laughter here than in any three John Landis' movies. People who understand Yiddish or Bavarian German will appreciate it even more as there are several jokes in Yiddish that score. Kilmer and Gutteridge are in a German restaurant and she orders a meal for them from the German waiter. What she is actually saying are several very rude remarks which we cannot translate here for fear of losing the family audience. Satirizing the teen musical or the spy film would have been enough. Combining the two was a bit much. Still, it's worth seeing and moves at a swift pace with loads of laughter. They could have called it "Beach Blanket Espionage."

p, Jon Davidson, Hunt Lowry; d, Jim Abrahams, David Zucker, Jerry Zucker; w, Abrahams, D. Zucker, J. Zucker, Martyn Burke; ph, Christopher Challis (Metrocolor); m, Maurice Jarre; ed, Bernard Gribble; prod d; Peter Lamont; art d, John Fenner, Michael Lamont; set d, Crispian Sallis; cos, Emma Porteous; spec eff, Nick Allder; ch, Gillian Gregory; m/l, "How Silly Can You Get," Phil Pickett, "Spend This Night with Me," Mike Moran, Abrahams, D. Zucker, J. Zucker, "Straighten Out the Rug," Paul Hudson, Abrahams, D. Zucker, J. Zucker, Martyn Burke.

Comedy/Spy/Musical Cas. (PR:C MPAA:PG)

TORCHLIGHT*½   (1984) 91m UCO/Film Ventures c

Pamela Sue Martin (*Lillian Gregory*), Steve Railsback (*Jake Gregory*), Ian McShane (*Sidney*), Al Corley (*Al*), Rita Taggart (*Rita*), Arnie Moore (*Richard*).

Martin, a television actress known for her appearances on "Nancy Drew" and "Dynasty," attempted a career move as writer-actress with this film but the results are far from satisfactory. She plays a successful artist commissioned to do a painting for Railsback, a rich owner of a Los Angeles construction firm. On their first meeting he practically undresses her with his eyes and before you know it the two are married. At their first anniversary Railsback gives Martin diamond earrings, then pierces her ears in an intense moment bordering on the sadomasochistic. At an art opening the two meet McShane. He takes them to a party at his home and introduces them to the art of freebasing cocaine. Though Martin dislikes the experience, Railsback is ent, rralled and quickly becomes a junkie. His entire life revolves around the water pipe used by freebasers. This slowly takes its toll on his marriage and eventually Martin leaves him. After several months the two meet again. Martin is now holding an important exhibition of her work while Railsback is a broken man, a slave to his cocaine addiction. This film, paved with good intentions, is marred by a poorly devised script. Character motivations are often unclear, resulting in a story that never seems to know what direction to take. That Martin would initially fall for Railsback after his smarmy come-on requres considerable tolerance by the viewer. Railsback's character is the most poorly devised: one moment he's a loving husband and the next he's an intense maniac. His irrational behavior is a given long before his cocaine abuse begins making one wonder what exactly was Martin's scripted intention. Eventually the story settles down but by then is no more effective than an average made-for-television social drama. As an actress, Martin fares better. Her character is the most realistic to emerge from the inconsistencies, though it's not much of an extension past Martin's television work. Her husband Manuel Rojas served as the film's executive producer.

p, Joel Douglas, Michael Schroeder; d, Tom Wright; w, Pamela Sue Martin, Eliza Moorman; ph, Alex Phillips; m, Michael Cannon; art d, Craig Stearns; m/l, "All the Love in the World," Cannon.

Drama   (PR:O MPAA:R)

TOY SOLDIERS*   (1984) 91m New World c

Jason Miller (Sarge), Cleavon Little (Buck), Rodolfo De Anda (Col. Lopez), Terri Garber (Amy), Tracy Scoggins (Monique), Willard Pugh (Ace), Jim Greenleaf (Tom), Mary Beth Evans (Buffy), Tim Robbins (Boe), Jay Baker (Jeff), Larry Poindexter (Trevor), Alejandro Arroyo (Rafael), Douglas Warhit (Larry).

The name conjures up Sugar Plum Fairies and memories of Laurel and Hardy, doesn't it? Well, forget that. This is the type of silly movie that one might only watch if the other choice on TV is an old "Brady Bunch" episode that you've seen 10 times and know that Cindy and Marcia will indeed be friends again by the end of the show. Garber, Scoggins, Evans, and Boe are rich Beverly Hills kids who are taking a relaxing cruise off the coast of an unnamed Central American country with a few pals. What they are doing in the area is not explained other than it's a search for some excitement and/or relaxation. The captain of their yacht is the wizened Miller. He steers their course through the kelp with considerable skill, his face crinkled by too much sun and not enough Paba #2 Skin Protection.

p, E. Darrell Hallenbeck; d, David A. Fisher; w, Fisher, Walter Fox; ph, Francisco Bojorquez (CFI color); m, Leland Bond; ed, Geoffrey Rowland.

Adventure   **Cas.**   (PR:O MPAA:R)

TREASURE OF THE YANKEE ZEPHYR**
   (1984) 90m Hemdale-Pact-Fay Richwhite First City/Film Ventures c
                     (GB: RACE FOR THE YANKEE ZEPHYR)

Ken Wahl (Barney), Lesley Ann Warren (Sally), Donald Pleasence (Gibbie), George Peppard (Theo Brown), Bruno Lawrence, Robert Bruce (Barkers), Grant Tilly (Coin Collector), Harry Rutherford-Jones (Harry), Dennis Hunt, Dick Jones, Steve Nicolle, Tony Sparks, Francis Taurua, Clark Walkington (Henchmen).

Wahl, Warren, and Pleasence set off across New Zealand on a search for a missing place... 40 years after it disappeared. The three hope to discover a missing cache of $50 million, but the villainous Peppard is on their trail. Peppard doesn't make for much of a villain, resulting in more camp than drama. There are some bright moments, however, including a hair-raising speedboat chase.

p, Anthony I. Ginnane, John Barnett, David Hemmings; d, Hemmings; w, Everett de Roche; ph, Vincent Morton (Panavision, Eastmancolor); m, Brian May; ed, John Laing; prod d, Bernard Hides; art d, Virginia Bieneman; cos, Aphrodite Kondos.

Adventure   **Cas.**   (PR:A-C MPAA:PG)

2019, I NUOVI BARBARI (SEE: WARRIORS OF THE WASTELAND, Ital.)

2010**½**   (1984) 114m MGM/UA c

Roy Scheider (Heywood Floyd), John Lithgow (Walter Curnow), Helen Mirren (Tanya Kirbuk), Bob Balaban (R. Chandra), Keir Dullea (Dave Bowman), Douglas Rain (Voice of HAL 9000), Madolyn Smith (Caroline Floyd), Dana Elcar (Dimitri Moisevitch), Taliesin Jaffe (Christopher Floyd), James McEachin (Victor Milson), Mary Jo Deschanel (Betty Fernandez), Elya Baskin (Maxim Brailovsky), Savely Kramarov (Vladimir Rudenko), Oleg Rudnik (Vasali Orlov), Natasha Shneider (Irina Yakunina), Vladimir Skomarovsky (Yuri Svetlanov), Victor Steinback (Mikolai Ternovsky), Jan Triska (Alexander Kovalev), Larry Carroll (Anchorman), Herta Ware (Jessie Bowman), Cheryl Carter (Nurse), Ron Recasner (Hospital Neurosurgeon), Robert Lesser (Dr. Hirsch), Olga Mallsnerd (Voice of SAL 9000), Delana Michaels, Gene McGarr (Commercial Announcers), Arthur C. Clarke (Man on Park Bench).

The sequel to a film that didn't need a sequel is just what it had to be–a disappointment. Stanley Kubrick's ground-breaking science fiction film 2001: A SPACE ODYSSEY, caused a sensation among audiences and critics for its obtuse, mystical impenetrableness. Its total refusal to clearly explain just what exactly was happening on screen in plain English has had moviegoers debating for years. 2001: A SPACE ODYESSY came to mean

different things to different people–everything from a new awaking of spirtuality to a dreadful, pretentious bore. The very fact that it stirred up such controversy is what made the film so wonderful. That was in 1968, this is 1984. The public would be interested in a sequel, but only if it answered the questions raised by the original. 2010 picks up the story nine years later. The American government learns that the Soviets intend to travel to Jupiter to investigate what happened on the Discovery which is still orbiting the huge planet. The Soviets approach the chief architect of the original mission, Scheider, and request that the Americans join them because of their knowledge of the HAL 9000 computer. The American government agrees and the two countries team up for the voyage to Jupiter. In addition to Scheider the American crew consists of Lithgow, and the creator of HAL, Balaban. The Russian crew is co-ed and the captain of the ship is a woman, Mirren, her second is a man, Baskin, there is another, younger, woman, Schneider, and a complement of indistinguishable Soviet men. The usual tension between the two countries is worked out into an amicable working relationship, though no one quite trusts Balaban who is a bit too creepy and cryptic when it comes to his beloved HAL 9000. Things are complicated for the crew by news from Earth stating that the situation in Central America has heated up between the U.S. and the Soviets and nuclear war is imminent. The ship finally makes it to its destination, and in an orgy of state-of- the-art special effects aided by the ghostly presence of Kier Dullea (last seen as the "star-child" in 2001), the monoliths reveal their secrets. Needless to say, the long-awaited secret is a bit of a letdown. As a standard science fiction film 2010 is pretty good. It has all the right plot elements, dramatic tension and eye-popping special effects, but one just can't get over the fact that the purpose of this film is to tear down all the awe-inspiring effect of the original. The performances are uniformly good, the space-adventure scenes are excitingly handled, and the reappearance of HAL 9000 and Dullea are downright eerie, but the film fails to fascinate, enthrall and awe us like the original did. Pseudo-Renaissance man, producer- writer-director Hyams (he also did his own cinematography and the mind boggles at the negotiations that must have taken place to get that past the strong film industry unions), is not Stanley Kubrick and never will be. Author Arthur C. Clarke (who made a rare appearance outside his home of Sri Lanka to be in a cameo on a park bench in Washington, D.C.) wrote the sequel as a novel in 1980 and it worked, more or less, on paper. But 2001 and 2010 are fundamentally a cinematic experience and always have been since their inception (Clarke wrote the novel 2001: A Space Odyssey after the film was made, not before). If the orginal film had flaws it was because it was just too obtuse. 2010 suffers from being too literal.

p,d&w, Peter Hyams (based on the novel 2010: Odyssey Two by Arthur C. Clarke); ph, Hyams (Panavision, Metrocolor); m, David Shire, Richard Strauss, Gyorgi Ligeti; ed, James Mitchell, Mia Goldman; prod d, Albert Brenner; set d, Rick Simpson; cos, Patricia Norris; spec eff, Henry Millar, Richard Edlund; makeup, Michael Westmore; stunts, M. James Arnett.

Science Fiction   **Cas.**   (PR:C MPAA:PG)

ULTIMATE SOLUTION OF GRACE QUIGLEY, THE**½**
             (1984) 102m MGM-UA-Cannon c (AKA: GRACE QUIGLEY)

Katharine Hepburn (Grace Quigley), Nick Nolte (Seymour Flint), Elizabeth Wilson (Emily Watkins), Chip Zien (Dr. Herman), Kit Le Fever (Muriel), William Duell (Mr. Jenkins), Walter Abel (Homer), Truman Gaige (Sam Pincus), Frances Pole (Sarah Hodgkins), Paula Trueman (Dorothy Truger), Christopher Murney (Max Putnam), William Cain (George Quigley), Howard Sherman (Alan), Jill Eikenberry (Faith), Michael Charters (Todd), Christopher Charters (Trevor), Harris Laskawy (Mr. Argo), Edward Marshall (Reverend), Sonny Landham (Driver No. 1).

An oddball pairing of Hepburn and Nolte works for about three quarters of this black comedy, then the whole thing falls apart. The writer, Zweiback, re-edited the picture after the first go-around and had members of the Writers Guild invited to a special screening of his version. It was somewhat better than the original. Hepburn is a poverty-stricken pensioner whose family has been dead for years. She sits by her Manhattan window and watches the world go by as she huddles in her sweater and shivers, rather than turn on the expensive gas. When she sees Nolte kill her rotten landlord, she realizes that he is a hit man. Nolte is that indeed but he is troubled about his work and spends regular sessions with his analyst, superbly played by Zien. Hepburn tracks Nolte down and makes him an offer. She thinks that they can open a business that will be beneficial as well as profitable. She has many aged friends, all of whom would like to end their existence on this earth, but they don't have the guts to do it themselves. With Hepburn running the financial end and Nolte doing the jobs, they can put the old folks out of their misery and make a few bucks at the same time. Nolte, whose girl friend is the delightful Le Fever, thinks Hepburn is nuts but he's fascinated by her and finds it intriguing that his potential victims are all for dying and willing to pay well for the privilege. The business begins and is going well until Hepburn gets a bit drunk with power, and when she is insulted by a rude cab driver, she orders Nolte to kill the man. Nolte sees what's happened to her and refuses. Not only did the man not pay for the murder, he doesn't want to die, and that's not in the deal. Zien listens to Nolte's complaints and says that he thinks Hepburn will probably blow the whistle. As the two of them are going to the funeral of four dead (and satisfied) clients, Nolte decides to kill Hepburn and the picture is resolved in a fashion that defies description and believability. Good supporting work from Murney, Abel, Trueman, Gaige, and Pole as pals of Hepburn who want to depart this vale of tears. Especially good moments for Wilson, who has made a career out of playing frustrated spinsters and reminds one of a taller U.S. version of Celia Johnson. Euthanasia is a delicate topic for a comedy but the film's creative team almost brings it off. They appeared to be trying for another picture like HAROLD AND MAUDE, with Hepburn in the Ruth Gordon role and Nolte playing a rough-hewn version of Bud Cort. It just wasn't madcap enough to be an all-out comedy. Originally released at more than 100 minutes, it plays much better in the truncated 87-minute version and probably could have used about 10 minutes more deleted.

p, Menahem Golan, Yoram Globus; d, Anthony Harvey; w, A. Martin Qweiback; ph, Larry Pizer (MGM Color); m, John Addison; ed, Robert Raetano; prod d, Gary Weist; art d, Jack Blackman; set d, Christopher Kelly; cos, Ruth Morley; m/l, "So Much More," Michel Herrey; makeup, Michael Bigger, Carla White, Edouard Henriques III.

Crime/Comedy   Cas.   (PR:C MPAA:PG-13)

UN AMOUR DE SWANN   (SEE: SWANN IN LOVE)

UN AMOUR EN ALLEMAGNE   (SEE: LOVE IN GERMANY, A, Fr./Ger.)

UN DIMANCHE A LA CAMPAGNE
          (SEE: SUNDAY IN THE COUNTRY, A, Fr.)

UNDER THE VOLCANO*½   (1984) 112m Ithaca-Conacine/UNIV c

Albert Finney (Geoffrey Firmin), Jacqueline Bisset (Yvonne Firmin), Anthony Andrews (Hugh Firmin), Ignacio Lopez Tarso (Dr. Vigil), Katy Jurado (Senora Gregoria), James Villiers (Brit), Dawson Bray (Quincey), Carlos Riquelme (Bustamante), Jim McCarthy (Gringo), Rene Ruiz (Dwarf), Eliazar Garcia, Jr. (Chief of Gardens), Salvador Sanchez (Chief of Stockyards), Sergio Calderon (Chief of Municipality), Araceli Ladewuen Castelun (Maria), Emilio Fernandez (Diosdado), Arturo Sarabia (Cervantes), Roberto Martinez Sosa (Few Fleas), Hugo Stiglitz (Sinarquista), Ugo Moctezuma (Latin Consul), Isabel Vasquez (Chicken Lady), Gustavo Fernandez (Transvestite), Irene Diaz de Davila (Concepta), Alberto Olvera (Matador), Eduardo Borbolla (Don Juan Tenorio), Alejandra Saurez (Dona Ines), Rodolfo De Alejandre (Bus Driver), Juan Angel Martinez Ramos (Passenger), Martin Palomares (Dead Indian), Mario Arevalo, Ramiro Ramirez Ramirez (Horsemen), Gunter Meisner, Alfonso Castro Valle.

A bizzare journey into a mystical underworld of Mexico, 1939, during the morbid holiday known as the Day of the Dead–a day on which the souls of the dead spew forth from hell amidst the colorful and lively festivities of village known as Cuernavaca. Finney, a former British Consul is in Cuernavaca for the celebration, drinking himself to death as skulls reflect in the void of his dark sunglasses. The spirit of celebration is alive, but Finney appears lifeless, almost zombie-like as he wanders the streets. His former wife, Bisset, arrives after trying, unsuccessfully, to reach Finney by letter. With the help of Finney's brother, Andrews, they try to get him away from Mexico to a farm in the U.S., hoping it will curb his drinking. Spouting half-coherent drunken soliloquies. After wandering about the village pathetically for hours on end (at one point laughing maniacally while riding in a wild, upside down, amusement ride), Finney slips away from the village, prompting Bisset and Andrews to chase after him. Finney winds up in a sleazy bar/whorehouse, drinking himself further into oblivion with a vile dwarf, Ruiz, who offers the drunken consul one of his many prostitutes. In the meantime, Bisset and Andrews arrive, only to have Bisset run off again after learning that Finney is with a prostitute. A gang of banditos, Garcia, Sanchez, and Calderon, accuse Finney of trying to steal their horse and begin taunting him. Finney, in a fit of suicidal drunken bravery, grabs a machete, but is brutally gunned down in the rain and mud. Hearing the gunshots, Bisset, runs back to the bar, but is struck down by a runaway horse, dying in Andrews arms. Based on the brilliant 1947 novel by Malcom Lowry (the only work of any acclaim the writer produced) which was begun by the writer in 1936 at the age of twenty-seven, UNDER THE VOLCANO has been a project kicked around Hollywood since its publication. Lowry, a suicidal alcoholic, wrote the novel without any clear narrative line, relying instead on marvelously visual images, thereby causing many people to label the novel "unfilmable." Lowry's personal writings state the exact opposite, however, making constant allusions to film, writing of the novel: "It is hot music, a poem, a song, a tragedy, a comedy, a farce, and so forth...a preposterous movie." Lowry had originally intended to write the screenplay himself, writing an adaptation for F. Scott Fitzgerald's Tender is the Night and sending it to MGM with the hope of garnering interest in Under the Volcano. Five years after Lowry's death in 1957, actor Zachary Scott bought the rights, which again changed hands in 1965 after Scott's death. Luis Bunuel was then the next to become involved, followed, in succession, by Jules Dassin, Joseph Losey, Gabriel Garcia Marquez, Ken Russell, and Jerzy Skolimowski. At which point, the "unfilmable novel" ended up in the lap of John Huston. The result is very much worth the wait, bringing to life the mysticism of Mexico with a superb script by 28-year-old Gallo, exquisite photography by Figueroa, and the unparalled performance by Finney, in a part which would probably have been masterfully tackled by Humphrey Bogart had the film been made by Huston thirty years earlier on. Huston's

eye for the absurd and exotic Mexican detail–an eye which is also seen in his 1948 Mexican- based masterpiece THE TREASURE OF SIERRA MADRE. In a small role as a bartender is Emilio Fernandez, once the most prolific of Mexican directors and an actor perhaps best known to American audiences as "Mapache" in THE WILD BUNCH. A short sequence from the 1935 Peter Lorre picture MAD LOVE (here billed under its Mexican title LOS MANOS DE ORLAC) is briefly seen.

p, Moritz Borman, Wieland Schulz-Keil; d, John Huston; w, Guy Gallo (based on the novel by Malcolm Lowry); ph, Gabriel Figueroa (Technicolor); m, Alex North; ed, Roberto Silvi; prod d, Gunther Gerzso; art d, Jose Rodriguez Granada; set d, Teresa Wachter, Martin Cardenas; cos, Angela Dodson.

Drama   Cas.   (PR:O MPAA:R)

UNFAITHFULLY YOURS**   (1984) 96m FOX c

Dudley Moore (Claude Eastman), Nastassja Kinski (Daniella Eastman), Armand Assante (Maxmillian Stein), Albert Brooks (Norman Robbins), Cassie Yates (Carla Robbins), Richard Libertini (Giuseppe), Richard B. Shull (Jess Keller), Jan Triska (Jerzy Czyrek), Jane Hallaren (Janet), Bernard Behrens (Bill Lawrence), Leonard Mann (Screen Lover), Estelle Omens (Celia), Penny Peyser (Jewelry Salesgirl), Nicholas Mele (Waiter), Benjamin Rayson (Judge), Art LaFleur (Desk Sergeant), Magda Gyenes (Hungarian Singer), Frederic Franklyn (Elevator Operator), Alison Price (Kissing Girl), Frank DiElsi (Kissing Man), Edward Zammit (Lobby Attendant), Tony Abatemarco (Repairman), Daniele Jaimes Worth (Autograph Seeker), Alexander B. Reed (Man at Plaza), Ralph Buckley (Nut Vendor), Steven Hirsch, Murray Franklyn (Movie Patrons), Betty Shabazz (Woman at Plaza), Ed Van Nuys (Doorman), Robin Allyn (Teenager at Plaza), Ricky Paull Goldin, Evan Hollister Miranda, Elana Beth Rutenberg (Teenagers with Masks), Rochelle L. Kravit (Woman Patron), Gabriel E. Gyorffy (Comic), Linda Stayer (Woman in Mink), Bob Larkin (Security Guard), Kim Leslie (Ballet Dancer), Camille Hagen (Trixie), Mary Alan Hokanson (Lady on 57th Street), Jacque Foti (Maitre D').

This remake of Preston Sturges' 1948 classic features Moore in the role originally essayed by Rex Harrison. Moore plays an orchestra conductor (the same profession he held in 1978's FOUL PLAY) who is married to Kinski, an internationally renowned actress. The two are madly in love, but Brooks, Moore's brother-in-law, informs the conductor that he thinks Kinski has been fooling around. The object of her affections appears to be Assante, a handsome young violinist who is to appear in concert with Moore. After meeting with the detective who had been following Kinski, Moore is convinced he's being cuckolded. He confronts Assante, who admitts to having an affair, though the violinist has really been sleeping with Yates, Brooks' wife. Moore misunderstands him and at their concert he imagines how he will kill Kinski and set up Assante as the murderer. As in Sturges' film, the camera closes in on the conductor's eye and the scenario plays out against a musical background. Later Moore tries to play out his fantasy, but the results are disasterous. As the story comes to a close, Moore learns the truth and makes up with his forgiving wife. There are a few sparkles of humor here, but this remake is an inferior product. Whereas Sturges played out his story wit and cinematic style, Zieff's direction is flat and uninspired. The film moves from one scene to another, with a broad comic style that often telegraphs exactly what will happen to the characters. Moore, a classically trained musician, brings some skill to the conducting sequences but otherwise his character isn't all that different from any of his other recent roles. Kinski looks good but is not particularly outstanding. As the whining, annoying brother-in-law, Brooks is uncharacteristically lifeless, proof that the comedian only works best when he is allowed to direct himself. Though rated "PG," some steamy encounters between Moore and Kinski make this inappropriate for children.

p, Marvin Worth, Joe Wizan; d, Howard Zieff; w, Valerie Curtin, Barry Levinson, Robert Klane (based on the screenplay by Preston Sturges); ph, David M. Walsh (Panavision, DeLuxe Color); m, Bill Conti, Tchaikovsky violin concerto; ed, Sheldon Kahn; prod d, Albert Brenner; md, Lionel Newman; set d, Rich Simpson; cos, Kristi Zea, Darryl Athons, Thalia C. MacArthur; m/l, "Unfaithfully Yours," Stephen Bishop; stunts, Richard Brown, Karyn Raymakers, Sorin Serene Pricopie; violin solo, Pinchas Zukerman.

Comedy   Cas.   (PR:C MPAA:PG)

UNTIL SEPTEMBER*½   (1984) 95m MGM-UA c

Karen allen (Mo Alexander), Thierry Lhermitte (Xavier De La Perouse), Christopher Cazenove (Philip), Hutton Cobb (Andrew), Michael Mellinger (Col. Viola), Nitza Saul (Sylvia), Rochelle Robertson (Carol), Raphaelle Spencer (Jenny), Johanna Pavlis (Marcia), Helene Desbiez (Sophie), Steve Gadler (Carry), Edith Perret (Mme. Durand), Jean Claude Montalban, Gerard Caillaud (Airline Officials), Marie-Catherine Conti (Isabelle De La Perouse), Tiphanie Spencer (Laurence De La Perouse), Oliver Spencer (David De La Perouse), Maurice Tuech (Bank Clerk), Patrick Braoude (Passerby), Jean-Gabriel Nordmann (Travel Agent), Marika Green, Lyle Joyce (Bankers), Maxime Dufeu, Fernand Guiot, Thierry Liagre (Cab Drivers), Mike Marshall, Anne Le Fol (Friends Of Xavier), Roland LaCoste (Small Person), Benoit Ferreux (Villager), Jacques Canselier (Pet Shop Man), Maryam D'Abo (Nathalie), Francoise Fleury (Xavier's Secretary),

Serge Berry (Guide), Simone Roche, Peggy Frankston (Tourists), Albert Augier (TWA Official), Jacques Francois (Mons. Mauriac), Marc Hadjadj (Bartender).

A sappy romance which stars Allen (of RAIDERS OF THE LOST ARK) as an American tourist who misses her flight out of France and is forced to prolong her stay. She tries to spend the night with a friend only to discover that she has left on vacation. Allen resorts to a hotel. She soon meets Lhermitte, a dashing banker who just happens to be married. A predictable romance that falls neatly into place, conveniently avoiding any honest emotions. It's at least nice to look at, thanks to Hilton McConnico who has done production designer chores on DIVA (1981), MOON IN THE GUTTER (1983), and LA BALANCE (1982). Director Marquand had better luck his next time out with the suspenseful JAGGED EDGE (1985).

p, Michael Gruskoff; d, Richard Marquand; w, Janice Lee Graham; ph, Philippe Welt (Metrocolor); m, John Barry; ed, Sean Barton; prod d, Hilton McConnico; art d, Regis Des Plas.

Romance   **Cas.**   **(PR:O MPAA:R)**

UP THE CREEK***   (1984) 95m Arkoff/Orion c

Tim Matheson (Bob McGraw), Jennifer Runyon (Heather Merriweather), Stephen Furst (Gonzer), Dan Monahan (Max), Sandy Helberg (Irwin), Jeff East (Rex), Blaine Novak (Braverman), James B. Sikking (Tozer), John Hillerman (Dean Burch), Mark Andrews (Rocky), Will Bledsoe (Roger), Grant Wilson (Reggie), Julie Montgomery (Lisa), Jeana Tomasina (Molly), Romy Windsor (Corky), Tom Nolan (Whitney), Jason Court (Powers), Jesse D. Goins (Brown), Tim Jones (Johnson), Robert Costanzo, Ken Gibbel (Campus Guards), Hap Lawrence (Gas Station Attendant), Lori Sutton (Cute Girl), Peggy Trentini (Co-Ed), Kathy Sunshine Soler (Buxom Blonde), Sandy Kuykendall (Girl in Bar), Julie Caspell, Gina Barbisan (Chesty Girls), Katha Feffer (Girl in Corridor), Michael T. Judge (Guide St. Martins), Patricia A. Whitcer, Gene Kilty, Felicity Mithen (Hot Tub Girls), Jake (Chuck the Wonder Dog).

It would be easy to dismiss this vulgar, silly film by making a play on words regarding the title but that's a cheat. As smarmy and dumb as this is, if you're willing to suspend your good taste, it's also very amusing. Sam Arkoff, the man who was half responsible for the BEACH PARTY pictures (with his late partner, James Nicholson) teams up with his son, Louis, to fund this college capers film that's distinguished by some witty lines and a few scenes which place it far above the usual undergrad movie and just below the superior REVENGE OF THE NERDS. Three college teams are set to compete in a raft race. The team worth rooting for is composed of likable maladroits from "Lepetomane University," described by their own dean as "the worst learning institution in the world." (The name of the school is an inside joke based on the stage monicker of a man who used to appear in turn-of-the-century Paris theaters and demonstrate his "talents" by passing gas in rhythm, at various pitches, etc. A famous book was written about the man and it can still be found at remainder counters.) The boys from LU are Matheson, Furst (both from ANIMAL HOUSE), Monahan (PORKY'S) and Helberg (HISTORY OF THE WORLD, PART ONE). They drive off to the race and Furst tosses a sandwich out the window which hits a motorcyclist and causes him to go off a cliff. So, right away, we know what kind of movie we are about to see. The two other teams are the bad guys. From the Ivy League comes a foursome of wealthy blond preppies headed by East and the last competitors are from a tough military school, neo-Nazis lead by Novak. They are the defending champs and will stop at nothing to repeat. The favorites are the flaxen-haired Yuppies, who are about as scrupulous as snake oil salesmen. Before the race, there's a huge beer bash. Although party scenes seem to be the norm in all of these pictures, this one is handled better than most and serves to set up the characters well and indicate the tension that is underlying the action. One of the good guys is kidnaped just before the race and the only creature who knows his whereabouts is the dog. In as fresh and inventive a scene as has ever been lensed, the dog tells the others, via a wild game of charades, what's happened and where the victim is! Naturally, the boys you want to win are victorious so that's no surprise. What is surprising is the superb river raft footage that is so real it's hard to tell if it was done with miniatures or not. Butler and his special effects people are to be congratulated. There was a credit in the crawl for "second unit direction" by Chris Hibler and "second unit cinematography" by Roger Shearman. If it was those two who did the race footage, then let them be covered with kudos for their efforts. UP THE CREEK doesn't have an ounce, nay, a dram, of subtlety. The situations are clearly marked and their solutions are easily guessed. But that's not a detriment here as we can take solace in the familiar and all we need wonder about is the path to the obvious conclusion. Other than the aforementioned members of the "Brat Pack," the only other familiar faces belong to Hillerman (from TV's "Magnum, P.I.") and Sikking. It won't win any awards, it will enrage bluenoses, and it will annoy intellectuals, but the truth is that this one is funny, and when a company sets out to make a comedy, it had better be funny.

p, Michael L. Metzer, Fred Baum; d, Robert Butler; w, Jim Kouf (based on a story by Kouf, Jeff Sherman, Douglas Grossman); ph, James Glennon (DeLuxe Color); m, William Goldstein; ed, Bill Butler; prod d, William M. Hiney; set d, Gary Morenmo; cos, Robert Turturice.

Comedy   **Cas.**   **(PR:O MPAA:R)**

UTU*½**   (1984, New Zealand) 104m Utu-New Zealand Film Commission/Glitteron c

Anzac Wallace (Te Wheke), Bruno Lawrence (Williamson), Kelly Johnson (Lt. Scott), Wi Kuki Kaa (Wiremu), Tim Elliot (Col. Elliot), Ilona Rodgers (Emily), Tania Bristowe (Kura), Martyn Sanderson (Vicar), Faenza Reuben (Henare), John Bach (Belcher), Merata Mita (Matu), Bill Juliff (Charlie), Stephen Tozer (Capt. Rogers), Robin Ruakere (George), Tom Poata (Puni), Dick Puanaki (Eru), Sean Duffy (Jones), Wayne Allan (Cronin), Awatea Mita (Wikitoria), Puni Rangiaho (Wikitoria's Mother), Gook Te Huia (Te Wheke's Uncle), Joe Malcolm (Tattooer), Tim Shadbolt (Photographer), Rawiri (Spy), Ian Watkin, Ian Stewart, Ronnie Smith, Connie Gilbert, George Waaka.

One of the best films yet to emerge from the budding New Zealand cinema, UTU (Maori for "retribution") deals with the British colonial presence on the islands in the 1870s. Wallace is a Maori in the service of the British army as a scout and guide. One day, while going about his scouting duties, he comes across a village that the British have wiped out in a massacre. It is Wallace's own village, and he then deserts the British to seek revenge against them. With a small group of similarly angry renegades, he launches a campaign of terror and murder against the British. At one point they invade a church during services and kill the minister with a hatchet in front of his congregation. When they attack an isolated farm, murdering the woman of the house and burning it to the ground, another person takes up the search for revenge, Lawrence. The two men stalk, but eventually the British army, under the command of Elliot, whose chief concern is the safety of the wine supply, captures Wallace. As the various factions who want him dead vie for the privilege of killing him, another Maori in the service of the crown (Kaa) steps forth to make a speech concerning the injustices committed on all sides. Wallace, his face covered with ritual tattoos, is a superb actor, and his conversion from loyal British subject to killer is quite believable. Lawrence, the star of most of the successful films to come from New Zealand (SMASH PALACE, QUIET EARTH) is similarly believable as he is driven to revenge for the same reasons. The most expensive film in New Zealand's history, this film was a major success at home and abroad. Originally released in 1983.

p, Geoff Murphy, Don Blakeney; d, Murphy; w, Murphy, Keith Aberdein; ph, Graeme Cowley (Fujicolor); m, John Charles; ed, Michael Horton, Ian John; prod d, Ron Highfield; art d, Rick Kofoed; cos, Michael Kane.

Drama   **(PR:O MPAA:R)**

VAMPING*½   (1984) 107m Vamping/Atlantic c

Patrick Duffy (Harry Baranski), Catherine Hyland (Diane Anderson), Rod Arrants (Raymond O'Brien), Fred A. Keller (Fat Man), David Booze (Benjamin), Jed Cooper (Lennie), Steve Gilborn (Jimmy), John McCurry (Sam), Wendel Meldrum (Rita), Henry Stram (Deacon), Nataljia Nogulich (Julie), Raymond Fleszar, Frank O'Hara (Old Men), Isabel Price, Sally Birkhead (Matrons), Lambros Touris (Huge Man), Elizabeth Klein (Shopping Cart Lady).

Duffy is a saxophonist down on his luck. In desperation he takes to crime and decides to rob a house for some much needed cash. However things don't go quite as he planned. Instead of ending up with loot, Duffy finds himself caught up in a rather strange menage a trois. It's this sort of nonsense that probably sent Duffy running back to the television series "Dallas," a show he left in order to stretch his skills as an artist.

p, Howard Kling, Stratton Rawson; d, Frederick King Keller; w, Michael Healy, Robert Seidman (based on a story by Keller); ph, Skip Roessel; m, Ken Kaufman; ed, Darren Kloomok; prod d, Kling, Karen Morse, Rawson; set d, Michael Morgan; cos, Elizabeth Haas.

Drama   **Cas.**   **(PR:O MPAA:R)**

VARIETY*½   (1984) 100m Variety/Horizon c

Sandy McLeod (Christine), Will Patton (Mark), Richard Davidson (Louie), Luis Guzman (Jose), Nan Goldin (Nan), Lee Tucker (Projectionist), Peter Rizzo (Driver), Mark Boone, Jr (Porn Customer), April Andrew, Suzanne Fletcher, Peyton Green, Cookie Mueller, Norma Rodriguez, Sally Rodwell, Scotty Snider, Spalding Gray, Dr. Usharbudh Arya.

An independent film loaded with potential, VARIETY falls far short of its intended goals. McLeod works as a cashier for the Variety Theater, a pornographic movie house. With no life of her own McLeod grows obsessive in watching the X-rated films at the Variety, then dates one of the theater's regulars. It turns out that the man is involved with crime and the lonely McLeod follows him about. She starts receiving obscene messages on her telephone answering machine, then takes to making up pornographic stories herself. The film clearly wants to say something about the relationships between women, pornography, and power, but just doesn't quite know how to accomplish it. Written and directed by women, the story is hampered by a nondescript visual style that infuses little into the often aimless story. McLeod isn't much better as the lead, never letting the audience know what is going on inside her. Cast in a minor part is Spalding Gray, an avant-garde New York monologist with a quickly rising reputation among film and theater goers.

p, Renee Schafransky; d, Bette Gordon; w, Kathy Acker (based on a story by Gordon); ph, Tom Dicillo, John Foster (DuArt Color); m, John Lurie; ed, Ila Von Hasperg.

Drama (PR:O MPAA:NR)

VIGIL* (1984, New Zealand) 90m First Blood-Last Rites-New Zealand Film Commission/Enterprise c

Penelope Stewart (Elizabeth), Frank Whitten (Ethan), Bill Kerr (Birdie), Fiona Kay (Toss), Gordon Shields, Arthur Sutton, Snow Turner, Bill Liddy, Maurice Trewern, Eric Griffin, Emily Haupapa, Debbie Newton, Bob Morrison, Lloyd Grundy, Joseph Ritai, Josie Herlihy, Sadie Marriner, Bill Brocklehurst, Rangitoheriri Teupokopakari.

In the farming country of New Zealand Kay is an 11-year-old girl living with her widowed mother Stewart and grandfather Kerr. Stewart is beginning to cope without her husband, not realizing how painful the marriage truly was. Whitten is a stranger who enters this small family and provides them all with certain needs. Kerr takes him on as a partner in his practical jokes and oddball inventions while Stewart learns once more what love is like. The story is seen through Kay's eyes as she learns to deal with her father's death and the involvement that Whitten has with her small family. This little film is beautifully photographed with a tight ensemble that handles the sensitive material with skill. Kay herself is natural in a difficult role for a child, carrying the burden of the story without resorting to any precocious tricks. However, like real ife, this story does have a few dull stretches, though not enough to distract from the overall quality. The relationships within the story are realistic, giving this a wonderful humanistic feeling. Director Ward, only 27-years-old, had made two award-winning short films before turning to features with this. Reportedly VIGIL had been in planning stages for four years before finally going before the camera in 1983.

p, John Maynard; d, Vincent Ward; w, Ward, Graeme Tetley; ph, Alun Bollinger (Eastmancolor); m, Jack Body; ed, Simon Reece; prod d, Kai Hawkins; cos, Glenys Jackson.

Drama (PR:C MPAA:NR)

WARRIOR AND THE SORCERESS, THE* (1984) 81m New Horizons/New World c

David Carradine (Kain), Luke Askew (Zeg), Maria Socas (Naja), Anthony DeLongis (Kief), Harry Townes (Bludge), William Marin (Bal Caz), Arthur Clark (Burgo), Daniel March (Blather), John Overby (Gabble), Richard Paley (Scarface), Mark Welles (Burgo's Captain), Cecilia North (Exotic Dancer), Ned Ivers (Slave), Lillian Cameron (Drowning Slave), Eve Adams (Woman At Well), Dylan Williams, Herman Cass, Joe Cass, Arthur Neal, Michael Zane, Herman Gere, Gus Parker (Zeg's Guards).

Carradine is a wandering warrior who sells his services to both sides in a village dispute over a well. Lame swords-and-sorcery film vaguely reworked from YOJIMBO (1961). Carradine is as stiff as usual but seems to be having some fun as he rehashes his old "Kung Fu" role from television (even his character's name is an echo of his name on the show).

p, Frank Isaac, John Broderick; d&w, Broderick (based on a story by Broderick, William Stout); ph, Leonard Solis; m, Louis Saunders; ed, Silvia Ripoll; art d, Emmett Baldwin; set d, Evan Alcott; cos, Mary Bertram; spec eff, Chris Biggs; makeup, Biggs, George Barry.

Adventure Cas. (PR:O MPAA:R)

WARRIORS OF THE WASTELAND* (1984, Ital.) 87m Dear International/New Line c (I NUOVI BARBARI; 2019, I NUOVI BAR-BARI)

Timothy Brent [Giancarlo Prete] (Skorpion), Fred Williamson (Nadir), Anna Kanakis (Alma), Venantino Venantini (Moses), George Eastman, Enzo G. Castellari, Massimo Vanni, Andrea Coppola, Zora Kerowa, Patsy May McLachlan, Mark Gregory, Luigi Montefiori, Thomas Moore.

In some post-nuclear war future, a band of pilgrims led by Venantini crosses a desert, constantly harrassed by a leather-clad gang of barbarians known as the Templars. Brent and Williamson are warriors who drive souped-up cars from the 1960s and protect the religious travelers. Ripping off everything from THE ROAD WARRIOR and DELIVERANCE (hero Brent gets raped) to A FISTFUL OF DOLLARS, the film still manages to be lifeless and boring.

p, Fabrizio De Angelis; d, Enzo Girolami Castellari; w, Tito Carpi, Castellari (based on a story by Carpi); ph, Fausto Zuccoli (Telecolor); m, Claudio Simonetti; ed, Gianfranco Amicucci; prod d, Antonio Visone; spec eff, Germano Natali; stunts, Riccardo Pitrazzi.

Science Fiction Cas. (PR:O MPAA:R)

WARRIORS OF THE WIND* (1984, Jap.) 95m NW c

This Japanese cartoon, dubbed with American voices, is yet another science fiction/fantasy adventure aimed directly at the younger set. The story opens as civilization is struggling to rebuild itself after a fiery holocaust. In the Valley of the Wind, Princess Zandra lives with King Zeal, her father. Zandra saves her uncle, Lord Yuppa, from being attacked by a monstrous insect, but the Valley soon has other problems to contend with. First, an enemy ship brings a murderous Fire Demon. The Valley is then attacked by Queen Selena, a nasty sort, who is accompanied by her soldiers. King Zeal is killed, the survivors are held as Selena's hostages, and forced to join her evil cause. Zandra and her friend Axel are able to escape to an area that was unaffected by the devestating firestorms. Zandra and Axel regroup, and while rebellion, war, and giant Gorgons all pose a threat to the Valley of the Wind, Zandra is able to save her people for a happy conclusion. Strictly for fantasy buffs. Due to some violent moments, this feature is questionable for the youngest viewers in the family.

p, Isao Takahata; d, Kazuo Komatsubara; w, Kazunori Ito; ed, Tomoko Kida; md, Shigeharu Shiba; art d, Mitsuki Nakamura; animators, Hidiaki Anno, Junko Ikeda, Tomihiko Okubo, Shuchi Obara, Ai Kagawa, Yoshinori Kanada, Shutaro Kosaka, Kazuyuki Kobayashi, Shunji Saida, Noboru Takano, Tsukasa Tannai, Takashi Nakamura, Osamu Nabeshima, Yukiyoshi Hane, Tadashi Fukuda, Masahiro Maeda, Takashi Watabe, Shojuro Yamanouch, Yoichi Kotabe, Tadakatsu Yoshida, Masahiro Yoshida.

Animated Feature Cas. (PR:C MPAA:PG)

WEEKEND PASS* (1984) 92m Marimark/Crown c

D. W. Brown (Paul Fricker), Peter Ellenstein (Lester Gidley), Patrick Hauser (Webster Adams), Chip McAllister (Bunker Hill), Pamela G. Kay (Tina Wells), Hilary Shapiro (Cindy Hazard), Graem McGavin (Tawny Ryatt), Daureen Collodel (Heidi Henderson), Annette Sinclair (Maxine), Grand L. Bush (Bertram), Sara Costa (Tuesday Del Mundo), Valerie McIntosh (Etta), Cheryl Song (Chop Suzi), Peter Bailey-Britton (Henri), Theodore Wilson (Nat), Bunny Summers (Sadie), Phil Hartman (Joe Chicago), Tony DeLia (Tony Twan), Lynne Stewart (Sookie Lane), John Graves (Chainsaw Comedian), Mona Charles (Roberta), Debbie Christoffersen (Candy), Joan Dykman (Pickles), Kirk Calloway (Squeenie), Henry G. Sanders (Officer Henry), Anthony Penya (Officer Anthony), Jacqueline Jacobs (Shady Lady).

Yet another member of the low-budget sex comedy genre, this film at least has the distinction of portraying some group other than hormonally charged high-school students as protagonists. This time it's a group of sailors who get the title leave from their station in San Diego. The four prototypes include McAllister, a black ex-gang member turned cleancut type; Hauser as the token all-American; Brown, a would-be stand-up comic; and Ellenstein as the group's lovable nerd. The quartet goes on the prowl in L.A. getting into predictable jams before ending up with a suitable female counterpart. Of course this film takes place in that special part of California where no one gets pregnant or catches any of the myriad of sexually transmitted diseases. There is also a fair amount of jingoism to grab the super-patriots in the audience. WEEKEND PASS, like so many films of its ilk, is movie making by numbers. It goes from one point to the next to complete the picture with no surprises as to what turn it will take. Songs, written by John and Robbie Baer, include "All Night Love," "Hard as a Rock," "Beach Nut," "L. A. Xtra (Read Abut Me)," "Free Me From the Night Life," and the title song.

p, Marilyn J. Tenser, Michael D. Castle; d&w, Lawrence Bassoff (based on a story by Mark Tenser), ph, Bryan England (DeLuxe Color); m, John Baer; ed, Harry B. Miller III; art d, Ivo G. Cristante; set d, Julia Kaye Towery; cos, Ellen Rome Shanahan.

Comedy Cas. (PR:O MPAA:R)

WHAT YOU TAKE FOR GRANTED* (1984) 75m Iris Feminist Collective c

Belinda Cloud (Dianna the Doctor), Donna Blue Lachman (Anna the Truck Driver), Mosetta Harris (Cable Splicer), Fran Hart (Philosophy Professor), Helen Larimore (Sculptor).

A tedious pseudo-documentary which dramatically reconstructs interviews with women working in jobs usually reserved for men. These interviews are then intercut with unconvincing fictional scenes of the women relating on and off the job. The film concentrates most on Cloud and Lachman and follows them to the end of the film when they embark on a lesbian relationship. Some audiences may find this picture telling, but most will quickly turn off. Photographed on 16mm and funded with grants from the National Endowment for the Arts and the Alumni Fund of Northwestern University's School of Speech.

p,d&w, Michelle Citron; ph, Frances Reid; m, Karen Pritikin; ed, Citron.

Drama (PR:O MPAA:NR)

WHERE IS PARSIFAL? zero (1984, Brit.) 84m Terence Young c

Tony Curtis (Parsifal Katzenellenbogen), Cassandra Domenica 'Berta Dominguez D.' (Elba), Erik Estrada (Henry Board II), Peter Lawford (Montague Chippendale), Ron Moody (Beersbohm), Donald Pleasence (Mackintosh), Orson Welles (Klingsor), Christopher Chaplin (Ivan), Nancy Roberts (Ruth).

An alleged comedy that substitutes frantic action for real wit. It was written by costar Cassandra Domenica under her pseudonym, and for good reason. Nobody would want to put their name on this. Curtis is a takeoff on

Moliere's "Imaginary Invalid" or "Tartuffe," a wild hypochondriac who has invented a laser skywriter that he hopes will bring him enough money to pay for his life style, which includes a corps of crazies who live with him in his castle. Among them is his Germanic assistant, Moody, and a few others. Curtis hopes to sell the patent for his invention to millionaire businessman Estrada (and if you can believe the "Chips" lad in that role, then maybe you'll believe the rest of the silly movie) or Welles, a gypsy who is also stuffed with cash (perhaps he earned it from a chain of empty stores). Pleasence is the villain in the sense that he is trying to get all of Curtis' assets because Curtis is in such debt. The whole plot has to do with Curtis selling his invention before Pleasence takes everything. The picture is done at such a breakneck speed that there is not one delicious "moment" to savor. The cast consisted of several superior farceurs and the shame of it was that they had nothing with which to work. Helman's direction was a combination of the worst of Richard Lester with the worst of Mack Sennett. The executive producer was the redoubtable Terence Young who directed DR. NO, FROM RUSSIA WITH LOVE, and several other action films. He should have known better. The film was backed by Alexander Salkind, who had coproduced Welles' picture THE TRIAL. Welles undertook his cameo role in the hope of getting Salkind's backing for his proposed production of Shakespeare's "King Lear."

p, Daniel Carrillo; d, Henri Helman; w, Berta Dominguez D.; ph, Norman Langley (Rank Color): m, Hubert Rostaing, Ivan Jullien; ed, Russell Lloyd, Peter Hollywood; prod d, Malcolm Stone.

Comedy   **(PR:C MPAA:PG)**

WHERE THE BOYS ARE '84*   (1984) 97m ITC/Tri-Star c

Lisa Hartman (Jennie), Wendy Schaal (Sandra), Lorna Luft (Carol), Lynn-Holly Johnson (Laurie), Russell Todd (Scott), Christopher McDonald (Tony), Howard McGillian (Chip), Daniel McDonald (Camden), Alana Stewart (Maggie), Louise Sorel (Barbara), Danny Harvey, Michael Osborn, Dibbs Preston, Barry Ryan, Smutty Smiff (The Rockats), Asher Brauner (Ernie), Glenn Super (Mr. Bullhorn), Barry Marder (Rappaport), Jude Cole (Jude), George Coutoupis (Ray), Toby Lyons (Himself), Stephen Moore (Jeff), Don Cox (Himself), Robert Goodman (Gary), Dara Sedaka (Christine), Frank Zagarino (Conan), Jerri Lynn Davis (Stripper at Party), Eduardo Corbe (Hector), Leigh Torlage (Victim), Eileen Ward (Girl in Boots), Glenn Maska (Bartender), Dan Fitzgerald (Sgt. Porter), Mal Jones, John Nittolo (Guys in Jail), Florence McGee, Dee Dee Deering (Dowagers), Jorge Gil (Ned), Joe Gerwin (Oberlin Student), Rand Woodbury (Boy with Cat), Susan Teesdale (Hot Bod Contest Winner), M. James Arnett, Betty Raymond (Stunt Doubles), Courtney Brown, Kelly Browning, Alex Edlin, Art Malesci (Stunts), Thomas Manning, Paul Alvarez (Skydivers).

This cinematic tripe bears as much resemblance to the original film WHERE THE BOYS ARE as Brian De Palma's miserable SCARFACE bore to the original. An absolute insult to the intelligence of America in general and college students in particular, it just goes to prove that ex-manager Carr was a lucky man to have become involved in GREASE and the stage musical of "La Cage Aux Folles," because his other projects, CAN'T STOP THE MUSIC and GREASE II, were as dumb as this. The original film made stars of George Hamilton, Connie Francis, Jim Hutton, and Paula Prentiss. The stars of this movie will be lucky if it doesn't drive them out of show business entirely. Hartman, Luft, Johnson, and Schaal are alleged to be a quartet of coeds on their spring break in Fort Lauderdale with fun and games in mind. Luft was already past 30 when she did this and while the sister of Liza Minnelli is a good singer and not a bad actress, there was no way she could cheat the years. The foursome are in no way plausible as collegians. Rather, they appear to be four fully grown hedonists who have taken graduate courses in Dr. Ruth Westheimer's College of Good Sex. There is no naivete here and that makes them all appear so smarmy that it's not easy to like them. Just in case anyone questions the sexual nature of the group, we are shown early in the film that the girls feel all they need to have fun are bikinis and diaphragms and, just in case they don't meet a man, they've brought an inflatable doll (named Dave) whose body parts are all in place. (By the way, Dave gets the applause as best actor in the movie when one of the girls bites him in an expected area and, like the old joke, he flies around the room as the air rushes out of his inflated body. That must have looked good on paper because it sure didn't look good on screen.) The women are searching for that elusive "romance" although they give everyone (and the audience) the indication that they are girls who just wanna have fun. Hartman meets two men and is wooed by both. The first is Daniel McDonald, a wimpy musician, and the other is Todd, a hitchhiking hunk. (Todd, by the way, was "discovered" by Carr when his photo was seen by the producer at a hair-dressing salon. He had been a high-fashion model and his performance was as exciting as an 8 x 10 glossy.) Hartman's big problem is trying to decide which of the boys she wants. Meanwhile, Luft's beau has trailed her to Florida, thus putting a crimp in her action. Schaal is a snobby type who thinks Fort Lauderdale is beneath her and so she's just come along for the ride. Her austerity continues until she falls for local police officer Christopher McDonald. Johnson is the nympho of the group, a far cry from the pure and chaste character she played in ICE CASTLES. So four story lines are played against each other but they really never register and the movie appears to be a feeble attempt to show hijinks by the sea and little else. The movie would have been better off if the casting were more believable, the acting more honest, the emphasis off the obvious sexuality,

and the script destroyed before production began. Carr tried to induce Hamilton, Francis, and Prentiss to make guest appearances in the film and since Hutton had passed away in 1979 after completing his TV series "Ellery Queen," Carr went after his Oscar-winning son, Tim. All four wisely turned down the portly, caftaned producer, a tribute to their taste. In small roles, note Alana Stewart–former wife of rocker Rod Stewart and George Hamilton–and Louise Sorel, former wife of Herb Edelman and Ken Howard.

p, Allan Carr; d, Hy Averback; w, Stu Krieger, Jeff Burkhart (based on the novel Where the Boys Are by Glendon Swarthout); ph, James A. Contner (Technicolor); m, Sylvester Levay; ed, Melvin Shapiro, Bobbie Shapiro; prod d, Michael Baugh; set d, Don K. Ivey; cos, Marla Denise Schlom; ch, Tony Stevens.

Comedy   **Cas.**   **(PR:O MPAA:R)**

WHITE ELEPHANT**   (1984, Brit.) 99m Worldoc c

Peter Firth (Peter Davidson), Peter Sarpong (Bishop Of Kumasi), Nana Seowg (High Priestess), Ejissu Jasantua (Fetish Priest), High Priest Of Lake Bosomtwe, Frederick Lawluwi (Reverend in Anloga), A.N.K. Mensah (Herbalist In Anloga), Asugebe and Jasantua (Patron Ghosts Of Ejissu Fetish-Priest School), Abi Adatsi, Kwabena Holm, Owusu Akyeaw, Sarfo Opoku, Toni Darko, Nana Abiri, Otchere Darko, Charles Annan, Klevor Abo, Samuel Amoah, People's Defense Committee.

An entertaining, though familiar, story of a white businessman, Firth, who travels to Ghana in the hopes of setting up a high-tech plastic furniture factory. He also has dreams of modernizing the country by introducing the population to the microchip. The locals resist the pressures of imperialism and modernization, however, and do their best to prevent Firth's plans from going into effect. Firth begins to sympathize with the opposition and eventually succumbs to the local charm. WHITE ELEPHANT is a fine film, but doesn't compare to the similar LOCAL HERO (1983) or THE COCA-COLA KID (1985). This picture's a real cross-cultural event–a British film, shot in Ghana, by an Austrian director.

p&d, Werner Grusch; w, Grusch, Ashley Pharoah (based on an idea by Grusch); ph, Tom D. Hurwitz; m, The African Brothers, George Frederick Handel, Franco, Tabu Ley; ed, Thomas Schwalm.

Drama   **(PR:C MPAA:NR)**

WILD HORSES**   (1984, New Zealand) 90m Endeavor-New Zealand Film Commission/Satori c

Keith Aberdein (Dan "Mitch" Mitchell), John Bach (Jack Sullivan), Kevin Wilson (Harry Sullivan), Kathy Rawlings (Mary Mitchell), Helena Wilson (Anne Mitchell), Robyn Gibbes (Sara), Tom Poata (Sam Richardson), Marshall Napier (Andy), Matiu Mareikura (Kingi), Martyn Sanderson (Jones), Peter Tait (Joe), Bruno Lawrence (Tyson), Michael Haig (Benson), Richard Poore (Ranger).

The picturesque New Zealand landscape is the star of this mediocre, but well-meaning, western. Aberdein is an unemployed logger who is hired by a national park to round up a herd of wild horses. Bach and Wilson join up, but the trio has no success. Complications arise when a venison company hires a group of men, led by Lawrence, to kill all the deer in the area. Lawrence's men soon grow impatient with Aberdein's inability to capture horses and his uncanny knack at scaring off the deer. Lawrence plays tough and begin killing the horses. In the meantime, Aberdein has noticed a gorgeous white stallion and is determined to catch him. To insure the horse's safety, Aberdein makes a pact with Lawrence, who agrees not to kill the stallion. Aberdein and his men continue to have no luck with the round-up. Finally they receive some help from Poata and Gibbes, a likable pair who live off the land. Thanks to their new teachers, the trio improves its success rate. The feud between the deerhunters and the horse wranglers reaches the boiling point when Gibbes is attacked by some of Lawrence's more savage henchmen. A showdown occurs at the film's climax and the heroic Aberdein walks away with his head held high. Reportedly based on a real-life situation in New Zealand's Tongariro National Park in the 1960s.

p, John Barnett; d, Derek Morton; w, Kevin O'Sullivan [Kevin J. Wilson]; ph, Doug Milsome (Eastmancolor); m, Dave Fraser; ed, Simon Reece; prod d, Jose Bleakley.

Western   **Cas.**   **(PR:C MPAA:NR)**

WILD LIFE, THE zero   (1984) 96m UNIV c

Christopher Penn (Tom Drake), Ilan Mitchell-Smith (Jim Conrad), Eric Stoltz (Bill Conrad), Jenny Wright (Eileen), Lea Thompson (Anita), Brin Berliner (Tony), Rick Moranis (Harry), Hart Bochner (David Curtiss), Susan Blackstone (Donna), Cari Anne Warder (Julie), Robert Ridgely (Craig Davis), Jack Kehoe (Mr. Parker), Jennifer White (Brenda), Beth McKinley (Robin), Michael Bowen (Vince), Angel Salazar (Benny), Randy Quaid (Charlie), Dick Rude (Eddie), Robert Chestnut (Eddie's Friend), Reginald Farmer (Reggie), Sherilyn Fenn (Penny Hallin), Leo Penn (Tom's Dad), Hildy Brooks (Mrs. Conrad), Lee Ving (Installer), William Bramley (Security Officer), Dean Devlin (Liquor Store Clerk), Brynja Willis, Leigh Lombardi (Stewardesses), Rande Worcester (Louie), Kim Vignal (Girl By the Pool), Nancy Wilson (David's Wife), Ben Stein (Surplus Salesman), Tommy

Swerdlow (*Dork*), Paul Wiggins, Frank Montiforte (*Jocks*), Keone Young (*Japanese Bowler*), Kevin Hall (*Bouncer*), Tony Epper, Ted White (*Redneck Drunks*), Ashley St. Jon, Kitten Natividad (*Strippers*), Gary Riley (*Kid*), John Linson, Jess Weinstein (*Donut Kids*), Jeff Savenick (*Guy in Bed*), Karen Haber (*Shoplifter*), Barbara M. London (*Salesgirl*), Jayne Walters (*Female Customer*), Inga Ojala (*Girl at Counter*), Edward Call (*Captain of the Plumbing Team*), Michael H. Stein (*Ricky*).

The first four notes of the old "Dragnet" theme sum up this movie. If you don't recall, they were C, D, D sharp, C, or "Dumb, Dumb, Dumb." It's a compendium of every element in every inane teenage movie you've ever seen and the only reason anyone would watch this would be if they were being punished for something or suffering from a heretofore incurable case of insomnia. Made by two of the creative team behind FAST TIMES AT RIDGEMONT HIGH, this missed the touch of director Heckerling and seems to be a rehash of that with none of the fun. Chris Penn is a dumb jock wrestler with dyed blond hair. His parents are Leo Penn (his and Sean Penn's father in real life) and Brooks. He's the main character but he seems to spend most of his time wrestling, not acting. He loves Wright but she doesn't return the adoration and her dialog mostly consists of telling him to take a hike. Stoltz is a recent graduate who leaves the bosom of his home to move into a singles building. His long-time girl friend, Thompson, has been jettisoned because he thinks he is too mature to have a high schooler so he tosses her in the lap of married cop Bochner and the two of them get together for fun and games in the local donut shop's rear room. (Bochner is the son of Lloyd Bochner, veteran movie and TV character actor.) Thompson doesn't know that Bochner has a wife who is expecting and a young son already on Earth and she only learns that when she shows up unexpectedly at his house. Stoltz's younger brother is Mitchell-Smith, a young man who is fixated on the Vietnam war and follows veteran Quaid around like a puppy dog. (Quaid's appearance in the film is as fleeting as a quarter-horse race.) The situation of Mitchell-Smith's mental problems and his magnetism toward Quaid is unbelievable, although it might have been true and culled from a real happening in the author's life. These are the activities and it takes 96 wasted minutes to introduce the twaddle and resolve the issues. The final few minutes are the requisite party at Stoltz's apartment. The place is demolished, bedlam prevails, and Stoltz and Thompson are reconciled. Stoltz was the boy in MASK and the only reason to see this is to realize that he's not a bad-looking young man under the makeup Bogdanovich put on his face. Penn had already appeared in FOOTLOOSE, RUMBLE FISH, and ALL THE RIGHT MOVES. The good work he showed in those movies may have been obliterated by the disaster here. In a small role, Moranis (from TV's "Second City") is outstanding as Wright's employer at a local department store. Moranis is so much better than everyone else that the others look amateurish by comparison. The only other decent performance is turned in by Ridgley, one of the most successful commercial voices in Hollywood, who will also be recalled for his excellent role as the toothy emcee in MELVIN AND HOWARD.

p, Art Linson, Cameron Crowe, Don Phillips; d, Linson; w, Crowe; ph, James Glennon (Technicolor); m, Edward Van Halen, Donn Landee; ed, Michael Jablow; prod d, William Sandell; md, Debbie Gold; set d, Robert Gould; cos, Winnie Brown, Marilyn Vance, Ronald I. Caplan.

Teenage Comedy   **Cas.**   **(PR:C-O   MPAA:R)**

WILD SIDE, THE   (SEE: SUBURBIA)

WINDY CITY**½   (1984) 102m CBS/WB c

John Shea (*Danny Morgan*), Kate Capshaw (*Emily Reubens*), Josh Mostel (*Sol*), Jim Borrelli (*Mickey*), Jeffrey DeMunn (*Bobby*), Eric Pierpoint (*Pete*), Lewis J. Stadlen (*Marty*), James Sutorius (*Eddie*), Niles McMaster (*Michael*), Lisa Taylor (*Sherry*), Nathan Davis (*Mr. Jones*), Louie Lanciloti (*Ernesto*), Wilbert Bradley (*Joe the Janitor*), Lisa Hella, Elaine Wilkes (*Barzini Sisters*), Denise Baske, Pamela Hudak (*Coeds*), Kathleen Jean Klein (*Maria the Nurse*), Robert York (*Young Danny*), Christopher Russo (*Young Sol*), Nancy Serlin (*Linda*), Dianne Derfner (*Anita*), William Vines (*Bridge Guard*), Howard Orr (*Bull Martin*), Valerie Gobos (*Cat Lady*).

A film with a lot of heart which unfortunately never gels as a whole. Shea is a postman-*cum*-struggling writer in love with two people: Capshaw, his ex-girl friend who is about to be married, and Mostel, his best friend slowly dying from leukemia. In the rambling story (told in a series of flashbacks), Shea learns to cope with his pal's impending death, his own angst, and his longing for Capshaw. Surrounding himself with his old gang from boyhood, Shea goes through a series of adventures, including an all-night limousine party and organizing a last hurrah for Mostel. Full of genuine warmth and humanity. Shea is excellent as a young man caught between his different loyalties, unsure of himself and yet knowing exactly what he wants. Mostel and Capshaw are equally fine as the two closest to him. Where the story falters is in the myriad of flashbacks. First-time director Bernstein (who had previously written Francis Ford Coppola's ONE FROM THE HEART) relies much too heavily on flashback, jumping back and forth in time, resulting in more confusion than anything else. Rather than trying to evoke feelings with cinematic style, he should have stuck with the story of his three leads. When he concentrates on the relationships, this is a sweet, never overly sentimental film. Bernstein shot this in his native Chicago, using locations all over town to evoke the feeling of one big neighborhood. This, along with the film's autumn setting, give a warm nostalgic feeling to the story. WINDY CITY is the sort of film one can't help but like despite the often confusing style.

p, Alan Greisman; d&w, Armyan Bernstein; ph, Reynaldo Villalobos (Technicolor); m, Jack Nitzsche; ed, Clifford Jones, Christophr Rouse; prod d, Bill Kenney; set d, Rick Gentz; cos, Betsy Cox; spec eff, Gunter W. Jennings; m/l, "Hit and Run Lovers," Nitzsche, Buffy Sainte-Marie, "Trick or Treat," Saint-Marie.

Drama   **Cas.**   **(PR:C   MPAA:R)**

WINTER FLIGHT**½   (1984, Brit.) 103m Enigma-Goldcrest c

Reece Dinsdale (*Mal Stanton*), Nicola Cowper (*Angie*), Gary Olsen (*Dave*), Sean Benn (*Hooker*), Beverly Hewitt (*Lara*), Shelagh Stephenson (*Kel*), Michael Percival (*Doctor*), Anthony Trent (*Sgt. Bowyer*), Tim Bentinck (*Jack*).

Dinsdale is a young man who is in charge of keeping seagulls off a Royal Air Force runway. He meets Cowper, a more sophisticated unmarried mother-to-be and develops a crush on her. Benn is a soldier on the base who gives Dinsdale a beating, then destroys his car in a fit of jealousy. Eventually a sort of love does blossom between Dinsdale and Cowper thanks to the young man's pluck and determination. Though the story is routine, Dinsdale's performance gives the film an added edge. His character is infused with life throughout, bringing out the movie's original quirks. The contrast between the harsh military life and the difficult ordeal of everyday civilian existence is nicely balanced without projecting any heavy-handed messages. A few slow scenes and Cowper's less than polished performance do mar the film in spots, but overall WINTER FLIGHT is a nice small film.

p, Susan Richards, Robin Douet; d, Roy Battersby; w, Alan Janes; ph, Chris Menges; m, Richard Harvey; ed, Lesley Walker; art d, Adrienne Atkinson; cos, Sue Yelland.

Drama   **(PR:C   MPAA:NR)**

WOMAN FLAMBEE, A   (SEE: WOMAN IN FLAMES, A, Ger.)

WOMAN IN FLAMES, A***   (1984, Ger.) 106m Van Ackeren-Geissler/Almi c (DIE FLAMBIERTE FRAU; A WOMAN FLAMBEE)

Gudrun Landgrebe (*Eva*), Mathieu Carriere (*Chris*), Hanns Zischler (*Kurt*), Gabriele Lafari (*Yvonne*), Matthias Fuchs, Christiane B. Horn, Rene Schonenberger, Magdalena Montezuma, Klaus Mikoleit, Georg Tryphon, Walther Busch, Carola Regnier, Johannes Grutzke, Salome, Catharina Zwerenz, Ute Gerhard, Joachim von Ulmann, Roland von Schulze, Ursula Tahiri, Achim E. Ruppel, Klaus Hoser, Rosemarie Heinze, Thomas Voborka, Shawn Lawton.

A bizarre picture about a middle-class housewife, Landgrebe, who leaves her husband and turns to prostitution. She is initially conservative in her choice of clients, but becomes more daring. She meets Carriere, a bisexual prostitute who invites her to his luxurious apartment. The pair fall in love and share his apartment, setting aside one room for their prostitution business–a business which rapidly becomes a highly organized chore of high-finance bookkeeping. Carriere continues entertaining both male and female clients, while Landgrebe begins to favor clients with strange fetishes. After their work is done, Carriere and Landgrebe then resume their romance for the remainder of the evening. These conditions naturally puts a strain on their relationship. The nearly surreal end of the film has Carriere soaking Landgrebe with alcohol at the dinner table and then setting her afire. In eerie slow-motion she stumbles down the hall, her dress blazing. But, in the next scene she is seen, unscarred, with a friend at a bar. A very weird entry from the eccentric Van Ackeren, who has been touted as the next Rainer Werner Fassbinder (he isn't), A WOMAN IN FLAMES went on to become one of Germany's top-grossing films, challenging Fassbinder's moneymaker THE MARRIAGE OF MARIA BRAUN (1979). (In German; English subtitles.)

p&d, Robert Van Ackeren; w, Van Ackeren, Catharina Zwerenz; ph, Jurgen Jurges; m, Peer Raben; ed, Tanja Schmidtbauer; prod d, Herbert Weinand, Heidrun Brandt; cos, Astrid Ruhr, Uschi Welter.

Drama   **Cas.**   **(PR:O   MPAA:R)**

WOMAN IN RED, THE*   (1984) 87m Woman in Red Productions/Orion c

Gene Wilder (*Theodore Pierce*), Charles Grodin (*Buddy*), Joseph Bologna (*Joe*), Judith Ivey (*Didi*), Michael Huddleston (*Michael*), Kelly Le Brock (*Charlotte*), Gilda Radner (*Ms. Milner*), Kyle T. Heffner (*Richard*), Michael Zorek (*Shelly*), Billy Beck (*Bartender*), Kyra Stempel (*Missy*), Robin Ingnico (*Becky*), Viola Kates Stimpson (*Mama Dell*), Danny Wells (*Waiter*), Buddy

Silberman (Gilbert), Monica Parker (Corrine), Ernest Harada (Doorman), Julann Griffin (Miss Griffin), Sandra Wilder (Blonde Photographer), Tammy Brewer, Noni White (Stewardesses), John McKinney (Buddy's Friend), Barbara Schweke (Theresa), Larry Gilman (Frank), Milt Kogan (Traffic Boss), Bob Balhatchet, Dan Magiera (Traffic Planners), Catherine Schreiber (Lucy), Barbara Andrews (Eileen), Sharon Moore (Sharon), Allen Gebhardt (Young Man), Sheldon Feldner (Firechief), George Johnson (Policeman), Ann Waterman (Woman), Steven Kravitz (Companion), Dale Kusch (Club Member), Kelly Andrus, Deborah Dalton, Elissa Leeds (Girls at Club), Stevie Myers (Wrangler), Freddie Dawson, Robert Krantz (Club Attendants), Maureen O'Connor (Waitress), James Higgins (Salesman), Elizabeth Norment (Hair Stylist), James Cavan (Fisherman), Roberta J. Smith (Ethel), Deborah May (Hostess).

Producing bad remakes of French films seems to be a growing tradition among American filmmakers, and taking his turn with the hatchet here is the dubiously talented Wilder. Based on the film PARDON MON AFFAIRE (1977), Wilder plays a happily married man whose life takes an unexpected turn after he encounters Le Brock. The beautiful young lady is standing over an air vent in the sidewalk that blows up her skirt just like Marilyn Monroe's in THE SEVEN YEAR ITCH. Wilder is hypnotized by Le Brock's red panties and begins an unrelenting pursuit of this mystery lady. Just a regular kinda guy, eh? Wilder spends the rest of the film running around like a sex-starved teenager, before finding out that Le Brock is married. He gets into her bedroom but is forced to crawl out on the ledge when Le Brock's husband arrives. Someone thinks he's a potential suicide, which brings out the rescue squad, as well as the media. After leaping into the safety net, Wilder is captivated by a beautiful news photographer, implying that he hasn't learned much in his experiences. Wilder continues to exhibit an unashamed display of his barely existent talent for comedy writing and directing in this sexist nonsense. Women are treated with little respect by him, while men are portrayed as bad little boys who mean no harm. The so-called farce is just degrading prattle that drags on much longer than it should. Songs include: "The Woman in Red," "It's You," "Moments Aren't Moments," "I Just Called to Say I Love You" (Stevie Wonder), "Let's Just..." (Larry Gittens, Ben Bridges).

p, Victor Drai; d&w, Gene Wilder (based on the screenplay "Pardon Mon Affair" by Jean-Loup Dabadie, Yves Robert); ph, Fred Schuler (DeLuxe Color); m, John Morris; ed, Christopher Greenbury; prod d, David L. Snyder; set d, Peg Cummings; cos, Ruth Meyers; stunts, Tom Huff.

Comedy   **Cas.**   **(PR:C   MPAA:PG-13)**

YELLOW HAIR AND THE FORTRESS OF GOLD*½
                                          (1984) 102m Crown c

Laurene Landon (Yellow Hair), Ken Roberson (Pecos Kid), John Ghaffari (Shayowteewah), Luis Lorenzo (Col. Torres), Claudia Gravi (Grey Cloud), Aldo Sambrel (Flores), Eduardo Fajardo (Man-Who-Knows), Ramiro Oliveros (Tortuga), Suzannah Woodside (Rainbow), Concha Marquez Piquer, Tony Tarruella (Gambling Couple), Daniel Martin (1st Comanche), Mario De Abros (Deputy), Roman Ariz-Navarreta, Pablo Garcia Ortega (Machine Gunners), Joaquin Lopez (Fighting Indian), Juan Gomez Fernandez (Young Soldier), Paloma Gomez, Jose Truchado, Jr (Newlyweds), Juan Garcia

Delgado (Barman), Alfonso Maria Delgado (Waiter).

A princess in search of hidden fortunes needs the help of a strange man who lives in the unlikely abode of an elk's horn. Once she finds the man she can continue her search for a fortress of gold. Uninspired exploitation adventure. Director Cimber had directed a few "sex instruction" films during the 1960s before graduating to this sort of stuff.

p, John Ghaffari, Diego G. Sempre; d, Matt Cimber; w, Cimber, John Kershaw (based on characters and story by Cimber); ph, John Cabrera (Metrocolor); m, Franco Piersanti; ed, Claudio Cutry; cos, Augustin Jimenez; spec eff, Carlo DeMarchis.

Adventure   **Cas.**   **(PR:O   MPAA:R)**

YR ALCOHOLIG LION**   (1984, Brit.) 109m Cine Cymru c

Dafydd Hywel (Alun), Gwenlliam Davies (Mam), Eluned Jones (Gwen), Eleri Evans (El), Glesni Williams (Auntie), David Lyn (Maestro), Reginald Mathias (Die).

Somewhat of an oddity, YR ALCOHOLIG LION (which translates as THE HAPPY ALCOHOLIC) is a British film which was, for some reason, filmed in Welsh. It tells a rather pedestrian tale of an average fellow, Hywel, who spends too much of his time downing booze. He spends many a night with his drinking buddies while his life is crumbling around him. By the film's end he has lost everything–wife, daughter, and job–before turning to a kindly friend who steers him toward Alcoholics Anonymous. This one is not likely to be seen by anyone but those in Wales who are fond of reviving near-dead languages. (In Welsh.)

p, Hayden Pearce; d&w, Karl Francis; ph, Roger Evans; m, Ifor Ab Gwilym; ed, Aled Evans; art d, Pearce.

Drama   **(PR:C   MPAA:NR)**

ZAPPA***   (1984, Den.) 103m Per Holst/International Spectrafilm c

Adam Tonsberg (Bjorn), Morton Hoff (Mulle), Peter Reichhardt (Sten), Lone Lindorff (Bjorn's Mother), Arne Hansen (Bjorn's Father), Thomas Nielsen (Henning), Solbjorg Hojfeldt (Sten's Mother), Willy Jacobsen (Bjorn's Grandfather), Rikke Bondo (Kirsten), Mette Knudsen (Sisse), Michael Shomacker (Asger), Jonas Elmer (Folke), Soren Frolund (Kalormen).

A moving tale of three young delinquents growing up during the 1960s in a suburb of Copenhagen. As their home lives sour and their parents grow increasingly less authoritative, the youngsters become unforgivably evil. They are mean to everyone they meet, steal from shopkeepers, and even kill. The most demonic of the three is Reichhardt, a boy who looks as frightening as he acts. Eventually, however, the reasons for Reichhardt's malevolence are exposed. Blame can be taken from his shoulders and placed on his parents and ultimately on the decadent Copenhagen society of the 1960s. (In Danish; English subtitles.)

d, Billie August; w, August, Bjarne Reuter (based on the novel by Reuter); ph, Jan Weincke; m, Bo Holten; ed, Janus Billeskov Jansen; cos, Gitte Kolvig.

Drama   **(PR:O   MPAA:NR)**

MISCELLANEOUS TALKIES

NOTE: The following A-Z miscellaneous compilation of talking films includes, for the sake of being definitive, all those films, from 1927 through 1984 which the editors consider to be of a minor nature. Many of these theatrical films have been shown briefly, some, perhaps only a single or few times before being pulled and shelved, some shown regionally, some shown not at all, never having been released and a few cannot be verified as having been completed, but all are included here for the purpose of presenting comprehensive information.

A*P*E (1976, U.S./Korea) 87m

lp: Rod Arrants, Joanna DeVarona, Alex Nicol.

d, Paul Leder.

ABAR--THE FIRST BLACK SUPERMAN (1977)

lp: J. Walter Smith, Tobar Mayo, Roxie Young, Odell Mack, Gladys Lum, Robert Williams, Tina James.

ABDUCTORS, THE (1972) 95m

lp: Cheri Caffaro, William Grinnell, Richard Smedley, Patrick Wright, Jennifer Brooks.

d, Don Schain.

ABRAHAM OUR PATRIARCH (1933) 62m

lp: Ruben Wendroff, Morris B. Samuylow, Ben Adler, Jacob Mestel, Abraham Teitelbaum, Leibele Waldman.

d,George Roland.

ABSURD--ANTROPOPHAGOUS 2 (1982)

lp: Laura Gemser, Van Johnson.

d, Aristide Massaccesi.

ACCESS CODE (1984) 90m

lp: Martin Landau, MacDonald Carey, Michael Ansara.

ACCIDENT (1983) 104m

lp: Terence Kelly, Fiona Reid, Frank Perry.

d, Donald Britain.

ACCUSED, THE (1953) 52m

lp: Clifford Evans, Ingeborg Wells, Mary Laura Wood, Jean Lodge.

d, Lawrence Huntington, Charles Saunders.

ACID EATERS, THE (1968) 65m

lp: Buckie Buck, Bric Wahl, Bob Wren, John McCloud, Judy Wood, Chico Vespa.

d, B. Ron Elliott.

ACT OF REPRISAL (1965) 87m

lp: Ina Balin, Jeremy Brett.

ADULTERESS, THE (1976) 85m

lp: Tyne Daly, Eric Braeden, Gregory Morton.

d, Norbert Meisel.

ADVENTURE GIRL (1934) 69m

lp: Joan Lowell, Captain Wagner.

ADVENTURE IN MUSIC (1944) 62m

lp: Jose Iturbi, Emanuel Feuermann, Mildred Dilling.

d, Ernest Matray, S.K. Winston, Reginald LeBorg.

ADVENTURES OF CHICO, THE (1938) 56m

d, Stacy Woodard, Horace Woodard..

ADVENTURES OF LUCKY PIERRE, THE (1961)

lp: Billy Falbo.

d, Herschell Gordon Lewis.

ADVENTURES OF PINOCCHIO. THE (1978)

d, Jesse Vogel..

ADVENTURES OF STAR BIRD (1978) 90m

lp: A. Martinez, Don Haggarty, Louise Fitch, Skip Homeier, Skeeter Vaughn.

d, Jack Hively.

ADVENTURES OF THE MASKED PHANTOM, THE (1939) 60m

lp: Monte Rawlins, Sonny LaMont, Larry Mason, Betty Burgess, Jack Ingram.

d, Charles Abbott.

ADVENTURES OF YOUNG ROBIN HOOD (1983) 105m

lp: Peter Demin, Amanda Jones.

ADVENTUROUS KNIGHTS (1935) 56m

lp: David Sharpe, Mary Kornman, Mickey Daniels, Gertrude Messinger.

d, C. Edward Roberts.

ADVERSARY, THE (1970) 75m

lp: Howard Lawrence, Vic Campos, Frank Mangiapane, Stephanie Waxman, Brian Roberts.

d, Larry Klein.

AERODROME, THE (1983, Brit.) 91m

lp: Peter Firth, Richard Johnson, Richard Briers, Natalie Ogle, Jill Bennett.

d, Giles Foster.

AFFAIRS OF ROBIN HOOD, THE (1981) 70m

lp: Ralph Jenkins, Dee Lockood, Danelle Carver.

d, Richard Kanter.

AFRICAN INCIDENT (1934) 61m

lp: Monte Blue, Virginia Brown Faire, Arthur Edmund Carewe, John Miltern, Claire McDowell.

d, Sam Newfield.

AFTERMATH, THE (1980) 95m

lp: Steve Barkett, Lynne Margulies, Sid Haig, Christopher Barkett, Larry Latham, Vincent Barbi.

d, Barkett.

AGE OF PISCES (1972) 95m

lp: Mark Damon, Oliver Reed, Nancy Gates.

ALABAMA'S GHOST (1972)

lp: Christopher Brooks, E. Kerrigan Scott, Turk Murphy Jazz Band.

d, Fredric Hobbs.

ALARM ON 83RD STREET (1965) 91m

lp: George Nader, Sylvia Pascal.

ALBINO (1980)

lp: Christopher Lee, Sybil Danning, James Faulkner, Trevor Howard, Horst Frank.

d, Jurgen Goslar.

ALCHEMIST, THE (1981) 84m

lp: Robert Ginty, Lucinda Dooling, John Sanderford, Viola Kate Stimpson, Robert Glaudini.

d, Charles Band.

ALEX JOSEPH & HIS WIVES (1978)

d, Ted V. Mikels..

ALF GARNETT SAGA, THE (1972) 90m

lp: Dandy Nichols, Warren Mitchell, Adrienne Posta, Mike Angelis, John Le Mesurier.

d, Bob Kellett.

ALI BABA NIGHTS (1953)

lp: George Robey, Fritz Kortner, Anna May Wong, John Garrick, Dennis Hoey, Gibb McLaughlin.

d, Walter Forde.

ALIAS MR. TWILIGHT (1946) 69m

lp: Michael Duane, Olaf Hytten, Lloyd Corrigan, Rosalind Ivan, Alan Bridge, GiGi Perreau.

d, John Sturges.

ALICE GOODBODY (1974) 80m

lp: Sharon Kelly, Daniel Kauffman, Arem Fisher, Norman Field, C.D. LaFleure.

d, Tom Scheuer.

ALICE IN WONDERLAND (1931) 55m

lp: Ruth Gilbert, Leslie King, Ralph Hertz.

d, Bud Pollard.

ALICE OF WONDERLAND IN PARIS (1966) 52m

lp: Carl Reiner, Norma MacMillan, Howard Morris, Allen Swift.

d, Gene Deitch.

ALIEN CONTAMINATION (1981) 100m

lp: Ian McCulloch, Louise Monroe, Martin Mase, Samuel Rauch, Lisa Hahn.

ALIEN ENCOUNTER (1979) 93m

d, Edward Hunt..

ALIEN FACTOR, THE (1978) 80m

lp: Don Leifert, Tom Griffith, Richard Dyszel, Mary Mertens, Richard Geiwitz.

d, Donald M. Dohler.

ALIEN ZONE (1978)

lp: Ivor Francis, Judith Novgrod, Burr DeBenning, Charles Aidman, Stefanie Auerbach, John King.

d, Sharron Miller.

ALIENS FROM ANOTHER PLANET (1967) 90m

lp: James Darren, Robert Colbert, Robert Duvall, Joe Ryan, Tris Coffin, Lew Gallo, Byron Foulger.

ALIENS FROM SPACESHIP EARTH (1977)

lp: Lynda Day George, Donovan.

ALIEN'S RETURN, THE (1980) 90m

lp: Jan-Michael Vincent, Cybill Shepherd, Martin Landau, Raymond Burr.

ALIKI--MY LOVE (1963, U.S./Gr.) 90m

lp: Aliki Vouyouklaki, Wifrid Hyde-White, Jess Conrad, Roland George, Paris Alexander.

d, Rudolph Mate.

ALISON'S BIRTHDAY (1979, Aus.)

lp: Joanne Samuel, Lou Brown, Bunney Brooke.

d, Ian Coughlan,.

ALL COPPERS ARE... (1972, Brit.) 87m

lp: Nicky Henson, Martin Potter, Julia Foster, Ian Hendry.

d, Sidney Hayers.

ALL HALLOWE'EN (1952)

lp: Sally Gilmour, Oleg Briansky, Jane Baxter, Diane Cilento, Clive Morton.

d, Michael Gordon.

ALL MEN ARE APES (1965)

lp: Mark Ryan, Grace Lynn, Steve Woods, Steve Vincent, Bonny Lee Noll, Mia Marlowe.

d, J.P. Mawra.

ALL THAT I HAVE (1951) 62m

lp: Donald Woods, Houseley Stevenson, Sr, Onslow Stevens, John Eldredge.

d, William F. Claxton.

ALL THE YOUNG WIVES (1975) 92m

lp: Gerald Richards, Linda Cook, Edmond Genest, Johnny Popwell, April Johnson.

d, Mike Ripps.

ALONG CAME SALLY (1933) 84m

lp: Cicely Courtneidge, Sam Hardy, Phyllis Clare, Billy Milton, Hartley Power.

d, Tim Whelan.

ALONG THE SUNDOWN TRAIL (1942)

lp: William Boyd, Art Davis, Lee Powell, Julie Duncan, Kermit Maynard, Charles King.

d, Sam Newfield.

ALPHA INCIDENT, THE (1976)

lp: Ralph Meeker, Stafford Morgan, Carol Irene Newell, John Goff, John Alderman.

d, Bill Rebane.

ALTERNATIVE (1976) 74m

lp: Wendy Hughes, Peter Adams, Carla Hoogeveen, Tony Bonner.

ALTERNATIVE MISS WORLD, THE (1980) 93m

lp: Andrew Logan, Ken Grant, Luciana Martinez, Richard Logan, Peter Logan, Kevin Whitney.

d, Richard Gayer.

AMANITA PESTILENS (1963)

lp: Genevieve Bujold.

d, Rene Bonniere.

AMAZING LOVE SECRET (1975)

lp: John Holmes, Sandy Dempsey, Mario Arnold, George Carey.

d, Tom Parker.

AMAZING TRANSPLANT, THE (1970) 80m

lp: Juan Fernandez, Linda Southern, Larry Hunter, Olive Denneccio, Sandy Eden.

d, Louis Silverman.

AMERICAN GAME, THE (1979) 89m

lp: Brian Walker, Stretch Graham, Dave Tawil, Gil Ferschtman.

d, Jay Freund, David Wolf.

AMERICAN MATCHMAKER (1940) 87m

lp: Leo Fuchs, Judith Abarbanel, Rosetta Bialis, Yudel Dubinsky, Anna Guskin.

d, Edgar G. Ulmer.

AMERICAN NIGHTMARE (1981, Can.) 95m

lp: Lawrence S. Day, Lora Staley, Neil Dainard, Michael Ironside, Lenore Zann.

d, Don McBrearty.

AMERICAN RASPBERRY (1980) 75m

lp: Wil Albert, Paul Ainsley, Royce D. Applegate, Gene Borkan, Meredith Baer.

d, Bradley R. Swirnoff.

AMOROUS ADVENTURES OF DON QUIXOTE AND SANCHO PANZA, THE (1976) 127m

lp: Hy Pyke, Corey John Fischer, Maria Aronoff.

d, Raphael Nussbaum.

AND NOW TOMORROW (1952) 70m

lp: Don DeFore, Earle Hodgins, Louise Arthur, Morris Ankrum, Stanley Andrews, Lumsden Hare.

d, William Watson.

AND THE WALL CAME TUMBLING DOWN (1984) 73m

lp: Barbi Benton, Gareth Hurt, Brian Deacon, Peter Wyngarde, Pat Hayes.

d, Paul Annett.

ANDREA (1979) 90m

lp: Marina Langner, Lawrence St. Marks, Richard Massey.

d, Leopold Pomes.

ANDY WARHOL'S DRACULA (1974) 93m

lp: Udo Kier, Arno Juerging, Maxime McKenory, Joe Dallesandro.

d, Paul Morrissey.

ANDY WARHOL'S FRANKENSTEIN (1974) 94m

lp: Udo Kier, Dalila di Lazzaro, Monique Van Vooren, Joe Dallesandro.

d, Paul Morrissey.

ANGEL FOR SATAN, AN (1966, Ital.) 93m

lp: Barbara Steele, Antonio De Teffe, Claudio Gora, Ursula Davis, Aldo Berti.

d, Camillo Mastrocinque.

ANGEL OF H.E.A.T. (1982)

lp: Marilyn Chambers, Mary Woronov, Gerald Okamura, Stephen Johnson, Milt Kogan.

d, Helen Sanford.

ANGELS (1976) 90m

lp: Vincent Schiavelli, Keith Berger, Marquita Callwood, David Bryant.

d, Spencer Compton.

ANGELS' WILD WOMEN (1972)

lp: Regina Carrol, Kent Taylor, Maggie Bemby, Ross Hagen, Vicki Volante.

d, Al Adamson.

ANGRY GOD, THE (1948) 57m

lp: Alicia Parla, Casimiro Ortega.

d, Van Campel Heilner.

ANNABELLE LEE (1972)

lp: Margaret O'Brien.

d, Harold Daniels.

ANONYMOUS AVENGER, THE (1976, Ital.) 88m

lp: Franco Nero, Barbara Bach, Renzo Palmer, Giancarlo Prete, Romano Puppo.

d, Anzo G. Castellari.

ANY BODY...ANY WAY (1968)

lp: Eve Reeves, Joyce Denner, Daniel Garth, Ivan Hagar, Irene Lawrence.

d, Charles Romine.

ANYBODY'S WAR (1930)

lp: Moran and Mack, Joan Peers, Neil Hamilton.

d, Richard Wallace.

APACHE KID'S ESCAPE, THE (1930) 53m

lp: Jack Perrin.

APARTMENT ON THE THIRTEENTH FLOOR (1973)

lp: Vincent Parra, Emma Cohen.

d, Eloy De La Iglesia.

APE CREATURE (1968, Ger.) 96m

lp: Herbert Fux, Hubert von Meyerinck, Inge Langen, Eric Vaesser, Maria Litto.

d, Alfred Vohrer.

APOCALYPSE 3:16 (1964) 110m

lp: Myron Van Brundt, Tom Kealiinohomoku, Dion Satterfield, Donald McCauley, Chester Gorman.

d, Martin Charlot.

APPOINTMENT WITH A SHADOW (1957) 72m

lp: George Nader, Joanna Moore, Brian Keith, Virginia Field, Frank de Kova.

d, Richard Carlson.

AQUARIAN, THE (1972) 95m

lp: Joan Collins, Richard Todd, Franco Nero, Jan Murray.

ARE YOU BEING SERVED? (1977) 95m

lp: John Inman, Frank Thornton, Mollie Sugden, Trevor Bannister.

d, Bob Kellett.

ARNOLD'S WRECKING CO. (1973) 85m

lp: Steve De Souza, Mike Ranshaw, Eddie Henderson, Shirley Kauffman, Byron Schauer.

d, De Souza.

AROUSED (1968)

lp: Janine Lenon, Steve Hollister, Fleurette Carter, Joanna Mills, Tony Palladino, Ted Gelanza.

d, Anton Holden..

AROUND THE CORNER (1930) 71m

lp: George Sidney, Joan Peers, Charlie Murray, Charles Delaney.

d, Bert Glennon.

ARSON RACKET SQUAD (1938) 54m

lp: Bob Livingston, Rosalind Keith, Jack LaRue.

d, Joe Kane.

ARTHUR!! ARTHUR? (1970) 94m

lp: Shelley Winters, Terry Thomas, Tammy Grimes.

ASHES AND EMBERS (1982) 120m

lp: John Anderson, Evelyn Blackwell, Norman Blalock, Kathy Flewellen.

d, Maile Gerima.

ASSASSIN OF YOUTH (1937)

lp: Luana Gardner.

d, Elmer Clifton.

ASSAULT WITH A DEADLY WEAPON (1983)

lp: Richard Holliday, Sandra Foley, Lamont Jackson, Rinaldo Rincon.

d, Walter Gaines.

ASSIGNMENT, THE (1978) 92m

lp: Christopher Plummer, Thomas Hellberg, Carolyn Seymour, Fernando Rey.

ASSIGNMENT ABROAD (1955) 73m

lp: Robert Alda, Kay Callard, Robert Haynes, Indra Kamajozo, Lies Franken.

d, Arthur Dreifuss.

ASTROLOGER, THE (1975) 96m

lp: Craig Denney, Jacqueline Day, Rocky Barbanica, Darien Earle, Arthur Chadbourne, Harvey Hunter.

d, Denney.

ASTROLOGER, THE (1979)

lp: Bob Byrd, Mark Buntzman, Monica Tidewell.

d, Jim Glickenhaus.

ASYLUM FOR A SPY (1967) 90m

lp: Robert Stack, Don Gordon, Felicia Farr, Victor Buono, George Macready, J.D. Cannon.

d, Stuart Rosenberg.

ASYLUM OF SATAN (1972)

lp: Charles Kissinger, Carla Borelli, Nick Jolly.

d, William Girdler.

ATOMIC AGENT (1959, Fr.) 85m

lp: Martine Carol, Felix Marten, Dany Saval, Dario Moreno.

d, Henri Decoin.

ATOMIC WAR BRIDE (1966) 77m

lp: Anton Vodak, Eva Krewskan.

ATOR: THE FIGHTING EAGLE (1983) 100m

lp: Miles O'Keeffe, Sabrina Siani, Ritza Brown, Edmund Purdom, Laura Gemser.

d, David Hills.

ATOR, THE INVINCIBLE (1984) 100m

lp: Miles O'Keeffe, Lisa Foster, David Cain, Charles Barromel, Chen Wong.

d, David Hills.

ATTACK AT NOON SUNDAY (1971) 93m

lp: Mark Leonard, John Russell, Linda Avery.

AU PAIR GIRLS (1973)

lp: Gabrielle Drake, Astrid Frank, Me Me Lay, Richard O'Sullivan, Ferdy Mayne.

d, Val Guest.

AUTOPSY (1980, Ital.) 125m

lp: Mimsy Farmer, Barry Primus, Ray Lovelock, Angela Goodwin.

d, Armando Crispini.

AVALANCHE (1975, Brit.) 60m

lp: Michael Portman, David Ronder.

d, Frederic Goode.

AVENGER OF THE SEVEN SEAS (1960) 94m

lp: Richard Harrison, Walter Barnes.

AVENGER OF VENICE (1965) 91m

lp: Brett Halsey.

AWOL (1973) 82m

lp: Russ Thacker, Glynn Turman, Isabella Kaliff, Lenny Baker, Dutch Miller, Stefan Ekman.

d, Herb Freed.

AXE (1977) 67m

lp: Frederick R. Friedel, Jack Canon, Ray Green, Leslie Lee, Douglas Powers.

d, Friedel.

"B"...MUST DIE (1973) 94m

lp: Darren McGavin, Patricia Neal, Burgess Meredith.

B.J. LANG PRESENTS (1971) 85m

lp: Mickey Rooney, Luana Anders, Keenan Wynn.

BABO 73 (1964) 60m

lp: Taylor Mead.

d, Robert Downey.

BABY DOLLS (1982)

lp: Mel Welles, Len Lesser, Leslie Ackerman, Ron Ross, Speed Stearns, Linda Gary.

d, Welles.

BABY NEEDS A NEW PAIR OF SHOES (1974)

lp: Paul Harris, Reginald Farmer, Frank DeKova, Frances Williams.

BABYSITTER, THE (1969) 90m

lp: George E. Carey, Patricia Wymer, Ann Bellamy, Ken Hooker, Cathy Williams, Robert Tessier.

d, Don Henderson.

BACCHANALE (1970)

lp: Darcy Brown, Uta Erickson, Chuck Federico, Pat Agers, Lydia Burns.

d, John Amaro, Lem Amaro.

BACK PAGE (1934) 64m

lp: Peggy Shannon, Russell Hopton, Edwin Maxwell, Sterling Holloway, Claude Gillingwater.

d, Anton Lorenze.

BAD BUNCH, THE (1976)

lp: Greydon Clark, Tom Johnigarn, Jock Mahoney, Pamela Corbett, Jacqueline Cole, Aldo Ray.

d, Clark.

BAD GEORGIA ROAD (1977) 86m

lp: Gary Lockwood, Carol Lynley, Royal Dano, John Wheeler, John Kerry.

d, John C. Broderick.

BALKAN EXPRESS (1983) 102m

BALLAD OF BILLIE BLUE (1972)

lp: Jason Ledger, Marty Allen, Ray Danton, Erik Estrada.

d, Kent Osborne.

BAMBOO GODS AND IRON MEN (1974) 96m

lp: James Iglehart, Shirley Washington, Chiquito, Marissa Delgado, Eddie Garcia.

d, Cesar Gallardo.

BANDITS IN ROME (1967, Ital.) 109m

lp: John Cassavetes, Gabriele Ferzetti, Nikos Kourkoulos, Anita Sanders.

d, Alberto deMartino.

BAR MITSVE (1935) 85m

lp: Boris Thomashefsky, Regina Zuckerberg, Anita Chayes, Peter Graf, Gertrude Bullman, Leah Noemi.

BARBARA (1970)

lp: Jack Rader, Nancy Boyle, Robert McLane, John Kuhner, Bill Haislip, Melba LaRose, Jr.

d, Walter Burns.

BARE KNUCKLES (1977) 90m

lp: Robert Viharo, Sherry Jackson, Gloria Hendry, Michael Heit, John Daniels.

d, Don Edmonds.

BARGAIN WITH BULLETS (1937)

lp: Ralph Cooper, Francis Turnham, Theresa Harris, Sam McDaniel, Les Hite and the Cotton Club Orchestra.

BATTLE OF BILLY'S POND (1976) 60m

lp: Ben Buckton, Linda Robson.

d, Harley Cokliss.

BATTLE OF EL ALAMEIN (1971)

lp: Frederick Stafford, George Hilton, Michael Rennie.

d, Calvin Jackson Paget.

BATTLE OF THE EAGLES (1981) 100m

lp: Bekim Fehmiu, George Taylor, Frank Phillips, Gloria Samara, Peter Roland.

BE CAREFUL, MR. SMITH (1935) 72m

lp: Bobbie Comber, Cecil Ramage, Bertha Belmore, C. Denier Warren, Bertha Ricardo, Frank Atkinson.

d, Max Mack.

BEACH BUNNIES (1977)

lp: Wendy Cavanough, Brenda Fogerty, Linda Gildersleeve, Mariwin Roberts.

d, A.C. Stephen.

BEACH HOUSE (1982) 76m

lp: Kathy McNeil, Richard Duggan, Ileana Seidel, John Cosola, Spence Waugh.

d, John Gallagher.

BEALE STREET MAMA (1946)

lp: Spencer Williams, Rosalie Larrimore, Joyce McElrath, Allen & Allen.

d, Williams.

BEARTOOTH (1978) 85m

lp: Dub Taylor, Buck Taylor.

BEAST OF BORNEO (1935) 65m

lp: John Preston, Mae Stuart, Eugene Sigaloff, Doris Brook, Val Durran, Alexander Schonberg.

d, Harry Garson.

BEAST OF THE YELLOW NIGHT (1971, U.S./Phil.) 87m

lp: Eddie Garcia, John Ashley, Mary Wilcox, Leopold Salcedo, Ken Metcalf, Vic Diaz.

d, Eddie Romero.

BEAST THAT KILLED WOMEN (1965) 61m

d, Barry Mahn..

BEASTS (1983) 92m

lp: Tom Babson, Kathy Christopher, Vern Porter.

BEAUTY AND THE BODY (1963) 62m

lp: Kip Behar, Judy Miller.

d, Paul Mart.

BEAUTY'S DAUGHTER (1935) 69m

lp: Claire Trevor, Ralph Bellamy, Jane Darwell, Warren Hymer, Ben Lyon, Kathleen Burke.

d, Allan Dwan.

BECAUSE OF THE CATS (1974) 90m

lp: Bryan Marshall, Alexandra Stewart, Alex Van Rooyen, Leo Bayers, Martin Van Zundert, George Baker.

d, Fons Rademakers.

BED OF VIOLENCE (1967) 95m

lp: Cleo Nova, Kip Rivas, Nick Dundas, Tony Giarratano, Sue Evans, Rip Atlanta.

d, Joe Sarno.

BEGGAR'S HOLIDAY (1934) 59m

lp: Hardie Albright, J. Farrell MacDonald, Sally O'Neil, George Grandee, Barbara Barondess.

d, Sam Newfield.

BEGGING THE RING (1979, Brit.) 55m

lp: Danny Simpson, Jon Croft, Janette Legge, Kenneth Midwood, Terence Coholey, Alan Penn.

d, Colin Gregg.

BEHIND PRISON BARS   (1937)

lp: Ralph Morgan, Kay Linaker, Edward Acuff, Charles Brokaw, Ben Alexander.

d, Raymond Cannon.

BEHIND SOUTHERN LINES   (1952) 51m

lp: Guy Madison, Andy Devine, Rand Brooks, Murray Alper, Jonathan Hale, Orley Lindgren.

d, Thomas Carr.

BEHIND THE HEADLINES   (1953) 51m

lp: John Fitzgerald, Gilbert Harding, Adrienne Scott, Vi Kaley, Michael McCarthy.

d, Maclean Rogers.

BEHIND THE SHUTTERS   (1976, Span.) 87m

lp: Jean Seberg, Barry Stokes, Marisol, Perla Cristal, Gerard Tichy.

d, Juan Antonio Bardem.

BELL OF HELL, THE   (1973)

d, Claudio Guerin Hill..

BELLAMY: MESSAGE GIRL MURDERS   (1980) 92m

lp: John Stanton, Tim Elston.

BELLE SOMMERS   (1962) 62m

lp: Polly Bergen, David Janssen, Warren Stevens, Carroll O'Connor, Jay Adler.

d, Elliot Silverstein.

BELOVED, THE   (1972) 87m

lp: Raquel Welch, Flora Robson, Richard Johnson, Jack Hawkins, Frank Wolf.

d, Yorgo Pan Cosmatos.

BELOW THE HILL   (1974) 105m

lp: Ray Bernier, Lita Anderson, Roger Sorel, Suzanne Mannion.

d, Angus Bailey.

BELT AND SUSPENDERS MAN, THE   (1970) 85m

lp: Donald J. Levy, Halcyon Makapagal.

d, Levy.

BEST, THE   (1979) 85m

lp: Gloria Guida, Patricia Welby, Loretta Pierson, Carl Goefrey.

d, M. Guerin.

BEST FRIENDS   (1975)

lp: Richard Hatch, Susanne Benton, Doug Chapin, Ann Noland, Renee Paul.

d, Noel Nosseck.

BETHUNE   (1977) 88m

lp: Donald Sutherland, Kate Nelligan, David Gardner.

d, Eric Till.

BEWARE MY BRETHREN   (1972, Brit.) 91m

lp: Ann Todd, Patrick Magee, Tony Beckley, Madeline Hinde, Suzanna Leigh.

d, Robert Hart-Davis.

BEWARE OF BACHELORS   (1928) 64m

lp: Audrey Ferris, William Collier, Jr, Clyde Cook, Andre Beranger, Dave Morris.

d, Roy del Ruth.

BEWARE THE BLACK WIDOW   (1968) 72m

lp: Sharon Kent, Luke St. Clair, Don Canfield, Gia Nina, Dean Larents, Danny Nugent.

d, Larry Crane.

BEYOND CONTROL   (1971) 89m

lp: William Berger, Anthony Baker, Georgia Moll, Helga Anders, Grit Botcher.

d, Baker.

BEYOND REASON   (1977)

lp: Telly Savalas, Diana Muldaur, Laura Johnson, Douglas Dirkson, Barney Phillips, Walter Brooke.

d, Savalas.

BEYOND THE LAW   (1930) 63m

lp: Robert Frazer, Louise Lorraine, Jimmy Kane, Lane Chandler, Charles L. King.

d, J.P. McGowan.

BEYOND THE MOON   (1964) 78m

lp: Richard Crane, Sally Mansfield, James Lydon, Maurice Cass.

d, William Beaudine, Hollingsworth Morse.

BEYOND THE UNIVERSE   (1981) 90m

lp: David Ladd, Jackie Ray.

BIBI   (1977)

lp: Maria Forsa, Annie Sebring, Nadia Phillips.

d, Joe Sarno.

BIG BAD WOLF, THE   (1968) 53m

nar: Paul Tripp.

BIG BOY RIDES AGAIN   (1935)

lp: Guinn "Big Boy Williams", Connie Bergen, Lafe McKee, Vic Potel, Frank Ellis.

d, Al Herman.

BIG BUST-OUT, THE   (1973) 75m

lp: Vonetta McGee, Monica Taylor, Linda Fox, Karen Carter, Gordon Mitchell, Christin Thorn.

d, Richard Jackson.

BIG CALIBRE   (1935)

lp: Bob Steele, Bill Quinn, Earl Dwire, Peggy Campbell, John Elliott, Georgia O'Dell.

d, Robert N. Bradbury.

BIG DOLL HOUSE, THE   (1971) 93m

lp: Judy Brown, Roberta Collins, Pam Grier, Brooke Mills, Pat Woodell, Sid Haig.

d, Jack Hill.

BIG FIGHT, THE   (1930) 65m

lp: Lola Lane, Ralph Ince, Guinn "Big Boy" Williams, Stepin Fetchit, Wheeler Oakman.

d, Walter Lang.

BIG FUN CARNIVAL, THE   (1957) 90m

lp: Marian Stafford, Jared Reed.

d, Marc Daniels.

BIG TIME   (1977) 96m

lp: Christopher Joy, Tobar Mayo, Jayne Kennedy, Art Evans, Roger E. Mosley.

d, Andrew Georgias.

BIG TIMER   (1932)

lp: Ben Lyon, Thelma Todd, Constance Cummings, Charles Delaney, Tommy Dugan.

d, Eddie Buzzell.

BIG TIMERS   (1947)

lp: Jackie "Moms" Mabley, Duke Williams, Stepin Fetchit, Francine Everett.

d, Bud Pollard.

BIG ZAPPER   (1974)

lp: Linda Marlow, Gary Hope, Sean Hewett, Michael O'Malley, Jack May.

d, Lindsey Shonteff.

BIJOU   (1972) 77m

lp: Bill Harrison, Lydia Black, Tom Bradford, Cable, Peter Fisk, Michael Green.

d, Wakefield Poole.

BIKINI PARADISE   (1967) 89m

lp: Janette Scott, John Baer, Kieron Moore, Kay Walsh, Sylvia Sorente, Alexander Knox.

d, Gregg Tallas.

BILLION DOLLAR THREAT, THE   (1979, Brit.)

lp: Dale Robinette, Patrick Macnee, Ralph Bellamy.

BILLY THE KID OUTLAWED   (1940) 52m

lp: Bob Steele, Al "Fuzzy" St. John, Louise Currie, Carleton Young, John Merton.

d, Sam Newfield.

BILLY THE KID'S GUN JUSTICE   (1940) 57m

lp: Bob Steele, Al "Fuzzy" St. John, Louise Currie, Carleton Young, Charles King.

d, Sam Newfield.

BILLY THE KID'S SMOKING GUNS   (1942) 58m

lp: Buster Crabbe, Al "Fuzzy" St. John, John Merton, Ted Adams, Dave O'Brien.

d, Sherman Scott.

BIM   (1976) 100m

lp: Ralph Maharaj, Hamilton Parris, Wilbert Holder, Anna Seerattan, Lawrence Goldstraw.

d, Hugh A. Robertson.

BIO-HAZARD   (1984) 90m

lp: Angelique Pettijohn, Carroll Borland, Richard Hench.

d, Fred Olen Ray.

BIRTHRIGHT   (1939)

lp: Ethel Moses, Alec Lovejoy, Carmen Newsome, Laura Bowman, George Vessey.

BITCH, THE   (1979) 90m

lp: Joan Collins, Michael Coby, Kenneth Haigh, Ian Hendry, Sue Lloyd, Carolyn Seymour.

d, Gerry O'Hara.

BIZARRE   (1969) 91m

lp: Richard Schulman, Dorothy Grumbar, Anthony Rowlands, Yvonne Quenet, Elliott Stein.

d, Anthony Balch.

BLACK BELT JONES   (1974) 87m

lp: Jim Kelly, Gloria Hendry, Scatman Crothers, Alan Weeks.

d, Robert Clouse.

BLACK BIRD DESCENDING: TENSE ALIGNMENT   (1977) 110m

lp: Tessa Adams, Josephine LeGrice, Jack Murray, Liz Rhodes.

d, Malcolm LeGrice.

BLACK CARRION   (1984) 73m

lp: Season Hubley, Leigh Lawson, Norman Bird, Alan Love, Diana King, Julian Littman.

d, John Hough.

BLACK CHARIOT   (1971) 90m

lp: Bernie Casey, Barbara O. Jones.

d, Robert L. Goodwin.

BLACK CONNECTION, THE   (1974)

lp: The Checkmates, Ltd, Bobby Stevens, Sweet Louie, Sonny Charles, Tommy Moe Raft.

d, Michael J. Finn.

BLACK FANTASY   (1974)

d, Lionel Rogosin..

BLACK FIST   (1977) 94m

lp: Richard Lawson, Annazette Chase, Philip Michael Thomas, Dabney Coleman, Robert Burr.

d, Timothy Galfas.

BLACK FOREST, THE   (1954) 63m

lp: Peggy Ann Garner, Akim Tamiroff, Gordon Howard.

d, Gene Martel.

BLACK GODFATHER, THE   (1974) 96m

lp: Rod Perry, Damu King, Jimmy Witherspoon, Don Chastain, Diane Summerfield.

d, John Evans.

BLACK HEAT   (1976)

lp: Timothy Brown, Russ Tamblyn, Jana Bellan, Geoffrey Land, Al Richardson, Regina Carrol.

d, Al Adamson.

BLACK HOOKER   (1974)

lp: Sandra Alexandra, Kathryn Jackson, Jeff Burton, Teddy Quinn, Durey Mason.

d, Arthur Robertson.

BLACK ISLAND   (1979, Brit.) 60m

lp: Martin Murphy, Michael Salmon.

d, Ben Bolt.

BLACK JESUS   (1971, Ital.)

lp: Woody Strode, Jean Servais, Franco Citti.

d, Valerio Zurlin.

BLACK LOLITA   (1975)

lp: Yolanda Love, Ed Cheatwood, Joey Ginza, Susan Ayres.

d, Stephen Gibson.

BLACK ORCHID   (1952) 60m

lp: Ronald Howard, Mary Laura Wood, Olga Edwardes, John Bentley, Patrick Barr.

d, Charles Saunders.

BLACK PEARL, THE   (1977)
lp: Gilbert Roland, Carl Anderson, Mario Custudio.
d, Saul Swimmer.

BLACK PLANET, THE   (1982, Aus.) 78m
d, Paul Williams..

BLACK RAINBOW   (1966) 60m
d, Michael Zuckerman..

BLACK ROOM, THE   (1983)
lp: Stephen Knight, Cassandra Gaviola, Jim Stathis.
d, Norman Thaddeus Vane.

BLACK SAMURAI   (1977)
lp: Jim Kelly.
d, Al Adamson.

BLACK STARLET   (1974) 90m
lp: Juanita Brown, Eric Mason, Rockne Tarkington, Damu King, Diane Holden, Noah Keen.
d, Chris Munger.

BLACK STREETFIGHTER   (1976)
lp: Richard Lawson, Annazette Chase, Robert Burr.
d, Timothy Galfas.

BLACK TIDE   (1958) 69m
lp: Joy Webster, Derek Bond, John Ireland, Sam Rockett, Maureen Connell.
d, C. Pennington-Richards.

BLACK TORMENT   (1984) 87m
lp: Heather Sears, John Turner.

BLACK TRASH   (1978)
lp: Nigel Davenport, Ken Gampu, Peter Dyneley, Bima Stagg, Madala Mphahlele.
d, Chris Rowley.

BLACKJACK   (1978) 104m
lp: Bill Smith, Tony Burton, Paris Earl, Damu King, Diane Sommerfield, Angela May.
d, John Evans.

BLACKSNAKE   (1973) 85m
lp: Anouska Hempel, David Warbeck, Percy Herbert, Milton McCollin, Thomas Baptiste.
d, Russ Meyer.

BLANCHEVILLE MONSTER   (1963)
lp: Joan Hills, Richard Davis.

BLAST-OFF GIRLS   (1967) 79m
lp: Dan Conway, Tom Tyrell, Ron Liace, Dennis Hickey, Chris Wolski.
d, Herschell Gordon Lewis.

BLAZING ACROSS THE PECOS   (1948) 56m
lp: Charles Starrett, Smiley Burnette, Patricia White, Chief Thunder Cloud, Paul Campbell.
d, Ray Nazarro.

BLAZING BULLETS   (1951) 51m
lp: Johnny Mack Brown, Lois Hall, House Peters, Jr, Stanley Price, Dennis Moore.
d, Wallace F. Fox.

BLAZING GUNS   (1935)
lp: Reb Russell, Marion Shilling, Lafe McKee, Joseph Girard, Frank McCarroll.
d, Ray Heinz.

BLAZING JUSTICE   (1936) 60m
lp: Bill Cody, Gertrude Messinger, Gordon Griffith, Milt Moranti, Budd Buster, Frank Yaconelli.
d, Al Herman.

BLAZING MAGNUM (1976) 99m
lp: Stuart Whitman, John Saxon, Martin Landau, Tisa Farrow, Gayle Hunnicutt, Carole Laure.
d, Martin Herbert.

BLAZING STEWARDESSES   (1975) 85m
lp: Yvonne DeCarlo, Bob Livingstone, Don "Red" Barry, Jimmy Ritz, Harry Ritz, Regina Carroll.
d, Al Adamson.

BLAZING THE WESTERN TRAIL   (1945) 60m
lp: Charles Starrett, Dub Taylor, Tex Harding, Carole Mathews, Alan Bridge, Nolan Leary.
d, Vernon Keays.

BLESS THIS HOUSE   (1972, Brit.) 88m
lp: Sidney James, Sally Geeson, Diana Coupland, Terry Scott, June Whitfield.
d, Gerald Thomas.

BLIND FOOLS   (1940, Brit.) 66m
lp: Herbert Rawlinson, Claire Whitney, Russell Hicks.

BLIND RAGE   (1978)
lp: Tony Ferrer, D'Urville Martin, Leo Fong, Dick Adair, Fred Williamson, Darnell Garcia.
d, Efren C. Pinion.

BLIND SPOT   (1947) 73m
lp: Chester Morris, Constance Dowling, Steven Geray, Sid Tomack, James Bell.
d, Robert Gordon.

BLINKER'S SPY-SPOTTER   (1971) 58m
lp: David Spooner, Sally-Ann Marlowe, Brent Oldfield, Edward Kemp.
d, Jack Stephens.

BLOCKED TRAIL, THE   (1943) 58m
lp: Bob Steele, Tom Tyler, Jimmie Dodd, Helen Deverell, George Lewis, Kermit Maynard.
d, Elmer Clifton.

BLONDE CONNECTION, THE   (1975) 84m
lp: Judy Winter, Werner Peters.

BLONDE GODDESS   (1982) 85m
lp: Susanna Britton, J. Ford, Loni Sanders, Ron Jeremy, Jane Kelton.
d, Bill Eagle.

BLOOD AND GUNS   (1979, Ital.)
lp: Orson Welles, Tomas Milian.
d, Giulio Petroni.

BLOOD COUPLE   (1974) 86m
lp: Duane Jones, Mabel King, Marlene Clark, Leonard Jackson, Candece Tarpley, Richard Harrow.
d, F.H. Novikov.

BLOOD DEBTS (1983) 90m

lp: Richard Harrison, Mike Manty, James Gaines, Anne Jackson, Anne Milhench.

BLOOD MONSTER (1972)

lp: Carolyn Brandt, Ron Haydock, Jason Wayne, Linda Steckler, Laura Steckler.

d, Ray Dennis Steckler.

BLOOD OF JESUS (1941) 68m

lp: Spencer Williams, James B. Jones, Juanita Riley, Cathryn Caviness.

d, Williams.

BLOOD OF THE IRON MAIDEN (1969)

lp: John Carradine, Carol Kane, Marvin Miller, Peter Duryea, Pat Heider, Barbara Mallory.

d, Ben Benoit.

BLOOD SEEKERS, THE (1971)

d, Al Adamson..

BLOOD SONG (1982) 90m

lp: Frankie Avalon, Donna Wilkes, Richard Jaeckel, Dane Clark, Antoinette Bower, L. Montana.

d, Alan J. Levi.

BLOOD THIRST (1965 Phil./U.S.)

lp: Robert Winston, Yvonne Nielson, Judy Dennis, Vic Diaz, Eddie Infante, Katherine Henryk.

d, Newt Arnold.

BLOODLESS VAMPIRE, THE (1965)

lp: Charles Macauley, Helen Thompson.

d, Michael du Pont.

BLOODRAGE (1979) 83m

lp: Lawrence Tierney, Ian Scott, James Johnston, Jerry McGee, Jimi Keys.

d, Joseph Bigwood.

BLOODSTALKERS (1976) 90m

lp: Kenny Miller, Jerry Albert.

BLOODY BIRTHDAY (1980) 85m

lp: Susan Strasberg, Jose Ferrer, Lori Lethin, Melinda Cordell, Joe Penny, Ellen Geer.

d, Ed Hunt.

BLOW BUGLES BLOW (1936) 74m

lp: George Hicks.

d, Rudolph Messel.

BLOWN SKY HIGH (1984) 107m

lp: Daniel Hirsch, Frank Schultz, Clayton Norcross.

BLUE MONEY (1975) 93m

lp: Alain-Patrick Chappuis, Barbara Caron, Inga Maria, Jeff Gall, Oliver Aubrey, Steve Roberson.

d, Chappuis.

BLUE SEXTET (1972) 90m

lp: John Damon, Peter Clune, Coco Sumaki, Margaret Cathell, Adrienne Jalbert.

d, David E. Durston.

BLUE SUMMER (1973)

lp: Darcey Hollingsworth, Bo White, Lilly Bo Beep, Joann Sterling, Melissa Evers.

d, Chuck Vincent.

BLUEBEARD'S CASTLE (1969, Brit.) 60m

lp: Norman Foster, Anna Raquel Sartre.

d, Michael Powell.

BOARDING HOUSE (1984) 89m

lp: Hawk Audley, Kalassu, Alexandra Day, Joel McGinnis Riordan, Brian Bruderlin.

d, John Wintergate.

BOARDING HOUSE BLUES (1948) 90m

lp: Jackie "Moms" Mabley, Dusty Fletcher, Lucky Millinder, Johnny Lee, Jr.

d, Josh Binney.

BOD SQUAD, THE (1976) 99m

lp: Tamar Elliot, Sonja Jeanine, Diane Drube, Debra Ralls, Gillian Bray.

BODY BENEATH, THE (1970) 85m

lp: Jackie Skarvellis, Emma Jones, Susan Clark, Colin Gordon, Gavin Reed, Susan Heard.

d, Andy Milligan.

BODY FEVER (1981) 78m

lp: Bernard Fein, Gary Kent, Herb Robbins.

BODY IS A SHELL, THE (1957)

lp: Andrea Farnese, Carla Faryll, April Lynn, Wesley La Violette, Paul Barry.

d, Merle S. Gould.

BODYGUARD, THE (1976) 86m

lp: Sonny Chiba, Aaron Banks, Bill Louie, Judy Lee.

d, Simon Nuchtern.

BOESMAN AND LENA (1976) 102m

lp: Yvonne Bryceland, Athol Fugard, Sandy Tube, Val Donald, Percy Sieff.

d, Ross Devenish.

BOMBAY WATERFRONT (1952, Brit.) 71m

lp: John Bentley, Peter Gawthorne, Patricia Dainton.

BONE (1972) 95m

lp: Yaphet Kotto, Andrew Duggan, Joyce Van Patten, Jeannie Berlin, Casey King.

d, Larry Cohen.

BONNIE'S KIDS (1973) 103m

lp: Tiffany Bolling, Steve Sandor, Robin Mattson, Scott Brady.

d, Arthur Marks.

BOOT HILL BANDITS (1942) 58m

lp: Ray Corrigan, John King, Max Terhune, Jean Brooks, John Merton, Glenn Strange.

d, S. Roy Luby.

BOOTS TURNER (1973)

lp: Terry Carter, Gwen Mitchell, Kyle Johnson, James Sikking, Art Lund.

d, J. Edward, J. Lasko.

BORDER CITY RUSTLERS (1953) 54m

lp: Guy Madison, Andy Devine, Gloria Talbott, Isabel Randolph, Steve Pendleton, George Lewis, Murray Alper.

BORDER FENCE (1951) 89m

lp: Walt Wayne, Lee Morgan, Mary Nord, Steve Raines, Harry Garcia.

d, Norman Sheldon, H.W. Kier.

BORDER GUNS (1934)

lp: Bill Cody, Blanche Mehaffey, Bill Cody, Jr, George Chesebro, Franklyn Farnum.

d, Jack Nelson.

BORDER LUST (1967) 60m

lp: Don Megowan, Jim Davis, Sandra Giles.

BORDER MENACE, THE (1934)

lp: Bill Cody, Miriam Rice, Ben Corbett, George Chesebro, James Aubrey, Frank Clark.

d, Jack Nelson.

BORDER ROUNDUP (1942) 57m

lp: George Houston, Al "Fuzzy" St. John, Dennis Moore, Patricia Knox.

d, Sam Newfield.

BORDER VENGEANCE (1935)

lp: Reb Russell, Mary Jane Carey, Kenneth MacDonald, Ben Corbett, Hank Bell, Glenn Strange.

d, Ray Heinz.

BORDERTOWN TRAIL (1944) 55m

lp: Smiley Burnette, Sunset Carson, Ellen Lowe, Weldon Heyburn, Addison Richards.

d, Lesley Selander.

BORN FOR TROUBLE (1955) 77m

lp: Joan Shawlee, Peter Reynolds, Greta Gynt, Elizabeth Allen, Stephen Boyd, Peter Illing.

d, Desmond Davis.

BORN TO BATTLE (1935)

lp: Tom Tyler, Jean Carmen, Earl Dwire, Julian Rivero, Nelson McDowell, William Desmond.

d, Harry S. Webb.

BOSS COWBOY (1934) 51m

lp: Buddy Roosevelt, Frances Morris, Sam Pierce, Fay McKenzie, Lafe McKee.

d, Victor Adamson.

BOSS LADY (1982) 80m

lp: Claudia Smith, John Nuzzo, Candy Townsend, Fay Williams, Robert Atwood.

d, Chris Warfield.

BOSS OF BOOMTOWN (1944) 56m

lp: Rod Cameron, Tom Tyler, Fuzzy Knight, Vivian Austin, Sam Flint, Jack Ingram.

d, Ray Taylor.

BOTH BARRELS BLAZING (1945) 57m

lp: Charles Starrett, Tex Harding, Dub Taylor, Pat Parrish, Emmett Lynn, Alan Bridge.

d, Derwin Abrahams.

BOURBON ST. SHADOWS (1962) 70m

lp: Richard Derr, Mark Daniels, Helen Westcott, Jeanne Neher, Dan Mullin, Lee Edwards.

d, Ben Parker.

BOY FROM STALINGRAD, THE (1943)

lp: Bobby Samarzich, Conrad Binyon, Mary Lou Harrington, Scotty Beckett, Steven Muller.

d, Sidney Salkow.

BOY OF TWO WORLDS (1970) 88m

lp: Jimmy Sterman, Edvin Adolphson.

d, Astrid Henning Jensen.

BOY WITH TWO HEADS, THE (1974, Brit.) 60m

lp: Leslie Ash, Lance Percival.

d, Jonathan Ingrams.

BRAIN MACHINE, THE (1972) 89m

lp: James Best, Barbara Burgess, Gil Peterson, Gerald McRaney, Anne Latham.

d, Joy N. Houck, Jr..

BRAINWASH (1982, Brit.) 98m

lp: Yvette Minieux, Christopher Allport, Cindy Pickett, John Considine.

d, Bobby Roth..

BRANCHES (1971)

lp: Bill Weidner, Connie Brady, Al Capogrossi, Richard Perlmutter, Erica Saxe, Christian Larson.

BRAND OF CAIN, THE (1935)

lp: Clarence Brooks, Alec Lovejoy, Dorothy Van Engle, Laura Bowman, Lionel Monagas, Eunice Wilson.

BRAND OF HATE (1934) 63m

lp: Bob Steele, Lucille Brown, George "Gabby" Hayes, Archie Ricks, James Flavin.

d, Lew Collins.

BRAND OF THE OUTLAWS (1936) 60m

lp: Bob Steele, Margaret Marquis, Virginia True Boardman, Jack Rockwell.

d, Robert N. Bradbury.

BRAND X (1970) 87m

lp: Taylor Mead, Sally Kirkland, Tally Brown, Frank Cavestani, Abbie Hoffman.

d, Win Chamberlain.

BRANDY IN THE WILDERNESS (1969) 72m

lp: Stanton Kaye, Michaux French.

d, Kaye.

BRASS RING, THE (1975)

lp: Earl Owensby, Doug Hale, Johnny Popwell, Elizabeth Upton, Fred Covington, Maurice Hunt.

d, Martin Beck.

BREAKFAST IN PARIS (1981) 85m

lp: Barbara Parkins, Rod Mullinar, Jack Lenoir.

BREAKING OF BUMBO (1972, Brit.) 102m

lp: Richard Warwyck, Joanna Lumley.

BREAKOUT (1959) 62m

lp: John Paul, Lee Patterson, Hazel Court, Terence Alexander, Billie Whitelaw.

d, Peter Graham Scott.

BREED OF THE WEST (1930) 63m

lp: Wally Wales, Virginia Brown Faire.

d, Alvin J. Neitz.

BRIDE OF THE GORILLA (1951)

lp: Lon Chaney, Jr, Raymond Burr, Tom Conway.

BRIDGE IN THE JUNGLE, THE   (1971)

lp: John Huston, Katy Jurado, Charles Robinson, Elizabeth G. Chauvet, Jose A. Espinoza.

d, Pancho Kohner.

BRIDGES TO HEAVEN   (1975) 80m

lp: Hugh Griffith, Rosemary Griffith, Ronnie Thompson, Jo Jo.

BRIG, THE   (1965) 68m

lp: Jim Anderson, Warren Finnerty, Henry Howard, Tom Lillard, James Tiroff, Gene Lipton.

d, Jonas Mekas, Adolfas Mekas.

BRIGHT COLLEGE YEARS   (1971) 52m

d, Peter Rosen..

BRIGHTHAVEN EXPRESS   (1950) 75m

lp: John Bentley, Carol Marsh.

BROAD COALITION, THE   (1972) 91m

lp: William C. Reilly, Anita Morris, Sloan Shelton, Mary Cass, Jack Berns.

d, Simon Nuchtern.

BROKEN DISHES   (1930)

lp: Loretta Young, J. Farrell MacDonald, Grant Withers, Emma Dunn, Richard Tucker.

d, Mervyn Leroy.

BROKEN HEARTED   (1929) 64m

lp: Agnes Ayres, Gareth Hughes, Eddie Brownell.

d, Frank S. Mattison.

BROKEN HEARTS   (1933) 72m

lp: Roger Pryor, Helen Twelvetrees, Frank Sheridan, Charles Quigley, Charles Hill Mailes.

d, Christy Cabanne.

BROKEN STRINGS   (1940) 60m

lp: Clarence Muse, Cyril Lewis, Stymie Beard, Tommie Moore, Buck Woods, Pete Webster.

d, Bernard B. Ray.

BROTHER CARL   (1972) 97m

lp: Laurent Terzieff, Gunnel Lindblom, Genevieve Page, Keve Hielm, Torsten Wahlund.

d, Susan Sontag.

BROTHER, CRY FOR ME   (1970)

lp: Steve Drexel, Larry Pennell, Leslie Parrish, Richard Davalos, Kahana.

d, William White.

BROTHER OF THE WIND   (1972) 87m

lp: Dick Robinson.

d, Robinson.

BROTHER ON THE RUN   (1973)

lp: Terry Carter, Gwenn Mitchell, Kyle Johnson, James Sikking, Diana Eden.

d, Hebert Strock.

BROTHERHOOD OF DEATH   (1976) 82m

lp: Roy Jefferson, Mike Thomas, Larry Jones, Frank Grant, Mike Bass, Dennis Johnson.

d, Bill Berry.

BROTHERLY LOVE   (1928) 67m

lp: Karl Dane, George K. Arthur, Jean Arthur, Richard Carlyle, Edward Connelly.

d, Charles F. Reisner.

BRUTAL JUSTICE   (1978)

lp: Arthur Kennedy, Tomas Milian, Rosemary Omaggio, Mike Merli.

d, Bert Lenzi.

BRUTE CORPS   (1972) 90m

lp: Paul Carr, Alex Rocco, Joseph Kaufmann, Jennifer Billingsley, Michael Pataki.

d, Jerry Jameson.

BUFFALO RIDER   (1978)

lp: Rick Quinn, John Freeman, Patricia Lauris, George Sager, Rich Scheeland.

d, George Lauris.

BULL BUSTER, THE   (1975) 82m

lp: Paul Smith, Uri Zohar.

BULLDOG COURAGE   (1935) 60m

lp: Tim McCoy, Joan Woodbury, Karl Hackett, John Cowells, Eddie Buzzard, John Elliott.

d, Sam Newfield.

BULLDOG DRUMMOND AT BAY   (1947) 70m

lp: Ron Randell, Anita Louise, Pat O'Moore, Terence Kilburn, Holmes Herbert.

d, Sidney Salkow.

BULLDOG DRUMMOND STRIKES BACK   (1947) 65m

lp: Ron Randell, Gloria Henry, Pat O'Moore, Anabel Shaw, Terence Kilburn.

d, Frank McDonald.

BULLET FOR BILLY THE KID   (1963) 61m

lp: Gaston Sands, Steve Brodie, Lloyd Nelson, Marla Blaine, Richard McIntyre.

d, Rafael Baledon.

BULLETS AND SADDLES   (1943) 54m

lp: Ray Corrigan, Dennis Moore, Max Terhune, Julie Duncan, Budd Buster, Rose Plummer.

d, Anthony Marshall.

BULLETS FOR BANDITS   (1942) 55m

lp: Bill Elliott, Tex Ritter, Frank Mitchell, Dorothy Short, Forrest Taylor, Ralph Theodore.

d, Wallace Fox.

BULLY   (1978) 120m

lp: James Whitmore.

d, Peter H. Hunt.

BUMMER   (1973)

lp: Carol Speed, Connie Strickland, Dennis Burkley, Kipp Whitman, David Buchanan.

d, William Allen Castleman.

BURNOUT   (1979) 90m

lp: Mark Schneider, Robert Louden, John Zenda, Nick Cirino, Crystal Ramar.

d, Graham Meech-Burkestone.

BUSH PILOT   (1947) 60m

lp: Rochelle Hudson, Jack LaRue, Austin Willis, Frank Perry, Florence Kennedy.

d, Sterling Campbell.

BUSTER AND BILLIE   (1974) 90m

lp: Jan-Michael Vincent, Joan Goodfellow, Pamela Sue Martin, Clifton James.

d, Daniel Petrie.

BUTTERFLY AFFAIR, THE   (1934, Brit.) 75m

lp: Richard Bird, Nancy Burne, Diana Napier.

d, Walter Summers.

BUZZY AND THE PHANTOM PINTO   (1941) 55m

lp: Buzzy Henry, Dave O'Brien, Dorothy Short, Sven Hugo Borg, George Morrell.

d, Richard C. Kahn.

BUZZY RIDES THE RANGE   (1940) 60m

lp: Buzzy Henry, Dave O'Brien, Claire Rochelle, George Morrell, George Eldridge.

d, Richard C. Kahn.

BYE-BYE BUDDY   (1929) 63m

lp: Agnes Ayres, Bud Shaw, Fred Shanley, Ben Wilson, John Orlando, Dave Henderson.

d, Frank S. Mattison.

C.B. HUSTLERS   (1978) 85m

lp: Edward Roehm, Jake Barnes, John Alderman, Valdesta, Tiffany Jones.

d, Stuart Segall.

C.O.D.   (1983) 94m

lp: Chris Lemmon, Olivia Pascal, Jennifer Richards, Teresa Ganzel, Corinne Alphen.

d, Chuck Vincent.

CACTUS KID, THE   (1934)

lp: Jack Perrin, Jayne Regan, Tom London, Slim Whitaker, Fred Humes, Philo McCullough.

d, Harry S. Webb.

CADETS ON PARADE   (1942) 64m

lp: Freddie Bartholomew, Jimmy Lydon, Joseph Crehan, Raymond Hatton, Minna Gombell.

d, Lew Landers.

CAFE FLESH   (1982) 76m

lp: Andrew Nichols, Paul McGibboney, Pia Snow, Marie Sharp.

d, Rinse Dream.

CAGED VIRGINS   (1972)

d, Jean Rollin..

CAIO   (1967) 95m

d, David Tucker..

CALIFORNIA GOLD RUSH   (1946) 56m

lp: Bill Elliott, Bobby Blake, Alice Fleming, Peggy Stewart, Russell Simpson.

d, R.G. Springsteen.

CALIGARI'S CURE   (1983)

d, Tom Palozola..

CALL ME BY MY RIGHTFUL NAME   (1973) 90m

lp: Don Murray, Otis Young, Kathy Crosby.

CALL OF THE FOREST   (1949) 74m

lp: Robert Lowery, Ken Curtis, Martha Sherrill, Chief Thunder Cloud, Charles Hughes.

d, John Link.

CALL OF THE ROCKIES   (1931) 60m

lp: Ben Lyon, Marie Prevost, Russell Simpson, Anders Randolph.

d, Ray Johnston.

CALL OF THE ROCKIES   (1944) 56m

lp: Sunset Carson, Smiley Burnette, Ellen Hall, Kirk Alyn, Frank Jacquet, Harry Woods.

d, Lesley Selander.

CALL OF THE WEST   (1930) 73m

lp: Dorothy Revier, Matt Moore, Kathrin Clare Ward, Tom O'Brien, Alan Roscoe.

d, Albert Ray.

CALLING ALL CARS   (1935) 60m

lp: Jack LaRue, Lillian Miles, Jack Morton, Harry Holman, Eddie Featherston.

d, Spencer G. Bennet.

CALLING OF DAN MATTHEWS, THE   (1936) 65m

lp: Richard Arlen, Mary Kornman, Douglas Dumbrille, Charlotte Wynters, Donald Cook.

d, Phil Rosen.

CALLIOPE   (1971) 81m

lp: Sherry Miles, Mark Gottlieb, Sherry Bain, Marty Huston, Lou Epton, Gwen Van Dam.

d, Matt Cimber.

CAMERONS, THE   (1974)

lp: Lois Marshall, Joseph McKenna, Paul Kelly, Elissa Watsman, Joan Fitzpatrick, Bill Denniston.

CAMPER JOHN   (1973)

lp: William Smith, Joe Flynn, Gene Evans, Barbara Luna.

d, Sean McGregor.

CAMPSITE MASSACRE   (1981) 84m

lp: John Friedrich, Adrian Zmed, Daryl Hannah, Rachel Ward, Ernest Harden, Mark Metcalf.

d, Andrew Davis.

CAMPY KIDS FROM BOOT CAMP   (1942) 88m

lp: James Gleason, Joe Sawyer.

CAN HIERONYMUS MERKIN EVER FORGET MERCY HUMPPE AND FIND TRUE HAPPINESS?   (1969) 104 m

lp: Anthony Newley, Joan Collins, Connie Kreski, George Jessel, Milton Berle, Stubby Kaye.

d, Newley.

CAN I DO IT 'TIL I NEED GLASSES?   (1977) 80m

lp: Moe Baker, Roger Behr, Robin Williams.

d, I. Robert Levy.

CANDY SNATCHERS, THE   (1974) 98m

lp: Tiffany Bolling, Ben Piazza, Vincent Martorano, Christofer Trueblood, Delores Dorn.

d, Guerdon Trueblood.

CANDY STRIPE NURSES   (1974) 80m

lp: Candice Rialson, Robin Mattson, Maria Rojo, Kimberly Hyde, Dick Miller, Stanley Ralph Ross.

d, Allan Holleb.

CANDY TANGERINE MAN, THE   (1975) 95m

lp: Tom Hankerson, Eli Haynes, John Daniels, Marva Farmer, Buck Flower.

d, Matt Cimber.

CAPTAIN CELLULOID VS THE FILM PIRATES   (1974) 65m

lp: Robert Clayton, Doris Burnell, Alan G. Barbour, Barney Noto, John Cullen.

d, Louis A. McMahon.

CAPTAIN SCARLET VS. THE MYSTERIONS   (1982) 90m

CAPTIVE   (1980) 90m

lp: Cameron Mitchell, David Ladd, Lori Saunders.

CAPTURE OF BIGFOOT, THE   (1979)

lp: Stafford Morgan, Katherine Hopkins, Richard Kennedy, John Goff, George "Buck" Flower.

d, Bill Rebane.

CAPTURED IN CHINATOWN   (1935) 50m

lp: Marion Shilling, Charles Delaney, Philo McCullough, Robert Ellis, Robert Walker.

d, Elmer Clifton.

CAREER BED   (1972) 79m

lp: Liza Duran, Honey Hunter, James David, Merle Miller, John Cardoza, Donald Walters.

d, Joel M. Reed.

CARESSED   (1965)

lp: Robert Howay, Angela Gann, Lannie Beckman, Carol Pastinsky.

d, Laurence L. Kent.

CARHOPS   (1980) 88m

lp: Kitty Carl, Lisa Farringer, Fay de Witt, Pamela Miller, Marcie Barkin, Jack DeLeon.

d, Peter Locke.

CARIB GOLD   (1955) 72m

lp: Ethel Waters.

d, Harold Young.

CARNAL MADNESS   (1975)

lp: Michael Pataki, Bob Minor, Sharon Kelly, Stephen Stucker.

d, Gregory Corarito.

CARRINGTON SCHOOL MYSTERY, THE   (1958, Brit.) 60m

lp: Jenny Jones, Derek Freeman.

d, William Hammond.

CARRY ON ABROAD   (1974, Brit.) 89m

lp: Sidney James, Joan Sims.

d, Gerald Thomas.

CARRY ON BEHIND   (1975, Brit.) 95m

lp: Sidney James, Joan Sims.

d, Gerald Thomas.

CARRY ON DICK   (1975, Brit.) 95m

lp: Sidney James, Joan Sims.

d, Gerald Thomas.

CARRY ON GIRLS   (1974, Brit.) 92m

lp: Sidney James, Joan Sims, Kenneth Connor.

CARRY ON MATRON   (1973, Brit.) 89m

lp: Sidney James, Kenneth Williams, Hattie Jacques.

d, Gerald Thomas.

CARRY ON 'ROUND THE BEND   (1972, Brit.) 89m

lp: Sidney James, Kenneth Williams, Joan Sims, Charles Hawthrey.

CASS   (1977) 76m

lp: Michell Fawden, John Waters, Judy Morris, Peter Carroll.

CATACLYSM   (1980)

lp: Cameron Mitchell, Marc Lawrence, Maurice Grandmaison.

d, Tom McGowan, Greg Tallas, Philip Marshak.

CATCH ME IF YOU CAN   (1959) 83m

lp: Gilbert Roland, Dina Merrill, Greta Thyssen, Cesare Danova, Jonathan Harris, Antonio Moreno.

CAXAMBU   (1968) 85m

lp: John Ireland, Carol Ohmart, Keith Larsen, Gordon Blackman.

CENTERFOLD GIRLS, THE   (1974) 90m

lp: Andrew Prine, Aldo Ray, Tiffany Bolling, Ray Danton, Francine York, Jeremy Slate.

d, John Peyser.

CHAIN GANG WOMEN   (1972) 85m

lp: Michael Stearns, Linda York, Robert Lott, Barbara Mills.

d, Lee Frost.

CHALLENGE OF MC KENNA, THE   (1983) 90m

lp: John Ireland, Robert Woods.

CHALLENGERS, THE   (1968) 120m

d, Leslie H. Martinson..

CHANDU ON THE MAGIC ISLAND   (1934)

lp: Bela Lugosi, Cyril Armbrister.

CHARLIE CHAN: HAPPINESS IS A WARM CLUE   (1971) 71m

lp: Ross Martin, Virginia Ann Lee, Rocky Gunn.

d, Leslie Martinson.

CHASING THROUGH EUROPE   (1929) 62m

lp: Sue Carol, Nick Stuart, Gavin Gordon, Gustav von Seyffertitz.

d, David Butler, Alfred L. Werker.

CHATTERBOX   (1977) 73m

lp: Candice Rialson, Larry Gelman, Jane Kean, Perry Bullington.

d, Tom De Simone.

CHEERING SECTION   (1977)

lp: Rhonda Foxx, Tom Leindecker, Greg D'Jah, Patricia Michelle, Jeff Laine.

d, Harry E. Kerwin.

CHEERLEADERS, THE   (1973) 84m

lp: Stephanie Fondue, Denise Dillaway, Jovita Bush, Debbie Lowe, Sandy Evans.

d, Paul Glickler.

CHEERLEADERS BEACH PARTY　　　　　(1978) 85m

lp: Stephanie Hastings, Linda Jenson, Mary Lou Loredan, Denise Upson.

d, Alex E. Goitein.

CHERRY HILL HIGH　　　　　(1977)

lp: Linda McInerney, Nina Carson, Lynn Hastings, Stephanie Lawlor, Carrie Olson.

d, Alex E. Goitein.

CHIFFY KIDS GANG, THE　　　　　(1983) 108m

lp: Luke Batchelor, Leslie Saunders.

CHILD BRIDE　　　　　(1937) 75m

d, Harry Revier..

CHILD'S PLAY　　　　　(1984, Brit.) 73m

lp: Mary Crosby, Nicholas Clay, Debbie Chasen, Suzanne Church, Joanna Joseph.

d, Val Guest.

CHILL, THE　　　　　(1981) 95m

lp: Diane McLean, Jon Blake.

CHOICES　　　　　(1981) 80m

lp: Paul Carafotes, Victor French, Val Avery, Leila Goldoni, Demi Moore.

d, Silvio Narizzano.

CHOPPER SQUAD　　　　　(1971) 74m

lp: Rebecca Gillaing, Robert Colby, Eric Oldfield, Tony Bonner, Dennis Week.

CHORUS CALL　　　　　(1979)

lp: Kay Parker, Darby Lloyd Rains, Beth Anne, Susan London.

d, Antonio Shepherd.

CINDY AND DONNA　　　　　(1971) 84m

lp: Debbie Osborne, Nancy Ison, Cheryl Powell, Max Manning.

d, Robert Anderson.

CIRCLE OF POWER　　　　　(1984) 90m

lp: Yvette Mimieux, Christopher Allport, Cindy Pickett, John Considine, Walter Olkewicz.

d, Bobby Roth.

CIRCUS SHADOWS　　　　　(1935) 66m

lp: Dorothy Wilson, Kane Richmond, Russell Hopton, Dorothy Revier.

d, Charles Hutchinson.

CITIZEN SOLDIER　　　　　(1984) 127m

lp: Bill Gray, Toni Basil, Dean Stockwell.

d, Michael Elsey.

CITY LIMITS　　　　　(1941) 63m

lp: Frank Albertson, Jed Prouty, Lorna Gray, Kathryn Sheldon, Frank Faylen, Charles Hall, John Dilson.

d, Jean Yarbrough.

CLASS OF '74　　　　　(1972) 82m

lp: Pat Woodell, Marki Bey, Sandra Currie, Barbara Caron.

d, Arthur Marks, Mack Bing.

CLAW MONSTERS, THE　　　　　(1966) 100m

lp: Phyllis Coates, Myron Healey.

d, Franklin Adreon.

CLAWS　　　　　(1977) 100m

lp: Jason Evers, Leon Ames, Anthony Caruso, Myron Healey.

d, Richard Bansbach, R.E. Pierson.

CLOSE SHAVE　　　　　(1981)

lp: Scott Gaba, Toni Benson, Harry Levinthal.

d, Robert Hendrickson.

CLOSET CASANOVA, THE　　　　　(1979) 76m

lp: Ted Roter, Genadee Cook, Diane Miller, Margo Hansen.

d, Roter.

COCAINE FIENDS　　　　　(1937) 74m

lp: Lois January, Noel Madison, Sheila Mannors.

d, W.A. Conner.

COCKTAIL HOSTESSES, THE　　　　　(1976)

lp: Rene Bond, Terri Johnson, Lynn Harris, Kathy Hilton, Forman Shane.

d, A.C. Stephen.

CODE OF THE PLAINS　　　　　(1947)

lp: Buster Crabbe, Al "Fuzzy" St. John, Lois Ranson, Karl Hackett, Ray Bennett.

d, Sam Newfield.

CODY　　　　　(1977) 86m

lp: Tony Becker, Terry Evans.

COLOSSUS AND THE AMAZONS　　　　　(1960)

lp: Gianna Maria Canale, Ed Fury, Rod Taylor, Daniella Rocca, Dorian Gray.

d, Vittorio Sala.

COME ON, COWBOY!　　　　　(1948)

lp: Mantan Moreland, Mauryne Brent, Johnny Lee, F.E. Miller.

COME ONE, COME ALL　　　　　(1970)

lp: Sebastian Gregory, Gina Montaine, Henry Dillon, Diane Lamport, Roberta Landis.

d, Gregory.

COMES MIDNIGHT　　　　　(1940)

lp: Eddie.Green, James Baskett, Elinor Seagures, Bonnie Skeet, Amanda Rudolph.

COMING, THE　　　　　(1983)

lp: Susan Swift, Tisha Sterling, Albert Salmi, Guy Stockwell.

d, Bert I. Gordon.

COMING APART　　　　　(1969) 110m

lp: Rip Torn, Viveca Lindfors, Sally Kirkland, Megan McCormick, Lois Markle.

d, Milton Moses Ginsberg.

COMMANDO CODY　　　　　(1953)

lp: Judd Holdren, Aline Towne, Gregory Gaye.

d, Fred C. Bannon, Harry Keller, Franklin Adreon.

COMMUTER HUSBANDS　　　　　(1974)

lp: Gabrielle Drake, Robin Bailey.

COMPANION, THE　　　　　(1976) 85m

lp: Jack Ging, Edith Atwater, Anjanette Bower, Kent Smith.

CONDEMNED MEN   (1940)

lp: Mantan Moreland, Dorothy Dandridge, Niel Webster, Jesse Lee Brooks.

d, William Beaudine.

CONDOR   (1984) 77m

lp: Carolyn Seymour, Ray Wise, Craig Stevens, Wendy Kilbourne.

CONFESSION, THE   (1964) 100m

lp: Ginger Rogers, Ray Milland, Barbara Eden, Carl Schell, Michael Ansara, Elliott Gould.

d, William Dieterle.

CONFESSIONS OF TOM HARRIS   (1972) 98m

lp: Don Murray, Linda Evans, David Brian, Gary Clarke, Logan Ramsey.

d, John Derek, David Nelson.

CONSTANT WOMAN, THE   (1933) 76m

lp: Conrad Nagel, Leila Hyams, Tommy Conlon, Claire Windsor, Stanley Fields.

d, Victor Schertzinger.

CONVENTION GIRLS   (1978) 95m

lp: Nancy Lawson, Anne Sward, Carol Linden, Roberta White, Clarence Thomas.

d, Joseph Adler.

CONVOY BUDDIES   (1977) 82m

lp: Terrence Hall, Bob Spencer, Karen Blake, Angel Del Page, Rick Peters.

d, Arthur Pitt.

COOL SOUND FROM HELL, A   (1959) 71m

d, Sidney J. Furie..

COP KILLERS   (1984) 99m

lp: Harvey Keitel, John Lydon.

d, Roberto Faenza.

COPTER KIDS, THE   (1976, Brit.) 60m

lp: Sophie Nelville, Jonathan Scott-Taylor.

d, Ronald Spencer.

CORRUPTION OF THE DAMNED   (1965) 55m

d, George Kuchar..

CORVINI INHERITANCE   (1984, Brit.) 73m

lp: David McCallum, Jan Francis, Terence Alexander, Stephen Yardley, Paul Bacon.

d, Gabrielle Beaumont.

COSMO JONES, CRIME SMASHER   (1943) 62m

lp: Frank Graham, Gale Storm, Edgar Kennedy, Richard Cromwell, Mantan Moreland, Tristram Coffin.

d, James Tinling.

COTTER   (1972) 94m

lp: Don Murray, Carol Lynley, Rip Torn, Sherry Jackson.

d, Paul Stanley.

COUNTRY BLUE   (1975) 95m

lp: Jack Conrad, Dub Taylor, Rita George, David Huddleston, Mildred Brown.

d, Conrad.

COUNTRY CUZZINS   (1972)

lp: Rene Bond, John Tull, Pamela Princess, Jack Richisen, Ellen Stephens, Mark Buckalew, Steven Hodge.

COUNTRY MUSIC   (1972) 94m

lp: Marty Robbins, Sammy Jackson, Barbara Mandrell, Dottie West.

d, Robert Hinkle.

COUNTRY TOWN   (1971) 90m

lp: Terry McDermott, Gary Gray, Lynette Curran, Gerard Maguire, Sue Parsons.

d, Peter Maxwell.

COURAGE OF THE NORTH   (1935)

lp: John Preston, June Love, William Desmond, Tom London, Jimmy Aubrey.

d, Robert Emmett [Tansey].

COVER GIRL MODELS   (1975) 82m

lp: Lindsay Bloom, Pat Anderson, John Kramer, Rhoda Leigh Hopkins, Mary Woronov.

d, Cirio Santiago.

CRACKLE OF DEATH   (1974) 94m

lp: Darren McGavin, Philip Carey, Simon Oakland, William Smith, Elaine Giftos.

d, Don Weis, Alex Grasshoff.

CRAWLING ARM, THE   (1973) 91m

lp: Deborah Walley, John Crawford, Marvin Kaplan, Paul Carr.

CRAWLING TERROR, THE   (1958, Brit.) 75m

lp: Forrest Tucker, Gaby Andre, Martin Benson, Alec Mango, Hugh Latimer.

d, Gilbert Gunn.

CREATURE OF DESTRUCTION   (1967)

lp: Aron Kincaid, Les Tremayne, Pat Delaney, Neil Fletcher, Ann McAdams.

d, Larry Buchanan.

CREATURES OF DARKNESS   (1969) 83m

lp: Bill Williams, Aron Kincaid.

d, Williams.

CRICKET OF THE HEARTH, THE   (1968) 57m

Voices: Roddy McDowall, Danny Thomas, Marlo Thomas, Ed Ames, Hans Conried, Abbe Lane, Paul Frees.

CRIMINAL INVESTIGATOR   (1942) 62m

lp: John Miljan, Robert Lowery, Edith Fellows.

d, Jean Yarbrough.

CROOKED ROAD   (1932) 67m

lp: Gaston Glass, Wanda Hawley, Richard Tucker, J. Frank Glendon, Eddie Featherston.

d, Louis King.

CRUISE MISSILE   (1978)

lp: Peter Graves, Curt Jurgens, Michael Dante.

p, Ted V. Mikels.

CRUISIN' 57   (1975) 65m

lp: Terry Winter, Mike Muni, David Larson, Gary Nelson, Peanuts, Mike Tennis.

d, Toby Ross.

CRUNCH   (1975, Brit.) 100m

lp: Robert Forster, Jean Walker, John Vernon, Norman Fell.

CRUZ BROTHERS AND MISS MALLOY, THE   (1979) 54m

d, Kathleen Collins..

CRY TO THE WIND   (1979)

lp: Sheldon Woods, Cameron Garnick, Aaron Card, Bonnie Card, Lamont Topaum.

d, Robert W. Davidson.

CRY UNCLE   (1973) 87m

lp: Allen Garfield, Madeline le Roux.

d, John G. Avildsen.

CRYPT OF DARK SECRETS   (1976) 71m

lp: Maureen Chan, Ronald Tanet.

CURSE OF KILIMANJARO   (1978) 82m

lp: Charles Baxter, Addison Powell, Margaret Andrews, Rene Bouve, Bryn Jones.

d, Edward A. Kuplerski.

CURSE OF THE HEADLESS HORSEMAN   (1972) 80m

lp: Don Carrara, Claudia Dean, B.G. Fisher, Margo Dean, Lee Byers, Joe Cody.

d, John Kirkland.

CURSE OF THE MAYAN TEMPLE   (1977)

d, Bill Burrud..

CURSE OF THE MOON CHILD   (1972)

lp: Adam West, Jeremy Slate, Sherry Jackson.

CUTTING LOOSE   (1980) 97m

lp: Harold Green, Phil Catelli, Rhonda Spitz.

CYCLES SOUTH   (1971)

lp: Don Marshall, Vaughn Everly, Bobby Garcia.

d, Marshall.

CYNTHIA'S SISTER   (1975) 86m

lp: Flanagan, Paul Kirby, Susan Bowen, Emmett Hennessy, Preben Mahrt, June Fremont.

d, Arnold Baxter.

CZECH MATE   (1984, Brit.) 73m

lp: Susan George, Patrick Mower, Richard Heffer, Peter Vaughan, Stephan Gryff.

d, John Hough.

DAMIEN'S ISLAND   (1976) 92m

lp: Humberto Almazan, Irene Tsu, Earl Kingston, Suesie Elene.

d, Don Murray.

DANCE HALL RACKET   (1956)

lp; Lenny Bruce, Honey Harlow [Bruce].

d, Phil Tucker.

DANDY   (1973) 82m

lp: Cynthia Denny, John Alderman, Ed Kelly, Steve Vincent.

DANGEROUS APPOINTMENT   (1934)

lp: Charles Starrett, Dorothy Wilson.

DANGEROUS RELATIONS   (1973) 90m

lp: Brooke Bundy, Ellen Weston, Kenneth Pogue, John Varnum, Sam Bell.

d, J. Ford Bell.

DANNY   (1979) 90m

lp: Rebecca Page, Janet Zarich, Barbara Jean Ehrhardt, Gloria Maddox, George Luce.

d, Gene Feldman.

DARK AUGUST   (1975)

lp: Kim Hunter, William Robertson.

d, Martin Goldman.

DARK DREAMS   (1971)

lp: Tina Russell, Tim Long.

DARK ENDEAVOUR   (1933) 72m

lp: Reed Howes, Carmelita Geraghty, Clarence Geldert, Ben Hendricks, Jr, Walter Long.

d, Elmer Clifton.

DARK EYES   (1980)

lp: Lana Wood, Kabir Bedi, John Carradine, Britt Ekland.

d, James Polakof.

DARK SUNDAY   (1978) 90m

lp: Earl Owensby, Monique Proulx, Phillip Lanier, Ron Lampkin.

d, Jimmy Huston.

DAUGHTER OF THE CONGO, A   (1930) 88m

lp: Kathleen Noisette, Lorenzo Tucker, Clarence Reed, Willor Lee Guilford, Joe Byrd.

d, Oscar Micheaux.

DAWN OF THE MUMMY   (1981)

lp: Joan Levy, Victoria Johnson, Eilen Falson, John Salvo, George Peck.

d, Armand Weston.

DAY IT CAME TO EARTH, THE   (1979) 84m

lp: Roger Manning, Wink Roberts, Bob Ginnaven, Rita Wilson, Delight De Bruine.

d, Harry Z. Thomazon.

DAY SANTA CLAUS CRIED, THE   (1980) 100m

lp: Christopher George, Gay Hamilton, Seven Valsecchi.

d, Philip Otto.

DAY THE EARTH GOT STONED, THE   (1978)

d, Richard Patterson..

DAY THE LORD GOT BUSTED, THE   (1976) 81m

lp: Fabian Forte, Larry Bishop, Tony Russel, Hal Bonner, Casey Kasem.

d, Burt Topper.

DEAD CERT   (1974, Brit.) 99m

lp: Scott Antony, Judi Dench, Michael Williams, Nina Thomas, Mark Dignam.

d, Tony Richardson.

DEAD MEN DON'T MAKE SHADOWS   (1970) 98m

lp: Hunt Powers, Chet Davis.

DEADLINE   (1984)

lp: Stephen Young, Cindy Hinds, Sharon Masters, Phillip Leonard.

d, Mario Azzopardi.

DEADLY AND THE BEAUTIFUL   (1974) 81m

lp: Nancy Kivan, Ross Hagen, Roberta Collins.

d, Robert O'Neill.

DEADLY AUGUST (1966)

lp: Macdonald Carey, Howard Duff, Mary Murphy.

DEADLY ENCOUNTER (1979) 90m

lp: Dina Merrill, Carl Betz, Leon Ames, Vicki Powers, Mark Featherstone-Witty.

d, R. John Hugh.

DEADLY GAME, THE (1974) 90m

lp: Michael Rennie, Barbara Bouchet, Richard Jaeckel.

d, Wray Davis.

DEADLY GAMES (l980) 95m

lp: Sam Groom, Steve Railsback, Denise Galin.

d, Scott Mansfield.

DEADLY GAMES (1982) 104m

lp: George Segal, Trevor Howard, Emlyn Williams, Robert Morley, Alan Webb.

d, George Schaefer.

DEADLY HARVEST (1972)

lp: Clint Walker, Nehemiah Persoff, Kim Cattrall, David Brown, Gary Davies.

d, Timothy Bond.

DEADLY HONEYMOON (1974) 86m

lp: Dack Rambo, Rebecca Dianna Smith, John Beck, Pat Hingle.

d, Elliott Silverstein.

DEADLY WEAPONS (1974)

lp: Chesty Morgan.

d, Doris Wishman.

DEAFULA (1975) 95m

lp: Peter Wechsberg, James Randall, Gary Holstrom.

d, Wechsberg.

DEATH BY INVITATION (1971)

d, Ken Friedman..

DEATH DRIVER (1977) 90m

lp: Earl Owensby, Mike Allen, Patty Shaw, Mary Ann Hearn.

d, Jimmy Huston.

DEATH FORCE (1978)

lp: James Iglehart, Carmen Argenziano, Leon Isaac, Jayne Kennedy, Roberto Gonzales.

d, Cirio H. Santiago.

DEATH IN THE AIR (1937)

lp: Lona Andre, John Carroll, Henry Hall, Leon Ames, Wheeler Oakman, Reed Howes.

d, Elmer Clifton.

DEATH JOURNEY (1976) 90m

lp: Fred Williamson, Bernard Kuby, Heidi Dobbs, D'Urville Martin, Stephanie Faulkner.

d, Williamson.

DEATH MAY BE YOUR SANTA CLAUS (1969) 50m

lp: Ken Gajadhar, Donnah Dolce, Merdel Jordine, Tom Syie, Kim Keelin.

d, Frankie Dymor, Jr..

DEATH OF A STRANGER (1976) 90m

lp: Jason Robards, Jr, Hardy Kruger, Gila Almagor.

DEATH ON CREDIT (1976) 81m

lp: Linda Boyce, Kent Bateman, Caesar Cordova, Joseph Lewis, Lucky Kargo.

d, Victor Petrashevich.

DEATH RIDERS (1976) 75m

lp: Floyd Reed, Sr, Russ Smith, Jim Cates, Joe Byars.

DEATH SCREAMS (1982)

lp: Susan Kiger, Jody Kay, Martin Tucker, Jennifer Chase.

d, David Nelson.

DEATH SMILES ON A MURDER (1974)

lp: Klaus Kinski, Ewa Aulin, Angela Bo.

d, Aristide Massaccesi.

DEATHGAMES (1981) 80m

lp: Lou Brown, David Clendinning, Jennifer Cluff.

DEATHHEAD VIRGIN, THE (1974)

lp: Jock Gaynor, Larry Ward, Diane McBain.

DEFYING THE LAW (1935)

lp: Ted Wells, Dick Cramer, Jimmy Aubrey, William Desmond, Allan Greer, George Chesebro.

d, Robert J. Horner.

DELIVER US FROM EVIL (1975) 104m

lp: Lloyd Bridges, Pat Hingle, Morgan Woodward, Gilbert Roland, R.G. Armstrong.

d, Robert McCahon.

DEMOLITION (1977) 87m

lp: John Waters, Belinda Giblin, Fred Steele, Keith Lee, Donald Macdonald, Vincent Ball.

d, Kevin Dobson.

DEMONS OF THE DEAD (1976, Brit.) 86m

lp: George Hilton.

DEVIL AND LEROY BASSETT, THE (1973) 92m

lp: Cody Bearpaw, John F. Goff, George "Buck" Flower.

DEVIL CHECKS UP (1944)

lp: Alan Mowbray.

DEVIL HAS SEVEN FACES, THE (1977)

lp: Carroll Baker, Stephen Boyd, George Hilton.

d, Osvaldo Civirani.

DEVIL MONSTER (1946, Brit.) 65m

lp: Barry Norton, Blanche Mehaffey.

d, S. Edwin Graham.

DEVIL ON DECK (1932) 70m

lp: Reed Howes, Molly O'Day, Wheeler Oakman, June Marlowe, A.S. Myron, Rolfe Sedan.

d, Wallace W. Fox.

DEVIL RIDER (1971) 75m

lp: Ross Kananza, Sharon Mahon.

DEVIL WOLF OF SHADOW MOUNTAIN, THE (1964)

lp: Johnny Cardoz, Gene Pollock.

d, Gary Kent.

DEVILS, THE (1971) 108m

lp: Vanessa Redgrave, Oliver Reed, Dudley Sutton, Max Adrian, Gemma Jones, Murray Melvin.

d, Ken Russell.

DEVIL'S CANYON (1935)

lp: Noah Beery, Jr, Mimi Alvarez, William Desmond, Pat Carlisle, Fred Church.

d, Cliff Smith.

DIABOLIC WEDDING (1972)

lp: Margaret O'Brien.

d, Gene Nash.

DIAMOND STUD (1970) 82m

lp: Robert Hall, John Alderman, Monika Henreid, Victoria Carbe, Michael Greer.

d, Greg Corarito.

DICK DEADEYE (1977, U.S./Brit.) 79m

d, Bill Melendez..

DIDN'T YOU HEAR (1983) 93m

lp: Dennis Christopher, Gary Busey, Cheryl Waters, John Kauffman, Anthony Victor.

d, Skip Sherwood.

DIE, BEAUTIFUL MARYANNE (1969)

d, Pete Walker..

DIE SISTER, DIE (1978)

lp: Jack Ging, Edith Atwater, Antoinette Bower, Kent Smith, Robert Emhardt, Burt Santos.

d, Randall Hood.

DIRTIEST GIRL I EVER MET, THE (1973)

lp: Janet Lynn, Robin Askwith, Peter Eliott, Jess Conrad, Stubby Kaye.

d, Pete Walker.

DIRTY GERTY FROM HARLEM, USA (1946) 65m

lp: Spencer Williams, Francinne Everette, Don Wilson, Katherine Moore, "Piano" Frank.

d, Williams.

DISCIPLES OF DEATH (1975) 75m

lp: Josh Bryant, Dave Cass, Irene Kelly, John Martin, Carl Bensen, Linda Rascoe.

d, Frank Q. Dobbs.

DISCO FEVER (1978)

lp: Fabian, Casey Kasem, Phoebe Dorin, Susette Carroll, George Barris, Michael Blodgett.

d, Lamar Card.

DISCO GODFATHER (1979)

lp: Rudy Ray Moore.

DISCO 9000 (1977) 94m

lp: John Poole, Cal Wilson, Jeanie Bell, Harold Nicholas, Nicholas Lewis, Beverly Anne.

d, D'Urville Martin.

DIVINE LADY, THE (1929) 110m

lp: Corinne Griffith, H.B. Warner, Ian Keith, Victor Varconi, Marie Dressler, William Conklin.

d, Frank Lloyd.

DIVORCE MADE EASY (1929) 60m

lp: Douglas MacLean, Marie Prevost, Johnny Arthur, Frances Lee, Dot Farley, Jack Duffy.

d, Walter Graham.

DO YOU KNOW THIS VOICE? (1964) 80m

lp: Dan Duryea, Isa Miranda, Gwen Watford, Alan Edwards, Shirley Cameron.

DOBBIN, THE (1939) 80m

lp: Isidore Cashier, Helen Beverly, David Opatoshu, Yudel Dubinsky, Rosetta Bialis.

d, Edgar G. Ulmer.

DOC HOOKER'S BUNCH (1978) 88m

lp: Dub Taylor, Buck Taylor.

DOCTORS AND NURSES (1983) 90m

lp: Rebecca Rigg, Drew Forsythe, Graeme Blundell.

d, Maurice Murphy.

DOLL'S EYE (1982) 75m

lp: Sandy Ratcliffe, Paul Copley, Bernice Stegers, Lynne Worth, Nick Ellsworth, Richard Tolan.

d, Jan Worth.

DON'T GO INTO THE WOODS (1980)

lp: Buck Carradine, Mary Gail Artz, James P. Hayden, Ken Carter.

d, Jim Bryan.

DON'T GO NEAR THE PARK (1981) 87m

lp: Aldo Ray, Meeno Peluce, Linnea Quigley.

d, Lawrence D. Foldes.

DON'T OPEN THE DOOR (1974) 90m

lp: Susan Bracken, Larry O'Dwyer, Gene Ross.

DON'T PLAY US CHEAP (1973)

d, Melvin Van Peebles..

DOUBLE AGENT 73 (1974)

lp: Chesty Morgan.

d, Doris Wishman.

DOUBLE DEAL (1939) 60m

lp: Monte Hawley, Jeni Legon, Eddie Thompson, Florence O'Brien, Freddie Jackson.

d, Arthur Dreifuss.

DOUBLE INITIATION (1970) 96m

lp: Janet Wass, Tobalina, Jeannie Anderson, Maria-Pia, Andy Roth, Luis Vargas.

d, Carlos Tobalina.

DOUBLE TAKE (1972, Brit.) 90m

lp: Reg Varney, Norman Rossington, Sue Lloyd.

d, Harry Booth.

DOWN TO THE SEA (1975) 89m

lp: Anne Warren, Robert Hutchinson.

DRACULA SUCKS (1979)

lp: Jamie Gillis, Reggie Nalder, Serena, Annette Haven, John Leslie.

d, Philip Marshak.

DRAGNET, THE (1936) 90m

lp: Rod LaRocque, Marian Nixon, Betty Compson, Jack Adair, Edward LeSaint, Donald Kerr, Edward Keane.

DRAGON DIES HARD, THE (1974)

lp: Bruce Lee.

DREAM NO EVIL (1984) 93m

lp: Edmond O'Brien, Brooke Mills, Marc Lawrence.

DREAMER, THE (1947)

lp: Mantan Moreland, June Richmond, Mabel Lee, Pat Rainey.

DRIFTING SOULS (1932) 63m

lp: Lois Wilson, Gene Gowling, Theodore Von Eltz, Raymond Hatton, Shirley Grey.

d, Louis King.

DUNCAN'S WORLD (1977) 93m

lp: Larry Tobias, Billy Tobias, Calvin Brown, Jr.

DYNAMITE (1972)

lp: Marcia Rivers, Steve Gould, Dolly Sharp, Kurt Mann, Jamie Goodman, Leon Oriana, Dee Brown.

DYNAMITE BROTHERS, THE (1974)

lp: Alan Tang, Timothy Brown, James Hong, Aldo Ray, Carolyn Ann Speed, Don Oliver.

d, Al Adamson.

EASY STREET (1930)

lp: Richard B. Harison, Willor Lee Guilford, Lorenzo Tucker.

d, Oscar Micheaux.

EBONY, IVORY AND JADE (1977)

lp: Rosanne Katon, Colleen Camp, Sylvia Anderson, Christie Mayuga, Ken Washington.

d, Cirio H. Santiago.

EL SUPER (1979)

lp: Raymundo Hidalgo-Gato, Zully Montero, Reynaldo Medina.

d, Leon Ichaso, Orlando Jimenez-Leal.

ELECTRIC CHAIR, THE (1977)

lp: Nita Patterson, Katherine Cortez, Barry Bell, Don Cummins, Martin McDonald.

d, Pat Patterson.

11 X 14 (1977) 81m

lp: Serafina Bathrick, Paddy Whannel, Tim Welsh, Rick Goodwin.

d, James Benning.

ELIMINATOR, THE (1982) 94m

lp: JoAnn Harris, Steve Railsback.

ELLIS ISLAND (1936) 70m

lp: Donald Cook, Jack LaRue, Peggy Shannon.

d, Phil Rosen.

ELMER (1977) 76m

lp: Phillip Swanson.

d, Christopher Cain.

ELYSIA (1933)

d, Bryan Foy..

ENCOUNTERS OF THE DEEP (1984) 90m

lp: Carol Andre, Andy Garcia, John Garko, Alan Boyd.

END OF AUGUST (1974)

lp: Diane Turley, Eric Matthews, Mary Millington.

d, Gary Alexander Young.

ENDGAME (1984) 96m

lp: Al Cliver, Bobby Rhodes, Jill Elliot.

d, Steven Benson.

ENFORCER FROM DEATH ROW, THE (1978)

lp: Leo Fong, Darnell Garcia, Booker T. Anderson, Mariwin Roberts, Johnny Hammond.

ENTER THE DEVIL (1975) 86m

lp: Josh Bryant, Irene Kelly, Dave Cass, John Martin, Carle Bensen, Norris Domingue, Willie Gonzalez.

ESCAPE FROM ANGOLA (1976) 95m

lp: Stan Brock, Ivan Tors, Anne Collings, Peter Tors, David Tors, Mackson Ngobeni.

d, Leslie Martinson.

ESCAPE FROM EL DIABLO (1983, U.S./Brit./Span.) 89m

lp: Jimmy McNichol, Timothy Van Patten, John Wayne, Jr.

d, Gordon Hessler.

ETHAN (1971) 86m

lp: Robert Sampson, Rosa Rosal, Joseph DeCardova.

EVERYDAY (1976) 84m

lp: David E. Michaels, Anthony Gulassa, Stephen McGuire, Maury Espelin, Barbara Freeman.

d, George B. Britton.

EVIDENCE OF POWER (1979) 92m

lp: Alan Hale, Jr, Gordon Jump, Steven Wayne Carry, James Matz.

d, Vern Piehl.

EVIL EYE OF KALINOR, THE (1934) 64m

lp: Rex Lease, Gwen Lee, Theodore Lorch, Duke R. Lee, Otis Harlan.

d, B. Reeves "Breezy" Eason.

EVIL FINGERS (1975)

lp: Franco Nero, Edmund Purdom, Pamela Tiffin.

d, Luigi Bazzoni.

EVILS OF THE NIGHT (1983)

lp: John Carradine, Aldo Ray, Neville Brand, Julie Newmar, Tina Louise, Karrie Emerson.

d, Mardi Rustam.

EXPOSURE (1932) 71m

lp: Lila Lee, Walter Byron, Mary Doran, Bryant Washburn, Tully Marshall, Spec O'Donnell.

d, Norman Houston.

EXTREME CLOSE-UP (1973)

lp: James McMullan, James A. Watson, Jr, Kate Woodville, Bara Byrnes, Al Checco.

d, Jeannot Szwarc.

EYE FOR AN EYE, AN (1975) 86m

lp: Tom Basham, Gene Carlson, Gretchen Kanne, David Carlile, Barbara Grover, Lance Larson.

d, Larry Brown.

EYES BEHIND THE STARS (1972)

lp: Martin Balsam, Robert Hoffman, Nathalie Delon.

EYES OF THE JUNGLE (1953) 79m

lp: Jon Hall, Ray Montgomery, Victor Millan, Edgar Barrier, Frank Fenton, Robert Shayne.

d, Paul Landres.

FABULOUS JOE, THE (1946) 59m

lp: Walter Abel, Margot Grahame, Donald Meek, Clarence Kolb, Marie Wilson.

d, Harve Foster.

FADE-IN (1968) 93m

lp: Burt Reynolds, Barbara Loden, Noam Pitlik, Patricia Casey, James Hampton.

d, Allen Smithee [Jud Taylor].

FAIRY TALES (1979)

lp: Don Sparks, Sy Richardson, Brenda Fogarty, Martha Reeves, Irwin Corey, Linnea Quigley.

d, Harry Tampa.

FAKE-OUT (1982) 96m

lp: Pia Zadora, Telly Savalas, Desi Arnaz, Jr.

d, Matt Cimber.

FAKING OF THE PRESIDENT, THE (1976) 80m

lp: Marshall Efron, Alan Barinholtz, Robert Staats, William Daprato, Richard Dixon.

d, Jeanne Abel, Alan Abel.

FALCON'S GOLD (1982) 90m

lp: John Marley, Simon MacCorkindale, Louise Vallance, Blanca Guerra, George Touliatos.

d, Bob Schulz.

FALLS, THE (1980, Brit.) 190m

lp: Peter Westley, Aad Wirtz, Michael Murray, Patricia Carr.

d, Peter Greenaway.

FAMILY ENFORCER (1978) 82m

lp: Joseph Cortese, Lou Criscuola, Joseph Pesci, Anne Johns, Keith Davis.

d, Ralph DeVito.

FAMILY KILLER (1975) 95m

lp: John Saxon, Arthur Kennedy, Agostina Belli.

d, Vittorio Schiraldi.

FANGS (1974) 90m

lp: Les Tremayne, Janet Wood, Bebe Kelly, Marvin Kaplan, Alice Nunn.

d, Arthur A. Names.

FAST COMPANY (1979) 90m

lp: William Smith, John Saxon, Claudia Jennings, Nicholas Campbell, Don Francks.

d, David Cronenberg.

FAST KILL (1973) 90m

lp: Tom Adams, Susie Hampton, Michael Culver, Peter Halliday.

d, Lindsay Shonteff.

FAT CHANCE (1982) 92m

lp: Franham Scott, January Stevens, Jack Aaron, Amy Steel, Robert Reynolds.

d, M. Summers.

FATAL GAMES (1983) 90m

lp: Sally Kirkland, Lynn Banashek, Sean Masterson.

FATHER DEAR FATHER (1973, Brit.) 98m

lp: Patrick Cargill, Natasha Pyne.

FATHER STEPS OUT (1941) 63m

lp: Frank Albertson, Jed Prouty, Lorna Gray, Frank Faylen, Mary Field, Kathryn Sheldon.

d, Jean Yarbrough.

FEELIN' UP (1983) 85m

lp: Malcolm Groome, Kathleen Seward, Rhonda Hansome, Tony Collado, Charles Douglass.

d, David Secter.

FERN, THE RED DEER (1977, Brit.) 60m

lp: Candida Prior, Craig McFarland.

d, Jan Darnley-Smith.

FEUDIN' RHYTHM (1949) 66m

lp: Eddy Arnold, Kirby Grant, Gloria Henry, Tommy Ivo, Isabel Randolph, Fuzzy Knight.

d, Edward Bernds.

FIEND, THE (1971, Brit.)

lp: Ann Todd, Patrick Magee, Tony Beckley, Percy Herbert, Suzanna Leigh.

d, Robert Hartford-Davis.

FIGHT FOR LIFE, THE (1940) 69m

d, Pare Lorentz..

FIGHT NEVER ENDS, THE (1947)

lp: Joe Louis, The Mills Brothers, Ruby Dee, William Greaves, Emmett "Babe" Wallace, Harrell Tillman.

FIGHTER PILOTS (1977) 80m

lp: Will Roberts, John Hardy.

FIGHTING BLACK KINGS (1977)

lp: William Oliver, Charles Martin, Willie Williams, Mas Oyama.

FIGHTING DEVIL DOGS (1938)

lp: Lee Powell, Herman Brix, Eleanor Stewart, Montagu Love, Sam Flint.

d, John English, William Witney.

FIGHTING FOR JUSTICE (1932) 61m

lp: Tim McCoy, Hooper Atchley, Joyce Compton, William Norton Bailey, Walter Brennan.

d, Otto Brower.

FIGHTING FRONTIERSMAN, THE (1946) 61m

lp: Charles Starrett, Smiley Burnette, Helen Mowery, George Chesebro, Zon Murray.

d, Derwin Abrahams.

FIGHTING LADY (1935) 50m

lp: Peggy Shannon, Jack Mulhall, Mona Lessing, Mary Carr, Edward Woods, Edward Earle.

d, Carlos Borcosque.

FIGHTING MUSTANG (1948) 56m

lp: Sunset Carson, Lee Roberts, Patricia Starling, Al Terry, Forrest Matthews.

d, Oliver Drake.

FIGHTING PILOT, THE (1935) 65m

lp: Richard Talmadge, Victor Mace, Gertrude Messinger, Eddie Davis, Robert Frazer.

d, Noel Mason.

FIGHTING THROUGH (1934) 55m

lp: Reb Russell, Yakima Canutt, Lucille Lund, Edward Hearn, Ben Corbett, Chester Gans.

d, Harry Fraser.

FIGHTING TO LIVE (1934) 60m

lp; Marion Shilling, Gaylord [Steve] Pendleton, Reb Russell, Eddie Phillips.

d, Edward F. Cline.

FIRE AND SWORD (1982, Brit.) 90m

lp: Christoph Waltz, Leigh Lawson, Peter Firth.

d, Veith von Furstenberg.

1ST NOTCH, THE (1977)

lp: Leo G. Willey, Jason Ward, Joe Warder, Julie Ward, Eddie Mynatt, Cindy Rusler.

d, Gil Ward.

FIRST TIME ROUND (1972) 110m

lp: Jason Walker, Aaron Bedford, Doug Williams, Eric Martin, Joe Markham, Dale Carpenter.

d, J. Brian.

FIVE ANGRY WOMEN (1975) 82m

lp: Carolyn Judd, Teri Gusman, Darlene Mattingly, Angel Colbert, Bonita Kalem.

d, Kent Osborne.

FIVE BAD MEN (1935)

lp: Noah Beery, Jr, Art Mix, Buffalo Bill, Jr, William Desmond, Sally Darling.

d, Cliff Smith.

FLAMING URGE, THE (1953) 67m

lp: Harold Lloyd, Jr, Cathy Downs.

FLAMINGO (1947)

lp: Herb Jeffries, Dorothy Dandridge.

FLESH GORDON (1974) 70m

d, Bill Osco..

FLICKER UP (1946)

lp: Billy Eckstine, Mary Lou Harris.

FLIGHT FROM TREASON (1960, Brit.) 60m

lp: John Gregson, Robert Brown.

FLUSH (1981, Brit.) 90m

lp: William Calloway, William Bronder, Jeannie Linero.

d, Andrew J. Kuehn.

FLY ME (1973) 80m

lp: Pat Anderson, Lenore Kasdorf, Lyllah Torena, Richard Young, Naomi Stevens.

d, Cirio Santiago.

FLYING LARIATS (1931) 60m

lp: Wally Wales, Buzz Barton, Bonnie Gray, Sam Garrett, Etta Dalmas, Joe Lawliss.

d, Alvin J. Neitz.

FLYING SQUADRON (1952) 60m

lp: Massimo Serato, Dina Sassoli.

d, Luigi Capuano.

FOLLOW ME (1969)

lp: Claude Codgen, Mary Lou McGinnis, Bob Purvey, Bonnie Hill, Andrea Kermot, Deborah Lee.

d, Gene McCabe.

FOOTSTEPS ON THE MOON (1973) 90m

lp: Florinda Bolkan.

FOR MEMBERS ONLY (1960)

lp: Brian Cobby, Shelley Martin, Natalie Lynn, Anthony Oliver, Jacqueline D'Orsay.

d, Ramsey Harrington.

FORBID THEM NOT (1961)

lp: Michael Cole, Pattie O'Neil, John Ehrin, Herb Niccolls, John Beers, Ann Dashner, Alex Gal.

FORBIDDEN LESSONS (1982) 78m

lp: Lola Felice, Barbara Roy.

FORBIDDEN UNDER THE CENSORSHIP OF THE KING

(1973) 84m

lp: Herb Kaplow, Marshall Anker, Bob Lavigne, Lee Rey, Perry Gerwitz, Alana Blue.

d, Barry R. Kerr.

FORCE FOUR (1975)

lp: Malachi Lee, Warhawk Tanzania, Owen Watson, Judy Soriano, Sydney Filson, Sam Schwartz.

d, Michael Fink.

FORTRESS IN THE SUN (1978)

lp: Nancy Kwan, Tony Ferrer, Fred Galang.

d, George Rowe.

FORTRESS OF THE DEAD (1965) 78m

lp: John Hackett, Conrad Parkham, Ana Corita.

FORTY-FIVE CALIBRE ECHO (1932) 60m

lp: Jack Perrin, Ben Corbett, Eleanor Fair, Olin Francis, George Chesebro.

d, Bruce Mitchell.

FOUR AGAINST THE DESERT (1979) 93m

lp: Hal Frederick, Karen Dor, Ron Hayes.

FOX AFFAIR, THE (1978)

lp: Kathryn Dodd, Robert Bosco, Yuri Alexis, Steve Lincoln, Sunny Collins.

d, Fereidun G. Jorjani.

FOX STYLE (1973) 88m

lp: Chuck Daniel, John Taylor, Juanita Moore, Denise Denise, Hank Rolike, Jovita Bush.

d, Clyde Houston.

FRANKENSTEIN'S ISLAND (1982)

lp: John Carradine, Cameron Mitchell, Robert Clarke.

d, Jerry Warren.

FREEZE BOMB (1980) 91m
lp: George Lazenby, Jim Kelly, Harold Sakata, Aldo Ray.
d, Al Adamson.

FRIDAY ON MY MIND (1970)
lp: Michael Scott, Con Covert, Aaron Bedford, Allen Rogers, John Romero, Mama Chuck, Andy Helman.
d, Wayne A. Schotten.

FRIEND OR FOE (1982, Brit.) 60m
lp: Mark Luxford, John Holmes.
d, John Kirsh.

FROM BROADWAY TO CHEYENNE (1932) 60m
lp: Rex Ball, Marceline Day, Robert Ellis, Mathew Betz, Huntley Gordon.
d, Harry Fraser.

FROM THE DESK OF MARGARET TYDING (1958) 54m
lp: Craig Stevens, Margaret Hayes, Don Murphy, Peggy McCay.

FRONTIER FIGHTERS (1947)
lp: Buster Crabbe, Al St. John, Marjorie Manners, Kermit Maynard, Karl Hackett.
d, Sam Newfield.

FRONTIER GUNLAW (1946) 60m
lp: Charles Starrett, Tex Harding, Dub Taylor, Jean Stevens, Weldon Heyburn.
d, Derwin Abrahams.

FRONTIER WOMAN (1956) 80m
lp: Cindy Carson, Lance Fuller, Ann Kelly, James Clayton, Rance Howard, Curtis Dorsett, Mario Galento.
d, Ron Ormond.

FROZEN SCREAM (1980) 85m
lp: Renee Harmon, Thomas Gowan, Lee James, Sunny Bartholomew.
d, Frank Roach.

FUGITIVE GIRLS (1975) 90m
lp: Jabee Abercrombe, Rene Bond, Talie Cochrane, Dona Desmond, Margie Lanier.
d, Stephen C. Apostolof.

FUGITIVE KILLER (1975) 90m
lp: Neil Patrick, Karen Hansen, John-Scott Schroeder, Cheryl Patton.
d, Emile A. Harvard.

FUGITIVE OF THE PLAINS (1943) 57m
lp: Buster Crabbe, Hal Price, Al St. John, Maxine Leslie, Kermit Maynard.
d, Sam Newfield.

FULLER REPORT, THE (1966) 96m
lp: Ken Clark, Beba Loncar, Lincoln Tate, Jess Hahn, Sarah Ross.
d, Terence Hathaway.

FUN AND GAMES (1973)
lp: Alice Spivak, David Drew, Bob Hodge, Calvin Culver.
d, Mervyn Nelson.

FUN HOUSE, THE (1977)
lp: Steven Morrison, Dennis Crawford, Lawrence Bornman, Janet Sorley, Paul Phillips.
d, Victor Janos.

FURY ON THE BOSPHOROUS (1965, Brit.) 106m
lp: Ken Clark, Margaret Lee.

FYRE (1979) 87m
lp: Allen Garfield, Lynn Theel, Tom Baker, Cal Haynes, Donna Wilkes, Bruce Kirby.
d, Richard Grand.

G.I. EXECUTIONER, THE (1971) 91m
lp: Vicki Racimo, Angelique Pettyjohn.
d, Joel M. Reed.

GALLOPING KID, THE (1932)
lp: Al Lane, Karla Cowan, Little Buck Dale, Fred Parker, Horace B. Carpenter, George Bates.
d, Robert Emmett.

GALLOPING THUNDER (1946) 54m
lp: Charles Starrett, Smiley Burnette, Adelle Roberts, Kermit Maynard, Edmund Cobb.
d, Ray Nazarro.

GAMBLING WITH SOULS (1936)
lp: Martha Chapin, Robert Frazer, Wheeler Oakman, Bryant Washburn, Gaston Glass.
d, Elmer Clifton.

GAME SHOW MODELS (1977) 89m
lp: John Vickery, Diane Summerfield, Thelma Houston, Gilbert De Rush, Sid Melton.
d, David Neil Gottlieb.

GANGSTER'S DEN (1945) 55m
lp: Buster Crabbe, Al "Fuzzy" St. John, Sidney Logan, Charles King, Emmett Lynn.
d, Sam Newfield.

GAS PUMP GIRLS (1979) 90m
lp: Kirsten Baker, Dennis Bowen, Huntz Hall, Steve Bond, Leslie King, Linda Lawrence.
d, Joel Bender.

GAY CAVALIER, THE (1946) 65m
lp: Gilbert Roland, Martin Garralaga, Nacho Galindo, Helen Gerald, Ramsey Ames.
d, William Nigh.

GEORGIA ROSE (1930)
lp: Clarence Brooks, Irene Wilson, Evelyn Preer, Roberta Hyson, Allegretti Anderson.
d, Harry A, Gant.

GET DOWN AND BOOGIE (1977) 83m
lp: Trina Parks, Roger E. Mosley, Edna Richardson, Bettye Sweet, Shirley Washington.
d, William Witney.

GETTING IT ON (1983) 96m
lp: Martin Yost, Heather Kennedy, Jeff Edmond, Kathy Rockmeier, Mark Alan Ferri.
d, William Olsen.

GETTING WASTED (1980) 98m
lp: Brian Kerwin, Stephen Furst, Cooper Huckabee.

GHOST DANCE (1982)

lp: Henry Ball, Julie Amato.

d, Peter Bufa.

GHOST IN THE NOONDAY SUN (1974) 95m

lp: Peter Sellers, Anthony Franciosa, Peter Boyle.

d, Peter Medak.

GHOST OF A CHANCE, A (1968, Brit.) 51m

lp: Jimmy Edwards, Patricia Hayes, Graham Stark, Bernard Cribbins, Terry Scott.

d, Jan Darnley-Smith.

GHOST OF CROSSBONES CANYON, THE (1952) 56m

lp: Guy Madison, Andy Devine, Betty Davison, John Doucette, Russell Simpson.

d, Frank McDonald.

GHOST RIDER, THE (1943) 58m

lp: Johnny Mack Brown, Raymond Hatton, Tim Seidel, Beverly Boyd, Milburn Morante.

d, Wallace Fox.

GHOSTS OF HANLEY HOUSE, THE (1974) 80m

lp: Elsie Baker, Barbara Chase, Cliff Scott.

GHOSTS THAT STILL WALK (1977)

lp: Ann Nelson, Matt Boston, Jerry Jenson, Caroline Howe, Rita Crafts.

d, James T. Flocker.

GIFT FOR HEIDI, A (1958) 71m

lp: Douglas Fowley, Sandy Descher, Van Dyke Parks.

d, George Templeton.

GINGER (1972) 102m

lp: Cheri Caffaro, William Grannell.

d, Don Schain.

GIRL FROM TOBACCO ROW, THE (1966) 87m

lp: Tex Ritter, Rachel Romen, Earl Richards, Tim Ormond, Rita Faye, Ralph Emery.

d, Ron Ormond.

GIRL IN BLUE, THE (1974)

lp: David Selby, Maud Adams, Gay Rowan, William Osler, Diane Dewey, Michael Kirby.

d, George Kaczender.

GIRL OF THE NILE, THE (1967, US/ Ger.)

lp: Rory Calhoun, James Philbrook.

d, Sidney Pink.

GIRL TROUBLE (1933)

lp: Jack Perrin, Ben Corbett, Lola Tate, Mary Draper, Wally Turner.

d, B.B. Ray.

GIRL WITH THE FABULOUS BOX, THE (1969)

d, Charles Nisbet..

GIRLS ARE FOR LOVING (1973) 95m

lp: Timothy Brown, Cheri Caffaro.

d, Don Schain.

GIRLS FOR RENT (1974)

lp: Georgina Spelvin, Susan McIver, Rosalind Miles, Preston Pierce, Kent Taylor.

d, Al Adamson.

GIRLS NEXT DOOR, THE (1979)

lp: Kirsten Baker, Perry Lang, Leslie Cederquist, Richard Singer.

d, James Hong.

GIRLS OF 42ND STREET (1974) 80m

lp: Diana Lewis, Lynn Flanagan, Bob Walters, Paul Matthews, Daniel Dietrich, Dorin McGough.

d, Andy Milligan.

GLEN AND RANDA (1971) 94m

lp: Steven Curry, Shelley Plimpton, Woodrow Chambliss, Garry Goodrow, Roy Fox.

d, Jim McBride.

GLOVE, THE (1979) 91m

lp: John Saxon, Rosey Grier, Joanna Cassidy, Joan Blondell, Jack Carter, Aldo Ray.

d, Ross Hagen.

GO DOWN DEATH (1944) 54m

lp: Myra D. Hemmings, Samuel H. James, Eddy L. Houston, Spencer Williams, Amos Droughan.

d, Williams.

GO FOR A TAKE (1972, Brit.) 90m

lp: Reg Varney, Norman Rossington, Sue Lloyd, Dennis Price, Julie Ege, Patrick Newell.

d, Harry Booth.

GO-GET-'EM HAINES (1936) 63m

lp: William Boyd, Sheila Terry, Eleanor Hunt, Leroy Mason, Lloyd Ingraham, Jimmy Aubrey.

d, Sam Newfield.

GOD BLESS DR. SHAGETZ (1977)

lp: Dean Jagger, James Keach, Dabbs Greer, Regis Toomey.

d, Edward Collins, Peter Traynor, Larry Spiegel.

GOD, MAN AND DEVIL (1949) 100m

lp: Michael Michalesco, Berta Gersten, Gustav Berger, Lucy Gehrman, Max Bozyk.

d, Joseph Seiden.

GOD'S BLOODY ACRE (1975) 87m

lp: Scott Lawrence, Jennifer Gregory, Sam Moree, Daniel Schweitzer, Thomas Wood.

d, Harry E. Kerwin.

GOD'S STEPCHILDREN (1937)

lp: Alice B. Russell, Carmen Newsome, Jacqueline Lewis, Alice Lovejoy, Ethel Moses.

d, Oscar Micheaux.

GOIN' ALL THE WAY (1982) 85m

lp: Dan Waldman, Deborah Van Rhyn, Joshua Cadman, Sherie Miller, Joe Colligan.

d, Robert Freedman.

GOLD DIGGERS, THE (1984, Brit.) 89m

lp: Julie Christie, Colette Laffont, Hilary Westlake, David Gale, Tom Osborn.

d, Sally Potter.

GOLD WEST, THE (1932)

lp: Hattie McDaniel.

GOLDEN HANDS OF KURIGAL, THE　　　(1949) 100m

lp: Kirk Alyn, Rosemary La Planche.

GONE TO GROUND　　　(1976) 90m

lp: Charles Tingwell, Elaine Lee, Marion Johns.

GONE WITH THE WEST　　　(1976) 92m

lp: James Caan, Stefanie Powers, Aldo Ray, Robert Walker, Jr, Barbara Werle, Sammy Davis, Jr.

d, Bernard Girard.

GOOD, THE BAD, AND THE BEAUTIFUL, THE　　　(1975) 82m

lp: Allan Garfield, Janis Young, Jennifer Welles, Harold Herbsman.

GOODBYE CRUEL WORLD　　　(1983) 90m

lp: Dick Shawn, Cynthia Sikes, Chuck Mitchell.

d, David Irving.

GOONA-GOONA　　　(1932) 70m

d, Andre Roosevelt, Armand Denis..

GOSH　　　(1974) 80m

lp: Sharon Kelly, Daniel Kauffman, Keith McConnell, Arem Fisher, Norma Field.

d, Tom Scheuer.

GRAD NIGHT　　　(1980) 85m

lp: Joe Johnson, Barry Stoltze, Suzanna Fagan, Sam Whipple, Caroline Bates.

d, John Tenorio.

GRAND JURY　　　(1977) 100m

lp: Bruce Davison, Meredith MacRae, Leslie Nielsen, Barry Sullivan, Sharon Thomas.

d, Christopher Cain.

GREAT CALL OF THE WILD, THE　　　(1976) 95m

lp: Larry Jones.

GREAT LESTER BOGGS, THE　　　(1975) 94m

lp: Bob Ridgely, Alex Karras, Scott McKenzie, Willie Jones, Susan Denbo, Dean Jagger.

d, Harry Thomason.

GREAT MONKEY RIP-OFF, THE　　　(1979) 90m

lp: Alan Hale, Jr, Robert J. Wilke, Ashay Chitre.

d, Tom Stobart.

GREAT MORGAN, THE　　　(1946) 56m

lp: Frank Morgan, Eleanor Powell, The King Sisters, Virginia O'Brien.

d, Nat Perrin.

GREAT RIDE, THE　　　(1978) 90m

lp: Perry Lang, Michael MacRae.

d, Donald Hulette.

GREAT RIVIERA BANK ROBBERY, THE　　　(1979) 98m

lp: Ian McShane, Warren Clarke, Stephen Greif.

d, Francis Megahy.

GREAT SKYCOPTER RESCUE, THE　　　(1982)

lp: Aldo Ray, William Marshall, Terry Michos, Terri Taylor, Alex Mann.

d, Lawrence D. Foldes.

GREATER ADVISOR, THE　　　(1940) 70m

lp: Irving Jacobson, Yetta Zwerling, Sol Dickstein, Max Beden, Muni Serebroff.

d, Joseph Seiden.

GREGORIO　　　(1968) 93m

lp: Broderick Crawford.

GROOVE ROOM, THE　　　(1974, Brit.) 83m

lp: Sue Longhurst, Diana Dors, Martin Ljung, Ollie Soltoft, Malou Cartwright.

d, Vernon P. Becker.

GROUP MARRIAGE　　　(1972) 85m

lp: Victoria Vetri, Claudia Jennings, Aimee Eccles, Zack Taylor, Milt Kamen.

d, Stephanie Rothman.

GUERILLAS IN PINK LACE　　　(1964) 96m

lp: George Montgomery, Valerie Varda, Roby Grace, Joan Shawlee.

d, Montgomery.

GUILTY OR NOT GUILTY　　　(1932)

lp: Betty Compson, Claudia Dell, Tom Douglas, George Irving, Luis Alberni, Wheeler Oakman.

d, Al Ray.

GUMS　　　(1976)

lp: Terri Hall, Brother Theodore.

d, Robert J. Kaplan.

GUN GRIT　　　(1936)

lp: Jack Perrin, Ethel Beck, David Sharpe, Budd Buster, Roger Williams, Ralph Peters.

d, Lester Williams.

GUN MOLL　　　(1938) 65m

lp: Nina Mae McKinney, Lawrence Criner, Monte Hawley, Edward Thompson, Mantan Moreland, Vernon McCalla.

GUN SMOKE　　　(1945) 57m

lp: Johnny Mack Brown, Raymond Hatton, Jennifer Holt, Riley Hill.

d, Howard Bretherton.

GUNFIRE　　　(1935)

lp: Rex Bell, Ruth Mix, Buzz Barton, Milburn Morante, William Desmond, Theodore Lorch.

d, Harry Fraser.

GUNMAN, THE　　　(1952) 52m

lp: Whip Wilson, Fuzzy Knight, Rand Brooks, Terry Frost, I. Stanford Jolley.

d, Lewis Collins.

GUNNERS AND GUNS　　　(1935) 57m

lp: Black King, Edna Aselin, Edmund Cobb, Eddie Davis, Ned Norton, Lois Glaze.

d, Jerry Callahan.

GUNNING FOR VENGEANCE　　　(1946) 56m

lp: Charles Starrett, Smiley Burnette, Marjean Neville, Robert Kortman, George Chesebro.

d, Ray Nazarro.

GUNS ALONG THE BORDER　　　(1952)

lp: Johnny Mack Brown, Lee Roberts, Phyllis Coates, Hugh Prosser, Dennis Moore.

d, Lewis Collins.

GUNS FOR HIRE (1932) 58m

lp: Lane Chandler, Sally Darling, Neal Hart, Yakima Canutt, John Ince, Slim Whitaker.

d, Lew Collins.

GUNSMOKE (1947)

lp: Nick Stuart, Carol Forman, Robert Garden, Craig Lawrence, Marie Harmon, Clark Bush.

d, Fred King.

GUNSMOKE ON THE GUADALUPE (1935)

lp: Buck Coburn, Marion Shilling, Henry Hall, Roger Williams, Dick Botiller.

d, Bartlett Carre.

GUY FROM HARLEM, THE (1977)

lp: Loye Hawkins, Cathy Davis, Patricia Fulton, Wanda Starr.

d, Rene Martinez, Jr..

H.M.S. PINAFORE (1951) 70m

lp: California Opera Company.

HAIR-TRIGGER CASEY (1936) 59m

lp: Jack Perrin, Betty Mack, Fred "Snowflake" Toones, Wally Wales, Phil Dunham.

d, Harry Fraser.

HALF A HOUSE (1979) 84m

lp: Anthony Eisley, Pat Delaney, Francine York, Kaz Garas, Angus Duncan, Mary Grace Canfield.

d, Brice Mack.

HALFWAY TO HELL (1957) 75m

lp: Lyle Felice, Caroll Montour.

HALLELUJAH AND SARTANA, SON OF...GOD (1972) 100m

lp: Robert Widmark, Ron Ely.

HANDS ACROSS THE ROCKIES (1941) 58m

lp: Bill Elliott, Dub Taylor, Mary Daily, Tom Moray, Slim Whitaker, Kenneth MacDonald.

d, Lambert Hillyer.

HANGING WOMAN, THE (1976)

lp: Vicki Nesbitt, Stanley Cooper.

HANG-UP, THE (1969) 82m

lp: Sharon Matt, Sebastian Gregory.

d, John Hayes.

HANNAH--QUEEN OF THE VAMPIRES (1972)

lp: Andrew Prine, Mark Damon, Theresa Gimpera, Patty Shepard, Francisco Brana.

d, Ray Danton.

HANS BRINKER AND THE SILVER SKATES (1969) 100m

lp: Eleanor Parker, Richard Basehart, John Gregson, Robin Askwith, Cyril Ritchard.

HARD FEELINGS (1981) 110m

lp: Carl Marotte, Charlaine Woodward, Grand Bush, Vincent Buffano, Allan Katz.

d, Daryl Duke.

HARD WAY, THE (1980, Brit.) 88m

lp: Patrick McGoohan, Lee Van Cleef, Donal McCann, Edna O'Brien.

d, Michael Dryhurst.

HARD WAY TO DIE, A (1980)

lp: Billy Chong, Carl Scott, Louis Neglia.

HARLEM AFTER MIDNIGHT (1934)

lp: Lorenzo Tucker, Alfred "Slick" Chester.

d, Oscar Micheaux.

HAUNTED MINE, THE (1946) 51m

lp: Johnny Mack Brown, Raymond Hatton, Raphael Bennett, Riley Hill, Claire Whitney.

d, Derwin Abrahams.

HAUNTED TRAILS (1949) 58m

lp: Whip Wilson, Andy Clyde, Reno Browne, William H. Ruhl, Dennis Moore, I. Stanford Jolley.

d, Lambert Hillyer.

HAUNTING OF ROSALIND, THE (1973)

lp: Pamela Payton-Wright, Susan Sarandon.

HAWK, THE (1935) 55m

lp: Yancey Lane, Betty Jordan, Dickie Jones, Rolls Dix, Don Orlando, Lafe McKee.

d, Edward Dmytryk.

HAY, HAY, HAY (1983, Brit.) 120m

lp: Sadie Frost, Wilfred Brambell.

HE IS MY BROTHER (1976)

lp: Bobby Sherman, Kathy Paulo, Keenan Wynn, Robbie Rist, Joaquin Martinez, Benson Fong.

d, Edward Dmytryk.

HEADING WEST (1946) 54m

lp: Charles Starrett, Smiley Burnette, Doris Houch, Norman Willis, Nolan Leary.

d, Ray Nazarro.

HEADLESS EYES, THE (1983) 79m

lp: Bo Brundin, Gordon Ramon, Kelley Swartz, Mary Jane Early.

d, Kent Bateman.

HEARTBREAK MOTEL (1978) 85m

lp: Leslie Uggams, Shelley Winters, Michael Christian, Ted Cassidy, Dub Taylor, Slim Pickens.

HEAT (1972) 100m

lp: Sylvia Miles, Joe Dallesandro, Andrea Feldman, Pat Ast, Ray Vestal.

d, Paul Morrissey.

HEAVY TRAFFIC (1974) 77m

Voices: Joseph Kaufman, Beverly Hope Atkinson, Frank DeKova, Terri Haven, Mary Dean Lauria.

d, Ralph Bakshi.

HELL HOUSE GIRLS (1975, Brit.) 95m

lp: Madeline Hinde, Renee Asherson, Dennis Waterman, Patrick Mower.

d, Robert Hartford-Davies.

HELL IN NORMANDY (1968, Brit.) 98m

lp: Peter Lee Lawrence, Guy Madison.

HELL RIVER (1977) 98m

lp: Rod Taylor, Adam West, Bata Zivajinovic, Xenia Gratsos.

d, Stole Jankovic.

HELL'S VALLEY (1931) 60m
lp: Wally Wales, Virginia Browne Faire, Walter Miller, Franklyn Farnum, Vivian Rich.
d, Alvin J. Neitz.

HELP ME...I'M POSSESSED (1976)
lp: Bill Greer, Deedy Peters.
d, Charles Nizet.

HENRY'S NIGHT IN (1969) 75m
lp: Barbara Kline, Forman Shane.

HER SECOND MOTHER (1940)
lp: Esta Salzman, Muni Serebroff, Yetta Zwerling, Max Baden, Jacob Zanger, Rose Greenfield.
d, Joseph Seiden.

HER SECRET (1933) 73m
lp: Sari Maritza, Buster Collier, Alan Mowbray, Ivan Simpson, Monaei Lindley.
d, Warren Millais.

HER UNBORN CHILD (1933) 65m
lp: Adele Ronson, Paul Clare, Pauline Drake, Doris Rankin, Elisha Cook, Jr.
d, Albert Wray.

HERCULES AND THE PRINCESS OF TROY (1966)
lp: Gordon Scott, Diana Hyland, Everett Sloane.

HERCULES AND THE TYRANTS OF BABYLON (1964)
lp: Rock Stevens.

HERCULES IN VALE OF WOE (1962)
lp: Kirk Morris.

HERCULES, PRISONER OF EVIL (1967)
lp: Reg Park.

HERCULES THE INVINCIBLE (1963)
lp: Dan Vadis.

HERO OF OUR TIME, A (1969) 67m
lp: Alfonso Gil.
d, J. Ferrater-Mora.

HEROES, THE (1975) 108m
lp: Rod Steiger, Rod Taylor, Yul Brynner, Terry-Thomas.
d, Duccio Tessari.

HEROES THREE (1984) 90m
lp: Lauren C. Postma, Laurence Tan, Mike Kelly.

HEROWORK (1977)
lp: Rod Browning, Robert Chapel, Tabi Cooper, Nancy Kandal, Milt Kogan, Hugh Gillin.
d, Michael Adrian.

HIDEOUT IN THE SUN (1960)
lp: Greg Conrad, Dolores Carlos, Earl Bauer, Carol Little, Ann Richards, Mary Jane Line, Pat Reilly.

HIGH COUNTRY CALLING (1975) 90m
lp: Lorne Greene.

HIJACK (1975, Brit.) 60m
lp: Richard Morant, Tracy Peel.
d, Michael Forlong.

HILARY'S BLUES (1983) 80m
lp: Melinda Marx, Diane Berghoff, Sean Berti, Alan Mann, Alan Dumont, Bill Wegney.
d, Peter Jensen.

HINDERED (1974)
lp: Steve Dwoskin, Carola Regnier.
d, Dwoskin.

HIRED GUN (1952)
lp: Whip Wilson, Tommy Farrell, Phyllis Coates, Henry Rowland, I. Stanford Jolley.
d, Thomas Carr.

HIS WIFE'S LOVER (1931) 77m
lp: Ludwig Satz, Michael Rosenberg, Isidore Cashier, Lucy Levine, Jacob Frank.
d, Sidney Goldin.

HIT OF THE SNOW (1928) 72m
lp: Joe E. Brown, Gertrude Olmstead, William Norton Bailey, Gertrude Astor, Lee Shumway.
d, Ralph Ince.

HITCHHIKE TO HELL (1978) 87m
lp: Robert Gribbin, Russell Johnson, John Harmon, Randy Echols, Dorothy Bennett, Jacquelyn Poseley.
d, Irv Berwick:.

HITTER, THE (1979)
lp: Ron O'Neal, Sheila Frazier, Adolph Caesar, Bill Cobbs, Dorothy Fox.
d, Christopher Leitch.

HOLD THAT RIVER (1936) 80m

HOLIDAY ON THE BUSES (1974, Brit.) 85m
lp: Reg Varney, Doris Hare.

HOLLYWOOD HIGH (1976)
lp: Marcy Albrecht, Sherry Hardin, Rae Sperling, Kevin Mead, John Young.
d, Patrick Wright.

HOLLYWOOD KNIGHT (1979) 84m
lp: Michael Christian, Josette Banzet, Keenan Wynn, Donna Wilkes, John Crawford.
d, David Worth.

HOLLYWOOD MAN, THE (1976) 90m
lp: Don Stroud, William Smith, Jennifer Billingsley, Ray Girardin, Jude Farese, Mary Waronov.
d, Jack Starrett.

HOLLYWOOD 90028 (1973) 90m
lp: Christopher Augustine, Jeanette Dilger, Dick Glass, Gayle Davis.
d, Christina Hornisher.

HOLLYWOOD STRANGLER MEETS THE SKIDROW SLASHER, THE (1979)
d, Ray Dennis Steckler..

HOLLYWOOD THRILL-MAKERS (1954)
lp: James Gleason, Bill Henry, Thelia Darin, Jean Holcombe, James Macklin.
d, Bernard Ray.

HOME IN SAN ANTONE (1949) 62m

lp: Roy Acuff, Jacqueline Thomas, Bill Edwards, George Cleveland, Lloyd Corrigan.

d, Ray Nazarro.

HOMEWARD BORNE (1957) 82m

lp: Linda Darnell, Richard Kiley, Keith Andes.

HONEYMOONS WILL KILL YOU (1966) 91m

lp: Tony Russell.

HOOCH (1977) 96m

lp: Gil Gerard, Erika Fox, Melody Rogers, Mike Allen, Ray Serra, Danny Aiello.

d, Ed Mann.

HORSE (1965) 105m

lp: Tosh Carillo, Larry Latrae, Gregory Battcock, Daniel Cassidy, Jr.

d, Andy Warhol.

HOT CHILD (1974) 80m

lp: Peggy Kramer, Burton Dunning.

HOT OFF THE PRESS (1935) 57m

lp: Jack LaRue, Virgina Pine, Monte Blue, Fuzzy Knight, Fred Kelsey, Ed Hearn.

d, Al Herman.

HOT PURSUIT (1981) 89m

lp: Bob Watson, Don Watson, Debbie Washington.

d, James I. West.

HOT SUMMER IN BAREFOOT COUNTY (1974) 90m

lp: Jane Sumner, Dick Smith.

d, Will Zenz.

HOT T-SHIRTS (1980) 86m

lp: Ray Holland, Stephanie Lawlor, Pauline Rose, Corinne Alphen.

d, Chuck Vincent.

HOTWIRE (1980)

lp: George Kennedy, Strother Martin, John Terry, Jean Sanders.

d, Frank Q. Dobbs.

HOUSE AND THE BRAIN, THE (1973)

lp: Keith Charles, Carol Williard, Hurd Hatfield.

HOUSE OF DREAMS (1933)

lp: Lester Matthews, Jean Adrienne, Margot Grahame, Alma Taylor, Sebastian Shaw.

d, Anthony Frenguelli.

HOUSE OF DREAMS (1963) 72m

lp: Robert Berry.

d, Berry.

HOUSE OF GOD, THE (1979) 108m

lp: Tim Matheson, Charles Haid, Bess Armstrong, Michael Sacks, Lisa Pelikan, Ossie Davis.

d, Donald Wrye.

HOUSE OF MYSTERY, THE (1938) 65m

lp: Jack Holt, Beverly Roberts, Craig Reynolds, Marjoreson Gateson, Dorothy Appleby.

d, Lewis D. Collins.

HOUSE OF SHADOWS (1977, Arg.) 103m

lp: John Gavin, Yvonne De Carlo, Leonor Manso, Mecha Ortiz, German Krauss.

d, Richard Wulicher.

HOUSE OF THE DEAD (1980) 100m

lp: John Erikson, Charles Aidman, Bernard Fox, Ivor Francis.

HOUSE OF THE MISSING GIRLS (1974)

lp: Anna Gael.

HOUSE ON STRAW HILL, THE (1976) 84m

lp: Udo Kier, Linda Hayden, Fiona Richmond.

HOUSE RENT PARTY (1946)

lp: Dewey "Pigmeat" Markham, John Murray, MacBeth's Calypso Band.

HOUSE WHERE DEATH LIVES, THE (1982) 83m

lp: Patricia Pearcy, David Hayward, John Dukakis, Joseph Cotten.

d, Alan Beattie.

HOW TO MAKE A DOLL (1967) 81m

lp: Robert Wood, Jim Vance, Bobbi West, Elizabeth Davis, Margie Lester.

d, Herschell Gordon Lewis.

HOW TO SCORE WITH GIRLS (1980) 82m

lp: Ron Osborne, Larry Jacobs, Richard Young, Sandra McKnight, Arlana Blue, Janice Fuller.

d, Ogden Lowell.

HOW TO UNDRESS IN FRONT OF YOUR HUSBAND (1937)

lp: Elaine Barrie.

d, Dwain Esper.

HOWDY BROADWAY (1929) 70m

lp: Ellabee Ruby, Lucy Ennis, Jack J. Clark, Tommy Christian and His Band.

HUGHES AND HARLOW: ANGELS IN HELL (1978) 93m

lp: Victor Holchak, Lindsay Bloom, Royal Dano, Adam Roarke, David McLean, Linda Cristal.

d, Larry Buchanan.

HUMAN GORILLA (1948) 65m

lp: Richard Carlson, Tor Johnson.

HURRAY FOR BETTY BOOP (1980) 89m

Voices: Victoria D'Orzai, Tom Smothers.

HUSSY (1979) 94m

lp: Helen Mirren, John Shea, Daniel Chasen, Jenny Runacre.

d, Matthew Chapman.

HUSTLER SQUAD (1976) 98m

lp: John Ericson, Karen Ericson, Lynda Sinclaire, Nory Wright, Ramon Revilla.

d, Cesar Gallardo.

I AM FRIGID...WHY? (1973)

lp: Sandra Julien, John Terrade.

d, Max Pecas.

I HATE WOMEN (1934) 70m

lp: Wallace Ford, June Clyde, Bradley Page, Fuzzy Knight, Barbara Rogers, Alexander Carr.

d, Aubrey H. Scotto.

I REMEMBER LOVE   (1981) 88m

lp: Matt Greene, Nona Jane Lim, Stephen Nicholson.

d, Norbert Meisel.

I WANT TO BE A MOTHER   (1937) 75m

lp: Leo Fuchs, Hanna Hollander, Yetta Zwerling, Leibele Waldman, Muni Serebroff.

d, George Roland.

I WAS A TEENAGE ALIEN   (1980) 50m

d, Bob Cooper..

I WAS A ZOMBIE FOR THE F.B.I.   (1982)

lp: Larry Raspberry, James Raspberry, Laurence Hall, John Gillick, Christina Wellford.

d, Marius Penczner.

I WONDER WHO'S KILLING HER NOW   (1975) 87m

lp: Bob Dishy, Joanna Barnes, Bill Dana, Vito Scotti.

d, Steven H. Stern.

IDEAL MARRIAGE, THE   (1970) 84m

lp: Eva Christine, Gunther Stoll.

IF YOU DON'T STOP IT, YOU'LL GO BLIND   (1977) 80m

lp: George Spencer, Patrick Wright, Jane Kellen, Dick Stuart.

d, Bob Levy, Keefe Brasselle.

I'LL NAME THE MURDERER   (1936) 72m

lp: Ralph Forbes, Marion Shilling.

d, Raymond K. Johnson.

ILSA, HAREM KEEPER OF THE OIL SHEIKS   (1976) 93m

lp: Dyanne Thorne, Michael Thayer.

ILSA, SHE WOLF OF THE SS   (1975) 95m

lp: Dyanne Thorne, Greg Knoph.

I'M GOING TO BE FAMOUS   (1981) 103m

lp: Dick Sargent, Roslyn Kind, Vivian Blaine, Meredith MacRae, Joe Terry, Greg Mullavey.

d, Paul Leder.

IMAGE OF DEATH   (1977, Brit.) 81m

lp: Cathey Paine, Cheryl Waters, Tony Bonner, Barry Pierce, Sheila Helpmann, Penny Hackforth-Jones.

d, Kevin Dobson.

IMAGO   (1970) 83m

lp: Barbara Douglas, Morgan Evans, Victoria Wales, Dick DeCoit, Jenie Jackson, Robert Webb.

d, Ned Bosnic.

IN LOVE   (1983) 100m

lp: Kelly Nichols, Jerry Butler, Tish Ambrose, Joanna Storm, Samantha Fox, Jack Wrangler.

d, Chuck Vincent.

IN OLD LOS ANGELES   (1948) 88m

lp: William "Bill" Elliott, John Carroll, Catherine McLeod, Andy Devine, Joseph Schildkraut, Estelita Rodriguez, Virginia Brissac.

d, Joseph Kane.

IN OLD MONTANA   (1939) 61m

lp; Fred Scott, Jean Cameron [Julia Thayer], Harry Harvey, John Merton.

d, Raymond K. Johnson.

IN PARIS, A.W.O.L.   (1936) 67m

lp: Lola Lane, Irene Ware, Lawrence Gray, Chic Chandler, George Meeker.

d, Roland Reed.

IN SEARCH OF GOLDEN SKY   (1984)

lp: Charles Napier, George "Buck" Flower, Cliff Osmond.

d, Jefferson Richard.

IN SELF DEFENSE   (1947) 66m

lp: Don Castle, Audrey Long, Peggy Knudson, Samuel S. Hinds, Gloria Holden, John Miljan.

d, Jack Bernhard.

IN THE RAPTURE   (1976) 90m

lp: Gwendolyn Parrish, Clifford Hatcher, Joe Folson, Andy Crim.

d, William H. Wiggins, Jr..

INCOMING FRESHMEN   (1979) 84m

lp: Leslie Blalock, Debralee Scott, Cheryl Gordon, Richard Harriman.

d, Eric Lewald, Glenn Morgan.

INSEMINOID   (1980) 92m

lp: Robin Clarke, Jennifer Ashley, Stephanie Beacham, Judy Geeson.

d, Norman J. Warren.

INSTANT COFFEE   (1974) 91m

lp: Rita Tushingham, Aldo Maccione.

INSTRUCTOR, THE   (1983) 91m

lp: Don Bendell, Bob Chaney, Bob Saal, Lynda Scharnott, Hank Gordon, Bruce Bendell.

d, Bendell.

INTERPLAY   (1970)

lp: Ed Moore, Zee Wilson, Gwen Saska, Sam Coppola, Phil Allen.

d, Albert T. Viola.

INTIMATE PLAYMATES, THE   (1976)

lp: Carole Parker, Lynn Ross.

INVASION FROM INNER EARTH   (1977)

lp: Nick Holt, Debbie Pick, Paul Bentzen, Karl Wallace.

d, Bill Rebane.

INVASION OF THE FLESH HUNTERS   (1981) 91m

lp: John Saxon, Elizabeth Turner.

d, Anthony M. Dawson.

IRISH GRINGO, THE   (1935)

lp: Pat Carlyle, William Farnum, Bryant Washburn, Elena Duran, Olin Francis, Ace Cain, Milburn Morante.

d, William L. Thompson.

IS THERE SEX AFTER DEATH   (1971) 97m

lp: Buck Henry, Marshall Efron, Alan Abel, Holly Woodlawn, Jim Moran.

d, Jeanne Abel, Alan Abel.

ISLAND OF LOST GIRLS   (1975) 85m

lp: Brad Harris, Tony Kendall, Monica Pardo.

ISLAND TRADER   (1982) 99m

lp: John Eward, Sancho Gracia, Eric Oldfield.

IT HAPPENED IN HARLEM (1945)

lp: Slick and Slack, Phil Gomez, Dotty Rhodes, Juanita Pitts, George Wiltshire.

d, Bud Pollard.

IT RAINED ALL NIGHT THE DAY I LEFT (1978)

lp: Tony Curtis.

IT'S ALL IN YOUR MIND (1938) 63m

lp: Byron Foulger, Constance Bergen, Betty Roadman, Lynton Brent.

d, Bernard B. Ray.

IVY LEAGUE KILLERS (1962, Can.) 70m

lp: Don Borisenko, Barbara Bricker.

d, William Davidson.

J.C. (1972) 101m

lp: William McGaha, Hannibal Penny, Joanna Moore, Burr De Benning, Slim Pickens, Pati Delany.

d, McGaha.

JACKPOT (1982) 90m

lp: James Lawless, Shirley Venard, Warren Frost, Paul Davies, Peter Goetz, Mikel Clifford.

d, John Goodell.

JAMAICAN GOLD (1971) 100m

lp: Rod Taylor, Stuart Whitman, Elke Sommer, Keenan Wynn, Jeremy Kemp.

d, Henry Levin.

JEKYLL AND HYDE PORTFOLIO, THE (1972) 85m

lp: Gray Daniels, Mady Maguire, Sebastian Brook, John Terry, Don Greer.

d, Eric Jeffrey Haims.

JENNIE, WIFE/CHILD (1968) 83m

lp: Jack Lester, Beverly Lunsford, Jim Reader, Virginia Wood.

d, James Landis, Robert Carl Cohen.

JESSE'S GIRLS (1975)

d, Al Adamson..

JEWISH DAUGHTER (1933) 75m

lp: Chaim Schneier, Joseph Greenberg, Michael Rosenberg, Ben Besenko, Helen Blay.

d, George Roland.

JEWISH FATHER (1934)

lp: Wolf Goldfaden, Gertrude Bullman, Sam Gertler, Boas Young, Dora Kashinskaya.

d, Henry Lynn.

JEWISH KING LEAR (1935) 80m

lp: Maurice Krohner, Fannie Levenstein, Jacob Bergreen, Miriam Grossman, Eddie Pascal.

d, Harry Thomashefsky.

JEWISH MELODY, THE (1940) 89m

lp: Isidore Cashier, Lazar Freed, Chaim Tauber, Seymour Rechtzeit, Dave Lubritsky.

d, Joseph Seiden.

JIG SAW (1979)

lp: Angie Dickinson, Lino Ventura.

JIGGS AND MAGGIE IN COURT (1948) 71m

lp: Joe Yule, Renie Riano, George McManus, Tim Ryan, Riley Hill, June Harrison.

d, William Beaudine.

JIGGS AND MAGGIE IN JACKPOT JITTERS (1949) 67m

lp: Joe Yule, Renie Riano, George McManus, Tim Ryan, Walter G. McCarty.

d, William Beaudine.

JIM THE MAN (1967) 77m

d, Max Katz..

JIMMY, THE BOY WONDER (1966)

d, Herschell Gordon Lewis..

JIVE TURKEY (1976)

lp: Paul Harris, Frank DeKova, Serene.

d, Bill Brame.

JOE AND MAXI (1980) 80m

lp: Joe Cohen, Maxi Cohen, Barry Cohen, Danny Cohen, Bea Metzman, Dan Metzman.

d, Joel Gold, Maxi Cohen.

JOE PALOOKA IN THE KNOCKOUT (1947) 72m

lp: Leon Errol, Joe Kirkwood, Morris Carnovsky, Elyse Knox, Billy House, Trudy Marshall.

d, Reginald LeBorg.

JOE'S BED-STUY BARBERSHOP: WE CUT HEADS (1983) 60m

lp: Monty Ross, Donna Bailey, Stuart Smith, Tommie Hicks, Horace Long, LeVerne Summer, Africanis Rocius.

JOEY (1977) 96m

lp: Danny Martin, Marie O'Henry, Renny Roker, Juanita Moore, Candi Keath.

d, Horace B. Jackson.

JOHNNY FIRECLOUD (1975) 90m

lp: Victor Mohica, Ralph Meeker, David Canary, Frank DeKova, Sacheen Littlefeather.

d, William Allen Castleman.

JOHNSTOWN MONSTER, THE (1971) 54m

lp: Connor Brennan, Simon Tully, Rory Baily, Kim McDonald, Amanda Jane Tully, Seamus Kelly.

d, Olaf Pooley.

JOKES MY FOLKS NEVER TOLD ME (1979)

d, Gerry Woolery..

JOLLY GENIE, THE (1964)

d, Wesley E. Barry..

JOSEPH IN THE LAND OF EGYPT (1932) 80m

lp; Ben Alder, Joseph Greenberg [Green], Sigmund Zuckerberg, Herman Sarotsky, Wolf Goldfaden.

d, George Roland.

JOY RIDE TO NOWHERE (1978) 86m

lp: Leslie Ackerman, Sandy Serrano, Len Lesser, Welles, Ron Ross.

d, Mel Welles.

JUDGMENT BOOK, THE (1935) 63m

lp: Conway Tearle, Bernadine Hayes, Howard H. Lang, Richard Cramer, William Gould.

d, Charles Hutchinson.

JUKE JOINT (1947)

lp: Spencer Williams, July Jones, Mantan Moreland.

d, Williams.

JUNCTION 88 (1940) 60m

lp: Noble Sissle and His Orchestra, Bob Howard.

JUNGLE HELL (1956)

lp: Sabu, David Bruce, George E. Stone, K.T. Stevens.

d, Norman A. Cerf.

JUNGLE QUEEN (1946)

lp: Dorothy Dandridge.

d, Ray Taylor, Lewis Collins.

JUPITER MENACE, THE (1982) 76m

lp: George Kennedy, Greg Michaels.

d, Peter Matulavich, Lee Auerbach.

JUST BE THERE (1977) 95m

lp: Michael Montgomery, Lynn Baker, Charley McCarty, Nancy Nelson.

d, David Feldshuh.

JUST FOR THE HELL OF IT (1968) 85m

lp: Ray Sager, Rodney Bedell, Nancy Lee Noble, Agi Gyenes, Steve White.

d, Herschell Gordon Lewis.

JUST MY LUCK (1936) 70m

lp: Charles Ray, Anne Grey, Eddie Nugent, Quentin R. Smith, Snub Pollard, Lee Prather.

d, Russell Ray Heinz.

JUST TELL ME YOU LOVE ME (1979) 90m

lp: Robert Heeyes, Lisa Hartman, Debralee Scott, June Lockhart, Ricci Martin.

d, Tony Mordente.

JUST THE TWO OF US (1975) 82m

lp: Elizabeth Plumb, Alicia Courtney, John Aprea, Marland Proctor, Wayne Want.

d, Barbara Peeters.

KAHUNA! (1981)

lp: Debbie Jones, Luana King, Pat Waid, Maria Cortez, Danielle Roe, Julie Rohde.

d, Frank Sillman.

KEEP IT UP, JACK! (1975)

lp: Mark Jones, Sue Longhurst, Maggi Burton, Steve Viedor.

d, Tom Parker.

KEEP OFF! KEEP OFF! (1975) 90m

lp: Micky Dolenz, Marcus J. Grapes, Gary Wood, Everette Addington, Louis Quinn.

d, Shelley Berman.

KEEP PUNCHING (1939)

lp: Henry Armstrong, Canada Lee, Dooley Wilson, Alvin Childress, Francine Everett, Lionel Monagas.

d, John Clein.

KEEPING ON (1981) 75m

lp: Dick Anthony Williams, Carol Kane, James Broderick, Marcia Rodd, Rosalind Cash.

d, Barbara Kopple.

KELLY (1981, Can.) 93m

lp: Robert Logan, Twyla-Dawn Vokins, George Clutesi, Elaine Nalee, Doug Lennox.

d, Christopher Chapman.

KENYA--COUNTRY OF TREASURE (1964) 90m

lp: William Sylvester, June Ritchie.

KID FROM NOT SO BIG, THE (1978) 90m

lp: Veronica Cartwright, Jennifer McAllister, Robert Viharo, Paul Tulley, Don Keefer.

d, Bill Crain.

KILL, THE (1973) 81m

lp: Richard Jaeckel, Henry Duval, Judy Washington.

KILL THE GOLDEN GOOSE (1979)

lp: Brad Von Beltz, Ed Parker, Master Bong Soo Han.

d, Elliot Hong.

KILLER DILLER (1948) 80m

lp: Dusty Fletcher, Moms Mabley, Nat "King" Cole, George Wiltshire, Butterfly McQueen.

d, Josh Binney.

KILLER'S CARNIVAL (1965) 95m

lp: Stewart Granger, Lex Barker, Pierre Brice.

d, Albert Cardiff, Robert Lynn, Sheldon Reynolds.

KILLER'S DELIGHT (1978)

lp: James Luisi, Susan Sullivan, John Karlan, Martin Speer.

d, Jeremy Hoenack.

KILLER'S MOON (1978)

lp: Anthony Forrest, Tom Marshall, Georgina Kean, Nigel Gregory, David Jackson.

d, Alan Birkinshaw.

KILLING GROUND, THE (1972) 100m

lp: Richard Harrison, Fern Hunter, James Colby.

KILLING AT OUTPOST ZETA, THE (1980) 92m

lp: Gordon DeVol, Jackie Ray, James A. Watson.

KILLING TOUCH, THE (1983)

lp: Sally Kirkland, Melissa Prophet, Sean Masterson, Nicholas Love.

KING FRAT (1979)

lp: John DiSanti, Dan Chandler, Dan Fitzgerald, Mike Grabow, Ray Mann, Charles Pitt.

d, Ken Wiederhorn.

KING MONSTER (1977) 78m

lp: Robert White, Basil Bradbury, K.K. Mohajan.

d, Richard Martin.

KINGFISHER, THE (1982) 78m

lp: Rex Harrison, Wendy Hiller, Cyril Cusack.

KINGS OF THE HILL (1976) 91m

lp: Jim Bohan, Jason Sommers, Jana Bellan, Robert Burton.

d, Michael Dmytryk.

KINKY COACHES & THE POM POM PUSSYCATS, THE
(1981, Can.)

d, Mark Warren..

KINO, THE PADRE ON HORSEBACK (1977) 116m

lp: Richard Egan, Ricardo Montalban, John Ireland, Cesar Romero, Joe Campanella.

d, Ken Kennedy.

KISS DADDY GOODBYE (1981) 100m

lp: Fabian Forte, Marilyn Burns, Jon Ceddar.

KISS HER GOODBYE (1959) 94m

lp: Elaine Stritch, Steven Hill.

d, Albert Lipton.

KISS MY GRITS (1982) 98m

lp: Bruce Davison, Susan George, Tony Franciosa, Bruno Kirby.

d, Jack Starrett.

KISS THE GIRLS AND SEE THEM DIE (1968) 77m

KITTY CAN'T HELP IT (1975)

lp: Kitty Carl, Fay DeWitt, Pamela Miller, Lisa Farringer, Walter Wonderman.

d, Peter Locke.

KNIFE FOR THE LADIES, A (1973)

lp: Jack Elam, Ruth Roman, Jeff Cooper, John Kellogg, Joe Santos, Gene Evans.

d, Larry G. Spangler.

KNOCKING AT HEAVEN'S DOOR (1980) 90m

lp: Kristina David, Sam Dibello, Glenn E. Sacos, Mary De La Mare, Max Golightly.

d, John Linton.

KOL NIDRE (1939) 82m

lp: Lili Liliana, Leon Liebgold, Leibele Waldman, Joel Feig Double Choir, Menashe Oppenheim.

d, Joseph Seiden.

KUNG FU HALLOWEEN (1981) 94m

lp: Law Lee, Ka Ling, Tien I, Chang Wang.

d, Lam Chi Kam, Liu San.

LABORATORY (1980) 93m

lp: Camille Mitchell, Corrine Michaels.

LADY CHATTERLY VS. FANNY HILL (1980) 91m

lp: Joanna Lumley, Penny Brahms, Richard Wattis.

d, Malcolm Leigh.

LADY COCOA (1975)

lp: Lola Falana, Gene Washington, Alex Dreier, "Mean" Joe Green, James R. Watson.

d, Matt Cimber.

LAND OF SIX GUNS (1940) 54m

lp: Jack Randall.

d, Raymond K. Johnson.

LARAMIE KID, THE (1935)

lp: Tom Tyler, Alberta Vaughn, Al Ferguson, Murdock McQuarrie, George Chesebro.

d, Harry S. Webb.

LARIATS AND SIXSHOOTERS (1931) 65m

lp: Jack Perrin, Ann Lee, George Chesebro, Art Mix, Virginia Bell, Lafe McKee.

d, Alvin J. Neitz.

LASSIE, THE VOYAGER (1966) 96m

lp: Med Flory, Lassie the Dog.

d, Dick Moder, Jack B. Hively.

LAST ALARM, THE (1940) 61m

lp: J. Farrell MacDonald, Warren Hull, Polly Ann Young, Mary Gordon, George Pembroke.

d, William West.

LAST ASSIGNMENT, THE (1936) 60m

lp: Ray Walker, Joan Woodbury, William Farnum, Clara Kimball Young, Syd Saylor.

d, Dan Milner.

LAST FEELINGS (1981) 98m

lp: Carlo Lupo, Angela Goodwin.

LAST FIGHT, THE (1983) 86m

lp: Fred Williamson, Willie Colon, Ruben Blades, Darianne Fluegel.

d, Williamson.

LAST GAME, THE (1983) 90m

lp: Howard Segal, Ed L. Grady, Terry Alden, Jerry Rushing.

d, Martin Beck.

LAST GENERATION, THE (1971)

lp: Stuart Whitman, Vera Miles, Lew Ayres, Mercedes McCambridge, Pearl Bailey.

d, William Graham.

LAST KIDS ON EARTH, THE (1983) 105m

lp: Jayne Collins, Ian Mune.

LAST MOMENT, THE (1976) 87m

lp: Tracy Olson, Melba Conway.

LAST MUSKETEER, THE (1952) 67m

lp: Rex Allen, Mary Ellen Kay, Slim Pickens, James Anderson, Boyd "Red" Morgan.

d, William Witney.

LAST OF THE AMERICAN HOBOES, THE (1974) 80m

lp: Titus Moody, Hal Jon Norman.

d, Moody.

LAST PLANE OUT (1983) 92m

lp: Jan-Michael Vincent, Julie Carmen, Mary Crosby, David Huffman, William Windom.

d, David Nelson.

LAST REUNION (1978) 93m

lp: Cameron Mitchell, Leo Fong.

LAST STOP ON THE NIGHT TRAIN (1976) 85m

lp: Kay Beal, Patty Edwards, Norma Knight, Delbert Moss, Richard Davis.

d, Evans Isle.

LAST TANGO IN ACAPULCO, THE (1975)

lp: Rebecca Sharpe, Bill Cable, Keith Erickson, Maria Pia, Linda Tobalina, Jake Monroy.

d, Carlos Tobalina.

LAST THREE (1942) 62m

lp: Bobby Watson, Joe Devlin, Johnny Arthur, Jean Poster.

LAST WINTER, THE   (1983) 90m
lp: Kathleen Quinlan, Yona Eilan, Stephen Macht, Zippora Peled, Michael Schneider.

d, Riki Shelach.

LAW COMES TO GUNSIGHT, THE   (1947) 56m
lp: Johnny Mack Brown, Raymond Hatton, Reno Blair, Lanny Rees, Zon Murray.

d, Lambert Hillyer.

LAW OF THE CANYON   (1947) 55m
lp: Charles Starrett, Smiley Burnette, Nancy Saunders, Buzz Henry, Fred Sears.

d, Ray Nazarro.

LAW OF THE 45'S   (1935) 57m
lp: Guinn "Big Boy" Williams, Molly O'Day, Al St. John, Ted Adams, Lafe McKee.

d, John P. McCarthy.

LAW OF THE WEST   (1932) 50m
lp: Bob Steele, Nancy Drexel, Ed Brady, Hank Bell, Charles West, Earl Dwire.

d, Robert N. Bradbury.

LAW OF THE WILD   (1941) 55m
lp: Dennis Moore, Luana Walters, George Chesebro, Stephen Clark, Jack Ingram.

d, Raymond K. Johnson.

LAWBREAKERS, THE   (1960) 79m
lp: Jack Warden, Robert Douglas.

d, Joseph M. Newman.

LAWLESS VALLEY   (1932)
lp: Lane Chandler, Gertrude Messinger, Richard Cramer, Si Jenks, Anne Howard, Art Mix.

d, J.P. McGowan.

LEFT HAND OF GEMINI, THE   (1972) 92m
lp: Ian McShane, Ursula Theiss, Richard Egan, Patricia Blair.

LEFT-HANDED   (1972)
lp: Ray Frank, Robert Rikas, Larry Burns, Teri Reardon, Sal Mineo.

d, Jack Deveau.

LEGACY   (1963) 92m
lp: Jessica Thomas, Dorie Zabriskie, Rick Yearry, Michael Pflueger, Mike Snodgrass.

d, Richard Snodgrass.

LEGACY OF HORROR   (1978) 82m
lp: Elaine Boies, Chris Brodcrick, Marilee Troncone, Jeannie Cusick.

d, Andy Milligan.

LEGACY OF SATAN   (1973)
lp: Lisa Christian, John Francis, Paul Barry.

d, Gerard Damiano.

LEGEND OF ALFRED PACKER, THE   (1979) 95m
lp: Patrick Dray, Ron Haines, Jim Dratfield, Bob Damon, Dave Ellingson, Ron Holiday.

d, Jim Roberson.

LEGEND OF BLOOD MOUNTAIN, THE   (1965) 61m
lp: George Ellis, Zenas Sears, Glenda Brunson, Erin Fleming, Sheila Stringer.

d, Massey Cramer.

LEGEND OF CHAMPIONS   (1983) 92m
lp: Stuart Damon, Alexandra Bastedo, William Gaunt.

LEGEND OF EARL DURAND, THE   (1974) 110m
lp: Peter Haskell, Slim Pickens, Keenan Wynn, Martin Sheen, Anthony Caruso.

d, John D. Patterson.

LEGEND OF FRANK WOODS, THE   (1977)
lp: Troy Donahue, Kitty Vallacher, Brad Stewart.

d, Hagen Smith.

LEGEND OF HORROR   (1972)
lp: Karin Field.

d, Bill Davies.

LEGEND OF THE JUGGLER   (1978) 83m
lp: Joey Ross.

LEGEND OF THE WEREWOLF   (1974) 87m
lp: Peter Cushing, David Rintoul, Hugh Griffith, Lynn Dalby, Ron Moody.

d, Freddie Francis.

LEGEND OF THE WILD   (1981) 93m
lp: Dan Haggerty, Denver Pyle, Dan Shanks, Ken Curtis, Jack Kruschen, Linda Arbizu, Kristen Curry.

LEO CHRONICLES, THE   (1972)
lp: George Montgomery, Scott Brady, Maria Perschy.

LET GEORGE DO IT   (1938, Aus.) 75m
lp: George Wallace, Letty Craydon, Joe Valli, Alec Kellaway, George Lloyd, Gwen Munro.

d, Ken G. Hall.

LET'S HAVE FUN   (1943) 63m
lp: Bert Gordon, Margaret Lindsay, John Beal, Dorothy Ann Seese, Constance Worth.

d, Charles Barton.

LICENSED TO LOVE AND KILL   (1979, Brit.)
lp: Gareth Hunt, Nick Tate, Geoffrey Keen, Fiona Curzon.

LIES   (1983) 100m
lp: Ann Dusenberry, Bruce Davison, Gail Strickland, Clu Gulager, Terence Knox.

d, Ken Wheat, Jim Wheat.

LIFE AND LEGEND OF BUFFALO JONES, THE   (1976)
lp: Rick Guinn, John Freeman, George Sager, Rich Scheeland.

LIFE GOES ON   (1938) 70m
lp: Louise Beavers, Edward Thompson, Reginald Fenderson, Lawrence Criner, Monte Hawley, Hope Bennett.

LIFE POD   (1980) 94m
lp: Joe Penny, Jordon Michaels, Kristine DeBell.

LIGHTNIN' SMITH RETURNS   (1931) 59m
lp: Buddy Roosevelt, Barbara Worth, Tom London, Pee Wee Holmes, Jack Richardson.

d, Jack Irwin.

LIGHTNING CARSON RIDES AGAIN   (1938) 59m
lp: Tim McCoy, Joan Barclay, Bob Terry, Frank Wayne, Ben Corbett, Ted Adams.

d, Sam Newfield.

LIGHTNING TRIGGERS (1935) 57m

lp: Reb Russell, Yvonne Pelletier, Fred Kohler, Jack Rockwell, Edmund Cobb.

d, S. Roy Luby.

LINDA LOVELACE FOR PRESIDENT (1975) 107m

lp: Linda Lovelace, Fuddly Bagley, Val Bisoglio, Jack De Leon, Mickey Dolenz.

d, Claudio Guzman.

LION MAN, THE (1936)

lp: Jon Hall, Kathleen Burke, Richard Carlyle, Eric Snowden, Ted Adams.

d, John P. McCarthy.

LIONHEART (1970) 57m

lp: Anthony Kemp, Mary Burleigh, Martin Beaumont.

LIONS FOR BREAKFAST (1977)

lp: Jim Henshaw, Sue Petrie, Jan Rubes, Paul Bradley.

LIONS OF ST. PETERSBURG, THE (1971) 100m

lp: Mark Damon.

LIPS OF BLOOD (1972)

d, Ken Ruder..

LISA (1977) 67m

lp: Friedel, Leslie Lee, Jack Canon, Ray Green, Douglas Power, Frank Jones.

d, Frederick Friedel.

LITTLE DETECTIVES, THE (1983) 120m

lp: Joe McKenna, Matthew Wright.

LITTLE FELLER, THE (1979) 90m

lp: Steve Bisley, Sally Conabere, Lorna Lesley.

d, Colin Eggleston.

LITTLE GIRL, BIG TEASE (1977)

lp: Jody Ray, Rebecca Brooke.

d, Roberto Mitrotti.

LITTLE MERMAID, THE (1979)

LITTLE MISS INNOCENCE (1973)

lp: John Alderman, Sandy Dempsey, Judy Medford.

d, Chris Warfield.

LITTLE SISTERS (1972) 68m

d, Alex de Renzy..

LIVE AND LAUGH (1933)

lp: Menasha Skulnick, Joseph Buloff, Pinchus Lavenda, Seymour Rechtzeit, Yudel Dubinsky.

d, Max Wilner.

LIVING ORPHAN, THE (1939) 90m

lp: Gustav Berger, Fania Rubina, Jerry Rosenberg, Harry Feld, Yetta Zwerling, Ida Dworkin.

d, Joseph Seiden.

LOADED GUNS (1975) 90M

lp: Ursula Andress, Woody Strode.

LOCH NESS HORROR, THE (1983)

lp: Sandy Kenyon, Barry Buchanan, Preston Hansen.

d, Larry Buchanan.

LONE BANDIT, THE (1934)

lp: Lane Chandler, Doris Brook, Wally Wales, Slim Whitaker, Ray Gallagher, Ben Corbett.

d, J.P. McGowan.

LONE RIDER, THE (1934)

lp; Wally Wales, Marla Bratton, Franklyn Farnum, James Sheridan [Sherry Tansey], Fred Parker.

d, Robert Emmett.

LONE RIDER IN BORDER ROUNDUP (1942) 56m

lp: Dennis Moore, Al "Fuzzy" St. John.

d, Sam Newfield.

LONE RIDER IN FRONTIER FURY, THE (1941)

lp: George Houston, Al "Fuzzy" St. John, Hillary Brooke, Karl Hackett, Ted Adams.

d, Sam Newfield.

LONE RIDER RIDES ON, THE (1941) 61m

lp: George Houston, Al "Fuzzy" St. John, Hillary Brooke, Lee Powell, Buddy Roosevelt.

d, Sam Newfield.

LONE STAR COUNTRY (1983) 90m

lp: Heather Gable, Alicia Alexander, Allison Hanes, J.D. Johnson.

d, Lee Thornburg, Caruth C. Byrd.

LONE STAR MOONLIGHT (1946) 67m

lp: Ken Curtis, Joan Barton, Guy Kibbee, Robert Stevens, Claudia Drake, Arthur Loft.

d, Ray Nazarro.

LONESOME TRAIL (1945) 57m

lp: Jimmy Wakely, Lee "Lasses" White, Lorraine Miller, Iris Clive, John James.

d, Oliver Drake.

LONGSHOT (1982) 80m

lp: Leif Garrett, Linda Manz, Ralph Seymour, Zoe Chauveau.

d, E.W. Swackhamer.

LOONEY, LOONEY, LOONEY BUGS BUNNY MOVIE, THE (1981) 80m

Voices: Mel Blanc, June Foray, Frank Nelson, Frank Welfer, Stan Freberg, Ralph James.

d, Friz Freleng.

LOSER'S END (1934)

lp: Jack Perrin, Tina Menard, Frank Rice, William Gould, Fern Emmett.

d, Bernard B. Ray.

LOSING GROUND (1982) 86m

lp: Seret Scott, Bill Gunn, Duane Jones, Billie Allen, Gary Bolling, Norberto Kerner

d, Kathleen Collins.

LOST (1983) 92m

lp: Sandra Dee, Don Stewart, Ken Curtis, Jack Elam, Shelia Newhouse.

LOST CITY, THE (1982)

lp: Bernadette Clark, David Cain Haughton, Margot Samson.

d, Robert Dukes.

LOST WORLD OF LIBRA, THE (1968)

lp: James Darren, Stuart Whitman, Telly Savalas.

LOVE AFTER DEATH   (1968) 72m

LOVE AND KISSES   (?) 87m

lp: Ruth Alda, Charles Napier, Paul Norman, Kathy Knight.

d, Don Dorsey.

LOVE AND LARCENY   (1983) 148m

lp: Jennifer Dale, Douglas Rain, Kenneth Welsh.

LOVE AND SACRIFICE   (1936) 75m

lp: Lazar Freed, Rose Greenfield, Leibele Waldman, Anna Thomashefsky, Louis Kramer.

d, George Roland.

LOVE COMES QUIETLY   (1974)

lp; Barbara [Hershey] Seagull, Sandy van der Linden, Ward De Ravet, Kitty Janssen, Ralph Meeker.

LOVE IN HIGH GEAR   (1932) 66m

lp: Harrison Ford, Alberta Vaughn, Tyrrel Davis, Arthur Hoyt, Ethel Wales, Nanette Vallon.

d, Frank Strayer.

LOVE PILL, THE   (1971) 82m

lp: Toni Sinclair, Melinda Churcher, Henry Woolf, David Pugh, Kenneth Waller.

d, Kenneth Turner.

LOVE THY NEIGHBOUR   (1973) 85m

lp: Jack Smethurst, Kate Williams, Rudolph Walker, Nina Baden-Semper, Bill Fraser.

d, John Robins.

LOVE UNDER THE ELMS   (1973) 94m

lp: Anne Heywood, Mark Lester, Claudio Cassinelli.

LOVE, VAMPIRE STYLE   (1971) 83m

lp: Eva Renzi, B. Skay, B. Valentine.

LOVE WANGA   (1942) 61m

LOVELETTERS FROM TERALBA ROAD   (1977) 50m

lp: Bryan Brown, Kris McQuade, Joy Hruby, Kevin Leslie, Gia Corides, Pat Jones.

d, Stephen Wallace.

LOVELY BUT DEADLY   (1983) 93m

lp: Lucinda Dooling, John Randolph, Richard Herd, Susan Mechsner, Mel Novak.

d, David Sheldon.

LOW BLOW, THE   (1970)

lp: Minnie the Mermaid, John Kent.

LUCIFER COMPLEX, THE   (1978) 91m

lp: Robert Vaughn, Keenan Wynn, Merrie Lynn Ross, Aldo Ray.

d, David L. Hewitt, Kenneth Hartford.

LUCIFER'S WOMEN   (1978) 88m

lp: Larry Hankin, Jane Brunel-Cohen, Emily Smith.

d, Paul Aratow.

LUST TO KILL   (1960)

lp: Jim Davis, Don Megowan, Gerald Milton, Allison Hayes, Toni Turner, Sandra Giles, Tom Hubbard.

LYING LIPS   (1939) 60m

lp: Edna Mae Harris, Carmen Newsome, Amanda Randolph, Frances Williams.

d, Oscar Micheaux.

LYNCHING   (1968) 85m

lp: Glenn Saxon, Gordon Mitchell, King McQueen.

M3: THE GEMINI STRAIN   (1980) 88m

lp: Daniel Pilon, Kate Reid, Celine Lomez, Michael J. Reynolds.

d, Ed Hunt.

MACBETH   (1950) 78m

lp: Barbara Hudson Sowers, Bob Jones, Jr.

d, Katherine Stenholm.

MAD BUTCHER, THE   (1972)

lp: Victor Buono, Karin Field, Brad Harris, John Ireland, Charles Ross.

MADHOUSE   (1982)

lp: Trish Everly, Michael Macrae, Dennis Robertson, Morgan Hart.

d, Ovidio G. Assonitis.

MAFIA JUNCTION   (1977)

lp: Ivan Rassimov, Stephanie Beacham, Patricia Hayes.

d, Massimo Dallamano.

MAG WHEELS   (1978) 81m

lp: Shelley Horner, John McLaughlin, Phoebe Schmidt, Steven Rose, Verkema Flower.

d, Bethel Buckalew.

MAGIC PONY   (1979) 80m

Voices: Jim Backus, Hans Conried, Johnny Whitaker, Erin Moran.

d, Ivan Ivanov-vano.

MAGNIFICENT ADVENTURE, THE   (1952) 80m

lp: Nelson Leigh, Jerome Cowan, Onslow Stevens.

MAMA'S DIRTY GIRLS   (1974) 80m

d, John Hayes..

MAMA'S GONE A-HUNTING   (1976) 90m

lp: Judy Morris, Gerard Kennedy, Vince Martin, Carmen Duncan.

MAN ABOUT THE HOUSE   (1974, Brit.) 90m

lp: Richard O'Sullivan, Paula Wilcox, Sally Thomsett, Yootha Joyce, Brian Murphy.

d, John Robins.

MAN EATER   (1958) 72m

lp: Rhodes Reason.

MAN FOR HANGING, A   (1972) 80m

lp: Peter Breck, Paul Carr, Brooke Bundy.

MAN FROM ARIZONA, THE   (1932) 58m

lp: Rex Bell, Charles King, George Nash, John Elliott, Naomi Judge, Nat Carr, Les Lindsay.

d, Harry Fraser.

MAN FROM NOWHERE, THE   (1976, Brit.)

lp: Sarah Hollis-Andrews, Ronald Adam, Shane Franklin.

d, James Hill.

MAN FROM SONORA (1951) 54m

lp: Johnny Mack Brown, Phyllis Coates, Lyle Talbot, House Peters, Jr, Lee Roberts.

d, Lewis Collins.

MAN FROM THE BLACK HILLS (1952) 51m

lp: Johnny Mack Brown, Jimmy Ellison, Rand Brooks, Lane Bradford, I. Stanford Jolley.

d, Thomas Carr.

MAN IN A LOOKING GLASS, A (1965, Brit.) 91m

lp: Steve Forrest, Sue Lloyd, Bernard Lee, Yvonne Furneaux, John Carson, Frank Wolff, Ken Warren.

MAN OF ACTION (1933) 60m

lp: Tim McCoy, Caryl Lincoln, Wheeler Oakman, Walter Brennan, Stanley Blystone, Charles K. French, Julian Rivero.

d, George Melford.

MAN ON A MISSION (1965)

d, Bob Gardner..

MAN ON THE SPYING TRAPEZE (1965) 90m

lp: Wayde Preston, Helga Summerfeld, Pamela Tudor.

MAN OUTSIDE (1965) 120m

lp: Joseph Marzano, Barbara Ellen, Gordon Spencer, Bob Stewart, Robert James, Beverly Tey.

d, Marzano.

MAN TRAILER, THE (1934) 59m

lp: Buck Jones, Cecilia Parker, Arthur Vinton, Clarence Geldert, Lew Meehan.

d, Lambert Hillyer.

MAN WHO SAW TOMORROW, THE (1981) 88m

lp: Orson Welles, Richard Butler, Ray Laska, P.L. Clarke.

MAN WHO TALKS TO WHALES, THE (197?) 91m

lp: Victor Jory.

MAN WITH THE ICY EYES, THE (1971) 97m

lp: Victor Buono, Keenan Wynn, Faith Domergue.

MANHANDLERS, THE (1975) 85m

lp: Cara Burgess, Judy Brown, Rosalind Miles, Vince Cannon, Henry Brandon.

d, Lee Madden.

MANHATTAN BUTTERFLY (1935) 73m

lp: Dorothy Grainger, William Bakewell, Betty Compson, Kenneth Thomson.

d, Louis Collins.

MANHUNT IN SPACE (1954) 79m

lp: Ken Howard, Gary Lockwood, Stefanie Powers, James Olson.

d, Walter Grauman.

MANHUNTER (1983) 90m

lp: Earl Owensby, Johnny Popwell, Doug Hale, Elizabeth Upton.

d, Martin Beck.

MANIPULATOR, THE (1972) 92m

lp: Stephen Boyd, Sylva Koscina.

MAN'S BEST FRIEND (1935) 62m

lp: Douglas Haig, Frank Brownlee, Mary McLaren, Patricia Chapman, Lightning the Horse.

d, Edward Kull.

MANSON MASSACRE, THE (1976) 65m

lp: Blaidsell Makee, Debbie Osborne, Sean Kenney, Candice Roman.

d, Kentucky Jones.

MARK OF THE GUN (1969) 85m

lp: Ross Hagen, Brad Thomas, Chris Carter, Wallace J. Campodanio, Erick Lindberg.

MARK OF THE SPUR (1932) 60m

lp: Bob Custer, Lillian Rich, Franklyn Farnum, Bud Osborne, Blackie Whiteford.

d, J.P. McGowan.

MARK TWAIN, AMERICAN (1976)

lp: Ed Trostle.

d, Robert Wilbor.

MARRIAGE BARGAIN, THE (1935) 62m

lp: Lila Lee, Creighton Chaney, Edmund Breese, Francis McDonald, Audrey Ferris.

d, Albert Ray.

MARSHALS IN DISGUISE (1954)

lp: Guy Madison, Andy Devine, Norma Eberhardt, Leonard Penn, Tris Coffin, Fred Kelsey.

d, Frank McDonald.

MASQUERADE OF THIEVES (1973) 103m

lp: Richard Widmark.

MASSACRE AT GRAND CANYON (1965) 90m

lp: James Mitchum, Jill Powers, Eduardo Ciannelli.

d, Albert Band.

MATTER OF LOVE, A (1979) 88m

lp: Michelle Harris, Marc Anderson, Christy Neal, Jeff Alin.

d, Chuck Vincent.

MAURIE (1973) 112m

lp: Bernie Casey, Bo Svenson, Janet MacLachlan.

d, Daniel Mann.

MAY MORNING (1970) 95m

lp: James Berkin, John Steiner, Alessio Orano.

d, Ugo Liberatore.

MAZEL TOV, JEWS (1941) 89m

lp: Michael Rosenberg, Leo Fuchs, Yetta Swerling, Chaim Tauber, Leibele Waldman.

d, Joseph Seiden.

MEAN MOTHER (1974)

lp: Clifton Brown, Dennis Safren, Luciana Paluzzi.

MEATEATER (1979) 100m

lp: Arch Jaboulian, Diane Davis, Emily Spencer.

MELON AFFAIR, THE (1979)

lp: Frank Corsentino, Haji, Michael Finn, Marius Mazhanian, Lee McLaughlin, Charles Knatt.

d, Art Lieberman.

MEMORY OF LOVE (1949) 82m

lp: George Nader, Anita Bjork.

MEN OF ACTION (1935) 61m

lp: Roy Mason, Frankie Darro, Barbara Worth, Fred Kohler, Gloria Shea, Edwin Maxwell.

d, Alan James.

METAL MESSIAH (1978)

lp: John Paul Young, Richard Allen, David Hensen.

d, Tibor Takacs.

METAMORPHOSIS (1951) 75m

lp: Dana Elcar, Ted Heusel, Bette Ellis.

d, William J. Hampton.

MIDDLE PASSAGE (1978)

d, Tom Fielding..

MIDNIGHT PHANTOM, THE (1935) 63m

lp: Reginald Denny, Claudia Dell, Lloyd Hughes, James Farley, Barbara Bedford.

d, B.B. Ray.

MIDNIGHT PLOWBOY (1973)

lp: John Tull, Nancee, Debbie Osborne, Christie Anna, Jack Richesim.

MIDNIGHT SHADOW (1939)

lp: Frances Redd, Buck Woods, Richard Bates, Ollie Ann Robinson, Clinton Rosemond.

d, George Randol.

MILLION DOLLAR HAUL (1935) 60m

lp: Janet Chandler, Reed Howes, Tarzan the Police Dog.

MILPITAS MONSTER, THE (1980) 90m

lp: Paul Frees, Residents of Milpitas, California.

d, Robert L. Burrill.

MIRELE EFROS (1939) 91m

lp: Berta Gersten, Michael Rosenberg, Ruth Elbaum, Albert Lipton, Sarah Krohner, Moishe Feder.

d, Joseph Berne.

MIRRORS (1978) 83m

lp: Kitty Wynn, Peter Donat, William Swetland, Mary-Robin Redd, William Burns.

d, Noel Black.

MISS LESLIE'S DOLLS (1972) 85m

lp: Salvadore Ugarte, Terry Juston, Marcelle Bichette, Kitty Lewis, Charles W. Pitts.

d, Joseph G. Prieto.

MISS MELODY JONES (1973) 86m

lp: Philomena Nowlin, Ronald Warden, Jackie Dalyea, Peter Jacob.

d, Bill Brame.

MISSION HILL (1982) 90m

lp: Brian Burke, Alice Barrett, Barbara Orson, Robert Kerman, Daniel Silver, Nan Mulleneaux.

d, Robert Jones.

MISSION IN MOROCCO (1959) 79m

lp: Lex Barker, Julie Reding.

MISSION: MONTE CARLO (1981, Brit.) 96m

lp: Tony Curtis, Roger Moore, Susan George, Anette Andre, Alfred Marks, Laurence Naismith.

d, Roy Ward Baker.

MISSION OF THE SEA HAWK (1962, Brit.) 83m

lp: Terence Morgan, Jean Kent.

MISSION TO DEATH (1966) 76m

lp: Jim Brewer, James E. McLarty, Jim Westerbrook, Robert Stolper, Dudley Hafner, Jerry Lasater.

MR. HORATIO KNIBBLES (1971) 60m

lp: Lesley Roach, Gary Smith, Rachel Brennock, John Ash, Nigel Chivers, Anthony Sheppard.

d, Robert Hird.

MR. KINGSTREET'S WAR (1973) 92m

lp: John Saxon, Tippi Hedren, Rossano Brazzi, Brian O'Shaughnessy.

d, Percival Rubens.

MISTER SCARFACE (1977)

lp: Jack Palance, Edmund Purdom, Al Cliver, Harry Baer, Gisela Hahn, Enzo Pulcrano.

d, Fernando Di Leo.

MR. SMITH GOES GHOST (1940)

lp: Dewey "Pigmeat" Markham, Monte Hawley, Lillian Randolph, Lawrence Criner, Vernon McCalla, Millie Monroe.

MISTRESS PAMELA (1974)

lp: Ann Michelle, Julian Barnes, Anna Quayle, Rosemary Dunham.

d, Jim O'Connor.

MODERN DAY HOUDINI (1983) 90m

lp: Bill Shirk, Milbourne Christopher, Peter Lupus, Dick the Bruiser, Gary Todd.

d, Eddie Beverly, Jr..

MONEY IN MY POCKET (1962)

lp: Robert Anson, Jan Brinker, Graham Archer, Anthony Rowse, Suzie William, Bill Anderson, Nancy Allen, Frank Faro.

d, Erven Jourdan.

MONEY TO BURN (1981) 100m

lp: Jack Kruschen, Phillip Pine, David Wallace, Meegan King.

MONSTROID (1980) 100m

lp: Jim Mitchum, Keenan Wynn, John Carradine.

MONTANA INCIDENT (1952) 54m

lp: Whip Wilson, Rand Brooks, Noel Neill, Bruce Edwards, Peggy Stewart, Bill Fawcett.

d, Lewis Collins.

MOON OVER HARLEM (1939) 67m

lp: Bud Harris, Cora Green, Alec Lovejoy, Sidney Bechet, Izinetta Wilcois.

d, Edgar G. Ulmer.

MOON OVER MONTANA (1946) 56m

lp: Jimmy Wakely, Lee "Lasses" White, Jennifer Holt, Terry Frost, Jack Ingram.

d, Oliver Drake.

MORALS SQUAD (1960) 57m

lp: Bob O'Connell, Beverly Bennett, Vince Marcellino, Maritza, Jeri Archer, Vince Barbi.

MOUNTAIN CHARLIE (1982) 96m

lp: Denise Neilson, Dick Robinson, Rick Guinn, Lynne Seus.

d, George Stapleford.

MOVIEMAKERS (1970) 75m

d, John Pearse..

MURDER AT SCOTLAND YARD (1952) 75m

lp: Tod Slaughter, Patrick Barr, Tucker McGuire, Dorothy Bramhall, Tom Macauley.

d, Victor M. Gover.

MURDER ON LENOX AVENUE (1941) 65m

lp: Mamie Smith, Alec Lovejoy.

d, Arthur Dreifuss.

MURDER ON THE HIGH SEAS (1938) 65m

lp: Jack Mulhall, Montagu Love.

MURDER WITH MUSIC (1941) 59m

lp: Bob Howard, Noble Sissle, Nellid Hill, Milton J. Williams.

d, George P. Quigley.

MUTHERS, THE (1976) 83m

lp: Jeanne Bell, Rosanne Katon, J. Antonio Carrion, Jayne Kennedy, Trina Parks.

d, Cirio Santiago.

MY DOG SHEP (1948) 71m

lp: Lannie Rees, Tom Neal, Flame the Movie Dog.

d, Ford Beebe.

MY FRIENDS NEED KILLING (1984) 72m

lp: Greg Mullavey, Meredith MacRae, Clayton Wilcox, Carolyn Ames.

d, Paul Leder.

MY GIRLFRIEND'S WEDDING (1969) 60m

d, James McBride..

MY NAME IS LEGEND (1975) 88m

lp: Duke Kelly, Tom Kirk, Stan Foster, Kerry Smith, Rand Porter, Curley Montana, Scott Kelly, Roberta Eaton, Bill Lear.

d, Kelly.

MY PLEASURE IS MY BUSINESS (1974, Can.) 85m

lp: Xaviera Hollander, Henry Ramer, Colin Fox, Kenneth Lynch, Jayne Eastwood.

d, Al Waxman.

MYRTE AND THE DEMONS (1948) 73m

lp: Myrte, John Moore, Sonia Gables.

d, Bruno Paul Schreiber.

MYSTERIOUS STRANGER (1982)

lp: Christopher Makepeace, Fred Gwynne, Lance Kerwin.

d, Peter Hunt.

MYSTERY IN SWING (1940) 76m

lp: F.E. Miller, Monte Hawley, Marguerite Whitten, Tommie Moore, Edward Thompson.

d, Arthur Dreifuss.

MYSTERY RANCH (1934) 56m

lp: Tom Tyler, Roberta Gale, Jack Perrin, Frank Hall Crane, Louise Gabo, Charles King.

d, Ray Bernard.

NAKED RIVER (1977)

lp: Gerald Richards, Edmund Genest, Linda Cook, Johnny Popwell, Philip Pleasants.

d, William Diehl, Jr..

NARCOTIC, THE (1937)

d, Dwain Esper..

NAUGHTY GIRLS ON THE LOOSE (1976) 87m

lp: Joanna Richards, Paula Martin.

d, Martin M. Lewis.

NAUGHTY NYMPHS (1974) 82m

lp: Eve Garden, Christina Maybeck, Clark Tinney, Sybil Danning, Elina Moon, Paul Lowinger.

d, Frank Antel.

NAUGHTY SCHOOL GIRLS (1977) 84m

lp: Rebecca Brooke, Sandra Gartner, Judy Rauch, Kim Schachel, Clare Waugh.

d, Jean Paul Scardino.

NAUGHTY STEWARDESSES, THE (1973)

d, Al Adamson..

NAUGHTY WIVES (1974) 84m

lp: Brendan Price, Graham Stark, Chic Murray, Felicity Devonshire, Sue Longhurst.

d, Wolf Rilla.

NEEKA (1968) 90m

lp: Lassie, Jed Allan, Mark Miranda, Jeff Pomerantz.

NEIGHBORHOOD HOUSE (1936) 58m

lp: Charley Chase, Darla Hood, Rosina Lawrence, Margaret Irving, Tom Dugan.

d, Alan Hale, Sr., Harold Law.

NEVADA BUCKAROO, THE (1931) 59m

lp: Bob Steele, Dorothy Dix, George Hayes, Ed Brady, Glen Cavendar, Billy Engle.

d, John P. McCarthy.

NEVER TOO LATE (1935) 59m

lp: Richard Talmadge, Thelma White, Robert Frazer, Mildred Harris, Vera Lewis.

d, Franklin Shamroy.

NEW DAY AT SUNDOWN (1957)

lp: George Montgomery, Randy Stuart, James Griffith, House Peters, Jr, Susan Cummings.

d, Paul Landres.

NEWMAN SHAME, THE (1977) 90m

lp: George Lazenby, Diane Craig, Joan Bruce, Alwyn Kurts, Judy Nunn.

NEXT VICTIM (1971) 90m

lp: George Hilton, Edwige French.

NICOLE (1972) 85m

lp: Leslie Caron, Ramon Berry.

NIGHT CARGOES (1963) 60m

lp: Hugh James, Stephen Marriot.

d, Ernest Morris.

NIGHT NURSE, THE   (1977) 74m
lp: Davina Whitehouse, Kay Taylor, Gary Day, Kate Fitzpatrick.
d, Igor Auzins.

NIGHT OF THE ASSASSIN, THE   (1972) 95m
lp: George Sanders, Michael Craig, Eve Renzi, Yvette Mimieux.

NIGHT OF THE DEMON   (1980)
lp: Mike Cutt, Joy Allen, Richard Fields.
d, Jim Wasson.

NIGHT OF THE HOWLING BEAST   (1977)
d, M.I. Bonns..

NIGHT OF THE SORCERORS   (1970) 90m
lp: Jack Taylor, Simon Andrue, Kali Hansa.
d, Amando De Ossorie.

NIGHT TO DISMEMBER, A   (1983)
lp: Diane Cummins, Saul Meth, Michael Egan.
d, Doris Wishman.

NIGHTINGALE SANG IN BERKELEY SQUARE, A   (1979) 102m
lp: Richard Jordan, David Niven, Oliver Tobias, Elke Sommer, Gloria Grahame.
d, Ralph Thomas.

NIGHTKILLERS   (1983)
lp: Belinda Montgomery, Viveca Lindfors, Sydney Lassick.
d, Simon Nuchtern.

NIGHTMARE BLOOD BATH   (1971)
lp: Regina Carrol, Scott Brady.

NIGHTMARE COUNTY   (1977)
lp: Sean McGregor, Gayle Hemingway.
d, McGregor.

NIGHTMARE WEEKEND
lp: Dale Midkiff, Deborah Midkiff.

NINE LIVES OF FRITZ THE CAT, THE   (1974) 76m
Voices: Skip Hinnant, Reva Rose, Bob Holt, Fred Smoot, Pat Harrington, Jr.
d, Robert Taylor.

1931, ONCE UPON A TIME IN NEW YORK   (1972) 87m
lp: Lionel Stander, Richard Conte, Irene Papas.

99 WOMEN   (1969, Brit./Span./Ger./Ital.) 86m
lp: Maria Schell, Luciana Paluzzi, Mercedes McCambridge, Herbert Lom.
d, Jess Franco.

NINJA MISSION   (1984) 104M
lp: Christopher Kolberg, Hanna Pola, Bo F. Munthe.
d, Mats Helge.

NO DIAMONDS FOR URSULA   (1967) 96m
lp: Dana Andrews, Jean Valery, John Elliot, Dan Harrison, Roger Beaumont.

NOON SUNDAY   (1971) 93m
lp: Mark Leonard, John Russell, Linda Avery.

NORTH OF ARIZONA   (1935) 60m
lp: Jack Perrin, Blanche Mehaffey, Lane Chandler, Al Bridge, Murdock McQuarrie.

d, Harry S. Webb.

NORTH OF THE ROCKIES   (1942) 60m
lp: Bill Elliott, Tex Ritter, Shirley Patterson, Frank Mitchell, Tristram Coffin.
d, Lambert Hillyer.

NORTHEAST TO SEOUL   (1974) 98m
lp: John Ireland, Anita Ekberg, Victor Buono.

NOT A LADIES MAN   (1942) 60m
lp: Paul Kelly, Douglas Croft, Fay Wray.
d, Lew Landers.

NOT MY DAUGHTER   (1975)
lp: James J. Griffith, Karen Arthur, Belinda Palmer, Jimmy Cavaretta, Joe Hooker.
d, Jerry Schafer.

NOT TONIGHT HENRY   (1961)
lp: Hank Henry, Valkyra, Babe McDonnell, Daurine Dare, Marge Welling, Betty Blue, Joanne Berges.

NOW OR NEVER   (1935) 63m
lp: Richard Talmadge, Janet Chandler, Robert Walker, Ed Davis, Otto Metzetti, Thomas Ricketts.
d, B.B. Ray.

NUMBERED WOMAN   (1938) 60m
lp: Sally Blane, Lloyd Hughes, Mayo Methot, Clay Clement, J. Farrell MacDonald, Ward Bond.
d, Karl Brown.

NURSES FOR SALE   (1977) 84m
lp: Curt Jurgens, Joan Kozian.
d, Rolf Olsen.

NUTCRACKER   (1984) 105m
lp: Joan Collins, Carol White, Paul Nicholas, Finola Hughes, William Franklyn.
d, Anwar Kawardi.

NYMPH   (1974) 80m
lp: Peggy Kramer, Burton Dunning.

OASIS OF FEAR   (1973)
lp: Irene Papas, Raymond Lovelock, Ornella Muti.

OATH OF VENGEANCE   (1944) 57m
lp: Buster Crabbe, Al "Fuzzy" St. John, Mady Lawrence, Jack Ingram, Charles King.
d, Sam Newfield.

OBEAH   (1935) 75m
lp: Phillips H. Lord, Jeane Kelly, Alice Wesslar.
d, F. Herrick Herrick.

OFF YOUR ROCKER   (1980) 92m
lp: Milton Berle, Red Buttons, Lou Jacobi, Dorothy Malone.
d, Morley Markson, Larry Pall.

OIL   (1977, Ital.) 95m
lp: Stuart Whitman, Woody Strode, Ray Milland, George Dinica, William Berger, Tony Kendall.
d, Mircea Dragan.

OIL RAIDER, THE (1934) 65m
lp: Buster Crabbe, Gloria Shea.
d, Spencer Gordon Bennet.

OLD TESTAMENT (1963, Ital.) 96m
lp: Susan Paget, John Heston, Brad Davis, Margaret Taylor.

OLE REX (1961) 80m
lp: Robert Hinkle, Billy Hughes, William Foster, Whitey Hughes, William Hughes, Richard McCarty.
d, Hinkle.

OMEGANS, THE (1968)
lp: Keith Larsen, Ingrid Pitt, Lucien Pan, Bruno Punzalan, John Yench.
d, W. Lee Wilder.

ON THE LAM (1972) 78m
lp: Mark LaMura, Jan Cobler.

ONE ARMED EXECUTIONER (1980) 95m
lp: Franco Guerrero, Jody Kay, Pete Cooper, Nigel Hogge, Mike Cohen, James Gaines.
d, Bobby A. Auarez.

ONE AWAY (1980) 83m
lp: Elke Sommer, Bradford Dillman, Dean Stockwell.

ONE CHANCE TO WIN (1976)
lp: Tony DiStefano, Pierre Karsmakers, Brad Lackey, Marty Smith, Jim Weinert.

ONE LAST RIDE (1980) 125m
lp: Ronny Cox, David Hollander, Andrew Duggan.

ONE MAN AGAINST THE ORGANIZATION (1977)
lp: Stephen Boyd.

ONE OF THOSE THINGS (1974, Brit.) 90m
lp: Judy Geeson, Roy Dotrice, Zena Walker.
d, Erik Balling.

ONE PAGE OF LOVE (1979) 89m
lp: Gena Lee, Nancy Hoffman, Anthony Richards, Tovia Israel, Diane Miller, Richard Booth.
d, Ted Roter.

ONE RUSSIAN SUMMER (1973) 112m
lp: Oliver Reed, John McEnery, Carol Andre, Raymond Lovelock, Claudia Cardinale.
d, Antonio Calenda.

ONLY WAY OUT IS DEAD, THE (1970) 89m
lp: Stuart Whitman, Sandy Dennis, Burl Ives, Tom Harvey.
d, John Trent.

OPERATION SNAFU (1970, Ital./Yugo.) 97m
lp: Peter Falk, Jason Robards, Jr, Martin Landau, Nino Manfredi, Scott Hylands, Slim Pickens.
d, Nanni Loy.

OPERATION STOGIE (1960, Brit.) 75m
lp: John Hewer, Anton Rogers, Susan Stephen, Peter Illing.

ORDER TO KILL (1974) 94m
lp: Helmut Berger, Jose Ferrer, Sydne Rome, Kevin McCarthy, Juan Luis Galiardo.
d, Jose Maesso.

ORIENT EXPRESS (1952) 98m
lp: Curt Jurgens, Eva Bartok, Silvana Pampanini.

ORPHAN, THE (1979) 80m
lp: Mark Evans, Joanna Miles, Peggy Feury.
d, John Ballard.

OUR MAN IN JAMAICA (1965) 96m
lp: Larry Pennell, Margarita Scherr, Brad Harris.

OUR MAN IN THE CARIBBEAN (1962) 85m
lp: Diana Rigg, Carlos Thompson, Clemence Bettany, Tracy Reed, Shirley Eaton.

OUR MEN IN BAGHDAD (1967, Ital.) 100m
lp: Rory Calhoun, Roger Hanin, Evi Marandi, Ralph Baldwin, Jean Gaven, Lea Padovani.
d, Paolo Bianchini.

OUT OF THIN AIR (1969) 93m
lp: George Sanders, Maurice Evans, Patrick Allen, Neil Connery.
d, Gerry Levy.

OUTBREAK OF HOSTILITIES (1979) 90m
lp: George Mallaby, Colleen Fitzpatrick, Scot Burgess, Cornelia Francis.
d, David Copping.

OUTLAW QUEEN (1957) 70m
lp: Andrea King, Harry James, Robert Clarke, Jim Harakas, Andy Ladas, Kenne Duncan.
d, Herbert Greene.

OUTLAW RIDERS (1971) 86m
lp: Bryan Sonny West, Darlene Duralia, Bambi Allen, Bill Bonner.
d, Tony Houston.

OUTLAW ROUNDUP (1944) 55m
lp: Dave O'Brien, Jim Newill, Guy Wilkerson, Helen Chapman, Jack Ingram, I. Stanford Jolley.
d, Harry Fraser.

OUTLAW RULE (1935)
lp: Reb Russell, Betty Mack, Yakima Canutt, Jack Rockwell, John McGuire, Al Bridge.
d, S. Roy Luby.

OUTLAW TAMER, THE (1934)
lp: J.P. McGowan, Lane Chandler, Janet Morgan, George Hayes, Ben Corbett, Slim Whitaker.
d, McGowan.

OUTLAWS' HIGHWAY (1934) 61m
lp: John King, Tom London, Philo McCullough, Bartlett Carre, Del Morgan, Jack Donovan.
d, Bob Hill.

OUTLAWS OF BOULDER PASS (1942) 61m
lp: George Houston, Al "Fuzzy" St. John, Dennis Moore, Marjorie Manners, Charles King.
d, Sam Newfield.

OUTLAWS OF THE RANGE (1936) 59m
lp: Bill Cody, Catherine Cotter, Bill Cody, Jr, William McCall, Wally West, Gordon Griffith.
d, Al Herman.

OUTLAW'S SON (1954)

lp: Guy Madison, Andy Devine, Anne Kimball.

d, Frank McDonald.

OUTRIDERS, THE (1950) 93m

lp: Joel McCrea, Arlene Dahl, Barry Sullivan, Claude Jarman, Jr, James Whitmore, Ramon Navarro.

d, Roy Rowland.

OUTSIDE CHANCE (1978) 94m

lp: Yvette Mimieux.

d, Michael Miller.

OUTSIDE THE LAW (1938) 66m

lp: Jack Holt, Beverly Roberts, Paul Everton, Noah Beery, Jr, John Qualen.

d, Lewis D. Collins.

OVER THE SANTA FE TRAIL (1947) 63m

lp: Ken Curtis, Jennifer Holt, Guy Kibbee, Guinn "Big Boy" Williams, The Hoosier Hotshots.

d, Ray Nazarro.

OVERLAND TO DEADWOOD (1942) 59m

lp: Charles Starrett, Russell Hayden, Leslie Brooks, Cliff Edwards, Norman Willis.

d, William Berke.

OVERLAND TRAILS (1948) 58m

lp: Johnny Mack Brown, Raymond Hatton, Virgina Belmont, Bill Kennedy, Virginia Carroll.

d, Lambert Hillyer.

OVERSEXED (1974)

lp: Veronica Parrish.

d, Joe Sarno.

PACO (1976) 100m

lp: Jose Ferrer, Allen Garfield, Pernell Roberts, Andre Marquis, Panchito Gomes.

d, Robert Vincent O'Neil.

PANAMA RED (1976) 87m

lp: Jim Wingert, Barbara Mills, Alain Patrick, Henry Sanders, Rene Bond.

d, Robert C. Chinn.

PAPA SOLTERO (1939)

lp: Tito Guizar, Carlos Villarias, Barry Norton, Paul Ellis, Amanda Varela.

d, Richard Harlan.

PAPER PEOPLE, THE (1969) 75m

lp: Marc Strange, Kate Reid.

PARADES (1972) 95m

lp: Russ Thacker, Brad Sullivan, David Doyle.

PARADISE IN HARLEM (1939) 85m

lp: Frank Wilson, Mamie Smith, Juanita Hall, Joe Joe Thomas, Perry Bradford, Edna Mae Harris.

d, Joseph Seiden.

PARTNERS IN CRIME (1961, Brit.) 54m

lp: Bernard Lee, John Van Eyssen, Moira Redmond, Gordon Boyd.

d, Peter Duffell.

PASSPORT TO HEAVEN (1943) 73m

lp: Albert Basserman, Eric Blore, Mary Brian, Herman Bing, Luis Alberni.

PASSPORT TO PARADISE (1932) 67m

lp: Jack Mulhall, Blanche Mehaffey, Eddie Phillips, William Burt, Gloria Joy.

d, George B. Seitz.

PAWN, THE (1968)

lp: Guy "Buz" Dillow, Lisa Jonson, Lou Steele, Jean Carmen Dillow.

d, Jean Carmen Dillow.

PAY OR DIE (1982) 95m

lp: Marrie Lee, Chito Guerrero, Florence Carvajal.

PECOS DANDY, THE (1934)

lp: George J. Lewis, Dorothy Gulliver, Betty Lee.

d, Horace B. Carpenter, Victor Adamson.

PECOS KID, THE (1935)

lp: Fred Kohler, Jr, Ruth Findlay, Roger Williams, Edward Cassidy.

d, William Berke.

PELVIS (1977)

lp: Luther Whaney, Mary Mitchell, Cindy Tree, Billy Padgett, Bobby Astyr.

d, Lew Mishkin.

PEOPLE THAT SHALL NOT DIE, A (1939)

lp: Ben Adler, Zina Goldstein, Lillian Blum, Leon Schechter, Herman Zorotzksy.

d, Henry Lynn.

PEPPER AND HIS WACKY TAXI (1972) 79m

lp: John Astin, Frank Sinatra, Jr, Jackie Gayle, Alan Sherman, Maria Pohji.

d, Alex Grasshof.

PERFECT CRIME 90m

lp: Joseph Cotten.

PERFECT KILLER, THE (1977, Span.) 85m

lp: Lee Van Cleef, Tita Barker, John Ireland, Richard Widmark.

PERFORMANCE (1970, Brit.) 105m

lp: James Fox, Mick Jagger, Anita Pallenberg, Michele Breton, Ann Sidney, John Bindon.

d, Nicolas Roeg.

PERILOUS JOURNEY (1983) 95m

lp: David Else, Janene Pearce, Karen Thomas.

PETTY STORY, THE (1974)

lp: Darren McGavin, Richard Petty, Kathie Brown, Noah Beery, Jr, Lynn Marta, Pierre Jalbert, L.Q. Jones.

PHANTOM COWBOY, THE (1935) 55m

lp: Ted Wells, Edna Aslin, Jimmy Aubrey, George Chesebro, Richard Cramer, William Desmond.

d, Robert J. Horner.

PHANTOM KID, THE (1983) 85m

lp: Michael Tough, Susan Stacey, Jeremy Kaplan, Kelly Frost, Price McLean, Barry Delaney.

d, Peter Hammond.

PHILADELPHIA HERE I COME   (1975) 95m

lp: Donal McCann, Des Cave, Siobhan McKenna, Eamon Kelly, Fieldma Murphy, Liam Redmond.

d, John Quested.

PHOELIX   (1979) 50m

d, Anna Ambrose..

PICK-UP   (1975) 80m

lp: Jill Senter, Alan Long, Gini Eastwood, Tom Quinn, Bess Douglass, Don Penny.

d, Bernie Hirschenson.

PINK ANGELS, THE   (1971) 81m

lp: John Alderman, Tom Basham.

PINOCCHIO'S GREATEST ADVENTURE   (1974)

lp: Nancy Belle Fuller, Sean Sullivan, Danny McIlravey.

PINOCCHIO'S STORYBOOK ADVENTURES   (1979) 80m

lp: John Fields, Armand MacKinnon, Owen Edward, Ellen Prince.

d, Ron Merk.

PIRANHA, PIRANHA   (1972) 96m

lp: Peter Brown, William Smith, Ahna Capri.

PIT, THE   (1984) 96m

lp: Sammy Snyders, Sonja Smits, Jeannie Elias, Laura Hollingsworth.

d, Lew Lehman.

PITY ME NOT   (1960) 95m

lp: Tony Anthony, Anne Hegiba, Brud Talbot, Michael Dunn.

PLACE CALLED TRINITY, A   (1975) 97m

lp: Richard Harrison, Anna Zinneman, Donal O'Brien.

PLACE WITHOUT PARENTS, A   (1974)

lp: Albert Salmi, Nicholas Wahler, Craig Horrall.

d, Ken Handler.

PLAGUE DOGS, THE   (1982) 103m

d, Marton Rosen..

PLAINS OF HEAVEN, THE   (1982) 80m

lp: Richard Moir, Reg Evans, Gerard Kennedy, John Flaus.

d, Ian Pringle.

PLAY IT COOLER   (1961)

lp: Anthony Newley, Anne Aubrey, Bernie Winters, James Booth, Harry Andrews, Niall MacGinnis.

d, Ken Hughes.

PLAYMATES   (1971) 85m

lp: Donna Michel.

d, Jean-Claude Dague.

PLAYTHINGS OF HOLLYWOOD   (1931) 81m

lp: Phyllis Barrington, Rita LaRoy, Sheila Manners, Edmund Breese, Donald Reed.

d, William O'Connor.

PLEASE DON'T EAT MY MOTHER   (1972)

lp: Buck Kartalian, Lyn Lundgren, Rene Bond, Alicia Friedland.

d, Carl Monson.

PLEASURE DOING BUSINESS, A   (1979) 86m

lp: Conrad Bain, Alan Oppenheimer, John Byner.

d, Steven Vagnino.

PLOTTERS, THE   (1966) 80m

lp: Jane Holden, Bill Edwards.

PLUNGE INTO DARKNESS   (1977) 74m

lp: Bruce Barry, Olivia Hamnett, Ashley Grenville, Wallace Eaton, Tom Richards.

d, Peter Maxwell.

POLK COUNTY POT PLANE   (1977)

lp: Bob Watson, Don Watson, Paul Benefield, Debbie Washington, Jan Jones, Randy Mewbourn.

d, Jim West.

POOR LITTLE RICH GIRL   (1965) 70m

lp: Edie Sedgwick.

d, Andy Warhol.

POOR PRETTY EDDIE   (1975) 86m

lp: Leslie Uggams, Shelley Winters, Michael Christian, Ted Cassidy, Dub Taylor, Slim Pickens.

d, Richard Robinson.

PORT OF MISSING GIRLS   (1938)

lp: Judith Allen, Milburn Stone, Harry Carey, Betty Compson, Matty Fain, Jane Jones.

d, Karl Brown.

PORTRAIT OF A HITMAN   (1984) 85m

lp: Jack Palance, Bo Svenson, Richard Roundtree, Ann Turkel, Rod Steiger.

d, Allan A. Buckhantz.

PORTRAIT OF JASON   (1967)

lp: Jason Holiday.

d, Shirley Clarke.

POSSE FROM HEAVEN   (1975) 87m

lp: Fanne Foxe, Todd Compton, Sherry Bain, Ward Wood, Rod Roddy, Dick Burch.

d, Philip Pine.

POT! PARENTS! POLICE!   (1975) 87m

lp: Phillip Pine, Robert Mantell, Madelyn Keen, Martin Margules, Arthur Batanides.

d, Pine.

POTLUCK PARDS   (1934)

lp: Wally Wales, Ben Corbett, Josephine Hill, Harry Myers, James Aubrey, Robert Walker.

d, B.B. Ray.

POWER OF LIFE, THE   (1938) 74m

lp: Michel Michalesko, Morris Strassberg, Charlotte Goldstein, Bertha Hart.

d, Henry Lynn.

PRAIRIE GUNSMOKE   (1942) 56m

lp: Bill Elliott, Frank Mitchell, Virginia Carroll, Hal Price, Tris Coffin.

d, Lambert Hillyer.

PRAIRIE RAIDERS   (1947) 54m

lp: Charles Starrett, Smiley Burnette, Nancy Saunders, Robert Scott.

d, Derwin Abrahams.

PRANKS (1982) 86m

lp: Laurie Lapinski, Stephen Sachs, David Snow, Pamela Holland.

d, Jeffrey Obrow, Stephen Carpenter.

PREACHERMAN MEETS WIDDERWOMAN (1973)

d, Albert T. Viola..

PRELUDE TO TAURUS (1972)

lp: Pamela Tiffin, Robert Walker, Michael Crawford.

PREMONITION (1972)

lp: Carl Crow, Tim Ray, Winfrey Hester Hill, Victor Izay, Judith Patterson, Jon Huss.

d, Alan Rudolph.

PRISM (1971) 80m

lp: Paul Geier, Dale Soules, Nancy Volkman, Ozzie Tortora, Robert Root.

d, Anita Pivnick.

PRISONER OF THE CANNIBAL GOD (1978, Ital.)

lp: Stacy Keach, Ursula Andress.

PRISONERS (1975) 88m

lp: Jesse Dizon, Robert Reece, Peter Hooten, Howard Hesseman, Mark Bramwell.

d, William H. Bushnell, Jr..

PROFESSOR CREEPS (1942) 63m

lp: F.E. Miller, Mantan Moreland, Arthur Ray, Florence O'Brien, Zack Williams.

d, William Beaudine.

PROPHET, THE (1976) 90m

lp: Ann-Margret, Vittorio Gassman.

d, Dino Risi.

PSI FACTOR (1980, Brit.)

lp: Peter Mark Richman, Gretchen Corbett, Tom Martin.

d, Quentin Masters.

PSYCHO LOVER (1969, Brit.) 80m

lp: Lawrence Montaigne, Joanne Meredith, Elizabeth Plumb, Frank Cuva.

d, Robert Vincent O'Neill.

PSYCHO SISTERS (1972) 85m

lp: Susan Strasberg, Faith Domergue, Sydney Chaplin, Steve Mitchell, Charles Knox Robinson.

PUEBLO TERROR (1931) 59m

lp: Buffalo Bill, Jr, Wanda Hawley, Yakima Canutt, Art Mix, Hank Bell.

d, Alvin J. Neitz.

PUMA MAN, THE (1980) 100m

lp: Donald Pleasence, Walter George Alton, Sydne Rome, Miguel Angel Fuentes.

d, Albert Demartino.

PUSHING UP DAISIES (1971) 94m

lp: Ross Hagen, Kelly Thordsen.

PYRAMID, THE (1976) 90m

lp: C.W. Brown, Ira Hawkins, Tomi Barrett.

QUEEN BOXER, THE (1973) 85m

lp: Judy Lee.

QUEEN OF SHEBA MEETS THE ATOM MAN, THE (1963) 70m

lp: Winifred Bryan, Taylor Mead, Jack Smith.

d, Ron Rice.

QUEEN OF THE SEAS (1960) 87m

lp: Lisa Gastoni, Jerome Courtland.

QUICK TRIGGER LEE (1931) 59m

lp: Bob Custer, Caryl Lincoln, Monte Montague, Lee Cordova, Richard Carlyle.

d, J.P. McGowan.

R.S.V.P. (1984) 89m

lp: Adam Mills, Lynda Wiesmeier, Veronica Hart, Ray Colbert, Harry Reems.

d, Lem Amero.

RACHEL'S MAN (1974) 116m

lp: Mickey Rooney, Rita Tushingham, Leonard Whiting.

d, Moshe Mizrahi.

RACKETEER ROUND-UP (1934) 50m

lp: Edmund Cobb, Edna Aslin, Edward Allen Bilby, Eddie Davis, Ned Norton, Lois Glaze.

d, Robert Hoyt.

RAGE (1984) 92m

lp: Conrad Nichols.

RAIDERS OF ATLANTIS (1983) 90m

lp: Christopher Connelly.

RAINBOW BRIDGE (1972) 108m

d, Chuck Wein..

RAISING THE ROOF (1971, Brit.) 54m

lp: Patricia Davis, David Lodge, Robertson Hare.

d, Michael Forlong.

RAKU FIRE 75m

lp: Eileen Atkins, Trudy Young, Les Carlson.

d, Ron Weyman.

RAMON (1972) 95m

lp: Robert Hundar, Wilma Lindmar, Jean Louis.

RANGE WARFARE (1935)

lp: Reb Russell, Lucille Lund, Wally Wales, Lafe McKee, Roger Williams, Slim Whitaker.

d, S. Roy Luby.

RAPE KILLER, THE (1976) 80m

lp: Dorothy Moore, Larry Daniels, Leslie Bowman, Angela Clianto, Anthony Carr.

d, Dacosta Carayan.

RATS (1984) 90m

lp: Paul Merlin, Vic Mitchell.

RATTLERS (1976) 82m

lp: Sam Chew, Elizabeth Chauvet, Dan Priest, Ron Gold, Tony Ballen.

d, John McCauley.

RAWHIDE MAIL (1934) 59m

lp: Jack Perrin, Nelson McDowell, Lillian Gilmore, Richard Cramer, Lafe McKee, George Chesebro.

d, B.B. Ray.

RAWHIDE ROMANCE   (1934)

lp: Buffalo Bill, Jr, Genee Boutell, Lafe McKee, Si Jenks, Bart Carre.

d, Victor Adamson.

RAWHIDE TERROR, THE   (1934) 52m

lp: Art Mix, William Desmond, Edmund Cobb, William Barrymore, Frances Morris.

d, Bruce Mitchell.

RAWHIDE TRAIL, THE   (1950)

lp: Rex Reason, Nancy Gates, Richard Erdman, Rusty Lane, Frank Chase, Ann Doran.

d, Robert Gordon.

REBELLION   (1936) 60m

lp; Tom Keene, Rita Cansino [Hayworth], Duncan Renaldo, William Royle.

d, Lynn Shores.

REBORN   (1978) 91m

lp: Dennis Hopper, Michael Moriarty, Francisco Rabal, Antonella Murgia.

REBUS   (1969, Ger./Ital./Span./Arg.) 95m

lp: Ann-Margret, Laurence Harvey.

RECKLESS BUCKAROO, THE   (1935) 57m

lp: Bill Cody, Bill Cody, Jr, Betty Mack, Roger Williams, Buzz Barton, Edward Cassidy.

d, Harry Fraser.

RECKLESS RIDER, THE   (1932)

lp: Lane Chandler, Phyllis Barrington, J. Frank Glendon, Neal Hart, Pat Rooney.

d, Armand Schaefer.

RED ROSES OF PASSION   (1967) 85m

lp: Judson Todd, Jean James, Carol Halleck, Helena Clayton, Steve Barton, Johnny Kuhl.

d, Joe Sarno.

RED ZONE CUBA   (1972) 95m

lp: John Carradine, Coleman Francis, Harold Saunders, Tony Cardozza.

REDNECK MILLER   (1977)

lp: Geoffrey Land, Sydney Rubin, Paul Walsh, Marcel Cobb, Paulette Gibson.

d, John Clayton.

REET, PETITE AND GONE   (1947) 75m

lp: Louis Jordan & His Tympany Five, June Richmond, Lorenzo Tucker, Milton Woods.

d, William Forest Crouch.

REFLECTIONS FROM A BRASS BED   (1976)

lp: Carl John, Betty Nielsen.

d, Richard Clausen.

RENEGADE, THE   (1943) 58m

lp: Buster Crabbe, Al "Fuzzy" St. John, Lois Ranson, Karl Hackett, Ray Bennett.

d, Sam Newfield.

RETURN OF 18 BRONZEMEN   (1984) 97m

lp: Polly Shang Kuan, Tien Peng.

d, Joseph Kuo.

RETURN OF GILBERT AND SULLIVAN   (1952)

lp: Melville Cooper, Tudor Owen, Billy Gray, Mara Lynn, Pat Hogan, Joe Graves, Scatman Crothers.

RETURN OF RUSTY, THE   (1946)

lp: Ted Donaldson, John Litel, Mark Dennis, Barbara Wooddell, Robert Stevens.

d, William Castle.

RETURN OF THE DURANGO KID   (1945) 58m

lp: Charles Starrett, Tex Harding, Jean Stevens, John Calvert, Betty Roadman.

d, Derwin Abrahams.

RETURN OF THE TIGER   (1979) 86m

lp: Paul Smith, Bruce Li, Angela Mao, Change Li.

d, Jimmy Shaw.

RETURN TO THE LAND OF OZ   (1971, U.S./Yugo.)

d, Boris Kolar..

REUNION, THE   (1977)

lp: Mike Talbot, Peter Isacksen, Danny J. Sheflin, William Wisher, Joanne Hicks, Louise Foster.

d, Talbot.

REVENGE IS MY DESTINY   (1971) 95m

lp: Sidney Blackmer, Chris Robinson, Elisa Ingram, Joe E. Ross.

d, Joseph Adler.

REVENGE OF THE DEAD   (1975) 87m

d, Evan Lee..

REVENGE OF THE GLADIATORS   (1962) 90m

lp: Mickey Hargitay, Jose Greco, Renato Baldini.

REVOLT IN CANADA   (1964) 107m

lp: George Marin, Pamela Tudor, Luis Marin.

RHYTHM ROUND-UP   (1945) 66m

lp: Ken Curtis, Cheryl Walker, Hoosier Hotshots, Guinn "Big Boy" Williams, Raymond Hatton.

d, Vernon Keays.

RIDDLE RANCH   (1936) 59m

lp: Black King, David Worth, June Marlowe, Charline Barry, Richard Cramer.

d, Charles Hutchison.

RIDE THE TIGER   (1971) 96m

lp: George Montgomery, Victoria Shaw, Marshall Thompson.

d, Montgomery.

RIDERS OF RIO   (1931)

lp: Lane Chandler, Karla Cowan, Sheldon Lewis, Bob Card, Sherry Tansey, Fred Parks.

d, Robert Tansey.

RIDERS OF THE LONE STAR   (1947) 55m

lp: Charles Starrett, Smiley Burnette, Virginia Hunter, Steve Darrell.

d, Derwin Abrahams.

RIDERS OF THE PONY EXPRESS   (1949) 60m

lp: Ken Curtis, Shug Fisher, Cathy Douglas, Billy Benedict, Eddie McLean, Truman Van Dyke.

d, Michael Salle.

RIDERS OF THE SAGE (1939) 57m

lp: Bob Steele, Claire Rochelle, Ralph Hoopers, James Whitehead, Earl Douglas.

d, Harry S. Webb.

RIDIN' FOOL, THE (1931) 58m

lp: Bob Steele, Frances Morris, Josephine Velez, Florence Turner, Eddie Fetherston.

d, J.P. McCarthy.

RIDIN' KID (1930)

lp: Wally Wales.

RIDIN' ON (1936) 56m

lp: Tom Tyler, Joan Barclay, Rex Lease, John Elliott, Earl Dwire, Bob McKenzie, Roger Williams.

d, B.B. Ray.

RIDIN' THE TRAIL (1940) 57m

lp: Fred Scott, Iris Lancaster, Harry Harvey, Jack Ingram, John Ward.

d, Raymond K. Johnson.

RIDIN' THRU (1935) 55m

lp: Tom Tyler, Ruth Hiatt, Lafe McKee, Philo McCullough, Lew Meehan, Bud Osborne.

d, Harry S. Webb.

RIDING THE CALIFORNIA TRAIL (1947) 59m

lp: Gilbert Roland, Martin Garralaga, Frank Yaconelli, Teala Loring, Inez Cooper.

d, William Nigh.

RIDING THROUGH NEVADA (1942) 61m

lp: Charles Starrett, Shirley Patterson, Arthur Hunnicutt, Clancy Cooper, Davison Clark.

d, William Berke.

RIDING WILD (1935) 57m

lp: Tim McCoy, Billie Seward, Niles Welch, Edward J. Le Saint, Dick Alexander, Dick Botiller.

d, David Selman.

RIDING WITH DEATH (1976) 96m

lp: Ben Murphy, Ed Nelson, Andrew Prine, Katherine Crawford.

RIEL (1979) 180m

lp: Raymond Cloutier, William Shatner, Christopher Plummer, Leslie Nielsen.

d, George Bloomfield.

RIM OF HELL (1970) 89m

lp: Jack Bell, Warren McClure.

RIO GRANDE (1949) 72m

lp: Sunset Carson, Evohn Keyes, Lee Morgan, Bobby Clark, Bob Deats, Henry Garcia.

d, Norman Sheldon.

RIO RATTLER (1935)

lp: Tom Tyler, Marion Shilling, Eddie Gribbon, William Gould, Tom London, Slim Whitaker.

d, B.B. Ray.

RIOT SQUAD (1933) 64m

lp: Madge Bellamy, Pat O'Malley, James Flavin, Addison Richards, Harrison Greene.

d, Harry Webb.

RIP OFF (1977)

lp: Michael Benet, James Masters, Barbara Bourbon, Johnny Dark, Stelios Manios.

d, Manolis Tsafos.

RISE AND RISE OF MICHAEL RIMMER, THE (1970, Brit.) 101m

lp: Peter Cook, Denholm Elliott, Ronald Fraser.

d, Kevin Billington.

RIVER OF EVIL (1964) 83m

lp: Barbara Rutting, Harold Leipnitz.

ROAD OF DEATH (1977)

lp: Carol Connors, Joe Banana, Jack Birch, Lea Vivot.

d, Rene Martinez.

ROAD REBELS (1963) 64m

lp: Julie Francis, Bernie Rose.

d, Reno Calarco.

ROAD TO NASHVILLE (1967) 109m

lp: Doodles Weaver, Marty Robbins, Richard Arlen, Connie Smith, The Carter Family.

d, Will Zenz.

ROAMIN' WILD (1936) 58m

lp: Tom Tyler, Carol Wyndham, Al Ferguson, George Chesebro, Max Davidson, Fred Parker.

d, B.B. Ray.

ROARING FRONTIERS (1941) 62m

lp: Bill Elliott, Tex Ritter, Ruth Ford, Frank Mitchell, Hal Taliaferro, Bradley Page.

d, Lambert Hillyer.

ROARING RANGERS (1946) 55m

lp: Charles Starrett, Smiley Burnette, Adelle Roberts, Jack Rockwell, Edward Cassidy.

d, Ray Nazarro.

ROBIN (1979)

lp: Monica Tidwell, Lee Dorsey, Louis Senesi.

d, Hank Aldrich.

ROBIN HOOD OF MONTEREY (1947) 55m

lp: Gilbert Roland, Chris-Pin Martin, Evelyn Brent, Jack LaRue, Pedro De Cordoba.

d, Christy Cabanne.

ROBINSON CRUSOE AND THE TIGER (1972) 109m

lp: Hugo Stiglitz, Ahui.

d, Rene Cardona, Jr..

ROCK 'N' RULE (1983) 85m

lp: Don Francks, Paul LeMat, Susan Roman, Catherine O'Hara, Sam Langevin.

d, Clive A. Smith.

ROGUE, THE (1976) 84m

lp: Milan Galvanic, Barbara Bouchet, Margaret Lee.

d, Gregory Simpson.

ROGUE AND GRIZZLY, THE (1982) 95m

lp: Dick Robinson, Don Shanks, Gordon Wilde, Carol Elasz.

ROGUE'S GALLERY (1968) 88m

lp: Roger Smith, Greta Baldwin, Dennis Morgan, Farley Granger, Edgar Bergen, Brian Donlevy.

d, Leonard Horn.

ROLLING HOME (1948) 69m

lp: Jean Parker, Russell Hayden, Pamela Blake.

d, William Berke.

ROSE OF SANTA ROSA (1947)

lp: Patricia White, Eduardo Noriega, Fortunio Bonanova, Eduardo Ciannelli, Ann Cordes.

d, Ray Nazarro.

ROSES BLOOM TWICE (1977) 87m

lp: Glynis McNicoll, Michael Craig, Diane Craig, John Allen, Jennifer West.

d, David Stevens.

ROUGH RIDIN' JUSTICE (1945) 58m

lp: Charles Starrett, Dub Taylor, Betty Jane Graham, Wheeler Oakman, Jack Ingram.

d, Derwin Abrahams.

RUDDIGORE (1967, Brit.) 54m

Voices: John Reed, Ann Hood, David Palmer, Peggy Ann Jones, Kenneth Sanford.

d, Joy Batchelor.

RUN, RUN, JOE! (1974)

lp: Keith Carradine, Tom Skerritt, Sybil Danning, Cyril Cusack.

RUNAWAY (1971) 85m

lp: William Smith, Gilda Texter, Rita Murray, Tom Baker, Beach Dickerson.

d, Bickford Otis Webber.

RUNNING SCARED (1980) 80m

lp: Ken Wahl, Judge Reinhold, Pat Himgle, Annie McEnroe, John Saxon, Bradford Dillman.

d, Paul Glicker.

RUNNING WITH THE DEVIL (1973)

lp: Sean Kenny, Donna Stanley, Reagon Wilson, Jane Peters.

RUSTLERS OF THE BADLANDS (1945) 55m

lp: Charles Starrett, Tex Harding, Dub Taylor, Sally Bliss, George Eldridge.

d, Derwin Abrahams.

S.O.S. COAST GUARD (1937)

lp: Bela Lugosi, Ralph Byrd, Lawrence Grant.

SADDLE ACES (1935) 56m

lp: Rex Bell, Ruth Mix, Buzz Barton, Stanley Blystone, Earl Dwire, Chuck Morrison.

d, Harry Fraser.

SADDLE LEATHER LAW (1944)

lp: Charles Starrett, Dub Taylor, Vi Athens, Lloyd Bridges, Reed Howes, Robert Kortman.

d, Ben Kline.

SADDLE SERENADE (1945) 57m

lp: Jimmy Wakely, Lee "Lasses" White, John James, Nancy Brinkman, Alan Foster, Jack Ingram.

d, Oliver Drake.

SADDLES AND SAGEBRUSH (1943)

lp: Russell Hayden, Dub Taylor, Bob Wills and the Texas Playboys, Ann Savage.

d, William Berke.

SAGEBRUSH HEROES (1945) 56m

lp: Charles Starrett, Dub Taylor, Constance Worth, Ozie Waters, Elvin Field.

d, Benjamin Kline.

SAGITTARIUS MINE, THE (1972)

lp: Steve Forrest, Diane Baker, Ray Danton, Richard Basehart.

SAINT AND THE BRAVE GOOSE, THE (1981, Brit.) 99m

lp: Ian Ogilvy, Gayle Hunnicutt, Stratford Johns, Derrin Nesbitt, Joe Lynch.

d, Cyril Frankel.

ST. LOUIS WOMAN (1935) 68m

lp: Jeanette Loff, Johnny Mack Brown, Earle Foxe, Roberta Gale.

d, Al Ray.

SALT IN THE WOUND (1972) 92m

lp: George Hilton, Klaus Kinski.

SAMMY SOMEBODY (1976)

lp: Zalman King, Susan Strasberg, Sarah Kennedy, Jan Sterling.

d, Joseph Adler.

SAMSON AND THE SEA BEAST (1960) 84m

lp: Kirk Morris, Margaret Lee.

SANTA FE RIDES (1937) 58m

lp: Bob Custer, Eleanor Stewart, Dave Sharpe, Lafe McKee, Snub Pollard, Nelson McDowell.

d, B.B. Ray.

SARAH AND THE SQUIRREL (1983) 75m

Voice of Mia Farrow.

SATANIST, THE (1968) 64m

d, Zoltan G. Spencer..

SATAN'S BLACK WEDDING (1976) 62m

SATAN'S CHILDREN (1975) 87m

lp: Kathy Archer, Stephen White, Joyce Molloy, Bob Ray, Rosemary Orlando.

d, Joe Wiezycki.

SATAN'S HARVEST (1970) 104m

lp: George Montgomery, Tippi Hedren, Matt Monro, Davy Kaye.

d, Montgomery.

SAVAGE! (1973)

lp: James Inglehart, Carol Speed, Lada Edmund, Jr, Sally Jordan, Ken Metcalf, Rossana Ortiz, Vic Diaz.

SAVAGE SEASON (1970) 93m

lp: Ron Harper, Diane McBain, Victor Buono, Slim Pickens.

SCALAWAG BUNCH, THE (1976) 103m

lp: Mark Damon.

SCALP MERCHANT, THE (1977) 95m

lp: Cameron Mitchell, John Waters, Elizabeth Alexander, Margaret Nelson.

d, Howard Rubie.

SCORCHING FURY (1952) 68m

lp: Richard Devon, William Leslie, Peggy Nelson, Sherwood Price, Audrey Dineen.

d, Rick Freers.

SCORE (1973)

lp: Carl Parker, Claire Wilbur, Calvin Culver, Lynn Lowry, Gerald Grant.

SCORING (1980) 90m

lp: Myra Taylor, Charles Fatone, Freya Crane, Gregg Perrie, "Pistol" Pete Maravich.

d, Michael DeGaetano.

SCORPIO SCARAB, THE (1972)

lp: Angie Dickinson, Simon Oakland, Richardo Montalban, George Hamilton.

SCORPION WITH TWO TAILS (1982) 97m

lp: Van Johnson, John Saxon.

SCREAM BLOODY MURDER (1973)

lp: Fred Holbert, Leigh Mitchell, Robert Knox, A. Maana Tanelah, Ron Bastone.

d, Marc B. Ray.

SCREAM IN THE STREETS, A (1972)

lp: John Kirkpatric, Frank Bannon, Rosie Stone, Brandy Lyman, Con Covert, Linda York, Tony Scaponi.

SCREAMTIME (1983, Brit.) 90m

lp: Jean Anderson, Robin Bailey, Dora Bryan.

d, Al Beresford.

SEARCH FOR THE EVIL ONE (1967)

lp: Lee Patterson, Lisa Pera, Henry Brandon.

d, Joseph Kane.

SEAWOLF (1974) 97m

lp: Edward Meeks, Raymond Haymstorf, Beatrice Cardon.

SECOND CHANCE (1950) 72m

lp: Ruth Warwick, John Hubbard, Hugh Beaumont, David Holt, Pat Combs, Ellye Marshall.

d, William Beaudine.

SECRET OF NAVAJO CAVE (1976) 87m

lp: Rex Allen, Holger Kasper, Steven Benally, Jr, Johnny Guerro.

d, James T. Flocker.

SECRET OF OUTLAW FLATS (1953) 54m

lp: Guy Madison, Andy Devine, Kristine Miller, Richard Avonde, Jane Adams.

d, Frank McDonald.

SECRET OF THE BLACK WIDOW (1964)

lp: O.W. Fischer, Karin Dor.

SECRET OF THE CHINESE CARNATION, THE (1965)

lp: Brad Harris.

SECRETARY, THE (1971) 85m

lp: Josh Gamble, Angela Gale.

SECRETS OF HOLLYWOOD (1933) 58m

lp: Mae Busch, Wally Wales, June Walters, George Cowl, Norbert Myles.

d, George M. Merrick, Holbrook Todd.

SECTOR 13 (1982)

lp: D.W. Brown, Kirsten Baker, Chip Frye, Wendy Grayson.

d, Robert Stone Jordan.

SELF DEFENSE (1933) 65m

lp: Pauline Frederick, Claire Windsor, Theodore Von Eltz, Barbara Kent, Robert Elliott.

d, Phil Rosen.

SELF-SERVICE SCHOOLGIRLS (1976)

lp: Georgette Pope, Margo Younger.

SENIORS, THE (1978) 87m

lp: Jeffrey Byron, Gary Imhof, Dennis Quaid, Lou Richards, Priscilla Barnes.

d, Rod Amateau.

SENOR JIM (1936)

lp: Conway Tearle, Barbara Bedford, Alberta Dugan, Fred Malatesta, Betty Mack.

d, Jacques Jaccard.

SEPARATION (1977, Brit.) 150m

lp: Emile Genest, Monique Lepage.

SEVEN DOORS OF DEATH (1983)

lp: Katherine MacColl, David Warbeck, Sarah Keller, Tony Saint John, Veronica Lazur.

d, Louis Fuller.

SEVEN TIMES SEVEN (1973, Ital.) 92m

lp: Terry-Thomas, Lionel Stander, Gaston Moschin, Gordon Mitchell, Adolfo Celi.

d, Michele Lupo.

SEVERED ARM (1973) 91m

lp: Marvin Kaplan, Deborah Walley, Paul Carr, John Crawford, David Cannon.

d, Thomas Alderman.

SEX DU JOUR (1976)

lp: Toni Roam, Shelly Dinah Myte, Peony Jones, Jennifer Jordon, Susan Barret.

d, Beau Buchanan.

SEX MADNESS (1937) 50m

SHADOW LAUGHS (1933) 67m

lp: Hal Skelly, Rose Hobart, Harry T. Morey, Geoffrey Bryant, Bran Nossen, Hal Short.

d, Arthur Hoerl.

SHADOWS ON THE RANGE (1946) 57m

lp: Johnny Mack Brown, Raymond Hatton, Jan Bryant, Marshall Reed, John Merton.

d, Lambert Hillyer.

SHALIMAR (1978, India) 116m

lp: Rex Harrison, Sylvia Miles, John Saxon.

SHAME OF THE JUNGLE (1980, Fr./Bel.)

Voices: Johnny Weissmuller, Jr, John Belushi, Bill Murray, Bryan-Doyle Murray.

d, Picha, Boris Szulzinger.

SHANTYTOWN HONEYMOON (1972) 85m

lp: Ashley Brooke, Jim Beck, George Ellis.

SHE (1983) 99m

lp: Sandahl Bergman, Harrison Muller, Quinn Kessler, David Gross.

d, Avi Nesher.

SHE CAME TO THE VALLEY (1979) 90m

lp: Ronee Blakley, Dean Stockwell, Scott Glenn, Freddy Fender.

d, Albert Band.

SHE DEVIL (1940) 62m

lp: Laura Bowman.

SHE SHOULD HAVE SAID NO (1949)

lp: Lila Leeds.

SHE'LL FOLLOW YOU ANYWHERE (1971)

lp: Keith Barron, Kenneth Cope, Richard Vernon, Philippa Gail, Hillary Pritchard, Penny Brahms.

d, David C. Rea.

SHERIFF OF MEDICINE BOW, THE (1948) 55m

lp: Johnny Mack Brown, Raymond Hatton, Max Terhune, Evelyn Finley, Bill Kennedy, George J. Lewis.

d, Lambert Hillyer.

SHERIFF'S SECRET, THE (1931) 58m

lp: Jack Perrin, Dorothy Bauer, George Chesebro, Jimmy Aubrey, Fred Hargreaves.

d, James P. Hogan.

SHE'S TOO MEAN TO ME (1948)

lp: Mantan Moreland, Johnny Lee, F.E. Miller.

SHOCK HILL (1966) 77m

lp: William Thourlby, Warren Kemmerling, Michael Fox.

SHOOT FIRST, DIE LATER (1973) 99m

lp: Richard Conte.

SHOOT THE SUN DOWN (1981) 93m

lp: Margot Kidder, Geoffrey Lewis, Bo Brundin, Christopher Walkin, Sacheen Littlefeather.

d, David Leeds.

SHULAMIS (1931) 50m

d, Sidney Goldin..

SHUT MY BIG MOUTH (1946) 63m

lp: Dewey "Pigmeat" Markham, John Murray.

SICKLE OR THE CROSS, THE (1951)

d, Frank R. Strayer..

SIGMA III (1966) 90m

lp: Jack Taylor, Silvia Solar, Diana Martin.

SILENT CODE, THE (1935) 60m

lp: Kane Richmond, Blanche Mehaffey, J.P. McGowan, Joe Girard, Barney Furey, Pat Harmon.

d, Stuart Paton.

SILENT MEN (1933) 58m

lp: Tim McCoy, Florence Britton, Wheeler Oakman, J. Carroll Naish, Walter Brennan.

d, D. Ross Lederman.

SILENT STRANGER, THE (1975)

lp: Tony Anthony, Lloyd Barrista, Kin Omae, Kenji Ohara, Kita Mura, Sato, Yoshio Nukano.

d, Vance Lewis.

SILKS AND SADDLES (1938) 63m

lp; Herman Brix [Bruce Bennett], Toby Wing, Fuzzy Knight, Frank Melton, Robert McClung.

d, Robert Hill.

SILVER BULLET, THE (1935) 58m

lp: Tom Tyler, Jayne Regan, Lafe McKee, Charles King, Slim Whitaker, Franklyn Farnum.

d, B.B. Ray.

SILVER RANGE (1946) 53m

lp: Johnny Mack Brown, Raymond Hatton, Jan Bryant, I. Stanford Jolley, Terry Frost.

d, Lambert Hillyer.

SIMPLY IRRESISTIBLE (1983) 100m

lp: Richard Pacheco, Samantha Fox, Gayle Sterling, Star Wood, Gina Gianetti, Nicole Black.

d, Edwin Brown.

SINFUL DWARF, THE (1973)

lp: Anne Sparrow, Tony Eades, Clara Keller, Gerda Madsen.

SING ME A SONG OF TEXAS (1945) 66m

lp: Tom Tyler, Rosemary Lane, Guinn "Big Boy" Williams, Slim Summerville, Pinky Tomlin.

d, Vernon Keays.

SINGING ON THE TRAIL (1946) 60m

lp: Ken Curtis, Jeff Donnell, Guy Kibbee, Dusty Anderson, The Hoosier Hotshots.

d, Ray Nazarro.

SINGING SPURS (1948) 62m

lp: The Hoosier Hotshots, Kirby Grant, Patricia Knox, Lee Patrick, Jay Silverheels.

d, Ray Nazarro.

SINGLE GIRLS (1973) 85m

lp: Claudia Jennings, Jean Marie Ingels, Joan Prather, Greg Mullavey.

d, Ferd Sebastian, Beverly Sebastian.

SINNER'S BLOOD (1970) 90m

lp: Nancy Sheldon, Julie Connors.

SINS OF DORIAN GRAY (1982)

lp: Joseph Bottoms, Belinda Bauer, Anthony Perkins.

d, Tony Maylam.

SINS OF RACHEL, THE (1975) 94m

lp: Ann Noble, Jerome Scott, Brett Marriott, Chase Cordell, Patricia Rees.

d, Richard Fontaine.

SINTHIA THE DEVIL'S DOLL (1970)

lp: Diane Webber, Maria Lease, Boris Balachoff, Shula Roan.

d, Ray Steckler.

SISTER TO JUDAS (1933) 64m

lp: Claire Windsor, John Harron, Holmes Herbert, Lee Moran, David Callis, Wilfred Lucas.

d, E. Mason Hooper.

SISTERS OF DEATH (1976) 87m

lp: Arthur Franz, Claudia Jennings, Cheri Howell, Sherry Boucher, Paul Carr.

d, Joseph Mazzuca.

SIX-GUN DECISION (1953) 54m

lp: Guy Madison, Andy Devine, Don Haydon, Gloria Saunders, Fred Kohler, Jr.

d, Frank McDonald.

SIX GUN JUSTICE (1935) 57m

lp: Bill Cody, Wally Wales, Ethel Jackson, Budd Buster, Donald Reed, Ace Cain, Frank Moran, Bert Young.

d, Robert Hill.

SIX GUN MESA (1950) 56m

lp: Johnny Mack Brown, Milburn Morante, Gail Davis, Holly Bane, Steve Clark, Carl Mathews.

d, Wallace Fox.

SIX-GUN TRAIL (1938) 59m

lp: Tim McCoy, Nora Lane, Alden Chase, Ben Corbett, Karl Hackett, Donald Gallagher.

d, Sam Newfield.

69 MINUTES (1977) 75m

lp: Joe Leahy, John Chambers, Cindy Allison, Twila Pollard, Bill Williams, Michael Davenport.

d, Ian Morrison.

SKATEBOARD MADNESS (1980) 92m

lp: Stacey Peralta, Kent Senatore, Gregg Ayres, Don "Mini Shred" Smith, Kurt "Mello Cat" Ledterman.

d, Julian Pene, Jr..

SKETCHES OF A STRANGLER (?) 92m

lp: Allen Goorwitz, Meredith MacRae, Frank Witeman, Clayton Wilcox, Jennifer Rhodes.

SKEZAG (1971)

lp: Wayne Shirley, Louis "Sonny" Berrios, Angel Sanchez.

SKY PIRATES (1977, Brit.) 60m

lp: Adam Richens, Michael McVey.

d, C.M. Pennington Richards.

SKYBOUND (1935) 55m

lp: Lloyd Hughes, Lona Andre, Eddie Nugent, Grant Withers, Mildred Clare.

d, Raymond K. Johnson.

SLAP IN THE FACE (1974) 90m

lp: Curt Jurgens, Alexandra Stuart.

SLAUGHTERDAY (1981) 86m

lp: Rita Tushingham, Michael Hausserman, Frederick Jaeger, William Berger, Gordon Mitchell.

d, Peter Patzak.

SLAVE GIRL OF BABYLON (1962, Ital.) 101m

lp: John Ericson, Yvonne Furneaux.

SLAVE GIRLS OF SHEBA (1960) 92m

lp: Linda Cristal, Jose Suarez.

SLINGSHOT (1971) 96m

lp: Royal Dano, Harry Guardino, France Nuyen.

SMOKE LIGHTNING (1933) 61m

lp: George O'Brien, Virginia Sale, Douglas Dumbrille, Betsy King Ross, Nell O'Day.

d, David Howard.

SMOKEY AND THE GOODTIME OUTLAWS (1978) 90m

lp: Jesse Turner, Dennis Fimple, Slim Pickens, Diane Sherrill, Marcie Barkin.

d, Alex Grasshoff.

SMOKEY AND THE HOTWIRE GANG (1980) 85m

lp: James Keach, Stanley Livingston, Tony Lorea, Carla Ziegfeld, Skip Young.

d, Anthony Cardoza.

SMOKY RIVER SERENADE (1947) 67m

lp: Paul Campbell, Ruth Terry, The Hoosier Hotshots, Billy Williams, Virginia Hunter.

d, Derwin Abrahams.

SOCIAL ERROR (1935) 60m

lp: David Sharpe, Gertrude Messinger.

SOLDIER NAMED JOE, A (1970) 92m

lp: Dennis Safran, Lang Jeffries, Luciana Paluzzi.

SOLDIER'S STORY, THE (1981) 96m

lp: Geoffrey Bowes, Tom Do-Trong Chau.

SOMETHING CREEPING IN THE DARK (1972, Ital.) 90m

lp: Farley Granger, Lucia Bose, Stan Cooper.

d, Mario Colucci.

SON OF RUSTY, THE (1947) 69m

lp: Ted Donaldson, Stephen Dunne, Tom Powers, Ann Doran, Thurston Hall, Matt Willis.

d, Lew Landers.

SONG OF SONGS (1935)

lp: Samuel Goldenberg, Dora Weissman, Max Kletter, Mirele Gruber, Seymour Rechtzeit.

d, Henry Lynn.

SONG OF THE PRAIRIE (1945) 62m

lp: Ken Curtis, June Storey, Guinn "Big Boy" Williams, Jeff Donnell, Andy Clyde.

d, Ray Nazarro.

SONG OF THE RANGE (1944) 55m

lp: Jimmy Wakely, Lee "Lasses" White, Dennis Moore, Cay Forrester, Bud Osborne, George Eldredge.

d, Wallace Fox.

SONGS AND SADDLES (1938) 65m

lp: Gene Austin, Lynne Berkeley, Henry Rocquemore, Walter Willis, Charles King.

d, Harry Fraser.

SORCERESS (1983) 81m

lp: Leigh Harris, Lynette Harris, Bob Helson, David Millbern, Bruno Rey, Ana DeSade, Robert Ballesteros.

d, Brian Stuart,.

SOULS OF SIN (1949)

lp: Savannah Churchill, William Greaves, Jimmy Wright, Billie Allen, Emery Richardson, Louise Jackson.

d, Powell Lindsay.

SOUNDS OF HORROR   (1968) 92m

lp: James Philbrook, Arturo Fernandez.

SOUTH OF HELL MOUNTAIN   (1971) 92m

lp: Anna Stewart, Martin J. Kelley.

d, William Sachs, Louis Lehman.

SOUTH OF MONTEREY   (1946) 63m

lp: Gilbert Roland, Martin Garralaga, Frank Yaconelli, Marjorie Riordan.

d, William Nigh.

SOUTH OF THE CHISHOLM TRAIL   (1947) 58m

lp: Charles Starrett, Smiley Burnette, Nancy Saunders, Frank Sully, Jim Diehl.

d, Derwin Abrahams.

SOUTHERN DOUBLE CROSS   (1973) 92m

lp: Robert Denison, Judy Lewis, Anne Jeffreys, Avery Schreiber.

d, Don Edmonds.

SPACE RIDERS   (1984) 99m

lp: Barry Sheene, Gavan O'Herlihy, Toshiya Ito, Stephanie McLean, Sayo Inaba.

d, Joe Massot.

SPASMO   (1976)

lp: Suzy Kendall, Robert Hoffman, Monica Monet, Ivan Rassimov, Guido Alberti.

d, Umberto Lenzi.

SPECIALIST, THE   (1975) 93m

lp: Ahna Capri, John Anderson, Adam West, Alvy Moore.

d, Howard [Hikmet] Avedis.

SPECTRE OF EDGAR ALLAN POE   (1973) 89m

lp: Robert Walker, Jr, Cesar Romero, Carol Ohmart.

d, Mohy Quandur.

SPEED DEMON   (1933) 64m

lp: William Collier, Jr, Joan Marsh, Wheeler Oakman, Robert Ellis, Georgie Ernest.

d, D. Ross Lederman.

SPIRAL BUREAU, THE   (1974) 90m

lp: Peter Sumner, Wendy Hughes, Vincent Ball, Kevin Miles.

d, Ian Coughlin.

SPITTIN' IMAGE   (1983) 92m

lp: Sunshine Parker, Trudi Cooper, Sharon Barr, Karen Barr.

d, Russell S. Kern.

SPORTS KILLER, THE   (1976) 86m

lp: James Luisi, Susan Sullivan.

SPRINGTIME IN TEXAS   (1945) 57m

lp: Jimmy Wakely, Lee "Lasses" White, Dennis Moore, Marie Harmon, Rex Lease, Horace Murphy, I. Stanford Jolley.

d, Oliver Drake.

SPY, THE   (1931) 65m

lp: Kay Johnson, Neil Hamilton, John Halliday, Freddie Burke Frederick, Milton Holmes.

d, Berthold Viertel.

SPY SQUAD   (1962) 81m

lp: Richard Miller, Dick O'Neill, Richard Jordahl.

SPY TODAY, DIE TOMORROW   (1967) 93m

lp: Lex Barker, Brad Harris, Eddi Arent.

SQUARE SHOOTER   (1935) 57m

lp; Tim McCoy, Jacqueline Wells [Julie Bishop], Erville Alderson, Charles Middleton, John Darrow.

d, David Selman.

STAGECOACH DRIVER   (1951) 52m

lp: Whip Wilson, Fuzzy Knight, Jim Bannon, Gloria Winters, Lane Bradford, Barbara Allen, John Hart, Leonard Penn.

d, Lewis Collins.

STAGEFRIGHT   (1983) 82m

lp: Jenny Neumann, Gary Sweet, Nina Landis.

STAIRWAY FOR A STAR   (1947) 74m

lp: Cornel Wilde, Helen Beverly, Dennis Brent, Linda Lee Hill, Robert Pitkin, Eileen Pollack, Sam Wolfe.

STAND BY ALL NETWORKS   (1942) 64m

lp: John Beal, Florence Rice, Alan Baxter.

d, Lew Landers.

STAR MAIDENS   (1976, Brit.)

lp: Judy Geeson, Christiane Kruger.

STAR ODYSSEY   (1978) 97m

lp: Sharon Baker, Chris Avran.

STARBIRD AND SWEET WILLIAM   (1975) 90m

lp: A. Martinez, Louise Fitch, Don Haggerty, Ancil Cook, Skip Homeier.

d, Jack B. Hively.

STARK RAVING MAD   (1983) 88m

lp: Russell Fast, Marcie Severson, B. Joe Medley, Mike Walter, Janet Galen.

d, George F. Hood.

STEFANIE IN RIO   (1963)

d, Curtis Bernhardt..

STEPMOTHER, THE   (1973) 94m

lp: Alejandro Rey, John Anderson, Katherine Justice, Larry Linville, Claudia Jennings.

d, Hikmet Avedis.

STEPPING OUT   (1931) 73m

lp: Charlotte Greenwood, Leila Hyams, Reginald Denny, Lillian Bond, Cliff Edwards.

d, Charles F. Reisner.

STEVIE, SAMSON AND DELILAH   (1975) 86m

lp: Steve Hawkes, Steven Hawkes, Jr, Chuck Hall.

d, Hawkes.

STOLEN PARADISE   (1941)

lp: Leon Janney, Eleanor Hunt, Esther Muir, Wilma Francis, Doris Blaine, Herbert Fisher.

d, Louis Gasnier.

STORM OVER THE ANDES   (1935) 85m

lp: Jack Holt, Gean Lockhart, Grant Withers.

d, Christy Cabanne.

STORM SIGNAL (1966) 53m
d, Robert L. Drew..

STORYVILLE (1974) 87m
lp: Tim Rooney, Jeannie Wilson, Michael Nahay, June Josey, Armand Hug.
d, Jack Weiss.

STRAIGHT JACKET (1980) 100m
lp: Aldo Ray, Kory Clark, Chuck Jamison, Bobby Holt.

STRANGE THINGS HAPPEN AT NIGHT (1979)
lp: Sandra Julien.

STRANGER FROM PONCA CITY, THE (1947) 56m
lp: Charles Starrett, Smiley Burnette, Virginia Hunter, Paul Campbell, Jim Diehl.
d, Derwin Abrahams.

STRANGER FROM SANTA FE (1945) 57m
lp: Johnny Mack Brown, Raymond Hatton, Beatrice Gray, Jo Ann Curtis, Jack Ingram.
d, Lambert Hillyer.

STRANGERS AT SUNRISE (1969) 99m
lp: George Montgomery, Deana Martin, Brian O'Shaughnessy, Tromp Terreblanche.
d, Percival Rubens.

STREET GIRLS (1975) 84m
lp: Carol Case, Christine Souder, Paul Pompian, Art Burke, Jimmy Smith, Michael Albert Weber.
d, Michael Miller.

STREET LAW (1981)
lp: Franco Nero, Barbara Bach, Reno Palmer.

STREET OF DARKNESS (1958) 60m
lp: Robert Keys, John Close, James Seay, Sheila Ryan, Julie Gibson.

STREETS OF HONG KONG (1979) 90m
lp: Gary Collins, Nancy Kwan.
d, Hilton Alexander.

STRIKE ME DEADLY (1963)
lp: Gary Clarke, Jeannine Riley.
d, Ted V. Mikels.

STRIKING BACK (1981) 91m
lp: Perry King, Tisa Farrow, Don Stroud, George Kennedy, Park Jong Soo.
d, William Fruet.

STRONG MEDICINE (1981) 84m
lp: Kate Manheim, Scotty Snyder, Bill Raymond, Harry Roskolenko, Ron Vawter.
d, Richard Foreman.

SUDDEN DEATH (1977)
lp: Robert Conrad, Don Stroud, Felton Perry, John Ashley, Nancy Conrad, Jenny Green.
d, Eddie Romero.

SUGAR COOKIES (1973)
lp: George Shannon, Mary Woronov, Maureen Byrnes, Daniel Sadur, Ondine, Jennifer Welles.

SUMMER RUN (1974) 96m
lp: Andy Parks, Tina Lund.
d, L. Capetanos.

SUN TAN RANCH (1948)
lp: Byron & Bean, Eunice Wilson, Mildred Boyd, Joel Fluellen, Austin McCoy, Bill Walker.

SUNBURST (1975)
lp: Peter Hooten, Kathrine Baumann, James Keach, Peter Brown, Rudy Vallee.
d, James Polakoff.

SUNDANCE CASSIDY AND BUTCH THE KID (1975)
lp: John Wade, Karen Blake, Robert Neuman.
d, Arthur Pitt.

SUNDAY SINNERS (1941) 65m
lp: Mamie Smith, Alec Lovejoy, Norman Astwood, Edna Mae Harris, Cristola Williams.
d, Arthur Dreifuss.

SUNDOWN RIDER (1933) 65m
lp: Buck Jones, Barbara Weeks, Pat O'Malley, Wheeler Oakman, Niles Welch.
d, Lambert Hillyer.

SUNDOWN TRAIL, THE (1975) 95m
lp: Wally Wales, Fay McKenzie, James Sheridan, Barney Beasley, Jack Kirk, Silver King the Horse.
d, Robert Emmett.

SUNSET CARSON RIDES AGAIN (1948)
lp: Sunset Carson, Pat Starling, Al Terry, Dan White, Pat Gleason, Bob Cason, Steven Keyes.
d, Oliver Drake.

SUNSHINE RUN (1979) 102m
lp: Chris Robinson, David Legge, Phyllis Robinson, Ted Cassidy, Robert Leslie.
d, Robinson.

SUPER BUG (1975) 83m
lp: Robert Mark, Sal Bogese, Walter Giller.

SUPER SEAL (1976)
lp: Foster Brooks, Sterling Holloway, Sarah Brown, Bob Shepard, Nada Rowland.
d, Michael Dugan.

SUPER WEAPON, THE (1976)
lp: Ron Van Clief, Charles Bonet, Jason Pai Pow.

SUPERBUG, THE WILD ONE (1977) 92m
lp: Richard Lynn, Constance Siech, Jim Brown, Bob Mackay.
d, David Mark.

SUPERCOCK (1975) 90m
lp: Ross Hagen, Nancy Kwan, Tony Lorea.
d, Gus Trikonis.

SUPER-JOCKS, THE (1980) 100m
lp: Joe Stewardson, Ken Leach, John Higgins, Richard Loring, Jenny Meyer.
d, Emil Nofal, Ray Sargeant.

SUPERSONIC SAUCER (1956, Brit.) 50m

lp: Marcia Monolescue, Fella Edmonds, Donald Gray, Gillian Harrison, Tony Lyons, Raymond Rollett.

d, S.G. Ferguson.

SURABAYA CONSPIRACY (1975) 90m

lp: Michael Rennie, Richard Jaeckel, Barbara Bouchet, Mike Preston.

d, Roy Davis.

SWANEE RIVER (1931) 50m

lp: Grant Withers, Thelma Todd, Philo McCullough, Walter Miller.

d, Raymond Cannon.

SWANEE SHOWBOAT (1939)

lp: Nina Mae McKinney, Dewey "Pigmeat" Markham, Mabel Lee, Helen Barys, The Eight Black Streaks, The Lindy Hoppers.

SWEATER GIRLS (1978)

lp: Harry Moses, Meegan King, Noelle North, Kate Sarchet, Carol Seflinger, Tamara Barkley, Julie Parsons.

d, Don Jones.

SWEET COUNTRY ROAD (1981) 95m

lp: Buddy Knox, Kary Lynn, Gordie Tapp, Johnny Paycheck, Jeanne Pruett.

SWEET DREAMERS (1981) 87m

lp: Richard Moir, Sue Smithers, Adam Bowen, Frankie Raymond, Richard Tipping.

d, Tom Cowan.

SWEET GENEVIEVE (1947) 68m

lp: Jean Porter, Jimmy Lydon, Gloria Marlen, Ralph Hodges, Lucien Littlefield, Tom Batten.

d, Arthur Dreifuss.

SWEET GEORGIA (1972)

lp: Marsha Jordan, Barbara Mills, Gene Drew, Chuck Lawson, Bill King, Jr, Al Wilkins.

SWEET SAVIOR (1971) 90m

lp: Troy Donahue, Renay Granville, Francine Middleton, Talie Cochrane, Matt Greene.

d, Bob Roberts.

SWEET SOUND OF DEATH (1965, U.S./Span.)

lp: Dianik Zurakowska, Emil Cape, Alba, Victor Israel, Sun Sanders, Daniel Blum.

d, Javier Seto.

SWIM TEAM (1979) 92m

lp: James Daughton, Stephen Furst, Richard Young, Buster Crabbe.

d, James Polakoff.

SWING (1938)

lp: Cora Green, Hazel Diaz, Carmen Newsome, Dorothy Van Engle, Alec Lovejoy.

d, Oscar Micheaux.

SWING, COWBOY, SWING (1944)

lp: Cal Shrum, Max Terhune, Alta Lee, Walt Shrum, Don Weston, I. Stanford Jolley.

d, Elmer Clifton.

SWING THE WESTERN WAY (1947) 66m

lp: The Hoosier Hotshots, Jack Leonard, Mary Dugan, Thurston Hall, Regina Wallace.

d, Derwin Abrahams.

SWINGIN' IN THE GROOVE (1960) 52m

d, Barry Shear..

SWINGING CHEERLEADERS, THE (1974) 94m

lp: Jo Johnston, Rainbeaux Smith, Colleen Camp, Ron Hajek, Ric Carrott, Jason Sommers.

d, Jack Hill.

SWINGING COEDS, THE (1976)

lp: Susan Justice, Judy Marlow, Mandy Chandler, Bianca Herr, Astrid Blythe.

d, Ross Meyers.

TAKE ME BACK TO OKLAHOMA (1940) 57m

lp: Tex Ritter, Slim Andrews, Terry Walker, Karl Hackett, George Eldridge, Bob McKenzie, Olin Francis.

d, Al Herman.

TAKE ONE (1977) 98m

lp: Jeff Addison, Phillip Borden, Tony Franco, Sal Guange, Richard Locke.

d, Wakefield Poole.

TALL, TAN AND TERRIFIC (1946) 60m

lp: Francine Everett, Monte Hawley, Milton Woods, Mantan Moreland, Dotts Johnson.

d, Bud Pollard.

TANGLED FORTUNES (1932)

lp: Buzz Barton, Francis X. Bushman, Jr, Caryl Lincoln, Edmund Cobb, Charles Hertzinger.

d, J.P. McGowan.

TANYA (1976)

lp: Marie Andrews, Sasha Gibson, Suzi Adams.

d, Nate Rogers.

TARGET EAGLE (1982) 99m

lp: George Rivero, Maud Adams, George Peppard, Chuck Connors, Susana Dosamates.

TARGET OF AN ASSASSIN (1978, S. Africa) 96m

lp: Anthony Quinn, John Philip Law, Simon Sabela.

TAUR THE MIGHTY (1960) 89m

lp: Joe Robinson, Bella Cortez.

TEAM-MATES (1978)

lp: Karen Corrado, Max Goff, Christopher Seppe, Ivy Sinclair, Michael Goldfinger.

d, Steven Jacobson.

TEASERS, THE (1977)

lp: Gloria Guida, Alice Ames, Sherry Wilson.

d, George Lancer.

TEENAGE GRAFFITI (1977) 90m

lp: Michael R. Driscoll, Jeanetta Arnette, Alden Sherry.

d, Christopher Casler.

TEENAGE HITCHHIKERS (1975) 74m

lp: Kathie Christopher, Sandra Peabody, Nikki Lynn, Claire Wilbur, Ric Mancini, Peter Carew.

d, Gerri Sedley.

TEENAGE TEASE (1983) 90m

lp: Peter Brown, Jo Ann Harris, Elsa Cardenas, Rene Auberjonois.

d, Richard Erdman.

TEENAGE TEASERS   (1982)

lp: Dany Daniel, Nadine Perles, Daniel Fawcett.

d, Jack Angel.

TEENAGER   (1975) 91m

lp: Joe Warfield, Andrea Cagan, Reid Smith, Sue Bernard.

d, Gerald Seth Sindell.

TELEPHONE BOOK, THE   (1971)

lp: Sarah Kennedy, Norman Rose, Jill Clayburgh, Barry Morse, William Hickey, Ondine.

d, Nelson Lyon.

TELL ME THAT YOU LOVE ME   (1983) 90m

lp: Nick Mancuso, Barbara Williams, Belinda Montgomery.

d, Tripi Trope.

TEMPEST, THE   (1980, Brit.) 95m

lp: Heathcote Williams, Karl Johnson, Toyah Wilcox, Peter Bull, Richard Warwick.

d, Derek Jarman.

TEMPTATION   (1930) 72m

lp: Lois Wilson, Lawrence Gray, Billy Bevan, Eileen Percy, Gertrude Bennett.

d, E. Mason Hooper.

TEN GLADIATORS, THE   (1960) 104m

lp: Roger Browne, Dan Vadis, Susan Paget.

TEN MILLION DOLLAR GRAB   (1966, Ital.) 100m

lp: Dana Andrews, Brad Harris, Elaine DeWitt.

TEN MINUTES TO KILL   (1933)

d, Oscar Micheaux..

TEN MINUTES TO LIVE   (1932) 65m

lp: Lawrence Chenault, Willor Lee Guilford, William A. Clayton, A.B. Comathiere.

d, Oscar Micheaux.

TENDER DRACULA OR CONFESSIONS OF A BLOOD DRINKER
                                              (1974, Fr.) 98m

lp: Peter Cushing.

d, Alain Robbe-Grillet.

TENDER LOVING CARE   (1974) 77m

lp: Donna Desmond, Michael Asher, Leah Simon, Tony Victor, Anita King, John Daniels.

d, Don Edmonds.

TERROR FROM THE UNKNOWN   (1983) 90m

lp: Don Leifert, Richard Nelson, Anne Frith.

d, Don Dohler.

TERROR IN THE CRYPT   (1963, Span./Ital.) 84m

lp: Christopher Lee, Aubrey Amber, Ursula Davis, Jose Campos.

d, Camillo Mastrocinque.

TERROR IN THE SWAMP   (1984) 87m

lp: Billy Holiday.

TERROR OF THE PLAINS   (1934) 57m

lp: Tom Tyler, Roberta Gale, Bill Gould, Charles Whitaker, Fern Emmett, Nelson McDowell, Frank Rice.

TERROR TRAIL   (1946) 55m

lp: Charles Starrett, Smiley Burnette, Barbara Pepper, Lane Chandler, Zon Murray.

d, Ray Nazarro.

TEXAN, THE   (1932)

lp: Buffalo Bill, Jr, Lucile Browne, Jack Mower, Yakima Canutt, Lafe McKee.

d, Cliff Smith.

TEXAN'S HONOR, A   (1929)

lp: Yakima Canutt.

TEXAS DETOUR   (1978) 92m

lp: Patrick Wayne, Mitch Vogel, Lindsay Bloom, R.G. Armstrong, Priscilla Barnes.

d, Hikmet Avedis.

TEXAS JACK   (1935) 52m

lp: Jack Perrin, Jayne Regan, Nelson McDowell, Robert Walker, Budd Buster, Cope Borden.

d, B.B. Ray.

TEXAS JUSTICE   (1942) 58m

lp: George Houston, Al "Fuzzy" St. John, Dennis Moore, Wanda McKay, Claire Rochelle.

d, Sam Newfield.

TEXAS PANHANDLE   (1945) 57m

lp: Charles Starrett, Tex Harding, Dub Taylor, Nanette Parks, Carolina Cotton, Forrest Taylor.

d, Ray Nazarro.

TEXAS RAMBLER, THE   (1935) 59m

lp: Bill Cody, Catherine Cotter, Earle Hodgins, Stuart James, Mildred Rogers, Budd Buster.

d, Bob Hill.

TEXAS RENEGADES   (1940) 59m

lp: Tim McCoy, Nora Lane, Harry Harvey, Kenne Duncan, Lee Prather, Earl Gunn, Hal Price.

d, Sam Newfield.

TEXAS TROUBLE SHOOTERS   (1942) 55m

lp: Ray Corrigan, John King, Max Terhune, Julie Duncan, Glenn Strange, Roy Harris.

d, S. Roy Luby.

THAT CURSED WINTER'S DAY, DJANGO & SARTANA TO THE LAST SHOT   (1970) 88m

lp: Hunt Powers.

THAT GIRL IS A TRAMP   (1974) 102m

lp: Bette Nielson, Laura Viala, Isabelle Coppens.

d, Jack Guy.

THAT I MAY SEE   (1953) 56m

lp: Ruth Hussey, Jeffrey Lynn.

THAT MAN OF MINE   (1947)

lp: Ruby Dee, Powell Lindsay, Hazel Tillman, Rhina Harris, Flow Hawkins, Betty Haynes.

d, William Alexander.

THAT TEXAS JAMBOREE   (1946) 59m

lp: The Hoosier Hotshots, Ken Curtis, Jeff Donnell, Andy Clyde, Guinn "Big Boy" Williams.

d, Ray Nazarro.

THAT'S YOUR FUNERAL (1974, Brit.) 82m
lp: Bill Fraser, Raymond Huntley, David Battley.
d, John Robbins.

THEIR MAD MOMENT (1931)
lp: Warner Baxter, ZaSu Pitts, Dorothy Mackaill, Lawrence Grant.
d, Hamilton MacFadden, Chandler Sprague.

THEIR ONLY CHANCE (1978) 90m
lp: Jock Mahoney, Steve Hoddy, Chris Jeffers, Mildred Watt.
d, J. David Siddon.

THEY CALL ME HALLELUJAH (1973) 91m
lp: George Hilton, Charlie Southwood, Agatha Florry.
d, Anthony Ascot.

THEY CALLED HIM AMEN (1972) 92m
lp: Sydne Rome, Luc Merenda.

THEY'RE COMING TO GET YOU (1976)
lp: George Hilton, Susan Scott.
d, Sergio Martino.

THIRTEENTH GREEN (1954, Brit.) 67m
lp: Ronald Howard, Barbara Kelly.

THIRTY YEARS LATER (1938)
lp: William Edmonson, A.B. Comathiere, Mabel Kelly, Ardella Dabney, Gertrude Snelson.
d, Oscar Micheaux.

THIS TIME FOREVER (1981) 95m
lp: Claire Pimpare, Vincent Van Patten, Cloris Leachman, Eddie Albert.

THOR AND THE AMAZON WOMEN (1960) 95m
lp: Joe Robinson, Susy Anderson.

THOROUGHBREDS, THE (1977)
lp: Vera Miles, Stuart Whitman, Sam Groom, Pat Renella.
d, Henry Levin.

THREE BULLETS FOR A LONG GUN (1973) 89m
lp: Beau Brummell, Keith Van Der Wat, Patrick Mynhardt, Tulio Moneta.
d, Peter Henkel.

THREE DAUGHTERS (1949)
lp: Michael Rosenberg, Sacha Shaw, Rebecca Weintraub, Charlotte Goldstein, Max Wilner.
d, Jospeh Seiden.

THREE DIMENSIONS OF GRETA (1973)
lp: Leena Skoog, Tristan Rogers, Karen Boyes, Alan Curtis.
d, Pete Walker.

THREE LIVES (1971)
lp: Mallory Millet-Jones, Lillian Shreve, Robin Mide.

THREE OF A KIND (1944)
lp: Billy Gilbert, Shemp Howard, Maxie Rosenbloom, Helen Gilbert, June Lang.
d, D. Ross Lederman.

THREE ON A MEATHOOK (1973)
lp: Charles Kissinger, James Pickett.
d, William Girdler.

THREE SERGEANTS OF BENGAL (1965) 100m
lp: Richard Harrison, Wandisa Guida.

THREE SWORDS OF ZORRO, THE (1960) 92m
lp: Guy Stockwell, Gloria Milland, Mikaela.

THREE WAY LOVE (1977) 86m
lp: Paul Paige, Janet Loncar.
d, Lewis Scott.

THREE WAY WEEKEND (1979) 78m
lp: Jody Lee Olhava, Blake Parrish, Jerry Zanitsch, Dan Diego, Richard Blye.
d, Emmett Alston.

THROW A SADDLE ON A STAR (1946) 60m
lp: Ken Curtis, Jeff Donnell, Adelle Roberts, Guinn "Big Boy" Williams, Andy Clyde.
d, Ray Nazarro.

THUNDERBIRDS 6 (1968)
lp: Peter Dyneley, Catherine Finn, Sylvia Anderson.
d, David Lane.

THUNDERGAP OUTLAWS (1947)
lp: Dave "Tex" O'Brien, Jim Newill, Guy Wilkerson, Janet Shaw, Jack Ingram.
d, Albert Herman.

THURSDAY MORNING MURDERS, THE (1976)
lp: Nahay, Gordon Austin, Lyle S. Wall, J.B. Young, Lawrence Harris, Jean Rapstead.
d, Michael Nahay.

TIFFANY MEMORANDUM (1966) 96m
lp: Ken Clark, Irene Demick.
d, Terence Hathaway.

TIGHTROPE TO TERROR (1977, Brit.) 60m
lp: Rebecca Lacey, Eloise Ritchie, Richard Owen.
d, Robert Kellett.

TIMBER TRAMPS (1975)
lp: Claude Akins, Tab Hunter, Cesar Romero, Eve Brent, Leon Ames, Rosie Grier, Joseph Cotten.

TIMBERESQUE (1937)
lp: Barry Norton, Vyola Von, Enrique DeRosas.
d, King Guidice.

TIMBERLAND TERROR (1940, Aus.) 56m
lp: Frank Leighton, Shirley Ann Richards, Campbell Copling, Frank Harvey.
d, Ken G. Hall.

TIME FOR LOVE, A (1974) 87m
lp: Rick Jason, Jane Merrow, Benson Fong.

TIME OF FURY (1968) 86m
lp: Robert Ward, Jeff Comeron.

TIME RUNNING OUT (1950)
lp: Dane Clark, Robert Duke, Simone Signoret.

TIME TO RUN (1974)

lp: Ed Nelson, Randall Carver, Barbara Sigel, Joan Winmill, Gordon Rigsby, Billy Graham.

TINKER (1950, Brit.) 67m

lp: Tom Stone, Herbert Marshall.

TO CHASE A MILLION (1967) 97m

lp: Richard Bradford, Yoko Tani, Ron Randall, Anton Rodgers, Norman Rossington.

TO DIE IN PARIS (1968) 100m

lp: Louis Jourdan, Kurt Krueger, Phillippe Forquet, Stuart Nesbet.

TO HELL YOU PREACH (1972) 76m

lp: Hagen Smith, Michael Christian, Tim Scott, Kitty Vallacher, Richard Hurst.

d, Richard Robinson.

TO LOVE, PERHAPS TO DIE (1975) 88m

lp: Sue Lyon, Chris Mitchum, Jean Sorel, Ramon Pons, Charly Bravo, Alfredo Alba, David Carpenter.

TOBO, THE HAPPY CLOWN (1965)

lp: Eddie Finn.

d, William Rowland.

TODAY WE KILL...TOMORROW WE DIE (1971)

lp: Montgomery Ford, Bud Spencer, Tatsuya Nakadai, William Berger, Wayde Preston, Stanley Gordon.

TOGETHER FOR DAYS (1972) 84m

lp: Clifton Davis, Lois Chiles.

d, Michael Schultz.

TOGETHERNESS (1970) 103m

lp: George Hamilton, Peter Lawford, John Banner, Olinka Berova, Jesse White.

d, Arthur Marks.

TOKOLOSHE (1973)

lp: Saul Pelle, Sidney James, Chief Butulezei, Cy Sacks, Jimmy Sabe.

TOMBS OF THE BLIND DEAD (1974) 100m

lp: Cesar Burner, Lone Fleming, Helen Harp.

TOMCATS (1977)

lp: Chris Mulkey, Polly King, Scott Lawrence.

d, Harry E. Kerwin.

TOMORROW MAN, THE (1979)

lp: Don Francks, Stephen Markle, Michelle Chicoine, Gail Dahms.

d, Tibor Takacs.

TOMORROW'S CHILDREN (1934)

lp: Sterling Holloway.

TONTO KID, THE (1935)

lp: Rex Bell, Ruth Mix, Buzz Barton, Theodore Lorch, Joseph Girard, Barbara Roberts, Jack Rockwell, Murdock McQuarrie.

d, Harry Fraser.

TOO HOT TO HANDLE (1976) 88m

lp: Cheri Caffaro, Aharon Ipale, Vic Diaz, Corinne Calvet, Butz Aquino.

d, Don Schain.

TOPA TOPA (1938) 74m

lp: Helen Hughes, James Bush, LeRoy Mason, Ruth Coleman, Jill L'Estrange.

d, Vin Moore, Charles Hutchinson.

TORNADO IN THE SADDLE, A (1942) 59m

lp: Russell Hayden, Dub Taylor, Alma Carroll, Bob Wills and the Texas Playboys, Tris Coffin, Don Curtis.

d, William Berke.

TOUCH OF SATAN, THE (1974) 89m

lp: Michael Berry, Emby Mellay, Lee Amber, Yvonne Winslow, Jeanne Gerson.

d, Don Henderson.

TOUCHABLES, THE (1968, Brit.) 97m

lp: Judy Huxtable, Esther Anderson, Marilyn Rickard, Kathy Simmonds, Harry Baird.

d, Richard Freeman.

TOUGH (1974) 87m

lp: Dion Gossett, Renny Roker, Sandy Reed, Rich Holmes, Christopher Townes.

d, Horace Jackson.

TOY BOX, THE (1971)

lp: Evan Steele, Ann Myers, Neal Bishop, Deborah Osborne, Marie Arnold.

d, Ron Garcia.

TOY SOLDIERS (1983) 85m

lp: Jason Miller, Cleavon Little.

d, David Fischer.

TRACY RIDES (1935) 60m

lp: Tom Tyler, Virginia Brown Faire, Edmund Cobb, Charles K. French, Carol Shandrew.

d, Harry S. Webb.

TRAIL BLAZERS (1953) 69m

lp: Alan Hale, Jr, Richard Tyler, Barney McCormack, Jim Flowers, Henry Blair.

d, Wesley Barry.

TRAIL OF THE ARROW (1952) 54m

lp: Guy Madison, Andy Devine, Wendy Waldron, Raymond Hatton, Terry Frost, Jack Reynolds.

d, Thomas Carr.

TRAIL OF THE HAWK (1935) 60m

lp: Yancie Lane, Dickie Jones, Betty Jordan, Lafe McKee, Don Orlando, Gaines Blevins.

d, Edward Dmytryk.

TRAIL OF THE RUSTLERS (1950) 55m

lp: Charles Starrett, Smiley Burnette, Gail Davis, Tommy Ivo, Myron Healey, Don Harvey.

d, Ray Nazarro.

TRAIL TO LAREDO (1948) 54m

lp: Charles Starrett, Smiley Burnette, Jim Bannon, Virginia Maxey, Tommy Ivo.

d, Ray Nazarro.

TRAIL TO MEXICO (1946) 56m

lp: Jimmy Wakely, Lee "Lasses" White, Julian Rivero, Delores Castelli, Dora Del Rio.

d, Oliver Drake.

TRAILING DANGER (1947) 58m

lp: Johnny Mack Brown, Raymond Hatton, Peggy Wynne, Marshall Reed, Patrick Desmond.

d, Lambert Hillyer.

TRAILING NORTH (1933) 61m

lp: Bob Steele, Doris Hill, George Hayes, Arthur Rankin, Fred Burns, Dick Dickinson.

d, J.P. McCarthy.

TRAIL'S END (1935) 57m

lp: Conway Tearle, Claudia Dell, Baby Charlene Barry, Fred Kohler, Ernie Adams.

d, Al Herman.

TRAILS OF ADVENTURE (1935) 57m

lp: Buffalo Bill, Jr, Edna Aslin, Harry Carter, Allen Holbrook, Raymond B. Wells.

d, Buffalo Bill, Jr..

TRAILS OF THE GOLDEN WEST (1931) 58m

lp: Buffalo Bill, Jr, Wanda Hawley, Tom London, George Reed, Horace B. Carpenter.

d, Leander de Cordova.

TRAP ON COUGAR MOUNTAIN (1972) 94m

lp: Keith Larsen, Karen Steele, Eric Larsen.

d, Keith Larsen.

TRAPPED (1982)

lp: Henry Silva, Nicholas Campbell, Barbara Gordon, Gina Dick, Joy Thompson.

d, William Fruet.

TREASON (1933) 61m

lp: Buck Jones, Shirley Grey, Robert Ellis, Edward J. Le Saint, Frank Lackteen.

d, George B. Seitz.

TREASURE OF TAYOPA (1974) 90m

lp: Gilbert Roland, Rena Winters, Bob Corrigan, Frank Hernandez.

d, Bob Cawley.

TREASURE OF THE AMAZON (1983) 100m

lp: Stuart Whitman, Bradford Dillman, Ann Sydney, Donald Pleasence, John Ireland.

d, Rene Cardona, Jr..

TRIANGLE (1971) 87m

lp: Dana Wynter, Ray Danton, Paul Richards, Charles Robinson, Tiffany Bolling.

TRICK OR TREATS (1983) 92m

lp: David Carradine, Jackelyn Giroux, Carrie Snodgress, Steve Railsback, Julian Kessner.

d, Gary Graver.

TRIGGER FINGERS (1946) 56m

lp: Johnny Mack Brown, Raymond Hatton, Jennifer Holt, Riley Hill, Steve Clark.

d, Lambert Hillyer.

TRIGGER LAW (1944) 56m

lp: Hoot Gibson, Bob Steele, Beatrice Gray, Ralph Lewis, Edward Cassidy.

d, Vernon Keyes.

TRIGGER TOM (1935)

lp: Tom Tyler, Al "Fuzzy" St. John, Bernadene Hayes, William Gould, John Elliott.

d, Harry S. Webb.

TRIGGERMAN (1948) 56m

lp: Johnny Mack Brown, Raymond Hatton, Virginia Carroll, Bill Kennedy, Marshall Reed.

d, Howard Bretherton.

TRINITY (1975) 92m

lp: Richard Harrison, Donal O'Brien, George Wang, Anna Zinneman.

d, James London.

TRINITY AND SARTANA (1972) 105m

lp: Robert Widmark.

TRIP WITH THE TEACHER (1975) 91m

lp: Zalman King, Brenda Fogarty, Robert Porter, Robert Gribbin, Jill Voigt, Dina Ousley.

d, Earl Barton.

TRIUMPH OF ROBIN HOOD, THE (1960) 92m

lp: Don Burnett, Gia Scala, Gerard Philippe Noel.

TROUBLE AT MELODY MESA (1949) 60m

lp: Brad King, Cal Shrum, Lorraine Michie, I. Stanford Jolley, Walt Shrum, Alta Lee.

d, W.M. Connell.

TROUBLE BUSTERS (1933) 55m

lp: Jack Hoxie, Lane Chandler, Kaye Edwards, Ben Corbett, Harry Todd, Slim Whitaker.

d, Lew Collins.

TROUBLE CHASERS (1945) 62m

lp: Billy Gilbert, Maxie Rosenbloom, Shemp Howard.

d, Lew Landers.

TROUBLE ON THE TRAIL (1954)

lp: Guy Madison, Andy Devine.

d, Frank McDonald.

TROUBLED WATERS (1964, Brit.)

lp: Tab Hunter, Zena Walker, Andy Myers, Michael Goodliffe.

d, Stanley Goulder.

TRUCKIN' (1975)

lp: Nicholas Wahler, Dorothy Tristan, Craig Horrall, Albert Salmi.

d, Ken Handler.

TRUCKIN' BUDDY McCOY (1983) 90m

lp: Terence Cox.

TRUCKIN' MAN (1975)

lp: Michael Hawkins, Mary Cannon, Doodles Weaver, Sid Rancer, Larry Drake, Lynne Bradley.

d, Will Zens.

TUCK EVERLASTING (1981) 114m

lp: Fred A. Keller, James McGuire, Paul Flessa, Margaret Chamberlain.

d, Frederick King Keller.

TUGBOAT PRINCESS (1936) 69m

lp: Walter C. Kelly, Valerie Hobson, Edith Fellows, Clyde Cook, Lester Mathews.

d, David Selman.

TUMBLEWEED TRAIL (1942) 57m

lp: Bill "Cowboy Rambler" Boyd, Art Davis, Lee Powell, Marjorie Manners, Jack Rockwell.

d, Sam Newfield.

TUXEDO WARRIOR (1982) 93m

lp: John Wyman, Carol Royle, Holly Palance.

$20 A WEEK (1935) 80m

lp: Pauline Strake, Owen Lee, Jimmy Murray, William Worthington, Dorothy Revier.

d, Wesley Ford.

TWISTED RAILS (1935)

lp: Jack Donovan, Alice Dahl, Philo McCullough, Donald Keith, Vic Potel, Buddy Shaw.

d, Al Herman.

TWO CATCH TWO (1979) 95m

lp: Sam DiBello, Steven W. Anderson, Alan Hansen, Darrell Minshall.

d, Gene Marshall, Dennis R. Lisonbee.

TWO FACES OF EVIL, THE (1981, Brit.) 101m

lp: Anna Calder-Marshall, Gary Raymond, Denholm Elliott, James Laurenson.

d, Alan Gibson, Peter Sasdy.

TWO-FISTED STRANGER (1946) 50m

lp: Charles Starrett, Smiley Burnette, Doris Houck, Charles Murray, Lane Chandler.

d, Ray Nazarro.

TWO GUN CABALLERO (1931) 58m

lp: Robert Fraser, Consuelo Dawn, Bobby Nelson, Carmen LaRoux, Pat Harmon, Diane Esmond.

d, Jack Nelson.

TWO-GUN MAN FROM HARLEM (1938) 60m

lp; Herbert Jeffrey [Jeffries], Mary Whitten, Mantan Moreland, Stymie Beard.

d, Richard C. Kahn.

TWO MUGS FROM BROOKLYN (1942) 73m

lp: William Bendix, Joe Sawyer, Grace Bradley.

TWO THOUSAND YEARS LATER (1969) 79m

lp: Terry-Thomas, Edward Everett Horton, Pat Harrington, Lisa Seagram, John Abbott.

d, Bert Tenzer.

TWO TONS OF TURQUOISE TO TAOS (1967)

d, Robert Downey..

TWO VIOLENT MEN (1964) 94m

lp: Alan Scott, Susy Anderson, George Martin.

TWO WORLDS OF ANGELITA, THE (1982) 73m

lp: Marien Perez Riera, Rosalba Rolon, Angel Domenech Soto, Delia Esther Quinones.

d, Jane Marrison..

TYRANT, THE (1972, Can.) 95m

lp: Richard Johnson, Martha Hyer.

UNCLE MOSES (1932) 80m

lp: Maurice Schwartz, Zvee Scooker, Judith Abarbanel, Mark Schweid.

d, Sidney Goldin, Aubrey Scotto.

UNCLE NICK (1938) 60m

lp: Val Vousden.

d, Tom Cooper.

UNCONQUERED BANDIT (1935) 60m

lp: Tom Tyler, Lillian Gilmore, Slim Whitaker, William Gould, John Elliott, Earl Dwire.

d, Harry S. Webb.

UNDEFEATED, THE (1951, Brit.)

lp: Kynaston Reeves, Mollie Palmer, Cyril Conway, Cyril Clensy, Leo Genn.

UNDER THE DOCTOR (1976) 86m

d, Gerry Poulson..

UNDER THE SIGN OF CAPRICORN (1971)

lp: Barry Sullivan, Martin Landau, Chuck Connors, Stella Stevens.

UNDER THE TABLE YOU MUST GO (1969) 52m

d, Arnold Miller; Voices, Murray Kash, Gordon Davis, Liam Nolan..

UNDERCOVER MEN (1935)

lp: Charles Starrett, Adrienne Dore, Kenneth Duncan, Wheeler Oakman, Eric Clavering.

d, Sam Newfield.

UNDERGROUND ACES (1981)

lp: Dirk Benedict, Melanie Griffith, Robert Hegyes, Jerry Orbach, Frank Gorshin.

d, Robert Butler.

UNDERWORLD TERROR (1936) 57m

lp: Nick Stuart, Nina Quartaro.

UNKISSED BRIDE (1966) 82m

lp: Tom Kirk, Anne Helm, Jacques Bergerac.

UNKNOWN POWERS (1979) 96m

lp: Samantha Eggar, Jack Palance, Will Geer, Roscoe Lee Browne.

d, Don Como.

UNMASKED (1929) 54m

lp: Lyons Wickland, Susan Conroy, Milton Krims, Waldo Edwards, Kate Roemer, William Corbett.

d, Edgar Lewis.

UP JUMPED THE DEVIL (1941) 62m

lp: Mantan Moreland, Shelton Brooks, Maceo Sheffield, Clarence Brooks, Florence O'Brien, Lawrence Criner.

UP RIVER (1979) 95m

lp: Morgan Stevens, Jeff Corey, Debbie AuLuce.

UP YOUR ALLEY (1975)

lp: Frank Corsentino, Haji, Gordon McGill.

d, Art Lieberman.

UPPERCRUST, THE (1982) 114m

lp: Frank Buchrieser, Frank Gorshin, Lukas Resetarits, Broderick Crawford, Pavel Landovsky.

d, Peter Patzak.

UPS AND DOWNS (1981) 97m

lp: Leslie Hope, Andrew Sabiston, Gavin Brannon, Colin Skinner, Margo Nesbit.

d, Paul Almond.

URUBU (1948) 66m

lp: George Breakston, Yorke Coplen.

d, Breakston.

UTAH KID, THE (1944) 55m

lp: Bob Steele, Hoot Gibson, Beatrice Gray, Evelyn Eaton, Ralph Lewis, Mike Letz.

d, Vernon Keyes.

VALLEY OF BLOOD (1973) 64m

lp: Penny DeHaven, Ernie Ashworth, Zeke Clements, Wayne Forsythe, Rita Cristinziano.

d, Dean Tucker.

VALLEY OF FEAR (1947) 54m

lp: Johnny Mack Brown, Raymond Hatton, Christine McIntyre, Tris Coffin, Edward Cassidy.

d, Lambert Hillyer.

VALLEY OF TERROR (1937) 58m

lp: Kermit Maynard, Harley Wood, John Merton, Jack Ingram, Dick Curtis, Roger Williams.

d, Al Herman.

VALLEY OF WANTED MEN (1935) 63m

lp: Frankie Darro, Grant Withers, LeRoy Mason, Paul Fix, Russell Hopton, Walter Miller.

d, Alan James.

VANISHING MEN (1932) 62m

lp: Tom Tyler, Adele Lacy, Raymond Keane, William L. Thorne, John Elliott.

d, Harry Fraser.

VANISHING RIDERS (1935) 58m

lp: Bill Cody, Ethel Jackson, Wally Wales, Bill Cody, Jr, Bud Buster, Milburn Morante.

d, Robert Hill.

VEILED ARISTOCRATS (1932)

lp: Lawrence Chenault, Walter Fleming, Lorenzo Tucker.

d, Oscar Micheaux.

VENGEANCE OF RANNAH (1936) 59m

lp: Bob Custer, Rin-Tin-Tin, Jr, John Elliott, Victoria Vinton, Roger Williams, Eddie Phillips, Edward Cassidy.

d, B.B. Ray.

VENGEANCE OF THE WEST (1942) 60m

lp: Bill Elliott, Tex Ritter, Frank Mitchell, Adele Mara, Dick Curtis, Robert Fiske.

d, Lambert Hillyer.

VENGEANCE OF VIRGO (1972)

lp: Christopher Lee, Joan Blackman, Dana Wynter, Cameron Mitchell.

VERNON, FLORIDA (1982) 60m

lp: Claude Register, Albert Bitterling, Henry Shipes, Snake Reynolds.

d, Errol Morris.

VIGILANTES RIDE, THE (1944) 56m

lp: Russell Hayden, Dub Taylor, Shirley Patterson, Tristram Coffin, Jack Rockwell.

d, William Berke.

VOICE OVER (1983) 105m

lp: Ian McNiece, Bish Nethercote, John Cassady, Sarah Martin, David Pearce, Stuart Hutton, Eira Moore, Paul Chandler.

d, Chris Monger.

VOICE WITHIN, THE (1929)

lp: Eve Southern, Walter Pidgeon, Montagu Love, J. Barney Sherry.

d, George Archainbaud.

VULTURES IN PARADISE (1984) 101m

lp: Meredith Macrae, Stuart Whitman, Yvonne De Carlo, Aldo Ray, Jim Bailey.

d, Paul Leder.

WAGES OF SIN, THE (1929)

lp: Lorenzo Tucker, Katherine Noisette, Gertrude Snelson, Bessie Gibbens, Ethel Smith, Alice Russel.

WANTED DEAD OR ALIVE (1951) 59m

lp: Whip Wilson, Fuzzy Knight, Jim Bannon, Christine McIntyre, Leonard Penn, Lane Bradford.

d, Thomas Carr.

WARHEAD (1974) 91m

lp: David Janssen, Karin Dor, Chris Stone, Art Metrano.

d, John O'Connor.

WARLOCK MOON (1973)

lp: Laurie Walters, Joe Spano.

d, Bill Herbert.

WASHINGTON AFFAIR, THE (1978) 90m

lp: Tom Selleck, Carol Lynley, Barry Sullivan, Arlene Banas.

d, Victor Stoloff.

WEAPONS OF DEATH (1982) 90m

lp: Eric Lee, Bob Ramos, Ralph Catellanos.

WEDDING ON THE VOLGA, THE (1929) 58m

lp: Mark Schweid, Mary Fowler.

WEEKEND LOVER (1969) 88m

lp: Vic Lance, Chris Mathis, Antoinette Maynard, Sydney Carlysle.

d, Dwayne Avery.

WELCOME HOME, BROTHER CHARLES (1975)

lp: Marlo Monte, Reatha Grey, Stan Kamber, Tiffany Peters, Ven Bigelow, Jake Carter.

d, Jamaa Fanaka.

WEST IS STILL WILD, THE (1977)

lp: Rory Calhoun, Richard Webb, Angela Richardson, Doodles Weaver, Noble "Kid" Chissell.

d, Don Von Mizener.

WEST OF DODGE CITY (1947) 57m

lp: Charles Starrett, Smiley Burnette, Nancy Saunders, Fred Sears, Glenn Stuart.

d, Ray Nazarro.

WEST OF THE RIO GRANDE (1944) 57m

lp: Johnny Mack Brown, Raymond Hatton, Dennis Moore, Christine McIntyre, Lloyd Ingraham.

d, Lambert Hillyer.

WEST ON PARADE (1934)

lp; Denny Meadows [Dennis Moore], Ben Corbett, Jayne Regan, Franklyn Farnum, Fern Emmett, Philo McCullough.

d, B.B. Ray.

WESTERN CODE (1932) 61m
lp: Tim McCoy, Nora Lane, Mischa Auer, Wheeler Oakman, Gordon DeMain, Matthew Betz.
d, J.P. McCarthy.

WESTERN RACKETEERS (1935)
lp: Bill Cody, Edna Aslin, Wally Wales, Ben Corbett, Bud Buster, George Chesebro.
d, Robert J. Horner.

WE'VE GOT THE DEVIL ON THE RUN (1934)
lp: Elder Micheaux.

WHAT DO I TELL THE BOYS AT THE STATION (1972) 91m
lp: William C. Reilly, Anita Morris, Sloane Shelton, Mary Cass, Jack Berns, George Harris.
d, Simon Nuchtern.

WHAT GOES UP (1939)
lp: Eddie Green.

WHAT MAISIE KNEW (1976) 58m
lp: Epp Kotkas, Kate Manheim, Saskia Noordhoek-Hegt.
d, Babette Mangolte.

WHEN THE NORTH WIND BLOWS (1974) 113m
lp: Henry Brandon, Herbert Nelson, Don Haggerty.
d, Stuart Raffill.

WHEN TIME RAN OUT (1980) 109m
d, James Goldstone..

WHERE TRAILS END (1942) 58m
lp: Tom Keene, Joan Curtis, Frank Yaconelli, Charles King, Donald Stewart.
d, Robert Tansey.

WHERE'S WILLIE? (1978) 91m
lp: Henry Darrow, Kate Woodville, Guy Madison, Marc Gilpin, Rock Montanio.
d, John Florea.

WHILE THOUSANDS CHEER (1940)
lp: Kenny Washington, Gladys Snyder, Jeni LeGon, Florence O'Brien, Ida Belle, Mantan Moreland, Joel Fluellen.

WHIRLWIND (1951) 70m
lp: Gene Autry, Smiley Burnette, Gail Davis, Thurston Hall, Harry Lauter.
d, John English.

WHIRLWIND, THE (1933) 62m
lp: Tim McCoy, Alice Dahl, Pat O'Malley, J. Carrol Naish, Matthew Betz.
d, D. Ross Lederman.

WHIRLWIND RIDER, THE (1935)
lp: Buffalo Bill, Jr, Jeanne Boutell, Jack Long, Frank Clark, Clyde McClary.
d, Robert Horner.

WHISKEY MOUNTAIN (1977)
lp: Christopher George, Preston Pierce, Linda Borgeson, Roberta Collins, Robert Leslie.
d, William Grefe.

WHITE COMANCHE (1967) 90m
lp: Joseph Cotten, William Shatner, Perla Cristal, Rossana Yanni.
d, Gilbert Kay.

WHITE LIONS (1981) 96m
lp: Michael York, Glynnis O'Connor, Donald Moffat, J.A. Preston, Roger Mosley.
d, Mel Stuart.

WHITE RENEGADE (1931)
lp: Tom Santschi, Blanche Mehaffey, Philo McCullough, Reed Howes, Ted Wells.
d, Jack Irwin.

WHO'S CRAZY (1965) 83m
d, Allan Zion, Tom White..

WHOSE CHILD AM I? (1976)
lp: Kate O'Mara, Paul Freeman, Edward Judd, Felicity Devonshire.
d, Lawrence Britten.

WHY KILL AGAIN? (1965) 92m
lp: Anthony Steffen, Evelyn Stewart, Pepe Calvo.

WIDOW IN SCARLET (1932) 64m
lp: Dorothy Revier, Kenneth Harlan, Lloyd Whitlock, Glenn Tyron.
d, George B. Seitz.

WILD HORSE RANGE (1940) 58m
lp: Jack Randall, Phyllis Ruth, Frank Yaconelli, Charles King.
d, Raymond K. Johnson.

WILDCAT SAUNDERS (1936) 60m
lp: Jack Perrin, Blanche Mehaffey, William Gould, Fred "Snowflake" Toones.
d, Harry Fraser.

WILLIE AND SCRATCH (1975) 88m
lp: Paul Vincent, Claudia Jennings, Mike Hatfield.
d, Robert J. Emery.

WINDS OF AUTUMN, THE (1976)
lp: Jack Elam, Jeanette Nolan, Andrew Prine, Dub Taylor.
d, Charles B. Pierce.

WINTER COMES EARLY (1972) 106m
lp: Art Hindke, Trudy Young, Derek Sanderson.
d, George McCowan.

WITCH WHO CAME FROM THE SEA, THE (1976) 98m
lp: Millie Perkins, Lonny Chapman, Vanessa Brown, Peggy Feury, Rick Jason.
d, Matt Cimber.

WITCHES' BREW (1980) 99m
lp: Lana Turner, Richard Benjamin, Teri Garr, Kathryn Leigh Scott.
d, Richard Shorr, Hebert L. Strock.

WOLF LAKE 87m (1979)
lp: Rod Steiger.
d, Burt Kennedy.

WOLF RIDERS (1935)
lp: Jack Perrin, Lillian Gilmore, Lafe McKee, Nancy DeShon, William Gould, George Chesebro, Earl Dwire.
d, Harry S. Webb.

WOMAN CONDEMNED (1934) 66m
lp: Claudia Dell, Lola Lane, Richard Hemingway, Jason Robards, Sr.
d, Mrs. Wallace Reid.

WOMAN FOR ALL MEN, A   (1975) 95m

lp: Keenan Wynn, Judith Brown, Andy Robinson, Alex Rocco, Don Porter, Peter Hooten.

d, Arthur Marks.

WOMAN IN THE RAIN   (1976) 90m

lp: Barbara Luna, Alex Nicol, Ron Masak, Mary Frann, Stanley Adams, Kyle Johnson.

d, Paul Hunt.

WOMAN PURSUED   (1931)

lp: Ivan Lebedeff, Genevieve Tobin, Betty Compson, Ilka Chase, Rita LeRoy.

d, Richard Boleslavsky.

WOMAN'S MAN, A   (1934) 70m

lp: Kitty Kelly, Wallace Ford, Marguerite de la Motte, Jameson Thomas.

d, Edward Ludwig.

WOMAN'S URGE, A   (1966) 83m

WOMEN FOR SALE   (1975) 86m

lp: Robert Woods, Veronique Vendell, Barbara Cappell, Joe Busse, Werner Puchath.

d, Ernest Farmer.

WOMEN IN CAGES   (1972) 78m

lp: Judy Brown, Pam Grier, Roberta Collins.

d, Gerry De Leon.

WON'T WRITE HOME, MOM--I'M DEAD   (1975, Brit.)

lp: Pamela Franklin, Ian Bannen, Suzanne Neve.

WRECK OF THE HESPERUS   (1948) 70m

lp: Willard Parker, Edgar Buchanan, Patricia White.

d, John Hoffman.

WRESTLING QUEEN, THE   (1975)

lp: Vivian Vachon, "Cowboy" Bill Watts, "Mad Dog" Vachon, "Grizzly" Smith, Marie "Fifi" Laverne.

WRONG MR. RIGHT, THE   (1939)

lp: Dewey "Pigmeat" Markham, John Murray.

WYOMING HURRICANE   (1944) 58m

lp: Russell Hayden, Dub Taylor, Alma Carroll, Bob Wills and his Texas Playboys.

d, William Berke.

WYOMING ROUNDUP   (1952) 53m

lp: Whip Wilson, Phyllis Coates, Tommy Farrell, Henry Rowland, House Peters, Jr.

d, Thomas Carr.

WYOMING WHIRLWIND   (1932) 63m

lp: Lane Chandler, Adele Tracy, Harry Todd, Loie Bridge, Yakima Canutt.

d, Armand Schaefer.

YELLOW HAIRED KID, THE   (1952) 72m

lp: Guy Madison, Andy Devine, Alan Hale, Jr, Marcia Mae Jones, Alice Rolph.

d, Frank McDonald.

YIN AND YANG OF DR. GO, THE   (1972) 98m

lp: Burgess Meredith, James Mason, Jeff Bridges.

d, Meredith.

YOU AND ME   (1975) 96m

lp; David Carradine, Richard Chadbourne II, Bobbi Shaw, Barbara [Hershey] Seagull.

d, Carradine.

YOUNG AND WILD   (1975) 90m

lp: Carl Monson, Angela Carnon, Maybe Smith, Sharon Masters, Christopher Culhane, Pepe Russo.

d, Dwayne Avery.

YOUNG DETECTIVE, THE   (1964, Brit.) 60m

lp: Neil McCarthy, Sam Kydd.

d, Gilbert Gunn.

YOUNG JACOBITES   (1959)

lp: Francesca Annis, Frazier Hines, Jeremy Bullock, John Pike, John Woodnut.

d, John Reeve.

YOUNG MAN'S BRIDE, THE   (1968)

lp: Patricia Moore, Ralph G. Edwards.

d, George Gunter.

YOUNG SEDUCERS, THE   (1974)

lp: Evelyn Traeger, Ingrid Steeger.

d, Michael Thomas.

YUM-YUM GIRLS   (1976) 93m

lp: Judy Landers, Tanya Roberts, Michelle Dawn, Carey Poe, Stan Bernstein.

d, Barry Rosen.

ZEBRA FORCE   (1977) 100m

lp: Mike Lane, Richard X. Slattery, Rockne Tarkington, Glenn Wilder.

d, Joe Tornatore.

ZEBRA KILLER, THE   (1974) 90m

lp: Austin Stoker, James Pickett, Hugh Smith, Charles Kissinger, Valerie Rogers.

d, William Girdler.

ZETA ONE   (1969)

lp: Robin Hawdon, Yutte Stensgaard, James Robertson Justice, Charles Hawtrey.

d, Michael Cort.

ZOMBIE ISLAND MASSACRE   (1984) 95m

lp: David Broadnax, Rita Jenrette, Tom Cantrell.

d, John N. Carter.

ZOO ROBBERY   (1973, Brit.) 64m

lp: Paul Gyngell, Denise Gyngell, Karen Lucas, Luke Batchelor, Walter McKone.

d, Matt McCarthy, John Black.